CASES AND MATERIALS
ON
PROPERTY

By

JOHN E. CRIBBET
Dean, Chancellor and
Corman Professor of Law Emeritus
University of Illinois at Urbana-Champaign

CORWIN W. JOHNSON
Edward Clark Centennial
Professor Emeritus in Law
University of Texas at Austin

ROGER W. FINDLEY
Professor of Law and Fritz B. Burns
Chair in Real Property
Loyola Law School, Los Angeles
University of Illinois at Urbana-Champaign

ERNEST E. SMITH
Rex G. Baker Centennial Chair in
Natural Resources Law
University of Texas at Austin

SIXTH EDITION

Westbury, New York
THE FOUNDATION PRESS, INC.
1990

615 Merrick Ave.
Westbury, N.Y. 11590

Printed in the United States of America

Library of Congress Cataloging-in-Publication Data

Cases and materials on property / by John E. Cribbet . . . [et al.]. —
6th ed.
p. cm. — (University casebook series)
At head of title: Cribbet, Johnson, Findley & Smith.
Rev. ed. of: Cases and materials on property / by John E. Cribbet
and Corwin W. Johnson. 5th ed. 1984.
ISBN 0-88277-782-3
1. Property—United States—Cases. I. Cribbet, John E.
II. Cribbet, John E. Cases and materials on property. III. Series.
KF560.C7 1990
346.7304—dc20
[347.3064] 89-49620
CIP

C., J., F. & S.—Cs. Prop. 6th Ed. UCB
5th Reprint—1994

Dedicated to the thousands of law students who were introduced to the law of property in the first five editions of this casebook.

*

PREFACE TO THE SIXTH EDITION

This is the thirtieth anniversary of the publication of Cribbet, Fritz and Johnson, Cases and Materials on Property (1960). New editions have appeared at six-year intervals since 1960, and a perusal of prior Prefaces plus the Tables of Contents discloses the slow evolution of property law over the past three decades. Despite the appearance of numerus uniform and model acts, which have had their influence on the developing law, there has been no revolution in the institution of property. Many incremental changes have occurred in both legislation and judicial decisions but most of the "ancient wisdom" has remained essentially intact. The most significant changes have occurred in the public regulation of land use, where many of the private rights in the famous "bundle of sticks" have been transferred to the public pile. But even here, there are many indications of a counter-evolution evidencing some augmentation of the private pile. Landlord-tenant law has been altered considerably and title insurance has moved apace to become the dominant method of title assurance. All of these developments have deep roots in the earlier law, however, and many of the changes were foreshadowed by materials that appeared in the first edition.

Property rights still have a reputation for permanence that ignores the changing economic factors and social conditions which are reflected in the mirror of the law. Nonetheless, this undeserved reputation does reveal a modicum of truth: property law is a relatively stable platform in the shifting sands of modern American jurisprudence. The key word is *relative* because the materials of this Sixth Edition, as compared to the First, clearly disclose changing concepts and new approaches to old problems. We are not reprinting the prefaces to the older editions, but we are reproducing the Preface to the Fifth Edition because it states the assumptions which still underlie this new Edition.

Professors Cribbet and Johnson, who were present at the creation, have reached the age of "statutory senility" although, for both, retirement has been more "official" than "real." They are now joined in this Sixth Edition by Professor Findley of the University of Illinois and Professor Smith of the University of Texas. It is our collective hope to continue this collection of materials well into the twenty-first century. Perhaps the Twelfth Edition will reflect even greater changes than the first six. In any case, relying on the changing Rule Against Perpetuities, we shall just have to wait and see!

PREFACE TO THE SIXTH EDITION

In this edition, Professor Cribbet assumed primary responsibility for Chapters 1–5 and 12–15; Professor Johnson for Chapters 6–11, 18–22 and Section 2D of Chapter 17; Professor Findley for Chapters 23–26; and Professor Smith for Chapters 16–17, except Section 2D of Chapter 17.

JOHN E. CRIBBETT
CORWIN W. JOHNSON,
ROGER W. FINDLEY
ERNEST E. SMITH

March, 1990

PREFACE TO THE FIFTH EDITION

Any book published in 1984 has a kind of historic significance. After all, we have now arrived at George Orwell's dour vision of the future and the world is not in *quite* as bad shape as he predicted. Private property still exists, although the historic fee simple absolute is much diminished, and Americans, at least, are still free to criticize its perceived evils and develop plans to make private and public property more amenable to the needs of the consumer of land and other forms of wealth, subsumed under the rubric "property." For the editors of this casebook, the Fifth Edition is also an historic event. We, along with our late colleague, Professor William Fritz, began work on the First Edition well over a quarter of a century ago. We were all relative neophytes then, daring to publish property materials in competition with the established scholars who had dominated the property field for decades. How quickly the scene changes; now it is our turn to present the latest edition of our view of the law of property to a younger audience and in competition with the scholars of the "new property."

In the Fifth Edition, we have largely retained the organization and scope of the Fourth. All of the material has been updated to cover the developments of the intervening six years, many new cases and materials have been added, some of the old have been deleted, errors have been corrected, suggestions made by professors and students who have used the coursebook over the years have been considered and, frequently, incorporated in the new edition. Some *limited* coverage has been added, such as materials on the role of the real estate broker, condominiums, time-share agreements, rent control, discrimination against children in housing, group homes, preservation of agricultural land, public trust, and deregulation of land use. The material on water is entirely new. Additional references have been made, throughout the book, to relevant economic analysis.

The Fifth Edition reflects our continuing belief in the importance of the "big picture" for the basic, first-year course in property. As we stated in the Preface to the Fourth Edition, "this course should provide the fundamentals of property and furnish a foundation on which specialized courses can build in the second and third years of law study. Legal education remains in a state of ferment, with experimentation a prime ingredient in curriculum planning. We believe, however, that a sound program of study should be anchored to a condensed core of basic material which will enable the student to wend his or her way through the specialized maze which modern law has become. Property, as an institution, is one key element in this basic core. These materials are consistent with that concept of legal education and, if fully mastered by the student, should be sufficient to provide the insights required of all lawyers, whether or not they ultimately practice in the property field. At the same time, they should furnish an understanding of the working tools of the property specialist."

The materials are so organized that the teacher can restructure the presentation to suit his or her own preferred approach to the course or can find ample coverage to carve out sub-courses if that best fits the needs of a given law school's curriculum.

Above all, despite the wealth of material that has accumulated during the course of five editions, this book remains essentially a teaching tool. Every case, new and old, has been selected with the classroom in mind. The materials are designed not only to present relevant doctrine and principles, both ancient and modern, but to raise issues and prod the student to puzzle about the past, present *and future* of one of society's most important institutions. We love (that is not too strong a word) the law of property, with all of its faults, and we see it as the ideal vehicle for instruction in the first year of law school. We want the teacher and the taught to love it as well and not view it as the dull, desiccated subject some used to think it to be. If these cases and materials of the Fifth Edition achieve that objective, then we are content with our labors over the intervening years since 1960 when the First Edition appeared. It *is* 1984, but the present and future are brighter than in 1066, when William the Bastard crossed the English Channel and laid the foundation for the Anglo-American law of property!

JOHN E. CRIBBET
CORWIN W. JOHNSON

May, 1984

ACKNOWLEDGMENTS

Permission to reprint portions of the following materials is gratefully acknowledged:

American Law Institute, Restatement of Property (1944);

American Law Institute, Restatement (Second) of Torts (1979);

American Law Institute, The Model Land Development Code (1976);

American Law of Property (A.J. Casner ed. 1952), published by Little, Brown & Co.;

Ardrey, The Territorial Imperative (1966), published by Atheneum Publishers (Alfred A. Knopf, Jr.);

Ausness, Water Rights Legislation in the East: A Program for Reform, 24 Wm. & Mary L.Rev. 547 (1983);

Basye, Clearing Land Titles (2d ed. 1970), published by West Publishing Co.;

Berger, Unification of the Law of Servitudes, 55 S.Cal.L.Rev. 1339 (1982);

Brown on Personal Property (3d ed. W. Raushenbush 1975), published by Callaghan & Co.;

Brown & Dauer, Planning by Lawyers (1978), published by The Foundation Press, Inc.;

Burby, Real Property (3d ed. 1965) published by West Publishing Co.;

Chafee & Re, Cases and Materials on Equity (4th ed. 1958), published by The Foundation Press, Inc.;

Cheshire, The Modern Law of Real Property (6th ed. 1949), published by Butterworths;

Cohen, Dialogue on Private Property, 9 Rut.L.Rev. 357 (1954);

Cohen, Property and Sovereignty, 13 Corn.L.Q. 8 (1927);

Cribbet and Johnson, Principles of the Law of Property (3d ed. 1989), published by The Foundation Press, Inc.;

Cross, The Record "Chain of Title" Hypocrisy, 57 Colum.L.Rev. 787 (1957);

Dunham, Statutory Reformation of Land Obligations, 55 S.Calif.L.Rev. 1345 (1982);

Ellickson, Alternatives to Zoning: Covenants, Nuisance Rules, and Fines as Land Use Controls, 40 U.Chi.L.Rev. 681 (1973);

Fitch, Abstracts and Titles to Real Property (1954), published by Callaghan & Co.;

Flick, Abstract and Title Practice (2d ed. 1958), published by West Publishing Co.;

Freedman, Crowding and Behavior (1975), published by The Viking Press, Inc.;

French, Toward a Modern Law of Servitudes: Reweaving the Ancient Strands, 55 S.Calif.L.Rev. 1261 (1982);

Freyfogle, Vagueness and The Rule of Law: Reconsidering Installment Land Contract Forfeitures, 1988 Duke L.J. 609;

Gunther, Inside Russia Today (1958), published by Harper & Brothers;

Johnson, Compensation for Invalid Land-Use Regulations, 15 Ga.L.Rev. 559 (1981);

Johnson, Purpose and Scope of Recording Statutes, 47 Iowa L.Rev. 237 (1962);

Kratovil, Real Estate Law (1969), published by Prentice-Hall, Inc.;

Lippman, The Method of Freedom (1934), published by The Macmillan Co.;

Lowie, Incorporeal Property in Primitive Society, 37 Yale L.J. 551 (1928);

McDougal, Municipal Land Policy and Control (1946), published by The Practising Law Institute;

Maggs, The Security of Individually-Owned Property Under Soviet Law, 1961 Duke L.J. 537;

Maley & Thuma, Legal Description of Land (1955), published by Chicago Title & Trust Co.;

Meyers, The Covenant of Habitability and the American Law Institute, 27 Stan.L.Rev. 879 (1975);

Nelson & Whitman, Real Estate Transfer, Finance, and Development (2d ed. 1981), published by West Publishing Co.;

Netherton, Control of Highway Access (1963), published by the University of Wisconsin Press;

Note, Imposing Tort Liability on Real Estate Brokers Selling Defective Housing, 99 Harv.L.Rev. 1861 (1986);

Note, Nonconforming Uses: A Rationale and an Approach, 102 U.Pa.L.Rev. 91 (1953);

Osborne, Secured Transactions (1967), published by West Publishing Co.;

Patton, Titles (2d ed. 1957), published by West Publishing Co.;

Posner, Economic Analysis of Law (1973), published by Little, Brown & Co.;

Pound, The Law of Property and Recent Juristic Thought, 25 A.B.A.J. 993 (1939);

Powell, The Law of Real Property (1977), published by Matthew Bender & Co.;

Reich, The New Property, 73 Yale L.J. 733 (1964);

Reichman, Toward a Unified Concept of Servitudes, 55 S.Calif.L.Rev. 1179 (1982);

Roberts, Title Insurance: State Regulation and the Public Perspective, 39 Ind.L.J. 1 (1962);

Seligman, Principles of Economics (1905), published by Longmans, Green & Co.;

Strum, Proposed Uniform Residential Landlord and Tenant Act: A Departure from Traditional Concepts, 8 Real Prop., Prob. & Trust J. 495 (1973);

Tiffany, Real Property (3d ed. 1939) (New Abr. Ed. 1940), published by Callaghan & Co.;

Vance, The Quest for Tenure in the United States, 33 Yale L.J. 248 (1924);

Ward, Illinois Law of Title Examination (2d ed. 1952), published by Burdette Smith Co.;

Warren, Cutting Off Claims of Ownership Under the Uniform Commercial Code, 30 U.Chi.L.Rev. 469 (1963);

Wenig, The Marital Property Act, 12 Prob. & Prop. 9 (1983);

Winokur, The Mixed Blessings of Promissory Servitudes: Toward Optimizing Economic Utility, Individual Liberty, and Personal Identity, 1989 Wisc.L.Rev. 1.

*

SUMMARY OF CONTENTS

	Page
PREFACE TO THE SIXTH EDITION	v
PREFACE TO THE FIFTH EDITION	vii
ACKNOWLEDGMENTS	ix
TABLE OF CASES	xx

PART ONE. PROPERTY AS AN INSTITUTION—AN OVERVIEW OF PROPERTY LAW

Chapter		
1.	What Is Property?	1
2.	Attributes of Property	32
3.	Objects and Classifications of Property	56
4.	Role of Property in Society	71
5.	The Practice of Property Law—What Do Lawyers Do?	88

PART TWO. THE ACQUISITION OF PROPERTY(HEREIN PRIMARILY OF PERSONAL PROPERTY)

6.	Finding	92
7.	Creation of Bailments	119
8.	Bona Fide Purchase	128
9.	Unauthorized Possession	139
10.	Improving Another's Property by Mistake (Accession)	157
11.	Donative Transfers	166

PART THREE. PRIVATE INTERESTS IN LAND

12.	A Brief Look at the Historical Development of Estates Doctrine	209
13.	Freehold Estates	221
14.	Future Interests	273
15.	Concurrent Ownership	322
16.	Non–Freehold Estates: Landlord and Tenant	426
17.	Interests in Land of Another and in Natural Resources Affecting Another's Land	580

PART FOUR. PUBLIC INTERESTS IN LAND (HEREIN PRIMARILY OF LAND USE)

18.	Introduction to the Traditional Land Use Controls	788
19.	Administration of Land Use Controls	820
20.	Regulatory Takings	877
21.	Land Use Planning—Or Exclusion of People?	934
22.	Deregulation?	973

PART FIVE. THE SALE OF LAND

Chapter	Page
23. The Real Estate Contract	980
24. The Deed	1141
25. The Recording System	1203
26. The Methods of Title Assurance	1268

PART SIX. A CONCLUDING NOTE [1434]

Index 1435

TABLE OF CONTENTS

	Page
Preface to the Sixth Edition	v
Preface to the Fifth Edition	vii
Acknowledgments	ix
Table of Cases	xx

PART ONE. PROPERTY AS AN INSTITUTION—AN OVERVIEW OF PROPERTY LAW

Chapter 1. What Is Property? 1

Chapter 2. Attributes of Property 32

Chapter 3. Objects and Classifications of Property 56

Chapter 4. Role of Property in Society 71

Chapter 5. The Practice of Property Law—What Do Lawyers Do? 88

PART TWO. THE ACQUISITION OF PROPERTY (HEREIN PRIMARILY OF PERSONAL PROPERTY)

Chapter 6. Finding 92

Chapter 7. Creation of Bailments 119

Chapter 8. Bona Fide Purchase 128

Chapter 9. Unauthorized Possession 139

Section

1. Possession Deemed Ownership as to Third Persons 139
2. Acquisition of Limitation Title by Adverse Possession 142

Chapter 10. Improving Another's Property by Mistake (Accession) 157

Chapter 11. Donative Transfers 166

PART THREE. PRIVATE INTERESTS IN LAND

Chapter 12. A Brief Look at the Historical Development of Estates Doctrine 209

Chapter 13. Freehold Estates 221

Section

1. The Fee Simple Absolute and The Life Estate 224
   - A. Testate And Intestate Succession At Common Law And Under Early English Statutes 228
   - B. Intestate Succession Under A Modern Statute 231

Section Page
1. The Fee Simple Absolute and The Life Estate—Continued
C. Rules Of The Civil Law For Determining Inheritance By Collaterals 235
D. Problems 235
2. Defeasible Estates 248
3. The Fee Simple Conditional and the Fee Tail 268

Chapter 14. Future Interests 273
Section
1. Vested and Contingent Remainders 273
2. The Rule in Shelley's Case 281
3. The Doctrine of Worthier Title 285
4. Executory Interests (Herein of the Statute of Uses and its Modern Significance) 291

Chapter 15. Concurrent Ownership 322
Section
1. Introduction to Concurrent Ownership 322
2. Marital Estates 332
A. The Husband's Interest In The Wife's Property 332
B. The Wife's Interest In The Husband's Property 334
C. Homestead Rights 336
D. Community Property 336
E. The Marital Property Act 338
3. General Aspects of Concurrent Ownership 342
4. Creation and Attributes of Concurrent Estates 371
5. Condominiums and Time–Share Arrangements 415

Chapter 16. Non–Freehold Estates: Landlord and Tenant 426
Section
1. Nature and Creation of Leasehold Estates 427
2. Discrimination in Selection of Tenants 436
3. Tenant's Right to Possession 446
4. Condition of the Premises 456
A. Suitability For Tenant's Use 456
(1) Habitability 457
(2) Suitability for Intended Commercial Use 477
B. Injuries To Persons Or Property 481
5. Provisions Governing Rent, Duration and Use 495
A. Rent 495
B. Duration 503
(1) The Holdover Tenant 503
(2) Right to Extended Occupancy of Certain Housing 508
C. Permissible Uses by Tenant 532
6. Lessor's Remedies Against Defaulting Tenant 540
A. Tenant's Default on Rental Obligations 540
B. Eviction 545
C. Abandonment by Tenant 551
D. Security Against Tenant Defaults 559
7. Transfers 564

Page

Chapter 17. Interests in Land of Another and in Natural Resources Affecting Another's Land 580

Section

1. Interests Created by Volition, Implication and Prescription 580
   A. Easements, Profits à Prendre And Licenses 580
      (1) Express Creation 582
      (2) Creation By Implication 601
      (3) Creation by Prescription 613
      (4) Scope and Transferability 630
      (5) Termination 644
   B. Real Covenants And Equitable Servitudes 648
      (1) The Traditional Elements of Real Covenants 649
      (2) Equitable Servitudes 667
      (3) Constitutional and Public Policy Limitations on Covenants and Servitudes 690
      (4) Construction, Administration and Termination 699
   C. Reform 713
2. Non-Volitional ("Natural") Interests 716
   A. Nuisance Doctrines 716
   B. Support Of Land 733
   C. Drainage 740
   D. Interests In Water 747
      (1) Water in Watercourses 748
      (2) Groundwater 758
   E. Interests In Airspace, Air, Sunlight and Clouds 764

PART FOUR. PUBLIC INTERESTS IN LAND (HEREIN PRIMARILY OF LAND USE)

Chapter 18. Introduction to the Traditional Land Use Controls 788

Section

1. Zoning 788
2. Regulation of the Subdivision of Land 801
3. Reservation of Land for Public Acquisition (Official Maps) 805
4. Public Ownership 813

Chapter 19. Administration of Land Use Controls 820

Section

1. Nonconforming Uses 820
2. The Comprehensive Plan, Rezoning and Judicial Review 829
3. Zoning Variances and Special Exceptions 848
4. Contract Zoning, Floating Zones and Planned Unit Developments 853
5. Zoning by Electorate 870

Chapter 20. Regulatory Takings 877

Chapter 21. Land Use Planning—Or Exclusion of People? 934

Section

1. Racial Discrimination 934

Section | Page
2. The Single-Family Neighborhood 943
3. Housing the Non-Affluent in the Suburbs 958
4. Size and Rate of Growth of Local Communities 965

Chapter 22. Deregulation? 973

PART FIVE. THE SALE OF LAND

Chapter 23. The Real Estate Contract 980

Section

1. The Oral Contract 981
   A. The Doctrines Of Part Performance and Equitable Estoppel 982
   B. The Written Memorandum 1001
   C. Parol Modification and Rescission 1016
2. The Standard Written Contract 1021
3. Construction and Performance 1021
   A. Time For Performance 1022
   B. Financing Arrangements—Mortgages and Installment Land Contracts 1032
   C. Merchantable Title 1059
   D. Tender 1071
   E. Assignment 1076
   F. Remedies For Breach Of Contract 1081
4. Status of Vendor and Purchaser—Equitable Conversion 1091
   A. General Nature Of the Vendor–Purchaser Relationship 1091
   B. Devolution On Death 1097
   C. Risk Of Loss 1107
5. The Role of the Real Estate Broker 1122

Chapter 24. The Deed 1141

Section

1. Conveyancing at Common Law and Under the Statute of Uses 1141
2. The Modern Deed—Types and Elements 1149
3. Execution of the Deed 1163
4. Subject Matter Conveyed 1177

Chapter 25. The Recording System 1203

Section

1. General Operation of the System 1211
2. Persons Protected by the System 1234
3. The Chain of Title 1260

Chapter 26. The Methods of Title Assurance 1268

Section

1. Implied Covenants of Habitability and Some Related Doctrines 1268
2. Covenants for Title and After–Acquired Title (Estoppel by Deed) 1305
3. Examination of the Records or of an Abstract of Title 1337

Section | Page
4. Title Registration (Torrens System)—an Alternative to the Recording System? 1355
5. Title Insurance 1367
6. Statutes of Limitation and Related Legislation as Aids to Title Assurance 1392

PART SIX. A CONCLUDING NOTE [1434]

Index 1435

TABLE OF CASES

Principal cases are in italic type. Non-principal cases are in roman type. References are to Pages.

A. B. C. Auto Parts, Inc. v. Moran, 1015
Abo Petroleum Corp. v. Amstutz, 277, 280, 310
Abrahamson v. Sundman, 1365
Abstract Corp. v. Fernandez Co., 1354
Adamson v. Brockbank, 603
Addesso v. Shemtob, 1067
Adjudication of the Water Rights of Upper Guadalupe Segment of Guadalupe River Basin, In re, 758
A. D. Juilliard & Co. v. American Woolen Co., 570
Adrian v. Rabinowitz, 446
Aero Spark Plug Co. v. B. G. Corp., 284
Aggregate Supply Co. v. Sewell, 647
Agricultural Labor Relations Bd. v. Superior Court of Tulare County, 19
Ailes v. Decatur County Area Planning Com'n, 825
Akin v. Business Title Corp., 1176
Albany, City of v. State, 1200
Alevizos v. Metropolitan Air. Com'n of Mpls. & St. P., 5
Alexander v. Andrews, 1239
Alexander v. United States Dept. of Housing and Urban Development, 473
Allen v. Kingdon, 1018
Allingham v. City of Seattle, 932
Allred v. Biegel, 115
Alpine Const. Corp. v. Fenton, 712
Ambler Realty Co. v. Village of Euclid, Ohio, 796
Amoco Prod. Co. v. Sims, 603
Ampco Auto Parks, Inc. v. Williams, 124
Anaheim Co. v. Holcombe, 1036
Anaheim Union Water Co. v. Fuller, 754
Anderson v. Gouldberg, 139
Andrews v. Andrews, 348
Anson v. Murphy, 326
Anthony v. Brea Glenbrook Club, 678
A–1 Garage v. Lange Inv. Co., 564
Application of (see name of party)
Arbenz v. Exley, Watkins & Co., 435
Arko Enterprises, Inc. v. Wood, 1121
Arlington Heights, Village of v. Metropolitan Housing Development Corp., 934
Armory v. Delamirie, 100, 102
Armstrong v. Francis Corp., 740
Arnel Development Co. v. City of Costa Mesa, 876
Aronsohn v. Mandara, 1277
Arthur Treacher's Fish & Chips of Fairfax, Inc. v. Chillum Terrace Ltd. Partnership, 430
Arvai v. Shaw, 1278
Associated Home Builders of Greater Eastbay, Inc. v. City of Livermore, 965
Aszmus v. Nelson, 590, 591
Attorney-General of the Duchy of Lancaster v. G.E. Overton (Farms) Ltd., 115
Austin, City of v. Teague, 932
Avco Community Developers, Inc. v. South Coast Regional Commission, 829

Bachewicz v. American Nat. Bank and Trust Co. of Chicago, 1087
Backhausen v. Mayer, 603
Bahler v. Doenges, 408
Baird v. Moore, 351
Baker v. City of Milwaukie, 835
Baker v. Ore–Ida Foods, Inc., 763
Baker v. Planning Bd. of Framingham, 747
Bakken v. Price, 1281
Barker v. Francis, 1009
Bartholomew v. Staheli, 637
Barton v. Mitchell Co., 456
Bartos v. Czerwinski, 1063, 1067
Baseball Pub. Co. v. Bruton, 593
Basket v. Hassell, 183
Bass v. Boetel & Co., 550
Batten v. United States, 770
Beall v. Beall, 407
Beaullieu v. Atlanta Title & Trust Co., 1387
Becker v. IRM Corp., 486
Bell v. Tsintolas Realty Co., 473
Bell v. Vaughn, 430
Bellamy v. Board of Appeals of City of Rochester, 852
Belle Terre, Village of v. Boraas, 943
Bennett v. Moring, 1015
Benser v. Johnson, 493
Bentel v. Bannock County, 637
Bergesen v. Clauss, 1410
Berman v. Parker, 797
Bernard v. Nantucket Boys' Club, Inc., 1200
Bernards v. Link, 592
Bessemer v. Gersten, 698
Bishop v. Beecher, 1051
Blackett v. Olanoff, 453
Blakeney v. Home Owners' Loan Corporation, 1175
Bleckley v. Langston, 1107
Boehmer v. Big Rock Creek Irr. Dist., 754
Boomer v. Atlantic Cement Co., 721
Boomer v. Atlantic Cement Co., Inc., 726
Borland's Lessee v. Marshall, 333

Boston Housing Authority v. Hemingway, 473
Boswell v. Lyon, 1080
Boyd v. Lefrak Organization, 446
Boyle v. D-X Sunray Oil Co., 1400
Bradler v. Craig, 1300
Bradley v. Fox, 414
Brant v. Hargrove, 397
Braswell v. Braswell, 285
Brewer v. Peatross, 1321
Brewster v. Hines, 1311
Briarcliffe West Townhouse Owners Ass'n v. Wiseman Const. Co., 1286
Bridges v. Hawkesworth, 101, 104
Bringle v. Board of Supervisors of County of Orange, 852
Bromley v. Lambert and Son, Inc., 611
Brooks v. Black, 1325
Brown v. Lober, 1306
Brown v. Southall Realty Co., 457
Brown v. Voss, 633
Brown's Tie & Lumber Co. v. Chicago Title Co. of Idaho, 1383
Bruce Farms, Inc. v. Coupe, 1275
Brunke v. Pharo, 1321
Builders Service Corp., Inc. v. Planning & Zoning Com'n of Town of East Hampton, 917, 964
Burns v. McCormick, 990
Butts v. Atlanta Federal Sav. & Loan Ass'n, 1301
Buzard, State ex rel. Scott v., 106
Bybee v. Hageman, 1184

Caccamo v. Banning, 270
Cameron, State v., 797
Canteen Corp. v. Republic of Texas Properties, Inc., 534
Capitol Federal Sav. and Loan Ass'n v. Smith, 310
Capper v. Poulsen, 1335
Carlsen v. Zane, 1123
Carpenter v. Donohoe, 1275
Carrion v. Singley, 739
Carver v. Gilbert, 346
Cary, State ex rel. v. Cochran, 757
Casper, City of v. J. M. Carey & Bros., 265
Cauble v. Hanson, 565
Causby, United States v., 764
Center Management Corp. v. Bowman, 493
Centex Homes Corp. v. Boag, 416, 1081
Central Bank of Little Rock v. Downtain, 1256
Cessna v. Hulce, 1259
Chaffin v. Ramsey, 1088
Chandler v. Kountze, 327
Chaney v. Haeder, 1326
Chapin v. Freeland, 143
Chaplin v. Sanders, 1400
Charlotte Park & Recreation Commission v. Barringer, 314
Charping v. J.P. Scurry & Co., Inc., 658
Chaudoir v. Witt, 205
Cheney v. Jemmett, 1079
Cheney v. Village 2 at New Hope, Inc., 859
Cherin v. R. & C. Company, 1071
Chicago Bar Association v. Quinlan and Tyson, Inc., 214 N.E.2d 771, p. 1131
Chicago Bar Ass'n v. Quinlan & Tyson, Inc., 203 N.E.2d 131, p. 1131
Childs v. Warner Bros. Southern Theatres, 576
Chillemi v. Chillemi, 206, 1169
Chun v. Park, 1354
City and County of (see name of city)
City of (see name of city)
Clapp v. Tower, 1102
Clark v. Covington, 350
Clarke v. Clarke, 350
Clay v. Landreth, 1091
Clayton v. Le Roy, 137
Cleburne, Tex., City of v. Cleburne Living Center, 951
Clevenger v. Moore, 1170
Coastal Industrial Water Auth. v. York, 95
Cochran v. Keeton, 1275
Cochran, State ex rel. Cary v., 757
Coffin v. Left Hand Ditch Co., 754, 756
Cohen v. Kranz, 1071
Cohn, In re, 167
Cole v. Hills, 515
Cole v. Lynn, 515
Cole v. Steinlauf, 224, 226
Coleman v. Dillman, 993
Collard v. Incorporated Village of Flower Hill, 853
College Block v. Atlantic Richfield Co., 540
Collins v. Binkley, 1156
Collins v. Dye, 207
Committee of Protesting Cit. v. Val Vue Sewer Dist., 1096
Commonwealth Building Corporation v. Hirschfield, 503
Connor v. Great Western Sav. & Loan Ass'n, 1287
Cook v. University Plaza, 427
Coombs v. Ouzounian, 988
Coons v. First Nat. Bank, 126
Cooper v. Casco Mercantile Trust Co., 559
Copart Industries, Inc. v. Consolidated Edison Co. of New York, Inc., 726
Cornell v. Heirs of Walik, 325
Corrado v. Montuori, 1007
Corrigan v. City of Scottsdale, 933
Cottom v. Kennedy, 1006
Cottrell v. Nurnberger, 994
Country Squire Homeowners Ass'n v. Crest Hill Development Corp., 1286
Cowell v. Armstrong, 752
Cowen v. Pressprich, 124
Cowling v. Colligan, 706
Crenshaw v. Williams, 1087
Cultum v. Heritage House Realtors, Inc., 1132
Current Creek Irr. Co. v. Andrews, 763

Danielson v. Roberts, 106, 113
Darby v. Johnson, 994
Dartnell v. Bidwell, 617
Daughters v. Preston, 1233

Davidow v. Inwood North Professional Group–Phase I, 477
Davis v. Rental Associates, Inc., 473
Davis v. Skipper, 259
Davis v. Smith, 1322
Davis v. Ward, 1239
Dawson Industries, Inc. v. Godley Const. Co., Inc., 1275
Delay v. Truitt, 1259
Dengler v. Fowler, 1256
Dennen v. Searle, 227
Dennis v. Northwestern National Bank, 113
Department of Public Works and Bldgs. v. Halls, 1355
D'Ercole v. D'Ercole, 401, 407
Devereux Foundation, Application of, 848
Diamond Oaks Terrace Apartments v. Spraggins, 564
Dixieland Realty Co. v. Wysor, 1335
Dixon v. Salvation Army, 1112
Doctorman v. Schroeder, 1026
Doherty v. Dolan, 1087
Donvito v. Criswell, 407
Downtown Realty, Inc. v. 509 Tremont Bldg., Inc., 456
Drake v. Claar, 1403
Druid Homes, Inc. v. Cooper, 1275
Dryden v. Bell, 1275
Drye v. Eagle Rock Ranch, Inc., 612
Dubin Paper Co. v. Insurance Co. of North America, 1121
Dudzick v. Lewis, 539
Dugan v. Jones, 1090
Dulin v. Williams, 1230
Dunbar, City of, State ex rel. Wells v., 709
Duncan v. Vassaur, 411
Durant v. Hamrick, 327
Durant v. Town of Dunbarton, 802
Durfee v. Jones, 107
Durst v. Daugherty, 1239
Dutcher v. Owens, 422
Dwyer v. Skyline Apartments, Inc., 487
Dykes v. City of Houston, 604

Eade v. Brownlee, 1096
Eads v. Brazelton, 97
Eagle Enterprises, Inc. v. Gross, 665
Earle v. Fiske, 1218
Eastlake, City of v. Forest City Enterprises, Inc., 870
Easton v. Montgomery, 1062
Eastwood v. Shedd, 1234
Ebbe v. Senior Estates Golf and Country Club, 678
Ebersold v. Wise, 1051
Eddington v. Turner, 1104
Edgerton v. Peckham, 1030
Edmonds v. Ronella, 107
Edwards v. Habib, 545
Edwards v. Sims, 60
Edwards v. Stewart Title & Trust of Phoenix, Inc., 1177
Egbert v. Duck, 1239
Eggers v. Busch, 1062
Ellenborough Park, In re, 612
Elliott v. Joseph, 452
Elwes v. Briggs Gas Company, 115
Erickson v. Sinykin, 106, 113
Erickson v. Wahlheim, 1336
Escher v. Bender, 1067
Eschete v. City of New Orleans, 747
Estate of (see name of party)
Euclid, Ohio, Village of v. Ambler Realty Co., 788
Evans v. Abney, 314
Evans v. Giles, 284
Evans v. J. Stiles, Inc., 1276
Evans v. Merriweather, 748
Ex parte (see name of party)

Fahmie v. Wulster, 1321
Failoni v. Chicago and North Western Railway Co., 1403
Fairclaw v. Forrest, 330
Fasano v. Board of County Com'rs of Washington County, 829
Father Flanagan's Boys' Home v. Graybill, 1104
Feiges v. Racine Dry Goods Co., 507
Ferguson v. Ray, 114
Ferrell v. Stinson, 199
Fifth Avenue Corp. v. Washington County, By and Through Bd. of County Com'rs, 847
Filbert v. Dechert, 752
Fine v. Scheinhaus, 329
Finke v. Woodard, 1276
Finn v. Williams, 601
First American Federal Sav. and Loan Ass'n v. Royall, 1321
First American Title Ins. Co., Inc. v. First Title Service Co. of the Florida Keys Inc., 1348, 1386
First English Evangelical Lutheran Church of Glendale v. County of Los Angeles, Cal., 919
First Nat. Bank of Oregon v. Townsend, 1154
First Sec. Bank of Idaho, Nat. Ass'n v. Rogers, 1096
Flack v. Sarnosa Oil Corporation, 507
Flamingo Terrace Mobile Home Park, Inc. v. Scott, 529
Fleckenstein v. Faccio, 1006
Flexter v. Woomer, 1217
Florida Land Co. v. City of Winter Springs, 876
Flynn v. City of Cambridge, 529
Follette v. Pacific Light & Power Corporation, 1365
Ford v. Guarantee Abstract & Title Co., Inc., 1354
Forrer v. Sather, 1326
Foss v. Berlin, 1131
Foster v. Reiss, 177
Fox, State ex rel. Haman for Kootenai County v., 629
Framingham Clinic, Inc. v. Board of Selectmen of Southborough, 798

Frank v. Jansen, 1089
Frankland v. City of Lake Oswego, 835, 867
Fred F. French Investing Co., Inc. v. City of New York, 899
French v. French, 1144
Fresh Pond Shopping Center, Inc., v. Acheson Callahan, 899
Fresh Pond Shopping Center, Inc., v. Rent Control Board of Cambridge, 899
Frickel v. Sunnyside Enterprises, Inc., 1276
Friendswood Development Co. v. Smith–Southwest Industries, Inc., 740
Fuller v. Fuller, 392
Fuston v. National Mut. Ins. Co., 401

Gabel v. Drewrys Limited, U.S.A., Inc., 1240
Gaito v. Auman, 1276, 1277
Galbraith v. Wood, 564
Gallagher v. Bell, 649
Ganz v. Clark, 452
Garcia v. Siffrin Residential Ass'n, 958
Gardiner v. William S. Butler & Co., 426
Gardner v. Padro, 1036
Garner v. Stubblefield, 988
Garrett v. City of Oklahoma City, 801
GDJS Corp. v. 917 Properties, Inc., 1025
Gee v. CBS, Inc., 155
Georgia Outdoor Advertising, Inc. v. City of Waynesville, 826
Gerruth Realty Co. v. Pire, 1032
Giannini v. First Nat. Bank of Des Plaines, 421
Gill v. Johnson, 1366
Gillespie v. Dew, 106
Gion v. City of Santa Cruz, 629
Glennon Heights, Inc. v. Central Bank & Trust, 958
Goergen v. Maar, 351
Goodard v. Winchell, 92
Goren v. Royal Investments Inc., 1014
Gorieb v. Fox, 810
Gorski v. Troy, 446
Grainger v. Hamilton, 227
Granite Properties Ltd. Partnership v. Manns, 604
Grayson v. Holloway, 1156
Green v. Chaffee Ditch Co., 758
Green v. Hayward, 839
Greenbrier–Cloverdale Homeowners Ass'n v. Baca, 701
Green Point Sav. Bank v. Litas Investing Co., Inc., 1067
Gregerson v. Jensen, 1015
Gregor v. City of Fairbanks, 1225
Griffen, Matter of Estate of, 227
Griggs v. Allegheny County, Pa., 770
Grimes v. Virginia Elec. & Power Co., 644
Groves v. First Nat. Bank of Valparaiso, 1326
Gruen v. Gruen, 174
Gryb v. Benson, 1089
Guel v. Bullock, 1008
Guzman v. McDonald, 564
G–W–L, Inc. v. Robichaux, 1282

Hackett v. Richards, 558
Hagenbuch v. Chapin, 1200
Hagensick v. Castor, 1335
Halpert v. Rosenthal, 1277
Hamaker v. Blanchard, 106
Haman for Kootenai County, State ex rel. v. Fox, 629
Hammonds v. Central Kentucky Natural Gas Co., 96
Handler v. Horns, 534
Handzel v. Bassi, 1076
Haner v. Bruce, 1226
Hanlon v. Hayes, 1014
Hannah v. Peel, 105
Hannum v. Bella Vista Village Property Owners Ass'n, 633
Hardy v. Burroughs, 163, 165
Harms v. Sprague, 398
Harris v. Woodard, 1186
Harris Trust and Sav. Bank v. Beach, 290
Harvest Queen Mill & Elevator Co. v. Sanders, 592
Hawaii Housing Authority v. Midkiff, 813
Hawk v. Rice, 593
Hawkinson v. Johnston, 559
Hawthorne v. Hawthorne, 398
Hay v. Bruno, 629
Hay, State ex rel. Thornton v., 621
Hayes v. Hayes, 1148
Hays v. Pumphrey, 1239
Haywood v. Briggs, 539
Heath v. Parker, 702
Hedding v. Schauble, 1162
Heifner v. Bradford, 1432
Herlihy v. Dunbar Builders Corp., 1278, 1285
Hermitage Co. v. Levine, 558
Hero Lands Company v. United States, 770
Herold v. Hughes and Hamilton Gas Corporation, 636
Hertel v. Woodard, 1008
Heyert v. Orange & Rockland Utilities, Inc., 636
Hickam v. Colorado Real Estate Com'n, 1124
Hickey v. Green, 995
Hickey v. Illinois Cent. R. Co., 1420
Highway Holding Co. v. Yara Engineering Corp., 604
Hill v. Bowen, 1148
Hill v. Jones, 1286
Hills Development Co. v. Bernards Tp. in Somerset County, 964
Hill's Estate, Matter of, 1101
Hillstrom v. Gosnay, 1007
Hi–Lo Oil Co., Inc. v. McCollum, 685
Hinchliffe v. Fischer, 1156
Hochard v. Deiter, 1031
Hocking v. Title Insurance & Trust Co., 1391
Hoffman v. Schroeder, 1366
Holden v. Garrett, 1249
Holland v. Sutherland, 1399
Honolulu, City and County of v. Bennett, 1409

Hopkins v. Hartman, 1276
Horn v. Wright, 1070
Houston, City of v. Emmanuel United Pentecostal Church, Inc., 977
Howard v. Kunto, 1393
Hudgens v. N. L. R. B., 19
Humber v. Morton, 1280
Humble Oil and Refining Company v. West, 97, 160
Hummelman v. Mounts, 1162
Huntington Branch, N.A.A.C.P. v. Town of Huntington, 942
Huntington, N.Y., Town of v. N.A.A.C.P., 943
Hurd v. Curtis, 658
Hurley v. City of Niagara Falls, 117
Hurst v. Picture Theatres, Ltd., 599

Illinois v. City of Milwaukee, Wis., 733
Illinois Nat. Bank v. Chegin, 1063
Imperator Realty Co. v. Tull, 1019
Indiana Real Estate Ass'n, State ex rel. Indiana State Bar Ass'n v., 1124
Indiana State Bar Ass'n, State ex rel. v. Indiana Real Estate Ass'n, 1124
Indiana Toll Road Commission v. Jankovich, 771
In re (see name of party)
International Paper Co. v. Ouellette, 733
Inwood North Homeowners' Ass'n, Inc. v. Harris, 698
Irvmor Corporation v. Rodewald, 1007
Isle Royale Mining Co. v. Hertin, 161
ITT Indus. Credit Co. v. R.T.M. Development Co., Inc., 1169
ITT Rayonier, Inc. v. Bell, 1401

Jaber v. Miller, 565
Jackson v. Jackson, 207
Jackson v. O'Connell, 379
Jackson v. River Pines, Inc., 1278
Jackson v. Steinberg, 205 P.2d 562, p. 114
Jackson v. Steinberg, 200 P.2d 376, p. 114
Jackson ex dem. Gouch v. Wood, 1164
Javins v. First Nat. Realty Corp., 459
Jeminson v. Montgomery Real Estate & Co., 1301
Jennings v. Bradfield, 348
J. J. Newberry Co. v. Shannon, 1101
Johnson v. Amstutz, 280
Johnson v. City of Wheat Ridge, 263
Johnson v. Geer Real Estate Co., 1139
Johnson v. McIntosh, 71, 77
Johnson v. State, 663
Joiner v. Elrod, 1019
Joint Tribal Council of Passamaquoddy Tribe v. Morton, 77
Jones v. Alfred H. Mayer Co., 49, 54
Jones v. Conn., 754
Jones v. Green, 390
Jones v. Park Lane for Convalescents, 701
Jones, State v., 797
Jones v. Stone, 284
Joslin v. Pine River Development Corp., 699
Jozefowicz v. Leickem, 1169

Kaiman Realty, Inc. v. Carmichael, 1030
Kaiser Steel Corp. v. W. S. Ranch Co., 603
Kannavos v. Annino, 1096
Kappler, Matter of Estate of, 390
Karches v. City of Cincinnati, 932
Kartchner v. State Tax Comn., 1249
Kasten Const. Co. v. Maple Ridge Const. Co., 1022
Kaufman and Gold Construction Co. v. Planning & Zoning Com'n of City of Fairmont, 805
Keamo, Matter of, 1410
Kean v. Dench, 371
Keeble v. Hickeringill, 100
Keith v. El-Kareh, 350
Kendall v. Ernest Pestana, Inc., 579
Kennedy v. Classic Designs, Inc., 702
Kenney v. Parks, 207
Keron v. Cashman, 107
Keyes v. Guy Bailey Homes, Inc., 1277
Keystone Bituminous Coal Ass'n v. DeBenedictis, 900
Killam v. March, 1365
Kimball v. Houston Oil Co., 1259
Kimball Laundry Co. v. United States, 932
Kindred v. Boalbey, 1121
Kindred v. Crosby, 1256, 1259
King v. Anderson, 1325
King v. Wenger, 1009
Kirby Lumber Co. v. Temple Lumber Co., 362
Klamath Falls, City of v. Bell, 315
Klopstock, People v., 578
Knapp v. Simmons, 481
Kniebbe v. Wade, 207
Kohlbrecher v. Guettermann, 1007
Korn v. Campbell, 690
Kossler v. Palm Springs Developments, Ltd., 1031
Kost v. Foster, 273
Kramer v. Mobley, 1081, 1087
Kramp v. Showcase Builders, 1278
Kruse v. Conklin, 1260
Kunstsammlungen Zu Weimar v. Elicofon, 156
Kunzman v. Thorsen, 1079

Laba v. Carey, 1062
Lake Arrowhead Community Club, Inc. v. Looney, 710
Lake Bluff, Village of v. Dalitsch, 647
Lake Wauwanoka, Inc. v. Spain, 709
Lakewood, Ohio Congregation of Jehovah's Witnesses, Inc. v. City of Lakewood, Ohio, 797
Larkin v. Grendel's Den, Inc., 797
Lassiter v. Bliss, 701
Laura v. Christian, 346
Leach v. Gunnarson, 1313
Leavitt v. Blohm, 1070
Lebowitz v. Mingus, 993
Leeco Gas & Oil Co. v. Nueces County, 266
Lehmann v. Arnold, 1278
Lehmann v. Wallace, 613, 684
Leidig v. Hoopes, 1162

Leo Sheep Co. v. United States, 603
Levine v. Lafayette Bldg. Corporation, 1014
Lewicki v. Marszalkowski, 1336
Lewis v. Gollner, 679
Lewis v. Searles, 238
Libman v. Levenson, 1111
Lichtenstein v. Lichtenstein Building Corporation, 370
Licker v. Gluskin, 407
Lighthorse v. Clinefelter, 590
Lincoln Fireproof Warehouse Co. v. Greusel, 558
Lindsey v. Clark, 644
Lindsey v. Normet, 550
Lippman v. Sears Roebuck & Co., 544
Little v. Linder, 590
Local 1330, United Steel Workers of America v. United States Steel Corp., 69
Lohmeyer v. Bower, 1320
Lomarch Corp. v. Mayor and Common Council of City of Englewood, 810
London Corp., City of v. Appleyard, 106
London County Council v. Allen, 669, 672
Lone Star Gas Co. v. Murchison, 96
Long v. Long, 272
Loretto v. Teleprompter Manhattan CATV Corp., 898
Los Angeles, City of v. Gage, 820
Lovell v. Rowan Mut. Fire Ins. Co., 274 S.E.2d 170, p. 402
Lovell v. Rowan Mut. Fire Ins. Co., 264 S.E.2d 743, p. 400
L. Smirlock Realty Corp. v. Title Guarantee Co., 1383
Lucas v. Brown, 1411
Luette v. Bank of Italy Nat. Trust & Savings Ass'n, 1068
Lugar v. Edmondson Oil Co., Inc., 559
Lunt v. Kitchens, 613
Lydick v. Tate, 285
Lykins v. Westinghouse Elec., 733, 736
Lynbrook Gardens v. Ullmann, 1067

Madrid v. Spears, 1327
Mahoney Grease Service, Inc. v. City of Joliet, 859
Mahrenholz v. County Bd. of School Trustees of Lawrence County, 254
Main v. Pratt, 1170
Maine Sav. Bank v. Bridges, 414
Malken v. Hemming Bros, 1019
Mallin v. Good, 1281
Malloy v. Boettcher, 591
Mancini v. Gorick, 1286
Manders, State ex rel. Miller v., 805
Mangold v. Barlow, 1226
Mann v. Bradley, 408
Manning v. New England Mut. Life Ins. Co., 1412
Marina Point, Ltd. v. Wolfson, 436
Marlowe Inv. Corp. v. Radmall, 1070
Marrone v. Washington Jockey Club of District of Columbia, 598
Martin v. City of Seattle, 765 P.2d 257, p. 263
Martin v. City of Seattle, 728 P.2d 1091, p. *259*
Martin v. Port of Seattle, 770
Martin v. Seigel, 1008
Martineau v. Gresser, 1131
Martinez v. Steinbaum, 564
Maryland Bank & Trust Co., United States v., 1302
Maser v. Lind, 1277
Masid v. First State Bank, 620
Masterson v. International & G. N. Ry. Co., 142
Mathers v. Texaco, Inc., 764
Matter of (see name of party)
Maxton Builders, Inc. v. Lo Galbo, 1088
Mayer v. Sumergrade, 1281
McAllister v. Stoeco Homes, Inc., 1277
McAvoy v. Medina, 108
McCord v. Big Bros. Movement, 752
McCree v. Jones, 1410
McCutcheon v. United Homes Corporation, 494
McDaniel v. Silvernail, 1008
McKenzie v. Carte, 533
McKeon v. Brammer, 648
McLain v. Real Estate Bd. of New Orleans, Inc., 1123
McLane v. Russell, 382
McLaurin v. McLaurin, 227
McMillan v. Ingolia, 1015
McMillan v. Iserman, 691
Melms v. Pabst Brewing Co., 248
Mercantile–Safe Deposit and Trust Co. v. Mayor and City Council of Baltimore, 658, 710
Mercer v. Wayman, 1406
Merchandising Corp. v. Marine Nat. Exchange Bank Bank, 1320
Messersmith v. Smith, 1216
Metromedia, Inc. v. City of San Diego, 797
Metropolitan Housing Development Corp. v. Village of Arlington Heights, 942
Metro Realty v. El Dorado County, 812
Meyers v. Meyers, 182
Michaels, In re Estate of, 187
Michael's Estate, In re, 342
Michalski v. Michalski, 363
Midland Val. R. Co. v. Arrow Indus. Mfg. Co., 591
Miles v. Shauntee, 472
Miller v. Cannon Hill Estates, Limited, 1275
Miller v. City of Beaver Falls, 810
Miller v. Craig, 1176
Miller v. Green, 1256
Miller v. Letzerich, 746
Miller v. Long Family Partnership, 1025
Miller v. Lutheran Conference & Camp Ass'n, 638
Miller v. Riegler, 371
Miller, State ex rel. v. Manders, 805
Milligan v. Milligan, 1170
Milwaukee, City of v. Illinois and Michigan, 733

Minton v. Richards Group of Chicago Through Mach, 1279
Miracle Construction Company v. Miller, 1186
Mitchell v. Castellaw, 582, 611
Mitchell v. W. T. Grant Co., 559
Mobil Oil Credit Corp. v. DST Realty, Inc., 481
Mohr v. Midas Realty Corp., 782
Monaco v. Levy, 1014
Montanaro v. Pandolfini, 1014
Montoya v. New Mexico Human Services Dept., Income Support Div., 1148
Moody v. White, 629
Moore v. City of East Cleveland, Ohio, 946
Moore v. Megginson, 703
Moore v. Phillips, 244
Morgan v. Haley, 1311
Morgan v. Malleson, 196
Morgan and Bros. Manhattan Storage Co., Inc. v. McGuire, 118
Morris v. Flores, 1090
Morris v. Wicks, 1239
Morse v. Aldrich, 658
Morse v. San Luis Obispo County, 771
Mortensen v. Lingo, 1223
Mosser v. Dolsay, 328
Mounce v. Coleman, 1186
Mountain States Telephone and Tel. Co. v. Kelton, 1211
Moynihan Associates, Inc. v. Hanisch, 163
Mugaas v. Smith, 1220

Nectow v. City of Cambridge, 277 U.S. 183, p. *798*
Nectow v. City of Cambridge, 157 N.E. 618, p. 800
Nelson v. American Telephone & Telegraph Co., 598
Nelson v. Hughes, 1260
Neponsit Property Owners' Ass'n v. Emigrant Industrial Sav. Bank, 659
Neuberger v. City of Portland, 607 P.2d 722, p. 835
Neuberger v. City of Portland, 603 P.2d 771, p. 834
Newell v. National Bank of Norwich, 183
New Jersey State Bar Ass'n v. New Jersey Ass'n of Realtor Boards, 1131
Newman v. Hinky Dinky Omaha–Lincoln, Inc., 579
Newport Associates, Inc. v. Solow, 867
New York, State of v. Shore Realty Corp., 733
Nicholas v. Cousins, 1410
Nicholls v. Pitoukkas, 1036
Niernberg v. Feld, 1016
Nixon v. Mr. Property Management Co., Inc., 494
Nogarr, People v., 392, 398
Nollan v. California Coastal Com'n, 908
Nols, In re Estate of, 183
Noone v. Price, 733
Nordman v. Rau, 1217
Northcutt v. State Road Dept., 771
Northwest Kansas Area Vocational–Technical School v. Wolf, 1090
Northwest Pipeline Corp. v. Forrest Weaver Farm, Inc., 636
Nunziato v. Planning Bd. of Borough of Edgewater, 918

Oak's Oil Service, Inc. v. Massachusetts Bay Transp. Authority, 276
O'Banion v. Borba, 617
O'Brine's Estate, In re, 220
O'Connor's Estate, In re, 218
O'Donnell, In re, 452
O'Dwyer v. Ream, 1186
O'Keeffe v. Snyder, 145, 155
Oldfield v. Stoeco Homes, Inc., 248
Olevson v. Zoning Board of Review of Town of Narragansett, 852
Opinion of the Justices, In re, 629
Orange County Taxpayers Council, Inc. v. City of Orange, 496
Osborn v. Osborn, 1176
Osin v. Johnson, 1244
Osten v. Shah, 1036
Owen v. Hendricks, 1009

Pabst v. Finmand, 753
Palmer v. Flint, 383
Palmer v. Thompson, 315
Palumbo v. James, 1000
Pandol & Sons v. Agricultural Labor Relations Bd. of California, 19
Panushka v. Panushka, 1101
Park v. Sohn, 1275
Parker v. British Airways Board, 104
Parking Management, Inc. v. Gilder, 119
Parr v. Worley, 1197
Passaic, City of v. Paterson Bill Posting, Advertising & Sign Painting Co., 797
Paterson v. Deeb, 493
Patterson v. Bryant, 1227
Payne, State ex rel. v. Walden, 559
Payne v. Williams, 1406
Pearson v. Gardner, 998
Pease v. Baxter, 1051
Peet v. Roth Hotel Co., 124
Pelletier v. Dwyer, 1075
Pendergast v. Board of Appeals of Barnstable, 852
Penn Cent. Transp. Co. v. City of New York, 881
Pennell v. City of San Jose, 500, 528
Pennsylvania Coal Co. v. Mahon, 877
People v. ___ (see opposing party)
Perkins v. Coleman, 1336
Perry v. Housing Authority of City of Charleston, 473
Petersen v. Beekmere, Inc., 668
Petersen v. Hartell, 1057
Petersen v. Hubschman Const. Co., Inc., 1269
Peterson v. Taylor, 1186
Petition of (see name of party)
Pettigrew v. Dobbelaar, 1186
Phelps v. McQuade, 128

Philippi v. City of Sublimity, 848
Phinizy v. Guernsey, 1109
Pierson v. Post, 100
Piotrowski v. Parks, 1403
Poletown Neighborhood Council v. City of Detroit, 819
Poplar Bluff, City of v. Knox, 1330
Porter v. Wertz, 129
Posner v. Davis, 1277
Post v. Weil, 690
Potomac Bldg. Corp. v. Karkenny, 1071
Prah v. Maretti, 771
Prather v. Eisenmann, 758
Prather v. Hoberg, 752
Pratte v. Balatsos, 132 A.2d 142, p. 678
Pratte v. Balatsos, 113 A.2d 492, p. 678
Presbytery of Southeast Iowa v. Harris, 1421
Prete v. Cray, 738
Pritchard v. Rebori, 1192
Producers Lumber & Supply Co. v. Olney Bldg. Co., 165
PruneYard Shopping Center v. Robins, 898
Puritan–Greenfield Imp. Ass'n v. Leo, 852
Putnam Lake Community Council Bathing Beaches v. Deputy Com'r of State of N.Y., 898
Pye, Ex parte, 196
Pyle v. Springfield Marine Bank, 104

Quality Plastics, Inc. v. Moore, 1071

Raintree Corp. v. Rowe, 678
Raplee v. Piper, 1118
Rasmuson, United States v., 1364
Rauscher v. Albert, 1326
Re v. Magness Construction Co., 1280
Redarowicz v. Ohlendorf, 1276, 1277
Reed v. King, 1287
Rehoboth Heights Development Co. v. Marshall, 1402
Reid v. Architectural Bd. of Review of City of Cleveland Heights, 797
Renner v. Johnson, 648
Renton, City of v. Playtime Theatres, Inc., 797
Resser v. Carney, 1336
Rhenish v. Deunk, 1281
Rhue v. Cheyenne Homes, Inc., 703
Richards v. Delbridge, 196
Richmond Homes, Inc. v. Lee–Mar, Inc., 1281
Rickel v. Energy Systems Holdings, Ltd., 1058
RKO–Stanley Warner Theatres, Inc. v. Mellon Nat. Bank & Trust Co., 620
Robben v. Obering, 1331
Roberts v. Rhodes, 255, 262
Robinson v. Diamond Housing Corp., 548
Robinson v. 12 Lofts Realty, Inc., 446
Rock Springs, City of v. Sturm, 1399
Roeder v. Nolan, 563
Roeder Co. v. Burlington Northern, Inc., 1186, 1199
Rose v. Chaikin, 716
Rose v. Rose, 272
Rosenthal v. Sandusky, 421
Rosewood Corp. v. Fisher, 1058
Rosson v. Cutshall, 1088
Rucker v. Harrington, 1019
Runions v. Runions, 326, 327
Russell v. Hill, 140
Russell v. Richards, 1051
Ryan, United States v., 1359
Ryczkowski v. Chelsea Title & Guaranty Co., 1267

Sabo v. Horvath, 1263
Sakansky v. Wein, 633
Samples v. Geary, 124
Sanborn v. McLean, 681
Sandy Ridge Oil Co., Inc., In re, 1218
Sanford v. Breidenbach, 1112
Santa Barbara, City of v. Adamson, 951
Sargent v. Ross, 481
Sawyer v. Kendall, 1399
Sayre v. Dickerson, 602
Schad v. Borough of Mount Ephraim, 797
Scherer v. Hyland, 184
Schimenz, State ex rel. Zupancic v., 859
Schley v. Couch, 109, 113
Schmidt v. Reed, 1026
Schodde v. Twin Falls Land & Water Co., 757
Schuman v. Roger Baker and Associates, Inc., 1267
Scott, State ex rel. v. Buzard, 106
Scott County Bd. of Ed. v. Pepper, 259
Scrutton v. Sacramento County, 859
Seattle, Petition of City of, 819
Seawall Associates v. City of New York, 520
Seaway Co. v. Attorney General, 629
Seidelman v. Kouvavus, 550, 567
Seligman v. First Nat. Investments, Inc., 1070
Semachko v. Hopko, 1432
S.E.S. Importers, Inc. v. Pappalardo, 1089
Sexauer v. Wilson, 658
Sexton & Abbott v. Graham, 127
Shack, State v., 13
Shalimar Ass'n v. D.O.C. Enterprises, Ltd., 613
Shamrock Hilton Hotel v. Caranas, 122
Sharts v. Walters, 684
Shaughnessy v. Eidsmo, 982
Shay v. Penrose, 1098
Sheffet v. Los Angeles County, 747
Shelley v. Kraemer, 77, 691
Shelton v. City of College Station, 852
Sher v. Leiderman, 782
Sheradsky v. Basadre, 435
Sheridan Suzuki, Inc. v. Caruso Auto Sales, Inc., 134
Shirk v. Thomas, 1250
Short v. Texaco, Inc., 1412, 1433
Shugan v. Colonial View Manor, 990
Shullo Const. Co. v. Miller, 1026
Siders v. Schloo, 1275
Sierra Club v. Morton, 19
Simis v. McElroy, 1402

Simmons v. Quick–Stop Food Mart, Inc., 1231
Simmons v. Stum, 1232
Simon v. Solomon, 487
Simpson v. Kistler Inv. Co., 591
Singletary v. Atlantic Coast Line R. Co., 487
Sinks v. Karleskint, 1063, 1311
Skelly Oil Co. v. Ashmore, 1111
Skendzel v. Marshall, 1044, 1051
Skidmore, Owings & Merrill v. Pathway Financial, 1267
Slutsky v. City of New York, 787
Smith v. Blackburn, 1051
Smith v. J. Weingarten, Inc., 564
Smith v. King, 1081
Smith v. McEnany, 451
Smith v. Warr, 1085
Smith v. Winhall Planning Commission, 828
Snow v. Van Dam, 685
Sobol v. Gulinson, 1201
Somers v. Kane, 160
Somerville v. Jacobs, 165
Sondin v. Bernstein, 410
Sorenson v. Wright, 1335
South Staffordshire Water Co. v. Sharman, 102
Southern Burlington County N.A.A.C.P. v. Mount Laurel Tp., 958
Southern Illinois Conference of Methodist Church v. City of Edwardsville, 313
Southwest Weather Research, Inc. v. Duncan, 786
Southwest Weather Research, Inc. v. Rounsaville, 783
Speelman v. Pascal, 174
Spencer's Case, 657
S. P. Growers Ass'n v. Rodriguez, 550
Spiller v. Mackereth, 350
Sprague v. Kimball, 679
Sprecher v. Adamson Companies, 739
Spring Lakes, Ltd. v. O.F.M. Co., 1267
Spur Industries, Inc. v. Del E. Webb Development Co., 727
S. S. Kresge Co. of Michigan v. Winkelman Realty Co., 630
Staley v. Stephens, 1420
Standard Livestock Co. v. Pentz, 452
State v. ____ (see opposing party)
State, by Pai v. Thom, 1168
State ex rel. v. ____ (see opposing party and relator)
State Highway Com'n v. Bauman, 630
State of (see name of state)
Stegall v. Robinson, 684
Steinman v. Clinchfield Coal Corp., 1259
Stephens County v. Mid–Kansas Oil & Gas Co., 96
Sternberger v. Ragland, 1250
Stewart Title Guaranty Co. v. Lunt Land Corp., 1386
Stith v. Williams, 1201, 1399
St. Lo Const. Co. v. Koenigsberger, 709
Stockman v. Yanesh, 1322
Stoeco Development, Ltd. v. Department of the Army Corps of Engineers of United States, 254
Stoeco Homes, Inc., United States v., 253
Stoller v. Doyle, 306
Stoltz v. Maloney, 349
Stone v. City of Wilton, 826
Stone v. French, 1212
Stoner v. Zucker, 595
St. Onge v. Donovan, 852
Stratton v. Mt. Hermon Boys' School, 752
Stricklin v. Rice, 127
Strong v. Shatto, 709
Strong v. Strong, 1255
Strong v. Whybark, 1236, 1238
Stroup v. Conant, 532
Strout Realty, Inc. v. Milhous, 1137
Suess Builders Co. v. City of Beaverton, 847
Suffolk Housing Services v. Town of Brookhaven, 964
Sunnen Products Co. v. Chemtech Industries, Inc., 1303
Suttle v. Bailey, 702
Swann v. Gastonia Housing Authority, 508
Swartzbaugh v. Sampson, 354
Sybert v. Sybert, 281

Tavares v. Horstman, 1276
Taylor v. Allen, 1325
Taylor v. Taylor, 326
Taylor v. Wallace, 1325
Tee–Hit–Ton Indians v. United States, 76
Tempe, City of v. Baseball Facilities, Inc., 259
Tenn v. 889 Associates, Ltd., 782
Terlinde v. Neely, 1277
Terminal Freezers, Inc. v. Roberts Frozen Foods, Inc., 990
Tetrault v. Bruscoe, 1365
Texaco, Inc. v. Short, 1419
Texas American Energy Corp. v. Citizens Fidelity Bank & Trust Co., 97
Thomas v. Campbell, 611
Thomson, Estate of v. Wade, 590
Thornton, State ex rel. v. Hay, 621
3,218.9 Acres of Land, More or Less, Situated in Warren County, State of Pa., United States v., 66
Tipton County Abstract Co., Inc. v. Heritage Federal Sav. and Loan Ass'n, 1354
Title & Trust Co. of Florida v. Barrows, 1391
Tolbird v. Howard, 1070
Toledo Trust Co. v. Simmons, 106
Torres v. Portillos, 563
Totten, In re, 195
Town of (see name of town)
Transamerica Title Ins. Co. v. Johnson, 1383
Transport Management Co. v. American Radiator & Standard Sanitary Corp., 994
Treasure Salvors, Inc. v. Unidentified Wrecked & Abandoned Sailing Vessel, 100

Tremayne v. Taylor, 1410
Trentacost v. Brussel, 487
Trimble v. Gordon, 236
Tristram's Landing, Inc. v. Wait, 1132
Trustees of Schools of Township No. 1 v. Batdorf, 1411
Tulk v. Moxhay, 667, 668
Tull v. Ashcraft, 1201
Turner v. Cochran, 1259
Turner v. Lyon, 563
Tusch Enterprises v. Coffin, 1276
219 Broadway Corp. v. Alexander's, Inc., 430
Tymon v. Linoki, 1062
Tzitzon Realty Co. v. Mustonen, 1006

Unger v. Nunda Tp. Rural Fire Protection Dist., 1112
Union Bond & Trust Co. v. Blue Creek Redwood Co., 1052
Union Planters Nat. Bank v. United States, 415
United States v. ____ (see opposing party)
United States Financial v. Sullivan, 1301
United States Nat. Bank of Oregon v. Homeland, Inc., 551

Val Verde Hotel Co. v. Ross, 1175
Vanasdal v. Brinker, 1401
Vanderschrier v. Aaron, 1275
Van Sant v. Rose, 672
Vesey v. Vesey, 414
Village of (see name of village)
Vogeler v. Alwyn Imp. Corporation, 689

Waggoner, Estate of v. Gleghorn, 603
Wagner v. Cutler, 1286
Waitman v. Waitman, 196
Walden, State ex rel. Payne v., 559
Waldrop v. Town of Brevard, 710
Walk v. Miller, 410
Walker v. Ireton, 993
Wallach v. Riverside Bank, 1059
Walters v. Michel, 1090
Walters v. Tucker, 1187
Ward v. Mattuschek, 1001
Watkins Land Co. v. Clements, 752
Watson v. Watson, 1101
Wells, State ex rel. v. City of Dunbar, 709
Welsh v. James, 414
Welton v. Hamilton, 851
West v. First Agr. Bank, 406
Westfall, State v., 1355
Wetherbee v. Green, 157
W. F. White Land Co. v. Christenson, 690
Wheeler v. City of Pleasant Grove, 932
Whitcomb v. Brant, 557
White v. Smyth, 354
White v. Western Title Ins. Co., 1373
White Plains, City of v. Ferraioli, 951
Whitinsville Plaza, Inc. v. Kotseas, 673
Whittemore v. Farrington, 1280
Wichita Great Empire Broadcasting, Inc. v. Gingrich, 1354
Will v. Will Products, Inc., 1031
Willard v. First Church of Christ, Scientist, Pacifica, 586, 1162
William J. Davis, Inc. v. Slade, 459
Williamson County Regional Planning Com'n v. Hamilton Bank of Johnson City, 932
Willow River Power Co., United States v., 5
Willsmore v. Oceola Tp., 115
Wilson v. Klein, 1075
Wilson v. Lewis, 1123
Wilson v. Manning, 876
Wilson v. O'Connor, 564
Wilson v. Wilson, 1008
Windward Partners v. Delos Santos, 550
Wineberg v. Moore, 1250
Wingfield v. Oakes, 1109
W. L. Schautz Co. v. Duncan Hosiery Mills, Inc., 1216
Womack v. Hyche, 431
Womack v. Stegner, 1160
Wood Bldg. Corp. v. Griffitts, 1170
Woolums v. Simonsen, 277
Wright v. Raftree, 990
Wykoff v. Barton, 637

Yee v. Okamoto, 173
Yonkers City Post No. 1666, V.F.W. v. Josanth Realty Corp., 1326
Young v. DeGuerin, 1278
Young v. Hamilton, 1259
Young v. Morrisey, 472, 486
Young v. Young, 196

Zendman v. Harry Winston, Inc., 128
Ziman v. Village of Glencoe, 852
Zupancic, State ex rel. v. Schimenz, 859

CASES AND MATERIALS

ON

PROPERTY

Part One

PROPERTY AS AN INSTITUTION *—AN OVERVIEW OF PROPERTY LAW

Chapter 1

WHAT IS PROPERTY?

We begin our search for an understanding of property law with a simple inquiry—what is property? Unfortunately, as in the case of most fundamental questions, the answer is complex.[1] To the layman, property is a thing (a physical *res*)—land, an automobile, stocks and bonds, a case of scotch. To the lawyer, it is not a thing at all but a concept—the legal relationship among people in regard to a *res* or even an intangible subject such as an idea, e.g., a patent or a copyright. In the development of this concept all property depends, in the final analysis, upon the enforcement mechanisms of the state. Professor Robert S. Hunt states that "the basic problem of property law in general is nothing more or less than determining the relation of the individual to the community with regard to the use and exploitation of resources."

We can best illustrate the problems of property and ownership by a brief look at a familiar object of property—an automobile.

Mary is very fond of the sports car which was given to her by her father upon Mary's graduation from college. Mary refers to the car as her "property" and asserts that she "owns" the car. What is the meaning of such statements? Do they mean that Mary is entitled to use the car without obtaining anyone's permission? To allow others to use it? To sell it? To mortgage it? To give it away? To dispose of it by will? To be assured it will belong to her next of kin if Mary fails to execute a will? To recover the car from a thief? To recover compensa-

* "The meaning of the term institution deserves attention. It is a term applied to such different things as the church, marriage, the money economy, democracy and property. Perhaps, in generalized language, it can be said that we have an 'institution' whenever we discover a cluster of social usages from which an individual may depart only at his peril. The result of an institution's existence is the setting of a pattern of behavior and the fixing of a zone of tolerance for some segment of human activity." 1 Powell on Real Property 7 (1976).

1. As to just how complex the answer can be, see Cribbet, Concepts in Transition: The Search for a New Definition of Property, 1986 U. of Ill. Law Rev. 1. The author begins: "What is property? Nearly every first-year property course begins and ends with this query. The instructor never answers the question, but in the asking, and in the quest for meaning, every student gains some glimpse of the variety of possible answers. The question is unanswerable because the meaning of the chameleon-like word property constantly changes in time and space." In one sense, this entire casebook *is* a quest for the answer to that key query. The student should keep the question in mind throughout the course and observe his or her own ever-changing answer as the cases and materials unfold.

tion from one who wrongfully injures the car? Speaking generally, affirmative answers would be given to each of these questions. It appears, then, that "ownership" consists of many disparate claims by Mary sanctioned by law against many persons—a "bundle of sticks," as legal scholars sometimes have put it.

Would Mary be regarded as "owner" of the car if one or more of the above claims were not sanctioned by law? Which ones? Would the law sanction some additional claims not included in the above list?

It is apparent that Mary's "ownership" is qualified in many respects. She will not be allowed to drive her car on public streets without obtaining a driver's license, complying with traffic regulations, attaching license tags to the car, and submitting the car for safety inspections. If she fails to pay taxes levied upon the car, the car may be seized and sold to satisfy the tax claim. The car may, in many states, be retained by a mechanic until the charge for repairs made by him is paid. Mary may, in many states, be denied a right to recover damages for injuries to the car if her negligence was a contributing cause of the injury. Mary can transfer her car by sale, gift, or will only by complying with certain formalities. If her car is stolen by a thief who sells it to a purchaser for value without notice (a bfp), Mary *may* not be able to recover the car. If Mary is married, and if the common law as it existed prior to the adoption of modern legislation were in force, Mary would have no enforceable claim to the car, which would in reality belong to her husband. Other qualifications of Mary's "ownership" may come to mind. New qualifications may be added by subsequent legislation or court decisions. The applicability of any of the numerous qualifications of ownership to specific situations may be affected by subtle factual distinctions. Litigation may be required in order to resolve some of the questions of law and fact which will arise.

In view of the above considerations, what is meant by referring to Mary as the "owner" of the car? Does that label have any practical significance? Is it not more realistic to refer to specific enforceable claims by Mary regarding the car?

One can imagine a society in which individuals would have such limited claims in automobiles that the term "ownership" would seem inappropriate as applied to such claims. Such would be the case if all automobiles were declared by law to be owned by the state and made available for individual use only for short periods of time, for limited purposes, upon issuance of a permit by some government official. But would not the permit itself constitute "property," if not "ownership"? What would be the relevant considerations in seeking an answer to this question? A more fundamental question is why a society would restrict private property to such a narrow ambit. A still more significant inquiry seeks to determine the ideal scope of private property in modern society. Is a satisfactory general answer to this question realistically attainable? Is the question simply too broad and too complex to be answered? Must we be content to seek answers to tiny bits of the big issue? If the meaning of Mary's "ownership" of her car cannot be simply stated, how difficult it must be merely to describe, let alone prescribe, the role of private property in a society! Consider some preliminary efforts in this direction manifested by the following excerpts.

BLACKSTONE, COMMENTARIES ON THE LAWS OF ENGLAND

Book II, Chap. 1, p. 2 (15th ed. 1809).

There is nothing which so generally strikes the imagination, and engages the affections of mankind, as the right of property; or that sole and despotic dominion which one man claims and exercises over the external things of the world, in total exclusion of the right of any other individual in the universe.

BENTHAM, THEORY OF LEGISLATION, PRINCIPLES OF THE CIVIL CODE

Part I, 111–113, Dumont, ed., Hildreth, Trans. (1864).

The better to understand the advantages of law, let us endeavour to form a clear idea of *property*. We shall see that there is no such thing as natural property, and that it is entirely the work of law.

Property is nothing but a basis of expectation; the expectation of deriving certain advantages from a thing which we are said to possess, in consequence of the relation in which we stand towards it.

There is no image, no painting, no visible trait, which can express the relation that constitutes property. It is not material, it is metaphysical; it is a mere conception of the mind.

To have a thing in our hands, to keep it, to make it, to sell it, to work it up into something else, to use it—none of these physical circumstances, nor all united, convey the idea of property. A piece of stuff which is actually in the Indies may belong to me while the dress I wear may not. The aliment which is incorporated into my very body may belong to another, to whom I am bound to account for it.

The idea of property consists in an established expectation; in the persuasion of being able to draw such or such an advantage from the thing possessed, according to the nature of the case. Now this expectation, this persuasion, can only be the work of law. I cannot count upon the enjoyment of that which guarantees it to me. It is law alone which permits me to forget my natural weakness. It is only through the protection of law that I am able to inclose a field, and to give myself up to its cultivation with the sure though distant hope of harvest.

But it may be asked, what is it that serves as a basis to law, upon which to begin operations, when it adopts objects which, under the name of property, it promises to protect? Have not men, in the primitive state, a *natural* expectation of enjoying certain things—an expectation drawn from sources anterior to law?

Yes. There have been from the beginning, and there always will be, circumstances in which a man may secure himself, by his own means, in the enjoyment of certain things. But the catalogue of these cases is very limited. The savage who has killed a deer may hope to keep it for himself, so long as his cave is undiscovered, so long as he watches to defend it, and is stronger than this rivals; but that is all. How miserable and precarious is such a possession! If we suppose the least agreement among savages to respect the acquisitions of each other, we see the introduction of a principle to which no name can be given but that of law. A feeble and momentary expectation may result from time to time from circumstances purely physical; but a strong and permanent expectation can result only from law. That which, in the natural state, was an almost invisible thread, in the social state becomes a cable.

Property and law are born together, and die together. Before laws were made there was no property; take away laws, and property ceases.

As regards property, security consists in receiving no check, no shock, no derangement to the expectation, founded on the laws, of enjoying such and such a portion of good. The legislator owes the greatest respect to this expectation which he has himself produced. When he does not contradict it, he does what is essential to the happiness of society; when he disturbs it, he always produces a proportionate sum of evil.

FELIX S. COHEN, DIALOGUE ON PRIVATE PROPERTY

9 Rutgers L.Rev. 357, 374 (1954).

Now, at this point, it may be useful to summarize our analysis of property in terms of a simple label. Suppose we say, that is property to which the following label can be attached:

To the world:

Keep off X unless you have my permission, which I may grant or withhold.

Signed: Private citizen
Endorsed: The state

Let me offer the caution that such a label does not remove the penumbra of ambiguity that attaches to every word that we use in any definition. As William James says, "The word 'and' trails along after every sentence." No definition can be more precise than the subject permits. Aristotle remarks that it is a mark of immaturity to expect the same degree of precision in human affairs as in mathematics. All of the terms of our definition shade off imperceptibly into other things. Private citizen: consider how many inperceptible shadings there are in the range from private citizen through corporate official, public utility employee, and government corporation and the state itself. Or consider the shadings between the state and various other types of organization. Consider the initial words, "To the world," and the large middle ground between a direction to the whole world and a direction to a specific individual.

Any definition of property, to be useful, must reflect the fact that property merges by imperceptible degrees into government, contract, force, and value.

If we were to put these relations in the form of a diagram, we can certainly draw the boundary lines of property at many different points, just as we can fix arbitrary points between day and night and yet understand each other when we draw these lines at different points.

Note how one state court analyzed the question of whether property had been taken, destroyed, or damaged.

"It should be pointed out initially that the Minnesota Constitution requires compensation where private property is taken, destroyed, or damaged. Any statement of what constitutes 'property' can only be nebulous at best. Not every economic, social, or other interest or advantage is a property right, the taking of which must be compensated. As the United States Supreme Court pointed out in United States v. Willow River Power Co., 324 U.S. 499, 502, 65 S.Ct. 761, 764, 89 L.Ed. 1101, 1107 (1945), only those economic advantages which have the law back of them are property rights. Thus, to begin by arguing that compensation must be paid because a property right has been taken really merely raises the question that must be ultimately answered. Property is more than the physical thing—it involves the group of rights inhering in a citizen's relation to the physical thing. Traditionally, that group of rights has included the rights to possess, use, and dispose of property." Alevizos v. Metropolitan Airports Commission of Minneapolis and St. Paul, 298 Minn. 471, 216 N.W.2d 651 (1974).

While the federal and state constitutions require just compensation for the taking of private property, these deceptively simple constitutional mandates raise some of the most difficult questions in modern property law. When is property taken, as opposed to being subject to regulation (which typically requires no compensation)? What is *just* compensation? Partial answers to these and related questions will be covered in Part Four (Public Interests in Land). For an excellent overall analysis, see Michelman, Property, Utility, and Fairness: Comments on the Ethical Foundations of "Just Compensation" Law, 80 Harv.L.Rev. 1165 (1968).

The Minnesota court states that "only those economic advantages which have the law back of them are property rights". Consider the following comments by Professor Richard Posner, a leading scholar in law and economics, now a federal Court of Appeals judge on the Seventh Circuit.

POSNER, ECONOMIC ANALYSIS OF LAW

Little, Brown and Company (1973).
Pages 10–15.

I. THE ECONOMIC THEORY OF PROPERTY RIGHTS

Imagine a society in which all property rights have been abolished. A farmer plants corn, fertilizes it, and erects scarecrows, but when the corn is ripe his neighbor reaps and sells it.[1] The farmer has no legal remedy against his neighbor's conduct since he owns neither the land that he sowed nor the crop. After a few such incidents the cultivation of land will be abandoned and the society will shift to methods of subsistence (such as hunting) that involve less preparatory investment.[2]

This example suggests that the legal protection of property rights has an important economic function: to create incentives to use resources efficiently. Although the value of the crop in our example, as measured by consumer willingness to pay, may have greatly exceeded the cost in labor, materials, and foregone alternative uses of the land, without property rights there is no incentive to incur these costs because there is no reasonably assured reward for incurring them. The proper incentives are created by the parceling out among the members of society of mutually exclusive rights to the use of particular resources. If every piece of land is owned by someone, in the sense that there is always an individual who can exclude all others from access to any given area, then individuals will endeavor by cultivation or other improvements to maximize the value of land.

The creation of exclusive rights is a necessary rather than sufficient condition for the efficient use of resources. The rights must be transferable. Suppose the farmer in our example owns the land that he sows but is a bad farmer; his land would be more productive in someone else's hands. The maximization of value requires a mechanism by which the farmer can be induced to transfer rights in the property to someone who can work it more productively. A transferable property right is such a mechanism.

An example will illustrate. Farmer A owns a piece of land that he anticipates will yield him $100 a year, in excess of labor and other costs, indefinitely. The value of the right to a stream of future earnings can be expressed as a present sum. Just as the price of a share of common stock expresses the present value of the anticipated earnings to which the shareholder will be entitled, so the present value of a parcel of land that yields an annual net income of $100 can be calculated and is the minimum price that A will accept in exchange for his property right. Farmer B believes that he can use A's land more productively than A. Stated another way, B thinks he could net more

1. The example is somewhat artificial: presumably the "buyer" could simply grab the corn and would be under no obligation to pay for it. [Footnotes by the author.]

2. Some interesting anthropological evidence relevant to this point may be found in Harold Demsetz, Toward a Theory of Property Rights, 57 Am.Econ.Rev.Papers & Proceedings 347 (1967).

than $100 a year from working A's land. The present value of B's higher expected earnings stream will, of course, exceed the present value calculated by A. Assume the present value calculated by A is $1000 and by B $1500. Then sale of the property right by A to B will yield benefits to both parties if the price is anywhere between $1000 and $1500. At a price of $1250, for example, A receives $250 more than the land is worth to him and B pays $250 less than the land is worth to him. Thus, there are strong incentives for the parties voluntarily to exchange A's land for B's money, and if B is as he believes a better farmer than A, the transfer will result in an increase in the productivity of the land. Through a succession of such transfers, resources are shifted to their highest valued, most productive uses and efficiency in the use of economic resources is maximized.

The foregoing discussion suggests three criteria of an efficient system of property rights. The first is *universality.* Ideally, all resources should be owned, or ownable, by someone, except resources so plentiful that everybody can consume as much of them as he wants without reducing consumption by anyone else (sunlight is a good, but not perfect, example—why?). No issue of efficient use arises in such a case.

The second criterion—but one that requires, as we shall see careful qualification—is *exclusivity.* We have assumed so far that either the farmer can exclude no one or he can exclude everyone, but of course there are intermediate stages: the farmer may be entitled to exclude private individuals from reaping his crop, but not the government in time of war. It might appear that the more exclusive the property right, the greater the incentive to invest the right amount of resources in the development of the property. Suppose our farmer estimates that he can raise a hog with a market value of $100 at a cost of only $50 in labor and materials. Suppose further that there is no alternative combination of resources and land use that would yield a greater excess of value over cost: in the next best use his net income from the land would be only $20. He will raise the hog. But now suppose his property right is less than exclusive in two respects. First, he has no right to prevent an adjacent railroad from accidentally emitting engine sparks that may set fire to the hog's pen, killing it prematurely. Second, he has no right to prevent the local government from rezoning his land from agricultural to residential use and compelling him to sell the hog at disadvantageous terms before it is grown. In light of these contingencies he must reevaluate the yield of his land: he must discount the $100 to reflect the probability that the yield may be much less, perhaps zero. Suppose, after discounting the expected revenue from raising the hog (market value times the probability that it will reach the market) is only $60. He will not raise the hog. He will shift to the next best use of the land, which we said was less valuable.[3]

The analysis, however, is incomplete. While the farmer will be induced, as a consequence of no longer enjoying an exclusive property

3. The profit from raising the hog is now $10, since his costs are $50. The next best use, we said, yields a profit of $20.

right, to shift to an alternative land use that *seems* less efficient, overall efficiency may be increased. The removal of the hog may result in an increase in the value of surrounding residential land greater than the reduction in the value of the farmer's parcel. The cost of preventing the emission of engine sparks may be larger than the reduction in the value of the farmer's land when he switches from hog raising to, say, growing radishes. To this, the very alert reader may be tempted to reply that if the increase in value to others from a different use of the farmer's land exceeds the decrease to him, they can buy his right: the railroad can purchase an easement to emit sparks; the surrounding homeowners can purchase a covenant from the farmer not to raise hogs. Often, however, the costs of effecting a transfer of rights—transaction costs—are prohibitive; but more on this shortly.

The third criterion of an efficient system of property rights is *transferability.* If a property right cannot be transferred,[4] there is no way of shifting a resource from a less productive to a more productive use through voluntary exchange. The costs of transfer may be high to begin with; a legal prohibition against transferring may, depending on the penalties for violation, make the costs utterly prohibitive. We shall see that when the costs of transferring property rights are high, the attempt to achieve our second criterion, exclusivity, may actually reduce the efficiency of the property rights system.

II. PROPERTY RIGHTS IN LAW AND ECONOMICS: THE CASE OF BROADCAST FREQUENCIES

Property rights in our society are not in fact universal, exclusive, or freely transferable. For example, the law has purported not to recognize property rights in broadcasting at all. This is a good place at which to begin our discussion of the property rights system because it illustrates the difference between the legal conception of property right and the broader economic conception.[5]

In the early days of radio, before comprehensive federal regulation was imposed, there was some judicial support for the proposition that the right to broadcast on a particular frequency in a particular area without interference from other users was a property right that could be protected by injunction. With the creation in 1928 of the Federal Radio Commission (forerunner of the Federal Communications Commission) Congress determined upon a different approach. Licenses authorizing the use of particular frequencies in particular areas were to be granted at nominal charge for renewable three-year terms to applicants who persuaded the commission that licensing them would promote the public interest. Congress expressly provided that licensees were to have no property rights in the use of the frequencies assigned them; the purpose of this provision was to foreclose any claim to compensa-

4. We use transfer in a broad sense: if sales in fee simple were forbidden, but leases allowed, A could lease his farm to B in our example and the objective of shifting it to its highest valued use would be achieved.

5. The classic study of public regulation of the broadcasting industry, on which this section draws heavily, is Ronald H. Coase, The Federal Communications Commission, 2 J.Law & Econ. 1 (1959).

tion by a licensee whose license was withdrawn at the end of the three-year term.

Some of the objections that were advanced to the recognition of private property rights in the use of radio frequencies have an odd ring, at least in an economist's ear. For example, it was said that if broadcasting rights could be bought and sold like other property, the broadcast media would come under the control of the wealthy. This confuses willingness to pay with ability to pay. The possession of money does not dictate the objects that will be purchased. The poor frequently bid goods away from the rich by being willing to pay more. To be sure, willingness to pay presupposes ability to pay, but a group of poor people may have much greater financial resources in the aggregate than one wealthy person or a small group of wealthy people.

In the actual administration of the federal regulatory scheme for broadcasting, willingness to pay has played a decisive role and a system of de facto property rights has emerged. The desirable radio and television licenses have been awarded in comparative proceedings in which, much as in a system of property rights, willingness to pay—not for the license as such but for the legal representation and political influence that typically determine the outcome—has probably decided in most cases who would control the resource at stake. However, this method of initially assigning broadcast rights is less efficient than an auction or other conventional private sale. First, since there is a good deal of uncertainty in the political regulatory process, the applicant who pays his lawyers, lobbyists, etc., the most money—thereby indicating that he attaches the greatest value to obtaining the right—will often not receive it. Second, the costs of this method of allocation are much greater than the cost of allocation through the market: participation in an auction of broadcast frequencies would not necessitate costly legal services.

The first source of inefficiency is transitory, for once broadcast rights have been obtained by the method just outlined they are thereafter salable as an incident to the sale of the physical assets of a radio or television station. When a television station having a transmitter and other physical properties worth only a few hundred thousand dollars is sold for $10 million, one can be confident that the major part of the purchase price is payment for the right to use the frequency. Given such transfers, we may presume that, as with land, broadcast rights end up in the hands of those who value them most highly (and are therefore willing to pay the most money for them), even if the initial "auction" may not have allocated the rights very efficiently. The willingness of broadcasters to pay tens of millions of dollars for a right terminable after three years may seem peculiar. In fact, broadcast licenses have been terminated only for misconduct, in much the same way that one can lose one's land for nonpayment of real estate taxes.

In economic if not in formal legal terms, then, there are property rights in broadcast frequencies. The right is obtained initially in a competition in which willingness to pay plays an influential, and quite possibly decisive, role. Once obtained the right is transferable. It is exclusive: interference with a licensee's use of his frequency will be enjoined. And it is for all practical purposes perpetual. The right holder is subject to various regulatory constraints, but less so than a public utility, the principal assets of which are private property in the formal legal sense.

III. FUTURE RIGHTS

The rights system in broadcasting is not only costly and sub rosa but also incomplete in important respects. One we discuss later under transferability. Another, which has an interesting parallel in the law of water rights, is the difficulty of obtaining rights for future use. To purchase vacant land with the intention of holding it for future development is a common type of transaction, while to disclose in a broadcast license application an intention to defer indefinitely the commencement of broadcast operations would guarantee denial. So also in the case of water rights under the appropriation system that prevails in the western states: one acquires property rights in water by the actual diversion and use of a stream and the right embraces only the amount of water actually used; one cannot obtain a right for exercise at some future date. Both the broadcast and water limitations are circumvented to some extent, in the case of broadcasting by deferring actual construction after the license has been obtained, in the case of water by obtaining a preliminary permit that establishes the applicant's prior right even though the construction of diversion works and use of the water diverted are postponed.

The hostility to recognizing rights for future use may be related to the apparent "windfall" element that is present in both the broadcasting and water contexts. In both cases the right is awarded without charge—although the applicant may have gone to considerable expense to obtain it—and often can be immediately resold at a considerable profit. This need not be evidence of a true windfall. The "windfall," however, would appear even larger if the profit were obtained by one who appeared not to be providing any service.

The objection is bound up with a general hostility, reflected in many corners of the law, to speculation. Speculation is the purchase of a good not to use but to hold in the hope that it will appreciate in value. The speculator performs a valuable economic function in the adjustment of prices to changing values. In the case of land, water, or broadcast frequencies he can (if permitted) perform the additional function of preventing the premature commitment of resources. Moreover, the principal effect of forbidding speculative purchases of water or broadcast frequencies is not to prevent speculation but to encourage uneconomical resource uses—uses not to meet a demand but to stake a claim.

NOTE

In footnote 2 of the preceding excerpt, Judge Posner refers to an excellent article, Toward a Theory of Property Rights, by Professor Demsetz. In that article, Professor Demsetz notes: "In the world of Robinson Crusoe property rights play no role. Property rights are an instrument of society and derive their significance from the fact that they help a man form those expectations which he can reasonably hold in his dealings with others. These expectations find expression in the laws, customs, and mores of society. An owner of property rights possesses the consent of fellow men to allow him to act in particular ways. An owner expects the community to prevent others from interfering with his actions, provided that these actions are not prohibited in the specification of his rights."

It has long been apparent that the institution of property is not the sole property of the law and lawyers. Property is studied and is the subject of extensive research in many disciplines. History, philosophy, psychology, sociology and, especially, economics have a great deal to tell us about the profound impact of the institution of property on any society. Law reflects, more than it shapes, society. To truly understand law one must, therefore, have some knowledge of how society *is* shaped. Some of that knowledge you bring to law school as a part of some sixteen years (or more) of formal education. Some of it you will find secreted in the interstices of three years of law school study. The rest you will have to acquire as a part of the life-long process of learning, since no one leaves a university with a closed briefcase of knowledge.

The brief excerpt from Judge Posner's Economic Analysis of Law should whet your appetite to learn more about the role which economic power relationships play in the institution of property. See, in this connection, Ackerman, Economic Foundations of Property Law (Little, Brown and Co., 1975). The introduction (pages vii-xvi) to this book of materials is of particular interest. In that introduction, Professor Ackerman argues that economic theory should be the unifying factor in a modern, first-year course in property. "The institution of private property, after all, serves as a linchpin of our economic organization, and it would be remarkable if its proper study could not enlighten the fundamental premises of a wide range of legal phenomena. . . . Moreover, while other fields should certainly have a place at least as important as economics in the overall legal curriculum, it seems fair to ask whether they deserve an equally prominent place in the first-year property course. After all, it is impossible to do *everything* in a single course, and it seems wise to deploy our interdisciplinary resources so that the student—by the time he graduates—has been exposed to something more than an endless series of courses in which a smattering of interdisciplinary lore is applied in a haphazard fashion."

While the editors of this casebook find considerable merit in Professor Ackerman's thesis, we have not structured these cases and materials around an economics' base. This is partly because of limitations of time and space; partly because we view economics more as a research tool than as a teaching device. We do raise economics issues with our own students at various points in the course and we do hope that other professors using this book will do the same. Professor Ackerman's collection of materials is a useful supplement to the more traditional presentation of first-year property law.

For a legal analysis of the traditional rights in property, consider the comments of the late Dean Pound of Harvard.

POUND, THE LAW OF PROPERTY AND RECENT JURISTIC THOUGHT

25 American Bar Association Journal 993, 996 (1939).

Rights, liberty, property, law, four ideas which grew up in contests with arbitrary personal rulers, are losing ground and as we are told by many, will disappear in the society of the future. It is significant that they are losing with the rise of the new absolutism . . . .

Absolutisms have always borne hard on liberty and property and rights, which are the guarantees of both. As we have seen in the history of the bills of rights it has borne on property quite as much as on liberty, so that the two came to be associated even to the point of identification. The administrative absolutism in America today bears equally hard on each. . . .

Duguit tells us that there are no such things as rights. There are only social functions. . . . "Liberty," says Duguit, "is a function." He adds: "Today each person is considered as having a social function to fulfil and therefore is under a social duty to develop to the greatest possible extent his physical, intellectual and moral personality in order to perform his function most effectively."

Note how property tied up with liberty in this theory of state enforcement of social functions. According to the civilians, property involves six rights: a *jus possidende* or right of possessing, a right in the strict sense; a *jus prohibendi* or right of excluding others, also a right in the strict sense; a *jus disponendi* or right of disposition, what we should now call a legal power; a *jus utendi* or right of using, what we should now call a liberty; a *jus fruendi* or right of enjoying the fruits and profits; and a *jus abutendi* or right of destroying or injuring if one likes—the two last also what today we should call liberties. Thus at least half of the content of a right of property is liberty—freedom of applying as one likes, free of legal restraint. But, says Duguit, "property is not a right; it is a social function. The owner, that is to say the possessor of wealth, by the fact of his possession, has a social function to perform." If he does not perform it, the state is to intervene and compel him to employ it "according to its nature."

What such ideas may mean in action is well illustrated in international relations. A small state, in the judgment of a powerful neighbor, is not performing its social function in its domain. In the absence of a supernational state, the powerful neighbor steps in to compel employment of the domain "according to its nature." Such things have been happening. Where rights are not recognized they are likely to continue to happen.

Now, study carefully your first full case in these materials and see if your initial impression of the correct answer to the simple inquiry—what is property?—is intact.

STATE v. SHACK

Supreme Court of New Jersey, 1971.
58 N.J. 297, 277 A.2d 369.

WEINTRAUB, C.J. Defendants entered upon private property to aid migrant farmworkers employed and housed there. Having refused to depart upon the demand of the owner, defendants were charged with violating N.J.S.A. 2A:170–31 which provides that "[a]ny person who trespasses on any lands . . . after being forbidden so to trespass by the owner . . . is a disorderly person and shall be punished by a fine of not more than $50." Defendants were convicted in the Municipal Court of Deerfield Township and again on appeal in the County Court of Cumberland County on a trial *de novo.* R. 3:23–8(a). We certified their further appeal before argument in the Appellate Division.

Before us, no one seeks to sustain these convictions. The complaints were prosecuted in the Municipal Court and in the County Court by counsel engaged by the complaining landowner, Tedesco. However, Tedesco did not respond to this appeal, and the county prosecutor, while defending abstractly the constitutionality of the trespass statute, expressly disclaimed any position as to whether the statute reached the activity of these defendants.

Complainant, Tedesco, a farmer, employs migrant workers for his seasonal needs. As part of their compensation, these workers are housed at a camp on his property.

Defendant Tejeras is a field worker for the Farm Workers Division of the Southwest Citizens Organization for Poverty Elimination, known by the acronym SCOPE, a nonprofit corporation funded by the Office of Economic Opportunity pursuant to an act of Congress, 42 U.S.C.A. §§ 2861–2864. The role of SCOPE includes providing for the "health services of the migrant farm worker."

Defendant Shack is a staff attorney with the Farm Workers Division of Camden Regional Legal Services, Inc., known as "CRLS," also a nonprofit corporation funded by the Office of Economic Opportunity pursuant to an act of Congress, 42 U.S.C.A. 2809(a)(3). The mission of CRLS includes legal advice and representation for these workers.

Differences had developed between Tedesco and these defendants prior to the events which led to the trespass charges now before us. Hence when defendant Tejeras wanted to go upon Tedesco's farm to find a migrant worker who needed medical aid for the removal of 28 sutures, he called upon defendant Shack for his help with respect to the legalities involved. Shack, too, had a mission to perform on Tedesco's farm; he wanted to discuss a legal problem with another migrant worker there employed and housed. Defendants arranged to go to the farm together. Shack carried literature to inform the migrant farmworkers of the assistance available to them under federal statutes, but no mention seems to have been made of that literature when Shack was later confronted by Tedesco.

Defendants entered upon Tedesco's property and as they neared the camp site where the farmworkers were housed, they were confronted by Tedesco who inquired of their purpose. Tejeras and Shack stated their missions. In response, Tedesco offered to find the injured worker, and as to the worker who needed legal advice, Tedesco also offered to locate the man but insisted that the consultation would have to take place in Tedesco's office and in his presence. Defendants declined, saying they had the right to see the men in the privacy of their living quarters and without Tedesco's supervision. Tedesco thereupon summoned a State Trooper who, however, refused to remove defendants except upon Tedesco's written complaint. Tedesco then executed the formal complaints charging violations of the trespass statute.

I.

The constitutionality of the trespass statute, as applied here, is challenged on several scores.

It is urged that the First Amendment rights of the defendants and of the migrant farmworkers were thereby offended. Reliance is placed on Marsh v. Alabama, 326 U.S. 501, 66 S.Ct. 276, 90 L.Ed. 265 (1946), where it was held that free speech was assured by the First Amendment in a company-owned town which was open to the public generally and was indistinguishable from any other town except for the fact that the title to the property was vested in a private corporation. Hence a Jehovah's Witness who distributed literature on a sidewalk within the town could not be held as a trespasser. Later, on the strength of that case, it was held that there was a First Amendment right to picket peacefully in a privately owned shopping center which was found to be the functional equivalent of the business district of the company-owned town in *Marsh*. [Citations omitted.] Those cases rest upon the fact that the property was in fact opened to the general public. There may be some migrant camps with the attributes of the company town in *Marsh* and of course they would come within its holding. But there is nothing of that character in the case before us, and hence there would have to be an extension of *Marsh* to embrace the immediate situation.

Defendants also maintain that the application of the trespass statute to them is barred by the Supremacy Clause of the United States Constitution, Art. VI, cl. 2, and this on the premise that the application of the trespass statute would defeat the purpose of the federal statutes, under which SCOPE and CRLS are funded, to reach and aid the migrant farmworker. The brief of the United States, *amicus curiae*, supports that approach. Here defendants rely upon cases construing the National Labor Relations Act, 29 U.S.C.A. § 151 et seq., and holding that an employer may in some circumstances be guilty of an unfair labor practice in violation of that statute if the employer denies union organizers an opportunity to communicate with his employees at some suitable place upon the employer's premises. See NLRB v. Babcock and Wilcox Co., 351 U.S. 105, 76 S.Ct. 679, 100 L.Ed. 975 (1956), and annotation, 100 L.Ed. 984 (1956). The brief of New Jersey State Office of Legal Services, *amicus curiae* asserts the workers' Sixth Amendment right to counsel in criminal matters is involved and suggests also that a right to counsel in civil matters is a "penumbra" right emanating from the whole Bill of Rights under the thinking of Griswold v. Connecticut, 381 U.S. 479, 85 S.Ct. 1678, 14 L.Ed.2d 510 (1965), or is a privilege of national citizenship protected by the privileges and immunities clause of the Fourteenth Amendment, or is a right "retained by the people" under the Ninth Amendment, citing a dictum in United Public Workers v. Mitchell, 330 U.S. 75, 94, 67 S.Ct. 556, 91 L.Ed. 754, 770 (1947).

These constitutional claims are not established by any definitive holding. We think it unnecessary to explore their validity. The reason is that we are satisfied that under our State law the ownership of real property does not include the right to bar access to governmental services available to migrant workers and hence there was no trespass within the meaning of the penal statute. The policy considerations which underlie that conclusion may be much the same as those which would be weighed with respect to one or more of the constitutional challenges, but a decision in nonconstitutional terms is more satisfactory, because the interests of migrant workers are more expansively served in that way than they would be if they had no more freedom than these constitutional concepts could be found to mandate if indeed they apply at all.

II.

Property rights serve human values. They are recognized to that end, and are limited by it. Title to real property cannot include dominion over the destiny of persons the owner permits to come upon the premises. Their well-being must remain the paramount concern of a system of law. Indeed the needs of the occupants may be so imperative and their strength so weak, that the law will deny the occupants the power to contract away what is deemed essential to their health, welfare, or dignity.

Here we are concerned with a highly disadvantaged segment of our society. We are told that every year farmworkers and their families numbering more than one million leave their home areas to fill the seasonal demand for farm labor in the United States. The Migratory Farm Labor Problem in the United States (1969 Report of Subcommittee on Migratory Labor of the United States Senate Committee on Labor and Public Welfare), p. 1. The migrant farmworkers come to New Jersey in substantial numbers. The report just cited places at 55,700 the number of man-months of such employment in our State in

1968 (p. 7). The numbers of workers so employed here in that year are estimated at 1,300 in April; 6,500 in May; 9,800 in June; 10,600 in July; 12,100 in August; 9,600 in September; and 5,500 in October (p. 9).

The migrant farmworkers are a community within but apart from the local scene. They are rootless and isolated. Although the need for their labors is evident, they are unorganized and without economic or political power. It is their plight alone that summoned government to their aid. In response, Congress provided under Title III–B of the Economic Opportunity Act of 1964 (42 U.S.C.A. § 2701 et seq.) for "assistance for migrant and other seasonally employed farmworkers and their families." Section 2861 states "the purpose of this part is to assist migrant and seasonal farmworkers and their families to improve their living conditions and develop skills necessary for a productive and self-sufficient life in an increasingly complex and technological society." Section 2862(b)(1) provides for funding of programs "to meet the immediate needs of migrant and seasonal farmworkers and their families, such as day care for children, education, health services, improved housing and sanitation (including the provision and maintenance of emergency and temporary housing and sanitation facilities), legal advice and representation, and consumer training and counseling." As we have said, SCOPE is engaged in a program funded under this section, and CRLS also pursues the objectives of this section although, we gather, it is funded under § 2809(a)(3), which is not limited in its concern to the migrant and other seasonally employed farmworkers and seeks "to further the cause of justice among persons living in poverty by mobilizing the assistance of lawyers and legal institutions and by providing legal advice, legal representation, counseling, education, and other appropriate services."

These ends would not be gained if the intended beneficiaries could be insulated from efforts to reach them. It is in this framework that we must decide whether the camp operator's rights in his lands may stand between the migrant workers and those who would aid them. The key to that aid is communication. Since the migrant workers are outside the mainstream of the communities in which they are housed and are unaware of their rights and opportunities and of the services available to them, they can be reached only by positive efforts tailored to that end. *The Report of the Governor's Task Force on Migrant Farm Labor* (1968) noted that "One of the major problems related to seasonal farm labor is the lack of adequate direct information with regard to the availability of public services," and that "there is a dire need to provide the workers with basic educational and informational material in a language and style that can be readily understood by the migrant" (pp. 101–102). The report stressed the problem of access and deplored the notion that property rights may stand as a barrier, saying "In our judgment, 'no trespass' signs represent the last dying remnants of paternalistic behavior" (p. 63).

A man's right in his real property of course is not absolute. It was a maxim of the common law that one should so use his property as not to injure the rights of others. Broom, Legal Maxims (10th ed. Kersley

1939), p. 238; 39 Words and Phrases, "Sic Utere Tuo ut Alienum Non Laedas," p. 335. Although hardly a precise solvent of actual controversies, the maxim does express the inevitable proposition that rights are relative and there must be an accommodation when they meet. Hence it has long been true that necessity, private or public, may justify entry upon the lands of another. For a catalogue of such situations, see Prosser, Torts (3d ed. 1964), § 24, pp. 127–129; 6A American Law of Property (A.J. Casner ed. 1954) § 28.10, p. 31; 52 Am.Jur., "Trespass," §§ 40–41, pp. 867–869. See also Restatement, Second, Torts (1965) §§ 197–211; Krauth v. Geller, 31 N.J. 270, 272–273, 157 A.2d 129 (1960).

The subject is not static. As pointed out in 5 Powell, Real Property (Rohan 1970) § 745, pp. 493–494, while society will protect the owner in his permissible interests in land, yet

". . . [S]uch an owner must expect to find the absoluteness of his property rights curtailed by the organs of society, for the promotion of the best interests of others for whom these organs also operate as protective agencies. The necessity for such curtailments is greater in a modern industrialized and urbanized society than it was in the relatively simple American society of fifty, 100, or 200 years ago. The current balance between individualism and dominance of the social interest depends not only upon political and social ideologies, but also upon the physical and social facts of the time and place under discussion."

Professor Powell added in § 746, pp. 494–496:

"As one looks back along the historic road traversed by the law of land in England and in America, one sees a change from the viewpoint that he who owns may do as he pleases with what he owns, to a position which hesitatingly embodies an ingredient of stewardship; which grudgingly, but steadily, broadens the recognized scope of social interests in the utilization of things. . . .

"To one seeing history through the glasses of religion, these changes may seem to evidence increasing embodiments of the golden rule. To one thinking in terms of political and economic ideologies, they are likely to be labeled evidences of 'social enlightenment,' or of 'creeping socialism' or even of 'communistic infiltration,' according to the individual's assumed definitions and retained or acquired prejudices. With slight attention to words or labels, time marches on toward new adjustments between individualism and the social interests."

This process involves not only the accommodation between the right of the owner and the interests of the general public in his use of his property, but involves also an accommodation between the right of the owner and the right of individuals who are parties with him in consensual transactions relating to the use of the property. Accordingly substantial alterations have been made as between a landlord and his tenant. See Reste Realty Corp. v. Cooper, 53 N.J. 444, 451–453, 251 A.2d 268 (1969); Marini v. Ireland, 56 N.J. 130, 141–143, 265 A.2d 526 (1970).

The argument in this case understandably included the question whether the migrant worker should be deemed to be a tenant and thus entitled to the tenant's right to receive visitors, Williams v. Lubbering, 73 N.J.L. 317, 319–320, 63 A. 90 (Sup.Ct.1906), or whether his residence on the employer's property should be deemed to be merely incidental and in aid of his employment, and hence to involve no possessory interest in the realty. . . .

We see no profit in trying to decide upon a conventional category and then forcing the present subject into it. That approach would be artificial and distorting. The quest is for a fair adjustment of the competing needs of the parties, in the light of the realities of the relationship between the migrant worker and the operator of the housing facility.

Thus approaching the case, we find it unthinkable that the farmer-employer can assert a right to isolate the migrant worker in any respect significant for the worker's well-being. The farmer, of course, is entitled to pursue his farming activities without interference, and this defendants readily concede. But we see no legitimate need for a right in the farmer to deny the worker the opportunity for aid available from federal, State, or local services, or from recognized charitable groups seeking to assist him. Hence representatives of these agencies and organizations may enter upon the premises to seek out the worker at his living quarters. So, too, the migrant worker must be allowed to receive visitors there of his own choice, so long as there is no behavior hurtful to others, and members of the press may not be denied reasonable access to workers who do not object to seeing them.

It is not our purpose to open the employer's premises to the general public if in fact the employer himself has not done so. We do not say, for example, that solicitors or peddlers of all kinds may enter on their own; we may assume for the present that the employer may regulate their entry or bar them, at least if the employer's purpose is not to gain a commercial advantage for himself or if the regulation does not deprive the migrant worker of practical access to things he needs.

And we are mindful of the employer's interest in his own and in his employees' security. Hence he may reasonably require a visitor to identify himself, and also to state his general purpose if the migrant worker has not already informed him that the visitor is expected. But the employer may not deny the worker his privacy or interfere with his opportunity to live with dignity and to enjoy associations customary among our citizens. These rights are too fundamental to be denied on the basis of an interest in real property and too fragile to be left to the unequal bargaining strength of the parties. [Citations omitted.]

It follows that defendants here invaded no possessory right of the farmer-employer. Their conduct was therefore beyond the reach of the trespass statute. The judgments are accordingly reversed and the matters remanded to the County Court with directions to enter judgments of acquittal.

For reversal and remandment: CHIEF JUSTICE WEINTRAUB and JUSTICES JACOBS, FRANCIS, PROCTOR, HALL and SCHETTINO—6.

For affirmance: None.

NOTES

1. Along similar lines, see Agricultural Labor Relations Board v. Superior Court, 16 Cal.3d 392, 128 Cal.Rptr. 183, 546 P.2d 687 (1976). California's Labor Relations Board had adopted a regulation requiring farm owners to permit union organizers to enter their farms to speak with workers. The California Supreme Court said that this was not an unconstitutional taking of the farm owner's property. An appeal to the United States Supreme Court was dismissed under the name of Pandol v. Agricultural Labor Relations Board, 429 U.S. 802, 97 S.Ct. 34, 50 L.Ed.2d 63 (1976).

2. The principal case is included here to broaden your concept of property but it contains constitutional overtones which you are not now equipped to appreciate. See Hudgens v. N.L.R.B., 424 U.S. 507, 96 S.Ct. 1029, 47 L.Ed.2d 196 (1976), where the United States Supreme Court held that warehouse employees of a company which operated a retail store in a shopping center had no First Amendment right to enter the shopping center for the purpose of advertising their strike against the employer. The first amendment does protect such activity in a company town but not in a private shopping center. How would the United States Supreme Court have reacted to State v. Shack? What are the limits of private property?

You should now have a better idea of what lawyers mean by the "nebulous" term, property. In a sense, we will be exploring the meaning of the word property throughout these materials and, at the end, you will find it to be a "chameleon-like concept of seductive simplicity." We hope you will understand the concept even though it defies ready definition.

It has been said that all substantive law is secreted in the interstices of procedure, i.e., the law of property, contracts, torts, et al. is shaped by the legal procedures used to define and narrow the issues. If property is the legal relationship among people in regard to a *res,* then it is important to know which individual or group of individuals can assert legal rights to a thing—land or chattels. The right to sue to protect a claimed interest casts further light on our initial question. Note how the United States Supreme Court dealt with that problem in an environmental case.

SIERRA CLUB v. MORTON

Supreme Court of the United States, 1972.
405 U.S. 727, 92 S.Ct. 1361, 31 L.Ed.2d 636.

MR. JUSTICE STEWART delivered the opinion of the Court.

I.

The Mineral King Valley is an area of great natural beauty nestled in the Sierra Nevada Mountains in Tulare County, California, adjacent to Sequoia National Park. It has been part of the Sequoia National Forest since 1926, and is designated as a National Game Refuge by special Act of Congress.[1] Though once the site of extensive mining activity, Mineral King is now used almost exclusively for recreational purposes. Its relative inaccessibility and lack of development have limited the number of visitors each year, and at the same time have preserved the valley's quality as a quasi-wilderness area largely uncluttered by the products of civilization.

The United States Forest Service, which is entrusted with the maintenance and administration of national forests, began in the late 1940's to give consideration to Mineral King as a potential site for recreational development. Prodded by a rapidly increasing demand for skiing facilities, the Forest Service published a prospectus in 1965, inviting bids from private developers for the construction and operation of a ski resort that would also serve as a summer recreation area. The proposal of Walt Disney Enterprises, Inc., was chosen from those of six bidders, and Disney received a three-year permit to conduct surveys and explorations in the valley in connection with its preparation of a complete master plan for the resort.

The final Disney plan, approved by the Forest Service in January, 1969, outlines a $35 million complex of motels, restaurants, swimming pools, parking lots, and other structures designed to accommodate 14,000 visitors daily. This complex is to be constructed on 80 acres of the valley floor under a 30-year use permit from the Forest Service. Other facilities, including ski lifts, ski trails, a cog-assisted railway, and utility installations, are to be constructed on the mountain slopes and in other parts of the valley under a revocable special use permit. To provide access to the resort, the State of California proposes to construct a highway 20 miles in length. A section of this road would traverse Sequoia National Park, as would a proposed high-voltage power line needed to provide electricity for the resort. Both the highway and the power line require the approval of the Department of the Interior, which is entrusted with the preservation and maintenance of the national parks.

Representatives of the Sierra Club, who favor maintaining Mineral King largely in its present state, followed the progress of recreational planning for the valley with close attention and increasing dismay. They unsuccessfully sought a public hearing on the proposed development in 1965, and in subsequent correspondence with officials of the Forest Service and the Department of the Interior, they expressed the Club's objections to Disney's plan as a whole and to particular features included in it. In June of 1969 the Club filed the present suit in the

1. Act of July 3, 1926, 44 Stat. 821, 16 U.S.C.A. § 688. [Footnotes in the case are by the court and numbered accordingly.]

United States District Court for the Northern District of California, seeking a declaratory judgment that various aspects of the proposed development contravene federal laws and regulations governing the preservation of national parks, forests, and game refuges[2] and also seeking preliminary and permanent injunctions restraining the federal officials involved from granting their approval or issuing permits in connection with the Mineral King project. The petitioner Sierra Club sued as a membership corporation with "a special interest in the conservation and sound maintenance of the national parks, game refuges, and forests of the country," and invoked the judicial review provisions of the Administrative Procedure Act, 5 U.S.C.A. § 701 et seq.

After two days of hearings, the District Court granted the requested preliminary injunction. It rejected the respondents' challenge to the Sierra Club's standing to sue, and determined that the hearing had raised questions "concerning possible excess of statutory authority, sufficiently substantial and serious to justify a preliminary injunction . . . ." The respondents appealed, and the Court of Appeals for the Ninth Circuit reversed. 433 F.2d 24. With respect to the petitioner's standing, the court noted that there was "no allegation in the complaint that members of the Sierra Club would be affected by the actions of [the respondents] other than the fact that the actions are personally displeasing or distasteful to them," id., at 33, and concluded:

"We do not believe such club concern without a showing of more direct interest can constitute standing in the legal sense sufficient to challenge the exercise of responsibilities on behalf of all the citizens by two cabinet level officials of the government acting under Congressional and Constitutional authority." Id., at 30.

Alternatively, the Court of Appeals held that the Sierra Club had not made an adequate showing of irreparable injury and likelihood of success on the merits to justify issuance of a preliminary injunction. The court thus vacated the injunction. The Sierra Club filed a petition for a writ of certiorari which we granted, 401 U.S. 907, 91 S.Ct. 870, 27 L.Ed.2d 805, to review the questions of federal law presented.

II.

The first question presented is whether the Sierra Club has alleged facts that entitle it to obtain judicial review of the challenged action. Whether a party has a sufficient stake in an otherwise justiciable controversy to obtain judicial resolution of that controversy is what has

2. As analyzed by the District Court, the complaint alleged violations of law falling into four categories. First, it claimed that the special use permit for construction of the resort exceeded the maximum acreage limitation placed upon such permits by 16 U.S.C.A. § 497, and that issuance of a "revocable" use permit was beyond the authority of the Forest Service. Second, it challenged the proposed permit for the highway through Sequoia National Park on the grounds that the highway would not serve any of the purposes of the park in alleged violation of 16 U.S.C.A. § 1, and that it would destroy timber and other natural resources protected by 16 U.S.C.A. §§ 41 and 43. Third, it claimed that the Forest Service and the Department of the Interior had violated their own regulations by failing to hold adequate public hearings on the proposed project. Finally, the complaint asserted that 16 U.S.C.A. § 45(c) requires specific congressional authorization of a permit for construction of a power transmission line within the limits of a national park.

traditionally been referred to as the question of standing to sue. Where the party does not rely on any specific statute authorizing invocation of the judicial process, the question of standing depends upon whether the party has alleged such a "personal stake in the outcome of the controversy," Baker v. Carr, 369 U.S. 186, 204, 82 S.Ct. 691, 703, 7 L.Ed.2d 663, as to ensure that "the dispute sought to be adjudicated will be presented in an adversary context and in a form historically viewed as capable of judicial resolution." Flast v. Cohen, 392 U.S. 83, 101, 88 S.Ct. 1942, 1953, 20 L.Ed.2d 947. Where, however, Congress has authorized public officials to perform certain functions according to law, and has provided by statute for judicial review of those actions under certain circumstances, the inquiry as to standing must begin with a determination of whether the statute in question authorizes review at the behest of the plaintiff.[3]

The Sierra Club relies upon § 10 of the Administrative Procedure Act (APA), 5 U.S.C. § 702, which provides:

> "A person suffering legal wrong because of agency action, or adversely affected or aggrieved by agency action within the meaning of a relevant statute, is entitled to judicial review thereof."

Early decisions under this statute interpreted the language as adopting the various formulations of "legal interest" and "legal wrong" then prevailing as constitutional requirements of standing. But, in Association of Data Processing Service Organizations, Inc. v. Camp, 397 U.S. 150, 90 S.Ct. 827, 25 L.Ed.2d 184, and Barlow v. Collins, 397 U.S. 159, 90 S.Ct. 832, 25 L.Ed.2d 192, decided the same day, we held more broadly that persons had standing to obtain judicial review of federal agency action under § 10 of the APA where they had alleged that the challenged action had caused them "injury in fact," and where the alleged injury was to an interest "arguably within the zone of interests to be protected or regulated" by the statutes that the agencies were claimed to have violated.

In *Data Processing,* the injury claimed by the petitioners consisted of harm to their competitive position in the computer servicing market through a ruling by the Comptroller of the Currency that national banks might perform data processing services for their customers. In *Barlow,* the petitioners were tenant farmers who claimed that certain regulations of the Secretary of Agriculture adversely affected their

3. Congress may not confer jurisdiction on Art. III federal courts to render advisory opinions, Muskrat v. United States, 219 U.S. 346, 31 S.Ct. 450, 55 L.Ed. 246, or to entertain "friendly" suits, United States v. Johnson, 319 U.S. 302, 63 S.Ct. 1075, 87 L.Ed. 1413, or to resolve "political questions," Luther v. Borden, 7 How. 1, 12 L.Ed. 581, because suits of this character are inconsistent with the judicial function under Art. III. But where a dispute is otherwise justiciable, the question whether the litigant is a "proper party to request an adjudication of a particular issue," Flast v. Cohen, 392 U.S. 83, 100, 88 S.Ct. 1942, 1952, 20 L.Ed.2d 947, is one within the power of Congress to determine. Cf. FCC v. Sanders Bros. Radio Station, 309 U.S. 470, 477, 60 S.Ct. 693, 698, 84 L.Ed. 869; Flast v. Cohen, *supra,* 392 U.S., at 120, 88 S.Ct., at 1963 (Harlan, J., dissenting); Associated Industries of New York State v. Ickes, 2 Cir., 134 F.2d 694, 704. See generally Berger, Standing to Sue in Public Actions: Is it a Constitutional Requirement?, 78 Yale L.J. 816, 827 et seq. (1969); Jaffe, The Citizen as Litigant in Public Actions: The Non-Hohfeldian or Ideological Plaintiff, 116 U.Pa.L.Rev. 1033 (1968).

economic position vis-à-vis their landlords. These palpable economic injuries have long been recognized as sufficient to lay the basis for standing, with or without a specific statutory provision for judicial review. Thus, neither *Data Processing* nor *Barlow* addressed itself to the question, which has arisen with increasing frequency in federal courts in recent years, as to what must be alleged by persons who claim injury of a noneconomic nature to interests that are widely shared.[4] That question is presented in this case.

III.

The injury alleged by the Sierra Club will be incurred entirely by reason of the change in the uses to which Mineral King will be put, and the attendant change in the aesthetics and ecology of the area. Thus, in referring to the road to be built through Sequoia National Park, the complaint alleged that the development "would destroy or otherwise affect the scenery, natural and historic objects and wildlife of the park and would impair the enjoyment of the park for future generations." We do not question that this type of harm may amount to an "injury in fact" sufficient to lay the basis for standing under § 10 of the APA. Aesthetic and environmental well-being, like economic well-being, are important ingredients of the quality of life in our society, and the fact that particular environmental interests are shared by the many rather than the few does not make them less deserving of legal protection through the judicial process. But the "injury in fact" test requires more than an injury to a cognizable interest. It requires that the party seeking review be himself among the injured.

The impact of the proposed changes in the environment of Mineral King will not fall indiscriminately upon every citizen. The alleged injury will be felt directly only by those who use Mineral King and Sequoia National Park, and for whom the aesthetic and recreational values of the area will be lessened by the highway and ski resort. The Sierra Club failed to allege that it or its members would be affected in any of their activities or pastimes by the Disney development. Nowhere in the pleadings or affidavits did the Club state that its members use Mineral King for any purpose, much less that they use it in any way that would be significantly affected by the proposed actions of the respondents.[5]

4. No question of standing was raised in Citizens to Preserve Overton Park, Inc. v. Volpe, 401 U.S. 402, 91 S.Ct. 814, 28 L.Ed.2d 136. The complaint in that case alleged that the organizational plaintiff represented members who were "residents of Memphis, Tennessee who use Overton Park as a park land and recreation area and who have been active since 1964 in efforts to preserve and protect Overton Park as a park land and recreation area."

5. The only reference in the pleadings to the Sierra Club's interest in the dispute is contained in paragraph 3 of the complaint, which reads in its entirety as follows:

"Plaintiff Sierra Club is a non-profit corporation organized and operating under the laws of the State of California, with its principal place of business in San Francisco, California since 1892. Membership of the Club is approximately 78,000 nationally, with approximately 27,000 members residing in the San Francisco Bay area. For many years the Sierra Club by its activities and conduct has exhibited a special interest in the conservation and sound maintenance of the national parks, game refuges and forests of the country, regularly serving as a responsible representative of persons similarly interested. One of the

The Club apparently regarded any allegations of individualized injury as superfluous, on the theory that this was a "public" action involving questions as to the use of natural resources, and that the Club's longstanding concern with and expertise in such matters were sufficient to give it standing as a "representative of the public."[6] This theory reflects a misunderstanding of our cases involving so-called "public actions" in the area of administrative law.

The origin of the theory advanced by the Sierra Club may be traced to a dictum in Scripps-Howard Radio, Inc. v. FCC, 316 U.S. 4, 62 S.Ct. 875, 86 L.Ed. 1229, in which the licensee of a radio station in Cincinnati, Ohio, sought a stay of an order of the FCC allowing another radio station in a nearby city to change its frequency and increase its range. In discussing its power to grant a stay, the Court noted that "these private litigants have standing only as representatives of the public interest." Id., at 14, 62 S.Ct., at 882. But that observation did not describe the basis upon which the appellant was allowed to obtain judicial review as a "person aggrieved" within the meaning of the statute involved in that case,[7] since Scripps-Howard was clearly "aggrieved" by reason of the economic injury that it would suffer as a result of the Commission's action.[8] The Court's statement was rather directed to the theory upon which Congress had authorized judicial review of the Commission's actions. That theory had been described earlier in FCC v. Sanders Bros. Radio Station, 309 U.S. 470, 477, 60 S.Ct. 693, 698, 84 L.Ed. 869, as follows:

"Congress had some purpose in enacting § 402(b)(2). It may have been of opinion that one likely to be financially injured by the issue of a license would be the only person having a sufficient interest to bring to the attention of the appellate court errors of law in the action of the Commission in granting the license. It is within the power of Congress to confer such standing to prosecute an appeal."

principal purposes of the Sierra Club is to protect and conserve the national resources of the Sierra Nevada Mountains. Its interests would be vitally affected by the acts hereinafter described and would be aggrieved by those acts of the defendants as hereinafter more fully appears."

In an *amici curiae* brief filed in this Court by the Wilderness Society and others, it is asserted that the Sierra Club has conducted regular camping trips into the Mineral King area, and that various members of the Club have used and continue to use the area for recreational purposes. These allegations were not contained in the pleadings, nor were they brought to the attention of the Court of Appeals. Moreover, the Sierra Club in its reply brief specifically declines to rely on its individualized interest, as a basis for standing. . . . Our decision does not, of course, bar the Sierra Club from seeking in the District Court to amend its complaint by a motion under Rule 15, Federal Rules of Civil Procedure.

6. This approach to the question of standing was adopted by the Court of Appeals for the Second Circuit in Citizens Committee for the Hudson Valley v. Volpe, 425 F.2d 97, 105:

"We hold, therefore, that the public interest in environmental resources—an interest created by statutes affecting the issuance of this permit—is a legally protected interest affording these plaintiffs, as responsible representatives of the public, standing to obtain judicial review of agency action alleged to be in contravention of that public interest."

7. The statute involved was § 402(b)(2) of the Communications Act of 1934, 48 Stat. 1064, 1093.

8. This much is clear from the *Scripps-Howard* Court's citation of FCC v. Sanders Bros. Radio Station, 309 U.S. 470, 60 S.Ct. 693, 84 L.Ed. 869, in which the basis for standing was the competitive injury that the appellee would have suffered by the licensing of another radio station in its listening area.

Taken together, *Sanders* and *Scripps-Howard* thus established a dual proposition: the fact of economic injury is what gives a person standing to seek judicial review under the statute, but once review is properly invoked, that person may argue the public interest in support of his claim that the agency has failed to comply with its statutory mandate.[9] It was in the latter sense that the "standing" of the appellant in *Scripps-Howard* existed only as a "representative of the public interest." It is in a similar sense that we have used the phrase "private attorney general" to describe the function performed by persons upon whom Congress has conferred the right to seek judicial review of agency action. See *Data Processing,* supra, at 154, 90 S.Ct., at 830.

The trend of cases arising under the APA and other statutes authorizing judicial review of federal agency action has been towards recognizing that injuries other than economic harm are sufficient to bring a person within the meaning of the statutory language, and towards discarding the notion that an injury that is widely shared is *ipso facto* not an injury sufficient to provide the basis for judicial review.[10] We noted this development with approval in *Data Processing,* supra, at 154, 90 S.Ct., at 830, in saying that the interest alleged to have been injured "may reflect 'aesthetic, conservational, and recreational' as well as economic values." But broadening the categories of injury that may be alleged in support of standing is a different matter from abandoning the requirement that the party seeking review must have himself suffered an injury.

Some courts have indicated a willingness to take this latter step by conferring standing upon organizations that have demonstrated "an organizational interest in the problem" of environmental or consumer protection. Environmental Defense Fund, Inc. v. Hardin, 138 U.S.App. D.C. 391, 395, 428 F.2d 1093, 1097.[11] It is clear that an or-

9. The distinction between standing to initiate a review proceeding, and standing to assert the rights of the public or of third persons once the proceeding is properly initiated, is discussed in 3 Davis, Administrative Law Treatise, §§ 22.05–22.07 (1958).

10. See, e.g., Environmental Defense Fund, Inc. v. Hardin, 428 F.2d 1093, 1097 (interest in health affected by decision of Secretary of Agriculture refusing to suspend registration of certain pesticides containing DDT); Office of Communication of the United Church of Christ v. FCC, 359 F.2d 994, 1005 (interest of television viewers in the programming of a local station licensed by the FCC); Scenic Hudson Preservation Conf. v. FPC, 354 F.2d 608, 615–616 (interests in aesthetics, recreation, and orderly community planning affected by FPC licensing of a hydroelectric project); Reade v. Ewing, 205 F.2d 630, 631–632 (interest of consumers of oleomargarine in fair labeling of product regulated by Federal Security Administration); Crowther v. Seaborg, 312 F.Supp. 1205, 1212 (interest in health and safety of persons residing near the site of a proposed atomic blast).

11. See Citizens Committee for the Hudson Valley v. Volpe, n. 6, supra; Environmental Defense Fund, Inc. v. Corps of Engineers, 325 F.Supp. 728, 734–736; Izaac Walton League v. St. Clair, 313 F.Supp. 1312, 1317. See also Scenic Hudson Preservation Conf. v. FPC, supra, at 616:

> "In order to ensure that the Federal Power Commission will adequately protect the public interest in the aesthetic, conservational, and recreational aspects of power development, those who by their activities and conduct have exhibited a special interest in such areas, must be held to be included in the class of 'aggrieved' parties under § 313(b) [of the Federal Power Act]."

In most, if not all of these cases, at least one party to the proceeding did assert an individualized injury either to himself or, in the case of an organization, to its members.

ganization whose members are injured may represent those members in a proceeding for judicial review. See, e.g., NAACP v. Button, 371 U.S. 415, 428, 83 S.Ct. 328, 335, 9 L.Ed.2d 405. But a mere "interest in a problem," no matter how longstanding the interest and no matter how qualified the organization is in evaluating the problem, is not sufficient by itself to render the organization "adversely affected" or "aggrieved" within the meaning of the APA. The Sierra Club is a large and long-established organization, with an historic commitment to the cause of protecting our Nation's natural heritage from man's depredations. But if a "special interest" in this subject were enough to entitle the Sierra Club to commence this litigation, there would appear to be no objective basis upon which to disallow a suit by any other bona fide "special interest" organization, however small or short-lived. And if any group with a bona fide "special interest" could initiate such litigation, it is difficult to perceive why any individual citizen with the same bona fide special interest would not also be entitled to do so.

The requirement that a party seeking review must allege facts showing that he is himself adversely affected does not insulate executive action from judicial review, nor does it prevent any public interests from being protected through the judicial process.[12] It does serve as at least a rough attempt to put the decision as to whether review will be sought in the hands of those who have a direct stake in the outcome. That goal would be undermined were we to construe the APA to authorize judicial review at the behest of organizations or individuals who seek to do no more than vindicate their own value preferences through the judicial process.[13] The principle that the Sierra Club would have us establish in this case would do just that.

As we conclude that the Court of Appeals was correct in its holding that the Sierra Club lacked standing to maintain this action, we do not

12. In its reply brief, after noting the fact that it might have chosen to assert individualized injury to itself or to its members as a basis for standing, the Sierra Club states:

> "The Government seeks to create a 'heads I win, tails you lose' situation in which either the courthouse door is barred for lack of assertion of a private, unique injury or a preliminary injunction is denied on the ground that the litigant has advanced private injury which does not warrant an injunction adverse to a competing public interest. Counsel have shaped their case to avoid this trap."

The short answer to this contention is that the "trap" does not exist. The test of injury in fact goes only to the question of standing to obtain judicial review. Once this standing is established, the party may assert the interests of the general public in support of his claims for equitable relief. See n. 9 and accompanying text, supra.

13. Every schoolboy may be familiar with de Tocqueville's famous observation, written in the 1830's, that "Scarcely any political question arises in the United States that is not resolved, sooner or later, into a judicial question." 1 Democracy in America 280 (Alfred A. Knopf, 1945). Less familiar, however, is de Tocqueville's further observation that judicial review is effective largely because it is not available simply at the behest of a partisan faction, but is exercised only to remedy a particular, concrete injury.

> "It will be seen, also, that by leaving it to private interest to censure the law, and by intimately uniting the trial of the law with the trial of an individual, legislation is protected from wanton assaults and from the daily aggressions of party spirit. The errors of the legislator are exposed only to meet a real want; and it is always a positive and appreciable fact that must serve as the basis for a prosecution." Id., at 102.

reach any other questions presented in the petition, and we intimate no view on the merits of the complaint. The judgment is

Affirmed.

MR. JUSTICE POWELL and MR. JUSTICE REHNQUIST took no part in the consideration or decision of this case.

MR. JUSTICE BRENNAN, dissenting.

I agree that the Sierra Club has standing for the reasons stated by my Brother Blackmun in Alternative No. 2 of his dissent. I therefore would reach the merits. Since the Court does not do so, however, I simply note agreement with my Brother Blackmun that the merits are substantial.

MR. JUSTICE BLACKMUN, dissenting.

Rather than pursue the course the Court has chosen to take by its affirmance of the judgment of the Court of Appeals, I would adopt one of two alternatives:

1. I would reverse that judgment and, instead, approve the judgment of the District Court which recognized standing in the Sierra Club and granted preliminary relief. I would be willing to do this on condition that the Sierra Club forthwith amend its complaint to meet the specifications the Court prescribes for standing. If Sierra Club fails or refuses to take that step, so be it; the case will then collapse. But if it does amend, the merits will be before the trial court once again. . . .

2. Alternatively, I would permit an imaginative expansion of our traditional concepts of standing in order to enable an organization such as the Sierra Club, possessed, as it is, of pertinent, bona fide and well-recognized attributes and purposes in the area of environment, to litigate environmental issues. This incursion upon tradition need not be very extensive. Certainly, it should be no cause for alarm. It is no more progressive than was the decision in *Data Processing* itself. It need only recognize the interest of one who has a provable, sincere, dedicated, and established status. We need not fear that Pandora's box will be opened or that there will be no limit to the number of those who desire to participate in environmental litigation. The courts will exercise appropriate restraints just as they have exercised them in the past. . . .

MR. JUSTICE DOUGLAS, dissenting.

I share the views of my Brother Blackmun and would reverse the judgment below.

The critical question of "standing" would be simplified and also put neatly in focus if we fashioned a federal rule that allowed environmental issues to be litigated before federal agencies or federal courts in the name of the inanimate object about to be despoiled, defaced, or invaded by roads and bulldozers and where injury is the subject of public outrage. Contemporary public concern for protecting nature's ecological equilibrium should lead to the conferral of standing upon environmental objects to sue for their own preservation. See Stone, Should

Trees Have Standing? Toward Legal Rights for Natural Objects, 45 S.Cal.L.Rev. 450 (1972). This suit would therefore be more properly labeled as Mineral King v. Morton.

Inanimate objects are sometimes parties in litigation. A ship has a legal personality, a fiction found useful for maritime purposes.[14] The corporation sole—a creature of ecclesiastical law—is an acceptable adversary and large fortunes ride on its cases.[15] The ordinary corporation is a "person" for purposes of the adjudicatory processes, whether it represents proprietary, spiritual, aesthetic, or charitable causes.[16]

So it should be as respects valleys, alpine meadows, rivers, lakes, estuaries, beaches, ridges, groves of trees, swampland, or even air that feels the destructive pressures of modern technology and modern life. The river, for example, is the living symbol of all the life it sustains or nourishes—fish, aquatic insects, water ouzels, otter, fisher, deer, elk, bear, and all other animals, including man, who are dependent on it or who enjoy it for its sight, its sound, or its life. The river as plaintiff speaks for the ecological unit of life that is part of it. Those people who have a meaningful relation to that body of water—whether it be a fisherman, a canoeist, a zoologist, or a logger—must be able to speak for the values which the river represents and which are threatened with destruction. . . .

The Solicitor General . . . takes a wholly different approach. He considers the problem in terms of "government by the Judiciary." With all respect, the problem is to make certain that the inanimate objects, which are the very core of America's beauty, have spokesmen before they are destroyed. It is, of course, true that most of them are under the control of a federal or state agency. . . .

14. *In rem* actions brought to adjudicate libellants' interests in vessels are well known in admiralty. Gilmore & Black, The Law of Admiralty 31 (1957). But admiralty also permits a salvage action to be brought in the name of the rescuing vessel. The Camanche, 8 Wall. 449, 476, 19 L.Ed. 397 (1869). And, in collision litigation, the first-libelled ship may counterclaim in its own name. The Gylfe v. The Trujillo, 209 F.2d 386 (CA2 1954). Our case law has personified vessels:

> "A ship is born when she is launched, and lives so long as her identity is preserved. Prior to her launching she is a mere congeries of wood and iron. . . . In the baptism of launching she receives her name, and from the moment her keel touches the water she is transformed. . . . She acquires a personality of her own." Tucker v. Alexandroff, 183 U.S. 424, 438, 22 S.Ct. 195, 201, 46 L.Ed. 264.

15. At common law, an office holder, such as a priest or the King and his successors constituted a corporation sole, a legal entity distinct from the personality which managed it. Rights and duties were deemed to adhere to this device rather than to the office holder in order to provide continuity after the latter retired. The notion is occasionally revived by American courts. E.g., Reid v. Barry, 93 Fla. 849, 112 So. 846 (1927), discussed in Note, 12 Minn.L.Rev. 295 (1928), and in Note, 26 Mich.L.Rev. 545 (1928); see generally 1 Fletcher, Cyclopedia Corporation, §§ 50–53; P. Potter, Law of Corporation 27 (1881).

16. Early jurists considered the conventional corporation to be a highly artificial entity. Lord Coke opined that a corporation's creation "rests only in intendment and consideration of the law." The Case of Suttons Hospital, 77 Eng.Rep. 937, 973 (K.B.1613). Mr. Chief Justice Marshall added that the device is "an artificial being, invisible, intangible, and existing only in contemplation of law." Trustees of Dartmouth College v. Woodward, 4 Wheat 518, 636, 4 L.Ed. 629 (1819). Today suits in the names of corporations are taken for granted.

Yet the pressures on agencies for favorable action one way or the other are enormous. The suggestion that Congress can stop action which is undesirable is true in theory; yet even Congress is too remote to give meaningful direction and its machinery is too ponderous to use very often. The federal agencies of which I speak are not venal or corrupt. But they are notoriously under the control of powerful interests who manipulate them through advisory committees, or friendly working relations, or who have that natural affinity with the agency which in time develops between the regulator and the regulated. . . .

The Forest Service—one of the federal agencies behind the scheme to despoil Mineral King—has been notorious for its alignment with lumber companies, although its mandate from Congress directs is to consider the various aspects of multiple use in its supervision of the national forests.[17]

The voice of the inanimate object, therefore, should not be stilled. That does not mean that the judiciary takes over the managerial functions from the federal agency. It merely means that before these priceless bits of Americana (such as a valley, an alpine meadow, a river, or a lake) are forever lost or are so transformed as to be reduced to the eventual rubble of our urban environment, the voice of the existing beneficiaries of these environmental wonders should be heard.[18] . . .

Those who hike the Appalachian Trial into Sunfish Pond, New Jersey, and camp or sleep there, or run the Allagash in Maine, or climb the Guadalupes in West Texas, or who canoe and portage the Quetico Superior in Minnesota, certainly should have standing to defend those natural wonders before courts or agencies, though they live 3,000 miles away. Those who merely are caught up in environmental news or propaganda and flock to defend these waters or areas may be treated differently. That is why these environmental issues should be tendered by the inanimate object itself. Then there will be assurances that all of the forms of life which it represents will stand before the court—the pileated woodpecker as well as the coyote and bear, the lemmings as well as the trout in the streams. Those inarticulate members of the ecological group cannot speak. But those people who have so fre-

17. The Forest Reserve Act of 1897, 30 Stat. 34, 16 U.S.C.A. § 551, imposed upon the Secretary of the Interior the duty to "preserve the [national] forests . . . from destruction" by regulating their "occupancy and use." In 1905 these duties and powers were transferred to the Forest Service created within the Department of Agriculture by the Act of Feb. 1, 1905, 33 Stat. 628, 16 U.S.C.A. § 472. The phrase "occupancy and use" has been the cornerstone for the concept of "multiple use" of national forests, that is, the policy that uses other than logging were also to be taken into consideration in managing our 154 national forests. This policy was made more explicit by the 1960 Multiple Use and Sustained Yield Act, 74 Stat. 215, 43 U.S.C.A. § 315, which provides that competing considerations should include outdoor recreation, range, timber, watershed, wildlife and fish purposes. The Forest Service, influenced by powerful logging interests, has, however, paid only lip service to its multiple use mandate and has auctioned away millions of timberland acres without considering environmental or conservational interests. . . .

18. Permitting a court to appoint a representative of an inanimate object would not be significantly different from customary judicial appointments of guardians *ad litem*, executors, conservators, receivers, or counsel for indigents. . . .

quented the place as to know its values and wonders will be able to speak for the entire ecological community.

Ecology reflects the land ethic; and Aldo Leopold wrote in A Sand County Almanac 204 (1949), "The land ethic simply enlarges the boundaries of the community to include soils, waters, plants, and animals, or collectively, the land."

That, as I see it, is the issue of "standing" in the present case and controversy.

NOTES

1. The critical issue of standing to sue is a complex one. Do not read the principal case too broadly or it will be misleading. The issue will be covered in more detail in your procedure courses. For now, we are concerned with the light it sheds on the question: "What is property?"

2. For an extended discussion of the problem presented by the principal case see Stone, Should Trees Have Standing? (Toward Legal Rights For Natural Objects) (1974). See also Stone, Should Trees Have Standing? Revisited: How Far Will Law and Morals Reach? A Pluralist Perspective, 59 So.Calif.L.Rev. 1 (1985). The latter article is too long and difficult for your analysis at this time but perhaps you will appreciate Footnote 9 in the article which is reprinted verbatim.

"9. One attorney, skeptical of the Trees thesis, rhymed his doubts:

If Justice Douglas has his way—
O come not that dreadful day—
We'll be sued by lakes and hills
Seeking a redress of ills.
Great mountain peaks of name prestigious
Will suddenly become litigious.
Our brooks will babble in the courts,
Seeking damages for torts.
How can I rest beneath a tree
If it may soon be suing me?
Or enjoy the playful porpoise
While it's seeking habeas corpus?
Every beast within his paws
Will clutch an order to show cause.
The courts, besieged on every hand,
Will crowd with suits by chunks of land.
Ah! But vengeance will be sweet,
Since this must be a two-way street.
I'll promptly sue my neighbor's tree
For shedding all its leaves on me.

"Naff, Reflections on the Dissent of Douglas, J., in Sierra Club v. Morton, 58 A.B.A.J. 820, 820 (1972). The style, although it fails to confront us natural object advocates head-on, prose to prose, took hold. In disposing of a suit by a tree owner to recover from a negligent driver for injuries to the tree, the Oakland, Michigan County Appeals Court affirmed dismissal with the following opinion in its entirety:

> We thought that we would never see
> A suit to compensate a tree.
> A suit whose claim in tort is prest
> Upon a mangled tree's behest;
> A tree whose battered trunk was prest
> Against a Chevy's crumpled crest,
> A tree that faces each new day
> With bark and limb in disarray;
> A tree that may forever bear
> A lasting need for tender care.
> Flora lovers though we three
> We must uphold the court's decree.

"Fisher v. Lowe, 122 Mich.App. 418, 333 N.W.2d 67 (1983), quoted in 69 A.B.A.J. 436 (1983)."

Chapter 2

ATTRIBUTES OF PROPERTY

Whatever our concept of property may be, it is clear that one of its attributes is the universality of the institution of property both in time and space. Different societies will, naturally, have differing views as to the role and rules of property but all must recognize the basic human urge to own "things". Indeed, this urge may be said to transcend the human instinct and the animal kingdom too *may* have its "territorial imperative."

ARDREY, THE TERRITORIAL IMPERATIVE

Dell Publishing Co., Inc. (1966).
Pages 3, 4.

A territory is an area of space, whether of water or earth or air, which an animal or group of animals defends as an exclusive preserve. The word is also used to describe the inward compulsion in animate beings to possess and defend such a space. A territorial species of animals, therefore, is one which all males, and sometimes females too, bear an inherent drive to gain and defend an exclusive property. . . .

The concept of territory as a genetically determined form of behavior in many species is today accepted beyond question in the biological sciences. But so recently have our observations been made and our conclusions formed that we have yet to explore the implications of territory in our estimates of man. Is *Homo sapiens* a territorial species? Do we stake out property, chase off trespassers, defend our countries because we are sapient, or because we are animals? Because we choose, or because we must? Do certain laws of territorial behavior apply as rigorously in the affairs of men as in the affairs of chipmunks? That is the principal concern of this inquiry, and it is a matter of considerable concern, I believe, to any valid understanding of our nature. But it is a problem to be weighed in terms of present knowledge, not past.

FREEDMAN, CROWDING AND BEHAVIOR

The Viking Press, Inc. (1975).
Pages 26–32.

Almost all animals seem to display territorial behavior under some circumstances. They will protect a certain amount of territory and act aggressively toward any member of the same species attempting to intrude on it. There is no arguing about this, but the important question is whether this behavior is due to instinctive need for territory. It is known that animals sometimes react aggressively when they are crowded, and a territorial instinct would account for this behavior. Otherwise, the idea of territoriality is not an explanation but simply a description of how they behave. It is therefore necessary to look for evidence as to whether or not territoriality is instinctive. . . .

If territoriality is instinctive, it should not disappear even when food supply is unlimited. If it is an instinctive, innate reaction of the organism, if animals "need" a certain amount of space and will defend it from others, this should occur whether or not food is available. True, it will have greater adaptive and survival value when food is limited, but it should occur under all circumstances. Although there is very little direct evidence bearing on this question, it seems quite clear that the presence of ample amounts of food and water greatly reduces and perhaps eliminates entirely any territorial response. . . .

The reasons for believing that most animals do not have a territorial instinct are: First, animals seem to like physical contact. This is anecdotal evidence, but it suggests that there is no instinctive need for the individual animals to have a certain amount of space around them. It leaves open the possibility that a group or family needs a minimum amount of space or that under some circumstances the individual will also react to a lack of space.

Second, controlled studies on reactions to lack of space have produced mixed results. Reducing space while holding number constant sometimes increased aggressiveness, sometimes not. If there is an instinct, the results should be consistent, as an instinct is always in operation and does not vary from situation to situation. These results suggest, therefore, either that no instinct exists or that it is found only in certain species. They also indicate that other factors in the situation are much more important in determining behavior than is a need for territory.

Finally, the experiments on relatively short-term confinement demonstrate that the amount of space has little or no effect, while the number of other animals present does. Once again, if there were an instinctive territorial reaction, animals in smaller areas should show more negative responses. That they do not argues strongly against the instinctive notion.

Therefore, it seems unlikely that animals have built-in instinctive territorial instincts in the sense that Ardrey and others means it. Some animals may have such an instinct, and many animals probably have it under conditions involving limited food supply or protection of the nest or family. But the evidence seems clear that territorial behavior depends on these other factors and is not absolute. Lack of space by itself does not trigger an aggressive or defensive response, nor does it have other negative effects.

Would it be fair to say that property, in a legal sense, has any meaning for species other than mankind? Why or why not?

Note, however, that even the most primitive human societies have some concept of property.

LOWIE, INCORPOREAL PROPERTY IN PRIMITIVE SOCIETY

37 Yale L.J. 551–554, 561 (1928).

Among the problems that exercised the minds of the earlier evolutionists who dealt with human society, that of property was one of the most important. Its influence in modern industrial civilization was potent; hence the evolutionary schematist naturally assumed that in the earliest phases of culture it had been nil. Lewis H. Morgan's views may be taken as representative. He distinguished three major periods—Savagery, Barbarism, and Civilization. The beginnings of Barbarism were defined by the invention of pottery, those of Civilization by the use of a phonetic alphabet and literary records. The two former periods were subdivided each in a Lower, Middle and Upper Status. It was not until the Middle Status of Barbarism—exemplified by the village life of our Southwestern Indians, of the aboriginal Mexicans and the Peruvians—that Morgan assumed property to have played an important part. Among "savages," he held, property was inconsiderable.

"Their ideas concerning its value, its desirability and its inheritance were feeble. Rude weapons, fabrics, utensils, apparel, implements of flint, stone and bone, and personal ornaments represent the chief items of property in savage life. A passion for its possession had scarcely been formed in their minds, because the thing itself scarcely existed."

In short, Morgan does not deny that pre-ceramic savages had chattels, but he minimizes the importance of the property held, and of the correlated acquisitive urge. His successors have generally followed his leadership and assumed as a matter of course that on primitive levels property rights were weakly developed, that land was not appropriated by individuals or even families in the hunting stage.

These propositions are no longer tenable. In part they rest on ignorance of the ethnographic data, often on a failure to discriminate between moral and legal prescriptions. To illustrate the latter point, it is unquestionably customary to share the necessaries of life in a manner that sometimes amounts to practical communism; yet as a rule, in strict aboriginal law the line is clearly drawn between what is one's actual due and what is merely an ethical claim. There are, indeed, extreme instances. In Northeastern Siberia a boat lying idle may be put to effective use without the "owner's" consent, nor is the borrower liable for damages in case of injury. Yet among these same populations, other forms of property are jealously guarded from encroachment. As for land, Seligman has shown that the Vedda of Ceylon not only own tracts individually but practice a form of conveyance; and the prominence of hunting-territories among our Northeastern Algonkians of New England and Eastern Canada has been extensively described by Professor Speck.

This position is fully borne out by data on two genuinely "savage" groups, in Morgan's sense—the Yamana (Yaghan), the most southerly of South American tribes, and the Semang, a Negrito people of the Malay Peninsula.

The Yamana in particular exemplify the mingling of ethical and legal principles that has sometimes in the past misled sociological interpretation. Here there does not happen to be individual or family ownership of an economically valuable area, which is held to belong to the entire territorial group. Certain raw materials, such as iron pyrites for fire-making and a species of tree whose bark was suitable for the native types of canoe, were restricted to definite localities; and in these instances, utilization was permitted to territorial groups other than those within whose normal range these natural resources happened to lie. Nevertheless, personal property rights were recognized, and, as usual, they rested on individual manufacture and effective use. Baskets must be bought from women, harpoons from men; as elsewhere in North and South America, even the children's claims to ownership are respected. While most of these chattels were burnt with the corpse, a dog was invariably inherited by the eldest son or some other kinsman or acquaintance. Food is treated in the quasi-communistic fashion often reported for primitive tribes. In a particular case a successful seal-hunter immediately divided his kill into seven portions, of which he retained two, dividing the remainder among the five tribesmen present. Similarly, it is considered self-evident that the discoverer of a stranded whale should not play the part of a miser but should forthwith spread the glad tidings. Yet it is interesting to note that he had a prior claim to the booty and might select favored pieces or direct the distribution. However, no one was privileged simply to appropriate the neighbor's food, and any one who abused the privilege of hospitality soon fell in public estimation. There was also a pronounced tendency to make presents, whether of food, necklaces, slings, spears, or other implements; and acceptance involved the obligation of making a suitable return gift. The very fact of this institution constitutes proof of individual property rights. . . .

In the Trobriands, myths are not owned quite so exclusively as in certain other areas, yet particular ones are associated with lineages who "are supposed to possess the most intimate knowledge of the mythical events, and to be an authorty in interpreting them." Dances are more definitely individual property, the original inventor having the right to perform it in his village. "If another village takes a fancy to this song and dance, it has to purchase the right to perform it." Similarly, magical power—the knowledge of formulae intrinsically potent to achieve desired ends—is rated as a form of property.

The rudimentary concepts of a primitive people are greatly expanded by modern civilizations whose articulate philosophers and molders of public thought must seek rationalizations for their views of so vital a social institution. Ponder the reflections of some of these commentators on public and private ownership of basic natural resources, primarily land.

SELIGMAN, PRINCIPLES OF ECONOMICS

Pages 131–134 (1905).

The earliest theory of private property as found in some of the Roman writers is *the occupation theory.* The doctrine that property belongs of right to him who first seizes it is, however, one that can apply, if at all, only to the earliest stages of development. Where no one has any interest in the property, no one will object to the assertion of a claim by a newcomer. When property is without any discoverable owner, we still today assign it to the lucky finder. The occupation theory may explain how the present legal title to certain forms of property originated; it cannot serve as a justification of private property, except in the rare case of previously unoccupied or unutilized wealth. The mere fact that a person has seized a thing is no reason why he should retain it.

The next doctrine was *the natural rights theory.* Private property, so we were told by the philosophers of antiquity and the publicists of the later middle ages, is a natural right, a part of the law of nature. It will at once be asked, however, what is denoted by nature? The great philosophers of antiquity upheld private property in slaves as a natural right. Much of what we today consider natural, our descendants will deem unnatural. Our conception of nature in this sense is essentially ephemeral and mutable.

Driven from this position, the natural rights school took refuge in *the labor theory,* and maintained that the real title to private property is derived from the toil and trouble experienced in creating it. Surely, it will be said, a thing belongs of right to him who produces it. But at once comes the reply: no one has created the land. As a consequence, we find thinkers of all ages, from Phaleas of antiquity to the disciples of Henry George today, who contend that private property in land is unjust, while maintaining that private property in everything else is defensible. These critics, however, overlook the fact that the difference between land and so-called labor products is in this respect, at all events, one only of degree, because nothing is the result of individual labor alone. The carpenter, it is said, rightfully owns the table which he has made. But to what extent has he made it? The tree which affords him the raw material was not created by him; the axe with which the tree is felled is the accumulated result of centuries of invention expended by his ancestors; the stream along which the log is floated is not of his making. To pass over all the other intermediate processes, how long would he be secure in the possession of the tools he has used or of the product he has finished, were it not for the protection afforded to him by the law? And finally, of what use would the tables be unless there were a demand for them on the part of the community? The value of the table is as little the result of individual labor as is the value of the land. Society holds a mortgage over everything that is produced or exchanged.

Since, therefore, neither occupation, natural law nor labor gives an indefeasible title to private property, some philosophers were led to frame the so-called *legal theory* of private ownership, which is in essence that whatever is recognized as such by the law is rightfully private property. Obviously, however, this is not an economic doctrine. Good law may be bad economics. The law generally follows at a respectful distance behind the economic conditions, and adjusts itself gradually to them. The legal theory tells us *what* property is, not *why* it is, nor what it should be.

Thus we are finally driven to *the social utility theory.* This is really implied in the preceding theories and supplies the link that binds them all together. In ancient as in modern communities, the individual is helpless as against society, however much under modern democracy society may see fit to extend the bounds of individual freedom. If we allow the individual to seize upon unoccupied wealth, if we recognize the existence of certain rights in what are deemed to be the products of labor, if we throw the mantle of the law around the elements of private property—in every case society is speaking in no uncertain voice and permits these things because it is dimly conscious of the fact that they redound to the social welfare. Private property is an unmistakable index of social progress. It originated because of social reasons; it has grown under continual subjection to the social sanction. It is a natural right only in the broad sense that all social growth is natural.

ELY, PROPERTY AND CONTRACT IN THEIR RELATION TO THE DISTRIBUTION OF WEALTH

Vol. I, 135–137 (1914).

Furthermore, *property is exclusive in its nature and not absolute.* A phrase is found in Roman law which, as a definition of property, is misleading. The phrase is, "*Dominium est jus utendi et abutendi re.*" Some have said that it means that the right of property carries with it the right to use or to abuse a thing, and so it has been actually claimed that property is the right to use or misuse a thing, and that the right of property carries with it the right to make a bad use of things. But such an idea comes from bad translation. *Abutendi* means to use up or consume a thing, not to abuse it, and that has been conclusively shown by Knies in his discussion of the subject. While it means the right of using up or consuming, the Roman law never intended to give anyone the right of misusing a thing. This right might have existed in spite of the intent of the law, but it was contrary to the spirit of the law to give the right. It might have existed because it could not be prevented, but it was never sanctioned. Wagner also calls attention to the fact that, added to the phrase, "*Jus utendi et abutendi re,*" is the generally ignored clause, "*quatenus juris ratio patitur,*" "in so far as the reason of law permits." But Wagner claims that while *abutendi* may mean simply to consume, it does carry with it at least a suggestion or implication of misuse.

The right of property is an exclusive right, but it has never been an absolute right. In so far as the right of property existed it was an exclusive right, that is, it excluded others; but it was not a right without limitations or qualifications. Notice the distinction between *exclusive* and *absolute.*

The truth is, there are two sides to private property, *the individual side and the social side.* The social side of property finds illustration in the right of eminent domain and in the right of taxation. If there were no such thing as the social side of private property, how could the right of taxation exist? Take whatever theory you please. Suppose you say that the right of taxation is payment for protection. I say, "I do not want any protection," and if my right in private property is an absolute right, is not that sufficient, provided, furthermore, that I ask no privileges? The fact that I do not want protection does not give me exemption, and it shows at once that there is another side to private property than the individual side.

So also with the right of eminent domain. It is utterly incompatible with the absolute right of private property. *Moreover, this social side of private property is not to be regarded as something exceptional.* On the contrary it is an essential part of the institution itself. It is just as much a part of private property, as it exists at the present time, as the individual side is a part of it. The two necessarily go together, so that if one perishes the other must perish. The social side limits the individual side, and as it is always present there is no such thing as absolute private property. An absolute right of property, as the great jurist, the late Professor von Ihering says, would result in the dissolution of society.

MORRIS R. COHEN, PROPERTY AND SOVEREIGNTY

13 Cornell L.Q. 8 (1927).

The traditional theory of rights, and the one that still prevails in this country, was molded by the struggle in the seventeenth and eighteenth centuries against restrictions on individual enterprise. These restrictions in the interest of special privilege were fortified by the divine (and therefore absolute) rights of kings. As is natural in all revolts, absolute claims on one side were met with absolute denials on the other. Hence the theory of the natural rights of the individual took not only an absolute but a negative form; men have *in*alienable rights, the state must never interfere with private property, etc. The state, however, must interfere in order that individual rights should become effective and not degenerate into public nuisances. To permit anyone to do absolutely what he likes with his property in creating noise, smells, or danger of fire, would be to make property in general valueless. To be really effective, therefore, the right of property must be supported by restrictions or positive duties on the part of owners, enforced by the state as much as the right to exclude others that is the essence of property. Unfortunately, however, whether because of the general decline of juristic philosophy after Hegel or because law has become more interested in defending property against attacks by socialists, the doctrine of natural rights has remained in the negative state and has never developed into a doctrine of the positive contents of rights based upon an adequate notion of the function of these rights in society.

Lawyers occupied with civil or private law have in any case continued the absolutistic conception of property; and in doing this, they are faithful to the language of the great eighteenth century codes, the French, Prussian, and Austrian, and even of the nineteenth century codes like the Italian and German, which also begin with a definition of property as absolute or unlimited, though they subsequently introduce qualifying or limiting provisions.

As, however, no individual rights can in fact be exercised in a community, except under public regulation, it has been left mainly to publicists, to writers on politics and constitutional and administrative law to consider the limitations of private property necessary for public safety, peace, health, and morals, as well as for those enterprises like housing, education, the preservation of natural resources, etc., which the community finds it necessary to entrust to the state rather than to private hands. The fact, however, that in the United States the last word on law comes from judges, who, like other lawyers, are for the most part trained in private rather than in public law, is one of the reasons why with us traditional conceptions of property prevail over obvious national interests such as the freedom of labourers to organize, the necessity of preserving certain standards of living, or preventing the future manhood and womanhood of the country from being sacrificed to individual profits, and the like. Our students of property law need, therefore, to be reminded that not only has the whole law since the industrial revolution shown a steady growth in ever new restrictions upon the use of private property, but that the ideal of absolute laissez faire has never in fact been completely operative.

(1) Living in a free land economy we have lost the sense of how exceptional in the history of mankind is the absolutely free power of directing what shall be done with our property after our death. In the history of the common law, wills as to land begin only in the reign of Henry VIII. On the Continent it is still restrained by the system of the reserve. In England no formal restriction has been necessary because of the system of entails or strict settlement. Even in the United States, we have kept such rules as that against perpetuities, which is certainly a restraint on absolute freedom of testamentary disposition.

Even as to the general power of alienating the land inter vivos history shows that some restrictions are always present. The persistence of dower rights in our own individualistic economy is a case in point. Land and family interest have been too closely connected to sacrifice the former completely to pure individualism.

(2) More important than the foregoing limitations upon the transfer of property are limitations of the use of property. Looking at the matter realistically few will question the wisdom of Holdsworth's remarks that "at no time can the state be wholly indifferent to the use which the owners make of their property." There must be restrictions on the use of property not only in the interests of other property owners but also in the interests of the health, safety, religion, morals, and general welfare of the whole community. No community can view with indifference the exploitation of the needy by commercial greed. As under the conditions of crowded life the reckless or unconscionable use of one's property is becoming more and more dangerous, enlightened jurists find new doctrines to limit the abuse of ancient rights. The French doctrine of abus de droit, the prohibition of chicanery in the German Civil Code, and the rather vague use of "malice" in the common law are all efforts in that direction.

(3) Of greatest significance is the fact that in all civilized legal systems there is a great deal of just expropriation or confiscation without any direct compensation. This may sound shocking to those who think that for the state to take away the property of the citizen is not only theft or robbery but even worse, an act of treachery, since the state avowedly exists to protect people in those very rights.

As a believer in natural rights, I believe that the state can, and unfortunately often does, enact unjust laws. But I think it is a sheer fallacy based on verbal illusion to think that the rights of the community against an individual owner are no better than the rights of a neighbour. Indeed, no one has in fact had the courage of his confusion to argue that the state has no right to deprive an individual of property to which he is so attached that he refuses any money for it. Though no neighbour has such a right the public interest often justly demands that a proprietor shall part with his ancestral home to which he may be attached by all the roots of his being.

When taking away a man's property, is the state always bound to pay a direct compensation? I submit that while this is generally advisable in order not to disturb the general feeling of security, no absolute principle of justice requires it. I have already suggested that there is no injustice in taxing an old bachelor to educate the children of others, or taxing one immune to typhoid for the construction of sewers or other sanitary measures. We may go further and say that the whole business of the state depends upon its rightful power to take away the property of some (in the form of taxation) and use it to support others, such as the needy, those invalided in the service of the state in war or peace, and those who are not yet able to produce but in whom the hope of humanity is embodied. Doubtless, taxation and confiscation may be actuated by malice and may impose needless and cruel hardship on some individuals or classes. But this is not to deny that taxation and confiscation are within the just powers of the state.

MARX AND ENGELS, THE COMMUNIST MANIFESTO

In this sense, the theory of the Communists may be summed up in the single sentence: Abolition of private property.

We Communists have been reproached with the desire of abolishing the right of personally acquiring property as the fruit of a man's own labor, which property is alleged to be the groundwork of all personal freedom, activity, and independence. . . .

You are horrified at our intending to do away with private property. But in your existing society, private property is already done away with for nine-tenths of the population; its existence for the few is solely due to its non-existence in the hands of those nine-tenths. You reproach us, therefore, with intending to do away with a form of property, the necessary condition for whose existence is the non-existence of any property for the immense majority of society.

In one word, you reproach us with intending to do away with your property. Precisely so; that is just what we intend.

The Communists disdain to conceal their views and aims. They openly declare that their ends can be attained only by the forcible overthrow of all existing social conditions. Let the ruling classes tremble at a Communistic revolution. The proletarians have nothing to lose but their chains. They have a world to win.

YNTEMA, FOREWORD IN GSOVSKI, SOVIET CIVIL LAW

Page ix (1948).

The present work is of especial interest in exhibiting the operation of this system upon private rights and the apparent revival of traditional conceptions under the restrictive conditions of a socialized state. Thus, the State was to "wither away," but this has been postponed indefinitely. There was to be a "classless society," but the official bureaucratic and military caste, resurrecting even the insignia of the Tsars, has appeared. Labor, industrial and rural, for whose benefit the revolution was announced, has been subjected to collectivization and to a system of forced service, with inequalities of wages and controls of regimentation, recalling, if not surpassing, the worst days of capitalistic "wage slavery." Private property was to be abolished, but the conception of property, both "personal" and in the form of land tenancies, is well on the way to being restored; the same is true of inheritance rights.

GUNTHER, INSIDE RUSSIA TODAY

Pages 374–375 (1958).

Ownership of private property is an involved subject. A Soviet citizen may own a house, a piano, clothes, a car, and so forth, but not (to choose one item) an airplane, and certainly not a mine, a forest, or a factory. Most socialists, in Russia or out, have no objection to the personal ownership of property, provided that this does not include any means of production. Marx had no objection to the accumulation of private property, and the right of contemporary citizens to possess private property is specifically safeguarded in the Soviet constitution.

Thousands of Soviet citizens own their own homes; I saw a notice in a Russian paper a few days ago offering 2,400 cottages for sale. The usual process for acquiring a house goes like this, and is not unmixed, to understate the case, with capitalist procedures. First, the worker must prove that he has been a good worker, and has fulfilled his "plan." He will need recommendation from his trade union or factory manager. He then goes to a bank, where he may borrow up to fifteen to twenty thousand rubles for fifteen years, at 3 or even 2 per cent. interest; he pays off the debt in small installments, usually through deductions from his wages. Next, he goes to a local building agency and, if lucky, receives an allocation for land, materials, and labor. Next, he builds his house on the plot assigned, pays the construction company, and moves in. Subsequently he may sell, rent, or bequeath this property. He does not, however, own the land, which belongs to the state in perpetuity and absolutely.

MAGGS, THE SECURITY OF INDIVIDUALLY-OWNED PROPERTY UNDER SOVIET LAW

1961 Duke L.J. 537.

The law affecting private ownership of property in the Soviet Union has entered a relatively stable period. The nation's wealth has been divided definitely into areas of individual control and areas of control by state organizations. The property owner need not fear that the range of items deemed suitable for private ownership will be narrowed in the near future. This stability will serve to build up the idea of the sanctity of private property in the minds of the people of the Soviet Union. Thus, the chance of change will be lessened still further.

Large scale seizure of property has been abolished. The average law-abiding citizen need not fear confiscation of his property on a criminal charge. The period of drastic manipulation of the monetary system appears to be over. One whose home is taken for public use will not receive adequate compensation, but he will be given another place to live.

By Western standards, Soviet property law suffers from a lack of certainty. There is no clear delineation of the extent to which the restrictions on private commercial activity limit the property-owner's freedom of action. In the absence of precise legal norms, isolated cases and rumors affect the security of property ownership and cause fluctuations in market value. Soviet jurists have given private property rights a new name.* The task remaining is the development of a legal system that will provide an adequate definition of those rights.

MAGGS, LAW, PROPERTY RIGHTS, AND THE ECONOMY

Excerpt from revised version of paper presented at the Workshop on Political Control of the Soviet Economy, Yale University, March 16–19, 1989.

Under Gorbachev, there appears to be a movement toward the expansion of private ownership of housing. Single-family homes in rural and suburban areas have long been subject to private ownership. Owners of single family homes have been free to buy and sell them at market prices. While the plot of land associated with each house in theory has been state property, the law has automatically assigned it to the new owner, subject to the payment of a token ground rent. However, the importance of single-family homes has decreased with the urbanization of the Soviet population, which has led to the abandonment of many rural homes and has led to the taking of many suburban houses by eminent domain (with compensation to the owners) to make way for new apartment complexes. (Soviet urban planning theory calls for discouraging private automobiles by providing high-quality public transportation, which in turn requires high-density apartment housing to supply the necessary passenger volume.) The predominant type of urban housing has been state-owned apartments, rented to lessees at extraordinarily low rents (so low that they do not cover the costs of routine maintenance). The law guarantees the lessees the right to indefinite renewal of leases at these nominal rents. The lessees thus effectively have two basic ownership rights, those of possession and use. Their right of disposition is very limited, however. Parents can pass apartments on to their children by having the children listed as co-lessees at the time of the parents' death. There has been no way, however, for state apartment lessees to sell their apartments at full value. In recent years, there have also been a large number of privately-owned "cooperative apartments." However, there have also been restrictions preventing the free sale of these apartments at market prices, though the owners may pass them on to heirs or sell them at below-market prices. The result has been serious restrictions on the freedom of movement of Soviet citizens, because of the absence of a housing market in major cities. Now, there is talk of something closer to market rents for state-owned housing in major cities. If implemented and combined with permission for sale of apartments at market prices, this could mean the substitution of economic for legal barriers on change of residence. More changes in residence could reduce ethnic tensions by creating a "melting pot" society. The first major step in implementing the new policy is a 1988 decree. This decree authorizes

* In the 1920's Soviet law referred to "private" property. Modern legal writers all agree that this designation is obsolete and say that the property in the hands of Soviet citizens should be called "personal" or "individual" property.

the sale of state-owned apartments to lessees, or in the case of new or vacant apartments, to the public.

LIPPMAN, THE METHOD OF FREEDOM

Pages 100–102 (1934).

It has been the fashion to speak of the conflict between human rights and property rights, and from this it has come to be widely believed that the cause of private property is tainted with evil and should not be espoused by rational and civilized men. In so far as these ideas refer to plutocratic property, to great impersonal corporate properties, they make sense. These are not in reality private properties. They are public properties privately controlled, and they have either to be reduced to genuinely private properties or to be publicly controlled. But the issue between the giant corporation and the public should not be allowed to obscure the truth that the only dependable foundation of personal liberty is the personal economic security of private property.

The teaching of history is very certain on this point. It was in the mediaeval doctrine that to kings belong authority, but to private persons, property, that the way was discovered to limit the authority of the king and to promote the liberties of the subject. Private property was the original source of freedom. It is still its main bulwark. Recent experience confirms this truth. Where men have yielded without serious resistance to the tyranny of new dictators, it is because they have lacked property. They dared not resist because resistance meant destitution. The lack of a strong middle class in Russia, the impoverishment of the middle class in Italy, the ruin of the middle class in Germany, are the real reasons, much more than the ruthlessness of the Black Shirts, the Brown Shirts, and the Red Army, why the state has become absolute and individual liberty is suppressed. What maintains liberty in France, in Scandinavia, and in the English-speaking countries is more than any other thing the great mass of people who are independent because they have, as Aristotle said, "a moderate and sufficient property." They resist the absolute state. An official, a teacher, a scholar, a minister, a journalist, all those whose business it is to make articulate and to lead opinion, will act the part of free men if they can resign or be discharged without subjecting their wives, their children, and themselves to misery and squalor.

For we must not expect to find in ordinary men the stuff of martyrs, and we must, therefore, secure their freedom by their normal motives. There is no surer way to give men the courage to be free than to insure them a competence upon which they can rely. Men cannot be made free by laws unless they are in fact free because no man can buy and no man can coerce them. That is why the Englishman's belief that his home is his castle and that the king cannot enter it, like the American's conviction that he must be able to look any man in the eye and tell him to go to hell, are the very essence of the free man's way of life.

FELIX S. COHEN, DIALOGUE ON PRIVATE PROPERTY

9 Rutgers L.Rev. 357–361 (1954).

PRIVATE PROPERTY AND COMMUNISM

C. Mr. Allen, do you believe in the American form of government?

A. I certainly do.

C. And do you disapprove of communism?

A. I do.

C. Then you must believe that there is an important difference between communism and our American form of government.

A. Yes. I believe there are many important differences. For one thing, we have a democratic form of government in this country, and under communism there is a dictatorship.

C. That is certainly an important difference, but it would be just as applicable to Fascist or feudal dictatorships as to a communist dictatorship. Can you be any more specific as to the important differences between our American form of government and communism which would not apply equally to other types of dictatorship?

A. I suppose that the most important point of difference is that we in the United States recognize rights of private property and communism abolishes private property.

C. You don't mean that communism is incompatible with private property in toothbrushes or other consumer goods?

A. No, I was thinking more of factories and railroads and such things, which are owned by the state under communism.

C. May not the state own factories or railroads or canals under our American form of government?

A. Yes, but that is exceptional under our form of government and normal under communism.

C. Would you say, then, that here in the United States we have a large degree of private property in capital goods, and that this is not generally the case in communist countries?

A. Yes, I think that would be a fair statement.

C. Certainly it would be a fairer statement than the statement we started with, that the United States recognizes and communism abolishes private property. In fact, any difference is clarified when we can reduce it to a question of degree, which is the starting point for measurement. Now it seems to me that we have come to a very important conclusion. We seem to be agreed that one of the significant facts of life today is that here in the United States we have a great deal of private property in capital goods.

C. Is there any dissent from this conclusion? Now, Mr. Black, do your really think that the existence of private property in capital goods is one of the facts of life? Or are you just being polite and agreeable in not objecting to our conclusion? Might it be that the existence of private property is just a matter of theory or words or semantics? Or to be more specific, suppose we took a factory that is owned by the United States Steel Corporation, and took another factory in Russia that is owned by the Soviet Government. Are there some objective facts by which you could determine that one of these factories is private property and the other is not private property?

B. I suppose that in the United States Steel Corporation plant some individual would have the right to dispose of the products of the plant, and in the case of the Russian factory, the government would make these decisions.

C. Well, now, in both cases, some individual or group of individuals will decide what happens to the product, where the raw materials will be secured from, what wages will be paid to what employees, and so on. And in both cases there will be certain general laws or directives limiting these decisions of management. You say in the one case the individuals who make these decisions will be acting as private individuals, and in the other case they will be acting as government officials.

B. Yes, I suppose it comes down to that.

C. Now, suppose we call the board of directors of the United States Steel Corporation a Commissariat for Heavy Industry, and suppose we call the Russian Commissariat for Heavy Industry the board of directors of the Soviet Steel Corporation. Would that mean that Russia would be capitalistic and that the United States would be communistic? Is this difference that we are searching for purely a matter of words or semantics or theory, or is there some underlying objective fact that will persist, no matter what words we use to describe the individuals who make these decisions?

B. I think there is more to the distinction than just a matter of words or theories.

C. Let me read to you what Walton Hamilton says about property: "Property is a euphonious collection of letters which serves as a general term for the miscellany of equities that persons hold in the commonwealth." That is what Walton Hamilton says in his article on property in the Encyclopedia of the Social Sciences. Mr. Black, would you say that Walton Hamilton is a euphonious collection of letters?

B. No, I think he is a real individual.

C. And you also think that private property, in so far as it distinguishes our American form of government from the Russian form of government, is more than just words, or theories, that it reflects some basic reality, perhaps some basic differences of attitude and social organization and legal structure?

B. Yes, I think it does.

C. And you think there is a real difference between the American factory and the Russian factory even though the difference would not show up in a photograph?

B. Yes, I think there is.

C. Does anyone disagree with that conclusion? If not, it seems to me that we have come to a second important conclusion; namely, that there are some legal facts which are not just matters of words or definitions or theories, but which are objective in the sense that the facts remain no matter what kind of language we use to describe them, and here, of course, while we are talking now about property we might as well be talking about contracts, or crimes, or constitutions, or rules of law. Or we might be talking about mathematics or music. Here we are dealing with realities which have their origin in human institutions, but they are objective facts in the sense that we have to recognize their existence or else bump our heads against them.

DOES PRIVATE PROPERTY EXIST?

Now, let us see if we can get a clearer notion of the kind of facts that we are dealing with when we talk about property. We have all agreed that there is such a thing as private property in the United States, but suppose we run into a skeptic who refuses to accept our agreement. What evidence, Mr. Black, can you produce to show that private property really exists?

B. Well, here is a book that is my property. You can see it, feel it, weigh it. What better proof could there be of the existence of private property?

C. I can see the shape and color of the book very well, but I don't see its propertiness. What sort of evidence can you put forward to show that the book is your property?

B. Well, I paid for it.

C. Did you pay for your last haircut?

B. Yes.

C. And did you pay for last year's tuition, and last month's board, and your last railroad trip?

B. Yes.

C. But these things are not your property just because you paid for them, are they?

B. No, I suppose not, but now you are talking about past events and I am talking about a material object, a book, that I bought and paid for, which is something quite different from last year's tuition, or last night's dinner.

C. You could cite in support of that distinction, the definition of property given by Aigler, Bigelow and Powell: "Human beings . . . have various needs and desires. Many of these relate to external objects with which they are in some way associated. . . . The law of property may be looked at as an attempt upon the part of the state, acting through its courts and administrative officers, to give a systematized recognition of and protection of these attitudes and desires on the part of individuals towards things."

B. Yes, I think that clarifies our idea of property.

C. But is the copyright to a song a material, external object?

B. No, I suppose not.

C. And what about a mortgage or a patent on a chemical process or a future interest? These things can be property without being material objects, can't they?

B. Yes, I suppose they can.

C. Then what makes something property may be something intangible, invisible, unweighable, without shape or color?

B. I suppose that may be true in some cases, at least with respect to certain forms of intangible property.

C. Well, let's take the simplest case of tangible property, a piece of real estate, an acre of land on the outskirts of New Haven that you, let us assume, own in fee simple absolute. Would you say that the soil and the rock and the trees are tangible?

B. Yes, they certainly are.

C. But if you cut down the trees and sell them for firewood, the real property is still there on the outskirts of New Haven?

B. Yes.

C. And if you cut the sod and sell that, and dig up the top soil and sand and gravel and rock and sell that, the real property is still there on the outskirts of New Haven and you still have your fee simple absolute?

B. Yes.

C. Then a fee simple absolute is a sector of space in time and no more tangible than a song or a patent?

B. I see no way of avoiding that conclusion.

C. But you are not happy with this conclusion?

B. No, your questions seem to make property vanish into empty space.

C. Perhaps that is because you are assuming that reality always has a position in space. It seems to me that you and Aigler, Bigelow and Powell, are all prisoners of common sense, which is usually the metaphysics of 500 years back. In this case the current common sense is the metaphysical doctrine of Duns Scotus, William of Occam, and other 14th and 15th century scholastics, who held that all reality is tangible and exists in space. That idea runs through a great deal of common-law doctrine. Take, for example, the ceremony of *livery of seizin,* by which in transferring a possessory estate in land you actually pick up a piece of the sod and soil and hand to the grantee; or take the old common-law rule that a mortgage consists of a piece of paper, and if this piece of paper is destroyed, the mortgage disappears. Why should we assume that all reality exists in space? Do our differences of opinion exist in space? Why not recognize that spatial existence is only one of many realms of reality and that in dealing with the law we cannot limit ourselves entirely to the realm of spatial or physical existence?

What does Ely mean when he states: "An absolute right of property . . . would result in the dissolution of society"? do you agree with him? What are the justifications for private ownership of things—land or chattels? Should these justifications yield to the public right to exploit or conserve scarce natural resources, such as minerals, water, air rights, timber, etc.? Does Blackstone's reference to the "sole and despotic dominion . . . over the external things of the world" have any modern relevance? Any further questions?

A second attribute of private property is said to be the right of disposition. Does this mean that an owner of land can refuse to sell or rent it to anyone except the person of his choice? Is this an unrestricted right or can the state impose certain limits on this attribute of private property? Consider the excerpts from the following landmark case in the United States Supreme Court.

JONES v. ALFRED H. MAYER CO.

Supreme Court of the United States, 1968.
392 U.S. 409, 88 S.Ct. 2186, 20 L.Ed.2d 1189.

STEWART, J. * In this case we are called upon to determine the scope and constitutionality of an Act of Congress, 42 U.S.C.A. § 1982, which provides that:

"All citizens of the United States shall have the same right, in every State and Territory, as is enjoyed by white citizens thereof to inherit, purchase, lease, sell, hold, and convey real and personal property."

On September 2, 1965, the petitioners filed a complaint in the District Court for the Eastern District of Missouri, alleging that the respondents had refused to sell them a home in the Paddock Woods community of St. Louis County for the sole reason that petitioner Joseph Lee Jones is a Negro. Relying in part upon § 1982, the petitioners sought injunctive and other relief. The District Court sustained the respondents' motion to dismiss the complaint, and the Court of Appeals for the Eighth Circuit affirmed, concluding that § 1982 applies only to state action and does not reach private refusals to sell. We granted certiorari to consider the questions thus presented. For the reasons that follow, we reverse the judgment of the Court of Appeals. We hold that § 1982 bars *all* racial discrimination, private as well as public, in the sale or rental of property, and that the statute, thus construed, is a valid exercise of the power of Congress to enforce the Thirteenth Amendment.

I.

At the outset, it is important to make clear precisely what this case does *not* involve. Whatever else it may be, 42 U.S.C.A. § 1982 is not a comprehensive open housing law. In sharp contrast to the Fair Hous-

* All of the court's footnotes have been omitted.

ing Title (Title VIII) of the Civil Rights Act of 1968, Pub.L. 90–284, 82 Stat. 81, the statute in this case deals only with racial discrimination and does not address itself to discrimination on grounds of religion or national origin. It does not deal specifically with discrimination in the provision of services or facilities in connection with the sale or rental of a dwelling. It does not prohibit advertising or other representations that indicate discriminatory preferences. It does not refer explicitly to discrimination in financing arrangements or in the provision of brokerage services. It does not empower a federal administrative agency to assist aggrieved parties. It makes no provision for intervention by the Attorney General. And, although it can be enforced by injunction, it contains no provision expressly authorizing a federal court to order the payment of damages.

Thus, although § 1982 contains none of the exemptions that Congress included in the Civil Rights Act of 1968, it would be a serious mistake to suppose that § 1982 in any way diminishes the significance of the law recently enacted by Congress. . . .

. . .

. . . [The enactment of the Civil Rights Act of 1968] had no effect upon § 1982 and no effect upon this litigation, but it underscored the vast differences between, on the one hand, a general statute applicable only to racial discrimination in the rental and sale of property and enforceable only by private parties acting on their own initiative, and, on the other hand, a detailed housing law, applicable to a broad range of discriminatory practices and enforceable by a complete arsenal of federal authority. Having noted these differences, we turn to a consideration of § 1982 itself.

II.

This Court last had occasion to consider the scope of 42 U.S.C.A. § 1982 in 1948, in Hurd v. Hodge, 334 U.S. 24, 68 S.Ct. 847, 92 L.Ed. 1187. That case arose when property owners in the District of Columbia sought to enforce racially restrictive covenants against the Negro purchasers of several homes on their block. A federal district court enforced the restrictive agreements by declaring void the deeds of the Negro purchasers. . . .

. . .

Hurd v. Hodge, supra, squarely held, therefore, that a Negro citizen who is denied the opportunity to purchase the home he wants "[s]olely because of [his] race and color," 334 U.S., at 34, 68 S.Ct., at 852, has suffered the kind of injury that § 1982 was designed to prevent. Accord, Buchanan v. Warley, 245 U.S. 60, 79, 38 S.Ct. 16, 19, 62 L.Ed. 149; Harmon v. Tyler, 273 U.S. 668, 47 S.Ct. 471, 71 L.Ed. 831; City of Richmond v. Deans, 281 U.S. 704, 50 S.Ct. 407, 74 L.Ed. 1128. The basic source of the injury in *Hurd* was, of course, the action of private individuals—white citizens who had agreed to exclude Negroes from a residential area. But an arm of the Government—in that case, a federal court—had assisted in the enforcement of that agreement. Thus Hurd v. Hodge, supra, did not present the question whether *purely* private discrimination, unaided by any action on the part of government, would violate § 1982 if its effect were to deny a citizen the right to rent or buy property solely because of his race or color.

The only federal court (other than the Court of Appeals in this case) that has ever squarely confronted that question held that a wholly private conspiracy among white citizens to prevent a Negro from leasing a farm violated § 1982. United States v. Morris, D.C., 125 F. 322. It is true that a dictum in *Hurd* said that § 1982 was directed only toward "governmental action," 334 U.S., at 31, 68 S.Ct., at 851, but neither *Hurd* nor any other case before or since has presented that precise issue for adjudication in this Court. Today we face that issue for the first time.

III.

We begin with the language of the statute itself. In plain and unambiguous terms, § 1982 grants to all citizens, without regard to race or color, "the same right" to purchase and lease property "as is enjoyed by white citizens." As the Court of Appeals in this case evidently recognized, that right can be impaired as effectively by "those who place property on the market" as by the State itself. For, even if the State and its agents lend no support to those who wish to exclude persons from their communities on racial grounds, the fact remains that, whenever property "is placed on the market for whites only, whites have a right denied to Negroes." So long as a Negro citizen who wants to buy or rent a home can be turned away simply because he is not white, he cannot be said to enjoy "the *same* right . . . as is enjoyed by white citizens . . . to . . . purchase [and] lease . . . real and personal property." 42 U.S.C.A. § 1982. (Emphasis added.)

On its face, therefore, § 1982 appears to prohibit *all* discrimination against Negroes in the sale or rental of property—discrimination by private owners as well as discrimination by public authorities. Indeed, even the respondents seem to concede that, if § 1982 "means what it says"—to use the words of the respondents' brief—then it must encompass every racially motivated refusal to sell or rent and cannot be confined to officially sanctioned segregation in housing. Stressing what they consider to be the revolutionary implications of so literal a reading of § 1982, the respondents argue that Congress cannot possibly have intended any such result. Our examination of the relevant history, however, persuades us that Congress meant exactly what it said.

IV.

In its original form, 42 U.S.C.A. § 1982 was part of § 1 of the Civil Rights Act of 1866. . . .

. . .

The crucial language for our purposes was that which guaranteed all citizens "the same right, in every State and Territory in the United States, . . . to inherit, purchase, lease, sell, hold, and convey real and personal property . . . as is enjoyed by white citizens . . . ."

To the Congress that passed the Civil Rights Act of 1866, it was clear that the right to do these things might be infringed not only by "State or local law" but also by "custom, or prejudice." Thus, when Congress provided in § 1 of the Civil Rights Act that the right to purchase and lease property was to be enjoyed equally throughout the United States by Negro and white citizens alike, it plainly meant to secure that right against interference from any source whatever, whether governmental or private.

Indeed, if § 1 had been intended to grant nothing more than an immunity from *governmental* interference, then much of § 2 would have made no sense at all. For that section, which provided fines and prison terms for certain individuals who deprived others of rights "secured or protected" by § 1, was carefully drafted to exempt private violations of § 1 from the criminal sanctions it imposed. There would, of course, have been no private violations to exempt if the only "right" granted by § 1 had been a right to be free of discrimination by public officials. Hence the structure of the 1866 Act, as well as its language, points to the conclusion urged by the petitioners in this case—that § 1 was meant to prohibit *all* racially motivated deprivations of the rights enumerated in the statute, although only those deprivations perpetrated "under color of law" were to be criminally punishable under § 2.

In attempting to demonstrate the contrary, the respondents rely heavily upon the fact that the Congress which approved the 1866 statute wished to eradicate the recently enacted Black Codes—laws which had saddled Negroes with "onerous disabilities and burdens, and curtailed their rights . . . to such an extent that their freedom was of little value . . . ." Slaughter-House Cases, 16 Wall. 36, 70, 21 L.Ed. 394. The respondents suggest that the only evil Congress sought to eliminate was that of racially discriminatory laws in the former Confederate States. But the Civil Rights Act was drafted to apply throughout the country, and its language was far broader than would have been necessary to strike down discriminatory statutes.

That broad language, we are asked to believe, was a mere slip of the legislative pen. We disagree. For the same Congress that wanted to do away with the Black Codes *also* had before it an imposing body of evidence pointing to the mistreatment of Negroes by private individuals and unofficial groups, mistreatment unrelated to any hostile state legislation. . . .

. . .

V.

The remaining question is whether Congress has power under the Constitution to do what § 1982 purports to do: to prohibit all racial discrimination, private and public, in the sale and rental of property. Our starting point is the Thirteenth Amendment, for it was pursuant to that constitutional provision that Congress originally enacted what is now § 1982. The Amendment consists of two parts. Section 1 states:

"Neither slavery nor involuntary servitude, except as a punishment for crime whereby the party shall have been duly convicted, shall exist within the United States, or any place subject to their jurisdiction."

Section 2 provides:

"Congress shall have power to enforce this article by appropriate legislation."

As its text reveals, the Thirteenth Amendment "is not a mere prohibition of state laws establishing or upholding slavery, but an absolute declaration that slavery or involuntary servitude shall not exist in any part of the United States." Civil Rights Cases, 109 U.S. 3, 20, 3 S.Ct. 18, 28, 27 L.Ed. 835. It has never been doubted, therefore, "that the power vested in Congress to enforce the article by appropriate legislation," ibid., includes the power to enact laws "direct and primary, operating upon the acts of individuals, whether sanctioned by state legislation or not." Id., at 23, 3 S.Ct., at 30.

Thus, the fact that § 1982 operates upon the unofficial acts of private individuals, whether or not sanctioned by state law, presents no constitutional problem. If Congress has power under the Thirteenth Amendment to eradicate conditions that prevent Negroes from buying and renting property because of their race or color, then no federal statute calculated to achieve that objective can be thought to exceed the constitutional power of Congress simply because it reaches beyond state action to regulate the conduct of private individuals. The constitutional question in this case, therefore, comes to this: Does the authority of Congress to enforce the Thirteenth Amendment "by appropriate legislation" include the power to eliminate all racial barriers to the acquisition of real and personal property? We think the answer to that question is plainly yes.

. . .

Representative Wilson of Iowa was the floor manager in the House for the Civil Rights Act of 1866. In urging that Congress had ample authority to pass the pending bill, he recalled the celebrated words of Chief Justice Marshall in McCulloch v. State of Maryland, 4 Wheat. 316, 421, 4 L.Ed. 579:

"Let the end be legitimate, let it be within the scope of the constitution, and all means which are appropriate, which are plainly adapted to that end, which are not prohibited, but consist with the letter and spirit of the constitution, are constitutional."

"The end is legitimate," the Congressman said, "because it is defined by the Constitution itself. The end is the maintenance of freedom . . . . A man who enjoys the civil rights mentioned in this bill cannot be reduced to slavery. . . . This settles the appropriateness of this measure, and that settles its constitutionality."

We agree. The judgment is reversed.

[The concurring opinion of MR. JUSTICE DOUGLAS and the dissenting opinions of MR. JUSTICE HARLAN and MR. JUSTICE WHITE, are omitted.]

As Jones v. Alfred H. Mayer Co. mentions, in 1968 Congress passed the first comprehensive federal fair housing legislation. (Civil Rights Act of 1968, tit. VIII, 42 U.S.C.A. §§ 3601–19 (1970). Similar state and local legislation has been passed throughout the country. It should not be supposed, however, that the battle against racial discrimination in housing has been won. See Note, Is the U.S. Committed to Fair Housing? Enforcement of the Fair Housing Act Remains a Crucial Problem, 29 Cath.U.L.Rev. 641 (1980). The writer argues that the enforcement authority under the Fair Housing Act is inadequate. Informal methods tend to fail because they lack legal sanctions; suits by the Attorney General have been few in number; and private suits are too expensive and time consuming to be effective. The writer proposes additional legislation that, among other things, would give cease and desist authority to the federal government. How far can the law go in this area? How much of the problem is social, economic, and even educational?

In 1988, two decades after the first federal Fair Housing Act, Congress broadened and strengthened the Act. See Fair Housing Amendments Act of 1988, 42 U.S.C.A. §§ 3601–19 (1988). The amendments broadened the Act by adding the disabled and families with children to those individuals previously protected against discrimination in housing. The original Act had prohibited discrimination on the basis of sex, race, color, religion or national origin. The amendments strengthened the Act by eliminating a ceiling of $1000 for punitive damages and by obligating the government to act as advocate and legal counsel for victims of housing discrimination, taking cases to court and seeking penalties, instead of simply mediating disputes and seeking to expedite out-of-court settlements.

This is not the time to dwell on these departures from the centuries-old attitudes toward private property but you should be aware of the struggle involved in the conflict between differing social philosophies and values. Property rights and individual rights take on a new perspective when viewed as a part of the massive national effort to end segregation in a free society. An individual's house may be a private castle for some purposes but clearly not for all. The law is a potent force, although not the only one, in developing a new concept of property.

A third basic attribute of private property is the right to use the "thing" as its owner sees fit. How absolute is this right? What limitations on use can you think of, based on your prior education and experience?

Among other limitations which will occur to you are the various land use controls—zoning, subdivision ordinances, environmental regulations, etc. These matters will be studied in detail in later portions of the course (see Part Four, page 788 infra). One such limitation which is both ancient and pervasive is the doctrine of nuisance—so use your own land as not to unreasonably injure that of another. You may, at this point, wish to read the case of Boomer v. Atlantic Cement Co., reprinted at page 721 infra.

Refer to the excerpt from Dean Pound on page 12 supra. How absolute are any of the six attributes (rights) of property which he mentions? Does this mean that these attributes are meaningless? If not, in what sense do they have modern validity?

Chapter 3

OBJECTS AND CLASSIFICATIONS OF PROPERTY

Returning to the lawyer's concept of property as the legal relationship among people in regard to a thing, what are the objects of property, i.e., in what things can an individual claim private ownership? The short answer is that most "external things" of the world may be viewed as objects of property. There are some exclusions, at least so far as individual ownership is concerned. Certain drugs, weapons, the oceans, the atmosphere, uranium, etc. are normally beyond the ken of private ownership; they may be possessed, albeit illegally, but the state does not extend its legal process to protect the individual's claim. Are they, then property and, if so, whose? Like a cannon fired in an empty desert with no human ear to be the recipient of the sound waves (was there a noise?), this limited category of things defies traditional analysis. Does anyone, for example, own the clouds? For some light on this question see Southwest Weather Research, Inc. v. Rounsaville, reprinted at page 783 infra.

The normal objects of property are chattels and intangibles, land surfaces, land-sub-surfaces, water, and air space. Since all of these categories will be covered in this collection of materials, only a brief overview is required at this time. You will note that the bulk of this book is devoted to the law of land, i.e., land surfaces, because that is the most important single object of property, has the most complex set of rules for its allocation and protection, and, in a very real sense, is the most basic of all the categories since all other objects are related to it.

An always troublesome question is the distinction between real and personal property—land and chattels. It is wise to understand that distinction early in your study of property law.

BROWN ON PERSONAL PROPERTY (3d Ed. RAUSHENBUSH)

Callaghan and Co. (1975). *
Pages 9–12.

CLASSES OF PROPERTY

Property rights may be classified generally according to the nature of the object concerning which the rights are claimed. The most natural of these classifications is that between immovables (land and those things that are permanently attached to it) and movables (commonly designated in the law as chattels). The law in respect to these two types of objects of ownership varies greatly. Commonly today in

* The author's footnotes have been omitted.

Anglo-American countries a different type of transfer is necessary in the case of land than in the case of chattels. Historically, land descended differently on the death of the owner than did his chattels, and this distinction persists in some states today, though recent revisions in laws of descent and probate have reduced the number of such states. Part of this distinction is due to the inherent differences between the two classes. Land is permanent and immovable. Chattels are often of a temporary character and can be easily moved about. Land can be possessed or controlled by its owner in only an incomplete or limited manner, whereas chattels may be handled, manually transferred, altered, and usually even destroyed. The distinction between the law of land and that of movables, which in common-law systems is much greater than in countries whose law is based on that of Rome, is due, however, in a large degree to the circumstance that feudalism, which, as a system of law, developed more fully in England than on the continent, was largely based on landholding. Upon the holding of land was based much of the structure of medieval English legal, political and economic society. It was natural therefore, that concerning land a large body of common law developed which found no counterpart in the law relating to chattels.

Roughly speaking, the distinction tenaciously drawn in the common law between real and personal property is that between rights in land and rights in chattels. At this point pause must be taken to consider these words, "real" and "personal," which in their origin denoted not the difference between the objects of property rights but that between the forms of action by which rights were vindicated. Real actions, or actiones in rem, were those actions in which the thing itself, the res, was recovered by the successful suitor, whereas in personal actions, actiones in personam, the successful plaintiff recovered not the thing itself, but only damages from the adverse party. Due to the importance, already mentioned, of landholding in the feudal system, the real action was reserved largely for actions relating to land, while the personal action was the customary remedy for wrongs relating to chattels. Since in feudal society the relation between man and man was usually determined by the manner in which particular tracts of land were held, it was important in case a holder of land was ousted from his domain that he recover that particular tract. This was not so in the case of chattels. Moreover, the typical chattel in medieval society was the beast. Our words "chattel" and "cattle" have a close affinity, and in many primitive civilizations cattle even served as money, as the medium of exchange. In the case of the wrongful taking of a beast therefore it was not essential that the identical animal be returned by means of the real action, but it was sufficient that its equivalent be secured by an action in personam against the wrongdoer. Then in the process of time (by a not-difficult transition) the terms "real" and "personal," referring originally to types of actions, came to denote the kinds of property, for causes concerning which these two types of actions were available. Real property is land, or more technically rights in land, and personal property consists of chattels, or rights in chattels.

This brings us to a curious anomaly in the common law. Not all rights in land are considered as real property. The English law subdivides rights in land according to the duration of the interest therein of their possessors. Certain of these interests therein are termed freeholds, that is, those interests that endure for the life of the holder or longer. For such interests the real actions are available. Other interests, however, those that endure for a term of years, however long, and those that endure at the will of the parties, are termed nonfreehold. Concerning these latter interests, during the formative period of the law no real action was available. The termor, or lessee as he is now commonly called, was considered to have no real interest in the land itself but to hold only at the will of the lessor, against whom his rights were purely of a contractual nature. His rights in the land were therefore not real but personal. While in early times he could not dispose of his freehold land interests by will, the restriction did not apply to chattels, and leasehold interests came within the latter class. The lessee's lack of a real action was later remedied, but the distinction previously drawn endured in the law, and today leasehold interests in land are for many purposes still treated as personalty. Such interests, technically known as chattels real to indicate their hybrid character, are not within the scope of this text . . . .

Another classification remains to be mentioned. In its broader sense the word "property" includes all rights which are of value. As we have seen, many of these rights relate to the tangible physical things of the world, to lands and movables. However, many rights do not thus concern specific tangible things but consist of claims against third persons which, since they may be enforced by action, and, if the law permits, be assigned for a price, are of value and thus entitled to be termed property in the broader sense. Bank accounts, debts generally, corporate stock, patents and copyrights are common instances of this class of property. To distinguish between these two classes, lawyers have from early times used the terms "choses (i.e., things) in possession," and "choses in action." Thus choses in possession refer to rights in definite tangible things over which possession may be taken, and choses in action to rights of property which, though they may be represented by a piece of paper, like a promissory note, are essentially intangible in that they can ultimately only be claimed or enforced by action, not by taking physical possession. As these terms have a long history antedating the development of our modern commercial life, the attempt to give to them exact definitions and to determine just what interests are allocable to each seems rather a futile task. The general distinction that is drawn cannot, however, be denied.

It is not the purpose of this text to deal with choses in action which are commonly treated at length under other course subjects. It is necessary, however, to note that certain written and printed instruments, which in their primary essence are mere evidences or representations of the obligation of the parties, have for historical reasons or for the practical exigencies of commerce assumed many of the qualities of tangible things. An obvious example is money, in the situations (increasingly common!) when it has no significant intrinsic value as gold or silver but has value because it represents the obligation of the state to stand behind it in some mysterious way. From earliest times a bond, that is a sealed obligation, was regarded as more than the evidence of the contract of the parties, and considered in law to be the contract itself, so that formerly any destruction of the paper or of the seal destroyed the obligation itself. Nevertheless, the criminal law continued to treat the bond, as well as negotiable commercial securities, and even bank notes, as choses in action, which could not be subjects of larceny. This unfortunate condition has, however, been generally remedied by statute. In the various phases of the law of personal property, as will be seen later in the course of this work, negotiable instruments such as promissory notes and bills of exchange, and other commercial documents, bills of lading, warehouse receipts, and certificates of stock, are often subjected to many of the rules which, strictly speaking, are applicable only to tangible physical things.

The distinction between real and personal property is usually easy to draw but not always—see, for example, the problem of fixtures, neither quite fish nor fowl.

BROWN ON PERSONAL PROPERTY (3d Ed. RAUSHENBUSH)

Callaghan and Co. (1975). *
Pages 514–515.

DEFINITION AND GENERAL CONSIDERATIONS

A fixture can best be defined as a thing which, although originally a movable chattel, is by reason of its annexation to, or association in use with land, regarded as a part of the land. The law of fixtures concerns those situations where the chattel annexed still retains a separate identity in spite of annexation, for example a furnace or a light fixture. Where the chattel annexed loses such identity, as in the case of nails, boards, etc., the problem becomes one of accession, ... The question whether a particular article, formerly a chattel, has become part of the realty may arise in several different ways. (I) The owner of land and building may buy and install therein a new improvement—a furnace, a water heater, a gas range. He later sells or mortgages the real estate. Does the purchaser of the land, in absence of specific exclusions, obtain the above articles or any of them, or do they remain the personal property of the grantor? A similar problem arises when the landowner dies. Do the above articles pass to his heirs as part of the real estate, or are they personal property passing to the administrator? A related question is whether the article is subject to levy of execution or attachment, or to replevin, as personalty, or has become part of the real estate. Also, can the unpaid vendor of an article annexed to the realty claim a statutory mechanic's or construc-

* [The author's footnotes have been omitted.]

tion lien for an improvement to the realty? (II) The owner of a chattel may annex it to the land of another, or to land in which another has an interest. The most common example of this is where a tenant for years attaches to the land of his landlord articles necessary or convenient for the tenant's trade or his domestic enjoyment. In this situation the question arises whether the tenant on the termination of his lease can remove from the premises those articles which he has attached, or whether they remain the property of the landlord. (III) Lastly the annexor of the chattel may not own the same, or his ownership may be encumbered by the security interest of another. When such a chattel is placed on the annexor's land or on land in which others have an interest, question inevitably arises as to the respective rights of the chattel owner and the landowner. . . . It is obvious that situation (I) above is the simplest one. Only when the rules relating to that are understood is it profitable to consider the more complicated situations in (II) and (III). Much of the confusion in the law of fixtures is due, it is believed, to the attempt to consider together as analogous these three different fact situations, when in fact they are quite dissimilar. To attempt to discover an all-inclusive definition for a "fixture" or to posit tests for fixtures in all circumstances is not a profitable undertaking. The important quest is the determination of the rights of the parties in the different type situations above outlined. Whether the particular article involved be denominated a fixture or not is of little importance.

Focussing for the moment on land law, as opposed to the law of personal property, note that the land can be divided vertically as well as horizontally, hence surface, subsurface, and air rights. A different individual may own each of these rights or they may all belong to a single owner of Blackacre (academic symbolism for any piece of real property). These three phases of the law of land can be illustrated initially by the struggles of a Kentucky court over the property rights in a cave. For further insights see pages 733 to 771 infra.

EDWARDS v. SIMS

Court of Appeals of Kentucky, 1929.
232 Ky. 791, 24 S.W.2d 619.

STANLEY, C. This case presents a novel question.

In the recent case of Edwards v. Lee, 230 Ky. 375, 19 S.W.(2d) 992, an appeal was dismissed which sought a review and reversal of an order of the Edmonson circuit court directing surveyors to enter upon and under the lands of Edwards and others and survey the Great Onyx Cave for the purpose of securing evidence on an issue as to whether or not a part of the cave being exploited and shown by the appellants runs under the ground of Lee. The nature of the litigation is stated in the opinion and the order set forth in full. It was held that the order was interlocutory and consequently one from which no appeal would lie.

Following that decision, this original proceeding was filed in this court by the appellants in that case (who were defendants below) against Hon. N.P. Sims, judge of the Edmonson circuit court, seeking a writ of prohibition to prevent him enforcing the order and punishing the petitioners for contempt for any disobedience of it. It is alleged by the petitioners that the lower court was without jurisdiction or authority to make the order, and that their cave property and their right of possession and privacy will be wrongfully and illegally invaded, and that they will be greatly and irreparably injured and damaged without having an adequate remedy, since the damage will have been suffered before there can be an adjudication of their rights on a final appeal. It will thus be seen that there are submitted the two grounds upon which this court will prohibit inferior courts from proceeding, under the provisions of section 110 of the Constitution, namely: (1) Where it is a matter in which it has no jurisdiction and there is no remedy through appeal, and (2) where the court possesses jurisdiction but is exercising or about to exercise its power erroneously, and which would result in great injustice and irreparable injury to the applicant, and there is no adequate remedy by appeal or otherwise. Duffin v. Field, Judge, 208 Ky. 543, 271 S.W. 596; Potter v. Gardner, 222 Ky. 487, 1 S.W.(2d) 537; Litteral v. Woods, 223 Ky. 582, 4 S.W.(2d) 395.

There is no question as to the jurisdiction of the parties and the subject-matter. It is only whether the court is proceeding erroneously within its jurisdiction in entering and enforcing the order directing the survey of the subterranean premises of the petitioners. There is but little authority of particular and special application to caves and cave rights. In few places, if any, can be found similar works of nature of such grandeur and of such unique and marvelous character as to give to caves a commercial value sufficient to cause litigation as those peculiar to Edmonson and other counties in Kentucky. The reader will find of interest the address on "The Legal Story of Mammoth Cave" by Hon. John B. Rodes, of Bowling Green, before the 1929 Session of the Kentucky State Bar Association, published in its proceedings. In Cox v. Colossal Cavern Co., 210 Ky. 612, 276 S.W. 540, the subject of cave rights was considered, and this court held there may be a severance of the estate in the property, that is, that one may own the surface and another the cave rights, the conditions being quite similar to but not exactly like those of mineral lands. But there is no such severance involved in this case, as it appears that the defendants are the owners of the land and have in it an absolute right.

Cujus est solum, ejus est usque ad coelum ad infernos (to whomsoever the soil belongs, he owns also to the sky and to the depths), is an old maxim and rule. It is that the owner of realty, unless there has been a division of the estate, is entitled to the free and unfettered control of his own land above, upon, and beneath the surface. So whatever is in a direct line between the surface of the land and the center of the earth belongs to the owner of the surface. Ordinarily that ownership cannot be interfered with or infringed by third persons. 17 C.J. 391; 22 R.C.L. 56; Langhorne v. Turman, 141 Ky. 809, 133 S.W. 1008, 34 L.R.A. (N.S.) 211. There are, however, certain limitations on the right of enjoyment of possession of all property, such as its use to the detriment or interference with a neighbor and burdens which it must bear in common with property of a like kind. 22 R.C.L. 77.

With this doctrine of ownership in mind, we approach the question as to whether a court of equity has a transcendent power to invade that right through its agents for the purpose of ascertaining the truth of a matter before it, which fact thus disclosed will determine certainly whether or not the owner is trespassing upon his neighbor's property. Our attention has not been called to any domestic case, nor have we found one, in which the question was determined either directly or by analogy. It seems to the court, however, that there can be little differentiation, so far as the matter now before us is concerned, between caves and mines. And as declared in 40 C.J. 947: "A court of equity, however, has the inherent power, independent of statute, to compel a mine owner to permit an inspection of his works at the suit of a party who can show reasonable ground for suspicion that his lands are being trespassed upon through them, and may issue an injunction to permit such inspection."

There is some limitation upon this inherent power, such as that the person applying for such an inspection must show a bona fide claim and allege facts showing a necessity for the inspection and examination of the adverse party's property; and, of course, the party whose property is to be inspected must have had an opportunity to be heard in relation thereto. In the instant case it appears that these conditions were met.

. . .

. . .

We can see no difference in principle between the invasion of a mine on adjoining property to ascertain whether or not the minerals are being extracted from under the applicant's property and an inspection of this respondent's property through his cave to ascertain whether or not he is trespassing under this applicant's property.

It appears that before making this order the court had before him surveys of the surface of both properties and the conflicting opinions of witnesses as to whether or not the Great Onyx Cave extended under the surface of the plaintiff's land. This opinion evidence was of comparatively little value, and as the chancellor (now respondent) suggested, the controversy can be quickly and accurately settled by surveying the cave; and "if defendants are correct in their contention this survey will establish it beyond all doubt and their title to this cave will be forever quieted. If the survey shows the Great Onyx Cave extends under the lands of plaintiffs, defendants should be glad to know this fact and should be just as glad to cease trespassing upon plaintiff's lands, if they are in fact doing so." The peculiar nature of these conditions, it seems to us, makes it imperative and necessary in the administration of justice that the survey should have been ordered and should be made.

It appearing that the circuit court is not exceeding its jurisdiction or proceeding erroneously, the claim of irreparable injury need not be given consideration. It is only when the inferior court is acting erroneously, *and* great or irreparable damage will result, *and* there is no adequate remedy by appeal, that a writ of prohibition will issue restraining the other tribunal, as held by authorities cited above.

The writ of prohibition is therefore denied.

Whole court sitting.

LOGAN, J. (dissenting). The majority opinion allows that to be done which will prove of incalculable injury to Edwards without benefiting Lee, who is asking that this injury be done. I must dissent from the majority opinion, confessing that I may not be able to show, by any legal precedent, that the opinion is wrong, yet having an abiding faith in my own judgment that it is wrong.

It deprives Edwards of rights which are valuable, and perhaps destroys the value of his property, upon the motion of one who may have no interest in that which it takes away, and who could not subject it to his dominion or make any use of it, if he should establish that which he seeks to establish in the new suit wherein the survey is sought.

It sounds well in the majority opinion to tritely say that he who owns the surface of real estate, without reservation, owns from the center of the earth to the outmost sentinel of the solar system. The age-old statement, adhered to in the majority opinion as the law, in truth and fact, is not true now and never has been. I can subscribe to no doctrine which makes the owner of the surface also the owner of the atmosphere filling illimitable space. Neither can I subscribe to the doctrine that he who owns the surface is also the owner of the vacant spaces in the bowels of the earth.

The rule should be that he who owns the surface is the owner of everything that may be taken from the earth and used for his profit or happiness. Anything which he may take is thereby subjected to his dominion, and it may be well said that it belongs to him. I concede the soundness of that rule, which is supported by the cases cited in the majority opinion; but they have no application to the question before the court in this case. They relate mainly to mining rights; that is, to substances under the surface which the owner may subject to his dominion. But no man can bring up from the depths of the earth the Stygian darkness and make it serve his purposes; neither can he subject to his dominion the bottom of the ways in the caves on which visitors tread, and for these reasons the owner of the surface has no right in such a cave which the law should, or can, protect because he has nothing of value therein, unless, perchance, he owns an entrance into it and has subjected the subterranean passages to his dominion.

A cave or cavern should belong absolutely to him who owns its entrance, and this ownership should extend even to its utmost reaches if he has explored and connected these reaches with the entrance. When the surface owner has discovered a cave and prepared it for purposes of exhibition, no one ought to be allowed to disturb him in his dominion over that which he has conquered and subjected to his uses.

It is well enough to hang to our theories and ideas, but when there is an effort to apply old principles to present-day conditions, and they will not fit, then it becomes necessary for a readjustment, and principles and facts as they exist in this age must be made conformable. For these reasons the old sophistry that the owner of the surface of land is the owner of everything from zenith to nadir must be reformed, and the reason why a reformation is necessary is because the theory was never true in the past, but no occasion arose that required the testing of it. Man had no dominion over the air until recently, and, prior to his conquering the air, no one had any occasion to question the claim of the surface owner that the air above him was subject to his dominion. Naturally the air above him should be subject to his dominion in so far as the use of the space is necessary for his proper enjoyment of the surface, but further than that he has no right in it separate from that of the public at large. The true principle should be announced to the effect that a man who owns the surface, without reservation, owns not only the land itself, but everything upon, above, or under it which he may use for his profit or pleasure, and which he may subject to his dominion and control. But further than this his ownership cannot extend. It should not be held that he owns that which he cannot use and which is of no benefit to him, and which may be of benefit to others.

Shall a man be allowed to stop airplanes flying above his land because he owns the surface? He cannot subject the atmosphere through which they fly to his profit or pleasure; therefore, so long as airplanes do not injure him, or interfere with the use of his property, he should be helpless to prevent their flying above his dominion. Should the waves that transmit intelligible sound through the atmosphere be allowed to pass over the lands of surface-owners? If they take nothing from him and in no way interfere with his profit or pleasure, he should be powerless to prevent their passage.

If it be a trespass to enter on the premises of the landowner, ownership meaning what the majority opinion holds that it means, the aviator who flies over the land of one who owns the surface, without his consent, is guilty of a trespass as defined by the common law and is subject to fine or imprisonment, or both, in the discretion of a jury.

If he who owns the surface does not own and control the atmosphere above him, he does not own and control vacuity beneath the surface. He owns everything beneath the surface that he can subject to his profit or pleasure, but he owns nothing more. Therefore, let it be written that a man who owns land does, in truth and in fact, own everything from zenith to nadir, but only for the use that he can make of it for his profit or pleasure. He owns nothing which he cannot subject to his dominion.

In the light of these unannounced principles which ought to be the law in this modern age, let us give thought to the petitioner Edwards, his rights and his predicament, if that is done to him which the circuit judge has directed to be done. Edwards owns this cave through right of discovery, exploration, development, advertising, exhibition, and conquest. Men fought their way through the eternal darkness, into the mysterious and abysmal depths of the bowels of a groaning world to discover the theretofore unseen splendors of unknown natural scenic wonders. They were conquerors of fear, although now and then one of them, as did Floyd Collins, paid with his life, for his hardihood in adventuring into the regions where Charon with his boat had never before seen any but the spirits of the departed. They let themselves down by flimsy ropes into pits that seemed bottomless; they clung to scanty handholds as they skirted the brinks of precipices while the flickering flare of their flaming flambeaux disclosed no bottom to the yawning gulf beneath them; they waded through rushing torrents, not knowing what awaited them on the farther side; they climbed slippery steeps to find other levels; they wounded their bodies on stalagmites and stalactites and other curious and weird formations; they found chambers, star-studded and filled with scintillating light reflected by a phantasmagoria revealing fancied phantoms, and tapestry woven by the toiling gods in the dominion of Erebus; hunger and thirst, danger and deprivation could not stop them. Through days, weeks, months, and years—ever linking chamber with chamber, disclosing an underground land of enchantment, they continued their explorations; through the years they toiled connecting these wonders with the outside world through the entrance on the land of Edwards which he had discovered; through the years they toiled finding safe ways for those who might come to view what they had found and placed their seal upon. They knew nothing, and cared less, of who owned the surface above; they were in another world where no law forbade their footsteps. They created an underground kingdom where Gulliver's people may have lived or where Ayesha may have found the revolving column of fire in which to bathe meant eternal youth.

When the wonders were unfolded and the ways were made safe, then Edwards patiently, and again through the years, commenced the advertisement of his cave. First came one to see, then another, then two together, then small groups, then small crowds, then large crowds, and then the multitudes. Edwards had seen his faith justified. The cave was his because he had made it what it was, and without what he had done it was nothing of value. The value is not in the black vacuum that the uninitiated call a cave. That which Edwards owns is something intangible and indefinable. It is his vision translated into a reality.

Then came the horse leach's daughters crying: "Give me," "give me." Then came the "surface men" crying, "I think this cave may run under my lands." They do not know they only "guess," but they seek to discover the secrets of Edwards so that they may harass him and take from him that which he has made his own. They have come to a court of equity and have asked that Edwards be forced to open his doors and his ways to them so that they may go in and despoil him; that they may lay his secrets bare so that others may follow their example and dig into the wonders which Edwards has made his own. What may be the result if they stop his ways? They destroy the cave, because those who visit it are they who give it value, and none will visit it when the ways are barred so that it may not be exhibited as a whole.

It may be that the law is as stated in the majority opinion of the court, but equity, according to my judgment, should not destroy that which belongs to one man when he at whose behest the destruction is visited, although with some legal right, is not benefited thereby. Any ruling by a court which brings great and irreparable injury to a party is erroneous.

For these reasons I dissent from the majority opinion.

NOTES

1. In United States v. 3,218.9 Acres of Land, 619 F.2d 288 (3d Cir. 1980), the United States Court of Appeals, Third Circuit, considered a condemnation case where land in Pennsylvania was acquired to promote and protect the navigation of streams, production of timber, and development and management of adequate outdoor recreation resources in connection with the Allegheny Reservoir Project. The land in question was not held in fee simple absolute by any one owner. There was no issue as to the U.S. government's statutory authority to take the land; the question was whether the taking of the surface, reserving a right of access for mining the subsurface limited by government regulations, constituted a taking of the subsurface mineral interests and therefore entitled the owners of such interests to compensation. The court held no compensation was due the owners of the subsurface until such time as there was an interference with their rights.

In the course of the opinion, the court said: "Pennsylvania law recognizes that there may be three separate estates in land: the surface, the right of support, and the subsurface mineral rights. . . . There may be situations where interests in a piece of land may be severed and owned by different persons. . . . 'The right of property in natural gas and oil ordinarily belongs to the owner of land. The oil and gas are a part of the land so long as they are on it or in it or are subject to control therein. In other words, they are part of the land while they are in place. *They can be severed from ownership of the surface by grant or exception as separate corporeal rights.* Accordingly, they may be the subject of a sale, separate and apart from the surface and from any minerals beneath it; they belong to the owner in fee, or his grantee, as long as they remain part of his property, although use of them is not possible until they are severed from the freehold exactly as done in the case of all other minerals beneath the surface. Hence, a freehold of inheritance may be created in oil and gas.

"In this case the interests of the mineral holders had been severed from the surface fee *prior* to the plaintiff's declaration of taking. As to these properties, the declaration sought only to condemn the surface estate, with the reservation to the owners of the right to mine, subject however to the imposition of the Secretary of Agriculture's rules on future drilling on the surface estate. The parties holding only subsurface estates retained the same condition and rights after the taking as they possessed previously."

2. Water must also be considered as an object of property. George Eliot once commented: "It's plain enough what's the rights and the wrongs of water, if you look at it straightforward . . . but, you see . . . Water's a very particular thing—you can't pickit up with a pitchfork. That's why it's been nuts to old Harry and the lawyers." Just so! Water is tangible enough but it refuses to stay in one place. In Ecclesiastes 1:7, it is written: "All the rivers run into the sea; yet the sea is not full; unto the place from whence the rivers come, thither they return again." With less poetry, but more accuracy, modern scientists call this the hydrologic cycle and recognize that water is like a living thing, in constant motion.

Can anyone own water? Ownership may be difficult in the same sense that one owns Blackacre but a person may have a usufructuary right in the water that flows across his other land and *may* have an absolute right to ground water (percolating water). In this sense, water may be a species of private property, subject to its own peculiar rules for allocation and use. Later, we will cover some of the basic material of water law (see pages 740 to 764, infra) but for now it is enough to know that water too may be an object of property.

To these traditional objects of property, some commentators would add another category, referred to as "the new property".

REICH, THE NEW PROPERTY

73 Yale L.J. 733 (1964).

The institution called property guards the troubled boundary between individual man and the state. It is not the only guardian; many other institutions, laws, and practices serve as well. But in a society that chiefly values material well-being, the power to control a particular portion of that well-being is the very foundation of individuality.

One of the most important developments in the United States during the past decade has been the emergence of government as a major source of wealth. Government is a gigantic syphon. It draws in revenue and power, and pours forth wealth: money, benefits, services, contracts, franchises, and licenses. Government has always had this function. But while in early times it was minor, today's distribution of largess is on a vast, imperial scale.

The valuables dispensed by government take many forms, but they all share one characteristic. They are steadily taking the place of traditional forms of wealth—forms which are held as private property. Social insurance substitutes for savings; a government contract replaces a businessman's customers and goodwill. The wealth of more and more Americans depends upon a relationship to government. Increasingly, Americans live on government largess—allocated by government on its own terms, and held by recipients subject to conditions which express "the public interest."

The growth of government largess, accompanied by a distinctive system of law, is having profound consequences. It affects the underpinnings of individualism and independence. It influences the workings of the Bill of Rights. It has an impact on the power of private interests, in their relation to each other and to government. It is helping to create a new society . . ..

Professor Reich lists among these new objects of property, created by an expanding state: income and benefits, jobs, occupational licenses, franchises, contracts, subsidies, use of public resources, and services. In Reich, Individual Rights and Social Welfare: The Emerging Legal Issues, 74 Yale L.J. 1245 (1965), Professor Reich explored further the concept of "the new property," noting that: "Society today is built around entitlement. The automobile dealer has his franchise, the doctor and lawyer their professional licenses, the worker his union membership, contract, and pension rights, the executive his contract and stock options; all are devices to aid security and independence. Many of the most important of these entitlements now flow from government; subsidies to farmers and business men, routes for airlines and channels for television stations; long-term contracts for defense, space, and education; social security pensions for individuals. Such sources of security, whether private or public, are no longer regarded as luxuries or gratuities; to the recipients they are essential, fully deserved, and in no sense a form of charity. It is only the poor whose entitlements, although recognized by public policy, have not been effectively enforced." In brief, it may be realistic today to regard these various "entitlements," including welfare payments, as more like property than as gratuities.

Professor Reich's seminal articles have spawned a number of comments in the law reviews and elsewhere. See, for example, Van Alstyne, Cracks in "The New Property": Adjudicative Due Process in the Administrative State, 62 Cornell L.Rev. (1977) and Chapter Twenty, "New Property," of Haar and Liebman's casebook, Property and Law (Little, Brown and Company, (1977)). The latter is an excellent collection of cases and materials grouped under the rubric, "new property" with section headings of: Property as Process, Process and Liberty, Property as Contract, and Property as Rights and as Politics. This material represents an area where constitutional law, administrative law, and property law intersect.

In addition to Professor Reich's "new property", other commentators are exploring concepts that go well beyond the traditional classification of property interests. For a good example of this genre, see Singer, The Reliance Interest in Property, 40 Stanford Law Review 614 (1988). Using the plant closing problem created when the United States Steel Company demolished two steel plants in Youngstown, Ohio, Professor Singer argues for a property interest in the union and, indeed, in the community, based on the reliance that the plant would continue in existence or that a fair settlement would be worked out if closing became necessary. Professor Singer analyzes traditional doctrine (most of which is covered by the materials in this casebook) to demonstrate how courts and legistatures have recognized a "reliance interest" where multiple parties are involved in property disputes.

Although the Court of Appeals for the Sixth Circuit (Local 1330, United Steel Workers v. United States Steel Corp., 631 F.2d 1264 (6th Cir.1980)) did not recognize such a "reliance interest" it did quote from the opinion of the district judge: "United States Steel should not be permitted to leave the Youngstown area devastated after drawing from the lifeblood of the community for so many years. Unfortunately, the mechanism to reach this ideal settlement, to recognize this new property right, is not now in existence in the code of laws of our nation." (Id. at 1266). Professor Singer urges that such a property interest should exist and clearly believes that property rights should not be viewed as closed categories.

While some of these matters will be referred to later in the casebook, particularly in Part Four, Public Interests in Land, the editors view Professor Reich's "new property" and Professor Singer's "reliance interest" as essentially beyond the scope of a first-year course in property and appropriate for further study later in the curriculum.

Apart from the objects of property, there is a further problem of initial classification of property interests. Lawyers live by classification. Do the raw facts as presented by the client fall in the area of contracts, torts, property, corporations, etc.? Is it a trespass problem, a nuisance matter, a zoning issue or all three? Once classified, the lawyer knows where to begin his research in the texts, cases, law reviews, or statutes. Until then, the problem is just a can of worms dumped on his desk. By education and experience, the lawyer thus tends to think in a kind of outline format, all too frequently missing the "big picture" in the process. The law is a seamless web and often the classification does not fit properly but it remains a necessary process.

We already know that the basic classification is between real and personal property but, particularly if the object is real property, one must look at the various classifications of interests in land as represented by the doctrine of freehold estates, concurrent estates, non-freehold estates, and interests in the land of another. These matters are covered in Part Three of these materials (pages 208 to 787, infra) but a quick perusal of the subject headings will indicate the complexities of these classifications and illustrate why property law is a sophisticated subject indeed.

Unfortunately, the categories listed in the previous paragraph do not exhaust the subject because of the peculiar historical bifurcation of law and equity. These two separate, but parallel, streams of law (in the broad sense) were developed in discrete courts of law and chancery (equity). Thus, we have legal interests in property and equitable interests in property, governed by separate but complementary doctrines. We will have to separate these strands of the seamless web and unravel the mysteries as we explore the nature of Anglo-American law.

Overriding all of these, and still other classifications, is another basic split between private and public interests in property. Given the Anglo-American historic preference for private rights over public rights, the fallout from the conflict between the two has produced some of the most fascinating problems in the law of property. Police power regulations (zoning and its brethren), eminent domain, and taxation have long formed much of the grist for the real estate practitioners' mill, but today they are threatening to become the dominant force in property law. We will deal with these matters throughout the course but most directly in Part Four (pages 788 to 977, infra).

Chapter 4

ROLE OF PROPERTY IN SOCIETY

The material in the first three chapters should cast considerable light on the role of property in society. You should now pause to reflect on the impact of the various concepts on the citizens of a modern democracy. For example, which of the various theories of private property discussed by Seligman accounts for the fact that the very land on which the United States built a powerful nation was taken from the original occupants of North America? Is there any doubt about the role which property (in this case land) played in the development of the United States into a world power? Could the adjustment of the Indians' claim of ownership have been handled in a different way? What would have been the consequences of the various solutions you may have in mind? Consider the following excerpts from Johnson v. McIntosh.

JOHNSON v. McINTOSH

Supreme Court of the United States, 1823.
21 U.S. (8 Wheat.) 543, 5 L.Ed. 681.

MARSHALL, CH. J., delivered the opinion of the court. The plaintiff in this cause claim the land in their declaration mentioned, under two grants, purporting to be made, the first in 1773, and the last in 1775, by the chiefs of certain Indian tribes, constituting the Illinois and the Piankeshaw nations; and the question is, whether this title can be recognised in the courts of the United States? The facts, as stated in the case agreed, show the authority of the chiefs who executed this conveyance, so far as it could be given by their own people; and likewise show, that the particular tribes for whom these chiefs acted were in rightful possession of the land they sold. The inquiry, therefore, is, in a great measure, confined to the power of Indians to give, and of private individuals to receive, a title, which can be sustained in the courts of this country.

As the right of society to prescribe those rules by which property may be acquired and preserved is not, and cannot, be drawn into question; as the title to lands, especially, is, and must be, admitted, to depend entirely on the law of the nation in which they lie; it will be necessary, in pursing this inquiry, to examine, not simply those principles of abstract justice, which the Creator of all things has impressed on the mind of his creature man, and which are admitted to regulate, in a great degree, the rights of civilized nations, whose perfect independence is acknowledged; but those principles also which our own government has adopted in the particular case, and given us as the rule for our decision.

On the discovery of this immense continent, the great nations of Europe were eager to appropriate to themselves so much of it as they could respectively acquire. Its vast extent offered an ample field to the ambition and enterprise of all; and the character and religion of its inhabitants afforded an apology for considering them as a people over whom the superior genius of Europe might claim an ascendency. The potentates of the old world found no difficulty in convincing themselves that they made ample compensation to the inhabitants of the new, by bestowing on them civilization and Christianity, in exchange for unlimited independence. But as they were all in pursuit of nearly the same object, it was necessary, in order to avoid conflicting settlements, and consequent war with each other, to establish a principle, which all should acknowledge as the law by which the right of acquisition, which they all asserted, should be regulated, as between themselves. This principle was, that discovery gave title to the government by whose subjects, or by whose authority, it was made, against all other European governments, which title might be consummated by possession. The exclusion of all other Europeans, necessarily gave to the nation making the discovery the sole right of acquiring the soil from the natives, and establishing settlements upon it. It was a right with which no Europeans could interfere. It was a right which all asserted for themselves, and to the assertion of which, by others, all assented. Those relations which were to exist between the discoverer and the natives, were to be regulated by themselves. The rights thus acquired being exclusive, no other power could interpose between them.

In the establishment of these relations, the rights of the original inhabitants were, in no instance, entirely disregarded; but were, necessarily, to a considerable extent, impaired. They were admitted to be the rightful occupants of the soil, with a legal as well as just claim to retain possession of it, and to use it according to their own discretion; but their rights to complete sovereignty, as independent nations, were necessarily diminished, and their power to dispose of the soil, at their own will, to whomsoever they pleased, was denied by the original fundamental principle, that discovery gave exclusive title to those who made it. While the different nations of Europe respected the right of the natives, as occupants, they asserted the ultimate dominion to be in themselves; and claimed and exercised, as a consequence of this ultimate dominion, a power to grant the soil, while yet in possession of the natives. These grants have been understood by all, to convey a title to the grantees, subject only to the Indian right of occupancy.

The history of America, from its discovery to the present day, proves, we think, the universal recognition of these principles. . . .

No one of the powers of Europe gave its full assent to this principle more unequivocally than England. The documents upon this subject are ample and complete. So early as the year 1496, her monarch granted a commission to the Cabots, to discover countries then unknown to Christian people, and to take possession of them in the name of the king of England. Two years afterwards, Cabot proceeded on this voyage, and discovered the continent of North America, along which he sailed as far south as Virginia. To this discovery, the English trace their title. In this first effort made by the English government to acquire territory on this continent, we perceive a complete recognition of the principle which has been mentioned. The right of discovery given by this commission, is confined to countries "then unknown to all Christian people;" and of these countries, Cabot was empowered to take possession in the name of the king of England. Thus asserting a right to take possession, notwithstanding the occupancy of the natives, who were heathens, and, at the same time, admitting the prior title of any Christian people who may have made a previous discovery. The same principle continued to be recognised. . . .

. . .

Thus has our whole country been granted by the crown, while in the occupation of the Indians. These grants purport to convey the soil as well as the right of dominion to the grantees. In those governments which were denominated royal, where the right to the soil was not vested in individuals, but remained in the crown, or was vested in the colonial government, the king claimed and exercised the right of granting lands, and of dismembering the government, at his will. . . .

These various patents cannot be considered as nullities; nor can they be limited to a mere grant of the powers of government. A charter intended to convey political power only, would never contain words expressly granting the land, the soil and the waters. Some of them purport to convey the soil alone; and in those cases in which the powers of government, as well as the soil, are conveyed to individuals, the crown has always acknowledged itself to be bound by the grant. Though the power to dismember regal governments was asserted and exercised, the power to dismember proprietary governments was not claimed; and in some instances, even after the powers of government were revested in the crown, the title of the proprietors to the soil was respected. . . .

Further proofs of the extent to which this principle has been recognised, will be found in the history of the wars, negotiations and treaties, which the different nations, claiming territory in America, have carried on, and held with each other. . . . Thus, all the nations of Europe, who have acquired territory on this continent, have asserted in themselves, and have recognised in others, the exclusive right of the discoverer to appropriate the lands occupied by the Indians. Have the American states rejected or adopted this principle?

By the treaty which concluded the war of our revolution, Great Britain relinquished all claim, not only to the government, but to the "proprietary and territorial rights of the United States," whose boundaries were fixed in the second article. By this treaty, the powers of government, and the right to soil, which had previously been in Great Britain, passed definitively to these states. We had before taken possession of them, by declaring independence; but neither the declaration of independence, nor the treaty confirming it, could give us more than that which we before possessed, or to which Great Britain was before entitled. It had never been doubted, that either the United

States, or the several states, had a clear title to all the lands within the boundary lines described in the treaty, subject only to the Indian right of occupancy, and that the exclusive power to extinguish that right, was vested in that government which might constitutionally exercise it.

. . .

. . . The magnificent purchase of Louisiana, was the purchase from France of a country almost entirely occupied by numerous tribes of Indians, who are in fact independent. Yet, any attempt of others to intrude into that country, would be considered as an aggression which would justify war. Our late acquisitions from Spain are of the same character; and the negotiations which preceded those acquisitions, recognise and elucidate the principle which has been received as the foundation of all European title in America.

The United States, then, have unequivocally acceded to that great and broad rule by which its civilized inhabitants now hold this country. They hold, and assert in themselves, the title by which it was acquired. They maintain, as all others have maintained, that discovery gave an exclusive right to extinguish the Indian title of occupancy, either by purchase or by conquest; and gave also a right to such a degree of sovereignty, as the circumstances of the people would allow them to exercise. The power now possessed by the government of the United States to grant lands, resided, while we were colonies, in the crown or its grantees. The validity of the titles given by either has never been questioned in our courts. It has been exercised uniformly over territory in possession of the Indians. The existence of this power must negative the existence of any right which may conflict with and control it. An absolute title to lands cannot exist, at the same time, in different persons, or in different governments. An absolute must be an exclusive title, or at least a title which excludes all others not compatible with it. All our institutions recognise the absolute title of the crown, subject only to the Indian right of occupancy, and recognise the absolute title of the crown to extinguish that right. This is incompatible with an absolute and complete title in the Indians.

We will not enter into the controversy, whether agriculturists, merchants and manufacturers, have a right, on abstract principles, to expel hunters from the territory they possess, or to contract their limits. Conquest gives a title which the courts of the conqueror cannot deny, whatever the private and speculative opinions of individuals may be, respecting the original justice of the claim which has been successfully asserted. The British government, which was then our government, and whose rights have passed to the United States, asserted a title to all the lands occupied by Indians, within the chartered limits of the British colonies. It asserted also a limited sovereignty over them, and the exclusive right of extinguishing the titles which occupancy gave to them. These claims have been maintained and established as far west as the river Mississippi, by the sword. The title to a vast portion of the lands we now hold, originates in them. It is not for the courts of this country to question the validity of this title, or to sustain one which is incompatible with it.

Although we do not mean to engage in the defence of those principles which Europeans have applied to Indian title, they may, we think, find some excuse, if not justification, in the character and habits of the people whose rights have been wrested from them. The title by conquest is acquired and maintained by force. The conqueror prescribes its limits. Humanity, however, acting on public opinion, has established, as a general rule, that the conquered shall not be wantonly oppressed, and that their condition shall remain as eligible as is compatible with the objects of the conquest. Most usually, they are incorporated with the victorious nation, and become subjects or citizens of the government with which they are connected. The new and old members of the society mingle with each other; the distinction between them is gradually lost, and they make one people. Where this incorporation is practicable, humanity demands, and a wise policy requires, that the rights of the conquered to property should remain unimpaired; that the new subjects should be governed as equitably as the old, and that confidence in their security should gradually banish the painful sense of being separated from their ancient connections, and united by force to strangers. When the conquest is complete, and the conquered inhabitants can be blended with the conquerors, or safely governed as a distinct people, public opinion, which not even the conqueror can disregard, imposes these restraints upon him; and he cannot neglect them, without injury to his fame, and hazard to his power.

But the tribes of Indians inhabiting this country were fierce savages, whose occupation was war, and whose subsistence was drawn chiefly from the forest. To leave them in possession of their country, was to leave the country a wilderness; to govern them as a distinct people, was impossible, because they were as brave and as high-spirited as they were fierce, and were ready to repel by arms every attempt on their independence. What was the inevitable consequence of this state of things? The Europeans were under the necessity either of abandoning the country, and relinquishing their pompous claims to it, or of enforcing those claims by the sword, and by the adoption of principles adapted to the condition of a people with whom it was impossible to mix, and who could not be governed as a distinct society, or of remaining in their neighborhood, and exposing themselves and their families to the perpetual hazard of being massacred. Frequent and bloody wars, in which the whites were not always the aggressors, unavoidably ensued. European policy, numbers and skill prevailed; as the white population advanced, that of the Indians necessarily receded; the country in the immediate neighborhood of agriculturists became unfit for them; the game fled into thicker and more unbroken forests, and the Indians followed. The soil, to which the crown originally claimed title, being no longer occupied by its ancient inhabitants, was parcelled out according to the will of the sovereign power, and taken possession of by persons who claimed immediately from the crown, or mediately, through its grantees or deputies.

That law which regulates, and ought to regulate in general, the relations between the conqueror and conquered, was incapable of application to a people under such circumstances. The resort to some new and different rule, better adapted to the actual state of things, was unavoidable. Every rule which can be suggested will be found to be attended with great difficulty. However extravagant the pretension of converting the discovery of an inhabited country into conquest may appear; if the principle has been asserted in the first instance, and afterwards sustained; if a country has been acquired and held under it; if the property of the great mass of the community originates in it, it becomes the law of the land, and cannot be questioned. So too, with respect to the concomitant principle, that the Indian inhabitants are to be considered merely as occupants, to be protected, indeed, while in peace, in the possession of their lands, but to be deemed incapable of transferring the absolute title to others. However this restriction may be opposed to natural right, and to the usages of civilized nations, yet, if it be indispensable to that system under which the country has been settled, and be adapted to the actual condition of the two people, it may, perhaps, be supported by reason, and certainly cannot be rejected by courts of justice.

. . . The absolute ultimate title has been considered as acquired by discovery, subject only to the Indian title of occupancy, which title the discoverers possessed the exclusive right of acquiring. Such a right is no more incompatible with a seisin in fee, than a lease for years, and might as effectually bar an ejectment.

. . .

It has never been contended, that the Indian title amounted to nothing. Their right of possession has never been questioned. The claim of government extends to the complete ultimate title, charged with this right of possession, and to the exclusive power of acquiring that right. The object of the crown was, to settle the sea-coast of America; and when a portion of it was settled, without violating the rights of others, by persons professing their loyalty, and soliciting the royal sanction of an act, the consequences of which were ascertained to be beneficial, it would have been as unwise as ungracious, to expel them from their habitations, because they had obtained the Indian title, otherwise than through the agency of government. . . .

. . .

After bestowing on this subject a degree of attention which was more required by the magnitude of the interest in litigation, and the able and elaborate arguments of the bar, than by its intrinsic difficulty, the court is decidedly of opinion, that the plaintiffs do not exhibit a title which can be sustained in the courts of the United States; and that there is no error in the judgment which was rendered against them in the district court of Illinois.

Judgment affirmed, with costs.

The courts have generally followed the principal case and denied Indian land titles, e.g., see Tee-Hit-Ton Indians v. United States, 348 U.S. 272, 75 S.Ct. 313, 99 L.Ed. 314 (1955). Congress, however, has followed a fairly consistent policy of making voluntary payments to the

Indians. See Cohen, Original Indian Title, 32 Minn.L.Rev. 28 (1947). Mr. Cohen concluded that: "The notion that America was stolen from the Indians is one of the myths by which we Americans are prone to hide our real virtues and make our idealism look as hard-boiled as possible." Myth or not, the story of our treatment of the Indians is not a pleasant one but we cannot develop it here. Note, however, that the conflict goes on. See, for example, Joint Tribal Council of the Passamaquoddy Tribe v. Morton, 388 F.Supp. 649 (D.Me.1975), affirmed 528 F.2d 370 (1st Cir. 1975) and Note, Indian Title: The Rights of American Natives in Lands They Have Occupied Since Time Immemorial, 75 Col. L.Rev. 655 (1975).

Does the case of Johnson v. McIntosh cast light on the treatment of other minorities in America, those once viewed as "lesser breeds without the law"? Have we progressed since Johnson v. McIntosh was decided? Consider the earlier cases in this part of the materials and ponder excerpts from the following case.

SHELLEY v. KRAEMER

Supreme Court of the United States, 1948.
334 U.S. 1, 68 S.Ct. 836, 92 L.Ed. 1161.

VINSON, C.J. *

These cases present for our consideration questions relating to the validity of court enforcement of private agreements, generally described as restrictive covenants, which have as their purpose the exclusion of persons of designated race or color from the ownership or occupancy of real property. Basic constitutional issues of obvious importance have been raised.

The first of these cases comes to this Court on certiorari to the Supreme Court of Missouri. On February 16, 1911, thirty out of a total of thirty-nine owners of property fronting both sides of Labadie Avenue between Taylor Avenue and Cora Avenue in the city of St. Louis, signed an agreement, which was subsequently recorded, providing in part:

". . . the said property is hereby restricted to the use and occupancy for the term of Fifty (50) years from this date, so that it shall be a condition all the time and whether recited and referred to as [sic] not in subsequent conveyances and shall attach to the land, as a condition precedent to the sale of the same, that hereafter no part of said property or any portion thereof shall be, for said term of Fifty-years, occupied by any person not of the Caucasian race, it being intended hereby to restrict the use of said property for said period of time against the occupancy as owners or tenants of any portion of said property for resident or other purpose by people of the Negro or Mongolian Race."

The entire district described in the agreement included fifty-seven parcels of land. The thirty owners who signed the agreement held title

* The Court's footnotes have been omitted.

to forty-seven parcels, including the particular parcel involved in this case. At the time the agreement was signed, five of the parcels in the district were owned by Negroes. One of those had been occupied by Negro families since 1882, nearly thirty years before the restrictive agreement was executed. The trial court found that owners of seven out of nine homes on the south side of Labadie Avenue, within the restricted district and "in the immediate vicinity" of the premises in question, had failed to sign the restrictive agreement in 1911. At the time this action was brought, four of the premises were occupied by Negroes, and had been so occupied for periods ranging from twenty-three to sixty-three years. A fifth parcel had been occupied by Negroes until a year before this suit was instituted.

On August 11, 1945, pursuant to a contract of sale, petitioners Shelley, who are Negroes, for valuable consideration received from one Fitzgerald a warranty deed to the parcel in question. The trial court found that petitioners had no actual knowledge of the restrictive agreement at the time of the purchase.

On October 9, 1945, respondents, as owners of other property subject to the terms of the restrictive covenant, brought suit in the Circuit Court of the city of St. Louis praying that petitioners Shelley be restrained from taking possession of the property and that judgment be entered divesting title out of petitioners Shelley and revesting title in the immediate grantor or in such other person as the court should direct. The trial court denied the requested relief on the ground that the restrictive agreement, upon which respondents based their action, had never become final and complete because it was the intention of the parties to that agreement that it was not to become effective until signed by all property owners in the district, and signatures of all the owners had never been obtained.

The Supreme Court of Missouri sitting *en banc* reversed and directed the trial court to grant the relief for which respondents had prayed. That court held the agreement effective and concluded that enforcement of its provisions violated no rights guaranteed to petitioners by the Federal Constitution. At the time the court rendered its decision, petitioners were occupying the property in question. [The facts of the second case, arising in Michigan have been omitted.]

. . .

Petitioners have placed primary reliance on their contentions, first raised in the state courts, that judicial enforcement of the restrictive agreements in these cases has violated rights guaranteed to petitioners by the Fourteenth Amendment of the Federal Constitution and Acts of Congress passed pursuant to that Amendment. Specifically, petitioners urge that they have been denied the equal protection of the laws, deprived of property without due process of law, and have been denied privileges and immunities of citizens of the United States. We pass to a consideration of those issues.

I.

Whether the equal protection clause of the Fourteenth Amendment inhibits judicial enforcement by state courts of restrictive covenants based on race or color is a question which this Court has not heretofore been called upon to consider. . . .

It cannot be doubted that among the civil rights intended to be protected from discriminatory state action by the Fourteenth Amendment are the rights to acquire, enjoy, own and dispose of property. Equality in the enjoyment of property rights was regarded by the framers of that Amendment as an essential pre-condition to the realization of other basic civil rights and liberties which the Amendment was intended to guarantee. Thus, § 1978 of the Revised Statutes, derived from § 1 of the Civil Rights Act of 1866 which was enacted by Congress while the Fourteenth Amendment was also under consideration, provides:

"All citizens of the United States shall have the same right, in every State and Territory, as is enjoyed by white citizens thereof to inherit, purchase, lease, sell, hold, and convey real and personal property."

This Court has given specific recognition to the same principle. Buchanan v. Warley, 1917, 245 U.S. 60, 38 S.Ct. 16, 62 L.Ed. 149, L.R.A.1918C, 210, Ann.Cas. 1918A, 1201.

It is likewise clear that restrictions on the right of occupancy of the sort sought to be created by the private agreements in these cases could not be squared with the requirements of the Fourteenth Amendment if imposed by state statute or local ordinance. We do not understand respondents to urge the contrary. In the case of Buchanan v. Warley, supra, a unanimous Court declared unconstitutional the provisions of a city ordinance which denied to colored persons the right to occupy houses in blocks in which the greater number of houses were occupied by white persons, and imposed similar restrictions on white persons with respect to blocks in which the greater number of houses were occupied by colored persons. During the course of the opinion in that case, this Court stated: "The Fourteenth Amendment and these statutes enacted in furtherance of its purpose operate to qualify and entitle a colored man to acquire property without state legislation discriminating against him solely because of color."

. . .

But the present cases, unlike those just discussed, do not involve action by state legislatures or city councils. Here the particular patterns of discrimination and the areas in which the restrictions are to operate, are determined, in the first instance, by the terms of agreements among private individuals. Participation of the State consists in the enforcement of the restrictions so defined. The crucial issue with which we are here confronted is whether this distinction removes these cases from the operation of the prohibitory provisions of the Fourteenth Amendment.

Since the decision of this Court in the Civil Rights Cases, 1883, 109 U.S. 3, 3 S.Ct. 18, 27 L.Ed. 835, the principle has become firmly embedded in our constitutional law that the action inhibited by the first section of the Fourteenth Amendment is only such action as may fairly be said to be that of the States. That Amendment erects no shield against merely private conduct, however, discriminatory or wrongful.

We conclude, therefore, that the restrictive agreements standing alone cannot be regarded as a violation of any rights guaranteed to petitioners by the Fourteenth Amendment. So long as the purposes of those agreements are effectuated by voluntary adherence to their terms, it would appear clear that there has been no action by the State and the provisions of the Amendment have not been violated. . . .

But here there was more. These are cases in which the purposes of the agreements were secured only by judicial enforcement by state courts of the restrictive terms of the agreements. The respondents urge that judicial enforcement of private agreements does not amount to state action; or, in any event, the participation of the State is so attenuated in character as not to amount to state action within the meaning of the Fourteenth Amendment. Finally, it is suggested, even if the States in these cases may be deemed to have acted in the constitutional sense, their action did not deprive petitioners of rights guaranteed by the Fourteenth Amendment. We move to a consideration of these matters.

II.

That the action of state courts and of judicial officers in their official capacities is to be regarded as action of the State within the meaning of the Fourteenth Amendment, is a proposition which has long been established by decisions of this Court. That principle was given expression in the earliest cases involving the construction of the terms of the Fourteenth Amendment. . . .

. . .

One of the earliest applications of the prohibitions contained in the Fourteenth Amendment to action of state judicial officials occurred in cases in which Negroes had been excluded from jury service in criminal prosecutions by reason of their race or color. These cases demonstrate, also, the early recognition by this Court that state action in violation of the Amendment's provisions is equally repugnant to the constitutional commands whether directed by state statute or taken by a judicial official in the absence of statute. Thus, in Strauder v. West Virginia, 1880, 100 U.S. 303, 25 L.Ed. 664, this Court declared invalid a state statute restricting jury service to white persons as amounting to a denial of the equal protection of the laws to the colored defendant in that case. In the same volume of the reports, the Court in Ex parte Virginia, supra, held that a similar discrimination imposed by the action of a state judge denied rights protected by the Amendment, despite the fact that the language of the state statute relating to jury service contained no such restrictions.

The action of state courts in imposing penalties or depriving parties of other substantive rights without providing adequate notice and opportunity to defend, has, of course, long been regarded as a denial of the due process of law guaranteed by the Fourteenth Amendment. Brinkerhoff-Faris Trust & Savings Co. v. Hill, supra. Cf. Pennoyer v. Neff, 1878, 95 U.S. 714, 24 L.Ed. 565.

In numerous cases, this Court has reversed criminal convictions in state courts for failure of those courts to provide the essential ingredients of a fair hearing. . . .

But the examples of state judicial action which have been held by this Court to violate the Amendment's commands are not restricted to situations in which the judicial proceedings were found in some manner to be procedurally unfair. It has been recognized that the action of state courts in enforcing a substantive common-law rule formulated by those courts, may result in the denial of rights guaranteed by the Fourteenth Amendment, even though the judicial proceedings in such cases may have been in complete accord with the most rigorous conceptions of procedural due process. . . .

The short of the matter is that from the time of the adoption of the Fourteenth Amendment until the present, it has been the consistent ruling of this Court that the action of the States to which the Amendment has reference, includes action of state courts and state judicial officials. Although, in construing the terms of the Fourteenth Amendment, differences have from time to time been expressed as to whether particular types of state action may be said to offend the Amendment's prohibitory provisions, it has never been suggested that state court action is immunized from the operation of those provisions simply because the act is that of the judicial branch of the state government.

III.

Against this background of judicial construction, extending over a period of some three-quarters of a century, we are called upon to consider whether enforcement by state courts of the restrictive agreements in these cases may be deemed to be the acts of those States; and, if so, whether that action has denied these petitioners the equal protection of the laws which the Amendment was intended to insure.

We have no doubt that there has been state action in these cases in the full and complete sense of the phrase. The undisputed facts disclose that petitioners were willing purchasers of properties upon which they desired to establish homes. The owners of the properties were willing sellers; and contracts of sale were accordingly consummated. It is clear that but for the active intervention of the state courts, supported by the full panoply of state power, petitioners would have been free to occupy the properties in question without restraint.

These are not cases, as has been suggested, in which the States have merely abstained from action, leaving private individuals free to impose such discriminations as they see fit. Rather, these are cases in which the States have made available to such individuals the full coercive power of government to deny to petitioners, on the grounds of race or color, the enjoyment of property rights in premises which petitioners are willing and financially able to acquire and which the grantors are willing to sell. The difference between judicial enforcement and nonenforcement of the restrictive covenants is the difference to petitioners between being denied rights of property available to other members of the community and being accorded full enjoyment of those rights on an equal footing.

The enforcement of the restrictive agreements by the state courts in these cases was directed pursuant to the common-law policy of the States as formulated by those courts in earlier decisions. In the Missouri case, enforcement of the covenant was directed in the first instance by the highest court of the State after the trial court had determined the agreement to be invalid for want of the requisite number of signatures. In the Michigan case, the order of enforcement by the trial court was affirmed by the highest state court. The judicial action in each case bears the clear and unmistakable imprimatur of the State. We have noted that previous decisions of this Court have established the proposition that judicial action is not immunized from the operation of the Fourteenth Amendment simply because it is taken pursuant to the state's common-law policy. Nor is the Amendment ineffective simply because the particular pattern of discrimination, which the State has enforced, was defined initially by the terms of a private agreement. State action, as that phrase is understood for the purposes of the Fourteenth Amendment, refers to exertions of state power in all forms. And when the effect of that action is to deny rights subject to the protection of the Fourteenth Amendment, it is the obligation of this Court to enforce the constitutional commands.

We hold that in granting judicial enforcement of the restrictive agreements in these cases, the States have denied petitioners the equal protection of the laws and that, therefore, the action of the state courts cannot stand. We have noted that freedom from discrimination by the States in the enjoyment of property rights was among the basic objectives sought to be effectuated by the framers of the Fourteenth Amendment. That such discrimination has occurred in these cases is clear. Because of the race or color of these petitioners they have been denied rights of ownership or occupancy enjoyed as a matter of course by other citizens of different race or color. The Fourteenth Amendment declares "that all persons, whether colored or white, shall stand equal before the laws of the States, and, in regard to the colored race, for whose protection the amendment was primarily designed, that no discrimination shall be made against them by law because of their color." Strauder v. West Virginia, supra, 100 U.S. at 307, 25 L.Ed. 664. Only recently this Court has had occasion to declare that a state law which denied equal enjoyment of property rights to a designated class of citizens of specified race and ancestry, was not a legitimate exercise of the state's police power but violated the guaranty of the equal protection of the laws. Oyama v. California, 1948, 332 U.S. 633, 68 S.Ct. 269. Nor may the discriminations imposed by the state courts in these cases be justified as proper exertions of state police power. Cf. Buchanan v. Warley, supra.

Respondents urge, however, that since the state courts stand ready to enforce restrictive covenants excluding white persons from the ownership or occupancy of property covered by such agreements, enforcement of covenants excluding colored persons may not be deemed a denial of equal protection of the laws to the colored persons who are thereby affected. This contention does not bear scrutiny. The parties have directed our attention to no case in which a court, state or federal, has been called upon to enforce a covenant excluding members of the white majority from ownership or occupancy of real property on grounds of race or color. But there are more fundamental considerations. The rights created by the first section of the Fourteenth Amendment are, by its terms, guaranteed to the individual. The rights established are personal rights. It is, therefore, no answer to these petitioners to say that the courts may also be induced to deny white persons rights of ownership and occupancy on grounds of race or color. Equal protection of the laws is not achieved through indiscriminate imposition of inequalities.

Nor do we find merit in the suggestion that property owners who are parties to these agreements are denied equal protection of the laws if denied access to the courts to enforce the terms of restrictive covenants and to assert property rights which the state courts have held to be created by such agreements. The Constitution confers upon no individual the right to demand action by the State which results in the denial of equal protection of the laws to other individuals. And it would appear beyond question that the power of the State to create and enforce property interests must be exercised within the boundaries defined by the Fourteenth Amendment. Cf. Marsh v. Alabama, 1946, 326 U.S. 501, 66 S.Ct. 276, 90 L.Ed. 265.

The problem of defining the scope of the restrictions which the Federal Constitution imposes upon exertions of power by the States has given rise to many of the most persistent and fundamental issues which this Court has been called upon to consider. That problem was foremost in the minds of the framers of the Constitution, and since that early day, has arisen in a multitude of forms. The task of determining whether the action of a State offends constitutional provisions is one which may not be undertaken lightly. Where, however, it is clear that the action of the State violates the terms of the fundamental charter, it is the obligation of this Court so to declare.

The historical context in which the Fourteenth Amendment became a part of the Constitution should not be forgotten. Whatever else the framers sought to achieve, it is clear that the matter of primary concern was the establishment of equality in the enjoyment of basic civil and political rights and the preservation of those rights from discriminatory action on the part of the States based on considerations of race or color. Seventy-five years ago this Court announced that the provisions of the Amendment are to be construed with this fundamental purpose in mind. Upon full consideration, we have concluded that in these cases the States have acted to deny petitioners the equal protection of the laws guaranteed by the Fourteenth Amendment. Having so decided, we find it unnecessary to consider whether petitioners have also been deprived of property without due process of law or denied privileges and immunities of citizens of the United States.

For the reasons stated, the judgment of the Supreme Court of Missouri and the judgment of the Supreme Court of Michigan must be reversed.

Reversed.

MR. JUSTICE REED, MR. JUSTICE JACKSON, and MR. JUSTICE RUTLEDGE took no part in the consideration or decision of these cases.

In terms of the broad view of property's role in society and the tough issues still to be resolved by your generation of lawyers, read the comments by the following legal writers.

POWELL, THE LAW OF REAL PROPERTY

Vol. I, pages 2, 3, 33, 34 (1977).

Busy lawyers and judges are properly concerned chiefly with questions of present-day law. They desire quick access to current guidance in recent decisions and presently operative statutes. . . . In the field of property law, however, what *is* law on many points cannot be fairly grasped except in the full light of how it came to be. The background, even of considerable remoteness in time, is essential to any real understanding of what today's rule really requires. Furthermore statesmanship in the law of land requires perspective, a comprehension of the workings of the whole social organism, an awareness of the processes of evolution which are constantly at work in even the least regenerate of the fields of law. An opportunity and a need for statesmanship in this branch of law exist. . . .

So then, the test of goodness must be some mean between the concept of the complete dominance of the individual and the idea of the all-importance of the state. It is an assumption of any society based on private property that it is good for the individuals to have liberty of a high order in the use of things they own. It is a postulate of any society which hopes to survive that there be limits imposed on the absoluteness of property so as to assure rules which will be accepted as fair for the distribution of scarcities. Whenever a change in the institution of property is being tested for its quality, the change is unadulteratedly bad if it restricts an individual and contributes nothing to the social welfare. If, however, as is usually the case, it restricts the individual but contributes something to the social welfare the disadvantage and the advantage must be weighed against each other and such action taken as the tipping of the scales thus found may dictate. This falls far short of a clear chart to wisdom, but it provides an approach which will force persons to face squarely questions of social values, while preserving the benefits of private property.

The institution of property is the embodiment of accidents, events and the wisdom of the past. It is before us as clay into which we can introduce the coloration and configuration representing our wisdom. How great, how useful this new ingredient may be will largely determine the future happiness, and perhaps the continued existence of our society.

McDOUGAL, MUNICIPAL LAND POLICY AND CONTROL

Practicing Law Institute (1946).
Pages 13–15.

One convenient way to describe the social process in a given community is to refer to it as a group of people applying institutions to resources for the production of values. In this total process different people use the word property with different meanings and for different purposes. . . . An anthropological observer noting how this wonder-working word, "property," is used might well describe it as the symbol of highest-level abstraction, or of top ambiguity, in a large body of tautological propositions customarily invoked by governmental officials and others to rationalize, explain, and justify decisions about such important problems as what claims to the control and exploitation of resources are to be protected, in whom, against whom, to what extent, how, under what conditions, and for what purposes. He would stress especially that the propositions invoked remain largely constant verbally, whether the resource under discussion is a bag of peanuts or a small farm or a vast factory system, and that few clear discriminations are made in terms of values sought.

To one interested not in passive observation but in actively increasing the basic values produced by a given community, the important question is, however, not so much how the *word* property is used as how the *resources* of the community are used and whether this is the most efficient use that can be devised. How the word property is used becomes important only when it is used to confuse rather than to clarify fundamental issues about how the resources of a community are to be used. It has this effect, for example, when it is used to contrapose the long-term values of the individual and of the community. The prime interest of the individual in the future of property is, of course, in how he can secure for himself, and for those with whom he identifies himself, a maximum share of the basic democratic values, including opportunity to mature latent capacities into personally enjoyable and socially valued expression. From the community perspective the critical question is: considering the existing resources of this community and probable changes in these and other relevant variables, what are the most efficient institutions and practices by which this community can use and develop its resources for the implementation of its total policy—the production of maximum values for the greatest number of citizens? What balance, in other words, of public ownership and control and of private claim will best promote this total policy? Yet despite this difference in verbal formulation, there is no antithesis in fact between the individual and community perspectives. The individual who really identifies himself with the community of which he is a member will want to handle his private claims in such a way as to increase the aggregate values of the community. It is basic that acceptance of democracy carries with it a consideration of the aggregate interest and of the aggregate view of how that interest can best be achieved. In a community whose members seek democratic values it may, on the other hand, be assumed that one major objective will be to leave free to private decision the widest possible zones of activity compatible with the common welfare. In any contemporary community, furthermore, the interdependence of all individuals and groups is such that, entirely apart from the individual's willingness or unwillingness to identify himself with the community, the long-term welfare of most individuals, and of the small groups with which they do identify themselves, is inescapably dependent upon the long-term welfare of the whole community. Whatever the verbal obfuscations that special pleaders may on occasion employ, one who is actively concerned with either the individual or general interest comes back finally, therefore, to the central problem of property as the problem of how the people of a community can best use their resources for the fullest achievement of their values. It is a principal function of the specialists we call lawyers to use their unique skills to increase this efficiency.

NETHERTON, CONTROL OF HIGHWAY ACCESS

University of Wisconsin Press (1963).
Page 80.

The demands which public use and private property may make upon each other are constantly changing. Thus, while "property rights" under American law enjoy a reputation for permanence, they are in fact more highly relative and more sensitive to changing economic factors and social opinion than most other legal concepts.[1] The law has occasionally been pictured as a vast substratum of society which is constantly in a state of change and a superstructure of legal rules adjusting, sometimes tardily, to shifts in the foundation below.[2] The obvious implications of this characteristic were pointed out in broad terms by Woodrow Wilson:

"Law is an effort to fix in definite practice what has been found to be convenient, expedient, adapted to the circumstances of the actual

1. This idea has been expressed many ways. Consider, for example, the following: . . .

"The fact is that the laws of the land have seldom if ever recognized absolute rights. It might almost be said today that the more absolute the control that the law grants, the less likely it is to mean very much: that is, the more important the thing in which property is claimed, the greater the probability that the law will also limit its use, enjoyment and disposal. For obviously unrestricted dominion of the things of the world means power, and no government consciously and willingly permits that power to be exercised for purposes or results which seriously threaten interests which those in political control deem of paramount social importance. On the other hand, dominion also means individual liberty, and it is hardly too much to say that the major internal problems of free government turn on deciding wisely where to strike the balance in the dominion accorded. . . . Nor can any decision taken by lawmakers ever be more than a temporary one, subject always to change as new facts call for reconsiderations." Horack and Nolan, Land Use Controls (St. Paul 1955), p. 4.

2. See Hamilton, "Property Rights in the Market," 1 Journal of Legislative and Political Science 10 (1943).

world. Law in a moving, vital society grows old, obsolete, impossible, item by item. It is not necessary to repeal it or to set it formally aside. It will die of itself,—for lack of breath,—because it is no longer sustained by the facts or by the moral or practical judgments of the community whose life it has attempted to embody." [3]

These materials on "property as an institution" are intended to raise questions, not provide answers. Indeed, there are no definitive or final answers to the ultimate questions facing any society. One is reminded of Gertrude Stein's final moments on earth. As she lay dying, she whispered: "What is the answer?" Receiving no reply, she responded: "In that case, what is the question?"

It is always important, however, to ask the right questions because the very asking will cast some light on the nature of the human condition. Moreover, thoughtful individuals will try to provide some answers and thus contribute to our understanding of life, law, and other things that matter. This is not a casebook on jurisprudence, but we hope that you will develop some sense of the importance of a philosophical undergirding for the institution of property—private or public. If you wish to explore these issues in greater depth, see Schlatter, Private Property: The History of an Idea (1951); Becker, Property Rights: Philosophic Foundations (1977); and Ryan, Property and Political Theory (1984). [4]

3. Wilson, "The Law and the Facts," 5 American Political Science Review 1 (1911) at 1.

4. The Ryan book is favorably reviewed in Perkin, Book Review, London Times Literary Supplement 59 (1985). The reviewer writes in pertinent part: "Property has traditionally been the bedrock of political philosophy and social history, for the obvious reason that the obsessive concern of both has been with the struggle between the have and have-nots. That men should join and remain in communities in which some, usually a small minority, possess more of the products of the earth and the labour which makes them available, and even of the earth itself than others, usually the large majority, who possess nothing much beyond the labour of their hands, has always been a puzzle. . . . Alan Ryan in this eminently readable and reasonable book has no [solution], but he neatly shows how leading philosophers from Locke to Hegel have tried to justify the institution of property and why, despite Marx and Mill's forecast of its imminent demise, modern men and women in his opinion have lost interest in replacing it with socialism. . . .

"Ryan's concern in his 'pamphlet', 'Why Are There so Few Socialists?,' the last chapter of [his] book, is to inquire empirically why Mill and Marx turned out to be wrong. His answers are familiar, commonsensical and right as far as they go: first, 'roast beef and apple pie', to quote Sombart, the incredible economic success of latter-day capitalism in America and elsewhere; second, the high value modern men, especially workers, place on security above all for their families; third, the not-to-be-despised delights of consumerism, which people will not easily exchange for the distant hope of something better; fourth, the lack of interest on the part of most workers in sharing control with managers; and finally, the intellectual disintegration of socialism as it has become clear that a change of ownership from private enterprise to the state does not by itself guarantee freedom from tyranny or even from exploitation by the new class of managers and bureaucrats."

Chapter 5

THE PRACTICE OF PROPERTY LAW—WHAT DO LAWYERS DO?

In a general way, lawyers must be prepared "to assume direction of all phases of the areas of personal conflict inherent in a complex society and economy" and "to provide a very large proportion of national leadership at all levels of authority".*

In a more specific way, the practice of property law involves litigation before trial and appellate courts and administrative agencies; the drafting of legal documents, such as contracts, deeds, mortgages, leases, and wills; examination of abstracts of title or analysis of title insurance policies; planning of real estate developments, condominiums, long term leases, etc.; negotiations; counselling and advising of real estate clients; work with governmental agencies, involving zoning, subdivision controls, eminent domain, environmental impact statements et al. In short, the property lawyer is a planner, a negotiator, an advisor, and a litigator in all those areas involving the legal relationships among people in regard to the external things of this planet. He or she must understand both the substantive and procedural law and have the ability to make abstract theory work in a concrete, practical way. Some of this work is routine, even mundane, but it is important for the protection of the client's interests and it must be carefully performed. Some of the work is exciting and complex, and allows the property lawyer to "make" new law or apply traditional theories in novel ways. It tends to fall more heavily in the category of office work than in litigation and, indeed, in most cases, it could be called preventive law, designed to keep the client out of court and reduce his risks to a minimum. It deals with "things", in one sense, but it is also "people" law and there need not be a conflict between property rights and personal rights. After all, property law is designed, or should be, to serve people at all levels of society.

There are specialists in property law, just as in most areas of the law, but the field is also one of the mainstays of the general practitioner. In any survey of what lawyers do, property law always ranks near the top. One of the largest groups in the American Bar Association is the Section on Real Property, Probate and Trust Law with many thousands of members. Specialized journals, treatises, textbooks, etc. abound and many of them will be cited in these materials. As we finish this overview of property law, it might be wise to look at the lawyer's role in one key area e.g. the commercial transfer of real property. It is clear, however, that any meaningful understanding of

* Casner and Leach, Cases and Text on Property 3, 4 (1950). Professor Casner and the late Professor Leach, both of Harvard, describe seven basic qualities which lawyers should possess and which law school can help them attain: fact consciousness, a sense of relevance, comprehensiveness, foresight, lingual sophistication, precision and persuasiveness of speech, and self-discipline in habits of thoroughness.

the lawyer's role requires greater knowledge of property law than you now possess, so we will postpone the subject until Part Five of the Casebook.

As the preceding paragraphs in this short chapter indicate, lawyers are heavily involved in working with the institution of property. This is especially true in regard to real property (land and the improvements attached to it). Why does the law of land loom so large on the lawyers' horizon? For initial light on this question, read the following excerpt and then continue to ponder the question throughout the course.

BROWN and DAUER, PLANNING BY LAWYERS

The Foundation Press, Inc. (1978).
Pages 519–520.

. . .

3. Transactions involving real property are ubiquitous. In many states lawyers are involved, in one way or another, in virtually all but the very simplest, and often in those as well. That the legal profession should be so intimately connected with the development and exchange of real estate is surely the result of a number of factors. Most obvious is the fact that such transactions are as heavily attended to by positive law as are any other forms or objects of private activity. It is therefore in part a "public interest" in the uses of land, and not merely the fact that land transactions involve larger stakes, that makes lawyers as useful (or necessary) as they are. It would be beyond our present scope to explore fully why the law of real property is as extensive as it is. One could reflect, however, on some casual observations about the matter: First, even today parts of our system of landholding and exchange can trace their lineage back to the time when, in England at least, the relationships among people inter se and with the state was to a considerable degree determined by the relationships of people to land. The system of land tenure was very much at the heart of the system of public legal order. Second, land is not merely a scarce resource or economic good—it is nonreproducible and nonmoveable. If, for example, a section of coastline is devoted to a private commercial use no public recreational use can be made of that unique place. Unlike other social resources, real property supply is almost totally inelastic. Third, real property is the sine qua non of where things exist. Thus if some large area is encumbered with privately-created covenants that—in the absence of positive law—restrict some usage such as industrial or extractive activity (or habitation by Blacks or Jews or Orientals), then no such activities (or people) will exist in that place. Private transactions which limit minimum lot size or preclude multiple family dwellings would have, again in the absence of law, public effects in terms of economic and social demography, with its attendant implications for education, employment, mobility and cultural evolution. Thus the uses of real property are attended to by Law. Thus too, the involvement of lawyers.

A second, related factor which tends to make lawyers become very deeply involved in real property transactions is the complexity and enormous variety of many of these activities. Consider for example some of the legal areas which are relevant for one who proposes the development of a shopping center: Real estate finance; construction finance (real *and* personal property security); title acquisition and clearance; zoning; building codes; environmental impact; traffic ingress and egress; artisans' and materialmen's liens; labor law; commercial leasing (and, recently, potential antitrust implications of exclusionary lease clauses); public utilities; insurance of various kinds; and so on and on.

The point, of course, is not to articulate all of the reasons why lawyers are involved. It is sufficient for present purposes to observe that they *are* involved. It is probably a truism that as any area of social activity becomes increasingly subject to positive law, so do lawyers become more relevant to that area of social activity. And, so long as positive law remains the primary vehicle for the expression of collective regulation, it may follow that lawyers—a private profession—expand their "jurisdiction" with each expansion of collective or public-order control. As an exercise, perhaps, in fantasizing, assess the recent past and extrapolate to the role of positive law in the future. Now extrapolate the present role of the lawyer. Does the residential real property context as it presently exists indicate anything about such futurist scenarios?

Part Two

THE ACQUISITION OF PROPERTY (HEREIN PRIMARILY OF PERSONAL PROPERTY)

Collected in this part of the book are materials, mostly court opinions, deemed suitable to introduce the large subject of the law of acquisition of property. In some respects, these materials are more easily comprehended than are some of the materials appearing later in the book. Nevertheless, they raise questions of considerable importance, some of which are not easily answered. Most of the cases selected here concern personal property, sometimes of little market value, and some are types of cases that do not come up often in law practice. For example, you may never run into a finding problem in your practice but the cases on lost and found articles have great pedagogical value at the outset of your study.

A recurring concept in this part of the book is possession. This concept continues to be significant in American property law. There is still some room in our relatively mature legal system, as well as in primitive ones, for acquisition of property simply by taking possession. Also, and this is more important, there are significant problems related to the distinction between possessory and non-possessory property interests. It is not too early to begin to develop an understanding of this concept and its roles in our legal system.

Both volitional and non-volitional acquisition are covered here. Our law accords great freedom of transfer to property owners, but there are some formal requisites and some substantive limitations of that freedom which are assumed to advance policies of greater importance than the policy of deferring to the volition of owners. Non-volitional transfers are exemplified by those instances in which courts and legislatures extinguish interests in some owners and create property in others. In some cases, courts are creating property that did not exist previously in anyone.

These materials raise questions concerning the proper roles of courts and legislatures. Although these questions arise frequently in the law school curriculum, they should be addressed now within the context of the problems at hand.

Students are urged to view the cases here from many perspectives, including those of the court deciding the case, the parties, counsel for the parties, others who may be affected by the decision, and the objective observer who is concerned that our legal system function well.

Chapter 6

FINDING

GODDARD v. WINCHELL

Supreme Court of Iowa, 1892.
86 Iowa 71, 52 N.W. 1124.

Action in replevin. The subject of the controversy is an aerolite. In the district court the cause was tried without the aid of a jury, and the court gave judgment for the plaintiff, from which the defendant appealed.

GRANGER, J. The district court found the following facts, with some others, not important on this trial: "That the plaintiff, John Goddard, is, and has been since about 1857, the owner in fee simple of the north half of section No. three, in township No. ninety-eight, range No. twenty-five, in Winnebago county, Iowa, and was such owner at the time of the fall of the meteorite hereinafter referred to. (2) That said land was prairie land, and that the grass privilege for the year 1890 was leased to one James Elickson. (3) That on the 2d day of May, 1890, an aerolite passed over northern and northwestern Iowa, and the aerolite, or fragment of the same, in question in this action, weighing, when replevied, and when produced in court on the trial of this cause, about 66 pounds, fell onto plaintiff's land, described above, and buried itself in the ground to a depth of three feet, and became imbedded therein at a point about 20 rods from the section line on the north. (4) That the day after the aerolite in question fell it was dug out of the ground with a spade by one Peter Hoagland, in the presence of the tenant, Elickson; that said Hoagland took it to his house, and claimed to own same, for the reason that he had found same and dug it up. (5) That on May 5, 1890, Hoagland sold the aerolite in suit to the defendant H.V. Winchell, for $105, and the same was at once taken possession of by said defendant, and that the possession was held by him until same was taken under the writ of replevin herein; that defendant knew at the time of his purchase that it was an aerolite, and that it fell on the prairie south of Hoagland's land. . . . (10) I find the value of said aerolite to be one hundred and one dollars ($101) as verbally stipulated in open court by the parties to this action; that the same weighs about 66 pounds, is of a black, smoky color on the outside, showing the effects of heat, and of a lighter and darkish gray color on the inside; that it is an aerolite, and fell from the heavens on the 2d of May, 1890; that a member of Hoagland's family saw the aerolite fall, and directed him to it."

As conclusions of law, the district court found that the aerolite became a part of the soil on which it fell; that the plaintiff was the owner thereof; and that the act of Hoagland in removing it was wrongful. It is insisted by appellant that the conclusions of law are erroneous; that the enlightened demands of the time in which we live call for, if not a modification, a liberal construction, of the ancient rule, "that whatever is affixed to the soil belongs to the soil," or, the more modern statement of the rule, that "a permanent annexation to the soil, of a thing in itself personal, makes it a part of the realty." In behalf of appellant is invoked a rule alike ancient and of undoubted merit, "that of title by occupancy;" and we are cited to the language of Blackstone, as follows: "Occupancy is the taking possession of those things which before belonged to nobody;" and "whatever movables are found upon the surface of the earth, or in the sea, and are unclaimed by any owner, are supposed to be abandoned by the last proprietor, and as such are returned into the common stock and mass of things; and therefore they belong, as in a state of nature, to the first occupant or finder."

In determining which of these rules is to govern in this case, it will be well for us to keep in mind the controlling facts giving rise to the different rules, and note, if at all, wherein the facts of this case should distinguish it. The rule sought to be avoided has alone reference to what becomes a part of the soil, and hence belongs to the owner thereof, because attached or added thereto. It has no reference whatever to an independent acquisition of title; that is, to an acquisition of property existing independent of other property. The rule invoked has reference only to property of this independent character, for it speaks of movables "found upon the surface of the earth or in the sea." The term "movables" must not be construed to mean that which can be moved for, if so, it would include much known to be realty; but it means such things as are not naturally parts of earth or sea, but are on the one or in the other. Animals exist on the earth and in the sea, but they are not, in a proper sense, parts of either. If we look to the natural formation of the earth and sea, it is not difficult to understand what is meant by "movables," within the spirit of the rule cited. To take from the earth what nature has placed there in its formation, whether at the creation or through the natural processes of the acquisition and depletion of its particular parts, as we witness it in our daily observations, whether it be the soil proper or some natural deposit, as of mineral or vegetable matter, is to take a part of the earth, and not movables.

If, from what we have said, we have in mind the facts giving rise to the rules cited, we may well look to the facts of this case to properly distinguish it. The subject of the dispute is an aerolite, of about 66 pounds weight, that "fell from the heavens" on the land of the plaintiff, and was found three feet below the surface. It came to its position in the earth through natural causes. It was one of nature's deposits, with nothing in its material composition to make it foreign or unnatural to the soil. It was not a movable thing "on the earth." It was in the earth, and in a very significant sense immovable; that is, it was only movable as parts of earth are made movable by the hand of man. Except for the peculiar manner in which it came, its relation to the soil would be beyond dispute. It was in its substance, as we understand, a stone. It was not of a character to be thought of as "unclaimed by any owner," and, because unclaimed, "supposed to be abandoned by the last proprietor," as should be the case under the rule invoked by appellant. In fact, it has none of the characteristics of the property contemplated by such a rule.

We may properly note some of the particular claims of appellant. His argument deals with the rules of the common law for acquiring real property, as by escheat, occupancy, prescription, forfeiture, and alienation, which it is claimed were all the methods known, barring inheritance. We need not question the correctness of the statement, assuming that it has reference to original acquisition, as distinct from acquisitions to soil already owned, by accretion or natural causes. The general rules of the law, by which the owners of riparian titles are made to lose or gain by the doctrine of accretions, are quite familiar. These rules are not, however, of exclusive application to such owners. Through the action of the elements, wind and water, the soil of one man is taken and deposited in the field of another; and thus all over the country, we may say, changes are constantly going on. By these natural causes the owners of the soil are giving and taking as the wisdom of the controlling forces shall determine. By these operations one may be affected with a substantial gain, and another by a similar loss. These gains are of accretion, and the deposit becomes the property of the owner of the soil on which it is made.

A scientist of note has said that from six to seven hundred of these stones fall to our earth annually. If they are, as indicated in argument, departures from other planets, and if among the planets of the solar system there is this interchange, bearing evidence of their material composition, upon what principle of reason or authority can we say that a deposit thus made shall not be of that class of property that it would be if originally of this planet and in the same situation? If these exchanges have been going on through the countless ages of our planetary system, who shall attempt to determine what part of the rocks and formations of especial value to the scientist, resting in and upon the earth, are of meteoric acquisition, and a part of that class of property designated in argument as "unowned things," to be the property of the fortunate finder instead of the owner of the soil, if the rule contended for is to obtain? It is not easy to understand why stones or balls of metallic iron, deposited as this was, should be governed by a different rule than obtains from the deposit of boulders, stones, and drift upon our prairies by glacier action; and who would contend that these deposits from floating bodies of ice belong, not to the owner of the soil, but to the finder? Their origin or source may be less mysterious, but they, too, are "telltale messengers" from far-off lands, and have value for historic and scientific investigation.

It is said that the aerolite is without adaptation to the soil, and only valuable for scientific purposes. Nothing in the facts of the case will warrant us in saying that it was not as well adapted for use by the owner of the soil as any stone, or, as appellant is pleased to denominate it, "ball of metallic iron." That it may be of greater value for scientific or other purposes may be admitted, but that fact has little weight in determining who should be its owner. We cannot say that the owner of the soil is not as interested in, and would not as readily contribute to, the great cause of scientific advancement, as the finder, by chance or otherwise, of these silent messengers. This aerolite is of the value of $101, and this fact, if no other, would remove it from uses where other and much less valuable materials would answer an equally good purpose, and place it in the sphere of its greater usefulness.

The rule is cited, with cases for its support, that the finder of lost articles, even where they are found on the property, in the building, or with the personal effects of third persons, is the owner thereof against all the world except the true owner. The correctness of the rule may be conceded, but its application to the case at bar is very doubtful. The subject of this controversy was never lost or abandoned. Whence, it came is not known, but, under the natural law of its government, it became a part of this earth, and, we think, should be treated as such. . . .

Affirmed.

NOTES

1. The court in the above case cited no prior court decisions, statutes or constitutions. What was the source of the law applied by the court?

2. Was the court's reasoning satisfactory? Was the court's reliance upon the physical similarity of this aerolite and other stones on Goddard's land justified? It would be conceded that Goddard owns stones on and in his land, but should the aerolite be distinguished on the ground that no claim identical to Winchell's claim has been, or could be, made to those stones? Should the court have considered the effect of its decision as a disincentive to track and recover aerolites?

Was the court's reliance upon the analogy of accretion sound? What types of controversies have produced the law of accretion? Are those types of controversies distinguishable from the principal case? Did they involve claims by finders? The court refers to "rules of law, by which the owners of riparian titles are made to lose or gain by the doctrine of accretions . . . ." According to these rules, if the title to a person's land is described as bounded by a stream or body of water, gradual deposits of soil over time by action of the water will belong to that person, even though these deposits may have originated on another's land and may now be resting upon land that formerly was the bed of the body of water and owned by still another person. Similarly, gradual losses by erosion cause shrinkage of the land owned by a riparian. However, sudden (avulsive) changes, such as the cutting of a new river channel by a single flood, usually will not affect existing land title boundaries. Can you supply a rationale for these rules? Would that rationale be relevant to the controversy in the principal case? Assuming the relevance of the riparian analogy, would not the arrival of an aerolite be similar to an avulsive change? An interesting case involving riparian title is Coastal Industrial Water Authority v. York, 532 S.W.2d 949 (Tex.1976).

3. What result would the Iowa court now reach in a case factually identical except that the object of the controversy is a remnant of a

space vehicle launched by one making no claim to it? The court stressed the natural origin of the aerolite, but the generalization "that which is affixed to the soil belongs to the soil" is not so limited. There is much law concerning fixtures, which typically are manufactured objects that have become part of land by annexation to it.

4. Was the trial court's finding of facts satisfactory? Is it clear whether Hoagland was a trespasser? Would that be relevant? Is it clear that Winchell purchased with notice of Goddard's claim? Would that be relevant?

5. One of the trial court's conclusions of law was that "the aerolite became a part of the soil on which it fell." Was this really a finding of fact rather than a conclusion of law?

6. Suppose that a valuable pool of oil lies under land owned by A and also under land owned by B, who drills a well and commences pumping oil, a consequence being that oil under A's land moves to B's well. Has B taken A's oil? Courts have answered this question in the negative, but have disagreed as to the rationale. Some have said that oil and gas underground, being migratory, are similar to wild animals and therefore are not the property of anyone until reduced to possession by extraction. E.g., Hammonds v. Central Kentucky Natural Gas Co., 255 Ky. 685, 75 S.W.2d 204 (1934). Another view is that the landowner owns the oil and gas under his land, but that this ownership is lost as to oil or gas that moves into another's well. E.g., Stephens County v. Mid-Kansas Oil & Gas Co., 113 Tex. 160, 254 S.W. 290 (1923). Do the same consequences flow from each of these rationales? Why are courts reluctant to impose liability upon the pumper who causes drainage of oil or gas from beneath another's land? See ch. 17, § 2F, herein.

7. Courts have held that the ownership acquired by a possessor of a wild animal is terminated if the animal escapes. What rationale supports this result? This analogy was leaned upon heavily by a Kentucky court in holding that one who obtained natural gas from one tract of land and stored it in an exhausted underground gas reservoir situated partially under another tract of land owned by him and partially under a tract of land owned by a neighbor was not liable for use of the neighbor's land for storage. Hammonds v. Central Kentucky Natural Gas Co., supra. The Court said:

"If one capture a fox in a forest and turn it loose in another, or if he catch a fish and put it back in the stream at another point, has he not done with that migratory, common property just what the appellee has done with the gas in this case? Did the company not lose its exclusive property in the gas when it restored the substance to its natural habitat? . . . We are of opinion, therefore, that if in fact the gas turned loose in the earth wandered into the plaintiff's land, the defendant is not liable to her for the value of the use of her property, for the company ceased to be the exclusive owner of the whole of the gas—it again became mineral ferae naturae."

The rationale of the Hammonds case was rejected in Lone Star Gas Co. v. Murchison, 353 S.W.2d 870 (Tex.Civ.App.1962), which involved a dispute as to title to gas stored underground. The court said: "Gas has no similarity to wild animals. Gas is an inanimate, diminishing non-reproductive substance lacking any will of its own, and, instead of running wild and roaming at large as animals do, is subject to be moved solely by pressure or mechanical means. . . . [T]he owner of gas does not lose title thereof by storing the same in a well-defined underground reservoir." This language was approved in Humble Oil and Refining Co. v. West, 508 S.W.2d 812 (Tex.1974). The Kentucky Court, severely limiting the Hammonds case, has held that in some circumstances injected natural gas remains personal property of the injector. Texas American Energy Corp. v. Citizens Fidelity Bank & Trust Co., 736 S.W.2d 25 (Ky.1987).

EADS v. BRAZELTON

Supreme Court of Arkansas, 1861.
22 Ark. 499, 79 Am.Dec. 88.

FAIRCHILD, J. . . . The bill in this case is founded upon a right of occupancy which Brazelton, the plaintiff, insists was vested in him by his discovery of the wreck of the steam-boat America and by his intentions and acts relating thereto. Because this right was not respected by the defendants, partners and servants of a firm of wreckers doing business in the Mississippi River and its tributaries under the style of Eads and Nelson, Brazelton filed his bill on the chancery side of the Circuit Court of Mississippi County, to obtain the protection of the court, to relieve him from the interference of the defendants in his own intended labors, to recover the property in the wreck, and to obtain compensation for what they had taken therefrom.

From what is before us it may be taken as shown in the case that in November, 1827, the boat named sank in the Mississippi River within the limits of Mississippi County; that, of her cargo, shot and bundles of bar lead of an unascertained quantity and lead in pigs to about the number of three thousand remained in the river, wholly abandoned by the owners; that Brazelton, having information of the place where the boat sank, proceeded in December, 1854, to ascertain its exact locality in the bed of the river with the view of raising the sunken lead; that in January, 1855, he arrived at the vicinity of the wreck with his diving boat to carry out his intention and fastened a buoy to a weight that rested upon the wreck with the expectation of putting his boat over it the next day; but that he was detained by other business and by the difficulties and dangers of the work in the existing state of water with boats like his and by the necessity for making repairs upon his boat and apparatus for raising the cargo, till the defendants, upon the 28th of September, 1855, caused one of their boats to stop at the shore near the wreck, to search for and find it, to place their boat over it, and to commence raising the lead. . . . [The lower court entered a decree enjoining interference by the defendants and awarding damages to the plaintiff.]

When Brazelton found the wreck he traced lines to it from different points on the Arkansas side of the river, so that their intersection would show the situation of the wreck, and the lines were indicated by marks upon the trees. It was upon the return of Brazelton from St. Louis with his bell boat that a float or buoy was placed by Brazelton over the wreck, and this was done with the intention of signifying the place to which the diving boat was to be dropped the next morning. It was not to be expected that such objects would remain permanent fixtures, as the wreck was in the main channel of the river, and it is evident that Brazelton considered them as guides to the situation of the wreck, as the marked trees were, as he stated to Seth Daniel, in the presence of Reese Bowen, that it would make no difference if they should be washed away, as he could find the wreck from the ranges of his lines. Brazelton does not pretend to have put his boat over the wreck, or to have had any claim to the wreck but by occupancy, which depended upon his finding it, upon his providing means for easy approaches to it by land-marks, and floats upon water, and upon his being in the neighborhood of the wreck from January to the last of September, without any other appropriation of the wreck, but with a continual assertion of his claim, and with the intention of making it good by future action. . . .

With reference to the tree marks of Brazelton it may be said that there is no satisfactory evidence that they were used on the part of the defendants in finding the wreck. . . .

It is not established that the defendants knew that Brazelton was about to work upon the America, although a witness so inferred from the conversation of the Captain and others of the boat, while there is no room for suspicion that they intended to interfere with any occupancy of the boat by Brazelton, and the whole case is, that they did not do so according to their understanding of Brazelton's right.

But what that right was remains to be determined.

Notwithstanding the point made by the defendants, that Brazelton had no right to the lead which the law would protect, it being the property of the original owners of the cargo, there is no room for doubt that the lead was abandoned by its owners; and even without the positive testimony of an owner of the boat and cargo in affirmation of the fact the law would so imply from the term of the loss and from the fact of its having been covered by an island formed upon it which sustained trees growing to a height of thirty or forty feet. All reasonable hope of acquiring the property must have been given up from the nature of the case; and the evidence shows that during the two years that intervened between the sinking of the boat and its being covered by the tow head and island no effort was made to save that part of the cargo. . . .

The occupation or possession of property lost, abandoned or without an owner must depend upon an actual taking of the property with the intent to reduce it to possession. . . .

Brazelton's act of possession need not have been manual; he was not obliged to take the wreck or the lead between his hands; he might take such possession of them as their nature and situation permitted; but that his circumstances should give a legal character to his acts, making that to be possession which the law declares not to be possession, assumes more than a court can sanction. Marking trees that extended across the wreck and affixing temporary buoys to it were not acts of possession; they only indicated Brazelton's desire or intention to appropriate the property. Placing his boat over the wreck, with the means to raise its vauables and with persistent efforts directed to raising the lead, would have been keeping the only effectual guard over it, would have been the only warning that intruders—that is, other longing occupants—would be obliged to regard, and would have been such acts of possession as the law would notice and protect. . . .

The decree of the Circuit Court of Mississippi County sitting in chancery is reversed. . . .

NOTES

1. What justifications might be advanced for the doctrine that ownership of abandoned things may be acquired by taking possession? What alternative doctrines are conceivable and what can be said in support of them? One alternative would be a doctrine that abandoned things belong to the state. Another alternative would leave title with the original owner, whose attempted abandonment would be ineffective. This is the rule generally applied to ownership of land in this country. Why are land and chattels treated differently in this respect?

2. The doctrine that ownership may be acquired by taking possession has been applied not only to abandoned goods, wild animals and underground liquid and gaseous natural resources, but also to western water rights. In addition, qualified ownership may be acquired by taking possession of lost articles and other things, as shown by subsequent materials in this book. The meaning of qualified ownership in this context is illuminated by the next case in this chapter and following cases. Why is prior possession deemed important? Is there a single comprehensive policy served by all manifestations of the prior appropriation doctrine? Or do the varying fact situations in which prior possession has conferred ownership raise varying policy issues? Consider, in addition to pertinent materials in this book, the following policy explorations: Epstein, Possession as the Root of Title, 13 Ga.L. Rev. 1221 (1979); Rose, Possession as the Origin of Property, 52 U.Chi. L.Rev. 73 (1985).

3. If the owner of this vessel at the time of its sinking now sues to recover the lead or its value from the victorious party in the principal case, what will be the outcome? Assume that the plaintiff can establish that he never intended to relinquish title to the cargo and that his delay in asserting title was unavoidable.

4. The court in the principal case stated that one could not acquire possession without an "actual taking," but it then declared that Brazelton would have had possession if he had placed his "boat over the wreck, with the means to raise its valuables and with persistent efforts directed to raising the lead . . .." How can these statements be reconciled? Why should not discovery and claim be sufficient? One court explained that "the law does not clothe mere discovery with an

exclusive right to the discovered property because such a rule would provide little encouragement to the discoverer to pursue the often strenuous task of actually retrieving the property and returning it to a socially useful purpose and yet would bar others from attempting to do so." Treasure Salvors, Inc. v. Unidentified Wrecked and Abandoned Sailing Vessel, 640 F.2d 560, 573 (5th Cir. 1981).

5. Suppose that a hunter and his hounds are pursuing a fox closely on public land when the fox happens to run near a person who shoots and kills the fox and carries it away. If the hunter sues that person to recover the fox or its value, what result would be anticipated in view of the Eads case? On similar facts, the hunter lost in Pierson v. Post, 3 Caines (N.Y.) 175, 2 Am.Dec. 264 (1805). This and other cases involving attempted capture of wild animals are discussed in R. Brown, Personal Property c. II (3d ed. W. Raushenbush 1975).

6. Would the court's decision in the principal case have been the same had it been established that the defendants had relied upon the plaintiff's buoys and tree markings? Or suppose that Brazelton, on the day after setting out the buoys, had returned with his salvage equipment only to discover that defendants had destroyed his buoys and that Brazelton was never able thereafter to locate the wreck. Would B have any remedy other than a suit to recover the value of the buoys? Consider the bearing, if any, upon these questions of Keeble v. Hickeringill, 11 East 574, 103 Eng.Rep. 1127 (K.B.1707), holding, in an action on the case, that a cause of action was stated in a declaration alleging that the defendant, intending to deprive the plaintiff of the opportunity of capturing wild ducks, had frightened the ducks away from a pond in the plaintiff's possession by shooting guns. Holt, C.J., declared: ". . . . he that hinders another in his trade or livelihood is liable to an action for so hindering him. . . . where a violent or malicious act is done to a man's occupation, profession, or way of getting a livelihood, there an action lies in all cases. But if a man doth him damage by using the same employment; as if Mr. Hickeringill had set up another decoy on his own ground near the plaintiff's, and that had spoiled the custom of the plaintiff, no action would lie, because he had as much liberty to make and use a decoy as the plaintiff."

ARMORY v. DELAMIRIE

King's Bench, 1722.
1 Strange 505.

The plaintiff being a chimney sweeper's boy found a jewel and carried it to the defendant's shop (who was a goldsmith) to know what it was, and delivered it into the hands of the apprentice, who under pretence of weighing it, took out the stones, and calling to the master to let him know it came to three halfpence, the master offered the boy the money, who refused to take it, and insisted to have the thing again; whereupon the apprentice delivered him back the socket without the stones. And now in trover against the master these points were ruled:

1. That the finder of a jewel, though he does not by such finding acquire an absolute property or ownership, yet he has such a property as will enable him to keep it against all but the rightful owner, and consequently may maintain trover.

2. That the action well lay against the master, who gives a credit to his apprentice, and is answerable for his neglect.

3. As to the value of the jewel several of the trade were examined to prove what a jewel of the finest water that would fit the socket would be worth; and the Chief Justice directed the jury, that unless the defendant did produce the jewel, and shew it not to be of the finest water, they should presume the strongest against him, and make the value of the best jewels the measure of their damages: which they accordingly did.

NOTES

1. One informed of the circumstances of the finding would not have paid the plaintiff the full market value of the jewel. Why should the plaintiff recover more in this action?

2. If, after the defendant goldsmith satisfies this judgment, the person who lost the jewel brings an action in trover against the goldsmith, should this action succeed?

BRIDGES v. HAWKESWORTH

Court of Queen's Bench, 1851.
21 L.J.,N.S., 75.

This was an appeal brought by the plaintiff from the Westminster County Court.

The plaintiff was a traveller for a large firm with which the defendant, who was a shopkeeper, had dealings. On one occasion (October 1847) the plaintiff, who had called at the defendant's on business, on leaving the defendant's shop noticed and picked up a small parcel which was lying on the shop floor. He immediately shewed it to the shopman, and on opening it found it contained bank notes. The plaintiff told the defendant who came in that he had found a parcel of notes, and requested the defendant to keep them to deliver to the owner. Three years having elapsed and no owner appearing to claim them, the plaintiff applied to the defendant for them. The defendant refused to deliver them up, and the plaintiff brought a plaint to recover the notes. The Judge decided that the defendant was entitled to keep them as against the plaintiff, and gave judgment for the defendant.

PATTESON, J. The general right of the finder to any article which has been lost as against all the world except the true owner, was established in the case of Armory v. Delamirie, which has never been disputed. This right would clearly have accrued to the plaintiff had the notes been picked up by him outside the shop of the defendant. . . . The case then resolves itself into the single point, on which it appears that the learned judge decided it: namely, whether the circumstance of the notes being found *inside* the defendant's shop, gives him, the defendant, the right to have them as against the plaintiff who found them. There is no authority to be found in our law directly in point. . . . It was well asked on the argument, if the defendant has the right, *when* did it accrue to him? If at all, it must have been antecedent to the finding by the plaintiff, for that finding could not give the defendant any right. If the notes had been accidentally kicked into the street, and then found by someone passing by, could it be contended that the defendant was entitled to them, from the mere fact of their having been originally dropped in his shop? If the discovery had not been communicated to the defendant, could the real owner have had any cause of action against him, because they were found in his house? Certainly not. The notes never were in the custody of the defendant, nor within the protection of his house before they were found, as they would have been had they been intentionally deposited there, and the defendant has come under no responsibility. We find, therefore, no circumstances in this case to take it out of the general rule of law, that the finder of a lost article is entitled to it as against all parties except the real owner.

Judgment reversed.

NOTE

Did this court read Armory v. Delamirie too broadly? What was "established" in that case? Did the court that decided Armory v. Delamirie even consider the validity of a claim by the owner of the premises where the jewel was found? Are broad generalizations in court opinions that go beyond the facts of the case "law"? What weight, if any, should be accorded such statements? Read Goodhart, Three Cases on Possession, 3 Camb.L.J. 195 (1928), reprinted in W. Fryer, Readings on Personal Property 72 (3d ed.1938).

SOUTH STAFFORDSHIRE WATER CO. v. SHARMAN

Court of Queen's Bench, 1896.
[1896] 2 Q.B. 44.

Appeal from the decision of the county court of Staffordshire holden at Lichfield.

In August, 1895, the plaintiffs, owners of the fee simple in possession of the land covered by the Minster Pool, employed the defendant, together with a number of workmen, to clean out the pool. During the operation several articles of interest were found, and the defendant, while so employed, found in the mud at the bottom of the pool two gold rings. The plaintiff demanded the rings; but he refused to deliver them up, and placed them in the hands of the police authorities, who, by advertisement and otherwise, endeavoured to find the owner of the rings. Ultimately, being unsuccessful in finding the real owner, the police authorities returned the rings to the defendant.

The plaintiffs then sued the defendant in detinue for the recovery of the rings. It was proved at the trial that there was no special contract between the plaintiffs and the defendant as to giving up any articles that might be found. The county court judge gave judgment for the defendant, holding, on the authority of Armory v. Delamirie and Bridges v. Hawkesworth, that the defendant had a good title against all the world except the real owner. The plaintiffs appealed.

LORD RUSSELL OF KILLOWEN, C.J. In my opinion, the county court judge was wrong, and his decision must be reversed and judgment entered for the plaintiffs.

The plaintiffs are the freeholders of the locus in quo, and as such they have the right to forbid anybody coming on their land or in any way interfering with it. They had the right to say that their pool should be cleaned out in any way that they thought fit, and to direct what should be done with anything found in the pool in the course of such cleaning out. It is no doubt right, as the counsel for the defendant contended, to say that the plaintiffs must show that they had actual control over the locus in quo and the things in it; but under the circumstances, can it be said that the Minster Pool and whatever might be in that pool were not under the control of the plaintiffs? In my opinion, they were. The case is like the case, of which several illustrations were put in the course of the argument, where an article is found on private property, although the owners of that property are ignorant that it is there. The principle on which this case must be decided, and the distinction which must be drawn between this case and that of Bridges v. Hawkesworth, 21 L.J. (Q.B.) 75, is to be found in a passage in Pollock and Wright's Essay on Possession in the Common Law, p. 41: "The possession of land carries with it in general, by our law, possession of everything which is attached to or under that land, and, in the absence of a better title elsewhere, the right to possess it also. And it makes no difference that the possessor is not aware of the thing's existence. . . . It is free to any one who requires a specific intention as a part of a de facto possession to treat this as a positive rule of law. But it seems preferable to say that the legal possession rests on a real de facto possession constituted by the occupier's general power and intent to exclude unauthorized interference." . . .

The case of Bridges v. Hawkesworth stands by itself, and on special grounds; and on those grounds it seems to me that the decision in that case was right. Some one had accidentally dropped a bundle of banknotes in a public shop. The shopkeeper did not know they had been dropped, and did not in any sense exercise control over them. The shop was open to the public, and they were invited to come there. A customer picked up the notes and gave them to the shopkeeper in order that he might advertise them. The owner of the notes was not found, and the finder then sought to recover them from the shopkeeper. It was held that he was entitled to do so, the ground of the decision being, as was pointed out by Patteson, J., that the notes, being dropped in the public part of the shop, were never in the custody of the shopkeeper, or "within the protection of his house."

It is somewhat strange that there is no more direct authority on the question; but the general principle seems to me to be that where a person has possession of house or land, with a manifest intention to exercise control over it and the things which may be upon or in it, then, if something is found on that land, whether by an employee of the owner or by a stranger, the presumption is that the possession of that thing is in the owner of the locus in quo.

WILLS, J. I entirely agree; and I will only add that a contrary decision would, as I think, be a great and most unwise encouragement to dishonesty.

Appeal allowed; judgment for plaintiffs.

NOTES

1. Did Lord Russell accurately state the rationale relied upon by Patteson, J., in Bridges v. Hawkesworth? Did Patteson, J., make a distinction between the public and private parts of a land? Does the distinction make sense? Is it realistic to say that a shopowner does not control and intend to control the entire shop, including those portions to which the public are invited? How does one apply the distinction? If only a portion of the public are invited, such as those who purchase tickets, is the place public? Would Pasadena's Rose Bowl be a private place? How about the room in a bank to which only renters of safe deposit boxes are admitted? Such a place was deemed private in Pyle v. Springfield Marine Bank, 330 Ill.App. 1, 70 N.E.2d 257 (1946). Is there a better rationale for holding for the bank? While a bond on the floor could hardly be said to have been entrusted to the possession of the bank, nevertheless the bank has undertaken to provide a secure area for the location of safety deposit boxes. Is this not much different from the shop in Bridges v. Hawkesworth?

2. In Parker v. British Airways Board, [1982] 1 All E.R. (C.A.1981) 834, a gold bracelet found on the floor of an executive lounge (available only to passengers who hold first class tickets or are members of the airline Executive Club) was held to belong to the finder rather than to the airline.

Donaldson L.J.: ". . . British Airways, for their part, cannot assert any title to the bracelet based on the rights of an occupier over chattels attached to a building. The bracelet was lying loose on the floor. Their claim must, on my view of the law, be based on a manifest intention to exercise control over the lounge and all things which might be in it. The evidence is that they claimed the right to decide who should and who should not be permitted to enter and use the lounge, but their control was in general exercised on the basis of classes or categories of user and the availability of the lounge in the light of the need to clean and maintain it. I do not doubt that they also claimed the right to exclude individual undesirables, such as drunks, and specific types of chattels such as guns and bombs. But this control has no real relevance to a manifest intention to assert custody and control over lost articles. There was no evidence that they searched for such articles regularly or at all."

HANNAH v. PEEL

King's Bench, 1945.
[1945] 1 K.B. 509.

Action tried by BIRKETT, J. On December 13, 1938, the freehold of Gwernhaylod House, Overton-on-Dee, Shropshire, was conveyed to the defendant, Major Hugh Edward Ethelston Peel, who from that time to the end of 1940 never himself occupied the house and it remained unoccupied until October 5, 1939, when it was requisitioned, but after some months was released from requisition. Thereafter it remained unoccupied until July 18, 1940, when it was again requisitioned, the defendant being compensated by a payment at the rate of 250. a year. In August, 1940, the plaintiff, Duncan Hannah, a lance-corporal, serving in a battery of the Royal Artillery, was stationed at the house and on the 21st of that month, when in a bedroom, used as a sick-bay he was adjusting the black-out curtains when his hand touched something on the top of a window-frame, loose in a crevice, which he thought was a piece of dirt or plaster. The plaintiff grasped it and dropped it on the outside window ledge. On the following morning he saw that it was a brooch covered with cobwebs and dirt. Later, he took it with him when he went home on leave and his wife having told him it might be of value, at the end of October, 1940, he informed his commanding officer of his find and, on his advice, handed it over to the police, receiving a receipt for it. In August, 1942, the owner not having been found the police handed the brooch to the defendant, who sold it on October, 1942, for 66., to Messrs. Spink & Son, Ltd., of London, who resold it in the following month for 88. There was no evidence that the defendant had any knowledge of the existence of the brooch before it was found by the plaintiff. The defendant had offered the plaintiff a reward for the brooch, but the plaintiff refused to accept this and maintained throughout his right to the possession of the brooch as against all persons other than the owner, who was unknown. By a letter, dated October 5, 1942, the plaintiff's solicitors demanded the return of the brooch from the defendant, but it was not returned and on October 21, 1943, the plaintiff issued his writ claiming the return of the brooch, or its value, and damages for its detention. By his defence, the defendant claimed the brooch on the ground that he was the owner of Gwernhaylod House and in possession thereof.

[Most of the court's review of the authorities is omitted.]

It has been said that [South Staffordshire Water Co. v. Sharman] establishes that if a man finds a thing as the servant or agent of another, he finds it not for himself, but for that other, and indeed that seems to afford a sufficient explanation of the case. . . .

It is fairly clear from the authorities that a man possesses everything which is attached to or under his land. Secondly, it would appear to be the law from the authorities I have cited, and particularly from Bridges v. Hawkesworth, that a man does not necessarily possess a thing which is lying unattached on the surface of his land even though the thing is not possessed by someone else. . . .

[The plaintiff's] conduct was commendable and meritorious. The defendant was never physically in possession of these premises at any time. It is clear that the brooch was never his, in the ordinary acceptation of the term, in that he had the prior possession. He had no knowledge of it, until it was brought to his notice, by the finder. A discussion of the merits does not seem to help, but it is clear on the facts that the brooch was "lost" in the ordinary meaning of that word; that it was "found" by the plaintiff in the ordinary meaning of that word, that its true owner has never been found, that the defendant was the owner of the premises and had his notice drawn to this matter by the plaintiff, who found the brooch. In those circumstances I propose to follow the decision in Bridges v. Hawkesworth, and to give judgment in this case for the plaintiff for 66.

NOTES

1. In City of London Corp. v. Appleyard [1963] 1 W.L.R. 982 (Q.B.), the facts essentially were as follows. The owner and occupier of a building entered into a contract with a construction firm for the destruction of the building and the erection of another in its place. As the building was being razed, an employee of the construction firm discovered a large sum of money in a secret wall safe. In view of the earlier English cases, who should have been entitled to this money? A similar American case is State ex rel. Scott v. Buzard, 235 Mo.App. 636, 144 S.W.2d 847 (1940).

2. Blackacre is owned by O, but has never been occupied by O or any other person. X enters Blackacre without O's consent and removes timber. O brings an action of trespass against X to recover damages for injury to Blackacre. This action can be maintained only by one in possession of the land. There is authority in the United States that O can bring the action. See Gillespie v. Dew, 1 Stew. 229 (Ala.1827), where the court said: "We are of opinion that, where there is no adverse possession, the title draws with it constructive possession, so as to sustain the action of trespass."

3. Finders have frequently prevailed despite their status as employees of the owner of the place of finding. E.g., Danielson v. Roberts, 44 Or. 108, 74 P. 913 (1904). In Toledo Trust Co. v. Simmons, 52 Ohio App. 373, 3 N.E.2d 661 (1935), an attendant employed by a safety deposit concern was allowed to keep money he found in the place of his employment. Holding for a finder employed to decorate hotel rooms, the court in Erickson v. Sinykin, 223 Minn. 232, 26 N.W.2d 172 (1947), distinguished cases of finding by hotel chambermaids: "It is a matter of common knowledge that a chambermaid's work is nothing like that of a painter or decorator. Chambermaids frequently find articles which their employers' guests have forgotten. Ordinarily, their duty is to report and deliver to their employers the article so found, in order that restoration to the owner may be made." Even a chambermaid was permitted to retain money found in a hotel parlor. Hamaker v. Blanchard, 90 Pa. 377, 35 Am.Rep. 664 (1879).

4. O purchased an old safe and soon thereafter delivered it to B, who agreed to display it for sale. While the safe was in B's possession, B discovered money that apparently had slipped between an inner and outer lining of the safe sometime prior to O's acquisition of the safe. Durfee v. Jones, 11 R.I. 588, 23 Am.Rep. 528 (1877), held that B's claim to the money was better than O's. The court said that O "never had any possession of the money, except, unwittingly, by having possession of the safe which contained it. Such possession, if possession it can be called, does not of itself confer a right. The case at bar is in this view like Bridges v. Hawkesworth . . . ."

5. Five boys were walking along a railway track when one of them, A, picked up an old stocking, knotted at both ends and stuffed with soft material. It then passed from hand to hand as a plaything until, as one boy was striking another with it, the stocking burst open, revealing its contents to be some worthless material and about $800 in currency. The money was turned over to a chief of police who was unable to locate its owner. A then contended that he should have the money; the other boys urged that it should be divided equally. Keron v. Cashman, 33 A. 1055 (N.J.Eq.1896), held that the money should be divided equally. The court, citing Durfee v. Jones, said: "[I]nasmuch as none of the boys treated the stocking when it was found as anything but a plaything or abandoned article, I am of the opinion that the money within the stocking must be treated as lost property, which was not 'found,' in a legal sense, until the stocking was broken open during the play. At that time . . . it was in the possession of all, and all the boys are therefore equally finders . . . ." The court indicated that the result might have been different had "the stocking been like a pocketbook, an article generally used for containing money . . . ."

6. Hammer, J., in Edmonds v. Ronella, 73 Misc.2d 598, 342 N.Y.S. 2d 408 (1973):

"The court has been called upon to determine the respective rights to found property, viz., $12,300 in cash. The story unfolded in the courtroom at the trial of the action that on the 19th day of September, 1971, little Eugene, then aged 12, and little Pat, then aged 9, were on their way home from attending church. As little children are wont to do, the two boys passed the parking lot of an A & P supermarket located at Rockaway Boulevard and 84th Street, in Ozone Park. Rummaging around, the children discovered a manila envelope (in a bag) containing a large bankroll of cash, amid the trash and the discarded clothing located in said parking lot. The young children became excited, confused and, in their immature way, sought the assistance of friends in order to determine what disposition should be made of this "treasure trove." Some friends, also on their way home from church, including the defendant in this case, Antoinette, a grown young lady then 15 years of age, came to their aid and assistance. Subsequently, the envelope in the bag was picked up by Antoinette and taken to her house for parental advice. The boys tagged along.

. . . [I]t is the determination of this court that the lost money was not found, in a legal sense, until the plaintiffs and the defendant had, together, removed it from the parking lot. Having thus obtained possession jointly, the court finds that each of the parties is entitled to an equal share of the money. Prior case law of this point, though meager, clearly establishes that if several persons participated in a finding, they are joint finders with equal rights in the property found. (See Keron v. Cashman . . ..) . . . .

McAVOY v. MEDINA

Supreme Judicial Court of Massachusetts, 1866.
11 Allen (Mass.) 548, 87 Am.Dec. 733.

Tort to recover a sum of money found by the plaintiff in the shop of the defendant.

At the trial in the superior court, before Morton, J., it appeared that the defendant was a barber, and the plaintiff, being a customer in the defendant's shop, saw and took up a pocket-book which was lying upon a table there, and said, "See what I have found." The defendant came to the table and asked where he found it. The plaintiff laid it back in the same place and said, "I found it right there." The defendant then took it and counted the money, and the plaintiff told him to keep it, and if the owner should come to give it to him; and otherwise to advertise it; which the defendant promised to do. Subsequently the plaintiff made three demands for the money, and the defendant never claimed to hold the same till the last demand. It was agreed that the pocket-book was placed upon the table by a transient customer of the defendant and accidentally left there, and was first seen and taken up by the plaintiff, and that the owner had not been found.

The judge ruled that the plaintiff could not maintain his action, and a verdict was accordingly returned for the defendant; and the plaintiff alleged exceptions.

DEWEY, J. It seems to be the settled law that the finder of lost property has a valid claim to the same against all the world except the true owner, and generally that the place in which it is found creates no exception to this rule. 2 Parsons on Con. 97. Bridges v. Hawkesworth, 7 Eng.Law & Eq.R. 424.

But this property is not, under the circumstances, to be treated as lost property in that sense in which a finder has a valid claim to hold the same until called for by the true owner. This property was voluntarily placed upon a table in the defendant's shop by a customer of his who accidentally left the same there and has never called for it. The plaintiff also came there as a customer, and first saw the same and took it up from the table. The plaintiff did not by this acquire the right to take the property from the shop, but it was rather the duty of the defendant, when the fact became thus known to him, to use reasonable care for the safekeeping of the same until the owner should call for it. In the case of Bridges v. Hawkesworth the property, although found in a shop, was found on the floor of the same, and had not been placed there voluntarily by the owner, and the court held that the finder was entitled to the possession of the same, except as to the owner. But the present case more resembles that of Lawrence v. The State, 1 Humph. (Tenn.) 228, and is indeed very similar in its facts. The court there distinguished between the case of property thus placed by the owner and neglected to be removed, and property lost. It was there held that "to place a pocket-book upon a table and to forget to take it away is not to lose it, in the sense in which the authorities referred to speak of lost property."

We accept this as the better rule, and especially as one better adapted to secure the rights of the true owner.

In view of the facts of this case, the plaintiff acquired no original right to the property, and the defendant's subsequent acts in receiving and holding the property in the manner he did does not create any.

Exceptions overruled.

NOTE

Suppose that defendant barber had declined to accept the pocketbook when handed to him by plaintiff, who then departed and disappeared. Would defendant be liable to the true owner if he returns? I.e., had defendant become a bailee? If so, on what theory? Had defendant manifested an intention to assume this obligation? Is the obligation imposed by law upon defendant by virtue of his possession of the pocketbook? Did defendant, under the assumed facts, have possession of the pocketbook? See cases on bailment, chapter 7.

SCHLEY v. COUCH

Supreme Court of Texas, 1955.
155 Tex. 195, 284 S.W.2d 333.

GRIFFIN, JUSTICE. July 7, 1952 petitioner was the owner of a tract of land near Hamilton, Texas, upon which was situated a dwelling house with an attached garage and storeroom. The petitioner had acquired these premises from a Mr. Adams about June 15, 1952. At the time petitioner moved upon the premises there was a concrete floor covering only the front half of the garage, and the remaining half was a dirt floor. A few days prior to July 7, 1952, petitioner employed a Mr. Tomlinson and his crew of workmen—among whom was respondent—to put a concrete floor in the rear half of the garage. Petitioner's son was removing the soil from that portion of the garage floor which was being covered with concrete with a tractor having a blade attached thereto. The garage faced east and the dwelling was immediately south of and adjoining the garage. The storeroom was immediately west of and adjoined the garage, and to enter the storeroom one had to come through the garage. Due to the construction of the tractor and the walls of the garage it was impossible to remove the soil adjacent to the west wall (and being the east wall of the storeroom) with the blade attached to the tractor. Respondent's employer directed respondent to take a pick and loosen up this hardpacked soil which the blade could not reach. While digging in this soil, respondent's pick struck a hard object and respondent found the $1,000 sued for buried in the ground. The money was in currency. Included in this currency were two Hawaiian bills issued during World War II. All bills were fresh, and well preserved and of the size of present currency. A glass jar top and some glass from a jar were found nearby and evidencing that the money had been buried in a glass jar. The erection of the garage had been begun by a Mr. Allen, a predecessor in title, who had sold the property in April or May of 1948 at which time the garage was in the process of being built but had not been completed. Only one of the prior owners of this land asserted that he had buried the money in the garage. After two trials before a jury wherein this claimant was unable to secure favorable findings, he took a nonsuit and urged no further claim to the money. The owner of the money is unknown.

After some preliminary happenings which do not affect the case, respondent sued petitioner for the money and certain damages. The trial court submitted the case to the jury upon two special issues. One inquired if the money were "lost" property, and the other inquired if the money were "mislaid" property. The jury answered the money was "mislaid" property, and upon that verdict the trial court rendered judgment in favor of the defendant as bailee for the true owner. Upon appeal the Court of Civil Appeals reversed the trial court's judgment and rendered judgment for the respondent against the defendant for the money. The Court of Civil Appeals held that the money constituted neither "lost" nor "mislaid" property, but fell into yet a third category known in some jurisdictions as "treasure trove." It accordingly held the right of possession to be in the finder. 272 S.W.2d 171.

Neither party claims to be the true owner of the money, but each claims the right to have possession of the money for the benefit of the true owner, should he ever appear and establish his claim. Title to the money is not involved, but only the right of possession thereof.

This is a case of first impression in Texas. If the money constitutes treasure trove the decision of the Court of Civil Appeals is correct and in accordance with the decided cases from other jurisdictions. However, we have decided not to recognize the "treasure trove" doctrine as the law in Texas, but that this case should be governed by the rules of law applicable to lost and mislaid property. There is no statutory law in Texas regarding the disposition of such property, or provisions defining the respective rights of various claimants. The rule of treasure trove is of ancient origin and arose by virtue of the concealment in the ground and other hiding places of coin, bullion, and plate of the Roman conquerors when they were driven from the British Isles. These Romans expected to return at a later date and reclaim their buried and hidden treasures. For a time laws were in effect which gave all this treasure trove which might be discovered to the sovereign, but it was later held to belong to the finder, and this regardless of whether he was in ownership or possession of the land where the treasure was found. The doctrine only applied to "money or coin, gold, silver, plate, or bullion found hidden in the earth or other private places, the owner thereof being unknown." Black, Law Dictionary. Such doctrine has never been officially recognized in Texas, although it has been recognized and applied under the common law in many states of the American Union. We can see no good reason at the present time and under present conditions in our nation, to adopt such a doctrine. Therefore, we treat the money involved herein as no different from other personal property and will adjudicate the possession thereof in accordance with the rules governing personal property generally. We think the proper rule regarding treasure trove is that stated by the Oregon Supreme Court in 1948 in the case of Jackson v. Steinberg, 186 Or. 129, 200 P.2d 376, 378, 205 P.2d 562, as follows: "With regard to plaintiff's contention that the bills constituted treasure trove, it has been held that the law of treasure trove has been merged with that of lost goods generally, at least so far as respects the rights of the finder. . . . In other words, under modern concepts, the finder of buried money, if allowed to retain it, is so allowed because the circumstances of the particular case determine the property to be "lost" property and not because it falls into a separate category called "treasure trove." Lost property is defined as "that which the owner has involuntarily parted with through neglect, carelessness or inadvertence." Note 170 A.L.R. 706 . . .. Lost property may be retained by the finder as against the owner or possessor of the premises where it is found.

On the other hand, "mislaid property is to be distinguished from lost property in that the former is property which the owner intentionally places where he can again resort to it, and then forgets. Mislaid property is presumed to be left in the custody of the owner or occupier of the premises upon which it is found, and it is generally held that the right of possession to mislaid property as against all except the owner is in the owner or occupant of such premises." 170 A.L.R. 707 . . .. The facts of this case show that the bills were carefully placed in the jar and then buried in the ground and further show that the owner did not part with them inadvertently, involuntarily, carelessly or through neglect. Rather it shows a deliberate, conscious and voluntary act of the owner desiring to hide his money in a place where he thought it was safe and secure, and with the intention of returning to claim it at some future date. All the evidence indicates that the money must have been buried in the garage after the garage had been built. That was only a scant four years prior to the finding of the money. In the case of Heddle v. Bank of Hamilton, 17 B.C. 306, 6 B.R.C. 256, 5 D.L.R. 11, a lapse of four years was not sufficient to establish that the property had been lost beyond possibility of restitution to the true owner. See also 34 Am.Jur. 635. The character of the property is to be determined from all the facts and circumstances present in the particular case involving property found.

The facts in this case show, as a matter of law, that the property is not to be classed in the category of lost property. Conceivably, there may be cases in which the issue as to whether the property is lost or mislaid property would be for determination by a jury under appropriate instructions by the court. The trial judge submitted the matter to a jury in the present case. There were no objections raised by either party to the definitions of "lost" and "mislaid" property as contained in the charge. The jury upon consideration of all the facts found that the property was mislaid rather than lost property.

Property which is found embedded in the soil under circumstances repelling the idea that it has been lost is held to have the characteristics of mislaid property. The finder acquires no rights thereto, for the presumption is that possession of the article found is in the owner of the locus in quo, and, accordingly it is held that the right to possession of such property is in the landowner. . . .

No proof having been made in the present case as to who is the true owner of money found, we will indulge the presumption that he has forgotten where he secreted it, or has died since he secreted the property. . . .

The judgment of the Court of Civil Appeals is reversed and the judgment of the trial court is affirmed.

CALVERT, JUSTICE (concurring). I can agree to the judgment rendered herein but there is much in the majority opinion to which I cannot agree. I suggest that in an effort to simplify the law of found property, as applied in other common law jurisdictions, by declining to approve and adopt the law of "treasure trove" in this state, the majority opinion has only succeeded in confusing it.

As pointed out in the majority opinion the law of treasure trove is of ancient origin and was a well established part of the common law of England when, in 1840, it was declared by statute in this state that "The common law of England, so far as it is not inconsistent with the Constitution and laws of this State, shall together with such Constitution and laws, be the rule of decision, and shall continue in force until altered or repealed by the Legislature." Article 1, R.C.S. of Texas. The law of treasure trove, except where abolished by statute, has been universally applied as a part of the common law in the other states of this union.

Assuming for the purposes of this opinion that we are justified in departing from the common-law doctrine of treasure trove because that doctrine is "inconsistent with the conditions and circumstances of our people," . . . a point of departure rarely to be taken, . . . we should depart from it only to the extent necessary to nullify that doctrine. The majority opinion goes much further. It not only nullifies the doctrine of treasure trove; it declares, in effect, that we will not recognize in this state any of the common-law rules dealing with the right to possession of found property other than those distinguishing between "lost" and "mislaid" property.

The majority opinion declares, as a matter of law, that the property involved in this case is not to be classed as "lost" property because the facts show conclusively it was not " 'involuntarily parted with through neglect, carelessness or inadvertence.' " It then declares the property to be "mislaid property" . . .. None of the cited cases declare property of this type to be mislaid property. [A brief summary of these cases is omitted.] In none of the cases analyzed did the courts treat the property involved as mislaid property. In no case cited to this court or found by us has it been held that property found imbedded in the soil fell in the category of mislaid property, or had the characteristics of mislaid property.

The majority opinion fails to recognize a fourth category of found property: . . . that is, the category of personal property found imbedded in the soil. See also 34 Am.Jur. 634, Lost Property, Sec. 5; 170 A.L.R. 706, 708. The majority opinion has adopted the rule applicable to this category of property but has defined it as mislaid property. There is no need for this departure from the common-law rules. The rule as stated in American Jurisprudence is as follows: "Where property, not treasure trove, is found imbedded in the soil under circumstances repelling the idea that it has been lost, the finder acquires no title thereto, for the presumption is that the possession of the article found is in the owner of the locus in quo." All we need do in order to achieve our objective of rejecting the law of treasure trove is to eliminate from the foregoing rule the words "not treasure trove," thus adopting the rule that all personal property or chattels found imbedded in the soil under circumstances repelling the idea that it has been lost will be held to be rightfully in the possession of the owner of the soil as against all the world except the true owner. . . .

HICKMAN, C.J., and WALKER, J., join in this opinion.

WILSON, JUSTICE (concurring). I concur in the result. In so far as money buried or secreted on privately owned realty is concerned, the old distinctions between treasure-trove, lost property, and mislaid property seem to be of little value and not worth preserving. . . . A simple solution for all of these problems is to maintain the continuity of possession of the landowner until the true owner establishes his title.

NOTES

1. Might this money have been considered abandoned? In Erickson v. Sinykin, 223 Minn. 232, 26 N.W.2d 172, 170 A.L.R. 697 (1947), the court approved the trial court's finding that money discovered under a hotel room carpet had been abandoned, though the only evidence of abandonment was the likelihood, in view of its age, that the money had been undisturbed for over fifteen years. But in Dennis v. Northwestern Nat. Bank, 249 Minn. 130, 81 N.W.2d 254 (1957), the court declared that "mere lapse of time is not enough" evidence of abandonment. Assuming that the money was abandoned, why should it follow that the finder will prevail over the owner of the place of finding?

2. In a case remarkably similar factually to Schley v. Couch, the Supreme Court of Oregon held for the finder. In this case, Danielson v. Roberts, 44 Or. 108, 74 P. 913 (1904), two boys employed by a landowner to clean a chicken house discovered in the rubble on the floor a rusted tin can containing gold coins. The court indicated that the coins might be considered to be either lost property or treasure trove, but that this distinction would be immaterial in this case, since the finder would prevail over the landowner as to either type of property. The court did

not address the question whether the money might have been mislaid. A few months later, the Supreme Court of Oregon in Ferguson v. Ray, 44 Or. 557, 77 P. 600 (1904), held for the landowner against a tenant who found the remains of a buried sack of gold quartz. The court concluded that gold bearing quartz is not the type of substance which can be considered treasure trove. The court also declined to treat the quartz involved in this case as lost or abandoned, since it appeared that the quartz had been intentionally deposited in the place where it was found. The court finally concluded that the landowner was entitled to the quartz on the ground, "as was announced by Lord Russell in South Staffordshire Waterworks v. Sharman, supra, that 'the presumption is that the possession of the article found is in the owner of the locus in quo.' "

Almost half a century later, the Oregon court held that a chambermaid in a hotel was not entitled to keep money found under a paper lining of a dresser drawer in a guest room in the hotel. In its initial opinion the court relied on the master-servant relationship, but in its opinion on rehearing, the court relied upon the general possession theory of the Sharman case. Jackson v. Steinberg, 186 Or. 129, 200 P.2d 376 (1948), 205 P.2d 562 (1949). These cases are discussed by Professor Ralph W. Aigler, 48 Mich.L.Rev. 352 (1950).

3. The Crown of England was entitled to other kinds of property, in addition to treasure trove. Land of one who died intestate without heirs belonged to the Crown by virtue of escheat, an incident of feudal tenure. The Crown was regarded as lord paramount of all land and therefore entitled to regain possession upon termination of lesser interests. The Crown also was entitled to personal property under such circumstances by virtue of bona vacantia, a general entitlement by the sovereign to certain kinds of unclaimed goods. Bona vacantia had nothing to do with feudal tenure; the Crown's claim was simply regarded as better than that of any other claimant. Types of goods claimed by the Crown by virtue of bona vacantia included shipwrecks, waifs (stolen goods discarded by fleeing thieves) and estrays (straying domestic animals whose owners were unknown). Treasure trove has been regarded as an aspect of bona vacantia.

Although, as Schley v. Couch indicates, American states have not asserted claims to treasure trove, they have claimed by statute some types of property embraced within the common law doctrines of bona vacantia and escheat. Modern statutes, often using the term "escheat," entitle the state to property, real and personal, of persons dying intestate without heirs or next of kin. Closely related to escheat statutes are unclaimed property acts. Typically, they authorize designated state officials to take custody of inactive bank accounts, contents of safe deposit boxes for which rent has ceased to be paid, and other dormant funds and claims, after a specified period of inactivity (commonly seven years). Such acts purport to be merely custodial, unlike escheat statutes, which transfer title to the state. However, the unclaimed property acts authorize deposit of unclaimed funds in the state's general fund; property other than money may be sold and the proceeds deposited in the general fund. A small trust fund is established to satisfy claims of former owners. See the Uniform Unclaimed Property Act (1981), 8A Uniform Laws Annotated 617 (1983). See also Note, Virginia's Acquisition of Unclaimed and Abandoned Personal Property, 27 Wm. & Mary L.Rev. 409 (1986).

Can it be persuasively argued that the unclaimed property acts should be broadened to embrace found property? An old statute authorizing division of found property between the finder and the township was applied in Willsmore v. Township of Oceola, 106 Mich. App. 671, 308 N.W.2d 796 (1981). That statute subsequently was repealed and replaced by a statute entitling the finder to the entire property. MICH.COMP.LAWS § 434.21 et. seq. (West.Supp.1989).

4. Judge Calvert would have applied a "rule that all personal property or chattels found embedded in the soil under circumstances repelling the idea that it has been lost will be held to be rightfully in the possession of the owner of the soil as against all the world except the true owner." What is the rationale for this rule? The general possession theory relied upon in Sharman? The fixture concept relied upon in Goddard? The latter concept would cut off the true owner of the article. It also would favor an absentee fee simple owner of the land over a lessee or life tenant in possession. Consider Allred v. Biegel, 240 Mo.App. 818, 219 S.W.2d 665 (1949), holding that finders of an ancient Indian canoe imbedded in the soil were not entitled to recover it, even though they also had purchased the interest in the canoe of the life tenant in possession. The court declared that the canoe was "part of the realty" and that "[t]his doctrine was applied in Goddard v. Winchell . . . ." The court in Allred deemed the case before it to be "on all fours" with an English case, Elwes v. Briggs Gas Company, 33 Ch. 562 (1886), holding that a lessee who discovered an imbedded ancient ship was not entitled to retain it. While the facts in Allred and Elwes may have been "circumstances repelling the idea that [the articles] had been lost," can the same be said of the jar of money in Schley?

5. It should not be inferred from the court's opinion in the principal case that the Crown is no longer entitled to treasure trove in England. It is so entitled. The modern practice is to offer treasure trove to the British Museum or some other museum. If the finder has reported the find promptly, he will be paid its market value or, if the museum rejects the offer, be given it. See Attorney-General of the Duchy of Lancaster v. G.E. Overton (Farms) Ltd., 2 W.L.R. 397, 404 (Court of Appeals 1981). This case held that the Roman coins in this controversy were not treasure trove because they did not contain a "substantial" amount of gold or silver. The court commented: "The reason for the small amount of silver was that, at that time, the Roman Empire—the Emperors—were debasing the coinage. They were having inflation, just as we have now." The court rejected Blackstone's statement that "any money or coin" would constitute treasure trove. Only gold or silver qualifies. The court awarded the coins to the landowner rather than to the Crown. The finder, who had not reported his find, had been convicted of theft and was not a party to this case.

LEGISLATION ON LOST AND FOUND ARTICLES

Is there a need for modern legislation dealing with claims to lost and found articles? Consider Shartel, Meanings of Possession, 16 Minn.L.Rev. 611 (1932) and Riesman, Possession and the Law of Finders, 52 Harv.L.Rev. 1105 (1939). Set forth below is a suggested statute, modeled upon a New York statute, N.Y.Pers.Prop.Law § 251 et seq. (McKinney 1962), which was based upon a study by the New York Law Revision Commission, reported at page 1699 of McKinney's 1958 Session Laws of New York. The New York statute is much longer and more detailed than the statute set forth here. In what respects does this statute depart from the law developed in the cases you have read? Are the apparent objectives of this statute sound? Is the statutory language adequate to achieve those objectives? Are any problems created by the choice of statutory language? Has any matter of significance been omitted?

§ 1. Definitions

(a) The term "lost property" as used in this statute includes lost or mislaid property.

(b) The term "owner" as used in this statute means any person entitled to possession of the lost property as against the finder and against any other person who has made a claim.

(c) The term "finder" as used in this statute means the person who first takes possession of lost property.

§ 2. Deposit With Police

Except as otherwise provided, any person who finds lost property of the value of ten dollars or more or comes into possession of property of the value of ten dollars or more with knowledge that it is lost property or found property shall, within ten days after the finding or acquisition of possession thereof, either return it to the owner or report such finding or acquisition of possession to the police and deposit such property in a police station of the city where the finding occurred or possession was acquired. Except as otherwise provided, any person who shall refuse or wilfully neglect to comply with this section shall be guilty of a misdemeanor and upon conviction shall be punished by a fine of not more than one hundred dollars or imprisonment not exceeding six months or both.

§ 3. Duties of Police

Except as otherwise provided, lost property shall be kept in the custody of the police for the following periods, unless sooner delivered to the owner: property having a value of five hundred dollars or less, six months; property having a value of more than five hundred dollars but less than five thousand dollars, one year; property having a value of five thousand dollars or more, three years.

§ 4. Disposition of Lost Property

If at the end of the period specified in section 3, the owner has not claimed the property, it shall be delivered to the finder or person entitled to assert the rights of the finder, upon his demand and payment of all reasonable expenses incurred in connection therewith.

§ 5. Exceptions

(a) If a finder takes possession of lost property while he is upon premises with respect to which his presence is a crime, the person in possession of the premises where the lost property was found shall have the rights of the finder if, before the property is delivered to the finder by the police, he shall file with the police having custody of the property a written notice asserting such rights.

(b) If the finder is an employee under a duty to deliver the lost property to his employer, the employer shall have the rights of the finder if, before the property is delivered to the finder by the police, he shall file with the police having custody of the property a written notice asserting such rights.

(c) If lost property was discovered upon the enclosed safe deposit premises of a safe deposit company or safe deposit department of a bank, the police shall return it to the safe deposit company or bank at the expiration of six months from the date of deposit. If not claimed by its owner within fifteen years, this property shall escheat to the state.

§ 6. Title to Lost Property

The title to lost property which has been deposited with the police shall vest in the finder or other person entitled to assert the rights of the finder when the property is delivered to him by the police.

NOTES

1. How should the following case be decided under the above statute? Hurley entered into a contract to remodel a house owned and occupied by Moraca. While engaged in remodeling, Hurley found $5,000 in bills concealed in a floor. Hurley showed the money to Moraca, who said that it had not belonged to him. Hurley then said that he would deposit the money in his safe deposit box at a bank, and Moraca did not object. Instead of depositing the money as he had said he would do, Hurley attempted to spend some of it at a department store. Employees of the store became suspicious and alerted the police, who interrogated Hurley, who at first lied about the source of the money but finally turned it over to the police. The true owner failed to appear during the statutory period. Who is entitled to the money? The New York courts had some difficulty with an essentially identical case. The finder finally prevailed, but three members of the New York Court of Appeals dissented. Hurley v. City of Niagara Falls, 25 N.Y.2d 687, 254 N.E.2d 917 (1969). The dissenting opinion argued: "Hurley's failure to comply with the statutory provisions precludes him from asserting any rights under the statute which he so flagrantly disregarded. . . . Of course, it is fundamental that one cannot establish title

in himself merely by showing someone else to have no rights in the property. It is therefore evident that . . . we could not, without more, hold that the Moracas have title to the property in question. It is our opinion, however, that even if we assume that compliance with the statute is not a prerequisite to obtaining rights thereunder, the Moracas' rights are superior to Hurley's under the statute. . . . While it is true that the trial court determined that Hurley was an independent contractor, we need not give the term 'employee' as used in the statute such a restrictive reading as to limit it to only those employees whose liability would be imputed to their employers. Rather the term should be construed broadly to encompass all persons engaged to perform tasks . . .."

2. What are the rights of the true owner who fails to present a claim prior to the running of the statutory period? If none, is the statute valid? The report of the New York Law Revision Commission, supra, recommended that title to lost property "vest in a finder to whom the property is returned by the police pursuant to the statute after being kept for the specified period. Such a rule should encourage finders to take responsible action . . .. If the steps to be taken by the finder are reasonably calculated to insure restoration of the property to an owner who makes an effort to recover it, the loss of title by the true owner who does not make timely claim may be justified by the advantages resulting to others from the statutory system of handling found property. These advantages include the benefits to owners who do recover their property promptly and in good condition, the public benefit resulting from an established custom of responsible action by finders, and the public interest in settling title to unclaimed articles."

3. Other issues concerning the New York statute were raised in Morgan and Brothers Manhattan Storage Co. v. McGuire, 114 Misc.2d 951, 452 N.Y.S.2d 986 (1982). Employees of a warehouse company removed from a trunk stored in the warehouse a huge sum of money, $340,770 of which was recovered by the police. The true owner of this money was unknown. The warehouse company's claim that it came within the definition of finder as one who "first takes possession of lost property" was rejected on the ground that this definition excludes constructive possession. The alternative claim as an employer of a finder "under a duty to deliver the lost property to his employer" might prevail, the court held, only if the opening of the trunk was lawful; otherwise the warehouse company would gain a benefit from tortious conduct of its employees.

4. Would sharing of the found property by landowner and finder be a satisfactory resolution of these cases? See Helmholz, Equitable Division and the Law of Finders, 52 Fordham L.Rev. 313 (1983).

Chapter 7

CREATION OF BAILMENTS

Bailees of chattels, as well as lessees and life tenants of land, have limited property interests. The details of such interests usually are spelled out in the bailment contract, but may be implied in fact or in law. No doubt the vast majority of bailees assume that status voluntarily. The following cases involve attempts to fasten the responsibilities of bailees upon persons who deny having assumed them.

PARKING MANAGEMENT, INC. v. GILDER

District of Columbia Court of Appeals, 1975.
343 A.2d 51.

GALLAGHER, ASSOCIATE JUDGE. This court decided to hear this case *en banc* after a divided division of the court had reversed a judgment awarding appellee damages after a nonjury trial. Parking Management, Inc. v. Gilder, D.C.App., 327 A.2d 323 (1974), vacated by order of the court, December 19, 1974.

Appellee parked his car at the Parking Management, Inc. parking area which is enclosed within the Washington Hilton Hotel in this city. He was directed to a space by an attendant. He locked his car and kept the keys. He then opened the trunk in plain view of a group of employees and placed his lady friend's cosmetic bag in it and then locked the trunk. The rear of the car was exposed to the aisle. Upon his return, he found the trunk lid damaged from being pried open and reported it to the management.

The principal question for the court, initially at least, is the nature of the legal relationship of the parties. More particularly, it must be determined at the outset whether the parking lot operator owed the car owner any duties and, if so, what they were. In order to resolve this, it is necessary to examine the nature of the parking operation. It is not enough simply to ascertain whether the car owner locked his car and kept the keys ("park and lock"). These are material factors to be considered, but they do not end the inquiry.

When the car owner entered, he was handed a ticket by one of three attendants and directed to a particular parking space. There were about 160 lined spaces on one level and about 150 lined spaces on a second level. These were self-service to the extent that the driver places the car in a space at the direction of an attendant. If additional spaces are needed, *the aisle spaces are utilized* and according to the parking operator (PMI) these are "not self-service," which may only be construed as meaning that the attendants park the cars in the aisles and retain the keys. There is thus a mixed arrangement here, one being self-service and the other non-self-service, depending upon the volume of customers. Under appellant's theory of the case, there would be the anomaly of a bailment for the cars parked in the aisle but not for those in the lined spaces on the same floor in the same garage.

When appellee entered the garage, a number of PMI employees were on duty including a manager, a cashier, and three attendants. According to the Supervisor of Plans and Operations for Parking Management, Inc. (PMI):

A PMI employee is a uniformed employee. He is a public relations man for our company. He is a service man for our company. . . . He is there to control the parking, guide the parking *and control whatever is necessary in respect to housekeeping and any general operations that might pertain to the parking industry.* (Emphasis added.)

In respect to thefts at the garage the Supervisor said there were some claims for thefts, but those were more than fifteen days before this incident. He said that thefts are "not necessarily a big problem, but, of course, damages and thefts, *security is a major concern*" (emphasis added). He also agreed that watching the area and acting as a "kind of security" is part of the employees' job.

The trial court in this nonjury case concluded that the evidence established either (a) a bailment or (b) that the protection which the patron was led to believe existed was not provided. The court thereupon entered judgment for the car owner [for damage to the car].

Appellant contends this was error since appellee parked his car in the parking enclosure and retained the car keys, and consequently a bailor-bailee relationship did not exist, citing Quinn v. Milner, D.C. Mun.App., 34 A.2d 259 (1943), and subsequent decisions of this court. Appellant does not address itself to the alternative finding of the court concerning the lack of protection which the car owner was led to believe existed.

Appellant is correct in its assertion that this court has stated in those cases that a bailment did not exist where the car owner (a) parked his car and (b) kept the car keys (but see 1420 Park Road Parking, Inc. v. Consolidated Mutual Insurance Co., D.C.Mun.App., 168 A.2d 900, 901–02 (1961) (Hood, J., dissenting)). However, those cases simply involved those two factors and nothing more. Here there was additional evidence on the parking arrangement involved, e.g., the presence of 5 employees to service the customers in an enclosed area of the hotel and the acknowledgment that security of the cars is a major concern of PMI, which, according to the PMI supervisor, includes watching for thefts and tampering with the vehicles, as well as the acknowledged exertion of "control . . . in respect to housekeeping and any general operations that might pertain to the parking industry." Although, strictly speaking, the finding that a bailment existed may be open to debate, we believe the trial court reached the correct result in any event by way of its alternative finding that the protection the car owner was entitled to believe existed was not provided.

The car owner was entitled under the circumstances to expect that reasonable care would be utilized to prevent tampering with his auto; and that this was not an unreasonable expectation on his part was demonstrated by testimony of the management of PMI to the effect that this was in fact among the duties of the employees. The evidence here permitted the court to find there was a lack of protection which the car owner was entitled to believe existed. This being so, we must accept this finding as it is not clearly erroneous. D.C.Code 1973, § 17–305(a).

While there has been a tendency to consider a showing of a "park and lock" arrangement as creating a lease agreement, we doubt the sophistication of this doctrine. Unlike the usual tenant of realty, the car owner has utterly no control of the so-called leased space as he is by definition always absent and helpless to protect his property, for all practical purposes. There is in most instances no fixed term, the duration of the parking being usually at the option of the car owner. Lastly, the car owner may not remove the car until the parking fee is paid.

The owner of the car cannot observe and protect the car since he is always absent from it. It is the operator, not the car owner, who is in a position to have the superior knowledge.

We do not consider the law of landlord-tenant to be an apt doctrine to apply in such cases; and we think the time has come to reject that outmoded theory with its unrealistic confines in this type of application. Nor do we think mechanical labels should be applied to the relationship in "park and lock" arrangements.

. . .

On the facts here presented, we believe an operator may be required to exercise reasonable care to avoid malicious mischief to, or theft of, vehicles parked on a commercial parking lot [1] (a going concern), even though the arrangement was "park and lock." The car owner was necessarily absent when the car damage occurred and should not be disadvantaged as a matter of law because of this reality. We do not feel that a car owner may fairly be regarded as a virtual stranger to the lot operator except for the payment of a parking fee.

This view is founded upon the principle that " [w]here a contract is implied from the surrounding circumstances, the law will derive its terms from the circumstances shown." Sparrow v. Airport Parking Company of America, 221 Pa.Super. 32, 289 A.2d 87, 92 (1972). "There are . . . situations in which the actor, as a reasonable man, is required to anticipate and guard against the intentional, or even criminal, misconduct of others. In general, these situations arise where the actor is under a special responsibility toward the one who suffers the harm, which includes the duty to protect him against such intentional misconduct . . .. Normally such a duty arises out of a contract between the parties, in which such protection is an express or

1. Cars parked massively at airports, for example, perhaps at a comparatively reduced rate, may present a different situation, based upon what a car owner may reasonably expect under the individual circumstances. A different view likewise may, upon consideration, be applied where there is paid parking to witness a specific event, i.e., where the parking arrangement is on an *ad hoc* basis only. The legal relationship depends upon the place, the conditions and the nature of the transaction.

implied term of the agreement." Restatement (Second) of Torts § 302B, comment (e) (1965).

The circumstances here were sufficient to create an implied duty of reasonable care by the lot operator to protect the car from malicious mischief, and we conclude the finding by the trial court that a violation of that duty occurred was not clearly erroneous. Consequently, the judgment is

Affirmed.

SHAMROCK HILTON HOTEL v. CARANAS

Court of Civil Appeals of Texas, 1972.
488 S.W.2d 151.

BARRON, JUSTICE. This is an appeal in an alleged bailment case from a judgment non obstante veredicto in favor of plaintiffs below.

Plaintiffs, husband and wife, were lodging as paying guests at the Shamrock Hilton Hotel in Houston on the evening of September 4, 1966, when they took their dinner in the hotel restaurant. After completing the meal, Mr. and Mrs. Caranas, plaintiffs, departed the dining area leaving her purse behind. The purse was found by the hotel bus boy who, pursuant to the instructions of the hotel, dutifully delivered the forgotten item to the restaurant cashier, a Mrs. Luster. The testimony indicates that some short time thereafter the cashier gave the purse to a man other than Mr. Caranas who came to claim it. There is no testimony on the question of whether identification was sought by the cashier. The purse allegedly contained $5.00 in cash, some credit cards, and ten pieces of jewelry said to be worth $13,062. The misplacement of the purse was realized the following morning, at which time plaintiffs notified the hotel authorities of the loss.

Plaintiffs filed suit alleging negligent delivery of the purse to an unknown person and seeking a recovery for the value of the purse and its contents.

The trial was to a jury which found that the cashier was negligent in delivering the purse to someone other than plaintiffs, and that this negligence was a proximate cause of the loss of the purse. The jury further found that plaintiffs were negligent in leaving the purse containing the jewelry in the hotel dining room, and that this negligence was a proximate cause of the loss.

A motion for judgment n.o.v. and to disregard findings with respect to the findings that plaintiffs' negligence was a proximate cause of the loss of the purse and its contents was granted, and judgment was entered by the trial court for plaintiffs in the amount of $11,252.00 plus interest and costs. Shamrock Hilton Hotel and Hilton Hotels Corporation have perfected this appeal.

. . .

Contrary to appellants' contention, we find that there was indeed a constructive bailment of the purse. The delivery and acceptance were evidenced in the acts of Mrs. Caranas' unintentionally leaving her purse behind in the hotel restaurant and the bus boy, a hotel employee, picking it up and taking it to the cashier who accepted the purse as a lost or misplaced item. The delivery need not be a knowingly intended act on the part of Mrs. Caranas if it is apparent that were she, the quasi or constructive bailor, aware of the circumstances (here the chattel's being misplaced) she would have desired the person finding the article to have kept it safely for its subsequent return to her. . . .

. . .

Further, this bailment was one for the mutual benefit of both parties. Appellees were paying guests in the hotel and in its dining room. Appellant hotel's practice of keeping patrons' lost personal items until they could be returned to their rightful owners, as reflected in the testimony, is certainly evidence of its being incidental to its business, as we would think it would be for almost any commercial enterprise which caters to the general public. Though no direct charge is made for this service there is indirect benefit to be had in the continued patronage of the hotel by customers who have lost chattels and who have been able to claim them from the management.

Having found this to have been a bailment for the mutual benefit of the parties, we hold that the appellants owed the appellees the duty of reasonable care in the return of the purse and jewelry, and the hotel is therefore liable for its ordinary negligence.

Appellants urge that if a bailment is found it existed only as to "the purse and the usual petty cash or credit cards found therein" and not to the jewelry of which the hotel had no actual notice. This exact question so far as we can determine has never been squarely put before the Texas Courts, but as appellants concede, the general rule in other jurisdictions is that a bailee is liable not only for lost property of which he has actual knowledge but also the property he could reasonably expect to find contained within the bailed property. . . .

. . .

. . . We cannot say as a matter of law that there is no evidence upon which a jury could reasonably find that it was foreseeable that such jewelry might be found in a purse under such circumstances as here presented. It is known that people who are guests in hotels such as the Shamrock Hilton, a well-known Houston hotel, not infrequently bring such expensive jewelry with them, and it does not impress us as unreasonable under the circumstances that one person might have her jewelry in her purse either awaiting a present occasion to wear it or following reclaiming it from the hotel safe in anticipation of leaving the hotel.

. . .

The judgment of the trial court is affirmed.

SAM D. JOHNSON (dissenting).

If, as found by the majority, the evidence conclusively showed facts from which there was established a bailment, it is well to examine the relationship of the parties. Mrs. Caranas is characterized as a quasi or constructive bailor. The bailment is characterized as a mutual benefit and as a constructive bailment. If a bailment was created it was certainly unintentional. Mrs. Caranas had no intention of creating a bailment. The hotel had no such intention. Neither, in fact, for a considerable period of time knew of its existence.

This, for two reasons forming the basis of this dissent, is at least true of the jewelry allegedly contained in the purse. First, it seems to be conceded that the hotel had no actual notice of the existence of the jewelry in the purse and there is no authority in this state for the proposition that a bailee is liable for property he could reasonably expect to find contained in the bailed property. Secondly, even if the foregoing were true it does not occur to this writer that it is reasonable to expect a purse, inadvertently left under a chair in a hotel's restaurant and not even missed by the owner until the next day, might contain ten pieces of jewelry valued at $13,062.00.

NOTES

1. Compare the following cases:

(a) Ampco Auto Parks, Inc. v. Williams, 517 S.W.2d 401 (Tex.Civ.App.1974) held that a commercial auto parking enterprise was not a bailee of the contents of the trunk of an auto, concededly bailed, which a jury had found would not reasonably be expected to be placed in the trunk. The items involved were clothing, silver coins, pictures, antique family heirlooms, jewelry and a "pre-Columbian bell (1,000 B.C.)," totaling a value of $4,086.10.

(b) Samples v. Geary, 292 S.W. 1066 (Mo.App.1927) held that a dancing school that maintained a checking service for outer wearing apparel was not a bailee of a fur piece wrapped inside a checked coat. The court said: "Since the relation of bailee and bailor is founded upon contract, there must be a meeting of minds to make the contract valid. In this case, the fur piece being concealed, the bailee did not know it was there, the minds of the parties did not meet, and there was no acceptance by defendant of the article in question."

(c) Peet v. Roth Hotel Co., 191 Minn. 151, 253 N.W. 546 (1934) held that one who accepted possession of a ring for delivery to another was a bailee even though he was unaware that the ring was very valuable. This was not a mistake, said the court, "of such character as to show no mutual assent and so no contract."

See Annotation, Liability of Owner or Operator of Parking Lot or Garage for Loss or Damage to Contents of Parked Motor Vehicle, 78 A.L.R.3d 1057 (1977).

2. Traditionally, misdelivery by a bailee has been regarded as conversion. Consider Cowen v. Pressprich, 117 Misc. 663, 192 N.Y.S. 242 (1922). In that case, an employee of a securities broker endeavored to return an unordered bond to a messenger who had deposited the bond at the broker's office, but mistakenly handed the bond to another

person. The court, holding that the broker was a bailee and liable for conversion, said:

"A person who has been put, through no act or fault of his own, in such a situation as that in which the defendants were put upon the delivery to them of the wrong bond, has come to be known as "involuntary bailee" (1 Halsbury, The Laws of England, 528; Heugh v. L. & N.W.R.R. Co., L.R. 5 Ex. 51 [1870]; 5 Cyc. 166, note 27; Story, Bailments [7th Ed.] §§ 44a, 83a), or bailee by casualty (T.J. Moss Tie Co. v. Kreilich, 80 Mo.App. 304), or constructive or quasi bailee (Schouler, Bailments [3d Ed.] par. 3).

In the field of voluntary bailments, whether they be for hire or be otherwise coupled with an interest on the part of the bailee, or whether they be merely gratuitous, no rule is better settled than that it is the duty of the bailee to deliver the bailed article to the right person, and that delivery to the wrong person is not capable of being excused by any possible showing of care or good faith or innocence. . . .

Such distinctions as have been drawn between the duties of voluntary bailees for compensation and voluntary gratuitous bailees relate solely to the degree of care the bailee should exercise in respect of the custody of the thing bailed. In respect of delivery to the proper person, no such distinction is drawn; the duty in both cases is absolute.

What, then, is the difference, if any, between the duty of a voluntary gratuitous bailee and that of a wholly involuntary bailee? There is an astonishing paucity of decision and text opinion upon the subject. I think, however, that all that can be found upon it points to the conclusion that the involuntary bailee, as long as his lack of volition continues, is not under the slightest duty to care for or guard the subject of the bailment, and cannot be held, in respect of custody, for what would even be the grossest negligence in the case of a voluntary bailment . . ., but that, in case the involuntary bailee shall exercise any dominion over the thing so bailed, he becomes as responsible as if he were a voluntary bailee. . . ."

Judge Lehman, whose dissent was relied upon by the Appellate Division of the Supreme Court in reversing the decision of the Appellate Term, 202 App.Div. 796, 194 N.Y.S. 926, said:

"In the present case the defendants were put in possession of the bond by mistake; they discovered the mistake promptly, and thereafter they committed no "overt act" of interference with the bond except that they attempted to divest themselves of this possession by delivering the bond to a person whom they believed to be the messenger of the plaintiffs. That act was not only consistent with the continued title and right of dominion in the plaintiffs, but was an honest attempt to restore possession to the true owners. It certainly cannot be contended that the defendants were bound at their peril to wait until the plaintiffs came to their office and physically took away their property; they could take proper steps to divest themselves of the possession thrust upon them by mistake without thereby impliedly agreeing, contrary to their clear intention, to accept possession as bailees with the consequent obligations flowing from such relation. It is quite immaterial whether we call these defendants bailees or not if we keep in mind the fact that the possession of these goods was thrust upon them by mistake of the plaintiffs and without their invitation or consent, and that therefore any liability for failure to return the goods to the true owner upon demand must be the result of some act voluntarily done by the defendant thereafter. An attempt to return the bond to the true owner or to the person who delivered it cannot be considered as inconsistent with a recognition of the complete ownership and right of dominion by the true owner, and certainly shows no intent to accept the possession thrust upon the defendants by plaintiffs' mistake, and I fail to see how, in the absence of such elements, any implied contract of bailment can arise. If in making an attempt to return the goods, which was lawful and proper in itself, the defendants used means which were not reasonable and proper, and as a result thereof the goods were lost or misdelivered, then the defendants would be liable for negligence or possibly for conversion, for every man is responsible for his own acts; but, if the defendants had a right to divest themselves of possession and attempt to return the goods, then, in the absence of some obligation resting upon contract to deliver the goods only to the true owner or upon his order, I do not see how the mere fact that through innocent mistake the defendants handed the bond to the wrong messenger could constitute a conversion. . . ."

3. O rents a safety deposit box located in the vault of X Bank. Access to the box is obtained by presenting identification to the vault attendant and by opening the box with a key given the renter. O places in the box securities owned by B. These are stolen. In an action against the bank by the owner of the securities, the bank contends: (1) No bailment existed because O had possession of the box; (2) No bailment existed between the bank and B because the contract was between the bank and O, not between the bank and B; and (3) No bailment existed because the bank was unaware that the securities were placed in the box. Evaluate these contentions. See Coons v. First National Bank of Philmont, 218 App.Div. 283, 218 N.Y.S. 189 (1926); Fryer, Readings on Personal Property 209–217 (3d ed. 1938).

4. There are situations where a bailment is not created even though possession is transferred; e.g., where the article is sold. It may be difficult to determine in some cases whether the transaction constitutes a sale or a bailment. Grain elevator transactions have raised this problem. Since the grain deposited by various farmers is mixed together, no farmer expects to receive the identical grain deposited. If the grain is destroyed by fire, the depositors will prefer that the transaction be considered a sale to the elevator owner. If the elevator owner becomes insolvent, the depositors will prefer to be bailors. Consider the soundness of the following contentions: (1) Since it is the duty of a bailee to return the subject matter of the bailment to the bailor, there can be no bailment where the nature of the transaction is such that the depositors cannot reasonably expect to receive the identical grain deposited. (2) The transaction is a sale at the time of deposit if the elevator operator reserves the option either to return the same quantity of grain or to pay the depositor the market value of that quantity of

grain upon demand by the depositor. (3) The transaction is a bailment if the elevator operator requires depositors to pay a "storage charge." See Sexton & Abbott v. Graham, 53 Iowa 181, 4 N.W. 1090 (1880); Stricklin v. Rice, 141 S.W.2d 748 (Tex.Civ.App.1940).

5. Liability standards for bailees are discussed in Note, Bailment Liability: Toward a Standard of Reasonable Care, 61 S.Calif.L.Rev. 2119 (1988).

Chapter 8

BONA FIDE PURCHASE

If O's diamond is stolen by T, who sells it to P, who pays cash and reasonably believes that T is the owner, should O be allowed to recover the diamond from T? No one can convey a better title than one has, English and American courts have declared repeatedly, but substantial deviations from this principle have occurred, by court decisions and legislation. Consider the following:

(1) Suppose that O delivers his diamond to J, a jeweler, with instructions to display it with J's diamonds and seek offers. J, without authority from O, sells the diamond to P, who reasonably believes that J is authorized to sell it. J absconds. A court might hold that O is estopped by O's conduct from asserting title against P. See Zendman v. Harry Winston, Inc., 305 N.Y. 180, 111 N.E.2d 871 (1953).

(2) Suppose that certain diamonds held in trust by T for B are wrongfully sold to P, a bona fide purchaser. Prior to this sale, the legal title was in T and the equitable title was in B. The English Court of Chancery, the protector of equitable claims appealing to the conscience of the Chancellor, declined to intervene in this situation as the claims of both parties seemed evenly balanced. The practical effect was that the bona fide purchaser prevailed. See G.G. Bogert & G.T. Bogert, Handbook of the Law of Trusts 600 (1973).

(3) Suppose that B, the beneficiary of a trust res consisting of diamonds, conveys B's equitable title twice—first to P and then to X, a bona fide purchaser. Here, Chancery declined to protect the bona fide purchaser; among competing equities, the senior prevails. Thus, it could hardly be generalized that Chancery deemed bona fide purchasers more worthy than original owners. Id.

(4) Suppose that O is induced by C's false representation to convey O's diamond to C, who then sells it to P, a bona fide purchaser. There is authority that P prevails over O, the explanation being that C had acquired a voidable title, which became absolute when transferred to a bona fide purchaser. Phelps v. McQuade, 220 N.Y. 232, 115 N.E. 441 (1917). O's right to rescind is similar to the equitable interest of the beneficiary of a trust.

(5) Suppose that O conveys certain land twice—first to P and then to X, a bona fide purchaser—and that P had not recorded the deed from O prior to O's conveyance to X. If X had recorded his deed promptly (and in some states even if he had not), X would be protected by the recording acts. This subject is treated elsewhere in this book.

(6) The smooth functioning of commercial transactions would seem to require that entrepreneurs who engage daily in a multitude of transactions involving sales of goods and transfers of documents have some protection against claims of ownership by those not parties to the transaction. A response to this concern is the Uniform Commercial

Code, first approved by its sponsors in 1952, subsequently revised, and now in force in all states, with variations. Section 2–403 of the code is set forth below.

"(1) A purchaser of goods acquires all title which his transferor had or had power to transfer except that a purchaser of a limited interest acquires rights only to the extent of the interest purchased. A person with voidable title has power to transfer a good title to a good faith purchaser for value. When goods have been delivered under a transaction of purchase the purchaser has such power even though

(a) the transferor was deceived as to the identity of the purchaser, or

(b) the delivery was in exchange for a check which is later dishonored, or

(c) it was agreed that the transaction was to be a 'cash sale', or

(d) the delivery was procured through fraud punishable as larcenous under the criminal law.

"(2) Any entrusting of possession of goods to a merchant who deals in goods of that kind gives him power to transfer all rights of the entruster to a buyer in ordinary course of business.

"(3) 'Entrusting' includes any delivery and any acquiescence in retention of possession regardless of any condition expressed between the parties to the delivery or acquiescence and regardless of whether the procurement of the entrusting or the possessor's disposition of the goods have been such as to be larcenous under the criminal law.

"(4) The rights of other purchasers of goods and of lien creditors are governed by the Articles on Secured Transactions (Article 9), Bulk Transfers (Article 6) and Documents of Title (Article 7)."

PORTER v. WERTZ

New York Supreme Court, Appellate Division, First Department, 1979. 68 A.D.2d 141, 416 N.Y.S.2d 254, affirmed 53 N.Y.2d 696, 439 N.Y.S.2d 105, 421 N.E.2d 500 (1981).

BIRNS, JUSTICE:

Plaintiffs-appellants, Samuel Porter and Express Packaging, Inc. (Porter's corporation), owners of a Maurice Utrillo painting entitled "Chateau de Lion-sur-Mer", seek in this action to recover possession of the painting or the value thereof from defendants, participants in a series of transactions which resulted in the shipment of the painting out of the country. The painting is now in Venezuela.

Defendants-respondents Richard Feigen Gallery, Inc., Richard L. Feigen & Co., Inc. and Richard L. Feigen, hereinafter collectively referred to as Feigen, were in the business of buying and selling paintings, drawings and sculpture.

The amended answer to the complaint asserted, *inter alia*, affirmative defenses of statutory estoppel (UCC, § 2–403) and equitable estoppel. The trial court, after a bench trial, found statutory estoppel inapplicable but sustained the defense of equitable estoppel and dismissed the complaint.

On this appeal, we will consider whether those defenses, or either of them, bar recovery against Feigen. We hold neither prevents recovery.[2]

Porter, the owner of a collection of art works, bought the Utrillo in 1969. During 1972 and 1973 he had a number of art transactions with one Harold Von Maker who used, among other names, that of Peter Wertz.[3] One of the transactions was the sale by Porter to Von Maker in the spring of 1973 of a painting by Childe Hassam for $150,000, financed with a $50,000 deposit and 10 notes for $10,000 each. At about that time, Von Maker expressed an interest in the Utrillo. Porter permitted him to have it temporarily with the understanding that Von Maker would hang it in his (Von Maker's) home, pending Von Maker's decision whether to buy the painting. On a visit to Von Maker's home in Westchester in May 1973, Porter saw the painting hanging there. In June 1973, lacking a decision from Von Maker, Porter sought its return, but was unable to reach Von Maker.

The first note in connection with Von Maker's purchase of the Childe Hassam, due early July 1973, was returned dishonored, as were the balance of the notes. Porter commenced an investigation and found that he had not been dealing with Peter Wertz—but with another man named Von Maker. Bishop reports, dated July 10 and July 17, 1973, disclosed that Von Maker was subject to judgments, that he had been sued many times, that he had an arrest record for possession of obscene literature, and for "false pretenses", as well as for "theft of checks", and had been convicted, among other crimes, of transmitting a forged cable in connection with a scheme to defraud the Chase Manhattan Bank and had been placed on probation for three years. Porter notified the FBI about his business transactions concerning the notes. He did not report that Von Maker had defrauded him of any painting, for, as will be shown, Porter did not know at this time that Von Maker had disposed of the Utrillo.

Porter did, however, have his attorney communicate with Von Maker's attorney. As a result, on August 13, 1973, a detailed agreement, drawn by the attorneys for Porter and Von Maker, the latter still using the name Peter Wertz, was executed. Under this agreement the obligations of Von Maker to Porter concerning several paintings delivered by Porter to Von Maker (one of which was the Utrillo) were covered. In paragraph 11, Von Maker acknowledged that he had

2. We note that the appeal is from the trial court's determination that equitable estoppel constitutes a bar to the action. However, because the enactment of statutory estoppel (UCC, § 2–403) was intended to embrace prior uniform statutory provisions and case law thereunder (so as "to continue unimpaired all rights acquired under the law of agency or of apparent agency or ownership or other estoppel"), and to state a unified and simplified policy on good faith purchase of goods (see Practice Commentary, Alfred A. Berger and William J. O'Connor, Jr., McKinney's Cons.Laws of N.Y., Book 62½, p. 395), we find it necessary to enter into some discussion of section 2–403 of the Uniform Commercial Code.

3. As will be seen, Peter Wertz was a real person, at least an acquaintance of Von Maker; who permitted Von Maker to use his name. . . .

received the Utrillo from Porter together with a certain book on Utrillo, that both "belong to (Porter)", that the painting was on consignment with a client of Von Maker's, that within 90 days Von Maker would either return the painting and book or pay $30,000 therefor, and that other than the option to purchase within said 90-day period, Von Maker had "no claim whatsoever to the Utrillo painting or Book."

Paragraph 13 provided that in the event Von Maker failed to meet the obligations under paragraph 11, i.e., return the Utrillo and book within 90 days or pay for them, Porter would immediately be entitled to obtain possession of a painting by Cranach held in escrow by Von Maker's attorney, and have the right to sell that painting, apply the proceeds to the amount owing by Von Maker under paragraph 11, and Von Maker would pay any deficiency. Paragraph 13 provided further that "[t]he above is in addition to all [Porter's] other rights and remedies which [Porter] expressly reserved to enforce the performance of [Von Maker's] obligations under this Agreement."

We note that the agreement did not state that receipt of the Cranach by Porter would be in full satisfaction of Porter's claim to the Utrillo and book. Title to the Utrillo and book remained in Porter, absent any payment by Von Maker of the agreed purchase price of $30,000. Indeed, no payment for the Utrillo was ever made by Von Maker.

At the very time that Von Maker was deceitfully assuring Porter he would return the Utrillo and book or pay $30,000, Von Maker had already disposed of this painting by using the real Peter Wertz to effect its sale for $20,000 to Feigen. Von Maker, utilizing Sloan and Lipinsky, persons in the art world, had made the availability of the Utrillo known to Feigen. When Wertz, at Von Maker's direction, appeared at the Feigen gallery with the Utrillo, he was met by Feigen's employee, Ms. Drew-Bear. She found a buyer for the Utrillo in defendant Brenner. In effecting its transfer to him, Feigen made a commission. Through a sale by Brenner the painting is now in Venezuela, S.A.

We agree with the conclusion of the trial court that statutory estoppel does not bar recovery.

The provisions of statutory estoppel are found in section 2–403 of the Uniform Commercial Code. Subsection 2 thereof provides that "any entrusting of possession of goods to a merchant who deals in goods of that kind gives him power to transfer all rights of the entruster to a buyer in the ordinary course of business." Uniform Commercial Code, section 1–201, subdivision 9, defines a "buyer in [the] ordinary course of business" as "a person who in good faith and without knowledge that the sale to him is in violation of the ownership rights or security interest of a third party in the goods buys in ordinary course from a person in the business of selling goods of that kind . . . ."

In order to determine whether the defense of statutory estoppel is available to Feigen, we must begin by ascertaining whether Feigen fits the definition of "[a] buyer in [the] ordinary course of business." (UCC, § 1–201[9.) Feigen does not fit that definition, for two reasons. First,

Wertz, from whom Feigen bought the Utrillo, was not an art dealer—he was not "a person in the business of selling goods of that kind." (UCC, § 1–201[9] .) If anything, he was a delicatessen employee.[6] Wertz never held himself out as a dealer. Although Feigen testified at trial that before he (Feigen) purchased the Utrillo from Wertz, Sloan, who introduced Wertz to Feigen told him (Feigen) that Wertz was an art dealer, this testimony was questionable. It conflicted with Feigen's testimony at his examination before trial where he stated he did not recall whether Sloan said that to him. Second, Feigen was not "a person . . . in good faith" (UCC, § 1–201[9]) in the transaction with Wertz. Uniform Commercial Code, section 2–103, subdivision (1)(b), defines "good faith" in the case of a merchant as "honesty in fact and the observance of reasonable commercial standards of fair dealing in the trade." Although this definition by its terms embraces the "reasonable commercial standards of fair dealing in the trade", it should not—and cannot—be interpreted to permit, countenance or condone commercial standards of sharp trade practice or indifference as to the "provenance", i.e., history of ownership or the right to possess or sell an object d'art, such as is present in the case before us.

We note that neither Ms. Drew-Bear nor her employer Feigen made any investigation to determine the status of Wertz, i.e., whether he was an art merchant, "a person in the business of selling goods of that kind." (UCC, § 1–201[9].) Had Ms. Drew-Bear done so much as call either of the telephone numbers Wertz had left, she would have learned that Wertz was employed by a delicatessen and was not an art dealer. Nor did Ms. Drew-Bear or Feigen make any effort to verify whether Wertz was the owner or authorized by the owner to sell the painting he was offering. Ms. Drew-Bear had available to her the Petrides volume on Utrillo which included "Chateau de Lion-sur-Mer" in its catalogue of the master's work.[8] Although this knowledge alone might not have been enough to put Feigen on notice that Wertz was not the true owner at the time of the transaction, it could have raised a doubt as to Wertz's right of possession, calling for further verification before the purchase by Feigen was consummated. Thus, it appears that statutory estoppel provided by Uniform Commercial Code, section 2–403(2), was not, as Trial Term correctly concluded, available as a defense to Feigen.

We disagree with the conclusion of the trial court that the defense of equitable estoppel (see Zendman v. Harry Winston, Inc., 305 N.Y. 180, 111 N.E.2d 871) raised by Feigen bars recovery.

We pause to observe that although one may not be a buyer in the ordinary course of business as defined in the Uniform Commercial Code, he may be a good-faith purchaser for value and enjoy the protection of pre-Code estoppel (see Tumber v. Automation Design &

6. Wertz is described as a seller of caviar and other luxury food items (because of his association with a Madison Avenue gourmet grocery) and over whom the Trial Term observed, Von Maker "cast his hypnotic spell . . . and usurped his name, his signature and his sacred honor."

8. Page 32 of that book clearly contained a reference to the fact that that painting, at least at the time of publication of the book in 1969, was in the collection of Mrs. Donald D. King of New York, supposedly the party from whom Porter obtained it.

Mfg. Corp., 130 N.J.Super. 5, 13, 324 A.2d 602, 616; UCC, § 1–103). We now reach the question whether the defense of equitable estoppel has been established here.

As the Court of Appeals reiterated in Zendman v. Harry Winston, Inc., supra, an " 'owner may be estopped from setting up his own title and the lack of title in the vendor as against a *bona fide* purchaser for value where the owner has clothed the vendor with possession and other indicia of title (46 Am.Jur., Sales, § 463).' " Indeed, "[t]he rightful owner may be estopped by his own acts from asserting his title. If he has invested another with the usual evidence of title, or an apparent authority to dispose of it, he will not be allowed to make claim against an innocent purchaser dealing on the faith of such apparent ownership (Smith v. Clews, 114 N.Y. 190, 194, 21 N.E. 160, 161)." . . .

In the case at bar, Porter's conduct was not blameworthy. When the first promissory note was dishonored, he retained Bishop's investigative service and informed the FBI of the financial transactions concerning the series of notes. His attorney obtained a comprehensive agreement covering several paintings, within which was the assurance (now proven false) by Von Maker that he still controlled the Utrillo. Although Porter had permitted Von Maker to possess the painting, he conferred upon Von Maker no other indicia of ownership. Possession without more is insufficient to create an estoppel (Zendman v. Harry Winston, Inc., supra, 305 N.Y. at 186–187, 111 N.E.2d 874–875).

We find that the prior art transactions between Porter and Von Maker justified the conclusion of the trial court that Porter knew that Von Maker was a dealer in art. Nevertheless, the testimony remains uncontradicted, that the Utrillo was not consigned to Von Maker for business purposes, but rather for display only in Von Maker's home (compare Zendman v. Harry Winston, Inc., supra). In these circumstances, it cannot be said that Porter's conduct in any way contributed to the deception practiced on Feigen by Von Maker and Wertz.

Finally, we must examine again the position of Feigen to determine whether Feigen was a purchaser in good faith.

In purchasing the Utrillo, Feigen did not rely on any indicia of ownership in Von Maker. Feigen dealt with Wertz, who did not have the legal right to possession of the painting. Even were we to consider Wertz as the agent of Von Maker or merge the identities of Von Maker and Wertz insofar as Feigen was concerned, Feigen was not a purchaser in good faith. As we have commented, neither Ms. Drew-Bear nor Feigen made, or attempted to make, the inquiry which the circumstances demanded.

The Feigen claim that the failure to look into Wertz's authority to sell the painting was consistent with the practice of the trade does not excuse such conduct. This claim merely confirms the observation of the trial court that "in an industry whose transactions cry out for verification of . . . title . . . it is deemed poor practice to probe . . .." Indeed, commercial indifference to ownership or the right to sell facilitates traffic in stolen works of art. Commercial indifference diminishes the integrity and increases the culpability of the apathetic merchant. In such posture, Feigen cannot be heard to complain.

In the circumstances outlined, the complaint should not have been dismissed. Moreover, we find (CPLR 4213[b] and 5712[c][2]) that plaintiffs-appellants are the true owners of the Utrillo painting and are entitled to possession thereof, that defendants-respondents wrongfully detained that painting and are obligated to return it or pay for its value at the time of trial . . ..

Judgment, Supreme Court, New York County entered on June 23, 1978, reversed, on the law and the facts, and vacated, the complaint reinstated, judgment entered in favor of plaintiffs-appellants on liability, and the matter remanded for an assessment of damages. Appellants shall recover of respondents $75 costs and disbursements of this appeal.

All concur.

NOTE

In its opinion affirming this judgment, the Court of Appeals declined to pass upon the good faith issue:

"The Appellate Division opined that even if Von Maker had duped Feigen into believing that Peter Wertz was an art dealer, subdivision (2) of section 2–403 of the Uniform Commercial Code would still not protect his defective title because as a merchant, Feigen failed to purchase in good faith. Among merchants good faith requires not only honesty in fact but observance of reasonable commercial standards. (Uniform Commercial Code, § 2–103, subd. [1], par. [b]). The Appellate Division concluded that it was a departure from reasonable commercial standards for the Feigen Gallery to fail to inquire concerning the title to the Utrillo and to fail to question Peter Wertz' credentials as an art dealer. On this appeal we have received *amicus* briefs from the New York State Attorney-General urging that the court hold that good faith among art merchants requires inquiry as to the ownership of an *object d'art,* and from the Art Dealers Association of America, Inc., arguing that the ordinary custom in the art business is not to inquire as to title and that a duty of inquiry would cripple the art business which is centered in New York. In view of our disposition we do not reach the good faith question." 421 N.E.2d at 502.

SHERIDAN SUZUKI, INC. v. CARUSO AUTO SALES

New York Supreme Court, Erie County, 1981.
110 Misc.2d 823, 442 N.Y.S.2d 957.

MEMORANDUM

JOSEPH J. SEDITA, JUSTICE. . . .

On May 26, 1981, the plaintiff, Sheridan Suzuki, Inc., (hereinafter Suzuki) "sold" a motorcycle to one Ronald Bouton. Incident to this sale they gave him possession of the motorcycle, a signed bill of sale marked paid in full and registration of the vehicle in said Bouton's name.

Additionally, they filed an application for an original Certificate of Title (pursuant to requirements of Article 46 of the New York State Vehicle and Traffic Law). Said certificate was never received by Bouton. Its processing in Albany was interrupted when they were notified by Suzuki of subsequent developments. In return for the subject motorcycle, the plaintiff was given Bouton's check for Three thousand five hundred fifty-nine dollars and forty-four cents ($3,559.44) in satisfaction of the purchase price. Said check was later dishonored. Bouton has disappeared from the area.

On May 27, 1981, (one day after the initial sale), Bouton offered to sell the vehicle to Caruso Auto Sales, Inc., (hereinafter Caruso). After examining the papers that Bouton had "in hand", but before Bouton had received the Certificate of Title from Albany, Caruso "purchased" the motorcycle from Bouton for Two thousand dollars ($2,000.00). Bouton gave Caruso possession of the motorcycle, signed over the registration and assured Caruso that he would transfer the Certificate of Title upon receipt of the title documents from the State. Before accepting the transaction, Caruso had called Suzuki and they had confirmed Bouton's assertion of prior purchase (not yet having notice of the dishonored check). Justice Norman Stiller has granted a preliminary order placing the motorcycle with Suzuki pending a determination of the legal issues raised herein. . . .

At common law, a thief could pass no title whatsoever to stolen goods. . . .

However, section 2–403(1) pars. [b], [d] of the Uniform Commercial Code supplanted the common law rule as to goods received "in exchange for a check which is later dishonored . . ." or "delivery was procured through fraud punishable as larcenous under the criminal law." This motorcycle was transferred as part of a transaction involving a bad check, rather than as a result of a direct larceny or burglary and therefore it cannot be asserted that any title received by a "bona fide purchaser for value" would be void. The law is clear that a person receiving goods incident to a transaction involving a dishonored check and a fraud receives only voidable title, at best. (See U.C.C. sec. 2–403, supra) A "bona fide purchaser for value" can receive good title from a person with "voidable" title under the Uniform Commercial Code. (See Atlas Auto Rental Corp. v. Weisberg, 54 Misc.2d 168, 281 N.Y.S.2d 400.)

The crucial question at this point becomes the effect of the State Uniform Vehicle Certificate of Title Act (hereinafter U.V.C.T.A.) on the species of "title" received by Bouton. The Courts have an obligation to give effect to all acts of the legislature and to avoid interpretations which result in a conflict between statutes. Where a general statute and a more particular statute overlap, the Courts will usually give greater effect to the more particularized statute. . . .

This Court takes note of the fact that the Uniform Commercial Code establishes a general rule for commercial transactions. The Uniform Vehicle Certificate of Title Act does not seek to abrogate the U.C.C., but merely seeks to add additional requirements for transactions involving this unique area of "goods", due to unique problems of fraud and theft experienced with motor vehicles. . . . Section 2113(c) of the U.V.C.T.A. expressly states in part:

> " . . . a transfer by an owner is not perfected so as to be valid against third parties generally until the provisions of this section . . . have been complied with."

Section 2105 of the U.V.C.T.A. sets forth the procedures for making an application for the first Certificate of Title. This section makes clear that the requirements of this act are more than ministerial record keeping. The commissioner is required to make a "quasi-judicial" determination as to ownership. (See section 2105(d) of the U.V.C.T.A.)

"Title" under this act is not an automatic result once the bureaucratic process is triggered, but is a result of a *determination* of the Department after examining the documents submitted to it. The process of obtaining title is not complete, and the provisions of this statute are not fully complied with until the Department is satisfied that title was in the alleged owner/applicant.

Since the Department suspended the issuance of a title certificate due to its knowledge of the fraud perpetrated herein, the voidable "title" received by Bouton was never perfected as required by the statute (sec. 2113(c), cited supra) and could not be successfully passed to a "bona fide purchaser for value." The object of this section is clearly to effectuate the intent of the U.V.C.T.A., which is to make transfers of improperly obtained motor vehicles more difficult by requiring a "perfected" title before a successful transfer of a vehicle can be made. An interpretation which avoids this requirement would in effect "extract" the "teeth" built into this legislation and circumvent its clear purpose.

If Bouton had obtained a valid Certificate of Title, his title would have still been voidable, but would have been "perfected" according to the requirements of the law. He could then have successfully passed good title to a "bona fide purchaser for value." (As for example in White v. Pike, 240 Iowa 596, 36 N.W.2d 761, where the perpetrator of the fraud had obtained a Certificate of Title in addition to the other usual indicia of ownership.)

Since Bouton never had a perfected title, he could not pass good title to Caruso.

Defendant alleges that Suzuki is equitably estopped from denying Caruso's title because of Suzuki's representation that Bouton had properly received ownership of the vehicle in question. Caruso alleges that he relied upon those representations to his detriment. Equitable estoppel, however does not operate to create rights which are nonexistent. It may only operate to preclude the denial of a right claimed otherwise to have arisen.

. . .

Since Bouton never received the Certificate of Title, he never had perfected title as required under New York Law to enable him to transfer good title. Caruso therefore never got any legal title or right to the vehicle, and therefore has no claim to assert in seeking equitable estoppel against Suzuki's claim.

Buyers who purchase from a seller who does not have a Certificate of Title, do so at their own risk. Caruso took that risk in the hope of making a substantial profit by obtaining a brand new three thousand five hundred dollar ($3,500.00) motorcycle for two thousand dollars ($2,000.00). The risk he took backfired, and this Court cannot protect him from his loss. The law is clear and intended to protect society against exactly the type of fraud perpetrated herein. The duty of this Court is to enforce the express mandate of that law.

Accordingly, plaintiff's motion for Summary Judgment is granted and defendant's motion for Summary Judgment is denied.

NOTES

1. There is conflict among the states concerning relationships between the Uniform Commercial Code and certificate of title acts. See the brief discussion in R. Speidel, R. Summers & J. White, Commercial and Consumer Law 1170 (1981).

2. In England, bona fide purchasers of goods in markets overt (i.e., open, public markets) obtain good title even to stolen goods. See Clayton v. Le Roy, [1911] 2 K.B. 1031.

WILLIAM D. WARREN, CUTTING OFF CLAIMS OF OWNERSHIP UNDER THE UNIFORM COMMERCIAL CODE

30 Univ. of Chicago L.Rev. 469 (1963).

In justifying the rule that good faith purchasers of goods from a market overt took free of certain claims of ownership, Blackstone wrote: "[I]t is expedient, that the buyer, by taking proper precautions, may, at all events be secure of his purchase, otherwise all commerce between man and man must soon be at an end." A generation ago, a California judge, in holding that a good faith purchaser from a bailee took subject to the true owner's claims, quoted: "Owners of goods for commercial and other purposes must frequently intrust others with the possession of them, and the affairs of men could not be conducted unless they could do so with safety." Thus, these two gentlemen urge, respectively, that we are doomed if we do and doomed if we do not honor claims of ownership.

Statements of this sort—predicting commercial chaos if one or the other of the conflicting doctrines for preferring or denying claims of ownership against good faith purchasers were not adopted—have rattled around in the law of sales for centuries. Blackstone doubtless fashioned his prediction of disaster from that incomparable vantage point of the realities of the commercial process, the library of an Oxford college, while the judge's insight into the impact of legal doctrine on mercantile practices was probably gained in such a nerve center of the commercial world as Bakersfield, California.

. . .

The widespread acceptance of the Code represents substantial progress in the long journey toward the attainment of a mercantile or commercial theory regarding goods, documents and instruments. When one buys in good faith and in the regular course of commerce he is now assured by the Code of broad protection against prior claims of ownership and defenses with respect to negotiable instruments, documents of title and investment securities. The Code's inclusion of section 2–403, granting a measure of negotiability to goods in a commercial setting, has been the most dramatic step forward. Conversely, when the buyer is out of the ordinary flow of commerce—purchasing goods from one not a merchant; taking a non-negotiable instrument; loaning money on a document of title outside the regular course of business—the Code offers no aid against claims of ownership.

The rise of the commercial theory has usually been depicted as an orderly progression of right winning out over wrong—of good over evil—not unlike the conversion of the Goths to Christianity. It is intriguing to note that many businessmen are quite unenthusiastic about this new source of solace, the commercial theory.. . .

Perhaps we should not wonder at the indifference of the business community to the extensions made in the Code toward the mercantile theory. Financiers, manufacturers and sellers of goods are not directly helped by giving goods a measure of negotiability. And they are quite sure that they are injured by the requirement that one can only take documents free of claims or defenses if he takes in the regular course of business. Their contention is that this provision introduces such uncertainty into the purchase or financing of documents that the basic objectives of the commercial doctrine—promotion of the free flow of commerce—is subverted. Thus the Code broadens the application of the commercial doctrine where businessmen believe they are not helped—goods—only to narrow the group protected by the doctrine where they believe they will be hurt—documents.

During the 1954 New York hearings on the Code, Professor Llewellyn was asked why he had chosen to prefer the good faith purchaser over those having prior claims of ownership. He replied: "The choice is hard, and it gives little satisfaction, either way; but the Code's choice fits more comfortably into the whole body of our commercial law." Until the impact of the Code on business transactions is studied, there is little more that can be said.

. . .

Chapter 9

UNAUTHORIZED POSSESSION

SECTION 1. POSSESSION DEEMED OWNERSHIP AS TO THIRD PERSONS

ANDERSON v. GOULDBERG

Supreme Court of Minnesota, 1892.
51 Minn. 294, 53 N.W. 636.

Appeal by defendants, Hans J. Gouldberg and D.O. Anderson, from an order of the District Court of Isanti County, Lochren, J., made November 14, 1892, refusing a new trial.

This action was brought by the plaintiff, Sigfrid Anderson, against the defendants, partners as Gouldberg & Anderson, to recover the possession of ninety-three pine logs, marked L S X, or for the value thereof. Plaintiff claimed to have cut the logs on section 22, township 27, range 25, Isanti County, in the winter of 1889–1890, and to have hauled them to a mill on section 6, from which place defendants took them. The title to section 22 was in strangers, and plaintiff showed no authority from the owners to cut logs thereon. Defendants claimed that the logs were cut on section 26, in the adjoining township, on land belonging to the Ann River Logging Company, and that they took the logs by direction of the Logging Company, who were the owners. The court charged that even if plaintiff got possession of the logs as a trespasser, his title would be good as against any one except the real owner or some one who had authority from the owner to take them, and left the case to the jury on the question as to whether the logs were cut on the land of the Logging Company, and taken by defendants under its authority. The jury found a verdict for the plaintiff and assessed his damages at $153.45. From an order denying their motion for a new trial, defendants appeal.

. . .

MITCHELL, J. It is settled by the verdict of the jury that the logs in controversy were not cut upon the land of the defendants, and consequently that they were entire strangers to the property.

For the purposes of this appeal, we must also assume the fact to be (as there was evidence from which the jury might have so found) that the plaintiffs obtained possession of the logs in the first instance by trespassing upon the land of some third party.

Therefore the only question is whether bare possession of property, though wrongfully obtained, is sufficient title to enable the party enjoying it to maintain replevin against a mere stranger, who takes it from him. We had supposed that this was settled in the affirmative as long ago, at least, as the early case of Armory v. Delamirie, 1 Strange, 505, so often cited on that point.

When it is said that to maintain replevin the plaintiff's possession must have been lawful, it means merely that it must have been lawful as against the person who deprived him of it; and possession is good title against all the world except those having a better title.

Counsel says that possession only raises a presumption of title, which, however, may be rebutted. Rightly understood, this is correct; but counsel misapplies it. One who takes property from the possession of another can only rebut this presumption by showing a superior title in himself, or in some way connecting himself with one who has. One who has acquired the possession of property, whether by finding, bailment, or by mere tort, has a right to retain that possession as against a mere wrongdoer who is a stranger to the property. Any other rule would lead to an endless series of unlawful seizures and reprisals in every case where property had once passed out of the possession of the rightful owner.

Order affirmed.

NOTE

Is this case authority for the proposition that T, who has stolen O's chattel, may recover it or its value from T–1, who stole it from T? Should the court leave evil doers as it finds them? Does not judicial abstention have the practical effect of favoring the last thief? A scholar has concluded that thieves should not recover and that courts do not allow them to do so. Helmholz, Wrongful Possession of Chattels: Hornbook Law and Case Law, 80 Nw.U.L.Rev. 1221 (1986). Does it follow that good faith converters also should be denied recovery?

RUSSELL v. HILL

Supreme Court of North Carolina, 1900.
125 N.C. 470, 34 S.E. 640.

MONTGOMERY, J. This case was heard upon an agreed state of facts, the material parts of which are as follows: In 1887, after entry and survey, F.H. Busbee, trustee, received a grant from the state for a tract of land in Swain county. Iowa McCoy made a subsequent entry and survey, and received a grant from the state for a part of the land embraced in the grant to Busbee, trustee. Busbee, trustee, was the owner of the land by virtue of his grant, which was properly registered, and registered before the entry, survey, and grant of Mrs. McCoy. Mrs. McCoy had no knowledge of Busbee's grant, except the notice which the law implies from the fact of registration. Mrs. McCoy sold to the plaintiff certain timber standing on the land embraced in her grant, and the plaintiff cut the timber, and carried the same, in the shape of logs, to the bank of Nantahalla river, a floatable stream, for the purpose of floating them to the Asheville Furniture Company. While the logs were lying on the river bank, the defendants, without any claim of right or title to them from Busbee, trustee, or from any one else, so far as the record shows, took possession of the logs without the consent of the plaintiff, and sold and delivered them to the Asheville Lumber Company for $686.84. The lumber company is insolvent. The court, upon the facts agreed, adjudged that the plaintiff could not recover, and rendered judgment accordingly.

We are of the opinion that there was no error in the ruling and judgment of the court. Busbee, trustee, was the legal owner of the land. Mrs. McCoy was not in possession. If she had been in adverse possession, the title to the logs would have passed to the plaintiff, and he could have maintained this action; and Busbee would have been compelled to proceed against Mrs. McCoy for damages to the freehold. Brothers v. Hurdle, 32 N.C. 490; Ray v. Gardner, 82 N.C. 454; Howland v. Forlaw, 108 N.C. 567, 13 S.E. 173. The present action is in the nature of the old action of trover, and, before the plaintiff could recover in an action of that nature, he had to show both title and possession, or the right of possession. . . .

So, in the case before us, the title to the land from which the timber was cut is shown by the agreed state of facts to have been in Busbee, trustee, and not in the plaintiff or Mrs. McCoy. The same point arose in Barwick v. Barwick, 33 N.C. 80, and was decided in the same way. The court said: "But if it appears on the trial that the plaintiff, although in possession, is not in fact the owner, the presumption of title inferred from the possession is rebutted, and it would be manifestly wrong to allow the plaintiff to recover the value of the property; for the real owner may forthwith bring trover against the defendant, and force him to pay the value the second time, and the fact that he paid it in a former suit would be no defense. . . . Consequently trover can never be maintained unless a satisfaction of the judgment will have the effect of vesting a good title in the defendant, except where the property is restored, and the conversion was temporary. Accordingly, it is well settled as the law of this state that, to maintain trover, the plaintiff must show title and the possession, or a present right of possession." In the last-mentioned case the court went on to say, in substance, that in some of the English books, and in some of the Reports of our sister states, cases might be found to the contrary, but that those cases were all founded upon a misapprehension of the principle laid down in the case of Armory v. Delamirie, 1 Strange, 505. There a chimney sweep found a lost jewel. He took it into his possession, as he had a right to do, and was the owner, because of having it in possession, unless the true owner should become known. That owner was not known, and it was properly decided that trover would lie in favor of the finder against the defendant, to whom he had handed it for inspection, and who refused to restore it. But the court said the case would have been very different if the owner had been known. . . . Affirmed.

DOUGLAS, J., dissents.

NOTE

O lends O's auto to B while O vacations in Europe. O's car is damaged in a collision with a car driven by X. Assuming that X is liable for the damage to O's car, should B, without authority from O, be able to recover in full from X? Would a settlement between X and B be binding upon O?

In the Winkfield, [1902] P. 42 (C.A.), the Postmaster-General, as bailee of mail lost in a collision of ships at sea, was allowed to recover from owners of the ship at fault the value of mail whose owners had not filed claims. The court said: "Why, as against a wrongdoer, should the nature of the plaintiff's interest in the thing converted be any more relevant to the inquiry, and therefore admissible in evidence, than in the case of a finder? It seems to me that neither in one case nor the other ought it to be competent for the defendant to go into evidence on that matter. . . . As between bailee and stranger, possession gives title—that is, not a limited interest, but absolute and complete ownership, and he is entitled to receive back a complete equivalent for the whole loss or deterioration of the thing itself. As between bailor and bailee the real interests of each must be inquired into, and, as the bailee has to account for the thing bailed, so he must account for that which has become its equivalent and now represents it. What he has received above his own interest he has received to the use of his bailor. The wrongdoer, having once paid full damages to the bailee, has an answer to any action by the bailor." In Masterson v. International & Great Northern Railroad Co., 55 S.W. 577 (Tex.Civ.App.1900), a suit by a bailor against a railroad for the negligent killing of four mules was held to be barred by the prior payment by the railroad of money to the bailee on the latter's claim for the full value of the mules. It did not appear that the bailor had authorized the bailee to present this claim. The money received by the bailee had not been turned over to the bailor.

SECTION 2. ACQUISITION OF LIMITATION TITLE BY ADVERSE POSSESSION

Under certain circumstances, long-continued possession of land or chattels may result in acquisition by a possessor of title that is good against the true owner. An essential circumstance is that the possession be adverse to the true owner. Possession as a tenant, for example, however long continued, would not extinguish the landlord's title in favor of the tenant. The requisite duration of adverse possession to effect a change of ownership is measured by statutes limiting the period of time within which one out of possession must sue to recover land or chattels. Acquisition of title by adverse possession (limitation title) has been an issue in a tremendous number of cases involving land, but rarely has been raised in cases involving chattels. Some of the land cases are reported in this book at page 1392, et seq.

CHAPIN v. FREELAND

Supreme Judicial Court of Massachusetts, 1886.
142 Mass. 383, 8 N.E. 128, 56 Am.Rep. 701.

HOLMES, J. This is an action of replevin for two counters. There was evidence that they belonged to the defendant in 1867, when one Warner built a shop, put the counters in, nailed them to the floor, and afterwards, on January 2, 1871, mortgaged the premises to one De Witt. In April, 1879, De Witt's executors foreclosed and sold the premises to the plaintiff. The defendant took the counters from the plaintiff's possession in 1881. The court found for the defendant. Considering the bill of exceptions as a whole, we do not understand this general finding to have gone on the ground either of a special finding that the counters remained chattels for all purposes, and were not covered by the mortgage, (see Carpenter v. Walker, 140 Mass. 416; S.C., 5 N.E.Rep. 160,) or that there was a fraudulent concealment of the cause of action within Gen.St. c. 155, § 12, (Pub.St. c. 197, § 14;) but we understand the court to have ruled or assumed that although the statute would have run in favor of Warner or De Witt before the transfer to the plaintiff, that circumstances would not prevent the defendant from taking possession if she could, or entitle the plaintiff to sue her for doing so if she was the original owner.

A majority of the court are of opinion that this is not the law, and that there must be a new trial. We do not forget all that has been said and decided as to the statute of limitations going only to the remedy, especially in cases of contract. We do not even find it necessary to express an opinion as to what would be the effect of a statute like ours if a chattel, after having been held adversely for six years, was taken into another jurisdiction by the originally wrongful possessor. What we do decide is that, when the statute would be a bar to a direct proceeding by the original owner, it cannot be defeated by indirection within the jurisdiction where it is law. If he cannot replevy, he cannot take with his own hand. A title which will not sustain a declaration will not sustain a plea.

It is true that the statute in terms only limits the bringing of an action. But, whatever importance may be attached to that ancient form of words, the principle we lay down seems to us a necessary consequence of the enactment. Notwithstanding the disfavor with which the statute of limitations was formerly regarded, all the decisions or dicta which we know of, directly bearing upon the point, favor or go beyond that principle. . . .

As we understand the statutory period to have run before the plaintiff acquired the counters, we do not deem it necessary to consider what would have been the law if the plaintiff had purchased or taken the counters, within six years of the original conversion, from the person who first converted them, and the defendant had taken them after the action against the first taker had been barred, but within six years of the plaintiff's acquisition. We regard a purchaser from one against whom the remedy is already barred as entitled to stand in as good a position as his vendor. Whether a second wrongful taker would stand differently, because not privy in title, we need not discuss. . . .

Exceptions sustained.

FIELD, J. (dissenting). I am unable to assent to the opinion of the court. . . .

As the plaintiff first took possession of the counters as his own in 1881, the statute of limitations would have been no defense to him if the defendant had brought trover against him. His only defense would have been title in himself, derived from his vendors, and this title rests ultimately upon the possession of Warner. . . . The effect of the statute of limitations of real actions upon the acquisition of title to real property is carefully discussed in Langdell, Eq.Pl. § 119 et seq. Our statute of limitations of real actions (Pub.St. c. 196, § 1) provides that "no person shall commence an action for the recovery of land, nor make any entry thereon, unless within twenty years after the right to bring such action, or to make such entry, first accrued, or within twenty years after he, or those by or under whom he claims, have been seized or possessed of the premises, except as hereinafter provided." Gen.St. c. 154, § 1; Rev.St. c. 119, § 1; St.1786, c. 13; St.1807, c. 75; Commissioner's Notes to Rev.St. c. 119. As writs of right and of formedon, and all writs of entry except those provided by Gen.St. c. 134, were abolished, (Gen.St. c. 134, § 48; Rev.St. c. 101, § 51,) it follows that, with certain exceptions not necessary to be noticed, after 20 years from the time when the right to bring a writ of entry, or to enter upon the land, first accrued, the former owner can neither maintain any action to recover a freehold, nor enter upon the land; and as all remedy, either by action or by taking possession, is gone, his title is held to have been lost. The effect of the statute has been to extinguish the right, as well as to bar the remedy, and this is the construction given to the English statute of 3 & 4 Wm. IV. c. 27. Our statute of limitations of personal actions was taken from St. 21 Jac. I. c. 16; and this statute has been held not to extinguish the right, but only to bar the remedy. . . .

Pub.St. c. 197, § 1, is that "the following actions shall be commenced within six years after the cause of action accrues, and not afterwards: . . . Actions of replevin, and all other actions for taking, detaining, or injuring goods or chattels." There is no statute and no law prohibiting the owner of personal chattels from peaceably taking possession of them wherever he may find them. It is established in this commonwealth that a debt barred by the statute of limitations of the place of the contract is not extinguished. The statute only bars the remedy by action within the jurisdiction where the defendant has resided during the statutory period. . . . There is nothing in the statute which suggests any distinction between actions to recover chattels and actions to recover debts, and it does not purport to be a statute relating to the acquisition of title to property, but a statute prescribing the time within which certain actions shall be brought. There is not a trace to be found in our reports of the doctrine that possession of chattels for the statutory period of limitations for personal actions creates a title, and I can find no such doctrine in the English reports, or in the reports of a majority of the courts of the states of the United States.

O'KEEFFE v. SNYDER

Supreme Court of New Jersey, 1980.
83 N.J. 478, 416 A.2d 862.

POLLOCK, J.

This is an appeal from an order of the Appellate Division granting summary judgment to plaintiff, Georgia O'Keeffe, against defendant, Barry Snyder, d/b/a Princeton Gallery of Fine Art, for replevin of three small pictures painted by O'Keeffe. O'Keeffe v. Snyder, 170 N.J. Super. 75, 405 A.2d 840 (1979). In her complaint, filed in March, 1976, O'Keeffe alleged she was the owner of the paintings and that they were stolen from a New York art gallery in 1946. Snyder asserted he was a purchaser for value of the paintings, he had title by adverse possession, and O'Keeffe's action was barred by the expiration of the six-year period of limitations provided by N.J.S.A. 2A:14–1 pertaining to an action in replevin. Snyder impleaded third party defendant, Ulrich A. Frank, from whom Snyder purchased the paintings in 1975 for $35,000.

The trial court granted summary judgment for Snyder on the ground that O'Keeffe's action was barred because it was not commenced within six years of the alleged theft. The Appellate Division reversed and entered judgment for O'Keeffe. *O'Keeffe,* supra, 170 N.J. Super. at 92, 405 A.2d 840. A majority of that court concluded that the paintings were stolen, the defenses of expiration of the statute of limitations and title by adverse possession were identical, and Snyder had not proved the elements of adverse possession. Consequently, the majority ruled that O'Keeffe could still enforce her right to possession of the paintings.

The dissenting judge stated that the appropriate measurement of the period of limitation was not by analogy to adverse possession, but by application of the "discovery rule" pertaining to some statutes of limitation. He concluded that the six-year period of limitations commenced when O'Keeffe knew or should have known who unlawfully possessed the paintings, and that the matter should be remanded to determine if and when that event had occurred. Id. at 96–97, 405 A.2d 840.

We granted certification to consider not only the issues raised in the dissenting opinion, but all other issues. 81 N.J. 406, 408 A.2d 800 (1979). We reverse and remand the matter for a plenary hearing in accordance with this opinion.

The record, limited to pleadings, affidavits, answers to interrogatories, and depositions, is fraught with factual conflict. Apart from the creation of the paintings by O'Keeffe and their discovery in Snyder's gallery in 1976, the parties agree on little else.

O'Keeffe contended the paintings were stolen in 1946 from a gallery, An American Place. The gallery was operated by her late husband, the famous photographer Alfred Steiglitz.

An American Place was a cooperative undertaking of O'Keeffe and some other American artists identified by her as Marin, Hardin, Dove, Andema, and Stevens. In 1946, Steiglitz arranged an exhibit which included an O'Keeffe painting, identified as Cliffs. According to O'Keeffe, one day in March, 1946, she and Steiglitz discovered Cliffs was missing from the wall of the exhibit. O'Keeffe estimates the value of the painting at the time of the alleged theft to have been about $150.

About two weeks later, O'Keeffe noticed that two other paintings, Seaweed and Fragments, were missing from a storage room at An American Place. She did not tell anyone, even Steiglitz, about the missing paintings, since she did not want to upset him.

Before the date when O'Keeffe discovered the disappearance of Seaweed, she had already sold it (apparently for a string of amber beads) to a Mrs. Weiner, now deceased. Following the grant of the motion for summary judgment by the trial court in favor of Snyder, O'Keeffe submitted a release from the legatees of Mrs. Weiner purportedly assigning to O'Keeffe their interest in the sale.

O'Keeffe testified on depositions that at about the same time as the disappearance of her paintings, 12 or 13 miniature paintings by Marin also were stolen from An American Place. According to O'Keeffe, a man named Estrick took the Marin paintings and "maybe a few other things." Estrick distributed the Marin paintings to members of the theater world who, when confronted by Steiglitz, returned them. However, neither Steiglitz nor O'Keeffe confronted Estrick with the loss of any of the O'Keeffe paintings.

There was no evidence of a break and entry at An American Place on the dates when O'Keeffe discovered the disappearance of her paintings. Neither Steiglitz nor O'Keeffe reported them missing to the New York Police Department or any other law enforcement agency. Apparently the paintings were uninsured, and O'Keeffe did not seek reimbursement from an insurance company. Similarly, neither O'Keeffe nor Steiglitz advertised the loss of the paintings in Art News or any other publication. Nonetheless, they discussed it with associates in the art world and later O'Keeffe mentioned the loss to the director of the Art Institute of Chicago, but she did not ask him to do anything because "it wouldn't have been my way." O'Keeffe does not contend that Frank or Snyder had actual knowledge of the alleged theft.

Steiglitz died in the summer of 1946, and O'Keeffe explains she did not pursue her efforts to locate the paintings because she was settling his estate. In 1947, she retained the services of Doris Bry to help settle the estate. Bry urged O'Keeffe to report the loss of the paintings, but O'Keeffe declined because "they never got anything back by reporting it." Finally, in 1972, O'Keeffe authorized Bry to report the theft to the Art Dealers Association of America, Inc., which maintains for its members a registry of stolen paintings. The record does not indicate whether such a registry existed at the time the paintings disappeared.

In September, 1975, O'Keeffe learned that the paintings were in the Andrew Crispo Gallery in New York on consignment from Bernard Danenberg Galleries. On February 11, 1976, O'Keeffe discovered that Ulrich A. Frank had sold the paintings to Barry Snyder, d/b/a Princeton Gallery of Fine Art. She demanded their return and, following Snyder's refusal, instituted this action for replevin.

Frank traces his possession of the paintings to his father, Dr. Frank, who died in 1968. He claims there is a family relationship by marriage between his family and the Steiglitz family, a contention that O'Keeffe disputes. Frank does not know how his father acquired the paintings, but he recalls seeing them in his father's apartment in New Hampshire as early as 1941–1943, a period that precedes the alleged theft. Consequently, Frank's factual contentions are inconsistent with O'Keeffe's allegation of theft. Until 1965, Dr. Frank occasionally lent the paintings to Ulrich Frank. In 1965, Dr. and Mrs. Frank formally gave the paintings to Ulrich Frank, who kept them in his residences in Yardley, Pennsylvania and Princeton, New Jersey. In 1968, he exhibited anonymously Cliffs and Fragments in a one day art show in the Jewish Community Center in Trenton. All of these events precede O'Keeffe's listing of the paintings as stolen with the Art Dealers Association of America, Inc. in 1972.

Frank claims continuous possession of the paintings through his father for over thirty years and admits selling the paintings to Snyder. Snyder and Frank do not trace their provenance, or history of possession of the paintings, back to O'Keeffe.

As indicated, Snyder moved for summary judgment on the theory that O'Keeffe's action was barred by the statute of limitations and title had vested in Frank by adverse possession. For purposes of his motion, Snyder conceded that the paintings had been stolen. On her cross motion, O'Keeffe urged that the paintings were stolen, the statute of limitations had not run, and title to the paintings remained in her. . . .

On the limited record before us, we cannot determine now who has title to the paintings. That determination will depend on the evidence adduced at trial. Nonetheless, we believe it may aid the trial court and the parties to resolve questions of law that may become relevant at trial.

Our decision begins with the principle that, generally speaking, if the paintings were stolen, the thief acquired no title and could not transfer good title to others regardless of their good faith and ignorance of the theft. Joseph v. Lesnevich, 56 N.J.Super. 340, 346, 153 A.2d 349 (App.Div.1959); Kutner Buick, Inc. v. Strelecki, 111 N.J.Super. 89, 97, 267 A.2d 549 (Ch.Div.1970); see Ashton v. Allen, 70 N.J.L. 117, 119, 56 A. 165 (Sup.Ct.1903). Proof of theft would advance O'Keeffe's right to possession of the paintings absent other considerations such as expiration of the statute of limitations.

Another issue that may become relevant at trial is whether Frank or his father acquired a "voidable title" to the paintings under N.J.S.A. 12A:2–403(1). That section, part of the Uniform Commercial Code

(U.C.C.), does not change the basic principle that a mere possessor cannot transfer good title. 2 Anderson, Uniform Commercial Code (2d ed. 1971) § 2–403:6 at 41 (*Anderson*). Nonetheless, the U.C.C. permits a person with voidable title to transfer good title to a good faith purchaser for value in certain circumstances. N.J.S.A. 12A:2–403(1). If the facts developed at trial merit application of that section, then Frank may have transferred good title to Snyder, thereby providing a defense to O'Keeffe's action. No party on this appeal has urged factual or legal contentions concerning the applicability of the U.C.C. Consequently, a more complete discussion of the U.C.C. would be premature, particularly in light of our decision to remand the matter for trial.

On this appeal, the critical legal question is when O'Keeffe's cause of action accrued. The fulcrum on which the outcome turns is the statute of limitations in N.J.S.A. 2A:14–1, which provides that an action for replevin of goods or chattels must be commenced within six years after the accrual of the cause of action.

The trial court found that O'Keeffe's cause of action accrued on the date of the alleged theft, March, 1946, and concluded that her action was barred. The Appellate Division found that an action might have accrued more than six years before the date of suit if possession by the defendant or his predecessors satisfied the elements of adverse possession. As indicated, the Appellate Division concluded that Snyder had not established those elements and that the O'Keeffe action was not barred by the statute of limitations.

Since the alleged theft occurred in New York, a preliminary question is whether the statute of limitations of New York or New Jersey applies. The New York statute, N.Y.Civ.Prac.Law § 214 (McKinney), has been interpreted so that the statute of limitations on a cause of action for replevin does not begin to run until after refusal upon demand for the return of the goods. . . . Here, O'Keeffe demanded return of the paintings in February, 1976. If the New York statute applied, her action would have been commenced within the period of limitations. . . . In the present case, none of the parties resides in New York and the paintings are located in New Jersey. On the facts before us, it would appear that the appropriate statute of limitations is the law of the forum, N.J.S.A. 2A:14–1. On remand, the trial court may reconsider this issue if the parties present other relevant facts.

On the assumption that New Jersey law will apply, we shall consider significant questions raised about the interpretation of N.J.S.A. 2A:14–1. The purpose of a statute of limitations it to "stimulate to activity and punish negligence" and "promote repose by giving security and stability to human affairs". . . . A statute of limitations achieves those purposes by barring a cause of action after the statutory period. In certain instances, this Court has ruled that the literal language of a statute of limitations should yield to other considerations. . . .

To avoid harsh results from the mechanical application of the statute, the courts have developed a concept known as the discovery rule. Lopez v. Swyer, 62 N.J. 267, 273–275, 300 A.2d 563 (1973); W. Prosser, The Law of Torts, § 30 at 144–145 (4 ed. 1971); 51 Am.Jur.2d, Limitation of Actions, § 146 at 716. The discovery rule provides that, in an appropriate case, a cause of action will not accrue until the injured party discovers, or by exercise of reasonable diligence and intelligence should have discovered, facts which form the basis of a cause of action. Burd v. New Jersey Telephone Company, 76 N.J. 284, 291–292, 386 A.2d 1310 (1978). The rule is essentially a principle of equity, the purpose of which is to mitigate unjust results that otherwise might flow from strict adherence to a rule of law. *Lopez,* supra, 62 N.J. at 273–274, 300 A.2d 563. . . .

Similarly, we conclude that the discovery rule applies to an action for replevin of a painting under N.J.S.A. 2A:14–1. O'Keeffe's cause of action accrued when she first knew, or reasonably should have known through the exercise of due diligence, of the cause of action, including the identity of the possessor of the paintings. See N. Ward, Adverse Possession of Loaned or Stolen Objects—Is Possession Still 9/10ths of the Law?, published in Legal Problems of Museum Administration (ALI–ABA 1980) at 89–90. . . .

In determining whether O'Keeffe is entitled to the benefit of the discovery rule, the trial court should consider, among others, the following issues: (1) whether O'Keeffe used due diligence to recover the paintings at the time of the alleged theft and thereafter; (2) whether at the time of the alleged theft there was an effective method, other than talking to her colleagues, for O'Keeffe to alert the art world; and (3) whether registering paintings with the Art Dealers Association of America, Inc. or any other organization would put a reasonably prudent purchaser of art on constructive notice that someone other than the possessor was the true owner.

The acquisition of title to real and personal property by adverse possession is based on the expiration of a statute of limitations. R. Brown, The Law of Personal Property (3d ed. 1975), § 4.1 at 33 (Brown). Adverse possession does not create title by prescription apart from the statute of limitations. Walsh, Title by Adverse Possession, 17 N.Y. U.L.Q.Rev. 44, 82 (1939) (Walsh); see Developments in the Law—Statutes of Limitations, 63 Harv.L.Rev. 1177 (1950) (*Developments*).

To establish title by adverse possession to chattels, the rule of law has been that the possession must be hostile, actual, visible, exclusive, and continuous. Redmond v. New Jersey Historical Society, 132 N.J. Eq. 464, 474, 28 A.2d 189 (E. & A.1942); 54 C.J.S. Limitations of Actions § 119 at 23. *Redmond* involved a portrait of Captain James Lawrence by Gilbert Stuart, which was bequeathed by its owner to her son with a provision that if he should die leaving no descendants, it should go to the New Jersey Historical Society. The owner died in 1887, when her son was 14, and her executors delivered the painting to the Historical Society. The painting remained in the possession of the Historical Society for over 50 years, until 1938, when the son died and his children, the legatees under his will, demanded its return. The Historical Society refused, and the legatees instituted a replevin action.

The Historical Society argued that the applicable statute of limitations, the predecessor of N.J.S.A. 2A:14–1, had run and that plaintiffs' action was barred. The Court of Errors and Appeals held that the doctrine of adverse possession applied to chattels as well as to real property, *Redmond,* supra, 132 N.J.Eq. at 473, 28 A.2d 189, and that the statute of limitations would not begin to run against the true owner until possession became adverse. Id. at 475, 28 A.2d 189. The Court found that the Historical Society had done nothing inconsistent with the theory that the painting was a "voluntary bailment or gratuitous loan" and had "utterly failed to prove that its possession of the portrait was 'adversary', 'hostile'." Id. at 474–475, 28 A.2d at 195. The Court found further that the Historical Society had not asserted ownership until 1938, when it refused to deliver the painting to plaintiff, and that the statute did not begin to run until that date. Consequently, the Court ordered the painting to be returned to plaintiffs.

The only other New Jersey case applying adverse possession to chattels is Joseph v. Lesnevich, 56 N.J.Super. 340, 153 A.2d 349 (App. Div.1949). In *Lesnevich,* several negotiable bearer bonds were stolen from plaintiff in 1951. In October, 1951, Lesnevich received an envelope containing the bonds. On October 21, 1951, Lesnevich and his business partner pledged the bonds with a credit company. They failed to pay the loan secured by the bonds and requested the credit company to sell the bonds to pay the loan. On August 1, 1952, the president of the credit company purchased the bonds and sold them to his son. In 1958, within one day of the expiration of six years from the date of the purchase, the owner of the bonds sued the credit company and its president, among others, for conversion of the bonds. The Appellate Division found that the credit company and its president held the bonds "as openly and notoriously as the nature of the property would permit". *Lesnevich,* supra, 56 N.J.Super. at 355, 153 A.2d at 357. The pledge of the bonds with the credit company was considered to be open possession.

As *Lesnevich* demonstrates, there is an inherent problem with many kinds of personal property that will raise questions whether their possession has been open, visible, and notorious. In *Lesnevich,* the court strained to conclude that in holding bonds as collateral, a credit company satisfied the requirement of open, visible, and notorious possession.

Other problems with the requirement of visible, open, and notorious possession readily come to mind. For example, if jewelry is stolen from a municipality in one county in New Jersey, it is unlikely that the owner would learn that someone is openly wearing that jewelry in another county or even in the same municipality. Open and visible possession of personal property, such as jewelry, may not be sufficient to put the original owner on actual or constructive notice of the identity of the possessor.

The problem is even more acute with works of art. Like many kinds of personal property, works of art are readily moved and easily concealed. O'Keeffe argues that nothing short of public display should be sufficient to alert the true owner and start the statute running. Although there is merit in that contention from the perspective of the original owner, the effect is to impose a heavy burden on the purchasers of paintings who wish to enjoy the paintings in the privacy of their homes.

In the present case, the trial court and Appellate Division concluded that the paintings, which allegedly had been kept in the private residences of the Frank family, had not been held visibly, openly, and notoriously. Notwithstanding that conclusion, the trial court ruled that the statute of limitations began to run at the time of the theft and had expired before the commencement of suit. The Appellate Division determined it was bound by the rules in *Redmond* and reversed the trial court on the theory that the defenses of adverse possession and expiration of the statute of limitations were identical. Nonetheless, for different reasons, the majority and dissenting judges in the Appellate Division acknowledged deficiencies in identifying the statute of limitations with adverse possession. The majority stated that, as a practical matter, requiring compliance with adverse possession would preclude barring stale claims and acquiring title to personal property. *O'Keeffe,* supra, 170 N.J.Super. at 86, 405 A.2d 840. The dissenting judge feared that identifying the statutes of limitations with adverse possession would lead to a "handbook for larceny". Id. at 96, 405 A.2d 840. The divergent conclusions of the lower courts suggest that the doctrine of adverse possession no longer provides a fair and reasonable means of resolving this kind of dispute.

The problem is serious. According to an affidavit submitted in this matter by the president of the International Foundation for Art Research, there has been an "explosion in art thefts" and there is a "worldwide phenomenon of art theft which has reached epidemic proportions."

The limited record before us provides a brief glimpse into the arcane world of sales of art, where paintings worth vast sums of money sometimes are bought without inquiry about their provenance. There does not appear to be a reasonably available method for an owner of art to record the ownership or theft of paintings. Similarly, there are no reasonable means readily available to a purchaser to ascertain the provenance of a painting. It may be time for the art world to establish a means by which a good faith purchaser may reasonably obtain the provenance of a painting. An efficient registry of original works of art might better serve the interests of artists, owners of art, and bona fide purchasers than the law of adverse possession with all of its uncertainties. L. DuBoff, The Deskbook of Art Law at 470–472 (Fed.Pub.Inc. 1977). Although we cannot mandate the initiation of a registration system, we can develop a rule for the commencement and running of the statute of limitations that is more responsive to the needs of the art world than the doctrine of adverse possession.

We are persuaded that the introduction of equitable considerations through the discovery rule provides a more satisfactory response than the doctrine of adverse possession. The discovery rule shifts the emphasis from the conduct of the possessor to the conduct of the owner. The focus of the inquiry will no longer be whether the possessor has met the tests of adverse possession, but whether the owner has acted with due diligence in pursuing his or her personal property.

For example, under the discovery rule, if an artist diligently seeks the recovery of a lost or stolen painting, but cannot find it or discover the identity of the possessor, the statute of limitations will not begin to run. The rule permits an artist who uses reasonable efforts to report, investigate, and recover a painting to preserve the rights of title and possession.

Properly interpreted, the discovery rule becomes a vehicle for transporting equitable considerations into the statute of limitations for replevin, N.J.S.A. 2A:14–1. In determining whether the discovery rule should apply, a court should identify, evaluate, and weigh the equitable claims of all parties. *Lopez,* supra, 62 N.J. at 274, 300 A.2d 563. If a chattel is concealed from the true owner, fairness compels tolling the statute during the period of concealment. See *Lopez,* supra, 62 N.J. at 275 n. 2, 300 A.2d 563; *Developments,* supra, 1220 (1950). That conclusion is consistent with tolling the statute of limitations in a medical malpractice action where the physician is guilty of fraudulent concealment. See Tortorello v. Reinfeld, 6 N.J. 58, 67, 77 A.2d 240 (1950); Bauer v. Bowen, 63 N.J.Super. 225, 164 A.2d 357 (App.Div.1960).

It is consistent also with the law of replevin as it has developed apart from the discovery rule. In an action for replevin, the period of limitations ordinarily will run against the owner of lost or stolen property from the time of the wrongful taking, absent fraud or concealment. Where the chattel is fraudulently concealed, the general rule is that the statute is tolled. 51 Am.Jur.2d, Limitation of Actions, § 124 at 693; 54 C.J.S. Limitations of Actions, § 119 at 23; Annotation, "When statute of limitations commences to run against action to recover, or for conversion of, property stolen or otherwise wrongfully taken," 136 A.L.R. 658, 661–665 (1942); see Dawson, Fraudulent Concealment and Statutes of Limitation, 31 Mich.L.Rev. 875 (1933); Annotation, "What constitutes concealment which will prevent running of statutes of limitations," 173 A.L.R. 576 (1948); Annotation, "When statute of limitations begins to run against action for conversion of property by theft," 79 A.L.R.3d 847, § 3 at 853 (1975); see also Dawson, Estoppel and Statutes of Limitation, 34 Mich.L.Rev. 1, 23–24 (1935).

A purchaser from a private party would be well-advised to inquire whether a work of art has been reported as lost or stolen. However, a bona fide purchaser who purchases in the ordinary course of business a painting entrusted to an art dealer should be able to acquire good title against the true owner. Under the U.C.C. entrusting possession of goods to a merchant who deals in that kind of goods gives the merchant the power to transfer all the rights of the entruster to a buyer in the ordinary course of business. N.J.S.A. 12A:2–403(2). In a transaction under that statute, a merchant may vest good title in the buyer as against the original owner. See *Anderson,* supra, § 2–403:17 et seq. The interplay between the statute of limitations as modified by the discovery rule and the U.C.C. should encourage good faith purchases from legitimate art dealers and discourage trafficking in stolen art without frustrating an artist's ability to recover stolen art works.

The discovery rule will fulfill the purposes of a statute of limitations and accord greater protection to the innocent owner of personal property whose goods are lost or stolen. Accordingly, we overrule Redmond v. New Jersey Historical Society, supra, and Joseph v. Lesnevich, supra, to the extent that they hold that the doctrine of adverse possession applies to chattels.

By diligently pursuing their goods, owners may prevent the statute of limitations from running. The meaning of due diligence will vary with the facts of each case, including the nature and value of the personal property. For example, with respect to jewelry of moderate value, it may be sufficient if the owner reports the theft to the police. With respect to art work of greater value, it may be reasonable to expect an owner to do more. In practice, our ruling should contribute to more careful practices concerning the purchase of art.

The considerations are different with real estate, and there is no reason to disturb the application of the doctrine of adverse possession to real estate. Real estate is fixed and cannot be moved or concealed. The owner of real property knows or should know where his property is located and reasonably can be expected to be aware of open, notorious, visible, hostile, continuous acts of possession on it.

Our ruling not only changes the requirements for acquiring title to personal property after an alleged unlawful taking, but also shifts the burden of proof at trial. Under the doctrine of adverse possession, the burden is on the possessor to prove the elements of adverse possession. Wilomay Holding Co. v. Peninsula Land Co., 36 N.J.Super. 440, 443, 116 A.2d 484 (App.Div.1955), certif. den. 19 N.J. 618, 118 A.2d 128 (1955). Under the discovery rule, the burden is on the owner as the one seeking the benefit of the rule to establish facts that would justify deferring the beginning of the period of limitations. See *Lopez,* supra, 62 N.J. at 276, 300 A.2d 563.

Read literally, the effect of the expiration of the statute of limitations under N.J.S.A. 2A:14–1 is to bar an action such as replevin. The statute does not speak of divesting the original owner of title. By its terms the statute cuts off the remedy, but not the right of title. Nonetheless, the effect of the expiration of the statute of limitations, albeit on the theory of adverse possession, has been not only to bar an action for possession, but also to vest title in the possessor. There is no reason to change that result although the discovery rule has replaced adverse possession. History, reason, and common sense support the conclusion that the expiration of the statute of limitations bars the remedy to recover possession and also vests title in the possessor. . . .

Before the expiration of the statute, the possessor has both the chattel and the right to keep it except as against the true owner. The only imperfection in the possessor's right to retain the chattel is the original owner's right to repossess it. Once that imperfection is removed, the possessor should have good title for all purposes. Ames,

The Disseisin of Chattels, 3 Harv.L.Rev. 313, 321 (1890) (Ames). As Dean Ames wrote: "An immortal right to bring an eternally prohibited action is a metaphysical subtlety that the present writer cannot pretend to understand." Id. at 319.

Recognizing a metaphysical notion of title in the owner would be of little benefit to him or her and would create potential problems for the possessor and third parties. The expiration of the six-year period of N.J.S.A. 2A:14–1 should vest title as effectively under the discovery rule as under the doctrine of adverse possession.

Our construction of N.J.S.A. 2A:14–1 is consistent with the construction of N.J.S.A. 2A:14–6, one of the statutes pertaining to title by adverse possession of real estate. That statute recites that one with right or title of entry into real estate shall make such entry within 20 years after the accrual of the right or be barred. It does not expressly state that the expiration of 20 years vests title in the possessor. Two other statutes pertaining to the adverse possession of real estate, N.J. S.A. 2A:14–30 and 31, expressly state that adverse possession for the statutory period shall vest title in the possessor. Notwithstanding the difference in wording between N.J.S.A. 2A:14–6 and N.J.S.A. 2A:14–30 and 31, the former statute has always been construed as vesting title in the adverse possessor at the end of the statutory period. See, e.g., Braue v. Fleck, 23 N.J. 1, 16, 127 A.2d 1 (1956).

To summarize, the operative fact that divests the original owner of title to either personal or real property is the expiration of the period of limitations. In the past, adverse possession has described the nature of the conduct that will vest title of a chattel at the end of the statutory period. Our adoption of the discovery rule does not change the conclusion that at the end of the statutory period title will vest in the possessor.

We next consider the effect of transfers of a chattel from one possessor to another during the period of limitation under the discovery rule. . . .

The majority and better view is to permit tacking, the accumulation of consecutive periods of possession by parties in privity with each other. . . .

Treating subsequent transfers as separate acts of conversion could lead to absurd results. As explained by Dean Ames:

> The decisions in the case of chattels are few. As a matter of principle, it is submitted this rule of tacking is as applicable to chattels as to land. A denial of the right to tack would, furthermore, lead to this result. If a converter were to sell the chattel, five years after its conversion, to one ignorant of the seller's tort, the disposed owner's right to recover the chattel from the purchaser would continue five years longer than his right to recover from the converter would have lasted if there had been no sale. In other words, an innocent purchaser from a wrong-doer would be in a worse position than the wrong-doer himself,—a conclusion as shocking in point of justice as it would be anomalous in law. [Ames, supra at 323, footnotes omitted]

It is more sensible to recognize that on expiration of the period of limitations, title passes from the former owner by operation of the statute. Needless uncertainty would result from starting the statute running anew merely because of a subsequent transfer. 3 American Law of Property, § 15.16 at 837. It is not necessary to strain equitable principles, as suggested by the dissent, to arrive at a just and reasonable determination of the rights of the parties. The discovery rule permits an equitable accommodation of the rights of the parties without establishing a rule of law fraught with uncertainty. . . .

We reverse the judgment of the Appellate Division in favor of O'Keeffe and remand the matter for trial in accordance with this opinion.

[The dissenting opinions of Sullivan, J., and Handler, J., are omitted.]

NOTES

1. "[A]ll but universally in the United States the expiration of the statutory period has the effect, not only of barring the legal remedy, but also of extinguishing the owner's title and of transferring it to the adverse possessor or possessors." R. Brown on Personal Property 33 (3d ed. W. Raushenbush 1975). Would you expect to see other courts move to the O'Keeffe v. Snyder position? Can the concerns of the court in that case be satisfied without jettisoning adverse possession?

2. Can title to intangible interests be acquired by adverse possession? Cases so hold. One is Gee v. CBS, Inc., 471 F.Supp. 600 (E.D.Pa. 1979), affirmed 612 F.2d 572 (3d Cir.1979). This was a multifaceted suit brought against CBS by the estate of Bessie Smith, the famous singer and composer ("Empress of the Blues"). One allegation was that a recording by Bessie Smith of "At the Christmas Ball" was her property and had been misappropriated by CBS, which issued it after Bessie Smith's death. It was first issued in 1951 and reissued in 1972. The court had no difficulty concluding that the cause of action for the 1951 issue was barred by statutes of limitation. But if the 1972 reissue was actionable, the suit based upon it might not be barred. The court held that CBS had acquired title to Bessie Smith's performance of this work by adverse possession prior to 1972. The court deemed it significant that the record jacket bore the statement that the recording was "the property of Columbia Records." Other matters related to the claim of limitation title were addressed by the court as follows, at page 656:

> "This assertion of ownership, followed by issuance of 'At the Christmas Ball' as one of the 160 recordings referred to, was also clearly 'hostile' in the sense that the issuance of the record was not consented to by Bessie Smith's estate. Moreover, not only did Columbia assert a claim of ownership, but it took actual possession of the recording in the only meaningful sense it could: by distributing the record and retaining for itself all monies received therefrom. Indeed our only real question is whether defendants' actions were 'continuous' and 'uninterrupted' during the entire statutory period—three years in New York, six in Pennsylvania. While that

concept has a readily ascertainable meaning in the case of land or tangible personalty like chattels, it is not obvious what constitutes 'continuous' and 'uninterrupted' use in the case of a singing performance embodied in a record. One criterion would be how long defendants continued to receive money from the sale of the record. Another criterion would be how long the record was listed in the record company's catalogue as available for distribution. Another possibility would be to focus on whether the 1951 four volume album became part of the permanent collection of libraries, including the Library of Congress. In that event, the duration of its listing in library catalogues might be dispositive."

3. A claim of limitation title to two Albrecht Durer paintings failed because the court applied the New York rule that an innocent purchaser of stolen goods becomes a wrongdoer only after refusing the owner's demand for their return. Kunstsammlungen Zu Weimar v. Elicofon, 678 F.2d 1150 (2d Cir.1982).

Chapter 10

IMPROVING ANOTHER'S PROPERTY BY MISTAKE (ACCESSION)

WETHERBEE v. GREEN

Supreme Court of Michigan, 1871.
22 Mich. 311, 7 Am.Rep. 653.

COOLEY, J. The defendants in error replevied of Wetherbee a quantity of hoops, which he had made from timber cut upon their land. . . . Wetherbee claimed that replevin could not be maintained for the hoops, because he had cut the timber in good faith, relying upon a permission which he supposed proceeded from the parties having lawful right to give it, and had, by the expenditure of his labor and money, converted the trees into chattels immensely more valuable than they were as they stood in the forest, and thereby he had made such chattels his own. And he offered to show that the standing timber was worth twenty-five dollars only, while the hoops replevied were shown by the evidence to be worth near seven hundred dollars. . . . The evidence offered to establish these facts was rejected by the court, and the plaintiffs obtained judgment.

The principal question which, from this statement, appears to be presented by the record, may be stated thus: Has a party who has taken the property of another in good faith, and in reliance upon a supposed right, without intention to commit wrong, and by the expenditure of his money or labor, worked upon it so great a transformation as that which this timber underwent in being transformed from standing trees into hoops, acquired such a property therein that it cannot be followed into his hands and reclaimed by the owner of the trees in its improved condition?

The objections to allowing the owner of the trees to reclaim the property under such circumstances are, that it visits the involuntary wrong-doer too severely for his unintentional trespass, and at the same time compensates the owner beyond all reason for the injury he has sustained. In the redress of private injuries the law aims not so much to punish the wrong-doer as to compensate the sufferer for his injuries; and the cases in which it goes farther and inflicts punitory or vindictive penalties are those in which the wrong-doer has committed the wrong recklessly, willfully, or maliciously, and under circumstances presenting elements of aggravation. Where vicious motive or reckless disregard of right are not involved, to inflict upon a person who has taken the property of another, a penalty equal to twenty or thirty times its value, and to compensate the owner in a proportion equally enormous, is so opposed to all legal idea of justice and right and to the rules which regulate the recovery of damages generally, that if permitted by the law at all, it must stand out as an anomaly and must rest upon peculiar reasons.

As a general rule, one whose property has been appropriated by another without authority has a right to follow it and recover the possession from any one who may have received it; and if, in the meantime, it has been increased in value by the addition of labor or money, the owner may, nevertheless, reclaim it, provided there has been no destruction of substantial identity. So far the authorities are agreed. A man cannot generally be deprived of his property except by his own voluntary act or by operation of law; and if unauthorized parties have bestowed expense or labor upon it that fact cannot constitute a bar to his reclaiming it, so long as identification is not impracticable. But there must, nevertheless, in reason be some limit to the right to follow and reclaim materials which have undergone a process of manufacture. Mr. Justice Blackstone lays down the rule very broadly, that if a thing is changed into a different species, as by making wine out of another's grapes, oil from his olives, or bread from his wheat, the product belongs to the new operator, who is only to make satisfaction to the former proprietor for the materials converted. 2 Bl. Com. 404. We do not understand this to be disputed as a general proposition, though there are some authorities which hold that, in the case of a willful appropriation, no extent of conversion can give to the willful trespasser a title to the property so long as the original materials can be traced in the improved article. The distinction thus made between the case of an appropriation in good faith and one based on intentional wrong, appears to have come from the civil law, which would not suffer a party to acquire a title by accession, founded on his own act, unless he had taken the materials in ignorance of the true owner, and given them a form which precluded their being restored to their original condition. 2 Kent 363. While many cases have followed the rule as broadly stated by Blackstone, others have adopted the severe rule of the civil law where the conversion was in willful disregard of right. . . .

The cases of confusion of goods are closely analogous. It has always been held that he who, without fraud, intentional wrong, or reckless disregard of the rights of others, mingled his goods with those of another person, in such manner that they could not be distinguished, should, nevertheless, be protected in his ownership so far as the circumstances would permit. The question of motive here becomes of the highest importance; for, as Chancellor Kent says, if the commingling of property "was willfully made without mutual consent, . . . the common law gave the entire property, without any account, to him whose property was originally invaded, and its distinct character destroyed. Popham's Rep. 38, pl. 2. If A willfully intermix his corn or hay with that of B, or casts his gold into another's crucible, so that it becomes impossible to distinguish what belonged to A from what belonged to B, the whole belongs to B. . . ."

The important question on this branch of the case appears to us to be, whether standing trees, when cut and manufactured into hoops, are to be regarded as so far changed in character that their identity can be said to be destroyed within the meaning of the authorities. And as we enter upon a discussion of this question, it is evident at once, that it is difficult, if not impossible, to discover any invariable and satisfactory test which can be applied to all the cases which arise in such infinite variety. "If grain be taken and made into malt, or money taken and made into a cup, or timber taken and made into a house, it is held in the old English law that the property is so altered as to change the title. . . ." But cloth made into garments, leather into shoes, trees hewn or sawed into timber, and iron made into bars, it is said may be reclaimed by the owner in their new and original shape. . . . Some of the cases place the right of the former owner to take the thing in its altered condition upon the question whether its identity could be made out by the senses. . . . But this is obviously a very unsatisfactory test, and in many cases would wholly defeat the purpose which the law has in view in recognizing a change of title in any of these cases. That purpose is not to establish any arbitrary distinctions, based upon mere physical reasons, but to adjust the redress afforded to the one party and the penalty inflicted upon the other, as near as circumstances will permit, to the rules of substantial justice.

It may often happen that no difficulty will be experienced in determining the identity of a piece of timber which has been taken and built into a house; but no one disputes that the right of the original owner is gone in such a case. A particular piece of wood might perhaps be traced without trouble into a church organ, or other equally valuable article; but no one would defend a rule of law which, because the identity could be determined by the senses, would permit the owner of the wood to appropriate a musical instrument, a hundred or a thousand times the value of his original materials, when the party who, under like circumstances, has doubled the value of another man's corn by converting it into malt, is permitted to retain it, and held liable for the original value only. Such distinctions in the law would be without reason, and could not be tolerated. When the right to the improved article is the point in issue, the question, how much the property or labor of each has contributed to make it what it is, must always be one of first importance. The owner of a beam built into the house of another loses his property in it, because the beam is insignificant in value or importance as compared to that to which it has become attached, and the musical instrument belongs to the maker rather than to the man whose timber was used in making it, not because the timber cannot be identified, but because in bringing it to its present condition the value of the labor has swallowed up and rendered insignificant the value of the original materials. The labor, in the case of the musical instrument, is just as much the principal thing as the house is in the other case instanced; the timber appropriated is in each case comparatively unimportant.

No test which satisfies the reason of the law can be applied in the adjustment of questions of title to chattels by accession, unless it keeps in view the circumstance of relative values. When we bear in mind the fact that what the law aims at is the accomplishment of substantial equity, we shall readily perceive that the fact of the value of the materials having been increased a hundred fold, is of more importance in the adjustment than any chemical change or mechanical transformation, which, however radical, neither is expensive to the party making it, nor adds materially to the value. There may be complete changes with so little improvement in value, that there could be no hardship in giving the owner of the original materials the improved article; but in the present case, where the defendant's labor—if he shall succeed in sustaining his offer of testimony—will appear to have given the timber in its present condition nearly all its value, all the grounds of equity exist which influence the courts in recognizing a change of title under any circumstances.

We are of opinion that the court erred in rejecting the testimony offered. The defendant, we think, had a right to show that he had manufactured the hoops in good faith, and in the belief that he had the proper authority to do so; and if he should succeed in making that showing, he was entitled to have the jury instructed that the title to the timber was changed by a substantial change of identity, and that the remedy of the plaintiff was an action to recover damages for the unintentional trespass. . . .

For the reasons given, the judgment must be reversed, with costs, and a new trial ordered.

NOTE

Compare confusion of goods. C mixes C's logs, grain, oil, gas or other fungible goods with like goods owned by V. Would C gain title to the whole if the commingling was innocent and if C's share is many times more valuable than V's? No, but C may lose title to C's goods. See R. Brown, Personal Property 62–75 (3d ed. W. Raushenbush 1975). A strict view would require C to identify C's goods, which of course C could not do. C probably would be able to recover the value of that portion of the mass which C can prove C contributed. See Humble Oil & Refining Co. v. West, 508 S.W.2d 812 (Tex.1974). Should C be allowed to do so if the commingling was negligent or in bad faith? Yes, according to Somers v. Kane, 168 Minn. 420, 210 N.W. 287 (1926). Conceding that defendant had commingled in bad faith, "there should not be so drastic a result as the verdict brings. The logs of the plaintiff could not be identified, log for log, after their mingling with those of the defendants, but their relative amount and value could be found with approximate correctness. The law intends compensation for wrong done, and not a penalty, except when a statute for reasons of policy chooses to have it so, and in the few instances where, apart from statute, it allows a jury to add punitive damages by way of discouraging arbitrary or malicious wrong. The plaintiff is compensated if he gets the equivalent of his own. The defendants should not be required, as a punishment, to lose all, nor should the plaintiff be rewarded by giving him all. . . .

"It was reasonably possible to put the plaintiff in as good a position as he would have been in if the logs had not been intermingled. True, there would be some difficulty and some uncertainty, but not more than we meet elsewhere in the ordinary administration of the law, and for practical purposes amount and relative value were ascertainable. . . .

"In making a finding of value or amount, when there has been a fraudulent confusion, every reasonable doubt is resolved in favor of the party wronged."

ISLE ROYALE MINING CO. v. HERTIN

Supreme Court of Michigan, 1877.
37 Mich. 332, 26 Am.Rep. 520.

COOLEY, C.J. The parties to this suit were owners of adjoining tracts of timbered lands. In the winter of 1873–4 defendants in error, who were plaintiffs in the court below, in consequence of a mistake respecting the actual location, went upon the lands of the mining company and cut a quantity of cord wood, which they hauled and piled on the bank of Portage Lake. The next spring the wood was taken possession of by the mining company, and disposed of for its own purposes. The wood on the bank of the lake was worth $2.87½ per cord, and the value of the labor expended by plaintiffs in cutting and placing it there was $1.87½ per cord. It was not clearly shown that the mining company had knowledge of the cutting and hauling by the plaintiffs while it was in progress. After the mining company had taken possession of the wood, plaintiffs brought this suit. [The plaintiffs sought the value of their labor. A quotation from the declaration is omitted.]

The circuit judge instructed the jury as follows:

"If you find that the plaintiffs cut the wood from defendant's land by mistake and without any willful negligence or wrong, I then charge you that the plaintiffs are entitled to recover from the defendant the reasonable cost of cutting, hauling and piling the same." This presents the only question it is necessary to consider on this record. The jury returned a verdict for the plaintiffs.

Some facts appear by the record which might perhaps have warranted the circuit judge in submitting to the jury the question whether the proper authorities of the mining company were not aware that the wood was being cut by the plaintiffs under an honest mistake as to their rights, and were not placed by that knowledge under obligation to notify the plaintiffs of their error. But as the case was put to the jury, the question presented by the record is a narrow question of law, which may be stated as follows: whether, where one in an honest mistake regarding his rights in good faith performs labor on the property of another, the benefit of which is appropriated by the owner, the person performing such labor is not entitled to be compensated therefor to the extent of the benefit received by the owner therefrom? The affirmative of this proposition the plaintiffs undertook to support, having first laid the foundation for it by showing the cutting of the wood under an honest mistake as to the location of their land, the taking possession of the wood afterwards by the mining company, and its value in the condition in which it then was and where it was, as compared with its value standing in the woods.

We understand it to be admitted by the plaintiffs that no authority can be found in support of the proposition thus stated. It is conceded that at the common law when one thus goes upon the land of another on an assumption of ownership, though in perfect good faith and under honest mistake as to his rights, he may be held responsible as a trespasser. His good faith does not excuse him from the payment of damages, the law requiring him at his peril to ascertain what his rights are, and not to invade the possession, actual or constructive, of another. If he cannot thus protect himself from the payment of damages, still less, it would seem, can he establish in himself any affirmative rights, based upon his unlawful, though unintentional encroachment upon the rights of another. Such is unquestionably the rule of the common law, and such it is admitted to be.

It is said, however, that an exception to this rule is admitted under certain circumstances, and that a trespasser is even permitted to make title in himself to the property of another, where in good faith he has expended his own labor upon it, under circumstances which would render it grossly unjust to permit the other party to appropriate the benefit of such labor. The doctrine here invoked is the familiar one of title by accession, and though it is not claimed that the present case is strictly within it, it is insisted that it is within its equity, and that there would be no departure from settled principles in giving these plaintiffs the benefit of it. . . .

But there is no such disparity in value between the standing trees and the cord wood in this case as was found to exist between the trees and the hoops in Wetherbee v. Green. The trees are not only susceptible of being traced and identified in the wood, but the difference in value between the two is not so great but that it is conceivable the owner may have preferred the trees standing to the wood cut. The cord wood has a higher market value, but the owner may have chosen not to cut it, expecting to make some other use of the trees than for fuel, or anticipating a considerable rise in value if they were allowed to grow. It cannot be assumed as a rule that a man prefers his trees cut into cord wood rather than left standing, and if his right to leave them uncut is interfered with even by mistake, it is manifestly just that the consequences should fall upon the person committing the mistake, and not upon him. Nothing could more encourage carelessness than the acceptance of the principle that one who by mistake performs labor upon the property of another should lose nothing by his error, but should have a claim upon the owner for remuneration. Why should one be vigilant and careful of the rights of others if such were the law? Whether mistaken or not is all the same to him, for in either case he has employment and receives his remuneration; while the inconveniences, if any, are left to rest with the innocent owner. Such a doctrine offers a premium to heedlessness and blunders, and a temptation by false evidence to give an intentional trespass the appearance of an innocent mistake.

A case could seldom arise in which the claim to compensation could be more favorably presented by the facts than it is in this, since it is highly probable that the defendant would suffer neither hardship nor inconvenience if compelled to pay the plaintiffs for their labor. But a general principle is to be tested, not by its operation in an individual case, but by its general workings. If a mechanic employed to alter over one man's dwelling house, shall by mistake go to another which happens to be unoccupied, and before his mistake is discovered, at a large expenditure of labor shall thoroughly overhaul and change it, will it be said that the owner, who did not desire his house disturbed, must either abandon it altogether, or if he takes possession, must pay for labor expended upon it which he neither contracted for, desired nor consented to? And if so, what bounds can be prescribed to which the application of this doctrine can be limited? The man who by mistake carries off the property of another will next be demanding payment for the transportation; and the only person reasonably secure against demands he has never assented to create, will be the person who, possessing nothing, is thereby protected against anything being accidentally improved by another at his cost and to his ruin.

The judgment of the circuit court must be reversed, with costs, and a new trial ordered.

The other Justices concurred.

NOTE

O delivers his auto to M, a mechanic, for repairs. When the repairs are completed, is M entitled to retain possession of the auto until the charges for repairs are paid? The matter may be covered by contract or statute, but if it is not (and possibly if it is), M is entitled to retain possession of the car until the charges are paid. A limited interest—a lien—in O's car is conferred upon M by the common law. An illustrative case: Moynihan Associates, Inc. v. Hanisch, 56 Wis.2d 185, 201 N.W.2d 534 (1972). See R. Brown, Personal Property c. XIII (3d ed. W. Raushenbush 1975); G. Gilmore, Security Interests in Personal Property § 33.2 (1965).

Burroughs = D

Hardy = P

HARDY v. BURROUGHS

Supreme Court of Michigan, 1930.
251 Mich. 578, 232 N.W. 200.

CLARK, J. The trial court on motion declined to dismiss the bill of complaint and defendants have appealed. The allegations of the bill, here taken as true, are that plaintiffs constructed on lot 234 of Carton Park in Flint a dwelling house, that the lot is owned by defendants Burroughs, subject to outstanding land contract in defendants Tanhersley, that plaintiffs so constructed by mistake, that defendants Tanhersley have taken possession of the house and occupy it, that defendants decline to make any adjustment with plaintiffs, and that the value of the house is $1,250.

facts

No fraud is alleged, nor is there allegation of any conduct on the part of defendants to constitute estoppel, such as standing by and knowingly permitting plaintiffs to put up the house on the wrong lot.

It is not contended there can be recovery at law, Isle Royale Mining Co. v. Hertin, 37 Mich. 332, 26 Am.Rep. 520, and, this not being ejectment, the statute providing of compensation for improvements (section 13211, 3 Comp.Laws 1915) is not applicable. Lemerand v. Flint, etc., R. Co., 117 Mich. 309, 75 N.W. 763. If the owners had invoked the aid of the court of equity in the premises as against the builders as defendants, the court might require the owners to compensate the builders on the maxim "that he who seeks equity must do equity." Rzeppa v. Seymour, 230 Mich. 439, 203 N.W. 62. Abundant authority sanctions the exercise of the jurisdiction in such cases in favor of defendants or as auxiliary to some other relief properly cognizable in equity. Union Hall Association v. Morrison, 39 Md. 281. The question is, May the plaintiffs, the builders, sustain the bill as plaintiffs, except upon some ground of fraud or estoppel growing out of the conduct of the owners of the land, which, as has been said, is not in the case. On this question the authorities are divided. In 31 C.J. 315 it is said: "According to some authorities a bona fide occupant's right, in equity, to compensation for his improvements applies to him as defendant only, and does not give him the right to recover the value of his improvements after eviction by a direct affirmative suit against the owner of the property, although he made them innocently or through mistake, unless the owner of the land has been guilty of fraud, or of acquiescence after knowledge of his legal rights, or unless the parties have agreed upon compensation for the improvements. But according to other authorities, where an occupant in good faith has made improvements and has been evicted by the true owner, he may sue in equity for the value of his improvements without reference to any fraud or other misconduct on the part of the true owner. . . ."

In 14 R.C.L. 18, the weight of authority is recognized as in accord with the rule first stated in the above quotation. But the author of a note in 53 L.R.A. 339, after reviewing cases on both sides, aptly concludes: "And it would, indeed, seem strange that a state of facts which will furnish a perfect affirmative defense in an equity action should not constitute a cause of action, when necessary, in a suit in equity. In other words, that accident shall determine the assertion of what is a conceded equitable right."

The better reasoning is that plaintiffs may maintain this bill. It is not equitable on the facts here before us that defendants profit by plaintiffs' innocent mistake, that defendants take all and plaintiffs nothing. The fact that defendants need no relief and therefore seek none ought not to bar plaintiffs' right to relief in equity. It was said by Judge Story in Bright v. Boyd, Fed.Cas. No. 1875, 1 Story, 478: "To me it seems manifestly unjust and inequitable, thus to appropriate to one man the property and money of another, who is in no default. The argument, I am aware, is, that the moment the house is built, it belongs to the owner of the land by mere operation of law; and that he may certainly possess and enjoy his own. But this is merely stating the technical rule of law, by which the true owner seeks to hold, what, in a just sense, he never had the slightest title to, that is, the house. It is not answering the objection; but merely and dryly stating, that the law so holds. But, then, admitting this to be so, does it not furnish a strong ground why equity should interpose, and grant relief?" . . .

If, upon the hearing, plaintiffs make a case for equitable relief, it will be proper to offer to defendants by decree the privilege of taking the improvements at the fair value found by the court, or to release to plaintiffs upon their paying the fair value of the lot found by the court, and this within a reasonable time limited by decree. If defendants decline or neglect to comply therewith, conveyance to plaintiffs upon payment made may be decreed. McKelway v. Armour, supra.

No other question calls for discussion.

Affirmed. Costs to plaintiffs.

NOTES

1. Is the remedy of self-help available in such situations? Consider Producers Lumber & Supply Co. v. Olney Building Co., 333 S.W.2d 619 (Tex.Civ.App.1960). In this case, one who mistakenly built a house on another's land and, after learning of his mistake and failing to negotiate a satisfactory settlement with the landowner, demolished the house was held liable to the landowner for the value of the house and for exemplary damages. This conduct being unlawful, the court explained, the builder "cannot now come into court, with unclean hands, and seek the equitable remedy of reimbursement . . .." In a dissenting opinion, one judge observed that, had the builder sought judicial relief, one of the judicial remedies available would have been a decree allowing the builder to remove the building.

2. In a case reaching the same result as Hardy v. Burroughs, a dissenting opinion included the following passage: "This is nothing less than condemnation of private property by private parties for private use. . . . It clearly is the accepted law that as between two parties in the circumstances of this case he who made the mistake must suffer the hardship rather than he who was without fault." Caplan, J., dissenting in Somerville v. Jacobs, 153 W.Va. 613, 170 S.E.2d 805 (1969).

3. See generally, Casad, The Mistaken Improver—A Comparative Study, 19 Hastings L.J. 1039 (1968).

Chapter 11

DONATIVE TRANSFERS

The dominant concept in the law of gifts is that of "delivery" as a sine qua non for an effective transfer of ownership. The concept seems to have roots in a period of legal history when for many purposes ownership was identified with possession, when lawyers and judges found difficulty in conceiving "ownership rights" apart from "possessory rights." But whether or not this is an accurate characterization of ancestral legal thinking, the concept of delivery in present-day law can be and is analyzed and rationalized in an altogether different manner. In the ordinary lay sense "delivery" connotes a manual tradition—a handing-over or transfer of immediate possession—from one person to another of a chattel or of some symbol or instrument evidencing ownership claims concerning goods or values of many kinds—real and personal, tangible and intangible. A transfer of immediate possession may, of course, constitute delivery in the legal sense—in fact, in the great bulk of instances delivery is thus accomplished—but the legal meaning of the term embraces more. Generalizing roughly, we may say that "delivery" comprehends any acts or conduct of the donor which a court will regard as legally sufficient to manifest an intention to transfer ownership from donor to donee. This generalization puts major emphasis on *intention* and properly so in view of the overwhelming importance which our law, in all its aspects, attaches to private volition. But not every manifestation of intent to transfer ownership is regarded as legally sufficient, and thereby hangs the tale of this chapter. In some circumstances little more than a declaration is required; in others, much more (sometimes particular formalities or ceremonies) may be demanded. The thoughtful student may well inquire why a system of law so greatly honoring private volition does not accept *any* manifestation sufficient to convince an impartial, judicious finder of fact that on a given occasion a property owner intended to transfer ownership to another. The cases which follow will provide at least partial answers. Judicial opinions, however, are seldom, if ever, written in the expectation that they will be used as vehicles of legal education; hence they often do not plainly reveal as much as students should like to know about the mainsprings of the law. In view of this we suggest tentative hypothetical answers to the inquiry mentioned above and suggest that the student attempt to ascertain whether or not these answers are reflected in judicial discourse.

First, it is possible that the law of gifts to some extent effects a policy of protecting would-be donors against their own folly, against unguarded, spur-of-the-moment impulses to donate which they would subsequently rue if the sudden impulse were given irrevocable effect. In this connection, it should be observed that donative transfers, once effective, are irrevocable, except those made in contemplation of impending death; the latter, by standard doctrine, are revocable, though cases are few in which the doctrine becomes a factor. Incidentally, does the doctrine simply mean that the transfer has no legal effect until the donor dies? Is it to be distinguished from a testamentary transfer?

Second, it is possible that the law of gifts effects a policy of protecting property owners, their heirs, and their representatives against false claims of donations supported by a semblance of proof. In this connection it should be noted that the typical litigated dispute in this area is one in which the alleged donor is dead and his personal representative or a successor to his estate is contesting the alleged donee's assertion of a gift.

Third, it is possible that in shaping the law of gifts the judges have more or less consciously taken account of their distrust of the whims and vagaries of juries. Judicial opinions sometimes express doubts about the wisdom of rules sustaining the asserted transfer of an unlimited quantity of wealth through informal oral transactions unattended by safeguards designed to eliminate claims founded upon doubtful manifestations of donative intent. Insistence upon the principle that not every such manifestation shall be legally sufficient permits the elimination of many such claims without submitting them to a jury's determination and permits the judges to proceed with caution in specifying the circumstances in which disputes turning upon doubtful issues of fact shall be resolved by a jury.

IN RE COHN

Supreme Court of New York, Appellate Division, 1919.
187 App.Div. 392, 176 N.Y.S. 225.

Appeal from Surrogate's Court, New York County.

In the matter of the judicial settlement of the account of Sara Cohn and another, as executrix of and trustees under the last will and testament of Leopold Cohn, deceased. From a decree judicially settling the accounts of the executrix and trustees, Herbert Cohn and another appeal. Affirmed.

SHEARN, J. This appeal involves the validity of a gift of certificates of stock, effected by the execution and delivery of an instrument of gift, unaccompanied by actual delivery of the certificates. On September 20, 1911, the decedent, Leopold Cohn, a resident of the city of New York, but then temporarily residing with his family at West End, N.J., wrote out and delivered to his wife, in the presence of his entire family, on his wife's birthday, the following paper:

"West End, N.J., Sept. 20, 1911.

"I give this day to my wife, Sara K. Cohn, as a present for her (46th) forty-sixth birthday (500) five hundred shares of American Sumatra Tobacco Company common stock.

Leopold Cohn."

The donor died six days after the delivery of this instrument. At the time of the gift, the donor was the owner of 7,213 shares of the common stock of the American Sumatra Tobacco Company, but the stock was in the name and possession of his firm of A. Cohn & Co. and deposited in a safe deposit box in the city of New York, which was in the name of and belonged to the firm. This firm consisted of the donor, his brother, Abraham, and his nephew, Leonard A. Cohn and was dissolved by the death of Abraham Cohn on August 30, 1911. Prior to that time, the firm had 18,033 shares of the Sumatra stock, in certificates of 100 shares each, standing in the firm name. On December 20, 1910, the stock had been charged off on the books and was not an asset of the firm after that time. The testator was entitled to 40 per cent., or 7,213 shares, of the stock held in the firm name, but there had never been an actual delivery of the certificates by the firm to the donor in his lifetime. Just prior to his death the donor had agreed to enter into a new partnership, and he was to contribute some of the shares to a new firm as an asset. On September 22, 1911, two days after the delivery of the instrument of gift, the donor directed his counsel to hurry the new partnership agreement, because he wished to get the Sumatra stock belonging to him, which was to be delivered when the new partnership agreement was signed, which matter was to be closed on September 26, 1911, the day the donor died. The execution and delivery of the instrument of gift was established by the testimony of the two daughters of the donor, who were present at the time of its delivery, and their testimony is to the effect that their father handed the paper to the mother, in the presence of the whole family, and said he gave it to her as a birthday present; that he had not possession of the stock, but as soon as he got it he would give it to her.

Some stress is laid by the appellants upon the testimony that the donor "said that he could not give her the stock, because it was in the company, but as soon as he could get it he would give it to her," which it is claimed evidences an intent to make a gift in the future, instead of a present gift. This contention is completely overborne by the wording of the instrument itself, which reads, "I give this day"; also by the plain intention of the donor to make a birthday gift to his wife, the birthday being the day on which the instrument of gift was executed and delivered. When the donor explained that he could not "give" her the stock that day, "because it was in the company," and said that "as soon as he could get it he would give it to her," it is quite obvious that he meant that he could not deliver the stock that day, but would as soon as he could get it.

There being no rights of creditors involved, no suggestion of fraud, the intention to make the birthday gift being conclusively established, the gift being evidenced by an instrument of gift executed and delivered to the donee on her birthday, and ever since retained by her, and the circumstances surrounding the making of the gift affording a reasonable and satisfactory excuse for not making actual delivery of the certificates at the time the gift was made, there was in my opinion a valid and effectual gift of the certificates mentioned in the instrument of gift.

There is no doubt that it has been held in a long line of cases in this state that delivery of the thing given is, as a general rule, one of the essential elements to constitute a valid gift. Beaver v. Beaver, 117 N.Y. 421, 22 N.E. 940, 6 L.R.A. 403, 15 Am.St.Rep. 531; Young v. Young, 80 N.Y. 422, 36 Am.Rep. 634. But it is equally true that the rule requiring actual delivery is not inflexible. Matter of Van Alstyne, 207 N.Y. 298, 100 N.E. 802; McGavic v. Cossum, 72 App.Div. 35, 76 N.Y.S. 305; Matter of Mills, 172 App.Div. 530, 158 N.Y.S. 1100, affirmed 219 N.Y. 642, 114 N.E. 1072. In Beaver v. Beaver, supra, it was said that the delivery may be symbolical, as where the donor gives to the donee a symbol which represents possession. It was held in McGavic v. Cossum, supra, where an instrument of gift of bonds was delivered, that actual delivery of the bonds was excused where the only reason for not making delivery was the feeble condition of the donor and the fact that the bonds were in the custody of a bank in a nearby city. It was said in Matter of Van Alstyne: "The delivery necessary to consummate a gift must be as perfect as the nature of the property and the circumstances and surroundings of the parties will reasonably permit. . . . It is true that the old rule requiring an actual delivery of the thing given has been very largely relaxed, but a symbolical delivery is sufficient only when the conditions are so adverse to actual delivery as to make a symbolical delivery as nearly perfect and complete as the circumstances will allow."

As the rule requiring delivery is clearly subject to exceptions, in order to apply it correctly in varying circumstances resort should be had to the reason for the rule. Under the civil law delivery was not requisite to a valid gift, but it was made a requisite by the common law as a matter of public policy, to prevent mistake and imposition. . . . The necessity of delivery where gifts resting in parol are asserted against the estates of decedents is obvious; but it is equally plain that there is no such impelling necessity when the gift is established by the execution and delivery of an instrument of gift. An examination of a large number of cases in this state discloses the significant facts that (1) in every case where the gift was not sustained, the gift rested upon parol evidence; and (2) in every case of a gift evidenced by the delivery of an instrument of gift, the gift has been sustained. . . .

In Young v. Young, supra, there was a writing, but it was not an instrument of gift; it was a mere declaration of the donor that the bonds were the property of the donee and expressly reserving an interest in the donor. While the court said in Ridden v. Thrall, 125 N.Y. 572, 26 N.E. 627, 11 L.R.A. 684, 21 Am.St.Rep. 758, in sustaining a gift causa mortis, where there was both a writing and delivery, that the writing alone was not sufficient, it is to be noted that the written instrument was not delivered to the donee. It is interesting to note that in Matson v. Abbey, supra, sustaining a gift evidenced by an instrument of assignment without delivery of the property assigned, the court quotes with approval the statement of the English law in Irons v. Smallpiece, 2 Barn. & Ald. 551, 552, made by Abbott, C.J.: "I am of opinion that by the law of England, in order to transfer property by gift, there must either be a deed or instrument of gift, or there must be an actual delivery of the thing to the donee."

Based upon decisions in numerous other jurisdictions, it is stated in 20 Cyc. 1197, that: "The general rule is that a gift of property evidenced by a written instrument executed by the donor is valid without a manual delivery of the property."

I am inclined to think that this is a broader statement than the New York cases would justify, especially in view of Matter of Van Alstyne, supra, for it does not assume a delivery of the instrument of gift. But in view of the decision of this court in McGavic v. Cossum, supra, it seems to me beyond serious question that the delivery of the instrument of gift in the instant case constituted a good symbolical delivery. . . .

In the instant case, on the day the gift was made at West End, N.J., the certificates of stock were in a safe deposit box in New York City. Furthermore, there were the complications above referred to, in the partnership relations and in the fact that the certificates were in the partnership strong box, made out in the name of the firm. These were circumstances and surroundings tending to excuse manual delivery and to make a symbolical delivery effective. . . .

The instrument of gift was a symbol which represented the donee's right of possession. It was no more revocable than an assignment. A gift has been judicially defined as a voluntary transfer of property by one to another, without any consideration or compensation therefor. . . . A voluntary transfer or assignment unaccompanied by manual delivery was upheld, as we have seen, in Matson v. Abbey, supra. It must therefore have been held irrevocable. There is no apparent reason why a gift evidenced by an instrument of gift duly delivered is any more revocable than an assignment without consideration. Both strip the donor of dominion over the subject of the gift and place in the hands of the donee evidence of right to possession.

Therefore, applying the rule of delivery in the light of the reason which gave birth to it, and finding here no possibility of fraud or imposition, and no doubt whatever concerning the intention of the donor, and finding full support in the precedent of McGavic v. Cossum, supra, it is my opinion that there was a good constructive or symbolical delivery, consisting of the delivery of the instrument of gift, and that the gift should be sustained.

[The court here considered and rejected a contention that the widow's claim was bad because certain actions she had taken as executrix and trustee were inconsistent with her claim.]

The decree of the surrogate should be affirmed, with costs and disbursements to the respondents executrix and trustees, and disbursements of the special guardian, respondent. Order filed.

CLARKE, P.J., and SMITH, J., concur.

PAGE, J. (dissenting). In my opinion there was not a valid gift inter vivos of the 500 shares of stock of the American Sumatra Tobacco Company by the testator to Sara K. Cohn.

[Page, J., here stated a summary of the facts somewhat more detailed than the summary given in the majority opinion. He stated that on December 28, 1910, before the partnership was dissolved by the death of Abraham Cohn, bookkeeping entries had been made, withdrawing the American Sumatra shares from the partnership capital account and allotting them proportionately to the credit of the individual partners; that the partners did not (as they could have done) cause transfers to be made to themselves individually on the books of the issuing corporation, but allowed the certificates to remain in a safe deposit box in the firm name because this facilitated their controlling the election of directors; and that in connection with the formation of the new partnership, which was to have been consummated on the day Leopold Cohn died, it was understood that Leopold Cohn's holdings were to be kept intact so that the new partnership would have the benefit of them in controlling the election of a director. Page, J., also emphasized the daughters' testimony that Cohn had told his wife he could not give her the stock immediately but would do so as soon as he could get it.]

There was no delivery of the stock, either actual or constructive. The testator still retained dominion and control over it, for use in the business of the new copartnership. . . .

In the present case, the writing, taken alone, would seem to show the intention of the donor to make an actual present gift, for he says, "I give this day to my wife." Yet the delivery of the writing was accompanied by the statement, "that he could not give her the stock, because it was in the company, but as soon as he could get it he would give it." There is, therefore, a clearly expressed intention to give at a future day, and the acts of the testator showed an intention to retain the dominion and control of the stock, meanwhile, in himself.

A gift inter vivos has no reference to the future, while a gift causa mortis has reference to a condition subsequent. The latter, before the happening of the condition, is revocable, while the former is irrevocable. Some confusion has arisen in the cases from a failure to recognize this distinction between these two forms of gift. A gift is a voluntary transaction, without consideration. Until the donor has divested himself absolutely and irrevocably of the title, dominion, and control of the subject of the gift, he has the power to revoke, and a court of equity will not compel him to complete his gift. . . . When a chose in action has been delivered to a purchaser in good faith and for a valuable consideration, he acquires a good title in equity, although no assignment has been made, and a court of equity will compel the transfer of the legal title. There is no such right in the donee of an incomplete gift. He has paid nothing for it, and as long as the donor retains the title, dominion, or possession of the subject of the proposed gift, the donee has no standing in any court to enforce the gift. . . .

The respondent claims, however, that the delivery of this paper writing was a constructive delivery of the stock, and argues that the above rules only apply to gifts inter vivos where the evidence of the gifts rests in parol, and that, where there is a writing which evidences the donor's intention, the courts will give effect to the delivery of the writing as a constructive delivery of the subject of the gift. This, however, in my opinion, is not the law. The writing must be such as to transfer the right of possession. There may be a symbolic delivery, or there may be a constructive delivery; but, whether it be symbolic or constructive, it must be such a delivery as divests the donor with title, dominion, and right of possession, and it must be the best delivery that can be made under the circumstances of the case, having due regard to the character of the property. . . .

In the instant case there was no physical or other impossibility to the actual delivery of the stock; it stood in the name of the company, but the stock to the extent of 7,213 shares was the property of the testator, and it had been so held merely as a matter of business convenience of the old copartnership, and at the time was so held, pending the formation of a new copartnership, when it might be desirable to hold all the certificates of the stock in solido for the same business advantages. This latter consideration, in my opinion, was the controlling cause of the failure to make an immediate delivery of the stock, and the reason why the testator retained possession, dominion, and control of the certificates. . . .

I have been unable to find that the courts in this jurisdiction have held, heretofore, that it is only where a parol gift is sought to be established that delivery is essential, and that, where the intention to give is evidenced by a writing, delivery is not necessary. Among the cases cited in the prevailing opinion as tending to sustain the proposition that the requirement for delivery of the thing given is limited to oral gifts will be found cases where gifts evidenced by a writing have been declared invalid. It will also be found that many of those cases relate to gifts causa mortis, and not to gifts inter vivos. . . .

The writing given to Mrs. Cohn did not purport to assign, transfer, or set over to her the stock. It was not a deed or instrument of gift that divested the testator of possession of and dominion over the stock. That it was not intended that it should do so is clearly shown by the subsequent acts of the testator.

In my opinion the decree should be modified, by declaring the attempted gift void, and sustaining the objections to the account to that extent, and the executors and trustees be surcharged with the proceeds of the said 500 shares of stock, and that the same forms a part of the principal of the trust estate.

DOWLING, J., concurs.

NOTE

Some of the discussion in the foregoing opinions suggests that the judges were dealing with the concepts of donative intent and of delivery as two independent elements of an effective gift, and most other opinions in cases involving gifts of personalty suggest that judges are similarly thinking of "delivery" wholly in the sense of a transfer of immediate physical possession of the subject-matter. Contrast the manner in which, in dealing with transfers of land ownership, some courts have conceived the requirement that an instrument evidencing the transfer be "delivered"; a good example is a statement in Yee v. Okamoto, 45 Hawaii 445, 370 P.2d 463 (1962): "A manual or formal tradition is not indispensable to an effective delivery. . . . Historically, the legal concept of delivery had its inception in the traditional practice of making a manual transfer of the instrument, which gave rise to the expression 'delivery.' That, however, has been largely superseded by the view that delivery is basically a question of intent, there being a sufficient delivery if an intention appears that the instrument shall be legally operative. Thus, more precisely defined, delivery of a document is merely the intent of the parties to have it become legally operative at some definite point in time, however such intent may be indicated."

Quite possibly medieval judges may have adhered to the view that physical delivery of the subject-matter itself is absolutely indispensable. It is plain that judges no longer do so, but their opinions frequently suggest that where physical delivery is lacking a gift can be sustained only by invoking a fictional physical delivery of the subject-matter. Why else should we find them resorting to such superfluous abstractions as "constructive" and "symbolic" delivery? It appears that thought in this area would gain much in clarity and flexibility, with no attendant impairment of desirable policy, if it were fully recognized that physical delivery is only one of various manners in which donative intent may be made effective in law, and that "delivery" in the legal sense comprehends all these various manners. The failure to recognize this doubtless is chargeable chiefly to the fact that we have evolved no term other than "delivery," clogged with its older sense of manual tradition, to connote the broader concept. This semantic misfortune is one of many which have plagued legal thought.

The opinions in the principal case also suggest that a presently-manifested intention to transfer ownership in the future, without more, cannot be given effect whether the intention be manifested by physical delivery of the subject-matter or otherwise. Such an intention is sometimes characterized as a promise to donate, which is legally ineffective, being unsupported by consideration. The point is sufficiently self-evident—a transfer of ownership cannot be given effect unless, at the moment when it is to occur, it is sustained by the owner's properly-manifested intent. This does not necessarily mean that his prior conduct must be disregarded, for it may furnish a proper basis for an inference that at the moment transfer is to occur he has the necessary contemporaneous intent. Suppose a man hands to his niece an item of jewelry saying, "I intend that this shall be yours when you are graduated from college." If he permits her to retain the jewelry until after her graduation, may we not infer that at the moment of graduation he intends a transfer to her? Is there any sufficient reason to insist upon an additional affirmation (apart from mere inaction) at that moment?

. . .

In 1952, Gabriel Pascal Enterprises, Ltd., by agreement with the representative of George Bernard Shaw's estate, obtained an exclusive world-wide license to prepare and produce a musical version of Shaw's "Pygmalion." The license agreement provided for its termination if Pascal Enterprises did not, within fixed periods, arrange with suitable persons for the necessary composition and production. In February, 1954, Gabriel Pascal, who owned 98% of the stock issued by the licensee corporation, wrote, signed, and sent the following letter to Marianne Z. Kingman: "Dear Miss Kingman—This is to confirm to you our understanding that I give you from my shares of profits of the Pygmalion Musical stage version five per cent in England, and two percent of my shares of profits in the United States. From the film version, five percent from my profit shares all over the world. As soon as the contracts are signed, I will send a copy of this letter to my lawyer, Edwin Davies, in London, and he will confirm to you this arrangement in a legal form. This participation in my shares of profits is a present to you, in recognition for your loyal work for me as my Executive Secretary." When the letter was written, Pascal Enterprises had not fulfilled the requirements of the license agreement, but after Pascal's death in July, 1954, arrangements with Lerner, Loewe, and Levin were made, through a New York bank as temporary administrator of Pascal's estate, for the writing and production of "My Fair Lady." Its phenomenal success resulted in a suit by Marianne Z. Speelman (formerly Kingman) against the administratrix of Pascal's estate, seeking judgment for the percentages of profits mentioned in Pascal's letter. What, if anything, was given to Miss Kingman? Was the letter anything more than an unenforceable promise to make a future gift out of profits which Pascal expected to receive through contracts to be formed in the future? See Speelman v. Pascal, 10 N.Y.2d 313, 222 N.Y.S.2d 324, 178 N.E.2d 723 (1961); 11 Catholic U.L.Rev. 115 (1962); 13 Syracuse L.Rev. 481 (1962).

GRUEN v. GRUEN

Court of Appeals of New York, 1986.
68 N.Y.2d 48, 505 N.Y.S.2d 849, 496 N.E.2d 869.

SIMONS, JUDGE.

Plaintiff commenced this action seeking a declaration that he is the rightful owner of a painting which he alleges his father, now deceased, gave to him. He concedes that he has never had possession of the painting but asserts that his father made a valid gift of the title in 1963 reserving a life estate for himself. His father retained possession of the painting until he died in 1980. Defendant, plaintiff's stepmother, has the painting now and has refused plaintiff's requests that she turn it over to him. She contends that the purported gift was testamentary in nature and invalid insofar as the formalities of a will were not met or, alternatively, that a donor may not make a valid inter vivos gift of a chattel and retain a life estate with a complete right of possession. Following a seven-day nonjury trial, Special Term found that plaintiff had failed to establish any of the elements of an inter vivos gift and that in any event an attempt by a donor to retain a present possessory life estate in a chattel invalidated a purported gift of it. The Appellate Division held that a valid gift may be made reserving a life estate and, finding the elements of a gift established in this case, it reversed and remitted the matter for a determination of value (104 A.D.2d 171, 488 N.Y.S.2d 401). That determination has now been made and defendant appeals directly to this court, pursuant to CPLR 5601(d), from the subsequent final judgment entered in Supreme Court awarding plaintiff $2,500,000 in damages representing the value of the painting, plus interest. We now affirm.

The subject of the dispute is a work entitled "Schloss Kammer am Attersee II" painted by a noted Austrian modernist, Gustav Klimt. It was purchased by plaintiff's father, Victor Gruen, in 1959 for $8,000. On April 1, 1963 the elder Gruen, a successful architect with offices and residences in both New York City and Los Angeles during most of the time involved in this action, wrote a letter to plaintiff, then an undergraduate student at Harvard, stating that he was giving him the Klimt painting for his birthday but that he wished to retain the possession of it for his lifetime. . . . Plaintiff never took possession of the painting nor did he seek to do so. Except for a brief period between 1964 and 1965 when it was on loan to art exhibits and when restoration work was performed on it, the painting remained in his father's possession, moving with him from New York City to Beverly Hills and finally to Vienna, Austria, where Victor Gruen died on February 14, 1980. Following Victor's death plaintiff requested possession of the Klimt painting and when defendant refused, he commenced this action.

The issues framed for appeal are whether a valid inter vivos gift of a chattel may be made where the donor has reserved a life estate in the chattel and the donee never has had physical possession of it before the donor's death and, if it may, which factual findings on the elements of a valid inter vivos gift more nearly comport with the weight of the evidence in this case, those of Special Term or those of the Appellate Division. . . .

There is an important distinction between the intent with which an inter vivos gift is made and the intent to make a gift by will. An inter vivos gift requires that the donor intend to make an irrevocable present transfer of ownership; if the intention is to make a testamentary disposition effective only after death, the gift is invalid unless made by will.

Defendant contends that the trial court was correct in finding that Victor did not intend to transfer any present interest in the painting to plaintiff in 1963 but only expressed an intention that plaintiff was to get the painting upon his death. The evidence is all but conclusive, however, that Victor intended to transfer ownership of the painting to plaintiff in 1963 but to retain a life estate in it and that he did, therefore, effectively transfer a remainder interest in the painting to plaintiff at that time. . . . Victor made several statements orally and in writing indicating that he had previously given plaintiff the painting and that plaintiff owned it. Victor Gruen retained possession of the property, insured it, allowed others to exhibit it and made necessary repairs to it but those acts are not inconsistent with his retention of a life estate. . . .

Defendant contends that even if a present gift was intended, Victor's reservation of a lifetime interest in the painting defeated it. . . .

Defendant recognizes that a valid inter vivos gift of a remainder interest can be made not only of real property but also of such intangibles as stocks and bonds. Indeed, several of the cases she cites so hold. That being so, it is difficult to perceive any legal basis for the distinction she urges which would permit gifts of remainder interests in those properties but not of remainder interests in chattels such as the Klimt painting here. The only reason suggested is that the gift of a chattel must include a present right to possession. . . . Insofar as some of our cases purport to require that the donor intend to transfer both title and possession immediately to have a valid inter vivos gift, they state the rule too broadly and confuse the effectiveness of a gift with the transfer of the possession of the subject of that gift. . . . As long as the evidence establishes an intent to make a present and irrevocable transfer of title or the right of ownership, there is a present transfer of some interest and the gift is effective immediately. . . . Thus, in *Speelman v. Pascal,* we held valid a gift of a percentage of the future royalties to the play "My Fair Lady" before the play even existed. There, as in this case, the donee received title or the right of ownership to some property immediately upon the making of the gift but possession or enjoyment of the subject of the gift was postponed to some future time.

Defendant suggests that allowing a donor to make a present gift of a remainder with the reservation of a life estate will lead courts to effectuate otherwise invalid testamentary dispositions of property. The two have entirely different characteristics, however, which make them distinguishable. Once the gift is made it is irrevocable and the donor is limited to the rights of a life tenant not an owner. Moreover, with the gift of a remainder title vests immediately in the donee and any possession is postponed until the donor's death whereas under a will neither title nor possession vests immediately. . . .

Defendant contends that when a tangible piece of personal property such as a painting is the subject of a gift, physical delivery of the painting itself is the best form of delivery and should be required. . . . Defendant's statement of the rule as applied may be generally true, but it ignores the fact that what Victor Gruen gave plaintiff was not all rights to the Klimt painting, but only title to it with no right of possession until his death. Under these circumstances, it would be illogical for the law to require the donor to part with possession of the painting when that is exactly what he intends to retain.

. . .

Acceptance by the donee is essential to the validity of an inter vivos gift, but when a gift is of value to the donee, as it is here, the law will presume an acceptance. . . .

Judgment appealed from and order of the Appellate Division brought up for review affirmed, with costs.

FOSTER v. REISS

Supreme Court of New Jersey, 1955.
18 N.J. 41, 112 A.2d 553, 48 A.L.R.2d 1391.

[It appears that in this case the facts stated below were established by admissions of the parties or by undisputed proof. Ethel and Adam Reiss were married March 28, 1940; no children were born of their marriage, but each had children by a prior marriage. In 1940 Ethel executed a will, duly probated after her death, in which she gave one dollar to Adam and the residue of her estate to her children and grandchildren. In 1946 the two separated and in doing so executed an agreement concerning their respective rights in certain land. In 1948 they became reconciled and thereafter cohabited until 1951, when Ethel died, aged 66. Other facts are stated in the opinion below. The plaintiffs were persons responsible for carrying out Ethel Reiss's wishes concerning her estate, as evidenced by her will and by the separation agreement.]

VANDERBILT, C.J. On April 30, 1951 the decedent, Ethel Reiss, entered a hospital in New Brunswick where she was to undergo major surgery. Just prior to going to the operating room on May 4, 1951, she wrote the following note in her native Hungarian language to her husband, the defendant herein:

"My Dearest Papa:

"In the kitchen, in the bottom of the cabinet, where the blue frying pan is, under the wine bottle, there is one hundred dollars. Along side the bed in my bedroom, in the rear drawer of the small table in the corner of the drawer, where my stockings are, you will find about seventy-five dollars. In my purse there is six dollars, where the coats are. Where the coats are, in a round tin box, on the floor, where the shoes are, there is two hundred dollars. This is Dianna's. Please put it in the bank for her. This is for her schooling.

"The Building Loan book is yours, and the Bank book, and also the money that is here. In the red book is my son's and sister's and my brothers address. In the letter box is also my bank book.

"Give Margaret my sewing machine and anything else she may want; she deserves it as she was good to me.

"God be with you. God shall watch your steps. Please look out for yourself that you do not go on a bad road. I cannot stay with you. My will is in the office of the former Lawyer Anekstein, and his successor has it. There you will find out everything.

"Your kissing, loving wife,
"Ethel Reiss 1951–5–4."

She placed the note in the drawer of a table beside her bed, at the same time asking Mrs. Agnes Tekowitz, an old friend who was also confined in the hospital, to tell her husband or daughter about it—"In case my daughter come in or my husband come in, tell them they got a note over there and take the note". That afternoon, while the wife was in the operating room unconscious under the effects of ether, the defendant came to the hospital and was told about the note by the friend. He took the note from the drawer, went home, found the cash, the savings account passbook, and the building and loan book mentioned in the note, and has retained possession of them since that time.

The wife was admittedly in a coma for three days after the operation and the testimony is in dispute as to whether or not she recovered consciousness at all before her death on the ninth day. Her daughter, her son-in-law, Mrs. Waldner, an old friend and one of her executrices who visited her every day, and Mrs. Tekowitz, who was in the ward with her, said that they could not understand her and she could not understand them. The defendant, on the other hand, testified that while she was "awful poor from ether" after the operation, "the fourth, fifth and sixth days I thought she was going to get healthy again and come home. She talked just as good as I with you." The trial judge who saw the witnesses and heard the testimony found that "After the operation and until the date of her death on May 13, 1951 she was in a coma most of the time; was unable to recognize members of her family; and unable to carry on intelligent conversation. . . . Mrs. Reiss was never able to talk or converse after coming out of the operation until her death."

The decedent's will gave $1 to the defendant and the residue of her estate to her children and grandchildren. The decedent's personal representatives and her trustees under a separation agreement with the defendant, brought this action to recover the cash, the passbook, and the building and loan book from the defendant, who in turn claimed ownership of them based on an alleged gift causa mortis from his wife. The trial court granted judgment for the plaintiffs, concluding that there had been no such gift. The Appellate Division of the Superior Court reversed, 31 N.J.Super. 496, 107 A.2d 24, and we granted the plaintiffs' petition for certification to the Appellate Division, 16 N.J. 221, 108 A.2d 211.

The doctrine of donatio causa mortis was borrowed by the Roman law from the Greeks, 2 Bl.Com. 514, and ultimately became a part of English and then American common law. . . . Blackstone has said that there is a gift causa mortis "when a person in his last sickness, apprehending his dissolution near, delivers or causes to be delivered to another the possession of any personal goods, to keep in case of his decease." 2 Bl.Com. 514.

Justinian offered this definition: "A gift causa mortis is one made in expectation of death; when a person gives upon condition that, if any fatality happen to him, the receiver shall keep the article, but that if the donor should survive, or if he should change his mind, or if the donee should die first, then the donor shall have it back again. These gifts causa mortis are in all respects put upon the same footing as legacies. . . . To put it briefly, a gift causa mortis is when a person wishes that he himself should have the gift in preference to the donee, but that the donee should have it in preference to the heir." Walker's Just., at 119.

The modern description is similar: "A donatio causa mortis is a gift of personal property made by a party in expectation of death, then imminent, and upon the essential condition that the property shall belong fully to the donee in case the donor dies as anticipated, leaving the donee surviving him, and the gift is not in the meantime revoked, but not otherwise. . . . To constitute a valid gift causa mortis, it must be made in view of the donor's impending death; the owner must die of the disorder or peril; and there must be a delivery of the thing given. The donor must be competent to make the gift; there must be an intent upon his part to do so; and an acceptance by the donee. . . . The delivery must be such as is actual, unequivocal and complete during the lifetime of the donor, wholly divesting him of the possession, dominion, and control thereof." Weiss v. Fenwick, 111 N.J. Eq. 385, 387–388, 162 A. 609, 610 (E. & A.1932).

There is some doubt in the New Jersey cases as to whether as a result of a gift causa mortis the property remains in the donor until his death . . . or whether the transfer is considered absolute even though it is defeasible . . .. In any event, a gift causa mortis is essentially of a testamentary nature and as a practical matter the doctrine, though well established, is an invasion into the province of the statute of wills. . . .

The first question confronting us is whether there has been "actual, unequivocal, and complete delivery during the lifetime of the donor, wholly divesting him [her] of the possession, dominion, and control" of the property, Weiss v. Fenwick, supra. . . . In Keepers v. Fidelity Title and Deposit Co., 56 N.J.L. 302, 28 A. 585, 586, 23 L.R.A. 184 (1893), the question was whether the delivery of the key to a box containing valuable papers was sufficient delivery to constitute a valid gift causa mortis of the papers therein, when the box, which was not in the presence or immediate control of the donor, did not pass into the actual possession of the donee during the lifetime of the donor. Justice Dixon in his opinion for the court reviewed the English and American authorities, and then concluded that there had not been that delivery required under New Jersey law. . . .

Thus, under New Jersey law actual delivery of the property is still required except where "there can be no actual delivery" or where "the situation is incompatible with the performance of such ceremony." In the case of a savings account, where obviously there can be no actual delivery, delivery of the passbook or other indicia of title is required. . . .

Here there was no delivery of any kind whatsoever. We have already noted the requirement so amply established in our cases, supra, 162 A. 609, "actual, unequivocal and complete delivery during the lifetime of the donor, wholly divesting her of the possession, dominion, and control" of the property. This requirement is satisfied only by delivery by the *donor,* which calls for an affirmative act on her part, not by the mere taking of possession of the property by the donee.

. . .

We must not forget that since a gift causa mortis is made in contemplation of death and is subject to revocation by the donor up to the time of his death it differs from a legacy only in the requirement of delivery. Delivery is in effect the only safeguard imposed by law upon a transaction which would ordinarily fall within the statute of wills. To eliminate delivery from the requirements for a gift causa mortis would be to permit any writing to effectuate a testamentary transfer, even though it does not comply with the requirements of the statute of wills.

Here we are concerned with three separate items of property—cash, a savings account represented by a bank passbook, and shares in a building and loan association represented by a book. There was no actual delivery of the cash and no delivery of the indicia of title to the savings account or the building and loan association shares. Rather, the donor set forth in an informal writing her desire to give these items to the defendant. Although the writing establishes her donative intent at the time it was written, it does not fulfill the requirement of delivery of the property, which is a separate and distinct requirement for a gift causa mortis. The cash, passbook, and stock book remained at the decedent's home and she made no effort to obtain them so as to effectuate a delivery to the defendant.

We disagree with the conclusion of the Appellate Division that the donee already had possession of the property, and therefore delivery was unnecessary. Assuming, but not deciding, the validity of this doctrine, we note that the house was the property of the deceased and, although defendant resided there with her, he had no knowledge of the presence of this property in the house, let alone its precise location therein; therefore it cannot be said that he had possession of the property.

Unlike some other jurisdictions New Jersey has resisted efforts to extend the doctrine of gifts causa mortis, recognizing it as a dangerous encroachment upon the policy embodied in the statute of wills. . . .

But it is argued that the decedent's note to her husband in the circumstances of the case was an authorization to him to take possession of the chattels mentioned therein which when coupled with his taking of possession thereof during her lifetime was in law the equivalent of the delivery required in the Roman and common law alike and by all the decisions in this State for a valid gift causa mortis. Without accepting this contention, it is to be noted that it has no application to the present case, because here at the time the defendant obtained her note the decedent was in the operating room under ether and, according to the finding of the trial court, supra, "after the operation and until the date of her death on May 13, 1951 she was in a coma most of the time; was unable to recognize members of her family; and unable to carry on intelligent conversation. . . . Mrs. Reiss was never able to talk or converse after coming out of the operation until her death."

In these circumstances the note clearly failed as an authorization to the defendant to take possession of the chattels mentioned therein, since at the time he took the note from the drawer the decedent was under ether and according to the findings of the trial court unable to transact business until the time of her death. See section 122 of the Restatement of the Law of Agency: "The authority of the agent to make the principal a party to a transaction is terminated or suspended upon the happening of an event which deprives the principal of capacity to become a party to the transaction or deprives the agent of capacity to make the principal a party to it." and comment (b) thereunder: "The power of the agent terminates although he has no notice of the principal's loss of capacity or of the event causing it. It also terminates although the contingency has been provided for and it has been agreed that the authority would not thereupon terminate." . . .

The judgment of the Appellate Division of the Superior Court is reversed and the judgment of the Chancery Division of the Superior Court will be reinstated.

JACOBS, J. (with whom WACHENFELD and WILLIAM J. BRENNAN, Jr., JJ., agree) dissenting.

. . .

The delivery requirement has, for the most part, been applied in like fashion to gifts causa mortis and gifts inter vivos. See Brown, Personal Property (1936), 76, 137; Atkinson, Wills, (1937), 157. Cf. 4 Page, Wills (1941), 757. And although some courts have suggested that a stricter attitude is called for in gifts causa mortis than in gifts inter vivos, other courts have adopted the opposite point of view. See e.g., In re Wasserberg (1915) 1 Ch. 195; Begovich v. Kruljac, 38 Wyo. 365, 267 P. 426, 60 A.L.R. 1046 (Sup.Ct.1928); Devol v. Dye, 123 Ind. 321, 24 N.E. 246, 7 L.R.A. 439 (Sup.Ct.1890). In the Begovich case, supra [38 Wyo. 365, 267 P. 429], the court said: ". . . gifts causa mortis are ordinarily resorted to by intending donors because the facilities for executing the more formal testamentary disposition are not available, or the death of the donor is so imminent in point of time as to preclude preparation of the formal documents. They are in their very nature emergency measures. Hence, though delivery cannot be dispensed with, since words may be easily misrepresented . . . still we should naturally expect the courts to hold the requirements as to such delivery to be less strict than in connection with gifts inter vivos, and that, in fact, is the holding of at least many of the courts. . . ." . . .

No helpful purpose would be served by further discussion of the history or wisdom of the delivery rule or its sympathetic or hostile application to gifts causa mortis; it would seem that under any reasoned point of view the particular facts in the instant matter should be deemed to constitute the required delivery. It must be remembered that the gift to Adam Reiss did not rest upon delivery of the note alone; it rested on the acknowledged fact that in accordance with the terms of the note the donee took physical possession of the donated articles and retained them until after the death of the donor. In his article on Gifts of Chattels without Delivery, 6 L.Quar.Rev. 446 (1890), Sir Frederick Pollock said: "On principle it would seem that where A by word of mouth purports to give B a certain chattel, this will have the effect of a license to B to take that chattel peaceably wherever he may find it. For it would not be reasonable for A to treat B as a trespasser for acting upon A's expressed intention. The license is no doubt revocable until executed, and may be revoked either by the communication to B, by word or act, of A's will to that effect, or by A's death (which was the case of Irons v. Smallpiece) or perhaps by A's becoming insane. If without any revocation the license is executed by B taking possession of the chattel, then, it is submitted, the property is irrevocably transferred to B. There would be great and obvious inconvenience in holding otherwise."

. . .

When Ethel Reiss signed the note and arranged to have her husband receive it, she did everything that could reasonably have been expected of her to effectuate the gift causa mortis; and while her husband might conceivably have attempted to return the donated articles to her at the hospital for immediate redelivery to him, it would have been unnatural for him to do so. It is difficult to believe that our law would require such wholly ritualistic ceremony and I find nothing in our decisions to suggest it. The majority opinion advances the suggestion that the husband's authority to take possession of the donated articles was terminated by the wife's incapacity in the operating room and thereafter. The very reason she wrote the longhand note when she did was because she knew she would be incapacitated and wished her husband to take immediate possession, as he did. Men who enter hospitals for major surgery often execute powers of attorney to enable others to continue their business affairs during their incapacity. Any judicial doctrine which would legally terminate such power as of the inception of the incapacity would be startling indeed—it would disrupt commercial affairs and entirely without reason or purpose.

. . .

I would affirm the judgment of the Appellate Division.

NOTES

1. How is a gift causa mortis to be distinguished from an attempted transfer by will which cannot be given effect as a testate transfer because of failure to comply with the statute of wills? Considering only what Ethel Reiss did, and the language of the message to her husband, is there anything to indicate that she had in mind a transfer prior to her death rather than a transfer coinciding with her death? Did her message indicate that she intended that her husband should take possession of the items mentioned before her death?

If Adam Reiss had come to his wife's hospital room before she had gone to the operating room, and if she had handed him the note she had written, would the court have sustained the gift? In Meyers v. Meyers, 99 N.J.Eq. 560, 134 A. 95 (1926), M, being ill and about to undergo surgery, signed and acknowledged a sealed instrument which purported to assign to his fifteen-year-old son a two-thirds interest in a bond, secured by a mortgage, which M owned. He retained the bond and mortgage and left the instrument of assignment with the lawyer who had drafted it, telling him to have it recorded "if anything happened." The lawyer knew that M was anticipating the possibility of death, which in fact occurred shortly after the operation. M's administratrix challenged the attempted transfer. Was it valid?

2. In Basket v. Hassell, 107 U.S. 602, 2 S.Ct. 415, 27 L.Ed. 500 (1882), C had deposited money with a bank. Being ill and apprehending death, he endorsed the certificate of deposit as follows: "Pay to Martin Basket, of Henderson, Ky.; no one else; then not till my death. My life seems to be uncertain. I may live through this spell. Then I will attend to it myself. H.M. Chaney." He then handed the certificate to Basket and died shortly thereafter. C's administrator challenged the attempted transfer. Was it valid? Compare In re Nols' Estate, 251 Wis. 90, 28 N.W.2d 360 (1947).

3. As the opinions in Foster v. Reiss indicate, courts have held that if the donee has previously acquired possession of the subject-matter with the donor's consent, the donor's oral manifestation of donative intent, without more, is sufficient. Does this proposition impair any policy served by the rule that mere oral declarations of donative intent are ordinarily insufficient? Is there good reason to relax this rule in behalf of a donee having prior possession? Suppose a donor manifests donative intent by an oral declaration and by handing the subject-matter to the donee—if the donee thereafter transfers possession of the subject-matter to the donor, is the attempted transfer of ownership from donor to donee rendered ineffective? If it is not, does the result conflict with any policy served by the rule that physical delivery of the subject-matter to the donee is necessary in the absence of some other legally sufficient manifestation of donative intent?

4. In Newell v. National Bank of Norwich, 214 App.Div. 331, 212 N.Y.S. 158 (1925), R, seriously ill with pneumonia and anticipating death, sent for N, an intimate friend for many years, and handed him a diamond ring, making statements which, as reported by his nurse's testimony, suggested an intent to make a gift in contemplation of death. R survived the illness and died more than four years later. After R recovered N expressed unwillingness to wear the ring and offered to return it to R for his use as long as he lived. Several months after his recovery, when he was in N's office, R called in a third person and said, "Frank (N) wants me to wear this ring, but I don't think I should do it. I gave him that ring and I want him to have it, but he insists upon my wearing it, now that I am able to be around again. Under only one consideration will I agree to wear it and I want it thoroughly understood that this ring belongs to Frank and when I die I want it understood that it belongs to him and that he shall have it." R thereafter wore the ring until his death. His executor challenged N's ownership. The court sustained N's claim: "Viewed as a gift causa mortis the gift cannot be sustained because it is well established that the recovery to health of the donor works per se a revocation of the

gift. . . . The question then is does the evidence sustain the finding that a gift inter vivos was intended. . . . The circumstances . . . indicate quite clearly that when during his illness he gave the ring to the plaintiff he did so irrespective of whether he lived or died. . . ."

Compare with the approach of the court in Newell the declaration in Restatement (Second) of Property, Donative Transfers, § 31.3 (Tent. Draft No. 11, April 12, 1988) that "A failure to revoke within a reasonable time after the donor is no longer in apprehension of imminent death eliminates the right of revocation."

A, being ill and anticipating death, hands a ring to B, expressing an intent to make a gift causa mortis to B. Subsequently, A executes a will in which he makes various bequests and devises and leaves the residue of his estate to C. His executor, in behalf of C, seeks to recover the ring from B. What result? If he cannot recover the ring in this instance, can he do so if A specifically bequeaths the ring to C? R. Brown, Personal Property, § 7.19 (3rd ed. W. Raushenbush 1975).

A statute provides that a widow is entitled to one-third of all personalty owned by her husband at his death. She cannot be deprived of this by his will, unless she consents by electing to take in lieu thereof what he leaves her by will. Shortly before his death H makes an otherwise effective gift causa mortis of certain bank stock. After his death intestate, W asserts that the value of the bank stock must be included in ascertaining her statutory share of H's personalty. What result? R. Brown Personal Property 135 (3d ed. W. Raushenbush 1975).

SCHERER v. HYLAND

Supreme Court of New Jersey, 1977.
75 N.J. 127, 380 A.2d 698.

PER CURIAM.

Defendant, the Administrator *ad litem* of the Estate of Catherine Wagner, appeals from an Appellate Division decision, one judge dissenting, affirming a summary judgment by the trial court holding that Ms. Wagner had made a valid gift *causa mortis* of a check to plaintiff. We affirm.

The facts are not in dispute. Catherine Wagner and the plaintiff, Robert Scherer, lived together for approximately fifteen years prior to Ms. Wagner's death in January 1974. In 1970, the decedent and plaintiff were involved in an automobile accident in which decedent suffered facial wounds and a broken hip. Because of the hip injury, decedent's physical mobility was substantially impaired. She was forced to give up her job and to restrict her activities. After the accident, plaintiff cared for her and assumed the sole financial responsibility for maintaining their household. During the weeks preceding her death, Ms. Wagner was acutely depressed. On one occasion, she attempted suicide by slashing her wrists. On January 23, 1974, she committed suicide by jumping from the roof of the apartment building in which they lived.

On the morning of the day of her death, Ms. Wagner received a check for $17,400 drawn by a Pennsylvania attorney who had represented her in a claim arising out of the automobile accident. The check represented settlement of the claim. Plaintiff telephoned Ms. Wagner at around 11:30 a.m. that day and was told that the check had arrived. Plaintiff noticed nothing unusual in Ms. Wagner's voice. At about 3:20 p.m., decedent left the apartment building and jumped to her death. The police, as part of their investigation of the suicide, asked the building superintendent to admit them to the apartment. On the kitchen table they found the check, endorsed in blank, and two notes handwritten by the decedent. In one, she described her depression over her physical condition, expressed her love for Scherer, and asked him to forgive her "for taking the easy way out." In the other, she indicated that she "bequeathed" to plaintiff all of her possessions, including "the check for $17,400.00 . . .." The police took possession of the check, which was eventually placed in an interest-bearing account pending disposition of this action.

Under our wills statute it is clear that Ms. Wagner's note bequeathing all her possessions to Mr. Scherer cannot take effect as a testamentary disposition. N.J.S.A. 3A:3–2. . . .

The primary issue here is whether Ms. Wagner's acts of endorsing the settlement check, placing it on the kitchen table in the apartment she shared with Scherer, next to a writing clearly evidencing her intent to transfer the check to Scherer, and abandoning the apartment with a clear expectation of imminent death constituted delivery sufficient to sustain a gift *causa mortis* of the check. Defendant, relying on the principles established in Foster v. Reiss, 18 N.J. 41, 112 A.2d 553 (1955), argues that there was no delivery because the donor did not unequivocally relinquish control of the check before her death. Central to this argument is the contention that suicide, the perceived peril, was one which decedent herself created and one which was completely within her control. According to this contention, the donor at any time before she jumped from the apartment roof could have changed her mind, reentered the apartment, and reclaimed the check. Defendant therefore reasons that decedent did not make an effective transfer of the check during her lifetime, as is required for a valid gift *causa mortis.*

. . .

There is general agreement that the major purpose of the delivery requirement is evidentiary. Proof of delivery reduces the possibility that the evidence of intent has been fabricated or that a mere donative impulse, not consummated by action, has been mistaken for a completed gift. Since "these gifts come into question only after death has closed the lips of the donor," the delivery requirement provides a substantial safeguard against fraud and perjury. See Keepers v. Fidelity Title and Deposit Co., 56 N.J.L. 302, 308, 28 A. 585 (E. & A.1893). In *Foster,* the majority concluded that these policies could best be fulfilled by a strict rule requiring actual manual tradition of the subject-matter of the gift except in a very narrow class of cases where "there can be no actual delivery" or where "the situation is incompatible with the performance of such ceremony." 18 N.J. at 50, 112 A.2d at 559. Justice Jacobs, in his dissenting opinion (joined by Justices Brennan and Wachenfeld) questioned the reasonableness of requiring direct physical delivery in cases where donative intent is "freely and clearly expressed in a written instrument." Id. at 56, 112 A.2d at 562. He observed that a more flexible approach to the delivery requirement had been taken by other jurisdictions . . .. In essence, this approach takes into account the purposes served by the requirement of delivery in determining whether that requirement has been met. It would find a constructive delivery adequate to support the gift when the evidence of donative intent is concrete and undisputed, when there is every indication that the donor intended to make a present transfer of the subject-matter of the gift, and when the steps taken by the donor to effect such a transfer must have been deemed by the donor as sufficient to pass the donor's interest to the donee. We are persuaded that this approach, which does not minimize the need for evidentiary safeguards to prevent frauds upon the estates of the deceased, reflects the realities which attend transfers of this kind.

In this case, the evidence of decedent's intent to transfer the check to Robert Scherer is concrete, unequivocal, and undisputed. The circumstances definitely rule out any possibility of fraud. The sole question, then, is whether the steps taken by the decedent, independent of her writing of the suicide notes, were sufficient to support a finding that she effected a lifetime transfer of the check to Scherer. We think that they were. First, the act of endorsing a check represents, in common experience and understanding, the only act needed (short of actual delivery) to render a check negotiable. The significance of such an act is universally understood. Accordingly, we have no trouble in viewing Ms. Wagner's endorsement of the settlement check as a substantial step taken by her for the purpose of effecting a transfer to Scherer of her right to the check proceeds. Second, we note that the only person other than the decedent who had routine access to the apartment was Robert Scherer. Indeed, the apartment was leased in his name. It is clear that Ms. Wagner before leaving the apartment placed the check in a place where Scherer could not fail to see it and fully expected that he would take actual possession of the check when he entered. And, although Ms. Wagner's subsequent suicide does not itself constitute a component of the delivery of this gift, it does provide persuasive evidence that when Ms. Wagner locked the door of the apartment she did so with no expectation of returning. When we consider her state of mind as it must have been upon leaving the apartment, her surrender of possession at that moment was complete. We find, therefore, that when she left the apartment she completed a constructive delivery of the check to Robert Scherer. In light of her resolve to take her own life and of her obvious desire not to be deterred from that purpose, Ms. Wagner's failure manually to transfer the check to Scherer is understandable. She clearly did all that she could do or thought necessary to do to surrender the check. Her donative intent has been conclusively demonstrated by independent evidence. The law should effectuate that intent rather than indulge in nice distinctions which would thwart her purpose. Upon these facts, we find that the constructive delivery she made was adequate to support a gift *causa mortis.*

Defendant's assertion that suicide is not the sort of peril that will sustain a gift *causa mortis* finds some support in precedents from other jurisdictions. . . . We are, however, not bound by those authorities nor do we find them persuasive. While it is true that a gift *causa mortis* is made by the donor with a view to impending death, death is no less impending because of a resolve to commit suicide. Nor does that fixed purpose constitute any lesser or less imminent peril than does a ravaging disease. Indeed, given the despair sufficient to end it all, the peril attendant upon contemplated suicide may reasonably be viewed as even more imminent than that accompanying many illnesses which prove ultimately to be fatal. Cf. Berl v. Rosenberg, 169 Cal.App. 2d 125, 336 P.2d 975, 978 (Dist.Ct.App.1959) (public policy against suicide does not invalidate otherwise valid gift *causa mortis*). And, the notion that one in a state of mental depression serious enough to lead to suicide is somehow "freer" to renounce the depression and thus the danger than one suffering from a physical illness, although it has a certain augustinian appeal, has long since been replaced by more enlightened views of human psychology. In re Van Wormer's Estate, 255 Mich. 399, 238 N.W. 210 (Sup.Ct.1931) (melancholia ending in suicide sufficient to sustain a gift *causa mortis*). We also observe that an argument that the donor of a *causa mortis* gift might have changed his or her mind loses much of its force when one recalls that a *causa mortis* gift, by definition, can be revoked at any time before the donor dies and is automatically revoked if the donor recovers.

Finally, defendant asserts that this gift must fail because there was no acceptance prior to the donor's death. Although the issue of acceptance is rarely litigated the authority that does exist indicates that, given a valid delivery, acceptance will be implied if the gift is unconditional and beneficial to the donee.

Judgment affirmed.

IN RE ESTATE OF MICHAELS

Supreme Court of Wisconsin, 1965.
26 Wis.2d 382, 132 N.W.2d 557.

Proceeding initiated by the administrator with the will annexed of the estate of Helen Michaels, deceased, for instructions as to whether certain assets should be treated as owned individually by the deceased at the time of her death or whether they were then owned by her in joint tenancy with one or more other persons. Included in these assets was Savings Account #1395 in the State Bank of Newburg, the passbook to which was registered in the name of Helen Michaels or Harry Michaels. Immediately below the written names was [were] stamped these words, "A joint and several account Payable to either or the survivor." At the time of death of Helen Michaels on September 22,

1961, the sum of $4,110.50 was on deposit in this account. Harry Michaels is the son of Helen Michaels and survived her.

A hearing was held on the petition for instructions of the administrator with the will annexed. By memorandum decision the county court determined that it was not the intent of Helen Michaels to create a joint ownership in this bank account with a right of survivorship in Harry Michaels; Harry Michaels' name had been included on the bank account passbook for the convenience of Helen Michaels; and the account was solely owned by her at the time of her death. An order was entered under date of July 6, 1964, that this savings account "remain and be considered as personal property individually owned by the deceased at the time of her death." Harry Michaels has appealed from this order. Further facts will be stated in the opinion.

CURRIE, C.J. The facts of this case make it unique among the many joint bank account cases which have come before this court. The account was originally opened in the State Bank of Newburg on September 8, 1942, in the names of Walter Michaels or Helen Michaels with a deposit of $500. The record does not disclose the source of this $500 deposit. At that time there were two Walter Michaels. One was the husband of Helen and the other the sixteen year old son of Walter, Sr. and his wife, Helen. Walter, Sr. and Helen resided and operated a tavern in the unincorporated village of Waubeka in Ozaukee county which is some six to eight miles distant from Newburg. Walter, Sr. died October 25, 1944. At the time of his death there was $508.77 on deposit in the joint savings account. His estate was probated in the county court of Ozaukee county and there also was a separate termination of joint tenancy proceeding with respect to certain property he had owned in joint tenancy with Helen. The joint savings account is not referred to in either the estate or joint tenancy proceeding. Nevertheless, we think the reasonable inference is that the Walter named as one of the two depositors when the original savings account was opened was Walter, Sr. and not Walter, Jr. There are two reasons for this: First, Walter, Jr. was then but sixteen years old and the record discloses no reason why at that time he should have been preferred over his three brothers and one sister, all of whom were older than he. Secondly, the name Walter precedes that of Helen in the bank passbook which is more consistent with Walter being the husband rather than the minor son of the codepositor, Helen.

Some time after the original opening of the account, "Jr." was written after the name of Walter in both the passbook and on the bank's ledger sheet. The reason that we conclude it was done after the opening of the account is because it is written with ink of a lighter color than the original words "Walter or Helen Michaels." The record is silent as to when this change was made. Thereafter, the word "Cancelled" was written in ink across "Walter Jr." in the passbook and "Cancelled" was also written in ink slightly below and to the left of "Walter Jr." A small arrow was also drawn in ink after this second "Cancelled" pointing toward the cancellation of "Walter Jr." Isselman, an officer of the bank, testified that the writing of the words "Cancelled" and the drawing of the arrow were done by him and that he made these changes in the passbook on December 16, 1950. He could not recall the incident but "presumed" it was done at the request of Helen Michaels. At the same time three horizontal lines were drawn through the name "Walter Jr." on the bank's ledger sheet and the word "Cancelled" was written in ink below and to the left thereof together with the date "12/16/50" and an arrow was drawn after the word "Cancelled" pointing to the "Walter Jr." with the three horizontal lines drawn through it.

Thereafter, the words "or Harry Michaels" were written in ink in the passbook below "Helen Michaels." Harry is the son of Helen Michaels, and the brother of Walter Jr. Mrs. Johnson, daughter of Isselman, testified that she was employed in the bank only in 1951 and 1952 and that these words "or Harry Michaels" were in her handwriting. She could not recall whether the stamped words appearing below "or Harry Michaels" which read, "A joint and several account Payable to either or the survivor", were placed there by her but presumed they were and that her father was the one who told her to do so. However, Mrs. Johnson did not add any name on the bank ledger sheet covering this account. Thus ever since December 16, 1950 the bank ledger sheets named only Helen Michaels as the depositor. This we deem to be immaterial because the passbook constituted the contract between the depositor and the bank; the ledger sheet was merely the private record of the bank. Isselman testified that bank employees always had been instructed to have the two records (passbook and ledger sheet) correspond.

At the conclusion of the taking of testimony at the hearing Judge Larson stated: "I would like the attorneys to look at Exhibit, Harry Michaels' Exhibit No. 1 [the passbook] and ask whether it does not look to them as though this book had on the page bearing the names of the owners the names Walter or Helen Michaels. That later a 'Jr.' was written behind Walter. That after that word 'cancelled' was written across 'Walter' and 'Jr.' and the word 'Harry Michaels' added to the book." Counsel for the administrator with the will annexed and for Walter Michaels, Jr. both agreed with this interpretation of the exhibit, while counsel for Harry Michaels stated he refused to speculate on the sequence of events.

Both Walter, Jr. and Harry testified that they did not learn of the existence of the account until after their mother's death. The passbook was found in a little safe in the tavern at Waubeka which Helen operated from the time of her husband's death in 1944 until her own death in 1961. All deposits and withdrawals after the death of Walter, Sr. had been made by Helen. Walter, Jr. married September 16, 1950, and then left his mother's home, which was in the first story of the tavern premises. Harry, who is eleven years older than Walter, Jr., had married in 1943 but lived upstairs in the tavern premises until 1957. There is testimony that Walter, Jr.'s wife had at least one serious quarrel with Helen Michaels. Thus Walter, Jr.'s marriage and leaving his mother's home, and possibly also the quarrel between his wife and mother, provide an explanation of why Helen had Walter, Jr.'s name removed from the passbook as a joint payee on December 16, 1950.

Harry testified that during the years he lived upstairs in the tavern premises he helped tend bar, cut the grass, and took his mother to the doctor and dentist. When asked whether he helped out at the tavern he replied, "Quite a bit. The most.", which apparently meant that he helped out more than Walter, Jr. or his other brothers and sister. The public administrator was present in person at the hearing and asked Harry this question and received this answer:

"Q. Mr. Michaels, did your mother ever tell you about setting up this bank account for you?

"A. Well what she said is that she says I'm going to get more. Every time I go over to West Bend to the foot doctor because I usually took her once or twice a week. But I never knew she had any money in the bank book in Newburg."

Walter, Jr. testified that he also helped tend bar for his mother in the tavern and took her to the doctor and to Milwaukee. Helen Michaels died testate, leaving a will dated January 28, 1958, which was duly admitted to probate. All of her estate except a $200 bequest for masses was bequeathed by the residuary clause, which reads: "Because of the extra services rendered to me by my sons Harry Michaels and Walter Michaels, I give, devise and bequeath to each of them one-third (1/3) of the residue of my estate, and the remaining one-third I divide equally among all of my children, to-wit: John Michaels, Harry Michaels, William Michaels, Walter Michaels, Jr., and Frances Michaels Witte." The total appraised value of her estate, exclusive of the bank account in question, is slightly in excess of $33,500.

The foregoing constitutes a summary of all the evidence which we consider of possible materiality on the issue of whether the administrator with the will annexed or Harry, as the survivor of the two joint payees named in the bank passbook, is entitled to the account. We now turn to the applicable statutes, case law authorities, and writings of experts in the field, to determine whether the result below must be affirmed or reversed.

The only applicable statute is sec. 221.45, Stats., which provides: "When a deposit has been made or shall hereafter be made, in any bank, trust company bank or mutual savings banks transacting business in this state in the names of 2 persons, payable to either, or payable to either or the survivor, such deposit, or any part thereof, or any interest or dividend thereon, may be paid to either of said persons whether the other be living or not; and the receipt or acquittance of the person so paid shall be a valid and sufficient release and discharge to the bank for any payment so made."

Estate of Staver (1935), 218 Wis. 114, 260 N.W. 655, is generally regarded as the landmark decision by this court in the field of joint bank accounts. That case broke sharply with prior decisions which had applied concepts of traditional joint tenancy law and of the law governing the creation of gifts. The opinion flatly stated (at p. 120, 260 N.W. at p. 658): "No question of transfer from the depositor to the intended donee is in any manner involved." The rationale of the decision was that the survivor donee payee succeeded to the account by reason of the contract between the donor depositor and the bank as implemented by sec. 221.45, Stats. Among the cases cited in support of the adoption of this contract theory were Chippendale, Adm'r v. North Adams Savings Bank (1916), 222 Mass. 499, 111 N.E. 371, and Battles v. Millbury Savings Bank (1924), 250 Mass. 180, 145 N.E. 55.

Of particular applicability to the instant case are these further statements made in Estate of Staver (218 Wis. at pp. 122, 124, 260 N.W. at pp. 658, 659):

"The legal title being in the survivor, it would be necessary to show by clear and satisfactory evidence a conscientious duty upon the part of the survivor to hold the title in trust for another. In the absence of such a showing, the complete ownership must be held to be in the survivor. . . . The legal ownership of instruments and the incidents of such ownership should generally depend upon their terms, leaving it to a court of equity to impose on the holder of the legal title such equitable obligations as the law of trusts warrants."

. . .

Estate of Staver, supra, holds legal title to a joint bank account is in the survivor donee payee upon the death of the donor depositor subject to equity imposing a trust upon the holder as the law of trusts warrants upon proof "by clear and satisfactory evidence." A logical and natural development of this theory would be to hold that a rebuttable presumption exists that the donor depositor intended the right of survivorship, which presumption can only be rebutted by clear and satisfactory evidence. . . .

In the instant case there is no direct evidence, such as statements made to the bank employees or to others by Helen Michaels, of the intent which motivated the changes she made in the savings account subsequent to her husband's death. The fact that she at all times retained possession of the passbook, and did not disclose its existence to Walter, Jr., and Harry, gives rise to either or both of two reasonable inferences. One is that she did not intend anyone but herself to have any right to make withdrawals from this account. The other is that she wanted to have the right to change or remove the name of any donee payee at will. However, it would be indulging in pure speculation to assume that, because she wished to retain this tight control over the account during her lifetime, she did not intend to be applicable the stamped and conspicuous survivorship provision appearing in the heading of the passbook immediately following the names of herself and Harry.

Her will made in 1958, in which she treated both Walter, Jr. and Harry alike, is some evidence that she did not then intend Harry should be preferred over Walter, Jr. However, she had made no further deposits in the account subsequent to September 12, 1952. It is the intent she had at the time she added Harry's name as a joint payee with right of survivorship which is controlling. There is no evidence of expressed intent that the account be not governed by the deposit agreement with the bank.

It is our considered judgment that no clear and convincing evidence was adduced in this record which would rebut the presumption of survivorship arising from the deposit contract with the bank as implemented by sec. 221.45, Stats. Legal title to the account passed to Harry upon his mother's death, and there exists no basis upon which a court can impress a constructive trust upon him in favor of the estate of his mother, Helen Michaels.

The county court found and determined that Harry was named as a joint codepositor for the convenience of Helen Michaels. A good illustration of a joint savings account created for the convenience of the depositor whose money constituted the source of the deposits is presented by Plainse v. Engle (1952), 262 Wis. 506, 56 N.W.2d 89, 57 N.W.2d 586. There a father placed money in a joint bank account in the names of himself and daughter. The evidence established that this was done pursuant to an understanding between father and daughter that, if he got ill and needed a lot of medical attention, she would be able to withdraw money for such purpose. The father became mentally incompetent, and it was held that the joint account had been created solely for convenience and, therefore, the father's guardian was entitled to the account.

. . .

In the instant case there is no direct evidence that Helen Michaels in 1951 or 1952 had the bank add Harry's name to the account as a joint payee with the right of survivorship so as to enable Harry to make withdrawals for her at some future time. This occurred nine or ten years before her death and she continued active in the management of her tavern business up until the week of her death. Under the evidence here presented it is possible to surmise that she may have had Harry's name added as a joint payee so that if she did become incapacitated at some future time he would be able to make withdrawals for her benefit. It is equally tenable to assume that because Harry was then rendering assistance to her in the tavern and about the premises that she had his name added so that he would receive the account upon her death as a reward for his services. Mere surmise and theorizing of possibilities falls far short of constituting the clear and convincing evidence required as a condition for equity imposing a trust to defeat Harry's legal title to the account as the surviving copayee.

One further issue should be explored and resolved: Whether the attempted creation of survivorship rights in Harry constituted an invalid testamentary disposition of property by Helen Michaels. There is no prior decision of this court since the enactment of sec. 221.45, Stats., which has directly passed on the question of whether the deposit of money by a donor depositor in a joint bank account, with the intention that the named donee payee is to have no right to make withdrawals during the lifetime of the donor depositor, violates our Statute of Wills, sec. 238.06, Stats.

. . .

There can be no denial of the fact that the survivorship feature of a joint bank account is testamentary in character. The fact that these accounts have been termed the "poor man's will" is an open acknowledgment of this. See In re Edwards' Estate (1932), 140 Or. 431, 436, 14 P.2d 274; Barbour v. First Citizens Nat. Bank (1957), 77 S.D. 106, 110, 86 N.W.2d 526; and Disposition of Bank Accounts: The Poor Man's Will, 53 Columbia Law Review (1953), 103. Where the donee depositor is intended by the donor depositor to have the right to withdraw during his lifetime, the survivorship feature has posed no problems to the courts since there has been a transfer of a present interest to support the survivorship. Thus the transaction squares with the traditional concepts of *inter vivos* gifts.

Courts have not been much concerned with the fact that even in such a situation the donor depositor can defeat the survivorship rights of the donee payee by withdrawing all the funds prior to death. 10 Am. Jur. (2d) Banks, pp. 346–347, sec. 381. It is the situation, where the donor depositor withholds from the donee codepositor any right to withdraw during the lifetime of the donor, which has caused some courts to hold the survivorship feature of the account to be an invalid testamentary disposition. See 10 Am.Jur. (2d) Banks, p. 348, sec. 382.

. . .

The thoughtful analyses of the problems arising in the field of joint bank accounts contained in the article by Professor Richard W. Effland, Estate Planning: Co-Ownership, 1958 Wisconsin Law Review, 507; and those by Professor Kepner, The Joint and Survivorship Bank Account—A Concept Without a Name, 41 California Law Review (1953), 596, and Five More Years of the Joint Bank Account Muddle, 26 University of Chicago Law Review (1959) 376, commend themselves to this court. Both authors advocate that the survivorship feature of these accounts be enforced by the courts even though the surviving donee named as codepositor has had no right of withdrawal during the lifetime of the donor. We quote their views as follows:

"It is submitted that frank judicial recognition of an account which confers no rights during lifetime (or, as to a checking account, rights which are revocable), but carries survivorship rights, is justified, serves the modern policy of carrying out intent, and is no more a violation of the Statute of Wills than presently exists." Effland, supra, 1958 Wisconsin Law Review, 507, at page 520.

"The fact that the donee cannot make withdrawals may be evidence of the donor's intention, but it should not be conclusive on the question of whether or not a gift was made. The joint bank account gift is actually not intended to be a donation of an unrestricted right to make withdrawals, but is a present gift of the balance of the account, with the donee's enjoyment postponed until the donor's death. It is intended to be a form of a testamentary disposition of property in that the gift is not perfected until the donor's death. The gift should not be invalidated because the donee cannot make withdrawals." Kepner, supra, 26 University of Chicago Law Review (1959), 376, at page 388.

However, in order for this court to achieve this socially desirable result here and not overrule Tucker v. Simrow (1946), 248 Wis. 143, 21 N.W.2d 252, it will be necessary to ground it upon sec. 221.45, Stats., rather than the contract between Helen Michaels and the bank. In the Tucker Case, the owner of a savings account and a checking account signed a written direction to the bank that, upon her death, the bank pay one-half of these accounts to the depositor's husband, and one-fourth thereof to each of her two children. The bank accepted this written direction and it became part of the deposit contract. Both the trial court and this court held that there was an ineffective testamentary disposition. The court distinguished Estate of Staver, supra, on the ground that in the latter case a present interest had been created in the person alleged to be a joint tenant while in the Tucker Case the depositor had retained complete control until death. We deem a better basis for distinguishing the two cases to be that in the one there existed a statute which vested legal title to the account in the named surviving donee depositor while in the other there is no such statute covering bank accounts standing in the sole name of the depositor but payable on death to another. . . .

This court has on occasion stated that sec. 221.45, Stats., was enacted for the protection of the banks and does not determine the rights of the named payees of a joint bank account as between themselves. Estate of Schley (1955), 271 Wis. 74, 80, 72 N.W.2d 767, and Estate of Kemmerer, supra, 16 Wis.2d at page 488, 114 N.W.2d 803. This does not mean, however, that this statute may not be pertinent on the issue of whether the attempted conferral of survivorship rights on the surviving donee payee is an ineffective testamentary disposition. It is this statute which implements the deposit contract and causes legal title to vest in the survivor payee even though equity in a proper case may intervene to impress a trust against such survivor payee. The passing of legal title is irreconcilable with the concept that such an attempted transfer is an ineffective testamentary disposition because of failure to comply with the requirements of the Statute of Wills. Thus it necessarily follows that sec. 221.45 is a statutory exception to sec. 238.06, Stats., the same as is sec. 215.14, Stats., which we were called upon to construe in Estate of Fucela, Wis., 132 N.W.2d 553.

We summarize our determination of the issues in this appeal as follows: Legal title to the joint bank savings account passed to appellant Harry Michaels upon the death of Helen Michaels. There is insufficient evidence of a contrary intent on the part of Helen Michaels to permit equity to impress a trust against Harry in favor of her estate. The reservation by Helen of full control over the account during her lifetime, thus excluding Harry from any right of withdrawal, did not invalidate the survivorship feature of the joint account so as to make it an ineffective testamentary disposition.

The joint bank account is a comparatively new device in the long development of the law. While the joint payees of such account are termed joint tenants for lack of a better terminology, the account has different attributes than a true joint tenancy. Such an account provides a useful technique for transferring property, and need not fit any of the historical and traditional property concepts associated with the law of *inter vivos* gifts and joint tenancy. It would be a mistake to ignore the deposit contract and the intent of the parties in order to apply such concepts.

Order reversed and cause remanded for further proceedings consistent with this opinion.

NOTES

1. Closely related to the type of joint bank account considered in the foregoing opinion is a device commonly known as the Totten trust, so called because the best-known case dealing with the device is Matter of Totten, 179 N.Y. 112, 71 N.E. 748 (1904). Typically, it involves a deposit of his own money by A to the account of "A, in trust for B." After careful consideration, the New York court concluded that such a deposit should be deemed the declaration of a "tentative trust"—one which the donor-depositor may revoke by withdrawing the fund or by changing the form of the account. The transfer of ownership becomes complete only upon the depositor's death; thereafter the donee may effectively claim any amount credited to the account, but he has no enforceable claim during the depositor's lifetime, nor may he recover any sum which the depositor has withdrawn from the account. Occasionally a court is candid enough to recognize such a device as the Totten trust or the joint bank account with right of survivorship as "the poor man's will." Does giving these devices legal effect seriously conflict with the policy underlying statutes regulating testamentary succession? In this connection, consider other methods whereby a donor may, without the execution and probate of a will, transmit beneficial ownership of wealth upon his death: (1) by a present transfer of a future interest of the kind briefly discussed heretofore; (2) by investing in United States bonds payable to the investor, or upon his death to a named beneficiary; (3) by a gift causa mortis; (4) by creating a joint tenancy of realty between himself and another, with right of survivorship; (5) by a partnership contract providing that upon the death of a partner his share of the partnership assets shall be owned by the surviving partner or partners; (6) by a life insurance contract naming a donee as beneficiary, subject to change as the donor-insured may wish. To what extent do these arrangements have the ambulatory quality of a will?

The Totten trust is a modern development of the trust concept evolved by the English Court of Chancery, whereby one person is regarded as having the "legal title" and another is regarded as having the beneficial ownership or "equitable title." Trusts are the subject-matter of a complex body of law which is dealt with in detail elsewhere in the curriculum. In simple form, a trust is created by a transaction in which a person (ordinarily called the "settlor") gratuitously transfers "legal" title or ownership of realty or personalty to a second person (the "trustee") directing that he shall manage it and pay its revenues to a third person (the "beneficiary" or "cestui que trust"). When the trust is terminated the trustee distributes the trust fund according to directions given by the settlor in creating the trust. To say that the cestui que trust has only "equitable" ownership is a shorthand way of saying that recognition and protection of his interest was evolved as part of the jurisdiction of the Court of Chancery. Upon the principle that A may create a trust merely by declaring A trustee for the benefit of another, that court in a series of three cases, beginning with Ex Parte Pye, 18 Ves. 140 (1811) and ending with Morgan v. Malleson, L.R. 10 Eq. 475 (1870), seemed disposed to treat almost any clear manifestation of donative intent as a sufficient declaration of trust. It is plain that this course, if pursued, might have reduced to naught the rules which the English law courts had laboriously developed with reference to gratuitous transfers, but the threat was dissipated by Richards v. Delbridge, L.R. 18 Eq. 11 (1874), in which Sir George Jessel, Master of the Rolls, in refusing to sustain an alleged declaration of trust, said, "A man may transfer his property, without valuable consideration, in one of two ways: he may either do such acts as amount in law to a conveyance or assignment of the property, and thus divest himself of the legal ownership, in which case the person who by those acts acquires the property takes it beneficially, or on trust, as the case may be; or the legal owner of the property may, by one or other of the modes recognized as amounting to a valid declaration of trust, constitute himself a trustee, and, without an actual transfer of the legal title, may so deal with the property as to deprive himself of its beneficial ownership, and declare that he will hold it from that time forward on trust for the other person. It is true he need not use the words, 'I declare myself a trustee,' but he must do something which is equivalent to it, and use expressions which have that meaning; for, however anxious the court may be to carry out a man's intention, it is not at liberty to construe words otherwise than according to their proper meaning."

. . .

The principles thus announced are everywhere accepted in the United States, and it does not appear that courts of equity in any state ever doubted their correctness. Many judicial statements approving them may be found; e.g., in Young v. Young, 80 N.Y. 422 (1880), the court said, "It is established as unquestionable law that a court of equity cannot by its authority render that gift perfect which the donor has left imperfect, and cannot convert an imperfect gift into a declaration of trust, merely on account of that imperfection." Applying the principles, however, is by no means so easy as stating them, since the problem is to ascertain, usually after the donor's death, an intent ambiguously manifested by a variety of words and acts; as always where the inquiry is of this character it is difficult to find a clear precedent, since each case must turn on its peculiar circumstances, and among the cases which have thus far been decided a consistent pattern of decision is hardly to be found.

2. Straight-forward arrangements with financial institutions to pay the balance of accounts to specified persons upon the depositor's death continue to encounter judicial hostility. For example, see Waitman v. Waitman, 505 P.2d 171 (Okl.1972), holding testamentary

and invlaid the transfer attempted by a deposit in a savings account at a bank in the form "Waitman, Daisy P.O.D. Albert Waitman."

3. Section 6–104 of the Uniform Probate Code provides:

"(a) Sums remaining on deposit at the death of a party to a joint account belong to the surviving party or parties as against the estate of the decedent unless there is clear and convincing evidence of a different intention at the time the account is created. If there are 2 or more surviving parties, their respective ownerships during lifetime shall be in proportion to their previous ownership interests under Section 6–103 augmented by an equal share for each survivor of any interest the decedent may have owned in the account immediately before his death; and the right of survivorship continues between the surviving parties.

"(b) If the account is a P.O.D. account;

(1) On death of one of 2 or more original payees the rights to any sums remaining on deposit are governed by subsection (a);

(2) On death of the sole original payee or of the survivor of two or more original payees, any sums remaining on deposit belong to the P.O.D. payee or payees if surviving, or to the survivor of them if one or more die before the original payee; if 2 or more P.O.D. payees survive, there is no right of survivorship in the event of death of a P.O.D. payee thereafter unless the terms of the account or deposit agreement expressly provide for survivorship between them.

"(c) If the account is a trust account;

(1) on death of one of 2 or more trustees, the rights to any sums remaining on deposit are governed by subsection (a);

(2) on death of the sole trustee or the survivor of 2 or more trustees, any sums remaining on deposit belong to the person or persons named as beneficiaries, if surviving, or to the survivor of them if one or more die before the trustee, unless there is clear evidence of a contrary intent; if 2 or more beneficiaries survive, there is no right of survivorship in event of death of any beneficiary thereafter unless the terms of the account on deposit agreement expressly provide for survivorship between them.

"(d) In other cases, the death of any party to a multiple-party account has no effect on beneficial ownership of the account other than to transfer the rights of the decedent as part of his estate.

"(e) A right of survivorship arising from the express terms of the account or under this section, a beneficiary designation in a trust account, or a P.O.D. payee designation, cannot be changed by will."

Definitions in Section 6–101 include:

"(1) 'account' means a contract of deposit of funds between a depositor and a financial institution, and includes a checking account, savings account, certificate of deposit, share account and other like arrangement; . . ..

"(4) 'joint account' means an account payable on request to one or more of two or more parties whether or not mention is made of any right of survivorship; . . ..

"(10) 'P.O.D. account' means an account payable on request to one person during lifetime and on his death to one or more P.O.D. payees, or to one or more persons during their lifetimes and on the death of all of them to one or more P.O.D. payees; . . ..

"(14) 'trust account' means an account in the name of one or more parties as trustee for one or more beneficiaries where the relationship is established by the form of the account and the deposit agreement with the financial institution and there is no subject of the trust other than the sums on deposit in the account; it is not essential that payment to the beneficiary be mentioned in the deposit agreement. A trust account does not include a regular trust account under a testamentary trust or a trust agreement which has significance apart from the account, or a fiduciary account arising from a fiduciary relation such as attorney-client; . . .."

Comment by the drafters on Section 6–104:

"The effect of (a) of this section, when read with the definition of 'joint account' in 6–101(4), is to make an account payable to one or more of two or more parties a survivorship arrangement unless 'clear and convincing evidence of a different contention' is offered.

"The underlying assumption is that most persons who use joint accounts want the survivor or survivors to have all balances remaining at death. This assumption may be questioned in states like Michigan where existing statutes and decisions do not provide any safe and wholly practical method of establishing a joint account which is not survivorship. See Leib v. Genesee Merchants Bank, 371 Mich. 89, 123 N.W.(2d) 140 (1962). But, use of a form negating survivorship would make (d) of this section applicable. Still, the financial institution which paid after the death of a party would be protected by 6–108 and 6–109. Thus, a safe nonsurvivorship account form is provided. Consequently, the presumption stated by this section should become increasingly defensible.

"The section also is designed to apply to various forms of multiple-party accounts which may be in use at the effective date of the legislation. The risk that it may turn nonsurvivorship accounts into unwanted survivorship arrangements is meliorated by various considerations. First of all, there is doubt that many persons using any form of multiple name account would not want survivorship rights to attach. Secondly, the survivorship incidents described by this section may be shown to have been against the intention of the parties. Finally, it would be wholly consistent with the purpose of the legislation to provide for a delayed effective date so that financial institutions could get notices to customers warning them of possible review of accounts which may be desirable because of the legislation.

"Subsection (c) accepts the New York view that an account opened by 'A' in his name as 'trustee for B' usually is intended by A to be an informal will of any balance remaining on deposit at his death. The section is framed so that accounts with more than one 'trustee,' or more than one 'beneficiary' can be accommodated. Section 6–103(c) would apply to such an account during the lifetimes of 'all parties.' 'Party' is defined by 6–101(7) so as to exclude a beneficiary who is not described by the account as having a present right of withdrawal.

"In the case of a trust account for two or more beneficiaries, the section prescribes a presumption that all beneficiaries who survive the last 'trustee' to die own equal and undivided interests in the account. This dovetails with Sections 6–111 and 6–112 which give the financial institution protection only if it pays to all beneficiaries who show a right to withdraw by presenting appropriate proof of death. . . ."

The Uniform Probate Code had been adopted wholly or substantially in sixteen states by 1989. Some other states have adopted portions of the code relating to will substitutes. Still others have other statutes allowing various will substitutes. These statutes are reviewed briefly in Restatement (Second) of Property, Donative Transfers, § 32.4, Statutory Note (Tent.Draft No. 12, March 28, 1989).

4. Even though will substitutes may be legally permissible, their use may encounter other legal and practical problems. Some of these problems are discussed in Wellman, Transfer–on–Death Securities Registration: A New Title Form, 21 Ga.L.Rev. 789 (1987).

FERRELL v. STINSON

Supreme Court of Iowa, 1953.
233 Iowa 1331, 11 N.W.2d 701.

Suit in equity by residuary devisee to quiet title to real estate and set aside a deed from testatrix to defendants which plaintiff claims was never legally delivered. Decree for plaintiff. Defendants appeal.

GARFIELD, J. The land in controversy is a farm of 220 acres in Franklin county, Iowa, subject to a mortgage of $2,500. Plaintiff asserts there was no valid delivery of the deed under which defendants claim. In her lifetime, the property was owned by Miss Mary Kamberling, who died on October 2, 1940, in Phoenix, Arizona. She was an only child who had inherited the farm from her parents. She had no near relatives. From early childhood Mary was a cripple who used crutches when she attended school in Iowa Falls, her girlhood home. She developed tuberculosis and about 1917 was taken to Phoenix where she continued to live as an invalid until her death.

In Iowa Falls, Mary formed a most intimate and enduring friendship with Mrs. Esgate, one of the defendants, a daughter of the late Justice Weaver of this court. In 1916 Mrs. Esgate also moved from Iowa Falls to Phoenix and lived there until 1932, when she moved to Washington, D.C. Mary lived with Mrs. Esgate part of that time. After moving to Washington, Mrs. Esgate returned to Phoenix for about six weeks on each of five occasions, during which she did what she could to relieve Miss Kamberling, whose condition grew progressively worse. Miss Kamberling was indebted to Mrs. Esgate and her husband for money loaned her.

The other two defendants, who, with Mrs. Esgate, were grantees of the deed, are Brooks Baughman of Cedar Falls, Iowa, a first cousin of the grantor (apparently her nearest living relative), and Mrs. I.W. Stinson of Mason City, Iowa, a distant cousin of Mary and a first cousin of plaintiff Mrs. Ferrell, also a distant cousin of the grantor-testatrix. Miss Kamberling was also attached to these three cousins, defendants Baughman and Mrs. Stinson and plaintiff Mrs. Ferrell, who visited and assisted her at times.

The deed under which the three defendants claim was executed on December 2, 1939, in Phoenix. Miss Kamberling, bedridden at the time, called in a young lady notary who lived next door, gave her a copy of a quitclaim deed she had filled in with pencil and asked her to copy it on a typewriter. As directed, the notary typed the deed on another form which was duly signed, witnessed by two witnesses and acknowledged. The grantor then handed the executed deed to her housekeeper, Mrs. Orbison, and asked her to put it in a little metal box in a closet opening into her bedroom. The servant did as directed and the deed remained in the box in the closet during the ten months until the grantor's death. The box was not locked and there is no evidence that there was a key for it.

About the time the deed was executed Miss Kamberling talked to the same notary about making a will. The notary, as requested, asked an attorney, Mr. Karz, to get in touch with Miss Kamberling. This attorney prepared a will and it was executed the following day, December 3. The will provides for payment of debts of the testatrix, directs the sale by her executrix of her real estate in Phoenix, describing it, in the event her debts are fully paid from her personal property, leaves two legacies of $400 each and some personal belongings, and bequeaths all the rest and residue of her estate to plaintiff Mrs. Ferrell. Following Miss Kamberling's death the will was admitted to probate both in Arizona and Franklin county, Iowa. Plaintiff claims the farm in question as residuary devisee.

Mrs. Flora Thompson was a close friend of Miss Kamberling who was named in the will as executrix. On December 3, the day the will was made, Miss Kamberling told Mrs. Thompson in substance, "I have made a deed of my Iowa farm to Mrs. I.W. Stinson, Brooks Baughman and Mrs. A.T. Esgate (the defendants), and the deed is placed in the box in the closet with other papers and after I am gone you are to take the deed out of the box and send it to Jane," meaning Mrs. Stinson. In this conversation Mrs. Thompson told testatrix she had always done everything she could for her while alive and would be very glad to do what she could after Miss Kamberling was gone. Mrs. Thompson had frequently seen the box in the closet before that time, but did not see it again till the day after Miss Kamberling's death. Mrs. Thompson then found the deed in the box in the closet, and on October 4, 1940, as directed by the grantor, mailed it to Mrs. Stinson at Mason City, who had it placed of record in Franklin county. When opened by Mrs.

Thompson, the box contained the deed, the will, some old canceled mortgages and checks and some tax receipts. The box in which the deed was kept apparently was not used for current papers. The lease to the farm and bills were kept in a folder in a table drawer in the sick room.

There is no doubt that Miss Kamberling desired and intended defendants should have this farm and believed she had effectively conveyed the farm to them. The equity in the Iowa farm is worth approximately three times her other property, her personalty and Arizona real estate. It is plain that she intended to divide her estate in four nearly equal shares between her three cousins and her devoted friend Mrs. Esgate. These four were the principal natural objects of her bounty.

The attorney who drew the will testified without objection: "At the time she gave me the information with respect to the will she told me she had disposed of her property in Iowa; that she had executed deeds to the people she wanted to have that property, and it would not be necessary to insert it in the will or be bothered with probate proceedings. . . . She told me specifically at that time she had disposed of the property by deed, and that all had been taken care of long before the will was drawn, that is, the property out of the State of Arizona."

There is competent evidence that Miss Kamberling told the grantees of the making of the deed. She also told intimate friends she had deeded her Iowa farm to the three defendants. Mrs. Smith, an acquaintance of twenty years who wrote letters for the invalid, testified: "Mary Kamberling had told me what disposition she had made of the Iowa land. . . . Shortly after Mary Kamberling made her will I was at her house and she told me she had made her will which covered her Phoenix property. She said, 'Not the farm, the Iowa property,' because that was deeded to Mrs. Esgate, her cousin Brooks (Baughman), and Mrs. Stinson; that she deeded it because they might break a will but a deed would secure the property and insure it going to the people she wanted it to go to."

Although the grantor lived ten months after making the deed and will, it fairly appears that she made them in contemplation of impending death. She was in the advanced stages of tuberculosis with many complications and was failing rapidly. There is no evidence she was able to or did leave her bed except to go to the hospital in January or February, 1940, for an operation in an attempt to prolong her life.

It was stipulated upon the trial that, until she died, Miss Kamberling rented the farm, received the rents and controlled its operation.

I. The deed having been duly executed and recorded, plaintiff has the burden of proving its nondelivery by evidence that is clear, satisfactory and convincing. This is true even though the recording was after the grantor's death. Plaintiff does not question the above rule but contends the presumption of delivery has been conclusively rebutted.

II. Delivery is of course essential to the validity of a deed. Our own and other decisions hold that delivery depends very largely upon the intent of the grantor, to be determined by his acts or words or both, and that a manual delivery is not essential if it appears that the grantor intended to relinquish dominion and control over the deed and have it take effect as a present conveyance of title. Anno. 129 A.L.R. 11, 12, and cases cited.

We have frequently said that actual manual transfer of the paper is not necessary and that acts and words evincing the grantor's intent to part with the deed and relinquish his right over it is a sufficient delivery. . . . We have declared time and again that the intent of the grantor is the controlling element in the delivery of a deed. . . .

This court has uniformly held that where an unrecorded deed is found in a box belonging to the grantor after his death, without more, there is no presumption of delivery. . . .

We have also frequently held that an effective delivery may be made by placing the deed in the hands of a third person, without reserving the right to recall it and with instructions to deliver to the grantee after the grantor's death. If the conveyance is beneficial to the grantee, the third person is presumed to act as the grantee's agent. The effect of thus placing the instrument with a third person is to reserve a life estate to the grantor with title immediately passing to the grantee but with the latter's right to possession and enjoyment postponed until the grantor's death. . . .

Davis v. John E. Brown College, 208 Iowa 480, 222 N.W. 858, and Boone Biblical College v. Forrest, 223 Iowa 1260, 275 N.W. 132, 116 A.L.R. 67, held there was a valid delivery where a deed was placed with a third party, in spite of an expressed reservation of the right to recall the instrument during the grantor's life, provided such reservation was never exercised. These decisions were contrary to the clear weight of authority and to the principles of some of our own cases, including Lathrop v. Knoop, 202 Iowa 621, 210 N.W. 764, and were overruled in Orris v. Whipple, 224 Iowa 1157, 280 N.W. 617, 129 A.L.R. 1. The Orris case also overruled Robertson v. Renshaw, 220 Iowa 572, 261 N.W. 645, which was based largely on Davis v. John E. Brown College. The three overruled cases were said to "stand alone as supporting the rule therein announced." [224 Iowa 1157, 280 N.W. 624, 129 A.L.R. 1.]

The trial court's decision in plaintiff's favor here is based entirely on Orris v. Whipple upon which plaintiff mainly relies. We are unable to agree that the Orris case, with which we are in entire accord, is controlling here. It was a suit at law in replevin by the grantees of an unrecorded deed, which had been executed and placed in the grantor's safety deposit box to which she alone had access. There was, to quote the opinion, "no semblance of a delivery either to the grantees or a third person." See Lawson v. Boo, 227 Iowa 100, 103, 287 N.W. 282. No instructions were given to the banker or anyone else to deliver the deed. The only evidence in the Orris case having any tendency to show delivery was that the grantor told some others she wanted plaintiffs, or one of them, to have the property and had prepared papers so providing. This court properly held that plaintiffs who had the burden, as the opinion points out, failed to prove delivery.

One important distinction between the case at bar and Orris v. Whipple is that here the deed was in the nature of a voluntary settlement among the principal natural objects of the grantor's bounty. In the cited case attention is called to the fact that the grantees were "not even collateral heirs" of the grantor.

The rule that a valid delivery may occur without actual transfer of possession of the deed is particularly true where as here the conveyance is one of voluntary settlement among the objects of the grantor's bounty. 26 C.J.S., Deeds, p. 239, § 42, subd. a; 18 C.J. p. 201, § 96. In such a case the mere fact that the grantor retains possession of the deed is not conclusive against its validity if there is no circumstance other than its retention to show the deed was not intended to be absolute. Annot. 129 A.L.R. 11, 40, and cases cited; 7 Thompson on Real Property, Perm.Ed., p. 639, § 4170, and cases cited; Leighton v. Leighton, 196 Iowa 1191, 1201, 194 N.W. 276.

Where there is a good faith voluntary conveyance to those who naturally have a claim upon the grantor's bounty, courts of equity are strongly inclined to uphold the deed and will do so unless impelled to the opposite conclusion by strong and convincing evidence. There is in such a case a high degree of mutual confidence between the parties. In this class of cases courts of equity do not put so much importance in the mere manual possession of the deed as in the intent of the grantor. If his intent to pass title presently to the grantee is satisfactorily shown, equity usually sustains such a conveyance, even where the grantor retained manual possession of the deed. . . .

Mary Kamberling executed this deed when she was in her last illness. By the deed and will she clearly made what she believed was a final and effective disposition of her property among the principal claimants to her bounty. She handed the deed to Mrs. Orbison and instructed her to put it in a box in the closet where it remained. It is a fair inference that the grantor in her weakened condition was physically unable to go to the box during the remainder of her life. The grantor, so far as shown by the evidence, never intended to exercise further control or dominion over the deed. She plainly told Mrs. Thompson where the deed was and would be at her death and asked her to mail it to Mrs. Stinson, giving the address, when the grantor died. Mrs. Thompson at least impliedly promised to do as requested and later made good her promise. The deed was found where the grantor had said it would be.

Miss Kamberling told her attorney that her will was not to include her Iowa property, which had been deeded to those she wanted to have it. On the testimony of the attorney, see McKemey v. Ketchum, 188 Iowa 1081, 1082, 175 N.W. 325, and Payne v. Henderson, 340 Ill. 160, 172 N.E. 173. She later told defendants and others of the deed in a way that clearly shows she believed she had made an effective delivery and intended that what she did would so operate. Evidence of statements by the grantor that he had executed the deed has been "considered a potent factor, in connection with other circumstances, in determining whether or not there has been a delivery." Anno. 129 A.L.R. 11, 27, and cases cited. It is true the belief of the grantor is not sufficient of itself to prove delivery. Heavner v. Kading, 209 Iowa 1271, 1274, 228 N.W. 311.

Let us suppose the grantor had handed the deed to Mrs. Thompson when instructing her as to its disposition, that Mrs. Thompson had agreed to do as directed and then herself placed the deed in this same box in the closet. In the light of the evidence in the case there would then clearly have been a valid constructive delivery of this deed under our decisions. Even if the grantor had access to the box, this would not invalidate a previously completed delivery. . . . Since the controlling consideration is the intent of the grantor, we think the failure to hand the deed to Mrs. Thompson is not fatal to the claim of delivery. Unless we are to sacrifice substance for form, the legal effect of what was done is the substantial equivalent of the supposed case.

Plaintiff relies on one piece of testimony which it is claimed negatives delivery. The housekeeper testified, "After she made a loan on her place of $2,000 she said she had every intention of changing her will or deed, I wouldn't say which, or if she made both, I don't know." On this subject, however, Mrs. Smith, friend and typist, testified: "I was at Mary Kamberling's home every afternoon while the housekeeper was gone. During that time she talked to me about changing her will. She said that the way the will was worded Mrs. Thompson would be unable to give away any of the household furniture or any of her personal things and that there were certain things in the house she wished to go to certain friends, and that was why she felt she should change the will so that Mrs. Thompson would have the privilege of giving those things away. She wanted to make lists of various things in the house to go to certain friends but she never got it done."

In view of Mrs. Smith's testimony about talk of changing the will and under the entire record showing the grantor's complete satisfaction with the deed, we think the housekeeper's uncertain statement does not tend to show the deed was not delivered. We find nothing to indicate that the grantor did not intend the deed to be absolute except its retention in the box in the closet. Under the authorities heretofore cited, where the deed as here is a voluntary settlement, this circumstance is insufficient to establish that the deed was not delivered.

From the standpoint of equity and justice there can be no doubt that defendants are entitled to prevail unless such a decision runs counter to some established rule of law. We think there is no legal principle or no decision of this court which requires an affirmance of the lower court. We hold there was a valid delivery of the deed.

In a case of this kind a plaintiff must recover on the strength of his own title. . . . Here it appears beyond question that the grantor intended not only that defendants should have this farm but also that plaintiff should not have it. It is undisputed that the will under which plaintiff claims was not intended to include the farm. Plaintiff is asking a court of equity to take the property from those whom the grantor intended to have it, holding as they do under a deed delivered in accordance with her expressed directions, and to vest title in one whom she intended not to have it. We hold the relief asked should be denied.

Reversed.

NOTES

1. Compare with Ferrell Restatement (Second) of Property, Donative Transfers, § 32.4 (Tent.Draft No. 12, March 28, 1989): "An inter vivos donative document of transfer is valid even though it is a substitute for a will, in that the donor's current beneficial enjoyment of the gift property is not significantly curtailed during the donor's lifetime and the donee's interest in the gift property can be revoked by the donor." Following criticism by members of the American Law Institute, this draft provision was referred back to the drafter for reconsideration. 57 U.S.L.W. 2690 (May 30, 1989). Is such a broad exemption from statutes of wills for transfers that purport to be inter vivos, but are testamentary in operation, justifiable? What policies would be served by frustrating the intent of such donors? Should such donors be treated differently from persons who attempt to execute wills but fail to comply with statutory formalities for wills?

2. There is authority to the effect that if a deed which on its face appears to be an unconditional conveyance is handed to the grantee named therein, with a statement to the effect that it is to be effective as a conveyance only upon the occurrence of some future event (e.g., consummation of an impending marriage) the instrument is effective even though the stipulated event does not occur. Such an instrument which, though it does not say so, is intended to be effective only upon the happening of a condition, is called an "escrow." Hence, the proposition in question is that an instrument of conveyance cannot be "delivered as an escrow" to the grantee named therein, though if it is handed to a third person, its character of escrow is provable. On the other hand, there is authority that, even though the instrument is handed to the grantee, evidence is admissible that the grantor at that time had no ascertainable intent that it should have legal effect, conditional or unconditional; e.g., his purpose in handing the paper to the grantee might be to give the grantee, or his attorney, an opportunity to determine whether or not it is in satisfactory form.

Is there any acceptable reason for holding that an instrument cannot be handled as an escrow to the grantee? One explanation offered is as follows: "The reason of the rule is quite obvious. If it were possible to prove in every case that parol conditions were attached to the formal delivery of a deed there would be no safety in accepting a deed. Titles would be open to attack at all times, and the practical result would be to defeat the solemn provisions of a duly executed and formally delivered deed by parol testimony." Chaudoir v. Witt, 170 Wis. 556, 170 N.W. 932, 174 N.W 925 (1919). This suggests that a false claim that an instrument was a mere escrow, which never became a fully effective conveyance because an alleged parol condition did not occur, may sometimes succeed—i.e., adherence to the rule in question is necessary to prevent fraud upon the grantee. But notice that it is equally possible that adherence to the rule may result in fraud upon the grantor—i.e., the grantee may use the rule to obtain ownership notwithstanding an agreement to the contrary with the grantor. If the contest is between the grantor and an innocent purchaser for value from the grantee, it may well be that the latter should be protected, but the need for doing so does not justify the rule in question, since the doctrine of estoppel furnishes an adequate rationale for the desired protection.

It has also been argued that to permit extrinsic proof of an escrow agreement would violate the parol evidence rule. But the proper view, it seems, is that the parol evidence rule—more meaningfully expressed as the rule excluding extrinsic evidence—has no function with reference to the question of whether or not a writing was intended to be legally operative as evidence of a contract or conveyance. The instrument itself commonly says nothing concerning this matter, and extrinsic evidence necessarily must be relied upon to answer the question. Once it is determined that the instrument was intended to have legally operative effect, the parol evidence rule becomes functional with reference to the question of whether or not extrinsic evidence is admissible, in addition to the writing, to establish the intent or understanding of the parties to the instrument.

If it is said that the parol evidence rule is the rationale for the rule that if a "deed" is handed to the grantee, evidence is inadmissible to show that it was intended as an escrow—i.e., that it was to be effective only upon the occurrence of a stipulated condition—would it not be logically necessary to say that if a "deed" is handed to the grantee, evidence is inadmissible to show that it was intended to have no effect whatever—that it was handed over for purposes of inspection only, or the like? But it does not appear that any court has adopted the latter position.

Finally, it may be noticed that some scholars have suggested that the rule in question—that if the instrument is handed to the grantee, it cannot be regarded as an escrow—is merely "a relic of the primitive formalism which attached some peculiar efficacy to the physical transfer of the deed as a symbolical transfer of the land"—that the handing over of the instrument is equivalent to a livery of seisin, a solemn, conclusive ceremony of conveyance. If this is the "explanation," no argument is needed to show its inadequacy in the context of today's society. Some courts have found ways of evading it, or have openly repudiated it, as in Chillemi v. Chillemi, 197 Md. 257, 78 A.2d 750 (1951).

3. Suppose that A executes a deed which, on its face, purports to be an unconditional conveyance of a possessory fee simple to A's son, B, then hands the instrument to C with an instruction that he is to turn it over to B if, within 90 days after A's death, B pays stated sums of money to A's other children. A thereafter dies, and within 90 days B offers to pay the money; the other children refuse to accept and contend that the deed is invalid. What are the relevant issues and arguments? Consider the questions stated in the paragraph above.

See Jackson v. Jackson, 67 Or. 44, 135 P. 201 (1913)—does the court adequately answer the questions?

Suppose that O, who has an invalid daughter, D, and a son, S, executes two deeds. One purports to be an unconditional conveyance of a possessory fee simple estate in land to D; the other purports to be an unconditional conveyance of a possessory fee simple estate in the same land to S. O hands both instruments to H, with an instruction that, upon the death of O, if D is then living, H is to turn over to D the instrument naming her as grantee and destroy the deed naming S as grantee; if D is not then living, H is to turn over to S the deed naming him as grantee and destroy the deed to D. O thereafter dies, D and S surviving, and a contest ensues between D and S concerning the land. What are the relevant issues and arguments?

Suppose that X executes a deed which purports to be an unconditional conveyance of a possessory fee simple estate in X's land to Y, and that Y executes a deed which purports to be an unconditional conveyance of a possessory fee simple in Y's land to X. They also jointly sign a written statement that their purpose is to make an irrevocable arrangement so that on the death of one of them the survivor shall be sole owner of the land described in both deeds—i.e., on the death of either, his deed shall be operative and the deed of the survivor shall be inoperative. The two deeds and the statement are then placed in a safe deposit box to which both have access, or are handed to a third person with instructions to hold the instruments until one of the parties dies, then turn them over to the survivor. X thereafter dies, and a dispute follows between his heirs and Y. What are the relevant issues and arguments? See Kniebbe v. Wade, 161 Ohio St. 294, 118 N.E.2d 833 (1954); Kenney v. Parks, 125 Cal. 146, 57 P. 772 (1899); Collins v. Dye, 94 F.2d 799 (9th Cir. 1938); 23 Minn.L.Rev. 94 (1938).

Can you draft granting clauses which would be likely to avoid the disputes in the hypothetical cases above?

Part Three

PRIVATE INTERESTS IN LAND

At this stage of your study, you are aware that "ownership" is a concept which has varied meanings, depending upon the relationship of the parties and the nature of their claims. Several persons may have simultaneous interests of similar or diverse nature in a particular thing or tract of land. An owner may split up his ownership into lesser interests and confer some or all of them upon others.

The array of interests recognized by American courts today did not come into existence overnight, or even in modern times. They are products of centuries of development, dating back at least to the eleventh century. It is difficult, if not impossible, to understand the modern scheme without some awareness of the historical factors which were most significant in the shaping of these interests. This does not mean that the student of property law must make a detailed study of every step in the long evolutionary process. It must suffice to glance backward briefly at a few high spots.

A forward view is also necessary. Some attempt should be undertaken to evaluate the established categories of interests within the context of modern conditions. You will encounter characteristics of some interests which serve no policies of contemporary society. For the lawyer, in drafting deeds, wills and other instruments, this situation gives rise to a responsibility to steer clear of the booby traps which lurk in this branch of the law. For the bar, courts and legislatures, here is a challenge to bring the law up to date.

Chapter 12

A BRIEF LOOK AT THE HISTORICAL DEVELOPMENT OF ESTATES DOCTRINE

One of Mr. Justice Holmes' choice aphorisms ran: "There are times when a page of history is worth a volume of logic." This could well be the text for a sermon on the law of real property. While the modern student does not need a long bath in feudalism, he or she must understand the roots of the Anglo-American law of estates in land. Those roots still nourish the contemporary plant and, while the "calculus of estates" has a peculiar logic of its own, it is the logic of history, not the designed concept of any single group of legal thinkers.

CHESHIRE, THE MODERN LAW OF REAL PROPERTY

Pages 9–27 (6th ed. 1949).

Feudalism in Europe. Feudalism is a word of some vagueness and ambiguity, and one which was certainly unknown to the peoples to whom it is applied. It is often expected to represent the history of Western Europe from the eighth to the fourteenth century, and like the modern use of the word *capitalism,* or in some countries *socialism,* to describe the social characteristics of the period. We, however, are concerned only with its tenurial aspect. To a lawyer feudalism means that the land of the country is not owned by the persons who to the outward eye appear to be owners, but is held by them from somebody else. It is the negation of independence. It implies subordination; it means that one man is deliberately made inferior to another.

Now when it is remembered that in pre-feudal days the land of Europe was owned absolutely, though subject to custom, by persons who were grouped together in village communities, it becomes a matter of interest to discover why it was that a great part of the world lapsed from a state of comparative freedom into one of servility, why land ownership disappeared and land tenure took its place. The change undoubtedly represented a retrogression in the history of the world, but in Europe it was one of the necessary consequences of the disruption of the Roman Empire by the Barbarian invaders. The overthrow of that Empire caused chaos and disorganisation in Europe and produced conditions in which it was necessary for private persons to procure for themselves a higher degree of protection than fell within the capabilities of their own unaided efforts. In those days interference with personal freedom or with the ownership of property might come from several different quarters, such as a revolt of the peasants, the arrogance of a powerful neighbour, the extortion of the government or the hostility of some tribe. The only method of obtaining security was mutual support, and so it came to pass that men deliberately subordinated themselves to the strong hand of some magnate, and were compensated for the diminution of personal independence and the loss of land ownership by acquiring the protection afforded by the forces of which he disposed. This process involved both a personal and a proprietary subordination, but it is only on the latter that we need dwell. . . .

One of the effects of the feudalisation of Europe was that from a legal aspect land became the exclusive bond of union between men. Individual or communal ownership was destroyed. The ownership of the whole of the land in any given district was vested in the overlord, and the persons who had formerly owned it in their own right now held it from the overlord. In return for the land which they held they were bound to render services, chiefly of a military nature, to the overlord, while the latter in his turn was bound to protect the holders. Feudalism implied a reciprocity of rights and duties. The lord gained in dignity and consequence and became entitled to personal services, while the tenant obtained security. . . .

Feudalism in England. We now come to consider the effect which this Continental feudalism had upon the land law of England. As the scope of this book precludes the desirability of entering at length into questions of legal history, it will not be necessary to discuss the difficult problem of the extent to which feudalism existed in England prior to the Conquest. That a system was in vogue which bore similarities to Continental feudalism cannot be doubted, but the only fact that we need notice here is that the Normans applied their own ideas to the conditions prevalent in this country, and succeeded in establishing an English variety of feudalism which, though differing in many respects from that of the Continent, became a striking and universal feature of English land law. The attitude and policy of William left England, whatever it may have been before, a highly feudalised state. His attitude was that, since the English landowners had denied his right to the Crown of England and had compelled him to assert it by force, their landed possession became his to dispose of as he chose. What he did was not so much to seize land and parcel it out among his Norman followers, as to allow all Englishmen who recognised him as King to redeem by money payments the estates which by right of conquest had momentarily passed to him. . . .

Every acre of land in the country was held of the King. The King himself was the owner of the land in the true sense of the word, and he was the sole owner. . . .

If a tenant held immediately of the King, he was said to hold of him in chief or *in capite.* But the position might be less simple. Instead of a tenant holding directly of the King he might hold immediately, as for instance where C held of B, who held of A, who held of the King. C, who stood at the bottom of the scale and who would look more like an owner than anybody else interested in the land, was called the *tenant in demesne—tenet terram in dominico suo.* The persons between him and the King were called *mesne lords,* and their lordships were called *seignories.* A held the land, not *in demesne,* but in service, since he was entitled to the services of B, and B similarly held in service, since he was entitled to the services of C. The services due from these tenants would not necessarily be of the same nature, for A might hold of the King by military service, B of A in return for a money rent, and C of B in return for some personal service. In such a case each grantee owed to his immediate grantor the service that he had agreed to render, and from this point of view the service was called *intrinsec.* Services were not merely personal, but were charged on the tenement, so that if A failed in the performance of his military duties the King could distrain upon the land in the hands of C, as could A if B fell into arrear with the rent. B could agree to perform the military service in place of A, but no private arrangement of this kind could free the land from the burden. From this point of view the service was called for *forinsec;* i.e., foreign to any bargain between other parties. Of course, if, for example, A failed to perform his military service and the King proceeded against the land in C's occupation, the latter had a remedy against A, called the writ of *mesne.*

Now the most striking fact about English feudalism was the universality of this doctrine of land tenure. On the Continent tenure applied only to those who held lands in return for military services, but in England it applied to every holder whether the services were military, pecuniary or agricultural. Moreover, a movement began by which the number of mesne lordships was increased to a bewildering extent. As each year passed, more and more sub-tenancies were created. A, who held of the King, would transfer his land or part of it to B, and B to C, and so on, but each transfer, instead of being an out-and-out grant by which the transferor got rid of his entire interest, would operate as a grant of land to be held by each transferee as tenant of his immediate transferor.

This process, which was termed subinfeudation, was so common that Maitland was able to discover a case where there were as many as eight sub-tenancies in the same piece of land. One explanation of this reluctance to part with one's entire interest in land must be sought in the exceptional importance which distinguished land in the centuries immediately succeeding the Conquest. Apart from cattle, land was practically the only form of wealth. Money was scarce, and something had to take its place as a medium of exchange.

It thus became clear that the exceptional position occupied by land made it advisable for tenants to keep as tenacious a hold upon it as possible, and, when a transfer was contemplated, to subinfeudate rather than dispose of it outright. But for reasons into which we need not enter, the practice of subinfeudation was obnoxious to the great lords, and was finally stopped in 1290 by the Statute *Quia Emptores.*

This statute, while recognising the right of every freeman to dispose of the whole or of part of his land, expressly provided that after such a transfer the transferee was to hold from the same lord as the transferor had held from previously to the sale. Every alienation of a fee simple estate in land that has taken place since this statute has therefore been an out-and-out transfer, so that, if the grantor held immediately of A, the grantee steps into the same position and holds of

A also. Thus, at a comparatively early date the power to create new tenancies in the case of the fee simple estate in lands was taken away, except in the case of the Crown. Since *Quia Emptores* did not bind the Crown, tenants *in capite* could not alienate without the license of the King, a disability which meant in effect that they would pay a fine for the privilege. Thus the statute prevented for the future the creation of new tenancies, but at the time of its passage the process of subinfeudation had gone to such lengths that English land was already overlaid by a network of tenures.

Forms of tenure. There was not one common kind of tenure. We have seen how in early days, if a man wanted work of a regular nature done for him, he would generally get it done in exchange for land granted by him to the workman. Considering the diversity of personal needs which require to be satisfied, it is obvious that the services due from tenants would vary considerably in nature, importance and dignity. One tenant had to fight, another to look after a household, or to provide arms, or to pray for the soul of his overlord, or to do such agricultural work as might be demanded of him. There were vast differences between the possible services. It was considered an honourable thing to fight, but not to plough, and thus it came to pass that there gradually arose different kinds or forms of tenure based upon the differences in the nature of the services. It would be out of place to discuss here the various forms which tenure took, but it may be convenient to set out a table showing the state of affairs in the time of Edward I, when the tenures had become stabilised.

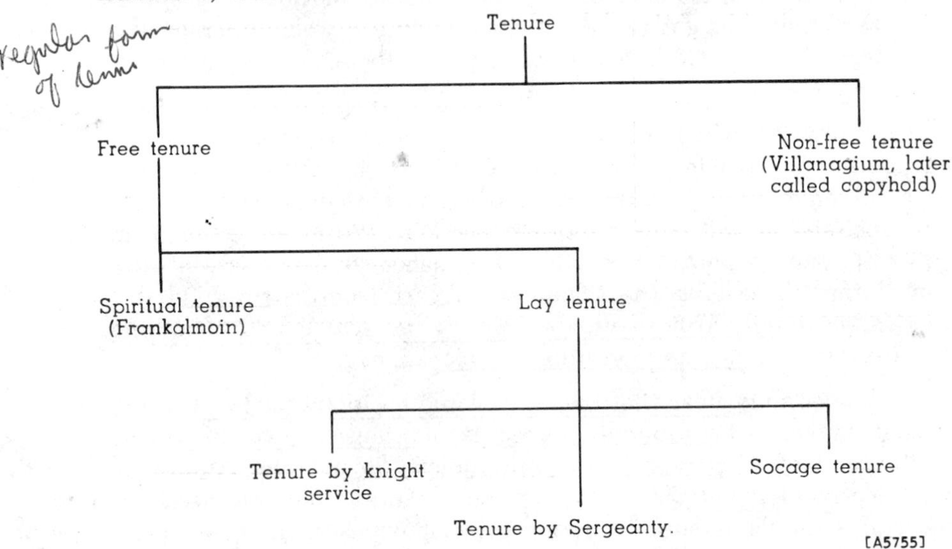

In addition to these regular tenures there also existed in certain districts a few customary methods of landholding under which the lands were subject in various respects to a number of abnormal incidents. Instances are gavelkind, borough-English, and ancient demesne. . . .

Knight service. The most important of the regular tenures in early days was knight service, or the tenure by which a man was obliged to render military services in return for the land that he held. . . . For about a hundred years after the Conquest the army—to the strength of about 5000 knights—was actually raised in this way, but it was soon discovered that such a short service as forty days was not conducive to the success of military operations, and the King began about 1166 to exact money payments called scutage from the tenants in chief instead of requiring the production of the fixed quota of knights. But by the time of Edward I even scutage had become useless as a means of providing an army, and it can be said that thenceforth the tenure ceased to be military in the sense that it no longer served to supply forces for the defence of the realm.

What at first sight seems remarkable is that knight service, instead of falling into oblivion after it had ceased to fulfil the function for which it was introduced, continued to develop, and ended by hardening into a legal system far stricter and more onerous than it had been originally. The reason for this unnatural continuance was that, quite apart from the duty of military service, the tenure carried with it certain feudal incidents which had such a high financial value for the lords of whom the lands were held that to foster and develop it became a matter of great personal interest. Subinfeudation led to the extension of knight service, and though the military sub-tenant had neither to fight nor to pay scutage, yet, being a military tenant, he was subject to a number of onerous claims from which he would have been free had his tenure been one of the other forms. As the matter is now merely of antiquarian interest, we must confine ourselves to the barest statement of the most valuable of the rights demandable from a military tenant, namely:—

1. **Relief.** The lord was entitled to the payment of a certain sum, called a relief, when a new tenant succeeded to the land on the death of the old tenant. Upon the death of the tenant payment of the relief entitled the heir to immediate possession, but this was not so where the land was held of the King. In this case the official escheator took possession and held an inquest as to who was next heir. It was only when the heir had done homage and paid the relief that he was entitled to enter the land. This royal privilege of first possession was called *primer seisin.*

2. **Aids.** The lord was entitled to demand in three special cases that his tenants should pay him a certain sum of money called an aid. The three cases arose when the lord was imprisoned and required a ransom; when he desired to make his eldest son a knight; and when he was obliged to supply his eldest daughter with a dowry on her marriage.

3. **Escheat propter delictum tenentis.** The commission by the tenant of a felony caused the land to escheat, that is to pass to the lord of whom it was held. Felony originally meant a breach of that faith and trust which ought to exist between lord and vassal; e.g., where the tenant laid violent hands on his lord. At an early date, however, "felony" lost its exclusively feudal signification and came to mean in effect any serious crime, such as murder. The result of this extended

meaning was to benefit the lords, and though it would seem incompatible with the interests of the Crown as custodian of the public peace that the land of a murderer or a thief should pass to a subject, the right of escheat was expressly confirmed by Magna Carta in 1215, subject to the proviso that the land should be held by the Crown for a year and a day. Forfeiture of the land was now said to occur because the felon's blood was attainted or corrupted.

4. **Wardship.** The most profitable right of the lord was that of wardship. If an existing tenant died leaving as his heir a male under 21 or a female under 14, the lord was entitled to the wardship of the heir, and as a consequence was free to make what use he liked of the lands during the minority without any obligation to render an account of his stewardship. Upon reaching the prescribed age the ward might sue for *livery* or *ousterlemain;* i.e., might enforce delivery of the land. For this privilege half a year's profits had to be paid, though relief was not exigible.

5. **Marriage.** Another privilege which the lord enjoyed in respect of infant tenants was the right of marriage. As Blackstone has said:

"While the infant was in ward, the guardian had the power of tendering him or her a suitable match, without disparagement, or inequality: which if the infants refused, they forfeited the value of the marriage, *valorem maritagii,* to their guardian: that is, so much as a jury would assess, or anyone would bona fide give to the guardian for such an alliance: and if the infants married themselves without the guardian's consent, they forfeited double the value, *duplicem valorem maritagii.*"

14th cent

Tenure by sergeanty was in early times, and from an economic point of view, of considerable importance, but it soon ceased to be anything more than a peculiarly dignified method of holding land. All tenures imply service of one kind or another, but the characteristic of sergeanty was that it required the tenant to perform services of an essentially personal nature. . . . A great lord would require that his accounts should be kept, his letters carried, his estates managed, armour provided, his food cooked, and so on, and he would in most cases grant lands to various sergeants to be held by them so long as the duties were faithfully performed. However, as time went on, it was realized that this was scarcely a convenient method of supplying the needs of life, and tenure by sergeanty began to decay as early as the fourteenth century. . . .

Abolition of military tenures. It is not necessary to describe these tenures further, because in 1660 a considerable simplification of the forms of landholding was effected by the legislature. The statute for the abolition of military tenures which was passed in that year, practically destroyed all the *free* lay tenures except socage. Tenure by knight service was destroyed altogether, and sergeanty was allowed to continue only in an emasculated form. Formerly it had rendered the tenant liable to onerous duties similar to those that might be exacted from a knight service tenant, but the effect of the Act was to abolish it as a separate tenure, and, where it existed, only to leave the privilege of performing those honorary services which, as we have seen, were peculiar to the higher ranks of sergeants. In other words, sergeanty was converted into socage, and the only peculiarity about socage land which had formerly been sergeanty was that the tenant might in some cases substantiate his right to perform certain honorary and dignified incidents.

Frankalmoin was the tenure by which a man made provision for the repose of his soul, and it arose where lands were granted to an ecclesiastical corporation on the implied understanding that the corporation as tenant would say prayers and masses for the souls of the grantor and his heirs. For various reasons the tenure fell into desuetude, and, though it was not formally abolished by the Act of 1660, it is seldom encountered at the present day.

We must now briefly describe the two tenures of socage and copyhold, which held the field until the legislation of 1925 abolished the latter.

Socage. As distinguished from knight service, socage was that species of tenure which represented a new aspect that the economic life of the country gradually began to wear. It was essentially nonmilitary and free from the worst features of knight service. At first it could not be defined in positive terms, but was described negatively as being that form of tenure which was neither spiritual, military, sergeanty, nor villeinage.

In early days the services due in respect of the land varied considerably. The tenant might pay a nominal rent sufficient to keep on record the fact that the lands were held of the lord, or a substantial rent equal to the economic value of the land, while sometimes his obligation would extend to the performance of agricultural services. Originally, no doubt, the socmanni, as they were called, belonged to the lower orders of society, but the tendency was for this mode of landholding to extend upwards for it was free from the worst of the feudal burdens incidental to knight service, and to escape those even the greater landowners were willing to sacrifice something of their dignity.

The next step was that it became usual to commute services, whatever these might have been, into money payments, and though these, when they were originally fixed, no doubt represented the economic value of the land, yet with the gradual fall in the value of money they became in course of time so insignificant in amount as not to be worth the trouble of collection.

So socage became the great residuary tenure. It included every tenure which was not knight service, sergeanty, frankalmoin or villeinage, and its outstanding characteristic came to be that it involved some service which was absolutely certain and fixed, and which in the vast majority of cases took the form of a money payment. It was free from the obnoxious rights of wardship and marriage that characterised knight service. The guardian of an infant socage tenant was the nearest relative who was incapable of inheriting the land. It was enacted by the Statute of Marlborough, 1267, that a guardian in socage must account for the profits of the land at the end of his stewardship, and must not give or sell the ward in marriage.

Copyhold tenure. To understand the character of copyhold tenure we must refer once more to the feudal manor, which was the unit of society in medieval England.

A typical manor consisted of

(a) the land belonging to the lord, which was called his demesne,

(b) the land held of the lord by free tenants whether in socage or knight service,

(c) the land held of the lord by persons called villein tenants,

(d) rights of jurisdiction exercisable by the lord over the free tenants, in the Court Baron, and over the villeins in the Court Customary,

(e) waste land on which the tenants were entitled to pasture their cattle.

The first point that emerges about the villeins is that it was they who cultivated the lord's demesne, a practice which originated in what has been termed the farm system. "Farm" in Anglo-Saxon times meant food, and the system in vogue was for the tenant, in return for his holding, to produce a farm—that is, enough food to sustain his lord for some given period, say a night, a week, or a fortnight.

In the thirteenth century this primitive system gave way to the labour service system, which meant that the villein tenant came under an obligation, often specified with the greatest detail, to cultivate by his own labour his lord's demesne. . . .

But in the fourteenth and fifteenth centuries this labour service system gave way to a money payment system under which the tenant in villeinage paid a rent to his lord instead of giving personal services, and the lord cultivated his demesne by hired labour. . . .

The term "copyhold" arose as follows: the copyhold tenant, like his predecessor the villein, held at the will of the lord, but yet at the same time he held on the conditions which had become fixed by the customs of his particular manor. The lord's will could not be exercised capriciously, but only in conformity with custom. The lord still held a court, and that court kept records of all transactions affecting the lands. These records were called the rolls of the court. When, for instance, a tenant sold his interest to a third party, the circumstances of the sale would be recorded, and the buyer would receive a copy of the court rolls in so far as they affected his holding. Inasmuch as he held his estate by copy of court roll, he came to be called a copyholder.

The change from villeinage to copyhold was of far-reaching importance to the tenant. He was rid of all traces of servility; he acquired an interest which in essentials was on all-fours with interests in land held by socage tenure, and above all he obtained recognition and protection from the King's courts. This protection was assured by the end of the fifteenth century.

Summary of tenures in 1925. If we now take stock of the feudal tenures as they existed in 1925 we shall find the position to have been as follows: the greater part of English land was held by socage tenure, a considerable part was subject to copyhold tenure, while the remainder was held either in grand sergeanty or in frankalmoin, or was affected by the peculiar customs of gavelkind, borough-English, or ancient demesne. Here was room for at least one form of simplification, and we shall see later that the Law of Property Acts, 1922 and 1925, seized the opportunity. They converted copyhold and ancient demesne into freehold tenure; they abolished gavelkind, borough-English, and all other customary modes of descent; and they purported to abolish frankalmoin. The honorary services incident to sergeanty were retained. Escheat, which was the right of a lord to take the land of his tenant who had died intestate without leaving heirs, was abolished and replaced by a right in the Crown to take the land as *bona vacantia* in the same way that it takes goods.

The result is that though the general theory of tenure is still a part of English law in the sense that all land is held of a superior and is incapable of absolute ownership, yet the law of tenure is both simpler and of less significance then it was before 1926. It is simpler because there is now only one form of tenure—namely, socage. It is of less significance because all the tenurial incidents (including escheat) which might in exceptional cases have brought profit to a mesne lord have been abolished, so that there is no inducement for a private person to prove that he is the lord of land. We can, in fact, now describe the theory of tenure, despite the great part that it has played in the history of English law, as a conception of merely academic interest. It is of so little practical importance that a fee simple tenant can fairly claim to be as complete an owner of the land as he is of his goods.

VANCE, THE QUEST FOR TENURE IN THE UNITED STATES

33 Yale Law Journal 248–250 (1924).

. . . Lands in Colonial America were undoubtedly granted by the English Crown to be held in free and common socage, "as our Manor at East-Greenwich, in the County of Kent" [1] or as in the patent given by Charles II to William Penn, "to bee holden of Us Our heires and Successors, Kings of England, as of Our Castle of Windsor in Our County of Berks, in free and common Socage, by fealty only for all Services, and not in Capite or by Knights Service: Yielding and paying therefore to Us, Our heires and Successors, Two Beaver Skins . . . ." Unquestionably there was land tenure in Colonial lands, even though of the mild and somewhat defeudalized type possible after the statute of 12 Car. II, c. 24. Then what has become of it? Look about as you may, you will see none of the familiar signs of English land tenure; no doing of homage, no swearing of fealty, no reliefs, no rent service or distress

1. As in the first charter of Virginia (1606).

in case of grants in fee (except in Pennsylvania), no escheat to the original grantor, even though such grantor be the Federal government, but only to the State in which the land lies.[2] There appears to be no tenure at all. . . . What can have become of that Colonial tenure, which was so very real and active as to keep the colonists in unceasing conflict and turmoil with the royal governors, or unhappy proprietaries, who attempted to take advantage of it and enforce the rendering of services reserved, here nearly always taking the form of quit rents, and which did so much to bring on the Revolution? The answer has puzzled our scholars and judges. Professor Gray thought it not probable that so "fundamental an alteration in the theory of property as the abolition of tenure would be worked by a change of political sovereignty." [3]

It is quite true that some of our states quickly took advantage of their newly-acquired independence to abolish all feudal tenures by legislative fiat, declaring that henceforth all lands should be allodial. Some others, while seeming to recognize the continuance of tenure, declared that thereafter all land tenure should be allodial, an expression that greatly pains some writers to whom the word allodium negatives *feud*, and therefore tenure. Yet others simply forgot it. And curiously enough, those which forgot about tenure have since been no more troubled by it than those which solemnly destroyed it. . . . Most lawyers are of the opinion, however, that, except possibly in Pennsylvania, it makes precious little difference in the practical working of our law whether tenure exists or not. . . .[4]

IN RE O'CONNOR'S ESTATE

Supreme Court of Nebraska, 1934.
126 Neb. 182, 252 N.W. 826.

YEAGER, DISTRICT JUDGE. This is an appeal by the state of Nebraska from the judgment of the district court for Adams county, Nebraska, in which county the estate of John O'Connor was probated. The estate escheated to the state of Nebraska for want of heirs. The county of Adams contends that the state is liable for the payment of an inheritance tax. This is the only question in the case. The county of Adams was successful in the action in district court and the state of Nebraska has appealed to this court.

It appears that this case must be determined on the true meaning of the term "escheat." In early England or during the feudal period, escheat meant the falling back or reversion of lands to the lord of the fee upon the failure of heirs capable of inheritance under the original

2. This fact, however, does not negative the feudal origin of modern escheat. The state merely succeeds the Federal Government as chief lord of the fee, just as the State of Texas succeeded the Mexican Government upon its declaration of independence.

3. Gray, Rule Against Perpetuities § 22 (3d ed. 1915).

4. [For a brief discussion of "three points at which it may be contended that the presence or absence of tenure between grantor and grantee in fee simple has some significance," see I Am.L.Prop. 59 (Casner ed. 1952).]

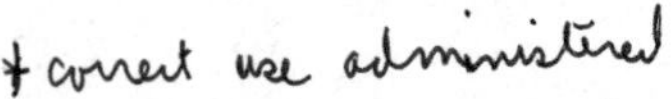

grant. In both England and the United States now, by escheat is meant the lapsing or reverting to the crown or the state as the original and ultimate proprietor of real estate, by reason of a failure of persons legally entitled to hold the same.

Clearly the theory of the law in the United States, then, is that first and originally the state was the proprietor of all real property and last and ultimately will be its proprietor, and what is commonly termed ownership is in fact but tenancy, whose continuance is contingent upon legally recognized rights of tenure, transfer, and of succession in use and occupancy. When this tenancy expires or is exhausted by reason of the failure of the state or the law to recognize any person or persons in whom such tenancy can be continued, then the real estate reverts to and falls back upon its original and ultimate proprietor, or, in other words, escheats to the state.

This state has never departed from the accepted meaning and interpretation of escheat in the United States. In our first Constitution (Const.1866, art. 6, § 3) it was provided: "All lands the title to which shall fail from a defect of heirs shall revert or escheat to the people." This provision is no longer to be found in our Constitution, but in section 3, art. 7, escheat is recognized. Though the above quoted provision has been taken out of the Constitution, it has never been removed from the statutes, where it has remained unchanged since 1875. Section 76–501, Comp.St.1929, being the provision referred to, is as follows: "Upon the failure of heirs the title shall vest at once in the state, without an inquest or other proceedings in the nature of office found." It then becomes apparent that in this state by "escheat" is meant a reversion of title to the state upon failure of heirs.

Section 6622, Rev.St.1913, contained the law providing for taxes upon inheritances. On account of its length we will not quote it here, but an analysis of its provisions clearly shows that what was intended was a tax upon a right of succession to property by inheritance, will, or by transfer made in contemplation of death, which is clearly distinguishable from a reversion, which can only take place where the title holder dies without will, without heirs, and without having made a transfer of the property in contemplation of death.

The appellee urges that, since escheat is mentioned in the seventh paragraph of the statutes providing the order and method of distribution of real estate in intestate estates (Comp.St.1929, § 30–102), the Legislature must therefore have intended to classify the state as a beneficiary. With this contention we cannot agree. The effect of such a theory would be the restriction and abridgment of the right of reversion which it had from earliest times, which right has been declared by Constitution and statute in such manner as to leave no doubt of the intention to retain it unimpaired. Escheat is one of the incidents of our state sovereignty and it cannot be surrendered unless the intention so to do is clearly and unequivocally expressed.

There are other questions suggested in the record of this case; but, since this one is decisive of the issue presented, no useful purpose would be served in their discussion. The judgment of the district court is reversed and the action dismissed.

Reversed and dismissed.

NOTES

1. Compare the result reached in In Re Estate of O'Brine, 37 N.Y.2d 81, 371 N.Y.S.2d 453, 332 N.E.2d 326 (1975), where the court held that the United States (through the Veterans Administration) was entitled only to those funds of an incompetent veteran that escheated, after deduction of New York state estate taxes. Three judges dissented, noting that "courts of other jurisdictions, when faced with similar situations, have held that the entirety of the funds is returnable, without being diminished by State imposed taxation, under the theory that the United States has retained a reversionary interest."

Strictly speaking, O'Brine is not contrary to O'Connor, since the funds involved in O'Brine were personal property rather than real property and the basis for the court's decision was statutory construction. Nonetheless, the approach of the two courts is different.

2. Feudalism is long dead but it should not be forgotten that, as a system, it functioned effectively in its time and place. It had a profound effect on the Anglo–American law of property and therefore is of more than historical interest. Indeed, Professor Reich sees elements of feudalism in the "new property" created by the growth of government largess. He sees in some of the entitlement cases a philosophy that resembles the philosophy of feudal tenure. "Wealth is not 'owned' or 'vested' in the holders. Instead, it is held conditionally, the conditions being ones which seek to ensure the fulfillment of obligations imposed by the state. Just as the feudal system linked lord and vassal through a system of mutual dependence, obligation, and loyalty, so government largess binds man to the state." [5]

5. Reich, The New Property, 73 Yale L.J. 733, 769 (1964).

Chapter 13

FREEHOLD ESTATES

Apart from the services and incidents of feudal tenure, what was the nature of the tenant's interest in the land? How long would his interest last? Could he transfer it during his lifetime or by a will taking effect at his death? Would his interest be inheritable? If so, by whom? How much freedom did the tenant have as to uses of the land? Answers to these questions came to depend largely upon the type of estate owned by the tenant. The types of estates which eventually were recognized in feudal England were: (1) the freehold estates—the fee simple, the fee tail and the life estate; and (2) the non-freehold estates [1]—the term for years, the periodic tenancy and the tenancy at will. In addition to these, there were non-possessory interests, such as easements,[2] which were not called "estates."

The word "estate" suggests a relationship between a man's social status and land ownership. Freehold estates were the estates which traditionally were owned by those who held by one of the "free" varieties of tenure. The villeins, at least for a time, were essentially tenants at will. The development of the term for years, said to have been employed in an early era mainly as an indirect means of evading the prohibition of usury, appears to have taken place outside the feudal heirarchy. The term for years not only failed to qualify as a freehold estate, but for many purposes was even considered personal property—a "chattel real."

Perhaps the most important distinction between freehold and non-freehold estates, at least in terms of its impact upon modern land law, involves the concept of seisin. The owner in possession of a freehold estate was said to have seisin. The owner of a non-freehold estate might have possession, but he could not have seisin. It is exceedingly difficult to define seisin, but certain important consequences were attributed to it. These will be examined in the materials which follow. One consequence was that the early remedies for the protection of landowners were available only to those who had seisin. As Pollock and Maitland have suggested, however, one may well ponder whether one was deemed to have seisin because he was entitled to those remedies.[3] One of the most striking aspects of seisin was the extreme

1. Non-freehold estates are considered in this book in chapter 16.

2. Easements and other non-possessory interests are considered in this book in chapter 17.

3. "The process by which words are specified, by which their technical meaning is determined, is at first glance a curious, illogical process. Legal reasoning seems circular:—for example, it is argued in one case that a man has an action of trespass because he has possession, in the next case that he has possession because he has an action of trespass; and so we seem to be running round from right to remedy and then from remedy to right. All the while, however, our law of possession is being more perfectly defined. Its course is not circular but spiral; it never comes back to quite the same point as that from which it started. This play of reasoning between right and remedy fixes the use of words.

extent to which it was a reification of the abstract concept of ownership. The notion that seisin was a "thing" was so strong that a present freehold estate could be transferred only by feoffment, a highly ceremonial transaction which took place on the land and in which "livery of seisin" was symbolized by handing over a twig or a clod in the presence of witnesses. The modern deed would not have sufficed.[4]

Assume that certain land is granted to B for his life, and then to C in fee simple. There are two basically different ways of looking at these interests. (1) It might appear that B and C are merely successive owners of the land: B owns the land during his life and upon B's death C becomes owner of the land. (2) Or, B and C may be regarded as owning separate estates in the land, rather than the land itself, both acquiring their estates at the same time, although C's right to possession is postponed until the termination of B's estate. The second approach was that taken by the English common law and is a characteristic which sharply distinguishes it from other legal systems.[5]

During its formative era in England, the law of estates was land law. Chattels and intangibles did not bulk large in the feudal economy and, in addition, many of them did not remain in existence for long periods of time. In modern American law, however, chattels and intangibles are most important forms of wealth, and owners may desire to create estates in such property. They are allowed to do so, the law of estates having been made applicable to chattels and intangibles by analogy. This is not to say that the law of estates in chattels is identical with the law of estates in land. Except during a very early period, the owner of a chattel was not deemed to have seisin. As you will see, this was an important distinction, though its modern significance has declined.

Before we begin our analysis of estates in land, you should be aware of the classification of interests in real property. This is an area in which it is difficult to tell one ball player from another without a score card. After we finish Part Three of the material, you should restudy this chart and notice how we have put flesh on the skeleton.

CLASSIFICATION OF INTERESTS IN REAL PROPERTY

I. Freehold Estates (these are real property)

  A. Fee Simple (always inheritable)

    1. fee simple absolute

A remedy, called an assize, is given to any one who is disseised of his free tenement:—in a few years lawyers will be arguing that X has been 'disseised of his free tenement,' because it is an established point that a person in his position can bring an assize. The word seisin becomes specified by its relation to certain particular remedies." Pollock and Maitland, The History of English Law 31 (2d ed. 1889).

4. See generally Bordwell, Seisin and Disseisin, 34 Harv.L.Rev. 604 (1921).

5. This feature of the common-law theory of estates was lauded and contrasted with the French system. Clauson, The Creative Use of Legal Concepts, 32 N.Y.U.L.R. 909 at 917, 918 (1957).

2. fee simple defeasible (also called base or qualified fee)
   a. fee simple subject to special limitation (also called fee simple subject to common law limitation; fee simple determinable)
   b. fee simple subject to condition subsequent
   c. fee simple subject to executory limitation

B. Fee Tail (successor to fee simple conditional—always inheritable)

C. Life Estates (never inheritable at common law but estates pur autre vie may be inheritable today—see page 237 infra)

1. created by deed or will (conventional life estates)
   a. life estate for the life of the grantee
   b. life estate for the life of one other than the grantee—called estate pur autre vie
2. created by operation of law (legal life estates)
   a. fee tail after possibility of issue extinct
   b. dower
   c. curtesy
   d. estate during coverture

II. Non-freehold Estates (chattels real—not inheritable at common law—treated as personal property)

A. Tenancy for years (for a term)

B. Tenancy from period to period (meaning year to year, month to month or week to week)—periodic tenancy

C. Tenancy at will

D. Tenancy at sufferance (not really an estate)

III. Concurrent Estates (meaning ownership or possession by two or more persons at the same time)

A. Joint tenancy

B. Tenancy by the entirety

C. Tenancy in common

D. Tenancy in coparcenary

IV. Incorporeal Interests in Real Property (these cannot be possessed physically because they consist of mere rights)

A. Easements

B. Profits

C. Covenants running with the land

D. Equitable servitudes

E. Licenses

V. Future Interests

A. Reversions

B. Possibilities of reverter

C. Rights of re-entry for condition broken (more recently called powers of termination)

D. Remainders

1. vested remainders

2. contingent remainders

E. Executory interests

1. executory limitations created by deed

a. springing uses

b. shifting uses

2. executory devises created by will

a. like springing uses

b. shifting uses

SECTION 1. THE FEE SIMPLE ABSOLUTE AND THE LIFE ESTATE

The most substantial estate which has gained recognition is the fee simple absolute. This estate has a potentially infinite duration. If the fee simple absolute is not conveyed away by its owner during his lifetime or by will at his death, it is inherited by his heirs. One wishing to convey a fee simple absolute to another traditionally uses the language "to A and his heirs." This does not mean that any interest is thereby conveyed to A's heirs. They inherit nothing if A conveys his fee simple absolute to another by deed or will. The explanation is that the words referring to heirs serve the function of describing or "limiting" A's estate rather than designating the heirs of A as owners also. Such words are termed words of "limitation" and are distinguished from words of "purchase." The words "to A" in the above phrase are words of purchase. In this sense, one may be a purchaser even though he is a donee.

Must the words "and his heirs" be used in order to convey a fee simple absolute? Would the phrase "to A in fee simple absolute" suffice? In the overwhelming majority of states, any form of expression of intention to convey a fee simple absolute is given effect.[6] Usually this result is based upon a statute. The lingering importance of the use of the exact phrase "and his heirs" is illustrated by the following case.

COLE v. STEINLAUF

Supreme Court of Errors of Connecticut, 1957.
144 Conn. 629, 136 A.2d 744.

WYNNE, CHIEF JUSTICE. There is no dispute as to the facts. The case presented a single question of law. It appears from the finding that it was submitted on the pleadings. The only evidence was the

6. The state of authority is reviewed in 2 Powell, Real Property ¶ 180 (1977).

deed which was part of the defendant's chain of title. The plaintiffs and the defendant entered into a contract for the sale of real estate situated in Norwalk. The plaintiffs were named as purchasers and the defendant as seller. The contract provided that if the seller was unable to convey title to the premises free and clear of any defect of title, the purchasers had the option of rejecting the seller's deed. In the event of such a rejection, all sums paid on account, together with reasonable fees for the examination of the title, were to be repaid to the purchasers. The plaintiffs paid the defendant $420 as a deposit when the contract was executed. They engaged an attorney to examine the title before the closing date of July 1, 1955. The attorney discovered that a deed had been executed in New York on October 22, 1945, to a predecessor in title of the defendant. It appears from the deed that it ran to the grantee "and assigns forever." No mention was made of "heirs" as would be customary and necessary in a fee simple conveyance made in Connecticut. The plaintiffs refused to accept the defendant's deed on the ground that the 1945 deed did not mention the heirs of the grantee. They made demand upon the defendant for a return of the $420 deposit plus expenses for the search of the title, which it was stipulated amounted to $50. The demand was refused, and the instant suit was thereafter brought.

The trial court found the issues for the defendant. . . . This result was reached on the theory that the 1945 conveyance was in law a conveyance of the full fee.

The issue for determination is whether the 1945 deed operated to convey the totality of the fee to the grantee without a flaw or defect which would render the title offered to the plaintiffs unmarketable. To create an estate of inheritance in land by deed, it is necessary to use the words "heirs." Chappell v. New York, N.H. & H.R. Co., 62 Conn. 195, 202, 24 A. 997, 17 L.R.A. 420. Where the common-law rule is in effect, as it is in Connecticut, a grant to a grantee "and his assigns forever" vests only a life estate in the grantee. 19 Am.Jur. 474. A deed can be reformed to vest a fee in a grantee where the word "heirs" is omitted if it can be determined from the clearly expressed intent of the parties that a fee was intended. Chamberlain v. Thompson, 10 Conn. 243, 253. It is impossible to determine the intent of the parties to the 1945 conveyance in this proceeding, for the reason that the necessary parties are not all before the court. It was not the function of the trial court to try the title. Rather, it was to determine whether the title offered was free from reasonable doubt, in law or in fact. Frank Towers Corporation v. Laviana, 140 Conn. 45, 53, 97 A.2d 567.

Another relevant factor is the fact that a title searcher must make his analysis of a title from the information appearing of record. The inquiry in the present case, therefore, should be whether the alleged defect in title is one which leaves the record title free from reasonable doubt or, on the contrary, is one which puts a purchaser to the test of proving intent from sources outside the record. . . .

However far the cases cited by the defendant may go in proving that the title conveyed was a fee simple, that is not the issue. It is not whether the property was in fact the defendant's to convey absolutely, but whether there is enough doubt in the chain of title to bring the plaintiffs up short and make them think twice before buying a lawsuit at a future time to determine title. Perhaps the court at a future time would find good title, but the plaintiffs do not have to gamble on that. The defendant quotes the case of Frank Towers Corporation v. Laviana, supra, 140 Conn. 52, 97 A.2d 567, for the proposition that a marketable title is one that could be mortgaged to a person of reasonable prudence as security for the loan of money. Considering the standards of title used by the lending institutions of this jurisdiction, would any of them lend money on the security of this piece of property, the face of the record being what it is? Would they be bound to go behind the land records and try to predict what a court would do if the issue of title arose in a subsequent proceeding? Although it seems a bit harsh to say a title is unmarketable because of the absence of two words in a deed twelve years old, where the rest of the deed is so unmistakably the conveyance of an estate in fee, it would put the plaintiffs to an intolerable burden at a future time to make them prove the intent of a prior grantor. The trial court erred in treating this as a title problem rather than as one to determine whether the plaintiffs were justified in refusing to take a chance on the title as revealed on the face of the Norwalk town records. It cannot be said that this title was marketable under our rule.

There is error, the judgment is set aside and the case is remanded with direction to render judgment for the plaintiffs for $470 and costs.

In this opinion DALY, KING and MURPHY, JJ., concurred.

BALDWIN, ASSOCIATE JUSTICE (concurring). . . .

While this deed in the defendant's chain of title may be at law inadequate upon its face to convey a fee simple estate in real property located in Connecticut, nevertheless the true intent of the parties to convey such an estate may be shown in equity. Anderson v. Colwell, 93 Conn. 61, 65, 104 A. 242; Chamberlain v. Thompson, 10 Conn. 243, 252. The province of the court in the instant case, however, was not to try a question of title but only to determine whether the title offered by the defendant was unmarketable, thereby furnishing a valid excuse for the refusal of the plaintiffs to accept it. Frank Towers Corporation v. Laviana, 140 Conn. 45, 53, 97 A.2d 567. No doubt a determination whether the parties to the deed in question intended that it should convey an estate in fee simple could be made in some appropriate action. Until that determination is made, the title offered by the defendant is sufficiently questionable to make it unmarketable and to justify the plaintiffs in refusing to accept it.

NOTES

1. In a subsequent case the same court stated: "In a number of our cases, the existence of a common-law requirement has been assumed. Fortunately, in no case have we directly so held. . . . Perhaps the case most nearly approaching such a holding is Cole v.

Steinlauf. . . . That case certainly strongly intimates that in a conveyance the use of the word 'heirs' is indispensable to the effective expression of an intention to create a fee simple estate in Connecticut and that the omission of the word necessarily reduces the estate granted to one for life. Such a rule is patently inconsistent with our settled rule that the construction of a conveyance is to be determined by the intention expressed therein. Actually, the case dealt with the marketability of title, and the holding went no further than correctly to recognize that under the then state of our case law, which we now clarify, a conveyance which did not make use of the word 'heirs' did not express an intention to grant a fee simple estate with sufficient certainty to create a marketable title. . . ." Dennen v. Searle, 149 Conn. 126, 137, 138, 176 A.2d 561, 568 (1961).

The requirement of words of inheritance for creation of a fee simple by deed is more firmly imbedded in the law of South Carolina, where it was reaffirmed in Grainger v. Hamilton, 228 S.C. 318, 90 S.E. 2d 209 (1955). Although that court acknowledged that this rule is intent-defeating, is not applied to wills or inter-vivos trusts, and seems to be supported by no modern policy, the court repeated the following words from an earlier opinion: " 'This is the rule of the common law from which the courts cannot escape. . . . [I]t has been so long established in this state that the courts cannot now overrule the cases laying it down, without imperiling vested rights.' " Id., 228 S.C. at 323, 90 S.E.2d at 211. See also McLaurin v. McLaurin, 265 S.C. 149, 217 S.E.2d 41 (1975) where the court continued to insist on "and his heirs" to create a fee simple absolute.

2. Since most jurisdictions have abolished the necessity for the use of "and his heirs" in the creation of a fee simple absolute, what is the modern result of a conveyance "to A and his heirs"? Almost universally, this language would create a fee simple absolute, the surplus words being viewed as a hangover from the past. In at least one case, however, involving a testamentary disposition, the court found this language created an interest in the heirs since A had predeceased the testator and otherwise there would have been a lapsed devise. See Matter of Estate of Griffen, 86 Wn.2d 223, 543 P.2d 245 (1975).

A BRIEF COMMENT ON THE MEANING OF THE WORD HEIRS

As the case of Cole v. Steinlauf illustrates, the word heirs is a word of art with a specific, legal meaning in the law of property. Since the word plays so large a part in the materials which follow, we must pause to explore its exact connotations. Heirs does *not* mean those individuals who take under a will (although this may be included in the layman's use of the term), they are devisees, if land is being transmitted, or legatees, if personal property is involved. Heirs are those who take the property under the relevant statutes of descent.

A. TESTATE AND INTESTATE SUCCESSION AT COMMON LAW AND UNDER EARLY ENGLISH STATUTES

Testamentary power over the fee simple estate in land, being inconsistent with concepts and policies of English law as it evolved in connection with feudalism, was never freely, directly, and generally exercisable before the middle of the sixteenth century. It was made so exercisable, subject to certain regulations designed to minimize the possibility of perjury, forgery, and other chicanery, by a series of statutes. The effects of the Statute of Wills (1540) and the Statute of Tenures (1660) have been noticed previously. With respect to formality, the former required only a written will; it did not specify that the testator himself write or sign the instrument. Reliable proof of authenticity was first prescribed by the Statute of Frauds (1677), which directed that the instrument be signed by the testator or, at his direction, by a person in his presence, and that it be attested and subscribed, in his presence, by "three or four credible witnesses." The Wills Act (1837) somewhat enlarged testamentary power and modified the requisite formality in ways which need not be detailed here.

In contrast, testamentary power over personalty (including non-freehold interests in land) has been recognized from very remote times. Indeed, intestacy was once regarded with horror, since according to the church's teaching, the making of a last testament, like the death-bed confession, was necessary for salvation and for burial in consecrated soil. It appears, however, that until the fourteenth century a testator's power was limited by a principle like one in Roman law whereby a surviving wife or child could enforce a claim to a share of his goods. Thereafter this "forced share" principle survived only by force of custom in some localities; it now has no significance with reference to children, but modern legislation abolishing or modifying dower and curtesy permits a surviving spouse to "disappoint" a will by claiming a statutory share of the estate.

The English law of testate and intestate succession was greatly complicated by the fact that for a long period jurisdiction over the administration of decedents' estates was divided between the ecclesiastical and the temporal courts. These rival tribunals, the one group following Roman legal traditions, the other English, were at times in open conflict; and though the ecclesiastical courts lost their power as the temporal influence of the Church waned, consequences of the ancient division of authority linger yet. "The ecclesiastical courts obtained jurisdiction over grants of Probate and Administration, and, to a certain degree, over the conduct of the executor and the administrator. All these branches of their jurisdiction could be exercised only over personal estate. This abandonment of jurisdiction to the ecclesiastical courts has tended, more than any other single cause, to accentuate the difference between real and personal property; for even when the ecclesiastical courts had ceased to exercise some parts of this jurisdiction, the law which they had created was exercised by their successors." 1 Holdsworth, History of English Law 625 (7th ed. 1956).

One consequence of the bifurcated system was that different rules of intestate succession were evolved for realty and personalty. Land was conceived as "descending" directly to the heir-at-law and was not subject to the decedent's debts other than obligations under seal in which the decedent had expressly bound the heir—the personalty was treated as the primary fund for creditors' satisfaction, and the heir was therefore entitled to reimbursement for his payment of any debt to which he was subject. Personalty was conceived as being transferred to the administrator—the "personal representative"—who was, in substantial effect, its owner until he had distributed it to the widow (if any) and next of kin. Similarly, if a decedent were testate, land was directly transferred to his devisee, but personalty was transferred to the executor—the "personal representative"—who in effect became a conduit of ownership between the testator and the legatees.

Apart from local custom, the primary principle of inheritance—i.e., succession to land—was primogeniture. The doctrine that inheritance was impartible—that a decedent had only a single heir-at-law—was obviously congenial to the feudal system, since feudal relations were disturbed as little as possible. For present purposes the complex rules whereby heirship was determined need not be examined; it is sufficient to note the following general characteristics:

1. Only a blood relative could inherit.

2. Among males and females who were equally closely related to the decedent females were excluded and the eldest male inherited.

3. If two or more females (equally closely related) were more nearly related to the decedent than any male, they inherited together "in coparcenary" (a type of joint tenancy), but in legal effect they constituted a single heiress.

4. A dead member of a group was represented by his issue; if a decedent's eldest son had died leaving a son or daughter, the grandchild would inherit though the decedent left surviving sons or daughters.

5. If the decedent had acquired the land in question by "purchase"—i.e., otherwise than by inheritance—a collateral relative on his father's side, however remote, would inherit rather than a collateral on his mother's side, however near. Thus, a distant cousin who traced descent from the decedent's paternal grandfather would displace a maternal uncle.

6. If the decedent had inherited the land from his father or someone related to him, it could not be inherited by a person related to the decedent only through his mother—e.g., a maternal uncle, aunt, or cousin. If he had inherited the land from his mother or someone related to her, it could not be inherited by a person related to the decedent only through his father. This rule may be regarded as simply an extension of the first rule stated above—i.e., when a person had acquired land by "purchase" its ownership could (and commonly did) pass thereafter from person to person by inheritance, but each of these persons must be related by blood to the "purchaser." Of course, one of these successive heirs might transfer the land by sale, by inter vivos gift, or by will; if this occurred, the transferee was a "purchaser" and

inheritance thereafter was traced from him. This rule that inheritance was confined to the "blood of the first purchaser" is commonly and conveniently referred to as the doctrine of "ancestral property" and is found in some modern statutes of descent and distribution.

In addition to the six general characteristics governing common-law inheritance, it should be noted that spouses were excluded as heirs, although certain other rights, such as dower and curtesy, were available to them. Moreover, lineal ancestors were excluded as heirs, despite their close blood relationship to the deceased. The policy of the common law was to pass land to the succeeding generations without undue concern for spouses, parents, or grandparents.

Intestate succession to personalty was not subject to the principle of primogeniture and the "canons of descent" summarized above. So long as the previously-mentioned religious sanction retained its force intestacy must have been relatively rare. When it occurred, in those days, it appears that a surviving wife took a third of the goods (half if no child survived), the children took a third (half if no wife survived), and the remaining part—the only part freely disposable by will—went to the church to be distributed to the poor or otherwise piously used for the benefit of the intestate's jeopardized soul. In the thirteenth century an ecclesiastical official exercised administrative power; a fourteenth-century statute required that administration be committed to the decedent's "next and most lawful friends," but the church courts retained the power of appointing administrators and supervising their functions.

Obviously, any acceptable scheme for obtaining administration of a decedent's estate or execution of his will must provide some safe-guard against the possibility that the representative will misuse his office for his own benefit or that of others, instead of faithfully and impartially settling the decedent's affairs and distributing his property. It appears that the ecclesiastical courts never solved this problem satisfactorily, and by the middle of the seventeenth century they found themselves essentially powerless in the matter, in part because the common-law judges were determined to hamper the rival jurisdiction in every way possible. Aimed at improving the situation, a bill was drafted by a leading church court lawyer, and from it Parliament evolved the Statute of Distribution (1670).

The effort to strengthen the ecclesiastical courts' jurisdiction failed, and in matters concerning administration they were subsequently displaced by Chancery. The statute is nevertheless significant for us, because its provisions for distribution, modified slightly by later legislation, shaped the modern law of intestate succession. The results of the legislation and of its judicial construction are summarized in 3 Holdsworth, History of English Law 561 (5th ed. 1942) as follows:

1. If the intestate were a married woman and her husband became administrator, he succeeded to the only personalty which was not already his by the marital right—i.e., her choses in action not possessed during marriage.

2. If a man were survived by his wife and by issue, the wife took a third of his personalty, the issue two-thirds. In default of issue, she took half and the next of kin—if none, the Crown—took half.

3. There being no surviving spouse, an intestate's personalty went to his or her issue if any; otherwise to the next of kin, if any; otherwise to the Crown.

4. In general, the degree of kinship between a decedent and a claimant was reckoned by taking the number of generative steps between them (in the case of ascendants or descendants) or by adding the numbers of such steps between each of them and their nearest common ancestor. Thus a decedent's parent would be one step removed, a grandparent, grandchild, brother, or sister two steps removed, a great-grandparent, great-grandchild, uncle, aunt, or nephew three steps removed, etc. The general idea that the personalty should go to the person or persons in the nearest degree of kinship was modified in some respects, most notably by the principle of representation. If children were distributees, the issue (however remote) of a dead member of the class took, by representation, the share which the dead member would have taken had he or she survived. This result of the principle seems proper enough—either to exclude the grandchildren entirely or to allow them to share equally with the children seems less acceptable—but by an extension of it the courts reached a result the propriety of which is more questionable; it was eventually held, where all the decedent's children had died, that the grandchildren took not per capita but per stirpes—i.e., the share each dead child would have taken if surviving went to his or her issue. Obviously this rule might yield a striking inequality of distribution among persons of the same degree of relationship to the decedent.

In modern law primogeniture and the canons of descent associated therewith have been swept away. Succession to land and succession to personalty still differ somewhat under a number of state statutes in this country, but in numerous other states and in England the two have been completely assimilated.

B. INTESTATE SUCCESSION UNDER A MODERN STATUTE

Analyze the meaning of the word heirs in a modern statute of descent. You should note that the statutes will vary from state to state and you must always consult the proper act before deciding who the heirs actually are.

DESCENT AND DISTRIBUTION

Illinois Revised Statutes, Chapter 110½ (1985).

Article II

§ 2–1. Rules of Descent and Distribution

The intestate real and personal estate of a resident decedent and the intestate real estate in this state of a non-resident decedent after all just claims against his estate are fully paid, descends and shall be distributed as follows:

(a) If there is a surviving spouse and also a descendant of the decendent: one-half of the entire estate to the surviving spouse and one-half to the decedent's descendants per stirpes.

(b) If there is no surviving spouse but a descendant of the decedent: the entire estate to the decedent's descendants per stirpes.

(c) If there is a surviving spouse but no descendant of the decedent: the entire estate to the surviving spouse.

(d) If there is no surviving spouse or descendant but a parent, brother, sister, or descendant of a brother or sister of the decedent: the entire estate to the parents, brothers, and sisters of the decedent in equal parts, allowing to the surviving parent, if one is dead, a double portion and to the descendants of a deceased brother or sister per stirpes the portion which the deceased brother or sister would have taken if living.

(e) If there is no surviving spouse, descendant, parent, brother, sister, or descendant of a brother or sister of the decedent, but a grandparent or descendant of a grandparent of the decedent: (1) one-half of the entire estate to the decedent's maternal grandparents in equal parts or to the survivor of them, or if there is none surviving, to their descendants per stirpes, and (2) one-half of the entire estate to the decedent's paternal grandparents in equal parts or to the survivor of them, or if there is none surviving, to their descendants per stirpes. If there is no surviving paternal grandparent or descendant of a paternal grandparent, but a maternal grandparent or descendant of a maternal grandparent of the decedent: the entire estate to the decedent's maternal grandparents in equal parts or to the survivor of them, or if there is none surviving, to their descendants per stirpes. If there is no surviving maternal grandparent or descendant of a maternal grandparent, but a paternal grandparent or descendant of a paternal grandparent of the decedent: the entire estate to the decedent's paternal grandparents in equal parts or to the survivor of them, or if there is none surviving, to their descendants per stirpes.

(f) If there is no surviving spouse, descendant, parent, brother, sister, descendant of a brother or sister or grandparent or descendant of a grandparent of the decedent: (1) one-half of the entire estate to the decedent's maternal great-grandparents in equal parts or to the survivor of them, or if there is none surviving, to their descendants per stirpes, and (2) one-half of the entire estate to the decedent's paternal great-grandparents in equal parts or to the survivor of them, or if there is none surviving, to their descendants per stirpes. If there is no surviving paternal great-grandparent or descendant of a paternal great-grandparent, but a maternal great-grandparent or descendant of a maternal great-grandparent of the decedent: the entire estate to the decedent's maternal great-grandparents in equal parts or to the survivor of them, or if there is none surviving, to their descendants per stirpes. If there is no surviving maternal great-grandparent or descendant of the maternal great-grandparent, but a paternal great-grandparent or descendant of a paternal great-grandparent of the decedent: the entire estate to the decedent's paternal great-grandparents in equal parts or to the survivor of them, or if there is none surviving, to their descendants per stirpes.

(g) If there is no surviving spouse, descendant, parent, brother, sister, descendant of a brother or sister, grandparent, descendant of a grandparent, great-grandparent, or descendant of a great-grandparent of the decedent: the entire estate in equal parts to the nearest kindred of the decedent in equal degree (computing by the rules of the civil law) and without representation.

(h) If there is no surviving spouse and no known kindred of the decedent: the real estate escheats to the county in which it is located; the personal estate physically located within this state and the personal estate physically located or held outside this state which is the subject of ancillary administration of an estate being administered within this state escheats to the county of which the decedent was a resident or, if the decedent was not a resident of this state, to the county in which it is located; all other personal property of the decedent of every class and character, wherever situate, or the proceeds thereof, shall escheat to this State and be delivered to the Director of Financial Institutions of the State pursuant to the Uniform Disposition of Unclaimed Property Act.

In no case is there any distinction between the kindred of the whole and the half blood. [Amended, effective Jan. 1, 1980, increasing spouses share in s. 2–1(a) from one-third to one-half and decreasing descendants share from two-thirds to one-half.]

§ 2–2. (Deals With Illegitimates)

§ 2–3. Posthumous Child

A posthumous child of a decedent shall receive the same share of an estate as if he had been born in his father's life time.

§ 2–4. (Deals With Adopted Child and Adopting Parent)

§ 2–5. (Deals With Advancements)

§ 2–6. Person Causing Death

Person causing death. A person who intentionally and unjustifiably causes the death of another shall not receive any property, benefit, or other interest by reason of the death, whether as heir, legatee, beneficiary, joint tenant, survivor, appointee or in any other capacity and whether the property, benefit, or other interest passes pursuant to any form of title registration, testamentary or nontestamentary instrument, intestacy, renunciation, or any other circumstance. The property, benefit, or other interest shall pass as if the person causing the death died before the decedent, provided that with respect to joint tenancy property the interest possessed prior to the death by the person causing the death shall not be diminished by the application of this Section. A determination under this Section may be made by any court of competent jurisdiction separate and apart from any criminal proceeding arising from the death, provided that no such civil proceeding shall proceed to trial nor shall the person be required to submit to discovery in such civil proceeding until such time as any criminal proceeding has been finally determined by the trial court or, in the event no criminal charge has been brought, prior to one year after the date of death. A person convicted of murder or voluntary manslaughter of the decedent is conclusively presumed to have caused the death intentionally and unjustifiably for purposes of this Section.

The holder of any property subject to the provisions of this Section shall not be liable for distributing or releasing said property to the person causing the death if such distribution or release occurs prior to a determination made under this Section.

Amended by P.A. 83–271, § 1, eff. Sept. 9, 1983.

§ 2–7. (Deals With Disclaimer)

§ 2–8. Renunciation of Will by Spouse

(a) If a will is renounced by the testator's surviving spouse, whether or not the will contains any provision for the benefit of the surviving spouse, the surviving spouse is entitled to the following share of the testator's estate after payment of all just claims: one-third of the entire estate if the testator leaves a descendant, or one-half of the entire estate if the testator leaves no descendant. (The remainder of the section deals with the method of renunciation.)

§ 2–9. Dower and Curtesy

There is no estate of dower or curtesy. All inchoate rights to elect to take dower existing on January 1, 1972, are extinguished.

§ 2–10. Waste by Surviving Spouse

Waste by surviving spouse. If the surviving spouse of a decedent commits waste in the real or personal estate of the decedent he is liable therefor to the representative, heir or legatee, as the case may be.

C. RULES OF THE CIVIL LAW FOR DETERMINING INHERITANCE BY COLLATERALS [7]

		Great grandfather (3)
Great Uncle (4)		Grandfather (2)
Child (5)		
Uncle (3)		Father (1)
1st cousin (4)	Brother (2)	Intestate
1st cousin (5) once removed	Nephew (3)	
1st cousin (6) twice removed	Grandnephew (4)	

Ascertain the closest common ancestor of intestate and claimant. Count steps from intestate to common ancestor and from common ancestor to claimant. Sum of the two figures represents degree of relationship between claimant and intestate. Claimant who stands in smallest numerical degree of relationship to the intestate takes the property.

D. PROBLEMS

A dies intestate. How will his property be handled in each of the following situations?

1. Survived by wife and one son.
2. By wife; one daughter; and two grandsons, children of a deceased son.
3. By a daughter; a son; and four grandchildren, children of the son.
4. By a wife only.
5. By a mother and a sister.
6. By a grandfather; a nephew, a son of a deceased sister; and an uncle.
7. By a great grandfather; an uncle; and a first cousin.
8. No wife; no lineal heirs; no collateral heirs.
9. What is dower?
10. What are the inheritance rights of illegitimate children?

The omitted Section 2–2 of the Illinois Revised Statutes deals with illegitimates. Until 1980, it concluded: "An illegitimate child is heir of his mother and of any maternal ancestor and of any person from whom his mother might have inherited, if living; and the lawful issue of an illegitimate person shall represent such person and take by descent any estate which the parent would have taken, if living. A child who was

7. For a detailed discussion see Atkinson, Law of Wills 41–50 (2d ed. 1953). It should be noted that the chart would have to be greatly expanded before it could be used to determine collateral heirs under an Illinois-type statute, since the civil law method of computation is effective only if the first six rules of descent and distribution fail to provide a taker. The chart is included solely to illustrate the principle of the civil law rules.

illegitimate whose parents intermarry and who is acknowledged by the father as the father's child is legitimate."

The Illinois pattern had been the general rule in the United States. "At common law, the bastard inherited from no one. Although statutes in nearly all states provide that an illegitimate child occupies the same position as a legitimate one with respect to inheritance from his *mother*, the illegitimate child generally cannot, except by will, inherit from his *father* unless the father has formally recognized or acknowledged him. Even a judgment in a paternity action only rarely gives the child the right to inherit from his father." Krause, Equal Protection For The Illegitimate, 65 Mich.L.Rev. 477 (1967).

In 1977, the United States Supreme Court declared the Illinois provision which allowed illegitimates to inherit by intestate succession only from their mothers, except where the parents intermarried and the child was acknowledged as legitimate by the father, invalid as a denial of equal protection. The Court said that a classification based on illegitimacy was required to bear a rational relationship to a legitimate state purpose and that the provision could not be justified on the ground that it promoted legitimate family relationships. The difficulties involved in proving paternity in some situations did not justify total statutory disinheritance of children born out of wedlock and the fact that the father could have provided for the child by making a will did not save the provision from invalidity. Mr. Justice Rehnquist dissented. Trimble v. Gordon, 430 U.S. 762, 97 S.Ct. 1459, 52 L.Ed.2d 31 (1977).

What new problems were created by the Supreme Court decision?

By an amendment, effective January 1, 1980, the Illinois General Assembly revised Section 2–2 on Illegitimates as follows: "An illegitimate person is heir of his mother and of any maternal ancestor and of any person from whom his mother might have inherited, if living; and the descendants of an illegitimate person shall represent such person and take by descent any estate which the parent would have taken, if living. If a decedent has acknowledged paternity of an illegitimate person or if during his lifetime or after his death a decedent has been adjudged to be the father of an illegitimate person, that person is heir of his father and of any paternal ancestor and of any person from whom his father might have inherited, if living; and the descendants of an illegitimate person shall represent that person and take by descent any estate which the parent would have taken, if living. If during his lifetime the decedent was adjudged to be the father of an illegitimate person by a court of competent jurisdiction, an authenticated copy of the judgment is sufficient proof of the paternity; but in all other cases paternity must be proved by clear and convincing evidence. A person who was illegitimate whose parents intermarry and who is acknowledged by the father as the father's child is legitimate." Amended by P.A. 81–400, § 1, eff. Jan. 1, 1980.

Does this amendment resolve the constitutional issue which caused the United States Supreme Court to invalidate the earlier Illinois statute? Why or why not?

The life estate[8] was probably the first estate to gain recognition. It is defined in the Restatement of Property § 18 (1936) as follows: "An estate for life is an estate which is not an estate of inheritance, and

"(a) is an estate which is specifically described as to duration in terms of the life or lives of one or more human beings, and is not terminable at any fixed or computable period of time; or

"(b) though not so specifically described as is required under the rule stated in Clause (a), is an estate which cannot last longer than the life or lives of one or more human beings, and is not terminable at any fixed or computable period of time or at the will of the transferor."[9]

If we assume that the life estate will terminate with the death of the owner of the life estate, it is obvious that the estate could not be inherited. But this assumption is unwarranted. A life estate may be measured by a life or lives of persons other than the owner. Land may be conveyed to "B for the life of C." Also, one who has a life estate for his own life may convey it inter vivos to another, in which event the conveyee has an estate measured by the life of the conveyor. What happens when the owner of the life estate predeceases the person whose life is the measuring life? Since the life estate by definition is not an inheritable estate, does it follow that no one is entitled to the land during this interval and that, accordingly, the first person who takes possession cannot be ousted? With undeniable logic, the English courts so held, though they permitted this unsatisfactory situation to be avoided by the designation of a "special occupant" in the instrument creating or transferring a life estate. E.g., if land was conveyed to "B and his heirs for the life of C," B's heir was entitled to the land as a special occupant. One of the numerous clauses of the Statute of Frauds (1677) provided that a life estate not ending with the death of its owner could be devised, and, if not devised, should pass as a chattel to the representative of the deceased owner's estate, in the absence of a special occupant. According to the Restatement of Property § 151 (1936), the common law rule in the United States is identical with the Statute of Frauds provision. Query: Is § 151 consistent with the declaration in § 18 that a life estate is not an estate of inheritance?

No words of art were required for the creation of a life estate, but it would be a mistake to conclude that the creation of life estates is free from difficulty.

In view of the interests of remaindermen or reversioners, the life tenant does not enjoy as broad rights to the use of land as does the owner of the fee simple. How broad they are is the subject of one case in this section.

---

8. Life estates are frequently classified in two broad categories—conventional and legal. Conventional life estates are created by the voluntary action of the owner of land, i.e., by deed or will. Legal life estates are created by operation of law and arise out of the marital relationship.

9. Copyright, 1936. Reprinted with the permission of the American Law Institute.

LEWIS v. SEARLES

Supreme Court of Missouri, 1970.
452 S.W.2d 153.

HENRY I. EAGER, SPECIAL COMMISSIONER. In this declaratory judgment suit plaintiff seeks to have the title to certain real estate quieted in her in fee and, in the process, to have a will construed. We have jurisdiction since the title to real estate is directly involved. The trial court adjudged that plaintiff had a life estate in the whole of the property, and a fee simple interest in an undivided one-third thereof, subject to the life estate. After an unavailing motion for a new trial plaintiff appealed. . . .

The will invoved here was that of Letitia G. Lewis (the owner of the land) who died on Sept. 27, 1926; this will was probated shortly thereafter. At the time of her death the testatrix left surviving her two nieces, the plaintiff and Letitia L. LaForge, and a nephew, James R. Lewis. At the time of the institution of this suit Letitia LaForge had died leaving three children; one of these children had died, also leaving three children. The nephew had also died leaving two sons, both of whom have entered their appearance and have actively contested the suit. The necessary defendants who reside in Missouri have been served with process and the others by publication. We have asked for and received certified copies of certain documents in order thus to verify the jurisdiction over the parties.

The facts, although somewhat scanty, are contained in a stipulation. No oral evidence was taken. The plaintiff was 95 years of age at the time of trial, and is presumably now about 96; she was thus approximately 53 years of age when the will was probated. We are told that the will was executed on May 31, 1911, when plaintiff was 38 years old. She has never been married. Since the death of the testatrix, plaintiff has been in continuous possession of the real estate.

Paragraph "Second" of the will was as follows: "Second, I devise to my niece, Hattie L. Lewis, all of my real and personal property of which I may die seized and possessed, so long as she remains single and unmarried. In the event that the said Hattie L. Lewis shall marry, then and in this event I desire that all of my property, both real and personal be divided equally between my nieces and nephews as follows, to the said Hattie L. Lewis, an undivided one third, to Letitia A. LaForge, wife of A.C. LaForge, an undivided one third, and to James R. Lewis an undivided one third." This is the only part in controversy.

In her petition plaintiff alleged the various relationships (including therein sundry unnecessary parties), described the real estate, attached a copy of the will, and prayed for an order of publication. She further alleged: that she had never been married; that she received an estate in fee under the will; that the restriction in the will against marriage was void; and that the other niece and the nephew of testatrix were deceased. The prayer was that a guardian ad litem be appointed for the minor defendants and others (which was done) and that title in fee to the land be quieted in her. The answer of J.R. (Dick) Lewis and

Lilbourn Z. Lewis (children of the nephew) admitted plaintiff's possession and her right to possession, but denied that she was the owner of the fee. In a counterclaim they prayed that title in fee to an undivided one-third of the land be quieted in each of them under the terms of the will, subject to a life estate in plaintiff. In a reply to the counterclaim plaintiff reaffirmed her position that she was the owner in fee of all the land.

The trial court found (aside from formal and admitted facts) that it was the intention of the testatrix to give to plaintiff a *life estate,* and that "upon the death of said plaintiff that the fee title to said real estate vest in fee simple one-third to plaintiff, Hattie L. Lewis, one-third to Letitia L. LaForge and one-third to James R. Lewis, or to their descendants, hereinabove named." Judgment was entered accordingly, providing that plaintiff was the owner of a life estate and also the owner in fee simple of an undivided one-third interest, subject to her life estate, with the remaining undivided two-thirds in fee vested as already indicated. Plaintiff's motion for a new trial was overruled.

Plaintiff's counsel raise two points on this appeal, simply stated, but not so simply decided: (1) that all provisions of the will concerning the marriage of plaintiff are void as against public policy and should be stricken; (2) that in any event it was not testatrix's intention to devise to plaintiff a life estate with a one-third remainder in fee, but to devise to her a determinable fee in the whole of the property, to be reduced only in the event of her marriage. Respondents simply converse these points, and the issues are clearly drawn.

There is no doubt that the older cases in Missouri and elsewhere held that a provision in general restraint of marriage was void as against public policy. Knost v. Knost, 229 Mo. 170, 129 S.W. 665, 49 L.R.A.,N.S., 627; Sullivan v. Garesche, 229 Mo. 496, 129 S.W. 949, 49 L.R.A.,N.S., 605; Williams v. Cowden, 13 Mo. 148 [211] ; 122 A.L.R. 7, Note. But, as stated by the author of the A.L.R. Annotation at loc. cit. 9, the courts have been reluctant to apply the rule and it has well-nigh been "eaten out with exceptions." One exception which has long been recognized is the right of a husband to terminate or decrease the extent of a devise to his wife upon her remarriage (subject, of course, to her statutory right to renounce the will). Knost, Sullivan, supra. As said by Judge Lamm in Knost, supra, it seems to be settled law that men "have a sort of mournful property right, so to speak, in the viduity of their wives, ..." 129 S.W. loc. cit. 667. The author of the A.L.R. Annotation says that "The preponderance of modern opinion seems to be that the right of a donor to attach such conditions as he pleases to his gift will outweigh the maxim that marriage should be free, except where such conditions are evidently attached through caprice rather than from a desire to carry out a reasonable purpose." (Loc. cit. 11–12.) The history of this most ancient rule is discussed in that Annotation. It is obvious that the cases on the subject are both conflicting and confusing, but that most, if not all, courts still give lip service to the doctrine. The tendency, however, is to consider whether, under the circumstances, the provision serves a legitimate purpose. And one reason which the author mentions as most commonly applied is the desire to furnish support to the devisee while single. Much confusion has developed in attempts to determine whether such a provision, in any given case, is a limitation or a condition. It has been indicated that generally a devise which is to be reduced in the event of marriage is held to be a condition subsequent. (Anno. loc. cit. 73.)

Into this welter of conflict and confusion came the case of Winget v. Gay, 325 Mo. 368, 28 S.W.2d 999 (1930). Plaintiff says that this case is not controlling because it was decided after the will in our case was probated. If that be the true rule, it would seem impossible ever to change the case law, since every such case is decided after the particular will involved has been probated. We follow Winget in part; in other respects it appears to be distinguishable. There the decedent had married a widow with three small children; the two born of his own marriage to her died, as did (later) the widow; two of her children were grown and living in their own homes. The other, the stepdaughter involved in the case, was a semi-invalid but she remained with him until his death. She was forty-four when his will was executed. He devised to her all the residue of his property "as long as she remains single, and if she marry it is my will that she share equally with the other heirs." His "other heirs" were brothers and sisters to whom he bequeathed one dollar each. Two essential questions were raised: (1) the validity of the provision concerning the stepdaughter's marriage, and (2) whether she got a determinable fee or a life estate in the residue. The Court initially recognized the rule that provisions in general restraint of marriage are void (citing the above Missouri cases) and then proceeded to impose its own exception. It held: that the testator's purpose, "when all the circumstances are considered," was merely to provide support for the stepdaughter while she was single and until such time as the obligation might be assumed by a husband; that, thus construed, his purpose *and the provision* did not "run counter" to public policy; and that he had the right to limit the duration of his bounty to the time of her probable dependency. The Court proceeded to hold, thereafter, that the devisee only took a life estate. We shall discuss that phase later.

It seems probable that there was, in the Winget case, some evidence of circumstances. Plaintiff says here that we may not reach a similar result with no such evidence. However, we find that the very wording of the will in our case expresses an intent of the testator to provide *support* for the plaintiff while she remained unmarried but, upon the happening of such a contingency, to require that she share with the other niece and the nephew. The provision did not constitute a penalty for marrying. This provision was obviously not inserted by whim or "caprice," for plaintiff was not to be cut off if she did marry. We conclude that the provision of the will concerning marriage was valid. We realize that this decision perhaps goes one step beyond the holding in Winget, but we find that the wording of the will itself justifies the result, and that it is more closely in accord with the tendency of the modern cases than it would be to hold otherwise.

The more difficult question remains: What estate did plaintiff take, a life estate or a determinable fee? The rule is very clear that each will must be construed as a whole to arrive at the intent of the testator, which, after all, is the ultimate guiding principle. We note: that testatrix said nothing about plaintiff's death; that there was no gift or limitation over upon plaintiff's death, and that this might result in total or partial intestacy if the will derived to her only a life estate; that plaintiff was to be given immediately one-third of the same property *in fee, if* she married; that it is not stated whether it is necessary for the nephew and the other niece to survive the plaintiff in order to receive one-third in fee upon plaintiff's marriage; that the devise to plaintiff was the only residuary clause in the will; that Section 474.480, RSMo 1959, V.A.M.S. (effective in substantially similar form at that time) eliminates the necessity for the words "heirs and assigns," if no intention appears to convey only an estate for life and if no further devise is made to take effect after the *death* of the devisee. It is clear that under Section 474.480, if the testator had stopped after merely devising to plaintiff all of her real and personal property, a fee simple estate would have been created. And it is also true that, in order to cut down a fee estate which has been granted, the words of a subsequent (and supposedly limiting provision) should be as clear and decisive as those of the preceding clause. Vaughan v. Compton, 361 Mo. 467, 235 S.W.2d 328; Middleton v. Dudding, Mo., 183 S.W. 443.

Defendants rely strongly on Winget, supra, to establish their claim that plaintiff took only a life estate, determinable on marriage. The Court so held there, holding also that the words "as long as she remains single," were words of limitation and duration, and that since the devisee might remain single until she died (which she did) she took a determinable life estate. It was apparently this construction to the particular wording of that will which was found to be decisive. The Court did not *mention* the predecessor statute of Section 474.480. We do not find that part of the opinion to be controlling here. One of the prime rules of construction is that a will must be construed as a *whole,* seeking to gain the testator's real intent from every sentence and every word. We also note that we are dealing here with specific real estate; if there was any personal property or any other real estate we do not know of it, and it is certainly not involved.

In Winget the "sharing" (upon marriage) was to be had generally with "the other heirs"; in our case the contingent sharing was to be expressly accomplished by the grant of "undivided" interests of one-third each in fee simple in this property to two named persons, with plaintiff retaining the other one-third. As we read and reread paragraph "Second" of the present will, we are convinced that the testatrix was thinking only in terms of *fee interests,* i.e., everything to plaintiff in fee conditioned upon her remaining single, and determinable (except for one-third) in the event of her marriage; and it was expressly provided that if she did marry, one-third (undoubtedly in fee, for there was no further limitation over) should go to each of the three (two nieces and a nephew). There is really no fairly expressed intent of *any* life estate in this will. If plaintiff's interest be held to be a terminable life estate only, it is a little difficult for us to see how she might succeed to a one-third fee interest in the event of her marriage, which intent was obviously expressed. The will contains no devise of plaintiff's interest to anyone after her death. In the Winget case, and in the case of Maddox v. Yoe, 121 Md. 288, 88 A. 225, upon which it relies, the courts have actually *written into* the wills the words "or upon her death" after the expressed contingency concerning marriage. Other authorities have done the same thing but to us it appears illogical. See cases cited on the "implication" theory in 73 A.L.R.2d, Note, at page 488. The argument sometimes made (Hutchinson's Est. v. Arnt, 210 Ind. 509, 1 N.E.2d 585, 4 N.E.2d 202) that unless the devise be construed as a terminable life estate an intestacy would result if the devisee died unmarried, does not bear scrutiny, for if the devise has become a fee absolute upon her death without marrying, her heirs, would take as in the case of the death of any other fee simple devisee. A testator does not and cannot pretend to fix the devolution beyond the quantum of a fee. The Annotation in 73 A.L.R.2d at loc. cit. 493 et seq. cites also certain cases as refusing "to imply (a) gift over on death unmarried."

There is a comment in Washington University Law Quarterly, 1951, 595 et seq. upon a Kentucky case (Taylor v. Farrow, Ky., 239 S.W.2d 73) ruling upon a somewhat similar provision for a widow. The Court there held that the language created a determinable fee, and in his comments the author said, in part: "In holding that the language created a fee simple determinable, the court stated that the words of the will, when considered as a whole, evinced an intent to pass the maximum possible estate consistent with the special limitation; and that if the testator had intended to give his widow less than a fee simple, he should have expressly limited the estate to her for life." The Court there decided the case upon the basis of the Kentucky statute which provided that unless a different purpose appeared by express words or by necessary inference, every estate in land created by deed or will, without words of inheritance, should be deemed a fee simple estate. (This is of the same essential substance as our § 474.480.) Cases from other states are cited as reaching the same result (loc. cit. 596).

In the above comment the factors are listed which mitigate for and against construing such a provision as creating a determinable fee. Among those listed as indicating an intent to devise a determinable fee simple are: the fact that the wife (in a case involving widowhood) has been given *part of the same property* in fee upon her remarriage (citing numerous cases from various states); the fact that there is neither a gift over upon death nor a residuary clause, thus resulting in partial intestacy if only a life estate was granted; the existence of a statute eliminating the necessity for words of inheritance as, "in the absence of the express words to the contrary." In his conclusion the author of the comment states, loc cit. 601–602: "It is submitted that in the absence of express language limiting the estate created to one for life, statutes such as the Kentucky act leave little room for the application of the other factors suggested above. The only problem for determination under such a statute is whether *express* words to the contrary are present. It is certainly true that words of limitation such as 'until remarriage' or 'so long as she remains unmarried' are not *express* words to the contrary within the meaning of those terms in the statute. Such words should not be regarded as words measuring the quantum of the estate, but rather as words relating only to the happening of a particular contingency, i.e., remarriage of the widow."

At this point we note again our Section 474.480. We quote it in full, as a matter of convenience. "In all devises of lands or other estate in this state, in which the words 'heirs and assigns', or 'heirs and assigns forever,' are omitted, and no expressions are contained in the will whereby it appears that the devise was intended to convey an estate for life only, and no further devise is made of the devised premises, to take effect after the death of the devisee to whom the same is given, it shall be understood to be the intention of the testator thereby to devise an absolute estate in the same, and the devise conveys an estate in fee simple to the devisee, for all of the devised premises." In essence, this says that all devises are in fee simple, if (1) no intent is expressed to create a life estate only, and (2) no further devise is made to take effect *after the death* of the devisee. The Winget case did not even mention this statute. We do not believe that we are justified in seeking to *force* from the words used an intent to create a life estate when the words do not clearly state such an intent; and certainly we may not substitute the words "death or marriage" for the word "death" as used in part (2) of the statute (as we have numbered it). It would seem that the will here contains neither of the requisites which would create a life estate. This statute evidences a policy of the state to liberalize the construction and effect of provisions in wills which are inartfully drawn, but in which there is no clear intent to devise less than a fee simple. We have concluded, after considerable difficulty, that there was no such intent here, either expressed or fairly to be inferred, and that plaintiff received a determinable fee in the real estate, subject to defeasance (of two-thirds) upon her marriage. This construction eliminates all possibility of an intestacy in whole or in part, it is consonant with what we believe to have been testatrix's thought and desire, namely, that she was dealing only with fee interests, and it constitutes a compliance with Section 474.480. . . .

So here, construing testatrix's intent from the words she used, we attach *much* importance to the fact that the *gift over* was only to be effective in the event of plaintiff's marriage; if she had intended to make the gift over effective on death, she should have said so, as various cases indicate. We decline to change the will, or the intent as we view it, by inserting the words "or death." We have also considered: the fact that plaintiff could not take one-third in fee after her own death, and that the testator apparently had no thought of plaintiff's heirs taking that interest; that if plaintiff's heirs could not take, there would be a partial intestacy; that there might be an issue as to whether or not the other niece and the nephew must survive the plaintiff in order to take one-third each, if plaintiff got only a life estate, at least unless Section 474.480 stepped in and supplied the deficiency; that plaintiff was devised a part of this identical property in fee in the event of her marriage, which indicates something more than the grant of a life estate prior to her marriage, for the testatrix clearly intended for plaintiff to have a greater estate if she did *not* marry; that the testatrix is presumed not to have intended a partial intestacy, but rather intended to dispose of the entire estate by granting a fee determinable on marriage. . . .

We thus hold that plaintiff took a fee simple estate in all the real estate, subject to divestiture of an undivided two-thirds interest in the event of her marriage; in such event that two-thirds would vest equally, per stirpes, in the heirs at law of the other niece and nephew. The construction of any will depends upon its own particular terms, and the intent evidenced thereby; it is our belief that the terms of the present will distinguish this case from Winget v. Gay . . . .

The judgment of the trial court is reversed, with directions to enter a judgment in accordance with this opinion.

PER CURIAM.

The foregoing opinion by Henry I. Eager, Special Commissioner, is adopted as the opinion of the Court.

All of the Judges concur.

MOORE v. PHILLIPS

Court of Appeals of Kansas, 1981.
6 Kan.App.2d 94, 627 P.2d 831.

PRAGER, JUSTICE PRESIDING:

This is a claim for waste asserted against the estate of a life tenant by remaindermen, seeking to recover damages for the deterioration of a farmhouse resulting from neglect by the life tenant. The life tenant was Ada C. Brannan. The defendant-appellant is her executrix, Ruby F. Phillips. The claimants–appellees are Dorothy Moore and Kent Reinhardt, the daughter and grandson of Ada C. Brannan.

The facts in the case are essentially as follows: Leslie Brannan died in 1962. By his will, he left his wife, Ada C. Brannan, a life estate in certain farmland containing a farmhouse, with remainder interests to Dorothy Moore and Kent Reinhardt. Ada C. Brannan resided in the farmhouse until 1964. She then rented the farmhouse until August 1, 1965, when it became unoccupied. From that point on, Ada C. Brannan rented all of the farmland but nobody lived in the house. It appears that from 1969 to 1971 it was leased to the remaindermen, but they did not live there. It is undisputed that the remaindermen inspected the premises from time to time down through the years. In 1973, Ada C. Brannan petitioned for a voluntary conservatorship because of physical infirmities. In 1976, Ada C. Brannan died testate, leaving her property to others. Dorothy Moore and Kent Reinhardt were not included in Ada's bounty. From the record, it is clear that Ada C. Brannan and her daughter, Dorothy Moore, were estranged from about 1964 on. This estrangement continued until Ada Brannan's death, although there was minimal contact between them from time to time.

After Ada Brannan's death, Dorothy Moore and Kent Reinhardt filed a demand against the estate of Ada Brannan on the theory of waste to recover damages for the deterioration of the farmhouse. The total damages alleged were in the amount of $16,159. Both the district magistrate and the district judge inspected the premises and found deterioration due to neglect by the life tenant. The district court found the actual damages to the house to be $10,433. The executrix of Ada's estate denied any neglect or breach of duty by Ada Brannan as life tenant. She asserted the defenses of laches or estoppel, the statute of limitation, and abandonment. These affirmative defenses were rejected by the district magistrate and the district judge, except the defense of laches or estoppel which the district magistrate sustained. On appeal, the district judge found that the defense of laches or estoppel was not applicable against the remaindermen in this case. Following entry of judgment in favor of the remaindermen, the executrix appealed.

It is important to note that the executrix does not contend, as points of error, that the life tenant was not responsible for deterioration of the farmhouse or that the action is barred by a statute of limitations. The amount of damages awarded is not contested. In her brief, the executrix-appellant asserts four points which essentially present a single issue: Whether the remaindermen, by waiting eleven years until the death of the life tenant before filing any claim or demand against the life tenant for neglect of the farmhouse, are barred by laches or estoppel?

The executrix contends, in substance, that laches and estoppel, although considered to be equitable defenses, are available in an action at law to recover damages. She points out that, under K.S.A. 58–2523, a remainderman may sue to prevent waste during the life of the tenant while the life tenancy is still in existence. She then notes that the remaindermen inspected the premises on numerous occasions during the eleven years the property was vacant; yet they made no demand that the farmhouse be kept in repair. They waited until the death of the life tenant to bring the action, because then they would not be faced with Ada's testimony which might defeat their claim.

The remaindermen, in their brief, dispute certain factual statements made by the executrix. They agree that the remaindermen had very limited contact with the life tenant after the estrangement. They contend that there is evidence to show the vast majority of the damage to the house occurred during the last two or three years of life tenancy and that Dorothy Moore did, in fact, express concern to her mother about the deterioration of the house 15 to 20 times during the eleven-year period. They contend that mere passage of time does not constitute laches and that, in order to have laches or estoppel, the person claiming the same must show a detrimental change of position or prejudice of some kind. They argue that the executrix has failed to show any prejudice, since the fact of waste and deterioration is clear and undisputed and there is nothing the testimony of the life tenant could have added on that issue had she been at the trial. As to the failure of the remaindermen to file an action in the lifetime of the life tenant, the remaindermen argue that claimants had been advised to avoid contact with Ada Brannan unless it was absolutely necessary and that they did not want to make a claim during her lifetime since it would have only made a bad situation worse. They maintain that they had good reasons to wait until Ada's death to assert the claim.

In order to place this case in proper perspective, it would be helpful to summarize some of the basic principles of law applicable where a remainderman asserts a claim of waste against a life tenant. They are as follows:

(1) A life tenant is considered in law to be a trustee or quasi-trustee and occupies a fiduciary relation to the remaindermen. The life tenant is a trustee in the sense that he cannot injure or dispose of the property to the injury of the rights of the remaindermen, but he differs from a pure trustee in that he may use the property for his exclusive benefit and take all the income and profits. Windscheffel v. Wright, 187 Kan. 678, 686, 360 P.2d 178 (1961); In re Estate of Miller, 225 Kan. 655, 594 P.2d 167 (1979).

(2) It is the duty of a life tenant to keep the property subject to the life estate in repair so as to preserve the property and to prevent decay or waste. 51 Am.Jur.2d, Life Tenants and Remaindermen § 259, pp. 546–548. Stated in another way, the law imposes upon a tenant the obligation to return the premises to the landlord or remaindermen at the end of the term unimpaired by the negligence of the tenant. Salina Coca-Cola Bottling Corp. v. Rogers, 171 Kan. 688, 237 P.2d 218 (1951); In re Estate of Morse, 192 Kan. 691, 391 P.2d 117 (1964).

(3) The term "waste" implies neglect or misconduct resulting in material damages to or loss of property, but does not include ordinary depreciation of property due to age and normal use over a comparatively short period of time. First Federal Savings & Loan Ass'n v. Moulds, 202 Kan. 557, 451 P.2d 215 (1969).

(4) Waste may be either voluntary or permissive. Voluntary waste, sometimes spoken of as commissive waste, consists of the commission of some deliberate or voluntary destructive act. Permissive waste is the failure of the tenant to exercise the ordinary care of a prudent man for the preservation and protection of the estate. 78 Am. Jr.2d, Waste § 3, p. 397.

(5) The owner of a reversion or remainder in fee has a number of remedies available to him against a life tenant who commits waste. He may recover compensatory damages for the injuries sustained. He may have injunctive relief in equity, or, in a proper case, may obtain a receivership. The same basic remedies are available against either a tenant for years or a life tenant. Kimberlin v. Hicks, 150 Kan. 449, 456, 94 P.2d 335 (1939).

(6) By statute in Kansas, K.S.A. 58–2523, "[a] person seized of an estate in remainder or reversion may maintain an action for waste or trespass for injury to the inheritance, notwithstanding an intervening estate for life or years." Thus a remainderman does not have to wait until the life tenant dies in order to bring an appropriate action for waste.

(7) Where the right of action of the remainderman or landlord is based upon permissive waste, it is generally held that the injury is continuing in nature and that the statute of limitations does not commence to run in favor of the tenant until the expiration of the tenancy. Under certain state statutes, it has been held that the period of limitation commences at the time the waste is committed. Prescott, Exor. of Mary E. Prescott v. Grimes, 143 Ky. 191, 136 S.W. 206 (1911); In Re Stout's Estate, 151 Or. 411, 50 P.2d 768 (1935).

(8) There is authority which holds that an action for waste may be lost by laches. Harcourt v. White, 28 Beavan's 303, 54 Eng.Reprint 382 (1860); 78 Am.Jur.2d, Waste § 38, p. 424. Likewise, estoppel may be asserted as a defense in an action for waste. The doctrine of laches and estoppel are closely related, especially where there is complaint of delay which has placed another at a disadvantage. Laches is sometimes spoken of as a species of estoppel. Laches is a wholly negative thing, the result of a failure to act; estoppel on the other hand may involve an affirmative act on the part of some party of the lawsuit. The mere passage of time is not enough to invoke the doctrine of laches. Each case must be governed by its own facts, and what might be considered a lapse of sufficient time to defeat an action in one case might be insufficient in another. Laches, in legal significance, is not mere delay, but delay that works a disadvantage to another. Clark v. Chipman, 212 Kan. 259, 510 P.2d 1257 (1973). The defense of laches may be applied in actions at law as well as in equitable proceedings. McDaniel v. Messerschmidt, 191 Kan. 461, 464, 382 P.2d 304 (1963). In Osincup v. Henthorn, 89 Kan. 58, 130 P. 652 (1913), it was held that laches is an equitable defense and will not bar a recovery from mere lapse of time nor where there is a reasonable excuse for nonaction of a party in making inquiry as to his rights or in *asserting* them.

The basic question for our determinaton is whether the district court erred in holding that the defense of laches or estoppel should not be applied in this case. We have concluded that the district court did not commit error in its rejection of the defense of laches or estoppel under the circumstances of this case. In reaching this conclusion, we have noted the following factors: The evidence is clear that the life tenant, Ada Brannan, failed to carry out her duty as life tenant and quasi-trustee to keep the property in reasonable repair. The claim of waste does not arise out of any act on the part of the remaindermen. Preservation of the property was the responsibility of the life tenant. There was evidence to show that the vast majority of the damage to the farmhouse occurred during the last two or three years of the life tenancy. The fact that permissive waste occurred was proved beyond question. If the life tenant had been alive, she could not very well have disputed the fact that the property has been allowed to deteriorate. Hence, any delay in filing the action until after Ada's death could not have resulted in prejudice to her executrix. There is no evidence in the record to support the defense of estoppel.

Furthermore, the evidence was undisputed that the life tenant was an elderly woman who died in August of 1976 at the age of 83. The position of Dorothy Moore was that she did not wish to file an action which would aggravate her mother and take funds which her mother might need during her lifetime. Even though Dorothy Moore was estranged from her mother, the law should not require her to sue her mother during her lifetime under these circumstances. As noted above, it was the tenant's obligation to see that the premises were turned over to the remaindermen in good repair at the termination of the life estate. Under all the circumstances in this case, we hold that the district court did not err in rejecting the defense of laches or estoppel.

The judgment of the district court is affirmed.

NOTE

In a classic case, Melms v. Pabst Brewing Co., 104 Wis. 7, 79 N.W. 738 (1899), the life tenant "improved" the property by razing a dwelling on the land and grading the surface down to street level so it would be more useful as part of a brewery. There was a dispute as to whether the interest was a life estate or a fee simple absolute, but it was held to be the former. The court traced the historical development of the doctrine of waste and agreed that "any material change in the nature and character of the buildings made by a tenant is waste, although the value of the property should be enhanced by the alteration." However, it recognized some limits to this broad principle. "Thus, the ancient English rule which prevented the tenant from converting a meadow into arable land was early softened down, and the doctrine of meliorating waste was adopted, which, without changing the legal definition of waste, still allowed the tenant to change the course of husbandry upon the estate if such change be for the betterment of the estate."

The court then asked two key questions. "Can it be reasonably or logically said that this entire change of condition is to be completely ignored, and the ironclad rule applied that the tenant can make no change in the uses of the property because he will destroy its identity? Must the tenant stand by, and preserve the useless dwelling house, so that he may at some future time turn it over to the reversioner, equally useless? Certainly, all the analogies are to the contrary." Judgment for the defendant life tenant was affirmed.

SECTION 2. DEFEASIBLE ESTATES

OLDFIELD v. STOECO HOMES, INC.

Supreme Court of New Jersey, 1958.
26 N.J. 246, 139 A.2d 291.

BURLING, J. This is a proceeding in lieu of prerogative writ. Suit was instituted by plaintiffs, residents and taxpayers of the City of Ocean City, with the object of having several resolutions of the City of Ocean City extending the time for performance of certain conditions in a deed declared invalid, and for the further relief of having lands owned by the defendants forfeited and returned to the city. The parties defendants are Stoeco Homes, Inc., the purchaser from Ocean City, Workshop, Inc., a subsequent grantee of a portion of the land from Stoeco, and Seaboard Fidelity Company, Workship's mortagee, and the City of Ocean City.

From an adverse determination in the Superior Court, Law Division, plaintiffs prosecuted an appeal. Prior to hearing in the Appellate Division, we certified the cause on our own motion.

The facts are not in dispute and have been stipulated by the parties. . . .

In 1951 Ocean City held title to a large number of lots of undeveloped land in a low-lying area of the city. The locale of the lots is roughly divisible into two large segments, with Bay Avenue forming a dividing line between east and west. . . . Ocean City, recognizing that an extensive redevelopment of these swampy areas would benefit the community, indicated its willingness to sell the lots, with the exception of 226 lots in the eastern tract which it desired to retain.

After receiving minimum bids for the two groups of lots, Ocean City advertised both tracts of land for public sale on February 14, 1951, setting forth in the advertisement various terms and conditions with which the the vendee was to comply. At the sale Stoeco was the only and therefore the highest bidder for both the eastern and western groups of lots, bidding $10,525 for the former and $100,000 for the latter. The sales were duly confirmed by two resolutions of the municipality dated February 16, 1951, and final settlement was made on both sales on June 29, 1951. Throughout, the sales were treated as separate transactions and no question is raised in this case concerning Stoeco's performance of the conditions imposed by the deeds to the lots on the western side.

While the deed from Ocean City to Stoeco contained various conditions and restrictions, the core provisions around which this dispute centers are:

"(a) Within one (1) year from the date of this Deed, the party of the second part shall fill all of the following listed lots of land now owned by the party of the first part and which are not being conveyed."

(Here follows a list of lots by lot number and block number.)

"(b) Within one (1) year following the date of this Deed, the party of the second part shall fill all of the lots of land sold to said party of the second part as a result of this sale."

"(d) All such lands shall be filled to at least the now established and existing grades of the City of Ocean City, New Jersey for the areas and lots to be filled."

"The City of Ocean City reserves the right to change or modify any restriction, condition or other requirements hereby imposed in a manner agreeable to or as permitted by law.

"A failure to comply with the covenants and conditions of paragraphs (a), (b) and (d) hereof will automatically cause title to all lands to revert to the City of Ocean City; and a failure of any other restrictions and covenants may cause title to revert to the City as to any particular land, lot or lots involved in any violation."

Thus, Stoeco was required to fill and grade not only the lots sold to them by the city, but also the lots retained by the city. . . .

These unfavorable dredging conditons, not orginally contemplated, created serious engineering and financial problems for Stoeco.

By June 29, 1952, one year after obtaining the deed, Stoeco had still not completed the substantial portion of filling and grading, nor had it done so by February of 1953. Ocean City, more interested in redevelopment than declaring a default, passed a resolution on February 20, 1953 to change and modify the terms and conditions of the sale of land. . . . The general import of the resolution was that Stoeco was to be given until December 31, 1954 to complete the filling and grading of all lots purchased between Bay and Haven Avenues and 20th and 24th Streets. . . .

On December 30, 1954, Ocean City passed the second of the disputed resolutions. . . . This resolution extended the time for performance of the original conditions of the sale as to land between 24th and 30th Streets until January 1, 1958, and as to the lots between 30th and 34th Streets until January 1, 1960. . . .

The legal issues projected by the pleadings and pre-trial order were: (1) whether the deed from Ocean City to Stoeco created an estate in fee simple subject to a condition subsequent or an estate subject to a limitation (a fee simple determinable, Restatement, Property § 44 (1936)). . . .

The court below held that the nature of the defeasible estate created was one in fee simple, subject to a condition subsequent; that the resolutions were neither unconstitutional nor ultra vires, and that the proceeding was barred on all the grounds advanced. The issues raised below are again urged on appeal.

First, we consider the issue relating to the nature of the estate created. It is said that a fee simple determinable differs from a fee simple subject to a condition subsequent in that, in the former, upon the happening of the stated event the estate "ipso facto" or "automatically" reverts to the grantor or his heirs, while in the latter the grantor must take some affirmative action to divest the grantee of his estate. Board of Chosen Freeholders of the County of Cumberland v. Buck, 79 N.J.Eq. 472, 82 A. 418 (Ch.1912); Carpender v. City of New Brunswick, 135 N.J.Eq. 397, 39 A.2d 40 (Ch.1944); Restatement, Property, §§ 44, 45 (1936). The interest remaining in the grantor in a fee simple determinable has been denominated a possibility of reverter, Restatement, Property, §§ 44, 154, while the interest remaining in the grantor of a fee simple subject to a condition subsequent, i.e., the right to re-enter upon the happening of the prescribed contingency, has been denominated a power of termination. Restatement, Property §§ 45, 155.

It is further alleged that a fee simple determinable estate is more onerous than an estate in fee simple subject to condition subsequent in that the defenses of waiver and estoppel which are applicable to the latter are unavailing in the former. But cf. Dunham, "Possibility of Reverter and Powers of Termination—Fraternal or Identical Twins?", 20 U.Chicago L.Rev. 215 (1952); McDougal and Haber, Property, Wealth, Land 286 (1948).[10] We can assume, without deciding the point, that such a distinction exists between the two estates, for the reason that, as will be hereafter developed, the estate created in the instant case was one subject to a condition subsequent. . . .

Plaintiffs assert that the language of automatic reverter in the deed indicates beyond cavil that the estate created was a fee simple determinable and that therefore the municipality's effort to waive the breach of performance was ineffectual.

While language is the primary guide for the ascertainment of whether a given deed attempts to condition or limit an estate, still it is the instrument as a whole, and not a particular phrase aborted from the context which provides the basis for the attainment of our ultimate task, which is to effectuate the intention of the parties. The particular words, upon which are predicated the right, or lack of it, to a forfeiture are often emphasized. Thus, it has been said that such words as "so long as," "until" or "during," followed by words of reverter, are appropriate to create a fee simple determinable, whereas such words as "upon condition that" or "provided that" are usual indicators of an estate upon condition subsequent. Board of Chosen Freeholders of the County of Cumberland v. Buck, supra; Carpender v. City of New Brunswick, supra; Restatement, Property § 44, comment (*l*); § 45, comment (j) (1936). But that particular forms of expression, standing alone and without resort to the purpose of the instrument in question, are not determinative is at once apparent to a discerning surveyor of the case authorities. . . .

The ancient land law imputed a thaumaturgic quality to language. . . . If the judicial eye in scanning the instrument chanced upon a pet phrase the inquiry was ended without resorting to the ardous effort of reconciling evident inconsistencies therein. The universal touchstone today is the intention of the parties to the instrument creating the interest in land.

If the four corners of the deed provide a coherent expression of the parties' intent, we need search no further, but if an ambiguity or a reasonable doubt appears from a perusal of the particular symbols of expression our horizons must be broadened to encompass the circumstances surrounding the transaction. . . . To the foregoing must be added certain constructional biases developed in a hierarchical fashion

10. [Professors McDougal and Haber declare: "It is, therefore, believed that the whole dichotomy, between determinable fees with possibilities of reverter and fees subject to condition subsequent with rights of entry, is just another example of needless double-talk, of obscure historical origins and unfortunate contemporary policy consequences, which might well disappear from the books. When the consequences a donor seeks are within the policy of the community, no informed draftsman will trust his donor's intent to so frail a carrier as the difference between 'so long as' and 'but if'; when the consequences a donor seeks are forbidden by community policy, no element of rationality suggests that he should be permitted to exceed the community's bounds by one verbal form and not by another." Professor Dunham, in his article, seeks to demonstrate that the distinction is not as significant in terms of actual consequences as it is commonly thought to be.]

and predicated upon the proposition that the law abhors a forfeiture. Thus, if the choice is between a condition subsequent and a restrictive covenant, the former [latter?] is preferred. Woodruff v. Woodruff, 44 N.J.Eq. 349, 16 A. 4, 1 L.R.A. 380 (Ch.1888); 2 Powell, Real Property § 188. And where the choice is between an estate in fee simple determinable and an estate on condition subsequent, the latter is preferred. Restatement, Property § 45, comment (m); 2 Powell, supra, § 188; 26 C.J.S. Deeds § 141.

To focus attention solely on the words "automatically cause title to revert" is to ignore and refuse effect to the following provisions: "This conveyance is also subject to the following *conditions*, requirements, reservations, covenants and restrictions:" (Emphasis supplied.) and "A failure to comply with the *covenants* and *conditions of paragraphs (a), (b) and (d) hereof* . . . ." (Emphasis supplied.) Moreover, the deed contained the following clause: "The City of Ocean City reserves the right to change or modify any restriction, condition or other requirements hereby imposed in a manner agreeable to or as permitted by law."

The repeated use of the word "condition" and the provision reserving the right to alter the arrangement in the clauses are sufficient to cast a reasonable doubt upon what was intended. Accordingly, we shall consider the surrounding circumstances in order to ascertain the intention of the parties in creating the estate.

Before proceeding to a determination of this question, however, it is well to keep in mind what condition in the deed was violated. The plaintiffs treat the condition as to the grading and filling within one year as a single condition. Thus, they contend that since by June 1952 the grading and filling was not complied with, the city, even if the clause be construed as a condition subsequent, had a right to reenter and terminate the estate. This power of termination for breach of a condition subsequent is in New Jersey an assignable and hence a saleable property interest. They therefore conclude that to extend the time for performance was in essence to donate a valuable property right to Stoeco without consideration. N.J.Const.1947, Art. VIII, Sec. III, par. 3. But the fault in analysis is that the language imposing the duty . . . is in reality two conditions and not one. First, Stoeco was to fill and grade according to specifications the various lots and secondly, they were to do it within one year. It is this latter condition which was modified by the city. There is a distinction recognized in the cases between a waiver of the time for performance and a waiver of the performance itself. . . . Annotation, "Condition Subsequent-Waiver-Estoppel," 39 A.L.R.2d 1116, at p. 1132. It may be that had the municipality waived the performance such action would be violative of the constitutional proscriptions. But that question is not before us. All the municipality did was to modify the original time for performance.

With this in mind, we proceed to a determination of whether the limitation as to time was a condition subsequent which could be waived by the city in its discretion or a limitation (fee simple determinable).

To hold that the condition as to time was so essential to the scheme of the parties that to violate it by a day would result in an immediate and automatic forfeiture of the estate is to distort beyond recognition what the parties intended. There is no indication that time was of the essence of the agreement. Ocean City was to receive two substantial considerations by this agreement. First, the 226 lots owned and retained by it were to be filled and graded, and hence their value greatly enhanced. Secondly, and perhaps more important, a large tract of land, hitherto the breeding place for mosquitoes, was to be developed for productive use. Indeed, an initial quid pro quo has already been received in the erection of 23 dwelling units in the area. No immediacy or sense of urgency in relation to the time within which this development was to take place is apparent. It may be fairly inferred that the one-year limitation was originally put in because Stoeco conceived that the fill from the drained lagoons on the west side would be of sufficient quantity and quality that the task could easily be completed within one year. But, as is often the case, difficulties were encountered with the plan, and at last it had to be discarded in favor of alternative and more expensive methods of grading and filling than those originally contemplated. In light of this impediment, the parties renegotiated for the time in which performance was to be made. To say that the parties intended a forfeiture irrespective of future contingencies impeding the original scheme is to ignore and refuse legal efficacy to the following language previously referred to in the resolutions and deed: "The City of Ocean City reserves the right to change or modify any restriction, condition or other requirements hereby imposed in a manner agreeable to or as permitted by law."

A certain amount of flexibility is inherent among such large-scale undertakings as the one under consideration. We might add here that the more one probes into the essence of this arrangement the more it becomes apparent that although deeds were utilized as the devices to accomplish the ultimate desired results, the transaction bears a closer resemblance to the law of contract than of real property. Cf. 3 Williston on Contracts § 845; Restatement, Contracts §§ 250, 276.

It is our conclusion that the parties contemplated that the estate created was not to expire automatically at the end of a year and that therefore it is one subject to a condition subsequent. . . .

Affirmed.

NOTES

1. Although the principal case is valuable for its analysis of defeasible estates in land, the problem of filling the marshland turned out to be no sport for the shortwinded. In United States v. Stoeco Homes, Inc., 498 F.2d 597 (3d Cir.1974), cert. denied 420 U.S. 927, 95 S.Ct. 1124, 43 L.Ed.2d 397 (1975) the dredge and fill operation was enjoined under the Rivers and Harbors Act. The saga was still ongoing in 1988 when Ocean City's 1951 useless marsh had become a 1988 still-unfilled, valuable wetland resource subject to the jurisdiction of the

Army Corps of Engineers. See Stoeco Development, Ltd. v. Department of the Army Corps of Engineers, 701 F.Supp. 1075 (D.N.J.1988).

2. In Mahrenholz v. County Board of School Trustees, etc., 93 Ill.App.3d 366, 48 Ill.Dec. 736, 417 N.E.2d 138 (1981) the court construed a deed which read "this land to be used for school purpose only; otherwise to revert to Grantors herein." The court held that this language created a fee simple determinable rather than a fee simple subject to a condition subsequent; therefore when the land was abandoned for school purposes the tract reverted automatically to the grantor or his heirs. (Under Illinois law neither possibilities of reverter nor powers of termination are alienable or devisable but both are inheritable—see Note *4* below.) Following the automatic reversion, the grantor or his heirs had a fee simple absolute and could convey that interest to a third party. If the deed had created a fee simple subject to a condition subsequent then there would have been no automatic reversion and, since the power of termination (right of re-entry for condition broken) had not been exercised at the time of the conveyance to a third party, no interest could have passed to him. "If the grantor had a possibility of reverter, he or his heirs become the owner of the property by operation of law as soon as the condition is broken. If he has a right of re-entry for condition broken, he or his heirs become the owner of the property only after they act to re-take the property."

The "Thaumaturgic quality of language" still plays a role in the modern cases and Professor Dunham's twins may be fraternal but they are not identical!

3. Prior to the enactment of the Statute of Uses in 1536, one could not provide that upon termination of a defeasible fee, some third person would be entitled to possession. It was said that no conditions could be created in strangers. This subject is treated in Section 4 of Chapter 14.

4. A number of states allow transfer inter vivos of the possibility of reverter, but not of the right of entry. In some states both are transferable inter vivos and in others neither is transferable inter vivos. There is even some authority that the attempt to alienate a right of entry has the effect of destroying it, but the more recent cases reject this view. Both types of interests are inheritable everywhere. They are also devisable in most states, but not in all—e.g., Illinois, where neither is alienable inter vivos or devisable. Ill.Rev. Stat. ch. 30, § 37b (1985). For discussion of the relevant policies, see I American Law of Property §§ 4.64–4.75 (Casner ed. 1952); 2 Powell, Real Property ¶¶ 280–284 (1977).

For an interesting recent case see Oak's Oil Service, Inc. v. Massachusetts Bay Transportation Authority, 15 Mass.App.Ct. 593, 447 N.E. 2d 27 (1983). The plaintiff was "relying on a line of cases which hold that an attempt to alienate a right of entry by conveyance inter vivos has the effect of destroying the right of entry and of vesting fee simple title in the holder of the estate theretofore defeasible by the exercise of the right of entry. Rice v. Boston and Worcester R.R., 12 Allen 141 (1866) . . . ." The court construed a 1954 Massachusetts statute limiting the duration of rights of entry and possibilities of reverter to thirty years as authorizing the transferability of rights of entry. "Under the new statute, if it is clear from the language of the deed and the attendant circumstances that the parties intended to create a right of entry in a person other than the grantor or to provide for the right of entry to be assignable with a conveyance of the grantor's remaining land, there is no reason not to give effect to that intention."

ROBERTS v. RHODES

Supreme Court of Kansas, 1982.
231 Kan. 74, 643 P.2d 116.

FROMME, JUSTICE:

This case is before this court on a Petition for Review of an unpublished opinion of the Court of Appeals filed November 13, 1981, reversing a decision of the Montgomery District Court. The case concerns title to two small adjacent tracts of land deeded to a school more than 70 years ago to be used for school purposes but without reversion or other language of limitation in the deeds. The district court held that when these tracts were no longer used for school purposes, the tracts reverted to the heirs and assigns of the original grantors. On appeal the Court of Appeals reversed the decision of the district court and held the deeds conveyed fee simple title to the school district.

The school district sold the land in 1971. The defendants Rhodes acquired the tracts by mesne conveyances from the school district. The plaintiffs Roberts claim title to these tracts by deed from the heirs of the original grantors and by reversion, since the land is no longer used for school purposes. We will now look at the wording in the original deeds to the school district, as set forth in the "Agreed Statement of Facts" appearing in the record:

> "1. That on the 29th day of September, 1902, D. W. Smith and Margaret Smith, husband and wife, made a quitclaim deed to School District No. 35 of Montgomery County, Kansas. The consideration for said deed was One ($1.00) Dollar and contains the following: 'WITNESSETH, That said parties of the first part, in consideration of the sum of One Dollar ($1.00), the receipt of which is hereby acknowledged, do by these presents, remise, release and quitclaim unto said parties of the second part, *their heirs and assigns*, all the following described Real Estate situated in the County of Montgomery and State of Kansas, to-wit: Beginning at the North West corner of the South Half of the Northwest Quarter of Section 10, Township 35, Range 14, running thence East 209 feet; South 418 feet; thence West 209 feet; thence North 418 feet to place of beginning, *it being understood that this grant is made only for school or cemetery purposes.*' That said deed was duly executed by the grantors and recorded in the office of the register of deeds of Montgomery County, Kansas, on the 30th day of September, 1902, at 8:00 o'clock A.M. That at the time of the execution of said deed, D. W. Smith and Margaret Smith were the owners in fee simple of

the South Half (S 1/2) of the Northwest Quarter (NW 1/4) of Section 10, Township 35, Range 14.

"2. That on the 9th day of April, 1908, T. A. Stevens and Louella Stevens, husband and wife, made, executed and delivered to School District No. 35 of Montgomery County, Kansas, a quitclaim deed. That said deed contains the following: 'WITNESSETH, That said parties of the first part, in consideration of the sum of Seventy Five and No/100 Dollars, the receipt of which is hereby acknowledged, do by these presents Remise, Release and Quitclaim unto said party of the second part, *its heirs and assigns,* all of the following described real estate, situated in the County of Montgomery and State of Kansas, to-wit: Beginning at a point 418 Feet South of the Northwest corner of the South Half of the Northwest Quarter of Section 10, Township 35, Range 14, running thence East 209 feet; South 209 feet; thence West 209 feet; thence North 209 feet to place of beginning. *It being understood that this grant is made for school and cemetery purposes only.*' That said deed was duly executed by the grantors and recorded in the office of the register of deeds of Montgomery County, Kansas, on April 11, 1908, at 8:00 o'clock A.M." Emphasis supplied.

As may be noted, the two deeds contain the ordinary verbiage of a quitclaim deed except for the following additional phrases:

"1. . . . [I]t being understood that this grant is made only for school or cemetery purposes."

"2. . . . It being understood that this grant is made for school and cemetery purposes only."

Under the agreed statement of facts, the two tracts of land were accepted and used for school purposes for over sixty years. They were not used for cemetery purposes. The understanding that the grant was made "for school *or* cemetery purposes" in the first deed, and "for school *and* cemetery purposes" in the second deed was clearly expressed. However, the grants were used for school purposes. A school district is not legally authorized to operate a cemetery. The difficulty in construing the deeds arises from a failure of the parties to provide for what should happen to the land after it has been used for school purposes for sixty years and then is no longer needed for such purpose. In the case of the second deed which provided the tract was to be used for school *and* cemetery purposes, there was no provision for reversion in case the tract was not used for cemetery purposes. Usually, if it is intended to limit the estate granted some form of limitation over is required.

The general rule for creation of an estate in fee simple determinable is set forth in the Restatement of Property § 44, p. 121 (1936) as follows:

"An estate in fee simple determinable is created by any limitation which, in an otherwise effective conveyance of land,

"(a) creates an estate in fee simple; and

> "(b) provides that the estate shall automatically expire upon the occurrence of a stated event."

The difficulty here is that neither deed made provision for the estate to revert or terminate on the occurrence of any stated events.

The statutory direction as to what interest generally should pass by conveyance is set out in K.S.A. 58–2202 as follows:

> "The term 'heirs,' or other words of inheritance, shall not be necessary to create or convey an estate in fee simple; and every conveyance of real estate shall pass all the estate of the grantor therein, unless the intent to pass a less estate shall expressly appear or be necessarily implied in the terms of the grant."

See Fast v. Fast, 209 Kan. 24, 26–27, 496 P.2d 171 (1972).

Where in the present conveyances to the school district can you find an intent to pass a less estate than one in fee simple? The conveyances run to heirs and assigns of the school district. It is true that it was understood by the parties that the grants were made for school purposes. It is also true that for over sixty years it was used for school purposes. The understanding under which these grants were made was fulfilled. In the absence of an intent to limit the title shown in the conveyance, either expressly or by necessary implication, the grantors pass all the interest they own in the real estate. The statute 58–2202 merely expresses the following accepted rules of real estate law. Forfeitures are not favored in the law. The general rule is well settled that the mere expression that property is to be used for a particular purpose will not in and of itself suffice to turn a fee simple into a determinable fee. 28 Am.Jur.2d, Estates § 29, p. 107; 2 Powell on Real Property § 188 (1981); Simes and Smith, Law of Future Interests § 248 (1956); Simes on Future Interests § 46 (1951); 4 Thompson on Real Property §§ 2063, 2064 (1979).

As pointed out in the Restatement, courts have in some cases recognized a special limitation on the interest conveyed which may cause the created interest to automatically expire upon the occurrence of a stated event. Words which are recognized as sufficient to express such automatic expiration include "until," "so long as," or "during," or those conveyances which contain a provision that "upon the happening of a stated event the land is to revert to the grantor." American Law Institute—Restatement of Property § 44, comment 1, p. 128. See also 28 Am.Jur.2d, Estates § 30, p. 109. The conveyances in our present case contained none of these words limiting the period or term for which the grant was made.

It appears safe to say as a general rule the mere statement of the purposes of a conveyance will not limit the extent of the grant. 28 Am. Jur.2d, Estates § 29, p. 107.

> "Mere expression of the purpose for which the property is to be used will not in and of itself suffice to limit the estate conveyed." Choctaw & Chickasaw Nations v. Board of County Com'rs, 361 F.2d 932, 934 (10th Cir. 1966).

"Although the purpose of the deeds is disclosed, words by which it is declared will not, without more, suffice to limit the estate granted." Cleary Petroleum Corp. v. Harrison, 621 P.2d 528, 532 (Okl. 1980).

"[T]he simple phrase, 'for school purposes,' under the circumstances of this case would be insufficient to create a determinable fee." Trone v. Nelson, 89 Ill.App.3d 1000, 1004, 45 Ill.Dec. 39, 412 N.E.2d 172 (1980).

Among the illustrations appearing in the Restatement of Property appear the following:

"A, owning Blackacre in fee simple absolute, transfers Blackacre 'to B and his heirs to and for the use of the C Church and for no other purpose.' B has an estate in fee simple absolute and not an estate in fee simple determinable." Restatement, § 44, comment *m*, illustration 18, p. 130.

Restatement, § 45, comment *o*, illustration 12, p. 143 is as follows:

"A, owning Blackacre in fee simple absolute, transfers Blackacre 'to B and his heirs in further consideration that the said grantee shall keep on said property a first class hotel, and shall not use the property for any other purpose than the hotel business.' B has an estate in fee simple absolute."

The early Kansas case of Curtis v. Board of Education, 43 Kan. 138, 23 P. 98 (1890), follows the general rule. The grantor conveyed property to School District No. 45 by warranty deed containing the provision *"for the erection of a school-house thereon, and for no other purposes."* 43 Kan. at 140, 23 P. 98. When this deed was challenged by the original grantor, this court as constituted in 1890 held an absolute estate in fee simple passed to the school district. *Curtis* has been followed by this court and remains the law in Kansas.

[The Court then discussed a series of Kansas cases dealing with the problem.]

. . .

After considering all the foregoing cases and authorities we conclude under the facts and circumstances of this case a quitclaim deed from the owner of property to a named school district by which a small tract of land is remised, released and quitclaimed to the school district, its heirs, and assigns, by metes and bounds description, "it being understood that this grant is made only for school or cemetery purposes" and without reversion or other language of limitation used, conveys fee simple title when the land has been accepted and used by the grantee for school purposes for more than sixty years.

Accordingly the judgment of the district court is reversed and the case is remanded with directions to enter judgment for the defendants. The judgment of the Court of Appeals is affirmed.

SCHROEDER, C.J., and HERD, J., dissent.

MCFARLAND, J., not participating.

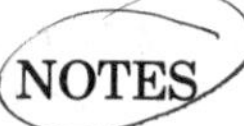

NOTES

1. For a consideration of $225, land was conveyed in 1915 to the Scott County Board of Education "for the purposes of a common school house, and for no other purpose." Held, in Scott County Board of Education v. Pepper, 311 S.W.2d 189 (Ky.App.1958), that this instrument conveyed a fee simple absolute.

See also City of Tempe v. Baseball Facilities, Inc., 23 Ariz.App. 557, 534 P.2d 1056 (1975) where the conveyances read: "Subject to the restriction that the . . . real property shall be operated and maintained solely for park, recreational and public accommodation, and convenience purposes." The court noted that the deed did not provide for a right of re-entry. "Therefore, it does not appear that a fee simple subject to a condition subsequent was created. The language could be construed as merely precatory . . . or as a restrictive covenant." What would be the consequences of treating the language as precatory? What would be the consequences of construing the language as creating a restrictive covenant? See pages 648 to 716, infra.

2. X conveyed land to trustees of a church and their successors "so long as the premises are used for church purposes." A church building was thereafter erected upon the land and church services are regularly conducted there. The church trustees recently drilled an oil and gas well on the land and are producing oil and gas. Church services are continuing. What action, if any, should be taken by X? See Davis v. Skipper, 125 Tex. 364, 83 S.W.2d 318 (1935).

MARTIN V. CITY OF SEATTLE

Court of Appeals of Washington, Division 1, 1986.
46 Wn.App. 1, 728 P.2d 1091.

DORE, JUSTICE.

C.B. Dodge Company owned some land in Seattle on the shore of Lake Washington. In 1908, the Dodge Company executed a quitclaim deed to a narrow strip of that property which bordered the lake so that the City could construct what is now Lake Washington Boulevard. The deed contained three conditions, one of which is to have the right, for itself and for its successors and assigns, to build and maintain a boathouse along the shore of Lake Washington. The City was responsible for acquiring the land necessary for the boathouse, as well as allowing the building and use of it. A breach of this condition allowed the grantor or his successors to reenter and forfeit the grant.

Between the time the quitclaim was executed in 1908, and 1983, the trial court found that neither C.B. Dodge nor any of its successors had asked the City to allow them to construct a boathouse on city land. This finding was challenged on appeal, but substantial evidence supports the conclusion that no boathouse was constructed, and this finding will not be overturned. Western Nat'l Assur. Co. v. Hecker, 43 Wash.App. 816, 822, 719 P.2d 954 (1986). In 1983, the Martins and two other successors to the Dodge land made such a demand on the City, but the City refused permission to construct a boathouse on July 29, 1983. The Martins then attempted to exercise their right to forfeit the City's interest in the land on which Lake Washington Boulevard is located. They brought this action to obtain a declaratory judgment as to the validity of the deed and their election to forfeit the land, as well as for damages in the alternative.

The trial court, after hearing testimony of the parties concerning the possibility of prior compliance of the conditions and value of the land, ruled that the deed was valid. Furthermore, it ruled that the condition of the deed was breached and the Martins were entitled to $50,000 in damages. The court specifically held the Martins did not have a right to reenter the land or forfeit the City's interest in the land. The trial court also denied the Martins their attorney fees.

The City appealed the decision, challenging the continuing validity of the 1908 deed and the condition subsequent. The Martins cross-appealed on the grounds that (a) the amount of damages was inadequate, (b) that they could not reenter the land, and (c) the denial of the attorney fees.

VALIDITY OF THE DEED

All parties admit that the deed created a condition subsequent. Breach of that condition subsequent, assuming it was still effective, would entitle the Martins to damages or to reenter the land in question. The City, however, asserts that the condition subsequent is no longer enforceable.

The City claims that the passage of time prevented the respondents from exercising their right to construct a boathouse. The City does not cite, and no case specifically addresses the issue of whether or not the passage of time can extinguish the right to exercise a condition subsequent in a deed. Nevertheless, the City proposes a number of theories which support its position that the passage of time does bar the respondents' rights in this case.

The City has cited a number of cases which hold that when a condition subsequent is created with a right of forfeiture given to the grantor, failure of the grantor to declare forfeiture within a reasonable time waives the grantor's right to declare a forfeiture. In Metropolitan Park Dist. v. Rigney, 65 Wash.2d 788, 399 P.2d 516 (1965), where a breach of a condition subsequent occurred in land granted to Tacoma and the grantor failed to declare forfeiture for over 30 years, the court held the ability to do so lapsed. See also Santa Monica v. Jones, 104 Cal.App.2d 463, 232 P.2d 55 (1951).

A similar result was reached in a number of cases not involving deeds. Contracts will be [illegible] ance within a reasonable time if no tin[illegible] v. Feider, 40 Wash.App. 589, 699 P.2d 8[illegible] ies, which the City argues is applicable, [illegible] e part of the party in exercising his or h[illegible] i, 75 Wash.2d 143, 437 P.2d 908, 449 P.[illegible] This doctrine however does not apply as the laches defense also requires resulting prejudice from the delay, and the trial court found specifically that no prejudice had resulted. Finding of fact 19. While this fact has been contested, the City cannot point to any resulting prejudice and this finding also will not be overturned on review.

Nevertheless, the language of the deed clearly contemplates that the right to build a boathouse should not run only to Dodge, but also to "its successors and assigns". No time period is mentioned, and had a boathouse been built in the 1910's, it is quite clear that the respondents could continue to maintain the boathouse today. While cases have held that failure to exercise the right to forfeit property extinguishes that right, no case has gone so far as to require a grantor to exercise an option under a deed to build a structure within a reasonable time. Furthermore, mere passage of time would not have extinguished the right to maintain the boathouse, and we do not believe it could extinguish the right to build it. The condition subsequent is still effective.

IMPOSSIBILITY

The City also argues that the subsequent lowering of Lake Washington has made compliance with the condition subsequent impossible. The City claims that because the State gave the newly uncovered land to it with the condition that the land be used as a park, it would be impossible for the City to allow construction of a private boathouse. This, the City asserts, excuses it from performance.

Impossibility of performance, in order to be a defense, requires more than just the occurrence of an unexpected, yet foreseeable, event. Liner v. Armstrong Homes of Bremerton, Inc. 19 Wash.App. 921, 579 P.2d 367 (1978). The lowering of Lake Washington, the event which the City relies on to escape performance, was anticipated by the parties involved, as a federal statute passed 2 years prior to the deed's execution authorized funds for that project. Finding of fact 5. Furthermore, the City has not demonstrated that it would be impossible to obtain permission from the State to allow the construction of a boathouse on the new shore of Lake Washington. Impossibility of performance is not a defense.

UNCONSTITUTIONAL TAKING

The Martins assert that they therefore have a vested right to build a boathouse on the shore of Lake Washington, and the city's unilateral denial of its construction amounted to an unconstitutional taking. We agree. A taking occurs whenever property owned by an individual is damaged or destroyed by governmental interference. Martin v. Port of Seattle, 64 Wash.2d 309, 391 P.2d 540 (1964), cert. denied, 379 U.S. 989, 85 S.Ct. 701, 13 L.Ed.2d 610 (1965). The term property includes the unrestricted right to use, enjoy and dispose of the land. Ackerman v. Port of Seattle, 55 Wash.2d 400, 348 P.2d 664, 77 A.R.R.2d 1344 (1960). The maintenance and use of a boathouse falls within this broad definition of property, and the City, by refusing to allow the boathouse's construction in 1983, committed an unconstitutional taking.

The Martins, by attempting to compel payment of just compensation, are bringing an action for inverse condemnation. The proper measure for damages is full and fair compensation for the loss of the property right. Highline School Dist. 401 v. Port of Seattle, 87 Wash.2d 6, 548 P.2d 1085 (1976). Expert testimony on both sides differed as to the value of the boathouse. The trial court valued the right to have a boathouse at $60,000, a valuation between the values testified to by the parties' appraisers. Finding of fact 23. This determination is supported by the record, and will not be disturbed on review. The trial court, however, erroneously reduced this award by $10,000 to account for any other party's interest in the boathouse. No evidence was introduced to reflect the value of any other interest in the boathouse, and absent such evidence, the trial court's unilateral reduction of $10,000 cannot be allowed.

The trial court also erred in refusing to award the Martins attorney fees.

. . .

CONCLUSION

The City of Seattle cannot prohibit the Martins from building a boathouse in the subject case without paying just compensation to the Martins. the City's denial constitutes the taking of Martin's property through inverse condemnation, which is an unconstitutional taking. The Martins are awarded judgment in the amount of $60,000 without any reduction. We remand to the trial court for reasonable attorney and expert witness fees to be awarded to the Martins.

MURPHY AND HOLTE, JJ., concur.

NOTES

1. How would you label the respective estates owned by the City of Seattle and the Martins? Why did the court in the principal case *not* decide that the City of Seattle owned the land in fee simple absolute? Compare Roberts v. Rhodes with the principal case. What is the distinction between the two cases?

Could the Martins have insisted on claiming the original land, now a public highway, or are they restricted to money damages? What is inverse condemnation? Why is this an unconstitutional taking? This is our first brush with the taking issue which will be discussed in depth later in the course. See pages 877 to 933 infra.

Why should the Martins and their predecessors in title be allowed to wait from 1908 to 1983 before claiming their rights under the old deed? What does this tell you about the problems involved in defeasible estates? How might some of these problems be resolved? Compare the next case, Johnson v. City of Wheat Ridge, and the Notes which follow.

2. The principal case was reversed in Martin v. Seattle, 111 Wn.2d 727, 765 P.2d 257 (1988). In holding for the City of Seattle, the Washington Supreme Court said (among other things) that the right to reenter and declare a forfeiture of the estate granted must be exercised within a reasonable period of time after breach of the condition. The Court then held that the breach did not occur in 1983 when the demand was made for permission to build a boathouse but rather in 1913 when the city acquired from the State for use as a public park the shoreland adjacent to the land conveyed by the grantor. "Since the breach occurred in 1913, the grantor had a reasonable amount of time after 1913 to declare a forfeiture and reenter the deeded property . . . Since no action was taken by the grantor or his successor until 1983, the power of termination had long since expired." There was a vigorous dissent on several grounds including the date of breach which Judge Callow felt did not occur until 1983.

JOHNSON v. CITY OF WHEAT RIDGE

Court of Appeals of Colorado, 1975.
532 P.2d 985.

ENOCH, JUDGE. Plaintiff, Paul Johnson, appeals from a judgment of the district court dismissing his quiet title action. We affirm.

The property at issue consists of land formerly owned by the late Judge Samuel W. Johnson which was conveyed by him in two parcels as a gift for use as a public park. These parcels were subsequently conveyed by the original donees to the City of Wheat Ridge (City).

Plaintiff, as executor and heir of the estate of Judge Johnson, alleges that the original conveyances by Judge Johnson were made under undue influence and additionally that the interest conveyed to the City had terminated by reason of the failure of the original donees and the City to satisfy certain conditions set forth in the deeds. At the conclusion of the evidence the court determined that all the conditions save one had been met, that the action was barred by the applicable statute of limitations, that plaintiff was barred by laches, and that there was insufficient evidence to support the charges of undue influence.

The property was conveyed by Judge Johnson in two transactions. A parcel of approximately five acres was conveyed to the Wheat Ridge Lions Foundation in 1955. A second parcel of approximately 14 acres was conveyed in 1957 to Jefferson County, for the custody and management of the Wheat Ridge Recreation District. In 1958 Judge Johnson consented in writing to the conveyance of the five acre parcel to Jefferson County on behalf of the Wheat Ridge Recreation District, subject to the conditions contained in the original deed. An interest in both parcels was transferred to the City when the City was incorporated in 1969.

The evidence shows that Judge Johnson was at an advanced age when he made the two conveyances. However, we agree with the trial court's conclusion that there is no evidence to support the claim that the grantor was under any undue influence at the time.

Each of the original deeds contains conditions that the property must be used for a public park to be named "Johnson Park." The 1957 deed contains additional conditions, i.e., that, within certain time limits, the grantee shall provide a road into the land, clear away fire hazards, and make available a public water supply and lavatories on the premises. Each deed also contains the following language:

> "In the event that any of the conditions set out above are not complied with the failure to comply shall constitute a condition subsequent terminating the estate of the Grantee and its assigns in and to all of the real property, land, above described, and the Grantor, his heirs and assigns may re-enter and take possession of said premises."

The court's determination that all of the conditions had been met except one is supported by the evidence and will not be disturbed on review. Broncucia v. McGee, 173 Colo. 22, 475 P.2d 336.

The one condition which had not been met was the installation of a public water supply and lavatory facilities on the larger of the two parcels within the required two years from the date of the conveyance. The breach of this condition, however, does not entitle plaintiff to relief. The breach of a condition subsequent does not cause title to revert automatically to the grantor or his heirs, and the use of judicial proceedings to enforce a resulting power to terminate is governed by the statute of limitations in C.R.S.1963, 118–8–4. Wolf v. Hallenbeck, 109 Colo. 70, 123 P.2d 412. C.R.S.1963, 118–8–4, provided that no action may be maintained,

> "to enforce the terms of any restriction concerning real property . . . unless said action be commenced within one year from the date of the violation for which the action is sought to be brought or maintained."

Although this statute has been amended, the change was not effective until May 10, 1972, and would not be applicable to this case which was filed in December 1971. See § 38–41–119, C.R.S.1973 (Colo.Sess.Laws 1972, ch. 100, 118–8–4 at 616). The applicable one year statute of limitations started to run from December 13, 1959, which was two years after the date of the deed and was the end of the period within which the conditions were to have been met. Therefore, though this one condition had not been met, the plaintiff's right of action is effectively barred by the statute of limitations.

Judgment affirmed.

BERMAN and VANCISE, JJ., concur.

NOTES

1. Most states have statutes of limitation which bar powers of termination or possibilities of reverter unless action is brought within a certain gross period of years after breach of the condition. See, for example, Ill.—S.H.A. ch. 110, ¶¶ 13–102, 13–103 (1985). The period in Illinois is seven years. What kind of estate does the owner of a defeasible fee have after these statutes of limitations have run?

2. A different kind of statute is one which bars the enforcement of a power of termination or a possibility of reverter after a certain

number of years from the creation of the defeasible fee (typically forty years). See Trustees of Schools of Township No. 1 v. Batdorf at page 1411, infra. What kind of estate does the owner of a defeasible fee have after this type of statute has run its course?

3. In the absence of statutes of limitation like those in the principal case and in Notes 1 and 2, how long will possibilities of reverter and powers of termination continue to exist? While the traditional answer was "forever," since the Rule Against Perpetuities did not apply to these future interests, some modern cases have taken a different view, even in absence of statutory change. See, for example, City of Casper v. J. M. Carey and Brothers, 601 P.2d 1010 (Wyo.1979), where the court held that the mere passage of time did not defeat the future interests but that a reasonable time should be implied. "[W]ith respect to conditions where no time limit is set by the grantor, the facts of any given case will be tested against a standard which asks whether such a period of time has passed as will satisfy the purpose of the condition subsequent in the context that the property is no longer suitable for the use contemplated by the condition. Where the property is found to no longer be reasonably suitable for such purpose, then the court can say that the condition has been satisfied by the passage of time."

The 1918 deed in question in City of Casper required the city to erect a city hall on the premises and thereafter use the property for the maintenance of a city hall *and* a public park. The city built the hall but was no longer using it for city purposes and, indeed, had demolished the original structure. The city was, however, using the rest of the land for a public park. The court indicated that the condition as it related to the city hall had been satisfied due to the changed circumstances and the passage of time but that the condition as to the use of the land for a park remained in full effect. "Public parks in the center of cities are desirable and essential. It is hard to conceive of a time span which would satisfy a condition subsequent dedicating land for public park purposes in the center of a thriving, active and growing city." See also Martin v. City of Seattle, page 259 supra.

Contrast the result reached by the statutes of limitation approach with that in City of Casper v. J. M. Carey and Brothers. Which approach seems better to you? Which is more in line with the presumed intent of the grantor? Which better promotes the free alienability of land? Which is easier to apply, thus reducing the probability of litigation?

4. As the previous cases indicate, the owner of a defeasible fee is frequently eager to be rid of the fetters of a possibility of reverter or a power of termination. Can a governmental agency, with the power of eminent domain, condemn the "fraternal twins"? If so, how would you determine just compensation for such interests in land? The next case casts some light on this perplexing problem.

LEECO GAS & OIL COMPANY v. COUNTY OF NUECES

Supreme Court of Texas, 1987.
736 S.W.2d 629.

GONZALEZ, JUSTICE:

This is a condemnation suit. The issue is whether Nueces County, as grantee in a deed, may condemn a possibility of reverter on land given to the County and pay mere nominal damages to the owner of the reversionary interest. The trial court answered this issue in the affirmative and the court of appeals affirmed the judgment of the trial court. 716 S.W.2d 615. We reverse and remand.

In 1960, Leeco gift deeded fifty acres of land on Padre Island to Nueces County for use as a park. Leeco retained a reversionary interest in the deed whereby the County would keep the property "so long as a public park is constructed and actively maintained" by the County on the property. The County dedicated and maintained a park on the property. However, in 1983, the County began condemnation proceedings against Leeco's interest. The commissioners awarded Leeco $10,000 for its reversionary interest. Leeco appealed to the county court at law where the trial judge granted a partial summary judgment against Leeco resolving all issues except damages. In a separate trial to determine compensation for Leeco, experts testified that the land was worth between $3,000,000 and $5,000,000. The trial court awarded Leeco $10 in nominal damages.

Leeco brings several points of error claiming that the County is estopped from condemning the property by its acceptance of a deed with knowledge of the reversionary interest. Leeco also challenges the measure of damages. We first address the estoppel argument.

The Texas Constitution provides that "[n]o person's property shall be taken . . . for . . . public use without adequate compensation being made, unless by the consent of such person. . . ." Tex. Const. art. I, § 17. Acquiring an interest in land to establish and maintain public parks involves a governmental function. See generally Schooler v. State, 175 S.W.2d 664, 669 (Tex.Civ.App.—El Paso 1943, writ ref'd w.o.m.) (acquisition of park land is a public use). When a governmental unit is exercising governmental powers it is not subject to estoppel. City of Hutchins v. Prasifka, 450 S.W.2d 829, 835 (Tex.1970). Therefore, we hold the County was not estopped from condemning the reversionary interest. We next consider whether the award of nominal damages by the trial court was proper.

Generally, under the Restatement of Property, a mere possibility of reverter has no ascertainable value when the event upon which the possessory estate in fee simple defeasible is to end is not probable within a reasonably short period of time. See generally, Restatement of Property § 53 comment b (1936). In affirming the $10 award of nominal damages, the court of appeals relied on City of Houston v. McCarthy, 464 S.W.2d 381 (Tex.Civ.App.—Houston [1st Dist.] 1971, writ ref'd n.r.e.). In McCarthy, the court found that when at the time of condemnation the property was being used as permitted under the deed and there was no evidence that the restrictive covenant would ever be broken, the value of the possibility of reverter was so speculative as to be nominal only. McCarthy, 464 S.W.2d at 384. The court of appeals pointed out that the McCarthy court cited Sabine River Auth. v. Willis, 369 S.W.2d 384 (Tex.1963) and Hamman v. City of Houston, 362 S.W.2d 402 (Tex.Civ.App.—Fort Worth 1962, writ ref'd n.r.e.) as authority to support its holding. The court of appeals then held that there was no evidence in this case that the County intended to violate the deed restrictions so long as Leeco retained the possibility of reverter and no evidence that the conditions were breached. This evidence is not determinative of the issue.

Here, one county official testified that there were "various ideas and proposals and schemes" about putting income producing activities on the land. The same official further stated that "it would be in the County's best interest" to own the park outright so that it "may in the future consider plans that are inconsistent with the present deed restrictions." Furthermore, in the County's Original Statement in Condemnation, the County pleaded that its plans for future development of the Park included "uses which could be construed to cause Plaintiff's determinable fee estate, to terminate and cease." The County further alleged that the "present use and operation of the Park" placed an "undue burden upon Plaintiff in its future development of the Park." Thus, this is not a case of condemning a "remote" possibility of reverter, but rather an attempt by the County to remove the "burden" of the reversionary interest by condemning the interest and paying nominal damages.

Also, in the McCarthy, Sabine and Hamman decisions, a governmental entity, which did not previously own the future interest or the possessory defeasible estate, was condemning the entire fee to the property. Although in McCarthy and Hamman the owner of the possessory defeasible estate was also a governmental entity, a different and "paramount" governmental entity was the condemnor. Hamman, 362 S.W.2d at 406. In each case, the condemning governmental entity paid actual damages for the taking. The issue was who would receive the damages—the owner of the possessory estate or the future interest. There were no prior indications that the restrictive covenants would ever be broken by the owners of the possessory defeasible state. Therefore, the value of the possibility of reverter was so speculative as to be nominal only and damages were rightfully awarded to the owner of the possessory estate. In this case the County, as owner of the defeasible estate, indicated that it "may in the future" break restrictions and condemned the possibility of reverter for nominal damages only.

There is a constitutional requirement that if the County is to condemn land, it must adequately compensate the landowner for the property interest taken. McCarthy, 464 S.W.2d at 387. Ten dollars in compensation for a multi-million dollar piece of property is not adequate as a matter of law. To allow a governmental entity, as grantee in a gift deed, to condemn the grantor's reversionary interest by paying only nominal damages would have a negative impact on gifts of real property to charities and governmental entities. It would discourage these types of gifts in the future. This is not in the best interests of the citizens of this State.

We hold that when a governmental entity is the grantee in a gift deed in which the grantor retains a reversionary interest, if the same governmental entity condemns the reversionary interest, it must pay as compensation the amount by which the value of the unrestricted fee exceeds the value of the restricted fee. See, e.g., Ink v. City of Canton, 212 N.E.2d 574, 579 (Ohio 1965).

We reverse the judgment of the court of appeals and remand this cause to the trial court to determine the amount by which the value of the unrestricted fee exceeds the value of the restricted fee.

CONCURRING OPINION

CAMPBELL, JUSTICE.

I concur in the result of this proceeding because there is some precedent for the court's holding. In future cases, however, I would hold that if a political subdivision has accepted a gift by deed that grants a fee simple determinable interest, implementation of condemnation proceedings by the grantee is a renunciation of the gift. The implementation is an act inconsistent with the granted authorized use and will cause the granted estate to terminate and revert to the grantor in fee simple absolute.

JUSTICE ROBERTSON and JUSTICE KILGARLIN join in this concurring opinion.

SECTION 3. THE FEE SIMPLE CONDITIONAL AND THE FEE TAIL

By various devices, the landed aristocracy in feudal England sought to keep land within the family for generation after generation. The most important technique was the conveyance of land "to A and the heirs of his body." The intent of the grantor who used such words probably was that A should enjoy the land until his death, A's eldest surviving son (or A's daughters jointly if no son survived) should occupy until his death, and so on until the line of descendants ended; that no collateral heirs (brothers, cousins, etc.) should inherit this land; and that no one in the line of owners should have the power to convey any more than an estate for his own life. However, the courts took a dim view of such extreme restraints upon alienation and sometime prior to 1285 construed them in a manner which frustrated the plan behind them. These words, it was held, created a *fee simple conditional;* i.e., they empowered A to convey a fee simple if and when a child should be born to him. This judicial victory for freedom of alienation was wiped out by the enactment in 1285 of the Statute De Donis Conditionalibus, which provided that "the will of the giver, according to the form in the deed of gift manifestly expressed shall be from henceforth observed, so that they to whom the land was given under such condition shall have no power to aliene the land so given, but that it shall remain unto the issue of them to whom it was given after their death or shall revert unto the giver and his heirs if issue fail either by reason that there is no issue at all, or if any issue be, it fail by death, the heir of such issue failing." Henceforth, a conveyance "to A and the heirs of his body" created an estate in *fee tail*—an estate inheritable only by lineal descendants, none of whom could convey more than an estate for his own life. The fee tail could even be restricted to male descendants (fee tail male) or to descendants of a particular spouse (fee tail special). Query: After the Statute De Donis, were the words "and the heirs of his body" words of limitation or words of purchase?

The policy of freedom of alienation (and no doubt other factors, too) eventually [11] led to circumvention of the Statute De Donis. By resorting to a lawsuit—called the *common recovery*—a tenant in tail in possession was permitted to convey a fee simple absolute. Another proceeding—the *fine*—had a similar effect. The highly fictitious nature of these suits is revealed in this brief description of the common recovery:[12] "The principle had already become established that a tenant in tail could convey a fee simple and so bar his heirs, providing he left assets equal in value to the land. This was then enlarged into the proposition that he could so convey if he left for his heirs a judgment for the value of the land so conveyed. These principles were combined in the common recovery in this fashion. If B, the tenant in tail, wished to convey the land to C in fee, C would bring by agreement a common recovery against B. B would allege that he had derived title in the land from X, and would ask that X be called in to defend the case. X, upon being called in, would, in accordance with the agreement between himself and B, admit that he had conveyed the land to B, but that he had no defense to C's action. Judgment would thereupon be given that C should recover the land in accordance with the terms of his allegation that he was entitled to it in fee simple. B and B's heirs would be given what in legal theory was an adequate recompense in the shape of a judgment against X for other lands of equal value in respect of which A's interest as reversioner would also theoretically attach. Since, however, X was always chosen for the part that he played, for the very reason that he was entirely irresponsible financially, the judgment against him, though adequate on the face of it, was, as was intended from the beginning, in fact worthless, and the net result of the transaction was that C obtained the land in fee simple and that the entailed line and the rights of the original donor of the land were barred."

Strange as it may seem, the phrase "to A and the heirs of his body" has appeared in numerous American conveyances. The consequences in the various states fall into six groups:[13]

(1) A fee simple conditional is created, the Statute De Donis not being deemed a part of the common law of those states.[14]

11. In 1472, in Taltarum's Case, Y.B. 12 Edw. IV, 19.

12. Bigelow, Introduction to the Law of Real Property 27 (1945).

13. For detailed treatment of these six groups, see Restatement, Property Ch. 5 (1936).

14. The fee simple conditional is a threatened species but it is not completely

(2) The fee tail is created, but is subject to disentailing conveyances, an ordinary deed usually being sufficient.

(3) Some states have constitutional or statutory provisions declaring that entailed estates shall not be recognized; e.g., Texas Constitution, Art. I, § 26. What is the effect of a conveyance which nevertheless purports to create a fee tail in such a state?

(4) Several statutes are similar to the Illinois statute providing that one who at common law would have been granted a fee tail shall have an estate "for . . . life only, and the remainder shall pass in fee simple absolute, to the person or persons to whom the estate tail" would have descended. Ill.Rev.Stat. ch. 30, § 5 (1985). Does such a remainder belong to all children or only those who survive the first taker? See 2 Powell, Real Property ch. 14 (1950).

(5) Some statutes preserve the estate tail for one generation and then convert it into a fee simple absolute.

(6) In several states, there is created by virtue of statute a fee simple absolute in the first taker.

CACCAMO v. BANNING

Superior Court of Delaware, 1950.
6 Terry 394, 75 A.2d 222.

WOLCOTT, JUDGE. Benjamin F. Potter, by his will, devised certain real estate to his wife for and during the term of her natural life and, upon her death, devised "all the same over unto my granddaughter, Anna Naomi Coverdale, in fee simple and absolutely forever; but in case the said Anna Naomi Coverdale should die without leaving lawful issue of her body begotten then and in that case I give, devise and bequeath all the same over unto" the children of William B. Potter in fee simple. By the codicil to his will, the testator added an additional person to the class of ultimate devisees.

Anna E. Potter, the widow of the testator, is now deceased.

Anna Naomi Coverdale, having inter-married with Carmen Caccamo, purported to bar the estate tail devised her by the terms of the will of Benjamin F. Potter, deceased, pursuant to Section 3698, R.C. 1935.[15]

extinct. See Third Nat. Bank in Nashville v. Stevens, 755 S.W.2d 459 (Tenn.App.1988) where the language used was "To A and his bodily issue." Said the Court: "A grant to the grantee and his heirs conveys a fee simple title, but a grant to the grantee and his bodily issue creates a fee conditional estate, which is a life estate convertible into a fee by the birth of bodily issue to the grantee. . . . The terms 'bodily issue' and 'bodily heirs' are synonymous." The grantee had no natural children but did have two adopted daughters. The court proceeded to hold that the words "bodily issue" expressed a clear intent that an adoption does not satisfy the condition of the fee. Query? What happens to the estate since the grantee never had any natural children? How would the result be altered if the court had held that a fee tail estate was created?

15. [This statute provides that an ordinary deed purporting to convey a fee simple absolute "shall have the same effect and operation for barring all estates tail" as a common recovery.]

Thereafter, on April 29, 1950, Anna Naomi Caccamo, at public auction, sold the lands in question to Delema W. Banning, the defendant, who was the high bidder, for the price of $2,025. The defendant paid to the plaintiff the sum of $405 and agreed to pay the balance of the purchase price on June 3, 1950 in exchange for a deed conveying good and sufficient title.

On June 3, 1950, the plaintiff tendered to the defendant a deed duly executed purporting to convey a fee simple title to the lands in question to the defendant, who declined to accept the deed and to pay the balance due on the ground that the plaintiff could not convey a good fee simple and marketable title to the lands in question.

It is agreed by the parties that if the plaintiff became seized of a fee simple estate in the lands in question under the will of Benjamin F. Potter, or if she became seized of an estate tail under the provisions of said will, and if that estate were barred, then judgment shall be entered in favor of the plaintiff and against the defendant for the sum of $1,620, but if the Court should not so find, then judgment should be entered in favor of the defendant and against the plaintiff for the sum of $405.

The case stated requires a construction of the provisions of Item I of the will of Benjamin F. Potter which have been quoted in part above.

The plaintiff contends that the effect of the provisions of Item I of the will was to devise a fee tail to the plaintiff and that, having by proper steps barred the fee tail, the plaintiff is able to convey a good fee simple marketable title to the defendant.

The defendant, on the other hand, contends that the proper construction to be placed on Item I of the will is that the plaintiff was devised a fee simple interest in the lands in question subject to being defeated if she should die without leaving a lineal descendant to survive her. In other words, the defendant contends that the phrase "die without leaving lawful issue" relates solely to the time of the death of the plaintiff and is, accordingly, a definite rather than an indefinite failure of issue.

It is well settled by a long line of decisions that at common law a gift to A for life and, upon his death, to the heirs of his body or his issue, was a gift of a fee tail. By a number of decisions, this rule has been consistently followed in this State. Similarly, in Roach v. Martin's Lessee, 1 Har. 548, 28 Am.Dec. 746, a gift to A and her heirs forever, "except she should die without heir born of her own body", with a remainder in that event over to B, was held to create an estate tail in A with a vested remainder in B. . . .

In the case at bar, the gift being to the plaintiff absolutely and in fee simple, subject to the provision that in case she died without leaving lawful issue of her body begotten, falls within the scope of the rule in Roach v. Martin's Lessee and, unless there is something in the will which evidences an intention to limit the dying without issue to the time of death of the plaintiff, thus making the contingency a definite rather than an indefinite failure of issue, the plaintiff took a fee tail under the will.

The full context of the will and codicil of Benjamin F. Potter does not appear in the case stated, but from that portion of the will which is included in the case stated, I can find nothing to indicate that the testator intended a definite rather than indefinite failure of issue in order for the ultimate gift over to take effect, unless the possible use of the word "leaving" in connection with issue can be said to be a relation of the failure of issue to the date of death of the plaintiff. However, in Re Reeves, 10 Del.Ch. 483, 94 A. 511, the Supreme Court construed a will which included a devise to A and the lawful heirs of his body forever, but if he died leaving no lawful issue of his body, then over to another, as having devised an estate tail to A. In that case, the use of the word "leaving" was not sufficient to make the failure of issue definite rather than indefinite. This ruling is controlling and, accordingly, I conclude that the proper construction of the will before me is that it devised a fee tail to the plaintiff and a vested remainder of the reversion to the collateral heirs of the testator.

The plaintiff having conveyed away by deed purporting to convey a fee simple interest, the lands in question and having had them conveyed back to her, is now, by reason of Section 3698, R.C.1935, seized of a fee simple interest in the lands in question, which could have been conveyed by her to the defendant on June 3, 1950.

Judgment will be entered for the plaintiff and against the defendant for the sum of $1,620 together with costs.

NOTES

1. Granted that a fee tail estate was created by the original conveyance, it is relatively easy to see how the disentailing act converts the estate into a fee simple absolute, but why was a fee tail created in the first instance? Note that the typical language creating a fee tail is "to A and the heirs of his body". That language was not used here yet the court construes the language as creating a fee tail.

2. Give the state of the title if the principal case had arisen in a state where a statute provides: "Whenever by any devise, gift or conveyance, an estate in fee tail would be created according to the common law, such devise, gift or conveyance shall be taken and construed to pass an estate in fee simple."

3. What is the effect of a conveyance "to A and his children and their children"? See Rose v. Rose, 191 Va. 171, 60 S.E.2d 45 (1950).

4. What kind of future interest is left in the grantor of a fee tail estate if the line of bodily heirs runs out? A reversion? A possibility of reverter? A power of termination? See Long v. Long, 45 Ohio St.2d 165, 343 N.E.2d 100 (1976). Said the court: "More importantly, for purposes of the present case, the statute *de donis* converted the donor's bare possibility of reversion or right of reverter into a reversion or fee simple expectant upon failure of issue. . . . This distinction is important because a reversion in fee is a vested interest or estate and is descendible, alienable or assignable by deed or conveyance, and is also devisable."

Chapter 14

FUTURE INTERESTS

A future interest is an estate which will (or may) become possessory at some future time. A consequence of the carving out of lesser estates from the fee simple absolute is that the right to enjoy the use of the land cannot be had simultaneously by owners of all estates. Each has to await termination of preceding estates before entering into possession. Of course, future interests may be of great value prior to that time. They are inheritable and most of them can be conveyed by deed or will. And, as you have seen, an owner of a future interest may be protected against waste by the owner of a present estate.

Future interests may be created either in the grantor or in a third person. When a grantor conveys a present estate smaller than the one he owns, the residue is a future interest. Usually this is a *reversion.* If A, the owner of a fee simple absolute, conveys a term for years, a life estate or a fee tail to B, A retains a reversion in fee simple. But you have already met future interests in the grantor which are not called reversions—*possibilities of reverter and rights of entry (powers of termination).* A *remainder* is a future interest created in a third person, but not all future interests in third persons are remainders. Some are designated *executory interests.* What these are and how they came to be is an involved story which will be told later.

SECTION 1. VESTED AND CONTINGENT REMAINDERS

KOST v. FOSTER

Supreme Court of Illinois, 1950.
406 Ill. 565, 94 N.E.2d 302.

DAILY, JUSTICE. This is an appeal in behalf of Oscar Durant Kost, one of the plaintiffs and counterdefendant, from a decree for partition entered on the counterclaim of counterplaintiff, Marshall C. Foster, in the circuit court of Fulton County.

The record discloses that on December 11, 1897, John Kost and his wife, Catherine, executed a warranty deed as follows: "The Grantors, John Kost and his wife Catherine Kost . . . Convey and Warrant to their son Ross Kost to have and to hold use and control for and during his natural life only, at his death to his lawful children, the lawful child or children of any deceased lawful child of Ross Kost to have and receive its or their deceased parent's share meaning and intending hereby to convey to Ross Kost a life estate only the following described real estate, to-wit:" and thereinafter describes the real estate in question. The deed was filed for record on September 18, 1909, in the recorder's office of Fulton County.

Ross Kost took possession of the real estate and occupied it until his death on March 8, 1949. The only lawful children ever born to him were Lether Page, Adah Charleroy, Fern Kost Rhodes, Harry L. Kost, Gladys Wilson, Gilbert Kost, Oscar Durant Kost and a child born in 1899, who died thirteen days after birth. Five of the children, including appellant, Oscar Durant Kost, were born prior to the execution of the deed of John and Catherine Kost. The others were born subsequently thereto. All of the children, except the one who died in infancy, are living and were parties plaintiff to the original complaint for partition.

On December 29, 1936, a trustee in bankruptcy of the estate of Oscar Durant Kost, bankrupt, executed a deed of conveyance of the interest of the bankrupt to Marshall C. Foster, defendant and counterplaintiff, pursuant to an order of the referee in bankruptcy for a private sale of the bankrupt's interest in and to the real estate here sought to be partitioned.

The original complaint alleges that the seven children of Ross Kost listed above are the sole owners in common of the real estate, subject only to easements acquired for railroad purposes and for highway purposes, and to the rights of Gilbert Kost as tenant in possession. It prays that the trustee's deed be declared void and removed as a cloud on the title, and that the real estate be partitioned according to the respective rights and interests of the parties.

An answer filed by Marshall C. Foster admits the material portion of the complaint but denies that the trustee's deed is void, and denies that the interests of the parties are correctly set forth. He avers that he purchased the interest of Oscar Durant Kost, and further avers that the decree of the District Court of the United States has never been reversed or modified and is not subject to collateral attack. The answer prayed that the complaint be dismissed. In addition Foster filed a counterclaim making all of the plaintiffs counterdefendants and reiterating the material portions of the complaint, but alleging that the counterplaintiff was the owner of the undivided one-seventh interest which Oscar Durant Kost had under the deed of John Kost. The counterclaim prays for partition of the premises and for general relief.

The trial court overruled motions of the plaintiff to dismiss the counterclaim and to strike the answer of the defendant, and thereupon plaintiffs filed a reply to the answer, and an answer to the counterclaim. The issues were tried before the court and a decree was entered for partition on the counterclaim of the counterplaintiff.

The principal question involved is whether or not the interest of Oscar Durant Kost was a vested remainder at the time of the purported sale by the trustee in bankruptcy. It is contended that Oscar Durant Kost had but a contingent remainder in the real estate, and that a contingent remainder does not pass to a trustee in bankruptcy of the remainderman.

We have frequently been called upon to define vested remainders and contingent remainders and to distinguish between them. The chief characteristic which distinguishes a vested from a contingent remainder is the present capacity to take effect in possession should the possession become vacant, with the certainty that the event upon which the vacancy depends will happen sometime, and not upon the certainty that it will happen or the possession become vacant during the lifetime of the remainderman. In the case of a vested remainder, there is a person in being ascertained and ready to take, who has a present right of future enjoyment which is not dependent upon any uncertain event or contingency, while in the case of a contingent remainder the right itself is uncertain. The uncertainty which distinguishes a contingent remainder is the uncertainty of the right and not of the actual enjoyment, for in this regard any remainder may be said to be uncertain, as the remainderman may die without heirs before the termination of the particular estate. . . .

Whether a remainder is vested or contingent depends upon the language employed. If the conditional element is incorporated into the description of or into the gift to the remainderman then the remainder is contingent, but if, after words giving a vested interest, a clause is added making it subject to being divested, the remainder is vested. Thus, on a devise to A for life, the remainder to his children, but if any child dies in the lifetime of A his share to go to those who survive, the share of each child is vested, subject to be divested by its death, but on a devise to A for life, remainder to such of his children as survive him, the remainder is contingent. Gray's Rule against Perpetuities; . . .. When a conveyance of a particular estate is made to support a remainder over, the tenant for the particular estate takes it, and if the remainderman is in being he takes the fee. In such a case the remainder is not contingent as to its becoming a vested remainder, because the title vests in the remainderman on the delivery of the deed. The title thus vested becomes an estate of inheritance. . . .

The language used by the grantors in the instant case is not conditional in nature. At the time of the execution of the deed there were five lawful children of Ross Kost in being, including the appellant, Oscar Durant Kost, and designated as remaindermen and capable of taking immediate possession upon the termination of the life estate. It is true that each of the estates in remainder was subject to being opened up and diminished in quantity by the birth of other children to the respective life tenants. . . . The remainders, while vested in the children already born to the life tenant, are contingent in quantity until the death of the life tenant because of the possibility of the birth of other children, who will have a right to share in the estate. . . . We find no authority for the contention that the rule as to the destruction of contingent remainders should be applied to a case where the estate is vested in quality but contingent in quantity. . . . The estate in remainder vested in the five lawful children of Ross Kost in esse upon the execution and delivery of the deed, and it vested in each of the other lawful children as each of them was born.

The words "at his death," as used in the deed of John and Catherine Kost, are similar in context to the language used in the case of Dustin v. Brown, 297 Ill. 499, 130 N.E. 859, 862, wherein we held that the language "after the death" of the life tenant referred to the time when the estate will vest in possession only, and we said, "it has, however, been so many times held in this and other states that the rule may be said to be well established, that the words 'after the death of A' and similar expressions, are to be construed as meaning at the termination (whenever and in whatever manner that may occur) of the particular estate of freehold and as referring to the time when the estate will vest in possession only. The remainder thus created 'after the death of A' is held to be a vested remainder unless there be that in the context which clearly takes it out of the rule."

It is urged by the appellant that the gift over to the lawful child or children of any deceased lawful child of Ross Kost indicated an intention of the grantors to create a contingent remainder in the children of Ross Kost; since if the remainders were vested it would descend to the issue of any child who might die during the lifetime of Ross Kost, and, therefore, no substitution would have been necessary. However, when we apply the test set forth by Professor Gray as stated above and approved by this court in Riddle v. Killian, 366 Ill. 294, 8 N.E.2d 629; Smith v. Chester, 272 Ill. 428, 112 N.E. 325, Ann. Cas.1917A, 925; Lachenmyer v. Gehlbach, 266 Ill. 11, 107 N.E. 202; Brechbeller v. Wilson, 228 Ill. 502, 81 N.E. 1094, and in numerous other decisions, we find that the gift over was in the nature of a condition subsequent, and no conditional limitation was incorporated into the description of or into the gift to the remaindermen. The remainder is subject to being divested on the contingency of one of the children of Ross Kost dying before the life tenant and leaving lawful children.

Nor can we agree with the argument of counsel for appellant that the words "meaning and intending hereby to convey to Ross Kost a life estate only" expressed an intention on the part of the grantors to create a contingent remainder in the lawful children of Ross Kost, so that he would be precluded from the possibility of inheriting any portion of the fee from any child who might predecease him without issue. Had it been the intention of the grantors to create a contingent remainder, the scriveners could have made the gift to the children of Ross Kost conditional upon their surviving him as stated above. They did not elect to do this, and used instead words which created a vested remainder in the children.

We have carefully studied the cases cited in the briefs of counsel for appellant and considered the arguments in support of their position, but are forced to the conclusion that the language employed in the deed of John and Catherine Kost meets every test for the creation of a vested remainder in the lawful children of Ross Kost. Since the appellant, Oscar Durant Kost, had a vested remainder, a trustee in bankruptcy could properly convey his interest pursuant to an order of the referee in bankruptcy, and the appellee, Foster, acquired an undivided one-seventh interest in the fee of the real estate, subject to the life estate in Ross Kost and subject to the easements hereinbefore set forth. . . .

Decree affirmed.

NOTES

1. Most courts, in line with a general policy of favoring alienability of interests in land, allow both types of remainders to be transferred by deed or will and to be subject to the claims of creditors. See, for example, Woolums v. Simonsen, 214 Kan. 722, 522 P.2d 1321 (1974) where the court stated: "Under the law of this state the general rule is that any interest a person may have in property, vested or contingent, legal or equitable, may, in a proper case, be subject to attachment and garnishment, and may be levied upon and sold under execution." Even courts in Illinois, and other states which adhere to the distinction where involuntary transfers are involved, manage to uphold most commercial transfers of contingent remainders on theories of estoppel and specific performance. See I American Law of Property §§ 4.65, 4.66 (A. Casner ed. 1952).

What difference would it make if the principal case had arisen in Kansas or any state following the Kansas view? Why do some states make a distinction between the involuntary transfer of vested interests and contingent interests?

2. An even more serious characteristic of contingent remainders is their destructibility. The position of the English common law, still adhered to by some American courts today, was that a contingent remainder which fails to vest at or before the termination of preceding freehold estates is destroyed. Thus, if A conveys land "to B for life, then to C's heirs," and B predeceases C, the contingent remainder in C's heirs is destroyed. C's heirs could not be ascertained until C's death, an event which occurred after termination of the preceding freehold estate. This rule of destructibility of contingent remainders, said to be based upon a policy of avoiding an "abeyance of seisin," is dealt with more fully in Section 4 of this Chapter. Many states have statutes either abolishing the doctrine of the destructibility of contingent remainders or declaring the complete absence of such a doctrine. For an analysis of these statutes see 2 Powell, Real Property ¶ 314 (1977).

The next case illustrates that the doctrine still has some vitality although modern courts are likely to reject it even in the absence of statutory change.

ABO PETROLEUM CORPORATION v. AMSTUTZ

Supreme Court of New Mexico, 1979.
93 N.M. 332, 600 P.2d 278.

PAYNE, JUSTICE.

This action was brought in the District Court of Eddy County by Abo Petroleum and others against the children of Beulah Turknett Jones and Ruby Turknett Jones to quiet title to certain property in Eddy County. Both sides moved for summary judgment. The district court granted Abo's motion, denied the children's motion, and entered a partial final judgment in favor of Abo. The children appealed, and we reversed the district court.

James and Amanda Turknett, the parents of Beulah and Ruby, owned in fee simple the disputed property in this case. In February 1908, by separate instruments entitled "conditional deeds," the parents conveyed life estates in two separate parcels, one each to Beulah and Ruby. Each deed provided that the property would remain the daughter's

> during her natural life, . . . and at her death to revert, vest in, and become the property absolute of her heir or heirs, meaning her children if she have any at her death, but if she die without an heir or heirs, then and in that event this said property and real estate shall vest in and become the property of the estate of . . . [her], to be distributed as provided by law at the time of her death. . . .

At the time of the delivery of the deed, neither daughter was married, nor were any children born to either daughter for several years thereafter.

In 1911, the parents gave another deed to Beulah, which covered the same land conveyed in 1908. This deed purported to convey "absolute title to the grantee . . . ." In 1916, the parents executed yet another deed to Beulah, granting a portion of the property included in her two previous deeds. A second deed was also executed to Ruby, which provided that it was a "correction deed" for the 1908 deed.

After all the deeds from the parents had been executed, Beulah had three children and Ruby had four children. These children are the appellants herein.

Subsequent to the execution of these deeds, Beulah and Ruby attempted to convey fee simple interests in the property to the predecessors of Abo. The children of Beulah and Ruby contend that the 1908 deeds gave their parents life estates in the property, and that Beulah and Ruby could only have conveyed life estates to the predecessors in interest of Abo. Abo argues that the 1911 and 1916 deeds vested Beulah and Ruby with fee simple title, and that such title was conveyed to Abo's predecessors in interest, thereby giving Abo fee simple title to the property.

We begin our inquiry by examining the nature of the estates James and Amanda Turknett conveyed in the 1908 deeds.

First, the deeds gave each of the daughters property "during her natural life." As Abo apparently concedes, these words conveyed only a life estate.

Second, each deed provided that upon the daughter's death, the property would pass to her "heir or heirs," which was specifically defined as "her children if she have any at her death." Because it was impossible at the time of the original conveyance to determine whether the daughters would have children, or whether any of their children would survive them, the deeds created contingent remainders in the daughters' children, which could not vest until the death of the daughter holding the life estate. C. Moynihan, Introduction to the Law of Real Property 123 (1962).

Third, each deed provided that if the contingent remainder failed, the property would become part of the daughter's estate, and pass "as provided by law at the time of her death." The effect of this language would be to pass the property to the heirs of the daughter upon the failure of the first contingent remainder. Because one's heirs are not ascertainable until death, (C. Moynihan, supra at 127), the grant over to the daughter's estate created a second, or alternative, contingent remainder.

The only issues that remain are whether the parents retained any interest, whether by their subsequent deeds to their daughters they conveyed any interest that remained, and whether those conveyances destroyed the contingent remainders in the children.

The grantor-parents divested themselves of the life estate and contingent remainder interest in the property upon delivery of the first deed. Because both remainders are contingent, however, the parents retained a reversionary interest in the property. C. Moynihan, supra at 124, n. 1.

Abo's position is that by the subsequent conveyances to the daughters, the parents' reversionary interest merged with the daughters' life estates, thus destroying the contingent remainders in the daughters' children and giving the daughters fee simple title to the property. This contention presents a question which this Court has not previously addressed—whether the doctrine of the destructibility of contingent remainders is applicable in New Mexico.

This doctrine, which originated in England in the Sixteenth Century, was based upon the feudal concept that seisin of land could never be in abeyance. From that principle, the rule developed that if the prior estate terminated before the occurrence of the contingency, the contingent remainder was destroyed for lack of a supporting freehold estate. The one instance in which this could happen occurred when the supporting life estate merged with the reversionary interest.

Although New Mexico has adopted the common law of England by statute, § 38–1–3, N.M.S.A.1978, it has been repeatedly held that "if the common law is not 'applicable to our condition and circumstances' it is not to be given effect." Flores v. Flores, 84 N.M. 601, 603, 506 P.2d 345, 347 (Ct.App.1973), cert. denied, 84 N.M. 592, 506 P.2d 336 (1973). See also Hicks v. State, 88 N.M. 588, 544 P.2d 1153 (1975). In *Hicks* this Court held that sovereign immunity—another doctrine of the common law—could be "put to rest by the judiciary" once it had reached a point of obsolescence. Id. at 590, 544 P.2d at 1155.

The doctrine of destructibility of contingent remainders has been almost universally regarded to be obsolete by legislatures, courts and legal writers. See, e.g., Whitten v. Whitten, 203 Okl. 196, 219 P.2d 228 (1950); 1 L. Simes and A. Smith, Law of Future Interests § 209 (2d ed. 1956). It has been renounced by virtually all jurisdictions in the United States, either by statute or judicial decision, and was abandoned in the country of its origin over a century ago. Section 240 of the Restatement of Property (1936) takes the position that the doctrine is based in history, not reason. Comment (d) to § 240 states that "complexity, confusion, unpredictability and frustration of manifested intent" are the demonstrated consequences of adherence to the doctrine of destructibility. Furthermore, because operation of the doctrine can be avoided by the use of a trust to support the contingent remainder, the doctrine places a premium on the drafting skills of the lawyer. 49 Mich.L.Rev. 762, 764 (1951).

The only tenable argument in support of the doctrine is that it promotes the alienability of land. It does so, however, only arbitrarily, and oftentimes by defeating the intent of the grantor. Land often carries burdens with it, but courts do not arbitrarily cut off those burdens merely in order to make land more alienable.

Because the doctrine of destructibility of contingent remainders is but a relic of the feudal past, which has no justification or support in modern society, we decline to apply it in New Mexico. As Justice Holmes put it:

> It is revolting to have no better reason for a rule of law than that so it was laid down in the time of Henry IV. It is still more revolting if the grounds upon which it was laid down have vanished long since, and the rule simply persists from blind imitation of the past.

Holmes, The Path of the Law, 10 Harv.L.Rev. 457 at 469 (1897).

We hold that the conveyances of the property to the daughters did not destroy the contingent remainders in the daughters' children. The daughters acquired no more interest in the property by virtue of the later deeds than they had been granted in the original deeds. Any conveyance by them could transfer only the interest they had originally acquired, even if it purported to convey a fee simple. Cook v. Daniels, 306 S.W.2d 573 (Mo.1957).

The summary judgment and partial final judgment entered in favor of Abo are reversed, and the cause is remanded for further proceedings consistent with this opinion.

IT IS SO ORDERED.

SOSA, C.J., and FELTER, J., concur.

NOTES

1. See Cohen, Contingent Remainders—Rule of Destructibility Abolished in New Mexico, 10 N.M.L.Rev. 471 (1980). The Doctrine of Destructibility of Contingent Remainders dies hard, even in New Mexico. See Johnson v. Amstutz, 101 N.M. 94, 678 P.2d 1169 (1984) where the argument was still being made that the doctrine *had* applied in New Mexico until abolished in ABO Petroleum Corporation v. Amstutz. The court disposed of that argument in a rather terse opinion, stating: "Therefore we specifically hold that the doctrine is not now and has never been the law in New Mexico."

2. Are the remainders created by the following phrases vested or contingent? Which phrases leave a reversion in A?

(1) A conveys "to B for life, then to C for life, and then to D and his heirs."

(2) A conveys "to B for life, then to C and his heirs, but if C fails to survive B, then to D and his heirs."

(3) A conveys "to B for life, then to C and his heirs if C survives B, but if C does not do so, then to D and his heirs."

SECTION 2. THE RULE IN SHELLEY'S CASE

SYBERT v. SYBERT

Supreme Court of Texas, 1953.
152 Tex. 106, 254 S.W.2d 999.

HICKMAN, CHIEF JUSTICE. The sole question for decision is the applicability of the rule in Shelley's Case to a devise in the will of J. H. Sybert. Mr. Sybert died February 4, 1942, leaving a will, which was duly probated, and by which he left all of his property to his wife, Mrs. Cora R. Sybert, for life "and after the death of my said wife I will and bequeath to my five (5) sons the following described pieces and parcels of land, to wit: '(a) To my son Fred Sybert I will and bequeath the following described tract of land (a life estate only, to manage, control and use for and during the term of his natural life and after the death of my said son, Fred Sybert, to vest in fee simple in the heirs of his body) . . . .'" This language was followed by a metes and bounds description of the tract of land in suit. Later Mrs. Cora R. Sybert died, leaving a will, which was duly probated, disposing of this land in the same manner and by the identical words copied above from the will of Mr. Sybert. Fred Sybert, the son to whom the land was devised, died childless and intestate on July 3, 1950, survived by respondent, his wife, Eunice Sybert. Two of his brothers are petitioners. Their contention is that the will vested a life estate only in Fred Sybert, while respondent contends that the rule in Shelley's Case operated to vest a fee simple estate in him. Her contention was sustained by the trial court and its judgment was affirmed by the Court of Civil Appeals. 250 S.W.2d 271.

There is no need for us at this late date to write a dissertation on the history and rationale of the ancient rule in Shelley's Case. It has perhaps been the subject of more writing in opinions, textbooks and law reviews than any other rule of property. Attorneys for petitioners, who have made an exhaustive and enlightening study of his subject, recognize that it is a positive rule of law in this State and not a rule of construction, and that, therefore, any abrogation of the rule must be made by the legislature and not by the courts. The legislatures in a majority of the states have abolished the rule in whole or in part, and it appears that in one state, Vermont, it was abolished by judicial decree. However, as observed in American Law of Property, Vol. 1, § 4.51, "The rule appears to be still in force in Arkansas, Delaware, Illinois, Indiana, North Carolina, Texas, and probably a few other states."

The rule in Shelley's Case has been variously stated. Since this court at an early date adopted Kent's definition, we need not substitute another one for it, even though some of the more modern expressions of the rule are stated in somewhat clearer language. We quote the rule from a landmark case, Hancock v. Butler, 21 Tex. 804, 808:

"'. . . when a person takes an estate of freehold, legally or equitably, under a deed, will, or other writing, and in the same instrument, there is a limitation, by way of remainder, either with or without the interposition of another estate, of an interest of the same legal or equitable quality, to his heirs, or heirs of his body, as a class of persons, to take in succession, from generation to generation, the limitation to the heirs entitles the ancestor to the whole estate.' 4 Kent, 215. This result would follow, although the deed might express that the first taker should have a life estate only. It is founded on the use of the technical words, 'heirs,' or 'heirs of his body,' in the deed or the will.

"The rule in Shelley's case is said to be a rule of law. It is really an organic rule, entering into the creation of the estate of inheritance."

The rule must inevitably apply in the instant case unless there is language qualifying the words "heirs of his body," showing that they were not used in their technical sense; that is, to signify an indefinite succession of takers from generation to generation. Turning now to an examination of the particular provisions of the will under construction we find that the only qualifying words contained therein modify the estate of Fred Sybert—not the words "heirs of his body." The language "a life estate only, to manage, control and use for and during the term of his natural life" is but a statement of the incidents of a life estate. The further language "and after the death of my said son, Fred Sybert, to vest in fee simple in the heirs of his body" does not indicate that the words "heirs of his body" were not used in their usual and technical sense. The expressions "vest in the heirs" and "vest in fee simple in the heirs" are identical in meaning. Crist v. Morgan, Tex.Com.App., 245 S.W. 659; Brown v. Bryant, 17 Tex.Civ.App. 454, 44 S.W. 399, writ refused. We concur in this conclusion of the Court of Civil Appeals [250 S.W.2d 273]: "We have diligently searched the wills of Mr. and Mrs. Sybert for some 'explanatory context,' qualification or modification of the words 'the heirs of his body,' as used in the wills, but none are present."

Petitioners place much reliance upon Wallace v. First National Bank of Paris, 120 Tex. 92, 35 S.W.2d 1036, 1037, and Robinson v. Glenn, 150 Tex. 169, 238 S.W.2d 169. The instruments construed in those cases are clearly distinguishable from the will before us. In the Wallace case the remainder was "to his bodily heirs equally," and it was held that the word "equally" qualified the word "heirs." We do not question the soundness of that holding. . . .

In Robinson v. Glenn two deeds were before us for construction. In one the remainder was "to the issue of her body" [238 S.W.2d 170] and we held that "issue" was a word of purchase, meaning children. That holding is in line with Hancock v. Butler, supra. In Lacey v. Floyd, 99

Tex. 112, 87 S.W. 665, 667, the holding of the court in Hancock v. Butler is stated in this language: "In that case Judge Roberts elaborately reviewed the rule in Shelley's Case in many of its phrases, but finally concluded his opinion, with this statement: 'What is decided now is, that the words "lawful issue," as they stand in this deed, are words of purchase, and not of limitation. No other question having been made, none other will be decided.' The question was correctly decided in that case, but it was based mainly upon the use of the word 'issue,' instead of the technical word 'heirs.' The distinction between that case and this is that in this case, instead of 'issue,' the word 'heirs' is used, to which the rule in Shelley's Case is peculiarly applicable."

In the other deed construed in Robinson v. Glenn the remainder was to "her bodily heirs, share and share alike." We held that "share and share alike" qualified the word "heirs" and took the case from out the rule. . . .

This court has said that the rule in Shelley's Case should be strictly construed. That is but to say that it should not be extended to apply to any instrument the language of which does not bring it within the rule as heretofore construed by this court. The language in the will in this case brings it squarely within the rule, and whether or not the testator so intended is immaterial. While the court may be liberal in construing explanatory language so that the words "heirs" or "heirs of his body" will not be read in their technical sense, we cannot supply that language when it is omitted from the instrument itself.

The judgment of the Court of Civil Appeals is affirmed.

GRIFFIN, JUSTICE (concurring). Under the well-settled decisions of this Court there is no question but that the wills under construction come within the Rule in Shelley's Case, and that we cannot decide this cause in any other manner than to affirm the judgments of both courts below.

This cause forcibly points out the anomaly brought about by the Rule in Shelley's Case. That rule is a relic, not of the horse and buggy days, but of the preceding stone cart and oxen days. The Rule was devised in feudal times to insure feudal landlords the receipt of their rents from their feoffs, or tenants. The reason for the Rule has long since passed, and it should be repealed.

A reading of these two wills can leave no doubt that it was the intention of these two testators to leave a life estate only in these lands to their son, Fred Sybert. The application of the Rule in Shelley's Case results in setting aside this intention of these testators. In fact, every case in which the Rule in Shelley's Case is applied results in setting aside the intention of the person making the instrument. No one intending to give a fee simple title to the first taker (generally called the ancestor) ever uses language that, in its ordinary meaning and significance, defines an estate for life only. This Rule is only a trap and snare for the unwary, and should be repealed.

England, where the Rule had its inception, repealed, the Rule some thirty years ago. As of 1948, thirty-seven of the states in our own union have set aside the Rule. In our own state the courts apply the Rule only when there is no escape from it.

Repeal is the duty of the legislative branch of our government, and the judiciary cannot legislate by refusing to follow the Rule. The Rule in Shelley's Case is a rule of property under which many citizens own property, and under its application titles have been passed and approved. For the courts to refuse to follow it in a case such as we have here would endanger all such titles and create uncertainty and endless confusion. The Legislature can remedy the situation by legislation to take effect at some definite future date, and secure all titles held by virtue of the Rule prior to the effective date of such act. By so doing, the courts will be able to give effect to the clear intention of those making instruments affecting title to real estate. I think this should be made possible.

NOTES

1. Why is abolition of the Rule in Shelley's Case a responsibility solely of the legislature? Courts often declare that, in view of supposed reliance upon property law by men in disposing of their land and other valuables, judicial reform should proceed more slowly in the property field than in some other fields of the law. But would any grantor or testator rely upon the Rule in Shelley's Case? Might grantees or devisees rely upon it? Assuming that persons have relied upon the Rule and that they should be protected, could not the court overrule its earlier decisions but give its new decision prospective application only? See Judge Jerome Frank's opinion in Aero Spark Plug Co. v. B. G. Corp., 130 F.2d 290, 294–299 (C.C.A.N.Y.1942).

The Texas Legislature finally abolished the Rule in Shelley's Case as to all conveyances becoming effective after January 1, 1964. Vernon's Ann.Tex.Civ.Stat. art. 1291a (1964).

2. It should not be inferred from judicial reluctance to abrogate the Rule that its application has been uniform and consistent, even in a single jurisdiction. Reviewing the Illinois cases, a writer asserted: "Every one of its principles has at one time or another been stretched beyond recognition. Reversal has followed reversal." Young, The Rule in Shelley's Case in Illinois: A New Analysis and Suggestion for Repeal, 45 Ill.L.Rev. 173 (1950). The Rule was finally abolished in Illinois in 1953 but the abolition has no retroactive effect. Ill.—S.H.A. ch. 30, §§ 186, 187 (1985).

Despite the abolition of the Rule in Shelley's Case and the Illinois statute dealing with the status of fee tail estates (see Note 4, Page 270, supra), both of these hangovers from our medieval past continue to cloud land titles in Illinois. For a particularly complicated case dealing with both doctrines, see Evans v. Giles, 80 Ill.App.3d 270, 35 Ill.Dec. 598, 399 N.E.2d 664 (1980).

The Rule in Shelley's Case lives on in some American jurisdictions. For a particularly good example, see Jones v. Stone, 52 N.C.App. 502, 279 S.E.2d 13 (1981) where the court observed: "This year marks the 400th anniversary of the formal pronouncement of the Rule in Shelley's

Case. The Rule is a vestige of feudal law and takes its name from an old English case, Wolfe v. Shelley, 1 Co.Rep. 93(b), 76th Eng.Rep. 206 (CB 1581) . . . Although the original objective of the Rule became outdated when feudal tenures were abolished in the seventeenth century, the Rule enjoyed prominence until the twentieth century. The Rule was abolished in England in 1925; it has never been repealed in North Carolina, however. Indeed, one year after the Rule was abolished in England, the North Carolina Supreme Court said: "'Today, the rule serves quite a different purpose, in that it prevents the tying up of real estate during the life of the first taker, facilitates its alienation a generation earlier, and at the same time, subjects it to the payment of the debts of the ancestor.'" The decision provides a scholarly analysis of the Rule and its application but the Court decided it did not apply in the case at hand because the words "heirs at law" were not used in a technical sense.

3. Consider the applicability of the Rule in Shelley's Case to the following:

(a) A conveys land "to B for 100 years if B so long live, then to B's heirs."

(b) A conveys 20 shares of General Motors common stock "to B for life, then to B's heirs."

(c) A conveys land "to B for life, then to C for life, then to B's heirs."

(d) A conveys land "to B for life, then to C for life, then to C's heirs."

(e) A conveys land "to B for C's life in trust for C, then to C's heirs."

(f) A executed a will devising land "to B during her widowhood, and upon B's death or remarriage to B's heirs." B remarried before A's death. See Lydick v. Tate, 380 Ill. 616, 44 N.E.2d 583 (1942).

SECTION 3. THE DOCTRINE OF WORTHIER TITLE

BRASWELL v. BRASWELL

Supreme Court of Appeals of Virginia, 1954.
195 Va. 971, 81 S.E.2d 560.

SMITH, JUSTICE. By deed dated May 2, 1903, James J. Braswell conveyed a tract of land containing 37 acres which he owned in fee simple to his son, Nathaniel T. Braswell, "during his natural life and to his lawful heirs at his death, and if the said Nathaniel T. Braswell should die leaving no lawful heir from his body, then the land herein conveyed shall revert back to the said James J. Braswell or to his lawful heirs."

The grantor, James J. Braswell, died intestate in 1932, leaving surviving him, as his sole heirs at law, three sons: S. J. Braswell, W. H. Braswell and Nathaniel T. Braswell, the life tenant. Nathaniel T.

Braswell died testate and without issue in 1952, devising all his real property to Charles Madison Braswell.

Charles Madison Braswell, devisee of Nathaniel T. Braswell, instituted this suit against S. J. and W. H. Braswell for partition under Code, § 8–690 et seq.; his bill alleged that he was the owner as tenant in common of a one-third undivided interest in the land conveyed in the deed of 1903. The trial court upheld this claim of ownership. The correctness of the claim and of the trial court's decision is to be determined from a proper construction of the quoted portion of the deed.

The first aspect of the limitation in the deed creates a life estate in Nathaniel T. Braswell with a contingent remainder in fee simple in his unborn issue. 1 Minor on Real Property, (2d Ed., Ribble) § 717, p. 941. This is a clear example of the type of limitation once controlled by the rule in Shelley's Case, which rule was finally abolished in Virginia in the code of 1887, long before the date of this deed. See Code, § 55–14. Here, however, the contingent remainder never vested because the life tenant died without issue, and therefore we need not be concerned with it further. It is the second aspect of the limitation, that the land "shall revert back to the said James J. Braswell or to his lawful heirs," if the life tenant should die without heirs of his body, that creates the difficult problem of construction; namely, whether the second aspect of the limitation is a reversion or remainder.

It is necessary to consider briefly the distinctions made by Mr. Minor in his work on real property and quoted with approval in Copenhaver v. Pendleton, 155 Va. 463, 477, 155 S.E. 802, 806, 77 A.L.R. 324, as follows: "'A remainder is defined to be "what is left" of an *entire grant* of lands or tenements after a *preceding part* of the *same grant or estate* has been disposed of in possession, whose regular *expiration* the remainder must await.' 1 Minor on Real Prop. (2d Ed.) § 702, p. 916. 'A reversion is the remnant of an estate *continuing in the grantor*, undisposed of, after the grant of a part of his interest. It differs from a *remainder* in that it arises by *act of the law*, whereas a remainder is by *act of the parties*. A reversion moreover, is the remnant *left in the grantor*, whilst a remainder is the remnant of the whole estate disposed of, after a preceding part of the same has been given away.' 1 Minor on Real Prop. (2d Ed.) § 769, p. 1005."

The common-law rule as to contingent remainders limited to the grantor's or testator's heirs, is stated in 1 Minor on Real Property, (2d Ed., Ribble) §§ 720, 721, pp. 947, 948, as follows: ". . . it is a rule of the common law, which is always eager to discriminate carefully between the acquisition of land *by descent* and *by purchase*, respectively, that if land is limited by way of remainder (so called) to the *heirs of the grantor* (or *testator*), this does not create a *contingent remainder* in the grantor's or testator's heirs, but is simply a reservation by the grantor or testator of the *reversion after the particular estate granted*. . . . But the reason for the rule as well as the rule itself ceases to apply, if we suppose other words added to the words *heirs, etc.*, which show that the grantor or testator did not have in mind the technical meaning of the word 'heirs,' etc., but employed it to describe and designate *certain definite persons in being.*"

This common-law rule, when applied to deeds, is sometimes referred to as the inter vivos branch of the doctrine of worthier title, sometimes as the rule against a remainder to the grantor's heirs and at other times as the conveyor-heir rule. [Citations omitted.]

An excellent statement of the rule and its present status is found in 16 A.L.R.2d 691, at page 693, as follows: "The doctrine of the English common law was that an inter vivos conveyance for life, with remainder to the heirs or next of kin of the conveyor is ineffective to create a remainder, but leaves in the conveyor a reversion which will pass by operation of law upon his death, unless he otherwise disposes of it. Although abrogated in England by the Inheritance Act of 1833 (3 & 4 Wm IV, ch 106, § 3), this common-law doctrine has been recognized and given effect in a substantial number of the American jurisdictions, usually, however, in the modified form of a rule or precept of construction rather than as an absolute rule of law."

It was this rule that Mr. Justice Eggleston was referring to in Bottimore v. First-Merchants Nat. Bank, 170 Va. 221, 230, 196 S.E. 593, 596, when he used the following language from Stephens v. Moore, 298 M. 215, 249 S.W. 601: " 'It is the generally accepted rule that, where there is a grant to one for life, with remainder to the heirs of the grantor, there is in fact no remainder; for the limitation, though denominated a remainder, continues in the grantor as his old reversion, and does not devolve upon his heirs as purchasers, as it would if it were a remainder, but as his heirs.' " . . .

This rule against a remainder to the grantor's heirs had its origin in feudal custom which preferred to have real property pass by the "worthier" channel of descent, rather than by the less worthy channel of purchase, and although the reason for the rule disappeared with the abolition of feudalism, the rule itself remained. The rule probably arose to prevent the overlord from being deprived of the fruits of his seigniory. . . . Further justification for the rule has been found in the rationalization that it ordinarily effectuates the intention of the grantor. . . . An additional reason is expressed in the maxim nemo est haeres viventis—no one is heir of the living. Doctor v. Hughes, 225 N.Y. 305, 122 N.E. 221.

Prior to its abolition in England, this doctrine seems to have been a rule of law rather than a rule of construction. The modern trend, however, is to regard it as a rule of construction rather than one of property. This view, as rationalized by Judge Cardozo in Doctor v. Hughes, supra, is supported by the best-considered opinions and by most of the text writers on the subject. . . . See, however, In re Brolasky's Estate, 302 Pa. 439, 153 A. 739, and Robinson v. Blankenship, 116 Tenn. 394, 92 S.W. 854, holding the rule one of property, to be applied regardless of intent.

The court in In re Burchell's Estate was speaking of the modern trend as expressed in the Doctor case, supra, when it said [299 N.Y. 351, 87 N.E.2d 296] that "The use of the old doctrine as a rule of construction results in either (1) a shift from an absolute rule against remainders to heirs of grantors to a rule that the grantor must expressly indicate his intention to create a remainder in his heirs; or (2) a presumption in favor of reversions which may be rebutted by indication of the grantor's contrary intent gathered from the instrument as a whole. The practice adopted in the majority of states falls into the second classification." (Citing cases.)

Hence, for the rule against remainders to heirs of grantors to be applied: (1) there must be an inter vivos transfer, (2) if the subject matter be realty there must be a limitation to the grantor's "heirs" (used in its technical meaning of indefinite succession) or an equivalent limitation. In applying the doctrine, the better view is that there is a presumption in favor of reversions which presumption may be rebutted by a contrary intent gathered from the instrument as a whole.

The rule does not apply if the limitation is construed to mean that the property was intended to pass to the heirs of the grantor, or upon an equivalent limitation, determined at some time other than the death of the grantor. . . . Here it is contended that the rule against remainders does not apply because by the use of the word "then" the grantor meant to fix the time of the ascertainment of his heirs at the date of the life tenant's death rather than the date of the grantor's death.

In support of this contention for an exception to the general rule that heirs of the grantor are usually determined as of the date of the grantor's death, we are referred to Driskill v. Carwile, 145 Va. 116, 118, 133 S.E. 773, in which the following provision of a will was under consideration: " 'The said property I give unto Nannie P. Moon during her life and that of her husband, Nathan S. Moon, and at their decease, I direct the same to be sold and equally divided between the living heirs of my brothers and sisters.' " It was held that by the use of the words "living heirs," under the circumstances of that case, the testator intended the beneficiaries to be those who were living at the time of the death of the last life tenant. Had the grantor in the deed before us had this in mind it would have been simple for him to have used the word "living."

We are also referred to Callis v. Ripley, 161 Va. 472, 474, 171 S.E. 497, in which the language used in a will there involved provided for a life estate and that if the life tenant should die leaving no lawful issue of his body, "then the said land and improvements shall be equally divided with my next surviving heirs." It was held that the use of the word "then" in connection with the words "my next surviving heirs" indicated that the testator intended the beneficiaries to be those who were living at the death of the life tenant. Again there is no such language used in the instant limitation.

On the other hand, there is the case of Allison v. Allison's Ex'rs, 101 Va. 537, 540, 44 S.E. 904, 905, in which the testator used this language following a life estate: " 'and at her [life tenant's] death to be equally divided among her children, should any survive her—if she should die without issue, or if her surviving child or children should die before becoming of age, then the property bequeathed for the benefit of my daughter is to be divided among my heirs at law according to the laws of the state of Virginia.'" It was held that the last clause referred to those persons who answered the description of the testator's heirs at the time of his death and not at the death of the life tenant. See review of cases in Snidow v. Day, 145 Va. 721, 134 S.E. 704. . . .

The only language used in the limitation before us which might tend to indicate the word "heirs" was not used to embrace those persons who corresponded to the description at the time of the grantor's death, is the word "then." The grantor said, ". . . if the said Nathaniel T. Braswell should die leaving no lawful heir from his body, *then* the land herein conveyed shall revert back to James J. Braswell or his lawful heirs." This use of the word "then" only fixes the time when it is determined whether the life tenant died without issue of his body and does not fix the time for ascertaining the heirs of the grantor. Also, there is significance to be accorded the word "revert." . . . By using the word "then" in conjunction with the word "revert," and without other language to the contrary, the grantor clearly intended that if the life tenant should die without issue of his body, "in that case" the land should "come back," and pass as if no conveyance had been made.

Thus under the construction most favorable to the appellants, we are unable to find in the language of this deed anything which would warrant us in disregarding the common-law rule against remainders to the grantor's heirs, nor any valid basis for holding the word "heirs" to signify anything other than its normal and technical meaning of indefinite succession as determined at the death of the grantor. The common-law rule, not having been abrogated in Virginia, is controlling. James J. Braswell upon the execution of the deed of 1903 retained a reversion in the 37 acre tract of land. Then upon his death intestate in 1932, his reversion passed to his three sons in equal shares, and upon Nathaniel T. Braswell's death testate and without issue in 1952, his one-third interest in the reversion which he inherited from James J. Braswell passed to his devisee, Charles Madison Braswell. The decision of the trial court so finding is correct.

Affirmed.

NOTES

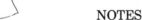

1. This rule, perhaps most accurately called the rule forbidding remainders to the grantor's heirs, exists in some form in nearly all states. Statutes abolishing the rule exist in a few states, an example being Illinois, which took this step in 1955. See L. Simes and A. Smith, Future Interests § 1612 (2d ed. 1956). But even in such states, the rule usually continues to apply to instruments executed before the effective date of the abolishing legislation. The nature of dissatisfaction with the rule is indicated in a résumé of the 1959 Report of the California Law Revision Commission appearing in 34 Cal.B.J. 84, 93 (1959); the Commission recommended that "the doctrine of worthier title be abol-

ished as to both inter vivos and testamentary transfers for the following basic reasons:

"(a) The doctrine is based upon a false premise, namely, the assumption that a person granting property to his own heirs or next of kin does not really intend to give the property to them or understand that he has done so but rather intends to retain a reversion in the property with full power to dispose of it again in the future.

"(b) The doctrine breeds litigation, since the presumption or rule of interpretation can be defeated by a showing that the grantor actually meant what he said.

"(c) The doctrine can easily operate as an estate and inheritance tax trap by creating a reversionary interest in the estate of a grantor who intended to avoid such taxes by making an inter vivos transfer of the property to his heirs or next of kin."

But compare Professor Powell's comment: "A statute prospectively operating either to weight the scales strongly in favor of a reversion or strongly in favor of a remainder would be helpful. It is believed that the statute should take the former of these two types because such a statute would be less likely to run counter to the real desires of settlors and would help to keep trusts readily revocable and property more easily alienable." 3 R. Powell, Real Property ¶ 269 (1952).

See also Johanson, Reversions, Remainders, and the Doctrine of Worthier Title, 45 Tex.L.Rev. 1 (1966).

2. The Doctrine of Worthier Title is deceptively easy to state but difficult to apply to concrete situations. See, for example, Harris Trust and Sav. Bank v. Beach, 145 Ill.App.3d 673, 99 Ill.Dec. 435, 495 N.E.2d 1170 (1 Dist.1986) where the court said: "We first address the issue of whether the doctrine of worthier title is applicable to the present case. Under the doctrine when the owner of a fee simple attempts to create a life estate with a remainder to his own heirs, the remainder is void. The grantor keeps a reversion. 'Thus, A conveys to B for life, and after B's death to the heirs of A. By virtue of the rule the state of the title is: life estate in B, reversion in fee simple in A' (Moynihan, Introduction to the Law of Real Property at 150 (1962)). The practical effect of the doctrine then, is that the heirs are prevented from taking anything at all, unless they later take the property under the intestacy statute or under the residuary clause of the grantor's will."

Although Illinois had abolished the doctrine in 1955, the statute was not retroactive and the two trusts being construed were established 60 years previously. The court correctly held that the Rule applied but also held that it was a rule of law (like the Rule in Shelley's Case) and hence could be intent-defeating. Said the court: "The common law applied the doctrine as a rule of Law. (Moynihan, p. 155). Thus, if the grantor clearly intended to give a remainder to his heirs, the doctrine applies so as to render that gift void. Then, in Doctor v. Hughes (1919), 225 N.Y. 305, 122 N.E. 221, the court applied the doctrine of worthier title as a rule of construction. The court held that the doctrine will result in a reversion unless the grantor clearly intended to create a contingent remainder in his heirs. However, the intention to transform the reversion into a remainder must be clearly expressed. (Doctor v. Hughes.) Many other jurisdictions followed the lead of New York and now accept the doctrine as a rule of construction. [Query, how would the intent be clearly expressed?] . . . Although some confusion exists in the Illinois cases as to whether the doctrine of worthier title is a rule of law or construction . . . we find that Illinois treats the doctrine as a rule of law for trusts created at the times of the Hixon trusts."

Now, do you see why the Doctrine is a litigation-breeder and why a number of states have abolished it entirely? Note again, however, that abolition is not retroactive and that the doctrine, though dead, may rule us from the grave.

3. Occasionally, the doctrine of worthier title is applied, or at least referred to, in fact situations which have nothing to do with the doctrine. For a prime example, see All Persons v. Buie, Miss., 386 So. 2d 1109 (1980) where the Supreme Court of Mississippi created confusion by invoking the doctrine even though there was no express limitation to the *grantor's* heirs. Nonetheless, the court did reach the right result in the case.

SECTION 4. EXECUTORY INTERESTS (HEREIN OF THE STATUTE OF USES AND ITS MODERN SIGNIFICANCE)

At this point in the materials we are primarily interested in completing our classification of future interests in real property. We now know something about reversions, remainders, possibilities of reverter and powers of termination. We have yet to explore another category—executory interests (springing and shifting uses). These interests can be understood only by another excursion into the past and an exploration of that perennial favorite of law students—the Statute of Uses. That Statute had consequences beyond the law of future interests, giving rise to the modern law of trusts and creating new methods for the conveyance of land. In order to make the Statute of Uses less opaque, the following text material provides a brief summary of the impact of the Statute of Uses on the law of property.

CRIBBET AND JOHNSON, PRINCIPLES OF THE LAW OF PROPERTY

Pages 69–85 (3d ed. 1989).

I. The Rise of the Use

The use was essentially a simple tool and not even a new one. For various purposes, the fee simple owner of land might convey it to another person to hold for certain specified uses. For example, the Franciscans, having taken a vow of poverty, could not own land, so religious followers would convey the necessary dwelling to some trusted individual to hold "for the use of" the friars. A similar transaction might be utilized to set up an estate for minor children while the father was on a crusade. The feudal lawyers were apparently as alert as contemporary ones and they hit upon the scheme of transferring Blackacre to two or more joint tenants to hold "for the use of" the grantor or such persons as he might specify. The transferee was called the "feoffee to uses" and the person for whose benefit he was to hold was called the *cestui que use.* Note that the feoffee to uses had the legal title, i.e., he was seised of the fee simple estate recognized by the courts while the *cestui que use* had only a beneficial interest, in reality a claim that the feoffee hold the proceeds of the estate for him.

Now comes the beauty of the scheme. The feudal incidents attached only to the legal estate, not to the beneficial interest which the law did not even recognize. Thus, if the *cestui que use* died no incidents were due and the feoffee to uses simply held Blackacre for the person or persons designated by the original grantor. Since wills were not permitted at this time,[1] probably because the king wanted all land to descend to the heir so he could have the feudal dues, the feoffment to uses also served as a method for passing the land at death to someone other than the heir at law. But suppose the feoffee to uses died, wouldn't he have to ante up the incidents since he had the legal title? He clearly would have had to do so but since two or more persons were used as joint tenants the land was held by the survivor and the feudal dues were defeated. Moreover, as soon as one joint tenant died a new one was introduced into the picture so that seldom would any obligations be incurred.

This conveyance to uses had one weak spot. If the feoffee to uses were dishonest or unfaithful to his "trust" the *cestui que use* was left without a remedy. The courts recognized that the feoffee was seised of Blackacre since a fee simple estate had been transferred to him and so they would not interfere to make him perform his promise. When the device was infrequently used this caused but little difficulty, but with its rapid growth in the fourteenth century the frauds began to multiply. A solution had to be found or the use abandoned.

In this dilemma the *cestui que uses* turned to the king who was the source of all justice in the realm. Most justice was dispensed by the common-law courts but the king retained a residue of power which he exercised through the chancellor and which could be utilized in extraordinary cases where there was no relief at the common law. Why the king should have intervened to help landowners who were engaged in depriving him of the cherished feudal incidents is not clear, but at any rate the chancellor did order the feoffee to uses to carry out the "trust" or be held in contempt of the royal prerogative. This is not the place to trace the rise of the court of chancery as a rival to the common-law courts[2] but a few comments must be made to clarify the operation of the feoffment to uses.

1. It was not until 1540 that the Statute of Wills, 32 Hen. 8, c. 1, made land generally devisable in England.

2. For a brief account of the role of equity in Anglo-American law see de

At first, the chancellor acted solely at his discretion and was not bound by any rules of precedent but eventually the chancery accumulated its own principles and equity became a separate system of "law" administered by an independent tribunal.[3] However, the chancery did not come into direct conflict with the common-law courts and did not attempt to interfere with the common-law estates. In fact, it adopted the same scheme of ownership so that you could have an equitable fee simple, fee tail, or life estate with the same consequences that we have already discussed. Equity went even further in permitting the creation of new interests in land and, since chancery was not bound by some of the more technical rules of the common law, it was possible to have springing and shifting uses as well as the more usual estates. Equity acted solely *in personam* by ordering the feoffee to uses to do certain things and then fining or imprisoning him for failure to do so. Thus, if O granted "to A and his heirs, to hold for the use of B for life, remainder for the use of C and his heirs", A had a legal fee simple while B had an equitable life estate followed by an equitable vested remainder in C. Equity recognized A's fee simple but if A refused to give the rents and profits to B during his lifetime or tried to sell Blackacre as his own, the chancellor, on request by B, would step in and see that the use was properly carried out. This power of the equity court extended to successors in interest of A and therefore an heir or devisee of A would take Blackacre subject to the use as would any purchaser from A who had notice (i.e., knew or should have known) of the use. The only person who could take free of the use would be a bona fide purchaser for value without notice (b.f.p.). Even in this last case, the *cestui que use* would have an action against the feoffee to uses for breach of confidence.

By the sixteenth century the use was a highly-developed device and vast quantities of English land were held to uses. Equitable titles were almost as common as legal ones and, since in each case the king was being deprived of his feudal incidents, it is not surprising to find an attempt being made to end the whole system.

II. The Statute of Uses

It was that multi-wived monarch, Henry VIII, who finally forced the issue. He seems to have been perpetually pressed for funds and a survey of the assets of the kingdom disclosed how the feudal incidents were slipping through the royal fingers. In 1535, he forced the Statute of Uses upon a reluctant parliament. It is a peculiar statute since it attacked the use only indirectly; it did not abolish the device or prohibit conveyances to uses but, rather, *executed* the use. It accom-

Funiak, Handbook of Modern Equity 1–26 (2d ed. 1956).

3. Equity has been defined as "that portion of remedial justice which is exclusively administered by courts of equity, as distinguished from courts of common law." Malone v. Meres, 91 Fla. 709, 109 So. 677 (1926).

plished this by providing that the seisin, and therefore the legal estate, should be vested in the *cestui que use*, passing right on through the feoffee to uses. Thus, the feudal incidents would become due to the lord of the fee as soon as the *cestui que use* died. The statute reads: "Where any person or persons stand or be seised . . . to the use, confidence or trust of any other person or persons or to any body politic . . . that in every such case all and every such person or persons and bodies politic that have . . . any such use in fee simple, fee tail, for term of life or for years . . . or in remainder or reverter shall stand and be seised . . . in lawful seisin estate and possession of the same . . . lands . . . to all intents of and in such like estates as they had or shall have in the use." [4]

The theory of the Statute was simple. Suppose *O* granted Blackacre "to *A* and his heirs for the use of *B* and his heirs." The statute executed the use and *B* received a *legal* estate in fee simple absolute. *A* did not receive anything but merely served as a conduit through which the legal title flowed from *O* to *B*. Moreover, the *cestui que use* received a legal estate of exactly the same type as the equitable one which he would have had before the passage of the Statute. Thus, if *O* grants "to *A* and his heirs to hold for the use of *B* for life, remainder for the use of *C* and his heirs", *A* takes nothing, *B* receives a legal life estate in possession and *C* a vested remainder in fee simple absolute (legal).

The immediate result of the Statute of Uses was to restore the feudal incidents to the overlord and nullify the point of a feoffment to uses. It had a side effect—destruction of the use as a method of devising property on death, the pre–1535 equivalent of a will. The latter effect seems to have caused the most immediate reaction because the habit of devising land to individuals other than, or in addition to, the heir was widespread. Henry VIII was forced to compromise on this issue and five years after the Statute of Uses, in 1540, the Statute of Wills was passed. It did not allow complete testation but it was adequate for the purpose and met the demands of the landowners. The Statute of Wills did not require the intervention of the use but allowed the testator to execute a document, under proper safeguards, which passed the legal title directly to the named devisees.

III. The Modern Significance of the Statute of Uses

The Statute of Uses has been called the most important single piece of legislation in the Anglo–American law of property. It is still on the statute books of many American states and is considered as a part of the adopted common law of England [5] in many more. Why

4. 27 Hen. 8, c. 10 (1535).

5. The Statute of Uses was repealed in England as a part of the property reform legislation of 1925. Speaking of the abolition of the Statute, the Lord Chancellor said: "I am told that there is one most respected practitioner, grown grey in the practice of the Chancery Law, sixty years of whose successful and brillant life has been spent in the exposition, not unremunerative exposition, of the Statute of Uses, who, when he heard, not from my lips but from lips perhaps less sympathetic, that at last the Statute of Uses was abolished, definitely and irrevocably announced his intention not to survive it, and that he resigned his practice at once."

should an essentially revenue-raising act of Henry VIII have had so profound an influence on property law? Paradoxically, it is because (1) the Statute was not successful in its primary aim and (2) the Statute had some totally unforeseen consequences. It is a perfect example of the unplanned growth of English law. The Statute's lack of success gave rise to the modern law of trusts, and the unforeseen consequences led to new methods of conveying real property and to the possibility of new estates in land. Let us look at each of these points in turn.

A. THE MODERN TRUST

It must have occurred to you that the ancient use bore many similarities to what we now call a trust. The feoffee to uses was the trustee, the *cestui que use* was the beneficiary, and the grantor of Blackacre was the settlor or trustor. In the modern trust, the trustee takes the legal title but must hold it for the benefit (use) of the beneficiary who thus has equitable title. In our modern courts, with their merger of law and equity, the trust is still the creature of equity and is handled on the chancery side of the court.[6] It is obvious that none of this could have come about if the Statute of Uses had been successful, for its avowed purpose was to destroy the split between legal and equitable ownership and return to the earlier concept of legal estates only. In fact, the Statute probably had this effect for nearly a century, but eventually loopholes were discovered in the legislation and through them crawled the equitable jurisdiction of chancery to fashion the modern trust. These loopholes were three in number: (1) the Statute did not apply to a use on a use; (2) it did not apply to personal property; and (3) it did not apply to active, as distinguished from passive, uses.

(1) Use on a Use

Suppose *O* granted Blackacre "to *A* and his heirs for the use of *B* and his heirs for the use of *C* and his heirs." Prior to the Statute of Uses, *A* would take the legal title and *B* would have the equitable one. *C* would take nothing, since *O* had exhausted his estate in the grant to *B* and the further limitation to *C* would be repugnant to it. After the Statute, you would normally assume that the legal title would pass to *C* since Blackacre was to be held to his ultimate use. The Statute should execute the two uses and *A* and *B* should both become mere conduits for the legal title. However, the chancellors finally decided that the Statute would operate only once and then, with its force spent, would retire from the scene. The state of the title would then be as follows: the Statute would execute the first use, so *A* would take nothing and *B*

6. See Karlen, Primer of Procedure 165–172 (1950) for a brief discussion of the fusion of law and equity in the modern judicial system.

would have the legal fee, but the Statute would not execute the second use, so *B* would hold Blackacre in trust for *C*, who now had the beneficial interest. By this bit of hocus pocus, equity was able to reassert its jurisdiction and in 1738 Lord Chancellor Hardwicke could claim that the Statute "has had no other effect than to add at most three words to a conveyance." If all of this seems, as the English say, "a bit much", you should remember that in 1660 the Statute of Tenures had finally ended the feudal incidents and the crown no longer cared whether the Statute of Uses was thwarted. Of course, the Statute could have been repealed, but why bother when the desirable results of a trust could be attained by the simple device of a use on a use?

The use *on* a use should be distinguished from the use *after* a use, for in the latter case the Statute was fully operational. Suppose *O* grants Blackacre "to *A* and his heirs for the use of *B* for life, remainder to the use of *C* and his heirs." This is a use *after* a use, first a use to *B* for life, followed by a use to *C* in remainder. As we have already pointed out, the Statute will operate to give *B* the legal life estate and *C* the legal vested remainder. Contrast this with the result in the previous paragraph where a use *on* a use was involved.

(2) Uses of Personal Property

The Statute of Uses was not concerned with personalty for no feudal incidents were involved. The Statute applied only where one person was *seised* to the use of another and seisin had no application outside of the freehold estates. If *O* gave a herd of cattle to *A* to hold for the use of *B*, you had a split between the legal and the equitable ownership and chancery would enforce the "trust" in favor of *B*, after, as well as before, the Statute. Suppose *O* granted Blackacre "to *A* for ninety-nine years, to hold for the use of *B* and his heirs." Would the Statute apply? It would not, because *A* was not *seised* to the use of *B*. *A* had only a non-freehold estate and, as we have already discussed, that was a species of personal property, a chattel real. Thus, *A* would be the trustee and *B* would have an equitable interest for the ninety-nine years, at the end of which time the land would revert to *O* or his heirs. Here, again, equity could retain its jurisdiction and while personal property did not bulk large in the seventeenth-century scheme of things, it makes up a large proportion of modern trust property. The most common ingredient of the contemporary trust *res* is likely to be stocks and bonds.

(3) Active Uses

Prior to the Statute of Uses, the feoffee to uses seldom had any duties to perform. After all, the use was only a scheme to evade the feudal incidents and perhaps to have the benefits of a will. The feoffee was in reality a straw man, holding a naked legal title for the true owner. Because of this fact, the common-law courts came to the conclusion that the Statute did not apply if, in fact, the feoffee was given some active duties to perform. It was reasoned that in such a case he was more than a straw man and must have the legal title if he were to successfully perform those duties. Moreover, the duties did not have to be very extensive before the court would say that the Statute had no application. Thus, if *O* granted Blackacre "to *A* and his heirs upon trust to collect the rents and profits and pay them to *B* ", the legal title remained in *A*, for how else could he justify his collection of the rents? Similarly, a trust for sale of the land by *A* was beyond the reach of the Statute, since *A* would have to hold the legal title in order to sell the estate. It was still possible to have a dry or passive trust where no duties were involved, but this became progressively less likely to happen. The typical, modern trust literally bristles with all sorts of duties for the trustee.

It should be clear that in these three areas where the Statute of Uses did not operate, there was sufficient room for the gigantic edifice which is the modern trust. Although the law of trusts is obviously a part of the law of property in the broad sense, it has become so specialized a subject that we will not spend further time on it in a book on the basic principles of property law. We will now turn our attention to two areas in which the Statute of Uses did operate, but with unforeseen consequences.

B. NEW METHODS OF CONVEYANCING

There were a number of methods of conveyancing at common law [7] but all of them were cumbersome and subject to various disadvantages. The most frequently used, the feoffment, involved the formal ceremony of livery of seisin and required the parties to be physically present on the land so that the clod of dirt or twig could be handed over to symbolize the transfer of seisin. Although a charter of feoffment was later given to memorialize the conveyance, the livery of seisin was the operative part of the feoffment. This bit of pageantry was undoubtedly appealing to the medieval mind but it was hardly the method on which to build the commercial use of land. Eventually, some simpler scheme for conveying real property was bound to be developed and the Statute of Uses happened to be the catalyst which called forth the modern deed.

7. Among those in normal use were the feoffment, the fine and common recovery, the lease, the grant, the lease and release, and the surrender. For a good, short discussion see Tiffany, Real Property 654–666 (New Abridged Edition, 1940).

Like most brief descriptions of legal phenomena, this is an oversimplification of what actually happened but it should clarify the importance of the Statute in the field of conveyancing. The two new methods of transferring title were the bargain and sale and the covenant to stand seised.

Before the passage of the Statute, the feoffment to uses had become so common that a presumption existed that any conveyance was for the use of the grantor unless there was evidence to the contrary. Thus, if *O* enfeoffed *A*, nothing more appearing, *A* received the legal title but he held it for the use of *O*. This was called a resulting use, since the use came back or resulted to *O*. It was a justifiable conclusion, since *O* was probably trying to put the legal title in *A* to avoid the feudal incidents. Of course, this presumption could be rebutted by showing that *A* paid value (consideration) to *O* or that there was an express declaration of use, such as "to *A* and his heirs for the use of *A* and his heirs" or "to *A* and his heirs for the use of *B* and his heirs." There was a corollary to this presumption in the case of the feoffment. Suppose *O* "bargained and sold Blackacre to *A* and his heirs", i.e., suppose *A* paid value to *O* for the land but did not take a common-law conveyance. This bargain and sale might be oral or it might be evidenced by a written contract, but in any case no formal conveyance was made and so the legal title to the land remained in *O*. Since value had been paid, however, it was presumed that the parties had intended *A* to become the beneficial owner and equity would treat *O* as holding to the use of *A*. What was the result after the passage of the Statute of Uses? The Statute executed the use, since *O* was seised to the use of *A*, and the legal as well as the beneficial interest passed to *A*.

The way had now been cleared for a simple, efficient method of land transfer. After the Statute, the parties could gather in the lawyer's office, he could draft a "deed" of bargain and sale, the purchaser could pay the money to the vendor, the Statute would automatically execute the use, and the purchaser could walk out of the office as the new owner of Blackacre. The bargain-and-sale form of deed is still much used in the United States and while most states have a simplified form of statutory conveyance [8] others still rely on the Statute of Uses to give vitality to their land transfers.

The effectiveness of the bargain and sale depended upon the payment of consideration to raise the presumption of use in the payor. A parallel development gave rise to the covenant to stand seised where no "valuable" consideration (money or money's worth) was involved but where "good" consideration (a legal relationship based on blood or marriage) was found to exist. If *O* covenanted to stand seised—promised under seal to hold Blackacre—to the use of *A*, and *A* was a stranger, the covenant had no legal consequence. There had been no legal conveyance to *A* and since value had not been paid there was no basis for a presumption of a use in *A*. But suppose *A* was the wife or son of *O*? Equity would now presume that, because of the close ties

8. 3 American Law of Property 221–224 (Casner ed. 1952).

between *O* and *A*,[9] the equitable title was in *A* while *O* continued to hold the legal title for the former's use. After the Statute, the use would, of course, be executed and the full legal title would be in *A* although no common-law conveyance of the land had been made.

Henry VIII and his advisors had never intended to affect the common-law conveyancing structure of England; the Statute was designed to be a reactionary, not a liberal reform, measure. But, due to the accidents of history and the adaptability of the common-law lawyers, a modern system of land transfer was born.

C. THE CREATION OF NEW ESTATES IN LAND

The permissible estates at common law were divided into two categories—freehold and non-freehold. The latter group was unaffected by the Statute of Uses but the freehold estates were expanded by the admission of certain types of future interests which had been impossible at common law. You will recall that the fees simple, the fee tail, and the life estate were the permissible freehold estates and the chancery court recognized equitable equivalents of each of them. The freehold estates could be further divided into present (possessory) estates and future interests. The future interests were also present estates but their owners were not entitled to possession until the preceding estate had ended, i.e., they were vested in interest but not in possession. These common-law future interests were the reversion, the vested remainder, the possibility of reverter, the right of entry for condition broken (power of termination), and the contingent remainder. Our prior discussion of these future interests pointed out that the first two were true estates in land, i.e., they represented interests that were certain to accrue to the holder or his heirs once the preceding possessory estate ended.[10] The latter three, however, were subject to further conditions and might, in fact, never become true estates. More accurately, they should be called expectancies but long usage has led to their classification generally as species of future interests.

In recognizing these future interests the common law was typically rigid and required a strict following of the rules. Earlier in this chapter some of these anachronistic rules—the Rule in Shelley's Case, the Doctrine of Worthier Title, and the destructibility of contingent remainders—were explored and it was pointed out that they have survived into modern times. The Statute of Uses should have affected some of these rules [11] but it did not do so and they were adopted by the

9. Just how close these ties must be is an open question. See Dawley v. Dawley's Estate, 60 Colo. 73, 152 P. 1171 (1915), where the court decided an agreement to hold property to the use of an *adopted* son was a good covenant to stand seised.

10. This is not strictly accurate since a reversion could be subject to a condition precedent, e.g., any reversion following a life estate and a contingent remainder. However, most reversions are of the vested type, i.e., following a life estate or an estate for years.

11. It clearly should have ended the destructibility of contingent remainders doctrine. Do you see why?

chancery, apparently as a part of the maxim that equity follows the law. But there were some further technical rules of the common-law courts that were not blindly followed in equity. These rules had to do mainly with seisin and the common-law insistence that seisin always be lodged in a specific person to whom the overlord could look for the feudal incidents. These rules were: (1) no freehold could be limited to begin *in futuro;* (2) no remainder could be limited after the grant of a fee simple; (3) no remainder could be limited so as to vest in possession prior to the normal ending of the preceding estate; and (4) no power of appointment could be used to vest in a third party an interest greater than that owned by the donee of the power.[12] It is necessary to look at each of these, in turn, and see the change wrought by the Statute of Uses.

(1) No freehold could be limited to begin *in futuro. O,* on January 1, grants "to *A* and his heirs from September 1." There might be many reasons why *O* would desire to do this, e.g., September 1 might be the marriage date of *A,* and *O,* going on a long journey, might want to make a present gift of Blackacre. At common law such a grant would be void because it must be made by a livery of seisin and once that was done *A* would be the owner. There could be no abeyance of seisin. (Of course, you realize that *O* could grant to *X* for eight months, then to *A,* but that was interpreted as a present grant to *A,* subject to an estate for years in *X*). This problem was easily solved by a use. *O* granted "to *X* and his heirs for the use of *A* and his heirs from September 1." The seisin passed to *X* immediately, thus no abeyance, and equity would enforce *A's* rights after September 1. Prior to that time, there would be a resulting use in *O* since *X* had given nothing of value and the language of grant was silent as to the intervening months. With the passage of the Statute of Uses, these equitable interests became legal ones and, in effect, *O* kept the legal estate until September 1 when the legal estate passed automatically to *A.* Thus, it was possible, after the Statute, to limit a freehold to begin *in futuro.* A new type of future interest had been added to the closed categories of the common law.

(2) No remainder could be limited after the grant of a fee simple. *O* could create a fee simple determinable or a fee simple subject to a condition subsequent and, if he did so, he would retain, respectively, a possibility of reverter or a power of termination. No other future interest was possible following a fee simple. Assume *O* granted "to *A* and his heirs, but if *A* shall marry a tradesman's daughter, then to *B* and his heirs." At common law, the limitation to *B* was void since it would result in shifting the seisin from *A* to *B* and would offend the rule under discussion. However, *O* could grant "to *X* and his heirs for the use of *A* and his heirs, but if *A* shall marry a tradesman's daughter, then to *B* and his heirs." Prior to the Statute, *X* would hold first for *A,* then if the condition occurred, he would hold for *B.* After the Statute, the use would be executed and both interests would be legal, the shift occurring automatically upon the happening of the contingency. Note,

12. Hargreaves, Introduction to Land Law 105–106 (3d ed. 1952).

however, that *B* would not have a contingent remainder but a shifting use or interest, called an executory devise if it appeared in a will. *A's* estate would be a defeasible fee, technically referred to as a fee simple subject to an executory limitation.[13]

To be accurate, it should be explained that the term executory interest (or executory limitation) is generic and includes the shifting use (interest) and the springing use (interest). The former has just been illustrated and arises whenever the happening of the condition destroys a legal estate vested in a grantee and shifts that estate over to another party. The latter term refers to an estate which springs out of the original grantor, i.e., where the happening of the condition destroys the original estate of the grantor. Thus, the estate in the immediately preceding subsection (1) is a springing use since it will spring into existence on September 1 and destroy the estate of *O*, the grantor. Similarly, *O* might grant "to *X* and his heirs for the use of *A* and his heirs when *A* shall attain the age of twenty-one." After the Statute, such a grant would leave *O* with a fee simple subject to an executory limitation and would give *A* a springing use.

(3) No remainder could be limited so as to vest in possession prior to the normal ending of the preceding estate. This rule is similar to the preceding one and, indeed, is another way of explaining why there could be no springing or shifting interests at common law. It is included here because it is a broader statement of the proposition and illustrates that any interest following a common-law estate had to wait for the natural end of its predecessor—"after you, my dear Alphonso!" Thus, if *O* granted "to *A* for life, but if he marries a tradesman's daughter, then to *B* for life", the grant to *B* was void since it might destroy *A's* estate prior to its normal termination on *A's* death. Again, it is apparent that this result could have been reached by a use and would now be possible because of the Statute of Uses.

(4) No power of appointment could be used to vest in a third party an interest greater than that owned by the donee of the power. Among the most flexible of the modern methods for the disposition of property

13. If you have been following this discussion closely, you will now see why the Statute of Uses should have ended the destructibility doctrine. Suppose, after 1536, *O* bargains and sells "to *A* for life, remainder to *A's* first son who shall reach twenty-one." *A* dies, survived by a minor son. The court should say that the land reverts to *O* in fee simple subject to an executory limitation and the minor son will take the land by a springing use when he reaches twenty-one. Such interests are now possible because of the Statute of Uses. Instead, in Purefoy v. Rogers, 2 Wms.Saund. 380 (1670) the court announced the rule: "No limitation capable of taking effect as a contingent remainder shall, if created inter vivos, be held to be a springing use under the Statute of Uses, or, if, created by will, be held to be an executory devise under the Statute of Wills." The quote is from White v. Summers, L.R. [1908] 2 Ch. 256 but it is known as the Rule of Purefoy v. Rogers. As you know from the previous discussion, the doctrine of destructibility has now been changed by statute in most states. For a case where the distinction between contingent remainders and executory interests determined the outcome see Stoller v. Doyle, 257 Ill. 369, 100 N.E. 959 (1913).

Since executory interests were non-destructible it became possible, after the Statute of Uses, to tie up property for an indefinite period and dead-hand control became a distinct reality. This gave rise to the Rule against Perpetuities as a common-law policy opposed to remoteness of vesting.

is the power of appointment. By this device, a power can be given to a trusted friend or a bank to designate a person or persons who will ultimately take the property, without the donee of the power having any interest in the property himself. This could not be done at common law. A grant "to *A* for life, remainder to such children of *A* as *X* shall appoint" would give *A* a life estate but the power would be void and *O* would have a reversion. But *O* could grant "to *X* and his heirs for the use of *A* for life then for the use of such children of *A* as *X* (or someone else) shall appoint." Equity would enforce such a use and after the Statute the interests were held to be legal, thus allowing the powers of appointment to be added to the arsenal of the property lawyer. These powers may be either general or special. The former allows the appointment to be exercised in favor of any one, including the donee of the power, while the latter restricts the exercise to members of a specified class.[14]

At the present time, all of these "new" estates in land are so well recognized that it is not necessary to follow the old formula, "to *X* and his heirs for the use of, etc.", in order to take advantage of the greater flexibility of equity. It is fair to say that the four rules just discussed no longer exist and that, in addition to the permissible common-law estates, executory interests and powers of appointment must be included in the list of estates in land.[15]

IV. The Rule Against Perpetuities and Restraints on Alienation

As the preceding material demonstrates, the Statute of Uses led to the creation of new estates in land. The distinction between contingent remainders and executory interests was a narrow one, based on the logic of history, but it had some significant consequences. Contingent remainders could be destroyed at common law but executory interests could not and hence they might vest at some indefinite (and remote) period in the future, thus tying up property interests in perpetuity. Since much of English law had been concerned with the free alienability of land, the courts viewed this prospect with alarm and set about (with all deliberate speed) the task of restraining too much "dead hand" control. The result was the Rule against Perpetuities—a deceptively stated Rule that has led to fantastic amounts of litigation and volumes of learned exegesis, expounding (and complicating) the application of the Rule. A little learning is a dangerous thing and no attempt will be made here to explain the full ramifications of the Rule, although you should be aware of its existence and should study it in detail in later courses in the curriculum. If you wish a short explanation at this time,

14. A full discussion of powers of appointment is beyond the scope of this text. For a brief discussion see Powell on Real Property 479–525. (Abridged Ed. Powell and Rohan (1968).

15. While executory interests, both springing and shifting, have full legal recognition today, they cannot be used to reach a result that is contrary to public policy. Thus, in Capitol Federal Savings & Loan Ass'n v. Smith, 136 Colo. 265, 316 P.2d 252 (1957) the court refused to enforce a shifting interest which would have prevented the sale of land to black persons.

you should read the justly popular article, "Perpetuities in a Nutshell" by the late Professor Leach of Harvard.[16] It will show something of the complex character of the Rule.

Professor Gray's classic statement of the Rule was as follows: "No interest is good unless it must vest, if at all, not later than twenty-one years after some life in being at the creation of the interest." It was a rule against remoteness of vesting and so long as the estate was vested in interest, even though not in possession, the Rule was not violated. After all, a fee simple absolute had a potentially infinite duration and that was no obstacle if someone had the power to alienate the land. The vice lay in tying up the land with non-destructible contingent interests in perpetuity. The Rule was designed to allow suspension of vesting for the lifetime or lifetimes of individuals living at the effective date of the deed, will, or trust plus the minority (hence twenty-one years) of someone not yet in being. (Later the twenty-one years was extended to include a period of gestation, twenty-one years plus nine months.) If the estate *might* vest in interest at a period more remote than that it was void for remoteness, being viewed as a perpetuity. The rest of the grant or devise was valid but the "gift over" failed and the intent of the grantor or testator was thwarted. Obviously, a devise to a living person for life, followed by a contingent interest in his issue (vesting on the death of the life tenant or within twenty-one years plus a period of gestation thereafter) was all right but attempts to keep the interest contingent through succeeding generations of the family would raise the spectre of the Rule.

One illustration, with which you are already acquainted, will demonstrate the complexities of the Rule. *O* devises Blackacre "to *A* and his heirs for so long as no liquor is sold on the premises." *A* has a fee simple determinable and *O* has a possibility of reverter. The Rule does not apply because a possibility of reverter, in common-law theory, is vested in interest (being a reversionary interest) and if liquor is ever sold on the premises (regardless of how long in the future, absent some special statute on the matter) *O* or his heirs will get the land, which will then vest in possession. If, however, *O* devises Blackacre "to *A* and his heirs for so long as no liquor is sold on the premises but if liquor shall ever be sold on the premises then to *B* and his heirs", the interest given to *B* is void as violating the Rule Against Perpetuities. *A* had a fee simple subject to an executory limitation and *B* had an executory interest of the shifting type, which does *not* vest in interest until liquor is, in fact, sold on the premises. Since this *might* be at a time more remote than lives in being plus twenty-one years it is void *ab initio.*[17]

16. Leach, Perpetuities in a Nutshell, 51 Harv.L.Rev. 638 (1938). Note Professor Leach's own *caveat.* "If this paper fails of its purpose it has, at least, eminent company. Lord Thurlow undertook to put the Rule in Shelley's case in a nutshell. 'But,' said Lord Macnaghten, 'it is one thing to put a case like Shelley's in a nutshell and another to keep it there.' Van Grutten v. Foxwell, [1897] A.C. 658, 671."

17. It will surely occur to the alert student that it might be wise to wait and see whether the future interest in fact vests within the period of the rule rather than declare it void *ab initio.* If it vests within that time frame well and good; if it does not, *then* declare it void. While the common law refused this more sensible approach, the wait-and-see method has been adopted by the American Law Institute's Restatement (Second) of Property (Donative Transfers Section 1.3 (1983)) and by the National Conference of Commissioners on Uniform State Laws when they ap-

A would still have his defeasible fee which he could lose if liquor is ever sold on the premises, but the future interest would be in *O* or his heirs not in *B*.[18] Of course, *O* could have saved the "gift over" to *B* by stipulating that if liquor is sold during the lifetime of *A* or twenty-one years thereafter then the land is to pass to *B* and his heirs.

Similarly, if *O* devised Blackacre "to *A* and his heirs at such time as liquor shall be sold on the premises", the interest in *A* would be void for violating the Rule. *A* would have had an executory interest of the springing type (springing out of *O*'s heirs if liquor is ever sold on the premises) but, since the interest cannot vest until liquor is in fact sold, that *might* occur at a time more remote than allowed by the Rule and it must fail. *O*'s heirs (or devisees) would take Blackacre freed of the executory interest in *A*.

This brief look at an intricate Rule should be sufficient to demonstrate why lawyers engaged in the property practice, especially in the drafting of wills and trusts, should have a thorough understanding of the subject. There is no reason why the client's interest cannot be adequately protected at the drafting stage (preventive law) but once the Rule has been violated it may require expensive litigation to settle the rights of the parties.

Somewhat related to the problems covered by Rule Against Perpetuities are the numerous attempts to place restraints on the alienation of land. True, the Rule is concerned solely with the remoteness of vesting but its objective is to allow freer alienability and prevent the accumulation of large interests which no one can transfer. Having been astute to frustrate the landowner's desire to tie up his property in perpetuity by creating non-destructible future interests, the courts could scarcely be expected to allow more direct restraints on alienation which would have the same effect. Thus, a conveyance "to *A* and his heirs, provided he never sells, mortgages, or otherwise transfers the land" is a direct restraint on alienation and hence void. The basic principle is clear enough but its application can be difficult. If the restraint is a reasonable one, e.g., prohibiting transfer to a small group or for a limited purpose, but leaving a wide range of volition in the grantee, it will be enforceable. The key issue is: what is reasonable? Like the Rule, the range of problems caused by attempted restraints is beyond the scope of this text and must be left to the student's initiative by a perusal of the excellent material on the subject[19] or to later courses in the property field.

---

proved the Uniform Statutory Rule Against Perpetuities, already adopted in at least three states—Minnesota, Nevada and South Carolina. The Uniform Act also adopts another wrinkle, substituting a flat period of 90 years rather than the use of actual measuring lives which has caused so much confusion in the law. The combination of a refined wait-and-see doctrine plus the flat 90-year period makes the statutory rule simple, fair, and workable, while still carrying out the policy of the law against remoteness of vesting. For an excellent discussion of this newest development in an ancient rule, see Waggoner, The Uniform Statutory Rule Against Perpetuities, 21 Real Property Probate and Trust Journal 569 (1986).

18. First Universalist Society of North Adams v. Boland, 155 Mass. 171, 29 N.E. 524 (1892).

19. See, for example, Schnebly, Restraints upon the Alienation of Legal Interests, 44 Yale L.J. 961, 1186, 1380 (1935).

V. OTHER ASPECTS OF EQUITY

Equity's principal impact on the law of property came through the ancient use, modified into the modern trust. It must not be supposed, however, that this was equity's sole contribution to property law. Chancery's jurisdiction depended, in the main, on the inadequacy of the remedy at law. Thus, you could expect that the chancellor would range across the whole field of the common law and that eventually equity would come to permeate most areas of contract, tort, and property. So extensive was this infiltration that today, following the merger of law and equity, it is often difficult to tell whether a particular rule was legal or equitable in origin. If it really makes a difference which it is, as in cases where the right to a jury trial is in dispute, the lawyer may have to undertake a sizable piece of historical research.

Aside from trusts, the principal areas of equitable concern in property matters are: (1) the specific performance of real estate contracts; (2) the cancellation and rescission of contracts and deeds for fraud, mistake, duress, undue influence, and lack of capacity to contract (insanity, infancy, etc.); (3) the enforcement of covenants relating to land under the doctrine of equitable servitudes; and (4) the equity of redemption and certain other features of the law of mortgages. Some of these points are beyond the scope of this book and so will not be mentioned again; others will receive further treatment in connection with later portions of our discussion.

NOTES

1. To test your understanding of the preceding text material consider each of the following problems. What would be the result in each instance before and after the Statute of Uses? Explain the reasoning behind the conclusions you reach.

SIGNIFICANCE OF THE STATUTE OF USES

I. *IN GENERAL*

1. O enfeoffed B and his heirs to the use of C and his heirs. What result before and after the Statute of Uses?

2. O enfeoffed B and his heirs. (No consideration paid; no use stated.) Resulting use in O.

3. O enfeoffed B and his heirs for the use of C for life. Resulting use in O.

II. *NEW METHODS OF CONVEYANCING*

4. O bargained and sold to B and his heirs (consideration paid).

5. O convenanted to stand seised to the use of B and his heirs. (B is a relative by blood or marriage to O.)

III. *NEW TYPES OF FUTURE INTERESTS—EXECUTORY INTERESTS*

6. O bargained and sold to B for life and one year after B's death to C and his heirs. Springing interest in C.

7. O bargained and sold to B and his heirs but if B dies without having had children then to C and his heirs. Shifting interest in C.

IV. *THE MODERN TRUST*

8. O enfeoffed B and his heirs to the use of C and his heirs to the use of D and his heirs. Use *on* a use.

9. O bargained and sold to B and his heirs to the use of C and his heirs. Another example of a use *on* a use.

10. O enfeoffed B and his heirs to the use of C for life and on C's death to the use of D and his heirs. Use *after* a use so statute executes and no trust is involved.

11. O bequeathed $25,000 to B for the use of C. Statute of Uses does not apply to personalty so a trust is created.

12. O enfeoffed B and his heirs to the use of C and his heirs with B having the duty to handle the renting of land, pay all bills, etc. and account to C for the net profits. Statute of Uses does not apply to active uses, only passive, so a trust is created.

2. Of course, the actual cases will be more complex than the simple problems set out above but the basic principle is the same. Now try your hand on the following three cases and see if you can understand the reasoning behind the courts' results.

STOLLER v. DOYLE

Supreme Court of Illinois, 1913.
257 Ill. 369, 100 N.E. 959.

CARTWRIGHT, J. On April 13, 1882, Lawrence Doyle and wife executed a warranty deed to Frank Doyle of the W. ½ of the S.E. ¼ of section 18, township 27, range 3, in Livingston county, in the form prescribed by section 9 of the conveyance act, but with the following restrictions and limitations: "Said Frank Doyle shall not have power to reconvey this land, unless it be to the grantor. He shall not have power to mortgage the land, and in case the said Frank Doyle should die before his wife dies, and any children survive him, the surviving children and his wife shall have the use of the land above described during the lifetime of his wife, when it shall go to his children, if any are living, but, if at the death of the grantee no children survive him, the title shall be in the grantors. Should any children survive the grantee and his wife also survive him, she shall have no [an?] interest in the land only so long as she remains unmarried and is his widow." On February 23, 1897, Lawrence Doyle, then a widower, executed a second deed of the same premises, in the same form, to Frank Doyle, omitting the restrictions and conditions, and containing the statement that it was made for the purpose of removing the restrictions contained in the former deed, and was meant to give the grantee an absolute title to the premises. On March 1, 1902, Frank Doyle and wife executed a warranty deed of that tract and other land to the defendant in error, John A. Stoller. On October 15, 1903, Stoller and Eilert Bauman made a contract by which Stoller agreed to convey to Bauman in fee simple, clear of all incumbrances, by a good and sufficient warranty deed, said tract of land and another tract of 80 acres. Bauman paid $1,500 cash, and there was, in the contract, a stipulation fixing $1,500 as liquidated damages to be paid by the party failing to perform. Stoller tendered a deed to Bauman, which Bauman refused to accept, because the abstract delivered in accordance with the contract did not show a merchantable title. Stoller, insisting that his title was a fee simple, filed a bill to compel specific performance of the contract; and, a demurrer to the bill having been sustained, it was dismissed without prejudice. Bauman then brought suit in the circuit court of Livingston county against Stoller to recover the cash payment of $1,500, with interest, and the $1,500 liquidated damages. The case was tried by the court, and the court held, on propositions of law, that by the first deed of April 13, 1882, a contingent interest in the real estate was conveyed to the children of Frank Doyle, the grantee, and that the later deed to him could not affect that interest, and therefore the abstract did not show a merchantable title. Accordingly there was a finding that the title was not merchantable, and a judgment for Bauman for $3,251.81 and costs. The Appellate Court for the Second District affirmed the judgment, and we affirmed the judgment of the Appellate Court, and that case came to an end on October 8, 1908. Bauman v. Stoller, 235 Ill. 480, 85 N.E. 657. These facts appear in the statement preceding the opinion in that case, but for convenience are repeated here.

After the decision, in the action at law, that the title of John A. Stoller was not merchantable, he filed his bill on April 10, 1909, in said circuit court of Livingston county against Doyle's children, alleging that by the first deed Frank Doyle did not take an estate in fee simple, but only an estate for life; that his wife took an estate for life, contingent upon her outliving him; that his children took a contingent remainder in fee; that there was an ultimate reversion in fee to the grantor in the event that no children survived Frank Doyle; and that the second deed to him conveyed the reversion, whereby the life estate was merged in the fee and the intervening contingent interests were destroyed. The prayer of the bill was that the defendant in error be declared the owner in fee simple of the premises, free and clear of any claims of the children, and that his title thereto should be quieted. The adult defendants were defaulted; but six of the children who were defendants were infants, and they answered by Steven R. Baker, who was appointed their guardian ad litem. The issue was referred to the master in chancery to take and report the evidence. The court heard the testimony taken by the master, made findings in accordance with the averments of the bill, and decreed that the defendant in error was the owner in fee simple of the premises, and quieted his title. Three of the defendants, who were still infants, John J. Doyle, Augustin D. Doyle, and Theresa Veronica Doyle, by Steven R. Baker (who had been their guardian ad litem in the circuit court), acting as their next friend, sued out a writ of error from this court to review the decree. We confirmed the action of the next friend, and appointed him guardian ad litem in this court. The adult defendants, who were defaulted in the trial court, and those who had reached their majority, whose names were used in suing out the writ of error, upon being brought into this court were content to abide by the decree, and refused to assign errors, whereupon an order of severance was entered, and it was ordered that the cause proceed in the name of the infants as plaintiffs in error.

When the deeds to Frank Doyle were under consideration in the former case on the appeal of the defendant in error, John A. Stoller, we decided that they did not give him a merchantable title; that the trial court did not err in holding propositions of law that, by the first deed, the children of Frank Doyle acquired a contingent interest in the real estate; and that the later deed to him could not affect that interest. The argument for the defendant in error at that time was that the first deed vested in Frank Doyle title in fee simple to the premises, and that the condition restricting alienation and the attempted limitations on the fee were repugnant to the estate granted, and therefore void. It was not then, and is not now, claimed that the restraint upon alienation was valid; but it was contended that there was no repugnancy between the granting clause and the conditional limitations, because the statutory form of deed did not include such words as were necessary to transfer an estate of inheritance at common law, and therefore the estate granted could be limited by express words or by construction or operation of law. We concurred in that view, and held that conditional limitations might be created in a deed made in the statutory form. The holding of the trial court that the later deed could not affect the interest of the children was approved, and the decision on these questions disposed of the case. The exact nature of the future interest was not the subject of argument; and, not being material, no attention was given to that question. In referring to the propositions of law, it was mentioned as a contingent interest, which the later deed could not affect, and this was equivalent to saying that it was indestructible, and in the last sentence of the opinion it was called a contingent remainder, but whether it could be designated by that name was of no importance. In this case, on account of the averments of the bill and the argument of counsel, the question whether there was a contingent remainder is material and controlling.

The defendant in error, by his bill of complaint in this case, alleged that the children by the first deed took a contingent remainder in the land; that Frank Doyle took a life estate; and that the second deed conveyed the reversion to him, so that the life estate merged in the fee, and the intervening contingent interests were extinguished.

A remainder is a remnant of an estate in land, depending upon a particular prior estate created at the same time and by the same instrument, and limited to arise immediately on the determination of that estate, and not in abridgment of it. 4 Kent's Com. 197, 2 Washburn on Real Prop. 585; 2 Blackstone's Com. 164; Viggerstaff v. Van Pelt, 207 Ill. 611, 69 N.E. 804. No remainder can be created without a precedent estate, which is said to support the remainder; and, where the particular estate, supporting a remainder, comes to an end before the happening of the event upon which the remainder is to take effect, the remainder is defeated. Under that rule, where the reversion and life estate come together in the same person, the life estate merges in the reversion and comes to an end, and a contingent remainder is destroyed. Bond v. Moore, 236 Ill. 576, 86 N.E. 386, 19 L.R.A.,N.S., 540.[20]

Looking at the deed of April 13, 1882, to determine what estate was granted, we find that, under sections 9 and 13 of the conveyance act (Hurd's Rev.St.1911, c. 30), a statutory warranty deed is to be deemed and held a conveyance in fee simple, although words formerly necessary to transfer an estate of inheritance are not contained in it. To create an estate in fee simple at common law, it was necessary that the grant should be to the grantee and his heirs without limitation. Lehndorf v. Cope, 122 Ill. 317, 13 N.E. 505. A deed in the statutory form, under the sections mentioned, is to be held a conveyance in fee simple; but a less estate may be limited by express words, or may appear to have been granted or conveyed by construction or operation of law. The estate granted to Frank Doyle was therefore a fee simple, except as limited by the deed. It was subject to conditional limitations, which might terminate it; but, unless the contingent events took place, it would last forever. There was one contingency, and but one, upon which it would cease to be a fee, and that was the event that the grantee's wife should survive him. If the contingent future event of the death of the grantee before his wife should occur, and any children should survive him, the wife and surviving children were to have the use of the land during the lifetime of the wife, the interest of the wife to terminate if she remarried, and after her death the fee was to go to the children; but, if at the death of the grantee no children should survive him, there was a reversion to the grantor. The grantor conveyed the whole estate, except a contingent reversion dependent on the grantee dying without leaving children surviving him. The future interest of the wife and children under that deed will take effect, if at all, in derogation of the estate of the grantee conveyed by the granting clause of the deed. Such a limitation could not be created by a deed at common law; but a deed of bargain and sale, such as the deed in this case, takes effect under the statute of uses, and such a limitation is valid. Although that question did not arise upon the record in Abbott v. Abbott, 189 Ill. 488, 59 N.E. 958, 82 Am.St.Rep. 470, it was argued by counsel, and it was held that the argument supported the proposition, "that where the fee in the first taker created by a deed is made determinable, as upon the happening of a valid condition subsequent, followed by a limitation over of the fee or use to another upon the happening of the prescribed event, the fee or use shifts from the first to

20. In 1921 Illinois abolished the destructibility doctrine in the following language: "No future interest shall fail or be defeated by the determination of any precedent estate or interest prior to the happening of the event or contingency on which the future interest is limited to take effect". Ill.Rev.Stat. ch. 30, § 40 (1985). This Act is prospective in operation only but what effect would such an Act have had on the present case if it had been operative when the deed in question was delivered?

the second taker, whereby the deed is a conveyance under the statute of uses, as all our American deeds are, and is a clear case of shifting use." The estate of the children was limited to take effect in derogation of the estate of the grantee, created by the granting clause. The deed operated as a conveyance of the fee, with the limitations over, which may terminate the estate granted upon the conditions specified in the deed, and did not create a contingent remainder destructible by the act of the grantor in subsequently conveying the reversion to the grantee. The conclusion in Bauman v. Stoller, supra, that the second deed to Doyle did not affect the contingent interest of his children was correct.

The adults being satisfied with the decree, a reversal will not affect their interests; but, as to the interests of the plaintiffs in error, the decree is reversed, and the cause is remanded to the circuit court, with directions to dismiss the bill as to them.

Reversed and remanded, with directions.[21]

NOTE

At this point, you should re-read Abo Petroleum Corp. v. Amstutz, 93 N.M. 332, 600 P.2d 278 (1979) page 277 supra. Illinois abolished the destructibility doctrine by statute in 1921, New Mexico did so by judicial decision in 1979. Do you see any difference in the legal effect of the two methods of abolition? What about retroactive versus prospective operation of the abolition? Why may statutory change have been desirable in Illinois but not necessary in New Mexico? What does this difference show about the relative impact of the English common law on the law of the various American states?

CAPITOL FEDERAL SAVINGS & LOAN ASSOCIATION v. SMITH

Supreme Court of Colorado, 1957.
136 Colo. 265, 316 P.2d 252.

KNAUSS, JUSTICE. For convenience we shall refer to the parties to this writ of error as they appeared in the trial court, where defendants in error were plaintiffs and plaintiffs in error were defendants.

Two claims were stated in plaintiff's amended complaint, one for a decree quieting title to real property, a second to obtain a declaratory judgment. Plaintiffs alleged that they were the owners of and in possession of certain lots in Block 6 Ashley's Addition to Denver and that on May 9, 1942 certain owners of lots in said Block, including plaintiffs' predecessors in title, entered into an agreement among themselves that the lots owned by them should not be sold or leased to colored persons and providing for forfeiture of any lots or parts of lots sold or leased in violation of the agreement to such of the then owners of other lots in said block who might place notice of their claims of record. Plaintiffs further alleged that they were colored persons of

21. See Dukeminier, Contingent Remainders and Executory Interests: A Requiem for the Distinction, 43 Minn.L.Rev. 13 (1958).

negro extraction and that any interest, or claim of any interest of defendants, under said agreement was without foundation of right and in violation of the Constitution of the United States and that said agreement was a cloud on plaintiffs' title which should be removed. Plaintiffs prayed for a complete adjudication of the rights of all parties to the action. Defendants placed of record in the office of the Clerk and Recorder of the City and County of Denver a Notice of Claim asserting that they were owners of lots in said Block 6 embraced in the agreement above mentioned and asserted title to the property which is the subject matter of the complaint by virtue of said agreement. By their answer and counterclaim defendants alleged that they were the owners and entitled to the possession of the real estate described in the complaint by virtue of the forfeiture provisions in the above mentioned agreement, and prayed for a complete adjudication of the rights of all parties and a decree quieting their title to the property in question.

All facts were stipulated and trial was to the court. The trial court entered a decree and declaratory judgment pursuant to Rules 105 and 57, R.C.P.Colo. The court found that the plaintiffs were the owners in fee simple of the property described in the complaint and quieted their title thereto free and clear of any right of enforcement or attempted enforcement of the restrictive covenant or the Notice of Claim filed by defendants. The court further adjudged and decreed that the restrictive covenant "may not be enforced by this court as a matter of law, as to enforce same by this court would be a violation of the equal protection clause of the Fourteenth Amendment of the United States Constitution, and the enforceability of same is hereby removed as a cloud upon the title of plaintiffs . . . ." From the judgment and decree so entered the defendants bring the case here on writ of error.

The covenant or agreement under consideration was dated May 9, 1942 and the several signatories to the contract agreed for themselves, their heirs and assigns "not to sell or lease the said above described lots and parcels of land owned by them respectively . . . to any colored person or persons, and covenant and agree not to permit any colored person or persons to occupy said premises during the period from this date to January 1, 1990." It further provided that if any of said property "shall be conveyed or leased in violation of this agreement" the right, title or interest of the owner so violating the agreement "shall be forfeited to and rest in such of the then owners of all of said lots and parcels of land not included in such conveyance or lease who may assert title thereto by filing for record notice of their claim . . . ."

The agreement also provided for an action to recover damages against any person or persons who violated the restriction, "or such owners may jointly or severally enforce or have their rights hereunder enforced by an action for specific performance, abatement, ejectment, or by injunction or any other proper judicial proceedings, which right shall be in addition to any and all right to the interest so conveyed or leased in violation of this agreement."

It is contended by counsel for defendants that the Supreme Court of the United States in Shelley v. Kraemer, 334 U.S. 1, 68 S.Ct. 836, 92 L.Ed. 1161, McGhee v. Sipes, 334 U.S. 1, 68 S.Ct. 836, 92 L.Ed. 1161 and Barrows v. Jackson, 346 U.S. 249, 73 S.Ct. 1031, 97 L.Ed. 1586, did not have before it an agreement "for automatic forfeiture, nor did any of them create a future interest in the land." Counsel assert that they have no quarrel with these decisions, stating that the Supreme Court "has been concerned solely with the question of judicial enforcement of restrictive covenants by injunction or by damages."

Covenants such as the one here considered, whether denominated "executory interests" or "future interests," as urged by counsel for defendants, cannot change the character of what was here attempted.

Counsel for defendants contend that the agreement in question entered into by the predecessors in interest of plaintiffs and defendants did not create a "private anti-racial restrictive covenant." Instead they claim that it created a future interest in the land known as an executory interest. They assert, "Such interest vested automatically in the defendants upon the happening of the events specified in the original instrument of grant, and the validity of the vesting did not in any way depend upon judicial action by the courts. The trial court's failure and refusal to recognize the vested interest of the defendants, and its ruling that the defendants have no title or interest in or to the property, deprived the defendants of their property without just compensation and without due process of law." We cannot agree.

In the amended complaint numerous persons, firms and corporations were named as defendants, but in designating the record to be filed in this court only the amended complaint, the answer and counterclaim of the defendants Whitney J. Armelin, Carmelita Armelin and Capitol Federal Savings and Loan Association, together with plaintiff's reply thereto, the stipulation of facts together with the judgment and decree of the trial court, are specified. The record was amended on motion of Midland Federal Savings and Loan Association to include its answer in which the allegations of the amended complaint were admitted and said association prayed that plaintiffs be awarded the relief demanded in their amended complaint. We are not advised as to pleadings filed by the other defendants, including Robert E. Lee, Public Trustee and the City and County of Denver, who with the Midland Federal Savings and Loan Association are named as defendants in error in the instant case.

We are unable to rid ourselves of a strong impression that this writ of error is being prosecuted in the interest of title examiners, rather than in that of the property owners in Block 6 Ashley's Addition to Denver. In the brief of counsel for plaintiffs in error we find this significant language: "Title examiners are in constant apprehension as to whether a title may be passed where these restrictive covenants prevail, and we feel that we should call upon this Honorable Body as to the doubts of this decision."

No matter by what ariose terms the covenant under consideration may be classified by astute counsel, it is still a racial restriction in violation of the Fourteenth Amendment to the Federal Constitution. That this is so has been definitely settled by the decisions of the Supreme Court of the United States. High-sounding phrases or outmoded common-law terms cannot alter the effect of the agreement embraced in the instant case. While the hands may seem to be the hands of Esau to a blind Isaac, the voice is definitely Jacob's. We cannot give our judicial approval or blessing to a contract such as is here involved.

In Shelley v. Kraemer, supra [334 U.S. 1, 68 S.Ct. 845], the Supreme Court of the United States said:

"We hold that in granting judicial enforcement of the restrictive agreements in these cases, the States have denied petitioners the equal protection of the laws and that, therefore, the action of the state courts cannot stand. We have noted that freedom from discrimination by the States in the enjoyment of property rights was among the basic objectives sought to be effectuated by the framers of the Fourteenth Amendment. That such discrimination has occurred in these cases is clear. Because of the race or color of these petitioners they have been denied rights of ownership or occupancy enjoyed as a matter of course by other citizens of different race or color. The Fourteenth Amendment declares 'that all persons, whether colored, or white, shall stand equal before the laws of the States, and, in regard to the colored race, for whose protection the amendment was primarily designed, that *no discrimination shall be made against them by law because of their color.*' " (Emphasis supplied.)

Because the language of the United States Supreme Court suggested that private racially restrictive covenants were not invalid per se, it was believed for some time that an action for damages might lie against one who violated such a covenant. A number of state courts adopted this position, and awarded damages against those who, contrary to their agreements, had made sales of property to negroes or other persons within the excluded classes. This problem came to the attention of the Supreme Court of the United States in Barrows v. Jackson, 346 U.S. 249, 253–254, 258, 259, 73 S.Ct. 1031, 97 L.Ed. 1586, where it was held that although such a grantor's constitutional rights were not violated, nevertheless the commodious protection of the Fourteenth Amendment extended to her and she could not be made to respond in damages for treating her restrictive covenant as a nullity.

Because the United States Supreme Court has extracted any teeth which such a covenant was supposed to have, no rights, duties or obligations can be based thereon.

The judgment is affirmed.

FRANTZ, J., not participating.

NOTES

1. For another example of an executory interest, designated by the court as a "springing executory interest" see Southern Illinois Conference of the Methodist Church v. The City of Edwardsville, 33 Ill. App.3d 642, 342 N.E.2d 315 (1975). The will in that case read:

"I give and devise my home property located at 918 St. Louis St., Edwardsville, Illinois to the City of Edwardsville as a site for a hospital, provided the said city accepts this devise for the purpose specified within one year after my death and if the city does not accept this devise within one year after my death, then said property shall go to the Southern Illinois Conference of the Methodist Church as a site for an old folk's home or in its discretion as a site for a Wesley Memorial for the benefit of the Edwardsville branch of Southern Illinois University, provided the Southern Illinois Conference of the Methodist Church accepts the devise for the purpose specified within two years after my death. If neither the City of Edwardsville nor the Southern Illinois Conference of the Methodist Church accepts this devise for the purposes indicated within the time specified, I give and devise said property to the city of Edwardsville for use as a public park."

The court said: "Acceptance of the property by the city within one year of [testatrix'] death was therefore the only condition precedent to the vesting of the city's interest. [There was no condition precedent that the hospital be actually built within a specific time.] The interest that the will gave to the city was a springing executory interest, which was to become a vested and possessory fee simple interest upon the city's timely acceptance."

(N.C. opinion) 2. The termination of a fee simple determinable was thought not to involve state action in Charlotte Park & Recreation Commission v. Barringer, 242 N.C. 311, 88 S.E.2d 114 (1955), certiorari denied 350 U.S. 983, 76 S.Ct. 469, 100 L.Ed. 851 (1956).

Similarly, a majority of the United States Supreme Court could find no state action in the reverter by operation of state law to the heirs of a devisor of land which he had devised in trust for a municipal park for whites only, the trust failing for want of a legitimate purpose. Evans v. Abney, 396 U.S. 435, 90 S.Ct. 628, 24 L.Ed.2d 634 (1970). For the court, Justice Black said: "When a city park is destroyed because the Constitution requires it to be integrated, there is reason for everyone to be disheartened. . . . Here, however, the action of the Georgia Supreme Court declaring the Baconsfield trust terminated presents no violation of constitutionally protected rights, and any harshness that may have resulted from the state court's decision can be attributed solely to its intention to effectuate as nearly as possible the explicit terms of Senator Bacon's will. . . . Similarly, the situation presented in this case is also easily distinguishable from that presented in Shelley v. Kraemer, 334 U.S. 1, 68 S.Ct. 836, 92 L.Ed. 1161 (1948), where we held unconstitutional state judicial action which had affirmatively enforced a private scheme of discrimination against Negroes. Here the effect of the Georgia decision eliminated all discrimination against Negroes in the park by eliminating the park itself, and the termination of the park was a loss shared equally by the white and Negro citizens . . .. The Baconsfield trust 'failed' under that law not because of any belief on the part of any living person that whites and Negroes might not enjoy being together but, rather, because Senator Bacon who died many years ago intended that the park remain forever for the exclusive use of white people. . . . [T]he loss of charitable trusts such as Baconsfield is part of the price we pay for permitting deceased persons to exercise continuing control over assets owned by them at death."

In a dissenting opinion, Justice Brennan found discriminatory state action:

"[A] state may not close down a public facility solely to avoid its duty to desegregate that facility. . . . Nothing in the record suggests that . . . the City of Macon retracted its previous willingness to manage Baconsfield on a nonsegregated basis, or that the white beneficiaries of Senator Bacon's generosity were unwilling to share it with Negroes, rather than have the park revert to his heirs. . . . Thus, so far as the record shows, this is a case of a state court's enforcement of a racial restriction to prevent willing parties from dealing with one another. The decision of the Georgia courts thus, under Shelley v. Kraemer, constitutes state action denying equal protection. . . ."

In a subsequent case, Palmer v. Thompson, 403 U.S. 217, 91 S.Ct. 1940, 29 L.Ed.2d 438 (1971), the court upheld the closing of public pools in Jackson, Mississippi.

THE CITY OF KLAMATH FALLS v. BELL

Court of Appeals of Oregon, 1971.
7 Or.App. 330, 490 P.2d 515.

SCHWAB, CHIEF JUDGE. In 1925, a corporation conveyed certain land to the city of Klamath Falls as a gift for use as the site for a city library. The deed provided, among other things, that the city should hold the land "so long as" it complied with that condition with regard to its use.

In 1969, the city terminated the use of the land for a library, and the question presented by this appeal is, "Does the title to the land remain in the city or did the termination of use as a library cause title to pass to the descendants of the shareholders of the donor-corporation (now dissolved)?"

The issue was presented to the trial court in the form of an agreed narrative statement, pertinent portions of which, in addition to the facts set forth above, are: the donor-corporation was known as the Daggett-Schallock Investment Company; the corporate deed provided that if at any time the city ceased to use the land for library purposes, title to the land should pass to Fred Schallock and Floy R. Daggett, their heirs and assigns; on September 19, 1927, the corporation was voluntarily dissolved, all creditors paid, and all assets (which we interpret as including the rights of the corporation, if any, in the land in question) were distributed in accordance with law to the sole shareholders Schallock and Daggett.

The city of Klamath Falls built a library on the land in 1926 in compliance with the conditions set out in the deed. The library continued in use from that date until July 1, 1969, when the books were moved to the County Library Building. Since that time, the city library services have been provided by Klamath County on a contract basis. The City Library building has not been used for any other purpose and now stands vacant.

After the library closure, the city of Klamath Falls filed a complaint against all the heirs of Schallock and Daggett for declaratory judgment pursuant to ORS ch. 28, asking the court to adjudicate the respective rights of the parties under the deed. The city joined Constance F. Bell, the sole heir of Fred Schallock, and Marijane Flitcraft and Caroline Crapo, the sole heirs of Floy R. Daggett, along with George C. Flitcraft, the husband of Marijane Flitcraft, and Paul Crapo, the husband of Caroline Crapo, as all the necessary parties to the suit.

The defendants Constance F. Bell, Caroline Crapo, and Paul Crapo conveyed their interests in the real property to the defendant Marijane Flitcraft in May and June 1970.

The trial court found that title to the real property was vested in the city of Klamath Falls. Its decision was based on a finding that the gift over to Fred Schallock and Floy R. Daggett was void under the rule against perpetuities.

The deed, in pertinent part, is as follows:

"KNOW ALL MEN BY THESE PRESENTS That Daggett-Schallock Investment Company a corporation organized and existing under the laws of the State of Oregon, for and as a gift and without any consideration, does hereby give, grant and convey unto the City of Klamath Falls, Oregon, so long as it complies with the conditions hereinafter set forth, and thereafter unto Fred Schallock and Floy R. Daggett, their heirs and assigns, the following described parcel of real estate, in Klamath County, Oregon, to-wit

". . .

"To have and to hold the same unto the said City of Klamath Falls, Oregon (and to any other municipal corporation which may lawfully succeed it) so long as it complies with the conditions above set forth, and thereafter unto Fred Schallock and Floy R. Daggett, their heirs and assigns forever.

". . .."

I.

We conclude that the estate that passed to the city under this deed was a fee simple on a special limitation, which is also known as a fee simple determinable, or a base or qualified fee.[1]

The "magic" words "so long as" have generally been held to create such an estate. Simes and Smith, The Law of Future Interests 345, § 287 (2d ed. 1956), states:

1. For a general discussion of Oregon law relevant to this case see O'Connell, Estates on Condition Subsequent and Estates on Special Limitation in Oregon, 18 Or.L.Rev. 63 (1939); Note, The Right of Entry and Possibility of Reverter: Traditional Uses—Subdivisions—Mineral Leases, 2 Will.L.J. 479 (1963). [Footnotes in the case are by the court and numbered accordingly.]

". . . The words of duration 'so long as' will almost certainly be judicially recognized as the distinctive insignia of such an estate, and, if coupled with a provision which clearly calls for an automatic termination of the estate granted, there is little room for construction. . . ."

O'Connell, Estates on Condition Subsequent and Estates on Special Limitation in Oregon, 18 Or.L.Rev. 63, 73 (1939), stresses the use of words:

. . . [T]he creation of an estate on a special limitation is characterized generally by the use of certain words. Typical words are 'so long as,' 'until,' or 'during.' However, any language in the instrument indicating an intent that the estate shall automatically end upon the occurrence of a designated event will be sufficient." See also, Magness v. Kerr et al., 121 Or. 373, 380, 254 P. 1012, 51 A.L.R. 1466 (1927).

One of the features of the fee simple on a special limitation thus created is that it terminates automatically upon breach of condition.[2] Fremont Lbr. Co. v. Starrell Pet. Co., 228 Or. 180, 186, 364 P.2d 773 (1961), and cases cited therein; Clark v. Jones, 173 Or. 106, 107, 144 P.2d 498 (1943); see Wagner v. Wallowa County, 76 Or. 453, 461–466, 148 P. 1140, L.R.A.1916F, 303 (1915).

II.

Upon breach of the condition, the deed provided for a gift over to Fred Schallock and Floy R. Daggett or their heirs and assigns. This gift over was an attempt to grant an executory interest since only an executory interest can follow an earlier grant in fee simple.

The rule against perpetuities applies to executory interests. Agan et al. v. United States National Bank, 227 Or. 619, 626, 363 P.2d 765 (1961); Closset et al. v. Burtchaell et al., 112 Or. 585, 604, 230 P. 554 (1924).

Gray's classic statement of the rule is as follows:

"NO INTEREST IS GOOD UNLESS IT MUST VEST, IF AT ALL, NOT LATER THAN TWENTY-ONE YEARS AFTER SOME LIFE IN BEING AT THE CREATION OF THE INTEREST." Gray, The Rule Against Perpetuities 191, § 201 (4th ed. 1942).

One of the main characteristics of a defeasible fee simple estate is that the first grantee might continue in possession in perpetuity. The city of Klamath Falls could have maintained a library on the site for an indefinite time in the future, or even forever. Therefore, the trial judge correctly found that the gift over to Fred Schallock and Floy R. Daggett, their heirs and assigns, was void *ab initio* under the rule against perpetuities.

2. There would be a different result if the interests of the city of Klamath Falls were characterized as a fee simple on a condition subsequent, which is also known as a fee simple conditional. When such an estate is created, there is no forfeiture until the grantor exercises his right of re-entry. Wagner v. Wallowa County, 76 Or. 453, 148 Pac. 1140 (1915); Raley v. Umatilla County, 15 Or. 172, 179–181, 13 Pac. 890, 3 Am.St.Rep. 142 (1887).

III.

The trial court's conclusion does not, however, dispose of the case at bar. Just because the gift over is invalid, it does not follow that the city of Klamath Falls now has an absolute interest in the property in question. There remains the question of whether under the deed a possibility of reverter remained in the grantor corporation.

When a deed reveals an unquestionable intent to limit the interest of the first grantee (here the city of Klamath Falls) to a fee simple on a special limitation, the courts of the United States do not create an indefeasible estate in the first grantee when a subsequent executory interest (here that of Schallock and Daggett) is void under the rule against perpetuities. Instead, the grantor (here the corporation) retains an interest known as a possibility of reverter.[3]

The general rule has been stated to be: ". . . [W]hen an executory interest, following a fee simple interest in land . . . is void under the rule against perpetuities, the prior interest becomes absolute unless the language of the creating instrument makes it very clear that the prior interest is to terminate whether the executory interest takes effect or not. . . ." Simes and Smith, The Law of Future Interests 316, 318, § 827 (2d ed. 1956).

All the jurisdictions in the United States which have dealt with a determinable fee and an executory interest void under the rule against perpetuities have followed this rule. Fletcher v. Ferrill, 216 Ark. 583, 227 S.W.2d 448, 449, 16 A.L.R.2d 1240 (1950); Brown v. Independent Baptist Church of Woburn, 325 Mass. 645, 91 N.E.2d 922 (1950) (which followed the earlier Massachusetts cases); Institution for Savings in Roxbury and its Vicinity v. Roxbury Home for Aged Women, 244 Mass. 583, 139 N.E. 301 (1923); First Universalist Society of North Adams v. Boland, 155 Mass. 171, 29 N.E. 524, 15 L.R.A. 231 (1892); Leonard v. Burr, 18 N.Y. 96 (1858); Yarbrough v. Yarbrough, 151 Tenn. 221, 269

3. It is well settled that the rule against perpetuities does not apply to possibilities of reverter. Gray, The Rule Against Perpetuities 46, 348, 349, §§ 41, 313, 314 (4th ed. 1942); Simes and Smith, The Law of Future Interests 311, § 825 (2d ed. 1956); Tiffany, Real Property 167, § 404 (3d ed. 1939). This historical anomaly has been criticized for allowing "dead hand rule" and creating "appalling practical results" when a possibility of reverter does fall in many years after the original grant. Leach, Perpetuities in Perspective: Ending the Rule's Reign of Terror, 65 Harv.L.Rev. 721, 739 (1952); Leach, Perpetuities: The Nutshell Revisited, 78 Harv.L.Rev. 973, 980 (1965).

However, as pointed out in 18 Or.L.Rev. supra, at 79:

". . . [A] rule restricting the alienation of such interests will tend to avoid a long-outstanding 'contingent' interest and thereby effectuate the policy behind the rule against perpetuities . . . it would be far more desirable to expressly make rights of entry and possibilities of reverter subject to the rule against perpetuities rather than accomplish the same result by indirection."

Where the rule against perpetuities has been applied to possibilities of reverter, it has always been done by legislative action. See, 78 Harv.L.Rev. 973, supra, at 989; Sparks, A Decade of Transition in Future Interests, 45 Va.L.Rev. 339, 362 (1959).

S.W. 36 (1924). This conclusion is favored by Restatement, 2 Property, app. 34–47, §§ 228, 229.

IV.

However, before this conclusion can be reached, an unusual Oregon rule must be considered. Oregon is one of a small minority of states that holds that a possibility of reverter cannot be alienated, Magness v. Kerr, 121 Or. 373, 383, 254 P. 1012, 51 A.L.R. 1466 (1927); see, Annotation, 53 A.L.R.2d 224 (1957), but the Oregon Supreme Court has never held that an attempt to alienate a possibility of reverter destroys it. In the case at bar, the grantor-corporation did attempt to alienate the possibility of reverter with its abortive gift over to Schallock and Daggett.[4] Thus, the question of whether an attempt to alienate a possibility of reverter destroys it is presented to an Oregon appellate court for the first time.

The Oregon Supreme Court has dealt with the consequences that follow a grantor's attempt to transfer the interest that remains in him when he grants a defeasible fee on two occasions.

Wagner v. Wallowa County, supra, involved a fee simple estate on a condition subsequent. The grantors gave land to the county for a high school. The county had taken possession of the land and had built and operated a high school on the property until the electorate voted to abolish the school. The election was held November 5, 1912. Prior to the election, during October 1912, the plaintiff and his wife had executed a deed to a Wallowa County school district. The court there applied a strict rule of construction and found that the grantors destroyed their right to re-enter when they attempted to convey it before the breach of the condition.

In Magness v. Kerr et al., supra, the Oregon Supreme Court dealt with a fee simple determinable:

> ". . . [T]he rule applied in the Wallowa County cases that an attempted conveyance by the grantor of his possibility of reverter, operates to destroy his right and vest an indefeasible estate in his first grantee, ought not to be applied in this case. First, the rule is a harsh one and produces a result not contemplated by the parties to the transaction, and therefore ought not to be applied unless required by some positive rule of law; secondly, in this case under the admitted facts in the case, the estate granted to the Equity Queen Canning Company had been determined by its failure to use the property for co-operative purposes, which was the contingency by which the estate was to be divested, and since by the happening of such a contingency the estate had been determined and the property had reverted. . . ." 121 Or. at 383, 254 P. at 1016.

While *Magness* criticizes the holding in *Wagner* as harsh, that portion of *Magness* is dictum, for *Magness* turned on the fact that the event

4. ORS 93.120 provides:

". . . Any conveyance of real estate passes all the estate of the grantor, unless the intent to pass a lesser estate appears by express terms, or is necessarily implied in the terms of the grant."

upon which the estate was to end had occurred before the transfer of the future interest.

Nothing in *Wagner* or *Magness* is conclusive in determining whether an attempt to alienate a possibility of reverter destroys it.

In Pure Oil Co. v. Miller-McFarland Drilling Co., 376 Ill. 486, 34 N.E.2d 854, 135 A.L.R. 567 (1941), the Illinois court held that a possibility of reverter is not destroyed when the grantor tries to transfer it, even though the possibility of reverter is not alienable under Illinois law. In Reichard v. Chicago, B. & Q. R. Co., 231 Iowa 563, 729, 1 N.W.2d 721 (1942), which involved a conveyance after termination of a fee simple subject to a special limitation, the same facts as in Magness v. Kerr et al., supra, the court said:

". . . It seems rather fantastic to us, that a conveyance which is ineffective to convey what it attempts to convey is nevertheless an effective means of destroying it. . . ." 231 Iowa at 576, 1 N.W.2d at 729.

We hold that an attempt by a grantor to transfer his possibility of reverter does not destroy it.

V.

The remaining issue is the city's contention that upon dissolution of the corporation in 1927, or at the latest, upon the post-dissolution, winding-up period, ORS 57.630(2),[5] the corporation was civilly dead and without a successor to whom the possibility of reverter could descend. As is pointed out in Addy and Errett v. Short et al., 8 Terry 157, 47 Del. 157, 162, 89 A.2d 136, 139 (1952), the statutory provision for distribution of corporate assets upon dissolution,

". . . is in effect a statutory expansion of the equitable doctrine that upon dissolution of a corporation its property, notwithstanding the technical rules of the early common law, does not escheat to the sovereign or revert to the original grantor, and will be administered . . . for the purpose of winding up the corporate affairs and distributing the assets to those equitably entitled to them. . . ."

In *Addy*, the corporation owning a possibility of reverter was dissolved and five years later the event (the abandonment of the use upon which the deed was conditioned) occurred. Delaware had only a three-year corporate dissolution winding-up period. The Delaware statutes did contain a provision that even after the three-year period, upon applica-

5. ORS 57.630(2) provides:

"Whenever any such corporation is the owner of real or personal property, or claims any interest or lien whatsoever in any real or personal property, such corporation shall continue to exist during such five-year period for the purpose of conveying, transferring and releasing such real or personal property or interest or lien therein, and such corporation shall continue after the expiration of such five-year period to exist as a body corporate for the purpose of being made a party to, and being sued in any action, suit or proceeding against it involving the title to any such real or personal property or any interest therein, and not otherwise; and any such action, suit or proceeding may be instituted and maintained against any such corporation as might have been had prior to the expiration of said five-year period. This section shall not be construed as affecting or suspending any statute of limitations applicable to any suit, action or proceeding instituted hereunder."

tion of creditors or shareholders of a dissolved corporation, the court could appoint a receiver to take charge of the estate of the corporation and to collect debts and property due and belonging to the company. *Addy* held that neither the dissolution of the corporation nor the expiration of the three-year dissolution period worked an extinguishment of the possibility of reverter retained by the deed in question, and that upon the abandonment of the land by the grantee, the possibility of reverter was enlarged to a fee simple title. It further held that as statutory successors to the rights and powers of the corporation the receivers were entitled to the land.

Oregon has no such receivership statute, but the Oregon statutes make it clear that corporate assets no longer escheat or revert to the original grantor upon dissolution. In this case, the parties agree that the corporation was lawfully dissolved, all the creditors paid, and that Daggett and Schallock, the sole shareholders of the corporation, were statutorily entitled to and did receive all of the remaining assets of the corporation. One such asset was the possibility of reverter of the land in question.

The parties further agree that the defendants in this case were all of the heirs of Daggett and Schallock. As is pointed out in 18 Or.L.Rev. 63, supra, there is no Oregon decision on the issue of the descendability of the possibility of reverter. However, the weight of authority recognizes that such an interest is descendable. Restatement, 2 Property 606, Comment *a*, § 164, and 3 Simes 144–45, § 707 (1936). We discern no sound policy considerations which lead us to a contrary conclusion.[6]

Marijane Flitcraft acquired all rights to the property when the other defendants conveyed their interests to her in 1970.

Reversed.

NOTE

This case illustrates an important distinction between executory interests and possibilities of reverter and powers of termination. The first future interest falls within the embrace of the Rule Against Perpetuities, the latter two do not (although they *may* be barred by relevant statutes of limitations—see page 264, supra). The full treatment of the complex Rule Against Perpetuities is reserved for a later course in the curriculum.

6. It is difficult to understand the reason for the rule that a future interest in the nature of a possibility of reverter should be inalienable. 18 Or.L.Rev. 63, supra, at 86.

Chapter 15

CONCURRENT OWNERSHIP

The term "concurrent ownership" might sensibly be used to refer to any situation in which two or more persons simultaneously may assert interests—socially-enforced claims—referable to an item of realty or personalty. As examples, consider lessor and lessee, bailor and bailee, mortgagor and mortgagee, pledgor and pledgee, life tenant and remainderman (or reversioner), owner of a possessory estate and owner of an easement, "true owner" and adverse possessor. In the narrower sense in which lawyers and judges ordinarily use the term, "concurrent ownership" is synonymous with "cotenancy" and refers only to situations in which two or more persons simultaneously have equal rights in the possession and use of land or chattels. Such a situation may be created in various ways; e.g., an owner may die intestate, survived by two or more persons who succeed to ownership in equal or unequal shares, in accordance with a statute of descent and distribution—or an owner may share his ownership with another person (or persons) by conveying whatever fractional "undivided interest (or interests)" he may choose.

This form of ownership may, of course, be satisfactory so long as the co-owners are in harmony concerning the use to be made of their common resource—the sharing of any revenue it may yield—the allocation of such costs of ownership as taxes, maintenance, and insurance—and perhaps other matters. If harmony is lacking and the opponents cannot agree upon truce or compromise, ordinarily the most attractive alternative is to compel termination of the cotenancy relationship through a judicial process termed "partition," but as subsequent materials will show, this solution is not always available.

SECTION 1. INTRODUCTION TO CONCURRENT OWNERSHIP

Except in special circumstances which will be considered hereafter, concurrent owners are termed "tenants in common"—this would be the proper term, for instance, where two or more persons share ownership of property as the result of an intestate succession. Tenants in common are conceived as owning fractional interests which may be equal or unequal—e.g., A, B, C, D may own a one-fourth interest; A may acquire the interests of B and C, so that he owns a three-fourths interest and D one-fourth. All these are termed "undivided interests." This means that none of the cotenants can be said to own an identifiable segment of the realty or personalty, though a partition in kind may result in his sole ownership of a segment. It also means that no cotenant can properly claim a paramount right of possession concerning any segment, however small; instead, each cotenant has a right of possession referable to the whole, coupled with a duty not to interfere with another cotenant's co-extensive right. Obviously, the foregoing statement presents a paradox—two persons cannot occupy the same space at the same time, or as a New Jersey court once put it, "Two men cannot plow the same furrow." If the tenants in common cannot agree upon a manner of allocating their rights of possession, two solutions are possible—one is partition in kind or by sale; or if that is not available or desirable, a somewhat similar device of leasing the entire property and apportioning the rents in accordance with the owners' fractional interests may be feasible. Other alternatives, of course, are conceivable—e.g., one cotenant's purchase of another's interest.

Similar conflicts may develop between cotenants concerning desirability of spending money or labor in improving the property; desirability of efforts to prevent dilapidation or depreciation; or willingness to prevent loss of the property through enforcement of a lien for unpaid taxes or for failure to discharge a mortgage debt. Likewise, there may be situations in which one cotenant occupies or makes some use of the property without the express or tacit consent of another who is not sharing the occupancy or use. The courts have not, in general, found these problems easy to deal with if conflicts result in litigation.

A second form of concurrent ownership, an ancient part of common-law jurisprudence known as "joint tenancy," is rooted in the concept that the cotenants comprise, for at least one purpose, not a number of individuals, each owning an undivided interest, but a corporate unity—a singular legal entity which owns the property. The consequence of this is that joint tenancy involves what is termed "right of survivorship." This signifies that upon the death of one joint tenant no interest can be transferred from him to any other person by testate or intestate succession. The surviving joint tenants (if two or more survive) continue to comprise the unity or entity which owns the property, and eventually the one who lives longest comprises the unit alone and is therefore sole owner. Since the concept is that upon the death of a joint tenant he simply ceases to be a part of the owning entity—i.e., no interest is "transferred" from him to anyone, it might be thought that death taxes and creditors' claims may thus be avoided. These matters will be considered further hereafter.

Before the nineteenth century an inter vivos or testamentary transfer of land in equal shares to two or more persons having no marital relationship created a joint tenancy, unless the transferor clearly manifested intent to create a tenancy in common. This rule of construction, giving effect to a preference of joint tenancy with its characteristic incident, the right of survivorship, is usually ascribed not to a presumption or inference of actual intent based upon probability, but to a feudal policy opposed to dividing the ownership of land held by military tenure—a policy which apparently contributed to the development of rules of inheritance based on primogeniture. Under those rules, despite this policy, two or more daughters, there being no surviving son, shared equally in the inheritance and were thus cotenants. It was early established that they did not hold as joint tenants;

they were not subject to procedural rules which governed joint tenancy, and each had a several interest which, upon her death, was not eliminated by operation of the doctrine of survivorship but was transmitted by inheritance. It was also early established that one of these "coparceners" could compel partition of the land; in contrast, though joint tenants could partition if all consented, no action lay to compel partition until legislation was enacted for the purpose in the reign of Henry VIII. Today there is almost never any need to distinguish coparcenary ownership as a form of cotenancy; though the term is still used occasionally, persons who share an inheritance are usually identified as tenants in common.

If ever there was rational justification for a rule promoting the principle of survivorship without regard to intent, it has long since vanished, and the old rule of construction has everywhere been reversed, either by judicial decision or by legislation. The relevant statutes will be considered briefly hereafter.

Notwithstanding the concept of joint tenants as comprising an entity, they are also regarded, for various purposes, as individuals, each owning an undivided interest—hence, the time-worn statement that joint tenants are "seised pur my et pur tout," meaning that each is both an owner of an undivided interest and an owner of the whole. One consequence is that any of two or more joint tenants can end his participation in the entity by compelling a partition. If the property can be properly partitioned "in kind"—i.e., physically divided, the proper portion will be awarded to the claimant as sole owner; assuming that there are two or more others who wish to continue as joint tenants, the remainder will be awarded to them in joint tenancy. If the property cannot equitably be partitioned in kind, it will be sold by judicial process, and the claimant's share will be paid to him.

A joint tenant can also end his participation in the entity by a deed conveying his undivided interest to any other person, thus effecting what is termed a "severance" of his interest. The grantee, since he cannot be regarded as being within the entity to which the property was originally conveyed, will be regarded as a tenant in common with reference to his interest; the doctrine of survivorship and any other rule (if any) peculiar to joint tenancy will be inapplicable to him. Similarly, a judgment creditor of a joint tenant, by writ of execution, can force a sale of the debtor's undivided interest, and the forced sale will effect a severance, just as a voluntary conveyance will do. It should be noticed that severance of one joint tenant's interest will not affect the relationship of two or more others—they will be treated as continuing to hold their interests in joint tenancy. It should also be noticed that, aside from the doctrine of survivorship, tenancy in common and joint tenancy do not differ in legal consequences; i.e., in many types of disputes between cotenants, the outcome will not be affected by the classification of their cotenancy.

A well-known passage in Blackstone's Commentaries elaborates the so-called fourfold unity of a joint tenancy: (1) the unity of interest means that the joint tenants have like interests, equal undivided shares, in the estate jointly held; (2) the unity of title means that their interests are derived through the same event or events—a single will or conveyance, or a single disseisin; (3) the unity of time means that their interests vest, says Blackstone, at the same time—hence a limitation in remainder or executory interest to the heirs of A and to the heirs of B will not create a joint tenancy if A and B die at different times—but herein lies a difficulty, since a limitation to a class (e.g., the children of A) may create a joint tenancy even though the members of the class come into being and thus acquire their individual interests at different times; (4) the unity of possession means that each joint tenant is seised of the whole estate, not merely of an undivided interest therein.

Though this formula has become widely current in discussion of joint tenancy, it is doubtful that it should be regarded as anything more than a detailed description of joint tenancy; for purposes of analysis it seems less helpful than the simpler concept that joint tenancy is ownership by an ideal unit comprising two or more persons. The notion that the "four unities" must be perfect has led a number of courts to adopt the dogma, hardly comprehensible to a layman, that a person owning land cannot, by a single conveyance, create a joint tenancy if the transferor is to be one of the cotenants—it is necessary to convey to a straw man who reconveys to the intended cotenants. The usual reasoning is that an owner cannot convey an interest (transfer ownership) to himself; hence, his conveyance naming himself and another as grantees is effective only to transfer an undivided interest to the other, so that a tenancy in common is effected but not a joint tenancy, since the unity of title and that of time are lacking. This conclusion might have been avoided by conceiving that the transferor is conveying to an ideal unit, and that his conveyance is effective for the purpose notwithstanding that he participates in the unit. Though this conception is supported by some authority, it has not been widely adopted.

Obviously, no considerations of public policy require that a grantor's manifested intent be denied effect unless he uses the device of a straw man, and some courts, willing to accept the view that mere conceptual difficulty should not be permitted to frustrate an otherwise unobjectionable intent, have held that by an appropriately worded conveyance a grantor may create a joint tenancy for himself and one or more others.[1] In states where the courts have found the conceptual difficulty insurmountable, it is not uncommon to find overriding statutes—see, e.g., the Maine statute quoted in Palmer v. Flint, reprinted at page 383 *infra*.

In some instances, courts unwilling to ignore the conceptual difficulty have managed to give at least partial effect to intent without recognizing a joint tenancy. If A, as grantor, purports to convey "to A and B and their heirs, and to the survivor of them," the deed may be

1. See, for example, Cornell v. Heirs of Walik, 306 Minn. 189, 235 N.W.2d 828 (1975), where the court upheld the creation of a joint tenancy without the use of a straw man. They based their decision on the intent of the parties, however, and declined to abolish the old four-unities' doctrine, observing that the decision might conceivably be to the contrary, given a different factual situation.

construed as conveying to B a life estate as tenant in common, plus a remainder in fee (or executory interest) if he survives A; or it may be held, as in Runions v. Runions, 186 Tenn. 25, 207 S.W.2d 1016, 1 A.L.R.2d 242 (1948), and in Anson v. Murphy, 149 Neb. 716, 32 N.W.2d 271 (1948), that the deed creates a tenancy in common in fee plus a somewhat anomalous "right of survivorship." Do these two constructions differ in effect? Considering the first, it seems plain that a voluntary conveyance or a subjection to execution of either cotenant's interest could not prevent the other, if he survived, from taking the fee simple free even from an execution purchaser's claim. Similarly, a dictum in Anson v. Murphy reads: "A survivorship attached to a tenancy in common is indestructible except by the voluntary action of all the tenants in common to do so." A further dictum declared, however, that a decedent cotenant's share would accrue to the survivor(s) burdened by the decedent's debts.

We may now consider the statutes referred to at the outset of this discussion as affecting the common-law rule of construction. Most of these statutes, varying somewhat in scope and detail, declare that a conveyance of land by deed or will to two or more persons other than fiduciaries shall be construed to create a tenancy in common unless an intent to create a joint tenancy is sufficiently manifested. Excepting fiduciaries—e.g., trustees and executors—is a sensible provision, since operation of the principle of survivorship facilitates performance of their duties.

Fairly typical is the Massachusetts statute: "A conveyance or devise of land to two or more persons or to husband and wife, except a mortgage or a devise or conveyance in trust, shall create an estate in common and not in joint tenancy, unless it is expressed in such conveyance or devise that the grantees or devisees shall take jointly, or as joint tenants, or in joint tenancy, or to them and the survivor of them, or unless it manifestly appears from the tenor of the instrument that it was intended to create an estate in joint tenancy. A devise of land to a person and his spouse shall, if the instrument creating the devise expressly so states, vest in the devisees a tenancy by the entirety." (Tenancy by the entirety will be considered hereafter.)

Unfortunately, laymen and other artless conveyancers often think of tenants in common as holding "jointly," and in several cases courts have considered the question of the significance of this word in a conveyance. The better opinions, recognizing that it is both a layman's term and a term of art, have concluded that unless it is supported by evidence of circumstances in which the conveyance was made, use of the word does not sufficiently manifest an intent to create a joint tenancy. See Taylor v. Taylor, 310 Mich. 541, 17 N.W.2d 745, 157 A.L.R. 559 (1945).

A few legislatures have adopted language such as the following: "In all estates, real and personal, held in joint tenancy, the part or share of any tenant dying shall not descend or go to the surviving tenant or tenants, but shall descend or be vested in the heirs, executors, or administrators, respectively, of the tenant so dying, in the same manner as estates held by tenancy in common." Tenn. Code Ann. § 64–107 (1955). Even such a statute as this is ordinarily construed to permit creation of a joint tenancy where the intent to do so is clearly manifested. Runions v. Runions, 186 Tenn. 25, 207 S.W.2d 1016, 1 A.L.R.2d 242 (1948); Chandler v. Kountze, 130 S.W.2d 327 (Tex.Civ.App. 1939). If there was evil in the common-law predilection in favor of construing instruments as creating joint tenancy, it lay in the possibility that the "right of survivorship" would be enforced even in situations where there was little or no reason to suppose that the grantor intended that it should be. It can hardly be said that intentional creation of a "right of survivorship" is immoral or outlawed by public policy, since the courts unquestionably will give effect to a conveyance to two or more persons for their joint lives, with a contingent remainder in fee to the survivor.

Notice that the effects of a conveyance to persons for their joint lives, with a contingent remainder to the survivor, differ sharply from the effects of a joint tenancy. Do you see how?[2] Naturally enough, situations will occur in which a lack of meticulous counselling and draftsmanship will leave room for dispute concerning a grantor's intent. An instrument may, for example, read "to A and B and to the survivor, his heirs and assigns forever." Can this language be construed as expressing an intent to create an estate for the joint lives of A and B, with a contingent remainder to the survivor? Keeping in mind the statutory rule that a conveyance to two or more will be construed to create a tenancy in common unless the instrument expresses a different intent, can the language be construed as expressing an intent to create a joint tenancy in fee simple? Notice that the "words of inheritance" are used with reference only to "the survivor"—should this be regarded as significant in a jurisdiction which has abolished the common-law rule that words of inheritance are essential in a transfer of a fee simple? Suppose the instrument reads "to A and B, their heirs and assigns, and to the survivor, his heirs and assigns forever"—is this language susceptible of both the interpretations suggested above?

The third form of concurrent ownership, available only to a married couple, is termed "tenancy by the entirety." Probably the concept was connected from the outset with the fiction, adopted in law because of religious doctrine, that husband and wife were one flesh, one personality. The analogy to the assumption of unity of joint tenants is obvious, but it appears that the concept was far more powerful in the husband-wife relationship because of the reinforcement furnished by ecclesiastical influence. For instance, as previously stated, joint tenants were regarded, for certain purposes, as owners of undivided interests, but this was not true of tenants by the entirety. In fact, the belief in the mystical union of husband and wife pervaded the law in many

2. Consider Durant v. Hamrick, Ala., 409 So.2d 731 (1982). A deed conveyed property to tenants in common with a contingent remainder in fee in the survivor. The court held that this differed from a joint tenancy with a right of survivorship since the right of survivorship in one tenant in common was not destructible by act of the other.

other ways. Her legal personality was, in effect, merged into her husband's—like an infant or imbecile, she was not sui juris but stood somewhat in the position of a ward who was represented in law by her guardian husband. Until amelioration of her position was wrought by developments in equity jurisprudence through the Court of Chancery, and much later and much more fully by legislation, her husband had essentially full dominion over chattels and choses which would have been under her dominion as a feme sole; even chattels real (leaseholds) were subject to his control and power of disposal while her coverture lasted. Moreover, he had, in effect, beneficial ownership of her freehold estates in realty, in that he controlled its use and could appropriate the rents and profits for his purposes with no obligation to account to her. These rights and powers ultimately became so well defined and established that they were dignified as the husband's estate by the marital right (estate jure uxoris). As its name implies, the estate would terminate upon dissolution of the marriage, so that it was, in effect, an estate for the joint lives of the spouses in times when absolute divorce was such a rarity that, as one court put it, it was no more to be anticipated than an earthquake. Given the required circumstances, a husband's right to beneficial use of his wife's land continued for his lifetime even though he outlived his wife, just as she had a right to beneficial use of a portion of his land for her lifetime if she survived him. These interests, termed curtesy and dower respectively, no longer have the significance they once had. In many, if not in all, states they have been either abolished or much modified by legislation; moreover, in any state statutes probably can be found providing more generously for a surviving spouse's support out of a decedent spouse's estate.

It has been suggested that the ancient mysticism of the marriage sacrament, embodying the avowal that the two were indissolubly joined as one flesh, is an inadequate explanation for the gross subordination—now almost inconceivable—of married women in law, but so long as it was enforced, it was hardly admissible that a conveyance of land by deed or will to husband and wife was a conveyance of an undivided interest to each of two persons. Indeed, the logical conclusion would be that tenancy by the entirety is not a cotenancy at all, since cotenancy by definition is ownership by two or more persons. In modern times the old fiction has lost most, but not all, of its force; it has been invoked in construing a deed which named X and H and W as grantees without clearly indicating how they were to share, the result being that X received one-half and H and W the other half jointly. Mosser v. Dolsay, 132 N.J.Eq. 121, 27 A.2d 155 (1942). The fiction may once have been so respected that it was impossible, by a conveyance to husband and wife, to create a cotenancy other than a tenancy by the entirety; nothing now prevents this in the twenty-odd states which still recognize tenancy by the entirety, though the usual rule of construction is such that only a clear expression of intent will accomplish it.

It has been noticed earlier in this discussion that the common-law predilection for joint tenancy has been displaced, probably in every state, by statutes favoring tenancy in common. The prevailing view, where tenancy by the entirety is recognized, is that a statute of this type affects a conveyance to husband and wife only if it is expressly mentioned, the common explanation being that such a conveyance is not one to "two or more persons." Observe that the Massachusetts statute, quoted previously, establishes the same rule of construction for "a conveyance or devise of land to two or more persons or to husband and wife." The wording of the last sentence in the statute is puzzling in that it requires giving effect to a declaration of intent to create a tenancy by the entirety in a "devise" but does not mention a "conveyance." The statute could be narrowly and literally construed to mean that it is no longer possible, in Massachusetts, to create a tenancy by the entirety by a "conveyance." It is conceivable that the legislature, having concluded that some of the incidents of ownership by the entirety are undesirable, wished to prevent one spouse, acting alone, or both, acting together, from acquiring ownership in this form by purchase, but did not feel that this policy warranted a hampering of freedom to make testamentary disposition. Whatever the proper view of the statute may be, it represents a recent (1954) and fairly radical change; in the past, the Massachusetts court has exhibited, perhaps more strongly than any other, a tendency to construe instruments as creating tenancy by the entirety and to deal with the estate in accordance with anachronistic rules antedating and inconsistent with modern legislation designed to eliminate the common-law effects of coverture upon a woman's property rights. See D'Ercole v. D'Ercole, reprinted at page 401, infra. In the Note which follows that case, the present status of tenancy by the entirety in Massachusetts is explored.

As the preceding sentence intimates, the days when "husband and wife were one, and the husband was the one" are gone. Nineteenth and twentieth century legislation and judicial action have left few, if any, of the common-law disabilities of women, married or unmarried; and in particular, statutes in every state, commonly referred to as "Married Women's Property Acts," have eliminated the wife's subordination to her husband in property law.

One consequence of this legislation was that courts were required to reconsider tenancy by the entirety. Some of them, perhaps feeling that in the new order property rights and powers of spouses must be worked out as if they were unmarried, went so far as to hold that the conceptual basis of the tenancy—the idea of the marital unity—had been eliminated, so that it was no longer possible to create a tenancy by the entirety; a conveyance to husband and wife would create the same kind of cotenancy as would a like conveyance to persons between whom there was no marital relationship. Other courts, refusing to find in the rather generalized language of the usual statute a legislative intent to abolish the concept of the marital unity, have sought to adapt the incidents of ownership by the entirety to the principle that neither spouse has rights or powers superior to those of the other. The prevailing view is that they have equal rights in the control and enjoyment of the land and its revenue. In this respect they do not differ from joint tenants or tenants in common owning equal undivided interests. Courts have seldom had to deal with disputes between spouses in this connection, but see Fine v. Scheinhaus, 202 Misc. 272,

109 N.Y.S.2d 307 (1952), a case apparently unique in legal history, in which H, seeking to evict his mother-in-law, was judicially told that a husband is no longer lord and master of a household held by the entirety.

A court's recognition of the estate necessarily implies, it seems, retention of the concept of absolute unity of the spouses for this purpose. The consequent prevailing doctrine is that the spouses are "seised pur tout et non pur my"—neither is recognized as an individual owning an undivided interest, and the estate therefore differs from joint tenancy in two respects: neither can effect a "severance" of the estate by conveying an undivided interest, and neither can compel a partition. Therefore, unless the estate is terminated in some manner, the surviving spouse will be sole owner, the decedent having no interest transmissible by will. It will be terminated if the marriage is ended by a divorce; what should be the result—a joint tenancy, or a tenancy in common? It will also be terminated, of course, if the spouses jointly convey otherwise than to another married couple, and by virtue of modern statutes abrogating the old rule that conveyances and contracts between spouses were impossible because of their unity in law, in many jurisdictions, if not all, it may be terminated by a direct conveyance of one spouse's interest to the other without the formality of a joint conveyance to a straw man who in turn reconveys to one of the spouses.

The chief problems presented have been those of creditors' rights. Formerly, these problems were much less troublesome since the wife, her legal personality being merged into that of her husband, had little or no capacity to incur debts. On the other hand, the husband was empowered to deal with the use and benefits of the land as he might wish, and his creditors could take advantage of this power, subject only to the wife's expectancy of survivorship. This power of the husband had been ascribed, not to any peculiar aspect of tenancy by the entirety, but to the general power, referred to previously in this discussion, conferred upon him by the common law, to control the use and benefits of his wife's estates in land. Now that Married Women's Property Acts have eliminated this power and have given married women full dominion over their property, a number of courts have held that the creditors of *neither* spouse can obtain satisfaction from land held by the entirety. The reason usually given is that to permit the creditor's action would improperly interfere with the other spouse's interest in its use and enjoyment. Though they do not say so, these courts may be influenced by the ancient concept of the spouses as one personality, so that the creditor may obtain satisfaction from the land only if the debt in question is an obligation of both spouses. On the basis of this concept, it may be said that a debt incurred by one spouse is not an obligation of the owning entity; thus, it would be no more proper to allow the creditor to use the owning entity's asset as a source of satisfaction than it would be to allow the creditor of one spouse to obtain satisfaction from property owned solely by the other.

Still another possible explanation—that of promoting stability and security of the family, the fundamental element in social organization—is suggested in Fairclaw v. Forrest, 76 U.S.App.D.C. 197, 130 F.2d

829 (1942): "The Married Woman's Property Statutes have changed the common-law principles of marital unity so that the husband cannot now assert an exclusive right to the rents and profits or divest the wife of her share directly by conveyance or indirectly by execution. Although it is said that no technical changes have been made in the estate by entirety, the results are different. Now each is entitled to the enjoyment and benefits of the whole and neither has a separate estate therein which may be subjected to a conveyance or execution. These are obvious advantages, some of which can be attained by no other form of tenancy. They are frequently the cause or motive of creating the entirety. The reason for this is no longer merely the fictional unity of husband and wife. The interest in family solidarity retains some influence upon the institution. It is available only to husband and wife. It is a convenient mode of protecting a surviving spouse from inconvenient administration of the decedent's estate and from the other's improvident debts. In that protection the estate finds its peculiar and justifiable function." Considered in this fashion, tenancy by the entirety serves the same purpose as does the homestead right and other property interests exempt by law from seizure by creditors. Notice, however, that in contrast with these exemptions, through the device of tenancy by the entirety realty of unlimited extent or value may be made inaccessible to creditors. The discrepancy is even greater in states where personalty—e.g., securities or a joint bank account—may be held by the entirety. Chiefly for this reason, after cataloguing a number of objections to retaining tenancy by the entirety, a committee of the American Bar Association in 1944 recommended that measures be adopted in all states to abolish it.

Other courts, perhaps taking a different view of the proper policy to follow in dealing with the debtor-creditor relationship, have taken the position that a creditor of either spouse, though he cannot compel a partition, or impair the other spouse's right of obtaining sole, unburdened ownership by surviving the debtor spouse, can take advantage of the debtor spouse's right to share in the benefits of the property while the marriage lasts. In effect, this view results in a tenancy in common between the creditor and the non-debtor spouse for the duration of the marriage or until the debt is extinguished. It may reasonably be expected that the courts would subject the two persons to the same rules that are ordinarily used in connection with tenancy in common.

The concurrent estates (tenancy in common, joint tenancy, and tenancy by the entirety) are most frequently utilized by husbands and wives, although, except for tenancy by the entirety, they are by no means restricted to the marital relationship. There are other concurrent interests in property, based on marriage, of which you should be aware—dower and curtesy (largely of historical importance), homestead rights, and community property (the latter being of major importance in eight states). It is especially difficult to deal, in a general way, with these interests because of the variations among the states. The following summary treatment is included to provide some understanding of these so-called marital estates before we turn to an analysis of the modern cases on concurent ownership.

SECTION 2. MARITAL ESTATES

A. THE HUSBAND'S INTEREST IN THE WIFE'S PROPERTY

It is hardly necessary to point out that during the past century or so revolutionary changes in the legal status of women—particularly married women—have occurred, culminating in legislation whereby they have been relieved of almost all the disabilities which they once suffered. Until these changes were wrought a married woman was not sui juris; i.e., like an infant or imbecile she had no legally recognized personalty for most purposes but stood somewhat in the position of a ward who was represented in matters legal by her guardian husband. It may be that the ancient mysticism of the marriage sacrament—the concept that the two were indissolubly joined as one flesh—had something to do with this, but it has been suggested that this "hackneyed fiction" is not an adequate explanation for the consequences of marriage as they evolved in the common law of property. It is worth noting that one of the incidents of feudal tenure was that if a tenant by knight service died, leaving an infant heir, the lord's right of wardship entitled him to take all the rents and profits of the ward's land during his minority, his only obligation being to provide proper care and tutelage of the ward. Similarly, a husband, as head and master of the family, had full dominion, with few exceptions, over chattels and choses which, if his wife were unmarried, would have been hers; even chattels real (leaseholds) were subject to his disposal as he wished while the marital relationship continued. Moreover he had, in effect, beneficial ownership of her realty in that he controlled its use and could appropriate the rents and profits for his purposes with no obligation to account to her. This interest, which in the course of time was dignified as the husband's estate by the marital right (jure uxoris), was alienable voluntarily or involuntarily—a judgment creditor or mortgagee could reach it by legal process to satisfy his claim. As its name implies, the estate would terminate upon dissolution of the marriage, so that it was, in effect, an estate for the joint lives of the spouses in times when absolute divorce was such a rarity that, as one court put it, it was no more to be anticipated than an earthquake.

The husband's interest was much like that of an ordinary life tenant—in his own right he had a remedy for deprivation of or injury to the usufruct (rents and profits) and it has been stated that, in principle at least, he was subject to the law of waste, though his wife's disability to sue him at law meant that her only remedy, if any, was equitable. On the other hand, both spouses were regarded as jointly seised of the freehold, as cotenants are; their joinder as plaintiffs or defendants was required in a suit for injury to or recovery of the freehold, and adverse possession for the necessary period resulted in a "limitation title" valid against both.

This withholding from married women the power to exercise the incidents of property ownership could not, of course, indefinitely survive the social conditions which engendered it. The common-law rules came to have such a rigidity that substantial reform could be effected only by legislation, but the greater flexibility of equity jurisprudence permitted innovations which reflected the growing pressure for greater economic independence of wives. During the eighteenth century an earlier protection was afforded whereby land could be conveyed to trustees for the "sole and separate use" of a married woman, and beneficial ownership could thus be conferred upon her free of her husband's control. This process of creating the married woman's "separate estate in equity" has been characterized as "a most remarkable piece of judicial legislation." Nineteenth and twentieth century legislation—the "Married Women's Property Acts"—has left few vestiges of the wife's subordination to her husband in property law.

If his wife gave birth to a living child (however short its life) and if she then held or thereafter acquired a fee simple (or a fee tail so limited as to be inheritable by the child) the husband acquired an interest therein exceeding the interest described above as the estate by the marital right. To his improved status a curious name was given—he was "tenant by the curtesy of England." Two differences between this estate and the estate jure uxoris are most notable: the husband was solely seised in his own right, and the estate was measured by his life rather by the joint lives of the spouses. Thus the wife's interest, which passed according to the ordinary law of succession if her husband survived her, was substantially the same as a reversion expectant upon a conventional life estate. A chief consequence was that a hostile possession would not affect this interest until the lapse of the appropriate period after the husband's death. According to the common law the husband had this interest only in an estate of which his wife (or he in her behalf) had acquired actual seisin—as opposed to seisin in law—during coverture. Hence, it did not extend to a future interest (reversion, remainder, or executory interest) expectant upon a freehold, or to a mere right to obtain seisin (e.g., as against a disseisor). Different explanations for this rule have been conjectured—would it be enough to say that the husband's interest as tenant by the curtesy was simply an extension of his right, jure uxoris, to take the rents and profits, and that the concept of actual seisin held (lawfully or unlawfully) by a stranger to the marital relationship involved the consequence, among others, that the stranger had the right to take the rents and profits? The decadence of the concept of seisin is marked by the prevalent American view that the husband has his curtesy interest in vacant or unimproved land without a showing that seisin in fact had been acquired by entry; and at least one court, rejecting as outmoded the justifications suggested by Blackstone and others for the contrary result, has held that the curtesy interest is recognizable in land occupied adversely to the spouses throughout the duration of the marriage. Borland's Lessee v. Marshall, 2 Ohio St. 308 (1853). In this connection it is also noteworthy that the curtesy interest was eventually extended to an equitable estate of inheritance, even where the trustee held to the wife's "sole and separate use."

Everywhere, statutes have either abolished or materially altered the curtesy interest. Because of Married Women's Property Acts it no longer can have any beneficial incidents while the marriage lasts and is reduced to an expectancy contingent upon the husband's surviving the wife. In some states where this expectancy (sometimes characterized as a remainder) is still recognized it cannot be avoided by a will or by a deed or mortgage executed by the wife alone; but the husband may, of course, release it by joining in a conveyance. By providing benefits in lieu of curtesy in her will the wife may require her surviving husband to elect between the testamentary benefits and the curtesy interest. In states where the interest has been abolished and in some where it has not been, statutes may be found making the surviving spouse a "forced heir"—i.e., providing that the survivor shall have a specified share of the decedent's real and personal estate after debts are paid, the size of the share typically depending upon the existence of surviving descendants. Again, however, provision of testamentary benefits may require an election between these and the statutory share, and in some states a surviving spouse may have an even more complicated problem of election, where a will provides benefits and the law permits the survivor to waive those and take either a statutory share or the common-law marital interest—curtesy or dower.

B. THE WIFE'S INTEREST IN THE HUSBAND'S PROPERTY

A wife's dower interest in her husband's property is analogous to his interest in hers as tenant by the curtesy—the incidents of the two, as developed in case law, are alike in many respects but not in all. It appears that in the twelfth and thirteenth centuries the husband's testamentary power over his personalty was restrained in that his wife (and children for whom he had not otherwise provided) had legally enforceable claims for fixed shares; but apart from this right, which subsequent developments eliminated, she had no interest in his personalty. However, she had then and continued to have a dower interest in his land. As it finally developed out of variant early stages, this was an interest for her life, commencing upon the husband's death, in one-third of all land in which, during the marriage, the husband was seised in fact or in law of a fee simple (or a fee tail inheritable by her issue). Several differences between dower and curtesy are apparent: (1) the wife had no beneficial interest in the husband's land while he lived—she had a mere expectancy contingent upon her surviving him, identified by the term "inchoate dower"; (2) her interest involved only one-third of the husband's land, and because of this the "assignment of dower" upon the husband's death might be a complex problem; (3) her interest did not depend upon birth of issue; (4) seisin in law was sufficient—the dower interest extended to land of which the husband had acquired ownership by devise or inheritance even though he had not acquired seisin in fact by entry, but by the same token it did not extend to a future interest expectant upon a freehold, to a mere right of entry for condition broken, or to a right to recover land occupied adversely to the husband throughout the period of coverture.

The ancient requirement of seisin, which was eliminated in England by the Dower Act of 1833, is doubtless related to a non-apparent fifth difference with respect to equitable estates. Before the Statute of Uses was enacted, it appears, the Chancellor recognized neither dower nor curtesy in land held to the use of a spouse, perhaps because it was customary, in accordance with an antenuptial agreement, to make a suitable provision for the prospective wife through a "jointure" as part of a family settlement—at any rate, among other evils of conveyances to uses the preamble of the Statute recited that husbands were denied their curtesy and wives their dower. (The preamble may seem a bit hypocritical in view of the fact that the Statute expressly provided for barring dower by means of a jointure.) When modern equity jurisdiction over interests in land flourished in the seventeenth century and later, the question was again presented whether or not to recognize dower and curtesy in equitable estates. Though curtesy was eventually allowed, as stated above, dower was not until the Dower Act (1833) was enacted. The distinction seemed invidious to judges and commentators alike—Blackstone asserted that disallowing dower resulted "more from a cautious adherence to some hasty precedents than from any well-grounded principle," and Lord Mansfield stated, perhaps regretfully, that the "wrong determination had misled in too many instances to be now altered and set right." Lord Mansfield may have meant what others have suggested—that the explanation of the matter lay not so much in the force of stare decisis as in the fact that allowance of dower would seriously disturb many family settlements made on the supposition that dower was excluded. It is notable that in the United States, where the importance of the ancestral domain was never so widely felt as in England, dower was much more freely recognized in equity.

As the foregoing discussion may suggest, much of legal history in connection with dower has to do with substitutes for or methods of avoiding it. The inchoate dower right was a clog upon the husband's power of alienation, since he could not, unless his wife joined in the conveyance, transfer land free of her right. In England the Dower Act (1833) empowered him to do so, but in a number of states inchoate dower continues to present problems and to be a nuisance for title examiners. Moreover, in a society where personalty forms an ever-increasing proportion of the total wealth, retention of dower as a means of providing security for widows seems anachronistic. It has been abolished in England (1925) and in several states. In all other states (other than those where the community property system operates) the legislatures have dealt haphazardly with dower, modifying its ancient incidents in various ways in efforts to cope with particular problems such as creditors' claims and the husband's power to alienate without a release of dower. Where dower has been eliminated, and in some states where it has not been, statutes of the type mentioned above in connection with curtesy may be found, making the wife a forced heir.

C. HOMESTEAD RIGHTS

Seeking to promote the stability and security of the family, all but a very few American jurisdictions have created a type of property interest which is primarily an incident of the marital relationship, though its benefits typically are not confined to that relationship. The interest seems to have originated in an 1839 act of the Republic of Texas, and since it rests altogether on constitutions or statutes, it is peculiarly a matter of local law, the scope and detail of its development varying widely from state to state. The following generalizations, therefore, are offered with the caveat that each of them is likely to be true for one or more states but not for others.

Any possessory interest in land which is used as a home or as a means of supporting a family may have a homestead character. As homestead it is protected from claims of the owner's general creditors, and it can be subjected only to certain liens (e.g., purchase money liens, mechanics' and materialmen's liens connected with improvements, tax liens). The interest may be owned by any member of the family; if it is owned (as is usual) by a husband or wife or both, it cannot be conveyed or subjected to a lien for improvements unless the necessary instrument is executed by both spouses in the manner prescribed by statute. Upon the death of an owner, his or her interest will devolve, like any other interest in land, in accordance with the local law of testate or intestate succession, but a surviving spouse (for life) or child (for minority) cannot be deprived of possession or use even though the survivor has no interest in the land save the homestead right. A homestead right in rural land is confined to a maximum number of acres; in a city or town it is confined to land of a maximum value to be ascertained (disregarding improvements) as of the time the right commenced. Whether or not a homestead right is recognizable depends primarily upon the intent of the head of a family as ascertained by objective manifestations; hence the right, once acquired may be terminated by abandonment. It is terminated, also, if spouses having no dependent children are divorced.

The foregoing statements obviously attempt no more than to convey a crude comprehension of major characteristics of the homestead right.

D. COMMUNITY PROPERTY

In eight states—Louisiana, Texas, New Mexico, Arizona, California, Nevada, Washington, and Idaho—property rights between husband and wife are regulated by a legal system derived from the Civil Law as it was developed in Spain and France. Before 1948, spouses domiciled in these states enjoyed a great advantage, with reference to the federal income tax, over spouses domiciled elsewhere, because of the theory that each owned half of all income classified as belonging to them "in community" and could report it accordingly for taxation, thus minimizing the effects of the graduated tax rates. Because of this, pressure developed for the adoption of the system in other states, and short-lived legislation to that end was enacted in five states (Michigan, Nebraska, Oklahoma, Oregon, Pennsylvania) and Hawaii before Congress made the change unnecessary, in 1948, by revising the tax scheme to permit spouses everywhere to divide their total income into halves in order to find the applicable tax rate. In 1947 the Pennsylvania Supreme Court had held the Pennsylvania legislation void, and that in the other jurisdictions was subsequently repealed; the net result of the excursion was a detritus of problems to be worked out concerning property acquisitions and transactions while the legislation was in effect. For detail see 50 Col.L.Rev. 332 (1950).

The incidents of ownership in community vary markedly in the states adhering to it, depending upon the extent to which the Civil Law institution has been modified by statutes and by decisions of judges whose thinking has been conditioned by doctrines, concepts, and practices native to Anglo-American law and society rather than to the legal and social order in which the community property system originated. The essence of the scheme is that whatever a spouse owns before marriage and whatever is acquired gratuitously thereafter—by gift or by testate or intestate succession—is classified as the spouse's separate property; all other property acquired during marriage is classified as community property. Logically this should mean that income derived from the use or investment of separate property should be treated as community property, and it is so treated—with variations—in Louisiana, Texas, and Idaho. In 1860, the California court nullified a statute to that effect, in an opinion which seems thoroughly imbued with the common-law point of view and oblivious of the fundamental principle of the community property scheme. Thereafter the legislature redefined separate property to include the "rents, issues, and profits" thereof, and Arizona, New Mexico, Nevada, and Washington have done likewise.

So long as the capital value of separate property can be traced and identified, it retains its separate character, notwithstanding mutations through exchange or reinvestment of proceeds of sale, and notwithstanding increases in value attributable to economic factors affecting market prices of comparable property. Ability to prove separate ownership of particular items is all-important in a dispute, however, since community property law characteristically involves a presumption that all property is owned in community.

Traditionally, the husband had sole legal power to manage the community property, to transfer it, and to incur obligations whereby it might be subjected to seizure through legal process. The wife had little contractual power, hence little power to subject community property to creditors' claims. In community-property states, as elsewhere, during the past century statutes have vastly enlarged the rights and powers of married women, and the tendency has been to give to them management of portions of the community property, as well as their separate property, with concomitant contractual power. This trend was greatly accelerated during the 1960's and 1970's, a period of heightened concern for reform of sexually discriminatory laws. See Barham, Equal Rights for Women v. the Civil Code, 48 Tul.L.Rev. 560 (1974); Bingaman, The Community Property Act of 1973: A Commentary and Quasi-Legislative History, 5 N.M.L.Rev. 1 (1974); Cross, Equality for Spouses in Washington Community Property Law—1972 Statutory Changes, 48 Wash.L.Rev. 527 (1973); Huie, Divided Management of Community Property in Texas, 5 Tex.Tech.L.Rev. 623 (1974); Reppy, Retroactivity of the 1975 California Community Property Reforms, 48 So.Cal.L.Rev. 977 (1975).

Upon dissolution of the marriage by death of a spouse, the predominant rule is that the decedent spouse has complete freedom to make a testamentary disposition of all separate property and half of the community property, subject to administration for the settlement of cognizable creditors' claims; otherwise the same interests devolve according to the local statutory scheme of descent and distribution, which may not be the same for community and separate property. Similarly, upon dissolution of the marriage by divorce, if there is no property settlement agreement the community property is likely to be divided equally between the spouses, though the court may have, in some or all circumstances, discretionary power to make an unequal division.

It should be borne in mind that the foregoing is no more than a very rough sketch of a few prominent incidents of community ownership—chiefly incidents which permit comparison with common-law marital property rights and with types of concurrent ownership outside the marital relationship. The law of the eight community-property states varies so much, both in general concepts and in particular rules, that it is hardly possible to generalize usefully. For a more detailed treatment, see W. de Funiak and M. Vaughn, Principles of Community Property (2d ed. 1971), but much has happened since publication of that book. A coursebook not limited to a single state is W. Reppy and C. Samuel, Community Property in the United States (2d ed. 1982). A useful survey is Greene, Comparison of the Property Aspects of the Community Property and Common-Law Marital Property Systems and Their Relative Compatibility with the Current View of the Marriage Relationship and the Rights of Women, 13 Creighton L.Rev. 71 (1979).

E. THE MARITAL PROPERTY ACT

The latest development in marital estates is the Uniform Marital Property Act, adopted by the National Conference of Commissioners on Uniform State Laws in 1983. The Act is too long to be reprinted here, but the following article from 12 Probate and Property 9 (1983) captures the spirit and principal "running gears" of this new look in marital estates. So far the Act has been adopted in only one state, Wisconsin, which, although modifying the Uniform Act, did accept the "heart" of the Act.[3] It is still too early to predict how influential this uniform act will be, but it may reflect the direction in which the law is moving.

THE MARITAL PROPERTY ACT

by Mary Moers Wenig *

It is news when William F. Buckley, Jr. and Phyllis Schlafly, on one end of the continuum, and the National Organization for Women on the other, agree. But agree they do. And in agreement with them, also, are others somewhere in between. For instance, the League of Women Voters of Wisconsin, The Older Women's League, Agri-Women, the 1963 President's Commission on the Status of Women, the 1976 National Commission on the International Women's Year, and the 1980 White House Conference on Families.

The concept that elicits this agreement is *sharing*—the equal sharing by husband and wife of the benefits and liabilities of the marriage partnership. The law which embodies this concept is community property law.

In a television program taped on November 30, 1982, William F. Buckley, Jr. stated that he "would welcome a change in the law that would grant community property rights, as they exist in eight states already, everywhere in the United States." A February 28, 1983 *Newsweek* interview with Phyllis Schlafly reported that she is working for passage of state community property laws. From the Wisconsin chapter of her Eagle Forum comes proof: a proposed community property act drafted for Phyllis Schlafly.

Judge Charles Sumner Lobingier, in an article in the *ABA Journal,* wrote that

> the introduction of the community [concept] would be a long step toward that juster and more equal status which the present condition of society demands. Moreover, it would relieve the state of diversity of marital property laws which is fast becoming intolerable. Here would seem to lie a promising field for the Commissioners on Uniform Laws.

The date of this article was 1928. Half a century later, the work was begun. . . .

Summary of the Act

Rather than the terms *community* and *separate* property, used by the eight community property states, the act uses the terms *marital property* and *individual property.* Use of this terminology is not intend-

3. A copy of the Wisconsin Act, together with UMPA (including official comments and several descriptive legislative memos is available from the Legislative Reference Bureau, 201 North, State Capitol, Madison, WI 53702. The compilation is entitled "Marital Property Act: Informational Bulletin 84–IB–1 April 1984).

* Co-Chair, Probate and Trust Division Committee H–5 on Marital Property, and ABA Advisor to the National Conference of Commissioners on Uniform State Laws Marital Property Act Drafting Committee.

ed to belittle the community property roots. But the term *marital property* evokes the property distribution provisions of the Uniform Marriage and Divorce Act and of comparable provisions for equitable distribution on marriage dissolution, now adopted by all but two of the common law states. In addition, the terms *marital property* and *individual property* are employed in recognition that the Marital Property Act attempts to meld concepts from both community property and common law.

The act provides that property acquired during marriage is marital property. Both husband and wife have a present undivided one-half interest in their marital property. Individual property includes property owned before marriage, or acquired at any time by gift or inheritance, and appreciation of individual property not resulting from substantial personal effort of the other spouse. Presumptions aid in the identification of marital property and simple rules, based on a time continuum, are provided for the sorting out of marital and individual property components of life insurance, pension and other deferred employee benefits which straddle the date of marriage.

The act applies prospectively only, affecting interests acquired after the act's effective date by married couples within the adopting state.

While title no longer governs the ownership of property acquired after the act's effective date, title bestows rights of management and control. Title can be in the name of one spouse or the other or both. If title is in the name of husband *and* wife, there is joint management and control; if in the name of husband *or* wife, either can manage and control. Third persons who rely on title are protected in their dealings with a spouse but gifts to third persons in excess of a certain annual amount or in excess of the standard of giving set by the spouses can be set aside by the nondonor spouse who acts promptly. If necessary, a spouse may obtain judicial aid to add his or her name to the title of marital property (except for partnership interests or assets of an unincorporated business of the other spouse). Other judicial remedies, if sought promptly, may protect the interest of either spouse in marital property.

Claims of third persons arising during an obligee's marriage can be satisfied from the obligee's individual property or from marital property; claims which antedate the marriage can be satisfied from the obligee's individual property and from his or her earnings during marriage. Broad scope is granted to husbands and wives to enter into marital property agreements which may vary the effect of the act. Marital property can be held in survivorship form or transferred to trust without losing its marital property characteristics if this is what the spouses want.

The act is a property act, not a divorce act. Therefore, to use Reporter Cantwell's metaphor, in the event of divorce the act takes the couple up to the steps of the courthouse, each with his or her undivided one-half interest in marital property in hand, and leaves them there. The divorce law, and whatever power of equitable distribution the state has given to the court, then takes over. Because the act is a property act, at death of either spouse, that spouse has power of testamentary disposition over his or her undivided one-half interest in the couple's marital property.

Because of the act's prospective application, couples who are married before the effective date of the act or married couples who move into an adopting state from a state which has not adopted the act may have considerable individual property, possibly all or substantially all owned by only one of the spouses. To protect the nonowning spouse on divorce, or to protect a surviving spouse, a deferred interest is given to that spouse in the other spouse's property which would have been marital property under the act's definition but for the fact that the property was acquired during the couple's marriage before the adoption of the act or before their move to the adopting state. . . .

The act may sound unfamiliar to lawyers accustomed to common law. But almost one-fourth of the population of the United States now lives in the eight community property states—Arizona, California, Idaho, Louisiana, New Mexico, Nevada, Texas and Washington. Married couples travel; their domiciles change as their jobs move or as their retirement plans direct. While the population of many of the community property states is growing, couples in these states also move. Should their rights in marital property turn on the accident of their choice of residence?

The variegated marital property regimes of the common law states have been moving in many ways in the past two decades toward community property. "Creeping community property" is reflected in piecemeal judicial decisions or legislation providing for equitable distribution on divorce; protection against disinheritance on death; increases in intestate shares of surviving spouses; presumptions classifying household effects and other family assets as joint and survivor property; recognition of husband-and-wife partnerships in family businesses and family farms; imposition of constructive trusts to aid one spouse's claim of interest in property held in the name of the other spouse; increasing validation of marital contracts; and the growing trend of the states, both before and after the federal adoption in 1981 of the unlimited marital deduction, toward tax-free interspousal transfers. In addition, federal law pertaining to public and private pensions has in recent years reinforced state law in giving increasing recognition to the necessity of permitting one spouse to share in the benefits earned by the other spouse.

Justified by the trend exemplified by the many illustrations of creeping community property, the Marital Property Act would bring order and symmetry to the law of marital property. By looking at the length of the marriage and assuming that husband and wife are economic partners and that they have been acting as such during the course of the marriage, unless they agree that they have not, the act gives equal weight to the contributions of both spouses. The act smooths the jagged edges of laws that in one state may give a larger share to the surviving spouse of a decedent who dies intestate than to the surviving spouse of a decedent who dies with a will and that, in a neighboring state, may do the reverse. The act deals with nonprobate assets that are such a large part of wealth today, in a manner that neither the intestate nor elective share laws can provide. The act differentiates between marriages of short duration and longer marriages, not only upon divorce but in the course of the marriage and upon death of one of the spouses.

In a recent National Institute on Divorce and Estate Planning in an Uncertain Marital Climate, held jointly by this Section and the Family Law Section, the panel moderator asked questions not of the panel but of the audience, ten dozen lawyers from twenty states. After listening to the chaotic range of answers to each question asked, the moderator summed up with a McLuhan paraphrase: The chaos *is* the message. Uniformity and consistency are the desiderata.

The "strange bedfellow" proponents of community property—Buckley, Schlafly and NOW—may indicate that the Marital Property Act is the correct culmination and embodiment of a demand that the law recognize that marital property is not "his" or "hers" but "ours." Another proponent may have been revealed by a wedding that occurred several years ago. The Church of England marriage ceremony contains the traditional vow, "with my worldly goods I thee endow." The old English separate property regime grant of the limited right of dower is thus embodied in the marriage ritual. But those who watched the televised wedding of Prince Charles and Princess Diana two summers ago heard Prince Charles speak not that traditional vow but instead the words: "All my goods, with thee I *share*."

That is what the Marital Property Act is about. Creeping community property and the sharing concept has crept up on Prince Charles as well as the rest of us. The ritual vow has changed, and the law can too. The concept of marriage as an economic partnership, in which the contributions of both partners are adjudged equal may, finally, with the aid or inspiration of the Marital Property Act, become the law of all of the states.

SECTION 3. GENERAL ASPECTS OF CONCURRENT OWNERSHIP

IN RE ESTATE OF MICHAEL

Supreme Court of Pennsylvania, 1966.
421 Pa. 207, 218 A.2d 338.

JONES, JUSTICE.

This is an appeal from a decree of the Orphans' Court of Lycoming County entered in a proceeding brought under the Uniform Declaratory Judgment Act. The purpose of the proceeding was to obtain an interpretation and construction of a deed to determine whether the decedent, Bertha W. Michael, died owning any interest in realty located in Wolf and Moreland Townships, Lycoming County, known as "King Farm."

On February 24, 1947, Joyce E. King deeded certain real estate in Lycoming County, known as "King Farm", to Harry L. Michael and Bertha M. Michael,[1] his wife, and Ford W. Michael (son of Bertha and Harry L. Michael) and Helen M. Michael, his wife. The pertinent provisions of the lawyer-drawn deed are as follows:

> "This Indenture Made the 24th day of February in the year of our Lord one thousand nine hundred forty-seven (1947).
>
> Between Joyce E. King, widow, of Milton, Northumberland County, State of Pennsylvania, party of the first part, Harry L. Michael and Bertha M. Michael, his wife, tenants by the entireties and Ford W. Michael and Helen M. Michael, his wife, as tenants by the entireties, *with right of survivorship,* of Hughesville, Lycoming County, Pennsylvania, parties of the second part." (Emphasis supplied.)
>
> ". . . [H]ave granted, bargained, sold, aliened, enfeoffed, released, conveyed and confirmed and by these presents does grant, bargain, sell, alien, enfeoff, release[,] convey and confirm unto the said parties of the second part, their heirs and assigns."
>
> . . .
>
> "To Have and To Hold the said hereditaments and premises hereby granted or mentioned and intended so to be with the appurtenances unto the said parties of the second part, their heirs and assigns to and for the only proper use and behoof of the said parties of the second part, their heirs and assigns forever."

Harry L. Michael died prior to February 20, 1962 leaving to survive him his wife, Bertha W. Michael and two sons, Ford W. Michael, one of the grantees, and Robert C. Michael, the appellant.

Bertha W. Michael died testate, November 26, 1963, leaving to survive her two sons, Ford W. and Robert C. Michael. By her will dated February 20, 1962, she provided inter alia as follows:

> "Second. It is my sincere wish and I hereby direct that my Executors settle my estate in such way that my sons Ford W. Michael and Robert C. Michael each receive an equal share of the same. Because of the fact that a good portion of my estate may be in the form of real estate, my Executors shall use their own discretion in the matter of the method to be used to make the division. The following, however, are my desires in this matter and these desires follow closely the wishes of their father, namely: . . . .
>
> (d) That my interest in the 'King Farm' situate partly in Wolf and partly in Moreland Townships go to Robert C. Michael and the sum of $1,000.00, be paid to Ford W. Michael to balance this gift."

The two sons were appointed executors of their mother's estate. Soon thereafter a dispute arose as to what, *if any,* interest Bertha W. Michael had in the real estate known as "King Farm." The answer to this question turns on the construction of the language, above-quoted,

1. It is stipulated that Bertha M. Michael and Bertha W. Michael are one and the same person. [Footnotes are by the court—and numbered accordingly.]

contained in the deed of 1947. The court below held that the deed created a joint tenancy with right of survivorship between the two sets of husbands and wives.

The appellant urges that the deed created a tenancy in common as between the two married couples, each couple holding its undivided one-half interest as tenants by the entireties.[2] The appellees, conceding that the respective one-half interests were held by husband and wife as tenants by the entireties, contend, however, that *as to each other* the couples held as joint tenants with a right of survivorship. The lower court, predicating its decision on the use in the deed of the phrase "with right of survivorship", held that there was a clear expression of an intended right of survivorship between the two couples. To further support its decision, the court found it significant that the phrase was not used twice in modification of each husband-wife-grantee designation, but rather was utilized after both couples had been named and had been designated severally as tenants by the entireties.

At common law, joint tenancies were favored, and the doctrine of survivorship was a recognized incident to a joint estate. The courts of the United States have generally been opposed to the creation of such estates, the presumption being that all tenants hold jointly as tenants in common, unless a clear intention to the contrary is shown.

In Pennsylvania, by the Act of 1812, the incident of survivorship in joint tenancies was eliminated unless the instrument creating the estate expressly provided that such incident should exist. The Act of 1812 has been repeatedly held to be a statute of construction; it does not *forbid* creation of a joint tenancy if the language creating it *clearly* expresses that intent. Whereas before the Act, a conveyance or devise to two or more persons (not husband and wife or trustees) was presumed to create a joint tenancy with the right of survivorship unless otherwise clearly stated, the presumption is reversed by the Act, with the result that now such a conveyance or devise carries with it no right of survivorship unless clearly expressed, and in effect it creates, not a joint tenancy, but a tenancy in common.

Since passage of the Act of 1812, the question of survivorship has become a matter of intent and, in order to engraft the right of survivorship on a co-tenancy which might otherwise be a tenancy in common, the intent to do so must be expressed with sufficient clarity to overcome the statutory presumption that survivorship is not intended. Whether or not survivorship was intended is to be gathered from the instrument and its language, but no particular form of words is required to manifest such intention. The incident of survivorship may be expressly provided for in a deed or a will or it may arise by necessary implication.

2. Appellant, in urging the creation of a tenancy in common, points to decedent's will (above-quoted in part) wherein she indicated that she expected her interest in the property to pass under her will. From this appellant argues that the interest was considered by the parties to be one of tenancy in common rather than joint tenancy. Such an argument is insufficient to establish the intention of the parties. The question must be answered solely by reference to the language employed in the conveying instrument.

Applying the above-stated principles to the instant facts, we fail to find a sufficiently *clear* expression of intent to create a right of survivorship, as required by the case law, to overcome the presumption against such a right arising from the Act of 1812. Neither the research of the parties involved nor our own has yielded any case involving language or involving facts similar to that in the present litigation.

The lower court found that the use in the deed of the phrase "with right of survivorship" and the location of that phrase in such deed (see quoted provision of deed, supra) constituted a clear expression of an intended right of survivorship. The inherent difficulty with such an interpretation is that it is purely conjectural and finds certainty in a totally ambiguous phrase.

The phrase, "with right of survivorship", is capable, as appellant properly urges, of at least three possible interpretations: (1) explanatory of the one of the incidents of the estate, known as tenancy by the entirety; (2) explanatory of the one tenancy by the entirety, the creation of which it follows or (3), as the appellee and the lower court contend, indicative of the creation of a right of survivorship as between the two sets of spouses. Any one of these interpretations is a *possibility* but deciding which was intended by the parties would involve nothing but a mere guess. Such ambiguous terminology falls far short of the *clear* expression of intent required to overcome the statutory presumption.

Nowhere in the deed is the term "joint tenants" employed. To create a right of survivorship the *normal* procedure is to employ the phrase "joint tenants, with a right of survivorship, and not as tenants in common" in describing the manner in which the grantees are to take or hold the property being conveyed or transferred.

The deed herein involved also uses the term "*their* heirs and assigns forever." (Emphasis supplied.) The use of the plural would tend to indicate a tenancy in common. If "*his* or *her*" heirs and assigns had been used a strong argument could be made that the grantor intended a right of survivorship and that the survivor of the four named grantees would have an absolute undivided fee in the property.

Both the Act of 1812 and our case law clearly dictate that joint tenancies with the incident right of survivorship are not to be deemed favorites of the law. We cannot find within the four corners of this deed a *clearly* expressed intention to create a joint tenancy with the right of survivorship. Having failed to find a *clear* intention to overcome the statutory presumption against such estates, the Act of 1812 compels us to find that the deed of 1947 created a tenancy in common as between the two sets of married couples, each couple holding its undivided one-half interest as tenants by the entireties.

Decree reversed. Each party to pay own costs.

NOTES

1. It may be that the original grantor, Joyce E. King, actually wanted to create a joint tenancy between the two family groups so that

the ultimate survivor of the four Michaels would take all of the "King Farm." If so, the lawyer who drafted the deed failed to carry out her purpose. How would you draft the deed to reach the desired result?

2. Note that in the principal case the original deed expressly created two tenancies by the entireties and the dispute centered on whether the two family groups held their respective one-half interests as tenants in common or as joint tenants. Suppose the original deed had been less explicit and had conveyed to "Harry and Bertha, husband and wife, and to Ford and Michael, husband and wife." Would this have made a difference in the concurrent estates created? "At common law it was presumed that a conveyance to husband and wife created a tenancy by the entirety even in the absence of language of survivorship or reference to that kind of tenancy." Carver v. Gilbert, 387 P.2d 928, 929 (Alaska 1963). Despite the modern preference for tenancy in common, some states, which still recognize tenancies by the entirety, continue this presumption. See, e.g., N.C.Gen.Stat. § 39–13.6 (1983 Supp.) Other states that still recognize tenancy by the entirety require that it be expressly declared. 4A Powell on Real Property s. 622 (1982).

LAURA v. CHRISTIAN

Supreme Court of New Mexico, 1975.
88 N.M. 127, 537 P.2d 1389.

OMAN, JUSTICE. This appeal is from a judgment quieting title in plaintiff-appellee (Laura) to a parcel of real property known as Fireside Lodge. We reverse as to appellant (Christian) and remand with directions.

There were several defendants, including Christian, named in the proceedings below, but only he has taken and perfected an appeal pursuant to Supreme Court Rules 5, 7, 10, 12, 14 and 15 [§§ 21–2–1(5), (7), (10), (12), (14) and (15), N.M.S.A. 1953 (Repl. Vol. 4, 1970)], which were applicable to this appeal but which have since been superseded. The other defendants are presumed to have been satisfied with the judgment of the district court. Chavez v. Myers, 11 N.M. 333, 68 P. 917 (1902). In any event, they have failed to perfect an appeal, and, therefore, are bound by the judgment.

Christian claims only a one-fourth interest as a tenant in common with Laura in the Fireside Lodge. Thus, this appeal and our decision relate only to this claim and to the admitted right of Laura as a cotenant to a lien upon Christian's interest to secure the payment by him of his proportionate share of all sums expended by Laura to protect and preserve their common property.

The property was subject to a mortgage lien at the times Laura and Christian acquired their respective interests. Thereafter, one payment on the principal and several payments of interest were made on the mortgage indebtedness which were contributed to by the cotenants. However, the subsequent payments as called for by the mortgage instruments were not paid, and the mortgagee instituted a foreclosure action on August 31, 1971. This suit proceeded to judgment in favor of the mortgagee, and a foreclosure sale was ordered for April 11, 1972.

On April 10, 1972, Laura, in order to protect the property from sale, paid the mortgagee the sum of $17,288.40, which represented the amount of the judgment, interest and expenses owing to the mortgagee.

Although Christian and other claimants to an interest in the property had knowledge as early as July, 1971, that foreclosure was being threatened, they failed to assume their respective obligations to pay their proportionate shares of the mortgage indebtedness as it became due, and failed to take any action to avoid the sale of the property. It was not until after it became apparent that the value of the property had been greatly enhanced by the execution on March 29, 1972 of what in effect amounted to an option to purchase adjoining lands and which was exercised by the optionee on July 19, 1972, that Christian demonstrated any real interest in the property and any willingness to pay any share of the indebtedness which was discharged by Laura on April 10, 1972.

However, the fact remains that Christian had and still has legal title to a one-fourth interest in the property, and on January 9, 1973, at the commencement of the trial in the cause now on appeal, agreed to the payment of his proportionate share of the expenditures made by Laura to protect the property and to the imposition by the district court of a lien upon his interest to secure payment thereof. The general rule as to reimbursement, or contribution, from a cotenant in a situation such as is here presented is as follows:

"As a general proposition, a cotenant who pays more than his share of a debt secured by a mortgage or other lien on the common property, or of interest falling due on such debt, is entitled to reimbursement (contribution) from his cotenants to the extent to which he paid their shares of the indebtedness." Annot., 48 A.L.R.2d 1295, 1308 (1956). . . .

It is also a general rule that the redemption or prevention from loss by one cotenant of common property by payment of an obligation or the purchase of an outstanding interest, which should be discharged or purchased proportionately by cotenants, inures to the benefit of the cotenants at their option, subject to the right of contribution. However the option must be exercised within a reasonable time, and what is reasonable depends upon the circumstances in each case. . . . We do not applaud the failure of Christian to promptly assume his obligation to pay his one-fourth of the amount paid by Laura in protecting their common property, or in waiting until after it became apparent that the payment thereof would be profitable to him before offering payment. However, under all the circumstances of this case, not all of which appear or can reasonably be detailed in this opinion, we conclude that his election to contribute was timely.

We are also mindful of the fact that the legal title to a one-fourth interest in the property was vested and still vests in Christian, and that we have previously held that a constructive trust cannot be imposed in a quiet title suit. Otero et al. v. Toti, 33 N.M. 613, 273 P. 917 (1928). See also Alston v. Clinton, 73 N.M. 341, 388 P.2d 64 (1963) and Clark v.

Primus, 62 N.M. 259, 308 P.2d 584 (1957), in which the holding in Otero was cited with approval.

The judgment of the district court should be reversed with instructions to enter a new judgment quieting title to a three-fourths interest in the property in Laura, establishing a one-fourth interest therein in Christian, subject to a lien thereon in favor of Laura to secure repayment to him of all amounts expended for the benefit of Christian, together with interest thereon from the date or dates of such expenditures to date of repayment by Christian, and, insofar as proper, granting Laura such other relief as is necessary to protect his right to contribution for all such expenditures and interest owing to him by Christian.

It is so ordered.

McMANUS, C.J., and MONTOYA, J., concur.

NOTES

1. The problem of the principal case arises in a wide variety of situations. For example, in Andrews v. Andrews, 155 Fla. 654, 21 So.2d 205 (1945) a wife redeemed property held in tenancy by the entireties from a tax sale. Despite the fact that the parties were divorced the court allowed the ex-husband to share the redeemed property, as a tenant in common, provided he reimbursed his former wife for one-half of the amount paid by her at the redemption. Said the court: "Each tenant by the entirety owes to the other the highest degree of confidence and trust. We repeat, if a tenant in common may not take advantage of his cotenant nor a parcener of his coparcener by purchasing a tax deed on the property they hold, there is all the more reason why the rule should be applied in the case of estate by the entirety."

2. The principle invoked by the Florida Court in the case referred to in Note 1 to the effect that the cotenants had a fiduciary relationship—a special basis for trust and confidence—has been relied upon to like effect in other opinions, but it should not be supposed that cotenants will always be regarded as having a fiduciary relationship which will prevent one from acting for himself to the possible disadvantage of another. It has been suggested that where the cotenants acquire their interests simultaneously by the same conveyance, or by a testate or intestate succession, the relationship should be recognized; otherwise not—e.g., where one cotenant conveys his undivided interest to an outsider, the latter may well be regarded as having no fiduciary duty to the other cotenant(s). It is also arguable that where the property is assessed as a whole for taxation, all the cotenants are equally in default if the tax is not paid when it is due, and none should be permitted to cure his own default by overdue payment, thus obtaining a "tax title," without allowing the others to do the same by reimbursing him. In Jennings v. Bradfield, 169 Colo. 146, 454 P.2d 81 (1969), allowing a tenant in common to acquire her two cotenants' shares by redeeming delinquent tax certificates, the Colorado Supreme Court relied upon the fact that the three undivided interests were separately assessed in the names of individual owners; hence, it could

not be said that the redeeming cotenant was in default with reference to taxes assessed against the others' interests.

According to one authority, "That principle [meaning fiduciary relationship] should not be applied to the purchase of the property by one of the tenants on the foreclosure of a mortgage on the entire property. The other cotenants, if adults, have the same opportunity to bid at the sale, and there is no basis for asserting that a duty exists in a cotenant to buy at the sale for the benefit of the others. In most of the cases holding to the contrary, there were special facts involving fraud on, or the taking of advantage of, the cotenants of the acquiring cotenant which justified the decision, but which did not justify the position that all purchases at such sales come under the rule." 2 Am. Law of Prop. 69 (1952). It may well be true that no general statements concerning the problem, including those just quoted, may safely be regarded as reliable guides; so much depends upon the circumstances of particular cases, including the length of time which has elapsed between the purported acquisition by one cotenant and the demand by another to be allowed to restore himself to his former position by contributing his share of cost of acquisition.

On this latter point, see also Stoltz v. Maloney, 129 Ariz. 264, 630 P.2d 560 (App.1981) where the court said: "We recognize the general rule that there exists a fiduciary relationship between tenants in common . . .. It is the general rule that tenants in common cannot buy the common property at a tax sale, except for the benefit of all . . .. An exception to this general rule arises where the land has been assessed upon the tax books in the names of the owners of the undivided interests separately, and when the owner of each undivided interest could have paid his own tax unaffected by the fact of the joint interest."

3. If one cotenant cannot take advantage of his fellows by redemption at a mortgage foreclosure or a tax sale, does it follow that a cotenant must account to his co-owners for rents and profits he receives in excess of his aliquot share?

"According to the early common law, an owner could not compel his co-owners to account for rents and profits derived from the common property. This rule was modified by the English Statute of 4 Anne, c. 16, enacted in 1705, which provides that a cotenant who *received* more than his just share of the rents and profits from the land could be compelled to account. According to the English decisions, however, this statute did not change the rule that a cotenant cannot be compelled to account for his own use and enjoyment of the common property. A cotenant is entitled to the right of possession; he may not be made to account for the exercise of a right which gives him only his just share of the rents and profits.

"In most of the American states, the Statute of 4 Anne, c. 16, is considered as a part of the common law, while in some states, a similar statute has been enacted. American jurisdictions differ on the point of accountability by a tenant in possession. However, the prevailing rule is that the language of the statute of Anne is subject to the interpretation that a cotenant may be compelled to account for rents and profits, if he derives from a third party more than his just share of the rents and profits, or if he derives a profit from the land through farming or mining operations. The tenant against whom an accounting is sought is entitled to an allowance for his labor: The liability to account extends only to the net profits. It is generally agreed that unless the cotenant has been ousted from possession, the one in possession is not, merely because of possession, required to account for the reasonable rental value of the land." Burby on Real Property 339–340 (2d ed. 1954) (The author's footnotes have been omitted.) See also Keith v. El-Kareh, 729 P.2d 377 (Colo.App.1986) where the court stated: "Moreover, in the absence of a written agreement, tenants in common are not entitled to rent from each other unless the tenant seeking rent has been ousted from possession. . . . Unless an actual ouster is shown, the law presumes that the possession of one tenant in common is the possession of all."

On Professor Burby's last point, compare Ill.—S.H.A., ch. 76, § 5 (1985). "When one or more joint tenants, tenants in common, or copartners in real estate, or any interest therein, shall take and use the profits *or benefits thereof,* in greater proportion than his or their interest, such person or persons, his or their executors and administrators, shall account therefore to his or their cotenants jointly or severally." [Emphasis added.] See Clarke v. Clarke, 349 Ill. 642, 183 N.E. 13 (1932). If the occupying cotenant is receiving the full benefit of the land himself, why shouldn't he be held to account to his non-occupying cotenants?

In Clark v. Covington, 107 Ill.App.3d 845, 63 Ill.Dec. 697, 438 N.E. 2d 628 (1982) the wife sought partition of real property owned in joint tenancy. The husband had occupied the premises alone since April, 1974, when the wife moved out. Although her complaint did not ask for rent for the period of the husband's sole occupancy, the appraiser found that the reasonable rental of $8,571.81 should be assessed against the husband as a part of the accounting. The court held against the wife, saying: "In order to render one cotenant liable to another cotenant for the rent or use of jointly owned property, there must be something more than mere occupancy of the property by one and forebearance from occupancy by another." The Appellate Court did not cite either the Illinois statute or Clarke v. Clarke. Did not the husband take and use the profits *or benefits thereof* in greater proportion than his interest? Would it have made a difference if the wife had sought this amount in her complaint for partition? Would it have made a difference if she had demanded the rent earlier and been refused?

See also Spiller v. Mackereth, 334 So.2d 859 (Ala.1976), where the court held an occupying cotenant could not be held liable for rent unless he had refused a demand of his cotenant to enter. A mere letter demanding the payment of rent or vacation of the land was not a sufficient demand to enter. What would be sufficient?

For further expositions of the duty to account see Baird v. Moore, 50 N.J.Super. 156, 141 A.2d 324 (1958) and Burby on Real Property 228–232 (3d ed. 1965).

GOERGEN v. MAAR

Supreme Court of New York, Appellate Division, 1956.
2 A.D.2d 276, 153 N.Y.S.2d 826.

HALPERN, J. In this action for partition, it appeared that the defendant-appellant and the plaintiff-respondent, together with the defendants-respondents, owned certain real property in the City of Albany, New York, as tenants in common. They all traced their title, by devise or inheritance, to a common source. The plaintiff-respondent was the owner of a 4/16ths interest; the defendant-appellant was the owner of a 6/16ths interest and the other two defendants were the owners of 3/16ths each. The defendant-appellant had been in sole possession of the property and had collected the rents from January 1, 1943, to the date of the commencement of the action, July 16, 1954. The other co-tenants sought to hold the appellant liable for the rents collected by her less the amounts disbursed for taxes, water rents and repairs. The appellant set up the bar of the six year statute of limitations. This objection was overruled by the Referee and by the Special Term and it presents the sole question raised upon this appeal.

The interlocutory judgment adjudges that the appellant be charged with the net balance of rents collected by her in the amount of $8,408.51 and directs that the Referee retain that amount out of her share of the proceeds of the sale and the judgment also directs that a personal judgment be rendered against the appellant for any deficiency, if her share of the proceeds of the sale should be insufficient to pay the amount owing by her. Presumably an adjustment is to be made, in carrying out the judgment, so that the appellant will be credited with the net share of the rents to which she is entitled as co-tenant.

Insofar as the judgment directed that an adjustment for the rents collected by the appellant be made upon the distribution of the proceeds of the sale, the Special Term was clearly correct in holding that the statute of limitations did not apply. Civil Practice Act, § 1075, provides that in an action for partition, the court "may adjust the rights of one or more of the parties as against any other party or parties, by reason of the receipt by the latter of more than his or their proper proportion of the rents or profits of a share or part of a share". This section was derived from section 1589 of Part II of the Code of Civil Procedure, Ch. 178, L.1880, without change of substance. The section was inserted in the Code, according to Throop's notes, "to avoid the possibility of affecting, by any of the previous provisions, the ruling in Scott v. Guernsey, 48 N.Y. 106". Scott v. Guernsey, which had been decided in 1871, had held that the court could make an equitable adjustment for rents collected by one co-tenant, in a partition action, and that it was not necessary to bring a separate action for an accounting and, furthermore, that "The rents, on a partition, are a lien upon the shares or interest of any co-tenants from whom they may be due", at page 124. While the court in Scott v. Guernsey, supra, mentioned only an adjustment of rents, the underlying principle was of course applicable to expenditures made by a co-tenant as well as to rents or profits collected by him. The Code section referred only to an adjustment of rents or profits, presumably because the draftsman of the section had the Scott case specifically in mind.

In a partition action, the court may adjust all the equities of the parties in determining the distribution of the proceeds of the sale. In the process of adjustment, the court is not concerned with the enforcement of any personal liability. Hence, there is no basis for applying any separate statute of limitations to the adjustment process. So long as the partition action itself is not barred by the running of the statute of limitations, C.P.A. § 41–a, there is no period of limitation beyond which the court is forbidden to go in making an equitable adjustment of the shares of the parties. The court may take into account the moneys received and the moneys expended by any of the co-tenants throughout the whole period of the co-ownership of the property. As was said many years ago, "There does not seem to be any provision limiting the time for which rents may be apportioned in actions for partition." Adams v. Bristol, 126 App.Div. 660, 664, 111 N.Y.S. 231, 234, affirmed 196 N.Y. 510, 89 N.E. 1095.

The legal theory seems to be that any item of rent received by a co-tenant, in excess of his share of the income of the property, is an equitable charge against his interest and any expenditure made by a co-tenant, in excess of his share of the obligation, is a charge against the interests of his co-tenants; the respective interests of the parties in the property are deemed to be reduced or increased accordingly. Each tenant in common "holds a contingent interest in the entire title until all equities relating to the tenancy are adjusted". The "respective interests" of the co-tenants are to be "equalized in a partition proceeding" and "the Statute of Limitations would not be a defense" to the adjustment of the equities. Matter of Wood's Estate, 68 Misc. 267, 269, 123 N.Y.S. 574, 575.

Insofar as the judgment appealed from provides that a personal judgment should be rendered against the appellant for any deficiency, a different question arises. In this respect, the judgment goes beyond an adjustment of the shares of the parties in the proceeds of the partition sale and undertakes to enforce a personal liability against the appellant. This liability is based upon section 532 of the Real Property Law under which a co-tenant "who has received more than his own just proportion" may be held liable for the excess in an action at law brought by his co-tenants. This statute goes back to the time of Queen Anne, 4 & 5 Anne, Ch. 16, § 27 (1705). The statute of Anne was re-enacted in New York State by Chapter 4 of the Laws of 1788, 1 Van Ness & Woodworth [1813 Rev.] 90, § 2, which was codified as section 9 of Title 5 of Chapter 1 of Part 2 of the Revised Statutes (1 Rev.Stat., of N.Y. [1st ed., 1829], part II. ch. 1, tit. V, § 9, p. 750). Minion v. Warner, 185 App.Div. 246, 173 N.Y.S. 69. Without change of substance, this statute subsequently became section 1666 of the Code of Civil Procedure, from which it was transferred to the Real Property Law.

The relationship of tenants in common "who hold their estate through descent or under a will" is "a quasi trust relationship". Minion v. Warner, 238 N.Y. 413, 417, 144 N.E. 665, 666. In such a case, the liability of the co-tenant receiving more than his just share of the rents may also be enforced by a suit in equity for an accounting. The statute of limitations is applicable to an action by one co-tenant against another, seeking a personal judgment, whether it is a common-law action on an account, under section 532 of the Real Property Law, or an action in equity for an accounting. The equity action would ordinarily be governed by a ten year statute of limitations, C.P.A. § 53, and the action at law by a six year statute of limitations, C.P.A. § 48. But, since this is a case of "concurrent jurisdiction in law and equity, equity is bound by the statute of limitations", which is applicable to the law action, Minion v. Warner, supra, 238 N.Y. 418, 144 N.E. 666. The six year statute of limitations is therefore applicable to the enforcement of the personal liability of the co-tenant.

However, the question remains as to when the statute of limitations begins to run against an action on an account or for an accounting. If there were an express agreement requiring the cotenant in possession to distribute the rents as soon as they were received or to render annual accountings, the statute of limitations would begin to run at the time of the receipt of the rents or at the end of the year in which the rents were received. But, in the absence of such an agreement, the statute of limitations does not ordinarily begin to run until the termination of the relationship of the cotenants, by a sale of the property. This conclusion may be reached by either of two approaches. First, it may be held that the relationship between the co-tenants is a fiduciary one, at least in a case in which the co-ownership originated in a devise by, or in inheritance from, a common source. Minion v. Warner, supra. A principle may then be applied analogous to that governing the running of the statute of limitations in an action against a trustee. Lammer v. Stoddard, 103 N.Y. 672, 9 N.E. 328; Spallholz v. Sheldon, 216 N.Y. 205, 110 N.E. 431. Under that theory, the statute of limitations would not begin to run until the termination of the relationship, unless the co-tenant in possession had theretofore openly repudiated his obligation to account, in which case the statute of limitations would begin to run at the time of the repudiation, Robinson v. Robinson, 173 Mass. 233, 53 N.E. 854; Bacon v. Bacon, 266 Mass. 462, 165 N.E. 485. The Robinson case was cited with approval by the Court of Appeals in Minion v. Warner, supra, 238 N.Y. at page 418, 144 N.E. at page 666, but the court chose to rest its conclusion that the statute of limitations had not begun to run until the termination of the relationship, in that case, upon a somewhat different ground. The court held that where "one tenant in common received rents and profits and paid, not merely for repairs and the ordinary running expenses of the property, but for taxes in respect to which he had a personal claim against his cotenants", there existed between the parties "mutual, open, and current accounts". Minion v. Warner, supra, 238 N.Y. at page 418, 144 N.E. at page 666. Accordingly, the court held, the statute of limitations did not begin to run "until the last item in 1916 when the property was . . . sold." 238 N.Y. at page 418, 144 N.E. at page 666. Civil Practice Act, § 56.

The same reasoning is applicable here. The appellant collected the rents of the property and became personally liable therefor, on the one hand, and, on the other, she paid the taxes for which all the co-tenants (all of whom resided in the tax district) were personally liable, Tax Law, § 71. There was therefore a "mutual, open, and current account" between the parties and the statute of limitations did not begin to run until the receipt of the last item of rent or the making of the last disbursement of taxes therefrom. The defendant-appellant was therefore properly required to account for all the rents collected by her from the time of her taking possession and the judgment properly provided for personal liability for any deficiency.

The judgment appealed from should be affirmed with costs.

NOTE

The cases in this Section deal with the general aspects of concurrent ownership, including the nature of the relationship between the co-owners, their right to partition, their duty to account, etc. One peculiarly perplexing set of problems arises when the land is used for mining, quarrying or timber operations. So long as all of the co-owners agree on how to exploit the land there is no problem, but that is like saying there is no problem when there is no problem. Inevitably, one co-owner will wish to use the land for these purposes, either by himself or through a lessee, and the other (or others) will refuse to consent. In some states, the co-owner who proceeds on his own is committing waste and he can be enjoined by the non-consenting co-owners or held liable for damages (in some instances treble damages). In other states, although the acts may be referred to as waste, the developing co-owner is merely held to a duty to account for net profits. In the former jurisdictions, a lease from the developing co-owner is void and the lessee can be ejected by the non-consenting co-owners. In the latter, the lease is valid although the lessor can be held to account. See, for example, Swartzbaugh v. Sampson, 11 Cal.App.2d 451, 54 P.2d 73 (1936). The duty to account for net profits sounds simple but can be extremely complex to apply. The following case illustrates some of those complexities.

WHITE v. SMYTH

Supreme Court of Texas, 1948.
147 Tex. 272, 214 S.W.2d 967, 5 A.L.R.2d 1348.

[In 1923, Mrs. Smyth and her children, tenants in common of approximately 30,000 acres of land, by lease conveyed to White the right to produce rock asphalt (limestone impregnated with asphalt) from the entire area. The lessors were to receive a royalty of twenty-five cents per ton on some of the rock produced and lesser amounts on other production. The lease term was 99 years, but White was empowered to terminate it at any time, whereupon he was to pay $1000, plus $13,222.22 as prepayment for 56,000 tons of rock to be produced after termination. White established a quarry and commenced production. In 1932 the cotenants effected a partition of the ranch, but the rock asphalt therein and a 200-acre tract surrounding the quarry were excluded from the partition and continued to be held in cotenancy.

In October, 1941, White terminated the lease and paid the lessors $14,222.22, notifying them that he would vacate when he had taken the rock paid for in advance. In October, 1942, White acquired the interests of two cotenants (one of whom was his wife) so that he then owned a one-ninth interest in the 200-acre tract and in the rock asphalt in the rest of the 30,000 acres. In November, 1942, he notified his cotenants by letter that he had removed the rock paid for in advance; that as owner of a one-ninth interest he would "now want to take out such part of my share of the rock as is practical before I move my machinery"; that he recognized "the right of all other interested parties to do likewise"; and that he would keep an accurate account of rock removed. His subsequent operations resulted in a suit by his cotenants. They sought a decree declaring that the 200-acre tract and the rock asphalt in the rest of the ranch could not be partitioned in kind and ordering partition by sale and division of the proceeds. They also asked judgment against White for their share of rock he had removed.

Answering special issues submitted, the jury found (a) that the rock asphalt could not properly by partitioned in kind; (b) that White's mining operations were not such as to exclude his cotenants from similar operations; (c) that White had not "mined more than one-ninth in value in the ground" of all the producible rock asphalt; (d) that the reasonable value, in the ground, of the 397,338.11 tons which White had taken during the period in question, October 29, 1942, to September 30, 1945, was $99,334.53 (twenty-five cents per ton); (e) that White's profit from his operations during this period was $250,180.56. On these findings the trial court ordered that the property in question be sold and the proceeds divided, and awarded the plaintiffs judgment against White for $222,382.72 (eight-ninths of his profits). On White's appeal the Court of Civil Appeals affirmed the judgment (214 S.W.2d 953), and White obtained a writ of error.]

SMEDLEY, J. . . .

The application for writ of error presents under several points three principal contentions: First, that petitioner White owes no duty to account to respondents, because he has not taken more than his fair share of the rock asphalt in place, has not excluded respondents from the premises and in mining has made merely normal use of the property, it having already been devoted to the mining of rock asphalt at the time petitioner acquired his undivided interest therein; second, that if he owes a duty to account, he is liable only for eight-ninths of the value in the ground of the rock asphalt he has mined and not for profits which he has realized; and third, that the jury's findings that the rock asphalt in certain surveys in the ranch and in all of the property outside of certain surveys cannot be equitably partitioned in kind are without evidence to support them. We consider first the points pertaining to partition, since the question whether the property is or is not capable of partition in kind has an important bearing upon the other questions.

[An extensive portion of the opinion, in which the court discussed and rejected the contentions concerning partition in kind, is omitted.]

The amount of the trial court's judgment in favor of respondents against petitioner represents eight-ninths of the net profits realized by petitioner from mining, processing and selling 397,381.11 tons of rock asphalt taken from the land during the period from October 29, 1942, to September 30, 1945. This amount of net profits was found by the jury after deducting from the gross proceeds all expenses incurred by petitioner, together with a reasonable compensation for his personal services and the reasonable value of the use of his plant and other property in the operation of the mine. The judgment follows the weight of authority and the general rule thus stated in American Jurisprudence: "Since any co-owner of a mine or mineral property is at liberty to work it, some courts have intimated that a co-owner who does not choose to avail himself of this right should have no claim upon the production of one who has elected to do so. But this view seems to be contrary to the weight of authority, and the prevailing rule appears to be that the producer must account to his cotenant for all profits made to the extent of his interest in the property." 14 Am.Jur., p. 104, Sec. 36. . . .

It seems that there are no decisions in this state as to the duty of a co-owner who takes solid minerals from the property to account to his cotenant. It is held, however, as in most of the other states, that one who takes oil without the consent of his cotenants must account to them for their share of the proceeds of the oil less the necessary and reasonable cost of producing and marketing it. . . .

Petitioner contends that the rule above stated does not apply to this case, and that he need not account to his cotenants, because he has mined no more than his fair share of the rock asphalt in place and has not excluded them from the premises. He relies primarily upon Kirby Lumber Co. v. Temple Lumber Co., 125 Tex. 284, 83 S.W.2d 638, and the text of Lindley (Lindley on Mines, 3rd Ed., Vol. 3, Secs. 789–789a, pp. 1933–1941) for what he insists is the applicable rule.

In the Kirby Lumber Company case the Temple Company owned an undivided two-thirds interest and the Kirby Company owned an undivided one-third interest in a 640 acre tract of land on which there was valuable standing timber. The Temple Company, believing that it owned the entire title to a specific 427 acres of the land, cut all of the timber standing on that tract, amounting to ten million feet, and manufactured it into lumber. There remained uncut on the 640 acres 2,783,325 feet of timber. The court's opinion states that the 640 acres was generally of uniform value as to timber and otherwise. The Kirby Company sued the Temple Company to recover the manufactured value of one-third of the timber that had been cut. The trial court found that the total amount of timber standing on the land before the cutting was 12,783,325 feet, of which the Kirby Company's one-third amounted to 4,261,108 feet, and that the amount left standing was 2,783,325 feet, which was treated as belonging to the Kirby Company, and that thus the Temple Company had cut 1,477,783 feet more than its share. Its judgment awarded to the Kirby Company $43,372.93, being the manufactured value of the 1,477,783 feet. The Court of Civil Appeals reversed and rendered the trial court's judgment, after holding that the Kirby Company was charged with notice that its predecessor in title had cut timber from part of the land. 42 S.W.2d 1070. The Supreme Court reversed the judgments of the two lower courts and rendered judgment in favor of the Kirby Company against the Temple Company for the stumpage value, $5.00 per thousand feet, of the 1,447,783 feet of excess timber cut by the Temple Company. Most of the Court's opinion is devoted to a discussion of the question whether the Kirby Company should be charged with notice that timber had been cut by its predecessor in title and of the question as to the amount of the recovery, that is whether stumpage value or manufactured value. Little is said in the approval of that part of the trial court's judgment which charged the Temple Company with only the amount of the timber cut in excess of its share. The authorities there cited relate to timber and to the question whether stumpage value or manufactured value may be recovered.

The important distinction between the Kirby Lumber Company case and the instant case, in respect to the ruling that the Temple Company need not account for the timber cut not in excess of its two-thirds share, is that in that case, as shown by the Court's statement that [125 Tex. 284, 83 S.W.2d 639] "the 640 acres was generally of uniform value as to timber and otherwise," the timber was fairly subject to partition in kind, whereas in the instant case the rock asphalt is not. The Temple Company's action in cutting the timber up to its share and the Court's approval of that action by the judgment rendered worked in effect a partition of the timber. Here there has not been, and there could not be, consistently with the finding that the rock asphalt is not capable of partition in kind, an approval by the court of White's action in taking for himself and disposing of a part of the rock asphalt. The ownership of all of the cotenants extends to all of the rock asphalt, and White was not authorized to make partition of it.

. . .

The facts of this case attest the obvious soundness of the rule that a cotenant cannot select and take for himself part of the property jointly owned and thus make partition. While he was lessee under the lease that covered the entire ranch, White selected the site for and developed the present pit, making extensive improvements, including the construction of roads, excavations and grading for private tracks, other excavations and grading, all at great cost and of very substantial value. The location of the plant site was favorable and valuable. The rock asphalt in the pit was both rich rock and lean rock, both of which were necessary to meet market demands and specifications. The east wall of the pit, which was rock asphalt, attained a height of about eighty feet. It was rich in asphalt at the top and lean at the bottom. From this wall much of the rock asphalt for which accounting is sought in this suit was mined and mixed by the simple process of blasting the rock from the face of the wall, so blasting it as to mix the rich rock with the lean rock. When White completed the mining of his prepaid rock the piled overburden was about two hundred feet east of the east wall of the pit, and he was able to mine the rock asphalt from the wall without moving more than the natural overburden, but at the time of the trial he had mined so far east that the toe of the piled overburden was reached and the overburden would have to be removed in order to mine farther east.

When White exercised the right to terminate the lease and completed the taking of his prepaid rock he had no further right or interest in the rock asphalt in the lands, the mine or the mine site, except that he was given by the lease the right to remove his machinery, tools, houses and implements. The rock asphalt estate in all of the lands belonged to all of the cotenants, as did also the added advantages and values to the entire mineral estate created and existing by reason of the developed pit and mine site; but White, taking advantage for himself of the added values, after acquiring the one-ninth interest of his wife and his wife's sister, mined from the pit about four hundred thousand tons of the rich, valuable and readily accessible rock asphalt.

It is true, as contended by petitioner, that in some of the cases cited above which required the producing tenant to account to his cotenants for their share of the profits, it does not affirmatively appear that the mining cotenant has not taken more than his share. In those cases the point made by petitioner seems not to have been made, and the rule is stated and applied that the producer must account, with no reference to the question whether he has taken more or has taken less than his share. In several of the cases, however, the point was made and rejected. . . .

Petitioner relies also upon Mr. Lindley's text in which the conclusion is expressed that, since cotenants are the owners of the substance of the estate, one of them may work a mine without accounting to his cotenants, even though it may consume the whole of the value of the estate, provided he does not exclude his cotenants. The reason for this conclusion is thus stated: "The taking of ore from the mine is rather the use than the destruction of the estate within the meaning of the general rule. The results of the tenant's labor and capital are in the nature of proceeds or profits, the partial exhaustion being but incidental consequence of the use. The same principle applies to the extraction of oil and gas." Lindley on Mines, 3rd Ed., Vol. 3, pp. 1933–1938, Secs. 789–789a. . . .

The rule announced by Mr. Lindley is an extension to cotenants of the common-law rule applied to life tenants who operate mines already opened on the property. It rests upon somewhat technical and artificial views of normal use and waste, and is unrealistic in treating the exhaustion of a mineral estate as but an incidental consequence of use.

It disregards the important fact that each cotenant's interest extends to all of the minerals. Its full application would permit a cotenant to take all of the minerals without being required to account. And, as has been shown, it is contrary to the weight of authority.

Kirby Lumber Co. v. Temple Lumber Co., 125 Tex. 284, 83 S.W.2d 638, is cited by petitioner to sustain his assignment of error that if he owes respondents the duty to account, he must account only for the value in the ground of the rock asphalt mined by him. That case is not an authority for this point. The plaintiff did not ask for an accounting for profits. There were no allegations as to profits and no issue as to profits was submitted. There is nothing to show that any profits were made. The question before the court was whether the defendant should be required to pay for the stumpage value of the timber cut or for its value after having been manufactured into lumber and without deduction for expenditures. The court held that the former, that is stumpage value, was the measure of recovery because the defendant had acted in good faith, believing that it owned all of the timber that it had cut. A fundamental difference between the facts of the Kirby case and the instant case, which has been noted herein, has an important bearing here. It is that in the Kirby case the standing timber was of uniform value and could readily be partitioned in kind, whereas in this case the rock asphalt cannot be fairly and equitably partitioned in kind.

Three cases are cited by petitioner in which the cotenant who had taken minerals was charged with their value in place: Appeal of Fulmer, 128 Pa. 24, 18 A. 493, 15 Am.St.Rep. 662; McGowan v. Bailey, 179 Pa. 470, 36 A. 325; and Clowser v. Joplin, W.D.Mo., Fed.Cas. No. 2,908a, 4 Dill. 469 note. While the opinions in the two Pennsylvania cases contain reasoning to justify the use of that measure, they also indicate that it was deemed just and equitable under the peculiar facts, and that it might not be applicable to all cases. In the Federal case a memorandum opinion adopts the measure of liability stated in the two Pennsylvania cases as appropriate under the Missouri statute. The three cases depart from the majority rule, supported by the authorities cited and discussed herein, which majority rule is stated in American Jurisprudence as follows:

"When it is claimed that a cotenant in possession of a mine or a mineral property has become liable to his cotenants for profits accruing from his productive operations, the usual mode of settling the account is to charge him with all his receipts and credit him with all his expenses, thereby ascertaining the net profits available for distribution. In other words, the usual basis of an accounting by a cotenant who works the common mine or develops the common oil and gas property is the value of the product, less the necessary expenses of production." 14 Am.Jur., p. 106, Sec. 38.

The text of American Jurisprudence contains also a statement that the weight of authority and the prevailing rule are that when a co-owner of mineral property works the property and disposes of the minerals produced, he must account to his cotenant for all profits made to the extent of his interest in the property. 14 Am.Jur., p. 104, Sec. 36.

The text of American Jurisprudence is supported by many decisions at the pages cited, and it is supported by the cases hereinabove cited where is discussed the duty of the producing tenant to account to his cotenant. It clearly appears from careful examination of the cases cited in American Jurisprudence, those cited herein and in the briefs of both parties, that the measure of accounting used by the trial court and approved by the Court of Civil Appeals accords with the great weight of authority.

It is argued by petitioner that his receipts have been from sales of a manufactured product, and that respondents should not be permitted, by sharing in the profits, to obtain the benefits of his personal skill and industry and of the flux oil and water used and the machinery, apparatus and equipment belonging to petitioner. We believe that the preparation of the rock asphalt for market, as described by petitioner's testimony and by that of other witnesses, is a processing rather than a manufacturing. The rock asphalt is rock asphalt in the ground; that is, limestone rock impregnated with asphalt. To make it ready for the market and for use in the building of roads it is mixed and crushed, and oil is mixed with it to give the small particles of rock a film of oil, and water is put in the mixture so that it will not become solid in transit. It is rock asphalt when it is sold and when it is used on the roads. The producing tenant is required to account to his cotenants for net profits realized from mining, smelting, crushing, processing or marketing solid minerals taken from the land. . . .

A statement of the expenses claimed by White as incident to the mining and marketing of the rock asphalt was prepared by him, furnished to respondents and introduced in evidence. With a few unimportant exceptions the statement was accepted and used by the jury as showing expenses to be deducted from the gross receipts in determining the net profits. The statement lists as expenses many items and large sums for flux oil, as well as charges for payrolls, salaries, depreciation, repairs, insurance, commissions, etc. In addition to these expenses, the jury, following the trial court's instructions, allowed substantial credits as reasonable compensation for White's personal services and as the reasonable value of the use of the plant and other property belonging to him. Examination of the evidence from which the jury's computation of the amount of net profits was made discloses that the jury was generous in the credits given for the expenses above referred to, and also in the credits for the use of petitioner's plant and other property and for his personal services. The trial court's judgment permits petitioner within six months after the sale by the receiver to remove the buildings, plant, property and equipment owned by him and situated on the premises. It is to be assumed that the jury which heard petitioner testify as to his experience and business ability, took these into consideration when in computing the net profits it gave credit for the value of his personal services.

The rock asphalt was owned in undivided interests by all of the cotenants. Their ownership extended to all of the rock asphalt and to all of the advantages and peculiar conditions and stages of development of the property at the time when petitioner terminated the lease. This ownership extended to the developed pit with its great wall of easily accessible rock asphalt and to the valuable mining site. It extended to the use value of the rock asphalt and to its profit possibilities. To limit the accounting to the value in place of the rock asphalt mined by petitioner would be to permit him to use for his own profit the property owned in common and the advantages and opportunities for profit inherent in that ownership and to deprive respondents of a substantial part of its value and benefits. In our opinion, the trial court's judgment, requiring petitioner to account to his co-owners according to their interests for the profits realized from the common property, after crediting him with all expenses and with the compensation above mentioned, assures to all of the co-owners the benefits and values of their ownership, is correct in principle and, as has been said, is supported by the decided weight of authority.

The judgments of the district court and the Court of Civil Appeals are affirmed.

SIMPSON, J. (dissenting). It is respectfully submitted that the measure of recovery allowed to respondents by the majority ruling is wrong, and is contrary to the applicable precedents under the established facts. It results in what is earnestly urged to be an unjust exaction of the petitioner White, who should have been required to account for $99,334.53, the value in place of the rock asphalt taken, and not $222,382.72, its net manufactured value.

[Most of this opinion is omitted. It described the process by which the rock asphalt was prepared for market, characterizing it pointedly as "manufacturing" and likening it to the refining of crude petroleum. It also reviewed the cases relied upon in the majority opinion, and other authorities, in an effort to demonstrate that "the virtually uncontradicted rule of decision, as well as the better reasoning, requires an accounting here on the basis of the crude rock asphalt in place or, what is the same thing, its value before being processed at White's mill less the reasonable cost of getting it there." It declared that this is the rule of accounting where innocent trespassers have converted minerals and that a cotenant should be in no worse stead.]

The respondents ought not to be allowed to share in the capital investment, the experience, enterprise and personal business acumen of the petitioner. To allow this sharing puts a grim penalty upon freedom of enterprise and the risk of one's own capital in a highly hazardous and competitive business. The respondents can be made whole by awarding them the value of their share in place of the crude rock asphalt which was mined. This is fair and just. It allows full compensation for what was taken. Respondents are entitled to this, but certainly not to more.

SHARP, BREWSTER, and FOLLEY, JJ., join in this opinion.

NOTE

It has been suggested that in dealing with a cotenant's claim for contribution because of repairs or improvements, the controlling principle should be that of preventing unjust enrichment. Another way of formulating the concept, in a situation where (as in the foregoing case) a plaintiff is seeking a remedy for conversion of his property is to say that the question is not what the defendant has gained, but what the plaintiff has lost. If an award of damages is intended to furnish full compensation to the plaintiff, and not to punish the defendant—this seems to be commonly accepted doctrine where there is no demand for exemplary (punitive) damages—the proposition above seems sound. As the dissenting opinion asserts, it has commonly been the basis of decision in suits against "innocent" converters of minerals or timber—i.e., those who apparently were not aware that they were acting wrongfully.

In this connection, several observations with reference to the foregoing case are noteworthy. First, in the original transaction the plaintiffs were willing to forego the profit-making opportunity which the rock asphalt in place presented—instead they were content to accept the value of the mineral in place (royalty) and to allow White to have the profit-making opportunity. Second, the opinion nowhere suggests that the plaintiffs alleged that White's activity, after terminating his position as a lessee and commencing operations as a cotenant, deprived them of a profit-making opportunity of which they would have availed themselves by joining in White's operations or by operating independently. Third, the opinion nowhere suggests that the plaintiffs sought to show that White was a willful converter—i.e., that he was conscious of wrongdoing—and in view of the intensely contested question of partitionability in kind, it appears doubtful that they could have shown that he was not acting with a reasonable belief that he was within his rights as a cotenant. Hence, it seems quite possible that if White had been a good faith trespasser, having no ownership interest in the land, he would have been liable only for the "royalty"—the value of the mineral in place—not for the net profit realized by the sale of the processed mineral. If so, can any satisfactory reason be given for subjecting him, as a cotenant, to a greater liability? Can the result be justified by taking the position that cotenants have a special, confidential, fiduciary relationship?

Finally, is the court's effort to distinguish Kirby Lumber Co. v. Temple Lumber Co. satisfactory? If the timber in question was partitionable in kind, as the court says, and if the Temple Co. had not cut more than its proper share, it would have had no liability at all. But in fact it cut part of the share owned by the Kirby Co., and surely the fact of partitionability in kind is irrelevant to the question of what the Kirby Co. should recover, just as it would have been if the Temple Co. had cut all the timber on the tract. Assume that the Kirby Co., like the Temple Co., was engaged in cutting timber and processing it into marketable lumber at a profit. Assume also that its share of the timber taken by the Temple Co. was not readily replaceable at stumpage value of what was wrongfully taken—what should be the proper measure of the Temple Co.'s liability?

MICHALSKI v. MICHALSKI

Superior Court of New Jersey, Appellate Division, 1958.
50 N.J.Super. 454, 142 A.2d 645.

FREUND, J.A.D. Defendant appeals from a judgment of the Superior Court, Chancery Division, granting plaintiff's demand that certain properties owned by the parties as tenants in common be sold in partition.

Plaintiff and defendant are husband and wife and are equal owners, as tenants in common, of the three properties with which we are concerned. The title to the properties was originally in the name of the defendant, and on July 1, 1949 they were conveyed by the defendant through an intermediary to the plaintiff and defendant as tenants in common. The validity of the conveyance to the plaintiff and defendant was established in Michalski v. Michalski, 20 N.J.Super. 258, 89 A.2d 722 (Ch.Div.1952) where the marital discord between the parties is defined.

Contemporaneously with the conveyance the parties executed the written agreement which forms the basis for the instant suit. It provided:

"Agreement made this 1st day of July, 1949, between Marion Michalski and Alexandra Otto Michalski, husband and wife.

"Whereas, certain domestic difficulties have arisen between the parties; and whereas, by deed bearing even date herewith and about to be recorded said Alexandra Otto Michalski has conveyed to said Marion Michalski a one-half interest and to certain properties known as 26 Pulaski Street, Bloomfield, 190–192 North Park Street, East Orange, 571 Liberty Street, Orange, and 123 Valley Road, West Orange, New Jersey, to the end that the same may be held by them as tenants in common; and whereas, said parties desire to make certain agreements in respect to the premises as hereinafter stated:

"In consideration of the premises, it is hereby agreed as follows:

"1. Each party shall treat the other with kindness and respect.

"2. Neither party shall transfer or mortgage his or her interest in and to said properties without the written consent of the other party, nor shall do or permit anything in respect thereto to defeat the common tenancy of said properties by said parties.

"3. Said Alexandra Otto Michalski shall, either personally or by said Marion Michalski as her agent, collect and take all the rents of said properties and pay all the taxes, insurance premiums, repairs and other charges thereon and maintain the same so long as she shall live, except that in the event said Marion Michalski becomes unable to pursue his usual business and engage in gainful occupation, one-half of the net rents shall be paid to him.

"4. In respect to the property known as No. 123 Valley Road, West Orange, New Jersey, it is understood and agreed that the parties propose to make this their home for occupancy by themselves, and by Jane Otto and Marianne Otto, daughters of said Alexandra Otto Michalski, and by Wladyslawa Michalski, mother of said Marion Michalski, and that all and each of them shall have the right to occupy said property as their home so long as they desire. Said Marion Michalski agrees to make a Will devising his interest in said property to said Alexandra Otto Michalski, her heirs and assigns, subject to the right of his mother to occupy the same as aforesaid; and said Alexandra Otto Michalski agrees to make a Will devising her interest in said property to her children, subject to the right of said Marion Michalski and his mother to occupy the same as aforesaid; and upon the death of either party, the occupants of said property shall pay the taxes, insurance premiums, repairs and other charges on said property in equal shares during their respective occupancy thereof.

"In Witness Whereof we hereunto set our hands and seals the day and year first above written.

"/s/ Marion Michalski (L.S.)
"/s/ Alexandra Otto
Michalski (L.S.)"

Of the original four properties mentioned in the agreement, the present appeal concerns only three, the fourth, at 123 Valley Road, West Orange, not being included in plaintiff's demand for partition.

As part of the record the parties stipulated the following facts which briefly describe the circumstances and living conditions of both plaintiff and defendant. At the time of the July 1, 1949 conveyance the plaintiff and defendant lived together as husband and wife in the common domicile on Liberty Street, Orange, one of the properties involved herein. Although their agreement contemplated that they were to live together in the property on Valley Road, the parties subsequently separated on February 6, 1952 and since then have continued to live separately. Plaintiff for the past three years has lived at 190 North Park Street, East Orange. Defendant, her daughters by a prior marriage, and the mother of the plaintiff lived at the Valley Road address, and, with the exception of the plaintiff's mother who died in September 1956, all have continued to live there. Plaintiff is now 69 years of age and his wife, the defendant, is 83 years of age.

The record further discloses that when the properties were conveyed to the plaintiff and defendant, as cotenants, and the agreement of July 1, 1949 executed, the marital relationship was harmonious. About a year after their agreement that "each party shall treat the other with kindness and respect," the defendant caused the plaintiff to be arrested on a complaint of assault and battery. He was indicted and acquitted by a jury. In February 1951 a similar complaint was made by the plaintiff against his wife, but it was withdrawn on the understanding that Mr. Michalski would leave the home, that he would collect the rents and divide the net profits. Several days later, on February 27, 1951, the defendant instituted suit to set aside the conveyances by which plaintiff obtained his interest, on the grounds that it was made under duress and without valid consideration. It was decided adversely to defendant in the case cited above. (20 N.J.Super. at page 258, 89 A.2d at page 722). In addition to the mentioned litigation between the parties, Mrs. Michalski in July 1952 filed a complaint to restrain her husband from collecting the rents and the matter of rents having been disposed of in the prior suit, the action was dismissed on the grounds of res judicata. In the original action Mr. Michalski was permitted to file a supplemental counterclaim seeking to recover one-half of the net rents. After a hearing, an amended judgment was entered on March 26, 1954 wherein it was ordered that Mrs. Michalski account to her husband for one-half of the net rents from and after February 1, 1954. Subsequently, he sought to have Mrs. Michalski held in contempt for her failure to obey the order to account. After several hearings Mrs. Michalski was ordered to restate her account for certain periods of time, keep proper records, and account in accordance with the order of the court. There has been additional litigation between the parties since. Suffice to say, the marital relationship has since 1949 been most discordant and distressing.

In the present partition action the defendant raises as a defense paragraph 2 of the agreement set forth above, which she claims effectively prohibits partition during the lifetime of both parties or at least during the period of the life of the shorter lived of the parties. The plaintiff countered on this issue by saying that paragraph 2 does not prohibit partition; that if it does, it is an unreasonable restraint on alienation and is invalid; the contract cannot now be relied upon by the defendant because she has breached it in several respects; and lastly, change of circumstances has made the present enforcement of the contract unfair to the plaintiff. The trial judge determined that the plaintiff was entitled to partition as a matter of right for the reason that paragraph 2 did not bar partition, and, if it did, it would be an unreasonable restraint on alienation lacking a definite time period. He declined to pass on the questions of whether the defendant had breached the agreement and whether the change of circumstances had made enforcement of the agreement unrealistic.

The trial judge in ruling that the agreement did not bar partition relied on the language in Drachenberg v. Drachenberg, 142 N.J.Eq. 127, 134, 58 A.2d 861, 865 (E. & A.1948), that "[t]he right of partition between co-tenants is an absolute right which should not be denied in the absence of an explicit agreement not to resort to partition . . . ." He further held that this agreement did not "expressly and with definiteness and certainty bar partition" and should therefore not be given that effect. The agreement, if construed to deny partition, was held "unreasonable and unenforceable and against public policy" even if interpreted to be a bar operative only for the parties' joint lives.

It is a well-established principle that the right of partition between cotenants is an absolute right. [Citations omitted.] Such right may, however, be subject to an agreement to refrain from partition, and such agreement, to be valid, must be reasonable. Yglesias v. Dewey, 60 N.J. Eq. 62, 47 A. 59 (Ch.1900); Roberts v. Jones, 307 Mass. 504, 30 N.E.2d

392, 132 A.L.R. 663 (Sup.Jud.Ct.1940); 2 American Law of Real Property (1952), § 6.26, p. 116; 40 Am.Jur., Partition, § 5, p. 5; Annotation, 132 A.L.R. 666 (1941).

In the Drachenberg case, 142 N.J.Eq. 127, 58 A. 2861, the five children of Alvine Drachenberg, who died intestate, became seized of her real estate as cotenants. Of these children Alvine was a minor, and Gottlieb in ill health. In order that these two might have a home, the four adult children executed a written agreement that Alvine, Gottlieb and Adolph, another of the children, should live in an apartment in one of the premises, without the payment of rent, in consideration of which Adolph would manage all the properties, collect the rents, pay the carrying charges, and account to his co-tenants. The agreement further provided that the properties inherited from their mother would not be sold, mortgaged or otherwise disposed of unless by unanimous consent. Gottlieb, Alvine and Adolph actually entered into possession of the apartment. Adolph managed the properties until he entered military service, at which time Alvine, the infant, assumed the management and collection of rents. Later Adolph returned and resumed management.

Albert, another of the cotenants, filed a complaint seeking an accounting of the management of the properties, and, by an amended complaint, sought to have the agreement declaired void and unenforceable as an unreasonable restraint on alienation, because uncertain in terms and conditions; to have an accounting of the rents, and to have the properties physically partitioned or sold and the proceeds of the sale divided among the five cotenants. The court had before it inter alia for determination the enforceability of that part of the agreement denying partition.

The Court of Errors and Appeals adopted the Chancery opinion which held that the agreement was not a bar to the sale of the property in the partition proceedings. Without setting out the actual agreement, the trial court held: "3. The purpose of the agreement was to provide a home in part of the property for Adolph, Gottlieb and Alvine. For Adolph as compensation for managing the property but he is no longer performing that service. For Alvine because she was a minor at the time but is now twenty-three years of age and employed. For Gottlieb because he was then somewhat of an invalid but the evidence shows he is competent and is employed. He is thirty-two years of age and considering his normal expectancy of life he may claim a right of use and occupancy for many years yet to come." (142 N.J.Eq. at page 130 et seq., 58 A.2d at page 864.)

The agreement was further unenforceable because: "The agreement was breached by the failure of Adolph and Alvine to account to complainant for his share of net rents, in which breach the co-tenants Martha and Gottlieb concurred, thus presenting an impelling reason why the agreement should now be regarded as of no binding effect on complainant." (142 N.J.Eq. at page 133, 58 A.2d at page 865.)

Additionally, the vice-chancellor stated that the agreement purported to bind a surviving spouse or children, then unborn, of a deceased cotenant, and, by thus prolonging the operation of the agreement, might violate the rule against perpetuities.

The court went on to say: "The right of partition between cotenants is an absolute right which should not be denied in the absence of an *explicit* agreement not to resort to partition . . .". (Emphasis added.) We consider the last quotation as obiter dicta. The true basis of the decision in Drachenberg in allowing partition by sale was the changed circumstances of the respective parties, the breach of the obligation to account for the net rents, and the fact that the agreement was for an unreasonable length of time, coupled with the fact that it was not binding on the infant cotenant—since she was not a party to the agreement. See Drachenberg v. Drachenberg, 4 N.J.Super. 510, 514, 67 A.2d 892 (App.Div.1949).

Although the first Drachenberg case, supra (142 N.J.Eq. 127, 58 A.2d 861) appears to enunciate a rule requiring the actual use of the word "partition" in any agreement purporting to prohibit partition, the weight of authority is opposed to such a view. Rosenberg v. Rosenberg, 413 Ill. 343, 108 N.E.2d 766 (Sup.Ct.1952); Roberts v. Jones, supra; 2 American Law of Real Property (1952), § 6.26, p. 116; 4 Powell, Real Property (1954), § 611, p. 626; 40 Am.Jur., Partition, § 7, p. 7; 68 C.J.S. Partition § 44, p. 67 (1950); Annotation, 132 A.L.R. 666, 670 (1941). We conclude that if the intention is sufficiently manifest from the language used, the court will hold that the parties may effectively bind themselves not to partition, even without express use of the word.

In addition to the requirement of a clear manifestation of intent, the rule has become established that the restraint must not be fixed for an unreasonable time. Drachenberg v. Drachenberg, supra, (142 N.J. Eq. 127, 58 A.2d 861); [other citations omitted]; 40 Am.Jur., Partition, § 5, p. 6, n. 2; 68 C.J.S. Partition § 44, p. 68, note 48; 6 American Law of Real Property (1952), § 26.74, p. 518; Simes, Future Interests (1951), § 105, pp. 356–357.

In the Yglesias case, supra, Vice-Chancellor Pitney held that a contract prohibiting partition for a period of five years was valid and enforceable as a bar to a partition action. In the Drachenberg case, supra, the court stated that it considered the limitation in restraint of alienation unreasonable as there was "no time limit fixed for the operation of the agreement . . . ." However, it is significant that in the same paragraph (142 N.J.Eq., at page 133, 58 A.2d at page 865) the vice-chancellor construed the potential duration of the restraint on partition as being greater than the period measured by the rule against perpetuities.

Our examination of the authorities indicates no firmly settled rule as to what constitutes a reasonable time for an agreement of cotenants not to partition. See Restatement, Property, § 173(c), p. 670, § 412, p. 2440; 6 American Law of Real Property (1952), § 26.74, p. 518; Simes, op. cit., supra, § 105, p. 357; cf. Roberts v. Jones, supra. In the present case we are required to go no further than to hold that with persons of the advanced age of these parties an agreement not to partition until one of them should die (as we interpret this agreement, infra) is not unreasonable.

It remains, then, to consider the application of these principles to the provision in the instant agreement. To define the problem, we repeat paragraph 2 of the agreement: "2. Neither party shall transfer or mortgage his or her interest in and to said properties without the written consent of the other party, *nor shall do or permit anything in respect thereto to defeat the common tenancy of said properties by said parties.*" (Emphasis added.)

The apparent intention of the parties is certain. The paragraph not only prohibits sale ("transfer") or mortgage, but also directs that nothing else should be done "to defeat the common tenancy." It is clear to us that the common tenancy referred to is that of the two parties as individuals. That partition would defeat such common tenancy is obvious. Further indication of this construction may be had from a reading of the entire agreement. The conveyance of the properties and the formulation of the contract was the culmination of the parties' efforts to restore domestic tranquility. They were to have a common domicile in one of the properties and partition would certainly defeat this expressed objective. The language used by the draftsman of the agreement was lucid and admits of no other interpretation than that it is a prohibition of compulsory partition, or any other alienation during the joint lifetime of "said parties."

We have not overlooked the possibility that since the contractual provision not only prohibits partition, but also sale or incumbrance of the interest of either party without the consent of the other, it may be attacked as an unreasonable restraint of alienation. See 6 American Law of Property, op. cit., supra, § 26.77, p. 522. The parties not having raised or argued the point, however, we do not decide it. Moreover, the question will become academic in view of our ultimate disposition of the appeal. R.R. 1:7–1(c).

Giving consideration to the duration of the instant restraint, it is to be observed that the quoted language of the agreement does not directly state the length of time the restraint is to be effective. However, the wording of the provision does indicate that it purports to bind only "said parties." The trial judge in his opinion stated that, as suggested by the defendant, the prohibition might be construed to last "during their respective lifetimes," or until the demise of one of the parties. Further, it could be contended that it is without limitation and he concluded that "[e]ach of the three possible interpretations represents an unreasonable period."

In our view the provision, standing alone, purporting to prevent sale, mortgage or partition (as construed by us) by "said parties," could only have lasted for a period of time no longer than a life in being, i.e., until the death of the first of the parties. We therefore reach the conclusion that, particularly having regard to the advanced age of the parties, the restraint upon partition here would not last for longer than a reasonable time.

Further, construing the agreement in its entirety, it is obvious that the intent of the parties was not to bind the heirs of either one, but rather to maintain and encourage marital harmony through ensuring financial security and peace of mind by providing against division of the property. That objective it was anticipated would have been fulfilled upon the demise of either. Indeed, paragraph 4 obligating the plaintiff to devise his interest in the Valley Road property to the defendant, her heirs and assigns, points directly to the conclusion that restraint of partition was to terminate, at least as to this property, upon the death of one of the parties. Thus the restraint on partition was to last for the shorter of the two lives.

Without considering the question of whether the restraint on sale coupled with the reasonable restraint on partition makes the entire provision void, we have concluded that the provision is a valid restraint on compulsory partition for the period of time measured by the death of the first cotenant In this we differ from the trial court.

However, two alternative reasons were advanced below by the plaintiff, and urged here, for the view that the prohibition against partition should not be enforced; that there has been a change in circumstances of the parties since the inception of the agreement so material as to have frustrated the purposes of the restraint, and that the defendant, having breached the agreement, may not now avail herself of its benefits. Although evidence was presented on these issues, the trial judge, as noted, did not rule on these points, but rested his determination in favor of plaintiff on his construction of the contract.

We have carefully reviewed the record and it is our opinion that since the circumstances of the parties upon the basis of which the agreement was made in 1949 have materially changed since that time, we should decline to enforce the restraint provision against the plaintiff to partition the properties held in common. Drachenberg v. Drachenberg, supra (142 N.J.Eq. at page 131, 58 A.2d at page 864).

Partition is inherently an equitable action, 2 American Law of Real Property (1952), § 6.21, p. 94 et seq.; 4 Pomeroy's Equity Jurisprudence (5th ed. 1941), § 1387, p. 1015 et seq., and hence general equitable principles should govern our determination. Where the defendant seeks to defeat plaintiff's right to partition, which is ordinarily an absolute right, relying upon such a contractual provision as the one here entered into, the defendant's responsibility is to establish that enforcement of the partition provision would be fair and equitable. The situation is not unlike one where, because of changed circumstances, equity will not enforce the provisions of a covenant creating an equitable servitude. [Citations omitted.]

Further, as is stated in Pomeroy, supra, the enforcement of such covenants is not an absolute right, but is controlled by the same equitable principles governing relief of specific performance of contracts. The following rule is particularly appropriate: "The contract and the situation of the parties must be such that the remedy of specific performance will not be *harsh or oppressive.* This rule generally operates in favor of defendants; but may be invoked by a plaintiff when a defendant demands the remedy by counter-claim or cross-complaint. The oppression or hardship may result from unconscionable provisions of the contract itself; or it may result from the situation of the parties, unconnected with the terms of the contract or with the circumstances of its negotiation and execution; that is, from external facts or events or circumstances which control or affect the situation of the defendant." (Emphasis added.) Pomeroy, op. cit., supra, § 1405a, p. 1944. [Citations omitted.]

Here the facts clearly establish that it would be manifestly unjust to enforce the agreement in bar of plaintiff's partition action. The parties have not lived together since 1951, nor have they jointly occupied the Valley Road premises as contemplated by their agreement. They have been continuously involved in litigation, both civil and criminal, since 1951. The plaintiff, aged 69 years, has become physically disabled and by a judgment in prior litigation he was awarded one-half of the net rents in the mentioned properties as of February 1, 1954. Obviously the circumstances have so changed that it would be inequitable to deny the partition. The intent of the parties has been entirely destroyed. Drachenberg v. Drachenberg, supra.

There was discussion at the argument concerning the effect of any determination as to whose fault it was that plaintiff ceased to reside with the defendant. We do not believe this issue has to be resolved. We are of the opinion that the evidence of the entire history of this couple and of the litigation indicates fault may have been partially in each. The general circumstances and conditions affecting the relationship are undoubtedly the result of actions of both parties and they are such as to make totally inappropriate the continued enforcement of the bar of partition. The judgment directing partition of the three properties is therefore affirmed.

NOTES

1. While the right to compel partition is an inherent aspect of a normal joint tenancy and tenancy in common, as opposed to a tenancy by the entirety, the problem is more complicated where future interests are involved. The rules for partition developed in equity did not allow the owner of a future interest to compel partition. Today, there are statutes on partition in most states but about half of the acts confine the power to persons who have present interests. Statutes in other states are less restrictive but the power is only partial and not as clear cut as in the present concurrent estates. See Powell on Real Property 264–275 (Abridged Edition, Powell and Rohan, 1968) for an extended analysis of these statutes. However, "present interests" include estates of freehold subject to an estate for years. This holdover from doctrines of seisin allows cotenants to partition land leased to a third party, even in a long term lease. Technically, the cotenants have only a reversion, a future interest, but they are seised presently and hence can partition. See, e.g., Lichtenstein v. Lichtenstein Building Corp., 442 S.W.2d 765 (Tex.App.1969).

Why should a present (possessory) interest be a necessary condition for a partition? Suppose that a landowner should devise a life estate to his wife and the fee simple estate in remainder to his children in equal shares. It is not difficult to conceive various reasons why one or more of the remaindermen might desire a partition judgment that would establish his or her sole ownership (subject to the life tenant's right, unless she were willing to relinquish it) of a definite portion of the land. What reasons can be given for denying effect to his or her desire?

2. While the power to compel a partition is inherent in a joint tenancy and a tenancy in common, it is an expensive procedure and should be utilized only where the parties cannot agree on their respective shares or on a proper accounting. It is much easier, and less costly, to handle the matter by voluntary conveyances. If a lawyer advises a partition suit when he knows the matter can be handled more simply he may be guilty of unethical conduct since he appears to be more interested in collecting a larger fee than in settling the problem with minimum cost to his client. His actions would be analogous to the doctor who recommends unnecessary surgery.

3. As these materials disclose, a tenant in common or a joint tenant can unilaterally convey his undivided interest to a third party, making him or her a cotenant with the other party or parties. Can he or she convey a specific interest, say by a metes and bounds description, or must it be an undivided interest, i.e., can one party, in effect, partition by self help? See Kean v. Dench, 413 F.2d 1 (3d Cir.1969) where the court said:

"On this appeal the plaintiff's first contention is that a tenant in common may not, without the consent of his cotenant, convey by metes and bounds his undivided interest in a portion of the common property to a third person. While some of the earlier authorities hold such a conveyance is void, we think that the better rule, which is followed by a majority of the states and which was applied by the district court in this case, is that such a conveyance is voidable only and as between the parties is valid and is to be given full effect if it can be done without prejudice or injury to the non-conveying cotenant."

SECTION 4. CREATION AND ATTRIBUTES OF CONCURRENT ESTATES

MILLER v. RIEGLER

Supreme Court of Arkansas, 1967.
243 Ark. 251, 419 S.W.2d 599.

HARRIS, C.J. Marjorie Miller, appellant herein, and Mary Jane Riegler, appellee, are sisters, and reside in Little Rock. Minnie Wagar, who died in Little Rock, testate, on August 8, 1963, was an aunt of these two sisters. In March, 1957, Mrs. Wagar lived in Long Beach, California. She had been ill, and Mrs. Riegler and her mother went to California and brought Mrs. Wagar back to this city. The latter lived with appellee, paying $100.00 per month for room and board, until January, 1958, when she went to a nursing home, staying there until her death. A joint checking account was opened with Mrs. Wagar's funds in the names of Minnie M. Wagar and Mary Jane Riegler, and a joint safe deposit box was taken in their names, and Mrs. Wagar's property was placed there. On July 23, 1957, Mrs. Wagar, then 81 years of age, executed her last will and testament and on July 25, she caused several hundred shares of stocks of the approximate value of $45,000.00 (representing about one-half of stocks owned by Mrs. Wagar) to be transferred to the joint names of Mrs. Riegler and herself. The new stock certificates reflected the owners of the stock to be "Mrs. Minnie W. Wagar and Mrs. Mary Jane Riegler, as joint tenants with right of survivorship and not as tenants in common." It was agreed that the aunt would receive the dividends for the balance of her life. Subsequently, the dividends from these stocks were placed in the joint checking account, and these dividends were reported on the Federal Income Tax returns of Mrs. Wagar. As previously stated, Mrs. Wagar departed this life in August, 1963, and her will was duly admitted to probate in Pulaski County. Mrs. Riegler, the executrix of the estate, recognized that the money in the joint checking account was a part of the estate, but she claimed absolute ownership of the stock as the survivor of the joint tenancy. Thereupon Mrs. Miller instituted suit, asserting that the stocks that were still held in the joint names at date of Mrs. Wagar's death actually belonged solely to the deceased (and accordingly were a part of her estate), and should be administered as such.[1] Appellant asked for judgment for one-half of the stocks and one-half of the value of any that had been converted.[2] Mrs. Riegler answered, denying that the transfer of the stock was for the convenience of Mrs. Wagar, asserted that it was a gift to Mrs. Riegler, and that Mrs. Miller accordingly had no interest. On trial, the Pulaski Chancery Court (1st Division) held: "That all of the stock certificates involved in this suit (including all stock certificates sold by Mary Jane Riegler prior to the institution of this suit and all stock certificates held by Mary Jane Riegler at the commencement of this suit which had been reissued in her name individually) were originally issued in the name of the testatrix and Mary Jane Riegler as joint tenants with right of survivorship and not as tenants in common, and all of said stocks are the sole property, in fee simple absolute of Mary Jane Riegler, individu-

1. Under Mrs. Wagar's will, after making some specific bequests, the residue and remainder of the estate was devised to Mrs. Riegler in trust, the income of the principal of the trust estate to be distributed in convenient installments to her brother, George Henry Miller, the father of appellant and appellee, during his lifetime. The trustee was also authorized to use any part of the principal as might be required to properly take care of the brother. The will further provided that, upon the death of George Henry Miller, or upon the death of Mrs. Wagar (if the brother died before the testatrix), the trust estate was to be divided equally between Mrs. Riegler and Marjorie Nicolini (Miller), or in event of the death of either niece, that share to the child or children of the deceased relative. [Footnotes in the case are by the Court and numbered accordingly.]

2. There was also a prayer in the complaint for certain items of personal property to which Mrs. Miller made claim, but the Chancellor's adverse decision on this point has not been appealed.

ally, and all dividends received from this stock are the sole property in fee simple absolute of Mary Jane Riegler, individually."

From the decree so entered, appellant brings this appeal. For reversal, it is asserted that the stocks involved in this case, which were held in the joint names of Minnie M. Wagar and Mary Jane Riegler at the time of the death of Mrs. Wagar, were the property of Minnie M. Wagar, and the 1957 transfer of the stocks into the joint names of Minnie M. Wagar and Mary Jane Riegler did not constitute or create a true joint tenancy, or gift, or otherwise vest any ownership rights in Mrs. Riegler.

It is first argued that the circumstances surrounding the transfer of the stocks clearly show that there was no intention by the aunt of making a gift to her niece. It is pointed out that, though reissued in the joint names of the two women, the stocks were returned to a joint safe deposit box (which had been acquired in their names on May 27, 1957), and that all other property in the box belonged to Mrs. Wagar. It is likewise pointed out that all of the dividends from all stocks including those held jointly, and those simply in Mrs. Wagar's name, were placed in the joint bank account at the Worthen Bank. Further, it is mentioned that the dividends from the joint stocks were reported solely on the federal income tax return of the aunt. Mrs. Wagar also received a $65.00 per month pension, which was placed in the joint bank account. No separate monies or funds of Mrs. Riegler were deposited in this account and all checks written on it were solely for the debts or expenditures of Mrs. Wagar. The checks were all written by appellee, with the exception of five or six of $100.00 each, which were given to Mrs. Riegler, and signed by Mrs. Wagar in payment of room and board. These facts are all argued by appellant as evidence that Mrs. Wagar had no intention, in creating the joint tenancy, of giving an interest in the transferred stock to Mrs. Riegler, but only made the transfer for the purpose of convenience, i.e., to enable Mrs. Riegler to handle financial transactions for the aunt with handiness. Appellant also calls attention to the fact that Mrs. Riegler recognized that funds in the joint bank account (with her aunt) were properly a part of the estate, and such funds were listed as assets. It is also argued that it simply isn't reasonable that Mrs. Wagar would give this amount of stock to a person (Mrs. Riegler) that she had only seen three or four times in her life before moving to Little Rock.[3] Mention is made of the fact that the deceased was apparently very devoted to her brother and that it was her principal intent, as evidenced by her will, that he be taken care of the rest of his life; that the will provided that, upon his death, the two daughters should take the residue of the estate. We see little, if any, significance to the fact that Mrs. Wagar held a high regard for her brother, as expressed in her will. The proof reflects that Mr. Miller had an income of over $200.00 per month, was older than Mrs. Wagar, and certainly the income, or even the principal, if needed, of the remaining $45,000.00 worth of stock (still held by Mrs. Wagar) would

3. The record indicates that this was about the same number of times that Mrs. Miller had seen her aunt.

have been considered adequate to take care of his needs. For that matter, however affectionately Mrs. Wagar might have felt toward her brother, she had made no provision for him until the will of July, 1957, was executed. At any rate, appellant's arguments, heretofore quoted, are all based on surmise and speculation. It is sometimes difficult to ascertain people's motives, but it is generally true, even with relatives, that a decedent feels closer to, or likes, one relative more than another. Here, one fact instantly stands out, viz., that Mrs. Wagar lived with Mrs. Riegler for nearly a year, and at the time of making the stock transfer, evidently planned to live with appellee for the balance of her life, this plan being altered because of illness suffered by the aunt following a fall in November of 1957. Not only that, but the very fact that the aunt would pick Mrs. Riegler to handle her business for her (which is not disputed) indicates that she had more confidence in, or closer ties with, appellee than with appellant. Still again, Mrs. Riegler was named Executrix of the Wagar estate, as well as Trustee. Of course, if the transfer was only made for convenience, one immediately wonders why all stocks were not transferred, instead of only half.

Be that as it may, litigation cannot be decided on surmise, or what someone else might have done under similar circumstances. It can only be decided on the evidence presented in court. The testimony heavily preponderates to the effect that the transfer was made at a time when Mrs. Wagar was fully possessed of all her faculties, and understood exactly what was being done. Only three people testified, Mrs. Riegler, Mrs. Miller, and Warren Bass, a certified public accountant of Little Rock, who handled tax matters for Mrs. Wagar.

Mrs. Miller testified that it was her "understanding" from a conversation with her sister that the latter was going to take care of the aunt's affairs, and the transfer of stock had been made for convenience only; she also stated that her sister said that, though part of the estate was in her (appellee's) name, everything would be divided "50–50." Mrs. Riegler denied making these statements, and said that she had informed Mrs. Miller that everything *in the estate* would be divided "50–50."

The strongest evidence introduced was that of Mr. Bass, who testified as follows: Mrs. Wagar was a small lady, quite bright, alert, knowledgeable, and very interesting to talk to. She knew the property she owned, and planned a transfer of stock along with executing the will. She stated that she intended to make her home with Mrs. Riegler the rest of her life; she also said that there were two people she cared for, one being Mrs. Riegler, and the other being the brother.

The witness made a list of the stocks which were to be transferred, such list being offered as an exhibit at the trial. He discussed the matter with Mrs. Wagar several times. Bass was very emphatic in stating that Mrs. Wagar knew exactly what she was doing, and that it was her intention to transfer the $45,000 worth of stock to Mrs. Riegler as a joint tenant. We think it was clearly established that the aunt, of her own free will and accord, made the transfer with full knowledge that the stocks transferred would not be a part of her estate, and the survivor of the joint tenancy created would take the full amount.

It is next contended that the requisites of a joint tenancy were not met, and accordingly, the gift must fail. It is first pointed out that there is no statutory provision here involved, such as those which cover savings and loan associations and banks; that accordingly, when a joint tenancy is created, the four "unities" must exist. These are set out in the case of Stewart v. Tucker, 208 Ark. 612, 188 S.W.2d 125, and are listed in a quote from 33 C.J. 907, as follows: "(1) Unity of interest. (2) Unity of title. (3) Unity of time. (4) Unity of possession. That is, each of the owners must have one and the same interest, conveyed by the same act or instrument to vest at one and the same time . . . and each must have the entire possession of every parcel of the property held in joint tenancy as well as of the whole."

Let it be first said that we have already, to some degree, departed from the rule of the four unities. In Ebrite v. Brookhyser, 219 Ark. 676, 244 S.W.2d 625, 44 A.L.R.2d 587, George Brookhyser conveyed real property, which he owned, from himself to his wife and himself as tenants by the entirety. The trial court held that an estate by the entirety had been created, and Ebrite appealed to this court. There too, Stewart v. Tucker, supra, was principally relied upon, and it was contended that essential requirements to create the estate had not been complied with, the wife's undivided half interest not having been acquired at the same time as the interest retained by her husband; that the husband could not convey to himself, and therefore could have acquired no new title by virtue of his own deed. In upholding the trial court, we stated that there was no reason why parties should not be able to do directly that which they could undoubtedly do indirectly through the device of a strawman. The late Justice J.S. Holt, writing for this court stated: "We cannot agree with this reasoning. A complete answer is given in what is now the leading case of In re Klatzl's Estate, 216 N.Y. 83, 110 N.E. 181, 185. There a majority of the judges, Bartlett, Collin, Hiscock, and Cardozo, agreed that under modern married women's property acts a husband may create a tenancy by the entirety by a conveyance to himself and his wife. The same argument as to the unity of time was presented there as here, but Judge Collin answered: 'The husband did not convey to himself but to a legal unity or entity which was the consolidation of himself and another.' "

This decision certainly has not been viewed as unsound for there can be no logic in preventing a spouse from directly giving to his or her marriage partner equal rights in property that is owned, when the same result was permitted by creating the estate through a third party who really held no interest in the property at all.

Likewise, it also appears that the same view is being widely followed with reference to joint tenancy. The landmark case is probably that of Colson v. Baker, et al., 42 Misc. 407, 87 N.Y.S. 238. The issue was stated in the opening line of the opinion, as follows: "The question to be determined on this motion is whether a person seised in fee of an estate can, by a direct grant, deed the property to another and himself in joint tenancy, instead of tenancy in common, without the intervention of a third party."

A part of the logic used by the court is interesting. It is pointed out that the unity of time refers to joint parties becoming joint tenants at the same time. As stated: ". . . When, therefore, he attempts to create for himself and his grantee an estate in joint tenancy out of his fee by a direct deed to the grantee, why does not the joint tenancy arise at the same time and by the same act? I think it does. Of course, each joint tenant has the same interest by such a deed, and each is in possession of the whole like tenants in common.

"In all references to the 'four unities' requisite to create a joint tenancy, I find nothing that prevents their existence or creation by the act of the grantor for himself and another as well as by his act for two other persons."

In the case of Kleemann v. Sheridan, 75 Ariz. 311, 256 P.2d 553, there is a succinct discussion of the issue with which we are here concerned. There, the question was whether a joint tenancy in personal property had been created by two sisters who, in leasing a safe deposit box, recited in writing that all property theretofore or thereafter placed in the box was the joint property of both and would pass to the survivor. The Arizona Supreme Court discussed the history of joint tenancy, saying: "Before entering upon a discussion of the points raised by appellant it will perhaps be pertinent to briefly recount the common-law essentials to create a joint tenancy. They are unity of time, unity of title, unity of interest, unity of possession. Such tenancy could not arise by descent or other operation of the law but may arise by grant, devise or contract. Of course, the right of survivorship is inherent in the joint tenancy estate and without which joint tenancy does not exist. At first joint tenancy under the common law involved only interest in land but at an early date it was recognized as applying to personal property as well. At common law a person could not make a conveyance to himself. An attempt to convey land to himself and to another resulted in a conveyance of only one-half of the property to the other and the grantor still held his moiety under his original title, thus destroying two essentials of joint tenancy, unity of time and of title. The result of such attempt was to create a tenancy in common.

"The same rule would seem to logically apply to personal property and is the rule of law relating to both real and personal property in many of the states of the Union including Maine, Illinois, Wisconsin and Nebraska but the majority of the state courts have held that common-law concept of the four unity essentials should give way to the intention of the parties and that a joint tenancy may be created by a conveyance from one to himself and another as joint tenants. California has passed a law making the rule applicable to husband and wife.

"We have apparently aligned ourselves with the majority rule insofar as personal property, the title to which passes by delivery, is concerned. . . .

"Another characteristic of joint tenancy is that it is not testamentary but 'is a present estate in which both joint tenants are seized in the case of real estate, and possessed in case of personal property, per my et per tout,' that is, such joint tenant is seized by the half as well as by the whole. The right of survivorship in a joint tenancy therefore does not pass anything from the deceased to the surviving joint tenant. Inasmuch as both cotenants in a joint tenancy are possessors and owners per tout, i.e., of the whole, the title of the first joint tenant who dies merely terminates and the survivior continues to possess and own the whole of the estate as before."

The court, mentioning that it was holding in line with the majority rule, and that it was the intention of the sisters to create a joint tenancy, held that the estate had been created. Numerous other cases also hold that the intention of the parties is controlling, rather than the common law concept of the four unities.[4]

Here, we think the intention of Mrs. Wagar is established, i.e., to create a joint tenancy, and we can see no more reason to hold to the old premise that the four unities must exist, than the jurisdictions (and numerous others) just quoted, particularly when we have already, as earlier pointed out, to some extent discarded that concept of the law.

However, appellant also relies upon the fact that Mrs. Wagar and Mrs. Riegler agreed that Mrs. Wagar was to retain—and did retain—the dividends[5] from the stocks jointly transferred. This, says appellant, is fatal to the creation of a joint tenancy for the reason that the two parties did not have equal rights to share in the enjoyment of the property during their lifetime. In connection with this argument, it is also urged that the retaining of the dividends from the transferred stock prevents the transfer from acquiring the status of a gift. We do not agree with these arguments. Joint tenants may agree between (or among) themselves as to the use to be made of the property. In 48 C.J.S. under Joint Tenancy § 10, page 933, we find: "Joint tenants may contract with each other concerning the use of the common property, as for the exclusive use of the property by one of them, or the division of the income from the property."

In Tindall, et al v. Yeats, et al, 392 Ill. 502, 64 N.E.2d 903, the question was whether a Mrs. Adams and Mrs. Yeats were joint tenants or tenants in common. The trial court held that they were joint tenants, and this holding was appealed to the Supreme Court. One of the points argued by appellant was that Mrs. Yeats had agreed that Mrs. Adams should have all rents from the land, as well as the possession thereof during the life of Mrs. Adams, and this, said appel-

4. See, inter alia, Greenwood v. Commissioner of Internal Revenue, 9 Cir., 134 F.2d 915; Switzer v. Pratt, 237 Iowa 788, 23 N.W.2d 837; Conlee v. Conlee, 222 Iowa 561, 269 N.W. 259; Creek v. Union National Bank in Kansas City (Mo.), 266 S.W.2d 737. These cases cite numerous others to the same effect.

5. It is also argued, though not forcefully, that Mrs. Wagar likewise retained an interest in the principal. This contention is based upon some answers given on cross-examination by Mrs. Riegler and Mr. Bass, but we think the evidence falls far short of establishing any retention by Mrs. Wagar of an interest in the principal. Actually, the testimony is confusing as to whether the dividends were to be, in all events, retained by Mrs. Wagar, or would only be retained if they were needed for her support. The legal question would be the same, but we treat the matter as though the withholding of the dividends was definite.

lant, prevented the estate from being one of joint tenancy. The Illinois Supreme Court disagreed, holding that it was clear that it was the intention of the parties that Mrs. Adams should enjoy the possession of the entire estate; that this was done with the permission and consent of Mrs. Yeats, and that the parties had the right to make this agreement.[6] And why should this not be permissible? Why should owners of property, real or personal, be prohibited from doing as they desire with that property, so long as the disposition is not for an immoral purpose, or against public policy?

Nor do we agree with appellant's argument with reference to the invalidity of the gift. Appellant states in her reply brief: "We submit it cannot be that there is any difference in the presumptions applicable to or the basic rules essential to the creation of a gift, whether in the form of outright ownership, joint tenancy, or otherwise, except such as might be inherent in the nature of the particular estate created. . . . If there is a retention of a right to income or principal, or both, inconsistent with the estate ostensibly donated, so that it is not made 'beyond recall,' then we submit it is incomplete and ineffectual as between the parties. . . . And, as pointed out in our brief in main, to permit a joint tenancy with retention of all income is nothing more than a void testamentary arrangement."

This stock was given to Mrs. Riegler, and placed in the lock box. We have shown, in the citations mentioned, that the joint tenancy was not affected, even though Mrs. Riegler was not to share in the dividend. We here point out that, in the creaton of the joint tenancy, Mrs. Riegler did not first become possessed of her interest or rights in the property when Mrs. Wagar died; rather, she acquired a *present* interest when the estate was created, i.e., her rights as a joint tenant had already vested before her aunt's death. This fact, of course, silences the argument that a joint tenancy with retention of income is nothing but a void testamentary arrangement.

Affirmed.

---

6. Incidentally, Illinois is one of the states that still hold that the four unities must be observed in creating a joint tenancy. [This is no longer true in Illinois, see Ill.Rev.Stat., ch. 76, § 2.1 (1985).] Mrs. Adams was the original owner of the property, and a conveyance from a third party was used in effecting the joint tenancy. At the time of the creation of the joint tenancy, Mrs. Adams and Mrs. Yeats entered into the following agreement:

> "Whereas the First Party has this day and date vested title in the parties hereto as joint tenants in the Marshall County, Illinois, farm owned by the First Party, all evidenced by certain deeds executed by the First Party and Martin A. Adams, her husband, and Walter C. Overbeck, all of the within date;
>
> "Now Therefore, in consideration of having vested title of said real estate as aforesaid, The Second Party herein, in consideration thereof, agrees with the First Party that said First Party shall have all the rentals from said real estate and the possession thereof during the term of her natural life, with power and authority to insure the buildings thereon, make repairs and do such other things thereon as she could or would do were she the sole and exclusive owner thereof. This Agreement shall not, however, in any manner affect the joint tenancy of said real estate nor the legal incidents accompanying same.
>
> "Dated this 31st day of May, A.D. 1939.
>
> "Grace M. Adams, (Seal)
>
> "Margaret Isabelle Yeats, (Seal)"

JACKSON v. O'CONNELL

Supreme Court of Illinois, 1961.
23 Ill.2d 52, 177 N.E.2d 194.

KLINGBIEL, JUSTICE. This appeal from a decree for partition entered by the circuit court of Cook County presents the question whether a conveyance by one of three joint tenants of real estate to another of the joint tenants destroyed the joint tenancy in its entirety or merely severed the joint tenancy with respect to the undivided third interest so conveyed, leaving the joint tenancy in force and effect as to the remaining two-thirds interest.

The controlling facts, as we viewed the case, are simple and uncontroverted. The various parcels of real estate in question are situated in Cook County and were formerly owned by Neil P. Duffy. The latter died testate in 1936 and by his will he devised the properties to his three sisters, Nellie Duffy, Anna Duffy, and Katherine O'Connell, as joint tenants. Thereafter Nellie Duffy, a spinster, by quitclaim deed dated July 21, 1948, conveyed and quitclaimed all her interest in the properties to Anna Duffy. The deed was in statutory form. It was duly delivered and recorded. Nellie Duffy died in 1949.

Some eight years later, in May 1957, Anna Duffy died testate. By her will she devised whatever interest she had in the real estate in question to four nieces, Beatrice Jackson, Eileen O'Barski, Catherine Young and Margaret Miller, plaintiffs herein.

Following the death of Anna Duffy, the plaintiffs commenced this suit against Katherine O'Connell (hereafter referred to as the defendant) and others to partition the real estate. Their suit is predicated on the theory that Nellie Duffy's quitclaim deed, dated July 21, 1948, to Anna Duffy severed in its entirety the joint tenancies existing between Nellie Duffy, Anna Duffy, and the defendant; that as a result, Anna Duffy became the owner of an undivided two-thirds interest and defendant an undivided one-third interest in the various parcels of real estate, as tenants in common; that plaintiffs, as successors in interest to Anna Duffy, accordingly each own an undivided one-sixth and defendant an undivided one-third interest as tenants in common. The defendant answered and filed a counterclaim on the theory that Nellie Duffy's quitclaim deed of July 21, 1948, to Anna Duffy severed the joint tenancies only so far as the grantor's one-third interest was concerned; that the joint tenancies between Anna Duffy and defendant continued in full force and effect as to the remaining two thirds; that upon Anna Duffy's death in 1957, defendant succeeded to that two-thirds interest as surviving joint tenant; and that plaintiffs are each entitled to a one-twelfth interest only, as devisees of the one-third interest which passed to Anna Duffy by reason of Nellie Duffy's quitclaim deed.

The cause was referred to a master who found the interests in accordance with defendant's contentions. The decree for partition appealed from confirmed the master's conclusions.

At the hearing before the master, plaintiffs adduced over defendant's objection testimony of the attorney who had drawn Nellie

Duffy's quitclaim deed for the purpose of showing that the grantor intended the deed to operate as a complete severance of the joint tenancy and that the attorney's advice was that the deed would have that legal effect. Such testimony cannot control the effect of the deed upon the joint tenancy but that issue must be determined as a matter of law. The deed was unambiguous and its legal effect cannot be changed by parol evidence that it was intended to have a legal operation different from that which would be imported by its terms. Fowler v. Black, 136 Ill. 363, 26 N.E. 596, 11 L.R.A. 670; Rockford Trust Co. v. Moon, 370 Ill. 250, 18 N.E.2d 447.

The problem then resolves itself down to the effect of Nellie Duffy's quitclaim deed upon the joint tenancy as a matter of law. The question appears to be one of first impression in Illinois.

The estate of joint tenancy comes down to us from the early English law and while the rules applicable to it have been modified in some particulars by statute in Illinois, most of the principles governing joint tenancies today are those which existed at common law. For example, it has been held from the earliest times that four co-existing unities are necessary and requisite to the creation and continuance of a joint tenancy; namely, unity of interest, unity of title, unity of time, and unity of possession. Any act of a joint tenant which destroys any of these unities operates as a severance of the joint tenancy and extinguishes the right of survivorship. American Law of Property, vol. II, sec. 6.2; Van Antwerp v. Horan, 390 Ill. 449, 61 N.E.2d 358, 161 A.L.R. 1133; Tindall v. Yeats, 392 Ill. 502, 64 N.E.2d 903.

It appears to have been well settled at common law that where there were three joint tenants, and one conveyed his interest to a third party, the joint tenancy was only severed as to the part conveyed; the third party grantee became a tenant in common with the other two joint tenants, but the latter still held the remaining two thirds as joint tenants with right of survivorship therein. Coke on Littleton, 189a (sec. 294); 2 Tiffany Real Property, 3rd ed., sec. 425; 2 Thompson on Real Property, sec. 1714. Counsel for plaintiffs argue that the rule should not apply where the conveyance is to a fellow joint tenant; that in such a case the interest of the grantee becomes different in quantity from that of the remaining joint tenant; that the unity of interest is destroyed and a severance of the entire joint tenancy necessarily results.

The early English authorities do not support such a view. Littleton stated the rule to be as follows: "And, if three joyntenants be, and the one release by his deed to one of his companions all the right which he hath in the land, then hath he to whom the release is made, the third part of the lands by force of the said release, and he and his companion shall hold the other two parts in joynture . . .. And as to the third part, which he has by force of the release, he holdeth that third part with himselfe and his companion in common." Coke on Littleton, 193a (sec. 304). Littleton goes on further to point out that if a disseisin should occur after such a transfer, the parties "shall have in both their names an assise of the two parts, &c. because the two parts they held jointly at the time of the disseisin: And as to the third part, he to whom the release was made, ought to have of that an assise in his own name, for that he (as to the same third part) is thereof tenant in common . . . because he commeth to this third part by force of the release, and not only by force of the joynture." Coke on Littleton, 196a (sec. 312).

Blackstone, after pointing out that a joint tenancy may be terminated by destroying the unity of interest, adds the following qualification: "Yet, if one of three joint-tenants alienes his share, the two remaining tenants still hold their parts by joint-tenancy and survivorship; and if one of three joint-tenants release his share to one of his companions, though the joint-tenancy is destroyed with regard to that part, yet the two remaining parts are still held in jointure; for they still preserve their original constituent unities." 2 Blackstone's Commentaries, (* 186,) Lewis's ed. p. 653.

Preston's statement of the rule accords with that of Littleton and Blackstone. 2 Preston on Abstracts, 61.

Modern-day writers support the same view. In American Law of Property, vol. II, sec. 6.2, it is said: "Where one joint tenant conveys to one of his cotenants, where there are more than two, the cotenant grantee holds the share conveyed as a tenant in common, taking it at a different time by a different title, while his original share is held with the remaining cotenants as a joint tenancy, the unity continuing to that extent." Other writers lay down the same rule. 2 Tiffany Real Property, 3rd ed., sec. 425, p. 211; 2 Walsh, Commentaries on the Law of Real Property, sec. 116, p. 11. There appears to be a dearth of case law on the subject, but no decisions have come to our attention which announce a doctrine contrary to that stated by the commentators mentioned above.

With respect to the contention that Nellie Duffy's quitclaim deed destroyed the joint tenancies in their entirety because as a result of that deed the undivided interests of the grantee, Anna Duffy, and the defendant in the various properties were rendered unequal, it is to be noted that their interests in the undivided two-thirds, which formed the subject matter of the joint tenancies here in question, remained the same. It is settled in Illinois that a valid joint tenancy may exist in an undivided interest. Klouda v. Pechousek, 414 Ill. 75, 110 N.E.2d 258; Ill.Rev.Stat.1959, chap. 76, par. 1. The requisite unity of interest is satisfied in such a case if it exists with respect to the undivided interest which forms the subject matter of the joint tenancy. In In re Galletto's Estate, 75 Cal.App.2d 580, 171 P.2d 152, a grantor conveyed an undivided half interest in certain real estate to a wife, individually. By separate deed, the grantor conveyed the remaining undivided half interest to the wife and her husband, as joint tenants. It was contended that a valid joint tenancy was not created for the reason that one of the essential unities was lacking, namely, unity of interest. In denying that contention, the court observed: "Once it is conceded that a joint tenancy may exist as to an undivided interest in property, and that rule is perfectly clear, the balance of the undivided interest may lawfully be held by one of the tenants as well as by a stranger. The equality of interest requirement simply means that the interests of the joint tenants in the subject or interest involved in the joint tenancy must be equal. The subject of the tenancy involved herein is an undivided one-half interest in the property. In that interest the respondent and wife owned equal and identical interests. They held one and the same interests in the subject of the joint tenancy." The principle stated is applicable to the situation presented in the case at bar.

It is contended that error was committed in the exclusion of testimony offered to show Anna Duffy's understanding of the legal effect of the quitclaim deed. This testimony was properly excluded for reasons previously stated.

The decree of the circuit court of Cook County was right and is affirmed.

Decree affirmed.

Would intent matter?

NOTE

In the principal case there was some evidence that the grantor intended the deed to operate as a complete severance of the joint tenancy and that the attorney's advice was that it would have that legal effect. Why did the court not follow that manifestation of intent? Would the attorney be liable for malpractice if he failed to carry out clear instructions by the client as to the desired legal effect? On this last point, see McLane v. Russell, 159 Ill.App.3d 429, 111 Ill.Dec. 250, 512 N.E.2d 366 (1987). In that case, two unmarried sisters owned a 240 acre farm, presumably as tenants in common. Earlier, they had executed wills in which they left all of their property to each other but, in 1958, they requested their attorney to place the farm in joint tenancy with right of survivorship. This was done and then, in 1971, one of the sisters was adjudged incompetent and the attorney was appointed her conservator. In 1975, the same attorney drafted a will for the other sister in which she devised a life estate in her interest in the farm to a long time tenant, with remainder interest to his son. The attorney neglected to sever the previous joint tenancy, however, and when the testatrix died in 1977 the farm passed to the surviving, incompetent sister. The tenants (father and son) sued the lawyer for malpractice since, as the named beneficiaries in the will, they had been deprived of a one-half interest in the land. The trial court awarded a judgment of $258,545, one half of the value of the farm, against the attorney. The Illinois Appellate Court affirmed and also held that the five year statute of limitations on malpractice began to run not from the date of the execution of the will but from the date of the testatrix's death. This latter point means that wills drafted by attorneys may have some very "long tails", i.e., the life of the testator plus five years. It isn't only doctors that have to worry about long-delayed lawsuits!

PALMER v. FLINT

Supreme Court of Maine, 1960.
156 Me. 103, 161 A.2d 837.

SIDDALL, J. This is a petition for a declaratory judgment to determine the right or status of the parties hereto in certain real estate located in Yarmouth, Cumberland County, Maine. On August 1, 1940, the Federal Land Bank of Springfield, one of the defendants, conveyed this real estate to Nathan H. Palmer and his wife, Alice E. Palmer (now Alice E. Flint), the other defendant. The granting and habendum clauses in this deed, with the exception of immaterial punctuation, both read as follows: "Unto the said Nathan H. Palmer and Alice E. Palmer as joint tenants, and not as tenants in common, to them and their assigns and to the survivor, and the heirs and assigns of the survivor forever." The deed contained a covenant of warranty that the grantor, its successors or assigns "shall and will warrant and defend the same to the said grantees, their heirs and assigns forever." Alice E. Palmer obtained a decree of divorce from Nathan H. Palmer on September 27, 1951, and by quitclaim deed without covenant dated September 29, 1951, she conveyed the premises to Nathan H. Palmer. Nathan H. Palmer conveyed the property to Frank L. Palmer, who reconveyed to Nathan and his sister, Roxa B. Palmer, the plaintiff herein, "as joint tenants and not as tenants in common, to them and their heirs and assigns, and to the survivor of them, and to the heirs and assigns of such survivor forever." Nathan H. Palmer died on May 21, 1957. The plaintiff asked that the Court determine (1) the rights or status of the parties in and to said premises, (2) that if it should appear that said deed from the Federal Land Bank of Springfield did not convey an estate of the true character which the grantor intended to convey and the grantees intended to receive, that the deed be reformed in accordance with the true intention of the parties.

The single justice hearing the case found and decreed that the parties in said deed did not purpose to grant or receive any form of conveyance other than that utilized by them; that the quitclaim deed of Alice E. Palmer to her former husband Nathan H. Palmer was inoperative to convey her contingent remainder; that the state of the title in the premises is an estate for the life of Alice E. Flint in Roxa B. Palmer, remainder in fee to Alice E. Flint (Palmer).

The real controversy in this case is between the plaintiff Roxa B. Palmer and the defendant Alice E. Flint. We summarize the contentions of these parties although the conclusions reached by us make a discussion of all of them unnecessary.

The plaintiff contends:

(1) That the deed from the Federal Land Bank of Springfield created in the grantees an estate in joint tenancy in fee simple with all the common-law incidents thereto.

(2) That it was the intention of the parties that the Federal Land Bank of Springfield should create in them an estate in joint tenancy in fee simple with all the common-law incidents thereto.

(3) In the event that it should be determined that the deed created a joint life estate in the grantees with the remainder over to the survivor, then such remainder is vested and not contingent.

(4) That the deed from Alice E. Palmer to Nathan H. Palmer was intended to convey and did convey all of her interest in the premises in the remainder or otherwise and that Nathan H. Palmer was thereby seized in fee simple of the entire interest in said premises so that upon his death Alice E. Flint acquired no interest therein.

The defendant contends:

(1) That the sitting justice was correct in his findings that the parties to the deed did not purpose to grant or receive any form of conveyance other than that utilized by them.

(2) That the conveyance from the Federal Land Bank of Springfield conveyed a joint life estate to the grantees with a contingent remainder in fee to the survivor.

(3) That the quitclaim deed of Alice E. Palmer to her former husband was inoperative to convey to him her contingent remainder.

There is no doubt that the entire fee in the property was conveyed by the Land Bank of Springfield. The necessary words of inheritance for that purpose were used. The problem before us is the determination of the respective estates of the grantees in the fee conveyed.

Under the common law of England, joint estates were favored. Conveyances to two or more persons were construed to create a joint tenancy unless a contrary intent was apparent from the wording of the instrument. With the substantial abolishment of tenures, however, joint tenancies became disfavored, and as a result statutes have been enacted in practically all of our states, either abolishing or changing the common-law rule. Our state as early as 1821 enacted legislation modifying this rule. The statute relating to conveyances to two or more persons, in effect on the date of the deed in question, August 1, 1940, reads as follows: "Conveyances to two or more. R.S. c. 78, § 13. Conveyances not in mortgage, and devises of land to two or more persons, create estates in common, unless otherwise expressed. Estates vested in survivors upon the principle of joint tenancy shall be so held." R.S.1930, Chap. 87, Sec. 13. This provision is now found in R.S.1954, Chap. 168, Sec. 13.

We note that the 96th Legislature in 1953 (P.L.1953, Chap. 301, now R.S.1954, Chap. 168, Sec. 13) amended this statutory provision by adding thereto the following: "A conveyance of real property by the owner thereof to himself and another or others as joint tenants or with the right of survivorship, or which otherwise indicates by appropriate language the intent to create a joint tenancy between himself and such other or others by such conveyance, shall create an estate in joint tenancy in the property so conveyed between all of the grantees, including the grantor. Estates in joint tenancy so created shall have and possess all of the attributes and incidents of estates in joint tenancy created or existing at common law and the rights and liabilities of the tenants in estates in joint tenancy so created shall be the same as in estates in joint tenancy created or existing at common law."

Joint tenancies have been entirely abolished by legislative action in some states, and courts in these states have at times been obliged to set up an estate of a different character in order to effectuate the intent of the parties to a deed to create an estate in survivors. In many cases the right of surviviorship as a necessary element of a joint tenancy has been discussed without reference to the principle of severance which seems of primary importance in the instant case. In some cases the word "survivor," without the use of the words "as joint tenants and not as tenants in common," as used in this case, has been the only indication of an intention to create a joint tenancy. In some jurisdictions estates by the entireties are recognized. Statutes modifying the common law differ in essential details in respect to the creation of joint tenancies and in respect to the necessity of the use of words of inheritance to create a fee. For these reasons an extensive review of the decisions in other jurisdictions is of little benefit. In the construction of the terms of the deed in the instant case we are concerned with factors, hereafter discussed, which appear to be peculiar to our own problem.

We note, however, some of the divergent views taken by the courts in the construction of deeds involving the issue of joint tenancy.

In some jurisdictions a conveyance to two persons and the survivor of them, in the absence of words of inheritance applying to both grantees, or other circumstances indicating an intention to create a fee simple in each, has been construed to create a cotenancy in the grantees for their lives, with a contingent remainder in the survivor. Tiffany on Real Estate, Sec. 191 (2nd Ed.); 1 Washburn on Real Property, Sec. 866 (6th Ed.). See also Rowerdink v. Carothers, 334 Mich. 454, 54 N.W.2d 715, containing a review of Michigan cases, among them the case of Jones v. Snyder, 218 Mich. 446, 188 N.W. 505, 506, in which the court held that a deed to four persons "as joint tenants, and to their heirs and assigns, and to the survivors or survivor of them, and to the heirs and assigns of the survivors or survivor of them, forever" created a joint tenancy for life in the grantees, with a contingent remainder in fee simple to the survivor; Ewing's Heirs v. Savary, 3 Bibb, Ky., 235; Finch v. Haynes, 144 Mich. 352, 107 N.W. 910, 911.

Many jurisdictions hold that where the language of a deed evidences an intention to create a right of survivorship, the deed will be given that effect, although it did not create a common-law joint tenancy by reason of the absence of one of the four unities of interest, time, title, and possession. See Annotation, 1 A.L.R.2d 247. In Therrien v. Therrien, 94 N.H. 66, 46 A.2d 538, 166 A.L.R. 1023, a warranty deed given by a wife to her husband recited in the granting clause that the property was "to be held by him with this grantor in joint tenancy with full rights of ownership vesting in the survivor," and the habendum clause contained the following language: "to him the said grantee as joint tenant." In a petition for a declaratory judgment brought by the surviving husband against the children of the deceased wife and grantor, the court held that this language clearly expressed an intention to create a joint tenancy, and it was so construed. It is noted that the technicalities of real estate conveyancing have been relaxed in New Hampshire, and this fact is emphasized by the court's reference to the following quotation from Dover Cooperative Bank v. Tobin's Estate, 86 N.H. 209, 219; 166 A. 247, 248: "'It is revolting to have no better reason for a rule of law than that so it was laid down in the time of Henry IV. It is still more revolting if the grounds upon which it was laid down have vanished long since, and the rule simply persists from blind imitation of the past.' Holmes, Collected Legal Papers (1920) 187. Even in the case of real estate, where the common-law presumption as to joint tenancy has been abolished by statute [R.L. c. 259 § 17], the language used . . . will be interpreted in the light of the circumstances surrounding the transaction. Dover, etc., Bank v. Tobin's Estate, 86 N.H. 209, 210, 166 A. 247, 248."

In Hart v. Kanaye Nagasawa, 218 Cal. 685, 24 P.2d 815, a conveyance was made to five grantees. The granting clause named the grantees "and to their heirs and assigns forever." The habendum clause, after the names of the parties, contained the following language: "in joint tenancy, with full and absolute title to him or her, the last survivor of the said parties of the second part, and to the longest liver of the said parties of the second part, and to his or her heirs, administrators or assigns forever." In construing the deed the court said: "We have no hesitancy in holding that the Harris deed conveyed the fee in joint tenancy. The granting clause purports to convey the fee-simple title to the five grantees without limitation. The habendum clause simply defines the estate granted as a joint tenancy, with right of survivorship. . . . Giving the words used their ordinary and usual meaning, they can be interpreted but one way—that is, they create a joint tenancy, with the right of survivorship expressly provided for. The estate contended for by appellant—a joint life estate with contingent remainder to the survivor—is of such an unusual nature that before a court would be justified in holding such an estate had been created, clear and unambiguous language to that effect would have to be used. Here there is no ambiguity or uncertainty in the words used. Nowhere in the deed did the grantors purport to be retaining or reserving any estate in themselves; nowhere in the deed is there any reference directly or indirectly to an estate in remainder; nowhere in the deed is there any reference at all to a life estate. Although not perhaps conclusive, these factors are of some importance in construing the words used. Another factor should be mentioned. Section 1105 of the Civil Code provides: 'A fee-simple title is presumed to be intended to pass by a grant of real property, unless it appears from the grant that a lesser estate was intended.' Nowhere in the deed her [sic] involved is there any reference to any such lesser estate, and so we must presume a fee was intended to pass."

In Hilborn v. Soale et al., 44 Cal.App. 115, 185 P. 982, 983, a deed of real estate to grantees, husband and wife, "as joint tenants with the right of survivorship, ... To have and to hold to the said grantees and to the survivor or [of] them forever," was held to create a joint tenancy, and not a life estate in the grantees and a contingent remainder in fee to the survivor. The court also held that an execution sale of the interest of one of the grantees severed the joint tenancy and left the purchaser at the execution sale and the other grantee as tenants in common.

In Shipley v. Shipley, 324 Ill. 560, 155 N.E. 334, 335, a conveyance to grantees "with full rights of survivorship, and not as tenants in common," was held to create an estate in joint tenancy. In construing the Illinois statute, similar to our own, modifying the common-law rule favoring joint tenancy, the court said: "It is not necessary to use the exact words of the statute, in order to indicate an intention to create a joint tenancy. It is sufficient if the language employed be such as to clearly and explicitly show that the parties to the deed intended that the premises were to pass in joint tenancy."

In Coudert et al. v. Earl, 45 N.J.Eq. 654, 18 A. 220, 221, the language used in the deed was as follows—the purchasers were described by name "as joint tenants." The granting part of the deed contained the following language: "as joint tenants, their heirs and assigns," and the habendum clause contained the following recitation, "in joint tenancy, their heirs and assigns, to them and their proper use." The court held that the language used was sufficient to create an estate in joint tenancy without the use of the words "and not an estate of tenancy in common."

Under statutes favoring the creation of tenancies in common but not abolishing joint tenancies it is generally held that any language clearly indicating an intention to create a joint tenancy will be sufficient regardless of where it appears in the deed. See 26 C.J.S. Deeds § 127, p. 968; 48 C.J.S. Joint Tenancy § 3, p. 918; 14 Am.Jur. pp. 85, 86. Difficulty arises, however, in those jurisdictions where such intent conflicts with technical rules of construction, particularly with reference to the creation of estates of inheritance.

In this jurisdiction any joint interest in either real or personal property is not recognized, except that of copartners, tenants in common, and joint tenants. Appeal of Garland, 126 Me. 84, 93, 136 A. 459. Tenancies in the entirety have not been recognized since the enactment of the statute authorizing married women to hold property. Appeal of Robinson, 88 Me. 17, 33 A. 652, 30 L.R.A. 331. An estate in joint tenancy is well recognized in this state. The statute does not abolish joint tenancies, but the intent to create such an estate must be clear and convincing. Appeal of Garland, supra. In the creation of joint tenancies, four essential elements are necessary, to wit: unity of time, unity of title, unity of interest, and unity of possession. Strout v. Burgess, 144 Me. 263, 268, 68 A.2d 241, 12 A.L.R.2d 939. The tenants must have one and the same interest, accruing by one and the same conveyance, commencing at one and the same time, and held by one and the same undivided possession. One of the characteristics of a joint tenancy is the right of survivorship. Strout v. Burgess, supra. Another incident of joint tenancy is the right of severance. Poulson v.

Poulson, 145 Me. 15, 70 A.2d 868; Strout v. Burgess, supra. Any joint tenant may convey his interest and a conveyance to a stranger destroys the unity of title, and also the unity of time, and the grantee becomes a tenant in common with the other cotenant. If there are more than two joint tenants and one conveys his interest to a third person, the grantee becomes a tenant in common with the others although the others remain joint tenants as between themselves. Tiffany, Real Property, 2d Ed., p. 637.

Undoubtedly having this statute in mind, as well as the technical nature of an estate in joint tenancy at common law, the legal profession of this state for many years has utilized the words "as joint tenants and not as tenants in common" when desiring to effectuate a conveyance of property in joint tenancy. In recent years this practice has become increasingly prevalent. A high percentage of conveyances to husband and wife, or to persons in close relationship, especially of residential property, have contained these words in some part of the instrument of conveyance. They have been placed in deeds with the obvious intention of creating an estate in joint tenancy with all of the well-recognized attributes and incidents of such an estate at common law. Indeed, it may well be said that joint tenancies in this jurisdiction, for many practical reasons, are now being looked upon with favor rather than with disfavor. These deeds, if possible, should be construed as joint tenancies in the entire estate parted with by the grantor.

Does the use of the word "heirs" in the phrase "and the heirs of the survivor forever," and in no other part of the granting or habendum clauses of the deed, preclude a severance of the property and thus create a life estate in the grantees with a contingent fee in the survivor, as claimed by the defendant? We believe not. The intention to create a joint tenancy, so clearly expressed in this deed, carries with it the intent to endow such tenancy with all of the well-recognized incidents of a joint tenancy at common law. If the intention of the parties to create a joint tenancy, clearly expressed as in this deed, is in conflict with technical rules of the common law in the construction of deeds, then that intent takes precedence over and overrides those technical rules which are attempted to be used to justify the creation of such an unusual estate as that claimed by the defendant. If the parties had desired to create the estate claimed by the defendant, they could have indicated such intent by apt language. They did not do so. The deed contained no reference to a life estate, nor did it refer to any estate in remainder.

We hold that the elements of unity of time, title, interest, and possession were present in the estate created by the deed, and that the deed conveyed the entire estate disposed of by the grantor, a fee, to the grantees as joint tenants with all of the incidents and attributes of such tenancy at common law. If our ruling in this respect be considered a departure from the technical rules of the common law, let it be said that it is made in the interest of the security of property titles and in accordance with the intention of the parties clearly expressed in the instrument of conveyance.

Reformation of the deed is unnecessary. The conveyance from the defendant Alice L. Palmer (Flint) to Nathan H. Palmer disposed of her entire interest in the property and he thereby became the owner of the fee, which is now in the plaintiff.

The entry will be

Appeal allowed. Bill of complaint sustained. Case remanded to sitting Justice for entry of a decree of declaratory judgment for plaintiff in accordance with this opinion.

NOTES

1. This case, like many others (some of them in this book) demonstrates that a lack of careful, thoughtful draftsmanship invites and sometimes produces litigation. Since the Palmers purchased the land from a Federal Land Bank, it is hardly questionable that the choice of the estate to be conveyed was theirs, not the grantor's. The terms of the deed warrant the inference that it was drafted by someone with experience in using legal terminology, or that its terms were copied from a book of legal forms. Assuming that the Palmers had no thought of obtaining an estate for their joint lives and a fee simple for the survivor, and that they told the draftsman that they desired a joint tenancy, he should have been aware that the deed should unambiguously show an intent that both of them, so long as both lived, were owners of the fee simple estate. His language did not do this—the words used in both the granting and habendum clauses, "to them and their assigns and to the survivor, and the *heirs and assigns* of the survivor forever" (emphasis added) suggest that the fee simple estate is conveyed only to the survivor, not to the two of them as an entity. Contrast the language of the subsequent conveyance whereby Nathan Palmer and his sister were made joint tenants, which, with reference to *both* of them used the traditional "words of inheritance" used to show an intent to convey a fee simple estate: "to them and *their heirs and assigns* and to the survivor of them, and to the heirs and assigns of such survivor forever." (Emphasis added.) One would like to know why this unambiguous language was not used in the deed from the Land Bank to the Palmers. One possibility is that the draftsman supposed that an estate in joint tenancy does not involve fee simple ownership by all the joint tenants together, but limits fee simple ownership only to the survivor. Quite possibly, the circumstances warranted a decree reforming the deed, but given its language as it stood, it is somewhat difficult to understand how the court could properly construe it as conveying a fee simple estate to the Palmers together.

2. As all of the cases in this Chapter indicate, the key issue is what type of concurrent estate was created by the language used in the operative legal instrument. Differing legal consequences will flow from the determination of that issue. Suppose, for example, the operative deed conveys to "Arthur Stone and Violet Stone, husband and wife, as tenants by the entireties" but that at no time were Arthur and Violet ever married to each other. In a state which recognizes the tenancy by the entireties, no such estate can result but how do the parties hold

title—as tenants in common or as joint tenants? In Matter of Estate of Kappler, 418 Mich. 237, 341 N.W.2d 113 (1983) held that the addition of the language "as tenants by the entireties" was not enough to create a joint tenancy and therefore the conveyance created a tenancy in common and Violet's interest passed to her son. Wouldn't it be just as plausible to hold that since the tenancy by the entireties carries with it a right of survivorship this was what the parties intended and the only estate which would carry out that purpose was a joint tenancy?

Suppose two parties purchase a residence "as joint tenants with full rights of survivorship and not as tenants in common." Isn't it clear that the parties intended to create a joint tenancy with the normal incidents thereof, including not only the right of survivorship but with the right of severance and partition? Before you answer that question too quickly read the next case.

JONES v. GREEN

Court of Appeals of Michigan, 1983.
126 Mich.App. 412, 337 N.W.2d 85.

PER CURIAM.

Defendant appeals by leave granted from a trial court order denying his motion for partial summary judgment.

Facts

Plaintiff and defendant purchased a residence on January 20, 1978. The deed conveying the residence stated in pertinent part that the seller "conveys and warrants to James A. Green and Dorothy J. Jones, as joint tenants with full rights of survivorship and not as tenants in common . . .". On August 4, 1981, plaintiff commenced the present action seeking, *inter alia,* to partition the property which she and defendant had purchased. On December 3, 1981, defendant moved for summary judgment under GCR 1963, 117.2(1), arguing that property conveyed to unmarried individuals as joint tenants with full right of survivorship and not as tenants in common cannot be partitioned under Michigan law. The trial court rejected defendant's arguments. Defendant now contends the trial court committed reversible error in denying his motion for partial summary judgment. . . .

All land held jointly is generally subject to partition. M.C.L. § 600.3304; M.S.A. § 27A.3304. *Henkel v. Henkel,* 282 Mich. 473, 276 N.W. 522 (1937); *Fuller v. Fuller,* 123 Mich.App. 592, 332 N.W.2d 623 (1983). In *Ames v. Cheyne,* 290 Mich. 215, 287 N.W. 439 (1939), however, the Supreme Court altered this principle, holding that where land is conveyed to parties as "joint tenants and not tenants in common, *and to the survivor thereof,* parties of the second part", a party to the joint tenancy may not deprive any other party of his right to survivorship and, accordingly, partition may not be granted. In *Ballard v. Wilson,* 364 Mich. 479, 481–484, 110 N.W.2d 751 (1961), the Supreme Court reaffirmed *Ames,* stating:

> "It is clear, however, that joint tenancy, as a property device, was not favored in the United States. Thus, in this State, although we have not gone so far as certain others (where the abolition has been accomplished) the legislature has provided that 'all grants and

devises of lands, made to 2 or more persons, . . . shall be construed to create estates in common, and not in joint tenancy, unless expressly declared to be in joint tenancy.' It has also provided that 'all persons holding lands as joint tenants or tenants in common, may have partition thereof.' Hence arises our problem: The 3 grantees before us hold the property as 'joint tenants with right of survivorship, and not as tenants in common.' Does such a deed create a mere joint tenancy, or something more? As a matter of original interpretation such language might be construed as doing no more than creating an ordinary joint tenancy, the words of survivorship being added merely out of an abundance of caution, to make doubly sure that by the recitation of this, the 'grand incident of joint estates,' there could be no doubt that the tenancy in common presumed by the statute was not intended to be created.

"But this conclusion is far from inevitable. Survivorship would follow as a matter of course in any joint tenancy. It is implicit in the concept. Hence, it may be argued *per contra*, that by the addition of express words of survivorship the grantor intended to create something more than a mere joint tenancy. Thus, it has been held repeatedly in a parallel situation, where a deed ran to 'A and B, and the survivor of them, his heirs and assigns,' that the intent of the grantor was to convey a moiety to A and B for life with remainder to the survivor in fee, and that neither grantee could convey the estate so as to cut off the remainder. Accordingly, and apparently upon parity of reasoning, we held in *Ames v. Cheyne, supra* [290 Mich] 218 [287 NW 439] that 'where property stands in the name of joint tenants with the right of survivorship, neither party may transfer the title to the premises and deprive the other of such right of survivorship' (citing the *Schultz [Schultz v Brohl,* 116 Mich 603; 74 NW 1012 (1898)] and *Finch* [*Finch v Haynes,* 144 Mich 352; 107 NW 910 (1906).] Cases, *supra,* note 9) and concluded that 'plaintiff may not have partition.'

"Under the rule of *Ames v. Cheyne* we hold that these parties intended to create and did create joint life estates followed by a contingent remainder in fee to the survivor, indestructible by the voluntary act of only one of the life tenants. Partition is denied." (Footnotes omitted.) 364 Mich. 482–484, 110 N.W.2d 751.

. . .

Plaintiff argues that the decisions in *Ames v. Cheyne* and *Ballard v. Wilson* do not apply here because those cases were decided before the enactment of M.C.L. § 600.3304; M.S.A. § 27A.3304. In support of this position, plaintiff relies on the following portion of the committee comment to the statute:

"The general rule that there is a right in a co-tenant to have the premises partitioned is not universally applicable. A co-tenant may do things which will limit this right. He may contract away his right to partition. *Avery v Payne* (1864) 12 Mich 540, *Eberts v Fisher* (1884) 54 Mich 294; 20 NW 80. The court probably went to the extreme limit of finding a contract against partition in the case of *Ames v Cheyne* (1939) 290 Mich 215, 287 NW 439, when it found that the parties by taking the land as joint tenants *with a right of survivorship* were contracting that they would not partition the premises. It seems quite likely that given a proper case reasonably argued the court would today find that property taken by persons as joint tenants with a right of survivorship was subject to partition since the statement 'with right of survivorship' would reasonably be considered merely a statement of an incident of joint tenancy rather than a contract." (Emphasis in original.)

Plaintiff's argument lacks merit. M.C.L. § 600.3304; M.S.A. § 27A.3304 is substantially the same as its predecessor, M.C.L. § 631.1; M.S.A. § 27.2012, which provided that "[a]ll persons holding lands as joint tenants or tenants in common, may have partition thereof. . . ." Furthermore, following the enactment of M.C.L. § 600.3304; M.S.A. § 27A.3304, the Supreme Court and this Court have reaffirmed the holding in *Ames. Mannausa v. Mannausa,* supra; Fuller v. Fuller, supra. We find that *Ames v. Cheyne* is controlling. *Fuller v. Fuller,* supra. Therefore, the real estate held by plaintiff and defendant cannot be partitioned. Accordingly, the trial court erred by denying defendant's motion for partial summary judgment.

Reversed.

NOTE

See also Fuller v. Fuller, 123 Mich.App. 592, 332 N.W.2d 623 (1983) to the same effect. Do not assume that all (or even most) courts would reach this same result. Indeed it is quite common in many states to use the language "To A and B not as tenants in common but as joint tenants *with right of survivorship.*" The italicized phrase is viewed as extra assurance, not as creating a non-severable estate. Once again, it is clear that legal language can be a "sticky wicket" and great care must be exercised to understand the results in a particular jurisdiction.

PEOPLE v. NOGARR

District Court of Appeal of California, 1958.
164 Cal.App.2d 591, 330 P.2d 858, 67 A.L.R.2d 992.

NOURSE, JUSTICE PRO TEM. This appeal presents but one question: Is a mortgage upon real property executed by one of two joint tenants enforceable after the death of that joint tenant?

The facts are not in dispute. The appellant, Elaine R. Wilson, hereinafter called "Elaine," and Calvert S. Wilson, hereinafter called "Calvert," were husband and wife. On April 10, 1950, they were the real property in question as joint tenants and the record title remained in them as joint tenants until the death of Calvert. In July 1954 Elaine and Calvert separated. On October 11, 1954, Calvert executed his promissory note to his parents, the respondents, Frank H. and Alice B. Wilson, hereinafter called "respondents." This note was in the sum of $6,440. At the same time he executed and delivered to respondents a mortgage upon the real property in question. Elaine did not have knowledge of or give her consent to the execution of this mortgage. On June 23, 1955, Calvert died. On May 8, 1956, the People of the State of California commenced an action to condemn the subject real property. By its complaint the condemner alleged that Elaine R. Wilson was the owner of the subject real property and that respondents were mortgagees thereof. By her answer Elaine alleged that she was the owner of the property, that respondents had no right, title or interest therein. Respondents by their answer alleged that they were the owners and holders of the mortgage executed by Calvert and prayed that the mortgage be satisfied from the proceeds of the condemnation award. By agreement the fair market value of the property was fixed at $13,800 and that amount together with interest was paid into court by the condemner. Thereafter trial was had as to the rights and interests of Elaine and the respondents. No formal findings were made by the court, but by a memorandum ruling the court found that there was owing to respondents the sum of $6,440 upon the promissory note executed by Calvert and secured by the aforesaid mortgage, and ordered that sum plus interest disbursed to respondents out of 50 per cent of the funds remaining in the hands of the trustee (the county clerk) after the payment of certain liens which were concededly a charge upon the joint estate. Judgment was entered accordingly. As a practical matter this resulted in distribution of 50 per cent of said balance to respondents, as the amount found due them was in excess of one-half of the balance remaining after the payment of other liens.

It is appellant's contention that execution of the mortgage by Calvert did not operate to terminate the joint tenancy and sever his interest from that of Elaine, but that the mortgage was a charge or lien upon his interest as a joint tenant only and that therefore upon his death, his interest having ceased to exist the lien of the mortgage terminated and that Elaine was entitled to the distribution of the entire award exclusive of the sums distributed to other lienholders.

We have reached the conclusion that appellant's contention must be sustained. In order that a joint tenancy may exist four unities are required; unity of interest, unity of title, unity of time and unity of possession. Hammond v. McArthur, 30 Cal.2d 512, 514, 183 P.2d 1 and authorities there cited. So long as these unities exist the right of survivorship is an incident of the tenancy, and upon the death of one joint tenant the survivor becomes the sole owner in fee by right of survivorship and no interest in the property passes to the heirs, devisees or personal representatives of the joint tenant first to die. King v. King, 107 Cal.App.2d 257, 236 P.2d 912; In re Estate of Zaring, 93 Cal.App.2d 577, 579–580, 209 P.2d 642.

It is undisputed in the present case that a joint tenancy in fee simple existed between Elaine and Calvert at the time of the execution of the mortgage, that at that time there existed all of the four unities, that consequently Elaine upon the death of Calvert became the sole owner of the property in question and under the doctrine of equitable conversion [entitled] to the entire award in condemnation, unless the execution by Calvert of the mortgage destroyed one of the unities and thus severed the joint tenancy and destroyed the right of survivorship.

Under the law of this state a mortgage is but a hypothecation of the property mortgaged. It creates but a charge or lien upon the property hypothecated, without the necessity of a change of possession and without any right of possession in the mortgagee, and does not operate to pass the legal title to the mortgagee. Civ.Code, § 2920; McMillan v. Richards, 9 Cal. 365, 406, 411; Dutton v. Warschauer, 21 Cal. 609, 621; 33 Cal.Jur.2d 423–424.

Inasmuch as the mortgage was but a lien or charge upon Calvert's interest, and as it did not operate to transfer the legal title or any title to the mortgagees or entitle the mortgagees to possession, it did not destroy any of the unities, and therefore the estate in joint tenancy was not severed and Elaine and Calvert did not become tenants in common. It necessarily follows that, as the mortgage lien attached only to such interest as Calvert had in the real property, when his interest ceased to exist the lien of the mortgage expired with it. Application of Gau, 230 Minn. 235, 41 N.W.2d 444; Power v. Grace, 1 D.L.R. 801; Zeigler v. Bonnell, 52 Cal.App.2d 217, 219–221, 126 P.2d 118, cited with approval in Hammond v. McArthur, supra, 30 Cal.2d 512, 183 P.2d 1.

In Zeigler v. Bonnell, supra, it was directly held that a judgment lien upon the interest of a joint tenant terminated on the death of the judgment debtor joint tenant. In so holding the court said (52 Cal.App. 2d at page 219, 126 P.2d at page 119): "The right of survivorship is the chief characteristic that distinguishes a joint tenancy from other interests in property. The surviving joint tenant does not secure that right from the deceased joint tenant, but from the devise or conveyance by which the joint tenancy was first created. (Citation.) While both joint tenants are alive each has a specialized form of a life estate, with what amounts to a contingent remainder in the fee, the contingency being dependent upon which joint tenant survives. The judgment lien of respondent could attach only to the interest of his debtor, William B. Nash. That interest terminated upon Nash's death. After his death there was no interest to levy upon. Although the title of the execution purchaser dates back to the date of his lien, that doctrine only applies when the rights of innocent third parties have not intervened. Here the rights of the surviving joint tenant intervened between the date of the lien and the date of the sale. On the latter date the deceased joint tenant had no interest in the property, and his judgment creditor has no greater rights. . . . This rule is sound in theory and fair in its operation. When a creditor has a judgment lien against the interest of one joint tenant he can immediately execute and sell the interest of his judgment debtor, and thus sever the joint tenancy, or he can keep his lien alive and wait until the joint tenancy is terminated by the death of one of the joint tenants. If the judgment debtor survives, the judgment lien immediately attaches to the entire property. If the judgment debtor is the first to die, the lien is lost. If the creditor sits back to await this contingency, as respondent did in this case, he assumes the risk of losing his lien."

We are unable to distinguish between the effect of a judgment lien and of a lien of a mortgage executed by one joint tenant only. The only distinction between the two liens is that the mortgage lien is a lien upon specific property while the judgment lien is a general lien upon all real property of the judgment debtor. McMillan v. Richards, supra, 9 Cal. 365, 409.

In Hammond v. McArthur, supra, in discussing the operation of a mortgage as a severance of joint tenancy, the Supreme Court, in what is undoubtedly dictum, as a mortgage was not there involved, said (30 Cal. 2d at page 515, 183 P.2d at page 3): "In jurisdictions where a mortgage ordinarily operates to transfer the legal title, a mortgage by a joint tenant causes a severance of the joint tenancy. (Citation.) Also, in some states where a mortgage is regarded as mere security, a mortgage by a joint tenant brings the tenancy to an end. (Citation.) However, that conclusion is not in accord with the common-law authorities to the effect that the creation by a joint tenant of a mere charge upon the land is a nullity as against the right of survivorship of the other joint tenant. (Citation.)"

Respondents have directed our attention to decisions of other jurisdictions which they assert support their contention that a joint tenant has a right to mortgage his interest and that this operates to sever the joint tenancy. Examination of each of the cases relied upon by respondents discloses that all except one of them were rendered in jurisdictions where a mortgage operated not merely as a lien or charge upon the mortgagor's interest but as a transfer or conveyance of his interest, the conveyance being subject to defeasance upon the payment of the mortgage debt. It is evident that in those jurisdictions where a mortgage operates to convey title to the mortgagee the unity of title is destroyed, and in those jurisdictions where it operates not only to transfer title but the right of possession to the mortgagee both the unity of title and of possession are destroyed; and that in either case there is a severance of the joint tenancy.

Respondents place their main reliance upon Wilken v. Young, 144 Ind. 1, 41 N.E. 68, 590, decided by the Supreme Court of the State of Indiana. At the time this decision was rendered Indiana adhered to the lien theory of mortgages and the case undoubtedly strongly tends to support respondents' position. We do not, however, feel bound by it. In the first place, the Supreme Court of Indiana based its holding that a joint tenant might mortgage his interest and that the lien of the mortgage survived his death upon two cases, York v. Stone, 1 Salk 158 and Simpson's Lessee v. Ammons, 1 Bin.Pa., 175. We will comment further on these opinions later in this opinion, but direct attention here to the fact that both of them were rendered in jurisdictions where a mortgage operated as a conveyance of the mortgagor's interest. In the second place, the Supreme Court of Indiana did not hold that the execution of the mortgage operated as a severance of the joint estate so as to destroy the right of survivorship, but expressly held that there was no severance and that upon the death of the mortgagor life tenant the surviving joint tenant took by virtue of the tenancy; but as to one-half of the property she took only the right of redemption from the mortgage created by the deceased joint tenant.

The decision seems to us entirely illogical and the result of it unjust, for under it one joint tenant might, as in the case at bar, mortgage and obtain the full value of an undivided one-half of the joint tenancy property and yet retain his right to the entire property as the surviving joint tenant should his cotenant be the first to die; while that cotenant, if the survivor, would take but the right to acquire from the mortgagee the one-half interest to which she had the right as the survivor. Further, the mortgagee would by the mortgage obtain a lien upon an undivided one-half interest which would not be defeated by the death of the mortgagor but also be a lien upon the whole property were the mortgagor to be the survivor.

York v. Stone, supra, was decided by the chancery court in England, and in that jurisdiction the mortgage operated to transfer the legal title to the mortgagee and gave the mortgagee the right to immediate possession. In Simpson's Lessee v. Ammon, supra, 1 Bin. 175, decided by the Supreme Court of Pennsylvania in 1806, the court, without citation of authority for the statement or the statement of any reason therefor, stated (at page 177): ". . . the court are of the opinion that the mortgage was a severance of the joint tenancy. The interest of Baynton and Morgan passed by it, but the interest of Wharton was not affected." While there is some conflict in the decisions of the Pennsylvania courts as to whether a mortgage operates merely as a charge or lien upon the property mortgaged or as a transfer of the title of the mortgagor, undoubtedly the Supreme Court of Pennsylvania in rendering its decision in the Simpson case considered a mortgage as vesting title in the mortgagee, for in Moliere's Lessee v. Noe, 4 Dall. 450, 1 L.Ed. 450, which was decided by the Supreme Court of Pennsylvania in the same year that it decided the Simpson case, Mr. Justice Tilghman, who was the author of the opinion in the Simpson case, said: "Before I dismiss this subject, I will give my opinion concerning debts due by mortgage, which were mentioned in the course of the argument. I conceive them to stand on a different footing from judgments, because the mortgagee is, strictly speaking, the owner of the land, and may recover it in an ejectment. The mortgagor has no more than an equity of redemption . . . ." See also Martin v. Jackson, 1856, 27 Pa. 504, 67 Am.Dec. 489.

Counsel have also directed our attention to Wolf v. Johnson, 157 Md. 112, 145 A. 363, 366. In the opinion, the question as to whether the execution of a mortgage by a joint tenant terminated the joint tenancy is not discussed but is assumed. The entire question discussed by the court was whether the estate there in question was one "by the entireties" or one of joint tenancy. We assume that the reason the question as to severance was not argued or discussed is that under the law of Maryland a mortgage operates to transfer the legal title to the mortgagee and in the absence of contract gives him the right to possession, and would therefore necessarily destroy the unities of both title and possession. Kramer v. United States, 4 Cir., 190 F.2d 712; Williams v. Safe Deposit & Trust Co., 167 Md. 499, 175 A. 331, 333.

Respondents also rely upon the decision of the Supreme Court of Wisconsin in Goff v. Yauman, 237 Wis. 643, 298 N.W. 179, 134 A.L.R. 952. There the court held that a statutory lien upon the interest of a joint tenant of real property, created under the old age assistance statutes of Wisconsin, survived the death of the joint tenant. The decision of the court was based entirely upon the construction of the statute, and the court expressly stated that it was not determining as to whether or not a severance would be created by the execution by a joint tenant of a mortgage. It may be pointed out that under a similar statute and in a much better reasoned decision the Supreme Court of Minnesota reached the opposite conclusion to that reached by the Supreme Court of Wisconsin and held that a statutory lien upon the interest of a joint tenant terminated with the death of that tenant. Application of Gau, 230 Minn. 235, 41 N.W.2d 444.

There is nothing inequitable in holding that the lien of respondents' mortgage did not survive the death of the mortgagor. Their note was payable upon demand, and they could have enforced the lien and mortgage by foreclosure and sale prior to the death of the mortgagor and thus have severed the joint tenancy. If they chose not to do so but to await the contingency of which joint tenant died first they did so at their own risk. Under that event the lien that they had expired. If the event had been otherwise and the mortgagor had been the survivor the security of their lien would have been doubled.

The judgment is reversed.

NOTE

1. A brief discussion of the mortgage, its historical development and modern consequences is set forth at page 1037 herein. According to the early English law a mortgage was regarded as a conveyance of the mortgagor's estate to the mortgagee with a defeasance clause to the effect that it would cease to be effective if the mortgagor repaid the borrowed money on the date set. Later, the Court of Chancery adopted the postition that the mortgagor could redeem the land even though he offered full payment long after the due date. This privilege, known as the "equity of redemption" made the mortgagee's title insecure, of course; hence, Chancery adopted a proceeding whereby he could "foreclose" the equity of redemption through a decree setting a time limit for payment.

This "title theory" of the mortgage as a defeasible conveyance was operative when Englishmen established colonies in North America, and as the foregoing opinion indicates, in much modified form it still persists in some states, particularly those derived from English colonial territory. In other states the theory became established that a mortgage has no effect as a conveyance of the mortgagor's estate subject to a condition subsequent; instead, it serves merely to give the mortgagee the security of a lien; i.e., the power to compel a sale of the property as a means of obtaining payment, if necessary.

2. In Brant v. Hargrove, 129 Ariz. 475, 632 P.2d 978 (App.1981) the court, in a case of first impression in Arizona, faced the converse

situation of the principal case. The husband gave a deed of trust on the subject property, apparently forging his wife's name. Her share of the joint tenancy was not subject to the lien but the court held that the deed of trust was valid to bind the husband's share. The husband survived and the wife's estate claimed that the trust deed worked a severance so that her heirs were entitled to one-half the estate free of the lien. The court held that there was no severance and that the husband took the property by right of survivorship and the lien attached to the whole. The court analyzed the issue in considerable detail, relying heavily on People v. Nogarr and California law, in the absence of Arizona precedent. The court reasoned that a deed of trust was in essence a mortgage, creating only a lien on the property and not conveying the title as a regular deed would do. "We do not believe that dogged adherence to the requirements of the four unities in the context of severance is required by our case law. Here there were no facts to indicate an intention to sever the relationship." See also Harms v. Sprague, 119 Ill.App.3d 503, 75 Ill.Dec. 155, 456 N.E.2d 976 (1983) where an Illinois Appellate Court, despite some Supreme Court dicta to the contrary, held a mortgage given by one joint tenant on his interest in the joint tenancy property did not sever the joint tenancy. On the death of the mortgagor, the other joint tenant took the whole estate. Said the court: "Courts in other jurisdictions have held that a mortgage executed by one joint tenant does not by itself sever the joint tenancy; the analytical instrument common to those cases is the conclusion that a mortgage creates only a lien and does not pass or interfere with the mortgaging joint tenant's title (citing People v. Nogarr among other authorities)."

HAWTHORNE v. HAWTHORNE

Court of Appeals of New York, 1963.
13 N.Y.2d 82, 242 N.Y.S.2d 50, 192 N.E.2d 20.

[The following statement is based upon, and in part quoted from, the trial court's opinion, 208 N.Y.S.2d 79. Plaintiff Edith Hawthorne (wife) and Wilson Hawthorne (husband) owned realty as tenants by the entirety. "They also were owners and holders of a standard fire insurance policy. . . ." (No basis for this statement was given—the opinion says nothing of how, when, or by whom the policy was procured or of source of premiums paid.) A fire destroyed a dwelling house, and in settlement the insurance company issued its draft, naming husband, wife, and a mortgagee as payees, for $12,500, "which was the total insurance in effect upon said destroyed premises under said policy." The plaintiff wife's suit, which made both the husband and the mortgagee defendants, sought a division of the insurance proceeds. The husband moved to dismiss the complaint, asserting that upon the facts stated therein the plaintiff was not entitled to relief. The trial court approved this motion and the Appellate Division affirmed the judgment of dismissal. The plaintiff requested and received permission to present the case to the Court of Appeals.]

BURKE, J. The question presented is whether the proceeds of a standard fire insurance policy insuring the interest of plaintiff wife and defendant husband as tenants by the entirety of real property must be divided at the demand of one of the owners or are impressed in equity with the inseverable quality of the ownership of the realty against whose loss they are payable.

The unity of person of husband and wife by reason of which we have entireties in realty is only an historical and not a functional explanation and itself gives no clue to the relationship that ought properly to obtain between the owners of the proceeds of insurance of such an interest. But if we must take the nature of the estate these parties had in the realty as we find it, so must we take the rule that there can be no holding by the entirety in personalty (Matter of Albrecht, 136 N.Y. 91, 32 N.E. 632, 18 L.R.A. 329; Matter of McKelway, 221 N.Y. 15, 116 N.E. 348, L.R.A.1917E, 1143; Matter of Blumenthal, 236 N.Y. 448, 141 N.E. 911, 30 A.L.R. 901). Both the proceeds and the contract under which they were paid are personal property (Brownell v. Board of Educ., 239 N.Y. 369, 374, 146 N.E. 630, 632, 37 A.L.R. 1319; Galante v. Hathaway Bakeries, 6 A.D.2d 142, 149, 176 N.Y.S.2d 87, 93). Since personalty cannot be held by the entirety this ends the question as far as a legal estate or title is concerned unless equity demands exact equivalence in both quantity and quality of ownership in all cases resembling "involuntary conversion." Special Term, as affirmed by the Appellate Division, has so held in dismissing the complaint.

Respondent and the courts below rely on the rule applied in Matter of City of New York (Jamaica Bay), 252 App.Div. 103, 297 N.Y.S. 415, in which a condemnation award for real property held by the entirety was made during the life of both owners but the husband died before payment thereof. The Appellate Division held that the wife was entitled to the full award by right of survivorship on the ground that the involuntary conversion from real property to an award of personal property should not affect the right of survivorship in the substituted *res*. Although this decision dealt solely with the right of survivorship, the continued existence of which would not bar the relief sought here,[1] there is dictum in this court which would indicate that the quality of inseverability also subsists in circumstances similar to the Jamaica Bay case. In Matter of Goodrich v. Village of Otego, 216 N.Y. 112, 116, 110 N.E. 162, 164, Judge Pound remarked that, where a parcel abutting a street was owned by the entirety, damages payable by reason of a change in the grade of the street "should be paid into court and

1. Admitting the right of survivorship arguendo (Scutella v. County Fire Ins. Co., 231 App.Div. 343, 247 N.Y.S. 689) only indicates that the proceeds of the insurance policy are held jointly. Absent the quality of inseverability unique to a holding by the entirety, joint ownership with right of survivorship is no barrier to a sale of the interest of one of the joint owners which destroys the reciprocal right of survivorship (Matter of Suter's Estate, 258 N.Y. 104, 179 N.E. 310; Matter of Polizzo's Estate, 308 N.Y. 517, 127 N.E.2d 316) and, accordingly, no barrier to invoking the power of equity to compel the indorsement and division of a jointly owned draft where it appears that the parties are unable to enjoy the benefits of a joint holding (Cooper v. Cooper, 225 Ark. 626, 284 S.W.2d 617; Loker v. Edmans, 204 App.Div. 223, 197 N.Y.S. 857; Rush v. Rush, 144 Misc. 489, 258 N.Y.S. 913). [Footnote by the Court.]

retained until death terminated the tenancy and then paid to the survivor, the income meanwhile being divided equally between them."

Without passing on the question raised by the dictum in the last-cited case, we believe that the insurance proceeds in dispute here are not the result of an involuntary conversion within the meaning of the cases relied upon by respondent. Unlike those cases neither these proceeds nor the right thereto are the result of an operation of law upon the extinguishment or diminution of an estate in real property. These proceeds have been paid pursuant to a personal contract of insurance entered into between these parties and the insurance company. Although it is quite true that this case is similar to the condemnation cases in respect to the involuntary character of the loss of the realty held by the entirety, mere involuntary loss is but one side of the coin of the insurance policy. Accordingly, the judgment appealed from should be reversed without costs, and the matter remitted to the Supreme Court for further proceedings not inconsistent with this opinion.

DESMOND, C.J., and DYE and FOSTER, JJ., concur with BURKE, J.

FULD, J., concurs in result.

VAN VOORHIS and SCILEPPI, JJ., dissent and vote to affirm.

NOTES

1. Suppose that joint tenants or tenants by the entirety contract to sell the land in a deferred payment transaction either (1) delivering a deed to the purchaser and receiving a mortgage as security for the promised price, or (2) agreeing to deliver the deed when the price is fully paid. Suppose also that a joint tenant, or one of the spouses, dies while part of the price is unpaid. What arguments may be offered concerning rights to the future payments, as between the surviving cotenant(s) and the heirs or devisees of the decedent?

2. In Lovell v. Rowan Mutual Fire Insurance Co., 46 N.C.App. 150, 264 S.E.2d 743 (1980), a case of first impression in North Carolina, the court held that an innocent wife could not recover under an insurance policy issued to the husband insuring property owned by them as tenants by the entirety, when the loss by fire was caused by the intentional burning of the property by the husband. If the arsonist had been a stranger there would have been no question as to the liability of the insurance carrier. At the time of the fire the wife was living apart from the husband and later brought an action for divorce. The arsonist husband apparently burned the jointly owned dwelling for spite, in retaliation against his wife and was later convicted in criminal court for his actions. The court said: "Since neither tenant in an estate by the entirety can insure his or her interest as a separate moiety apart from the estate owned by the two of them as an indivisible estate without the insurance inuring to the benefit of the entirety, it follows that each tenant must accept as an act of both of them any act of the other affecting the estate. The fact that the husband was the named insured is of no consequence. . . . While the plaintiff may have an

action against her husband, she cannot recover her loss from the defendant insurer." There was a dissenting opinion. The case was reversed by the Supreme Court of North Carolina, 302 N.C. 150, 274 S.E.2d 170 (1981). In light of the principal case, can you think of at least one reason for reversal?

See also Fuston v. National Mutual Insurance Co., 440 N.E.2d 751 (Ind.App.1982). Under similar facts, the court held that although Indiana adheres to the common law fiction that a husband and wife are one person for the purposes of owning real estate as tenants by the entireties, a felonious act will sever and dissolve the tenancy and convert it into a tenancy in common. The wife was entitled to one-half of the insurance proceeds.

D'ERCOLE v. D'ERCOLE

United States District Court, D.Massachusetts, 1976.
407 F.Supp. 1377.

TAURO, DISTRICT JUDGE. This is an action brought under 42 U.S.C.A. § 1983 in which the plaintiff seeks declaratory and injunctive relief for deprivation of rights allegedly secured to her under the Fifth and Fourteenth Amendments. Jurisdiction is claimed under 28 U.S.C.A. § 1343(3) and (4).

Basically, plaintiff's complaint states that the common law concept of tenancy by the entirety, as formulated and enforced by case law, and as recognized by the statutes of the Commonwealth of Massachusetts, deprives her of due process and equal protection of the law in that it gives the defendant, her husband, the right of possession and control during his lifetime of their home, owned by them as tenants by the entirety. Defendant's position is that plaintiff's complaint fails to state a claim upon which relief can be granted. Fed.R.Civ.P. 12(b)(6).[1]

I.

The plaintiff and the defendant have been married for some thirty five years. In November of 1962 they bought a residence at 61 Stone Road, Waltham, Massachusetts, for $20,000. The percentage of down payment provided by each party for the home is disputed.[2] Plaintiff used her own funds to purchase some $3500 in new furnishings for the home at the time of purchase. She has been steadily employed during the entire thirty-five years of her marriage and, by agreement with the defendant, assumed financial responsibility for all household expenses, except for mortgage payments and real property taxes. Defendant

1. Injunctive relief is sought only against the defendant husband. . . . Since the complaint does not seek to enjoin the enforcement of any state statute, a three-judge court is not required. See 28 U.S.C.A. §§ 2281–2284. [Footnotes in the case are by the court and numbered accordingly.]

2. Plaintiff in her complaint alleges that she provided one half of the $1,000 down payment. Defendant has denied this allegation, but his version of the truth in this matter is not in the record. The parties have agreed, and the court concurs, that the exact details of this transaction are not critical to this court's ruling.

further concedes that plaintiff has paid for all the preparatory and college expenses of her son.[3]

In 1971, the plaintiff and defendant determined they could no longer live together. When the defendant refused to leave the marital home, plaintiff departed, moving to a relative's home where she still resides.

Proceedings for legal separation and for divorce are now pending in the Middlesex County Probate Court. The defendant husband is seeking a divorce. The plaintiff wife is seeking a separation and is vehemently opposing the divorce on factual issues and because of religious beliefs.

Defendant has refused to share the marital home with plaintiff by allowing her sole occupancy for part of the year, by selling the house and dividing the proceeds, by paying plaintiff her share in the equity of the house, or by renting the premises and dividing the proceeds. In support of his position, defendant points out that the property in question is held under a tenancy by the entirety, which gives both him and the plaintiff an indefeasible right of survivorship, but gives him exclusive right to possession and control in his lifetime. He has stated that he will grant plaintiff one-half the equity in the house if she will grant him an uncontested divorce.[4]

II.

When two or more persons wish to hold property together in Massachusetts they may select one of three common law forms of ownership: the tenancy in common, joint tenancy or tenancy by the entirety.

The tenancy in common is the holding of land "by several and distinct titles."

Each tenant owns an undivided fraction, being entitled to an interest in every inch of the property. With respect to third persons the entire tenancy constitutes a single entity. There is no right of survivorship as between tenants in common. Upon the death of a tenant in common his undivided interest in the property is transferred to his heirs or devisees, subject to liens, claims and dower.

28 Mass.Practice (Park) § 125, at 119–120. (Footnotes omitted). There is a presumption in favor of the tenancy in common over the joint tenancy as a matter of construction in Massachusetts. Each tenant in common has a right to free usage of the whole parcel and may freely convey out his share of the property to a third party, who then becomes a tenant in common in relation to the remaining cotenants.

3. This child is referred to in plaintiff's complaint and in the parties' joint pre-trial memorandum as "her son." It is not clear, therefore, whether or not the defendant is the child's father.

4. Divorce would, in any case, terminate the tenancy by the entirety and thus allow the plaintiff to seek partition of the property. Campagna v. Campagna, 337 Mass. 599, 605, 150 N.E.2d 699, 703 (1958). Separation, even when ratified by a formal decree, does not end the tenancy by the entirety.

The joint tenancy is "a single estate in property owned by two or more persons under one instrument or act."

A joint tenancy is similar to a tenancy in common in that all tenants have an equal right to possession, but the joint tenants hold the property by one joint title and in one right, whereas the tenants in common hold by several titles or by one title and several rights.

The joint tenancy differs also in that there is a right of survivorship in a joint tenancy but not in a tenancy in common. On the death of one of the joint tenants his interest does not descend to his heirs or pass under his will as in a tenancy in common. . . . The widow of the deceased tenant has no dower rights and his creditors have no claim against the enlarged interest of the surviving tenants.

28 Mass.Practice (Park) § 126, at 121–122. (Footnotes omitted). A joint tenant may convey out his share in the property via a legal partition. See Mass.Gen.L. ch. 241, § 1.

The tenancy by the entirety is designed particularly for married couples and may be employed only by them. Until 1973 unless there was clear language to the contrary a conveyance to a married couple was presumed to create a tenancy by the entirety.[5] This form of property ownership differs from the joint tenancy in two respects. First, each tenant has an indefeasible right of survivorship in the *entire* tenancy, which cannot be defeated by any act taken individually by either spouse during his or her lifetime. There can be no partition. Second, the spouses do not have an equal right to control and possession of the property. The husband during his lifetime has paramount rights in the property. In the event of divorce the tenancy by the entirety becomes a tenancy in common unless the divorce decree reflects that a joint tenancy is intended.

III.

The stage was set for the instant case by this court's decision in Klein v. Mayo, 367 F.Supp. 583 (1973) aff'd 416 U.S. 953, 94 S.Ct. 1964, 40 L.Ed.2d 303 (1974). In *Klein* a three-judge panel[6] heard a challenge to the constitutionality of Mass.Gen.L. ch. 241, § 1. This statute states that:

Any person, except a tenant by the entirety, owning a present undivided legal estate in land, not subject to redemption, shall be entitled to have partition in the manner hereinafter provided.

The plaintiff in that case was in precisely the same position as the present plaintiff, having separated from her husband without dissolving her marriage and desiring an equal share in their property which was held under a tenancy by the entirety. She contended that, given the bias of the tenancy by the entirety, the quoted statute barring partition discriminated against her on the basis of sex. In ordering judgment for the defendant, *Klein* separated the issue of partition from the issue of

5. See note 8, infra.

6. The members of this panel were: Campbell, Circuit Judge; Julian, Senior District Judge; and Tauro, District Judge.

any underlying bias in the common law tenancy by the entirety. Finding that partition was equally unavailable to men and women holding property by the entirety, the court concluded that the challenged statute was non-discriminatory, while leaving open the possibility of future direct challenges to the tenancy by the entirety itself.

The statute which is the subject of plaintiff's complaint deals solely with the right to partition, and that right is denied to both husbands and wives. The issue concerning right to possession and control is separate and distinct from that concerning the right to partition.

We are mindful that, in the future, certain common-law aspects of tenancy by the entirety may be subject to judicial review in the light of recent decisions concerning sex discrimination. See, e.g., Frontiero v. Richardson, 411 U.S. 677 [93 S.Ct. 1764, 36 L.Ed.2d 583] (1973); Reed v. Reed, 404 U.S. 71 [92 S.Ct. 251, 30 L.Ed.2d 225] (1971). We are mindful as well that such a challenge may or may not be met by the fact that tenancy by the entirety is but one option open to married persons, and is in no way compelled by the state. 367 F.Supp. 586.

This action presents the challenge referred to in *Klein*, a direct attack on the common law tenancy by the entirety. No challenge to a statute is involved here. Plaintiff's original claim for an order of partition and sale by this court has been waived. Plaintiff asks this court to "restrain and enjoin the defendant from collecting any rents or profits from the above described premises," and to "restrain and enjoin the defendant from continuing to exercise exclusive possession and control over the above described premises."[7]

IV.

Defendant has not contested the court's jurisdiction in this case,[8] but defends on the merits, contending that the Massachusetts' tenancy by the entirety does not discriminate against women.[9]

7. In a third claim for relief plaintiff asks this court to "declare that upon physical separation of a husband and wife, the wife on her behalf, has the absolute right to file a petition for partition of the property held by her as tenants [sic] by the entirety." Such contention, however, was foreclosed by *Klein*.

8. An issue might have been raised as to the existence of state action in this case, but in any event this court concludes that the tenancy by the entirety is a "custom of usage" enforced by the "persistent practices of state officials" sufficient to satisfy the state action prerequisite for suits brought under 42 U.S.C.A. § 1983. Adickes v. S.H. Kress & Co., 398 U.S. 144, 167, 90 S.Ct. 1598, 26 L.Ed. 2d 142 (1970). In Adickes the Supreme Court clearly suggested that a common law creation can constitute a "custom or usage" for purposes of § 1983. Id., at 165, 90 S.Ct. 1598, quoting Cong.Globe, 42d Cong., 1st Sess., App. 216 (remarks of Senator Thurmond). The presumption favoring the tenancy by the entirety in property holdings by married persons has been upheld by a line of Massachusetts cases, unbroken until 1973, when the presumption was eliminated by statute. See Pray v. Stebbins, 141 Mass. 219, 4 N.E. 824 (1886); Hoag v. Hoag, 213 Mass. 50, 99 N.E. 521 (1912); Childs v. Childs, 293 Mass. 67, 199 N.E. 383 (1935); Finn v. Finn, 348 Mass. 443, 204 N.E.2d 293 (1965); Maddams v. Maddams, 352 Mass. 32, 223 N.E.2d 519 (1967). See also, Gould v. Gould, 359 Mass. 29, 267 N.E.2d 652 (1971). The presumption in favor of tenancies by the entirety was eliminated by an amendment to Mass. Gen.L. ch. 184, § 7, April 23, 1973, ch. 210 of the Acts of 1973.

In addition, as noted above, the common law tenancy by the entirety is enforced in the Commonwealth by Mass.Gen.L. ch. 241, § 1 which bars partition of property so held.

9. Defendant also contends that Massachusetts' statutes already provide plaintiff

As was conceded in *Klein*, the common law concept of tenancy by the entirety is male oriented.

It is true that the only Massachusetts tenancy tailored exclusively for married persons appears to be balanced in favor of males. There is no equivalent female-biased tenancy, nor is there a "neutral" married persons' tenancy providing for indefeasible survivorship but not vesting paramount lifetime rights in the male. Married couples may, it is true, elect a joint tenancy, a tenancy in common, or a sole tenancy. However, the survivorship feature of a joint tenancy may be destroyed by partition. A wife who wants the security of indefeasible survivorship can achieve it only by means of a male-dominated tenancy.

367 F.Supp. at 585.

But, the dispositive issue is not merely whether the tenancy by the entirety favors males. Rather, the issue is whether it does so in a manner that creates a constitutionally impermissible classification. On the specific facts of this case, this court holds that tenancy by the entirety, being but one option open to married persons seeking to take title in real estate, is constitutionally permissible.

It may be possible in some future case for a plaintiff wife to demonstrate factually that a selection of tenancy by the entirety was made through coercion, ignorance or misrepresentation. But no such facts were presented here, nor does plaintiff advance such a theory. Rather, this record makes almost inescapable the conclusion that plaintiff freely entered into a contract along with her husband in 1961, selecting one among several options open to her. Events have not transpired as she expected and now she seeks to revise the terms of her contract, because she now feels that her husband got the better end of the bargain.[10]

Without greater justification than plaintiff's unsubstantiated allegations of prejudice, this court will not declare unconstitutional a form of property ownership selected by and presently relied upon by thousands of Massachusetts residents, including this plaintiff and defendant. As was noted in *Klein,*

[t]he state does not compel husbands and wives to hold their property as tenants by the entirety. Undoubtedly, that choice is knowingly made in many instances despite or even, perhaps, because of its male oriented aspects. The choice would have been the same whether or not alternatives were available.

Id., at 585.

The Commonwealth permits tenancy by the entirety as one available option of property ownership. The plaintiff now complains of its

with the relief she seeks here. He cites Mass.Gen.L. ch. 209, §§ 32 and 32D and ch. 208, § 34B, which give the state probate court discretionary power to grant the plaintiff a share, or a constructive share, in the subject property. Since the court is of the opinion that the tenancy by the entirety does not discriminate against women, it is not necessary to reach this defense.

10. It is of more than passing significance to note that if plaintiff prevailed in this case, she would hold the property as a tenant in common, or possibly a joint tenant, with a right of partition. These are both options the Commonwealth afforded her back in 1961.

consequences. But, as indicated in *Klein,* this is not to say that other married women would not prefer a vehicle giving husbands the right to possession, while at the same time foreclosing the possibility of partition, thereby preserving the family homestead even during bitter but temporary periods of separation.[11]

This case is readily distinguishable from Reed v. Reed, 404 U.S. 71, 92 S.Ct. 251, 30 L.Ed.2d 225 (1971). There, the challenged statute barred forever a wife from acting as administratrix of her child's estate if her husband sought appointment as administrator. Here, the plaintiff has made her own choice. The state did not compel her current status. Moreover, if the effects of the tenancy are too onerous or inequitable, she may apply to the probate court for appropriate relief.

This court is sympathetic with plaintiff's concern that the tenancy by the entirety is to some degree a legal artifact, formerly justified by the presumed incompetence of women to manage property. But this decision is not based on such an archaic and patently invalid stereotype. Rather, the fact is that, regardless of its roots, the tenancy by the entirety exists today as one of several options open to married persons seeking to purchase real estate. Its existence constitutes a matter of choice not discrimination. If there is a classification, it is one selected by the plaintiff, not one imposed by the Commonwealth. She is entitled to the benefit of her bargain, no more and no less. There being no evidence that the plaintiff in this case made her choice among then existing options other than freely, this court will not step in to re-write the agreement between her and her husband.

The court orders entry of judgment for the defendant.

NOTES

1. How realistic is the court's assumption that the plaintiff had an option among several categories of concurrent ownership and freely chose tenancy by the entirety? Is this but another example of the law creating (or allowing) a pitfall for the unwary?

2. In West v. First Agricultural Bank, 382 Mass. 534, 419 N.E.2d 262 (1981) the Supreme Judicial Court of Massachusetts revisited the entire issue of the status of the tenancy by the entirety in that state. It pointed out that of the twenty-odd states in which tenancies by the entirety still exist, only Massachusetts, North Carolina, and Michigan have reserved into modern times the tenancy's traditional husband-oriented form. Michigan amended the tenancy in 1975 but North Carolina, to this date, apparently had not. Massachusetts finally resolved the matter in 1980 but, in the instant case, neither party claimed that the 1980 legislation applied retroactively.

11. It could be argued that the legislature has not abolished the common law tenancy by the entirety as a vehicle for acquiring the title, because it serves as an effective means for the Commonwealth to quiet disputes as to possession pending a determination of that issue by the probate court. After reviewing the circumstances of a particular case, the probate court may well award possession and control of the premises to the wife, among other similar options. Mass.Gen.L. ch. 209, §§ 32 and 32D and ch. 208, § 34B.

The case was argued on constitutional grounds, attacking, as in D'Ercole v. D'Ercole (cited in the West case) the validity of an estate which was based on sex discrimination. The court rejected arguments based on the equal protection clause of the Fourteenth Amendment and on Pt. 1, Art. 1, of the Massachusetts Declaration of Rights, as amended, which states in part, "Equality under the law shall not be denied or abridged because of sex. . . ."—the Equal Rights Amendment. The court was obviously bothered by an estate that "appeared to be a reflection of discredited stereotypes" but was unwilling to hand down a decision which would have retroactive consequences because so many land titles in Massachusetts were based on Licker v. Gluskin, 265 Mass. 403, 164 N.E. 613 (1929), "a monument to the conventional attitudes." This view was strengthened by the 1980 legislation in the state which covers conveyances from and after February 11, 1980. It amended G.L.C. 209, sect. 1, to provide: "A husband and wife shall be equally entitled to the rents, products, income or profits and to the control, management and possession of property held by them as tenants by the entirety." And further: "The interest of a debtor spouse in property held as tenants by the entirety shall not be subject to seizure or execution by a creditor of such debtor spouse so long as such property is the principal residence of the non debtor spouse" (with a proviso regarding liability of the spouses for necessaries). Said the court: "From these provisions the whole shape of the new tenancy will be extrapolated." The court was unwilling to muddy the waters by altering the nature of the tenancy as it existed prior to 1980.

The full opinion, too long and complicated to reprint here, is well worth reading as an example of how difficult it is to eradicate archaic doctrines of property law, even when nearly everyone agrees that the doctrines are more a reflection of the past than a reliable guide for the future.

3. Despite the attacks on the tenancy by the entireties, it is a hardy survivor in many states. For example, the Court of Appeals of Maryland has recently stated that: "Maryland retains the estate of tenancy by the entirety in its traditional form." Beall v. Beall, 291 Md. 224, 434 A.2d 1015 (1981). The court then proceeded, in what it called a case of first impression in the United States and Great Britain, to hold that an option to purchase land given by a husband and wife, as tenants by the entirety, lapsed upon the death of one tenant and thereafter could not be accepted by the offeree. The court reasoned that the offer was made by the tenants by the entirety as a team rather than as two individuals. The continuation of the offer depended upon the continuous assent of both members of the team. There was a dissent by two judges who obviously thought that the estate should be abolished rather than extended and that the offer survived the death of the husband and hence the widow should have been bound.

4. Ohio is a good example of the hardihood of the tenancy by the entireties and the litigation which it can generate. That state had no common law tenancy by the entireties but in 1972 the estate was authorized by statute, or at least the courts so held in interpreting an ambiguous new statute dealing with survivorship rights. In Donvito v.

Criswell, 1 Ohio App.2d 53, 439 N.E.2d 467 (1982), the court construed the new statute to prevent the creditor of only one spouse from attaching or levying upon the interest of that spouse in property held by tenancy by the entireties. [Note that the debtor protection applied to both spouses under the Ohio interpretation.] This shield against creditors apparently appealed to a significant number of married couples and the estate was widely used. Then, in 1985, the General Assembly by amendments to R.C. 5302.17, effective April 4, 1985, radically changed the character and content of the statute, apparently abolishing the legislatively created estate and removing the debtor protection aspect, thus leaving the estate as, in effect, a joint tenancy. In Bahler v. Doenges, 26 Ohio App.3d 172, 499 N.E.2d 35 (1986) the court recognized the change but refused to apply the statute retroactively noting that the Doenges "owned the real estate sold at foreclosure as tenants by the entireties, that neither spouse could alienate the property without the other's consent, that the property is therefore immune from one spouse's creditors."

This Ohio excursion into troubled waters has left a detritus of problems and not a few unanswered questions. See Reedy, Legislative Note, 11 U.Dayton L.Rev. 481 (1986). The moral of this tale may well be that the committee of the American Bar Association which, in 1944, recommended that measures be adopted in all states to abolish tenancy by the entireties was on the right track.

MANN v. BRADLEY

Supreme Court of Colorado, 1975.
188 Colo. 392, 535 P.2d 213.

HODGES, JUSTICE. A petition for writ of certiorari was granted to review the opinion of the Colorado Court of Appeals in Bradley v. Mann, Colo.App., 525 P.2d 492 (1974). The issue is unique in Colorado case law, and its resolution is significant in the law relating to joint tenancy ownership of real property. Specifically, the issue is whether certain provisions in the divorce property settlement agreement in this case effectuated a termination of a joint tenancy ownership and converted it into a tenancy in common. Bradley v. Mann, supra, is a well reasoned opinion and correctly holds that the joint tenancy ownership was terminated. We therefore affirm.

The real property involved is a family residence which was in 1954 acquired in joint tenancy by Betty Rea Mann and Aaron C. Mann during their marriage. They were divorced in 1971. In connection therewith, an agreement, which was adopted as an order of the court in the divorce action, was entered into by the parties. Among other things, it provided that the family residence should be sold and that the proceeds be equally divided between them upon the occurrence of any one of the three following events:

(1) The remarriage of Mrs. Mann;

(2) When the youngest child of the couple attains the age of 21; or

(3) The mutual agreement of the parties to sell.

Betty Rea Mann continued to reside in the family residence with her children until her death in October of 1972. A short time after her death, Mr. Mann, the petitioner herein, informed his children that the family residence now belonged to him by virtue of the right of survivorship in the joint tenancy ownership with their mother. Thereupon, the administratrix of the estate of Mrs. Mann and the children, the respondents herein, filed an action in the district court of Morgan County to quiet title to the property on the theory that the divorce property settlement agreement had the legal effect of converting the joint tenancy into a tenancy in common with the result that Mrs. Mann's interest passed to the children upon her death. After trial in the district court, judgment was entered quieting title in the children as tenants in common in fee simple of an undivided one-half interest in the family residence. Mr. Mann appealed to the court of appeals which, as indicated previously, affirmed that judgment.

Petitioner argues that the provisions of the agreement demonstrate a clear intent that the property remain in joint tenancy until the occurrence of one of the three contingencies. Since none of these contingencies occurred prior to Mrs. Mann's death, petitioner reasons that the property passed to him by right of survivorship. Under the facts here, this contention has no merit.

The modern tendency is to not require that the act of the co-tenant be destructive of one of the essential four unities of time, title, possession or interest before a joint tenancy is terminated. Comment, 8 Hastings L.J. 294 (1957); Note, 25 Ala.L.Rev. 851 (1973). The joint tenancy may be terminated by mutual agreement, as here, where the parties treated their interests as belonging to them in common. McDonald v. Morley, 15 Cal.2d 409, 101 P.2d 690 (1940); 48 C.J.S. Joint Tenancy § 4. An agreement between the joint tenants to hold as tenants in common may be inferred from the manner in which the parties deal with the property. Thomas v. Johnson, 12 Ill.App.3d 302, 297 N.E.2d 712 (1973); Mamalis v. Bornovas, 112 N.H. 423, 297 A.2d 660 (1972); Wardlow v. Pozzi, 170 Cal.App.2d 208, 338 P.2d 564 (1959); O'Connor v. Dickerson, 188 So.2d 241 (Miss.1966); Robertson v. United States, 281 F.Supp. 955 (N.D.Ala.(1968)).

The district court and the court of appeals properly applied these tenets to the facts of this case. The intent of the parties as shown in the property settlement agreement is central to the issue presented. This agreement provided for the ultimate sale of the property and the division of the proceeds, which evinces the intent to no longer hold the property in joint tenancy from the effective date of the agreement. The entire tenor of those provisions of the agreement pertaining to this property is inconsistent with any purpose of the parties to continue the right of survivorship, which is the *sine qua non* of joint tenancy.

Nor does the provision of the agreement which stipulates that the property "shall remain in the joint names of the parties" dictate a different result. This wording is consistent with any form of continued concurrent ownership of the property. Konecny v. Von Gunten, 151

Colo. 376, 379 P.2d 158 (1963). In our view, this language in fact strongly supports the proposition that the parties intended to change the ownership from joint tenancy, and that since they were, by the provisions of the agreement, going to sell and divide the proceeds, the property would remain in their joint names, which is precisely the way tenants in common hold property.

When faced with a similar issue in Wardlow v. Pozzi, supra, the reviewing court commented:

". . . it is hard to see how two persons in domestic difficulties, and desirous of settling their domestic problems as well as those relating to property, would have intentionally entered into an agreement such as the one before us which would have left the bulk of his or her estate to the other. . . ."

This statement has salient applicability in this case.

The judgment of the Court of Appeals is affirmed.

PRINGLE, C.J., dissents.

NOTES

1. Suppose the parties in the principal case had not been divorced but were estranged and living separate and apart? Suppose there is a clear manifestation of intent that joint tenants no longer wish the survivorship feature to be in effect? Will proof of that fact be sufficient or must there be a deed of severance?

See also Sondin v. Bernstein, 126 Ill.App.3d 703, 81 Ill.Dec. 804, 467 N.E.2d 926 (1984) where the court stated the general rule that a divorce decree alone does not sever a joint tenancy of real estate. The court noted that a divorce terminates only those property rights not actually vested and, since the right of survivorship of a joint tenant does not arise out of the marriage relationship, the divorce itself could not destroy a vested right. However, in that case there had been a property settlement agreement that the proceeds of a sale should be split between the husband and wife and the court looked to that agreement to find an intent to sever. Therefore, even if the wife was the surviving joint tenant, the sale of the house meant that the husband's estate was entitled to enforce the valid settlement agreement to split the proceeds of sale.

2. In Walk v. Miller, 650 P.2d 1286 (Colo.App.1981), a husband and wife owned property in joint tenancy. The husband attempted to give an option to purchase to a lessee but the wife refused to join in the option. The husband contended that even if the option could not affect his wife's rights, it should be construed as a severance because the unity of title was destroyed when certain rights were carved out by the signing joint tenant. The court found there was no intent to sever the joint tenancy because the husband negotiated with the tenant for sale of the entire interest and only fell back on the severance issue when his wife refused to consent. The proposed agreement never ripened into a contract. Is there any way by which the husband could have affected

the wife's interest? Is there any way by which he could have worked a severance and given an option on his half?

DUNCAN v. VASSAUR

Supreme Court of Oklahoma, 1976.
550 P.2d 929.

DAVISON, JUSTICE. The real estate involved herein are lots 20, 21, 22, 23 and 24, block 16, in Checote Addition to the City of Okmulgee, Oklahoma. This property was owned by Edgar Vassaur, Jr., prior to his marriage to Betty E. Vassaur and was by him conveyed to Edgar Vassaur, Jr. and Betty E. Vassaur as joint tenants by Warranty Deed dated June 30, 1969, and remained in joint tenancy when on August 9, 1971, the wife, Betty Elaine Vassaur, shot and killed her husband.

On September 30, 1971, after she had been charged with first degree manslaughter for killing her husband, Betty E. Vassaur, as a widow, conveyed the involved property to her father, William M. Duncan, the appellee.

Edgar Vassaur, Sr., is the administrator of his deceased son's estate. As such, he claimed ownership of one-half the property, a lien on the balance in the amount of the proceeds of a credit life insurance policy on the victim's life, and another lien in the amount of a home improvement loan which had been repaid by the estate. These claims were asserted in an answer and cross petition filed by the administrator in the action to quiet the title to the realty brought by Duncan against the estate. Duncan interposed a demurrer to the answer and cross petition and moved for judgment on the pleadings. The trial judge sustained the demurrer, dismissed the cross petition and granted Duncan's motion for judgment on the pleadings.

At issue here is the interpretation and applicability of the Oklahoma "slayer statute," 84 O.S.1971 § 231, which provided in parts here pertinent as follows:

"No person who is convicted of murder or manslaughter in the first degree under the laws of this State . . . of having taken . . . the life of another, shall inherit from such person, or receive any interest in the estate of the decedent, or take by devise or legacy, or descent or distribution, from him, or her, any portion of his or her, estate . . . ."

This statute very clearly relates to the manner in which property devolves, whether by will or under the statute of descent and distribution, a subject which the Oklahoma Supreme Court has held to be exclusively within the province of the legislature. Holloway v. McCormick, et al., 41 Okl. 1, 136 P. 1111 (1913); Cox v. Cox, 95 Okl. 14, 217 P. 493 (1923).

The facts in the instant case present a question of first impression in this jurisdiction.

We have held that the fee simple title to property held in joint tenancy by a husband and wife vested in the husband upon the death of the wife. Mercer v. Mercer, Okl., 365 P.2d 554. However, it was unnecessary in such a case to consider or interpret Title 84 O.S.1971 § 231, supra.

We have held that a joint tenant can terminate the joint tenancy by any act which is inconsistent with its continued existence. Shackleton v. Sherrard, Okl., 385 P.2d 898. We are of the opinion that the murder here involved was inconsistent with the continued existence of the joint tenancy and that at the time the murder was committed, the joint tenancy was terminated and separated.

The question before us has been the subject for determination by a number of states with a number of different and contrary views, such as: (1) Some jurisdictions hold that the murderer is deprived of the entire interest except for a life interest in one-half. (2) The murderer is entitled to keep all the property. (3) The murderer holds upon a constructive trust to the extent of the computed value of one-half of the property as of the date of the victim's death for the period of the victim's expectancy. (4) The murderer is chargeable as constructive trustee of the entire property for the benefit of his victim's estate. (5) The murderer is chargeable as constructive trustee of one-half of the property for the benefit of the victim's estate. (6) By the murder, the joint tenancy has separated and terminated and one-half of the property should go to the heirs of the deceased (murdered person) and the other one-half to the murderer, or to his heirs, when deceased.

We believe it unnecessary to attempt to discuss all of the various theories expressed in opinions on the present subject.

We are of the opinion that the most equitable solution of the question is to hold that by the murder, the joint tenancy is separated and terminated and one-half of the property should go to the heirs of the deceased husband (murdered person) and the other one-half to the murderer, wife, or to her heirs, when deceased. By such holding, the joint tenancy is changed to a tenancy in common. We so hold.

In adopting the above theory, we are guided by 84 O.S.Supp.1975 § 231, effective June 12, 1975, and by several cases from other jurisdictions.

In the case of Bradley v. Fox, 7 Ill.2d 106, 129 N.E.2d 699, the following language was used:

"It is our conclusion that Fox by his felonious act, destroyed all rights of survivorship and lawfully retained only the title to his undivided one-half interest in the property in dispute as a tenant in common with the heir-at-law of Matilda Fox, deceased.

. . .

In so construing the rights of the parties to deny a murderer the fruits of his crime, this court is functioning, not as a 'theological institution,' as suggested in the Ohio case cited by defendants, but as a tribunal dedicated to the adjudication of law, for effecting justice is not a novel role for the courts, nor one transcending the sphere of other institutions."

In the case of Grose v. Holland, 357 Mo. 874, 211 S.W.2d 464, it was held that one-half of the property held in joint tenancy by husband and wife should go to the heirs of the deceased (murdered person) and that the other half of the property should go to the murderer.

In the last cited opinion, it was said:

"When William Edgar Holland murdered his wife he did acquire a practical, substantial benefit by that act. Prior to that murder, both he and his wife were each entitled to enjoy the whole, and each had a chance of survivorship and consequent acquisition of the whole as a tenant in severalty. The practical benefit that he acquired by the death of his wife does satisfy the conditions imposed by the common law relative to estate by entirety so that the survivor may take all. One must not only be a survivor in fact but also a survivor in contemplation of law. Indispensable is the prerequisite that decease must be in the ordinary course of events and subject only to the vicissitudes of life. The killer can assert no right to complete ownership as survivor. Equity will not allow him to profit by his own crime."

Also see Cowan v. Pleasant, Ky., 263 S.W.2d 494.

In defendant's (appellant's) answer to plaintiff's (appellee's) petition, in addition to praying for a one-half interest in the property, also asked for additional relief as follows:

1. For one-half of the rent collected by plaintiff from the rental of the property on which is located a business building.

2. That at the time of the death of the deceased, he was the owner of a credit life insurance policy on his life for the balance due on a real estate mortgage to the Okmulgee Savings and Loan Association on the involved property for which the estate was liable. That on the death of decedent, the mortgage of $2,402.25 was paid and mortgage released. Defendant asks that a lien be placed on plaintiff's interest in the property for one-half of this amount in favor of the estate of the deceased.

3. For one-half the amount the estate paid on an improvement loan made for improvement of the involved property and which the deceased was legally obligated to pay. Defendant asks that one-half of this amount paid by the estate be declared to be a lien on plaintiff's interest in the property.

Since the trial court originally decided the case on the pleadings, it will be necessary that evidence be taken on the above items and judgment entered thereon accordingly.

Lastly, it will be noted in plaintiff's petition that it was not claimed that plaintiff was an innocent purchaser for value, without notice of the fact that his grantor, Betty E. Vassaur, had been charged with murdering her husband at the time of the execution and delivery of the deed to him.

It is inconceivable that plaintiff did not know of the fact that his daughter had murdered her husband on August 9, 1971, when on the 30th day of September, 1971, he received the deed in question. However, the plaintiff should be given an opportunity to prove that he was a bona fide innocent purchaser for a valuable consideration and that he was without knowledge that his grantor, daughter, had murdered her husband at the time of the execution and delivery of the deed.

It follows that the judgment must be reversed and the cause remanded with directions to set aside the judgment of dismissal and in the absence of proper proof of plaintiff being an innocent purchaser for a valuable consideration and without knowledge that his daughter had murdered her husband at the time of the execution and delivery of the deed, then in that event, the trial court is directed to enter judgment in favor of the defendant, administrator as follows: That one-half of the property should go to the plaintiff and the other one-half to the administrator of the deceased to be distributed to the heirs of the deceased. Also the plaintiff should account to the administrator for one-half the rents collected by him less necessary money paid out for upkeep and taxes. Also that a lien should be fixed on plaintiff's one-half of the property for one-half of the insurance paid to release the mortgage and also one-half of the amount paid by the estate for release of the improvement mortgage. It is so ordered.

WILLIAMS, C.J., HODGES, V.C.J., and IRWIN, BERRY, LAVENDER, BARNES, and SIMMS, JJ., concur.

NOTES

1. For two interesting Illinois cases developing the same theme see Welsh v. James, 408 Ill. 18, 95 N.E.2d 872 (1951) and Bradley v. Fox, 7 Ill.2d 106, 129 N.E.2d 699 (1955). Note that the second case reverses a position taken just four years earlier. Why so rapid a reversal in judicial doctrine?

See also Vesey v. Vesey, 237 Minn. 295, 54 N.W.2d 385, 32 A.L.R.2d 1090 (1952). And Maine Savings Bank v. Bridges, 431 A.2d 633 (Me. 1981). In the former case, the court allowed the heirs of the allegedly murdered husband to take *all* of the proceeds of two joint accounts. In the latter case, the court held that the husband's intentional or knowing killing of his wife effected a severance of the joint tenancy and the husband became an owner of the property as a tenant in common with the wife's heirs other than himself. Which view seems the better to you?

3. The tax consequences of the various forms of concurrent ownership are beyond the scope of these materials. Now that you understand the basic running gears of concurrent estates you will be able to relate that knowledge to the taxation courses which will follow later in the curriculum. For a good preview of the problems in the tax area, see Severing Joint Property Interests, 16 Real Property, Probate, and Trust Journal 435 (1981). That Report of the Committee on Estate Planning and Drafting: Inter Vivos Transfers and Property Ownership concludes: "The advisability of severing joint property interests should be an important agenda item in the estate planner's review of the client's affairs. The substantive advantages and disadvantages of automatic transmission to the survivor upon the death of a joint tenant and the estate tax consequences thereof should be weighed carefully against the desirability of a severance prior to death with the possible gift tax

consequences of such action." For an interesting case involving tenancy by the entireties and federal tax policy see Union Planters National Bank v. United States, 361 F.2d 662 (6th Cir.1966).

SECTION 5. CONDOMINIUMS AND TIME-SHARE ARRANGEMENTS

It will have struck the observant student that there are forms of concurrent ownership or, at least, of related interests that have not so far been mentioned in these materials. Both the condominium and the time-share agreement have caught the fancy of the American public and the practice of nearly every real estate lawyer will be involved with the special problems these newer forms of real estate holding create. It is impossible, however, even in a "big picture" casebook, to cover all relevant doctrine without increasing the size of the materials beyond all reason. Moreover, the legal doctrines involved in both arrangements are based on the principles that are covered in this book—concurrent ownership, landlord and tenant, covenants running with the land, the real estate contract, etc. The specialized legal problems are reserved for advanced courses or seminars which will allow a more leisurely approach to these rapidly developing property tools.

There is a rich lode of legal material on condominiums and the inquiring student may wish to consult the leading treatise, Rohan and Reskin, Condominium Law and Practice (1965 plus annual supplements). For a more elementary treatment of the basic principles involved, see Cribbet and Johnson, Principles of the Law of Property 118–140 (3d ed. 1989). Of course, in a condominium the individual has title to his own unit but he has concurrent ownership of the common elements and many of the problems are similar to those covered in this chapter. It should be noted that condominiums are, in a sense, a new type of subdivision—vertical rather than horizontal—and they have the same potential for development that has occurred in subdivision growth generally since the end of World War II. They have the same vulnerability to exploitation that unregulated growth of traditional subdivisions has already disclosed but also the identical opportunity for decent housing if properly planned and controlled.

All of the states now have condominium statutes governing this form of concurrent ownership and condominium law represents a rich blend of common-law principles and legislative policy. In 1978, the National Conference of Commissioners on Uniform State Laws adopted a Uniform Condominium Act and, if past experience with uniform acts is a reliable guide, this Act should be influential in the years ahead. See Judy and Wittie, Uniform Condominium Act: Selected Key Issues, 13 Real Property, Probate and Trust Law Journal 437 (1978).

There has been a recent trend toward the conversion of rental apartments into condominiums. This development raises a whole cluster of legal and public policy issues since it withdraws units from the rental market at a time when there is very little construction of new rental housing. For a discussion of some of these issues, see Note, the Condominium Conversion Problem: Causes and Solution, 1980 Duke

L.J. 306. Obviously, the problem is most pronounced in the major urban areas and several cities have passed ordinances designed to slow down the rate of conversion. These ordinances, in turn, raise serious legal questions. For example, do they represent a taking of private property without just compensation, if the owner of the apartment must have the consent of the tenants prior to conversion? See Note, The Validity of Ordinances Limiting Condominium Conversion, 78 Mich.L.Rev. 124 (1979).

Time-share agreements are an even more recent development than condominiums. At a 1979 time-sharing conference in Houston, Texas, it was said that possibly one-quarter million American families would purchase time-shares in that year alone. The popularity of this arrangement continues unabated as Americans seek vacation-land residences across the country and abroad, with Mexico being a particularly attractive winter spa. As the time-share industry has developed into big business, several states have recognized the need for regulation and some have amended their condominium acts to include time shares. For a brief overview of the time-share arrangement, see Burek, Uniform Real Estate Time-Share Act, 14 Real Property, Probate, and Trust Journal 683 (1979).

In its simplest terms, a time-sharing agreement involves the division of ownership of a condominium into a number of fixed time periods, during which each purchaser has the exclusive right of occupation and use. In other words, it is a further split of ownership with the co-owners having a kind of fee simple (or term of years, depending on the agreement) for a specific week, month, etc., extending forward into time. So far, only a few states have enacted time-share laws and common-law principles must be used to work out agreements among the parties. For some insight into the present state of the art, see Comment, Time-Share Condominiums: Property's Fourth Dimension, 32 Maine L.Rev. 181 (1980) and Note, Legal Challenges to Time-Sharing Ownership, 45 Mo.L.Rev. 423 (1980).

We have included two cases involving condominium projects to illustrate the nature of this form of concurrent ownership and to demonstrate that courts may look rather closely at the unique characteristics of condominiums as they deal with the legal problems that inevitably arise between the developer and the consumer.

CENTEX HOMES CORP. v. BOAG

Superior Court of New Jersey, Chancery Division, 1974.
128 N.J.Super. 385, 320 A.2d 194.

GELMAN, J.S.C., Temporarily Assigned.

Plaintiff Centex Homes Corporation (Centex) is engaged in the development and construction of a luxury high-rise condominium project in the Boroughs of Cliffside Park and Fort Lee. The project when completed will consist of six 31-story buildings containing in excess of 3600 condominium apartment units, together with recreational buildings and facilities, parking garages and other common elements associated with this form of residential development. As sponsor of the project Centex offers the condominium apartment units for sale to the public and has filed an offering plan covering such sales with the appropriate regulatory agencies of the States of New Jersey and New York.

On September 13, 1972 defendants Mr. & Mrs. Eugene Boag executed a contract for the purchase of apartment unit No. 2019 in the building under construction and known as "Winston Towers 200." The contract purchase price was $73,700, and prior to signing the contract defendants had given Centex a deposit in the amount of $525. At or shortly after signing the contract defendants delivered to Centex a check in the amount of $6,870 which, together with the deposit, represented approximately 10% of the total purchase of the apartment unit. Shortly thereafter Boag was notified by his employer that he was to be transferred to the Chicago, Illinois, area. Under date of September 27, 1972 he advised Centex that he "would be unable to complete the purchase" agreement and stopped payment on the $6,870 check. Centex deposited the check for collection approximately two weeks after receiving notice from defendant, but the check was not honored by defendants' bank. On August 8, 1973 Centex instituted this action in Chancery Division for specific performance of the purchase agreement or, in the alternative, for liquidated damages in the amount of $6,870. The matter is presently before this court on the motion of Centex for summary judgment.

Both parties acknowledge, and our research has confirmed, that no court in this State or in the United States has determined in any reported decision whether the equitable remedy of specific performance will lie for the enforcement of a contract for the sale of a condominium apartment. The closest decision on point is Silverman v. Alcoa Plaza Associates, 37 A.D.2d 166, 323 N.Y.S.2d 39 (App.Div.1971), which involved a default by a contract-purchaser of shares of stock and a proprietary lease in a cooperative apartment building. The seller, who was also the sponsor of the project, retained the deposit and sold the stock and the lease to a third party for the same purchase price. The original purchaser thereafter brought suit to recover his deposit, and on appeal the court held that the sale of shares of stock in a cooperative apartment building, even though associated with a proprietary lease, was a sale of personalty and not of an interest in real estate. Hence, the seller was not entitled to retain the contract deposit as liquidated damages.[1]

As distinguished from a cooperative plan of ownership such as involved in *Silverman,* under a condominium housing scheme each condominium apartment unit constitutes a separate parcel of real property which may be dealt with in the same manner as any real estate. Upon closing of title the apartment unit owner receives a recordable deed which confers upon him the same rights and subjects him to the same obligations as in the case of traditional forms of real estate ownership, the only difference being that the condominium

1. Under New York law, if the contract was deemed to be for the sale of realty, the seller could retain the deposit in lieu of damages. [Footnotes by the Court.]

owner receives in addition an undivided interest in the common elements associated with the building and assigned to each unit. See the Condominium Act, N.J.S.A. 46:8B–1 et seq.; 15 Am.Jur.2d, Condominiums and Cooperative Apartments, at 977 et seq.; Note, 77 Harv.L.Rev. 777 (1964).

Centex urges that since the subject matter of the contract is the transfer of a fee interest in real estate, the remedy of specific performance is available to enforce the agreement under principles of equity which are well-settled in this state. . . .

The principle underlying the specific performance remedy is equity's jurisdiction to grant relief where the damage remedy at law is inadequate. The text writers generally agree that at the time this branch of equity jurisdiction was evolving in England, the presumed uniqueness of land as well as its importance to the social order of that era led to the conclusion that damages at law could never be adequate to compensate for the breach of a contract to transfer an interest in land. Hence specific performance became a fixed remedy in this class of transactions. See 11 Williston on Contracts (3d ed. 1968) § 1418A; 5A Corbin on Contracts § 1143 (1964). The judicial attitude has remained substantially unchanged . . . .

While the inadequacy of the damage remedy suffices to explain the origin of the vendee's right to obtain specific performance in equity, it does not provide a *rationale* for the availability of the remedy at the instance of the vendor of real estate. Except upon a showing of unusual circumstances or a change in the vendor's position, such as where the vendee has entered into possession, the vendor's damages are usually measurable, his remedy at law is adequate and there is no jurisdictional basis for equitable relief. But see Restatement, Contracts § 360, comment c.[2] The early English precedents suggest that the availability of the remedy in a suit by a vendor was an outgrowth of the equitable concept of mutuality, i.e., that equity would not specifically enforce an agreement unless the remedy was available to both parties. . . .

So far as can be determined from our decisional law, the mutuality of remedy concept has been the prop which has supported equitable jurisdiction to grant specific performance in actions by vendors of real estate.[3] . . . The first reported discussion of the question occurs in

2. The Restatement's reasoning, as expressed in § 360, comment c amounts to the inconsistent propositions that (1) because the vendor may not have sustained any damage which is actionable at law, specific performance should be granted, and (2) he would otherwise sustain damage equal to the loss of interest on the proceeds of the sale. Yet loss of interest is readily measurable and can be recovered in an action at law, and to the extent that the vendor has sustained no economic injury, there is no compelling reason for equity to grant to him the otherwise extraordinary remedy of specific performance. At the end of the comment, the author suggests that the vendor is entitled to specific performance because that remedy should be mutual, a concept which is substantially rejected as a decisional basis in §§ 372 and 373 of the Restatement.

3. Another theory has been suggested as a basis for equity's jurisdiction to grant specific performance to a vendor: the vendee's breach constitutes an "equitable conversion" of the purchase price of which the vendee is deemed to be a trustee. See Comment, 10 Villanova L.Rev. 557, 569 (1965); 1 Pomeroy, Equity Jurisprudence, (5th ed. 1941), § 221(b). . . .

Hopper v. Hopper, 16 N.J.Eq. 147 (Ch.1863), which was an action by a vendor to compel specific performance of a contract for the sale of land. In answer to the contention that equity lacked jurisdiction because the vendor had an adequate legal remedy, Chancellor Green said (at p. 148):

> "It constitutes no objection to the relief prayed for, that the application is made by the vendor to enforce the payment of the purchase money, and not by the vendee to compel a delivery of the title. The vendor has not a complete remedy at law. Pecuniary damages for the breach of the contract is not what the complainant asks, or is entitled to receive at the hands of a court of equity. He asks to receive the price stipulated to be paid in lieu of the land. The doctrine is well established that the remedy is mutual, and that the vendor may maintain his bill in all cases where the purchaser could sue for a specific performance of the agreement."

No other *rationale* has been offered by our decisions subsequent to *Hopper,* and specific performance has been routinely granted to vendors without further discussion of the underlying jurisdictional issue.[4] . . .

Our present Supreme Court has squarely held, however, that mutuality of remedy is not an appropriate basis for granting or denying specific performance. Fleischer v. James Drug Store, 1 N.J. 138, 62 A.2d 383 (1948). . . . The test is whether the obligations of the contract are mutual and not whether each is entitled to precisely the same remedy in the event of a breach. In *Fleischer* plaintiff sought specific performance against a cooperative buying and selling association although his membership contract was terminable by him on 60 days' notice. Justice Heher said:

> And the requisite mutuality is not wanting. The contention *contra* rests upon the premise that, although the corporation "can terminate the contract only in certain restricted and unusual circumstances, any 'member' may withdraw at any time by merely giving notice."
>
> Clearly, there is mutuality of obligation, for until his withdrawal complainant is under a continuing obligation of performance in the event of performance by the corporation. It is not essential that the remedy of specific performance be mutual. . . . The modern view is that the rule of mutuality of remedy is satisfied if the decree of specific performance operates effectively against both parties and gives to each the benefit of a mutual obligation. . . .
>
> The fact that the remedy of specific enforcement is available to one party to a contract is not in itself a sufficient reason for making the remedy available to the other; but it may be decisive when the adequacy of damages is difficult to determine and there is no other reason for refusing specific enforcement. It is not neces-

4. The doctrine of mutuality is discussed in later specific performance cases where the vendor either lacked title to the property at the time of the contract or there was an infirimity in the vendor's title. E.g., Ten Eyck v. Manning, 52 N.J. Eq. 47, 27 A. 900 (Ch.1893).

> sary, to serve the ends of equal justice, that the parties shall have identical remedies in case of breach. [at 149, 62 A.2d at 388]

The disappearance of the mutuality of remedy doctrine from our law dictates the conclusion that specific performance relief should no longer be automatically available to a vendor of real estate, but should be confined to those special instances where a vendor will otherwise suffer an economic injury for which his damage remedy at law will not be adequate, or where other equitable considerations require that the relief be granted. . . . As Chancellor Vroom noted in King v. Morford, 1 N.J.Eq. 274, 281–282 (Ch.Div.1831), whether a contract should be specifically enforced is always a matter resting in the sound discretion of the court and

> . . . considerable caution should be used in decreeing the specific performance of agreements, and . . . the court is bound to see that it really does the complete justice which it aims at, and which is the ground of its jurisdiction.

Here the subject matter of the real estate transaction—a condominium apartment unit—has no unique quality but is one of hundreds of virtually identical units being offered by a developer for sale to the public. The units are sold by means of sample, in this case model apartments, in much the same manner as items of personal property are sold in the market place. The sales prices for the units are fixed in accordance with a schedule filed by Centex as part of its offering plan, and the only variance as between apartments having the same floor plan (of which six plans are available) is the floor level or the building location within the project. In actuality, the condominium apartment units, regardless of their realty label, share the same characteristics as personal property.

From the foregoing one must conclude that the damages sustained by a condominium sponsor resulting from the breach of the sales agreement are readily measurable and the damage remedy at law is wholly adequate. No compelling reasons have been shown by Centex for the granting of specific performance relief and its complaint is therefore dismissed as to the first count.

Centex also seeks money damages pursuant to a liquidated damage clause in its contract with the defendants. It is sufficient to note only that under the language of that clause (which was authored by Centex) liquidated damages are limited to such moneys as were paid by defendant at the time the default occurred. Since the default here consisted of the defendant's stopping payment of his check for the balance of the down-payment, Centex's liquidated damages are limited to the retention of the "moneys paid" prior to that date, or the initial $525 deposit. Accordingly, the second count of the complaint for damage relief will also be dismissed.

NOTES

1. The court states: "In actuality, the condominium apartments units, regardless of their realty label, share the same characteristics as personal property." This statement should not be taken out of context.

It relates to the availability of the remedy of specific performance to the developer and in most other situations condominiums are governed by real property principles. Incidentally, could the Boags have successfully sought specific performance against Centex, if the developer had been in breach? Could the vendor-owner of an individual unit successfully seek specific performance against a purchaser of that unit?

In answer to the two questions in the preceding paragraph, consider Giannini v. First Nat. Bank of Des Plaines, 136 Ill.App.3d 971, 91 Ill. Dec. 438, 483 N.E.2d 924 (1 Dist.1985) where the court granted specific performance to the purchaser of a specific condominium unit over the objection of the vendor that the same condominium units were available in other buildings owned by the vendor. The vendor argued that a condominium unit is not so unique as to require the equitable remedy of specific performance and relied heavily on Centex Homes Corp. v. Boag. The Illinois court distinguished the Centex case and added: "In any event it is the decision of a trial court of another jurisdiction and as such is not binding precedent on this court." The Illinois court held that a condominium is real property for purposes of the action of specific performance and stated: "Illinois courts have long held that where the parties have fairly and understandingly entered into a valid contract for the sale of real property, specific performance of the contract is a matter of right and equity will enforce it, absent circumstances of oppression and fraud."

2. Most courts grant specific performance to either the vendor or the purchaser of real property without much discussion of the rationale for extending this important equitable remedy to the vendor. Typically, the purchaser can even get specific performance with abatement of the price against a vendor who cannot fully perform due to an outstanding encumbrance, a deficiency in the quantity of the land, etc. See, for example, Rosenthal v. Sandusky, 35 Colo.App. 220, 533 P.2d 523 (1975) and Note, Specific Performance with Abatement, 24 Okl.L.Rev. 495 (1971). However, there does appear to be a trend against automatically giving the vendor specific performance of real estate contracts. The Uniform Land Transactions Act, sect. 2–506(b) gives the vendor the right to the purchase price "only if the seller is unable after a reasonable effort to resell it at a reasonable price or the circumstances reasonably indicate the effort will be unavailing." It remains to be seen how influential this uniform act will be in the face of equitable doctrine that is centuries old.

The principal case should be restudied in connection with the materials on Remedies for Breach of Contract appearing at pages 1081 to 1090 infra.

DUTCHER v. OWENS

Supreme Court of Texas, 1983.
647 S.W.2d 948.

RAY, JUSTICE.

This is a case of first impression concerning the allocation of liability among condominium co-owners for tort claims arising out of the ownership, use and maintenance of "common elements." The defendant was found to be vicariously liable for the homeowners' association's negligence. The trial court ordered that the plaintiffs recover from the defendant an amount based upon the defendant's proportionate ownership in the condominium project. The court of appeals reversed in part the judgment of the trial court, holding "that each unit owner, as a tenant in common with all other unit owners in the common elements, is jointly and severally liable for damage claims arising in the common elements." 635 S.W.2d 208, 211. We reverse the judgment of the court of appeals and affirm the trial court's judgment.

J.A. Dutcher, a resident of San Diego, California, owned a condominium apartment in the Eastridge Terrace Condominiums, located in Dallas County, which he leased to Ted and Christine Owens. Ownership of the apartment includes a 1.572% *pro rata* undivided ownership in the common elements of the project. The Owenses suffered substantial property loss in a fire which began in an external light fixture in a common area.

The Owenses filed suit in Tarrant County against Dutcher, the Eastridge Terrace Condominium Association, Joe Hill Electric Company, IHS–8 Ltd. (the developer) and a class of co-owners of condominiums in Eastridge Terrace represented by the officers of the homeowners' association. All defendants with the exception of Dutcher obtained a change of venue to Dallas County. The case was tried before a jury, which found the following:

(1) The fire was proximately caused by the lack of an insulating box behind the light fixture in the exterior wall air space;

(2) The homeowners' association knew of this defect;

(3) The homeowners' association alone was negligent in failing to install an insulating box with knowledge of the defect; and

(4) The negligence of homeowners' association resulted in damage to the Owens' property in the amount of $69,150.00.

The trial court rendered judgment against Dutcher on the jury's verdict in the amount of $1,087.04. The award represents the amount of damages multiplied by Dutcher's 1.572% *pro rata* undivided ownership in the common elements of the Eastridge Terrace Condominium project.

By an agreed statement of facts filed with the court of appeals, the parties stipulated that the sole issue for determination on appeal was whether a condominium co-owner is jointly and severally liable or is liable only for a *pro rata* portion of the damages. Tex.R.Civ.P. 377(d).

In enacting the Texas Condominium Act (the Act), Tex.Rev.Civ. Stat.Ann. art. 1301a, the Texas Legislature intended to create "a new method of property ownership." [1] 1963 Tex.Gen.Laws, Ch. 191, § 26 at 512. A condominium is an estate in real property consisting of an undivided interest in a portion of a parcel of real property together with a separate fee simple interest in another portion of the same parcel. In essence, condominium ownership is the merger of two estates in land into one: the fee simple ownership of an apartment or unit in a condominium project and a tenancy in common with other co-owners in the common elements. Scott v. Williams, 607 S.W.2d 267, 270 (Tex.Civ.App.—Texarkana 1980, writ ref'd n.r.e.); Tex.Rev.Civ.Stat. Ann. art. 1301a; see also White v. Cox, 17 Cal.App.3d 824, 95 Cal.Rptr. 259, 45 A.L.R.3d 1161 (1971); Comment, "The Condominium and the Corporation—A Proposal for Texas," 11 Hous.L.Rev. 454 (1974).

"General common elements" consist of, *inter alia,* the land upon which the building stands, the "foundations, bearing walls and columns, roofs, halls, lobbies, stairways, and entrances and exits or communication ways; . . . [a]ll other elements of the building desirable or rationally of common use or necessary to the existence, upkeep and safety of the condominium regime, and any other elements described in the declaration . . . ." Tex.Rev.Civ.Stat.Ann. art. 1301a, § 2(*l*), subsections (1), (2) & (7). An individual apartment cannot be conveyed separately from the undivided interest in the common elements and *vice versa.* Id. § 9.

A condominium regime must be established according to the Act. The declaration must be filed with the county clerk, who must record the instrument in the Condominium Records. Once the declarant has complied with the provisions of the Act, each apartment in the project is treated as an interest in real property. Id. §§ 3, 4, & 7. Administration of the regime is established by the Act. Id. §§ 13, 14 & 15.

The condominium association or council is a legislatively created unincorporated association of co-owners having as their common purpose a convenient method of ownership of real property in a statutorily created method of ownership which combines both the concepts of separateness of tenure and commonality of ownership. The California Supreme Court has concluded that "the concept of separateness in the condominium project carries over to any management body or association formed to handle the common affairs of the project, and that both the condominium project and the condominium association must be considered separate legal entities from its unit owners and association members." White v. Cox, 95 Cal.Rptr. at 262.

Given the uniqueness of the type of ownership involved in condominiums, the onus of liability for injuries arising from the management of condominium projects should reflect the degree of control exercised by the defendants. We agree with the California court's conclusion that to rule that a condominium co-owner had any effective control

1. Condominium ownership is a tenure unknown at common law. Provisions for a form of condominium ownership can be found in the Roman civil law and the Napoleonic Code. 4B Powell on Real Property (Part III) ¶¶ 599, 633.1 et seq. (1976).

over the operation of the common areas would be to sacrifice "reality to theoretical formalism," for in fact a co-owner has no more control over operations than he would have as a stockholder in a corporation which owned and operated the project. White v. Cox, 95 Cal.Rptr. at 263. This does not limit the plaintiff's right of action. The efficiency found in a suit directed at the homeowners' association and its board of directors representing the various individual homeowners, as well as any co-owner causally or directly responsible for the injuries sustained, benefits both sides of the docket as well as the judicial system as a whole.

Such a result is not inconsistent with the legislative intent. While the Act creates a new form of real property ownership, it does not address the issue of the allocation of tort liability among co-owners. Nevertheless, we are guided in our decision by the other provisions in the Act which appear *in pari materia,* and which proportionately allocate various financial responsibilities. For example, the Act provides for *pro rata* contributions by co-owners toward expenses of administration and maintenance, insurance, taxes and assessments. *Pro rata* provisions also exist for the application of insurance proceeds. Tex. Rev.Civ.Stat.Ann. art. 1301a, §§ 15, 18, 19, & 20.

Respondents have cited us to two bills submitted in the legislature in 1981.[2] The bills, which did not pass, included provisions for reapportionment of liability on a *pro rata* basis. Inasmuch as each bill involved a complete revision of the Act, we cannot draw inferences of the legislature's intent from the failure of the bills to pass. Any such inference would involve little more than conjecture. The legislative history of the Act is so scant that the most that can be said is that the Act is silent as to the matter, and hence the legislative intent is unknown. Cf. Marmon v. Mustang Aviation, Inc., 430 S.W.2d 182, 186 (Tex.1968).

The theories of vicarious and joint and several liability are judicially created vehicles for enforcing remedies for wrongs committed. Justified on public policy grounds, they represent a deliberate allocation of risk. See Newspapers, Inc. v. Love, 380 S.W.2d 582, 588–89 (Tex.1964); Landers v. East Texas Salt Water Disposal Co., 151 Tex. 251, 248 S.W.2d 731, 733 (1952); W. Prosser, Law of Torts, § 69 at 459 (4th ed. 1971).

Texas follows the rule that statutes in derogation of the common law are not to be strictly construed. Tex.Rev.Civ.Stat.Ann. art. 10, § 8. Nevertheless, it is recognized that if a statute creates a liability unknown to the common law, or deprives a person of a common law right, the statute will be strictly construed in the sense that it will not be extended beyond its plain meaning or applied to cases not clearly within its purview. Satterfield v. Satterfield, 448 S.W.2d 456, 459 (Tex. 1969); see also 3 C. Sands, Sutherland Statutory Construction § 61.02 (4th ed. 1973). Since the Act is silent as to tort liability, we are dealing with rights and liabilities which are not creatures of statute but with the common law, which is our special domain. Hence, the rule we have

2. House Bills 439 and 2233.

reached is not a usurpation of the legislative prerogative. To the contrary, it is one reached in the public interest.

We hold, therefore, that because of the limited control afforded a unit owner by the statutory condominium regime, the creation of the regime effects a reallocation of tort liability. The liability of a condominium co-owner is limited to his *pro rata* interest in the regime as a whole, where such liability arises from those areas held in tenancy-in-common. The judgment of the court of appeals is reversed and the judgment of the trial court is affirmed.

Chapter 16

NON-FREEHOLD ESTATES: LANDLORD AND TENANT

The tendency of judges to adhere to concepts and doctrines familiar to past ages is hardly anywhere more evident than it is in the law relating to the relationships, widely varying in their factual settings, connoted by such terms as "leasehold," "landlord," and "tenant." As Justice Holmes said in Gardiner v. Wm. S. Butler & Co., 245 U.S. 603, 38 S.Ct. 214, 62 L.Ed. 505 (1918), "But the law as to leases is not a matter of logic in vacuo; it is a matter of history that has not forgotten Lord Coke." The relevant segment of legal history presents many curiosities. Though apparently it was not so regarded in the early stages of its development, the lessee's interest has long been conceived as an "estate in land," and the concept that a lease is a conveyance, creating an estate, underlies much of the doctrine with which we are here concerned. In employing the concept, however, one must be constantly wary of confusing it with the historically different concept of "freehold estates." The distinctions made between them are perhaps most vividly illustrated in the fact that for ages the lessee's interest has been categorized as personalty—a "chattel real"—not as realty, and is still treated accordingly for certain purposes. Assimilation of leasehold and freehold interests through statutes and judicial decisions has blurred but has by no means obliterated the ancient diversities.

The law relating to leases presents another aspect, centering upon the fact that virtually every lease instrument includes numerous promises (commonly called "covenants" even though the instrument is not sealed) between lessor and lessee. In a measure this reflects the parties' felt need for complex arrangements concerning various matters—e.g., rent and modes of securing its payment; the lessee's right to renew the lease or purchase the lessor's estate; restrictions of the lessee's power to use the premises, transfer the leasehold, or execute subleases; protection of the lessee against competition by the lessor or other lessees; and allocation of such burdens as maintenance, taxes, and insurance. It also reflects their desire to avoid the operation of certain more or less anachronistic rules of law which would regulate their relationship in the absence of manifested agreement. Covenants are unquestionably useful as determinants of the parties' rights and liabilities, but it is hardly possible, even by the most careful negotiation and draftsmanship, to eliminate all possibility of dispute; unforeseen problem situations constantly appear and even in situations which have been more or less clearly anticipated, litigation may be necessary to resolve conflicts involving the interpretation of covenants.

Since a formal lease commonly has the dual character of conveyance and contract, it becomes important to consider the extent to which, in dealing with litigation between landlord and tenant, courts will employ rules and doctrines which govern contractual relationships in other contexts. Several of the cases which follow bear in various ways upon this inquiry.

See generally Restatement (Second) of Property, Landlord and Tenant (1977) and R. Schoshinski, American Law of Landlord and Tenant (1980).

SECTION 1. NATURE AND CREATION OF LEASEHOLD ESTATES

COOK v. UNIVERSITY PLAZA

Appellate Court of Illinois, Second District, 1981.
100 Ill.App.3d 752, 56 Ill.Dec. 325, 427 N.E.2d 405.

SEIDENFELD, PRESIDING JUSTICE:

In this appeal, we consider the applicability of the statute providing payment of interest on security deposits to a tenant (Ill.Rev.Stat. 1979, ch. 74, pars. 91–93), to particular contracts. The parties to the agreements are the plaintiffs, the residents of University Plaza as a class, who entered into residence hall contracts with University Plaza and its general partners, defendants, a privately owned university dormitory which serves students of Northern Illinois University in DeKalb. Plaintiffs appeal from the dismissal of their class action suit. The defendants' motion was sustained on the basis that the statute is inapplicable because no tenant-landlord relationship has been created by the contracts and thus that no cause of action was stated.

The individual contracts with the students are entitled "Residence Hall Contract Agreement". The introductory paragraph states that the agreement governs the use of the University Plaza facilities and services by the resident. In Clause I the dormitory agrees to furnish accommodations and services, including basic furniture, carpeting and draperies, local telephone service, cleaning service, social and recreational facilities, and parking facilities. Clause III requires a $50 security deposit and spells out the rights that the resident has in that deposit. University Plaza reserves the right to cancel the contract for default, although the resident has no right to cancel once it has accepted the agreement. If the resident has not vacated the premises at the end of seven days following a written notice of intent to cancel the contract, University Plaza may take possession of the premises and remove the resident. University Plaza provides meal service for the residents. It also reserves the right to make assignments of space, to authorize or deny room and roommate changes and to require the resident to move from one room to another. There is also a provision that the dormitory is closed and meals are not served during Thanksgiving and spring recess as well as during semester breaks; and that no one is allowed to remain in the residence hall during these stated periods or beyond the established academic year closing date.

Clause IV states:

"Notwithstanding anything to the contrary which may herein be contained, expressly, impliedly or otherwise, it is specifically understood and agreed by and between the parties hereto, that it is not the intention of the parties hereto to create a landlord-tenant relationship, and that the intention hereof is strictly contractual in nature; for bed and board, ancillary service, the use of certain recreational facilities, and participation in student social programs promoted at University Plaza, all of which are for the most part in concert with others. The resident may not assign any rights hereunder and may not sublet the room assigned."

Whether a contract is a lease or a license is not to be determined from the language that the parties choose to call it but from the legal effect of its provisions. Illinois Cent. R. Co. v. Michigan Cent. R. Co., 18 Ill.App.2d 462, 473–74, 152 N.E.2d 627 (1958). See, also, Holladay v. Chicago Arc Light & Power Co., 55 Ill.App. 463, 466 (1894).

. . .

In In re Application of Rosewell, 69 Ill.App.3d 996, 26 Ill.Dec. 36, 387 N.E.2d 866 (1979), the court considered whether agreements between the City of Chicago and certain individuals under which the individuals were permitted to operate city owned parking garages or lots, constituted leases or licenses. The court held that the essence of a lease was transfer of possession (at 1000–1001, 26 Ill.Dec. 36, 387 N.E.2d 866) while a license is "an agreement which merely entitles one party to use property subject to the management and control of the other party." (1001, 26 Ill.Dec. 36, 387 N.E.2d 866). Thus, it concluded that since the City retained the right to control how the parking lots were operated the agreement constituted a license, even though the City surrendered exclusive possession of the lots to the parking lot operators. In People v. Chicago Metro Car Rentals, Inc., 72 Ill.App.3d 626, 28 Ill.Dec. 843, 391 N.E.2d 42 (1979), the issue was whether an agreement between the City of Chicago and a car rental agency, which permitted the agency to operate a rent-a-car business at O'Hare airport, constituted a lease or a license. In finding that the agreement constituted a lease the court noted that the document was written using traditional terms; that it contained all of the essential requirements of a lease, including a definite agreement as to the extent and bounds of the leased property; and that the agreement granted Metro exclusive possession of a designated service area and designated counter space amounting to a particular number of square feet, legally described and diagramed in the agreement. 72 Ill.App.3d at 629, 28 Ill.Dec. 843, 391 N.E.2d 42.

While the agreement before us contains certain aspects normally associated with leases, a definite and agreed term and a definite and agreed price of rental and manner of payment, (see, *Metro* at 629, 28 Ill. Dec. 843, 391 N.E.2d 42), we conclude that it lacks the essential requirement of being a definite agreement as to the extent and bounds of the property to be used. The fact that the students may be moved during the term from room to room at the will of the contracting party is the principal feature of the agreement which we find persuasive in our determination that the parties did not intend to enter into a landlord and tenant relationship since the agreement failed to pass a possessory interest in specific property.

The question remains as to whether the legislature intended the statute on security deposits to apply to dormitories which provide bed and board to students. Paragraph 93 of the statute excludes only public housing units from the application of the act. (Ill.Rev.Stat.1979, ch. 74, par. 93). However, parties are only covered by the statute if the agreement between the residents and the dormitory can be considered a lease. We find nothing in either the legislative history of the act or in its terms which would support the view that the legislature intended to include security deposits paid by students in dormitories in which they reside without reference to whether their agreement is a license or a lease.

We would note that there appears to be no public policy which would prevent the legislature from enacting a statute which would require that interest be paid on deposits made by persons in the class of the plaintiffs or others similarly situated. However, we conclude that the legislature has not done so and that the remedy in these circumstances is within the legislative domain. . . .

Affirmed.

NOTES

1. Compare Restatement (Second) of Property, Landlord and Tenant (1977) § 1.1, for which the following illustration is given:

"L leases a described portion of a building to T for five years. The lease contains a provision that gives L the right to relocate T in the building at any time during the five-year period by giving him thirty days' notice, the relocation space to contain approximately the same number of square feet. This arrangement is one with respect to a space that is intended to have a fixed location for the duration of the lease. The fact that the fixed location may be varied within a predetermined area from time to time during the lease does not prevent the arrangement from creating a landlord-tenant relationship."

2. There are requirements for the creation of a lease in addition to the requirement that the lessor transfer the right to possession of a definite space for the duration of the lease. In some instances a writing is necessary.

The original Statute of Frauds, enacted by Parliament in 1677, during the reign of Charles II, declared, in effect, that a parol lease for three years or less "from the making thereof" should be valid, but a lease for more than three years, to be valid as such, must be evidenced by a written instrument—otherwise it should have the effect of a tenancy at will; i.e., one terminable by either party at any time without prior notice. Another section of the statute declared that no action could be maintained upon a parol contract which was not performable within one year "from the making thereof." Similar statutes are in force throughout the United States. Typically they shorten the period for permissible parol leases to one year (a few retain the three-year period and a few require a writing for a lease of any fixed duration) and do not specify, as the English statute did, that the period shall be measured "from the making thereof," but they retain the provision concerning contracts not performable within a year from their formation.

In a state having a statute with the typical provisions mentioned above, L and T orally agree upon a lease for one year, the term to commence sixty days after the date of their agreement. What arguments could be urged for and against the validity of the lease? Bell v. Vaughn, 46 Ariz. 515, 53 P.2d 61, 111 A.L.R. 1460 (1935); notes, 20 Minn.L.Rev. 833 (1935); 19 U. of Chi.L.Rev. 529 (1950); 111 A.L.R. 1465.

Delivery may also be a prerequisite to creating a leasehold estate. Consider the following statement by the court in 219 Broadway Corp. v. Alexander's, Inc., 46 N.Y.2d 506, 414 N.Y.S.2d 889, 387 N.E.2d 1205 (1979):

> The underlying justification for viewing delivery as fundamental to the conveyance of an interest in land is not grounded in the blind application of what some may consider archaic principles of property law. On the contrary, delivery serves a very practical end. It is a common practice in the contemporary business world for parties to draft and sign instruments of conveyance prior to the time at which they intend their contemplated transaction to become irrevocable. By requiring delivery, the law facilitates the true expectations of the parties by ensuring that the interest in the property is not conveyed until that moment when the parties so intend. . . .
>
> The due signature of the lease instrument is but one step in the process of conveying an interest in land. Delivery requires something more. There must be evidence of an unequivocal intent that the interest intended to be conveyed is, in fact, being conveyed. The mere signing of the instrument by parties not in the presence of each other, without more, does not evince such intent. . . .

3. Although there is a contractual relationship between the lessor and lessee as soon as they sign the lease, the leasehold estate may not exist until the tenant actually takes possession of the premises. In Arthur Treacher's Fish & Chips of Fairfax, Inc. v. Chillum Terrace Ltd. Partnership, 272 Md. 720, 327 A.2d 282 (1974) a tenant who repudiated a lease prior to entry successfully argued that it was liable only for breach of contract and not for rent. The court reasoned as follows:

> Under the common law, until the lessee enters, he has no estate [in land], but only an *interesse termini,* a right to enter. *Interesse termini* applies in two situations, where the term stated in the lease has commenced but the lessee has not taken possession, and where there is a lease to take effect in the future. American Law of Property, supra, § 3.22. Thus, one who is a lessee under a

validly executed lease to commence in the future immediately becomes the owner of a future interest, a right of entry, which will ripen into a possessory estate when the term commences and when the lessee enters. The lessee acquires no possessory estate until the term commences and he enters upon the land.

Consequently, when a lessee breaches a lease agreement prior to entering into possession, he cannot be held liable for rent, because the leasehold estate has never come into existence as a present possessory interest, and rent is an incident of the leasehold estate. In Simon v. Kirkpatrick, supra, where the lessee refused to take possession when it was tendered, the court held that the tenant could not be held liable for rent, since the landlord-tenant relationship had never commenced and the estate had not come into existence. The court, however, apparently relying upon the contract facet of the lease, held the lessee liable for breach of contract and awarded appropriate damages.

WOMACK v. HYCHE

Supreme Court of Alabama, 1987.
503 So.2d 832.

JONES, JUSTICE.

This is an appeal from a judgment for the defendant in a dispute between lessor (the plaintiff) and lessee (the defendant). We reverse and remand.

The plaintiff, Billye Womack, is the owner of real property in Shelby County fronting on Waxahatchee Creek. On that property are a store/cafe, five piers, a gas pumping facility, a concrete boat launch, and a parking lot. This property, its improvements, and 11 aluminum fishing boats (all the property of Womack) are used as a commercial fishing camp known as Camp Waxahatchee.

In January of 1979, Womack and the defendant, Lillian Hyche, executed a written lease memorandum as follows:

> "I BILLYE WOMACK, LEASE TO LILLIAN HYCHE THE PROPERTY KNOWN AS 'CAMP WAXAHATCHEE', FOR THE SUM OF ($300.00) THREE HUNDRED DOLLARS PER YEAR, WITH THE OPTION TO RENEW THE LEASE AS LONG AS THE CAMP IS RUN AS A BUSINESS FOR A PROFIT. I WILL ALSO DEFEND ANY PREVIOUS CLAIMS AGAINST THIS PROPERTY."

This written agreement, "with further oral understandings," allowed Hyche to lease Camp Waxahatchee from Womack in return for the $300.00 per year rental fee plus one-half of the funds received from boat rentals and launch fees and for the further concession of free use of the boat launch and piers for Womack and her "tenants."

By 1984 friction between Womack and Hyche had become a serious dispute as to the essentials of the lease and as to each party's performance under the lease. Womack instituted a declaratory judgment action in the Shelby County Circuit Court.

In her complaint, Womack alleged that the written lease agreement was void (1) for vagueness and uncertainty; (2) for unfairness to Womack because Hyche had violated the terms of the parties' oral "understandings" and the camp was no longer run as a business for profit; (3) for lack of mutuality; (4) for violation of the rule against perpetuities; (5) for improper execution; and (6) for uncertainty of the lease term. . . .

Womack requested that the trial court hold either that the lease had been breached by Hyche or that the lease was void and that Hyche was occupying the camp as a tenant at will and "subject to immediate removal . . . by process of law."

After a non-jury trial, the court entered judgment in favor of the defendant, Mrs. Hyche. The trial court's order read, in part:

. . .

> "It is the finding of this Court that the parties entered into a valid lease agreement on January 10, 1979, for a term of 1 year for the sum of $300.00 per year, with an option to renew each year as long as the camp is run as a business for a profit but not to be valid for a term in excess of 20 years in accordance with the provisions of Title 35–4–6, Code of Alabama, 1975.
>
> "It is therefore ORDERED, ADJUDGED, AND DECREED by the Court that the lease agreement between the parties, dated January 10, 1979, is valid and is binding on the parties for a term of year to year for the sum of $300.00 per year, with the option to renew the lease, as long as the camp is run as a business for profit for no longer term than 20 years from January 10, 1979."

The trial court denied Womack's motion for amendment or alteration of judgment, or for a new trial, and Womack filed this appeal.

Womack's argument on appeal centers on the terms of the lease itself. The language, "with the option to renew the lease as long as the camp is run as a business for profit," created a lease with an uncertain ending; therefore, the lease is void under the holding of *Industrial Machinery, Inc. v. Creative Displays, Inc.,* 344 So.2d 743 (Ala.1977):

> "A lease for a term of years must have a term certain. There must be a certain beginning and a certain ending. [Cites omitted.] The lease [in dispute] began on January 1, 1973, for a term of 'indefinite years,' ending 'year to year thereafter.' Thus, there was no certain ending, thereby rendering the lease void for a term of years." *Industrial Machinery,* 344 So.2d at 745.

Womack also cites the case of *National Bellas Hess, Inc. v. Kalis,* 191 F.2d 739 (8th Cir.1951), cert. denied, 342 U.S. 933, 72 S.Ct. 377, 96 L.Ed. 695 (1952), wherein a lease containing the provision, "for a term commencing October 1, 1943, and ending sixty (60) days after the signing of the treaty of peace upon the close of the war with Germany and/or with Japan, whichever treaty of peace is the latest," was found to be of uncertain duration. The Eighth Circuit Court of Appeals held that "it is not the certainty of the happening of the event (which is to end the term) but the certainty of the date on which the termination of the lease will take place that is the determinative factor"; therefore, the lease had no fixed ending and was held to be void.

Hyche argues that her lease with Womack has a definite ending because the lease is effective for only one year at a time. After each year the lessee is given the option to renew the lease, as long as the camp has been "run as a business for a profit." Hyche cites, as authority for her contentions, the holding in *Copiah Hardware Co. v. Johnson,* 123 Miss. 624, 86 So. 369 (1920). There, the Mississippi Supreme Court considered a one-year lease which contained the following covenant:

> " 'With the privilege and right of the parties of the second part or their assigns to renew the lease for one year at a time or after November 1, 1918, as long as they may desire to do so at the same rental as aforesaid and on the same terms and conditions embraced in this lease.' " *Copiah Hardware Co. v. Johnson,* 123 Miss. at 633, 86 So. at 369.

The lease had been once renewed, and the lessee had claimed the right to continue such renewals as long as it desired. The lessor argued that a lease renewal covenant granted no more than one renewal unless the terms of the covenant expressly provided otherwise. The court agreed with the lessor, but held:

> "That renewal covenants in a lease should be so construed is undoubtedly the law, but that can avail this [lessor] nothing, for the covenant of the lease here in question in clear and unambiguous language grants to the lessees the right to renew the lease as many times as they may desire to do so. Each renewal is to run for one year, and the right to renew annually is to continue 'as long as they may desire to do so;' that is, throughout such an extent of time as they may desire to do so." *Copiah Hardware Co. v. Johnson,* 123 Miss. at 633, 86 So. at 369.

. . .

In *Industrial Machinery, supra,* the questioned provision, that the lease was for a term of "indefinite years" and that it was to begin on January 1, 1973, and end "year to year thereafter," was no more than a general covenant to renew, there being no clear or express provision for the terms of any multiple renewals. So, too, was the renewal provision in the *National Bellas Hess* lease. That lease's renewal provision, which was to be determined by the duration of World War II, was clearly too uncertain and indefinite to be enforceable. The statement from that case upon which Hyche places great reliance, while setting out a valid legal concept, did not change the holding in that case—nor does it here. Just as the date of the signing of a peace treaty was uncertain to the contracting parties in 1943, so was the time at which the books of Camp Waxahatchee could begin to show a loss uncertain to the instant parties.

The Mississippi Supreme Court did enforce the renewal clause in the *Copiah Hardware* lease, but expressly held that the provision in question had been drafted in "clear and unambiguous language" which could not be "disregarded" in ascertaining the intention of the parties. "[A]s long as the camp is run as a business for a profit" does not reach the level of the "clear and unambiguous language" required to save the renewal clause at issue in the instant case and make it enforceable.

The lease for Camp Waxahatchee contains a renewal clause which provides no clear expression of the terms of further renewals; rather, it is so indefinite and uncertain in its terms as to be unenforceable. Further, perpetual leases and the covenants which create such leases are not favored, and courts will not enforce such covenants unless the parties have, by plain and unambiguous terms, expressed their intention to create such a lease. *Waldrop v. Siebert,* 286 Ala. 106, 237 So.2d 493 (1970); 51C C.J.S., *Landlord and Tenant, supra.*

The terms of the renewal provision at issue here, because they are ambiguous, tend to create a perpetuity without that requisite plain expression of the parties that a perpetuity was intended. Therefore, the lease is to be construed as having given to Womack and Hyche the right of one renewal; and, under Alabama law, the provision for renewal was completely performed upon the parties' first renewal of the lease at the end of Hyche's first year of operating the camp (January 1980).

Because the Womack/Hyche lease had no certain ending, thus rendering the lease void as a tenancy for years, a tenancy at will was created. "Where the end of the term is indefinite and uncertain there is no valid lease for a term of years, but an estate at will is thereby created. 3 Thompson on Real Property § 1088 (1959); *National Bellas Hess, Inc. [supra].* The question, therefore, is for what period of time was the tenancy at will in existence." *Industrial Machinery, Inc.,* 344 So.2d at 745. The tenancy at will resulting from the void lease between Womack and Hyche began at the close of the first renewal term of the lease, that is, in January 1981.

. . .

We find that the lease agreement between Womack and Hyche, by its terms, ended at the close of the year following the parties' first yearly renewal of the lease. After January, 1981, the parties continued under a tenancy at will, and Womack is now entitled to an order requiring Hyche's immediate vacation of the premises known as Camp Waxahatchee. The judgment is reversed, and this cause is remanded for entry of an order requiring Hyche to vacate the leased premises within such time as the trial court shall determine to be reasonable.

REVERSED AND REMANDED WITH INSTRUCTIONS.

TORBERT, C.J., and SHORES and STEAGALL, JJ., concur.

ADAMS, J., concurs specially.

NOTES

1. The tenancy for years and the tenancy at will, which are discussed in the preceding case, are two of the three basic types of non-freehold estates recognized at common law. The third is the periodic

tenancy. A periodic tenancy is a form of lease which continues from year to year, month to month, or other specified period until proper notice of termination is given. At common law notice six months prior to the end of a yearly period was necessary to terminate a tenancy from year to year, and notice one full period in advance was required to terminate a periodic tenancy for a shorter period. Alternatively, the parties could provide in the lease for the requisite period of advance notice necessary to end the tenancy. Many states have now codified required periods of notice, and these may be different from the common law notice requirements. Such statutes often shorten the advance notice required to terminate a year-to-year tenancy. See, for example, Colo.Rev.Stat. 13–40–107 (1982) (3 months); N.C.Gen.Stat. § 42–14 (1984) (one month).

According to the tenant's argument in the Womack case, what sort of lease was created by operation of the renewal clause?

2. Can a renewal clause operate to keep a lease in existence forever? In construing a renewal clause providing for an automatic renewal "under the same terms and conditions" as the original five-year lease "unless either party by written notice within 60 days of expiration date, declines to renew said lease," the court in Sheradsky v. Basadre, 452 So.2d 599 (Fla.App.1984) rejected the tenant's argument that the lease could be renewed for a series of successive five year terms. The court stated that "leases in perpetuity are universally disfavored, and if there is any uncertainty as to whether the parties intended a perpetual lease, the agreement should be construed so as to provide for only one renewal."

3. In Arbenz v. Exley, Watkins & Co., 57 W.Va. 580, 50 S.E. 813 (1905), a written lease for five years and three months, beginning January 1, 1896, and ending March 31, 1902, was ineffective under West Virginia law, because it was unsealed, to create an estate for years; but occupancy and payment of rent at the rate of $700 per year, payable in monthly installments, resulted in a year-to-year tenancy. On September 15, 1898, a fire totally destroyed the building on the premises, so that the tenant could no longer usefully occupy. There being no agreement or statute relieving the tenant firm, its rent liability, according to the common law, was unaffected by this disaster. The firm paid the rent for September and October and with the October payment sent the following letter: "October 31st, 1898. Mr. John Arbenz, City. Dear Sir: We beg to advise that we have vacated the premises known as West Building on 20th Street, destroyed by fire September 15th, last, and hereby surrender possession of same. Yours truly, Exley, Watkins & Co." An applicable statute provided: "A tenancy from year to year may be terminated by either party giving notice in writing to the other, prior to the end of any year, for three months, of his intention to terminate the same." Having vacated the premises, the tenant firm refused to pay any further rent. In November, 1899, Arbenz sued and obtained judgment for rent from November 1, 1898, to October 31, 1899. On August 1, 1903, he sued to recover rent for thirty-eight more months, from November 1, 1899, to December

31, 1902. What principles and arguments should counsel for the respective parties rely upon?

SECTION 2. DISCRIMINATION IN SELECTION OF TENANTS

MARINA POINT, LTD. v. WOLFSON

Supreme Court of California, 1982.
30 Cal.3d 721, 180 Cal.Rptr. 496, 640 P.2d 115, cert. denied 459 U.S. 858, 103 S.Ct. 129, 74 L.Ed.2d 111.

TOBRINER, JUSTICE.

In this case we must determine whether, under California law, an owner of an apartment complex may lawfully refuse to rent any of its apartments to a family solely because the family includes a minor child. In the landlord's action to eject the family, the municipal court found, inter alia, that "[c]hildren are rowdier, noisier, more mischievous and more boisterous than adults," and upheld the landlord's policy of excluding all families with minor children. The tenants now appeal from the judgment in favor of the landlord, contending that the exclusionary policy violates their statutory rights under the Unruh Civil Rights Act (Civ.Code, § 51 et seq.) and the California Fair Housing Law (Health & Saf.Code, § 35700 et seq., now Gov.Code, § 12955) and, in addition, impermissibly infringes upon their state and federal constitutional rights of familial privacy (U.S. Const., 9th & 14th Amends., Cal. Const. art, I, § 1) and equal protection of the law. (U.S. Const., 14th Amend; Cal. Const., art. I, § 7.)

For the reasons discussed below, we have concluded that the landlord's broad, class-based exclusionary practice violates the Unruh Civil Rights Act (hereafter Unruh Act or act); in light of this conclusion, we have no occasion in this case to address any of the tenants' more sweeping and far-reaching constitutional contentions. . . .

Plaintiff Marina Point, Ltd. (hereafter landlord or Marina Point) is a privately owned apartment complex, which, at the time of trial, consisted of 846 separate apartment units. The apartment complex, located in Marina del Rey, an unincorporated area in the County of Los Angeles, stands on land owned, and leased by the county to Marina Point. The master lease between the county and Marina Point specifically forbids Marina Point from discriminating on the basis of race, religion or national ancestry, but contains no provision with respect to other forms of discrimination.

In January 1974, defendants Stephen and Lois Wolfson signed a one-year lease for an apartment in the Marina Point complex with occupancy to begin on February 1 of that year. Although the printed form lease that the Wolfsons then signed contained a clause which provided that no minors under the age of 18 could reside in the leased premises without the landlord's written permission, Marina Point acknowledges that at that time it followed a policy of renting its apartments to families with children as well as to families without children.

In October 1974, Marina Point altered its rental policy with the objective of ultimately excluding all children from the apartment complex. At that time, well over 60 families with children lived in apartments in the complex, and Marina Point decided that while it would allow the children already there to remain, it would not rent any apartments to new families with children or with pregnant women.

In February 1975, the Wolfsons renewed their lease for a one-year period; the form lease again contained the same clause with respect to children as had appeared in the initial lease. In September 1975, Lois Wolfson gave birth to a son, Adam, who thereafter resided with his parents in the family apartment in Marina Point. In February 1976, the Wolfsons renewed their lease for another year; although the lease again contained the identical clause as to written consent for children, the Wolfsons apparently did not specifically inform the landlord of Adam's presence, and the lease made no reference to him.

In the fall of 1976, the landlord's manager learned that the Wolfsons had a child living in the apartment; shortly thereafter, the landlord informed them that their lease, due to expire on January 31, 1977, would not be renewed, and that the sole reason for such nonrenewal was Adam's presence on the premises.

After some negotiation between the parties, Marina Point agreed to a three-month extension of the Wolfsons' lease; the new lease agreement, which again contained the same provision as to children, specified that the premises would be occupied by the Wolfsons and their son. Thereafter, upon the Wolfsons' request, the landlord agreed to an additional one-month extension of the lease to May 31, 1977.

When the Wolfsons failed to vacate the premises on May 31, the landlord commenced the present unlawful detainer action in municipal court. In their answer, the Wolfsons maintained that the landlord's policy of discriminating against families with children violated both statutory constitutional prescriptions, and, as such, did not provide a lawful basis for their eviction. The landlord acknowledges that if its exclusion of the Wolfsons does in fact contravene statutory or constitutional strictures, such illegality would indeed provide a valid defense to the unlawful detainer action. . . .

At trial, the landlord conceded that its nonrenewal of the Wolfsons' lease rested solely on its current general policy of refusing to rent any of its apartments to families with children, but the landlord denied that this policy violated any statutory or constitutional principle. In defense of its exclusionary policy, the landlord's apartment manager testified that the decision to bar families with children rested in part on a number of past instances in which young tenants had engaged in annoying or potentially dangerous activities, ranging from acts of arson to roller skating and batting practice in the hallways to the attempted solicitation of snacks from the landlord's office staff.

The manager did not indicate, however, what proportion of the tenant children engaged in such activities or what steps, short of the blanket exclusionary policy, the landlord had implemented to deal with the problem, such as promulgating general rules as to permissible and impermissible conduct or excluding from the complex those families whose children repeatedly committed disruptive or destructive acts. Moreover, the landlord introduced no evidence that the Wolfsons' child had ever engaged in any such activity and, indeed, two of the Wolfsons' immediate neighbors testified that Adam's presence was not annoying to them at all.

As an additional explanation for the exclusionary policy, the apartment manager testified that the Marina Point complex had no special facilities for children, such as playground equipment, and no suitable area for children to play. The manager conceded, however, that the facilities of the complex had remained unaltered since the landlord had implemented its "no children" policy. In additon, the evidence revealed that, even at the time of trial, seven children were still living in apartments in the Marina Point complex.

Finally, the landlord presented testimony of two expert witnesses who had been in the real estate business for many years. These witnesses testified that in their opinion children, as a class, generally cause more wear and tear on property than adults do, and that as a consequence, landlords who rent to families with children generally have higher maintenance costs than landlords who exclude children. The witnesses presented no statistical data in support of their conclusion, but simply testified on the basis of their general experience.

As already noted, two immediate neighbors of the Wolfsons, one living next door and one living overhead, testified on behalf of the Wolfsons that they had not been disturbed by Adam's presence in the apartment. In addition to these neighbors' testimony, the Wolfsons presented one expert witness, a professor of real estate finance at California State University at Fullerton, who testified that the basic profitability of operating an apartment complex does not generally vary with the type or age of its tenants. Finally, the Wolfsons introduced a number of recent studies by various groups documenting the extensive nature of the practice of discrimination against families with children in rental housing that currently exists throughout California. As these and more recent studies reveal, in many of the major metropolitan areas of the state, families with children are excluded from 60 to 80 percent of the available rental housing.[1]

At the conclusion of the trial, the municipal court ruled in favor of Marina Point, rejecting the Wolfsons' contention that the landlord's policy of excluding all families with children violated their statutory or

1. See, for example, Note, Landlord Discrimination Against Children (1978) 11 Loyola L.A.L.Rev. 609, 611–613; Ashford & Eston, The Extent and Effects of Discrimination Against Children in Rental Housing: A Study of Five California Cities (1979); City of Campbell, Survey of Rental Policies Relating to Families with Children (1979); City of Mountain View, Children in the Housing Market (1978).

Similar discrimination in rental housing against families with children apparently exists in many regions throughout the country. (See, e.g., Reid et al., Patterns of Discrimination Against Children in Rental Housing in the Metro-Atlanta Area (1979); Greene, Child Discrimination in Rental Housing: A Comparative Analysis of Apartment Policies in Dallas, Texas (1979); Travalio, Suffer the Little Children—But Not in My Neighborhood: A Constitutional View of Age-Restrictive Housing (1979) 40 Ohio St.L.J. 295, 296–297; O'Brien & Fitzgerald, Apartment for Rent-Children Not Allowed (1975) 25 DePaul L.Rev. 64, 74–86.)

constitutional rights. The court's formal findings of fact contain findings, inter alia, that the landlord's "exclusion of children . . . proceeds from a reasonable economic motive to promote a quiet and peaceful environment free from noise and damage caused by children." Yet the court's memorandum opinion reveals that the court's *legal* conclusion that the practice in question did not violate any prohibited discrimination rested on the erroneous belief that the statutory proscription of discrimination applied only to a limited number of specifically designated "protected classes." [2] Because the municipal court could find "no decision to include children, parents with children, or families with children, as a protected class by the wording of the statutes themselves, or by judicial determination," the court concluded that the exclusionary practice challenged in this case fell beyond the reach of the state's existing anti-discrimination statutes. The court accordingly entered judgment in favor of the landlord, awarding it possession of the premises, $1,903.50 in damages, $3,000 in attorney fees and costs.[3]

The Wolfsons now appeal from the judgment, asserting that both the Unruh Act and the Fair Housing Law bar the landlord's admitted policy of discriminating against families with children. They additionally contend that the exclusion violates their rights to familial privacy and equal protection of the law guaranteed by the state and federal Constitutions. As noted above, because we conclude that the landlord's exclusionary policy violates the Unruh Act we need not, and do not, reach the Wolfsons' additional contentions.

. . .

2. The municipal court's memorandum opinion states in relevant part:

"The Unruh and Rumford Acts, taken collectively establish a classification of person[s] protected from discrimination in housing and business establishments. This classification includes persons discriminated against on the basis of race, religion, [national] origin, ancestry, sex and marital status. By judicial construction, this protection has been extended to homosexuals, long hairs, persons of unusual dress, persons of unusual political views, and unmarried couples living together. [Citation.]

"Not every class or person is protected. It is only such class or person that is protected as is set forth in the Statutes or who come under the Statutes by judicial determination. There is no decision to include children, parents with children, or families with children, as a protected class by the wording of the Statutes themselves, or by judicial determination. [¶] . . . The Court finds that the California Statutes do not extend protection to persons in the class of defendants who are refused housing on the ground that they have a child . . . .

"[T]he Court . . . is not indifferent to the plight of the defendants and other similarly situated persons as parents or families with children. The Court is satisfied that there is a problem of major importance; that there is difficulty in obtaining housing where one has a child. The judgment of the Court in no way is to be interpreted as 'Closing one's eyes to the problem.' However, the Court is restricted to a judicial determination as the law now exists under the provisions of the applicable statutes and case law. The Court finds that there is no case law or statute placing defendants in any protected class as parents of children."

3. After judgment was entered in favor of the landlord, the Wolfsons sought a stay of execution from the trial court pending appeal. The trial court issued a temporary stay for six months, and at the expiration of that period the Wolfsons vacated the premises. This vacation of the apartment does not render the appeal moot, however, in light of the outstanding judgment for damages, attorneys' fees and costs, as well as the general importance of the underlying issue. (See Green v. Superior Court (1974) 10 Cal.3d 616, 622, fn. 6, 111 Cal. Rptr. 704, 517 P.2d 1168.)

In evaluating the legality of the challenged exclusionary policy in this case, we must recognize at the outset that in California, unlike many other jurisdictions, the Legislature has sharply circumscribed an apartment owner's traditional discretion to accept and reject tenants on the basis of the landlord's own likes or dislikes. California has brought such landlords within the embrace of the broad statutory provisions of the Unruh Act, Civil Code section 51.[4] Emanating from and modeled upon traditional "public accommodations" legislation, the Unruh Act expanded the reach of such statutes from common carriers and places of public accommodation and recreation, e.g., railroads, hotels, restaurants, theaters and the like, to include "all business establishments of every kind whatsoever." (See generally, Horowitz, *The 1959* California Equal Rights in "Business Establishments" Statute—A Problem in Statutory Application (1960) 33 So.Cal.L.Rev. 260, 272–294.)

For nearly two decades the provisions of the Unruh Act, in light of its broad application to "all business establishments," have been held to apply with full force to the business of renting housing accommodations. . . . Indeed, in the case at bar, Marina Point apparently concedes that, like other business establishments that deal with the public, its freedom or authority to exclude "customers," i.e., prospective tenants, from the goods and services it offers, i.e., rental units, is limited by the provisions of the Unruh Act.

The municipal court properly recognized that Marina Point, as a "business establishment," was generally subject to the Unruh Act. It concluded, however, that the act provided no protection to the Wolfsons because it found that the subjects, i.e., "victims," of the discriminatory practice in this case, described variously as "children" or "families with children," did not fall within what the court believed to be a limited set of "protected classes" shielded from discriminatory treatment by the act. As already noted, the court, in elaborating upon its understanding of the Unruh Act, stated in this regard: "Not every class is protected. It is only such class or person that is protected as is set forth in the Statutes or who come under the Statutes by judicial determination." Because discrimination against children or against families with children was not in explicit terms proscribed by the language of section 51 or by any prior judicial decision, the court determined that any such discrimination was beyond the scope of the act.

The municipal court's interpretation of the act directly conflicts with this court's interpretation of the Unruh Act a decade ago in In re Cox, supra, 3 Cal.3d 205, 90 Cal.Rptr. 24, 474 P.2d 992. In *Cox*, an individual who claimed that he had been excluded from a shopping center because a friend with whom he was talking "wore long hair and dressed in an unconventional manner" (3 Cal.3d at p. 210, 90 Cal.Rptr.

4. Section 51 presently provides: "All persons within the jurisdiction of this state are free and equal, and no matter what their sex, race, color, religion, ancestry or national origin are entitled to the full and equal accommodations, advantages, facilities, privileges or services in all business establishments of every kind whatsoever.

"This section shall not be construed to confer any right or privilege on a person which is conditioned or limited by law or which is applicable alike to persons of every sex, color, race, religion, ancestry or national origin."

Unless otherwise noted, all statutory references are to the Civil Code.

24, 474 P.2d 992), asserted that such exclusion was barred by the Unruh Act. Relying upon the fact that the act, by its terms, expressly referred only to discrimination on the basis of "race, color, religion, ancestry or national origin,"[6] the city argued in response that the act's proscriptions were limited to discrimination which was based on the specifically enumerated forbidden criteria, and did not encompass the alleged discrimination against "hippies" or their associates.

After reviewing the common law origin, the legislative history and the past judicial interpretations of the act and its statutory predecessors, our court unanimously concluded in *Cox* that the "identification of particular bases of discrimination—color, race, religion, ancestry, and national origin— . . . *is illustrative rather than restrictive.* [Citation.] Although the legislation has been invoked primarily by persons alleging discrimination on racial grounds, its language and its history compel the conclusion that the Legislature intended to prohibit *all arbitrary discrimination by business establishments.*" (Italics added.) (3 Cal.3d at p. 216, 90 Cal.Rptr. 24, 474 P.2d 992.)

In reaching this conclusion, we relied, inter alia, upon the fact that the Unruh Act had emanated from the venerable common law doctrine which "attached [to various 'public' or 'common' callings] 'certain obligations including—at various stages of doctrinal development—*the duty to serve* all customers on reasonable terms without discrimination . . .'" (italics added) (id., at p. 212, 90 Cal.Rptr. 24, 474 P.2d 992), and upon the fact that prior judicial decisions construing the predecessors of the Unruh Act had clearly held that the statutory protections were not limited to discrimination based on race, religion, or national origin but also barred, for example, the exclusion of homosexuals from a public bar or restaurant (Stoumen v. Reilly (1951) 37 Cal.2d 713, 716, 324 P.2d 969) or the exclusion of persons with the reputation of immoral character from a public race track. (Orloff v. Los Angeles Turf Club (1951) 36 Cal.2d 734, 227 P.2d 449.) Because we could find absolutely no evidence to suggest that the Legislature intended to contract the reach of the statutory protections when it enacted the expansive Unruh Act in 1959, we concluded that the act must properly be interpreted "to interdict all arbitrary discrimination by a business enterprise." (3 Cal. 3d at p. 212, 90 Cal.Rptr. 24, 474 P.2d 992.)

. . .

The landlord maintains, however, that even if the municipal court erred in concluding that the Unruh Act did not apply because children or families with children were not a "protected class" under the act, the judgment in its favor should nonetheless be affirmed. It asserts that the trial court's findings of fact demonstrate that its policy of excluding all families with children from its apartment complex is "reasonable" and not "arbitrary" and, as such, is not barred by the Unruh Act.

6. Subsequent to our decision in *Cox*, the Legislature added "sex" to the bases of discrimination specifically listed in the statute. (Stats.1974, ch. 1193, § 1, p. 2568.) The purpose and legislative history of the 1974 legislation is discussed below. (See post, p. 504 of 180 Cal.Rptr., p. 123 of 640 P.2d.) With the exception of this single addition, the current statute is identical to the provision as construed in *Cox*.

In this regard, the landlord correctly points out that in *Cox* we explained that while the Unruh Act prohibits a business establishment from engaging in any form of arbitrary discrimination, the act does not absolutely preclude such an establishment from excluding a patron in all circumstances. As we stated in *Cox*: "In holding that the Civil Rights Act forbids a business establishment generally open to the public from arbitrarily excluding a prospective customer, we do not imply that the establishment may never insist that a patron leave the premises. Clearly, an entrepreneur need not tolerate customers who damage property, injure others or otherwise disrupt his business. A business establishment may, of course, promulgate reasonable deportment regulations that are rationally related to the services performed and the facilities provided. [Citation.]" (3 Cal.3d at p. 217, 90 Cal.Rptr. 24, 474 P.2d 992.)

The landlord contends that the exclusionary policy at issue here falls within the category of permissible regulations to which *Cox* adverted. Marina Point acknowledges that its blanket policy of excluding all families with children cannot properly be characterized as a "deportment regulation" since it does not focus on the conduct of the individuals or families who are actually excluded by the rule. (Cf. Hales v. Ojai Valley Inn and Country Club (1977) 73 Cal.App.3d 25, 28–29, 140 Cal.Rptr. 555 (restaurant rule requiring men to wear ties).) The landlord contends, however, that in light of the trial court's factual finding that "[c]hildren are rowdier, noisier, more mischievous and more boisterous than adults," its exclusion of all children bears a rational relation to its legitimate interest in preserving an appropriate environment.

. . .

As we recognized in *Cox,* of course, an individual may forfeit his statutory right of access to the services of a business enterprise if he conducts himself improperly or disrupts the operations of the enterprise. But . . . the Unruh Act does not permit a business enterprise to exclude an *entire class* of individuals on the basis of a generalized prediction that the class "as a whole" is more likely to commit misconduct than some other class of the public.

. . .

Finally, the landlord argues that even if the potential misbehavior of children as a class does not justify its exclusionary practice under the Unruh Act, its "no children" policy may nonetheless be sustained as reasonable on the ground that the presence of children basically does not accord with the nature of its business enterprise and of the facilities provided. In this regard, the landlord attempts to analogize its contemplated "adults only" apartment complex to such businesses as bars, adult book stores and theaters, or senior citizen convalescent homes or housing facilities which routinely exclude children from their premises or services.

In our view, the suggested analogy clearly fails. Stated simply, nothing in the nature of an ordinary apartment complex is incompatible with the presence of families with children. Indeed, as the record in this case indicates, prior to its decision to exclude children in 1974, the landlord freely rented its apartments to families with children and, even at the time of trial, several families with children continued to reside in the complex.

Unlike the exclusion of children from bars or adult book stores or movie theaters, the Marina Point complex's exclusionary policy cannot, of course, be defended by reference to any statutorily sanctioned restriction on the activities of children. (Cf., e.g., Bus. & Prof.Code, § 25658 (furnishing alcoholic beverages to person under 21); Pen.Code, § 313.1 (distributing "harmful matter" to a minor).)

Moreover, the exclusionary practice at issue in this case is also clearly distinguishable from the age-limited admission policies of retirement communities or housing complexes reserved for older citizens. Such facilities are designed for the elderly and in many instances have particular appurtenances and exceptional arrangements for their specified purposes. The special housing needs of the elderly in contemporary American society have been extensively chronicled,[10] and both the state and federal governments have enacted specific "age-conscious" legislative measures addressed to this problem. (See, e.g., Health & Saf.Code, § 51230 (reserving proportion of state-financed low income housing for occupancy by elderly); 12 U.S.C. § 1701q (federal loan program for housing for elderly families); 42 U.S.C. § 1485 (same).)

10. See, for example, 2 White House Conference on Aging, Toward a National Policy on Aging (1971) 29–36; President's Task Force on Aging, Toward a Brighter Future for the Elderly (1970) 38–40; Hearings on Condominium Conversions and the Elderly before the California Assembly Committee on Aging (1978).

In Taxpayers Ass'n of Weymouth Tp. v. Weymouth Tp. (1976) 71 N.J. 249, 364 A.2d 1016, 1026–1028, the New Jersey Supreme Court, in a thoughtful and well-documented opinion, explained at some length the numerous factors underlying the special housing needs of the elderly. The Court stated: "In part the need of the elderly for specialized housing results from the fixed and limited incomes upon which many older persons are dependent. . . . [¶] In part, though, the needs for specialized housing transcends economic status and results from the particular physical and social problems of the elderly . . . '. . . To the elderly, accidents in the home are a real danger. Falls, for example, are the leading cause of accidental death for those 65 and over. . . . [Housing p] lans should include more and wider walkways with fewer stairs, an interior and exterior designed to permit easy social contact, provision for common rooms, short distances between buildings, easy refuse collection, light maintenance and well-lighted walkways and halls. . . .' "Though special social and psychological needs of the elderly are perhaps less obvious than their physical needs, they are no less real. The elderly are apt to be less mobile than younger persons. They may have lost friends and relatives of comparable age and background. As a result, readily accessible companionship becomes increasingly important to them. In addition, the fact that children may have moved away sometimes causes elderly persons to seek an age-homogeneous environment to replace broken family ties. . . . Such an environment also helps older citizens to adjust to the social and psychological effects of retirement . . .. In addition, age-homogeneous communities afford a sense of security to their residents and thereby reduce the fear of criminal victimization. . . . Finally, these communities facilitate social relations and increase opportunities for the peer contact which many older persons need and desire." (364 A.2d at pp. 1026–1028 [citations omitted].) (See also Teaff et al., Impact of Age Integration on the Well-Being of Elderly Tenants in Public Housing (1978) 33 J. Gerontology 126 (empirical study finding that elderly tenants "living in age-segregated environments . . . participate more in organized activities within the housing environment, . . . have higher morale, higher housing satisfaction, and greater mobility in their neighborhoods").)

In light of the public policy reflected by these legislative enactments, age qualifications as to a housing facility reserved for older citizens can operate as a reasonable and permissible means under the Unruh Act of establishing and preserving specialized facilities for those particularly in need of such services or environment. (See, e.g., Taxpayers Ass'n. of Weymouth Tp. v. Weymouth Tp., supra. 71 N.J. 249, 364 A.2d 1016, 1026–1030; 58 Ops.Cal.Atty.Gen. 608, 613 (1975).)[11] Such a specialized institution designed to meet a social need differs fundamentally from the wholesale exclusion of children from an apartment complex otherwise open to the general public.[12]

Marina Point cannot plausibly claim that its exclusionary policy serves any similarly compelling societal interest. It can hardly contend, for example, that the class of persons for whom Marina Point seeks to reserve its housing accommodation, i.e., single adults or families without children, are more in need of housing than the class of persons whom the landlord has excluded from its apartment complex; indeed, precisely the opposite is true. As the Legislature stated in 1979: "The Legislature finds and declares that the state's housing problems are substantial, complex and now of crisis proportions . . . The Legislature finds and declares that the greatest need for housing is experienced by residents at the lower end of the economic scale. Many moderate and low income households *with children* cannot normally find decent, safe and suitable housing at prices they can afford. . . ." (Italics added.) (Stats.1979, ch. 1043, §§ 1, 2, pp. 3643–44.) Thus, unlike the case of special housing for the elderly, the exclusionary policy at issue here exacerbates, rather than alleviates, the state's specialized housing needs.

Finally, apartment house living is by no stretch of the imagination the type of dangerous or hazardous activity as to which the exclusion of children might be defended on health or safety grounds. Although certain facilities offered by an apartment complex may possibly be withheld from children pursuant to such a safety rationale, a landlord cannot seize upon the availability of such incidental facilities as a justification for closing off all of its principal services, i.e., housing

11. In light of the housing special needs of older citizens, the New Jersey Supreme Court, in the *Weymouth* case quoted at length in footnote 10, upheld the validity of a municipal zoning ordinance setting aside a portion of land for use as a mobile home park for older citizens. In reaching its conclusion, the court observed: "The role which mobile home developments can play in satisfying the special needs of the State's senior citizens is evident. First, mobile homes provide a relatively inexpensive form of housing at a time when the demand for such housing is great and its availability is limited . . . Second, mobile home developments afford the elderly the age-homogeneous environments which many older persons now seek and desire. Finally, the size of mobile homes is ideal for older persons with both physical and financial limitations. . . ." (364 A.2d at p. 1029.)

These special features of mobile home parks, which corrolate closely with the special needs of older citizens, may well explain the fact that mobile home parks constitute the only housing facilities in which the California Legislatuıe has explicitly authorized "adult only" restrictions. (See Civ.Code, §§ 798.76, 799.5.)

12. Thus, contrary to the suggestion of the dissent (dis. opn., post, pp. 510–511 of 180 Cal.Rptr., pp. 129–130 of 640 P.2d), this opinion does not bar age-limited admission policies of retirement communities or housing complexes reserved for older citizens.

accommodations, to the broad class of families with children.[13] If the rule were otherwise, of course, a proprietor could easily circumvent the Unruh Act's prohibitions simply by adding some incidental facility which posed a special danger to an undesired class of potential patrons. The fundamental right of equal access to public business enterprises established by the Unruh Act cannot be so readily defeated.

. . .

The judgment is reversed.

RICHARDSON, JUSTICE, dissenting.

. . .

Our sole inquiry, under *Cox,* is to determine whether the landlord has acted reasonably—i.e., whether in initiating and enforcing its new policy, it has done so by regulations which are reasonable in light of the circumstances and "rationally related to the services performed and facilities provided." (*Cox,* supra, at p. 212, 90 Cal.Rptr. 24, 474 P.2d 992.) The trial court's conclusion that plaintiff's action met this standard is fully supported by the court's express findings of fact and substantial evidence in this record. . . . In the matter before us, however, the majority simply disagrees with the explicit fact findings of a trial court which listened to the witnesses, examined the evidence, and expressly found as a fact that the premises in question were planned and built for all-adult tenants and not for children. On the basis of these findings, there is nothing in the Unruh Act which prohibits limitations here imposed. It is not unreasonable that the rental policies of an apartment complex be tailored and fashioned to match its planned design and character. . . .

NOTES

1. A provision of the federal Fair Housing Act, 42 U.S.C.A. § 3601 et seq. (1989 Supp.) prohibits discrimination in selling or renting housing "because of race, color, religion, sex, familial status, or national origin." "Familial status" is defined as meaning one or more persons under the age of 18 domiciled with a parent, a person having legal

13. Although one argument urged in defense of the exclusion of families with children from Marina Point rests upon the presence of swimming pools on the premises, the landlord's own actions reveals the hollowness of the contention. The swimming pools were part of the apartment complex long before the landlord instituted its "adults only" program. If the pools were not incompatible with the presence of children during the period before the new program, the pools could hardly become prohibitively dangerous after the institution of that program.

Moreover, the landlord's ostensible concern for the safety of children has never led it to adopt the less restrictive practice of simply excluding children from the use of the pools. Instead, the evidence at trial established that the landlord has routinely permitted both the remaining resident children and children of guests to use its swimming facilities. Under these circumstances, the presence of the swimming pools cannot possibly justify the landlord's broad exclusionary policy.

Finally, we note that the asserted "special features" on which the dissent relies—swimming pools with no shallow ends, no playgrounds, ungated gangplanks to the ocean—are hardly the kind of amenities which would suggest that this apartment complex was intended solely for "our middle aged or older citizens" on whose behalf the dissent defends the complex's exclusionary policy. (See dis. opn. post, pp. 510–511 of 180 Cal.Rptr., pp. 129–130 of 640 P.2d.)

custody, or a person designated in writing by the parent or legal custodian. Discrimination against pregnant women or a person seeking legal custody of a minor is also prohibited.

Can foster parents invoke the protection of the act, even though the state retains legal custody of the children in their care? Does the act apply to persons who have qualified under state guidelines to become foster parents but have not yet had a child entrusted to them? See Gorski v. Troy, 714 F.Supp. 367 (N.D.Ill.1989).

2. The Fair Housing Act also contains prohibitions against discriminating in the sale or rental of housing because of a handicap. 42 U.S.C.A. § 3604(f)(1989 Supp.). Discrimination is defined to include refusal to permit the handicapped person to pay for modifying the premises if modification is necessary to afford him full enjoyment of the premises. In such a situation the lessor can condition permission for modification upon the tenant's agreement to restore the premises to their original condition at the end of the tenancy.

3. A tenant may find it difficult to prove that a lessor has refused to rent to her because of her race, sex, religion or other basis set out in an anti-discrimination statute or ordinance. The federal Fair Housing Act was held not to forbid a landlord from following a practice of renting only to applicants whose net weekly income equals 90% of the monthly rent, even though the effect of this practice is exclusion of more blacks than whites, unless a racially discriminatory motive can be established. Boyd v. Lefrak Organization, 509 F.2d 1110 (2d Cir.1975), rehearing denied 517 F.2d 918, cert. denied 423 U.S. 896, 96 S.Ct. 197, 46 L.Ed.2d 129. Compare Robinson v. 12 Lofts Realty, Inc., 610 F.2d 1032 (2d Cir.1979), holding that a prima facie case of racially discriminatory motive may be established by showing: "(1) that [the applicant] is Black; (2) that he applied for and was qualified to rent or purchase the housing; (3) that he was rejected; and (4) that the housing opportunity remained available." Id. at 1038.

SECTION 3. TENANT'S RIGHT TO POSSESSION

ADRIAN v. RABINOWITZ

Supreme Court of New Jersey, 1936.
116 N.J.L. 586, 186 A. 29.

HEHER, J. On April 30, 1934, defendant [Rachel Rabinowitz], by an indenture, leased to plaintiff [Goodwin Adrian] certain store premises in the main business district of the city of Paterson, for the term of six months, commencing on June 15th next ensuing, at a stipulated monthly rent payable in advance; and the gravamen of this action is the breach of an obligation thereby imposed upon the lessor, as is said, to deliver to the lessee possession of the demised premises at the beginning of the term so prescribed. The state of demand is in two counts: The first seems to be grounded upon an asserted implied duty "to give and deliver possession" of the demised premises on the first day of the term; and the second, upon what plaintiff conceives to be an express covenant to put the lessee in possession on that day.

The lessee stipulated to devote the premises to the conduct of the shoe business; and he was given an option to renew the lease for an additional term of six months. Rent for the first month of the term was paid upon delivery of the lease, and the payment was acknowledged therein.

At the time of the execution of the contract, the premises were tenanted by another, who failed to respond to the landlord's notice to vacate on June 15. The landlord deemed himself [herself] obliged to institute dispossess proceedings, which terminated in a judgment of removal. This judgment was executed on July 7, 1934, and plaintiff took possession two days later.

The district court judge, sitting without a jury, found for the plaintiff on the basic issue, and measured the damages at $500, "the loss sustained by plaintiff in the resale of the seasonable merchandise." He also ruled that plaintiff was not liable for rent for the portion of the term he was deprived of possession and, making allowance for this, he awarded $25 to defendant on her set-off for rent due for the month beginning July 15, 1934.

It is apparent that the tenant in possession when the lease was executed wrongfully held over after the termination of the tenancy; and the primary question, raised by motions to nonsuit and direct a verdict in defendant's favor, is whether, expressly or by implication, the contract imposed upon the lessor the duty of putting the lessee in actual and exclusive possession of the demised premises at the beginning of the term.

It seems to be the rule in this state that a covenant for quiet enjoyment, as one of the covenants of title, is not to be implied from the mere relation of landlord and tenant, even when that relation springs from a deed. May v. Levy, 88 N.J.Law, 351, 95 A. 999, Ann.Cas.1917C, 619; [other citations omitted]. But here the lessor expressly covenanted that the lessee, "on paying the said monthly rent, and performing the covenants aforesaid, shall and may peaceably and quietly have, hold and enjoy the said demised premises for the term aforesaid." And it has been held elsewhere that a covenant for quiet enjoyment, similarly phrased, imposed upon the lessor the obligation to deliver possession of the premises on the first day of the term. Clark, Adm'r, v. Butt, 26 Ind. 236; King v. Reynolds, 67 Ala. 229, 42 Am.Rep. 107. Yet a covenant for quiet enjoyment is generally interpreted to secure the lessee against the acts or hindrances of the lessor, and persons deriving their right or title through him, or from paramount title, and does not protect the lessee from interference by strangers with his possession. Compare Prospect Point Land Improvement Co. v. Jackson, 109 N.J.Law, 385, 162 A. 576; O'Neil v. Pearse, 87 N.J.Law, 382, 94 A. 312; Playter v. Cunningham, 21 Cal. 229; Hannan v. Dusch, 154 Va. 356, 153 S.E. 824, 70 A.L.R. 141; Rice v. Biltmore Apartments Co., 141 Md. 507, 514, 119 A. 364.

It remains to consider whether the lessor, in the absence of an express undertaking to that effect, is under a duty to put the lessee in actual as well as legal possession of the demised premises at the commencement of the term. We are of the view that he is. There seems to be no dissent from the doctrine that the lessor impliedly covenants that the lessee shall have the legal right of possession at the beginning of the term. But there is a contrariety of view as to whether this implied obligation extends as well to actual possession, especially where, as here, the prior tenant wrongfully holds over. See 70 A.L.R. 151 et seq.

In some of our American jurisdictions, the rule obtains that, while the lessee is entitled to have the legal right of possession, there is no implied covenant to protect the lessee against wrongful acts of strangers. Gardner v. Keteltas, 3 Hill (N.Y.) 330, 38 Am.Dec. 637; Snider v. Deban, 249 Mass. 59, 144 N.E. 69; Hannan v. Dusch, supra; Gazzolo v. Chambers, 73 Ill. 75. The English rule is that, where the term is to commence in futuro, there is an implied undertaking by the lessor that the premises shall be open to the lessee's entry, legally and actually, when the time for possession under the lease arrives. Coe v. Clay, 5 Bing. 440, 130 Eng.Reprint. 113; [other citations omitted]. This rule has the support of respectable American authority. [Citations of cases in ten states omitted.] And in an early case in this state, where the premises, while tenanted, were let for a term to begin on a fixed day in the future, and the lessor, in an action of covenant brought by the lessee for failure to deliver possession on the first day of the term, or any time thereafter, pleaded inability to deliver possession because of the wrongful holding over by the tenant, this court construed the stipulation for possession at the commencement of the term "as an express covenant to let the premises, and give possession" on the first day of the term, and held that the lessor, having failed in the performance of the duty thus undertaken, was liable to the action. Kerr v. Whitaker, 3 N.J.Law, 670.

The English rule, so-called, is on principle much the better one. It has the virtue, ordinarily, of effectuating the common intention of the parties—to give actual and exclusive possession of the premises to the lessee on the day fixed for the commencement of the term. This is what the lessee generally bargains for; and it is the thing the lessor undertakes to give. Such being the case, there is no warrant for placing upon the lessee, without express stipulation to that effect, the burden of ousting, at his own expense, the tenant wrongfully holding over, or the trespasser in possession of the premises without color of right at the commencement of the term; and thus to impose upon him who is not in possession of the evidence the burden of establishing the respective rights and duties of the lessor and the possessor of the lands inter se, as well as the consequences of the delay incident to the adjudication of the controversy, and the obligation to pay rent during that period. As was said by Baron Vaughan in Coe v. Clay, supra: "He who lets agrees to give possession, and not merely to give a chance of a law suit." This doctrine is grounded in reason and logic. The underlying theory is that the parties contemplated, as an essential term of their undertaking, without which the lease would not have been made, that the lessor should, at the beginning of the term, have the premises open to the entry and exclusive possession of the lessee. This is certainly the normal course of dealing, and in the absence of stipulation to the contrary, is to be regarded as the parties' understanding of the lessor's covenant to deliver possession of the demised premises at the time prescribed for the commencement of the term.

There is an obvious distinction, which seems to have been overlooked in some of the cases rejecting the English doctrine, e.g., Snider v. Deban, supra, between a wrongful possession at the time fixed for the commencement of the term and the acts of trespassers who intrude after the lessee has been given the possession provided by the contract. 16 R.C.L. 724 et seq.

It is worthy of note that here the lessor, apparently conscious of a contractual obligation in the premises, initiated and prosecuted to a conclusion the proceedings requisite for dispossession of the hold-over tenant. She interpreted the contract as imposing the duty.

Therefore, the motions for a nonsuit and a direction of a verdict in defendant's favor on the ground that there was no evidence of a breach of defendant's undertaking to deliver possession of the demised premises at the stipulated time were rightly denied.

But there was error in the admeasurement of the damages claimed to have ensued from the breach of the undertaking. The judge found as a fact that the "plaintiff would have disposed of at least $2,800 worth of seasonable merchandise," purchased in anticipation of delivery of possession of the demised premises at the commencement of the prescribed term, "had he had possession in accordance with the terms of" the lease, and that he was thereafter compelled to sacrifice his merchandise at 25 per cent. below cost.

The measure of damages for the breach of an undertaking to lease is, in the absence of special circumstances attending the making of the contract, and communicated by the party asserting the breach to the one charged therewith, the difference between the actual rental value and the rent reserved for the period of the deprivation of possession. Weiss v. Revenue Building & Loan Ass'n, 116 U.J.Law, 208, 182 A. 891; Drischman v. McManemin, 68 N.J.Law, 337, 53 A. 548. The damages recoverable are those fairly and reasonably within the contemplation of the parties to the contract, at the time of its making, as the probable consequence of the breach; and this principle likewise obtains when the contract is made under special circumstances known to the party charged with the breach. The injured party is entitled to have the damages ordinarily flowing from the breach of a contract made under the known special circumstances, i.e., the direct and immediate result of the nonfulfillment of the contract. But the law, in the estimation of the damages consequent upon the breach, applies that formula which makes for the greater definiteness and certainty; and, in a case such as this, the difference between the rental value and the rent reserved measures the damages with that degree of certainty which the law terms reasonable, while evidence of possible profits during the period in question, and, by the same reasoning, losses resulting from the depreciation in value of seasonable merchandise which might have been sold, do not provide a definite and trustworthy standard. The hazards, contingencies, and uncertainties incident to the operation of a newly-established business preclude the consideration of such factors in the appraisement of the injury. They are too remote and speculative to serve as a satisfactory guide. Compare Weiss v. Revenue Building & Loan Ass'n, supra; Cramer v. Grand Rapids Show Case Co., 223 N.Y. 63, 119 N.E. 227, 1 A.L.R. 154; [other citations omitted].

But, granting that that depreciation in the value of the merchandise may fairly and reasonably be supposed to have been within the contemplation of the parties to the contract as the probable result of the breach, and that the making of the contract under the asserted special circumstances may be established by parol . . ., the proofs offered do not warrant the application of that standard. Plaintiff was permitted to estimate the quantum of probable sales of merchandise during the period in question upon the basis of "the amount of business did (sic) after" he took possession, and the business done in another store located eight blocks away. He did not produce his books of account, or introduce testimony from his accountant, even after promising to do so during the course of the trial. His own evidence upon this point was vague and uncertain, although concededly capable of precise and exact proof. Justification for the application of such a rule in the admeasurement of damages must necessarily rest upon the hypothesis of the existence of provable data furnished by experience as the basis for an estimation of the quantum of the loss with a reasonable degree of certainty. There was no proof of such data here, assuming its existence, and therefore no basis for the award made. Weiss v. Revenue Building & Loan Ass'n, supra; [other citations omitted].

It is to be presumed that seasonal goods would be offered during the period in question at prices calculated to yield a reasonable profit, and the sale thereof below cost deferred until the season had ended. And it is significant that plaintiff disposed of the business before the expiration of the relatively short term granted by the lease. From this, it is fairly inferable that he was engaged in an experiment that did not prove successful. But however this may be, it furnishes an added reason for the introduction of all provable data bearing upon this issue.

Judgment reversed, and a venire de novo awarded; costs to abide the event.

NOTES

1. Several states have enacted statutes requiring a lessor to deliver possession to the tenant on the first day of the lease term. The Maryland statute, Md.Code, Real Prop., § 8–204 (1988), applies only to residential tenants. What reasons, if any, are there for not including commercial lessees?

2. Arguments in favor of the "American" rule that the landlord is not responsible for interference by a holdover tenant or other wrongful possessor are detailed in Hannan v. Dusch, cited in the foregoing

opinion. In summary: by force of the new lease, the lessee has the right of possession, not the lessor—hence, occupancy by another is a wrong toward the lessee only; when the new lease was being negotiated, both parties were chargeable with knowledge that a wrongful occupancy at the beginning of the term was possible, and either could have insisted upon an express covenant dealing with the possibility—hence, its omission may be regarded as significant, and to say that a covenant concerning occupancy is implied is tantamount to the court's "making a contract for the parties"; the general rule is that a party to a bargain, himself without fault, is not responsible for tortious interference by a stranger—the "English rule" invokes against lessors an arbitrary, unjustifiable exception to the general principle; it is unanimously agreed that after a lessee takes possession his only cause of action for trespass by a stranger lies against the trespasser—there is no substantial difference between a trespass which interrupts a possession and a trespass which precludes taking possession initially. In Hannan v. Dusch the court also relied upon the fact that, by the terms of the Virginia wrongful detainer statute, the lessee alone could employ the simple and speedy statutory remedy for invasion of possessory rights. On this basis, the doctrine of avoidable consequences could be regarded as relevant, the lessee having failed to minimize his loss by enforcing his possessory right against the holdover tenant. Notice that in New Jersey the summary statutory action (termed "dispossess proceedings" in the Adrian opinion above) is evidently available to the lessor.

3. The generally accepted doctrine is that an actual partial eviction by the *landlord* relieves the tenant of all obligation to pay for use of the leased premises, even though he is deprived of possession of only a small portion. The relationship is not terminated unless the tenant chooses (as he may) so to treat it; other covenants of the lease are enforceable, but the tenant's obligation to pay is suspended so long as the ouster continues. This rule is perhaps difficult to rationalize, save in terms of ancient concepts. In Smith v. McEnany, 170 Mass. 26, 48 N.E. 781 (1897), where a brick wall built upon adjoining land encroached, by the lessor's permission, upon a narrow strip of the leased premises, the court (per Holmes, J.) said, "It is settled in this State, in accordance with the law of England, that a wrongful eviction of the tenant by the landlord from a part of the premises suspends the rent under the lease. The main reason which is given for the decisions is, that the enjoyment of the whole consideration is the foundation of the debt and the condition of the covenant, and that the obligation to pay cannot be apportioned. [Citations omitted.] It also is said that the landlord shall not apportion his own wrong, following an expression in some of the older English books. [Citations omitted.] But this does not so much explain the rule as suggest the limitation that there may be an apportionment when the eviction is by title paramount, or when the lessor's entry is rightful. [Citations omitted.] It leaves open the question why the landlord may not show that his wrong extended only to a part of the premises. No doubt the question equally may be asked why the lease is construed to exclude apportionment, and it may be that this is partly due to the traditional doctrine that the rent issues

out of the land, and that the whole rent is charged on every part of the land. Gilbert, Rents, 178, 179, gives this as one ground why the lessor shall not discharge any part from the burden and continue to charge the rest, coupled with considerations partly of a feudal nature. [Citations omitted.] But the same view naturally would be taken if the question arose now for the first time. The land is hired as one whole. If by his own fault the landlord withdraws a part of it, he cannot recover either on the lease or outside of it for the occupation of the residue. [Citations omitted.]" This position is rejected by the Restatement (Second) of Property, Landlord and Tenant § 6.1, Reporter's Note 6 (1977).

4. A covenant of quiet enjoyment is frequently expressed in a lease, but if it is omitted the prevailing view, contrary to what the Adrian opinion says concerning New Jersey law, is that the covenant is implied in every lease unless terms in the lease are construed to exclude the implication. The covenant provides a contractual basis for a remedy if the lessee is adversely affected by the lessor's lack of an unencumbered fee simple title. See, e.g., In re O'Donnell, 240 N.Y. 99, 147 N.E. 541 (1925), in which the lessor, having only a life estate, leased for seven years and died before the term expired; Ganz v. Clark, 252 N.Y. 92, 169 N.E. 100 (1929) and Standard Live Stock Co. v. Pentz, 204 Cal. 618, 269 P. 645, 62 A.L.R. 1239 (1928), in which realty was leased subject to a mortgage, and default in payment resulted in a foreclosure action and eviction of the lessee.

Condemnation of land pursuant to the power of eminent domain is not a breach of the covenant of quiet enjoyment, as this is not a consequence of any defect in landlord's title. Must the tenant continue to pay the stipulated rent even though all or part of the leased premises have been taken by eminent domain? If all of the leased premises are condemned, the leasehold (including the covenant to pay rent) is extinguished by merger of the leasehold and the fee simple in the condemnor. If, however, only a portion of the leased premises are condemned, the traditional rule is that the rent obligation is unaffected. See, e.g., Elliott v. Joseph, 163 Tex. 71, 351 S.W.2d 879 (1961). If, as is probably the case, the tenant is entitled to share in the eminent domain award to the extent of the value of the leasehold interest taken, is the traditional rule unfair to the tenant? Might it be unfair to the landlord?

5. The covenant of quiet enjoyment also may protect a tenant against conduct by a landlord interfering with enjoyment of the premises. If the interference is sufficiently severe, the tenant may vacate the premises and claim that a constructive eviction has occurred, the legal consequences being the same as those of an actual eviction. This remedy may be preferred by the tenant to tort actions that may be available. Consider the following case.

BLACKETT v. OLANOFF

Supreme Judicial Court of Massachusetts, 1977.
371 Mass. 714, 358 N.E.2d 817.

WILKINS, JUSTICE.

The defendant in each of these consolidated actions for rent successfully raised constructive eviction as a defense against the landlords' claim. The judge found that the tenants were "very substantially deprived" of quiet enjoyment of their leased premises "*for a substantial* time" (emphasis original). He ruled that the tenants' implied warranty of quiet enjoyment was violated by late evening and early morning music and disturbances coming from nearby premises which the landlords leased to others for use as a bar or cocktail lounge (lounge). The judge further found that, although the landlords did not intend to create the conditions, the landlords "had it within their control to correct the conditions which . . . amounted to a constructive eviction of each [tenant]." He also found that the landlords promised each tenant to correct the situation, that the landlords made some attempt to remedy the problem, but they were unsuccessful, and that each tenant vacated his apartment within a reasonable time. Judgment was entered for each tenant; the landlords appealed; and we transferred the appeals here. We affirm the judgments.

The landlords argue that they did not violate the tenants' implied covenant of quiet enjoyment because they are not chargeable with the noise from the lounge. The landlords do not challenge the judge's conclusion that the noise emanating from the lounge was sufficient to constitute a constructive eviction, if that noise could be attributed to the landlords.[3] Nor do the landlords seriously argue that a constructive eviction could not be found as matter of law because the lounge was not on the same premises as the tenants' apartments. See 1 American Law of Property § 3.51 at 281 (A.J. Casner ed. 1952). The landlords' principal contention, based on the denial of certain requests for rulings, is that they are not responsible for the conduct of the proprietors, employees, and patrons of the lounge.

Our opinions concerning a constructive eviction by an alleged breach of an implied covenant of quiet enjoyment sometimes have stated that the landlord must perform some act with the intent of depriving the tenant of the enjoyment and occupation of the whole or part of the leased premises. See Katz v. Duffy, 261 Mass. 149, 151–152, 158 N.E. 264 (1927), and cases cited. There are occasions, however, where a landlord has not intended to violate a tenant's rights, but there was nevertheless a breach of the landlord's covenant of quiet enjoyment which flowed as the natural and probable consequence of what the

3. There was evidence that the lounge had amplified music (electric musical instruments and singing, at various times) which started at 9:30 P.M. and continued until 1:30 A.M. or 2 A.M., generally on Tuesdays through Sundays. The music could be heard through the granite walls of the residential tenants' building, and was described variously as unbelievably loud, incessant, raucous, and penetrating. The noise interfered with conversation and prevented sleep. There was also evidence of noise from patrons' yelling and fighting.

landlord did, what he failed to do, or what he permitted to be done. Charles E. Burt, Inc. v. Seven Grand Corp., 340 Mass. 124, 127, 163 N.E.2d 4 (1959) (failure to supply light, heat, power, and elevator services). Westland Housing Corp. v. Scott, 312 Mass. 375, 381, 44 N.E.2d 959 (1942) (intrusions of smoke and soot over a substantial period of time due to a defective boiler). Shindler v. Milden, 282 Mass. 32, 33–34, 184 N.E. 673 (1933) (failure to install necessary heating system, as agreed). Case v. Minot, 158 Mass. 577, 587, 33 N.E. 700 (1893) (landlord authorizing another lessee to obstruct the tenant's light and air, necessary for the beneficial enjoyment of the demised premises). Skally v. Shute, 132 Mass. 367, 370–371 (1882) (undermining of a leased building rendering it unfit for occupancy). Although some of our opinions have spoken of particular action or inaction by a landlord as showing a presumed intention to evict, the landlord's conduct, and not his intentions, is controlling. See Westland Housing Corp. v. Scott, supra, 312 Mass. at 382–383, 44 N.E. 959.

The judge was warranted in ruling that the landlords had it within their control to correct the condition which caused the tenants to vacate their apartments. The landlords introduced a commercial activity into an area where they leased premises for residential purposes. The lease for the lounge expressly provided that entertainment in the lounge had to be conducted so that it could not be heard outside the building and would not disturb the residents of the leased apartments. The potential threat to the occupants of the nearby apartments was apparent in the circumstances. The landlords complained to the tenants of the lounge after receiving numerous objections from residential tenants. From time to time, the pervading noise would abate in response to the landlords' complaints. We conclude that, as matter of law, the landlords had a right to control the objectionable noise coming from the lounge and that the judge was warranted in finding as a fact that the landlords could control the objectionable conditions.

This situation is different from the usual annoyance of one residential tenant by another, where traditionally the landlord has not been chargeable with the annoyance. See Katz v. Duffy, 261 Mass. 149, 158 N.E. 264 (1927) (illegal sale of alcoholic beverages); DeWitt v. Pierson, 112 Mass. 8 (1873) (prostitution).[4] Here we have a case more like Case

4. The general, but not universal, rule in this country is that a landlord is not chargeable because one tenant is causing annoyance to another (A.H. Woods Theatre v. North American Union, 246 Ill.App. 521, 526–527, [1927] [music from one commercial tenant annoying another commercial tenant's employees]), even where the annoying conduct would be a breach of the landlord's covenant of quiet enjoyment if the landlord were the miscreant. See Paterson v. Bridges, 16 Ala.App. 54, 55, 75 So. 260 (1917); Thompson v. Harris, 9 Ariz. App. 341, 345, 452 P.2d 122 (1969), and cases cited; 1 American Law of Property § 3.53 (A.J. Casner ed. 1952); Annot., 38 A.L.R. 250 (1925). Contra Kesner v. Consumers Co., 255 Ill.App. 216, 228–229 (1929) (storage of flammables constituting a nuisance); Bruckner v. Helfaer, 197 Wis. 582, 585, 222 N.W. 790 (1929) (residential tenant not liable for rent where landlord, with ample notice, does not control another tenant's conduct).

The rule in New York appears to be that the landlord may not recover rent if he has had ample notice of the existence of conduct of one tenant which deprives another tenant of the beneficial enjoyment of his premises and the landlord does little or nothing to abate the nuisance. See Cohen v. Werner, 85 Misc.2d 341, 342, 378 N.Y.S.2d 868 (N.Y.App.T.1975); Rockrose Associates v. Peters, 81 Misc.2d 971, 972, 366 N.Y.S.2d 567 (N.Y.Civ.Ct.1975) (office

v. Minot, 158 Mass. 577, 33 N.E. 700 (1893), where the landlord entered into a lease with one tenant which the landlord knew permitted that tenant to engagein activity which would interfere with the rights of another tenant. There, to be sure, the clash of tenants' rights was inevitable, if each pressed those rights. Here, although the clash of tenants' interests was only a known potentiality initially, experience demonstrated that a decibel level for the entertainment at the lounge, acoustically acceptable to its patrons and hence commercially desirable to its proprietors, was intolerable for the residential tenants.

Because the disturbing condition was the natural and probable consequence of the landlords' permitting the lounge to operate where it did and because the landlords could control the actions at the lounge, they should not be entitled to collect rent for residential premises which were not reasonably habitable. Tenants such as these should not be left only with a claim against the proprietors of the noisome lounge. To the extent that our opinions suggest a distinction between nonfeasance by the landlord, which has been said to create no liability (P. Hall, Massachusetts Law of Landlord and Tenant §§ 90–91 [4th ed. 1949]), and malfeasance by the landlord, we decline to perpetuate that distinction where the landlord creates a situation and has the right to control the objectionable conditions.

Judgments affirmed.

NOTES

1. A tenant leased space in a large shopping center for use as a retail store selling patio furniture. Adjacent space was later leased to Body Electric, an exercise studio. "Loud music, screams, shouts and yells" from the exercise studio made it virtually impossible for the furniture store to conduct business. In spite of repeated complaints by the offended tenant, the lessor did nothing to remedy the problem, and the tenant vacated the premises with more than two years remaining in the term of her lease. The tenant urged constructive eviction as a defense to the lessor's suit for rent for the remainder of the term. She relied in part upon a paragraph of her lease stating that

> Tenant, upon paying the rents and performing all of the terms on its part to be performed, shall peaceably and quietly enjoy the Demised Premises. . . .

In response the lessor pointed to another lease paragraph providing:

> Landlord shall not be liable to Tenant or any other person for any damage or injury caused to any person or property by reason of the failure of Landlord to perform any of its covenants or agreements

lease); Home Life Ins. Co. v. Breslerman, 168 Misc. 117, 118, 5 N.Y.S.2d 272 (N.Y. App.T.1938). But see comments in Trustees of the Sailors' Snug Harbor in the City of New York v. Sugarman, 264 App.Div. 240, 241, 35 N.Y.S.2d 196 (N.Y.1942) (no nuisance).

A tenant with sufficient bargaining power may be able to obtain an agreement from the landlord to insert and to enforce regulatory restrictions in the leases of other, potentially offending, tenants. See E. Schwartz, Lease Drafting in Massachusetts § 6.33 (1961).

hereunder, . . . or for any damage arising from acts or negligence of other tenants or occupants of the Shopping Center.

What result? See Barton v. Mitchell Co., 507 So.2d 148 (Fla.App. 1987).

2. A tenant who moves out as a result of a constructive eviction may be able to recover damages. See Downtown Realty, Inc. v. 509 Tremont Bldg., 748 S.W.2d 309 (Tex.App.1988) (constructive eviction by lessor's failure to repair heating and air-conditioning system; commercial tenant entitled to damages for lost profits.) Suppose, however, the tenant prefers to remain in possession. Is she still entitled to damages? The traditional negative answer is rejected by the Restatement (Second) of Property, Landlord and Tenant § 6.1.

SECTION 4. CONDITION OF THE PREMISES

The traditional characterization of a lease as a conveyance negated the lessor's responsibility for the condition of the premises. Since the lessee was viewed as being in essentially the same position as a purchaser of land in fee simple, he was responsible for inspecting the property to determine its suitability for his use and, in most instances, its safety. The lessor's liability for defects was usually limited to situations where he had made misrepresentations concerning the property or had failed to reveal hidden defects of which he knew but which would not be discovered by the prospective lessee's reasonable inspection.

Within the last two decades this body of law has undergone a sweeping transformation. Although not every state court has adopted these developments, the law today is distinctly more favorable to the tenant.

A. SUITABILITY FOR TENANT'S USE

Traditional doctrine afforded scant protection to a tenant from conditions rendering the premises unsuitable for their intended use. As a purchaser of a leasehold estate, a tenant was subject to the strictures of caveat emptor. In addition, the duty to repair was upon the tenant, unless the lease provided otherwise. In the absence of a duty of the landlord to make the premises suitable, even the remedy of constructive eviction was not available. If a tenant managed to obtain inclusion in the lease of a covenant by the landlord to repair, constructive eviction would be available, as would the remedy of damages, but the tenant could not resort to the remedy most likely to be effective—withholding of the rent until performance by the landlord. Covenants in leases, it was said, are independent. This situation has changed dramatically during recent years, as the following cases show.

(1) HABITABILITY

BROWN v. SOUTHALL REALTY CO.

District of Columbia Court of Appeals, 1968.
237 A.2d 834.

QUINN, J. This appeal arises out of an action for possession brought by appellee-landlord, against appellant-tenant, Mrs. Brown, for nonpayment of rent. The parties stipulated, at the time of trial, that the rent was in the arrears in the amount of $230.00. Mrs. Brown contended, however, that no rent was due under the lease because it was an illegal contract. The court held to the contrary and awarded appellee possession for nonpayment of rent.

Although counsel for appellant stated at oral argument before this court that Mrs. Brown had moved from the premises and did not wish to be returned to possession, she asserts that this court should hear this appeal because the judgment of the court below would render certain facts res judicata in any subsequent suit for rent. In Bess v. David, supra, a suit by a landlord against a tenant for recovery of rent owed, defendant contended that he did not owe rent because he was not a tenant during the time alleged. The defendant was, however, denied that defense, this court stating on appeal that ". . . we think *any* question of appellant's tenancy is foreclosed by the judgment in the previous *possessory* action." (Emphasis supplied.) 140 A.2d 317.

Thus, because the validity of the lease and the determination that rent is owing will be irrevocably established in this case if the judgment of the trial court is allowed to stand, we feel that this appeal is timely made.

Although appellant notes a number of errors, we consider the allegation that the trial court erred in failing to declare the lease agreement void as an illegal contract both meritorious and completely dispositive, and for this reason we reverse.

The evidence developed, at the trial, revealed that prior to the signing of the lease agreement, appellee was on notice that certain Housing Code violations existed on the premises in question. An inspector for the District of Columbia Housing Division of the Department of Licenses and Inspections testified that the violations, an obstructed commode, a broken railing and insufficient ceiling height in the basement, existed at least some months prior to the lease agreement and had not been abated at the time of trial. He also stated that the basement violations prohibited the use of the entire basement as a dwelling place. Counsel for appellant at the trial below elicited an admission from the appellee that "he told the defendant after the lease had been signed that the back room of the basement was habitable despite the Housing Code Violations." In addition, a Mr. Sinkler Penn, the owner of the premises in question, was called as an adverse witness by the defense. He testified that "he had submitted a sworn statement to the Housing Division on December 8, 1964 to the effect that the basement was unoccupied at that time and would continue to be kept vacant until the violations were corrected."

This evidence having been established and uncontroverted, appellant contends that the lease should have been declared unenforceable because it was entered into in contravention to the District of Columbia Housing Regulations, and knowingly so.

Section 2304 of the District of Columbia Housing Regulations reads as follows: No persons shall rent or offer to rent any habitation, or the furnishings thereof, unless such habitation and its furnishings are in a clean, safe and sanitary condition, in repair, and free from rodents or vermin. Section 2501 of these same Regulations, states: Every premises accommodating one or more habitations shall be maintained and kept in repair so as to provide decent living accommodations for the occupants. This part of the Code contemplates more than mere basic repairs and maintenance to keep out the elements; its purpose is to include repairs and maintenance designed to make a premises or neighborhood healthy and safe.

It appears that the violations known by appellee to be existing on the leasehold at the time of the signing of the lease agreement were of a nature to make the "habitation" unsafe and unsanitary. Neither had the premises been maintained or repaired to the degree contemplated by the regulations, i.e., "designed to make a premises . . . healthy and safe." The lease contract was, therefore, entered into in violation of the Housing Regulations requiring that they be safe and sanitary and that they be properly maintained.

In the case of Hartman v. Lubar, 77 U.S.App.D.C. 95, 96, 133 F.2d 44, 45 (1942), cert. denied, 319 U.S. 767, 63 S.Ct. 1329, 87 L.Ed. 1716 (1943), the court stated that, "[t]he general rule is that an illegal contract, made in violation of the statutory prohibition designed for police or regulatory purposes, is void and confers no right upon the wrongdoer." The court in Lloyd v. Johnson, 45 App.D.C. 322, 327 (1916), indicated: To this general rule, however, the courts have found exceptions. For the exception, resort must be had to the intent of the legislature, as well as the subject matter of the legislation. The test for the application of the exception is pointed out in Pangborn v. Westlake, 36 Iowa 546, 549, and approved in Miller v. Ammon, 145 U.S. 421, 426, 36 L.Ed. 759, 762, 12 Sup.Ct.Rep. 884, as follows: "We are, therefore, brought to the true test, which is, that while, as a general rule, a penalty implies a prohibition, yet the courts will always look to the subject matter of it, the wrong or evil which it seeks to remedy or prevent, and the purpose sought to be accomplished in its enactment; and if, from all these, it is manifest that it was not intended to imply a prohibition or to render the prohibited act void, the court will so hold and construe the statute accordingly."

Applying this general rule to the Housing Regulations, it may be stated initially that they do provide for penalties for violations. A reading of Sections 2304 and 2501 infers that the Commissioners of the District of Columbia, in promulgating these Housing Regulations, were endeavoring to regulate the rental of housing in the District and to insure for the prospective tenants that these rental units would be "habitable" and maintained as such. The public policy considerations are adequately stated in Section 2101 of the District of Columbia Housing Regulations, entitled "Purpose of Regulations." To uphold the validity of this lease agreement in light of the defects known to be existing on the leasehold prior to the agreement (i.e., obstructed commode, broken railing, and insufficient ceiling height in the basement) would be to flout the evident purposes for which Sections 2304 and 2501 were enacted. The more reasonable view is therefore, that where such conditions exist on a leasehold prior to an agreement to lease the letting of such premises constitutes a violation of Sections 2304 and 2501 of the Housing Regulations, and that these Sections do indeed "imply a prohibition" so as "to render the prohibited act void." Neither does there exist any reason to treat a lease agreement differently from any other contract in this regard.

Thus, for this reason and those stated above, we reverse.

Reversed.

NOTE

Should the landlord in the principal case be permitted to recover the reasonable value of the use of the premises during the tenant's occupancy? This was allowed in William J. Davis, Inc. v. Slade, 271 A.2d 412 (D.C.App.1970), although the court observed that "as a general rule" a quasi-contractual theory would not be available in such a case. The distinguishing factor here, as viewed by the court, was the judicially recognized status in the District of Columbia of a tenant under a lease invalid due to housing code violations as a tenant at sufferance rather than a trespasser. As a tenant at sufferance, the tenant could remain in possession at least for 30 days following a proper notice to quit, and possibly longer.

JAVINS, SAUNDERS, AND GROSS v. FIRST NATIONAL REALTY CORP.

United States Court of Appeals, District of Columbia Circuit, 1970.
138 U.S.App.D.C. 369, 428 F.2d 1071, cert. denied 400 U.S. 925, 91 S.Ct. 186, 27 L.Ed.2d 185.

Before WRIGHT, MCGOWAN and ROBB, CIRCUIT JUDGES.

J. SKELLY WRIGHT, CIRCUIT JUDGE. These cases present the question whether housing code [1] violations which arise during the term of a lease have any effect upon the tenant's obligation to pay rent. The Landlord and Tenant Branch of the District of Columbia Court of General Sessions ruled proof of such violations inadmissible when proffered as a defense to an eviction action for nonpayment of rent. The District of Columbia Court of Appeals upheld this ruling. Saunders v. First National Realty Corp., 245 A.2d 836 (1968).

Because of the importance of the question presented, we granted appellants' petitions for leave to appeal. We now reverse and hold that a warranty of habitability, measured by the standards set out in the

1. Housing Regulations of the District of Columbia (1956).

Housing Regulations for the District of Columbia, is implied by operation of law into leases of urban dwelling units covered by those Regulations and that breach of this warranty gives rise to the usual remedies for breach of contract.

I.

The facts revealed by the record are simple. By separate written leases,[2] each of the appellants rented an apartment in a three-building apartment complex in Northwest Washington known as Clifton Terrace. The landlord, First National Realty Corporation, filed separate actions in the Landlord and Tenant Branch of the Court of General Sessions on April 8, 1966, seeking possession on the ground that each of the appellants had defaulted in the payment of rent due for the month of April. The tenants, appellants here, admitted that they had not paid the landlord any rent for April. However, they alleged numerous violations of the Housing Regulations as "an equitable defense or [a] claim by way of recoupment or setoff in an amount equal to the rent claim," as provided in the rules of the Court of General Sessions.[3] They offered to prove "[t]hat there are approximately 1500 violations of the Housing Regulations of the District of Columbia in the building at Clifton Terrace, where Defendant resides some affecting the premises of this Defendant directly, others indirectly, and all tending to establish a course of conduct of violation of the Housing Regulations to the damage of Defendants . . .."

Settled Statement of Proceedings and Evidence, p. 2 (1966). Appellants conceded at trial, however, that this offer of proof reached only violations which had arisen since the term of the lease had commenced. The Court of General Sessions refused appellants' offer of proof[4] and entered judgment for the landlord. The District of Columbia Court of Appeals affirmed, rejecting the argument made by appellants that the

2. A clause in the lease provided that the tenant waived the statutory 30-day notice to quit. 45 D.C.Code § 908 (1967) expressly permits waiver of this notice. Appellants' answer put in issue the validity of the waivers. In view of our disposition, we have no occasion to pass upon this aspect of the case.

3. Rule 4(c) of the Landlord and Tenant Branch of the Court of General Sessions provides: "In suits in this branch for recovery of possession of property in which the basis of recovery of possession is nonpayment of rent, tenants may set up an equitable defense or claim by way of recoupment or set-off in an amount equal to the rent claim. No counterclaim may be filed unless plaintiff asks for money judgment for rent. The exclusion of prosecution of any claims in this branch shall be without prejudice to the prosecution of any claims in other branches of the court." Appellants have sought only to defeat the landlord's action; they have not as yet claimed any money damages for the landlord's alleged breach of contract. Under Rule 4(c) supra, they may not counterclaim for money damages if the landlord seeks only possession and no money judgment, as it has done here. For the considerations to be applied in determining whether this rule conforms "as nearly as may be practicable" to the Federal Rules of Civil Procedure as required by 13 D.C.Code § 101 (1967). See McKelton v. Bruno, 138 U.S.App.D.C. 366, 428 F.2d 718 (decided February 17, 1970).

4. According to established procedure, this case was submitted to both the District of Columbia Court of Appeals and this court on the basis of a sparse "Settled Statement of Proceedings and Evidence," as approved by both parties and the trial judge. Unfortunately, the court's ruling on the offer of proof was made from the bench, and the basis of the ruling is not reflected in the "Settled Statement." We have recently noted the inadequacy of such records for review by an appellate court. Lee v. Habib, 137 U.S.App.D.C. 403, 424 F.2d 891 (1970).

landlord was under a contractual duty to maintain the premises in compliance with the Housing Regulations. Saunders v. First National Realty Corp., supra, 245 A.2d at 838.[5]

II.

Since, in traditional analysis, a lease was the conveyance of an interest in land, courts have usually utilized the special rules governing real property transactions to resolve controversies involving leases. However, as the Supreme Court has noted in another context, "the body of private property law . . ., more than almost any other branch of law, has been shaped by distinctions whose validity is largely historical."[6] Courts have a duty to reappraise old doctrines in the light of the facts and values of contemporary life—particularly old common law doctrines which the courts themselves created and developed.[7] As we have said before, "[T]he continued vitality of the common law . . . depends upon its ability to reflect contemporary community values and ethics."[8]

The assumption of landlord-tenant law, derived from feudal property law, that a lease primarily conveyed to the tenant an interest in land may have been reasonable in a rural, agrarian society; it may continue to be reasonable in some leases involving farming or commercial land. In these cases, the value of the lease to the tenant is the land itself. But in the case of the modern apartment dweller, the value of the lease is that it gives him a place to live. The city dweller who seeks to lease an apartment on the third floor of a tenement has little interest in the land 30 or 40 feet below, or even in the bare right to possession within the four walls of his apartment. When American city dwellers, both rich and poor, seek "shelter" today, they seek a well known package of goods and services[9]—a package which includes not merely walls and ceilings, but also adequate heat, light and ventilation, serviceable plumbing facilities, secure windows and doors, proper sanitation, and proper maintenance.

Professor Powell summarizes the present state of the law: ". . . The complexities of city life, and the proliferated problems of modern society in general, have created new problems for lessors and lessees and these have been commonly handled by specific clauses inserted in

5. In the District of Columbia Court of Appeals, appellee urged that these cases were moot on the basis of events occurring since the landlord initiated this litigation. The D.C. Court of Appeals held that the cases were not moot. Saunders v. First National Realty Co., 245 A.2d 836, 837 (1968). Appellee has not argued mootness here, and in any event we follow the ruling of the D.C. Court of Appeals on this point.

6. Jones v. United States, 362 U.S. 257, 266, 80 S.Ct. 725, 733, 4 L.Ed.2d 697 (1960).

7. See Spencer v. General Hospital of the District of Columbia, 138 U.S.App.D.C. 48, 53, 425 F.2d 479, 484 (1969) (*en banc*); Schipper v. Levitt & Sons, Inc., 44 N.J. 70, 90, 207 A.2d 314, 325 (1965). Cf. 11 S. Williston Contracts § 1393A at 461 (3d ed. W. Jaeger 1968) ("Most of the leading jurisdictions have not hesitated to undo a judicially committed blunder . . . by employing the same means—judicial decisions") and cases cited therein at n. 20.

8. Whetzel v. Jess Fisher Management Co., 108 U.S.App.D.C. 385, 388, 282 F.2d 943, 946 (1960).

9. See, e.g., National Commission on Urban Problems, Building the American City 9 (1968). The extensive standards set out in the Housing Regulations provide a good guide to community expectations.

leases. This growth in the number and detail of specific lease covenants has reintroduced into the law of estates for years a predominantly contractual ingredient. In practice, the law today concerning estates for years consists chiefly of rules determining the construction and effect of lease covenants. . . ." [10] Ironically, however, the rules governing the construction and interpretation of "predominantly contractual" obligations in leases have too often remained rooted in old property law.

Some courts have realized that certain of the old rules of property law governing leases are inappropriate for today's transactions. In order to reach results more in accord with the legitimate expectations of the parties and the standards of the community, courts have been gradually introducing more modern precepts of contract law in interpreting leases.[11] Proceeding piecemeal has, however, led to confusion where "decisions are frequently conflicting, not because of a healthy disagreement on social policy, but because of the lingering impact of rules whose policies are long since dead." [12]

In our judgment the trend toward treating leases as contracts is wise and well considered. Our holding in this case reflects a belief that leases of urban dwelling units should be interpreted and construed like any other contract.[13]

III.

Modern contract law has recognized that the buyer of goods and services in an industrialized society must rely upon the skill and honesty of the supplier to assure that goods and services purchased are of adequate quality.[14] In interpreting most contracts, courts have sought to protect the legitimate expectations of the buyer and have steadily widened the seller's responsibility for the quality of goods and services through implied warranties of fitness and merchantability.[15]

10. 2 R. Powell, Real Property ¶ 221[1] at 179 (1967).

11. E.g., Medico-Dental Building Co. v. Horton & Converse, 21 Cal.2d 411, 418, 132 P.2d 457, 462 (1942). See also 1 American Law of Property § 3.11 at 202–205 (A. Casner ed. 1952); Note, The California Lease—Contract or Conveyance?, 4 Stan.L. Rev. 244 (1952); Friedman, The Nature of a Lease in New York, 33 Cornell L.Q. 165 (1947).

12. Kessler, The Protection of the Consumer Under Modern Sales Law, 74 Yale L.J. 262, 263 (1964).

13. This approach does not deny the possible importance of the fact that land is involved in a transaction. The interpretation and construction of contracts between private parties has always required courts to be sensitive and responsive to myriad different factors. We believe contract doctrines allow courts to be properly sensitive to all relevant factors in interpreting lease obligations.

We also intend no alteration of statutory or case law definitions of the term "real property" for purposes of statutes or decisions on recordation, descent, conveyancing, creditors' rights, etc. We contemplate only that contract law is to determine the rights and obligations of the parties to the lease agreement, as between themselves. The civil law has always viewed the lease as a contract, and in our judgment that perspective has proved superior to that of the common law. See 2 M. Planiol, Treatise on the Civil Law § 1663 et seq. (1959); 11 La.Stat.Ann., Civil Code, Art. 2669 (1952).

14. See generally 8 S. Williston, Contracts §§ 983–989 (3d ed. W. Jaeger 1964); W. Prosser, Torts § 95 (3d ed. 1964).

15. See Jaeger, Warranties of Merchantability and Fitness for Use, 16 Rutgers L.Rev. 493 (1962); Uniform Commercial Code §§ 2–314, 2–315 (1968).

Thus without any special agreement a merchant will be held to warrant that his goods are fit for the ordinary purposes for which such goods are used and that they are at least of reasonably average quality. Moreover, if the supplier has been notified that goods are required for a specific purpose, he will be held to warrant that any goods sold are fit for that purpose. These implied warranties have become widely accepted and well established features of the common law, supported by the overwhelming body of case law.[16] Today most states as well as the District of Columbia [17] have codified and enacted these warranties into statute, as to the sale of goods, in the Uniform Commercial Code.

Implied warranties of quality have not been limited to cases involving sales. The consumer renting a chattel, paying for services, or buying a combination of goods and services must rely upon the skill and honesty of the supplier to at least the same extent as a purchaser of goods. Courts have not hesitated to find implied warranties of fitness and merchantability in such situations.[18] In most areas product liability law has moved far beyond "mere" implied warranties running between two parties in privity with each other.[19]

The rigid doctrines of real property law have tended to inhibit the application of implied warranties to transactions involving real estate.[20] Now, however, courts have begun to hold sellers and developers of real property responsible for the quality of their products.[21] For example, builders of new homes have recently been held liable to purchasers for improper construction on the ground that the builders had breached an implied warranty of fitness.[22] In other cases courts have held builders of new homes liable for breach of an implied warranty that all local building regulations had been complied with.[23] And following the developments in other areas, very recent decisions [24] and commentary [25]

16. Ibid.

17. 28 D.C.Code Subtitle I (1967).

18. Farnsworth, Implied Warranties of Quality in Non-Sales Cases, 57 Colum.L. Rev. 653 (1957). See Cintrone v. Hertz Truck Leasing & Rental Service, 45 N.J. 434, 212 A.2d 769 (1965); 2 F. Harper & F. James, Torts § 28.19 at 1577, n. 5 and n. 6 (1956).

19. See, e.g., Henningsen v. Bloomfield Motors, Inc., 32 N.J. 358, 161 A.2d 69 (1960); Goldberg v. Kollsman Instrument Corp., 12 N.Y.2d 432, 240 N.Y.S.2d 592, 191 N.E.2d 81 (1963). See generally Prosser, The Assault Upon the Citadel (Strict Liability to the Consumer), 69 Yale L.J. 1099 (1960); Jaeger, Product Liability: The Constructive Warranty, 39 Notre Dame Lawyer 501 (1964).

20. See Fegeas v. Sherill, 218 Md. 472, 147 A.2d 223 (1958); 7 S. Williston, Contracts § 926 at 800–801, § 926A (3d ed. W. Jaeger 1963).

21. See generally Bearman, Caveat Emptor in Sale of Realty—Recent Assaults Upon the Rule, 14 Vand.L.Rev. 541 (1961); Dunham, Vendor's Obligation as to Fitness of Land for a Particular Purpose, 37 Minn. L.Rev. 108 (1953).

22. See Waggoner v. Midwestern Development, Inc., S.D., 154 N.W.2d 803 (1967); Bethlahmy v. Bechtel, 91 Idaho 55, 415 P.2d 698 (1969); Schipper v. Levitt & Sons, Inc., supra, note 7; Carpenter v. Donohoe, 154 Colo. 78, 388 P.2d 399 (1964); Loraso v. Custom Built Homes, Inc., La.App., 144 So. 2d 459 (1962). Other cases still continue the older limitation on the vendor's liability to homes sold before construction is complete. See e.g., Hoye v. Century Builders, 52 Wash.2d 830, 329 P.2d 474 (1958).

23. See Schiro v. W.E. Gould & Co., 18 Ill.2d 538, 165 N.E.2d 286 (1960); Annot., 110 A.L.R. 1048 (1937).

24. Connor v. Great Western Savings and Loan Ass'n, 69 Cal.2d 850, 73 Cal.Rptr. 369, 447 P.2d 609 (1968) (in bank) (Traynor, Ch. J.). Chief Justice Traynor's excellent opinion utilizes tort doctrines to extend liability beyond the immediate seller.

25. Comment, Liability of the Institutional Lender for Structural Defects in New Housing, 35 U.Chi.L.Rev. 739 (1968).

suggest the possible extension of liability to parties other than the immediate seller for improper construction of residential real estate.

Despite this trend in the sale of real estate, many courts have been unwilling to imply warranties of quality, specifically a warranty of habitability into leases of apartments. Recent decisions have offered no convincing explanation for their refusal [26]; rather they have relied without discussion upon the old common law rule that the lessor is not obligated to repair unless he covenants to do so in the written lease contract.[27] However, the Supreme Courts of at least two states, in recent and well reasoned opinions, have held landlords to implied warranties of quality in housing leases. Lemle v. Breeden, S.Ct. Hawaii, 462 P.2d 470 (1969); Reste Realty Corp. v. Cooper, 53 N.J. 444, 251 A.2d 268 (1969). See also Pines v. Perssion, 14 Wis.2d 590, 111 N.W.2d 409 (1961). In our judgment, the old no-repair rule cannot coexist with the obligations imposed on the landlord by a typical modern housing code, and must be abandoned [28] in favor of an implied warranty of habitability.[29] In the District of Columbia, the standards of this warranty are set out in the Housing Regulations.

IV.

A. In our judgment the common law itself must recognize the landlord's obligation to keep his premises in a habitable condition. This conclusion is compelled by three separate considerations. First, we believe that the old rule was based on certain factual assumptions which are no longer true; on its own terms, it can no longer be justified. Second, we believe that the consumer protection cases discussed above require that the old rule be abandoned in order to bring residential landlord-tenant law into harmony with the principles on which those cases rest. Third, we think that the nature of today's urban housing market also dictates abandonment of the old rule.

The common law rule absolving the lessor of all obligation to repair originated in the early Middle Ages.[30] Such a rule was perhaps well suited to an agrarian economy; the land was more important [31] than whatever small living structure was included in the leasehold, and the

26. E.g., Kearse v. Spaulding, 406 Pa. 140, 176 A.2d 450 (1962); Susskind v. 1136 Tenants Corp., 43 Misc.2d 588, 251 N.Y.S.2d 321 (1964); Rubinger v. Del Monte, N.Y.S.Ct., App.T., 217 N.Y.S.2d 792 (1961).

27. The cases which recite this old rule are legion. A representative sampling is cited in 32 Am.Jur. Landlord and Tenant § 655 n. 14 (1941).

28. As far as tort liability is concerned, we have previously held that the old common law rule has been changed by passage of the housing code and that the landlord has a duty to maintain reasonably safe premises. See note 52, infra.

29. Although the present cases involve written leases, we think there is no particular significance in this fact. The landlord's warranty is implied in oral and written leases for all types of tenancies.

30. The rule was "settled" by 1485. 3 W. Holdsworth, A History of English Law 122–123 (6th ed. 1934). The common law rule discussed in text originated in the even older rule prohibiting the tenant from committing waste. The writ of waste expanded as the tenant's right to possession grew stronger. Eventually, in order to protect the landowner's reversionary interest, the tenant became obligated to make repairs and liable to eviction and damages if he failed to do so. Ibid.

31. The land was so central to the original common law conception of a leasehold that rent was viewed as "issuing" from the land: "[T]he governing idea is that the land is bound to pay the rent . . .. We

tenant farmer was fully capable of making repairs himself.[32] These historical facts were the basis on which the common law constructed its rule; they also provided the necessary prerequisites for its application.[33]

Court decisions in the late 1800's began to recognize that the factual assumptions of the common law were no longer accurate in some cases. For example, the common law, since it assumed that the land was the most important part of the leasehold, required a tenant to pay rent even if any building on the land was destroyed.[34] Faced with such a rule and the ludicrous results it produced, in 1863 the New York Court of Appeals declined to hold that an upper story tenant was obliged to continue paying rent after his apartment building burned down.[35] The court simply pointed out that the urban tenant had no interest in the land, only in the attached building.

Another line of cases created an exception to the no-repair rule for short term leases of furnished dwellings.[36] The Massachusetts Supreme Judicial Court, a court not known for its willingness to depart from the common law, supported this exception, pointing out: ". . . [A] different rule should apply to one who hires a furnished room, or a furnished house, for a few days, or a few weeks or months. Its fitness for immediate use of a particular kind, as indicated by its appointments, is a far more important element entering into the contract than when there is a mere lease of real estate. One who lets for a short term a house provided with all furnishings and appointments for immediate residence may be supposed to contract in reference to a well-understood purpose of the hirer to use it as a habitation. . . . It would be unreasonable to hold, under such circumstances, that the landlord does not impliedly agree that what he is letting is a house suitable for occupation in its condition at the time. . . ." [37]

may almost go to the length of saying that the land pays it through [the tenant's] hand." 2 F. Pollock & F. Maitland, The History of English Law 131 (2d ed. 1923).

32. Many later judicial opinions have added another justification of the old common law rule. They have invoked the time-worn cry of caveat emptor and argued that a lessee has the opportunity to inspect the premises. On the basis of his inspection, the tenant must then take the premises "as is," according to this reasoning. As an historical matter, the opportunity to inspect was not thought important when the rule was first devised. See note 30, supra. To the extent the no-repair rule rests on caveat emptor, see page 453, infra.

33. Even the old common law courts responded with a different rule for a landlord-tenant relationship which did not conform to the model of the usual agrarian lease. Much more substantial obligations were placed upon the keepers of inns (the only multiple dwelling houses known to the common law). Their guests were interested solely in shelter and could not be expected to make their own repairs. "The modern apartment dweller more closely resembles the guest in an inn than he resembles an agrarian tenant, but the law has not generally recognized the similarity." J. Levi, P. Hablutzel, L. Rosenberg & J. White, Model Residential Landlord-Tenant Code 6–7 (Tent.Draft 1969).

34. Paradine v. Jane, Aleyn 26, 82 Eng. Rep. 897 (K.B.1947); 1 American Law of Property, supra, note 11, § 3.103.

35. Graves v. Berdan, 26 N.Y. 498 (1863).

36. 1 American Law of Property, supra, note 11, § 3.45 at 267–268, and cases cited therein.

37. Ingalls v. Hobbs, 156 Mass. 348, 31 N.E. 286 (1892).

These as well as other similar cases [38] demonstrate that some courts began sometime ago to question the common law's assumptions that the land was the most important feature of a leasehold and that the tenant could feasibly make any necessary repairs himself. Where those assumptions no longer reflect contemporary housing patterns, the courts have created exceptions to the general rule that landlords have no duty to keep their premises in repair.

It is overdue for courts to admit that these assumptions are no longer true with regard to all urban housing. Today's urban [39] tenants, the vast majority of whom live in multiple dwelling houses, are interested, not in the land, but solely in "a house suitable for occupation." Furthermore, today's city dweller usually has a single, specialized skill unrelated to maintenance work; he is unable to make repairs like the "jack-of-all-trades" farmer who was the common law's model of the lessee.[40] Further, unlike his agrarian predecessor who often remained on one piece of land for his entire life, urban tenants today are more mobile than ever before. A tenant's tenure in a specific apartment will often not be sufficient to justify efforts at repairs. In addition, the increasing complexity of today's dwellings renders them much more difficult to repair than the structures of earlier times. In a multiple dwelling repair may require access to equipment and areas in the control of the landlord. Low and middle income tenants, even if they were interested in making repairs, would be unable to obtain any financing for major repairs since they have no long-term interest in the property.

Our approach to the common law of landlord and tenant ought to be aided by principles derived from the consumer protection cases referred to above.[41] In a lease contract, a tenant seeks to purchase from his landlord shelter for a specified period of time. The landlord sells housing as a commercial businessman and has much greater opportunity, incentive and capacity to inspect and maintain the condition of his building. Moreover, the tenant must rely upon the skill and *bona fides* of his landlord at least as much as a car buyer must rely upon the car manufacturer. In dealing with major problems, such as heating, plumbing, electrical or structural defects, the tenant's position corresponds precisely with "the ordinary consumer who cannot be expected to have the knowledge or capacity or even the opportunity to make adequate inspection of mechanical instrumentalities, like automobiles, and to decide for himself whether they are reasonably fit for the

38. The cases developing the doctrines of "quiet enjoyment" and "constructive eviction" are the most important. See 2 R. Powell, supra, note 10, ¶ 225[3]. See also Gladden v. Walker & Dunlop, 83 U.S.App. D.C. 224, 168 F.2d 321 (1948) (landlord has duty to maintain portions of apartment "under his control" including plumbing, heating and electrical systems); J.D. Young Corp. v. McClintic, Tex.Civ.App., 26 S.W.2d 460 (1930) (implied covenant of fitness in lease of building under construction); Steefel v. Rothschild, 179 N.Y. 273, 72 N.E. 112 (1904) (duty to disclose latent defects).

39. In 1968 more than two thirds of America's people lived in the 228 largest metropolitan areas. Only 5.2% lived on farms. The World Almanac 1970 at 251 (L. Long ed.). More than 98% of all housing starts in 1968 were non-farm. Id. at 313.

40. See J. Levi et al., supra, note 33, at 6.

41. See Part III, supra.

designed purpose." Henningsen v. Bloomfield Motors, Inc., 32 N.J. 358, 375, 161 A.2d 69, 78 (1960).[42]

Since a lease contract specifies a particular period of time during which the tenant has a right to use his apartment for shelter, he may legitimately expect that the apartment will be fit for habitation for the time period for which it is rented. We point out that in the present cases there is no allegation that appellants' apartments were in poor condition or in violation of the housing code at the commencement of the leases.[43] Since the lessees continue to pay the same rent, they were entitled to expect that the landlord would continue to keep the premises in their beginning condition during the lease term. It is precisely such expectations that the law now recognizes as deserving of formal, legal protection.

Even beyond the rationale of traditional products liability law, the relationship of landlord and tenant suggests further compelling reasons for the law's protection of the tenants' legitimate expectations of quality. The inequality in bargaining power between landlord and tenant has been well documented.[44] Tenants have very little leverage to enforce demands for better housing. Various impediments to competition in the rental housing market, such as racial and class discrimination [45] and standardized form leases,[46] mean that landlords place tenants in a take it or leave it situation. The increasingly severe shortage [47] of adequate housing further increases the landlord's bargaining power and escalates the need for maintaining and improving the existing stock. Finally, the findings by various studies of the social impact of bad housing has led to the realization that poor housing is detrimental to the whole society, not merely to the unlucky ones who must suffer the daily indignity of living in a slum.[48]

Thus we are led by our inspection of the relevant legal principles and precedents to the conclusion that the old common law rule imposing an obligation upon the lessee to repair during the lease term was really never intended to apply to residential urban leaseholds. Contract principles established in other areas of the law provide a more rational framework for the apportionment of landlord-tenant responsi-

42. Nor should the average tenant be thought capable of "inspecting" plaster, floorboards, roofing, kitchen appliances, etc. To the extent, however, that some defects *are* obvious, the law must take note of the present housing shortage. Tenants may have no real alternative but to accept such housing with the expectation that the landlord will make necessary repairs. Where this is so, caveat emptor must of necessity be rejected.

43. In Brown v. Southall Realty Co., 237 A.2d 834 (1968), the District of Columbia Court of Appeals held that unsafe and unsanitary conditions existing at the beginning of the tenancy and known to the landlord rendered any lease of those premises illegal and void.

44. See Edwards v. Habib, 130 U.S.App. D.C. 126, 140, 397 F.2d 687, 701 (1968); 2 R. Powell, supra, note 10, ¶ 221[1] at 183; President's Committee on Urban Housing, A Decent Home 96 (1968).

45. President's Committee, supra, note 44, at 96; National Commission, supra, note 9, at 18–19; G. Sternlieb, The Tenement Landlord 71 (1966).

46. R. Powell, supra, note 10, ¶ 221[1], at 183, n. 13.

47. See generally President's Committee, supra, note 44.

48. A. Schorr, Slums and Insecurity (1963); J. Levi, et al., supra, note 33, at 7–8.

bilities; they strongly suggest that a warranty of habitability be implied into all contracts [49] for urban dwellings.

B. We believe, in any event that the District's housing code requires that a warranty of habitability be implied in the leases of all housing that it covers. The housing code—formally designated the Housing Regulations of the District of Columbia—was established and authorized by the Commissioners of the District of Columbia on August 11, 1955.[50] Since that time, the code has been updated by numerous orders of the Commissioners. The 75 pages of the Regulations provide a comprehensive regulatory scheme setting forth in some detail: (a) the standards which housing in the District of Columbia must meet; [51] (b) which party, the lessor or the lessee, must meet each standard; and (c) a system of inspections, notifications and criminal penalties. The Regulations themselves are silent on the question of private remedies.

Two previous decisions of this court, however, have held that the Housing Regulations create legal rights and duties enforceable in tort by private parties. In Whetzel v. Jess Fisher Management Co., 108 U.S.App.D.C. 385, 282 F.2d 943 (1960), we followed the leading case of Altz v. Lieberson, 233 N.Y. 16, 134 N.E. 703 (1922), in holding (1) that the housing code altered the common law rule and imposed a duty to repair upon the landlord, and (2) that a right of action accrued to a tenant injured by the landlord's breach of this duty. As Judge Cardozo wrote in Lieberson: ". . . We may be sure that the framers of this statute, when regulating tenement life, had uppermost in thought the care of those who are unable to care for themselves. The Legislature must have known that unless repairs in the rooms of the poor were made by the landlord, they would not be made by any one. The duty imposed became commensurate with the need. The right to seek redress is not limited to the city or its officers. The right extends to all whom there was a purpose to protect. . . ." 134 N.E. at 704. Recently, in Kanelos v. Kettler, 132 U.S.App.D.C. 133, 135, 406 F.2d 951, 953 (1968), we reaffirmed our position in Whetzel, holding that "the Housing Regulations did impose maintenance obligations upon appellee [landlord] which he was not free to ignore." [52]

The District of Columbia Court of Appeals gave further effect to the Housing Regulations in Brown v. Southall Realty Co., 237 A.2d 834 (1968). There the landlord knew at the time the lease was signed that housing code violations existed which rendered the apartment "unsafe and unsanitary." Viewing the lease as a contract, the District of Columbia Court of Appeals held that the premises were let in violation

49. We need not consider the provisions of the written lease governing repairs since this implied warranty of the landlord could not be excluded. See Henningsen v. Bloomfield Motors, Inc., supra, note 19; Kay v. Cain, 81 U.S.App.D.C. 24, 25, 154 F.2d 305, 306 (1946). See also note 58, infra.

50. 2 D.C.Register 47 (1955).

51. These include standards for nursing homes and other similar institutions. The full scheme of the Regulations is set out in Whetzel v. Fisher Management Co., supra, note 8.

52. Kanelos and Whetzel have effectively overruled, on the basis of the enactment of the housing code, Bowles v. Mahoney, 91 U.S.App.D.C. 155, 202 F.2d 320 (1952) (two to one decision, Judge Bazelon dissenting).

of Sections 2304[53] and 2501[54] of the Regulations and that the lease, therefore, was void as an illegal contract. In the light of Brown, it is clear not only that the housing code creates privately enforceable duties as held in Whetzel, but that the basic validity of every housing contract depends upon substantial compliance with the housing code at the beginning of the lease term. The Brown court relied particularly upon Section 2501 of the Regulations which provides: "Every premises accommodating one or more habitations shall be maintained and kept in repair so as to provide decent living accommodations for the occupants. This part of this Code contemplates more than mere basic repairs and maintenance to keep out the elements; its purpose is to include repairs and maintenance designed to make a premises or neighborhood healthy and safe."

By its terms, this section applies to maintenance and repair during the lease term. Under the Brown holding, serious failure to comply with this section before the lease term begins renders the contract void. We think it untenable to find that this section has no effect on the contract after it has been signed. To the contrary, by signing the lease the landlord has undertaken a continuing obligation to the tenant to maintain the premises in accordance with all applicable law.

This principle of implied warranty is well established. Courts often imply relevant law into contracts to provide a remedy for any damage caused by one party's illegal conduct.[55] In a case closely analogous to the present ones, the Illinois Supreme Court held that a builder who constructed a house in violation of the Chicago building code had breached his contract with the buyer: ". . . [T]he law existing at the time and place of the making of the contract is deemed a part of the contract, as though expressly referred to or incorporated in it. . . .

"The rationale for this rule is that the parties to the contract would have expressed that which the law implies 'had they not supposed that it was unnecessary to speak of it because the law provided for it.' . . . Consequently, the courts, in construing the existing law as part of the express contract, are not reading into the contract provisions different from those expressed and intended by the parties, as defendants contend, but are merely construing the contract in accordance with the intent of the parties."[56]

(Principle of implied warranty)

53. "No person shall rent or offer to rent any habitation, or the furnishings thereof, unless such habitation and its furnishings are in a clean, safe and sanitary condition, in repair, and free from rodents or vermin."

54. See infra.

55. See cases cited in Annot., 110 A.L.R. 1048 (1937).

56. Schiro v. W.E. Gould & Co., supra Note 23, 18 Ill.2d at 544, 165 N.E.2d at 290. As a general proposition, it is undoubtedly true that parties to a contract intend that applicable law will be complied with by both sides. We recognize, however, that reading statutory provisions into private contracts may have little factual support in the intentions of the particular parties now before us. But, for reasons of public policy, warranties are often implied into contracts by operation of law in order to meet generally prevailing standards of honesty and fair dealing. When the public policy has been enacted into law like the housing code, that policy will usually have deep roots in the expectations and intentions of most people. See Costigan, Implied-in-Fact Contracts and Mutual Assent, 33 Harv.L.Rev. 376, 383–385 (1920).

We follow the Illinois court in holding that the housing code must be read into housing contracts—a holding also required by the purposes and the structure of the code itself.[57] The duties imposed by the Housing Regulations may not be waived or shifted by agreement if the Regulations specifically place the duty upon the lessor.[58] Criminal penalties are provided if these duties are ignored. This regulatory structure was established by the Commissioners because, in their judgment, the grave conditions in the housing market required serious action. Yet official enforcement of the housing code has been far from uniformly effective.[59] Innumerable studies have documented the desperate condition of rental housing in the District of Columbia and in the nation. In view of these circumstances, we think the conclusion reached by the Supreme Court of Wisconsin as to the effect of a housing code on the old common law rule cannot be avoided: ". . . [T]he legislature has made a policy judgment—that it is socially (and politically) desirable to impose these duties on a property owner—which has rendered the old common law rule obsolete. To follow the old rule of no implied warranty of habitability in leases would, in our opinion, be inconsistent with the current legislative policy concerning housing standards. . . ."[60]

We therefore hold that the Housing Regulations imply a warranty of habitability measured by the standards which they set out, into leases of all housing that they cover.

V.

In the present cases, the landlord sued for possession for nonpayment of rent. Under contract principles,[61] however, the tenant's obligation to pay rent is dependent upon the landlord's performance of his obligations, including his warranty to maintain the premises in habitable condition. In order to determine whether any rent is owed to the landlord, the tenants must be given an opportunity to prove the housing code violations alleged as breach of the landlord's warranty.[62]

57. "The housing and sanitary codes, especially in light of Congress' explicit direction for their enactment, indicate a strong and pervasive congressional concern to secure for the city's slum dwellers, decent, or at least safe and sanitary, places to live." Edwards v. Habib, supra, note 44, 130 U.S.App.D.C. at 139, 397 F.2d at 700.

58. Any private agreement to shift the duties would be illegal and unenforceable. The precedents dealing with industrial safety statutes are directly in point: ". . . [T]he only question remaining is whether the courts will enforce or recognize as against a servant an agreement express or implied on his part to waive the performance of a statutory duty of the master imposed for the protection of the servant, and in the interest of the public, and enforceable by criminal prosecution. We do not think they will. To do so would be to nullify the object of the statute. . . ." Narramore v. Cleveland, C., C. & St. L. Ry. Co., 6 Cir., 96 F. 298, 302 (1899). See W. Prosser, Torts § 67 at 468–469 (3d ed. 1964) and cases cited therein.

59. See Gribetz & Grad, Housing Code Enforcement: Sanctions and Remedies, 66 Colum.L.Rev. 1254 (1966); Note, Enforcement of Municipal Housing Codes, 78 Harv.L.Rev. 801 (1965).

60. Pines v. Perssion, 14 Wis.2d 590, 596, 111 N.W.2d 409, 412–413 (1961). Accord, Buckner v. Azulai, 251 Cal.App.2d Supp. 1013, 59 Cal.Rptr. 806 (1967).

61. In extending all contract remedies for breach to the parties to a lease, we include an action for specific performance of the landlord's implied warranty of habitability.

62. To be relevant, of course, the violations must affect the tenant's apartment or common areas which the tenant uses.

At trial, the finder of fact must make two findings: (1) whether the alleged violations[63] existed during the period for which past due rent is claimed, and (2) what portion, if any or all, of the tenant's obligation to pay rent was suspended by the landlord's breach. If no part of the tenant's rental obligation is found to have been suspended, then a judgment for possession may issue forthwith. On the other hand, if the jury determines that the entire rental obligation has been extinguished by the landlord's total breach, then the action for possession on the ground of nonpayment must fail.[64]

The jury may find that part of the tenant's rental obligation has been suspended but that part of the unpaid back rent is indeed owed to the landlord.[65] In these circumstances, no judgment for possession should issue if the tenant agrees to pay the partial rent found to be due.[66] If the tenant refuses to pay the partial amount, a judgment for possession may then be entered.

The judgment of the District of Columbia Court of Appeals is reversed and the cases are remanded for further proceedings consistent with this opinion.[67]

Moreover, the contract principle that no one may benefit from his own wrong will allow the landlord to defend by proving the damage was caused by the tenant's wrongful action. However, violations resulting from inadequate repairs or materials which disintegrate under normal use would not be assignable to the tenant. Also we agree with the District of Columbia Court of Appeals that the tenant's private rights do not depend on official inspection or official finding of violation by the city government. Diamond Housing Corp. v. Robinson, 257 A.2d 492, 494 (1969).

63. The jury should be instructed that one or two minor violations standing alone which do not affect habitability are de minimis and would not entitle the tenant to a reduction in rent.

64. As soon as the landlord made the necessary repairs rent would again become due. Our holding, of course, affects only eviction for nonpayment of rent. The landlord is free to seek eviction at the termination of the lease or on any other legal ground.

65. In George Y. Worthington & Son Management Corp. v. Levy, 204 A.2d 334, 336 (1964), the District of Columbia Court of Appeals approved a similar procedure: "In actions for possession of real property by reason of default in rent, where no money judgment for the back rent is sought, it is nevertheless proper practice for the trial court to specifically find the amount of rent in arrears. . . ."

66. Compare Molyneaux v. Town House, Inc., D.C.C.A., 195 A.2d 744 (1963). A jury finding that the landlord had failed to live up to all of his obligations would operate as a conclusive finding that the tenant was entitled to equitable relief under Molyneaux.

67. Appellants in the present cases offered to pay rent into the registry of the court during the present action. We think this is an excellent protective procedure. If the tenant defends against an action for possession on the basis of breach of the landlord's warranty of habitability, the trial court may require the tenant to make future rent payments into the registry of the court as they become due; such a procedure would be appropriate only while the tenant remains in possession. The escrowed money will, however, represent rent for the period between the time the landlord files suit and the time the case comes to trial. In the normal course of litigation, the only factual question at trial would be the condition of the apartment during the time the landlord alleged rent was due and not paid.

As a general rule, the escrowed money should be apportioned between the landlord and the tenant after trial on the basis of the finding of rent actually due for the period at issue in the suit. To insure fair apportionment, however, we think either party should be permitted to amend its complaint or answer at any time before trial, to allege a change in the condition of the apartment. In this event the finder of fact should make a separate finding as to the condition of the apartment at the time at which the amendment was filed. This new finding will have no effect upon the original action; it will only affect the distribution of the escrowed rent paid after the filing of the amendment.

NOTES

1. Contrast the position of the court in Miles v. Shauntee, 664 S.W.2d 512 (Ky.1983):

> Appellants argue that an implied warranty of habitability should arise from local housing or health codes absent an express provision in the contract of lease and absent such a provision in the ordinance or regulation in question. Absent an expression to the contrary such provisions do not create an implied warranty of habitability, or create a cause of action in the tenants. The remedies for violations are found within the codes, ordinances or regulations themselves. It is for the legislature to create rights and duties nonexistent under the common law. Absent legislation to the contrary the established doctrine in effect in Kentucky is that the tenant takes possession of the premises as he first finds them, and the landlord, absent an express covenant to the contrary, has no obligation to repair the premises. . . . No implied warranty of habitability exists under Kentucky Law.

2. With remarkable haste, since Javins, courts and legislatures have rushed to read into residential leases an implied warranty of habitability, or its equivalent. By legislation, court decision, or a combination of both, over forty states have taken this step. This development is thoroughly surveyed and analyzed in Cunningham, The New Implied and Statutory Warranties of Habitability in Residential Leases: From Contract to Status, 16 Urban L.Ann. 3 (1979). Professor Cunningham reports that legislation generally falls into three categories:

"(1) Statutes that, without expressly creating any new rights, build on existing housing codes by detailing new tenant-initiated private remedies for the landlord's failure to provide a habitable dwelling.

(2) Statutes that expressly impose a new duty on landlords to provide tenants with a habitable dwelling, usually stated in terms of a 'warranty' or 'covenant' of habitability, but without describing any duty or remedy in detail.

(3) Statutes that detail both the landlord's duty to provide a habitable dwelling and the tenants' remedies for breach. All but one of these statutes are embodied in comprehensive new codes of landlord-tenant law, and most of them are similar—though not identical—because based on either the Uniform Residential Landlord and Tenant Act (URLTA) or the Model Residential Landlord-Tenant Code."

URLTA and the Model Code provisions on this matter are summarized by Professor Cunningham at pages 66–74 of his article.

Is legislative or judicial action on this issue preferable?

3. If a jurisdiction implies a warranty of fitness for use in the sale of a new house, is the implication of a warranty of habitability in residential leases logically inescapable? See Young v. Morrisey, 285 S.C. 236, 329 S.E.2d 426 (1985).

4. What objections, if any might reasonably be made to a court order requiring a tenant resisting landlord's suit for recovery of possession to pay into the registry of the court the full rent accruing during the litigation? Should it be relevant that tenant's defense is apparently meritorious? Or that tenant had expended substantial sums for repairs? Or that tenant's financial condition had deteriorated greatly? Or that landlord's financial condition is not precarious? Consult Bell v. Tsintolas Realty Corp., 139 U.S.App.D.C. 101, 430 F.2d 474 (1970).

If tenant fails to comply with an order to pay accruing rent into the registry of the court pending litigation, is landlord entitled to judgment awarding him possession? Such a judgment was approved in Davis v. Rental Associates, Inc., 456 A.2d 820 (D.C.App.1983).

5. Should a warranty of habitability be implied in a lease of a dwelling unit of a public housing project? No—according to Alexander v. United States Department of Housing and Urban Development, 555 F.2d 166 (7th Cir.1977), affirmed on other grounds 441 U.S. 39, 99 S.Ct. 1572, 60 L.Ed.2d 28 (1979), the court declaring: "In contrast to housing projects in the private sector, the construction and operation of public housing are projects established to effectuate a stated national policy 'to remedy the unsafe and insanitary housing conditions and the acute shortage of decent, safe, and sanitary dwellings for families of low income'. 42 U.S.C.A. § 1401. As such, the implication of a warranty of habitability in leases pertaining to public housing units is a warranty that the stated objectives of national policy have been and are being met. We feel that the establishment of any such warranty that national policy goals have been attained or that those goals are being maintained is best left to that branch of government which established the objectives."

Accord: Perry v. Housing Authority of Charleston, 664 F.2d 1210 (4th Cir.1981), which also rejected other claims by tenants of public housing for relief from an alleged state of disrepair posing major hazards to their health, safety and welfare.

Support for the contrary position is found in Note, 19 B.C.L.Rev. 343 (1978) ("The implication of a warranty of habitability is not a guarantee that federal housing policy goals are being met . . . .") and Boston Housing Authority v. Hemingway, 363 Mass. 184, 293 N.E.2d 831 (1973).

6. Recognition of implied warranty of habitability by the American Law Institute in its Restatement of the Law (Second) of Property, Landlord and Tenant (1977), is qualified by allowing agreement of the parties to the contrary unless such agreement is "unconscionable or significantly against public policy." Section 5.6. The provisions of housing codes and the relative bargaining positions of the parties are relevant factors. See Comment e, § 5.6.

7. The proposal that the American Law Institute adopt the doctrine of implied warranty of habitability was adopted over vigorous objections by the late Dean Charles J. Meyers of Stanford Law School, who expressed his views orally at the annual meeting of the Institute and also in writing, The Covenant of Habitability and the American

Law Institute, 27 Stan.L.Rev. 897 (1975). Briefly stated, Dean Meyers' position is that the practical effect of the ALI provisions is that a landlord's warranty of habitability is judicially imposed contrary to the agreement of the parties and that this is an ineffective means of accomplishing the questionable goal of requiring landlords to provide suitable housing for the poor. A few excerpts from Dean Meyers' article are reprinted here.

CHARLES J. MEYERS, THE COVENANT OF HABITABILITY AND THE AMERICAN LAW INSTITUTE

27 Stanford L.Rev. 879 (1975).

. . . On the basis of the limited empirical evidence available, one can question the portrayal of the owners of dilapidated property as rich and rapacious, the notorious slumlord so vital to the middle-class reformer's iconography of villainy. But if it is true that rich slumlords are the typical owners of dilapidated rental property, it does not follow that placing the nonwaivable duty of repair upon them will improve urban housing conditions. The rich slumlord may be rich because as a profit-maximizing man he does not invest his money in losing properties. If improving slum property is uneconomical, the *Restatement* rule is hardly likely to change a landlord's behavior. Hence, though housing may be in short supply and though tenants may be poor and landlords rich, the duty of habitability may not change the bargaining position of tenants or improve the condition of rental housing. Whether or not it will do so depends on other considerations, primarily the rents that can be collected and the cost of repairs. In short, the *Restatement's* rationale for the habitability duty is based on moral philosophy and distributive justice, but the objectives it seeks to achieve cannot be accomplished outside the narrow and perhaps selfish confines of economic behavior.

. . .

In summary, the economic consequences of the *Restatement* rules on habitability are likely to be the following:

(1) Some proportion of the substandard rental housing stock would be upgraded and rents would be raised to cover the added costs. Tenants formerly occupying the housing would either be forced out or be required to pay a higher proportion of their income for rent. Those tenants who are unable or unwilling to pay for the upgraded housing will move out, creating an increased demand for lower-priced, lower-quality housing.

(2) For some proportion of the substandard rental housing stock, rents could not be raised, but landlords could still upgrade the housing without incurring a deficit. In these cases the tenants would enjoy a short-term wealth transfer, for they would enjoy better housing at no increase in rent. But low-income tenants as a class would not benefit in the long run, for the covenant of habitability will retire this compo-

nent of the housing stock sooner than would otherwise be the case and will discourage new investment in low-rent housing.

(3) The third portion of the substandard housing stock will be abandoned as soon as the owner determines that income will not cover the expenses of *Restatement* repairs and concludes that this deficit is likely to persist.

The conclusions reached above are based on theory; that is, on the assumption that landlords, along with the rest of mankind, are rational economic beings who seek to maximize profits and minimize losses. If landlords do in fact fit this model, then the prediction that some portion of the housing stock will be abandoned seems to be well-founded. Moreover, under this model, the *Restatement*'s assertions that there is a housing shortage and that landlords enjoy excessive bargaining power relative to tenants, even if true, are simply irrelevant to the consequences that can be expected from the adoption of the *Restatement* rules. A landlord owning rental housing in category (1) will raise rents and will abandon housing in category (3), unless he is altruistic, in which case the housing would meet code standards in the first place.

Lawyers, however, are loath to base action on anyone's theories except their own. A lawyer will confidently write an opinion letter predicting what courts will do on the basis of legal theory, but will take the stance of the man from Missouri when it comes to predictions of behavior based on economic theory. This is a curious posture, for the behavioral assumptions of economic theory seem far better supported by every day experience than the assumptions of legal theory.

It is fortunate, therefore that the case against the *Restatement* rules need not rest on economic theory alone. In his pioneering studies of slum tenements, George Sternlieb has gathered empirical data on landlord behavior in the slums. His two books, The Tenement Landlord and Residential Abandonment: The Tenement Landlord Revisited deserve to be read in full by anyone concerned with low-rental housing. Sternlieb's principal conclusions relevant to our inquiry may be summarized:

(1) "Actual abandonment of blighted neighborhoods by landlords has reached shockingly high levels."

(2) The classic view of the rapacious slumlord waxing fat as he milks the property is a myth.

. . .

(3) Code enforcement, even of the conventional sort resulting in modest fines, is counterproductive. . . .

(4) Landlords in slum areas do not believe that repairs can be economically justified by increased rentals or resale potential. . . .

Abandonment figures alone do not prove much, but when combined with the reasons for abandonment, they forcefully support the argument that increasing the repair costs of slum housing or, in the alternative, reducing rental income by allowing tenants to withhold rent, will raise the abandonment rate. Sternlieb reports that the combination of low rents, collection difficulties, high taxes, high maintenance costs (in part due to tenant vandalism and in part to price levels), and the unavailability of insurance cause the abandonment of his sampled residential buildings. . . .

If the question is whether enforcement of the *Restatement* covenant of habitability will raise the quality of low-rental housing and improve the condition of the low-income tenant, both theory and the available evidence indicate a negative answer. In fact, conditions are likely to worsen.

. . .

The Reporter advances another argument in support of the *Restatement* rules; he contends that the housing codes establish a legislative policy which the judiciary merely implements when it applies the *Restatement* rules. The argument is hard to sustain, however, if the housing code is taken as a whole and not artificially separated into two independent, unrelated parts consisting of (1) standards of housing quality and (2) enforcement. Viewed in its totality, the code prescribes housing standards which, if violated, may result in the penalty of a fine. Enforcement of the code is committed to a building inspector who has the equivalent of prosecutorial discretion. Further discretion is vested in courts with respect to the size of fines. In short, the policy underlying the code is discretionary administration: if better housing can be obtained through enforcement of the code, citations may be issued. But if code enforcement will increase the abandonment rate or will price the poor out of the housing market, enforcement can be stayed. Discretionary enforcement is delegated to public officials who know the housing market and who are expected to, and do, proceed with enforcement cautiously and prudently. Unlike the *Property Restatement*, the code does *not* provide for rent abatement and rent withholding, for those remedies frustrate the achievement of the code's objective, which is the maintenance of the housing stock and its improvement where economically feasible in the judgment of knowledgeable public officials.

. . .

The fundamental reason offered here against assigning judges the rule-making power endorsed by the *Restatement* is that the rules are too closely tied to basic social and economic policies to emanate from the judiciary. The quality of housing that the poor can afford to rent or buy is the product of political decisions on income distribution on the purchasers' side and the organization and operation of the market on the sellers' side. Raise the income of the poor and they can afford better housing. Reduce such restrictions on housing output as labor monopoly and land-use controls and the poor will have better housing. But each of those changes involves basic political choices that must be made by the society in order to gain acceptance. When courts intrude on a problem of such dimension, without the political base or the political tools, especially the spending power, to effect significant change, they have both in theory and in practice exceeded the powers confided in them by the people. [Copyright 1975 by the Board of Trustees of the Leland Stanford Junior University.]

. . .

NOTE

Theoretical and empirical studies of the effectiveness of the implied warranty of habitability and related legislation are reviewed in Cunningham, The New Implied and Statutory Warranties of Habitability in Residential Leases: From Contract to Status, 16 Urban L.Ann. 3, 138 (1979). Sternlieb's studies include the following: G. Sternlieb, The Tenement Landlord (1966); G. Sternlieb & R. Burchell, Residential Abandonment: The Tenement Landlord Revisited (1973); G. Sternlieb & J. Hughes, The Future of Rental Housing (1981).

(2) Suitability for Intended Commercial Use

DAVIDOW v. INWOOD NORTH PROFESSIONAL GROUP—PHASE I

Supreme Court of Texas, 1988.
747 S.W.2d 373.

Spears, Justice.

This case presents the question of whether there is an implied warranty by a commercial landlord that the leased premises are suitable for their intended commercial purpose. Respondent Inwood North Professional Group—Phase I sued petitioner Dr. Joseph Davidow for unpaid rent on medical office space leased by Dr. Davidow. The jury found that Inwood materially breached the lease agreement and that the defects rendered the office space unsuitable for use as a medical office. The trial court rendered judgment that Inwood take nothing and that Dr. Davidow recover damages for lost time and relocation expenses. The court of appeals reversed the trial court judgment and rendered judgment that Inwood recover unpaid rents for the remainder of the lease period and that Dr. Davidow take nothing. 731 S.W.2d 600. We affirm in part and reverse and render in part.

Dr. Davidow entered into a five-year lease agreement with Inwood for medical office space. The lease required Dr. Davidow to pay Inwood $793.26 per month as rent. The lease also required Inwood to provide air conditioning, electricity, hot water, janitor and maintenance services, light fixtures, and security services. Shortly after moving into the office space, Dr. Davidow began experiencing problems with the building. The air conditioning did not work properly, often causing temperatures inside the office to rise above eighty-five degrees. The roof leaked whenever it rained, resulting in stained tiles and rotting, mildewed carpet. Patients were directed away from certain areas during rain so that they would not be dripped upon in the waiting room. Pests and rodents often infested the office. The hallways remained dark because hallway lights were unreplaced for months. Cleaning and maintenance were not provided. The parking lot was constantly filled with trash. Hot water was not provided, and on one occasion Dr. Davidow went without electricity for several days because Inwood failed to pay the electric bill. Several burglaries and various acts of vandalism occurred. Dr. Davidow finally moved out of the premises and discontinued rent payments approximately fourteen months before the lease expired.

Inwood sued Dr. Davidow for the unpaid rent and costs of restoration. Dr. Davidow answered by general denial and the affirmative defenses of material breach of the lease agreement, a void lease, and breach of an implied warranty that the premises were suitable for use as a medical office. The jury found that Inwood materially breached the lease, that Inwood warranted to Dr. Davidow that the lease space was suitable for a medical office, and that the lease space was not suitable for a medical office. One month after the jury returned its verdict, but before entry of judgment, the trial court allowed Dr. Davidow to amend his pleadings to include the defense of constructive eviction. The trial court then rendered judgment that Inwood take nothing and that Dr. Davidow recover $9,300 in damages.

With one justice dissenting, the court of appeals reversed the trial court judgment and rendered judgment in favor of Inwood for unpaid rent. The court of appeals held that because Inwood's covenant to maintain and repair the premises was independent of Dr. Davidow's covenant to pay rent, Inwood's breach of its covenant did not justify Dr. Davidow's refusal to pay rent. The court of appeals also held that the implied warranty of habitability does not extend to commercial leaseholds and that Dr. Davidow's pleadings did not support an award of affirmative relief.

Inwood contends that the defense of material breach of the covenant to repair is insufficient as a matter of law to defeat a landlord's claim for unpaid rent. In Texas, the courts have held that the landlord's covenant to repair the premises and the tenant's covenant to pay rent are independent covenants. . . . Thus, a tenant is still under a duty to pay rent even though his landlord has breached his covenant to make repairs.

This theory of independent covenants in leases was established in early property law prior to the development of the concept of mutually dependent covenants in contract law. At common law, the lease was traditionally regarded as a conveyance of an interest in land, subject to the doctrine of *caveat emptor.* The landlord was required only to deliver the right of possession to the tenant; the tenant, in return, was required to pay rent to the landlord. Once the landlord delivered the right of possession, his part of the agreement was completed. The tenant's duty to pay rent continued as long as he retained possession, even if the buildings on the leasehold were destroyed or became uninhabitable. The landlord's breach of a lease covenant did not relieve the tenant of his duty to pay rent for the remainder of the term because the tenant still retained everything he was entitled to under the lease—the right of possession. All lease covenants were therefore considered independent. *See* 3 G. Thompson, *Thompson on Real Estate*

§§ 1110, 1115 (1980); *cf. Kamarath v. Bennett,* 568 S.W.2d 658, 659–60 (Tex.1978).

In the past, this court has attempted to provide a more equitable and contemporary solution to landlord-tenant problems by easing the burden placed on tenants as a result of the independence of lease covenants and the doctrine of *caveat emptor.* See, e.g., *Kamarath v. Bennett,* 568 S.W.2d 658 (Tex.1978); *Humber v. Morton,* 426 S.W.2d 554 (Tex.1968). In *Kamarath v. Bennett,* we reexamined the realities of the landlord-tenant relationship in a modern context and concluded that the agrarian common-law concept is no longer indicative of the contemporary relationship between the tenant and landlord. The land is of minimal importance to the modern tenant; rather, the primary subject of most leases is the structure located on the land and the services which are to be provided to the tenant. The modern residential tenant seeks to lease a dwelling suitable for living purposes. The landlord usually has knowledge of any defects in the premises that may render it uninhabitable. In addition, the landlord, as permanent owner of the premises, should rightfully bear the cost of any necessary repairs. In most instances the landlord is in a much better bargaining position than the tenant. Accordingly, we held in *Kamarath* that the landlord impliedly warrants that the premises are habitable and fit for living. We further implicitly recognized that the residential tenant's obligation to pay rent is dependent upon the landlord's performance under his warranty of habitability. *Kamarath,* 568 S.W.2d at 660–61.

When a commercial tenant such as Dr. Davidow leases office space, many of the same considerations are involved. A significant number of commentators have recognized the similarities between residential and commercial tenants and concluded that residential warranties should be expanded to cover commercial property. See, e.g., Chused, *Contemporary Dilemmas of the Javins Defense: A Note on the Need for Procedural Reform in Landlord–Tenant Law,* 67 Geo.L.J. 1385, 1389 (1979); Greenfield & Margolies, *An Implied Warranty of Fitness in Nonresidential Leases,* 45 Albany L.Rev. 855 (1981); Levinson & Silver, *Do Commercial Property Tenants Possess Warranties of Habitability?,* 14 Real Estate L.J. 59 (1985); Note, *Landlord–Tenant—Should a Warranty of Fitness be Implied in Commercial Leases?,* 13 Rutgers L.J. 91 (1981); see also Restatement (Second) of Property § 5.1 reporter's note at 176 (1977).

It cannot be assumed that a commercial tenant is more knowledgeable about the quality of the structure than a residential tenant. A businessman cannot be expected to possess the expertise necessary to adequately inspect and repair the premises, and many commercial tenants lack the financial resources to hire inspectors and repairmen to assure the suitability of the premises. Note, supra, at 111. Additionally, because commercial tenants often enter into short-term leases, the tenants have limited economic incentive to make any extensive repairs to their premises. Levinson & Silver, supra, at 68. Consequently, commercial tenants generally rely on their landlords' greater abilities to inspect and repair the premises. Id.

. . .

There is no valid reason to imply a warranty of habitability in residential leases and not in commercial leases. Although minor distinctions can be drawn between residential and commercial tenants, those differences do not justify limiting the warranty to residential leaseholds. Therefore, we hold there is an implied warranty of suitability by the landlord in a commercial lease that the premises are suitable for their intended commercial purpose. This warranty means that at the inception of the lease there are no latent defects in the facilities that are vital to the use of the premises for their intended commercial purpose and that these essential facilities will remain in a suitable condition. If, however, the parties to a lease expressly agree that the tenant will repair certain defects, then the provisions of the lease will control.

We recognized in *Kamarath* that the primary objective underlying a residential leasing arrangement is "to furnish [the tenant] with quarters suitable for living purposes." *Kamarath,* 568 S.W.2d at 661. The same objective is present in a commercial setting. A commercial tenant desires to lease premises suitable for their intended commercial use. A commercial landlord impliedly represents that the premises are in fact suitable for that use and will remain in a suitable condition. The tenant's obligation to pay rent and the landlord's implied warranty of suitability are therefore mutually dependent.

. . .

The jury found that Inwood leased the space to Dr. Davidow for use as a medical office and that Inwood knew of the intended use. The evidence and jury findings further indicate that Dr. Davidow was unable to use the space for the intended purpose because acts and omissions by Inwood rendered the space unsuitable for use as a medical office. The jury findings establish that Inwood breached the implied warranty of suitability. Dr. Davidow was therefore justified in abandoning the premises and discontinuing his rent payments.

. . .

[The court affirmed the denial of damages to Dr. Davidow on procedural grounds.]

NOTES

1. Dr. Davidow's office space would have been highly unsatisfactory for any type of commercial or professional use. Should the result have been the same if he had been unable to use the premises solely because the nature of his practice required special facilities, such as special wiring or plumbing, not typically found in an office building?

2. Is the court correct in suggesting that there is little reason to distinguish between residential and commercial tenants in implying a warranty of fitness of use? Arguments in favor of making this distinction are set out in Note, The Unwarranted Implication of a Warranty of Fitness in Commercial Leases—An Alternative Approach, 41 Vanderbilt L.Rev. 1057 (1988). The author contends that the commercial tenant is in a better position than the residential tenant to make a

meaningful inspection of the premises and to take care of necessary repairs. Moreover, the commercial tenant can pass the cost of repairs and inspections on to his customers. Most significantly, there is likely to be a greater equality of bargaining power between a lessor and commercial lessee. In addition to the lack of policy justifications for implying a warranty in commercial leases, the author argues that there are potential disadvantages in extending an implied warranty of suitability to commercial leases.

> Rental costs will increase as the lessor passes on the expected outlays because of the implication of the warranty to the tenant. Assuming that the lessor's estimates are accurate, this increase in rent roughly will translate into the lessee paying for his own repairs on an installment plan. There is no need for the warranty if this occurs. Additionally, the tenants who arguably need the protection of an implied warranty the most would be hit the hardest. Smaller commercial lessees with less capital to start up their companies or keep them running would be forced to allocate a disproportionate amount of their resources to rental payments. These tenants' choice to utilize scarce capital resources on nonrepair expenses effectively would be curtailed. Finally, to the extent that the landlord could not pass on all of the cost of this warranty protection to the tenant, his margin of profit would decrease. Property that is on the edge of profitability would be abandoned as unrentable. In turn, urban decay would accelerate, forcing current tenants to relocate.

3. Section 5.1 of the Restatement (Second) of Property, Landlord and Tenant (1977) provides remedies for premises which are unsuitable for use only in the case of residential tenancies. The reason stated for the limitation was that existing judicial and statutory law did not warrant extension of the rule to commercial tenancies. States remain split on this issue. For recent decisions refusing to extend an implied warranty of fitness beyond residential tenancies see Knapp v. Simmons, 345 N.W.2d 118 (Iowa 1984); Mobil Oil Credit Corp. v. DST Realty, Inc., 689 S.W.2d 658 (Mo.App.1985).

B. INJURIES TO PERSON OR PROPERTY

SARGENT v. ROSS

Supreme Court of New Hampshire, 1973.
113 N.H. 388, 308 A.2d 528, 64 A.L.R.3d 329.

KENISON, CHIEF JUSTICE. The question in this case is whether the defendant landlord is liable to the plaintiff in tort for the death of plaintiff's four-year-old daughter who fell to her death from an outdoor stairway at a residential building owned by the defendant in Nashua. The defendant resided in a ground-floor apartment in the building, and her son and daughter-in-law occupied a second story apartment serviced by the stairway from which the child fell. At the time of the accident the child was under the care of the defendant's daughter-in-law who was plaintiff's regular baby-sitter.

Plaintiff brought suit against the daughter-in-law for negligent supervision and against the defendant for negligent construction and maintenance of the stairway which was added to the building by the defendant about eight years before the accident. There was no apparent cause for the fall except for evidence that the stairs were dangerously steep, and that the railing was insufficient to prevent the child from falling over the side. The jury returned a verdict for the daughter-in-law but found in favor of the plaintiff in her action against the defendant landlord. The defendant seasonably excepted to the denial of her motions for a nonsuit, directed verdict, judgment n.o.v., and to have the verdict set aside, and all questions of law were reserved and transferred to this court by Dunfey, J.

Claiming that there was no evidence that the defendant retained control over the stairway, that it was used in common with other tenants, or that it contained a concealed defect, defendant urges that there was accordingly no duty owing to the deceased child for the defendant to breach. This contention rests upon the general rule which has long obtained in this and most other jurisdictions that a landlord is not liable, except in certain limited situations, for injuries caused by defective or dangerous conditions in the leased premises. E.g., Black v. Fiandaca, 98 N.H. 33, 93 A.2d 663 (1953); Towne v. Thompson, 68 N.H. 317, 44 A. 492 (1895); 2 Powell, Real Property ¶ 234 (rev. ed. 1971); Prosser, Torts § 63 (4th ed. 1971); 1 Tiffany, Real Property §§ 104, 107 (3d ed. 1939). The plaintiff does not directly attack this rule of nonliability but instead attempts to show, rather futilely under the facts, defendant's control of the stairway. She also relies upon an exception to the general rule of nonliability, to wit, that a landlord is liable for injuries resulting from his negligent repair of the premises. . . . The issue, as framed by the parties, is whether the rule of nonliability should prevail or whether the facts of this case can be squeezed into the negligent repair or some other exception to the general rule of landlord immunity.

General principles of tort law ordinarily impose liability upon persons for injuries caused by their failure to exercise reasonable care under all the circumstances. . . . A person is generally negligent for exposing another to an unreasonable risk of harm which foreseeably results in an injury. . . . But, except in certain instances, landlords are immune from these simple rules of reasonable conduct which govern other persons in their daily activities. This "quasi-sovereignty of the landowner" (2 Harper and James, Law of Torts 1495 (1956) finds its source in an agrarian England of the dark ages. . . . Due to the untoward favoritism of the law for landlords, it has been justly stated that "the law in this area is a scandal." Quinn and Phillips, The Law of Landlord-Tenant: A Critical Evaluation of the Past with Guidelines for the Future, 38 Ford.L.Rev. 225 (1969). "For decades the court persistently refused to pierce the hardened wax that preserved the landlord-tenant relationship in its agrarian state." Note, 59 Geo.L.J. 1153, 1163 (1971). But courts and legislatures alike are beginning to reevaluate the rigid rules of landlord-tenant law in light of current needs and principles of law from related areas. See Kline v. Burns supra; . . .

One court recognized at an early date that ordinary principles of tort liability ought to apply to landlords as other persons. "The ground of liability upon the part of a landlord when he demises dangerous property has nothing special to do with the relation of landlord and tenant. It is the ordinary case of liability for personal misfeasance, which runs through all the relations of individuals to each other." Wilcox v. Hines, 100 Tenn. 538, 548–549, 46 S.W. 297, 299 (1898). Most courts, however, while recognizing from an early date that "the law is unusually strict in exempting the landlord from liability" (Bowe v. Hunking, 135 Mass. 380, 386 (1883)), sought refuge from the rigors of the rule by straining other legal principles such as deceit (Cummings v. Prater, 95 Ariz. 20, 23 n. 1, 386 P.2d 27, 29 n. 1 (1963); Note, Landlord and Tenant: Defects Existing at the Time of the Lease, 35 Ind.L.J. 361 (1960)) and by carving out exceptions to the general rule of nonliability. 2 Harper and James, supra at 1510. Thus, a landlord is now generally conceded to be liable in tort for injuries resulting from defective and dangerous conditions in the premises if the injury is attributable to (1) a hidden danger in the premises of which the landlord but not the tenant is aware, (2) premises leased for public use, (3) premises retained under the landlord's control, such as common stairways, or (4) premises negligently repaired by the landlord. . . .

As is to be expected where exceptions to a rule of law form the only basis of liability, the parties in this action concentrated at trial and on appeal on whether any of the exceptions applied, particularly whether the landlord or the tenant had control of the stairway. . . . The determination of the question of which party had control of the defective part of the premises causing the injury has generally been considered dispositive of the landlord's liability. . . . This was a logical modification to the rule of nonliability since ordinarily a landlord can reasonably be expected to maintain the property and guard against injuries only in common areas and other areas under his control. A landlord, for example, cannot fairly be held responsible in most instances for an injury arising out of the tenant's negligent maintenance of the leased premises. . . . But the control test is insufficient since it substitutes a facile and conclusive test for a reasoned consideration of whether due care was exercised under all the circumstances. . . .

There was evidence from which the jury could find that the landlord negligently designed or constructed a stairway which was dangerously steep or that she negligently failed to remedy or adequately warn the deceased of the danger. A proper rule of law would not preclude recovery in such a case by a person foreseeably injured by a dangerous hazard solely because the stairs serviced one apartment instead of two. But that would be the result if the control test were applied to this case, since this was not a "common stairway" or otherwise under the landlord's control. . . . While we could strain this test to the limits and find control in the landlord . . ., as plaintiff suggests, we are not inclined to so expand the fiction since we agree that "it is no part of the general law of negligence to exonerate a defendant simply because the condition attributable to his negligence has passed beyond his control before it causes injury . . . ." 2 Harper and James, Law of Torts § 27.16, at 1509 (1956); see id. at 207 (Supp. to vol. 2 (1968)).

The anomaly of the general rule of landlord tort immunity and the inflexibility of the standard exceptions, such as the control exception, is pointedly demonstrated by this case. A child is killed by a dangerous condition of the premises. Both husband and wife tenants testify that they could do nothing to remedy the defect because they did not own the house nor have authority to alter the defect. But the landlord claims that she should not be liable because the stairs were not under her control. Both of these contentions are premised on the theory that the other party should be responsible. So the orthodox analysis would leave us with neither landlord nor tenant responsible for dangerous conditions on the premises. This would be both illogical and intolerable, particularly since neither party then would have any legal reason to remedy or take precautionary measures with respect to dangerous conditions. In fact, the traditional "control" rule actually discourages a landlord from remedying a dangerous condition since his repairs may be evidence of his control. . . . Nor can there be serious doubt that ordinarily the landlord is best able to remedy dangerous conditions, particularly where a substantial alteration is required.

In Wiggin v. Kent McCray, Inc., 109 N.H. 342, 252 A.2d 418 (1969), which involved an injury from a defective door in a shopping center, we considered the control question but analyzed the problem in ordinary negligence terms. In fact, the issue of control is relevant to the determination of liability only insofar as it bears on the question of what the landlord and tenant reasonably should have believed in regard to the division of responsibility for *maintaining* the premises in a safe condition. The basic claim in this case involves only the design or construction of the steps; the maintenance of the stairs was not seriously in issue, except perhaps concerning the lack of precautions, since the evidence was clear that the stairway was dry and free of debris. The inquiry should have centered upon the unreasonableness of the pitch of the steps and the unreasonableness of failing to take precautionary measures to reduce the danger of falls.

Similarly, the truly pertinent questions involved in determining who should bear responsibility for the loss in this case were clouded by the question of whether the accident was caused by a hidden defect or secret danger. . . . The mere fact that a condition is open and obvious, as was the steepness of the steps in this case, does not preclude it from being unreasonably dangerous, and defendants are not infrequently "held liable for creating or maintaining a perfectly obvious danger of which plaintiffs are fully aware." 2 Harper and James, supra at 1493; . . . Additionally, while the dangerous quality of the steps might have been obvious to an adult, the danger and risk would very likely be imperceptible to a young child such as the deceased. . . . The obviousness of the risk is primarily relevant to the basic issue of a plaintiff's contributory negligence. . . . Here, the trial court properly withdrew the issue of the contributory negligence of the deceased from the jury because of the child's very young age. . . .

Finally, plaintiff's reliance on the negligent repairs exception to the rule of nonliability . . . would require us to broaden the exception to include the negligent construction of improvements to the premises. We recognize that this would be no great leap in logic (see Bohlen, Landlord and Tenant, 35 Harv.L.Rev. 633, 648 (1922)), but we think it more realistic instead to consider reversing the general rule of nonliability (Note, 62 Harv.L.Rev. 669 (1949)) since "[t]he exceptions have . . . produced a twisting of legal concepts which seems undesirable." Id. at 676. And "it appears to us that to search for gaps and exceptions in a legal doctrine . . . which exists only because of the somnolence of the common law and the courts is to perpetuate further judicial fictions when preferable alternatives exist. . . . The law of landlord-tenant relations cannot be so frail as to shatter when confronted with modern urban realties and a frank appraisal of the underlying issues." Lemle v. Breeden, 51 Haw. 426, 435, 462 P.2d 470, 475 (1969) (establishing an implied warranty of habitability in dwelling leases). The emphasis on control and other exceptions to the rule of nonliability, both at trial and on appeal, unduly complicated the jury's task and diverted effort and attention from the central issue of the unreasonableness of the risk.

In recent years, immunities from tort liability affording "special protection in some types of relationships have been steadily giving way" in this and other jurisdictions. 2 Harper and James, supra at 1508. . . . We think that now is the time for the landlord's limited tort immunity to be relegated to the history books where it more properly belongs.

This conclusion springs naturally and inexorably from our recent decision in Kline v. Burns, 111 N.H. 87, 276 A.2d 248 (1971). *Kline* was an apartment rental claim suit in which the tenant claimed that the premises were uninhabitable. Following a small vanguard of other jurisdictions, we modernized the landlord-tenant contractual relationship by holding that there is an implied warranty of habitability in an apartment lease transaction. As a necessary predicate to our decision, we discarded from landlord-tenant law "that obnoxious legal cliché, *caveat emptor*." Pines v. Perssion, 14 Wis.2d 590, 596, 111 N.W.2d 409, 413 (1961). In so doing, we discarded the very legal foundation and justification for the landlord's immunity in tort for injuries to the tenant or third persons. . . .

To the extent that Kline v. Burns did not do so, we today discard the rule of "caveat lessee" and the doctrine of landlord nonliability in tort to which it gave birth. We thus bring up to date the other half of landlord-tenant law. Henceforth, landlords as other persons must exercise reasonable care not to subject others to an unreasonable risk of harm. . . . A landlord must act as a reasonable person under all of the circumstances including the likelihood of injury to others, the probable seriousness of such injuries, and the burden of reducing or avoiding the risk. . . . The questions of control, hidden defects and common or public use, which formerly had to be established as a prerequisite to even considering the negligence of a landlord, will now be relevant only inasmuch as they bear on the basic tort issues such as the foreseeability and unreasonableness of the particular risk of harm. . . .

Our decision will shift the primary focus of inquiry for judge and jury from the traditional question of "who had control?" to a determination of whether the landlord, and the injured party, exercised due care under all the circumstances. . . .

Although the trial court's instructions to the jury in the instant case were cast according to the traditional exceptions of control and hidden danger, the charge clearly set forth the elements of ordinary negligence which were presented by the court as prerequisite to a finding of liability on either issue. Thus, the jury could find that the defendant was negligent in the design or construction of the steep stairway or in failing to take adequate precautionary measures to reduce the risk of injury. We have carefully reviewed the record and conclude that there is sufficient evidence, on the basis of the principles set forth above, to support the verdict of the jury which had the benefit of a view. . . . Both plaintiff and the wife tenant testified that the stairs were too steep, and the husband tenant testified that his wife complained to him of this fact. While the defendant landlord did not testify, the jury could find that she knew that this steep stairway was frequently used by the young children for whom her daughter-in-law was the regular, daily babysitter. In any event, the use of these steps by young children should have been anticipated by the defendant. . . .

The verdict of the jury is sustained, and the order is

Exceptions overruled; judgment on the verdict.

GRIMES, J., did not participate; DUNCAN, J., concurred in the result; the others concurred.

NOTES

1. Arguments in favor of making lessors strictly liable for tenant injuries are advanced in Love, Landlord's Liability for Defective Premises: Caveat Lessee, Negligence, or Strict Liability? 1975 Wis.L.Rev. 19, and at least one court has imposed strict liability for injuries resulting from a latent defect in the premises. Becker v. IRM Corp., 38 Cal.3d 454, 213 Cal.Rptr. 213, 698 P.2d 116 (1985). Generally, however, courts have been reluctant to take this step. Consider the reasoning in Young v. Morrisey, 285 S.C. 236, 329 S.E.2d 426 (1985), a wrongful death action against the owners of an apartment house which had caught fire because of defective wiring in the control box of the furnace.

> A New Jersey court listed numerous compelling reasons for refusing to impose strict liability on landlords.
>
> > (1) A landlord is not engaged in mass production whereby he places his product—the apartment—in a stream of commerce exposing it to a large number of consumers; (2) he has

> not created the product with a defect which is preventable by greater care at the time of manufacture or assembly; (3) he does not have the expertise to know and correct the condition, so as to be saddled with responsibility for a defect regardless of negligence; (4) an apartment includes several rooms with many facilities constructed by many artisans with differing types of expertise, and subject to constant use and deterioration from many causes; (5) it is a commodity wholly unlike a product which is expected to leave a manufacturer's hands in a safe condition with an implied representation upon which the consumer relies; (6) the tenant may expect that at the time of letting there are no hidden dangerous defects known to the landlord of which the tenant has not been warned, but he does not expect that all will be perfect in his apartment for all the years of his occupancy; (7) to apply strict liability would impose an unjust burden on property owners; how can a property owner prevent a latent defect or repair when he has no way of detecting it? And if he can't prevent the defect, why should he be liable?

Dwyer v. Skyline Apartments, Inc., 123 N.J.Super. 48, 301 A.2d 463 (1973), *affirmed mem.* 63 N.J. 577, 311 A.2d 1 (1973).

This Court has rejected the insurer concept in numerous similar settings. Merchants are not insurers of the safety of their customers. *See* cases collected at 14 S.C. Digest *Negligence* Key No. 32(1). Common carriers are not insurers of the safety of their passengers. *Singletary v. Atlantic Coast Line Ry. Co.*, 217 S.C. 212, 60 S.E.2d 305 (1950). Innkeepers are not insurers of their guests' safety. *See* cases collected at 11 S.C. Digest *Innkeepers* Key Nos. 10.1, 10.3. Amusement operators do not insure their patrons' safety. *See* cases collected at 17A S.C. Digest *Theaters and Shows* Key No. 6. Nor do we hold landlords insurers of the safety of tenants and guests from injuries caused by latent defects.

2. In Simon v. Solomon, 385 Mass. 91, 431 N.E.2d 556 (1982), noted 6 Suffolk U.L.Rev. 865 (1982), a tenant was permitted to recover $35,000 for emotional distress due to repeated flooding of her basement apartment. The court declined to pass upon tenant's claim that recovery could be based upon strict liability for breach of the implied warranty of habitability. Instead, it relied upon the jury's finding that landlord's conduct had been reckless, which the court said could have been based upon the landlord's long-continued indifference.

TRENTACOST v. BRUSSEL

Supreme Court of New Jersey, 1980.
82 N.J. 214, 412 A.2d 436.

PASHMAN, J.

Once again this Court is asked to examine the contours of the relationship between residential landlords and their tenants. Specifically, the question is whether a landlord who provides inadequate security for common areas of rental premises may be liable for failing to prevent a criminal assault upon a tenant. The trial court entered judgment for the tenant upon a jury's award of damages. The Appellate Division affirmed. 164 N.J.Super. 9, 395 A.2d 540 (App.Div.1978). We granted defendant's petition for certification. 81 N.J. 48, 404 A.2d 1148 (1979), to consider whether the landlord was obligated to secure the entrance to the common areas of plaintiff's building. We now affirm.

I

Facts

On the afternoon of December 21, 1973, plaintiff, Florence Trentacost, returned to her apartment at 273 Monroe Street, Passaic, New Jersey, from an afternoon of shopping. After she had entered her building and reached the top of a flight of stairs leading to her apartment, someone grabbed her ankles from behind and dragged her down the stairs. Her attacker, who remains unknown, left her bleeding in the ground floor hallway but returned almost immediately to steal her purse. Conscious yet unable to speak, she lay helpless for several minutes until a tenant leaving the building noticed her. Another neighbor then called the police, who took plaintiff to a nearby hospital.

Mrs. Trentacost was hospitalized for 15 days. Her injuries included a dislocated right shoulder, fractures of the left shoulder, left ankle and jaw, lacerations about the mouth and broken teeth. She wore casts on her arms and leg for about a month and a half, and at the time of trial in late 1976 still suffered from pain and loss of mobility.

At the time of the attack, plaintiff was 61 years old and a widow. She had rented her four-room apartment for more than ten years from defendant, Dr. Nathan T. Brussel. The building consisted of eight dwelling units located over street level stores with access provided by front and rear entrances. A padlock secured the back entrance, but there was no lock on the front door, which both plaintiff and apparently her assailant had used to enter the premises.

There was considerable evidence at trial regarding criminal and other suspicious activity in the vicinity of plaintiff's residence. A Passaic city detective testified that in the three years preceding the incident, the police had investigated from 75 to 100 crimes in the neighborhood, mostly burglaries and street muggings. Another policeman stated that "civil disturbances" had occurred in the area between 1969 and 1971. Two months before she was attacked, Mrs. Trentacost had herself reported to defendant an attempt to break into the building's cellar. At other times she had notified the landlord of the presence of unauthorized persons in the hallways. Plaintiff claimed the defendant had promised to install a lock on the front door, but he denied ever discussing the subject prior to the assault on plaintiff.

At the close of evidence, the trial court granted plaintiff's motion to strike the defense of contributory negligence. The judge instructed the jury in part as follows:

> A landlord owes to his tenants the duty of exercising reasonable care to guard against foreseeable dangers arising from the use of premises in connection with those portions which remain within

the landlord's control. . . . The relationship between a landlord and his tenant does not impose upon the landlord the duty to protect a tenant from the crime of third persons. Only upon proper proof that the landlord unreasonably enhanced the risk of the criminal activity by failing to take reasonable measures to safeguard the tenants from foreseeable criminal conduct and a showing of suitable notice of existing defects to the landlord can a tenant recover damages from his landlord.

After the jury returned a verdict for plaintiff of $3,000, the trial court denied defendant's motion for judgment notwithstanding the verdict. R. 4:40–2. When defendant refused to consent to an *additur* of $15,000, the court granted plaintiff's motion for a new trial as to damages. A second jury found damages in the sum of $25,000. Defendant then appealed.

In discussing the extent of the landlord's obligation to provide security measures for his tenants, the Appellate Division found our decision in Braitman v. Overlook Terrace Corp., 68 N.J. 368, 346 A.2d 76 (1975), to be controlling. 164 N.J.Super. at 14, 395 A.2d 540, 543. According to the court, "[t]he keynote of the decision in *Braitman* was simply that the liability of the landlord was properly posited upon familiar negligence concepts." Id. Examining the evidence, the court concluded there was sufficient support for finding that the absence of a lock on the entrance to the building, which was located in a high-crime neighborhood, created a foreseeable risk of harm to tenants. It was therefore a jury question whether the landlord had failed to take reasonable security measures to protect the tenants. Id. at 16, 395 A.2d 540. Rejecting defendant's other arguments regarding the sufficiency and admissibility of evidence, the Appellate Division affirmed.

II

Liability for Foreseeable Criminal Conduct

As the Appellate Division correctly recognized, *Braitman* supplies the focal point of controversy regarding the landlord's duty. In that case the tenants had suffered property loss resulting from theft because of a defective "dead bolt" lock on the apartment door. See 68 N.J. at 371–372, 346 A.2d 76. The trial court found that the remaining slip lock had not provided adequate security and that the landlord had received sufficient notice of the defective dead lock. Id. at 373, 346 A.2d 76. Since the robbery was within the scope of the foreseeable risks created by the inadequate security, the court found the landlord liable for negligence.

After the Appellate Division affirmed judgment for the tenants, 132 N.J.Super. 51, 332 A.2d 212 (App.Div.1974), this Court examined in detail the various evolving theories concerning the responsibilities of a landlord. We began by noting the traditional rule: "[T] he relationship between a landlord and his tenant does not, without more, impose upon the landlord a duty to protect the tenant from the crime of third persons." 68 N.J. at 374, 346 A.2d at 79 (citations omitted). We went on, however, to cite with approval Kline v. 1500 Massachusetts Ave.

Apartment Corp., 141 U.S.App.D.C. 370, 439 F.2d 477 (D.C.Cir.1970), as the leading case in the trend away from that tradition.

In fashioning a duty to provide tenant security, the court in *Kline* drew upon three sources. The first, described as "the logic of the situation itself," id. at 376, 439 F.2d at 483, was the recognition that the landlord was in a better economic position than the tenant to take precautionary measures. The court adopted this as a predicate for the landlord's tort liability. Id. at 377, 439 F.2d at 484. Relying on existing law in the District of Columbia, the court noted as a second source an implied contractual undertaking to maintain those protective measures in effect at the beginning of the lease term. Id. at 378, 439 F.2d at 485. A third source was the law governing an innkeeper's duties towards his guests. The court thought this doctrine provided a more appropriate analogy than that of a medieval agrarian lease—the formal predecessor of the modern urban residential lease—for determining the landlord's obligations. See id. at 375, 378, 439 F.2d at 482, 485; see also Javins v. First Nat'l Realty Corp., 138 U.S.App.D.C. 369, 375–377, 428 F.2d 1071, 1077–1079 (D.C.Cir.1970), cert. den., 400 U.S. 925, 91 S.Ct. 186, 27 L.Ed.2d 185 (1970). These three bases provided a foundation for enlarging the landlord's duty to maintain common areas of rental premises so as to safeguard tenants from foreseeable criminal conduct of third parties. *Kline*, 141 U.S.App.D.C. at 380, 439 F.2d at 487.

Although a majority of the Court in *Braitman* did not embrace the reasoning of *Kline*, see *Braitman*, 68 N.J. at 387–388, 346 A.2d 76 (separate views of Hughes, C. J., Sullivan and Pashman, JJ.), we did acknowledge "a developing judicial reluctance to allow landlords to insulate themselves from liability to their tenants for the criminal conduct of third parties," id. at 378, 346 A.2d at 81. We then turned to the development of negligence liability for foreseeable criminal conduct in New Jersey. We held that "upon a logical extension of the principles of our own case law," a landlord could be held liable for creating an "unreasonably enhanced" risk of loss resulting from foreseeable criminal conduct. Id. at 382–383, 346 A.2d 76, 84. See *Zinck v. Whelan*, 120 N.J.Super. 432, 445, 294 A.2d 727 (App.Div.1972). As in *Braitman*, here the landlord was confronted with the existence of a high level of crime in the neighborhood, see ante at 218–219. Yet he failed to install a lock on the front door leading in to the building's lobby. By failing to do anything to arrest or even reduce the risk of criminal harm to his tenants, the landlord effectively and unreasonably enhanced that risk. See *Braitman*, 68 N.J. at 381–382, 346 A.2d 76.

We reiterate that our holding in *Braitman* lies well within traditional principles of negligence law. . . .

Application of these principles in *Braitman* led to the imposition of liability for a landlord's failure to provide adequate security against foreseeable criminal conduct. . . . They also support affirmance of plaintiff's judgment in the present case. . . . Since there was sufficient evidence for concluding that the mugging was a foreseeable result of the landlord's negligence, the jury's finding of liability was warranted.

III

Theories of Landlord Liability

Although we need go no further to affirm the judgment for the tenant, we choose not to ignore the alternative theories of landlord liability discussed in *Braitman*. A majority of that Court found that a violation of an administrative regulation governing the condition of multiple dwellings was independent evidence of negligence, 68 N.J. at 385–386, 346 A.2d 76, while two members considered that breach to establish negligence conclusively, id. at 389, 346 A.2d 76 (Clifford and Schreiber, JJ., concurring). Three members raised the possibility of imposing liability for unsafe premises based on the landlord's implied warranty of habitability. Id. at 387–388, 346 A.2d 76 (separate views of Hughes, C.J., Sullivan and Pashman, JJ.). There was also mention of liability based on a covenant implied in fact to furnish adequate security. Id. at 389, 346 A.2d 76 (Clifford and Schreiber, JJ., concurring).

Over four years have passed since we decided *Braitman*. During this period the need for judicial guidance regarding landlord liability has grown. See generally Note, "The 1975–1976 New Jersey Supreme Court Term," 30 Rut.L.Rev. 492, 696–702 (1977). Although we need not reconcile the alternative theories of *Braitman* to resolve this case, we nevertheless take this opportunity to clarify the scope of a residential landlord's duty to his tenant. . . .

A

Implied Warranty of Habitability

. . .

In *Braitman* we considered but declined to resolve whether the implied warranty is "flexible enough to encompass appropriate security devices." 68 N.J. at 388, 346 A.2d at 87 (separate opinion of Hughes, C.J., Sullivan and Pashman, JJ.). We now conclude that it is and therefore hold that the landlord's implied warranty of habitability obliges him to furnish reasonable safeguards to protect tenants from foreseeable criminal activity on the premises.

The "premises" which the landlord must secure necessarily encompass the common areas of multiple dwellings. There is no doubt that the rent charged by a landlord includes a portion for maintaining such areas. That these areas are used by all the tenants does not require a different result. Viewing "premises" as restricted to the individual dwelling units would render common areas a "no man's land" for the purposes of assessing habitability. We consider the provision of some measure of security in these areas to be "vital to the use of the premises."

Examining the facts of this case, we find that defendant breached his implied warranty by failing to secure in any way the front entrance of the building. The absence of even a simple slip lock—the most elementary of safeguards—permitted the halls and stairwells to become virtually public ways, completely accessible to the criminal element. Defendant did nothing to protect against the threat of crime which seriously impaired the quality of residential life in his building. Since the landlord's implied undertaking to provide adequate security exists independently of his knowledge of any risks, there is no need to prove notice of such a defective and unsafe condition to establish the landlord's contractual duty. It is enough that defendant did not take measures which were in fact reasonable for maintaining a habitable residence.

By failing to provide adequate security, the landlord has impaired the habitability of the tenant's apartment. He has therefore breached his implied warranty of habitability and is liable to the tenant for the injuries attributable to that breach.

B

Violations of Administrative Regulations

. . .

In *Braitman* we noted that "the violation of a statutory duty of care is not conclusive on the issue of negligence . . . but it is a circumstance which the trier of fact should consider in assessing liability." 68 N.J. at 385, 346 A.2d at 85. It is entirely appropriate in an action to establish civil liability to consider the landlord's statutory and administrative responsibilities to his tenants to furnish habitable residential premises. As we stated in *Michaels*, 26 N.J. at 386, 140 A.2d 199, and reiterated in *Braitman*, 68 N.J. at 383–386, 346 A.2d 76, the statutory and regulatory scheme governing the habitability of multifamily dwellings establishes a standard of conduct for landlords. It is thus available as evidence for determining the duty owed by landlords to tenants. Defendant's eight-unit building was a "multiple dwelling" subject to the requirements of the regulations. Regulation 602.3(f)(2)(i) of the "Regulations for the Construction and Maintenance of Motels and Multiple Dwellings" effective July 19, 1968, provided that "[b] uilding entrance doors and exterior exit doors shall be equipped with heavy duty lock sets." The absence of a lock at the time of Mrs. Trentacost's assault was contrary to the Legislature's standard of care. Since the violation was clearly established it constitutes evidence of defendant's negligence.

IV

Conclusion

. . .

Our analysis has led to the conclusion that a landlord has a legal duty to take reasonable security measures for tenant protection on the premises. His obligation to provide safe and habitable premises gives rise to potential liability on alternative grounds of conventional negligence and the implied warranty of habitability. Together these theories will serve to protect the otherwise precarious position of the individual tenant in a manner consistent with modern conceptions of public policy.

For the foregoing reasons, the judgment of the Appellate Division is affirmed.

CLIFFORD, J., dissenting in part.

. . .

I take this opportunity to register disagreement with the notion that liability can be imposed on the defendant landlord on the theory of implied warranty of habitability. Emphasizing the growing presence of crime in society the Court declares today that "the landlord's implied warranty of habitability obliges him to furnish reasonable safeguards to protect tenants from foreseeable criminal activity on the premises", ante at 218; and that "[s]ince [this] undertaking exists independently of [the landlord's] knowledge of any risks, there is no need to prove notice of a defective and unsafe condition." Ante at 218.

The harsh realities of modern life are all too well-known. I share the majority's concern with them. But novel application of the implied warranty of habitability to the baleful conditions reflected in those realities is unwarranted and ill-advised. . . . In practical effect this exercise predicates what amounts to absolute liability solely upon the relationship between the landlord and tenant and upon loose notions of foreseeability. In my view the existence of a duty here should not be grounded simply on a special relationship between the parties but rather should arise from the particular circumstances of the case, including foreseeability. . . . Clearly the inquiry must involve a fair balancing of the relative interests of the parties, the nature of the risk, and the public interest in the proposed solution. . . . This process has been well served in the past through the application of traditional negligence principles. I perceive no compelling reason for departing from that practice.

NOTES

1. The lessor's failure to provide adequate security against break-ins and sexual assaults is an increasingly common basis for finding tort liability. See, for example, Center Management Corp. v. Bowman, 526 N.E.2d 228 (Ind.App.1988) (lessor's failure to restrict access to master keys was proximate cause of burglary of tenant's apartment); Benser v. Johnson, 763 S.W.2d 793 (Tex.App.1988) (landlord's negligence in failing to provide workable locks on windows was proximate cause of tenant's rape). Many states have statutes requiring a lessor to provide locks and keys for apartments. Is proof that the lessor failed to comply with this statutory duty sufficient to impose liability for a tenant's rape by an intruder, or must the tenant also establish that the attack was reasonably foreseeable as a result of the breach? See Paterson v. Deeb, 472 So.2d 1210 (Fla.App.1985).

2. The minor plaintiff, while playing on the sidewalk outside her own home, was abducted, dragged into a vacant apartment in an apartment building across the street, and raped. The glass in the windows of the vacant apartment was broken and the front door was off its hinges. A city ordinance required a building owner to "keep the doors and windows of a vacant structure or vacant portion of a structure securely closed to prevent unauthorized entry."

The plaintiff sued the owner of the building in which the sexual assault occurred. There was testimony that one reason for securing vacant units was to prevent this type of crime from happening and that numerous crimes had been committed in the apartment building prior to the rape of the plaintiff. The defendant moved for summary judgment. How should the trial judge have ruled on the motion? See Nixon v. Mr. Property Management, 690 S.W.2d 546 (Tex.1985) (two judges filing separate concurring opinions; three judges dissenting).

3. What is the effect of a clause in a lease stating: "Lessor shall not be liable to lessee, his family, guests or employees or any person for any personal injury suffered on the premises"? Would it be relevant that the person injured did not sign the lease? A similar exculpatory clause was held not to bar suits by two tenants for their injuries in McCutcheon v. United Homes Corp., 79 Wn.2d 443, 486 P.2d 1093 (1971). The court said:

"The importance of 'freedom of contract' is clear enough. However, the use of such an argument for avoiding the affirmative duty of a landlord to its residential tenant is no longer compelling in light of today's multi-family dwelling complex wherein a tenant merely rents some space with appurtenant rights to make it more usable or livable. Under modern circumstances the tenant is almost wholly dependent upon the landlord to provide reasonably for his safe use of the 'common areas' beyond the four walls demised to him. . . .

"When a lessor is no longer liable for the failure to observe standards of affirmative conduct, or for *any* conduct amounting to negligence, by virtue of an exculpatory clause in a lease, *the standard ceases to exist.* In short, such a clause *destroys* the concept of negligence in the landlord-tenant relationship. Neither the standard nor negligence can exist in abstraction.

"It is no answer to argue that the rental agreement relates exclusively to the 'personal and private affairs of two parties on equal footing' and thus is 'not a matter of public interest.' . . .

"We no longer live in an era of the occasional rental of rooms in a private home or over the corner grocery. In the relatively short span of 30 years the public's use of rental units in this state has expanded dramatically. In the past 10 years alone, in the state of Washington, there has been an increase of over 77,000 rental units. It takes no imagination to see that a business which once had a minor impact upon the living habits of the citizenry has developed into a major commercial enterprise directly touching the lives of hundreds of thousands of people who depend upon it for shelter.

"Thus, we are not faced merely with the theoretical duty of construing a provision in an isolated contract specifically bargained for by *one landlord and one tenant* as a 'purely private affair.' Considered realistically, we are asked to construe an exculpatory clause, the generalized use of which may have an impact upon thousands of potential tenants."

See also Restatement (Second) of Torts § 496B (1965).

SECTION 5. PROVISIONS GOVERNING RENT, DURATION, AND USE

The clauses of a lease may cover a wide variety of matters, especially in a commercial setting. In all instances, however, a written lease will normally contain clauses dealing with the rent owed by the tenant, the duration of the tenancy, and the permissible uses which the tenant can make of the premises. In theory, these clauses represent the agreement of the parties. In many instances, however, the tenant, especially the tenant of residential premises, may have little ability to bargain for terms different than those set out in a form document. As the preceding section has indicated, courts and legislatures have become increasingly willing to imply a covenant that the premises are suitable for the use intended. Other provisions of the lease, including those dealing with rent and duration, have also occasionally been the subject of judicial, statutory and regulatory action which has the effect of modifying or even superseding the language of the lease.

A. RENT

Residential leases typically provide for a set rental amount, payable monthly. The rent clauses of commercial leases may follow this straight-forward format, but commonly they are more complex. For example, leases of space in a shopping center commonly provide for a rent based upon a percentage of store sales in addition to a minimum fixed rental amount based on floor space. Additional charges, such as contributions to advertising funds and common area maintenance fees, may also be imposed as part of the rent obligation. The following is an example of the kind of rental provision which may be found in a shopping mall lease.

Minimum Rentals:

A Minimum Rental as herein defined at the rate of Thirty Five Thousand Five Hundred Eighty-seven and 50/100 ($35,587.50) Dollars per annum, payable at the rate of Two Thousand Nine Hundred Sixty-five and 63/100 ($2,965.63) Dollars per month.

Percentage Rentals:

In the event that the gross sales (as herein defined) made by Tenant upon the leased premises during any quarter of the lease term hereof, are in excess of One Hundred Six Thousand Seven Hundred Sixty-two and 50/100 ($106,762.50) Dollars, then Tenant will pay as "Additional Rental" hereunder a sum equal to Six (6%)

percent of all gross sales in excess of One Hundred Six Thousand Seven Hundred Sixty-two and 50/100 ($106,762.50) Dollars, if any.

Is a tenant under such a lease under an implied obligation to continue business operations? Material dealing with this question can be found in Section 6 of this chapter.

ORANGE COUNTY TAXPAYERS COUNCIL, INC. v. CITY OF ORANGE

Supreme Court of New Jersey, 1980.
83 N.J. 246, 416 A.2d 353.

PASHMAN, J.

This is the third of three related cases challenging municipal power to prevent the deterioration of rented residental housing.[1] Here we consider the validity of a rent control ordinance which prohibits increases in rent without a certification that a dwelling is in "substantial compliance" with municipal housing regulations.

On November 15, 1976, the City of Orange enacted Ordinance MCD 27–76 "to regulate, control and stabilize rents and to create a Rent Control Board within the City of Orange . . .." The enactment codified and replaced the various ordinances regarding rent control which had been passed since 1972. It applied to all rented housing besides hotels, motels, one- and two-family dwellings and three-family, owner-occupied dwellings. The ordinance prohibited increases in rentals except under three sets of circumstances. When a lease expired or a periodic lease terminated, a landlord could charge an increase in rent proportionate to the increase in the Consumer Price Index[2] over the period of the former lease. Such periodic increases were originally limited to an annual rate of 4%.[3] A landlord could also petition for an increase to avoid economic hardship if he could not meet his "usual[,] customary and normal" operating expenses, including mortgage payments and maintenance costs. Finally, the ordinance permitted a landlord to seek additional rent for "major capital improvements or service [improvements]." An increase by reason of hardship or capital improvements was limited to 15% of a tenant's rent.

While no further official authorization was needed for periodic increases, each proposed increase in rentals due to hardship or capital improvements required the approval of the city's Rent Leveling Board. The board consisted of five members and two alternates appointed by the City Council for three-year terms. The ordinance granted the board authority to promulgate rules and regulations to implement the ordinance. Such regulations would "have the force of law." An aggrieved landlord or tenant could appeal decisions of the Rent Level-

1. The other cases, also decided today, are Dome Realty Inc. v. City of Paterson, 83 N.J. 212, 416 A.2d 334 (1980), and State v. C.I.B. International, 83 N.J. 262, 416 A.2d 362 (1980).

2. Specifically, the ordinance employed the Consumer Price Index of all items for the New York City metropolitan area, as compiled by the Bureau of Labor Statistics, United States Department of Labor.

3. Amendments to the rent control ordinance raised that ceiling to 7% on September 7, 1979, and lowered it to 5% on November 9, 1979.

ing Board to the City Council within 20 days of the date of determination.

The ordinance contains several provisions designed to insure a multiple dwelling's compliance with municipal standards for safety and habitability. When seeking a periodic increase in rents, a landlord must give formal notice to his tenants of the calculations involved in the increase, "and a certification that said dwelling and housing space as in *substantial compliance* with the applicable Property Maintenance Codes." Petitions for increases due to hardship or capital improvements required "a certification from the Property Maintenance Department of the City of Orange that the building and grounds are in Substantial Compliance with the Property Maintenance Code." The ordinance provided that the landlord must apply for official certification no more than one month prior to filing his petition with the Rent Leveling Board.

The ordinance defined "substantial compliance" as follows:

> "Substantial Compliance" means that the housing space and dwelling are free from all heat, hot water, elevator and all health, safety and fire hazards as well as 90% qualitatively free of all other violations of the Orange Property Maintenance Code and the Property Maintenance Code of the State of New Jersey[4] where applicable. [footnote added]

As written, the definition appeared to mandate compliance with both the State and municipal housing codes. After the Appellate Division's decision in this case, however, the Rent Leveling Board issued regulations requiring substantial compliance with only the municipal housing code for the issuance of certificates.

Orange Taxpayers Council, Inc., a coalition of owners of rental properties in Orange, and several individual landlords instituted this challenge to the rent control ordinance on March 10, 1977. Filing a verified complaint in lieu of prerogative writs, R. 4:69, plaintiffs named as defendants the City of Orange, its Rent Leveling Board, each of the board's members and its secretary, the Orange Tenants Association, an unincorporated association of tenants residing in Orange, and Barbara Davis, the association's president. Plaintiffs alleged numerous grounds for the invalidation of Orange's rent control scheme. Among them were challenges to the requirements that a landlord provide or obtain a certification of "substantial compliance" as a condition for any increase in rents.

The parties filed cross motions for summary judgment on the legality of the certification scheme. In a letter opinion the trial court held it invalid. According to the court, the requirement that an apartment be in "substantial compliance" with housing regulations was unrelated to the purposes of rent control. . . .

Defendants sought and were granted leave to appeal this decision to the Appellate Division. Finding no facial defect in the certification

4. This is undoubtedly a reference to the Regulations for Construction and Maintenance of Hotels and Multiple Dwellings promulgated by the State Department of Community Affairs, N.J.A.C. 5:10-1.1 et seq. See N.J.S.A. 55:13A-7, -8.

requirement, the Appellate Division reversed the trial court. Orange Taxpayers Council, Inc. v. City of Orange, 169 N.J.Super. 288, 404 A.2d 1186 (App.Div.1979). . . .

We granted plaintiffs' petition for certification, but limited our review to whether a municipality could require the production of a certificate of "substantial compliance" as a prerequisite to an increase in controlled rents. 81 N.J. 399, 408 A.2d 793 (1979). As to that issue we now affirm.

The power of a municipality to control rents within its borders, in the absence of specific legislative authorization by the State, was recognized in the landmark case of Inganamort v. Borough of Fort Lee, 62 N.J. 521, 303 A.2d 298 (1973). Writing for the Court, Chief Justice Weintraub observed, "The police power is vested in local government to the very end that the right of property may be restrained when it ought to be because of sufficient local need." Id. at 538, 303 A.2d at 307. The Court in *Inganamort* found that a shortage of rental housing and the consequent risk that landlords would exploit tenants presented a proper occasion for local government "to devise measures tailored to the local scene[,] . . . to meet varying conditions or to achieve the ultimate goal more effectively." Id. at 528, 303 A.2d at 302. The "reservoir of police power" conferred by N.J.S.A. 40:48–2 was held to contain a delegation of legislative authority sufficient to support rent control by municipalities. See 62 N.J. at 536, 303 A.2d 298.

While *Inganamort* acknowledged the existence of municipal police power to regulate rents, the scope of that power remained largely unexplored until 1975. At that time, in a series of three decisions, Hutton Park Gardens v. West Orange Town Council, 68 N.J. 543, 350 A.2d 1 (1975); Brunetti v. Borough of New Milford, 68 N.J. 576, 350 A.2d 19 (1975); Troy Hills Village v. Parsippany-Troy Hills Tp., 68 N.J. 604, 350 A.2d 34 (1975), the Court addressed various questions concerning the manner in which a municipality may exercise its police power to control rents. The fundamental principle enunciated in these decisions was that municipal rent control ordinances "are subject to the same narrow scope of review under principles of substantive due process as are other [forms of legislative price regulations]." . . .

Application of this principle led to a three-part analysis for assessing local rent control provisions. The first part is "whether the legislative body could rationally have concluded that the unrestrained operation of the competitive market was not in the public interest." . . . The second inquiry is whether the regulatory scheme when examined in its entirety permits a "just and reasonable return" to the owners of rental properties. . . . Finally, the means adopted to accomplish regulation in the public interest must be rationally related to the purposes of the rent control ordinance. . . .

When a plaintiff attacks a legislative enactment as simply arbitrary and unreasonable—a violation of his substantive due process rights—his claim is that he has been deprived of property for reasons unrelated to the welfare of the community. Judicial deference to the judgment of elected lawmakers requires that municipal rent control ordinances, like other legislative enactments, carry a presumption of validity. Although the presumption is not irrebuttable, it places a heavy burden upon the proponent of invalidity.

When confiscation is the issue, and the attack is upon the terms of the enactment itself and not the consequence of its application, the plaintiff's task is equally onerous. Only if a rent leveling ordinance is "so restrictive as to facially preclude any possibility of a just and reasonable return" may a court declare it invalid without considering the actual effects of the ordinance upon landlords. Hutton Park Gardens, 68 N.J. at 571, 350 A.2d 1; see *Brunetti*, 68 N.J. at 592, 350 A.2d 19.[13]

When these principles are applied to the case before us, it becomes clear that we must reject plaintiffs' claims. As their principal argument, plaintiffs challenge as arbitrary and unreasonable the requirement that an apartment be in "substantial compliance" with local housing regulations before a landlord can charge higher rents. Thus, they contend that the enforcement of minimum standards of safety and habitability is completely unrelated to the goals of rent control. This proposition cannot be accepted.

We have ourselves described as "possible rationales for adopting [a rent control] ordinance . . . a housing shortage, widespread imposition of exorbitant rents, monopoly control of the rental housing market or *prevalence of substandard housing.*" *Brunetti*, 68 N.J. at 594, 350 A.2d at 28 (emphasis added). See Hutton Park Gardens, 68 N.J. at 564, 394 A.2d 65. Both "the problems of substandard dwellings and exorbitant rentals . . . stem from the critical condition of the housing market." *Inganamort v. Borough of Fort Lee*, 120 N.J.Super. 286, 310, 293 A.2d 720, 733 (Law Div.1972), aff'd, 62 N.J. 521, 303 A.2d 298 (1973). No one would applaud the wisdom of lawmakers who by controlling the price of rental housing but not its quality, insured that their constituents could live in affordable dwellings that are unsafe, unsanitary and harmful to health. A municipality's authority to act "for the preservation of the public health, safety and welfare" of its residents, N.J.S.A. 40:48–2, permits it to go beyond mere regulation of price. There is no doubt that a municipality can employ its delegated police power to regulate the forces of the marketplace to help its residents obtain decent housing within their means.

This was precisely the goal of the City of Orange when it imposed a requirement of "substantial compliance" in its rent control ordinance. The preamble to the ordinance under scrutiny expressed official concern about both "increases in rents and subsequent deterioration of [residential] dwelling units." The same concerns were expressed in the city's original rent control ordinance in 1972. It appears that by enacting the "substantial compliance" requirement, the city could have acted—and indeed, did act—upon a rational perception of the "health, safety and welfare" of its citizens. We therefore find that the require-

13. When the *operation* of a rent control ordinance is challenged, "plaintiffs must show by clear and convincing evidence that the ordinance had a widespread confiscatory impact upon efficient landlords." *Helmsley*, 78 N.J. at 218, 394 A.2d at 73; . . .

ment is not an arbitrary and unreasonable feature of Orange's rent control ordinance. . . .

The only feature of the ordinance which on its face gives rise to a claim of confiscation is the requirement that a dwelling be in "substantial compliance" with housing regulations before the Rent Leveling Board grants an increase in rents for economic hardship or capital improvements. As the trial court noted, "[t]he landlord seeking an increase to cure violations by a capital improvement or hardship increase cannot even file the petition because such a landlord could not get the certificate." The effect of this requirement, however, is not the preclusion of "any possibility of a just and reasonable return," Hutton Park Gardens, 68 N.J. at 571, 350 A.2d at 16. The purpose of requiring substantial compliance before granting an increase is to insure that tenants will not finance indirectly, by way of rent increases, those repairs which housing regulations and the landlord's implied warranty of habitability, see Trentacost v. Brussel, 82 N.J. 214, 412 A.2d 436 (1980), already obligate him to undertake. In the past we have recognized a tenant's right to receive reductions or rebates of rent when premises violate minimum standards of safety and health. See Berzito v. Gambino, 63 N.J. 460, 308 A.2d 17 (1973); see also N.J.S.A. 2A:42–85 et seq. Since the notion of a "just and reasonable return" embraces a landlord's responsibilities to his tenants as well as his right to receive sufficient income, we perceive no inherent defect in an ordinance that prevents increases in rent for defective premises. . . .

For the foregoing reasons, the judgment of the Appellate Division is affirmed.

NOTES

1. Determining what constitutes a "just and reasonable return" is difficult. Rent control boards, even within a single state, have not adhered to the same formula. See Note, Rethinking Rent Control: An Analysis of "Fair Return," 12 Rutgers L.J. 617 (1981). Practices and litigation in California are reviewed in Brom, Courts Consider Limits on Landlords' Profits, Calif. Lawyer, Sept. 1983, p. 14.

2. The factors which can properly be considered in determining whether a rent increase is appropriate were in dispute in Pennell v. City of San Jose, 485 U.S. 1, 109 S.Ct. 849, 99 L.Ed.2d 1 (1988). The plaintiffs, including an apartment house owners' association, challenged the constitutionality of a city ordinance which listed hardship to the tenant as one of seven factors to be taken into account in determining the reasonableness of a rent increase. A majority of the Court ruled that the suit was premature, since there was no evidence that tenant hardship had ever been used to set rents below a reasonable level. Justice Scalia, dissenting in part, would have held the ordinance facially invalid because of the tenant-hardship provision. He reasoned as follows:

> When commodities have been priced at a level that produces exorbitant returns, the owners of those commodities can be viewed as responsible for the economic hardship that occurs. Whether or

not that is an accurate perception of the way a free-market economy operates, it is at least true that the owners reap unique benefits from the situation that produces the economic hardship, and in that respect singling them out to relieve it may not be regarded as "unfair." That justification might apply to the rent regulation in the present case, apart from the single feature under attack here.

. . .

Once the other six factors [cost of debt servicing, rental history of the unit, physical condition of the unit, changes in housing services, other financial information provided by the landlord, and market value rents for similar units] of the ordinance have been applied to a landlord's property, so that he is receiving only a reasonable return, he can no longer be regarded as a "cause" of exorbitantly priced housing; nor is he any longer reaping distinctively high profits from the housing shortage. The seventh factor, the "hardship" provision, is invoked to meet a quite different social problem: the existence of some renters who are too poor to afford even reasonably priced housing. But *that* problem is no more caused or exploited by landlords than it is by the grocers who sell needy renters their food, or the department stores that sell them their clothes, or the employers who pay them their wages, or the citizens of San Jose holding the higher-paying jobs from which they are excluded. . . .

The traditional manner in which American government has met the problem of those who cannot pay reasonable prices for privately sold necessities—a problem caused by the society at large—has been the distribution to such persons of funds raised from the public at large through taxes, either in cash (welfare payments) or in goods (public housing, publicly subsidized housing, and food stamps). Unless we are to abandon the guiding principle of the Takings Clause that "public burdens . . . should be borne by the public as a whole," Armstrong, supra, 364 U.S., at 49, 80 S.Ct., at 1569, this is the only manner that our Constitution permits. The fact that government acts through the landlord-tenant relationship does not magically transform general public welfare, which must be supported by all the public, into mere "economic regulation," which can disproportionately burden particular individuals. Here the City is not "regulating" rents in the relevant sense of preventing rents that are excessive; rather, it is using the occasion of rent regulation (accomplished by the rest of the Ordinance) to establish a welfare program privately funded by those landlords who happen to have "hardship" tenants.

THE REPORT OF THE PRESIDENT'S COMMISSION ON HOUSING

Pages 91–93 (1982).

The most evident interference in the ability of the private market to supply rental housing is rent control, which is now in use in over 200 cities and affects a substantial percentage of the nation's multifamily rental housing stock.[3] Rent control is not simply an attempt to protect lower income persons. More generally it has been a device for redistributing inflation-induced capital gains from landlords to tenants, regardless of tenant incomes. As rents rise, pressure for the local regulation of rents will increase from tenants of all income levels.

Rent control acts as a severe disincentive to investment and mortgage lending and therefore inhibits the provision of rental housing in the private market, a point forcefully made at the Commission public hearings in Los Angeles, Washington, D.C., and New York. Frequently, it is not just the enactment of rent control that deters rental investment; even the discussion of potential enactment can create a disincentive. Rental housing is a long-lived commitment. Investors make decisions about new construction or the rehabilitation of rental housing based on their expectations. If investors anticipate the future enactment of rent control, even in a relatively nonbinding form, it will affect their predictions about future income flows and expenses as well as their decision to invest.

After rent control is enacted, landlords tend to disinvest from their real estate ventures. This disinvestment either takes the form of conversion to cooperative or condominium forms of ownership, deferred maintenance, or, in extreme cases, abandonment. The Commission finds that rent control causes a reduction in the quality of existing rental housing stock and discourages the investment of capital in new rental property.

Moreover, rent control essentially yields an income redistribution from landlords to tenants by implicitly taxing landlords for the benefit of tenants. In general such a tax is inefficient and inequitable. Rental property owners are often small-scale investors who do not have large financial resources. More importantly, such a tax ignores the fact that individuals can move to another area to avoid or take advantage of local redistribution programs. Over time, a tax on landlords in the form of rent control will cause landlords and investors to leave areas with rent control. The result will be a lack of new construction and a deteriorating stock of existing rental housing. In the long run, tenants lose. Tenants may also move to try to take advantage of rent-controlled units; this may create an excess demand for controlled units and perhaps a black market method of allocation. For example, a new tenant may be required to buy furniture from the previous tenant at a highly inflated price.

The Commission does recognize that there are special circumstances in which rent control is warranted. For example, in 1974 the Alaskan cities of Fairbanks, Anchorage, and Valdez enacted rent control to protect residents from dramatic rent increases occurring as a result of the influx of workers for the Alaska pipeline. The controls were terminated when the pipeline was completed in 1977. By contrast, New York City imposed rent controls under "emergency" legisla-

3. Thomas Thibodeau, "Rent Regulation and the Market for Rental Housing Services" (Washington, D.C.: Urban Institute, November 1981), p. 9; background paper prepared for the Commission.

tion passed in 1943. The Commission finds such long term allegations of "emergency" to be a serious abuse of the term. We doubt that the original wartime conditions giving rise to the legislative finding of an "emergency" have persisted. The nature of an emergency which gives rise to rent control should be periodically reviewed. Only if this is done can rent control be justified as an explicitly short-term measure to prevent excess profits from accruing to existing landlords. In most cases, the adoption and continuation of rent control does not coincide with emergency conditions and has deleterious effects on the housing market. . . .

B. DURATION

As discussed in the first section of this chapter, the duration of a lease for either a fixed or a renewable period determines its classification as a term for years or a periodic tenancy. These common law categories do not provide answers to all questions concerning the duration of a lessee's possession. What is the relationship of the lessor and lessee if a tenant remains in possession past the end of the term? To what extent may statutes or regulations create a right to possession which extends beyond the stated term of the lease? The following material deals with some of the issues raised by these questions.

(1) THE HOLDOVER TENANT

COMMONWEALTH BUILDING CORP. v. HIRSCHFIELD

Appellate Court of Illinois, 1940.
307 Ill.App. 533, 30 N.E.2d 790.

MATCHETT, JUSTICE. In a suit for rent to the amount of $3,300, on trial by jury, there was a verdict for plaintiff in the sum of $1,100. There were motions by each of the parties for judgment non obstante veredicto, which were in each case denied, and a motion by defendant for a new trial, which was allowed on August 1, 1940. This appeal is by leave from that order.

The material (and as we think uncontradicted) facts are that the defendant with his family was in possession of an apartment used for residence purposes, under a written lease with the plaintiff, which by its terms expired September 30, 1938. The lease contained a clause (paragraph 11 not abstracted) providing that if defendant held over he would become liable for double rent. Mr. Kishin was the bookkeeper for plaintiff. He was also an attorney employed by the firm of Pennish and Rashbaum, and Mr. Pennish was managing director of this building. It contained thirteen floors comprising twenty-four apartments, twelve of seven rooms each and twelve of nine rooms each. The apartment leased by defendant was known as 3–A. It contained nine rooms, and the rent paid by defendant under his lease was $275 per month. The business office of defendant was at 544 N. Wells street.

Mr. Fleury was engineer in charge of the building, and Mr. Danny was his assistant. Mr. Zeri was a janitor-helper. There was an elevator in the front of the building used exclusively by passengers and an elevator in the back of the building used exclusively for deliveries and general service. The passenger elevator was operated by an attendant. The freight elevators were operated without an attendant by the use of electricity applied by pushing buttons.

Defendant determined to move at the expiration of his lease, and about two months before the lease expired so notified plaintiff by registered mail. Defendant employed the Federal Storage and Moving Company to do the necessary work and transportation of goods to that end. Two packers delivered boxes and barrels and necessary material for the packing of breakables on September 27. The breakable goods were packed in boxes and barrels and September 29 part of the household goods (including large items of furniture) were moved out by way of the elevator in the rear. Six to ten van loads were moved out on September 29; forty to fifty barrels (including cases). The moving continued for three days, the 28th, 29th and 30th of September.

While this was going on Danny was washing the walls and removing trash and garbage. Most of the goods had been moved out by the 30th, the day on which the lease expired. The work was, however, not quite completed. There had been some delay in getting the use of the elevators. Defendant gave evidence tending to show that the servants of plaintiff were responsible for this, but the evidence is denied by them and they on the contrary say they gave assistance. This would seem to be true as Mrs. Hirschfield testified she tipped them as a reward for their help. At any rate, when the lease expired at 12 o'clock on the night of September 30, the family was not yet out and with the servants slept in the apartment. Carpets and the bedroom furniture had not been removed but were promptly taken out on the following day, October 1.

At about ten o'clock on the morning of October 1, Mr. Pennish, for plaintiff, served upon defendant at his office in Wells street, a notice as follows: "In view of the fact that you did not vacate possession of your apartment within the time provided for in your lease, the undersigned has elected, and does hereby elect, to treat you as a hold-over tenant for another year, and you are accordingly requested to pay October rent immediately."

While the law is otherwise in England (16 R.C.L., § 684, p. 1163) it was decided in New York in the early case of Conway v. Starkweather, 1 Denio 113, 114, that a tenant who holds over after the expiration of his term may, at the election of the landlord, be held to be either a trespasser or tenant for another similar term. Later New York decisions adhere to that rule . . . although the later case of Herter v. Mullen, 159 N.Y. 28, 53 N.E. 700, 44 L.R.A. 703, 70 Am.St.Rep. p. 517, seems to decide that the holding must be voluntary on the part of the tenant.

The New York rule was adopted by the Illinois Supreme Court in the case of Clinton Wire Cloth Co. v. Gardner et al., 99 Ill. 151, and has been followed in subsequent cases based upon the theory, however, that the rule is to be applied only where the holding is voluntary. United Cigar Stores Co. v. Worth–Gyles Co., 212 Ill.App. 26.

The argument for strict adherence to the New York rule is based upon the necessity for certainty as between landlords and tenants with regard to their respective rights. In a note to Herter v. Mullen, supra, in the American State Reports, it is said: "It is a universal rule that if premises are let for a year or from year to year, and the tenant holds over, the landlord may elect to treat him as a tenant from year to year, or when the renting is for a shorter period and the tenant holds over, he may be deemed to hold upon the terms upon which he entered, and the landlord may recover rent of him according to the terms of the original contract or lease. . . . or the landlord may at his election treat the tenant holding over as a trespasser and may bring ejectment against him without any previous notice, unless the holding over has been such that it may be presumed that the landlord has assented thereto. . . ."

The trial court in granting defendant's motion for a new trial stated that it would be sustained "only upon the error the court made in the giving of plaintiff's instruction No. 7." But on an appeal of this kind we are not limited in our review of the appeal to the reasons stated by the trial court. . . . Upon a consideration of the whole record we are of the opinion that the motion for an instructed verdict in favor of defendant should have been given, and that after the trial the motion of defendant for a judgment in his favor notwithstanding the verdict should have been allowed.

An examination of the cases discloses that usually they proceed upon one of two theories. First, that the voluntary action of the tenant is such as to disclose the right of the landlord to assume an intention on the tenant's part to create a second tenancy, or secondly, that the action of the tenant is such that the court will as a matter of law hold the tenant liable for a second lease upon the principle of quasi contract that justice may prevail. Williston on Contracts, Vol. 6, § 1836.

On the undisputed facts of this case we think plaintiff is not entitled to recover upon either theory. The uncontradicted evidence recited above shows no grounds on which a voluntary agreement for a new tenancy could be inferred. Defendant was vacating the premises with reasonable speed and in good faith. The representatives of the landlord were present, knew and assisted them in getting their goods out of the apartment and were given extra pay for doing so. There is not a scintilla of evidence from which the jury could reasonably find there was any intention on the part of defendant to continue the lease. Unfortunately, notwithstanding good faith, the removal of the last piece of furniture was delayed for a few hours. The tenant and his family did not arise at midnight and move out. They waited until the rising of the sun. Shortly thereafter the landlord availed himself of this supposed ancient rule of law and served notice of his intention to collect from defendant $3,300 for his delict. There is nothing either in word or deed of the tenant that indicates an intention on his part to renew. Every action indicated the contrary intention. Defendant, therefore, cannot be held on the theory of a voluntary contract. Nor in our opinion can defendant be held on the theory of quasi contract that justice required an absolute presumption of a contract for another tenancy. The lease provided for precisely such a contingency. The provision was in substance (paragraph 11 not abstracted) that if the tenant failed to move at the expiration of the lease, he should pay double the usual rent for the actual time of his occupancy. This is the agreement of the parties and is reasonable. The claim of plaintiff is highly penal in its nature. It has been held in New York that the rule is not applicable in such a case. Pickett v. Bartlett, 107 N.Y. 277, 14 N.E. 301. In Green v. Kroeger, 67 Mo.App. 621, under similar circumstances the court said: "In this case the lease by express terms provides for the rights of the parties in the contingency of a holding over after its expiration. By the clause to that effect it is distinctly provided that the continued occupancy of the premises after the end of the term shall entitle the lessor to recover double rent from the occupiers 'for all such time.' This clause did not deprive the lessor of his option to retake the premises at the expiration of the lease, but in case of his failure so to do or to make a new agreement with the lessees, it deprived him of the power to do more than recover double rent for the time he should permit the lessees to hold over after the expiration of the lease."

There are no Illinois decisions so far as we are informed to the contrary. We hold the motion of defendant for judgment in his favor notwithstanding the verdict should have been allowed. Under § 92 of the Civil Practice Act, Smith–Hurd Anno.Stats. ch. 110, par. 216, p. 419, the order allowing a new trial will be reversed and judgment entered in this court for the defendant notwithstanding the verdict.

Reversed with judgment here for the defendant.

McSurely, J., concurs.

O'Connor, Presiding Justice (specially concurring).

I agree with what is said in the foregoing opinion and the result reached but I think it ought to be said that the claim made by plaintiff for $3,300 shocks the conscience of the court. It is wholly without merit and ought not to be entertained by any court of justice. As stated in the opinion, defendant had the right to remain in the premises all day of the 30th of September and it is common knowledge in Chicago, of which we take judicial notice, that some leases of apartments expire on the 30th of April and others on the 30th of September, and that a lease to a succeeding tenant begins the first of May and others on the first of October. And everyone knows that tenants who are vacating on the 30th of April or on the 30th of September, as the case might be, have not completed their moving on the last day covered by their respective leases, there being a great many persons moving at those times so that it is physically impossible to do so. But in such cases the "rule of reason" must constantly be kept in mind. . . . Under this rule which is in every case whether we realize it or not, it is not every dereliction however slight which will give rise to a cause of action.

NOTES

1. Somewhat in contrast with legislative and judicial amelioration of the effects of holding over are statutes to be found in some states (their prototypes being two English statutes enacted in 1730 and 1737) which purport to impose liability for double rent upon a holdover tenant. Similarly, a tenant who holds over may be subject to an unlawful detainer statute which imposes a penalty. The courts tend to construe these statutes, like all penal statutes, strictly and to hold them inapplicable where the tenant has a decent excuse for holding over against the landlord's wishes—e.g., a good faith, though erroneous, claim of right. In Feiges v. Racine Dry Goods Co., 231 Wis. 270, 285 N.W. 799, 122 A.L.R. 272 (1939), the tenant firm was unable to move because its striking employees picketed the premises. Holding the tenant not liable for treble damages in an unlawful detainer action, the court said, in part, "To impose treble damages for not doing something that the defendant intended and had arranged and wished to do and that he was prevented from doing by conduct of others beyond his power to control would be so severe that it can not be the basis of an unlawful detainer action wherein the recovery of possession ipso facto imposes the imposition of such penalty. The infliction of a penalty and a judgment that leads to such result can only be warranted by a holding over that is intentional, voluntary and within the defendant's power to prevent or avoid. Only a tortious act by the tenant, at least tortious in the sense that it is an intentional failure to perform an obligation or duty can constitute basis for an action in which such a judgment must be rendered. The plaintiffs herein are demanding damages which trebled amount to over $12,000 because of the judgment for recovery of possession of the leased premises. Manifestly such mulcting of the defendant for a holding over that was involuntary, against its will and beyond its power to prevent, is not within the contemplation of the statute that provides the summary action of unlawful detainer. To hold that the legislature entertained intent of imposition of such a penalty would convict them of unreasonableness and oppression."

2. During the interim between termination of a leasehold and creation of a new tenancy or eviction, a holdover tenant is referred to as a "tenant at sufferance." One so classified is a wrongful possessor, distinguishable from a trepasser only in that the entry into possession by the holdover had been lawful. This distinction once had important procedural implications. See R. Schoshinski, American Law of Landlord & Tenant § 2.20 (1980). It may still be viable today in other contexts.

(2) Right to Extended Occupancy of Certain Housing

SWANN v. GASTONIA HOUSING AUTHORITY

United States Court of Appeals, Fourth Circuit, 1982.
675 F.2d 1342.

Harrison L. Winter, Chief Judge:

Defendants in a class action appeal from a judgment of the district court ordering that tenants in the Gastonia Section 8 Existing Housing Program not be evicted unless the Gastonia Housing Authority (GHA) has determined after a full-fledged hearing that good cause exists for the eviction. We affirm the portion of the district court's judgment holding (1) that the GHA must make a finding of good cause before approving the termination of a tenancy, (2) that a tenant in this program has a constitutionally protected expectation of remaining in his home in the absence of good cause for eviction, and (3) that the eviction constitutes state action. We disagree with the district court, however, that a full-fledged hearing before GHA is required. The statute which requires GHA to make a good cause determination does not go so far as to require a hearing, and the requirements of the due process clause are met by the hearing available in state court if the eviction is brought, as it now must be, for good cause.

Accordingly, we affirm in part and reverse in part and remand.

I.

GHA is a public housing agency which administers a Section 8 Existing Housing Program in Gastonia, North Carolina, under the provisions of 42 U.S.C. § 1437f and 24 C.F.R. part 882. In 1978, the City of Gastonia acquired for demolition the home of James and Jonell Swann. The City fulfilled its statutory duty to provide the Swanns with relocation assistance by helping them obtain a Certificate of Family Participation from GHA. This certificate entitled the Swanns to a rent subsidy from GHA if they rented from a landlord who would participate in the Section 8 Existing Housing Program.

Such a landlord, William Huffstetler, was located. On September 15, 1978, the Swanns and Huffstetler entered into a one-year lease and GHA and Huffstetler entered into a Housing Assistance Payment Contract. The lease provides that either party may terminate at any time by giving thirty days' notice. A feature of the Section 8 Existing Housing Program in Gastonia is that leases are automatically renewed at the end of their terms unless this same termination procedure is followed.

In May 1979, Huffstetler brought a summary eviction action against the Swanns, but they obtained assistance from a legal aid clinic and Huffstetler dismissed the action because he was persuaded that adequate notice to vacate had not been given. In August 1979, Huffstetler informed the Swanns that their one-year lease would not be renewed and asked them to vacate by October 1. The Swanns believed that this was in retaliation for their use of the services of the legal aid clinic.

The version of § 1437f(d)(1)(B) then in effect required all Housing Assistance Payment Contracts to provide that "the agency shall have the sole right to give notice to vacate, with the owner having the right to make representation to the agency for termination of tenancy." See 42 U.S.C. § 1437f(d)(1)(B) (1976).[1] The regulation implementing that version of the statute, 24 C.F.R. § 882.215 (1981), provided that the landlord should send the notice to vacate to the tenant and a copy to the agency for its approval. The regulation also provided that the tenant may present his objections to the agency and that failure by the agency to act within twenty days constitutes approval of the termination. The Swanns requested GHA to disapprove the termination of their tenancy or at least to hold a hearing before making a decision. An informal conference was held, but GHA refused to deviate from its policy of allowing landlords to evict tenants at the end of their lease terms with or without good cause.

On September 22, the Swanns filed a class action founded on 42 U.S.C. § 1983 (1976), in which they alleged that their eviction violated the version of § 1437f then in effect and the due process clause of the Fourteenth Amendment. GHA, a number of its officers in their official capacities and Huffstetler were joined as defendants. The Swanns claimed to represent a class of all present and future participants in the Gastonia Section 8 Existing Housing Program. They sought only declaratory and injunctive relief. The landlord agreed to let the Swanns remain in their home pending the completion of the litigation. In early 1980, James Swann died and was dropped as a named plaintiff. The parties stipulated to the facts and filed cross motions for summary judgment.

On November 25, 1980, an order was entered granting the plaintiff's motion and denying the defendants' motion. The district court ruled that the old version of § 1437f required that GHA make a finding of good cause before approving the termination of any tenancy. With respect to the due process claim, the district court ruled that the old version of § 1437f and prevailing custom gave a tenant a constitutionally protected expectation of remaining in his home in the absence of good cause for eviction and that the eviction constituted state action. 502 F.Supp. 362.

At the end of the year, the class was certified. On April 8, 1981, a final judgment was entered. The court repeated its earlier conclusions and then, without further discussion, held that the process due is a hearing by GHA with the following elements: (a) the hearing should be conducted by an impartial decision maker who would issue a written

1. An amended version of § 1437f(d)(1)(B) is applicable to leases entered into on or after October 1, 1981. It provides for no agency involvement in the eviction but, unlike the version it supplanted, it explicitly requires that there be good cause for the termination of a tenancy. See Omnibus Budget Reconciliation Act of 1981, Pub.L. No. 97–35, § 326(e), 95 Stat. 357, 407 (1981). We express no opinion, of course, on the procedures to be followed for the termination of tenancies entered into on or after October 1, 1981.

decision, and (b) both the landlord and the tenant should have the right to counsel, the right to call witnesses, and the right to cross-examine the other side's witnesses. As a predicate to such a hearing, the judgment provided that the tenant would have to receive adequate notice of the alleged grounds for the termination of his tenancy.

II.

We begin with the question of whether the statute requires that GHA make a finding of good cause before approving the termination of a tenancy. We think that it does.

The old version of § 1437f contained no explicit good cause requirement, but we think that one was implied by the language of § 1437f(d)(1)(B). That portion of the old version required all Housing Assistance Payment Contracts to provide that "the agency shall have the sole right to give notice to vacate, with the owner having the right to make representation to the agency for termination of tenancy." See 42 U.S.C. § 1437f(d)(1)(B) (1976). This provision was pointless if the housing authority was not to exercise some judgment before an eviction occurs.

The old version of § 1437f(d)(1)(B) was applicable only to Section 8 programs involving existing housing. A different provision governed Section 8 programs involving newly constructed or substantially rehabilitated housing, and it expressly required all Housing Assistance Payment Contracts to provide "that all ownership, management, and maintenance responsibilities, including the selection of tenants and the *termination of tenancy*, shall be assumed by the owner." 42 U.S.C. § 1437f(e)(2) (1976) (emphasis added). This language with respect to new or rehabilitated housing supports the conclusion that the particular approval scheme provided for in the old version of § 1437f(d)(1)(B) with regard to existing housing was adopted for a reason.

It certainly is possible that the agency was meant to do nothing more than determine that evictions covered by the provision met the requirements of state law and the lease. That, of course, is all that 24 C.F.R. § 882.215 (1981) provided for. It is difficult to imagine, however, why Congress would have thought it necessary for someone other than the state courts to make that determination. We think that the most reasonable interpretation of the statute is that it was meant to require the agency to determine that good cause existed before approving the termination of a tenancy.[2]

The district court gave no indication that it based the hearing requirement that it prescribed on the statute, and we think that was proper. If the agency must make a good cause determination, it follows necessarily that the landlord must state his reason for wanting to

2. We note that several courts have declared illegal the procedure set out in 24 C.F.R. § 882.215 (1981), whereby the *landlord* sends the notice to vacate. See Jeffries v. Georgia Residential Finance Authority, 503 F.Supp. 610 (N.D.Ga.1980); Brown v. Harris, 491 F.Supp. 845 (N.D.Cal. 1980). These courts deemed the old version of § 1437f(d)(1)(B) ("the agency shall have the sole right to give notice to vacate") to mean what it says. The present suit did not challenge the procedure set out in the regulation, and we express no opinion on the subject.

terminate the tenancy, and that the tenant must be informed of the reason and given an opportunity to respond. There is simply no basis in the statute, however, for requiring a full-fledged hearing like that ordered by the district court. Cf. S.Rep. No. 871, 95th Cong., 2d Sess. (1978), *reprinted in* [1978] U.S.Code Cong. & Ad.News 4773, 4788 (a later Congress's expression of opinion that the statute required a good cause determination but not a hearing). We therefore must consider plaintiff's claim that the due process clause of the Fourteenth Amendment affords her a right to a full and complete hearing before GHA.

III.

For the due process clause of the Fourteenth Amendment to dictate the procedure to be followed before a tenant is evicted, two conditions must be met. First, the tenant must have an expectation, rising to the status of a property interest, of remaining in his home in the absence of good cause for eviction. Second, an eviction must constitute state action.

We have already indicated that a tenant in this Section 8 Existing Housing Program is assured by statute that he will continue in occupancy in the absence of good cause for eviction. It is now beyond question that such statutory entitlements are protected by the due process clause. See Goldberg v. Kelly, 397 U.S. 254, 261–62, 90 S.Ct. 1011, 1016–17, 25 L.Ed.2d 287 (1970) (statutory entitlement to welfare benefits).[3]

We think also that the eviction constitutes state action. To begin, there is substantial continuing agency involvement in the tenancy. The government pays a major portion of each month's rent directly to the landlord and it will pay eighty percent of the rent for up to sixty days of the tenant vacates in violation of the lease. See 24 C.F.R. § 882.105 (1981). The landlord submits to significant regulation. See, e.g., id. § 882.109 (housing quality standard); id. § 882.111 (equal opportunity requirements). More importantly, GHA must determine on a case-by-case basis whether good cause exists for terminations of tenancies. We think that this government involvement is significantly more indicative of state action than that deemed insufficient to constitute state action in Jackson v. Metropolitan Edison Co., 419 U.S. 345, 95 S.Ct. 449, 42 L.Ed.2d 477 (1974) (state utility commission approved utility's general tariff, which included procedures for terminating service to customers). We also think that the government involvement in the present case is significantly more indicative of state action than the mere grant to all landlords of access to state eviction proceedings, which has generally been held insufficient to constitute state action. See, e.g., Weigand v. Afton View Apartments, 473 F.2d 545 (8 Cir.1973); McGuane v. Chenango Court, Inc., 431 F.2d 1189 (2 Cir.1970) (per curiam), cert. denied, 401 U.S. 994, 91 S.Ct. 1238, 28 L.Ed.2d 532 (1971).

3. Since we hold that the statute is sufficient to give a tenant a constitutionally protected expectation, we need not consider the validity of the district court's partial reliance on prevailing custom. See generally Meachum v. Fano, 427 U.S. 215, 96 S.Ct. 2532, 49 L.Ed.2d 451 (1976); Bishop v. Wood, 426 U.S. 341, 96 S.Ct. 2074, 48 L.Ed.2d 684 (1976); Joy v. Daniels, 479 F.2d 1236, 1241 (4 Cir.1973).

Accordingly, we hold that the two conditions requisite to application of the due process clause are met and that the due process clause of the Fourteenth Amendment dictates the procedure to be followed before a tenant in this Section 8 Existing Housing Program may be evicted.

IV.

The question of whether a hearing before GHA is required is governed, we think, by Joy v. Daniels, 479 F.2d 1236 (4 Cir.1973). Dealing with a different quasi-public housing program from the one involved in the present case,[4] we held in *Joy* that, even though the lease provided that it was terminable at the expiration of the term, a tenant had a constitutionally protected expectation of remaining in his home in the absence of good cause for eviction, that an eviction constituted state action, but that any process that was due was adequately provided in the state eviction proceeding. We directed that the landlord be enjoined from attempting to evict the tenant except for cause.

The differences between various quasi-public housing programs may be crucial when a court must determine the scope of a tenant's constitutionally protected expectations and whether an eviction constitutes state action. As for whether the state eviction proceeding adequately provides the process that is due, however, we think that the present case raises a question that is identical to the one that was answered in *Joy*.

Joy arose in South Carolina. The eviction statute then in effect in that state provided that a "tenant may be ejected upon application of the landlord or his agent when (a) such tenant fails or refuses to pay the rent when due or demanded, (b) the term of tenancy or occupancy has ended or (c) the terms and conditions of the lease have been violated." S.C.Code § 41–101 (1962). In an earlier case, Johnson v. Tamsberg, 430 F.2d 1125 (4 Cir. 1970), we had held that where a tenant in a public housing project was evicted in South Carolina for violating the terms and conditions of her lease, the state eviction proceeding adequately provided any process that was constitutionally due, since the landlord was required to prove the truth of his accusations. Reasoning that the imposition of a good cause requirement recast all end-of-term evictions as evictions for violating the terms and conditions of the lease, we followed *Johnson* in *Joy* and held that the process that was constitutionally due would be adequately provided in the eviction proceeding in state court.

The present case arose in North Carolina. The eviction statute in effect in that state is indistinguishable in any relevant respect from the statute involved in *Johnson* and *Joy*. See N.C.Gen.Stat. § 42–26 (1976). The conclusion is thus inescapable, we think, that the process that is due in the present case is adequately provided by the state court in the eviction proceeding if, as we have held, the tenant may be evicted only for cause and not merely for expiration of term.

4. The landlord in *Joy* received federal mortgage benefits under 12 U.S.C. § 1715*l*(d)(3) (1971) and federal rent subsidies under 12 U.S.C. § 1701s(b) (1971).

The plaintiff-appellees contend that the matter is governed instead by Caulder v. Durham Housing Authority, 433 F.2d 998 (4 Cir. 1970), cert. denied, 401 U.S. 1003, 91 S.Ct. 1228, 28 L.Ed.2d 539 (1971). That case, like the present one, arose in North Carolina. It involved an eviction statute indistinguishable in any relevant respect from the one at issue in *Joy* and *Johnson* and the one at issue in the present case. See N.C.Gen.Stat. § 42–26 (1966).

In *Caulder*, the public housing authority held a summary proceeding at which it determined that the tenant should be evicted because of immoral acts allegedly committed by her children. The tenant denied the allegations, but was not allowed to cross-examine her children's accusers or even to know their names. The tenant then brought suit in federal court under 42 U.S.C. § 1983 (1964), claiming that she had been denied her constitutional right to due process in the summary proceeding just described. She asked that the public housing authority be enjoined from evicting her. Meanwhile, the public housing authority brought an end-of-term eviction proceeding in state court. The federal district court dismissed the tenant's action and she appealed.

The first issue on appeal was whether the anti-injunction statute, 28 U.S.C. § 2283 (1964), barred the tenant's action. We held that it did not. The "in-aid-of-its-jurisdiction" exception to the anti-injunction statute was applicable, we said, because the end-of-term eviction proceeding in state court did not give the tenant an adequate forum for her constitutional claim. *See* 433 F.2d at 1001–02.[5] The only issue in the state proceeding, we pointed out, was whether or not the tenant was holding over. See id. at 1002. Turning to the tenant's constitutional claim, we held that the tenant was entitled to a full-fledged hearing before being evicted on the basis of the allegations on which the public housing authority had relied. See id. at 1002–04.

The important thing to note for present purposes is that there was no claim in *Caulder* that a tenant could never be evicted except for good cause. In other words, there was no claim that the landlord should not be permitted to bring an end-of-term eviction proceeding in state court. All we held in *Caulder* was that when a public landlord determined to evict a tenant by reason of her family's conduct, the tenant was entitled to a hearing. Since it was uncontested that the public housing authority could avail itself of a summary end-of-term eviction proceeding in state court, it followed that the required hearing had to be held by the public authority itself.[6]

5. This question would not arise today. The Supreme Court has held that the "expressly-authorized-by-Act-of-Congress" exception to the anti-injunction statute applies to injunctions under § 1983. See Mitchum v. Foster, 407 U.S. 225, 92 S.Ct. 2151, 32 L.Ed.2d 705 (1972). At the time *Caulder* was decided, however, this circuit had ruled to the contrary. See Baines v. City of Danville, 337 F.2d 579 (4 Cir. 1964) (in banc), cert. denied sub nom. Chase v. McCain, 381 U.S. 939, 85 S.Ct. 1772, 14 L.Ed.2d 702 (1965).

6. HUD responded to *Caulder* by requiring that all publicly-owned housing projects under its jurisdiction hold a full-fledged hearing before every termination. See U. S. Department of Housing and Urban Development, Grievance Procedure in Low Rent Public Housing Projects, HUD Circular RHM 7465.9 (Feb. 22, 1971).

Joy and the present case are distinguishable from *Caulder* because we held in *Joy*, and we now hold in the present case, that the landlord can never avail himself of a summary end-of-term eviction proceeding in state court. The eviction proceeding in state court must be brought, if at all, for cause. That proceeding will provide the tenant with all the process that is due. A hearing before the housing agency therefore is not constitutionally required.

The judgment of the district court is affirmed in part and reversed in part and the case is remanded for the entry of a modified decree consistent with the views expressed herein.

Affirmed in part; reversed in part; and remanded.

CHAPMAN, CIRCUIT JUDGE, dissenting:

I do not think that 42 U.S.C. § 1437f or the Fourteenth Amendment require a showing of good cause prior to termination of a lease in the § 8 Existing Housing Program, therefore, I respectfully dissent.

The majority bases its holding that a good cause determination is required solely on the language of 42 U.S.C. § 1437f(d)(1)(B) that "the agency has the sole right to give notice to vacate, with the owner having the right to make representation to the agency for termination of the tenancy." The majority reasons that the agency's role is meaningless if its function was to do nothing more than determine that evictions applied for meet requirements of state law and the lease. I do not agree with this narrow view.

The proper function of the Public Housing Authority (PHA), as evinced by the regulations applying thereto, is to examine the sufficiency of the grounds for eviction under the terms of the lease. This is far from pointless. Participants in § 8 Existing Housing Projects are, on the whole, poorly suited to determine their own rights under a lease. Recognizing this fact, Congress placed the PHA between the tenant and the landlord as interpreter of the lease. By preventing terminations not proper under the lease the PHA protects the rights of tenants without the expense and embarrassment of defending an eviction action in state court. The proper interpretation of the statute is in my view that the PHA examine the sufficiency of the grounds for termination under the terms of the lease. This interpretation provides substantial protection to the tenant and protects the expectation of the private landlord that he will be able to take his property out of the program if he desires upon expiration of the lease. The majority would impose upon the landlord a mandatory renewal term, to which he has not agreed. His agreement with the PHA specifically prvides that the term of his commitment shall be one year (the term of the lease).

The federal agency assigned the task of implementing § 8 programs has taken the view expressed in this dissent. Title 24 C.F.R. § 882.215 provides that the PHA shall examine the sufficiency of the grounds for eviction under the terms of the lease, imposing no requirement of a good cause showing. Moreover, 24 C.F.R. § 882.107 states that the lease term be for not less than one year nor more than three. The majority would apparently require a showing of good cause at the end of the third year of a three year lease making it extremely difficult for a landlord to ever remove his property from the § 8 Existing Housing Program.

For the reasons stated above, I would hold that a determination of good cause for termination is not implied by 42 U.S.C. § 1437f. For reasons hereafter stated I would also hold that such a determination is not required by the Fourteenth Amendment. Joy v. Daniels, 479 F.2d 1236 (1973) teaches that in determining whether a tenant has an expectation of renewal sufficient to create a "property interest" protected by due process "we must look to applicable statutes, governmental regulations and the custom and understanding of public landlords . . . ." As I stated above, it is my view that applicable statutes and regulations do not create an expectation of renewal. To the contrary, the language of the statutes and regulations create an expectation that lease terms will be honored. Moreover, the custom and understanding of a private landlord is different from that of a public landlord found in *Joy*.[1] The private landlord, and the private tenant as well, enter a lease expecting to be bound by its terms, especially terms dealing with duration, termination and renewal.

One purpose of the § 8 Existing Housing Program is to promote economically mixed housing, 42 U.S.C. § 1437f(a). That is, to inject qualified tenants into areas of single family dwellings rather than into massive apartment projects like the one involved in *Joy*. Because it is intended to put those who might not otherwise be able to afford it into areas of privately owned residences, the program should be governed by the rules and expectations applicable to private sector property owners and tenants. It is difficult to imagine how a § 8 tenant could have an expectation of renewal based on the applicable statutes, regulations, and understandings of private landlords. I would hold, therefore, that § 8 Existing Housing Tenants do not have a property interest in renewal of a lease and, therefore, that no good cause showing is mandated by the Fourteenth Amendment.

NOTE

Tenants who vacated a housing project owned by HUD following HUD's decision to demolish the project as economically infeasible were held entitled to a preliminary injunction requiring HUD to discontinue demolition, restore already demolished units to minimally habitable conditions existing as of the date of HUD's decision to demolish, and permit former tenants to return on the same terms. Cole v. Lynn, 389 F.Supp. 99 (D.D.C.1975), enforced and modified Cole v. Hills, 396 F.Supp. 1235. HUD's decision to demolish was deemed flawed by failure to consider fully alternatives to demolition and to afford a hearing to tenants.

---

1. *Joy* involved a project with a number of apartments. The present action covers one freestanding residence.

SENIOR CITIZENS AND DISABLED PROTECTED TENANCY ACT

N.J. Stat.Ann. 2A:18–61.22 et seq. (West Supp.1983).

2A:18–61.23 Legislative Findings and Declarations

The Legislature finds that research studies have demonstrated that the forced eviction and relocation of elderly persons from their established homes and communities harm the mental and physical health of these senior citizens, and that these disruptions in the lives of older persons affect adversely the social, economic and cultural characteristics of communities of the State, and increase the costs borne by all State citizens in providing for their public health, safety and welfare. These conditions are particularly serious in light of the rising costs of home ownership, and are of increasing concern where rental housing is converted into condominiums or cooperatives which senior citizens on fixed limited incomes cannot afford, an occurrence which is becoming more and more frequent in this State under prevailing economic circumstances. The Legislature, therefore, declares that it is in the public interest of the State to avoid the forced eviction and relocation of senior citizen tenants wherever possible, specifically in those instances where rental housing market conditions and particular financial circumstances combine to diminish the ability of senior citizens to obtain satisfactory comparable housing within their established communities, and where the eviction action is the result not of any failure of the senior citizen tenant to abide by the terms of a lease or rental agreement, but of the owner's decision advantageously to dispose of residential property through the device of conversion to a condominium or cooperative.

The Legislature further finds that it is in the public interest of the State to avoid the forced eviction and the displacement of the handicapped wherever possible because of their limited mobility and the limited number of housing units which are suitable for their needs.

The Legislature further declares that in the service of this public interest it is appropriate that qualified senior citizen tenants and disabled tenants be accorded a period of protected tenancy, during which they shall be entitled to the fair enjoyment of the dwelling unit within the converted residential structure, to continue for such time, up to 40 years, as the conditions and circumstances which make necessary such protected tenancy shall continue.

The Legislature further finds that the promotion of this public interest is possible only if senior citizen tenants and disabled tenants are protected during this period from alterations in the terms of the tenancy or rent increases which are the result solely of an owner's decision to convert.

2A:18–61.24 Definitions

As used in this amendatory and supplementary act:

a. "Senior citizen tenant" means a person who is at least 62 years of age on the date of the conversion recording for the building or structure in which is located the dwelling unit of which he is a tenant, or the surviving spouse of such a person if the person should die after the owner files the conversion recording; provided that the building or structure has been the principal residence of the senior citizen tenant or the spouse for the 2 years immediately preceding the conversion recording or the death, as the case may be;

b. "Disabled tenant" means a person who is, on the date of the conversion recording for the building or structure in which is located the dwelling unit of which he is a tenant, totally and permanently unable to engage in any substantial gainful activity by reason of any medically determinable physical or mental impairment, including blindness; provided that the building or structure has been the principal residence of the disabled tenant for the 2 years immediately preceding the conversion recording. For the purposes of this subsection, "blindness" means central visual acuity of 20/200 or less in the better eye with the use of correcting lens. An eye which is accompanied by a limitation in the fields of vision such that the widest diameter of the visual field subtends an angle no greater than 20 degrees shall be considered as having a central visual acuity of 20/200 or less;

c. "Tenant's annual household income" means the total income from all sources during the last full calendar year for all members of the household who reside in the dwelling unit at the time the tenant applies for protected tenant status, whether or not such income is subject to taxation by any taxing authority;

d. "Application for registration of conversion" means an application for registration filed with the Department of Community Affairs in accordance with "The Planned Real Estate Development Full Disclosure Act," P.L.1977, c. 419 (C. 45:22A–21 et seq.);

e. "Registration of conversion" means an approval of an application for registration by the Department of Community Affairs in accordance with "The Planned Real Estate Development Full Disclosure Act," P.L.1977, c. 419 (C. 45:22A–21 et seq.);

f. "Convert" means to convert one or more buildings or structures or a mobile home park containing in the aggregate not less than 5 dwelling units or mobile home sites or pads from residential rental use to condominium, cooperative, planned residential development or separable fee simple ownership of the dwelling units or of the mobile home sites or pads;

g. "Conversion recording" means the recording with the appropriate county officer of a master deed for condominium or a deed to a cooperative corporation for a cooperative or the first deed of sale to a purchaser of an individual unit for a planned residential development or separable fee simple ownership of the dwelling units;

h. "Protected tenancy period" means, except as otherwise provided in section 11 of this amendatory and supplementary act, the 40 years following the conversion recording for the building or structure in which is located the dwelling unit of the senior citizen tenant or disabled tenant.

2A:18–61.25 Protected Tenancy Status; Conversion of Dwelling Unit of Eligible Senior Citizen or Disabled Tenant

Each eligible senior citizen tenant or disabled tenant shall be granted a protected tenancy status with respect to his dwelling unit whenever the building or structure in which that unit is located shall be converted. The protected tenancy status shall be granted upon proper application and qualification pursuant to the provisions of this amendatory and supplementary act.

. . .

2A:18–61.27 Notice of Intention to Register for Conversion to Administrative Agency or Officer and to Tenants; Contents: Affidavit of Proof of Notice to Tenants

The owner of any building or structure who, after the effective date of this amendatory and supplementary act, seeks to convert any premises, shall, prior to his filing of the application for registration of conversion with the Department of Community Affairs, notify the administrative agency or officer responsible for administering this amendatory and supplementary act of his intention to so file. The owner shall supply the agency or officer with a list of every tenant residing in the premises, with stamped envelopes addressed to each tenant and with sufficient copies of the notice to tenants and application form for protected tenancy status. Within 10 days therefter, the administrative agency or officer shall notify each residential tenant in writing of the owner's intention and of the applicability of the provisions of this amendatory and supplementary act and shall provide him with a written application form. The agency's or officer's notice shall be substantially in the following form: . . .

2A:18–61.28 Application for Eligibility; Determination; Grounds; Written Notice of Eligibility to Tenant and to Owner

Within 30 days after receipt of an application for protected tenancy status by a tenant, the administrative agency or officer shall make a determination of eligibility. It shall send written notice of eligibility to each senior citizen tenant or disabled tenant who:

a. Applied therefor on or before the date of registration of conversion by the Department of Community Affairs; and,

b. Qualifies as an eligible senior citizen tenant or disabled tenant pursuant to this amendatory and supplementary act; and

c. Has an annual household income that does not exceed an amount equal to three times the County per capita personal income, as last reported by the Department of Labor and Industry on the basis of the U.S. Department of Commerce's Bureau of Economic Analysis data; and,

d. Has occupied the premises as his principal residence for the past 2 years. . . .

2A:18–61.31 Rent Increases; Limitations

In a municipality which does not have a rent control ordinance in effect, no evidence of increased costs which are solely the result of the conversion, including but not limited to any increase in financing or carrying costs, and which do not add services or amenities not previously provided shall be used as a basis to establish the reasonableness of a rent increase under section 2f. of P.L.1974, c. 49 (C. 2A:18–61.1).

In a municipality which has a rent control ordinance in effect, a rent increase for a tenant with a protected tenancy status, or for any tenant to whom notice of termination pursuant to section 3g. of P.L. 1974, c. 49 (C. 2A:18–61.2) has been given, shall not exceed the increase authorized by the ordinance for rent controlled units. Increased costs which are solely the result of a conversion, including but not limited to any increase in financing or carrying costs, and which do not add services or amenities not previously provided shall not be used as a basis for an increase in a fair return or hardship hearing before a municipal rent board or on any appeal from such determination.

2A:18–61.32 Termination of Protected Tenancy Status; Grounds; Removal; Procedures

The administrative agency or officer shall terminate the protected tenancy status immediately upon finding that:

a. The dwelling unit is no longer the principal residence of the senior citizen tenant or disabled tenant; or

b. The tenant's annual household income, or the average of the tenant's annual household income for the current year, computed on an annual basis, and the tenant's annual household income for the 2 preceding years, whichever is less, exceeds an amount equal to three times the county per capita personal income as last reported by the Department of Labor and Industry on the basis of the U.S. Department of Commerce's Bureau of Economic Analysis data.

Upon the termination of the protected tenancy status by the administrative agency or officer, the senior citizen tenant or disabled tenant may be removed from the dwelling unit pursuant to P.L.1974, c. 49 (C. 2A:18–61.1 et seq.), except that all notice and other times set forth therein shall be calculated and extend from the date of the expiration or termination of the protected tenancy period, or the date of the expiration of the last lease entered into with the senior citizen tenant or disabled tenant during the protected tenancy period, whichever shall be later.

. . .

2A:18–61.36 Modification or Waiver of Provisions of Act Void and Unenforceable; Exceptions

Except as otherwise provided in this section, any provision in a lease or other agreement which waives or modifies any provision of this amendatory and supplementary act shall be void and unenforceable as against public policy. An owner and a tenant may, however, agree to a modification or waiver of some or all of the protections afforded to the tenant pursuant to the provisions of this amendatory and supplemental act provided that:

a. The modification or waiver is encompassed in written contract separate from the lease;

b. The modification or waiver is voluntarily entered into without duress;

c. The modification or waiver is entered into with full understanding of the terms by each party;

d. The modification or waiver is for adequate consideration; and,

e. The tenant's signature on the modification or waiver is affixed and notarized after the tenant moves into the apartment.

In any action involving a modification or waiver, the owner shall have the burden of proof to establish that the requirements of this section have been met. . . .

SEAWALL ASSOCIATES v. CITY OF NEW YORK

Court of Appeals of New York, 1989.
74 N.Y.2d 92, 544 N.Y.S.2d 542, 542 N.E.2d 1059.

HANCOCK, JUDGE.

Local Law No. 9 prohibits the demolition, alteration, or conversion of single-room occupancy (SRO) properties and obligates the owners to restore all units to habitable condition and lease them at controlled rents for an indefinite period. Plaintiffs, real estate developers who own SRO properties, challenge the law as an unconstitutional taking of private property without just compensation. Defendants, the City of New York and various officials, contend that the law is a valid effort to help prevent homelessness by preserving the stock of low-rent SRO housing. In our view, Local Law No. 9 is facially invalid as both a physical and regulatory taking in violation of the Federal and State Constitutions and we, therefore, declare it null and void.

I.

After years of encouraging the demolition and redevelopment of SRO properties—which the City of New York considered substandard housing—the City abandoned its policy when it found that the stock of low-cost rental housing was shrinking at an alarming rate (see, Blackburn, Single Room Occupancy in New York City, at 1–4 to 1–7). On August 5, 1985, the City enacted Local Law No. 59 which imposed an 18–month moratorium on the demolition of conversion of structures containing SRO units. Thereafter, Local Law No. 22 was enacted to extend the moratorium through the end of 1986. Local Law No. 22 added the requirement that owners of SRO properties rehabilitate all vacant units and offer them for rent, and it provided for substantial monetary penalties for noncompliance.

Plaintiffs commenced separate actions challenging Local Law No. 22 as violative of the "Takings" Clauses of the Federal and State Constitutions. Supreme Court consolidated the actions and declared the law invalid to the extent that it imposed affirmative obligations on property owners to rehabilitate and then rent vacant units (134 Misc.2d 187). The City did not perfect an appeal; it did, however, alter the provisions of Local Law No. 22 by enacting Local Law No. 1 on February 2, 1987, which, in turn, was amended and reenacted as Local Law No. 9 on March 5, 1987. Local Law No. 9 extended the prior moratorium for an initial five-year period with the possibility of unlimited renewals.

The main provisions of Local Law No. 9 are as follows:

Moratorium. The conversion, alteration and demolition of SRO multiple dwellings are prohibited (Administrative Code of City of New York § 27–198.2); the moratorium extends for five years and is renewable for additional five-year periods as the City Council deems necessary (Local Laws, 1987, No. 9 of City of New York § 7).

Rehabilitation and Antiwarehousing. SRO property owners must rehabilitate and make habitable every SRO unit in their buildings, and lease every unit to a "bona fide" tenant ("rent-up" obligation) at controlled rents (Administrative Code § 27–2151(a)); an owner is presumed to have violated these requirements if any unit remains vacant for a period of 30 days (§ 27–2152(d)).

Penalties. Noncompliance is punishable by fines including $150,000 for each dwelling unlawfully altered, converted or demolished, with an additional $45,000 per unit for reducing the total number of units (§ 27–198.2(g)(2), (5)); a $500 per unit penalty is provided for each unit unrented to a bona fide tenant (§ 27–2152(e)).

Buy–Out and Replacement Exemptions. An owner may purchase an exemption from the moratorium by payment of $45,000 per unit (or such other amount as the Commission of the Department of Housing Preservation and Development determines would equal the cost of a replacement unit; or by providing an equal number of replacement units approved by the Commissioner (§ 27–198.2(d)(4)(a)(i), (ii)).

Hardship Exemption. The amount of payment or the number of replacement units required for an exemption may be reduced at the discretion of the Commissioner, in whole or in part, if there is no reasonable possibility that such owner can make a reasonable rate of return, defined as a net annual return of 8½% of the assessed value of the property as an SRO multiple dwelling (§ 27–198.2(d)(4)(b)).

. . . Supreme Court . . . held that the so-called "buy-out," "replacement," and "hardship" exemptions failed to save Local Law No. 9 . . . and concluded that the law was invalid as a taking without just compensation in violation of both the Federal and State Constitutions. The Appellate Division disagreed, declaring the law constitutional in all respects. 142 A.D.2d 72, 534 N.Y.S.2d 958. For the following reasons, we now reverse.

II.

"The Fifth Amendment's guarantee that private property shall not be taken for the public use without just compensation was designed to bar Government from forcing some people alone to bear public burdens which, in all fairness and justice, should be borne by the public as a whole." (Armstrong v. United States, 364 U.S. 40, 49, 80 S.Ct. 1563, 1569, 4 L.Ed.2d 1554). The corollary to this oft-quoted proposition is that "government action that works a taking of property rights necessarily implicates the 'constitutional obligation to pay just compensation.'" (First Lutheran Church v. Los Angeles County, 482 U.S. 304, 315, 107 S.Ct. 2378, 2386, 96 L.Ed.2d 250, quoting Armstrong v. United States, supra, 364 U.S. at 49, 80 S.Ct. at 1569). The question here, as in any case where government action is challenged as violative of the right to just compensation, is whether the uncompensated obligations and restrictions imposed by the governmental action force individual property owners to bear more than a just share of obligations which are rightfully those of society at large.

In our opinion, the provisions of Local Law No. 9, which not only prevent the SRO property owners from developing their properties by replacing the existing structures, but also compel them to refurbish the structures and keep them fully rented, impose on the property owners more than their just share of such societal obligations. Whether viewed as effecting a physical or regulatory taking, Local Law No. 9, we believe, violates the "Takings" Clauses of the Fifth Amendment of the Federal Constitution and article I, § 7 of the New York State Constitution.

. . .

The rent-control and other landlord-tenant regulations that have been upheld by the Supreme Court and this court merely involved restrictions imposed on existing tenancies where the landlords had voluntarily put their properties to use for residential housing. Unlike Local Law No. 9, however, those regulations did not force the owners, in the first instance, to subject their properties to a use which they neither planned nor desired. The local law at issue in Loab Estates [v. Druhe, 300 N.Y. 176, 90 N.E.2d 25 (1949)], for example, barred the eviction of residential tenants unless provisions had been made for their relocation (300 N.Y., at 179, 90 N.E.2d 25). And the Federal rent-control statute in Bowies explicitly did not require "any person . . . to offer any accommodations for rent" (321 U.S. at 517, 64 S.Ct. at 648). By sharp contrast to the statutes in Loab Estates and Bowies, Local Law No. 9 compels owners to be residential landlords; it requires owners to rehabilitate and offer their properties for rent, as SRO units, to persons with whom they have no existing landlord-tenant relationship.

The City, however, argues that, although the owners are compelled to rent their units, there can be no physical taking here because they have not been divested of all control over the selection of tenants and the rental terms. But this minimal authority retained by the owners over their own properties does not distinguish the City's action here from other physical takings. It is forced occupation by strangers under the rent-up provisions of the law, not the identities of the new tenants or the terms of the leases, which deprives the owners of their possessory interests and results in physical takings.

We conclude that Local Law No. 9 has effected a per se physical taking because it "interfere(s) so drastically" (Nollan v. California Coastal Commn., supra, 483 U.S. at 836, 107 S.Ct. at 3148) with the SRO property owners' fundamental rights to possess and to exclude (see, Loretto v. Teleprompter Manhattan CATV Corp., supra, 458 U.S. at 435–436, 102 S.Ct. at 3175–3176). The law requires nothing less of the owners than "to suffer the physical occupation of (their) building(s) by third parties" (id. at 440, 102 S.Ct. at 3178; see also, Kaiser Aetna v. United States, supra, 444 U.S. at 179–180, 100 S.Ct. at 392–393).

. . .

Even if Local Law No. 9 were not held to effect a physical taking, it would still be facially invalid as a regulatory taking. "Suffice it to say that government regulation—by definition—involves the adjustment of rights for the public good. Often this adjustment curtails some potential for the use or economic exploitation of private property." (Andrus v. Allard, 444 U.S. 51, 65, 100 S.Ct. 318, 326, 62 L.Ed.2d 210). But the constitutional guarantee against uncompensated takings is violated when the adjustment of rights for the public good becomes so disproportionate that it can be said that the governmental action is "forcing some people alone to bear public burdens which, in all fairness and justice, should be borne by the public as a whole." (Armstrong v. United States, supra, 564 U.S. at 49, 80 S.Ct. at 1569.) There is no "set formula" for determining in all cases when an adjustment of rights has reached the point when "justice and fairness" require that compensation be paid (see, Penn Cent. Transp. Co. v. New York City, 438 U.S. 104, 124, 98 S.Ct. 2646, 2659, 57 L.Ed.2d 631). It is basic, however, that such a burden-shifting regulation of the use of private property will, without more, constitute a taking: (1) if it denies an owner economically viable use of his property, or (2) if it does not substantially advance legitimate State interests. . . . We turn first to whether the law denies owners the economically viable use of their properties.

. . .

As previously discussed, the coerced rental provisions deprive owners the fundamental right to possess their properties. Moreover, these mandatory rental provisions—together with the prohibition against demolition, alteration and conversion of the properties to other uses, and the requirement that uninhabitable units be refurbished—deny owners of SRO buildings any right to use their properties as they see fit. Unquestionably, the effect of the law is to strip owners of SRO buildings—who may have purchased their properties solely to turn them into profitable investments by tearing down and replacing the existing structures with new ones (as plaintiffs claim they have)—of the very right to use their properties for any such purpose. Owners are forced to devote their properties to another use which, albeit one which might serve the City's interests, bears no relation to any economic purpose which could be reasonably contemplated by a private investor.

Finally, Local Law No. 9, particularly in those provisions prohibiting redevelopment and mandating rental, inevitably impairs the ability of owners to sell their properties for any sums approaching their investments. Thus, the local law must also negatively affect the owners' right to dispose of their properties. By any test, we think these restrictions deny the owners "economically viable use" of their properties.

. . .

There can be no question that the development rights which have been totally abrogated by the local law are, standing alone, valuable components of the "bundle of rights" making up their fee interests (see, Michelman, [Property, Utility and Fairness: Comments on the Ethical Foundations of "Just Compensation" Law] 80 Harv.L.Rev. [1165] at 1233 [1967] (prospective continuing use "is a discrete twig out of (the owner's) fee simple bundle" of rights)). Indeed, in French Investing Co. v. City of New York, 39 N.Y.2d 587, 385 N.Y.S.2d 5, 350 N.E.2d 381, we recognized that development rights "are an essential component of the value of the underlying property" and that "they are a potentially valuable and even a transferable commodity and may not be disregarded in determining whether the ordinance has destroyed the economic value of the underlying property" (id., at 597, 385 N.Y.S.2d 5, 350 N.E.2d 381).

. . .

We agree with plaintiffs, moreover, that Local Law No. 9 does not pass the other threshold test for constitutional validity of regulatory takings: that the burdens imposed substantially advance legitimate State interests (see, Nollan v. California Coastal Commn., supra; Agins v. Tiburon, supra; Penn Cent. Transp. Co. v. New York City, supra).

Of course, the end sought to be furthered by Local Law No. 9 is of the greatest societal importance—alleviating the critical problems of homelessness. The question here, however, concerns the means established by the local law purportedly to achieve this end. In other words, can it be said that imposing the burdens of the forced refurbishing and rent-up provisions of the owners of SRO properties substantially advances the aim of alleviating the homelessness problem? . . .

Defendants contend that by increasing the availability of SRO units the antiwarehousing and moratorium measures will provide more available low-cost housing and, thereby, further the aim of alleviating homelessness; this relationship between means and ends, they argue, supplies the required "close nexus." The City's own Blackburn study, however, acknowledges that a ban on converting, destroying and warehousing SRO units would do little to resolve the homeless crisis. Indeed, the SRO units are not earmarked for the homeless or for potentially homeless low-income families, and there is simply no assurance that the units will be rented to members of either group (see, Blackburn, Single Room Occupancy in New York City, op. cit., at 5–6). While, of course, any increase in the supply of low-cost housing would benefit some prospective tenants, it is by no means clear that it would actually benefit the homeless.

. . .

The question remains whether the added features of Local Law No. 9—the buy-out, replacement, and hardship exemptions—in some way mitigate the invidious effects of the law so that it becomes constitutionally acceptable. We agree with Justice Saxe that they do not (Seawall Assocs. v. City of New York, 134 Misc.2d 187, 510 N.Y.S.2d 435, supra). The reasons, we think, are evident.

If, as we hold, the effect of the moratorium and antiwarehousing measures is unconstitutionally to deprive owners of their basic rights to possess and to make economically viable use of their properties, merely allowing them to purchase exemptions from the law cannot alter this conclusion. In effect, the City, in the buy-out and replacement exemptions, is saying no more to the owners than that it will not do something unconstitutional if they pay the City not to do it. But if the initial act amounts to an unlawful taking, then permitting the owners to avoid the illegal confiscation by paying a "ransom" cannot make it lawful. Indeed, the stark alternatives offered by Local Law No. 9—either submit to an uncompensated and, therefore, unconstitutional appropriation of your properties or pay the price (in cash or in replacement units)—amount to just the sort of exaction which could be classified, not as "a valid regulation of land use but 'an out-and-out plan of extortion.' "

Nor can the hardship exemption make a difference. It can do no more than permit the Commissioner—in the event that an owner could ever come within its provisions—to exercise his discretion and lower the purchase price of escape from the law. If Local Law No. 9 creates an illegal taking notwithstanding the buy-out and replacement options—as we hold it does—it certainly does not become legal simply because an owner may, in some cases, buy his way out of the law by paying a lesser sum.

. . .

Because the owners are, by the terms of the law, afforded no compensation, Local Law No. 9, we hold, is facially invalid, under the "Takings" Clauses of both the Federal and State Constitutions (U.S. Const. 5th, 14th Amends.; N.Y. Const., art. I, § 7).

. . .

No one minimizes the tragic reality of homelessness. But the City's response—to foist its responsibilty on certain private property owners, by requiring them to remain in the SRO business or ransom their property rights—simply does not meet the requirements of the Federal and State Constitutions.

The order of the Appellate Division should be reversed, with costs, Local Law No. 9 declared to be unconstitutional as stated in this opinion, and defendants enjoined from implementing the law's provisions.

BELLACOSA, JUDGE (dissenting).

. . .

In 1904, Justice Holmes wrote the quintessential dissenting opinion in Lochner v. New York, 198 U.S. 45, 74, 25 S.Ct. 539, 551, 40 L.Ed. 937, which presciently warned against his own court declaring unconstitutional an act of the New York State Legislature attempting to limit the working hours of children. The historical, economic, social, legal, policy and constitutional parallels to the facial jettisoning of New York City's SRO law suggest that it would be far better to harken to that history instead of being condemned to relive it.

Justice Holmes eloquently and cogently sums up the relevancy: "(A) constitution is not intended to embody a particular economic (or property) theory, whether of paternalism and the organic relation of the citizen to the State or of *laissez faire. It is made for people of fundamentally differing views* . . . General propositions do not decide concrete cases. The decision will depend on a judgment or intuition more subtle than any articulate major premise. . . . I think that the word *liberty* in the Fourteenth Amendment *is perverted when it is held to prevent the natural outcome of a dominant opinion, unless it can be said that a rational and fair man necessarily would admit that the statute proposed would infringe fundamental principles* as they have been understood by the traditions of our people and our law. *It does not need research to show that no such sweeping condemnation can be passed upon the statute before us.*" (id. at 75–76, 25 S.Ct. at 546–547 [Emphasis added]). Nor on the local law before us either!

Eighty-five years after Lochner, we observe property rights, like the contract rights of that bygone era, being exalted over the Legislature's assessment of social policy. Like the economic theories underlying Lochner, we, as judges, should not inquire into the wisdom or wholesomeness of SRO's as shelter for potentially 52,000 new, displaced homeless persons—that policy choice belongs to the elected officials who enacted the law.

. . .

The legislation enjoys a presumptive threshold of constitutionality. Research reveals no cases in which the Supreme Court or our court have used the regulatory taking theory to undo a legislative act on a facial attack. Also, no precedents in the orbit of this case have previously ventured into the per se physical taking universe to declare a legislative act facially unconstitutional. It could well be that, due to the need to assess the real economic impact of this kind of law upon different property owners before a regulatory taking is decreed, no such doctrine as a facial challenge to a law as a regulatory taking will be recognized. But even if such a proposition is possible, it certainly has not been found to and should not be allowed to be applied against a law such as the challenged one which inherently impacts on widely diverse and different property owners.

. . .

Statutes undergoing constitutional challenge as facially invalid in a takings context enjoy even greater deference because there is "an important distinction between a claim that the mere enactment of a statute constitutes a taking and a claim that the particular impact of government action on a specific piece of property requires the payment of just compensation." (Keystone Bituminous Coal Assn. v. DeBenedictis, 480 U.S. 470, 494, 107 S.Ct. 1232, 1247, 94 L.Ed.2d 472.) The Supreme Court routinely rejects preenforcement taking challenges—conceptually and functionally equivalent to facial attacks—to the constitutionality of legislative enactments. Relevantly and bluntly, that court recently rejected a facial challenge to a rent-control law, stating: "We have found it particularly important in takings cases to adhere to our admonition that 'the constitutionality of statutes ought not to be decided except in an actual factual setting that makes such a decision necessary.'" (Pennell v. San Jose, 485 U.S. 1, ___, 108 S.Ct. 849, 856, 99 L.Ed.2d 1, supra, quoting Hodel v. Virginia Surface Min. & Reclamation Assn., 452 U.S. 264, 294–295, 101 S.Ct. 2352, 2369–2370, 69 L.Ed.2d 1; see also, Ruckelhaus v. Monsanto Co., 467 U.S. 986, 1005, 104 S.Ct. 2862, 2874, 81 L.Ed.2d 815; Kaiser Aetna v. United States, 444 U.S. 164, 175, 100 S.Ct. 383, 390, 62 L.Ed.2d 332, citing Penn Cent. Transp. Co. v. New York City, 438 U.S. 104, 124, 98 S.Ct. 2646, 2659, 57 L.Ed.2d 631, supra).

The Supreme Court's "admonition" is particularly pertinent in this case where the declaration of facial unconstitutionality is overinclusive and rooted in a record devoid of specific and relevant facts. The conclusion that the antiwarehousing and rental provisions are a forced occupation, effecting a per se physical taking, contradicts the way high courts have treated their functionally and conceptually equivalent rent-control and regulatory statutes—by repeatedly finding them constitutional, at least facially. . . .

. . .

When it is clear—as in this case—that a law substantially advances a self-evidently legitimate governmental interest, the test to be applied in considering a facial challenge is simplified: "(a) statute regulating the uses that can be made of property effects a taking if it 'denies an owner economically viable use of his land.'" (Hodel v. Virginia Surface Min. & Reclamation Assn., 452 U.S. 264, 295–296, 101 S.Ct. 2352, 2370–2371, 69 L.Ed.2d 1, supra; see, Keystone Bituminous Coal Assn. v. DeBenedictis, supra; Agins v. Tiburon, supra.) The SRO moratorium law effects no such deprivation. Indeed, it guarantees a fair minimum return, among a whole host of other economic balancing features. Government regulation almost always limits the maximization of the economic aggrandizement from private property ownership. Local Law No. 9 concededly places substantial restraints on the destruction or redevelopment of SRO buildings. But I would find dispositive of this takings challenge that the law leaves the owners in possession and guarantees them a whole web of economic concessions or "give-backs," including the minimum profit of 8½% of the assessed value of the property per year. . . .

Appellant owners and some amici argue nevertheless that properties could be put to more profitable uses if their destruction or redevelopment options were unimpeded. The simple answer to that proposition is that a property owner is not constitutionally guaranteed the most profitable use. (Andrus v. Allard, supra; Penn Cent. Transp. Co. v. New York City, 438 U.S. 104, 125, 98 S.Ct. 2646, 2659, 57 L.Ed.2d 631, supra.)

. . .

Peripherally, the court also decides today that one particular known person may not be ousted from his habitation because that would violate a legislated antieviction policy in a rent-control situation. (Braschi v. Stahl Assocs. Co., 74 N.Y.2d 201, — N.Y.S.2d ——, — N.E.2d —— (decided today).) To be sure, the statutes and the issues have some differences, but they have one essential feature in common: Local Law No. 9's genesis and purpose are founded in the identical social policy as the antieviction regulation—securing shelter for people—only in the instant case the statute tries to protect the most disadvantages members of our society who truly have no where else to go. The court, contradictorily in my view, authorizes the expulsion of 52,000 people to allow, in the main, for commercial redevelopment of their former less-than-modest dwellings while keeping one known individual in his rent-controlled apartment. The decisional compass seems to be oscillating between opposite poles.

In sum, the Constitution, the authorities and the policies do not support the conclusion that the legislated emergency moratorium against the elimination of SRO dwelling units, societally critical to the temporary preservation of some housing for low-income persons, is a facially impermissible governmental taking, i.e., an inverse condemnation of property. . . .

NOTES

1. Contrast the holding of the U.S. Supreme Court in Pennell v. City of San Jose, 485 U.S. 1, 109 S.Ct. 849, 99 L.Ed.2d 1 (1988). A city ordinance which authorized a hearing officer to take seven factors into account in determining the reasonableness of a rent increase was attacked as unconstitutional because one of the factors to be considered was "hardship to the tenant." The plaintiffs, who included a lessors' association, argued that the only legitimate purpose of rent control was the elimination of excessive rents resulting from the city's housing shortage. They contended that consideration of hardship to a tenant would reduce rentals below the reasonable amount objectively established by the other six factors set out in the ordinance and thus constitute a taking of their property. A majority of the court, speaking through Mr. Justice Rehnquist, held that the attack was premature because there was no evidence that the tenant-hardship clause had ever been relied upon to reduce a rent below the level set by the other factors. The Court rejected the plaintiffs' argument that the mere authorization to consider tenant hardship rendered the ordinance facially invalid "because we have long recognized that a legitimate and rational goal of price or rate regulation is the protection of consumer welfare. . . . [The ordinance] represents a rational attempt to ac-

commodate the conflicting interest of protecting tenants from burdensome rent increases while at the same time ensuring that landlords are guaranteed a fair return on their investment."

2. In Flynn v. City of Cambridge, 383 Mass. 152, 418 N.E.2d 335 (1981) the court upheld an ordinance prohibiting housing subject to rent control from being converted to condominiums. In rejecting the plaintiffs' claims that the ordinance was an unconstitutional taking of their property, the court reasoned as follows:

> The ordinance does deny a condominium owner the right to occupy his unit if it was used for rental housing on and not converted before the effective date of the ordinance. There are two classes of owners who are affected. The first class, those owners who purchase their condominium units after the effective date of the ordinance, are on notice that they have no right to use their property as owner-occupied housing. They are fairly warned that they are purchasing property which may be used for rental housing only, and presumably the purchase price reflects this use restriction. Since these owners were notified that they had no right to occupy their unit, they were not denied a right to which they had a legitimate expectation. Clearly the government is not required to compensate an individual for denying him the right to use that which he has never owned.
>
> The second class of owners is comprised of those owners whose units were purchased prior to, and which were being used for rental housing on, the effective date of the ordinance. These owners, under prior law, did have a right to occupy their unit. That right is now denied them. However, "the submission that [plaintiffs] may establish a 'taking' simply by showing that they have been denied the ability to exploit a property interest that they heretofore had believed was available for development is quite simply untenable. . . . 'Taking' jurisprudence does not divide a single parcel into discrete segments and attempt to determine whether rights in a particular segment have been entirely abrogated. In deciding whether a particular governmental action has effected a taking, [the focus is] rather both on the character of the action and on the nature and extent of the interference with rights in the parcel as a whole" (emphasis added). Penn Central Transp. Co. v. New York City, 438 U.S. 104, 130–131, 98 S.Ct. 2646, 2662–63, 57 L.Ed.2d 631 (1978). . . . While the use restrictions subsequently enacted undeniably diminish the value of the property, this alone does not establish a taking. . . .

3. Termination of leases to occupants of mobile homes has been the subject of legislation. Minnesota legislation is summarized in Flamingo Terrace Mobile Home Park v. Scott, 317 N.W.2d 697, 699 (Minn.1981):

"The Minnesota legislature has addressed the problems associated with the development and expanded use of mobile home parks. It is obvious that the term 'mobile' is inappropriate in describing the general operation of most trailer parks. In today's society these are the permanent homes of most of the tenants of these parks. This situation created a need to protect such individuals from being forced from their locations on short term notice. . . . Minn.Stat. § 327.44(f) requires the lease term to be of one year duration. The effect of this legislation is to create year-to-year tenancies with the right of the lessor to terminate the year-to-year tenancy by giving the lessee 60–days notice as required by Minn.Stat. § 327.42, subd. 2 and by seeking to recover possession within 15 days of the end of the annual lease term."

THE REPORT OF THE PRESIDENT'S COMMISSION ON HOUSING

Pages 81–83 (1982).

Conversion of multifamily units to cooperatives or condominiums enables many people to become homeowners who otherwise would not have this opportunity. The Commission believes that homeownership is beneficial not only for those who occupy the units, but also to the community as well. The substantial numbers of units that have been purchased under this form of ownership provides evidence of public awareness of the benefits. As the size and nature of households change, the attraction to condominiums and cooperatives is expected to grow.

There are, however, conflicting interests here. The Commission believes that potential homebuyers must continue to be served by the conversion option. Public policy must also protect the rights of apartment owners to dispose of their property. At the same time, the Commission recognizes that there may be important social consequences for those low-income tenants, particularly the elderly, who cannot afford homeownership and therefore must relocate. The Commission supports governmental policies that permit owners to convert while protecting tenants against undue disruption. Public policy should not interfere with free choice in the marketplace. The recommendations here are intended to allow conversions in response to market pressure.

Nationwide, 366,000 rental units were converted to condominiums and cooperatives during the 1970–79 period; 71 percent of these conversions (260,000) occurred during 1977–79. The number of condominiums and cooperatives increased annually through 1979, during which 135,000 units were converted. Compared to the entire rental stock, the number of conversions is relatively small (1.3 percent). Although concentrated in larger metropolitan areas, where conversions are roughly split evenly between the central cities and the suburbs, some evidence shows that the conversion phenomenon may be increasing in smaller metropolitan areas.

The benefits of conversion to the community as well as to homebuyers are considerable, but many demands have been made for imposition of government restrictions on conversions. One reason is the concern that rental housing is being removed, with adverse consequences to renters, who tend to be lower-income people. However, the mere number of gross conversions overstates the impact on the rental market. The conversion of rental units to ownership coincides with a movement of renters to ownership, which in large part is a voluntary movement. In addition, many units are purchased by investors and rerented. Therefore, some conversions do not represent reductions in the rental housing supply. In fact, the HUD report on condominium conversions indicated that the net impact of conversion—the reduction in the stock of rental housing relative to the number of remaining renters—is 5 units or less per 100 preconversion units.[4]

Although evidence indicates that most people moving from converted buildings experience little long-run hardship, the process of conversion can be stressful—especially for the elderly. Although great variation exists, tenants of converting buildings typically are given about 70-days notice to decide whether to buy. Nearly three-fourths of those who moved from converting buildings—but only one-fourth of those who remained—have stated that they felt pressured by the conversion experience.

In response to these concerns, by 1981 about one-half of the States had taken at least limited action to regulate conversions, and about one in five localities with conversions had adopted regulatory ordinances. Such regulations include those designed to protect tenants of converted buildings, those intended to protect buyer/owners of converted units, and those developed to preserve the supply of rental housing and/or housing for low-and moderate-income households. The most common regulations are those requiring advance notice to tenants and granting them the right to purchase before the units are offered to the public. Also common are provisions designed to protect tenants from disturbance during conversion, to protect buyers against possible unfair sales practices, and to provide assistance in moving if necessary.

Aside from the various procedural safeguards that might be afforded tenants during the conversion process, consideration has been given by some States—and should be given by all States—to relocation assistance or in-place financial assistance, in particular for the low-income elderly. Although the Commission recognizes that equity considerations may require this form of compensation, State legislatures should determine the nature and amount of such assistance, provided that any such requirements do not unreasonably constrain the right of the owner to convert.

. . .

---

4. U.S. Department of Housing and Urban Development, Office of Policy Development and Research, "The Conversion of Rental Housing to Condominiums and Cooperatives," June 1980.

C. PERMISSIBLE USES BY TENANT

STROUP v. CONANT

Supreme Court of Oregon, 1974.
268 Or. 292, 520 P.2d 337.

TONGUE, JUSTICE. This is a suit to rescind a lease of space in a building in which the tenant undertook to operate the "Birds & Bees Adult Book Store." Plaintiff's complaint alleged that she was induced to enter into the lease in reliance upon the false representation by defendant that he intended to use the leased premises for the sale of watches, wallets, chains, novelties and a few books and magazines and imported items. Defendant appeals from a decree rescinding the lease. We affirm.

Defendant contends that there was no evidence of misrepresentation, reliance or damage. It thus becomes necessary to summarize the evidence, although not in completely unexpurgated form.

Defendant states in his brief that he informed plaintiff of his intent to sell "a variety of items," including magazines, "for adults only." Plaintiff, however, denies any such conversation. Plaintiff's son, who represented her in negotiating the lease, testified that defendant called him by telephone in response to a newspaper advertisement for lease of the premises, located on S.E. Division Street in Portland; that he asked defendant what his business was and was told that defendant intended to conduct "a variety type operation" and to sell watches, wallets, chains, trinkets and a few books and novelties, but did not say that he intended to operate an "adult book store" or to sell pornographic material.

Plaintiff's attorney then prepared a one year lease, with an option to renew for one additional year. The lease provided, among other things, that the premises were to be used "for the sale of gifts, novelties, etc." Defendant then went to the lawyer's office and signed the lease. He was not present when plaintiff later signed the lease. The lease, as thus executed, was dated March 25, 1973.

On April 6, 1973, plaintiff's son received a telephone call from another tenant who operated a gun shop in the same building complaining that "you've ruined me" and informing him of the adult book store in the adjacent premises. Plaintiff testified that her son had reported to her that the premises had been rented for a variety and gift store and that she would not have signed the lease if she had known of defendant's intent to operate an adult book store on the premises. Upon visiting the premises, plaintiff's son found large signs in the store windows, and upon going inside he saw no watches, wallets, chains or novelties for sale, but only racks of pornographic magazines and books. He then called plaintiff's lawyer.

During the next few days one of the residents in the neighborhood, after going into the store and purchasing three magazines whose titles had best be left unstated, circulated a petition of "protest" upon which he secured 300 signatures in the neighborhood, which he described as "predominantly residential." The two other tenants in the building, the operators of a meat market and a paint store, also complained to plaintiff that the adjacent adult book store "spoils their business," and plaintiff was "deluged" with telephone calls.

On April 10, 1973, plaintiff's attorney wrote a letter to defendant charging him with violating the terms of the lease and demanding that he vacate the premises immediately. At that time, however, plaintiff did not tender the return of the first and last months' rent, as previously paid by defendant, claiming that she was entitled to that money.

On May 4, 1973, after defendant had apparently refused to move out, plaintiff filed a complaint seeking to rescind the lease and offering to "do complete equity and restore the status quo." Defendant filed a general denial and awaited trial, which was held on August 8, 1973. . . .

Based upon this record we have no hesitation in holding that there was ample basis to support the decision by this trial court in its decree rescinding this lease, dated September 17, 1973.

Even assuming that one who seeks to rent premises for the operation of such an "adult book store" and who does not disclose the nature of his intended operation may, by remaining silent, be able to acquire a binding lease from either an unsuspecting or a willing landlord, regardless of neighborhood protests, this is not such a case.

. . .

There was ample evidence of misrepresentation by "half-truths and concealment of special knowledge" in this case, as well as reliance thereon by plaintiff, despite defendant's testimony to the contrary.

. . .

. . . There was ample evidence that plaintiff suffered damage not only in the form of humiliation and embarrassment, but also by the potential loss of other tenants . . . .

. . .

For these reasons we affirm the decree of the trial court.

NOTES

1. Assuming that tenant has not misrepresented his anticipated use of the premises, what rights and remedies would the landlord have with respect to illegal activities conducted on the premises? See McKenzie v. Carte, 385 S.W.2d 520 (Tex.Civ.App.1964), the court stating: "At common law, the lessee does not forfeit his lease by using the demised premises for illegal purposes in the absence of a provision in the lease contract for a forfeiture in such cases." A contrary view is taken by the Restatement of Property, Second, Landlord and Tenant § 12.5 (1977), based, according to the reporter's note to this section, upon common statutory policy and also upon the adoption by the Restatement of the dependence of obligations doctrine generally for leases.

2. Tenant entered into a commercial lease providing that it would use space in an office building "only for the purpose of a restaurant." The lessee further agreed that it would "operate its business in an efficient, high class and reputable manner" and would keep the restaurant open during office hours in the building. Tenant ceased operating as a delicatessen style restaurant and installed vending machines serving hot and cold food and beverages. Is the lessor entitled to an injunction prohibiting the tenant from operating vending machines? To specific performance of an obligation to operate a restaurant? See Canteen Corp. v. Republic of Texas Properties, Inc., 773 S.W.2d 398 (Tex.App.1989).

3. Physical alterations of the premises by the tenant are governed by the law of waste. See page 244, herein. See also Restatement of Property, Second, Landlord and Tenant § 12.2 (1977), adopting the position that the tenant may make changes that are "reasonably necessary" for the tenant's "reasonable" uses. This position, the reporter states, "is probably a minority position (although the precise state of the law in this area is unclear)."

HANDLER v. HORNS

Supreme Court of New Jersey, 1949.
2 N.J. 18, 65 A.2d 523.

ACKERSON, J. Defendants appeal from a decree of the former Court of Chancery in a suit instituted for partition of certain real estate, and the sole question presented is whether or not certain fixtures installed therein by a tenant are removable as chattels.

In 1929, Henry Horns and his wife Augusta leased to their son, Fred Horns, the premises in question consisting of a five story brick building on Mulberry Street, Newark, New Jersey, theretofore occupied by a dealer in seeds and garden supplies, who used the first floor as a store and the upper floors for storage. The lease to Fred Horns was for a term beginning September 1, 1929 and continuing until "the first day of the sixth month" following the death of the survivor of the two lessors, at a rental of $500 per month. This lease gave Fred Horns the privilege of installing a new front in the building and otherwise altering it for use as a plant for the processing, refrigeration and sale of meat, and he covenanted to keep the building and its appurtenances "in as good and sufficient repair as at the date of the execution hereof . . . and at the end or other expiration of the term, will deliver up the demised premises and its fixtures in as good condition as on the date hereof"—ordinary wear and tear excepted. Additionally the tenant was given the option to purchase the premises any time before the expiration of the lease for $75,000.

The lessee, Fred Horns, promptly installed a refrigeration system in a considerable portion of the leased building. He placed in the basement refrigeration compressors, machinery, ammonia tanks, and piping which extended to the second, third, fourth and fifth floors. Partitions insulated with cork and fitted with refrigerator doors were built across the rear end of each of these floors. All windows in each of the refrigeration rooms thus formed were filled up with brick and the walls and floors were insulated with cork and properly covered. Inside these refrigeration rooms steel "I" beams were installed along the ceiling from wall to wall and between the "I" beams were suspended wooden beams to which in turn were bolted tracks or rails for meat hangers, and above the beams and resting on them refrigerating coils were built in wooden troughs. So that, in effect, each floor above the first was a complete cold storage room with tracks for the meat hangers continuing on out from within the room to an elevator in the small service room to the rear. The ground floor of the building was not materially altered, and was at that time, and is still used as a store. The entire cost of the alterations and improvements was approximately $89,000.

Augusta Horns, who survived her husband, died on October 11, 1937, and by will devised the aforesaid premises to her three children, Hulda Muller, now deceased, Fred Horns, the tenant then in possession, and Clara Horns, who thereby became seized thereof as tenants in common. The complainant Hazel H. Handler is the only child and sole devisee of Hulda Muller, deceased.

After his mother's death, Fred Horns' lease expired according to its terms, on the "first day of the sixth month" thereafter, which was on April 1, 1938, and his option to purchase was never exercised. Nevertheless he continued on in possession as a hold over tenant paying the same rental and on April 14, 1939, he and the corporation which he had formed to carry on his business under the name of Fred Horns, Inc. (later changed to Fred Horns & Son), entered into a new lease with the then owners of the premises, who were himself and his two sisters, for a term of two years, from May 1, 1939 to April 30, 1941, at the same rental with an option of renewal for an additional term of three years. That lease provided, inter alia, as follows:

"Sixth: That no alterations, additions or improvements shall be made . . . without the consent of the Landlords . . ., and all additions and improvements made by the Tenant shall belong to the Landlords. . . .

"Twenty-Seventh: It is further . . . agreed between the parties hereto that at the expiration of this lease or any renewal thereof, the Tenant shall have the right to remove any and all trade fixtures that may belong to it or which it may have installed in the premises, with the exception, however, of any fixtures that may be so affixed to the building as to become a part of the realty and not removable without causing material damage to the premises."

When the term of this lease expired, the tenants continued on under a tenancy from year to year at the same rental. Fred Horns died in 1945 bequeathing his meat business and any interest in the fixtures on the premises in question, and all shares of stock of the defendant corporation, Fred Horns & Son, through which he was conducting said business, to his son, the defendant, Henry W. Horns. The premises are still occupied by that corporation as tenant from year to year, which corporation is apparently owned by said Horns by virtue of his father's will.

The complainant Hazel Handler, who owns an undivided one-third interest in the premises, claims that all of the improvements made by Fred Horns were annexed to and became part of the realty and therefore may not be removed by the tenant. Defendant, Henry W. Horns, who is also the owner of an undivided one-third interest in the premises, claims to be the owner of the improvements installed by his father with the right to remove them as trade fixtures, which right is conceded by the defendant, Clara Horns, the owner of the remaining one-third interest in the premises. Such concession, however, made during the progress of the suit and under the circumstances here presented, is not controlling so far as the plaintiffs are concerned.

The subject of the litigation was referred to a Special Master who reported that the premises could not be partitioned but should be sold in one parcel and that all of the fixtures placed in the building by the tenant had become a part thereof and were to be sold therewith. Exceptions having been taken to this report in so far as it applied to the fixtures, the matter came before a Vice Chancellor who concluded that it was the intention of the tenant that the fixtures should become a part of the realty. He considered, inter alia, that the whole installation made "one economic unit, the greater part of which could not be advantageously removed" and, applying the institutional theory, confirmed the master's report.

It is an ancient maxim, which in the language of antiquity is expressed quicquid plantatur solo, solo cedit, that whatsoever is fixed to the realty is thereby made a part of the realty to which it adheres, and partakes of all of its incidents and properties. . . . But through the advancing years that old maxim has given way to numerous exceptions. One of the most conspicuous modifications of this rule is exhibited in the instance of fixtures put upon property by a tenant. As between landlord and tenant the presumption is that the tenant's motive in placing fixtures on the demised premises is for his own benefit not to enhance his landlord's realty, and this is so even though the lease is silent on the subject. Particularly is this true where the personalty is annexed or appropriated to the demised premises for the purpose of carrying on a trade or business for profit thereon. . . . It is also considered sound public policy to allow the tenant the greatest latitude to remove fixtures to encourage trade and industry. . . . These considerations have led the courts to place special emphasis upon the element of intention as to the ownership of fixtures where the claimants are landlord and tenant. Vide 22 Am.Jur., Fixtures, § 40, p. 749.

So today it is the general rule, in the absence of an agreement to the contrary, that a tenant may remove whatever he has erected or installed for the purpose of carrying on trade, usually referred to as trade fixtures, provided they can be severed from the freehold without material injury thereto, and that such removal is effected before he yields possession of the premises. 36 C.J.S., Fixtures, § 38, p. 973; 1 Thompson on Real Property, Per.Ed., § 208, p. 336. As a general rule, an article may be regarded as a "trade fixture" if annexed for the purpose of aiding in the conduct by the tenant of a trade or business exercised on the demised premises for the purpose of pecuniary profit, it being accessory to the enjoyment of his term. To constitute any chattel that has been attached to the freehold a "trade fixture," it is only necessary that it be devoted to what is known as a trade purpose, and the form or size of the annexed chattel is immaterial. . . .

In holding that the installations in question had become a part of the real estate and not removable, the court below leaned heavily upon the institutional theory exemplified in Smyth Sales Corp. v. Norfolk B. & L. Ass'n, Err. & App.1935, 116 N.J.L. 293, 298, 184 A. 204, 111 A.L.R. 357, but that principle is applicable to owner, mortgagee and conditional seller situations and has not been extended as a governing principle to the landlord-tenant relationship, where the subject is still a matter of bargain and intention. Furthermore, with the exception of the store on the ground floor, the building in question was to all intents and purposes an empty warehouse at the time of the original lease, and although the tenant adapted it as a plant for the processing, refrigeration and sale of meat, yet there is persuasive evidence that a part at least of the fixtures installed therein can be removed without material damage to the freehold, and if so removed the building again could be devoted effectually to its original use.

Referring to the second lease of the premises, made on April 14, 1939, the defendants [complainant?] ask us to apply the rule invoked in Gerbert v. Trustees, Err. & App.1896, 59 N.J.L. 160, 35 A. 1121, 69 L.R.A. 764, 59 Am.St.Rep. 578, that if a tenant, at the end of his term, renews his lease, and thereby acquires a new interest in the premises, his right to remove improvements is forfeited, unless he takes the precaution to reserve such right in the renewal lease. There, however, the improvement was a sizable building which had been erected by the tenant during the term, and which under the old common law, as the court observed, became a part of the freehold. The rule stated in the cited case is generally referred to as the forfeiture rule which has been much criticized in modern judicial literature, and in many cases has been either repudiated or limited in its application. The strongest denunciation of it was made by Justice Cooley in Kerr v. Kingsbury, 1878, 39 Mich. 150, 33 Am.Rep. 362. . . .

In any event it is commonly accepted today that trade fixtures are removable by a tenant so long as he remains in possession of the leasehold, provided they are capable of removal without material injury to the realty, notwithstanding his failure to preserve such right in a renewal lease. . . . Furthermore we think that the second lease made between the parties on April 14, 1939, adequately protected the tenants in the foregoing respects for reasons presently to be stated.

We note in the original lease of 1929 the provision that at the end of the term the tenant "will deliver up the demised premises and its fixtures in as good condition *as on the date hereof* (wear and tear arising from a reasonable use of the same excepted)" (italics supplied). Obviously this does not apply to fixtures installed by the tenant after the date of the lease, but only to those on the premises "on the date" of the making of the lease. Covenants restricting tenants in the removal of ordinary trade fixtures are always strictly construed and cannot be extended by implication. . . .

The sixth paragraph of the second lease which provides that "additions and improvements" shall belong to the landlords, is not only confined to those thereafter made, but also distinguishes this type of permanent structural addition to the building from the trade fixtures placed therein by the tenant which, according to the twenty-seventh paragraph of the same lease, may be removed by him if such removal "does not materially damage the premises".

Since there was no prohibition against the removal of such fixtures by the tenant contained in the original lease, and the second lease provides for such removal under the stated condition, we conclude that this establishes the lessee's right to such trade fixtures as can be so removed.

Therefore, inasmuch as it appears from the testimony of the experts that much of the fixtures in question could be removed without causing material damage to the freehold, the decree below is modified so as to exclude from the sale of the premises thereby ordered to be sold, such of the trade fixtures as can be so removed. And to that end this cause is remanded to the Chancery Division of the Superior Court for the purpose of determining, according to its practice, the fixtures so to be excluded from said sale, the terms of their removal from the premises, the requirements necessary for otherwise returning the premises to the condition required by the letting, and for further proceedings in conformity with this opinion.

NOTE

Problems with reference to fixtures involve many relationships other than that of landlord and tenant. Two general types of situations should be distinguished. In one, which can be conveniently termed the "common ownership" situation, the owner of a fee simple estate equips the land for a particular use with some appurtenance (e.g., a building, machinery, tanks or vats, piping, a furnace or kiln, an ornamental statue or fountain) which he also owns, and thereafter, in connection with some event (e.g., a contract to sell the land, a levy of execution, a condemnation proceeding, a mortgage foreclosure, an intestate succession, a tax assessment) one person asserts that the appurtenance shall be treated as part of the land and another the contrary. In the other situation, termed the "divided ownership" one, a person who, whether he is aware of it or not, has no ownership of the land or only a limited interest (e.g., a tenant for life or for years, an adverse possessor, a licensee, a cotenant, a mortgagee in possession) equips the land with some appurtenance at his own expense and thereafter desires to remove it over the objection of someone owning the land or an interest therein, who asserts that through the doctrine of accession he has acquired partial or total ownership of the appurtenance. The problem is often further complicated because it involves the claim of a third person who has had no part in the annexation of the appurtenance to the realty; the annexor may have stolen the item in question, or may have acquired it under a conditional sale contract, or may have given a chattel mortgage covering it before or after annexing it to the realty. In the latter two instances a statute requiring that the instrument be recorded and possibly defining the rights of the vendor or mortgagee after recordation, is likely to be important.

The foregoing rough sketch may serve to suggest the widely varying types of disputes with which courts may be faced, and it may well be doubted that they are sufficiently homogeneous that any single principle or unified set of principles will serve satisfactorily for the treatment of all. Nonetheless, perhaps beguiled by the notion that any particular appurtenance has, somehow, an inherent, essential character either of realty or personalty, and that this character can—and must—be treated as controlling, whoever the disputants and whatever the context of the dispute may be, the courts frequently seem hopelessly tangled in semantic difficulties. The English courts, in particular, have had the greatest difficulty in escaping the implications of a maxim to which they have felt committed by very early precedents contemporaneous with the initial formation of this branch of English law—the maxim that whatever is planted in the soil belongs to the soil. For example, they have been unable to rationalize, satisfactorily to themselves, the rule they evolved, that a tenant may remove "trade fixtures" which he has installed—especially in connection with an ancient rule that his right of removal is lost if he does not take the fixtures with him when he leaves the premises upon the termination of his tenancy. Does the rule permitting removal mean that a tenant's trade fixtures planted in the soil do not—contrary to the maxim—belong to the soil? To admit this is to say that the essential character of a thing as realty or personalty depends upon who annexes it to the soil—a manifestly absurd proposition? Moreover, if the fixture is mere personalty, belonging to the tenant, how can the rule be rationalized that his ownership is lost if he does not take the fixture with him upon departure? But if, as the maxim says, the fixture becomes part of the soil, the freehold, the conclusion is inescapable that the landlord owner of the freehold, has acquired ownership of it by accession, and if so it is anomalous, to say the least, to permit the tenant to deprive the landlord of it.

American courts, fortunately have escaped most of the maxim's hampering effects upon thought, but they, like the English courts, apparently feeling a necessity to find some formula whereby all fixtures can be classified, for all purposes, as realty or personalty, have tended to ignore relevant factors differentiating the problems confronting them, and to indulge in question-begging statements in support of unsatisfactory solutions. For examples, see Dudzick v. Lewis, 175 Tenn. 246, 133 S.W.2d 496 (1939); Haywood v. Briggs, 227 N.C. 108, 41 S.E.2d 289 (1947). A good elementary discussion of fixtures problems, on which the foregoing comments are based, may be found in 5 Am.Law of Prop. 3–68 (1952).

SECTION 6. LESSOR'S REMEDIES AGAINST DEFAULTING TENANT

A. TENANT'S DEFAULT IN RENTAL OBLIGATIONS

COLLEGE BLOCK v. ATLANTIC RICHFIELD COMPANY

Court of Appeal, Second District, 1988.
206 Cal.App.3d 1376, 254 Cal.Rptr. 179.

OPINION ON REHEARING

ASHBY, ACTING PRESIDING JUSTICE.

In this matter the trial court held as a matter of law that in the parties' lease there was an implied covenant of continued operation. We find that although the parties intended the lessee to continually operate a gasoline service station for the entire leasehold period, the trial court acted prematurely and a further factual determination must be made before the covenant is implied.

STATEMENT OF CASE AND FACTS

In 1965, respondent, The College Block (College Block) owned a parcel of undeveloped real property. College Block signed a 20–year lease with appellant Atlantic Richfield Company (ARCO) in which ARCO agreed to build and operate a gasoline service station on the property.[1] Other provisions of the lease allowed ARCO to build, maintain and replace any buildings ARCO desired in operating a station, obligated ARCO to pay all applicable taxes, prohibited College Block from operating a gasoline station on other properties it owned or controlled, limited ARCO's use of the property to that of a service station, and allowed ARCO the right to cancel the lease if it could not obtain permits required in running a station. Pursuant to the lease, ARCO constructed and then operated for approximately 17 years a gasoline service station on the property.

The rent, pursuant to the lease, was determined by a percentage of the gasoline delivered, and irrespective of the gallons delivered, College Block was to receive a minimum of $1,000 per month.[2]

1. The original lease was between College Block's predecessor and ARCO's predecessor.

2. Article 3 of the lease states, in pertinent part, as follows:

"Lessee shall pay as full rental for the premises during the effective term of this lease the following amounts at the following times:

"A sum equal to ONE AND ONE–QUARTER CENTS (1¼¢) per gallon for each gallon of gasoline, irrespective of grade, delivered to the herein described premises; or

"A sum equal to SIX AND FIVE-TENTHS PER CENT (6.5%) of the gross price . . . of all gasoline delivered to the demised premises; WHICHEVER IS GREATER provided, however, that in no event, and irrespective of the number of gallons of gasoline so delivered, shall Lessor receive less than ONE THOUSAND DOLLARS ($1,000.00) per month for each month during which this lease remains in effect. For fractional monthly periods the minimum guaranteed rental herein specified shall be duly prorated. All rent shall be paid on or about the 20th day of each calendar month following the calendar month in which deliveries are made."

On January 1, 1983, 39 months prior to the expiration of the lease, ARCO closed the station. When ARCO ceased operations, it paid College Block $1,000 per month for the months remaining on the lease. ARCO contended that it was responsible only for the minimum monthly rental because the lease did not contain an express covenant requiring it to operate the station. College Block brought suit alleging that ARCO was also responsible for additional sums College Block would have received had the station remained in business. College Block contended that it was entitled to damages because as a matter of law a covenant of continued operation was implied into the lease.

College Block presented its case. There was no evidence presented as to whether, at the time the lease was entered into, the parties considered the $1,000 minimum rent to be a "substantial" minimum. Before ARCO proceeded, the court ruled as a matter of law that there was an implied covenant in the lease which required ARCO to operate a gasoline station for the entire twenty (20) year lease period. Based upon this ruling, the parties subsequently stipulated that had the station been in operation, College Block would have received approximately $3,250 per month. A judgment based on this amount was subsequently entered.

. . .

DISCUSSION

The issue of whether there is an implied covenant of continued operation arises because the lease did not fix the rent, but guaranteed a minimum payment plus a percentage based upon the gasoline delivered. In having a percentage lease, the parties contemplated a lengthy association (20 years) during which rents would periodically be established by the market place.

A percentage lease provides a lessor with a hedge against inflation and automatically adjusts the rents if the location becomes more valuable. (*Resolving Disputes Under Percentage Leases* (1967) 51 Minn. L.R. 1139, 1139; see also *Powell on Real Property* (1986) vol. 2, § 242[1], pp. 372.15–372.20.) It is advantageous to the lessee if the "location proves undesirable or his enterprise proves unsuccessful." (Id.) Thus, both parties share in the inherent business risk. (51 Minn.L.R., *supra*, at p. 1150, fn. 62.) Inherent within all percentage leases is the fundamental idea that the business must continually operate if it is to be successful. To make a commercial lease mutually profitable when the rent is a minimum plus a percentage, or is based totally on a percentage, a covenant to operate in good faith will be implied into the contract if the minimum rent is not substantial. (*Lippman v. Sears, Roebuck & Co.* (1955) 44 Cal.2d 136, 280 P.2d 775.)

In interpreting contracts, "[t]he whole of a contract is to be taken together, so as to give effect to every part . . . each clause helping to interpret the other." (Civ.Code, § 1641.) Further, contracts are to be interpreted so as to make them reasonable without violating the intention of the parties. (Civ.Code, § 1643.) To effectuate the intent of the parties, implied covenants will be found if after examining the contract as a whole it is so obvious that the parties had no reason to state the covenant, the implication arises from the language of the agreement, and there is a legal necessity. (*Lippman,* supra, 44 Cal.2d at p. 142, 280 P.2d 775.) A covenant of continued operation can be implied into commercial leases containing percentage rental provisions in order for the lessor to receive that for which the lessor bargained. (*Lippman v. Sears, Roebuck & Co.,* supra; *Cordonier v. Central Shopping Plaza Associates,* supra, 82 Cal.App.3d 991, 147 Cal.Rptr. 558; cf. *Prins v. Van Der Vlugt* (1959) 215 Or. 682, 337 P.2d 787, 796.)

We first examine the lease to determine that to which the parties bargained. The lease between ARCO and College Block required ARCO to build and operate a gasoline service station on the undeveloped property owned by College Block. Other provisions in the lease allowed ARCO to build and maintain any edifices ARCO desired in operating a service station, obligated ARCO to pay all applicable property and taxes and insurance, prohibited College Block from conducting a gasoline station on other properties College Block owned or controlled, gave ARCO the right of first refusal if College Block received an offer to sell the property, and limited ARCO's use of the property to that of the gasoline service station.[5]

In addition, the rent was tied to the operation of the station. The rent provision, an essential part of the lease, did not set a minimum payment irrespective of whether the property was utilized as a service station, but rather "irrespective of the number of gallons . . . delivered." "Without an on-going service station operation, no basis would exist to calculate the rent." (*Continental Oil Co. v. Bradley* (1979) 198 Colo. 331, 602 P.2d 1, 2.) The wording of this provision suggests that continued operation of the business was contemplated.

Further, it is incongruent to limit College Block's abilities to lease properties it owned or controlled for use as another gasoline station under the noncompetition clause, thus foreclosing College Block from securing another station if ARCO abandoned the premises, and to limit ARCO's ability to operate any other type of business on the property, yet to conclude that ARCO could cease operations when it desired. Contrary to ARCO's suggestion, the fact that ARCO and not College Block was obligated to build the gasoline service station is not control-

5. Article 6 of the lease grants ARCO the right and privilege of erecting and maintaining structures for the purpose of operating a gasoline service station. The original draft of the lease contained a provision which would have allowed ARCO to utilize the property for a gasoline station as well as for any lawful purpose. This provision was deleted by the parties. We need not consider the deleted provision to conclude that ARCO was prohibited from utilizing the property for any purpose other than a gasoline station. Even though "a statement as to the purpose for which premises are leased does not imply a covenant by the lessee that he will engage in that use. . . ." (*Lippman v. Sears, Roebuck & Co., supra,* 44 Cal.2d at p. 142, 280 P.2d 775), here the parties' intent to limit Arco's use of the property is implicit within the totality of the contract. In examining the contract as a whole, all important provisions refer to a gasoline station. For example, the contract provisions required ARCO to build a station, allowed ARCO the option of cancelling the lease if ARCO could not obtain permits necessary to run the station and determined the amount of rent based upon the number of gallons delivered. To suggest that ARCO could utilize the property for any other purpose would be contrary to the spirit of the entire contract.

ling. Both parties were entitled to the expectations as bargained for in the lease.

ARCO's contention that there is no implied covenant of continued operation is based on Article 7 of the lease. ARCO's two arguments based upon this provision have no merit. Article 7 allows ARCO "[a]t any time during the term of this lease . . . [to] remove from said premises any and all buildings, structures, improvements, . . ." ARCO argues that "[s]ince it is impossible for ARCO to operate a service station while simultaneously exercising its right to remove all buildings and equipment from the leased property" it therefore could cease operating the station at any time as long as College Block was paid the specified minimum rent. ARCO's interpretation of this provision is inconsistent with the spirit of the entire contract. Article 7 is the only contract clause which raises a hint of ambiguity. As shown above, when this provision is viewed in conjunction with all other provisions of the contract, the party's intent becomes evident—ARCO was expected to continually operate a station for the entire length of the lease. (See e.g., *Lilac Variety, Inc. v. Dallas Texas Company* (Tex. 1964) 383 S.W.2d 193, 196.) Article 7 was an obvious recognition that ARCO would need the right to refurbish, replace, and upgrade its station over the 20–year lease period. However, leaving this property idle was not in the contemplation of the parties. ARCO could tear down the gasoline station, replace it, and refurbish it. However, ARCO was still obligated to operate a station for the entire leasehold period.[7]

Article 6 gave ARCO the "right and privilege of erecting . . . structures . . . that it may require or desire to use in operating . . . and conducting . . . business of . . . a gasoline and oil filling and service station. . . ." Relying on *Hicks v. Whelan Drug Co.* (1955) 131 Cal.App.2d 110, 280 P.2d 104, ARCO contends that this language did not obligate ARCO to maintain a station, but merely gave it the "privilege" of doing so. In *Hicks* the court held that a tenant who leased property to operate a drug store and in addition had the "privilege" of operating a restaurant or soda fountain within the drug store could not be forced to operate the soda fountain. The court based its ruling on the fact that the soda fountain was an incidental function of the primary purpose of the lease, i.e., the drug store. Unlike *Hicks* and another case relied upon by appellant, *Masciotra v. Harlow* (1951) 105 Cal.App.2d 376, 233 Cal.Rptr. 586, when ARCO closed the gasoline service station it completely frustrated the purpose of the contract. The entire purpose of the lease between College Block and ARCO was to enable ARCO to operate a gasoline station on property owned by College Block. Thus, neither *Hicks* nor *Masciotra* is controlling.

7. ARCO cites three cases from other jurisdictions to support its argument that a removal provision indicates that a lessee may cease operations. *Williams v. Safeway Stores, Incorporated* (1967) 198 Kan. 331, 424 P.2d 541 is inapplicable because the case deals with a lessee's right to sublet property. *Stevens v. Mobil Oil Corp.* (Mich.1976) 412 F.Supp. 809 is inapplicable because a removal clause included in the pertinent lease only mentions the business purpose (gasoline station) in two other places and provides a maximum rental in addition to the guaranteed minimum rental payment. *Stemmler v. Moon Jewelry Company* (Fla.1962) 139 So.2d 150 is inapplicable because it deals with a short lease (five years) and the removal provision relates to fixtures.

We now turn to whether the $1,000 rent minimum was "substantial." . . . If both parties contemplated continued operations of the business, a covenant of continued operation will be implied into commercial lease containing a specified minimum plus a percentage when the guaranteed minimum is not substantial or adequate. In this way, the lessor will receive the benefit of the lessor's bargain.

"A substantial minimum" cannot be precisely defined and factual information on this issue must be examined before a covenant will be implied. By evaluating the facts surrounding the formulation of the contract, the courts determine if the specified sum provides the lessor with what was reasonably expected.

Here, the court erred by ruling that there was an implied covenant of continued operation in the lease prior to receiving evidence on this factual issue. The lease between ARCO and College Block was executed approximately 17 years prior to the cessation of operations. In the interim, great changes in property values, gasoline prices, and the amount of sales could have occurred. Before finding, as a matter of law, that a covenant of continued operation will be implied, the trier of fact must find that the $1,000, the guaranteed minimum, was not substantial and did not provide College Block with a fair return on its investment. The parties should be given an opportunity to submit evidence as to the facts and circumstances surrounding the contract to determine if, at the time the contract was entered into, the guaranteed rent was "substantial." We remand to the trial court so evidence may be heard on this issue.

. . .

NOTES

1. The court in the principal case stated in a footnote that if a covenant of continued operation is implied, the measure of damages will be the difference between the amount the lessor would have received had the service station been operated in its usual and customary manner and the minimum rent actually paid by ARCO.

2. In Lippman v. Sears, Roebuck & Co., 44 Cal.2d 136, 280 P.2d 775 (1955) a tenant under a lease providing for a percentage rent based upon net sales ceased all retail operations in the premises and used them as a warehouse instead. The lease contained provisions stipulating that if the tenant assigned or sublet the premises the lessor would receive "the average monthly rental paid . . . during the twelve months' period last preceding" the subletting or assignment and that if the lessee abandoned the premises prematurely, the tenant would pay as damages the difference between the best rent obtainable by a reletting and "the rent herein reserved." The court treated these clauses as providing for liquidated damages for the loss of the lessor's percentage rent if the tenant ceased occupying the premises and concluded that the parties must have intended the same measure of damages to apply when that loss resulted from abandoning retail sales.

B. EVICTION

EDWARDS v. HABIB

United States Court of Appeals, District of Columbia Circuit, 1968.
397 F.2d 687, cert. denied 393 U.S. 1016, 89 S.Ct. 618, 21 L.Ed.2d 560 (1969).

J. SKELLY WRIGHT, CIRCUIT JUDGE. In March 1965 the appellant, Mrs. Yvonne Edwards, rented housing property from the appellee, Nathan Habib, on a month-to-month basis. Shortly thereafter she complained to the Department of Licenses and Inspections of sanitary code violations which her landlord had failed to remedy. In the course of the ensuing inspection, more than 40 such violations were discovered which the Department ordered the landlord to correct. Habib then gave Mrs. Edwards a 30–day statutory notice [1] to vacate and obtained a default judgment for possession of the premises.[2] Mrs. Edwards promptly moved to reopen this judgment, alleging excusable neglect for the default and also alleging as a defense that the notice to quit was given in retaliation for her complaints to the housing authorities. Judge Greene, sitting on motions in the Court of General Sessions, set aside the default judgment and, in a very thoughtful opinion, concluded that a retaliatory motive, if proved, would constitute a defense to the action for possession. At the trial itself, however, a different judge apparently deemed evidence of retaliatory motive irrelevant and directed a verdict for the landlord.

Mrs. Edwards then appealed to this court for a stay pending her appeal to the District of Columbia Court of Appeals, and on December 3, 1965, we granted the stay, provided only that Mrs. Edwards continue to pay her rent. Edwards v. Habib, 125 U.S.App.D.C. 49, 366 F.2d 628 (1965). She then appealed to the DCCA, which affirmed the judgment of the trial court. 227 A.2d 388 (1967). In reaching its decision the DCCA relied on a series of its earlier decisions holding that a private landlord was not required, under the District of Columbia Code, to give a reason for evicting a month-to-month tenant and was free to do so for any reason or for no reason at all. The court acknowledged that the landlord's right to terminate a tenancy is not absolute, but felt that any limitation on his prerogative had to be based on specific statutes or very special circumstances. Here, the court concluded, the tenant's right to

1. 45 D.C.Code § 902 (1967), Notices to quit—Month to month:

"A tenancy from month to month, or from quarter to quarter, may be terminated by a thirty days' notice in writing from the landlord to the tenant to quit, or by such a notice from the tenant to the landlord of his intention to quit, said notice to expire, in either case on the day of the month from which such tenancy commenced to run."

2. 45 D.C.Code § 910 (1967), Ejectment or summary proceedings:

"Whenever a lease for any definite term shall expire, or any tenancy shall be terminated by notice as aforesaid, and the tenant shall fail or refuse to surrender possession of the leased premises, the landlord may bring an action of ejectment to recover possession in the United States District Court for the District of Columbia: or the landlord may bring an action to recover possession before the District of Columbia Court of General Sessions, as provided in Sections 11–701 to 11–749."

See also 16 D.C.Code § 1501 (1967).

report violations of law and to petition for redress of grievances was not protected by specific legislation and that any change in the relative rights of tenants and landlords should be undertaken by the legislature, not the courts. We granted appellant leave to appeal that decision to this court. We hold that the promulgation of the housing code by the District of Columbia Commissioners at the direction of Congress impliedly effected just such a change in the relative rights of landlords and tenants and that proof of a retaliatory motive does constitute a defense to an action of eviction. Accordingly, we reverse the decision of the DCCA with directions that it remand to the Court of General Sessions for a new trial where Mrs. Edwards will be permitted to try to prove to a jury that her landlord who seeks to evict her harbors a retaliatory intent.

Appellant has launched a constitutional challenge to the judicial implementation of 45 D.C.Code §§ 902 and 910 in aid of a landlord who is evicting because his tenant has reported housing code violations on the premises. . . .

But we need not decide whether judicial recognition of this constitutional defense is constitutionally compelled. We need not, in other words, decide whether 45 D.C.Code § 910 could validly compel the court to assist the plaintiff in penalizing the defendant for exercising her constitutional right to inform the government of violations of the law; for we are confident that Congress did not intend it to entail such a result.

45 D.C.Code § 910, in pertinent part, provides:

"Whenever . . . any tenancy shall be terminated by notice as aforesaid [45 D.C.Code § 902, see note 1, supra], and the tenant shall fail or refuse to surrender possession of the leased premises, . . . the landlord may bring an action to recover possession before the District of Columbia Court of General Sessions, as provided in sections 11–701 to 11–749."

And 16 D.C.Code § 1501, in pertinent part, provides:

"When a person detains possession of real property . . . after his right to possession has ceased, the District of Columbia Court of General Sessions . . . may issue a summons to the party complained of to appear and show cause why judgment should not be given against him for restitution of possession."

These provisions are simply procedural. They neither say nor imply anything about whether evidence of retaliation or other improper motive should be unavailable as a defense to a possessory action brought under them. It is true that in making his affirmative case for possession the landlord need only show that his tenant has been given the 30-day statutory notice, and he need not assign any reason for evicting a tenant who does not occupy the premises under a lease. But while the landlord may evict for any legal reason or for no reason at all, he is not, we hold, free to evict in retaliation for his tenant's report of housing code violations to the authorities. As a matter of statutory construction and for reasons of public policy, such an eviction cannot be permitted.

The housing and sanitary codes, especially in light of Congress' explicit direction for their enactment, indicate a strong and pervasive congressional concern to secure for the city's slum dwellers decent, or at least safe and sanitary, places to live. Effective implementation and enforcement of the codes obviously depend in part on private initiative in the reporting of violations. Though there is no official procedure for the filing of such complaints, the bureaucratic structure of the Department of Licenses and Inspections establishes such a procedure, and for fiscal year 1966 nearly a third of the cases handled by the Department arose from private complaints.[43] To permit retaliatory evictions, then, would clearly frustrate the effectiveness of the housing code as a means of upgrading the quality of housing in Washington.

As judges, "we cannot shut our eyes to matters of public notoriety and general cognizance. When we take our seats on the bench we are not struck with blindness, and forbidden to know as judges what we see as men." Ho Ah Kow v. Nunan, C.C.D.Cal., 12 Fed.Cas. 252, 255 (No. 6546) (1879). In trying to effect the will of Congress and as a court of equity we have the responsibility to consider the social context in which our decisions will have operational effect. In light of the appalling condition and shortage of housing in Washington, the expense of moving, the inequality of bargaining power between tenant and landlord, and the social and economic importance of assuring at least minimum standards in housing conditions, we do not hesitate to declare that retaliatory eviction cannot be tolerated. There can be no doubt that the slum dweller, even though his home be marred by housing code violations, will pause long before he complains of them if he fears eviction as a consequence. Hence an eviction under the circumstances of this case would not only punish appellant for making a complaint which she had a constitutional right to make, a result which we would not impute to the will of Congress simply on the basis of an essentially procedural enactment, but also would stand as a warning to others that they dare not be so bold, a result which, from the authorization of the housing code, we think Congress affirmatively sought to avoid.

The notion that the effectiveness of remedial legislation will be inhibited if those reporting violations of it can legally be intimidated is so fundamental that a presumption against the legality of such intimidation can be inferred as inherent in the legislation even if it is not expressed in the statute itself. Such an inference was recently drawn by the Supreme Court from the federal labor statutes to strike down under the supremacy clause a Florida statute denying unemployment insurance to workers discharged in retaliation for filing complaints of federally defined unfair labor practices. While we are not confronted with a possible conflict between federal policy and state law, we do have

43. Of 47,701 cases handled, almost 15,000 were initiated by private complaint. See Hearings Before the Subcommittee on Business and Commerce of the Senate Committee on the District of Columbia on S. 2331, S. 3549 and S. 3558, 89th Cong., 2d Sess., at 52 (1966). And the need for increased private and group participation in code enforcement has been widely recognized. Gribetz and Grad, Housing Code Enforcement: Sanctions and Remedies, 66 Colum.L.Rev. 1254 (1966); Note, Enforcement of Municipal Housing Codes, 78 Harv.L.Rev. 801, 843–860 (1965). See also Sax and Hiestand, Slumlordism as a Tort, 65 Mich.L.Rev. 869 (1967).

the task of reconciling and harmonizing two federal statutes so as to best effectuate the purposes of each.[50] The proper balance can only be struck by interpreting 45 D.C.Code §§ 902 and 910 as inapplicable where the court's aid is invoked to effect an eviction in retaliation for reporting housing code violations.

This is not, of course, to say that even if the tenant can prove a retaliatory purpose she is entitled to remain in possession in perpetuity. If this illegal purpose is dissipated, the landlord can, in the absence of legislation or a binding contract, evict his tenants or raise their rents for economic or other legitimate reasons, or even for no reason at all.[53] The question of permissible or impermissible purpose is one of fact for the court or jury, and while such a determination is not easy, it is not significantly different from problems with which the courts must deal in a host of other contexts. . . .

Reversed and remanded.

NOTES

1. In Robinson v. Diamond Housing Corp., 150 U.S.App.D.C. 17, 463 F.2d 853 (1972) the lessor's initial attempt to evict a tenant for nonpayment of rent was defeated when she successfully invoked the Brown v. Southal Realty argument (see p. 457) that she owed no rent because a lease of premises that violated the D.C. Housing Code was void. The lessor then instituted a second eviction suit alleging that the tenant was not entitled to possession because the lease was void. This action was defeated because the lessor had failed to give 30 days' notice as required by statute. In response to the lessor's third action for eviction, which was filed after the requisite period of notice, the tenant argued that she was being evicted in retaliation for having asserted Brown v. Southal Realty as a defense to the lessor's first action. The court of appeals reversed the lower courts' holdings that the retaliatory eviction defense of Edwards v. Habib was inapplicable to the facts of the case.

> Since *Edwards* involved reporting of code violations to city officials while this case involves setting up those violations as a defense to an action for eviction, it is contended that *Edwards* does not compel reversal here. Moreover, Diamond argues that, even if

50. See, e.g., United States v. Borden Co., 308 U.S. 188, 198, 60 S.Ct. 182, 84 L.Ed. 181 (1939); Rawls v. United States, 8 Cir., 331 F.2d 21, 28 (1964). When Congress enacted 45 D.C.Code §§ 902 and 910, it did not have in mind their possible use in effectuating retaliatory evictions. Indeed, when they were enacted there was no housing code at all. And in all probability Congress did not attend to the problem of retaliatory evictions when it directed the enactment of the housing code. Our task is to determine what Congress would have done, in light of the purpose and language of the statute, had it confronted the question now before the court. And where there is a possible conflict, the more recent enactment, the housing code, should be given full effect while leaving an area of effective operation for the earlier statute. International Union of Electrical, Radio, etc., Workers v. N.L.R.B., 110 U.S.App.D.C. 91, 95, 289 F.2d 757, 761 (1960). This task, we think, our resolution of the issue accomplishes.

53. Of course, because of his prior taint the landlord may not be able to disprove an illicit motive unless he can show a legitimate affirmative reason for eviction.

Edwards is more broadly read, it still should not be applied to a case such as this where the landlord is prevented from collecting rent by *Southall Realty,* refuses to repair the premises, and wishes to take the housing off the market altogether. Closely allied to this contention is the further argument that Mrs. Robinson is precluded from remaining in possession by Section 2301 of the Housing Regulations which makes it illegal to occupy premises which are in violation of the Regulations. Finally, Diamond argues that in any event this case is now moot since Mrs. Robinson has voluntarily surrendered possession and Diamond has chosen to forego any claim it might have to back rent.

We have carefully examined each of these arguments and have concluded that none of them sufficiently distinguishes this case from *Edwards* or precludes application of the District of Columbia law against retaliatory evictions. If we resolve all reasonable doubts in favor of appellant—as we must when reviewing a summary judgment, it becomes plain that a jury might find Diamond Housing to be using the eviction machinery to punish Mrs. Robinson for exercising her legal rights. . . .

. . .

It must nonetheless be conceded that implementing the legislative will in this fact situation leads to some difficulties and ambiguities. For example, Diamond Housing argues that permitting a retaliatory eviction defense here may mean that it will never be able to recover possession of its property. Nonreceipt of rent is a continuing injury, Diamond argues, and it will always want to remove the tenant so as to remove the source of injury. Yet ironically, so long as it is motivated by this goal, the *Edwards* defense will prevent achievement of it.

. . .

. . . Diamond Housing is correct when it asserts it will never be able to evict Mrs. Robinson so long as it is motivated by a desire to rid itself of a tenant who is not paying rent. But it does not follow that Diamond will be burdened by its unwanted tenant forever. If Diamond comes forward with a legitimate business justification—other than the mere desire to get rid of a tenant exercising *Southall Realty* rights—it may be able to convince a jury that it is motivated by this proper concern. For example, if Diamond brought the premises up to housing code standards so that rent was again due and then evicted the tenant for some unrelated, lawful reason, the eviction would be permissible. Similarly, if Diamond were to make a convincing showing that it was for some reason impossible or unfeasible to make repairs, it would have a legitimate reason for evicting the tenant and taking the unit off the market.

It does not follow, however, that mere desire to take the unit off the market is by itself a legitimate business reason which will justify an eviction.

2. Over 30 legislatures have enacted statutes addressing retaliatory eviction. Note, 1979 Wash.U.L.Q. 1168, 1170. For what reasons might legislation be desired? What drafting difficulties might be encountered? How should the burden of persuasion on the factual question of the existence of a retaliatory motive be handled? How should the matter of mixed motives be addressed? Should statutory retaliatory eviction be exclusive of common law retaliatory eviction? Compare Windward Partners v. Delos Santos, 59 Haw. 104, 577 P.2d 326 (1978) and Seidelman v. Kouvavus, 57 Ill.App.3d 350, 14 Ill.Dec. 922, 373 N.E.2d 53 (1978). See Statutory Comment, 61 Minn.L.Rev. 523 (1977). See also Article V of the Uniform Residential Landlord and Tenant Act. Compare Restatement (Second) of Property, Landlord and Tenant §§ 14.8, 14.9 (1977).

3. To allow tenants to raise issues of habitability and retaliatory eviction in summary proceedings instituted by landlords to recover possession tends to make those proceedings less summary—and thus to defeat their purpose. That purpose was summarized by Justice White in Lindsey v. Normet, 405 U.S. 56, 71, 92 S.Ct. 862, 873, 31 L.Ed.2d 36, 49 (1972):

"At common law, one with the right to possession could bring an action for ejectment, a 'relatively slow, fairly complex, and substantially expensive procedure.' But, . . . the common law also permitted the landlord to 'enter and expel the tenant by force, without being liable to an action of tort for damages, either for his entry upon the premises, or for an assault in expelling the tenant, provided he uses no more force than is necessary, and do[es] no wanton damage.' . . . The landlord-tenant relationship was one of the few areas where the right to self-help was recognized by the common law of most States, and the implementation of this right has been fraught with 'violence and quarrels and bloodshed.' . . . An alternative legal remedy to prevent such breaches of the peace has appeared to be an overriding necessity to many legislators and judges."

4. Some courts have manifested concern about the extent to which the summary nature of the FED remedy may be impaired by allowing tenants to raise issues of habitability and retaliatory motive in such proceedings. See, for example, S.P. Growers Association v. Rodriguez, 17 Cal.3d 719, 131 Cal.Rptr. 761, 763, 552 P.2d 721, 723 (1976) ("[W]e must engage in a balancing process. We must determine whether the public policies furthered by protecting defendants from eviction outweigh the interests in preserving the summary nature of unlawful detainer proceedings.").

5. If landlords perceive that the FED remedy is not sufficiently summary, they may be tempted to insert provisions in their leases entitling them to recover possession by self-help. Are such provisions valid? The cases are not in agreement. See, for example, Bass v. Boetel & Co., 191 Neb. 733, 217 N.W.2d 804 (1974). The court held such a clause void: To uphold it "would scuttle our forcible entry and detainer statute. Self-help, relating to the repossession of real estate, has long been contrary to the public policy of Nebraska and is not to be

condoned." But a dissenting judge stated: "The right of a landlord to reenter for default in payment of rent or a wrongful holding over should be permitted where the lease provides for reentry and it can be accomplished without violence. This is similar to the right of a conditional sale vendor to take possession of the security on default by peaceful means. See § 9–503, U.C.C." See also Annotation, 6 A.L.R.3d 177 (1966); Restatement (Second) of Property § 14.2, Reporter's Note (1977); R. Schoshinski, § 6.5 et seq. (1980).

C. ABANDONMENT BY TENANT

UNITED STATES NATIONAL BANK OF OREGON v. HOMELAND, INC.

Supreme Court of Oregon, 1981.
291 Or. 374, 631 P.2d 761.

PETERSON, JUSTICE.

Homeland, Inc., leased office space from Ralph D. Schlesinger and Bernice W. Schlesinger (hereinafter referred to as "lessor"). Prior to the expiration of the lease, Homeland abandoned the premises, after which lessor relet the premises to a new tenant for a longer term and at a higher rental. The new tenant also defaulted on the second lease. Two issues are presented:

1. When a leasehold tenant of commercial premises[1] abandons the premises prior to the expiration of the lease, and the lessor relets the premises for a term extending beyond the expiration of the original lease and at a higher rent, does such reletting constitute a termination of the lease, as a matter of law, thus freeing the tenant from any claim for damages accruing subsequent to the reletting?

2. When a lease of commercial premises provides that if a receiver is appointed, the lessor may, without notice, terminate the lease, does the lessor's reletting of the premises terminate the tenant's obligation to pay damages arising subsequent to the reletting?

Lessor owns an office building in downtown Portland. Homeland leased 3,000 square feet of office space from lessor for a five-year term, April 1, 1971 to March 31, 1976. The monthly rental for the first six months was $1,175 per month; for the second six months, $1,275 per month; and for the remaining 48 months, $1,415 per month. Homeland vacated the premises on July 31, 1973, with 32 months remaining on the lease and thereafter paid no more rent. In due course, a receiver, Paul C. Diegel, was appointed for Homeland. This case involves a claim by lessor against the Homeland receiver for unpaid rent accruing following Homeland's abandonment of the premises in July, 1973.

Between the Homeland default in July of 1973 and the reletting to Sebastian's International, Inc., in February of 1974, lessor attempted to lease the premises to other tenants on the same terms and conditions as

1. This case does not involve a dwelling unit. In leases of dwelling units, the landlord's duty to mitigate is covered by statute. See ORS 91.825(3).

other premises in the lessor's office building. At all times, the rental terms were competitive with those offered for similar office premises in Portland, Oregon. At the time in question, there was an excess of office space of this type in downtown Portland, Oregon, with the vacancy factor being between 10 percent and 12 percent. There were other vacancies in the lessor's building.

On February 1, 1974, lessor leased the premises to Sebastian's for a term commencing February 1, 1974, and ending January 31, 1977. The term of this lease extended 10 months longer than the Homeland lease, and the rent was $1,500 per month, $85 per month more than under the Homeland lease. Sebastian's subsequently defaulted and vacated the premises on July 14, 1974, after having paid a total rent of $7,500.

After the Sebastian's default, lessor continued to attempt to lease the premises but was unable to do so until August 1, 1975. Lessor relet the office space to another party effective August 1, 1975. Lessor's claim against the receiver is for the period August 1, 1973, though July 31, 1975, 24 months at a monthly rate of $1,415, less the rent paid by Sebastian's in the amount of $7,500, lessor's net claim being $26,460.

The receiver urged the trial court to limit the claim to the period from the date that Homeland vacated until February 1, 1974, when the premises were leased to Sebastian's. Without explanation or opinion, the trial court so limited the claim and denied the remainder of lessor's claim. The Court of Appeals affirmed. 47 Or.App. 745, 615 P.2d 380 (1980).

The receiver asserts (1) that the reletting to Sebastian's for a longer term and at a higher rent than that provided in the original lease terminated the Homeland lease as a matter of law, and (2) that the reletting operated to terminate Homeland's lease in accordance with one of the terms of that lease. The resolution of this case turns, in part, upon rules of law enunciated in three recent Oregon cases. We will first discuss the legal framework within which this case arose and then turn to the specific issues.

Prior to Wright v. Baumann, 239 Or. 410, 398 P.2d 119 (1965), Oregon subscribed to the view that a lessor is not required to mitigate damages when the tenant abandons the leasehold premises. The theory was that a lease was a conveyance of an interest in real property, that the tenant "becomes the owner of the premises for a term and therefore the lessor need not concern himself with lessee's abandonment of his own property." 239 Or. at 413, 398 P.2d 119.

In Wright v. Baumann, however, this view was rejected. We held that such a transaction is essentially a contract rather than a conveyance. Justice O'Connell, speaking for the court, observed that

> ". . . covenants in a modern business lease, particularly where only a part of the space in a building is leased, relate for the most part to the use of the space. The lessor's duties do not end with the execution of the lease. The case of Whitaker v. Hawley, 25 Kan. 674, 687 (1881) expresses this view as follows: '. . . a lease is in one sense a running rather than a completed contract. It is an agreement for a continuous interchange of values between

landlord and tenant, rather than a purchase single and completed of a term or estate in lands.'" 239 Or. at 413–414, 398 P.2d 119.

In reference to the landlord's duty to mitigage damages, the court stated:

> ". . . Writing in 1925, McCormick predicted that eventually 'the logic, inescapable according to the standards of a "jurisprudence of conceptions" which permits the landlord to stand idly by the vacant, abandoned premises and treat them as the property of the tenant and recover full rent, will yield to the more realistic notions of social advantage which in other fields of the law have forbidden a recovery for damages which the plaintiff by reasonable efforts could have avoided.' We believe that it is time for McCormick's prediction to become a reality." (Footnote omitted.) 239 Or. at 415, 398 P.2d 119.[2]

The discussion of the issue concluded with this statement:

> ". . . And whether they are regarded as arising out of contract or conveyance, a court of equity should require the plaintiff seeking equity to do equity by making a reasonable effort to avoid damages." 239 Or. at 417, 398 P.2d 119.

Two years later, Kulm v. Coast-to-Coast Stores, 248 Or. 436, 432 P.2d 1006 (1967), held that the landlord has the duty to mitigate damages. By analogy to claims for breach of contract for the sale of goods, we adopted the rule that in the event of the tenant's abandonment, the lessor's measure of damages was ". . . not the full amount of the stipulated rent but an amount which represents the difference between the stipulated rent and the rent which [landlord] would receive upon leasing the premises to others." 248 Or. at 442, 432 P.2d 1006.

The result of this rule of damages was to give the landlord the benefit of the bargain, on the theory that if the fair rental value was less than the agreed rent, the landlord could relet the premises at fair rental value, and the landlord would be made whole by receiving the fair rental value from the new tenant, *plus* the difference between the fair rental value and the abandoning tenant's agreed rental.

Kulm also held that if, after a reasonable effort, the landlord was unable to relet the premises, the landlord would be entitled to receive the entire amount of the rent reserved for the period during which the premises could not be rented.[3]

2. The McCormick quotation is from McCormick, The Rights of the Landlord Upon Abandonment of the Premises by the Tenant, 23 Mich.L.Rev. 211, 221–22 (1925).

3. ". . . In ordinary circumstances property which is the subject matter of a contract to execute or renew a lease can be leased to others upon the promissor's failure to accept the lease. Under such circumstances it is reasonable to assume, in the absence of proof to the contrary, that the lessor's loss is not the full amount of the stipulated rent but an amount which represents the difference between the stipulated rent and the rent which plaintiff would receive upon leasing the premises to others. If the plaintiff can show that there is no market for the leasehold, he can, of course, recover the entire amount of the rent reserved, but it is his burden to show this and if he does not, he has not made out his case. . . . ." 248 Or. at 442, 432 P.2d 1006.

The holdings of Wright v. Baumann, supra, and Kulm v. Coast-to-Coast Stores, supra, were affirmed in Foggia v. Dix, 265 Or. 315, 509 P.2d 412 (1973). In *Foggia*, the landlord was unable to relet the premises (a dental clinic) at the same rental that the abandoning tenant had agreed to pay. The tenant claimed that the landlord had an obligation to mitigate damages by reletting at less than the fair rental value and for a use other than as a dental clinic. The court stated:

> "In order to mitigate the damages occasioned by a lessee's breach of a lease, the landlord should not be required to substantially alter his obligations as established in the pre-existing lease. Thus in the present case plaintiff was not required to rent the premises to persons not working in dentistry or related fields, since the offices were part of a dental clinic occupied by two other dentists and were designed for that special use. Nor should plaintiff be required to rent the premises below their fair rental value. Defendant did not produce any evidence that $375 per month was not the fair rental value of the dental offices. Under all these circumstances we are of the opinion that plaintiff fulfilled his obligation to mitigate the damages." 265 Or. at 321, 509 P.2d 412.

The resolution of this case turns upon the application of rules of law derived from the cases discussed above, a consideration of the nature of the tenant's interest in the property following abandonment, and the determination of the landlord's responsibility following the tenant's abandonment.

Following abandonment of the leased premises, the landlord cannot stand idly and look to the tenant for damages in the amount of the rent which would accrue during the remainder of the leasehold term. The lessor has a duty to make a reasonable effort to mitigate damages by finding a suitable tenant.

The tenant, by abandoning the leased premises,[4] forfeits his *estate* in the real property, but remains liable for damages for breach of contract under the rule of *Kulm*, supra. In a physical sense, the tenant has surrendered the possession of the premises to the landlord; and by virtue of Wright v. Baumann, supra, and Kulm v. Coast-to-Coast Stores, supra, the landlord has a duty to accept the surrendered premises and make a reasonable effort to relet the premises.[5]

It follows that mere acceptance and reletting of the surrendered premises does not release the tenant from contractual liability for breach of contract.[6] The tenant is in the position of one who has

4. See G. Weissenberger, The Landlord's Duty to Mitigate Damages on the Tenant's Abandonment: A Survey of Old Law and New Trends, 53 Tem.L.Q. 1, 2 n. 5 (1980).

5. As will be seen below, in a jurisdiction such as Oregon, which treats such situations within the framework of breach of contract rather than within the pre-Wright v. Baumann, conveyance theory, consideration of the older "acceptance of surrender" cases is inappropriate, for the lessor, under *Kulm* and *Wright*, must, in a physical sense, accept the surrender.

6. Compare this language from footnote 7 of Wright v. Baumann, 239 Or. 410, 416, 398 P.2d 119 (1965):

> ". . . In Oregon, however, it has long been the rule that 'a landlord may relet for the benefit of an original lessee who has abandoned the premises, and that the act of reletting does not of itself necessarily effect a termination of the lease,' Meagher v. Eilers Music House,

anticipatorily breached a contract for the sale of goods. The tenant remains liable for the difference between the agreed price (the stipulated rent) and the fair rental value of the premises (which is the amount the law presumes the lessor can obtain by making a reasonable effort to relet the premises). In addition, the tenant remains liable for the entire amount of the rent, at the agreed rate, for such period of time that the lessor (if a reasonable effort is made) is unable to relet the premises. Kulm v. Coast-to-Coast Stores, supra, 148 Or. at 442, 432 P.2d 1006. Upon reletting, the tenant is in a situation similar to that of a tenant who assigns a lease. The tenant remains responsible for the rent for the remainder of the term, if the second tenant fails to pay.[7] We turn then to a consideration of the effect of the landlord's reletting or attempting to relet the premises (1) for a different term than the unexpired portion of the abandoning tenant's lease or (2) at a higher rent than under the abandoning tenant's lease.

The facts of this case are undisputed. There is no claim or suggestion that the lessor was attempting to rent other space in the building so as to protect any claim for damages against the receiver.[8] The receiver's sole claim is that the lessor's ". . . attempt to relet the premises for a term and rent in excess of that provided for in the original lease [terminated any claim for damages] as a matter of law."

We have no hesitancy in concluding that attempting to relet for a longer or shorter term does not, of itself, bar the lessor's claim for damages as a matter of law, for to insist that the lessor relet only for the unexpired term of the lease might well inhibit marketability of the premises, particularly when a short term remained on the original lease. A new tenant might prefer or demand a shorter term or a longer term, depending on need. Here, the Sebastian's lease was for a term slightly longer than the unexpired term of the Homeland lease. There is no evidence that the reletting or the attempts to relet which preceded the relettings inhibited the marketability of the premises or otherwise operated to the receiver's prejudice.[9]

84 Or. 33, 39, 164 P. 373 (1917). Consequently, there is no substantial difference between the instant case and one involving a sublessee insofar as the danger of an unintended surrender is concerned."

The term reletting "for the benefit of the original lessee" is commonly found in opinions discussing the doctrine of "surrender by operation of law" under the "conveyance" theory, which Wright v. Baumann disavowed. See, for example, Phegley v. Enke's City Dye Works, 127 Or. 539, 545, 272 P. 898 (1928).

7. See C. Updegraff, The Element of Intent in Surrender by Operation of Law, 38 Harv.L.Rev. 64, 79 (1925).

8. Sommer v. Kridel, 74 N.J. 446, 459, 378 A.2d 767, 774 (1977), stands for the proposition that the landlord is not required to grant the abandoning tenant preferential treatment vis-a-vis other similar property owned by the landlord. There being no evidence other than that the landlord offered the premises ". . . on the same terms and conditions as other premises in the building . . .," we need not decide what specific circumstances would support a finding that the lessor failed to act with due diligence by preferring other property in order to maintain a damage claim against an abandoning tenant.

9. The receiver relies on Casper National Bank v. Curry, 51 Wyo. 284, 65 P.2d 1116, 1118 (1937); In re Goldburg's Estate, 148 Misc. 607, 266 N.Y.S. 106, 109 (1933); Eidelman v. Walker & Dunlop, Inc., 265 Md. 538, 290 A.2d 780 (1972); and Wilson v. Ruhl, 277 Md. 607, 356 A.2d 544 (1976).

The Wyoming and New York cases relied upon by receiver follow the view that a lease term is an estate in lands and that lessor's interference with tenant's possessory interest is an eviction which releases

Although reletting or attempting to relet at a higher rent poses a more challenging inquiry, we also conclude that reletting or attempting to relet at a higher rate does not, as a matter of law, bar the landlord's claim for damages. Although any increase in rent may have a theoretical effect in limiting marketability, a lessor's duty to mitigate damages does not compel the reletting at less than the then fair rental value.

Mr. Schlesinger's affidavit states:

> "At all times we attempted to lease the premises to other tenants, and showed the premises to anyone who might be interested. The premises were offered on the same terms and conditions as other premises in the building, and at all times the rental terms were competitive with those offered for similar premises in Portland, Oregon. During the term reserved in the lease between my wife and me and Homeland, Inc., there was an excess of office space in older buildings in downtown Portland, Oregon. I would estimate that the vacancy factor was approximately 10% to 12%. We had other vacancies in our building also."

The rent that similar premises then receive is relevant to the fair rental value of the subject premises. The premises were relet to Sebastian's at a rate of $1,500 per month. The Homeland rental rate was $1,415 per month. The rental under the Sebastian's lease, executed nearly three years later than the Homeland lease, exceeded the rental under the Homeland lease by but six percent. The receiver points to no evidence that the effort to relet at $1,500 per month inhibited the reletting or that $1,500 per month was other than fair rental value.[10]

While each case is, to a degree, dependent on its facts, this case is not remarkably different from Foggia v. Dix, 265 Or. 315, 509 P.2d 412 (1972), which held that the lessor's duty to mitigate damages does not

tenant. For example, Casper National Bank v. Curry, 51 Wyo. 284, 65 P.2d 1116 (1937), stated that ". . . it is necessary, if the second lease, given without the tenant's consent, is to be regarded as valid to confer present rights of possession, that the operation of the former lease shall have come to an end, since two distinct persons cannot each be entitled to the exclusive possession of the same premises." In further explanation of its position, the Wyoming court cited Welcome v. Hess, 90 Cal. 507, 27 P. 269 (1891), in which the California court stated that a "[lease] term is an estate in lands. The tenant . . . is the owner for the term. If he . . . [abandons], his title still continues . . . ." 27 P. at 371.

Under this view, because lessee has a continued right to possession, when lessor relets the premises, he "interfere[s] with the right of the tenant to the absolute dominion and control [of the premises] ." 27 P. at 371. This interference amounts to a constructive eviction and lessee is released.

Receiver's cases are distinguishable because, as noted above, Wright v. Baumann, 239 Or. 410, 398 P.2d 119 (1965), rejected the view that a lease term was a purchase of an estate in lands; instead we concluded that such a transaction is essentially a contract.

Moreover, in the most recent Maryland case cited by receiver, Millison v. Clarke, 287 Md. 420, 403 A.2d 384 (1980), the court held that re-leasing the premises for a term in excess of the abandoned original lease did not operate to terminate the original lease as a matter of law. 403 A.2d at 389.

10. In his brief the receiver virtually concedes that $1,500 per month was fair rental value, for he states:

> ". . . Thus, the only evidence regarding the fair rental value at or near the time of surrender was the rent specified in the Sebastian's lease, $1,500, which was greater than the amount specified in the Homeland lease."

require reletting at less than fair rental value. 265 Or. at 321, 509 P.2d 412. In the case at bar, there is substantial evidence that similar premises were then renting at $1,500 per month, and that $1,500 per month was "competitive." In the absence of any claim or evidence that $1,500 per month is not fair rental value, we conclude that the increase in rent from $1,415 per month to $1,500 per month is consistent with a "reasonable effort" on the lessor's part.[11]

. . .

Reversed and remanded for entry of judgment in favor of lessor in the sum of $26,460.

NOTES

1. Certain conceptual difficulties have hampered solution of this problem. To say that no surrender is effected by a reletting is to say that the former estate continues. Should it be conceived that the landlord, in reletting, is making a sublease or assignment as the tenant's agent? One difficulty with this conception is that the landlord usually acts in his own name and at least partially in his own interest; probably neither he nor the defaulting tenant ordinarily regards their relationship as one of agency. Moreover, though the landlord usually acts without written authorization, it is improbable that a court would treat the new arrangement as unenforceable on the ground that an agent's authority to convey an interest in land must, by the Statute of Frauds, be in writing. Still further, if the landlord is conceived to be acting as the tenant's agent, he would be required to account to the tenant for the surplus, if he managed to relet at a figure higher than the original rent; but, unless the landlord has covenanted to do so in the lease, it is improbable that any court would require him to account for a surplus. See Whitcomb v. Brant, 90 N.J.L. 245, 100 A. 175 (1917), questioned in 30 Harv.L.Rev. 766 (1917). It is possible, of course, to provide in a lease that the landlord may relet as agent for an abandoning tenant, but this is risky at best, for a court may find that in reletting on different terms the landlord has acted in his own interest rather than that of the tenant and has thereby effected an unintended surrender. See Flack v. Sarnosa Oil Corp., 293 S.W.2d 688 (Tex.Civ. App.1956), critically examined in 35 Tex.L.Rev. 869 (1957). Could these difficulties, including the Statute of Frauds, be avoided by conceiving the situation as one in which the landlord is exercising a power conferred by law to deal with the tenant's estate? See Schnebly, Operative Facts in Surrenders, 22 Ill.L.Rev. 117, 130 (1927). Suppose the landlord combines the premises in question with other premises he owns, leasing the whole for a period exceeding the remaining portion of the original term—how is it possible to rationalize the conclusion that

11. Compare: Consolidated Sun Ray, Inc. v. Oppenstein, 335 F.2d 801, 811 (8th Cir.1964); Irving Trust Co. v. American Silk Mills, Inc., 93 F.2d 667 (2d Cir.1938); Payne v. Hall, 82 N.J.L. 362, 82 A. 518 (1912); Weeks v. International Trust Co., 125 F. 370 (1st Cir.1903), error dismissed for want of jurisdiction, 193 U.S. 667, 24 S.Ct. 853, 48 L.Ed. 839 (1904); Benson v. Iowa Bake-Rite Co., 207 Iowa 410, 221 N.W. 464 (1928).

the original estate continues; i.e., that no surrender by operation of law has occurred?

2. It is standard practice to include in the lease a clause providing that if the tenant abandons and repudiates his obligations, or is evicted for failure to perform, he shall be liable for any loss incurred by the landlord in reletting for the rest of the term. Does such a clause solve the problem of rationalizing the tenant's liability for loss resulting from reletting? What of the situation where the defaulting tenant is an assignee, who is obligated to pay rent only by privity of estate? See Lincoln Fireproof Warehouse Co. v. Greusel, 199 Wis. 428, 224 N.W. 98, 227 N.W. 6 (on rehearing), 70 A.L.R. 1096 (1929).

Unless the covenant of indemnity is carefully drafted, the landlord may find that he has no remedy against the defaulting tenant until the end of the term. In Hermitage Co. v. Levine, 248 N.Y. 333, 162 N.E. 97, 59 A.L.R. 1015 (1928), a lease made in 1924 for 21 years provided that upon the tenant's abandonment or eviction for default, the landlord might relet the premises "as agent for the tenant, and the tenant shall remain liable for all damages which the landlord may sustain. . . ." Five months after the term began the tenant was evicted for failure to pay rent. Exercising due diligence, the landlord relet portions of the building to three different tenants for varying periods, all of which would expire before the terminal date of the original term. About fifteen months after the tenant's eviction the landlord sued for the deficiency in rent to that time. Affirming a judgment for the tenant, the court (per Cardozo, C.J.) said, "No doubt a damage clause can be drawn in such a way as to make a tenant responsible for monthly deficits after the re-entry of his landlord, and this without charging the landlord with a duty to account for a surplus in other seasons. . . . Nonetheless, in the absence of a provision that points with reasonable clearness to a different construction, a liability for damages resulting from a reletting is single and entire, not multiple and several. The deficiency is to be ascertained when the term is at an end. [Citations omitted.] The tenant when ejected ceases to be a tenant. What he covenants to pay is the damage, not the rent. To hold him for monthly deficits is to charge him with the obligations of a tenant without any of the privileges. He must pay in the lean months, without recouping in the fat ones. He must do this, though it may turn out in the end that there has been a gain and not a loss. A liability so heavy may not rest upon uncertain inference. We do not overlook the landlord in postponing the cause of action until October, 1945. . . . If the damage clause as drawn gives inadequate protection, the fault is with the draftsman. The courts are not at liberty to supply its omissions at the expense of a tenant whose liability for the future ended with the cancellation of the lease except in so far as he bound himself by covenant to liability thereafter." If the landlord had been able to relet for the entire remaining portion of the term, could he have recovered at once for the entire deficiency in rent? If so, would he thereby have relieved the original tenant from any further obligation to pay in the event the new tenant defaulted? See Hackett v. Richards, 13 N.Y. 138 (1855).

3. Damages for repudiation of a long-term lease may be difficult to establish. See Hawkinson v. Johnston, 122 F.2d 724 (8th Cir.1941), involving a lease having an unexpired term of 67 years at the time of repudiation. The court approved the trial court's determination that damages could be predicted with sufficient certainty for a period of ten years following breach.

4. In some states the courts have refused to permit a landlord to use the doctrine of breach by anticipatory repudiation, relying upon the conception current in Lord Coke's time that a covenant to pay rent creates no obligation enforceable in advance of the time when the promised payment is due. See, e.g., Cooper v. Casco Mercantile Trust Co., 134 Me. 372, 186 A. 885, 111 A.L.R. 548 (1936). This rule was established, of course, long before the doctrine of breach by repudiation was clearly formulated in the nineteenth century.

D. SECURITY AGAINST TENANT DEFAULTS

The landlord normally desires security for his rent claim, so that he will not have to seek satisfaction of a judgment through the ordinary channels. To some extent the law may provide this, independently of agreement. Stemming from the feudal tenurial relationship is the landlord's ancient right to distrain—to seize chattels which the tenant had brought upon the premises and to hold them until accrued rent was paid. An English statute of 1690 empowered landlords to sell distrained chattels. This right of distress has been much disfavored; with modifications it finds some recognition in the United States, but a landlord is more likely to have a high-priority statutory lien on the tenant's chattels within the premises or on crops grown thereon. Not infrequently a lease will provide a contractual lien.

Even as modified, distress statutes may encounter challenges to their constitutionality. A few cases have held such statutes invalid as denying due process of law to the extent that they authorize seizure of a tenant's property without prior notice and hearing. See, e. g., State ex rel. Payne v. Walden, 156 W.Va. 60, 190 S.E.2d 770 (1972). But see Restatement of Property (Second) Landlord and Tenant, Statutory Note to Section 13.1 (1977), suggesting that "it is very questionable whether other states will follow their lead" in view of the subsequent case of Mitchell v. W.T. Grant Co., 416 U.S. 600, 94 S.Ct. 1895, 40 L.Ed.2d 406 (1974), upholding a Louisiana sequestration statute on the rationale that where "only property rights are involved, postponement of the judicial inquiry is not a denial of due process, if the opportunity given for ultimate judicial determination of liability is adequate." See also Lugar v. Edmonson Oil Co., 457 U.S. 922, 102 S.Ct. 2744, 73 L.Ed. 482 (1982).

In order to have more adequate or more conveniently available security the landlord may require that the tenant deposit cash or its equivalent with him or with a depositary. The attempt to adjust the conflicting interests of the landlord and tenant in connection with these deposits has involved a number of problems which obviously call for careful thought in the negotiation and drafting of a lease. For general discussion see Wilson, Lease Security Deposits, 34 Col.L.Rev. 426 (1934). In the absence of express agreement, where the courts must attempt to ascertain an unexpressed intent, shall the relationship be treated as that of debtor and creditor, as that of pledgee and pledgor, or as that of trustee and beneficiary? The question is important if the landlord has become insolvent. Will the landlord's rights in the deposit be altered if the leasehold is assigned and the original tenant thus becomes a quasi surety for the assignee's performance? How shall the matter be managed if the landlord transfers his reversionary estate? Will the transferee be obliged to refund the deposit, whether or not it has been transferred to him? May the original landlord, by transferring the deposit along with his reversionary estate, relieve himself of liability to reimburse the tenant, even though the transferee's reliability or solvency is doubtful? If the tenant defaults, or if the leasehold is prematurely terminated through no fault of his, what protection has he against an attempt by the landlord to retain the whole deposit even though it may exceed his actual loss?

UNIFORM RESIDENTIAL LANDLORD AND TENANT ACT (1972)

. . .

2.101 [Security Deposits; Prepaid Rent]

(a) A landlord may not demand or receive security, however denominated, in an amount or value in excess of [1] month[s] periodic rent.

(b) Upon termination of the tenancy property or money held by the landlord as security may be applied to the payment of accrued rent and the amount of damages which the landlord has suffered by reason of the tenant's noncompliance with Section 3.101 all as itemized by the landlord in a written notice delivered to the tenant together with the amount due [14] days after termination of the tenancy and delivery of possession and demand by the tenant.

(c) If the landlord fails to comply with subsection (b) or if he fails to return any prepaid rent required to be paid to the tenants under this Act the tenant may recover the property and money due him together with damages in an amount equal to [twice] the amount wrongfully withheld and reasonable attorney's fees.

(d) This section does not preclude the landlord or tenant from recovering other damages to which he may be entitled under this Act.

(e) The holder of the landlord's interest in the premises at the time of the termination of the tenancy is bound by this section.

. . .

2.105 [Limitation of Liability]

(a) Unless otherwise agreed, a landlord who conveys premises that include a dwelling unit subject to rental agreement in a good faith sale to a bona fide purchaser is relieved of liability under the rental agreement and this Act as to events occurring after written notice to the tenant of the conveyance. However, he remains liable to the tenant for all security recoverable by the tenant under Section 2:101 and all prepaid rent.

STRUM,* PROPOSED UNIFORM RESIDENTIAL LANDLORD AND TENANT ACT: A DEPARTURE FROM TRADITIONAL CONCEPTS

8 Real Property, Probate and Trust Journal 495–498 (1973).

. . .

The continuation of the original landlord's liability to the tenant for the security deposit, however, would seem to be an impediment to sales of multi-unit houses. For example, the selling landlord, desiring to relieve himself of this liability, must return the security deposit and demand that the tenant redeposit that money with the new landlord or perhaps obtain a written release of liability from the tenant. It would have been less cumbersome to provide that the selling landlord would be relieved of liability if he transferred the security deposit to the new landlord, sent notice of that transfer to the tenant and also obtained and sent to the tenant the new landlord's acknowledgement of receipt of the security deposit and assumption of the landlord's duties with respect thereto.[10] Admittedly, the tenant would not have a choice as to whether to accept the credit of the new landlord, and the selling landlord's credit may be far more acceptable to the tenant than that of the new landlord. But it is submitted that the tenant was not influenced by the original landlord's credit when he entered into the original rental agreement. Why then should he now measure the credit of his landlord who will, at least on the surface, have the same assets as the original landlord, i.e., the building? Furthermore, the amount of the security deposit is small[11] compared to the size of the

* Member of the New York and New Jersey Bars.

In light of Mr. Justice Douglas' recommendations (Douglas, Law Reviews and Full Disclosure, 40 Wash.L.Rev. 227 (1965)), the author wishes to point out that he is Assistant General Counsel of The Prudential Insurance Company of America. Prudential has extensive investments in real estate and is often in the position of owner-landlord or mortgagee of multi-unit residential property. The views expressed in this article are those of the author and not any institution with which he is affiliated.

10. A separate release of liability obtained from the tenant may not be enforceable. Section 1.301(11) provides such a broad definition of "rental agreement" that it may include this release instrument, and section 1.403(a) states that a limitation of landlord's liability contained in a rental agreement is unenforceable. Some states have provided that the transfer of the security deposit to the new owner plus notice to the tenant will relieve the selling landlord from further liability. Cal.Civ.Code § 1950.5(d) (Supp.1973); N.J. Stat.Ann. § 46:8–21 (Supp.1973); N.Y.Gen. Obligations Law § 7–105 (McKinney Supp. 1973).

11. The smallness of the security deposit raises other problems. The Act does not present an adequate procedure to ensure

transaction, which may not be consummated because of failure to obtain a tenant's consent to the transfer of the security deposit. Indeed, by continuing the selling landlord's liability for return of the security deposit and forcing him to deal with the tenant in order to relieve himself of that liability, the Commissioners are allowing the tenant to renegotiate the rental agreement before expiration of the term and are modifying, to a great extent, the right of the landlord to demand security.

If protection of the tenant's security were the Commissioner's intent, they have failed to implement that concept. They have refused to treat the security deposit as an escrow fund not to be commingled with the other funds of the landlord, nor to be used by the landlord for his own benefit. Security deposits are required to protect the landlord against possible future damage to the property by the tenant. Until that event, the deposit should be treated as the tenant's property. In this regard, the security deposits are closely related to escrow funds. Therefore, some states have viewed the landlord's duty with regard to handling these deposits as a fiduciary duty and have prohibited commingling.[12] Indeed some states have gone further and recognized that the tenant rightfully may claim any benefit or profit derived from the use of those funds while in the possession of the landlord.[13] Perhaps treatment of these deposits as true escrow funds and the recognition of the landlord's new fiduciary duties would have served to allay the fears of the Commissioners with regard to transfer of the security deposit.

The security deposit provision of the Act departs from the well accepted concept that the deposit is security against injuries to the premises or waste committed by the tenant; it is not normally to be used for the payment of rent.[14] Only after the tenant has surrendered the premises and the damages to the premises are measured is the remaining balance of the deposit to be applied to the amount of rent owed. By allowing the security deposit to "be applied to the payment of accrued rent," [15] the Commissioners seem to condone the practice of tenants who forego payment of the last month's rent by treating their security deposit as payment thereof. As a result, at the end of the

the return of the deposit, nor to ensure the collection by landlord of damages in excess of the deposit. The amount of money involved may be very small when compared to the cost of obtaining a just determination of the issue. . . .

12. Some states treat the security deposit as escrow funds. E.g., Md.Code Ann. Art. 21, § 8–213 (1973); N.Y.Gen.Obligations Law § 7.103(1) (McKinney Supp. 1973); N.J.Stat.Ann. § 46:8–19 (Supp. 1973). Pa.Stat.Ann. tit. 68, § 250.511a (Supp.1973). California provides that the security is held by the landlord for the tenant, but apparently the tenant's claim is not superior to the claim of a trustee in bankruptcy. Cal.Civ.Code § 1950.5(b) (Supp.1973).

13. Some states require interest to be paid to the tenant. E.g., Mass.Ann.Law ch. 186, § 15B (Supp.1972). Others require interest payments only after allowing the landlord to deduct an amount for expenses incurred in administering these security deposits. E.g., N.Y.Gen.Obligations Law § 7–103(2a) (McKinney Supp.1973); Pa. Stat.Ann. tit. 68, § 250.511b (Supp.1973) (on funds held more than two years); N.J. Stat.Ann. § 46:8–19 (Supp.1973).

14. Many lease forms specifically prohibit the tenant's use of the security deposit as the payment of the last month's rent. See Modern Legal Forms § 5097 (Supp. 1972).

15. Section 2.101(b). The Commissioners may have intended that use of the security deposit for unpaid rent was at the option of the landlord, but the wording employed does not prohibit the tenant from forcing that result.

term, the tenant will have fled leaving a security deposit sufficient only to make the last payment of rent. The landlord will then have to bring suit against the tenant in order to recover the cost of damages caused by the tenant. The Commissioners have apparently ignored the entire rationale behind the landlord's requirement of security deposits. They leave the landlord where he would have been if he merely required payment of rent in advance without any security deposit.

. . . [Copyright 1973 American Bar Association. Reprinted by permission from Fall issue of Real Property, Probate and Trust Journal. Nothing contained herein shall be deemed to represent the opinion or views of the American Bar Association or the Section of Real Property, Probate and Trust Law, unless and until adopted pursuant to the By-Laws of the Association and of the Section.]

NOTES

1. Section 38–12–103(2) of Colorado's Security Deposit Act provides that landlord's failure to provide the required written statement listing reasons for retention of a security deposit shall work a forfeiture, not only of landlord's rights to retain the deposit, but also of landlord's rights to "bring suit against the tenant for damages to the premises." The latter provision was held invalid in Turner v. Lyon, 189 Colo. 234, 539 P.2d 1241 (1975), on the ground that it, not being applicable to unsecured landlords, "imposes an unreasonable and discriminatory class distinction between landlords."

But a provision of the Colorado statute authorizing recovery of attorney fees and court costs by tenants establishing willful illegal withholding of security deposits was upheld even though landlords are not entitled to such recovery for successful defense of such suits. Torres v. Portillos, 638 P.2d 274 (Colo.1981).

2. Where is the burden of persuasion on the issue of landlord's bad faith? Consider Roeder v. Nolan, 321 N.W.2d 1, 4 (Iowa 1982):

"Roeder argues at length that to make meaningful a landlord's duty to refund deposits under section 562.10 of the Code of 1977, the landlord who retains a deposit without right should have the burden of persuading the fact finder that he did so in good faith. The argument has appeal but the statute contains no such clause, although it does have a clause placing the burden on the landlord to show the reason for withholding. § 562.10. We hold that under the 1977 Code, when a landlord withholds a deposit in whole or in part, he has the burden of persuasion of showing the right to withhold, but if he fails to carry that burden and is thus liable for the deposit, the tenant has the burden of persuasion that the landlord withheld in bad faith, before punitive damages may be awarded the tenant. The tenant is demanding the punitive damages, and placing the burden on him accords with the general principle on placement of the burden of proof on an exemplary damage claim. 22 Am.Jur.2d Damages § 303 (1965); 25A C.J.S. Damages § 144d (1966).

The uniform landlord-tenant act as proposed by the commissioners provides for a penalty on the landlord of a sum (or twice the sum, at the choice of the legislature) equal to the amount wrongfully withheld, plus attorney fees. Unif. Residential Landlord and Tenant Act § 2.101(c), *reprinted in* 7A U.L.A. 524 (1978). Apparently this penalty is automatic when wrongful withholding is found. The Iowa General Assembly did not choose to enact that provision of the uniform act. Some states have statutory provisions expressly placing the burden of proof on the landlord to establish that his retention of a deposit was not 'wrongful,' Martinez v. Steinbaum, Colo., 623 P.2d 49, 54 (1981); Guzman v. McDonald, 194 Colo. 160, 162, 570 P.2d 532, 533 (1977), or creating a presumption of bad faith on the part of the landlord who wrongfully withholds. Diamond Oaks Terrace Apartments v. Spraggins, 561 S.W. 2d 612, 613 (Tex.Civ.App.1978); Wilson v. O'Connor, 555 S.W.2d 776, 780 (Tex.Civ.App.1977). We apply our statute as we find it."

4. In Smith v. J. Weingarten, Inc., 120 S.W.2d 878 (Tex.Civ.App. 1938), the lease provided, "As a part of the consideration for the execution of this lease, and to secure its performance, the Lessee has paid Lessor $3000, being the rental due for the first three months, and Lessee obligates itself to pay the stipulated monthly rental every thirty days, in this manner keeping the rent paid three months in advance in lieu of furnishing Lessor with a security bond." The lease also provided, "In the event the building shall be totally destroyed by fire, it is agreed that the rights of the parties shall be at an end, . . . and the Lessee shall be released from any further obligation to pay rent." The building was destroyed by fire, and in the lessee's suit to recover the deposit the court invoked the prevailing doctrine that rent paid in advance, as contrasted with a security deposit, cannot be recovered despite termination of the lease before commencement of the period for which the rent was paid. To the same effect where the lessor exercised a power of termination for breach of condition see Galbraith v. Wood, 124 Minn. 210, 144 N.W. 945 (1914). For criticism of an opinion in a similar case see 25 Ill.L.Rev. 716 (1931). Attorneys have sometimes been successful, where a straight-forward agreement for forfeiture of a deposit as liquidated damages would be unenforceable, in disguising the agreement. In A–1 Garage v. Lange Investment Co., 6 Cal.App.2d 593, 44 P.2d 681 (1935), discussed in 45 Yale L.J. 537 (1936), the court gave literal effect to a carefully-drafted provision that a deposit should be treated as "consideration" paid for the leasehold in addition to rent, even though the deposit, in effect, was refundable with interest upon the lessee's full performance.

5. See generally Yee, Tenant Protection Through Security Deposit Legislation, 8 Real Estate L.J. 136 (1979).

SECTION 7. TRANSFERS

If the landlord conveys his interest in the land to another, his transferee generally is bound by the lease and may enforce it. [One exception to this generalization is that lease covenants that do not "run with the land" may not be enforceable by or against the new landlord. The criteria for the running of covenants are considered elsewhere in this book. See Chapter 17.] A common law vestige of feudal tenure conditioned the creation of the new landlord-tenant relationship upon tenant's manifestation of willingness to accept the transferee as the landlord. This condition, referred to as attornment, is now generally abolished by statute or repudiated by court decisions. See R. Schoshinski, American Law of Landlord and Tenant 539 et seq. (1980).

In the absence of enforceable lease provisions to the contrary, tenants may transfer their leasehold estates. They do not, however, thereby escape their contractual obligations, including the covenant to pay rent (unless the landlord has released them from this obligation), even though the landlord could recover rent from the new tenant. In such a situation, the landlord may recover judgments against either or both of these parties, but is entitled to only one satisfaction of his rent claim. See, e.g., Cauble v. Hanson, 249 S.W. 175 (Tex.App.1923).

The tenant's transferee may, or may not, become a tenant of the landlord. This depends upon whether the transfer is a sublease or an assignment. If the transfer is merely a sublease, the transferee is a tenant of the transferor, not of the landlord.

JABER v. MILLER

Supreme Court of Arkansas, 1951.
219 Ark. 59, 239 S.W.2d 760.

GEORGE ROSE SMITH, J. This is a suit brought by Miller to obtain cancellation of fourteen promissory notes, each in the sum of $175, held by the appellant, Jaber. The plaintiff's theory is that these notes represent monthly rent upon a certain business building in Fort Smith for the period beginning January 1, 1950, and ending March 1, 1951. The building was destroyed by fire on December 3, 1949, and the plaintiff contends that his obligation to pay rent then terminated. The defendant contends that the notes were given not for rent but as deferred payments for the assignment of a lease formerly held by Jaber. The chancellor, in an opinion reflecting a careful study of the matter, concluded that the notes were intended to be rental payments and therefore should be canceled.

In 1945 Jaber rented the building from its owner for a five-year term beginning March 1, 1946, and ending March 1, 1951. The lease reserved a monthly rent of $200 and provided that the lease would terminate if the premises were destroyed by fire. Jaber conducted a rug shop in the building until 1949, when he sold his stock of merchandise at public auction and transferred the lease to Norber & Son. Whether this instrument of transfer is an assignment or a sublease is the pivotal issue in this case.

In form the document is an assignment rather than a sublease. It is entitled "Contract and Assignment." After reciting the existence of the five-year lease the instrument provides that Jaber "hereby transfers and assigns" to Norber & Son "the aforesaid lease contract . . . for the remainder of the term of said lease." It also provides that "in consideration of the sale and assignment of said lease contract" Norber

& Son have paid Jaber $700 in cash and have executed five promissory notes for $700 each, due serially at specified four-month intervals. Norber & Son agree to pay to the owner of the property the stipulated rental of $200 a month, and Jaber reserves the right to retake possession if Norber & Son fail to pay the rent or the notes. The instrument contains no provision governing the rights of the parties in case the building is destroyed by fire.

Later on the plaintiff, Miller, obtained a transfer of the lease from Norber & Son. Miller, being unable to pay the $700 notes as they came due, arranged with Jaber to divide the payments into monthly installments of $175 each. He and the Norbers accordingly executed the notes now in controversy, which Jaber accepted in substitution for those of the original notes that were still unpaid. When the premises burned Miller contended that Jaber's transfer to Norber & Son had been a sublease rather than an assignment and that the notes therefore represented rent. Miller now argues that, under the rule that a sublease terminates when the primary lease terminates, his sublease ended when the fire had the effect of terminating the original lease.

In most jurisdictions the question of whether an instrument is an assignment or a sublease is determined by principles applicable to feudal tenures. In a line of cases beginning in the year 1371 the English courts worked out the rules for distinguishing between an assignment and a sublease. See Ferrier, "Can There Be a Sublease for the Entire Term?" 18 Calif.L.Rev. 1. The doctrine established in England is quite simple: If the instrument purports to transfer the lessee's estate for the entire remainder of the term it is an assignment, regardless of its form or of the parties' intention. Conversely, if the instrument purports to transfer the lessee's estate for less than the entire term—even for a day less—it is a sublease, regardless of its form or of the parties' intention.

The arbitrary distinction drawn at common law is manifestly at variance with the usual conception of assignments and subleases. We think of an assignment as the outright transfer of all or part of an existing lease, the assignee stepping into the shoes of the assignor. A sublease, on the other hand, involves the creation of a new tenancy between the sublessor and the sublessee, so that the sublessor is both a tenant and a landlord. The common law distinction is logical only in the light of feudal property law.

In feudal times everyone except the king held land by tenure from someone higher in the hierarchy of feudal ownership. "The king himself holds land which is in every sense his own; no one else has any proprietary right in it; but if we leave out of account this royal demesne, then every acre of land is 'held of' the king. The person whom we may call its owner, the person who has the right to use and abuse the land, to cultivate it or leave it uncultivated, to keep all others off it, holds the land of the king either immediately or mediately. In the simplest case he holds it immediately of the king; only the king and he have rights in it. But it well may happen that between him and the king there stand other persons; *Z* holds immediately of *Y*, who holds of

X, who holds of *V*, who holds . . . of *A*, who holds of the king." Pollock and Maitland, History of English Law (2d Ed.), vol. I, p. 232. In feudal law each person owed duties, such as that of military service or the payment of rent, to his overlord. To enforce these duties the overlord had the remedy of distress, being the seizure of chattels found on the land.

It is evident that in feudal theory a person must himself have an estate in the land in order to maintain his place in the structure of ownership. Hence if a tenant transferred his entire term he parted with his interest in the property. The English courts therefore held that the transferee of the entire term held of the original lessor, that such a transferee was bound by the covenants in the original lease, and that he was entitled to enforce whatever duties that lease imposed upon the landlord. The intention of the parties had nothing to do with the matter; the sole question was whether the first lessee retained a reversion that enabled him to hold his place in the chain of ownership.

The injustice of these inflexible rules has often been pointed out. Suppose that *A* makes a lease to *B* for a certain rental. *B* then executes to *C* what both parties intend to be a sublease as that term is generally understood, but the sublease is for the entire term. If *C* in good faith pays his rent to *B*, as the contract requires, he does so at his peril. For the courts say that the contract is really an assignment, and therefore *C*'s primary obligation is to *A* if the latter elects to accept *C* as his tenant. Consequently *A* can collect the rent from the subtenant even though the sublessor has already been paid. For a fuller discussion of this possibility of double liability on the part of the subtenant see Darling, "Is a Sublease for the Residue of a Lessee's Term in Effect an Assignment?" 16 Amer.L.Rev. 16, 21.

Not only may the common law rule operate with injustice to the subtenant; it can be equally harsh upon the sublessor. Again suppose that *A* makes a lease to *B* for a certain rental. *B* then makes to *C* what *B* considers a profitable sublease for twice the original rent. But *B* makes the mistake of attempting to sublet for the entire term instead of retaining a reversion of a day. The instrument is therefore an assignment, and if the original landlord acquires the subtenant's rights there is a merger which prevents *B* from being able to collect the increased rent. That was the situation in Webb v. Russell, 3 T.R. 393, 100 Eng.Reprint 639. The court felt compelled to recognize the merger, but in doing so Lord Kenyon said: "It seems to me, with all the inclination which we have to support the action (and we have hitherto delayed giving judgment in the hopes of being able to find some ground on which the plaintiff's demand might be sustained), that it cannot be supported. The defence which is made is of a most unrighteous and unconscious nature; but unfortunately for the plaintiff the mode which she has taken to enforce her demand cannot be supported." Kent, in his Commentaries (14th Ed.), p. 105, refers to this case as reaching an "inequitable result"; Williams and Eastwood, in their work on Real Property, p. 206, call it an "unpleasant result." Yet when the identical question arose in California the court felt bound to hold that the same distasteful merger had taken place. Smiley v. Van Winkle, 6 Cal. 605.

A decided majority of the American courts have adopted the English doctrine in its entirety. Tiffany, Landlord & Tenant, § 151. A minority of our courts have made timid but praiseworthy attempts to soften the harshness of the common law rule. In several jurisdictions the courts follow the intention of the parties in controversies between the sublessor and the sublessee, thus preserving the inequities of feudal times only when the original landlord is concerned. . . .

In other jurisdictions the courts have gone as far as possible to find something that might be said to constitute a reversion in what the parties intended to be a sublease. In some states, notably Massachusetts, it has been held that if the sublessor reserves a right of re-entry for nonpayment of rent this is a sufficient reversionary estate to make the instrument a sublease. Dunlap v. Bullard, 131 Mass. 161; Davis v. Vidal, 105 Tex. 444, 151 S.W. 290, 42 L.R.A.,N.S., 1084. But even these decisions have been criticized on the ground that at common law a right of re-entry was a mere chose in action instead of a reversionary estate. See, for example, Tiffany, supra, § 151.

The appellee urges us to follow the Massachusetts rule and to hold that since Jaber reserved rights of re-entry his transfer to Norber & Son was a sublease. We are not in sympathy with this view. It may be true that a right of re-entry for condition broken has now attained the status of an estate in Arkansas. . . . Even so, the Massachusetts rule was adopted to carry out the intention of parties who thought they were making a sublease rather than an assignment. Here the instrument is in form an assignment, and it would be an obvious perversion of the rule to apply it as a means of defeating intention.

In Arkansas the distinction between a sublease and an assignment has been considered in only one case, and then in such circumstances that the litigants were in agreement as to the law. In Pennsylvania Min. Co. v. Bailey, 110 Ark. 287, 161 S.W. 200, the transcript in this court at first contained an instrument purporting to transfer possession for only ten years out of a term of about eighteen years. The appellant accordingly argued that the instrument was a sublease under the orthodox common law rule. The appellee then had the transcript amended to show that the original lessee had later executed an instrument purporting to transfer the entire remaining term. In view of this amendment to the transcript the appellee merely adopted the appellant's argument as to the distinction between an assignment and a sublease. It was therefore to be expected that the court would announce the traditional view, since both parties were urging that position. In one other case, Crump v. Tolbert, 210 Ark. 920, 198 S.W.2d 518, we adverted by dictum to the customary distinction between the two instruments.

In this state of the law we do not feel compelled to adhere to an unjust rule which was logical only in the days of feudalism. The execution of leases is a very practical matter that occurs a hundred times a day without legal assistance. The layman appreciates the common sense distinction between a sublease and an assignment, but he would not even suspect the existence of the common law distinction. As Darling, supra, puts it: "Everyone knows that a tenant may in turn let to others, and the latter thereby assume no obligations to the owner of the property; but who would guess that this could only be done for a time falling short by something—a day or an hour is sufficient—of the whole term? And who, not familiar with the subject of feudal tenures, could give a reason why it is held to be so?" It was of such a situation that Holmes was thinking when he said: "It is revolting to have no better reason for a rule than that so it was laid down in the time of Henry IV. It is still more revolting if the grounds upon which it was laid down have vanished long since, and the rule simply persists from blind imitation of the past." The Path of the Law, 10 Harv.L.Rev. 457, 469. The rule now in question was laid down some years before the reign of Henry IV.

The English distinction between an assignment and a sublease is not a rule of property in the sense that titles or property rights depend upon its continued existence. A lawyer trained in common law technicalities can prepare either instrument without fear that it will be construed to be the other. But for the less skilled lawyer or for the layman the common law rule is simply a trap that leads to hardship and injustice by refusing to permit the parties to accomplish the result they seek.

For these reasons we adopt as the rule in this State the principle that the intention of the parties is to govern in determining whether an instrument is an assignment or a sublease. If, for example, a tenant has leased an apartment for a year and is compelled to move to another city, we know of no reason why he should not be able to sublease it for a higher rent without needlessly retaining a reversion for the last day of the term. The duration of the primary term, as compared to the length of the sublease, may in some instances be a factor in arriving at the parties' intention, but we do not think it should be the sole consideration. The Bailey case, to the extent that it is contrary to this opinion, is overruled.

In the case at bar it cannot be doubted that the parties intended an assignment and not a sublease. The document is so entitled. All its language is that of an assignment rather than that of a sublease. The consideration is stated to be in payment for the lease and not in satisfaction of a tenant's debt to his landlord. The deferred payments are evidenced by promissory notes, which are not ordinarily given by one making a lease. From the appellee's point of view it is unfortunate that the assignment makes no provision for the contingency of a fire, but the appellant's position is certainly not without equity. Jaber sold his merchandise at public auction, and doubtless at reduced prices, in order to vacate the premises for his assignees. Whether he would have taken the same course had the contract provided for a cancellation of the deferred payments in case of a fire we have no way of knowing. A decision either way works a hardship on the losing party. In this situation we do not feel called upon to supply a provision in the assignment which might have been, but was not, demanded by the assignees.

Reversed.

HOLT, J., not participating.

NOTE

Legislation treating all transfers of leases as assignments is recommended in Jaccard, The Scope of Liability Between Landlord and Tenant, 16 Colum.J. of Law & Social Probs. 365 (1981).

A.D. JUILLIARD & CO. v. AMERICAN WOOLEN CO.

Supreme Court of Rhode Island, 1943.
69 R.I. 215, 32 A.2d 800, 148 A.L.R. 187.

CAPOTOSTO, J. This is an action in assumpsit to recover installments of rent and taxes in the total amount of $2,935.83, allegedly due for the period between September, 1940, and March, 1941, under a lease of certain premises in the city of Providence. A justice of the superior court, sitting without a jury, rendered a decision for the defendant. The case is before us on plaintiff's exception to this decision and also on certain other exceptions to rulings in the case.

Unless otherwise specified, all parties to transactions hereinafter mentioned are corporations. . . .

On May 12, 1893, the Atlantic Mills leased certain premises in the city of Providence to the Riverside Worsted Mills for the term ending September 1, 1955. In this lease the specific covenant which the plaintiff asserts the defendant has assumed is to pay rent and certain other charges as therein set forth. This lease contains no restrictions whatever against assignment, nor does it provide that, upon an assignment of the lease, the assignee should assume and be bound for the entire unexpired term by the covenant just mentioned. The plaintiff succeeded to the rights of the lessor in this lease on December 4, 1936.

On April 15, 1899, the lessee, Riverside Worsted Mills, assigned the lease to the American Woolen Company, a New Jersey corporation, which in turn assigned it, on February 15, 1916, to the defendant American Woolen Company, a Massachusetts corporation. Four assignments of the lessee's interests occurred between 1916 and the bringing of this suit on April 14, 1941. The names of the successive assignees and the dates of such assignments are as follows: National & Providence Worsted Mills, a subsidiary of the defendant, December 22, 1931; American Woolen Company, the present defendant, December 26, 1934; Textile Realty Company, also a subsidiary of the defendant, June 1, 1939; and Reo Realty Company, November 21, 1939. The defendant admits that it was virtually the lessee until the lease was assigned to the Reo Realty Company, but denies that in this assignment it retained any beneficial interest in or control of the lease or premises covered thereby. In no one of these assignments did the assignee agree to assume the obligation to pay rent for the unexpired term of the lease.

The plaintiff's first contention raises a question of law, which appears not to have been heretofore considered by this court, so far as we have been able to ascertain. Broadly stated, this contention is that the assignee of a lease of real property, as here, is liable for the payment of the stipulated rent for the entire unexpired term, notwithstanding that the assignee did not agree to assume such obligation and assigned the lease before the expiration of the term.

This contention is contrary to the overwhelming weight of authority both in England and this country. Excepting certain decisions by the Texas civil court of appeals, which we will presently consider, the courts in this country have consistently held that, in the absence of the assumption by the assignee of the obligations of the lease, the liability of such assignee to the lessor rests in privity of estate which is terminated by a new assignment of the lease made by the assignee. This firmly established principle of law is subject to an exception which we will consider later in this opinion in connection with plaintiff's third main contention. . . .

The plaintiff urges that as this court is "unfettered by prior decisions" on the subject, it should reject the "archaic doctrine" which has been "blindly followed" by most of the American courts since 1797, and adopt the "progressive rule" of the Texas court. In support of this progressive rule, so-called, the plaintiff cites three decisions by the Texas court of civil appeals of three different districts: Waggoner v. Edwards, Tex.Civ.App., 68 S.W.2d 655, 83 S.W.2d 386; Marathon Oil Co. v. Rone, Tex.Civ.App., 83 S.W.2d 1028; Stark v. American National Bank of Beaumont, Tex.Civ.App., 100 S.W.2d 208.

In the Waggoner case, upon which the plaintiff most strongly relies, it was held that notwithstanding "the absence of an express agreement on the part of an assignee of the unexpired term of a lease of real property to assume and pay the rentals contracted to be paid by the original lessee . . . the assignee under such circumstances becomes primarily liable for the debt, and the original lessee only secondarily liable. The lessee having enjoyed and exercised his right to dispose of such leasehold estate, the assignee is held to take the estate subject to all the terms and conditions expressed in the original lease contract, and is bound to the original lessor for the performance of the obligations which were imposed upon his assignor, or, in other words, he simply stands in the shoes of the original lessee." 68 S.W.2d 655, 662. The Marathon Oil Co. and Stark cases are to the same effect.

But at page 212 of 100 S.W.2d of its opinion on motion for rehearing in the Stark case, which is the latest of the three Texas cases cited to us by the plaintiff, the court frankly says that it decided that case as it did "solely because the holding follows the present rule of decision in this state", although it was "firmly convinced that the rule is not sound and that it is contrary to the holdings of the vast majority of other jurisdictions." The court there urges the supreme court of that state to promulgate a rule of decision "in keeping with the great weight of authority and which it is believed is more consistent with the principles of justice." It then gives its reasons for suggesting such a change. In view of the cogency of these reasons against the Texas rule, we think that a somewhat extensive quotation from that opinion is justified here.

At page 213 of 100 S.W.2d of the opinion under consideration the court says that the effect of the Texas rule is to "place an assignee in complete privity of contract with the original lessor as a matter of law by reason of the assignment alone, without any stipulation or agreement on his part to become so bound. . . . When a property owner leases his property to another and confers upon such lessee the right to assign to whomsoever he pleases, he impliedly relies upon his lessee for the performance of the covenants of the lease. In addition to that he has the personal obligation of each assignee so long as he keeps the estate and also the right at all times to repossess his property for a breach of covenant. And while the lessee, when he assigns, may impose upon his assignee the obligations of the original lease contract, that matter should be left to the contract of the parties. It should not be read into an assignment as a mere legal implication."

Apparently the Texas rule has never been squarely considered by the supreme court of that state, for no decision of that court to that effect has been cited to us by either party in this case, nor have we been able to find one in our own investigation. It seems that what is termed as "the present rule of decision" in the Stark case, with reference to a situation like the one in the instant case, finds its origin in Davis v. Vidal, 1912, 105 Tex. 444, 151 S.W. 290, 42 L.R.A.,N.S., 1084, which is clearly distinguishable in its facts from the three Texas cases upon which the plaintiff relies and from the case at bar.

The plaintiff here further argues that the majority rule under consideration, which makes an assignee who does not expressly assume to pay the rent stipulated in the original lease liable only for such rent as accrues while privity of estate exists, may not operate unfairly in cases of short term leases, but that in long term leases, as in the instant case, it results in "an artificially induced lack of mutuality", which "should not commend itself to a court which is not bound by the precedent of its own decisions." In the Stark case, the court, at page 213 of 100 S.W.2d of that opinion, takes a contrary view and says that the Texas rule, which makes an assignee liable by mere legal implication in the circumstances above stated "is unnecessarily harsh and unjust and may, in its operation, tend to hamper the assignment of long term leases." But, whatever may be the practical result under either rule, the plain answer to the plaintiff's argument on this point is that the lessor has it within his power to protect himself against any detriment to him by incorporating adequate provisions in the lease concerning assignments thereof. If he chooses to execute a lease without adequately protecting his rights as lessor thereunder, he cannot thereafter complain if, by force of law, he is deprived of a benefit that he might otherwise have secured for himself.

After careful examination and consideration of the majority rule and of the Texas rule, our conclusion is that the former of these rules is not the blind following of an old English doctrine, as the plaintiff would like to have us believe, but that it is the embodiment of the considered judgment of American courts whose opinions should not be cast aside by mere summary characterization. In our opinion, the majority rule, which, in the absence of any restrictions in the lease governing its assignment, has the effect of leaving the matter of the assumption by an assignee of future rentals for the unexpired term of the lease to the contract between him and his assignor, is the sounder rule. We therefore cannot agree with the plaintiff's first contention.

Plaintiff's second and third contentions raise issues of fact. In our opinion the evidence on those issues is reasonably open to different conclusions, and in such case this court will not disturb the findings of fact made by a trial justice sitting without a jury unless such findings are clearly wrong. This rule is so well established with us that it requires no citation of authority. It is not possible to set forth in any detail the evidence in connection with the issues of fact raised by these contentions. Suffice it therefore to say that we have read the transcript and the numerous exhibits in the case, and have carefully considered, in all its aspects, the evidence upon which the plaintiff relies.

The plaintiff's second contention is that even though the defendant, as assignee, did not expressly assume to pay rent for the entire unexpired term of the lease, it nevertheless "indirectly" assumed to pay such rent by its course of dealing with the plaintiff's predecessor in title. In support of this contention, the plaintiff relies upon the effect, both singly and collectively, of the four incidents that follow. [Several paragraphs, in which the court stated and briefly discussed the separate incidents, are omitted.]

We have discussed, in a summary manner, the four incidents upon which the plaintiff relies because, as hereinbefore indicated, the space at our command does not permit a detailed refutation of the inferences that the plaintiff seeks to draw as the only inferences that can be drawn from the evidence on the points thus raised. In our opinion, such evidence is not consistent only with an assumption of the lease by the defendant. Whether that evidence is considered with reference to any one incident or to all of them collectively, it is fairly open to a conclusion contrary to that urged by the plaintiff. Our answer to plaintiff's second contention therefore is that the plaintiff has failed to show that the trial justice was clearly wrong in finding that the defendant had not bound itself to pay rent to the plaintiff for the entire unexpired term of the lease through its course of dealing with plaintiff's predecessor in title, the Atlantic Mills.

Plaintiff's third main contention is that the assignment of the lease from the Textile Realty Company, which was admittedly a subsidiary of the defendant, to the Reo Realty Company was "colorable" and therefore did not terminate defendant's liability, even though it had not assumed the obligations of the lease.

The law on this point is also well settled. As early as 1780, in Eaton v. Jaques, Douglas 455, at page 460, Lord Mansfield said: "In leases, the lessee, being a party to the original contract, continues always liable, notwithstanding any assignment; the assignee is only liable in respect of his possession of the thing. He bears the burden while he enjoys the benefit, and no longer . . . ." Unless fraudulent or colorable, a new assignment of the lease terminates the assignee's liability to the lessor for rent subsequently accruing. See authorities hereinbefore cited by us in discussing plaintiff's first main contention. If such assignee, by a new assignment, fairly relinquishes not only possession of the leased premises but also all benefits therefrom, it is immaterial that the new assignee may be financially irresponsible, or that he gave no consideration, or even that he received a bonus as an inducement to accept the assignment of the lease. . . .

The case is different, however, where such assignee makes an assignment which, though proper in form, leaves him as a matter of fact in possession of the leased premises or in receipt of benefits therefrom. In such case the assignment is colorable and will not terminate his liability to the lessor for rent, while he, in reality, continues in possession of the premises covered by the lease or enjoys any benefits from the use of such property. . . .

The plaintiff here contends that the assignment by the Textile Realty Company to the Reo Realty Company was colorable. The defendant admits that it created the Textile Realty Company to serve as a medium for the sale of certain properties that it considered either useless or unprofitable, but it vigorously denies that the assignment to the Reo Realty Company was not in good faith.

Among the properties that the defendant desired to sell and which it transferred to the Textile Realty Company for that purpose were the lease under consideration and some vacant land with a railroad siding, which vacant land it had been unable to sell in the open market. In July, 1939, one Aaron J. Oster, who was in the scrap metal business, became interested in those properties and bought them the following November for $630.30, taking title thereto in the name of the Reo Realty Company, a corporation controlled by him and in which the defendant, according to the record before us, had no interest whatever. Oster, who testified that he purchased the property for "the sole reason of using it and making money with it", then tried to secure from the plaintiff a reduction of the rent payable under the lease but was unsuccessful. There is evidence that the Reo Realty Company paid one installment of rent and expended some money in repairs. We have thus summarized our understanding of the evidence because it is impossible to refer specifically in this opinion to the large amount of correspondence, memoranda and agreements which bear upon this aspect of the case.

The plaintiff claims that the transaction between the defendant, through the Textile Realty Company, and Oster, through the Reo Realty Company, was nothing more than a scheme by the former's officials "to procure a rent reduction and in effect a new lease." It draws this conclusion mainly from the fact that the Reo Realty Company was a new corporation without known assets and that it paid so small a sum for an assignment of the lease and a deed of the vacant land.

The trial justice found that the transaction under consideration was in good faith; that on or about November 29, 1939, the Reo Realty Company "entered into exclusive control and possession of the leased premises", and that since that date "neither the American Woolen Company, the defendant, nor the Textile Realty Company has exercised any control over the leased premises; nor have they or either of them, had possession of such premises." We have found no competent evidence in contradiction of these findings of the trial justice. Unless resort is had to speculation or unwarranted suspicion, there is nothing to show, as the plaintiff states in its brief, that the transaction "envisaged", in the event that Oster failed to obtain a reduction of the rent, "the collapse of the dummy, Reo Realty Company, and the leaving of the property in the same status as if that company had never been formed and no assignment had been attempted." A fair consideration of the record before us shows that each of the parties in interest was assisted by able counsel and dealt with each other at arm's length in effecting a business transaction, which each party considered beneficial to itself.

Granting, as the plaintiff argues, that the amount paid by Oster for the leasehold and the vacant land was relatively small, yet according to the authorities hereinbefore cited on the point under consideration, this fact was not enough to render the assignment from the Textile Realty Company to the Reo Realty Company colorable, so as to continue the liability, to the plaintiff, of the defendant as an assignee of the lease in constructive possession of the premises. In the absence of collusion, and we find none in the circumstances of this case, the defendant, which was not bound contractually to the contrary, could sell or dispose of its property on such terms as it chose in order to relieve itself of the burden resulting from the possession of property that had become useless or unprofitable, so long as it relinquished all benefits therefrom. For the reasons stated, the trial justice was not in error in finding that the assignment of the lease to the Reo Realty Company terminated defendant's liability for rent under the lease.

Plaintiff's other exceptions have been considered and found to be without merit.

The plaintiff's exceptions are all overruled, and the case is remitted to the superior court for the entry of judgment on the decision.

CHILDS v. WARNER BROTHERS SOUTHERN THEATRES, INC.

Supreme Court of North Carolina, 1931.
200 N.C. 333, 156 S.E. 923.

Action by R.A. Childs and others against the Warner Bros. Southern Theatres, Inc. Judgment for plaintiffs, and defendant appeals.

The agreed facts are substantially as follows: Prior to February 1, 1923, the Berkley Company, a corporation, owned certain property in the city of Columbia, known as No. 1426 Main street, fronting on said street approximately 26 feet, and having a depth of approximately 125 feet. The property was used for the purpose of conducting a moving picture theater. On February 1, 1923, the Berkley Company leased said property to R.D. Craver for a period of five years, commencing February 1, 1923, and ending January 31, 1928. Thereafter the Berkley Company conveyed the property to the plaintiffs in this action. Subsequently, on or about June 10, 1925, Craver, the lessee, "transferred and assigned said lease to Warner Bros. Southern Theatres, Inc." The transfer or assignment by Craver purported to convey "all right, title and interest of the undersigned" in and to said lease. The plaintiffs assented to said assignment. Thereafter Warner Bros. Southern Theatres, Inc., took charge of the property and occupied it until about January 28, 1926, when they reassigned said lease to Carolina Theatres, Inc. The Carolina Theatres, Inc., took possession of the property and occupied the same until said corporation was placed in the hands of a receiver. Warner Bros. Southern Theatres, Inc., paid all rent that accrued up to the time they reassigned said lease to Carolina Theatres. When Warner Bros. Southern Theatres, Inc., assigned the lease to Carolina Theatres they notified the plaintiff of such assignment; whereupon the plaintiff notified said Warner Bros. Southern Theatres, Inc., as follows: "If it is your desire to have the Carolina Theatres, Inc., remit the rent direct to me, that will be satisfactory, but I shall continue to recognize you as the lessee of the property now occupied by the Broadway Theatres and expect you to see that the payments are made promptly in accordance with the lease." The amount of rent accrued and unpaid is $450.

The original lease between the Berkley Company and Craver specified: (a) "That said Berkley Co., Inc., has granted and leased, and by these presents does grant and lease unto the said R.D. Craver, lessee, the two story building situate, lying and being on the eastern side of Main Street," etc.; (b) "to have and to hold the said premises unto the said R.D. Craver, his executors, administrators and assigns for the full term of five years." etc.; (c) "said R.D. Craver, his executors, administrators and assigns for and in consideration of the above letten premises hereby covenant and agree to pay to the said Berkley Co., Inc., its successors and assigns the above stipulated rent in the manner herein required"; (d) "if the said lessee shall at any time fail or neglect to perform any of the covenants hereunto contained and on his part to be performed, or shall be adjudged a bankrupt or insolvent, then and in that event the lessor shall have the right to re-enter into and upon the demised premises," etc.; (d) "lastly, it is agreed that the said R.D. Craver shall not convey this lease or underlet the premises without the written consent of the lessors," etc.

Upon the foregoing facts the trial judge was of the opinion that the defendant assignee was liable for the rent and so adjudged, from which judgment the defendant appealed.

BROGDEN, J. If a lessor executes a lease to a given lessee, and the lease provides that the lessee shall not convey the lease nor underlet the premises without the written consent of the lessor, and thereafter the lessor consents to an assignment of the lease, can such assignee subsequently make a valid reassignment of the lease without the consent of the lessor?

In 1603, the English courts decided Dumpor's Case, which is reported in 4 Coke, 119, Smith Leading Cases (8th Ed.) 95. In that case a lease was made to a lessee, and the lease provided that the lessee or his assigns should not alienate the premises to any one without special license of the lessors. Subsequently the lessors consented that the lessee might assign the lease, and in consequence thereof the lessee assigned to one Tubbe. It was held that the assignee Tubbe had a right to assign the remainder of the term to any person whomsoever, irrespective of the consent of the lessors upon the ground that the condition in the lease prohibiting assignment without the consent of the lessor was entire, and consequently, the assent to assignment having once been given, the whole condition was wiped out, and the assignee was at liberty to assign the lease to whomsoever he pleased. In other words, if a lessor once gives his assent to an assignment, such assent is deemed to be a waiver of the provision prohibiting assignment, and the control of the lessor over his property is forever gone. The Dumpor Case was followed in England and perhaps crossed the Atlantic in the Mayflower and took root in America, because many of the earlier cases in the American courts followed the reasoning and applied the doctrine announced by the English courts. However, some of the courts in order to avoid the application of the principles in the Dumpor Case, began to draw a distinction between covenants in a lease which were single and covenants which were multiple; that is to say, if the covenant against assignment operated only upon the lessee and did not extend to his heirs and assigns, the covenant or condition was said to be single, but if the covenant against assignment without the written assent of the lessor operated not only upon the lessee but upon his heirs and assigns, the covenant is properly deemed to be multiple. Many courts took the position that, if the covenant were single, Dumpor's Case applied; but, if the covenant were not single, Dumpor's Case did not apply. The whole question is discussed and the authorities assembled in Investors' Guaranty Corporation v. Thompson, 31 Wyo. 264, 225 P. 590, 32 A.L.R. 1071. See, also Spitz v. Nunn, 34 Ohio App. 397, 171 N.E. 117; Klein v. Niezer (Ind.App.) 169 N.E. 688; Gusman v. Mathews, 29 Ohio App. 402, 163 N.E. 636. See also, Keith v. McGregor, 163 Ark. 203, 259 S.W. 725, 36 A.L.R. 311.

In the case at bar the lease in the habendum clause expressly included the lessee and his assigns. Moreover, the lessee and his assigns agreed to pay the rent, and, upon failure to pay the rent, the lessor expressly reserved the right of re-entry upon the premises. Without entering into any discussion of the distinctions which may exist between single and multiple covenants and the great learning with which various views are elaborated, it is deemed sufficient to say that a reasonable construction of the lease involved in this case leads to the conclusion that the restriction against assignment and subletting operated upon the heirs and assigns of the lessee as well as upon the lessee himself. The covenant to pay rent is continuous in its nature, and such covenant is binding by express provision upon the assigns of the lessee, and all persons occupying the premises under the assignment from the lessee were charged with notice of the conditions imposed by the writing under which they held title to the premises. Therefore we hold that, by consenting to one assignment, the lessor did not waive the conditions of the lease and did not consent that thereafter any subsequent assignee could turn his property over to the use and occupancy of any undesirable or irresponsible person without his approval. Indeed, when the defendant notified the plaintiff of its purpose to reassign the lease, the plaintiff gave express notice that it would still hold the defendant liable for the rent. Krider v. Ramsay, 79 N.C. 354; Alexander v. Harkins, 120 N.C. 452, 27 S.E. 120; Garbutt & Donovan v. Barksdale-Pruitt Junk Co., 37 Ga.App. 210, 139 S.E. 357; Cornell Millinery Co. v. Little-Long Co., 197 N.C. 168, 148 S.E. 26.

Affirmed.

NOTES

1. What doctrinal basis did the court have for holding that the defendant was liable for the rent, notwithstanding its attempted reassignment of the leasehold? May it be said that the court held the reassignment, without the landlord's consent, ineffective to transfer the leasehold, so that there remained a privity of estate between the landlord and the defendant? Cf. People v. Klopstock, 24 Cal.2d 897, 151 P.2d 641 (1944), holding that though an assignment was in breach of a covenant not to assign without the landlord's consent, it was not void; the landlord could elect either to approve it or to invoke one of the remedies available to him for the breach under the terms of the lease and the applicable law. On this theory the result reached in the Childs case might be rationalized by saying that the amount of rent which the second assignee failed to pay was the proper measure of damages for the defendant's breach of covenant. Does the opinion indicate that the court acted upon this theory?

2. A lease contains a clause prohibiting assignment or sublease without lessor's consent. Is lessor entitled to withhold consent in the absence of a reasonable ground? Courts traditionally have not inquired into lessor's motives for non-consent to transfers by tenant. Recently, however, several courts have held that a lessor cannot withhold its consent to an assignment in the absence of a good faith, reasonable

objection. See Kendall v. Ernest Pestana, Inc., 40 Cal.3d 488, 709 P.2d 837, 220 Cal.Rptr. 818 (1985); Newman v. Hinky Dinky Omaha-Lincoln, Inc., 229 Neb. 382, 427 N.W.2d 50 (1988).

Professor Alex Johnson argues that the treatment of clauses requiring the lessor's consent to an assignment should depend upon the form of the transaction. While generally approving the approach of the minority jurisdictions where short-term, residential leases are involved, he suggests that this approach is inappropriate for long-term commercial leases. Consider the following comments in Johnson, Correctly Interpreting Long-Term Leases Pursuant to Modern Contract Law: Toward a Theory of Relational Leases, 74 Va.L.Rev. 751, 804–805 (1988).

> Unfortunately, those courts and commentators adopting the minority position have focused on the "status" of the parties to the tranaction, as either lessors or lessees, rather than on the type of the transaction. The minority position effectively treats the commercial lessee's right as akin to his residential counterpart because of their parallel status, and the courts view the commercial lessee as prey to all the negative consequences, such as the absence of bargaining and freedom of contract, connoted by the status of "lessee." As they mistakenly apply to the commercial lessor and lessee incompatible contract principles that mandate the use of certain status rights, the courts have reduced the freedom to contract by implying terms that the sophisticated parties to the contract cannot waive, even if both believe a waiver to be in their best interests. This rigidity forecloses negotiations between the parties that might result in a better deal for both parties.

Chapter 17

INTERESTS IN LAND OF ANOTHER AND IN NATURAL RESOURCES AFFECTING ANOTHER'S LAND

Although Doe owns the fee simple absolute in Blackacre, the value of that ownership may be greatly affected by uses of neighboring parcels of land. Some uses may enhance the value of Blackacre. Others may impair it. Some examples of harmful uses: a rendering plant that emits foul odors making Blackacre unsuited for residential use; topographical alterations that cause Blackacre to be flooded; excavation which results in a falling away of a portion of Blackacre. Some examples of beneficial uses: exterior design of buildings that is compatible with the exterior design of buildings on Blackacre; the establishment of utility lines across neighboring parcels to serve Blackacre.

Doe and his neighbors (or their predecessors) may seek to deal with these relationships by various arrangements. Some may appear to be conveyances of interests in land. Others may resemble contracts more than conveyances. Still others may be stated as conditions in conveyances of the fee. Finally, some may purport to do no more than give permission for use of another's land. What are the consequences of choosing one of these forms rather than another? To what extent are persons allowed by the law to restrict use of another's land? These questions are addressed in the materials that follow.

When conflicting land uses are not covered by some volitional arrangement, courts may seek to resolve the conflict. When they do so, the practical consequence in many instances is that a non-volitional interest has been created in a parcel for the benefit of another. What policies and procedures guide this process? What policies and procedures should guide this process? These questions also are addressed in the materials that follow.

SECTION 1. INTERESTS CREATED BY VOLITION, IMPLICATION AND PRESCRIPTION

A. EASEMENTS, PROFITS A PRENDRE AND LICENSES

Easements. One can readily point to many familiar examples of easements—the right to use a roadway across another's land, the right to place pipelines under another's land, and the right to flood another's land. It is not as easy to define an easement. The definition adopted in the Restatement of Property § 450 (1944) is: "An easement is an interest in land in the possession of another which (a) entitles the owner of such interest to a limited use or enjoyment of the land in which the interest exists; (b) entitles him to protection as against third persons from interference in such use or enjoyment; (c) is not subject to the will of the possessor of the land; (d) is not a normal incident of the possession of any land possessed by the owner of the interest, and (e) is capable of creation by conveyance." [1]

Most easements are affirmative easements; i.e., they entitle one to do acts upon the burdened land or which affect the burdened land. Less common are negative easements, which entitle the owner of the easement to prevent the owner of the burdened land from making certain uses of his land; e.g., an easement entitling one to the free flow of light and air from adjoining land has the effect of restricting the erection of structures on the burdened land. Might an easement also entitle one to the performance of some act by the owner of the burdened land, such as maintaining a fence or a party wall? Traditional terminology classifies such a right as a covenant, rather than an easement, but it has also been called a "spurious easement." Perhaps in the materials which follow you can discover a reason which would impel courts to use the easement label here.

An easement may be either appurtenant or in gross. The former benefits its owner in connection with his ownership of neighboring land, the easement being said to be appurtenant to that land. An easement in gross benefits one without regard for his ownership of any land. The common law of England did not recognize easements in gross. An apparent easement in gross was viewed as a contract affecting only the parties. M. Bowles, Gale on Easements 13 (13th ed. 1959). Thus, a purported grant of a right of way to a railroad for its tracks would not be enforceable by the railroad against the grantor's successors, nor could the railroad transfer its "right of way." What policies supported the English position? How have railroads and utilities managed to function in the face of the common-law rule? Concerning the last question, in this instance (as will be developed later in this coursebook) equity jurisprudence failed to come to the rescue. Parliament did, by conferring upon individuals and entities "statutory easements in gross." Sturley, The "Land Obligation"; An English Proposal for Reform, 55 S.Calif.L.Rev. 1417, 1422 (1982).

Profits à Prendre. A profit is a right to use another's land by removing a portion of the land or its products. Common examples are rights to remove gravel, minerals and timber. The Restatement of Property does not state the law of profits apart from the rules applicable to easements. The explanation: "In phrasing the rules applicable to each of these interests it has been found, however, that in no case was there a rule applicable to one of these interests which was not also applicable to the other. This is not true with respect to English law. Under that law the interest designated as an easement can exist only as an appurtenance of a dominant tenement, while a profit may exist independently of such a tenement, or, as it is commonly expressed, in

1. Copyright, 1944, Reprinted with permission of The American Law Institute.

gross. . . . This difference does not exist in this country." § 450, Special Note.

Licenses. A license differs from an easement most importantly in that "a license is, in general, subject to termination at the will of the possessor of the land subject to the privilege of use while an easement is not. . . . Licenses are subject to few if any conveyancing rules, and in explaining why this is true it is often said that a license is not an interest in land at all. For some purposes it must, however, be admitted that any privilege to use land constitutes an interest in land." 2 American Law of Property § 8.110 (A.J. Casner ed. 1952). If this definition seems crystal clear, you should consider Hohfeld's much-quoted statement that "the chameleon-hued term, 'license' . . may be said to be a word of convenient and seductive obscurity." Hohfeld, Faulty Analysis in Easement and License Cases, 27 Yale L.J. 66, 92 (1917).

---

(1) Express Creation

MITCHELL v. CASTELLAW

Supreme Court of Texas, 1952.
151 Tex. 56, 246 S.W.2d 163.

GARWOOD, JUSTICE. The defendants, Mitchell and Powers, petition for relief from the judgment of both courts below, establishing easements in favor of the plaintiff-respondents, Castellaw et vir., as owners of a corner filling station lot, over two small strips upon the two adjoining lots of the petitioners, all in Block 42 of the City of Gilmer. The trial was by the court, and no fact findings appear in the record. For further details of the proceedings below, see the opinion of the Court of Civil Appeals, 241 S.W.2d 946.

The location of the strips and lots in question is, for our purposes, sufficiently indicated by the following sketch (with arbitrary lot numbers):

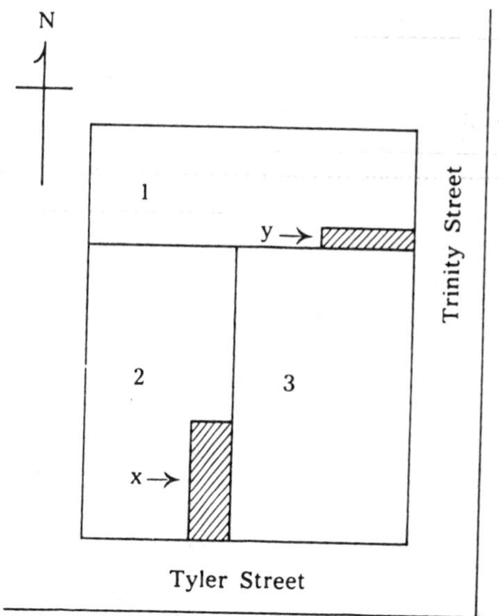

Legend:

1 — Mitchell and Powers North Lot
2 — Mitchell and Powers West Lot
3 — Filling Station Lot
x — 9′ x 23′ Driveway strip
y — 2½′ x 16½′ Wash Rack strip

[B7186]

As indicated, the alleged servitudes are (x) a driveway connecting the filling station (lot 3) with Tyler Street via lot 2 and (y) the northerly two and a half feet of a wash shed or rack of the station which projects from its main location on lot 3 onto lot 1 to that extent. As decreed by the courts below, the driveway is to be without limit in point of time, but the other is to expire on removal of the projecting part of the wash shed for any cause. The easements derive respectively from two 1938 conveyances of a Mrs. Sallie Stapp, who then owned all three lots, the driveway being said to arise by way of express reservation in her deed of lot 2 to Malcolm Smith and wife, while the temporary wash shed easement is implied from circumstances incident to her deed of lot 1 to her daughter, Mrs. Isabelle Anderson.

Throughout 1938 and for many years previously and subsequently, lot 3 was leased out by Mrs. Stapp and has been continuously used as a filling station under those leases, the last of which was apparently still in effect when she died sometime between 1945 and 1948. Respondent, Mrs. Castellaw, who is another daughter of Mrs. Stapp, succeeded to ownership of the filling station as her devisee and, in effect, renewed the last lease made by Mrs. Stapp, so that the term will expire in late 1953.

As to the driveway easement, Mrs. Stapp's conveyance of lot 2 to Smith and wife was by general warranty deed, . . . Obviously, the only words suggestive of a reservation are those following the metes and bounds description of the full lot and reading as follows: " 'It is expressly agreed and understood that grantors, their heirs or

assigns, shall not build or permit any one else to construct any type of building or anything else on the portion of lot described as follows; and that grantor shall have the right to use this part of said lot as a driveway.'" (followed by metes and bounds description of the driveway strip).

Clearly, if this single provision, which itself contains no words of inheritance or other words of art, were lifted out of the instrument, the latter would be a grant of complete and exclusive dominion over the lot. The word "grantors" in the very first part of the provision obviously was intended to mean "grantees." The grantees, Smith and wife, conveyed the lot to petitioners Mitchell and Powers in 1947 (some ten years later) and in their deed changed "grantors" to read "grantees," but otherwise used the exact "reservation" clause of the Stapp deed.

The view of petitioners is that the provision in question either amounted to nothing more than a so-called easement "in gross," that is, a merely personal right of Mrs. Stapp, which did not pass by her devise of the filling station lot to respondent, Mrs. Castellaw, or that the provision is repugnant to the grant of the whole lot and should therefore be treated as if never written. Further consideration of the matter confirms our original conclusion that the courts below properly rejected these contentions.

That an easement of this kind may be validly reserved in a deed of the fee simple title is beyond question. Stuart v. Larrabee, Tex.Civ. App., 14 S.W.2d 316, er. ref.; Hansen v. Bacher, Tex.Com.App., 299 S.W. 225; Word v. Kuykendall, Tex.Civ.App., 246 S.W. 757. And petitioners apparently concede—as they should—that the easement here would so have arisen if only the deed had been somewhat more artfully drawn as to (1) an intent that the "reservation" clause and the other provisions of the instrument should be read together and (2) the relationship of the "reserved" rights with the filling station lot as an appurtenance of the latter, rather than as rights purely personal to Mrs. Stapp.

So far as the point of repugnance goes, if the granting, habendum or warranty clause had contained the mere phrase "subject to the reservation elsewhere made herein," or if the reservation clause had but included the words "notwithstanding any other provision of this instrument," there would be little doubt from the whole instrument that a reservation was intended. The situation is clearly different from one in which, for example, the usage were for very general purposes, or for a specific purpose but purportedly applicable to every part of the lot conveyed. In Hansen v. Bacher, supra, which upheld a reservation for temporary occupancy by the grantor in an otherwise fee simple, general warranty deed, and is quoted from at length in the opinion below, Judge Powell aptly points out that in a sense every reservation conflicts with the grant, and the real question is whether there is such a clear conflict that the grantor could not reasonably have intended both provisions to stand as written. See also Word v. Kuykendall, supra; Cravens v. White, 73 Tex. 577, 579, 11 S.W. 543, 544; 14 Tex.Jur., "Deeds" §§ 179–180. Here, it is quite unlikely that the ordinary reader of the whole instrument would be puzzled about what the grantor meant to alienate and what she intended to keep, and we see no good reason to require in addition that she expressly disclaim the possibility of a conflict. . . .

As suggested in Hansen v. Bacher, supra, where both the grant and the reservation are general, or both are specific, a true repugnance is far more probable than where the grant is general and the reservation specific. In the two former situations, the intent of the grantor may well be, as a practical matter, a hopeless enquiry. In the latter, there is ordinarily a common sense inference that the grant is meant to be qualified by the specific reservation, and accordingly to that extent both should be allowed to stand. See also Word v. Kuykendall, supra; 14 Tex.Jur., supra. In the present case the specific character of the reservation relative to the grant is evident from the limited physical area affected, the exact description thereof, its location at the very edge of the lot, the limited number of rights reserved and no doubt also the fact that such rights were consistent with a substantial usage of the same area by the grantee.

We consider equally unfounded the contention of an easement in gross or—what in result here would be the same thing—the inadequacy of the reservation for lack of words such as "reserve" or "and her heirs." In Stuart v. Larrabee, supra, A reserved in her deed to B a right of way for C and D "as owners of" certain tracts adjoining the land conveyed. In holding the easement to be appurtenant to the mentioned tracts, the court considered "not only the terms of the grant itself, but the nature of the right and the surrounding circumstances." 14 S.W.2d 316, 320. . . . Beyond question such a test on the record before us results in an appurtenance. Even were there a doubt, which apparently there is not, that Malcolm Smith himself (as sublessee of Magnolia Petroleum Company) was and had long been using the driveway on lot 2 for access to lot 3, when Mrs. Stapp conveyed the former to him, it is yet plain that an easement of such purpose, location, area and shape could be useful only with reference to lot 3, which Mrs. Stapp then owned. Under such circumstances the easement will be considered an appurtenance to lot 3. It would seem to be the better rule that neither words of inheritance nor other words of art are essential to the valid reservation of an appurtenant easement of even unlimited duration. . . . [The portion of the opinion involving the claimed wash shed easement is discussed at p. 611.]

NOTE

Prior to the Statute of Uses, when present freehold estates were transferable only by livery of seisin, easements and other incorporeal interests were transferable by a "grant," and instrument under seal. Is the seal still required? And is "grant" a word of art? These questions are answered by the Restatement of Property § 467 (1944) as follows: "The formal requisites for the creation of an easement by conveyance inter vivos are (a) those required in a conveyance of an estate in land of like duration, and (b) subject to statutory modification, a written instrument under seal." As to the extent of "statutory modification," see 3 R. Powell, Real Property 397 (1977).

WILLARD v. FIRST CHURCH OF CHRIST, SCIENTIST, PACIFICA

Supreme Court of California, 1972.
7 Cal.3d 473, 102 Cal.Rptr. 739, 498 P.2d 987.

PETERS, ASSOCIATE JUSTICE. In this case we are called upon to decide whether a grantor may, in deeding real property to one person, effectively reserve an interest in the property to another. We hold that in this case such a reservation vests the interest in the third party.

Plaintiffs Donald E. and Jennie C. Willard filed an action to quiet title to a lot in Pacifica against the First Church of Christ, Scientist (the church). After a trial judgment was entered quieting the Willards' title. The church has appealed.

Genevieve McGuigan owned two abutting lots in Pacifica known as lots 19 and 20. There was a building on lot 19, and lot 20 was vacant. McGuigan was a member of the church, which was located across the street from her lots, and she permitted it to use lot 20 for parking during services. She sold lot 19 to one Petersen, who used the building as an office. He wanted to resell the lot, so he listed it with Willard, who is a realtor. Willard expressed an interest in purchasing both lots 19 and 20, and he and Petersen signed a deposit receipt for the sale of the two lots. Soon thereafter they entered into an escrow, into which Petersen delivered a deed for both lots in fee simple.

At the time he agreed to sell lot 20 to Willard, Petersen did not own it, so he approached McGuigan with an offer to purchase it. She was willing to sell the lot provided the church could continue to use it for parking. She therefore referred the matter to the church's attorney, who drew up a provision for the deed that stated the conveyance was "subject to an easement for automobile parking during church hours for the benefit of the church on the property at the southwest corner of the intersection of Hilton Way and Francisco Boulevard . . . such easement to run with the land only so long as the property for whose benefit the easement is given is used for church purposes." Once this clause was inserted in the deed, McGuigan sold the property to Petersen, and he recorded the deed.

Willard paid the agreed purchase price into the escrow and received Petersen's deed 10 days later. He then recorded this deed, which did not mention an easement for parking by the church. While Petersen did mention to Willard that the church would want to use lot 20 for parking, it does not appear that he told him of the easement clause contained in the deed he received from McGuigan.

Willard became aware of the easement clause several months after purchasing the property. He then commenced this action to quiet title against the church. At the trial, which was without a jury, McGuigan testified that she had bought lot 20 to provide parking for the church, and would not have sold it unless she was assured the church could thereafter continue to use it for parking. The court found that McGuigan and Petersen intended to convey an easement to the church, but that the clause they employed was ineffective for that purpose because it was invalidated by the common law rule that one cannot "reserve" an interest in property to a stranger to the title.

The rule derives from the common law notions of reservations from a grant and was based on feudal considerations. A reservation allows a grantor's whole interest in the property to pass to the grantee, but revests a newly created interest in the grantor.[1] (4 Tiffany, The Law of Real Property (3d ed. 1939) § 972.) While a reservation could theoretically vest an interest in a third party, the early common law courts vigorously rejected this possibility, apparently because they mistrusted and wished to limit conveyance by deed as a substitute for livery by seisin. (See Harris, Reservations in Favor of Strangers to the Title (1953) 6 Okla.L.Rev. 127, 132–133). Insofar as this mistrust was the foundation of the rule, it is clearly an inapposite feudal shackle today. Consequently, several commentators have attacked the rule as groundless and have called for its abolition. (See, e.g., Harris, supra, 6 Okla.L. Rev. at p. 154; Meyers & Williams Oil and Gas Conveyancing; Grants and Reservations by Owners of Fractional Mineral Interests (1957) 43 Va.L.Rev. 639, 650–651; Comment, Real Property: Easements: Creation by Reservation or Exception (1948) 36 Cal.L.Rev. 470, 476; Annot., Reservation or Exception in Deed in Favor of Stranger, 88 A.L.R.2d 1199, 1202; cf. 4 Tiffany, supra, § 974, at p. 54; 2 American Law of Property (Casner ed. 1952) § 8.29, at p. 254.)

California early adhered to this common law rule. (Eldridge v. See Yup Company (1860) 17 Cal. 44.) In considering our continued adherence to it, we must realize that our courts no longer feel constricted by feudal forms of conveyancing. Rather, our primary objective in construing a conveyance is to try to give effect to the intent of the grantor. . . . In general, therefore, grants are to be interpreted in the same way as other contracts and not according to rigid feudal standards. . . . The common law rule conflicts with the modern approach to construing deeds because it can frustrate the grantor's intent. Moreover, it produces an inequitable result because the original grantee has presumably paid a reduced price for title to the encumbered property. In this case, for example, McGuigan testified that she had discounted the price she charged Petersen by about one-third because of the easement. Finally, in some situations the rule conflicts with section 1085 of the Civil Code.[3]

1. The effect of a reservation should be distinguished from an exception, which prevents some part of the grantor's interest from passing to the grantee. The exception cannot vest an interest in the third party, and the excepted interest remains in the grantor. (6 Powell, The Law of Real Property (Rohan ed. 1971) § 892.)

3. Section 1085 provides that "[a] present interest, and the benefit of a condition or covenant respecting property, may be taken by any natural person under a grant, although not named a party thereto." We have been unable to find a California case that cites the section. Similar provisions in the codes of other states have also lain unused on the books. (See Mont. Rev.Codes Ann. (1962) § 67–1524; N.D. Cent.Code (1962) § 47–09–17; R.I.Gen. Laws Ann. (1956) § 34–11–10.) The language of the section clearly does not apply

In view of the obvious defects of the rule, this court has found methods to avoid it where applying it would frustrate the clear intention of the grantor. In Butler v. Gosling (1900) 130 Cal. 422, 62 P. 596, the court prevented the reserved title to a portion of the property from vesting in the grantee by treating the reservation as an exception to the grant. In Boyer v. Murphy (1927) 202 Cal. 23, 259 P. 38, the court, noting that its primary objective was to give effect to the grantor's intention (id., at pp. 28–29, 259 P. 38), held that the rule was inapplicable where the third party was the grantor's spouse. (See Fleming v. State Bar (1952) 38 Cal.2d 341, 345, fn. 2, 239 P.2d 866.) Similarly, the lower courts in California [4] and the courts of other states [5] have found ways of circumventing the rule.[6]

The highest courts of two states have already eliminated the rule altogether, rather than repealing it piecemeal by evasion. In Townsend v. Cable (Ky.1964) 378 S.W.2d 806, the Court of Appeals of Kentucky abandoned the rule. It said: "We have no hesitancy in abandoning this archaic and technical rule. It is entirely inconsistent

in this case because the church is a corporation and not a natural person.

4. In Sutter Butte Canal Co. v. Richvale Land Co. (1919) 40 Cal.App. 451, 181 P. 98, a developer provided, in its subdivision proposal, that certain easements for streets were reserved to its assigns and successors. Faced with a challenge to the easement based on the rule against reservation to a stranger, the court noted that it was "not justified in resorting to technical refinement as to the meaning of 'reversions' to defeat the manifest intent of the parties . . . ." (Id., at pp. 456–457, 181 P. at p. 100.) It held that the complaining landowner was estopped to object to the easement because of his express consent to it. Similarly, in Smith v. Kraintz (1962) 201 Cal.App.2d 696, 20 Cal.Rptr. 471, the court upheld a reservation to the general public because the intent to dedicate can be shown by even an ineffective instrument.

5. (See generally Harris, Reservations in Favor of Strangers to the Title, supra, 6 Okla.L.Rev. 127, 139–150.) Some courts, like the court in *Butler*, supra, mitigate the harshness of the rule by treating the reservation as an exception that retained the interest in the grantor. (See Lemon v. Lemon (1918), 273 Mo. 484, 201 S.W. 103.) While this approach did prevent the reserved interest from passing to the grantee, it did not achieve the grantor's intention of vesting that interest in the third party. Other courts gave effect to the grantor's intention by estopping those who claimed under a chain of title including the deed containing the reservation from challenging it on the basis of the common law rule. (See Beinlein v. Johns (1898) 102 Ky. 570, 44 S.W. 128; Hodge v. Boothby (1861) 48 Me. 68; Dalton v. Eller (1926) 153 Tenn. 418, 284 S.W. 68. This approach has the effect of emasculating the common law rule without expressly abandoning it. One court found that a reservation created a trust in favor of the stranger (Burns v. Bastien (1935) 174 Okl. 40, 50 P.2d 377), but this approach seems unduly elaborate to achieve the grantor's intent. Finally, several courts, like the court in *Boyer*, supra, will disregard the rule entirely when the stranger is the grantor's spouse. (See Saunders v. Saunders (1940) 373 Ill. 302, 26 N.E.2d 126; DuBois v. Judy (1920) 291 Ill. 340, 126 N.E. 104; Derham v. Hovey (1917) 195 Mich. 243, 161 N.W. 883; Glasgow v. Glasgow (1952) 221 S.C. 322, 70 S.E.2d 432.) Thus, as in California, the rule has been riddled with exceptions in other states.

6. Mott v. Nardo (1946) 73 Cal.App.2d 159, 166 P.2d 37, is the only appellate decision in California since 1860 to apply the rule. In that case, however, application of the rule did not defeat the grantor's intention. A bank owned the subject property and was joined in conveying it by one Avery, who was a trustee of the bank but who had no interest in the property. The deed reserved a right-of-way for construction of water conduits, and Avery quitclaimed his interest to a water company. Finding that the deed did not purport to convey an interest to Avery (id., at p. 162, 166 P.2d 37), and that the bank was unaware Avery believed he had acquired some interest (id., at p. 163, 166 P.2d 37), the court held that he had no interest because he was a stranger to the title. Since the bank apparently did not intend to vest an interest in Avery, the holding is not inconsistent with the general effort to effectuate the grantor's intention.

with the basic principle followed in the construction of deeds, which is to determine the intention of grantor as gathered from the four corners of the instrument." (Id., at p. 808.) (See also Blair v. City of Pikeville (Ky.1964) 384 S.W.2d 65, 66; Combs v. Hounshell (Ky.1961) 347 S.W.2d 550, 554.) Relying on *Townsend*, the Supreme Court of Oregon, in Garza v. Grayson (1970) 255 Or. 413, 467 P.2d 960, rejected the rule because it was "derived from a narrow and highly technical interpretation of the meaning of the terms 'reservation' and 'exception' when employed in a deed" (id., at p. 961), and did not sufficiently justify frustrating the grantor's intention. Since the rule may frustrate the grantor's intention in some cases even though it is riddled with exceptions, we follow the lead of Kentucky and Oregon and abandon it entirely.

Willard contends that the old rule should nevertheless be applied in this case to invalidate the church's easement because grantees and the title insurers have relied upon it. He has not, however, presented any evidence to support this contention,[7] and it is clear that the facts of this case do not demonstrate reliance on the old rule. There is no evidence that a policy of title insurance was issued, and therefore no showing of reliance by a title insurance company. Willard himself could not have relied upon the common law rule to assure him of an absolute fee because he did not even read the deed containing the reservation. This is not a case of an ancient deed where the reservation has not been asserted for many years. The church used lot 20 for parking throughout the period when Willard was purchasing the property and after he acquired title to it, and he may not claim that he was prejudiced by lack of use for an extended period of time.

The determination whether the old common law rule should be applied to grants made prior to our decision involves a balancing of equitable and policy considerations. We must balance the injustice which would result from refusing to give effect to the grantor's intent against the injustice, if any, which might result by failing to give effect to reliance on the old rule[8] and the policy against disturbing settled titles. The record before us does not disclose any reliance upon the old common law rule, and there is no problem of an ancient title. Although in other cases the balancing of the competing interests may warrant application of the common law rule to presently existing deeds, in the instant case the balance falls in favor of the grantor's intent, and the old common law rule may not be applied to defeat her intent.

Willard also contends that the church has received no interest in this case because the clause stated only that the grant was "subject to" the church's easement, and not that the easement was either excepted or reserved. In construing this provision, however, we must look to the clause as a whole which states that the easement "is given." Even if

7. Although there was testimony at the trial as to the chain of title by an employee of a title insurance company, there was no evidence that a policy of title insurance was actually issued, or what its terms were.

8. In weighing claims of reliance, the court must, of course, give consideration to the several exceptions to the common law rule developed by the courts and partial abrogation of the rule by section 1085 of the Civil Code.

we assume that there is some ambiguity or conflict in the clause, the trial court found on substantial evidence that the parties to the deed intended to convey the easement to the church. (Coast Bank v. Minderhout, 61 Cal.2d 311, 315, 38 Cal.Rptr. 505, 392 P.2d 265; see Estate of Russell, 69 Cal.2d 200, 206–214, 70 Cal.Rptr. 561, 444 P.2d 353.)

The judgment is reversed.

NOTES

1. In many instances a deed lists both spouses as grantors even though only one owns the property. Should a reservation in such a deed be deemed to create an interest in the non-owning spouse? See Lighthorse v. Clinefelter, 36 Ohio App.3d 204, 521 N.E.2d 1146 (1987); Little v. Linder, 651 S.W.2d 895 (Tex.App.1983). What reasons, other than an intent to give the other spouse an interest in the land, might prompt the parties to include the names of both spouses as grantors?

There are other situations where the grantor's intent to create an interest in a third party referred to in the deed is unclear. For example, a grant may be made "subject to" an easement in a named party who owns no easement. Such language is equally consistent with creating an easement in the named party and with protecting the grantor against a claim for breach of warranty in the event the named party has a valid claim to an implied or prescriptive easement. See Smith, "The 'Subject to' Clause," 30 Rocky Mt.Min.L.Inst. 15–1 (1985). In Aszmus v. Nelson, 743 P.2d 377 (Alaska 1987) the court relied upon the explicit description of the easement as evidence that the seller might have intended something more than merely protecting itself against claims for breach of deed warranties and remanded the case for a factual determination of the grantor's intent.

2. Not all courts have agreed with the reasoning of the Willard decision. The court in Estate of Thomson v. Wade, 69 N.Y.2d 570, 516 N.Y.S.2d 614, 509 N.E.2d 309 (1987) pointed out that the creation of an easement in a third party can easily be accomplished by a prior conveyance to the third party, and while recognizing that the "stranger-to-the-deed rule" may frustrate the grantor's intent, the court concluded that

> The overriding considerations of the "public policy favoring certainty in title to real property, both to protect bona fide purchasers and to avoid conflicts of ownership, which may engender needless litigation" (Matter of Violo, 65 N.Y.2d 392, 492 N.Y.S.2d 550, 482 N.E.2d 29) persuade us to decline to depart from our settled rule. We have previously noted that in this area of law, "where it can reasonably be assumed that settled rules are necessary and necessarily relied upon, stability and adherence to precedent are generally more important than a better or even a 'correct' rule of law. . . ." 65 N.Y.2d 574, 310 N.E.2d 310.

Do you find the reasoning of Willard or Estate of Thomson to be the more convincing?

3. Although the court in Estate of Thomson characterizes the Willard decision as representing the minority view, an increasing number of courts have adopted it. See, for example, Aszmus v. Nelson, 743 P.2d 377 (Alaska 1987); Malloy v. Boettcher, 334 N.W.2d 8 (N.D.1983); Simpson v. Kistler Investment Co., 713 P.2d 731 (Wyo. 1986).

MIDLAND VALLEY RAILROAD CO. v. ARROW INDUSTRIAL MFG. CO.

Supreme Court of Oklahoma, 1956.
297 P.2d 410.

PER CURIAM. The parties will be referred to as they appeared in the trial court, Midland Valley Railroad Company, a corporation, plaintiff, and Arrow Industrial Manufacturing Company, a corporation and St. Louis-San Francisco Railway Company, a corporation, defendants. The only question presented in this appeal is: Did the following described instrument convey a fee simple title or merely an easement?

"RIGHT OF WAY DEED

"Know all Men by these Presents: That for and in consideration of the sum of one dollar, in hand paid, the receipt of which is hereby acknowledged, and the benefits to accrue to the undersigned by reason of the construction and operation of the railroad, of the grantee herein, the Constantin Refining Company, a corporation, hereby conveys and warrants to the Midland-Valley Railroad Company a strip of land for a right of way over and across the following described tract of land, situated in Tulsa County, State of Oklahoma, as follows, to-wit:"

(Here is described a particular 30 foot strip of land).

The deed is not in statutory form and contains no habendum clause.

The defendant, Arrow Industrial Manufacturing Company, is now the owner of the property from which this strip of land was conveyed by the parties' common grantor in the chain of title, and if the instrument conveyed only an easement, they are the owners of the reversion upon an abandonment of the easement. After the issue was made by the pleadings, upon pre-trial conference the trial court construed the instrument to be an easement and thereafter rendered judgment for the defendants.

It is now axiomatic that the intent of the parties to a conveyance is to be determined from the four corners of the instrument, unless it is ambiguous, and that railroad corporations may acquire and hold the fee simple title to their right of way either by private contract or condemnation. It is likewise settled that a conveyance need not be in the exact terms as those set forth in the statutes, but that a substantial compliance is sufficient if the requisite intent be adequately expressed. Walker v. Renegar, 178 Okl. 82, 61 P.2d 666.

By express statutory provision in Oklahoma, every estate in land which shall be conveyed by deed, shall be deemed an estate in fee simple and of inheritance, unless limited by express words. 16 O.S. 1951 § 29. This statutory rule accounts for the apparent difference in the construction of instruments in this jurisdiction from that given in many of the cases cited as authority by the defendants. See 132 A.L.R. 142 for an annotation covering the subject. . . .

In Higgins v. Oklahoma City, 191 Okl. 16, 127 P.2d 845, 847, an instrument denominated a " 'Right of Way Deed' " and whose operative words were " 'grant, bargain, quitclaim and relinquish and convey to . . . the following described lands for a right of way for its railroad, . . . viz.: A strip of land 100 feet wide over, through and across the lands owned . . .' ", was construed to convey an estate in fee simple to the grantee therein. The language in the instrument now under consideration is quite similar to that used in the Higgins' deed, and we are of the opinion that the decision there is controlling here. It has been pointed out that where the instrument purports to convey a described strip of land rather than a right of way over a strip of land the conveyance is considered a fee estate instead of an easement. Aubert v. St. Louis-San Francisco Ry. Co., 207 Okl. 537, 251 P.2d 190. Here, stripped of verbiage and analyzed, the deed by express terms attempts to convey to the plaintiff a strip of land some thirty feet in width. The direct object of the verb "convey" is "a strip of land." In view of the authorities heretofore cited, the additional language, acknowledging the use to which the land is to be placed, is insufficient to limit the estate granted.

The judgment is reversed with directions to proceed in conformity with the views herein expressed. . . .

NOTES

1. Contrast Bernards v. Link, 199 Or. 579, 248 P.2d 341 (1952), adhered to on rehearing in 199 Or. 579, 263 P.2d 794 (1953), where a "Right of Way Deed" of a "strip of land . . . for its use as a right of way for a railroad" was construed as creating an easement. Contrast also Harvest Queen Mill & Elevator Co. v. Sanders, 189 Kan. 536, 370 P.2d 419 (1962), holding that a deed conveying to a railroad a "strip of land . . . for the purpose of building or constructing its roadbed" passed only an easement. The court thought that more was involved than construction. Since the statute conferring eminent domain upon railroads limited that power to acquisition of easements, the same policy should apply to voluntary conveyances, the court said. The court quoted from an earlier opinion: " 'May a railroad company purchase a strip of land extending a great distance through the country and over many farms, abandon the enterprise, and then sell the strip to those who will put it to a wholly different use—one which might be both obnoxious and menacing to the adjoining owners?' " See Annotations, 132 A.L.R. 142 (1941); 136 A.L.R. 379 (1942); 6 A.L.R.3d 973 (1966).

2. A deed purporting to convey a "right of way for the railroad" provides in its habendum clause that "if the described land ceases permanently to be used for railroad purposes, said land shall revert to grantor, his heirs or assigns." A similar deed was construed as conveying an easement rather than a defeasible fee in Hawk v. Rice, 325 N.W.2d 97 (Iowa 1982). Why would it matter? It matters in Iowa because a statute bars termination of defeasible fees, but not easements, under certain circumstances.

BASEBALL PUBLISHING CO. v. BRUTON

Supreme Judicial Court of Massachusetts, 1938.
302 Mass. 54, 18 N.E.2d 362, 119 A.L.R. 1518.

LUMMUS, JUSTICE. The plaintiff, engaged in the business of controlling locations for billboards and signs and contracting with advertisers for the exhibition of their placards and posters, obtained from the defendant on October 9, 1934, a writing signed but not sealed by the defendant whereby the defendant "in consideration of twenty-five dollars . . . agrees to give" the plaintiff "the exclusive right and privilege to maintain advertising sign one ten feet by twenty-five feet on wall of building 3003 Washington Street" in Boston, owned by the defendant, "for a period of one year with the privilege of renewal from year to year for four years more at the same consideration." It was provided that "all signs placed on the premises remain the personal property of the plaintiff." The writing was headed "Lease No. —." It was not to be effective until accepted by the plaintiff.

It was accepted in writing on November 10, 1934, when the plaintiff sent the defendant a check for $25, the agreed consideration for the first year. The defendant returned the check. The plaintiff nevertheless erected the contemplated sign, and maintained it until February 23, 1937, sending the defendant early in November of the years 1935 and 1936 checks for $25 which were returned. On February 23, 1937, the defendant caused the sign to be removed. On February 26, 1937, the plaintiff brought this bill for specific performance, contending that the writing was a lease. The judge ruled that the writing was a contract to give a license, but on November 2, 1937, entered a final decree for specific performance, with damages and costs. The defendant appealed. It is stipulated that on November 3, 1937, the plaintiff tendered $25 for the renewal of its right for another year beginning November 10, 1937, but the defendant refused the money.

The distinction between a lease and a license is plain, although at times it is hard to classify a particular instrument. A lease of land conveys an interest in land, requires a writing to comply with the statute of frauds though not always a seal (Alfano v. Donnelly, 285 Mass. 554, 557, 189 N.E. 610; Mayberry v. Johnson, 15 N.J.L. (3 Green) 116), and transfers possession. Roberts v. Lynn Ice Co., 187 Mass. 402, 406, 73 N.E. 523. A license merely excuses acts done by one on land in possession of another that without the license would be trespasses, conveys no interest in land, and may be contracted for or given orally.

Cook v. Stearns, 11 Mass. 533, 538; Grasselli Dyestuff Corp. v. John Campbell & Co., 259 Mass. 103, 107, 156 N.E. 17; Nelson v. American Telephone & Telegraph Co., 270 Mass. 471, 479, 170 N.E. 416. A lease of a roof or a wall for advertising purposes is possible. Alfano v. Donnelly, 285 Mass. 554, 557, 189 N.E. 610. The writing in question, however, giving the plaintiff the "exclusive right and privilege to maintain advertising sign . . . on wall of building," but leaving the wall in the possession of the owner with the right to use it for all purposes not forbidden by the contract and with all the responsibilities of ownership and control, is not a lease. Gaertner v. Donnelly, Mass., 5 N.E.2d 419; and cases cited. Reynolds v. Van Beuren, 155 N.Y. 120, 49 N.E. 763, 42 L.R.A. 129. The fact that in one corner of the writing are found the words, "Lease No. —," does not convert it into a lease. Those words are merely a misdescription of the writing. . . .

Subject to the right of a licensee to be on the land of another for a reasonable time after the revocation of a license, for the purpose of removing his chattels . . ., it is of the essence of a license that it is revocable at the will of the possessor of the land. . . . The revocation of a license may constitute a breach of contract, and give rise to an action for damages. But it is none the less effective to deprive the licensee of all justification for entering or remaining upon the land. . . .

If what the plaintiff bargained for and received was a license, and nothing more, then specific performance that might compel the defendant to renew the license, leaving it revocable at will, would be futile and for that reason should not be granted. 5 Williston, Contracts (Rev. Ed.) § 1442; Am.Law.Inst.Restatement: Contracts, § 377. Specific performance that might render the license irrevocable for the term of the contract would convert it into an equitable estate in land and give the plaintiff more than the contract gave. . . . There can be no specific performance of a contract to give a license, at least in the absence of fraud or estoppel. . . .

The writing in the present case, however, seems to us to go beyond a mere license. It purports to give "the exclusive right and privilege to maintain" a certain sign on the defendant's wall. So far as the law permits, it should be so construed as to vest in the plaintiff the right which it purports to give. Kaufman v. Federal National Bank of Boston, 287 Mass. 97, 100, 101, 191 N.E. 422. That right is in the nature of an easement in gross, which, whatever may be the law elsewhere, is recognized in Massachusetts. . . . We see no objection to treating the writing as a grant for one year and a contract to grant for four more years an easement in gross thus limited to five years. Similar writings have been so treated in other jurisdictions. . . .

An easement, being inconsistent with seisin in the person owning it, always lay in grant and could not be created by livery of seisin. Randall v. Chase, 133 Mass. 210, 214. It is an interest in land within the statute of frauds and, apart from prescription, requires a writing for its creation. G.L.(Ter.Ed.) c. 183, § 3. Cook v. Stearns, 11 Mass. 533. Indeed, the creation of a legal freehold interest in an easement, apart from prescription, requires a deed. Stevens v. Stevens, 11 Metc. 251, 256; Morse v. Copeland, 2 Gray 302, 305; Curtis v. Noonan, 10 Allen 406, 409; Brady v. Blackinton, 174 Mass. 559, 562, 55 N.E. 474. And differing from a lease of land for not more than seven years (Alfano v. Donnelly, 285 Mass. 554, 557, 189 N.E. 610), a grant of an easement for as short a term as five years apparently requires a deed in order to create a legal interest. . . . But in equity a seal is not necessary to the creation of an easement. Since equity treats an act as done where there is a duty to do it enforceable in equity, or, as more tersely phrased, equity treats that as done which ought to be done, an enforceable unsealed contract such as the writing in this case, providing for the creation of an easement, actually creates an easement in equity. . . .

There is no error in the final decree granting specific performance. The affirmance of this decree will not prevent an assessment of the damages as of the date of the final decree after rescript. Rudnick v. Rudnick, 281 Mass. 205, 208, 183 N.E. 348.

Interlocutory decree overruling demurrer affirmed.

Final decree affirmed, with costs.

STONER v. ZUCKER

Supreme Court of California, 1906.
148 Cal. 516, 83 P. 808.

HENSHAW, J. Plaintiff pleaded that defendants had entered upon his land in 1899, under license, and had constructed thereon and thereover a ditch for the carrying of water; that he never conveyed or agreed to convey to the defendants any right of way, easement, or interest in the land for the purpose, and their right to construct and maintain the ditch rested wholly upon this license; that in 1900 he served notice upon them that the license to construct and operate the ditch had been revoked and abrogated by him. Notwithstanding this notice of revocation and abrogation, the defendants, disregarding it, have continuously entered upon plaintiff's land, making repairs upon the ditch and restoring the same where it was broken and washed away, and defendants threaten to continue this trespass upon the lands of the plaintiff. Plaintiff therefore prayed that the defendants be adjudged trespassers and be enjoined from the use of the ditch or from in any manner entering upon the lands of the plaintiff to repair or other wise maintain it. The evidence established, without controversy, that defendants constructed the ditch for the purpose of carrying water for irrigation to their own and other lands, and had expended upon the ditch the sum of seven thousand and more dollars. The court found that "a right of way for the construction and maintenance of the ditch for the purpose of taking water from Santa Ana river for use in connection with and upon defendants' lands was given and granted by the plaintiff to the defendants, and that the defendants are the owners of a right of way for said ditch for the purpose aforesaid." The court further found that there was a consideration for the "granting of said right of way, in that defendants contracted and agreed with the plaintiff to deliver to and for the use of the plaintiff on his land lying under said canal sufficient water to irrigate the land, and the defendants have at all times delivered said water so agreed to be delivered." This last finding derives no support from the evidence, and the first finding, to the effect that the plaintiff "granted" a right of way, can be supported only upon the understanding that the court by "grant" meant that "permission" was given to defendants for the construction and maintenance of the ditch. So construing the findings, the question is squarely presented as to the revocability or nonrevocability of an executed parol license, whose execution has involved the expenditure of money, and where, from the very nature of the license given, it was to be continuous in use.

Appellant contends that a parol license to do an act upon the land of the licensor, while it justifies anything done by the licensee before revocation, is revocable at the option of the licensor, so that no further acts may be justified under it, and this, although the intention was to confer a continuing right, and money has been expended by the licensor upon the faith of the license, and that such a license cannot be changed into an equitable right on the ground of equitable estoppel. To the support of this proposition is offered authority of great weight and of the highest respectability. The argument in brief is that a license in its very nature is a revocable permission, that whoever accepts that permission does it with knowledge that the permission may be revoked at any time; that the rule cannot be changed, therefore, because the licensee has foolishly or improvidently expended money in the hope of a continuance of a license, upon the permanent continuance of which he has no right in law or in equity to rely; that to convert such a parol license into a grant or easement under the doctrine of estoppel is destructive of the statute of frauds, which was meant to lay down an inflexible rule; and, finally, that there is no room or play for the operation of the doctrine of estoppel, since the licensor has in no way deceived the licensee by revocation, has put no fraud upon him, and has merely asserted a right which had been absolutely reserved to him by the very terms of his permission. No one has stated this argument more clearly and cogently than Judge Cooley, who, holding to this construction of the law, has expressed it in his work on Torts. Cooley, Torts (2d Ed.) 364. But that the same eminent jurist recognized the injustice and the hardship which followed such a conclusion is plainly to be seen from his opinion in Maxwell v. Bay City Bridge Co., 41 Mich. 453, 2 N.W. 639, where, discussing this subject he says: "But the injustice of a revocation after the licensee, in reliance upon the license, has made large and expensive improvements, is so serious that it seems a reproach to the law that it should fail to provide some adequate protection against it. Some of the courts have been disposed to enforce the license as a parol contract which has been performed on one side." Indeed, the learned jurist, with equal accuracy, might have stated that the majority of courts have so decided, in accordance with the leading case of Rerick v. Kern, 14 Serg. & R. 267, 16 Am.Dec. 497. That case was carefully considered, and it was held that it would be to countenance a fraud upon the part of the licensor if he were allowed after expenditure of money by the licensees upon the faith of the license, to cut short by revocation the natural term of its continuance and existence, and that under the doctrine of estoppel, the licensor would not be allowed to do this. The decision was that the licensor would be held to have conveyed an easement commensurate in its extent and duration with the right to be enjoyed. In that case there was a parol license without consideration to use the waters of a stream for a sawmill, and it was held it could not be revoked at the grantor's pleasure, where the grantee, in consequence of the license, had erected a mill. The court in that case says, after discussion: "It is to be considered as if there had been a formal conveyance of the right, and nothing remains but to determine its duration and extent. A right under a license, when not specifically restricted, is commensurate with the thing of which the license is an accessory." And the court said further: "Having in view an unlimited enjoyment of the privilege, the grantee has purchased by the expenditure of money, a right indefinite in point of duration, which cannot be forfeited by a nonuser unless for a period sufficient to raise the presumption of a release. The right to rebuild in case of destruction or dilapidation and to continue the business on its original footing may have been in fact as necessary to his safety, and may have been an inducement of the particular investment in the first instance."

It will not be necessary to multiply citations of authority upon this point. It is sufficient to refer to the very instructive comment of Prof. Freeman to the case of Rerick v. Kern, reported in 16 Am.Dec., at page 497. The learned author of the note concludes his review by saying, as he shows, that "it will be seen that the doctrine of the principal case, though not recognized in some of our state courts, is, nevertheless, expressive of the law as administered by the majority of them, and that the preponderance of recent judicial opinions is in harmony with the views of Judge Gibson." This court in the case of Flickinger v. Shaw, 87 Cal. 126, 25 P. 268, 11 L.R.A. 134, 22 Am.St.Rep. 234, discussed and approved the case of Rerick v. Kern, supra. It was not called upon there to pass upon the precise question here presented, because in that case defendant had entered and expended money upon a parol agreement to convey a right of way, and the court was called upon merely to decide in consonance with undisputed equitable principles that that parol agreement was enforceable, but in Smith v. Green, 109 Cal. 234, 41 P. 1024, the exact principle here announced is distinctly recognized, and it is said: "The general rule, no doubt, is that one who rests his claim to an easement on a verbal contract alone, unexecuted and unaccompanied by any other facts, has no rights thereto which he can enforce. But there are many cases where a mere parol license which has been executed, and where investments have been made upon the faith of it, has been held irrevocable. Gould on Waters, §§ 232, 324." The recognized principle, therefore, is that where a licensee has entered under a parol license and has expended money, or its equivalent in labor, in the execution of the license, the license becomes irrevocable, the licensee will have a right of entry upon the lands of the licensor for the purpose of maintaining his structures or, in general, his rights under his license, and the license will continue for so long a time as the nature of it calls for. Thus, for example, where the license was to erect a lumber mill, the license came to an end when the timber available for use at that mill had been worked up into lumber. The same has been held as to a milldam, the right to maintain the dam continuing so long as there was use for the mill, and the right being lost by abandonment and disuse only when the non-user had continued for a period sufficient to raise the presumption of release. In the case of irrigating ditches, drains, and the like, the license becomes, in all essentials, an easement, continuing for such length of time, under the indicated conditions, as the use itself may continue.

For these reasons the judgment and order appealed from are affirmed.

We concur: McFarland, J., Lorigan, J.

NOTES

1. Compare Nelson v. American Telephone & Telegraph Co., 270 Mass. 471, 170 N.E. 416 (1930): In 1893, landowner A executed a document reciting that for twenty dollars consideration "I hereby grant unto [the telephone company] its successors and assigns, the right to construct, operate and maintain its lines over and along the property. . . ." Being unsealed, this document did not satisfy the formal requirements for creation of an easement. Soon thereafter the telephone company erected poles and wires on the land. In 1923, B a purchaser of the land who had notice that the poles and wires were on the land with A's permission, notified the company to remove its equipment. Removal would cost over $4,000. The court held that the telephone company had only a license and that it had been revoked.

2. Concerning licenses which would be easements but for failure to comply with formal requirements, the position taken in the Restatement of Property § 519(4) (1944) is that a licensee "who has made expenditures of capital or labor in the exercise of his license in reasonable reliance upon representations by the licensor as to the duration of the license, is privileged to continue the use permitted by the license to the extent reasonably necessary to realize upon his expenditures." A vigorous critic of the Restatement has said of this provision, "Concededly there is no authority for this principle; and it is quite undesirable, as adding greatly to the uncertainty of property titles, without any real connection with the parties' intent or natural expectations under the circumstances." C. Clark, Covenants and Interests Running With Land 64 (2d ed. 1947).

MARRONE v. WASHINGTON JOCKEY CLUB

Supreme Court of the United States, 1912.
227 U.S. 633, 33 S.Ct. 401, 57 L.Ed. 679.

Holmes, J. This is an action of trespass for forcibly preventing the plaintiff from entering the Bennings Race Track in this District after he had bought a ticket of admission, and for doing the same thing, or turning him out, on the following day, just after he had dropped his ticket into the box. There was also a count charging that the defendants conspired to destroy the plaintiff's reputation, and that they excluded him on the charge of having "doped" or drugged a horse entered by him for a race a few days before, in pursuance of such conspiracy. But as no evidence of a conspiracy was introduced, and as no more force was used than was necessary to prevent the plaintiff from entering upon the race track, the argument hardly went beyond an attempt to overthrow the rule commonly accepted in this country from the English cases, and adopted below, that such tickets do not create a right in rem. 35 App.D.C. 82. Wood v. Leadbitter, 13 Mees. & W. 838, 14 L.J.Exch.N.S. 161, 9 Jur. 187, 16 Eng.Rul.Cas. 49. . . .

We see no reason for declining to follow the commonly accepted rule. The fact that the purchase of the ticket made a contract is not enough. A contract binds the person of the maker, but does not create an interest in the property that it may concern, unless it also operates as a conveyance. The ticket was not a conveyance of an interest in the race track, not only because it was not under seal, but because by common understanding it did not purport to have that effect. There would be obvious inconveniences if it were construed otherwise. But if it did not create such an interest, that is to say, a right in rem, valid against the landowner and third persons, the holder had no right to enforce specific performance by self-help. His only right was to sue upon the contract for the breach. It is true that if the contract were incidental to a right of property either in the land or in goods upon the land, there might be an irrevocable right of entry; but when the contract stands by itself, it must be either a conveyance or a license, subject to be revoked.

Judgment affirmed.

NOTES

1. Hurst v. Picture Theatres, Ltd., [1915] 1 K.B. 1, affirmed recovery of damages by an ejected patron against a theatre for assault and false imprisonment. Buckley L.J. declined to apply Wood v. Leadbitter. An excerpt from his opinion, at page 11:

"The defendants had, I think, for value contracted that the plaintiff should see a certain spectacle from its commencement to its termination. They broke that contract and it was a tort on their part to remove him. They committed an assault upon him in law. It was not of a violent kind, because, like a wise man, the plaintiff gave way to superior force and left the theatre. They sought to justify the assault by saying that they were entitled to remove him because he had not paid. He had paid, the jury have so found. Failing on that question of fact, they say that they were entitled to remove him because his license was revocable. In my opinion, it was not. There was, I think, no justification for the assault here committed. Under the circumstances it was for the jury to give him such a sum as was right for the assault which was committed upon him, and for the serious indignity to a gentleman of being seized and treated in this way in a place of public resort."

2. Holmes indicates that a license coupled with an interest might be irrevocable. Can you think of examples? If a neighbor permits me to park my car on his land, can he revoke my license to enter that land to remove my car? Might the license to enter the race track have been viewed as coupled with the contractual right to view the race? In another part of his opinion in the Hurst case, Buckley L.J. manifested support for this rationale.

3. See Conard, The Privilege of Forcibly Ejecting an Amusement Patron, 90 U.Pa.L.Rev. 809 (1942) and Turner and Kennedy, Ejection and Segregation of Theatre Patrons, 32 Iowa L.Rev. 625 (1947).

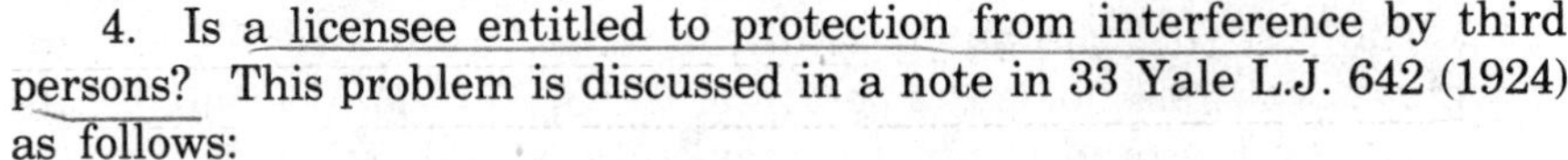

4. Is a licensee entitled to protection from interference by third persons? This problem is discussed in a note in 33 Yale L.J. 642 (1924) as follows:

"That licenses with respect to real estate carry with them no rights to protection against interference has been frequently stated with unhesitating precision. Yet as to the justice of the rule or the policy on which it is based little seems even to have been thought. A license has been defined innumerable times to be a mere personal revocable privilege to do an act or series of acts upon the land of another without possessing any interest or estate in that land. From this conception as a major premise, the decision in Taft v. Bridgeton Worsted Co., 246 Mass. 444, 141 N.E. 119 (1923), follows logically enough. The plaintiffs, owners of part of the land under a pond created by the defendant's dam, cut ice on the entire pond. The defendant, unreasonably and with intent to injure the plaintiffs, drew down the water at a time when the ice was ready to be cut. The court allowed damages for the injury only to the ice over the plaintiffs' own soil and not for that over the land of a third party which they had a mere gratuitous parol license to cut. The court said that 'the damage to their right to exercise their revocable license was a damage which the law does not recognize as an injury to their property.' . . .

"Between the parties the power of revocation is no doubt important, but as against third parties it should be immaterial. In other fields of law one person can create in another, even gratuitously, rights against a third party, although retaining the power to extinguish the relations he has created. The settlor of a revocable trust creates in the cestui que trust rights against the trustee, and creates in the trustee (if not in the cestui) rights in rem with respect to the trust property as long as the trust remains unrevoked. Even in property law an owner of land may create in a tenant at will a right of possession against third parties, though it may be terminated at the pleasure of the owner. The privilege is personal in the sense that it is non-assignable; but, by the majority rule, this is true of an easement in gross. A license is an insufficient interest in land to come within the statute of frauds, but it nevertheless has value to the licensee. . . ."

"Easements of necessity" (Right of way easement appurtenant to estate)

(2) Creation By Implication

FINN v. WILLIAMS

Supreme Court of Illinois, 1941.
376 Ill. 95, 33 N.E.2d 226, 133 A.L.R. 1390.

Wilson, Justice. February 16, 1895, Charles H. Williams owned a tract of land in Salisburg township, in Sangamon county, consisting of approximately 140 acres. On the day named, Williams conveyed 39.47 acres to Thomas J. Bacon. In 1937, the plantiffs, Eugene E. Finn and Curtis Estallar Finn, acquired the title to this tract. The defendant, Zilphia Jane Williams, inherited the remaining 100 acres. By their complaint filed in the circuit court of Sangamon county, plaintiffs charge that the nearest and only available means of egress from and ingress to their land to a highway and to any market for their livestock and crops is by means of a right of way over defendant's tract immediately to the north; that their tract is not located or situated on any public highway and is entirely surrounded by land of strangers and the defendant's tract; that prior to and during all the time the 40 acres and the 100 acres constituted one tract and were owned by defendant's husband, the only means of ingress and egress to and from the single tract to a highway was by right of way in a northerly direction through a third tract of land north and adjacent to the present tract of defendant, and that this open road is still used by defendant as her only means of egress and ingress from and to the highway. The relief sought was the declaration of a right of way easement of necessity from the north line of plaintiffs' tract through the defendant's tract, to the beginning of the right of way road through the third tract mentioned. Answering, the defendant admitted that plaintiffs' land is not located or situated on any public highway but averred that since its severance from her land it is and has been located on a private road leading to the south to a public highway. This averment, plaintiffs denied. Evidence was heard, and a decree rendered adjudging the plaintiffs to be the owners of a right of way easement of necessity over defendant's 100 acres, as alleged. Defendant appeals directly to this court, a freehold being involved. . . .

Private permissive ways of ingress and egress over the land of strangers both to the east and to the south have been available to the successive owners, including plaintiffs, of the 40-acre tract since its severance from the 100-acre tract of the defendant in 1895, but each of the private ways over the lands of the adjoining strangers has been closed and, as defendant concedes, these permissive means of ingress and egress do not now exist. Two witnesses for defendant who had lived near the property in controversy for about sixty years testified to roads leading to the south and to the east from the 40-acre tract over the land of strangers. These roads were private roads over the property of strangers, and are now closed. Nathan Woodrum, defendant's son-in-law, testified that he had until recently lived on the 100-acre tract, and that a road through defendant's land connects with the road through the tract at the north, and that the road through this third tract is the only mode of access to the highway unless permission be obtained to go through the land of strangers. Since May, 1939, defendant has refused to permit plaintiffs to travel further over the right of way through her tract. As a result of defendant's action, the plaintiffs have been unable to take their livestock and farm products to market, have had no means of egress from or ingress to their 40 acres on which they live, and have had to walk to the township highway, a distance of about three-quarters of a mile, carrying such produce as they could.

The evidence does not sustain defendant's averment that plaintiffs have the use of a private road leading to the south to a public highway and defendant, by her concession that a present necessity exists, has apparently abandoned this claim. She maintains, however, that the necessity has arisen by reason of changed circumstances since the severance of the two tracts. Firmly established principles control. Where an owner of land conveys a parcel thereof which has no outlet to a highway except over the remaining lands of the grantor or over the land of strangers, a way by necessity exists over the remaining lands of the grantor. 17 Am.Jur., (Easements) sec. 48; Trapp v. Gordon, 366 Ill. 102, 7 N.E.2d 869; Gilfoy v. Randall, 274 Ill. 128, 113 N.E. 88. If, at one time, there has been unity of title, as here, the right to a way by necessity may lie dormant through several transfers of title and yet pass with each transfer as appurtenant to the dominant estate and be exercised at any time by the holder of the title thereto. 17 Am.Jur., (Easements) sec. 49, 127; Logan v. Stogsdale, 123 Ind. 372, 24 N.E. 135, 8 L.R.A. 58. Plaintiffs' land is entirely surrounded by property of strangers and the land of the defendant from which it was originally severed. A right of way easement of necessity was necessarily implied in the conveyance severing the two tracts in 1895, and passed by mesne conveyances to plaintiffs in 1937. The fact that the original grantee and his successors in interest have been permitted ingress to and egress from the 40 acres over the land owned by surrounding strangers is immaterial. When such permission is denied, as in the present case, the subsequent grantees may avail themselves of the dormant easement implied in the deed severing the dominant and servient estates.

The decree of the circuit court is right, and it is affirmed.

Decree affirmed.

NOTES

1. Is the implication of an easement by necessity for ingress and egress based upon inferred intention? Or is it based upon a policy of promoting a public interest in efficient utilization of natural resources? Support for the latter view is found in 3 R. Powell, Real Property ¶ 410 (P.Rohan ed. 1981). What effect does the choice of one of these views over the other have upon the outcome of cases? Suppose that a conveyance that creates a landlocked tract expressly negates implication of an easement for access. Sayre v. Dickerson, 278 Ala. 477, 179 So.2d 57 (1965), indicates that the express negation would be effective. If the implied easement of necessity cases are really based upon a policy of serving the public interest, should not the way be situated so as to

provide the most satisfactory access, even though this would burden land that had never been in unity of title with the benefited land? Also, if this is the true basis for the doctrine, should not the burdened landowner be entitled to compensation?

Even if compensation were to be awarded, the doctrine being treated as a kind of eminent domain, is it clear that the "public use" or "public purpose" constitutional requirement for eminent domain is satisfied? A statute purporting to authorize any person "who claims the right to use land which is either wholly or partially surrounded by land owned by another" to obtain (without compensation) a "reasonable route" over that land by giving written notice to the owner was held invalid for lack of public use as required by a state constitution. Estate of W.T. Waggoner v. Gleghorn, 378 S.W.2d 47 (Tex.1964). However, statutes or constitutional provisions similar to the Texas statute (but entitling the burdened landowner to compensation) are applied in many states. The Wyoming statute and cases concerning it are discussed in Note, 16 Land & Water L. Rev. 281 (1981). In New Mexico, a mine owner can acquire by eminent domain an easement for piping water, but not for a road, to his mine. Kaiser Steel Corp. v. W.S. Ranch Co., 81 N.M. 414, 467 P.2d 986 (1970), the explanation given for this curious result being the importance accorded water resources by the state constitution.

If access to an enclosed parcel can be obtained by eminent domain, does it follow that an easement of necessity should not be implied? The position against implication was taken in Leo Sheep Co. v. United States, 440 U.S. 668, 99 S.Ct. 1403, 59 L.Ed.2d 677 (1979). But some courts have not regarded these two modes of creation of easements as equivalents. E.g. Backhausen v. Mayer, 204 Wis. 286, 234 N.W. 904 (1931), noting that public officials have discretion to deny a request for condemnation of a way, and Adamson v. Brockbank, 112 Utah 52, 185 P.2d 264 (1947), noting that the cost of condemnation might be prohibitive.

Does the implication of easements of necessity really promote efficient use of land? Is not the eminent domain approach more likely to do so, since an easement probably would not be condemned unless the value of the easement at least equals the required compensation?

2. X's land is entirely surrounded by A's lan[illegible]ot entitled to an implied easement of necessity for i[illegible]d no statute authorizes condemnation of [illegible] A refuses to grant an easement. X disco[illegible]nveyed to A a small part of the landlocke[illegible]erved "the oil and gas mineral rights anc[illegible] to develop same." X argues that this cl[illegible]rant from A of an easement of ingress a[illegible] land, at least for the purpose of develop[illegible]ts. This argument was rejected in Amoc[illegible]Sims, 97 N.M. 324, 639 P.2d 1178 (1981).

3. "When lands are sold with reference to a map upon which lots and streets are delineated, there is a dedication of such streets to the

public, . . . and such dedication continues and cannot be revoked except by consent of the municipality, ... After such dedication of streets to the public use, the public has the right to appropriate them at any time it wants or convenience requires, . . . no matter how long delayed, . . . and these public rights can only be destroyed by proper municipal action, . . . usually by vacation. A resolution vacating a street does not take away, or in the least impair, the private rights of an abutting owner; it is only a surrender or extinction of the public easement. . . ." Highway Holding Co. v. Yara Engineering Corp., 22 N.J. 119, 123 A.2d 511, 515 (1956), dealing with the question whether the existence of such easements in a street never accepted by the city would render title unmerchantable and giving a negative answer under the circumstances of this case.

Suppose that a city refuses to open a "paper" street, that an abutting landowner attempts to do so by bulldozing a crude path barely wide enough for two cars to meet, and that the city then erects a barricade preventing use of the street. What issues are suggested? How would they probably be resolved? See Dykes v. City of Houston, 406 S.W.2d 176 (Tex.1966).

GRANITE PROPERTIES LIMITED PARTNERSHIP v. MANNS

Supreme Court of Illinois, 1987.
117 Ill.2d 425, 111 Ill.Dec. 593, 512 N.E.2d 1230.

JUSTICE RYAN delivered the opinion of the court:

The plaintiff, Granite Properties Limited Partnership, brought this suit in the circuit court of Madison County, seeking to permanently enjoin the defendants, Larry and Ann Manns, from interfering with the plaintiff's use and enjoyment of two claimed easements over driveways which exist on the defendants' property. One driveway provides ingress to and egress from an apartment complex and the other to a shopping center. Both the apartment complex and the shopping center are situated on the plaintiff's property. Following a bench trial, the circuit court entered judgment against the plaintiff and in favor of the defendants as to both claimed easements. Following argument of the plaintiff's post-trial motion, the circuit court granted permanent injunctive relief as to the claimed apartment complex easement, but reaffirmed its decision denying the claimed shopping center easement. Both parties appealed from that portion of the judgment adverse to them. The appellate court, with one justice dissenting, held that the plaintiff was entitled to easements by implication over the driveways in question. (140 Ill.App.3d 561, 94 Ill.Dec. 353, 487 N.E.2d 1230.) We granted the defendants' petition for leave to appeal (94 Ill.2d R. 315).

The relative location of the subject properties and the claimed easements may be seen by reference to the following rough diagram adapted from the defendants' petition for leave to appeal.

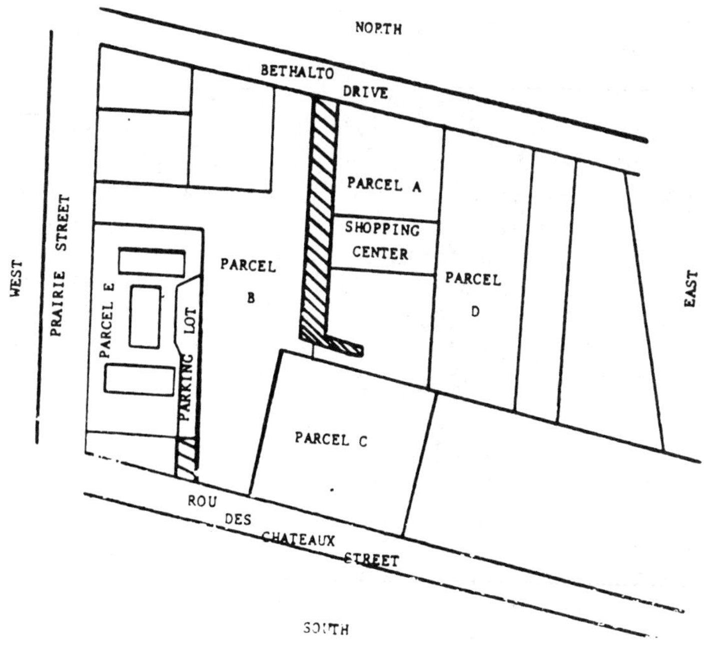

As indicated, the parcels which are the subject of this appeal are adjoining tracts located to the south of Bethalto Drive and to the north of Rou des Chateaux Street in Bethalto, Illinois. The plaintiff and its predecessors in title owned all of the subject properties from 1963 or 1964 until 1982, at which time the parcel labeled "B" was conveyed by warranty deed to the defendants. The plaintiff currently owns the parcels labeled "A" and "E," which are on the opposite sides of parcel B. The shopping center situated on the parcel designated "A" extends from lot line to lot line across the east-west dimension of that property. To the north of the shopping center is an asphalt parking lot with approximately 191 feet of frontage on Bethalto Drive. . . . To the south of parcel A on the parcel denominated "C" are five four-family apartment buildings. The distance between the back of the shopping center and the property line of parcel C is 50 feet. . . .

An apartment complex, known as the Chateau des Fleurs Apartments, is located on the parcel labeled "E." Both of the plaintiff's properties were developed prior to the time parcel B was sold to the defendants. Parcel B remains undeveloped.

The first claimed easement provides access to the rear of the shopping center which is located on parcel A. The center, which was built in 1967, contains several businesses, including a grocery store, a pharmacy, and doctors' offices. The rear of the center is used for deliveries, trash storage and removal, and utilities repair. To gain access to the rear of the shopping center for these purposes, trucks use a gravel driveway which runs along the lot line between parcel A and parcel B. A second driveway, located to the east of the shopping center on parcel D, enables the trucks to circle the shopping center without having to turn around in the limited space behind the stores.

Robert Mehann, the owner of the Save–A–Lot grocery store located in the shopping center, testified on direct examination that groceries, which are delivered to the rear of the store, are loaded by forklift on a concrete pad poured for that purpose. Mehann indicated that there are large, double steel doors in the back of the store to accommodate items which will not fit through the front door. Mehann testified that semitrailer trucks make deliveries to the rear of the grocery store four days a week, with as many as two or three such trucks arriving daily. An average of 10 to 12 trucks a day, including semitrailer trucks, make deliveries to the grocery store. Mehann further explained on direct examination that because the area behind the Save–A–Lot building extends only 50 feet to the rear property line, it would be difficult, if not impossible, for a semitrailer truck to turn around in the back and exit the same way it came in. In response to a question as to whether it would be feasible to have trucks make front-door deliveries, Mehann suggested that such deliveries would be very disruptive; pallets that would not fit through the front door would have to be broken down into parts, requiring extra work, and there would not be adequate space in the front of the store to do such work during business hours. Mehann admitted on cross-examination that he had not investigated the cost of installing a front door which would be big enough for pallets of groceries to be brought in by forklift. Further cross-examination revealed that there would not be enough space to manipulate the forklift around the front of the store, although it could be run between the shelves of food to the back of the store.

. . .

The other claimed easement concerns ingress and egress over a driveway which leads into the parking area of the apartment complex situated on parcel E. The complex, which was erected in the 1960's prior to the conveyance of parcel B to the defendants, consists of three buildings containing 36 units. The parking lot, which is situated to the rear of the buildings, provides 72 parking spaces. The only access to the parking lot is by a driveway from Rou des Chateaux, a public street located to the south of the properties. The driveway, which cuts across a small panhandle on the southwestern corner of parcel B, has been in existence since the apartment complex was constructed. . . .

Although there was a distance of 20 feet between the apartment buildings, Layman [a witness for the plaintiff] opined that it would not be enough "usable space" to accommodate a driveway from Prairie Street to the existing parking lot because such driveway would interfere with stairways which lead to the basement apartments. Although he admitted that he did not investigate the cost of installing a driveway either between the buildings or adjacent to the end building on the north, Layman concluded that, based on his experience in the layout and design of apartment buildings, "it would be a dangerous situation" for the tenants of the apartments if a driveway were to be run between the buildings or next to their sides.

. . .

In affirming the circuit court's judgment granting injunctive relief as to the claimed apartment complex easement, the appellate court majority concluded that the circuit court's finding that such easement was highly convenient and reasonably necessary for the use and enjoyment of the complex was amply supported by the evidence at trial. 140 Ill.App.3d 561, 573–74, 94 Ill.Dec. 353, 487 N.E.2d 1230. In reversing the circuit court's judgment denying injunctive relief as to the claimed shopping center easement, the appellate majority concluded that the circuit court, in focusing upon the degree of necessity required to sustain the implication of an easement, placed inordinate emphasis upon this requirement, thus failing to give proper consideration to the element of prior use. In light of the strong showing of prior use, the appellate majority further concluded that the evidence was sufficient to fulfill the requirement of necessity of the claimed shopping center easement. 140 Ill.App.3d 561, 573, 94 Ill.Dec. 353, 487 N.E.2d 1230.

The plaintiff contends in this court that it acquired, by implied reservation, easements over the driveways which provide access to the rear of the shopping center located on parcel A and to the parking lot of the apartment complex situated on parcel E. Plaintiff alleges that parcels A, B and E were held in common ownership by the plaintiff and its predecessors in title until 1982, at which time the defendants received a warranty deed to parcel B, that the driveways in question were apparent and obvious, permanent, and subject to continuous, uninterrupted, and actual use by the plaintiff and its predecessors in title until the time of severance of unity of ownership, and that the driveways are highly convenient and reasonably necessary for the beneficial use and enjoyment of the shopping center and the apartment complex. Therefore, the plaintiff maintains that, upon severance of unity of title, the defendants took parcel B subject to the servitudes then existing, as the parties are presumed to convey with reference to the existing conditions of the property.

. . .

There are two types of implied easements—the easement by necessity and the easement implied from a pre-existing use. The easement by necessity usually arises when an owner of land conveys to another an inner portion thereof, which is entirely surrounded by lands owned either by the grantor or the grantor plus strangers. Unless a contrary intent is manifested, the grantee is found to have a right-of-way across the retained land of the grantor for ingress to, and egress from, the land-locked parcel. Similarly, an easement is implied by way of necessity in the deed when the owner of lands retains the inner portion, conveying to another the balance.

The easement implied from a prior existing use, often characterized as a "quasi-easement," arises when an owner of an entire tract of land or of two or more adjoining parcels, after employing a part thereof so that one part of the tract or one parcel derives from another a benefit or advantage of an apparent, continuous, and permanent nature, conveys or transfers part of the property without mention being made of these incidental uses. In the absence of an expressed agreement to the contrary, the conveyance or transfer imparts a grant of property with all the benefits and burdens which existed at the time of the conveyance of the transfer, even though such grant is not reserved or specified in the deed. . . . This court has stated on numerous occasions that an easement implied from a preexisting use is established by proof of three elements: first, common ownership of the claimed dominant and servient parcels and a subsequent conveyance or transfer separating that ownership; second, before the conveyance or transfer severing the unity of title, the common owner used part of the united parcel for the benefit of another part, and this use was apparent and obvious, continuous, and permanent; and third, the claimed easement is necessary and beneficial to the enjoyment of the parcel conveyed or retained by the grantor or transferrer.

As the above discussion indicates, easements created by implication arise as an inference of the intention of the parties to a conveyance of land. This inference, which is drawn from the circumstances surrounding the conveyance alone, represents an attempt to ascribe an intention to parties who had not thought or had not bothered to put the intention into words, or to parties who actually had formed no intention conscious to themselves. To fill these common gaps resulting in incomplete thought, courts find particular facts suggestive of intent on the part of the parties to a conveyance. In the case of an easement implied from a preexisting use, proof of the prior use is evidence that the parties probably intended an easement, on the presumption that the grantor and the grantee would have intended to continue an important or necessary use of the land known to them that was apparently continuous and permanent in its nature. Where an easement by necessity is claimed, however, there is no requirement of proof of a known existing use from which to draw the inference of intention. This leaves proof of necessity alone to furnish the probable inference of intention, on the presumption that the grantor and the grantee do not intend to render the land unfit for occupancy.

This essentially is the position taken by the Restatement of Property. The Restatement describes a doctrine creating easements "by implication from the circumstances under which the conveyance was made." (Restatement of Property sec. 474 (1944).) This implication "arises as an inference of the intention of those making a conveyance." (Restatement of Property sec. 474, comment *b* (1944).) The Restatement operates on the basis of eight "important circumstances" from which the inference of intention may be drawn: whether the claimant is the conveyor or the conveyee; the terms of the conveyance; the consideration given for it; whether the claim is made against a simultaneous conveyee; the extent of necessity of the easement to the claimant; whether reciprocal benefits result to the conveyor and the conveyee; the manner in which the land was used prior to its conveyance; and the extent to which the manner of prior use was or might have been known to the parties. (Restatement of Property sec. 476 (1944).) These eight factors vary in their importance and relevance according to whether the claimed easement originates out of necessity or for another reason.

In applying the Restatement's eight important circumstances to the present case, the fact that the driveways in question had been used by the plaintiff or its predecessors in title since the 1960's, when the respective properties were developed, that the driveways were permanent in character, being either rock or gravel covered, and that the defendants were aware of the driveways' prior uses before they purchased parcel B would tend to support an inference that the parties intended easements upon severance of the parcels in question. (See Restatement of Property sec. 476, comments *i*, *j* (1944).) Although the prior uses which the plaintiff seeks to continue existed during the common ownership of the parcels in question, under circumstances where the defendants were fully informed by physical appearance of their existence, the defendants, nevertheless, argue that there are two factors which overwhelmingly detract from the implication of an easement: that the claimant is the conveyor and that the claimed easement can hardly be described as "necessary" to the beneficial use of the plaintiff's properties. Relying on the principle that a grantor should not be permitted to derogate from his own grant, the defendants urge this court to refuse to imply an easement in favor of a grantor unless the claimed easement is absolutely necessary to the beneficial use and enjoyment of the land retained by the grantor. The defendants further urge this court not to cast an unreasonable burden over their land through imposition of easements by implication where, as here, available alternatives affording reasonable means of ingress to and egress from the shopping center and the apartment complex allegedly exist.

While the degree of necessity required to reserve an easement by implication in favor of the conveyor is greater than that required in the case of the conveyee (Restatement of Property sec. 476, comment *c* (1944)), even in the case of the conveyor, the implication from necessity will be aided by a previous use made apparent by the physical adaptation of the premises to it. (Restatement of Property sec. 476, comment *j* (1944).) Moreover, the necessity requirement will have a different meaning and significance in the case involving proof of prior use than it will in a case in which necessity alone supports the implication; otherwise, proof of prior use would be unnecessary. (Restatement of Property sec. 476, comment *g* (1944).) Thus, when circumstances such as an apparent prior use of the land support the inference of the parties' intention, the required extent of the claimed easement's necessity will be less than when necessity is the only circumstance from which the inference of intention will be drawn. While some showing of necessity for the continuance of the use must be shown where a prior use has been made, to the extent that the prior use strengthens the implication, the degree or extent of necessity requisite for implication is reduced. (Restatement of Property sec. 476, comment *i* (1944).) As one treatise concludes:

> "If a previous use is continuous and apparent, an easement may be created by implication even though the need for the use to be made is not sufficiently great to meet the test of necessity as

applied in the absence of such a previous use. Hence, the test is phrased in terms of *reasonable necessity* rather than in terms of unqualified necessity. A use is necessary, it is often said, when without it no effective use could be made of the land to be benefited by it. *Where, because of a continuous and apparent previous use, the test of necessity becomes that of reasonable necessity, it is said that a use is reasonably necessary when it is reasonably convenient to the use of the land benefited.* In fact, however, reasonable necessity too is a flexible test. *The more pronounced a continuous and apparent use is, the less the degree of convenience of use necessary to the creation of an easement by implication.*" (Emphasis added.) (2 American Law of Property sec. 8.43 (A.J. Casner ed. 1952).)

As the above quote demonstrates, the "degree or extent of necessity" rubric suggests a concept with variable parameters. Professor Thompson notes the various phrases courts have used to describe the "extent of necessity" in cases in which there is proof of prior use:

> "Basically, three things are essential to the creation of an easement upon the severance of an estate, upon the ground that the owner before the severance made use of an improvement in one part of the estate for the benefit of another: first, there must be a separation of the title, for, so long as there is unity of ownership, there can be no easement; second, it must appear that before the separation took place the use which gives rise to the easement shall have been so long continued and so obvious or manifest as to show that it was meant to be permanent; and, third, *the easement shall be necessary to the proper enjoyment of the land or to its reasonable, convenient or beneficial enjoyment, 'reasonably necessary' to its enjoyment or use, 'convenient use,' or 'clearly necessary' to its beneficial use.*" (Emphasis added.) 2 G. Thompson, Commentaries on the Modern Law of Real Property sec. 352, at 305–07 (rep. ed. 1980).

Professor Powell, in his treatise, offers an alternative solution to the problem of stating the "extent of necessity" concept for the prior use situation that distinguishes it from the similar concept in the easement by necessity. Powell suggests that in a case with proof of prior use, the word "necessity" should be replaced by the phrase "important to the enjoyment of the conveyed quasi-dominant [or quasi-servient] parcel." As Powell explains:

> "The requirement that the quasi-easement must have been 'important for the enjoyment of the conveyed quasi-dominant [or quasi-servient] parcel' is highly elastic. Some courts say that the use must be one which is 'reasonably necessary to the enjoyment of the [conveyed or retained] land.' Others demand a use which is necessary for the beneficial, convenient, comfortable or reasonable enjoyment of such land. *When this prerequisite is phrased in terms of 'necessity,' a court is no longer properly considering the problem of implication from a quasi-easement but has crossed over (perhaps unwittingly) into the domain of easements by necessity (see supra par. 410).* The English courts have avoided this possible confusion

by dispensing completely with this third requirement, finding easements by implication from a quasi-easement which is both 'apparent' and 'continuous,' and without proof of its 'importance.' In the American courts, *'importance' strengthens the inference that the claimed easement was intended by the parties.*" (Emphasis added.) 3 R. Powell, The Law of Real Property sec. 411[2] (P. Rohan ed. 1987).

Notwithstanding their difference in use of terminology, the authorities agree that the degree or extent of necessity required to create an easement by implication differs in both meaning and significance depending on the existence of proof of prior use. Hence, given the strong evidence of the plaintiff's prior use of the driveways in question and the defendants' knowledge thereof, we must agree with the appellate court majority that the evidence in this case was sufficient to fulfill the elastic necessity requirement. We approve of the appellate court majority's application of the facts of this case to the law as we have described it herein.

. . .

For the above reasons, the judgment of the appellate court is affirmed. The cause is remanded to the circuit court of Madison County.

Affirmed and remanded.

NOTES

1. In 1968 a tract of land was divided into two parcels, with the only access to the plaintiff's parcel being by a dirt road crossing the other property. Subsequently a public street was built which provided access to the plaintiff's land. In upholding the plaintiff's continued right to use the dirt road, the court in Bromley v. Lambert and Son, Inc., 752 P.2d 595 (Colo.App.1988) concluded that the time of severance of the original property into two parcels was the relevant date for determining whether the easement was necessary. Should the result have been different if there had been no pre-existing dirt road at the time plaintiff's tract was created?

2. Not all courts would agree with the approach of the court in the Granite Properties case. In Mitchell v. Castellaw, page 582, the court rejected the plaintiff's claim to an implied easement over the portion of the adjacent lot occupied by a service station wash shed. Pointing out that the whole theory of implied easements was in derogation of both the recording statutes and the Statute of Frauds, the court took a stricter approach toward implied reservations of easements than implied grants and refused to recognize the former in the absence of a showing of strict necessity.

3. A subdivider erects a house with a panoramic view of the city. Does the purchaser have an implied scenic easement which will enable her to enjoin the subdivider from blocking her view by a building on the adjacent lot? What do you think of the argument that such an easement is too vague to be enforceable? See Thomas v. Campbell, 107 Idaho 398, 690 P.2d 333 (1984). For a discussion of analogous issues

which arise when a landowner asserts a right to access to sunlight and air, see the material dealing with rights in airspace, air, sunlight and clouds in Section 2 of this chapter.

4. In Drye v. Eagle Rock Ranch, Inc., 364 S.W.2d 196 (Tex.1962), the court rejected a claim by purchasers of building lots in a rustic resort area of implied easements for recreation activities in an adjoining 1000-acre ranch. The plat did not show the ranch, but a brochure displayed to prospective purchasers of lots did do so and contained the assertion that purchasers of lots would have "an easement over the entire ranch. In other words, . . . all the pleasure rights over the entire ranch property." The court said: "At common law, it was considered that a written easement to wander about over the land of another was invalid. It was referred to as a 'jus spatiandi,' which was a contraction of a part of a Latin phrase (taken from the Roman law), which when translated was: 'A praedial servitude cannot be created so as to give me permission to pick an apple, to wander about or to picnic on another's land.' [1] Only as late as 1955, the English Court of Appeals upheld a written easement in a park, a relatively small square, surrounded on three sides by homeowners and on the fourth side by the sea. The deed to the lot owners contained the written easements to use the park, subject to a fee for upkeep. It was held that the area *was* subject to easements appurtenant to the lot owners, the *jus spatiandi* notwithstanding. The park was likened to a garden which traditionally (as an appurtenance) adjoined to a residence. The area and all its uses were well defined. In re Ellenborough Park, 3 All E.R. 667 (1955).

"Thus, in England it was stated that easements, even in writing, were traditionally limited to six categories: air, light, ways or roads, support, water, and fences.[2] Probably because of this restricted view, the legislatures in several states, including California, Montana, Oklahoma, North Dakota and South Dakota, enacted statutes to permit servitudes or easements for rights of pasture, fishing, hunting, conducting lawful sports, and similar purposes.[3] Texas has no similar statute. Apparently the policy of those jurisdictions limiting easements appurtenant was that the land should be left free for development and not burdened with uses which were less important to the economic development of the community.

"This Court does not take the view that the types of permissible easements have been, or are, limited to the prescribed few listed above. Assuming that this Court will uphold express written easements appurtenant to land for pleasure and recreational purposes, this historical development influences our thinking on whether such easements will be implied by the courts under circumstances such as are here presented in the absence of a written agreement or deed of the parties.

1. "Jus Spatiandi,—a Valid Easement, re Ellenborough Park," 2 Sidney Law Review (1956–58) 370; "Re Ellenborough Park," 3 All England Law Reports Annotated (1955) 667; "The Right to Use a Private Pleasure Ground," 221 The Law Times (1956) 34.

2. Behan, Covenants Affecting Land (1924) 45; and see Alfred Conard, "Easement Novelties," 30 California Law Review (1942) 125, at 126.

3. 1 Thompson, Real Property (Perm.ed.) 523, Easements, § 327.

". . . For the easement appurtenant to be implied, some degree of definiteness in the scope or extent of the interest is essential to its recognition as an interest in land or a property interest. . . .

"Easements for pleasure and recreation over a 1000-acre ranch including the right to study nature, picnic, hike, ride horseback, camp out, bird watch and other similar activities fall within the general category of 'novelty easements.' They present problems even when they are created in writing. Supervision and enforcement by a court of an implied easement of this nature are difficult. . . .

"Viewing the problem from the State as a whole, to impose indefinite servitudes for pleasure and recreation on so large an area would tend to fetter estates, retard building and improvements thereon, and hinder the use of the land."

5. Other courts have been more receptive to the argument that a subdivider should be held to representations made to purchasers concerning the use of other land in the subdivision. In Shalimar Ass'n v. D.O.C. Enterprises, Inc., 142 Ariz. 36, 688 P.2d 682 (App.1984) the court concluded that the original developer, who had shown prospective purchasers brochures, maps and plats representing that an existing golf course adjacent to the residential lots would be maintained as such, was bound by an "implied restrictive covenant" to continue using the land as a golf course. The covenant was also deemed binding on persons who had bought the golf course with a view to developing it.

Also, compare with the Eagle Rock Ranch case a more recent holding by a lower court in the same jurisdiction. Lehmann v. Wallace, 510 S.W.2d 675 (Tex.Civ.App.1974) held that a developer's representations to purchasers that only one residence could be built on any one tract, regardless of the size of the tract, created restrictive covenants binding on the developers and all lot purchasers. The court stated that "where the owners of a tract subdivide it and sell distinct parcels thereof to separate grantees, imposing restrictions upon its use pursuant to a general plan of development or improvement, such restrictions may be enforced by any grantee against any other grantee, either upon the theory that there is a mutuality of covenants and consideration, or upon the ground that mutual negative equitable easements are created." 510 S.W.2d 681.

Are the courts' decisions in Shalimar Ass'n and Lehmann inconsistent with the Eagle Rock case? Reconsider this question after your study of equitable servitudes.

---

(3) Creation by Prescription

LUNT v. KITCHENS

Supreme Court of Utah, 1953.
123 Utah 488, 260 P.2d 535.

McDonough, Justice. This is a suit brought by a landowner to have defendants enjoined from using a driveway on her property.

Defendants entered a counterclaim to have an easement by prescription declared in them. The lower court found that defendants and their predecessors in interest had used the claimed right of way openly, adversely, continuously, uninterruptedly, and under claim of right for a period of more than twenty-five years and granted the counterclaim. Plantiffs appeal.

Appellant Lunt, the original plaintiff, is the owner of property located at 418 East Fourth South in Salt Lake City; appellant Strasser was joined as party plaintiff when his interest under a contract of sale with plaintiff Lunt appeared. Appellant's predecessor in interest, Carrie E. Weidner, and her husband were owners in possession of the property when respondents' predecessor in interest, Willie Ann Kitchens, bought and occupied the property to the west of the Weidner property, known as 414 East Fourth South, in the year 1920. There is no evidence in the record of an adverse user or claim to use the driveway on the Weidner property between the two houses before that time. The two families, the Weidners and the Kitchenses, lived in accord and there is in evidence a showing on both sides of complete harmony and friendship. There were never any objections as to the use of the driveway by the Kitchenses for delivery of coal and wood to the coal shed on the east side of their property, for parking their cars, and for foot passengers. The Weidners also used the driveway, although probably to a lesser extent since their family was smaller.

In 1934, Mrs. Weidner executed a warranty deed to her entire property to her children, Fred E. Weidner and Bessie Evelyn Ferguson. In 1936, she executed a quit-claim deed to the driveway, a strip 10 feet wide and 99 feet deep, to her friend, Mrs. Kitchens. Respondents do not claim under this abortive attempt to convey a right of way, nor do they say that this deed originated their claim of right beginning their adverse use, but rather that this deed was a recognition of a valid claim in the respondents. The only evidence of challenge and dispute over the driveway appears in 1946, when Clarence James Evans, a tenant of the Weidners, placed a gate across the driveway and George Kitchen took it down.

The question here involved is whether there is sufficient evidence of adverse user for a period of twenty years to sustain the trial court's finding of a prescriptive easement.

In order to settle rights in land to the benefit of the persons profitably using the land and to avoid the impossible burden of proving an ancient, actual grant to use the property, the courts of this country early adopted the legal fiction of a lost grant, whereby proof of continuous use for the prescriptive period, openly and with knowledge of the landowner, was sufficient to raise a presumption of grant, which in effect was a positive rule of law. The fact that the grantor with knowledge of such use, makes no protest against it is proof of his recognition of a claim of right in the grantee. In other words, it is conclusively presumed from the landowner's acquiescence for the defined period of time in the other's user of his land, he having the right and power to stop such user, that it is a rightful user. Tiffany on Real

Property, §§ 1191–1196. If, of course, the landowner consents to the use of his land, then the right created is a license and a prescriptive right cannot arise from a license unless the licensee renounces openly his claim under the license.

This court has defined the difference between consent and acquiescence in Zollinger v. Frank, 110 Utah 514, 175 P.2d 714, 170 A.L.R. 770. The distinction, we said, lies in whether the use was "against" the owner or "under" the owner, regardless of whether the use is described as peaceable, hostile, adverse to, or as acquiesced in by the servient owner. Because of the presumption that the use of another's land is adverse to him, the owner has the burden to show that the use was under his permission as distinguished from against it. Cache Valley Banking Company v. Cache County Poultry Growers Association, 116 Utah 258, 209 P.2d 251. Big Cottonwood Tanner Ditch Company v. Moyle, 109 Utah 197, 159 P.2d 596. American Law Institute, Restatement of Property, § 458d.

However, it is obvious that where a special relationship such as a license exists, the owner of the land is entitled to more notice than the mere use of his land not inconsistent with the license. Thus it is said the Restatement of Property § 458j:

"Where a user of land and one having an interest affected by the use have a relationship to each other sufficient in itself to justify the use, the use is not adverse unless knowledge of its adverse character is had by the one whose interest is affected. The responsibility of bringing this knowledge to him lies in the one making the use."

In other words, the presumption of adversity will not arise under mere use by a licensee and knowledge of such use on the part of the licensor. Yeager v. Woodruff, 17 Utah 361, 53 P. 1045. The use cannot be adverse when it rests upon license or mere neighborly accommodation. Jensen v. Gerrard, 85 Utah 481, 39 P.2d 1070. Sdrales v. Rondos, 116 Utah 288, 209 P.2d 562.

The failure of the Weidners to object to the use of their property by the Kitchenses in the case at hand must have been because of an implied consent in order to accommodate their neighbors. The use by the Kitchenses added no burden to the driveway; they did not attempt to widen it, nor to interfere with the use by the Weidners. Where a person opens the way for use of his own premises and another uses it without interfering with the landowner's use or causing him damage, the presumption is that the use was permissive and in absence of proof to the contrary, the person so using it does not acquire a right of way by prescription. . . . Since the use is presumed to have been with consent in 1920, unless respondents in the present case have presented sufficient evidence to show that it became adverse and that the claim of use against permission was known to the Weidners, the decree of the lower court must be reversed.

An unsigned will by Mrs. Weidner and the quit-claim deed to the driveway indicate her intent to give the right of way to Mrs. Kitchens, but obviously these were insufficient to convey any interest. They each would present adequate knowledge of an adverse claim necessary to start the running of a prescriptive period under these circumstances, but the will was dated 1935 and the deed was delivered in 1936 and the necessary 20 years had not accrued when this action was filed in 1950. Respondents claim that the will and deed are recognition of the claim which had existed previously, but the interpretation that these documents were an attempt to make a gift of property in which the donor recognized only her own interest is more plausible.

When the driveway became muddy and rutty, the Kitchenses repaired it by dumping ashes in the roadway. If the Kitchenses claimed an easement, they would be interested in keeping the premises in repair, but also their repairing would not be inconsistent with duties under a license, particularly in view of the fact that no great amount of money or labor was expended and no major repairs were made. In the case of Zollinger v. Frank, supra, this court considered evidence of replacement of a bridge along with other evidence of a claim to an easement, but in that case the landowner notified the claimant that the bridge was down, implying acknowledgment of claimant's easement. On the other hand, use of a ditch for the necessary period plus continuous repairs did not amount to notice of adverse possession where such activity was consistent with a license in Yeager v. Woodruff, supra. So it is in the present case.

The fact that, as witness for the respondents testified, the driveway was used "constantly as ours [the Kitchenses]" is also insufficient to give notice to a licensor of an adverse claim. The tearing down of a gate erected by the Weidners' tenant, of course, would give actual notice of a claim of right, but this act did not occur until 1946.

This case is similar to that presented in Cache Valley Banking Company v. Cache County Poultry Growers Association, supra, wherein there was no evidence of communication between the adjoining owners as to the usage of the way, no permission was expressly sought nor claimed and none was expressly given or denied. No evidence was introduced contrary to the premise that this usage was with permission and not against it; in fact, the plaintiff, as in the present case, produced evidence that defendant considered the use permissive and not adverse. This court found no adverse claim. Where the use begins as permissive, . . . it is incumbent upon the party asserting that it has afterward become adverse to show at what point this occurred in order to show a twenty-year hostile period. "We are not justified in conjecturing as to when or if such a hostile period began." Savage v. Nielsen, 114 Utah 22, 197 P.2d 117, 124.

The respondents have not introduced evidence of a claim of right renouncing the use of the driveway under permission nor have they met their responsibility of showing actual knowledge of the claim on the part of appellant's predecessors to rebut the presumption that the use continued with the permission of the landowner. The findings and decree of the trial court cannot be sustained on the facts and evidence adduced and must be set aside. The decree is reversed and the case remanded to the lower court with instructions to enter a decree in conformity with the views herein expressed.

Costs to appellant.

WOLFE, C.J., and CROCKETT, HENRIOD, and WADE, JJ., concur.

NOTE

"There has been considerable confusion in the cases involving the acquisition of easements by prescription, concerning the presence or absence of a presumption that the use is under a claim of right adverse to the owner of the servient tenement, and of which he has constructive notice, upon the showing of an open, continuous, notorious and peaceable use for the prescriptive period. Some cases hold that from that showing a presumption arises that the use is under a claim of right adverse to the owner. . . . It has been intimated that the presumption does not arise when the easement is over unenclosed and unimproved land. . . . Other cases hold that there must be specific direct evidence of an adverse claim of right, and in its absence, a presumption of permissive use is indulged. . . . The preferable view is to treat the case the same as any other; that is, the issue is ordinarily one of fact, giving consideration to all the circumstances and the inferences that may be drawn therefrom. The use may be such that the trier of fact is justified in inferring an adverse claim and user and imputing constructive knowledge thereof to the owner. There seems to be no apparent reason for discussing the matter from the standpoint of presumptions. For the trial court the question is whether the circumstances proven do or do not justify an inference showing the required elements. In the appellate court the issue is merely whether there is sufficient evidence to support the judgment of the trial court." Carter, J., in O'Banion v. Borba, 32 Cal.2d 145, 147–150, 195 P.2d 10, 12, 13 (1948).

. . .

DARTNELL v. BIDWELL

Supreme Judicial Court of Maine, 1916.
115 Me. 227, 98 A. 743, 5 A.L.R. 1320.

SAVAGE, C. J. Trespass quare clausum. In defense, it was contended that the defendant had a right of way over the plaintiff's premises, and that the acts complained of, or some of them, at least, were done in making necessary and reasonable repairs of the way. A portion of the way was acquired by grant. The remainder was claimed by prescription. Whether she had such a prescriptive right was contested. The verdict was for the defendant. The plaintiff brings the case here on exceptions to refusals to give requested instructions, and on a motion for a new trial.

One of the issues in the case, and perhaps one decisive of the case, is whether the prescriptive easement claimed by the defendant was interrupted by the plaintiff while it was yet inchoate. The presiding justice was requested to instruct the jury that:

"The defendant must not only prove the use of the way claimed by prescription, for 20 years, but that it was continued, uninterrupted, and adverse; that is, under a claim of right, with the knowledge and acquiescence of the owner, and not as a matter of favor or courtesy on his part."

This language seems to have been taken from the opinion in Sargent v. Ballard, 9 Pick. (Mass.) 251. The presiding justice declined to give this instruction. In declining to do so he said:

"It is true that the use must be for 20 years, that it must be continued, uninterrupted, and adverse, under a claim of right, but it need not be under an acquiescence of the owner."

The plaintiff excepted. While the easement was still inchoate as claimed by the plaintiff, the plaintiff wrote a letter to the defendant, in which she said:

"You are hereby notified that that portion of my land . . . which you have recently plowed and made into a road is across my private property. . . . No person has or ever had any right to pass in or over this field, and you are liable to me in damages for trespass. . . . I hereby notify you to at once go back to the original location and the original cartroad width as given in deed Hussey to Myers in 1856. . . . I hereby forbid you or any one in your behalf to pass in or travel over any portion of my land whatsoever and especially that portion which you have unlawfully and without any right made into a road, and you are notified to hereafter travel only in the single cartroad. . . ."

This letter related to the prescriptive way in question. The plaintiff at the trial contended that this letter was an interruption of the defendant's inchoate easement, and requested an instruction to that effect. A third request differently phrased was to the same effect. These requests were refused, and the plaintiff excepted. All the exceptions so far may be considered together.

A prescriptive easement is created only by a continuous use for at least 20 years under a claim of right adverse to the owner, with his knowledge and acquiescence, or by a use so open, notorious, visible, and uninterrupted that knowledge and acquiescence will be presumed. Each of the elements is essential and each is open to contradiction. The existence of all the elements for the requisite period creates a right conclusive against attack. Rollins v. Blackden, 112 Me. 459, 92 A. 521, and cases cited. The present controversy concerns the element of acquiescence, and the question is whether the plaintiff's acquiescence was interrupted in law by the letter from which we have quoted. It is not claimed that the defendant's use was interrupted by it.

Acquiescence is used in its ordinary sense. It does not mean license or permission in the active sense. It means passive assent, or submission. It means quiescence. It is consent by silence. Pierce's Adm'r v. Pierce, 66 Vt. 369, 29 A. 364; Cass County Commissioners v. Plotner, 149 Ind. 116, 48 N.E. 635; Scott v. Jackson, 89 Cal. 258, 26 P. 898. See Webster's Dictionary, tit. "Acquiescence." Proof of acquiescence by the owner is held essential by all authorities. It raises the presumption of a grant. Rollins v. Blackden, supra. Where the adverse use has continued for 20 years without interruption or denial on the part of the owner, and with his knowledge, his acquiescence is conclusively presumed. It was error then to rule that proof of acquiescence was unnecessary.

The distinction between the creation of an easement by adverse use and the gaining of a title to land by adverse possession is not always borne in mind. We said in Rollins v. Blackden, supra, that:

"In the matter of acquiescence, the creation of a prescriptive easement logically differs from the acquisition of a title to real estate by adverse possession. In the former the possession continues in the owner of the servient estate, and the prescriptive right arises out of adverse use. In the latter, the owner is ousted from possession, and the right or title arises out of adverse possession; and nothing short of making entry, or legal action, will break the continuity of possession."

See Workman v. Curran, 89 Pa. 226.

If the case at bar had been one of claimed adverse possession, the request would have been erroneous, and the ruling would have been right.

Anything which disproves acquiescence rebuts the presumption of a grant. Smith v. Miller, 11 Gray (Mass.) 145. It interrupts the inchoate easement. So far there is no dispute. The question now is: In what manner may acquiescence by disproved? And upon the question the authorities are divided. Upon one side is the leading case of Powell v. Bagg, 8 Gray (Mass.) 441, 69 Am.Dec. 262, in which it was said that if the owner of the land before the lapse of 20 years, "by a verbal act upon the premises in which the easement is claimed, resists the exercise, . . . and denies its existence, . . . his acquiescence . . . is disproved, and the essential elements of a title . . . by adverse use are shown not to exist." In C. & N.W. Ry. Co. v. Hoag, 90 Ill. 339, which was a case where the owner orally remonstrated against the use, the court approved the doctrine of Powell v. Bagg, and went further, and held that it was not material where the remonstrance was made, whether on or off the land. The doctrine that denials and remonstrances, on or off the land, are sufficient to rebut acquiescence, and work an interruption is supported by Workman v. Curran, supra; . . .

On the other hand, there are courts which hold that mere denials of the right, complaints, remonstrances, or prohibitions of user, unaccompanied by physical interference to some degree, will not prevent the acquisition of a right by prescription. The leading case, perhaps, on this side, is Lehigh Valley R.R. Co. v. McFarlan, 43 N.J.Law, 605. See other cases referred to in Rollins v. Blackden, supra. In the New Jersey case, the court seemed to follow by analogy the doctrine of adverse possession, and did not mark the distinction, which we have pointed out, between creating an easement and acquiring title by adverse possession.

When we consider what acquiescence means, and that nonacquiescence defeats an easement, but alone does not defeat title by adverse possession, we are persuaded that the doctrine in the former class of cases is founded upon the better reason. If acquiescence is consented by silence, to break the silence by denials and remonstrances ought to afford evidence of nonacquiescence, rebutting the presumption of a grant. In Rollins v. Blackden, supra, we held that the grant of an easement to A. effectually interrupted the inchoate easement to B. because it was an act of the strongest potency to rebut the presumption of acquiescence. In that aspect, there was no physical interruption nor disturbance. In the case at bar, we think that the letter of the plaintiff to the defendant expressly denying the latter's right, protesting its present, and forbidding its future, exercise, ought, in reason, to be held sufficient evidence of the plaintiff's nonacquiescence, and of an interruption of the defendant's inchoate easement. And we do hold it to be such. In fact, the statute (R.S. c. 107, § 12) provides expressly that an easement may be interrupted by a notice in writing served and recorded. That the notice should be served or delivered is necessary to bring knowledge of the interruption home to the claimant. Otherwise it is not notice to him. The provision for recording is to perpetuate the evidence of the interruption and give notice to third parties. But we think the statutory method is not exclusive. A notice in writing, served or delivered, but not recorded, is sufficient if proved. The plaintiff's requested instructions should have been given. . . . Exceptions and motion sustained.

NOTES

1. Is not the better view expressed in the following excerpt from Masid v. First State Bank, 213 Neb. 431, 329 N.W.2d 560, 563 (1983): "The use and enjoyment which will give title by prescription to an easement is substantially the same in quality and characteristics as the adverse possession which will give title to real estate. It must be exclusive, adverse, under a claim of right, continuous and uninterrupted, and open and notorious for the full prescriptive period. While some of our earlier opinions have included a requirement that the use also be with "the knowledge and acquiescence of the owner of the servient tenement," upon further reflection we now determine that such a requirement is neither necessary nor proper and is now specifically deleted as a requirement for establishing a prescriptive easement."

What issues are suggested by the following statement in RKO-Stanley Warner Theatres, Inc. v. Mellon National Bank & Trust Co., 436 F.2d 1297 (3d Cir. 1970), and how should they be resolved?

"The complaint charges that the plaintiff, RKO, owns and operates a motion picture theatre in Pittsburgh, Pennsylvania. The theatre building, with a marquee extending over the sidewalk in front of it, was erected in 1912. One of the defendants, Mellon Bank, owned and operated a bank adjacent to the theatre from 1935 until 1968. Prior to demolition of Mellon Bank's building in 1968, the theatre and the bank building existed on a common building line. Paragraph 6 of the complaint alleges:

"From the time the said theater and marquee were erected and the time when said bank building was erected the Plaintiff, and the predecessor operators of said theater, have used the sidewalk in front of said bank building and the air space above the same for the maintenance of and the changing of signs on, the said marquee; the use of said sidewalk and said air space has been uninterrupted, continuous and adverse for a period in excess of twenty-one (21) years.

"In May 1969 the defendant City of Pittsburgh vacated the sidewalk in front of the bank building. Vacation of the sidewalk relieved Mellon Bank of an easement in favor of the public and gave Mellon Bank a fee simple title, free of all encumbrances, to the 10-foot wide strip of land that formerly constituted the public sidewalk. In August 1969 RKO learned that Mellon Bank planned to construct a new building on its property that would extend over this 10-foot wide strip, and that the City of Pittsburgh would issue a building permit for the building as planned. Construction of a building over the 10-foot wide strip that formerly constituted the public sidewalk would physically block one side of RKO's marquee from public view and would prevent RKO from maintaining its marquee and changing the signs thereon."

STATE EX REL. THORNTON v. HAY

Supreme Court of Oregon, 1969.
254 Or. 584, 462 P.2d 671.

GOODWIN, JUSTICE. William and Georgianna Hay, the owners of a tourist facility at Cannon Beach, appeal from a decree which enjoins them from constructing fences or other improvements in the dry-sand area between the sixteen-foot elevation contour line and the ordinary high-tide line of the Pacific Ocean.

The issue is whether the State has the power to prevent the defendant landowners from enclosing the dry-sand area contained within the legal description of their ocean-front property.

The state asserts two theories: (1) the landowners' record title to be disputed area is encumbered by a superior right in the public to go upon and enjoy the land for recreational purposes; and (2) if the disputed area is not encumbered by the asserted public easement, then the state has power to prevent construction under zoning regulations made pursuant to ORS 390.640.

The defendant landowners concede that the State Highway Commission has standing to represent the rights of the public in this litigation, ORS 390.620, and that all tideland lying seaward of the ordinary, or mean high-tide line is a state recreation area as defined in ORS 390.720.

From the trial record, applicable statutes, and court decisions, certain terms and definitions have been extracted and will appear in this opinion. A short glossary follows:

ORS 390.720 refers to the "ordinary" high-tide line, while other sources refer to the "mean" high-tide line. For the purposes of this case the two lines will be considered to be the same. The mean high-tide line in Oregon is fixed by the 1947 Supplement to the 1929 United States Coast and Geodetic Survey data.

The land area in dispute will be called the dry-sand area. This will be assumed to be the land lying between the line of mean high tide and the visible line of vegetation.

The vegetation line is the seaward edge of vegetation where the upland supports vegetation. It falls generally in the vicinity of the sixteen-foot-elevation contour line, but is not at all points necessarily identical with that line. Differences between the vegetation line and the sixteen-foot line are irrelevant for the purposes of this case.

The sixteen-foot line, which is an engineering line and not a line visible on the ground, is mentioned in ORS 390.640, and in the trial court's decree.

The extreme high-tide line and the high-water mark are mentioned in the record, but will be treated as identical with the vegetation line. While technical differences between extreme high tide and the high-water mark, and between both lines and the sixteen-foot line, might have legal significance in some other litigation, such differences, if any, have none in this case. We cite these variations in terminology only to point out that the cases and statutes relevant to the issues in this case, like the witnesses, have not always used the same words to describe similar topographical features.

Below, or seaward of, the mean high-tide line, is the state-owned foreshore, or wetland area, in which the landowners in this case concede the public's paramount right, and concerning which there is no justiciable controversy.

The only issue in this case, as noted, is the power of the state to limit the record owner's use and enjoyment of the dry-sand area, by whatever boundaries the area may be described.

The trial court found that the public had acquired, over the years, an easement for recreational purposes to go upon and enjoy the dry-sand area, and that this easement was appurtenant to the wet-sand portion of the beach which is admittedly owned by the state and designated as a "state recreation area."

Because we hold that the trial court correctly found in favor of the state on the rights of the public in the dry-sand area, it follows that the state has an equitable right to protect the public in the enjoyment of those rights by causing the removal of fences and other obstacles.

It is not necessary, therefore, to consider whether ORS 390.640 would be constitutional if it were to be applied as a zoning regulation to lands upon which the public had not acquired an easement for recreational use.

In order to explain our reasons for affirming the trial court's decree, it is necessary to set out in some detail the historical facts which lead to our conclusion.

The dry-sand area in Oregon has been enjoyed by the general public as a recreational adjunct of the wet-sand or foreshore area since the beginning of the state's political history. The first European settlors on these shores found the aboriginal inhabitants using the foreshore for clam-digging and the dry-sand area for their cooking fires. The newcomers continued these customs after statehood. Thus, from the time of the earliest settlement to the present day, the general public has assumed that the dry-sand area was a part of the public beach, and the public has used the dry-sand area for picnics, gathering wood, building warming fires, and generally as a headquarters from which to supervise children or to range out over the foreshore as the tides advance and recede. In the Cannon Beach vicinity, state and local officers have policed the dry sand, and municipal sanitary crews have attempted to keep the area reasonably free from man-made litter.

Perhaps one explanation for the evolution of the custom of the public to use the dry-sand area for recreational purposes is that the area could not be used conveniently by its owners for any other purpose. The dry-sand area is unstable in its seaward boundaries, unsafe during winter storms, and for the most part unfit for the construction of permanent structures. While the vegetation line remains relatively fixed, the western edge of the dry-sand area is subject to dramatic moves eastward or westward in response to erosion and accretion. For example, evidence in the trial below indicated that between April 1966 and August 1967 the seaward edge of the dry-sand area involved in this litigation moved westward 180 feet. At other points along the shore, the evidence showed, the seaward edge of the dry-sand area could move an equal distance to the east in a similar period of time.

Until very recently, no question concerning the right of the public to enjoy the dry-sand area appears to have been brought before the courts of this state. The public's assumption that the dry sand as well as the foreshore was "public property" had been reinforced by early judicial decisions. See Shively v. Bowlby, 152 U.S. 1, 14 S.Ct. 548, 38 L.Ed. 331 (1894), which affirmed Bowlby v. Shively, 22 Or. 410, 30 P. 154 (1892). These cases held that landowners claiming under federal patents owned seaward only to the "high-water" line, a line that was then assumed to be the vegetation line.

In 1935, the United States Supreme Court held that a federal patent conveyed title to land farther seaward, to the mean high-tide line. Borax Consolidated, Ltd. v. Los Angeles, 296 U.S. 10, 56 S.Ct. 23, 80 L.Ed. 9 (1935). While this decision may have expanded seaward the record ownership of upland landowners, it was apparently little noticed by Oregonians. In any event, the *Borax* decision had no discernible effect on the actual practices of Oregon beachgoers and upland property owners.

Recently, however, the scarcity of ocean-front building sites has attracted substantial private investment in resort facilities. Resort owners like these defendants now desire to reserve for their paying guests the recreational advantages that accrue to the dry-sand portions of their deeded property. Consequently, in 1967, public debate and political activity resulted in legislative attempts to resolve conflicts between public and private interests in the dry-sand area:

(Statute)

ORS 390.610 "(1) The Legislative Assembly hereby declares it is the public policy of the State of Oregon to forever preserve and maintain the sovereignty of the state heretofore existing over the seashore and ocean beaches of the state from the Columbia River on the North to the Oregon-California line on the South so that the public may have the free and uninterrupted use thereof.

"(2) The Legislative Assembly recognizes that over the years the public has made frequent and uninterrupted use of lands abutting, adjacent and contiguous to the public highways and state recreation areas and recognizes, further, that where such use has been sufficient to create easements in the public through dedication, prescription, grant or otherwise, that it is in the public interest to protect and preserve such public easements as a permanent part of Oregon's recreational resources.

"(3) Accordingly, the Legislative Assembly hereby declares that all public rights and easements in those lands described in subsection (2) of this section are confirmed and declared vested exclusively in the State of Oregon and shall be held and administered in the same manner as those lands described in ORS 390.720.

. . .

The state concedes that such legislation cannot divest a person of his rights in land, Hughes v. Washington, 389 U.S. 290, 88 S.Ct. 438, 19 L.Ed.2d 530 (1967), and that the defendants' record title, which includes the dry-sand area, extends seaward to the ordinary or mean high-tide line. Borax Consolidated, Ltd. v. Los Angeles, supra.

The landowners likewise concede that since 1899 the public's rights in the foreshore have been confirmed by law as well as by custom and usage. Oregon Laws 1899, p. 3, provided:

"That the shore of the Pacific ocean, between ordinary high and extreme low tides, and from the Columbia river on the north to the south boundary line of Clatsop county on the south, is hereby declared a public highway, and shall forever remain open as such to the public."

The disputed area is *sui generis*. While the foreshore is "owned" by the state, and the upland is "owned" by the patentee or record-title holder, neither can be said to "own" the full bundle of rights normally connoted by the term "estate in fee simple." 1 Powell, Real Property § 163, at 661 (1949).

In addition to the *sui generis* nature of the land itself, a multitude of complex and sometimes overlapping precedents in the law confronted the trial court. Several early Oregon decisions generally support the trial court's decision, i.e., that the public can acquire easements in private land by long-continued user that is inconsistent with the owner's exclusive possession and enjoyment of his land. A citation of the cases could end the discussion at this point. But because the early cases do not agree on the legal theories by which the results are reached, and because this is an important case affecting valuable rights in land, it is appropriate to review some of the law applicable to this case.

One group of precedents relied upon in part by the state and by the trial court can be called the "implied-dedication" cases. The doctrine of implied dedication is well known to the law in this state and elsewhere. See cases collected in Parks, The Law of Dedication in Oregon, 20 Or.L.Rev. 111 (1941). Dedication, however, whether express or implied, rests upon an intent to dedicate. In the case at bar, it is unlikely that the landowners thought they had anything to dedicate, until 1967, when the notoriety of legislative debates about the public's rights in the dry-sand area sent a number of ocean-front landowners to the offices of their legal advisers.

A second group of cases relied upon by the state, but rejected by the trial court, deal with the possibility of a landowner's losing the exclusive possession and enjoyment of his land through the development of prescriptive easements in the public.

In Oregon, as in most common-law jurisdictions, an easement can be created in favor of one person in the land of another by uninterrupted use and enjoyment of the land in a particular manner for the statutory period, so long as the user is open, adverse, under claim of right, but without authority of law or consent of the owner. Feldman et ux. v. Knapp et ux., 196 Or. 453, 476, 250 P.2d 92 (1952); Coventon v. Seufert, 23 Or. 548, 550, 32 P. 508 (1893). In Oregon, the prescriptive period is ten years. ORS 12.050. The public use of the disputed land in the case at bar is admitted to be continuous for more than sixty years. There is no suggestion in the record that anyone's permission was sought or given; rather, the public used the land under a claim of right. Therefore, if the public can acquire an easement by prescription, the requirements for such an acquisition have been met in connection with the specific tract of land involved in this case.

The owners argue, however, that the general public, not being subject to actions in trespass and ejectment, cannot acquire rights by prescription, because the statute of limitations is irrelevant when an action does not lie.

While it may not be feasible for a landowner to sue the general public, it is nonetheless possible by means of signs and fences to prevent or minimize public invasions of private land for recreational purposes. In Oregon, moreover, the courts and the Legislative Assembly have both recognized that the public can acquire prescriptive easements in private land, at least for roads and highways. See, e.g., Huggett et ux. v. Moran et ux., 201 Or. 105, 266 P.2d 692 (1954), in which we observed that counties could acquire public roads by prescription. And see ORS 368.405, which provides for the manner in which counties may establish roads. The statute enumerates the formal governmental actions that can be employed, and then concludes: "This section does not preclude acquiring public ways by adverse user."

Another statute codifies a policy favoring the acquisition by prescription of public recreational easements in beach lands. See ORS 390.610. While such a statute cannot create public rights at the expense of a private landowner the statute can, and does, express legislative approval of the common-law doctrine of prescription where the facts justify its application. Consequently, we conclude that the law in Oregon, regardless of the generalizations that may apply elsewhere,[9] does not preclude the creation of prescriptive easements in beach land for public recreational use.

Because many elements of prescription are present in this case, the state has relied upon the doctrine in support of the decree below. We believe, however, that there is a better legal basis for affirming the decree. The most cogent basis for the decision in this case is the English doctrine of custom. Strictly construed, prescription applies only to the specific tract of land before the court, and doubtful prescription cases could fill the courts for years with tract-by-tract litigation. An established custom, on the other hand, can be proven with reference to a larger region. Ocean-front lands from the northern to the southern border of the state ought to be treated uniformly.

The other reason which commends the doctrine of custom over that of prescription as the principal basis for the decision in this case is the unique nature of the lands in question. This case deals solely with the dry-sand area along the Pacific shore, and this land has been used by the public as public recreational land according to an unbroken custom running back in time as long as the land has been inhabited.

A custom is defined in 1 Bouv.Law Dict., Rawle's Third Revision, p. 742 as "such a usage as by common consent and uniform practice has become the law of the place, or of the subject matter to which it relates."

In 1 Blackstone, Commentaries * 75–* 78, Sir William Blackstone set out the requisites of a particular custom.

Paraphrasing Blackstone, the first requirement of a custom, to be recognized as law, is that it must be ancient. It must have been used so long "that the memory of man runneth not to the contrary." Professor Cooley footnotes his edition of Blackstone with the comment that "long and general" usage is sufficient. In any event, the record in the case at bar satisfies the requirement of antiquity. So long as there has been an institutionalized system of land tenure in Oregon, the public has freely

9. See, e.g., Sanchez v. Taylor, 377 F.2d 733, 738 (10th Cir. 1967), holding that the general public cannot acquire grazing rights in unfenced land. Among other reasons assigned by authorities cited in Sanchez v. Taylor are these: prescription would violate the rule against perpetuities because no grantee could ever convey the land free of the easement; and presciption rests on the fiction of a "lost grant," which state of affairs cannot apply to the general public. The first argument can as well be made against the public's acquiring rights by express dedication; and the second argument applies equally to the fictional aspects of the doctrine of implied dedication. Both arguments are properly ignored in cases dealing with roads and highways, because the utility of roads and the public interest in keeping them open outweighs the policy favoring formal over informal transfers of interests in land.

exercised the right to use the dry-sand area up and down the Oregon coast for the recreational purposes noted earlier in this opinion.

The second requirement is that the right be exercised without interruption. A customary right need not be exercised continuously, but it must be exercised without an interruption caused by anyone possessing a paramount right. In the case at bar, there was evidence that the public's use and enjoyment of the dry-sand area had never been interrupted by private landowners.

Blackstone's third requirement, that the customary use be peaceable and free from dispute, is satisfied by the evidence which related to the second requirement.

The fourth requirement, that of reasonableness, is satisfied by the evidence that the public has always made use of the land in a manner appropriate to the land and to the usages of the community. There is evidence in the record that when inappropriate uses have been detected, municipal police officers have intervened to preserve order.

The fifth requirement, certainly, is satisfied by the visible boundaries of the dry-sand area and by the character of the land, which limits the use thereof to recreational uses connected with the foreshore.

The sixth requirement is that a custom must be obligatory; that is, in the case at bar, not left to the option of each landowner whether or not he will recognize the public's right to go upon the dry-sand area for recreational purposes. The record shows that the dry-sand area in question has been used, as of right, uniformly with similarly situated lands elsewhere, and that the public's use has never been questioned by an upland owner so long as the public remained on the dry sand and refrained from trespassing upon the lands above the vegetation line.

Finally, a custom must not be repugnant, or inconsistent, with other customs or with other law. The custom under consideration violates no law, and is not repugnant.

Two arguments have been arrayed against the doctrine of custom as a basis for decision in Oregon. The first argument is that custom is unprecedented in this state, and has only scant adherence elsewhere in the United States. The second argument is that because of the relative brevity of our political history it is inappropriate to rely upon an English doctrine that requires greater antiquity than a newly-settled land can muster. Neither of these arguments is persuasive.

The custom of the people of Oregon to use the dry-sand area of the beaches for public recreational purposes meets every one of Blackstone's requisites. While it is not necessary to rely upon precedent from other states, we are not the first state to recognize custom as a source of law. See Perley et ux'r v. Langley, 7 N.H. 233 (1834).

On the score of the brevity of our political history, it is true that the Anglo-American legal system on this continent is relatively new. Its newness has made it possible for government to provide for many of our institutions by written law rather than by customary law.[10] This

10. The English law on customary rights grew up in a small island nation at a time when most inhabitants lived and died without traveling more than a day's walk

truism does not, however, militate against the validity of a custom when the custom does in fact exist. If antiquity were the sole test of validity of a custom, Oregonians could satisfy that requirement by recalling that the European settlers were not the first people to use the dry-sand area as public land.

Finally, in support of custom, the record shows that the custom of the inhabitants of Oregon and of visitors in the state to use the dry sand as a public recreation area is so notorious that notice of the custom on the part of persons buying land along the shore must be presumed. In the case at bar, the landowners conceded their actual knowledge of the public's long-standing use of the dry-sand area, and argued that the consensual elements present in the relationship between the landowners and the public precluded the application of the law of prescription. As noted, we are not resting this decision on prescription, and we leave open the effect upon prescription of the type of consent that may have been present in this case. Such consensual elements are, however, wholly consistent with the recognition of public rights derived from custom.

Because so much of our law is the product of legislation, we sometimes lose sight of the importance of custom as a source of law in our society. It seems particularly appropriate in the case at bar to look to an ancient and accepted custom in this state as the source of a rule of law. The rule in this case, based upon custom, is salutary in confirming a public right, and at the same time it takes from no man anything which he has had a legitimate reason to regard as exclusively his.

For the foregoing reasons, the decree of the trial court is affirmed.

DENECKE, JUSTICE (specially concurring).

I agree with the decision of the majority; however, I disagree with basing the decision upon the English doctrine of "customary rights." In my opinion the facts in this case cannot be fitted into the outlines of that ancient doctrine. . . .

I base the public's right upon the following factors: (1) long usage by the public of the dry sands area, not necessarily on all the Oregon beaches, but wherever the public uses the beach; (2) a universal and long held belief by the public in the public's right to such use; (3) long and universal acquiescence by the upland owners in such public use; and (4) the extreme desirability to the public of the right to the use of

from their birthplace. Most of the customary rights recorded in English cases are local in scope. The English had many cultural and language groups which eventually merged into a nation. After these groups developed their own unique customs, the unified nation recognized some of them as law. Some American scholars, looking at the vast geography of this continent and the freshness of its civilization, have concluded that there is no need to look to English customary rights as a source of legal rights in this country. See, e.g., 6 Powell, Real Property § 934, note 5, at 362 (1949). Some of the generalizations drawn by the text writers from English cases would tend to limit customary rights to specific usages in English towns and villages. See Gray, The Rule Against Perpetuities §§ 572–588 (1942). But it does not follow that a custom, established in fact, cannot have regional application and be enjoyed by a larger public than the inhabitants of a single village.

the dry sands. When this combination exists, as it does here, I conclude that the public has the right to use the dry sands.

Admittedly, this is a new concept as applied to use of the dry sands of a beach . . ..

NOTES

1. The Hays later failed to persuade a federal court that the Oregon beach legislation, as interpreted and applied to the Hays, was an "unpredictable change of property law" that constituted a taking of property in violation of the United States Constitution. Hay v. Bruno, 344 F.Supp. 286 (D.Or.1972). A somewhat different view was taken in In re Opinion of the Justices, 356 Mass. 681, 313 N.E.2d 561 (1974), an advisory opinion that a proposed statute recognizing and protecting a "public on-foot right-of-passage" on coastal beaches would be an unconstitutional taking, despite its provision that it should not be construed as altering existing rights.

2. Compare State ex rel. Haman v. Fox, 100 Idaho 140, 594 P.2d 1093 (1979). This was a suit by a county attorney on behalf of the people of Idaho to establish public recreational rights in two lots abutting Lake Coeur d'Alene. The suit failed. Concerning prescription, the court said: "Under the lost grant rationale, courts have held that the general public, considered apart from legally organized or political entities, could not acquire prescriptive rights because they could not receive a grant. . . . Although Idaho long ago abandoned the fiction of the lost grant, we reach the same result . . .. [T]he rights contended for here are in the nature of an easement in gross. Being a personal right, the rule is that one individual's prescriptive use cannot inure to the benefit of anyone else . . . absent some express statutory authority. The one situation where the legislature has allowed such public prescriptive rights is in public highways." Concerning implied dedication, the court said: "The intent of the owner to dedicate his land to public use must be clearly and unequivocally shown and must never be presumed." Concerning custom, the court said: "Virtually all commentators are agreed that, until recently, the law of custom was a dead letter in the United States. . . . The doctrine was exhumed, however, by the Supreme Court of Oregon in State ex rel. Thornton v. Hay . . .. [T]his court is of opinion that the doctrine does obtain in Idaho . . .. [However,] of the seven essential elements of a customary right, the trial court found adversely to appellant on six of them." The court also quickly rejected an argument that the claimed public rights could be supported by the public trust doctrine.

3. Some courts have based public recreational rights in coastal beaches upon implied dedication. Gion v. City of Santa Cruz, 2 Cal.3d 29, 84 Cal.Rptr. 162, 465 P.2d 50 (1970); Moody v. White, 593 S.W.2d 372 (Tex.Civ.App.1979); Seaway Co. v. Attorney General, 375 S.W.2d 923 (Tex.Civ.App.1964). The court in Moody v. White explained: "The mere fact that the prior owner stood by and watched the public use 'his' beach for many years indicates that he intended to give the beachfront to the public . . .. The final act of accomplishing dedication is that

there must be an acceptance of the dedication. This acceptance does not require a formal or express act. By general and customary use, the public can accept a dedication." That court also upheld jury findings that the public rights had been established by prescription and custom. See Annot., Implied Acceptance, by Public Use, of Dedication of Beach or Shoreline Adjoining Public Waters, 24 A.L.R. 4th 294 (1983).

4. An attempt to extend State ex rel Thornton v. Hay beyond the vegetation line to a dune area failed. State v. Bauman, 16 Or.App. 275, 517 P.2d 1202 (1974).

5. For commentary, see Roberts, Beaches: The Efficiency of the Common Law and Other Fairy Tales, 28 U.C.L.A.L.Rev. 169 (1980). A major burden of this article is to determine "whether decisions to increase public access to beaches are 'efficiency producing.' "

---

(4) Scope and Transferability

S.S. KRESGE CO. v. WINKELMAN REALTY CO.

Supreme Court of Wisconsin, 1952.
260 Wis. 372, 50 N.W.2d 920.

This action involves an easement across a small tract of land located in block number 13 of the original plat of the village (now city) of Wausau, Wisconsin. This block is bounded on the north by Jefferson street, on the west by Second street, on the south by Washington street, and on the east by Third street. The block consists of eight lots. Lots 1, 2, 3 and 4 are located in the south half of the block and are numbered in that order from west to east. Lots 5, 6, 7 and 8 are in the north half of the block and are numbered in that order from east to west.

The plaintiff is the owner of the south half of lots 5 and 6. The west eleven and one-half feet of the plaintiff's property consists of an alleyway. The defendant Winkelman Realty Company is the owner of lot 2 and the west half of lot 3, the south 96.85 feet of the east half of lot 3, and the south 96.85 feet of lot 4. The defendant Winkelman Department Store leases all of its real estate from Winkelman Realty Company, and in turn subleases lot 2 and a portion of the west half of lot 3 to Winkelman's Men's Store. All of the defendant corporations are controlled by the same group and will be referred to as the defendants. They operate a department store on the east half of lot 3 and on lot 4, and an appliance store on the west half of lot 3, and a men's store on lot 2.

For several years prior to 1936, one Max Tisch was the owner of lot 2 and had a commercial building thereon, consisting of a plumbing shop, garage, and retail plumbing store. One Albert Dern was the owner of the west half of lot 3 and used the lower floor of the building thereon for a barber shop and the second floor for living quarters. In 1934, Tisch bought the Dern property. He remodelled the building thereon and leased it with the building on lot 2 to Sears Roebuck &

Company, which used the entire property as a retail store. In 1936 the Kresge Company tried to close the alleyway which extends across the west eleven and one-half feet of its property. Tisch thereupon brought an action to establish his right to use the alleyway in question against the Kresge Company, and judgment was entered in said action on September 16, 1936, wherein Tisch was adjudged to have a perpetual right of way for all purposes of ingress and egress across said alleyway to and from the west half of lot 3. In 1943, the defendants purchased the Tisch property with the appurtenant easement. Thereafter the basement of the Tisch buildings, the area under the alleyway from Washington street, and the area under the sidewalks were treated as one store room for all of the buildings. Merchandise consigned to the different Winkelman stores was delivered across the plaintiff's alleyway to the former Dern building, from which it was distributed to the other stores.

The complaint herein sets forth two causes of action: the first, to establish the claim of the plaintiff against any claim of the defendants except their easement for ingress and egress to the west half of lot 3; and second, to enjoin the defendants from using any portion of plaintiff's real estate except as a right of way for ingress and egress to the west half of lot 3, and to enjoin defendants from conveying or transporting merchandise to or from the Men's Store or the Department Store by way of the former Dern property.

The trial court found that the easement acquired by the defendants from Tish is appurtenant only to the west half of lot 3 and is not appurtenant to any of the other property owned by the defendants, but that the defendants had made regular and substantial use of said easement for the transportation of merchandise for the other stores. The trial court further found that such use was not within the contemplation of the owners of the premises at the time the easement was acquired by prescription, and that said unauthorized use is an added burden upon the servient estate owned by the plaintiff.

The judgment quieted title to the alleyway in question in the plaintiff, but recognized the easement for ingress and egress to the west half of lot 3 in the defendant Winkelman Realty Company. The judgment further enjoined the defendants from imposing a different kind of use or species of burden upon said easement right than was acquired by prescription and established by the judgment of September 16, 1936, and defendants were specifically enjoined and restrained from using said easement for the purpose of bringing or taking goods, merchandise, supplies or other articles to and from lot 2, the east half of lot 3, and lot 4 in said block across the alleyway of the plaintiff.

The defendants appeal from the judgment entered January 20, 1951, and the plaintiff served notice of review thereof and asked for modification of said judgment to enjoin any use of the easement by the defendants.

BROADFOOT, JUSTICE. The defendants claim that the owner of land has a right to use it to its fullest economic value. With this general statement there can be no quarrel. However, the plaintiff is the owner of the alleyway in question, subject to the easement established by the judgment of 1936. There is another general statement of law that an easement can be used only in connection with the estate to which it is appurtenant. Reise v. Enos, 76 Wis. 634, 45 N.W. 414, 8 L.R.A. 617; Guse v. Flohr, 195 Wis. 139, 217 N.W. 730. A prescriptive right acquired by a particular use of the property cannot ordinarily justify an added use in connection with the dominant estate in a manner far different from that employed under the original use. Defendants' easement was established because of use of the alleyway by the owner of a building used for a barber shop and living quarters. The fact that in 1934 the property was used in connection with lot 2 as a retail store had not established any prescriptive rights in 1936. In this case the defendants have greatly changed the use of the dominant estate in that it is now used as a retail outlet for appliances and as a storage warehouse for other merchandise that is not to be sold upon the premises. The trial court's finding that this was an added burden upon the servient estate is clearly supported by the evidence.

The facts in this case are similar to those in the case of McCullough v. Broad Exchange Co., 101 App.Div. 566, 92 N.Y.S. 533. In that case an easement permitted the use of an alley for ingress and egress over a servient estate. Later the dominant estate was included as part of a larger tract of land upon which an office building was erected. The building was heated by a single plant on the dominant estate, which was located so that the alley could be used in hauling coal to and removing ashes from the building. The court there held that the owner of the office building had no right to use the dominant estate to generate heat which he transmitted to portions of the building not located on the dominant estate. This was held to be an added burden upon the servient estate and an improper attempt to enlarge upon the original easement.

The defendants further contend that they have not unreasonably burdened or changed the nature of the use of the alleyway. It was held in the case of Lindokken v. Paulson, 224 Wis. 470, 272 N.W. 453, 110 A.L.R. 910 that an easement for a specified purpose may be enlarged by subsequent adverse user. The owner of the servient estate is not required to wait until his property has been unreasonably burdened and thereby permit additional rights to be gained by prescription but he may proceed when any additional burden is placed upon his property and whenever the defendants improperly attempt to increase their rights under their easement.

The plaintiff, by motion for review, asks for modification of the judgment to enjoin any use of the easement by the defendants on the ground that it is difficult to distinguish the increased burden from the lawful use of the easement to which the defendants are entitled. The judgment granted all of the relief prayed for by the plaintiff in its complaint. Sec. 270.57, Stats. provides: "The relief granted to the plaintiff, if there be no answer, cannot exceed that which he shall have demanded in his complaint; but in any other case the court may grant him any relief consistent with the case made by the complaint and embraced within the issue."

The defendants having answered, the court could have granted any relief consistent with the allegations of the complaint. He did not choose to enjoin the defendants from making any use of their easement, and since there was no abuse of judicial discretion, there is no basis for plaintiff's motion for review.

Judgment affirmed.

NOTES

1. In Brown v. Voss, 105 Wash.2d 366, 715 P.2d 514 (1986) the court upheld the trial court's refusal to enjoin the holder of an express easement from using it for the benefit of both the original dominant estate and other adjacent property which he subsequently acquired. While adhering to the rule that any extension of an easement to benefit nondominant property is a misuse of the easement, the court held that the trial judge had properly exercised his discretion in refusing to grant an equitable remedy. The owner of the servient estate had suffered no substantial injury because the defendant's use of the easement for a house which straddled the boundary line of the dominant and nondominant properties did not increase the burden on the servient estate.

2. Purchasers of lots in a resort community acquired easements entitling them to use recreational facilities owned by a property owners association. May the association prevent a lessee of a residence from using those facilities? Is the easement appurtenant to the fee only? The association prevailed on this issue in Hannum v. Bella Vista Village Property Owners Association, 272 Ark. 49, 611 S.W.2d 756 (1981). In that case, the Declaration and Protective Covenants of the association provided that the easements in the "Common Properties" shall be "appurtenant to and shall pass with the title to every Lot or Living Unit." Should this reference to "title" be decisive?

SAKANSKY v. WEIN

Supreme Court of New Hampshire, 1933.
86 N.H. 337, 169 A. 1.

Petition for injunction. The facts were found by a master.

At the time of the filing of the petition, the plaintiff Sakansky was the owner of a certain parcel of land with the buildings thereon, situated on the westerly side of Main street in Laconia. The deed by means of which he took title also conveyed to him a right of way, eighteen feet in width, over land which for the purposes of this case may be regarded as belonging to the defendants. Before trial Sakansky conveyed this property, together with the right of way, to the plaintiff J.J. Newberry Company, and took back a mortgage thereon. This right of way, with no expressed limitation as to mode of use, originated in a deed to the plaintiff's ancestor in title in 1849. This deed gave the right of way definite location upon the ground.

The defendants wish to develop their servient estate by erecting a building over the land subjected to the plaintiff's easement. They proposed to leave an opening in their new building at the place where it crosses the way; this opening to allow headroom of eight feet for the way where it passes under the defendant's building. They also propose to lay out a new way over level ground around the westerly end of the new building, which new way will give access to the same point on the dominant estate as the old way. This new way is free from obstruction and affords an easy means of access for vehicles whose height would prevent them from continuing to use the old way. The plaintiff objected and excepted to the introduction of evidence concerning the proposed new way.

The master ruled that neither party had any absolute or unlimited rights in the old right of way, but that the rights of each were to be determined by the rule of reasonableness. He further ruled that what was reasonable was a question of fact, to be determined by considering all the circumstances of all of the property, including the advantages accruing to the defendants and the disadvantages to be suffered by the plaintiff.

Applying the above principles he found that, considering the proposed additional right of way, the defendants' proposed reduction in height of the old right of way was not an unreasonable interference with the plaintiff's rights. But he found further that if it was not proper for him to take into consideration the proposed new way, then a reduction in height of the old way, as proposed, would be an unreasonable interference with the plaintiff's rights. On the basis of the above rulings of law and findings of fact, and giving consideration to the proposed new way, he recommended a decree permitting the defendants to build over the old way upon condition that they provide the plaintiff with the new way as proposed by them.

The plaintiff's exception to the admission of evidence concerning the new right of way, and the question of whether the plaintiff is entitled to an injunction, were transferred without ruling by Burque, J.

WOODBURY, JUSTICE. In this state the respective rights of dominant and servient owners are not determined by reference to some technical and more or less arbitrary rule of property law as expressed in some ancient maxim . . ., but are determined by reference to the rule of reason. The application of this rule raises a question of fact to be determined by consideration of all the surrounding circumstances, including the location and uses of both dominant and servient estates, and taking into consideration the advantage to be derived by one and the disadvantage to be suffered by the other owner. . . . The same rule has been applied to easements other than rights of way; for example, to aqueduct rights . . . to rights of flowage, both as to surface water . . . and as to water in a stream . . .. In the somewhat analogous cases involving the reciprocal rights of adjoining owners the same principle has been applied. . . . The master's general rulings of law are in accordance with the foregoing and are therefore correct.

The error arises in the application of the above principle to the situation presented in the case at bar.

Implicit in the master's findings of fact is the finding that it is reasonable for the plaintiff to have access to the rear of its premises for vehicles over eight feet high. The master has applied the rule of reason to deflect this reasonable use over the new way which the defendants propose to create. This may not be done under the circumstances of this case.

The rule of reason is a rule of interpretation. Its office is either to give a meaning to words which the parties or their ancestors in title have actually used, as was done in Farmington, etc., Ass'n v. Trafton, 84 N.H. 29, 146 A. 169, in which the word "necessary" was held to mean "reasonably necessary," or else to give a detailed definition to rights created by general words either actually used, or whose existence is implied by law. . . . This rule of reason does not prevent the parties from making any contract regarding their respective rights which they may wish, regardless of the reasonableness of their wishes on the subject. The rule merely refuses to give unreasonable rights, or to impose unreasonable burdens, when the parties, either actually or by legal implication, have spoken generally.

In the case at bar the parties are bound by a contract which not only gave the dominant owner a way across the servient estate for the purpose of access to the rear of its premises, but also gave that way definite location upon the ground. The use which the plaintiff may make of the way is limited by the bounds of reason, but within those bounds it has the unlimited right to travel over the land set apart for a way. It has no right to insist upon the use of any other land of the defendants for a way, regardless of how necessary such other land may be to it, and regardless of how little damage or inconvenience such use of the defendants' land might occasion to them. No more may the defendants compel the plaintiff to detour over other land of theirs.

The rule of reason is to be applied to determine whether or not the plaintiff has the right to approach the rear of its building with vehicles over eight feet high. This question having been answered in the affirmative, the plaintiff, by virtue of the grant, has the right to use that land, and only that land, which was set apart for the purpose of a way, and it may insist upon that right regardless of whether such insistence on its part be reasonable or not.

This does not mean that the defendants may not build over the old way at all. The plaintiff has no absolute right to have the way remain open to the sky. What, if any, structure the defendants may build over the way depends upon what is reasonable. Tiffany on Real Property (2d Ed.) vol. 2, § 371; 19 C.J. § 239. . . . The master has already found that a height of only eight feet for the old way is not reasonable. The defendants must provide more headroom. How much more is a question of fact, which may be determined later in further proceedings before the master if the defendants wish for a definition of the extent of this right.

In view of the fact that the rule of reason may not be invoked to deflect the plaintiff's reasonable travel over the new way, evidence concerning that way becomes immaterial and irrelevant, and hence it was error for the master to have admitted it. Had the rule of reason been applicable, it would not have been error to have admitted evidence regarding this other means of access, since it was one of the surrounding circumstances affecting the situation . . . and the fact that the defendants proposed to lay it out over their own land for the plaintiff's benefit does not render it any the less one of the surrounding circumstances.

The argument advanced that what is reasonable must be considered in the light of the situation as it was at the time the way was granted in 1849 is without merit. What is or is not a reasonable use of a way does not become crystallized at any particular moment of time. Changing needs of either owner may operate to make unreasonable a use of the way previously reasonable, or to make reasonable a use previously unreasonable. There is an element of time as well as of space in this question of reasonableness. In the absence of contract on the subject, the owner of the dominant estate is not limited in his use of the way to such vehicles only as were known at the time the way was created, but he may use the way for any vehicle which his reasonable needs may require in the development of his estate. Abbott v. Butler, supra. In this respect the use of the way is analogous to the use of a highway. State v. Scott, 82 N.H. 278, 279, 132 A. 685.

Case discharged.

All concurred.

NOTES

1. A deed purports to grant "the right to place oil and gas pipelines in the described land." The deed is silent as to the time and location of construction of the pipelines. Servient owner argues that this deed should be held void for vagueness and because it unreasonably restricts use of the fee by precluding construction of buildings pending installation of the pipelines. How should this argument be answered? A divided court upheld a similar deed in Northwest Pipeline Corp. v. Forrest Weaver Farm, Inc., 103 Idaho 180, 646 P.2d 422 (1982).

2. In Herold v. Hughes, 141 W.Va. 182, 90 S.E.2d 451 (1955), an easement acquired by the State Road Commission for "public road purposes" was held to include the right to locate a gas transmission pipe line beneath the road. The court said: "We cannot assume that the grant was made and accepted for any limited purposes or methods of travel or transportation." A contrary conclusion was reached in Heyert v. Orange & Rockland Utilities, Inc., 17 N.Y.2d 353, 218 N.E.2d 263, 269 (1966), the court explaining: "Many a town highway is donated through dedication by abutting owners, and the equivalent of many dollars is thus obtained for public use from private owners who might hesitate to do so if they were aware that, without mentioning them, they were also conveying pole and wire easements for telephone and power, and for conduits below ground, as well as for mains for

sewer, water and gas for the service of private customers." Cases involving similar problems are collected in Note, 58 A.L.R.2d 525 (1958).

3. "When an easement is acquired by prescription, the extent of the right is fixed and determined by the manner of use in which it originated." Thompson, J., in Bartholomew v. Staheli, 86 Cal.App.2d 844, 195 P.2d 824 (1948), involving a prescriptive easement in a roadway for the benefit of dominant land the use of which was changed from farming to the establishment and maintenance of a nudist colony. In the words of the court, "The easement for access to a tranquil home and farm was converted into a turbulent route to reach a hilarious nudist colony." Does it follow that the court would have permitted no change in the character of use of the dominant land (e.g., lumbering to grazing)? How about a change in the type of vehicles traveling the way (horse-drawn wagons to motor vehicles)? Or an increase in the volume of traffic which either does, or does not, diminish the enjoyment of the servient land (by increasing dust or noise, for example)? See 4 Tiffany, Real Property § 1209 (3d ed. 1939).

4. A county has acquired a prescriptive easement based upon a public use of a road for transportation. Does this easement entitle the county to place utility lines under the road surface? To authorize a private company to install under the road surface a pipeline for transmission of effluent from that company's fertilizer plant, for the purpose of promoting the public interest in stream water quality? Affirmative answers were given to both questions in Bentel v. County of Bannock, 104 Idaho 130, 656 P.2d 1383 (1983).

5. A deed conveying a portion of grantor's land provided: "RESERVING unto the grantor, its successors and assigns, a right of way for ingress and egress over the Easterly 25.0 feet of said property." The servient land was used for cattle grazing. It appeared that grantor intended to use the way for ingress and egress to his residence and for transport of some farm animals. For a number of years, use of the way was sufficiently non-intensive that servient owner was able to graze cattle on the way. The present dominant owner now plans to subdivide his tract into residential lots and put an all-weather surface on the way. Servient owner asserts the right to erect gates at both ends of the way, to prevent the escape of cattle. These gates would be locked and keys given to lawful users. The dominant owner objects to the gates, but is willing to erect a fence separating the easement from the balance of the servient tract. Servient owner objects to the fence because it would interfere with possessory rights incident to the fee. A divided court held for the servient owner in Wykoff v. Barton, 646 P.2d 756 (Utah 1982).

6. Restatement of Property § 488 (1944): "Except as limited by the terms of its transfer, or by the manner [1] or terms of the creation of the easement appurtenant, those who succeed to the possession of each

1. The term "manner" is "particularly applicable to creation by prescription." Restatement, Property § 487. Comment c (1944). Copyright, 1944. Portions reprinted with permission of The American Law Institute.

of the parts into which a dominant tenement may be subdivided thereby succeed to the privileges of use of the servient tenement authorized by the easement." In the Comment on this section, it is said: "The burden upon a servient tenement frequently will not be greatly increased by permitting an easement appurtenant to attach to each of the parts into which the dominant tenement may be subdivided. Though some increase in burden may result from the fact that the number of users is increased by the subdivision, the extent of the use is still measured by the needs of the land which constituted the original dominant tenement. Moreover, dominant tenements are ordinarily divisible and their division is so common that it is assumed that the possibility of their division is contemplated by their creation. . . . Indications to the contrary may be implicit in the use authorized by the easement. The use may be of such a character that division of it will increase the burden caused by it beyond what can reasonably be assumed to have been contemplated in its creation. If so, a division of the use will not be permitted."

7. Restatement of Property § 487, Comment b (1944): "There is nothing to prevent a transferor from effectively providing that the benefit of an easement appurtenant shall not pass to the transferee of the dominant tenement. Such a provision contravenes no rule of law. If its purpose is to extinguish the easement it will have this effect. If the purpose of the provision is to change the easement appurtenant into an easement in gross, it will have this effect if, and only if, the manner or the terms of the creation of the easement permit such a change to be made. If they do not permit this to be done, the result will be either that the provision against transfer is ineffective or that the easement is extinguished. Which of these results will occur depends upon whether the provision against transfer is construed to be conditioned upon the effective accomplishment of the purpose to change the easement into one in gross." [2]

MILLER v. LUTHERAN CONFERENCE & CAMP ASSOCIATION

Supreme Court of Pennsylvania, 1938.
331 Pa. 241, 200 A. 646, 130 A.L.R. 1245.

STERN, JUSTICE. This litigation is concerned with interesting and somewhat novel legal questions regarding rights of boating, bathing and fishing in an artificial lake.

Frank C. Miller, his brother Rufus W. Miller, and others, who owned lands on Tunkhannock Creek in Tobyhanna Township, Monroe County, organized a corporation known as the Pocono Spring Water Ice Company, to which, in September 1895, they made a lease for a term of ninety-nine years of so much of their lands as would be covered by the backing up of the water as a result of the construction of a 14-foot dam which they proposed to erect across the creek. The company was to

2. Copyright, 1944. Reprinted with permission of The American Law Institute.

have "the exclusive use of the water and its privileges." It was chartered for the purpose of "erecting a dam . . ., for pleasure, boating, skating, fishing and the cutting, storing and selling of ice." The dam was built, forming "Lake Naomi," somewhat more than a mile long and about one-third of a mile wide.

By deed dated March 20, 1899, the Pocono Spring Water Ice Company granted to "Frank C. Miller, his heirs and assigns forever, the exclusive right to fish and boat in all the waters of the said corporation at Naomi Pines, Pa." On February 17, 1900, Frank C. Miller (his wife Katherine D. Miller not joining) granted to Rufus W. Miller, his heirs and assigns forever, "all the one-fourth interest in and to the fishing, boating, and bathing rights and privileges at, in, upon and about Lake Naomi . . .; which said rights and privileges were granted and conveyed to me by the Pocono Spring Water Ice Company by their indenture of the 20th day of March, A.D. 1899." On the same day Frank C. Miller and Rufus W. Miller executed an agreement of business partnership, the purpose of which was the erection and operation of boat and bath houses on Naomi Lake and the purchase and maintenance of boats for use on the lake, the houses and boats to be rented for hire and the net proceeds to be divided between the parties in proportion to their respective interests in the bathing, boating and fishing privileges, namely, three-fourths to Frank C. Miller and one-fourth to Rufus W. Miller, the capital to be contributed and the losses to be borne in the same proportion. In pursuance of this agreement the brothers erected and maintained boat and bath houses at different points on the lake, purchased and rented out boats, and conducted the business generally, from the spring of 1900 until the death of Rufus W. Miller on October 11, 1925, exercising their control and use of the privileges in an exclusive, uninterrupted and open manner and without challenge on the part of anyone.

Discord began with the death of Rufus W. Miller, which terminated the partnership. Thereafter Frank C. Miller, and the executors and heirs of Rufus W. Miller, went their respective ways, each granting licenses without reference to the other. Under date of July 13, 1929, the executors of the Rufus W. Miller estate granted a license for the year 1929 to defendant, Lutheran Conference and Camp Association, which was the owner of a tract of ground abutting on the lake for a distance of about 100 feet, purporting to grant to defendant, its members, guests and campers, permission to boat, bathe and fish in the lake, a certain percentage of the receipts therefrom to be paid to the estate. Thereupon Frank C. Miller and his wife, Katherine D. Miller, filed the present bill in equity,[3] complaining that defendant was placing diving floats on the lake and "encouraging and instigating visitors and boarders" to bathe in the lake, and was threatening to hire out boats and canoes and in general to license its guests and others to boat, bathe and fish in the lake.[4] The bill prayed for an injunction to prevent defendant from trespassing on the lands covered by the waters of the lake,

3. Plaintiffs died during the pendency of the suit and their executors were substituted as parties plaintiff.

4. In 1904 Frank C. Miller, Rufus W. Miller and others had conveyed to the Pocono Pines Assembly and Summer

from erecting or maintaining any structures or other encroachments thereon, and from granting any bathing licenses. The court issued the injunction.

It is the contention of plaintiffs that, while the privileges of boating and fishing were granted in the deed from the Pocono Spring Water Ice Company to Frank C. Miller, no *bathing* rights were conveyed by that instrument. In 1903 all the property of the company was sold by the sheriff under a writ of fi. fa. on a mortgage bond which the company had executed in 1898. As a result of that sale the Pocono Spring Water Ice Company was entirely extinguished, and the title to its rights and property came into the ownership of the Pocono Pines Ice Company, a corporation chartered for "the supply of ice to the public."[5] In 1928 the title to the property of the Pocono Pines Ice Company became vested in Katherine D. Miller. Plaintiffs therefore maintain that the bathing rights, never having passed to Frank C. Miller, descended in ownership from the Pocono Spring Water Ice Company through the Pocono Pines Ice Company to plaintiff Katherine D. Miller, and that Frank C. Miller could not, and did not, give Rufus W. Miller any title to them. They further contend that even if such bathing rights ever did vest in Frank C. Miller, all of the boating, bathing and fishing privileges were easements in gross which were inalienable and indivisible, and when Frank C. Miller undertook to convey a one-fourth interest in them to Rufus W. Miller he not only failed to transfer a legal title to the rights but, in attempting to do so, extinguished the rights altogether as against Katherine D. Miller, who was the successor in title of the Pocono Spring Water Ice Company. It is defendant's contention, on the other hand, that the deed of 1899 from the Pocono Spring Water Ice Company to Frank C. Miller should be construed as transferring the bathing as well as the boating and fishing privileges, but that if Frank C. Miller did not obtain them by grant he and Rufus W. Miller acquired them by prescription, and that all of these rights were alienable and divisible even if they be considered as easements in gross, although they might more properly, perhaps, be regarded as licenses which became irrevocable because of the money spent upon their development by Frank C. Miller and Rufus W. Miller.[6] . . .

Schools the lot of ground which by mesne conveyances was subsequently acquired by defendant. In the deed there was reserved the right to build a road 100 feet in width along the lake front, and the parties also entered into an agreement contemplating the construction of a similar strip around the entire lake for purposes of a park road and pleasure ground. This development apparently was never carried out, but in the present bill plaintiffs alleged that defendant threatened to build bath houses and erect a diving board on this strip, and prayed injunctive relief from any violation of the restrictions in the deed and the agreement. This phase of the litigation, however, is apparently of minor importance and is therefore not discussed herein.

5. There being some question as to whether the 99-year leasehold interest passed under the sheriff's levy and sale, Frank C. Miller, Rufus W. Miller, and others, in July, 1911, confirmed the title thereto in the Pocono Pines Ice Company, and in September, 1911, the Pocono Pines Ice Company confirmed to Frank C. Miller the boating and fishing rights which had been granted to him in 1899 by the Pocono Spring Water Ice Company.

6. Shortly before the present action was begun the executors of the Rufus W. Miller estate brought a bill in equity against Frank C. Miller, as surviving partner, for an accounting of the assets of the partnership, and the attempt was there made to raise the questions which are now present-

We are thus brought to a consideration of the next question, which is whether the boating, bathing and fishing privileges were assignable by Frank C. Miller to Rufus W. Miller. What is the nature of such rights? In England it has been said that easements in gross do not exist at all, although rights of that kind have been there recognized. In this country such privileges have sometimes been spoken of as licenses, or as contractual in their nature, rather than as easements in gross. These are differences of terminology rather than of substance. We may assume, therefore, that these privileges are easements in gross, and we see no reason to consider them otherwise. It has uniformly been held that a profit in gross—for example, a right of mining or fishing—may be made assignable. Funk v. Haldeman, 53 Pa. 229; Tinicum Fishing Co. v. Carter, 61 Pa. 21, 39, 100 Am.Dec. 597; see cases cited 19 C.J. 870, note 25. In regard to easements in gross generally, there has been much controversy in the courts and by textbook writers and law students as to whether they have the attribute of assignability. There are dicta in Pennsylvania that they are non-assignable. Tinicum Fishing Co. v. Carter, supra, pages 38, 39; Lindenmuth v. Safe Harbor Water Power Corporation, 309 Pa. 58, 63, 64, 163 A. 159, 89 A.L.R. 1180; Commonwealth v. Zimmerman, 56 Pa.Super. 311, 315, 316. But there is forcible expression and even definite authority to the contrary. Tide Water Pipe Co. v. Bell, 280 Pa. 104, 112, 113, 124 A. 351, 40 A.L.R. 1516; Dalton Street Railway Co. v. Scranton, 326 Pa. 6, 12, 191 A. 133. Learned articles upon the subject are to be found in 32 Yale Law Journal 813; 38 Yale Law Journal 139; 22 Michigan Law Review 521; 40 Dickinson Law Review 46. There does not seem to be any reason why the law should prohibit the assignment of an easement in gross if the parties to its creation evidence their intention to make it assignable. Here, as in Tide Water Pipe Company v. Bell, supra, the rights of fishing and boating were conveyed to the grantee—in this case Frank C. Miller— "his heirs and assigns," thus showing that the grantor, the Pocono Spring Water Ice Company, intended to attach the attribute of assignability to the privileges granted. Moreover, as a practical matter, there is an obvious difference in this respect between easements for personal enjoyment and those designed for commercial exploitation; while there may be little justification for permitting assignments in the former case, there is every reason for upholding them in the latter.

The question of assignability of the easements in gross in the present case is not as important as that of their divisibility. It is argued by plaintiffs that even if held to be assignable such easements are not divisible, because this might involve an excessive user or "surcharge of the easement" subjecting the servient tenement to a greater burden than originally contemplated. The law does not take

ed to this court. That case went to the Superior Court: Miller v. Miller, 118 Pa. Super. 38, 179 A. 248. An account was stated covering the relations between the parties down to October 11, 1925, the date of the death of Rufus W. Miller, from which it appeared he was at that time indebted according to the partnership accounts, to Frank C. Miller, and accordingly the plaintiffs in that action were not entitled to receive anything from the partnership assets. The Superior Court held that the boating, bathing and fishing rights had not been conveyed by the two Millers to the partnership, but remained in their common ownership, and therefore could not be adjudicated in those proceedings.

that extreme position. It does require, however, that if there be a division, the easements must be used or exercised as an entirety. This rule had its earliest expression in Mountjoy's Case, which is reported in Co.Litt. 164b, 165a. It was there said, in regard to the grant of a right to dig for ore, that the grantee, Lord Mountjoy, "might assign his whole interest to one, two, or more; but then, if there be two or more, they could make no division of it, but work together with one stock." In Caldwell v. Fulton, 31 Pa. 475, 477, 478, 72 Am.Dec. 760, and in Funk v. Haldeman, 53 Pa. 229, that case was followed, and it was held that the right of a grantee to mine coal or to prospect for oil might be assigned, but if to more than one they must hold, enjoy and convey the right as an entirety, and not divide it in severalty. There are cases in other jurisdictions which also approve the doctrine of Mountjoy's Case, and hold that a mining right in gross is essentially integral and not susceptible of apportionment; an assignment of it is valid, but it cannot be aliened in such a way it may be utilized by grantor and grantee, or by several grantees, separately; there must be a joint user, nor can one of the tenants alone convey a share in the common right. Grubb v. Bayard, Fed.Cas.No. 5,849, C.C.E.D.Pa.; Harlow v. Lake Superior Iron Co., 36 Mich. 105, 121; Stanton v. T.L. Herbert & Sons, 141 Tenn. 440, 211 S.W. 353.

These authorities furnish an illuminating guide to the solution of the problem of divisibility of profits or easements in gross. They indicate that much depends upon the nature of the right and the terms of its creation, that "surcharge of the easement" is prevented if assignees exercise the right as "one stock," and that a proper method of enjoyment of the easement by two or more owners of it may usually be worked out in any given instance without insuperable difficulty.

In the present case it seems reasonably clear that in the conveyance of February 17, 1900, it was not the intention of Frank C. Miller to grant, and of Rufus W. Miller to receive, a separate right to sub-divide and sub-license the boating, fishing and bathing privileges on and in Lake Naomi, but only that they should together use such rights for commercial purposes, Rufus W. Miller to be entitled to one-fourth and Frank C. Miller to three-fourths of the proceeds resulting from their combined exploitation of the privileges. They were to hold the rights, in the quaint phraseology of Mountjoy's Case, as "one stock." Nor do the technical rules that would be applicable to a tenancy in common of a corporeal hereditament apply to the control of these easements in gross. Defendant contends that, as a tenant in common of the privileges, Rufus W. Miller individually was entitled to their use, benefit and possession and to exercise rights of ownership in regard thereto, including the right to license third persons to use them, subject only to the limitation that he must not thereby interfere with the similar rights of his cotenant. But the very nature of these easements prevents their being so exercised, inasmuch as it is necessary, because of the legal limitations upon their divisibility, that they should be utilized in common and not by two owners severally, and, as stated, this was evidently the intention of the brothers.

Summarizing our conclusions, we are of opinion (1) that Frank C. Miller acquired title to the boating and fishing privileges by grant and he and Rufus W. Miller to the bathing rights by prescription; (2) that he made a valid assignment of a one-fourth interest in them to Rufus W. Miller; but (3) that they cannot be commercially used and licenses thereunder granted without the common consent and joinder of the present owners, who with regard to them must act as "one stock." It follows that the executors of the estate of Rufus W. Miller did not have the right, in and by themselves, to grant a license to defendant.

The decree is affirmed; costs to be paid by defendant.

NOTE

Restatement of Property § 493 (1944): "The apportionability of an easement in gross is determined by the manner or the terms of its creation." Comment: ". . . If the owners of the undivided shares or the owners of the divided parts proceed to use the servient tenement independently of each other, the result may be to increase greatly the total use over the use which would probably be made were the easement to continue to be regarded by its owners, and operations under it made by them, as a unit." If the easement is exclusive, there is an "inference in the usual case that the easement was intended in its creation to be apportionable. This inference is very strong in cases where an increase in use is in fact advantageous to the possessor of the servient tenement. *Illustration*: 1. A, the owner and possessor of Blackacre, grants to B, his heirs and assigns, the exclusive privilege of mining iron in Blackacre. B agrees to pay for the privilege a specified amount for each ton of ore mined. B assigns his right to mine in the east one-half of Blackacre to C and in the west one-half to D. C and D are entitled to mine independently of each other in the tracts assigned to them respectively." But in the case of a nonexclusive easement in gross, "the owner and possessor of the servient tenement has not only the privilege himself to make the use authorized by the easement, but he retains the power to create like privileges in others. The apportionability of the easement by its owner would be inconsistent with such a power in the owner and possessor of the servient tenement. Because of this, the apportionability of the easement will not be assumed in the absence of a clear indication to the contrary in the manner or terms of its creation."

A landowner granted to X Power Company, "its successors and assigns, the perpetual easement to construct, operate, and maintain one or more pole or tower lines . . . for the purpose of transmitting electricity", over a strip of land 50 feet wide and 2,500 feet long. Subsequently X Power Company authorized Y Power Company to attach a limited number of its wires to poles of X Power Company located on the described strip. Holding that the landowner was entitled to compensation for an increased burden on his land, the court said: "The additional lines . . . place an additional burden on plaintiff's land without his consent. Two power companies enjoy an easement over his land. He granted only one." Grimes v. Virginia Electric & Power Co., 245 N.C. 583, 96 S.E.2d 713 (1957).

For a recent assessment of the easement in gross, see Note, The Easement in Gross Revisited: Transferability and Divisibility Since 1945, 39 Vanderbilt L.Rev. 109 (1986).

---

(5) Termination

LINDSEY v. CLARK

Supreme Court of Appeals of Virginia, 1952.
193 Va. 522, 69 S.E.2d 342.

Buchanan, Justice. This suit was instituted by the Lindseys to enjoin the Clarks from using a driveway along the north side of the Lindsey lots and to have themselves adjudged the fee simple owners of the two lots claimed by them. The trial court held that the Clarks owned a right of way on the south side of the Lindsey lots and, in effect, put the Lindseys on terms to make it available to them or else allow the Clarks to continue using the one on the north side.

There is no controversy about the controlling facts.

In 1937 the Clarks were the owners of four adjoining lots, Nos. 31, 32, 33 and 34, each fronting 25 feet on the east side of Magnolia avenue in West Waynesboro, and running back 150 feet to a 20-foot alley. The Clark residence was on Nos. 31 and 32.

By deed dated July 24, 1937, the Clarks conveyed to C. W. Six and Mabel G. Six, his wife, the latter being a daughter of the Clarks, the front two-thirds of Lots 33 and 34, being a frontage of 50 feet and extending back 100 feet. On the rear one-third of these two lots Clark erected a dwelling and garage for rental purposes. After this conveyance the Sixes built a house on their property, approximately 15 feet from the Clark line on the north and about 8 feet from their own line on the south. The Clark deed to the Sixes contained this reservation: "There is reserved, however, a right-of-way ten (10) feet in width, along the South side of the two lots herein conveyed for the benefit of the property in the rear."

By deed of January 16, 1939, the Sixes conveyed their property to William H. McGhee and wife, with the same reservation; and by deed of March 16, 1944, the McGhees conveyed the property to the Lindseys, without any reservation.

These three deeds were all made with general warranty and both the deed to the Sixes and the deed to the McGhees were duly recorded prior to the date of the deed to the Lindseys.

Notwithstanding that the 10-foot right of way was reserved by Clark along the south side of the property conveyed to the Sixes, now owned by the Lindseys, Clark proceeded to use it along the north side of the Six property, and has so used it ever since, without objection by the Sixes, or by the McGhees, or by the Lindseys until a few months before this suit was brought. There is no explanation of this change of location. Six, a witness for the Lindseys, testified that Clark stood in the driveway on the north and said, "I am reserving this driveway to get to my back property." The time of that statement is not shown, but the words suggest it was at or before the time of the conveyance to the Sixes. When the McGhees bought the property in 1939, Six pointed out to them the driveway on the north, but the reservation in the deed he made to the McGhees was, as stated, on the south.

In 1946 the Lindseys had their attorney write to Clark, referring to the right of way in the deed to the McGhees, their grantors, and complaining, not of its location, but of its being used for parking purposes. Again, on November 7, 1949, they had their attorney write Clark, calling attention to the fact that the reservation was along the south side of their property and complaining about the use of a water line on their property which had not been reserved. The Lindseys, the letter stated, wanted to erect a line fence and suggested a discussion of the matter before this was done.

The Lindseys contend that the Clarks now have no right of way across their property because none was reserved along the north side and the one reserved on the south side has been abandoned and thereby extinguished. The trial court held it had not been abandoned and that holding was clearly right.

Abandonment is a question of intention. A person entitled to a right of way or other easement in land may abandon and extinguish such right by acts *in pais*; and a cessation of use coupled with acts or circumstances clearly showing an intention to abandon the right will be as effective as an express release of the right. Scott v. Moore, 98 Va. 668, 687, 37 S.E. 342, 348; Daniel v. Doughty, 120 Va. 853, 858, 92 S.E. 848, 850; Magee v. Omansky, 187 Va. 422, 430, 46 S.E.2d 443, 448.

But mere non-user of an easement created by deed, for a period however long, will not amount to abandonment. In addition to the non-user there must be acts or circumstances clearly manifesting an intention to abandon; or an adverse user by the owner of the servient estate, acquiesced in by the owner of the dominant estate, for a period sufficient to create a prescriptive right. Watts v. C. F. Johnson &c. Corp., 105 Va. 519, 525, 54 S.E. 317, 319; 28 C.J.S., Easements, § 60, p. 724. Nor is a right of way extinguished by the habitual use by its owner of another equally convenient way unless there is an intentional abandonment of the former way. Scott v. Moore, supra, 98 Va. at page 686, 37 S.E. at page 348. 17 Am.Jur., Easements, § 144, p. 1029.

The burden of proof to show the abandonment of an easement is upon the party claiming such abandonment, and it must be established by clear and unequivocal evidence. Daniel v. Doughty, supra, 120 Va. at page 858, 92 S.E. at page 850; Blanford v. Trust Co., 142 Va. 73, 82, 128 S.E. 640, 643.

Clark specifically reserved a right of way over the lots now owned by the Lindseys. Very clearly he had no intention of abandoning that right of way. He was evidently mistaken as to where it was located; but his grantees, the Sixes, were likewise mistaken, as were also their grantees, the McGhees. Clark's use on the wrong location of the right of way reserved by him did not establish an intention on his part to abandon his right of way on the right location. He could not have intended to abandon his easement on the south of the Lindsey lots when he did not know that that was where his easement was.

The residence built by the Sixes, and now occupied by the Lindseys, encroaches by about two feet on the 10-foot alley when located on the south side, and the Lindsey property on that side within the 10-foot space is terraced and planted with shrubbery and a tree. The Lindseys argue that the Clarks are estopped from claiming a right of way on that side because Clark knew where the Sixes were building the house. The only testimony about that is from Six, who said that Clark was away at work when the house was being built but came and went every day to and from his home on the adjoining property, saw where the house was located and made no objection; but Six also said that Clark had nothing to do with locating the house. There is no evidence that Clark knew, any more than Six knew, that the house was encroaching on the right of way. Clark did not think the right of way was on that side. Even if he had known it was there, he would not likely have known that Six was building on it. The location of the house was not influenced by anything Clark did or said. Clark knew nothing about the matter that Six did not know.

"It is essential to the application of the principles of equitable estoppel or estoppel in pais, that the party claiming to have been influenced by the conduct or declarations of another to his injury, was not only ignorant of the true state of facts, but had no convenient and available means of acquiring such information, and where the facts are known to both parties, and both had the same means of ascertaining the truth, there can be no estoppel." Lindsay v. James, 188 Va. 646, 659, 51 S.E.2d 326, 332, 7 A.L.R.2d 597.

The Lindseys had both actual and constructive knowledge of the situation. The driveway was there on the north side when they bought the property and Lindsey testified he could see where cars had been using it. They negligently failed to have their title examined but they are, of course, chargeable with the information contained in the recorded deeds. Pillow v. Southwest &c. Imp. Co., 92 Va. 144, 152, 23 S.E. 32, 34; Florence v. Morien, 98 Va. 26, 33, 34 S.E. 890, 891; 15 M.J., Recording Acts, § 15, p. 561.

The suit therefore developed this situation: The Clarks were entitled to a 10-foot right of way along the south side of the Lindsey property. That right of way was partially blocked by the Lindsey house with its terraces and shrubbery. To require their removal would be very expensive to the Lindseys and damaging to their property. The Clarks were willing to let their right of way continue to be located on the north side.

The court was well warranted in resolving the matter by applying the maxim "He who seeks equity must do equity." That means that "he who seeks the aid of an equity court subjects himself to the imposition of such terms as the settled principles of equity require, and that whatever be the nature of the controversy between the parties, and whatever be the nature of the remedy demanded, the court will not confer its equitable relief on the party seeking its interposition and aid, unless he has acknowledged and conceded, or will admit and provide for, all the equitable rights, claims, and demands justly belonging to the adversary party, and growing out of, or necessarily involved in, the subject matter of the controversy." 30 C.J.S. Equity, § 91, p. 461. 2 Pom.Eq.Jur., 5th ed., § 385, pp. 51–2.

A court of equity may in a case in which the principles and rules of equity demand it, condition its granting of the relief sought by the complainant upon the enforcement of a claim or equity held by the defendant which the latter could not enforce in any other way. United Cigarette Mach. Co. v. Brown, 119 Va. 813, 825, 89 S.E. 850, 855, L.R.A.1917F, 1100; 2 Pom.Eq.Jur., supra, § 386a, p. 57; 19 Am.Jur., Equity, § 463, p. 319.

The decree of the trial court provided: "The Court will not require the expensive removal of the obstruction, so long as the right-of-way along the north side of the property is made available. However, it is ordered that the defendants desist from the use of the right-of-way for any purpose other than the use of the rear one-third portion of Lots 33 and 34, and only for the right of passage over and across the said right-of-way to and from the property in the rear." And, further, "Should the complainants make an election under this order, a further order will be entered fixing the rights of the respective parties."

The decree appealed from is affirmed and the cause is remanded for further decree as indicated.

Affirmed and remanded.

NOTES

1. In Aggregate Supply Co. v. Sewall, 217 Ga. 407, 122 S.E.2d 580 (1961), the court took the position that a right to remove sand and gravel from the land of another is a profit a prendre, which is a corporeal interest, which is not subject to termination by abandonment. Recall the observation in the Restatement of Property that there is no significant distinction in American law between easements and profits à prendre. Section 450, Special Note.

2. A subdivider dedicated Lillian Dells Drive to the City of Lake Bluff upon condition that the city keep the road in repair and maintain it as a pleasure drive only. The city contended that it was not subject to these conditions, inasmuch as it had acquired, prior to the dedication, an easement to use this road as a public way. The court said: "It is settled law that where there is a unity of title to and possession of the dominant and servient estates in the same owner, that fact operates to extinguish the servient estate absolutely and forever. No one may have an easement in his own land. . . . Here, the city held an easement for public use of this roadway, the servient estate. Subsequently it obtained a conveyance of the roadway in fee, the dominant estate. By application of the general rule above, the easement is merged in the fee, extinguishing the servient estate." Lake Bluff v.

Dalitsch, 415 Ill. 476, 114 N.E.2d 654, 659 (1953). Is this reasoning sound? Termination of easements by merger and estoppel is discussed in 3 Powell, Real Property ¶ 425 (1977).

3. "An easement created by express written grant is, if recorded, operative against subsequent purchasers for value without notice. . . . But when the easement is not based upon any written instrument such as an easement by prescription or implication, it would seem that the recording acts should have no application. It is the law that a purchaser of the servient estate will be charged with notice of all apparent easements, and the purchaser is bound where a reasonably careful inspection of the premises would disclose the existence of the easement. But what will we say as to an easement that is created by implication or prescription, and hence not subject to recordation, and is of such nature that it cannot be seen or is not apparent from any marks on the servient land? . . . There is a clear distinction between the rule of law that requires apparency of an unrecorded easement for its creation and the rule with respect to the extinction of an established easement. . . . It is our holding that such an easement is not terminated by such a sale, and the purchaser takes subject to the easement." Mulroney, J., in McKeon v. Brammer, 238 Iowa 1113, 29 N.W.2d 518, 174 A.L.R. 1229 (1947).

Compare Renner v. Johnson, 2 Ohio St.2d 195, 207 N.E.2d 751 (1965), where the court said: "The implied easement is based upon the equitable right to reform the grant. Hence, such an equitable right should not be enforceable against a bona fide purchaser for value who has no notice of such easement. . . . The owner of the dominant parcel could request a deed for the easement from the owner of the servient parcel. If given, he could record it. If refused, he could bring an action in equity to establish his legal right to the easement."

B. REAL COVENANTS AND EQUITABLE SERVITUDES

Suppose that Cribbet and Johnson, owners of adjoining vacant lots on a bluff above a scenic lake, executed a written agreement in which each covenanted "for the protection of scenic views from these lots to erect no structure on the rear half of his lot and to contribute the sum of $1,000 annually to keep all vegetation on the rear half of his lot cut to a maximum height of five feet." The agreement was recorded properly and promptly. Subsequently, Cribbet conveyed his lot to Findley, and Johnson conveyed his lot to Smith. Is the Cribbet-Johnson agreement enforceable against Findley by Smith?

Is there any good reason to deny such enforcement? Is there any doubt that Cribbet and Johnson intended that this agreement bind and benefit subsequent owners of the respective lots? Would such enforcement by contrary to any policy that should override the intent of Cribbet and Johnson? Do these covenants impair alienability of land to any greater extent than would the same restrictions in the form of a special limitation? A condition? An easement? If Findley refuses to abide by the agreement, can Smith enforce the agreement to pay $1,000 for the lot's upkeep against Cribbet?

In addition to the above questions, one must consider the applicability of a cluster of time-honored doctrines that tend to prevent a subsequent owner of a covenantee's land from enforcing a covenant against a subsequent owner of a covenantor's land. These fetters on volition, which have been substantially loosened in equity, are not easily justified by contemporary policy. Possibly their existence can by explained by noting that they emerged during an era when the assignment of choses in action was not permitted: to allow covenants to run with the land at all may have been viewed as an exceptional development that should be cautiously confined. What, if any, are the relevant policy considerations today?[1]

---

(1) THE TRADITIONAL ELEMENTS OF REAL COVENANTS

GALLAGHER v. BELL

Court of Special Appeals of Maryland, 1986.
69 Md.App. 199, 516 A.2d 1028.

WILNER, JUDGE.

In 1960, appellants George and Judith Gallagher bought a charming Eighteenth Century tenant house situated on about a half acre of land in Montgomery County. It was, unfortunately, in the middle of a larger tract owned by appellees that was intended for eventual development. . . .

All the land involved in this case—something more than 34½ acres—was once owned by the Sisters of Mercy of the Union in the United States of America, Incorporated (the Sisters). The land lies generally to the north and east of Bradley Boulevard and had access to that road by means of Kendale Road, an 18–foot private road that ran just over a mile from Bradley Boulevard to the Sisters' "Villa Marie" Mansion House. Kendale Road also served the old tenant house on the land.

In 1959, the Sisters sold the Mansion House and some immediately surrounding acreage to the Franciscans, retaining the balance of the tract. . . . Later in 1959, the Sisters sold the remainder of the tract, save only the half-acre parcel on which the tenant house was situate, to appellees F. Meade Bell and David P. Bell. It was understood that the Bells, who are developers, were buying the 34½–acre tract in order to subdivide and develop it, for the contract mentions "the proposed subdivision." The last clause of the contract dealt with the excepted parcel; it provided: "The existing house and lot in Section 4 shall be excluded from this contract. Subsequent purchaser of said lot and house shall agree to dedicate half of street bounding said lot and share

1. The drafting of the Restatement provisions on this subject evoked sharply conflicting views. See Clark, Covenants and Interests Running With Land (2d ed. 1947); Rundell, Judge Clark on the American Law Institute's Law of Real Covenants: A Comment, 53 Yale L.J. 312 (1944). See also on this subject Berger, A Policy Analysis of Promises Respecting the Use of Land, 55 Minn.L.Rev. 167 (1970).

pro-rata cost of installing street and utilities by this purchaser of Section 4."

In April, 1960, the Gallaghers purchased the half-acre parcel and tenant house from the Sisters. In the contract, Mr. Gallagher agreed "to dedicate half of streets bounding said lot and shall share pro-rata cost of installing street and utilities by F.M. and D.P. Bell." It was further agreed that the contract would be binding on the principals and their respective heirs, successors, and assigns and that its provisions would "survive the execution and delivery of the deed . . . and shall not be merged therein."

. . .

. . . [O]n June 16, 1961, the Gallaghers entered into an agreement with the Bells under which:

> (1) the Bells granted to the Gallaghers "a temporary right of way over that portion of the existing private road now known as Kentsdale Drive leading to Bradley Boulevard from [the Gallaghers' property] which crosses the [Bells' property] until such time as said portion of said private road is supplanted by a dedicated and paved road giving access from the [Gallaghers' property] to Aldershot Drive as now dedicated, at which time the right to the use of said portion of said private road by [the Gallaghers] shall terminate" and
>
> (2) "[A]s part of the consideration for this agreement the [Gallaghers] do hereby covenant and agree for themselves, their heirs and assigns, that they will dedicate one-half of the streets bounding on their said property and shall share pro-rata the cost of the installation of said streets and the utilities by [the Bells]."

. . .

. . . [I]n October, 1979, the Gallaghers sold their property to Deborah Camalier. Ms. Camalier, who became aware of the recorded 1961 agreement between the Gallaghers and the Bells, apparently insisted on an indemnity from the Gallaghers.

. . .

The Bells finally got started on the roads in the area of the Gallagher/Camalier property in 1983. In July of that year, they made demand on Ms. Camalier for some $18,000. When Ms. Camalier refused payment, relying on her indemnity agreement, the Bells made demand on the Gallaghers, and, when they rejected the demand, the Bells filed this lawsuit. It is undisputed that, at the time the suit was filed, the streets for which contribution was sought had not yet been completed.

The Gallaghers defended the action on a number of bases, including that the covenant they made in 1961 was a covenant running with the land and that their liability on it terminated when they conveyed the property to Ms. Camalier in 1980. If there is any continuing liability on the covenant, they argued, it is that either of Ms. Camalier or Mr. and Mrs. Sindelar, to whom Ms. Camalier conveyed the property in December, 1983. Regarding the nature of the covenant to be a factual matter, however, the court submitted the issue to a jury, which returned a verdict for the Bells in the amount of $7,000.

From the judgment entered on that verdict and the court's refusal to grant a judgment n.o.v., the Gallaghers have brought this appeal. The Gallaghers contend that the nature of the covenant was an issue of law to be decided by the court, that it should not have been submitted to the jury, and that, on this record, the court should have declared the covenant to run with the land. If it ran with the land, they continue, their liability under it ended when they conveyed the property. . . .

Nature of the Covenant

Covenants made by parties to the conveyance of an interest in land may be regarded as being either personal in nature or as running with the land. The difference, as observed in 5 R. Powell, *The Law of Real Property,* § 673[1], p. 60–36, "hinges upon whether the original covenanting parties' respective rights or duties can devolve upon their successors."

Normally, the question of whether a covenant runs with the land arises when either the party seeking to enforce the covenant is someone other than the original covenantee or when the party against whom enforcement is sought is someone other than the original covenantor. The issue then becomes whether the non-covenantee who has in some manner succeeded to the interest of the covenantee can enforce the covenant or, conversely, whether the non-covenantor who has succeeded to the interest of the covenantor is liable on it. This case is different. Here, the plaintiffs and the defendants are the original contracting parties. The Gallaghers are being asked to perform on a promise they made directly to the Bells.

. . . [A]lthough the courts are not unanimous in this view, there is a body of law to the effect that, if the covenant runs with the land, the liability of the covenantor ends when he conveys the burdened land.

The earliest source generally cited for the concept of a covenant running with the land and being enforceable by or against persons other than the original contracting parties is *Spencer's Case,* 5 Co.Rep. 16a, 77 Eng.Rep. 72 (QB 1583). The plaintiff there leased certain property to S for a term of 21 years. S, for himself and his executors and administrators, promised in the lease that he, his executors, administrators, or assigns would build a brick wall on the premises. S assigned his leasehold interest to J, who then assigned it to Clark. When the wall was not built, Spencer sued Clark on the covenant. Although the Court denied recovery, it set out in its opinion a number of principles for determining when such extended liability would accrue. The two major criteria, known generally as the "in esse" and "touch and concern" tests, were summarized nearly three centuries later in *Lynn v. Mount Savage Iron Co.,* 34 Md. 603, 634–35 (1871), as follows:

> "1st. That when the covenant extends to a thing in *esse,* parcel of the demise, the thing to be done by force of the covenant is in a manner annexed and appurtenant to the thing demised, and shall

run with the land, and shall bind the assignee, although he be not bound by *express words;* as if the lessee covenant to repair the houses, this is parcel of the contract, and extends to the supporting of the thing demised; but, because the covenant in that case was in respect of a thing which was not in *esse* at the time of the demise made, but to be newly built after, and therefore bound only the covenantor, his executors or administrators, *and not the assignee,* the covenant did not, by the law, annex. 2nd. But if the lessee had covenanted for himself *and his assigns,* that they would make a new wall upon some part of the thing demised, that forasmuch as it is to be done upon the land demised, that it should bind the assignee; for although the covenant doth extend to a thing to be newly made, yet it is to be made upon the thing demised, and the assignee is to take the benefit of it, and therefore shall bind the assignee *by express words.*"

(Emphasis in original.)

The questions addressed in *Spencer's Case* have been before the courts many times and in many different contexts over the past 400 years, and, not unexpectedly, the principles laid down in that case have undergone some refinement. Powell notes that "[t]he elements most often said to be required for covenants to run at law are that: (1) the covenant 'touch and concern' the land; (2) the original covenanting parties intend the covenant to run; and (3) there be some form of privity of estate." A fourth requirement, "sometimes mentioned," is that the covenant be in writing. § 673[1], pp. 60–37, 60–38.

. . .

(a) Touch and Concern

The "touch and concern" test is a key one. As early as *Glenn v. Canby,* [24 Md. 127, 130 (1866)], the Court announced as "established doctrine" that "a covenant to run with the land must extend to the land, so that the thing required to be done will affect the quality, value, or mode of enjoying the estate conveyed, and thus constitute a condition annexed, or appurtunent to it. . . ." See also *Whalen v. Balto. & Ohio R. Co.,* supra, 108 Md. at 20, 69 A. 390: "The question as to whether the covenant runs with the land does not depend on its being performed on the land itself, but its performance must touch and concern the land, or some right or easement annexed or appurtenant thereto. . . ."

. . .

. . . That, of course, looks at the issue essentially from the benefit point of view. Powell, at § 673[2], p. 60–41, states that the generally accepted test for the "touch and concern" test is that proposed by Dean Harry Bigelow; i.e.,

"[I]f the covenantor's legal interest in land is rendered less valuable by the covenant's performance, then the burden of the covenant satisfies the requirement that the covenant touch and concern land. If, on the other hand, the covenantee's legal interest in land is rendered more valuable by the covenant's performance, then the benefit of the covenant satisfies the requirement that the covenant touch and concern land."

Both Tiffany (3 H. Tiffany, *The Law of Real Property,* (3d ed. (1939)) and the *Restatement of Property* (§ 537 (1944)) generally adopt this more complete way of viewing the criterion.[8] . . .

Here, of course, we are concerned only with the running of the burden, for the party seeking to enforce the covenant is the original covenantee. There is no doubt that the covenantees would be benefited by performance of the promise; their interest in their land is obviously rendered more valuable by it. It is equally true that, in terms of Dean Bigelow's test, the Gallaghers' interest in their property was immediately and continually rendered less valuable by the covenant. Even under the *Restatement* benefit-oriented test, the fact is that, while the particular covenant was a detriment to the Gallaghers, the transaction from which that covenant arose was of benefit to them. In return for their promise, they received a right-of-way that, at least arguably, they did not otherwise have and that was essential to avoid their being landlocked. Appellees throughout have regarded the extension of that right-of-way as valuable consideration and have not suggested that it does not bear a reasonable relation to the burden imposed on the Gallaghers.

Covenants to pay money have often been found to run with the land. . . . [T]he Court of Appeals has found covenants to pay rent and taxes, to keep demised or mortgaged property insured, to repair or rebuild such premises, and to build and maintain railroad depots and facilities on conveyed land to "touch and concern" the land. . . . Certainly, this covenant has no lesser connection to the land. Under any of the tests noted, it clearly "touches and concerns" the land owned by the Gallaghers.

(b) Intent

The second factor mentioned by Powell is whether the parties intended the covenant to run with the land. Both the *Restatement* (§ 531, pp. 3196–98) and Powell (§ 673[2][b], pp. 60–47, 60–48) make

8. The *Restatement* test is not quite the same as that espoused by Dean Bigelow or Tiffany. It provides, in § 537, p. 3218:

"The successors in title to land respecting the use of which the owner has made a promise can be bound as promisors only if

(a) the performance of the promise will benefit the promisee or other beneficiary of the promise in the physical use or enjoyment of the land possessed by him, or

(b) the consummation of the transaction of which the promise is a part will operate to benefit and is for the benefit of the promisor in the physical use or enjoyment of land possessed by him, and the burden on the land of the promisor bears a reasonable relation to the benefit received by the person benefited."

This requires that some aspect of the promise be of benefit in the use and enjoyment of land. Either the promisee must be benefited in the enjoyment of his land or the transaction spawning the promise must benefit the promisor in the enjoyment of the servient land. It would seem that subsection (a) concerns the running of the benefit, whereas subsection (b) sets the standard for the running of the burden. Comment b, for example, states, in relevant part, that "[f]or the burden of a promise to run the promise must be one respecting the use of the land of the promisor." *Restatement, supra,* at p. 3219.

clear that the benefit or the burden of a covenant will not pass to a successor in interest unless the parties intended that result. Unlike the "touch and concern" test, which looks objectively at the nature and quality of the covenant and seeks to measure the relationship between its performance and someone's enjoyment of land, the intention requirement "focuses on the subjective state of mind of the original covenanting parties." Powell, supra, at p. 60–49.

Subjective intent is generally a question of fact for resolution by a jury, and, thus, if the issue is in dispute, it is ordinarily inappropriate for a court to decide it on motion. But that is not an absolute prohibition. Like any other question of fact, if, after viewing the evidence and all *reasonable* inferences from it in favor of the non-moving party, the court is able to determine an answer as a matter of law, it may do so by granting a motion for judgment under Md.Rule 2–519 or a motion for judgment n.o.v. under Rule 2–532.

. . .

The record here reveals the following: (1) by inserting this same requirement in their contract with the Sisters, appellees made clear their intent to impose the obligation on whoever purchased the half-acre lot, not the Gallaghers in particular; (2) the covenant at issue was in conformance with that requirement and simply confirmed the obligation imposed on Mr. Gallagher by his contract with the Sisters; (3) the covenant at issue expressly extends to the assigns of the Gallaghers; (4) that covenant was intended to benefit adjacent land retained by the covenantee; (5) the time for performance was uncertain and would not necessarily occur while the Gallaghers were in title; (6) the Gallaghers have consistently maintained that the covenant ran with the land; (7) on July 20, 1983—before commencement of this litigation—appellees filed among the Land Records of Montgomery County a Declaration of Covenant reciting the Gallaghers' sale to Ms. Camalier, asserting that "by virtue of said conveyance, Deborah N. Camalier became the assignee of the Gallaghers *and bound by the aforesaid Agreement regarding pro rata payment of the cost of installation of streets and utilities*" and attesting that the purpose of the Declaration was "to memorialize the pro rata costs *attributable to the Property now owned by the said Deborah N. Camalier*" (emphasis added); (8) at trial, counsel for appellees specifically characterized the 1961 agreement as "a document that constitutes a covenant and runs with the land"; and (9) also at trial, F. Meade Bell, one of the appellees, acknowledged that, because of the inclusion of "heirs and assigns" in the 1961 agreement, he initially sought recovery from Ms. Camalier and that he set his sight on the Gallaghers only because of the indemnity agreement between her and the Gallaghers.

Each of these facts indicates that the covenant was intended to run with the land. Indeed, the last three enumerated above, taken together, constitute a virtual concession by appellees to that effect. Against that, appellees seek to draw an inference that the 1961 covenant was a personal one from (1) the "fact" that they already had a similar covenant running with the land by virtue of the clause in Mr. Gallagher's contract with the Sisters, and (2) the indemnity agreement between the Gallaghers and Ms. Camalier.

We do not regard such an inference as a *reasonable* one. As noted, the contract with the Sisters was not signed by Mrs. Gallagher, and the covenant therein was not included in the deed. It therefore did not directly bind her or her assigns. She became directly bound only by virtue of the 1961 agreement with appellees. If there is an inference to be drawn from the indemnity agreement, it seems to us that it is an unfavorable one to appellees. On this record, the only reasonable inference that can be drawn from the agreement is that Ms. Camalier recognized that, by taking title with knowledge of the recorded 1961 agreement, she would become liable on the covenant and that she desired to have recourse to the original covenantors. As noted, appellees, in their 1983 Declaration of Covenant, shared that view.

On this record, therefore, we think it clear as a matter of law that the parties intended the covenant at issue to run with the land and to bind the assigns of the Gallaghers.

(c) Privity

The requirement that there be privity of estate between the parties in order that a covenant run with the land appears to stem not from *Spencer's Case,* which mentions the concept of privity only in passing and in connection with leases and conveyances of personalty, but rather from Webb v. Russell, 3 T.R. 393, 100 Eng.Rep. 639 (KB 1789). The facts of that case were a bit complex and are not especially germane to what is now before us; what is important is Lord Kenyon's pronouncement that "[i]t is not sufficient that a covenant is concerning the land, but, in order to make it run with the land, there must be privity of estate between the covenanting parties." That requirement of privity, which in fact was present in *Spencer's Case,* became firmly ingrained in the Maryland law.. . . . The question is, what kind of privity is required?

Powell points out that there are at least three kinds of privity of estate that have been mentioned by the courts—mutual privity, requiring that the original parties have had a mutual and continuing interest in the same land; horizontal privity, requiring that the covenant be made in connection with the conveyance of an estate in fee from one of the parties to the other; and vertical privity, requiring only that "the person presently claiming the benefit, or being subjected to the burden, is a successor to the estate of the original person so benefited or burdened." Powell, supra, § 673[2], p. 60–64. He further observes that:

> "Many modern cases still require some type of privity for covenants to run at law. Unfortunately, there is frequently no consistency as to the type of privity required even within a jurisdiction, and many courts just do not state which type of privity they require. According to one authority, as of 1970, six states which formerly required horizontal privity had abolished the requirement, and it had been expressly adopted in only one state in the

twenty-seven years previous to 1970. Modern legal writers unanimously favor the abolition of at least mutual and horizontal privity."

The modern view, rather clearly, is that no more than vertical privity is required. That is also the view of Judge Charles E. Clark, formerly of the Court of Appeals for the Second Circuit and one of the preeminent authorities on the law of covenants. *See* Clark, *Covenants and Interests Running with Land* (2d ed. 1947), p. 117; . . .

We see nothing in the Maryland cases heretofore decided precluding our adoption of this modern and, to us, more rational view. Focusing on the precise relationship of the original contracting parties can create artificial results, causing covenants to be regarded as personal (and thus binding on persons who have long since conveyed the land or, conversely, unenforceable by successors to the covenantee) when the covenant touches and concerns the land and the parties clearly intended for it to run with the land. The "vertical privity" concept avoids that problem and focuses instead on the devolutional relationships, where, we think, the focus should be.

(d) Conclusion

Holding

Upon this analysis, we conclude that the covenant in question—to pay a pro rata share of the cost of installing the streets adjacent to the property—was one that runs with the land.

Consequence

The essence of a covenant running with the land was described in Donelson v. Polk, supra, 64 Md. at 504:

> "The principle of law is a familiar one, that the liability of an assignee of a term to the original lessor, or those claiming under him, grows out of the privity of estate, and that such liability continues only so long as such privity of estate exists. So long as the privity of estate continues, the assignee is liable upon all covenants that *run with the land* . . .; and for any breach of such covenants, the lessor may sue him during the continuance of the assignment. *But as his liability springs altogether from his relation to the land, it follows that when he severs that relation he puts an end to his liability for any future breaches of the covenant contained in the lease,* whether such covenants be expressed or implied. In regard to this there is no question or conflict of authority."

(Emphasis added.) See also Union Trust Co. v. Rosenburg, supra, 171 Md. at 415–20, 189 A. 421; Com. Bldg. Ass'n v. Robinson, supra, 90 Md. at 618, 45 A. 449; Nickel v. Brown, supra, 75 Md. at 184–85, 35 A. 1086; 5 Powell, supra, § 673[3], pp. 60–73, –74.

Those cases, however, involved actions against assignees of the original covenantor. Whether a different rule is applied where, as here, the original covenantor is the defendant is not altogether clear.

Noting that the question has "not been extensively litigated," Powell observes, at § 673[3], that

> "A liability continuing after the original covenantor had lost control of the burdened land would be harsh, and might well lessen the willingness of people to utilize covenants. It is not surprising, therefore, to find several courts holding that the conveyance of the burdened land ends the covenantor's liability. A few states have enacted statutes to this same effect. This result normally embodies the intention of the original parties reasonably inferable from the circumstances of the original covenant, giving due emphasis to the nature of the conduct promised. This is particularly true with respect to covenants to render services or to curtail the use of the burdened land; but is less likely to be true in the case of covenants to pay money, where the personal credit of the original covenantor is an important factor."

. . .

. . . In that regard, the record here clearly indicates that the Bells were not relying especially upon the credit of the Gallaghers in extracting the covenant. They wanted, and insisted upon, the undertaking from whomever purchased the burdened tract, and indeed turned to the Gallaghers only when they mistakenly concluded that Ms. Camalier was not liable because of her indemnity agreement. . . .

We need not, in this case, go so far as to announce such a rule as a matter of law, or indeed as to every kind of covenant that may run with the land. It will suffice to conclude only that the continuing liability of an original covenantor on a covenant of the type involved here will end upon his conveyance of the burdened property if the parties intended for that to be the case, and that the record here demonstrates such an intent. . . .

. . . Any liability they may have under their indemnity agreement—a matter not now before us and upon which we express no opinion—would flow to Ms. Camalier and not to appellees. The court therefore erred in not entering judgment in favor of the Gallaghers, as it was thrice requested to do.

JUDGMENT REVERSED; . . . .

NOTES

1. As the principal case suggests, the law of real covenants has roots deep in English common law, and many of the traditional elements required for a real covenant have been modified or abandoned over time. The *in esse* rule, mentioned by the court early in its opinion, is an example. It originated in Spencer's Case, 5 Co. 16a, 77 Eng.Rep. 72 (K.B.1583) and required the covenantor expressly to bind his assigns if the covenant dealt with something which was not yet in existence. If the requisite language was missing, the covenant would not run with the land. Most courts have repudiated this doctrine on the grounds that (1) Lord Coke's resolutions in Spencer's Case may not actually have been the holding of the court in that case and (2) the rule is

supported by no good reason. Sexauer v. Wilson, 136 Iowa 357, 113 N.W. 941 (1907).

Nonetheless, the absence of any reference to the covenantor's "heirs, successors and assigns" should not be ignored. The *in esse* rule may still be the law in some states. See Mercantile–Safe Deposit & Trust Co. v. Baltimore, 308 Md. 627, 521 A.2d 734 (1987); Williams, Restrictions on the Use of Land, 27 Tex.L.Rev. 419, 423 (1949). Moreover, the phrase may be relevant in determining whether the parties intended the covenant to run with the land. See Charping v. J.P. Scurry & Co., 296 S.C. 312, 372 S.E.2d 120 (1988).

2. A student is unlikely to have trouble with a requirement that the covenanting parties must intend for a covenant to run with the land in order for it to bind their successors. The remaining requirements discussed in the principal case—privity and "touch and concern"—may be less comprehensible. Even courts occasionally have some difficulty, especially with the concept of privity. Part of the problem stems from the variety of meanings which the term has been given.

The position of the original Restatement of Property on horizontal and mutual privity is stated in § 534: "The successors in title to land respecting the use of which the owner has made a promise are not bound as promisors upon the promise unless (a) the transaction of which the promise is a part includes a transfer of an interest either in the land benefited by or in the land burdened by the performance of the promise; or (b) the promise is made in the adjustment of the mutual relationships arising out of the existence of an easement held by one of the parties to the promise in the land of the other." The following example of clause (b) is given: "A conveys to B, the owner and possessor of Blackacre, an easement giving to B the privilege of taking mud deposits from a pond on Whiteacre, neighboring land owned by A, to be used as a fertilizer upon Blackacre. Two months later A and B enter into a supplemental but independent contract whereby A agrees on behalf of himself, his successors and assigns, that he will draw the water out of the pond under certain stipulated conditions for the purpose of enabling B to secure the mud deposit." Massachusetts recognizes only this latter type of privity. Morse v. Aldrich, 36 Mass. 449 (1837); Hurd v. Curtis, 36 Mass. 459 (1837).

3. The final type of privity, which is sometimes referred to as "vertical" privity, concerns the relationship between a party to the covenant and his or her successor. The apparent meaning of this requirement is that one who seeks to enforce a covenant on the theory that it runs with the land must show that he or she has succeeded to ownership of land owned by the covenantee and, similarly, that the one against whom enforcement is sought succeeded to land owned by the covenantor.

The "vertical" privity of estate concept has been encountered previously in this book. Recall the distinction between assignment and sublease of leaseholds. A sublessee, not being in privity of estate with lessor, is not liable to lessor on the covenant to pay rent. The sublessee has an interest in the leased land, but has not succeeded to the tenant's estate. Does it follow that the grantee of a life estate from an owner of the fee would be unaffected by real covenants binding or benefitting the grantor? In other words, do covenants run only with the entire estate originally bound thereby, or will they also run with a lesser interest. See the Restatement of Property, §§ 535, 547 (1944).

4. The enforcement of real covenants is frequently at issue in residential subdivisions. Can a homeowners' association enforce covenants, even though the association itself owns no interest in land benefitted by the covenant? In this regard consider the following case.

NEPONSIT PROPERTY OWNERS' ASS'N v. EMIGRANT INDUSTRIAL SAV. BANK

Court of Appeals of New York, 1938.
278 N.Y. 248, 15 N.E.2d 793, 118 A.L.R. 973.

LEHMAN, J. The plaintiff, as assignee of Neponsit Realty Company, has brought this action to foreclose a lien upon land which the defendant owns. The lien, it is alleged, arises from a covenant, condition or charge contained in a deed of conveyance of the land from Neponsit Realty Company to a predecessor in title of the defendant. The defendant purchased the land at a judicial sale. The referee's deed to the defendant and every deed in the defendant's chain of title since the conveyance of the land by Neponsit Realty Company purports to convey the property subject to the covenant, condition or charge contained in the original deed. The answer of the defendant contains, in addition to denials of some of the allegations of the complaint, seven separate affirmative defenses and a counterclaim. The defendant moved for judgment on the pleadings, dismissing the complaint pursuant to rule 112 of the Rules of Civil Practice. The plaintiff moved to dismiss the counterclaim pursuant to rule 109, subdivision 6, and to strike out the affirmative defenses contained in the answer pursuant to rule 103, as well as pursuant to rule 109, subdivision 6, of the Rules of Civil Practice. The motion of the plaintiff was granted and the motion of the defendant denied. The Appellate Division unanimously affirmed the order of the Special Term and granted leave to appeal to this court upon certified questions. . . .

Upon this appeal the defendant contends that the land which it owns is not subject to any lien or charge which the plaintiff may enforce. . . .

It appears that in January, 1911, Neponsit Realty Company, as owner of a tract of land in Queens county, caused to be filed in the office of the clerk of the county a map of the land. The tract was developed for a strictly residential community, and Neponsit Realty Company conveyed lots in the tract to purchasers, describing such lots by reference to the filed map and to roads and streets shown thereon. In 1917, Neponsit Realty Company conveyed the land now owned by the defendant to Robert Oldner Deyer and his wife by deed which contained the covenant upon which the plaintiff's cause of action is based.

That covenant provides:

"And the party of the second part for the party of the second part and the heirs, successors and assigns of the party of the second part further covenants that the property conveyed by this deed shall be subject to an annual charge in such an amount as will be fixed by the party of the first part, its successors and assigns, not, however, exceeding in any year the sum of four ($4.00) Dollars per lot 20 × 100 feet. The assigns of the party of the first part may include a Property Owners' Association which may hereafter be organized for the purposes referred to in this paragraph, and in case such association is organized the sums in this paragraph provided for shall be payable to such association. The party of the second part for the party of the second part and the heirs, successors and assigns of the party of the second part covenants that they will pay this charge to the party of the first part, its successors and assigns on the first day of May in each and every year, and further covenants that said charge shall on said date in each year become a lien on the land and shall continue to be such lien until fully paid. Such charge shall be payable to the party of the first part or its successors or assigns, and shall be devoted to the maintenance of the roads, paths, parks, beach, sewers and such other public purposes as shall from time to time be determined by the party of the first part, its successors or assigns. And the party of the second part by the acceptance of this deed hereby expressly vests in the party of the first part, its successors and assigns, the right and power to bring all actions against the owner of the premises hereby conveyed or any part thereof for the collection of such charge and to enforce the aforesaid lien therefor.

"These covenants shall run with the land and shall be construed as real covenants running with the land until January 31st, 1940, when they shall cease and determine."

Every subsequent deed of conveyance of the property in the defendant's chain of title, including the deed from the referee to the defendant, contained, as we have said, a provision that they were made subject to covenants and restrictions of former deeds of record.

There can be no doubt that Neponsit Realty Company intended that the covenant should run with the land and should be enforceable by a property owners association against every owner of property in the residential tract which the realty company was then developing. The language of the covenant admits of no other construction. Regardless of the intention of the parties, a covenant will run with the land and will be enforceable against a subsequent purchaser of the land at the suit of one who claims the benefit of the covenant, only if the covenant complies with certain legal requirements. These requirements rest upon ancient rules and precedents. The age-old essentials of a real covenant, aside from the form of the covenant, may be summarily formulated as follows: (1) It must appear that grantor and grantee intended that the covenant should run with the land; (2) it must appear that the covenant is one "touching" or "concerning" the land with which it runs; (3) it must appear that there is "privity of estate" between the promisee or party claiming the benefit of the covenant and the right to enforce it, and the promisor or party who rests under the burden of the covenant. Clark on Covenants and Interests Running with Land, p. 74. Although the deeds of Neponsit Realty Company conveying lots in the tract it developed "contained a provision to the effect that the covenants ran with the land, such provision in the absence of the other legal requirements is insufficient to accomplish such a purpose." Morgan Lake Co. v. New York, N.H. & H.R.R. Co., 262 N.Y. 234, 238, 186 N.E. 685, 686. . . .

. . . Though between the grantor and the grantee there was privity of estate, the covenant provides that its benefit shall run to the assigns of the grantor who "may include a Property Owners' Association which may hereafter be organized for the purposes referred to in this paragraph." The plaintiff has been organized to receive the sums payable by the property owners and to expend them for the benefit of such owners. Various definitions have been formulated of "privity of estate" in connection with covenants that run with the land, but none of such definitions seems to cover the relationship between the plaintiff and the defendant in this case. The plaintiff has not succeeded to the ownership of any property of the grantor. It does not appear that it ever had title to the streets or public places upon which charges which are payable to it must be expended. It does not appear that it owns any other property in the residential tract to which any easement or right of enjoyment in such property is appurtenant. It is created solely to act as the assignee of the benefit of the covenant, and it has no interest of its own in the enforcement of the covenant.

The arguments that under such circumstances the plaintiff has no right of action to enforce a covenant running with the land are all based upon a distinction between the corporate property owners association and the property owners for whose benefit the association has been formed. If that distinction may be ignored, then the basis of the arguments is destroyed. How far privity of estate in technical form is necessary to enforce in equity a restrictive covenant upon the use of land, presents an interesting question. Enforcement of such covenants rests upon equitable principles (Tulk v. Moxhay, 2 Phillips, 774; Trustees of Columbia College v. Lynch, 70 N.Y. 440, 26 Am.Rep. 615; Korn v. Campbell, 192 N.Y. 490, 85 N.E. 687, 37 L.R.A.,N.S., 1, 127 Am.St.Rep. 925), and at times, at least, the violation "of the restrictive covenant may be restrained at the suit of one who owns property or for whose benefit the restriction was established, irrespective of whether there were privity either of estate or of contract between the parties, or whether an action at law were maintainable." Chesebro v. Moers, 233 N.Y. 75, 80, 134 N.E. 842, 843, 21 A.L.R. 1270. The covenant in this case does not fall exactly within any classification of "restrictive" covenants, which have been enforced in this State (Cf. Korn v. Campbell, 192 N.Y. 490, 85 N.E. 687, 37 L.R.A.,N.S., 1, 127 Am.St.Rep. 925), and no right to enforce even a restrictive covenant has been sustained in this State where the plaintiff did not own property which would benefit by such enforcement so that some of the elements of an equitable servitude are present. In some jurisdictions it has been held that no action may be maintained without such elements. But cf. Van Sant v. Rose, 260 Ill. 401, 103 N.E. 194, 49 L.R.A.,N.S., 186. We do not attempt to decide now how far the rule of Trustees of Columbia College v. Lynch, supra, will be carried, or to formulate a definite rule as to when, or even whether, covenants in a deed will be enforced, upon equitable principles, against subsequent purchasers with notice, at the suit of a party without privity of contract or estate. Cf. "Equitable Rights and Liabilities of Strangers to a Contract," by Harlan F. Stone, 18 Columbia Law Review, 291. There is no need to resort to such a rule if the courts may look behind the corporate form of the plaintiff.

The corporate plaintiff has been formed as a convenient instrument by which the property owners may advance their common interests. We do not ignore the corporate form when we recognize that the Neponsit Property Owners' Association, Inc., is acting as the agent or representative of the Neponsit property owners. As we have said in another case: when Neponsit Property Owners' Association, Inc., "was formed, the property owners were expected to, and have looked to that organization as the medium through which enjoyment of their common right might be preserved equally for all." Matter of City of New York, Public Beach, Borough of Queens, 269 N.Y. 64, 75, 199 N.E. 5, 9. Under the conditions thus presented we said: "It may be difficult, or even impossible, to classify into recognized categories the nature of the interest of the membership corporation and its members in the land. The corporate entity cannot be disregarded, nor can the separate interests of the members of the corporation" (page 73, 199 N.E. page 8). Only blind adherence to an ancient formula devised to meet entirely different conditions could constrain the court to hold that a corporation formed as a medium for the enjoyment of common rights of property owners owns no property which would benefit by enforcement of common rights and has no cause of action in equity to enforce the covenant upon which such common rights depend. Every reason which in other circumstances may justify the ancient formula may be urged in support of the conclusion that the formula should not be applied in this case. In substance if not in form the covenant is a restrictive covenant which touches and concerns the defendant's land, and in substance, if not in form, there is privity of estate between the plaintiff and the defendant. . . .

The order should be affirmed, with costs. . . .

NOTES

1. As lawyer for the Neponsit Realty Company, could you have suggested ways for setting up the subdivision and the homeowners' association that would have avoided the privity issue? How?

2. Traditionally, a covenant would not run unless it benefitted land as well as burdening land. In other words, the benefit of the covenant could not be in gross. A covenant by a landowner that she, her heirs, successors and assigns will not build on a strip of her

property abutting a highway would not bind a purchaser with notice of the covenant because the benefit of the covenant runs to the state and its inhabitants rather than to any identifiable parcel of land owned by the state. See Johnson v. State, 27 Or.App. 581, 556 P.2d 724 (1976).

Opponents of the requirement that both ends of a covenant must touch and concern specific tracts point out that it is inconsistent with the American rule allowing easements in gross and that there is no convincing reason for prohibiting in-gross real covenants and equitable servitudes. See Cribbet and Johnson, Principles of the Law of Property 384–385 (3d ed. 1989). Contrast the following argument advanced against the recognition of private in-gross conservation servitudes:

> One difference between classic easements and privately held conservation servitudes in gross is that easements usually do not involve veto power over the land of another. Typical easements in gross involve the grant of sewer lines, railroad corridors, oil and gas pipelines, water lines, and rights of ways—clearly defined, limited interests, affecting only a portion of the servient land. They are usually affirmative easements, which allow the easement owner to act on the servient land, rather than negative easements, which allow the easement owner to prohibit the servient owner from acting. Thus, although the servient owner's use is controlled to some extent, there is usually no limitation on the fundamental rights to use of the property. Korngold, Privately Held Conservation Servitudes: A Policy Analysis in the Context of in Gross Real Covenants and Easements, 63 Tex.L.Rev. 433, 477–478 (1984).

Does the requirement that the benefit of a covenant must be tied to some other tract of land address Professor Korngold's concern that the broad scope and permanence of certain types of servitudes will make it difficult to meet changing land use needs?

3. The requirement that a real covenant "touch and concern" the land was also an issue in the Neponsit case. The defendant argued that an affirmative covenant to pay money for maintenance work which would not be performed upon its own lot did not touch or concern the land. While recognizing that the New York courts had not abandoned the traditional distinction between deed covenants to pay money or perform other affirmative acts, which were treated as personal covenants, and those which impose restrictions on the use of property, the court concluded that the provision for annual charges contained in the original deed to the lot was enforceable against the defendant. It reasoned as follows:

> It has been suggested that a covenant which runs with the land must affect the legal relations—the advantages and the burdens—of the parties to the covenant, as owners of particular parcels of land and not merely as members of the community in general, such as taxpayers or owners of other land. Clark, op. cit. p. 76. Cf. Professor Bigelow's article on The Contents of Covenants in Leases, 12 Mich.L.Rev. 639; 30 Law Quarterly Review, 319. That method of approach has the merit of realism. The test is based on the effect of the covenant rather than on technical distinctions. Does

the covenant impose, on the one hand, a burden upon an interest in land, which on the other hand increases the value of a different interest in the same or related land?

Even though we accept that approach and test, it still remains true that whether a particular covenant is sufficiently connected with the use of land to run with the land, must be in many cases a question of degree. A promise to pay for something to be done in connection with the promisor's land does not differ essentially from a promise by the promisor to do the thing himself, and both premises constitute, in a substantial sense, a restriction upon the owner's right to use the land, and a burden upon the legal interest of the owner. On the other hand, a covenant to perform or pay for the performance of an affirmative act disconnected with the use of the land cannot ordinarily touch or concern the land in any substantial degree. Thus, unless we exalt technical form over substance, the distinction between covenants which run with land and covenants which are personal, must depend upon the effect of the covenant on the legal rights which otherwise would flow from ownership of land and which are connected with the land. The problem then is: Does the covenant in purpose and effect substantially alter these rights?

. . .

. . . Stressing the intent and substantial effect of the covenant rather than its form, it seems clear that the covenant may properly be said to touch and concern the land of the defendant and its burden should run with the land. True, it calls for payment of a sum of money to be expended for "public purposes" upon land other than the land conveyed by Neponsit Realty Company to plaintiff's predecessor in title. By that conveyance the grantee, however, obtained not only title to particular lots, but an easement or right of common enjoyment with other property owners in roads, beaches, public parks or spaces and improvements in the same tract. For full enjoyment in common by the defendant and other property owners of these easements or rights, the roads and public places must be maintained. In order that the burden of maintaining public improvements should rest upon the land benefited by the improvements, the grantor exacted from the grantee of the land with its appurtenant easement or right of enjoyment a covenant that the burden of paying the cost should be inseparably attached to the land which enjoys the benefit. It is plain that any distinction or definition which would exclude such a covenant from the classification of covenants which "touch" or "concern" the land would be based on form and not on substance.

EAGLE ENTERPRISES, INC. v. GROSS

Court of Appeals of New York, 1976.
39 N.Y.2d 505, 384 N.Y.S.2d 717, 349 N.E.2d 816.

GABRIELLI, JUSTICE. In 1951, Orchard Hill Realties, Inc., a subdivider and developer, conveyed certain property in the subdivision of Orchard Hill in Orange County to William and Pauline Baum. The deed to the Baums contained the following provision:

"The party of the first part shall supply to the party of the second part, seasonably from May 1st to October 1st, of each year, water for domestic use only, from the well located on other property of the party of the first part, and the party of the second part agrees to take said water and to pay the party of the first part, a fee of Thirty-five ($35.00) dollars per year, for said water so supplied."

In addition, the deed also contained the following:

"It is expressly provided that the covenants herein contained shall run with the land . . . and shall bind and shall enure to the benefit of the heirs, distributees, successors, legal representatives and assigns of the respective parties hereto".

Appellant is the successor in interest of Orchard Hill Realties, Inc., and respondent, after a series of intervening conveyances, is the successor in interest of the Baums. The deed conveying title to respondent does not contain the aforementioned covenant to purchase water and, in fact none of the deeds following the original deed to the Baums contained the mutual promises regarding water supply. While some of the deeds in the chain of title from Baum contained a provision that they were made subject to the restrictions in the deed from Orchard Hill Realties to Baum, the deed to respondents contained no such covenants, restrictions or "subject to" clause.

According to the stipulated facts, respondent has refused to accept and pay for water offered by appellant since he has constructed his own well to service what is now a year-round dwelling. Appellant, therefore, instituted this action to collect the fee specified in the covenant (contained only in the original deed to Baum) for the supply of water which, appellant contends, respondent is bound to accept. The action was styled as one "for goods sold and delivered" even though respondent did not utilize any of appellant's water. Two of the lower courts found that the covenant "ran" with the land and, hence, was binding upon respondent as successor to the Baums, but the Appellate Division reversed and held that the covenant could not be enforced against respondent. We must now decide whether the promise of the original grantees to accept and make payment for a seasonal water supply from the well of their grantor is enforceable against subsequent grantees and may be said to "run with the land." We agree with the determination of the Appellate Division and affirm its order.

. . .

A close examination of the covenant in the case before us leads to the conclusion that it does not substantially affect the ownership interest of landowners in the Orchard Hill subdivision. The covenant provides for the supplying of water for only six months of the year; no claim has been advanced by appellant that the lands in the subdivision would be waterless without the water it supplies. Indeed, the facts here point to the converse conclusion since respondent has obtained his own source of water. The record, based on and consisting of an agreed stipulation of facts, does not demonstrate that other property owners in the subdivision would be deprived of water from appellant or that the price of water would become prohibitive for other property owners if respondent terminated appellant's service. Thus, the agreement for the seasonal supply of water does not seem to us to relate in any significant degree to the ownership rights of respondent and the other property owners in the subdivision of Orchard Hill. The landowners in *Neponsit* received an easement in common to utilize public areas in the subdivision; this interest was in the nature of a property right attached to their respective properties. The obligation to receive water from appellant resembles a personal, contractual promise to purchase water rather than a significant interest attaching to respondent's property. It should be emphasized that the question whether a covenant is so closely related to the use of the land that it should be deemed to "run" with the land is one of degree, dependent on the particular circumstances of a case . . . . Here, the meager record before us is lacking and woefully insufficient to establish that the covenant "touches and concerns" the land, as we have interpreted that requirement.

There is an additional reason why we are reluctant to enforce this covenant for the seasonal supply of water. The affirmative covenant is disfavored in the law because of the fear that this type of obligation imposes an "undue restriction on alienation or an onerous burden in perpetuity" (Nicholson v. 300 Broadway Realty Corp., 7 N.Y.2d 240, 246, 196 N.Y.S.2d 945, 950, 164 N.E.2d 832, 835, supra). In *Nicholson,* the covenant to supply heat was not interdicted by this concern because it was conditioned upon the continued existence of the buildings on both the promisor's and the promisee's properties. Similarly, in *Neponsit,* the original 1917 deed containing the covenant to pay an annual charge for the maintenance of public areas expressly provided for its own lapse in 1940. Here, no outside limitation has been placed on the obligation to purchase water from appellant. Thus, the covenant falls prey to the criticism that it creates a burden in perpetuity, and purports to bind all future owners, regardless of the use to which the land is put. Such a result militates strongly against its enforcement. On this ground also, we are of the opinion that the covenant should not be enforced as an exception to the general rule prohibiting the "running" of affirmative covenants.

Accordingly, the order of the Appellate Division should be affirmed, with costs.

---

(2) EQUITABLE SERVITUDES

English courts at law have been far less willing than American courts to allow a covenant to run with the land. Concerned about restraints on alienation of estates, they refused to enforce covenants attached to a fee simple against anyone other than the original covenantor. Under the English view privity of estate was lacking unless each party to the covenant had an interest in the land involved. The concept of runnability was thereby effectively limited to covenants contained in leases.

Placed in this context, the following case dealing with the enforcement of a covenant in equity is clearly of utmost importance. Moreover, its importance is not limited to England. It has had a significant impact on American law, especially in those states that have traditionally taken a strict view toward the running of covenants with the land.

TULK v. MOXHAY

Court of Chancery, England, 1848.
2 Phillips 774.

In the year 1808 the plaintiff, being then the owner in fee of the vacant piece of ground in Leicester Square, as well as of several of the houses forming the Square, sold the piece of ground by the description of "Leicester Square Garden or Pleasure Ground, with the equestrian statue then standing in the centre thereof, and the iron railing and stone work round the same," to one Elms in fee: and the deed of conveyance contained a covenant by Elms, for himself, his heirs, and assigns, with the plaintiff, his heirs, executors, and administrators, "that Elms, his heirs, and assigns should, and would from time to time, and at all times thereafter at his and their own costs and charges, keep and maintain the said piece of ground and Square Garden, and the iron railing round the same in its then form, and in sufficient and proper repair as a Square Garden and Pleasure Ground, in an open state, uncovered with any buildings, in neat and ornamental order; and that it should be lawful for the inhabitants of Leicester Square, tenants of the Plaintiff, on payment of a reasonable rent for the same, to have keys at their own expense and the privilege of admission therewith at any time or times into the said Square Garden and Pleasure Ground."

The piece of land so conveyed passed by divers mesne conveyances into the hands of the defendant, whose purchase deed contained no similar covenant with his vendor; but he admitted that he had purchased with notice of the covenant in the deed of 1808.

The defendant having manifested an intention to alter the character of the Square Garden, and asserted a right, if he thought fit, to build upon it, the plaintiff, who still remained owner of several houses in the Square, filed this bill for an injunction; and an injunction was granted by the Master of the Rolls, to restrain the defendant from converting or using the piece of ground and Square Garden, and the iron railing round the same, to or for any other purpose than as a

Square Garden and Pleasure Ground in an open state, and uncovered with buildings.

On a motion, now made, to discharge that order.

THE LORD CHANCELLOR. . . .

That this court has jurisdiction to enforce a contract between the owner of land and his neighbour purchasing a part of it, that the latter shall either use or abstain from using the land purchased in a particular way, is what I never knew disputed. Here there is no question about the contract: the owner of certain houses in the Square sells the land adjoining, with a covenant from the purchaser not to use it for any other purpose than as a Square Garden. And it is now contended, not that the vendee could violate that contract, but that he might sell the piece of land, and that the purchaser from him may violate it without this court having any power to interfere. If that were so, it would be impossible for an owner of land to sell part of it without incurring the risk of rendering what he retains worthless. It is said that, the covenant being one which does not run with the land, this court cannot enforce it; but the question is, not whether the covenant runs with the land, but whether a party shall be permitted to use the land in a manner inconsistent with the contract entered into by his vendor, and with notice of which he purchased. Of course, the price would be affected by the covenant, and nothing could be more inequitable than that the original purchaser should be able to sell the property the next day for a greater price, in consideration of the assignee being allowed to escape from the liability which he had himself undertaken.

That the question does not depend upon whether the covenant runs with the land, is evident from this, that if there was a mere agreement and no covenant, this court would enforce it against a party purchasing with notice of it; for if an equity is attached to the property by the owner, no one purchasing with notice of that equity can stand in a different situation from the party from whom he purchased. . . .

I think the cases cited before the Vice-Chancellor and this decision of the Master of the Rolls perfectly right, and, therefore, that this motion must be refused with costs.

NOTE

Should this case be read as supporting the position that affirmative, as well as negative, covenants may run in equity? Subsequent English cases confining Tulk v. Moxhay to negative covenants are criticized by Bell, Tulk v. Moxhay Revisited, [1981] The Conveyancer and Property Lawyer 55, who laments the difficulties posed by this rule for modern conveyancing. Bell's views, in turn, have been criticized by Griffith, Tulk v. Moxhay Reclarified, [1983] The Conveyancer and Property Lawyer 29.

This issue was addressed in Petersen v. Beekmere, Inc., 117 N.J. Super. 155, 283 A.2d 911 (1971):

"This is a class action to construe a covenant compelling purchasers of property in a subdivision, known as Allison Acres, to purchase a share of stock in a community association, Beekmere, Inc. Said action has been consolidated with a county district court suit instituted by Beekmere against each of the plaintiffs herein for $100 for a required stock subscription, and for $75 representing the 1969 annual assessment as against each of them.

. . .

"The threshold question for the court is whether this covenant, being affirmative in nature, can be enforced at law through the medium of the county district court action, or in equity, by plaintiffs' action to construe the covenant. . . .

. . .

"Thus, although the question whether an affirmative covenant is enforceable at law as a covenant running with the land is here expressly left open, it is the conclusion of this court that such a covenant is, in equity, enforceable as an equitable servitude against a subsequent grantee who takes with notice."

LONDON COUNTY COUNCIL v. ALLEN

Court of Appeal, 1914.
L.R. [1914] 3 K.B. 642, Ann.Cas.1916C 932.

SCRUTTON, J. read the following judgment: In this case the London County Council, on January 24, 1907, entered into an indenture with one Morris Joseph Allen, a builder, describing himself as "the owner in fee simple of certain land," by which he "doth hereby for himself, his heirs and assigns, and other the persons claiming under him, and so far as practicable to bind the land and hereditaments herein mentioned into whosoever hands the same may come, covenant and agree with the council that he and they will not erect or place, or cause or permit to be erected or placed, any building, structure, or other erection upon the land shewn by green colour on the said plan, without the previous consent in writing of the council so to do, and that on every conveyance, sale, charge, mortgage, lease, assignment, or other dealing with the land herein mentioned or any part thereof he will give notice of the aforesaid covenant in every conveyance, transfer, mortgage, charge, lease, assignment, or other document by which such dealing is effected." The plots coloured green were two plot intended to be reserved for the making of roads. On plot No. 1, in July, 1911, three houses were built by Mrs. Allen; on plot No. 2 a wall was built by Allen. The London County Council thereupon issued a writ claiming a mandatory injunction to pull down the houses and wall respectively. Thereupon it was alleged that as to plot No. 1 the legal estate was in one Norris as mortgagee, and the equity of redemption in Mrs. Allen, who had taken title from Mr. Allen and Willcocks, his mortgagee, who had no notice of the restrictive covenant; and it was contended (1.) by way of demurrer that as the London County Council were not neighbouring landowners, or grantors of the plot in question, a covenant by Allen in their favour was only a personal covenant, and could not affect the land when in the hands of assigns of Allen, whether they had notice of the covenant or not. It was said that to affect them the right must be in the nature of a negative easement; that an easement required both a dominant and a servient tenement; and that as the council had no land to which the benefit of the covenant could attach, there could be no dominant tenement, and therefore no negative easement binding on a servient tenement, but only an easement in gross, which did not bind assigns of the land. (2.) It was alleged that the defendants Mrs. Allen and Norris could prove they were purchasers for value of the legal estate without notice of the covenant, and therefore not bound by it. Avory, J. found on the second contention as a fact that Mrs. Allen and Norris had not satisfied him they had not notice, actual or constructive, of the covenant. On the first contention he said: "It was contended before me that this restrictive covenant, being in the nature of a negative easement, the action would not lie except at the suit of a covenantee who was at the time of the covenant in possession of land which required protection, and that the plaintiffs were not at the time in possession of any such land. But having regard to the powers vested in the London County Council under ss. 7 and 9 of the London Building Act, 1894, and to the admission made in the argument before me that the conditions imposed in this case were not ultra vires, I think this contention fails." He apparently treated the duty and interest of the county council in the matter of new streets as sufficient to make the covenant bind the land in the hands of assigns from Allen. This Court determined to decide the first contention before hearing argument on the second, and we have now to decide on the first contention.

Counsel on each side agreed that the burden of this covenant would not run with the land at law, so as to bind assigns, for the reason stated in the notes to Spencer's Case [5] that "there appears to be no authority which has decided, apart from the equitable doctrine of notice" (by which is meant, as hereinafter explained, the doctrine identified with the case of Tulk v. Moxhay [6]) "that the burden of a covenant will run with land in any case except that of landlord and tenant." This opinion appears to be justified by the judgments of the Court of Appeal in Austerberry v. Oldham Corporation,[7] especially that of Lindley, L.J. at p. 781 and of Fry, L.J. at p. 784.

The question then is whether it is essential to the doctrine of Tulk v. Moxhay that the covenantee should have at the time of the creation of the covenant, and afterwards, land for the benefit of which the covenant is created, in order that the burden of the covenant may bind assigns of the land to which it relates. It is clear that the covenantee may sue the covenantor himself though the former has parted with the land to which the covenant relates: Stokes v. Russell.[8] To answer the question as to the assigns of the covenantor, and the land in their hands, requires the investigation of the historical growth of the doctrine of Tulk v. Moxhay. Though the covenantee in that case did hold adjacent land, there is no trace in the judgment of Lord Cottenham of

5. 1 Sm.L.C., 11th ed., at p. 88.

6. 2 Ph. 774.

7. 29 Ch.D. 750.

8. 3 T.R. 678.

the requirement that the covenantee should have and continue to hold land to be benefited by the covenant. I read Lord Cottenham's judgment as proceeding entirely on the question of notice of the covenant, and on the equitable ground that a man purchasing land with notice that there was a covenant not to use it in a particular way would not be allowed to violate the covenant he knew of when he bought the land. Lord Cottenham states the question, "Whether a party shall be permitted to use the land in a manner inconsistent with the contract entered into by his vendor and with notice of which he purchased," and answers it: "If there was a mere agreement and no covenant, this Court would enforce it against a party purchasing with notice of it; for if an equity is attached to the property by the owner, no one purchasing with notice of that equity can stand in a different situation from the party from whom he purchased." . . .

I think the result of this long chain of authorities is that, whereas in my view, at the time of Tulk v. Moxhay and for at least twenty years afterwards, the plaintiffs in this case would have succeeded against an assign on the ground that the assign had notice of the covenant, since Formby v. Barker,[9] In re Nisbet and Potts' Contract,[10] and Millbourn v. Lyons,[11] three decisions of the Court of Appeal, the plaintiffs must fail on the ground that they have never had any land for the benefit of which this "equitable interest analogous to a negative easement" could be created, and therefore cannot sue a person who bought the land with knowledge that there was a restrictive covenant as to its use, which he proceeds to disregard, because he is not privy to the contract. I think the learned editors of Dart on Vendors and Purchasers, 7th ed., vol. ii, p. 769, are justified by the present state of the authorities in saying that "the question of notice to the purchaser has nothing whatever to do with the question whether the covenant binds him, except in so far as the absence of notice may enable him to raise the plea of purchaser for valuable consideration without notice." If the covenant does not run with the land in law, its benefit can only be asserted against an assign of the land burdened, if the covenant was made for the benefit of certain land, all or some of which remains in the possession of the covenantee or his assign, suing to enforce the covenant. It may be, if the matter is considered by a higher tribunal, that tribunal may see its way to revert to what I think was the earlier doctrine of notice, or at any rate to treat it as co-existing with the later refinement of "an equitable interest analogous to a negative easement" binding on persons who are ignorant of it. The remarks of Lord Selborne in Earl of Zetland v. Hislop[12] are not favourable to the too rigid development or enforcement of the latter alternative; and the observations of Lord Macnaghten (p. 32), Lord Davey (p. 35), and Lord Lindley (p. 36) in Noakes & Co. v. Rice[13] seem to suggest that the doctrine of Tulk v. Moxhay may well be reconsidered and put on a proper footing. For I regard it as very regrettable that a public body should be prevented from enforcing a restriction on the use of property imposed for the

9. [1903] 2 Ch. 539.

10. [1905] 1 Ch. 391; [1906] 1 Ch. 386.

11. [1914] 1 Ch. 34; 2 Ch. 231.

12. 7 App.Cas. 427, at pp. 446, 447.

13. [1902] A.C. 24.

public benefit against persons who bought the property knowing of the restriction, by the apparently immaterial circumstance that the public body does not own any land in the immediate neighbourhood. But, after a careful consideration of the authorities, I am forced to the view that the later decisions of this Court compel me so to hold.

In my opinion, therefore, the demurrer of Mr. Norris and of Mrs. Allen succeeds. The action against Mr. Norris must be dismissed with costs. I regret that I do not see my way to depriving Mrs. Allen of her costs, as, whatever may be her equitable rights, I am not at all favourably impressed with her conduct as a good citizen. I see no reason for interfering with the judgment against Mr. Allen in respect of plots No. 1 or No. 2, and his appeal must be dismissed with costs.

Appeal of Norris and Emily Allen allowed; appeal of M.J. Allen dismissed.

NOTES

1. In view of the English courts' refusal to recognize easements in gross, the decision in the principal case is said to be "logical" but subject to criticism because of "its tacit admission that equity's concept of property interests must be restricted to the categories established by courts of law." 2 American Law of Property § 9.32 (1952). Despite the general approval of easements in gross by American courts, the few American cases in point are in conflict concerning running of the burden in equity when there is no benefit to other land. Ibid.; 5 Powell, Real Property ¶ 675 (1956). According to the Restatement of Property § 537, comment c, and § 539, comment k (1944), where the benefit is in gross the burden will not run at law, but will run in equity.

2. G conveyed land to E, who covenanted that he would erect thereon only single-family dwellings. G owned no other land in the neighborhood, and there was no apparent reason for his putting the restrictive covenant in the deed. E conveyed the land to X, who commenced to erect an apartment house, although he had notice of the covenant. Assuming that the doctrine of London County Council v. Allen is unsound, does it follow that G may obtain an injunction? An affirmative answer was given in Van Sant v. Rose, 260 Ill. 401, 103 N.E. 194 (1913), but the decision is severely criticized in Leesman, Covenants Running With the Land in Illinois, 14 Ill.L.Rev. 480, 486–500 (1920).

3. Parliament has authorized London County to enforce agreements of the type involved in London County Council v. Allen. See Sturley, The "Land Obligation"; An English Proposal for Reform, 55 S.Calif.L.Rev. 1417, 1423 (1982).

WHITINSVILLE PLAZA, INC. v. KOTSEAS

Massachusetts Supreme Judicial Court, 1979.
378 Mass. 85, 390 N.E.2d 243.

QUIRICO, JUSTICE.

These are civil actions commenced by Whitinsville Plaza, Inc. (Plaza), against Charles H. Kotseas and Paul Kotseas (Kotseas) and against Whitinsville CVS, Inc. (CVS). In its further amended complaint against Kotseas, Plaza alleged imminent violations of certain anticompetitive deed restrictions and requested declaratory, injunctive, and monetary relief under theories of breach of contract and unfair acts or practices within the meaning of G.L. c. 93A, § 2. Plaza's amended complaint against CVS likewise alleged imminent violations of the deed restrictions, and it requested declaratory, injunctive, and monetary relief on theories of breach of contract, unfair trade practices, and interference with contractual relations. A judge of the Superior Court granted the defendants' motions to dismiss for failure to state a claim. See Mass.R.Civ.P. 12(b)(6), 365 Mass. 754 (1974).

Plaza appealed from the dismissal of its actions, and we granted its application for direct appellate review in both cases. See Mass.R.A.P. 11(a), 365 Mass. 854 (1974). We hold that dismissal for failure to state a claim was erroneous as to some counts of each complaint.

In ruling on a motion to dismiss, "the allegations of the complaint [and annexed exhibits], as well as such inferences that may be drawn therefrom in the plaintiff's favor, are to be taken as true." . . . These are as follows. In 1968, Kotseas conveyed certain land identified as "Parcel A" to four individuals as trustees of the "122 Trust" (Trust), a wholly owned subsidiary of Plaza. The deed set forth numerous, detailed, reciprocal restrictions and covenants designed to assure the harmonious development of a shopping center on Parcel A and on abutting land retained by Kotseas. In particular, Kotseas promised (a) not to use the retained land in competition with the discount store contemplated by the grantee and (b) to use the retained land only for enumerated business purposes.[3] Among the permitted business uses of the land retained by Kotseas was a "drug store," defined in an appendix to the deed as a store selling prescribed types of merchandise. In addition, the deed recited that "[t]he foregoing restrictions shall be considered as covenants running with the land to which they are applicable and shall bind and inure to the benefit of the heirs and assigns of the respective parties to whom any part of the lands made subject to the above restrictions covenants and conditions shall at any time become or belong during the period hereinbefore set forth."[4]

3. The deed also purported to restrict land later acquired by Kotseas within a one-half mile radius. Except as this provision may bear on the intent of the parties to bind Kotseas personally rather than as landowner, we need not consider it because the actions complained of have occurred and will occur on land that Kotseas owned in 1968.

4. The deed also provided that the restrictions would terminate when a certain adjacent area ceased to be used for parking or when the parties or their successors should so agree in a recorded instrument.

In 1975, the Trust conveyed Parcel A to Plaza and, thereafter, ceased operations. The deed to Plaza expressly made Plaza subject to, and gave it the benefit of, the restrictions and covenants in the 1968 deed from Kotseas to the Trust. At some later time, Kotseas leased a portion of its abutting land to CVS for use as a "discount department store and pharmacy." Plaza's complaints state that the lease to CVS, dated May 10, 1977, was expressly subject to the 1968 deed restrictions and that operation of the contemplated CVS store would violate those restrictions. Although the defendants controvert these allegations, we must, as we have said, accept them as true in ruling on the motion to dismiss.[5]

As against Kotseas, Plaza sought (a) an injunction prohibiting the use of the retained land in violation of the restrictions and (b) damages suffered because of the alleged violations. In the alternative, Plaza prayed for a declaration that its own land was no longer subject to the anticompetitive restrictions. Plaza also requested the court to find that Kotseas had knowingly and wilfully violated G.L. c. 93A, § 2, and to award double or treble damages and counsel fees. As against CVS, Plaza requested similar relief and also requested damages on the theory that CVS had tortiously interfered with Plaza's contract by inducing Kotseas to violate its restrictions. The defendants filed motions to dismiss, stating as grounds that Plaza lacked standing to sue on the covenants and that the covenants were, in any event, unreasonable and in restraint of trade.

The granting of the motions to dismiss raises a number of complex and somewhat interrelated issues. . . . We are, therefore, obligated to consider each of the alternative theories of law—namely, that the covenants run with the land, that the covenants constitute contractual promises, and that the defendants have engaged in unfair trade practices—on which Plaza's action might be maintained. . . . Underlying all the issues in this case, of course, is the question whether, notwithstanding Plaza's right to sue on one or more legal theories, the 1968 restrictions are unenforceable as unreasonable restraints of trade. With this understanding of the breadth of the present appeal, we turn to examination of the several issues.

A. *Real covenant analysis.* Plaza has primarily sought to maintain its actions on the theory that the covenants contained in the 1968 deed run with the land. In our view, Plaza has alleged sufficient facts to be entitled to a hearing on its claims for legal and equitable relief on this theory. . . . The covenants in question are evidenced by a writing signed by Kotseas, the covenantor. . . . The language of the 1968 deed aptly expresses the intention of the original parties that the covenants run with the land. . . . The deed also grants mutual easements sufficient to satisfy the requirement that Plaza and CVS be in privity of estate. . . . Plaza's complaint alleges that CVS had actual knowledge of the restrictions and shows, in any event, that the restrictions were recorded with the deed. . . .

5. Because the lease was not annexed to the complaint, it is not open in the present posture of the case for the defendants to argue for or against any particular interpretation of it. See Mass.R.Civ.P. 12(b), 365 Mass. 754 (1974).

One additional prerequisite for either legal or equitable relief is, however, arguably lacking in this case on the present state of our case law. It is essential that both the benefit and the burden of a real covenant "touch and concern" the affected parcels of land before it will be considered to run. . . . This court has long held that a covenant not to compete contained in a deed, such as is involved in this case, does not "touch and concern" the land to be benefited and that, in consequence, such a covenant does not run with the land. Shade v. M. O'Keefe, Inc., 260 Mass. 180, 183, 156 N.E. 867 (1927); Norcross v. James, 140 Mass. 188, 192, 2 N.E. 946 (1885). In Shell Oil Co. v. Henry Ouellette & Sons, 352 Mass. 725, 227 N.E.2d 509 (1967), we intimated that we might overrule *Norcross* and *Shade* in an appropriate case. Id. at 730–731 & n. 8, 227 N.E.2d 509. We believe this is such a case.

It is essential to our task that we identify precisely the holding and rationale of the cases we propose to overrule. *Norcross* was an action seeking specific performance of a covenant not to quarry stone from a parcel of land. The covenant in question was contained in a deed by which one Kibbe conveyed a stone quarry to one Flynt, and it concerned adjoining land retained by Kibbe. The defendant James, a successor to Kibbe's interest, began operating a quarry on the restricted land. The plaintiff Norcross, a successor to Flynt's interest, sought an injunction to halt that operation. 140 Mass. at 188, 2 N.E. 946. In an opinion by Justice Holmes, this court denied relief. Id. at 192, 2 N.E. 946.

Justice Holmes analyzed the case before him in two steps. He first noted a distinction drawn in early English decisions between promises resembling warranties of title and those resembling grants of easements. Warranty-like covenants ran "with the estate" to grantees from the covenantee, but were enforceable only against the covenantor. Easement-like covenants, on the other hand, ran "with the land" in favor of and against subsequent owners. Id. at 188–190, 2 N.E. 946. See also O.W. Holmes, The Common Law 371–409 (1881) (developing historical analysis summarized later in *Norcross* opinion).

Having traced the development of the law of real covenants, Justice Holmes proceeded to determine whether the covenant could be encompassed within the easement-like class.[6] He stated that a real covenant must "touch or concern" the land by conferring "direct physical advantage in the occupation of the dominant estate." 140 Mass. at 192, 2 N.E. at 949. The covenant against operating a quarry did not do so because "[i]t does not make the use or occupation of [the dominant estate] more convenient. It does not in any way affect the use or occupation; it simply tends indirectly to increase its value, by excluding a competitor from the market for its products." Id. In addition, the covenant transgressed a supposed rule against attaching "new and unusual incidents" to land, for it attempted to create "an easement of monopoly,—an easement not be be competed with" not theretofore recognized. Id.

6. Because Kibbe, the original covenantor, was not a party to the *Norcross* case, it was obvious that classifying the covenant with warranties of title would not assist the plaintiff.

Two observations about *Norcross* are appropriate before we consider later developments. First of all, the benefit of the covenant surely touched and concerned the dominant estate within the ordinary sense and meaning of the phrase "touch and concern." Justice Holmes's analysis has been described as "overlook[ing] the purpose of all building restrictions, which is to enhance the market value of the promisee's land, whether for residential or for business purposes." 2 American Law of Property § 9.28, at 414 (Casner ed. 1952). It has been suggested that Justice Holmes's "real objection to [the covenant was] the policy against monopolies, and not any policy with reference to real covenants as such." C. Clark, Real Covenants and Other Interests Which "Run with Land" 84 n. 26 (1929). Cf. 140 Mass. at 193, 2 N.E. 946 (unnecessary to decide whether covenant would be invalid restraint of trade if enforcement attempted against Kibbe). If free-competition policies were indeed the basis for the *Norcross* decision, it would now seem preferable for us to deal with them explicitly rather than to condemn all anticompetitive covenants regardless of reasonableness.

Second, *Norcross* seems to turn on an assumption that there could be no other class of covenants, differing both from easements and from warranties, but which might nevertheless run with the land. Justice Holmes reasoned that neither the benefit nor the burden of the covenant could run because the benefit was personal to the original covenantee and was therefore inconsistent with the existence of any easement-like right appurtenant to the dominant land. Underlying such reasoning is the peculiar Massachusetts requirement of privity of estate, created by the existence of an easement between the parties to an action on a real covenant. . . . Yet, privity of estate in this sense had never been thought essential to an action *in equity* for specific performance of a covenant. Beals v. Case, 138 Mass. 138, 139–140 (1884); Parker v. Nightingale, 6 Allen 341, 344 (1863).

Notwithstanding the questions inherent in the *Norcross* decision, this court uncritically followed that case in Shade v. M. O'Keefe, Inc., 260 Mass. 180, 156 N.E. 867 (1927). Like *Norcross, Shade* was a suit in equity by a successor to the promisee against a successor to the promisor seeking specific performance of an anticompetitive covenant. The covenant in question prohibited the operation of a grocery store on the defendant's land for ninety-nine years after 1902, the date of the original deed. 260 Mass. at 181–182, 156 N.E. 867. The court reiterated that, for a covenant to be enforceable in equity, it must accompany or create "an esement or *quasi* easement" in the promisor's land for the benefit of the promisee's land. Id. at 183, 156 N.E. 867. It thus followed the rule stated by Justice Holmes in *Norcross.* Without further analysis the court stated that the case before it was indistinguishable from *Norcross,* and it concluded that the action should be dismissed. . . .

Massachusetts has been practically alone in its position that covenants not to compete do not run with the land to which they relate. It has long been the opinon of text writers that our rule is anachronistic and in need of change. See 2 American Law of Property § 9.28, at 414 (Casner ed. 1952); 5 Powell, supra par. 678, at 197. The American Law

Institute has suggested that an otherwise enforceable covenant not to compete should be held enforceable in the same manner as an equitable servitude. Restatement of Property § 539, Comment k (1944). Reasonable anticompetitive covenants are enforceable in the great majority of States where the issue has arisen. See Comment, Covenants Not to Compete—Do They Pass?, 4 Cal.W.L.Rev. 131, 133–134 (1968). Modern judicial analysis of cases like the one at bar appears to concentrate on the effects of particular covenants on competition and to avoid the esoteric convolutions of the law of real covenants. See, e.g., Hall v. American Oil Co., 504 S.W.2d 313, 316 n. 3 (Mo.App.1973); Quadro Stations, Inc., v. Gilley, 7 N.C.App. 227, 231–235, 172 S.E.2d 237 (1970).

In addition to the doctrinal questions about the *Norcross* rule and the preference of most authorities for a more flexible approach, we may note the unfairness that would result from applying that rule to the facts of this case. In what appears to have been an arm's-length transaction, Kotseas agreed in 1968 not to use retained land in competition with the Trust. We may assume (a) that Kotseas received compensation for thus giving up part of his ownership rights by limiting the uses he could make of the retained land, and (b) that freedom from destructive, next-door competition was part of the inducement for the Trust's purchase and of the price paid by the Trust. Plaza, a closely associated business entity, succeeded to the Trust's interest in 1975. One of these entities established a business, presumably at great cost to itself and in reliance on the contractually obtained limitation of competition in its own narrow market area. Notwithstanding the promise not to do so, Kotseas proceeded to lease land to CVS for the purpose of carrying on the business that it knew would, at least in part, compete with Plaza and divert customers from Plaza's premises. Acting with full knowledge of the 1968 arrangement, CVS participated in this inequitable conduct by Kotseas. If we assume for the moment that the 1968 covenants are reasonable in their application to the present facts, we cannot condone the conduct of Kotseas and CVS. Yet, if *Norcross* remains the law, we are powerless to prevent Kotseas and CVS from indirectly destroying or diminishing the value of Plaza's investment in its business.

We think the time has come to acknowledge the infirmities and inequities of *Norcross*. Prior decisions by this court established what we believe is the proper direction. . . . In short, our decisions support what we hereby state to be the law: reasonable covenants against competition *may* be considered to run with the land when they serve a purpose of facilitating orderly and harmonious development for commercial use. To the extent they are inconsistent with this statement, *Norcross, Shade,* and *Ouellette* are hereby expressly overruled. . . .

What we have said should not be construed as an invitation to legal draftsmen to insert unlimited, "boilerplate"-type covenants against competition in real estate documents. As we have said, an enforceable covenant will be one which is consistent with a reasonable overall purpose to develop real estate for commercial use. In addition, the ordinary requirements for creation and enforcement of real covenants must be met. We have summarized many of these requirements earlier in this opinion. Others are found in G.L. c. 184, §§ 27, 30, which regulate enforcement of land-use restrictions generally. Within these limits, however, commercial developers may control the course of development by reasonable restrictive covenants free from resort to devious subterfuges in their attempts to avoid the doubts created by the *Norcross* rule and our efforts to apply or reconcile it in later cases.

. . .

To the extent that they dismiss Plaza's claims under c. 93A, the judgments are affirmed without prejudice to Plaza's right to amend its complaints within a reasonable time hereafter. To the extent they dismiss Plaza's claims for violation of real covenants or for interference with contractual relations, the judgments are erroneous and must be vacated. The cases are remanded to the Superior Court for further proceedings consistent with this opinion.

NOTES

1. R contracted for himself, his "heirs, successors and assigns," to allow M to install and maintain a juke box of described type at the "Joy Bar Cafe, 130 State Street," for fifteen years, R to receive forty per cent. of the gross receipts. R sold his cafe (land, building, fixtures and business) to P. They had no express agreement concerning the juke box contract, but P knew about it. May P remove the juke box? Would it be material that his reason for doing so is (1) M's refusal to increase the cafe owner's share of the gross receipts to fifty per cent.; or (2) P's desire to convert his cafe into a highclass restaurant and substitute a string ensemble for the juke box? Suppose P moves his restaurant business to a new location—will he have to take the juke box with him? See Chafee, The Music Goes Round and Round: Equitable Servitudes and Chattels, 69 Harvard L.Rev. 1250 (1956), criticizing Pratte v. Balatsos, 99 N.H. 430, 113 A.2d 492 (1955). The New Hampshire Supreme Court was unmoved by this criticism. Pratte v. Balatsos, 101 N.H. 48, 132 A.2d 142 (1957).

2. Some types of fees imposed by property owners associations continue to run afoul of the touch and concern requirement. Ebbe v. Senior Estates Golf and Country Club, 61 Or.App. 398, 657 P.2d 696 (1983) held void on this ground a covenant requiring subsequent owners to pay an "initation fee" of $1,000 to the association golf club, even though such persons may be denied membership in the club. The same result was reached in Raintree Corp. v. Rowe, 38 N.C.App. 664, 248 S.E.2d 904 (1978), despite the provision that subsequent owners automatically become members of the club. The court noted that such persons might not use the club facilities. But compare Anthony v. Brea Glenbrook Club, 58 Cal.App.3d 506, 130 Cal.Rptr. 32 (1976), finding that the touch and concern requirement was satisfied even as to non-users of club facilities on the ground that the club facilities enhanced the value of their lots.

3. Bales owned a vacant tract of land adjacent to a neighborhood of expensive, single-family dwellings. Bales undertook to develop on

his tract a ten-story apartment building. His application for rezoning to allow this development was opposed by the neighbors, but was granted. Bales' tract was not subject to any restrictive covenants. Before Bales commenced construction, the neighbors offered to purchase his tract. They came to an agreement and Bales conveyed the tract to the neighbors. As a part of this transaction, Bales also promised in writing that he would not develop any other land he then owned or might acquire in the vicinity for any purpose other than single-family residences.

Bales did not then own any other land near this site, but a few weeks after his agreement with the neighbors, he purchased another vacant tract nearby. Bales commenced to carry out a plan to build a high-rise apartment on this tract, but abandoned this plan when the neighbors threatened suit. Bales then conveyed this tract to Cox, who was aware of Bales' agreement with the neighbors. Cox then commenced construction of a high-rise apartment on this tract. The neighbors bring suit to obtain an injunction restraining Cox from building the apartment.

What result should be reached? Consider Lewis v. Gollner, 129 N.Y. 227, 29 N.E. 81 (1891), which supports a decision for the neighbors. Possibly a distinguishing fact in that case, however, was the fact that the person in Cox' position was the covenantor's wife, and the transfer may have been colorable. The court said:

"In other words, when he bought the land the plaintiff's equitable rights at once attached to it, and became a burden upon it so long as Gollner owned it, so that apparently the contract ceases to be merely and purely personal because it affects and was intended to affect the use and occupation of Gollner's after-acquired land in that neighborhood. But, if the contract remains technically a personal one, I think the reasonable and settled doctrine is that the contract equity is so attached to the use of the land which is its subject-matter as to follow the land itself into the hands of a purchaser with full knowledge of all the facts, who buys with his eyes open to the existing equity, and more especially when he buys for the express purpose of defeating and evading that equity."

SPRAGUE v. KIMBALL

Supreme Judicial Court of Massachusetts, 1913.
213 Mass. 380, 100 N.E. 622.

BRALEY, J. The question for decision is whether the provision of R.L. c. 74, § 1, that a contract for the sale of lands "or of any interest in or concerning them must be in writing signed by the party to be charged therewith," requires us to reverse the decree. The deeds poll from the defendant Kimball, hereafter referred to as the defendant, under which the plaintiffs respectively derive title to the second, third, fourth and part of the fifth lot shown on the plan which the defendant caused to be prepared and recorded, contain this clause: "The premises are conveyed subject to the following restrictions which shall remain in force for twenty years from the date hereof, viz.: That no building shall be erected or maintained upon the granted premises within twenty-three feet of said Bassett street, and no stable within fifty feet of said street, provided however, that steps, bay windows, verandas, cornices and other usual projections may project into said reserved space; that no public or livery stable shall be maintained thereon; that they shall not be used for mechanical, manufacturing or mercantile business, nor for any trade or occupation offensive to a neighborhood for dwelling houses only." The plaintiffs, even if thus restrained in the use of their own estates, did not gain a corresponding right as against their common grantor in the remaining land exhibited by the plan unless the burden of the restrictions was annexed thereto under a contemporaneous enforceable agreement. . . .

The lots were sold from time to time as purchasers could be obtained and more than three years elapsed after the first and before the last conveyance, while apparently seven years intervened between the last conveyance and the defendant's agreement for the sale of the remainder of lot 5 to the defendant Grossman without restrictions, which the bill seeks to enjoin. The plan incorporated by reference in the deeds, with the exception of the conveyance of lot 2, upon which the defendant before the transfer had built a dwelling in conformity with the building line, contains no reference to the restrictions, while the deeds are silent as to any express covenant or stipulation on the part of the defendant purporting that in future sales similar restrictions were to be imposed. But the restrictions upon the mode of occupation as expressed in the deeds are uniform and the judge finds that the defendant intended, and so informed the plaintiffs at the time of their respective purchases, to subject the lots as they were sold to similar restrictions for their mutual advantage and protection. It is moreover plain from the evidence that each plaintiff was induced by the defendant's promise to buy and build, being assured that the entire neighborhood would be restricted to residential purposes. It would be a forced conclusion, in view of the general scheme originated by the defendant, as shown by the plan, the deeds and the circumstances under which the plaintiffs severally bought, that the restrictions were intended as the mere reservation of personal rights to be enforced for the sole benefit of the defendant or her heirs so long as any portion of the tract remained unsold. The right invoked by the plaintiffs accordingly attached to each lot as it was granted for the mutual benefit of the grantees, although the grantor while he owned the remainder and observed the conditions of the contract of sale, could have compelled in equity a compliance with the restrictions by the lot owners or their successors in title. . . .

It is not a covenant running with the land at law, but it is an equitable easement or servitude passing with a conveyance of the premises to subsequent grantees. . . . While only the mode of use is regulated and the fee passed, yet the estate is encumbered with the inherent restrictions which create an equitable, enforceable interest. It is settled by our decisions, that under R.L. c. 74, § 1, and chapter 127,

§ 3, an equitable as well as a legal interest in land must be evidenced by some sufficient instrument in writing or it is unenforceable. . . .

If the front building line, with any language indicating the nature of the restrictions, had appeared on the plan, the defendant would have been estopped to deny an implied grant with covenants coextensive with the scope of the plan, or if by any appropriate wording of the deeds it appeared that the remaining lots as they were sold should be subject to the restrictions, the statute would have been satisfied. . . . The proposed restrictions undoubtedly formed part of the consideration for the purchase, and each plaintiff would have had the right to demand that the defendant insert in the title deed a stipulation or covenant in accordance with the terms of sale. The judge, however, has found, and the evidence warranted the finding, that the agreement to restrict lot 5 rested wholly in parol, and even if executed as to the other lots, and a small portion of lot 5, it remained wholly executory as to her ownership of the residue.

To prevent the statutory bar the plaintiffs urge that, as there has been full performance on their part, relief should be decreed or the statute would be converted into a shield for fraud; a result not countenanced by a court of equity. But the mere nonperformance of an oral contract, within the statute which is pleaded, as in the case at bar, and where no relation of trust and confidence exists, does not constitute fraud. . . .

Nor did the plaintiffs, on whom and not on the defendant the burden of part performance rests where this ground for relief is sought, by taking title, entering into occupation and making improvements on their own estates in reliance upon the parol agreement, acquire any legal or equitable interest in the defendant's remaining land. . . . The suit cannot be maintained, and the bill must be dismissed.

Ordered accordingly.

SANBORN v. McLEAN

Supreme Court of Michigan, 1925.
233 Mich. 227, 206 N.W. 496, 60 A.L.R. 1212.

WIEST, J. Defendant Christina McLean owns the west 35 feet of lot 86 of Green Lawn subdivision, at the northeast corner of Collingwood avenue and Second boulevard, in the city of Detroit, upon which there is a dwelling house, occupied by herself and her husband, defendant John A. McLean. The house fronts Collingwood avenue. At the rear of the lot is an alley. Mrs. McLean derived title from her husband, and, in the course of the opinion, we will speak of both as defendants. Mr. and Mrs. McLean started to erect a gasoline filling station at the rear end of their lot, and they and their contractor, William S. Weir, were enjoined by decree from doing so and bring the issues before us by appeal. Mr. Weir will not be further mentioned in the opinion.

Collingwood avenue is a high grade residence street between Woodward avenue and Hamilton boulevard, with single, double, and apartment houses, and plaintiffs, who are owners of land adjoining and in the vicinity of defendants' land, and who trace title, as do defendants, to the proprietors of the subdivision, claim that the proposed gasoline station will be a nuisance per se, is in violation of the general plan fixed for use of all lots on the street for residence purposes only, as evidenced by restrictions upon 53 of the 91 lots fronting on Collingwood avenue, and that defendants' lot is subject to a reciprocal negative easement barring a use so detrimental to the enjoyment and value of its neighbors. Defendants insist that no restrictions appear in their chain of title and they purchased without notice of any reciprocal negative easement, and deny that a gasoline station is a nuisance per se. We find no occasion to pass upon the question of nuisance, as the case can be decided under the rule of reciprocal negative easement.

How do we know

This subdivision was planned strictly for residence purposes, except lots fronting Woodward avenue and Hamilton boulevard. The 91 lots on Collingwood avenue were platted in 1891, designed for and each one sold solely for residence purposes, and residences have been erected upon all of the lots. Is defendants' lot subject to a reciprocal negative easement? If the owner of two or more lots, so situated as to bear the relation, sells one with restrictions of benefit to the land retained, the servitude becomes mutual, and, during the period of restraint, the owner of the lot or lots retained can do nothing forbidden to the owner of the lot sold. For want of a better descriptive term this is styled a reciprocal negative easement. It runs with the land sold by virtue of express fastening and abides with the land retained until loosened by expiration of its period of service or by events working its destruction. It is not personal to owners, but operative upon use of the land by any owner having actual or constructive notice thereof. It is an easement passing its benefits and carrying its obligations to all purchasers of land, subject to its affirmative or negative mandates. It originates for mutual benefit and exists with vigor sufficient to work its ends. It must start with a common owner. Reciprocal negative easements are never retroactive; the very nature of their origin forbids. They arise, if at all, out of a benefit accorded land retained, by restrictions upon neighboring land sold by a common owner. Such a scheme of restriction must start with a common owner; it cannot arise and fasten upon one lot by reason of other lot owners conforming to a general plan. If a reciprocal negative easement attached to defendants' lot, it was fastened thereto while in the hands of the common owner of it and neighboring lots by way of sale of other lots with restrictions beneficial at that time to it. This leads to inquiry as to what lots, if any, were sold with restrictions by the common owner before the sale of defendants' lot. While the proofs cover another avenue, we need consider sales only on Collingwood.

December 28, 1892, Robert J. and Joseph R. McLaughlin, who were then evidently owners of the lots on Collingwood avenue, deeded lots 37 to 41 and 58 to 62, inclusive, with the following restrictions:

"No residence shall be erected upon said premises which shall cost less than $2,500, and nothing but residences shall be erected upon said premises. Said residences shall front on Helene (now Collingwood) avenue and be placed no nearer than 20 feet from the front street line."

July 24, 1893, the McLaughlins conveyed lots 17 to 21 and 78 to 82, both inclusive, and lot 98 with the same restrictions. Such restrictions were imposed for the benefit of the lands held by the grantors to carry out the scheme of a residential district, and a restrictive negative easement attached to the lots retained, and title to lot 86 was then in the McLaughlins. Defendants' title, through mesne conveyances, runs back to a deed by the McLaughlins dated September 7, 1893, without restrictions mentioned therein. Subsequent deeds to other lots were executed by the McLaughlins, some with restrictions and some without. Previous to September 7, 1893, a reciprocal negative easement had attached to lot 86 by acts of the owners, as before mentioned, and such easement is still attached and may now be enforced by plaintiffs, provided defendants, at the time of their purchase, had knowledge, actual or constructive, thereof. The plaintiffs run back with their title, as do defendants, to a common owner. This common owner, as before stated, by restrictions upon lots sold, had burdened all the lots retained with reciprocal restrictions. Defendants' lot and plaintiff Sanborn's lot, next thereto, were held by such common owner, burdened with a reciprocal negative easement, and, when later sold to separate parties, remained burdened therewith, and right to demand observance thereof passed to each purchaser with notice of the easement. The restrictions were upon defendants' lot while it was in the hands of the common owners, and abstract of title to defendants' lot showed the common owners, and the record showed deeds of lots in the plat restricted to perfect and carry out the general plan and resulting in a reciprocal negative easement upon defendants' lot and all lots within its scope, and defendants and their predecessors in title were bound by constructive notice under our recording acts. The original plan was repeatedly declared in subsequent sales of lots by restrictions in the deeds, and, while some lots sold were not so restricted, the purchasers thereof, in every instance, observed the general plan and purpose of the restrictions in building residences. For upward of 30 years the united efforts of all persons interested have carried out the common purpose of making and keeping all the lots strictly for residences, and defendants are the first to depart therefrom.

When Mr. McLean purchased on contract in 1910 or 1911, there was a partly built dwelling house on lot 86, which he completed and now occupies. He had an abstract of title which he examined and claims he was told by the grantor that the lot was unrestricted. Considering the character of use made of all the lots open to a view of Mr. McLean when he purchased, we think he was put thereby to inquiry, beyond asking his grantor, whether there were restrictions. He had an abstract showing the subdivision and that lot 86 had 97 companions. He could not avoid noticing the strictly uniform residence character given the lots by the expensive dwellings thereon, and the least inquiry would have quickly developed the fact that lot 86 was subjected to a reciprocal negative easement, and he could finish his house, and, like the others, enjoy the benefits of the easement. We do not say Mr. McLean should have asked his neighbors about restrictions, but we do say that with the notice he had from a view of the premises on the street, clearly indicating the residences were built and the lots occupied in strict accordance with a general plan, he was put to inquiry, and, had he inquired, he would have found of record the reason for such general conformation, and the benefits thereof serving the owners of lot 86 and the obligations running with such service and available to adjacent lot owners to prevent a departure from the general plan by an owner of lot 86. . . .

We notice the decree in the circuit directed that the work done on the building be torn down. If the portion of the building constructed can be utilized for any purpose within the restrictions, it need not be destroyed.

With this modification, the decree in the circuit is affirmed, with costs to plaintiffs.

NOTES

1. The doctrine of implied reciprocal negative easements (or servitudes) is frequently asserted when a subdivider begins to sell or develop land for uses other than those authorized in the restrictive covenants imposed in the earlier deeds. The existence and geographic extent of a common plan for development can be established from such things as the grantor's representations to the buyers, statements in sales brochures, maps, advertisements and recorded declarations of restrictive covenants. See Sharts v. Walters, 107 N.M. 414, 759 P.2d 201 (App.1988); Lehmann v. Wallace, 510 S.W.2d 675 (Tex.Civ.App.1974).

Arguments against the enforceability of such covenants often involve claims that the defendant had no notice of restrictions on his land. In Stegall v. Robinson, 81 N.C.App. 617, 344 S.E.2d 803 (1986) the court held that the defendant had record notice of a restriction against placing a house trailer on his lot, even though the restriction did not appear in any of the deeds in the chain of title to his land. The court pointed out that the subdivider had included a page of restrictions applicable to all lots in the subdivision in its first recorded conveyance. What are the arguments for and against a rule which requires a title examiner to read all deeds made by any grantor in a purchaser's chain of title, including those which convey different lots than that being purchased?

2. A grantor who owned considerable highway frontage sold part of its land to the plaintiff oil company and included in the deed a covenant that the grantor "shall restrict its [remaining] property . . . from use for sale of petroleum products." The grantor later sold another portion of its land to the defendant, but did not include within the deed any restriction prohibiting the sale of petroleum products. The defendant built a truck stop and began selling diesel fuel. In plaintiff's suit to enjoin the sale of diesel products, the defendant argued that the plaintiff's remedy, if any, was against the grantor for breach of contract. He contended that the language in the deed to plaintiff did not impose a covenant on the land retained by the grantor,

but was merely a promise by the grantor to impose covenants in future deeds. Who should win this argument? See Hi–Lo Oil Co., Inc. v. McCollum, 38 Ohio App.3d 12, 526 N.E.2d 90 (1987).

SNOW v. VAN DAM

Supreme Judicial Court of Massachusetts, 1935.
291 Mass. 477, 197 N.E. 224.

LUMMUS, JUSTICE. This suit although brought in Middlesex county, relates to land on the seashore at Brier Neck in Gloucester in Essex county, title to which, after the decision in Luce v. Parsons, 192 Mass. 8, 77 N.E. 1032, was registered on September 5, 1906, in the name of one Luce, from whom title soon passed to one Shackelford. The tract so registered was bounded northerly by a line through a pond not far northerly from a county road called Thatcher Road, which ran through the tract from west to east; easterly by land of other owners; southerly by the Atlantic Ocean, where there was a fine bathing beach; and westerly by Witham Road. The entrance to the tract was at the northwesterly corner, where is situated the lot now owned by the defendant Van Dam, which is the larger part of a triangular piece of land lying north of Thatcher Road and enclosed by Thatcher Road, Witham Road and another road.

The northerly part of the tract, including the lot of the defendant Van Dam, is low and marshy. When the tract was registered in 1906, this northerly part was deemed unsuitable for building, and worthless, and consequently was not divided into lots on the earlier plans. Thatcher Road is a public way on which electric cars used to run. There is no summer residence on the north side of that way, and only one bounding on that way on the south side.

From Thatcher Road, going south, there is a fairly sharp ascent to the top of a low hill, from which there is a gentle slope southward to the beach. This hill and slope were in 1906, and still are, well adapted to summer residences. In 1907 the whole tract, except the part north of Thatcher Road, was divided into building lots. By later plans some of the lots were further subdivided and the boundaries of others were changed. In all, about a hundred building lots were laid out. Each of the plaintiffs owns one of these building lots, either on the hill or on the southerly slope, on which he has built a summer residence.

Between July 8, 1907, and January 23, 1923, almost all the lots into which the part of the tract south of Thatcher Road was divided, including the lots of most of the plaintiffs, were sold at various times by the general owner of the tract to various persons. With negligible exceptions, the deeds contained uniform restrictions, of which the material one is that "only one dwelling house shall be erected or maintained thereon at any given time which building shall cost not less than $2500 and no outbuilding containing a privy shall be erected or maintained on said parcel without the consent in writing of the grantor or their [sic] heirs." The entire unsold remainder of the land south of Thatcher Road was conveyed, on June 15, 1923, by Shackelford, the general owner of the unsold parts of the tract, to J. Richard Clark, subject to similar restrictions.

The low and marshy land north of Thatcher Road was first divided, on a revised plan of 1919, into three parcels, called C, D and E. The revised plan covered the whole Brier Neck tract. On January 23, 1923, about five months before the deed to J. Richard Clark, already mentioned, said Shackelford conveyed said lots C, D and E to one Robert C. Clark, subject to the following restrictions: "Only one dwelling house may be maintained on each of said parcels of land at any given time, which dwelling house shall cost not less than Twenty-five Hundred Dollars ($2500) unless plans and specifications for a dwelling house of less cost shall be approved in writing by the grantor of said parcels of land, and no outbuilding containing a privy shall be maintained on either of said parcels of land without the consent in writing of the grantor. . . ." Lot D is the last of which the larger part is now owned by the defendant Van Dam, having been conveyed to him by Robert C. Clark on February 18, 1933, subject to the restrictions contained in the deed to him "in so far as the same may be now in force and applicable." This phrase did not purport to create any new restriction, and could have no such effect. The defendants have erected on lot D a large building to be used for the sale of ice cream and dairy products and the conducting of the business of a common victualler. The plaintiffs bring this suit for an injunction, claiming a violation of the restrictions. We think that the erection of a building to be used for business purposes was a violation of the language of the restriction. The zoning of the land for business in 1927 by the city of Gloucester could not operate to remove existing restrictions.

Prior to the conveyance from Shackelford to Robert C. Clark on January 23, 1923, there could not have been, under the law of this commonwealth, any enforceable restriction upon lot D. Sprague v. Kimball, 213 Mass. 380, 100 N.E. 622, Ann.Cas.1914A, 431. If any now exists in favor of the lands of the plaintiffs, it must have been created by that deed.

. . . A restriction, to be attached to land by way of benefit, must not only tend to benefit that land itself, but must also be intended to be appurtenant to that land. . . . If not intended to benefit an ascertainable dominant estate, the restriction will not burden the supposed servient estate, but will be a mere personal contract on both sides. . . .

In the absence of express statement, an intention that a restriction upon one lot shall be appurtenant to a neighboring lot is sometimes inferred from the relation of the lots to each other. . . . But in many cases there has been a scheme or plan for restricting the lots in a tract undergoing development to obtain substantial uniformity in building and use. The existence of such a building scheme has often been relied on to show an intention that the restrictions imposed upon the several lots shall be appurtenant to every other lot in the tract included in the scheme. . . . In some cases the absence of such a scheme has made it impossible to show that the burden of the restriction was intended to be appurtenant to neighboring land. . . . In the present case, unless the lots of the plaintiffs and the defendant Van Dam were included in one scheme of restrictions, there is nothing to show that the restrictions upon the lot of the defendant Van Dam were intended to be appurtenant to the lots of the plaintiffs.

What is meant by a "scheme" of this sort? In England, where the idea has been most fully developed, it is established that the area covered by the scheme and the restrictions imposed within that area must be apparent to the several purchasers when the sales begin. The purchasers must know the extent of their reciprocal rights and obligations, or, in other words, the "local law" imposed by the vendor upon a definite tract. Reid v. Bickerstaff, [1909] 2 Ch. 305; Kelly v. Barrett, [1924] 2 Ch. 379, 399 et seq. Where such a scheme exists, it appears to be the law of England and some American jurisdictions that a grantee subject to restrictions acquires by implication an enforceable right to have the remaining land of the vendor, within the limits of the scheme, bound by similar restrictions. . . . But it was settled in this commonwealth by Sprague v. Kimball, 213 Mass. 380, 100 N.E. 622, Ann. Cas.1914A, 431, that the statute of frauds prevents the enforcement against the vendor, or any purchaser from him of a lot not expressly restricted, of any implied or oral agreement that the vendor's remaining land shall be bound by restrictions similar to those imposed upon lots conveyed. Only where . . . the vendor binds his remaining land by writing, can reciprocity of restriction between the vendor and the vendee be enforced.

Nevertheless, the existence of a "scheme" continues to be important in Massachusetts for the purpose of determining the land to which the restrictions are appurtenant. Sometimes the scheme has been established by preliminary statements of intention to restrict the tract, particularly in documents of a public nature or in a recorded plan. More often it is shown by the substantial uniformity of the restrictions upon the lots included in the tract. In some jurisdictions the logic of the English rule, that the extent and character of the scheme must be apparent when the sale of the lots begins, has led to rulings that the restrictions imposed in later deeds are not evidence of the existence or nature of the scheme. In the present case there is no evidence of a scheme except a list of conveyances of different lots from 1907 to 1923 with substantially uniform restrictions. Although the point has not been discussed by this court, the original papers show, more clearly than the reports, that subsequent deeds were relied on to show a scheme existing at the time of the earlier conveyances to the parties or their predecessors in title, in Hills v. Metzenroth, 173 Mass. 423, 53 N.E. 890; Bacon v. Sandberg, 179 Mass. 396, 60 N.E. 936; Stewart v. Finkelstone, 206 Mass. 28, 92 N.E. 37, 28 L.R.A.,N.S., 634, 138 Am.St. Rep. 370; and Storey v. Brush, 256 Mass. 101, 152 N.E. 225. See, also, Hazen v. Mathews, 184 Mass. 388, 393, 68 N.E. 838. Apparently in Massachusetts a "scheme" has legal effect if definitely settled by the common vendor when the sale of lots begins, even though at that time evidence of such settlement is lacking and a series of subsequent conveyances is needed to supply it. In Bacon v. Sandberg, 179 Mass.

396, 398, 60 N.E. 936, 937, it was said, "the criterion in this class of cases is the intent of the grantor in imposing the restrictions."

Neither the restricting of every lot within the area covered, nor absolute identity of restrictions upon different lots, is essential to the existence of a scheme. . . . But extensive omissions or variations tend to show that no scheme exists, and that the restrictions are only personal contracts.

The existence of a "scheme" is important in the law of retrictions for another purpose, namely, to enable the restrictions to be made appurtenant to a lot within the scheme which has been earlier conveyed by the common vendor. In the present case the lots of some of the plaintiffs were sold before, and the lots of others after, the conveyance from Shackelford to Robert C. Clark on January 23, 1923, which first imposed a restriction upon the lot now owned by the defendant Van Dam. The plaintiffs whose lots were sold before January 23, 1923, cannot claim succession to any rights of Shackelford or of land then retained by him. In general, an equitable easement or restriction cannot be created in favor of land owned by a stranger. Hazen v. Mathews, 184 Mass. 388, 68 N.E. 838. Compare Vogeler v. Alwyn Improvement Corp., 247 N.Y. 131, 159 N.E. 886; Lister v. Vogel, 110 N.J.Eq. 35, 158 A. 534. Nevertheless an earlier purchaser in a land development has long been allowed to enforce against a later purchaser the restrictions imposed upon the latter by the deed to him in pursuance of a scheme of restrictions. . . . Earlier as well as later purchasers of lots within the area covered by the scheme acquire such an interest in the restrictions that the common vendor cannot release them.

The rationale of the rule allowing an earlier purchaser to enforce restrictions in a deed to a later one pursuant to a building scheme, is not easy to find. The simple explanation that the deed to the earlier purchaser, subject to restrictions, implied an enforceable agreement on the part of the vendor to restrict in like manner all the remaining land included in the scheme (Dean Stone, now Mr. Justice Stone, in 19 Colum.L.Rev., 177, 187), cannot be accepted in Massachusetts without conflict with Sprague v. Kimball, 213 Mass. 380, 100 N.E. 622, Ann.Cas. 1914A, 431. In Bristol v. Woodward, 251 N.Y. 275, 288, 167 N.E. 441, 446, Cardozo, C.J., said, "If we regard the restriction from the point of view of contract, there is trouble in understanding how the purchaser of lot A can gain a right to enforce the restriction against the later purchaser of lot B without an extraordinary extension of Lawrence v. Fox, 20 N.Y. 268. . . . Perhaps it is enough to say that the extension of the doctrine, even if illogical has been made too often and too consistently to permit withdrawal or retreat."

It follows from what has been said, that if there was a scheme of restrictions, existing when the sale of lots began in 1907, which scheme included the lands of the plaintiffs and of the defendant Van Dam, and if the restrictions imposed upon the land of the defendant Van Dam in 1923 were imposed in pursuance of that scheme, then all the plaintiffs are entitled to relief, unless some special defense is shown. The burden is upon the plaintiffs to show the existence of such a scheme. In our opinion they have done so. Unquestionably there was a scheme which included all the land south of Thatcher Road. The real question is, whether in its origin it included the land north of that road, where is situated the lot of the defendant Van Dam. That lot lies at the gateway of the whole development. One must pass it to visit any part of Brier Neck. The use made of that lot tends strongly to fix the character of the entire tract. It is true, that the land north of Thatcher Road was not divided into lots until 1919, but it was shown on all the plans from the beginning. The failure to divide it sooner was apparently due to a belief that it could not be sold, not to an intent to reserve it for other than residential purposes. We think that the scheme from the beginning contemplated that no part of the Brier Neck tract should be used for commercial purposes. When the lot of the defendant Van Dam was restricted in 1923, the restriction was in pursuance of the original scheme and gave rights to earlier as well as to later purchasers. . . .

G.L.(Ter.Ed.) c. 184, § 23, provides that "restrictions, unlimited as to time, . . . shall be limited to the term of thirty years after the date of the deed or other instrument . . . creating them. . . ." The defendants contend that the restrictions in question were created in 1907, and therefore will expire in 1937 under the statute. But it has already been shown that no restriction existed upon the lot of the defendant Van Dam until January 23, 1923, when the conveyance to his grantor was made. Although the deed was dated January 19, 1923, the registration, which was the operative act of conveyance (G.L. c. 185, § 57), took place on January 23, 1923. The latter date is the one from which the period of thirty years runs. The final decree is to be modified by striking out the word "permanently" in paragraphs 4 and 5, and by inserting a provision limiting the period of the injunction to the time prior to and including January 23, 1953. As thus modified, the final decree is affirmed, with costs.

Ordered accordingly.

NOTES

1. A deed from A to B of a lot contained a covenant by B restricting the height of structures to be erected on this lot, the restriction being for the stated benefit of an adjoining lot owned by C. Held, C may enforce the restriction against a grantee from B. Vogeler v. Alwyn Improvement Corp., 247 N.Y. 131, 159 N.E. 886 (1928). The court said: "In some cases there are expressions in the opinions which standing alone might seem to indicate that the right of a prior grantee of one parcel to enforce a restriction imposed upon a subsequent conveyance of another parcel by the same grantor is limited to cases where both parcels were embraced in a general plan for development of a larger tract. A critical examination of these opinions will demonstrate that these considerations have been regarded as decisive only where on the face of the subsequent deed no covenant or restriction is found in favor of prior grantees or where the action has been brought

in jurisdictions where courts have been compelled to create an exception to a general rule prevailing there that a third party may not enforce a contract made for his benefit.

"In the present case no such questions exist. The restriction was imposed for the defendant's benefit under circumstances where the beneficiary of a promise may sue for its enforcement in accordance with the general doctrines prevailing here."

2. A conveyed one acre of urban land to B by a recorded deed with a covenant restricting use of the land to residential purposes. A owned no other land in the neighborhood. B subdivided the tract into four lots, erected a house on each of them, and conveyed them to various grantees by deeds without restrictions. C, the present owner of one of these lots, is undertaking to convert the residence to a structure suitable for commercial use. D, the present owner of another of these lots, seeks an injunction. What probable result? See Korn v. Campbell, 192 N.Y. 490, 85 N.E. 687 (1908).

3. Deeds from the common grantor of lots in a residential subdivision refer to residential restrictions as "covenants and conditions" and declare that the grantor reserves a right of entry for breach of any restriction. Can grantor, while he still owns some lots in the subdivision, assert his right of entry successfully? Consider W.F. White Land Co. v. Christenson, 14 S.W.2d 369 (Tex.Civ.App.1928). The court there said:

"It is our conclusion that what purported to be conditions subsequent in the deed are merely building restrictions denoting covenants, for the violation of which injunctive relief was provided in the instrument. . . . It was said by Chief Justice Phillips, in Decker v. Kirlicks, 110 Tex. 90, 216 S.W. 385, that: 'Forfeitures are harsh and punitive in their operation. They are not favored by the law, and ought not to be. The authority to forfeit a vested right or estate should not rest in provisions whose meaning is uncertain and obscure. It should be found only in language which is plain and clear—whose unequivocal character may render its exercise fair and rightful.' . . . It cannot be doubted that by that language the grantor was given a remedy for a violation of any of the restrictions contained in the deed, which are there designated as covenants. In view of the right so given, the grantor is in no position to claim the harsher remedy of forfeiture of title. . . ."

Suppose that the restrictions were referred to simply as "conditions." Who could enforce those? Could grantor obtain forfeiture? See Post v. Weil, 115 N.Y. 361, 22 N.E. 145 (1889), which construed such language as creating a covenant.

---

(3) CONSTITUTIONAL AND PUBLIC POLICY LIMITATIONS ON COVENANTS AND SERVITUDES

The enforceability of covenants and servitudes does not depend solely upon compliance with common law doctrines. Like other private arrangements, covenants and servitudes are subject to limitations imposed by statutes, constitutional doctrines, and public policy. They cannot be used to accomplish purposes that are clearly contrary to such laws or policies.

SHELLEY v. KRAEMER

[Reprinted herein at page 76.]

NOTE

Does it follow that court enforcement of private land use restrictions not relating to race would constitute "state action"? If so, what is the distinction between private and state action? Shelley v. Kraemer has not yet been extended by the United States Supreme Court beyond racial restrictions. See discussion in L. Tribe, American Constitutional Law § 18–6 (2d ed.1988).

Racial discrimination in the sale and use of land is also forbidden by legislation. See Jones v. Alfred H. Mayer Co., herein at page 49.

McMILLAN v. ISERMAN

Michigan Court of Appeals, 1983.
120 Mich.App. 785, 327 N.W.2d 559.

CAVANAGH, PRESIDING JUDGE.

Plaintiffs sued the defendants, alleging that the defendants' proposed use of property in their subdivision violated an amended deed restriction which prohibited the use of any subdivision lots for a state-licensed group residential facility, as that term is defined in M.C.L. § 125.216a; M.S.A. § 5.2961(16a), and M.C.L. § 125.583b; M.S.A. § 5.2933(2). The trial court granted the defendants' motion for summary judgment on the basis that the amended deed restriction discriminates against mentally impaired persons and thereby violates the Fourteenth Amendment to the United States Constitution. Plaintiffs appealed by right. Defendants cross-appealed, challenging the trial court's findings regarding the retroactive effect of the amended deed restriction and state public policy.

The issue which we must decide is whether the amended deed restriction prohibiting the use of subdivision property for a state-licensed group residential facility is valid and binding upon the defendants. The parties agree that the property in the subdivision is subject to a 1958 restrictive covenant which also provides that three-fourths of the property owners in the subdivision have the power to amend the restrictions at any time. We find our analysis somewhat hampered by the parties' failure to make the 1958 restrictive covenant a part of this record, especially since the defendants argue that they are not bound by the amended deed restriction which was amended pursuant to the provisions of the 1958 covenant. Although the trial court ruled in the defendants' favor on constitutional grounds, we will first examine the retroactive effect of the amended deed restriction and its conflict, if any, with state public policy.

Defendants argue that the amended deed restriction may not be applied retroactively because to do so would subject the defendants to an impermissible retroactive reciprocal negative easement. . . . In this case, the reciprocal negative easements consist of the 1958 deed restrictions, which apparently were validly imposed at a time when the subdivision property was in the hands of a common owner. The amended restriction is not, as such, an impermissible retroactive reciprocal negative easement; such a term implies an independent new restriction placed on land and applied retroactively rather than a new restriction stemming from an amendment passed pursuant to an amending clause found in the original deed restrictions.

Courts in this state and in other jurisdictions generally recognize that land use covenants containing restrictions such as reciprocal negative easements may include a clause giving the grantees or lot owners the power to amend, modify, extend or revoke the restrictions and that any such action taken by the property owners applies to all of the properties which are subject to the restrictions. Sampson v. Kaufman, 345 Mich. 48, 75 N.W.2d 64 (1956); Ardmore Park Subdivision v. Simon, 117 Mich.App. 57, 323 N.W.2d 591 (1982); Riley v. Boyle, 6 Ariz. App. 523, 434 P.2d 525 (1967); Montoya v. Barreras, 81 N.M. 749, 473 P.2d 363 (1970); Valdes v. Moore, 476 S.W.2d 936 (Tex.Civ.App.1972), and Anno: Validity, construction and effect of contractual provision regarding future revocation or modification of covenant restricting use of real property, 4 A.L.R.3d 570, 582–586, § 4(b). Cases concerning the issue of amended deed restrictions have generally dealt with parties opposing the amendment on the basis that it was not properly adopted (i.e., less than the required number agreed to the amendment) or that the amendment would apply only to a portion of the restricted area. None of the cases we have found address a factual scenario similar to the one presented here, i.e., relying upon the absence of any relevant deed restriction, defendants Iserman entered into a binding lease agreement with defendant Alternate Living Program and Health Assistance and subsequently the land use contracted for became impermissible because of a new amendment to the original deed restrictions. Thus, we are concerned here with an amendment which imposes a harsher restriction than any imposed in the original deed restrictions and which becomes effective *after* a lot owner has detrimentally relied on the absence of such a restriction.

This Court has not previously been faced with the issue of whether amended deed restrictions may be more restrictive than those contained in the original deed restrictions. The facts in other cases dealing with challenges to amended deed restrictions usually involved an amendment which is less restrictive. See Couch v. Southern Methodist University, 10 S.W.2d 973 (Tex.Comm.App.1928), Valdes v. Moore, supra. In Johnson v. Three Bays Properties # 2, Inc., 159 So.2d 924 (Fla.App.1964), the Court considered an amendment that was indisputably less restrictive yet the Court broadly held that amended deed restrictions may be more or less restrictive than the original deed restrictions. In Van Deusen v. Ruth, 343 Mo. 1096, 125 S.W.2d 1 (1938), the Court held that the word "amend" contained in the original deed restrictions could not be construed as permitting the imposition of harsher restrictions than those which had been originally imposed. Recently in *Ardmore Park Subdivision,* supra, a contested amendment imposed a harsher restriction prohibiting fences over four feet in height, but the propriety of imposing subsequent restrictions which are more restrictive was apparently not at issue.

We are not prepared to say that a clause permitting original deed restrictions to be amended must be limited to allow for only the imposition of restrictions which are less restrictive than those originally imposed. As the plaintiffs point out, defendants Iserman were on notice that the restrictions originally imposed and applicable to their land when they bought it were not absolute and could be amended at a later date. Presumably there was nothing in the amending clause which led defendants Iserman to believe that an amendment to the restrictions could only serve to lessen the original restrictions; the language of the clause itself has not been disputed by the parties. Although imposing a harsher restriction by amendment in and of itself does not trouble us, we are concerned with such an amendment when it seeks to affect a lot owner who has detrimentally relied on the absence of any such restriction.

Here we have lot owners who, in the absence of a deed restriction to the contrary, bind themselves by contract to a particular use of their land. After making this commitment, they are suddenly faced with an amendment to the deed restrictions, passed after they had bound themselves by contract, prohibiting such use of their land. To comply with the amended restriction would force them to be in breach of contract. We find this result to be manifestly unfair. Even with the knowledge that deed restrictions can be amended, lot owners have a right to rely on those restrictions in effect at the time they embark on a particular course of action regarding the use of their land, and subsequent amended deed restrictions should not be able to frustrate such action already begun.

For example, it certainly would be manifestly unfair to permit a subsequent amended deed restriction to force a lot owner to modify a preexisting use or structure which does not conform to the amendment. If a lot owner builds a garage, a subsequent amended deed restriction prohibiting garages could not force the owner to tear down his or her garage, which had been built when the owner relied on the absence of any such deed restriction. We see only a difference in degree between an amendment which seeks to affect a lot owner with a completed garage, a partially completed garage, or a contract to build a garage. In each case the lot owner would have, without notice to the contrary, relied on existing deed restrictions when embarking on the particular course of action, and a subsequent amendment should not be permitted to impose a hardship on such reliance.

We thus hold that an amended deed restriction does not apply to a lot owner who has, prior to the amendment, committed himself or herself to a certain land use which the amendment seeks to prohibit, providing: (1) the lot owner justifiably relied on the existing restrictions (i.e., had no notice of the proposed amendment), and (2) the lot owner will be prejudiced if the amendment is enforced as to his or her lot. Since we find that defendants Iserman justifiably relied on existing deed restrictions when they contracted with defendant Alternate Living Programs and Health Assistance, Inc., and since to enforce the amended deed restriction would result in forcing defendants Iserman to breach that contract, we hold that plaintiffs are estopped from asserting that the amended deed restriction applies to the lot owned by defendants Iserman.

Not only do we conclude that this amended deed restriction does not apply to the lot owned by defendants Iserman, but we also find that it is unenforceable on public policy grounds. We are not unmindful of the fact that courts should be wary of voiding a contract on the basis that it is contrary to public policy. Skutt v. Grand Rapids, 275 Mich. 258, 264, 266 N.W. 344 (1936). On the other hand, such caution must give way when the court is faced with a contract provision which is "manifestly against the public interest". 275 Mich. 265.

We recognize the fact that it is the established public policy of this state to permit and uphold certain restrictions upon the use and occupancy of real property. Wood v. Blancke, 304 Mich. 283, 287–288, 8 N.W.2d 67 (1943). However, it is also the settled public policy of our state to promote "the development and maintenance of quality programs and facilities for the care and treatment of the mentally handicapped". Bellarmine Hills Ass'n v. The Residential Systems Co., 84 Mich.App. 554, 558, 269 N.W.2d 673 (1978), lv. den. 405 Mich. 836 (1979). This policy is based in part upon Const.1963, art. 8, § 8, which provides:

> "Institutions, programs and services for the care, treatment, education or rehabilitation of those inhabitants who are physically, mentally or otherwise seriously handicapped shall always be fostered and supported."

This policy also finds legislative support in our zoning statutes, which state in pertinent part:

> "*In order to implement the policy of this state that persons in need of community residential care shall not be excluded by zoning from the benefits of normal residential surroundings,* a state licensed residential facility providing supervision or care, or both, to 6 or less persons shall be considered a residential use of property for the purposes of zoning and a permitted use in all residential zones, including those zoned for single family dwellings, and shall not be subject to a special use or conditional use permit or procedure different from those required for other dwellings of similar density in the same zone." (Emphasis added.) M.C.L. § 125.216a(2); M.S.A. § 5.2961(16a)(2).

The fact that a zoning statute limits its declaration of policy to zoning does not lessen to any degree the policy of this state to protect and foster facilities for the mentally handicapped.

With two such competing public policies in the scales and being faced with having to make a choice, we find that the scales in this case tip decidedly in favor of protecting the state-licensed residential facility for the mentally handicapped. As Judge McGregor stated, dissenting in Jayno Heights Landowners Ass'n v. Preston, 85 Mich.App. 443, 454–455, 271 N.W.2d 268 (1978):

> "In applying with the utmost caution the principle that restrictive covenants which violate public policy may not be enforced, I would find that the public policy favoring the establishment of residential adult foster care facilities outweighs the policy supporting the enforcement of residential restrictive covenants and that the covenant in question may not be enforced to enjoin defendants' use of this property as a licensed foster care facility. In reaching this result, it should be noted that the balance between the competing policies in this case is exceedingly close and that M.C.L. § 331.688(1); M.S.A. § 16.610(8)(1) serves to prohibit the excessive concentration of such facilities in any community. Residential homeowners are therefore protected from any detriments which may result from such a situation."

We conclude that the amended deed restriction here, specifically prohibiting state-licensed residential facilities for the mentally handicapped, is manifestly against the public interest and thus unenforceable on public policy grounds.

In light of our resolution of the two foregoing issues, we need not address the constitutional argument raised by the parties.

Affirmed.

MACKENZIE, JUDGE (dissenting).

I respectfully dissent. The parties agree that the property at issue is covered by a restrictive covenant dating back to 1958 which, among other things, permits three-fourths of the property owners within the subdivision to amend the restrictive covenant at any time. The covenant was amended on November 3, 1980, to include the following restrictions:

> "1. All of the lots of this subdivision shall be owned, described and used for strictly private residential purposes only.
>
> "2. No lot may be used for the operation of any business, enterprise, activity or service, profit or nonprofit, where the gross revenues, payments or other remuneration received by such businesses, enterprises, activities or services, or by the owners and/or operators of such businesses, enterprises, activities or services, exceed three thousand dollars ($3,000.00) per annum.
>
> "3. No lot may be used for the operation of any state licensed residential facility, as that term is defined by Sections 125.216a, 125.286a and 125.583b of the Michigan Compiled Laws on January 1, 1980, such laws being more commonly referred to as M.C.L.A. Sections 125.216a, 125.286a and 125.583b. This restriction is to be liberally construed and is meant to exclude the operation of any State of Michigan-licensed facility that provides resident services for six (6) or less persons under 24-hour supervision or care for persons in need of that supervision or care, whether such residen-

tial facility is licensed pursuant to Public Act 287 of 1972, as amended, Public Act 218 of 1979, as amended, or pursuant to any Public Act of the State of Michigan that may be adopted in the future which supersedes or amends Public Act 287 of 1972 or Public Act 218 of 1979 in any way.

"4. No lot may be used for the operation of any business, enterprise, activity or service where the primary purpose of such business, enterprise, activity or service is to provide shelter, supervision and/or care to other persons in exchange for remuneration of any sort. This restriction shall not be interpreted so as to prevent any property owner within the Huron Woods Subdivision from renting or leasing his home to another person or persons, providing that the person or persons do not then use the home to provide shelter, supervision and/or care to other persons in exchange for remuneration of any kind."

Defendants Iserman acquired the property at issue before the 1980 amendments. Defendants argue that the 1980 amendments were invalid because they imposed retroactive reciprocal negative easements. . . .

The difficulty with defendants' argument is that the provision of the restrictive covenant permitting amendment predates defendants' acquisition of the property at issue and apparently dates back to the time when all the property in the subdivision was in the hands of a common owner. Thus, the provision for amendment was itself a valid nonretroactive reciprocal negative easement.

Defendants rely on Sampson v. Kaufman, 345 Mich. 48, 75 N.W.2d 64 (1956). In that case the Court held that the renewal of certain provisions of a restrictive covenant by a vote of two-thirds of the property owners within a subdivision was invalid as creating retroactive reciprocal negative easements; however, in *Sampson,* renewal took place 21 months after the date specified in the original restrictive covenant for renewal. *Sampson* cannot be read as prohibiting renewal or amendment of provisions of a restrictive covenant in accordance with the provisions in the original restrictive covenant for renewal or amendment.

As the majority correctly points out, other jurisdictions which have considered the issue have generally recognized as valid the amendment of a restrictive covenant in accordance with the provisions in the original covenant for amendment. . . .

The majority proffers a theory of estoppel and detrimental reliance. However, an examination of the record discloses that none of the elements of estoppel are present here. . . .

By what conduct of plaintiffs were defendants misled? The restrictive covenant in effect at the time defendants acquired the property gave defendants notice that the covenant might be amended at any time by three-fourths of the property owners in the subdivision. There is no claim of any explicit or implicit representation by plaintiffs that the right to amend the covenant would not be exercised. There is no claim that plaintiffs failed to act promptly on learning of defendants' plans. There is no claim that plaintiffs knew that defendants had entered into a lease when they acted to amend the covenant.

How have defendants suffered prejudice? This is not a case in which defendants claim to have made substantial improvements to the property on the supposition that their proposed use of the property would be permitted. Compare Boston-Edison Protective Ass'n v. Teahen, 337 Mich. 353, 358–359, 60 N.W.2d 162 (1953). Defendants have entered into a lease, but defendants have never claimed that they will suffer damages if the land use they envisioned when they entered the lease is forbidden. In this connection it should be noted that frustration of purpose and impossibility of performance are well-established defenses to an action for breach of contract; see 17 Am.Jur.2d, Contracts, §§ 401, 402, 404, pp. 847–850, 851–853.

Defendants also argue that the restrictions were contrary to public policy and therefore void. . . .

Courts should act with caution in determining whether contracts are contrary to public policy and therefore void. Contracts should be declared void only in cases plainly within the reasons on which the doctrine rests. . . .

Defendants first seek an applicable public policy in certain zoning statutes. The following language appears as M.C.L. § 125.216a(2), M.S.A. § 5.2961(16a)(2), M.C.L. § 125.286a(2), M.S.A. § 5.2963(16a)(2), and M.C.L. § 125.583b(2), M.S.A. § 5.2933(2)(2):

> "In order to implement the policy of this state that *persons in need of community residential care shall not be excluded by zoning from the benefits of normal residential surroundings,* a state licensed residential facility providing supervision of care, or both, to 6 or less persons shall be considered a residential use of property *for the purposes of zoning* and a permitted use in all residential zones, including those zoned for single family dwellings, and shall not be subject to a special use or conditional use permit or procedure different from those required for other dwellings of similar density in the same zone." (Emphasis added.)

The emphasized language shows that the Legislature expressly limited its declaration of policy to zoning. To apply the statutes to void a restrictive covenant would be to ignore the plain language of the statute.

Defendants also seek an applicable public policy in a line of decisions of this Court which includes Bellarmine Hills Ass'n v. The Residential Systems Co., 84 Mich.App. 554, 269 N.W.2d 673 (1978), lv. den. 405 Mich. 836 (1979); . . . The issue in these cases was not whether restrictive covenants were valid or void; rather, each case presented a dispute as to interpretation of a restrictive covenant. . . .

Defendants argue and the circuit judge held that judicial enforcement of the restrictive covenant would amount to a denial of equal protection. In Shelley v. Kraemer, 334 U.S. 1, 10–11, 68 S.Ct. 836, 840–41, 92 L.Ed. 1161 (1948), the Court held that judicial enforcement of a restrictive covenant was state action and therefore judicial enforcement of a covenant requiring racial discrimination amounted to a denial of the equal protection of laws guaranteed by U.S. Const., Am. XIV. . . .

In contrast to the restrictions at issue in *Shelley,* the restrictions here proscribe a particular use of the affected properties, use as a state-licensed residential facility. No designated class of persons is excluded from ownership or use of the properties. Moreover, the restrictions here would not amount to a denial of equal protection if imposed by statute or ordinance. Compare Village of Belle Terre v. Boraas, 416 U.S. 1, 94 S.Ct. 1536, 39 L.Ed.2d 797 (1974), in which the Court upheld a zoning ordinance which restricted land use to one-family dwellings excluding lodging houses, boarding houses, fraternity houses, or multiple dwelling houses. The ordinance specified that more than two persons living together but not related by blood, marriage, or adoption did not constitute one family. The Court found the ordinance to be reasonable rather than arbitrary and to bear a rational relationship to a permissible state objective, namely, preservation of the single family character of the neighborhood.

In view of the foregoing, I would reverse and remand for entry of an appropriate injunction.

NOTES

1. Laws and policies that render covenants and servitudes unenforceable are commonly applicable to other types of arrangements as well. Several examples may be found elsewhere in this casebook. Attempts to exclude group homes from residential areas by zoning are treated at page 934. Jones v. Alfred H. Mayer Co., at page 49, involves the application of constitutional and statutory prohibitions against racial discrimination to sales and rentals of housing. The legality of private restrictions of occupancy to certain age groups is treated at page 436.

2. Some state constitutions contain provisions protecting a homestead against all debts except those for the purchase money of the home, home improvements and taxes. The lots in many residential subdivisions are subject to covenants imposing an annual assessment for the maintenance of common areas and declaring such assessments secured by a lien against the land. If a homeowner defaults in paying an assessment, should foreclosure of the lien be barred by the homestead provisions? See Bessemer v. Gersten, 381 So.2d 1344 (Fla.1980); Inwood North Homeowners' Ass'n v. Harris, 736 S.W.2d 632 (Tex.1987).

(4) CONSTRUCTION, ADMINISTRATION AND TERMINATION

(Relationship of bldg. + use restriction)

JOSLIN v. PINE RIVER DEVELOPMENT CORP.

Supreme Court of New Hampshire, 1976.
116 N.H. 814, 367 A.2d 599.

KENISON, CHIEF JUSTICE. This is an appeal from an order of the Superior Court (King, J.) granting a permanent injunction enjoining the defendants, their successors and all persons acting under their authority from using Lot # 26 in the Scribner Park Subdivision at Pine River Pond in Wakefield, New Hampshire as a common boating or beach area, or a common ingress or egress to and from the beach. The defendants were also enjoined from using Lot # 26 in any manner inconsistent with or in contravention of the restrictions in the deed conveying the lots on Pine River Pond. All exceptions were reserved and transferred. P.H.

The original developers, the Scribners, laid out forty-eight shore lots including Lot # 26 and many more back lots which together constitute the Scribner Park Subdivision. They conveyed some of the shore parcels to the plaintiffs or their predecessors in title. The defendant corporation purchased Lot # 26 and a large tract with no frontage. The corporation subdivided the large tract into 161 lots and sold 147 of them to various buyers, some of whom formed the defendant Pine River Association, Inc. The corporation conveyed Lot # 26 to the association so that association members would have access to the water and could use the area for swimming, docking their boats, and for other recreational purposes. The land was conveyed because the owners of back lots "ran into trouble" attempting to use other routes to the water. The defendants entered upon Lot # 26 and cleared the land for the admitted purpose of making it a docking, beach and recreational area.

All of the deeds to the frontage lots including Lot # 26 contain four restrictions limiting the number of cottages to be built on the lots, prohibiting mobile homes, requiring permanent buildings, finished exteriors, modern plumbing facilities and imposing set back requirements. Two other restrictions concern utility easements and drainage rights.

The defendants do not dispute that Lot # 26 is subject to the six restrictions imposed upon the rest of the parcels of land in the subdivision. The parties disagree only upon the meaning or effect of those covenants. In determining whether the restrictions concerning the construction of a cottage on Lot # 26 prevent the defendants from using the lot for common beach and boating purposes, we confront the general issue of whether restrictions on dwellings or residences limit the use of the land itself apart from any building. 5 R. Powell, Real Property § 673, at 158–62 (1968). The conclusions reached in cases posing this issue are so dependent upon the particular phraseology of the covenants involved that no sufficient general rules can be stated. Annot., Restrictive Covenants as Applicable to Land Itself Apart from Buildings, 155 A.L.R. 528 (1945). Issue

. . .

According to the defendants, the proper rule of law to be applied in this case is that restrictive covenants are strictly construed to permit the free use of land, that all doubts must be resolved in favor of free use, and that no restrictions may be implied from those expressly stated. . . .

. . .

The former prejudice against restrictive covenants which led courts to strictly construe them is yielding to a gradual recognition that they are valuable land use planning devices. 7 G. Thompson, Real Property § 3158 (J. Grimes ed. Supp.1976). In Traficante v. Pope, 115 N.H. 356, 358, 341 A.2d 782, 784 (1975), we noted that private land use restrictions "have been particularly important in the twentieth century when the value of property often depends in large measure upon maintaining the character of the neighborhood in which it is situated." They are particularly useful in the development of lake communities. Vogel, Lake Community Developments with Property Owners' Associations: Selected Problems for Lot Owners, 8 Urb.L.Ann. 169, 172 (1974). The modern viewpoint is that the former policy of strictly construing restrictive covenants is no longer operative. 7 G. Thompson, supra at § 3166 (J. Grimes ed. Supp.1976).

Even some of those courts that speak in terms of strict construction have mitigated the harshness of the rule. They give great weight to the intent of the parties and will not defeat the purpose for which the covenant was established. Stockdale v. Lester, 158 N.W.2d 20 (Iowa 1968); Hanley v. Misischi, 111 R.I. 233, 302 A.2d 79 (1973). All the surrounding circumstances existing at the time of the creation of the covenants are taken into account in determining the intent of the parties. 5 R. Powell, supra at § 673; 7 G. Thompson, supra at § 3160, at 108–10 (J. Grimes ed. 1962). In determining whether building restrictions constitute use restrictions on the land itself, courts often consider the location and character of the entire tract of land, the purpose of the limitation, whether it was imposed for the sole benefit of the grantor or for the grantee and subsequent purchasers as well and whether the restriction is pursuant to a general building plan for the development of the property. Annot., 155 A.L.R. 528, 529 (1945); see Annot., Construction and Application of Covenant Restricting Use of Property to "Residence" or "Residential Purposes," 175 A.L.R. 1191, 1193 (1948). The rule of law proposed by the defendant is too mechanical and rigid and is not the law in this State.

. . . We cannot say as a matter of law that in the instant case the trial judge, who heard all the testimony, reviewed all the evidence and made findings of fact, erred in granting the injunction.

The restrictive covenants imposed upon Lot # 26, although explicitly referring only to buildings are obviously part of a general plan to prevent the use of property in the Scribner Park Subdivision for any purpose other than residential. . . . Given the surrounding circumstances and the conduct and intent of the parties, the court was not required to find that the use of Lot # 26 by potentially hundreds of people at all hours of the day and night for docking their boats, sunbathing, swimming and other recreational activities was within the scheme of residential development of the Pine River Pond area. . . .

. . .

Defendants' exceptions overruled.

NOTES

1. Compare Jones v. The Park Lane for Convalescents, Inc., 384 Pa. 268, 120 A.2d 535 (1956), holding that a covenant that the land "shall be used only for the purpose of erecting thereon private dwellings" did not prevent the owner from using a residence for a convalescent and nursing home and making interior alterations to accommodate the new use. The court said:

"In order properly to consider and determine the question involved it is important at the outset to have in mind the applicable legal principles that have been enunciated, frequently reiterated, and consistently applied, through a long succession of cases decided by this court. . . . However variously phrased, they are, in substance, that restrictions on the use of land are not favored by the law because they are an interference with an owner's free and full enjoyment of his property; that nothing will be deemed a violation of a restriction that is not in plain disregard of its express words; that there are no implied rights arising from a restriction which the courts will recognize; that a restriction is not to be extended or enlarged by implication; that every restriction will be construed most strictly against the grantor and every doubt and ambiguity in its language resolved in favor of the owner. Restrictions limiting the right of the owner to deal with his land as he may desire fall naturally into two distinct classes, the one consisting of restrictions on the type and number of buildings to be erected thereon, and the other on the subsequent use of such buildings. The restrictions in the former class are concerned with the physical aspect or external appearance of the buildings, those in the latter class with the purposes for which the buildings are used, the nature of their occupancy, and the operations conducted therein as affecting the health, welfare and comfort of the neighbors. A building restriction and a use restriction are wholly independent of one another, and, in view of the legal principles above stated, the one is not to be extended so as to include the other unless the intention so to do is expressly and plainly stated; to doubt is to deny enforcement."

Similar reasoning was used in Greenbrier–Cloverdale Homeowners Association v. Baca, 763 P.2d 1 (Colo.App.1988) to support the conclusion that a covenant prohibiting buildings "other than single-family dwellings" did not preclude use of a house in the subdivision as a home for developmentally disabled adults. What other rationale might the courts have relied on to reach the same result? See McMillan v. Iserman, reprinted herein at p. 691.

2. Several cases have involved the applicability of restrictions to mobile homes and modular homes. Would you anticipate that courts would be sympathetic to such housing? They disagree. Compare Lassiter v. Bliss, 559 S.W.2d 353 (Tex.1977) (construing a covenant

excluding "trailers" as also excluding mobile homes) with Heath v. Parker, 93 N.M. 680, 604 P.2d 818 (1980) (contra). Modular homes have been treated somewhat more favorably. In Kennedy v. Classic Designs, Inc., 239 Kan. 540, 722 P.2d 504 (1986) the court construed a prohibition against moving buildings into the subdivision as inapplicable to modular homes. In distinguishing among mobile homes, "stick-built" homes constructed entirely on the premises, and modular homes the court suggested that the construction of modular homes differed only in degree from the construction of "stick-built" homes, which often contain preformed or prebuilt components. It concluded that "[t]he construction of the proposed dwelling by utilizing new components built off the premises and then moving those components onto the lot and assembling them into a completed building does not constitute moving a building into the addition."

SUTTLE v. BAILEY

Supreme Court of New Mexico, 1961.
68 N.M. 283, 361 P.2d 325.

CARMODY, JUSTICE. The defendants in the court below appeal from the granting of an injunction restraining them from using their real estate as business property in violation of certain restrictions.

In about 1937, a Mr. Dickason and his wife platted and dedicated an addition to the City of Albuquerque known as the Mesa Verde Addition. The entire property was subdivided into lots and restrictive covenants placed thereon. These covenants, as to at least a certain portion of the addition, restricted the use of the property to residential uses only. The actual restrictions themselves are not pertinent, but the covenant which was contained in the deeds detailed certain prohibitions as to building and use, and closed with the following sentence:

". . . The said covenants shall run with the land, and shall be construed as real covenants until January 1st, 1970, when they shall cease and terminate, except, however, it is mutually understood and agreed that the above covenants and restrictions or any of them, may be altered, or annulled at any time prior to said January 1st, 1970, by written agreement by and between the first party, his successors, or assigns, and the owner for the time being of the premises in respect of which it is agreed to alter, or annul, the said covenants and restrictions; and the said written agreement, if made, shall be effectual to alter, or annul, said covenants and restrictions as to the said premises without the consent of the owner, or owners, of any adjacent premises."

The plaintiffs are the present owners of two of the lots in the addition and the defendants are purchasing two of the adjoining lots from the now record owners thereof, a Mr. and Mrs. Thomas. The contract to purchase provides that the property is being sold subject to the restrictions of record. The defendants have placed an office building nearer to the property line than allowed by the restrictions and have constructed improvements for the operation of an insulation business.

Although other questions are raised, the only matter that we need to determine is whether a general reservation of the power to dispense with restrictions negatives the purpose of uniform development from which the right of mutuality among lot owners in a platted subdivision is deemed to arise. To state the proposition in another way, is a reservation by the grantor of a general power to dispense with restrictions a personal covenant, or one which runs with the land? . . .

The right was reserved to the grantor, and the fact that it was not exercised except in the one instance does not destroy the substance of the right. No subsequent grantee had any assurance, other than the personal integrity of the original grantor, that the restrictions on any adjacent lot or lots in the subdivision might not be altered or annulled at any time without his consent. Therein lies the lack of mutuality or reciprocity so necessary to create a covenant which will run with the land and inure to the benefit of all subsequent owners. We, therefore, hold that the reservation included in the covenant made it a personal covenant between the grantor and his individual grantees, and that there is no right as between the individual grantees to enforce the restrictive covenants; that the right is one which is vested only in the grantor, and does not run with the land. . . .

The judgment of the district court will be reversed and the cause remanded, with direction to set aside its judgment and decree and to enter judgment denying the injunctive relief sought and dismissing the complaint.

It is so ordered.

COMPTON, C. J., and CHAVEZ and MOISE, JJ., concur.

NOBLE, J., not participating.

NOTE

Compare Moore v. Megginson, 416 So.2d 993 (Ala.1982), approving a reservation in subdivider of authority to modify or terminate restrictions, but requiring that this power be exercised reasonably. See also Annot., 4 A.L.R.3d 570, 573 (1965).

RHUE v. CHEYENNE HOMES, INC.

Supreme Court of Colorado, 1969.
168 Colo. 6, 449 P.2d 361.

PRINGLE, JUSTICE. In the trial court, Cheyenne Homes, Inc., obtained an injunction prohibiting Leonard Rhue and Family Homes, Inc., hereinafter referred to as plaintiffs in error, from moving a thirty year old Spanish style house into a new subdivision which was about 80% improved and which contained only modern ranch style or split level homes.

At the time that the subdivision in which the plaintiffs in error seek to locate this house was platted, the owner placed upon the entire area certain restrictive covenants contained in a "Declaration of Protective Covenants," which was duly recorded. As recited in the document, these protective covenants were for the purpose of "protecting the present and future values of the properties located" in the subdivision. Admittedly, the house which the plaintiffs in error wish to put in the subdivision does not violate any of the few specific restrictions contained in the protective covenants. However, paragraph C–2 of the recorded protective covenants contains the following declaration:

"C–2 No building shall be erected, placed or altered on any lot until the construction plans and specifications and a plan showing the location of the structure shall have been approved by the architectural control committee . . .."

Plaintiffs in error failed to submit their plans to the architectural control committee, and the trial court, in entering its injunction, held (1) that such failure constituted a breach of the restrictive covenants, and (2) that the placing of the house would not be in harmony with the existing neighborhood and would depreciate property values in the area.

Plaintiffs in error contend that restriction C–2 is not enforceable because no specific standards are contained therein to guide the committee in determining the approval or disapproval of plans when submitted. We disagree.

It is no secret that housing today is developed by subdividers who, through the use of restrictive covenants, guarantee to the purchaser that his house will be protected against adjacent construction which will impair its value, and that a general plan of construction will be followed. Modern legal authority recognizes this reality and recognizes also that the approval of plans by an architectural control committee is one method by which guarantees of value and general plan of construction can be accomplished and maintained.

So long as the intention of the covenant is clear (and in the present case it is clearly to protect present and future property values in the subdivision), covenants such as the one before us have been upheld against the contention that they lacked specific restrictions providing a framework within which the architectural committee must act. Winslette v. Keeler, 220 Ga. 100, 137 S.E.2d 288; Kirkley v. Seipelt, 212 Md. 127, 128 A.2d 430; Fairfax Community Assoc. v. Boughton, 127 N.E.2d 641 (Ohio Com.Pl.); Hannula v. Hacienda Homes, 34 Cal.2d 442, 211 P.2d 302, 19 A.L.R.2d 1268. In Kirkley v. Seipelt, supra, the plaintiff in error argued unsuccessfully that a covenant requiring approval of plans failed in the test of reasonableness because there were no standards to guide the approving party.

. . .

. . . While we have here enunciated the proposition that the covenant requiring approval of the architectural committee before erection of a house in the subdivision is enforceable, we point out that there is a corollary to that proposition which affords protection and due process of law to a purchaser of a lot in the subdivision, namely, that a refusal to approve plans must be reasonable and made in good faith and must not be arbitrary or capricious. . . .

Since two of the three committee members testified that they would disapprove the plans if they were presented to them, we examine the evidence to determine if such refusal is warranted under the rules we have laid down. There was testimony that the house was about thirty years old, and that the other houses were no older than two years. The house of plaintiffs in error has a stucco exterior and a red tile roof. The other houses are commonly known as ranch style or split level, and are predominantly of brick construction with asphalt shingle roofs. There was further testimony that the style of the house would devalue the surrounding properties because it was "not compatible" with the houses already in place.

One member of the committee expressed concern that the house of plaintiffs in error would devalue surrounding property. The other added that he thought the covenant gave the architectural committee the authority to refuse approval of plans for property which would seriously affect the market value of other homes in the area. Clearly, a judgment of disapproval of the plans by the committee is reasonable and in good faith and in harmony with the purposes declared in the covenant.

The judgment is affirmed.

NOTE

The liberalized enforcement of covenants has helped to maintain the uniform character and quality of residential areas, but the resulting homogeneity may have serious drawbacks both for individuals and for society as a whole. Consider the comments by Winokur in The Mixed Blessings of Promissory Servitudes: Toward Optimizing Economic Utility, Individual Liberty, and Personal Identity, 1989 Wisc.L.Rev. 1, 3–5:

> By so strictly segregating land uses, these servitudes often exclude not only all nonresidential uses, but also residential uses which vary in density, in cost, or in caliber of improvements. Neighborhood servitude restrictions can effectively segregate social classes, isolating residents of one neighborhood from outsiders who neither live, shop nor work with residents of these exclusive districts. In contrast to some uniquely beautiful servitude-restricted neighborhoods, much of the suburban sprawl controlled by association-administered servitude regimes has become aesthetically undifferentiated and culturally desolate. . . . [T]he domination of housing markets by potentially perpetual, uniform servitude regimes has begun to undercut both the economic efficiency of these servitudes and the personal liberties of existing residents and potential buyers. Enforcement of all restrictions imposed by servitude regimes, limiting neither the duration nor the content of servitudes, can also undermine the availability of neighborhoods conducive to human flourishing, where each individual's identity can be based on personal control of a unique place in the residential environment.

Are these criticisms justified? Would legislation limiting the enforceability of covenants to a specified number of years adequately remedy the problems mentioned? Are there other reforms you can suggest?

COWLING v. COLLIGAN

Supreme Court of Texas, 1958.
312 S.W.2d 943.

CALVERT, JUSTICE. This class suit was brought by R.E. Cowling and some seventeen other owners of lots in Post Oak Gardens subdivision, an addition to the City of Houston, against Mrs. R.M. Colligan as owner and J. Terry Falkenbury as tenant or lessee of Tract No. 2 in the subdivision. The purpose of the suit was to obtain a declaratory judgment that certain restrictive covenants, and particularly a covenant restricting use of the lots in the subdivision "for residence purposes only" were still valid, binding and enforceable restrictions on the use of all lots or tracts in the subdivision and to enjoin the defendants from using Tract No. 2 for business or commercial purposes. Falkenbury died before trial and his interest, if any, went out of the case.

The case was tried without a jury. Judgment was entered declaring the restrictive covenants contained in a certain instrument of record, including the covenant limiting the use of the lots for residence purposes only, to be "valid, subsisting and enforceable restrictive covenants" which had "not been waived, breached or abandoned to such an extent that they are no longer enforceable." However, the court recited in its judgment that there had been such a change of conditions and of uses of lands in the vicinity of Tract No. 2 as to make it unjust and inequitable to enforce the covenants against that tract and ordered it removed from their effect. The Court of Civil Appeals affirmed. 307 S.W.2d 841.

Pursuant to request of plaintiffs the trial judge filed findings of fact and conclusions of law. The appeal of the plaintiffs was predicated solely on the transcript containing the findings and conclusions. No statement of facts was filed in the Court of Civil Appeals.

Other restrictive covenants are involved in the declaratory judgment but issue is joined by the parties on the covenant restricting the use of Tract No. 2 for residence purposes only.

There is no map or plat of the Post Oak Gardens subdivision in the record before us and we have no descriptive information with respect to the division other than that which is found in the findings of fact filed by the trial court.

The findings of fact pertinent to the issue before us establish that the subdivision contains 49 tracts or lots ranging in size from 4 to 7.81 acres; that a church is located on the east three acres of Tract No. 1, to the west of Tract No. 2, and immediately across Bering Drive; that churches have been built upon two other tracts in the subdivision, and several other tracts have been sold to church bodies who contemplate the erection of church buildings; that one-half of the remaining building sites in the sudivision have residences erected upon them; that

Tract No. 2, owned by the defendant, contains 5 acres, is bounded on the south by Westheimer Road and on the west by Bering Drive, has no improvements upon it except for one small frame building which is easily removable, and has never been devoted to any business or commercial use except for the storage of pipe and related items upon it; that the property adjoining Tract No. 2 on the east also fronts on Westheimer Road, is outside of the subdivision, is unrestricted, and is devoted to business and commercial uses; that the property abutting Westheimer Road on the south is outside the subdivision, is unrestricted, and is devoted to business and commercial uses; that Westheimer Road was a quiet country road at the time the subdivision was platted and the restrictions laid, but is now a heavily-traveled main thoroughfare; that the reasonable market value of Tract No. 2, restricted, is $10,000 per acre, whereas, if unrestricted, it is from $35,000 to $43,000 per acre. What may be said to be an "ultimate" fact finding of the trial court is as follows: "Tract No. 2, by reason of all of said matters, is no longer suitable for exclusively residential purposes."

The trial court concluded that the restrictions laid by the instrument of record are "valid, subsisting and enforceable restrictive covenants, and the same have not been waived, breached and abandoned to such an extent that the same are no longer enforceable in accordance with their terms." The trial court further concluded, however, that "it is no longer just and equitable to enforce said restrictive covenants against Tract No. 2 and to prevent the use of it for business and commercial purposes."

The plaintiffs contended in the Court of Civil Appeals, and contend here, that, as a matter of law, the facts found by the trial court do not support its second conclusion and that the court erred in removing Tract No. 2 from the effect of the restrictive covenant. We agree.

There are certain rules of law by which a court of equity must be guided in determining whether to enforce a residential-only restriction. It may refuse to enforce it because of the acquiescence of the lot owners in such substantial violations within the restricted area as to amount to an abandonment of the covenant or a waiver of the right to enforce it. 5 Restatement of the Law of Property § 561; 2 American Law of Property § 9.38; 14 Am.Jur. 644–646, Covenants, Conditions and Restrictions §§ 295–298; 12 Tex.Jur. 172–174, Covenants and Conditions § 108. It may also refuse to enforce it because there has been such a change of conditions in the restricted area or surrounding it that it is no longer possible to secure in a substantial degree the benefits sought to be realized through the covenant. 5 Restatement of the Law of Property § 564; 2 American Law of Property § 9.39; 14 Am.Jur. 648, § 305.

As heretofore indicated, the trial court found that the restrictions in Post Oak Gardens had not been waived or abandoned. Whether that conclusion be treated as an ultimate finding of fact or as a conclusion of law, the only contrary evidentiary fact found by the trial court is the erection and existence of churches in the subdivision. In the absence of a statement of facts we must presume that the other evidence heard supports the finding or conclusion.

The authorities are uniform in declaring that the erection of a church violates a covenant restricting the use of property for residential purposes. . . . . It has been held, however, that the violation is so trivial in character that the failure of other property owners in the restricted area to complain does not operate as a waiver of their right to enforce the covenant against business or commercial development, or as an abandonment of the covenant. Mechling v. Dawson, 234 Ky. 318, 28 S.W.2d 18, 19. We approve that holding.

A court may not refuse to enforce a residential-only restriction against a particular lot on the sole ground that a change of conditions has rendered the lot unsuitable for residential purposes and it would therefore be inequitable to enforce it. The equities favoring the particular owner is only one facet of the judicial inquiry. Those equities must be weighed against the equities favoring the lot owners who, having acquired their property on the strength of the restriction, wish to preserve the residential character of the area. The judgment must arise out of a balancing of equities or of relative hardships. 5 Restatement of the Law of Property § 563. In paragraph c of § 563 it is said: "It is not sufficient to create the disproportion [of harm] that will justify refusing to grant injunctive relief that the harm ensuing from granting such relief will be greater than the benefit gained thereby. When the disproportion between harm and benefit is the sole reason for refusing relief, the disproportion must be one of considerable magnitude."

The trial court made no finding that the removal of Tract No. 2 from the restriction would not prove harmful to the plaintiffs who wish to preserve the residential character of the subdivision, and we may not presume such a finding. Rule 299, Texas Rules of Civil Procedure. Other than the advent of churches into the subdivision the only changed conditions found by the court lie outside the subdivision. Tract No. 2 is a border tract and is openly exposed to those changed conditions but the majority view is that "if the benefits of the original plan for a restricted subdivision can still be realized for the protection of the interior lots, the restriction should be enforced against the border lots, notwithstanding that such lot owners are deprived of the most valuable use of their lots." 2 American Law of Property 447. See also 4 A.L.R.2d 115. We are committed to that view. Bethea v. Lockhart, Tex.Civ.App., 127 S.W.2d 1029, writ refused. . . .

The reasoning of the courts is that if because of changed conditions outside the restricted area one lot or tract were permitted to drop from under the protective cover of residential-only restrictions, the owner of the adjoining lot would then have an equal claim on the conscience of the court, and, in due course, all other lots would fall like ten-pins, thus circumventing and nullifying the restriction and destroying the essentially residential character of the entire area. It is no answer to that reasoning to say that the trial court's judgment has declared the restriction enforceable against all other lots and thus will prevent such a disastrous result. The judgment is res adjudicata only of present and not of future conditions. 14 Am.Jur. 648. . . .

We can see no reason why our normal procedure should not be followed in this case. Accordingly, the judgment of the Court of Civil Appeals is reversed and the judgment of the trial court is reformed by striking from it the following:

". . . provided, however, by reason of the change of conditions and uses of lands in the vicinity of Tract Two (2) Post Oak Gardens, both in the immediate area within said subdivision, as well as adjoining and abutting lands without, it is no longer just and equitable to enforce said restrictive covenants against said Tract Two (2), and the said Tract Two (2) is hereby ordered removed from the effect of such restrictive covenants."

As reformed the judgment of the trial court is affirmed, and that court is directed to issue a writ of injunction in appropriate terms restraining and enjoining the defendant from devoting Tract No. 2 to business or commercial uses.

All costs are taxed against defendant.

NOTES

1. If a court refuses, because of neighborhood changes, to enjoin violation of a covenant, could damages for its breach be recovered? See St. Lo Construction Co. v. Koenigsberger, 174 F.2d 25 (D.C.Civ.1949); Strong v. Shatto, 45 Cal.App. 29, 187 P. 159 (1919); Pound, The Progress of the Law, 1918–1919, 33 Harv.L.Rev. 813, 820 (1920).

2. What is the effect of a change of conditions in the neighborhood upon possibilities of reverter and rights of entry? See Goldstein, Rights of Entry and Possibilities of Reverter as Devices to Restrict the Use of Land, 54 Harvard L.Rev. 248 (1940).

3. Deeds to lots in a resort subdivision contained a covenant to pay assessments for maintenance of roads and other facilities, subject to the limitation that "no assessment for any one year shall exceed the sum of fifty-five (.55) cents per front foot . . .." The entity entitled to levy these assessments seeks a court decree terminating the limitation on the ground that changed conditions have made it impossible to continue the community as planned unless the limitation on assessments is terminated. What result? See Lake Wauwanoka, Inc. v. Spain, 622 S.W.2d 309 (Mo.App.1981).

4. A few lots in a subdivision restricted to residential uses are condemned for a highway. Are owners of other lots entitled to compensation for extinction of their interests in the lots taken? Holding that they are not, the court in State ex rel. Wells v. Dunbar, 142 W.Va. 332, 95 S.E.2d 457, 461 (1956) explained: "To hold otherwise would enable those having title to real estate often to greatly inconvenience and, perhaps, defeat the proper and orderly exercise by the government of the right of eminent domain . . .. [T]hose who enter into such covenants do so with the knowledge that the government has the absolute right to acquire lands for governmental purposes . . .."

Compare the reasoning of the Maryland Court of Appeals in Mercantile–Safe Deposit & Trust Co. v. Baltimore, 308 Md. 627, 521 A.2d 734 (1987) in construing a typical state constitutional provision requiring compensation when private property is taken for public use: " '[P]roperty' clearly encompasses more than a tangible thing; it 'extends to easements and other incorporeal hereditaments, which, though without tangible or physical existence, may become the subject of private ownership.' Thus, DeLauder [v. Baltimore County, 50 A. 427 (Md.1901)] held that an easement for ingress and egress is compensable property. So is a scenic easement, and a leasehold interest. More to the point, the Supreme Court of California has reasoned that '[t]o establish a substantive distinction by merely labeling one [an easement for ingress and egress] a property interest for which compensation must be made and the other [a restrictive covenant] a mere contractual right which may be appropriated by a condemnor without any compensation is inequitable and rationally indefensible.' "

The Mercantile–Safe Deposit & Trust Co. case involved a claim for compensation by a landowner whose lessees had covenanted to make substantial modifications to the buildings which were taken in condemnation proceedings. Is the argument for compensation as strong when it is asserted by landowners whose lots are not taken, but who assert that they are entitled to compensation for the termination of restrictive covenants binding other lots in the subdivision? Most courts would apparently now treat such covenants as compensable property rights. See Nichols, The Law of Eminent Domain § 5.15 (3d ed. 1985).

5. To what extent are private restrictions terminated by zoning ordinances? See Berger, Conflicts Between Zoning Ordinances and Restrictive Covenants, 43 Neb.L.Rev. 449 (1964); Note, 24 Vand.L.Rev. 1031 (1971); Comment, 48 Mich.L.Rev. 103 (1949). How about the effect of a tax sale of the servient land? See Lake Arrowhead Community Club, Inc. v. Looney, 748 P.2d 649 (Wash.App.1988).

WALDROP v. TOWN OF BREVARD

Supreme Court of North Carolina, 1950.
233 N.C. 26, 62 S.E.2d 512.

This is an action in which the plaintiffs seek to have abated as a private and public nuisance the presently maintained garbage dump of the Town of Brevard, and to recover special damages resulting from its operation since October 1, 1946.

In 1938 the Town of Brevard purchased from I.F. Shipman and wife a tract of land, consisting of five acres, for a garbage dump. The land purchased was near the middle of a 120-acre tract owned by the grantors. At the time the appellees purchased this land, only the grantors and one other family lived on the Shipman lands.

The duly recorded deed from Shipman and wife to the Town of Brevard, in addition to conveying the five-acre tract of land, contains the following provisions:

"Together with a right of way across the lands of the parties of the first part 16 feet in width, extending from the road from Rocky Hill to Camp Illahee along the present road leading from said road to the property herein described. With the right to construct, reconstruct, repair or maintain said road in any manner which the party of the second part may see fit.

"It is understood and agreed that the party of the second part is purchasing the property hereinabove described for use as a dumping ground for garbage, waste, trash, refuse, and other materials and products which the party of the second part desires to dispose of. And as a part of this conveyance the parties of the first part do hereby grant and convey unto the said party of the second part, its successors and assigns, the right, without limit as to time and quantity, to use the lands hereinabove described as a dumping ground for the Town of Brevard for garbage, waste, trash, refuse and other materials and products of any and every kind which the said party of the second part desires to dispose of by dumping on said lands and burning or leaving thereon, and the said parties of the first part do hereby release, discharge, waive and convey unto the said party of the second part, its successors or assigns, any or all rights of action, either legal or equitable which they have or ever might or may have by reason of any action of the party of the second part in using the lands hereinabove described as a dumping ground for the Town of Brevard, or by reason of any fumes, odors, vapors, smoke or other discharges into the atmosphere by reason of such location and use of a dumping ground on the lands hereinabove described.

"The agreements and waiver hereinabove set out shall be covenants running with the remainder of the lands owned by the parties of the first part, and binding on said parties as the owners of said lands, and their heirs and assigns, and anyone claiming under them, or any of them, as owners or occupants thereof."

After the Town of Brevard began using the land referred to herein as a garbage dump, I.F. Shipman and wife began selling other portions of the original 120-acre tract. Now some 35 or 40 families live in the neighborhood.

In 1939 Van R. Tinsley and wife purchased a lot from I.F. Shipman and wife, the lot being a portion of the original 120-acre tract and situate approximately 300 yards or more from the land used by the defendant as a garbage dump. The Tinsleys constructed a house on the lot and conveyed the property to the plaintiffs in 1940. They have owned and resided on the premises since that time. . . .

At the close of plaintiffs' evidence, the defendant moved for judgment as of nonsuit. The motion was denied, but upon renewal thereof at the close of all the evidence, the motion was allowed. Plaintiffs except, appeal and assign error.

DENNY, JUSTICE. If it be conceded that the normal operation of the defendant's garbage dump in a reasonably careful and prudent manner constitutes a nuisance, in our opinion these plaintiffs are estopped from asserting any claim for damages or for other relief by reason thereof, in view of the grant and covenants contained in the conveyance from I.F. Shipman and wife to the Town of Brevard. . . .

"A covenant or agreement may operate as a grant of an easement if it is necessary to give it that effect in order to carry out the manifest intention of the parties." 17 Am.Jur., Sec. 27, p. 940.

The grant and release or waiver contained in the deed from I.F. Shipman and wife to the Town of Brevard, in our opinion, created a right in the nature of an easement in favor of the Town of Brevard, upon the remainder of the lands owned by the grantors. And the waiver or release of any right to make a future claim for damages or other relief, resulting from the use of the premises conveyed to the defendant as a garbage dump, constitutes a covenant not to sue and is binding on the grantors, their heirs and assigns. . . .

The plaintiffs' contention that conditions have changed to such an extent, in the neighborhood adjacent to the defendant's garbage dump, that the covenants in the defendant's deed should not be enforced, is without merit. Changed conditions may, under certain circumstances, justify the non-enforcement of restrictive covenants, but a change, such as that suggested by the plaintiffs here, will not in any manner affect a duly recorded easement previously granted.

We do not construe the plaintiffs' complaint to allege that the nuisance complained of was the result of negligent conduct on the part of the defendant, its agents or employees. Therefore, in view of the interpretation we have given to the provisions contained in the defendant's conveyance from I.F. Shipman and wife, plaintiffs' predecessors in title, the judgment as of nonsuit entered below should be upheld.

Affirmed.

NOTE

A 1950 deed contained a clause reserving to the grantors, their heirs, successors and assigns "all coal and asphalt . . . with right of ingress and egress to go upon said land and remove said coal and asphalt by stripmining method . . ., and said grantors, their heris[sic] successors or assigns shall pay to the grantees herein, their heirs successors or assigns the sum of $25.00 per acre as surface damages. . . ." The grantors' successor began stripmining the land 38 years later. Setting aside the trial court's ruling that it would be inequitable to allow a compensation amount set in 1950 to apply to land values in 1988, the court in Alpine Construction Corp. v. Fenton, 764 P.2d 1340 (Okl.1988) held that the provision establishing surface damages was not a covenant complete in itself, but was part of the mineral reservation and not subject to the doctrine of changed circumstances. The court also stated that the surface owners were presumed to have taken the reservation of the stripmining rights into consideration when they negotiated the purchase price of the property.

C. REFORM

REICHMAN, TOWARD A UNIFIED CONCEPT OF SERVITUDES

55 S.Calif.L.Rev. 1179 (1982).

Servitudes provide the legal foundation of many of today's comprehensive private planning schemes that determine the physical layout, regulation, and operation of large residential and commercial developments. The market's sophistication is not matched, however, by an adequate analytical process in the courts. The American law of servitudes remains a murky subject burdened with obsolete forms and rules that have caused confusion and uncertainty.

Students of property law are initially confronted with three concepts: easements, real covenants, and equitable servitudes, all of which fit into the generic group of servitudes. Different rules apply to each of these forms. . . .

The thesis of this Article is that the three forms of servitudes should be considered as one concept. The normative distinctions indicated above would therefore almost entirely disappear. It is unimportant whether the unified concept is entitled a servitude, a land obligation, or any other term. The importance is in understanding that only a single concept is necessary—a concept which primarily partakes the qualities of what is presently described as an easement. In fact, the proposed approach accords with today's practices. All servitudes appear in the same documents and substantially serve the same function. By clarifying the subject, the problems mentioned above will be alleviated and private land use planning will gain greater flexibility. In most jurisdictions the reform called for could be implemented by the judiciary without the need to resort to legislation. . . .

NOTE

Professor Reichman's article and another, French, Toward a Modern Law of Servitudes: Reweaving the Ancient Strands, 55 S.Calif.L. Rev. 1261 (1982), are the lead articles in a symposium issue on servitudes. Both articles are in general agreement. Professor French proposes:

"Once the courts possess the means to terminate obsolete agreements, the parties should be free to make any agreements that suit their purpose. If the agreement is otherwise valid, its burdens and benefits should run with the land or with interests in the land as the parties intended. Thus, individuals should be able to create running burdens with benefits in gross and running benefits with burdens in gross. They should be free to enter agreements to create powers to sever running interests from the land. They should also be able to make interests assignable. Adoption of the basic principle that the law will give effect to the intent of the parties so long as the agreement itself is enforceable will simplify the law enormously."

In a more recent article containing a design proposal for the new Restatement of the Law of Property, Professor French argues that the new Restatement should reflect a new conceptual basis which emphasizes the doctrinal unity of servitudes rather than the diversity in the land use arrangements implemented by servitudes. Similarly, vocabulary should be adopted using the term "servitude" as "the generic description of devices tying rights and obligations to land ownership and occupancy." She further suggests that lease covenants, other than those such as the warranty of habilitability which are implied because of the landlord-tenant relationship and those such as the rent covenant which are unique to leases, should be included within the coverage of servitudes. French, Design Proposal for the New Restatement of the Law of Property—Servitudes, 21 U.C. Davis L.Rev. 1213, 1226–1229 (1988).

Is the Reichman-French thesis sound? Excerpts from two critical symposium articles are set forth below. All excerpts from articles in this symposium have been reprinted with permission of the Southern California Law Review.

LAWRENCE BERGER, UNIFICATION OF THE LAW OF SERVITUDES

55 S.Calif.L.Rev. 1339 (1982).

"At first blush, the notion of unifying the law of servitudes into one coherent whole sounds both attractive and superficially plausible. After all, easements, equitable servitudes, and real covenants all involve the limited rights of one person in the land of another. Specifically, they are respectively rights to use or to control the use of another's land or at least to insist that he perform some land-related affirmative duty. So why not have one body of law to govern them? The answer, I suppose, is that it really does not matter whether one labels the structure as one, two, or three bodies of law. The real issues are whether the rules in the structure make good policy sense and whether they are unnecessarily inconsistent. I say this because it is absolutely clear that the law about the various servitudes cannot be "unified" in the sense that the same rules should always apply to each of them. The rules are different and many of the variances make good sense. . . ."

DUNHAM, STATUTORY REFORMATION OF LAND OBLIGATIONS

55 S.Calif.L.Rev. 1345 (1982).

An underlying premise of the Reichman and French articles is that consensual transactions involving property interests are "good" and that the complicated terminology and unnecessary requirements associated with the creation of such interests are "bad." Professor Reichman proposes that the terminology should be standardized by calling all fragmented property interests "land obligations" or merely "servitudes." In support of standardization Professor Reichman describes vividly the tendency in Anglo-American law to create a new legal institution through the use of a new term. This description is preparatory to his argument that the integration he proposes can occur through judicial decision and resulting "precedent."

Neither Professor Reichman nor Professor French, however, speculate as to why the change in terminology has not been matched by a change in substance. If the picture is as bad as they paint it, then why, in a regime where private volition creates "interests," has not some California developer or enterprising lawyer invented a new institution? The "conditional sales contract" and the "trust receipt" were consciously invented by lawyers as a technique for financing the acquisition and production of many "big ticket" items for personal and household use; in this way, the business shortcomings of the "chattel mortgage" were overcome. If it is indeed possible to create a unified concept of servitudes through judicial activism, one is hard pressed to explain why creative lawyering has not produced a similar result in this area. . . .

The modern trend in reforming property law is to use statutes. . . .

I agree with Professors Reichman and French to the extent that they argue for substantive integration of the legal rules governing land obligations. Neither Professor Reichman nor Professor French, however, adequately address the impact of their proposal on the recent trend to simplify land transfers. Specifically, they fail to discuss the problem of title examination. Their proposal to extend the doctrine of changed circumstances to cover easements, rights of entry, and the like, fails to provide a solution to the title search problem. The caution of the title examining industry will allow no examiner to conclude that an encumbrance is removed by reason of changed circumstances without an official determination that circumstances have indeed changed.

Thus, given the constraints of the title assuring system, invalidating servitudes through application of the changed circumstances doctrine will have the same effect on marketability as invalidating them through the privity and touch and concern requirements; only complete elimination of the common-law servitude system can achieve title simplification objectives. The recommendations of Professors Reichman and French regarding the termination problem will produce only more judicial supervision and, therefore, more uncertainty.

If this conclusion is correct, as I believe it is, then reform cannot be accomplished by any system short of a means for the elimination of restrictions with absolute certainty. To realize this objective, legislation is necessary; only two types of legislation seem appropriate:

(1) a limit on the duration of restrictions, calculated from the *time* of recordation (a certain point of beginning), or

(2) a provision that, on application by the owner of a servient estate and on payment to the owner of the dominant estate of a sum equal to the loss suffered by reason of the release, the servient estate is released from the restriction.

NOTE

For a critical evaluation of the modern law of promissory servitudes, see Winokur, "The Mixed Blessings of Promissory Servitudes: Toward Optimizing Economic Utility, Individual Liberty, and Personal Identity, 1989 Wis.L.Rev. 1 (1989). Professor Winokur's conclusions are similar to those of Professor Dunham in that he views the inflexibility of servitudes over a long time span as being especially troublesome. This is not, however, the sole problem with servitudes. He suggests that "[a]s presently structured and enforced, promissory servitude regimes impose economic inefficiencies and excessive restraints of individual liberty and self expression. Association-administered servitude regimes have generated growing dissatisfaction and conflict among neighbors, many of whom come to regret the servitude relationships."

SECTION 2. NON-VOLITIONAL ("NATURAL") INTERESTS

A. NUISANCE DOCTRINES

ROSE v. CHAIKIN

Superior Court of New Jersey, Chancery Division, Atlantic County, 1982.
187 N.J.Super. 210, 453 A.2d 1378.

GIBSON, J.S.C.

This action seeks to enjoin the operation of a privately owned windmill. Plaintiffs occupy neighboring properties and allege that the unit constitutes both a private nuisance and a violation of local zoning laws. Defendants deny the allegations and have counterclaimed. Based on the evidence presented at trial, the following factual findings may be made.

All of the parties are residents and/or owners of single-family homes located in a contiguous residential neighborhood in Brigantine, New Jersey. On or about June 18, 1981 defendants, in an effort to save on electric bills and conserve energy, obtained a building permit for the construction of a windmill. Pursuant to that permit they erected a 60-high tower on top of which was housed a windmill and motor. The unit is located ten feet from the property line of one of plaintiffs. Shortly after the windmill became operational it began to produce offensive noise levels, as a result of which plaintiffs experienced various forms of stress-related symptoms, together with a general inability to enjoy the peace of their homes.

Relief was initially sought through city council. Although certain orders were issued reducing the times when the windmill could operate, the problem continued more or less until an action was instituted in this court. Following an initial hearing here, there was a preliminary finding of a nuisance and a temporary restraining order was issued restricting the use of the machine except for a period of no more than two hours a day, that being the time claimed to be needed for maintenance purposes. By consent, those restraints were continued up through the time of trial and still continue.[1]

Although the evidence was in sharp dispute concerning the impact of the noise levels existing when the windmill is operational, this court is satisfied that those levels are of such a nature that they would be offensive to people of normal sensibilities and, in fact, have unreasonably interfered with plaintiffs' use and enjoyment of their properties. Measurements at the site reveal that the sound levels produced by the windmill vary, depending on the location, but generally show a range of 56 to 61 decibels (dBA). In all instances those levels exceed the 50 dBA permissible under the controlling city ordinance. Ordinance 11–1981, § 906.6.3., City of Brigantine. Although there are other sources of sounds in the area, for the most part they are natural to the site. These background (or ambient) sounds include the ocean, the sounds of sea gulls, the wind and the distant sounds of occasional boat traffic in the adjacent inlet. An exception to these "natural" sounds is the heat pump owned by plaintiffs Joel and Isadora Rose, of which more will be said later.

The sounds of the windmill have been variously described. Generally, however, they most resemble those produced by a large motor upon which there is superimposed the action of blades cutting through the air. The sounds are distinguishable not just by the level of the noise produced (noise being defined as unwanted sound) but because they are unnatural to the scene and are more or less constant. Although a reduction in the wind speed to below eight m.p.h. will automatically shut down the unit, the prevailing winds at this site are generally above that. Given the proximity of the homes involved, the net result is a noise which is both difficult to ignore and almost impossible to escape.

The impact on plaintiffs is significant. Both the lay and expert testimony support the conclusion that, in varying degrees, all of them experienced tension and stress-related symptoms when the windmill was operational. Those symptoms included nervousness, dizziness, loss of sleep and fatigue. The sounds disturbed many of the activities associated with the normal enjoyment of one's home, including reading, eating, watching television and general relaxation.

Defendants counterclaim and seek to enjoin the operation of the Rose heat pump. Although the unrebutted testimony indicated that it, too, produced sound levels in excess of 50 dBA, the impact on defendants was relatively small. Complaints were limited to some disturbance of certain activities, such as causing a distraction during reading and dinner. There is no evidence that it unreasonably interferes with defendants' health and comfort. What disturbance does occur is limit-

1. Following the issuance of the TRO, the manufacturer, the installer and the city were joined as third-party defendants. Each elected not to participate in the trial and agreed to be bound by the result.

ed not only in duration but in frequency. The unit is rarely used by the Roses, and when used is on for relatively short periods of time.

The basic standards for determining what constitutes a private nuisance were set forth by our Supreme Court in Sans v. Ramsey Golf & Country Club, 29 N.J. 438, 149 A.2d 599 (1959). The court made clear that a case-by-case inquiry, balancing competing interests in property, is required.

> The essence of a private nuisance is an unreasonable interference with the use and enjoyment of land. The elements are myriad. . . . The utility of the defendant's conduct must be weighed against the *quantum* of harm to the plaintiff. The question is not simply whether a person is annoyed or disturbed, but whether the annoyance or disturbance arises from an unreasonable use of the neighbor's land. . . . [at 448–49, 149 A.2d 599]

Unreasonableness is judged

> ". . . 'not according to exceptionally refined, uncommon or luxurious habits of living, but according to the simple tastes and unaffected notions generally prevailing among plain people.' " 50 N.J.Super. 127, at page 134, 141 A.2d 335, citing Stevens v. Rockport Granite Co., 216 Mass. 486, 104 N.E. 371 (Sup.Jud.Ct.1914). [at 449, 149 A.2d 599]

Defendants resist plaintiffs' claim by advancing three basic arguments: first, that noise, standing alone, cannot constitute a private nuisance; second, that even if noise can amount to a nuisance, the noise from their windmill does not exceed the applicable threshold, and third, that in any event the circumstances of this case do not warrant the "extraordinary relief" of an injunction.

The first argument is without merit. New Jersey case law makes it clear that noise may, under the principles of unreasonable use, constitute an actionable private nuisance. . . . Noise is an actionable private nuisance if two elements are present: (1) injury to the health and comfort of ordinary people in the vicinity, and (2) unreasonableness of that injury under all the circumstances. . . . The "circumstances" may be multiple and must be proven by "clear and convincing" evidence. . . .

> Broadly stated, the noises which a court of equity normally enjoins are those which affect injuriously the health and comfort of ordinary people in the vicinity to an unreasonable extent. . . . *Thus, the character, volume, frequency, duration, time, and locality are relevant factors in determining whether the annoyance materially interferes with the ordinary comfort of human existence.* [Lieberman v. Saddle River Tp., 37 N.J.Super. at 67, 116 A.2d 809; emphasis supplied]

To the factors listed in *Lieberman* may be added several others gleaned from New Jersey cases and cases in other jurisdictions applying a "reasonableness under the circumstances" test. For example, the availability of alternative means of achieving the defendant's objective has been found to be relevant. See *Sans,* supra 29 N.J. at 448, 149 A.2d

599 (change in location of golf tee feasible); Malhame, supra 162 N.J. Super. at 264–266, 392 A.2d 652 (plaintiffs failed to prove that alternative fire-siren system wouldn't just transfer nuisance elsewhere). So, also, might the social utility of defendant's conduct, judged in light of prevailing notions of progress and the demands of modern life, be relevant. See Protokowicz v. Lesofski, 69 N.J.Super. 436, 443, 174 A.2d 385 (Ch.Div.1961) (in light of scientific progress, noise from Diesel engine cannot be considered nuisance *per se*). Whether a given use complies with controlling governmental regulations, while not dispositive on the question of private nuisance, Monzolino v. Grossman, 111 N.J.L. 325, 328, 168 A. 673 (E. & A. 1933), does impact on its reasonableness. See, e.g., Desruisseau v. Isley, 553 P.2d 1242, 1245–46 (Ariz. App.1976); 58 Am.Jur.2d, Nuisances, § 30 (1971).

An application of these factors to the present case supports the conclusion that defendants' windmill constitutes an actionable nuisance. As indicated, the noise produced is offensive because of its character, volume and duration. It is a sound which is not only distinctive, but one which is louder than others and is more or less constant. Its intrusive quality is heightened because of the locality. The neighborhood is quiet and residential. It is well separated, not only from commercial sounds, but from the heavier residential traffic as well. Plaintiffs specifically chose the area because of these qualities and the proximity to the ocean. Sounds which are natural to this area—the sea, the shore birds, the ocean breeze—are soothing and welcome. The noise of the windmill, which would be unwelcome in most neighborhoods, is particularly alien here.

The duration of the windmill noise is also significant. Since the prevailing winds keep the unit operating more or less constantly, the noise continues night and day. Interfering, as they do, with the normal quiet required for sleep, nighttime noises are considered particularly intrusive. . . . Since ambient sounds are normally reduced at night, an alien sound is even more offensive then. The sound levels are well documented and clearly exceed permissible limits under the zoning ordinance. Ordinance 11–1981. Independent of the ordinance, the evidence supports the conclusion that the noise is disturbing to persons of ordinary sensibilities. It can and does affect injuriously the health and comfort of ordinary people in the vicinity to an unreasonable extent. . . .

When consideration is given to the social utility of the windmill and the availability of reasonable alternatives, the conclusion supporting an injunction is the same. Defendants' purpose in installing the windmill was to conserve energy and save on electric bills. Speaking to the latter goal first, clearly the court can take judicial notice that alternative devices are available which are significantly less intrusive. Evid.R. 9(1). As to its social utility, a more careful analysis is required. Defendants argue that the windmill furthers the national need to conserve energy by the use of an alternate renewable source of power. See, generally, Wind Energy Systems Act of 1980, 42 U.S.C.A. §§ 9201–13, and Public Utility Regulatory Policies Act of 1978, 16 U.S.C.A. § 824a–3. The social utility of alternate energy sources cannot be denied; nor should the court ignore the proposition that scientific and social progress sometimes reasonably require a reduction in personal comfort. Protokowitz v. Lesofski, supra 69 N.J.Super. at 443, 174 A.2d 385; Annotation, "Nuisance—Operation of Air Conditioner," 79 A.L.R.3d 320, 328 (1977). On the other hand, the fact that a device represents a scientific advance and has social utility does not mean that it is permissible at any cost. Such factors must be weighed against the quantum of harm the device brings to others. . . .

In this case the activity in question substantially interferes with the health and comfort of plaintiffs. In addition to the negative effect on their health, their ability to enjoy the sanctity of their homes has been significantly reduced. The ability to look to one's home as a refuge from the noise and stress associated with the outside world is a right to be jealously guarded. Before that right can be eroded in the name of social progress, the benefit to society must be clear and the intrusion must be warranted under all of the circumstances. Here, the benefits are relatively small and the irritation is substantial. On balance, therefore, the social utility of this windmill is outweighed by the quantum of harm that it creates.

That is not to say that all windmills constitute a nuisance or even that this windmill cannot be modified in a way to justify a different conclusion. Every case must be examined on an individual basis. Given the circumstances here, however, the evidence clearly and convincingly establishes a nuisance and the imposition of an injunction is warranted. Although defendants assert defenses of estoppel, laches and unclean hands, these claims are without factual support and need not be treated further.

With respect to the counterclaim, defendants have failed to prove that plaintiffs' heat pump constitutes an actionable nuisance. While the noise of the pump may at times be as loud as that of the windmill, several factors distinguish it. The operation of the pump is limited in duration and frequency, as it is rarely used and then only for short periods; also, the sound is less alien. In addition, defendants' proofs have failed to clearly and convincingly prove that the pump "unreasonably affects their health and comfort." They complain only of minor disturbances and distractions, rather than nuisances. That is not to say that a heat pump can never be a nuisance, or even that, given more substantial evidence, this particular heat pump could not be deemed a nuisance. It is only to say that in this case, given these proofs, defendants did not meet their burden.

. . .

In conclusion, it is the view of this court that, for a variety of reasons, defendants' windmill constitutes an actionable nuisance. Under the same analysis plaintiffs' heat pump does not. An alternative basis for granting injunctive relief is defendants' violation of the municipal zoning ordinance. An order should be entered accordingly.

NOTES

1. May it be said that the injunction created a property interest in defendant's land for the benefit of plaintiffs similar to that created by a restrictive covenant? Should defendant have been compensated?

2. Do you agree that the "social utility of this windmill is outweighed by the quantum of harm that it creates"? Does it appear that the court gave sufficient weight to society's interests in encouraging development of non-fossil energy sources? What criteria guide a judge in assessing social utility?

3. See Note, Regulating Wind Access in California: Legal Drafting, 13 Pac.L.J. 1301 (1982).

BOOMER v. ATLANTIC CEMENT CO.

Court of Appeals of New York, 1970.
26 N.Y.2d 219, 309 N.Y.S.2d 312, 257 N.E.2d 870.

BERGAN, JUDGE. Defendant operates a large cement plant near Albany. These are actions for injunction and damages by neighboring land owners alleging injury to property from dirt, smoke and vibration emanating from the plant. A nuisance has been found after trial, temporary damages have been allowed; but an injunction has been denied.

The public concern with air pollution arising from many sources in industry and in transportation is currently accorded ever wider recognition accompanied by a growing sense of responsibility in State and Federal Governments to control it. Cement plants are obvious sources of air pollution in the neighborhoods where they operate.

But there is now before the court private litigation in which individual property owners have sought specific relief from a single plant operation. The threshold question raised by the division of view on this appeal is whether the court should resolve the litigation between the parties now before it as equitably as seems possible; or whether, seeking promotion of the general public welfare, it should channel private litigation into broad public objectives.

A court performs its essential function when it decides the rights of parties before it. Its decision of private controversies may sometimes greatly affect public issues. Large questions of law are often resolved by the manner in which private litigation is decided. But this is normally an incident to the court's main function to settle controversy. It is a rare exercise of judicial power to use a decision in private litigation as a purposeful mechanism to achieve direct public objectives greatly beyond the rights and interests before the court.

Effective control of air pollution is a problem presently far from solution even with the full public and financial powers of government. In large measure adequate technical procedures are yet to be developed and some that appear possible may be economically impracticable.

It seems apparent that the amelioration of air pollution will depend on technical research in great depth; on a carefully balanced consideration of the economic impact of close regulation; and of the actual effect on public health. It is likely to require massive public expenditure and to demand more than any local community can accomplish and to depend on regional and interstate controls.

A court should not try to do this on its own as a by-product of private litigation and it seems manifest that the judicial establishment is neither equipped in the limited nature of any judgment it can pronounce nor prepared to lay down and implement an effective policy for the elimination of air pollution. This is an area beyond the circumference of one private lawsuit. It is a direct responsibility for government and should not thus be undertaken as an incident to solving a dispute between property owners and a single cement plant—one of many—in the Hudson River valley.

The cement making operations of defendant have been found by the court at Special Term to have damaged the nearby properties of plaintiffs in these two actions. That court, as it has been noted, accordingly found defendant maintained a nuisance and this has been affirmed at the Appellate Division. The total damage to plaintiffs' properties is, however, relatively small in comparison with the value of defendant's operation and with the consequences of the injunction which plaintiffs seek.

The ground for the denial of injunction, notwithstanding the finding both that there is a nuisance and that plaintiffs have been damaged substantially, is the large disparity in economic consequences of the nuisance and of the injunction. This theory cannot, however, be sustained without overruling a doctrine which has been consistently reaffirmed in several leading cases in this court and which has never been disavowed here, namely that where a nuisance has been found and where there has been any substantial damage shown by the party complaining an injunction will be granted.

The rule in New York has been that such a nuisance will be enjoined although marked disparity be shown in economic consequence between the effect of the injunction and the effect of the nuisance.

The problem of disparity in economic consequence was sharply in focus in Whalen v. Union Bag & Paper Co., 208 N.Y. 1, 101 N.E. 805. A pulp mill entailing an investment of more than a million dollars polluted a stream in which plaintiff, who owned a farm, was "a lower riparian owner". The economic loss to plaintiff from this pollution was small. This court, reversing the Appellate Division, reinstated the injunction granted by the Special Term against the argument of the mill owner that in view of "the slight advantage to plaintiff and the great loss that will be in inflicted on defendant" an injunction should not be granted (p. 2, 101 N.E. p. 805). "Such a balancing of injuries cannot be justified by the circumstances of this case", Judge Werner noted (p. 4, 101 N.E. p. 805). He continued: "Although the damage to the plaintiff may be slight as compared with the defendant's expense of abating the condition, that is not a good reason for refusing an injunction" (p. 5, 101 N.E. p. 806).

Thus the unconditional injunction granted at Special Term was reinstated. The rule laid down in that case, then, is that whenever the damage resulting from a nuisance is found not "unsubstantial", viz., $100 a year, injunction would follow. This states a rule that had been followed in this court with marked consistency (McCarty v. Natural Carbonic Gas Co., 189 N.Y. 40, 81 N.E. 549; Strobel v. Kerr Salt Co., 164 N.Y. 303, 58 N.E. 142; Campbell v. Seaman, 63 N.Y. 568).

There are cases where injunction has been denied. McCann v. Chasm Power Co., 211 N.Y. 301, 105 N.E. 416 is one of them. There, however, the damage shown by plaintiffs was not only unsubstantial, it was non-existent. Plaintiffs owned a rocky bank of the stream in which defendant had raised the level of the water. This had no economic or other adverse consequence to plaintiffs, and thus injunctive relief was denied. Similar is the basis for denial of injunction in Forstmann v. Joray Holding Co., 244 N.Y. 22, 154 N.E. 652 where no benefit to plaintiffs could be seen from the injunction sought (p. 32, 154 N.E. 655). Thus if, within Whalen v. Union Bag & Paper Co., supra which authoritatively states the rule in New York, the damage to plaintiffs in these present cases from defendant's cement plant is "not unsubstantial", an injunction should follow.

Although the court at Special Term and the Appellate Division held that injunction should be denied, it was found that plaintiffs had been damaged in various specific amounts up to the time of the trial and damages to the respective plaintiffs were awarded for those amounts. The effect of this was, injunction having been denied, plaintiffs could maintain successive actions at law for damages thereafter as further damage was incurred.

The court at Special Term also found the amount of permanent damage attributable to each plaintiff, for the guidance of the parties in the event both sides stipulated to the payment and acceptance of such permanent damage as a settlement of all the controversies among the parties. The total of permanent damages to all plaintiffs thus found was $185,000. This basis of adjustment has not resulted in any stipulation by the parties.

This result at Special Term and at the Appellate Division is a departure from a rule that has become settled; but to follow the rule literally in these cases would be to close down the plant at once. This court is fully agreed to avoid that immediately drastic remedy; the difference in view is how best to avoid it.[1]

One alternative is to grant the injunction but postpone its effect to a specified future date to give opportunity for technical advances to permit defendant to eliminate the nuisance; another is to grant the injunction conditioned on the payment of permanent damages to plaintiffs which would compensate them for the total economic loss to their

1. Respondent's investment in the plant is in excess of $45,000,000. There are over 300 people employed there.

property present and future caused by defendant's operations. For reasons which will be developed the court chooses the latter alternative.

If the injunction were to be granted unless within a short period—e.g., 18 months—the nuisance be abated by improved methods, there would be no assurance that any significant technical improvement would occur.

The parties could settle this private litigation at any time if defendant paid enough money and the imminent threat of closing the plant would build up the pressure on defendant. If there were no improved techniques found, there would inevitably be applications to the court at Special Term for extensions of time to perform on showing of good faith efforts to find such techniques.

Moreover, techniques to eliminate dust and other annoying by-products of cement making are unlikely to be developed by any research the defendant can undertake within any short period, but will depend on the total resources of the cement industry nationwide and throughout the world. The problem is universal wherever cement is made.

For obvious reasons the rate of the research is beyond control of defendant. If at the end of 18 months the whole industry has not found a technical solution a court would be hard put to close down this one cement plant if due regard be given to equitable principles.

On the other hand, to grant the injunction unless defendant pays plaintiffs such permanent damages as may be fixed by the court seems to do justice between the contending parties. All of the attributions of economic loss to the properties on which plaintiffs' complaints are based will have been redressed.

The nuisance complained of by these plaintiffs may have other public or private consequences, but these particular parties are the only ones who have sought remedies and the judgment proposed will fully redress them. The limitation of relief granted is a limitation only within the four corners of these actions and does not foreclose public health or other public agencies from seeking proper relief in a proper court.

It seems reasonable to think that the risk of being required to pay permanent damages to injured property owners by cement plant owners would itself be a reasonable effective spur to research for improved techniques to minimize nuisance.

The power of the court to condition on equitable grounds the continuance of an injunction on the payment of permanent damages seems undoubted. (See, e.g., the alternatives considered in McCarty v. Natural Carbonic Gas Co., supra, as well as Strobel v. Kerr Salt Co., supra.) . . . .

Thus it seems fair to both sides to grant permanent damages to plaintiffs which will terminate this private litigation. The theory of damage is the "servitude on land" of plaintiffs imposed by defendant's nuisance. (See United States v. Causby, 328 U.S. 256, 261, 262, 267, 66 S.Ct. 1062, 90 L.Ed. 1206, where the term "servitude" addressed to the land was used by Justice Douglas relating to the effect of airplane noise on property near an airport.)

The judgment, by allowance of permanent damages imposing a servitude on land, which is the basis of the actions, would preclude future recovery by plaintiffs or their grantees (see Northern Indiana Public Serv. Co. v. W.J. & M.S. Vesey, supra, p. 351, 200 N.E. 620.)

This should be placed beyond debate by a provision of the judgment that the payment by defendant and the acceptance by plaintiffs of permanent damages found by the court shall be in compensation for a servitude on the land.

Although the Trial Term has found permanent damages as a possible basis of settlement of the litigation, on remission the court should be entirely free to re-examine this subject. It may again find the permanent damage already found; or make new findings.

The orders should be reversed, without costs, and the cases remitted to Supreme Court, Albany County to grant an injunction which shall be vacated upon payment by defendant of such amounts of permanent damage to the respective plaintiffs as shall for this purpose be determined by the court.

JASEN, JUDGE (dissenting).

I agree with the majority that a reversal is required here, but I do not subscribe to the newly enunciated doctrine of assessment of permanent damages, in lieu of an injunction, where substantial property rights have been impaired by the creation of a nuisance. . . .

I see grave dangers in overruling our long-established rule of granting an injunction where a nuisance results in substantial continuing damage. In permitting the injunction to become inoperative upon the payment of permanent damages, the majority is, in effect, licensing a continuing wrong. It is the same as saying to the cement company, you may continue to do harm to your neighbors so long as you pay a fee for it. Furthermore, once such permanent damages are assessed and paid, the incentive to alleviate the wrong would be eliminated, thereby continuing air pollution of an area without abatement.

It is true that some courts have sanctioned the remedy here proposed by the majority in a number of cases, but none of the authorities relied upon by the majority are analogous to the situation before us. In those cases, the courts, in denying an injunction and awarding money damages, grounded their decision on a showing that the use to which the property was intended to be put was primarily for the public benefit. Here, on the other hand, it is clearly established that the cement company is creating a continuing air pollution nuisance primarily for its own private interest with no public benefit.

This kind of inverse condemnation (Ferguson v. Village of Hamburg, 272 N.Y. 234, 5 N.E.2d 801) may not be invoked by a private person or corporation for private gain or advantage. Inverse condemnation should only be permitted when the public is primarily served in the taking or impairment of property. (Matter of New York City Housing Auth. v. Muller, 270 N.Y. 333, 343, 1 N.E.2d 153, 156; Pocantico Water Works Co. v. Bird, 130 N.Y. 249, 258, 29 N.E. 246, 248.) The promotion of the interests of the polluting cement company has, in my opinion, no public use or benefit. . . .

I would enjoin the defendant cement company from continuing the discharge of dust particles upon its neighbors' properties unless, within 18 months, the cement company abated this nuisance.

It is not my intention to cause the removal of the cement plant from the Albany area, but to recognize the urgency of the problem stemming from this stationary source of air pollution, and to allow the company a specified period of time to develop a means to alleviate this nuisance.

I am aware that the trial court found that the most modern dust control devices available have been installed in defendant's plant, but, I submit, this does not mean that *better* and more effective dust control devices could not be developed within the time allowed to abate the pollution.

Moreover, I believe it is incumbent upon the defendant to develop such devices, since the cement company, at the time the plant commenced production (1962), was well aware of the plaintiffs' presence in the area, as well as the probable consequences of its contemplated operation. Yet, it still chose to build and operate the plant at this site.

In a day when there is growing concern for clear air, highly developed industry should not expect acquiescence by the courts, but should, instead, plan its operations to eliminate contamination of our air and damage to its neighbors.

Accordingly, the orders of the Appellate Division, insofar as they denied the injunction, should be reversed, and the actions remitted to Supreme Court, Albany County to grant an injunction to take effect 18 months hence, unless the nuisance is abated by improved techniques prior to said date.

FULD, C.J., and BURKE and SCILEPPI, JJ., concur with BERGAN, J.

JASEN, J., dissents in part and votes to reverse in a separate opinion.

BREITEL and GIBSON, JJ., taking no part.

In each action: Order reversed, without costs and the case remitted to Supreme Court, Albany County, for further proceedings in accordance with the opinion herein.

NOTES

1. On remand, the lower court had much difficulty in measuring the damages to be awarded. Boomer v. Atlantic Cement Co., 72 Misc.2d 834, 340 N.Y.S.2d 97 (Sup.Ct.1972).

2. In a subsequent case factually similar to Boomer, a jury finding of no nuisance was upheld. Copart Industries, Inc. v. Consolidated Edison, 41 N.Y.2d 564, 394 N.Y.S.2d 169, 362 N.E.2d 968 (1977). The trial court's charge to the jury, approved on appeal, instructed the jury

to find that there was a nuisance only if defendant's conduct was an "intentional invasion of plaintiff's rights" or negligent. Fuchsberg, dissenting, viewed the charge as misleading by diverting the jury's attention from the crucial task of balancing harms and benefits: "[P]laintiff in this case should be permitted to sustain its action for damages on proof that the harm is substantial and that the financial burden of compensating for the harm does not render 'infeasible' the continuation of the defendant's business activity."

SPUR INDUSTRIES, INC. v. DEL E. WEBB DEVELOPMENT CO.

Supreme Court of Arizona, 1972.
108 Ariz. 178, 494 P.2d 700.

[In 1956, Spur's predecessor established cattle feedlots in a rural area several miles from Phoenix. In 1959, Del E. Webb commenced nearby a residential development known as Sun City. Both enterprises expanded during the years that followed.]

CAMERON, VICE CHIEF JUSTICE. From a judgment permanently enjoining the defendant, Spur Industries, Inc., from operating a cattle feedlot near the plaintiff Del E. Webb Development Company's Sun City, Spur appeals. Webb cross-appeals. . . .

. . .

Del Webb's suit complained that the Spur feeding operation was a public nuisance because of the flies and the odor which were drifting or being blown by the prevailing south to north wind over the southern portion of the Sun City. . . .

. . .

The difference between a private nuisance and a public nuisance is generally one of degree. A private nuisance is one affecting a single individual or a definite small number of persons in the enjoyment of private rights not common to the public, while a public nuisance is one affecting the rights enjoyed by citizens as a part of the public. To constitute a public nuisance, the nuisance must affect a considerable number of people or an entire community or neighborhood. City of Phoenix v. Johnson, 51 Ariz. 115, 75 P.2d 30 (1938).

. . .

We have no difficulty, however, in agreeing with the conclusion of the trial court that Spur's operation was an enjoinable public nuisance as far as the people in the southern portion of Del Webb's Sun City were concerned.

§ 36–601, subsec. A reads as follows:

"§ 36–601. **Public Nuisances Dangerous to Public Health**

"A. The following conditions are specifically declared public nuisances dangerous to the public health:

"1. Any condition or place in populous areas which constitutes a breeding place for flies, rodents, mosquitoes and other insects which are capable of carrying and transmitting disease-causing organisms to any person or persons."

. . .

It is clear that as to the citizens of Sun City, the operation of Spur's feedlot was both a public and a private nuisance. They could have successfully maintained an action to abate the nuisance. Del Webb, having shown a special injury in the loss of sales, had a standing to bring suit to enjoin the nuisance. Engle v. Clark, 53 Ariz. 472, 90 P.2d 994 (1939); City of Phoenix v. Johnson, supra. The judgment of the trial court permanently enjoining the operation of the feedlot is affirmed.

. . .

Were Webb the only party injured, we would feel justified in holding that the doctrine of "coming to the nuisance" would have been a bar to the relief asked by Webb, and, on the other hand, had Spur located the feedlot near the outskirts of a city and had the city grown toward the feedlot, Spur would have to suffer the cost of abating the nuisance as to those people locating within the growth pattern of the expanding city . . ..

. . .

In addition to protecting the public interest, however, courts of equity are concerned with protecting the operator of a lawfully, albeit noxious, business from the result of a knowing and willful encroachment by others near his business.

In the so-called "coming to the nuisance" cases, the courts have held that the residential landowner may not have relief if he knowingly came into a neighborhood reserved for industrial or agricultural endeavors and has been damaged thereby . . ..

. . .

There was no indication in the instant case at the time Spur and its predecessors located in western Maricopa County that a new city would spring up, full-blown, alongside the feeding operation and that the developer of that city would ask the court to order Spur to move because of the new city. Spur is required to move not because of any wrongdoing on the part of Spur, but because of a proper and legitimate regard of the courts for the rights and interests of the public.

Del Webb, on the other hand, is entitled to the relief prayed for (a permanent injunction), not because Webb is blameless, but because of the damage to the people who have been encouraged to purchase homes in Sun City. It does not equitably or legally follow, however, that Webb, being entitled to the injunction, is then free of any liability to Spur if Webb has in fact been the cause of the damage Spur has sustained. It does not seem harsh to require a developer, who has taken advantage of the lesser land values in a rural area as well as the availability of large tracts of land on which to build and develop a new town or city in the area, to indemnify those who are forced to leave as a result.

Having brought people to the nuisance to the foreseeable detriment of Spur, Webb must indemnify Spur for a reasonable amount of the cost of moving or shutting down. It should be noted that this relief to Spur is limited to a case wherein a developer has, with foreseeability, brought into a previously agricultural or industrial area the population which makes necessary the granting of an injunction against a lawful business and for which the business has no adequate relief.

It is therefore the decision of this court that the matter be remanded to the trial court for a hearing upon the damages sustained by the defendant Spur as a reasonable and direct result of the granting of the permanent injunction. Since the result of the appeal may appear novel and both sides have obtained a measure of relief, it is ordered that each side will bear its own costs.

Affirmed in part, reversed in part, and remanded for further proceedings consistent with this opinion.

NOTES

1. Over 35 states have adopted "right to farm" statutes. One such statute provides that "no nuisance action shall be brought against an agricultural operation which has lawfully been in operation for one year or more prior to the date of bringing such action, where the conditions or circumstances complained of as constituting the basis of the nuisance action have existed substantially unchanged since the established date of operation." One who brings such a suit "is liable to the agricultural operator for all costs and expenses incurred in defense of such action . . . ." Vernon's Tex.Code Ann., Agric.Code § 251.004 (1982). See Hanna, "Right to Farm" Statutes—The Newest Tool in Agricultural Land Preservation, 10 Fla.St.L.Rev. 415 (1982); Thompson, Defining and Protecting the Right to Farm, 5 Zon. & Pl.Law Rep. 57, 65 (1982).

2. There is an extensive literature on economic analysis of nuisance law. The leading article is Coase, The Problem of Social Cost, 3 J.Law & Econ. 1 (1960). Most of the writing stimulated by it is cited in Gjerdingen, The Coase Theorem and the Psychology of Common-Law Thought, 56 S.Calif.L.Rev. 711 (1983), and Hoffman and Spitzer, The Coase Theorem: Some Experimental Tests, 25 J.Law & Econ. 73 (1982). An excellent survey of economic analysis of land-use conflicts appears in R. Ellickson and D. Tarlock, Land-Use Controls 547–563 (1981). Particularly relevant to the Spur Industries Case is Calabresi and Melamed, Property Rules, Liability Rules, and Inalienability: One View of the Cathedral, 85 Harv.L.Rev. 1089 (1972). The following excerpts from an article by Professor Ellickson provide an introduction to the subject.

ELLICKSON, ALTERNATIVES TO ZONING: COVENANTS, NUISANCE RULES, AND FINES AS LAND USE CONTROLS

40 U.Chi.L.Rev. 681, 683, 684, 720–724 (1973).

. . .

Economists assert that if the market remains free of imperfections, market transactions will optimally allocate scarce resources. They do not maintain that the distribution of these optimally-allocated resources among specific individuals will necessarily be just. If injustices in distribution arise, most economists urge that they be corrected by direct cash transfer payments, rather than through more indirect attempts at redistribution. According to this economic model, optimally efficient patterns of city development would evolve naturally if urban land development markets were to operate free of imperfections; city planning or public land use controls would only make matters worse from an efficiency standpoint. Since market forces would generate the most efficient land use, the basic decision for policy makers would be the distribution of urban pleasures among residents, with adjustments preferably made through cash transfer payments. . . .

Land development markets, however, are not perfect and in reality city development is far from optimal. Economists regularly use land markets to illustrate that where transactions or activities entail "externalities" or "spillovers"—that is, impacts on nonconsenting outsiders—suboptimal resource allocation will often result. Although beneficial externalities can also impair efficient allocation, this article deals primarily with externalities harmful to nonconsenting outsiders. Welfare economists have urged that harmful externalities be "internalized" to eliminate excessive amounts of nuisance activity. Internalization is said to be accomplished through devices that force a nuisance-maker to bear the true costs of his activity. Internalization of harmful spillovers in land development often requires some departure from what this article calls a laissez faire distribution of property rights, an imaginary legal world where each landowner can choose to pursue any activity within the boundaries of his parcel without fear of liability to his neighbors or governmental sanction. These departures range from those that are compatible with the continuance of private markets to those that seek to supplant the market mechanism altogether; thus, systems for internalizing harmful spillovers range from relatively decentralized ones that emphasize private ordering to others that are highly collectivized and rely on mandatory decrees. . . .

Many of the doctrinal difficulties in nuisance law have arisen when courts have tried to avoid granting injunctive relief, the traditional remedy in nuisance cases. An injunction often imposes prevention costs that exceed the reduction in nuisance costs it achieves; the closing of a factory may be more costly to the economy than the losses caused to neighbors by its operation. As courts became sensitive to this danger they responded by limiting the circumstances in which they were willing to find a nuisance, rather than denying injunctive relief while still allowing damages. Nuisance law thus came to provide no relief in many cases where the risk of loss could appropriately have been shifted to the landowner carrying out the damaging activity.

In many instances courts avoided finding actionable nuisances by applying a type of balancing test; the social utility of the actor's conduct was compared to the total amount of harm caused. This test is proper for deciding whether to grant injunctive relief. Unfortunately most courts applied the test to the initial question of whether a nuisance existed at all, incorrectly limiting the availability of damage awards that would internalize the harmful externalities. That a grocery in the Santa Monica Mountains is shown to have high utility is a good reason to refuse to enjoin its construction, but it is not good grounds for allowing it to avoid paying for its external costs. Illogical doctrines of this type have greatly reduced the value of nuisance law as a land use control system.

The use of nuisance law reached a height in the United States during the 1920's and 1930's as landowners invoked it to relieve actual or threatened noxious uses in their neighborhoods, with gas stations and funeral parlors generating the greatest volume of cases. In virtually all of these cases the plaintiff asked for only injunctive relief; damages were sought only from a government, charity, public utility, or other defendant against whom courts would not be likely to issue an injunction. The courts were thus forced to make difficult all-or-nothing decisions about whether a particular use should be allowed to continue.

Because courts had so limited their remedy options, one party was likely to be highly aggrieved whatever the trial court's decision, and appeals were common. Nuisance litigation thus became an expensive process. In addition, courts were hardly an expert institution for making difficult resource allocation decisions.

These administrative flaws of nuisance law combined with its doctrinal weaknesses to fuel the belief that public regulation systems such as zoning would be superior. As zoning began to flourish, nuisance law became less important. The decline of nuisance law is perhaps not surprising in light of its doctrinal and administrative shortcomings. If these underlying weaknesses were remedied, however, for example by curtailing availability of injunctive relief and transferring nuisance adjudications to specialized bodies, nuisance law might return to prominence as a system for internalizing external costs. . . .

In an important economic analysis of the problem of external cost, Professor R.H. Coase showed that if administrative costs are zero, the same resource allocation will result regardless of the initial distribution of rights. Assume, for example, that there is a grocery in the Santa Monica Mountains, the only external harm to the neighbors is added noise, and administrative costs are zero. The Coase theorem states that if the cost to the grocer of going out of business is less than his neighbors' gains from the reduction in noise resulting from the termination of his enterprise, the grocer will shut down regardless of the initial distribution of rights. If homeowners have the right to recover for injury caused by the noise, the grocer will choose to absorb the smaller loss of going out of business rather than pay for the damage he causes by staying open. If the law does not require the grocer to compensate the homeowners for noise, the homeowners will combine to pay the grocer to close. The grocer will agree if the bounty is larger than his losses from closing, and the homeowners will be willing to offer more than the amount of his loss if their total damage exceeds that amount.

On the other hand, when the cost to the grocer of closing exceeds the resulting benefit to the homeowners, the grocer will continue to operate. If the homeowners have the right to recover, the grocer will pay damages rather than absorb the larger costs of terminating his business. If the grocer need not pay damages, the homeowners will not pay him to adopt a more neighborly course of action, because the minimum payment he would insist on to shut down exceeds the value of the damage they are currently suffering. In brief, the Coase theorem states that private bargaining will tend to reduce the sum of nuisance and prevention costs over time, regardless of assignment of rights.

The Coase theorem does not imply that the policy maker need not be concerned about how rights are assigned. First, as Coase reminds us, administrative costs in bargaining situations are not zero, and consequently the assignment of rights does affect resource allocation. Second, the policy maker cannot ignore the equities of resource distribution, as Coase intentionally does, to focus solely on the efficiency of resource allocation. Any unexpected alteration of the distribution of rights among landowners is almost certain to affect their relative shares of wealth. Decisions on the distribution of rights in cases of external cost thus must accommodate the complex considerations of administrative costs and fairness. . . .

NOTES

1. The harm to adjacent land and landowners caused by toxic waste dumps is an example of the "harmful externalities" discussed by Ellickson. One of the most notorious instances of such harm was the leakage of highly toxic wastes from a dumpsite in Niagra Falls, N.Y., which forced the permanent abandonment of many homes and resulted in the first declaration of a national disaster that was not the result of natural causes. Passage of the Comprehensive Environmental Response, Compensation and Liability Act (CERCLA) was, in part, a response to the "Love Canal" incident.

CERCLA, as amended in 1986, sets up a fund in excess of $8 billion for governmental or private clean up of hazardous substances. Commonly referred to as the "Superfund," the Hazardous Substance Response Fund is financed through excise taxes on petroleum and chemical feedstocks, a surtax on businesses with annual incomes over $2 million, and through general appropriations. Although private-cost recovery actions are authorized by CERCLA, most of the legislation deals with government-sponsored clean-up efforts.

2. The U.S. Supreme Court has recognized the existence of a federal common law of nuisance which is applicable to the pollution of interstate air and waters. State of Illinois v. City of Milwaukee, 406 U.S. 91, 92 S.Ct. 1385, 31 L.Ed.2d 712 (1972). The federal common law may be preempted by comprehensive federal regulatory programs. In City of Milwaukee v. States of Illinois, 451 U.S. 304, 101 S.Ct. 1784, 68 L.Ed.2d 114 (1981) the Court rejected Illinois' claim to abate a nuisance caused by Milwaukee's untreated sewage overflowing into Lake Michigan on the ground that federal common law remedies had been superseded by the Federal Water Pollution Control Act Amendments of 1972. Similarly, CERCLA has been held to preempt the federal common law of nuisance in its application to the interstate transportation and storage of toxic wastes. Lykins v. Westinghouse Electric, 27 ERC 1590, 18 Envt'l L.Rep. 21,498 (E.D.Ky.1988). State nuisance law, however, is not preempted by CERCLA. See State of New York v. Shore Realty Corp., 759 F.2d 1032 (2d Cir.1985). In instances of interstate pollution the applicable nuisance law is that of the state where the source of the pollution is located. International Paper Co. v. Ouellette, 479 U.S. 481, 107 S.Ct. 805, 93 L.Ed.2d 883 (1987).

3. Imposition of liability under CERCLA is not limited to the companies that generated, transported or stored hazardous substances. The statute also imposes liability for clean-up costs on owners of contaminated property unless they exercised "environmental due diligence" in acquiring already contaminated property. The implications of potential CERCLA liability for persons buying or selling land are discussed in Chapter 26 at pages 1301–1305.

B. SUPPORT OF LAND

NOONE v. PRICE

West Virginia Court of Appeals, 1982.
298 S.E.2d 218.

NEELY, JUSTICE:

In 1960 the plaintiffs below, and appellants in this Court, Mr. and Mrs. William H. Noone, bought a house located on the side of a mountain in Glen Ferris, West Virginia. This house had been constructed in 1928 or 1929 by Union Carbide, and in 1964, four years after plaintiffs purchased the house, plaintiffs became aware that the wall under their front porch was giving way and that the living room plaster had cracked.

The defendant below, appellee in this Court, Mrs. Marion T. Price, lived directly below the plaintiffs at the foot of the hill in a house that was built in 1912. Sometime between 1912 and 1919 a wall of stone and concrete was constructed along the side of the hill, ten to twelve feet behind the defendant's house. This wall was a hundred to a hundred and twenty-five feet long, approximately four feet high, and of varying degrees of thickness. The wall lay entirely on the defendant's property, and was approximately ten to twelve feet from the property line that divided the defendant's property from the plaintiffs' property. The defendant purchased her house in 1955 and lived there until 1972, when she sold the property. Before the defendant's purchase, the wall had fallen into disrepair.

When the plaintiffs discovered that their house was slipping down the hill, they complained to the defendant that their problem was the result of deterioration in the defendant's retaining wall. The defendant did nothing to repair the wall and the plaintiffs repaired the damage to their house at a cost of approximately $6,000.

The action before us now was filed in 1968 for damages of $50,000 for failure of the defendant to provide lateral support for the plaintiffs' land, and her negligent failure to provide lateral support for their house. Plaintiffs alleged that the wall was constructed to provide support to the slope upon which their house was built, and that the disrepair and collapse of the wall caused the slipping and eventual damage to their property.

The defendant denied that the wall on her property provided support to the slope, or that the condition of her wall caused the slipping and damage to the plaintiffs' property. In addition, the defendant asserted that the plaintiffs were negligent in failing to take reasonable precautions to protect their own property and were estopped from suing her because the wall on her property was erected by her predecessor in title and the plaintiffs had purchased their property with knowledge of the wall's deteriorating condition.

Defendant made a motion for summary judgment that the circuit court granted in part. The circuit court concluded that the plaintiffs had no right to recover for damage to their dwelling house and buildings, but the court left open the question of whether plaintiffs could recover for damage to their land. The circuit court stated on the record that "there is a duty of lateral support to the land but not to a structure on the land." Unfortunately, while the circuit court stated an entirely correct principle of law, his disposition of this case on summary judgment was inappropriate. While an adjacent landowner has an obligation only to support his neighbor's property in its raw or natural condition, if the support for land in its raw, natural condition is insufficient and the land slips, the adjacent landowner is liable for both the damage to the land and the damage to any buildings that might be on the land. Consequently, we reverse and remand.

This case provides an opportunity that we have not had for many years to address the obligations of adjoining landowners to provide lateral support to each other's land. Support is lateral when the supported and supporting lands are divided by a vertical plane. The withdrawal of lateral support may subject the landowner withdrawing the support to strict liability or to liability for negligence. We have recognized both forms of liability in Walker v. Strosnider, 67 W.Va. 39, 67 S.E. 1087 (1910) and this case, remarkably enough, is still in harmony with the modern weight of authority as articulated in the Restatement (Second) of Torts.

As a general rule, "[a] landowner is entitled, *ex jure naturae,* to lateral support in the adjacent land for his soil." Point 2, syllabus, McCabe v. City of Parkersburg, 138 W.Va. 830, 79 S.E.2d 87 (1953). Therefore, as we said in syllabus point 2 of Walker, supra:

> "An excavation, made by an adjacent owner, so as to take away the lateral support, afforded to his neighbor's ground, by the earth so removed, and cause it, of its own weight, to fall, slide or break away, makes the former liable for the injury, no matter how carefully he may have excavated. Such right of support is a property right and absolute."

An adjacent landowner is strictly liable for acts of commission and omission on his part that result in the withdrawal of lateral support to his neighbor's property. This strict liability, however, is limited to land in its natural state; there is no obligation to support the added weight of buildings or other structures that land cannot naturally support. However, the majority of American jurisdictions hold that if land in its natural state would be capable of supporting the weight of a building or other structure, and such building or other structure is damaged because of the subsidence of the land itself, then the owner of the land on which the building or structure is constructed can recover damages for both the injury to his land and the injury to his building or structure.[2] The West Virginia cases are largely consistent with this position, although none has expressly so held.

The converse of the preceding rule is also the law: where an adjacent landowner provides sufficient support to sustain the weight of the land in its natural state, but the land slips as a direct result of the additional weight of a building or other structure, then in the absence of negligence on the part of the adjoining landowner, there is no cause of action against such adjoining landowner for damage either to the land, the building, or other structure.[4]

The issue in the case before us concerns the proper application of the strict liability rule. The circuit court improperly awarded summary judgment because the plaintiffs should have been allowed to prove that their land was sufficiently strong in its natural state to support the weight of their house, and that their house was damaged as a result of a chain reaction that began when the land in its natural state, toward the bottom of the hill, slipped as a result of the withdrawal of lateral support occasioned by the deterioration of the retaining wall, causing, in turn, successive parts of the hillside to subside until the ripple effect reached the foundation of the plaintiffs' house.

The cases recognize that lateral support sufficient to hold land in its natural state may be insufficient to support the additional weight of

2. See, e.g., Williams v. Anderson Construction Co., 105 F.Supp. 497 (D.Alaska, 1952); Gladin v. Von Engeln, 195 Colo. 88, 575 P.2d 418 (1978); Smith v. Howard, 201 Ky. 249, 256 S.W. 402 (1923); Busby v. Holthaus, 46 Mo. 161 (1870); Riley v. Continuous Rail Joint Co., 110 App.Div. 787, 97 N.Y.S. 283 (1906), aff'd, 193 N.Y. 643, 86 N.E. 1132 (1908); Prete v. Cray, 49 R.I. 209, 141 A. 609 (1928); Stearns v. City of Richmond, 88 Va. 992, 14 S.E. 847 (1892); Williams v. Southern Railway Co., 55 Tenn.App. 81, 396 S.W.2d 98 (1965); and Restatement (Second) of Torts § 817 comment n (1979).

4. Walker v. Strosnider, 67 W.Va. 39, 67 S.E. 1087 (1910); . . .

a building or other structure. If, therefore, as a result of the additional weight of a building or other structure, so much strain is placed upon existing natural or artificial lateral support that the support will no longer hold, then in the absence of negligence, there is no liability whatsoever on the part of an adjoining landowner. In the case before us, this means that if the weight of the plaintiffs' house placed so much pressure on the soil that the house itself caused the subsidence, and the land would not have subsided without the weight of the house, then the plaintiffs cannot recover.

A theoretical problem that presents itself in all of these cases is the extent to which the obligation of support runs with the land. The weight of authority appears to be that where an actor, whether he be an owner, possessor, lessee, or third-party stranger, removes necessary support he is liable, and an owner cannot avoid this liability by transferring the land to another.[5] Nevertheless, when an actor who removes natural lateral support substitutes artificial support to replace it, such as a retaining wall, the wall then becomes an incident to and a burden on the land upon which it is constructed, and subsequent owners and possessors have an obligation to maintain it.[6]

In the case *sub judice,* the plaintiffs' land had no buildings erected on it at the time the defendant's predecessor in title built the retaining wall on his property; therefore, he needed only to erect a retaining wall sufficient to provide support for their soil. He was not required to furnish a wall sufficient to support any structure which they might erect upon their property. The defendant, as his successor, merely had the obligation to maintain the wall to support the plaintiffs' land in its natural condition. Defendant was not required to strengthen the wall to the extent that it would provide support for the weight of plaintiffs' buildings.

Since the pleadings in the case before us make reference to negligence, it is appropriate here to address the scope of a negligence theory. In general, it has been held that while an adjoining landowner has no obligation to support the buildings and other structures on his neighbor's land, nonetheless, if those structures are *actually being supported,* a neighbor who withdraws such support must do it in a non-negligent way. In an action predicated on strict liability for removing support for the land in its natural state, the kind of lateral support withdrawn is material, but the quality of the actor's conduct is immaterial; however, in a proceeding based upon negligence, the kind of lateral support withdrawn is immaterial, and the quality of the actor's conduct

5. E.g., Frederick v. Burg, 148 F.Supp. 673 (W.D.Pa.1957); Paul v. Bailey, 109 Ga. App. 712, 137 S.E.2d 337 (1964); First National Bank & Trust Co. v. Universal Mortg. and Realty Trust, 38 Ill.App.3d 345, 347 N.E.2d 198 (1976); and Restatement (Second) of Torts § 817 comment j (1979).

6. Urosevic v. Hayes, 267 Ark. 739, 590 S.W.2d 77 (1979); Sager v. O'Connell, 67 Cal.App.2d 27, 153 P.2d 569 (1944); Vennard v. Morrison, 3 Conn.Cir. 120, 209 A.2d 202 (Conn.Cir.Ct.App.Div., 1964); Gorton v. Schofield, 311 Mass. 352, 41 N.E.2d 12 (1942); Salmon v. Peterson, 311 N.W.2d 205 (S.D.1981); Foster v. Brown, 55 D.L.R. 143, 48 Ont.L.R. 1, 10 B.R.C. 918 (Ont.App. Div.1920); see also Annot., 139 A.L.R. 1267 (1942); cf. Restatement (Second) of Torts § 817 comment k (1979) [later withdrawal of artificial support subjects one who withdraws it to liability].

is material.[7] Comment e, Restatement (Second) of Torts § 819 succinctly explains the nature of liability for negligence.

> "The owner of land may be unreasonable in withdrawing lateral support needed by his neighbor for artificial conditions on the neighbor's land in either of two respects. First, he may make an unnecessary excavation, believing correctly that it will cause his neighbor's land to subside because of the pressure of artificial structures on the neighbor's land. If his conduct is unreasonable either in the digging or in the intentional failure to warn his neighbor of it, he is subject to liability to the neighbor for the harm caused by it. The high regard that the law has by long tradition shown for the interest of the owner in the improvement and utilization of his land weighs heavily in his favor in determining what constitutes unreasonable conduct on his part in such a case. Normally the owner of the supporting land may withdraw lateral support that is not naturally necessary, for any purpose that he regards as useful provided that the manner in which it is done is reasonable. But all the factors that enter into the determination of the reasonableness or unreasonableness of the actor's conduct must be considered, and in a particular case the withdrawal itself may be unreasonable. Thus, if the actor's sole purpose in excavating his land is to harm his neighbor's structures, the excavation itself is unreasonable. Furthermore, although for the purpose of permanently leveling the land it may be reasonable to withdraw support that is not naturally necessary, it may be unreasonable to make an excavation for a building that will itself require a foundation, without providing for the safeguarding of the neighbor's structures during the progress of the work. Likewise it is normally unreasonable not to notify an adjacent landowner of excavations that certainly will harm his structures, unless the neighbor otherwise has notice.
>
> "Secondly, the owner of land may be negligent in failing to provide against the risk of harm to his neighbor's structures. This negligence may occur either when the actor does not realize that any harm will occur to his neighbor's structures or when the actor realizes that there is a substantial risk to his neighbor's land and fails to take adequate provisions to prevent subsidence, either by himself taking precautions or by giving his neighbor an opportunity to take precautions. Although the law accords the owner of the supporting land great freedom in withdrawing from another's land support that is not naturally necessary in respect to the withdrawal itself, it does not excuse withdrawal in a manner that involves an unreasonable risk of harm to the land of another. The owner in making the excavation is therefore required to take reasonable precautions to minimize the risk of causing subsidence of his neighbor's land. In determining whether a particular precaution is reasonably required, the extent of the burden that the taking of it will impose upon the actor is a factor of great importance."

7. Restatement (Second) of Torts § 819 comment c, p. 75 (1979).

In the case of Walker v. Strosnider, supra, Judge Poffenbarger, speaking for a unanimous court, explained the law of West Virginia in a way completely in accord with the modern Restatement. . . .

The plaintiffs contend that the defendant should be held liable for negligence in removing the support required by their dwelling, in addition to the strict liability for removing support for their soil, relying on Walker v. Strosnider, supra; Beaver v. Hitchcock, 151 W.Va. 620, 153 S.E.2d 886 (1967); and Weaver Mercantile Co. v. Thurmond, 68 W.Va. 530, 70 S.E. 126 (1911). The latter case dealt with maintaining a nuisance, and has no application to the right of lateral support. *Walker* and *Beaver* imposed liability for damages to structures caused by negligent excavation and failure to shore up an excavation; however, they involved situations where the structures were already in existence at the time of the acts that deprived them of lateral support, and the owner of the property was the actor who caused the excavation to be made. If there are no structures on the land at the time of the excavation, the excavator owes no further duty than to refrain from removing the lateral support for the soil, or to substitute artificial support for that which is removed. His duty of support cannot be enlarged by the addition of artificial structures to the land; therefore, the duty of his successor in title cannot be greater, where she has done no act to deprive the structures of their support.

It would appear that the case before us either stands or falls on a question of strict liability. It is admitted that the retaining wall on the defendant's property was constructed at least sixty years ago, before the construction of the plaintiffs' house, and that all parties to this action were aware of the condition of the wall. Furthermore, there is no allegation that the defendant did anything to cause the collapse of the wall, but rather only failed to keep it in repair. Therefore, if the plaintiffs can recover, they must do so by proving that the disrepair of the retaining wall would have led ineluctably to the subsidence of their land in its natural condition. If, on the other hand, the land would not have subsided but for the weight of the plaintiffs' house, then they can recover nothing.

Since the proper resolution of this issue will require the development of an appropriate factual record, the judgment of the Circuit Court of Fayette County is reversed and the case is remanded for further proceedings consistent with this opinion.

NOTES

1. Is strict liability for withdrawal of lateral support justified? Why are nuisance doctrines not applied? To say, as the court did in the Noone case, that each landowner has a property interest similar to an easement in adjoining land for support tells us nothing about the relevant policy considerations. Does the strict liability rule unduly favor the neighbor who builds first? See Rathbun, J., dissenting in Prete v. Cray, 49 R.I. 209, 141 A. 609, 613 (1928). What are other logical consequences of the easement concept of the right to support? Suppose that collapse of the supported land does not occur until several

years after removal of the supporting land—a longer period than the applicable statute of limitations. When would the statute begin to run? If suit is brought before collapse, what would be the measure of damages? See Restatement (Second) of Torts, Scope and Introductory Note to Ch. 39 (1977).

2. The court in *Noone* refers to the obligation to support a neighbor's property "in its raw or natural condition." Does it follow that the duty of lateral support is inapplicable if the contour of the land has been changed? In Carrion v. Singley, 614 S.W.2d 916 (Tex.Civ.App. 1981) a developer had terraced a slope and obtained level building lots by cutting the ground beneath its natural grade on the east side of the lots and filling the ground above its natural grade on the west side. A retaining wall on the defendant's land, which supported the plaintiff's higher land to the east, was allowed to deteriorate and the resulting subsidence of plaintiff's lot endangered the foundation of his house. The appellate court reversed a trial court judgment ordering the defendant to repair or replace the wall, pointing out that neither lot "remotely resembled the natural state as existed prior to the beginning of construction on the properties."

3. Due to unstable soil conditions and a prolonged period of heavy rain, soil on the upper side of a hill on D's land slides down and destroys P's house. Assuming that D's acts have not contributed to the landslide, but that D had been aware of the danger and could have prevented the damage to P by the exercise of reasonable care, should D be liable? Sprecher v. Adamson Companies, 30 Cal.3d 358, 178 Cal. Rptr. 783, 636 P.2d 1121 (1981), rejected the traditional common law immunity of a landowner from liability for harm caused by natural conditions, and adopted a negligence standard. A concurring opinion noted, however, that "it is exceedingly difficult to imagine what respondents *reasonably* could have done to prevent or reduce the damage caused by the natural conditions here present"—i.e., the extensive landslide problems in the Malibu region.

4. When ownership of the subsurface has been severed from the surface, as is customary in mining operations, liability for removal of subjacent support may become an issue. This area of law, especially as it relates to coal mining, is subject to extensive regulation at the state and federal levels. See Hunt & Jones, Subsidence Regulation Under the Surface Mining Control and Reclamation Act of 1977, 2 J.Min.L. & Policy 63 (1986–87); Ingram, Regulation of Mine Subsidence—Legal Issues Raised by Governmental Intervention in Historically Private Arrangements, 5 Eastern Min.L.Inst. 6–1 (1984). Traditionally, the surface owner could waive the absolute right to subjacent support, either in the severance deed or by subsequent agreement. The extent to which federal and state statutes may have altered the effect of a waiver is discussed in Palmore & McGuire, Avoidance of Disputes Between the Surface Owner and the Coal Owner/Operator Through Properly Drafted Severance Deeds, Leases, Subsidence Agreements and Other Instruments, 9 Eastern Min.L.Inst. 6–1 (1988).

5. Subsidence may also occur as the result of pumping out underground water. In Friendswood Development Co. v. Smith–Southwest Industries, Inc., 576 S.W.2d 21 (Tex.1978) the court held that landowners who withdrew percolating ground waters from wells located on their own land were not liable for the subsidence which resulted on the plaintiffs' land. The court relied on its earlier adoption of the common law rule giving a landowner an absolute interest in all the ground water which he can draw to the surface of his own land without regard to the effect on other wells in the same area. The dissenting judge argued that the majority was applying the wrong body of law. Arguing that the doctrines requiring subjacent and lateral support should apply, he stated that "[I]t is no more logical to say that this is a case concerning the right to groundwater than it would be correct in a case in which an adjoining landowner removed lateral support by a caterpillar [tractor] to say that the case would be governed by the law of caterpillars." His position is consistent with the present stance of the American Law Institute. Compare Restatement of Torts § 818 (1939) with Restatement (Second) of Torts § 818 (1977). The majority of the Texas court in Friendswood announced that in the future it would apply a negligence standard in cases of land subsidence caused by pumping of water.

C. DRAINAGE

ARMSTRONG v. FRANCIS CORP.

Supreme Court of New Jersey, 1956.
20 N.J. 320, 120 A.2d 4.

WILLIAM J. BRENNAN, JR., J. The Chancery Division, after trial, entered a final judgment against the defendant, the Francis Corporation. Francis appealed to the Appellate Division, and we certified the appeal here on our own motion.

A small natural stream rose in Francis' 42-acre tract, which lies immediately south of Lake Avenue in Rahway. The stream flowed in a northerly direction 1200 feet across the Francis lands through a seven-foot box culvert under Lake Avenue and emptied into Milton Lake, 900 feet north of the avenue. It was the natural drainway for the larger 85-acre area south of Lake Avenue which includes the Francis tract.

Francis stripped its tract and erected 186 small homes thereon in a development known as Duke Estates, Section 2. It also built some 14 houses on an adjacent small tract known as Duke Estates, Section 1, lying in another drainage area. It constructed a drainage system of streets, pavements, gutters, ditches, culverts and catch basins to serve both developments. The system emptied into a corrugated iron pipe laid by Francis below the level of the natural stream bed on its lands. The pipe followed the course of the stream bed to the box culvert under Lake Avenue, although deviating from the course at some places. The pipe was covered with fill on Francis' tract and all evidence of the natural stream there has disappeared.

The drainage of the original 85 acres was thus augmented not only by the drainage of some 2½ acres of the Duke Estates, Section 1, but also by waters percolating into the joints of the pipe where it lay below the level of the water table of the Francis tract. The pipe joints were expressly designed to receive such percolating waters, and, to the extent that the percolation lowered the level of the water table, the result was to provide a drier terrain more suitable to housing development.

Where the stream passes north of Lake Avenue en route to Milton Lake after leaving the box culvert it remains largely in its natural state and forms the boundary line between the residential tracts of the plaintiffs Armstrong and the defendants Klemp. The Klemps were made parties defendant by Francis' cross-claim but prevailed thereon and were allowed the same relief as the Armstrongs. The stream passes through a 36-inch culvert under the Klemp driveway and thence, across lands of the Union County Park Commission, to the Lake.

The Francis improvement resulted in consequences for the Armstrongs and the Klemps fully described by Judge Sullivan in his oral opinion as follows:

"Now the stream, as it emerges from the underground pipe, goes under Lake Avenue and then flows past and through the Armstrong and Klemp properties, is no longer the 'babbling brook' that Mr. Klemp described. Now there is a constant and materially increased flow in it. The stream is never dry. The water is now discolored and evil smelling and no longer has any fish in it. A heavy deposit of silt or muck up to eighteen inches in depth now covers the bottom of the stream. After a heavy rainstorm the stream undergoes a remarkable change for several hours. All of the upstream rain water that used to be absorbed or held back is now channeled in undiminished volume and at great speed into this stream. This causes a flash rise or crest in the stream, with a tremendous volume of water rushing through at an accelerated speed. As a result, the stream has flooded on several occasions within the last year, although this was unheard of previously. More distressing, however, is the fact that during these flash situations the body of water moving at the speed it does tears into the banks of the brook particularly where the bed may turn or twist. At a point even with the plaintiff's [Armstrong] house the stream makes a sharp bend. Here the effect of the increased flow of water is most apparent since the bank on plaintiff's side of the stream has been eaten away to the extent of about ten feet. This erosion is now within fifteen feet of the Armstrong septic tank system. It is difficult to say where it will stop, where the erosion will stop. The silting has, of course, raised the bed of the stream up to eighteen inches in places and the raising of the stream results in water action against different areas of the bank so that the erosion problem while unpredictable is ominous. The eating away of the banks in several places has loosened rocks or boulders which have been rolled downstream by the force of the water. Those stones, however, as they rolled through the Klemp culvert cracked and broke the sides and bottom of the culvert and the water is now threatening to undermine the entire masonry. There is no doubt but that the defendant's activities have caused all of the condition just related.

"A matter of some concern is that defendant's housing development occupies only about one-half of the area which drains into this brook. At the present time there is a forty acre undeveloped section to the south of the defendant and it is reasonable to assume that it, too, will be improved and built upon at some future time. Defendant's underground trunk sewer was built to accommodate any possible runoff from this tract. If and when that section is developed, Armstrong and Klemp will have that much more erosion, silting and flooding to deal with."

Judge Sullivan concluded that the Armstrongs and the Klemps were plainly entitled to relief in these circumstances and "that the only sensible and permanent solution to the problem is to pipe the rest of the brook," that is, from the culvert outlet at Lake Avenue the entire distance to Milton Lake. A plan for that purpose had been prepared by Francis' engineer and approved by the Armstrongs and the Klemps at a time when efforts were being made to compromise the dispute before the trial. The final judgment orders Francis, at its expense forthwith to proceed with and complete within 60 days the work detailed on that plan. The Union County Park Commission has given its formal consent to the doing of the work called for by the plan on its lands.

The important legal question raised by the appeal is whether the damage suffered by the Armstrongs and the Klemps is *damnum absque injuria,* namely, merely the non-actionable consequences of the privileged expulsion by Francis of waters from its tract as an incident to the improvement thereof. Francis argues, however, that, even if the injuries caused are actionable, Judge Sullivan's findings are against the weight of the evidence, that there was prejudicial error in the admission of evidence dealing with the offer of compromise, and that the relief granted was excessive, improper and unwarranted. We find no merit in any of these contentions.

The findings are fully and amply supported by competent evidence. The controverted questions lie principally in the opposing interpretations of the facts by the expert witnesses, and we are not persuaded that Judge Sullivan should have accepted the opinion of the Francis experts in preference to the opinion of the expert who testified for the Armstrongs and the Klemps. And there is nothing in the record as we read it to suggest that Judge Sullivan weighed the evidence of the offer of compromise in reaching his conclusions. His finding that the completion of the piping to Milton Lake was the sensible thing to do in no wise refers to the compromise offer, and in the context of his oral opinion that finding seems plainly to be predicated upon his view of what was needful to save the Armstrongs and the Klemps from further harm. The prescription in the judgment that the piping plan developed by Francis' own engineer be completed does not point to a contrary conclusion. Having decreed that piping was necessary to afford adequate relief, ordering its accomplishment according to the plan which reflected Francis' own concept of that need was wholly logical. Like considerations also answer Francis' other point that the relief allowed was excessive,—or, at least, point up the absence of any basis for the intrusion of appellate judgment into the question of its reasonableness.

Turning, then, to the basic question for decision, appellant grounds its argument upon the following statement of the Appellate Division in Yonadi v. Homestead Country Homes, 35 N.J.Super. 514, 521, 114 A.2d 564, 567 (1955):

"While the New Jersey cases do not deal with the matter explicitly, we conclude that where surface water is concentrated through a drain or other artificial means and is conducted to some place substantially where it otherwise would have flowed, the defendant will not be liable even though by reason of improvements he has made in the land, the water is brought there in larger quantities and with greater force than would have incurred prior to the improvements. The policies underlying the general rule come to bear here. What reasonably could the upland proprietor or occupant do in the present case with this excess water? Rather than require him to dispose of it—and so perhaps require him to secure the cooperation of a number of lowland properties through which the water must eventually be brought—the burden is cast on each lowland proprietor to protect his own land."

We might summarily dispose of this point against the appellant upon the ground that more than the surface water drained from the 85-acre tract is involved here. Appellant has augmented the volume of water passing through the Lake Avenue culvert with water from another drainage area and with water percolating into its pipe where the level of the natural water table on its tract is higher,—and so the cited proposition would not in any event apply. See Town of Union v. Durkes, 38 N.J.L. 21 (Sup.Ct.1875). But, because we do not agree that the quoted proposition, in the form stated, which makes no allowance for differences in factual situations, is or should be the law governing the liability of the landowner who alters the flow of surface waters with resulting material harm to other landowners, we shall treat the case as if only the disposal of surface water from the 85-acre tract was involved and determine appellant's point upon that premise.

In their article, "Interferences with Surface Waters", 24 Minn.L. Rev. 891, 899 (1940) Professor Kinyon and Mr. McClure have convincingly demonstrated that there was no true common law of surface waters and that the law in that respect has been largely developed since 1850, both in England and in the United States.

The casting of surface waters from one's own land upon the land of another, in circumstances where the resultant material harm to the other was foreseen or foreseeable, would appear on the face of it to be tortious conduct, as actionable, where the consequence is an unreasonable use of the possessor's land, as in the case of the abstraction or diversion of water from a stream which unreasonably interferes with the use of the stream below, Prosser, Torts (1951), p. 586, and as in the case of the unreasonable use of percolating or subterranean waters,

Meeker v. City of East Orange, 77 N.J.L. 623, 74 A. 379, 25 L.R.A.,N.S., 465 (E. & A.1909), and as in the case of artificial construction on one's land which unreasonably speeds the waters of a stream past one's property onto that of an owner below, causing harm, Kidde Manufacturing Co. v. Bloomfield, 20 N.J. 52, 118 A.2d 535 (1955); Hughes v. Knight, 33 N.J.Super. 519, 111 A.2d 69 (App.Div.1955). Yet only the courts of the states of New Hampshire and Minnesota have expressly classified the possessor's liability, where imposed, for harm by the expulsion of surface waters to be a tort liability. Those courts have evolved the "reasonable use" rule laying down the test that each possessor is legally privileged to make a reasonable use of his land, even though the flow of surface waters is altered thereby and causes some harm to others, but incurs liability when his harmful interference with the flow of surface waters is unreasonable. Franklin v. Durgee, 71 N.H. 186, 51 A. 911, 58 L.R.A. 112 (S.Ct.1901); Sheehan v. Flynn, 59 Minn. 436, 61 N.W. 462, 26 L.R.A. 632 (S.Ct.1894); 24 Minn.L.Rev., supra, 909.

All other states have treated the legal relations of the parties as a branch of property law—that is, have done so, if we emphasize only the language of the decisions and ignore the actual results reached. Two rules have been evolved which, in their statement, are directly opposed, for under one the possessor would not be liable in any case and under the other he would be liable in every case. But an analysis of the results reached under both rules shows that neither is anywhere strictly applied. The first rule, purportedly applicable in our own State, stems from the view that surface waters are the common enemy. The "common enemy" rule emphasizes the possessor's privilege to rid his lands of surface waters as he will. That rule "is, in substance, that a possessor of land has an unlimited and unrestricted legal privilege to deal with the surface water on his land as he pleases, regardless of the harm which he may thereby cause others." 24 Minn.L.Rev., supra, 898. . . . The other rule, borrowed from the civil law of foreign nations and called the "civil law" rule, emphasizes not the privileges of the possessor but the duties of the possessor to other landowners who are affected by his expulsion of surface waters from his lands. That rule is to the effect that "a person who interferes with the *natural* flow of surface waters so as to cause an invasion of another's interests in the use and enjoyment of his land is subject to liability to the other." 24 Minn.L.Rev., supra, 893.

The quoted statement from the Yonadi opinion implies that what Francis did here was absolutely privileged, which is the clear import of the common enemy rule. But our decisions have invariably refused to apply the rule according to its letter where it works injustice. . . . Nor have states which are said to follow the civil law rule held that the possessor may not under any circumstances rid his lands of surface water without incurring liability if harm is caused to another. In sum, the courts here and elsewhere, in terms of results, have actually come out at the "reasonable use" doctrine, Prosser, supra. Professor Kinyon and Mr. McClure have summarized the course of the decisions as follows (24 Minn.L.Rev., supra, pp. 916, 920, and 913):

"From the rationale of the common enemy rule, it would seem that a possessor of land has an unlimited privilege to rid his land of the surface water upon it or to alter its course by whatever means he wishes, irrespective of the manner of doing it or the harm thereby caused to others. However, in substantially all of the jurisdictions purportedly committed to that rule, the courts have refused to go that far. Most of these courts have developed a qualifying rule which is, in substance, that a possessor of land is not privileged to discharge upon adjoining land, by artificial means, large quantities of surface water in a concentrated flow otherwise than through natural drainways, regardless of the means by which the surface water is collected and discharged. The scope of this qualifying rule varies from jurisdiction to jurisdiction, but it has been adopted in one form or another . . ..

"In jurisdictions purportedly committed to the civil law rule, one would expect from the rationale of that rule to find that a possessor has no privilege, under any circumstances, to interfere with the surface water on his land so as to cause it to flow upon adjoining land in a manner or quantity substantially different from its natural flow. An examination of the cases in these jurisdictions, however, reveals that the courts have refused to follow the rationale of the rule to that extent. In most of these jurisdictions the courts have recognized that a possessor must have a privilege, under certain circumstances, to make minor alterations in the natural flow of surface water where necessary to the normal use and improvement of his land, even though such alterations cause the surface water to flow upon adjoining land in a somewhat unnatural manner. This is especially true where the possessor disposes of the surface water by depositing it in existing natural drainways. Consequently, the courts . . ., with variations from state to state, have held that a possessor has a limited privilege to discharge surface water on other lands, by artificial means in a non-natural manner . . .."

The authors conclude:

". . . [Thus] even though the broad principle of reasonable use has not made much headway as an articulate basis of decision, substantially all of the jurisdictions which purport to follow the civil law or common enemy rules have engrafted upon them numerous qualifications and exceptions which, in actual result, produce decisions which are not as conflicting as would be expected, and which would generally be reached under the reasonable use rule."

We therefore think it appropriate that this court declare, as we now do, our adherence in terms to the reasonable use rule and thus accord our expressions in cases of this character to the actual practice of our courts. Indeed, Judge Sullivan did so in his oral opinion below when he pronounced his judgment as based upon his finding that what Francis did was not "done in the reasonable use of his [its] land," relying for authority upon the decision of the former Court of Chancery in Smith v. Orben, supra. And it is significant of the true state of the law that the Restatement on Torts, sec. 833, has adopted the reasonable use test as the rule actually prevailing.

The rule of reasonableness has the particular virtue of flexibility. The issue of reasonableness or unreasonableness becomes a question of fact to be determined in each case upon a consideration of all the relevant circumstances, including such factors as the amount of harm caused, the foreseeability of the harm which results, the purpose or motive with which the possessor acted, and all other relevant matter. 93 C.J.S., Waters, § 116; Enderson v. Kelehan, 226 Minn. 163, 32 N.W.2d 286 (S.Ct.1948). It is, of course, true that society has a great interest that land shall be developed for the greater good. It is therefore properly a consideration in these cases whether the utility of the possessor's use of his land outweighs the gravity of the harm which results from his alteration of the flow of surface waters. Sheehan v. Flynn, supra. But while today's mass home building projects, of which the Francis development is typical, are assuredly in the social good, no reason suggests itself why, in justice, the economic costs incident to the expulsion of surface waters in the transformation of the rural or semi-rural areas of our State into urban or suburban communities should be borne in every case by adjoining landowners rather than by those who engage in such projects for profit. Social progress and the common wellbeing are in actuality better served by a just and right balancing of the competing interests according to the general principles of fairness and common sense which attend the application of the rule of reason.

Affirmed.

NOTES

1. The judicial evolution of doctrine in this field should be compared with legislative change, which may be subject to attack on the ground that property rights are taken or damaged without due process of law. Upholding a Texas statute which apparently adopted the civil-law rule in the face of prior court decisions applying the common-enemy rule, the Supreme Court of Texas relied in part upon this reasoning: "As to lands granted since 1840, the proprietors had no vested right in the rule of decision prescribed by the adoption of the common law. No easement or servitude of any character was created or intended by the so-called 'common-law rule.' It merely permitted the respective owners of contiguous estates to use their own property in a certain way, for which we said under the common law no cause of action existed, even though injury might be done to the adjacent properties. The act of 1915 changed the rule and gave a cause of action where the owner of one estate so used his property as to injure an adjacent tenement." Miller v. Letzerich, 121 Tex. 248, 49 S.W.2d 404, 85 A.L.R. 451 (1932). In describing the civil-law rule, the court said: "These rights of the owners of estates under the civil law are appurtenant to and a part of the land itself, and passed to them with the grants. The right of the owner of the upper estate to have the surface waters falling thereon to pass in their natural condition onto the lands of the lower estate is a servitude or natural right in the nature of an easement over the lower estate of his neighbor. It is a right of property, which inheres in the estate entitled to its benefit independent of any contractual or prescriptive right." Does it follow that a legisla-

ture lacks power to change from the civil-law rule to the common-enemy rule?

2. Unfortunately, the judgment in Armstrong did not restore the babbling brook. Proper design of a subdivision or other land development, incorporating such features as maximum impervious cover, detention areas and drainage-oriented street layout, might be able to preserve streams and other natural features of the landscape. Municipal regulations of subdivisions commonly include such elements. If a subdivision plat is approved by municipal officials without making adequate provision for drainage, the municipality may be liable. See Sheffet v. County of Los Angeles, 3 Cal.App.3d 720, 84 Cal.Rptr. 11 (1970); Eschete v. City of New Orleans, 258 La. 133, 245 So.2d 383 (1971). Suppose that O's land in its natural condition serves as a detention area for runoff of water from higher land and thereby protects lower land from flooding. Could O lawfully be denied permission to develop his land as a residential subdivision if the unavoidable consequence of development would be termination of the water-detention function of O's land? No, according to Baker v. Planning Board of Framingham, 353 Mass. 141, 228 N.E.2d 831 (1967). See also the treatment of subdivision regulation herein, page 869.

3. In developing legal doctrines courts have traditionally distinguished between the drainage of diffuse surface water, such as that produced by rain and melting snow, and rights in water which flows in established watercourses. Is such a distinction realistic? What policies support it? For a critique of the distinction see Comment, Toward a Unified Reasonable Use Approach to Water Drainage in Washington, 59 Wash.L.Rev. 61 (1983). Consider also the material in the following section.

D. INTERESTS IN WATER

"Water is like a living thing. Essentially all of it that is usable is in motion—a part of the vast circulatory system known as the hydrologic cycle. In this cycle water evaporates wherever it is exposed to the air, but especially from the oceans; rises into the atmosphere; travels as a part of vast air masses over ocean and land; is condensed when an air mass rises to pass over another or over a mountain range; and falls as rain or snow. . . . Water is water—it is vapor at one time, rain, snow, or dew at another, surface or ground water at another. It may be surface water one moment and ground water the next, and vice versa. But it is all water, and it must be considered as a whole—each phase in relation to the others and to the entire hydrologic cycle." C.L. McGuinness, The Water Situation in the United States With Special Reference to Ground Water 3–6 (United States Geological Survey, 1951).

Despite the constant movement of water through the hydrologic cycle, rights to the use of water may depend upon the position of the water in the cycle at any particular time. Thus, when water is in a stream or a lake, the law of riparian rights or prior appropriation applies; when the same water seeps underground, it becomes subject to a different set of legal rules as to its use; and a still different legal framework governs water while it is flowing in a diffused state upon the earth's surface. (You have already encountered legal problems concerning this last situation, which involves mainly the problem of unwanted water.)

---

(1) WATER IN WATERCOURSES

EVANS v. MERRIWEATHER

Supreme Court of Illinois, 1842.
4 Ill. 492.

LOCKWOOD, JUSTICE, delivered the opinion of the court:

This was an action on the case, brought in the Greene Circuit Court, by Merriweather against Evans, for obstructing and diverting a water course. The plaintiff obtained a verdict, and judgment was rendered thereon. On the trial the defendant excepted to the instructions asked for and given, at the instance of the plaintiff. The defendant also excepted, because instructions, that were asked by him, were refused. After the cause was brought into this court, the parties agreed upon the following statement of facts, as having been proved on the trial, to wit: "It is agreed between the parties to this suit, that the following is the statement of facts proved at the trial in this case, and that the same shall be considered as part of the record by the court, in the adjudication of this cause. Smith & Baker, in 1834, bought of T. Carlin six acres of land, through which a branch ran, and erected a steam mill thereon. They depended upon a well and the branch for water in running their engine. About one or two years afterwards, John Evans bought of T. Carlin six acres of land, on the same branch, above and immediately adjoining the lot owned by Smith & Baker, and erected thereon a steam mill, depending upon a well and the branch for water in running his engine.

"Smith & Baker, after the erection of Evans' mill, in 1836 or 1837, sold the mill and appurtenances to Merriweather for about $8000. Evans' mill was supposed to be worth $12,000. Ordinarily there was an abundance of water for both mills; but in the fall of 1837, there being a drought, the branch failed, so far that it did not afford water sufficient to run the upper mill continually. Evans directed his hands not to stop, or divert the water, in the branch; but one of them employed about the mill did make a dam across the branch, just below Evans' mill, and thereby diverted all the water in the branch into Evans' well. Evans was at home, half a mile from the mill, and was frequently about his mill, and evidence was introduced conducing to prove that he might have known that the water of the branch was diverted into his well. After the diversion of the water into Evans' well, as aforesaid, the branch went dry below, and Merriweather's mill could not and did not run, in consequence of it, more than one day in a week, and was then supplied with water from his well. Merriweather then brought this suit, in three or four weeks after the putting of the dam across the branch, for the diversion of the water, and obtained a verdict for $150. This suit, it is admitted, is the first between the parties litigating the right as to the use of the water. It is further agreed, that the branch afforded usually sufficient water for the supply of both mills, without materially affecting the size of the current, though the branch was not depended upon exclusively for that purpose. Furthermore, that at the time of the grievances complained of by the plaintiff below, the defendant had water hauled in part for the supply of his boilers. That the dam was made below the defendant's well, across the branch, which diverted as well the water hauled and poured out into the branch above the well, as the water of the branch, into the defendant's well."

Upon this state of facts, the question is presented, as to what extent riparian proprietors, upon a stream not navigable, can use the water of such stream? The branch mentioned in the agreed statement of facts is a small natural stream of water, not furnishing, at all seasons of the year, a supply of water sufficient for both mills. There are no facts in the case showing that the water is wanted for any other than milling purposes, and for those purposes to be converted into steam, and thus entirely consumed. In an early case decided in England, it is laid down that "A water course begins 'ex jure naturae,' and having taken a certain course naturally, cannot be diverted." The language of all the authorities is, that water flows in its natural course, and should be permitted thus to flow, so that all through whose land it naturally flows, may enjoy the privilege of using it. The property in the water, therefore, by virtue of the riparian ownership, is in its nature usufructuary, and consists, in general, not so much of the fluid itself as of the advantage of its impetus. A riparian proprietor, therefore, though he has an undoubted right to use the water for hydraulic or manufacturing purposes, must so use it as to do no injury to any other riparian proprietor. Some decisions, in laying down the rights of riparian proprietors of water courses, have gone so far as to restrict their right in the use of water flowing over their land, so that there shall be no diminution in the quantity of the water, and no obstruction to its course. The decisions last referred to cannot, however, be considered as furnishing the true doctrine on this subject. Mr. Justice Story, in delivering the opinion of the court, in the case of Tyler v. Wilkinson, says, "I do not mean to be understood as holding the doctrine that there can be no diminution whatever, and no obstruction or impediment whatever, by a riparian proprietor in the use of water as it flows; for that would be to deny any valuable use of it. There may be, and there must be of that which is common to all, a reasonable use. The true test of the principle and extent of the use is, whether it is to the injury of the other proprietors or not. There may be diminution in quantity, or a retardation or acceleration of the natural current, indispensable for the general and valuable use of the water, perfectly consistent with the use of the common right. The diminution, retardation, or acceleration, not positively and sensibly injurious, by diminishing the value of the common right, is an implied element in the right of using the stream at all. The law here, as in many other cases, acts with a reasonable reference to public convenience and general good, and is not betrayed into a narrow strictness, subversive of common use, nor into an extravagant looseness, which would destroy private rights." The same learned judge further says, "That of a thing common by nature, there may be an appropriation by general consent or grant. Mere priority of appropriation of running water, without such consent or grant, confers no exclusive right." This doctrine is fully sustained by English and American cases. In the case of Arnold v. Foot, it was held, where a defendant had diverted the water from a spring rising on his land, to irrigate his meadow, "that he had a right to use so much as is necessary for his family and his cattle, but he has no right to use it for irrigating his meadow, if thereby he deprive the plaintiff of the reasonable use of the water in its natural channel."

Each riparian proprietor is bound to make such a use of running water, as to do as little injury to those below him, as is consistent with a valuable benefit to himself. The use must be a reasonable one. Now the question fairly arises, is that a reasonable use of running water by the upper proprietor, by which the fluid itself is entirely consumed? To answer this question satisfactorily, it is proper to consider the wants of man in regard to the element of water. These wants are either natural or artificial. Natural are such as are absolutely necessary to be supplied, in order to his existence. Artificial, such only, as by supplying them, his comfort and prosperity are increased. To quench thirst, and for household purposes water is absolutely indispensable. In civilized life, water for cattle is also necessary. These wants must be supplied, or both man and beast will perish.

The supply of man's artificial wants is not essential to his existence; it is not indispensable; he could live if water was not employed in irrigating lands, or in propelling his machinery. In countries differently situated from ours, with a hot and arid climate water doubtless is absolutely indispensable to the cultivation of the soil, and in them, water for irrigation would be a natural want. Here it might increase the products of the soil, but it is by no means essential, and cannot therefore be considered a natural want of man. So of manufactures, they promote the prosperity and comfort of mankind, but cannot be considered absolutely necessary to his existence; nor need the machinery which he employs be set in motion by steam.

From these premises would result this conclusion: that an individual owning a spring on his land, from which water flows in a current through his neighbor's land, would have the right to use the whole of it if necessary to satisfy his natural wants. He may consume all the water for his domestic purposes, including water for his stock. If he desires to use it for irrigation or manufactures, and there be a lower proprietor to whom its use is essential to supply his natural wants, or for his stock, he must use the water so as to leave enough for such lower proprietor. Where the stream is small, and does not supply water more than sufficient to answer the natural wants of the different proprietors living on it, none of the proprietors can use the water for either irrigation or manufactures. So far then as natural wants are concerned, there is no difficulty in furnishing a rule by which riparian proprietors may use flowing water to supply such natural wants. Each proprietor in his turn may, if necessary, consume all the water for these purposes. But where the water is not wanted to supply natural wants, and there is not sufficient for each proprietor living on the stream to carry on his manufacturing purposes, how shall the water be divided? We have seen that without a contract or grant, neither has a right to use all the water; all have a right to participate in its benefits. Where all have a right to participate in a common benefit, and none can have an exclusive enjoyment, no rule, from the very nature of the case, can be laid down, as to how much each may use without infringing upon the rights of others. In such cases, the question must be left to the judgment of the jury, whether the party complained of has used, under all the circumstances, more than his just proportion.

It appears from the facts agreed on, that Evans obstructed the water by a dam, and diverted the whole into his well. This diversion, according to all the cases, both English and American, was clearly illegal. For this diversion, an action will lie. It, however, was contended that Evans forbade the construction of the dam by which the water was diverted into his well. If a servant do an act against the consent of the master, the latter is not liable. In this case, however, a jury might fairly infer from the fact that as Evans lived near the mill, and was frequently at it, he must have been conversant of the manner in which his mill was supplied with water, and that he either countermanded the instructions, or acquiesced in the construction of the dam, after it was erected. Having availed himself of the illegal act of his servant, the law presumes he authorized it. Having arrived at the conclusion that an action will lie in behalf of Merriweather against Evans for obstructing and diverting the water course mentioned in the plaintiff's declaration, I have not deemed it necessary to examine the instructions given by the court, to see if they accord with the principles above laid down. Having decided that the plaintiff below has a right to recover on the facts, whether the instructions were right or wrong would not vary that result. It is possible that if the true principles which govern this action had been correctly given to the jury, the damages might have been either less or more than the jury have given; but in this case, as the damages are small, the court ought not, where justice has upon the whole been done, to send the case back, to see if a jury, upon another trial, would not give less.

NOTES

1. The Restatement (Second) of Torts, Introductory Note, ch. 41 (1979), discusses the distinctions between the "natural flow" theory and the "reasonable use" theory. The former is defined as entitling each riparian to a right "to have the body of water flow as it was wont to flow in nature, qualified only by the privilege of each to make limited uses of the water." The latter is defined as according each riparian a "right to be free from unreasonable uses that would cause harm to his own reasonable use of the water." Which theory was adopted by the Supreme Court of Illinois in Evans v. Merriweather? As explained in

this Restatement note, the logical consequences to the two theories differ markedly. The practical significance of this doctrinal dichotomy today, however, is minimal, because, as this Restatement note observes: "The reasonable use theory has won an almost complete victory in the American courts, although a considerable amount of natural flow language may be found." Section 850A of this Restatement lists the following factors relevant to a determination of reasonableness: "(a) The purpose of the use, (b) the suitability of the use to the watercourse or lake, (c) the economic value of the use, (d) the social value of the use, (e) the extent and amount of the harm it causes, (f) the practicality of avoiding the harm by adjusting the use or method of use or method of use of one proprietor or the other, (g) the practicality of adjusting the quantity of water used by each proprietor, (h) the protection of existing values of water uses, land, investment and enterprises, and (i) the justice of requiring the user causing harm to bear the loss." Copyright 1979. Reprinted with permission of the American Law Institute.

2. Would irrigation in arid or semi-arid regions of this country be a "natural" use, entitled to preference over "artificial" uses? No, held Watkins Land Co. v. Clements, 98 Tex. 578, 86 S.W. 733, 70 L.R.A. 964 (1905).

3. Riparian A diverts water from the stream for the use of its guests at a resort maintained on the riparian land. During the summer months there are usually about 200 guests at the resort each day. The water diverted for their benefit is used for purposes of drinking, food preparation, laundering, and bathing. Riparian B is a farmer downstream who diverts water from the stream for household needs and for about 100 head of stock. During periods of low flow, insufficient water reaches B for B's needs. Is B entitled to any relief against A? See Prather v. Hoberg, 24 Cal.2d 549, 150 P.2d 405 (1944); Cowell v. Armstrong, 210 Cal. 218, 290 P. 1036 (1930); McCord v. Big Brothers Movement, 120 N.J.Eq. 446, 185 A. 480 (1936); Filbert v. Dechert, 22 Pa.Super. 362 (1903).

STRATTON v. MT. HERMON BOYS' SCHOOL

Supreme Judicial Court of Massachusetts, 1913.
216 Mass. 83, 103 N.E. 87.

RUGG, C.J. The plaintiff, the owner of a mill upon a small stream, sues the defendant, an upper riparian proprietor upon the same stream, for wrongful diversion of water therefrom to his injury. The material facts are that the defendant owns a tract of land through which the stream flows and upon which also is a spring confluent to the stream. Upon this land it has established pumping apparatus whereby it diverts about 60,000 gallons of water each day from the spring and stream to another estate belonging to it and not contiguous to its land adjacent to this stream, but located about a mile away in a different watershed, for the domestic and other uses of a boys' school with dormitories, gymnasium and other buildings and a farm. The number of students increased from 363 in 1908 to 525 in 1911, while the number of teachers, employés and other persons on the estate was over 100. During the latter year there were kept on the farm 103 cattle, 28 horses and 90 swine. There was a swimming pool, laundry, canning factory and electric power plant, for the needs of all of which water was supplied from this source. There was evidence tending to show that this diversion caused a substantial diminution in the volume of water which otherwise in the natural flow of the stream would have come to the plaintiff's land and in the power which otherwise might have been developed upon his wheel by the force of the current.

The defendant requested the court to rule in effect that diversion of water to another nonriparian estate owned by it was not conclusive evidence that the defendant was liable, but that the only question was whether it had taken an unreasonable quantity of water under all the circumstances. This request was denied and the instruction given that the defendant's right was confined to a reasonable use of the water for the benefit of its land adjoining the water course, and of persons properly using such land, and did not extend to taking it for use upon other premises, and that if there was such use the plaintiff was entitled to recover at least nominal damages even though he had sustained no actual loss. The exceptions raise the question as to the soundness of the request and of the instruction given. . . .

The governing principle of law in a case like the present is this: A proprietor may make any reasonable use of the water of the stream in connection with his riparian estate and for lawful purposes within the watershed, provided he leave the current diminished by no more than is reasonable, having regard for the like right to enjoy the common property by other riparian owners. If he diverts out of the watershed or upon a disconnected estate the only question is whether there is actual injury to the lower estate for any present or future reasonable use. The diversion alone without evidence of such damage does not warrant a recovery even of nominal damages.

The charge of the court below was not in conformity to this principle. It would have permitted the recovery of nominal damages in any event, quite apart from the possibility of real injury to the plaintiff. But the defendant has suffered no harm by this error. The verdict of the jury was for substantial damages and there was ample evidence to support such a conclusion. . . .

Exceptions overruled.

NOTES

1. Compare the following: "Against a person who seeks to divert water to nonriparian lands, the riparian owner is entitled to restrain any diversion, and he is not required to show any damage to his use. Although no damage to the present use of the riparian owner results from the diversion, yet damage to the future use may result, and an injunction will be granted to prevent the diversion from growing into a right by the lapse of the statutory period." Pabst v. Finmand, 190 Cal. 124, 211 P. 11, 14 (1922).

2. Would the court in the Stratton case have reached the same result if the defendant had owned no riparian land? If so, can it be

said that any person is entitled to take water from a stream so long as no riparian suffers actual harm? If a trespasser who causes no actual harm may be held liable for nominal damages or enjoined, why is an unauthorized user of stream water not dealt with similarly? The Restatement (Second) of Torts § 856, Comment on Subsection (1) declares that a nonriparian user has a "privilege" that "is to some extent a legally protected interest. A nonriparian who is making a reasonable and beneficial use of water that causes no harm to a riparian is entitled to protection from intentional or unintentional conduct, other than the exercise of a riparian right, which may constitute a tort under the rules stated in other Chapters." Copyright, 1979. Reprinted with permission of the American Law Institute.

3. What is riparian land? The principal case indicates that, to be riparian, land must not only be contiguous to a watercourse, but also within the watershed of that watercourse. What rationale supports this limitation? How is "watershed" to be defined? Suppose D, who owns land riparian to Rapid River, diverts water from that stream for irrigation of a portion of D's farm situated in the watershed of Slow River, which joins Rapid River to form Grand River. Is this wrongful as to P, who irrigates a farm riparian to Grand River and is deprived of needed water by D's diversion? See Anaheim Union Water Co. v. Fuller, 150 Cal. 327, 88 P. 978 (1907). Is riparian status of land fixed by the boundaries of the original grant from the sovereign? If other land contiguous to riparian land is acquired by the owner of the riparian land, does the newly acquired land also become riparian? If a riparian conveys away a portion of the riparian tract having no contact with the watercourse, does the conveyed land lose its riparian status? Courts have disagreed. Consult Boehmer v. Big Rock Creek Irrigation Dist., 117 Cal. 19, 48 P. 908 (1897) and Jones v. Conn., 39 Or. 30, 64 P. 855 (1901). What are the relevant policy considerations?

COFFIN v. LEFT HAND DITCH CO.

Supreme Court of Colorado, 1882.
6 Colo. 443.

HELM, J. Appellee, who was plaintiff below, claimed to be the owner of certain water by virtue of an appropriation thereof from the south fork of the St. Vrain creek. It appears that such water, after its diversion, is carried by means of a ditch to the James creek, and thence along the bed of the same to Left Hand creek, where it is again diverted by lateral ditches and used to irrigate lands adjacent to the last named stream. Appellants are the owners of lands lying on the margin and in the neighborhood of the St. Vrain below the mouth of said south fork thereof, and naturally irrigated therefrom.

In 1879 there was not a sufficient quantity of water in the St. Vrain to supply the ditch of appellee and also irrigate the said lands of appellant. A portion of appellee's dam was torn out, and its diversion of water thereby seriously interfered with by appellants. The action is brought for damages arising from the trespass, and for injunctive relief to prevent repetitions thereof in the future. . . .

It is contended by counsel for appellants that the common law principles of riparian proprietorship prevailed in Colorado until 1876, and that the doctrine of priority of right to water by priority of appropriation thereof was first recognized and adopted in the constitution. But we think the latter doctrine has existed from the date of the earliest appropriations of water within the boundaries of the state. The climate is dry, and the soil, when moistened only by the usual rainfall, is arid and unproductive; except in a few favored sections, artificial irrigation for agriculture is an absolute necessity. Water in the various streams thus acquires a value unknown in moister climates. Instead of being a mere incident to the soil, it rises, when appropriated, to the dignity of a distinct usufructuary estate, or right of property. It has always been the policy of the national, as well as the territorial and state governments, to encourage the diversion and use of water in this country for agriculture; and vast expenditures of time and money have been made in reclaiming and fertilizing by irrigation portions of our unproductive territory. Houses have been built, and permanent improvements made; the soil has been cultivated, and thousands of acres have been rendered immensely valuable, with the understanding that appropriations of water would be protected. Deny the doctrine of priority or superiority of right by priority of appropriation, and a great part of the value of all this property is at once destroyed.

. . .

We conclude, then, that the common law doctrine giving the riparian owner a right to the flow of water in its natural channel upon and over his lands, even though he makes no beneficial use thereof, is inapplicable to Colorado. Imperative necessity, unknown to the countries which gave it birth, compels the recognition of another doctrine in conflict therewith. And we hold that, in the absence of express statutes to the contrary, the first appropriator of water from a natural stream for a beneficial purpose has, with the qualifications contained in the constitution, a prior right thereto, to the extent of such appropriation.

. . .

It is urged, however, that even if the doctrine of priority or superiority of right by priority of appropriation be conceded, appellee in this case is not benefited thereby. Appellants claim that they have a better right to the water because their lands lie along the margin and in the neighborhood of the St. Vrain. They assert that, as against them, appellee's diversion of said water to irrigate lands adjacent to Left Hand creek, though prior in time, is unlawful.

In the absence of legislation to the contrary, we think that the right to water acquired by priority of appropriation thereof is not in any way dependent upon the *locus* of its application to the beneficial use designed. And the disastrous consequences of our adoption of the rule contended for, forbid our giving such a construction to the statutes as will concede the same, if they will properly bear a more reasonable and equitable one.

The doctrine of priority of right by priority of appropriation for agriculture is evoked, as we have seen, by the imperative necessity for artificial irrigation of the soil. And it would be an ungenerous and inequitable rule that would deprive one of its benefit simply because he has, by large expenditure of time and money, carried the water from one stream over an intervening watershed and cultivated land in the valley of another. It might be utterly impossible, owing to the topography of the country, to get water upon his farm from the adjacent stream; or if possible, it might be impracticable on account of the distance from the point where the diversion must take place and the attendant expense; or the quantity of water in such stream might be entirely insufficient to supply his wants. It sometimes happens that the most fertile soil is found along the margin or in the neighborhood of the small rivulet, and sandy and barren land beside the larger stream. To apply the rule contended for would prevent the useful and profitable cultivation of the productive soil, and sanction the waste of water upon the more sterile lands. It would have enabled a party to locate upon a stream in 1875, and destroy the value of thousands of acres, and the improvements thereon, in adjoining valleys, possessed and cultivated for the preceding decade. Under the principle contended for, a party owning land ten miles from the stream, but in the valley thereof, might deprive a prior appropriator of the water diverted therefrom whose lands are within a thousand yards, but just beyond an intervening divide.

. . .

Affirmed.

NOTES

1. The prior appropriation system of water rights in streams and lakes exists in seventeen western states and Mississippi. In some of these states it is the exclusive system, while in others it has been combined with the riparian system. State constitutions and statutes have played a dominant role in the development of prior appropriation law. Appropriative rights today are acquired in nearly all states by permits issued by state administrative agencies. Thus, unlike riparian rights, appropriative rights do not originate as incidents of land ownership. For some purposes, however, they may become incidents of land ownership. Thus, a deed conveying land irrigated with water based upon an appropriation permit may also transfer the permit, despite absence of reference in the deed to the permit. In addition, in a few states such a water right cannot be severed from the land to which it has been applied. For more extended coverage of prior appropriation law, see A. Tarlock, Law of Water Rights and Resources, ch. 5 (1988).

2. Coffin v. Left Hand Ditch Co. extolls the virtues of prior appropriation doctrine. This doctrine also has weaknesses. The principal shortcoming is overemphasis of priority in time of use. Consider the following situation:

> (1) The senior appropriator on a stream is S, who irrigates farm land. J, a junior appropriator, supplies water for household use of residents of a private subdivision. During a drought, according to traditional doctrine, J is entitled to no water so long as S's needs

are unsatisfied. Courts and legislatures have required that uses be "beneficial" in order to be protected as appropriative rights, but this does not mean that a more beneficial junior use would be preferred over a less beneficial senior use during a period of shortage. The beneficial use requirement is applied most often at the inception of an appropriative right; an application for a permit to appropriate may be denied on the ground that the proposed use is not beneficial, or is not as beneficial as a use contemplated by a competing application. Statutes commonly provide a list of water uses ranked as to their relative importance.

(2) S, the senior appropriator on a stream, irrigates land near the mouth of the stream. Extreme losses of water upstream occur due to seepage into the bed. It has been held that upstream junior appropriators nevertheless must leave sufficient water in the stream to reach S. State ex rel. Cary v. Cochran, 138 Neb. 163, 292 N.W. 239 (1940).

(3) S, a senior appropriator, continues to divert water through unlined canals and to use antiquated irrigation devices that consume much more water than do modern devices. Is S required by prior appropriation doctrine to line the canals with impervious materials and to utilize modern irrigation devices? In the absence of relevant legislation, courts have been reluctant to require appropriators to adopt more efficient means of diversion or use of water, but have done so in extreme cases. In a much-cited decision, a senior appropriator who relied upon the current of a stream to turn a water wheel to lift water was denied relief against one who built a dam downstream, slowing the current and thereby rendering the wheel ineffective. Schodde v. Twin Falls Land & Water Co., 224 U.S. 107, 32 S.Ct. 470, 56 L.Ed. 686 (1912). The court recognized that the senior appropriator had a right to remove a certain quantity of water from the stream, but rejected as unreasonable the contention that this right embraced a right to use a means of diversion that denied substantial amounts of water to others.

(4) A state agency has declared a stream fully appropriated and refuses to issue new permits, but some appropriators are not using all of the water to which they are entitled. This problem may be addressed by authorizing temporary permits, but investments in enterprises based upon such permits would be risky. Appropriative rights may be lost by abandonment, but this requires proof of intent to abandon. Statutes also commonly authorize forfeiture of appropriative rights for stated periods of nonuse (often five years), but recognition of certain excuses and lax enforcement weaken this remedy.

(5) Reliance upon the market to allocate appropriative rights to more valuable uses is fraught with difficulties. Although such rights are transferable, in some states they cannot be severed from the land. There are also other legal impediments to transfers of appropriative rights. Some of these impediments should be removed, but others protect significant interests. For example,

should an upstream senior appropriator using water for irrigation be allowed to convey its full water right to an enterprise that will return less flow to the stream, depriving downstream juniors of flow upon which they have relied? Juniors are protected in this situation. E.g., Green v. Chaffee Ditch Co., 150 Colo. 91, 371 P.2d 775 (1962). The general problem is addressed in A. Tarlock, Law of Water Rights and Resources § 5.17 (1988).

3. How can riparian and appropriative rights coexist on the same stream, as they do in several western states? Coordination typically is accomplished by legislation confining riparian rights to actual uses prior to a specified date. Such legislation has been upheld against constitutional challenges. In re the Adjudication of the Water Rights of the Upper Guadalupe Segment of the Guadalupe River Basin, 642 S.W.2d 438 (Tex.1982).

4. Although eastern states, with the exception of Mississippi, have not adopted the prior appropriation system, many of them have subjected riparian rights to regulation. Some of these eastern regulatory programs require permits and have other features similar to prior appropriation. See Ausness, Water Rights Legislation in the East: A Program for Reform, 24 Wm. & Mary L.Rev. 547 (1983).

(2) GROUNDWATER

PRATHER v. EISENMAN

Supreme Court of Nebraska, 1978.
200 Neb. 1, 261 N.W.2d 766.

SPENCER, JUSTICE.

This is an action brought by domestic well owners to enjoin the pumping of ground water from an irrigation well owned by defendants, and for damages. The District Court found defendants' withdrawal caused a loss of artesian pressure in plaintiffs' wells, interfering with their domestic appropriation.

The court found the water was sufficient for all users if plaintiffs lowered their pumps to below the aquifer and defendants did not lower their pump. It permanently enjoined defendants from lowering their pump and from pumping for the period of time reasonably required by plaintiffs to lower their pumps. The court awarded plaintiffs the necessary costs of providing an assured alternative method of water supply, or a total recovery of $5,346.58. We affirm.

Plaintiffs Prather are the owners of a 9–acre tract upon which they maintain their residence. The residence is supplied with water by an artesian well located on the premises. The artesian pressure was normally sufficient to force water in the well to a level 5 to 6 feet above the ground. The well was 121 feet 10 inches deep and 2 inches in diameter.

Two other landowners, Furleys and Zessins, assigned their claims to Prathers. Unless designated by name hereafter, they are included in the title "plaintiffs." The Furleys are the owners of a 2–acre tract. The residence on the premises is supplied with water from an artesian well 111 feet deep and 2 inches in diameter. The artesian pressure was sufficient to raise the water above the ground.

The Zessins are the owners of a tract of land in the same area which is occupied by their daughter. The residence upon the premises is supplied with water by a 160–foot well with 4–inch casing and a submersible pump. The water in the Zessin well did not rise above the surface of the ground.

Defendants Eisenmanns purchased a 90–acre tract of land in the area in March of 1976. On July 9, 1976, they completed an irrigation well on the premises. The well was 179 feet deep and had a capacity of 1,250 gallons per minute on a 2–hour test.

On July 9, 1976, Eisenmanns commenced pumping from the well at an estimated rate of 650 gallons per minute. Prathers and Furleys lost the use of their wells on July 10, 1976. Zessins lost the use of their well between the evening of July 12 and the morning of July 13 when the water level dropped below the level of the submersible pump. Because of the loss of water, the Zessins' pump overheated and welded itself to the casing. Zessins were unable to dislodge the pump and were forced to drill a new well to a depth of 164 feet.

Following a stipulation by the parties, a temporary injunction was issued on July 20, 1976, to permit the University of Nebraska Conservation and Survey Division to conduct certain tests on the wells. The tests consisted of pumping the irrigation well at a rate of 375 gallons per minute for 3 days, then measuring the draw down of the Eisenmanns' well and a number of other observation wells which included the three domestic wells. At the end of the pumping period the measured draw down on the Prathers' well was 61.91 feet; the Furleys' well, 65.45 feet; and the Zessins' well, 65.6 feet. The draw down of the Eisenmanns' well was 97.92 feet. All the wells recovered to the prepumping level within 11 days after cessation of pumping from the irrigation well.

The two hydrologists who conducted the tests made certain findings: (1) The irrigation well and the domestic wells were drawing from the same aquifer. (2) The aquifer could be defined with reasonable scientific certainty. (3) The pumping by Eisenmanns depressed the artesian head of the domestic wells. (4) The cone of influence caused by Eisenmanns' pumping intercepted or affected the plaintiffs' wells. (5) The common aquifer from which the domestic and irrigation wells draw water is sufficient to supply both domestic and irrigation needs. (6) For plaintiffs to obtain water from their wells during periods when Eisenmanns were pumping, they would have to pump water from the top of the shale.

Section 46–635, R.R.S.1943, defines "ground water" as: ". . . that water which occurs or moves, seeps, filters, or percolates through the ground under the surface of the land." The existence of ground water in any particular area is dependent not only on the source of the water but also on the geologic formation of the earth. The earth materials with sufficient porosity to contain significant amounts of ground water and sufficient permeability to allow its withdrawal in significant quantities are called "aquifers." The upper surface of the water-saturated material is called "the water table."

Aquifers are almost always underlain by an impervious layer which prevents the water from percolating and seeping downward to such a level that it would be beyond economical reach. Two of the domestic wells involved were dependent upon artesian pressure. This results when ground water is not only underlain by impervious material but is confined between or underneath impervious layers as well. A well penetrating through one of the surrounding impervious layers provides an escape valve through which water will flow without external force so long as sufficient artesian pressure exists.

Before restating the current Nebraska law, it is well to note the various common law views concerning rights to ground water. The nonstatutory theories are classified as: (1) The common law, or English rule; (2) the reasonable use, or American rule; and (3) the correlative rights doctrine, or California rule.

Under the English or common law rule, a landowner had absolute ownership of the waters under his land. He could, therefore, without liability, withdraw any quantity of water for any purpose even though the result was to drain all water from beneath surrounding lands.

The American rule of reasonable use also recognized a proprietary interest of an overlying owner in the waters under his lands. " ' "The American, as distinguished from the English rule, is that, while the owner of the land is entitled to appropriate subterranean or other waters accumulating on his land, which thereby become a part of the realty, he cannot extract and appropriate them in excess of a reasonable and beneficial use upon the land he owns, unconnected with the beneficial use of the land, especially if the exercise of such use in excess of the reasonable and beneficial use is injurious to others, who have substantial rights to the water." ' " Metropolitan Utilities Dist. v. Merritt Beach Co., 179 Neb. 783, 140 N.W.2d 626 (1966). There is no preference as to use under the American rule.

The California or correlative rights rule essentially provides the rights of all landowners over a common aquifer are coequal or correlative and one cannot extract more than his share of the water even for use on his own land where others' rights are injured thereby.

Nebraska has had few decisions dealing with underground water problems. In Olson v. City of Wahoo, 124 Neb. 802, 248 N.W. 304, our court, in 1933, enunciated a modified reasonable use rule. It said: "The American rule is that the owner of land is entitled to appropriate subterranean waters found under his land, but he cannot extract and appropriate them in excess of a reasonable and beneficial use upon the land which he owns, especially if such use is injurious to others who have substantial rights to the waters, *and if the natural underground supply is insufficient for all owners, each is entitled to a reasonable proportion of the whole,* and while a lesser number of states have adopted this rule, it is, in our opinion, supported by the better reasoning." (Italics supplied.) The portion emphasized was not a part of the American rule as enunciated in a majority of the states. Nebraska, in

Olson, adopted the rule of reasonable use with the addition of the California doctrine of apportionment in time of shortage. . . .

The question the instant case presents is one of first impression in this state. The three domestic wells of the plaintiffs do not contribute significantly to a reduction in the artesian pressure or water level of the underground aquifer. It was not until the defendants subsequently sunk and operated their irrigation well that plaintiffs lost the artesian pressure and the use of their wells.

The evidence indicates defendants had a runoff of approximately 15 to 25 gallons of water per minute above the water utilized on their land. The trial court found this was in excess of a reasonable and beneficial use on their own land. It is not necessary for us to reach this issue. We do not deem it material in view of the decision we reach herein. This case must be analyzed in reference to section 46–613, R.R.S.1943, the preferential use statute.

Under the reasonable use doctrine, two neighboring landowners, each of whom is using the water on his own property overlying the common supply, can withdraw all the supply he can put to beneficial and reasonable use. What is reasonable is judged solely in relationship to the purpose of such use on the overlying land. It is not judged in relation to the needs of others. Harnsberger, Oeltjen, & Fischer, Groundwater: From Windmills to Comprehensive Public Management, 52 Neb.L.Rev. 179 at p. 205 (1973).

Our preference statute points the way to a solution of the present controversy. It is apparent the trial court used it with an adaptation of the rule proposed in the Tentative Draft No. 17 of section 858A of Restatement, Torts 2d (1971). That rule provides in part: "S. 858A. Non-liability for use of ground water—exceptions. A possesser of land or his grantee who withdraws ground water from the land and uses it for a beneficial purpose is not subject to liability for interference with the use of water by another, unless (a) the withdrawal of water causes unreasonable harm through lowering the water table or reducing artesian pressure, * * *." The District Court found defendants' appropriation of water "caused unreasonable harm to plaintiffs by lowering the water table and reducing artesian pressure."

The comment in Restatement, Torts 2d, suggests the tentative rule is the American rule with its protection broadened. It is not so broad, however, as the Nebraska rule. As the comment notes, it gives more or less unrestricted freedom to the possessor of overlying land to develop and use ground water. It does not attempt to apportion the water among users except to the extent that special conditions permit it to be done on a rational basis. It gives the protection of the American rule to owners of small wells harmed by large withdrawals for use elsewhere, but extends that protection in proper cases to harm done by large withdrawals for operation on overlying lands.

Much of the litigation involving users of ground water has involved the collateral effects of a withdrawal of the water rather than a division of it. There was no problem here with the artesian pressure until defendants withdrew in excess of 350 gallons per minute and lowered the water beyond the reach of the domestic wells.

There is sufficient water in the aquifer for all the parties if defendants' irrigation well remains at its present level and the domestic wells are lowered to the top of the shale. The trial court found plaintiffs had been damaged to the extent of the expense necessary to lower their wells to the shale.

The term reasonable use, as contemplated in the American rule, relates to the manner in which water is used upon the land of the appropriator. The interests of adjacent landowners are in issue only when the appropriator uses water in excess of the reasonable and beneficial use of it upon his land, and that excess use is injurious to the adjacent landowner.

The term "reasonable use" as defined in the correlative rights doctrine means reasonable share of the whole. Under the correlative rights doctrine, the overlying owners have no proprietary interest in the water, and in times of shortage each overlying owner has an equal and correlative right to make beneficial use of his proportionate share of the water.

Reasonable use, as defined in the proposed Restatement doctrine, means a balancing of the equities between the use made of the water by the subsequent appropriator versus the injury caused by that use to the prior appropriator.

The Nebraska rule, as previously pointed out, is a combination of the American and the correlative rights doctrine. It must be construed, however, in the light of our preference statute, section 46–613, R.R.S.1943. This statute provides as follows: "Preference in the use of underground water shall be given to those using the water for domestic purposes. They shall have preference over those claiming it for any other purpose. Those using the water for agricultural purposes shall have the preference over those using the same for manufacturing or industrial purposes.

"As used in this section, domestic use of ground water shall mean all uses of ground water required for human needs as it relates to health, fire control, and sanitation and shall include the use of ground water for domestic livestock as related to normal farm and ranch operations."

It is our statute which distinguishes the Nebraska rule from other rules. Under the statute, the use of underground water for domestic purposes has first preference. It takes priority over all other uses. As between domestic users, however, there is no preference or priority. Every overlying owner has an equal right to a fair share of the underground water for domestic purposes. If the artesian head in the present situation had been lowered by other domestic users, plaintiffs would be entitled to no relief so long as they still could obtain water by deepening their wells. If the water became insufficient for the use of all domestic users, each domestic user would be entitled to a proportionate share of the water. All domestic users, regardless of priority in time, are entitled to a fair share of the water in the aquifer.

That, however, is not the present problem. We are dealing with plaintiffs who have preferential rights. We are confronted with the situation where the appropriation by the defendants rendered the plaintiffs' well useless during the pumping period and the period of time after the pumping ceased to recharge the area so the water again reached plaintiffs' pumps. In the case of the 3–day test conducted by the hydrologists, this recharge period was 11 days. In the case of the Zessin well, the appropriation by defendants also froze the pump to the pipe and required the drilling of a new well.

Plaintiffs can still obtain sufficient water for domestic purposes by drilling wells to the shale. It would not have been necessary for them to incur the necessary expense to do so except for the action of defendants. Without question, plaintiffs have been damaged by the operation of defendants' well. As the trial court found, defendants' withdrawal of water caused unreasonable harm to plaintiffs by lowering the water table or reducing the artesian pressure. Plaintiffs had obtained a property right in that use so they should have a remedy for their damage.

The remedy devised by the trial court presents a very equitable solution. It reimburses the plaintiffs only for the expense they were forced to incur because of the action of the defendants. Plaintiffs' wells were very adequate for their own purposes. Their use of water for domestic purposes took precedence over the appropriation for agricultural purposes by the defendants. Plaintiffs had a valuable property right in the extraction of water for domestic purposes. It was solely defendants' action which deprived them of their right. Defendants, by pumping large quantities of water from the same aquifer, destroyed the artesian pressure for two of the wells. For the other well, which was deeper and used a pump, defendants' action lowered the water below the reach of the pump and the resultant heat froze the pump to the pipe. The only way plaintiffs could be assured of water for domestic purposes was to drill wells to the shale. This expense was thrust upon plaintiffs solely as a consequence of defendants' action in destroying plaintiffs' artesian pressure and lowering the water below the reach of their domestic wells. Plaintiffs' right to the extraction of water from their existing wells was appropriated or destroyed by the action of defendants. What should be the extent of plaintiffs' damage? Certainly it should be the cost of restoring or obtaining what plaintiffs had before it was appropriated by defendants' action. . . .

Affirmed.

NOTES

1. The prior appropriation doctrine is applied to groundwater in some states, but with substantial modification. What would be the consequences of strict application to groundwater? Consider Current Creek Irrig. Co. v. Andrews, 9 Utah 2d 324, 344 P.2d 528 (1959). See also Baker v. Ore–Ida Foods, Inc., 95 Idaho 575, 513 P.2d 627 (1973), applying a statutory provision that "while the doctrine of 'first in time is first in right' is recognized, a reasonable exercise of this right shall

not block full economic development of underground water resources, but early appropriators of underground water shall be protected in the maintenance of reasonable ground water pumping levels as may be established by" a designated official. This statute is applicable to aquifers that have substantial natural recharge. Some aquifers do not. Pumping from those constitutes mining. What policies should govern such pumping? For one approach, see Mathers v. Texaco, Inc., 77 N.M. 239, 421 P.2d 771 (1966).

2. Economists have addressed the problem of achieving optimum development of groundwater resources. A standard reference is Hirshleifer, De Haven & Milliman, Water Supply: Economics, Technology, and Policy 59 (1960).

E. INTERESTS IN AIRSPACE, AIR, SUNLIGHT AND CLOUDS

UNITED STATES v. CAUSBY

United States Supreme Court, 1946.
328 U.S. 256, 66 S.Ct. 1062, 90 L.Ed. 1206.

MR. JUSTICE DOUGLAS delivered the opinion of the Court.

This is a case of first impression. The problem presented is whether respondents' property was taken, within the meaning of the Fifth Amendment, by frequent and regular flights of army and navy aircraft over respondents' land at low altitudes. The Court of Claims held that there was a taking and entered judgment for respondents, one judge dissenting. 60 F.Supp. 751. The case is here on a petition for a writ of certiorari which we granted because of the importance of the question presented.

Respondents own 2.8 acres near an airport outside of Greensboro, North Carolina. It has on it a dwelling house, and also various outbuildings which were mainly used for raising chickens. The end of the airport's northwest-southeast runway is 2,220 feet from respondents' barn and 2,275 feet from their house. The path of glide to this runway passes directly over the property—which is 100 feet wide and 1,200 feet long. The 30 to 1 safe glide angle [1] approved by the Civil Aeronautics Authority [2] passes over this property at 83 feet, which is 67 feet above the house, 63 feet above the barn and 18 feet above the highest tree.[3] The use by the United States of this airport is pursuant to a lease executed in May, 1942, for a term commencing June 1, 1942 and ending June 30, 1942, with a provision for renewals until June 30, 1967, or six months after the end of the national emergency, whichever is the earlier.

1. A 30 to 1 glide angle means one foot of elevation or descent for every 30 feet of horizontal distance.

2. Military planes are subject to the rules of the Civil Aeronautics Board where, as in the present case, there are no Army or Navy regulations to the contrary. Cameron v. Civil Aeronautics Board, 7 Cir., 140 F.2d 482.

3. The house is approximately 16 feet high, the barn 20 feet, and the tallest tree 65 feet.

Various aircraft of the United States use this airport—bombers, transports and fighters. The direction of the prevailing wind determines when a particular runway is used. The northwest-southeast runway in question is used about four per cent of the time in taking off and about seven per cent of the time in landing. Since the United States began operations in May, 1942, its four-motored heavy bombers, other planes of the heavier type, and its fighter planes have frequently passed over respondents' land and buildings in considerable numbers and rather close together. They come close enough at times to appear barely to miss the tops of the trees and at times so close to the tops of the trees as to blow the old leaves off. The noise is startling. And at night the glare from the planes brightly lights up the place. As a result of the noise, respondents had to give up their chicken business. As many as six to ten of their chickens were killed in one day by flying into the walls from fright. The total chickens lost in that manner was about 150. Production also fell off. The result was the destruction of the use of the property as a commercial chicken farm. Respondents are frequently deprived of their sleep and the family has become nervous and frightened. Although there have been no airplane accidents on respondents' property, there have been several accidents near the airport and close to respondents' place. These are the essential facts found by the Court of Claims. On the basis of these facts, it found that respondents' property had depreciated in value. It held that the United States had taken an easement over the property on June 1, 1942, and that the value of the property destroyed and the easement taken was $2,000.

I. The United States relies on the Air Commerce Act of 1926, 44 Stat. 568, 49 U.S.C. § 171, as amended by the Civil Aeronautics Act of 1938, 52 Stat. 973, 49 U.S.C. § 401. Under those statutes the United States has "complete and exclusive national sovereignty in the air space" over this country. 49 U.S.C. § 176(a). They grant any citizen of the United States "a public right of freedom of transit in air commerce[4] through the navigable air space of the United States." 49 U.S.C. § 403. And "navigable air space" is defined as "airspace above the minimum safe altitudes of flight prescribed by the Civil Aeronautics Authority." 49 U.S.C. § 180. And it is provided that "such navigable airspace shall be subject to a public right of freedom of interstate and foreign air navigation." Id. It is, therefore, argued that since these flights were within the minimum safe altitudes of flight which had been prescribed, they were an exercise of the declared right of travel through the airspace. The United States concludes that when flights are made within the navigable airspace without any physical invasion of the property of the landowners, there has been no taking of property. It says that at most there was merely incidental damage occurring as a consequence of authorized air navigation. It also argues that the landowner does not own superadjacent airspace which he has not subjected to possession by the erection of structures or other

4. "Air commerce" is defined as including "any operation or navigation of aircraft which directly affects, or which may endanger safety in, interstate, overseas, or foreign air commerce." 49 U.S.C. § 401(3).

occupancy. Moreover, it is argued that even if the United States took airspace owned by respondents, no compensable damage was shown. Any damages are said to be merely consequential for which no compensation may be obtained under the Fifth Amendment.

It is ancient doctrine that at common law ownership of the land extended to the periphery of the universe—*Cujus est solum ejus est usque ad coelum.*[5] But that doctrine has no place in the modern world. The air is a public highway, as Congress has declared. Were that not true, every transcontinental flight would subject the operator to countless trespass suits. Common sense revolts at the idea. To recognize such private claims to the airspace would clog these highways, seriously interfere with their control and development in the public interest, and transfer into private ownership that to which only the public has a just claim.

But that general principle does not control the present case. For the United States conceded on oral argument that if the flights over respondents' property rendered it uninhabitable, there would be a taking compensable under the Fifth Amendment. It is the owner's loss, not the taker's gain, which is the measure of the value of the property taken. United States v. Miller, 317 U.S. 369, 63 S.Ct. 276, 87 L.Ed. 336, 147 A.L.R. 55. Market value fairly determined is the normal measure of the recovery. Id. And that value may reflect the use to which the land could readily be converted, as well as the existing use. United States v. Powelson, 319 U.S. 266, 275, 63 S.Ct. 1047, 1053, 87 L.Ed. 1390, and cases cited. If, by reason of the frequency and altitude of the flights, respondents could not use this land for any purpose, their loss would be complete.[6] It would be as complete as if the United States had entered upon the surface of the land and taken exclusive possession of it.

We agree that in those circumstances there would be a taking. Though it would be only an easement of flight which was taken, that easement, if permanent and not merely temporary, normally would be the equivalent of a fee interest. It would be a definite exercise of complete dominion and control over the surface of the land. The fact that the planes never touched the surface would be as irrelevant as the absence in this day of the feudal livery of seisin on the transfer of real estate. The owner's right to possess and exploit the land—that is to say, his beneficial ownership of it—would be destroyed. It would not be a case of incidental damages arising from a legalized nuisance such as was involved in Richards v. Washington Terminal Co., 233 U.S. 546, 34 S.Ct. 654, 58 L.Ed. 1088, L.R.A.1915A, 887. In that case, property owners whose lands adjoined a railroad line were denied recovery for damages resulting from the noise, vibrations, smoke and the like, incidental to the operations of the trains. In the supposed case, the

5. 1 Coke, Institutes (19th ed. 1832) ch. 1, § 1(4a); 2 Blackstone, Commentaries (Lewis ed. 1902) p. 18; 3 Kent, Commentaries (Gould ed. 1896) p. 621.

6. The desctruction of all uses of the property by flooding has been held to constitute a taking. Pumpelly v. Green Bay Co., 13 Wall. 166, 20 L.Ed. 557; United States v. Lynah, 188 U.S. 445, 23 S.Ct. 349, 47 L.Ed. 539; United States v. Welch, 217 U.S. 333, 30 S.Ct. 527, 54 L.Ed. 787, 28 L.R.A.,N.S., 385, 19 Ann.Cas. 680.

line of flight is over the land. And the land is appropriated as directly and completely as if it were used for the runways themselves.

There is no material difference between the supposed case and the present one, except that here enjoyment and use of the land are not completely destroyed. But that does not seem to us to be controlling. The path of glide for airplanes might reduce a valuable factory site to grazing land, an orchard to a vegetable patch, a residential section to a wheat field. Some value would remain. But the use of the airspace immediately above the land would limit the utility of the land and cause a diminution in its value.[7] That was the philosophy of Portsmouth Co. v. United States, 260 U.S. 327, 43 S.Ct. 135, 67 L.Ed. 287. In that case the petition alleged that the United States erected a fort on nearby land, established a battery and a fire control station there, and fired guns over petitioner's land. The Court, speaking through Mr. Justice Holmes, reversed the Court of Claims, which dismissed the petition on a demurrer, holding that "the specific facts set forth would warrant a finding that a servitude has been imposed."[8] 260 U.S. at page 330, 43 S.Ct., at page 137, 67 L.Ed. 287. And see Delta Air Corp. v. Kersey, 193 Ga. 862, 20 S.E.2d 245, 140 A.L.R. 1352. Cf. United States v. 357.25 Acres of Land, D.C., 55 F.Supp. 461.

The fact that the path of glide taken by the planes was that approved by the Civil Aeronautics Authority does not change the result. The navigable airspace which Congress has placed in the public domain is "airspace above the minimum safe altitudes of flight prescribed by the Civil Aeronautics Authority." 49 U.S.C. § 180. If that agency prescribed 83 feet as the minimum safe altitude, then we would have presented the question of the validity of the regulation. But nothing of the sort has been done. The path of glide governs the method of operating—of landing or taking off. The altitude required for that operation is not the minimum safe altitude of flight which is the downward reach of the navigable airspace. The minimum prescribed by the Authority is 500 feet during the day and 1,000 feet at night for air carriers (Civil Air Regulations, Pt. 61, §§ 61.7400, 61.7401, Code Fed.Reg.Cum.Supp., Tit. 14, ch. 1), and from 300 feet to 1,000 feet for other aircraft, depending on the type of plane and the character of the terrain. Id., Pt. 60, §§ 60.350–60.3505, Fed.Reg.Cum.Supp., supra. Hence, the flights in question were not within the navigable airspace which Congress placed within the public domain. If any airspace needed for landing or taking off were included, flights which were so

7. It was stated in United States v. General Motors Corp., 323 U.S. 373, 378, 65 S.Ct. 357, 359, 89 L.Ed. 311, 156 A.L.R. 390, "The courts have held that the deprivation of the former owner rather than the accretion of a right or interest to the sovereign constitutes the taking. Governmental action short of acquisition of title or occupancy has been held, if its effects are so complete as to deprive the owner of all or most of his interest in the subject matter, to amount to a taking." The present case falls short of the *General Motors* case. This is not a case where the United States has merely destroyed property. It is using a part of it for the flight of its planes.

Cf. Warren Township School Dist v. Detroit, 308 Mich. 460, 14 N.W.2d 134; Smith v. New England Aircraft Co., 270 Mass. 511, 170 N.E. 385; Burnham v. Beverly Airways, Inc., 311 Mass. 628, 42 N.E.2d 575.

8. On remand the allegations in the petition were found not to be supported by the facts. 64 Ct.Cl. 572.

close to the land as to render it uninhabitable would be immune. But the United States concedes, as we have said, that in that event there would be a taking. Thus, it is apparent that the path of glide is not the minimum safe altitude of flight within the meaning of the statute. The Civil Aeronautics Authority has, of course, the power to prescribe air traffic rules. But Congress has defined navigable airspace only in terms of one of them—the minimum safe altitudes of flight.

We have said that the airspace is a public highway. Yet it is obvious that if the landowner is to have full enjoyment of the land, he must have exclusive control of the immediate reaches of the enveloping atmosphere. Otherwise buildings could not be erected, trees could not be planted, and even fences could not be run. The principle is recognized when the law gives a remedy in case overhanging structures are erected on adjoining land.[9] The landowner owns at least as much of the space above the ground as he can occupy or use in connection with the land. See Hinman v. Pacific Air Transport, 9 Cir., 84 F.2d 755. The fact that he does not occupy it in a physical sense—by the erection of buildings and the like—is not material. As we have said, the flight of airplanes, which skim the surface but do not touch it, is as much an appropriation of the use of the land as a more conventional entry upon it. We would not doubt that, if the United States erected an elevated railway over respondents' land at the precise altitude where its planes now fly, there would be a partial taking, even though none of the supports of the structure rested on the land.[10] The reason is that there would be an intrusion so immediate and direct as to subtract from the owner's full enjoyment of the property and to limit his exploitation of it. While the owner does not in any physical manner occupy that stratum of airspace or make use of it in the conventional sense, he does use it in somewhat the same sense that space left between buildings for the purpose of light and air is used. The superadjacent airspace at this low altitude is so close to the land that continuous invasions of it affect the use of the surface of the land itself. We think that the landowner, as an incident to his ownership, has a claim to it and that invasions of it are in the same category as invasions of the surface.[11]

9. Baten's Case, 9 Coke R. 53b; Meyer v. Metzler, 51 Cal. 142; Codman v. Evans, 89 Mass. 431; Harrington v. McCarthy, 169 Mass. 492, 48 N.E. 278. See Ball, The Vertical Extent of Ownership in Land, 76 U.Pa.L.Rev. 631, 658–671.

10. It was held in Butler v. Frontier Telephone Co., 186 N.Y. 486, 79 N.E. 716, 11 L.R.A.,N.S., 920, 116 Am.St.Rep. 563, 9 Ann.Cas. 858, that ejectment would lie where a telephone wire was strung across the plaintiff's property, even though it did not touch the soil. The court stated, pp. 491–492: ". . . an owner is entitled to the absolute and undisturbed possession of every part of his premises, including the space above, as much as a mine beneath. If the wire had been a huge cable, several inches thick and but a foot above the ground, there would have been a difference in degree, but not in principle. Expand the wire into a beam supported by posts standing upon abutting lots without touching the surface of plaintiff's land, and the difference would still be one of degree only. Enlarge the beam into a bridge, and yet space only would be occupied. Erect a house upon the bridge, and the air above the surface of the land would alone be disturbed."

11. See Bouvé, Private Ownership of Navigable Airspace Under the Commerce Clause, 21 Amer. Bar Assoc. Journ. 416, 421–422; Hise, Ownership and Sovereignty of the Air, 16 Ia.L.Rev. 169; Eubank, The Doctrine of the Airspace Zone of Effective Possession, 12 Boston Univ.L.Rev. 414.

In this case, as in Portsmouth Co. v. United States, supra, the damages were not merely consequential. They were the product of a direct invasion of respondents' domain. As stated in United States v. Cress, 243 U.S. 316, 328, 37 S.Ct. 380, 385, 61 L.Ed. 746, " . . . it is the character of the invasion, not the amount of damage resulting from it, so long as the damage is substantial, that determines the question whether it is a taking."

We said in United States v. Powelson, supra, 319 U.S. at page 279, 63 S.Ct. at page 1054, 87 L.Ed. 1390, that while the meaning of "property" as used in the Fifth Amendment was a federal question, "it will normally obtain its content by reference to local law." If we look to North Carolina law, we reach the same result. Sovereignty in the airspace rests in the State "except where granted to and assumed by the United States." Gen.Stats.1943, § 63–11. The flight of aircraft is lawful "unless at such a low altitude as to interfere with the then existing use to which the land or water, or the space over the land or water, is put by the owner, or unless so conducted as to be imminently dangerous to persons or property lawfully on the land or water beneath." Id., § 63–13. Subject to that right of flight, "ownership of the space above the lands and waters of this State is declared to be vested in the several owners of the surface beneath . . . " Id., § 63–12. Our holding that there was an invasion of respondents' property is thus not inconsistent with the local law governing a landowner's claim to the immediate reaches of the superadjacent airspace.

The airplane is part of the modern environment of life, and the inconveniences which it causes are normally not compensable under the Fifth Amendment. The airspace, apart from the immediate reaches above the land, is part of the public domain. We need not determine at this time what those precise limits are. Flights over private land are not a taking, unless they are so low and so frequent as to be a direct and immediate interference with the enjoyment and use of the land. We need not speculate on that phase of the present case. For the findings of the Court of Claims plainly establish that there was a diminution in value of the property and that the frequent, low-level flights were the direct and immediate cause. We agree with the Court of Claims that a servitude has been imposed upon the land.

. . .

III. The Court of Claims held, as we have noted, that an easement was taken. But the findings of fact contain no precise description as to its nature. It is not described in terms of frequency of flight, permissible altitude, or type of airplane. Nor is there a finding as to whether the easement taken was temporary or permanent. Yet an accurate description of the property taken is essential, since that interest vests in the United States. . . .

Since on this record it is not clear whether the easement taken is a permanent or a temporary one, it would be premature for us to consider whether the amount of the award made by the Court of Claims was proper.

The judgment is reversed and the cause is remanded to the Court of Claims so that it may make the necessary findings in conformity with this opinion.

Reversed.

MR. JUSTICE BLACK, dissenting.

. . .

No greater confusion could be brought about in the coming age of air transportation than that which would result were courts by constitutional interpretation to hamper Congress in its efforts to keep the air free. Old concepts of private ownership of land should not be introduced into the field of air regulation. I have no doubt that Congress will, if not handicapped by judicial interpretations of the Constitution, preserve the freedom of the air, and at the same time, satisfy the just claims of aggrieved persons. The noise of newer, larger, and more powerful planes may grow louder and louder and disturb people more and more. But the solution of the problems precipitated by these technological advances and new ways of living cannot come about through the application of rigid constitutional restraints formulated and enforced by the courts. What adjustments may have to be made, only the future can reveal. It seems certain, however, that courts do not possess the techniques or the personnel to consider and act upon the complex combinations of factors entering into the problems. The contribution of courts must be made through the awarding of damages for injuries suffered from the flying of planes, or by the granting of injunctions to prohibit their flying. When these two simple remedial devices are elevated to a constitutional level under the Fifth Amendment, as the Court today seems to have done, they can stand as obstacles to better adapted techniques that might be offered by experienced experts and accepted by Congress. Today's opinion is, I fear, an opening wedge for an unwarranted judicial interference with the power of Congress to develop solutions for new and vital national problems. In my opinion this case should be reversed on the ground that there has been no "taking" in the constitutional sense.

NOTES

1. In Griggs v. Allegheny County, 369 U.S. 84, 82 S.Ct. 531, 7 L.Ed.2d 585 (1962), a county, as owner-operator of an airport was held to have taken avigation easements by virtue of noisy overflights caused by the location of runways.

2. Assume that in Causby the military flights had not penetrated the airspace above claimants' lands. Same result? Compare Batten v. United States, 306 F.2d 580 (10th Cir.1962), cert. denied 371 U.S. 955, 83 S.Ct. 506 (1963) (no compensation) with Martin v. Port of Seattle, 64 Wn.2d 309, 391 P.2d 540 (1964), cert. denied 379 U.S. 989, 85 S.Ct. 701, 13 L.Ed.2d 610 (1965). If the Causby's land had been unimproved, would the government have been liable for a "taking" as a result of the impermissibly low flights, even though there was no substantial interference with the use and enjoyment of the land? See Hero Lands Co. v.

United States, 554 F.Supp. 1262 (Ct.Cl.1983), affirmed 727 F.2d 1118 (Fed.Cir.1983). For discussion of these and related problems, see Lesser, The Aircraft Noise Problem: The Past Decade—Still Federal Power and, at Least for a While Longer, Local Liability, 13 Urb.Law. 285 (1981). See also Dolley & Carroll, Airport Noise Pollution Damages: The Case for Local Liability, 15 Urb.Law. 621 (1983).

3. Can liability for inverse condemnation be avoided by land use regulation which prevents residential use of land near airports? Severe restrictions on the height of structures near airports ("airport zoning") have been held invalid. E.g., Indiana Toll Road Commission v. Jankovich, 244 Ind. 574, 193 N.E.2d 237 (1963), cert. dismissed 379 U.S. 487, 85 S.Ct. 493, 13 L.Ed.2d 439 (1965). Density controls, such as large lot zoning, on the other hand, have been upheld. Morse v. County of San Luis Obispo, 247 Cal.App.2d 600, 55 Cal.Rptr. 710 (1967). If land use regulation is held to be a "taking," does it follow that the landowner is entitled to compensation on the inverse condemnation theory? See p. 991, et seq. herein.

4. Other, and more promising, approaches to handling noise and other adverse environmental impacts of airports include comprehensive planning of airport location and design, improvement of traffic control systems, coordination with other forms of transportation, construction of sound-resistent dwellings, and development of quieter aircraft engines. See Airport and Airway Development Act of 1970, 49 U.S.C.A. § 1712 et seq.; Environmental Studies Board, National Academy of Sciences—National Academy of Engineering, Jamaica Bay and Kennedy Airport (1971).

5. Rights in airspace, as well as rights to minerals underground, may be severed from ownership in the surface. Any foreseeable problems? See Schnidman & Roberts, Municipal Air Rights: New York City's Proposal To Sell Air Rights over Public Buildings and Public Spaces, 15 Urb.Law. 347 (1983).

6. Compare with Causby the judicial treatment accorded claims of residents near major highways for compensation for similar interferences. Northcutt v. State Road Department, 209 So.2d 710 (Fla.App. 1968), denying compensation, is typical.

PRAH v. MARETTI

Supreme Court of Wisconsin, 1982.
108 Wis.2d 223, 321 N.W.2d 182.

ABRAHAMSON, JUSTICE.

This appeal from a judgment of the circuit court for Waukesha county, Max Raskin, circuit judge, was certified to this court by the court of appeals, sec. (Rule) 809.61, Stats.1979–80, as presenting an issue of first impression, namely, whether an owner of a solar-heated residence states a claim upon which relief can be granted when he asserts that his neighbor's proposed construction of a residence (which conforms to existing deed restrictions and local ordinances) interferes with his access to an unobstructed path for sunlight across the neighbor's property. This case thus involves a conflict between one landowner (Glenn Prah, the plaintiff) interested in unobstructed access to sunlight across adjoining property as a natural source of energy and an adjoining landowner (Richard D. Maretti, the defendant) interested in the development of his land.

The circuit court concluded that the plaintiff presented no claim upon which relief could be granted and granted summary judgment for the defendant. We reverse the judgment of the circuit court and remand the cause to the circuit court for further proceedings.

According to the complaint, the plaintiff is the owner of a residence which was constructed during the years 1978–1979. The complaint alleges that the residence has a solar system which includes collectors on the roof to supply energy for heat and hot water and that after the plaintiff built his solar-heated house, the defendant purchased the lot adjacent to and immediately to the south of the plaintiff's lot and commenced planning construction of a home. The complaint further states that when the plaintiff learned of defendant's plans to build the house he advised the defendant that if the house were built at the proposed location, defendant's house would substantially and adversely affect the integrity of plaintiff's solar system and could cause plaintiff other damage. Nevertheless, the defendant began construction. The complaint further alleges that the plaintiff is entitled to "unrestricted use of the sun and its solar power" and demands judgment for injunctive relief and damages.[1]

After filing his complaint, the plaintiff moved for a temporary injunction to restrain and enjoin construction by the defendant. In ruling on that motion the circuit court heard testimony, received affidavits and viewed the site.

The record made on the motion reveals the following additional facts: Plaintiff's home was the first residence built in the subdivision, and although plaintiff did not build his house in the center of the lot it was built in accordance with applicable restrictions. Plaintiff advised defendant that if the defendant's home were built at the proposed site it would cause a shadowing effect on the solar collectors which would reduce the efficiency of the system and possibly damage the system. To avoid these adverse effects, plaintiff requested defendant to locate his home an additional several feet away from the plaintiff's lot line, the exact number being disputed. Plaintiff and defendant failed to reach

1. As part of his amended answer to the complaint the defendant asserts that "the plaintiff's complaint fails to state a claim or cause of action against the defendant upon which relief can be granted and that the plaintiff is without legal or equitable rights with respect to his claim that he is entitled to the unrestricted use of the sun and its solar power and that the plaintiff's action is frivolous and without merit."

For a discussion of protecting solar access, see Note, Obtaining Access to Solar Energy: Nuisance, Water Rights, and Zoning Administration, 45 Bkyn.L.Rev. 357 (1979); Comment, Obstruction of Sunlight as a Private Nuisance, 65 Cal.L.Rev. 94 (1977); Comment, Solar Rights: Guaranteeing a Place in the Sun, 57 Ore.L.Rev. 94 (1977); Note, The Allocation of Sunlight; Solar Rights and the Prior Appropriation Doctrine, 47 U.Colo.L.Rev. 421 (1976).

an agreement on the location of defendant's home before defendant started construction. The Architectural Control Committee of the subdivision and the Planning Commission of the City of Muskego approved the defendant's plans for his home, including its location on the lot. After such approval, the defendant apparently changed the grade of the property without prior notice to the Architectural Control Committee.[2] The problem with defendant's proposed construction, as far as the plaintiff's interests are concerned, arises from a combination of the grade and the distance of defendant's home from the defendant's lot line.

The circuit court denied plaintiff's motion for injunctive relief, declared it would entertain a motion for summary judgment and thereafter entered judgment in favor of the defendant.

. . .

The plaintiff presents three legal theories to support his claim that the defendant's continued construction of a home justifies granting him relief: (1) the construction constitutes a common law private nuisance; (2) the construction is prohibited by sec. 844.01, Stats.1979–80; [3] and (3) the construction interferes with the solar easement plaintiff acquired under the doctrine of prior appropriation.[4]

As to the claim of private nuisance the circuit court concluded that the law of private nuisance requires the court to make "a comparative evaluation of the conflicting interests and to weigh the gravity of the harm to the plaintiff against the utility of the defendant's conduct." The circuit court concluded: "A comparative evaluation of the conflicting interests, keeping in mind the omissions and commissions of both Prah and Maretti, indicates that defendant's conduct does not cause the

2. There appears to be some dispute over the facts that immediately preceded the initiation of construction concerning the granting of building permits, approval of the Architectural Control Committee and subsequent initiation of construction at a grade level not approved by the Committee. The specific dispute over this sequence of events is not relevant to this appeal, but suffice it to say that such facts will become relevant to the question of the reasonableness of the defendant's construction in light of our decision that the plaintiff has stated a claim on the issue of private nuisance.

3. Sec. 844.01, Stats.1979–80, provides:

"(1) Any person owning or claiming an interest in real property may bring an action claiming physical injury to, or interference with, the property or his interest therein; the action may be to redress past injury, to restrain further injury, to abate the source of injury, or for other appropriate relief.

(2) Physical injury includes unprivileged intrusions and encroachments; the injury may be surface, subsurface or suprasurface; the injury may arise from activities on the plaintiff's property, or from activities outside the plaintiff's property which affect plaintiff's property.

(3) Interference with an interest is any activity other than physical injury which lessens the possibility of use or enjoyment of the interest.

(4) The lessening of a security interest without physical injury is not actionable unless such lessening constitutes waste."

We can find no reported cases in which sec. 844.01 has been interpreted and applied, and the parties do not cite any.

4. Under the doctrine of prior appropriation the first user to appropriate the resource has the right of continued use to the exclusion of others.

The doctrine of prior appropriation has been used by several western states to allocate water, Paug Vik v. Wards Cove, 633 P.2d 1015 (Alaska 1981), and by the New Mexico legislature to allocate solar access, secs. 47–3–1 to 47–3–5, N.M.Stats.1978. See also Note, The Allocation of Sunlight: Solar Rights and the Prior Appropriation Doctrine, 47 Colo.L.Rev. 421 (1976).

gravity of the harm which the plaintiff himself may well have avoided by proper planning." The circuit court also concluded that sec. 844.01 does not apply to a home constructed in accordance with deed and municipal ordinance requirements. Further, the circuit court rejected the prior appropriation doctrine as "an intrusion of judicial egoism over legislative passivity."

We consider first whether the complaint states a claim for relief based on common law private nuisance. This state has long recognized that an owner of land does not have an absolute or unlimited right to use the land in a way which injures the rights of others. The rights of neighboring landowners are relative; the uses by one must not unreasonably impair the uses or enjoyment of the other. VI–A American Law of Property sec. 28.22, pp. 64–65 (1954). When one landowner's use of his or her property unreasonably interferes with another's enjoyment of his or her property, that use is said to be a private nuisance. Hoene v. Milwaukee, 17 Wis.2d 209, 214, 116 N.W.2d 112 (1962); Metzger v. Hochrein, 107 Wis. 267, 269, 83 N.W. 308 (1900). See also Prosser, Law of Torts sec. 89, p. 591 (2d ed. 1971).

The private nuisance doctrine has traditionally been employed in this state to balance the conflicting rights of landowners, and this court has recently adopted the analysis of private nusiance set forth in the Restatement (Second) of Torts. CEW Mgmt. Corp. v. First Federal Savings & Loan Association, 88 Wis.2d 631, 633, 277 N.W.2d 766 (1979). The Restatement defines private nuisance as "a nontrespassory invasion of another's interest in the private use and enjoyment of land." Restatement (Second) of Torts sec. 821D (1977). The phrase "interest in the private use and enjoyment of land" as used in sec. 821D is broadly defined to include any disturbance of the enjoyment of property. The comment in the Restatement describes the landowner's interest protected by private nuisance law as follows:

> "The phrase 'interest in the use and enjoyment of land' is used in this Restatement in a broad sense. It comprehends not only the interests that a person may have in the actual present use of land for residential, agricultural, commercial, industrial and other purposes, but also his interests in having the present use value of the land unimpaired by changes in its physical condition. Thus the destruction of trees on vacant land is as much an invasion of the owner's interest in its use and enjoyment as is the destruction of crops or flowers that he is growing on the land for his present use. 'Interest in use and enjoyment' also comprehends the pleasure, comfort and enjoyment that a person normally derives from the occupancy of land. Freedom from discomfort and annoyance while using land is often as important to a person as freedom from physical interruption with his use or freedom from detrimental change in the physical condition of the land itself." Restatement (Second) of Torts, Sec. 821D, Comment *b*, p. 101 (1977).

Although the defendant's obstruction of the plaintiff's access to sunlight appears to fall within the Restatement's broad concept of a private nuisance as a nontrespassory invasion of another's interest in the private use and enjoyment of land, the defendant asserts that he has a right to develop his property in compliance with statutes, ordinances and private covenants without regard to the effect of such development upon the plaintiff's access to sunlight. In essence, the defendant is asking this court to hold that the private nuisance doctrine is not applicable in the instant case and that his right to develop his land is a right which is *per se* superior to his neighbor's interest in access to sunlight. This position is expressed in the maxim "cujus est solum, ejus est usque ad coelum et ad infernos," that is, the owner of land owns up to the sky and down to the center of the earth. The rights of the surface owner are, however, not unlimited. U.S. v. Causby, 328 U.S. 256, 260–1, 66 S.Ct. 1062, 1065, 90 L.Ed. 1206 (1946). See also 114.03, Stats.1979–80.

The defendant is not completely correct in asserting that the common law did not protect a landowner's access to sunlight across adjoining property. At English common law a landowner could acquire a right to receive sunlight across adjoining land by both express agreement and under the judge-made doctrine of "ancient lights." Under the doctrine of ancient lights if the landowner had received sunlight across adjoining property for a specified period of time,[7] the landowner was entitled to continue to receive unobstructed access to sunlight across the adjoining property. Under the doctrine the landowner acquired a negative prescriptive easement and could prevent the adjoining landowner from obstructing access to light.[8]

Although American courts have not been as receptive to protecting a landowner's access to sunlight as the English courts, American courts have afforded some protection to a landowner's interest in access to sunlight. American courts honor express easements to sunlight. American courts initially enforced the English common law doctrine of ancient lights, but later every state which considered the doctrine repudiated it as inconsistent with the needs of a developing country. Indeed, for just that reason this court concluded that an easement to light and air over adjacent property could not be created or acquired by prescription and has been unwilling to recognize such an easement by implication. Depner v. United States National Bank, 202 Wis. 405, 408, 232 N.W. 851 (1930); Miller v. Hoeschler, 126 Wis. 263, 268–69, 105 N.W. 790 (1905).

Many jurisdictions in this country have protected a landowner from malicious obstruction of access to light (the spite fence cases) under the common law private nuisance doctrine.[9] If an activity is

7. The specified time period of uninterrupted enjoyment required to create a right to receive light across adjoining property varied in English legal history. Thomas, Miller & Robbins, Overcoming Legal Uncertainties About Use of Solar Energy Systems 23 (Am. Bar Foundation 1978).

8. Pfeiffer, Ancient Lights: Legal Protection of Access to Solar Energy, 68 ABAJ 288 (1982). No American common law state recognizes a landowner's right to acquire an easement of light by prescription. Comment, Solar Lights: Guaranteeing a Place in the Sun, 57 Ore.L.Rev. 94, 112 (1977).

9. In several of the spite fence cases courts have recognized the property owner's interest in sunlight. Hornsby v. Smith, 191 Ga. 491, 500, 13 S.E.2d 20 (1941) ("the air and light no matter from which direction they come are God-given, and are essential to the life, comfort, and happiness of everyone"); Burke v. Smith, 69 Mich. 380, 389, 37 N.W. 838 (1888) ("the

motivated by malice it lacks utility and the harm it causes others outweighs any social values. VI–A Law of Property sec. 28.28, p. 79 (1954). This court was reluctant to protect a landowner's interest in sunlight even against a spite fence, only to be overruled by the legislature. Shortly after this court upheld a landowner's right to erect a useless and unsightly sixteen-foot spite fence four feet from his neighbor's windows, Metzger v. Hochrein, 107 Wis. 267, 83 N.W. 308 (1900), the legislature enacted a law specifically defining a spite fence as an actionable private nuisance.[10] Thus a landowner's interest in sunlight has been protected in this country by common law private nuisance law at least in the narrow context of the modern American rule invalidating spite fences. See, e.g., Sundowner, Inc. v. King, 95 Idaho 367, 509 P.2d 785 (1973); Restatement (Second) of Torts, sec. 829 (1977).

This court's reluctance in the nineteenth and early part of the twentieth century to provide broader protection for a landowner's access to sunlight was premised on three policy considerations. First, the right of landowners to use their property as they wished, as long as they did not cause physical damage to a neighbor, was jealously guarded. Metzger v. Hochrein, 107 Wis. 267, 272, 83 N.W. 308 (1900).

Second, sunlight was valued only for aesthetic enjoyment or as illumination. Since artificial light could be used for illumination, loss of sunlight was at most a personal annoyance which was given little, if any, weight by society.

Third, society had a significant interest in not restricting or impeding land development. Dillman v. Hoffman, 38 Wis. 559, 574 (1875). This court repeatedly emphasized that in the growth period of the nineteenth and early twentieth centuries change is to be expected and is essential to property and that recognition of a right to sunlight would hinder property development. The court expressed this concept as follows:

> "As the city grows, large grounds appurtenant to residences must be cut up to supply more residences. . . . The cistern, the outhouse, the cesspool, and the private drain must disappear in deference to the public waterworks and sewer; the terrace and the garden, to the need for more complete occupancy. . . . Strict limitation [on the recognition of easements of light and air over adjacent premises is] in accord with the popular conception upon which real estate has been and is daily being conveyed in Wisconsin and to be essential to easy and rapid development at least of our municipalities." Miller v. Hoeschler, supra, 126 Wis. at 268, 270, 105 N.W. 790; quoted with approval in *Depner*, supra, 202 Wis. at 409, 232 N.W. 851.

Considering these three policies, this court concluded that in the absence of an express agreement granting access to sunlight, a land-

right to breathe the air and enjoy the sunshine, is a natural one"); Barger v. Barringer, 151 N.C. 433, 437, 66 S.E. 439 (1909) ("light and air are as much a necessity as water, and all are the common heritage of mankind").

10. The legislature specifically overruled Metzger, ch. 81, Laws of 1903; sec. 280.08 Stats.1925. Cf. Steiger v. Nowakowski, 67 Wis.2d 355, 227 N.W.2d 104 (1975).

owner's obstruction of another's access to sunlight was not actionable. Miller v. Hoeschler, supra, 126 Wis. at 271, 105 N.W. 790; Depner v. United States National Bank, supra, 202 Wis. at 410, 232 N.W. 851. These three policies are no longer fully accepted or applicable. They reflect factual circumstances and social priorities that are now obsolete.

First, society has increasingly regulated the use of land by the landowner for the general welfare. Euclid v. Ambler Realty Co., 272 U.S. 365, 47 S.Ct. 114, 71 L.Ed. 303 (1926); Just v. Marinette, 56 Wis.2d 7, 201 N.W.2d 761 (1972).

Second, access to sunlight has taken on a new significance in recent years. In this case the plaintiff seeks to protect access to sunlight, not for aesthetic reasons or as a source of illumination but as a source of energy. Access to sunlight as an energy source is of significance both to the landowner who invests in solar collectors and to a society which has an interest in developing alternative sources of energy.[11]

Third, the policy of favoring unhindered private development in an expanding economy is no longer in harmony with the realities of our society. State v. Deetz, 66 Wis.2d 1, 224 N.W.2d 407 (1974). The need for easy and rapid development is not as great today as it once was, while our perception of the value of sunlight as a source of energy has increased significantly.

Courts should not implement obsolete policies that have lost their vigor over the course of the years. The law of private nuisance is better suited to resolve landowners' disputes about property development in the 1980's than is a rigid rule which does not recognize a landowner's interest in access to sunlight. As we said in Ballstadt v. Pagel, 202 Wis. 484, 489, 232 N.W. 862 (1930), "What is regarded in law as constituting a nuisance in modern times would no doubt have been tolerated without question in former times." We read State v. Deetz, 66 Wis.2d 1, 224 N.W.2d 407 (1974), as an endorsement of the application of common law nuisance to situations involving the conflicting interests of landowners and as rejecting *per se* exclusions to the nuisance law reasonable use doctrine.

In *Deetz* the court abandoned the rigid common law common enemy rule with respect to surface water and adopted the private nuisance reasonable use rule, namely that the landowner is subject to

11. State and federal governments are encouraging the use of the sun as a significant source of energy. In this state the legislature has granted tax benefits to encourage the utilization of solar energy. See Ch. 349, 350, Laws of 1979. See also Ch. 354, Laws of 1981 (eff. May 7, 1982) enabling legislation providing for local ordinances guaranteeing access to sunlight.

The federal government has also recognized the importance of solar energy and currently encourages its utilization by means of tax benefits, direct subsidies and government loans for solar projects. Energy Tax Act of 1978, Nov. 9, 1978, P.L. 95–618, 92 Stat. 3174, relevant portion codified at 26 U.S.C.A. sec. 44(c) (1982 Supp.); Energy Security Act, June 30, 1980, P.L. 96–294, 94 Stat. 611, relevant portion codified at 12 U.S.C.A. sec. 3610 (1980); Small Business Energy Loan Act, July 4, 1978, P.L. 95–315, 92 Stat. 377, relevant portion codified within 15 U.S.C.A. secs. 631, 633, 636, and 639 (1982 Supp.); National Energy Conservation Policy Act, Nov. 9, 1978, P.L. 95–619, 92 Stat. 3206, relevant portion codified at 42 U.S.C.A. secs. 1451, 1703–45 (1982 Supp.); Energy Conservation and Production Act, Aug. 14, 1976, P.L. 94–385, 90 Stat. 1125, relevant portion codified at 42 U.S.C.A. sec. 6881 (1977).

liability if his or her interference with the flow of surface waters unreasonably invades a neighbor's interest in the use and enjoyment of land. Restatement (Second) of Torts, sec. 822, 826, 829 (1977). This court concluded that the common enemy rule which served society "well in the days of burgeoning national expansion of the mid-nineteenth and early-twentieth centuries" should be abandoned because it was no longer "in harmony with the realities of our society." *Deetz*, supra, 66 Wis.2d at 14–15, 224 N.W.2d 407. We recognized in *Deetz* that common law rules adapt to changing social values and conditions.[12]

Yet the defendant would have us ignore the flexible private nuisance law as a means of resolving the dispute between the landowners in this case and would have us adopt an approach, already abandoned in *Deetz*, of favoring the unrestricted development of land and of applying a rigid and inflexible rule protecting his right to build on his land and disregarding any interest of the plaintiff in the use and enjoyment of his land. This we refuse to do.[13]

12. This court has recognized "that the common law is susceptible of growth and adaptation to new circumstances and situations, and that courts have power to declare and effectuate what is the present rule in respect of a given subject without regard to the old rule. . . . The common law is not immutable, but flexible, and upon its own principles adapts itself to varying conditions." Dimick v. Schiedt, 293 U.S. 474, 487, 55 S.Ct. 296, 301, 79 L.Ed. 603 (1935), quoted with approval in Schwanke v. Garlt, 219 Wis. 367, 371, 263 N.W. 176 (1935).

In Bielski v. Schulze, 16 Wis.2d 1, 11, 114 N.W.2d 105 (1962), this court said: "Inherent in the common law is a dynamic principle which allows it to grow and to tailor itself to meet changing needs within the doctrine of *stare decisis*, which, if correctly understood, was not static and did not forever prevent the courts from reversing themselves or from applying principles of common law to new situations as the need arose. If this were not so, we must succumb to a rule that a judge should let others 'long dead and unaware of the problems of the age in which he lives, do his thinking for him.' Mr. Justice Douglas, Stare Decisis, 49 Columbia Law Review (1949), 735, 736."

"The genius of the common law is its ability to adapt itself to the changing needs of society." Moran v. Quality Aluminum Casting Co., 34 Wis.2d 542, 551, 150 N.W.2d 137 (1967). See also State v. Esser, 16 Wis.2d 567, 581, 115 N.W.2d 505 (1962).

13. Defendant's position that a landowner's interest in access to sunlight across adjoining land is not "legally enforceable" and is therefore excluded *per se* from private nuisance law was adopted in Fontainebleau Hotel Corp. v. Forty-five Twenty-five, Inc., 114 So.2d 357 (Fla.App. 1959), cert. den. 117 So.2d 842 (Fla.1960). The Florida district court of appeals permitted construction of a building which cast a shadow on a neighboring hotel's swimming pool. The court asserted that nuisance law protects only those interests "which [are] recognized and protected by law," and that there is no legally recognized or protected right to access to sunlight. A property owner does not, said the Florida court, in the absence of a contract or statute, acquire a presumptive or implied right to the free flow of light and air across adjoining land. The Florida court then concluded that a lawful structure which causes injury to another by cutting off light and air—whether or not erected partly for spite—does not give rise to a cause of action for damages or for an injunction. See also People ex rel. Hoogasian v. Sears, Roebuck & Co., 52 Ill.2d 301, 287 N.E.2d 677 (1972).

We do not find the reasoning of *Fontainebleau* persuasive. The court leaped from rejecting an easement by prescription (the doctrine of ancient lights) and an easement by implication to the conclusion that there is no right to protection from obstruction of access to sunlight. The court's statement that a landowner has no right to light should be the conclusion, not its initial premise. The court did not explain why an owner's interest in unobstructed light should not be protected or in what manner an owner's interest in unobstructed sunlight differs from an owner's interest in being free from obtrusive noises or smells or differs from an owner's interest in unobstructed use of water. The recognition of a *per se* exception to private nusiance law may invite unreasonable behavior.

Private nuisance law, the law traditionally used to adjudicate conflicts between private landowners, has the flexibility to protect both a landowner's right of access to sunlight and another landowner's right to develop land. Private nuisance law is better suited to regulate access to sunlight in modern society and is more in harmony with legislative policy and the prior decisions of this court than is an inflexible doctrine of non-recognition of any interest in access to sunlight across adjoining land.[14]

We therefore hold that private nuisance law, that is, the reasonable use doctrine as set forth in the Restatement, is applicable to the instant case. Recognition of a nuisance claim for unreasonable obstruction of access to sunlight will not prevent land development or unduly hinder the use of adjoining land. It will promote the reasonable use and enjoyment of land in a manner suitable to the 1980's. That obstruction of access to light might be found to constitute a nuisance in certain circumstances does not mean that it will be or must be found to constitute a nuisance under all circumstances. The result in each case depends on whether the conduct complained of is unreasonable.

Accordingly we hold that the plaintiff in this case has stated a claim under which relief can be granted. Nonetheless we do not determine whether the plaintiff in this case is entitled to relief. In order to be entitled to relief the plaintiff must prove the elements required to establish actionable nuisance, and the conduct of the defendant herein must be judged by the reasonable use doctrine.

The defendant asserts that even if we hold that the private nuisance doctrine applies to obstruction of access to sunlight across adjoining land, the circuit court's granting of summary judgment should be affirmed.

Although the memorandum decision of the circuit court in the instant case is unclear, it appears that the circuit court recognized that the common law private nuisance doctrine was applicable but concluded that defendant's conduct was not unreasonable. The circuit court apparently attempted to balance the utility of the defendant's conduct with the gravity of the harm. Sec. 826, Restatement (Second) of Torts (1977). The defendant urges us to accept the circuit court's balance as adequate. We decline to do so.

The circuit court concluded that because the defendant's proposed house was in conformity with zoning regulations, building codes and deed restrictions, the defendant's use of the land was reasonable. This court has concluded that a landowner's compliance with zoning laws does not automatically bar a nuisance claim. Compliance with the law "is not the controlling factor though it is, of course, entitled to some weight." Bie v. Ingersoll, 27 Wis.2d 490, 495, 135 N.W.2d 250 (1965). The circuit court also concluded that the plaintiff could have avoided any harm by locating his own house in a better place. Again, plaintiff's

14. For a discussion of nuisance law, see Ellickson, Alternatives to Zoning: Covenants, Nuisance Rules, and Fines as Land Use Controls, 40 U.Chi.L.Rev. 681 (1973); Comment, Nuisance as a Modern Mode of Land Use Control, 46 Wash.L.Rev. 47 (1970).

ability to avoid the harm is a relevant but not a conclusive factor. See secs. 826, 827, 828, Restatement (Second) of Torts (1977).

Furthermore, our examination of the record leads us to conclude that the record does not furnish an adequate basis for the circuit court to apply the proper legal principles on summary judgment. The application of the reasonable use standard in nuisance cases normally requires a full exposition of all underlying facts and circumstances. Too little is known in this case of such matters as the extent of the harm to the plaintiff, the suitability of solar heat in that neighborhood, the availability of remedies to the plaintiff, and the costs to the defendant of avoiding the harm. Summary judgment is not an appropriate procedural vehicle in this case when the circuit court must weigh evidence which has not been presented at trial. 6 (Pt. 2) Moore's Federal Practice, 56.15[7], pp. 56–638 (1982); 10 Wright and Miller, Federal Practice and Procedure—Civil, secs. 2729, 2731 (1973).

Because the plaintiff has stated a claim of common law private nuisance upon which relief can be granted, the judgment of the circuit court must be reversed. We need not, and do not, reach the question of whether the complaint states a claim under sec. 844.01, Stats.1979–80, or under the doctrine of prior appropriation. Attoe v. Madison Professional Policemen's Assoc., 79 Wis.2d 199, 205, 255 N.W.2d 489 (1977).

For the reasons set forth, we reverse the judgment of the circuit court dismissing the complaint and remand the matter to circuit court for further proceedings not inconsistent with this opinion.

. . .

CALLOW, JUSTICE (dissenting).

. . . Because I believe the facts of this case clearly reveal that a cause of action for private nuisance will not lie, I dissent. . . .

I would submit that any policy decisions in this area are best left for the legislature. . . .

The legislature has recently acted in this area. Chapter 354, Laws of 1981 (effective May 7, 1982), was enacted to provide the underlying legislation enabling local governments to enact ordinances establishing procedures for guaranteeing access to sunlight. This court's intrusion into an area where legislative action is being taken is unwarranted, and it may undermine a legislative scheme for orderly development not yet fully operational.

Chapter 354, Laws of 1981, sec. 66.032, provides specific conditions for solar access permits. In part that section provides for impermissible interference with solar collectors within specific limitations:

"66.032 Solar access permits.

"(f) 'Impermissible interference' means the blockage of solar energy from a collector surface or proposed collector surface for which a permit has been granted under this section during a collector use period if such blockage is by any structure or vegetation on property, an owner of which was notified under sub. (3)(b). *'Impermissible interference' does not include:*

"1. Blockage by a narrow protrusion, including but not limited to a pole or wire, which does not substantially interfere with absorption of solar energy by a solar collector.

"2. *Blockage by any structure constructed, under construction or for which a building permit has been applied for before the date the last notice is mailed or delivered under sub. (3)(b).*

"3. Blockage by any vegetation planted before the date the last notice is mailed or delivered under sub. (3)(b) unless a municipality by ordinance under sub. (2) defines impermissible interference to include such vegetation." (Emphasis added.)

Sec. 66.032(3)(b) provides for notice:

"(3) PERMIT APPLICATIONS.

"(b) An agency shall determine if an application is satisfactorily completed and shall notify the applicant of its determination. If an applicant receives notice that an application has been satisfactorily completed, *the applicant shall deliver by certified mail or by hand a notice to the owner of any property which the applicant proposes to be restricted by the permit under* sub. (7). The applicant shall submit to the agency a copy of a signed receipt for every notice delivered under this paragraph. The agency shall supply the notice form. The information on the form may include, without limitation because of enumeration:

"1. The name and address of the applicant, and the address of the land upon which the solar collector is or will be located.

"2. That an application has been filed by the applicant.

"3. That the permit, if granted, may affect the rights of the notified owner to develop his or her property and to plant vegetation.

"4. The telephone number, address and office hours of the agency.

"5. That *any person may request a hearing* under sub. (4) within 30 days after receipt of the notice, and the address and procedure for filing the request." (Emphasis added.)

This legislative scheme would deal with the type of problem presented in the present case and precludes the need for judicial activism in this area.

I examine with interest the definition of nuisance as set out in the Restatement (Second) of Torts and adopted in the majority opinion: "A private nuisance is a nontrespassory *invasion* of another's interest in the private use and enjoyment of land." Restatement (Second) of Torts sec. 821D (1977) (emphasis added). The majority believes that the defendant's obstruction of the plaintiff's access to sunlight falls within the broad definition of "use and enjoyment of land." Supra, at 187–188. I do not believe the defendant's "obstruction" of the plaintiff's access to sunlight falls within the definition of "invasion," as it applies to the private use and enjoyment of land. Invasion is typically synonymous with "entry," "attack," "penetration," "hostile entrance," "the incoming or spread of something unusually hurtful." Webster's Third International Dictionary, 1188 (1966). Most of the nuisance cases arising under this definition involve noxious odors, smoke, blasting, flooding, or *excessive light* invading the plaintiff's right to the use of enjoyment of his property. See Prosser, Law of Torts, sec. 89, 591–92 (4th ed. 1971).[4] *See* Williams, Solar Access and Property Rights: A Maverick Analysis, 11 Conn.L.Rev. at 441 (there are significant practical differences between dust and noise, on the one hand, and solar access blockage on the other). Clearly, an owner who merely builds his home in compliance with all building code and municipal regulations is not "invading" another's right to the use and enjoyment of his property. To say so is to acknowledge that all construction may be an "invasion" because all construction has some restrictive impact on adjacent land. A "view," for example, is modified by any construction simply because it is there.

. . .

NOTES

1. Other courts have also questioned the traditional American rule refusing to recognize interests in access to light and air, but they have generally analyzed a plaintiff's claim to injury from nearby construction in terms of the private nuisance doctrine rather than the English doctrine of ancient lights. Why might a court prefer to use the latter doctrine? See Tenn v. 889 Associates, Ltd., 127 N.H. 321, 500 A.2d 366 (1985). Would either doctrine support a plaintiff's action to enjoin a neighboring landowner from building so close to the street that he will block passing motorists' view of the plaintiff's business? See Mohr v. Midas Realty Corp., 431 N.W.2d 380 (Iowa 1988).

2. In Sher v. Leiderman, 181 Cal.App.3d 867, 226 Cal.Rptr. 698 (1986) the plaintiffs objected to shade from overgrown trees on neighboring property which had adversely affected the thermal efficiency of their passive solar home and had transformed its "formerly cheerful and sunny ambience" into an interior "now dark and dismal in the winter months." In rejecting the approach of the Prah case the court recognized that regulation of building height and density had significantly limited the rights of property owners, but stated that limitations imposed for the public good did not justify a judicial imposition of restrictions for the private benefit of a particular homeowner. However the court's principal reason for rejecting the private nuisance doctrine was its concern that recognizing such an action would improperly infringe upon the province of the legislature, which had already enacted a Solar Shade Control Act prohibiting a property owner from allowing trees on his property to interfere with solar collectors. The court reasoned that the legislature might have intended either to limit recourse for excessive shade to the situation described in the act or,

4. Dean Prosser also includes disturbances with peace of mind occasioned by "bawdy houses," stored explosives, or fire hazards within the purview of the definition of nuisance. I submit these indicia of nuisance relate to a defendant's unreasonable or unlawful use of his property.

alternatively, to enact subsequent legislation detailing further rights of solar access.

3. Property in solar access may be created by legislation. New Mexico's Solar Rights Act, N.M.Stat.Ann.1978, § 47–3–4, declares that "the right to use the natural resource of solar energy is a property right" and that in "disputes involving solar rights, priority in time shall have the better right. . . ." Related legislation, the Solar Recordation Act, N.M. Stat.Ann.1978, § 47–3–6, requires recordation of solar right claims and notice to affected property owners as "a necessary condition precedent to enforcing a solar right." An affected property owner may contest the claim by filing a declaration of contest within 60 days. If such a declaration is filed, "the solar right shall not be enforceable against the property covered by the declaration unless agreed to by contract or ordered by a court of competent jurisdiction, and any claim of a solar right shall expire one year from the date of declaration, unless the parties agree by contract to settle the solar rights dispute or unless court action has commenced by that date to establish a claim of the solar right."

SOUTHWEST WEATHER RESEARCH, INC. v. ROUNSAVILLE

Court of Civil Appeals of Texas, 1958.
320 S.W.2d 211.

PER CURIAM. This is an appeal from an injunction issued by the Eighty-third District Court, Jeff Davis County, Texas, which said injunction commands the appellants "to refrain from seeding the clouds by artifical nucleation or otherwise and from in any other manner or way interfering with the clouds and the natural condition of the air, sky, atmosphere and air space over plaintiffs' lands and in the area of plaintiffs' lands to in any manner, degree or way affect, control or modify the weather conditions on or about said lands, pending final hearing and determination of this cause; and from further flying over the above-described lands of plaintiffs and discharging any chemicals or other matter or material into the clouds over said lands." Appellees are ranchmen residing in West Texas counties, and appellants are owners and operators of certain airplanes and equipment generally used in what they call a "weather modification program," and those who contracted and arranged for their services.

It is not disputed that appellants did operate their airplanes at various times over portions of lands belonging to the appellees, for the purpose of and while engaged in what is commonly called "cloud seeding." Appellants do not deny having done this, and testified through the president of the company that the operation would continue unless restrained. He stated, "We seeded the clouds to attempt to suppress the hail." The controversy is really over appellants' right to seed clouds or otherwise modify weather conditions over appellees' property; the manner of so doing; and the effects resulting therefrom. Appellants stoutly maintain that they can treat clouds in such manner as will prevent the clouds from precipitating hail, and that such operation does not and cannot decrease either the present or ultimate rainfall from any cloud or clouds so treated. Appellants were hired on a hail suppression program by a large number of farmers in and around Fort Stockton and other areas generally east, or easterly, of Jeff Davis County. It was developed that the farmers' land was frequently ravaged by damaging hail storms, which appellants claim originated in and over the Davis Mountains in the Jeff Davis County area.

The appellees' testimony, on the other hand, which was elicited from several witnesses, was to the effect that this program of cloud seeding destroyed potential rain clouds over their property.

The trial court, in granting the temporary injunction, found as a matter of fact that appellants were engaging in day-to-day flying airplanes over appellees' lands and into the clouds over appellees' lands, and expelling a foreign substance into the clouds above appellees' lands in such a manner that there was a change in the contents of the clouds, causing them to be dissipated and scattered, with the result that the clouds over plaintiffs' lands were prevented from following their natural and usual course of developing rain upon and over and near plaintiffs' lands, thereby resulting in retarded rainfall upon plaintiffs' properties. The court further held that such was injurious to appellees and was in interference of their property rights, and would cause irreparable damage if not restrained.

It has long been decided that in cases of this sort we must affirm the decision of the trial court unless it is clearly shown that he abused his discretion in granting the temporary injunction: Rudd v. Wallace, Tex.Civ.App., 232 S.W.2d 121; 24–A, Tex.Juris., ¶ 265, p. 382. Therefore, we must now examine the evidence to see if the trial court's action was proper. . . .

So, summing up the fact situation or the evidence that was before the trial court, we find that the three appellees and other witnesses testified that they had visually observed the destruction of potential rain clouds over their own property by the equipment of the appellants. They testified that they had seen this happen more than once. The experts differed sharply in the probable effect of a hail suppression program accomplished by the cloud seeding methods used here. The trial court apparently, as reflected by his findings included in the judgment, believed the testimony of the lay witnesses and that part of the expert testimony in harmony with his judgment. This he had a right to do as the trier of facts.

We have carefully considered the voluminous record and exhibits that were admitted in evidence, and have concluded that the trial court had ample evidence on which to base his findings and with which to justify the issuance of the injunction.

Now we must turn to the objections of the appellants, who protest the issuance of the injunction on the grounds, generally, that appellants had every right to do what they were doing in order to protect their crops from hail, and that the facts or credible evidence did not justify the issuance of the injunction. Appellants maintain that appellees have no right to prevent them from flying over appellees lands; that no one owns the clouds unless it be the State, and that the trial court was without legal right to restrain appellants from pursuing a lawful occupation; also, that the injunction is too broad in its terms.

First of all, it must be noted that, here, we do not have any governmental agency, State or Federal, and find no legislative regulation. This is exclusively a dispute between private interests. It has been said there is no precedent and no legal justification for the trial court's action. It has long been understood that equity was created for the man who had a right without a remedy, and, as later modified, without an adequate remedy. Appellees urge here that the owner of land also owns in connection therewith certain so-called "natural rights," and cite us the following question from Spann v. City of Dallas, 111 Tex. 350, 235 S.W. 513, 514, in which Chief Justice Nelson Phillips states: "Property in a thing consists not merely in its ownership and possession, but in the unrestricted right of use, enjoyment and disposal. Anything which destroys any of these elements of property, to that extent destroys the property itself. The substantial value of property lies in its use. If the right of use be denied, the value of the property is annihilated and ownership is rendered a barren right. . . .

"The very essence of American constitutions is that the material rights of no man shall be subject to the mere will of another. Yick Wo v. Hopkins, 118 U.S. 356, 6 S.Ct. 1064, 30 L.Ed. 220."

In Volume 34, Marquette Law Review, at Page 275, this is said: "Considering the property right of every man to the use and enjoyment of his land, and considering the profound effect which natural rainfall has upon the realization of this right, it would appear that the benefits of natural rainfall should come within the scope of judicial protection, and a duty should be imposed on adjoining landowners not to interfere therewith."

In the Stanford Law Review, November 1948, Volume 1, in an article entitled, "Who Owns the Clouds?", the following statements occur: "The landowner does have rights in the water in clouds, however. The basis for these rights is the common-law doctrine of natural rights. Literally, the term 'natural rights' is well chosen; these rights protect the landowner's use of his land in its natural condition. . . .

"All forms of natural precipitation should be elements of the natural condition of the land. Precipitation, like air, oxygen, sunlight, and the soil itself, is an essential to many reasonable uses of the land. The plant and animal life on the land are both ultimately dependent upon rainfall. To the extent that rain is important to the use of land, the landowner should be entitled to the natural rainfall."

In California Law Review, December 1957, Volume 45, No. 5, in an article, "Weather Modification", is found the following statement: "What are the rights of the landowner or public body to natural rainfall? It has been suggested that the right to receive rainfall is one of those 'natural rights' which are inherent in the full use of land from the fact of its natural contact with moisture in the air." . . .

Appellees call our attention to various authorities that hold that, although the old ad coelum doctrine has given way to the reality of present-day conditions, an unreasonable and improper use of the air space over the owner's land can constitute a trespass: Guith v. Consumers Power Co., D.C., 36 F.Supp. 21; Restatement of the Law of Torts, paragraph 194, etc.; United States v. Causby, 328 U.S. 256, 66 S.Ct. 1062, 90 L.Ed. 1206. Other cases are cited, also, and apparently hold that the land owner, while not owning or controlling the entire air space above his property, is entitled to protection against improper or unreasonable use thereof or entrance thereon.

We believe that under our system of government landowner is entitled to such precipitation as Nature deigns to bestow. We believe that the landowner is entitled, therefore and thereby, to such rainfall as may come from clouds over his own property that Nature, in her caprice, may provide. It follows, therefore, that this enjoyment of or entitlement to the benefits of Nature should be protected by the courts if interfered with improperly and unlawfully. It must be noted that defendant's planes were based at Fort Stockton, in Pecos County, and had to fly many miles to seed clouds over defendants' lands in Jeff Davis County. We do not mean to say or imply at this time or under the conditions present in this particular case that the landowner has a right to prevent or control weather modification over land not his own. We do not pass upon that point here, and we do not intend any implication to that effect.

There is ample evidence here to sustain the fact findings of the trial court that clouds were destroyed over property of appellees by operations of the appellants. The trial court chose to believe the evidence to that effect, and we hold there was ample evidence to support him in so holding and finding. We further hold that the trial court was justified in restraining appellants from modifying or attempting to modify any clouds or weather over or in the air space over lands of the appellees.

However, we do find that the temporary injunction granted by the trial court was too broad in its terms, in that it purports to restrain appellants from any activity with reference to land in the area of "plaintiffs' lands." The trial court's injunction is, therefore, modified so as to restrain appellants from the activities therein described only as they apply to the lands of appellees. . . .

All other points of appellants are accordingly overruled, and, with the above modification, the judgment of the trial court is affirmed.

ABBOTT, J., not sitting.

NOTES

1. Affirming this judgment and that in a companion case, Southwest Weather Research, Inc. v. Duncan, 319 S.W.2d 940 (1958), the Supreme Court of Texas said: "These causes involve complicated scientific problems, as well as the legal determination of the property rights of both the landowners on one hand and those engaged in a business

enterprise on the other. Admittedly the case is not fully developed. It has not been tried upon the merits and the sole purpose of the temporary injunctions was to preserve the status quo until these complicated scientific problems and attendant legal questions can be fully considered and a final judgment rendered delineating and determining the rights of litigating parties." 327 S.W.2d 417 (1959). Noted, 73 Harv.L.Rev. 790 (1960).

2. Compare Slutsky v. City of New York, 197 Misc. 730, 97 N.Y.S. 2d 238 (1950), denying a vacation resort owner a permanent injunction against rain-making attempts by New York City in the region. The court contrasted the "speculative" harm to the resort with New York City's need for water.

3. For background and discussion of the issues, see: Controlling the Weather (H. Taubenfeld ed. 1970); Ball, Shaping the Law of Weather Control, 58 Yale L.J. 213 (1949); Corbridge and Moses, Weather Modification: Law and Administration, 8 Nat.Res.J. 207 (1968); Davis, State Regulation of Weather Modification, 12 Ariz.L.Rev. 35 (1970); Fischer, Weather Modification and the Right of Capture, 8 Nat. Res.Lawyer 639 (1975); Oppenheimer, The Legal Aspects of Weather Modification, 1948 Ins.L.J. 314 (1958).

Part Four

PUBLIC INTERESTS IN LAND (HEREIN PRIMARILY OF LAND USE)

Examples of recognition of public interests in property law are found in most, if not all, subdivisions of the field. Indeed, one may generalize that every statute, regulation or judicial doctrine that restrains volition of private owners either protects some public interest or is unjustified. The law of land use, however, consists to an unusually great extent of regulation by statutes, local ordinances and administrative actions for the asserted benefit of the public. Salient features of this public law of land use will be examined in this part of the book.

Chapter 18

INTRODUCTION TO THE TRADITIONAL LAND USE CONTROLS

SECTION 1. ZONING

VILLAGE OF EUCLID v. AMBLER REALTY CO.

Supreme Court of the United States, 1926.
272 U.S. 365, 47 S.Ct. 114, 71 L.Ed. 303.

MR. JUSTICE SUTHERLAND delivered the opinion of the Court.

The village of Euclid is an Ohio municipal corporation. It adjoins and practically is a suburb of the city of Cleveland. Its estimated population is between 5,000 and 10,000, and its area from 12 to 14 square miles, the greater part of which is farm lands or unimproved acreage. It lies, roughly, in the form of a parallelogram measuring approximately 3½ miles each way. East and west it is traversed by three principal highways: Euclid avenue, through the southerly border, St. Clair avenue, through the central portion, and Lake Shore boulevard, through the northerly border, in close proximity to the shore of Lake Erie. The Nickel Plate Railroad lies from 1,500 to 1,800 feet north of Euclid avenue, and the Lake Shore Railroad 1,600 feet farther to the north. The three highways and the two railroads are substantially parallel.

Appellee is the owner of a tract of land containing 68 acres, situated in the westerly end of the village, abutting on Euclid avenue to the south and the Nickel Plate Railroad to the north. Adjoining this tract, both on the east and on the west, there have been laid out restricted residential plats upon which residences have been erected.

On November 13, 1922, an ordinance was adopted by the village council, establishing a comprehensive zoning plan for regulating and restricting the location of trades, industries, apartment houses, two-family houses, single family houses, etc., the lot area to be built upon, the size and height of buildings, etc.

The entire area of the village is divided by the ordinance into six classes of use districts, denominated U–1 to U–6, inclusive; three classes of height districts, denominated H–1 to H–3, inclusive; and four classes of area districts, denominated A–1 to A–4, inclusive. The use districts are classified in respect to the buildings which may be erected within their respective limits, as follows: U–1 is restricted to single family dwellings, public parks, water towers and reservoirs, suburban and interurban electric railway passenger stations and rights of way, and farming, noncommercial greenhouse nurseries, and truck gardening; U–2 is extended to include two-family dwellings; U–3 is further extended to include apartment houses, hotels, churches, schools, public libraries, museums, private clubs, community center buildings, hospitals, sanitariums, public playgrounds, and recreation buildings, and a city hall and courthouse; U–4 is further extended to include banks, offices, studios, telephone exchanges, fire and police stations, restaurants, theaters and moving picture shows, retail stores and shops, sales offices, sample rooms, wholesale stores for hardware, drugs, and groceries, stations for gasoline and oil (not exceeding 1,000 gallons storage) and for ice delivery, skating rinks and dance halls, electric substations, job and newspaper printing, public garages for motor vehicles, stables and wagon sheds (not exceeding five horses, wagons or motor trucks), and distributing stations for central store and commercial enterprises; U–5 is further extended to include billboards and advertising signs (if permitted), warehouses, ice and ice cream manufacturing and cold storage plants, bottling works, milk bottling and central distribution stations, laundries, carpet cleaning, dry cleaning, and dyeing establishments, blacksmith, horseshoeing, wagon and motor vehicle repair shops, freight stations, street car barns, stables and wagon sheds (for more than five horses, wagons or motor trucks), and wholesale produce markets and salesrooms; U–6 is further extended to include plants for sewage disposal and for producing gas, garbage and refuse incineration, scrap iron, junk, scrap paper, and rag storage, aviation fields, cemeteries, crematories, penal and correctional institutions, insane and feeble-minded institutions, storage of oil and gasoline (not to exceed 25,000 gallons), and manufacturing and industrial operations of any kind other than, and any public utility not included in, a class U–1, U–2, U–3, U–4, or U–5 use. There is a seventh class of uses which is prohibited altogether.

Class U–1 is the only district in which buildings are restricted to those enumerated. In the other classes the uses are cumulative—that is to say, uses in class U–2 include those enumerated in the preceding class U–1; class U–3 includes uses enumerated in the preceding classes, U–2 and U–1; and so on. In addition to the enumerated uses, the ordinance provides for accessory uses; that is, for uses customarily incident to the principal use, such as private garages. Many regulations are provided in respect of such accessory uses.

The height districts are classified as follows: In class H–1, buildings are limited to a height of 2½ stories, or 35 feet; in class H–2, to 4 stories, or 50 feet; in class H–3, to 80 feet. To all of these, certain exceptions are made, as in the case of church spires, water tanks, etc.

The classification of area districts is: In A–1 districts, dwellings or apartment houses to accommodate more than one family must have at least 5,000 square feet for interior lots and at least 4,000 square feet for corner lots; in A–2 districts, the area must be at least 2,500 square feet for interior lots, and 2,000 square feet for corner lots; in A–3 districts, the limits are 1,250 and 1,000 square feet, respectively; in A–4 districts, the limits are 900 and 700 square feet, respectively. The ordinance contains, in great variety and detail, provisions in respect to width of lots, front, side, and rear yards, and other matters, including restrictions and regulations as to the use of billboards, signboards, and advertising signs.

A single family dwelling consists of a basement and not less than three rooms and a bathroom. A two-family dwelling consists of a basement and not less than four living rooms and a bathroom for each family, and is further described as a detached dwelling for the occupation of two families, one having its principal living rooms on the first floor and the other on the second floor.

Appellee's tract of land comes under U–2, U–3 and U–6. The first strip of 620 feet immediately north of Euclid avenue falls in class U–2, the next 130 feet to the north, in U–3, and the remainder in U–6. The uses of the first 620 feet, therefore, do not include apartment houses, hotels, churches, schools, or other public and semipublic buildings or other uses enumerated in respect of U–3 to U–6, inclusive. The uses of the next 130 feet include all of these, but exclude industries, theaters, banks, shops, and the various other uses set forth in respect of U–4 to U–6, inclusive.

Annexed to the ordinance, and made a part of it, is a zone map, showing the location and limits of the various use, height, and area districts, from which it appears that the three classes overlap one another; that is to say, for example, both U–5 and U–6 use districts are in A–4 area districts, but the former is in H–2 and the latter in H–3 height districts. The plan is a complicated one, and can be better understood by an inspection of the map, though it does not seem necessary to reproduce it for present purposes.

The lands lying between the two railroads for the entire length of the village area and extending some distance on either side to the north and south, having an average width of about 1,600 feet, are left open, with slight exceptions, for industrial and all other uses. This includes the larger part of appellee's tract. Approximately one-sixth of the area of the entire village is included in U–5 and U–6 use districts. That part of the village lying south of Euclid avenue is principally in U–1 districts. The lands lying north of Euclid avenue and bordering on the long strip just described are included in U–1, U–2, U–3, and U–4 districts, principally in U–2.

The enforcement of the ordinance is intrusted to the inspector of buildings, under rules and regulations of the board of zoning appeals. Meetings of the board are public, and minutes of its proceedings are kept. It is authorized to adopt rules and regulations to carry into effect provisions of the ordinance. Decisions of the inspector of buildings may be appealed to the board by any person claiming to be adversely affected by any such decision. The board is given power in specific cases of practical difficulty or unnecessary hardship to interpret the ordinance in harmony with its general purpose and intent, so that the public health, safety and general welfare may be secure and substantial justice done. Penalties are prescribed for violations, and it is provided that the various provisions are to be regarded as independent and the holding of any provision to be unconstitutional, void or ineffective shall not affect any of the others.

The ordinance is assailed on the grounds that it is in derogation of section 1 of the Fourteenth Amendment to the federal Constitution in that it deprives appellee of liberty and property without due process of law and denies it the equal protection of the law, and that it offends against certain provisions of the Constitution of the state of Ohio. The prayer of the bill is for an injunction restraining the enforcement of the ordinance and all attempts to impose or maintain as to appellee's property any of the restrictions, limitations or conditions. The court below held the ordinance to be unconstitutional and void, and enjoined its enforcement, 297 F. 307.

Before proceeding to a consideration of the case, it is necessary to determine the scope of the inquiry. The bill alleges that the tract of land in question is vacant and has been held for years for the purpose of selling and developing it for industrial uses, for which it is especially adapted, being immediately in the path of progressive industrial development; that for such uses it has a market value of about $10,000 per acre, but if the use be limited to residential purposes the market value is not in excess of $2,500 per acre; that the first 200 feet of the parcel back from Euclid avenue, if unrestricted in respect of use, has a value of $150 per front foot, but if limited to residential uses, and ordinary mercantile business be excluded therefrom, its value is not in excess of $50 per front foot.

It is specifically averred that the ordinance attempts to restrict and control the lawful uses of appellee's land, so as to confiscate and destroy a great part of its value; that it is being enforced in accordance with its terms; that prospective buyers of land for industrial, commercial, and residential uses in the metropolitan district of Cleveland are deterred from buying any part of this land because of the existence of the ordinance and the necessity thereby entailed of conducting burdensome and expensive litigation in order to vindicate the right to use the land for lawful and legitimate purposes; that the ordinance constitutes a cloud upon the land, reduces and destroys its value, and has the effect of diverting the normal industrial, commercial, and residential development thereof to other and less favorable locations.

The record goes no farther than to show, as the lower court found, that the normal and reasonably to be expected use and development of that part of appellee's land adjoining Euclid avenue is for general trade and commercial purposes, particularly retail stores and like establishments, and that the normal and reasonably to be expected use and development of the residue of the land is for industrial and trade purposes. Whatever injury is inflicted by the mere existence and threatened enforcement of the ordinance is due to restrictions in respect to these and similar uses, to which perhaps should be added—if not included in the foregoing—restrictions in respect of apartment houses. Specifically there is nothing in the record to suggest that any damage results from the presence in the ordinance of those restrictions relating to churches, schools, libraries, and other public and semipublic buildings. It is neither alleged nor proved that there is or may be a demand for any part of appellee's land for any of the last-named uses, and we cannot assume the existence of facts which would justify an injunction upon this record in respect to this class of restrictions. For present purposes the provisons of the ordinance in respect to these uses may therefore be put aside as unnecessary to be considered. It is also unnecessary to consider the effect of the restrictions in respect of U–1 districts, since none of appellee's land falls within that class.

We proceed, then, to a consideration of those provisions of the ordinance to which the case as it is made relates, first disposing of a preliminary matter.

A motion was made in the court below to dismiss the bill on the ground that, because complainant (appellee) had made no effort to obtain a building permit or apply to the zoning board of appeals for relief, as it might have done under the terms of the ordinance, the suit was premature. The motion was properly overruled; the effect of the allegations of the bill is that the ordinance of its own force operates greatly to reduce the value of appellee's lands and destroy their marketability for industrial, commercial and residential uses, and the attack is directed, not against any specific provision or provisions, but against the ordinance as an entirety. Assuming the premises, the existence and maintenance of the ordinance in effect constitutes a present invasion of appellee's property rights and a threat to continue it. Under these circumstances, the equitable jurisdiction is clear. . . .

The ordinance now under review, and all similar laws and regulations, must find their justification in some aspect of the police power, asserted for the public welfare. The line which in this field separates the legitimate from the illegitimate assumption of power is not capable of precise delimitation. It varies with circumstances and conditions. A regulatory zoning ordinance, which would be clearly valid as applied to the great cities, might be clearly invalid as applied to rural communities. In solving doubts, the maxim "sic utere tuo ut alienum non laedas," which lies at the foundation of so much of the common law of nuisances, ordinarily will furnish a fairly helpful clew. And the law of nuisances, likewise, may be consulted, not for the purpose of controlling, but for the helpful aid of its analogies in the process of ascertaining the scope of, the power. Thus the question whether the power exists to forbid the erection of a building of a particular kind or for a particular use, like the question whether a particular thing is a nuisance, is to be determined, not by an abstract consideration of the building or of the thing considered apart, but by considering it in connection with the circumstances and the locality. A nusiance may be merely a right thing in the wrong place, like a pig in the parlor instead of the barnyard. If the validity of the legislative classification for zoning purposes be fairly debatable, the legislative judgment must be allowed to control.

There is no serious difference of opinion in respect of the validity of laws and regulations fixing the height of buildings within reasonable limits, the character of materials and methods of construction, and the adjoining area which must be left open, in order to minimize the danger of fire or collapse, the evils of overcrowding and the like, and excluding from residential sections offensive trades, industries and structures likely to create nuisances.

Here, however, the exclusion is in general terms of all industrial establishments, and it may thereby happen that not only offensive or dangerous industries will be excluded, but those which are neither offensive nor dangerous will share the same fate. But this is no more than happens in respect of many practice-forbidding laws which this court has upheld, although drawn in general terms so as to include individual cases that may turn out to be innocuous in themselves. The inclusion of a reasonable margin, to insure effective enforcement, will not put upon a law, otherwise valid, the stamp of invalidity. Such laws may also find their justification in the fact that, in some fields, the bad fades into the good by such insensible degrees that the two are not capable of being readily distinguished and separated in terms of legislation. In the light of these considerations, we are not prepared to say that the end in view was not sufficient to justify the general rule of the ordinance, although some industries of an innocent character might fall within the proscribed class. It cannot be said that the ordinance in this respect "passes the bounds of reason and assumes the character of a merely arbitrary fiat." Moreover, the restrictive provisions of the ordinance in this particular may be sustained upon the principles applicable to the broader exclusion from residential districts of all business and trade structures, presently to be discussed.

It is said that the village of Euclid is a mere suburb of the city of Cleveland; that the industrial development of that city has now reached and in some degree extended into the village, and in the obvious course of things will soon absorb the entire area for industrial enterprises; that the effect of the ordinance is to divert this natural development elsewhere, with the consequent loss of increased values to the owners of the lands within the village borders. But the village, though physically a suburb of Cleveland, is politically a separate municipality, with powers of its own and authority to govern itself as it sees fit, within the limits of the organic law of its creation and the state and federal Constitutions. Its governing authorities, presumably representing a majority of its inhabitants and voicing their will, have determined, not that industrial development shall cease at its boundaries, but that the course of such development shall proceed within definitely fixed lines. If it be a proper exercise of the police power to relegate industrial establishments to localities separated from residential sections, it is not easy to find a sufficient reason for denying the power because the effect of its exercise is to divert an industrial flow from the course which it would follow, to the injury of the residential public, if left alone, to another course where such injury will be obviated. It is not meant by this, however, to exclude the possibility of cases where the general public interest would so far outweigh the interest of the municipality that the municipality would not be allowed to stand in the way.

We find no difficulty in sustaining restrictions of the kind thus far reviewed. The serious question in the case arises over the provisons of the ordinance excluding from residential districts apartment houses, business houses, retail stores and shops, and other like establishments. This question involves the validity of what is really the crux of the more recent zoning legislation, namely, the creation and maintenance of residential districts, from which business and trade of every sort, including hotels and apartment houses, are excluded. Upon that question this court has not thus far spoken. The decisions of the state courts are numerous and conflicting; but those which broadly sustain the power greatly outnumber those which deny it altogether or narrowly limit it, and it is very apparent that there is a constantly increasing tendency in the direction of the broader view. . . .

The matter of zoning has received much attention at the hands of commissions and experts, and the results of their investigations have been set forth in comprehensive reports. These reports, which bear every evidence of painstaking consideration, concur in the view that the segregation of residential, business and industrial buildings will make it easier to provide fire apparatus suitable for the character and intensity of the development in each section; that it will increase the safety and security of home life, greatly tend to prevent street accidents, especially to children, by reducing the traffic and resulting confusion in residential sections, decrease noise and other conditions which produce or intensify nervous disorders, preserve a more favorable environment in which to rear children, etc. With particular reference to apartment houses, it is pointed out that the development of detached house sections is greatly retarded by the coming of apartment houses, which has sometimes resulted in destroying the entire section for private house purposes; that in such sections very often the apartment house is a mere parasite, constructed in order to take advantage of the open spaces and attractive surroundings created by the residential character of the district. Moreover, the coming of one apartment house is followed by others, interfering by their height and bulk with the free circulation of air and monopolizing the rays of the sun which otherwise would fall upon the smaller homes, and bringing, as their necessary accompaniments, the disturbing noises incident to increased traffic and business, and the occupation, by means of moving and parked automobiles, of larger portions of the streets, thus detracting from their safety and depriving children of the privilege of quiet and open spaces for play, enjoyed by those in more favored localities—until, finally, the residential character of the neighborhood and its desirability as a place of detached residences are utterly destroyed. Under these circumstances, apartment houses, which in a different environment would be not only entirely unobjectionable but highly desirable, come very near to being nuisances.

If these reasons, thus summarized, do not demonstrate the wisdom or sound policy in all respects of those restrictions which we have indicated as pertinent to the inquiry, at least the reasons are sufficiently cogent to preclude us from saying, as it must be said before the ordinance can be declared unconstitutional, that such provisions are clearly arbitrary and unreasonable, having no substantial relation to the public health, safety, morals, or general welfare.

It is true that when, if ever, the provisions set forth in the ordinance in tedious and minute detail, come to be concretely applied to particular premises, including those of the appellee, or to particular conditions, or to be considered in connection with specific complaints, some of them, or even many of them, may be found to be clearly arbitrary and unreasonable. But where the equitable remedy of injunction is sought, as it is here, not upon the ground of a present infringement or denial of a specific right, or of a particular injury in process of actual execution, but upon the broad ground that the mere existence and threatened enforcement of the ordinance, by materially and adversely affecting values and curtailing the opportunities of the market, constitute a present and irreparable injury, the court will not scrutinize its provisions, sentence by sentence, to ascertain by a process of piecemeal dissection whether there may be, here and there, provisions of a minor character, or relating to matters of administration, or not shown to contribute to the injury complained of, which, if attacked separately, might not withstand the test of constitutionality. In respect of such provisions, of which specific complaint is not made, it cannot be said that the landowner has suffered or is threatened with an injury which entitles him to challenge their constitutionality. . . .

Decree reversed.

MR. JUSTICE VAN DEVANTER, MR. JUSTICE MCREYNOLDS, and MR. JUSTICE BUTLER dissent.

NOTES

1. Were the court's arguments for exclusion of apartments from residential neighborhoods of single-family homes persuasive? Are apartment buildings necessarily bad neighbors of single-family residences? Could not all of the adverse impacts of apartment buildings mentioned by the court be prevented by regulations of height, design,

lot size, siting on the lot, off-street parking, and other troublesome aspects of apartments? Is the concept of allowing in separate districts specified uses sounder than some other approach, such as siting of various uses on the basis of performance standards? Do the latter pose unreasonable administrative problems? Modern zoning ordinances rely upon performance standards to some extent. A much more extensive use of them is proposed by L. Kendig, Performance Zoning (1980).

2. What would the court have said about Euclid's exclusion of duplexes from single-family zones, had it faced that issue? See Babcock, The Egregious Invalidity of the Single-Family Zone, Land Use Law & Zoning Dig., July 1983, p. 4.

3. The lower court's view of the Euclid ordinance:

> "The purpose to be accomplished is really to regulate the mode of living of persons who may hereafter inhabit it. In the last analysis, the result to be accomplished is to classify the population and segregate them according to their income or situation in life. The true reason why some persons live in a mansion and others in a shack, why some live in a single-family dwelling and others in a double-family dwelling, why some live in a two-family dwelling and others in an apartment, or why some live in a well-kept apartment and others in a tenement, is primarily economic. It is a matter of income and wealth, plus the labor and difficulty of procuring adequate domestic service. Aside from contributing to these results and furthering such class tendencies, the ordinance has also an esthetic purpose; that is to say, to make this village develop into a city along lines now conceived by the village council to be attractive and beautiful. The assertion that this ordinance may tend to prevent congestion, and thereby contribute to the health and safety, would be more substantial if provision had been or could be made for adequate east and west and north and south street highways. Whether these purposes and objects would justify the taking of plaintiff's property as and for a public use need not be considered. It is sufficient to say that, in our opinion, and as applied to plaintiff's property, it may not be done without compensation under the guise of exercising the police power."

Ambler Realty Co. v. Village of Euclid, 297 Fed. 307, 316 (N.D. Ohio 1924).

4. If the Euclid ordinance was intended to divert the "industrial flow from the course which it would follow," that purpose appears not to have been achieved, at least wholly. See R. Ellickson and A.D. Tarlock, Land-Use Controls 51 (1981), who report that apparently all of the realty company's land was rezoned later for heavy industrial use, and that parts of Euclid Avenue have been devoted to commercial uses.

5. Would, as is indicated in the lower court opinion in Euclid, zoning solely for aesthetic purposes be invalid? In a pre-Euclid case, a state court invalidated an ordinance regulating billboards on the ground that aesthetic considerations are a "matter of luxury and indulgence rather than of necessity, and it is necessity alone which justifies the exercise of the police power to take private property

without compensation." City of Passaic v. Paterson Bill Posting, Advertising & Sign Painting Co., 73 N.J.L. 285, 62 A. 267, 268 (1905). Judicial support for that position has declined markedly. See State v. Jones, 305 N.C. 520, 290 S.E.2d 675, 681 (1982), upholding an ordinance regulating junkyards and overuling "our previous cases to the extent that they prohibited regulation based upon aesthetic considerations alone." The modern judicial view is probably represented by Justice Douglas' declaration in a case upholding exercise of the eminent domain power for urban renewal that it "is within the power of the legislature to determine that the community should be beautiful as well as healthy, spacious as well as clean, well-balanced as well as carefully patrolled." Berman v. Parker, 348 U.S. 26, 33, 75 S.Ct. 98, 99 L.Ed. 27 (1954).

However, some kinds of aesthetic regulations pose difficult problems. Ordinances authorizing a local agency to prevent construction of unattractive buildings, though usually upheld, are challenged on the grounds that standards are insufficiently precise to prevent arbitrary decisions and that the community's aesthetic views are not demonstrably better than than those of individuals. See Reid v. Architectural Board of Review of the City of Cleveland Heights, 119 Ohio App. 67, 192 N.E.2d 74 (1963), upholding disapproval of construction of a single-story home of unusual design in a multi-story neighborhood. A dissenting opinion pointed out that "there is an important principle of eclecticism in architecture that implies freedom on the part of the architect or client or both to choose among the styles of the past and present which seems to them most appropriate." Id., 192 N.E.2d at 81. See also Costonis, Law and Aesthetics: A Critique and a Reformulation of the Dilemmas, 80 Mich.L.Rev. 355 (1982). Some regulations of signs and billboards may infringe freedom of speech protected by the First Amendment of the United States Constitution. See Metromedia, Inc. v. City of San Diego, 453 U.S. 490, 101 S.Ct. 2882, 69 L.Ed.2d 800 (1981).

Other types of land use controls have been challenged, sometimes successfully, as infringing speech and other rights protected by the First Amendment. A zoning ordinance prohibiting location of "adult" motion picture theatres within 1,000 feet of any residential zone, single- or multiple-family dwelling, church, park or school was upheld in City of Renton v. Playtime Threatres, Inc., 475 U.S. 41, 106 S.Ct. 925, 89 L.Ed.2d 29 (1986). But total exclusion from a local community of all "live" entertainment, including nude dancing, was held invalid in Schad v. Borough of Mount Ephraim, 452 U.S. 61, 101 S.Ct. 2176, 68 L.Ed.2d 671 (1981). Courts are divided as to whether exclusion of churches from residential zones is prohibited by constitutional protection of the exercise of religious freedom. See the discussion in State v. Cameron, 184 N.J.Super. 66, 445 A.2d 75 (1982), affirmed 189 N.J.Super. 404, 460 A.2d 191 (1983) and Lakewood, Ohio Congregation of Jehovah's Witnesses, Inc. v. City of Lakewood, 699 F.2d 303 (6th Cir.1983), cert denied 464 U.S. 815, 104 S.Ct. 72, 78 L.Ed.2d 85 (1983), both of which cases upheld the exclusion. In Larkin v. Grendel's Den, Inc., 459 U.S. 116, 103 S.Ct. 505, 74 L.Ed.2d 297 (1983), the court held that the establishment of religion clause of the First Amendment was violated by a statute providing that premises "located within five hundred feet of a church or school shall not be licensed for the sale of alcoholic beverages if the governing body of such church or school files written objection thereto." The court conceded that an absolute ban of sales of alcoholic beverages within a stated distance of a church would be valid. Total exclusion of abortion clinics from a local community was held invalid as infringing constitutionally protected rights of privacy in Framingham Clinic, Inc. v. Board of Selectmen, 373 Mass. 279, 367 N.E.2d 606 (1977).

NECTOW v. CITY OF CAMBRIDGE

Supreme Court of the United States, 1928.
277 U.S. 183, 48 S.Ct. 447, 72 L.Ed. 842.

MR. JUSTICE SUTHERLAND delivered the opinion of the Court.

A zoning ordinance of the city of Cambridge divides the city into three kinds of districts, residential, business, and unrestricted. Each of these districts is subclassified in respect of the kind of buildings which may be erected. The ordinance is an elaborate one, and of the same general character as that considered by this court in Euclid v. Ambler Co., 272 U.S. 365, 47 S.Ct. 114, 71 L.Ed. 303. In its general scope it is conceded to be constitutional within that decision. The land of plaintiff in error was put in district R–3, in which are permitted only dwellings, hotels, clubs, churches, schools, philanthropic institutions, greenhouses and gardening, with customary incidental accessories. The attack upon the ordinance is that, as specifically applied to plaintiff in error, it deprived him of his property without due process of law in contravention of the Fourteenth Amendment.

The suit was for a mandatory injunction directing the city and its inspector of buildings to pass upon an application of the plaintiff in error for a permit to erect any lawful buildings upon a tract of land without regard to the provisions of the ordinance including such tract within a residential district. The case was referred to a master to make and report findings of fact. After a view of the premises and the surrounding territory, and a hearing, the master made and reported his findings. The case came on to be heard by a justice of the court, who, after confirming the master's report, reported the case for the determination of the full court. Upon consideration, that court sustained the ordinance as applied to plaintiff in error, and dismissed the bill. 157 N.E. 618.

A condensed statement of facts, taken from the master's report, is all that is necessary. When the zoning ordinance was enacted plaintiff in error was and still is the owner of a tract of land containing 140,000 square feet, of which the locus here in question is a part. The locus contains about 29,000 square feet, with a frontage on Brookline street, lying west, of 304.75 feet, on Henry street, lying north, of 100 feet, on the other land of the plaintiff in error, lying east, of 264 feet, and on land of the Ford Motor Company, lying southerly, of 75 feet. The territory lying east and south is unrestricted. The lands beyond Henry street to the north and beyond Brookline street to the west are within a restricted residential district. The effect of the zoning is to separate from the west end of plaintiff in error's tract a strip 100 feet in width. The Ford Motor Company has a large auto assembling factory south of the locus; and a soap factory and the tracks of the Boston & Albany Railroad lie near. Opposite the locus, on Brookline street, and included in the same district, there are some residences; and opposite the locus, on Henry street, and in the same district, are other residences. The locus is now vacant, although it was once occupied by a mansion house. Before the passage of the ordinance in question, plaintiff in error had outstanding a contract for the sale of the greater part of his entire tract of land for the sum of $63,000. Because of the zoning restrictions, the purchaser refused to comply with the contract. Under the ordinance, business and industry of all sorts are excluded from the locus, while the remainder of the tract is unrestricted. It further appears that provision has been made for widening Brookline street, the effect of which, if carried out, will be to reduce the depth of the locus to 65 feet. After a statement at length of further facts, the master finds:

"That no practical use can be made of the land in question for residential purposes, because among other reasons herein related, there would not be adequate return on the amount of any investment for the development of the property."

The last finding of the master is:

"I am satisfied that the districting of the plaintiff's land in a residence district would not promote the health, safety, convenience, and general welfare of the inhabitants of that part of the defendant city, taking into account the natural development thereof and the character of the district and the resulting benefit to accrue to the whole city and I so find."

It is made pretty clear that because of the industrial and railroad purposes to which the immediately adjoining lands to the south and east have been devoted and for which they are zoned, the locus is of comparatively little value for the limited uses permitted by the ordinance.

We quite agree with the opinion expressed below that a court should not set aside the determination of public officers in such a matter unless it is clear that their action "has no foundation in reason and is a mere arbitrary or irrational exercise of power having no substantial relation to the public health, the public morals, the public safety or the public welfare in its proper sense." Euclid v. Ambler Co., supra, p. 395 (47 S.Ct. 121).

An inspection of a plat of the city upon which the zoning districts are outlined, taken in connection with the master's findings, shows with reasonable certainty that the inclusion of the locus in question is not indispensable to the general plan. The boundary line of the residential district before reaching the locus runs for some distance along the streets, and to exclude the locus from the residential district requires only that such line shall be continued 100 feet further along Henry street and thence south along Brookline street. There does not appear to be any reason why this should not be done. Nevertheless, if that were all, we should not be warranted in substituting our judgment for that of the zoning authorities primarily charged with the duty and responsibility of determining the question. But that is not all. The governmental power to interfere by zoning regulations with the general rights of the land owner by restricting the character of his use, is not unlimited, and, other questions aside, such restriction cannot be imposed if it does not bear a substantial relation to the public health, safety, morals, or general welfare. Euclid v. Ambler Co., supra, p. 395 (47 S.Ct. 114). Here, the express finding of the master, already quoted, confirmed by the court below, is that the health, safety, convenience, and general welfare of the inhabitants of the part of the city affected will not be promoted by the disposition made by the ordinance of the locus in question. This finding of the master, after a hearing and an inspection of the entire area affected, supported, as we think it is, by other findings of fact, is determinative of the case. That the invasion of the property of plaintiff in error was serious and highly injurious is clearly established; and, since a necessary basis for the support of that invasion is wanting, the action of the zoning authorities comes within the ban of the Fourteenth Amendment and cannot be sustained.

Judgment reversed.

NOTES

1. Compare the language of the Supreme Judicial Court of Massachusetts: "If there is to be zoning at all, the dividing line must be drawn somewhere. There cannot be a twilight zone. If residence districts are to exist, they must be bounded. In the nature of things, the location of the precise limits of the several districts demands the exercise of judgment and sagacity. There can be no standard susceptible of mathematical exactness in its application. Opinions of the wise and good well may differ as to the place to put the separation between different districts. Seemingly there would be great difficulty in pronouncing a scheme for zoning unreasonable and capricious because it embraced land on both sides of the same street in one district instead of making the center of the street the dividing line. . . . No physical features of the locus stamp it as land improper for residence. Indeed, its accessibility to means of transportation, to centers of business, and to seats of learning, as well as its proximity to land given over to residence purposes, give to it many of the attributes desirable for land to be used for residence. . . . Courts cannot set aside the decision of public officers in such a matter unless compelled to the conclusion that it has no foundation in reason and is a mere arbitrary or irrational exercise of power having no substantial relation to the public health, the public morals, the public safety, or the public welfare in its proper sense. These considerations cannot be weighed with exactness. That they demand the placing of the boundary of a zone one hundred feet one way or the other in land having similar material features would be hard to say as a matter of law. . . . The case at bar is close to the line. But we do not feel justified in holding that the zoning line established is whimsical and without foundation in reason." Nectow v. Cambridge, 260 Mass. 441, 447, 448, 157 N.E. 618, 620 (1927).

2. Does it follow from the invalidation of the zoning of Nectow's land that Nectow should be entitled to a building permit? Should the city have a reasonable time to rezone Nectow's land lawfully? Consider Garrett v. City of Oklahoma City, 594 P.2d 764 (Okl.1979).

SECTION 2. REGULATION OF THE SUBDIVISION OF LAND

NATIONAL COMMISSION ON URBAN PROBLEMS, BUILDING THE AMERICAN CITY

Pages 201, 203 (1968).

The regulation of land subdivision existed in this country from its earliest days and survived in some form even during the 19th century. Much of the 19th century regulation, however, was mainly designed to assure the adequacy of engineering data and the accurate recording of plats. Gradually, however, the objectives were broadened. Some States required that new streets be designed to tie into existing ones and that streets be dedicated to the public. Enforcement was achieved by requiring governmental approval of street layouts before plats could be officially recorded and lots sold.

The present form of subdivision regulation, like that of zoning, bears the stamp of the 1920's. At that time, subdivision regulation began to be widely considered as a means of guiding urban growth. In 1928, the Department of Commerce issued the Standard City Planning Enabling Act, a model act that made subdivision regulation one of the tools of comprehensive planning and placed major responsibility for administering subdivision regulations in local planning boards. While the Standard City Planning Enabling Act did not take State legislatures by storm in quite the fashion of its zoning predecessor, many States did enact planning statutes that bore some resemblance to the Standard Act.

Local subdivision regulations were becoming widespread by the time the depression halted most subdivision activity. A 1934 survey found 269 municipal planning commissions in 29 States with power to regulate land subdivision, and an additional 156 commissions empowered to act in an advisory capacity on such regulations. . . .

While conventional zoning normally applies to individual lots, subdivision regulations govern the process by which those lots are created out of larger tracts.

a. *Regulated subjects.* Site design and relationships: Subdivision regulations typically seek to assure that subdivisions are appropriately related to their surroundings. Commonly, they require that the subdivision be consistent with a comprehensive plan for the area (e.g., by reserving land for proposed highways or parks). Requirements normally assure that utilities (local streets, sewers) tie into those located or planned for adjoining property. Other requirements are intended to assure that the subdivision itself is related to its own site and that it will work effectively. The widths of streets, the length of blocks, the size of lots, and the handling of frontage along major streets, are among commonly regulated subjects.

Allocation of facilities cost—dedications and fees: Second, subdivision regulations may contain provisions that effectively allocate costs of public facilities between the subdivider and local taxpayers. Commonly, regulations require subdividers to dedicate land for streets and to install, at their own expense, a variety of public facilities to serve the development. These often include streets, sidewalks, storm and sanitary sewers, and street lights. In recent years, more and more subdivision regulations have also been requiring subdividers to dedicate parkland, and sometimes school sites, or to make cash payments in lieu of such dedication. Some regulations go further still, requiring payment of fees to apply toward such major public costs as the construction of sewage disposal plants.

b. *Administration.* Subdivision regulations contemplate a more sophisticated administrative process than do conventional zoning regulations. Instead of prescribing the precise location of future lot lines, for example, subdivision regulations provide more general design standards (based in part on local plans). The local planning commission or governing body then applies these standards, at the time of subdivision, to preliminary and final plats submitted by property owners.

NOTE

Courts have disagreed as to the validity of mandatory dedications and fees exacted as a condition for approval of a subdivision plat. See pp. 908–919, infra.

DURANT v. TOWN OF DUNBARTON

Supreme Court of New Hampshire, 1981.
121 N.H. 352, 430 A.2d 140.

DOUGLAS, JUSTICE.

The plaintiff, Pearl Durant, appeals from the Dunbarton Planning Board's denial of her subdivision plan. The Superior Court (*Cann,* J.) affirmed the denial. We find no error.

In April 1977, the plaintiff requested that the defendant planning board approve her subdivision plan for a tract of land in Dunbarton. The proposed plan divided the tract into eight lots, each of which fronted on Jewett Road, a State highway. The New Hampshire Water Supply and Pollution Control Commission approved the plan, and the plaintiff submitted the certificate of approval to the planning board with her request. After a hearing and several views, the board refused to approve the subdivision plan for three reasons: (1) potential disruption of natural water courses; (2) potential sight distance problems from the driveways exiting onto a State highway; and (3) potential problems with subsurface septic systems due to an extremely high water table in the area.

The essence of the plaintiff's first argument on appeal is that the planning board did not have authority under its subdivision regulations to deny the plan for the reasons given. If any of the board's reasons for denial support its decision, then the plaintiff's appeal must fail. Blakeman v. Planning Commission, 152 Conn. 303, 306, 206 A.2d 425, 427 (1965).

. . .

RSA 36:19 authorizes municipalities to grant to their planning boards discretionary authority to approve or disapprove subdivision plans. Before a board may exercise that authority, however, it must adopt subdivision regulations. RSA 36:21 (Supp.1979). The scope of those regulations may be quite broad and "generally may include provisions which will tend to create conditions favorable to health, safety, convenience, or prosperity." RSA 36:21 (Supp.1979). In 1965, pursuant to the provisions of RSA 36:19 to :29 then in effect, the Dunbarton Planning Board adopted the subdivision regulations under which it denied approval of the plaintiff's plan. The specific regulations on which the board based its denial read in part as follows:

> "V. B. Land of such character that it cannot be *safely* used for building purposes because of exceptional *danger to health* or peril from fire, flood *or other menace* shall not be platted for residential occupancy, nor for such other uses as may increase danger to health, life or property or aggravate the flood hazard, until appropriate measures have been taken by the subdivider to eliminate such hazards. . . .
>
> Q. It shall be the responsibility of the subdivider to provide adequate information to prove that the area of each lot is *adequate* to permit the installation and operation of an individual sewage disposal system (septic tank and drain field not a cesspool). . . .
>
> R. It shall be the responsibility of the subdivider to provide adequate information to prove that the area of each lot is adequate to permit the installation and operation of both individual on-lot water and sewerage systems. . . ."

(Emphasis added). The statutory delegation under RSA 36:21 (Supp. 1979) is quite broad, and the regulation of septic tanks and sewerage systems falls within the purview of the statute.

The plaintiff argues that the regulations are impermissibly vague because they do not contain standards for the evaluation of on-site septic systems. We have previously held that broad regulations are not necessarily vague even if they do not "precisely apprise one of the standards by which an administrative board will make its decision." Town of Freedom v. Gillespie, 120 N.H. 576, 580, 419 A.2d 1090, 1092 (1980); see Carbonneau v. Town of Rye, 120 N.H. 96, 98, 411 A.2d 1110, 1112 (1980). In this case, the regulations, when read as a whole, inform a subdivider that his plan must provide adequate information to enable the board to conclude that future development of the land will not pose an exceptional danger to health. We find that this language provides sufficient notice to developers of what is expected of them.

The plaintiff raises a similar argument with respect to the board's disapproval of the plan based on potential disruption of water courses. Although the regulations are less specific with regard to such criteria, we also find them to be adequate. . . .

Under its subdivision regulations a planning board may consider any characteristics of the land that relate to "the current and future fitness of the land for building purposes." Patenaude v. Town of Meredith, 118 N.H. 616, 621, 392 A.2d 582, 585 (1978); see Town of Seabrook v. Tra-Sea Corp., 119 N.H. at 941, 410 A.2d at 243. Water courses over land clearly affect the desirability and suitability of construction on a particular piece of property, and consideration of such factors is within the ambit of the board's delegated authority.

The plaintiff also questions the authority of the planning board to evaluate a subdivision plan for sight distance problems with driveways that exit onto a State highway. We need not discuss that issue because the other two reasons given by the board for denial of the plaintiff's plan support the action. But see J.E.D. Assoc. Inc. v. Town of Sandown, 121 N.H. 317, 430 A.2d 129 (1981).

We next consider the plaintiff's argument that the board's findings of "potential" problems with water courses and waste disposal systems are inadequate in view of the fact that the regulations require a finding of "*exceptional* danger to health or peril from fire, flood, or other menace." Town of Dunbarton, Land Subdivision Control Regulations § V. B. (1965). (Emphasis added.) Subdivision regulations are a tool for "promoting the orderly and planned growth of a municipality." In re Estate of Sayewich, 120 N.H. 237, 240, 413 A.2d 581, 583 (1980); see 4 A. Rathkopf, The Law of Zoning and Planning, ch. 71, § 2, at 71–11 (4th ed. 1980). In evaluating a subdivision plan a board "must consider current as well as anticipated realities." Patenaude v. Town of Meredith, 118 N.H. at 621, 392 A.2d at 585. A board may, therefore, deny approval of a plan based on "potential" conflicts with its regulations. Although in this case the board did not state that those potential dangers were exceptional, the record indicates that it found them to be so. We agree with the master's conclusion that there is evidence of danger to health "of a degree meeting the required standard, regardless of the adjective used."

The plaintiff argues that the record does not support the board's findings. . . . The record reveals that the board took several views of the lot in question. They walked the land and twice examined the depth of water in test pits. They evaluated the topography of the land and subsurface conditions to determine whether the land would be suited for development of the proposed density. All of these considerations are permissible and desirable in subdivision review. J. Rose, Legal Foundations of Land Use Planning, 323 (1979). From its observations, the board concluded that the high water table in the area created the potential for groundwater contamination and flooding. The plaintiff makes much of the fact that the New Hampshire Water Supply and Pollution Control Commission approved the plan. However, the planning board is entitled to rely in part on its own judgment and experience in acting upon applications for subdivision approval.

After a review of the record, we find no error of law and conclude that the record supports the trial court's decision that the plaintiff had not established by a balance of probabilities that the board's action was unreasonable.

Affirmed.

NOTE

Compare Kaufman & Gold Construction Co. v. Planning & Zoning Commission of the City of Fairmont, 298 S.E.2d 148 (W.Va.1982), reversing a planning commission's denial of approval of a subdivision plat. Neighbors had objected to the proposed development, which was to consist in part of houses owned by a local housing authority and rented to low-income persons. The court said: "The Commission admitted that it found no technical flaws in the plat proposal. It justified its action by finding that the development would not be in harmony with other subdivisions in the area, that construction would depreciate local property values, and that the influx of new residents would burden highway and school systems. . . . Much of the argument in this case has treated the decision as a zoning matter. However, planning and zoning are not identical . . .. Although the concerns expressed by the intervenors may be legitimate, the fact remains that the developer complied with every statute and ordinance enacted by the state and the city. When an applicant meets all requirements, plat approval is a ministerial act and a planning commission has no discretion in approving the submitted application."

SECTION 3. RESERVATION OF LAND FOR PUBLIC ACQUISITION (OFFICIAL MAPS)

STATE EX REL. MILLER v. MANDERS

Supreme Court of Wisconsin, 1957.
2 Wis.2d 365, 86 N.W.2d 469.

Mandamus to compel the issuance of a building permit. The defendants are the building inspector and the members of the zoning and planning board of appeals of the city of Green Bay.

Under the date of July 1, 1947, the common council of the city of Green Bay, pursuant to sec. 62.23(6), Wis.Stats.1945, by ordinance adopted an official map of the city showing established and proposed streets, highways, parkways, parks and playgrounds. Later in July, 1950, the common council by further ordinance reaffirmed the adoption of such official map.

On May 29, 1953, the relator Miller purchased a tract of land lying to the north of Velp avenue in said city, which had a frontage of 384.17 feet on such street and a depth of 1330 feet. The southerly portion of the premises fronting on Velp avenue was suitable as building sites for various businesses, while the northerly portion was low land which the relator hoped to devote to industrial purposes. Shortly after the relator acquired such premises he leased a rectangular tract thereof to the Clark Oil & Refining Corporation for a service station. Such leased parcel had a frontage on Velp avenue of 200 feet and a depth of 100 feet, and was so situated that it left the relator with 92.17 feet of street frontage to the west thereof and 92 feet of street frontage to the east.

The city official map showed the location of a proposed street having a width of 80 feet extending in a general northerly direction from Velp avenue. As a result, 80 feet of the 92 feet of frontage of relator's property located to the east of the Clark service station lies within the bed of such proposed street.

On August 13, 1953, relator applied to the defendant building inspector Manders for a building permit to erect a drive-in service lunch stand on a nearly triangular shaped parcel of his property fronting on Velp avenue, which lies immediately to the east of the parcel leased to the Clark Oil & Refining Corporation. The building itself was to be located on land lying within the bed of such proposed street. Manders refused the application, and the relator appealed therefrom to the zoning and planning board of appeals. In his written appeal the relator challenged the constitutionality of sec. 62.23(6), Stats., and of the city ordinances, establishing the official map enacted pursuant to such statute. After a hearing the board of appeals sustained the building inspector's denial of the application for a building permit.

The relator then instituted mandamus proceedings in the circuit court to compel issuance of the building permit, in which the constitutionality of such statute and ordinances was again attacked. The circuit court determined that the statute and ordinances were constitutional, and under date of April 25, 1957, judgment was entered dismissing the proceedings. From such judgment the relator has appealed.

CURRIE, JUSTICE. The issue before us on this appeal is whether Wisconsin's Official Map Law (sec. 62.23(6), Stats.), and the ordinances of the city of Green Bay enacted pursuant thereto, are unconstitutional as being a taking by the city of the relator's property for public use without just compensation.

A comprehensive history of such statute is to be found in an article entitled, "Wisconsin's Official Map Law" by Joseph C. Kucirek and J. H. Beuscher appearing in 1957 Wis.Law Review 176. Edward M. Bassett and Frank B. Williams, experts in the field of municipal planning, drafted the original offical map statute enacted by the state of New York in 1926, General City Law, McKinney's Consol. Laws, c. 21, § 26 et seq. Our official map statute, which was enacted by the 1941 Wisconsin legislature, was substantially copied from that of New York. As of the time of the writing of the article by Kucirek and Beuscher, thirty-three Wisconsin cities and villages had adopted official map ordinances pursuant to sec. 62.23(6), Stats. Among such municipalities is the city of Green Bay.

Subds. (a) and (b) of sec. 62.23(6) provide for the adoption by the common council of any city by ordinance or resolution of an official map showing existing streets, highways, parkways, parks and playgrounds, and also "the exterior lines of planned new streets, highways, parkways, parks or playgrounds". Subd. (d) of sec. 62.23(6), which is the subsection with which we are particularly concerned on this appeal reads:

"(d) For the purpose of preserving the integrity of such official map, no permit shall hereafter be issued for any building in the bed of any street, highway or parkway, shown or laid out on such map except as provided in this section. . . . Any person desiring to construct a building in the bed of a street, highway or parkway so shown as extended may apply to the authorized official of the city or village for a building permit. Unless such application is made, and the permit granted or not denied within 30 days, such person shall not be entitled to compensation for damage to such building in the course of construction of the street, highway or parkway. If the land within such mapped street, highway or parkway is not yielding a fair return, the board of appeals in any municipality which has established such a board having power to make variances or exceptions in zoning regulations, shall have power in a specific case, by the vote of a majority of its members, to grant a permit for a building in such street, highway or parkway, which will as little as practicable increase the cost of opening such street, highway or parkway or tend to cause a change of such official map; and such board may impose reasonable requirements as a condition of granting such permit, which requirements shall be designated to promote the health, convenience, safety or general welfare of the community. Such board shall refuse a permit where the applicant will not be substantially damaged by placing his building outside the mapped street, highway or parkway."

The first question to be considered is whether the enactment of sec. 62.23(6) by the legislature can be sustained as a valid exercise of the police power on the ground that it tends to promote the general welfare.

One of the objectives of the statute is to promote orderly city growth and development so as to prevent the haphazard erection of buildings, and the installation of service facilities, which bear no relationship to future streets. There are practical reasons why municipalities, such as cities, should have the right to enforce such planning in advance of the actual acquiring title to the land underlying proposed streets in areas undergoing improvement and development. This was emphasized by the New York court of appeals in Headley v. City of Rochester, 1936, 272 N.Y. 197, 5 N.E.2d 198, 200, in which it was considering the New York Official Map Law. We quote from such opinion as follows:

"A statutory requirement that a city must acquire title to the land in the bed of the streets shown on the general map or plan, and provide compensation for the land taken, would create practical difficulties which would drastically limit, if, indeed, they did not render illusory, any power conferred upon the city to adopt a general map or plan which will make provision for streets which will be needed only if present anticipations of the future development of the city are realized."

There would seem to be little doubt that an objective which seeks to achieve better city planning is embraced within the concept of promoting the general welfare. 1 Metzenbaum, Law of Zoning, 2d Ed., p. 484. A broad reading of the recent decision by the United States supreme court in Berman v. Parker, 1954, 348 U.S. 26, 75 S.Ct. 98, 99 L.Ed. 27, is that the constitution will accommodate a wide range of community planning devices to meet the pressing problems of community growth, deterioration, and change. Constitutional Law and Community Planning by Prof. Corwin W. Johnson, 20 Law and Contemporary Problems 199, at p. 208.

A second objective of sec. 62.23(6) is made manifest by the afore-quoted provision of subd. (d) thereof, that authorizes the board of appeals to grant a permit to erect a building within the lines of a proposed street shown on the official map "which will as little as practicable increase the cost of opening such street." Such objective is to protect the financial interests of taxpayers of the city. This court has previously held that the protection of economic interests of the general public falls within the scope of promotion of the general welfare, and thereby affords a basis for the exercise of the police power. State v. Ross, 1951, 259 Wis. 379, 384, 48 N.W.2d 460, and State ex rel. Saveland Park Holding Corp. v. Wieland, 1955, 269 Wis. 262, 267, 69 N.W.2d 217.

In Vangellow v. City of Rochester, 1947, 190 Misc. 128, 71 N.Y.S.2d 672, an action for declaratory judgment was instituted by the plaintiff property owners to have declared unconstitutional an ordinance of the defendant city enacted pursuant to New York's Official Map Law. Such ordinance contained provisions similar to those set forth in subd. (d) of sec. 62.23(6), Wis.Stats. The New York court . . . clearly indicates that the right to exercise the police power to protect a municipality against added costs, which might have to be incurred in case of future condemnation or purchase of property needed for a public improvement, is subject to rather narrow limits. The draftsmen of the original New York Official Map Law, from which our Wisconsin statute was substantially copied, recognized this. That is why the saving clause was inserted therein which is duplicated in subd. (d) of sec. 62.23(6), Wis.Stats. Without such a saving clause it is extremely doubtful if an official map statute would be constitutional.

Such saving clause, as found in our own statute, requires that the board of appeals shall refuse a building permit "where the applicant will not be substantially damaged by placing his building outside the mapped street, highway or parkway". We deem that subd. (d) of sec. 62.23(6) must be so construed that the converse of this is true, viz., it is the duty of the board of appeals to grant the permit if the applicant property owner would be substantially damaged, if the permit were to be denied. This is because this court must so construe the official map law as to sustain its constitutionality if possible to do so.

Subd. (d) of sec. 62.23(6) authorizes the board to "impose reasonable requirements as a condition of granting" a building permit to erect a building within the boundary lines of a proposed street shown on the official map.

If the board of appeals should deny a permit under circumstances which would result in substantial damage to the applicant property owner, or should grant the permit subject to condition which would result in such substantial damage, the aggrieved applicant may secure court review by certiorari. . . .

. . .

The mere fact that the relator in the instant case was denied a building permit thus preventing him from erecting a building upon that part of his land lying in the bed of the proposed street, does not establish the unconstitutionality of sec. 62.23(6). This court nearly thirty years ago upheld the set-back provisions of a zoning ordinance in Bouchard v. Zetley, 1928, 196 Wis. 635, 220 N.W. 209, basing such determination upon the precedent of Gorieb v. Fox, 1927, 274 U.S. 603, 47 S.Ct. 675, 71 L.Ed. 1228. . . .

We cannot spell out of the . . . statute any legislative motive to depress existing property values. Furthermore, the saving clause contained in subd. (d) protects a property owner against any substantial damage that might be inflicted upon him in the future operation of the statute by denial of a building permit.

It is our considered judgment that sec. 62.23(6), Stats., is a valid exercise of the police power and is constitutional. We further determine that the relator has failed to establish that the Green Bay official map ordinances, as applied to his property, are unconstitutional. However, we do not rule out the possibility that under certain circumstances a municipal official map ordinance drafted pursuant to, and in compliance with, sec. 62.23(6) might be invalid as applied to particular lands. For a situation where this might be the result, see Roer Construction Corp. v. City of New Rochelle, 1954, 207 Misc. 46, 136 N.Y.S.2d 414.

We do not consider any arguments addressed to the merits of the issue, of whether the denial of a building permit by the building inspector and board of appeals caused substantial damage to the relator, to be germane to this appeal. Such issue must be raised by certiorari as provided by subd. (f) of sec. 62.23(6), Stats.

Judgment affirmed.

NOTES

1. An official street map ordinance precludes the erection of a building within a 25-foot strip along the front of X's lot. A zoning ordinance area requirement precludes the erection of a building within a 25-foot strip along the front of Y's lot. In separate suits, X and Y assert the invalidity of these ordinances. Will the same arguments be

relevant in both actions? See Gorieb v. Fox, 274 U.S. 603, 47 S.Ct. 675, 71 L.Ed. 1228 (1927).

2. "It has long been well settled that the mere plotting of a *street* upon a city plan without anything more does not constitute a taking of land in a constitutional sense so as to give an abutting owner the right to have damages assessed. The doctrine is said to be founded upon equitable considerations and a wise public policy. . . . Shall this principle relating to streets, which are narrow, well defined and absolutely necessary, be extended to parks and playgrounds which may be very large and very desirable but not necessary?" Miller v. City of Beaver Falls, 368 Pa. 189, 82 A.2d 34 (1951) (giving a negative answer to its question.)

LOMARCH CORP. v. MAYOR AND COMMON COUNCIL OF CITY OF ENGLEWOOD

Supreme Court of New Jersey, 1968.
51 N.J. 108, 237 A.2d 881.

HANEMAN, J. This action in lieu of prerogative writs tests the constitutionality of N.J.S.A. 40:55–1.32 and N.J.S.A. 40:55–1.38, a part of what is commonly known as the Official Map Act, as well as an ordinance adopted by the Common Council of Englewood pursuant thereto. The Law Division found the Act unconstitutional and the defendant appealed to the Appellant Division. While pending there we certified the case on motion of both parties. R.R. 1:10–1A.

In April of 1967, plaintiff, who was and is the owner of some sixteen acres situate in Englewood, applied for approval of its plans to subdivide the property in order to construct single family dwellings. While consideration of the application was pending, the Common Council of Englewood adopted what is Ordinance # 1724 pursuant to N.J.S.A. 40:55–1.32 and N.J.S.A. 40:55–1.34 which placed the land on the Official Map of the City and designated it land reserved for use as a park.

N.J.S.A. 40:55–1.32 provides that a municipality may designate land uses upon an official map and that

". . . Upon the application for approval of a plat, the municipality may reserve for future public use the location and extent of public parks and playgrounds shown on the official map, or any part thereof and within the area of said plat for a period of one year after the approval of the final plat or within such further time as agreed to by the applying party. Unless within such one year period or extension thereof the municipality shall have entered into a contract to purchase, or instituted condemnation proceedings, for said park or playground according to law, such applying party shall not be bound to observe the reservation of such public parks or playgrounds. During such period of one year or any extension thereof the applicant for the plat approval, and his assigns and successors in interest, may use the area so reserved for any purpose other than the location of buildings or improvements thereon, except as provided in [N.J.S.A. 40:55–1.38]."

Read in connection with N.J.S.A. 40:55–132, the practical effect of the ordinance was to "freeze", for a one year period, any attempt to develop the designated land.

On May 23, 1967 plaintiff's subdivision plan was granted initial approval. At the same time plaintiff was notified by letter that the land in question had been reserved for park land acquisition. Subsequently, the resolution granting final approval provided

"The approval granted by this Resolution does not in any way obligate the City of Englewood, and the applicant is acting solely at its own peril since the applicant is on notice that this property has been reserved by the City of Englewood on the offical map under the Green Acres Program and the applicable Statutes of the State of New Jersey."

Eight days before final approval was granted, plaintiff brought this suit to challenge the statutory authority by which it had been denied the right to develop its lands for a period of one year. Such a denial it argues constitutes a taking of property without compensation as the statute makes no provision for payment and therefore violates both the Fourteenth Amendment to the Federal Constitution and Art. I ¶ 20 of the State Constitution. The defendant denies that the statute violates the constitutional prohibitions and further argues that plaintiff is prevented from bringing the suit, since it has not availed itself of the relief provisions of the Act (N.J.S.A. 40:55–1.38) which provides:

"For the purpose of preserving the integrity of the official map of a municipality, no permit shall be issued for any building in the bed of any street or drainage right of way shown on the official map, or on a plat filed pursuant to the Municipal Planning Act (1953) before adoption of the official map, except as herein provided. Whenever one or more parcels of land upon which is located the bed of such a mapped street or drainage right of way, or any park or playground location reserved pursuant to [n.j.s.a. 40:55–1.32] hereof, cannot yield a reasonable return to the owner unless a building permit be granted, the board of adjustment, in any municipality which has established such a board, may, in a specific case by the vote of a majority of its members, grant a permit for a building in the bed of such mapped street or drainage right of way or within such reserved location of a public park or playground, which will as little as practicable increase the cost of opening such street, or tend to cause a minimum change of the official map, and the board shall impose reasonable requirements as a condition of granting the permit, so as to promote the health, morals, safety and general welfare of the public and shall inure to the benefit of the municipality. In any municipality in which there is no board of adjustment, the governing body shall have the same powers and be subject to the same restrictions as provided in this section."

Plaintiff's answer is that this provision is inadequate and cannot serve to save the statutory scheme. We agree that the above provision pays but token service to the landowner's right to use his land and is of little practical value. . . .

In construing a statute the presumption is that the legislature acted with existing constitutional law in mind and intended the act to function in a constitutional manner. Jardine v. Borough of Rumson, 30 N.J.Super. 509, 105 A.2d 420 (App.Div.1954). Thus, it follows, in light of our decision in Morris County Land Improvement Co. v. Parsippany-Troy Hills Tp., 40 N.J. 539, 193 A.2d 232 (1963), that the legislature understood that any attempt to deprive a landowner of the use of his property for one year would be unconstitutional absent an intent to compensate the landowner.

The question now becomes whether that intent need be explicitly set forth in the statutory language. A statute oftens speaks as plainly by inference as by express words. Juzek v. Hackensack Water Co., 48 N.J. 302, 225 A.2d 335 (1966). The details for the accomplishment of a statutory objective do not have to be specifically spelled out with particularity. It is not always essential in order to avoid unconstitutionality that provisions to insure compliance with the Federal or State constitution be spelled out in detail. Whenever the legislature authorizes municipal action which, if taken, would require, under the Constitution, that just compensation be paid, it follows that if the municipality wishes to exercise that power it must comply with the constitutional mandate and pay. The statute is not constitutionally defective for failure to expressly provide for compensation.

Consonant with the foregoing, we conclude that the "option" for the purchase of land upon the unilateral action of the municipality without any consensual action of the landowner, was statutorily granted to the municipality only upon the implied duty and obligation to make payment of adequate compensation to the landowner for the temporary taking and his deprivation of use.

Although the question is not formally before us, in anticipation of further proceedings concerning the establishment of reasonable compensation to plaintiff for this taking and for future guidance of the parties, we suggest that fair compensation would be attained in the following manner: The landowner should receive the value of an "option" to purchase the land for the year. The "option" price should, among other features, reflect the amount of taxes accruing during the "option" period. This sum can be established by expert advice and opinion. If the municipality decides to purchase the lands, he shall be compensated, not only for the value of the land, but for reasonable amount of engineering expenses necessarily incurred in connection with obtaining municipal approval of the plat. If the municipality does not eventually take title no compensation shall be made for such expenses as the landowner has the continued benefit thereof.

Judgment reversed. Costs to plaintiff.

NOTE

Compare Metro Realty v. County of El Dorado, 222 Cal.App.2d 508, 35 Cal.Rptr. 480 (1963), upholding a county ordinance prohibiting subdivision and construction of buildings for a period of from one to three years within thirty-one potential reservoir sites being studied. The court said: "It appears to us that plaintiff in blaming defendant's ordinance for his asserted hardship forgets that it is not just the ordinance but the fact that a plan is under contemplation which, if adopted, will place plaintiff's lands beneath a dam or under water that causes the depression in value to such lands for the time being."

SECTION 4. PUBLIC OWNERSHIP

Public ownership of land is a means for controlling or influencing development of land in private ownership. The siting of public facilities such as schools, parks, highways, points of access to limited-access highways, and water and sewer mains exerts strong, often compelling, influence upon the nature and timing of development of private lands. A more direct approach is acquisition by the regulating government of title to the land to be regulated and subsequent conveyance of that land with restrictions to private grantees. A constitutional issue posed by this approach is addressed in the following case.

HAWAII HOUSING AUTHORITY v. MIDKIFF

Supreme Court of the United States, 1984.
467 U.S. 229, 104 S.Ct. 2321, 81 L.Ed.2d 186.

JUSTICE O'CONNOR delivered the opinion of the Court.

The Fifth Amendment of the United States Constitution provides, in pertinent part, that "private property [shall not] be taken for public use, without just compensation." These cases present the question whether the Public Use Clause of that Amendment, made applicable to the States through the Fourteenth Amendment, prohibits the State of Hawaii from taking, with just compensation, title in real property from lessors and transferring it to lessees in order to reduce the concentration of ownership of fees simple in the State. We conclude that it does not.

The Hawaiian Islands were originally settled by Polynesian immigrants from the western Pacific. These settlers developed an economy around a feudal land tenure system in which one island high chief, the ali'i nui, controlled the land and assigned it for development to certain subchiefs. The subchiefs would then reassign the land to other lower ranking chiefs, who would administer the land and govern the farmers and other tenants working it. All land was held at the will of the ali'i nui and eventually had to be returned to his trust. There was no private ownership of land.

Beginning in the early 1800's, Hawaiian leaders and American settlers repeatedly attempted to divide the lands of the kingdom among the crown, the chiefs, and the common people. These efforts proved largely unsuccessful, however, and the land remained in the hands of a few. In the mid-1960's, after extensive hearings, the Hawaii Legislature discovered that, while the State and Federal Governments owned almost 49% of the State's land, another 47% was in the hands of only 72 private landowners. The legislature further found that 18 landholders, with tracts of 21,000 acres or more, owned more than 40% of this land and that on Oahu, the most urbanized of the islands, 22 landowners owned 72.5% of the fee simple titles. The legislature concluded that concentrated land ownership was responsible for skewing the State's residential fee simple market, inflating land prices, and injuring the public tranquility and welfare.

To redress these problems, the legislature decided to compel the large landowners to break up their estates. The legislature considered requiring large landowners to sell lands which they were leasing to homeowners. However, the landowners strongly resisted this scheme, pointing out the significant federal tax liabilities they would incur. Indeed, the landowners claimed that the federal tax laws were the primary reason they previously had chosen to lease, and not sell, their lands. Therefore, to accommodate the needs of both lessors and lessees, the Hawaii Legislature enacted the Land Reform Act of 1967 (Act), Haw.Rev.Stat., ch. 516, which created a mechanism for condemning residential tracts and for transferring ownership of the condemned fees simple to existing lessees. By condemning the land in question, the Hawaii Legislature intended to make the land sales involuntary, thereby making the federal tax consequences less severe while still facilitating the redistribution of fees simple.

Under the Act's condemnation scheme, tenants living on single-family residential lots within developmental tracts at least five acres in size are entitled to ask the Hawaii Housing Authority (HHA) to condemn the property on which they live. Haw.Rev.Stat. §§ 516–1(2), (11), 516–22 (1977). When 25 eligible tenants,[1] or tenants on half the lots in the tract, whichever is less, file appropriate applications, the Act authorizes HHA to hold a public hearing to determine whether acquisition by the State of all or part of the tract will "effectuate the public purposes" of the Act. § 516–22. If HHA finds that these public purposes will be served, it is authorized to designate some or all of the lots in the tract for acquisition. It then acquires, at prices set either by condemnation trial or by negotiation between lessors and lessees, the former fee owners' full "right, title, and interest" in the land. § 516–25.

After compensation has been set, HHA may sell the land titles to tenants who have applied for fee simple ownership. HHA is authorized to lend these tenants up to 90% of the purchase price, and it may condition final transfer on a right of first refusal for the first 10 years following sale. §§ 516–30, 516–34, 516–35. If HHA does not sell the lot to the tenant residing there, it may lease the lot or sell it to someone else, provided that public notice has been given. § 516–28. However, HHA may not sell to any one purchaser, or lease to any one tenant, more than one lot, and it may not operate for profit. §§ 516–28, 516–

1. An eligible tenant is one who, among other things, owns a house on the lot, has a bona fide intent to live on the lot or be a resident of the State, shows proof of ability to pay for a fee interest in it, and does not own residential land elsewhere nearby. Haw.Rev.Stat. §§ 516–33(3), (4), (7) (1977).

32. In practice, funds to satisfy the condemnation awards have been supplied entirely by lessees. See App. 164. While the Act authorizes HHA to issue bonds and appropriate funds for acquisition, no bonds have issued and HHA has not supplied any funds for condemned lots. See ibid.

In April 1977, HHA held a public hearing concerning the proposed acquisition of some of appellees' lands. HHA made the statutorily required finding that acquisition of appellees' lands would effectuate the public purposes of the Act. Then, in October 1978, it directed appellees to negotiate with certain lessees concerning the sale of the designated properties. Those negotiations failed, and HHA subsequently ordered appellees to submit to compulsory arbitration.

Rather than comply with the compulsory arbitration order, appellees filed suit, in February 1979, in United States District Court, asking that the Act be declared unconstitutional and that its enforcement be enjoined. The District Court temporarily restrained the State from proceeding against appellees' estates. Three months later, while declaring the compulsory arbitration and compensation formulae provisions of the Act unconstitutional,[3] the District Court refused preliminarily to enjoin appellants from conducting the statutory designation and condemnation proceedings. Finally, in December 1979, it granted partial summary judgment to appellants, holding the remaining portion of the Act constitutional under the Public Use Clause. See 483 F.Supp. 62 (Haw.1979). The District Court found that the Act's goals were within the bounds of the State's police powers and that the means the legislature had chosen to serve those goals were not arbitrary, capricious, or selected in bad faith.

The Court of Appeals for the Ninth Circuit reversed. 702 F.2d 788 (CA9 1983). First, the Court of Appeals decided that the District Court had permissibly chosen not to abstain from the exercise of its jurisdiction. Then, the Court of Appeals determined that the Act could not pass the requisite judicial scrutiny of the Public Use Clause. It found that the transfers contemplated by the Act were unlike those of takings previously held to constitute "public uses" by this Court. The court further determined that the public purposes offered by the Hawaii Legislature were not deserving of judicial deference. The court concluded that the Act was simply "a naked attempt on the part of the state of Hawaii to take the private property of A and transfer it to B solely for B's private use and benefit." Id., at 798. One judge dissented.

On applications of HHA and certain private appellants who had intervened below, this Court noted probable jurisdiction. 464 U.S. 932, 104 S.Ct. 334, 78 L.Ed.2d 304 (1983). We now reverse.

3. As originally enacted, lessor and lessee had to commence compulsory arbitration if they could not agree on a price for the fee simple title. Statutory formulae were provided for the determination of compensation. The District Court declared both the compulsory arbitration provision and the compensation formulae unconstitutional. No appeal was taken from these rulings, and the Hawaii Legislature subsequently amended the statute to provide only for mandatory negotiation and for advisory compensation formulae. These issues are not before us.

We begin with the question whether the District Court abused its discretion in not abstaining from the exercise of its jurisdiction. . . . We do not believe that abstention was required.

. . .

The majority of the Court of Appeals next determined that the Act violates the "public use" requirement of the Fifth and Fourteenth Amendments. On this argument, however, we find ourselves in agreement with the dissenting judge in the Court of Appeals.

The starting point for our analysis of the Act's constitutionality is the Court's decision in Berman v. Parker, 348 U.S. 26, 75 S.Ct. 98, 99 L.Ed. 27 (1954). In *Berman,* the Court held constitutional the District of Columbia Redevelopment Act of 1945. That Act provided both for the comprehensive use of the eminent domain power to redevelop slum areas and for the possible sale or lease of the condemned lands to private interests. In discussing whether the takings authorized by that Act were for a "public use," id., at 31, 75 S.Ct., at 101, the Court stated:

> "We deal, in other words, with what traditionally has been known as the police power. An attempt to define its reach or trace its outer limits is fruitless, for each case must turn on its own facts. The definition is essentially the product of legislative determinations addressed to the purposes of government, purposes neither abstractly nor historically capable of complete definition. Subject to specific constitutional limitations, when the legislature has spoken, the public interest has been declared in terms well-nigh conclusive. In such cases the legislature, not the judiciary, is the main guardian of the public needs to be served by social legislation, whether it be Congress legislating concerning the District of Columbia . . . or the States legislating concerning local affairs. . . . This principle admits of no exception merely because the power of eminent domain is involved. . . ." Id., at 32, 75 S.Ct., at 102 (citations omitted).

The Court explicitly recognized the breadth of the principle it was announcing, noting:

> "Once the object is within the authority of Congress, the right to realize it through the exercise of eminent domain is clear. For the power of eminent domain is merely the means to the end. . . . Once the object is within the authority of Congress, the means by which it will be attained is also for Congress to determine. Here one of the means chosen is the use of private enterprise for redevelopment of the area. Appellants argue that this makes the project a taking from one businessman for the benefit of another businessman. But the means of executing the project are for Congress and Congress alone to determine, once the public purpose has been established." Id., at 33, 75 S.Ct. at 102.

The "public use" requirement is thus coterminous with the scope of a sovereign's police powers.

There is, of course, a role for courts to play in reviewing a legislature's judgment of what constitutes a public use, even when the eminent domain power is equated with the police power. But the Court in *Berman* made clear that it is "an extremely narrow" one. Id., at 32, 75 S.Ct., at 102. The Court in *Berman* cited with approval the Court's decision in Old Dominion Co. v. United States, 269 U.S. 55, 66, 46 S.Ct. 39, 40, 70 L.Ed. 162 (1925), which held that deference to the legislature's "public use" determination is required "until it is shown to involve an impossibility." The *Berman* Court also cited to United States ex rel. TVA v. Welch, 327 U.S. 546, 552, 66 S.Ct. 715, 718, 90 L.Ed. 843 (1946), which emphasized that "[a]ny departure from this judicial restraint would result in courts deciding on what is and is not a governmental function and in their invalidating legislation on the basis of their view on that question at the moment of decision, a practice which has proved impracticable in other fields." In short, the Court has made clear that it will not substitute its judgment for a legislature's judgment as to what constitutes a public use "unless the use be palpably without reasonable foundation." United States v. Gettysburg Electric R. Co., 160 U.S. 668, 680, 16 S.Ct. 427, 429, 40 L.Ed. 576 (1896).

To be sure, the Court's cases have repeatedly stated that "one person's property may not be taken for the benefit of another private person without a justifying public purpose, even though compensation be paid." Thompson v. Consolidated Gas Corp., 300 U.S. 55, 80, 57 S.Ct. 364, 376, 81 L.Ed. 510 (1937). Thus, in Missouri Pacific R. Co. v. Nebraska, 164 U.S. 403, 17 S.Ct. 130, 41 L.Ed. 489 (1896), where the "order in question was not, *and was not claimed to be,* . . . a taking of private property for a public use under the right of eminent domain," id., at 416, at 135 (emphasis added), the Court invalidated a compensated taking of property for lack of a justifying public purpose. But where the exercise of the eminent domain power is rationally related to a conceivable public purpose, the Court has never held a compensated taking to be proscribed by the Public Use Clause.

On this basis, we have no trouble concluding that the Hawaii Act is constitutional. . . . Regulating oligopoly and the evils associated with it is a classic exercise of a State's police powers. We cannot disapprove of Hawaii's exercise of this power.

Nor can we condemn as irrational the Act's approach to correcting the land oligopoly problem. The Act presumes that when a sufficiently large number of persons declare that they are willing but unable to buy lots at fair prices the land market is malfunctioning. When such a malfunction is signalled, the Act authorizes HHA to condemn lots in the relevant tract. The Act limits the number of lots any one tenant can purchase and authorizes HHA to use public funds to ensure that the market dilution goals will be achieved. This is a comprehensive and rational approach to identifying and correcting market failure.

Of course, this Act, like any other, may not be successful in achieving its intended goals. . . . When the legislature's purpose is legitimate and its means are not irrational, our cases make clear that empirical debates over the wisdom of takings—no less than debates over the wisdom of other kinds of socioeconomic legislation—are not to be carried out in the federal courts. Redistribution of fees simple to correct deficiencies in the market determined by the state legislature to be attributable to land oligopoly is a rational exercise of the eminent domain power. Therefore, the Hawaii statute must pass the scrutiny of the Public Use Clause.[6]

The Court of Appeals read our cases to stand for a much narrower proposition. First, it read our "public use" cases, especially *Berman,* as requiring that government possess and use property at some point during a taking. Since Hawaiian lessees retain possession of the property for private use throughout the condemnation process, the court found that the Act exacted takings for private use. 702 F.2d, at 796–797. Second, it determined that these cases involved only "the review of . . . *congressional* determination[s] that there was a public use, *not* the review of . . . state legislative determination[s]." Id., at 798 (emphasis in original). Because state legislative determinations are involved in the instant cases, the Court of Appeals decided that more rigorous judicial scrutiny of the public use determinations was appropriate. The court concluded that the Hawaii Legislature's professed purposes were mere "statutory rationalizations." Ibid. We disagree with the Court of Appeals' analysis.

The mere fact that property taken outright by eminent domain is transferred in the first instance to private beneficiaries does not condemn that taking as having only a private purpose. The Court long ago rejected any literal requirement that condemned property be put into use for the general public. "It is not essential that the entire community, nor even any considerable portion, . . . directly enjoy or participate in any improvement in order [for it] to constitute a public use." Rindge Co. v. Los Angeles, 262 U.S., at 707, 43 S.Ct., at 692. "[W]hat in its immediate aspect [is] only a private transaction may . . . be raised by its class or character to a public affair." Block v. Hirsh, 256 U.S., at 155, 41 S.Ct., at 459. As the unique way titles were held in Hawaii skewed the land market, exercise of the power of eminent domain was justified. The Act advances its purposes without the State's taking actual possession of the land. In such cases, government does not itself have to use property to legitimate the taking; it is only the taking's purpose, and not its mechanics, that must pass scrutiny under the Public Use Clause.

Similarly, the fact that a state legislature, and not the Congress, made the public use determination does not mean that judicial deference is less appropriate.[7] Judicial deference is required because, in our system of government, legislatures are better able to assess what public

6. We similarly find no merit in appellees' Due Process and Contract Clause arguments. The argument that due process prohibits allowing lessees to initiate the taking process was essentially rejected by this Court in New Motor Vehicle Board v. Fox Co., 439 U.S. 96, 108–109, 99 S.Ct. 403, 411–412, 58 L.Ed.2d 361 (1978). Similarly, the Contract Clause has never been thought to protect against the exercise of the power of eminent domain. See United States Trust Co. v. New Jersey, 431 U.S. 1, 19, and n. 16, 97 S.Ct. 1505, 1516, and n. 16, 52 L.Ed.2d 92 (1977).

7. It is worth noting that the Fourteenth Amendment does not itself contain an independent "public use" requirement. Rather, that requirement is made binding on the States only by incorporation of the Fifth Amendment's Eminent Domain Clause through the Fourteenth Amendment's Due Process Clause. See Chicago, B. & Q.R. Co. v. Chicago, 166 U.S. 226, 17 S.Ct. 581, 41 L.Ed. 979 (1897). It would be

purposes should be advanced by an exercise of the taking power. State legislatures are as capable as Congress of making such determinations within their respective spheres of authority. Thus, if a legislature, state or federal, determines there are substantial reasons for an exercise of the taking power, courts must defer to its determination that the taking will serve a public use.

The State of Hawaii has never denied that the Constitution forbids even a compensated taking of property when executed for no reason other than to confer a private benefit on a particular private party. A purely private taking could not withstand the scrutiny of the public use requirement; it would serve no legitimate purpose of government and would thus be void. But no purely private taking is involved in these cases. The Hawaii Legislature enacted its Land Reform Act not to benefit a particular class of identifiable individuals but to attack certain perceived evils of concentrated property ownership in Hawaii—a legitimate public purpose. Use of the condemnation power to achieve this purpose is not irrational. Since we assume for purposes of these appeals that the weighty demand of just compensation has been met, the requirements of the Fifth and Fourteenth Amendments have been satisfied. Accordingly, we reverse the judgment of the Court of Appeals, and remand these cases for further proceedings in conformity with this opinion.

It is so ordered.

NOTE

Similar provisions in state constitutions may be construed by state courts similarly to, or differently from, construction of the Fifth Amendment taking clause by the United States Supreme Court. Compare the following cases. Poletown Neighborhood Council v. City of Detroit, 410 Mich. 616, 304 N.W.2d 455 (1981), allowed the City of Detroit to condemn private land for the purpose of transferring it to General Motors Corporation for use as an industrial plant. Two judges dissented. The court said: "The power of eminent domain is to be used in this instance primarily to accomplish the essential public purposes of alleviating unemployment and revitalizing the economic base of the community. The benefit to a private interest is merely incidental." In re City of Seattle, 96 Wn.2d 616, 638 P.2d 549 (1981), disapproved condemnation by the city of land to be transferred to private owners for retail commercial uses, even though a stated purpose was to forestall inner-city decay and the land was to be developed according to a plan approved by the city containing a public park, other public open spaces, a public parking garage, a monorail terminal, and an art museum. Three judges dissented. The court said: "If a private use is combined with a public use in such a way that the two cannot be separated, the right of eminent domain cannot be invoked."

ironic to find that state legislation is subject to greater scrutiny under the incorporated "public use" requirement than is congressional legislation under the express mandate of the Fifth Amendment.

Chapter 19

ADMINISTRATION OF LAND USE CONTROLS

SECTION 1. NONCONFORMING USES

Consider the status of land uses that are not allowed in the zoning district in which they are situated, but existed prior to that zoning, such as a gasoline station in a neighborhood zoned for residential use. Most zoning ordinances allow existing nonconforming uses to continue, but burden such uses with restrictions designed to bring about their eventual termination. They commonly limit both expansion of a nonconforming use and substantial alteration of facilities associated with it. Thus, an owner of a nonconforming gasoline station might not be permitted to enlarge the structure so as to accommodate additional pumps. This could lead to unprofitability of the enterprise and closing of the station. If, after a change in demand for gasoline, the owner decided to reopen the station, it is likely that a provision of the zoning ordinance forbidding resumption of abandoned nonconforming uses would thwart the owner's plan. Such ordinance provisions are usually upheld by the courts, but many cases have raised issues concerning their application. Some ordinances contain amortization provisions, requiring termination of certain types of nonconforming uses, typically billboards and junkyards, after lapse of a stated period of time. Judicial reaction to amortization of nonconforming uses has varied.

CITY OF LOS ANGELES v. GAGE

District Court of Appeal, California, 1954.
127 Cal.App.2d 538, 274 P.2d 34.

VALLEE, JUSTICE. This appeal involves the constitutionality of the provisions of a zoning ordinance which require that certain nonconforming existing uses shall be discontinued within five years after its passage, as they apply to defendants' property.

Plaintiff brought this suit for an injunction to command defendants to discontinue their use of certain property for the conduct of a plumbing business and to remove various materials therefrom, and to restrain them from using the property for any purpose not permitted by the comprehensive zoning plan provisions of the Los Angeles Municipal Code. The cause was submitted to the trial court on admissions in the pleadings and a stipulation of facts. Defendants will be referred to as "Gage."

In 1930 Gage acquired adjoining lots 220 and 221 located on Cochran Avenue in Los Angeles. He constructed a two-family residential building on lot 221 and rented the upper half solely for residential purposes. He established a wholesale and retail plumbing supply business on the property. He used a room in the lower half of the residential building on lot 221 as the office for the conduct of the business, and the rest of the lower half for residential purposes for himself and his family; he used a garage on lot 221 for the storage of plumbing supplies and materials; and he constructed and used racks, bins, and stalls for the storage of such supplies and materials on lot 220. Later Gage incorporated defendant company. The realty and the assets of the plumbing business were transferred to the company. The case is presented as though the property had been owned continuously from 1930 to date by the same defendant. The use of lots 220 and 221 begun in 1930, has been substantially the same at all times since.

In 1930 the two lots and other property facing on Cochran Avenue in their vicinity were classified in "C" zone by the zoning ordinance then in effect. Under this classification the use to which Gage put the property was permitted. Shortly after Gage acquired lots 220 and 221, they were classified in "C–3" zone and the use to which he put the property was expressly permitted. In 1936 the city council of the city passed Ordinance 77,000 which contained a comprehensive zoning plan for the city. Ordinance 77,000 re-enacted the prior ordinances with respect to the use of lots 220 and 221. In 1941 the city council passed Ordinance 85,015 by the terms of which the use of a residential building for the conduct of an office in connection with the plumbing supply business was permitted. Ordinance 85,015 prohibited the open storage of materials in zone "C–3" but permitted such uses as had been established to continue as nonconforming uses. The use to which lots 220 and 221 were put by defendants was a nonconforming use that might be continued. In 1946 the city council passed Ordinance 90,500. This ordinance reclassified lots 220 and 221 and other property fronting on Cochran Avenue in their vicinity from zone "C–3" to zone "R–4" (Multiple dwelling zone). Use of lots 220 and 221 for the conduct of a plumbing business was not permitted in zone "R–4." At the time Ordinance 90,500 was passed, and at all times since, the Los Angeles Municipal Code (§ 12.23 B & C) provided: "(a) The nonconforming use of a conforming building or structure may be continued, except that in the 'R' Zones any nonconforming commercial or industrial use of a residential building or residential accessory building shall be discontinued within five (5) years from June 1, 1946, or five (5) years from the date the use becomes nonconforming, whichever date is later. . . .

"(a) The nonconforming use of land shall be discontinued within five (5) years from June 1, 1946, or within five (5) years from the date the use became nonconforming, in each of the following cases: (1) where no buildings are employed in connection with such use; (2) where the only buildings employed are accessory or incidental to such use; (3) where such use is maintained in connection with a conforming building."

Prior to the passage of Ordinance 90,500 about 50% of the city had been zoned. It was the first ordinance which "attempted to zone the entire corporate limits of the city." Prior to its passage, several thousand exceptions and variances were granted from restrictive provisions of prior ordinances, some of which permitted commercial use of property zoned for residential use, "and in some cases permitted the use of land for particular purposes like or similar to use of subject property which otherwise would have been prohibited." Under Ordinance 90,500, the uses permitted by these exceptions and variances that did not carry a time limit may be continued indefinitely.

The business conducted by Gage on the property has produced a gross revenue varying between $125,000 and $350,000 a year. If he is required to abandon the use of the property for his business, he will be put to the following expenses: "(1) The value of a suitable site for the conduct of its business would be about $10,000, which would be offset by the value of $7,500 of the lot now used. (2) The cost incident to removing of supplies to another location and construction of the necessary racks, sheds, bins and stalls which would be about $2,500. (3) The cost necessary to expend to advertise a new location. (4) The risk of a gain or a loss of business while moving, and the cost necessary to reestablish the business at a new location, the amount of which is uncertain."

The noise and disturbance caused by the loading and unloading of supplies, trucking, and the going and coming of workmen in connection with the operation of a plumbing business with an open storage yard is greater than the noise and disturbance that is normal in a district used solely for residential purposes.

The court found: the business conducted by Gage has a substantial value; he could not, either prior to June 1, 1951, or at any time thereafter or in the future, remove the business without substantial loss or expense; the value of Gage's property has not been increased or stabilized by the passage of Ordinance 90,500, nor will observance or enforcement of the ordinance increase the value of the property; the use of the property for the purpose that it has been used continuously since 1930 will not adversely and detrimentally affect the use or value of other property in the neighborhood thereof; the use to which the property has been put by Gage has not been unsanitary, unsightly, noisy, or otherwise incompatible with the legal uses of adjoining property; Gage has not, nor will he in the future, operate to disturb the peace and quiet of the residents of the neighborhood as long as the property is operated substantially as it was operated at the date of the filing of the complaint; the use to which the property has been put does not interfere with the lawful and reasonable use of the streets and alleys in the vicinity by the residents in the neighborhood or others entitled thereto.

The court concluded: Gage became vested with the right to use the property for the purpose that it was used; insofar as the Los Angeles Municipal Code purports to require the abandonment of the use of the building on lot 221 as an office for the plumbing and plumbing supply business or the use of lot 220 for the open storage of plumbing supplies in the manner that it has been and is being used by Gage, it is void and of no legal effect; Ordinance 90,500 is void insofar as it affects Gage's use of the property in that it deprives him of a vested right to use the property for the purpose it has been used continuously since 1930 and deprives him of property without due process of law. Judgment was that plaintiff take nothing. Plaintiff appeals.

Plaintiff contends that the mandatory discontinuance of a nonconforming use after a fixed period is a reasonable exercise of the police power, and that on the agreed facts the Los Angeles ordinance is a valid exercise of such power as applied to Gage's property. Gage does not question the validity of the ordinance as a whole, but he contends it may not be constitutionally applied to require the removal of his existing business. He asserts that under Jones v. City of Los Angeles, 211 Cal. 304, 295 P. 14, the decision of the trial court was correct. . . .

A nonconforming use is a lawful use existing on the effective date of the zoning restriction and continuing since that time in nonconformance to the ordinance. A provision permitting the continuance of a nonconforming use is ordinarily included in zoning ordinances because of the hardship and doubtful constitutionality of compelling the immediate discontinuance of nonconforming uses. . . . It is generally held that a zoning ordinance may not operate to immediately suppress or remove from a particular district an otherwise lawful business or use already established therein. 58 Am.Jur. 1022, § 148.

No case seems to have been decided in this state squarely involving the precise question presented in the case at bar. Until recently zoning ordinances have made no provision for any systematic and comprehensive elimination of the nonconforming use. The expectation seems to have been that existing nonconforming uses would be of little consequence and that they would eventually disappear. See 9 Minn.L.Rev. 593, 598. The contrary appears to be the case, 35 Va.L.Rev. 348, 352; Wis.L.Rev. (1951) 685; 99 Univ.Pa.L.Rev. 1019, 1021. It is said that the fundamental problem facing zoning is the inability to eliminate the nonconforming use. 17 Ill.Munic.Rev. 221, 232. The general purpose of present-day zoning ordinances is to eventually end all nonconforming uses. Ricciardi v. County of Los Angeles, 115 Cal.App.2d 569, 576, 252 P.2d 773. There is a growing tendency to guard against the indefinite continuance of nonconforming uses by providing for their liquidation within a prescribed period. County of San Diego v. McClurken, 37 Cal. 2d 683, 686, 234 P.2d 972. It is said, "The only positive method of getting rid of nonconforming uses yet devised is to amortize a nonconforming building. That is, to determine the normal useful remaining life of the building and prohibit the owner from maintaining it after the expiration of that time." Crolly and Norton, Termination of Nonconforming Uses, 62 Zoning Bulletin 1, Regional Plan Assn., June 1952.

Amortization of nonconforming uses has been expressly authorized by recent amendments to zoning enabling laws in a number of states. Ordinances providing for amortization of nonconforming uses have been passed in a number of large cities. The length of time given the owner to eliminate his nonconforming use or building varies with the city and with the type of structure. . . .

Exercise of the police power frequently impairs rights in property because the exercise of those rights is detrimental to the public interest.

Every zoning ordinance effects some impairment of vested rights either by restricting prospective uses or by prohibiting the continuation of existing uses, because it affects property already owned by individuals at the time of its enactment. People v. Miller, 304 N.Y. 105, 106 N.E.2d 34, 35. In essence there is no distinction between requiring the discontinuance of a nonconforming use within a reasonable period and provisions which deny the right to add to or extend buildings devoted to an existing nonconforming use, which deny the right to resume a nonconforming use after a period of nonuse, which deny the right to extend or enlarge an existing nonconforming use, which deny the right to substitute new buildings for those devoted to an existing nonconforming use—all of which have been held to be valid exercises of the police power. See County of Orange v. Goldring, 121 Cal.App.2d 442, 263 P.2d 321; 58 Am.Jur. 1026, 1029, §§ 156, 158, 162; annotation 147 A.L.R. 167; 1 Yokley, Zoning Law and Practice, 2d ed., §§ 151–157.

The distinction between an ordinance restricting future uses and one requiring the termination of present uses within a reasonable period of time is merely one of degree, and constitutionality depends on the relative importance to be given to the public gain and to the private loss. Zoning as it affects every piece of property is to some extent retroactive in that it applies to property already owned at the time of the effective date of the ordinance. The elimination of existing uses within a reasonable time does not amount to a taking of property nor does it necessarily restrict the use of property so that it cannot be used for any reasonable purpose. Use of a reasonable amortization scheme provides an equitable means of reconciliation of the conflicting interests in satisfaction of due process requirements. As a method of eliminating existing nonconforming uses it allows the owner of the nonconforming use, by affording an opportunity to make new plans, at least partially to offset any loss he might suffer. The loss he suffers, if any, is spread out over a period of years, and he enjoys a monopolistic position by virtue of the zoning ordinance as long as he remains. If the amortization period is reasonable the loss to the owner may be small when compared with the benefit to the public. Nonconforming uses will eventually be eliminated. A legislative body may well conclude that the beneficial effect on the community of the eventual elimination of all nonconforming uses by a reasonable amortization plan more than offsets individual losses.

The ordinance in question provides, according to a graduated periodic schedule, for the gradual and ultimate elimination of all commercial and industrial uses in residential zones. These provisions require the discontinuance of nonconforming uses of land within a five-year period, and the discontinuance of nonconforming commercial and industrial uses of residential buildings in the "R" zones within the same five-year period. These provisions are the only ones pertinent to the decision in this case. However, it may be noted that other provisions of the ordinance require the discontinuance of nonconforming billboards and, in residential zones, the discontinuance of nonconforming buildings and of nonconforming uses of nonconforming buildings, within specified periods running from 20 to 40 years according to the type of building construction.

We have no doubt that Ordinance 90,500, in compelling the discontinuance of the use of defendants' property for a wholesale and retail plumbing and plumbing supply business, and for the open storage of plumbing supplies within five years after its passage, is a valid exercise of the police power. Lots 220 and 221 are several blocks from a business center and it appears that they are not within any reasonable or logical extension of such a center. The ordinance does not prevent the operation of defendants' business; it merely restricts its location. Discontinuance of the nonconforming use requires only that Gage move his plumbing business to property that is zoned for it. Such property can be found within a half mile of Gage's property. The cost of moving is $5,000, or less than 1% of Gage's minimum gross business for five years, or less than half of 1% of the mean of his gross business for five years. He has had eight years within which to move. The property is usable for residential purpose. Since 1930 lot 221 has been used for residential purposes. All of the land within 500 feet of Gage's property is now improved and used for such purposes. Lot 220, now unimproved, can be improved for the same purposes.

We think it apparent that none of the agreed facts and none of the ultimate facts found by the court justify the conclusion that Ordinance 90,500, as applied to Gage's property, is clearly arbitrary or unreasonable, or has no substantial relation to the public's health, safety, morals, or general welfare, or that it is an unconstitutional impairment of his property rights.

It is enough for us to determine and we determine only that Ordinance 90,500 of the city of Los Angeles, insofar as it required the discontinuance of Gage's wholesale and retail plumbing business on lots 220 and 221 within five years from the date of its passage, is a constitutional exercise of the police power.

The judgment is reversed, and the superior court is directed to render judgment for plaintiff as prayed for in the complaint.

SHINN, P.J. and PARKER WOOD, J., concur.

NOTES

1. Some courts regard amortization of nonconforming uses, under any circumstances, as unconstitutional. E.g., Ailes v. Decatur County Area Planning Commission, 448 N.E.2d 1057 (Ind.1983). That court reasoned: "The factors to be considered [by courts approving amortization regulations if reasonable] appear to be the length of time given to phase out the use, the type of business or endeavor exercised, and the nature of the business or use and its relationship to the neighborhood or area involved. From a constitutional standpoint, it does not appear that a resolution of any of these factors can make reasonable which is basically and from the outset unreasonable." Id. at 1059. Invalidating a four-year amortization ordinance for billboards, another court viewed that ordinance as merely "reducing the dog's pain by cutting off his tail

an inch at a time." Georgia Outdoor Advertising, Inc. v. City of Waynesville, 690 F.Supp. 452, 458 (W.D.N.C.1988).

2. The American Law Institute's Model Land Development Code (1975) departs from the policy of encouraging the termination of nonconforming uses. See Article 4. The Commentary on this article states that the traditional goal of districting of homogeneous land uses is becoming increasingly questionable, that the task of defining nonconformity is unreasonably difficult, that enforcement of termination provisions is lax, and that landowners are often confused as to the significance of the nonconforming status of their property. The code restricts the power to eliminate nonconforming uses to instances where there is an expressly manifested policy that a "specifically-defined neighborhood character should be maintained over a substantial period of time."

3. Under some circumstances, developers are allowed to establish nonconforming uses that did not exist at the time such uses were prohibited. These are situations in which projects have been initiated in reliance upon ordinances or official action. Courts speak of vested rights and estoppel in such cases. They disagree as to the circumstances that entitle an incipient development to continue. The following case represents one view.

STONE v. CITY OF WILTON

Supreme Court of Iowa, 1983.
331 N.W.2d 398.

McGIVERIN, JUSTICE.

Plaintiffs Alex and Martha Stone appeal from the dismissal of their petition for declaratory judgment, injunctive relief and damages in an action regarding defendant City of Wilton's rezoning from multi-family to single-family residential of certain real estate owned by plaintiffs. The issues raised by plaintiffs focus on the validity of the rezoning ordinance and the trial court's striking of plaintiffs' claim for lost profits. We find no error in trial court's rulings and affirm its decision.

This appeal is a zoning dispute involving approximately six acres of land in the city of Wilton, Iowa. Plaintiffs purchased the undeveloped land in June 1979 with the intent of developing a low income, federally subsidized housing project. The project was to consist of several multi-family units; therefore, feasibility of the project depended upon multi-family zoning of the tract. At the time of purchase approximately one-fourth of plaintiffs' land was zoned R–1, single-family residential, and the remainder was zoned R–2, multi-family residential.

After the land was purchased, plaintiffs incurred expenses for architectural fees and engineering services in the preparation of plans and plats to be submitted to the city council and its planning and zoning commission. In addition, plaintiffs secured a Farmers' Home Administration (FHA) loan commitment for construction of the project.

This suit is based primarily on actions of city officials between December 1979 and June 1980. We will discuss only the most pertinent events now and will relate other facts later when we consider the issues raised by plaintiffs.

In December 1979 plaintiffs filed a preliminary plat for the project with the city clerk. In March 1980, following a public meeting, the planning and zoning commission recommended to the city council that land in the northern part of the city be rezoned to single-family residential due to alleged inadequacies of sewer, water and electrical services. The rezoning recommendation affected all of plaintiffs' property plus tracts owned by two other developers. Plaintiffs' application on May 21, 1980, for a building permit to construct multi-family dwellings was denied due to the pending rezoning recommendation.

In May 1980, plaintiffs filed a petition against the city seeking a declaratory judgment invalidating any rezoning of their property, temporary and permanent injunctions to prohibit passage of any rezoning ordinance, and in the event of rezoning, $570,000 damages for monies expended on the project, anticipated lost profits and alleged reduction in the value of plaintiffs' land. The temporary injunction was denied.

In accordance with the recommendation of the planning and zoning commission, the city council passed an ordinance rezoning the land from R–2 to R–1 in June 1980. Following the council's rezoning decision, the planning and zoning commission approved plaintiffs' preliminary plat.

This action proceeded to trial in November 1980. . . .

As stated earlier, the inevitable restrictions on individual uses of property which accompany zoning normally do not constitute a taking. Plaintiffs, however, claim to have had a vested right in developing their property as subsidized, multi-family housing and, therefore, the rezoning allegedly amounted to a taking of this right. Consequently, they contend the zoning ordinance should be inapplicable to their project. We disagree.

The record shows that a factor in the Stones' choice of property was zoning which permitted multi-family residences. Immediately after purchasing the property in Wilton, plaintiffs made certain expenditures in preparation for obtaining the necessary government financing and in order to comply with city ordinances for platting and building permits. These expenditures totaled approximately $7,900, plus the time and effort expended personally by the plaintiffs.

The standard for determining if a property owner has vested rights in a zoning classification was set forth in Board of Supervisors of Scott County v. Paaske, 250 Iowa 1293, 1300, 98 N.W.2d 827, 831 (1959):

> It is impossible to fix a definite percentage of the total cost which establishes vested rights and applies to all cases. It depends on the type of the project, its location, ultimate cost, and *principally the amount accomplished under conformity.* Each case must be decided on its own merits, taking these elements into consideration.

(Emphasis added.) Prior to rezoning, Paaske purchased a parcel of land onto which he planned to move five houses. The county granted him a permit to move the houses. Paaske excavated the basements for four houses; placed a septic tank underground for the fifth house; laid concrete footings for the basement of two houses; entered into a contract for the building of the foundations under all five houses, and placed a substantial amount of building materials on the property before the land was rezoned. We concluded that Paaske's endeavors prior to rezoning were so substantial that he had a vested right in completing his project. See also Crow v. Board of Adjustment of Iowa City, 227 Iowa 324, 288 N.W. 145 (1939) (contract for construction of new building, purchase of material and partial completion of excavation and foundation work prior to revocation of building permit created vested rights); c.f., Brackett v. City of Des Moines, 246 Iowa 249, 261–62, 67 N.W.2d 542, 548 (1954) (while owned by plaintiff, land zoned commercial and approximately twenty-five years later rezoned residential; just prior to rezoning plaintiff obtained a building permit for a commercial building, had plans drawn up and took bids for construction but no work done prior to revocation of permit; "in the absence of any actual construction by plaintiff under his building permit its revocation was not in violation of his vested rights").

In the present case, one of the factors leading to the purchase of this land in Wilton was the fact that it was zoned for multi-family residences. Plaintiffs secured funding from the FHA and engaged the services of an architect and engineer who drew up plans and plats. But these were only the most preliminary steps towards construction. The architect's plans were not the working blueprints of a contractor. The trial court stated they were "the kind [of plans] that one could find in Better Homes and Gardens [magazine]." No construction bids were sought and no construction contracts were let. No materials were placed on the site and no construction or earth work was started. We agree with the trial court that plaintiffs' efforts and expenditures prior to rezoning were not so substantial as to create vested rights in the completion of the housing project on that particular tract of land in Wilton.

. . .

AFFIRMED.

NOTES

1. Compare Smith v. Winhall Planning Commission, 140 Vt. 178, 436 A.2d 760, 761 (1981):

> "We are fully cognizant that the majority rule, so-called, supports appellant's position that neither the filing of an application for a permit nor issuance of the permit, even though valid and conforming to regulations, vest rights in the applicant against future changes in zoning regulations. Two major exceptions seem to be recognized, the first where there has been a substantial change of position, and the second where the amendment was enacted primarily to thwart the applicant's plans for development.

See Annot., 50 A.L.R.3d 596 (1973). Both exceptions involve a factual determination virtually impossible to arrive at short of litigation, a feature which, in our view, emphasizes the undesirability of the rule generally. The minority rule, vesting rights under the then existing regulations as of the time when proper application is filed, is not without substantial support. See Western Land Equities, Inc. v. City of Logan, 617 P.2d 388 (Utah 1980); Ben Lomond, Inc. v. City of Idaho Falls, 92 Idaho 595, 448 P.2d 209, 215 (1968); Gibson v. City of Oberlin, 171 Ohio St. 1, 167 N.E.2d 651 (1960). The minority rule is, we feel, the more practical one to administer. It serves to avoid a great deal, at least, of extended litigation. It makes for greater certainty in the law and its administration. It avoids much of the protracted maneuvering which too often characterizes zoning controversies in our communities. It is, we feel, the more equitable rule in long run application, especially where no amendment is pending at the time of the application, as here."

2. These and other judicial views are discussed in D. Mandelker, Land Use Law 213–221 (2d ed. 1988). Developers may seek "development agreements" purporting to obligate officials not to alter regulations applicable to a particular pending project. Do these really bind the contracting officials and their successors? "[I]t is settled that the government may not contract away its right to exercise the police power in the future." Avco Community Developers v. South Coast Regional Commission, 17 Cal.3d 785, 132 Cal.Rptr. 386, 396, 553 P.2d 546, 556 (1976). Assurance also has been sought through definitions of "vested rights" in ordinances and statutes. A Colorado statute that became effective in 1988 defines such a right as established by approval of a "site specific development plan," the definition of which, however, is expressly left to the discretion of local governments. See the discussion of this act, Colo.Rev.Stat. 24–68–101 (1988), in Campanella, Elliott and Merriam, New Vested Property Rights Legislation: States Seek to Steady a Shaky Judicial Doctrine, 11 Zoning and Planning L.Rep. 81 (1988).

SECTION 2. THE COMPREHENSIVE PLAN, REZONING AND JUDICIAL REVIEW

FASANO v. BOARD OF COUNTY COMMISSIONERS OF WASHINGTON COUNTY

Supreme Court of Oregon, 1973.
264 Or. 574, 507 P.2d 23.

HOWELL, JUSTICE. The plaintiffs, homeowners in Washington county, unsuccessfully opposed a zone change before the Board of County Commissioners of Washington County. Plaintiffs applied for and received a writ of review of the action of the commissioners allowing the change. The trial court found in favor of plaintiffs, disallowed the zone change, and reversed the commissioners' order. The Court of Appeals affirmed, 489 P.2d 693 (1971), and this court granted review.

The defendants are the Board of County Commissioners and A.G.S. Development Company. A.G.S., the owner of 32 acres which had been zoned R–7 (Single Family Residential), applied for a zone change to P–R (Planned Residential), which allows for the construction of a mobile home park. The change failed to receive a majority vote of the Planning Commission. The Board of County Commissioners approved the change and found, among other matters, that the change allows for "increased densities and different types of housing to meet the needs of urbanization over that allowed by the existing zoning."

The trial court, relying on its interpretation of Roseta v. County of Washington, 254 Or. 161, 458 P.2d 405, 40 A.L.R.3d 364 (1969), reversed the order of the commissioners because the commissioners had not shown any change in the character of the neighborhood which would justify the rezoning. The Court of Appeals affirmed for the same reason, but added the additional ground that the defendants failed to show that the change was consistent with the comprehensive plan for Washington county.

According to the briefs, the comprehensive plan of development for Washington county was adopted in 1959 and included classifications in the county for residential, neighborhood commercial, retail commercial, general commercial, industrial park and light industry, general and heavy industry, and agricultural areas.

The land in question, which was designated "residential" by the comprehensive plan, was zoned R–7, Single Family Residential.

Subsequent to the time the comprehensive plan was adopted, Washington county established a Planned Residential (P–R) zoning classification in 1963. The P–R classification was adopted by ordinance and provided that a planned residential unit development could be established and should include open space for utilities, access, and recreation; should not be less than 10 acres in size; and should be located in or adjacent to a residential zone. The P–R zone adopted by the 1963 ordinance is of the type known as a "floating zone," so-called because the ordinance creates a zone classification authorized for future use but not placed on the zoning map until its use at a particular location is approved by the governing body. The R–7 classification for the 32 acres continued until April 1970 when the classification was changed to P–R to permit the defendant A.G.S. to construct the mobile home park on the 32 acres involved.

The defendants argue that (1) the action of the county commissioners approving the change is presumptively valid, requiring plaintiffs to show that the commissioners acted arbitrarily in approving the zone change; (2) it was not necessary to show a change of conditions in the area before a zone change could be accomplished; and (3) the change from R–7 to P–R was in accordance with the Washington county comprehensive plan.

We granted review in this case to consider the questions—by what standards does a county commission exercise its authority in zoning matters; who has the burden of meeting those standards when a request for change of zone is made; and what is the scope of court review of such actions?

Any meaningful decision as to the proper scope of judicial review of a zoning decision must start with a characterization of the nature of that decision. The majority of jurisdictions state that a zoning ordinance is a legislative act and is thereby entitled to presumptive validity.

. . .

At this juncture we feel we would be ignoring reality to rigidly view all zoning decisions by local governing bodies as legislative acts to be accorded a full presumption of validity and shielded from less than constitutional scrutiny by the theory of separation of powers. Local and small decision groups are simply not the equivalent in all respects of state and national legislatures. There is a growing judicial recognition of this fact of life:

. . .

Ordinances laying down general policies without regard to a specific piece of property are usually an exercise of legislative authority, are subject to limited review, and may only be attacked upon constitutional grounds for an arbitrary abuse of authority. On the other hand, a determination whether the permissible use of a specific piece of property should be changed is usually an exercise of judicial authority and its propriety is subject to an altogether different test. . . .

We reject the proposition that judicial review of the county commissioners' determination to change the zoning of the particular property in question is limited to a determination whether the change was arbitrary and capricious.

In order to establish a standard of review, it is necessary to delineate certain basic principles relating to land use regulation.

The basic instrument for county or municipal land use planning is the "comprehensive plan." Haar, In Accordance with a Comprehensive Plan, 68 Harv.L.Rev. 1154 (1955); 1 Yokley, Zoning Law and Practice, § 3–2 (1965); 1 Rathkopf, The Law of Zoning and Planning, § 9–1 (3d ed. 1969). The plan has been described as a general plan to control and direct the use and development of property in a municipality. Nowicki v. Planning and Zoning Board, 148 Conn. 492, 172 A.2d 386, 389 (1961).

In Oregon the county planning commission is required by ORS 215.050 to adopt a comprehensive plan for the use of some or all of the land in the county. Under ORS 215.110(1), after the comprehensive plan has been adopted, the planning commission recommends to the governing body of the county the ordinances necessary to "carry out" the comprehensive plan. The purpose of the zoning ordinances, both under our statute and the general law of land use regulation, is to "carry out" or implement the comprehensive plan. 1 Anderson, American Law of Zoning, § 1.12 (1968). Although we are aware of the analytical distinction between zoning and planning, it is clear that under our statutes the plan adopted by the planning commission and the zoning ordinances enacted by the county governing body are closely related; both are intended to be parts of a single integrated procedure for land use control. The plan embodies policy determinations and guiding principles; the zoning ordinances provide the detailed means of giving effect to those principles.

ORS 215.050 states county planning commissions "shall adopt and may from time to time revise a comprehensive plan." In a hearing of the Senate Committee on Local Government, the proponents of ORS 215.050 described its purpose as follows:

". . . The intent here is to require a basic document, geared into population, land use, and economic forecasts, which should be the basis of any zoning or other regulations to be adopted by the county. . . ."[1]

In addition, ORS 215.055 provides:

"215.055 Standards for plan. (1) The plan and all legislation and regulations authorized by ORS 215.010 to 215.233 shall be designed to promote the public health, safety and general welfare and shall be based on the following considerations, among others: The various characteristics of the various areas in the county, the suitability of the areas for particular land uses and improvements, the land uses and improvements in the areas, trends in land improvement, density of development, property values, the needs of economic enterprises in the future development of the areas, needed access to particular sites in the areas, natural resources of the county and prospective needs for development thereof, and the public need for healthful, safe, aesthetic surroundings and conditions."

We believe that the state legislature has conditioned the county's power to zone upon the prerequisite that the zoning attempt to further the general welfare of the community through consciousness, in a prospective sense, of the factors mentioned above. In other words, except as noted later in this opinion, it must be proved that the change is in conformance with the comprehensive plan.

In proving that the change is in conformance with the comprehensive plan in this case, the proof, at a minimum, should show (1) there is a public need for a change of the kind in question, and (2) that need will be best served by changing the classification of the particular piece of property in question as compared with other available property.

. . .

Because the action of the commission in this instance is an exercise of judicial authority, the burden of proof should be placed, as is usual in judicial proceedings, upon the one seeking change. The more drastic the change, the greater will be the burden of showing that it is in conformance with the comprehensive plan as implemented by the ordinance, that there is a public need for the kind of change in question, and that the need is best met by the proposal under consideration. As the degree of change increases, the burden of showing that the

1. Hearing on Senate Bill 129 before the Senate Committee on Local Government, 52nd Legislative Assembly, February 14, 1963.

potential impact upon the area in question was carefully considered and weighed will also increase. If other areas have previously been designated for the particular type of development, it must be shown why it is necessary to introduce it into an area not previously contemplated and why the property owners there should bear the burden of the departure.[3]

By treating the exercise of authority by the commission in this case as the exercise of judicial rather than of legislative authority and thus enlarging the scope of review on appeal, and by placing the burden of the above level of proof upon the one seeking change, we may lay the court open to criticism by legal scholars who think it desirable that planning authorities be vested with the ability to adjust more freely to changed conditions. However, having weighed the dangers of making desirable change more difficult against the dangers of the almost irresistible pressures that can be asserted by private economic interests on local government, we believe that the latter dangers are more to be feared.

What we have said above is necessarily general, as the approach we adopt contains no absolute standards or mechanical tests. We believe, however, that it is adequate to provide meaningful guidance for local governments making zoning decisions and for trial courts called upon to review them. With future cases in mind, it is appropriate to add some brief remarks on questions of procedure. Parties at the hearing before the county governing body are entitled to an opportunity to be heard, to an opportunity to present and rebut evidence, to a tribunal which is impartial in the matter—i.e., having had no pre-hearing or ex parte contacts concerning the question at issue—and to a record made

3. For example, if an area is designated by the plan as generally appropriate for residential development, the plan may also indicate that some high-density residential development within the area is to be anticipated, without specifying the exact location at which that development is to take place. The comprehensive plan might provide that its goal for residential development is to assure that residential areas are healthful, pleasant and safe places in which to live. The plan might also list the following policies which, among others, are to be pursued in achieving that goal:

1. High-density residential areas should be located close to the urban core area.

2. Residential neighborhoods should be protected from any land use activity involving an excessive level of noise, pollution or traffic volume.

3. High trip-generating multiple family units should have ready access to arterial or collector streets.

4. A variety of living areas and housing types should be provided appropriate to the needs of the special and general groups they are to serve.

5. Residential development at urban densities should be within planned sewer and water service areas and where other utilities can be adequately provided.

Under such a hypothetical plan, property originally zoned for single family dwellings might later be rezoned for duplexes, for garden apartments, or for high-rise apartment buildings. Each of these changes could be shown to be consistent with the plan. Although in addition we would require a showing that the county governing body found a bona fide need for a zone change in order to accommodate new high-density development which at least balanced the disruption shown by the challengers, that requirement would be met in most instances by a record which disclosed that the governing body had considered the facts relevant to this question and exercised its judgment in good faith. However, these changes, while all could be shown to be consistent with the plan, could be expected to have differing impacts on the surrounding area, depending on the nature of that area. As the potential impact on the area in question increases, so will the necessity to show a justification.

and adequate findings executed. Comment, Zoning Amendments—The Product of Judicial or Quasi-Judicial Action, 33 Ohio St.L.J. 130–143 (1972).

When we apply the standards we have adopted to the present case, we find that the burden was not sustained before the commission. The record now before us is insufficient to ascertain whether there was a justifiable basis for the decision. The only evidence in the record, that of the staff report of the Washington County Planning Department, is too conclusory and superficial to support the zoning change. It merely states:

"The staff finds that the requested use does conform to the residential designation of the Plan of Development. It further finds that the proposed use reflects the urbanization of the County and the necessity to provide increased densities and different types of housing to meet the needs of urbanization over that allowed by the existing zoning. . . ."

Such generalizations and conclusions, without any statement of the facts on which they are based, are insufficient to justify a change of use. Moreover, no portions of the comprehensive plan of Washington County are before us, and we feel it would be improper for us to take judicial notice of the plan without at least some reference to its specifics by counsel.

As there has not been an adequate showing that the change was in accord with the plan, or that the factors listed in ORS 215.055 were given proper consideration, the judgment is affirmed.

NOTES

1. The Fasano approach has been adopted wholly or partially in some states and rejected in others. See the survey in Rose, Planning and Dealing: Piecemeal Land Controls as a Problem of Local Legitimacy, 71 Calif.L.Rev. 839, 845 n. 18, 19 (1983).

2. Neuberger v. City of Portland, 288 Or. 155, 603 P.2d 771 (1979), upheld the rezoning of a 601-acre parcel of undeveloped land for higher density residential development. The court concluded that the rezoning was quasi-judicial, but would be approved even though applicants for the change had not shown that the public need for residential development would best be served by changing the classification in question as compared with other available property. Such a showing is not required in rezoning cases, said the court, which stressed that since Fasano much planning legislation had been enacted by the legislature, which had not seen fit to impose this requirement. On the issue of characterization of the rezoning in this case, the court rejected the contention that the rezoning constituted the creation rather than the application of policy. The policy alleged to have been created was that "on large vacant land areas close to the central business district moderate cost housing, affordable by middle income family [sic] should be encouraged." The court conceded that "Large-scale decisions of specific applicability frequently, if not inevitably, require of the decision-maker both the creation and the application of policy," but insisted

that the challenge to the rezoning in this case was to application of policies rather than to the policies applied.

3. Neuberger v. City of Portland, 288 Or. 585, 607 P.2d 722 (1980) (Neuberger II), explained that the Fasano condemnation of ex parte contacts disqualifies a tribunal acting quasi-judicially only if "the evidence shows that the tribunal or its members were biased."

4. The interest of a landowner in the zoning of neighboring land was discussed by the same court in another case, Frankland v. City of Lake Oswego, 267 Or. 452, 517 P.2d 1042 (1973):

"The nature of the right of an adjoining landowner to bring suit to enjoin the violation of a zoning ordinance has been variously described by the courts, but all seem to reflect the policy consideration expressed in 3 Anderson, American Law of Zoning 636, § 23.11 (1968), where the author states:

"Since many municipalities lack sufficient personnel to carry out an effective program of zoning inspection and enforcement, actions commenced by private persons to enjoin violation of the zoning ordinance are an important part of the enforcement program. In these actions, which are more numerous than those commenced by taxpayers or by municipalities, the person who institutes the proceedings acts in his private capacity, not as a taxpayer seeking to vindicate a taxpayer's interest in law enforcement. . . .

"Four theories have been advanced: (1) that a zoning ordinance is similar to a third party beneficiary contract; (2) that the zoning ordinance is similar to a covenant running with the land; (3) that the cause of action is similar to a nuisance action; and (4) that a zoning ordinance creates rights in favor of individuals as well as public authorities which are enforceable in a civil suit.

. . .

"The court, in lieu of granting a mandatory injunction, may award damages to the adjoining owners for a depreciation in value of their property resulting from the ordinance violation. . . ."

Another portion of this opinion is reprinted at page 953, herein. For another view, see Krasnowiecki, Planned Unit Development: A Challenge to Established Theory and Practice of Land Use Control, 114 U.Pa.L.Rev. 47, 55–63, 72–72 (1965).

BAKER v. CITY OF MILWAUKIE

Supreme Court of Oregon, 1975.
271 Or. 500, 533 P.2d 772.

HOWELL, JUSTICE. This is an appeal from the dismissal of a writ of mandamus. The plaintiff sought to compel the City of Milwaukie to conform a zoning ordinance to its comprehensive plan, to cancel a variance approved by the Milwaukie Planning Commission, and to suspend the issuance of building permits in areas of the city where the zoning ordinance allows a more intensive use than the set forth in the comprehensive plan. The trial court sustained the City's demurrer to the alternative writ. The plaintiff refused to plead further and the court dismissed the writ. The Court of Appeals reversed the action of the trial court but on grounds not substantially in favor of the plaintiff, and plaintiff's petition for review to this court was allowed.

Basically, the petition for the alternative writ states that plaintiff is a landowner in the City of Milwaukie. On October 17, 1968, the City of Milwaukie adopted a zoning ordinance which designated plaintiff's land and the surrounding area "A 1 B" (residential apartment-business office). This category allowed 39 units per acre. On November 11, 1969, a comprehensive plan for the City of Milwaukie was adopted by the Planning Commission. This comprehensive plan designated plaintiff's land and the surrounding area as high density residential, allowing 17 units per acre. On January 12, 1970, the Milwaukie City Council passed a resolution adopting the above plan as the comprehensive plan for the City of Milwaukie.

On February 27, 1973, without public hearing and against staff recommendation, the Milwaukie City Planning Commission granted a variance authorizing a proposed 95-unit apartment complex near plaintiff's property with one and one-half parking spaces per unit rather than the required two.

Subsequent to the granting of the variance, an application was made for a building permit for the construction of a 102-unit apartment on property immediately adjacent to plaintiff's property. This 102-unit complex would result in 26 units per acre—less than the 39 units allowed by the zoning ordinance but substantially more than the 17 units allowed by the comprehensive plan.

After demand was made on the City Council and the Building Inspector to conform the zoning ordinance to the comprehensive plan, to cancel the variance previously granted, and to suspend the issuance of building permits where the zoning in the city did not conform to the comprehensive plan, the plaintiff brought this proceeding. Her petition alleged, in relevant part:

"VIII

"Even though obligated to do so and even though more than three years have expired between approval of the comprehensive plan and the present, Defendants City Councilmen have not even though they have a duty to do so, taken steps to modify the zoning in the area of concern to conform to the comprehensive plan for such area. Defendant inspector has failed or refused to indicate that he will suspend issuance of a building permit for the area of concern until such time as the zoning of the City of Milwaukie conforms to the comprehensive plan for such city."

The defendants filed a return to the alternative writ in which they state:

"The defendants have not done as they were herein commanded, and the cause of their omission is that there is no obligation that the zoning ordinance of the city of Milwaukie be conformed to the comprehensive plan subsequently adopted by resolution."

At the same time the defendants demurred to the petition on the grounds that several causes of action were improperly united and that the petition did not state facts sufficient to constitute a cause of action. The trial court sustained the demurrer on the grounds that the "facts set forth in the petition are insufficient to sustain the relief prayed for in the petition." The trial court did not rule on defendants' demurrer that several causes of action were improperly united.

The Court of Appeals reversed solely on the ground that the plaintiff had alleged sufficient facts to support her claim with regard to the improper granting of the variance.[4] In all other respects the Court of Appeals held that the facts stated in the petition were insufficient. Baker v. City of Milwaukie, 17 Or.App. 89, 520 P.2d 479 (1974). We granted review to consider the effect of the adoption, by a municipality, of a comprehensive plan on pre-existing and conflicting zoning ordinances.

The defendants argue that "the zoning ordinance would govern land use with a definite and precise requirement, and would control over the comprehensive plan." Thus the defendants contend that although the City has passed a comprehensive plan, there is no duty to effectuate it through the enactment of conforming zoning ordinances. They further argue that the present conflicting zoning ordinances remain in effect until the City decides to replace them with ordinances which are in accord with the comprehensive plan.

We agree with the plaintiff and the amici curiae (Northwest Environmental Defense Center, Oregon Environmental Council, and Oregon Chapter of the American Institute of Planners) that the position of defendants evidences a fundamental misunderstanding of the relationship between planning and zoning.

. . .

In the instant case, as noted above, the zoning ordinance was passed in October, 1968. The comprehensive plan was adopted by the Planning Commission in November, 1969, and adopted by the City Council in January, 1970. The plan recites:

"The City of Milwaukie had adopted a new zoning ordinance [apparently referring to the ordinance enacted in october, 1968] that was developed in conjunction with the Comprehensive Plan. Basic features of the new ordinance as adopted are consistent with the Plan described in this report."

Plaintiff alleges that an examination of the ordinance and the plan shows that a conflict exists, at least in the area in question in this case.[7]

4. The variance issue has not been appealed by the defendants to this court.

7. The fact that the zoning ordinance was "developed in conjunction with the Comprehensive Plan" and yet conflicts with that very plan is itself strong evidence that proper planning did not go into the development of the zoning ordinance and that that ordinance is not "in accord with a well considered plan." ORS 227.240(1).

The defendants argue, and the Court of Appeals held, that there is no duty [8] to adopt a written comprehensive plan such as that adopted by the City of Milwaukie. However, this begs the question. The fact is that the City of Milwaukie *has* adopted a comprehensive plan. . . . If that plan is to have any efficacy as the basic planning tool for the City of Milwaukie, it must be given preference over conflicting prior zoning ordinances. To hold otherwise would allow a city to go through the motions and expense of formulating a comprehensive plan and then relegating that document to oblivion through continued reliance on the older zoning ordinances.[9]

In summary, we conclude that a comprehensive plan is the controlling land use planning instrument for a city. Upon passage of a comprehensive plan a city assumes a responsibility to effectuate that plan and conform prior conflicting zoning ordinances to it. We further hold that the zoning decisions of a city must be in accord with that plan and a zoning ordinance which allows a more intensive use than that prescribed in the plan must fail.[14]

In the instant case, we agree with the Court of Appeals that the plaintiff has stated a cause of action with regard to the granting of the variance. We further hold that the plaintiff has stated a cause of action in seeking to compel the City of Milwaukie to conform its zoning ordinances to the comprehensive plan and to suspend the issuance of

8. Prior to 1973 there was some disagreement as to whether municipalities were required to adopt a comprehensive plan. Or.Laws 1969, ch. 324 (ORS 215.505 et seq.) at least express a state policy in favor of comprehensive planning at all levels of government. Any ambiguity in this area has been cleared up through the passage of Or.Laws 1973, ch. 80 (ORS ch. 197). ORS 197.175(2) provides:

> "(2) Pursuant to ORS 197.005 to 197.430, 215.055, 215.510, 215.515, 215.535 and 453.345, each city and county in this state shall:
>
> "(a) Prepare and adopt comprehensive plans consistent with state-wide planning goals and guidelines approved by the commission; and
>
> "(b) Enact zoning, subdivision and other ordinances or regulations to implement their comprehensive plans."

ORS 197.015(4) provides:

> "(4) 'Comprehensive plan' means a generalized, coordinated land use map and policy statement of the governing body of a state agency, city, county or special district that interrelates all functional and natural systems and activities relating to the use of lands, including but not limited to sewer and water systems, transportation systems, educational systems, recreational facilities, and natural resources and air and water quality management programs. 'Comprehensive' means all-inclusive, both in terms of the geographic area covered and functional and natural activities and systems occurring in the area covered by the plan. 'General nature' means a summary of policies and proposals in broad categories and does not necessarily indicate specific locations of any area, activity or use. A plan is 'coordinated' when the needs of all levels of governments, semi-public and private agencies and the citizens of Oregon have been considered and accommodated as much as possible. 'Land' includes water, both surface and subsurface, and the air."

See Macpherson and Paulus, Senate Bill 100: The Oregon Land Conservation and Development Act, 10 Will.L.J. 414 (1974); 36 Op.Or. AG 960, 972 (1974).

9. The petition in the instant case alleges:

> "VI
>
> "Petitioner Baker and her husband purchased their property in reliance on the comprehensive plan."
>
> . . .

14. In deciding that the ordinance must be in conformance with the comprehensive plan we do not indicate what should or should not be included in such ordinance or the precise time that the ordinance should be enacted.

building permits in violation of the plan. This case must go beyond the pleading stages to determine whether, in fact, the zoning ordinance is in accord with the comprehensive plan, whether the comprehensive plan was validly enacted, and whether the variance was properly granted.

Defendants' demurrer should have been overruled.

Affirmed as modified.

LEAVY, JUSTICE PRO TEM. (dissenting).

. . .

I know of no authority, nor has any been cited by the majority, which holds that the adoption of a comprehensive plan makes a prior ordinance invalid, nor would I treat adoption of a plan to be of such legislative magnitude that by its very nature it telescopes implementary legislation into planning. . . .

GREEN v. HAYWARD

Supreme Court of Oregon, 1976.
275 Or. 693, 552 P.2d 815.

O'CONNELL, JUSTICE. This case comes to us on a petition for review from the Court of Appeals, which held invalid two orders of the Lane County Board of County Commissioners, one rezoning a 50-acre tract of land owned by Bohemia, Inc., and the other declaring the Board's intent to rezone an adjacent 90-acre parcel upon which Bohemia held an option to purchase.[1] That option has since been exercised. We granted review because the case raises significant questions concerning judicial review of local government rezoning determinations in light of our decisions in Fasano v. Washington Co. Comm., 264 Or. 574, 507 P.2d 23 (1973) and Baker v. City of Milwaukie, 271 Or. 500, 533 P.2d 772 (1975).

The two parcels lie approximately two miles north of the City of Coburg, and were zoned AGT (agricultural, grazing and timber raising) in 1966. At that time there was a veneer plant in operation on the 50-acre parcel. That plant continued in operation as a nonconforming use, and was purchased by Bohemia in 1972.

Also in 1972 the Lane County Board of County Commissioners adopted the "Eugene-Springfield Metropolitan Area 1990 General Plan," a document which

". . . consists of statements of goals and recommendations and accompanying illustrations to guide the development of the metropolitan area. The plan indicates how the various elements of the metropol-

1. The "declaration of intent to rezone" is apparently a procedure sanctioned by the Lane County zoning ordinances by which the Board commits itself to a later rezoning provided the applicant submits detailed plans which meet with the Board's approval. See Green v. Hayward, 23 Or. App. 310, 542 P.2d 144 (1975) at note 1. For purposes of this opinion we will refer generally to the two orders of the Board as "rezoning" decisions.

itan community can be developed in order to attain the compact growth form consistent with achievement of the General Plan goals." [2]

The text of the 1990 Plan does not indicate the precise geographic area of its coverage. There are frequent references to the "metropolitan area," the "metropolitan community" and the "outlying" or "satellite" communities. None of these terms is defined in the Plan, but Coburg is described as one of the satellite communities.

In 1973 Bohemia applied for a rezoning of its mill site, and also of the 90 acres lying immediately north of the mill, from AGT to M–3 (heavy industrial). The rezoning was requested in part because Bohemia needed to expand its existing facilities to provide increased space for log storage and improved sewage disposal capacity in connection with its current activities and in part because Bohemia wished to construct a bark-processing plant where it could utilize a new process which it had developed for converting bark, which was a waste product of its mill operations, into saleable products.

Bohemia's rezoning requests were opposed by a number of residents of the area. After notice and public hearing, the Board of County Commissioners made its decisions in favor of Bohemia's requests. Some of the opponents then applied to the circuit court for a writ of review of the Board's action on the ground, among others, that the zone changes did not conform to the 1990 Plan. Bohemia was made a party by intervention and, after appropriate proceedings, the circuit court enterd judgment affirming the action of the Board.

The Court of Appeals, citing Baker v. City of Milwaukie, 271 Or. 500, 533 P.2d 772 (1975), held that the zone change was invalid because it failed in two respects to comply with the 1990 Plan. In the first place, the court held,

". . . The plan designates that the tracts of land in controversy are for agricultural use only. Zoning ordinances allowing the much more intensive industrial use manifestly do not comply with that designation." 542 P.2d at 148.

Apparently the Court of Appeals found the designation of these tracts for agricultural use on the "Metropolitan Area Plan Diagram" which is a part of the 1990 Plan. That diagram uses color designations to indicate different types of land uses. All of the land surrounding the City of Coburg, from the Willamette River on the west and south to the foothill area on the east, and extending northward as far as the map shows, is colored brown. According to the key provided with the diagram, brown means:

"AGRICULTURAL. Primarily reserved for agriculture and related activities, some localized areas within may be considered as 'rural' provided they do not conflict with adjoining agricultural uses." [3]

2. Eugene-Springfield Metropolitan Area 1990 General Plan ["1990 Plan"] at p. 5.

3. According to the key, a "rural" designation means: "General agriculture, open space, woodland, rural residential (average parcel size of five acres or greater based on development patterns, soil types and other natural conditions). Urban level of service not likely within the current planning period. Portions of these areas may also provide needed space for urban develop-

Industrial areas are colored magenta. An "Industrial" designation on the diagram means, according to the key, "Major centers for manufacturing, warehousing, and wholesaling." The industrial areas shown on the diagram are all approximately four miles or more from these tracts. A note to the diagram key, however, states:

> "In interpreting proposals shown on this plan diagram, it is necessary to refer to the findings, goals, objectives, recommendations and descriptive analyses contained in the text to gain a complete understanding of the General Plan."

Moreover, that portion of the text which introduces the diagram refers to it as "Illustrative" and points out that the diagram does not include all detailed land use specifications.[4] If the opinion of the Court of Appeals relfects or creates an understanding that our decision in Baker v. City of Milwaukie, supra, was intended to hold that a local government's zoning map must coincide in detail with the map portion of the comprehensive plan, that misunderstanding should be corrected. In *Baker* this court did not have to interpret or apply a comprehensive plan. That case was before use for review of the dismissal of a writ of mandamus. The writ alleged, in essence, that the city had adopted a comprehensive plan, but that for a period exceeding three years had taken no steps to amend the zoning ordinances to conform to the plan, and was proceeding under pre-existing inconsistent ordinances to grant building permits for development more intensive than permitted by the plan. The city's defense in that case was that it had no obligation to conform its zoning to the plan. In effect, it admitted the allegations that the zoning ordinances and building permits were in violation of the plan. . . .

We were not called upon to determine, nor did we attempt to do so, whether the zoning was, in fact, inconsistent with the plan, or the form in which a comprehensive plan should prescribe permissible uses of land. *Baker* does not hold that a diagram or map which constitutes a part of a comprehensive plan is necessarily the controlling land use document.

At times relevant to this case, Oregon law did not prescribe the format of the comprehensive plan.[5] In fact, there is as yet no agreement within the planning profession as to the form which a good comprehensive plan should take.[6]

ment after 1990 or sooner in the event that urban growth occurs at a faster rate than projected."

4. "Finally, note that the plan does not offer detailed proposals related to neighborhood and community facilities. Such proposals properly belong in more detailed community and area plans. The emphasis of this metropolitan area General Plan is on the broad allocation of land for urban use." 1990 Plan at p. 17.

5. ORS 215.050, prior to its amendment in 1973, provided: "The commission shall adopt and may from time to time revise a comprehensive plan for the use of some or all of the land in the county. The plan may be adopted and revised part by part."

6. See, e.g., Plager, "The Planning Land-Use Control Relationship: A Look at Some Alternatives," Land-Use Controls Q., 26, 28 (Winter 1969) quoted in Hagman, Public Planning and Control of Urban and Land Development (1973) at 337:

> ". . . The understanding in the profession ranges along a continuum with, at the one end, a plan that must appear in mapped form, to, at the other end, the policies plan that does not use maps at all. . . . [t]he problem of determining 'accordness' is a difficult one and is relat-

The 1973 legislature did address the question with a statutory definition of a comprehensive plan. Although not directly applicable to this controversy, that statute illustrates that even a very recent legislative definition does not attempt to describe the plan format in detail. Although it calls for both a map and a policy statement, the statute addresses primarily questions of content, leaving the problem of form to those responsible for the creation and adoption of the plan. ORS 197.015(4). In light of the freedom given local governments, both in the past and for the future, to design the form of their comprehensive plans, we refrain from statements of general application about how such plans are to be read or interpreted. The relationship between the text and the maps within a particular plan must be determined from the plan document itself, considered as a whole.

In the present case, the Plan itself tells us that neither the text nor the illustrative diagram was intended to provide advance answers to the kinds of questions involved in this case.[8] We conclude that in the 1990 Plan, the plan map or diagram was intended to illustrate what the text calls the "broad allocation" of land within the area shown, but not to put a limit on the permissible uses of each and every tract within that area.[9] In order to determine whether a particular zoning decision is in compliance with the Plan, we must look to other portions of the Plan in addition to the diagram.

One of the central policies of the Plan is that of discouraging urban sprawl by implementing a "compact growth pattern" for the Eugene-Springfield metropolitan area. By implementing such a pattern, the plan aims to achieve the following objectives:

ed to the problem of what a plan is. To the extent that the plan itself is a detailed map of the land indicating specific uses, it differs hardly at all from the zoning map itself. Under these circumstances, while it is possible to measure 'accordness' with some degree of accuracy, the plan becomes rigid and of little use in dealing with dynamic community growth. The planners generally reject such an interpretation of what a comprehensive plan is. If on the other hand the plan is displayed graphically as large blobs of bright colors with no clear boundary lines—sort of a planner's Rorschach test—the decision-making process finds little to aid it in dealing with specific land uses at the edge of the blobs. And as one gets away from graphics altogether and into the area of broad policy statements, the plan provides even less by way of guidelines for specific land-use decisions . . .."

8. The notes to the diagram refer the reader to the text for a complete understanding of the "proposals" shown on the diagram. The text, in the Introduction, says:

"In terms of form, the General Plan is not a zoning ordinance or a blueprint for the specific development of particular buildings, highways and so on. Such specific recommendations would soon be outdated. Instead, the General Plan presents a number of broad development guidelines. Some specific details are provided, but they serve as illustrative examples as possible applications of the guideline policies rather than as fixed decisions. The policies can be applied to individual projects or area plans conceived by local government agencies or private developers. In other words, the General Plan, which is long-range, comprehensive and focused on physical development, provides a flexible guide for specific development decision making. It does not, in itself, set down the decisions." 1919 Plan at p. 2.

9. In addition to the text of the Plan, we find further support for this conclusion in the fact that the diagram contains many large single-color areas which appear to be undifferentiated as to uses. Moreover, counsel agreed at oral argument that the Coburg Industrial Park is not shown on the diagram as an industrial area.

(1) "Preservation of prime, agricultural land from urban development.

(2) "Elimination of urban development in the flood plain area.

(3) "Reduction of scatteration and urban sprawl.

(4) "Reduction of the amount of public utilities which will not be used efficiently for many years.

(5) "Encouragement of development of vacant land where services are available thus capitalizing on the public expenditures already made for these services.

(6) "Shaping and regulating urban form and growth and preservation of the special character of the area.

(7) "Protection of open space.

(8) "Minimize the need for more outer beltline roads.

(9) "Making urban mass transit more economically feasible thus lessening the need for an auto-dominated transportation system." 1990 Plan at p. 11.

The Court of Appeals held that the rezoning in this case failed to conform to the Plan because it "notably failed to comply with several essential objectives of the plan's design for growth," specifying objectives (1), (3), (5) and (6) as quoted above. 23 Or.App. at ___, 542 P.2d at 148.

As to objective (1), Commissioner Elliott expressly found that the land involved was not prime agricultural land, and Commissioner Omlid found:

"Soil ranges from good to poor, therefore it is difficult to class that as essentially prime agricultural land."

The evidence before the Board relating to the suitability of the land for agriculture was conflicting, but there was substantial evidence to support the above findings and the Court of Appeals was therefore bound by them. As to objectives (3), (5) and (6), the statement of the Court of Appeals appears to be accurate. However, the Plan contains other policy statements with which the rezoning decisions can reasonably be said to be consistent. Commissioner Omlid made the following findings:

"The Plant expansion itself will contribute to the attainment of goals cited in the 1990 Plan in that it will:

"Enhance the economic health of a small rural community.

"The production process brings a greater utilization of our basic industrial resource.

"The process will aid in enhancing our environment by using that part of the resource that must now be burned or put into the sanitary landfills or somehow gotten rid of.

"The traffic problem which presently exists is more likely to be alleviated than aggravated.

"The lagoons for waste treatment and the drainage system proposed around the area will be an important improvement over what presently exists."

And Commissioner Elliott made the following finding, among others:

"The Coburg City Council and the Coburg Planning Commission has [sic] recommended approval. The 1990 Plan suggests that satellite communities should develop on a balance basis."

The Board has thus found that the rezoning would further some of the objectives of the Plan. The Court of Appeals has concluded that other important objectives would be violated by this rezoning decision. Both conclusions find some support in the record of the hearing before the Board.

. . .

The record contains substantial evidence to support the specific findings of Commissioners Omlid and Elliott which are quoted above. The more difficult question is whether the findings and the evidence are sufficient to support the rezoning decisions themselves. As we have noted the Plan contains a number of goals, objectives, and recommendations, stated in general terms. We are reluctant to hold that one or a few of those general statements may be severed from the Plan as a whole and used in isolation as justification for a rezoning decision. To hold that a zoning amendment is placed beyond judicial review by a finding, supported by substantial evidence, that the rezoning furthers *some* policy in the comprehensive plan would place these decisions beyond the reach of meaningful judicial scrutiny. Nearly every individual zoning decision could reasonably be said to conform to or support one or more of the generally-stated goals or objectives in a typical modern comprehensive plan. On the other hand, we are not authorized, and do not wish, to prescribe de novo court review of these decisions on the merits. The proper concern of the courts in these cases is to ascertain whether adequate procedures were followed and proper legal standards were applied. The difficulty in this case arises because we have not been provided with an adequate statement of the reasons for the decisions of the Board—a statement which would have informed us of the portions of the Plan which the Board considered relevant and the reasons why a zone change which is consistent with some of the Plan's goals but violates others is considered to be in compliance with the Plan.

Moreover, we find in the Plan a set of "minimum location standards for industrial parks, research, and development, and other restrictive industrial development in areas not otherwise shown for industrial development in the '1990 General Plan Diagram' . . .." These minimum standards are quoted in the margin.[12] There is,

12. "a. Access to an arterial road is immediately available without the generation of traffic through areas planned for residential use.

"b. Sufficient natural or man-made features exist or can be provided in the development process so as to otherwise insure compatability with adjacent areas, considering, among other factors: (1) prevailing winds; (2) noise, water, and air pollution; (3) physical character of the proposed development, such as off-street parking facilities; openness and attractiveness of the setting; bulk, height, and setting of structure; landscaping; (4) natural hazards

however, nothing in the record, the findings, or the decision to indicate why these standards were not expressly applied. We do not know whether the Board considered them inapplicable to this type of industrial development, considered them advisory only because they are cast in the form of a "recommendation," believed all the standards were met, or simply overlooked them.

As we find these "minimum standards" to be the only specific guidance given by the Plan for the decision to permit industry in areas not designated industrial on the diagram, and as there has been no showing that the standards are not applicable to this case, a showing of conformity to the Plan requires a showing that these standards have been met. The findings and order of the Board are far from clear on this point. We realize that the public hearing on Bohemia's requests took place not long after the publication of the *Fasano* decision, and that the Board was justifiably uncertain about the procedures which it was required by that decision to observe. Finding itself in the unfamiliar situation of conducting a hearing on the record, in light of *Fasano's* rather general procedural admonitions, the Board made considerable and commendable efforts to assure fairness and a proper hearing, aided by the advice of counsel. Because we are convinced that the parties were afforded a fair hearing and that the Board conscientiously addressed itself to the underlying problems of public policy in reaching its decision on Bohemia's requests, we have examined the record to determine whether its decision could reasonably have been based on substantial evidence that the minimum locational standards, specified in the Plan, were met.

We are, however, unwilling to make this a practice. The appropriate place for both an initial interpretation of a comprehensive plan and a determination whether a proposed change complies with the specifics of the plan as properly interpreted is at the local level where the governing body is familiar with the plan and its implementation, and has heard the evidence at first hand. The chances of misunderstanding and of inconsistent land-use decisions are greatly enhanced when the courts are forced, because of inadequacies in the record, to undertake a search for evidence to support findings which were not made and reasons which were not given. Judicial review in these cases should be limited to a consideration of whether a properly documented decision finds support in the record. If necessary in the future, we would be justified in returning cases such as this to the local body for a complete statement of the basis for the decision.

. . .

such as flooding, drainage and geological conditions.

"c. Those utilities and services necessary for the category of industrial development are available or planned for the site (and for other adjacent sites of the same characteristics and logical for the same type of development) without creating: (1) excessive burdens on such services, (2) the lowering of service levels in the general vicinity, or (3) excessive or unreasonable financial burdens on other properties in the general vicinity.

"d. Use of the area for non-residential purposes would not disrupt the continuity of a neighborhood or community (such as the utilization of land planned for residential development to the extent that an existing or planned school facility for the area would be under-utilized or could not be justified.)"

With some misgivings on these grounds we have, nevertheless, examined the record to determine whether the evidence will support the Board's decision to rezone. There is evidence in the record before the Board which would support findings that: (1) the proposed facility, by enabling Bohemia to utilize a waste product on the site, would reduce traffic problems rather than generate additional traffic; (2) the "intent to rezone" procedure, together with permit requirements of other agencies, will insure compatibility of Bohemia's expansion with adjacent areas; (3) no additional utilities and services will have to be provided; and (4) because of its association with an existing industrial facility, the new plant would not disrupt the continuity of a neighborhood or community. Although much of this evidence was controverted, a determination by the Board that the minimum location standards were met would not be arbitrary.

. . .

It is contended that there was no showing of necessity for change in this case, as much of the land in Lane County which had been previously zoned for heavy industrial development had not been used for that purpose. It is also argued that Bohemia's desire to build its new plant on land which it already owned (or had an option to purchase) was not a proper consideration. Ordinarily this argument would carry considerable weight. The integrity of comprehensive planning would be seriously compromised if a property owner could obtain a zone change on the ground that he did not own any of the land that was already zoned for the type of development he had in mind, or that his proposed development would be less profitable in an appropriately zoned area. In this case, however, there was evidence before the Board that the new plant was to utilize a process which had been developed by Bohemia, that the plant, to be economically feasible, had to be constructed close to an existing mill, and that it was in the public interests as well as in the interest of Bohemia to permit the construction of such a plant in order to utilize the quantities of old-growth bark which would otherwise constitute a solid-waste disposal problem. The Board could reasonably have concluded that if the plant were not built adjacent to Bohemia's existing mill, no such plant would be built within the county, and that it was in the public interest to have such a plant constructed. We think the record is adequate to support a finding of necessity for the zoning changes.

As we have found the record adequate to support the Board's decisions, we do not need to reach petitioner's contention that the 1990 Plan was not a legally sufficient comprehensive plan for the Coburg area. Assuming that the Plan is legally sufficient, the Board was justified in concluding that the rezoning was in conformance with the Plan.

The decision of the Court of Appeals is reversed and the judgment of the circuit court is reinstated.

NOTES

1. Mandelker & Netter, Comprehensive Plans and the Law, in Land-Use Law: Issues for the Eighties 55, 70 (1981) report: "As of February 1981, 18 states have adopted mandatory planning legislation. In 10 of these states, zoning must be consistent with local plans. In two states, planning is optional, but consistency is required if there is a local comprehensive plan. In still other states, courts measure the reasonableness of local land-use regulations by their conformity to the plan."

Is this trend desirable? Consider Tarlock, Consistency with Adopted Land Use Plans as a Standard of Judicial Review: The Case Against, 9 Urb.L.Ann. 69 (1975). Professor Tarlock summarizes his position at p. 101:

"No persuasive reason exists to require that zoning changes be consistent with adopted comprehensive plans. First, the legitimacy of planning choices has not been established. Secondly, the lack of a consistent rationale for advance allocation of land development opportunities creates a substantial risk that these allocations will be both arbitrary and inefficient."

For other views, see J. DiMento, The Consistency Doctrine and the Limits of Planning (1980); Rose, Planning and Dealing: Piecemeal Land Controls as a Problem of Local Legitimacy, 71 Cal.L.Rev. 839 (1983).

2. Suppose that a comprehensive plan designates O's land as the site of a public park. Unlike official maps, this designation does not purport to impose any legal restriction upon O's land. The practical effect, however, may be deterrence of development or sale pending governmental acquisition, which may never occur. To what relief, if any, should O be entitled? O would have no remedy in most states, but would the new significance of the comprehensive plan in Oregon and some other states lead to a different result? Not unless special circumstances are present, according to Fifth Avenue Corp. v. Washington County, 282 Or. 591, 581 P.2d 50 (1978) and Suess Builders Co. v. City of Beaverton, 294 Or. 254, 656 P.2d 306 (1982). The court in Fifth Avenue Corp. stated that "the owner is not entitled to compensation for inverse condemnation unless: (1) he is precluded from all economically feasible private uses pending eventual taking for public use; or (2) the designation results in such governmental intrusion as to inflict irreversible damage." In Suess Builders Co., a complaint alleging a taking was deemed sufficient to survive a motion to dismiss, the language of the complaint being "broad enough to encompass a hypothetical claim that defendants told plaintiffs that the property was certain to be acquired, that it would be useless to pursue any proposals for private development, and that defendants began to acquire easements for certain facilities. If that were the case, and the defendants later abandoned their plans, a court could find that one or perhaps both of the governmental bodies had temporarily taken all economic use of plaintiffs' property."

3. In still another of an apparently endless line of cases on the role of the comprehensive plan, the Oregon Supreme Court upheld the denial of a subdivision development permit for single-family residences, even though both the zoning ordinance and the comprehensive plan of the local government designated the land as "single family." The denial was based upon an "agricultural retention policy" set forth in the local comprehensive plan. The court explained that a "plan policy to retain agriculturally productive land in that use until such time as it is needed for the zoned use is not inconsistent with the concept of zoning designations." Philippi v. City of Sublimity, 294 Or. 730, 662 P.2d 325 (1983).

SECTION 3. ZONING VARIANCES AND SPECIAL EXCEPTIONS

APPLICATION OF DEVEREUX FOUNDATION, INC.

Supreme Court of Pennsylvania, 1945.
351 Pa. 478, 41 A.2d 744.

HORACE STERN, JUSTICE. We are here called upon to deal with a type of controversy in which two interests, each in itself legitimate and wholly commendable, come into conflict merely by reason of the proximity of their locations. The one interest is that of a school devoted to the education of mentally deficient, weak and abnormal children, and the other that of the inhabitants of a fine residential suburban section who oppose the housing therein of the pupils of such an institution.

The Devereux School, begun in 1918, was incorporated in 1938 as a non-profit corporation of the first class under the title of "The Devereux Foundation, Inc.," for the purpose of "studying, treating, engaging in and carrying on research and educational work in connection with functional and nervous disorders and for the educating, developing, and advancing of boys and girls of any age under required direction in addition to their intellectual and vocational needs along psychological and psychiatric lines . . .."

The school now has a staff of 74 teachers and an enrollment of 366 pupils. In 1939 it purchased a large residential property in Devon, Easttown Township, Chester County, containing approximately 14 acres of land. This property, known as the "Academy," is used by it as a girls' dormitory and for other purposes.

On August 6, 1940, Easttown Township, in pursuance of the authority granted by the Act of July 1, 1937, P.L. 2624, 53 P.S. § 19093–2201 et seq., adopted a zoning ordinance under which the "Academy" was included within an "A residence District"; however, as this property was already in use by the Foundation, it was not affected by the restrictions imposed by the ordinance. The ordinance provided that in an "A residence District" a building might be used, inter alia, for an "educational or religious use, including dormitory of an educational institution, but excluding cemeteries, hospital, homes, sanitarium, correctional institution or structure or other place for accommodating the insane or other persons mentally deficient, weak or abnormal, except as provided in Article X." Article X, thus referred to, provided that the Board of Adjustment should have the power ". . . (b) To hear and decide special exceptions to the terms of this Ordinance in such cases as are herein expressly provided for, in harmony with the general purpose and intent of this Ordinance, with power to impose appropriate conditions and safeguards. (c) To authorize, upon appeal, in specific cases, such variance from the terms of this Ordinance as will not be contrary to the public interest, where, owing to special conditions, a literal enforcement of the provisions of this Ordinance will result in unnecessary hardship, and so that the spirit of this Ordinance shall be observed and substantial justice done."

In 1943 the Foundation purchased an additional tract known as the "Ilsley" property consisting of a private residence and 4 acres of land, all included within the same road boundaries as the "Academy" and the same "A residence District" under the ordinance. The Foundation intended to use this property, not for educational work, but as a dormitory for boys. It applied for a certificate of occupancy, which application was denied by the Zoning Administrative Officer of the township. Upon appeal to the Board of Adjustment that body, after hearing testimony, found that the contemplated use of the property was a violation of the terms of the ordinance but that "the circumstances of this case warrant the granting of an exception which is hereby allowed," and accordingly directed that an occupancy permit be issued. Thereupon residents of the District who had appeared before the Board of Adjustment in opposition to the application appealed to the Court of Common Pleas of Chester County. The court supported the conclusion of the Board that the proposed use of the property was prohibited by the ordinance, but overruled the action of the Board in granting an exception. The Foundation now appeals from that order of the court.

. . .

We come to the question whether the Board of Adjustment was warranted in granting what it terms an "exception," and on that basis permitting the issuance of the certificate of occupancy requested by the Foundation. The Act of July 1, 1937, P.L. 2624, which authorizes townships of the second class to adopt and enforce zoning ordinances, provides in Section 7 that the board of township supervisors may appoint a board of adjustment and may provide that "said board of adjustment may in appropriate cases, and subject to appropriate conditions and safeguards, make special exceptions to the terms of the ordinance in harmony with its general purpose and intent and in accordance with general or specific rules therein contained." As far as the terms of the Easttown Township ordinance appear in the record there are no rules therein contained in accordance with which special exceptions may be made. An "exception" in a zoning ordinance is one allowable where facts and conditions detailed in the ordinance, as those upon which an exception may be permitted, are found to exist. But zoning ordinances usually provide, as does the present one, for another kind of dispensation, also permitted by the statute, by which a "variance" from the terms of the ordinance may be authorized in cases where a literal enforcement of its provisions would result in unnecessary hardship. Presumably, therefore, it is such a variance which the Board of Adjustment intended here to authorize.

Was it justified in so doing? It was said in Kerr's Appeal, 294 Pa. 246, 253, 144 A. 81, 84: "The difficulties and hardships, which move the board of adjustment to depart from the strict letter of the ordinance, should be substantial and of compelling force." And in Valicenti's Appeal, 298 Pa. 276, 283, 148 A. 308, 310, 311, it was said: "It is true that variations may be permitted, but only in cases of practical necessity, and for reasons that are 'substantial, serious and compelling.' " To the same effect is Jennings' Appeal, 330 Pa. 154, 159, 160, 198 A. 621, 623. In Junge's Appeal (No. 1), 89 Pa.Super. 543, 546, the late, lamented Judge Keller said: "The authority thus placed in the Board is not an arbitrary one. The discretion vested in the Board is subject to review if abused or not exercised in accordance with the provisions of the Act. The statute does not give the Board power to do whatever they feel inclined to, regardless of the provisions of the statute. . . . The strict letter of the ordinance may be departed from only where there are practical difficulties or unnecessary hardships in the way of carrying it out; and in such manner that the spirit of the ordinance may be observed, the public health, safety and general welfare secured and substantial justice done. No other considerations should enter into the decision." This case was cited, and the principle which it enunciated was followed, in Appeal of Heman Johnson, 93 Pa.Super. 599, and Huebner v. Philadelphia Saving Fund Society, 127 Pa.Super. 28, 192 A. 139. It is true that ordinarily the grant or the refusal by the Board of Adjustment of a variance from the terms of a zoning ordinance should not be reversed unless its action was "a manifest and flagrant abuse of discretion": Jennings' Appeal, 330 Pa. 154, 157, 198 A. 621, 622; Perelman v. Yeadon Borough Board of Adjustment, 144 Pa.Super. 5, 10, 18 A.2d 438, 440. But we agree with the court below that in this case the Board of Adjustment did abuse its discretion in allowing a so-called "exception" or variance, for there was no evidence to support such a grant. It is of some significance that the Board did not state facts or advance reasons for its action. Mere hardship is not sufficient; there must be *unnecessary* hardship, and there is nothing in the record to indicate that the Foundation will be subjected to such hardship by denial of the right to use the Ilsley property as a dormitory for its pupils. It bought the property with full knowledge of the terms of the ordinance, and certainly the mere curtailment of its ambition to expand its work over forbidden territory is not an unnecessary hardship within the statutory meaning of that phrase; to hold otherwise would be to nullify the entire purpose and effect of the zoning regulations. Moreover, the power given by the statute and by the ordinance to authorize a variance is limited by the provision that it must be such "as will not be contrary to the public interest"; this presumably is intended to insure protection of the interests of that portion of the public which is affected by the variance, namely, the owners and occupants of the neighboring properties. The objections raised by the latter cannot be dismissed as capricious or unduly selfish. While it is true that the Foundation will, in any event, continue to operate its school, on the "Academy" property, it is natural that the creation of a dormitory on the Ilsley tract should arouse added apprehension among the neighbors, for the close presence of persons who are below the normal standards of mental capacity and are subject to psychological and psychiatric aberrations not only constitutes a depressing factor calculated to interfere with the enjoyment of home life but even involves the potential danger of physical disturbances.

We do not believe that it was the intention of the legislature, nor of the township supervisors, to empower a board of adjustment to set at naught the zoning statute and ordinance under the guise of a variance. The power to authorize such a variance is to be sparingly exercised and only under peculiar and exceptional circumstances, for otherwise there would be little left of the zoning law to protect public rights; prospective purchasers of property would hesitate if confronted by a tribunal which could arbitrarily set aside the zoning provisions designed to establish standards of occupancy in the neighborhood. Indeed, if such power were to be interpreted as a grant to the board of the right to amend or depart from the terms of the ordinance at its uncontrolled will and pleasure, it might well be challenged as being an unconstitutional delegation of legislative authority to a purely administrative tribunal.

Order affirmed; costs to be paid by appellant.

[the dissenting opinion of JONES, J., is omitted.]

NOTES

1. There is considerable evidence that zoning boards of adjustment tend to be too lenient in granting variances, especially as to use, and thereby endanger the integrity of the zoning plan. See Anderson, The Board of Zoning Appeals—Villain or Victim? 13 Syracuse L.Rev. 353 (1962); Dukeminier and Stapleton, The Zoning Board of Adjustment: A Case Study in Misrule, 50 Ky.L.J. 273 (1952). Judicial reaction has ranged from tolerance to extreme hostility. The grant of power to zoning boards of adjustment, to allow variances, in some statutes and ordinances has been held void as a delegation of legislative power. E.g., Welton v. Hamilton, 344 Ill. 82, 176 N.E. 333 (1931). The Illinois statute was later amended. In other cases courts have construed these grants of power very narrowly. Some courts, unable to see any real distinction between amendments and use variances, have been unwilling to believe that it was intended that an administrative agency have power to amend the ordinance, and have held that the variance power does not include uses, but is limited to area, height and density provisions. Green, The Power of the Zoning Board of Adjustment to Grant Variances from the Zoning Ordinance, 29 N.C.L.Rev. 245 (1951). Other courts have indicated that use variances are to be granted more sparingly than dimensional variances and that the burden of establishing "unnecessary hardship" for the latter may be very onerous, proof being required that the hardship is more than loss of financial gain,

that the applicant has made reasonable efforts to sell, that the hardship is unique (i.e., not suffered also by applicant's neighbors), that the hardship is not self-inflicted, and that granting the variance will not alter the character of the neighborhood. Puritan-Greenfield Improvement Association v. Leo, 7 Mich.App. 659, 153 N.W.2d 162 (1967); Bellamy v. Board of Appeals, 32 Misc.2d 520, 223 N.Y.S.2d 1017 (1962). Similar proof requirements have also been written into enabling acts and ordinances and made applicable to dimensional, as well as use, variances. Ziman v. Village of Glencoe, 132 Ill.App.2d 399, 270 N.E.2d 537 (1971). Almost uniformly, decisions by zoning boards of adjustment have been reviewed by courts as they review other administrative decisions. They are not accorded the presumption of validity accorded legislation. A remarkable exception is Shelton v. City of College Station, 780 F.2d 475 (5th Cir.1986).

2. Zoning boards of adjustment sometimes grant variances subject to conditions, typically calculated to minimize harm to neighboring land uses. Would explicit statutory authorization of this practice be required? Consider the sufficiency of the ordinance in Devereux, supra. How can this practice be reconciled with the theoretical basis of the variance device? Is this a desirable practice? What types of conditions would clearly be beyond the power of the board to impose? How about a requirement that one granted renewal for five years of a use variance for storage of excavation machinery dedicate without compensation a permanent easement for street widening? This was upheld in Bringle v. Board of Supervisors of Orange County, 54 Cal.2d 86, 4 Cal.Rptr. 493, 351 P.2d 765 (1960). How about a use variance to allow a rooming house on condition that it continue to be owned and managed by applicant, who has convinced the board that he will do nothing to harm the neighborhood? This was held invalid in Olevson v. Zoning Board of Review of Town of Narragansett, 71 R.I. 303, 44 A.2d 720 (1954). Accord: St. Onge v. Donovan, 71 N.Y.2d 507, 527 N.Y.S.2d 721, 722, 522 N.E.2d 1019, 1020 (1988): "[C]onditions imposed on the grant of a variance must relate only to the use of the property . . . without regard to the person who owns or occupies the property." See generally Strine, The Use of Conditions in Land-Use Control, 67 Dick.L. Rev. 109 (1963).

3. When an application for a special exception or variance is denied by the board, what relief may be obtained on appeal to a court? See Pendergast v. Board of Appeals, 331 Mass. 555, 559–560, 120 N.E.2d 916, 919 (1954), Qua, C.J., declaring: "Both parties and the judge at the hearing seem to have treated this statute as practically substituting the court for the board of appeals and giving the court the same power to grant variances that the board possesses. We do not think that is the meaning of the statute. The vesting in a court of authority to grant or order licenses, permits, or similar privileges of any kind is to say the least unusual. Especially would it be unusual to vest such authority where the granting or refusal of the license, permit, or privilege is in the nature of the exercise of administrative discretion and where the law gives no one a right to such license, permit, or privilege. It is the usual function of courts to secure and defend legal rights. The exercise

by a court of licensing powers apart from questions of legal right would involve grave constitutional doubts. The statute should be so construed if reasonably possible, as to avoid such doubts. . . .

"We think no one has a legal right to a variance. If a case should come to us in which an owner had been denied a variance solely upon a legally untenable ground and the board should indicate that except for that ground the variance would have been granted, perhaps the court could give relief. But no such case is before us. Neither have we before us a case where the decision of the board is unreasonable, whimsical, capricious, or arbitrary and so illegal. We make no implication, as to such a case, if such a case can arise."

In St. Onge v. Donovan, supra paragraph 2, the court invalidated a condition attached to a variance, but allowed the variance to stand. Should the court have done so?

SECTION 4. CONTRACT ZONING, FLOATING ZONES AND PLANNED UNIT DEVELOPMENTS

COLLARD v. INCORPORATED VILLAGE OF FLOWER HILL

Court of Appeals of New York, 1981.
52 N.Y.2d 594, 439 N.Y.S.2d 326, 421 N.E.2d 818.

JONES, JUDGE.

Where a local municipality conditions an amendment of its zoning ordinance on the execution of a declaration of covenants providing, in part, that no construction may occur on the property so rezoned without the consent of the municipality, absent a provision that such consent may not be unreasonably withheld the municipality may not be compelled to issue such consent or give an acceptable reason for failing to do so.

Appellants now own improved property in the Village of Flower Hill. In 1976, the then owners of the subject premises and appellants' predecessors in title, applied to the village board of trustees to rezone the property from a General Municipal and Public Purposes District to a Business District.[1] On October 4 of that year the village board granted the rezoning application by the following resolution:

"RESOLVED that the application of Ray R. Beck Company for a change of Zone of premises known and designated as Section 6, Block

1. Prior to 1964 the subject premises, then vacant, had been zoned for single-family dwellings with a minimum lot size of 7,500 square feet. In that year the then owners applied to the village board to rezone a portion of the property and place it in the General Municipal and Public Purposes District so that a private sanitarium might be constructed. Concurrently with that application a declaration of covenants restricting the use of the property to a sanitarium was recorded in the county clerk's office. The village board then granted the rezoning application, but limited the property's use to the purposes set forth in the declaration of covenants. The 1976 rezoning application, which as conditionally granted is the subject of this suit, was made because the private sanitarium had fallen into disuse and it was asserted that without rezoning the property could neither be sold nor leased.

73, Lots 9, 12 and 13 on the land and tax map of Nassau County from General Municipal and Public Purposes District be and the same hereby is granted upon the following conditions:

"(a) The Subject Premises and any buildings, structures and improvements situated or to be situated thereon, will be erected, altered, renovated, remodelled, used, occupied and maintained for the following purposes and no other;

"(i) Offices for the practice of the professions of medicine, dentistry, law, engineering, architecture or accountancy;

"(ii) Executive offices to be used solely for the management of business concerns and associations and excluding therefrom, but without limitation, retail or wholesale sales offices or agencies, brokerage offices of all types and kinds, collection or employment agencies or offices, computer programming centres or offices, counseling centres or offices and training offices or business or trade schools.

"(b) No more than four separate tenancies or occupancies are to be permitted on the subject premises or in any building, structure or improvement situated therein at any one time.

"(c) No building or structure or any portion thereof situated or to be situated on the Subject Premises is to be occupied by more than one person (excluding visitors, clients or guests of any tenant or occupant of such building or structure) for each 190 square feet of the gross floor area of such building or structure;

"(d) No building or structure situated on the Subject Premises on the date of this Declaration of Covenants will be altered, extended, rebuilt, renovated or enlarged without the prior consent of the Board of Trustess of the Village.

"(e) There will be maintained on the Subject Premises at all times, no less than twenty-six paved off-street, onsite parking spaces for automobiles and other vehicles, each such parking space to be at least 9″ × 20″ in dimensions and will be served by aisles and means of ingress and egress of sufficient width to permit the free movement and parking of automobiles and other vehicles.

"(f) Trees and shrubs installed on the Subject Premises pursuant to a landscape plan heretofore filed with the Village in or about 1964, will be maintained in compliance with said landscape plan."

Subsequently, appellants' predecessors in title entered into the contemplated declaration of covenants which was recorded in the office of the Clerk of Nassau County on November 29, 1976. Consistent with paragraph (d) of the board's resolution, that declaration provided that "[n]o building or structure situated on the Subject Premises on the date of this Declaration of Covenants will be altered, extended, rebuilt, renovated or enlarged without the prior consent of the Board of Trustees of the Village."

Appellants, after acquiring title, made application in late 1978 to the village board for approval to enlarge and extend the existing structure on the premises. Without any reason being given that application was denied. Appellants then commenced this action to have the board's determination declared arbitrary, capricious, unreasonable, and unconstitutional and sought by way of ultimate relief an order directing the board to issue the necessary building permits.

Asserting that the board's denial of the application was beyond review as to reasonableness, respondent moved to dismiss the complaint for failure to state a cause of action. Special Term denied the motion, equating appellants' allegation that the board's action was arbitrary and capricious with an allegation that such action was lacking in good faith and fair dealing—an allegation which it found raised triable issues of fact. The Appellate Division, 75 A.D.2d 631, 427 N.Y.S.2d 301, reversed and dismissed the complaint, holding that the allegation of arbitrary and capricious action by the board was not the equivalent of an allegation that the board breached an implied covenant of fair dealing and good faith. We now affirm.

At the outset this case involves the question of the permissibility of municipal rezoning conditioned on the execution of a private declaration of covenants restricting the use to which the parcel sought to be rezoned may be put. Prior to our decision in Church v. Town of Islip, 8 N.Y.2d 254, 203 N.Y.S.2d 866, 168 N.E.2d 680 in which we upheld rezoning of property subject to reasonable conditions, conditional rezoning had been almost uniformly condemned by courts of all jurisdictions—a position to which a majority of States appear to continue to adhere. Since *Church,* however, the practice of conditional zoning has become increasingly widespread in this State, as well as having gained popularity in other jurisdictions (see, e.g., Scrutton v. County of Sacramento, 275 Cal.App.2d 412, 79 Cal.Rptr. 872; Goffinet v. County of Christian, 30 Ill.App.3d 1089, 333 N.E.2d 731; City of Greenbelt v. Bresler, 248 Md. 210, 236 A.2d 1; Sylvania Elec. Prods. v. City of Newton, 344 Mass. 428, 183 N.E.2d 118; Gladwyne Colony v. Lower Merion Twp., 409 Pa. 441, 187 A.2d 549).

Because much criticism has been mounted against the practice, both by commentators and the courts of some of our sister States,[3] further exposition is in order.

Probably the principal objection to conditional rezoning is that it constitutes illegal spot zoning, thus violating the legislative mandate requiring that there be a comprehensive plan for, and that all condi-

3. (See, e.g., Babcock, The Zoning Game, chs. 1, 3; Basset, Zoning, ch. 9; Crolly, The Rezoning of Properties Conditioned on Agreements with Property Owners—Zoning by Contract, N.Y.L.J., March 9, 1961, p. 4, col. 1; Scott, Toward a Strategy for Utilization of Contract and Conditional Zoning, 51 J. Urban L. 94; Trager, Contract Zoning, 23 Md.L.Rev. 121; Note, Three Aspects of Zoning: Unincorporated Areas—Exclusionary Zoning—Conditional Zoning, 6 Real Prop., Prob. & Tr. J. 178 (1971); Comment, The Use and Abuse of Contract Zoning, 12 U.C.L.A.L.Rev. 897. For judicial criticism, see, e.g., Allred v. City of Raleigh, 277 N.C. 530, 178 S.E.2d 432; Baylis v. City of Baltimore, 219 Md. 164, 148 A.2d 429; City of Farmers Branch v. Hawnco, Inc., 435 S.W.2d 288 [tex.civ. app.]; Ford Leasing Dev. Co. v. Board of County Comrs., 186 Colo. 418, 528 P.2d 237; Hartnett v. Austin, 93 So.2d 86 [fla.]; Haymon v. City of Chattanooga, 513 S.W.2d 185 [tenn.app.] ; Houston Petroleum Co. v. Automotive Prods. Credit Assn., 9 N.J. 122, 87 A.2d 319; Sandenburgh v. Michigamme Oil Co., 249 Mich. 372, 228 N.W. 707; Ziemer v. County of Peoria, 33 Ill.App.3d 612, 338 N.E.2d 145.

tions be uniform within, a given zoning district. When courts have considered the issue . . ., the assumptions have been made that conditional zoning benefits particular landowners rather than the community as a whole and that it undermines the foundation upon which comprehensive zoning depends by destroying uniformity within use districts. Such unexamined assumptions are questionable. First, it is a downward change to a less restrictive zoning classification that benefits the property rezoned and not the opposite imposition of greater restrictions on land use. Indeed, imposing limiting conditions, while benefiting surrounding properties, normally adversely affects the premises on which the conditions are imposed. Second, zoning is not invalid per se merely because only a single parcel is involved or benefited (Matter of Mahoney v. O'Shea Funeral Homes, 45 N.Y.2d 719, 408 N.Y.S.2d 470, 380 N.E.2d 297); the real test for spot zoning is whether the change is other than part of a well-considered and comprehensive plan calculated to serve the general welfare of the community (Rodgers v. Village of Tarrytown, 302 N.Y. 115, 96 N.E.2d 731). Such a determination, in turn, depends on the reasonableness of the rezoning in relation to neighboring uses—an inquiry required regardless of whether the change in zone is conditional in form. Third, if it is initially proper to change a zoning classification without the imposition of restrictive conditions notwithstanding that such change may depart from uniformity, then no reason exists why accomplishing that change subject to condition should automatically be classified as impermissible spot zoning.

Both conditional and unconditional rezoning involve essentially the same legislative act—an amendment of the zoning ordinance. The standards for judging the validity of conditional rezoning are no different from the standards used to judge whether unconditional rezoning is illegal. If modification to a less restrictive zoning classification is warranted, then a fortiori conditions imposed by a local legislature to minimize conflicts among districts should not in and of themselves violate any prohibition against spot zoning.

Another fault commonly voiced in disapproval of conditional zoning is that it constitutes an illegal bargaining away of a local government's police power . . .. Because no municipal government has the power to make contracts that control or limit it in the exercise of its legislative powers and duties, restrictive agreements made by a municipality in conjunction with a rezoning are sometimes said to violate public policy. While permitting citizens to be governed by the best bargain they can strike with a local legislature would not be consonant with notions of good government, absent proof of a contract purporting to bind the local legislature in advance to exercise its zoning authority in a bargained-for manner, a rule which would have the effect of forbidding a municipality from trying to protect landowners in the vicinity of a zoning change by imposing protective conditions based on the assertion that that body is bargaining away its discretion, would not be in the best interests of the public. The imposition of conditions on property sought to be rezoned may not be classified as a prospective commitment on the part of the municipality to zone as requested if the conditions are met; nor would the municipality necessarily be precluded on this account from later reversing or altering its decision (cf. Matter of Grimpel Assoc. v. Cohalan, 41 N.Y.2d 431, 393 N.Y.S.2d 373, 361 N.E.2d 1022).

Yet another criticism leveled at conditional zoning is that the State enabling legislation does not confer on local authorities authorization to enact conditional zoning amendments (see, e.g., Houston Petroleum Co. v. Automotive Prods. Credit Assn., 9 N.Y. 122, 87 A.2d 319, supra; Baylis v. City of Baltimore, 219 Md. 164, 148 A.2d 429, supra). On this view any such ordinance would be *ultra vires.* While it is accurate to say there exists no explicit authorization that a legislative body may attach conditions to zoning amendments (see, e.g., Village Law, § 7–700 et seq.), neither is there any language which expressly forbids a local legislature to do so. Statutory silence is not necessarily a denial of the authority to engage in such a practice. Where in the face of nonaddress in the enabling legislation there exists independent justification for the practice as an appropriate exercise of municipal power, that power will be implied. Conditional rezoning is a means of achieving some degree of flexibility in land-use control by minimizing the potentially deleterious effect of a zoning change on neighboring properties; reasonably conceived conditions harmonize the landowner's need for rezoning with the public interest and certainly fall within the spirit of the enabling legislation (see Church v. Town of Islip, 8 N.Y.2d 254, 203 N.Y.S.2d 866, 168 N.E.2d 680, supra).

One final concern of those reluctant to uphold the practice is that resort to conditional rezoning carries with it no inherent restrictions apart from the restrictive agreement itself. This fear, however, is justifiable only if conditional rezoning is considered a contractual relationship between municipality and private party, outside the scope of the zoning power—a view to which we do not subscribe. When conditions are incorporated in an amending ordinance, the result is as much a "zoning regulation" as an ordinance, adopted without conditions. Just as the scope of all zoning regulation is limited by the police power, and thus local legislative bodies must act reasonably and in the best interests of public safety, welfare and convenience . . ., the scope of permissible conditions must of necessity be similarly limited. If, upon proper proof, the conditions imposed are found unreasonable, the rezoning amendment as well as the required conditions would have to be nullified, with the affected property reverting to the preamendment zoning classification.

Against this backdrop we proceed to consideration of the contentions advanced by appellants in the appeal now before us. It is first useful to delineate arguments which they do not advance. Thus, they do not challenge the conditional zoning change made in 1976 at the behest of their predecessors in title; no contention is made that the village board was not authorized to adopt the resolution of October 4, 1976, conditioned as it was on the execution and recording of the declaration of covenants, or that the provisions of that declaration were in 1976 arbitrary, capricious, unreasonable or unconstitutional.[4] The reason may be what is apparent, namely, that any successful challenge to the adoption of the 1976 resolution would cause appellants' premises to revert to their pre-1976 zoning classification—a consequence clearly unwanted by them.

The focus of appellants' assault is the provision of the declaration of covenants that no structure may be extended or enlarged "without the prior consent of the Board of Trustees of the Village". Appellants would have us import the added substantive prescription—"which consent may not be unreasonably withheld". Their argument proceeds along two paths: first, that as a matter of construction the added prescription should be read into the provision; second, that because of limitations associated with the exercise of municipal zoning power the village board would have been required to include such a prescription.

Appellants' construction argument must fail. The terminology employed in the declaration is explicit. The concept that appellants would invoke is not obscure and language to give it effect was readily available had it been the intention of the parties to include this added stipulation. Appellants point to no canon of construction in the law of real property or of contracts which would call for judicial insertion of the missing clause. Where language has been chosen containing no inherent ambiguity or uncertainty, courts are properly hesitant, under the guise of judicial construction, to imply additional requirements to relieve a party from asserted disadvantage flowing from the terms actually used (cf. Dress Shirt Sales v. Martinque Assoc., 12 N.Y.2d 339, 239 N.Y.S.2d 660, 190 N.E.2d 10).

The second path either leads nowhere or else goes too far. If it is appellants' assertion that the village board was legally required to insist on inclusion of the desired prescription, there is no authority in the court to reform the zoning enactment of 1976 retroactively to impose the omitted clause. Whether the village board at that time would have enacted a different resolution in the form now desired by appellants is open only to speculation; the certainty is that they did not then take such legislative action. On the other hand, acceptance of appellants' proposition would produce as the other possible consequence the conclusion that the 1976 enactment was illegal, throwing appellants unhappily back to the pre-1976 zoning of their premises, a destination which they assuredly wish to sidestep.

Finally, we agree with the Appellate Division that the allegation of the complaint that the village board in denying appellants' application acted in an arbitrary and capricious manner is not an allegation that the board acted in bad faith or its equivalent.

For the reasons stated the Board of Trustees of the Incorporated Village of Flower Hill may not now be compelled to issue its consent to the proposed enlargement and extension of the existing structure on

4. Inasmuch as no contention is made that the adoption of the 1976 resolution by the village board constituted impermissible spot zoning or that the action of the board at that time was otherwise unreasonable or constituted an impermissible exercise of its zoning powers, we do not reach or consider such issues.

the premises or in the alternative give an acceptable reason for failing to do so. Accordingly, the order of the Appellate Division should be affirmed, with costs.

NOTES

1. Compare State ex rel. Zupancic v. Schimenz, 46 Wis.2d 22, 174 N.W.2d 533 (1970): "We hold that when a city itself makes an agreement with a landowner to rezone the contract is invalid; this is contract zoning. However, when the agreement is made by others than the city to conform the property in a way or manner which makes it acceptable for the requested rezoning and the city is not committed to rezone, it is not contract zoning in the true sense and does not vitiate the zoning if it is otherwise valid."

2. Would there be any sound objection to including in the rezoning ordinance and the deed restriction provisions a declaration that breach of any restriction will automatically restore the prior zoning? Consider Scrutton v. County of Sacramento, 275 Cal.App.2d 412, 79 Cal. Rptr. 872 (1969).

3. Should a contract to rezone ever bind the local government? A city was held bound in Mahoney Grease Service, Inc. v. City of Joliet, 85 Ill.App.3d 578, 40 Ill.Dec. 708, 406 N.E.2d 911 (1980). As part of a settlement of a condemnation suit, the city had agreed, in exchange for landowner's consent to annexation, to rezone. The court explained: "The city retained the benefits of dismissal of the condemnation proceedings. . . . Where municipalities have received and accepted the benefits of a contract, they are estopped to deny its validity."

4. The varying positions of courts on contract zoning are surveyed in Kramer, Contract Zoning—Old Myths and New Realities, Land Use L., August 1982, p. 4.

CHENEY v. VILLAGE OF NEW HOPE, INC.

Supreme Court of Pennsylvania, 1968.
429 Pa. 626, 241 A.2d 81.

ROBERTS, JUSTICE. Under traditional concepts of zoning the task of determining the type, density and placement of buildings which should exist within any given zoning district devolves upon the local legislative body. In order that this body might have to speak only infrequently on the issue of municipal planning and zoning, the local legislature usually enacts detailed requirements for the type, size and location of buildings within each given zoning district, and leaves the ministerial task of enforcing these regulations to an appointed zoning administrator, with another administrative body, the zoning board of adjustment, passing on individual deviations from the strict district requirements, deviations known commonly as variances and special exceptions. At the same time, the overall rules governing the dimensions, placement, etc. of primarily public additions to ground, e.g., streets, sewers, playgrounds, are formulated by the local legislature through the passage of subdivision regulations. These regulations are enforced and applied to individual lots by an administrative body usually known as the planning commission.

This general approach to zoning fares reasonably well so long as development takes place on a lot-by-lot basis, and so long as no one cares that the overall appearance of the municipality resembles the design achieved by using a cookie cutter on a sheet of dough. However, with the increasing popularity of large scale residential development, particularly in suburban areas, it has become apparent to many local municipalities that land can be more efficiently used, and developments more aesthetically pleasing, if zoning regulations focus on density requirements rather than on specific rules for each individual lot. Under density zoning, the legislature determines what percentage of a particular district must be devoted to open space, for example, and what percentage used for dwelling units. The task of filling in the particular district with real houses and real open spaces then falls upon the planning commission usually working in conjunction with an individual large scale developer. See Chrinko v. South Brunswick Twp., Planning Bd., 77 N.J.Super. 594, 187 A.2d 221 (1963). The ultimate goal of this so-called density or cluster concept of zoning is achieved when an entire self-contained little community is permitted to be built within a zoning district, with the rules of density controlling not only the relation of private dwellings to open space, but also the relation of homes to commercial establishments such as theaters, hotels, restaurants, and quasi-commercial uses such as schools and churches. The present controversy before this Court involves a frontal attack upon one of these zoning districts, known in the trade as a Planned Unit Development (hereinafter PUD).

Spurred by the desire of appellant developer to construct a Planned Unit Development in the Borough of New Hope, in December of 1964 Borough Council began considering the passage of a new zoning ordinance to establish a PUD district in New Hope. After extensive consultation with appellant, council referred the matter to the New Hope Planning Commission for further study. This body, approximately six months after the project idea was first proposed, formally recommended to council that a PUD district be created. Council consulted with members of the Bucks County Planning Commission on the text of the proposed ordinance, held public hearings, and finally on June 14, 1965 enacted ordinance 160 which created the PUD district, and ordinance 161 which amended the Borough zoning map, rezoning a large tract of land known as the Rauch farm from low density residential to PUD. Pursuant to the procedural requirements of ordinance 160, appellant presented plans for a Planned Unit Development on the Rauch tract to the Borough Planning Commission. These plans were approved on November 8, 1965, and accordingly four days later two building permits, known as zoning permits 68 and 69, were issued to appellant. (Some question exists as to the current status of these permits, see text infra.) Subsequently, permit number 75 was issued. Appellees, all neighboring property owners opposing the issuance of these permits, appealed to the zoning board of adjustment. The board, after taking extensive testimony, upheld ordinances 160 and 161 and accordingly affirmed the issuance of the permits. Appellees then appealed to the Bucks County Court of Common Pleas. That tribunal took no additional testimony but reversed the board, holding the ordinances invalid for failure to conform to a comprehensive plan and for vesting too much discretion in the New Hope Planning Commission. This Court granted certiorari under Supreme Court Rule 68½. . . .

I.

Approximately one year before the PUD seed was planted in New Hope, Borough Council had approved the New Hope Comprehensive Plan. This detailed land use projection clearly envisioned the Rauch tract as containing only single family dwellings of low density. The court below therefore concluded that the enactment of ordinance 160, and more specifically the placing of a PUD district on the Rauch tract by ordinance 161 was not "in accordance with a comprehensive plan," as required by the Act of February 1, 1966, P.L. (1965)—§ 3203, 53 P.S. § 48203. See also Eves v. Zoning Bd. of Adjustment, 401 Pa. 211, 164 A.2d 7 (1960).

The fallacy in the court's reasoning lies in its mistaken belief that a comprehensive plan, once established, is forever binding on the municipality and can never be amended. Cases subsequent to *Eves* have made it clear, however, that these plans may be changed by the passage of new zoning ordinances, provided the local legislature passes the new ordinance with some demonstration of sensitivity to the community as a whole, and the impact that the new ordinance will have on this community. As Mr. Chief Justice Bell so artfully stated in Furniss v. Lower Merion Twp., 412 Pa. 404, 406, 194 A.2d 926, 927 (1963): "It is a matter of common sense and reality that a comprehensive plan is not like the law of the Medes and the Persians; it must be subject to reasonable change from time to time as conditions in an area or a township or a large neighborhood change." This salutary rule that comprehensive plans may be later amended by the passage of new zoning ordinances has been approved not only in *Furniss,* but also in Donahue v. Zoning Bd. of Adjustment, 412 Pa. 332, 194 A.2d 610 (1963) and Key Realty Co. Zoning Case, 408 Pa. 98, 182 A.2d 187 (1962).

Given this rule of law allowing post-plan zoning changes, and the presumption in favor of an ordinance's validity, see *National Land,* supra, 421 Pa. at 521–522, 215 A.2d at 607, we are not in a position, having reviewed the record in the present case, to say that the zoning board committed an abuse of discretion or an error of law when it concluded that ordinances 160 and 161 were properly passed. Presented as it was with evidence that the PUD district had been under consideration by council for over six months and had been specifically recommended by the borough planning commission, a body specially equipped to view proposed ordinances as they relate to the rest of the community, we hold that the board, within its sound discretion, could have concluded that council passed the ordinances with the proper overall considerations in mind. The PUD district established by ordinance 160 is not the type of use which by its very nature could have no place in the middle of a predominantly residential borough. It is not a steel mill, a fat rendering plant, or a desiccated egg factory. It is, in fact, nothing more than a miniature residential community.

Closely tied to the comprehensive plan issue is the argument raised by appellees that ordinances 160 and 161 constitute spot zoning outlawed by *Eves,* supra. Given the fact situation in *Eves,* however, as well as the post-*Eves* cases, we do not believe that there is any spot zoning here. In *Eves,* the municipality created a limited industrial district, F–1, which, by explicit legislative pronouncement, was not to be applied to any particular tract until the individual land owner requested that his own tract be so re-zoned. The obvious evil in this procedure did *not* lie in the fact that a limited industrial district might be placed in an area previously zoned, for example, residential. The evil was the *pre-ordained* uncertainty as to where the F–1 districts would crop up. The ordinance all but invited spot zoning where the legislature could respond to private entreaties from land owners and re-zone tracts F–1 without regard to the surrounding community. In *Eves,* it was almost impossible for the F–1 districts to conform to a comprehensive plan since tracts would be re-zoned on a strictly ad hoc basis.

Quite to the contrary, no such "floating zone" exists in the present case. On the very day that the PUD district was created by ordinance 160, it was brought to earth by ordinance 161; and, as discussed supra, this *was* done "in accordance with a comprehensive plan." Speaking of a similar procedure in Donahue v. Zoning Bd. of Adjustment, 412 Pa. 332, 194 A.2d 610 (1963), this court faced squarely an attack based upon *Eves* and responded thusly:

"It was this case by case review [in *Eves*] which demonstrated the absence of a comprehensive plan and which sought to enable the Board of Supervisors [the local legislative body] to exercise powers they did not statutorily possess.

"In the instant case, the new classification was established and the zoning map amended within a very short period of time [in the case at bar, on the same day]. Under the rules of statutory construction which are likewise applicable to ordinances, see Cloverleaf Trailer Sales Co. v. Pleasant Hills Borough, 366 Pa. 116, 76 A.2d 872 (1950); Philadelphia to Use of Polselli v. Phillips, 179 Pa.Super. 87, 116 A.2d 243 (1955); these ordinances should be read together as one enactment. See Statutory Construction Act, May 28, 1937, P.L. 1019, § 62, 46 P.S. § 562, 1952. So construed, Ordinances 151 [creating new zone] and 155 [amending zoning map] do not create the 'floating zone', anchored only upon case by case application by landowners, which we struck down in *Eves.* While it is true that the change here was made upon request of a particular landowner, this does not necessarily create the evils held invalid in *Eves* where the defects were specifically created by the very terms of the ordinances. It is not unusual for a zoning change to be made on request of a landowner, and such change is not invalid if made in accordance with a comprehensive plan." 412 Pa. at 334–335, 194 A.2d at 611.

We think *Donahue* is completely controlling on the issue of alleged spot zoning and compels the conclusion that ordinances 160 and 161 do not fall on that ground. See also the excellent discussion of *Eves* and its progeny in Krasnowiecki, Legal Aspects of Planned Unit Development, Technical Bull. 52, Urban Land Institute, pp. 20–22 (1965).

II.

The court below next concluded that even if the two ordinances were properly *passed,* they must fall as vesting authority in the planning commission greater than that permitted under Pennsylvania's zoning enabling legislation. More specifically, it is now contended by appellees that complete project approval by the planning commission under ordinance 160 requires that commission to encroach upon legislative territory whenever it decides where, within a particular PUD district, specific types of building should be placed.

In order to appreciate fully the arguments of counsel on both sides it is necessary to explain in some detail exactly what is permitted within a PUD district, and who decides whether a particular land owner has complied with these requirements. Admittedly the range of permissible uses within the PUD district is greater than that normally found in a traditional zoning district. Within a New Hope PUD district there may be: single family attached or detached dwellings; apartments; accessory private garages; public or private parks and recreation areas including golf courses, swimming pools, ski slopes, etc. (so long as these facilities do not produce noise, glare, odor, air pollution, etc., detrimental to existing or prospective adjacent structures); a municipal building; a school; churches; art galleries; professional offices; certain types of signs; a theatre (but not a drive-in); motels and hotels; and a restaurant. The ordinance then sets certain overall density requirements. The PUD district may have a maximum of 80% of the land devoted to residential uses, a maximum of 20% for the permitted commercial uses and enclosed recreational facilities, and must have a minimum of 20% for open spaces. The residential density shall not exceed 10 units per acre, nor shall any such unit contain more than two bedrooms. All structures within the district must not exceed maximum height standards set out in the ordinance. Finally, although there are no traditional "set back" and "side yard" requirements, ordinance 160 does require that there be 24 feet between structures, and that no townhouse structure contain more than 12 dwelling units.

The procedure to be followed by the aspiring developer reduces itself to presenting a detailed plan for his planned unit development to the planning commission, obtaining that body's approval and then securing building permits. Of course, the planning commission may not approve any development that fails to meet the requirements set forth in the ordinance as outlined above.

We begin with the observation that there is nothing in the borough zoning enabling act which would prohibit council from creating a zoning district with this many permissible uses. The applicable section of the borough code is the Act of February 1, 1966, P.L. (1965)—§ 3201, 53 P.S. § 48201. Under this section, council is given the power to regulate and restrict practically all aspects of buildings themselves, open spaces, population density, location of structures, etc., the only limitation on this power being that it be exercised so as to promote the "health, safety, morals or the general welfare" of the borough. Under the same act, section 1601, 53 P.S. § 46601, empowers council to adopt ordinances to govern the use of public areas, such as streets, parks, etc., again with the only limitation being that such ordinances create "conditions favorable to the health, safety, morals, and general welfare of the citizens." Thus, if council reasonably believed that a given district could contain *all* types of structures, without *any* density requirements whatsoever, so long as this did not adversely affect health, safety and morals, such a district could be created. In fact, it is common knowledge that in many industrial and commercial districts just such a wide range of uses is permitted. Given such broad power to zone, we cannot say that New Hope Borough Council abrogated its legislative function by creating a PUD district permitting the mixture of uses outlined supra, especially given the density requirements.

We must next examine the statutory power of the borough planning commission to determine whether such an administrative body may regulate the internal development of a PUD district. The Act of February 1, 1966, P.L. (1965)—§ 1155, 53 P.S. § 46155 requires that all plans for land "laid out in building lots" be approved by the planning commission before they may be recorded. Thus, the traditional job of the commission has been to examine tract plans to determine whether they conform to the applicable borough ordinances. The ordinances most frequently interpreted and applied by the planning commission are those dealing with streets, sewers, water and gas mains, etc., i.e., the so-called public improvements. However, the statute contains no language which would prohibit the planning commission from approving plans with reference to ordinances dealing with permissible building uses as well. The primary reason that planning commissions have not traditionally interpreted this type of ordinance is that such regulations do not usually come into play until the landowner wishes to begin the actual construction of a particular building. By this time, the relevant subdivision plan has already been approved by the commission; thus the task of examining the plans for a particular structure to see whether it conforms to the regulations for the zoning district in which it will be erected devolves upon the local building inspector who issues the building permit.

However, in the case of PUD the entire development (including specific structures) is mapped out and submitted to the administrative agency at once. Accordingly, the requirements set forth in a PUD ordinance must relate not only to those areas traditionally administered by the planning commission, but also to areas traditionally administered by the building inspector. Therefore, quite logically, the job of approving a particular PUD should rest with a single municipal body. The question then is simply which one: Borough Council (a legislative body), the Planning Commission (an administrative body), or the Zoning Board of Adjustment (an administrative body)?

There is no doubt that it would be statutorily permissible for council itself to pass a PUD ordinance and simultaneous zoning map amendment so specific that no details would be left for an administrator. The ordinance could specify where each building should be placed, how large it should be, where the open spaces are located, etc. But what would be the practical effect of such an ordinance? One of the most attractive features of Planned Unit Development is its flexibility; the chance for the builder and the municipality to sit down together and tailor a development to meet the specific needs of the community and the requirements of the land on which it is to be built. But all this would be lost if the Legislature let the planning cement set before any developer could happen upon the scene to scratch his own initials in that cement. Professor Krasnowiecki has accurately summed up the effect on planned unit development of such legislative planning. The picture, to be sure, is not a happy one:

> "The traditional refuge of the courts, the requirement that all the standards be set forth in advance of application for development, does not offer a practical solution to the problem. The complexity of pre-established regulations that would automatically dispose of any proposal for planned unit development, when different housing types and perhaps accessory commercial areas are envisaged, would be quite considerable. Indeed as soon as various housing types are permitted, the regulations that would govern their design and distribution on every possible kind of site, their relationship to each other and their relationship to surrounding properties must be complex unless the developer's choice in terms of site, site plan, and design and distribution of housing is reduced close to zero. It is not likely . . . that local authorities would want to adopt such a set of regulations." Krasnowiecki, Planned Unit Development: A Challenge to Established Theory and Practice of Land Use Control, 114 U.Pa.L.Rev. 47, 71 (1965).

Left with Professor Krasnowiecki's "Hobson's choice" of no developer leeway at all, or a staggering set of legislative regulations sufficient to cover every idea the developer might have, it is not likely that Planned Unit Development could thrive, or even maintain life, if the local legislature assumed totally the role of planner.

The remaining two municipal bodies which could oversee the shaping of specific Planned Unit Developments are both administrative agencies, the Zoning Board of Adjustment and the Planning Commission. As this Court views both reality and zoning enabling act, the Zoning Board of Adjustment is not the proper body. The Act of February 1, 1966, P.L. (1965)—§ 3207, 53 P.S. § 48207(g) specifically sets forth the powers of a borough zoning board of adjustment. These powers are three in number, and only three. The board may (1) hear and decide appeals where there is an alleged error made by an administrator in the enforcement of the enabling act or any ordinance enacted pursuant thereto; (2) hear and decide special exceptions; and (3) authorize the grant of variances from the terms of existing ordinances.

These powers in no way encompass the authority to review and approve the plan for an entire development when such plan is neither at variance with the existing ordinance nor is a special exception to it; nor does (1) above supply the necessary power since the board would not be reviewing an alleged administrative error.

Moreover, from a practical standpoint, a zoning board of adjustment is, of the three bodies here under discussion, the one least equipped to handle the problem of PUD approval. Zoning boards are accustomed to focusing on one lot at a time. They traditionally examine hardship cases and unique uses proposed by landowners. As Professor Krasnowiecki has noted: "To suggest that the board is intended, or competent, to handle large scale planning and design decisions is, I think, far fetched." Technical Bulletin 52, Urban Land Institute, p. 38 (1965). We agree.

Thus, the borough planning commission remains the only other body both qualified and statutorily permitted to approve PUD. Of course, we realize that a planning commission is not authorized to engage in actual re-zoning of land. But merely because the commission here has the power to approve more than one type of building for a particular lot within the PUD district does not mean that the commission is usurping the zoning function. Indeed, it is acting in strict *accordance* with the applicable zoning ordinance, for that ordinance, No. 160, *permits* more than one type of building for a particular lot. To be sure, if the commission approved a plan for a PUD district where 30% of the land were being used commercially, *then* we would have an example of illegal re-zoning by an administrator. But no one argues in the present case that appellant's plan does not conform to the requirements of ordinance 160.

Nor is this Court sympathetic to appellees' argument that ordinance 160 permits the planning commission to grant variances and special exceptions. We fail to see how a development such as appellant's that meets every single requirement of the applicable zoning ordinance can be said to be the product of a variance or a special exception. The very essence of variances and special exceptions lies in their *departure* from ordinance requirements, not in their compliance with them. We therefore conclude that the New Hope Planning Commission has the power to approve development plans submitted to it under ordinance 160. . . .

BELL, C.J., took no part in the consideration or decision of this case.

NOTE

The developer is permitted to exceed traditional building density requirements in some portions of the PUD tract, so long as he does not exceed overall building density requirements for the entire tract. Consider the possibility that such "transfers" of density might be made between tracts not within a single project. Would a developer be allowed to exceed the allowable density for his tract by transferring unused allowable density from an adjoining tract owned by him? This has been permitted in some downtown centers, notably in New York

City. See Newport Associates, Inc. v. Solow, 30 N.Y.2d 263, 332 N.Y.S.2d 617, 283 N.E.2d 600 (1972). This case involved floor area ratios (FAR), which limit the total floor area which may be built upon a lot. The lot owner is allowed great freedom in arranging his allowable floor area anywhere on his lot. He may build a tall, narrow building or a short, wide one. To allow transfer of unused allowable floor space from an adjoining lot owned by the developer to the lot upon which he proposes to build would not exceed overall density in the downtown center. Should a developer be allowed to transfer unused density allowable from a lot he owns in another part of the city? Can you imagine circumstances in which city officials would encourage, or require, a developer to do this? See pages 881 to 889, herein.

FRANKLAND v. CITY OF LAKE OSWEGO

Supreme Court of Oregon, 1973.
267 Or. 452, 517 P.2d 1042.

HOWELL, JUSTICE. Plaintiffs filed this action for a declaratory judgment seeking an injunction or, alternatively, an award of monetary damages as remedies for the construction of an apartment building by the defendant Dave Christensen, Inc. At the close of plaintiffs' case, the trial court allowed defendants' motion to dismiss. On appeal, the Court of Appeals reversed and remanded the case to the trial court, 8 Or.App. 224, 493 P.2d 163 (1972). We granted review.

The plaintiffs, adjoining property owners, challenge the validity of the construction of the apartment building which was erected pursuant to a planned unit development ordinance enacted by the City of Lake Oswego. Plaintiffs contend that the construction was not accomplished according to the planned unit development plan as submitted to the City, and that they are entitled to have the apartment building removed or be awarded damages for the depreciation in value of their property resulting from such construction.

. . .

The planned unit development concept necessarily allows for a great deal of discretion in the hands of planning authorities in implementing a PUD ordinance, but that discretion is properly in their hands and not those of the developers. Obviously, in order to guarantee a well conceived and well designed planned unit development, the planning authorities must have the necessary plans and information from the developer before making a decision. Once approved, the developer should be bound by the plans unless any changes are approved by the planning authorities in accordance with the PUD ordinance.

The ordinance delineates the procedure to be followed for a planned unit development:

The developer is required to submit to the Planning Commission a preliminary plan showing *inter alia* the building types and coverage of the real property, the proposed land use and densities, open spaces, and vehicular and pedestrian traffic plans. After submission of the preliminary plan, the City Planning Director is required to submit to the Planning Commission a staff report showing the existing zoning of the subject property and the "adjoining properties within or without the boundaries" of the City, plus comments on the proposed PUD.

After receiving the Planning Director's report, the Planning Commission is required to hold a public hearing on the application. After the hearing, the Planning Commission may approve in principle the preliminary plan, modify or reject it. Within six months from approval of the preliminary plan, the developer is required to file a final development plan showing land use, contours and drainage, traffic circulation, and landscaping. Section 53.330 of the PUD ordinance also requires, as part of the final plan, the submission of architectural sketches of the buildings proposed to be built in the PUD area. That section of the ordinance which is important to this case states:

"53.330. In planned-unit developments containing less than twenty-five acres the developer shall submit preliminary architectural sketches depicting the types of buildings and their approximate location on lots. The sketches to also depict the general height, bulk and type of construction and proximity of structures on lots.

"In planned-unit developments containing more than twenty-five acres the developer shall submit architectural sketches as required above for each phase of development containing less than twenty-five acres before the time such phase begins actual construction. For a planned-unit development or phase thereof in excess of twenty-five acres the developer shall submit architectural sketches depicting the types of buildings (single family, duplex, multi-family, commercial, etc.) and their prospective locations in the development showing their general height and bulk in relationship to the other improvements in the development and upon adjacent land."

At the time the applicant submits his final development plan, he is required to submit an application for a zone change. Thereafter, after notice is given, a public meeting is held and the Planning Commission considers the final plan and application for a zone change.

Finally, the City Council, after notice, holds a public hearing on the final plan and zone change, and if the Council approves the plan and change, an ordinance to that effect is adopted. The developer is then required to file with the City Recorder and the City Planning Director the final approved development plan.

Section 53.330 of the PUD ordinance requires, *inter alia,* a developer to submit architectural sketches showing the type of buildings to be constructed, their prospective locations in the development, and their general height and bulk characteristics.

Implicit in this requirement is that the developer build in accordance with these sketches so that the City's approval of the sketches acts as a device to control development. Thus, if a developer fails to comply with the sketches he has submitted, he is in noncompliance with the final plan and the zoning ordinance which was passed to implement that final plan.

. . .

The sketches submitted to the Planning Commission and the City Council . . . bear no resemblance, either generally or specifically, to the apartment building constructed. . . .

. . .

We conclude that the defendants Mountain Park and Christensen failed to build the apartment in accordance with the final plan submitted pursuant to Section 53.330 of the ordinance.

A requirement in a PUD ordinance that a developer submit final plans showing with some particularity the various features involved in his planned unit development, and that thereafter he is bound to these plans, serves at least two desirable purposes. First, it gives the planning authorities and the City Council full knowledge of what they are asked to approve before they grant a zone change. Secondly, it gives any opponent complete information about the project. It serves no worthwhile purpose for an ordinance to allow a full public hearing on a proposed planned unit development and zone change if the facts are not available. There is nothing to debate. Neither the opponents nor the proponents would know the issues, and the governing body charged with making a decision would be doing so in a vacuum. In so holding, we are aware of the need for flexibility in planning, but flexible planning does not, in our view, justify delegation of the planning function to a private developer, nor does it allow a developer to build without regard to plans as presented to the appropriate planning authorities.

. . .

While it might be said that the term "sketches" in the ordinance should not be read so expansively, we note that this is the only tool which the City can use to oversee the type, height, and bulk of structures to be built in advance of construction and thus has enhanced importance under the scheme of development envisaged by the general Lake Oswego PUD ordinance.

. . .

The decision of the Court of Appeals is affirmed as modified herein, and this cause is remanded to the circuit court for further proceedings consistent with this opinion.

O'CONNELL, CHIEF JUSTICE (dissenting).

. . .

The principal vice of the opinion is that it magnifies out of all proportion one aspect of planning (the architectural design of a building) at the cost of many other more important considerations in formulating a good land use plan.

NOTE

The Model Land Development Code adopted by the American Law Institute in 1975 (a state enabling act) represents a substantial departure from traditional American land use planning and control. These changes are summarized by the drafters as follows (page 29):

"1. It requires that zoning and subdivision regulations be combined in a single 'development ordinance' (§ 2–101(1)).

"2. It requires that the development ordinance be administered by a single 'Land Development Agency' (§ 2–102) but grants the local government great flexibility in designating who shall act as the Land Development Agency (§ 2–301(1)) and grants the Agency great flexibility in delegating functions to other officers, boards or committees (§ 2–301(2)).

"3. It establishes in some detail the administrative procedures to be used by the Land Development Agency (§§ 2–303–6).

"4. It attempts to discourage the local legislative body from becoming involved in individual development proposals (§ 2–312)."*

A central feature of the code is the development permit, which is required for "development" unless exempted by the local development ordinance (§ 2–102). "Development" is defined broadly (§ 1–202).

Another very significant aspect of the code is the larger-than-traditional role it accords the state in land use regulation, particularly with respect to "areas of critical state concern" and to "development of regional impact" (Art. 7).

SECTION 5. ZONING BY ELECTORATE

CITY OF EASTLAKE v. FOREST CITY ENTERPRISES, INC.

Supreme Court of the United States, 1976.
426 U.S. 668, 96 S.Ct. 2358, 49 L.Ed.2d 132.

MR. CHIEF JUSTICE BURGER delivered the opinion of the Court.

The question in this case is whether a city charter provision requiring proposed land use changes to be ratified by 55% of the voters violates the due process rights of a landowner who applies for a zoning change.

The city of Eastlake, Ohio, a suburb of Cleveland, has a comprehensive zoning plan codified in a municipal ordinance. Respondent, a real estate developer, acquired an eight-acre parcel of real estate in Eastlake zoned for "light industrial" uses at the time of purchase.

In May 1971, respondent applied to the City Planning Commission for a zoning change to permit construction of a multi-family, high-rise apartment building. The Planning Commission recommended the pro-

* [Copyright 1976. Reprinted with the permission of the American Law Institute.]

posed change to the City Council, which under Eastlake's procedures could either accept or reject the Planning Commission's recommendation. Meanwhile, by popular vote, the voters of Eastlake amended the City Charter to require that any changes in land use agreed to by the Council be approved by a 55% vote in a referendum.[1] The City Council approved the Planning Commission's recommendation for reclassification of respondent's property to permit the proposed project. Respondent then applied to the Planning Commission for "parking and yard" approval for the proposed building. The Commission rejected the application, on the ground that the City Council's rezoning action had not yet been submitted to the voters for ratification.

Respondent then filed an action in state court, seeking a judgment declaring the charter provision invalid as an unconstitutional delegation of legislative power to the people. While the case was pending, the City Council's action was submitted to a referendum, but the proposed zoning change was not approved by the requisite 55% margin. Following the election, the Court of Common Pleas and the Ohio Court of Appeals sustained the charter provision.

The Ohio Supreme Court reversed. Concluding that enactment of zoning and rezoning provisions is a legislative function, the court held that a popular referendum requirement, lacking standards to guide the decision of the voters, permitted the police power to be exercised in a standardless, hence arbitrary and capricious manner. Relying on this Court's decisions in Washington ex rel. Seattle Title Trust Co. v. Roberge, 278 U.S. 116, 49 S.Ct. 50, 73 L.Ed. 210 (1928), Thomas Cusack Co. v. Chicago, 242 U.S. 526, 37 S.Ct. 190, 61 L.Ed. 472 (1917), and Eubank v. Richmond, 226 U.S. 137, 33 S.Ct. 76, 57 L.Ed. 156 (1912), but distinguishing James v. Valtierra, 402 U.S. 137, 91 S.Ct. 1331, 28 L.Ed. 2d 678 (1971), the court concluded that the referendum provision constituted an unlawful delegation of legislative power.[4]

We reverse.

The conclusion that Eastlake's procedure violates federal constitutional guarantees rests upon the proposition that a zoning referendum involves a delegation of legislative power. A referendum cannot, however, be characterized as a delegation of power. Under our constitutional assumptions, all power derives from the people, who can delegate

1. As adopted by the voters, Art. VII, § 3, of the Eastlake City Charter provides in pertinent part:

> "That any change to the existing land uses or any change whatsoever to any ordinance . . . cannot be approved unless and until it shall have been submitted to the Planning Commission, for approval or disapproval. That in the event the city council should approve any of the preceding changes, or enactments, whether approved or disapproved by the Planning Commission it shall not be approved or passed by the declaration of an emergency, and it shall not be effective, but it shall be mandatory that the same be approved by a 55% favorable vote of all votes cast of the qualified electors of the City of Eastlake at the next regular municipal election, if one shall occur not less than sixty (60) or more than one hundred and twenty (120) days after its passage, otherwise at a special election falling on the generally established day of the primary election. . . ."

4. Respondent did not challenge the 55%-majority requirement as such. Instead, respondent contended that any mandatory referendum provision, regardless of the requisite margin for approval, violated due process as applied to its rezoning application.

it to representative instruments which they create. See, e.g., Federalist Papers, No. 39. In establishing legislative bodies, the people can reserve to themselves power to deal directly with matters which might otherwise be assigned to the legislature. Hunter v. Erickson, 393 U.S. 385, 392, 89 S.Ct. 557, 561, 21 L.Ed.2d 616 (1969).

The reservation of such power is the basis for the town meeting, a tradition which continues to this day in some States as both a practical and symbolic part of our democratic processes. The referendum, similarly, is a means for direct political participation, allowing the people the final decision, amounting to a veto power, over enactments of representative bodies. The practice is designed to "give citizens a voice on questions of public policy." James v. Valtierra, 402 U.S., at 141, 91 S.Ct., at 1333.

In framing a state constitution, the people of Ohio specifically reserved the power of referendum to the people of each municipality within the State.

"The initiative and referendum powers are hereby reserved to the people of each municipality on all questions which such municipalities may now or hereafter be authorized by law to control by legislative action . . . ." Ohio Const. Art. II, § 1f (1955).

To be subject to Ohio's referendum procedure, the question must be one within the scope of legislative power. The Ohio Supreme Court expressly found that the City Council's action in rezoning respondent's eight acres from light industrial to high-density residential use was legislative in nature.[7] Distinguishing between administrative and legislative acts, the court separated the power to zone or rezone, by passage or amendment of a zoning ordinance, from the power to grant relief from unnecessary hardship.[8] The former function was found to be legislative in nature.[9] . . .

The Ohio Supreme Court further concluded that the amendment to the City Charter constituted a "delegation" of power violative of federal constitutional guarantees because the voters were given no standards to

7. The land use change requested by respondent would likely entail the provision of additional city services, such as schools, police and fire protection. Cf. James v. Valtierra, 402 U.S., at 137 n. 4, 91 S.Ct., at 1334. The change would also diminish the land area available for industrial purposes, thereby affecting Eastlake's potential economic development.

8. By its nature, zoning "interferes" significantly with owners' uses of property. It is hornbook law that "[m]ere diminution of market value or interference with the property owner's personal plans and desires relative to his property is insufficient to invalidate a zoning ordinance or to entitle him to a variance or rezoning." 8 McQuillan, Municipal Corporations § 25.44, at 111. There is, of course, no contention in this case that the existing zoning classification renders respondent's property valueless or otherwise diminishes its value below the value when respondent acquired it.

9. The power of initiative or referendum may be reserved or conferred "with respect to any matter, legislative or administrative, within the realm of local affairs. . . ." 5 McQuillan, Municipal Corporations, § 16.54, at 208. However, the Ohio Supreme Court, concluded that only land use changes granted by the City Council when acting in a *legislative* capacity were subject to the referendum process. Under the court's binding interpretation of state law, a property owner seeking relief from unnecessary hardship occasioned by zoning restrictions would not be subject to Eastlake's referendum procedure. For example, if unforeseeable future changes give rise to hardship on the owner, the holding of the Ohio Supreme Court provides avenues of administrative relief not subject to the referendum process.

guide their decision. Under Eastlake's procedure, the Ohio Supreme Court reasoned, no mechanism existed, nor indeed could exist, to assure that the voters would act rationally in passing upon a proposed zoning change. This meant that "appropriate legislative action [would] be made dependent upon the potentially arbitrary and unreasonable whims of the voting public." 41 Ohio St.2d 137, 324 N.E.2d 740 (1975). The potential for arbitrariness in the process, the court concluded, violated due process.

Courts have frequently held in other contexts that a congressional delegation of power to a regulatory entity must be accompanied by discernible standards, so that the delegatee's action can be measured for its fidelity to the legislative will. . . . Assuming, *arguendo*, their relevance to state governmental functions, these cases involved a delegation of power by the legislature to regulatory bodies, which are not directly responsible to the people; this doctrine is inapplicable where, as here, rather than a delegation of power, we deal with a power reserved by the people to themselves.[10]

In basing its claim on federal due process requirements, respondent also invokes Euclid v. Ambler Realty Co., 272 U.S. 365, 47 S.Ct. 114, 71 L.Ed. 303 (1926), but it does not rely on the direct teaching of that case. Under *Euclid*, a property owner can challenge a zoning restriction if the measure is "clearly arbitrary and unreasonable, having no substantial relation to the public health, safety, morals, or general welfare." 272 U.S., at 395, 47 S.Ct., at 121. If the substantive result of the referendum is arbitrary and capricious, bearing no relation to the police power, then the fact that the voters of Eastlake wish it so would not save the restriction. As this Court held in invalidating a charter amendment enacted by referendum:

"The sovereignty of the people is itself subject to those constitutional limitations which have been duly adopted and remain unrepealed." Hunter v. Erickson, 393 U.S., at 392, 89 S.Ct., at 561.

. . .

But no challenge of the sort contemplated in Euclid v. Ambler is before us. The Ohio Supreme Court did not hold, and respondent does not argue, that the present zoning classification under Eastlake's comprehensive ordinance violates the principles established in Euclid v. Ambler. If respondent considers the referendum result itself to be unreasonable, the zoning restriction is open to challenge in state court, where the scope of the state remedy available to respondent would be determined as a matter of state law, as well as under Fourteenth

10. The Ohio Supreme Court's analysis of the requirements for standards flowing from the Fourteenth Amendment also sweeps too broadly. Except as a legislative history informs an analysis of legislative action, there is no more advance assurance that a legislative body will act by conscientiously applying consistent standards than there is with respect to voters. For example, there is no certainty that the City Council in this case would act on the basis of "standards" explicit or otherwise in Eastlake's comprehensive zoning ordinance. Nor is there any assurance that townspeople assembling in a town meeting, as the people of Eastlake could do, Hunter v. Erickson, 393 U.S., at 392, 89 S.Ct., at 561, will act according to consistent standards. The critical constitutional inquiry, rather, is whether the zoning restriction produces arbitrary or capricious results.

Amendment standards. That being so, nothing more is required by the Constitution.

Nothing in our cases is inconsistent with this conclusion. Two decisions of this Court were relied on by the Ohio Supreme Court in invalidating Eastlake's procedure. The thread common to both decisions is the delegation of legislative power, originally given by the people to a legislative body, and in turn delegated by the legislature to a *narrow segment* of the community, not to the people at large. In Eubank v. City of Richmond, 226 U.S. 137, 33 S.Ct. 76, 57 L.Ed. 156 (1912), the Court invalidated a city ordinance which conferred the power to establish building setback lines upon the owners of two-thirds of the property abutting any street. Similarly, in Washington ex rel. Seattle Title Trust Co. v. Roberge, 278 U.S. 116, 49 S.Ct. 50, 73 L.Ed. 210 (1928), the Court struck down an ordinance which permitted the establishment of philanthropic homes for the aged in residential areas, but only upon the written consent of the owners of two-thirds of the property within 400 feet of the proposed facility.[12]

Neither *Eubank* nor *Roberge* involved a referendum procedure such as we have in this case; the standardless delegation of power to a limited group of property owners condemned by the Court in *Eubank* and *Roberge* is not to be equated with decisionmaking by the people through the referendum process. The Court of Appeals for the Ninth Circuit put it this way:

"A referendum, however, is far more than an expression of ambiguously founded neighborhood preference. It is the city itself legislating through its voters—an exercise by the voters of their traditional right through direct legislation to override the views of their elected representatives as to what serves the public interest." Southern Alameda Spanish Speaking Organization v. City of Union City, California, 424 F.2d 291, 294 (CA9 1970).

Our decision in James v. Valtierra, 402 U.S. 137, 91 S.Ct. 1331, 28 L.Ed.2d 678 (1971), upholding California's mandatory referendum requirement, confirms this view. Mr. Justice Black, speaking for the Court in that case, said:

"This procedure ensures that *all the people* of a community will have a voice in a decision which may lead to large expenditures of local governmental funds for increased public services . . . ."

Id., at 143, 91 S.Ct., at 1334 (Emphasis added).

12. The Ohio Supreme Court also treated this Court's decision in Thomas Cusack Co. v. Chicago, 242 U.S. 526, 37 S.Ct. 190, 61 L.Ed. 472 (1917). In contrast to *Eubank* and *Roberge*, the *Cusack* Court upheld a neighborhood consent provision which permitted property owners to waive a municipal restriction prohibiting the construction of billboards. This Court in *Cusack* distinguised *Eubank* in the following way:

"[The ordinance in *Eubank*] left the establishment of the building line untouched until the lot owners should act and then . . . gave to it the effect of law. The ordinance in the case at bar absolutely prohibits the erection of any billboards . . . but permits this prohibition to be modified with the consent of the persons who are to be most affected by such modification." 242 U.S., at 531, 37 S.Ct., at 192.

Since the property owners could simply waive an otherwise applicable legislative limitation, the Court in *Cusack* determined that the provision did not delegate legislative power at all. Ibid.

Mr. Justice Black went on to say that the referendum procedure at issue here is a classic demonstration of "devotion to democracy . . . ." 402 U.S., at 141, 91 S.Ct., at 1333. As a basic instrument of democratic government, the referendum process does not, in itself, violate the Due Process Clause of the Fourteenth Amendment when applied to a rezoning ordinance.[13] Since the rezoning decision in this case was properly reserved to the People of Eastlake under the Ohio Constitution, the Ohio Supreme Court erred in holding invalid, on federal constitutional grounds, the charter amendment permitting the voters to decide whether the zoned use of respondent's property could be altered.

The judgment of the Ohio Supreme Court is reversed and the case is remanded for further proceedings not inconsistent with this opinion.

Reversed and remanded.

MR. JUSTICE POWELL, dissenting.

There can be no doubt as to the propriety and legality of submitting generally applicable legislative questions, including zoning provisions, to a popular referendum. But here the only issue concerned the status of a single small parcel owned by a single "person." This procedure, affording no realistic opportunity for the affected person to be heard, even by the electorate, is fundamentally unfair. The "spot" referendum technique appears to open disquieting opportunities for local government bodies to by-pass normal protective procedures for resolving issues affecting individual rights.

MR. JUSTICE STEVENS, with whom MR. JUSTICE BRENNAN joins, dissenting.

. . .

I have no doubt about the validity of the initiative or the referendum as an appropriate method of deciding questions of community policy. I think it is equally clear that the popular vote is not an acceptable method of adjudicating the rights of individual litigants. The problem presented by this case is unique, because it may involve a three-sided controversy, in which there is at least potential conflict between the rights of the property owner and the rights of his neighbors, and also potential conflict with the public interest in preserving the city's basic zoning plan. If the latter aspect of the controversy were predominant, the referendum would be an acceptable procedure. On

13. The fears expressed in dissent rest on the proposition that the procedure at issue here is "fundamentally unfair" to landowners; this fails to take into account the mechanisms for relief potentially available to property owners whose desired land use changes are rejected by the voters. First, if hardship is occasioned by zoning restrictions, *administrative* relief is potentially available. Indeed, the very purpose of "variances" allowed by zoning officials is to avoid "practical difficulties and unnecessary hardship." 8 McQuillan, Municipal Corporations § 25.159, at 511. As we noted, ante, at 8, remedies remain available under the Ohio Supreme Court's holding and provide a means to challenge unreasonable or arbitrary action. Euclid v. Ambler, supra.

The situation presented in this case is not one of a zoning action denigrating the use or depreciating the value of land; instead, it involves an effort to *change* a reasonable zoning restriction. No existing rights are being impaired; new use rights are being sought from the City Council. Thus, this case involves an owner seeking approval of a new use free from the restrictions attached to the land when it was acquired.

the other hand, when the record indicates without contradiction that there is no threat to the general public interest in preserving the city's plan—as it does in this case, since respondent's proposal was approved by both the Planning Commission and the City Council and there has been no allegation that the use of this eight-acre parcel for apartments rather than light industry would adversely affect the community or raise any policy issue of citywide concern—I think the case should be treated as one in which it is essential that the private property owner be given a fair opportunity to have his claim determined on its merits.

. . .

NOTES

1. Some state courts have held that rezonings were not "legislative" and therefore not subject to the referendum process. See e.g., Wilson v. Manning, 657 P.2d 251 (Utah 1982). Contra: Florida Land Co. v. City of Winter Springs, 427 So.2d 170 (Fla.1983).

2. Rezoning by initiative has been upheld. Arnel Development Co. v. City of Costa Mesa, 28 Cal.3d 511, 169 Cal.Rptr. 904, 620 P.2d 565 (1980). A neighborhood association, seeking to prevent proposed development of Arnel's land, had begun the initiative process. The court declared that all zoning ordinances, "whatever the size of parcel affected," are legislative. This no-exceptions policy promotes certainty, said the court, which also reaffirmed that in California all approvals of subdivision plats are adjudicatory.

3. For commentary, see Glenn, State Law Limitations on the Use of Initiatives and Referenda in Connection with Zoning Amendments, 51 S.Cal.L.Rev. 265 (1978).

Chapter 20

REGULATORY TAKINGS

PENNSYLVANIA COAL CO. v. MAHON

Supreme Court of the United States, 1922.
260 U.S. 393, 43 S.Ct. 158, 67 L.Ed. 322.

MR. JUSTICE HOLMES delivered the opinion of the Court.

This is a bill in equity brought by the defendants in error to prevent the Pennsylvania Coal Company from mining under their property in such way as to remove the supports and cause a subsidence of the surface and of their house. The bill sets out a deed executed by the Coal Company in 1878, under which the plaintiffs claim. The deed conveys the surface, but in express terms reserves the right to remove all the coal under the same, and the grantee takes the premises with the risk, and waives all claim for damages that may arise from mining out the coal. But the plaintiffs say that whatever may have been the Coal Company's rights, they were taken away by an Act of Pennsylvania, approved May 27, 1921, P.L. 1198, commonly known there as the Kohler Act. The Court of Common Pleas found that if not restrained the defendant would cause the damage to prevent which the bill was brought, but denied an injunction, holding that the statute if applied to this case would be unconstitutional. On appeal the Supreme Court of the State agreed that the defendant had contract and property rights protected by the Constitution of the United States, but held that the statute was a legitimate exercise of the police power and directed a decree for the plaintiffs. A writ of error was granted bringing the case to this Court.

The statute forbids the mining of anthracite coal in such way as to cause the subsidence of, among other things, any structure used as a human habitation, with certain exceptions, including among them land where the surface is owned by the owner of the underlying coal and is distant more than one hundred and fifty feet from any improved property belonging to any other person. As applied to this case the statute is admitted to destroy previously existing rights of property and contract. The question is whether the police power can be stretched so far.

Government hardly could go on if to some extent values incident to property could not be diminished without paying for every such change in the general law. As long recognized, some values are enjoyed under an implied limitation and must yield to the police power. But obviously the implied limitation must have its limits, or the contract and due process clauses are gone. One fact for consideration in determining such limits is the extent of the diminution. When it reaches a certain magnitude, in most if not in all cases there must be an exercise of eminent domain and compensation to sustain the act. So the question depends upon the particular facts. The greatest weight is given to the judgment of the legislature, but it always is open to interested parties to contend that the legislature has gone beyond its constitutional power.

This is the case of a single private house. No doubt there is a public interest even in this, as there is in every purchase and sale and in all that happens within the commonwealth. Some existing rights may be modified even in such a case. But usually in ordinary private affairs the public interest does not warrant much of this kind of interference. A source of damage to such a house is not a public nuisance even if similar damage is inflicted on others in different places. The damage is not common or public. The extent of the public interest is shown by the statute to be limited, since the statute ordinarily does not apply to land when the surface is owned by the owner of the coal. Furthermore, it is not justified as a protection of personal safety. That could be provided for by notice. Indeed the very foundation of this bill is that the defendant gave timely notice of its intent to mine under the house. On the other hand the extent of the taking is great. It purports to abolish what is recognized in Pennsylvania as an estate in land—a very valuable estate—and what is declared by the Court below to be a contract hitherto binding the plaintiffs. If we were called upon to deal with the plaintiffs' position alone, we should think it clear that the statute does not disclose a public interest sufficient to warrant so extensive a destruction of the defendant's constitutionally protected rights.

But the case has been treated as one in which the general validity of the act should be discussed. The Attorney General of the State, the City of Scranton, and the representatives of other extensive interests were allowed to take part in the argument below and have submitted their contentions here. It seems, therefore, to be our duty to go farther in the statement of our opinion, in order that it may be known at once, and that further suits should not be brought in vain.

It is our opinion that the act cannot be sustained as an exercise of the police power, so far as it affects the mining of coal under streets or cities in places where the right to mine such coal has been reserved. . . . To make it commercially impracticable to mine certain coal has very nearly the same effect for constitutional purposes as appropriating or destroying it. This we think that we are warranted in assuming that the statute does.

It is true that in Plymouth Coal Co. v. Pennsylvania, 232 U.S. 531, it was held competent for the legislature to require a pillar of coal to be left along the line of adjoining property, that, with the pillar on the other side of the line, would be a barrier sufficient for the safety of the employees of either mine in case the other should be abandoned and allowed to fill with water. But that was a requirement for the safety of employees invited into the mine, and secured an average reciprocity of advantage that has been recognized as a justification of various laws.

The rights of the public in a street purchased or laid out by eminent domain are those that it has paid for. If in any case its representatives have been so short sighted as to acquire only surface rights without the right of support, we see no more authority for supplying the latter without compensation than there was for taking the right of way in the first place and refusing to pay for it because the public wanted it very much. The protection of private property in the Fifth Amendment presupposes that it is wanted for public use, but provides that it shall not be taken for such use without compensation. A similar assumption is made in the decisions upon the Fourteenth Amendment. When this seemingly absolute protection is found to be qualified by the police power, the natural tendency of human nature is to extend the qualification more and more until at last private property disappears. But that cannot be accomplished in this way under the Constitution of the United States.

The general rule at least is, that while property may be regulated to a certain extent, if regulation goes too far it will be recognized as a taking. It may be doubted how far exceptional cases, like the blowing up of a house to stop a conflagration, go—and if they go beyond the general rule, whether they do not stand as much upon tradition as upon principle. . . . We are in danger of forgetting that a strong public desire to improve the public condition is not enough to warrant achieving the desire by a shorter cut than the constitutional way of paying for the change. As we already have said, this is a question of degree—and therefore cannot be disposed of by general propositions. But we regard this as going beyond any of the cases decided by this Court. . . .

We assume, of course, that the statute was passed upon the conviction that an exigency existed that would warrant it, and we assume that an exigency exists that would warrant the exercise of eminent domain. But the question at bottom is upon whom the loss of the changes desired should fall. So far as private persons or communities have seen fit to take the risk of acquiring only surface rights, we cannot see that the fact that their risk has become a danger warrants the giving to them greater rights than they bought.

Decree reversed.

MR. JUSTICE BRANDEIS, dissenting.

. . .

Every restriction upon the use of property imposed in the exercise of the police power deprives the owner of some right theretofore enjoyed, and is, in that sense, an abridgement by the State of rights in property without making compensation. But restriction imposed to protect the public health, safety or morals from dangers threatened is not a taking. The restriction here in question is merely the prohibition of a noxious use. The property so restricted remains in the possession of its owner. The State does not appropriate it or make any use of it. The State merely prevents the owner from making a use which interferes with paramount rights of the public. Whenever the use prohibited ceases to be noxious,—as it may because of further change in local or social conditions,—the restriction will have to be removed and the owner will again be free to enjoy his property as heretofore.

The restriction upon the use of this property can not, of course, be lawfully imposed, unless its purpose is to protect the public. But the purpose of a restriction does not cease to be public, because incidentally some private persons may thereby receive gratuitously valuable special benefits. Thus, owners of low buildings may obtain, through statutory restrictions upon the height of neighboring structures, benefits equivalent to an easement of light and air. Furthermore, a restriction, though imposed for a public purpose, will not be lawful, unless the restriction is an appropriate means to the public end. But to keep coal in place is surely an appropriate means of preventing subsidence of the surface; and ordinarily it is the only available means. Restriction upon use does not become inappropriate as a means, merely because it deprives the owner of the only use to which the property can then be profitably put. The liquor and the oleomargarine cases settled that. Mugler v. Kansas, 123 U.S. 623, 668, 669; Powell v. Pennsylvania, 127 U.S. 678, 682. Nor is a restriction imposed through exercise of the police power inappropriate as a means, merely because the same end might be effected through exercise of the power of eminent domain, or otherwise at public expense. Every restriction upon the height of buildings might be secured through acquiring by eminent domain the right of each owner to build above the limiting height; but it is settled that the State need not resort to that power. If by mining anthracite coal the owner would necessarily unloose poisonous gasses, I suppose no one would doubt the power of the State to prevent the mining, without buying his coal fields. And why may not the State, likewise, without paying compensation, prohibit one from digging so deep or excavating so near the surface, as to expose the community to like dangers? In the latter case, as in the former, carrying on the business would be a public nuisance.

It is said that one fact for consideration in determining whether the limits of the police power have been exceeded is the extent of the resulting diminution in value; and that here the restriction destroys existing rights of property and contract. But values are relative. If we are to consider the value of the coal kept in place by the restriction, we should compare it with the value of all other parts of the land. That is, with the value not of the coal alone, but with the value of the whole property. The rights of an owner as against the public are not increased by dividing the interests in his property into surface and subsoil. The sum of the rights in the parts can not be greater than the rights in the whole. The estate of an owner in land is grandiloquently described as extending *ab orco usque ad coelum.* But I suppose no one would contend that by selling his interest above one hundred feet from the surface he could prevent the State from limiting, by the police power, the height of structures in a city. And why should a sale of underground rights bar the State's power? For aught that appears the value of the coal kept in place by the restriction may be negligible as compared with the value of the whole property, or even as compared with that part of it which is represented by the coal remaining in place and which may be extracted despite the statute. . . .

It is said that this is a case of a single dwelling house; that the restriction upon mining abolishes a valuable estate hitherto secured by a contract with the plaintiffs; and that the restriction upon mining cannot be justified as a protection of personal safety, since that could be provided for by notice. The propriety of deferring a good deal to tribunals on the spot has been repeatedly recognized. May we say that notice would afford adequate protection of the public safety where the legislature and the highest court of the State, with greater knowledge of local conditions, have declared, in effect, that it would not? If public safety is imperiled, surely neither grant, nor contract, can prevail against the exercise of the police power. . . .

NOTE

It has been argued that, in view of increasing pressures upon "our limited and natural resources," the United States Supreme Court should "re-examine its earlier precedents," "recognize that Justice Brandeis was right," and "return to the strict construction of the taking clause by declaring that a regulation of the use of land, if reasonably related to a valid purpose, can never constitute a taking." F. Bosselman, D. Callies and J. Banta, The Taking Issue 238, 253 (1973).

According to The Origins and Original Significance of the Just Compensation Clause of the Fifth Amendment, 94 Yale L.J. 694 (1985), the just compensation clause was not viewed at the time of its adoption as applicable to regulation.

PENN CENTRAL TRANSPORTATION CO. v. CITY OF NEW YORK

United States Supreme Court, 1978.
438 U.S. 104, 98 S.Ct. 2646, 57 L.Ed.2d 631.

MR. JUSTICE BRENNAN delivered the opinion of the Court.

The question presented is whether a city may, as part of a comprehensive program to preserve historic landmarks and historic districts, place restrictions on the development of individual historic landmarks—in addition to those imposed by applicable zoning ordinances—without effecting a "taking" requiring the payment of "just compensation." Specifically, we must decide whether the application of New York City's Landmarks Preservation Law to the parcel of land occupied by Grand Central Terminal has "taken" its owners' property in violation of the Fifth and Fourteenth Amendments.

I

A

Over the past 50 years, all 50 States and over 500 municipalities have enacted laws to encourage or require the preservation of buildings and areas with historic or aesthetic importance. These nationwide legislative efforts have been precipitated by two concerns. The first is recognition that, in recent years, large numbers of historic structures, landmarks, and areas have been destroyed without adequate consideration of either the values represented therein or the possibility of preserving the destroyed properties for use in economically productive ways. The second is a widely shared belief that structures with special historic, cultural, or architectural significance enhance the quality of life for all. Not only do these buildings and their workmanship represent the lessons of the past and embody precious features of our heritage, they serve as examples of quality for today. "[h] istoric conservation is but one aspect of the much larger problem, basically an environmental one, of enhancing—or perhaps developing for the first time—the quality of life for people." [4]

New York City, responding to similar concerns and acting pursuant to a New York State enabling Act, adopted its Landmarks Preservation Law in 1965. See N.Y.C. Admin. Code, ch. 8–A, § 205–1.0 et seq. (1976). The city acted from the conviction that "the standing of [new york city] as a world-wide tourist center and world capital of business, culture and government" would be threatened if legislation were not enacted to protect historic landmarks and neighborhoods from precipitate decisions to destroy or fundamentally alter their character. § 205–1.0(a). The city believed that comprehensive measures to safeguard desirable features of the existing urban fabric would benefit its citizens in a variety of ways: e.g., fostering "civic pride in the beauty and noble accomplishments of the past"; protecting and enhancing "the city's attractions to tourists and visitors"; "support[ing] and stimul[ating] business and industry"; "strengthen[ing] the economy of the city"; and promoting "the use of historic districts, landmarks, interior landmarks and scenic landmarks for the education, pleasure and welfare of the people of the city." § 205–1.0(b).

The New York City law is typical of many urban landmark laws in that its primary method of achieving its goals is not by acquisitions of historic properties,[6] but rather by involving public entities in land-use decisions affecting these properties and providing services, standards, controls, and incentives that will encourage preservation by private owners and users. While the law does place special restrictions on landmark properties as a necessary feature to the attainment of its larger objectives, the major theme of the law is to ensure the owners of any such properties both a "reasonable return" on their investments and maximum latitude to use their parcels for purposes not inconsistent with the preservation goals.

The operation of the law can be briefly summarized. The primary responsibility for administering the law is vested in the Landmarks Preservation Commission (Commission), a broad based, 11-member

4. Gilbert, Introduction, Precedents for the Future, 36 Law & Comtemp. Prob. 311, 312 (1971), quoting address by Robert Stipe, 1971 Conference on Preservation Law, Washington D.C., May 1, 1971 (unpublished text, pp. 6–7).

6. The consensus is that widespread public ownership of historic properties in urban settings is neither feasible nor wise. Public ownership reduces the tax base, burdens the public budget with costs of acquisitions and maintenance, and results in the preservation of public buildings as museums and similar facilities, rather than as economically productive features of the urban scene. See Wilson & Winkler, The Response of State Legislation to Historic Preservation, 36 Law & Contemp. Prob. 329, 330–331, 339–340 (1971).

agency assisted by a technical staff. The Commission first performs the function, critical to any landmark preservation effort, of identifying properties and areas that have "a special character or special historical or aesthetic interest or value as part of the development, heritage or cultural characteristics of the city, state or nation." § 207–1.0(n); see § 207–1.0(h). If the Commission determines, after giving all interested parties an opportunity to be heard, that a building or area satisfies the ordinance's criteria, it will designate a building to be a "landmark," § 207–1.0(n), situated on a particular "landmark site," § 207–1.0(*o*), or will designate an area to be a "historic district," § 207–1.0(h). After the Commission makes a designation, New York City's Board of Estimate, after considering the relationship of the designated property "to the master plan, the zoning resolution, projected public improvements and any plans for the renewal of the area involved," § 207–2.0(g)(1), may modify or disapprove the designation, and the owner may seek judicial review of the final designation decision. Thus far, 31 historic districts and over 400 individual landmarks have been finally designated, and the process is a continuing one.

Final designation as a landmark results in restrictions upon the property owner's options concerning use of the landmark site. First, the law imposes a duty upon the owner to keep the exterior features of the building "in good repair" to assure that the law's objectives not be defeated by the landmark's falling into a state of irremediable disrepair. See § 207–10.0(a). Second, the Commission must approve in advance any proposal to alter the exterior architectural features of the landmark or to construct any exterior improvement on the landmark site, thus ensuring that decisions concerning construction on the landmark site are made with due consideration of both the public interest in the maintenance of the structure and the landowner's interest in use of the property. See §§ 207–4.0 to 207–9.0.

In the event an owner wishes to alter a landmark site, three separate procedures are available through which administrative approval may be obtained. First, the owner may apply to the Commission for a "certificate of no effect on protected architectural features": that is, for an order approving the improvement or alteration on the ground that it will not change or affect any architectural feature of the landmark and will be in harmony therewith. See § 207–5.0. Denial of the certificate is subject to judicial review.

Second, the owner may apply to the Commission for a certificate of "appropriateness." See § 207–6.0. Such certificates will be granted if the Commission concludes—focusing upon aesthetic, historical, and architectural values—that the proposed construction on the landmark site would not unduly hinder the protection, enhancement, perpetuation, and use of the landmark. Again, denial of the certificate is subject to judicial review. Moreover, the owner who is denied either a certificate of no exterior effect or a certificate of appropriateness may submit an alternative or modified plan for approval. The final procedure—seeking a certificate of appropriateness on the ground of "insufficient return," see § 207–8.0—provides special mechanisms, which vary depending on whether or not the landmark enjoys a tax exemption, to ensure that designation does not cause economic hardship.

Although the designation of a landmark and landmark site restricts the owner's control over the parcel, designation also enchances the economic position of the landmark owner in one significant respect. Under New York City's zoning laws, owners of real property who have not developed their property to the full extent permitted by the applicable zoning laws are allowed to transfer development rights to contiguous parcels on the same city block. See New York City, Zoning Resolution Art. I, ch. 2, § 12–10 (1978) (definition of "zoning lot"). A 1968 ordinance gave the owners of landmark sites additional opportunities to transfer development rights to other parcels. Subject to a restriction that the floor area of the transferee lot may not be increased by more than 20% above its authorized level, the ordinance permitted transfers from a landmark parcel to property across the street or across a street intersection. In 1969, the law governing the conditions under which transfers from landmark parcels could occur was liberalized, see New York City Zoning Resolutions 74–79 to 74–793, apparently to ensure that the Landmarks Law would not unduly restrict the development options of the owners of Grand Central Terminal. See Marcus, Air Rights Transfers in New York City, 36 Law & Contemp. Prob. 372, 375 (1971). The class of recipient lots was expanded to include lots "across a street and opposite to another lot or lots which except for the intervention of streets or street intersections f[or]m a series extending to the lot occupied by the landmark building[, provided that] all lots [are] in the same ownership." New York City Zoning Resolution 74–79 (emphasis deleted). In addition, the 1969 amendment permits, in highly commercialized areas like midtown Manhattan, the transfer of all unused development rights to a single parcel. Ibid.

B

This case involves the application of New York City's Landmarks Preservation Law to Grand Central Terminal (Terminal). The Terminal, which is owned by the Penn Central Transportation Co. and its affiliates (Penn Central), is one of New York City's most famous buildings. Opened in 1913, it is regarded not only as providing an ingenious engineering solution to the problems presented by urban railroad stations, but also as a magnificent example of the French beaux-arts style.

The Terminal is located in midtown Manhattan. Its south facade faces 42d Street and that street's intersection with Park Avenue. At street level, the Terminal is bounded on the west by Vanderbilt Avenue, on the east by the Commodore Hotel, and on the north by the Pan-American Building. Although a 20-story office tower, to have been located above the Terminal, was part of the original design, the planned tower was never constructed. The Terminal itself is an eight-story structure which Penn Central uses as a railroad station and in which it rents space not needed for railroad purposes to a variety of commercial interests. The Terminal is one of a number of properties owned by appellant Penn Central in this area of midtown Manhattan. The others include the Barclay, Biltmore, Commodore, Roosevelt, and Waldorf-Astoria Hotels, the Pan-American Building and other office buildings along Park Avenue, and the Yale Club. At least eight of these are eligible to be recipients of development rights afforded the Terminal by virtue of landmark designation.

On August 2, 1967, following a public hearing, the Commission designated the Terminal a "landmark" and designated the "city tax block" it occupies a "landmark site." The Board of Estimate confirmed this action on September 21, 1967. Although appellant Penn Central had opposed the designation before the Commission, it did not seek judicial review of the final designation decision.

On January 22, 1968, appellant Penn Central, to increase its income, entered into a renewable 50-year lease and sublease agreement with appellant UGP Properties, Inc. (UGP), a wholly owned subsidiary of Union General Properties, Ltd., a United Kingdom corporation. Under the terms of the agreement, UGP was to construct a multistory office building above the Terminal. UGP promised to pay Penn Central $1 million annually during construction and at least $3 million annually thereafter. The rentals would be offset in part by a loss of some $700,000 to $1 million in net rentals presently received from concessionaires displaced by the new building.

Appellants UGP and Penn Central then applied to the Commission for permission to construct an office building atop the Terminal. Two separate plans, both designed by architect Marcel Breuer and both apparently satisfying the terms of the applicable zoning ordinance, were submitted to the Commission for approval. The first, Breuer I, provided for the construction of a 55-story office building, to be cantilevered above the existing facade and to rest on the roof of the Terminal. The second, Breuer II Revised,[17] called for tearing down a portion of the Terminal that included the 42d Street facade, stripping off some of the remaining features of the Terminal's facade, and constructing a 53-story office building. The Commission denied a certificate of no exterior effect on September 20, 1968. Appellants then applied for a certificate of "appropriateness" as to both proposals. After four days of hearings at which over 80 witnesses testified, the Commission denied this application as to both proposals.

The Commission's reasons for rejecting certificates respecting Breuer II Revised are summarized in the following statement: "To protect a Landmark, one does not tear it down. To perpetuate its architectural features, one does not strip them off." Record 2255. Breuer I, which would have preserved the existing vertical facades of the present structure, received more sympathetic consideration. The Commission first focused on the effect that the proposed tower would have on one desirable feature created by the present structure and its surroundings: the dramatic view of the Terminal from Park Avenue South. Although

17. Appellants also submitted a plan, denominated Breuer II, to the Commission. However, because appellants learned that Breuer II would have violated existing easements, they substituted Breuer II Revised for Breuer II, and the Commission evaluated the appropriateness only of Breuer II Revised.

appellants had contended that the Pan-American Building had already destroyed the silhouette of the south facade and that one additional tower could do no further damage and might even provide a better background for the facade, the Commission disagreed, stating that it found the majestic approach from the south to be still unique in the city and that a 55-story tower atop the Terminal would be far more detrimental to its south facade than the Pan-American Building 375 feet away. Moreover, the Commission found that from closer vantage points the Pan Am Building and the other towers were largely cut off from view, which would not be the case of the mass on top of the Terminal planned under Breuer I. In conclusion, the Commission stated:

> "[we have] no fixed rule against making additions to designated buildings—it all depends on how they are done . . .. But to balance a 55-story office tower above a flamboyant Beaux-Arts facade seems nothing more than an aesthetic joke. Quite simply, the tower would overwhelm the Terminal by its sheer mass. The 'addition' would be four times as high as the existing structure and would reduce the Landmark itself to the status of a curiosity.
>
> "Landmarks cannot be divorced from their settings—particularly when the setting is a dramatic and integral part of the orginal concept. The Terminal, in its setting, is a great example of urban design. Such examples are not so plentiful in New York City that we can afford to lose any of the few we have. And we must preserve them in a meaningful way—with alterations and additions of such character, scale, materials and mass as will protect, enhance and perpetuate the original design rather than overwhelm it." Id., at 2251.

Appellants did not seek judicial review of the denial of either certificate. Because the Terminal site enjoyed a tax exemption, remained suitable for its present and future uses, and was not the subject of a contract of sale, there were no further administrative remedies available to appellants as to the Breuer I and Breuer II Revised plans. See n. 13, supra. Further, appellants did not avail themselves of the opportunity to develop and submit other plans for the Commission's consideration and approval. Instead, appellants filed suit in New York Supreme Court, Trial Term, claiming, *inter alia*, that the application of the Landmarks Preservation Law had "taken" their property without just compensation in violation of the Fifth and Fourteenth Amendments and arbitrarily deprived them of their property without due process of law in violation of the Fourteenth Amendment. Appellants sought a declaratory judgment, injunctive relief barring the city from using the Landmarks Law to impede the construction of any structure that might otherwise lawfully be constructed on the Terminal site, and damages for the "temporary taking" that occurred between August 2, 1967, the designation date, and the date when the restrictions arising from the Landmarks Law would be lifted. The trial court granted the injunctive and declaratory relief, but severed the question of damages for a "temporary taking." [20]

Appellees appealed, and the New York Supreme Court, Appellate Division, reversed. 50 A.D.2d 265, 377 N.Y.S.2d 20 (1975). The Appellate Division held that the restrictions on the development of the Terminal site were necessary to promote the legitimate public purpose of protecting landmarks and therefore that appellants could sustain their constitutional claims only by proof that the regulation deprived them of all reasonable beneficial use of the property. . . . The Appellate Division concluded that all appellants had succeeded in showing was that they had been deprived of the property's most profitable use, and that this showing did not establish that appellants had been unconstitutionally deprived of their property.

The New York Court of Appeals affirmed. 42 N.Y.2d 324, 397 N.Y.S.2d 914, 366 N.E.2d 1271 (1977). That court summarily rejected any claim that the Landmarks Law had "taken" property without "just compensation," id., at 329, 397 N.Y.S.2d, at 917, 366 N.E.2d, at 1274, indicating that there could be no "taking" since the law had not transferred control of the property to the city, but only restricted appellants' exploitation of it. In that circumstance, the Court of Appeals held that appellants' attack on the law could prevail only if the law deprived appellants of their property in violation of the Due Process Clause of the Fourteenth Amendment. Whether or not there was a denial of substantive due process turned on whether the restrictions deprived Penn Central of a "reasonable return" on the "privately created and privately managed ingredient" of the Terminal. Id., at 328, 397 N.Y.S.2d, at 916, 366 N.E.2d, at 1273.[23] The Court of Appeals concluded that the Landmarks Law had not effected a denial of due process because: (1) the landmark regulation permitted the same use as had been made of the Terminal for more than half a century; (2) the appellants had failed to show that they could not earn a reasonable return on their investment in the Terminal itself; (3) even if the Terminal proper could never operate at a reasonable profit some of the

20. Although that court suggested that any regulation of private property to protect landmark values was unconstitutional if "just compensation" were not afforded, it also appeared to rely upon its findings: first, that the cost to Penn Central of operating the Terminal building itself, exclusive of purely railroad operations, exceeded the revenues received from concessionaires and tenants in the Terminal; and second, that the special transferable development rights afforded Penn Central as an owner of a landmark site did not "provide compensation to plaintiffs or minimize the harm suffered by plaintiffs due to the designation of the Terminal as a landmark."

23. The Court of Appeals suggested that in calculating the value of the property upon which appellants were entitled to earn a reasonable return, the "publicly created" components of the value of the property—i.e., those elements of its value attributable to the "efforts of organized society" or to the "social complex" in which the Terminal is located—had to be excluded. However, since the record upon which the Court of Appeals decided the case did not, as that court recognized, contain a basis for segregating the privately created from the publicly created elements of the value of the Terminal site and since the judgment of the Court of Appeals in any event rests upon bases that support our affirmance see infra, this page, we have no occasion to address the question whether it is permissible or feasible to separate out the "social increments" of the value of property. See Costonis, The Disparity Issue: A Context for the Grand Central Terminal Decision, 91 Harv.L.Rev. 402, 416–417 (1977).

income from Penn Central's extensive real estate holdings in the area, which include hotels and office buildings, must realistically be imputed to the Terminal; and (4) the development rights above the Terminal, which had been made transferable to numerous sites in the vicinity of the Terminal, one or two of which were suitable for the construction of office buildings, were valuable to appellants and provided "significant, perhaps 'fair,' compensation for the loss of rights above the terminal itself." Id., at 333–336, 397 N.Y.S.2d, at 922, 366 N.E.2d, at 1276–1278.

. . .

II

The issues presented by appellants are (1) whether the restrictions imposed by New York City's law upon appellants' exploitation of the Terminal site effect a "taking" of appellants' property for a public use within the meaning of the Fifth Amendment, which of course is made applicable to the States through the Fourteenth Amendment, see Chicago, B. & Q. R. Co. v. Chicago, 166 U.S. 226, 239, 17 S.Ct. 581, 585, 41 L.Ed. 979 (1897), and (2), if so, whether the transferable development rights afforded appellants constitute "just compensation" within the meaning of the Fifth Amendment. We need only address the question whether a "taking" has occurred.[25]

A

Before considering appellants' specific contentions, it will be useful to review the factors that have shaped the jurisprudence of the Fifth Amendment injunction "nor shall private property be taken for public use, without just compensation." The question of what constitutes a "taking" for purposes of the Fifth Amendment has proved to be a problem of considerable difficulty. While this Court has recognized that the "Fifth Amendment's guarantee . . . [is] designed to bar Government from forcing some people alone to bear public burdens which, in all fairness and justice, should be borne by the public as a whole," Armstrong v. United States, 364 U.S. 40, 49, 80 S.Ct. 1563, 1569, 4 L.Ed.2d 1554 (1960), this Court, quite simply, has been unable to develop any "set formula" for determining when "justice and fairness" require that economic injuries caused by public action be compensated by the government, rather than remain disproportionately concentrated on a few persons. See Goldblatt v. Hempstead, 369 U.S. 590, 594, 82 S.Ct. 987, 990, 8 L.Ed.2d 130 (1962). Indeed, we have frequently observed that whether a particular restriction will be rendered invalid by the government's failure to pay for any losses proximately caused by it depends largely "upon the particular circumstances [in that] case." United States v. Central Eureka Mining Co., 357 U.S. 155, 168, 78 S.Ct. 1097, 1104, 2 L.Ed.2d 1228 (1958); see United States v. Caltex, Inc., 344 U.S. 149, 156, 73 S.Ct. 200, 203, 97 L.Ed. 157 (1952).

25. As is implicit in our opinion, we do not embrace the proposition that a "taking" can never occur unless government has transferred physical control over a portion of a parcel.

In engaging in these essentially ad hoc, factual inquiries, the Court's decisions have identified several factors that have particular significance. The economic impact of the regulation on the claimant and, particularly, the extent to which the regulation has interfered with distinct investment-backed expectations are, of course, relevant considerations. See Goldblatt v. Hempstead, supra, 369 U.S., at 594, 82 S.Ct., at 990. So, too, is the character of the governmental action. A "taking" may more readily be found when the interference with property can be characterized as a physical invasion by government, see, e.g., United States v. Causby, 328 U.S. 256, 66 S.Ct. 1062, 90 L.Ed. 1206 (1946), than when interference arises from some public program adjusting the benefits and burdens of economic life to promote the common good.

"Government hardly could go on if to some extent values incident to property could not be diminished without paying for every such change in the general law," Pennsylvania Coal Co. v. Mahon, 260 U.S. 393, 413, 43 S.Ct. 158, 159, 67 L.Ed. 322 (1922), and this Court has accordingly recognized, in a wide variety of contexts, that government may execute laws or programs that adversely affect recognized economic values. Exercises of the taxing power are one obvious example. A second are the decisions in which this Court has dismissed "taking" challenges on the ground that, while the challenged government action caused economic harm, it did not interfere with interests that were sufficiently bound up with the reasonable expectations of the claimant to constitute "property" for Fifth Amendment purposes. See, e.g., United States v. Willow River Power Co., 324 U.S. 499, 65 S.Ct. 761, 89 L.Ed. 1101 (1945) (interest in high-water level of river for run-off for tailwaters to maintain power head is not property); United States v. Chandler-Dunbar Water Power Co., 229 U.S. 53, 33 S.Ct. 667, 57 L.Ed. 1063 (1913) (no property interest can exist in navigable waters); see also Demorest v. City Bank Co., 321 U.S. 36, 64 S.Ct. 384, 88 L.Ed. 526 (1944); Muhlker v. Harlem R. Co., 197 U.S. 544, 25 S.Ct. 522, 49 L.Ed. 872 (1905); Sax, Takings and the Police Power, 74 Yale L.J. 36, 61–62 (1964).

More importantly for the present case, in instances in which a state tribunal reasonably concluded that "the health, safety, morals, or general welfare" would be promoted by prohibiting particular contemplated uses of land, this Court has upheld land-use regulations that destroyed or adversely affected recognized real property interests. See Nectow v. Cambridge, 277 U.S. 183, 188, 48 S.Ct. 447, 448, 72 L.Ed. 842 (1928). Zoning laws are, of course, the classic example, see Euclid v. Ambler Realty Co., 272 U.S. 365, 47 S.Ct. 114, 71 L.Ed. 303 (1926) (prohibition of industrial use); Gorieb v. Fox, 274 U.S. 603, 608, 47 S.Ct. 675, 677, 71 L.Ed. 1228 (1927) (requirement that portions of parcels be left unbuilt); Welch v. Swasey, 214 U.S. 91, 29 S.Ct. 567, 53 L.Ed. 923 (1909) (height restriction), which have been viewed as permissible governmental action even when prohibiting the most beneficial use of the property. See Goldblatt v. Hempstead supra, 369 U.S., at 592–593, 82 S.Ct., at 988–989, and cases cited; see also Eastlake v. Forest City

Enterprises, Inc., 426 U.S. 668, 674, n. 8, 96 S.Ct. 2358, 2362 n. 8, 49 L.Ed.2d 132 (1976).

Zoning laws generally do not affect existing uses of real property, but "taking" challenges have also been held to be without merit in a wide variety of situations when the challenged governmental actions prohibited a beneficial use to which individual parcels had previously been devoted and thus caused substantial individualized harm. Miller v. Schoene, 276 U.S. 272, 48 S.Ct. 246, 72 L.Ed. 568 (1928), is illustrative. In that case, a state entomologist, acting pursuant to a state statute, ordered the claimants to cut down a large number of ornamental red cedar trees because they produced cedar rust fatal to apple trees cultivated nearby. Although the statute provided for recovery of any expense incurred in removing the cedars, and permitted claimants to use the felled trees, it did not provide compensation for the value of the standing trees or for the resulting decrease in market value of the properties as a whole. A unanimous Court held that this latter omission did not render the statute invalid. The Court held that the State might properly make "a choice between the preservation of one class of property and that of the other" and since the apple industry was important in the State involved, concluded that the State had not exceeded "its constitutional powers by deciding upon the destruction of one class of property [without compensation] in order to save another which, in the judgment of the legislature, is of greater value to the public." Id., at 279, 48 S.Ct., at 247.

Again, Hadacheck v. Sebastian, 239 U.S. 394, 36 S.Ct. 143, 60 L.Ed. 348 (1915), upheld a law prohibiting the claimant from continuing his otherwise lawful business of operating a brickyard in a particular physical community on the ground that the legislature had reasonably concluded that the presence of the brickyard was inconsistent with neighboring uses. See also United States v. Central Eureka Mining Co., supra (Government order closing gold mines so that skilled miners would be available for other mining work held not a taking); Atchison, T. & S. F. R. Co. v. Public Utilities Comm'n, 346 U.S. 346, 74 S.Ct. 92, 98 L.Ed. 51 (1953) (railroad may be required to share cost of constructing railroad grade improvement); Walls v. Midland Carbon Co., 254 U.S. 300, 41 S.Ct. 118, 65 L.Ed. 276 (1920) (law prohibiting manufacture of carbon black upheld); Reinman v. Little Rock, 237 U.S. 171, 35 S.Ct. 511, 59 L.Ed. 900 (1915) (law prohibiting livery stable upheld); Mugler v. Kansas, 123 U.S. 623, 8 S.Ct. 273, 31 L.Ed. 205 (1887) (law prohibiting liquor business upheld).

Goldblatt v. Hempstead, supra, is a recent example. There, a 1958 city safety ordinance banned any excavations below the water table and effectively prohibited the claimant from continuing a sand and gravel mining business that had been operated on the particular parcel since 1927. The Court upheld the ordinance against a "taking" challenge, although the ordinance prohibited the present and presumably most beneficial use of the property and had, like the regulations in *Miller* and *Hadacheck,* severely affected a particular owner. The Court assumed that the ordinance did not prevent the owner's reasonable use of the property since the owner made no showing of an adverse effect on the value of the land. Because the restriction served a substantial public purpose, the Court thus held no taking had occurred. It is, of course, implicit in *Goldblatt* that a use restriction on real property may constitute a "taking" if not reasonably necessary to the effectuation of a substantial public purpose, see Nectow v. Cambridge, supra; cf. Moore v. East Cleveland, 431 U.S. 494, 513–514, 97 S.Ct. 1932, 1943, 52 L.Ed.2d 531 (1977) (Stevens, J., concurring), or perhaps if it has an unduly harsh impact upon the owner's use of the property.

Pennsylvania Coal Co. v. Mahon, 260 U.S. 393, 43 S.Ct. 158, 67 L.Ed. 322 (1922), is the leading case for the proposition that a state statute that substantially furthers important public policies may so frustrate distinct investment-backed expectations as to amount to a "taking." There the claimant had sold the surface rights to particular parcels of property, but expressly reserved the right to remove the coal thereunder. A Pennsylvania statute, enacted after the transactions, forbade any mining of coal that caused the subsidence of any house, unless the house was the property of the owner of the underlying coal and was more than 150 feet from the improved property of another. Because the statute made it commercially impracticable to mine the coal, id., at 414, 43 S.Ct., at 159, and thus had nearly the same effect as the complete destruction of rights claimant had reserved from the owners of the surface land, see id., at 414–415, 43 S.Ct., at 159–160, the Court held that the statute was invalid as effecting a "taking" without just compensation. See also Armstrong v. United States, 364 U.S. 40, 80 S.Ct. 1563, 4 L.Ed.2d 1554 (1960) (Government's complete destruction of a materialman's lien in certain property held a "taking"); Hudson Water Co. v. McCarter, 209 U.S. 349, 355, 28 S.Ct. 529, 531, 52 L.Ed. 828 (1908) (if height restriction makes property wholly useless "the rights of property . . . prevail over the other public interest" and compensation is required). See generally Michelman, Property, Utility, and Fairness: Comments on the Ethical Foundations of "Just Compensation" Law, 80 Harv.L.Rev. 1165, 1229–1234 (1967).

Finally, government actions that may be characterized as acquisitions of resources to permit or facilitate uniquely public functions have often been held to constitute "takings." United States v. Causby, 328 U.S. 256, 66 S.Ct. 1062, 90 L.Ed. 1206 (1946), is illustrative. In holding that direct overflights above the claimant's land, that destroyed the present use of the land as a chicken farm, constituted a "taking," *Causby* emphasized that Government had not "merely destroyed property [but was] using a part of it for the flight of its planes." Id., 328 U.S., at 262–263, n. 7, 66 S.Ct., at 1066. See also Griggs v. Allegheny County, 369 U.S. 84, 82 S.Ct. 531, 7 L.Ed.2d 585 (1962) (overflights held a taking); Portsmouth Co. v. United States, 260 U.S. 327, 43 S.Ct. 135, 67 L.Ed. 287 (1922) (United States military installations' repeated firing of guns over claimant's land is a taking); United States v. Cress, 243 U.S. 316, 37 S.Ct. 380, 61 L.Ed. 746 (1917) (repeated floodings of land caused by water project is taking); but see YMCA v. United States, 395 U.S. 85, 89 S.Ct. 1511, 23 L.Ed.2d 117 (1969) (damage caused to building when federal officers who were seeking to protect building were attacked by rioters held not a taking). See generally Michelman, supra, at 1226–1229; Sax, Takings and the Police Power, 74 Yale L.J. 36 (1964).

B

In contending that the New York City law has "taken" their property in violation of the Fifth and Fourteenth Amendments, appellants make a series of arguments, which, while tailored to the facts of this case, essentially urge that any substantial restriction imposed pursuant to a landmark law must be accompanied by just compensation if it is to be constitutional. Before considering these, we emphasize what is not in dispute. Because this Court has recognized, in a number of settings, that States and cities may enact land-use restrictions or controls to enhance the quality of life by preserving the character and desirable aesthetic features of a city, see New Orleans v. Dukes, 427 U.S. 297, 96 S.Ct. 2513, 49 L.Ed.2d 511 (1976); Young v. American Mini Theatres, Inc., 427 U.S. 50, 96 S.Ct. 2440, 49 L.Ed.2d 310 (1976); Village of Belle Terre v. Boraas, 416 U.S. 1, 9–10, 94 S.Ct. 1536, 39 L.Ed.2d 797 (1974); Berman v. Parker, 348 U.S. 26, 33, 75 S.Ct. 98, 102, 99 L.Ed. 27 (1954); Welch v. Swasey, 214 U.S., at 108, 29 S.Ct., at 571, appellants do not contest that New York City's objective of preserving structures and areas with special historic, architectural, or cultural significance is an entirely permissible governmental goal. They also do not dispute that the restrictions imposed on its parcel are appropriate means of securing the purposes of the New York City law. Finally, appellants do not challenge any of the specific factual premises of the decision below. They accept for present purposes both that the parcel of land occupied by Grand Central Terminal must, in its present state, be regarded as capable of earning a reasonable return, and that the transferable development rights afforded appellants by virtue of the Terminal's designation as a landmark are valuable, even if not as valuable as the rights to construct above the Terminal. In appellants' view none of these factors derogate from their claim that New York City's law has effected a "taking."

They first observe that the airspace above the Terminal is a valuable property interest, citing United States v. Causby, supra. They urge that the Landmarks Law has deprived them of any gainful use of their "air rights" above the Terminal and that, irrespective of the value of the remainder of their parcel, the city has "taken" their right to this superadjacent airspace, thus entitling them to "just compensation" measured by the fair market value of these air rights.

Apart from our own disagreement with appellants' characterization of the effect of the New York City law, the submission that appellants may establish a "taking" simply by showing that they have been denied the ability to exploit a property interest that they heretofore had believed was available for development is quite simply untenable. Were this the rule, this Court would have erred not only in upholding laws restricting the development of air rights, see Welch v. Swasey, supra, but also in approving those prohibiting both the subadjacent, see Goldblatt v. Hempstead, 369 U.S. 590, 82 S.Ct. 987, 8

L.Ed.2d 130 (1962), and the lateral, see Gorieb v. Fox, 274 U.S. 603, 47 S.Ct. 675, 71 L.Ed. 1228 (1927), development of particular parcels.[27] "Taking" jurisprudence does not divide a single parcel into discrete segments and attempt to determine whether rights in a particular segment have been entirely abrogated. In deciding whether a particular governmental action has effected a taking, this Court focuses rather both on the character of the action and on the nature and extent of the interference with rights in the parcel as a whole—here, the city tax block designated as the "landmark site."

Secondly, appellants, focusing on the character and impact of the New York City law, argue that it effects a "taking" because its operation has significantly diminished the value of the Terminal site. Appellants concede that the decisions sustaining other land-use regulations, which, like the New York City law, are reasonably related to the promotion of the general welfare, uniformly reject the proposition that diminution in property value, standing alone, can establish a "taking," see Euclid v. Ambler Realty Co., 272 U.S. 365, 47 S.Ct. 114, 71 L.Ed. 303 (1926) (75% diminution in value caused by zoning law); Hadacheck v. Sebastian, 239 U.S. 394, 36 S.Ct. 143, 60 L.Ed. 348 (1915) (87½% diminution in value); cf. Eastlake v. Forest City Enterprises, Inc., 426 U.S., at 674 n. 8, 96 S.Ct., at 2362 n. 8, and that the "taking" issue in these contexts is resolved by focusing on the uses the regulations permit. See also Goldblatt v. Hempstead, supra. Appellants, moreover, also do not dispute that a showing of diminution in property value would not establish a taking if the restriction had been imposed as a result of historic-district legislation, see generally Maher v. New Orleans, 516 F.2d 1051 (CA5 1975), but appellants argue that New York City's regulation of individual landmarks is fundamentally different from zoning or from historic-district legislation because the controls imposed by New York City's law apply only to individuals who own selected properties.

Stated baldly, appellants' position appears to be that the only means of ensuring that selected owners are not singled out to endure financial hardship for no reason is to hold that any restriction imposed on individual landmarks pursuant to the New York City scheme is a "taking" requiring the payment of "just compensation." Agreement with this argument would, of course, invalidate not just New York City's law, but all comparable landmark legislation in the Nation. We find no merit in it.

It is true, as appellants emphasize, that both historic-district legislation and zoning laws regulate all properties within given physical communities whereas landmark laws apply only to selected parcels. But, contrary to appellants' suggestions, landmark laws are not like

27. These cases dispose of any contention that might be based on Pennsylvania Coal Co. v. Mahon, 260 U.S. 393, 43 S.Ct. 158, 67 L.Ed. 322 (1922), that full use of air rights is so bound up with the investment-backed expectations of appellants that governmental deprivation of these rights invariably—i.e., irrespective of the impact of the restriction on the value of the parcel as a whole—constitutes a "taking." Similarly, *Welch, Goldblatt,* and *Gorieb* illustrate the fallacy of appellants' related contention that a "taking" must be found to have occurred whenever the land-use restriction may be characterized as imposing a "servitude" on the claimant's parcel.

discriminatory, or "reverse spot," zoning: that is, a land-use decision which arbitrarily singles out a particular parcel for different, less favorable treatment than the neighboring ones. See 2 A. Rathkopf, The Law of Zoning and Planning 26–4, and n. 6 (4th. ed. 1978). In contrast to discriminatory zoning, which is the antithesis of land-use control as part of some comprehensive plan, the New York City law embodies a comprehensive plan to preserve structures of historic or aesthetic interest wherever they might be found in the city,[28] and as noted, over 400 landmarks and 31 historic districts have been designated pursuant to this plan.

Equally without merit is the related argument that the decision to designate a structure as a landmark "is inevitably arbitrary or at least subjective, because it is basically a matter of taste," Reply Brief for Appellants 22, thus unavoidably singling out individual landowners for disparate and unfair treatment. The argument has a particularly hollow ring in this case. For appellants not only did not seek judicial review of either the designation or of the denials of the certificates of appropriateness and of no exterior effect, but do not even now suggest that the Commission's decisions concerning the Terminal were in any sense arbitrary or unprincipled. But, in any event, a landmark owner has a right to judicial review of any Commission decision, and, quite simply, there is no basis whatsoever for a conclusion that courts will have any greater difficulty identifying arbitrary or discriminatory action in the context of landmark regulation than in the context of classic zoning or indeed in any other context.[29]

Next, appellants observe that New York City's law differs from zoning laws and historic-district ordinances in that the Landmarks Law does not impose identical or similar restrictions on all structures located in particular physical communities. It follows, they argue, that New York City's law is inherently incapable of producing the fair and equitable distribution of benefits and burdens of governmental action which is characteristic of zoning laws and historic-district legislation and which they maintain is a constitutional requirement if "just compensation" is not to be afforded. It is, of course, true that the Landmarks Law has a more severe impact on some landowners than on others, but that in itself does not mean that the law effects a "taking." Legislation designed to promote the general welfare commonly burdens some more than others. The owners of the brickyard in *Hadacheck*, of

28. Although the New York Court of Appeals contrasted the New York City Landmarks Law with both zoning and historic-district legislation and stated at one point that landmark laws do not "further a general community plan," 42 N.Y.2d 324, 330, 397 N.Y.S.2d 914, 918, 366 N.E.2d 1271, 1274 (1977), it also emphasized that the implementation of the objectives of the Landmarks Law constitutes an "acceptable reason for singling out one particular parcel for different and less favorable treatment." Ibid., 397 N.Y.S.2d, at 918, 366 N.E.2d, at 1275. Therefore, we do not understand the New York Court of Appeals to disagree with our characterization of the law.

29. When a property owner challenges the application of a zoning ordinance to his property, the judicial inquiry focuses upon whether the challenged restriction can reasonably be deemed to promote the objectives of the community land-use plan, and will include consideration of the treatment of similar parcels. See generally Nectow v. Cambridge, 277 U.S. 183, 48 S.Ct. 447, 72 L.Ed. 842 (1928). When a property owner challenges a landmark designation or restriction as arbitrary or discriminatory, a similar inquiry presumably will occur.

the cedar trees in Miller v. Schoene, and of the gravel and sand mine in Goldblatt v. Hempstead, were uniquely burdened by the legislation sustained in those cases.[30] Similarly, zoning laws often affect some property owners more severely than others but have not been held to be invalid on that account. For example, the property owner in *Euclid* who wished to use its property for industrial purposes was affected far more severely by the ordinance than its neighbors who wished to use their land for residences.

In any event, appellants' repeated suggestions that they are solely burdened and unbenefited is factually inaccurate. This contention overlooks the fact that the New York City law applies to vast numbers of structures in the city in addition to the Terminal—all the structures contained in the 31 historic districts and over 400 individual landmarks, many of which are close to the Terminal. Unless we are to reject the judgment of the New York City Council that the preservation of landmarks benefits all New York citizens and all structures, both economically and by improving the quality of life in the city as a whole—which we are unwilling to do—we cannot conclude that the owners of the Terminal have in no sense been benefited by the Landmarks Law. Doubtless appellants believe they are more burdened than benefited by the law, but that must have been true, too, of the property owners in *Miller, Hadacheck, Euclid,* and *Goldblatt.* [32]

Appellants' final broad-based attack would have us treat the law as an instance, like that in United States v. Causby, in which government, acting in an enterprise capacity, has appropriated part of their property for some strictly governmental purpose. Apart from the fact that *Causby* was a case of invasion of airspace that destroyed the use of the farm beneath and this New York City law has in nowise impaired the present use of the Terminal, the Landmarks Law neither exploits appellants' parcel for city purposes nor facilitates nor arises from any

30. Appellants attempt to distinguish these cases on the ground that, in each, government was prohibiting a "noxious" use of land and that in the present case, in contrast, appellants' proposed construction above the Terminal would be beneficial. We observe that the uses in issue in *Hadacheck, Miller,* and *Goldblatt* were perfectly lawful in themselves. They involved no "blameworthiness, . . . moral wrongdoing or conscious act of dangerous risk-taking which induce[d society] to shift the cost to a pa[rt]icular individual." Sax, Takings and the Police Power, 74 Yale L.J. 36, 50 (1964). These cases are better understood as resting not on any supposed "noxious" quality of the prohibited uses but rather on the ground that the restrictions were reasonably related to the implementation of a policy—not unlike historic preservation—expected to produce a widespread public benefit and applicable to all similarly situated property.

Nor, correlatively, can it be asserted that the destruction or fundamental alteration of a historic landmark is not harmful. The suggestion that the beneficial quality of appellants' proposed construction is established by the fact that the construction would have been consistent with applicable zoning laws ignores the development in sensibilities and ideals reflected in landmark legislation like New York City's. Cf. West Bros. Brick Co. v. Alexandria, 169 Va. 271, 282–283, 192 S.E. 881, 885–886, appeal dismissed for want of a substantial federal question, 302 U.S. 658, 58 S.Ct. 369, 82 L.Ed. 508 (1937).

32. It is, of course, true that the fact the duties imposed by zoning and historic-district legislation apply throughout particular physical communities provides assurances against arbitrariness, but the applicability of the Landmarks Law to a large number of parcels in the city, in our view, provides comparable, if not identical, assurances.

entrepreneurial operations of the city. The situation is not remotely like that in *Causby* where the airspace above the property was in the flight pattern for military aircraft. The Landmarks Law's effect is simply to prohibit appellants or anyone else from occupying portions of the airspace above the Terminal, while permitting appellants to use the remainder of the parcel in a gainful fashion. This is no more an appropriation of property by government for its own uses than is a zoning law prohibiting, for "aesthetic" reasons, two or more adult theaters within a specified area, see Young v. American Mini Theatres, Inc., 427 U.S. 50, 96 S.Ct. 2440, 49 L.Ed.2d 310 (1976), or a safety regulation prohibiting excavations below a certain level. See Goldblatt v. Hempstead.

C

Rejection of appellants' broad arguments is not, however, the end of our inquiry, for all we thus far have established is that the New York City law is not rendered invalid by its failure to provide "just compensation" whenever a landmark owner is restricted in the exploitation of property interests, such as air rights, to a greater extent than provided for under applicable zoning laws. We now must consider whether the interference with appellants' property is of such a magnitude that "there must be an exercise of eminent domain and compensation to sustain [it]." Pennsylvania Coal Co. v. Mahon, 260 U.S., at 413, 43 S.Ct., at 159. That inquiry may be narrowed to the question of the severity of the impact of the law on appellants' parcel, and its resolution in turn requires a careful assessment of the impact of the regulation on the Terminal site.

Unlike the governmental acts in *Goldblatt, Miller, Causby, Griggs,* and *Hadacheck,* the New York City law does not interfere in any way with the present uses of the Terminal. Its designation as a landmark not only permits but contemplates that appellants may continue to use the propety precisely as it has been used for the past 65 years: as a railroad terminal containing office space and concessions. So the law does not interfere with what must be regarded as Penn Central's primary expectation concerning the use of the parcel. More importantly, on this record, we must regard the New York City law as permitting Penn Central not only to profit from the Terminal but also to obtain a "reasonable return" on its investment.

Appellants, moreover, exaggerate the effect of the law on their ability to make use of the air rights above the Terminal in two respects.[33] First, it simply cannot be maintained, on this record, that appellants have been prohibited from occupying *any* portion of the airspace above the Terminal. While the Commission's actions in denying applications to construct an office building in excess of 50 stories above the Terminal may indicate that it will refuse to issue a certificate of appropriateness for any comparably sized structure, nothing the

33. Appellants, of course, argue at length that the transferable development rights, while valuable, do not constitute "just compensation." Brief for Appellants 36–43.

Commission has said or done suggests an intention to prohibit *any* construction above the Terminal. The Commission's report emphasized that whether any construction would be allowed depended upon whether the proposed addition "would harmonize in scale, material and character with [the terminal]." Record 2251. Since appellants have not sought approval for the construction of a smaller structure, we do not know that appellants will be denied any use of any portion of the airspace above the Terminal.

Second, to the extent appellants have been denied the right to build above the Terminal, it is not literally accurate to say that they have been denied *all* use of even those pre-existing air rights. Their ability to use these rights has not been abrogated; they are made transferable to at least eight parcels in the vicinity of the Terminal, one or two of which have been found suitable for the construction of new office buildings. Although appellants and others have argued that New York City's transferable development-rights program is far from ideal, the New York courts here supportably found that, at least in the case of the Terminal, the rights afforded are valuable. While these rights may well not have constituted "just compensation" if a "taking" had occurred, the rights nevertheless undoubtedly mitigate whatever financial burdens the law has imposed on appellants and, for that reason, are to be taken into account in considering the impact of regulation. Cf. Goldblatt v. Hempstead, 369 U.S., at 594 n. 3, 82 S.Ct., at 990 n. 3.

On this record, we conclude that the application of New York City's Landmarks Law has not effected a "taking" of appellants' property. The restrictions imposed are substantially related to the promotion of the general welfare and not only permit reasonable beneficial use of the landmark site but also afford appellants opportunities further to enhance not only the Terminal site proper but also other properties.[36]

Affirmed.

MR. JUSTICE REHNQUIST, with whom THE CHIEF JUSTICE and MR. JUSTICE STEVENS join, dissenting.

. . . The question in this case is whether the cost associated with the city of New York's desire to preserve a limited number of "landmarks" within its borders must be borne by all of its taxpayers or whether it can instead be imposed entirely on the owners of the individual properties.

Only in the most superficial sense of the word can this case be said to involve "zoning." Typical zoning restrictions may, it is true, so limit the prospective uses of a piece of property as to diminish the value of that property in the abstract because it may not be used for the forbidden purposes. But any such abstract decrease in value will more than likely be at least partially offset by an increase in value which

36. We emphasize that our holding today is on the present record, which in turn is based on Penn Central's present ability to use the Terminal for its intended purposes and in a gainful fashion. The city conceded at oral argument that if appellants can demonstrate at some point in the future that circumstances have so changed that the Terminal ceases to be "economically viable," appellants may obtain relief. See Tr. of Oral Arg. 42–43.

flows from similar restrictions as to use on neighboring properties. All property owners in a designated area are placed under the same restrictions, not only for the benefit of the municipality as a whole but also for the common benefit of one another. In the words of Mr. Justice Holmes, speaking for the Court in Pennsylvania Coal Co. v. Mahon, 260 U.S. 393, 415, 43 S.Ct. 158, 160, 67 L.Ed. 322 (1922), there is "an average reciprocity of advantage."

Where a relatively few individual buildings, all separated from one another, are singled out and treated differently from surrounding buildings, no such reciprocity exists. The cost to the property owner which results from the imposition of restrictions applicable only to his property and not that of his neighbors may be substantial—in this case, several million dollars—with no comparable reciprocal benefits. And the cost associated with landmark legislation is likely to be of a completely different order of magnitude than that which results from the imposition of normal zoning restrictions. Unlike the regime affected by the latter, the landowner is not simply prohibited from using his property for certain purposes, while allowed to use it for all other purposes. Under the historic-landmark preservation scheme adopted by New York, the property owner is under an affirmative duty to *preserve* his property *as a landmark* at his own expense. . . .

. . .

NOTES

1. Compare the court's approach to the taking issue in Kaiser Aetna v. United States, supra, p. 822, and in Loretto v. Teleprompter Manhattan CATV Corp., 458 U.S. 419, 102 S.Ct. 3164, 73 L.Ed.2d 868 (1982). In neither case was the multi-factor balancing approach followed. The right to exclude, deemed to have been taken in Kaiser Aetna, is a "fundamental" attribute of ownership, said the court. Should the court have attached greater significance to the fact that the landowner had opened the land to such numbers of persons as to make it scarely distinguishable from a small city? In PruneYard Shopping Center v. Robins, 447 U.S. 74, 100 S.Ct. 2035, 64 L.Ed.2d 741 (1980), decided later during the same term, the court held that a state law forbidding a shopping center to exclude pamphleteers was not a taking. See also Putnam Lake Community Council v. Deputy Commissioner, 90 A.D.2d 850, 456 N.Y.S.2d 100 (1982), holding that a private lake was "public" for the purpose of application of the state sanitary code, in view of the use of the lake by 1,400 landowners, their families and friends.

In the Loretto case, the court held that a statute requiring landlords to allow installation of cable television wiring and related facilities, in order that tenants might obtain access to cable television, constituted a taking. The court said that "we have long considered a physical intrusion by government to be a property restriction of an unusually serious character for purposes of the Takings Clause. Our cases further establish that when the physical intrusion reaches the extreme form of a permanent physical occupation, a taking has occurred. In such a case, 'the character of the government action' not only is an important factor in resolving whether the action works a taking but is determinative."

Justice Rehnquist regarded as a physical invasion a rent control regulation that prevented a landlord from removing an apartment building from the rental market, in order that it could be razed to enable use of the land as a parking lot. See his dissent in Fresh Pond Shopping Center, Inc. v. Acheson Callahan, ___ U.S. ___, 104 S.Ct. 218, 78 L.Ed.2d 215 (1983), dismissing for want of a substantial federal question an appeal from Fresh Pond Shopping Center, Inc. v. Rent Control Board of Cambridge, 338 Mass. 1051, 446 N.E.2d 1060 (1983). Justice Rehnquist argued that since the landlord is "unable to possess the property" until "tenant decides to leave of his own volition," the ordinance effects a "transfer of control over the reversionary interest" to the tenant, thereby depriving the landlord of the right to exclude. What is the answer to this argument?

2. Compare with the principal case Fred F. French Investing Co. v. City of New York, 39 N.Y.2d 587, 385 N.Y.S.2d 5, 350 N.E.2d 381, (1976), cert. denied, 429 U.S. 990, 97 S.Ct. 515, 50 L.Ed.2d 602. This case held invalid as a denial of due process, but not as a taking, zoning of private parks as public parks. This zoning was not saved by coupling it with a transferable development right (TDR) feature allowing the landowner to transfer his development rights lost by the zoning to land he might acquire in a designated "receiving area" elsewhere in the city.

3. Costonis, The Disparity Issue: A Context for the Grand Central Terminal Decision, 91 Harv.L.Rev. 402 (1977), argues that a TDR program allowing transfers to receiving areas distant from the regulated land can be, if properly devised, less burdensome to the regulated landowner than a TDR program allowing transfers only to adjacent sites.

4. Richards, Transferable Development Rights: Corrective, Catastrophe, or Curiosity? 12 Real Estate L.J. 26 (1983), reports that the reliance upon TDR in New York City has encouraged excessive concentration of development, but has preserved few landmarks. For other appraisals and applications of the TDR device, see Transferring Density (F. Schnidman ed. 1980); F. James & D. Gale, Zoning for Sale (1977); Randle, The National Reserve System and Transferable Development Rights: Is the New Jersey Pinelands Plan an Unconstitutional "Taking"? 10 B.C.Env.Aff.L.Rev. 183 (1982).

5. Similar to TDR, and also to development exactions, is incentive or bonus zoning. Regulations, particularly of density, may provide that a developer can exceed the prescribed standard if he provides some amenity for the public, typically open space such as plazas. See The New Zoning (Marcus & Groves eds. 1970). Critics of this device maintain that in practice it provides the community with amenities of doubtful value and encourages excessive density. See Cook, Incentive Zoning, Land Use Law, Sept. 1982, p. 4; Costonis, Law & Aesthetics: A Critique and A Reformulation of the Dilemmas, 80 Mich. L.Rev. 355, 363 (1982).

KEYSTONE BITUMINOUS COAL ASSOCIATION v. DE BENEDICTIS

Supreme Court of the United States, 1987.
480 U.S. 470, 107 S.Ct. 1232, 94 L.Ed.2d 472.

JUSTICE STEVENS, delivered the opinion of the Court.

In Pennsylvania Coal Co. v. Mahon, the Court reviewed the constitutionality of a Pennsylvania statute that admittedly destroyed "previously existing rights of property and contract."

Now, 65 years later, we address a different set of "particular facts," involving the Pennsylvania Legislature's 1966 conclusion that the Commonwealth's existing mine subsidence legislation had failed to protect the public interest in safety, land conservation, preservation of affected municipalities' tax bases, and land development in the Commonwealth. Based on detailed findings, the legislature enacted the Bituminous Mine Subsidence and Land Conservation Act (the "Subsidence Act" or the "Act"), Pa.Stat.Ann., Tit. 52, § 1406.1 et seq. (Purdon Supp.1986). Petitioners contend, relying heavily on our decision in *Pennsylvania Coal,* that § 4 and § 6 of the Subsidence Act and certain implementing regulations violate the Takings Clause, and that § 6 of the Act violates the Contracts Clause of the Federal Constitution. The District Court and the Court of Appeals concluded that *Pennsylvania Coal* does not control for several reasons and that our subsequent cases make it clear that neither § 4 nor § 6 is unconstitutional on its face. We agree. . . .

Pennsylvania's Subsidence Act authorizes the Pennsylvania Department of Environmental Resources (DER) to implement and enforce a comprehensive program to prevent or minimize subsidence and to regulate its consequences. Section 4 of the Subsidence Act, Pa.Stat. Ann., Tit. 52, § 1406.4 (Purdon Supp.1986), prohibits mining that causes subsidence damage to three categories of structures that were in place on April 17, 1966: public buildings and noncommercial buildings generally used by the public; dwellings used for human habitation; and cemeteries.[6] Since 1966 the DER has applied a formula that generally requires 50% of the coal beneath structures protected by § 4 to be kept in place as a means of providing surface support. Section 6 of the Subsidence Act authorizes the DER to revoke a mining permit if the

6. Section 4 provides:

"Protection of surface structures against damage from cave-in, collapse, or subsidence

"In order to guard the health, safety and general welfare of the public, no owner, operator, lessor, lessee, or general manager, superintendent or other person in charge of or having supervision over any bituminous coal mine shall mine bituminous coal so as to cause damage as a result of the caving-in, collapse or subsidence of the following surface structures in place on April 27, 1966, overlying or in the proximity of the mine:

"(1) Any public building or any noncommercial structure customarily used by the public, including but not being limited to churches, schools, hospitals, and municipal utilities or municipal public service operations.

"(2) Any dwelling used for human habitation; and

"(3) Any cemetery or public burial ground; unless the current owner of the structure consents and the resulting damage is fully repaired or compensated." . . .

removal of coal causes damage to a structure or area protected by § 4 and the operator has not within six months either repaired the damage, satisfied any claim arising therefrom, or deposited a sum equal to the reasonable cost of repair with the DER as security.

In 1982, petitioners filed a civil rights action in the United States District Court for the Western District of Pennsylvania seeking to enjoin officials of the DER from enforcing the Subsidence Act and its implementing regulations. The petitioners are an association of coal mine operators, and four corporations that are engaged, either directly or through affiliates, in underground mining of bituminous coal in western Pennsylvania. The members of the association and the corporate petitioners own, lease, or otherwise control substantial coal reserves beneath the surface of property affected by the Subsidence Act. The defendants in the action, respondents here, are the Secretary of the Commonwealth of Pennsylvania, the Chief of DER's Division of Mine Subsidence, and the Chief of DER's Section on Mine Subsidence Regulation.

The complaint alleges that Pennsylvania recognizes three separate estates in land: The mineral estate; the surface estate; and the "support estate." Beginning well over 100 years ago, land owners began severing title to underground coal and the right of surface support while retaining or conveying away ownership of the surface estate. It is stipulated that approximately 90% of the coal that is or will be mined by petitioners in western Pennsylvania was severed from the surface in the period between 1890 and 1920. When acquiring or retaining the mineral estate, petitioners or their predecessors typically acquired or retained certain additional rights that would enable them to extract and remove the coal. Thus, they acquired the right to deposit wastes, to provide for drainage and ventilation, and to erect facilities such as tipples, roads, or railroads, on the surface. Additionally, they typically acquired a waiver of any claims for damages that might result from the removal of the coal.

In the portions of the complaint that are relevant to us, petitioners alleged that both § 4 of the Subsidence Act, as implemented by the 50% rule, and § 6 of the Subsidence Act, constitute a taking of their private property without compensation in violation of the Fifth and Fourteenth Amendments. They also alleged that § 6 impairs their contractual agreements in violation of Article I, § 10 of the Constitution. The parties entered into a stipulation of facts pertaining to petitioners' facial challenge, and filed cross motions for summary judgment on the facial challenge. The District Court granted respondent's motion. . . .

The Court of Appeals affirmed, agreeing that *Pennsylvania Coal* does not control because the Subsidence Act is a legitimate means of "protect[ing] the environment of the Commonwealth, its economic future, and its well-being." . . .

Petitioners assert that disposition of their takings claim calls for no more than a straightforward application of the Court's decision in *Pennsylvania Coal Co. v. Mahon.* Although there are some obvious similarities between the cases, we agree with the Court of Appeals and the District Court that the similarities are far less significant than the differences, and that *Pennsylvania Coal* does not control this case. . . .

The holdings and assumptions of the Court in *Pennsylvania Coal* provide obvious and necessary reasons for distinguishing *Pennsylvania Coal* from the case before us today. The two factors that the Court considered relevant, have become integral parts of our takings analysis. We have held that land use regulation can effect a taking if it "does not substantially advance legitimate state interests, . . . or denies an owner economically viable use of his land." . . . Application of these tests to petitioners' challenge demonstrates that they have not satisfied their burden of showing that the Subsidence Act constitutes a taking. First, unlike the Kohler Act, the character of the governmental action involved here leans heavily against finding a taking; the Commonwealth of Pennsylvania has acted to arrest what it perceives to be a significant threat to the common welfare. Second, there is no record in this case to support a finding, similar to the one the Court made in *Pennsylvania Coal,* that the Subsidence Act makes it impossible for petitioners to profitably engage in their business, or that there has been undue interference with their investment-backed expectations.

Unlike the Kohler Act, which was passed upon in *Pennsylvania Coal,* the Subsidence Act does not merely involve a balancing of the private economic interests of coal companies against the private interests of the surface owners. The Pennsylvania Legislature specifically found that important public interests are served by enforcing a policy that is designed to minimize subsidence in certain areas. . . .

The District Court and the Court of Appeals were both convinced that the legislative purposes set forth in the statute were genuine, substantial, and legitimate, and we have no reason to conclude otherwise.

. . .

As the cases discussed above demonstrate, the public interest in preventing activities similar to public nuisances is a substantial one, which in many instances has not required compensation. The Subsidence Act, unlike the Kohler Act, plainly seeks to further such an interest. Nonetheless, we need not rest our decision on this factor alone, because petitioners have also failed to make a showing of diminution of value sufficient to satisfy the test set forth in Pennsylvania Coal and our other regulatory takings cases.

The second factor that distinguishes this case from Pennsylvania Coal is the finding in that case that the Kohler Act made mining of "certain coal" commercially impracticable. In this case, by contrast, petitioners have not shown any deprivation significant enough to satisfy the heavy burden placed upon one alleging a regulatory taking. For this reason, their takings claim must fail. . . .

The posture of the case is critical because we have recognized an important distinction between a claim that the mere enactment of a statute constitutes a taking and a claim that the particular impact of government action on a specific piece of property requires the payment of just compensation. . . . Petitioners thus face an uphill battle in making a facial attack on the Act as a taking.

The hill is made especially steep because petitioners have not claimed, at this stage, that the Act makes it commercially impracticable for them to continue mining their bituminous coal interests in western Pennsylvania. Indeed, petitioners have not even pointed to a single mine that can no longer be mined for profit. The only evidence available on the effect that the Subsidence Act has had on petitioners' mining operations comes from petitioners' answers to respondents' interrogatories. Petitioners described the effect that the Subsidence Act had from 1966–1982 on 13 mines that the various companies operate, and claimed that they have been required to leave a bit less than 27 million tons of coal in place to support § 4 areas. The total coal in those 13 mines amounts to over 1.46 billion tons. See App. 284. Thus § 4 requires them to leave less than 2% of their coal in place. But, as we have indicated, nowhere near all of the underground coal is extractable even aside from the Subsidence Act. The categories of coal that must be left for § 4 purposes and other purposes are not necessarily distinct sets, and there is no information in the record as to how much coal is actually left in the ground *solely* because of § 4. We do know, however, that petitioners have never claimed that their mining operations, or even any specific mines, have been unprofitable since the Subsidence Act was passed. Nor is there evidence that mining in any specific location affected by the 50% rule has been unprofitable.

Instead, petitioners have sought to narrowly define certain segments of their property and assert that, when so defined, the Subsidence Act denies them economically viable use. They advance two alternative ways of carving their property in order to reach this conclusion. First, they focus on the specific tons of coal that they must leave in the ground under the Subsidence Act, and argue that the Commonwealth has effectively appropriated this coal since it has no other useful purpose if not mined. Second, they contend that the Commonwealth has taken their separate legal interest in property—the "support estate."

Because our test for regulatory taking requires us to compare the value that has been taken from the property with the value that remains in the property, one of the critical questions is determining how to define the unit of property "whose value is to furnish the denominator of the fraction." Michelman, Property, Utility, and Fairness: Comments on the Ethical Foundations of "Just Compensation" Law, 80 Harv.L.Rev. 1165, 1192 (1967). In *Penn Central* the Court explained:

> " 'Taking' jurisprudence does not divide a single parcel into discrete segments and attempt to determine whether rights in a particular segment have been entirely abrogated. In deciding whether a particular governmental action has effected a taking, this Court focuses rather both on the character of the action and on

the nature of the interference with rights *in the parcel as a whole*—here the city tax block designated as the 'landmark site.'"

Similarly, in Andrus v. Allard, 444 U.S. 51, 100 S.Ct. 318, 62 L.Ed.2d 210 (1979), we held that "where an owner possesses a full 'bundle' of property rights, the destruction of one 'strand' of the bundle is not a taking because the aggregate must be viewed in its entirety." Although these verbal formulization do not solve all of the definitional issues that may arise in defining the relevant mass of property, they do provide sufficient guidance to compel us to reject petitioners' arguments.

The parties have stipulated that enforcement of the DER's 50% rule will require petitioners to leave approximately 27 million tons of coal in place. Because they own that coal but cannot mine it, they contend that Pennsylvania has appropriated it for the public purposes described in the Subsidence Act.

This argument fails for the reason explained in *Penn Central* and *Andrus.* The 27 million tons of coal do not constitute a separate segment of property for takings law purposes. Many zoning ordinances place limits on the property owner's right to make profitable use of some segments of his property. A requirement that a building occupy no more than a specified percentage of the lot on which it is located could be characterized as a taking of the vacant area as readily as the requirement that coal pillars be left in place. Similarly, under petitioners' theory one could always argue that a set-back ordinance requiring that no structure be built within a certain distance from the property line constitutes a taking because the footage represents a distinct segment of property for takings law purposes. Cf. Gorieb v. Fox, 274 U.S. 603, 47 S.Ct. 675, 71 L.Ed. 1228 (1927) (upholding validity of set-back ordinance) (per Holmes, J.). . . .

When the coal that must remain beneath the ground is viewed in the context of any reasonable unit of petitioners' coal mining operations and financial-backed expectations, it is plain that the petitioners have not come close to satisfying their burden of proving that they have been denied the economically viable use of that property. The record indicates that only about 75% of petitioners' underground coal can be profitably mined in any event, and there is no showing that petitioners' reasonable "investment-backed expectations" have been materially affected by the additional duty to retain the small percentage that must be used to support the structures protected by § 4.

Pennsylvania property law is apparently unique in regarding the support estate as a separate interest in land that can be conveyed apart from either the mineral estate or the surface estate. Petitioners therefore argue that even if comparable legislation in another State would not constitute a taking, the Subsidence Act has that consequence because it entirely destroys the value of their unique support estate. It is clear, however, that our takings jurisprudence forecloses reliance on such legalistic distinctions within a bundle of property rights. For example, in *Penn Central,* the Court rejected the argument that the "air rights" above the terminal constituted a separate segment of property for Takings Clause purposes. Likewise, in *Andrus v. Allard,* we viewed the right to sell property as just one element of the owner's property interest. In neither case did the result turn on whether state law allowed the separate sale of the segment of property.

The Court of Appeals, which is more familiar with Pennsylvania law than we are, concluded that as a practical matter the support estate is always owned by either the owner of the surface or the owner of the minerals. . . .

Thus, in practical terms, the support estate has value only insofar as it protects or enhances the value of the estate with which it is associated. Its value is merely a part of the entire bundle of rights possessed by the owner of either the coal or the surface. Because petitioners retain the right to mine virtually all of the coal in their mineral estates, the burden the Act places on the support estate does not constitute a taking. Petitioners may continue to mine coal profitably even if they may not destroy or damage surface structures at will in the process.

But even if we were to accept petitioners' invitation to view the support estate as a distinct segment of property for "takings" purposes, they have not satisfied their heavy burden of sustaining a facial challenge to the Act. Petitioners have acquired or retained the support estate for a great deal of land, only part of which is protected under the Subsidence Act, which, of course, deals with subsidence in the immediate vicinity of certain structures, bodies of water, and cemeteries. The record is devoid of any evidence on what percentage of the purchased support estates, either in the aggregate or with respect to any individual estate, has been affected by the Act. Under these circumstances, petitioners' facial attack under the takings clause must surely fail.

In addition to their challenge under the Takings Clause, petitioners assert that § 6 of the Subsidence Act violates the Contracts Clause by not allowing them to hold the surface owners to their contractual waiver of liability for surface damage. Here too, we agree with the Court of Appeals and the District Court that the Commonwealth's strong public interests in the legislation are more than adequate to justify the impact of the statute on petitioners' contractual agreements.

. . .

The judgment of the Court of Appeals is *Affirmed.*

CHIEF JUSTICE REHNQUIST, with whom JUSTICE POWELL, JUSTICE O'CONNOR, and JUSTICE SCALIA, join, dissenting. . . .

The Court opines that the decision in *Pennsylvania Coal* rested on the fact that the Kohler Act was "enacted solely for the benefit of private parties," and "served only private interests." A review of the Kohler Act shows that these statements are incorrect. The Pennsylvania legislature passed the statute "as remedial legislation, designed to cure existing evils and abuses." 274 Pa., at 495, 118 A., at 492 (quoting the Act). These were *public* "evils and abuses," identified in the preamble as "wrecked and dangerous streets and highways, collapsed public buildings, churches, schools, factories, streets, and private dwellings, broken gas, water and sewer systems, the loss of human life. . . ." Id., at 496, 118 A., at 493. . . .

Though several aspects of the Kohler Act limited its protection of these interests, this Court did not ignore the public interests served by the Act. . . . The strong public interest in the stability of streets and cities, however, was insufficient "to warrant achieving the desire by a shorter cut than the constitutional way of paying for the change."

The Subsidence Act rests on similar public purposes. . . . Thus, it is clear that the Court has severely understated the similarity of purpose between the Subsidence Act and the Kohler Act. The public purposes in this case are not sufficient to distinguish it from *Pennsylvania Coal.* . . .

This statute is not the type of regulation that our precedents have held to be within the "nuisance exception" to takings analysis.

The ease with which the Court moves from the recognition of public interests to the assertion that the activity here regulated is "akin to a public nuisance" suggests an exception far wider than recognized in our previous cases. . . . A broad exception to the operation of the Just Compensation Clause based on the exercise of multifaceted health, welfare, and safety regulations would surely allow government much greater authority than we have recognized to impose societal burdens on individual landowners, for nearly every action the government takes is intended to secure for the public an extra measure of "health, safety and welfare."

Thus, our cases applying the "nuisance" rationale have involved at least two narrowing principles. First, nuisance regulations exempted from the Fifth Amendment have rested on discrete and narrow purposes. The Subsidence Act, however, is much more than a nuisance statute. The central purposes of the Act, though including public safety, reflect a concern for preservation of buildings, economic development, and maintenance of property values to sustain the Commonwealth's tax base. We should hesitate to allow a regulation based on essentially economic concerns to be insulated from the dictates of the Fifth Amendment by labeling it nuisance regulation.

Second, and more significantly, our cases have never applied the nuisance exception to allow complete extinction of the value of a parcel of property. . . .

Here, petitioners' interests in particular coal deposits have been completely destroyed. By requiring that defined seams of coal remain in the ground, § 4 of the Subsidence Act has extinguished any interest one might want to acquire in this property. . . .

The Court's conclusion that the restriction on particular coal does not work a taking is primarily the result of its view that the 27 million tons of coal in the ground "do not constitute a separate segment of property for takings law purposes." This conclusion cannot be based on the view that the interests are too insignificant to warrant protection by the Fifth Amendment, for it is beyond cavil that government appropriation of "relatively small amounts of private property for its own use" requires just compensation. Instead, the Court's refusal to recognize the coal in the ground as a separate segment of property for takings purposes is based on the fact that the alleged taking is "regulatory," rather than a physical intrusion. On the facts of this case, I cannot see how the label placed on the government's action is relevant to consideration of its impact on property rights.

Our decisions establish that governmental action short of physical invasion may constitute a taking because such regulatory action might result in "as complete [a loss] as if the [government] had entered upon the surface of the land and taken exclusive possession of it." United States v. Causby, 328 U.S. 256, 261, 66 S.Ct. 1062, 1065, 90 L.Ed. 1206 (1946). . . . Our observation that "[a] 'taking' may more readily be found when the interference with property can be characterized as a physical invasion by government," Penn Central Transportation Co. v. New York City, 438 U.S., at 124, 98 S.Ct., at 2659, was not intended to alter this perspective merely because the claimed taking is by regulation. Instead, we have recognized that regulations—unlike physical invasions—do not typically extinguish the "full bundle" of rights in a particular piece of property. . . . This characteristic of regulations frequently makes unclear the breadth of their impact on identifiable segments of property, and has required that we evaluate the effects in light of the "several factors" enumerated in *Penn Central Transportation Co.:* "[t]he economic impact of the regulation on the claimant, . . . the extent to which the regulation has interfered with investment-backed expectations, [and] the character of the governmental action." 438 U.S., at 124, 98 S.Ct., at 2659.

No one, however, would find any need to employ these analytical tools where the government has physically taken an identifiable segment of property. Physical appropriation by the government leaves no doubt that it has in fact deprived the owner of all uses of the land. Similarly, there is no need for further analysis where the government by regulation extinguishes the whole bundle of rights in an identifiable segment of property, for the effect of this action on the holder of the property is indistinguishable from the effect of a physical taking. . . .

In this case, enforcement of the Subsidence Act and its regulations will require petitioners to leave approximately 27 million tons of coal in place. There is no question that this coal is an identifiable and separable property interest. . . . From the relevant perspective—that of the property owners—this interest has been destroyed every bit as much as if the government had proceeded to mine the coal for its own use. The regulation, then, does not merely inhibit one strand in the bundle, but instead destroys completely any interest in a segment of property. In these circumstances, I think it unnecessary to consider whether petitioners may operate individual mines or their overall mining operations profitably, for they have been denied all use of 27 million tons of coal. I would hold that § 4 of the Subsidence Act works a taking of these property interests.

Petitioners also claim that the Subsidence Act effects a taking of their support estate. . . .

When held by owners of the mineral estate, the support estate "consists of the right to remove the strata of coal and earth that undergird the surface . . ." 771 F.2d, at 715. Purchase of this right, therefore, shifts the risk of subsidence to the surface owner. Section 6 of the Subsidence Act, by making the coal mine operator strictly liable for any damage to surface structures caused by subsidence, purports to place this risk on the holder of the mineral estate regardless of whether the holder also owns the support estate. Operation of this provision extinguishes the petitioners' interests in their support estates, making worthless what they purchased as a separate right under Pennsylvania law. Like the restriction on mining particular coal, this complete interference with a property right extinguishes its value, and must be accompanied by just compensation. . . .

NOLLAN v. CALIFORNIA COASTAL COMMISSION

Supreme Court of the United States, 1987.
483 U.S. 825, 107 S.Ct. 3141, 97 L.Ed.2d 677.

JUSTICE SCALIA delivered the opinion of the Court.

James and Marilyn Nollan appeal from a decision of the California Court of Appeal ruling that the California Coastal Commission could condition its grant of permission to rebuild their house on their transfer to the public of an easement across their beachfront property. 177 Cal. App.3d 719, 223 Cal.Rptr. 28 (1986). The California Court rejected their claim that imposition of that condition violates the Takings Clause of the Fifth Amendment, as incorporated against the States by the Fourteenth Amendment. . . .

The Nollans own a beachfront lot in Ventura County, California. A quarter-mile north of their property is Faria County Park, an oceanside public park with a public beach and recreation area. Another public beach area, known locally as "the Cove," lies 1,800 feet south of their lot. A concrete seawall approximately eight feet high separates the beach portion of the Nollans' property from the rest of the lot. The historic mean high tide line determines the lot's oceanside boundary.

The Nollans originally leased their property with an option to buy. The building on the lot was a small bungalow, totaling 504 square feet, which for a time they rented to summer vacationers. After years of rental use, however, the building had fallen into disrepair, and could no longer be rented out.

The Nollans' option to purchase was conditioned on their promise to demolish the bungalow and replace it. In order to do so, under California Public Resources Code §§ 30106, 30212, and 30600 (West 1986), they were required to obtain a coastal development permit from the California Coastal Commission. On February 25, 1982, they submitted a permit application to the Commission in which they proposed to demolish the existing structure and replace it with a three-bedroom house in keeping with the rest of the neighborhood.

The Nollans were informed that their application had been placed on the administrative calendar, and that the Commission staff had recommended that the permit be granted subject to the condition that they allow the public an easement to pass across a portion of their property bounded by the mean high tide line on one side, and their seawall on the other side. This would make it easier for the public to get to Faria County Park and the Cove. The Nollans protested imposition of the condition, but the Commission overruled their objections and granted the permit subject to their recordation of a deed restriction granting the easement.

On June 3, 1982, the Nollans filed a petition for writ of administrative mandamus asking the Ventura County Superior Court to invalidate the access condition. They argued that the condition could not be imposed absent evidence that their proposed development would have a direct adverse impact on public access to the beach. The court agreed, and remanded the case to the Commission for a full evidentiary hearing on that issue.

On remand, the Commission held a public hearing, after which it made further factual findings and reaffirmed its imposition of the condition. It found that the new house would increase blockage of the view of the ocean, thus contributing to the development of "a 'wall' of residential structures" that would prevent the public "psychologically . . . from realizing a stretch of coastline exists nearby that they have every right to visit." The new house would also increase private use of the shorefront. These effects of construction of the house, along with other area development, would cumulatively "burden the public's ability to traverse to and along the shorefront." Therefore the Commission could properly require the Nollans to offset that burden by providing additional lateral access to the public beaches in the form of an easement across their property. . . .

The Court of Appeal . . . ruled that the requirement did not violate the Constitution . . .

Had California simply required the Nollans to make an easement across their beachfront available to the public on a permanent basis in order to increase public access to the beach, rather than conditioning their permit to rebuild their house on their agreeing to do so, we have no doubt there would have been a taking. . . . We have repeatedly held that, as to property reserved by its owner for private use, "the right to exclude [others is] 'one of the most essential sticks in the bundle of rights that are commonly characterized as property.'" Loretto v. Teleprompter Manhattan CATV Corp., 458 U.S. 419, 433, 102 S.Ct. 3164, 3175, 73 L.Ed.2d 868 (1982), quoting Kaiser Aetna v. United States, 444 U.S. 164, 176, 100 S.Ct. 383, 391, 62 L.Ed.2d 332 (1979). In Loretto we observed that where governmental action results in "[a] permanent physical occupation" of the property, by the government itself or by others, "our cases uniformly have found a taking to the extent of the occupation, without regard to whether the action achieves an important public benefit or has only minimal economic impact on the owner." We think a "permanent physical occupation" has occurred, for purposes of that rule, where individuals are given a permanent and continuous right to pass to and fro, so that the real property may continuously be traversed, even though no particular individual is permitted to station himself permanently upon the premises. . . .

. . .

Given, then, that requiring uncompensated conveyance of the easement outright would violate the Fourteenth Amendment, the question becomes whether requiring it to be conveyed as a condition for issuing a land use permit alters the outcome. We have long recognized that land use regulation does not effect a taking if it "substantially advance[s] legitimate state interests" and does not "den[y] an owner economically viable use of his land," . . . Our cases have not elaborated on the standards for determining what constitutes a "legitimate state interest" or what type of connection between the regulation and the state interest satisfies the requirement that the former "substantially advance" the latter.[3] They have made clear, however, that a broad range of governmental purposes and regulations satisfies these requirements. . . . The Commission argues that among these permissible purposes are protecting the public's ability to see the beach, assisting the public in overcoming the "psychological barrier" to using the beach created by a developed shorefront, and preventing congestion on the public beaches. We assume, without deciding, that this is so—in which case the Commission unquestionably would be able to deny the Nollans their permit outright if their new house (alone, or by reason of the cumulative impact produced in conjunction with other construction) would substantially impede these purposes, unless the denial would interfere so drastically with the Nollans' use of their property as to constitute a taking.

The Commission argues that a permit condition that serves the same legitimate police-power purpose as a refusal to issue the permit should not be found to be a taking if the refusal to issue the permit would not constitute a taking. We agree. Thus, if the Commission attached to the permit some condition that would have protected the public's ability to see the beach notwithstanding construction of the new house—for example, a height limitation, a width restriction, or a

3. Contrary to Justice BRENNAN's claim, *post*, at 3150, our opinions do not establish that these standards are the same as those applied to due process or equal-protection claims. To the contrary, our verbal formulations in the takings field have generally been quite different. We have required that the regulation "substantially advance" the "legitimate state interest" sought to be achieved, Agins v. Tiburon, 447 U.S. 255, 260, 100 S.Ct. 2138, 2141, 65 L.Ed.2d 106 (1980), not that "the State '*could rationally have decided*' the measure adopted might achieve the State's objective." Post, at —, quoting Minnesota v. Clover Leaf Creamery Co., 449 U.S. 456, 466, 101 S.Ct. 715, 725, 66 L.Ed.2d 659 (1981). Justice BRENNAN relies principally on an equal protection case, Minnesota v. Clover Leaf Creamery Co., supra, and two substantive due process cases, Williamson v. Lee Optical of Oklahoma, Inc., 348 U.S. 483, 487–488, 75 S.Ct. 461, 464–465, 99 L.Ed. 563 (1955) and Day-Brite Lighting, Inc. v. Missouri, 342 U.S. 421, 423, 72 S.Ct. 405, 407, 96 L.Ed. 469 (1952), in support of the standards he would adopt. But there is no reason to believe (and the language of our cases gives some reason to disbelieve) that so long as the regulation of property is at issue the standards for takings challenges, due process challenges, and equal protection challenges are identical; any more than there is any reason to believe that so long as the regulation of speech is at issue the standards for due process challenges, equal protection challenges, and First Amendment challenges are identical. Goldblatt v. Hempstead, 369 U.S. 590, 82 S.Ct. 987, 8 L.Ed.2d 130 (1962), does appear to assume that the inquiries are the same, but that assumption is inconsistent with the formulations of our later cases.

ban on fences—so long as the Commission could have exercised its police power (as we have assumed it could) to forbid construction of the house altogether, imposition of the condition would also be constitutional. Moreover (and here we come closer to the facts of the present case), the condition would be constitutional even if it consisted of the requirement that the Nollans provide a viewing spot on their property for passersby with whose sighting of the ocean their new house would interfere. Although such a requirement, constituting a permanent grant of continuous access to the property, would have to be considered a taking if it were not attached to a development permit, the Commission's assumed power to forbid construction of the house in order to protect the public's view of the beach must surely include the power to condition construction upon some concession by the owner, even a concession of property rights, that serves the same end. If a prohibition designed to accomplish that purpose would be a legitimate exercise of the police power rather than a taking, it would be strange to conclude that providing the owner an alternative to that prohibition which accomplishes the same purpose is not.

The evident constitutional propriety disappears, however, if the condition substituted for the prohibition utterly fails to further the end advanced as the justification for the prohibition. When that essential nexus is eliminated, the situation becomes the same as if California law forbade shouting fire in a crowded theater, but granted dispensations to those willing to contribute $100 to the state treasury. While a ban on shouting fire can be a core exercise of the State's police power to protect the public safety, and can thus meet even our stringent standards for regulation of speech, adding the unrelated condition alters the purpose to one which, while it may be legitimate, is inadequate to sustain the ban. Therefore, even though, in a sense, requiring a $100 tax contribution in order to shout fire is a lesser restriction on speech than an outright ban, it would not pass constitutional muster. Similarly here, the lack of nexus between the condition and the original purpose of the building restriction converts that purpose to something other than what it was. The purpose then becomes, quite simply, the obtaining of an easement to serve some valid governmental purpose, but without payment of compensation. Whatever may be the outer limits of "legitimate state interests" in the takings and land use context, this is not one of them. In short, unless the permit condition serves the same governmental purpose as the development ban, the building restriction is not a valid regulation of land use but "an out-and-out plan of extortion."

The Commission claims that it concedes as much, and that we may sustain the condition at issue here by finding that it is reasonably related to the public need or burden that the Nollans' new house creates or to which it contributes. We can accept, for purposes of discussion, the Commission's proposed test as to how close a "fit" between the condition and the burden is required, because we find that this case does not meet even the most untailored standards. The Commission's principal contention to the contrary essentially turns on a play on the word "access." The Nollans' new house, the Commission found, will interfere with "visual access" to the beach. That in turn (along with other shorefront development) will interfere with the desire of people who drive past the Nollans' house to use the beach, thus creating a "psychological barrier" to "access." The Nollans' new house will also, by a process not altogether clear from the Commission's opinion but presumably potent enough to more than offset the effects of the psychological barrier, increase the use of the public beaches, thus creating the need for more "access." These burdens on "access" would be alleviated by a requirement that the Nollans provide "lateral access" to the beach.

Rewriting the argument to eliminate the play on words makes clear that there is nothing to it. It is quite impossible to understand how a requirement that people already on the public beaches be able to walk across the Nollans' property reduces any obstacles to viewing the beach created by the new house. It is also impossible to understand how it lowers any "psychological barrier" to using the public beaches, or how it helps to remedy any additional congestion on them caused by construction of the Nollans' new house. We therefore find that the Commission's imposition of the permit condition cannot be treated as an exercise of its land use power for any of these purposes.[6] Our conclusion on this point is consistent with the approach taken by every other court that has considered the question, with the exception of the California state courts. . . .

Justice BRENNAN argues that imposition of the access requirement is not irrational. In his version of the Commission's argument, the reason for the requirement is that in its absence, a person looking toward the beach from the road will see a street of residential structures including the Nollans' new home and conclude that there is no public beach nearby. If, however, that person sees people passing and repassing along the dry sand behind the Nollans' home, he will realize that there is a public beach somewhere in the vicinity. The Commission's action, however, was based on the opposite factual finding that the wall of houses completely blocked the view of the beach and that a person looking from the road would not be able to see it at all.

Even if the Commission had made the finding that Justice BRENNAN proposes, however, it is not certain that it would suffice. We do not share Justice BRENNAN's confidence that the Commission "should

6. As Justice BRENNAN notes, the Commission also argued that the construction of the new house would " 'increase private use immediately adjacent to public tidelands,' " which in turn might result in more disputes between the Nollans and the public as to the location of the boundary. That risk of boundary disputes, however, is inherent in the right to exclude others from one's property, and the construction here can no more justify mandatory dedication of a sort of "buffer zone" in order to avoid boundary disputes than can the construction of an addition to a single-family house near a public street. Moreover, a buffer zone has a boundary as well, and unless that zone is a "no-man's land" that is off-limits for both neighbors (which is of course not the case here) its creation achieves nothing except to shift the location of the boundary dispute further on to the private owner's land. It is true that in the distinctive situation of the Nollans' property the sea-wall could be established as a clear demarcation of the public easement. But since not all of the lands to which this land-use condition applies have such a convenient reference point, the avoidance of boundary disputes is, even more obviously than the others, a made-up purpose of the regulation.

have little difficulty in the future in utilizing its expertise to demonstrate a specific connection between provisions for access and burdens on access" that will avoid the effect of today's decision. We view the Fifth Amendment's property clause to be more than a pleading requirement, and compliance with it to be more than an exercise in cleverness and imagination. As indicated earlier, our cases describe the condition for abridgement of property rights through the police power as a "*substantial* advanc[ing]" of a legitimate State interest. We are inclined to be particularly careful about the adjective where the actual conveyance of property is made a condition to the lifting of a land use restriction, since in that context there is heightened risk that the purpose is avoidance of the compensation requirement, rather than the stated police power objective.

We are left, then, with the Commission's justification for the access requirement unrelated to land use regulation:

> "Finally, the Commission notes that there are several existing provisions of pass and repass lateral access benefits already given by past Faria Beach Tract applicants as a result of prior coastal permit decisions. The access required as a condition of this permit is part of a comprehensive program to provide continuous public access along Faria Beach as the lots undergo development or redevelopment."

That is simply an expression of the Commission's belief that the public interest will be served by a continuous strip of publicly accessible beach along the coast. The Commission may well be right that it is a good idea, but that does not establish that the Nollans (and other coastal residents) alone can be compelled to contribute to its realization. Rather, California is free to advance its "comprehensive program," if it wishes, by using its power of eminent domain for this "public purpose," see U.S. Const., Amdt. V; but if it wants an easement across the Nollans' property, it must pay for it.

Reversed.

JUSTICE BRENNAN, with whom JUSTICE MARSHALL joins, dissenting.

. . .

The Court's conclusion that the permit condition imposed on appellants is unreasonable cannot withstand analysis. First, the Court demands a degree of exactitude that is inconsistent with our standard for reviewing the rationality of a state's exercise of its police power for the welfare of its citizens. Second, even if the nature of the public access condition imposed must be identical to the precise burden on access created by appellants, this requirement is plainly satisfied.

There can be no dispute that the police power of the States encompasses the authority to impose conditions on private development. It is also by now commonplace that this Court's review of the rationality of a State's exercise of its police power demands only that the State "*could rationally have decided*" that the measure adopted might achieve the State's objective. Minnesota v. Clover Leaf Creamery Co., 449 U.S. 456, 466, 101 S.Ct. 715, 725, 66 L.Ed.2d 659 (1981) (emphasis in original).[1] In this case, California has employed its police power in order to condition development upon preservation of public access to the ocean and tidelands. The Coastal Commission, if it had so chosen, could have denied the Nollans' request for a development permit, since the property would have remained economically viable without the requested new development. Instead, the State sought to accomodate the Nollans' desire for new development, on the condition that the development not diminish the overall amount of public access to the coastline. Appellants' proposed development would reduce public access by restricting visual access to the beach, by contributing to an increased need for community facilities, and by moving private development closer to public beach property. The Commission sought to offset this diminution in access, and thereby preserve the overall balance of access, by requesting a deed restriction that would ensure "lateral" access: the right of the public to pass and repass along the dry sand parallel to the shoreline in order to reach the tidelands and the ocean. In the expert opinion of the Coastal Commission, development conditioned on such a restriction would fairly attend to both public and private interests.

The Court finds fault with this measure because it regards the condition as insufficiently tailored to address the precise type of reduction in access produced by the new development. The Nollans' development blocks visual access, the Court tells us, while the Commission seeks to preserve lateral access along the coastline. Thus, it concludes, the State acted irrationally. Such a narrow conception of rationality, however, has long since been discredited as a judicial arrogation of legislative authority. . . .

The Commission is charged by both the state constitution and legislature to preserve overall public access to the California coastline. . . . The Commission has sought to discharge its responsibilities in a flexible manner. It has sought to balance private and public interests and to accept tradeoffs: to permit development that reduces access in some ways as long as other means of access are enhanced. In this case, it has determined that the Nollans' burden on access would be offset by a deed restriction that formalizes the public's right to pass along the shore. In its informed judgment, such a tradeoff would preserve the

1. . . .

Notwithstanding the suggestion otherwise, our standard for reviewing the threshold question whether an exercise of the police power is legitimate is a uniform one. . . .

Our phraseology may differ slightly from case to case—e.g., regulation must "substantially advance," Agins v. Tiburon, 447 U.S. 255, 260, 100 S.Ct. 2138, 2141, 65 L.Ed.2d 106 (1980) or be "reasonably necessary to" Penn Central Transportation Co. v. New York City, 438 U.S. 104, 127, 98 S.Ct. 2646, 2660, 57 L.Ed.2d 631 (1978) the government's end. These minor differences cannot, however, obscure the fact that the inquiry in each case is the same.

Of course, government action may be a valid exercise of the police power and still violate specific provisions of the Constitution. Justice SCALIA is certainly correct in observing that challenges founded upon these provisions are reviewed under different standards. Our consideration of factors such as those identified in *Penn Central,* supra, for instance, provides an analytical framework for protecting the values underlying the Takings Clause, and other distinctive approaches are utilized to give effect to other constitutional provisions. This is far different, however, from the use of different standards of review to address the threshold issue of the rationality of government action.

net amount of public access to the coastline. The Court's insistence on a precise fit between the forms of burden and condition on each individual parcel along the California coast would penalize the Commission for its flexibility, hampering the ability to fulfill its public trust mandate.

. . .

Even if we accept the Court's unusual demand for a precise match between the condition imposed and the specific type of burden on access created by the appellants, the State's action easily satisfies this requirement. First, the lateral access condition serves to dissipate the impression that the beach that lies behind the wall of homes along the shore is for private use only. It requires no exceptional imaginative powers to find plausible the Commission's point that the average person passing along the road in front of a phalanx of imposing permanent residences, including the appellants' new home, is likely to conclude that this particular portion of the shore is not open to the public. If, however, that person can see that numerous people are passing and repassing along the dry sand, this conveys the message that the beach is in fact open for use by the public. Furthermore, those persons who go down to the public beach a quarter-mile away will be able to look down the coastline and see that persons have continuous access to the tidelands, and will observe signs that proclaim the public's right of access over the dry sand. The burden produced by the diminution in visual access—the impression that the beach is not open to the public—is thus directly alleviated by the provision for public access over the dry sand. The Court therefore has an unrealistically limited conception of what measures could reasonably be chosen to mitigate the burden produced by a diminution of visual access.

The second flaw in the Court's analysis of the fit between burden and exaction is more fundamental. The Court assumes that the only burden with which the Coastal Commission was concerned was blockage of visual access to the beach. This is incorrect. The Commission specifically stated in its report in support of the permit condition that "[t]he Commission finds that the applicants' proposed development would present an increase in view blockage, *an increase in private use of the shorefront,* and that this impact would burden the public's ability to traverse to and along the shorefront." It declared that the possibility that "the public may get the impression that the beachfront is no longer available for public use" would be "due to *the encroaching nature of private use immediately adjacent to the public use, as well as* the visual 'block' of increased residential build-out impacting the visual quality of the beachfront." . . .

The fact that the Commission's action is a legitimate exercise of the police power does not, of course, insulate it from a takings challenge, for when "regulation goes too far it will be recognized as a taking." . . .

The physical intrusion permitted by the deed restriction is minimal. The public is permitted the right to pass and re-pass along the coast in an area from the seawall to the mean high tide mark. This area is at its *widest* 10 feet, which means that *even without the permit condition,* the public's right of access permits it to pass on average within a few feet of the seawall. Passage closer to the 8–foot high rocky seawall will make the appellants even less visible to the public than passage along the high tide area farther out on the beach. The intrusiveness of such passage is even less than the intrusion resulting from the required dedication of a sidewalk in front of private residences, exactions which are commonplace conditions on approval of development. . . .

Examination of the economic impact of the Commission's action reinforces the conclusion that no taking has occurred. Allowing appellants to intensify development along the coast in exchange for ensuring public access to the ocean is a classic instance of government action that produces a "reciprocity of advantage." Pennsylvania Coal, supra, 260 U.S., at 415, 43 S.Ct., at 160. Appellants have been allowed to replace a one-story 521–square-foot beach home with a two-story 1,674–square-foot residence and an attached two-car garage, resulting in development covering 2,464 square feet of the lot. Such development obviously significantly increases the value of appellants' property; appellants make no contention that this increase is offset by any diminution in value resulting from the deed restriction, much less that the restriction made the property less valuable than it would have been without the new construction. Furthermore, appellants gain an additional benefit from the Commission's permit condition program. They are able to walk along the beach beyond the confines of their own property only because the Commission has required deed restrictions as a condition of approving other new beach developments. Thus, appellants benefit both as private landowners and as members of the public from the fact that new development permit requests are conditioned on preservation of public access. . . .

With respect to the permit condition program in general, the Commission should have little difficulty in the future in utilizing its expertise to demonstrate a specific connection between provisions for access and burdens on access produced by new development. Neither the Commission in its report nor the State in its briefs and at argument highlighted the particular threat to lateral access created by appellants' development project. In defending its action, the State emphasized the general point that *overall* access to the beach had been preserved, since the diminution of access created by the project had been offset by the gain in lateral access. This approach is understandable, given that the State relied on the reasonable assumption that its action was justified under the normal standard of review for determining legitimate exercises of a State's police power. In the future, alerted to the Court's apparently more demanding requirement, it need only make clear that a provision for public access directly responds to a particular type of burden on access created by a new development. Even if I did not believe that the record in this case satisfies this requirement, I would have to acknowledge that the record's documentation of the impact of coastal development indicates that the Commission should have little problem presenting its findings in a way that avoids a takings problem.

Nonetheless it is important to point out that the Court's insistence on a precise accounting system in this case is insensitive to the fact that increasing intensity of development in many areas calls for farsighted, comprehensive planning that takes into account both the interdependence of land uses and the cumulative impact of development. . . .

I dissent.

JUSTICE BLACKMUN, dissenting. [omitted]

JUSTICE STEVENS, with whom JUSTICE BLACKMUN joins, dissenting. [omitted]

NOTES

1. Does this case mean that henceforth all regulations of land use, when challenged as takings, will be subject to a stricter standard of judicial review than heretofore? Professor Frank Michelman views the case as no basis for extending heightened judicial scrutiny of land use regulations beyond instances of conditional imposition of permanent physical occupation. In view of the Loretto decision, he says, the stricter scrutiny in Nollan "is hardly a novelty at all." Michelman, Takings, 1987, 88 Colum.L.Rev. 1600, 1608, 1609 (1988). A state court rejected a contention that due process review was altered by *Nollan*: "[C]ontrary to the plaintiffs' claims . . ., the *Nollan* majority was not, as Justice Brennan claimed, advancing a new standard of review of land use regulation cases and abandoning the reasonable relationship standard." Builders Service Corporation, Inc. v. Planning & Zoning Commission of the Town of East Hampton, 208 Conn. 267, 545 A.2d 530, 539, n. 12 (1988).

2. Local governments commonly condition approval of subdivision plats and other development proposals upon dedication of land or payment of money to help meet needs generated by the proposed development for public services. To what extent are such development exactions affected by Nollan? See Freilich & Morgan, Municipal Strategies for Imposing Valid Development Exactions: Responding to *Nollan,* 10 Zoning & Planning L.Rep. 169 (1987), concluding that the effects are minimal or non-existent. See also Symposium, Exactions: A Controversial New Source for Municipal Funds, 50 Law & Contemp.Probs. 1 (1987). The following excerpt briefly summarizes state court reactions to development exactions.

J. CRIBBET & C. JOHNSON, PRINCIPLES OF THE LAW OF PROPERTY

Pages 452, 453 (3d ed. 1989).

Several state court cases have considered the validity of development exactions of various sorts. The most common and traditional exactions are dedication of streets and utility easements within a proposed subdivision as a condition for approval of the plat. This requirement is not likely to be challenged, as the subdivider is benefited by assumption by the local government of responsibility for maintenance of streets and easements. There also is no serious doubt about the validity of a requirement that the subdivider provide improvements that serve only the subdivision, such as paving of internal streets and installation of on-site utility facilities. Requiring the subdivider to dedicate a portion of land within the subdivision for a public park or school site, or alternatively pay a sum of money for development of a public park or school site elsewhere, has received mixed reviews by the courts. One court, invalidating such an exaction, declared that a developer can be required to assume only those costs that are "specifically and uniquely attributable to his activity and which would otherwise be cast upon the public."[84] Most, courts, however, approve such exactions if the subdivision would merely contribute to municipal growth, thereby generating needs for parks or school sites.[85] One court has also required assurance that money paid in lieu of dedication be earmarked for the benefit of the subdivision.[86]

In addition to mandated dedication of land or payment of in-lieu fees, some local governments have imposed "impact fees" for connections with utility systems or for building permits, to defray part of the cost of community facilities such as water plants.[87] Residential developers also have been required in some states and localities to set aside a portion of the project for housing affordable by persons with low or moderate incomes or make an in-lieu donation. These are referred to as "inclusionary zoning." One state court held such a program constitutes a taking,[88] but the highest court of New Jersey not only views such programs as lawful, but has ordered local governments under certain circumstances to adopt them.[89] Developers of offices have been required in some localities to pay "linkage fees" into a fund to be used to provide affordable housing, to balance displacement of such housing by the office project or creation by it of additional need for such housing.[90]

NOTE

Ad hoc development exactions resulting from bargaining between regulatory agencies and developers may render the development permission vulnerable to attack by third parties. Nunziato v. Edgewater Planning Bd, 225 N.J.Super. 124, 541 A.2d 1105 (1988) invalidated as

84. Pioneer Trust and Savings Bank v. Village of Mount Prospect, 22 Ill.2d 375, 176 N.E.2d 799 (1961). But cf. Krughoff v. City of Naperville, 68 Ill.2d 352, 12 Ill.Dec. 185, 369 N.E.2d 892 (1977).

85. E.g., Jordan v. Village of Menomonee Falls, 28 Wis.2d 608, 137 N.W.2d 442 (1965).

86. City of College Station v. Turtle Rock Corp., 680 S.W.2d 802 (Tex.1984).

87. E.g., Contractors & Bldrs. Ass'n of Pinellas County v. City of Dunedin, 329 So. 2d 314 (Fla.1976).

88. Board of Supervisors of Fairfax County v. Degroff Enterprises, Inc., 214 Va. 235, 198 S.E.2d 600 (1973).

89. Southern Burlington County NAACP v. Township of Mount Laurel, 92 N.J. 158, 456 A.2d 390 (1983).

90. E.g., San Telmo Assoc. v. City of Seattle, 108 Wash.2d 20, 735 P.2d 673 (1987). See generally, Symposium on Exactions: A Controversial New Source for Municipal Funds, 50 Law & Contemp.Prob. 1 (1987); Bray, Caudill & Owen, New Wave Land Use Regulation: The Impact of Impact Fees on Texas Lenders, 19 St. Mary's L.J. 319 (1987).

capricious approval of construction of a high rise condominium apartment building conditioned upon a contribution by the developer of $203,000 for affordable housing, after informal bargaining, despite continued willingness by the developer to pay this sum. The court said: "Without legislated standards the possibilities for abuse in such negotiations between an applicant and a regulatory body, no matter how worthy the cause, are unlimited. Approvals would be granted or withheld depending upon the board members' arbitrary sense of how much an applicant should pay. Cases can be visualized in which neighboring land owners file competing applications for site plan approval of shopping center developments and where the applicant promising the larger contribution is granted approval and the other is not. Or others in which a homeowner offers $1000 to obtain a variance, but his neighbor defeats the application by offering $2000." 541 A.2d at 1110.

FIRST ENGLISH EVANGELICAL LUTHERAN CHURCH OF GLENDALE v. COUNTY OF LOS ANGELES

Supreme Court of the United States, 1987.
482 U.S. 304, 107 S.Ct. 2378, 96 L.Ed.2d 250.

CHIEF JUSTICE REHNQUIST delivered the opinion of the Court.

In this case the California Court of Appeal held that a landowner who claims that his property has been "taken" by a land-use regulation may not recover damages for the time before it is finally determined that the regulation constitutes a "taking" of his property. We disagree, and conclude that in these circumstances the Fifth and Fourteenth Amendments to the United States Constitution would require compensation for that period.

In 1957, appellant First English Evangelical Lutheran Church purchased a 21-acre parcel of land in a canyon along the banks of the Middle Fork of Mill Creek in the Angeles National Forest. The Middle Fork is the natural drainage channel for a watershed area owned by the National Forest Service. Twelve of the acres owned by the church are flat land, and contained a dining hall, two bunkhouses, a caretaker's lodge, an outdoor chapel, and a footbridge across the creek. The church operated on the site a campground, known as "Lutherglen," as a retreat center and a recreational area for handicapped children.

In July 1977, a forest fire denuded the hills upstream from Lutherglen, destroying approximately 3,860 acres of the watershed area and creating a serious flood hazard. Such flooding occurred on February 9 and 10, 1978, when a storm dropped 11 inches of rain in the watershed. The runoff from the storm overflowed the banks of the Mill Creek, flooding Lutherglen and destroying its buildings.

In response to the flooding of the canyon, appellee County of Los Angeles adopted Interim Ordinance No. 11,855 in January 1979. The ordinance provided that "[a] person shall not construct, reconstruct, place or enlarge any building or structure, any portion of which is, or will be, located within the outer boundary lines of the interim flood protection area located in Mill Creek Canyon. . . ." App. to Juris.

Statement A31. The ordinance was effective immediately because the county determined that it was "required for the immediate preservation of the public health and safety. . . ." Id., at A32. The interim flood protection area described by the ordinance included the flat areas on either side of Mill Creek on which Lutherglen had stood.

The church filed a complaint in the Superior Court of California a little more than a month after the ordinance was adopted. As subsequently amended, the complaint alleged two claims against the county and the Los Angeles County Flood Control District. The first alleged that the defendants were liable under Cal.Gov't Code Ann. § 835 (West 1980) [1] for dangerous conditions on their upstream properties that contributed to the flooding of Lutherglen. As a part of this claim, appellant also alleged that "Ordinance No. 11,855 denies [appellant] all use of Lutherglen." App. 12, 49. The second claim sought to recover from the Flood District in inverse condemnation and in tort for engaging in cloud seeding during the storm that flooded Lutherglen. Appellant sought damages under each count for loss of use of Lutherglen. The defendants moved to strike the portions of the complaint alleging that the county's ordinance denied all use of Lutherglen, on the view that the California Supreme Court's decision in Agins v. Tiburon, 24 Cal.3d 266, 157 Cal.Rptr. 372, 598 P.2d 25 (1979), aff'd on other grounds, 447 U.S. 255, 100 S.Ct. 2138, 65 L.Ed.2d 106 (1980), rendered the allegation "entirely immaterial and irrelevant[, with] no bearing upon any conceivable cause of action herein." App. 22. See Cal.Civ.Proc. Code Ann. § 436 (West Supp.1987) ("The court may . . . strike out any irrelevant, false, or improper matter inserted in any pleading").

In *Agins v. Tiburon,* supra, the Supreme Court of California decided that a landowner may not maintain an inverse condemnation suit in the courts of that State based upon a "regulatory" taking. 24 Cal.3d, at 275–277, 157 Cal.Rptr., at 376–78, 598 P.2d, at 29–31. In the court's view, maintenance of such a suit would allow a landowner to force the legislature to exercise its power of eminent domain. Under this decision, then, compensation is not required until the challenged regulation or ordinance has been held excessive in an action for declaratory relief or a writ of mandamus and the government has nevertheless decided to continue the regulation in effect. Based on this decision, the trial court in the present case granted the motion to strike the allegation that the church had been denied all use of Lutherglen. It explained that "a careful re-reading of the *Agins* case persuades the Court that when an ordinance, even a non-zoning ordinance, deprives a person of the total use of his lands, his challenge to the ordinance is by way of declaratory relief or possibly mandamus." App. 26. Because the appellant alleged a regulatory taking and sought only damages, the allegation that the ordinance denied all use of Lutherglen was deemed irrelevant.[2]

1. Section 835 of the California Government Code establishes conditions under which a public entity may be liable "for injury caused by a dangerous condition of its property. . . ."

2. The trial court also granted defendants' motion for judgment on the pleadings on the second cause of action, based on cloud seeding. It limited trial on the first cause of action for damages under Cal.

On appeal, the California Court of Appeal read the complaint as one seeking "damages for the uncompensated taking of all use of Lutherglen by County Ordinance No. 11,855. . . ." App. to Juris. Statement A13–A14. It too relied on the California Supreme Court's decision in *Agins* in rejecting the cause of action, declining appellant's invitation to reevaluate *Agins* in light of this Court's opinions in San Diego Gas & Electric Co. v. San Diego, 450 U.S. 621, 101 S.Ct. 1287, 67 L.Ed.2d 551 (1981). The court found itself obligated to follow *Agins* "because the United States Supreme Court has not yet ruled on the question of whether a state may constitutionally limit the remedy for a taking to nonmonetary relief. . . ." App. to Juris. Statement A16. It accordingly affirmed the trial court's decision to strike the allegations concerning appellee's ordinance. The Supreme Court of California denied review.

This appeal followed, and we noted probable jurisdiction. 478 U.S. ___, 106 S.Ct. 3292, 92 L.Ed.2d 708. Appellant asks us to hold that the Supreme Court of California erred in *Agins v. Tiburon* in determining that the Fifth Amendment, as made applicable to the States through the Fourteenth Amendment, does not require compensation as a remedy for "temporary" regulatory takings—those regulatory takings which are ultimately invalidated by the courts. Four times this decade, we have considered similar claims and have found ourselves for one reason or another unable to consider the merits of the *Agins* rule. See MacDonald, Sommer & Frates v. Yolo County, 477 U.S. ___, 106 S.Ct. 2561, 91 L.Ed.2d 285 (1986); Williamson County Regional Planning Comm'n v. Hamilton Bank, 473 U.S. 172, 105 S.Ct. 3108, 87 L.Ed.2d 126 (1985); *San Diego Gas & Electric Co., supra; Agins v. Tiburon, supra.* For the reasons explained below, however, we find the constitutional claim properly presented in this case, and hold that on these facts the California courts have decided the compensation question inconsistently with the requirements of the Fifth Amendment.

I

Concerns with finality left us unable to reach the remedial question in the earlier cases where we have been asked to consider the rule of *Agins.* See MacDonald, Sommer & Frates, supra, 477 U.S., at ___, 106 S.Ct., at ___ (summarizing cases). In each of these cases, we concluded either that regulations considered to be in issue by the state court did not effect a taking, Agins v. Tiburon, supra, 24 Cal.3d, at 263, 157 Cal.Rptr. 372, 598 P.2d 25, or that the factual disputes yet to be resolved by state authorities might still lead to the conclusion that no taking had occurred. MacDonald, Sommer & Frates, supra, 477 U.S., at ___, 106 S.Ct., at ___; Williamson County, supra, 473 U.S., at ___, 105 S.Ct., at ___; San Diego Gas & Electric Co., supra, 450 U.S., at 631–632, 101 S.Ct., at 1293–1294. Consideration of the remedial question in those circumstances, we concluded, would be premature.

Gov't Code Ann. § 835 (West 1980), rejecting the inverse condemnation claim. At the close of plaintiff's evidence, the trial court granted a nonsuit on behalf of defendants, dismissing the entire complaint.

The posture of the present case is quite different. Appellant's complaint alleged that "Ordinance No. 11,855 denies [it] all use of Lutherglen," and sought damages for this deprivation. App. 12, 49. In affirming the decision to strike this allegation, the Court of Appeal assumed that the complaint sought "damages for the uncompensated *taking* of all use of Lutherglen by County Ordinance No. 11,855." App. to Juris. Statement A13–A14 (emphasis added). It relied on the California Supreme Court's *Agins* decision for the conclusion that "the remedy for a *taking* [is limited] to nonmonetary relief. . . ." Id., at A16 (emphasis added). The disposition of the case on these grounds isolates the remedial question for our consideration. The rejection of appellant's allegations did not rest on the view that they were false. Cf. MacDonald, Sommer & Frates, supra, at ___, n. 8, 106 S.Ct., at 2568, n. 8 (California court rejected allegation in the complaint that appellant was deprived of all beneficial use of its property); Agins v. Tiburon, 447 U.S., at 259, n. 6, 100 S.Ct., at 2141, n. 6 (same). Nor did the court rely on the theory that regulatory measures such as Ordinance No. 11,855 may never constitute a taking in the constitutional sense. Instead, the claims were deemed irrelevant solely because of the California Supreme Court's decision in *Agins* that damages are unavailable to redress a "temporary" regulatory taking. The California Court of Appeal has thus held that regardless of the correctness of appellants' claim that the challenged ordinance denies it "all use of Lutherglen" appellant may not recover damages until the ordinance is finally declared unconstitutional, and then only for any period after that declaration for which the county seeks to enforce it. The constitutional question pretermitted in our earlier cases is therefore squarely presented here.[6]

We reject appellee's suggestion that, regardless of the state court's treatment of the question, we must independently evaluate the adequacy of the complaint and resolve the takings claim on the merits before we can reach the remedial question. However "cryptic"—to use appellee's description—the allegations with respect to the taking were, the California courts deemed them sufficient to present the issue. We accordingly have no occasion to decide whether the ordinance at issue actually denied appellant all use of its property or whether the county might avoid the conclusion that a compensable taking had occurred by establishing that the denial of all use was insulated as a part of the State's authority to enact safety regulations. These questions, of course, remain open for decision on the remand we direct today. We now turn to the question of whether the Just Compensation Clause requires the government to pay for "temporary" regulatory takings.

6. Our cases have also required that one seeking compensation must "seek compensation through the procedures the State has provided for doing so" before the claim is ripe for review. Williamson County Regional Planning Comm'n v. Hamilton Bank, 473 U.S. 172, 194, 105 S.Ct. 3108, 3121, 87 L.Ed.2d 126 (1985). It is clear that appellant met this requirement. Having assumed that a taking occurred, the California court's dismissal of the action establishes that "the inverse condemnation procedure is unavailable. . . ." Id., at 197, 105 S.Ct., at 3122. The compensation claim is accordingly ripe for our consideration.

II

Consideration of the compensation question must begin with direct reference to the language of the Fifth Amendment, which provides in relevant part that "private property [shall not] be taken for public use, without just compensation." As its language indicates, and as the Court has frequently noted, this provision does not prohibit the taking of private property, but instead places a condition on the exercise of that power. This basic understanding of the Amendment makes clear that it is designed not to limit the governmental interference with property rights *per se,* but rather to secure *compensation* in the event of otherwise proper interference amounting to a taking. Thus, government action that works a taking of property rights necessarily implicates the "constitutional obligation to pay just compensation." Armstrong v. United States, 364 U.S. 40, 49, 80 S.Ct. 1563, 1569, 4 L.Ed.2d 1554 (1960).

We have recognized that a landowner is entitled to bring an action in inverse condemnation as a result of " 'the self-executing character of the constitutional provision with respect to compensation. . . .' " United States v. Clarke, 445 U.S. 253, 257, 100 S.Ct. 1127, 1130, 63 L.Ed.2d 373 (1980), quoting 6 P. Nichols, Eminent Domain § 25.41 (3d rev. ed. 1972). . . .

It has also been established doctrine at least since Justice Holmes' opinion for the Court in Pennsylvania Coal Co. v. Mahon, 260 U.S. 393, 43 S.Ct. 158, 67 L.Ed. 322 (1922) that "[t]he general rule at least is, that while property may be regulated to a certain extent, if regulation goes too far it will be recognized as a taking." Id., at 415, 43 S.Ct., at 160. While the typical taking occurs when the government acts to condemn property in the exercise of its power of eminent domain, the entire doctrine of inverse condemnation is predicated on the proposition that a taking may occur without such formal proceedings. . . .

While the Supreme Court of California may not have actually disavowed this general rule in *Agins,* we believe that it has truncated the rule by disallowing damages that occurred prior to the ultimate invalidation of the challenged regulation. The Supreme Court of California justified its conclusion at length in the *Agins* opinion, concluding that:

> "In combination, the need for preserving a degree of freedom in the land-use planning function, and the inhibiting financial force which inheres in the inverse condemnation remedy, persuade us that on balance mandamus or declaratory relief rather than inverse condemnation is the appropriate relief under the circumstances." Agins v. Tiburon, 24 Cal.3d, at 276–277, 157 Cal.Rptr., at 378, 598 P.2d, at 31.

We, of course, are not unmindful of these considerations, but they must be evaluated in the light of the command of the Just Compensation Clause of the Fifth Amendment. The Court has recognized in more than one case that the government may elect to abandon its intrusion or discontinue regulations. See e.g., Kirby Forest Industries,

Inc. v. United States, 467 U.S. 1, 104 S.Ct. 2187, 81 L.Ed.2d 1 (1984); United States v. Dow, 357 U.S. 17, 26, 78 S.Ct. 1039, 1046, 2 L.Ed.2d 1109 (1958). Similarly, a governmental body may acquiesce in a judicial declaration that one of its ordinances has affected an unconstitutional taking of property; the landowner has no right under the Just Compensation Clause to insist that a "temporary" taking be deemed a permanent taking. But we have not resolved whether abandonment by the government requires payment of compensation for the period of time during which regulations deny a landowner all use of his land.

In considering this question, we find substantial guidance in cases where the government has only temporarily exercised its right to use private property. In United States v. Dow, supra, at 26, 78 S.Ct., at 1046, though rejecting a claim that the Government may not abandon condemnation proceedings, the Court observed that abandonment "results in an alteration in the property interest taken—from [one of] full ownership to one of temporary use and occupation. . . . In such cases compensation would be measured by the principles normally governing the taking of a right to use property temporarily. See Kimball Laundry Co. v. United States, 338 U.S. 1, 69 S.Ct. 1434, 93 L.Ed. 1765 [1949]; United States v. Petty Motor Co., 327 U.S. 372, 66 S.Ct. 596, 90 L.Ed. 729 [1946]; United States v. General Motors Corp., 323 U.S. 373, 65 S.Ct. 357, 89 L.Ed. 311 [1945]." Each of the cases cited by the Dow Court involved appropriation of private property by the United States for use during World War II. Though the takings were in fact "temporary," see Petty Motor Co., supra, 327 U.S., at 375, 66 S.Ct., at 598, there was no question that compensation would be required for the Government's interference with the use of the property; the Court was concerned in each case with determining the proper measure of the monetary relief to which the property holders were entitled.

These cases reflect the fact that "temporary" takings which, as here, deny a landowner all use of his property, are not different in kind from permanent takings, for which the Constitution clearly requires compensation. Cf. San Diego Gas & Electric Co., 450 U.S., at 657, 101 S.Ct., at 1307 (BRENNAN, J., dissenting) ("Nothing in the Just Compensation Clause suggests that 'takings' must be permanent and irrevocable"). It is axiomatic that the Fifth Amendment's just compensation provision is "designed to bar Government from forcing some people alone to bear public burdens which, in all fairness and justice, should be borne by the public as a whole." Armstrong v. United States, 364 U.S., at 49, 80 S.Ct., at 1569. In the present case the interim ordinance was adopted by the county of Los Angeles in January 1979, and became effective immediately. Appellant filed suit within a month after the effective date of the ordinance and yet when the Supreme Court of California denied a hearing in the case on October 17, 1985, the merits of appellant's claim had yet to be determined. The United States has been required to pay compensation for leasehold interests of shorter duration than this. The value of a leasehold interest in property for a period of years may be substantial, and the burden on the property owner in extinguishing such an interest for a period of years may be great indeed. See, e.g., *United States v. General Motors,* supra. Where this burden results from governmental action that amounted to a taking, the Just Compensation Clause of the Fifth Amendment requires that the government pay the landowner for the value of the use of the land during this period. Cf. United States v. Causby, 328 U.S., at 261, 66 S.Ct., at 1065–1066 ("It is the owner's loss, not the taker's gain, which is the measure of the value of the property taken"). Invalidation of the ordinance or its successor ordinance after this period of time, though converting the taking into a "temporary" one, is not a sufficient remedy to meet the demands of the Just Compensation Clause.

Appellee argues that requiring compensation for denial of all use of land prior to invalidation is inconsistent with this Court's decisions in Danforth v. United States, 308 U.S. 271, 60 S.Ct. 231, 84 L.Ed. 240 (1939), and Agins v. Tiburon, 447 U.S. 255, 100 S.Ct. 2138, 65 L.Ed.2d 106 (1980). In *Danforth,* the landowner contended that the "taking" of his property had occurred prior to the institution of condemnation proceedings, by reason of the enactment of the Flood Control Act itself. He claimed that the passage of that Act had diminished the value of his property because the plan embodied in the Act required condemnation of a flowage easement across his property. The Court held that in the context of condemnation proceedings a taking does not occur until compensation is determined and paid, and went on to say that "[a] reduction or increase in the value of property may occur by reason of legislation for or the beginning or completion of a project," but "[s]uch changes in value are incidents of ownership. They cannot be considered as a 'taking' in the constitutional sense." Danforth, supra, 308 U.S., at 285, 60 S.Ct., at 236. *Agins* likewise rejected a claim that the city's preliminary activities constituted a taking, saying that "[m]ere fluctuations in value during the process of governmental decisionmaking, absent extraordinary delay, are 'incidents of ownership.'" See 447 U.S., at 263, n. 9, 100 S.Ct., at 2143, n. 9.

But these cases merely stand for the unexceptional proposition that the valuation of property which has been taken must be calculated as of the time of the taking, and that depreciation in value of the property by reason of preliminary activity is not chargeable to the government. Thus, in *Agins,* we concluded that the preliminary activity did not work a taking. It would require a considerable extension of these decisions to say that no compensable regulatory taking may occur until a challenged ordinance has ultimately been held invalid.[10]

10. *Williamson County Regional Planning Comm'n* is not to the contrary. There, we noted that "no constitutional violation occurs until just compensation has been denied." 473 U.S., at 194, n. 13, 105 S.Ct., at 3121, n. 13. This statement, however, was addressed to the issue of whether the constitutional claim was ripe for review and did not establish that compensation is unavailable for government activity occurring before compensation is actually denied. Though, as a matter of law, an illegitimate taking might not occur until the government refuses to pay, the interference that effects a taking might begin much earlier, and compensation is measured from that time. See Kirby Forest Industries, Inc. v. United States, 467 U.S. 1, 5, 104 S.Ct. 2187, 2191, 81 L.Ed.2d 1 (1984) (Where Government physically occupies land without condemnation proceedings, "the owner has a right to bring an 'inverse condemnation' suit to recover the value of the land *on the date of the intrusion by the Government*").

Nothing we say today is intended to abrogate the principle that the decision to exercise the power of eminent domain is a legislative function, " 'for Congress and Congress alone to determine.' " Hawaii Housing Authority v. Midkiff, 467 U.S. 229, 240, 104 S.Ct. 2321, 2329, 81 L.Ed.2d 186 (1984), quoting Berman v. Parker, 348 U.S. 26, 33, 75 S.Ct. 98, 103, 99 L.Ed. 27 (1954). Once a court determines that a taking has occurred, the government retains the whole range of options already available—amendment of the regulation, withdrawal of the invalidated regulation, or exercise of eminent domain. Thus we do not, as the Solicitor General suggests, "permit a court, at the behest of a private person, to require the . . . Government to exercise the power of eminent domain. . . ." Brief for United States as *Amicus Curiae* 22. We merely hold that where the government's activities have already worked a taking of all use of property, no subsequent action by the government can relieve it of the duty to provide compensation for the period during which the taking was effective.

We also point out that the allegation of the complaint which we treat as true for purposes of our decision was that the ordinance in question denied appellant all use of its property. We limit our holding to the facts presented, and of course do not deal with the quite different questions that would arise in the case of normal delays in obtaining building permits, changes in zoning ordinances, variances, and the like which are not before us. We realize that even our present holding will undoubtedly lessen to some extent the freedom and flexibility of land-use planners and governing bodies of municipal corporations when enacting land-use regulations. But such consequences necessarily flow from any decision upholding a claim of constitutional right; many of the provisions of the Constitution are designed to limit the flexibility and freedom of governmental authorities and the Just Compensation Clause of the Fifth Amendment is one of them. . . .

Here we must assume that the Los Angeles County ordinances have denied appellant all use of its property for a considerable period of years, and we hold that invalidation of the ordinance without payment of fair value for the use of the property during this period of time would be a constitutionally insufficient remedy. The judgment of the California Court of Appeals is therefore reversed, and the case is remanded for further proceedings not inconsistent with this opinion.

It is so ordered.

JUSTICE STEVENS, with whom JUSTICE BLACKMUN and JUSTICE O'CONNOR join as to Parts I and III, dissenting.

One thing is certain. The Court's decision today will generate a great deal of litigation. Most of it, I believe, will be unproductive. But the mere duty to defend the actions that today's decision will spawn will undoubtedly have a significant adverse impact on the land-use regulatory process. . . .

There is no dispute about the proposition that a regulation which goes "too far" must be deemed a taking. When that happens, the Government has a choice: it may abandon the regulation or it may continue to regulate and compensate those whose property it takes. In the usual case, either of these options is wholly satisfactory. Paying compensation for the property is, of course, a constitutional prerogative of the sovereign. Alternatively, if the sovereign chooses not to retain the regulation, repeal will, in virtually all cases, mitigate the overall effect of the regulation so substantially that the slight diminution in value that the regulation caused while in effect cannot be classified as a taking of property. We may assume, however, that this may not always be the case. There may be some situations in which even the temporary existence of a regulation has such severe consequences that invalidation or repeal will not mitigate the damage enough to remove the "taking" label. This hypothetical situation is what the Court calls a "temporary taking." But, contrary to the Court's implications, the fact that a regulation would constitute a taking if allowed to remain in effect permanently is by no means dispositive of the question whether the effect that the regulation has already had on the property is so severe that a taking occurred during the period before the regulation was invalidated.

A temporary interference with an owner's use of his property may constitute a taking for which the Constitution requires that compensation be paid. At least with respect to physical takings, the Court has so held. Thus, if the Government appropriates a leasehold interest and uses it for a public purpose, the return of the premises at the expiration of the lease would obviously not erase the fact of the Government's temporary occupation. Or if the Government destroys a chicken farm by building a road through it or flying planes over it, removing the road or terminating the flights would not palliate the physical damage that had already occurred. These examples are consistent with the rule that even minimal physical occupations constitute takings which give rise to a duty to compensate.

But our cases also make it clear that regulatory takings and physical takings are very different in this, as well as other, respects. While virtually all physical invasions are deemed takings, a regulatory program that adversely affects property values does not constitute a taking unless it destroys a major portion of the property's value. This diminution of value inquiry is unique to regulatory takings. Unlike physical invasions, which are relatively rare and easily identifiable without making any economic analysis, regulatory programs constantly affect property values in countless ways, and only the most extreme regulations can constitute takings. . . .

Regulations are three dimensional; they have depth, width, and length. As for depth, regulations define the extent to which the owner may not use the property in question. With respect to width, regulations define the amount of property encompassed by the restrictions. Finally, and for purposes of this case, essentially, regulations set forth the duration of the restrictions. It is obvious that no one of these elements can be analyzed alone to evaluate the impact of a regulation, and hence to determine whether a taking has occurred. For example, in *Keystone Bituminous* we declined to focus in on any discrete segment of the coal in the petitioners' mines, but rather looked to the effect that the restriction had on their entire mining project. Similarly, in *Penn*

Central, the Court concluded that it was error to focus on the nature of the uses which were prohibited without also examining the many profitable uses to which the property could still be put. Both of these factors are essential to a meaningful analysis of the economic effect that regulations have on the value of property and on an owner's reasonable investment-based expectations with respect to the property.

Just as it would be senseless to ignore these first two factors in assessing the economic effect of a regulation, one cannot conduct the inquiry without considering the duration of the restriction. See generally, Williams, Smith, Siemon, Mandelker, & Babcock, The White River Junction Manifesto, 9 Vt.L.Rev. 193, 215–218 (Fall 1984). For example, while I agreed with the Chief Justice's view that the permanent restriction on building involved in *Penn Central* constituted a taking, I assume that no one would have suggested that a temporary freeze on building would have also constituted a taking. Similarly, I am confident that even the dissenters in *Keystone Bituminous* would not have concluded that the restriction on bituminous coal mining would have constituted a taking had it simply required the mining companies to delay their operations until an appropriate safety inspection could be made.

On the other hand, I am willing to assume that some cases may arise in which a property owner can show that prospective invalidation of the regulation cannot cure the taking—that the temporary operation of a regulation has caused such a significant diminution in the property's value that compensation must be afforded for the taking that has already occurred. For this ever to happen, the restriction on the use of the property would not only have to be a substantial one, but it would have to remain in effect for a significant percentage of the property's useful life. In such a case an application of our test for regulatory takings would obviously require an inquiry into the duration of the restriction, as well as its scope and severity. See Williamson Planning Comm'n v. Hamilton Bank, 473 U.S. 172, 190–191, 105 S.Ct. 3108, 3119, 87 L.Ed.2d 126 (1985) (refusing to evaluate taking claim when the long-term economic effects were uncertain because it was not clear that restrictions would remain in effect permanently).

The cases that the Court relies upon for the proposition that there is no distinction between temporary and permanent takings are inapposite, for they all deal with physical takings—where the diminution of value test is inapplicable.[8] None of those cases is controversial; the state certainly may not occupy an individual's home for a month and then escape compensation by leaving and declaring the occupation

8. In United States v. Dow, 357 U.S. 17, 78 S.Ct. 1039, 2 L.Ed.2d 1109 (1958), the United States had "entered into physical possession and began laying the pipe line through the tract." Id., at 19, 78 S.Ct., at 1043. In Kimball Laundry Co. v. United States, 338 U.S. 1, 69 S.Ct. 1434, 93 L.Ed. 1765 (1949), the United States Army had taken possession of the laundry plant including all "the facilities of the company, except delivery equipment." Id., at 3, 69 S.Ct., at 1436. In United States v. Petty Motor Co., 327 U.S. 372, 66 S.Ct. 596, 90 L.Ed. 729 (1946), the United States acquired by condemnation a building occupied by tenants and ordered the tenants to vacate. In United States v. General Motors Corp., 323 U.S. 373, 65 S.Ct. 357, 89 L.Ed. 311 (1945), the Government occupied a portion of a leased building.

"temporary." But what does that have to do with the proper inquiry for regulatory takings? Why should there be a constitutional distinction between a permanent restriction that only reduces the economic value of the property by a fraction—perhaps one-third—and a restriction that merely postpones the development of a property for a fraction of its useful life—presumably far less than a third? In the former instance, no taking has occurred; in the latter case, the Court now proclaims that compensation for a taking must be provided. The Court makes no effort to explain these irreconcilable results. Instead, without any attempt to fit its proclamation into our regulatory takings cases, the Court boldly announces that once a property owner makes out a claim that a regulation would constitute a taking if allowed to stand, then he or she is entitled to damages for the period of time between its enactment and its invalidation.

Until today, we have repeatedly rejected the notion that all temporary diminutions in the value of property automatically activate the compensation requirement of the Takings Clause. In *Agins,* we held:

> "The State Supreme Court correctly rejected the contention that the municipality's good-faith planning activities, which did not result in successful prosecution of an eminent domain claim, so burdened the appellants' enjoyment of their property as to constitute a taking. . . . Even if the appellants' ability to sell their property was limited during the pendency of the condemnation proceeding, the appellants were free to sell or develop their property when the proceedings ended. Mere fluctuations in value during the process of governmental decisionmaking, absent extraordinary delay, are 'incidents of ownership. They cannot be considered as a "taking" in the constitutional sense.'" 447 U.S., at 263, n. 9, 100 S.Ct., at 2143, n. 9, quoting Danforth v. United States, 308 U.S. 271, 285, 60 S.Ct. 231, 236, 84 L.Ed. 240 (1939).
>
> Our more recent takings cases also cut against the approach the Court now takes. In *Williamson,* supra, and MacDonald, Sommer & Frates v. County of Yolo, 477 U.S. ____, 106 S.Ct. 2561, 91 L.Ed.2d 285 (1986), we held that we could not review a taking claim as long as the property owner had an opportunity to obtain a variance or some other form of relief from the zoning authorities that would permit the development of the property to go forward. Implicit in those holdings was the assumption that the temporary deprivation of all use of the property would not constitute a taking if it would be adequately remedied by a belated grant of approval of the developer's plans. See Sallet, Regulatory "Takings" and Just Compensation: The Supreme Court's Search for a Solution Continues, 18 Urb.Law. 635, 653 (1986).

The Court's reasoning also suffers from severe internal inconsistency. Although it purports to put to one side "normal delays in obtaining building permits, changes in zoning ordinances, variances and the like," the Court does not explain why there is a constitutional distinction between a total denial of all use of property during such "normal delays" and an equally total denial for the same length of time in order to determine whether a regulation has "gone too far" to be sustained unless the Government is prepared to condemn the property. Precisely the same interference with a real estate developer's plans may be occasioned by protracted proceedings which terminate with a zoning board's decision that the public interest would be served by modification of its regulation and equally protracted litigation which ends with a judicial determination that the existing zoning restraint has "gone too far," and that the board must therefore grant the developer a variance. The Court's analysis takes no cognizance of these realities. Instead, it appears to erect an artificial distinction between "normal delays" and the delays involved in obtaining a court declaration that the regulation constitutes a taking.[10]

In my opinion, the question whether a "temporary taking" has occurred should not be answered by simply looking at the reason a temporary interference with an owner's use of his property is terminated.[11] Litigation challenging the validity of a land-use restriction gives rise to a delay that is just as "normal" as an administrative procedure seeking a variance or an approval of a controversial plan.[12] Just because a plaintiff can prove that a land-use restriction would constitute a taking if allowed to remain in effect permanently does not mean that he or she can also prove that its temporary application rose to the level of a constitutional taking. . . .

There is, of course, a possibility that land-use planning, like other forms of regulation, will unfairly deprive a citizen of the right to develop his property at the time and in the manner that will best serve his economic interests. The "regulatory taking" doctrine announced in *Pennsylvania Coal* places a limit on the permissible scope of land-use restrictions. In my opinion, however, it is the Due Process Clause rather than that doctrine that protects the property owner from improperly motivated, unfairly conducted, or unnecessarily protracted governmental decisionmaking. Violation of the procedural safeguards mandated by the Due Process Clause will give rise to actions for damages under 42 U.S.C. § 1983, but I am not persuaded that delays in the development of property that are occasioned by fairly conducted administrative or judicial proceedings are compensable, except perhaps in the most unusual circumstances. On the contrary, I am convinced that the public interest in having important governmental decisions made in an orderly, fully informed way amply justifies the temporary

10. Whether delays associated with a judicial proceeding that terminates with a holding that a regulation was not authorized by state law would be a "normal delay" or a temporary taking depends, I suppose, on the unexplained rationale for the Court's artificial distinction.

11. "[T]he Constitution measures a taking of property not by what a State says, or what it intends, but by what it does." Hughes v. Washington, 389 U.S. 290, 298, 88 S.Ct. 438, 443, 19 L.Ed.2d 530 (1967) (Stewart, J., concurring). The fact that the effects of the regulation are stopped by judicial, as opposed to administrative decree, should not affect the question of whether compensation is required.

12. States may surely provide a forum in their courts for review of general challenges to zoning ordinances and other regulations. Such a procedure then becomes part of the "normal" process. Indeed, when States have set up such procedures in their courts, we have required resort to those processes before considering takings claims. See Williamson, Planning Comm'n v. Hamilton Bank, 473 U.S. 172, 105 S.Ct. 3108, 87 L.Ed.2d 126 (1985).

burden on the citizen that is the inevitable by-product of democratic government.

. . .

The policy implications of today's decision are obvious and, I fear, far reaching. Cautious local officials and land-use planners may avoid taking any action that might later be challenged and thus give rise to a damage action. Much important regulation will never be enacted,[17] even perhaps in the health and safety area. Were this result mandated by the Constitution, these serious implications would have to be ignored. But the loose cannon the Court fires today is not only unattached to the Constitution, but it also takes aim at a long line of precedents in the regulatory takings area. It would be the better part of valor simply to decide the case at hand instead of igniting the kind of litigation explosion that this decision will undoubtedly touch off.

I respectfully dissent.

NOTES

1. Local governments sometimes impose moratoria on land development, pending completion of studies or provision of municipal services, such as sewage treatment plants. Will such moratoria for reasonable periods of time, reasonably related to proper police power goals, now be upheld, as they were prior to First English? The impacts of moratoria on landowners and developers may be identical to the interim impacts of regulations held invalid as takings. But the same can be said about the impacts of "normal delays" incident to valid regulations. See Ziegler, Interim Zoning and Building Moratoria: Temporary Takings Claims After First English, 12 Zoning & Planning L.Rep. 97 (1989).

17. It is no answer to say that "[a]fter all, if a policeman must know the Constitution, then why not a planner?" San Diego Gas & Electric Co. v. San Diego, 450 U.S. 621, 661, n. 26, 101 S.Ct. 1287, 1309, n. 26, 67 L.Ed.2d 551 (1981) (BRENNAN, J., dissenting). To begin with, the Court has repeatedly recognized that it itself cannot establish any objective rules to assess when a regulation becomes a taking. See Hodel v. Irving, 481 U.S. ___, ___, 107 S.Ct. 2076, ___, 95 L.Ed.2d ___ (1987); Andrus v. Allard, 444 U.S. 51, 65, 100 S.Ct. 318, 326, 62 L.Ed.2d 210 (1979); Penn Central, 438 U.S., at 123–124, 98 S.Ct., at 2658–2659. How then can it demand that land planners do any better? However confusing some of our criminal procedure cases may be, I do not believe they have been as open-ended and standardless as our regulatory takings cases are. As one commentator concluded: "The chaotic state of taking law makes it especially likely that availability of the damages remedy will induce land-use planning officials to stay well back of the invisible line that they dare not cross." Johnson, Compensation for Invalid Land–Use Regulations, 15 Ga.L.Rev. 559, 594 (1981); see also Sallet, The Problem of Municipal Liability for Zoning and Land–Use Regulation, 31 Cath.U.L.Rev. 465, 478 (1982); Charles v. Diamond, 41 N.Y.2d 318, 331–332, 392 N.Y.S.2d 594, 604, 360 N.E.2d 1295, 1305 (1977); Allen v. City and County of Honolulu, 58 Haw. 432, 439, 571 P.2d 328, 331 (1977).

Another critical distinction between police activity and land-use planning is that not every missed call by a policeman gives rise to civil liability; police officers enjoy individual immunity for actions taken in good faith. See Harlow v. Fitzgerald, 457 U.S. 800, 102 S.Ct. 2727, 73 L.Ed.2d 396 (1982); Davis v. Scherer, 468 U.S. 183, 104 S.Ct. 3012, 82 L.Ed.2d 139 (1984). Moreover, municipalities are not subject to civil liability for police officers' routine judgment errors. See Monell v. New York City Dept. of Social Services, 436 U.S. 658, 98 S.Ct. 2018, 56 L.Ed.2d 611 (1978). In the land regulation context, however, I am afraid that any decision by a competent regulatory body may establish a "policy or custom" and give rise to liability after today.

2. Litigants may encounter judicial reluctance to pass upon taking claims. Courts may insist that the challenger demonstrate that the regulatory agency's decision was final ("ripe") and that all administrative remedies had been exhausted. It appears that federal courts have been more insistent on this than have state courts. In one case, the United States Supreme Court held that a claim for compensation for an alleged taking was not ripe because the claimant had neither sought a variance nor brought a suit for inverse condemnation available under state law. Williamson County Regional Planning Commission v. Hamilton Bank, 473 U.S. 172, 105 S.Ct. 3108, 87 L.Ed.2d 126 (1985). Some commentators view the ripeness requirement as an extremely formidable obstacle, at least in federal courts. See Mandelker & Blaesser, Applying the Ripeness Doctrine in Federal Land Use Litigation, 11 Planning L.Rep. 49 (1988). But consider two state court cases in which finality and exhaustion requirements did not prevent the court from deciding taking issues. In Karches v. City of Cincinnati, 38 Ohio St.3d 12, 526 N.E.2d 1350 (1988), the challenger had neither sought a variance nor applied for a building permit, but the circumstances convinced the court that such moves would have been futile. In Allingham v. City of Seattle, 109 Wn.2d 947, 749 P.2d 160 (1988), exhaustion of administrative remedies was not required because, had they succeeded, the ordinance itself would still have had such severe impact on the landowner as to constitute a taking (as viewed by the court).

3. What is the proper measure of damages for interim regulatory takings? Kimball Laundry Co. v. United States, 338 U.S. 1, 69 S.Ct. 1434, 93 L.Ed. 1765 (1949) held that the proper measure of compensation for condemnation of a plant for use by the United States Army for a short period was the "rental that probably could have been obtained." The court expressly rejected the measure that would obligate the government to pay only "the difference between the market value of the fee on the date of the taking and its market value on the date of its return." Should the Kimball standard apply to interim regulatory takings? Unlike the Army there, regulatory governments have not taken possession; at most, they have a negative servitude. Wheeler v. City of Pleasant Grove, 833 F.2d 267 (11th Cir.1987), ruled that for an interim regulatory taking the landowner should be awarded the "market rate return computed over the period of the temporary taking on the difference between the property's fair market value without the regulatory restriction and its fair market value with the restriction." Id. at 271. The lower court in that case had concluded that "since the [landowners] could now sell the property on the market at a sizeable profit, they had suffered no actual injury." Id. at 269. A state court declared that "[l]oss of rentals is an appropriate measure of damages for the temporary loss of use of land," but reversed a judgment awarding damages for an interim regulatory taking because the plaintiff did not prove with reasonable certainty that the unimproved tract would have produced any return at all." City of Austin v. Teague, 570 S.W.2d 389, 395 (Tex.1978). Another state court manifested reluctance to adopt any single standard for measuring compensation for all cases of regulatory takings, but emphasized that "no matter what measure of

damages is appropriate in a given case, the award must only be for *actual damages.*" Corrigan v. City of Scottsdale, 149 Ariz. 538, 720 P.2d 513, 519 (1986).

4. A litigant may prefer, instead of suing directly for a violation of the taking clause of the Fifth Amendment, to sue under Section 1983 of the Civil Rights Act of 1871, authorizing suits for deprivation of constitutional rights. One reason for doing so is that legal costs and attorney fees incurred by the prevailing party may be reimbursed. But the decision to allege direct violation of the Fifth Amendment or to invoke the statute should be made only after careful consideration of several matters. See D. Mandelker, Land Use Law 342–351 (2d ed. 1988).

Chapter 21

LAND USE PLANNING—OR EXCLUSION OF PEOPLE?

SECTION 1. RACIAL DISCRIMINATION

VILLAGE OF ARLINGTON HEIGHTS v. METROPOLITAN HOUSING DEVELOPMENT CORP.

Supreme Court of the United States, 1977.
429 U.S. 252, 97 S.Ct. 555, 50 L.Ed.2d 450.

MR. JUSTICE POWELL delivered the opinion of the Court.

In 1971 respondent Metropolitan Housing Development Corporation (MHDC) applied to petitioner, the Village of Arlington Heights, Ill., for the rezoning of a 15-acre parcel from single-family to multiple-family classification. Using federal financial assistance, MHDC planned to build 190 clustered townhouse units for low and moderate income tenants. The Village denied the rezoning request. MHDC, joined by other plaintiffs who are also respondents here, brought suit in the United States District Court for the Northern District of Illinois.[1] They alleged that the denial was racially discriminatory and that it violated, *inter alia,* the Fourteenth Amendment and the Fair Housing Act of 1968, 42 U.S.C.A. § 3601 et seq. Following a bench trial, the District Court entered judgment for the Village, 373 F.Supp. 208 (1974), and respondents appealed. The Court of Appeals for the Seventh Circuit reversed, finding that the "ultimate effect" of the denial was racially discriminatory, and that the refusal to rezone therefore violated the Fourteenth Amendment. 517 F.2d 409 (1975). We granted the Village's petition for certiorari, 423 U.S. 1030, 96 S.Ct. 560, 46 L.Ed.2d 404 (1975), and now reverse.

I.

Arlington Heights is a suburb of Chicago, located about 26 miles northwest of the downtown Loop area. Most of the land in Arlington Heights is zoned for detached single-family homes, and this is in fact the prevailing land use. The Village experienced substantial growth during the 1960's, but, like other communities in northwest Cook County, its population of racial minority groups remained quite low. According to the 1970 census, only 27 of the Village's 64,000 residents were black.

1. Respondents named as defendants both the Village and a number of its officials, sued in their official capacity. The latter were the Mayor, the Village Manager, the Director of Building and Zoning, and the entire Village Board of Trustees. For convenience, we will occasionally refer to all the petitioners collectively as "the Village."

The Clerics of St. Viator, a religious order (the Order), own an 80-acre parcel just east of the center of Arlington Heights. Part of the site is occupied by the Viatorian high school, and part by the Order's three-story novitiate building, which houses dormitories and a Montessori school. Much of the site, however, remains vacant. Since 1959, when the Village first adopted a zoning ordinance, all the land surrounding the Viatorian property has been zoned R–3, a single-family specification with relatively small minimum lot size requirements. On three sides of the Viatorian land there are single-family homes just across a street; to the east the Viatorian property directly adjoins the back yards of other single-family homes.

The Order decided in 1970 to devote some of its land to low and moderate income housing. Investigation revealed that the most expeditious way to build such housing was to work through a nonprofit developer experienced in the use of federal housing subsidies under § 236 of the National Housing Act, 12 U.S.C.A. § 1715z–1.

MHDC is such a developer. It was organized in 1968 by several prominent Chicago citizens for the purpose of building low and moderate income housing throughout the Chicago area. In 1970 MHDC was in the process of building one § 236 development near Arlington Heights and already had provided some federally assisted housing on a smaller scale in other parts of the Chicago area.

After some negotiation, MHDC and the Order entered into a 99-year lease and an accompanying agreement of sale covering a 15-acre site in the southeast corner of the Viatorian property. MHDC became the lessee immediately, but the sale agreement was contingent upon MHDC's securing zoning clearances from the Village and § 236 housing assistance from the Federal Government. If MHDC proved unsuccessful in securing either, both the lease and the contract of sale would lapse. The agreement established a bargain purchase price of $300,000, low enough to comply with federal limitations governing land acquisition costs for § 236 housing.

MHDC engaged an architect and proceeded with the project, to be known as Lincoln Green. The plans called for 20 two-story buildings with a total of 190 units, each unit having its own private entrance from outside. One hundred of the units would have a single bedroom, thought likely to attract elderly citizens. The remainder would have two, three or four bedrooms. A large portion of the site would remain open, with shrubs and trees to screen the homes abutting the property to the east.

The planned development did not conform to the Village's zoning ordinance and could not be built unless Arlington Heights rezoned the parcel to R–5, its multiple-family housing classification. Accordingly, MHDC filed with the Village Plan Commission a petition for rezoning, accompanied by supporting materials describing the development and specifying that it would be subsidized under § 236. The materials made clear that one requirement under § 236 is an affirmative marketing plan designed to assure that a subsidized development is racially integrated. MHDC also submitted studies demonstrating the need for housing of this type and analyzing the probable impact of the development. To prepare for the hearings before the Plan Commission and to assure compliance with the Village building code, fire regulations, and related requirements, MHDC consulted with the Village staff for preliminary review of the development. The parties have stipulated that every change recommended during such consultations was incorporated into the plans.

During the Spring of 1971, the Plan Commission considered the proposal at a series of three public meetings, which drew large crowds. Although many of those attending were quite vocal and demonstrative in opposition to Lincoln Green, a number of individuals and representatives of community groups spoke in support of rezoning. Some of the comments, both from opponents and supporters, addressed what was referred to as the "social issue"—the desirability or undesirability of introducing at this location in Arlington Heights low and moderate income housing, housing that would probably be racially integrated.

Many of the opponents, however, focused on the zoning aspects of the petition, stressing two arguments. First, the area always had been zoned single-family, and the neighboring citizens had built or purchased there in reliance on that classification. Rezoning threatened to cause a measurable drop in property value for neighboring sites. Second, the Village's apartment policy, adopted by the Village Board in 1962 and amended in 1970, called for R–5 zoning primarily to serve as a buffer between single-family development and land uses thought incompatible, such as commercial or manufacturing districts. Lincoln Green did not meet this requirement, as it adjoined no commercial or manufacturing district.

At the close of the third meeting, the Plan Commission adopted a motion to recommend to the Village's Board of Trustees that it deny the request. The motion stated: "While the need for low and moderate income housing may exist in Arlington Heights or its environs, the Plan Commission would be derelict in recommending it at the proposed location." Two members voted against the motion and submitted a minority report, stressing that in their view the change to accommodate Lincoln Green represented "good zoning." The Village Board met on September 28, 1971, to consider MHDC's request and the recommendation of the Plan Commission. After a public hearing, the Board denied the rezoning by a 6–1 vote.

The following June MHDC and three Negro individuals filed this lawsuit against the Village, seeking declaratory and injunctive relief. A second nonprofit corporation and an individual of Mexican-American descent intervened as plaintiffs. The trial resulted in a judgment for petitioners. Assuming that MHDC had standing to bring the suit, the District Court held that the petitioners were not motivated by racial discrimination or intent to discriminate against low income groups when they denied rezoning, but rather by a desire "to protect property values and the integrity of the Village's zoning plan." 373 F.Supp., at 211. The District Court concluded also that the denial would not have a racially discriminatory effect.

A divided Court of Appeals reversed. It first approved the District Court's finding that the defendants were motivated by a concern for the integrity of the zoning plan, rather than by racial discrimination. Deciding whether their refusal to rezone would have discriminatory effects was more complex. The court observed that the refusal would have a disproportionate impact on blacks. Based upon family income, blacks constituted 40% of those Chicago area residents who were eligible to become tenants of Lincoln Green, although they comprised a far lower percentage of total area population. The court reasoned, however, that under our decision in James v. Valtierra, 402 U.S. 137, 91 S.Ct. 1331, 28 L.Ed.2d 678 (1971), such a disparity in racial impact alone does not call for strict scrutiny of a municipality's decision that prevents the construction of the low-cost housing.

There was another level to the court's analysis of allegedly discriminatory results. Invoking language from Kennedy Park Homes Association v. City of Lackawanna, 436 F.2d 108, 112 (C.A.2 1970), cert. denied, 401 U.S. 1010, 91 S.Ct. 1256, 28 L.Ed.2d 546 (1970), the Court of Appeals ruled that the denial of rezoning must be examined in light of its "historical context and ultimate effect." Northwest Cook County was enjoying rapid growth in employment opportunities and population, but it continued to exhibit a high degree of residential segregation. The court held that Arlington Heights could not simply ignore this problem. Indeed, it found that the Village had been "exploiting" the situation by allowing itself to become a nearly all white community. 517 F.2d, at 414. The Village had no other current plans for building low and moderate income housing, and no other R–5 parcels in the Village were available to MHDC at an economically feasible price.

Against this background, the Court of Appeals ruled that the denial of the Lincoln Green proposal had racially discriminatory effects and could be tolerated only if it served compelling interests. Neither the buffer policy nor the desire to protect property values met this exacting standard. The court therefore concluded that the denial violated the Equal Protection Clause of the Fourteenth Amendment.

II.

At the outset, petitioners challenge the respondents' standing to bring the suit. It is not clear that this challenge was pressed in the Court of Appeals, but since our jurisdiction to decide the case is implicated, Jenkins v. McKeithen, 395 U.S. 411, 421, 89 S.Ct. 1843, 1848, 23 L.Ed.2d 404 (1969) (plurality opinion), we shall consider it.

In Warth v. Seldin, 422 U.S. 490, 95 S.Ct. 2197, 45 L.Ed.2d 343 (1975), a case similar in some respects to this one, we reviewed the constitutional limitations and prudential considerations that guide a court in determining a party's standing, and we need not repeat that discussion here. The essence of the standing question, in its constitutional dimension, "is whether the plaintiff has 'alleged such a personal stake in the outcome of the controversy' [as] to warrant *his* invocation of federal-court jurisdiction and to justify exercise of the court's remedial powers on his behalf." Id., at 498–499, 95 S.Ct. at 2205, quoting

Baker v. Carr, 369 U.S. 186, 204, 82 S.Ct. 691, 703, 7 L.Ed.2d 663 (1962). The plaintiff must show that he himself is injured by the challenged action of the defendant. The injury may be indirect, see United States v. SCRAP, 412 U.S. 669, 688, 93 S.Ct. 2405, 2416, 37 L.Ed.2d 254 (1973), but the complaint must indicate that the injury is indeed fairly traceable to the defendant's acts or omissions.

A.

Here there can be little doubt that MHDC meets the constitutional standing requirements. The challenged action of the petitioners stands as an absolute barrier to constructing the housing MHDC had contracted to place on the Viatorian site. If MHDC secures the injunctive relief it seeks, that barrier will be removed. An injunction would not, of course, guarantee that Lincoln Green will be built. MHDC would still have to secure financing, qualify for federal subsidies, and carry through with construction. But all housing developments are subject to some extent to similar uncertainties. When a project is as detailed and specific as Lincoln Green, a court is not required to engage in undue speculation as a predicate for finding that the plaintiff has the requisite personal stake in the controversy. MHDC has shown an injury to itself that is "likely to be redressed by a favorable decision." Simon v. Eastern Kentucky Welfare Rights Org., 426 U.S., at 38, 96 S.Ct., at 1924.

Petitioners nonetheless appear to argue that MHDC lacks standing because it has suffered no economic injury. MHDC, they point out, is not the owner of the property in question. Its contract of purchase is contingent upon securing rezoning. MHDC owes the owners nothing if rezoning is denied.

We cannot accept petitioners' argument. In the first place, it is inaccurate to say that MHDC suffers no economic injury from a refusal to rezone, despite the contingency provisions in its contract. MHDC has expended thousands of dollars on the plans for Lincoln Green and on the studies submitted to the Village in support of the petition for rezoning. Unless rezoning is granted, many of these plans and studies will be worthless even if MHDC finds another site at an equally attractive price.

Petitioners' argument also misconceives our standing requirements. It has long been clear that economic injury is not the only kind of injury that can support a plaintiff's standing. MHDC is a nonprofit corporation. Its interest in building Lincoln Green stems not from a desire for economic gain, but rather from an interest in making suitable low-cost housing available in areas where such housing is scarce. This is not mere abstract concern about a problem of general interest. The specific project MHDC intends to build, whether or not it will generate profits, provides that "essential dimension of specificity" that informs judicial decisionmaking.

B.

Clearly MHDC has met the constitutional requirements and it therefore has standing to assert its own rights. . . . As a corporation, MHDC has no racial identity and cannot be the direct target of the petitioners' alleged discrimination. In the ordinary case, a party is denied standing to assert the rights of third persons. But we need not decide whether the circumstances of this case would justify departure from the prudential limitation and permit MHDC to assert the constitutional rights of its prospective minority tenants. For we have at least one individual plaintiff who has demonstrated standing to assert these rights as his own.

Respondent Ransom, a Negro, works at the Honeywell factory in Arlington Heights and lives approximately 20 miles away in Evanston in a 5-room house with his mother and his son. The complaint alleged that he seeks and would qualify for the housing MHDC wants to build in Arlington Heights. Ransom testified at trial that if Lincoln Green were built he would probably move there, since it is closer to his job.

The injury Ransom asserts is that his quest for housing nearer his employment has been thwarted by official action that is racially discriminatory. If a court grants the relief he seeks, there is at least a "substantial probability," Warth v. Seldin, 42 U.S., at 504, 95 S.Ct., at 2208, that the Lincoln Green project will materialize, affording Ransom the housing opportunity he desires in Arlington Heights. His is not a generalized grievance. Instead, as we suggested in *Warth,* id., at 507, 508 n. 18, 95 S.Ct., at 2210, it focuses on a particular project and is not dependent on speculation about the possible actions of third parties not before the court. Unlike the individual plaintiffs in *Warth,* Ransom has adequately averred an "actionable causal relationship" between Arlington Heights' zoning practices and his asserted injury. Warth v. Seldin, 422 U.S., at 507, 95 S.Ct., at 2209. We therefore proceed to the merits.

III.

Our decision last Term in Washington v. Davis, 426 U.S. 229, 96 S.Ct. 2040, 48 L.Ed.2d 597 (1976), made it clear that official action will not be held unconstitutional solely because it results in a racially disproportionate impact. "Disproportionate impact is not irrelevant, but it is not the sole touchstone of an invidious racial discrimination." Id., at 242, 96 S.Ct., at 2049. Proof of racially discriminatory intent or purpose is required to show a violation of the Equal Protection Clause. Although some contrary indications may be drawn from some of our cases, the holding in *Davis* reaffirmed a principle well established in a variety of contexts. E.g., Keyes v. School District No. 1, 413 U.S. 189, 208, 93 S.Ct. 2686, 2697, 37 L.Ed.2d 548 (1973) (schools); Wright v. Rockefeller, 376 U.S. 52, 56–57, 84 S.Ct. 603, 605, 11 L.Ed.2d 512 (1964) (election districting); Akins v. Texas, 325 U.S. 398, 403–404, 65 S.Ct. 1276, 1279, 89 L.Ed. 1692 (1945) (jury selection).

Davis does not require a plaintiff to prove that the challenged action rested solely on racially discriminatory purposes. Rarely can it be said that a legislature or administrative body operating under a broad mandate made a decision motivated solely by a single concern, or even that a particular purpose was the "dominant" or "primary" one. In fact, it is because legislators and administrators are properly concerned with balancing numerous competing considerations that courts refrain from reviewing the merits of their decisions absent a showing of arbitrariness or irrationality. But racial discrimination is not just another competing consideration. When there is a proof that a discriminatory purpose has been a motivating factor in the decision, this judicial deference is no longer justified.

Determining whether invidious discriminatory purpose was a motivating factor demands a sensitive inquiry into such circumstantial and direct evidence of intent as may be available. The impact of the official action—whether it "bears more heavily on one race than another," Washington v. Davis, 426 U.S., at 242, 96 S.Ct., at 2049—may provide an important starting point. Sometimes a clear pattern, unexplainable on grounds other than race, emerges from the effect of the state action even when the governing legislation appears neutral on its face. Yick Wo v. Hopkins, 118 U.S. 356, 6 S.Ct. 1064, 30 L.Ed. 220 (1886); Guinn v. United States, 238 U.S. 347, 35 S.Ct. 926, 59 L.Ed. 1340 (1915); Lane v. Wilson, 307 U.S. 268, 59 S.Ct. 872, 83 L.Ed. 1281 (1939); Gomillion v. Lightfoot, 364 U.S. 339, 81 S.Ct. 125, 5 L.Ed.2d 110 (1960). The evidentiary inquiry is then relatively easy. But such cases are rare. Absent a pattern as stark as that in *Gomillion* or *Yick Wo,* impact alone is not determinative, and the Court must look to other evidence.

The historical background of the decision is one evidentiary source, particularly if it reveals a series of official actions taken for invidious purposes. The specific sequence of events leading up to the challenged decision also my shed some light on the decisionmaker's purposes. Reitman v. Mulkey, 387 U.S. 369, 373–376, 87 S.Ct. 1627, 1629–1631, 18 L.Ed.2d 830 (1967); Grosjean v. American Press, 297 U.S. 233, 250, 56 S.Ct. 444, 449, 80 L.Ed. 660 (1936). For example, if the property involved here always had been zoned R–5 but suddenly was changed to R–3 when the town learned of MHDC's plans to erect integrated housing, we would have a far different case. Departures from the normal procedural sequence also might afford evidence that improper purposes are playing a role. Substantive departures too may be relevant, particularly if the factors usually considered important by the decisionmaker strongly favor a decision contrary to the one reached.

The legislative or administrative history may be highly relevant, especially where there are contemporary statements by members of the decisionmaking body, minutes of its meetings, or reports. In some extraordinary instances the members might be called to the stand at trial to testify concerning the purpose of the official action, although even then such testimony frequently will be barred by privilege.

The foregoing summary identifies, without purporting to be exhaustive, subjects of proper inquiry in determining whether racially discriminatory intent existed. With these in mind, we now address the case before us.

IV.

This case was tried in the District Court and reviewed in the Court of Appeals before our decision in Washington v. Davis, supra. The respondents proceeded on the erroneous theory that the Village's refusal to rezone carried a racially discriminatory effect and was, without more, unconstitutional. But both courts below understood that at least part of their function was to examine the purpose underlying the decision. In making its findings on this issue, the District Court noted that some of the opponents of Lincoln Green who spoke at the various hearings might have been motivated by opposition to minority groups. The court held, however, that the evidence "does not warrant the conclusion that this motivated the defendants." 373 F.Supp., at 211.

On appeal the Court of Appeals focused primarily on respondents' claim that the Village's buffer policy had not been consistently applied and was being invoked with a strictness here that could only demonstrate some other underlying motive. The court concluded that the buffer policy, though not always applied with perfect consistency, had on several occasions formed the basis for the Board's decision to deny other rezoning proposals. "The evidence does not necessitate a finding that Arlington Heights administered this policy in a discriminatory manner." 517 F.2d, at 412. The Court of Appeals therefore approved the District Court's findings concerning the Village's purposes in denying rezoning to MHDC.

We also have reviewed the evidence. The impact of the Village's decision does arguably bear more heavily on racial minorities. Minorities comprise 18% of the Chicago area population, and 40% of the income groups said to be eligible for Lincoln Green. But there is little about the sequence of events leading up to the decision that would spark suspicion. The area around the Viatorian property has been zoned R–3 since 1959, the year when Arlington Heights first adopted a zoning map. Single-family homes surround the 80-acre site, and the Village is undeniably committed to single-family homes as its dominant residential land use. The rezoning request progressed according to the usual procedures. The Plan Commission even scheduled two additional hearings, at least in part to accommodate MHDC and permit it to supplement its presentation with answers to questions generated at the first hearing.

The statements by the Plan Commission and Village Board members, as reflected in the official minutes, focused almost exclusively on the zoning aspects of the MHDC petition, and the zoning factors on which they relied are not novel criteria in the Village's rezoning decisions. There is no reason to doubt that there has been reliance by some neighboring property owners on the maintenance of single-family zoning in the vicinity. The Village originally adopted its buffer policy long before MHDC entered the picture and has applied the policy too consistently for us to infer discriminatory purpose from its application in this case. Finally, MHDC called one member of the Village Board to the stand at trial. Nothing in her testimony supports an inference of invidious purpose.

In sum, the evidence does not warrant overturning the concurrent findings of both courts below. Respondents simply failed to carry their burden of proving that discriminatory purpose was a motivating factor in the Village's decision. This conclusion ends the constitutional inquiry. The Court of Appeals' further finding that the Village's decision carried a discriminatory "ultimate effect" is without independent constitutional significance.

V.

Respondents' complaint also alleged that the refusal to rezone violated the Fair Housing Act, 42 U.S.C.A. § 3601 et seq. They continue to urge here that a zoning decision made by a public body may, and that petitioners' action did, violate § 3604 or § 3617. The Court of Appeals, however, proceeding in a somewhat unorthodox fashion, did not decide the statutory question. We remand the case for further consideration of respondents' statutory claims.

Reversed and remanded.

MR. JUSTICE STEVENS took no part in the consideration or decision of this case.

MR. JUSTICE MARSHALL, with whom MR. JUSTICE BRENNAN joins, concurring in part and dissenting in part. [omitted]

MR. JUSTICE WHITE, dissenting. [omitted]

NOTES

1. On remand of this case, the Seventh Circuit held that "under some circumstances a violation of section 3604(a) [of the Fair Housing Act] can be established by a showing of a discriminatory effect without a showing of discriminatory intent," and remanded to the district court for clarification of the discriminatory effect. Metropolitan Housing Development Corp. v. Village of Arlington Heights, 558 F.2d 1283 (7th Cir.1977), cert. denied 434 U.S. 1025, 98 S.Ct. 752, 54 L.Ed.2d 772 (1978). The district court approved a settlement allowing some multiple-family development on land which the village agreed to annex. Id., 469 F.Supp. 836 (N.D.Ill.1979), affirmed 616 F.2d 1006 (7th Cir. 1980). The principal case is discussed in Mandelker, Racial Discrimination and Exclusionary Zoning: A Perspective on Arlington Heights, 55 Tex.L.Rev. 1217 (1977).

2. Huntington Branch, NAACP v. Town of Huntington, 844 F.2d 926 (2d Cir.1988) held that proof of discriminatory intent is not required to show a violation of the Fair Housing Act. The court said that when land use controls of a local government are shown to have a disparate effect upon a racial minority, there is a *prima facie* violation of the act, and the burden is then upon the local government to show that its actions "furthered, in theory and in practice, a legitimate, bona fide governmental interest and that no alternative would serve that interest

with less discriminatory effect." Huntington was found not to have met this burden in attempting to justify its refusal to rezone so as to allow an integrated housing project for low-income families in a neighborhood where 98% of the residents were white, there being inadequate opportunities for such housing elsewhere in the town. In a *per curiam* opinion, the United States Supreme Court agreed that the town had not met the disparate effect test, but concluded that it was not necessary to decide whether the proper test is disparate effect or discriminatory intent, as the town had conceded that it be judged by the disparate effect test. Town of Huntington v. NAACP, ___ U.S. ___, 109 S.Ct. 276, 102 L.Ed.2d 180 (1988).

3. The standing issue is discussed in Sager, Insular Minorities Unabated: Warth v. Seldin and City of Eastlake v. Forest City Enterprises, Inc., 91 Harv.L.Rev. 1373 (1978); Note, Standing to Challenge Exclusionary Land Use Devices in Federal Courts after Warth v. Seldin, 29 Stan.L.Rev. 323 (1977).

SECTION 2. THE SINGLE-FAMILY NEIGHBORHOOD

VILLAGE OF BELLE TERRE v. BORAAS

Supreme Court of the United States, 1974.
416 U.S. 1, 94 S.Ct. 1536, 39 L.Ed.2d 797.

MR. JUSTICE DOUGLAS delivered the opinion of the Court.

Belle Terre is a village on Long Island's north shore of about 220 homes inhabited by 700 people. Its total land area is less than one square mile. It has restricted land use to one-family dwellings excluding lodging houses, boarding houses, fraternity houses, or multiple-dwelling houses. The word "family" as used in the ordinance means, "[o]ne or more persons related by blood, adoption, or marriage, living and cooking together as a single housekeeping unit, exclusive of household servants. A number of persons but not exceeding two (2) living and cooking together as a single housekeeping unit though not related by blood, adoption, or marriage shall be deemed to constitute a family."

Appellees, the Dickmans, are owners of a house in the village and leased it in December 1971 for a term of 18 months to Michael Truman. Later Bruce Boraas became a colessee. Then Anne Parish moved into the house along with three others. These six are students at nearby State University at Stony Brook and none is related to the other by blood, adoption, or marriage. When the village served the Dickmans with an "Order to Remedy Violations" of the ordinance, the owners plus three tenants thereupon brought this action under 42 U.S.C.A. § 1983 for an injunction and a judgment declaring the ordinance unconstitutional. The District Court held the ordinance constitutional, 367 F.Supp. 136, and the Court of Appeals reversed, one judge dissenting. 2 Cir., 476 F.2d 806. The case is here by appeal, 28 U.S.C.A.

§ 1254(2); and we noted probable jurisdiction, 414 U.S. 907, 94 S.Ct. 234, 38 L.Ed.2d 145.

. . .

The present ordinance is challenged on several grounds: that it interferes with a person's right to travel; that it interferes with the right to migrate to and settle within a State; that it bars people who are uncongenial to the present residents; that it expresses the social preferences of the residents for groups that will be congenial to them; that social homogeneity is not a legitimate interest of government; that the restriction of those whom the neighbors do not like trenches on the newcomers' rights of privacy; that it is of no rightful concern to villagers whether the residents are married or unmarried; that the ordinance is antithetical to the Nation's experience, ideology, and self-perception as an open, egalitarian, and integrated society.

We find none of these reasons in the record before us. It is not aimed at transients. Cf. Shapiro v. Thompson, 394 U.S. 618, 89 S.Ct. 1322, 22 L.Ed.2d 600. It involves no procedural disparity inflicted on some but not on others such as was presented by Griffin v. Illinois, 351 U.S. 12, 76 S.Ct. 585, 100 L.Ed. 891. It involves no "fundamental" right guaranteed by the Constitution, such as voting, Harper v. Virginia State Board, 383 U.S. 663, 86 S.Ct. 1079, 16 L.Ed.2d 169; the right of association, NAACP v. Alabama ex rel. Patterson, 357 U.S. 449, 78 S.Ct. 1163, 2 L.Ed.2d 1488; the right of access to the courts, NAACP v. Button, 371 U.S. 415, 83 S.Ct. 328, 9 L.Ed.2d 405; or any rights of privacy, cf. Griswold v. Connecticut, 381 U.S. 479, 85 S.Ct. 1678, 14 L.Ed.2d 510; Eisenstadt v. Baird, 405 U.S. 438, 453–454, 92 S.Ct. 1029, 1038–1039, 31 L.Ed.2d 349. We deal with economic and social legislation where legislatures have historically drawn lines which we respect against the charge of violation of the Equal Protection Clause if the law be " 'reasonable, not arbitrary' " (quoting F.S. Royster Guano Co. v. Virginia, 253 U.S. 412, 415, 40 S.Ct. 560, 561, 64 L.Ed. 989) and bears "a rational relationship to a [permissible] state objective." Reed v. Reed, 404 U.S. 71, 76, 92 S.Ct. 251, 254, 30 L.Ed.2d 225.

It is said, however, that if two unmarried people can constitute a "family," there is no reason why three or four may not. But every line drawn by a legislature leaves some out that might well have been included. That exercise of discretion, however, is a legislative, not a judicial, function.

It is said that the Belle Terre ordinance reeks with an animosity to unmarried couples who live together. There is no evidence to support it; and the provision of the ordinance bringing within the definition of a "family" two unmarried people belies the charge.

The ordinance places no ban on other forms of association, for a "family" may, so far as the ordinance is concerned, entertain whomever it likes.

The regimes of boarding houses, fraternity houses, and the like present urban problems. More people occupy a given space; more cars rather continuously pass by; more cars are parked; noise travels with crowds.

A quiet place where yards are wide, people few, and motor vehicles restricted are legitimate guidelines in a land-use project addressed to family needs. This goal is a permissible one . . . . The police power is not confined to elimination of filth, stench, and unhealthy places. It is ample to lay out zones where family values, youth values, and the blessings of quiet seclusion and clean air make the area a sanctuary for people.

The suggestion that the case may be moot need not detain us. A zoning ordinance usually has an impact on the value of the property which it regulates. But in spite of the fact that the precise impact of the ordinance sustained in *Euclid* on a given piece of property was not known, 272 U.S., at 397, 47 S.Ct., at 121, the Court, considering the matter a controversy in the realm of city planning, sustained the ordinance. Here we are a step closer to the impact of the ordinance on the value of the lessor's property. He has not only lost six tenants and acquired only two in their place; it is obvious that the scale of rental values rides on what we decide today. . . . When Mr. Justice Holmes said for the Court in Block v. Hirsh, 256 U.S. 135, 155, 41 S.Ct. 458, 459, 65 L.Ed. 865, "property rights may be cut down, and to that extent taken, without pay," he stated the issue here. As is true in most zoning cases, the precise impact on value may, at the threshold of litigation over validity, not yet be known.

Reversed.

MR. JUSTICE BRENNAN, dissenting.

The constitutional challenge to the village ordinance is premised *solely* on alleged infringement of associational and other constitutional rights of *tenants.* But the named tenant appellees have quit the house, thus raising a serious question whether there now exists a cognizable "case or controversy" that satisfies that indispensable requisite of Art. III of the Constitution. . . .

MR. JUSTICE MARSHALL, dissenting.

. . . In my view, the disputed classification burdens the students' fundamental rights of association and privacy guaranteed by the First and Fourteenth Amendments. Because the application of strict equal protection scrutiny is therefore required, I am at odds with my Brethren's conclusion that the ordinance may be sustained on a showing that it bears a rational relationship to the accomplishment of legitimate governmental objectives.

. . .

A variety of justifications have been proffered in support of the village's ordinance. It is claimed that the ordinance controls population density, prevents noise, traffic and parking problems, and preserves the rent structure of the community and its attractiveness to families. As I noted earlier, these are all legitimate and substantial interests of government. But I think it clear that the means chosen to accomplish these purposes are both overinclusive and underinclusive, and that the asserted goals could be as effectively achieved by means of an ordinance that did not discriminate on the basis of constitutionally protected choices of lifestyle. The ordinance imposes no restriction whatsoever on the number of persons who may live in a house, as long as they are related by marital or sanguinary bonds—presumably no matter how distant their relationship. Nor does the ordinance restrict the number of income earners who may contribute to rent in such a household, or the number of automobiles that may be maintained by its occupants. In that sense the ordinance is underinclusive. On the other hand, the statute restricts the number of unrelated persons who may live in a home to no more than two. It would therefore prevent three unrelated people from occupying a dwelling even if among them they had but one income and no vehicles. While an extended family of a dozen or more might live in a small bungalow, three elderly and retired persons could not occupy the large manor house next door. Thus the statute is also grossly overinclusive to accomplish its intended purposes.

There are some 220 residences in Belle Terre occupied by about 700 persons. The density is therefore just above three per household. The village is justifiably concerned with density of population and the related problems of noise, traffic, and the like. It could deal with those problems by limiting each household to a specified number of adults, two or three perhaps without limitation on the number of dependent children. The burden of such an ordinance would fall equally upon all segments of the community. It would surely be better tailored to the goals asserted by the village than the ordinance before us today, for it would more realistically restrict population density and growth and their attendant environmental costs. Various other statutory mechanisms also suggest themselves as solutions to Belle Terre's problems—rent control, limits on the number of vehicles per household, and so forth, but, of course, such schemes are matters of legislative judgment and not for this Court. Appellants also refer to the necessity of maintaining the family character of the village. There is not a shred of evidence in the record indicating that if Belle Terre permitted a limited number of unrelated persons to live together, the residential familial character of the community would be fundamentally affected.

. . .

MOORE v. CITY OF EAST CLEVELAND

Supreme Court of the United States, 1977.
431 U.S. 494, 97 S.Ct. 1932, 52 L.Ed.2d 531.

MR. JUSTICE POWELL announced the judgment of the Court, and delivered an opinion in which MR. JUSTICE BRENNAN, MR. JUSTICE MARSHALL, and MR. JUSTICE BLACKMUN joined.

East Cleveland's housing ordinance, like many throughout the country, limits occupancy of a dwelling unit to members of a single family. § 1351.02.[1] But the ordinance contains an unusual and com-

1. All citations by section number refer to the Codified Ordinances of the City of East Cleveland, Ohio.

plicated definitional section that recognizes as a "family" only a few categories of related individuals, § 1341.08.[2] Because her family, living together in her home, fits none of those categories, appellant stands convicted of a criminal offense. The question in this case is whether the ordinance violates the Due Process Clause of the Fourteenth Amendment.[3]

Appellant, Mrs. Inez Moore, lives in her East Cleveland home together with her son, Dale Moore Sr., and her two grandsons, Dale, Jr., and John Moore, Jr. The two boys are first cousins rather than brothers; we are told that John came to live with his grandmother and with the elder and younger Dale Moores after his mother's death.[4]

In early 1973, Mrs. Moore received a notice of violation from the city, stating that John was an "illegal occupant" and directing her to comply with the ordinance. When she failed to remove him from her home, the city filed a criminal charge. Mrs. Moore moved to dismiss, claiming that the ordinance was constitutionally invalid on its face. Her motion was overruled, and upon conviction she was sentenced to five days in jail and a $25 fine. The Ohio Court of Appeals affirmed after giving full consideration to her constitutional claims,[5] and the

2. Section 1341.08 provides:

" 'Family' means a number of individuals related to the nominal head of the household or to the spouse of the nominal head of the household living as a single housekeeping unit in a single dwelling unit, but limited to the following:

"(a) Husband or wife of the nominal head of the household.

"(b) Unmarried children of the nominal head of the household or of the spouse of the nominal head of the household, provided, however, that such unmarried children have no children residing with them.

"(c) Father or mother of the nominal head of the household or of the spouse of the nominal head of the household.

"(d) Notwithstanding the provisions of subsection (b) hereof, a family may include not more than one dependent married or unmarried child of the nominal head of the household or of the spouse of the nominal head of the household and the spouse and dependent children of such dependent child. For the purpose of this subsection, a dependent person is one who has more than fifty percent of his total support furnished for him by the nominal head of the household and the spouse of the nominal head of the household.

"(e) A family may consist of one individual."

3. Appellant also claims that the ordinance contravenes the Equal Protection Clause, but it is not necessary for us to reach that contention.

4. Brief for Appellant 4, 25. John's father, John Moore, Sr., has apparently been living with the family at least since the time of trial. Whether he was living there when the citation was issued is in dispute. Under the ordinance, his presence too probably would be a violation. But we take the case as the city has framed it. The citation that led to prosecution recited only that John Moore, Jr., was in the home in violation of the ordinance.

5. The dissenting opinion of The Chief Justice suggests that Mrs. Moore should be denied a hearing in this Court because she failed to seek discretionary administrative relief in the form of a variance, relief that is no longer available. There are sound reasons for requiring exhaustion of administrative remedies in some situations, but such a requirement is wholly inappropriate where the party is a *criminal defendant* in circumstances like those present here. See generally McKart v. United States, 395 U.S. 185, 89 S.Ct. 1657, 23 L.Ed.2d 194 (1969). Mrs. Moore defends against the State's prosecution on the ground that the ordinance is facially invalid, an issue that the zoning review board lacks competency to resolve. In any event, this Court has never held that a general principle of exhaustion could foreclose a criminal defendant from asserting constitutional invalidity of the statute under which she is being prosecuted. See, e.g., Yakus v. United States, 321 U.S. 414, 446–447, 64 S.Ct. 660, 677–678, 88 L.Ed. 834 (1944).

Ohio Supreme Court denied review. We noted probable jurisdiction of her appeal, 425 U.S. 949, 96 S.Ct. 1723, 48 L.Ed.2d 193 (1976).

The city argues that our decision in Village of Belle Terre v. Boraas, 416 U.S. 1, 94 S.Ct. 1536, 39 L.Ed.2d 797 (1974), requires us to sustain the ordinance attacked here. Belle Terre, like East Cleveland, imposed limits on the types of groups that could occupy a single dwelling unit. Applying the constitutional standard announced in this Court's leading land-use case, Euclid v. Ambler Realty Co., 272 U.S. 365, 47 S.Ct. 114, 71 L.Ed. 303 (1926), we sustained the Belle Terre ordinance on the ground that it bore a rational relationship to permissible state objectives.

But one overriding factor sets this case apart from *Belle Terre.* The ordinance there affected only *unrelated* individuals. It expressly allowed all who were related by "blood, adoption, or marriage" to live together, and in sustaining the ordinance we were careful to note that it promoted "family needs" and "family values." 416 U.S., at 9, 94 S.Ct., at 1541. East Cleveland, in contrast, has chosen to regulate the occupancy of its housing by slicing deeply into the family itself. This is no mere incidental result of the ordinance. On its face it selects certain categories of relatives who may live together and declares that others may not. In particular, it makes a crime of a grandmother's choice to live with her grandson in circumstances like those presented here.

When a city undertakes such intrusive regulation of the family, neither *Belle Terre* nor *Euclid* governs; the usual judicial deference to the legislature is inappropriate. "This Court has long recognized that freedom of personal choice in matters of marriage and family life is one of the liberties protected by the Due Process Clause of the Fourteenth Amendment." Cleveland Board of Education v. LaFleur, 414 U.S. 632, 639–640, 94 S.Ct. 791, 796, 39 L.Ed.2d 52 (1974). A host of cases, tracing their lineage to Meyer v. Nebraska, 262 U.S. 390, 399–401, 43 S.Ct. 625, 626–627, 67 L.Ed. 1042 (1923), and Pierce v. Society of Sisters, 268 U.S. 510, 534–535, 45 S.Ct. 571, 573–574, 69 L.Ed. 1070 (1925), have consistently acknowledged a "private realm of family life which the state cannot enter." Prince v. Massachusetts, 321 U.S. 158, 166, 64 S.Ct. 438, 442, 88 L.Ed. 645 (1944). . . . Of course, the family is not beyond regulation. See Prince v. Massachusetts, supra, 321 U.S. at 166, 64 S.Ct. at 442. But when the government intrudes on choices concerning family living arrangements, this Court must examine carefully the importance of the governmental interests advanced and the extent to which they are served by the challenged regulation. . . .

Moreover, those cases that have denied certain nonconstitutional defenses to criminal defendants for failure to exhaust remedies did so pursuant to statutes that implicitly or explicitly mandated such a holding. See, e.g., Falbo v. United States, 320 U.S. 549, 64 S.Ct. 346, 88 L.Ed. 305 (1944); Yakus v. United States, supra; McGee v. United States, 402 U.S. 479, 91 S.Ct. 1565, 29 L.Ed.2d 47 (1971). Because of the statutes the defendants were on notice that failure to pursue available administrative relief might result in forfeiture of a defense in an enforcement proceeding. But here no Ohio statute or ordinance required exhaustion or gave Mrs. Moore any such warning. Indeed, the Ohio courts entertained all her claims, perceiving no denigration of state administrative process in according full judicial review.

When thus examined, this ordinance cannot survive. The city seeks to justify it as a means of preventing overcrowding, minimizing traffic and parking congestion, and avoiding an undue financial burden on East Cleveland's school system. Although these are legitimate goals, the ordinance before us serves them marginally, at best.[7] For example, the ordinance permits any family consisting only of husband, wife, and unmarried children to live together, even if the family contains a half-dozen licensed drivers, each with his or her own car. At the same time it forbids an adult brother and sister to share a household, even if both faithfully use public transportation. The ordinance would permit a grandmother to live with a single dependent son and children, even if his school-age children number a dozen, yet it forces Mrs. Moore to find another dwelling for her grandson John, simply because of the presence of his uncle and cousin in the same household. We need not labor the point. Section 1341.08 has but a tenuous relation to alleviation of the conditions mentioned by the city.

. . .

. . . Our decisions establish that the Constitution protects the sanctity of the family precisely because the institution of the family is deeply rooted in this Nation's history and tradition. It is through the family that we inculcate and pass down many of our most cherished values, moral and cultural.

Ours is by no means a tradition limited to respect for the bonds uniting the members of the nuclear family. The tradition of uncles, aunts, cousins, and especially grandparents sharing a household along with parents and children has roots equally venerable and equally deserving of constitutional recognition. . . .

Reversed.

MR. JUSTICE BRENNAN, with whom MR. JUSTICE MARSHALL joins, concurring. [omitted]

. . .

MR. JUSTICE STEVENS, concurring in the judgment.

In my judgment the critical question presented by this case is whether East Cleveland's housing ordinance is a permissible restriction on appellant's right to use her own property as she sees fit.

. . .

There appears to be no precedent for an ordinance which excludes any of an owner's relatives from the group of persons who may occupy his residence on a permanent basis. Nor does there appear to be any justification for such a restriction on an owner's use of his property. The city has failed totally to explain the need for a rule which would allow a homeowner to have two grandchildren live with her if they are

7. It is significant that East Cleveland has another ordinance specifically addressed to the problem of overcrowding. See Department of Agriculture v. Moreno, 413 U.S. 528, 536-537, 93 S.Ct. 2821, 2826-2827, 37 L.Ed.2d 782 (1973). Section 1351.03 limits population density directly, tying the maximum permissible occupancy of a dwelling to the habitable floor area. Even if John Jr., and his father both remain in Mrs. Moore's household, the family stays well within these limits.

brothers, but not if they are cousins. Since this ordinance has not been shown to have any "substantial relation to the public health, safety, morals or general welfare" of the City of East Cleveland, and since it cuts so deeply into a fundamental right normally associated with the ownership of residential property—that of an owner to decide who may reside on her property—it must fall under the limited standard of review of zoning decisions which this Court preserved in *City of Euclid* and *Nectow,* supra. Under that standard, East Cleveland's unprecedented ordinance constitutes a taking of property without due process and without just compensation.

For these reasons, I concur in the Court's judgment.

MR. CHIEF JUSTICE BURGER, dissenting.

It is unnecessary for me to reach the difficult constitutional issue this case presents. Appellant's deliberate refusal to use a plainly adequate administrative remedy provided by the City should foreclose her from pressing in this Court any constitutional objections to the City's zoning ordinance.

. . .

MR. JUSTICE STEWART, with whom MR. JUSTICE REHNQUIST joins, dissenting.

. . .

To suggest that the biological fact of common ancestry necessarily gives related persons constitutional rights of association superior to those of unrelated persons is to misunderstand the nature of the associational freedoms that the Constitution has been understood to protect. Freedom of association has been constitutionally recognized because it is often indispensable to effectuation of explicit First Amendment guarantees.

The "association" in this case is not for any purpose relating to the promotion of speech, assembly, the press, or religion. And wherever the outer boundaries of constitutional protection of freedom of association may eventually turn out to be, they surely do not extend to those who assert no interest other than the gratification, convenience, and economy of sharing the same residence.

. . .

The appellant also challenges the single-family occupancy ordinance on equal protection grounds. Her claim is that the city has drawn an arbitrary and irrational distinction between groups of people who may live together as a "family" and those who may not. While acknowledging the city's right to preclude more than one family from occupying a single dwelling unit, the appellant argues that the purposes of the single-family occupy law would be equally served by an ordinance that did not prevent her from sharing her residence with her two sons and their sons.

This argument misconceives the nature of the constitutional inquiry. In a case such as this one, where the challenged ordinance intrudes upon no substantively protected constitutional right, it is not the Court's business to decide whether its application in a particular case seems inequitable, or even absurd. . . .

[MR. JUSTICE WHITE'S dissenting opinion is omitted.]

NOTE

Many state courts, applying state law, have held inapplicable or invalid restrictive definitions of "family" in zoning ordinances. A leading case is City of White Plains v. Ferraioli, 34 N.Y.2d 300, (357 N.Y.S.2d 449), 313 N.E.2d 756 (1974), holding that the following zoning ordinance definition did not preclude occupancy by an adult couple, their two children and ten foster children: "A 'family' is one or more persons limited to the spouse, parents, grandparents, grandchildren, sons, daughters, brothers or sisters of the owner or the tenant or of the owner's spouse or tenant's spouse living together as a single housekeeping unit with kitchen facilities." The court rationalized: "So long as the group home bears the generic character of a family unit as a relatively permanent household, and is not a framework for transients or transient living, it conforms to the purpose of the ordinance . . . . [n]either by express provision nor construction may it limit the definition of family to exclude a household which in every but a biological sense is a single family." City of Santa Barbara v. Adamson, 27 Cal.3d 123, 164 Cal.Rptr. 539, 610 P.2d 436 (1980), held that an ordinance defining family as limited to related persons or no more than five unrelated persons violated a state constitutional protection of "inalienable rights" of "enjoying life and liberty, . . . possession . . . property, and pursuing and obtaining . . . happiness, and privacy," and therefore could not prevent occupancy of a house by 12 unrelated adults.

CITY OF CLEBURNE V. CLEBURNE LIVING CENTER, INC.

Supreme Court of the United States, 1985.
473 U.S. 432, 105 S.Ct. 3249, 87 L.Ed.2d 313.

JUSTICE WHITE delivered the opinion of the Court.

A Texas city denied a special use permit for the operation of a group home for the mentally retarded, acting pursuant to a municipal zoning ordinance requiring permits for such homes. The Court of Appeals for the Fifth Circuit held that mental retardation is a "quasi-suspect" classification and that the ordinance violated the Equal Protection Clause because it did not substantially further an important governmental purpose. We hold that a lesser standard of scrutiny is appropriate, but conclude that under that standard the ordinance is invalid as applied in this case.

I

In July 1980, respondent Jan Hannah purchased a building at 201 Featherston Street in the city of Cleburne, Texas, with the intention of leasing it to Cleburne Living Center, Inc. (CLC), for the operation of a group home for the mentally retarded. It was anticipated that the home would house 13 retarded men and women, who would be under the constant supervision of CLC staff members. The house had four bedrooms and two baths, with a half bath to be added. CLC planned to comply with all applicable state and federal regulations.

The city informed CLC that a special use permit would be required for the operation of a group home at the site, and CLC accordingly submitted a permit application. In response to a subsequent inquiry from CLC, the city explained that under the zoning regulations applicable to the site, a special use permit, renewable annually, was required for the construction of "[h]ospitals for the insane or feeble-minded, or alcoholic [*sic*] or drug addicts, or penal or correctional institutions." [3] The city had determined that the proposed group home should be classified as a "hospital for the feeble-minded." After holding a public hearing on CLC's application, the City Council voted 3 to 1 to deny a special use permit.

CLC then filed suit in Federal District Court against the city and a number of its officials, alleging, *inter alia,* that the zoning ordinance was invalid on its face and as applied because it discriminated against the mentally retarded in violation of the equal protection rights of CLC and its potential residents. The District Court found that "[i]f the potential residents of the Featherston Street home were not mentally retarded, but the home was the same in all other respects, its use would be permitted under the city's zoning ordinance," and that the City Council's decision "was motivated primarily by the fact that the residents of the home would be persons who are mentally retarded." App. 93, 94. Even so, the District Court held the ordinance and its application constitutional. Concluding that no fundamental right was implicated and that mental retardation was neither a suspect nor a quasi-suspect classification, the court employed the minimum level of judicial scrutiny applicable to equal protection claims. The court deemed the ordinance, as written and applied, to be rationally related to the city's

3. The site of the home is in an area zoned "R–3," an "Apartment House District." App. 51. Section 8 of the Cleburne zoning ordinance, in pertinent part, allows the following uses in an R–3 district:

"1. Any use permitted in District R–2.

"2. Apartment houses, or multiple dwellings.

"3. Boarding and lodging houses.

"4. Fraternity or sorority houses and dormitories.

"5. Apartment hotels.

"6. Hospitals, sanitariums, nursing homes or homes for convalescents or aged, *other than for the* insane or *feeble-minded* or alcoholics or drug addicts."

"7. Private clubs or fraternal orders, except those whose chief activity is carried on as a business.

"8. Philanthropic or eleemosynary institutions, other than penal institutions.

"9. Accessory uses customarily incident to any of the above uses. . . ."

Id., at 60–61 (emphasis added).

Section 16 of the ordinance specifies the uses for which a special use permit is required. These include "[h]ospitals for the insane or feeble-minded, or alcoholic [*sic*] or drug addicts, or penal or correctional institutions." Id., at 63. Section 16 provides that a permit for such a use may be issued by "the Governing Body, after public hearing, and after recommendation of the Planning Commission." All special use permits are limited to one year, and each applicant is required "to obtain the signatures of the property owners within two hundred (200) feet of the property to be used." Ibid.

legitimate interests in "the legal responsibility of CLC and its residents, . . . the safety and fears of residents in the adjoining neighborhood," and the number of people to be housed in the home. Id., at 103.

The Court of Appeals for the Fifth Circuit reversed, determining that mental retardation was a quasi-suspect classification and that it should assess the validity of the ordinance under intermediate-level scrutiny. 726 F.2d 191 (1984). Because mental retardation was in fact relevant to many legislative actions, strict scrutiny was not appropriate. But in light of the history of "unfair and often grotesque mistreatment" of the retarded, discrimination against them was "likely to reflect deep-seated prejudice." Id., at 197. In addition, the mentally retarded lacked political power, and their condition was immutable. The court considered heightened scrutiny to be particularly appropriate in this case, because the city's ordinance withheld a benefit which, although not fundamental, was very important to the mentally retarded. Without group homes, the court stated, the retarded could never hope to integrate themselves into the community. Applying the test that it considered appropriate, the court held that the ordinance was invalid on its face because it did not substantially further any important governmental interests. The Court of Appeals went on to hold that the ordinance was also invalid as applied. Rehearing en banc was denied with six judges dissenting in an opinion urging en banc consideration of the panel's adoption of a heightened standard of review. We granted certiorari, 469 U.S. 1016, 105 S.Ct. 427, 83 L.Ed.2d 354 (1984).

II

The general rule is that legislation is presumed to be valid and will be sustained if the classification drawn by the statute is rationally related to a legitimate state interest. When social or economic legislation is at issue, the Equal Protection Clause allows the States wide latitude and the Constitution presumes that even improvident decisions will eventually be rectified by the democratic processes.

The general rule gives way, however, when a statute classifies by race, alienage, or national origin. These factors are so seldom relevant to the achievement of any legitimate state interest that laws grounded in such considerations are deemed to reflect prejudice and antipathy—a view that those in the burdened class are not as worthy or deserving as others. For these reasons and because such discrimination is unlikely to be soon rectified by legislative means, these laws are subjected to strict scrutiny and will be sustained only if they are suitably tailored to serve a compelling state interest. Similar oversight by the courts is due when state laws impinge on personal rights protected by the Constitution. Kramer v. Union Free School District No. 15, 395 U.S. 621, 89 S.Ct. 1886, 23 L.Ed.2d 583 (1969); Shapiro v. Thompson, 394 U.S. 618, 89 S.Ct. 1322, 22 L.Ed.2d 600 (1969); Skinner v. Oklahoma ex rel. Williamson, 316 U.S. 535, 62 S.Ct. 1110, 86 L.Ed. 1655 (1942).

Legislative classifications based on gender also call for a heightened standard of review.

We have declined, however, to extend heightened review to differential treatment based on age:

> "While the treatment of the aged in this Nation has not been wholly free of discrimination, such persons, unlike, say, those who have been discriminated against on the basis of race or national origin, have not experienced a 'history of purposeful unequal treatment' or been subjected to unique disabilities on the basis of stereotyped characteristics not truly indicative of their abilities." Massachusetts Board of Retirement v. Murgia, 427 U.S. 307, 313, 96 S.Ct. 2562, 2567, 49 L.Ed.2d 520 (1976).

The lesson of *Murgia* is that where individuals in the group affected by a law have distinguishing characteristics relevant to interests the State has the authority to implement, the courts have been very reluctant, as they should be in our federal system and with our respect for the separation of powers, to closely scrutinize legislative choices as to whether, how, and to what extent those interests should be pursued. In such cases, the Equal Protection Clause requires only a rational means to serve a legitimate end.

III

Against this background, we conclude for several reasons that the Court of Appeals erred in holding mental retardation a quasi-suspect classification calling for a more exacting standard of judicial review than is normally accorded economic and social legislation. First, it is undeniable, and it is not argued otherwise here, that those who are mentally retarded have a reduced ability to cope with and function in the everyday world. Nor are they all cut from the same pattern: as the testimony in this record indicates, they range from those whose disability is not immediately evident to those who must be constantly cared for. They are thus different, immutably so, in relevant respects, and the States' interest in dealing with and providing for them is plainly a legitimate one. How this large and diversified group is to be treated under the law is a difficult and often a technical matter, very much a task for legislators guided by qualified professionals and not by the perhaps ill-informed opinions of the judiciary. Heightened scrutiny inevitably involves substantive judgments about legislative decisions, and we doubt that the predicate for such judicial oversight is present where the classification deals with mental retardation.

Second, the distinctive legislative response, both national and state, to the plight of those who are mentally retarded demonstrates not only that they have unique problems, but also that the lawmakers have been addressing their difficulties in a manner that belies a continuing antipathy or prejudice and a corresponding need for more intrusive oversight by the judiciary. . . . The State of Texas has similarly enacted legislation that acknowledges the special status of the mentally retarded by conferring certain rights upon them, such as "the right to live in the least restrictive setting appropriate to [their] individual needs and abilities," including "the right to live . . . in a group home." Mentally Retarded Persons Act of 1977, Tex.Rev.Civ.Stat.Ann., Art. 5547–300, § 7 (Vernon Supp.1985).[11]

Third, the legislative response, which could hardly have occurred and survived without public support, negates any claim that the mentally retarded are politically powerless in the sense that they have no ability to attract the attention of the lawmakers. Any minority can be said to be powerless to assert direct control over the legislature, but if that were a criterion for higher level scrutiny by the courts, much economic and social legislation would now be suspect.

Fourth, if the large and amorphous class of the mentally retarded were deemed quasi-suspect for the reasons given by the Court of Appeals, it would be difficult to find a principled way to distinguish a variety of other groups who have perhaps immutable disabilities setting them off from others, who cannot themselves mandate the desired legislative responses, and who can claim some degree of prejudice from at least part of the public at large. One need mention in this respect only the aging, the disabled, the mentally ill, and the infirm. We are reluctant to set out on that course, and we decline to do so.

. . .

Our refusal to recognize the retarded as a quasi-suspect class does not leave them entirely unprotected from invidious discrimination. To withstand equal protection review, legislation that distinguishes between the mentally retarded and others must be rationally related to a legitimate governmental purpose. . . .

IV

. . .

The constitutional issue is clearly posed. The city does not require a special use permit in an R–3 zone for apartment houses, multiple dwellings, boarding and lodging houses, fraternity or sorority houses, dormitories, apartment hotels, hospitals, sanitariums, nursing homes for convalescents or the aged (other than for the insane or feebleminded or alcoholics or drug addicts), private clubs or fraternal orders, and other specified uses. It does, however, insist on a special permit for the Featherston home, and it does so, as the District Court found, because it would be a facility for the mentally retarded. May the city require the permit for this facility when other care and multiple-dwelling facilities are freely permitted? . . .

Because in our view the record does not reveal any rational basis for believing that the Featherston home would pose any special threat

11. CLC originally sought relief under the Act, but voluntarily dismissed this pendent state claim when the District Court indicated that its presence might make abstention appropriate. The Act had never been construed by the Texas courts. App. 12, 14, 84–87.

A number of States have passed legislation prohibiting zoning that excludes the retarded. See, e.g., Cal. Health & Safety Code Ann. § 1566 et seq. (West 1979 and Supp.1985); Conn.Gen.Stat. § 8–3e (Supp. 1985); N.D.Cent.Code § 25–16–14(2) (Supp. 1983); R.I.Gen.Laws § 45–24–22 (1980). See also Md. Health Code Ann. § 7–102 (Supp.1984).

to the city's legitimate interests, we affirm the judgment below insofar as it holds the ordinance invalid as applied in this case.

The District Court found that the City Council's insistence on the permit rested on several factors. First, the Council was concerned with the negative attitude of the majority of property owners located within 200 feet of the Featherston facility, as well as with the fears of elderly residents of the neighborhood. But mere negative attitudes, or fear, unsubstantiated by factors which are properly cognizable in a zoning proceeding, are not permissible bases for treating a home for the mentally retarded differently from apartment houses, multiple dwellings, and the like. . . .

Second, the Council had two objections to the location of the facility. It was concerned that the facility was across the street from a junior high school, and it feared that the students might harass the occupants of the Featherston home. But the school itself is attended by about 30 mentally retarded students, and denying a permit based on such vague, undifferentiated fears is again permitting some portion of the community to validate what would otherwise be an equal protection violation. The other objection to the home's location was that it was located on "a five hundred year flood plain." This concern with the possibility of a flood, however, can hardly be based on a distinction between the Featherston home and, for example, nursing homes, homes for convalescents or the aged, or sanitariums or hospitals, any of which could be located on the Featherston site without obtaining a special use permit. The same may be said of another concern of the Council—doubts about the legal responsibility for actions which the mentally retarded might take. If there is no concern about legal responsibility with respect to other uses that would be permitted in the area, such as boarding and fraternity houses, it is difficult to believe that the groups of mildly or moderately mentally retarded individuals who would live at 201 Featherston would present any different or special hazard.

Fourth, the Council was concerned with the size of the home and the number of people that would occupy it. The District Court found, and the Court of Appeals repeated, that "[i]f the potential residents of the Featherston Street home were not mentally retarded, but the home was the same in all other respects, its use would be permitted under the city's zoning ordinance." App. 93; 726 F.2d, at 200. Given this finding, there would be no restrictions on the number of people who could occupy this home as a boarding house, nursing home, family dwelling, fraternity house, or dormitory. The question is whether it is rational to treat the mentally retarded differently. It is true that they suffer disability not shared by others; but why this difference warrants a density regulation that others need not observe is not at all apparent. . . .

In the courts below the city also urged that the ordinance is aimed at avoiding concentration of population and at lessening congestion of the streets. These concerns obviously fail to explain why apartment houses, fraternity and sorority houses, hospitals and the like, may freely locate in the area without a permit. So, too, the expressed worry about fire hazards, the serenity of the neighborhood, and the avoidance of danger to other residents fail rationally to justify singling out a home such as 201 Featherston for the special use permit, yet imposing no such restrictions on the many other uses freely permitted in the neighborhood.

The short of it is that requiring the permit in this case appears to us to rest on an irrational prejudice against the mentally retarded, including those who would occupy the Featherston facility and who would live under the closely supervised and highly regulated conditions expressly provided for by state and federal law.

The judgment of the Court of Appeals is affirmed insofar as it invalidates the zoning ordinance as applied to the Featherston home. The judgment is otherwise vacated, and the case is remanded.

It is so ordered.

JUSTICE STEVENS, with whom THE CHIEF JUSTICE joins, concurring. [omitted]

JUSTICE MARSHALL, with whom JUSTICE BRENNAN and JUSTICE BLACKMUN join, concurring in the judgment in part and dissenting in part.

. . .

The Court holds the ordinance invalid on rational-basis grounds and disclaims that anything special, in the form of heightened scrutiny, is taking place. Yet Cleburne's ordinance surely would be valid under the traditional rational-basis test applicable to economic and commercial regulation. In my view, it is important to articulate, as the Court does not, the facts and principles that justify subjecting this zoning ordinance to the searching review—the heightened scrutiny—that actually leads to its invalidation. Moreover, in invalidating Cleburne's exclusion of the "feebleminded" only as applied to respondents, rather than on its face, the Court radically departs from our equal protection precedents. . . .

In light of the importance of the interest at stake and the history of discrimination the retarded have suffered, the Equal Protection Clause requires us to do more than review the distinctions drawn by Cleburne's zoning ordinance as if they appeared in a taxing statute or in economic or commercial legislation. The searching scrutiny I would give to restrictions on the ability of the retarded to establish community group homes leads me to conclude that Cleburne's vague generalizations for classifying the "feeble-minded" with drug addicts, alcoholics, and the insane, and excluding them where the elderly, the ill, the boarder, and the transient are allowed, are not substantial or important enough to overcome the suspicion that the ordinance rests on impermissible assumptions or outmoded and perhaps invidious stereotypes. . . .

NOTES

1. The locating of some types of group homes in residential areas may be encouraged by state statutes, which may impliedly or expressly preempt local zoning ordinances purporting to exclude such facilities.

Glennon Heights, Inc. v. Central Bank & Trust, 658 P.2d 872 (Colo.1983) upheld a statute providing that a "state-licensed group home for eight developmentally disabled persons" must be allowed in single-family zones. But compare Garcia v. Siffrin Residential Association, 63 Ohio St. 259, 407 N.E.2d 1369 (1980), cert. denied 450 U.S. 911, 101 S.Ct. 1349, 67 L.Ed.2d 334 (1981). In this case, a non-profit corporation was held not entitled to use a residence in a two-family residential zone as a half-way house for discharged mental patients. The zoning ordinance defined "family" as "one or more persons occupying a dwelling unit and living as a single housekeeping unit, whether or not related to each other by birth or marriage, as distinguished from a group occupying a boarding house, motel, hotel, fraternity or sorority house." The court concluded that the proposed half-way house would not be a "single housekeeping unit" because it would be established primarily for "habilitation" rather than for "sharing a dwelling." The court then held that this "ban" of group homes was not preempted by a statute providing that any "person may operate a licensed family home as a permitted use in any residential district" because it was a "special law" prohibited by the state constitution. Do the Colorado and Ohio courts have different attitudes toward group homes?

2. Statutes supportive of group homes also may override restrictive covenants, expressly or by implication. See McMillan v. Iserman, supra, p. 691.

3. For commentary, see Jaffe, Group Homes and Family Values, Land Use L., March 1982, p. 4; Lippincott, "A Sanctuary for People": Strategies for Overcoming Zoning Restrictions on Community Homes for Retarded Persons, 31 Stan.L.Rev. 767 (1979); Note, City of Santa Barbara v. Adamson: An Associational Right of Privacy and the End of Family Zones, 69 Calif.L.Rev. 1052 (1981); Note, Can the Mentally Retarded Enjoy "Yards that are Wide?" 28 Wayne L.Rev. 1349 (1982).

SECTION 3. HOUSING THE NON-AFFLUENT IN THE SUBURBS

SOUTHERN BURLINGTON COUNTY NAACP v. TOWNSHIP OF MOUNT LAUREL

Supreme Court of New Jersey, 1983.
92 N.J. 158, 456 A.2d 390.

WILENTZ, C.J.

This is the return, eight years later, of Southern Burlington County N.A.A.C.P. v. Township of Mount Laurel, 67 N.J. 151, 336 A.2d 713 (1975) (Mount Laurel I). We set forth in that case, for the first time, the doctrine requiring that municipalities' land use regulations provide a realistic opportunity for low and moderate income housing. The doctrine has become famous. The *Mount Laurel* case itself threatens to become infamous. After all this time, ten years after the trial court's initial order invalidating its zoning ordinance, Mount Laurel remains afflicted with a blatantly exclusionary ordinance. Papered over with studies, rationalized by hired experts, the ordinance at its core is true to nothing but Mount Laurel's determination to exclude the poor. Mount Laurel is not alone; we believe that there is widespread non-compliance with the constitutional mandate of our original opinion in this case.

To the best of our ability, we shall not allow it to continue. This Court is more firmly committed to the original *Mount Laurel* doctrine than ever, and we are determined, within appropriate judicial bounds, to make it work. The obligation is to provide a realistic opportunity for housing, not litigation. We have learned from experience, however, that unless a strong judicial hand is used, *Mount Laurel* will not result in housing, but in paper, process, witnesses, trials and appeals. We intend by this decision to strengthen it, clarify it, and make it easier for public officials, including judges, to apply it.

This case is accompanied by five others, heard together and decided in this opinion. All involve questions arising from the *Mount Laurel* doctrine. They demonstrate the need to put some steel into that doctrine. The deficiencies in its application range from uncertainty and inconsistency at the trial level to inflexible review criteria at the appellate level. . . .

A brief statement of the cases may be helpful at this point. *Mount Laurel II* results from the remand by this Court of the original *Mount Laurel* case. The municipality rezoned, purportedly pursuant to our instructions, a plenary trial was held, and the trial court found that the rezoning constituted a bona fide attempt by Mount Laurel to provide a realistic opportunity for the construction of its fair share of the regional lower income housing need. Reading our cases at that time (1978) as requiring no more, the trial court dismissed the complaint of the N.A. A.C.P. and other plaintiffs but granted relief in the form of a builder's remedy, to a developer-intervenor who had attacked the total prohibition against mobile homes. Plaintiffs' appeal of the trial court's ruling sustaining the ordinance in all other respects was directly certified by this Court, as ultimately was defendant's appeal from the grant of a builder's remedy allowing construction of mobile homes. We reverse and remand to determine Mount Laurel's fair share of the regional need and for further proceedings to revise its ordinance; we affirm the grant of the builder's remedy.

[The court's review of the other cases is omitted]

I.

Background

A. *History of the Mount Laurel Doctrine*

In *Mount Laurel I,* this Court held that a zoning ordinance that contravened the general welfare was unconstitutional. We pointed out that a developing municipality violated that constitutional mandate by excluding housing for lower income people; that it would satisfy that constitutional obligation by affirmatively affording a realistic opportunity for the construction if its fair share of the present and prospective regional need for low and moderate income housing. 67 N.J. at 174,

336 A.2d 713.[3] This is the core of the *Mount Laurel* doctrine. Although the Court set forth important guidelines for implementing the doctrine, their application to particular cases was complex, and the resolution of many questions left uncertain. Was it a "developing" municipality? What was the "region," and how was it to be determined? How was the "fair share" to be calculated within that region? Precisely what must that municipality do to "affirmatively afford" an opportunity for the construction of lower income housing? Other questions were similarly troublesome. When should a court order the granting of a building permit (i.e., a builder's remedy) to a plaintiff-developer who has successfully challenged a zoning ordinance on *Mount Laurel* grounds? How should courts deal with the complicated procedural aspects of *Mount Laurel* litigation, such as the appointment of experts and masters, the joinder of defendant municipalities, and the problem of interlocutory appeals? These have been the principal questions that New Jersey courts have faced in attempting to implement the *Mount Laurel* mandate, and the principal questions dealt with in this opinion. . . .

. . .

C. *Summary of Rulings*

Our rulings today have several purposes. First, we intend to encourage voluntary compliance with the constitutional obligation by defining it more clearly. We believe that the use of the State Development Guide Plan and the confinement of all *Mount Laurel* litigation to a small group of judges, selected by the Chief Justice with the approval of the Court, will tend to serve that purpose. Second, we hope to simplify litigation in this area. While we are not overly optimistic, we think that the remedial use of the SDGP may achieve that purpose, given the significance accorded it in this opinion. Third, the decisions are intended to increase substantially the effectiveness of the judicial remedy. In most cases, upon determination that the municipality has not fulfilled its constitutional obligation, the trial court will retain jurisdiction, order an immediate revision of the ordinance (including, if necessary, supervision of the revision through a court appointed master), and require the use of effective affirmative planning and zoning devices. . . .

The following is a summary of the more significant rulings of these cases:

3. Several other state courts have held that municipalities have an obligation to consider regional needs in their zoning decisions. See, e.g., Surrick v. Zoning Bd. of Providence Twp., 476 Pa. 182, 382 A.2d 105, 108–10 (Pa.1977); Associated Home Builders v. Livermore, 18 Cal.3d 582, 599–601, 557 P.2d 473, 483, 135 Cal.Rptr. 41, 51 (Cal.1976); Berenson v. Town of New Castle, 38 N.Y.2d 102, 378 N.Y.S.2d 672, 341 N.E.2d 236, 242 (N.Y.1975), aff'd as modified, 67 A.D.2d 506, 415 N.Y.S.2d 669 (App. Div.1979), enforced sub nom. Blitz and Locker v. Town of New Castle, — N.Y.2d —, — N.Y.S. —, — N.E.2d —, (N.Y.1982) appeal filed __82; see also Manatee County v. Estech Gen. Chem. Corp., 402 So.2d 1251 (Fla.Dist.Ct.App.1981). None of these decisions, however, requires municipalities to provide their fair share of low and moderate income housing needs. For a general discussion of the case law in this area, see Blumstein, "A Prolegomenon to Growth Management and Exclusionary Zoning Issues," 43 Law & Contemp. Prob. 5 (Spring 1979); Note, "Developments in the Law-Zoning," 91 Harv.L.Rev. 1427, 1635–59 (1978).

(1) *Every* municipality's land use regulations should provide a realistic opportunity for decent housing for at least some part of its resident poor who now occupy dilapidated housing. . . .

(2) The existence of a municipal obligation to provide a realistic opportunity for a fair share of the region's present and prospective low and moderate income housing need will no longer be determined by whether or not a municipality is "developing." . . .

(3) *Mount Laurel* litigation will ordinarily include proof of the municipality's fair share of low and moderate income housing in terms of the number of units needed immediately, as well as the number needed for a reasonable period of time in the future. "Numberless" resolution of the issue based upon a conclusion that the ordinance provides a realistic opportunity for *some* low and moderate income housing will be insufficient. . . .

(4) Any future *Mount Laurel* litigation shall be assigned only to those judges selected by the Chief Justice with the approval of the Supreme Court. . . .

(5) The municipal obligation to provide a realistic opportunity for the construction of its fair share of low and moderate income housing may require more than the elimination of unnecessary cost-producing requirements and restrictions. Affirmative governmental devices should be used to make that opportunity realistic, including lower-income density bonuses and mandatory set-asides. Furthermore the municipality should cooperate with the developer's attempts to obtain federal subsidies. For instance, where federal subsidies depend on the municipality providing certain municipal tax treatment allowed by state statutes for lower income housing, the municipality should make a good faith effort to provide it. Mobile homes may not be prohibited, unless there is solid proof that sound planning in a particular municipality requires such prohibition.

(6) The lower income regional housing need is comprised of both low and moderate income housing. A municipality's fair share should include both in such proportion as reflects consideration of all relevant factors, including the proportion of low and moderate income housing that make up the regional need.

(7) Providing a realistic opportunity for the construction of least-cost housing will satisfy a municipality's *Mount Laurel* obligation if, and only if, it cannot otherwise be satisfied. In other words, it is only after *all* alternatives have been explored, *all* affirmative devices considered, including, where appropriate, a reasonable period of time to determine whether low and moderate income housing is produced, only when everything has been considered and tried in order to produce a realistic opportunity for low and moderate income housing that least-cost housing will provide an adequate substitute. Least-cost housing means what it says, namely, housing that can be produced at the lowest possible price consistent with minimal standards of health and safety.

(8) Builder's remedies will be afforded to plaintiffs in *Mount Laurel* litigation where appropriate, on a case-by-case basis. Where the plaintiff has acted in good faith, attempted to obtain relief without litigation,

and thereafter vindicates the constitutional obligation in *Mount Laurel*-type litigation, ordinarily a builder's remedy will be granted, provided that the proposed project includes an appropriate portion of low and moderate income housing, and provided further that it is located and designed in accordance with sound zoning and planning concepts, including its environmental impact.

(9) The judiciary should manage *Mount Laurel* litigation to dispose of a case in all of its aspects with one trial and one appeal, unless substantial considerations indicate some other course. . . .

(10) The *Mount Laurel* obligation to meet the prospective lower income housing need of the region is, by definition, one that is met year after year in the future, throughout the years of the particular projection used in calculating prospective need. In this sense the affirmative obligation to provide a realistic opportunity to construct a fair share of lower income housing is met by a "phase-in" over those years; it need not be provided immediately. Nevertheless, there may be circumstances in which the obligation requires zoning that will provide an immediate opportunity—for instance, zoning to meet the region's present lower income housing need. In some cases, the provision of such a realistic opportunity might result in the immediate construction of lower income housing in such quantity as would radically transform the municipality overnight. Trial courts shall have the discretion, under those circumstances, to moderate the impact of such housing by allowing even the present need to be phased in over a period of years. Such power, however, should be exercised sparingly. . . .

. . .

E. *Judicial Remedies*

If a trial court determines that a municipality has not met its *Mount Laurel* obligation, it shall order the municipality to revise its zoning ordinance within a set time period to comply with the constitutional mandate; if the municipality fails adequately to revise its ordinance within that time, the court shall implement the remedies for noncompliance outlined below; and if plaintiff is a developer, the court shall determine whether a builder's remedy should be granted.

1. *Builder's Remedy*

Builder's remedies have been one of many controversial aspects of the *Mount Laurel* doctrine. Plaintiffs, particularly plaintiff-developers, maintain that these remedies are (i) essential to maintain a significant level of *Mount Laurel* litigation, and the only effective method to date of enforcing compliance; (ii) required by principles of fairness to compensate developers who have invested substantial time and resources in pursuing such litigation; and (iii) the most likely means of ensuring that lower income housing is actually built. Defendant municipalities contend that even if a plaintiff-developer obtains a judgment that a particular municipality has not complied with *Mount Laurel*, that municipality, and not the developer, should be allowed to determine how and where its fair share obligation will be met.

In *Madison*, this Court, while granting a builder's remedy to the plaintiff appeared to discourage such remedies in the future by stating that "such relief will ordinarily be rare." 72 N.J. at 551–52 n. 50, 371 A.2d 1192. Experience since *Madison*, however, has demonstrated to us that builder's remedies must be made more readily available to achieve compliance with *Mount Laurel*. We hold that where a developer succeeds in *Mount Laurel* litigation and proposes a project providing a substantial amount of lower income housing, a builder's remedy should be granted unless the municipality establishes that because of environmental or other substantial planning concerns, the plaintiff's proposed project is clearly contrary to sound land use planning. We emphasize that the builder's remedy should not be denied solely because the municipality prefers some other location for lower income housing, even if it is in fact a better site. Nor is it essential that considerable funds be invested or that the litigation be intensive.

. . .

2. *Revision of the Zoning Ordinance: the Master*

If the trial court determines that a municipality's zoning ordinance does not satisfy its *Mount Laurel* obligation, it shall order the defendant to revise it. . . .

3. *Remedies for Non-Compliance*

If within the time allotted by the trial court a revised zoning ordinance is submitted by the defendant municipality that meets the municipality's *Mount Laurel* obligations, the trial court shall issue a judgment of compliance. If the revised ordinance does not meet the constitutional requirements, or if no revised ordinance is submitted within the time allotted, the trial court may issue such orders as are appropriate, including any one or more of the following:

(1) that the municipality adopt such resolutions and ordinances, including particular amendments to its zoning ordinance, and other land use regulations, as will enable it to meet its *Mount Laurel* obligations;

(2) that certain types of projects or construction as may be specified by the trial court be delayed within the municipality until its ordinance is satisfactorily revised, or until all or part of its fair share of lower income housing is constructed and/or firm commitments for its construction have been made by responsible developers;

(3) that the zoning ordinance and other land use regulations of the municipality be deemed void in whole or in part so as to relax or eliminate building and use restrictions in all or selected portions of the municipality (the court may condition this remedy upon failure of the municipality to adopt resolutions or ordinances mentioned in (1) above); and

(4) that particular applications to construct housing that includes lower income units be approved by the municipality, or any

officer, board, agency, authority (independent or otherwise) or division thereof. . . .

When the court orders that an ordinance be amended, it does very little different from ordering that a variance be granted, actions taken by our courts in New Jersey for many years. It does very little different from declaring that a zoning ordinance is invalid on equal protection grounds, the effect of that often being not simply to allow a plaintiff to use his property in a manner not permitted by the ordinance, but to give the same right to an entire class. The ordinance is effectively amended to permit a use explicitly excluded, or in some cases to exclude one explicitly permitted. . . .

NOTES

1. The Mount Laurel decisions generated great public controvery, culminating in enactment in 1985 of legislation transferring most of the responsibility for administering the "fair share" obligations of municipalities from the courts to an administrative agency, the Council on Affordable Housing. In Hills Development Co. v. Township of Bernards in Somerset County, 103 N.J. 1, 510 A.2d 621 (1986), the Supreme Court of New Jersey upheld the act, against allegations that it was inconsistent with the constitutional obligations of municipalities as outlined in the Mount Laurel case. The court declared, however, that if the act "achieves nothing but delay, the judiciary will be forced to resume its appropriate role." See Franchese, Mount Laurel III: The New Jersey Supreme Court's Judicious Retreat, 18 Seton Hall L.Rev. 30 (1988), applauding the "supreme court's zealous and controversial iniative," without which needed comprehensive legislation "would not have been forthcoming." The work of the Council is criticized in Payne, Rethinking Fair Share: Enforcement of Affordable Housing Policies, 16 Real Est.L.J. 20 (1987).

2. The judicial role in the Mount Laurel decisions was rejected by the New York Court of Appeals in Suffolk Housing Services v. Town of Brookhaven, 70 N.Y.2d 122, 517 N.Y.S.2d 924, 511 N.E.2d 67 (1987), in which the court manifested willingness to invalidate exclusionary practices, but not to order inclusionary remedies. Decisions in various states addressing exclusionary practices are concisely reviewed in D. Mandelker, Land Use Law 287–304 (2d ed. 1988). A recent relevant case is Builders Service Corporation, Inc. v. Planning & Zoning Commission of the Town of East Hampton, 208 Conn. 267, 545 A.2d 530 (1988), invalidating minimum floor area requirements that failed to contain a "per person occupancy based component." For critical commentary, see Ellickson, The Irony of Inclusionary Zoning, 54 S.Cal.L. Rev. 1167 (1981).

SECTION 4. SIZE AND RATE OF GROWTH OF LOCAL COMMUNITIES

. . .

ASSOCIATED HOME BUILDERS v. CITY OF LIVERMORE

Supreme Court of California, 1976.
18 Cal.3d 582, 135 Cal.Rptr. 41, 557 P.2d 473.

TOBRINER, JUSTICE. We face today the question of the validity of an initiative ordinance enacted by the voters of the City of Livermore which prohibits issuance of further residential building permits until local educational, sewage disposal, and water supply facilities comply with specified standards.[1] Plaintiff, an association of contractors, subdividers, and other persons interested in residential construction in Livermore, brought this suit to enjoin enforcement of the ordinance. The superior court issued a permanent injunction, and the city appealed.

. . .

Finally, we reject plaintiff's suggestion that we sustain the trial court's injunction on the ground that the ordinance unconstitutionally attempts to bar immigration to Livermore. Plaintiff's contention symbolizes the growing conflict between the efforts of surburban communities to check disorderly development, with its concomitant problems of air and water pollution and inadequate public facilities, and the increasing public need for adequate housing opportunities. We take this opportunity, therefore, to reaffirm and clarify the principles which govern validity of land use ordinances which substantially limit immigration into a community; we hold that such ordinances need not be sustained by a compelling state interest, but are constitutional if they are reasonably related to the welfare of the region affected by the ordinance. Since on the limited record before us plaintiff has not demonstrated that the Livermore ordinance lacks a reasonable relationship to the regional welfare, we cannot hold the ordinance unconstitutional under this standard. The initiative ordinance in question was enacted by a majority of the voters at the Livermore municipal election of April 11, 1972, and became effective on April 28, 1972. The ordinance, set out in full in the margin,[2] states that it was enacted to

1. For the history of the events leading to the enactment of the Livermore ordinance see Stanford Environmental Law Society, A Handbook for Controlling Local Growth (1973), pages 90–96; Deutsch, Land Use Growth Controls: A Case Study of San Jose and Livermore, California (1974) 15 Santa Clara Law. 1, 12–14.

2. The initiative provides as follows:

"INITIATIVE ORDINANCE RE BUILDING PERMITS

"An ordinance to control residential building permits in the City of Livermore:

"A. The people of the City of Livermore hereby find and declare that it is in the best interest of the City in order to protect the health, safety, and general welfare of the citizens of the city, to control residential building permits in the said city. Residential building permits include single-family residential, multiple residential, and trailer court building permits within the meaning of the City Code of Livermore and the General Plan of Livermore. Additionally, it is the purpose of this initiative measure to contribute to the solution of air pollution in the City of Livermore.

further the health, safety, and welfare of the citizens of Livermore and to contribute to the solution of air pollution. . . .

Plaintiff association filed suit to enjoin enforcement of the ordinance and for declaratory relief. After the city filed its answer, all parties moved for judgment on the pleadings and stipulated that the court, upon the pleadings and other documents submitted, could determine the merits of the cause. On the basis of that stipulation the court rendered findings and entered judgment for plaintiff. The city appeals from that judgment.

. . .

Plaintiff urges that we affirm the trial court's injunction on a ground which it raised below, but upon which the trial court did not rely. Plaintiff contends that the ordinance proposes, and will cause, the prevention of nonresidents from migrating to Livermore, and that the ordinance therefore attempts an unconstitutional exercise of the police power, both because no compelling state interest justifies its infringement upon the migrant's constitutionally protected right to travel, and because it exceeds the police power of the municipality.

The ordinance on its face imposes no absolute prohibition or limitation upon population growth or residential construction. It does provide that no building permits will issue unless standards for educational facilities, water supply and sewage disposal have been met, but plaintiff presented no evidence to show that the ordinance's standards were unreasonable or unrelated to their apparent objectives of protecting the public health and welfare. Thus, we do not here confront the question of the constitutionality of an ordinance which limits or bars population growth either directly in express language or indirectly by the imposition of prohibitory standards; we adjudicate only the validity of an ordinance limiting building permits in accord with standards that reasonably measure the adequacy of public services.

As we shall explain, the limited record here prevents us from resolving that constitutional issue. We deal here with a case in which a land use ordinance is challenged solely on the ground that it assertedly exceeds the municipality's authority under the police power; the challenger eschews any claim that the ordinance discriminates on a basis of race or wealth. Under such circumstances, we view the past decisions of this court and the federal courts as establishing the

"B. The specific reasons for the proposed position are that the undersigned believe that the resulting impact from issuing residential building permits at the current rate results in the following problems mentioned below. Therefore no further residential permits are to be issued by the said city until satisfactory solutions, as determined in the standards set forth, exist to all the following problems:

"1. *Educational facilities.* No double sessions in the schools nor over-crowded classrooms as determined by the California Education Code.

"2. *Sewage.* The sewage treatment facilities and capacities meet the standards set by the Regional Water Quality Control Board.

"3. *Water supply.* No rationing of water with respect to human consumption or irrigation and adequate water reserves for fire protection exist.

"C. This ordinance may only be amended or repealed by the voters at a regular municipal election.

"D. If any portion of this ordinance is declared invalid the remaining portions are to be considered valid."

following standard: the land use restriction withstands constitutional attack if it is fairly debatable that the restriction in fact bears a reasonable relation to the general welfare. For the guidance of the trial court we point out that if a restriction significantly affects residents of surrounding communities, the constitutionality of the restriction must be measured by its impact not only upon the welfare of the enacting community, but upon the welfare of the surrounding region. We explain the process by which the court can determine whether or not such a restriction reasonably relates to the regional welfare. Since the record in the present case is limited to the pleadings and stipulations, and is devoid of evidence concerning the probable impact and duration of the ordinance's restrictions, we conclude that we cannot now adjudicate the constitutionality of the ordinance. Thus we cannot sustain the trial court judgment on the ground that the ordinance exceeds the city's authority under the police power; that issue can be resolved only after trial.

We turn now to consider plaintiff's arguments in greater detail. Seeking to capitalize upon the absence of an evidentiary record, plaintiff contends that the challenged ordinance must be subjected to strict judicial scrutiny; that it can be sustained only upon a showing of a compelling interest, and that the city has failed to make that showing.

Many writers have contended that exclusionary land use ordinances tend primarily to exclude racial minorities and the poor, and on that account should be subject to strict judicial scrutiny. (See e.g., Davidoff & Davidoff, Opening the Suburbs: Toward Inclusionary Land Use Controls (1971) 22 Syracuse L.Rev. 509; Sager, Tight Little Islands: Exclusionary Zoning, Equal Protection, and the Indigent (1969) 21 Stan. L.Rev. 767; Note, op. cit., supra, 26 Stan.L.Rev. 585, 597, fn. 45 and authorities there cited; Note, The Equal Protection Clause and Exclusionary Zoning after Valtierra and Dandridge (1971) 81 Yale L.J. 61.) These writers, however, are concerned primarily with ordinances which ban or limit less expensive forms of housing while permitting expensive single family residences on large lots. The Livermore ordinance is not made from this mold; it impartially bans all residential construction, expensive or inexpensive. Consequently plaintiff at bar has eschewed reliance upon any claim that the ordinance discriminates on a basis of race or wealth.

Plaintiff's contention that the Livermore ordinance must be tested by a standard of strict scrutiny, and can be sustained only upon a showing of a compelling state interest, thus rests solely on plaintiff's assertion that the ordinance abridges a constitutionally protected right to travel. As we shall explain, however, the indirect burden imposed on the right to travel by the ordinance does not warrant application of the plaintiff's asserted standard of "compelling interest."[19]

In asserting that legislation which burdens a right to travel requires strict scrutiny, and can be sustained only upon proof of compel-

19. For analysis of the constitutional origins of the right to travel, see Note, Municipal Self-Determination: Must Local Control of Growth Yield to Travel Rights? (1975) 17 Ariz.L.Rev. 145, 148–152.

ling need, plaintiff relies on recent decisions of this court (In re King (1970) 3 Cal.3d 226, 90 Cal.Rptr. 15, 474 P.2d 983) and the United States Supreme Court (Memorial Hospital v. Maricopa County (1974) 415 U.S. 250, 94 S.Ct 1076, 39 L.Ed.2d 306; Dunn v. Blumstein (1972) 405 U.S. 330, 92 S.Ct. 995, 31 L.Ed.2d 274; Shapiro v. Thompson (1969) 394 U.S. 618, 89 S.Ct. 1322, 22 L.Ed.2d 600). The legislation held invalid by those decisions, however, directly burdened the right to travel by distinguishing between nonresidents or newly arrived residents on the one hand and established residents on the other, and imposing penalties or disabilities on the former group.[20]

Both the United States Supreme Court and this court have refused to apply the strict constitutional test to legislation, such as the present ordinance, which does not penalize travel and resettlement but merely makes it more difficult for the outsider to establish his residence in the place of his choosing.[21] (See Village of Belle Terre v. Boraas (1973) 416 U.S. 1, 7, 94 S.Ct. 1536, 39 L.Ed.2d 797; Ector v. City of Torrance (1973) 10 Cal.3d 129, 135, 109 Cal.Rptr. 849, 514 P.2d 433; see also McCarthy v. Philadelphia (1976) 424 U.S. 645, 96 S.Ct. 1154, 47 L.Ed.2d 366; Construction Ind. Ass'n, Sonoma County v. City of Petaluma, supra, 522 F.2d 897, 906–907, fn. 13; Note, 50 N.Y.U.L.F. (1975) 1163, 1168.) The only contrary authority, the decision of the federal district court in Construction Ind. Ass'n, Sonoma Cty. v. City of Petaluma (N.D.Cal. 1974) 375 F.Supp. 574 holding that an ordinance limiting residential construction must be supported by a compelling state interest has now been reversed by the Court of Appeals for the Ninth Circuit. (Construction Ind. Ass'n, Sonoma Cty. v. City of Petaluma, supra, 522 F.2d 897, cert. den., 424 U.S. 934, 96 S.Ct. 1148, 47 L.Ed.2d 342.)

Most zoning and land use ordinances affect population growth and density. As commentators have observed, to insist that such zoning laws are invalid unless the interests supporting the exclusion are compelling in character, and cannot be achieved by an alternative method, would result in wholesale invalidation of land use controls and endanger the validity of city and regional planning. . . .

We conclude that the indirect burden upon the right to travel imposed by the Livermore ordinance does not call for strict judicial scrutiny. The validity of the challenged ordinance must be measured by the more liberal standards that have traditionally tested the validity of land use restrictions enacted under the municipal police power.

20. In re King struck down a penal code provision which declared that failure of a father to support his child was a misdemeanor when the father was a California resident, but decreed that it was a felony when the father resided out of the state. The United States Supreme Court cases overturned residency requirements imposed to restrict eligibility for medical care (Memorial Hospital v. Maricopa County), voting (Dunn v. Blumstein), or welfare (Shapiro v. Thompson). For analysis of these decisions, see generally Comment, A Strict Scrutiny of the Right to Travel (1975) 22 UCLA L.Rev. 1129).

21. For discussion of the application of the right to travel to land use regulations see Comment, The Right to Travel: Another Constitutional Standard for Local Land Use Regulations? (1972) 39 U.Chi.L.Rev. 612; Note, The Right to Travel and Exclusionary Zoning (1975) 26 Hastings L.J. 849.

This conclusion brings us to plaintiff's final contention: that the Livermore ordinance exceeds the authority conferred upon the city under the police power. . . .

. . .

These considerations impel us to the conclusion that the proper constitutional test is one which inquires whether the ordinance reasonably relates to the welfare of those whom it significantly affects. If its impact is limited to the city boundaries, the inquiry may be limited accordingly; if, as alleged here, the ordinance may strongly influence the supply and distribution of housing for an entire metropolitan region, judicial inquiry must consider the welfare of that region.

. . .

We explain the process by which a trial court may determine whether a challenged restriction reasonably relates to the regional welfare. The first step in that analysis is to forecast the probable effect and duration of the restriction. In the instant case the Livermore ordinance posits a total ban on residential construction, but one which terminates as soon as public facilities reach specified standards. Thus to evaluate the impact of the restriction, the court must ascertain the extent to which public facilities currently fall short of the specified standards, must inquire whether the city or appropriate regional agencies have undertaken to construct needed improvements, and must determine when the improvements are likely to be completed.

The second step is to identify the competing interests affected by the restriction. We touch in this area deep social antagonisms. We allude to the conflict between the environmental protectionists and the egalitarian humanists; a collision between the forces that would save the benefits of nature and those that would preserve the opportunity of people in general to settle. Suburban residents who seek to overcome problems of inadequate schools and public facilities to secure "the blessing of quiet seclusion and clean air" and to "make the area a sanctuary for people" (Village of Belle Terre v. Boraas, supra, 416 U.S. 1, 9, 94 S.Ct. 1536, 1541, 39 L.Ed.2d 797) may assert a vital interest in limiting immigration to their community. Outsiders searching for a place to live in the face of a growing shortage of adequate housing, and hoping to share in the perceived benefits of suburban life, may present a countervailing interest opposing barriers to immigration.

Having identified and weighed the competing interests, the final step is to determine whether the ordinance, in light of its probable impact, represents a reasonable accommodation of the competing interests. We do not hold that a court in inquiring whether an ordinance reasonably relates to the regional welfare, cannot defer to the judgment of the municipality's legislative body.[27] But judicial deference is not

27. The reconciliation and accommodation of the competing interests can reasonably take a variety of forms, depending upon the needs and characteristics of the community and its surrounding region. Courts have upheld restrictive zoning ordinances of limited duration (see Builders Assn. of Santa Clara-Santa Cruz Counties v. Superior Court (1974) 13 Cal.3d 225, 118 Cal.Rptr. 158, 529 P.2d 582 (app. dismissed, 427 U.S. 901, 96 S.Ct. 3184, 49 L.Ed.2d 1195 (1976); Metro Realty v. County of El Dorado (1963) 222 Cal.App.2d 508, 35 Cal. Rptr. 480), an ordinance aimed at diverting

judicial abdication. The ordinance must have a *real and substantial* relation to the public welfare. . . .

The burden rests with the party challenging the constitutionality of an ordinance to present the evidence and documentation which the court will require in undertaking his constitutional analysis. Plaintiff in the present case has not yet attempted to shoulder that burden. Although plaintiff obtained a stipulation that as of the date of the trial the ordinance's goals had not been fulfilled, it presented no evidence to show the likely duration or effect of the ordinance's restriction upon building permits. We must presume that the City of Livermore and appropriate regional agencies will attempt in good faith to provide that community with adequate schools, sewage disposal facilities, and a sufficient water supply; plaintiff, however, has not presented evidence to show whether the city and such agencies have undertaken to construct the needed improvements or when such improvements will be completed. Consequently we cannot determine the impact upon either Livermore or the surrounding region of the ordinance's restriction on the issuance of building permits pending achievement of its goals.

With respect to the competing interests, plaintiff asserts the existence of an acute housing shortage in the San Francisco Bay Area, but presents no evidence to document that shortage or to relate it to the probable effect of the Livermore ordinance. Defendants maintain that Livermore has severe problems of air pollution and inadequate public facilities which make it reasonable to divert new housing, at least temporarily, to other communities but offer no evidence to support that claim. Without an evidentiary record to demonstrate the validity and significance of the asserted interests, we cannot determine whether the instant ordinance attempts a reasonable accommodation of those interests.

. . .

The judgment of the superior court is reversed, and the cause remanded for further proceedings consistent with the views expressed herein.

WRIGHT, C.J. and MCCOMB, SULLIVAN and RICHARDSON, JJ., concur.

CLARK, JUSTICE (dissenting). [omitted]

MOSK, JUSTICE (dissenting).

Limitations on growth may be justified in resort communities, beach and lake and mountain sites, and other rural and recreational areas; such restrictions are generally designed to preserve nature's environment for the benefit of all mankind. They fulfill our fiduciary obligation to posterity. As Thomas Jefferson wrote, the earth belongs to the living, but in usufruct.[1]

growth to less impacted areas of a city (Builders Assn. of Santa Clara-Santa Cruz Counties v. Superior Court, supra), and phased growth ordinances (see Construction Ind. Ass'n, Sonoma Cty. v. City of Petaluma, supra, 522 F.2d 897; Golden v. Planning Board of Town of Ramapo (1972) 30 N.Y.2d 359, 334 N.Y.S.2d 138, 285 N.E.2d 291).

1. Jefferson called this principle "self-evident." (Laing, Jefferson's Usufruct Principle (July 3, 1976) 223 The Nation Magazine, p. 7.)

But there is a vast qualitative difference when a suburban community invokes an elitist concept to construct a mythical moat around its perimeter, not for the benefit of mankind but to exclude all but its fortunate current residents.

The majority, somewhat desultorily, deny that the ordinance imposes an absolute prohibition upon population growth or residential construction. It is true that the measure prohibits the issuance of building permits for single-family residential, multiple residential and trailer residential units until designated public services meet specified standards. But to see such restriction in practicality as something short of total prohibition is to employ ostrich vision.

First of all, the ordinance provides no timetable or dates by which the public services are to be made adequate. Thus the moratorium on permits is likely to continue for decades, or at least until attrition ultimately reduces the present population. Second, it is obvious that no inducement exists for *present* residents to expend their resources to render facilities adequate for the purpose of accommodating *future* residents. It would seem more rational, if improved services are really contemplated for any time in the foreseeable future, to admit the new residents and compel them to make their proportionate contribution to the cost of the educational, sewage and water services. Thus it cannot seriously be argued that Livermore maintains anything other than total exclusion.

The trial court found, inter alia, that the ordinance prohibited the issuance of building permits for residential purposes until certain conditions are met, but the measure does not provide that any person or agency is required to expend or commence any efforts on behalf of the city to meet the requirements. Nor is the city itself obliged to act within any specified time to cure its own deficiencies. Thus, in these circumstances procrastination produces its own reward: continued exclusion of new residents.

The significant omissions, when noted in relation to the ordinance preamble, reveal that the underlying purpose of the measure is "to control residential building permits in the City of Livermore"—translation: to keep newcomers out of the city—and not to solve the purported inadequacies in municipal educational, sewage and water services. Livermore concedes no building permits are now being issued and it relates no current or prospective schedule designed to correct its defective municipal services.

. . .

Communities adopt growth limits from a variety of motives. There may be conservationists genuinely motivated to preserve general or specific environments. There may be others whose motivation is social exclusionism, racial exclusion, racial discrimination, income segregation, fiscal protection, or just fear of any future change; each of these purposes is well served by growth prevention.

Whatever the motivation, total exclusion of people from a community is both immoral and illegal. (Cal.Const. art. I, §§ 1, 7, subds. (a) &

(b).) Courts have a duty to prevent such practices, while at the same time recognizing the validity of genuine conservationist efforts.

The problem is not insoluble, nor does it necessarily provoke extreme results. Indeed, the solution can be relatively simple if municipal agencies would consider the aspirations of society as a whole, rather than merely the effect upon their narrow constituency. (See, e.g., A.L.I. Model Land Development Code, art. 7.) Accommodation between environmental preservation and satisfaction of housing needs can be reached through rational guidelines for land-use decision-making. Ours, of course, is not the legislative function. But two legal inhibitions must be the benchmark of any such guidelines. First, any absolute prohibition on housing development is presumptively invalid. And second, local regulations, based on parochialism, that limit population densities in growing suburban areas may be found invalid unless the community is absorbing a reasonable share of the region's population pressures.

Under the foregoing test, the Livermore ordinance is fatally flawed. I would affirm the judgment of the trial court.

NOTE

See D. Mandelker, Land Use Law ch. 10 (2d ed.1988); Ellickson, Suburban Growth Controls: An Economic and Legal Analysis, 86 Yale L.J. 385 (1977); Roberts, An Appropriate Economic Model of Judicial Review of Suburban Growth Control, 55 Ind. L.J. 441 (1980); Stone, The Prevention of Urban Sprawl Through Utility Extension Control, 14 Urb.Law. 357 (1982); Symposium on Growth Policy in the Eighties, 43 L. & Contemp.Prob. 3 (Spring 1979).

Chapter 22

DEREGULATION?

THE REPORT OF THE PRESIDENT'S COMMISSION ON HOUSING

Pages 180, 200–202 (1982).

The Need for Regulatory Reform

In hearings held across the country, the Commission was told repeatedly that unnecessary regulations at all levels of government have seriously hindered the production of housing, increased its cost, and restricted opportunities for mobility. (See Methodology in appendix.) Some testimony, however, expressed support of regulation to achieve social (e.g., environmental) or economic (e.g., energy conservation) benefits. Nevertheless, the Commission believes that unnecessary regulation of land use and buildings has increased so much over the past two decades that Americans have begun to feel the undesirable consequences: fewer housing choices, limited production, high costs, and lower productivity in residential construction. Based on these hearings and other research and consultation, the Commission found that:

- Regulation can hinder the efficient operation of the marketplace by denying consumers a wide range of housing choices and denying owners and developers the freedom to use property efficiently;
- Overregulation has hampered the production of housing, particularly for people of average or lower income;
- Regulation has unnecessarily pushed up costs in some localities by as much as 25 percent of the final sales price; and
- Regulation often limits flexibility in housing construction, both by inhibiting the substitution of available materials, labor, land, and capital in response to changes in relative prices, and by impeding the rate at which new products and building systems can be introduced.

With these findings in mind, the Commission concluded that government should substantially cut back its regulation of housing to give freer play to the marketplace, leaving to government its traditional responsibility to protect public health and safety and other vital and pressing governmental interests. Regulatory reform and a more robust private market should provide greater housing opportunities not only for those living within the community, but for prospective residents as well.

Housing Choices

Government regulations can unnecessarily restrict housing choices by limiting locations where construction can occur, by driving up the cost of housing and thereby placing new housing beyond the financial reach of increasing numbers of people, and by arbitrarily placing absolute limits on the amount and type of housing built. Location limitations may arise from such land-use policies as zoning, growth controls, and farmland preservation policies, which either prohibit housing development in certain areas or direct growth away from some areas and into others. Prohibitions on multifamily housing or mobile homes restrict the choices available to consumers, as to requirements that multifamily housing include units with only a few bedrooms.

Owners are similarly denied the full use of their property as a consequence of these restrictions. While the Commission does not advocate unrestricted use of property in a way that is harmful to others, it is concerned that regulations impose unjustified restrictions on property interests. . . .

General Zoning Regulations

General Standard

To protect property rights and to increase the production of housing and lower its cost, all State and local legislatures should enact legislation providing that no zoning regulations denying or limiting the development of housing should be deemed valid unless their existence or adoption is necessary to achieve a vital and pressing governmental interest. In litigation, the governmental body seeking to maintain or impose the regulation should bear the burden for proving it complies with the foregoing standard.

Under the Federal system, States have primary responsibility for zoning regulation. Virtually all States, however, have chosen to delegate this authority to local governments, and many municipalities have used this power in ways that unnecessarily restrict the production of housing and increase its costs.

To correct improper use of this power, States should adopt constitutional or legislative enabling provisions that prohibit restrictive local zoning—except where land-use regulation is necessary to satisfy a "vital and pressing" governmental interest. Where States fail to act, localities should enact their own ordinances to correct improper zoning.

Generally, a vital and pressing governmental interest will involve protecting health and safety, remedying unique environmental problems, preserving historic resources, or protecting investments in existing public infrastructure resources.[5] This new standard for zoning is

5. Vital and pressing governmental interests that zoning ordinances should serve include adequate sanitary sewer and water services; flood protection; topographical conditions that permit safe construction and accommodate septic tank effluence; protection of drinking-water aquifers; avoidance of nuisance or obnoxious uses; off-street parking; prohibition of residential construction amidst industrial development; and avoidance of long-term damage to the vitality of historically established neighborhoods.

intended to limit substantially the imposition of exclusionary land-use policies, since exclusion is clearly not an acceptable governmental interest.

In enacting the proposed new standard, the States should give this standard specific content to assure it is not abused. State statutes (or local ordinances, where applicable) should specifically define what constitutes vital and pressing governmental interests, thereby leaving to the genius of federalism the ultimate contours of this standard. However, a locality should have the burden of proving that any zoning restriction it imposes on housing meets the new standard in later judicial review.

The Commission's proposed standard would apply only to housing. Thus, all decisions related to size of lot, size or type of housing, percentage of multifamily, or other housing types and locations would be left to the market, unless government intervention is justified by the locality as serving a vital and pressing governmental interest.

A possible problem of deregulation is that it may adversely affect those who in good faith made their purchase or investments in reliance on the old rules. A change to the proposed "vital and pressing" standard would pose such a problem. Persons who purchase a home or a lot for construction of a home near vacant land assume that it will not be arbitrarily reclassified to allow other uses. The reasonable investment expectations of these homeowners should be protected. When vacant land is proposed for a use that would have required rezoning, homeowners entitled to notice under the old rules should be protected under the requirements and procedures of the old rules.

Nor is the proposed standard intended to limit a municipality's power to plan and build streets, parks, public buildings, schools, storm and sanitary sewers, and water mains and other public facilities or to designate homes or districts for historic preservation—unless those powers are used intentionally to limit the production of housing. (Historic preservation generally is not regulated under zoning ordinances.) Finally, the standard would not affect reasonable community-imposed development fees, dedications, servitudes, parking requirements, or other exactions that are not intended to limit production of housing. Municipalities should, of course, limit production if vital and pressing governmental interests require.

Constitutional Validity of Zoning Restrictions

The President should direct the Attorney General to analyze the constitutional validity and jurisprudential ramifications of the "vital and pressing" standard for judicially determining the validity of zoning ordinances and related standards that strike a balance between legitimate governmental interest and individuals' rights to property; if the Attorney General then concludes that a change should be sought in the existing Euclid standard, he should seek an appropriate case for urging the Supreme Court to adopt a new test.

The Commission believes that in recent years our legal system has weakened the property rights of owners of real property and largely ignored the implicit rights of newcomers deprived of affordable housing by excessive or exclusionary zoning. This imbalance should be redressed by State legislatures. But there is another potential source of protection—the courts.

In the past 25 years, the courts and legislatures have expanded the traditional meanings of property in applying due process protections. Yet the ownership of real property continues to be governed by a 50-year-old precedent that constitutes a significant departure from the traditional judicial role of protecting such property rights against government interference.

The framers of the Constitution were clearly concerned with property rights—the most obvious, in that era, being the right to own and use real property.[6] . . .

Euclid was controversial in its day and still has critics. Experience indicates that the broad land-use charter it afforded localities has been abused—often at the expense of housing. At the time *Euclid* was decided, zoning was an appropriate governmental response to the need to separate noncompatible land uses within the community. In today's more complex environment, zoning has been employed to do far more. It is used not only to separate land uses but also to exclude people from the community. The promising line of State court decisions on exclusionary zoning represents a valuable response to this abuse of zoning.

The Commission believes the pendulum has swung too far away from the right to enjoy the ownership of real property and the important societal interests of increasing mobility and access to housing opportunities. Accordingly, the Commission believes the *Euclid* doctrine should be reexamined. The Commission recommends that the Attorney General seek an appropriate case in which to request review of the *Euclid* doctrine in the context of modern land-use issues and the due process protections afforded other property rights in the 50 years since *Euclid* was decided. Most Commissioners believe that the "vital and pressing governmental interest" standard, described elsewhere in this report, represents an appropriate redress of the balance.[13] Nonetheless, the Commission suggests the Attorney General consider the "vital and pressing" and other potential standards in his review.

Several Commissioners are concerned that adoption of this proposed new standard as a constitutional doctrine raises serious dangers of an expanded role for the judiciary and believe that judges are ill-equipped to balance the social and environmental concerns inherent in zoning. These commissioners are concerned that the police power, of which zoning is an example, not be so constrained; rather, it should be

6. A detailed discussion of the historical context of constitutional protections of property rights appears in Bernard H. Siegan, Economic Liberties and the Constitution (Chicago, Ill.: University of Chicago Press, 1980), pp. 3–59; see also Vanhorne's Lessee v. Dorrance, 2 U.S. (2 Dall.) 304 (1795); Fletcher v. Peck, 10 U.S. (6 Cranch) 87 (1810); Terrett v. Taylor, 13 U.S. (9 Cranch) 43 (1815).

13. The proposed change to a vital and pressing standard would substantially elevate the level of judicial scrutiny similar to that utilized for reviewing gender classifications. Craig v. Boren, 429 U.S. 190, 50 L.Ed.2d 397, 97 S.Ct. 451 (1976); Califano v. Westcott, 443 U.S. 76, 61 L.Ed.2d 382, 99 S.Ct. 2655 (1979).

dynamic, and able to adjust as economic and social conditions vary. They would rely on the legislation recommended by the Commission to confine the exercise of discretionary local land-use decisions.

. . .

NOTES

1. Are these recommendations sound? Commentary supportive of them: Resolving the Housing Crisis: Government Policy, Decontrol and the Public Interest (M.B. Johnson ed. 1982); Kmiec, Deregulating Land Use: An Alternative Free Enterprise Development System, 130 U.Pa.L.Rev. 28 (1981); Pulliam, Brandeis Brief for Decontrol of Land Use: A Plea for Constitutional Reform, 13 Sw.U.L.Rev. 435 (1983).

2. The City of Houston, Texas, has never adopted zoning. Advocates of deregulation maintain that Houston has benefited from non-zoning. See Siegan, Non-Zoning in Houston, 13 J.Law & Econ. 71 (1970); Siegan, The Houston Solution: The Case for Removing Land-Use Controls, 4 Land-Use Controls Q. 1 (1970). For another view, see Babcock, Houston: Unzoned, Unfettered, and Most Unrepentant, Planning Magazine, March 1982, p. 21. It should be noted that Houston has various controls of land other than zoning. An ordinance adopted in 1982 requires approval by the planning commission of all plats for residential and commercial development, which must meet standards for street layout, building setbacks, off-street parking, open space and other matters. 5 Zon. & Pl. Law Rep. 72 (1982). The city also enforces residential restrictive covenants. See City of Houston v. Emmanuel United Pentecostal Church, Inc., 429 S.W.2d 679 (Tex.Civ.App.1968); Comment, Municipal Enforcement of Private Restrictive Covenants: An Innovation in Land-Use Control, 44 Tex.L.Rev. 741 (1966).

Part Five

THE SALE OF LAND

As you are aware at this stage of your study, Anglo-American land law is complex and diverse. It follows that the commercial transfer (sale) of land is more complicated than the corresponding transfer of personal property. Unfortunately, it has become even more difficult than it needs to be, due to a variety of factors—historical development, local practices and customs, and the omnipresent problems of a federal system with its fifty separate states plus the federal jurisdiction. Most of the relevant doctrine in this area is state law; there is no national law governing the sale of land although various federal statutes do impinge on real estate transactions. See, for example, the Federal Interstate Land Sales Full Disclosure Act, 15 U.S.C.A. § 1701 et seq. and HUD's regulations implementing the Act, published in 38 Fed.Reg. 23866 (Sept. 4, 1973), 24 C.F.R. Ch. IX. The problems are discussed in a Note, Regulation of Interstate Land Sales, 25 Stan.L.Rev. 605 (1973). See also the Real Estate Settlement Procedures Act of 1974 (RESPA), 12 U.S.C.A. § 2601 et seq. For a discussion of some of the problems created by the latter legislation read Whitman, RESPA: How to Comply, Problems and Prospects, 4 Real Estate L.J. 223 (1976). While the federal legislation is of great importance in the sale of land, a full scale treatment of its impact is beyond the scope of the first-year property course and must be reserved for later courses in the curriculum.

Since the sale of land is largely a matter of state law, the National Conference of Commissioners on Uniform State Laws has given the subject careful attention in an effort to simplify and improve the modern land transaction. Two significant acts have been drafted by the National Conference: (1) the Uniform Land Transactions Act, approved and recommended for enactment in all states at the August, 1975 meeting of the Commissioners and (2) the Uniform Simplification of Land Transfers Act, similarly approved and recommended in August, 1976. Neither of these acts has thus far been adopted in any state but they have had nationwide publicity among the members of the legal profession and may help chart the development of the law in the years ahead. The former act deals with contractual transfers of real estate, including transfers for security and transfers of limited interests such as leases, easements, restrictions, etc. As to these matters, it provides comprehensive provisions as to the relationship between the parties to the contract. The latter act, among other things, contains provisions designed to supplant existing recording statutes.

Several of the most relevant sections from the two acts have been incorporated in the material which follows in this part of the book. Even greater use of the new acts would have been made but for space limitations. If the acts are widely adopted by the states, the next edition will necessarily reflect that development in more detail. Fortunately, both acts are easily understood in the light of existing law and the transition to practice under either of them should not be difficult if the materials which follow are fully mastered. For example, the prefatory note to The Uniform Land Transactions Act states: "Perhaps the most important example of modernization of real estate law by this Act is Section 2–309 which imposes implied warranties of quality on persons in the business of selling real estate. For a substantial period of years the nearly universal opinion of writers on the subject has been that the old rules of caveat emptor were totally out of date and pernicious in effect. In spite of that, judicial overthrow of the rule has been slow." See pages 1268 to 1287, infra, which cover this same subject under existing case law, as it is being changed by the courts themselves. See also page 1048, infra, where an Indiana court cites Section 3–102(a) of the act with approval, even though the act has not been adopted in the state.

The official text of the Uniform Land Transactions Act and the Uniform Simplification of Land Transfers Act, together with helpful comments by the reporters, are available from West Publishing Co. at a modest price. These acts can be used as supplemental materials to demonstrate the effect which statutory intervention can have on the modern land transaction.

Chapter 23

THE REAL ESTATE CONTRACT

A thoroughly logical treatment of the law would cover the commercial transfer of all types of property in this part of the book. But, as you know by now, the development of the law has not been tied too closely to logic, and personal and real property have followed divergent paths. The sale of goods raises many tough legal problems but their solution lies principally in the Uniform Commercial Code and related legislation. Hence, you will study those materials in a separate course usually called Sales. This part of the book, then, is confined to the legal tangles resulting from the sale of real property and involves a study of the real estate contract, the role of the real estate broker, the deed of conveyance, the recording system, and the methods of title assurance. However, throughout this part you should bear in mind the contrast between the sale of Blackacre and the sale of an automobile, a television set, or a barrel of Puerto Rican rum.

The cases and materials in this chapter are those traditionally embodied in the law of vendor and purchaser.[1] A definitive treatment of this branch of the law would require the duplication of most of the course in Contracts, but we will incorporate those materials by reference and ask you to bear in mind that offer, acceptance, consideration, etc. are an important part of this phase of the law of property. However, some special attention must be given to the real estate contract, both because it is a matter of almost daily concern to many lawyers and because it has some peculiar twists which are not sufficiently covered in general contracts courses. These peculiarities of the law of vendor and purchaser will be stressed in the present chapter.

The most important single fact about the contract for the sale of land is the remedy available in event of breach. Since equity regards all land as unique, the legal remedy is never adequate, and specific performance is usually available at the instance of the nonbreaching party, whether he be vendor or purchaser. The jurisdiction of chancery has resulted in numerous doctrines, the most significant of which are part performance (Section 1) and equitable conversion (Section 4). In the materials which follow you should note the role of equity in shaping the law of vendor and purchaser. We have included a brief analysis of the role of the real estate broker (Section 5) because of the frequent conflict between brokers and lawyers and because you should understand the nature of the legal relationship between the broker and the parties to the contract.

The overwhelming bulk of the contracts will be in writing, and the lawyer's role will be concerned with the proper draftsmanship of what is to be the blueprint for the real estate transaction (Section 2) or with

1. For a detailed practice book see Holtzschue, Real Estate Contracts (1985).

problems of construction and performance of a contract already drafted by himself, another lawyer, or (horrors) a layman (Section 3). But occasionally the parties will fail to reduce a contract to writing, will do nothing more than sign a sketchy memorandum, or will try to modify or rescind a contract that has been carefully drafted. Then the lawyer must become an advisor, after the harm has been done, and he may have to resort to litigation to settle the controversy. Thus we begin this chapter with that perennial favorite—The Statute of Frauds.

SECTION 1. THE ORAL CONTRACT

AN ACT FOR PREVENTION OF FRAUDS AND PERJURIES

Statute 29 Charles II, Chapter 3 (1677).

IV. And be it further enacted by the authority aforesaid that no action shall be brought . . . (4) or upon any contract or sale of lands, tenements or hereditaments, or any interest in or concerning them; (5) or upon any agreement that is not to be performed within the space of one year from the making thereof; (6) unless the agreement upon which such action shall be brought, or some memorandum or note thereof, shall be in writing, and signed by the party to be charged therewith, or some other person thereunto by him lawfully authorized.

XVII. And be it further enacted by the authority aforesaid that from and after the said four and twentieth day of June, no contract for the sale of any goods, wares, and merchandises, for the price of ten pounds sterling or upwards shall be allowed to be good, except the buyer shall accept part of the goods so sold, and actually receive the same, or give something in earnest to bind the bargain or in part of payment, or that some note or memorandum in writing of the said bargain be made and signed by the parties to be charged by such contract, or their agents thereunto lawfully authorized.[2]

The American statutes are based on the English model, and while they vary in phraseology they are similar in substance. There are three principal points of divergence: (a) some statutes follow the New York style and make the oral agreement *void*; others simply say *no action* shall be brought; (b) some statutes require that the agreement be *subscribed*, others only that it be signed; (c) some statutes require that the agreement be signed by the party to be charged, others that it be signed by the vendor, and at least one state (Idaho) has held the agreement unenforceable unless signed by both parties.

Since the statute was first passed in 1677 and has been but little changed to date, you might suppose that its meaning is well settled.

2. Sections 1, 2, and 3 of the Act dealt with the conveyancing and leasing of land as opposed to the contract to convey. See pages 429 and 1149 herein, where the necessity for a written instrument is discussed in connection with the formal requirements of leases and deeds respectively. Section 17 is devoted to personal property and is covered in the course in Sales, but the student should note that it expressly provided for a type of part performance.

But note the following statement from the annual survey of New York law published in 25 N.Y.U.L.Rev. 1201 (1950): "More than a score of *reported* cases deal with the Statute of Frauds. The quantity of litigation required to construe a seventeenth-century statute recalls Chancellor Kent's statement more than a century ago that the cost of explaining the statute has been a million dollars or more. And the decisions themselves lend support to the Lord Chancellor's committee proposal in 1937 that the statute be repealed." [3]

The legal literature on the Statute of Frauds is a massive monument to man's attempt to reconcile the irreconcilable. Suffice it to say that in the Index to Legal Periodicals you can find an essay on any conceivable aspect of the subject. Obviously you would never handle a real estate transaction without reducing the contract to writing along the lines we will study later, *but* your clients may not always be so circumspect. The Statute of Frauds has been a fruitful litigation producer; the key to understanding the litigation lies in the reported cases. The statute says that no action shall be brought on an oral contract, but the legislative draftsman reckoned without the chancellor and the doctrine of part performance.

A. THE DOCTRINES OF PART PERFORMANCE AND EQUITABLE ESTOPPEL

SHAUGHNESSY v. EIDSMO

Supreme Court of Minnesota, 1946.
222 Minn. 141, 23 N.W.2d 362.

MATSON, J.

[The court's footnotes, consisting chiefly of citations, have been omitted.]

In an action for specific performance, defendant Bernt Eidsmo appeals from an order denying his motion for a new trial.

Plaintiffs, husband and wife, on April 5, 1943, by oral agreement, leased from the defendant Bernt Eidsmo a dwelling house and lot described as follows: The north 28 feet of lot 3 and the south 24 feet of lot 2, both in block 18, Roslyn Park Addition, also known as and numbered 4852 N.E. 6th Street, Columbia Heights, Anoka county, Minnesota, for a term of one year from May 1, 1943, at a rental of $47.50 per month, and, in consideration for the making of said lease and as a part thereof, defendant agreed to give, and gave, plaintiffs an option to purchase said property at the expiration of the lease term at a price between $4,750 and $5,000 on a contract for deed, subject to the proviso that plaintiffs should be allowed as a credit on the purchase price the total rent paid for the lease term with the balance of the purchase price to be paid in monthly installments of $32.50, inclusive of

3. England has now repealed most of the Statute of Frauds. Act 1954, 2 and 3 Eliz. 2, c. 34. However, the sections dealing with land and suretyship still remain.

unpaid taxes and five percent interest per annum on the unpaid balance. Defendant also agreed to sell plaintiffs a stove for $119.50, payable in installments of $4 per month without interest. Plaintiffs entered into possession May 1, 1943, and continued in possession throughout the one-year lease term ending April 30, 1944, and paid during said term a total rental of $570 and a total of $48 on the purchase price of the stove. At and before the expiration of said lease term, plaintiffs notified defendant that they wished to exercise their option of purchase according to the terms thereof, and on several occasions they demanded of defendant that he deliver a contract for deed as agreed. On each of these occasions, defendant told plaintiffs that he did not have time to have a contract drawn, but that his word was good and they should not worry. Plaintiffs fully performed their part of the option agreement and have at all times been ready, willing, and able to execute a contract for deed. Since the expiration of the lease term, plaintiffs have continued in possession, and from May 1, 1944, to May 1, 1945, have paid an additional $570 on the purchase of said property and a further sum on the purchase of the stove. When the option and lease agreement were made, the premises were subject to a $4,200 mortgage of which no mention was made to the plaintiffs and in regard to which no agreement was made that plaintiffs should assume said mortgage or take the property subject to the same.

Contrary to the above facts as established by the findings of the trial court, defendant contends that he had given no option, but that he had assured plaintiffs that at the end of the lease term he would give them the first opportunity to buy the premises for something in excess of $5,200, subject to a certain mortgage, on which the monthly payments were about $32, and that he would give them credit for the rent paid after making deductions for interest, taxes, and insurance. Defendant alleges that plaintiffs have done nothing to exercise any option, but that they merely asked him for a written lease and not for a contract for deed.

The trial court decreed that plaintiffs have a vendees' interest in the property and that they were entitled to a contract for deed from defendant specifying a purchase price of $5,000, subject to a credit on said price for the gross sum of all rents and purchase money paid, with a proviso that the balance of the price should be paid in monthly installments of $32.50 each, inclusive of taxes and interest at five percent per annum.

Two issues arise for consideration, namely, (1) whether the findings of the trial court are supported by the evidence, and (2) whether the oral agreements involved are within the statute of frauds.

Defendant's evidence contradicted that of plaintiffs to produce an issue of fact for determination by the trial court. Conflicts in evidence are not to be resolved on appeal, and the trial court's findings will not be disturbed unless they are manifestly and palpably contrary to the evidence. We find here ample evidence to sustain the findings. . . .

The oral agreement to lease the premises to plaintiffs for a term of one year embodied a provision giving to plaintiffs an option to purchase the premises upon the expiration of the lease term. This option, prior to its execution or acceptance, did not of itself contribute anything to bring the agreement under the statute of frauds. In the first place, a contract conferring an option to purchase is nothing more than an irrevocable and continuing offer to sell, and conveys no interest in land to the optionee, but vests in him only a right in personam to buy at his election. At best it is but an irrevocable right or privilege of purchase and does not come within Minn.St.1941, § 513.04, Mason St.1927, § 8459.

In the second place, an option agreement is a unilateral contract and as such it is, however long the time for the exercise of the option may run, not within the statute of frauds. By its very nature it is, from its inception, fully performed by the optionee as far as the acquirement of an irrevocable right of purchase is concerned. Obviously, it does not therefore fall within the provision of § 513.01 (§ 8456) that no action shall be maintained on any agreement "that by its terms is not to be performed within one year from the making thereof." The result is the same even though the option of purchase is a part of an oral lease. Place v. Johnson, 20 Minn. 219, 20 Gil. 198; Willard v. Tayloe, 8 Wall. 557, 19 L.Ed. 501; Richanbach v. Ruby, 127 Or. 612, 271 P. 600, 61 A.L.R. 1441; Rease v. Kittle, 56 W.Va. 269, 49 S.E. 150.

The oral lease, however, aside from the option contained therein, as a bilateral contract, was not capable of performance within one year from the date of its making on April 5, 1943, and was therefore subject to §§ 513.01, 513.04 (§§ 8456, 8459), unless taken out of the statute by part performance. § 513.06 (§ 8461). An oral lease of real estate for a term of one year, to commence in futuro, is within the statute of frauds. Here, however, the entire oral lease agreement had been fully performed when plaintiffs exercised the option, and the statute was no longer applicable. Bjornstad v. Northern States Power Co., 195 Minn. 439, 442, 263 N.W. 289, 290; Theopold v. Curtsinger, 170 Minn. 105, 108, 212 N.W. 18, 19; Nelson v. McElroy, 140 Minn. 429, 431, 168 N.W. 179, 180, 587; 6 Dunnell, Dig. & Supp. § 8852.

The instant, however, plaintiffs exercised their option by notifying defendant of their election to buy the premises a new contract, an oral contract for the purchase and sale of land, came into being. It was clearly within the statute of frauds (§ 513.04 [§ 8459]), unless taken therefrom by part performance, § 513.06 (§ 8461). According to Restatement, Contacts, § 197, the applicable rule is as follows:

"Where, acting under an oral contract for the transfer of an interest in land, the purchaser with the assent of the vendor [(a) makes valuable improvements on the land or] (b) takes possession thereof or retains possession thereof existing at the time of the bargain, and also pays a portion or all of the purchase price, the purchaser or the vendor may specifically enforce the contract."

In other words, the acts of taking possession and of making part payment, when they are performed under or in reliance upon the oral contract as to be unequivocally referable to the vendor-vendee relationship and not referable to any other relation between the parties, are sufficient to remove the contract from the statute of frauds. The doctrine of part performance, exemplifed by the above rule, was followed by this court in Wentworth v. Wentworth, 2 Minn. 277, 2 Gil. 238, 72 Am.Dec. 97; Gill v. Newell, 13 Minn. 462, 13 Gil. 430; and Bresnahan v. Bresnahan, 71 Minn. 1, 73 N.W. 515. In Brown v. Hoag, 35 Minn. 373, 375, 29 N.W. 135, 137, however, the court expressly rejected the unequivocal reference theory upon which the earlier cases were based and adopted the fraud theory under which the plaintiff must show that his acts of part performance in reliance upon the contract so altered his position that he would incur an unjust and irreparable injury in the event the defendant were permitted to rely on the statute of frauds. This latter decision, though apparently overlooked in Bresnahan v. Bresnahan, supra, has been followed in subsequent cases. We now adopt the Restatement principle to the effect that the taking of possession, coupled with the making of part payment, in reliance upon and with unequivocal reference to the vendor-vendee relationship, *without proof of irreparable injury through fraud,* is sufficient to avoid the statute. Brown v. Hoag, supra, and subsequent decisions based thereon, in so far as they require proof of irreparable injury or great hardship in addition to part performance, are expressly overruled. In other jurisdictions, as well as our own, in losing sight of historical antecedents considerable confusion has resulted in determining the basis for the removal of cases from purview of the statute of frauds. See 13 Minn.L.Rev. 744; Annotation, 101 A.L.R. 923, 943.

"The origin of the doctrine of the part performance as applied to permit the specific performance of an oral contract for the sale of real estate may be traced to a rule of equity which, antedating the English statute of frauds, required as a prerequisite of the enforcement of parol contracts concerning land that the plaintiff show that the contract had been partly performed, *or* that he had so altered his position in reliance on the agreement that a refusal to enforce it would amount to a fraud upon him." (Italics supplied.) 49 Am.Jur., Statute of Frauds, § 420.

Dean Pound, The Progress of the Law, in 33 Harv.L.Rev. 929, 937, with clarity explains the basis for the confusion that has arisen in so many American jurisdictions:

". . . It is important to insist that the taking of cases out of the statute is a historical anomaly, only to be understood by reference to seventeenth-century and eighteenth-century legal institutions and modes of thought in equity and that, like all historical anomalies of the sort, it defies logically satisfactory analytical treatment.

"What is the actual situation? We say that for the purposes of courts of equity, cases are taken out of the purview of the statute in either of two ways: by fraud *or* by part performance. Recently there has been a tendency to run the two together, largely under the influence of Pomeroy's doctrine of 'equitable fraud.' But they had an independent origin and have developed along independent lines. Hence they call first for independent consideration." (Italics supplied.)

. . .

"Before a decade had passed after its [statute of frauds] enactment, the Court of Chancery began to take cases out of the operation of the statute where purchaser had been put in possession under the contract. Sugden [Vendor and Purchaser (14 ed.) 152, note p] long ago called attention to some old cases which indicate that this was the result of ideas as to livery of seisin. *Putting the purchaser in possession was taken to be the substance of a common-law conveyance.* The rule thus derived became established in England and in a majority of American jurisdictions. But its original basis was soon overlooked and attempts to rationalize the subject led writers and courts to turn to the idea of 'fraud' in order to make a reasoned doctrine of 'part performance' on the basis of the old cases where the chancellor had dispensed with the statute. Different developments of this idea gave rise to many varieties of doctrine. Thus we get to-day cases taken out by possession alone; cases taken out by possession coupled with something else, arbitrarily prescribed by judicial decision or by statute; cases taken out by possession when joined to circumstances of great hardship upon purchaser; cases of part performance other than by taking possession, where there are acts solely referable to a contract as to the very land or showing a change in the character of the pre-existing possession, and cases where it is not possible to take possession but relief is given on a theory of fraud or of irreparable injury to purchaser, without more." (Italics supplied.)

Equitable relief has usually been denied where the court in its discretion has found the common-law remedy to be adequate. Where, however, an interest in land is involved, we have an exception to this rule that is significant in illustrating the special status accorded to land as distinguished from other forms of property. Clark, in his Principles of Equity, § 42, says: ". . . damages for the breach of a contract for the sale and purchase of any interest in land is always considered inadequate, without regard to the size, value or location of the land or the possibility of getting other land substantially equivalent. The crystallization of this rule is probably due historically to the peculiar respect and consideration which has been accorded to land in the English law; its modern justification is that because there is no open market for land either for seller or buyer, the number of instances where the buyer could get land substantially as satisfactory or where the vendor could make a ready sale to another purchaser is so small as to be negligible."

In short, inadequacy of damages is presumed, and proof thereof is not required. This presumption is sound. In order to effect complete justice, there is, after all, no adequate substitute for specific performance. It is submitted, where relief is sought to prevent the statute of frauds from itself becoming an instrument of fraud, that, in the light of historical development and consistent with the purpose of the statute, there has been no occasion for requiring, in addition to part performance, a proof of irreparable injury. See 1 Pomeroy, Equity Jurisprudence, 5th Ed., § 221b; 4 Id. § 1402; Gartrell v. Stafford, 12 Neb. 545, 11 N.W. 732, 41 Am.Rep. 767.

Samuel Williston, under whose direction Restatement, Contracts, § 197, was drafted, in Commentaries on Contracts, Restatement No. 4, pp. 14, 15, dated February 23, 1928, states: ". . . Courts of equity early adopted the doctrine that such acts as the taking of possession, making of improvements, and the like by the purchaser with consent of the vendor make the contract enforceable though there is no written memorandum. This doctrine has been rested upon two main reasons: (1) that the rule of the Statute of Frauds is an evidential rule and that any acts clearly and solely referable to the existence of the contract satisfy in equity the purpose of the Statute; (2) that equity should relieve against the operation of the Statute in cases where it would be unconscionable for the vendor to rely upon it in defense."

These two main reasons given by Williston correspond to Dean Pound's analysis that "cases are taken out of the purview of the statute in either of two ways: by fraud *or* by part performance." (Italics supplied.) Obviously, the evidential purpose of the statute is fully satisfied by adequate part performance without proof of irreparable injury. See 13 Minn.L.Rev. 744; Kingsley, Some Comments on the Section of the Minnesota Statute of Frauds Relating to Contracts, 14 Minn.L.Rev. 746, 753, 754.

Whether the acts of part performance are unequivocally referable to the vendor-vendee relationship under the oral contract is (in this case) a question of fact for the trier of fact. See Seitz v. Sitze, 215 Minn. 452, 10 N.W.2d 426; Ritchie v. Jennings, 181 Minn. 458, 233 N.W. 20; Place v. Johnson, 20 Minn. 219, 20 Gil. 198.

In the instant case, the two essential elements of possession and part payment are present. Defendant contends, however, that possession is not unequivocally referable to the vendor-vendee relationship, but is equally referable to the relation of landlord and tenant. The entire record, however, is pregnant with indications of a dominant intent of the parties from the inception of their transaction that a purchase-and-sale relation should be established upon the expiration of the lease term. The purchase of the stove also indicated an understanding that plaintiffs were to occupy the premises permanently. After plaintiffs exercised their option and an oral contract of purchase and sale then came into being, defendant's conduct and statements were consistent only with a mutual understanding that plaintiffs' possession of the premises was no longer that of a tenant but that of a vendee with unequivocal reference to the oral contract. When plaintiffs, on several occasions, requested the preparation of a contract for deed, defendant, instead of rejecting the vendor-vendee relationship, affirmed it by stating "that he did not have time to have a contract drawn; that his word was good; that plaintiff Mark Shaughnessy was not to worry about getting his contract." In fact, defendant finally presented to plaintiffs a written memorandum to be used as a basis for drawing a contract for deed. The conduct of the parties indicated no misunderstanding as to the nature of their transaction and the relation that each bore to the other. There was a dispute as to the amount of the purchase price and the terms of payment, but as to these matters the findings of the court are sustained by the evidence. Similar considerations support the findings that the payments made by plaintiffs were solely referable to the oral contract of purchase and sale.

The order denying a new trial is affirmed.

Affirmed.

NOTES

1. Although the principal case states that an option is not within the Statute of Frauds, a little analysis will show that this dictum is meaningless. The option must, at some point, ripen into a contract of sale and that must be in writing or there must be sufficient part performance to allow its enforcement. In Coombs v. Ouzounian, 24 Utah 2d 39, 465 P.2d 356 (1970), the court held that an option is an interest in real estate and is within the Statute of Frauds.

2. Some courts, while feeling bound by precedent to follow the doctrine of part performance, have cast doubt on the validity of making any exceptions to the Statute of Frauds. See, for example, Garner v. Stubblefield, 5 Tex. 552, 553 (1851).

"It will be perceived that the statute inhibits all actions upon contracts for the sale of lands unless the agreement, or some memorandum thereof, shall be in writing; and were this law enforced according to its letter, there would be an end to this suit and to litigation upon contracts of this character. . . .

"But eminent judges in more modern times have regretted that full effect was not given to the statute. They have doubted the wisdom of departing from the rule therein prescribed, however plausible the pretexts which seemed to justify the exceptions. In Lindsay v. Lynch (2 Sch. & Lef.R. 4, 5, 7), the Chancellor expresses his disapprobation of the course of decisions in the following terms: 'The statute was made for the purpose of preventing frauds and perjuries; and nothing can be more manifest to any person who has been in the habit of practicing in the Courts of Equity, than that the relaxation of the statute has been the ground of much perjury and much fraud. If the statute had been rigorously observed, the result would probably have been that few instances of parol agreements would have occurred. Agreements would, from the necessity of the case, have been reduced to writing; whereas, it is manifest that the decisions on the subject have opened a new door to fraud; and that under the pretence of part execution, if possession is had in any way whatever, means are frequently found to put a Court of Equity in such a situation, that, without departing from its rule, it feels obliged to break through the statute,' . . .

"It may be said that the mischiefs produced by temporizing with the statute are obvious to all, but that the beneficent effects of a rigorous construction have not been tested by experience; that they exist only in theory, and that there is no certainty that much fraud might not be perpetrated by an unconscientious and perverse use of the statute.

"However this may be, and it is not my design to discuss the subject, one result of the relaxation of the statute is beyond doubt: an uncertain and perplexing rule of action has been substituted for one which was plain, easily understood, and the hardships of which would be attributed rather to the negligence of the party, than to the doubtful state of the law. (2 Story, Eq. 765–6; Rob'ts on Frauds 137–8; 1 Bibb, R. 203; 4 Id. 59).

"These observations are thrown out to induce discussion in cases where it is sought to enforce parol agreements within the reach of the statute. The question is left open, and we proceed to examine whether the facts presented in this case are such as to bring the contract within any of the equitable exceptions which have been allowed to the statute."

Garner v. Stubblefield is an old case but it discusses a valid point and expresses an attitude toward the Statute of Frauds which is the, often unarticulated, premise of some modern decisions. Should the Statute be strictly construed? What would be the consequences of refusing to enforce *any* oral contract for the sale of land? What are the relevant policy considerations?

3. "Possession, Payment and Improvements as Part Performance in the United States.

"There are at least five different views in the United States as to what acts of part performance by the purchaser under an oral land contract who takes possession of the land will take the case out of the Statute of Frauds:

"(1) That *possession alone* is sufficient. . . .

"(2) That *possession accompanied by payment* is sufficient. . . .

"(3) That *possession accompanied by the making of valuable and lasting improvements* is sufficient. . . .

"(4) That there must be *both possession and such a change of position by the purchaser* (usually the result of making valuable improvements which cannot be fairly compensated in money) *that irreparable injury will result* unless the oral contract is enforced. . . .

"(5) That *no acts of part performance will be recognized* to take an oral land contract out of the Statute of Frauds. . . .

"The law of many states as to part performance is quite doubtful, and that of some extremely confused both in theory and in application." Chafee and Re, Cases and Materials on Equity 609 (4th ed. of Chafee and Simpson's Cases on Equity) (1958).

The authors' references to which states follow which of the five views have been omitted. The modern decisions are in flux and it is somewhat misleading to put a particular state in a given category. It *is* important to note the variety of ways in which the fifty states have analyzed a common problem.

In a few states the part performance doctrine has been adopted legislatively. The Alabama Statute of Frauds provides that an oral agreement for the sale of land is void "unless the purchase money, or a portion thereof is paid and the purchaser is put in possession of the land by the seller." Alabama Code 1975, § 8–9–2.

4. It is not enough to show the acts of part performance discussed in the principal case and the previous note. The plaintiff must also clearly prove that an oral contract existed. This proof can be by oral evidence, however, and the contract can then be enforced if the requisite acts of part performance are shown. Moreover, the acts of possession, payment, and improvement must have been made pursuant to the contract itself. If they are explainable on some other basis specific performance will be denied. See Wright v. Raftree, 181 Ill. 464, 54 N.E. 998 (1899).

In many states the Statute of Frauds must be specifically pleaded if it is to be a valid defense. See, for example, Terminal Freezers, Inc. v. Roberts Frozen Foods, Inc., 41 Ill.App.3d 981, 354 N.E.2d 904 (1976), where the court stated: "The Illinois Civil Practice Act requires that all affirmative defenses, such as the statute of frauds, must be specifically pleaded. . . . Failure to specifically plead the statute of frauds constitutes a waiver of the statute as a defense, even though the defense may appear to be within the evidence. . . . Plaintiff contends that its general denial of the contract was sufficient to raise the statute of frauds. We fail to see how a general denial of the existence of the contract can comply with the requirements . . .". See also, Shugan v. Colonial View Manor, 107 Ill.App.3d 458, 63 Ill.Dec. 82, 437 N.E.2d 731 (1982).

BURNS v. McCORMICK

Court of Appeals of New York, 1922.
233 N.Y. 230, 135 N.E. 273.

CARDOZO, J. In June, 1918, one James A. Halsey, an old man, and a widower, was living, without family or housekeeper, in his house in Hornell, New York. He told the plaintiffs, so it is said, that if they gave up their home and business in Andover, New York, and boarded and cared for him during his life, the house and lot, with its furniture and equipment, would be theirs upon his death. They did as he asked, selling out an interest in a little draying business in Andover, and boarding and tending him till he died, about five months after their coming. Neither deed nor will, nor memorandum subscribed by the promisor, exists to authenticate the promise. The plaintiffs asked specific performance. The defense is the statute of frauds (Real Property Law [Consol.Laws, c. 50] § 259).

We think the defense must be upheld. Not every act of part performance will move a court of equity, though legal remedies are inadequate, to enforce an oral agreement affecting rights in land. There must be performance "unequivocally referable" to the agreement, performance which alone and without the aid of words of promise is unintelligible or at least extraordinary unless as an incident of ownership, assured, if not existing.

"An act which admits of explanation without reference to the alleged oral contract or a contract of the same general nature and purpose is not, in general, admitted to constitute a part performance." Woolley v. Stewart, 222 N.Y. 347, 351, 118 N.E. 847, 848.

What is done must itself supply the key to what is promised. It is not enough that what is promised may give significance to what is done. The housekeeper who abandons other prospects of establishment in life and renders service without pay upon the oral promise of her employer to give her a life estate in land must find her remedy in an action to recover the value of the service. Maddison v. Alderson, L.R. 8 App.Cas. 467, 475, 476. Her conduct, separated from the promise, is not significant of ownership, either present or prospective. Maddison v. Alderson, supra, L.R. 8 App.Cas. at pages 478, 481. On the other hand, the buyer who not only pays the price, but possesses and improves his acre, may have relief in equity without producing a conveyance. Canda v. Totten, 157 N.Y. 281, 51 N.E. 989; McKinley v. Hessen, 202 N.Y. 24, 95 N.E. 32. His conduct is itself the symptom of a promise that a conveyance will be made. Laxer tests may prevail in other jurisdictions. We have been consistent here. . . .

Promise and performance fail when these standards are applied. The plaintiffs make no pretense that during the lifetime of Mr. Halsey they occupied the land as owners or under claim of present right. They did not even have possession. Cooley v. Lobdell, 153 N.Y. 596, 601, 602, 47 N.E. 783. The possession was his; and those whom he invited to live with him were merely his servants or his guests. Pollock & Wright on Possession, pp. 56, 58; Holmes, Common Law, p. 226; Kerslake v. Cunnings, 180 Mass. 65, 67, 61 N.E. 760; Mygatt v. Coe, 142 N.Y. 78, 85, 36 N.E. 870, 24 L.R.A. 850. He might have shown them the door, and the law would not have helped them to return. Whatever rights they had were executory and future. The tokens of their title are not, then, to be discovered in acts of possession or dominion. The tokens must be found elsewhere if discoverable at all. The plaintiffs did, indeed, while occupants of the dwelling, pay the food bills for the owner as well as for themselves, and do the work of housekeepers. One who heard of such service might infer that it would be rewarded in some way. There could be no reasonable inference that it would be rewarded at some indefinite time thereafter by a conveyance of the land. Woolley v. Stewart, supra, 222 N.Y. at page 353, 118 N.E. 847. The board might be given in return for lodging. The outlay might be merely an advance to be repaid in whole or part. "Time and care" might have been bestowed "From a vague anticipation that the affection and gratitude so created would, in the long run, insure some indefinite reward." Maddison v. Alderson, supra, L.R. 8 App.Cas. at page 486. This was the more likely since there were ties of kinship between one of the plaintiffs and the owner. Even if there was to be a reward, not merely as of favor, but as of right, no one could infer, from knowledge of the service, without more, what its nature or extent would be. Mr. Halsey paid the taxes. He paid also for the upkeep of the land and building. At least, there is no suggestion that the plaintiffs had undertaken to relieve him of those burdens. He was the owner while he lived. Nothing that he had accepted from the plaintiffs evinces an agreement that they were to be the owners when he died.

We hold, then, that the acts of part performance are not solely and unequivocally referable to a contract for the sale of land. Since that is so, they do not become sufficient because part of the plaintiffs' loss is without a remedy at law. At law the value of board and services will not be difficult of proof. The loss of the draying business in Andover does not permit us to disregard the statute, though it may go without requital. We do not ignore decisions to the contrary in other jurisdictions. . . . Cf. 1 Williston on Contracts, § 494. They are not law for us. Inadequacy of legal remedies, without more, does not dispense with the requirement that acts, and not words, shall supply the framework of the promise. That requirement has its origin in something more than an arbitrary preference of one form over others. It is "intended to prevent a recurrence of the mischief" which the statute would suppress. Maddison v. Alderson, supra, L.R. 8 App.Cas. at page 478. The peril of perjury and error is latent in the spoken promise. Such, at least, is the warning of the statute, the estimate of policy that finds expression in its mandate. Equity, in assuming what is in substance a dispensing power, does not treat the statute as irrelevant, nor ignore the warning altogether. It declines to act on words, though the legal remedy is imperfect, unless the words are confirmed and illuminated by deeds. A power of dispensation, departing from the letter in supposed adherence to the spirit, involves an assumption of jurisdiction easily abused, and justified only within the limits imposed by history and precedent. The power is not exercised unless the policy of the law is saved. Pound, Equity and the Statute of Frauds, 33 Harvard Law Review, 933, 944.

In conclusion, we observe that this is not a case of fraud. No confidential relation has been abused. Goldsmith v. Goldsmith, 145 N.Y. 313, 39 N.E. 1067; Wood v. Rabe, 96 N.Y. 414, 48 Am.Rep. 640. No inducement has been offered with the preconceived intention that it would later be ignored. Maddison v. Alderson, supra, L.R. 8 App.Cas. at page 490; Wheeler v. Reynolds, supra, 66 N.Y. at page 234. The most that can be said against Mr. Halsey is that he made a promise which the law did not compel him to keep, and that afterwards he failed to keep it. Woolley v. Stewart, supra, 222 N.Y. at page 351, 118 N.E. 847; Wheeler v. Reynolds, supra. We cannot even say of his failure that it was willful. He had made a will before the promise. Negligence or mere inertia may have postponed the making of another. The plaintiffs left the preservation of their agreement, if they had one, to the fallible memory of witnesses. The law exacts a writing.

The judgment of the Appellate Division and that entered on the report of the referee should be reversed, and the complaint dismissed, with costs in all courts.

HISCOCK, C.J., and HOGAN, POUND, MCLAUGHLIN, CRANE, and ANDREWS, JJ., concur.

Judgments reversed, etc.

NOTES

1. In the principal case the plaintiffs sold their draying business in another community in alleged reliance on the oral contract of the

defendant. This change in position was not enough to move the conscience of the court in absence of specific acts of part performance unequivocally referable to the contract. This attitude is typical of many cases. See, e.g., Walker v. Ireton, 221 Kan. 314, 559 P.2d 340 (1977) where the purchaser sold his own farm in reliance on an oral contract and the vendor repeated a promise that he would perform the oral contract. Said the court: "Generally an act which is purely collateral to an oral contract, although done in reliance on such contract is not such a reliance as to authorize the enforcement of the contract by a court of equity. An exception is recognized, however, where the agreement was made to induce the collateral act or where the collateral act was contemplated by the parties as a part of the entire transaction." See the case for a good discussion of the doctrine of part performance.

The doctrine of unequivocal referability so clearly enunciated in the principal case continues to be decisive across the country. See, for example, Coleman v. Dillman, 624 P.2d 713 (Utah 1981) where the court noted: "In the instant case, plaintiff's possession of the property was not exclusively referable to a contract of purchase, but was also equally consonant with defendant's allegation of a rental agreement. The same is true of the so-called improvements to the property made by plaintiff during his occupancy thereof. Nothing was accomplished which could not be characterized as routine household maintenance by a renter . . . ." The court denied specific performance. See also Lebowitz v. Mingus, 100 A.D.2d 816, 474 N.Y.S.2d 748 (1984), where plaintiff entered into a three-year lease of defendant's cooperative apartment in New York City and expended $50,000 to renovate it. The court held that the Statute of Frauds was applicable to a contract for sale of the shares of a cooperative apartment, and that the improvements in question were not unequivocally referable to an alleged oral contract by defendant either to sell the apartment to plaintiff or to permit plaintiff to remain in possession beyond the expiration of the lease. "[P]laintiff's expenditures may be satisfactorily explained by her desire to improve the surroundings in which she was to live and work for a period of several years. Moreover, the expenditures may also be attributable to plaintiff's belief, based upon the right of first refusal [in the lease], that it was likely that she would in fact be permitted at some point to purchase the apartment."

2. "No less than twenty-three cases during the past year turned on alleged oral contracts to leave property by will, or to adopt and leave property to the adopted person as to a child. As one reads these cases he cannot but have an uneasy feeling that general expectations of becoming the object of a testator's bounty often ripen into a contract after testator's death. Where the courts do not require the acts of part performance relied upon to take the case out of the Statute of Frauds to be unequivocal and indubitably referable to a contract as to the very land in question, but are content with a case of great hardship upon plaintiff, it is not hard to do for the deceased by proof of his casual 'admissions' in conversation over a series of years what the law would not have permitted him to do in person otherwise than by jealously

guarded formalities." Pound, The Progress of the Law, Equity, 33 Harv.L.Rev. 933 (1920).

3. Judicial attitudes toward the Statute of Frauds continue to vary widely. Contrast the California approach with that in West Virginia. "Hardship alone, according to the Supreme Court of California, may remove an oral contract from the Statute of Frauds by estoppel. . . . California courts have been clearly progressing toward abrogation of the Statute of Frauds." Note, 3 Stan.L.Rev. 281, 297 (1951). "The Statute of Frauds is a time honored statute. The need of a statute of that character became evident in England during the reign of Charles II and it was enacted in 1676. In some form it has been the law of this state and of the Commonwealth of Virginia since the beginning of the statehood of each. . . . The dangerous consequences which would follow the relaxation of the requirements of these wise and salutary statutes to permit the creation and the transfer of various interests and estates in land by parol would inevitably produce intolerable confusion and destructive instability in the law of real property. To sanction the substitution of verbal declarations for written instruments . . . is to reject the wholesome experience of the past for uncertain memory and unrecorded expression and, in so doing, to adopt a course which is necessarily fraught with danger. This risk should never be undertaken except to prevent, in a clear case, the injustice which results from fraud or inequitable conduct, and whenever doubt on this point exists the requirements of these statutes should be strictly adhered to and enforced. . . ." Cottrell v. Nurnberger, 131 W.Va. 391, 411, 47 S.E.2d 454, 463 (1948).

4. Many cases treat part performance in terms of estoppel. In Transport Management Company v. American Radiator and Standard Sanitary Corporation, 326 F.2d 62, 65 (3d Cir.1963), the plaintiff argued equitable estoppel because the agents of the defendant had allegedly assured the plaintiff a written contract was unnecessary. The court found both parties were aware that the oral discussions were to be reduced to writing before a binding agreement would be executed. "There is no indication in the New Jersey authorities that the bar of the statute of frauds may be avoided on the theory of estoppel by circumstances which would not qualify as part performance. . . . In any event, estoppel requires the showing of an assumption of a position by representation or act by one party upon which the other has rightfully relied, to an extent which would render unjust its repudiation by the first party."

5. Near the end of the principal case, Justice Cardozo noted that it was "not a case of fraud. . . . No inducement has been offered with the preconceived intention that it would later be ignored." In Darby v. Johnson, 477 So.2d 322 (Ala.1985), the court said, "[E]quity may intervene, even though the part performance requirement is not met, when fraud operates from the beginning—that is, when the breaching party procured the land or purchase money with no intent to perform the oral agreement admitted to have been made. The cases further require that this fraud be clearly shown. Equity will not intervene when the party merely refuses to perform."

HICKEY [1] v. GREEN

Appeals Court of Massachusetts, Plymouth, 1982.
14 Mass.App.Ct. 671, 442 N.E.2d 37.

CUTTER, JUSTICE.

This case is before us on a stipulation of facts (with various attached documents). A Superior Court judge has adopted the agreed facts as "findings." We are in the same position as was the trial judge (who received no evidence and saw and heard no witnesses).[2]

Mrs. Gladys Green owns a lot (Lot S) in the Manomet section of Plymouth. In July, 1980, she advertised it for sale. On July 11 and 12, Hickey and his wife discussed with Mrs. Green purchasing Lot S and "orally agreed to a sale" for $15,000. Mrs. Green on July 12 accepted a deposit check of $500, marked by Hickey on the back, "Deposit on Lot . . . Massasoit Ave. Manomet . . . Subject to Variance from Town of Plymouth." Mrs. Green's brother and agent "was under the impression that a zoning variance was needed and [had] advised . . . Hickey to write" the quoted language on the deposit check. It turned out, however, by July 16 that no variance would be required. Hickey had left the payee line of the deposit check blank, because of uncertainty whether Mrs. Green or her brother was to receive the check and asked "Mrs. Green to fill in the appropriate name." Mrs. Green held the check, did not fill in the payee's name, and neither cashed nor endorsed it. Hickey "stated to Mrs. Green that his intention was to sell his home and build on Mrs. Green's lot."

"Relying upon the arrangements . . . with Mrs. Green," the Hickeys advertised their house on Sachem Road in newspapers on three days in July, 1980, and agreed with a purchaser for its sale and took from him a deposit check for $500 which they deposited in their own account.[3] On July 24, Mrs. Green told Hickey that she "no longer intended to sell her property to him" but had decided to sell to another for $16,000. Hickey told Mrs. Green that he had already sold his house and offered her $16,000 for Lot S. Mrs. Green refused this offer.

The Hickeys filed this complaint seeking specific performance. Mrs. Green asserts that relief is barred by the Statute of Frauds contained in G.L. c. 259, § 1. The trial judge granted specific performance.[4] Mrs. Green has appealed.

The present rule applicable in most jurisdictions in the United States is succinctly set forth in Restatement (Second) of Contracts,

1. His wife Patricia E. Hickey.

2. This record presents what, at least under our prior practice, would have been regarded as a "case stated." See Quinton Vespa Co., Inc. v. Construction Serv. Co., 343 Mass. 547, 551–552, 179 N.E.2d 895 (1962); Robbins v. Department of Pub. Works, 355 Mass. 328, 244 N.E.2d 577 (1969). Compare Mass.R.A.P. 8(d), as amended, 378 Mass. 934 (1979).

3. On the back of the check was noted above the Hickeys' signatures endorsing the check "Deposit on Purchase of property at Sachem Rd. and First St., Manomet, Ma. Sale price, $44,000."

4. The judgment ordered Mrs. Green to convey Lot S to the Hickeys but, probably by inadvertence, it failed to include an order that it be conveyed only upon payment by the grantees of the admittedly agreed price of $15,000.

§ 129 (1981).[5] The section reads, "A contract for the transfer of an interest in land may be specifically enforced notwithstanding failure to comply with the Statute of Frauds if it is established that the party seeking enforcement, *in reasonable reliance on the contract* and on the continuing assent of the party against whom enforcement is sought, *has so changed his position that injustice can be avoided only by specific enforcement*" (emphasis supplied).[6] The earlier Massachusetts decisions laid down somewhat strict requirements for an estoppel precluding the assertion of the Statute of Frauds. . . . Frequently there has been an actual change of possession and improvement of the transferred property, as well as full payment of the full purchase price, or one or more of these elements.

It is stated in Park, Real Estate Law, § 883, at 334, that the "more recent decisions . . . indicate a trend on the part of the [supreme judicial c]ourt to find that the circumstances warrant specific performance." This appears to be a correct perception. . . .

The present facts reveal a simple case of a proposed purchase of a residential vacant lot, where the vendor, Mrs. Green, knew that the Hickeys were planning to sell their former home (possibly to obtain funds to pay her) and build on Lot S. The Hickeys, relying on Mrs. Green's oral promise, moved rapidly to make their sale without obtaining any adequate memorandum of the terms of what appears to have been intended to be a quick cash sale of Lot S. So rapid was action by the Hickeys that, by July 21, less than ten days after giving their deposit to Mrs. Green, they had accepted a deposit check for the sale of their house, endorsed the check, and placed it in their bank account. Above their signatures endorsing the check was a memorandum probably sufficient to satisfy the Statute of Frauds under A.B.C. Auto Parts, Inc. v. Moran, 359 Mass. 327, 329–331, 268 N.E.2d 844 (1971). Cf. Guarino v. Zyfers, 9 Mass.App. 874, 401 N.E.2d 857 (1980). At the very least, the Hickeys had bound themselves in a manner in which, to avoid a transfer of their own house, they might have had to

5. The late Mr. Justice Braucher, prior to his appointment to the Supreme Judicial Court, was the reporter for the Restatement (Second) of Contracts when the language of what is now § 129 was drafted; see Tent. Draft No. 4, § 197 (1968). The section appears to be consistent with Massachusetts law.

6. Comments *a* and *b* to § 129, read (in part): "*a* . . . This section restates what is widely known as the 'part performance doctrine.' Part performance is not an accurate designation of such acts as taking possession and making improvements when the contract does not provide for such acts, but such acts regularly bring the doctrine into play. The doctrine is contrary to the words of the Statute of Frauds, but it was established by English courts of equity soon after the enactment of the Statute. Payment of purchase-money, without more, was once thought sufficient to justify specific enforcement, but a contrary view now prevails, since in such cases restitution is an adequate remedy . . . . Enforcement has . . . been justified on the ground that repudiation after 'part performance' amounts to a 'virtual fraud.' A more accurate statement is that courts with equitable powers are vested by tradition with what in substance is a dispensing power based on the promisee's reliance, *a discretion to be exercised with caution* in the light of all the circumstances . . . [emphasis supplied].

"*b* . . . Two distinct elements enter into the application of the rule of this Section: first, the extent to which the evidentiary function of the statutory formalities is fulfilled by the conduct of the parties; second, the reliance of the promisee, providing a compelling substantive basis for relief in addition to the expectations created by the promise."

engage in expensive litigation. No attorney has been shown to have been used either in the transaction between Mrs. Green and the Hickeys or in that between the Hickeys and their purchaser.

There is no denial by Mrs. Green of the oral contract between her and the Hickeys. This, under § 129 of the Restatement, is of some significance.[9] There can be no doubt (a) that Mrs. Green made the promise on which the Hickeys so promptly relied, and also (b) she, nearly as promptly, but not promptly enough, repudiated it because she had a better opportunity. The stipulated facts require the conclusion that in equity Mrs. Green's conduct cannot be condoned. This is not a case where either party is shown to have contemplated the negotiation of a purchase and sale agreement. If a written agreement had been expected, even by only one party, or would have been natural (because of the participation by lawyers or otherwise), a different situation might have existed. It is a permissible inference from the agreed facts that the rapid sale of the Hickeys' house was both appropriate and expected. These are not circumstances where negotiations fairly can be seen as inchoate. Compare Tull v. Mister Donut Development Corp., 7 Mass.App. 626, 630–632, 389 N.E.2d 447 (1979).

We recognize that specific enforcement of Mrs. Green's promise to convey Lot S may well go somewhat beyond the circumstances considered in the *Fisher* case, 332 Mass. 727, and in the *Orlando* case, 337 Mass. 157, 148 N.E.2d 373, where specific performance was granted. It may seem (perhaps because the present facts are less complicated) to extend the principles stated in the *Cellucci* case (see esp. 2 Mass.App. at 728, 320 N.E.2d 919). We recognize also the cautionary language about granting specific performance in comment *a* to § 129 of the Restatement (see note 6, supra). No public interest behind G.L. 259, § 1, however, in the simple circumstances before us, will be violated if Mrs. Green fairly is held to her precise bargain by principles of equitable estoppel, subject to the considerations mentioned below.

Over two years have passed since July, 1980, and over a year since the trial judge's findings were filed on July 6, 1981. At that time, the principal agreed facts of record bearing upon the extent of the injury to the Hickeys (because of their reliance on Mrs. Green's promise to convey Lot S) were those based on the Hickeys' new obligation to convey their house to a purchaser. Performance of that agreement had been extended to May 1, 1981. If that agreement has been abrogated or modified since the trial, the case may take on a different posture. If enforcement of that agreement still will be sought, or if that agreement

9. Comment *d* of Restatement (Second) of Contracts, § 129, reads "*d*. . . . Where specific enforcement is rested on a transfer of possession plus either part payment of the price or the making of improvements, it is commonly said that the action taken by the purchaser must be unequivocally referable to the oral agreement. But this requirement is not insisted on *if the making of the promise is admitted or is clearly proved.* The promisee *must act in reasonable reliance on the promise, before the promisor has repudiated* it, and the action must be such that the remedy of restitution is inadequate. If these requirements are met, *neither taking of possession nor payment of money nor the making of improvements is essential* . . ." (emphasis supplied).

has been carried out, the conveyance of Lot S by Mrs. Green should be required now.

The case, in any event, must be remanded to the trial judge for the purpose of amending the judgment to require conveyance of Lot S by Mrs. Green only upon payment to her in cash within a stated period of the balance of the agreed price of $15,000. The trial judge, however, in her discretion and upon proper offers of proof by counsel, may reopen the record to receive, in addition to the presently stipulated facts, a stipulation or evidence concerning the present status of the Hickeys' apparent obligation to sell their house. If the circumstances have changed, it will be open to the trial judge to require of Mrs. Green, instead of specific performance, only full restitution to the Hickeys of all costs reasonably caused to them in respect of these transactions (including advertising costs, deposits, and their reasonable costs for this litigation) with interest. The case is remanded to the Superior Court Department for further action consistent with this opinion. The Hickeys are to have costs of this appeal.

So ordered.

NOTE

Was there a sufficient memorandum to take this oral contract out of the Statute of Frauds without invoking the doctrines of part performance and equitable estoppel? (See cases in the next sub-section.) How significant is the fact that Mrs. Green did not deny the existence of the oral contract? How can she admit the contract and still hope to succeed by pleading the Statute of Frauds? Were the Hickeys legally bound to complete the oral contract for the sale of *their* house?

PEARSON v. GARDNER

Supreme Court of Michigan, 1918.
202 Mich. 360, 168 N.W. 485, L.R.A.1918F, 384.

BROOKE, J. Bill for specific performance. On June 6, 1917, defendants entered into an oral contract with the plaintiff for the purchase of a house and lot in the village of Hamburg. At the time of the purchase the plaintiff gave the defendants the following receipt:

"Hamburg, Michigan, June 6 [there is a 6 and a 7 over it], 1917. Received of Edd Gardner and Della Gardner one hundred dollars ($100) on purchase price of house and lot in Hamburg village. Balance of eighteen hundred dollars ($1,800) to be paid and deed given in five days.

A. H. Pearson."

The $100 mentioned in said receipt was paid by defendants to plaintiff. Under the oral contract the plaintiff, a physician and surgeon, agreed to rent from the defendants a small office building located on one corner of the lot for a period of one year with an option for one additional year at $5 per month. The $60 for the first year's rent to be deducted from the purchase price. Plaintiff immediately vacated the house and three days later on the morning of the 10th defendants took possession of the house and the barn located on the premises.

It is the claim of plaintiff that he and his wife had executed a deed of the property, and on the 5th day after the agreement told defendants it was ready, but that he was advised by them that their money was in a bank in Detroit and would not be available for a few days; that shortly thereafter defendant Della Gardner was called away because of the illness of a relative, and remained absent for some time. This was denied by the defendants. The record shows that there was considerable discussion between the parties about carrying out the deal up to the latter part of July, when the defendants finally refused to further proceed. Thereupon plaintiff prepared a new deed, the former one having been destroyed, and on the first day of August made a tender of the deed, the unexpired insurance policy and the abstract of title. A second tender was made on August 10th, in the presence of a witness. Performance on the part of the defendants was again refused. In the meantime the defendants had continued in the possession of the property, had removed one of the partitions on the lower floor of the dwelling house, making two rooms into one, changed the location of the kitchen sink, trimmed the lower limbs from a couple of shade trees in front of the house, and had harvested the vegetables from the garden. They continued in possession and retained the same at the time of the trial in the court below on the 12th day of December, 1917.

It is conceded by counsel for plaintiff that the written evidence of the contract is insufficient under the statute of frauds. The only question involved is whether the defendants by their acts in making partial payment, taking possession, reaping the fruits of the garden, and changing the character of the premises, have done sufficient to take the case out of the statute and to equitably entitle plaintiff to the decree for specific performance which was awarded by the court below. Partial payment of the purchase price alone is not sufficient to take the case out of the statute. Possession alone is insufficient, but where there is partial payment and possession accompanied by acts of ownership of the vendee changing the character of the freehold, and lessening its value, a court of equity may award a decree for specific performance. Peckham v. Balch, 49 Mich. 179, 13 N.W. 506; Cole v. Cole Realty Co., 169 Mich. 347, 135 N.W. 329. It is true that in the case cited the action was brought by the vendee rather than the vendor, but it is well settled that specific performance is granted in favor of the vendor of land as freely as in favor of the vendee, though the relief actually obtained by him is the recovery of money, the purchase price. The rule is stated in 36 Cyc. p. 686, as follows:

"The vendor or lessor may have specific performance of a contract which has been part performed. This is in part because the delivery of possession by him to the vendee involves a change of condition on his part as well as on the part of the vendee, and points to a contract concerning the land; chiefly because, in cases where the remedy is available to the vendee, it should, on the ground of mutuality, be available to the vendor likewise"—citing cases in note 24.

See, also, Pomeroy's Equitable Remedies, vol. 2, § 747, and Langdell, Brief Survey of Equity Jurisdiction, pp. 50–52.

The parties agree as to the exact terms of the oral contract. The defendants entered into possession thereunder and still retain such possession. They paid a portion of the purchase price, and have exercised such rights and acts of dominion over the property in changing its character as would in our opinion make it inequitable for them now to decline full performance of the oral contract.

The decree is affirmed.

NOTES

1. The vendor sought specific performance of an agreement to sell real estate. A memorandum had been signed by the vendor but not by the purchaser. Deeds were executed by the vendor and placed in escrow to be delivered upon payment of the purchase price. The purchaser made part payment, entered into possession, planted a substantial garden, and by separate contract purchased the household furniture. Later the purchaser abandoned the premises and returned the key. Decree for the vendor. *Reversed.* "There was no such part performance on the part of the defendant as would give the plaintiff the right to demand specific performance of the unwritten contract. The defendant entered into possession and planted the garden, but he made no substantial repairs on the premises, and did nothing that amounted sufficiently to part performance to take the case out of the statute of frauds . . . ."

"Even if there were evidence of part performance by the defendant, this would not entitle the plaintiff to specific performance. Equity will not permit the statute of frauds to become an instrument of fraud, and to prevent injustice it will decree specific performance in favor of one who, acting on an oral agreement for the conveyance of land, enters into possession and makes substantial improvements. In such circumstances it would be a fraud on the purchaser to deprive him of the benefit of the contract. But the other party to the contract cannot rely on the part performance of the buyer to enforce performance. 'If the party who resists the enforcement of the contract chooses not to stand on what he has done under and in pursuance of it, the other party cannot be aided by it.'" Palumbo v. James, 266 Mass. 1, 3, 164 N.E. 466, 467 (1929), discussed in 38 Yale L.J. 821 (1929), 13 Minn.L.Rev. 519 (1929).

2. What do the cases of Pearson v. Gardner and Palumbo v. James add to your understanding of the rationale behind the doctrines of part performance and equitable estoppel? Why should the non-performing party *ever* be able to rely on the acts of part performance of the other party? In Hickey v. Green, could Mrs. Green have enforced the oral contract against the Hickeys if *they* had decided not to perform? Consider whether the rationale of these exceptions to the strict language of the Statute of Frauds is based on some proof that a contract must have existed or is based on Pomeroy's "equitable fraud" or the Hickey v. Green doctrine of equitable estoppel. Are these rationales

mutually exclusive or do they overlap? Does it make any difference which rationale a court adopts?

B. THE WRITTEN MEMORANDUM

WARD v. MATTUSCHEK

Supreme Court of Montana, 1958.
134 Mont. 307, 330 P.2d 971.

VICTOR H. FALL, DISTRICT JUDGE (sitting in place of BOTTOMLY, JUSTICE).

The facts presented by this appeal are:

Otto and Frank Mattuschek are bachelors, owners of and reside on a ranch in Fergus County, Montana, consisting of about 3,540 acres. For many years past they have operated the ranch as a grain and stock enterprise.

E. F. Carnell is a licensed real estate broker at Lewistown, Montana, the county seat of Fergus County. Having heard that the Mattuschek ranch might be for sale, he drove out to the place on or about May 14, 1953, and talked to the Mattuschek "boys". As a result of that conversation the following instrument was executed:

"Plaintiff's Exhibit 'A'
"Appointment of Agent

"I hereby appoint E. F. Carnell of Lewistown, Montana whose office is located in said City and State, my agent with the exclusive right to sell the following property:

"Our Ranch property 3540 acres, T. 23 & 22–R–19 & 20–Fergus County Mont. ______

"For the sum of $30,000.

"Conditions and terms of the sale are as follows:

"Cash to seller. possession Dec. 1–1953, seller retain 5% landowner Royalty. seller pay 1953 taxes, seller transfers all lease land to Buyer.

"And I agree to furnish a title as outlined in the following paragraph A ______

"A. An abstract of title showing a good merchantable title to said property together with a warranty deed properly executed

~~"B. A Tax Title~~
~~"C. A Bargain and Sales Title~~

"Said sale may be made for a less amount if hereafter authorized by me; you are further authorized to receive a deposit on the sale price. I agree to pay a commission of $1000–on the sale price and the commission shall be payable as soon as the sale is made and a down payment has been made, or sale price paid in full at the time of sale, and, or as soon as a binder fee has been collected on the sale, whichever be first.

"This authorization is to remain in effect and full force for 30 days and thereafter until revoked by me in writing.

"Dated at Lewistown, Montana this 14th day of May 1953—

"x Otto Mattuschek

"x Frank Mattuschek"

A few days later Carnell met a party by the name of Ward with whom he was acquainted and attempted to "sell" the Mattuschek ranch to Ward. After some discussion, and on May 20, 1953, Ward agreed to buy the place for $30,000 and gave his check to Carnell for $2,500 as a "binder". The check, Plaintiff's Exhibit "B", is as follows:

"Plaintiff's Exhibit 'B'

"1st Bank Stock Corporation

93–73
921

First National Bank of Lewistown

Lewistown, Montana, May 20 1953

No. ______

Pay To The Order of ______ Red Carnell ______ $2500xx 00

______ twenty five hundred and no/100 ______ Dollars

"s/s E. E. Ward

"For down payment on land

"Mattuschek

"(Endorsement E. F. Carnell)"

At the same time he executed Plaintiff's Exhibit "C" which reads as follows:

"Plaintiff's Exhibit 'C'

"(Defendant's Exhibit No. 1)

Real Estate	Fergus Realty	City Property
Insurance	213 Main St. Phone 598	Farms
Rentals	Lewistown, Montana	Ranches

May 20–1953—

"I hereby agree to buy the Mattuschek place in accordance with the terms of the agreement between E. F. Carnell and the Mattuschecks Dated May 14, 1953.

"/s/E. E. Ward

"To Buy Or Sell—See 'Red' Carnell"

Immediately thereafter, Carnell drove out to the ranch and advised Frank and Otto Mattuschek that he had "closed" a deal and sold the ranch to Ward. Otto then asked Carnell if Ward would lease back to them the "farm" land. Carnell returned to town and asked Ward about this and after learning that such arrangement was agreeable, drove back again to the ranch and advised the Mattuscheks that Ward would lease them the farm land. A meeting was then arranged to be held in Carnell's office in Lewistown to close the mechanics of the sale to Ward and the lease back to the Mattuscheks. Out of this meeting a disagreement arose resulting in the refusal of the Mattuscheks to convey to Ward. An action was brought by Ward against the Mattuscheks seeking specific performance and for damages. The action was tried to the court sitting without a jury. Upon conclusion of the trial, the court refused the proposed findings and conclusions of each party and made and entered its own. The facts recited above were all found by the court to be true, and in addition, there was a finding that the reasonable annual rental value of the Mattuschek ranch is $2,500.

The court, among others, made the following conclusion of law: "That the plaintiff has failed to produce any note or memorandum in writing which is subscribed by the defendants or their authorized agent sufficient to satisfy the requirements of Sections 13–606 and 93–1401–7 R.C.M. of 1947 with respect to the agreement or sale of real property alleged by plaintiff." And as a result held that plaintiff is not entitled to relief. Judgment and decree was entered accordingly. This appeal is from such judgment.

One of the questions presented is whether the writings (Plaintiff's Exhibits "A", "B" and "C") are sufficient to take the case out of the Statute of Frauds.

R.C.M.1947, § 13–606, insofar as pertinent here, reads as follows:

"What contracts must be in writing. The following contracts are invalid, unless the same, or some note or memorandum thereof, be in writing and subscribed by the party to be charged, or his agent: . . ..

"5. An agreement . . . for the sale of real property, or of an interest therein; and such agreement, if made by an agent of the party sought to be charged, is invalid, unless the authority of the agent be in writing, subscribed by the party sought to be charged.

"6. An agreement authorizing or employing an agent or broker to purchase or sell real estate for compensation or a commission."

R.C.M.1947, § 93–1401–7, insofar as pertinent, reads as follows:

"Agreement not in writing—when invalid. In the following cases the agreement is invalid, unless the same or some note or memorandum thereof be in writing, and subscribed by the party charged, or by his agent; evidence, therefore, of the agreement cannot be received without the writing or secondary evidence of its contents: . . ..

"5. An agreement for . . . the sale of real property, or of an interest therein; and such agreement, if made by an agent of the party sought to be charged, is invalid, unless the authority of the agent be in writing, subscribed by the party sought to be charged."

Few more fruitful sources of litigation can be found than that arising out of brokerage contracts relating to the sale of real estate. The annotations found at 48 A.L.R. 634, and 43 A.L.R.2d 1014, illustrate the point.

Much of the briefs and a great part of oral argument was directed toward the question of the right of a real estate broker to enter into a contract for the sale of the seller's land. As we view it, for reasons hereinafter stated, that is not before this court on this appeal.

The note or memorandum must name the parties. It may consist of several writings. Johnson v. Elliot, 123 Mont. 597, 605, 218 P.2d 703.

The note or memorandum must contain all the essentials of the contract but may be stated in general terms. Dineen v. Sullivan, 123 Mont. 195, 213 P.2d 241.

With the foregoing principles of law in mind, an examination of Plaintiff's Exhibits "A", "B" and "C" shows the following:

The respondents Mattuscheks unqualifiedly and exclusively agreed in writing to permit Carnell for a period of thirty days to sell their ranch for $30,000 for which they agreed to pay Carnell a commission of $1,000. The terms of sale were succinctly but adequately stated in these words: "Cash to seller. possession Dec. 1–1953, seller retain 5% land-owner, Royalty. seller pay 1953 taxes, seller transfers all lease land to buyer."

The acceptance of Ward was in writing (Plaintiff's Exhibit "C"), and accompanied by a check (Plaintiff's Exhibit "B") as a down payment. It was unqualified. It is difficult to conceive of a more clear-cut offer and acceptance in writing than is evidenced in the exhibits above set forth. This is not a situation of a broker making a contract for the seller at all—it is simply a situation of a buyer executing, in writing, an unqualified acceptance of a seller's offer to sell.

This court said in Steen v. Rustad, Mont.1957, 313 P.2d 1014, 1018: "It is well established that a court, in interpreting a written instrument, will not isolate certain phrases of that instrument in order to garner the intent of the parties, but will grasp the instrument by its four corners and in the light of the entire instrument, ascertain the paramount and guiding intention of the parties. Mere isolated tracts, clauses and words will not be allowed to prevail over the general language utilized in the instrument. [citing cases.]"

The further question has been presented that the offer executed by the Mattuscheks fails insofar as this plaintiff is concerned because of lack of mutuality, i.e., that Ward did not sign the contract executed by the Mattuscheks. Ordinarily, both parties to a written agreement execute it, but that is not always necessary. "While an agreement signed by one party only, without other evidence of obligation on, or acceptance by, the other party, will ordinarily be regarded as unilateral, mutuality does not require that both parties sign the contract, and if a contract signed by one party is acted upon by the other a binding agreement may result." 17 C.J.S. Contracts § 100, pp. 443, 454. In support of this statement this court's opinion in Orem v. Hansen Packing Co., 91 Mont. 222, 7 P.2d 546, 549, is cited. In that case this court said: " . . . plaintiff contends that the letter, Defendant's Exhibit 1, is not a contract because it is signed by only one party, and hence lacking in mutuality. It is signed, however, by the only party affected and bound by it, and it constituted a written offer by plaintiff."

Again, in 37 C.J.S. Frauds, Statute of § 206, p. 698, we find the following language: "The two general rules as to the party or parties who must sign the memorandum are that a party not signing the memorandum cannot be charged on the contract, and that the only signature made necessary by the statute [of frauds] is that of the party to be charged, or, in other words, defendant in the action or the party against whom the contract is to be enforced. Mutuality of obligation is not essential to the validity of a contract, in so far as its compliance with the statute of frauds is concerned, and the fact that the contract may not be enforceable against one party, because not subscribed by him, is no defense to the other, by whom it is signed."

Under the topic Specific Performance, 81 C.J.S. § 12, pp. 434, 435, we find the following language: "The rule was established soon after the enactment of the statute of frauds, that a contract, the memorandum of which was signed by the defendant, *may be specifically enforced by a plaintiff who has not signed,* notwithstanding because of the lack of such signature the contract could not be enforced against plaintiff, either in law or in equity, up to the time of the commencement of the suit, since the requisite mutuality is supplied by complainant's filing of his bill." This is supported by the citing of cases from several jurisdictions and among them the case of Johnson v. Elliot, 123 Mont. 597, 604, 218 P.2d 703, 707, wherein this court said: "The plaintiff who had not signed the contract supplied the necessary mutuality of obligation by the institution of the action on the contract." . . .

Nor can objection be made on the part of the defendants that their offer was not intended for this particular plaintiff and hence, fails for lack of mutuality. It is the rule that if the memorandum is otherwise sufficient it is binding for the purpose of satisfying the statute of frauds, "even though it is not intended for, or addressed, delivered, or known to, the other contracting party." 37 C.J.S. Frauds, Statute of § 173 d, p. 651.

However, all this is somewhat beside the point for the reason that the plaintiff, as pointed out above, accepted the offer of defendants, in writing and without qualification.

. . .

The judgment of the court below is reversed with instructions to enter "Conclusions of Law" in accordance with the views expressed herein; to enter judgment and decree for specific performance, and to award damages.

HARRISON, C. J., and CASTLES and ANGSTMAN, JJ., concur.

ADAIR, JUSTICE.

I dissent.

The instrument designated "Appointment of Agent" between the real estate agent, E. F. Carnell, and signed by Otto and Frank Mattuschek is simply a thirty day listing agreement. It does not constitute a power of attorney. It does not authorize the real estate agent to execute or deliver in the name of the Mattuscheks any deed of conveyance or any contract for sale and purchase. It is purely and simply an agreement between the real estate agent and the owners of the 3,540 acre ranch. Should the Mattuscheks wrongfully fail to perform their part of the agreement, the only loss to the real estate agent would be his commission of $1,000 to become due him upon a sale by the Mattuscheks of their property. Such would be the extent of the real estate agent's damage and it could be fully satisfied by the payment of money so that the extraordinary remedy of specific performance would neither be authorized nor available.

The Mattuscheks' listing agreement was with the real estate agent Carnell and not with Carnell's prospective purchaser for the property, and in my opinion Carnell's prospective purchaser, E. E. Ward, has no right of action for specific performance against the Mattuscheks to compel them by court decree to make an involuntary conveyance to him of their ranch and holdings.

In my opinion, the judgment of the district court was correct and it should be affirmed.

NOTES

1. Many cases involve the necessity for a proper signature. In Tzitzon Realty Co. Inc. v. Mustonen, 352 Mass. 648, 227 N.E.2d 493 (1967) the court held that a land contract did not violate the Statute of Frauds where the memorandum was signed only by the vendor-husband and not by the vendor-wife, since the husband signed in the wife's presence, with her consent, and since it was the intention of both that his signature represented her as well. To the same effect, see Fleckenstein v. Faccio, Alaska, 619 P.2d 1016 (1980).

In Cottom v. Kennedy, 140 Ill.App.3d 290, 94 Ill.Dec. 683, 488 N.E.2d 682 (1986), defendant buyers claimed that plaintiff sellers could not specifically enforce a land contract because the person who signed the contract for plaintiffs lacked authority to bind them. The court rejected the argument, saying, "[T]he only signature made necessary by the statute [of frauds] is that of the party to be charged. . . . It is no defense . . . that such a contract lacks mutuality of obligation in that it is not enforceable against the other, non-signing party. Rather, by bringing suit on the contract to enforce it, the non-signing party has bound himself and thereby rendered the contract mutual."

Even though properly signed, the memorandum may fail if both the vendor and the purchaser are not properly identified. Thus, in

Kohlbrecher v. Guettermann, 329 Ill. 246, 251, 160 N.E. 142, 144 (1928) the memo read: "Dec. 9, 1921. For the sum of forty-four hundred dollars, I, the undersigned, agree to sell my property, located at the corner of Second and Washington known as No. 102 South Second, paid in hand fifty dollars as earnest money." This writing was signed by the vendor by her son, in her presence and by her direction. Although the memo was properly signed by the party to be charged the court held it insufficient for failure to identify the purchaser. " 'The memorandum must state who are the parties to the contract, either by naming them or by so designating or describing them that they may be recognized or identified without fair or reasonable doubt or dispute. It must contain the names or sufficient descriptions of both parties to the contract, not only the person to be charged but also the person in whose favor he is to be charged.' . . . 'The reason upon which this rule is founded is that unless the names of both parties appear the contract may be foisted upon any one by perjury, which is the very thing that the Statute of Frauds was enacted to prevent.' " Justice Cardozo, in his characteristic style, wrote in a similar case, "There is nothing more than an offer lanced into the void." Irvmor Corp. v. Rodewald, 253 N.Y. 472, 476, 171 N.E. 747, 748, 70 A.L.R. 192 (1930).

Suppose the "signature" of one party is the typewritten signature on a telegram, is that sufficient? Yes, according to Hillstrom v. Gosnay, 188 Mont. 388, 614 P.2d 466 (1980). The telegram sent by the vendor to the purchaser stated, "please consider this my written acceptance," and the wording of the telegram was dictated by the purchaser to the real estate agent and then to the vendor. This established the vendor's intent to authenticate her typewritten name on the telegram and the Statute of Frauds was satisfied.

2. It is clear that a sufficient memorandum must describe the land adequately. But what is an adequate description? In Corrado v. Montuori, 49 R.I. 78, 81, 139 A. 791, 792 (1928) the following was held sufficient: "December 30, 1925. Providence, R. I. We, the undersigned, agree to sell to Antonio Corrado and Maria Corrado and they agree to buy a certain lot situated on Gillen Street in Providence, Rhode Island, for the sum of $1,525.00 (fifteen hundred twenty-five dollars) free and clear of all incumbrances; Warranty Deed to be given for the said lot on January 2, 1927."

"Nicola Montuori

Carmela Montuori

Anthony Corrado"

"Signed in the presence of T. De Cesare."

The evidence showed that the vendor owned no other land on Gillen Street. Said the court: "When two men, not dealers in real estate, negotiate for the sale of a certain lot on a definite street in a named city, of which lot one of them is the owner, and carry their bargain to the point where the purchaser pays the seller the full purchase price, it may reasonably be inferred that the seller is intending to deal with land which he owns and not with some indefinite parcel which he may later purchase."

In Guel v. Bullock, 127 Ill.App.3d 36, 82 Ill.Dec. 264, 468 N.E.2d 811 (1984), the contract described the subject property only as "8427 S. Euclid," with no reference to city or state. The trial court granted defendant seller summary judgment, but the appellate court reversed: "If it is apparent from the writing that a term has been agreed upon, parol evidence may be introduced to clear up any ambiguity. . . . [P]laintiff may be able to establish that defendant Bullock has an interest in only one parcel of real estate which is designated as '8427 S. Euclid' and that that parcel is located in Chicago, Illinois."

Contrast the memo in Hertel v. Woodard, 183 Or. 99, 101, 191 P.2d 400, 401 (1948). "May 10, 1947. Received from Lucky Hertel $80.00 Eighty Dollars earnest money on lot and house number 960 Union Street. Price $5000 Five Thousand and—balance of $4,920.00 to be paid when papers and title insurance are completed. It is understood this deal would be closed and house vacated on or before June the 10th. All furniture except personal belongings included in this transaction." The court sustained a demurrer based on the inadequacy of the memo. "It will be observed that the paper does not mention the city, county or state in which the property is located. . . . Possibly it may be argued that since people normally do not sell property which they do not own, and since this court has sustained such descriptions as 'my farm' . . . and 'my property' . . ., the word 'my' should be inserted by implication in front of 'lot and house' where that term appears in the writing. 'The general opinion is that no such implication is permissible' says Wigmore on Evidence, 3d Ed., § 2476. It is clear that we cannot indulge in the implication which is needed to sustain the writing."

This strict approach to the description requirement continues to be followed in some recent cases. See for example Martin v. Seigel, 35 Wash.2d 223, 212 P.2d 107 (1949) commented on in 27 Wash.L.Rev. 166 (1952), where the court required the description of the property by lot number, block, addition, city, county, and state. In Wilson v. Wilson, 134 Ind.App. 655, 190 N.E.2d 667 (1963) the court held insufficient a description of land as 137 acres in a certain township in a particular county of the state which failed to identify the exact 137 acres. "Though the recent trend is for American courts to liberally interpret the Statute of Frauds, we believe that a decision to the contrary would completely abrogate a statute of our legislative branch. . . ."

See also McDaniel v. Silvernail, 37 Ill.App.3d 884, 346 N.E.2d 382 (1976) where the court held the following memo inadequate: "I agree to sell to George McDaniel the house on R. R. 2 in which he now lives, plus two acres, xxx for $6,000. to be agreed.

Alfreda Silvernail

Rent of $70 monthly to be applied as purchase price—less taxes and Ins."

The description was too indefinite because the vendor owned 600 acres at the time the contract was made. The court refused to allow parol evidence to cure a "patent ambiguity".

In Barker v. Francis, 741 P.2d 548 (Utah App.1987), Barker was to receive the Francises' ranch—except for 40 acres to be designated by the Francises, which they were to retain—in exchange for $600,000 and 80 acres of Barker's 150–acre farm. In holding that there was an enforceable contract, the appellate court said, "The trial court properly received extrinsic evidence to show that the parties had agreed upon which 80 acres owned by Barker were intended to be transferred to" the Francises. With respect to the 40 unspecified acres to be retained by Barker, the court stated, "If a contract grants one party the exclusive right to select the land involved, the contract is sufficiently definite to enforce."

3. In most states the Statute of Frauds applies to real estate brokerage contracts and many of the same problems covered in this section on the real estate contract arise in the broker's agreement. For example, the adequacy of the description or designation of the property is often in issue. See Owen v. Hendricks, 433 S.W.2d 164, 30 A.L.R.3d 929 (Tex.1968). In some states, the Statute does not apply to real estate brokerage contracts and the broker's agreement may be oral although the contract between the vendor and purchaser remains subject to the provisions of the Statute.

KING v. WENGER

Supreme Court of Kansas, 1976.
219 Kan. 668, 549 P.2d 986.

FROMME, JUSTICE. This is an action for specific performance of an agreement for the sale of real estate. The action was tried to the court and judgment was rendered in favor of all defendants. The plaintiff Ward E. King has appealed.

The real estate in controversy consists of approximately 160 acres of land in Brown County, Kansas. The defendants Loraine Wenger and Lorene Ralston each owned an undivided half interest in the property subject to a life estate in their mother, Ethel Wenger. Ethel Wenger's health was failing and she discussed the advisability of selling this land with her daughters. They agreed it should be sold and Loraine Wenger approached the plaintiff to have him appraise the land for sale. The plaintiff declined but expressed a desire to purchase the property.

The mother, Ethel Wenger, was hospitalized in Holton, Kansas. The plaintiff visited her in the hospital on December 26, 1972, and discussed his prospects for purchasing the land. The daughter, Loraine Wenger, also visited her mother in Holton on that day and met the plaintiff at the hospital. All three discussed the sale of the property and the mother, Ethel Wenger, indicated that she was willing to release her interest so the land might be sold.

The sale of the land to plaintiff was further considered and a purchase price of $16,000.00 was agreed on. The plaintiff and Loraine decided it would be helpful to contact the other sister, Lorene Ralston, by telephone. She lived in Colorado. Both the plaintiff and Loraine spoke with Mrs. Ralston over the telephone and the terms of the sale were discussed and agreed on in a general way.

Immediately following the telephone conversation the plaintiff King and Loraine Wenger sat in Loraine Wenger's car while she wrote out an agreement in longhand on a piece of paper. This agreement which gives rise to the present action is as follows:

"Agreed date 12–26–72

"N ½, NW ¼, Sec. 14, Twp. 4, Range 15
"W ½, NE ¼ " " " 4, " 15

"Sale price $16,000.00 + maximum of $250.00 closing costs for 160 acres of land as situated above.

"Earnest payment of $1,000.00 made of this date which would be returned to purchaser in case of failure to clear abstract or deliver merchantable title.

"Additional down payment of $3,000.00 to be made as date of delivery of acceptable title to buyer.

"Payments of $2,000.00 annually commencing one year from date of down payment plus five percent annual interest on unpaid balance until paid in full.

Seller:
x Loraine E. Wenger
Ward King buyer x Loraine E. Wenger for Lorene E. Ralston"

It was agreed at the time the agreement was signed that the parties would meet that same afternoon in the office of the plaintiff's attorney, Robert Gernon, where a formal contract for sale of the property would be drawn and executed. The earnest payment of $1,000.00 mentioned in the handwritten agreement was not made to Loraine Wenger.

When the two parties arrived at Gernon's law office they discussed details of the sale with Mr. Gernon. He advised them that he did not have time that day to draw a formal contract. He suggested that he be permitted to prepare and forward such a contract to the parties for their signatures at a later date. Mr. Gernon advised plaintiff not to deliver the earnest money to Loraine Wenger at that time. Plaintiff did make out two checks totaling $1,000.00 and naming Loraine as payee, but the checks were retained by plaintiff's attorney.

The formal written contract was never signed by the Wengers. It was drafted and mailed to Loraine on January 9, 1973, but Mr. Gernon was advised that the contract as drawn was not in accordance with their previous understanding. The sellers would not agree to stipulate the exact number of acres covered in the legal description. The formal contract did not require the purchaser to pay the first $250.00 of closing costs as specified in the hand written agreement and there were other terms in the formal contract which were not agreeable to the sellers.

On January 19, 1973, Mr. Gernon replied by mail and enclosed a revised contract for signatures. In the letter Mr. Gernon stated:

". . . It was never my understanding that the whole agreement between the parties was to be ironed out in black and white on the day you were in the office. As a matter of fact it seemed that all the parties were in a rush that date, and that the written real estate contract would be drawn by me to conform with standard real estate contract procedures that we use here in the office. . . ."

The revised contract was rejected by Loraine and returned to plaintiff's attorney, Gernon, on January 29, at which time she advised that the property had been sold to other parties.

A formal written contract had been entered into by the Wengers on January 20, 1973, agreeing to convey this land to Donald L. Vandover, Dottie O. Vandover, Raymond J. Harrison and Melva J. Harrison. The sale price was $16,000.00 payable in installments. The contract was signed individually by Loraine E. Wenger, Ethel H. Wenger and Lorene E. Ralston. Their signatures were acknowledged by notary publics.

After tendering a down payment on February 15, 1973, plaintiff filed this action for specific performance against Loraine Wenger, Ethel Wenger and Lorene Ralston. The new purchasers, Vandovers and Harrisons, were subsequently joined in the action as interested parties.

Ethel Wenger died prior to trial and Lorene Ralston's motion for summary judgment was sustained by the trial court. The plaintiff King proceeded in a trial to the court against Loraine Wenger and the new purchasers of the property. No appeal has been taken from the order granting summary judgment to Lorene Ralston. From the evidence at the trial the court made findings of fact and conclusions of law. The findings include those facts previously narrated and the court concluded:

"The plaintiff has never made any payment for purchase of the land to defendants, and has never been in possession of this real estate.

"The plaintiff has failed to meet the burden of proof and his prayer for specific performance of the instrument dated December 26, 1972, the same being defendants exhibit one, is hereby denied."

On appeal, although numerous points of error are listed by appellant, only one question need be considered. This court must determine whether the written memorandum of December 26, 1972, constitutes a binding contract for sale of property upon which an action for specific performance will lie.

Rule

Whether parties to an informal agreement become bound prior to the drafting and execution of a contemplated formal writing is largely a question of intent on their part. The intent of the parties is to be determined by the surrounding facts and circumstances of each case. (17 C.J.S. Contracts § 49, p. 697; 17 Am.Jur.2d, Contracts, §§ 28, 29, pp. 363–368; Anno.: 122 A.L.R. 1219, Contract—When Deemed Closed; 165 A.L.R. 756, Contract—When Deemed Closed.)

This court has held that the mere intention to reduce an informal agreement to a formal writing is not of itself sufficient to show that the parties intended that until the formal writing was executed the informal agreement should be without binding force. (Storts v. Eby Construction Co., 217 Kan. 34, 535 P.2d 908; Phillips & Easton Supply Co., Inc. v. Eleanor International, Inc., 212 Kan. 730, 512 P.2d 379; Miles v. City of Wichita, 175 Kan. 723, 267 P.2d 943.)

However, the fact that the parties contemplate the execution of a formal document is some evidence, not in itself conclusive, that they intend not to be bound until it is executed. And where formal contracts are normally executed because of the complexity and importance of the transaction involved the more likely it is that the informal agreement is intended to be only preliminary. (1 Corbin on Contracts [1963], § 30, p. 97.)

Rule

The subsequent conduct and interpretation of the parties themselves may be decisive of the question of whether a contract has been made even though a document was contemplated and has never been executed. For that reason in Miles v. City of Wichita, supra, where the parties to an oral lease of property had begun performance and the preparation and execution of a written agreement which remained uncompleted was little more than a clerical act it was held that a valid contract existed under the oral agreement.

But where the intent of the parties is clear that they are negotiating with an understanding that the terms of the contract are not fully agreed upon and a written formal agreement is contemplated a binding contract does not come into existence in the absence of execution of the formal document. (Weil & Associates v. Urban Renewal Agency, 206 Kan. 405, 479 P.2d 875.)

RA

At the time the parties in this case drew up their tentative written agreement they both contemplated adjourning to Mr. Gernon's office to work out additional details of the land transaction and upon completion of that task to draft and execute a formal contract. Discussion at the attorney's office involved a number of matters which Gernon later said had not been clearly settled. In a letter to Loraine Wenger he remembered that all of the contract terms had not been agreed to during the meeting at his office. Neither party began performance under the informal agreement. King withheld payment of $1,000.00 earnest money upon his attorney's advice entrusting the checks for payment to his counsel rather than tendering them to Loraine Wenger.

The informal agreement was executed by only one of the three co-owners of the property, Loraine Wenger. Although she presumed to sign for her sister, Lorene Ralston, she had no written authorization to do so. K.S.A. 33–105 provides that an interest in real estate shall not be granted unless the grant be in writing signed by the grantor or the grantor's agent lawfully authorized in writing to do so. K.S.A. 33–106 states that no action shall be brought to charge a party upon any contract for the sale of lands ". . . unless the agreement upon which such action shall be brought, or some memorandum or note thereof, shall be in writing and signed by the party to be charged therewith, or some other person thereunto by him or her lawfully authorized in writing."

Therefore it is apparent in this case, where the parties contemplated a sale of all interests in the property, that the temporary agreement would not suffice to complete the transaction and govern the rights of all parties in this sale regarding Lorene Ralston's interest in the real estate. Especially was this true since the sale agreement contemplated a purchase of the land on installment payments over a six year period.

Although the plaintiff admits the $1,000.00 earnest money payment was not delivered to Loraine Wenger in accordance with the terms of the handwritten agreement, he argues that in reliance on the agreement he made expenditures for attorney's and abstractor's fees and has partially performed the agreement. The record indicates he was reimbursed for the abstractor's fees and the expenses of his attorney must be considered normal business expenses incurred on the expectancy of ultimate success, not performance of his obligations under a completed agreement. (See Weil & Associates v. Urban Renewal Agency, supra, at p. 416, 479 P.2d 875.) Plaintiff makes some further contention that he changed his position as a result of the agreement by selling his trucking business in anticipation of increasing his farming operation. Without regard to the legal sufficiency of such a claim, the record indicates he was in the process of selling his trucking business prior to his negotiations for the purchase of this land.

Under the facts and circumstances of this case the trial court was correct in holding that the parties did not enter into a binding contract. The parties did not intend to become legally bound until a formal contract was drawn by appellant's attorney and approved by the owners of the property. The evidence clearly indicates the earnest money was never paid to Loraine Wenger and that the owners did not agree to all the terms set forth in the formal contract. The owner's rejection of these terms was properly communicated to plaintiff's attorney and no binding contract was made by the parties.

Judgment affirmed.

SCHROEDER, J., not participating.

NOTES

1. As the preceding cases illustrate, the Statute of Frauds can become important in various types of real estate transactions and at

differing stages of the negotiations. Probably the bulk of the problems arise out of family settlements and similar friendly (in the inception) deals where the parties never think of consulting a lawyer or of drawing up a formal document. However, the commercial transaction also furnishes a fair amount of difficulty. Real estate agents are usually eager to close a sale and lawyers are not always available to draft the contract at a moment's notice. As a result the lawyer is sometimes left out of the process completely or is called in at a late date after the damage has been done. Frequently the real estate broker will use an informal memorandum or receipt as a binder until a formal contract can be drafted and signed.

Does the use of such a binder raise any additional legal problems? What minimum standards must the binder meet? Suppose the informal memorandum meets the required minimum but contains the phrase, "Formal contract to be signed on or before September 1, 19__." On this last point see the principal case and Levine v. Lafayette Building Corp., 103 N.J.Eq. 121, 142 A. 441 (1928), *rev'd,* 105 N.J.Eq. 532, 148 A. 772 (1929). In Goren v. Royal Investments Inc., 25 Mass.App.Ct. 137, 516 N.E.2d 173 (1987), the court held that there was a binding contract even though the "Offer to Purchase" signed by the parties provided, "A mutually acceptable Purchase and Sale Agreement shall be executed within four weeks of the acceptance of this offer." The court said, "If . . . the parties have agreed upon all material terms, it may be inferred that the purpose of the final document which the parties agree to execute is to serve as a polished memorandum of an already binding contract."

2. The memo should contain the terms of the contract, but it is far from clear just how much detail may be required. Obviously, it will not contain all of the items to be found in a standard contract. Moreover, the court can imply certain terms if the parties have failed to include them in their agreement. Thus, the court may imply a reasonable time for performance, that the consideration will be paid in cash when no agreement was reached as to terms, and even that a reasonable price will be paid where the parties have failed to agree on this item. If, however, the parties have agreed upon the key terms but have failed to include them in the memo, the Statute of Frauds will probably bar enforcement. This can lead to some peculiar results; e.g., if the parties in fact agree upon a certain price per acre, but the memo is silent as to the consideration, could the vendor use oral testimony to prove the terms, and then plead the Statute of Frauds on the basis of an insufficient memo? For some light on this point see Hanlon v. Hayes, 404 Ill. 362, 89 N.E.2d 51 (1949), commented on in [1950] U.Ill.L.F. 309.

Much of the difficulty concerning terms relates to financing provisions. Some courts are quite strict while others are very liberal in their requirements. Contrast Montanaro v. Pandolfini, 148 Conn. 153, 168 A.2d 550 (1961) (contract unenforceable for failure to specify when the monthly payments are to commence or the amount of each payment in a purchase money mortgage) with Monaco v. Levy, 12

A.D.2d 790, 209 N.Y.S.2d 555 (1961) (contract on its face satisfied the Statute of Frauds, despite its silence as to the mortgage maturity date and the mortgage interest rate).

If the memo contains all of the necessary items but some of them are erroneously stated because of a mutual mistake of fact by the parties, the equitable remedy of reformation can probably be used to correct the errors. But reformation is not available to fill in essential items which are missing entirely. To permit the remedy in the latter situation would allow the complaining party to hoist himself by his own bootstraps and reform nothing into something.

3. While the memo must contain certain key elements in order to be adequate, it is not necessary that these elements appear in a single memo. A series of documents, including the check for down payment, may be construed together if they relate to each other. See A.B.C. Auto Parts, Inc. v. Edward Moran, 359 Mass. 327, 268 N.E.2d 844 (1971). See also Bennett v. Moring, 33 Colo.App. 390, 522 P.2d 741 (1974). The court noted: "Where more than one writing is used to satisfy the requirements of the statute of frauds, some nexus between the writings must be shown. . . . While the phrase 'internal reference' is often used to describe the requisite nexus, it need not be in the form of express cross-references between the writings. Instead, the requirement may be satisfied by parol evidence, where, as here, it is apparent that the memoranda referred to the same subject matter or transaction."

In Gregerson v. Jensen, 617 P.2d 369 (Utah 1980), the Supreme Court indicated specific performance should have been granted of a contract based on a check inscribed by the purchaser "½ payment on land as agreed—other ½ payment when deed delivered." The deed was discovered *after the trial* and expressly referred to the parties in question and specifically described the property. The two writings were held to evidence a single transaction and were read together to fulfill the requirements of the Statute of Frauds. The district court erred in denying a motion for a new trial based upon the newly discovered deed. There was a dissent.

Can an undelivered deed, standing alone, serve as an adequate memo of a contract? McMillan v. Ingolia, 87 Ill.App.3d 727, 43 Ill. Dec. 162, 410 N.E.2d 162 (1980) held no. "The deed in the instant case, which is the only writing evidencing the essential terms of the repurchase option, does not constitute a memorandum sufficient to satisfy the requirements of the Statute. Although the deed was signed by the grantor plaintiffs, it was not signed by the grantee defendants or by their agent . . . ." Note that most deeds are signed by the grantor only (deeds poll). Suppose it were an indenture, signed by both parties, would that be sufficient?

4. Compare the cases and notes in this, and the preceding, subsection with Section 2–201 of the Uniform Land Transactions Act:

Section 2–201. [formal requirements; Statute of Frauds]

(a) Notwithstanding agreement to the contrary and except as provided in subsection (b), a contract to convey real estate is not enforceable by judicial proceeding unless there is a writing signed by or on behalf of the party against whom enforcement is sought which describes the real estate and is sufficient to indicate that a contract to convey has been made by the parties.

(b) A contract not evidenced by a writing satisfying the requirements of subsection (a), but which is valid in other respects, is enforceable if:

(1) it is for the conveyance of real estate for one year or less;

(2) the buyer has taken possession of the real estate and has paid all or a part of the price;

(3) the buyer has accepted a deed from the seller;

(4) either party, in reasonable reliance upon the contract and upon the continuing assent of the party against whom enforcement is sought, has changed his position to the extent that an unreasonable result can be avoided only by enforcing the contract; or

(5) the party against whom enforcement is sought admits in his pleading, testimony, or otherwise in court that the contract for conveyance was made.

If the act were adopted in the specific jurisdictions involved would it affect the decisions of the courts? Explain how.

C. PAROL MODIFICATION AND RESCISSION

NIERNBERG v. FELD

Supreme Court of Colorado, 1955.
131 Colo. 508, 283 P.2d 640.

HOLLAND, J. Philip and Melba Niernberg, husband and wife, defendants in the trial court, as owners of certain real estate entered into a sales agreement with Nathan B. and Esther Feld, which agreement was designated as "Receipt and Option." The Felds paid $1,500 as a deposit on the agreed purchase price of $27,000, the balance to be paid on or before May 5, 1952, part in cash and part by a note secured by deed of trust on the property. Abstract of title was to be furnished the buyers on or before April 25, and, provided payment was made or tendered by the buyers on or before May 1, the sellers were to convey the property by warranty deed and the agreement provided that if payment was not made or tendered as provided, then the money paid and receipted for was to be held as liquidated damages, and in either case, both purchaser and seller were to be released from all further obligations. Arrangements were made for the Felds, the buyers, to secure a first loan on the property and the sellers furnished an abstract within the time provided in the agreement. Prior to May 1, the Felds decided they "couldn't go through with the deal," and so advised their attorney, who notified the sellers, and on the same day Nathan Feld advised Philip Niernberg to the same effect.

Apprehension by the Felds, as to the matter of a return of the deposit, caused them to arrange for a conference with the Niernbergs in their attorney's office, which was held prior to May 1, 1952, at which conference Nathan B. Feld, Philip Niernberg and the Felds' attorney were present. Neither Mrs. Feld nor Mrs. Niernberg attended this conference. It was orally agreed by those present that the Niernbergs might retain the $1,500 deposit and procure a buyer for the property, and if they were able to sell the property for the same or better price, than the Felds had agreed to pay, then the $1,500 deposit was to be returned to the Felds, the buyers; however, if the owners were forced to sell the property for less, they were to deduct the difference between the price obtained and the price the Felds had agreed to pay from the deposit, and if there was any difference it was to be paid to the Felds.

Philip Niernberg denied that there was such a meeting held before May 1, 1952, and that he made any such oral agreement. About ninety days thereafter, the property was sold for a price equal to or in excess of what the Felds had proposed to pay and the Niernbergs refused to refund the deposit, whereupon the present suit was instituted by complainant. . . .

The jury returned a verdict in favor of plaintiffs against defendant Philip Niernberg for the amount of the deposit, together with interest accrued thereon. To the judgment entered on this verdict, error is specified and the argument summarized as follows:

1. An attempted executory rescission or modification of a prior written agreement is invalid as being in violation of the statute of frauds.

2. That a subsequent oral promise was without consideration and therefore void, because no benefit was conferred or detriment suffered.

3. The oral promise of defendant Philip Niernberg given to plaintiffs did not constitute a rescission of the written agreement, because one of the parties to the written agreement was not a party to the subsequent oral agreement, and one joint obligor could not agree to a rescission without the consent of the other obligor.

The applicability of the statute of frauds in the present action arises in connection with the question of whether or not the rescission agreement entered into was required to be in writing. We believe this question to be one of first impression in this jurisdiction and we find the decisions of other jurisdictions to be in serious conflict. Defendants in their motions to dismiss relied upon either section 6 or 8, or both, chapter 71, '35 C.S.A., which are as follows:

Section 6: "No estate or interest in lands, other than leases for a term not exceeding one year, nor any trust or power over or concerning lands, or in any manner relating thereto, shall hereafter be created, granted, assigned, surrendered or declared, unless by act or operation of law, or by deed or conveyance in writing, subscribed by the party creating, granting, assigning, surrendering or declaring the same, or by his lawful agent, thereunto authorized by writing."

Section 8: "Every contract for the leasing for a longer period than one year, or for the sale of any lands or any interest in lands, shall be void, unless the contract, or some note or memorandum thereof, expressing the consideration, be in writing, and be subscribed by the party by whom the lease or sale is to be made."

There can be no doubt that the original agreement concerning the sale and purchase of an interest in land was required to be in writing in compliance with the above statute. It is well to note at the outset that this original written agreement was never performed. The authorities upon which plaintiff in error relies generally, have to do with executed contracts. It seems to be the better-reasoned rule that an executory contract involving title to, or an interest in, lands may be rescinded by an agreement resting in parol. The statute of frauds concerns the making of contracts only, and does not apply to the matter of their revocation. The requirements for the making of a contract is one thing, and the revocation or rescission thereof is another, and we are satisfied to announce as the law in this jurisdiction that such executory contracts may be rescinded by the mutual consent of the parties thereto.

As to the question of lack of consideration, we find that in the instant case there was a promise for a promise involving the release of each party from further performance, and this mutual consideration is sufficient to support the agreement. Further, we find that in this instance, the party here relying upon the statute of frauds has accepted a benefit to the detriment of the other party, the buyer, in that, the seller did sell the property for a price equal to, or in excess of, what plaintiffs had contracted to pay, thereby receiving a substantial benefit; besides, he had all of plaintiffs' money that was on deposit, and after making the agreement—although denied by him, but sufficiently established—he should not, as a matter of right and wrong, retain a full deposit from one party and then sell the property to another for a higher price. Neither is he in position to successfully contend as a reason for escape, that he is not liable, because his wife was not a party to the rescission. If he assumed to act in her absence and she was dismissed from the case, he should be bound by his own actions and declarations. Notwithstanding his denial that he entered into the subsequent oral agreement, the jury resolved this question against him upon the facts presented. We perceive no reversible error in the trial record nor in the instructions given the jury; and the verdict is amply supported by the evidence; accordingly the judgment based thereon should be, and is, affirmed.

NOTES

1. A comment on the principal case in 28 Rocky Mt.L.Rev. 268 (1956) indicates that most American decisions agree with Niernberg v. Feld, although there are numerous holdings to the contrary. Allen v. Kingdon, 723 P.2d 394 (Utah 1986), expressly declined to follow Niernberg v. Feld in a case of an "entirely executory rescission," but the court said that oral rescissions had been recognized in Utah where

there was "part performance" of the rescission agreement or where buyer or seller had substantially changed position in reliance on the rescission agreement. See note 3 below.

2. V and P executed a valid written contract for the sale of land. Before the date set for performance there was a parol modification of the contract, so that P, instead of giving a note secured by a mortgage for the balance of the purchase price, would convey a parcel of land to V. The court held the modified contract unenforceable although the original contract could still be enforced as written. "If the original contract was modified and changed by subsequent agreement, the contract as changed became a new contract. . . . The original contract, being for the sale of real estate, was within the statute of frauds; and no action could be maintained upon it, unless it, or some memorandum thereof, was made in writing, signed by the parties. The modified contract, as alleged and attempted to be proved, was equally within the statute." Malken v. Hemming Bros., 82 Conn. 293, 296, 73 A. 752, 753 (1909).

"The great weight of authority favors the proposition that subsequent verbal changes or modifications are not allowed to affect the original writing. . . . It should be apparent that if the original contract must be in writing, to be capable of enforcement, any subsequent change therein must likewise be in writing. It is difficult to find argument to sustain this proposition, simply from the fact that it is self-evident." Rucker v. Harrington, 52 Mo.App. 481, 488, 494 (1893).

However, since the memorandum evidencing a land contract "does not need to contain all of the stipulations on which the parties have agreed," it follows that "[i]f neither the portion of the written contract affected by the subsequent modification nor the matter encompassed by the modification itself is required by the Statute of Frauds to be in writing, then the oral modification will not render the contract unenforceable." Joiner v. Elrod, 716 S.W.2d 606 (Tex.App.1986).

3. As the principal case and the preceding notes indicate, the weight of American authority holds that a total rescission of a written contract for the sale of land is permissible on the theory that the Statute of Frauds applies only to the enforcement of the contract, not to the release of rights under it by the parties. On the other hand, a parol modification of some of the contract terms is ineffective because you cannot enforce a land contract which is partly written and partly oral. The original contract stands, as written, and the changes fail *unless* it is possible to enforce them on a theory of estoppel. In Imperator Realty Co., Inc. v. Tull, 228 N.Y. 447, 127 N.E. 263 (1920), the parties agreed to an oral change in the manner of performance (a cash deposit was to be acceptable in lieu of the discharge of certain claims against the property). On the day set for performance—final payment and delivery of the deed—the defendant failed to appear and later asserted that the plaintiff was in breach for failure to comply with the contract as written. The court held that he was estopped to deny the oral change on which the plaintiff had relied or, at least, he would be required to allow a reasonable period of time to permit compliance with

the written contract. Said Judge Cardozo: "The defendant might have retracted his oral promise an hour after making it, and the plaintiff would have been helpless. He might have retracted a week before closing, and, if a reasonable time remained within which to remove the violations, the plaintiff would still have been helpless. Retraction at the very hour of closing might not have been too late if coupled with the offer of extension which would neutralize the consequences of persuasion and reliance . . . . The difficulty with the defendant's position is that he did none of these things. He had notified the plaintiff in substance that there was no need of haste in removing the violations, and that title would be accepted on deposit of adequate security for their removal in the future. He never revoked that notice. He gave no warning of a change of mind. He did not even attend the closing. He abandoned the contract, treated it as at an end, held himself absolved from all liability thereunder, because the plaintiff had acted in reliance on a consent which, even in the act of abandonment, he made no effort to recall . . . . The principle is fundamental and unquestioned . . . . Sometimes the resulting disability has been characterized as an estoppel, sometimes as a waiver . . . . We need not go into the question of the accuracy of the description . . . . The truth is that we are facing a principle more nearly ultimate than either waiver or estoppel, one with roots in the yet larger principle that no one shall be permitted to found any claim upon his own inequity or take advantage of his own wrong . . . . The Statute of Frauds was not intended to offer an asylum of escape from that fundamental principle of justice."

4. Compare the principal case and notes in this sub-section with Section 1–310 of the Uniform Land Transactions Act:

Section 1–310. [modification, rescission and waiver]

(a) An agreement modifying a contract needs no consideration to be binding.

(b) A signed agreement excluding modification or rescission except by a signed writing cannot otherwise be modified or rescinded.

(c) The requirements of the provisions on formal requirements and statute of frauds (Sections 2–201 and 3–203) must be satisfied if the contract as modified is within those provisions.

(d) An attempted modification or rescission may operate as a waiver although it does not satisfy the requirements of subsection (b) or (c).

(e) Unless the retraction would be unjust in view of a material change of position in reliance upon the waiver, a party who has made a waiver affecting an executory portion of a contract may retract the waiver as to future performance by seasonable notification received by the other party that strict performance will be required of any term previously waived.

Would the adoption of the act affect the result in either of these cases?

SECTION 2. THE STANDARD WRITTEN CONTRACT

In contrast with the oral understanding or the sketchy memorandum, the typical written contract for the sale of real estate is a detailed document covering all aspects of the transaction. Actually, there is no "standard" contract, since the forms vary throughout the country to meet the peculiarities of local law and the customs of the community. Moreover, the details of individual transactions differ widely and no one form can possibly meet all demands. It is preferable to prepare a tailor-made instrument for each client and avoid the use of printed forms. However, the principal points are present in nearly every sale, and tested forms should be used as a guide. In most localities the bar relies heavily on forms prepared by bar associations, title insurance companies, or real estate boards.

In order to make the materials which follow in this chapter more meaningful, you should obtain one of the standard form contracts in use in your state and relate the stock clauses to the cases you will be studying. How well do those clauses cover the issues which have resulted in litigation? Are they successful as tools for "preventive law?" This is not a course in legal drafting but it would be helpful to read some material on the drafting of real estate contracts at this juncture or after you have finished Section 3. Some good examples for your guidance are: Holtzschue, Real Estate Contracts (Prac.Law Inst.1985); Friedman, Contracts and Conveyances of Real Property (4th ed.1984); Friedman, Buying a Home: Representing the Purchaser, 47 A.B.A.J. (1961); and Friedman, Buying and Selling a House: Some Considerations in the Drafting of the Contract of Sale, 23 Record of Assoc. of the Bar of City of New York (1968).

SECTION 3. CONSTRUCTION AND PERFORMANCE

In a dispute concerning the meaning of the contractual terms, it is axiomatic that the court will have the last conjecture. In general, the problem of construing real estate agreements is the same as that of construing other contracts. However, certain clauses habitually appear in contracts for the sale of land and have been the subject of frequent interpretation. The lawyer should be aware of the full significance of such clauses.

A. TIME FOR PERFORMANCE

KASTEN CONSTRUCTION CO. v. MAPLE RIDGE CONSTRUCTION CO.

Court of Appeals of Maryland, 1967.
245 Md. 373, 226 A.2d 341.

HORNEY, JUDGE. The question presented by this appeal is whether the Maple Ridge Construction Company (Maple Ridge), as buyer, is entitled to require the Kasten Construction Company (Kasten), as seller, to specifically perform a contract in which settlement for the sale for certain building lots was to have been made in sixty days but the time was not stipulated as being of the essence.

The contract of sale, dated December 4, 1964, provided for the sale and purchase of a tract of land in Section 4 of the Maple Ridge Subdivision in Anne Arundel County consisting of thirty-four "finished" lots [4] designated as 20–A and 20–B through 36–A and 36–B. The contract further provided that Maple Ridge was to have an option to purchase ninety-four other lots in the subdivision within twelve months from the date of the contract of sale and was given the first refusal to purchase approximately five hundred of the remaining lots in Sections 3 and 4. Subsequently, when financing difficulties were encountered, the settlement date was extended in writing to on or before March 19, 1965, but again time was not stated to be of the essence. Maple Ridge had requested a longer extension, but it was refused by Kasten and later requests for extensions were also refused.

Although Kasten in the interim between the making of the contract of sale and the extended settlement date had bulldozed several of the streets or roads and stabilized them with gravel, it had made little progress toward providing Maple Ridge with the finished or completed lots it needed to begin constructing homes. No agreement had been made between Kasten and the County with respect to street and drainage easements and there had been delays in connection with the construction of the curbs and gutters and the installation of public utilities. And while a proposed agreement and bond was completed by the County department of public works on March 3, 1965 and delivered to Kasten promptly, it was never executed and returned. Moreover, although Kasten recorded a deed of "covenants, restrictions and conditions" purporting to cover Sections 3 and 4 of Maple Ridge, which it was agreed was required before the houses to be thereafter constructed would be eligible for FHA financing, Maple Ridge was never consulted or afforded an opportunity to participate in formulating the specifications contained in the restrictions. Maple Ridge, however, in addition to engaging an architect to prepare plans for houses to be constructed in the development and the renting of a trailer to be used on location as an office at a total outlay of $12,000, had continued trying to obtain the

4. By "finished" it was meant that utilities, streets, curbs, gutters and water and sewerage lines were to be completed before final settlement was made. [Footnotes 4 & 5 by the Court.]

type of financing it hoped to get before the extended settlement date expired without having to use such of the personal funds of its president as were available to the corporation. In the meantime the settlement date came and went and neither party made a demand on the other. But when Maple Ridge notified Kasten five days after the expiration of the extension that it had applied for a title examination and it would take about three weeks to complete it, Kasten in turn notified Maple Ridge that the contract of sale had expired, as had the extension, and that it considered the contract null and void and no longer in force. Subsequent negotiations were unsuccessful and this suit for specific performance was brought.

On the evidence and the exhibits produced at the hearing, the chancellor, having found that although the buyer was dilatory in making the necessary financial arrangements and in applying for a title examination, it had tendered full performance of the terms of the contract within a reasonable time after the expiration of the extended settlement date; that the seller, besides acting as if time was not of the essence, had been somewhat lackadaisical in the performance of its part of the contract; and that the seller had suffered no loss that could not be compensated by the payment of interest, decreed specific performance of the contract of sale.[5]

On appeal, Kasten, claiming that the chancellor erred in decreeing specific performance, contends that its refusal to grant further extensions was a clear indication that time was of the essence and should therefore have been inferred from the circumstances. Maple Ridge, however, claiming that a specified date for settlement did not mean that the parties intended time to be of the essence, contends that it was not and that the delay in making settlement was reasonable under the circumstances.

In a case involving specific performance, where the intention of the parties is always the controlling factor, the general rule is that time is not of the essence of the contract of sale and purchase of land unless a contrary purpose is disclosed by its terms or is indicated by the circumstances and object of its execution and the conduct of the parties. Of course, one may lose his right to specific performance by gross laches and unreasonable delay in paying the purchase money. Ordinarily, however, time is held to be of the essence only when it is clear that the parties have expressly so stipulated or their intention is inferable from the circumstances of the transaction, the conduct of the parties or the purpose for which the sale was made. . . .

Applying these tests to the facts of this case, we think the chancellor was correct in decreeing that Maple Ridge was entitled to specific performance. Under the circumstances, it was not necessary to regard the stipulation fixing the original and extended times for payment of the purchase price as imposing a condition requiring strict and punctual compliance in order to entitle the buyer to specific performance.

5. There were other decretal orders affecting the deed of covenants, restrictions and conditions, the option to purchase other lots and the right of refusal to purchase still other lots, but we are not concerned here with any of these things.

. . . Nor, even though the buyer was somewhat neglectful in not paying the balance of the purchase money on the day it was due, can it be said that the delay, particularly in view of the fact that the seller was in no hurry to perform its part of the contract, was unreasonable. Derrett v. Bowman, supra; Jaeger v. Shea, supra. In any event, the buyer was required to compensate the seller for whatever loss it sustained by the payment of interest. Moreover, the mere fixing of a particular date for the completion of a contract for the sale and purchase of land is not regarded as being of the essence with respect to payment but treats the provision as formal rather than essential. . . .

Although the seller relies principally on Stern v. Shapiro, supra, Doering v. Fields, 187 Md. 484, 50 A.2d 553 (1947) and Levy v. Baetjer, 198 Md. 240, 81 A.2d 644 (1951), to support the claim that the chancellor erred in granting specific performance, all of these cases are distinguishable on the facts from the case at bar. In *Stern,* the provision that the down payment was to be forfeited in the event settlement was not made within the time specified, warranted the inference that time was of the essence. Here, a forfeiture was neither provided nor contemplated. In *Doering,* the buyers not only made no effort to settle within the agreed time, but despite an extension were still unable to pay the balance of the purchase money at the expiration of the extended period. Here, although the extended time had expired, the president of the corporate buyer had tendered full performance within a reasonable time thereafter. In *Levy,* the express provision that time was of the essence was held not to have been waived by the extension of the settlement date. Here, the very absence of the essentialness of time without more distinguishes that case from this.

The further claim that the presence of a stipulated settlement date in the contract of sale impels an inference that time was to be of the essence is likewise without merit. In Soehnlein v. Pumphrey, supra, it was said (at p. 338 of 183 Md., at p. 845 of 37 A.2d):

"The accepted doctrine is that in the ordinary case of contract for the sale of land, even though a certain period of time is stipulated for its consummation, equity treats the provision as formal rather than essential, and permits the purchaser who has suffered the period to elapse to make payments after the prescribed date, and to compel performance by the vendor notwithstanding the delay, unless it appears that time is of the essence of the contract by express stipulation, or by inference from the conduct of the parties, the special purpose for which the sale was made, or other circumstances surrounding the sale."

. . . The rule, of course, is subject to certain qualifications, but none of them, as is herein pointed out, is applicable to the facts and circumstances of this case. When there has been a delay, as there was in this case, the important question is whether it was reasonable. The chancellor found that it was and we cannot say that he erred in so doing. . . .

Decree affirmed; appellants to pay the costs.

NOTES

1. "The general opinion has always been, that the day fixed was imperative on the parties at law. This was so laid down by Lord Kenyon, and has never been doubted in practice. The contrary rule would lead to endless difficulties. . . . The effect of this rule would be, that the appointment of a day would have no effect, and in every case it must be referred to a jury to consider whether the act was done within a reasonable time. The precise contract of the parties would be avoided, in order to introduce an uncertain rule, which would lead to endless litigation. . . . But *equity*, which from its peculiar jurisdiction is enabled to examine into the cause of delay in completing a purchase, and to ascertain how far the day named was deemed material by the parties, will in certain cases carry the agreement into execution, notwithstanding that the time appointed be elapsed; . . . for, as Lord Eldon remarks, the title to an estate requires so much clearing and enquiry, that unless substantial objections appear, *not merely as to the time,* but an alteration of circumstances affecting the value of the thing; or objections arising out of circumstances, *not merely as to the time,* but the conduct of the parties during the time; unless the objection can be so sustained, many of the cases go the length of establishing, that the objections cannot be maintained. Perhaps there is cause to regret that even *equity* assumed this power of dispensing with the literal performance of contracts in cases like these." Sugden, Law of Vendors and Purchasers 335–339 (7th American ed. 1851).

In GDJS Corp. v. 917 Properties Inc., 99 A.D.2d 998, 473 N.Y.S.2d 453 (1984), plaintiff buyers sued to recover their $50,000 downpayment and other damages resulting from defendant seller's alleged breach of a land contract. The court said that although "in an action at law . . . it is generally held that the time for performance stipulated in the contract is of the essence unless a contrary intent appears . . ., the parties, by their conduct, may evince an intent that time not be of the essence and, in such instances, . . . the refusal to grant a reasonable adjournment may amount to a repudiation of the agreement. On this record, we are in agreement that these parties did not intend that time be of the essence, evidenced by their discussion to exclude such a provision when the contract was executed and their subsequent conduct, thereby entitling plaintiffs to a reasonable adjournment of the closing." See also Miller v. Long Family Partnership, 151 Ariz. 306, 727 P.2d 359 (App.1986), an action at law in which buyer was denied recovery of his deposit after offering to perform on the closing date specified in the contract and refusing seller's tender of a deed one or two days later.

2. "The parties to a contract may by its terms make the time of performance essentially important and its observance in that respect requisite to relief. . . . And when that is not so either of the parties to the contract may, by a reasonable notice to the other party for that purpose, render the time of performance as of the essence of the contract and avail himself of forfeiture on default. . . . Time was not necessarily of the essence of the contract in question. But the trial

court found that the plaintiff notified the defendants on the twelfth of November, 1888, that the mortgage would mature on the 1st of November, 1889, and that he would not accept a deed of the premises unless the defendants procured for him at the time fixed for the passing of the title, a proper and sufficient extension of the mortgage until November, 1891, and upon that fact the court determined that such notice made time of the essence of the contract." Schmidt v. Reed, 132 N.Y. 108, 113, 30 N.E. 373 (1892). Can parties generally change the terms of a contract by unilateral action of this sort? Are the terms of a contract changed when the vendor tells the purchaser that time shall be of the essence even though it was not made so originally? Consider the following statement by Professor Walsh in commenting on Schmidt v. Reed: "It is clear that the notice before breach could not have made time of the essence without modifyng the contract. The case is a doubtful one, to be supported, if at all, only because of the subsequent purchase by the plaintiff elsewhere coupled with the defendant's silence." See generally Walsh, Equity 361–377 (1930).

Despite Professor Walsh's attack on "unilateral modification" the cases seem to support the following statement from Shullo Construction Co. v. Miller, 2 Ohio App.2d 177, 207 N.E.2d 393, 395 (1965). "[t]he sales agreement did not specifically state that time was of the essence. It stated only—'This sale to be closed on or before November 30, 1963.' 91 C.J.S. Vendor and Purchaser 104(c), at page 1003, treats of a similar situation as follows: 'Although time is not of the essence of a contract for the sale of realty as originally made it may be made so by the subsequent conduct of the parties, as by one party giving notice to the other that he will insist on a strict performance, or, if the time of performance has arrived or is past, that he will insist on performance by a certain date, provided the time allowed by the notice is reasonable, which is a question of fact depending on the circumstances of the particular case.' "

DOCTORMAN v. SCHROEDER

Court of Errors and Appeals of New Jersey, 1921.
92 N.J.Eq. 676, 114 A. 810.

Appeal from Court of Chancery.

Bill by Solomon Doctorman and others against Walter L. Schroeder and others. Bill dismissed, and complainants appeal. Affirmed.

The following is the opinion of Vice Chancellor Leaming in the court below:

I think it would be conceded by any one that the aim of a court of equity appropriately would be always to relieve a purchaser, who had failed to comply strictly with the terms of a contract, from the forfeiture of his right to purchase a property, if it should be in the power of the court to do so. That is especially so in a case of this nature where the failure consisted of a neglect to make a tender of purchase money at the hour named in the contract, and where the purchaser was prepared to pay the money approximately a half-hour after the expiration of the time limit agreed upon. If there can be said to be lodged in a court of equity power to relieve the complainant in this case from that default, obviously it should be done; such a default could only be a source of substantial damage to an owner in case a new purchaser on more favorable terms could be found during the period of default, or new conditions had led the owner to wish to be relieved of the duty of sale.

The single question, then, which is presented for consideration to my mind is whether this court has the power, after parties have deliberately and solemnly contracted to the time when a payment should fall due under a contract, and equally deliberately and solemnly agreed upon the consequences that should flow from a failure to pay at the time, to say that different consequences shall flow from such a default, even though the default is only a matter of minutes. Obviously, if the default has been waived a different situation exists, but in the absence of a waiver it seems to me a court of equity is powerless to come to the relief of a purchaser of property who has failed to pay at the time specified in the agreement, when the agreement distinctly and clearly provides that that time is essential, and that the purchaser's rights as purchaser shall cease and become void unless payment is made at the time stipulated.

In this case the contract for the sale of this land provided for the second payment, a payment of $1,500, on the 19th of December, 1919, $500 having been prior to that time paid down by the purchaser. On that day Mrs. Doctorman, the purchaser, was unable to raise the $1,500 which she was required to pay by the terms of the contract. In that contract the parties had specifically stipulated that unless that specific $1,500 should be paid on that day then all moneys paid on account "shall be forfeited and this agreement shall be null and void, otherwise to remain in full force and effect." And in a subsequent part of the agreement it is again, in another form, stipulated to the same effect, by a clause stating that time shall be considered the essence of the contract. I am mistaken. That clause appears in the fore part of the clause I was first reading from.

Clearly, there is nothing unlawful in a purchaser agreeing that she shall lose her right to buy a property if she fails to pay on a given day. I am not now discussing, and shall not discuss, because it is not involved in this case, the question of the rights of the purchaser under such circumstances in the event of a default to recover back the money already paid, but so far as the agreement relates to the loss of the right of the purchaser to buy the property in the event of failure to pay an installment at a time agreed upon, it seems to me there can be no doubt of the rights of the parties to so contract, and of either party to stand upon his rights under such a contract; and when that time has arrived and the payment has not been made it is the privilege of the owner of the property to either accept the payment at a later day or to treat the contract as null and void. I cannot see that there is the slightest doubt about that.

In this case, the purchaser, the complainant in this suit, being unable to pay on the 19th of December the entire $1,500, induced the owner of the property to accept $500 and extend the time for the payment of the remaining $1,000 of that installment, and the parties entered into a supplemental agreement to that effect, and in that agreement, in language which is probably as apt and as powerful and explicit as can be drawn, it is stipulated that the $500 is received—referring now to the language of the agreement—"upon condition that the further sum of $1,000 cash is to be paid by said Fannie Doctorman, the purchaser, to the said owners not later than the hour of 2:30 p.m. on Saturday, December 20, 1919, at the Rooms 30–32 Real Estate & Law Building, Atlantic City, N.J." And at the end of that agreement there is added this further clause: "It is further distinctly understood and agreed that time shall be the essence of this receipt." The agreement is written in the general form of a receipt, although it contains these stipulations. The concluding part of what I was reading is as follows: "The said sum of $500 is received with the further understanding that the said Walter L. Schroeder and Anna M. Schroeder do not in any way waive their rights or interest in said agreement, and if the said balance of $1,000 is not paid as herein mentioned then all moneys paid upon account of said agreement and this sum of $500 shall be forfeited by said Fannie Doctorman, and said agreement of sale shall immediately become null and void."

Now, there it is stipulated in language as plain as the English can be written that the extension of time is conditional, and that the rights of the purchaser of that property shall be null and void unless the $1,000 which should have been paid on the 19th is paid on the 20th, not later than the hour of 2:30 in the afternoon of that day.

All I have said touching such an agreement, when I was commenting upon the original agreement, is equally applicable to the supplemental agreement. There is nothing unlawful or illegal in such an extension, in such an agreement, in such covenants, or in such stipulations. If the parties see fit to provide that default of payment by a certain hour of a given day shall terminate the rights of the purchaser, I know no reason why they cannot agree to it. I can see no possible legal objection to it. It is in their power, as all of the authorities hold, to make time the essence of the contract. The parties have clearly done so in this supplemental agreement in every way that can be done.

It transpired that the purchaser defaulted at 2:30 on the afternoon of the day named in the supplemental contract, the hour when payment should have been made under the terms of the supplemental contract. Now, what was the effect of that default. I do not recall of ever having seen any case which has discussed the subject of a stipulated hour for payment with the consequence stipulated for failure to pay upon that hour or minute, but the principle must be the same as a stipulation to pay on a given day. The time limit is fixed, and the contract between these parties is that the payment must not be made later than that hour, whereas in fact the purchaser undertook to make the payment later than the time stated. That attempt, it seems to me, was entirely ineffectual, unless, of course, there was some waiver upon the part of the owner of the property.

It is contended here, however, that there was such a waiver. I have listened with great interest to Mr. Coulomb's argument to the effect that the circumstances that the owners of the property remained at the place appointed for some half hour after the hour designated in the contract amounted to a waiver, because it indicated a condition of mind upon their part showing their intention to permit the purchaser to perform should she come in during the period that they determined to wait. I may almost say that I regret that I am unable to reach the conclusion that counsel urges; but I see no element in that situation that contains the necessary requisites of a waiver.[6]

When the time expired within which payment should be made the rights of the owners were to accept payment at a later hour or refuse to accept payment at a later hour, according as they might choose, no matter what their motives and purposes were. It may be that had the purchaser arrived 5 minutes after the appointed time that they would have been inclined to have accepted payment. Who knows? It may be that 10 minutes after they would not have done so. But, whether they would or whether they would not, their rights, if they have any rights in the matter, were to accept payment or to refuse to accept it. The latter they did. Approximately a half an hour after the time, probably about 40 minutes after, an effort was made upon the part of the purchaser to induce them to take the money, and they refused to do so. Now, how is it material what their reasons were? I think I know what the reasons were. There are no two witnesses who have testified to the same things; a large number of people were present at that time, and every one of them has narrated what transpired in more or less modified form, but I think I know the truth.

I am very well convinced that the facts are that the owners of the property before the hour named for the payment on the 20th had become more or less dissatisfied with the purchaser; they had become pretty well convinced that the purchaser was not responsible. Her failure the day before to meet her engagement looked to them as though she was not responsible, and altogether they were not pleased with the person whom their agent had found as purchaser for this property, and with whom they had entered into this contract. That, of course, was no ground for them repudiating the contract, and they went to the appointed place with the intention of performing, providing the

6. Waiver is a frequent defense by the purchaser in "time of the essence" cases. Repeated acceptance of late payments by a vendor often leads to a successful waiver plea. "The vendor who has, by a practice of accepting late payment, permitted the purchaser to rely on this course of conduct, need only give reasonable notice that thereafter he will insist on strict performance of the contract. Further defaults would entitle him to his foreclosure remedy." Stinemeyer v. Wesco Farms, Inc., 487 P.2d 65 (Or.1971). See also, Fisher v. Tiffen, 275 Or. 437, 551 P.2d 1061 (1976) holding that a non-waiver provision in a contract could itself be waived by the vendor's action in accepting late payments; and Gordon v. Schumacher, 83 Or.App. 544, 733 P.2d 35 (1987), in which vendor waived the time of the essence clause by accepting several late payments but reinstated it by sending two letters to that effect. For further discussion of the waiver doctrine as it applies to time of the essence clauses, see Hart v. Lyons, 106 Ill.App.3d 803, 62 Ill. Dec. 697, 436 N.E.2d 723 (1982).

payment was made as it should have been made. After the appointed hour they waited—perhaps under some persuasion upon the part of Mr. Campbell; perhaps because they were not entirely apprised of what their rights might be, and were a little fearful to go off and ignore the possibility of the purchaser appearing later, so they waited. They waited for nearly half an hour, when a statement was made by the agent that if the purchaser did not appear there would not be any harm done, because he knew another man who would take the property. That is what probably happened. And it was then that the owners saw a chance to get rid of the proposed purchaser that they were dissatisfied with, and they grasped at that opportunity. Accordingly, a little later, perhaps about 3 o'clock, when the purchaser came in and went into the other room, and returned after a short period with a proposal to pay the money, the owners had determined to avail themselves of the opportunity which they had to get rid of the purchaser, because she was behind in the time of performance. And there was then probably said all that some of the witnesses have referred to. Some of the witnesses have quoted what was said with reference to the reason why the owners would not accept the money. The real reason, however, to my mind, was that they saw the opportunity—the owners saw the opportunity—to get rid of a purchaser they did not like, and they availed themselves of it.

Now, I hold that it was their right to avail themselves of such an opportunity; they lawfully did it. . . .

I therefore base my decision in the case entirely upon the theory that, when the hour for performance arrived, and complainant failed to perform, her rights under the contract ceased at the option of the owner.

I will advise a decree dismissing the bill.

PER CURIAM. The decree appealed from will be affirmed, for the reasons stated in the opinion filed in the court below by Vice Chancellor Leaming.

NOTES

1. "But it is equally clear that there is a class of cases where time is of the essence of the contract; and where a disregard of the conditions of the contract will deprive a party of relief, both at law and in equity.

"1st. Time may have become the essence of the contract by the rise or depreciation of the value of the premises contracted to be sold. . . .

"2d. Time may be of the essence of the contract, by reason of the nature of the interest in the property which is to be conveyed. . . .

"3d. Time may be of the essence of the contract when there is an express stipulation to that effect. . . ." Edgerton v. Peckham, 11 Paige (N.Y.) 352, 354 (1844).

The case of Edgerton v. Peckham states ancient dogma but it is still valid today. See, for example, Kaiman Realty, Inc. v. Carmichael, 2

Hawaii App. 499, 634 P.2d 603 (1981) where the court said: "Time may be made of the essence of the contract by express stipulations, or even without an express stipulation to that effect where such intention is clearly manifested from the agreement as a whole, construed in the light of the surrounding facts." See also Will v. Will Products, Inc., 109 Ill.App.3d 778, 65 Ill.Dec. 430, 441 N.E.2d 343 (1982) and Kossler v. Palm Springs Developments, Ltd., 101 Cal.App.3d 88, 161 Cal.Rptr. 423 (1980). The court in the Kossler case, during the course of an interesting but lengthy opinion, noted: "Professor Pomeroy, in his treatise on Specific Performance, states, 'the prescribing a day at or before which, or a period within which, an act must be done, even with a stipulation that it shall be done at or before the day named, . . . does not render the time essential with respect to such an act.' . . . The general rule in equity is that time is not of the essence unless it has been made so by . . . express terms or is necessarily so from the nature of the contract.' "

2. In connection with the first point in Edgerton v. Peckham, see Hochard v. Deiter, 219 Kan. 738, 549 P.2d 970 (1976), where the court allowed specific performance after three and one-half years. Time had not been made of the essence and the facts did not indicate it was a material factor. The contract price was $11,200 and there was testimony that the fair market value of the property was $32,500 at the time of suit but the court held this change in value was not a sufficient reason for denying specific performance.

Why did not the rise in value make time of the essence? Apparently, the "rise or depreciation in value" must be very rapid, i.e., a highly volatile market, in order to trigger the first rule. An inflationary or deflationary economy over a course of time is not enough to make time of the essence by implication where the parties have not done so expressly.

3. The Uniform Land Transactions Act makes the following provisions for the time of performance:

Section 2–302. [time of performance; Time of Essence]

(a) The time for performance is a reasonable time after the making of the contract and tender must be at a reasonable hour and after reasonable notice to the other party of intention to tender. If the contract does not fix the time for performance, either party may fix a time for performance if the time is not unreasonable and is fixed in good faith.

(b) Except as provided in subsection (d), even though the contract specifies a particular time for performance, the failure of one of the parties to tender his performance at the specified time does not discharge the other party from his duties under the contract unless:

(1) the failure to perform, under the circumstances, is a material breach, or

(2) the contract explicitly provides that failure to perform at the time specified discharges the duties of the other party.

(c) The phrase "time is of the essence" or other similar general language does not of itself provide explicitly that failure to perform at the time specified discharges the duties of the other party.

(d) If the contract specifies a particular time for performance, either party, by reasonable and good faith notice to the other before that date, may specify effectively that failure to perform on the specified date will discharge him from his own duties under the contract.

(e) If the contract specifies a particular time for performance, and a failure to tender performance at the specified time does not discharge the other party (subsections (b) and (d)):

(1) the time for performance is a reasonable time thereafter; and

(2) the rules of subsection (a) as to time for tender and fixing of time for performance apply.

(f) If a seller's delay in tender is a breach of contract, buyer, as specified in the provisions on deduction of damages from the price (Section 2–515), may deduct his damages from the amount due the seller upon seller's tender.

B. FINANCING ARRANGEMENTS—MORTGAGES AND INSTALLMENT LAND CONTRACTS

GERRUTH REALTY CO. v. PIRE

Supreme Court of Wisconsin, 1962.
17 Wis.2d 89, 115 N.W.2d 557.

This is a suit to recover on a $5,000 promissory note given to the plaintiff by the defendants as a down payment on the purchase of real estate under an offer of purchase.

The defendants were interested in purchasing two commercial properties in Beloit, Wisconsin, one owned by Mayer Putterman and the other owned by the plaintiff Gerruth Realty Co. On June 15, 1960, the defendants Walter E. Pire and Emily Pire, his wife, signed an instrument designated "Deposit Receipt and Purchase Agreement" on a printed form of the Beloit Real Estate Board which was accepted by the plaintiff. This form which is substantially an offer to purchase, was filled out by the real estate broker for the plaintiff, and provided for the usual details. The purchase price for the plaintiff's property was $30,000; $5,000 of which was the down payment, evidenced by a note payable at the time of closing. The balance of the purchase price was to be paid in cash. The offer to purchase contained a typewritten paragraph to the effect the offer was conditioned upon the defendants' buying the Putterman property for $40,000 and the offer was void unless the closing of the purchase of the two properties took place simultaneously. During the negotiations, there was some talk of financing. The defendants were under the impression they would have no difficulty financing the purchase but insisted upon a clause for their protection. The real estate broker inserted the following clause in the offer: "This offer to purchase is further contingent upon the purchaser obtaining the proper amount of financing."

On the trial, it was proven the defendant Walter E. Pire attempted to borrow $75,000 from the Second National Bank in Beloit with whom he did business and which had mortgages on his house and business. No formal application was made, but in discussing the matter the defendant was told that a borrowing limit to one person was $100,000, which would be exceeded because of his other loans. In order to come within this limit, it was suggested the defendant might incorporate his business. There was testimony [that] the usual and customary commercial loans by banks in Beloit on commercial property for holders of good credit could not exceed 66⅔ per cent of the value of the property. The defendant notified the plaintiff he could not go through with the contract because of his inability to obtain the proper amount of financing. The plaintiff and the Puttermans offered to finance the purchase of the properties to the extent of $45,000, which was refused by the defendants.

The case was tried to the court without a jury. The court found the "subject to financing" clause was a condition precedent to the performance of the contract on the part of the defendants, who in good faith had attempted to obtain the financing which they would require to consummate the purchase but were unable to do so. The court concluded the defendants were entitled to a dismissal of the complaint. From the judgment dismissing the complaint, the plaintiff appeals.

HALLOWS, JUSTICE. [Footnotes by the court have been omitted.]

Contracts of purchase or offers to purchase containing "subject to financing" clauses are fairly common and the clauses have been construed frequently as constituting a condition precedent to the buyer's performance. The initial question in reference to such a contract is whether it is definite enough to be sustained or if indefinite, whether it may be given a meaning which renders the contract certain. Courts are not inclined to strike down such a contract for uncertainty if the deficiency can be supplied consistent with reasonableness in the interest of preserving the contract which parties thought they made. A contract is certain which may be made certain from the surrounding circumstances.

In Locke v. Bort, supra, this court pointed out "subject to financing" clauses could not be construed solely by the language of the contract and without consideration of the surrounding circumstances. On this theory, the plaintiff argues the clause "contingent upon the purchaser obtaining the proper amount of financing" must be construed in the light of current practices in the community with respect to financing of similar transactions. The defendants contend the clause in the light of the circumstances gave the option to the defendants to determine what the proper amount of financing was in relation to his [sic] particular needs. It was this latter view which the trial court adopted. However, any interpretation, which allows one party to a contract to determine without limitation and in a subjective manner the meaning of an ambiguous term, comes dangerously close to an illusory or aleatory contract [see 3a corbin on contracts, p. 399, ch. 38], if it does not in fact reach it.

The evidence does not disclose what was said concerning the amount and details of the financing of the purchase excepting the defendants thought they would have no difficulty in arranging financing. An inference might be drawn from the fact the down payment was not cash but in the form of a promissory note for $5,000 payable on the closing and the offer was also conditioned upon the purchase and simultaneous closing of the Putterman property, that the defendant would need to borrow a large part, if not the total amount, of the purchase price of both properties. The transcript of the evidence is barren of any communicated details of the amount or terms of the financing which the defendants had in mind, if they had any, or tentative ones, or what was understood by the real estate broker representing the plaintiff. Apparently both parties had something in mind when this clause was inserted in the offer to purchase for the benefit of the defendants. The real estate broker presumably familiar with the difficulties, details and terms of financing, might have asked the defendants for more details, but was apparently content with putting something in writing and having it signed by the purchasers.

The problem presented is whether there is sufficient evidence upon which this court can ascertain the intention of the parties, i.e., whether there was a meeting of the minds, even objectively, concerning the meaning of this clause. If it is impossible to fairly ascertain such intention, the contract must fail for indefiniteness. The facts of this case are distinguishable from Kovarik v. Vesely (1958), 3 Wis.2d 573, 89 N.W.2d 279, 280 in that an essential term (the amount of financing) is not designated. In Kovarik, the clause "contingent upon buyer's ability to arrange 'above described financing,'" referring to his $7,000 purchase money mortgage from the Fort Atkinson Savings and Loan Association was held to give the purchaser the option to select the terms of financing, which he exhausted upon making an application to the Fort Atkinson Savings and Loan Association. The court construed, in view of the evidence, that the particular lending institution was not an essential term of the clause and it made no difference from whom the buyer obtained his loan.

In the two cases which we were able to find in which the amount of the financing was not stated in the contract, the court did not hold the contract void. In Reese v. Walker (Ohio Mun., 1958), 151 N.E.2d 605, the facts are somewhat analogous. There, the contract for the purchase of real estate contained the clause "contingent upon securing necessary financing." The court held the buyers had the right to determine the terms of financing they needed and the seller was in no position to complain if the buyers' honesty [sic] determined what kind of a loan they needed. A similar view was taken in Zigman v. McMackin (1958), 6 A.D.2d 907, 177 N.Y.S.2d 723, wherein the contract obligated the purchaser to apply for a purchase money mortgage loan of not more than $10,000 at 5% due in 15 years or longer. In both these cases, the court found a meaning from the circumstances surrounding the execution of the contract and from the purposes the parties sought to accomplish, namely, a loan in such amount or on such terms as the buyer in good faith considered necessary for his purposes.

We do not reach the question of good faith on the part of the defendants in the instant case in determining the amount of the financing because we believe the contract can not be made certain by the surrounding circumstances. In our view, the good faith issue arises only after the determination of the meaning of the ambiguous phrase. True, if we could interpret the contract from the surrounding circumstances that it was intended to give the defendant buyers the sole right to determine the amount of financing, then they would be required to determine in good faith the amount of the loan which they honestly needed. Since financing is such an important element in the purchase of real estate, it is to be wondered why so little attention is paid to this important element in the contract or offer of purchase by those dealing in the sale of real estate.

We cannot find in the evidence any indication upon which even a reasonable inference can be drawn that the parties contracted knowingly and in light of any current practices in the community of Beloit with respect to financing of similar transactions. The evidence sets forth what the current practices were but there is no evidence both parties had them in mind at the time the offer to purchase was executed. Likewise, we cannot agree this clause gave the defendants the exclusive or absolute option or privilege to determine the proper amount of financing, without holding the contract illusory. The contract, and the evidence also, are silent as to all the other terms and conditions of the loan, many of which terms and conditions are interrelated and vary with the security and the borrower. The evidence shows the defendant Walter E. Pire attempted to or at least desired to borrow from his bank \$5,000 more than the combined purchase price of the two properties, which the court inferred the defendant intended to use for remodeling. Such a loan was beyond the limit of current practices in the community. The defendant met other difficulties in attempting to finance the purchase which he had not anticipated, namely, the bank's policy of not loaning in excess of \$100,000 to a customer. If this evidence is taken as indicating what the defendants had in mind at the time they signed the offer of purchase, it was not communicated to the agent of the plaintiff.

It seems to us, if we were to adopt either the interpretation contended for by the plaintiff or that urged by the defendants, we would be making, in fact, a contract for the parties by supplying an essential term thereof rather than interpreting what they mutually meant by an ambiguous term. We find the task of interpreting this contract, on the evidence presented, impossible and must hold the contract void for indefiniteness.

Judgment affirmed.

NOTES

1. See Raushenbush, Problems and Practices with Financing Conditions in Real Estate Purchase Contracts, 1963 Wis.L.Rev. 566.

In Anaheim Co. v. Holcombe, 246 Or. 541, 426 P.2d 743 (1967) the case turned on a phrase in the contract, "This offer is contingent on obtaining a loan of $25,000." The court held that an implied condition was imposed on the purchaser to use reasonable diligence in procuring a loan. The question of reasonable diligence was for the trial court and the burden of proof was on the purchaser. Since the burden was not sustained the purchaser could not recover a $5,000 earnest money payment.

Clauses related to efforts by the purchaser to secure adequate financing, not resolved at the time the contract was signed, continue to be a rich source of litigation. In Osten v. Shah, 104 Ill.App.3d 784, 60 Ill.Dec. 497, 433 N.E.2d 294 (1982) the financing clause read: "This offer is subject to the buyer being able to secure a first mortgage loan with any reputable lending institution in the amount of $92,000. Buyer agrees to make application for said loan immediately upon acceptance of said offer." The court said both parties in every contract impliedly promise to act in good faith. Whether the purchasers employed reasonable efforts to obtain a first mortgage as a condition of the contract and whether their single attempt to obtain a first mortgage was done in good faith were questions of fact precluding a summary judgment. Similar problems were encountered with financing clauses in Gardner v. Padro, 164 Ill.App.3d 449, 115 Ill.Dec. 445, 517 N.E.2d 1131 (1987) (holding that vendors were not a "lending institution" for purposes of the contract, so that purchaser was under no obligation to accept the private financing they offered); and Nicholls v. Pitoukkas, 491 N.E.2d 574 (Ind.App.1986) (holding that, although purchasers failed to apply for financing as required by contract, the breach was immaterial because their income was so low that an application would have been futile). How can the financing clause be drafted in order to avoid most of the difficulties represented by these (and all too similar) cases? How many of these cases can be traced to overzealous real estate agents, eager to have a contract signed before the parties fully understand the very real difficulties involved in securing the required financing?

2. Purchasers seldom pay the full amount of the contract price for the sale of land in cash. Typically, a mortgage or an installment land contract is the method of financing. Although the mortgage, along with the contract of sale, the lease, and the deed, is one of the basic documents in the commercial land transaction, it cannot be treated extensively in a first-year property course. Most law schools offer separate courses in the subject, frequently under the heading of property security or real estate financing, and the materials are too long and complex to be incorporated at this point. The principal student text is Nelson & Whitman, Real Estate Finance Law (2d ed.1985). The following excerpts are included to give you some background in mortgage theory and practice. The cases and notes demonstrate the legal distinctions between the mortgage and the installment land contract and illustrate how the two methods are converging in the modern law.

KRATOVIL, REAL ESTATE LAW

Pages 203–212, 220 (5th ed. 1969).

Mortgage defined. A mortgage may be defined as a conveyance of land given as security for the payment of a debt. On analysis, this definition discloses the existence of two elements: (1) Like a deed, a mortgage is a conveyance of land. (2) However, the object of the document is not, as in the case of a deed, to effect a sale of land, but to provide security for the payment of a debt.

History of mortgage law. The history of mortgage law is the history of hundreds of years of ceaseless struggle for advantage between borrowers and lenders, and the lawbooks reflect the constantly shifting fortunes of this war. Occasionally the battle has gone in favor of the lenders. More recently, however, many laws favorable to the borrowers have been passed, and the battle has usually gone in their favor. To understand how the modern mortgage developed out of these centuries of struggle is to take a long step forward toward understanding modern mortgage law.

Much of our mortgage law comes to us from England. In that country, mortgage arrangements of various kinds existed even in the Anglo-Saxon times before the conquest of England by William the Conqueror in 1066. However, it will suffice for our purposes to begin with the mortgage of the fourteenth century. This document was a simple deed of the land, running from the borrower (mortgagor) to the lender (mortgagee). All the ceremonies needed for a full transfer of ownership took place when the mortgage was made. The mortgagee became the owner of the land just as if a sale had taken place. However, this ownership was subject to two qualifications:

1. The mortgagee, as owner, could oust the mortgagor, take immediate possession of the property, and collect the rents. However, the rents so collected had to be applied on the mortgage debt. For this reason, the mortgagee often permitted the mortgagor to remain in possession.

2. The mortgage described the debt it secured and stated a date of payment, known as the *law day.* The mortgage gave the mortgagor the right to pay the debt on the law day. If he did so, the mortgage provided that it was thereby to become void. This provision was known as the *defeasance clause,* for payment of the debt on the law day defeated the mortgage and put ownership back in the mortgagor.

In early times, the courts enforced the mortgage as it was written. Foreclosure proceedings did not exist. Failure to pay the mortgage debt when due, termed a *default,* automatically extinguished all the mortgagor's interest in the land.

The equity of redemption. For many years no one dreamed of questioning this scheme of things. Then slowly at first, and later n greater numbers, borrowers who had lost their property through default began to seek the assistance of the king by presenting *petitions* to him. A typical petition by such a borrower would set forth the borrowing of the money, the making of the mortgage, the default in payment, and the resulting loss of the land. The petition would continue with the statement that the borrower now had funds and offered to pay the mortgage debt in full, with interest. The petition would then ask that the king order the mortgagee, who now owned the land, to accept the proffered money and to convey the land back to the borrower. The king had little time or inclination to tend to these petitions personally, and so he habitually referred them to a high official, the Lord Chancellor. Since the king was the fountain of all justice, it was the Chancellor's duty to dispose of these petitions justly and equitably, according to good conscience, and this he did. In cases of hardship or accident, for example, where the mortgagor had been robbed while on his way to pay the debt, the Chancellor would order the mortgagee to accept payment of the debt from the borrower and to convey the land back to the borrower. A mortgagee who refused to do as he was told was sent to jail. In time, by about the year 1625, what had begun as a matter of grace on the part of the king had developed into the purest routine. Borrowers filed their petitions directly with the Chancellor, who was now functioning as the judge of a court, and with routine regularity his order was issued commanding the mortgagee to reconvey. Thus a new and very important right was born, the right of the mortgagor to pay his debt even after default and in this manner to recover his property. This right came to be known as the *equitable right of redemption,* or the *equity of redemption.* Later the courts held that the mortgagor could sell this equitable right of redemption, that he could dispose of it by his will, and that if he died leaving no will, the right could be exercised by his heirs. You will perceive that as a result of these developments, the mortgagor, even after default, retained very important rights in the land. Technically the mortgagee became full owner of the land upon default, but practically the mortgagor could now be regarded as the owner even after default, since he could reacquire ownership by exercising his equitable right of redemption.

Waiver of right of redemption. The mortgagees reacted to the development of the equitable right of redemption by inserting in their mortgages clauses reciting that the mortgagor waived and surrendered all his equitable rights of redemption. The courts, however, nipped this idea in the bud by holding that all such clauses were void, since a needy borrower will sign anything and it is up to the courts to protect him. This rule flourished and exists in full vigor today. Any provision in the mortgage purporting to terminate the mortgagor's ownership in case of failure to make payments when due is against public policy and is void. *Once a mortgage, always a mortgage.* It cannot be converted into an outright deed by the mere default of the mortgagor. And no matter how the mortgage seeks to disguise an attempted waiver of the equitable right of redemption, the courts will strike it down.

Example. At the time the mortgage was made the mortgagor signed a deed conveying the property to the mortgagee as grantee. He then delivered the deed to a third person in escrow with directions to deliver the deed to the mortgagee in case of default in the mortgage payments. This deed and escrow were held invalid as an attempted waiver of the equitable right of redemption. Plummer v. Ilse, 41 Wash. 5, 82 Pac. 1009; Hamod v. Hawthorne, 52 Cal.2d 78, 338 P.2d 387.

Development of foreclosure. The efforts of the courts to rescue the mortgagor in turn placed the mortgagee at a disadvantage. The mortgagee, it is true, became the owner of the land when the mortgagor defaulted, but he could not be certain he would remain the owner, for the mortgagor might choose to redeem. To remedy this situation a new practice sprang up. Immediately upon default in payment of the mortgage debt, the mortgagee would file a petition in court, and the judge would enter an order, called a decree, allowing the mortgagor additional time to pay the debt. If he failed to pay within this time, usually six months or a year, the decree provided that his equitable right of redemption was thereby barred and foreclosed. Thereafter he could not redeem his property. Thus developed the *foreclosure suit,* a suit to bar or terminate the equitable right of redemption.

The method of foreclosure just described is known today as *strict foreclosure.* It is still used in Connecticut and Vermont and occasionally elsewhere.

The next development was foreclosure through public sale. The idea emerged that in mortgage foreclosures, justice would best be served by offering the land for sale at public auction, for if at such sale the property sold for more than the mortgage debt, the mortgagee would be paid his debt in full and the surplus proceeds of the sale would be salvaged for the mortgagor. This method of *foreclosure by sale* is the most common method of foreclosure in America today. This development constituted another major victory for the mortgagor. More important still, it led to another and even greater victory for the borrowers. As the practice of foreclosure by sale grew more common, the view began to emerge that *the mortgage, despite its superficial similarity to a deed, was really not a deed of conveyance but only a lien on the land—that is, merely a means of bringing about a public sale to raise money for the payment of the mortgage debt.*

Title and lien theories. The relatively recent view that the mortgage is not really a conveyance of land but only a lien, has reached its fullest development in the agricultural and western states. Certain states, called *title theory states,* still take the older view that a mortgage gives the mortgagee some sort of legal title to the land. In other states, called *lien theory states,* the view that the mortgagee has the legal title is entirely superseded by the view that he has merely a lien to secure his debt. Some states take a position midway between these two views. These are called *intermediate states.*

It is not possible, however, to draw any hard and fast line between these groups of states, since vestiges of title theory will be found in lien theory states, and many title theory states have adopted rules developed by lien theory courts. The differences in point of view are of importance in determining the mortgagee's rights with respect to possession and rents of the mortgaged property.

Statutory redemption. When a mortgage foreclosure sale is held, the equitable right of redemption ends. Indeed, the whole object of the foreclosure suit is to put an end to the mortgagor's equitable right of redemption. In the last hundred years, however, laws have been enacted giving the mortgagor an additional concession. Under these laws, the mortgagor is given one last chance to get his property back.

Explanation. Suppose, for example, that a farmer whose farm is mortgaged has a bad crop year. He cannot meet his mortgage payments, and the mortgage is foreclosed. Perhaps next year the weather and crops will be good, and he will have enough to pay all of his debts. To afford farmers and other mortgagors one last opportunity to salvage their properties, many legislatures have passed laws allowing additional time, often one year, after the foreclosure sale during which the mortgagor can by paying the amount of the foreclosure sale price, get his property back from the mortgagee. This right is called the *statutory right of redemption. Thus the equitable right of redemption ends and the statutory right of redemption begins with the holding of the foreclosure sale.*

Types of mortgages. There are several different types of mortgage instruments. Those commonly encountered are *regular mortgages, deeds of trust, equitable mortgages, and deeds absolute given as security for debts.*

Regular mortgages. The ordinary printed form of mortgage encountered in most states today is referred to herein as the regular mortgage. It is, in form a deed or conveyance of the land by the borrower to the lender followed or preceded by a description of the debt and including a provision to the effect that such mortgage shall be void on full payment of such debt. The content of the additional paragraphs of "fine print" varies considerably.

Deeds of trust. The regular mortgage involves only two parties, the borrower and the lender. In the *trust deed,* also known as the *deed of trust,* the borrower conveys the land, not to the lender, but to a third party, in trust for the benefit of the holder of the note or notes that represent the mortgage debt.

The trust deed form of mortgage has certain advantages, the chief one being that in a number of states it can be foreclosed by trustee's sale under the *power of sale clause* without any court proceedings. The power of sale trust deed is used in Alabama, Alaska, California, Colorado, District of Columbia, Mississippi, Missouri, Montana, Nebraska, Nevada, New Mexico, North Carolina, Oregon, South Carolina, Tennessee, Texas, Virginia, Washington, and West Virginia.

Equitable mortgages. As a general rule, any instrument in writing by which the parties show their intention that real estate be held as security for the payment of a debt will constitute an equitable mortgage, which can be foreclosed in a court of equity.

. . .

An instrument intended as a regular mortgage, but which contains some defect, may operate as an equitable mortgage.

. . .

Deeds absolute given as security. Often when a landowner borrows money he gives as security an absolute deed to the land. By absolute deed is meant an ordinary quitclaim or warranty deed such as is used in sales of land. On its face the transaction looks like a sale and conveyance of the land. Nevertheless the courts treat such a deed as a mortgage, although they require convincing evidence that the deed was really intended only as security for a debt. But if such proof is available, the borrower is entitled to pay the debt and to demand a reconveyance from the lender, just as in the case of an ordinary mortgage; whereas if the debt is not paid, the grantee must foreclose just as if a regular mortgage had been made.

. . .

The mortgage note. After the mortgagee has given his commitment to make the loan, the mortgagor signs a promissory note and mortgage. The mortgage stands as security for payment of the note. *The chief function of the note is to make the mortgagor personally liable for payment of the mortgage debt.* If the mortgagor signs such a note and then decides that he does not want the building, he cannot simply abandon the property and move elsewhere. Wherever he goes he takes his personal liability with him, and if the mortgage is foreclosed, the mortgagee can obtain a personal judgment against him for any deficiency between the foreclosure sale price and the amount of the mortgage debt. Armed with such a judgment, the mortgagee can garnishee the mortgagor's wages or have his other property sold to pay the balance due.

. . .

Prepayment of mortgage debt. In the absence of an agreement to the contrary, the mortgagee has a contractual right to have his money out earning the stipulated interest. Unless there is an agreement to that effect, the mortgagor has no right to insist upon making payment before maturity, even by offering to pay the principal and all interest to the maturity date. Fuller v. Manchester Bank, 102 N.H. 117, 152 A.2d 179. Accordingly, it is to the mortgagor's advantage to provide in the mortgage and mortgage note that the debt is payable *on or before* the due date, or that the debt is payable in monthly payments of a stated sum *or more.* Or a specific clause may be inserted conferring on the mortgagor the privilege of prepaying the mortgage debt. This is known as a *prepayment privilege.* In corporate trust deeds securing issues of bonds, the comparable provision is that providing for *redemption* of bonds prior to their stated maturity dates. Such provisions enable the mortgagor to refinance when money is cheaper or to retire the mortgage where he has entered into a contract of sale that requires him to deliver title free and clear of any mortgage.

OSBORNE, SECURED TRANSACTIONS

Page 224 (1967).

LAND CONTRACTS

The device which is the most serious rival of the mortgage in cases where the obligation is an agreement to pay the purchase price is the long term land sale contract in which the vendor has not conveyed title but the vendee, ordinarily, has been given possession. The similarity is obvious: the vendor under the land contract is the analogue of the mortgagee under a purchase-money mortgage; the vendee occupies the same relative position as does the mortgagor. The rules governing the two sorts of transactions, while parallel in some respects, are strikingly dissimilar in others.

It is outside the scope of this [excerpt] to explore in detail the law governing these executory contracts, that law being embedded in the doctrines of equity applying to the subject of specific performance of contracts and strongly influenced by ideas of "freedom of contract" and the inviolability of obligations based upon agreement. The most important difference is that the vendor in a land contract, on default by the vendee, by summary proceedings analogous to strict foreclosure, may keep the land, all installments paid, and sue for installments due, if the contract so provides, with the vendee having no right of redemption—a situation completely repugnant to mortgage law ever since the original creation of the redemption right. Because of this advantageous treatment accorded the vendor, increasing numbers of sellers prefer to use the land contract, and by the same token, a purchaser prefers the mortgage as security for the payment of purchase money. . . .

FREYFOGLE, VAGUENESS AND THE RULE OF LAW: RECONSIDERING INSTALLMENT LAND CONTRACT FORFEITURES

1988 Duke L.J. 609, 610–621.

The law of installment land contract forfeitures is amazingly muddled these days. . . . Decades ago the law was relatively clear. Courts enforced forfeiture clauses with few questions asked, except perhaps when a forfeiture was shocking in amount or otherwise grossly unfair. . . .

. . . Courts now show greater solicitude toward the purchaser, a person whom they perceive as poorly informed, inadequately represented, and relatively low in income. New rules give the purchaser additional time to reinstate the contract and redeem the property, while diminishing the adverse consequences when forfeiture is unavoidable.

. . .

As courts have developed sympathy for the installment purchaser, they have begun to reassess the wisdom of denying installment purchasers the numerous protections of mortgage law. A few states . . . have reversed direction in full and have decided to treat the installment contract as the functional equivalent of a mortgage, at least in certain categories of cases. In these states, installment purchasers can require foreclosure and claim the other rights of mortgagors. Most jurisdictions, however, have tailored a separate set of protections for installment purchasers, protections that echo mortgage law but in weakened form. In state after state, these separate rules have become more extensive and complex. . . .

The Pitfalls of Declaring a Forfeiture

1. *The Need for Notice*. . . . The terms of many installment contracts allow a vendor to declare a default and to accelerate the unpaid balance with no notice to the purchaser. But in nearly all states, common law rules and statutory provisions override these contract terms and require vendors to give fair notice of a possible forfeiture. . . .

A vendor must properly phrase a notice of default, but courts again are vague in defining what constitutes proper phrasing. Generally, the notice of forfeiture must specify the nature of the default, the action needed to cure, and the time by which the cure must take place. The notice must state clearly that a forfeiture *will* occur *if* the cure is not performed. Vendors often err at this stage. The notice cannot *declare* a forfeiture, and if it does, it will be ineffective even as a notice of intent to declare a forfeiture in the future. Moreover, a notice that specifies one ground for forfeiture can preclude the vendor from later seeking forfeiture on another ground.

. . .

2. *Waiving the Vendor's Rights.* As courts scrutinize forfeiture measures in particular cases, they are quick to conclude that a vendor has waived the right to declare a forfeiture by accepting late payments or otherwise delaying the right's enforcement. . . .

. . .

3. *The Purchaser's Right to Redeem.* The principal right that states have extended to defaulting purchasers is the right to redeem an installment contract by paying the entire purchase price. In a few states, statutes grant an express right of redemption. In more states, courts use notice rules to this end, allowing a purchaser to redeem during the required notice period prior to forfeiture. California and a few other states employ a somewhat different method, granting purchasers a right to specific performance for a reasonable period after a default and forfeiture declaration. . . .

. . .

4. *The Right to Reinstate.* A few states, typically by statute, give defaulting purchasers an additional right that can be quite valuable—the right to reinstate the contract by paying only the past-due installments (rather than, as in redemption, the entire unpaid debt). . . .

SKENDZEL v. MARSHALL

Supreme Court of Indiana, 1973.
261 Ind. 226, 301 N.E.2d 641.

HUNTER, JUSTICE. Petitioners seek transfer to this Court as a result of an adverse ruling by the Court of Appeals. Plaintiff-respondents originally brought suit to obtain possession of certain real estate through the enforcement of a forfeiture clause in a land sale contract. Plaintiff-respondents suffered a negative judgment, from which they appealed. The Court of Appeals reversed, holding that the defendant-petitioners had breached the contract and that the plaintiff-respondents had not waived their right to enforce the forfeiture provisions of the contract.

In December of 1958, Mary Burkowski, as vendor, entered into a land sale contract with Charles P. Marshall and Agnes P. Marshall, as vendees. The contract provided for the sale of certain real estate for the sum of $36,000.00, payable as follows:

"$500.00, at the signing, execution and delivery of this contract, the receipt whereof is hereby acknowledged; $500.00 or more on or before the 25th day of December, 1958, and $2500.00 or more on or before the 15th day of January, 1960, and $2500.00 or more on or before the 15th day of January of each and every year thereafter until the balance of the contract has been fully paid, all without interest and all without relief from valuation and appraisement laws and with attorney fees."

The contract also contained a fairly standard section which provided for the treatment of prepayments—but which the Court of Appeals found to be of particular importance. It provided as follows:

"Should Vendees have made prepayments or paid in advance of the payments herein required, said prepayments, if any, shall at any time thereafter be applied in lieu of further principal payments required as herein stated, to the extent of such prepayments only."

The following is the forfeiture/liquidated damages provision of the land sale contract:

"It is further agreed that if any default shall be made in the payment of said purchase price or any of the covenants and/or conditions herein provided, and if any such default shall continue for 30 days, then, after the lapse of said 30 days' period *all moneys and payments previously paid shall, at the option of the Vendor without notice or demand, be and become forfeited and be taken and retained by the Vendor as liquidated damages* and thereupon this contract shall terminate and be of no further force or effect; provided, however, that nothing herein contained shall be deemed or construed to prevent the Vendor from enforcing specific performance of this agreement in the event of any default on the part of the Vendees in complying, observing and performing any of the conditions, covenants and terms herein contained. . . ." (Emphasis added.)

The vendor, Mary Burkowski, died in 1963. The plaintiffs in this action are the assignees (under the vendor's will) of the decedent's interests in the contract. They received their assignment from the executrix of the estate of the vendor on June 27, 1968. One year after this assignment, several of the assignees filed their complaint in this action alleging that the defendants had defaulted through non-payment.

The schedule of payments made under this contract was shown by the evidence to be as follows:

"Date	Amount Paid	Total of Paid Principal
12/1/1958	$ 500.00	$ 500.00
12/25/1958	500.00	1,000.00
3/26/1959	5,000.00	6,000.00
4/5/1960	2,500.00	8,500.00
5/23/1961	2,500.00	11,000.00
4/6/1962	2,500.00	13,500.00
1/15/1963	2,500.00	16,000.00
6/30/1964	2,500.00	18,500.00
2/15/1965	2,500.00	21,000.00"

No payments have been made since the last one indicated above—$15,000.00 remains to be paid on the original contract price.

In response to the plaintiff's attempt to enforce the forfeiture provision, the defendants raised the affirmative defense of waiver. The applicable rule is well established and was stated by the Court of Appeals as follows:

"Where a contract for the sale and purchase of land contains provisions similar to those in the contract in the case at bar, *the vendor may waive strict compliance with the provisions of the contract by accepting overdue or irregular payments,* and having so done, equity requires the vendor give specific notice of his intent that he will no longer be indulgent and that he will insist on his right of forfeiture unless the default is paid within a reasonable and specified time." (Emphasis citing) . . . .

. . .

It follows that where the vendor has not waived strict compliance by acceptance of late payments, no notice is required to enforce its provisions. (289 N.E.2d at 771, *citing* Conner v. Fisher, supra; Clayton v. Fletcher Savings & Trust Co., supra.)

In essence, the Court of Appeals found that there was no waiver because the vendors were obligated to accept prepayment, and, "the payments made, although irregular in time and amount, were prepayments on the unpaid balance through and including the payment due on January 15, 1965." (289 N.E.2d at 771.) The Court concluded that up to January 15, 1966, "the vendors waived no rights under the contract, because they were obliged to accept prepayment" and that, "[t]he vendors could not have insisted on forfeiture prior to January 15, 1966, the date of the first missed payment." (We believe the Court of Appeals miscalculated here; the vendors could not have insisted on forfeiture until January 16, 1968.)

If forfeiture is enforced against the defendants, they will forfeit outright the sum of $21,000, or well over one-half the original contract price, as liquidated damages *plus possession.*

Forfeitures are generally disfavored by the law. Carr v. Troutman (1954), 125 Ind.App. 151, 123 N.E.2d 243. In fact, ". . . [e]quity abhors forfeitures and beyond any question has jurisdiction, which it will exercise in a proper case to grant relief against their enforcement." 30 C.J.S. Equity § 56 (1965) and cases cited therein. This jurisdiction of equity to intercede is predicated upon the fact that "the loss or injury occasioned by the default must be susceptible of exact compensation." 30 C.J.S., supra.

. . .

Paragraph 17 of the contract, supra, provides that all prior payments "become forfeited and be taken and retained by the Vendor as liquidated damages." "Reasonable" liquidated damage provisions are permitted by the law. See 22 Am.Jur., 2d Damages § 212 (1965). However, the issue before this Court, is whether a $21,000 forfeiture is a "reasonable" measure of damages. If the damages are unreasonable, i.e., if they are disproportionate to the loss actually suffered, they must be characterized as penal rather than compensatory. See Melfi v. Griscer Industries, Inc. (1967), 141 Ind.App. 607, 231 N.E.2d 54; Czeck v. Van Helsland (1968), 143 Ind.App. 460, 241 N.E.2d 272. Under the facts of this case, a $21,000 forfeiture is clearly excessive.

The authors of American Law Reports have provided an excellent analysis of forfeiture provisions in land contracts:

"As is frequently remarked, there is no single rule for the determination of whether a contractual stipulation is one for liquidated damages or a penalty, each case depending largely upon its own facts and equities, and this apothegm is fully applicable to the decisions involving provisions in land contracts for the forfeiture of payments.

"There is a plethora of abstract tests and criteria for the determination of the nature of a contractual provision as one for a penalty or liquidated damages, and in most instances the courts struggle valiantly to make the result reached by them accord reasonably well with one or more of the more prominent of these abstract tests. But it must be observed that in the last analysis, these factors and criteria are so vague and indefinite that it is doubtful if they are of much aid in construing a specific contractual provision, even assuming that the court makes a conscious and conscientious effort to apply them. At any rate, a reading of the cases collected herein conveys the impression that the ultimate catalyst is the court's belief as to the equities of the case before it.

"Granting this, however, certain tendencies of decision are clearly discernible in the cases. If, for example, the contract involved calls for deferred payments of the purchase price which are relatively small in amount and extend over a number of years, and if it appears that at the time of the purchaser's breach and the consequent invocation of the forfeiture clause by the vendor a comparatively small proportion of the total price remains unpaid, the courts are prone to find that the forfeiture clause was one for a penalty, at least if, as is usually the case, such a holding will tend to give the purchaser another chance to complete the purchase.

"On the other hand, if the amount of the payments received by the vendor at the time the purchase was abandoned represents but a small percentage of the total purchase price, and if the purchaser's breach occurred soon after the execution of the agreement (and particularly if the circumstances indicate that the purchase was made for speculative purposes or that the breach represented an effort on the part of the purchaser to escape an unfortunate turn in the market), the courts tend to hold that the forfeiture clause was one for liquidated damages, with the result that the purchaser cannot recover back the payments made." 6 A.L.R.2d 1401 (1949).

If we apply the specific equitable principle announced above—namely, that the amount paid be considered in relation to the total contract price—we are compelled to conclude that the $21,000 forfeiture as liquidated damages is inconsistent with generally accepted principles of fairness and equity. The vendee has acquired a substantial interest in the property, which, if forfeited, would result in substantial injustice.

Under a typical conditional land contract, the vendor retains legal title until the total contract price is paid by the vendee. Payments are generally made in periodic installments. *Legal* title does not vest in the vendee until the contract terms are satisfied, but equitable title vests in the vendee at the time the contract is consummated. When the parties enter into the contract, all incidents of ownership accrue to the vendee. Thompson v. Norton (1860), 14 Ind. 187. The vendee assumes the risk of loss and is the recipient of all appreciation in value. *Thompson,* supra. The vendee, as equitable owner, is responsible for taxes. Stark v. Kreyling (1934), 207 Ind. 128, 188 N.E. 680. The vendee has a sufficient interest in land so that upon sale of that interest, he holds a vendor's lien. Baldwin v. Siddons (1910), 46 Ind. App. 313, 90 N.E. 1055, 92 N.E. 349.

This Court has held, consistent with the above notions of equitable ownership, that a land contract, once consummated constitutes a present sale and purchase. The vendor " 'has, in effect, exchanged his property for the unconditional obligation of the vendee, the performance of which is secured by the retention of the legal title.' " Stark v. Kreyling, supra, 207 Ind. at 135, 188 N.E. at 682. The Court, in effect, views a conditional land contract as a sale with a security interest in the form of legal title reserved by the vendor. Conceptually, therefore, the retention of the title by the vendor is the same as reserving a lien or mortgage. Realistically, vendor-vendee should be viewed as mortgagee-mortgagor. To conceive of the relationship in different terms is to pay homage to form over substance. See Principles of Equity, Clark, 4th edition, Sec. 9, p. 23.

. . .

It is also interesting to note that the drafters of the Uniform Commercial Code abandoned the distinction between a conditional sale and a security interest. Section 1–201 of the UCC (IC 1971, 26–1–1–201 (Ind.Ann.Stat. § 19–1–201 [1964 repl.])) defines "security interest" as "an interest in personal property or fixtures which secures payment or performance of an obligation . . . retention or reservation of title by a seller of goods notwithstanding shipment or delivery to the buyer is limited in effect to a reservation of 'security interest.'" We can conceive of no rational reason why conditional sales of real estate should be treated any differently.[7]

A conditional land contract in effect creates a vendor's lien in the property to secure the unpaid balance owed under the contract. This lien is closely analogous to a mortgage—in fact, the vendor is commonly referred to as an "equitable mortgagee." D.S.B. Johnston Land Co. v. Whipple, supra; Harris v. Halverson, supra. In view of this characterization of the vendor as a lienholder, it is only logical that such a lien be enforced through foreclosure proceedings. Such a lien "[has] all the incidents of a mortgage" (D.S.B. Johnston Land Co. v. Whipple, supra, 234 N.W. at 61), one of which is the right to foreclose.

. . .

Forfeiture is closely akin to strict foreclosure—a remedy developed by the English courts which did not contemplate the equity of redemption. American jurisdictions, including Indiana, have, for the most part, rejected strict foreclosure in favor of foreclosure by judicial sale: "The doctrine of strict foreclosure developed in England at a time when real property had, to a great extent, a fixed value; the vastly different conditions in this country, in this respect, led our courts to introduce modifications to the English rules of foreclosure. Generally, in consonance with equity's treatment of a mortgage as essentially a security for the payment of the debt, foreclosure by judicial sale supplanted strict foreclosure as the more equitable mode of effectuating the mutual rights of the mortgagor and mortgagee; and there is at the present time, in the majority of the American states, no strict foreclosure as developed by the English courts—either at law or in equity—by which a mortgagee can be adjudged absolute owner of the mortgaged property. The remedy of the mortgagee is by an action for the sale of the mortgaged premises and an application of the proceeds of such sale to the mortgage debt, and although usually called an action to foreclose, it is totally different in its character and results from a strict foreclosure. The phrase 'foreclosure of a mortgage' has acquired, in general, a different meaning from that which it originally bore under the English practice and the common law imported here from England. In this country, the modern meaning of the term 'foreclosure' denotes an equitable proceeding for the enforcement of a lien against property in satisfaction of a debt."

7. In fact, the Commissioners on Uniform State Laws have recognized the transparency of any such distinctions. Section 3–102 of the Uniform Land Transactions Code (working draft of first tentative draft) reads as follows:

"This Article applies to security interests created by contract, including mortgage . . . land sales contract . . . and any other lien or title retention contract intended as security."

We believe this position is entirely consistent with the evolving case law in the area. [footnote by the court.]

55 Am.Jur.2d, Mortgages, § 549 (1971).

Guided by the above principles we are compelled to conclude that judicial foreclosure of a land sale contract is in consonance with the notions of equity developed in American jurisprudence. A forfeiture—like a strict foreclosure at common law—is often offensive to our concepts of justice and inimical to the principles of equity. This is not to suggest that a forfeiture is an inappropriate remedy for the breach of all land contracts. In the case of an abandoning, absconding vendee, forfeiture is a logical and equitable remedy. Forfeiture would also be appropriate where the vendee has paid a minimal amount on the contract at the time of default and seeks to retain possession while the vendor is paying taxes, insurance, and other upkeep in order to preserve the premises. Of course, in this latter situation, the vendee will have acquired very little, if any, equity in the property. However, a court of equity must always approach forfeitures with great caution, being forever aware of the possibility of inequitable dispossession of property and exorbitant monetary loss. We are persuaded that forfeiture may only be appropriate under circumstances in which it is found to be consonant with notions of fairness and justice under the law.

In other words, we are holding a conditional land sales contract to be in the nature of a secured transaction, the provisions of which are subject to all proper and just remedies at law and in equity.

Turning our attention to the case at hand, we find that the vendor-assignees were seeking forfeiture, including $21,000 already paid on said contract as liquidated damages and immediate possession. They were, in fact, asking for strict application of the contract terms at law which we believe would have led to unconscionable results requiring the intervention of equity. "Equity delights in justice, but that *not* by halves." (Story, Eq.Pl. § 72.) On the facts of this case, we are of the opinion that the trial court correctly refused the remedy sought by the vendor-assignees, but in so refusing it denied all remedial relief to the plaintiffs. Equity will "look upon that as done which ought to have been done." (Story, Eq.Jur. § 64(g)). Applying the foregoing maxims to the case at bar, where such parties seek unconscionable results in such an action, equity will treat the subject matter as if the final acts and relief contemplated by the parties were accomplished exactly as they should have been in the first instance. Where discretionary power is not exercised by a trial court, under the mistaken belief that it was without this power, a remand and direction by a court of review is necessary and proper. 5 Am.Jur.2d § 773, p. 216, n. 3 (cases cited therein). This is not an unwarranted interference with the trial court's function. Upon appeal to this Court, we have the judicial duty to *sua sponte* direct the trial court to apply appropriate equitable principles in such a case. 5 Am.Jur.2d, § 656, p. 107, citing: Mark v. Kahn (1956), 333 Mass. 517, 131 N.E.2d 758, 53 A.L.R.2d 908. Consistent with such abovestated rules, this Court has the undeniable authority to remand with guidelines which will give substantial relief to plaintiffs under their secured interests and will prevent the sacrifice of the vendees' equitable lien in the property.

For all of the foregoing reasons, transfer is granted and the cause is reversed and remanded with instructions to enter a judgment of foreclosure on the vendors' lien, pursuant to Trial Rule 69(C) and the mortgage foreclosure statute (IC 1971, 32–8–16–1 (Ind.Stat.Ann., § 3–1801 [1968 repl.])) as modified by Trial Rule 69(C). Said judgment shall include an order for the payment of the unpaid principal balance due on said contract, together with interest at 8% per annum from the date of judgment. The order may also embrace any and all other proper and equitable relief that the court deems to be just, including the discretion to issue a stay of the judicial sale of the property, all pursuant to the provisions of Trial Rule 69(C). Such order shall be consistent with the principles and holdings developed within this opinion.

Reversed and remanded with instructions.

ARTERBURN, C.J., and DEBRULER and PRENTICE, JJ., concur in this opinion on the merits.

PRENTICE, J., filing an additional statement.

GIVAN, J., dissents.

PRENTICE, JUSTICE (concurring).

I have some concern that our opinion herein might be viewed by some as indicating an attitude of indifference towards the rights of contract vendors. Such a view would not be a true reflection.

Because the installment sales contract, with forefeiture provisions, is a widely employed and generally accepted method of commerce in real estate in this state, it is appropriate that a vendee seeking to avoid the forfeiture, to which he agreed, be required to make a clear showing of the inequity of enforcement. In any given transaction anything short of enforcing the forfeiture provision may be a denial of equity to the vendor. It has been set forth in the majority opinion that if the vendee has little or no real equity in the premises, the court should have no hesitancy in declaring a forfeiture. It follows that the vendee has indicated his willingness to forego his equity, if any, whether by mere abandonment of the premises, by release or deed or by a failure to make a timely assertion of his claim, he should be barred from thereafter claiming an equity.

If the court finds that forfeiture, although provided for by the terms of the contract, would be unjust, it should nevertheless grant the vendor the maximum relief consistent with equity against a defaulting vendee. In so doing, it should consider that, had the parties known that the forfeiture provision would not be enforceable, other provisions for the protection of the vendor doubtlessly would have been incorporated into the agreement. Generally, this would require that the transaction be treated as a note and mortgage with such provisions as are generally included in such documents customarily employed in the community by prudent investors. Terms customarily included in such notes and mortgages but frequently omitted from contracts include provisions for increased interest during periods of default, provision for the acceleration of the due date of the entire unpaid principal and interest upon a default continuing beyond a reasonable grace period, provisions for attorneys' fees and other expenses incidental to foreclosure, for the waiver of relief from valuation and appraisement laws and for receivers.

NOTES

1. Skendzel v. Marshall has been followed in subsequent Indiana cases. See, for example, Ebersold v. Wise, 412 N.E.2d 802 (Ind.App.1980), where the court said: "Under the doctrine of Skendzel v. Marshall . . . forfeiture is inappropriate when the vendee has acquired a substantial interest in the property and a forfeiture would result in substantial injustice. In certain cases, forfeiture is still permitted." The principal case indicates that forfeiture provisions in installment land contracts will be enforced if it is not inequitable to do so, i.e., not all such contracts will be treated as equitable mortgages with the attendant safeguards for the purchaser. For a typical case following this view see Bishop v. Beecher, 67 N.M. 339, 355 P.2d 277 (1960). The contract was in the usual installment form with a forfeiture provision, the down payment was small, the monthly payments were $60 (about like rent), and the purchaser had been in possession for almost six years at the time of default. Said the court: "Appellants also ask that we consider the equities because they have paid approximately one-third of the total of the contract. . . . However, under the circumstances of this case, we do not feel that the equities warrant such a result. . . . [w]e will not rewrite the contract into which the parties freely entered. Appellants failed to comply with their agreement, and, absent unfairness which shocks the conscience of the court, the appellees are entitled to enforce the contract as written." In Russell v. Richards, 103 N.M. 48, 702 P.2d 993 (1985), the New Mexico court said, "To determine whether a forfeiture shocks the conscience of the court, this Court has applied the following equitable considerations: the amount of money already paid by the buyer to the seller; the period of possession of the real property by the buyer; the market value of the real property at the time of default compared to the original sales price; and the rental potential and value of the real property."

Under an Ohio statute, R.C. § 5313.07, when purchaser has paid in accordance with the terms of the contract for at least five years, or has paid at least twenty percent of the purchase price, seller's remedy for default lies in foreclosure and not in forfeiture. Smith v. Blackburn, 31 Ohio App.3d 251, 511 N.E.2d 132 (1987), held that the portion of buyer's payments constituting interest must be excluded in determining whether the twenty percent standard has been met.

2. The traditional attitude of the courts toward forfeiture clauses in installment land contracts was harsh indeed. In Pease v. Baxter, 12 Wash. 567, 570, 41 P. 899 (1895) the contract price was $26,000 of which $13,000 had been paid and several thousand dollars expended in permanent improvements on the land when the purchaser failed to pay a $52.08 installment of interest and allowed the insurance coverage to fall below the amount covenanted. The court granted strict enforce-

ment of the forfeiture clause and denied relief on the theory of "equitable mortgages."

UNION BOND & TRUST CO. v. BLUE CREEK REDWOOD CO.

United States District Court, N.D.California, 1955.
128 F.Supp. 709.

GOODMAN, DISTRICT JUDGE.

[The court's footnotes, consisting chiefly of citations, have been omitted.]

This diversity case poses the troublesome question of the nature and extent of the power of this Court, under uncertain California law, to mold a just and appropriate equity decree.

The assignors of the parties litigant, in May of 1946, entered into a timber purchase contract. The contract vendee agreed to purchase from the vendor certain timber lands for a price of $750,000 to be paid out of the proceeds of timber cut, with certain fixed minimum payments.

Their assignees proceeded under the contract. All went *reasonably* well until $585,000 had been paid by vendees. Then certain defaults of the vendee (found by the Court to be wilful) occurred.

Plaintiff, assignee of the vendee, filed this action for a judgment declaring the contract to be in full force and effect and requiring specific performance of the vendor. Defendants, assignees of vendor, by answer, prayed that plaintiff be declared in default under the contract, and, by cross-complaint, prayed for damages caused by the default and also that their title to the timber land be quieted.

At the trial, the evidence showed that plaintiff was in default and that the default had continued for more than 60 days after plaintiff had been notified in writing by defendants of the default. The evidence further showed that on May 12, 1954, defendants notified plaintiff by letter that the contract was cancelled. The notice of cancellation accorded with paragraph 12 of the contract which provided that in the event the vendee should continue in default for more than 60 days after written demand by the vendor for performance, the vendor was entitled to resume possession of the property, retain all payments made by the vendee and cancel the contract by notice. The contract also provided that time was of the essence.

It is clear, and the parties agree, that under California law, which governs by express stipulation of the contract and because this is a diversity suit, plaintiff is entitled to relief from any forfeiture imposed by the contract for his default. The point in issue is the form such relief should take. Plaintiff urges that relief can best be afforded by ordering a conveyance of the land to him upon his immediate payment of the balance of the purchase price as well as any damages to defendants resulting from the default. Defendants contend that plaintiff's default was wilful, and that a vendee in wilful default cannot be given the benefit of his bargain, but at most is entitled to restitution of any payments made in excess of the damages to the vendor.

Three California Civil Code sections are pertinent:

"§ 1492. *Compensation after delay in performance.* Where delay in performance is capable of exact and entire compensation, and time has not been expressly declared to be of the essence of the obligation, and offer of performance, accompanied with an offer of such compensation, may be made at any time after it is due, but without prejudice to any rights acquired by the creditor, or by any other person, in the meantime."

"§ 3275. *Relief in case of forfeiture.* Whenever, by the terms of an obligation, a party thereto incurs a forfeiture, or a loss in the nature of a forfeiture, by reason of his failure to comply with its provisions, he may be relieved therefrom, upon making full compensation to the other party, except in case of a grossly negligent, willful, or fraudulent breach of duty."

"§ 3369.

"1. Neither specific nor preventive relief can be granted to enforce a penalty or forfeiture in any case . . .."

Section 1492 specifically authorizes the kind of relief requested by plaintiff. But it is unavailing here, because, by its terms, it is not applicable to contracts which declare time to be of the essence, as is the case here.

Whether Sections 3275 and 3369 are applicable here, depends upon how they have been construed by the California Courts.

The early California cases, either overlooking or ignoring these Code sections, applied a strict rule of forfeiture against vendees defaulting under contracts declaring time to be of the essence. In 1898, the case of Glock v. Howard, 123 Cal. 1, 55 P. 713, 43 L.R.A. 199, without reference to either Code section, established the rule that a defaulting vendee seeking restitution of payments made under a contract declaring time to be of the essence could not recover in the absence of an equitable showing of surprise, mistake, or fraud. Similarly in quiet title actions, the Courts, without consideration of Section 3369, which prohibits granting specific relief to enforce a forfeiture, quieted title against defaulting vendees without requiring restitution of payments made. Significantly, however, in these quiet title actions, the Courts, although not requiring restitution, in some instance conditioned the decree quieting title upon the vendee's failure to complete performance under the contract and compensate the vendor for damages within a specific period. Thus even in the days when the rights of defaulting vendees were at their lowest ebb in California, it apparently was within the Court's discretion to afford the vendee an opportunity to carry out the contract before quieting title against him.

The California Courts soon modified their strict rule of forfeiture by holding it inapplicable when the vendor had waived or was estopped to assert the time provisions of the contract, or had allowed the entire price to become due without declaring a forfeiture. In some cases, the

Courts invoked Section 3275 to grant relief to the vendee. But even in these cases, the Courts justified the application of the statute by a finding that the vendor had waived or was estopped to assert the time provisions of the contract, or that the vendee had breached a condition subsequent rather than a condition precedent as in the Glock case supra.

In 1949, in Barkis v. Scott, 34 Cal.2d 116, 208 P.2d 367, 368, the California Supreme Court applied Section 3275 to relieve a vendee who had breached a condition precedent under a "time of the essence" contract, in the absence of a waiver by the vendor. The Court distinguished the Glock case on the ground that it appeared from the facts of that case that the vendee could not have qualified for relief under Section 3275. Thus Barkis has established the rule that a defaulting vendee, who meets the requirements of Section 3275, can be relieved from forfeiture even though the vendee has breached a condition precedent and there has been no waiver of provisions of the contract making time of the essence. Moreover, the Supreme Court did not grant relief merely by ordering restitution of the payments made, but rather it sanctioned the restoration of the vendee to his rights under the contract. Indeed, the Court indicated that this form of relief would ordinarily be preferable to restitution. The Court said in this regard, at 34 Cal.2d 121, 208 P.2d 270, "A vendee in default who is seeking to keep the contract alive, however, is in a better position to secure relief than one who is seeking to recover back the excess of what he has paid over the amount necessary to give the vendor the benefit of his bargain after performance under the contract has terminated. In the latter situation it may be so difficult to compute the vendor's damages that the vendee will be unable to prove that the vendor will be unjustly enriched by allowing him to keep all the money that has been paid. (Cases cited.) . . . On the other hand, when the default has not been serious and the vendee is willing and able to continue with his performance of the contract, the vendor suffers no damage by allowing the vendee to do so. In this situation, if there has been substantial part performance or if the vendee has made substantial improvements in reliance on his contract, permitting the vendor to terminate the vendee's right under the contract and keep the installments that have been paid can result only in the harshest sort of forfeitures. Accordingly, relief will be granted whether or not time has been made of the essence."

Thus it is clear that a vendee who meets the requirements of Section 3275 may be relieved from any forfeiture either by restoring him to his rights under the contract, or, as cases subsequent to Barkis have established, by awarding him restitution of payments made in excess of the vendor's damage. Had the plaintiff here been able to qualify for relief under Section 3275, the form of relief which he seeks could be granted under that Section. But, as defendants assert and as the evidence showed, plaintiff fails to qualify because his default was wilful within the meaning of Section 3275.

An alternative basis for the relief sought by plaintiff is indicated, however, by the decision of the California Supreme Court in Freedman

v. Rector, 1951, 37 Cal.2d 16, 230 P.2d 629, 632, 31 A.L.R.2d 1, some two years after the Barkis decision. In the Freedman case, the vendee under an installment contract for the purchase of land sued for specific performance. The trial Court found that the vendee was in wilful default and therefore not entitled to relief under Section 3275 and gave judgment for the defendant vendor. On appeal, the Supreme Court agreed that relief under Section 3275 was precluded, but held that Section 3275 was not exclusive, but merely permissive, and that an alternative basis for the relief of a vendee in wilful default is provided by the damage provisions of the Civil Code and by the policy of the law against penalties and forfeitures.

The damage provisions of the Civil Code referred to by the Court are Section 3294, which provides for exemplary damages for the breach of certain obligations *not* arising from contract, and Sections 1670 and 1671, which validate contractual provisions for liquidated damages in situations where it would be impracticable or extremely difficult to fix the actual damage. It would be inconsistent with these provisions, the Court said, to permit what are, in effect, punitive damages merely because a party has partially performed his contract before his breach. Section 3294 expresses the policy of the law against the allowance of exemplary damages for breach of contract regardless of the nature of the breach. Sections 1670 and 1671 prevent the enforcement of a provision for the forfeiture of installment payments as a valid provision for liquidated damages, when it would not be impracticable or extremely difficult to fix the actual damages.

The Court in Freedman also stated that to deny the vendee relief, because his breach is wilful, would create an anomalous situation when considered with Section 3369 of the Civil Code, supra, which provides that "Neither specific nor preventive relief can be granted to enforce a penalty or forfeiture in any case." That Section, the Court said, "precludes the court from quieting the vendor's title unless he refunds the excess of the part payments over the damage caused by the vendee's breach. . . . Unless the same rule is adopted when the vendee seeks restitution, the rights of the parties under identical fact situations will turn on the chance of which one first seeks the aid of the court."

In Freedman, the Supreme Court held that the defaulting vendee was entitled to restitution of payments made in excess of the vendor's damage. Relief in the form of specific performance was necessarily denied the vendee, however, since the trial court had found that the vendee had, apart from his default, rescinded the contract, and that, before the rescission was revoked, the vendor had sold the property to another.

Under the Freedman rule it is clear that the plaintiff here, even though in wilful default, is at least entitled to relief in the form of restitution of payments made in excess of the defendants' damage. The pertinent remaining question is whether the Freedman rule is broad enough to permit relief in the form of an opportunity to complete the contract, upon compensating the defendants for their damage. The refusal of the court to grant such relief in the Freedman case does not preclude it here since in Freedman the vendee had, apart from his default, rescinded the contract and the property was thereupon sold to another. The grounds upon which the Court in Freedman allowed restitution should equally justify relief in the form of an opportunity to complete the contract in a proper case.

The basis upon which the Court afforded relief in Freedman was the Code sections expressing a policy against permitting forfeitures or exemplary damages for breach of contract. These sections, the Court said, require that a vendee in wilful default be relieved from any forfeiture, just as Section 3275 permits relief to be accorded a vendee whose default is not wilful. But these Code sections do not prescribe the form such relief should take any more than does Section 3275. In granting relief from forfeiture under Section 3275, in Barkis, supra, the Supreme Court seemed to take it for granted that a proper method, and indeed the preferable one, was to permit the vendee to carry out the contract.

Defendants here urge that a vendee in wilful default should not be relieved from a forfeiture by permitting him to complete performance under the contract because he would then be receiving the benefit of his bargain. But, this argument amounts to no more than the contention that the Court should punish a vendee in wilful default by denying him an opportunity to complete the contract, even though in some manner it must relieve him from the forfeiture. Yet the *policy* against the imposition of a penalty for breach of contract is the very basis for the holding in Freedman that a vendee in wilful default must be relieved from any forfeiture. Certainly, then, the determination of the form such relief should take should not be conditioned by a purpose to penalize the vendee.

The California Supreme Court also said in Freedman that the rights of the vendor and vendee should not turn on the chance of which one first seeks the aid of Court. The Court stated that Section 3369 of the Civil Code prohibiting the enforcement of forfeiture precludes a Court from quieting the vendor's title unless he refunds the excess of the part payments over his damages. The same rule, the Court said, should be followed when the vendee seeks restitution.

But, as has been noted, the California Courts previously had paid no heed to Section 3369 in quiet title actions and had entered decrees quieting title without requiring restitution. They had, however, in some instances given the vendee an opportunity to complete the contract, and it appears to be the established rule that it is within the discretion of the Court to do so. Thus, if the vendee is to have the same rights when he invokes the aid of the Court, as when the vendor seeks to quiet title, the Court should have the discretion in either situation to give the vendee an opportunity to complete the contract.

While this view has not been precisely stated by the highest Courts of California, I am of the opinion that they would so hold if called upon to resolve the facts of this case. Barkis and Freedman point the way towards that end.

Some of the considerations which might enter into the exercise of the Court's discretion were indicated by the Supreme Court in Barkis. The Court noted that in some cases it would be difficult to compute the vendor's damages if the contract were terminated. The Court suggested, that if the vendee were able and willing to complete the contract, and had made substantial part performance, or substantial improvements on the property, completion of the contract would best protect the rights of the parties.

In the present case, the plaintiff has made substantial payments under the contract and has made substantial improvements on the property. Because of conflicting estimates of value, the vendor's damages may be difficult to determine, if the contract is terminated. Consequently the just and equitable course would appear to be to enter a preliminary decree permitting plaintiff to complete the contract within a specified time by paying the entire purchase price together with the defendants' damages resulting from the delay in performance.

Accordingly, an interlocutory decree will be entered as follows:

(1) The plaintiff may complete the contract of purchase by paying the entire unpaid purchase price within 60 days from date hereof.

(2) Within 10 days thereafter the Court will hear evidence as to defendants' damage, limited to

(a) interest on past due payments;

(b) cost of investigating plaintiff's defaults; and

(c) costs and expenses of suit and trial including reasonable attorney's fees.

Final decree will then enter adjudging the amount of damages due defendant.

(3) In the event plaintiff fails to pay the unpaid purchase price within the time specified in (1), the Court will enter an interlocutory decree quieting vendor's title to the property and within 10 days thereafter will hear any further evidence and/or argument the parties wish to present as to the amount of restitution to be made to the plaintiff and will thereupon enter final decree adjudging the rights and liabilities of the parties.

Counsel will present findings and interlocutory decree within 10 days.

[Affirmed 243 F.2d 476, 9th Cir. 1957.]

NOTES

1. In Petersen v. Hartell, 40 Cal.3d 102, 219 Cal.Rptr. 170, 707 P.2d 232 (1985), the Supreme Court of California held that "where the seller of land retains title only as security for amounts payable under an installment sale contract, a vendee who wilfully defaults in one or more payments after having paid a substantial part of the purchase price nonetheless retains an absolute right to redeem the property by paying the entire balance of the price and any other amounts [interest and damages] due." Chief Justice Bird, in a separate opinion, urged

that the right of redemption be extended to vendees who have not paid a substantial part of the purchase price, and that vendors' remedy be limited to foreclosure by sale, subject to vendees' right to reinstate the contract by paying only the delinquent amounts plus costs and attorneys' fees. The majority of the court noted that these major changes in the law were not sought by plaintiff vendees, and chose to limit its holding to the issues necessarily presented for decision. Compare Rickel v. Energy Systems Holdings, Ltd., 114 Idaho 585, 759 P.2d 876 (1988), where purchaser failed to pay an installment under a contract which did not provide for acceleration of future payments in the event of such a default. The court ordered that purchaser be given 120 days to pay the $400,000 installment and that if purchaser failed to do so, the trial court should impose a vendor's lien on the property for the $1.7 million unpaid balance of the original $2.2 million price, and order foreclosure by judicial sale.

2. Some of the difficulties with the installment land contract stem from a failure to distinguish the purposes for which the contract is employed. To paraphrase Gertrude Stein, the courts tend to say "the contract is a contract is a contract . . . ." Professor Hetland makes this point clear in The California Land Contract, 48 Calif.L.Rev. 729 (1960). "A 'land contract' often is a security device in lieu of a mortgage or deed of trust. To the extent this is the meaning of 'land contract', security remedies may be appropriate; perhaps the judicial sale, redemption period and deficiency judgment prohibition should replace the traditional action for specific performance or for damages. But a 'land contract' also is an earnest money contract, or a deposit receipt, or occasionally mutual escrow instructions; in other words, it is often the basic buy-sell agreement rather than a security device. And if this is what 'land contract' means, the security debtor's protections should not interfere with the vendor's action for damages, his retention of liquidated damages, or his action for specific performance."

3. The form of action chosen by a vendor may limit the defenses available to a defaulting purchaser. In a highly publicized case, Rosewood Corp. v. Fisher, 46 Ill.2d 249, 263 N.E.2d 833 (1970), plaintiff land developers instituted hundreds of forcible entry and detainer actions to recover possession of houses from defaulting purchasers, all of whom were black. Defendants, for the most part, had complied with their contracts for several years and accumulated equities in their respective properties. In 1968, a general feeling of dissatisfaction arose among the purchasers, stemming from a belief that they had been overcharged for their houses and that unfair advantage and discrimination, made possible by the social and economic problems encountered by members of their race in the purchase of suitable residences, had been practiced against them. Rather than seeking judicial relief from allegedly unconscionable contracts, purchasers embarked upon a concerted course of self-help, for the purpose of securing modification and renegotiation of their contracts, and stopped making their installment payments. They thus exposed themselves to forfeiture of their contract rights and equities and to suits for possession.

The trial court entered judgments for possession in favor of plaintiff vendors in all of the cases, relying upon a provision in the Forcible Entry and Detainer Acts that "defendant may under a general denial of the allegations of the complaint give in evidence any matter in defense of the action. No matters not germane to the distinctive purpose of the proceeding shall be introduced by joinder, counterclaim or otherwise. . . ." The trial court concluded that the statute allowed defendants to deny that they had defaulted on their contracts, but not to introduce by way of answer, counterclaim or affirmative defense other matters going to the validity and enforceability of the contracts.

On appeal, the state Supreme Court reversed all of the judgments, holding that the purchasers' defenses were "germane" to the distinctive purpose of the proceedings. "Should a contract purchaser not be permitted to defend upon the very contract upon which the seller relies, . . . the result could be, as argued, a direct denial of constitutional rights and an indirect denial of civil rights."

For more about the Contract Buyers League litigation, see McPherson, In My Father's House There Are Many Mansions—And I'm Going to Get Me Some of Them Too, 229 The Atlantic Monthly 51–82 (April, 1972).

4. For an excellent discussion of the current state of the law regarding installment land contract forfeitures, see Freyfogle, Vagueness and the Rule of Law: Reconsidering Installment Land Contract Forfeitures, 1988 Duke L.J. 609.

C. MERCHANTABLE TITLE

WALLACH v. RIVERSIDE BANK

Court of Appeals of New York, 1912.
206 N.Y. 434, 100 N.E. 50.

By a contract made on the 4th of February, 1905, the defendant agreed to sell to the plaintiff "all the premises known as Nos. 165 and 167 East 108th street in the city of New York," bounded and described by definite and certain metes and bounds. The sale was stated to be subject to existing leases expiring on May 1, 1905, and to "existing restrictions of record if any." The plaintiff, on his part, agreed to purchase said premises and to pay therefor the sum of $22,000, part in cash and the balance by a purchase-money mortgage. Upon receipt of the money and mortgage the defendant agreed to execute, acknowledge, and deliver to the plaintiff a "quitclaim deed of said premises." On the law day the defendant tendered to the plaintiff a quitclaim deed in the usual form of such instruments and demanded performance from him according to his covenant. The plaintiff declined to accept title and take the deed tendered because "the wife of William G. Wood did not join in the execution of the deed to George T. Leaird made by the said William G. Wood and recorded in Liber 23, section 16, of Conveyances, page 464." In the defendant's chain of title said deed is an essential part, yet the wife of the grantor did not join therein, although she was living when it was given and is living still with the marriage in full force. The plaintiff duly tendered performance on his part and offered to comply with the contract in all respects "provided a marketable title could be conveyed to him by the defendant." The defendant refused to perform other than as stated, and the plaintiff, after demanding the sum paid down and a further sum for the reasonable expense of examining the title, commenced this action to recover the same. The trial justice found the facts thus stated, and also found "that prior to the execution by plaintiff of the agreement between him and defendant of date February 4, 1905, plaintiff objected to the word 'quitclaim' in the agreement and refused at first to sign the agreement because of the use of the word 'quitclaim.'" As conclusions of law he found that the title of the defendant was unmarketable and that the plaintiff was entitled to judgment for the amounts claimed. From the judgment of affirmance rendered by the Appellate Division, this appeal is brought.

Vann, J. (after stating the facts as above). The main question presented by this appeal is whether the defendant met its covenant to convey the premises by tendering a quitclaim deed thereof under the circumstances found by the trial court. The subject of the contract was a certain parcel of land, and the object of the plaintiff was to buy, and of the defendant to sell, "all the premises," which were carefully described. The means prescribed by the parties to carry the contract into effect on the part of the defendant was a quitclaim deed. The defendant, however, did not have a perfect title free from incumbrances, for the premises were subject to an inchoate right of dower vested by statute in the wife of a prior grantor. As it could not convey that outstanding right, it could not convey the premises, except by leaving them subject to that right. The covenant was to convey a certain parcel of land, not to convey all the right, title, and interest of the defendant in that land. A contract to sell land implies ownership and power to give good title on the law day. The plaintiff did not agree to accept a defective title. He agreed to buy "all the premises" described by clear and unmistakable boundaries, and by implication of law this means in an executory contract a good title to the whole thereof, free and clear from incumbrances. Although the writing does not say so, the law says so, and the law is part of the writing.

When a vendor agrees to sell a piece of land, the law imputes to him a covenant that he will convey a marketable title unless the vendee stipulates to accept something less. While, owing to a statute, no covenant can be implied in a deed, in an executory contract to convey land the vendor always covenants by implication to give a good title, unless such a covenant is expressly made or is expressly excluded by the terms of the agreement. Even if the conveyance is to be made without warranties, still the land itself is to be conveyed, and, as the grantor can convey only that which he has, unless he has title to the land he cannot convey the land. If his title is subject to a right which may take away part of the land, he cannot in the full legal sense convey the land, for there is an outstanding interest which his deed does not touch. If the plaintiff was bound to accept the deed tendered with a partial defect of title, he would have been bound to accept it even if it conveyed nothing whatever, although the consideration named was $22,000.

These views are supported by the authorities, both ancient and modern. In the leading case in this state, decided in 1854, Judge Samuel L. Selden, upon a careful review of the previous cases and after an able discussion of the principles involved, with the concurrence of all his associates, held that "in every executory contract for the sale of lands there is an implied warranty on the part of the vendor that he has a good title which continues until merged in the deed of conveyance." Burwell v. Jackson, 9 N.Y. 535. This case has been frequently cited, but never questioned, and the opinion shows such perfection of learning and reasoning as to make it a landmark in the law. . . .

The agreement of the plaintiff to accept a quitclaim deed as the means of transfer was not a waiver of the defect. A quitclaim deed is as effective as any to convey all the title the grantor has, and a deed with all the covenants known cannot strengthen a defective title, but can simply protect from loss on account thereof.

The sale was subject to existing liens and to existing restrictions of record, and it could be subject to no other defect unless it was also specified. As was said in Moore v. Williams, 115 N.Y. at page 592, 22 N.E. at page 234, 5 L.R.A. 654, 12 Am.St.Rep. 844, supra: "The express stipulation that he (the vendee) was to take the lot subject to an incumbrance specified shows that in the minds of the parties there was to be no other incumbrance upon the lot. But, aside from the language used in the contract, it is familiar law that an agreement to make a good title is always implied in executory contracts for the sale of land, and that a purchaser is never bound to accept a defective title, unless he expressly stipulates to take such title, knowing its defects. His right to an indisputable title, clear of defects and incumbrances, does not depend upon the agreement of the parties, but is given by the law."

If the plaintiff knew of the defect when the contract was signed, he had the right to presume from its terms that a good title would be made before the law day. It is a somewhat common practice to agree to sell land without limitation, although both parties know at the time that some outstanding right must be acquired by the vendor in order to enable him to perform his covenant when the law day arrives.

The defendant insists that the court erred in refusing to find upon its request that the plaintiff knew what a quitclaim deed was and the title it would convey; that before the agreement was executed he had been told by the defendant that the only title it could give was such as it had and no more; and that he knew when he signed the contract that there were existing questions respecting the title.

Assuming, without holding, that there was sufficient uncontradicted evidence to warrant these findings, the written agreement could not be cut down or limited by such facts. Whatever was said before the instrument was signed being merged therein became wholly immaterial, and it is not an error of law to refuse to find an immaterial fact even upon uncontradicted evidence.

The judgment should be affirmed, with costs.

CULLEN, C.J., and GRAY, HAIGHT, WERNER, WILLARD BARTLETT, and HISCOCK, JJ., concur.

NOTES

1. For further light on this problem see Tymon v. Linoki, 16 N.Y. 2d 293, 213 N.E.2d 661 (1965) where the court carefully distinguishes between the *title* to be conveyed and the kind of *deed* to be used for the conveyance. See also Laba v. Carey, 29 N.Y.2d 302, 327 N.Y.S.2d 613, 277 N.E.2d 641 (1971) where the court said: "It is axiomatic that a purchaser is entitled to marketable title unless the parties provide otherwise in the contract (citing Wallach v. Riverside Bank, among other authorities) . . . . A seller is required to tender a title which is readily subject to resale and free from reasonable doubt." On the other hand, a purchaser is not entitled to a warranty deed unless his contract expressly calls for one.

2. A typical contract clause reads as follows: "Vendor agrees to furnish the purchaser a complete abstract[8] of title brought down to date showing merchantable title to the premises. In the event there are objections to such title the purchaser shall, within a reasonable time, submit in writing a statement of all objections which he deems material." Even in the absence of such a clause, the burden is on the purchaser to point out defects in the title. While the vendor cannot force an unmerchantable title on the purchaser by a suit for specific performance, neither can the latter bring suit for defects until he specifically points them out to the seller and gives him an opportunity to correct them. Nor can the vendee wait until the day of closing to raise objections; doing so will have the effect of prolonging the time for performance by the vendor. See Easton v. Montgomery, 90 Cal. 307, 27 P. 280, 25 Am.St.Rep. 123 (1891).

3. While there is general agreement that the vendor must furnish a merchantable title, unless the parties contract for something more (a title satisfactory to a third party or an insurable title) or less (such interest as the vendor may have), it is most difficult to define merchantability. Most definitions beg the question and sound like the following: A merchantable title is "a title not subject to such reasonable doubt as would create a just apprehension of its validity in the mind of a reasonable, prudent and intelligent person; one that persons of reasonable prudence and intelligence, guided by competent legal advice, would be willing to take and pay the fair value of the land for." Eggers v. Busch, 154 Ill. 604, 607, 39 N.E. 619, 620 (1895). Any more questions?

Perhaps the best indication of what the term means can be found by listing the types of defects which may make a title unmerchantable. Some seventy Illinois cases involving this phase of the contract turned on the following points: will construction, deed construction, necessary

8. See page 1337 for a discussion of the abstract of title. While the contract usually provides that the vendor will furnish the abstract, the purchaser must provide his own if the contract is silent. See 24 Mich. L.Rev. 318 (1925).

party omitted in a proceeding, break in chain of record title, mortgage, dower, lease, taxes, special assessments, judgments, claims against a decedent's estate, building restrictions, easements, encroachments, title based on judicial or tax sale, defectively executed instruments, variation in names, defect in description of realty, lack of possession by vendor, competency of the grantor, lost deed, outstanding contract of purchase, title tainted with fraud, no patent or land grant from government, and suits pending against the vendor. See Reeve, Defining the Undefinable—Marketability (1954), published by the Chicago Title and Trust Co., 111 West Washington Street, Chicago, Illinois. The point can be summed up best by the maxim, "Equity will not force a man to buy a lawsuit."

Lack of access to a tract of land does not render the owner's title unmerchantable. "Merchantability does not equate with market value or [saleability]. Numerous factors may affect the market value of land and unquestionably access to a public way is such a factor; however, if the title is secure against defects in the statutory warranties, the title is merchantable." Sinks v. Karleskint, 130 Ill.App.3d 527, 85 Ill.Dec. 807, 474 N.E.2d 767 (1985).

4. Frequently criminal statutes provide for penalties against a landowner and then make a fine a lien against the land but make no provision for recording the lien. Do these liens make the title unmerchantable? The Illinois Supreme Court held "no " in Illinois National Bank v. Chegin, 35 Ill.2d 375, 220 N.E.2d 226 (1966). "Here, it is evident that the forfeiture provisions in the Criminal Code were enacted for the purpose of encouraging property owners and occupants to eliminate illicit activities from their premises, and to provide an effective method for abating the nuisance and reimbursing injured parties if the person maintaining the nuisance fails in his responsibilities. At the same time, however, there is no indication that the legislature . . . intended or desired to impede the ease of land conveyance which has long been enjoyed in this State, or to abrogate the various recording statutes which have made freedom of conveyance possible. To the contrary, legislative history reflects a policy and desire on the part of our lawmakers to encourage such commerce and to this end they have by statute established public records which may be relied upon by a purchaser in determining the status of real estate titles." What result if the legislature made provision for recording the liens?

BARTOS v. CZERWINSKI

Supreme Court of Michigan, 1948.
323 Mich. 87, 34 N.W.2d 566.

CARR, JUSTICE. Plaintiffs brought this action to compel the specific performance of a written agreement for the sale of certain real estate in the city of Detroit. The instrument in question, which was dated October 3, 1945, was in the form of an offer and acceptance. Plaintiffs undertook to pay the sum of $6,300 for the property described with the sum of $200 down to apply on the purchase price, such amount "to be returned should proposition be rejected by owner, or prior sale, of said property; or should the title be found unmarketable." The offer further provided for closing the deal within ten days from the date of delivery of an abstract of title. The acceptance agreed to the terms of the offer and contained an express provision that defendant would furnish "abstract of title certified to date, showing marketable title."

Following execution of the agreement an abstract was delivered to plaintiffs for their examination. It was submitted to an attorney who gave his opinion to the effect that the title shown by the abstract was marketable. Thereafter plaintiffs submitted it to their attorney, Mr. Piotrowski, who came to the conclusion that there was a flaw in the record of title of such character as to render it not marketable in the ordinary acceptance of the term. The abstract in question is not in the record, in this court, and it does not appear that it was introduced in evidence on the hearing in the trial court. However, a witness on behalf of the plaintiffs, an employee of the Wayne County Tract Index Department, testified with reference to the title as shown by the records of said department. It is a fair inference from the record here that the alleged defect in title shown by the abstract arose from certain conveyances to which the witness testified, and concerning which there seems to be no dispute. In 1922 the property in question was conveyed by warranty deed to Richard S. Hickey and Derk Eppinga, said deed being recorded October 30, 1922. In January, 1923, by warranty deed recorded January 25th of said year, the grantees in the previous deed conveyed to the Peoples State Bank of Detroit. By a quitclaim deed dated December 28, 1927, Eppinga conveyed his interest in the property to Hickey, the instrument being recorded January 7, 1928. The record further disclosed a quitclaim deed dated December 29, 1927, from the Peoples State Bank to Hickey and Eppinga, recorded January 10, 1928. Thereafter Hickey made conveyance of his interest in the property, but it does not appear that Eppinga did so. Plaintiffs' attorney came to the conclusion that there was, or might be, an outstanding undivided one-half interest in the property, held by Eppinga or others claiming under him, and advised plaintiffs accordingly.

It appears that the plaintiff Frank Bartos became ill and went to Arizona while the matter was pending. Subsequent negotiations were carried on between Mrs. Bartos and her attorney on one side, and defendant and her son, on the other. On behalf of plaintiffs, it was insisted that some action should be taken to clear the title, plaintiffs clearly indicating that they would not accept a conveyance unless the alleged defect was obviated or protection afforded them in some manner against a possible subsequent attack on the title to the property. A quitclaim deed was prepared for Eppinga's signature, and defendant's son contacted him, presumably for the purpose of having the deed executed if that action could be brought about. However, Eppinga stated, in substance, that he did not care to be bothered, and it does not appear that any further attempt was made to procure from him a release of any interest that he might have in the property in question. No further action was taken by defendant with reference to the matter. The record shows, however, that, in a conversation between them, defendant and Mrs. Bartos reached an agreement with reference to the return of the deposit; but the agreement was not carried out for the reason that defendant insisted on a return of the preliminary contract for the purchase of the property or some form of receipt for the money that would release defendant from liability.

In their bill of complaint plaintiffs alleged that defendant was in position to convey good title to the land. On the trial, however, they reasserted their prior position that they would not accept a conveyance unless such action was taken by the defendant as would render the title marketable. It thus appears that plaintiffs sought not merely a conveyance of the property as the averments of the bill of complaint would suggest, but rather a decree that would require defendant to clear the title to the property to the satisfaction of the plaintiffs, and then make conveyance in accordance with the preliminary agreement. The trial court came to the conclusion that plaintiffs were not entitled to such relief, that there was a variance between the bill of complaint and the proofs offered by plaintiffs on the trial, and that the alleged defect in defendant's title to the property was not of serious character. Accordingly relief was denied. From the decree entered, plaintiffs have appealed.

Whether defendant's title to the property was actually not marketable is not clearly shown on this record. The deed from the Peoples State Bank to Hickey and Eppinga was dated December 29, 1927, while the conveyance from Eppinga to Hickey was dated on December 28th preceding, but there is nothing otherwise in the record to indicate when the instruments were actually delivered. It is conceivable, of course, that the conveyance by Eppinga was actually consummated after the deed to him had been delivered and accepted. If it be assumed, however, that each conveyance was delivered on the date appearing thereon, then the abstract indicated, as plaintiffs' attorney concluded, that there was, or might, be an outstanding interest in Eppinga or in someone claiming under him. If such was the case, then the title that defendant had was not a marketable one in the ordinary acceptance of the term. In Barnard v. Brown, 112 Mich. 452, 70 N.W. 1038, 1039, 67 Am.St.Rep. 432, it was said:

"A marketable title, however, is one of such character as should assure to the vendee the quiet and peaceable enjoyment of the property, and one which is free from incumbrance." . . .

A title may be regarded as unmarketable if a reasonably careful and prudent man, familiar with the facts, would refuse to accept the title in the ordinary course of business. It is not necessary that the title be actually bad in order to render it unmarketable. It is sufficient if there is such a doubt or uncertainty as may reasonably form the basis of litigation. Williams v. Bricker, 83 Kan. 53, 109 P. 998, 30 L.R.A.,N.S., 343. A purchaser of property entitled to a "marketable title" may not be required to accept a conveyance if the title is in such condition that he may be required to defend litigation challenging his possession and interest. . . .

Assuming that defendant's title was, as claimed by plaintiffs, not a marketable one because of a possible outstanding interest in the property in another, the remedy of specific performance must nevertheless be denied. Plaintiffs are in effect asking that the court compel defendant to obtain a proper conveyance or release from Eppinga, or in the alternative to institute and carry through to a successful termination proceedings to quiet title to the property. This the court may not properly do. There is no assurance that defendant can obtain a conveyance from Eppinga, and certainly it cannot be said that a suit to quiet title would be a mere formal matter that would result in accomplishing the desired purpose. Neither may the court require defendant to furnish title insurance for the benefit of plaintiffs. The contract made no provision therefor and the court may not add any such requirement.

In Lingemann v. Naoumson, 237 Mich. 557, 212 N.W. 955, 957, it was said:

"Courts of equity are loathe to impose and supervise the performance and execution of contracts freighted with contingencies or uncertainties, but leave the plaintiff to his remedy at law."

The case of Ogooshevitz v. Arnold, 197 Mich. 203, 163 N.W. 946, 165 N.W. 633, to which counsel for plaintiffs has called attention, presented an entirely different situation. There the defendants were unquestionably in position to remedy the defect in title. As above pointed out, such is not the situation in the case at bar. The equitable remedy by specific performance is not one of right, but rather rests in the sound discretion of the court. Viewing the situation in the light most favorable to plaintiffs, it must be held that they are not entitled to the relief that they are seeking.

It is apparent from the record that plaintiffs knew when they started their suit that defendant could not convey to them a satisfactory marketable title without taking action to clear that title. They must have realized also that there was no certainty as to defendant's ability to obtain a conveyance from Eppinga, or to quiet title as against him or others claiming under him. It was their position on the trial, as it had been previously, that they would not accept a conveyance from defendant unless the doubt as to the sufficiency of the record title were in some way removed. . . .

Under the proofs in the instant case there is no basis for equitable jurisdiction. The trial court correctly held that plaintiffs were not entitled to specific performance of the contract involved in the suit. Dismissal of the bill of complaint should, however, be without prejudice to the right of the plaintiffs to pursue such remedy on the law side as they may think proper for the recovery of the money paid by them to defendant. Decree will enter here modifying in this respect, and otherwise affirming, the decree of the trial court. Defendant may have costs.

BUSHNELL, C.J., and SHARPE, BOYLES, REID, NORTH, DETHMERS, and BUTZEL, JJ., concur.

NOTES

1. If vendor's title is unmarketable because it is subject to a mortgage which he lacks the resources to pay, can the purchaser obtain specific performance? In Addesso v. Shemtob, 122 A.D.2d 754, 505 N.Y.S.2d 642 (1986), the court said yes because "defendants could pay the mortgage out of the proceeds of the purchase price." In Green Point Savings Bank v. Litas Investing Co., 124 A.D.2d 555, 507 N.Y.S.2d 700 (1986), vendor voluntarily encumbered the property with a mortgage after contracting to sell and then pleaded inability to convey marketable title. The court awarded purchaser specific performance, saying, "We see no establishment of considerable hardship preventing the defendant from raising the money to pay off the . . . mortgage . . . and conveying clear title to the plaintiff in accordance with the contract."

2. It has been said that a merchantable title is that title which a court of equity will force an unwilling purchaser to take in a suit for specific performance. While such a definition begs the question, it does raise a valid point. If the court decides that the title is merchantable doesn't that make it so? Why was the court in the principal case unwilling to decide that the defect was minor and force the purchaser to accept the title without a release from Eppinga? Suppose the alleged defect is based on the asserted invalidity of a tax lien law under both the state and federal constitutions. Can the state court decide the issue and grant specific performance? In Lynbrook Gardens, Inc. v. Ullman, 291 N.Y. 472, 477, 53 N.E.2d 353, 354 (1943) the Court of Appeals of New York refused to do so, saying, "Even though this court were to sustain the validity of the statute, the Supreme Court of the United States might still reach a different conclusion. A subsequent purchaser could at any time reject title on that ground and litigate that question in a different forum. A title which can be challenged in that manner is not marketable and a decree of specific performance may not be rendered under such circumstances." There was a vigorous dissent.

3. The suit to quiet title is the classic remedy for the unmerchantable title. It is designed to bring all possible claimants within the jurisdiction of the court of equity so that their claims may be eliminated as clouds on the title, *if* they are found to be without merit. Would such a suit have been an effective remedy in a case like Bartos v. Czerwinski? Is a title based on adverse possession merchantable? Consider Escher v. Bender, 338 Mich. 1, 7, 61 N.W.2d 143, 147 (1953) where the court said: "By the terms of defendant's agreement to sell the premises, he was bound to convey to the plaintiff a good marketable title as shown by the abstract. Title established through adverse possession is free from encumbrance and of a character to assure quiet and peaceful enjoyment of the property by the owner, . . . but it is not a marketable title of record until there has been a judicial determination of such title." See also pages 1453 to 1496 infra. For a critical analysis of the remedial problem see Note, Enhancing the Marketability of Land: The Suit to Quiet Title, 68 Yale L.J. 1245 (1959).

LUETTE v. BANK OF ITALY NAT. TRUST & SAVINGS ASS'N

Circuit Court of Appeals, Ninth Circuit, 1930.
42 F.2d 9.

KERRIGAN, DISTRICT JUDGE. This is an appeal from an order dismissing a third amended and supplemental bill of complaint and from the decree of dismissal entered thereon.

The complaint alleges that the plaintiffs entered into a contract in June, 1926, with the predecessor in interest of the defendant for the purchase of a certain parcel of real property. The purchase price was $6,500, $1,625 of which was paid at the time of the execution of the contract. The balance was to be paid in monthly installments, which plaintiffs paid to July, 1928; the complaint showing that such payments would continue to May, 1933, under the contract. Plaintiffs allege in effect, construing all of the allegations as to defendant's title together, that defendant has record title to the property in question, and that an adverse claim has been asserted through the filing of homestead claims upon the theory that title to the land is in the United States, the outcome of which claims is uncertain; the matter being now before the Department of the Interior on appeal. It may be fairly concluded from the description of the present state of these homestead proceedings that the decision in the first instance in the Land Office was unfavorable to the homestead right, and that the appeal is that of the claimants; in other words, that the Land Office has held that the land in question is not part of the public domain.

Plaintiffs allege that, on discovery of the existence of the homestead claims, they demanded of defendant that it exhibit its title, and offered, if and when defendant should do so, to pay the amount due under the contract, but that defendant has refused to exhibit its title and, on demand, has refused to repay to plaintiffs the sums already paid upon the contract. The prayer of the complaint is that defendant be enjoined from canceling the contract of plaintiffs and forfeiting plaintiffs' rights thereunder, and that plaintiffs be relieved from paying further installments pending the outcome of the proceedings before the Department of the Interior. Plaintiffs further pray that, in the event the court is unable to grant the relief prayed for, the contract between plaintiffs and defendant be rescinded, and that plaintiffs have judgment for the moneys already paid under the contract. In seeking to rescind, plaintiffs allege that the only thing of value received by them is the contract of sale itself, which they tender.

In considering whether this complaint states a cause of action, its aspect as a bill for an injunction must be disregarded, as plaintiffs state no ground for the intervention of equity to preserve all of their rights under the contract pending the determination of defendant's title, while at the same time relieving them from the duty of performing their part of the bargain. There is no allegation that defendant is, or is likely to become, insolvent, nor any pleading of other equities to justify such relief. The question therefore is whether the complaint states grounds for rescission of the contract.

The vendees under an executory contract here seek to rescind on account of an uncertainty as to the state of the vendor's title, at a time long prior to the date when the vendor will be required to convey title under the installment contract. The complaint shows that the plaintiffs attempted to put the vendor in default by demanding that the title be exhibited and tendering the balance due. The rule has long been settled in California that there can be no rescission by a vendee of an executory contract of sale merely because of lack of title in the vendor prior to the date when performance is due. Joyce v. Shafer, 97 Cal. 335, 32 P. 320; Shively v. Semi-Tropic Land & Water Co., 99 Cal. 259, 33 P. 848; Brimmer v. Salisbury, 167 Cal. 522, 140 P. 30. And the vendee cannot place the vendor in default by tendering payment and demanding a deed in advance of the time and under circumstances not contemplated by the contract. Garberino v. Roberts, 109 Cal. 126, 41 P. 857; Hanson v. Fox, 155 Cal. 106, 99 P. 489, 20 L.R.A.(N.S.) 338, 132 Am.St.Rep. 72. In the present case the pleading does not show the vendor to be in default, as under the contract, assuming a defect to exist, the time within which title must be perfected does not expire until May, 1933.

In this connection an attempt is made to strengthen plaintiffs' position by averring that, in the event that the homestead claims are allowed and the whole tract in which plaintiffs' lot is situated is declared to be part of the public domain, defendant will be financially unable to procure title to the whole tract, and hence can never perform its obligation to convey title to plaintiffs. The whole tract contains over 16,000 acres. Plaintiffs' lot comprises about one-fourth of an acre. The complaint does not show that defendant would be unable, for financial or other reasons, to procure title to the one-fourth acre which it has contracted to convey to plaintiffs and with which alone plaintiffs are concerned.

There remains to be considered the question as to whether certain allegations of fraud bring this case within the rule that, even though the vendor is not in default, the vendee may rescind an executory contract for material fraudulent misrepresentations of the vendor as to a matter of title upon which the vendee was justified in relying. Crane v. Ferrier-Brock Development Co., 164 Cal. 676, 130 P. 429; Brimmer v. Salisbury, 167 Cal. 522, 530, 140 P. 30. Plaintiffs allege that they are inexperienced in business and relied upon the defendant for fair treatment, being accustomed to put complete trust in and rely upon banks and bankers. The latter allegation is insufficient to establish a fiduciary relationship between plaintiffs and defendant, as there is no suggestion that defendant voluntarily assumed a relation of personal confidence with plaintiffs. Ruhl v. Mott, 120 Cal. 668, 53 P. 304. The parties to the contract must therefore be regarded as having dealt at arm's length. Viewing the pleading in this light and looking to the averments as to the state of the title referred to above, it appears that plaintiffs have not charged defendant with material misrepresentations, unequivocally averred to be false, upon which plaintiffs relied to their injury.

The orders appealed from are affirmed.

NOTES

1. For an interesting case in which the court acknowledged "that the vendor in a real estate contract is generally not obliged to have full and clear marketable title at all times during the pendency of his contract of sale because, ordinarily, title need not be conveyed until the final payment is made or tendered . . . .", but still allowed the purchaser to treat the contract as rescinded see Leavitt v. Blohm, 11 Utah 2d 220, 223, 357 P.2d 190, 192 (1960). The vendor had interfered with the purchaser's "right to the quiet and peaceable enjoyment" of a motel by failing to make necessary payments to the party from whom the vendor was buying the property. See also Tolbird v. Howard, 101 Ill.App.2d 236, 242 N.E.2d 468 (1968) where the court held that, unless required by the terms of the installment land contract, the vendor need not have merchantable title prior to the time for conveyance nor can he be compelled to furnish an abstract showing merchantable title before that date.

In Marlowe Investment Corp. v. Radmall, 26 Utah 2d 124, 485 P.2d 1402 (1971) the court noted: "The trial court's analysis and conclusion are supported by sound principles of law. The first relates to the subject of impossibility of performance by the vendor. It is true that ordinarily such a vendor does not necessarily have to have marketable title until the purchaser has made his payments. Nevertheless, if it plainly appears that he has so lost or encumbered his ownership or his title that he will not be able to fulfill his contract, he cannot insist that the purchaser continue to make payments when it is obvious that his own performance will not be forthcoming." How can the lawyer for the purchaser avoid the difficulties raised in these cases?

2. On a closely related point as to the validity of a real estate contract where the vendor does not own any or all of the land, see Horn v. Wright, 157 Ga.App. 408, 278 S.E.2d 66 (1981) where the court noted: "One may, however, contract to sell property not owned by himself, taking his chances on obtaining title prior to the date of consummation of the sale or responding in damages if he fails to do so. 'Whether or not the seller could have delivered a good title on the closing date is not a question which addresses itself to the validity of the contract.'" In that case, the purchaser had contended that the contract was a nullity because the vendor was at most only a tenant in common, sharing with the other heirs of an estate. Why would a person contract to sell property which he does not own? Would a purchaser enter into such a contract if he knew the full facts as to the title?

In Seligman v. First National Investments, Inc., 184 Ill.App.3d 1053, 133 Ill.Dec. 191, 540 N.E.2d 1057 (1989), defendant was negotiating to purchase a building when he contracted to sell it to plaintiff, with conveyance of marketable title to occur one month later. Upon learning that defendant did not have title, plaintiff declined to proceed to a closing and sued for breach of contract. The court held for defendant, saying that "the evidence merely showing that [defendant] did not hold title . . . did not prove that [he] could not convey a good and merchantable title when he was required to do so under the contract, i.e., at the time of closing."

3. As the preceding materials indicate, a large number of claims, liens, and defects can cause a title to be unmerchantable. One troublesome question is whether a tax deed conveys a merchantable title, providing, of course, the defaulting taxpayer had such a title at the time of the tax sale. In most states, there are statutes which provide for annual tax sales if the taxes on real estate are delinquent. Ultimately, if the taxpayer does not redeem as provided in the act, a government official is empowered to give a tax deed to the purchaser who buys at the sale. The purchaser typically pays the back taxes plus interest and receives the land for less than it is worth. The legislatures have viewed the tax sale as a convenient method of real estate tax collection; the courts have viewed it as an unfair interference with the "true" owner's rights and have been less than kindly toward the tax purchaser. The result has been that tax deeds could be set aside by the courts for the slightest technical error in issuance and that few tax titles were considered merchantable. In recent years, this attitude has changed, helped by new legislation which provides greater safeguards for the taxpayer, and the tax title has acquired a higher status. See, for example, Cherin v. R. & C. Co., 11 Ill.2d 447, 143 N.E.2d 235 (1957). For a good analysis of this trend see Young, the Tax Deed—Modern Movement Towards Respectability, 34 Rocky Mt.L.Rev. 181 (1962). The problem still remains a real one, however, as see Potomac Building Corp. v. Karkenny, 364 A.2d 809 (D.C.1976). One of two required notices of a tax sale was not published due to an error on the part of a newspaper. The trial court held that there had been substantial compliance with the statute and that was sufficient. The appellate court reversed, holding that substantial compliance was not enough for a valid sale.

It has long been recognized that even an invalid tax deed may constitute color of title and that if the purchaser takes possession and pays the taxes for the requisite period he will obtain title under a short term statute of limitations. For a recent case to this effect, see Quality Plastics, Inc. v. Moore, 131 Ariz. 238, 640 P.2d 169 (1982). See also, page 1555 infra.

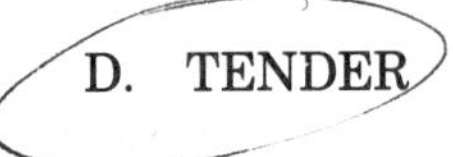

D. TENDER

COHEN v. KRANZ

Court of Appeals of New York, 1963.
12 N.Y.2d 242, 189 N.E.2d 473.

BURKE, JUDGE. On September 22, 1959 plaintiff contracted to purchase defendants' one-family house in Nassau County for $40,000.

Four thousand dollars was paid on the signing of the contract and the balance due upon delivery of the deed was in the form of $24,500 cash and the assumption of an $11,500 first mortgage. Closing was set for November 15. Plaintiff obtained an adjournment of the closing date to December 15 without any indication that title would be rejected. On November 30, plaintiff's attorney sent defendants' attorney a letter stating: "An investigation has disclosed that the present structure of the premises is not legal and thus title is unmarketable. Unless a check to the order of Lester Cohen, as attorney in fact, for Sarah Cohen is received in five days, we shall be obligated to commence proceedings against your client."

Plaintiff's attorney appeared at the office of defendants' attorney on the adjourned law date and demanded return of the $4,000 deposit, which was refused by the latter. Neither party was then able to perform and neither made any tender. Plaintiff thereafter commenced this action for return of the deposit plus the costs of searching title; defendants counterclaimed for damages for breach of contract.

Trial Term, Nassau County, gave judgment for plaintiff. The court found that the premises were subject to protective covenants filed in the Nassau County Clerk's office and that the insurability clause of the contract was not complied with because a swimming pool on the premises, installed under a permit, lacked a certificate of occupancy from the Oyster Bay Architectural Control Committee. Further, a split rail fence projected beyond the front line of the dwelling. The court also found that plaintiff had notified defendants of the claimed defects prior to the December 15 closing date and that defendants had taken no steps to remedy the defects, nor had it been established that the violations were minor. The court held, therefore, that the defective title excused plaintiff from tender of payment and awarded plaintiff judgment in the amount of her deposit.

The Appellate Division, Second Department [5 App.Div.2d 938, 226 N.Y.S.2d 509], unanimously reversed Trial Term on the law and facts and directed judgment on the counterclaim for $1,500. It is from this judgment that plaintiff appeals.

In reversing Trial Term's findings of fact, the Appellate Division expressly found that plaintiff's letter of November 30 rejecting title and demanding return of the deposit failed to specify the claimed illegality, and that specific objections to title were not raised until January 25, 1960. The letter speaks for itself and the Appellate Division is obviously correct. Plaintiff's arguments directed at the Appellate Division's finding of January 25th as the date when specific objections were first communicated to defendants are unavailing inasmuch as the earliest further communication of objections supported by the evidence took place upon the commencement of this action by plaintiff on December 31st, still more than two weeks after the law date. It was also found, contrary to the trial court, that the objections to title were curable upon proper and timely notice and demand. We think the weight of the evidence supports the Appellate Division here too. The swimming pool was constructed with a permit and lacked only a certificate of occupancy (which was in fact obtained before defendants sold the house to a third person).[9] The fence projection likewise could clearly be found to be a readily curable objection. These were the only two objections that possibly violated the "Declaration of Protective Covenants" recorded in the Nassau County Clerk's office and to which the title insurer excepted.

The Appellate Division also found that defendants had not waived a tender by plaintiff and that plaintiff's rejection of title in advance was a default precluding her from recovery of the deposit. Since it is undisputed that defendants made no tender, the Appellate Division's award of damages for breach of contract necessarily implies that no such tender was required. We agree.

While a vendee can recover his money paid on the contract from a vendor who defaults on law day without a showing of tender or even of willingness and ability to perform where the vendor's title is incurably defective (Greene v. Barrett, Nephews & Co., 238 N.Y. 207, 144 N.E. 503), a tender and demand are required to put the vendor in default where his title could be cleared without difficulty in a reasonable time. . . . Further, the vendor in such a case is entitled to a reasonable time beyond law day to make his title good (Ballen v. Potter, 251 N.Y. 224, 167 N.E. 424). It is, therefore, clear that plaintiff's advance rejection of title and demand for immediate return of the deposit was unjustified and an anticipatory breach of contract. This position, adhered to throughout, prevented defendants' title defects from ever amounting to a default. Consequently, plaintiff is barred from recovering the deposit from a vendor whose title defects were curable and whose performance was never demanded on law day. (Higgins v. Eagleton, supra). Ansorge v. Belfer, 248 N.Y. 145, 150, 161 N.E. 450, 452, is not to the contrary. It merely holds that a vendee may recover his deposit from a clearly defaulting vendor despite his own unjustified refusal to agree to an adjournment of the law date. It does not deny the doctrine that a vendor whose title defects are curable is not automatically in default but, rather, must be put in default by the vendee's tender of performance and demand for a good title deed. The vendor was there put in default by the vendee's tender. The vendor simply never retrieved his default by curing the defects and tendering a good title (as he could have—Harris v. Shorall, 230 N.Y. 343, 130 N.E. 572). True, defendants here never offered to clear their title and perform; but they were never put in default in the first place by a demand for good title. So Ansorge merely holds with respect to curable title defects what Greene v. Barrett, Nephews & Co., supra, held with respect to incurable defects—namely, that where the vendor is in default the deposit can be recovered even though the vendee himself is in default or breach, e.g., no showing of performance of conditions precedent or excuse for nonperformance (the Greene case); or an

9. The opinion in the Appellate Division pointed out that the vendors actually sold the house to the third person for $34,000, thus suffering a $6,000 loss. $4,000 was paid down. Does the vendor get to keep this $4,000 plus the $1,500 allowed on his counter claim? If so, shouldn't the judgment have been for $2,000 to give the vendor the benefit of his bargain?

unjustified refusal to adjourn the closing date (the Ansorge case). The difference is that a vendor with incurable [10] title defects is automatically in default, whereas a vendor with curable title defects must be placed in default by a tender and demand, which was not done here.

Defendants obtained an affirmative recovery on their counterclaim for breach of contract based on the loss they sustained when they sold the house to a third person for what the courts below found to be its fair market value. This recovery stands on a different footing from their right to retain the deposit. As Judge Andrews pointed out, in speaking of a vendee, in Greene v. Barrett, Nephews & Co., supra, while the vendee's right to recover the deposit from a defaulting vendor can rest solely upon the latter's default, an action for *damages* for breach of contract requires a showing that the plaintiff himself (the vendee in the Greene case) has performed all conditions precedent and concurrent, unless excused. In the case of a purchase of real estate, this would be a showing of tender and demand or, if that be unnecessary, an idle gesture, because of the incurable nature of the title defect, then at least a showing at the trial that the plaintiff vendee was in a position to perform had the vendor been willing and able to perform his part. (Greene v. Barrett, Nephews & Co., supra; Stern v. McKee, 70 App.Div. 142, 75 N.Y.S. 157; Norris v. McMechen, 134 Misc. 866, 236 N.Y.S. 486; Restatement, Contracts, § 306.) Likewise, a vendor such as the defendants here must show a basic ability to perform even if actual tender and demand is unnecessary. However, while it cannot be denied that defendants did not have a title conformable to the contract at law date, an applicable corollary of the above rule excuses even inability to perform conditions precedent or concurrent where such inability is caused by advance notice from the other party that he will not perform his part. (Clarke v. Crandall, 27 Barb. 73; Kotcher v. Edelblute, 250 N.Y. 178, 164 N.E. 897; Restatement, Contracts, §§ 270, 284, 306). Not only did plaintiff's unjustified attempt to cancel the contract and recover her deposit before the adjourned law date render unnecessary and wasteful any attempt by defendants to cure the minor defects before that date, but the failure to specify the objections rendered it impossible. The finding of the Appellate Division, supported by the weight of the evidence, that the defects were curable means that defendants were basically able to perform and whatever technical inability existed in this regard on the law date was caused by plaintiff and is excused fully as much as the lack of formal tender.

The judgment should be affirmed, without costs.

DESMOND, C.J., and DYE, FULD, VAN VOORHIS, FOSTER and SCILEPPI, JJ., concur.

Judgment affirmed.

10. We use "incurable" to mean not within the vendor's power to remedy within a reasonable time. (See Greene v. Barrett, Nephews and Co., supra, 238 N.Y. pp. 211–212, 144 N.E. pp. 504–505.) (Footnote by the Court.)

NOTES

1. In Pelletier v. Dwyer, 334 A.2d 867 (Me.1975), the vendor did not have title at the time he contracted to sell real estate to the purchaser for $83,000. A $5,000 deposit was made with provision for forfeiture. The vendor had himself contracted to buy the property and received a deed the morning of law day. He did not, however, make a tender to the purchaser and the court allowed the latter to recover his $5,000 down payment. Said the court: "The tender need not be absolute, in the sense of a delivery to the actual possession of the other party; but the tender must be such as to manifest a willingness to perform in compliance with the agreement and must be reasonably necessary to apprise the other party of the tender and the overt willingness to perform."

In Wilson v. Klein, 715 S.W.2d 814 (Tex.App.1986), plaintiff contracted to purchase several tracts of land from defendant at a price of $18,000 per acre. The contract stated that time was of the essence. A dispute then arose over whether plaintiff was required to pay for 6.6 acres located within the bounds of dedicated roadways. On law day plaintiff tendered payment calculated on a formula which excluded the 6.6 acres. Defendant was prepared to perform but refused to do so on that basis. Plaintiff sued for specific performance, offering in his pleading to pay for the roadways if it was judicially determined that he was obligated to do so. The court found that plaintiff was so obligated but denied him specific performance because he had not made "an actual tender of the correct purchase price" at the time specified in the contract for performance. The court said that "the word 'tender' generally implies *an unconditional* offer by an obligor to pay a sum *not less than what is due* his obligee."

2. The Uniform Land Transactions Act handles the tender requirements, in cases where the contract is silent on the issue, as follows:

Section 2–301. [Seller's Tender of Conveyance; Buyer's Tender of Purchase Price]

(a) If a recording is necessary to protect a buyer against another conveyance of the real estate, the seller's tender of a recordable instrument conveying the real estate agreed to be conveyed and the buyer's tender of the purchase price are concurrent obligations. The seller's performance of the obligations imposed by the provisions on title obligations in other than leasehold transactions (Section 2–304), if applicable, and his substantial performance of other obligations are conditions to the buyer's duty to tender the purchase price.

(b) The buyer, upon reasonable notice to the seller, may inspect the real estate before tender of the purchase price or acceptance of the instrument of conveyance. The buyer must exercise good faith in selecting a time for inspection.

(c) The buyer may inspect the instrument of conveyance before making the payment required at the time of tender of the instrument.

(d) Tender of payment is sufficient if made in any manner conforming to applicable usage (Section 1–303).

E. ASSIGNMENT

HANDZEL v. BASSI

Appellate Court of Illinois, Second District, 1951.
343 Ill.App. 281, 99 N.E.2d 23.

DOVE, JUSTICE. The complaint in this case which was filed on June 9, 1950, alleged that on September 18, 1948, the plaintiffs entered into a written contract with defendants for the purchase of certain described property located in Lake County for $21,500.00. A photostatic copy of the contract was attached to and made a part of the complaint. The contract provided for a down payment of $5000.00, and the balance of the purchase price was to be paid in installments of $3500.00 each on October 1, 1949, October 1, 1950, October 1, 1951, October 1, 1952, and a final payment of $2500.00 was to be made on October 1, 1953. All deferred payments were to draw 4% interest. The contract further provided that after one-half of the purchase price had been paid, defendants would convey the property to plaintiffs and plaintiffs would deliver to defendants a purchase money mortgage for the balance.

Among other things, the contract provided: "that the Purchaser shall not transfer or assign this agreement or any interest therein, without the previous written consent of the Seller, and that any such assignment or transfer, without such previous written consent, shall not vest in the transferee or assignee any right, title or interest herein or hereunder or in said premises, but shall render this contract null and void, at the election of the Seller; and that the Purchaser will not sublet or lease said premises, or any part thereof, for any purpose, except upon the previous written consent of the Seller."

The complaint further alleged that the purchasers paid $5000.00 upon the execution of the contract and $3500.00, plus interest, on October 1, 1949, and have fully complied with the contract and kept the premises in excellent condition and spent money in improving and maintaining the premises; that on February 3, 1950, the plaintiffs entered into a written agreement with Josephine Bellcom by which they agreed to sell the real estate involved herein to her for $23,500.00, of which amount $6000.00 was paid down and further payments were to be made of $200.00 per month beginning May 10, 1950; it was further alleged that on March 21, 1950, defendants served a notice on plaintiffs setting out certain portions of the contract and alleging that they had violated these provisions and had transferred or assigned their interest in their contract without previous written consent of the defendants and had made certain structural changes by changing a window into a door and constructing an outside wooden stairway and notifying them that unless all these defaults were corrected by April 22, 1950, defendants would declare the contract null and void and that the payments already made would be retained as liquidated damages.

It was further alleged that on May 8, 1950, defendants served a notice on plaintiffs to the effect that inasmuch as plaintiffs had failed to correct these defaults, defendants declared the contract null and void, forfeited and determined, and that all payments which plaintiffs had made were forfeited and would be retained by defendants as liquidated damages and that defendants would proceed to recover possession of the premises.

The complaint further alleged that on May 8, 1950, plaintiffs were served with another notice to the effect that the contract of September 18, 1948, had been cancelled and demanding that possession of the premises be surrendered to defendants on or before June 10, 1950. It was further alleged that on June 1, 1950, one of the plaintiffs tendered to one of the defendants a money order in the amount of $4020.00, representing $3500.00 which would become payable October 1, 1950, plus interest on $13,000.00 at 4% to October 1, 1950, and demanded a warranty deed from defendants and offered to execute a purchase money mortgage for the unpaid balance. It was further alleged that the plaintiffs were ready, willing and able to pay said sum of $4020 and continue said offer and tender. The prayer of the complaint was that a temporary injunction issue forthwith restraining defendants from forfeiting or attempting to forfeit the original contract and that upon the hearing the temporary injunction be made permanent and that the original contract be declared to be in full force and effect and defendants ordered to specifically perform the same.

On June 19, 1950, upon notice and a hearing, a preliminary injunction was issued as prayed. Thereafter, on September 28, 1950, a motion was made by appellants to dissolve the temporary injunction. This motion was, on October 19, 1950, denied, and this appeal seeks to reverse that interlocutory order.

The record further shows that on September 29, 1950, before the denial of the motion to dissolve the injunction, appellees deposited with the Clerk of the Court $4,219.28 representing $3500.00 principal due October 1, 1950, plus interest and taxes. The record further discloses that on November 27, 1950, appellees notified appellants that appellees had a commitment and had borrowed sufficient money to pay appellants the contract price in full if appellants would give plaintiffs a deed and good title as required by the contract.

It is insisted by counsel for appellants that the allegations of the complaint show that appellees had violated their contract with appellants by assigning the contract without appellants' consent, and, because of this violation of the contract, appellants had properly forfeited the contract and appellees are not entitled to an injunction.

Counsel for appellees argue that the contract of sale by them to Josephine Bellcom, as set forth in the complaint, is a separate, independent transaction and does not violate any of the provisions of the contract with appellants. Counsel for appellees also contend that under the facts alleged in the complaint and applying thereto the general principle of law that equity abhors a forfeiture, the chancellor very properly issued the temporary injunction.

The temporary injunction is based on the complaint, and the question is whether or not the facts set up in the complaint authorize the injunction granted by the trial court. Counsel for appellants insist that the separate contract entered into by appellees with Josephine Bellcom was in effect an assignment of the contract which it is now sought to specifically enforce. Counsel cite and rely on the case of Kew v. Trainor, 150 Ill. 150, 37 N.E. 223, which held that a provision forbidding the assignment of a lease without the consent of the lessor was a condition and not merely a covenant and that the right of re-entry on violation of that provision was enforceable. Counsel also calls to our attention Traders Safety Building Corporation v. Shirk, 237 Ill. App. 1. The court there states the general principles of law with reference to covenants against assignments in leases, and at page 11 of 237 Ill.App. says: "That courts both of law and equity abhor forfeitures and that covenants against assignments are not favored and will be strictly construed in order to prevent forfeitures, are propositions which may well be considered elementary. . . . That the unauthorized assignment of lease in breach of its covenants gives a landlord the right to terminate it and that equity will not grant relief against such forfeiture is also settled." . . .

The policy of the law with reference to restraints on alienation is stated in Postal Telegraph Co. v. Western Union Telegraph Co., 155 Ill. 335, 40 N.E. 587, a case involving the construction of a lease. The court stated at pages 347–348 of 155 Ill., at page 590 of 40 N.E.: "Restrictions on the power of alienation have long been unfavored, and the policy of this state has ever been hostile to them, and this principle is [so] firmly engrafted on our polity that such covenants will be construed with the utmost strictness [to the end that the restraint shall not be extended], beyond the express stipulation; and all doubts, as a general rule, must be resolved in favor of a free use of property, and against restrictions."

In Waukegan Times Theatre Corp. v. Conrad, 324 Ill.App. 622, at page 631, 59 N.E.2d 308, at page 312, another case involving a lease, this court stated: "That covenants against assignments will be strictly construed in order to prevent forfeitures, is an elementary proposition of law."

Under the contract in this case appellants were to receive $21,500.00 for this property and after $10,750.00 had been paid, appellants were to deliver appellees a warranty deed and appellees were to give appellants a purchase money mortgage for the remaining unpaid balance. Appellants' basic right under the contract was to get the money contracted to be paid for the property. Appellees offered to do this before the complaint was filed and repeated the offer in the complaint and appellees later paid into court the amount due.

[The court then discussed several cases involving prohibitions of assignments.]

In the instant case, the agreement of appellees to sell the property to Josephine Bellcom was an independent contract. Under it appellees were to convey their title to the property to Josephine Bellcom, if, as and when they acquired it. The contract with Josephine Bellcom in no way released them from their original contract with appellants. They were still bound to perform the original contract and this, the record shows, they have offered and are able to do.

If, however, the contract with Josephine Bellcom be treated as an assignment of the original contract with appellants, the provision for a forfeiture in the original contract on account of such an assignment is a harsh one. It should not be enforced where the appellees offer and are able to complete the performance of the contract. The stipulation against an assignment in the contract with appellants was intended to safeguard performance on the part of the appellees and when it appears that full performance is offered by appellees under the terms of the contract it is no abuse of discretion for the Chancellor to protect the rights of appellees pending the hearing of the case on its merits.

Under the authorities cited, we are clearly of the opinion that the Chancellor did not err in granting the preliminary injunction in this case and properly denied the motion to dissolve it. The order appealed from is therefore affirmed.

Order affirmed.

NOTES

1. The assignment of real estate contracts involves the same principles as the assignment of leases and you should incorporate by reference the materials previously covered in non-freehold estates.

In Cheney v. Jemmett, 107 Idaho 829, 693 P.2d 1031 (1984), vendor sued to compel purchasers to pay the balance due on a land sale contract, claiming that purchasers were in default under a clause prohibiting assignment without vendor's consent. The court dismissed vendor's complaint. "[W]hen a contract grants the purchaser the right to assign his interest in the contract, or in the property in issue, conditioned upon obtaining the consent of the seller, the seller must act reasonably and in good faith in withholding his consent to a proposed assignment. [In this case] plaintiff's refusal was not given in good faith and was totally unreasonable." The court also said, "As to those contracts which absolutely prohibit the right of assignment, we express no opinion."

If a land contract purchaser assigns to a third party "all of the vendee's right, title and interest in and to" the contract "and to the real estate described therein," does the assignment impose upon assignee all of the assignor's *duties* as well as his rights under the original contract? Kunzman v. Thorsen, 303 Or. 600, 740 P.2d 754 (1987), awarded the original vendors a decree of specific performance against the assignee. "Where a party accepts a broadly worded assignment of a land sale contract, 'steps into the shoes' of the assignor and asserts the interests the contract conveys, the presumption arises that the assignee intended also to assume the duties the contract imposes." See American Law Institute, Restatement (Second) Contracts § 328 (1981).

In Boswell v. Lyon, 401 N.E.2d 735 (Ind.App.1980), Boswell purchased an apartment building on an installment contract from Hadley. The contract provided that the interest in the real estate could not be sold, assigned or pledged without Hadley's consent. Boswell assigned his interest under the contract to Batties and Hadley consented. Hadley then sold the real estate to Lyon. Batties assigned his interest under the contract to Roberts. Lyon consented. Roberts defaulted and judgment was entered against Boswell, Batties and Roberts. Boswell argued that: (1) the conduct of the parties surrounding the assignment created a question of fact as to whether there was an intent creating novation and, therefore, summary judgment should not have been granted against him, and (2) when Boswell's assignee assigned the contract without the consent of Boswell, that resulted in a change in the principal and surety relationship and Boswell was discharged. The court held that a mere assignment, even with the consent of the creditor, does not operate as a novation. An assignment under a land sale contract establishes a surety relationship between the vendee-assignor who becomes surety and the assignee who becomes principal. Vendee's liability continues even though his assignee makes a subsequent assignment. Had the vendor changed the terms or manner of payment, the obligation of Boswell would have been discharged.

2. The typical real estate contract ends with this boilerplate: "It is mutually agreed by and between the parties hereunto, that the covenants and agreements herein contained shall extend to and be obligatory upon the heirs, executors, administrators, and assigns of the respective parties." What, if anything, does this add to the legal rights of the contracting parties?

3. Owner contracted to sell an apartment building to P for $57,000 under an installment contract. P subsequently contracted to sell the building for $90,000 to D, who expressly assumed and agreed to pay as part of the $90,000 all amounts still due to Owner under the first contract. Except for a $9,000 downpayment to P, D made no payments to P or Owner, and owner successfully sued to enforce a forfeiture of P's and D's interests. P sued D for $24,000, the unpaid principal still due *to P* under the second contract, plus interest and attorneys' fees. D argued that P should receive only the difference between "the contract price still owing to [P] and the market price of the property at the time of [D's] breach," a formula which would have denied P any recovery. The court adopted the measure of damages urged by P, noting that it gave him the benefit of his bargain with D, and that D's formula wrongly presupposed that P was still free to sell the building and realize its market value. Because D's breach "caused [P's] entire interest in the property to be forfeited," the value of the property to P "was reduced to zero." However, three dissenting judges sided with D on the ground that P voluntarily elected to default on his contract with Owner, rather than continuing to make payments under the first contract (e.g., by using funds from D's $9,000 downpayment) and suing D for damages or forfeiture. "[T]he decision of [P] can only be de-

scribed as an election to forfeit the interest of [D] and therefore precludes any additional recovery against him. . . . [T]he result the majority countenances is a marked departure from well settled law in this state. The breach of a real estate contract allows the vendor either to sue for damages or to forfeit the purchaser's interest in the property. The vendor, however, cannot get both remedies." Smith v. King, 106 Wn.2d 443, 722 P.2d 796 (1986).

For an extended discussion of the election-of-remedies doctrine, see Freyfogle, Vagueness and the Rule of Law: Reconsidering Installment Land Contract Forfeitures, 1988 Duke L.J. 609, 622–627. The article, which also is relevant to section F below, examines a variety of remedies available to vendors and vendees. See note 2, page 1088 infra.

F. REMEDIES FOR BREACH OF CONTRACT

CENTEX HOMES CORP. v. BOAG

Superior Court of New Jersey, Chancery Division, 1974.
128 N.J.Super. 385, 320 A.2d 194.
[reprinted at page 416 supra.]

KRAMER v. MOBLEY

Court of Appeals of Kentucky, 1949.
309 Ky. 143, 216 S.W.2d 930.

REES, JUSTICE. V.H. Mobley, appellee here and plaintiff below, brought this action against T.J. Kramer to recover damages for the breach of a contract for the sale of 745½ acres of land located in Ballard County. The plaintiff alleged in his petition that the land was reasonably worth $10 an acre more than the agreed price, and that the difference between the agreed price plaintiff was to pay and the actual market value of the land was, at least, $7,455. He sought to recover that amount and, in addition thereto, the sum of $250, the alleged expenses incurred by him including the cost of an investigation of the title. By agreement of the parties, the case was submitted to the court without the intervention of a jury, and the court found that the land was actually worth $67 an acre, or $2 an acre more than the agreed price of $65. The court also found that the plaintiff had incurred some expense which he should be compensated for by the defendant by reason of the defendant's refusal to complete the transaction. It was adjudged that the plaintiff recover the sum of $2,000, and the defendant appeals.

T.J. Kramer purchased 901 acres of land, including the 745½ acres involved in this controversy, from C.E. Gordon and Bertha F. Gordon. The deed executed by the Gordons was dated September 30, 1943, and recited a consideration of $1 cash and the payment of $22,750 on or before January 1, 1944, the deferred payment being evidenced by a note secured by a lien retained on the land. On March 27, 1944, Bertha F. Gordon signed a release on the margin of the deed book which recited that $20,612 had been paid on the note. In December, 1944, Kramer listed the land with King C. Dunn, a real estate broker, for sale. V.H. Mobley became interested as a prospective purchaser, and on April 21, 1945, met Kramer and Dunn on the land. After considerable negotiations, Kramer agreed to sell the 745½-acre tract of land to Mobley for $65 an acre, or a total of $48,457. The sale price included all of the personal property on the farm except a saddle mare. The value of the personal property included in the sale was less than $1,000. A written contract, signed by Mobley and King C. Dunn, agent, provided that $15,457 should be paid upon execution and delivery of the deed and $33,000 should be paid at the rate of $5,000 a year, the deferred payments to be evidenced by notes secured by a vendor's lien. Mobley delivered to Dunn a check for $5,000, the proceeds to be applied on the cash payment. The contract provided that the deed should be delivered within ten days. Kramer and his wife executed two deeds to Mobley on April 23, 1945, one providing for payment of the purchase price in cash and one providing for a cash payment of $1 and the balance on terms in accordance with the written contract of sale. It appears that Mobley had expressed a desire to pay all of the purchase price in cash if he could secure a mortgage loan from his bank. The parties met at Dunn's office on April 24 to conclude the transaction, and Mobley informed Kramer that an examination of the records disclosed a lien on the land for $2,138 in favor of Gordon. Mobley testified that the encumbrance upon the property was unknown to him when he executed his agreement to purchase, and that he learned of it for the first time two days later when he had the title examined by an abstractor. Kramer testified that he informed Dunn, the real estate broker, when the agency contract was executed that the validity of the $2,138 lien was in dispute, and that the purchaser must accept deed with indemnification against loss by reason of the lien until its validity could be determined in a court proceeding. Dunn, who was a witness for appellee, was unable to remember whether he so informed Mobley. At the meeting on April 24 Kramer explained that the validity of this lien was in dispute since he claimed that Gordon wrongfully moved from the land property of the value of $2,138 when he gave possession. Kramer stated that he would bring an action against Gordon to have the validity of the claim determined and the title cleared, and proposed to deliver to Mobley a certified check for $3,000 to indemnify him against loss by reason of the lien. There is evidence that this arrangement was substantially agreed to, and that it was satisfactory to the banker who had agreed to make a loan to Mobley to be secured by a mortgage on the land. However, before the negotiations were concluded the parties recessed for lunch with the understanding that they would meet again after lunch. During the recess period Mobley encountered Gordon who informed him that he would have trouble if he accepted the deed without requiring a release of the lien. The negotiations broke down at the afternoon meeting, but another meeting was held at a bank in Benton on Monday, April 30. At that meeting

Kramer tendered to Mobley a general warranty deed and a certified check for $3,000, but Mobley refused to accept the deed unless Kramer paid off Gordon's claim of $2,138 and obtained a release of the lien. Kramer insisted that he owed no part of the claim and promised to clear the title in an action which he would institute against Gordon. Mobley refused to agree to this arrangement, his $5,000 check was returned to him, and the negotiations were dropped. Later Mobley brought this action.

Appellant first argues that the real estate agent, Dunn, was without authority to bind his principal, Kramer, and that the contract of sale was not enforceable since it was not signed by Kramer. Huddleston v. Disney, 304 Ky. 164, 200 S.W.2d 109, is cited in support of the argument. In that case we approved the holding in Speiss v. Martin, 192 Ky. 211, 232 S.W. 615, that in the absence of a special authorization a real estate broker has no power to enter into a contract for a purchase or sale of land so as to bind his principal, and we held that the agent in the Huddleston case was without such special authorization in view of the language of the contract between Huddleston and the real estate broker. In the present case the agency contract between appellant and Dunn, which was in writing, contained this: "I hereby appoint you exclusive agent to make sale of real property herein described . . . and you are hereby authorized to accept a deposit to be applied on the purchase price and to execute a binding contract for sale on my behalf." Thus the agent, Dunn, had explicit authorization to enter into a written contract of sale binding on his principal.

The main question presented for our determination is: What are the rights of the purchaser of real estate under an executory contract where the sale fails by reason of a defect of title, or what is the proper measure of damages? It is the general rule that where the seller under an executory contract for the sale of personal property breaches his contract by failing to deliver the property, the measure of damages is the difference, if any, between the contract price and the market value of the property either at the time of the breach or at the time fixed for delivery. King v. Herbert Bauman Lumber Company, 223 Ky. 782, 4 S.W.2d 699; Elder v. Florsheim Shoe Company, 209 Ky. 509, 273 S.W. 60. The same rule as to the measure of damages is usually applied where the vendor in an executory contract for the sale of real estate wilfully refuses to convey to the vendee a good or marketable title as required by the contract. New Domain Oil & Gas Co. v. McKinney, 188 Ky. 183, 221 S.W. 245; Gordon v. Wanless, 231 Ky. 498, 21 S.W.2d 815. However, it is the rule in this and many other jurisdictions that if the sale fails by reason of a defect in the vendor's title and the vendor is guilty of no bad faith or fraud, the measure of the vendee's damage is substantially the same as in the case of an executed sale; that is, the vendee may recover any consideration he has paid, with interest, and any legitimate expense incurred by him, but he can recover nothing for the loss of his bargain. The leading case on the subject in this jurisdiction is Crenshaw v. Williams, 191 Ky. 559, 231 S.W. 45, 48 A.L.R. 5, where the cases are collected and the reason for the rule is elaborately discussed. The question was again thoroughly considered in Potts v. Moran's Ex'rs, 236 Ky. 28, 32 S.W.2d 534, and the rule announced in Crenshaw v. Williams was approved. In the course of the opinion it was said:

"After an examination of the decisions of this and other courts, we announced the rule that a vendee of real estate is not entitled to damages for the loss of his bargain upon the inability of the vendor to make a good title, where the vendor acted in good faith and was guilty of no active nor positive fraud in the transaction. We also held that mere failure of a vendor of real estate to refer the vendee to his record of title, or the judicial decisions bearing upon it, was not such fraud as to deprive him of the benefit of the rule that damages for loss of bargain will not be awarded against a good-faith vendor who is unable to convey a good title. In reaching this conclusion we called attention to the fact that we had uniformly ruled that the measure of damages upon a breach of warranty of title was the value of the land lost as fixed by the consideration paid or agreed to be paid. We further pointed out that, with respect to the measure of damages, there was no substantial difference between a breach of warranty of title, and the breach of a covenant to convey where the vendor acted in good faith, and quoted with approval the following excerpt from the opinion of this court in Goff v. Hawks, 5 J.J.Marsh. 341: 'Since the decision in the case of Cox's Heirs v. Strode, 2 Bibb. [273], 276, 5 Am.Dec. 603, the criterion of damages upon a covenant to convey land, which has been violated, but without fraud on the part of the covenantor, is the purchase money and interest thereon, or in the language of the case of Rutledge v. Lawrence, 1 A.K.Marsh. [396], 397, it is, the "value of the land at the time of the sale, to be ascertained by the consideration fixed or other evidence." If, however, the covenantor has been guilty of fraud, a different rule may govern the case. Then, he would be responsible for the increased value of the land, at the time his covenant should have been performed.' "

In the Potts case the vendor's wife refused to unite in the deed conveying the property, and, in discussing the question of bad faith, the court said:

"Here no bad faith on the part of Moran was charged or proved. On the contrary, he evinced his good faith by an offer in his answer to convey the land and deduct therefrom the value of his wife's inchoate right of dower, and to pay Potts all the expense to which he had been put. All that we have is the wife's refusal to join in the deed."

A collection of authorities on the subject may be found in the annotations in 48 A.L.R. 12 and 68 A.L.R. 137.

In the present case a good title could have been conveyed if appellant had paid the disputed debt and had obtained a release of the lien. His refusal did not constitute fraud or bad faith. He made a fair offer to indemnify appellee against loss pending an action to determine the validity of the lien. It is true that appellee could not have been compelled to accept the proffered deed in an action for specific performance, but this has no bearing on the question of appellant's good faith. The vendor is not compelled to make a substantial sacrifice in order to avoid the charge of fraud or bad faith. In Crenshaw v. Williams, supra, it was said [191 Ky. 559, 231 S.W. 46]:

". . . our investigation has shown that the courts generally, including this one, deny such recovery (damages for loss of one's bargain) in the sale of real estate where the vendor acts in good faith, and is guilty of no positive or active fraud in the transaction."

The appellant was guilty of no positive or active fraud in the transaction, and the court erred in awarding as damages the difference between the contract price and the market value. The court allowed as damages in this respect the sum of $1,491, leaving the sum of $509 allowed as expenses incurred by appellee. The latter allowance is excessive in the light of the pleadings and the proof. Appellee alleged in his petition that he had incurred expenses in the sum of $250, but the only expense concerning which proof was introduced was the cost of the examination of the title. Appellee testified that he had not paid any amount on this account, but the abstractor had informed him the cost would be $30 to $50.

Judgment is reversed for further proceedings.

SMITH v. WARR

Supreme Court of Utah, 1977.
564 P.2d 771.

WILKINS, JUSTICE. This appeal involves a breach of contract for the sale of real estate.

On August 20, 1973, buyer (appellant) contracted with sellers (respondents) to purchase the property in question. The Uniform Real Estate Contracts they executed provided that title was to be passed by special warranty deed upon full payment. Within four months of the signing, an action in adverse possession was initiated by plaintiffs below (not parties to the present appeal) to quiet title against sellers. On June 16, 1975, plaintiffs joined buyer as a party defendant in said action. In his answer, buyer filed a cross complaint against sellers for breach of contract. Buyer, however, continued to make payments on the contract throughout the adverse possession proceeding.

The District Court of Salt Lake County entered judgment in favor of the plaintiffs, the adverse possessors. Subsequently, on January 16, 1976, the Court ruled in favor of buyer on his cross complaint against sellers. Damages were awarded, however, only in the amount of buyer's out-of-pocket loss, and both attorney's fees and costs were denied. Buyer is appealing from the judgment in his favor below claiming that the court erred in awarding him only his out-of-pocket loss, rather than the larger amount of the benefit-of-the-bargain damages, i.e., the market value of the property at the time of the breach less the amount of the unpaid purchase money (as part of the contract price had been paid).

The issue on appeal, therefore, is whether the correct measure of damages for a breach of contract for the sale of real property in the State of Utah is out-of-pocket loss or benefit-of-the-bargain damages.

There is a split of authority among the states as to which measure of damages is appropriate for a breach of contract for the sale of land. Some states award benefit-of-the-bargain damages only if the breach was committed in bad faith. Others consistently award benefit-of-the-bargain damages whether or not the breaching party had good faith cause for failing to convey.

Sellers argue that, although Utah has never expressly articulated which of these two positions it adheres to, case law in this state indicates that the good faith-bad faith distinction is required, and that only out-of-pocket loss is to be awarded in the case of good faith breach. Since the District Court made a finding of good faith on sellers' part, sellers contend it would then follow that out-of-pocket loss would be the correct measure of damages.

Sellers' contention that benefit-of-the-bargain damages have only been awarded in this state when the breach was in bad faith, however, is not well-founded. Sellers rely, for example, on Bunnell v. Bills, 13 Utah 2d 83, 368 P.2d 597 (1962). In that case the seller had contracted to sell to the buyer property that he did not yet own, but which he had contracted to buy. The seller was financially unable to proceed with the purchase of the property, and his contract with the owner was consequently rescinded, whereupon the buyer sued for breach of contract. There is no mention of bad faith in this Court's decision in *Bunnell,* nor is bad faith apparent from the facts of the case, yet this Court stated there:

> The measure of damages where the vendor has breached a land sale contract is the market value of the property at the time of the breach less the contract price to the vendee. Id. 368 P.2d at 601.

Other cases cited by sellers in support of their position that Utah has implicitly followed the rule that awards benefit-of-the-bargain damages only in case of a bad faith breach are similarly unconvincing. In Dunshee v. Geoghegan, 7 Utah 113, 25 P. 731 (1891), for example, where bad faith was apparent, the court awarded benefit-of-the-bargain damages and then stated by way of dictum: "and it does not excuse the vendor that he may have acted in good faith . . . ." Id. 25 P. at 732. Sellers also cited good faith cases, in which only out-of-pocket loss was awarded the buyer. In these cases, however, the buyers had only sought out-of-pocket losses, and the court expressly recognized that damages on the contract would also have been an available remedy. See e.g., McBride v. Stewart, 68 Utah 12, 249 P. 114 (1926).

The rule followed by Utah is that benefit-of-the-bargain damages are to be awarded for breach of contract for the sale of real estate, regardless of the good faith of the party in breach. We therefore reverse, and remand to the District Court for a determination of damages consistent with this opinion, for an award of reasonable attorney's fees as required by the contract, and for costs below in the discretion of the Court. Costs on appeal to Buyer-Appellant Warr.

Ellett, C.J., and Crockett and Maughan, JJ., concur.

Hall, J., does not participate herein.

NOTES

1. The Kramer v. Mobley case represents the so-called English rule and is followed in about half the states. The American rule, well stated in the leading case of Doherty v. Dolan, 65 Me. 87, 20 Am.Rep. 677 (1876), follows the rule in personal property. In Crenshaw v. Williams, 191 Ky. 559, 567, 231 S.W. 45, 49, 48 A.L.R. 5 (1921) the court gave the following reasons for the English rule: "If it should be asked why there should be a different rule, governing the measurement of damages for failure to comply with a contract relating to real estate, than the one applying to a contract for the sale of personalty, we might find it difficult to give a satisfactory answer. The English courts put the distinction upon the ground of the intricate involvement of titles to real estate growing out of the variously worded deeds, wills, and other muniments of title, so that a vendor might innocently believe that he could convey a good title when a learned attorney or a court might determine otherwise. Another reason suggesting itself to us is that real property is the only character of property absolutely essential to human existence, and that it is the policy of the law for it to remain in the hands of home builders and home maintainers, and not to encourage speculative or chance bargaining in it, but to adjust the rights of the parties concerning its transfer, in the absence of fraud or bad faith, placing them *in statu quo,* which in the absence of a contrary showing will be presumed to have been in their contemplation. Furthermore, land values oscillate, because of rapidly occurring events which the parties at the time of making the contract could not possibly contemplate; illustrations of which are the discovery of minerals in the land or in the neighborhood of it, the existence of which were wholly unknown at the time of the contract, and perhaps other equally unanticipated developments. But whatever the reason may be, it is our duty to administer the law as it is and not as we might have written it at the beginning." For a good discussion of this and related problems in damages see McCormick, Damages 680–700 (1935).

In Bachewicz v. American National Bank & Trust Co. of Chicago, 126 Ill.App.3d 298, 81 Ill.Dec. 294, 466 N.E.2d 1096 (1984), reversed on other grounds 111 Ill.2d 444, 95 Ill.Dec. 827, 490 N.E.2d 680 (1986), purchaser sought to recover not only the difference between the market value of the property (an apartment building) at the time of vendor's breach and the stipulated contract price, but also the profits which purchaser allegedly would have made in converting the building and selling it as condominiums. The court denied recovery of the claimed lost profits because they were not reasonably within the contemplation of vendor at the time it entered into the land contract, and because the amount of such profits was too speculative.

The foregoing discussion, and the principal cases, have involved the measure of damages payable by a breaching vendor. If it is the purchaser who breaches, can the vendor get the benefit of his bargain? See the notes which follow.

2. Even the most careful drafting of the real estate contract will not prevent occasional breaches. A skillfully handled transaction may result in the rights of the respective parties being so clear that an easy settlement can be reached without litigation. Even so, there will always be cases that can be terminated only by resort to the courts. When a lawsuit becomes inevitable the attorney must choose among a variety of judicial remedies, including actions for damages at law, specific performance, specific performance with compensation, damages given by an equity court in lieu of specific performance, enforcement of a vendor's or a vendee's lien, actions for the recovery of possession (ejectment, forcible entry and detainer), or a suit to quiet title.

The doctrine of election of remedies was cited previously. See note 3, pages 1080–81 supra. In Rosson v. Cutshall, 11 Kan.App.2d 267, 719 P.2d 23 (1986), the trial court awarded vendor both forfeiture of the defaulting purchaser's interest in the land contract and damages in the amount of the reasonable rental value of the property from the time when purchaser stopped making payments under the contract. The appellate court reversed the award of damages, holding that although there is judicial authority in other states for allowing this combination of remedies, see 77 Am.Jur.2d, Vendor and Purchaser § 324, p. 486, Kansas' position is that they are inconsistent.

3. One common, and troublesome, damages question relates to the nature of the down payment (earnest money). In event of breach, the purchaser will naturally wish its return but he may well fail if it is viewed as liquidated damages and he is in default. In Maxton Builders, Inc. v. Lo Galbo, 68 N.Y.2d 373, 509 N.Y.S.2d 507, 502 N.E.2d 184 (1986), the court rejected the "modern rule" which permits a breaching purchaser to recover a down payment to the extent that it exceeds vendor's actual damages; the court followed the "majority rule" allowing vendor to retain the entire down payment, even if the contract does not refer to it as liquidated damages, especially where it does not exceed 10% of the contract price. Moreover, a liquidated damage clause may be for a larger amount than the down payment and still be sustained. See, for example, Chaffin v. Ramsey, 276 Or. 429, 555 P.2d 459 (1976), where the court allowed a ten per cent ($13,000) liquidated damage clause ($1,000 was paid down) as against a claim that it was a penalty. Said the court: "The trial court's finding has the effect of categorizing the agreement to pay ten per cent of the sale price in case of breach as a provision for 'a penalty' rather than as a provision for 'liquidated damages'. In order for such a clause to be construed as one for liquidated damages, the sum provided, at the time of the making of the contract, must seem to bear a reasonable relationship to anticipated damages and the actual damages must be difficult or impossible to ascertain." The court held that the provision in question met both tests and reversed the trial court. There was a vigorous dissent.

In some instances, the purchaser may desire to have the down payment treated as liquidated damages so that he will have no further liability for compensatory damages. See Frank v. Jansen, 303 Minn. 86, 226 N.W.2d 739 (1975), where the court refused to treat a $2,000 down payment as liquidated damages and held the purchaser liable for a larger amount. In the syllabus by the court it was noted: "Whether a provision in a contract for the sale of real property calling for the forfeiture of the buyer's earnest money in the event of breach constitutes a liquidated damage clause and limits the buyer's liability to the amount of the earnest money must be gleaned from the language of the contract and the evidence as to the intention of the parties, and where the evidence did not support a finding that the parties intended the stipulated amount to be in lieu of compensatory damages, the trial court's finding of a liquidated damages agreement could not stand."

In Gryb v. Benson, 84 Ill.App.3d 710, 40 Ill.Dec. 423, 406 N.E.2d 124 (1980), the court held the vendors were entitled to recover their actual damages even though the contract contained an optional liquidated damages provision allowing the vendors to retain the earnest money in event of breach by the purchasers. The vendors chose not to exercise that option. The vendors were entitled to recover the difference between the contract price and the resale price but other losses, which arose from their attempts to finance the purchase of a second house upon learning that the expected proceeds from sale of the first house would not be forthcoming, were remote rather than proximate and reasonably foreseeable and thus were not recoverable.

4. Of course, the parties can make their intent clear in the original contract by stipulating that forfeiture of the earnest money is not in lieu of such other remedies (specific performance and suit for compensatory damages) as may be appropriate. If this is not done, the actual intent may be difficult to determine.

Even a careful stipulation in the contract of the remedies available in event of breach will not necessarily avoid litigation. See, for example, S.E.S. Importers, Inc. v. Pappalardo, 53 N.Y.2d 455, 442 N.Y.S.2d 453, 425 N.E.2d 841 (1981) where the purchaser's remedies were clearly stated in the event that the vendor, for any reason, not his fault, could not convey title in accordance with the terms of the contract. Specific performance was not included, nonetheless the Court of Appeals granted specific performance in a situation where the title was defective, due to outstanding leases, at the time for performance but where the defect was resolved by the time the litigation began. The majority of the court believed that the contract provision related only to procedural remedies and not to substantive rights. "Thus, nothing therein operated to deprive this buyer of its right to go to court for a judicial resolution of the critical substantive issue—whether the seller could give good title—and in that action to seek specific performance by way of remedy should the court conclude that the seller could do so." There was a vigorous dissent on the theory that the court was re-writing the contract for the parties. "It is elementary that equity enforces contracts; it neither reviews nor rewrites them."

In Walters v. Michel, 745 P.2d 913 (Wyo.1987), the contract provided that if buyer breached, seller "may elect to either retain the deposit [as] liquidated damages . . . or to maintain an action to enforce specific performance." Buyer argued that the remedies specified were exclusive and that, because no deposit was paid and because seller made specific performance impossible by selling the property to a third party (to mitigate damages in a falling market), seller was entitled to no relief. The court disagreed, awarding seller damages in the amount of the difference between the contract price and the value of the property at the time of breach. "Remedies mentioned in a contract generally are not exclusive [but are] merely some of several remedies which might be pursued by an injured party. The contract . . . did not include a limiting 'exclusive remedy' clause." However, in Morris v. Flores, 174 Ill.App.3d 504, 124 Ill.Dec. 122, 528 N.E.2d 1013 (1988), where purchaser had paid only a $100 deposit, seller was denied additional compensatory damages despite a contractual stipulation that "this provision [allowing seller to retain the deposit in case of default by purchaser] with respect to liquidated damages shall not be the exclusive remedy of Seller, and Seller shall retain all monies deposited without prejudice to his other remedies." The court said that "the 'other' remedies refers to rights of a kind and character other than money damages . . ., such as injunctive relief."

5. In many instances, the purchaser would prefer to rescind the contract, following breach by the vendor, rather than seek damages, i.e., he no longer wishes to buy the property and wants out of what he now views as a bad bargain. For example, in Northwest Kansas Area Vocational-Technical School v. Wolf, 6 Kan.App.2d 817, 635 P.2d 1268 (1981) a purchaser contracted to buy a solar-heated house built as part of a school curriculum. A malfunctioning valve caused 750 to 900 gallons of water to escape, damaging the ceiling, floors and walls of the house. Most of the damage was covered by insurance, but the vendor refused to correct a design defect which cost $500 out of a $93,000 purchase price. The court denied rescission, saying: "It is not every breach which gives rise to the right to rescind a contract. In order to warrant rescission of a contract the breach must be material and the failure to perform so substantial as to defeat the object of the parties in making the agreement." The court granted specific performance of the contract but allowed the purchaser $500 for the cost of the design defect. What would have been a material breach in this case? Suppose the purchaser's principal losses had not been covered by insurance?

Even if a purchaser obtains rescission, she may have to compensate the vendor to restore him to the status quo. In Dugan v. Jones, 724 P.2d 955 (Utah 1986), the court said that vendor should receive the fair rental value of the premises for the time the purchaser had possession, plus compensation for permissive waste allowed by the purchaser.

SECTION 4. STATUS OF VENDOR AND PURCHASER—EQUITABLE CONVERSION

If real property were sold in the same manner as most personal property, there would be no need for this section. That is, if the agreement to sell and the transfer of legal title were virtually simultaneous acts, we would not be much concerned about the rights of the parties pending title transfer. But in nearly every case the land contract involves what real estate men call "the gap," the period between the making of the contract and the delivery of the deed. This gap exists chiefly because the purchaser must determine whether or not the vendor has a merchantable title, and this requires both time and effort.[11] The time lapse is usually a matter of a few weeks but in installment land contracts may be several years. What happens if the improvements are destroyed during this period; if the land is condemned for public use; or if the parties die, marry, become legally incapacitated, or run into financial difficulties and are successfully sued by their creditors? These and similar problems form the heart of the present section.

A. GENERAL NATURE OF THE VENDOR-PURCHASER RELATIONSHIP

CLAY v. LANDRETH

Court of Appeals of Virginia, 1948.
187 Va. 169, 45 S.E.2d 875, 175 A.L.R. 1047.

GREGORY, JUSTICE. Pearl C. Clay filed his bill in chancery against the defendants, Landreth and Tysinger, the purpose of which was to have the court decree the specific performance of a certain contract made between the parties for the sale and purchase of a certain lot. An answer was filed by the defendants, and the case was heard upon the bill, answer and an agreed statement of facts. The trial court denied the relief requested and delivered a written opinion which is made a part of the record.

The defense set forth in the answer is that the parties had agreed to sell and purchase the said lot for the purpose of erecting thereon a storage plant for ice cream and frozen fruits, at a time when this particular use was not prohibited by the zoning ordinances of the city of Roanoke for the reason that the lot was then zoned for business uses. It was averred that between the time the contract was made and the time for the delivery of the deed the city council rezoned this lot so that it could be used only for residence purposes; that at the time of making the contract it was contemplated and known by both the vendor and the vendee that it was to be used for the purpose of erecting a storage

11. The methods of title assurance are covered in detail in Chapter 26 of Part Five.

plant for ice cream and frozen fruits; that the rezoning of the lot has caused a very substantial depreciation in its value; that it would be inequitable and produce results not within the intent or understanding of the parties when the contract was made if specific performance should be decreed; and that to enforce the contract under such circumstances would be harsh and oppressive to the defendants.

From the agreed statement of facts it is clear that there is no question of fraud, misrepresentation, unfair dealing, or inequitable conduct on the part of either the complainant or the defendants, and that the defendants agreed to buy and the complainant agreed to sell the lot with the mutual intent that it would be usable for the purpose of erecting a storage plant thereon, but before the transaction was closed the intent and purpose of the sale failed through no fault of either party.

The issue here is whether the contract for the sale of the lot should have been enforced specifically when the agreed purpose for which it was purchased and sold was defeated by the subsequent unanticipated enactment by the city council of a rezoning ordinance changing the lot from what is known as business property to residential property.

The appellant argues here that the doctrine of equitable conversion applies; that this court should consider done what ought to have been done; and that in equity the complainant or vendor should be considered the owner of the purchase money and the defendants or vendees the owners of the lot as of the date of the contract, namely, March 13, 1946. The resultant loss of the intended use of the property and the loss in value of the lot sustained by the rezoning would fall on the defendants if this theory were applied.

That the doctrine of equitable conversion exists in Virginia cannot be doubted. In the early case of Dunsmore v. Lyle, 1891, 87 Va. 391, at page 392, 12 S.E. 610, 611, the doctrine was stated thus: "The principles upon which courts of equity decree specific performance of contracts for the sale of real estate are well understood and familiar to the profession; yet it will be convenient, in the view we have taken of this case, to briefly recur to first principles. And we will remark that it is one of the principles of equity that it looks upon things agreed to be done as actually performed; and consequently, as soon as a valid contract is made for the sale of an estate, equity considers the buyer as the owner of the land, and the seller as a trustee for him; and, on the other hand, it considers the seller as the owner of the money, and the buyer as a trustee for him." See also Digest of Va. & W.Va. Reports (Michie), Vol. 2, at p. 966.

The rule, however, is limited in its application to cases where the enforcement of the contract is in accord with the intention of the parties, free from fraud, misrepresentation and the like, and where it will not produce inequitable results. Principles similar to those which govern the enforcement of specific performance underlie the application of equitable conversion. In both cases the equitable doctrines and their limitations are well defined and stem from the same equitable source. Neither will specific performance of a contract be decreed, nor equitable conversion applied if, by doing so, hardship and injustice are forced upon one of the parties through a change in circumstances not contemplated by them when the contract was made. This equitable principle applies equally whether the case involves a will or a contract for the sale of land. . . .

In the early case of Craig v. Leslie, 3 Wheat. 563, 16 U.S. 563, 4 L.Ed. 460, the Supreme Court defined the doctrine of equitable conversion thus: "The doctrine of conversion is based on the principle that equity regards things directed or agreed to be done as having been actually performed *where nothing has intervened which ought to prevent a performance.* Hence money directed to be employed in the purchase of land, and land directed to be sold and converted into money are to be considered as that species of property into which they are directed to be converted; and this is whatever manner the direction is given,—whether by will, contract, marriage settlement or otherwise." (Italics supplied.)

If something has intervened which ought to prevent it, the doctrine of equitable conversion will not be applied. It does not exist as a matter of right and is not applicable to all circumstances. It is a fiction invented by courts of equity to be applied only when necessity and justice require its exercise. When it arises from a contract, as distinguished from a will, the general rule is that the legal fiction is based upon the presumed intent of the parties. National Bank of Topeka v. Saia, 154 Kan. 740, 121 P.2d 251, 138 A.L.R. 1290; Eddington v. Turner, Del., 38 A.2d 738, 155 A.L.R. 562. In Ingraham v. Chandler, 179 Iowa 304, 161 N.W. 434, 435, L.R.A.1917D, 713, is found this clear statement of the rule: "The doctrine of equitable conversion is altogether a doctrine of equity and depends wholly upon the rules of equity. Its real purpose is to give effect to the manifest intent of a testator or vendor and to treat that as done which by will the testator has directed to be done, or that which by previous contract with another both have mutually bound themselves to do."

And again at page 437 of 161 N.W. this is stated: "As already indicated, the doctrine of equitable conversion is a doctrine of equity, and not a rule of law. Its intent is to lengthen the arm of the court of equity to do justice in a particular case by giving effect to the intention of a testator. Its application is always withheld if it should appear to foil the intent of the testator or to work injustice in the particular case."

When the agreed facts are considered it is apparent that, in the case at bar, the legal fiction of equitable conversion should not be applied because to do so would set at naught the intent and purpose of the parties with resultant hardship and injustice to the defendants. The sole intent of the vendor in the contract was to sell to the vendees and the vendees intended to purchase a lot usable for the erection of a storage plant. This intent has been defeated by the supervening act of the council of Roanoke in rezoning the property, which has effected such a substantial change of conditions and loss in value that it would be inequitable to apply the doctrine of equitable conversion . . . .

The question presented in the case at bar is a novel one in this jurisdiction. It does not appear that a similar case in point of facts has been decided by our court although the general equitable principles involved have been frequently adjudicated.

In Anderson v. Steinway & Sons, 178 App.Div. 507, 165 N.Y.S. 608, affirmed in 221 N.Y. 639, 117 N.E. 575, specific performance was refused in a case almost identical with the one at bar because it would have been inequitable to have required performance. The court ruled that neither party to the contract when it was made could have reasonably anticipated that before closing the transaction the lawmaking power would step in and impose such restrictions upon the use of the property as would render it useless to the defendant for the only purpose for which he sought to acquire it. Like considerations obtain in the case at bar. From our research the logical and sound principle announced in the Anderson case is still the law of New York.

In Williston on Contracts, Rev.Ed., Vol. 4, at p. 2587, the author states, in speaking of zoning ordinances, that "if a restriction precludes use of the land for the purpose for which, as the vendor knows, it is bought, specific performance will not be granted." The case of Anderson v. Steinway & Sons, supra, is cited as support for that proposition.

In addition to the case of Anderson v. Steinway & Sons, supra, the only other case which we have found that is similar to the one at bar on the facts is Kend et al. v. Crestwood Realty Co., 210 Wis. 239, 246 N.W. 311, 312. There an action was brought by the plaintiffs for the *cancellation* and *rescission* of a land contract entered into between the plaintiffs and the realty company. The realty company had represented to the plaintiffs that the land was restricted for business purposes, and, relying upon this representation, the plaintiffs were induced to enter into the contract. A subsequent zoning law was enacted forbidding the use of the premises for business. This change in the use of the premises was the basis of the plaintiff's action for the cancellation of the contract. The court held that there was no basis for a cancellation and rescission and that there was no breach of the contract on the part of the defendants which would warrant the relief sought by the plaintiffs. The Wisconsin court, however, recognized the principle applied in Anderson v. Steinway & Sons, supra, and in speaking of that case, said, that the New York court "recognizing that the title was marketable and unincumbered in a legal sense, held that under all of the circumstances the relief of specific performance could not conscionably be given. This case amounts merely to an application of the ordinary rule that when circumstances subsequent to a contract have so changed the situation as to render the equitable relief of specific performance unfair or unjust, the chancellor will follow his conscience and deny such relief."

And the Wisconsin court concluded: "Nor does the fact that a court of equity might decline its assistance in the direction of specific performance compel the conclusion that the same court should permit or assist plaintiffs to rescind."

What has been quoted is sufficient to show that a court of equity may refuse specific performance when a subsequent change of circumstances not contemplated by the parties, occurring after the contract has been made, would render it inequitable. There is a difference between rescission of a contract and the specific performance of it. Rescission is the counterpart of a suit for specific performance. Hagan v. Taylor, 110 Va. 9, 65 S.E. 487. If the former is granted, the contract is terminated for all purposes, while if the latter is refused, the contract is not terminated. The court of equity simply refuses to enforce it but for other purposes the contract is still in force. This principle was recognized in the decree in the case at bar when it provided that it was "without prejudice to his (complainant's) right to bring an action at law."

If the Wisconsin case had been one to enforce specifically the contract instead of one for rescission, no doubt the court would have followed the principle in the case of Anderson v. Steinway & Sons, supra, and denied the relief.

Finally, the appellant contends that the defendants were guilty of an inequity in that they did not actively oppose the rezoning of the lot in question. Counsel for the defendants was in the council chamber when the question of rezoning was brought up but he took no part in the discussion. He expressed no opposition to the rezoning. Under these circumstances it is difficult to see how any bad faith could be imputed to the defendants from counsel's conduct. The agreed facts contain nothing that would show any inequitable conduct on the part of either the complainant or the defendants.

The intervening of governmental authority, entirely unanticipated, has vitiated the purpose which was the foundation for the contract. It rendered the property useless to the defendants in that they could not use it for the intended purpose. The complainant cannot convey to the defendants what they agreed to purchase and he agreed to convey.

We think the decree should be affirmed.

Affirmed.

NOTES

1. In the principal case the tract in question was rezoned while the contract was executory, thus bringing into issue the doctrine of equitable conversion. A different issue arises if the zoning remains unchanged but the purchaser is ignorant of the land use status. Normally, the purchaser is deemed to have notice of the zoning classification and can't rescind because of his own mistake of law. If the vendor is guilty of deliberate fraud the purchaser should have the right to rescind. Close cases are certain to develop and the facts will be decisive. For example, in a Massachusetts case the original advertisements offered houses for investment properties and the broker expressly asserted that the houses were being rented to the public for multifamily purposes. The vendors knew that the purchasers planned to use the buildings for apartments. The court held that the vendors were bound to disclose to the purchasers that a multi-family use of houses

violated zoning provisions and their failure to do so constituted fraud entitling the purchasers to rescind. Kannavos v. Annino, 356 Mass. 42, 247 N.E.2d 708 (1969).

2. The concept of equitable conversion cannot be carried to its logical extreme in all cases and it presents inconsistencies, as do most legal concepts, but it has had a profound influence on the development of the law. Note, however, that although the purchaser is said to have equitable title, after an enforceable contract has been made, he does not have the right of possession, unless the contract expressly or impliedly gives it to him, until the delivery of the deed. Possession, in other words, follows the legal title. Moreover, even if the purchaser is entitled to possession, he is not free to treat the land in such a fashion that the vendor's security for the remainder of the purchase price is threatened. A court of equity may even enjoin the cutting of timber, the removal of minerals, etc., by using the mortgagor-mortgagee analogy. In any long-term contract involving land which must be denuded in order to be useful, it is essential that rather exact limits be set for activities by the purchaser.

3. When real estate is under a valid contract of sale, a question frequently arises as to who is the "owner" for a wide variety of legal purposes. See, for example, Committee of Protesting Citizens, etc. v. Val Vue Sewer District, 14 Wn.App. 838, 545 P.2d 42 (1976), where, applying the logic of equitable conversion, the court held that the purchaser, not the vendor, was "owner" for the purpose of protesting the formation of a local improvement district under a Washington statute.

4. Who is the "owner" of the land for the purposes of a creditor seeking to reach the assets of his debtor? "The rights of creditors of the vendor and purchaser to reach the interest of their debtor in the land contracted to be sold or purchased depend in large part on the theory of equitable conversion. Since on that theory, the purchaser is regarded as owner of the land and debtor for the purchase money and the vendor as holding legal title as security for payment by the purchaser, it logically follows that the creditors of the purchaser should be able to reach the land subject to the vendor's lien thereon, while creditors of the vendor should be able to reach the land only to the extent of the vendor's security interest. This is the underlying conception on the basis of which the law in this field has developed; but that development has been shaped to a very considerable extent by the existence of statutes as to executions and judgment liens, so that the practical applications of the underlying principle are intelligible only upon a somewhat detailed examination of this legislation." Simpson, Legislative Changes in the Law of Equitable Conversion by Contract: I, 44 Yale L.J. 559, 575 (1935). See also Comment, 1955 U.Ill.L.F. 754; Annot., 1 A.L.R.2d 727 (1948). For an example of how this theory works in practice see First Security Bank of Idaho, National Association v. Rogers, 91 Idaho 654, 429 P.2d 386 (1967).

5. Under the logic of equitable conversion a purchaser can mortgage his equitable title as security for a loan. However, in Eade v.

Brownlee, 29 Ill.2d 214, 218, 193 N.E.2d 786, 789 (1963), the contract provided: "5. That no right, title or interest, legal or equitable, in the premises aforesaid, or any part thereof, shall vest in the Purchaser until the delivery of the deed aforesaid by the Seller, or until the full payment of the purchase price at the times and in the manner herein provided." The court held that the doctrine of equitable conversion evolved to carry out the intention of the parties to the contract and those who claim under them. In view of the above clause the purchaser had no interest which he could mortgage. If the purchaser has no interest which he can subject to the voluntary lien of a mortgage does it follow that he has no interest which can be reached by the involuntary lien of a judgment and execution?

B. DEVOLUTION ON DEATH

The doctrine of equitable conversion by contract finds its principal application in those cases where either the vendor or the purchaser dies while the contract is still executory. If the vendor dies the legal title devolves by testate or intestate succession. But who is entitled to the beneficial interest under the contract; i.e., the remaining payments owed by the purchaser? Who can enforce the contract if the purchaser defaults? If the purchaser dies, his estate is liable for the rest of the purchase price, but whose share of the estate must be used to pay it, where those who succeed to his realty and those who succeed to his personalty are not the same? Who gets the land after the payments have been made?

Equity answered these questions by applying the doctrine of equitable conversion with the results suggested by the following cases. You should note that the doctrine formerly made a great difference in case of intestate succession, since realty and personalty did not devolve alike. With the abolition of primogeniture and the adoption of modern statutory schemes of descent and distribution, those who succeed to the personalty usually succeed also to the realty. Thus, legislation which was not directed at equitable conversion had a profound effect on the significance of the doctrine. (Incidentally, this phenomenon occurs quite frequently when common-law or equitable rules are changed by legislation.) The statutes of descent and distribution have no effect, however, on testate succession, and the doctrine of equitable conversion may be significant where a vendor or a purchaser leaves a will disposing of realty and personalty differently.

SHAY v. PENROSE [12]

Supreme Court of Illinois, 1962.
25 Ill.2d 447, 185 N.E.2d 218.

HOUSE, JUSTICE. This is an appeal from a final order of the city court of Sterling in an action for the partition of real estate, striking certain affirmative defenses and dismissing the amended, counterclaim of the defendant, Grace Penrose. A freehold is involved.

Carol M. Shay individually acquired six parcels of real estate in her lifetime. Between 1955 and 1960 she executed contracts for deed to separate purchasers of four of the properties. None of the contracts is set out in full but it appears from the pleadings that they are the type of contract for deed in common usage by the profession. Each provided for a down payment with the balances payable in his contract. Provisions were made for delivery of abstracts of title varying amounts per month together with interest on the balances from time to time unpaid. Each buyer went into possession under showing merchantable title in seller, title examination by the buyers, methods of perfecting any title defects, and delivery of warranty deeds upon receipt of final payment. The seller retained an option of forfeiture in the event the buyer failed to perform his covenants, including that of making the specified payments.

On July 31, 1960, Carol M. Shay died intestate and was survived by her husband Arthur R. Shay, the plaintiff, who is also made a party as administrator, and her sister Grace Penrose. The husband filed a complaint for partition of the two unsold tracts. The sister answered admitting the allegations with respect to the two tracts but alleged that plaintiff should have included the four parcels sold under contract. By her counterclaim the sister alleged that she and the surviving husband were each entitled to a one-half interest in the four parcels and prayed for partition of them as well as the two tracts described in the complaint. This is based upon her theory that she is entitled to one-half of each of the four tracts of real estate under section 11 of the Probate Act. Ill.Rev.Stat.1961, chap. 3, par. 11.

The trial court held that equitable conversion had occurred at the time of execution of the contracts so that the four tracts were not subject to partition by heirs of the seller. Defendant's basic contention is that equitable conversion does not apply to a long term contract for the sale of real estate prior to the time that both parties have performed all acts necessary to complete the contract except tender of final payment and delivery of the deed.

Equitable conversion is the treating of land as personalty and personalty as land under certain circumstances. Hence, as between the parties and those claiming through them, when the owner of land enters into a valid and enforceable contract for its sale he continues to hold the legal title, but in trust for the buyer; and the buyer becomes the equitable owner and holds the purchase money in trust for the

12. See also In re Estate of McDonough, 113 Ill.App.2d 437, 251 N.E.2d 405 (1969).

seller. The conversion takes place at the time of entering into the contract. It stems from the basic equitable principle that equity regards as done that which ought to be done. The doctrine of equitable conversion has been recognized in Illinois, as it has in practically every other jurisdiction, since earliest times. Lombard v. Chicago Sinai Congregation, 64 Ill. 477; Fuller v. Bradley, 160 Ill. 51, 43 N.E. 732; Lewis v. Shearer, 189 Ill. 184, 59 N.E. 580; Rhodes v. Meredith, 260 Ill. 138, 102 N.E. 1063; Ward v. Williams, 282 Ill. 632, 118 N.E. 1021; Knights v. Knights, 300 Ill. 618, 133 N.E. 377; Smith v. Smith, 340 Ill. 34, 172 N.E. 32; see Pomeroy, Equity Jurisprudence, 5th ed. vol. 2, sec. 368.

We would be less than candid if we said that this court has been consistent in applying the doctrine. Much of the confusion in this area arose from language in the early case of Chappell v. McKnight, 108 Ill. 570. It was there said that the contract to convey at a future time did not create an equitable title and that the buyer's estate would not ripen into an equitable title until he had performed all acts necessary to entitle him to a deed. While the Chappell case was one at law (ejectment) and therefore the equitable doctrine did not apply, nevertheless, it was cited with approval in some subsequent equity cases. (See e.g., Walters v. Walters, 132 Ill. 467, 23 N.E. 1120; Gall v. Stoll, 259 Ill. 174, 102 N.E. 225.) We believe the correct view to be that expressed in the majority of the cases which hold equitable conversion takes place at the instant a valid and enforceable contract is entered into and that the buyer at that time acquires an equitable title. To the extent that the Chappell case and those following it are inconsistent with this view they are hereby expressly overruled.

The defendant seeks, in effect, a definitive rule of application of the doctrine in the several fields where it may be invoked, such as dower, insurance, joint tenancy and the like. The issue here presented is devolution of title at the death of the seller and we concern ourselves in this opinion only with that issue.

It is suggested that a hearing is necessary to determine whether these contracts for deed are valid and enforceable, a prerequisite to application of the doctrine of equitable conversion. Since neither lack of validity nor lack of enforceability was properly raised by the pleadings, the chancellor was not required to hear evidence on these matters. The terms of the contracts were sufficiently set out and their existence admitted in the counterclaim, so that the trial court had enough information to pass upon the question of whether the counterclaim stated a cause of action.

The defendant seems to read special significance into the long term nature of these contracts and suggests that a seller needs the protection of the courts. The simple answer is that a seller voluntarily enters into such a contract and is deemed to know the legal implication of his acts. To base application of the doctrine of equitable conversion upon the length of time the contracts have to run would leave titles in an utter state of confusion. It is a matter of common knowledge, admitted by defendant, that contracts for deed are useful to and increasingly used in our society. As a matter of policy, entirely aside from the legal desirability of a doctrine almost universally accepted, certainty and stability of titles dictate that application of the doctrine cannot depend upon the flexible element suggested by defendant.

Thus far we have treated all four contracts in their general aspects, and now turn to special circumstances with respect to two of them. The DeWitt contract was two months in arrears at the date of the seller's death. The Horton contract provided that it was not assignable without the written consent of the seller, and the plaintiff, individually and as administrator of the seller's estate, consented to an assignment after seller's death. The answer applies to both situations. Equitable conversion took place at the time of execution of the contracts, so that upon the death of the seller the plaintiff became entitled to the entire unpaid balance of the purchase prices as personal representative of the decedent, since it was personal property under the doctrine of equitable conversion. The option to declare the contract in default and the right to consent to the assignment were therefore vested in the plaintiff as administrator.

We find no error in the order of the city court of the city of Sterling striking part of the answer and dismissing the counterclaim and it is, therefore, affirmed.

Order affirmed.

NOTES

1. When the principal case was decided the relevant portion of the Rules of Descent and Distribution read as follows: "Third, when there is no descendant but a surviving spouse and also a parent, brother, sister, or descendant of a brother or sister of the decedent: the entire personal estate and one-half of each parcel of real estate to the surviving spouse and one-half of each parcel of real estate to the parents, brothers, and sisters . . . ." Ill.Rev.Stat. ch. 3, § 11 (1961). In 1963, the Illinois statute was revised to read: "Third, when there is a surviving spouse but no descendant of the decedent: the entire estate to the surviving spouse. . . ." How does this change in the statute affect the impact of the doctrine of equitable conversion on decedent's estates?

2. In the principal case, the court refused to discuss dower, insurance, joint tenancy, etc. Equitable conversion has made its influence felt in all of these areas but with far from uniform results. The insurance problems will be covered in the next section but a few words are necessary as to dower and concurrent estates.

Dower. "As before explained, one to whom another has contracted to convey land has what is regarded as an equitable estate in the land, and this view has been applied, in some jurisdictions, to the extent of giving the widow of such vendee dower in land purchased and paid for by the husband, but which had not been conveyed to him at the time of his death. Though there is authority to the contrary, some decisions hold that the husband must have paid all, and not merely a part, of the purchase price, before his death, in order that his widow be endowed.

And even in states where this view does not obtain, the widow is given dower only as to the surplus value of the land after payment of the balance of the purchase money due. Nor is there usually any dower right if, before the purchase price was entirely paid, the husband transferred to another his interest under the contract of purchase." 2 Tiffany, Real Property 357–358 (3d ed. 1939). For an application of this doctrine see J.J. Newberry Co. v. Shannon, 268 Mass. 116, 167 N.E. 292, 63 A.L.R. 133 (1929).

Concurrent estates. In Panushka v. Panushka, 221 Or. 145, 166, 349 P.2d 450, 460 (1960), H and W owned a motel as tenants by the entirety. They signed an executory contract to sell the motel, the purchasers went into possession and H died intestate before the full price was paid. W claimed the remaining amount due by right of survivorship while her stepson insisted that one-half belong to H's estate. The court applied the doctrine of equitable conversion, plus the Oregon rule forbidding tenancy by the entirety in personal property, and held that while the wife succeeded to the entire legal estate as trustee for benefit of the purchasers she was a tenant in common with H's estate as to the unpaid purchase price. There was a vigorous dissent. "How does the contract for the sale of the land work a change in this right of survivorship incident to an estate by the entirety? The majority of the court takes the position that the doctrine of equitable conversion forces the conclusion. That is the fundamental error upon which the majority builds its opinion. The doctrine . . . originated out of a need to adjust the traditional categories of property interests so that a just result could be reached through the application of accepted principles of law. The doctrine does not demand that contracts for the sale of land shall in all instances convert the interest of the vendor from real to personal property. 'When we speak of conversion we are not describing a condition of the property for all purposes with respect to everybody but are giving a name to a situation resulting from the application of equitable doctrines to a state of facts between certain parties.' Pound, The Progress of the Law 1918–1919, 33 Harv.L.Rev. 813 at 831 (1920)."

Under similar facts involving a joint tenancy the Illinois courts have concluded that a contract signed by both H and W (suppose only one signs?) does not work a severance and that the surviving joint tenant is entitled to the remaining payments. Watson v. Watson, 5 Ill. 2d 526, 126 N.E.2d 220 (1955). Is there anything inherent in the difference between tenancy by the entirety and joint tenancy which should lead to this difference in result?

3. For a decision similar to the principal case see Matter of Estate of Hills, 222 Kan. 231, 564 P.2d 462 (1977), where the court noted: "A contract for the sale of real estate works an equitable conversion of the land into personalty *from the time when it was made,* and the purchase-money becomes, thereupon, a part of the vendor's personal estate, and, as such, distributable, upon his death, to his widow and next-of-kin." (Emphasis added.)

CLAPP v. TOWER

Supreme Court of North Dakota, 1903.
11 N.D. 556, 93 N.W. 862.

YOUNG, J. This is an action to quiet title to a section of land situated in Cass county, which was conveyed to the plaintiff by the executors of the last will and testament of Charlemange Tower, deceased. The complaint alleges that the plaintiff is the owner of said real estate, and that the defendants claim an interest therein adverse to the plaintiff, and prays that they be required to set forth their claims, to the end that their validity may be determined, and that title be quieted in the plaintiff. Defendants, in their answer, allege that they are the next of kin and all of the heirs at law of said Charlemange Tower, deceased, and all the surviving legatees under his will; that said Charlemange Tower died in, and a resident of, the city of Philadelphia, Pa., and that his will was probated there; that the land in question was sold by said deceased to one Hadley upon a contract which provided for the execution and delivery of a deed to him upon the making of certain deferred payments specified in said contract; that subsequent to the death of Charlemange Tower the executors of his will foreclosed said contract by reason of the default of said Hadley in making payments according to its terms, and that said land became a part of the estate of said deceased; that thereafter the executors, acting upon the theory that said land was subject to the principle and rule of equitable conversion, and was for the purposes of administration to be treated as personal property, sold and conveyed the same to the plaintiff, who has ever since been in possession of the same, claiming the ownership and possession thereof by virtue of said deed from said executors; that the defendants are the owners of said real estate by virtue of their heirship, and ask that the title be quieted in them. The plaintiff demurred to the answer upon the ground that it does not state facts sufficient to constitute a defense or counterclaim. The trial court sustained the demurrer, and the defendants appeal from the order sustaining the same.

The will of Charlemange Tower was before this court in the case of Penfield v. Tower, 1 N.D. 216, 46 N.W. 413. This court held that, so far as its provisions related to real estate situated in this state, it was inoperative and void, and that the real estate of said deceased in this state must be distributed according to the law of succession of this state and that the personal property should be distributed according to the terms of the will. The only question involved upon the issue raised by the demurrer is whether the land in question should, under the facts pleaded in the answer, be treated as real estate or as personal property. If, for the purposes of administration, it retains the character of real estate, the will not being operative, it descended directly to the heirs, the defendants in this action. This is conceded. If, on the other hand, it is to be considered as personal property, it then went to the executors for the purposes of distribution, and they had full right and authority to sell and convey the same in the manner and form pursued, and to account for the proceeds to the orphans' court of the state of Pennsylvania, from which they received their appointment. It is very properly conceded by both parties that under the rule and doctrine of equitable conversion land may be treated as money and money as land, whenever, in equity, it is proper to invoke and apply the principle of that doctrine. "Equitable conversion is defined as a constructive alteration in the nature of property by which, in equity, real estate is regarded as personalty or personal estate as realty." 7 Amer. & Eng. Enc. of Law (2d Ed.) p. 464. And the doctrine has its origin in the maxim of equity that that is regarded as done which should be done. Penfield v. Tower, supra. There is no room for doubt that upon the facts pleaded in the defendants' answer the rule of equitable conversion is applicable, and that the execution and delivery of the contract of sale of the real estate in question by Charlemange Tower during his lifetime—and the same was valid and enforceable at the time of his death—worked a conversion of the land into personalty. His interest, after the execution of the contract and at the time of his death, was the money contracted to be paid by the purchaser, and the purchaser's interest was the land contracted to be conveyed. In such cases, says Pomeroy, in his work on Equity Jurisprudence (section 105), "the vendor still holds the legal title, but only as a trustee, and he in turn acquires an equitable ownership of the purchase money. His property, as viewed by equity, is no longer real estate, in the land, but personal estate, in the price; and, if he dies before payment, it goes to his administrators, and not to his heirs. In short, equity regards the contracting parties as having changed positions, and the original estate of each as having been 'converted'—that of the vendee from personal into real property, and that of the vendor from real into personal property."

The doctrine is laid down in Williams et al. v. Haddock, 145 N.Y. 144, 39 N.E. 825, as follows: "Courts of equity regard that as done which ought to be done. They look at the substance of things, and not at the mere form of agreements, to which they give the precise effect which the parties intended. It is presumed that the vendor, in agreeing to sell his land, intends that his property shall assume the character of the property in which it is to be converted, and it cannot be denied that it is competent for the owner of land thus to make such land into money at his sole will and pleasure. If the vendor die prior to the completion of the bargain, provided there has been no default, the heir of the vendor may be compelled to convey, and the proceeds of the land will go to the executors as personal property." The rule is uniform, we think, that, where a valid and binding contract of sale of land has been entered into, such as a court of equity will specifically enforce against an unwilling purchaser, the contract operates as a conversion. Keep et al. v. Miller, 42 N.J.Eq. 100, 6 A. 495. See, also, 7 Am. & Eng.Enc. of Law (2d Ed.) 471, cases cited in note 1. The only authority cited by appellants in opposition to this general rule which can be said to be at all in point is Kerr v. Day, 14 Pa. 112, 53 Am.Dec. 526. That case, however, cannot be considered as an authority in their favor, for in that case the contract of sale was not enforceable, and for that reason it was held that a conversion was prevented. Had the contract been valid and enforceable, as the contract in the case at bar, it is evident that the decision would have been otherwise.

The real estate in question, having assumed the character of personalty, went to the executors, and it continued as personalty for the purposes of administration, so that the executors could, after the cancellation of the contract, sell and convey the same to the plaintiff in the manner and form pursued.

The demurrer to the answer was, therefore, properly sustained, and the order will be affirmed.

MORGAN, J., concurs. COCHRANE, J., did not hear the argument or participate in the decision.

NOTE

In the typical case the will precedes the contract of sale and, under the logic of equitable conversion, equity will treat the realty as personalty in distributing the estate. Suppose, however, the contract is signed first and, while it is still executory, the vendor makes a will devising the land being sold to plaintiff while bequeathing the personal property to defendant. Which party should receive the proceeds of the sale? That plaintiff should be preferred see Father Flanagan's Boys' Home v. Graybill, 178 Neb. 79, 132 N.W.2d 304, 309 (1964). "It seems clear to us that testator, under such circumstances, intended that his interest in the Logan County farm, . . . was to pass to the plaintiffs under the will. The fact that he believed that his retention of the bare legal title and its devise by the will would accomplish his purpose will not operate to defeat his intent to devise and bequeath his interest in the Logan County farm to the plaintiffs. . . . A general or specific devise of land passes the interest of the testator in the land which he had contracted to sell, unless the intent of the testator as demonstrated by the will and the attendant circumstances is shown otherwise."

EDDINGTON v. TURNER

Supreme Court of Delaware, 1944.
27 Del.Ch. 411, 38 A.2d 738, 155 A.L.R. 562.

Thomas W. Turner, of Sussex County, Delaware, owning certain real estate in said County made his will dated October 17, 1938. By this will he devised certain land to his sister, Sallie B. Turner, for life. There was no devise of the lands after the death of Sallie B. Turner, and no residuary clause in the will. The testator left as his only heirs at law, under the intestate law of the State of Delaware, two sons, Arthur D. Turner, and Thomas H. Turner, who were also Executors of his will.

After making the will, and on October 20, 1938, Thomas W. Turner, for the consideration of $100 entered into an agreement giving to one J. Robert Eddington "the exclusive right or option to purchase at any time within 60 days from the date hereof" a large tract of land, including all of the land devised in his will to Sallie B. Turner, together with some additional land. Time was made the essence of the option and it was agreed that if Eddington should not elect "to take, accept and purchase said property at the price and terms aforesaid, at or before the expiration of 60 days from the date hereof then this agreement shall forthwith become null and void and of no effect."

Within the 60 day period, and on December 16, 1938, Thomas W. Turner died, not having changed his will in any respect. Within the life of the option, and on December 19, 1938, Eddington elected to exercise his option.

Subsequently, Eddington filed his bill for specific performance, and eventually a deed was made to Eddington for the property, and the purchase money deposited in Court. Upon petition to draw the money out of Court the Chancellor held that Sallie B. Turner was entitled to a life interest in such portion of the proceeds as the land devised to her for life bore to the amount of land conveyed under the option to purchase. This proportion was ascertained by a Special Master appointed for the purpose, and such proportion, less costs, was ordered paid to Sallie B. Turner, upon her entering into a bond conditioned upon the payment of said sum at her death to Arthur D. Turner and Thomas H. Turner.

From this decree the present appeal was taken, and the appellants contend that the proceeds of sale received from the exercise of the option constituted personal property, and that they, as Executors and distributees, are entitled to the entire fund, and that the devisee of the real estate for life is entitled to nothing.

RODNEY, JUDGE, delivering the opinion of the Court:

The foregoing facts give rise to three questions so intimately blended together that it is difficult to keep them separate, for in some particulars they impinge closely on each other, and yet contain elements of dissimilarity. These questions are:

(1) Does the granting of the option to purchase, made after the execution of the will and the subsequent exercise of the option after the death of the optionor, operate as an equitable conversion of the property relating back to the date of the option, so that the proceeds of sale would pass to the personal representatives rather than to the specific devisee of the land? . . .

Equitable conversion is, of course, a well established principle of equity, arising from consideration of a will or contract. While there is some authority holding that equitable conversion by contract, as distinguished from that arising by will depends upon the operation of law regardless of the intent of the parties, yet the prevailing view is that it includes a legal fiction based upon the presumed intent of the parties, and embodying the equitable maxim that equity considers that to have been done which should have been done. By the application of the doctrine and upon the entering into a mutually obligatory contract the nature of the property is considered as having been changed. Equity thereafter considers the vendor as holding the land subject to the call of the vendee, and as security for the payment of the purchase price, and considers the vendee as holding the purchase price for the vendor. Either can require the other to specifically perform the contract, and by the doctrine the parties upon the entering upon the contract are deemed to be entitled to that which he will receive when the contract is carried out. The matter has chief application in determining the interests of persons claiming under the vendor or vendee.

Any difficulties surrounding the application of equitable conversion are increased when considered with relation to a mere option to purchase, as contrasted with a mutually binding contract of sale, and these difficulties are again intensified when the option is not exercised until after the death of the person giving the option.

Most of the facts indicated were present in the case of Lawes v. Bennett, Ch., 1 Cox 167, 29 Eng.Reprint 1111, from which case stems all thought that where the option is exercised after the death of the optionor the equitable conversion relates in some way back to the date of the option, and not to the date of its exercise, and consequently the proceeds of sale are treated as personalty, passing to the personal representatives rather than to the specific devisees of the real estate itself. . . .

The theory of the relation back of the equitable conversion as held in Lawes v. Bennett, does not appeal to us as either embodying the intent of the testator or embodying any sound principle of law or equity. In the present case the testator evidenced his desire that his sister should have a portion of the land for life. He then granted an option for the limited period of 60 days. He could not tell whether the option would or would not be exercised. He knew, of course, if it should be exercised and he made the conveyance, that there would then be nothing left as a basis for the devise. He knew equally that if the option was not exercised he would continue as the owner of the land as if the option had never been given. He had no enforceable right to the purchase money, or control over the exercise of the option. He simply held the land under the obligation to convey if the optionee should so require. He then died. The devisee received by the will the land subject to the same obligation imposed upon it by the testator. The devisee received for her own use the rents and profits, and if the option was not exercised, would continue to do so for life. The devisee has taken the land under the will and held it under precisely the same terms and obligations as the testator, and continued so to hold it until the contingency happened which required her to make a deed for the property—viz. the exercise of the option. If there be any equitable conversion at all it could not occur prior to the exercise of the option, for until then no duty rested on anyone in connection with the land. There having been no conversion of the land during the testator's life, he had no claim for the purchase price transmissible to his personal representatives. To us it seems that the devisee took the land subject to the obligation to convey it upon the exercise of the option. The land is at that point converted into money, and as she had the life interest in the land with its rents and profits prior to conversion, so she should have the life interest in the proceeds of the land. . . .

The decree of the Chancellor is affirmed.

NOTE

"It is to be noted that the application of the conversion theory assumes a specifically enforceable contract. If neither vendor nor purchaser is entitled to specific performance, as, for example, where neither party has signed a memorandum in writing sufficient to satisfy the Statute of Frauds, the devolution of rights and duties upon the death of either party is the same as if no contract had ever been made. If one party is not entitled to specific performance but the other party is, as, for example, in a case where partial performance with compensation could be obtained by the purchaser only, devolution on the side of the party who cannot enforce the contract is not affected, nor, according to the authorities, is devolution on the side of the party who can compel specific performance. It is immaterial that the party who can enforce the contract in fact elects, after the death of the other, to do so. On the other hand, if there is a mutually specifically enforceable contract at the time when a party dies, his rights and duties devolve in accordance with the principles of equitable conversion even though the contract is not in fact specifically enforced. Thus, where the vendor dies while the contract is subsisting and specifically enforceable by and against him, his executor or administrator becomes entitled to the unpaid purchase money for the benefit of the legatees or next-of-kin; and if the purchaser fails to complete and the contract is not specifically enforced against him, the vendor's executor or administrator can enforce payment of this money out of the land in the hands of the vendor's devisee or heir. On the same principle, an option which is exercised and so becomes a binding contract before either party dies effects a conversion although the contract is never in fact specifically enforced; but if the option is not exercised until after the death of the optionor, there is no conversion (although the English decisions regarding this point are, erroneously, to the contrary); and if the option is not exercised until after the death of the optionee, there is no conversion on the optionee's side even in the English view." Chafee and Re, Cases and Materials on Equity 488–489 (4th ed. of Chafee and Simpson's Cases on Equity, 1958).

C. RISK OF LOSS

BLECKLEY v. LANGSTON

Court of Appeals of Georgia, 1965.
112 Ga.App. 63, 143 S.E.2d 671.

HALL, JUDGE. In this case the defendant assigns error on judgments of the trial court overruling its general demurrers to the plaintiffs' petition, sustaining the plaintiffs' general demurrer to the defendants' cross action, and granting the plaintiffs' motion for summary judgment.

The plaintiffs' petition and the parties' agreed statement of facts show: On December 23, 1963, the parties entered into a contract in which the plaintiffs agreed to purchase described real estate from the defendants for $120,000, and the plaintiffs paid $10,000 as earnest money, the contract specifying the terms for payment of the balance of the purchase price. On December 31, 1963, and January 1, 1964, while the defendants were still in possession of the property and before they had tendered or executed a deed to the plaintiffs, an ice storm damaged all the pecan trees upon the real estate, which reduced the fair market value of the real estate by at least $32,000. The contract provided that the sale was to be consummated, an additional cash payment made by the vendee, and the property conveyed to the vendee before February 1, 1964, and that the vendor should have the right to retain possession until February 1, 1964, for the purpose of gathering pecans. Before February 1, 1964, the vendee notified the vendor that it elected to rescind and would not consummate the contract because of the damage to the pecan trees, and demanded the return of their earnest money. The defendants notified the plaintiffs that they were willing and able to perform and called upon the vendee to perform the contract, and did not return the earnest money. The petition prayed for rescission of the contract and recovery of the earnest money.

The cross action contends that the defendants are entitled to damages for the plaintiffs' failure to perform their contract, by retention of the $10,000 earnest money and judgment for an additional $22,000 against the plaintiffs.

The facts show a destruction of a substantial part of the real estate constituting the subject matter of the contract occurring between the date of the contract and the time fixed for performance without the fault of either party. The question where the loss must fall in these circumstances can be determined by the parties themselves by provisions in the contract. In this case the contract did not contain an agreement between the parties upon this subject and the court must decide the question.

It was established in England in 1801 that after a contract for the sale of realty and acceptance of title the risk of loss is upon the vendee. Paine v. Meller, 6 Ves. 349, 31 Eng.Rep. 1088; cited with approval in Phinizy v. Guernsey, 111 Ga. 346, 349, 36 S.E. 796, 50 L.R.A. 680; 3 American Law of Property 90, § 11.30; 92 C.J.S. Vendor and Purchaser § 295, p. 174. "The rule is based on the principle that the contract gives to the purchaser in fact and substance the real ownership of the land, the vendor retaining in his own right possession, rents and profits for the brief interval before performance, and the legal title as security for the purchase money." Walsh on Equity 440, § 96. As a result of the rule, the vendee is entitled to the proceeds arising from condemnation proceedings. Fulton County v. Amorous, 89 Ga. 614(3), 61 S.E. 201. "This rule, however, is not applicable unless there is an ability as well as a willingness on the part of the vendor to convey; the purchaser not being considered as the owner from the date of the contract unless the vendor is prepared to convey a clear title and is not in default." Phinizy v. Guernsey, 111 Ga. 346, 348, 36 S.E. 796, 797, supra; Mackey v. Bowles, 98 Ga. 730, 25 S.E. 834.

There is a minority view in this country, known as the Massachusetts rule, which holds that there is a failure of consideration which turns the vendee loose and leaves the vendor with his ruins. Libman v. Levenson, 236 Mass. 221, 128 N.E. 13. As a practical matter, the latter rule is more expedient, and more in accord with practical common sense and business practices. The inaccuracy of the theory of "Equitable Conversion" was exposed by the late Chief Justice, then Dean Stone, in his oft-cited article, "Equitable Conversion by Contract," 13 Col.L. Rev. 369, 386–388 (1913). And its inconsistency with natural justice, practical advantage, and the principles of law in analogous cases was exposed by Williston in "The Risk of Loss After An Executory Contract of Sale in the Common Law," 9 Harvard L.Rev. 106, 118–123. It is also interesting that the Massachusetts rule was eventually adopted in England by Parliament in the Law of Property Act of 1925, § 47. Nevertheless, the prevailing law of this country and in this State is that the risk of loss is normally upon the vendee who is in substance the owner of the property.

The vendee in this case takes the position that possession of the property at the time of loss should be the criterion for determining whether the loss should be borne by the vendee or the vendor. This was not true at common law nor "has any court of last resort ever reached this result." See Agnor, "Risk of Loss In The Vendor and Purchaser Relation," 11 Ga.B.J. 401, 405. "Casual statements, that the loss falls on the purchaser who has taken possession as in Mackey v. Bowles, 98 Ga. 730, 734 (25 S.E. 834) (1896) [also Phinizy v. Guernsey, 111 Ga. 346, (36 S.E. 746) and Wingfield v. Oakes, 96 [93] Ga.App. 783 [92 s.e.2d 820]] do not mean that he does not assume the risk until he has taken possession." Walsh on Equity 446, § 97, fn. 78. This is also in accord with the view of the late Dean Pound who, referring to possession at the time of loss as a criterion says: "There is practically no authority for this view . . . . Possession is not material with respect to the passing or existence of either legal or equitable title to land. Why then should it be material as to the incidents of equitable title." Pound "The Progress of the Law," 33 Harvard L.Rev. 813, 826, fn. 68. Though it may reasonably be argued that possession as well as equitable title in the vendee should be necessary to place upon him losses which the party in possession has the power to protect against, this reasoning is not necessarily applicable to losses caused by an act of God. DeFuniak, Handbook of Modern Equity 218, § 93. Professor Agnor's article, supra, takes the position that the English Rule of Paine v. Meller, supra, is the law of Georgia and can only be changed by a statute similar to the Uniform Vendor and Purchaser Risk Act.

Neither party has referred us to a case and we have found none in which a Georgia court has decided which party—vendor or vendee—takes the loss when improvements on realty are substantially damaged after a binding contract of sale, when the vendor is still in possession and is able to convey title. The Georgia Supreme Court has decided or held as the basis for decision that the loss falls on the vendor when the contract between the parties is not binding (Walker v. General Insurance Co., 214 Ga. 758, 107 S.E.2d 836), or when the vendor is not able to convey title (Mackey v. Bowles, 98 Ga. 730, 25 S.E. 834; Phinizy v. Guernsey, 111 Ga. 346, 349, 36 S.E. 796), and that the loss falls upon the vendee when the vendor is able to convey title. Bruce v. Jennings, 190 Ga. 618, 620, 10 S.E.2d 56. Accord Wingfield v. Oakes, 93 Ga.App. 783, 92 S.E.2d 820. Only in the Phinizy case, supra, was the vendor in possession at the time of the loss. Opinions in Georgia cases contain the following statement: It is the general rule that, where the purchaser goes into possession under a binding executory contract for the sale of improved realty which the seller is able to convey, but where, before the transfer of the legal title is consummated, the improvements are destroyed by fire without the fault of either party, the loss falls on the purchaser as the owner of the equitable title." Bruce v. Jennings, supra, 190 Ga. 620, 10 S.E.2d 57; Mackey v. Bowles, supra, 98 Ga. 734, 25 S.E. 834; Wingfield v. Oakes, supra, 93 Ga.App. 785, 92 S.E.2d 820. The reason for the statement of the rule in this language may be that each of the earlier cases (Mackey, Phinizy, Bruce, supra) involved a bond for title. "The most common form taken by transactions of this kind is for the vendor to receive from the vendee purchase-money notes and to execute to him a bond for title, i.e., a written agreement to convey him good and sufficient title to the land when the purchase-money notes have been paid." Powell on Land Actions, 443, § 373. The vendee would normally always be in possession after the execution of the bond for title and this relationship would exist for a considerable time depending upon the period of the loan.

The opinion in the Phinizy case supra, 111 Ga. p. 349, 36 S.E. p. 797, states: "If the contract has been so far completed that the vendee is to be treated as the owner of the premises, then the loss falls upon him, as was the case in Paine v. Meller, 6 Ves. [jr.] 349, where it was held that when there was a contract for the sale of houses, which, on account of defects in the title, could not be completed,—the treaty, however, proceeding upon a proposal to waive the objections upon certain terms,—and the houses were burned before the conveyance, the purchaser was bound if he accepted the title; and the fact that the vendor allowed insurance on the houses to expire on the day on which the contract was originally to have been completed, without notice to the vendee, made no difference." This dictum appears to be regarded as an adoption by the Georgia Supreme Court of the view that when there is a binding agreement and the vendor is able to convey title "equity regards the vendor as a trustee of the legal title for the benefit of the vendee, while the latter is looked upon as a trustee of the purchase-money for the benefit of the former," and that "if the contract of sale is so far completed that the vendors would have held the legal title as trustees for the vendee," the vendee would take the loss, whether or not he was in possession. Bruce v. Jennings, supra; Agnor, Ga. Bar Journal, 401, 402. See Maddox v. Rowe, 23 Ga. 431, 435, 68 Am.Dec. 535; 55 Am.Jur. 782, § 356.

Accordingly, since it appears in this case that the parties had entered into a binding contract for the sale of real estate, which the vendor was willing and able to consummate at the time of the destruction of a substantial part of the realty, the loss falls on the vendee.

The cases cited in the plaintiffs' brief do not support their argument that the contract was not binding.

The trial court erred in overruling the defendants' general demurrer to the petition, in sustaining the plaintiffs' general demurrer to the defendants' cross action, and in granting the plaintiffs' motion for summary judgment.

Judgment reversed.

BELL, P.J., and FRANKUM, J., concur.

NOTES

1. The numerical majority of American courts, following the logic of equitable conversion, have placed the risk of loss on the purchaser. Not surprisingly, there are cases holding the opposite view. Libman v. Levenson, 236 Mass. 221, 128 N.E. 13 (1920), is an outstanding example. Said the court: "It is now settled . . . that the contract is to be construed as subject to the implied condition that it no longer shall be binding if, before the time for the conveyance to be made, the buildings are destroyed by fire. The loss by the fire falls upon the vendor, the owner; and if he has not protected himself by insurance, he can have no reimbursement of this loss; but the contract is no longer binding upon either party. If the purchaser has advanced any part of the price, he can recover it back." For a later case purporting to follow the Massachusetts rule, although the dissent felt the majority shifted back to equitable conversion in mid-stream, see Skelly Oil Co. v. Ashmore, 365 S.W.2d 582 (Mo.1963).

2. This troublesome problem has been the subject of statutory tinkering. A uniform act drafted by Professor Williston and approved by the Commissioners on Uniform State Laws has been adopted, with minor revisions, in California, Hawaii, Illinois, Michigan, Nevada, New York, North Carolina, Oklahoma, Oregon, South Dakota, and Wisconsin.

Uniform Vendor and Purchaser Risk Act

1. Any contract hereafter made in this State for the purchase and sale of realty shall be interpreted as including an agreement that the parties shall have the following rights and duties, unless the contract expressly provides otherwise:

(a) If, when neither the legal title nor the possession of the subject matter of the contract has been transferred, all or a material part thereof is destroyed without fault of the purchaser or is taken by eminent domain, the vendor cannot enforce the contract, and the purchaser is entitled to recover any portion of the price that he has paid;

(b) If, when either the legal title or the possession of the subject matter of the contract has been transferred, all or any part thereof is destroyed without fault of the vendor or is taken by eminent domain, the purchaser is not thereby relieved from a duty to pay the price, nor is he entitled to recover any portion thereof that he has paid.

2. This act shall be so interpreted and construed as to effectuate its general purpose to make uniform the law of those states which enact it.

3. This act may be cited as the Uniform Vendor and Purchaser Risk Act.

In Unger v. Nunda Township Rural Fire Protection District, 135 Ill.App.3d 758, 90 Ill.Dec. 416, 482 N.E.2d 123 (1985), purchaser sought damages from an adjacent landowner for destruction by fire of trees on the land which purchaser was buying under an installment contract. Under the contract, which did not expressly allocate the risk of loss by fire, purchaser had the right of possession and had been exercising it by removing trees. The court held that in light of section 1(b) of the Uniform Act, purchaser could recover the value of the burned trees although defendant already had paid $4,000 to and obtained a release from vendors, "their heirs, executors and administrators."

In Dixon v. Salvation Army, 142 Cal.App.3d 463, 191 Cal.Rptr. 111 (1983), one of three buildings on the land under contract was destroyed by fire while vendor still retained legal title and possession. Rejecting contrary decisions in New York, the court denied purchaser the remedy of specific performance with abatement of the price for the fire damage, holding that under section 1(a) of the Uniform Act he was entitled only to the return of any consideration paid. A dissenting opinion accused the majority of protecting vendor only because it had carried inadequate fire insurance.

SANFORD v. BREIDENBACH

Court of Appeals of Ohio, 1960.
111 Ohio App. 474, 173 N.E.2d 702.

HUNSICKER, JUDGE. Three appeals, all arising from the same judgment below, have been submitted on the same briefs and arguments; the details of which are hereinafter set out at length.

On January 14, 1959, James R. Sanford and Bianchi R. Sanford, his wife, herein known as "Sanford," agreed in writing to sell to Frederic (herein impleaded as "Frederick") R. Breidenbach, herein known as "Breidenbach," certain lands in the village of Hudson, Summit County, Ohio, upon which lands was an 8-room, 1½ story, house and separate outbuilding. The agreed purchase price was $26,000. According to the terms of the contract, possession of the premises was to be delivered on transfer of the title, although Breidenbach did receive two keys to the house prior to its destruction by fire. He did enter the house with certain others, preparatory to having the heating system changed from oil heat to gas, to plan the location of furniture, and to show the new home to friends. Breidenbach also checked the oil tank to see if there was fuel to heat the house.

The written contract to purchase these premises had, on the reverse side thereof, the following provisions:

"The following paragraphs are an essential part of the contract on the reverse side hereof.

"January 14, 1959.

"1. A proper legal agreement signed by all owners concerned shall be furnished by the sellers giving permenent [sic] permission to use of the present septic system by the purchasers and their successors and assigns.

"2. It is understood that legal agreements covering driveway easement, easement for water line, etc., are in effect covering the thirty-acre properties. Said agreements shall be submitted to the purchasers for their approval prior to deposit of funds in escrow."

The parties who had signed the contract on its face also signed these provisions at the end thereof.

On February 16, 1959, while the papers necessary to a transfer of title were being prepared, the 8-room house on the lands was totally destroyed by fire. Breidenbach immediately instructed the Evans Savings Association, that was to loan him a part of the money needed to buy the home, not to file the deed for record. This deed, transferring the premises from Sanford to Breidenbach, had been prepared and placed in escrow with the Evans Savings Association pending a title search.

When Breidenbach executed the contract of purchase, he secured from Northwestern Mutual Insurance Company a policy of insurance to protect him against loss in the event the 8-room house was destroyed by fire. The amount of this insurance was $22,000.

Sanford had maintained insurance on these premises in the sum of $20,000. The agent from whom Sanford purchased insurance, in accord with standing instructions from Sanford, renewed this insurance coverage on December 26, 1958. On learning that the premises were being sold, this agent, through his employee, cancelled this policy without authority from Sanford, and without notice to Sanford. There seems to be no great question herein that the terms of such policy were in full force and effect at the time of the fire.

On April 29, 1959, Sanford brought an action in the Common Pleas Court of Summit County, Ohio, against Breidenbach, Northwestern Mutual Insurance Company, and Hudson Village Real Estate Co., Inc. Breidenbach had deposited, with the real estate company, $12,000 as a partial payment for the premises. This sum has been, by arrangement of the parties, placed in escrow with a third party, and the real estate company is to all intents and purposes no longer involved herein. The principal relief sought by this action was specific performance of the contract to purchase the lands of Sanford.

Breidenbach, by way of cross-petition, brought Insurance Company of North America into the action by alleging that such company had insured the Sanford home against fire, and that such company should be made responsible for the loss suffered by Sanford, or, if the premises are decreed to be the property of Breidenbach, then his interest in the proceeds of the policy should be declared.

The Insurance Company of North America says, by way of answer, that it did, on December 26, 1958, renew the policy of insurance on these premises, but that, by agreement between the company and the insured, it was cancelled on January 26, 1959. It further alleged that Breidenbach never had any interest in such policy. As stated above, there seems to be no question now that this policy was in full force and effect at the time of the fire. The attempted cancellation of such policy was of no force or effect.

After a trial of the issues herein, the court determined that Sanford was not entitled to specific performance, but that he should recover from each insurance company for the loss of the premises.

The judgment against Northwestern Mutual Insurance Company is $11,523.81 being 22/42 of the loss, and the judgment against Insurance Company of North America is $10,476.19, being 20/42 of the loss. The court added the amounts of the two policies, and then proportioned the loss in accord with the ratio which each policy bears to such total. . . .

We shall first direct our attention to the question of whether Sanford is entitled to specific performance, and shall therein consider whether Breidenbach was, under the doctrine of equitable conversion, the owner of the premises at the time the house was destroyed by fire. After a disposition of those questions, we shall then pass to the matter of the liability of the two insurance companies.

"A decree for the specific performance of a contract is not a matter of right, but of grace, granted on equitable principles, and rests in the sound discretion of the court." 37 Ohio Jurisprudence, Specific Performance, Section 20, at pp. 24 and 25, and authorities there cited.

The rule above set out is so well known that no authorities need be cited and it is such rule that must be applied in the instant case. We have a contract herein for the sale and purchase of real property, which made definite mention of a septic tank easement. The easement is, by the language used by the parties, an essential part of the contract. At the time of trial, August 3, 1959, a satisfactory septic tank easement had not been submitted to the purchaser, Breidenbach. The septic tank agreement submitted in May, 1959, provided that under certain conditions the right to use this facility terminated, whereas the provision of the contract made no such exception.

It is apparent, therefore, that at the time when specific performance was sought in the trial court, one of the material parts of the agreement had not been complied with, and hence we had an uncompleted contract. . . .

We therefore determine that specific performance cannot be decreed under the facts of this case.

Sanford insists that, even though specific performance may not lie, Breidenbach is to be considered in equity the owner of the premises; and, under the doctrine of equitable conversion, the loss, if any has ensued as a result of the destruction of the house by fire, must be placed upon Breidenbach and his insurer, Northwestern Mutual Insurance Company.

There are few cases in Ohio in which, in contracts for the sale and purchase of real property, the doctrine of equitable conversion has been discussed. Counsel have brought to our attention Gilbert & Ives v. Port, 28 Ohio St. 276; and Oak Building and Roofing Co. v. Susor, 32 Ohio App. 66, 166 N.E. 908; in which latter case the court, in following the pronouncement in Gilbert & Ives v. Port, supra, said:

"Where contract for exchange of real estate contained no provision as to who should bear the loss in case any building on either of properties should be destroyed before deeds were executed, the purchaser must be regarded as equitable owner of property and loss by reason of fire destroying building before execution of deed falls on him."

This court, in a matter not similar to the instant case, said, in Oberholtz v. Oberholtz, 79 Ohio App. 540, at page 547, 74 N.E.2d 574, at page 579, with reference to the doctrine of equitable conversion, as follows:

"We recognize the rule of equitable conversion as applied to contracts for the sale of real property—viz., that under certain circumstances equity looks upon things agreed to be done as actually done, and that, when a contract is made for the sale of real property, the vendor, from the execution of such contract, holds the legal title to the lands as a trustee for the vendee, and the vendor's beneficial interest in the contract is treated for purposes of descent as personalty and as an asset of the vendor's estate to be administered by his executor or administrator."

An excellent collation of the authorities on the subject of "Vendor and purchaser: risk of loss by casualty pending contract for conveyance," with a discussion of the rules adopted by the courts in the several states, may be found in 27 A.L.R.2d 444 et seq.

In general, the rule under the doctrine of equitable conversion is that a contract to sell real property vests the equitable ownership of the property in the purchaser; and thus, where there is any loss by a destruction of the property through casualty during the pendency of the contract (neither party being guilty of causing the destruction), such loss must be borne by the purchaser.

We do not find herein that possession had been given to Breidenbach. The incidental checking of the oil level in the heating system, and the acceptance of the key to the premises, do not constitute a surrender of possession to the purchaser in this case.

The courts of Ohio have spoken with reference to the rights of a vendor and purchaser where the purchaser has gone into possession of the premises agreed to be conveyed, for in the case of Coggshall v. Marine Bank Co., 63 Ohio St. 88, at pages 96 and 97, 57 N.E. 1086, at page 1088, Judge Spear cites with approval the statement from Jaeger v. Hardy, 48 Ohio St. 335, 27 N.E. 863—

". . . to the effect that a vendor's interest before conveyance 'is the legal title and a beneficial estate in the lands to the extent of the unpaid purchase money,' while that of the vendee is 'an equitable estate in the land equal to the amount of the purchase money paid by him, and which, upon full payment, may ripen into a complete equity entitling him to conveyance of the legal title according to the terms of the contract,'" and then says:

"This language cannot be reconciled with the proposition that the purchaser is the full owner and the vendor a mere naked trustee, and if we adhere to the principle above quoted, as we must, the latter proposition must fail. Every just right of the vendee is protected by the rule that his ownership extends to the amount of the purchase money paid, and the right to receive a deed upon payment of the balance of the purchase money in compliance with the contract. Possession by the purchaser gives notice of his right to all the world, and of nothing more. . . ."

The better rule in cases such as that now before us, we believe, is that equitable conversion by the purchaser, in a contract to convey real property, does become effective in those cases in which the vendor has fulfilled all conditions and is entitled to enforce specific performance, and the parties, by their contract, intend that title shall pass to the vendee upon the signing of the contract of purchase. The case before us does not meet any of these requirements.

In 4 Pomeroy's Equity Jurisprudence (5 Ed.), Section 1161a, the author, quoting from "Chafee and Simpson, Cases on Equity," gives five rules concerning the risk of loss in contracts for the sale of real estate.

One of such rules, which we believe sustains our position herein, is stated by the author as follows:

"'That the risk of loss should be on the vendor until the time agreed upon for the conveyance of the legal title, and thereafter on the purchaser, unless the vendor is then in such default as to be unable specifically to enforce the contract.'"

See, also, Coolidge & Sickler, Inc. v. Regn, 7 N.J. 93, 80 A.2d 554, 27 A.L.R.2d 437, at page 443.

It is hence our judgment that, since Sanford could not specifically enforce the contract of sale, and there was no intention expressed in the contract of purchase that the risk of loss should be on the vendee when the contract was executed by the parties, there is no basis to claim that equitable conversion existed, thereby placing the burden of loss by fire upon Breidenbach.

We now pass to the question of the liability of the respective insurance companies. As we have heretofore stated, Sanford had fire loss coverage in the amount of $20,000, with Insurance Company of North America as the insurer; Breidenbach, in order to protect whatever interest he had in such premises, secured a policy with a fire loss coverage of $22,000 with Northwestern Mutual Insurance Company.

It is our heretofore stated judgment that the policy of Insurance Company of North America is a valid and subsisting contract to indemnify Sanford for the loss he might sustain, if, as a result of fire, the house described in the policy was destroyed. This contract of insurance was not cancelled by the unilateral action of the agent for Insurance Company of North America.

At the time of the loss, Sanford was the owner of the premises, and hence the risk of loss must, in this case, fall upon him. With this view of the matter, it follows naturally that his insurer must respond under the terms of the policy for the face amount thereof.

Since we have determined that Sanford and not Breidenbach was the owner of the premises at the time of the fire, what, if any, interest did Breidenbach have in these premises?

It is true that he could have waived any defect in the title or a failure to give a septic tank agreement and insisted that the contract of sale be completed by a delivery to him of a deed to the lands. He did not, however, choose this course of action, but, since the subject matter of the contract was destroyed, he refused to accept delivery of a deed to the land. We have said, in effect, that he had a legal right to take this position.

Up to the moment when Breidenbach refused to complete the contract of purchase, he had an insurable interest in the premises. The contract of insurance with Northwestern Mutual Insurance Company insured Breidenbach and his legal representatives for loss by fire and other casualty; it did not insure Sanford or any other person except those "named in the policy." This policy which Breidenbach purchased was for his protection in the event he suffered a loss. Breidenbach did not suffer a loss: first, because all of the money he deposited in escrow, as a part of the purchase price for the premises, has been, or will be, returned to him under an agreement to that effect, made by the parties and Hudson Village Real Estate Company, Inc., the realtor herein; and, second, because by the judgment of this court he is not required to perform his contract. Inasmuch as Breidenbach suffered no indemnifiable loss in this matter, his insurer need not respond by way of money payment under the policy of insurance.

We do not believe that Section 3929.26, Revised Code, which covers the situation where there is more than one policy of insurance on the same property, is applicable to the facts of this case.

There can be no apportionment of loss between insurers in this case, because there was no loss applicable to an insurable interest held by Breidenbach which inured to the benefit of Sanford. The interest of Breidenbach in the property, we have indicated above, ceased, or was not effective, at the time of the loss; hence the insurance ended at the same moment. There being no loss to Breidenbach, and no interest of Sanford to be protected by the Northwestern Mutual Insurance Company policy, there can be no prorata division of the proceeds of that policy. . . .

Judgments accordingly.

DOYLE, P.J., and GRIFFITH, J., concur.

RAPLEE v. PIPER

Court of Appeals of New York, 1957.
3 N.Y.2d 179, 164 N.Y.S.2d 732, 143 N.E.2d 919, 64 A.L.R.2d 1397.

DESMOND, JUDGE. When a land purchase contract requires the vendee to keep the property insured against fire and there is a fire loss before performance of the contract is completed, any such insurance received by the vendor is to be applied on any remaining balance of the purchase price. Every appellate decision in New York so holds. . . . If, however, the vendor at his own cost, for his own protection and not because of any agreement, has taken out fire insurance, then such contract is personal to him and he need not credit the proceeds against the price (Brownell v. Board of Educ., 239 N.Y. 369, 146 N.E. 630, 37 A.L.R.1319). Such is the rule in New York as in some other States (5 Appleman on Insurance Law and Practice, § 3366; 8 Couch's Cyclopedia of Insurance Law, § 1937). Nor can there be any doubt, under the brief stipulation of facts on which this case was tried, that the rule insofar as it credits the vendee with the insurance is applicable here. That stipulation says that, while plaintiff was in possession as vendee under the contract, a fire occurred, defendant vendor received $4,650 as the fire loss under a policy, premiums for which had been paid by plaintiff vendee as required by the contract, plaintiff tendered to defendant the difference between the amount actually unpaid on the contract and the insurance proceeds, but defendant refused plaintiff's demand that $4,600 be credited on the balance of the purchase price. In the Persico case, supra, the courts held in a situation like the present one that the insurance proceeds form a trust fund for the benefit of both purchaser and seller (see, likewise, Williams v. Lilley, 67 Conn. 50, 34 A. 765, 37 L.R.A. 150; Brakhage v. Tracy, 13 S.D. 343, 83 N.W. 363). The reason why the purchaser lost in the Brownell case, supra, was as explained by Judge Pound at page 374, of 239 N.Y., at page 632 of 146 N.E., that under the facts there "vendor took out his own insurance". The insurance money was not "a part of the *res* bargained for and no trust relation exists in regard to it."

It would be most unjust if a contract vendee, although complying with the contract by keeping the property insured in the name of the vendor, should get no benefit from the insurance. A situation would result where the vendor would be entitled to the full purchase price even though the building was destroyed, plus the insurance proceeds, but the vendee, although deprived of the destroyed building, would nonetheless pay the full price. The courts have refused to adopt so inequitable a result. Whether we say that these insurance moneys were "a trust fund" or describe the relationship in some other way, the simple analysis of the situation is that the insurance was taken out at the cost of the vendee in the name of the vendor for the protection of the contract and of both parties to the contract.

Section 240–a of the Real Property Law, Consol.Laws, c. 50, has nothing to do with the present case. Under common law the risk of fire loss during the pendency of the contract and before passing of title was on the purchaser in all cases. Under the "Uniform Statute" which

New York has adopted as section 240–a, the risk of destruction by fire is on those vendees only who are in possession at the time of the fire or have taken legal title. Thus either at common law or under section 240–a this vendee would be in the same position. He must take the damaged property and pay the full purchase price but he is entitled to credit thereon for the insurance proceeds since he and the vendor have so agreed.

The judgment should be affirmed, with costs.

BURKE, JUDGE (dissenting). The issue presented is whether, in the absence of an agreement so providing, a contract vendee of real property is entitled to have the proceeds of a fire insurance policy, in the vendor's name only, applied in reduction of the purchase price where the contract of sale required the vendee to pay the insurance premiums, the fire occurring intermediate the execution of the contract and the passing of title while the vendee was in possession of the premises. We think not. This court took advantage of the opportunity afforded by the case of Brownell v. Board of Educ., 239 N.Y. 369, 146 N.E. 630, to adopt the doctrine of Rayner v. Preston (18 Ch.D. 1) and unanimously and unequivocally laid down the flat and positive rule that by its nature a policy of property insurance is a personal contract of indemnity which runs solely to the named insured and not with the land, and, in the absence of a specific agreement, a vendee is not entitled to the proceeds of the vendor's policy because it is not part of the *res* bargained for and no trust relation exists in regard to it (see Brownell case, supra, 239 N.Y. at pages 373–374, 146 N.E. at pages 631–632). This court reiterated that rule without qualification four years later (see Reife v. Osmers, 252 N.Y. 320, 324, 169 N.E. 399, 400, 67 A.L.R. 1101).

That the bench and bar have recognized the rule laid down by the Brownell case as such is attested to by the numerous references in the volumes of legal citations which fail to distinguish or depart from it. That this was the legislature's understanding of the significance of the Brownell case is clear beyond question (see N.Y.Legis.Doc., 1936, No. 65 [m], p. 13; 1936 Report of N.Y.Law Rev.Comm., p. 767). The legislature was not only aware of the fact that in following this rule this court adopted a minority view, but it was also aware of the fact that it could readily be changed by making appropriate amendments to the Insurance Law as the English Parliament had done to alter the rule of Rayner v. Preston (see 12 & 13 Geo. V, ch. 16, § 105 [1922] mod. and re-enacted as statute 15 Geo. V, ch. 20, § 47 [1925]; Macgillivray on Insurance Law [2d ed.] , pp. 939–940). But it was convinced of the basic soundness of the rule and eschewed the adoption of such amendatory legislation (see N.Y.Legis.Doc., 1936, No. 65 [m] pp. 9–26; 1936 Report of N.Y.Law Rev.Comm., pp. 763–780).

Since the Brownell case there have been only two reported decisions in this State which deal with the issue presented by this case. One, Persico v. Guernsey, 129 Misc. 190, 220 N.Y.S. 689, affirmed without opinion 222 App.Div. 719, 225 N.Y.S. 890, which reached the same result that the majority reaches in this case, and the other, Cowan v. Sutherland, 6 Misc.2d 71, 117 N.Y.S.2d 365, which holds to directly the opposite. As the only opinion in the Guernsey case indicates, it was decided upon the erroneous theory that the vendor was the trustee of the insurance proceeds because he was trustee of the legal title to the property once the contract of sale was made (see Persico v. Guernsey, 129 Misc. 190, 193, 220 N.Y.S. 689, 692). In view of this we do not think that the Guernsey case is sound authority upon which to predicate the decision of the present appeal. Of course, as the other cases cited by the majority were decided before the Brownell case and were on the books at the time the rule in that case was adopted, they do not provide a sound basis for altering the rule.

The majority opinion suggests that we may ignore the rule laid down in the Brownell case, supra, by describing the insurance proceeds as something other than a trust fund, for example, by saying that the contract was insured for the benefit of all the parties concerned. This is not a novel suggestion. Lord Justice James in his dissenting opinion in Rayner v. Preston, supra, 18 Ch.D. at page 15, made a similar suggestion: "I believe it to be considered by the universal consensus of mankind, to be a policy for the benefit of all persons interested in the property". However, it was not only rejected by the majority in that case because it was not the law and failed to take into consideration the nature of a policy of property insurance, but the same argument was also rejected by the unanimous bench of this court in the Brownell case, supra, 239 N.Y. at page 374, 146 N.E. at page 632, when it declared: "These reasons may savor of layman's ideas of equity, but they are not law. The majority of the court in Rayner v. Preston were sound in principle. Insurance is a mere personal contract to pay a sum on money by way of indemnity to protect the interest of the insured. (Cromwell v. Brooklyn Fire Ins. Co., 44 N.Y. 42, 47; The City of Norwich, 118 U.S. 468, 504, 505, 6 S.Ct. 1150, 30 L.Ed. 134.) In common parlance the buildings are insured, but everyone who stops to consider the nature of the insurance contract understands that they are not. Both in the forum and the market place it is known that the insurance runs to the individual insured and not with the land. The vendor has a beneficial interest to protect, i.e., his own. The vendee has an insurable interest and may protect himself."

In light of these circumstances we think that this court should adhere to the rule established by the Brownell case. Such adherence, it seems to us, is imperative, not only because this is a well-recognized rule which the legislature has not undertaken to change, but also because many businessmen and their lawyers may have entered into contracts in reliance upon it (see City of New York v. Bedford Bar & Grill, 2 N.Y.2d 429, 161 N.Y.S.2d 67, 141 N.E.2d 575).

Accordingly, we believe that the judgment should be reversed and the complaint dismissed.

DYE, FULD and FROESSEL, JJ., concur with DESMOND, J.

BURKE, J., dissents in an opinion in which CONWAY, C.J., and VAN VOORHIS, J. concur.

Judgment affirmed.

NOTES

1. In Dubin Paper Co. v. Insurance Co. of North America, 361 Pa. 68, 85, 63 A.2d 85, 94 (1949), the court said: "The problem before us is clarified if the fact is noted that as between the insured and the insurance companies the insured remains the owner of the property until the sale is completed, but as between the vendor and the vendee, the vendor holds only the legal title and if he receives the proceeds of the insurance policy on his property he holds these as trustee for the buyer. The vendee's interest was not insured by the defendants; the vendor's was. The vendee's right to a part of the policy's proceeds in the vendee's [sic] hands is derived from the agreement of sale when that is given the meaning which under the circumstances of this case the 'conscience of equity' says it must be given." For an excellent collection of the numerous law review articles on the problems of risk of loss and insurance see Chafee and Re, Cases and Materials on Equity 514–530 (4th ed. of Chafee and Simpson's Cases on Equity) (1958). As a legal advisor and draftsman how can you avoid the pitfalls represented by the last three cases?

2. In Kindred v. Boalbey, 73 Ill.App.3d 37, 29 Ill.Dec. 77, 391 N.E.2d 236 (1979) property was sold on an installment land contract which required the purchaser to insure the buildings against loss by fire with the proceeds payable to the parties as their interests might appear. The purchaser did insure, the residence on the land was damaged by fire, and the vendor claimed the $15,998.00 insurance check although the balance due on the contract was only $12,000.61. The vendor also attempted to forfeit the contract for various breaches by the purchaser, thus reclaiming the land and keeping the insurance proceeds. The court gave the usual analysis of equitable conversion, saying that the vendor became the trustee of the legal title for the purchaser with a lien on the land as security for the purchase money. Forfeiture was denied under the facts of the case (the purchaser's failure to perform was, at least partly, due to the dispute over the insurance proceeds) and the vendor was held entitled to the balance due on the installment land contract ($12,000.61) while the purchaser was entitled to the remainder of the insurance proceeds less certain court costs. The Illinois Appellate Court cited Raplee v. Piper, along with other cases, and said: "Equity demands that the plaintiff (vendor) not be unjustly enriched by receiving a double recovery in this instance."

3. In the preceding cases the loss occurred due to fire or to an "Act of God". Suppose the loss is due to an act of the state, i.e.: a taking under the power of eminent domain. Does the doctrine of equitable conversion apply and, if so, how? For an interesting case on this problem see Arko Enterprises, Inc. v. Wood, 185 So.2d 734 (Fla. App.1966). The court said: "[it] appears to be the law of this state that where land subject to a vendor's lien is appropriated under the power of eminent domain, the condemnation proceeding does not destroy the lien nor does it affect the right of the vendor to seek enforcement of his lien against the vendee for the full amount of the unpaid purchase price.

"The general rule governing the relationship of parties to an executory contract of purchase and sale involving land which is appropriated under the power of eminent domain before the contract is fully executed is stated by Nichols in his work on Eminent Domain as follows:

" 'Where the vendee of the land under an executory contract is in possession, and having made the payments agreed upon, is entitled to a deed, although he has not yet received one, it is generally held that he is the owner in respect to eminent domain proceedings.

" 'A more difficult question arises when a contract has been made for the sale of land at a certain price which is less than its fair market value as subsequently fixed, and the intending purchaser has made an initial payment but before the date fixed for conveyance the land is taken by eminent domain. The contract is, of course, rendered impossible of performance and the purchaser is not entitled to damages from the vendor for his failure to carry out his agreement. It would seem, however, that the purchaser is entitled to compensation from the condemnor for the taking of his equitable interest in the land, and, if the award is greater than the contract price, the vendor should receive the exact amount for which he had agreed to sell the property and the purchaser should be awarded the balance. The reasoning of the court is predicated upon the fact that such executory contract is considered, in effect, an assignment of the award to the purchaser who is considered the equitable owner.' "

Chief Judge Rawls, dissenting, felt that equitable conversion should not have been applied *as a matter of law* to the special facts in the case since the doctrine is based on equitable principles and should not be used to reach an unfair result.

SECTION 5. THE ROLE OF THE REAL ESTATE BROKER

It is impossible to deal extensively with the role of the real estate broker in a basic, first-year course on property. On the other hand, you should have some understanding of the role played by this important member of the land-transfer team. Most real estate on the market today is listed with a broker. The listing process involves a contract between the broker and the vendor which obligates the latter to pay a commission, typically a percentage of the sales price, if the broker is successful in selling the property. This contract may take a variety of forms and, of course, the listing can be tailor-made for the needs of the vendor, if he or she is astute enough to really negotiate a special contract. Typically, however, the listing is on a prepared form which gives the broker an exclusive right to sell the property. (In a non-exclusive listing, the broker may be only one of several people who are authorized to seek a buyer.)

"Exclusive listing agreements are of two types. An 'exclusive agency' agreement is interpreted as prohibiting the owner from selling the property through the agency of another broker during the listing period, but the owner may sell the property through his own efforts. However, an 'exclusive right to sell' agreement (exclusive sales contract) prohibits the owner from selling both personally and through another broker without incurring liability for a commission to the original broker. In the event the owner breaches this type of agreement, he is liable for the commission which would have accrued if the broker had procured a purchaser during the period of listing. The broker need not show that he could have performed by tendering a satisfactory buyer or that he was the procuring cause of the sale. The owner may breach the agreement by negotiating a sale in violation of the agreement or by action which renders the broker's performance impossible." Carlsen v. Zane, 261 Cal.App.2d 399, 67 Cal.Rptr. 747 (1968). Most listing agreements are of the second, "exclusive right to sell", type.

Today, many brokers participate in a local multiple listing service (MLS) which makes the listing available to all broker members of the service. MLS speeds up the marketing of real estate by giving maximum publicity to the availability of the listed property. Non-members of the MLS do not have access to the listing and, of course, non-brokers, such as the vendor himself, are excluded. There are antitrust problems involved in MLS—see, for example, McLain v. Real Estate Board of New Orleans, Inc., 444 U.S. 232, 100 S.Ct. 502, 62 L.Ed.2d 441 (1980)—but those problems are reserved for the course in anti-trust law. Incidentally, it is possible for a broker to represent both buyer and seller but it is rarely done and carries with it an almost impossible duty to make full disclosure to both vendor and purchaser. See, for example, Wilson v. Lewis, 106 Cal.App.3d 802, 165 Cal.Rptr. 396 (1980).

Real estate brokers are often highly professional and frequently understand more about the sale of real property, particularly the financing aspects, than the lawyer who may be a non-specialist in real estate transactions. Usually, however, the broker will know relatively little law outside the narrow confines of his expertise and title problems, for example, are not his responsibility. Breathes there a broker with soul so dead that he knows the intricacies of the Rule in Shelley's Case? Are brokers, like lawyers, subject to licensure and to regulation by the state?

In partial answer to the last question, note the comment by Professors Nelson and Whitman in Real Estate Transfer, Finance and Development, p. 11 (West Publishing Co., 1981). "In every state, brokers and their sales personnel are licensed by some state agency, usually a Real Estate Commission or the like. In most states there are two levels of licensure. The *salesperson's* license requires (beyond proof of good character) only the passing of an examination which can usually be managed with a modest amount of rote memorization. Salespeople, however, cannot work on their own, but must be supervised by a licensed *broker.* To become a broker one must accrue some period of experience as a salesperson and pass a harder examination. Some states have added to the foregoing various educational requirements for obtaining or keeping one's license. In many states members of the bar are permitted to do everything a licensed real estate broker can do, except perhaps to employ others as salespeople.

"The regulation of brokers and salespeople in many states is not especially vigorous, but what the Real Estate Commissioner giveth, he may also take away." For an example of Professors Nelson's and Whitman's last point see Hickam v. Colorado Real Estate Commission, 36 Colo.App. 76, 534 P.2d 1220 (1975).

STATE EX REL. INDIANA STATE BAR ASSOCIATION v. INDIANA REAL ESTATE ASSOCIATION, INC.

Supreme Court of Indiana, 1963.
244 Ind. 214, 191 N.E.2d 711.

ACHOR, JUDGE. This is an original action brought by The Indiana State Bar Association, and others, under Rule 3–26 of this court, to enjoin the alleged unlawful practice of law by the respondents, Indiana Real Estate Association, Inc., and all licensed real estate brokers and salesmen in the state of Indiana.

We have held that this court has jurisdiction to entertain the proceedings for the reason that, inherently, and under Acts 1951, ch. 143, § 1, p. 382, being § 4–3605, Burns' 1962 Supp., this court is charged with the duty of supervising and controlling the practice of law in this state, and of issuing restraining orders and injunctions against the unauthorized practice of law, whether in or out of our courts.[1]

The practice of law, in the broad sense, both in and out of the courts, is such a necessary part of, and so inexorably connected with, the exercise of the judicial power of this court, that this court is charged with the continuing responsibility of exercising its supervisory control of such practice of law.

The questions presented in this case are whether or not the use of forms of legal instruments prepared by attorneys, the selection of such forms to be used, and the insertion of words within the printed forms in connection with the real estate transactions in which they are involved, constitutes the unauthorized practice of law by respondents who are not attorneys and [whether] such action [can] be enjoined as against public interest.

The respondents are duly licensed by the Indiana Real Estate Commission under Acts 1949, ch. 44, §§ 1–24, inclusive, being §§ 63–2401—63–2423, Burns' 1961 Repl. Section 9 of the above Act [§ 63–2409] provides, in part:

"Every person acting for himself, every member of a firm, partnership, association or corporation participating or engaged in the real estate brokerage or as a real estate salesman therefor shall obtain and keep renewed and wholly unrevoked a license as a real estate broker or real estate salesman as herein required."

1. State ex rel. Ind. State Bar Ass'n v. Osborne (1961), 241 Ind. 375, 172 N.E.2d 434; State ex rel. Gary Bar Ass'n, etc. v. Dudak, etc. (1955), 234 Ind. 413, 127 N.E.2d 522. [Footnotes in the case are by the court and numbered accordingly.]

The act further provides that the commission shall hold examinations to determine the qualifications of those asking for a license, and shall promulgate rules and regulations for the conduct of such agents and brokers.

The respondents admit that they use the forms, as alleged in the petition, but deny that they are giving legal advice, directly or indirectly, in connection with their use. They further deny that they undertake to draw or prepare documents in connection with real estate transactions, "but merely fill in the blank spaces in the forms referred to in the petition," stating in their response that such does not constitute the practice of law.

The respondents further state that the forms referred to in the petition have been in all cases, prepared by attorneys who are members of the bar of the state of Indiana; and that although not all the forms have been approved by The Indiana State Bar Association, these forms have been used since 1950 when an agreement was made with The Indiana State Bar Association, wherein they agreed to the use of certain of such forms by the real estate brokers, and further agreed to "approve and promulgate" other forms for use by both attorneys and realtors. This agreement was originally made in 1942, and amended in 1950, and reads in part as follows:

"2. The Realtor shall not undertake to draw or prepare documents fixing and defining the legal rights of parties to a transaction. However, when acting as broker, a Realtor may use an earnest money contract form for the protection of either party against unreasonable withdrawal from the transaction, provided that such earnest money contract form, as well as *any other standard legal forms used by the broker in transacting such business shall first have been approved and promulgated for such use by the Bar Association and the Real Estate Board in the locality where the forms are to be used.*" [Our italics.]

Although the "other standard legal forms," referred to in the above agreement, were never drafted, "approved and promulgated" by the parties to this action, it is contended by the respondents that The Indiana State Bar Association has impliedly approved the use of forms, such as those specified in its petition, by the respondents; and that by reason of the prolonged failure of The Indiana State Bar Association to consummate their agreement, the Association is now estopped to object to the use of forms here placed in issue, which forms have been unilaterally prepared and approved by competent legal counsel for the respondents.

Since the court has elected to decide the case upon its merits, a ruling upon the issue of estoppel is not necessary. However, the fact of the long standing negotiations between the parties upon the issue before us is indicative of the fact that a just solution of the problem, as it relates to the parties and the general public, probably lies within the area of agreement reached by the parties, as above recited.

In our consideration of the case, we make plain that the question presented here is narrowly limited to the use of forms [prepared by attorneys], the selection of such forms to be used, and the filling in of blanks in such forms by licensed real estate brokers and agents in transactions in which they are authorized by statute to perform. There is no issue here presented with reference solely to the offering or giving of legal advice.

In some of the briefs, an attempt is made to make the issue turn upon definitions of "the practice of law." In any event, we believe that the real question here at issue is whether the selection, completion, and use of the standardized forms by brokers, in connection with real estate transactions for their clients, and here sought to be enjoined, is prohibited to them, as being the practice of law. Although the practice of law is one of the oldest and most honored professions, the law itself is by no means an absolute science, the practice of which can be accurately and unequivocally defined. For example, under the early English law, some instruments were prepared by scriveners, who were neither barristers nor solicitors, although the preparation of such instruments is now universally considered to constitute the practice of law. On the other hand, persons not admitted to the practice of law are now permitted to represent clients before tax courts, etc., where formerly only attorneys were authorized to appear. These changes have come about because of the exigencies of the particular situation. So it is today with regard to the practice of law. There is a twilight zone between the area of activity which is clearly permitted to the layman, and that which is denied him. Generally, it can be said that the filling in of blanks in legal instruments, prepared by attorneys, which require only the use of common knowledge regarding the information to be inserted in said blanks, and general knowledge regarding the legal consequences involved, does not constitute the practice of law. However, when the filling in of such blanks involves considerations of significant legal refinement, or the legal consequences of the act are of great significance to the parties involved, such practice may be restricted to members of the legal profession.

As stated by the Supreme Judicial Court of Massachusetts in Lowell Bar Association v. Loeb (1943), 315 Mass. 176, 186, 52 N.E.2d 27, 34:

"But though the difference is one of degree, it may nevertheless be real. [Citing cases.] There are instruments that no one but a well trained lawyer should ever undertake to draw. But there are others, common in the commercial world, and fraught with substantial legal consequences, that lawyers seldom are employed to draw, and that in the course of recognized occupations other than the practice of law are often drawn by laymen for other laymen, as has already been shown. The actual practices of the community have important bearing on the scope of the practice of law. [Citing cases.]" See also: Cain v. Merchants Nat. Bank & Trust Co. of Fargo (1936), 66 N.D. 746, 268 N.W. 719; Hulse v. Criger (1952), 363 Mo. 26, 247 S.W.2d 855.

Thus, the question which this court must determine is where, within this "twilight zone", it is proper to draw the line between those acts which are and are not permissible to persons who are not lawyers. Obviously, the drawing of such line must be, in some respects, arbitrary, as is true of a law which fixes the permissible age at which a person may drive an automobile, or speed at which it may be driven within a particular zone, or specified time of day. Nevertheless, the issue presented is one which requires determination.

We are presented with arguments by relators as to the potential danger to the public if the real estate brokers and salesmen, who are not technicians of the law, are permitted to utilize legal forms and fill blanks therein. We are aware of the dire consequences which might, in isolated instances, result from the use of an improper form, by persons not skilled in law, but such speculative consequences cannot be made to outweigh the practicalities of the situation.

We judicially know that both the relators and respondents are sensitive to the normal needs of the business society. It cannot be urged, with reason, that a lawyer must preside over every transaction where written legal forms must be selected and used by an agent acting for one of the parties. Such a restriction would so paralyze business activities that very few transactions could be expeditiously consummated. This is especially true with regard to transactions by real estate brokers, which transactions are frequently not made during generally established office hours. The Bar Association, in its brief, has expressed great concern as to the consequences of permitting the filling in of blanks in legal forms by persons not members of the bar. The possibility of an occasional improvident act in the use of such forms may not, with reason, be made the basis for denying the right to perform the same act in a thousand instances where the public convenience and necessity would seem to require it. Lawyers, themselves, on rare occasions have been known to make errors in the drafting of such forms.

The legislature has, by Acts 1949, ch. 44, §§ 1–23, p. 129 [§§ 63-2401—63-2423, Burns' 1961 Repl.], supra, recognized that the real estate brokers and salesmen perform an approved function in our business society, and has established a procedure whereby their qualification is ascertained. No issue has been raised as to the sufficiency of this examination. By this method, the legislature has attempted to establish reasonable standards for the safeguard of the public in their real estate transactions. We consider it expedient that we attempt a reconciliation of the overlapping services performed by the real estate brokers and members of the bar. We should, if possible, permit each to do those acts within their respective professions and established abilities which public convenience and necessity requires.

In reviewing the cases of other states upon the narrow issue of the use of forms incidental to the real estate brokers' business, we find that the majority have been decidedly in favor of the respondent real estate brokers. In eight states which have given expression upon this issue, it is permissible for real estate brokers and agents to use and fill in the following forms, prepared by attorneys, incidental to their real estate transactions:

ARKANSAS: Ark. Bar Assn. v. Block (1959), 230 Ark. 430, 323 S.W.2d 912.

Offers and Acceptances.

COLORADO: Conway–Bogue v. Bar Assn. (1957), 135 Colo. 398, 213 P.2d 998.

Receipts; options for purchase; contracts of sale; deeds; promissory notes, deeds of trust; real estate mortgages; releases of deeds of trust and mortgages; leases; notices terminating tenancy; demands to pay rent, demands to vacate.

FLORIDA: Keyes Company v. Dade County Bar Assn. (1950), [Fla.] 46 So.2d 605.

Memorandum of agreement; deposit receipt, contract of sale.

MICHIGAN: Ingham Co. Bar Ass'n v. Neller Co. (1955), 342 Mich. 214, 69 N.W.2d 713.

Purchase and sale; deeds; land contracts; mortgages; assignments of mortgages, notices to quit, et cetera, as printed by stationers.

MINNESOTA: Cowern v. Nelson (1940), 207 Minn. 642, 290 N.W. 795.

Purchase money contracts; contracts for deeds; leases, notes, mortgages; chattel mortgages; bills of sale; deeds; assignments; satisfactions, and any other instruments of conveyance.

MISSOURI: Hulse v. Criger (1952), 363 Mo. 26, 247 S.W.2d 855.

Warranty deeds; quit claim deeds; trust deeds; notes; chattel mortgages, short term leases.

VIRGINIA: Commonwealth v. Jones & Robins, Inc. (1947), 186 Va. 30, 31 S.W. 720.

Contracts of sale; options, leases.

WISCONSIN: State ex rel. Reynolds v. Dinger (1961), 14 Wis.2d 193, 109 N.W.2d 685.

Deeds; land contracts; leases; options; mortgages; assignments of mortgages and land contracts; releases of mortgages, chattel mortgages; bills of sale; conditional sales contracts, and other instruments of a similar nature.

In Hulse v. Criger (1952), 363 Mo. 26, 45–46, 247 S.W.2d 855, 862, the court outlined in very succinct terms the limits placed upon such real estate brokers and agents, and what they may and may not do, which statement, we feel, in the main is a wise guide to our course of conduct. In that case the court stated:

"First: A real estate broker, in transactions in which he is acting as a broker, may use a standardized contract in a form prepared or approved by counsel and may complete it by filling in the blank spaces to show the parties and the transaction which he has procured.

"Second: A real estate broker, in transactions in which he is acting as a broker, may use standardized forms of warranty deeds, quit claim deeds, trust deeds, notes, chattel mortgages and short term leases, prepared or approved by counsel and may complete them by filling in the blank spaces to show the parties, descriptions and terms necessary to close the transaction he has procured.

"Third: A real estate broker may not make a separate charge for completing any standardized forms, and he may not prepare such forms for persons in transactions, in which he is not acting as a broker, unless he is himself one of the parties to the contract or instrument.

"Fourth: The required approval by counsel of standardized forms to be used in real estate transactions properly may be made either by lawyers selected by real estate brokers individually or selected by real estate boards of which they are members.

"Fifth: Even in transactions in which he is acting as a broker, a real estate broker may not give advice or opinions as to the legal rights of the parties, as to the legal effect of instruments to accomplish specific purposes or as to the validity of title to real estate; and he may not prepare reservations or provisions to create estates for life or in remainder or any limited or conditional estates or any other form of conveyance than a direct present conveyance between the parties, as provided for in standardized approved forms, to be effective upon delivery.

"Sixth: A real estate broker in conferring with parties to obtain facts and information about their personal and property status, other than is necessary to fill in the blank spaces in standardized forms necessary to complete and close transactions in which he is acting as a broker, for the purpose of advising them of their rights and the action to be taken concerning them, is engaging in the practice of law."

It is our judgment that the opinion of the Supreme Court of Missouri, in that case, is a proper guide to follow, and that the conclusions therein stated will reach the fairest and the most just result, except with respect to the execution of deeds. The execution of a deed usually follows the finalizing of the agreement of the parties and is at their convenience. Ordinarily, it is preceded by the examination of an abstract of title by an attorney. Often it involves the life savings and/or years of future income of the parties. Therefore, there seems to be no reason, in time or convenience, why this important legal instrument should not be executed by persons of the highest possible skill in the practice of law. Therefore, we make this exception to the Missouri rule, the execution of deeds is restricted to attorneys.

For the reasons hereinbefore stated, it is our opinion that the real estate brokers and agents should, within the limitations heretofore specified, be, and hereby are permitted to fill in the forms of the following legal instruments prepared by attorneys, the use of which is here placed in issue: Listing Agreement; Earnest Money Contract; Proposition; Offer to Purchase; Option; Option [with listing clause]; Affidavit [real estate vendor]; Purchase Agreement; Exchange Agreement; Bill of Sale; Lease [short form], Contracts of Sale.

Furthermore, it is our opinion that the execution of legal instruments, other than those listed above, by persons other than the parties to the transaction,[2] should be limited to members of the legal profession.

2. The decision in this case does not limit or restrict the rights of parties, in transactions involving any or all of the legal instruments herein considered, to ex-

For the reasons hereinabove stated, the injunction is granted, insofar as "standard legal forms," now used by respondent realtors, and made exhibits in the pleadings, are not within the list of those hereinabove enumerated, and the injunction is denied as to the use of the above enumerated forms by respondents.

MYERS, C.J., and LANDIS, J., concur.

ARTERBURN, J., concurs, with opinion.

JACKSON, J., concurs in part and dissents in part, with opinion. [Omitted]

ARTERBURN, JUDGE (concurring).

I concur in the majority opinion because I believe it correctly states the law; yet I make the following comment because as a lawyer I am vitally interested in the welfare of my profession. I feel that the bringing of an action of this type was ill-considered from a public relations viewpoint. The image of the lawyer in the public eye is not enhanced by this proceeding. Most lawyers care little for the kind of legal work that is the subject of this litigation. The charges are relatively small and the time distracting from more important work in most law offices. It would have been better to have left "well enough alone". For example, the medical profession is too sensible to launch a crusade against or proceed against everyone encroaching upon its precincts.

Of course, one may conjure up dire consequences flowing from untrained persons engaging either in law or in medicine, but such speculation should not outweigh the practicalities of everyday life. It is by a conceptualistic, rather than a realistic, approach to the problem of just what constitutes the practice of law that it can be said that the realtors are engaged in the unauthorized practice of law. The public reaction to such a course as this is well demonstrated by what happened in the State of Arizona where a very stringent Supreme Court decision, almost totally restricting real estate agents in their activities, was cancelled out immediately by a constitutional amendment.

The American Bar Association has intervened in this case. It is interesting to note, however, that nothing of any considerable importance is being done by that association in the federal area, where persons who are not members of the bar are permitted to practice before the gigantic federal bureaus, such as the Interstate Commerce Commission, Federal Power Commission, Patent Bureau, Federal Trade Commission, Treasury Department, to mention but a few.[3] At the same time these administrative agencies assume the power to deny a

ecute such instruments on their own behalf, as every man is entitled to act as his own attorney, whether it be within or outside a court of law, and to assume the consequences of his acts so performed.

3. One of the rules for admission to practice before the Interstate Commerce Commission reads as follows:

"(b) *Persons not attorneys.* Any person not an attorney at law who is a citizen or resident of the United States, and who shall satisfy the Commission that he is possessed of the *necessary legal* and technical qualifications to enable him to render valuable service before the Commission, and that he is otherwise competent to advise and assist in the presentation of matters before the Commission." (Our italics)

member of the bar the right to represent a client before them without their permission.

There seems to be some delicacy and hesitancy in any effort to resist such unwarranted arrogance where it assumes a magnitude of some importance in the federal bureaucracy. On the other hand, attention, as here, is directed to petty practices in the state area. If the image of the attorney in the public eye is to be improved, we could very well spend more time cleaning up our own house rather than to discipline other organizations [sic].

NOTES

1. Granting the basic point that the filling in of blanks in a form contract is the practice of law, how can such practice by unauthorized personnel be effectively prevented? For an interesting possibility see Martineau v. Gresser, 19 O.O.2d 374, 182 N.E.2d 48 (1962). In that case a licensed salesman for a licensed real estate broker went beyond the limits allowed by the Ohio legislature and courts in drafting a contract. The court held she was engaged in the illegal practice of law so that the contract itself was void and unenforcible and the real estate broker could not recover the $918.00 commission.

However effective this approach might be, it has not been widely followed. Indeed, Ohio appears to have abandoned it. See Foss v. Berlin, 3 Ohio App.3d 8, 443 N.E.2d 197 (1981) where the court said: "Although a real estate broker's drafting of a real estate sales contract constituted the unauthorized practice of law, such conduct did not void the contract as illegal and, hence, relieve a defendant from his obligation to pay the broker his commission." The court did not cite the earlier Martineau v. Gresser case.

2. Chicago Bar Association v. Quinlan & Tyson, Inc., 53 Ill.App.2d 388, 203 N.E.2d 131 (1964), reached a conclusion contrary to the principal case. The Illinois Appellate Court said that "the public interest must be the guiding principle for this court in deciding this case" and held that only lawyers could perform the services which the Indiana decision had opened to realtors. This result was the most stringent to that date in its protection of the lawyers' role. Only Arizona had previously gone so far and the consequences in that state are referred to in Judge Arterburn's concurring opinion. However, the Illinois Supreme Court reversed the Appellate Court in a decision similar to the principal case. Chicago Bar Association v. Quinlan & Tyson, Inc., 34 Ill.2d 116, 214 N.E.2d 771 (1966). As a result of the Supreme Court decision, the Illinois lawyers and real estate brokers worked out an agreement as to their respective roles in real estate transactions. See Foreman, The Illinois Real Estate Broker—Lawyer Accord, 55 Ill.B.J. 284 (1966).

3. In New Jersey State Bar Association v. New Jersey Association of Realtor Boards, 93 N.J. 470, 461 A.2d 1112 (1983), modified 94 N.J. 449, 467 A.2d 577 (1983), the court approved a consent judgment allowing licensed real estate brokers and salespersons not only to fill in forms but also to negotiate and draft entire contracts for the sale of

residential properties containing up to four dwelling units as well as leases of any duration for residential units. However, each such contract was required to provide at the top of the first page, "This is a legally binding contract that will become final within three business days. During this period you may choose to consult an attorney who can review and cancel the contract. See section on attorney review for details." The required attorney-review section dealt with methods of—but not reasons for—giving notices of cancellation. A dissenting judge noted, "[T]he attorney is the only one who can cause revocation of the contract or lease. Why the attorney, and not the party, should be given that power is unclear. . . . Indeed, the clause is unclear as to whether the right of revocation depends upon the attorney's reason, if any. If that reason may simply be the client's desire to withdraw from the transaction, why must the individual engage an attorney and why should that not be made clear on the face of the instrument?"

In Cultum v. Heritage House Realtors, Inc., 103 Wn.2d 623, 694 P.2d 630 (1985), the court held that "a real estate broker or salesperson is permitted to complete simple printed standardized real estate forms, which forms must be approved by a lawyer." Nevertheless, the defendant brokerage firm, which had completed an earnest money agreement, was held liable to its client, the purchaser, because the firm's agent had "failed to exercise the reasonable care and skill of a practicing attorney."

TRISTRAM'S LANDING, INC., et al.[1] v. WAIT

Supreme Court of Massachusetts, 1975.
367 Mass. 622, 327 N.E.2d 727.

TAURO, CHIEF JUSTICE.

This is an action in contract seeking to recover a brokerage commission alleged to be due to the plaintiffs from the defendant. The case was heard by a judge, sitting without a jury, on a stipulation of facts. The judge found for the plaintiffs in the full amount of the commission. The defendant filed exceptions to that finding and appealed.

The facts briefly are these: The plaintiffs are real estate brokers doing business in Nantucket. The defendant owned real estate on the island which she desired to sell. In the past, the plaintiffs acted as brokers for the defendant when she rented the same premises.

The plaintiffs heard that the defendant's property was for sale, and in the spring of 1972 the plaintiff Van der Wolk telephoned the defendant and asked for authority to show it. The defendant agreed that the plaintiffs could act as brokers, although not as exclusive brokers, and told them that the price for the property was $110,000. During this conversation there was no mention of a commission. The

1. D.P. Van der Wolk. (Footnotes by the Court.)

defendant knew that the normal brokerage commission in Nantucket was five per cent of the sale price.

In the early months of 1973, Van der Wolk located a prospective buyer, Louise L. Cashman (Cashman), who indicated that she was interested in purchasing the defendant's property. Her written offer of $100,000 dated April 29, was conveyed to the defendant. Shortly thereafter, the defendant's husband and attorney wrote to the plaintiffs that "a counter-offer of $105,000 with an October 1st closing" should be made to Cashman. Within a few weeks, the counter offer was orally accepted, and a purchase and sale agreement was drawn up by Van der Wolk.

The agreement was executed by Cashman and was returned to the plaintiffs with a check for $10,500, representing a ten per cent down payment. The agreement was then presented by the plaintiffs to the defendant, who signed it after reviewing it with her attorney. The down payment check was thereafter turned over to the defendant.

The purchase and sale agreement signed by the parties called for an October 1, 1973, closing date. On September 22, the defendant signed a fifteen day extension of the closing date, which was communicated to Cashman by the plaintiffs. Cashman did not sign the extension. On October 1, 1973, the defendant appeared at the registry of deeds with a deed to the property. Cashman did not appear for the closing and thereafter refused to go through with the purchase. No formal action has been taken by the defendant to enforce the agreement or to recover damages for its breach, although the defendant has retained the down payment.

Van der Wolk presented the defendant with a bill for commission in the amount of $5,250, five per cent of the agreed sales price. The defendant, through her attorney, refused to pay, stating that "[t] here has been no sale and consequently the 5% commission has not been earned." The plaintiffs then brought this action to recover the commission.[2]

In the course of dealings between the plaintiffs and the defendant there was no mention of commission. The only reference to commission is found in the purchase and sale agreement signed by Cashman and the defendant, which reads as follows: "It is understood that a broker's commission of five (5) per cent on the said sale is to be paid to . . . [the broker] by the said seller." The plaintiffs contend that, having produced a buyer who was ready, willing and able to purchase the property, and who was in fact accepted by the seller, they are entitled to their full commission. The defendant argues that no commission was earned because the sale was not consummated. We agree with the defendant, and reverse the finding by the judge below.

2. The plaintiffs brought this action in four counts, two by the corporate plaintiff and two by the individual plaintiff. One count by each plaintiff was for recovery on the contract and the other stated a count in quantum meruit. At the hearing before the judge, the counts in quantum meruit were waived.

1. The general rule regarding whether a broker is entitled to a commission from one attempting to sell real estate is that, absent special circumstances, the broker "is entitled to a commission if he produces a customer ready, able, and willing to buy upon the terms and for the price given the broker by the owner." Gaynor v. Laverdure, 362 Mass. 828, 831, 291 N.E.2d 617 (1973), quoting Henderson & Beal, Inc. v. Glen, 329 Mass. 748, 751, 110 N.E.2d 373 (1953). In the past, this rule has been construed to mean that once a customer is produced by the broker and accepted by the seller, the commission is earned, whether or not the sale is actually consummated. . . . Furthermore, execution of a purchase and sale agreement is usually seen as conclusive evidence of the seller's acceptance of the buyer. . . .

Despite these well established and often cited rules, we have held that "[t]he owner is not helpless" to protect himself from these consequences. "He may, by appropriate language in his dealings with the broker, limit his liability for payment of a commission to the situation where not only is the broker obligated to find a customer ready, willing and able to purchase on the owner's terms and for his price, but also it is provided that no commission is to become due until the customer actually takes a conveyance and pays therefor." Gaynor v. Laverdure, supra, at 835, 291 N.E.2d at 622.

In the application of these rules to the instant case, we believe that the broker here is not entitled to a commission. We cannot construe the purchase and sale agreement as an unconditional acceptance by the seller of the buyer, as the agreement itself contained conditional language. The purchase and sale agreement provided that the commission was to be paid "on the said sale," and we construe this language as requiring that the said sale be consummated before the commission is earned.

While we recognize that there is a considerable line of cases indicating that language providing for payment of a commission when the agreement is "carried into effect" or "when title is passed" does not create a condition precedent, but merely sets a time for payment to be made, Alvord v. Cook, 174 Mass. 120, 121, 54 N.E. 499 (1899); Rosenthal v. Schwartz, 214 Mass. 371, 372, 101 N.E. 1070 (1913); Lord v. Williams, 259 Mass. 278, 156 N.E. 421 (1927); Canton v. Thomas, 264 Mass. 457, 162 N.E. 769 (1928), we do not think the course of events and the choice of language in this case fall within the *Alvord* case and its progeny. This is not a case, like Canton v. Thomas, where a separate agreement was made between the seller and the broker wherein the broker would receive a commission " 'in consideration of . . . procuring a purchaser.' " 264 Mass. at 458, 162 N.E. at 769 (1928). Similarly, Rosenthal v. Schwartz, supra, is distinguishable on its facts, as there the seller himself defaulted, thus depriving the broker of a commission by his own acts. Maher v. Haycock, 301 Mass. 594, 18 N.E.2d 348 (1938), cited by the defendant here and by the court in the *Gaynor* case, is not necessarily to the contrary, as there the words "if . . . sold" were construed to require other than the consummation of the sale in order to avoid the prohibition against Sunday contracts, and not merely to determine whether the broker was entitled to a commission.[3]

To the extent that there are cases (such as those collected in the *Gaynor* case), unique on their facts, which may appear inconsistent with this holding and seem to indicate a contrary result, we choose not to follow them.

In light of what we have said, we construe the language "on the said sale" as providing for a "special agreement," Gaynor v. Laverdure, supra, at 832, 291 N.E.2d 617, or as creating "special circumstances," Henderson & Beal, Inc. v. Glen, 329 Mass. 748, 751, 110 N.E.2d 373 (1953), wherein consummation of the sale became a condition precedent for the broker to earn his commission. Cf. McCarthy v. Daggett, 344 Mass. 577, 579, 183 N.E.2d 502 (1962).[4] Accordingly, since the sale was not consummated, the plaintiffs were not entitled to recover the amount specified in the purchase and sale agreement.[5]

2. Although what we have said to this point is determinative of the rights of the parties, we note that the relationship and obligations of real estate owners and brokers inter se has been the "subject of frequent litigation," Henderson & Beal, Inc. v. Glen, supra, 329 Mass. at 751, 110 N.E.2d 373. See Note, 23 Rutgers L.Rev. 83, 85 (1968). In two of the more recent cases where we were faced with this issue, we declined to follow the developing trends in this area, holding that the cases presented were inappropriate for that purpose. See LeDonne v. Slade, 355 Mass. 490, 492, 245 N.E.2d 434 (1969); Gaynor v. Laverdure, 362 Mass. 828, 838–839, 291 N.E.2d 617. We believe, however, that it is both appropriate and necessary at this time to clarify the law, and we now join the growing minority of States who have adopted the rule of Ellsworth Dobbs, Inc. v. Johnson, 50 N.J. 528, 236 A.2d 843 (1967).[6]

In the *Ellsworth* case, the New Jersey court faced the task of clarifying the law regarding the legal relationships between sellers and brokers in real estate transactions. In order to formulate a just and proper rule, the court examined the realities of such transactions. The

3. In Remington v. Pattison, 264 Mass. 249, 251, 162 N.E. 347 (1928), there was language in the purchase and sale agreement like that in the present case, and recovery was denied on the basis of a local usage.

4. Our holding here is not inconsistent with our recent decision in the *Gaynor* case, as there no language was present which would take the case out of the general rule. In that case, the purchase and sale agreement stated merely that "[a] brokerage commission of $9,000 shall be paid by the seller to Lucy K. Gaynor." 362 Mass. at 830, 291 N.E.2d at 619 (1973).

5. We note here that the count of quantum meruit was waived at trial, and the action proceeded on the written contract only.

6. Both Kansas and Oregon have adopted the *Ellsworth* rule in its entirety. See Winkelman v. Allen, 214 Kansas 22, 519 P.2d 1377 (1974); Brown v. Grimm, 258 Or. 55, 59–61, 481 P.2d 63 (1971). Additionally, Vermont, Connecticut and Idaho have cited the case with approval. See also Potter v. Ridge Realty Corp., 28 Conn.Supp. 304, 311, 259 A.2d 758 (1969); Rogers v. Hendrix, 92 Idaho 141, 438 P.2d 653 (1968); Staab v. Messier, 128 Vt. 380, 384, 264 A.2d 790 (1970). Other States and the District of Columbia also have similar, but more limited, rules which were adopted prior to the *Ellsworth* case. See generally Gaynor v. Laverdure, 362 Mass. 836 n. 2, 291 N.E.2d 617 (1973).

court noted that "ordinarily when an owner of property lists it with a broker for sale, his expectation is that the money for the payment of commission will come out of the proceeds of the sale." Id. at 547, 236 A.2d at 852. It quoted with approval from the opinion of Lord Justice Denning, in Dennis Reed, Ltd. v. Goody, [1950] 2 K.B. 277, 284–285, where he stated: "When a house owner puts his house into the hands of an estate agent, the ordinary understanding is that the agent is only to receive a commission if he succeeds in effecting a sale . . .. The common understanding of men is . . . that the agent's commission is payable out of the purchase price. . . . The house-owner wants to find a man who will actually buy his house and pay for it. He does not want a man who will only make an offer or sign a contract. He wants a purchaser 'able to purchase and able to complete as well.'" Id. at 549, 236 A.2d at 853.

The court went on to say that the principle binding "the seller to pay commission if he signs a contract of sale with the broker's customer, regardless of the customer's financial ability, puts the burden on the wrong shoulders. Since the broker's duty to the owner is to produce a prospective buyer who is financially able to pay the purchase price and take title, a right in the owner to assume such capacity when the broker presents his purchaser ought to be recognized." Id. at 548, 236 A.2d at 853. Reason and justice dictate that it should be the broker who bears the burden of producing a purchaser who is not only ready, willing and able at the time of the negotiations, but who also consummates the sale at the time of closing.

Thus, we adopt the following rules: "When a broker is engaged by an owner of property to find a purchaser for it, the broker earns his commission when (a) he produces a purchaser ready, willing and able to buy on the terms fixed by the owner, (b) the purchaser enters into a binding contract with the owner to do so, and (c) the purchaser completes the transaction by closing the title in accordance with the provisions of the contract. If the contract is not consummated because of lack of financial ability of the buyer to perform or because of any other default of his . . . there is no right to commission against the seller. On the other hand, if the failure of completion of the contract results from the wrongful act or interference of the seller, the broker's claim is valid and must be paid." Id. at 551, 236 A.2d at 855.

Accordingly, we hold that a real estate broker, under a brokerage agreement hereafter made, is entitled to a commission from the seller only if the requirements stated above are met. This rule provides necessary protection for the seller and places the burden with the broker, where it belongs. In view of the waiver of the counts in quantum meruit, we do not now consider the extent to which the broker may be entitled to share in a forfeited deposit or other benefit received by the seller as a result of the broker's efforts.

We recognize that this rule could be easily circumvented by language to the contrary in purchase and sale agreements or in agreements between sellers and brokers. In many States a signed writing is required for an agreement to pay a commission to a real estate broker.

See Restatement 2d: Contracts, 418, 420 (Tent. drafts Nos. 1–7, 1973). Such a requirement may be worthy of legislative consideration, but we do not think we should establish such a requirement by judicial decision. Informal agreements fairly made between people of equal skill and understanding serve a useful purpose. But many sellers, unlike brokers, are involved in real estate transactions infrequently, perhaps only once in a lifetime, and are thus unfamiliar with their legal rights. In such cases agreements by the seller to pay a commission even though the purchaser defaults are to be scrutinized carefully. If not fairly made, such agreements may be unconscionable or against public policy.

Exceptions sustained.

Judgment for the defendant.

NOTE

In Strout Realty, Inc. v. Milhous, 107 Idaho 330, 689 P.2d 222 (1984), broker brought purchasers and sellers together, and they entered into an agreement by which purchasers obligated themselves to pay $255,000 for certain property over a period of two years. Sellers agreed to pay broker a $15,300 sales commission, of which $2,250 was paid immediately. Purchasers took possession of the land but then defaulted after paying only $5,500. Broker sued sellers to recover the balance of his commission, but sellers denied liability on the ground that broker had failed to procure an "able" buyer. The trial court awarded broker an amount equal to the $5,500 paid by purchasers to sellers, but the Court of Appeals remanded for entry of judgment for broker in the amount of $13,050. "What is the relevant point in time for evaluating a buyer's ability to perform? Neither party has urged us to support the traditional estoppel rule, which would fix the relevant time as the signing of the earnest money agreement. [Broker] maintains that the buyer's ability to perform must be determined at or before the time of closing. [Sellers] believe the ability of the buyer can be examined even after the transaction is closed. . . . By closing the transaction, we believe the seller has demonstrated an acceptance of the buyer's ability to perform, sufficient to support a finding that the broker has produced an able buyer."

NOTE, IMPOSING TORT LIABILITY ON REAL ESTATE BROKERS SELLING DEFECTIVE HOUSING

99 Harvard Law Review 1861, 1862–1866 (1986).

Traditionally, buyers have been able to recover damages from brokers only in actions based on intentional misrepresentation, under which redress is granted only if the broker knowingly made a false statement and the buyer relied on it to her detriment. But buyers usually have lost intentional misrepresentation actions against brokers, because of the difficulty of proving some of the tort's elements. Buyers often have found it difficult to prove that brokers made statements, that they knowingly lied, or that they intended the buyers to rely on the statements. Buyers are barred from recovery if the court finds that the brokers' false statements reflected opinions or misrepresented the state of the law; only misrepresentations of fact are actionable. Moreover, buyers traditionally have been able to recover only when brokers affirmatively misrepresented the condition of property; nondisclosure was not actionable even when brokers intended to mislead buyers. Even when buyers have met these proof requirements, they often have been denied recovery if they could have discovered the truth of statements by themselves.

Because of the difficulty of proving that a broker has lied knowingly, some courts have allowed recovery by buyers who prove that brokers negligently misrepresented the value of property to them. Under negligent misrepresentation, a broker who honestly believes in the truth of a representation may be held liable for failing to use reasonable care in ascertaining the facts. A minority of courts have gone a step further by imposing liability under the doctrine of innocent misrepresentation, which relieves a buyer of the need to prove the broker's knowledge and intent. Under this formulation, it is irrelevant whether the broker knew that the information she provided was false or intended that the buyer rely upon it; the buyer need prove only that she justifiably relied on a misrepresentation of material fact.

In addition, to circumvent the traditional rule that only brokers who have made explicit misrepresentations are liable, some jurisdictions have moved closer to holding that silence may constitute a misrepresentation.[15] Although courts in the past have refused to impose a duty to disclose known defects because brokers are not in privity of contract with buyers, many jurisdictions now recognize that such a duty arises when the broker voluntarily enters a relationship with a buyer. Some courts have determined the scope of a broker's duty to disclose by examining the process by which brokers are licensed and the ethical code regulating broker conduct.

Alternatively, some courts have relieved buyers of the need to prove the elements of misrepresentation by allowing buyers to sue under the general doctrine of negligence. To prevail on a claim of negligence, the buyer need only prove that 1) the broker owed the buyer a legal duty to take reasonable care to protect her from harm; 2) the broker breached this duty; and 3) the breach proximately caused actual loss or injury to the buyer. Because negligence doctrine requires brokers to prevent foreseeable harm to buyers, brokers will be held liable for remaining silent when they know about potentially dangerous defects.

15. *Compare* Swinton v. Whitinsville Savings Bank, 311 Mass. 677, 42 N.E.2d 808 (1942) (holding that there was no duty to disclose that a home was infested with termites), *with* Obde v. Schlemeyer, 56 Wash.2d 449, 353 P.2d 672 (1960) (imposing liability for failure to disclose that a home was infested with termites). Although such rulings place nondisclosure cases within the doctrinal framework of misrepresentation, courts may reach the same result under negligence theory by holding that silence breaches an implied duty to warn of defects.

Some jurisdictions have afforded buyers additional protection by enacting legislation regulating broker conduct.[21] Where statutes require brokers to disclose known information to potential buyers, courts have allowed buyers to maintain tort actions against brokers breaching such a duty. Where no statute explicitly requires brokers to disclose information or to avoid misrepresentation, some courts have implied such a duty from the more general provisions of existing consumer protection statutes.

Although most courts have imposed liability on brokers only for failing to disclose known defects, two recent decisions have imposed liability on brokers who failed to disclose the existence of defects of which they were unaware. In Easton v. Strassburger,[25] a California appellate court relied on negligence doctrine to hold that real estate brokers have an "affirmative duty to conduct a reasonably competent and diligent inspection of the residential property listed for sale and to disclose to prospective purchasers all facts materially affecting the value or desirability of the property that such an investigation would reveal." In imposing this duty, the court noted that the Code of Ethics of the National Association of Realtors includes the provision that "a broker must not only 'avoid . . . concealment of pertinent facts,' but 'has an affirmative obligation to discover adverse factors that a reasonably competent and diligent investigation would disclose.'" In Berman v. Watergate West, Inc.,[28] the District of Columbia Court of Appeals held that strict liability may be imposed on a broker for selling a defective cooperative apartment. The *Berman* court drew an analogy to the strict liability imposed on sellers of new homes, which in turn was based on an analogy to strict product liability. To date, only the *Berman* court has based broker liability on the act of selling defective housing, rather than on failure to warn the buyer about the home's condition.

NOTE

You should relate the foregoing discussion of brokers' liability for sales of defective housing to the materials in section 1 of Chapter 26, pages 1268–1301 infra, concerning vendors' implied covenants of habitability and construction lenders' liability.

In Johnson v. Geer Real Estate Company, 239 Kan. 324, 720 P.2d 660 (1986), vendors mistakenly believed, and so informed their listing broker, that their house was connected to the city sanitary sewer system, when in fact it was not but was served by a septic tank. Before contracting to buy the house, plaintiffs told the broker that they did not want a house with a septic tank, and broker told them that this house was connected to a public sewer. After taking possession of the house, plaintiffs suffered damages and incurred expenses because the septic tank malfunctioned. At trial, the jury absolved vendors of liability but

21. Such statutes often apply to a variety of consumer transactions. See, e.g., Texas Deceptive Trade Practices and Consumer Protection Act, TEX.BUS & COM.CODE ANN. §§ 17.41–.63 (Vernon Supp.1986).

25. 152 Cal.App.3d 90, 199 Cal.Rptr. 383 (1984).

28. 391 A.2d 1351 (D.C.1978).

held the broker liable for $10,000 actual damages and $17,500 punitive damages. On appeal by the broker, the state Supreme Court found that the evidence—"several indications which, to the eye of an experienced realtor, would indicate that the property was not served by the public sewer system"—was "sufficient to establish ordinary negligence" on the part of the realtor. The court held that this evidence supported the jury's finding that broker "should have known that the property was on a septic tank instead of a city sewer line and breached its duty to disclose this material fact to the plaintiffs. This finding of negligent misrepresentation would support an award of actual but not punitive damages. . . . Under the facts of this case, the nonliability of the sellers does not absolve the broker of liability."

Chapter 24

THE DEED

The cases and materials in this and the following two chapters have been traditionally covered in courses labeled Conveyances or Titles. The contract for the sale of land and the deed conveying the legal title to the land are closely related. However, it is vital that you understand that they are two separate legal transactions, represented by two distinct documents. Chronologically, the deed follows the contract and we are therefore using that order of study. Logically, many of the technical points concerning deeds must be mentally digested before the law of vendor and purchaser becomes clear. Note, then, how the present materials tend to illuminate our prior discussions.

In the present chapter we will take a look at the history of conveyancing (Section 1), at the characteristics of the modern deed (Section 2), at the formalities required to make a deed effective (Section 3), and at the description necessary to convey an interest in land (Section 4). The intricacies of the recording system and the methods of making sure that the deed actually conveys something we will leave to succeeding chapters.

SECTION 1. CONVEYANCING AT COMMON LAW AND UNDER THE STATUTE OF USES

PATTON, TITLES

Vol. 1, pages 3–8 (2d ed. 1957).

HISTORY OF ENGLISH SYSTEM OF CONVEYANCING

We do not know the origin of the practice of transferring title to real estate by a written instrument. It may have been in existence and quite highly developed at the very dawn of written history. It appears to have passed from one predominating civilization to the next till it reached the Roman era, and from the latter into the legal systems of continental Europe. But Roman law did not, directly at least, exercise any appreciable influence on English land law. Instead, therefore, of finding transfers of title in England made from the time of the Roman occupation by the execution and delivery of a deed, we find that at no very remote date, possession was the only evidence of title and that proof of a transfer of title existed solely in the memory of witnesses present at the time when the change of possession occurred. As to estates for years, a transfer of title was effected by a mere entry of the new owner, but in the case of freehold estates the change had to be in the form of a symbolic ceremony known as livery of seisin. This was a ceremony consisting of a symbolical delivery of the corporeal possession of land by the grantor, or "feoffor," as he was called, to the grantee, or "feoffee." The parties, with their witnesses, went upon the land, and the feoffor gave to the feoffee a stick, twig, piece of turf, or a handful of earth taken from the land. Sometimes a ring, a cross, or a knife was handed over, anything, in fact, as a token of the delivery. As a further part of the ceremony the feoffor used proper and technical, words which were to show that he intended to transfer the land to the feoffee, and which also marked out, or limited, the estate, or the interest, in the land which the feoffor intended the feoffee to have. The words "I give" (Latin, "do") were the proper words to use for the conveyance, while the words "to him" (i.e., the feoffee) "and his heirs," or "to him and the heirs of his body," (designating the limitation, either as a fee simple or a fee tail) indicated the estate conveyed. A distinction was made between livery in deed and livery in law. The former arose when the livery of seisin took place on the land itself; the latter when the parties were not actually on the land—as when the transfer was made in sight of the premises, but without an actual entry on them. In the latter case, the feoffor, pointing out the land, bade the feoffee enter and take possession of it. Should the feoffee do so within the lifetime of the parties, the feoffment was valid in law. Livery of seisin also required an abjuration of the land by the donor, or feoffor; that is, he had to leave, or vacate, the land, leaving the feoffee in possession. No writing was necessary to give evidence to livery of seisin, although writings became customary in very early times. In later times, however, livery of seisin was usually accompanied by a written deed, especially when the limitations of the estate granted were numerous. Such a deed was, however, only an evidence of title, and not a conveyance itself. A writing was not legally required till the statute of frauds.

Later, as the art of writing became common among our ancestors, there might also have been a deed in order to more definitely designate the nature and extent of the estate granted, and its various conditions and limitations. But the use of a writing remained optional with the parties till the passage in 1677 of the Statute of Frauds. It was only incorporeal interests and future estates, which were not capable of livery of seisin because of an absence of the element of possession, as to which a transfer of title could be made by a deed alone. The latter was called a deed of grant and was responsible for the common-law distinction between things which "lie in livery" and those which "lie in grant." In the case of freehold estates in corporeal real property, the deed required by the Statute of Frauds did not operate to transfer the title, and livery of seisin remained essential in England, theoretically at least, till dispensed with by the Real Property Act 1845, § 3. But the enactment of the Statute of Uses in 1535 had practically that effect in that it brought into almost universal use modes of alienation which did not require the symbolic ceremony. Aside from a more common form of conveyance which indirectly resulted from the statute, as set forth in the next paragraph, those directly resulting from the statute were, (1) a contract in the form of a covenant to stand seized of property for the benefit of a beneficiary related to the covenantor by blood or marriage, and (2) a contract, or deed, of bargain and sale of lands "whereby the bargainor for some pecuniary consideration bargains and sells, that is, contracts to convey, the land to the bargainee; and becomes by such bargain, a trustee for, or seised to the use of the bargainee." The statute executed the contract in both cases, and thus the purchaser acquired the seisin and possession of the same as though there had been a livery of seisin.

But since the statute enabled a landowner by a mere contract of sale to vest the title in another without livery of seisin or other publicity, the same parliament passed a companion act for the express purpose of preventing clandestine conveyances. This was the Statute of Enrollments. It made a deed of bargain and sale of a freehold interest void unless within six months it was enrolled in a court of record at Westminster, or in certain other public offices. These two statutes were merely part of a plan to provide a general scheme for the transfer of title by deed, and for the recording or registry of land conveyances. But because of a general disposition of the landholding aristocracy to withdraw the details of their family settlements and domestic arrangements from the curiosity of the public, their conveyancers welcomed the first part of the plan and set themselves to work to frustrate the second. A common-law deed of "lease and release" had previously been somewhat used to effect a transfer of title without the formal livery of seisin; it was now brought into general use to effect a conveyance which would not be within the terms of the Statute of Enrollments. . . . All that the conveyancer had to do was to have the owner execute a lease (usually in the form of a bargain and sale deed of an estate for one year), followed at once by a release of the reversion to the lessee. This cumbersome use of two instruments for every transfer continued in England till the necessity for the fictitious lease was abolished in 1841. Four years later the Real Property Act was passed, making a simple deed of grant sufficient to convey all estates.

CONVEYANCING IN THE UNITED STATES

Though livery of seisin was necessarily recognized as effective to transfer title in the few instances in which it was employed in the early days of this country, and though the statute of uses has been frequently relied upon to give effect to an instrument which might otherwise be ineffective to operate as a conveyance, most of the states early adopted statutes authorizing the transfer of title by simple forms of deeds of conveyance without livery of seisin or other ceremony. Many of these follow substantially the wording of the deeds of bargain and sale which came into use with the statute of uses, others resemble common-law deeds of grant (though no longer confined to incorporeal things or future estates), with or without the addition of covenants of warranty, and some are patterned after the early common-law release. In Louisiana, conveyance has always been by deed but by forms derived from those of France rather than of England.

FRENCH v. FRENCH

Supreme Court of New Hampshire, 1825.
3 N.H. 234.

This was a writ of entry, in which the demandant counted upon his own seisin of land in Pembroke, in this county, and upon a disseisin by the tenant; and was submitted to the decision of the court upon the following facts:

The tenant, being seised of the demanded premises, on the 13th January, 1812, made and executed a deed as follows:

"Know all men, that this indenture of lease witnesseth, that I, George French, of Pembroke, &c. do hereby lease, and release, and quitclaim to my honored father, Andrew French, the use and improvement during his natural life, of that half of his farm, which he hath this day given a deed of to me: the true meaning of this is, that I, the said George, shall not convey the land, he hath given me a deed of, during his natural life.

"Dated Pembroke, Jan. 13, 1812.

"George French, & seal.

"Attest—Nathaniel Head."

. . .

RICHARDSON, C.J. The tenant's claim to judgment in this case is rested by his counsel upon two propositions.

In the first place, he has urged, that under the statute of February 10, 1791, entitled "An act declaring the mode of conveyance by deed," nothing will pass by a deed, unless it be "signed by two or more witnesses."

In the second place, he has contended, that every deed, which is not a valid conveyance under the said statute, is wholly inoperative.

To the truth of the first proposition, we, without any hesitation, accede. The language of the statute is too plain and explicit to admit a doubt. In addition to this, it is understood to have been solemnly decided in this court, at November term, in the county of Strafford, 1813, in the case of Thompson vs. Bennet, that a deed, attested by one witness only, was not sufficient to pass real estate under the statute. This decision was recognized as law in the case of Smith vs. Chamberlain, (2 N.H.Rep. 440,) and the correctness of it has not been questioned in this case by the demandant's counsel.

But the second proposition is so new, so extraordinary, and so repugnant to what is believed to be the general opinion of the profession on the subject, that we should not have deemed it worthy of a moment's consideration, had it not been urged upon our attention by counsel with an earnestness, which seemed to evince a deep conviction, that the proposition might be maintained. We have thought it due to the very able and ingenious argument, which has been urged in its support, to examine it with attention; and we have considered it in every point of view, in which it has been presented to us. The result of our examination of the question we shall now endeavor to state.

At the common law, feoffments and grants were the usual modes of transferring property. A feoffment was defined as a conveyance of corporeal hereditaments, by delivery of the possession upon or within view of the land. No charter of feoffment was necessary; and when it was used, the lands were supposed to be transferred, not by the charter, but by the livery. A grant, in the original signification of the word, is a conveyance of an incorporeal hereditament. As livery of seisin could not be had of incorporeal hereditaments, the transfer of them was always made by writing, in order to give to them that notoriety, which was produced in the transfer of corporeal hereditaments by delivery of possession.

The statute of the 27 Hen. VIII. cap. 10, commonly called the statute of uses, produced a great revolution in the modes of transferring landed property. It is, however, unnecessary to notice, on the present occasion, more than two new modes of conveyance, introduced by that statute. These are bargains and sales, and covenants to stand seised to uses.

There is no doubt, that a species of conveyance by bargain and sale existed before the statute of uses, and originated from an equitable construction of the court of chancery. A bargain was made for the sale of an estate; the purchase money was paid; but there was either no conveyance at all of the legal interest, or a conveyance defective at law, by reason of the omission of livery of seisin, or attornment; the court of chancery properly thought that the estate ought in conscience to belong to the person, who paid the money, and therefore considered the bargainor as a trustee for him. But the cestui que trust had only an equitable interest. The statute of uses enacted, that, "where any person or persons, &c. stand or are seised of any honors, &c. lands, tenements, &c. to the use, confidence, or trust of any other person, or persons, &c. by reason of any bargain, sale, feoffment, &c. such person, or persons, &c. that have any such use, shall be deemed and adjudged in lawful seisin, estate, and possession thereof, to all intents and purposes, of or in such like estates as they have in the use, &c. and the estate, right, and possession of him and them, so seised to any use, &c. shall be deemed and adjudged in him or them, which have the use, &c. after such quality, manner, &c. as they had before in or to the use." On this statute the conveyance, which has been called a bargain and sale, is founded. The bargainer contracts to sell the land, and receives the purchase money; after this, he is, in equity, considered as seised of the land to the use of the bargainee; and this statute unites the possession to the use, so that the very instant the use is raised, the possession is joined to it, and the bargainee becomes seised of the land. The words of transfer, applicable to this conveyance, are *bargain and sell*; but they are by no means necessary nor material to its operation. There must be a pecuniary consideration. But if a man, for such a consideration, covenants to stand seised to the use of another person, a use is thereby raised, which the statute will execute.

Covenants to stand seised are another species of conveyance founded upon the statute of uses. The consideration of this conveyance is the foundation of it. The words *covenant to stand seised* are, therefore, not absolutely necessary to its operation. Uses can only be raised upon a covenant to stand seised in consideration of blood or marriage. If the consideration appear, though it be not particularly expressed, yet it is sufficient to raise a use upon this conveyance. Thus, if a man covenant to stand seised to the use of his wife, son, or cousin, without saying in consideration of natural love, the covenant will raise the use, and the statute execute it.

When our ancestors first came to this country, they brought with them and adopted the various modes of conveying real estate, then in use in England. This is very apparent from the language of several ancient statutes. Thus, a statute of the colony of Massachusetts, passed in 1652, enacted, that "henceforth no sale or alienation of houses and lands, within this jurisdiction, shall be holden good in law, except the same be done by deed in writing, under hand and seal, and delivered, and possession given upon part in the name of the whole by the seller, or his attorney, so authorized, under hand and seal, unless the said deed be acknowledged and recorded according to law." Mass.Col. & Prov.Laws 85.

Here a feoffment is distinctly recognized, as a valid conveyance.

In 1697, a provincial act of Massachusetts declared, "that henceforth all deeds or conveyances of any houses or lands, within this province, signed and sealed by the party or parties granting the same, having good and lawful right and authority thereto, and acknowledged by such grantor or grantors, before a justice of the peace, and recorded at length in the registry of the county, where such houses or lands do lie, shall be valid to pass the same, without any other act or ceremony in the law whatever.

"And that no bargain, sale, mortgage, or other conveyance of houses or lands, &c. shall be good and effectual in law, to hold such houses and lands against any other person or persons, but the grantor or grantors, and their heirs only; unless the deed or deeds thereof be acknowledged and recorded in manner as is before expressed." Mass. Col. & Prov.Laws 303.

Here a bargain and sale is distinctly recognized as a mode of conveyance in use.

Our provincial act of the 13 W. 3, cap. 12 (Prov.Laws 19,) was copied verbatim from the said provincial act of Massachusetts, and of course mentions a bargain and sale as a mode of conveyance in use.

Our statute, entitled "an act declaring the mode of conveyance," sec. 4, which is now in force, enacts, "that all deeds or other conveyances of any lands, tenements, or hereditaments lying in this state, signed and sealed by the party granting the same, having good and lawful authority thereto, and signed by two or more witnesses, and acknowledged by such grantor or grantors, before a justice of the peace, and recorded at length in the registry of deeds in the country, &c. shall be valid to pass the same, without any other act or ceremony in law whatever. And no deed of bargain and sale, mortgage, or other conveyance, &c. shall be good and effectual in law to hold such lands, tenements, or hereditaments, against any other person or persons, but the grantor or grantors, and their heirs only, unless the deed or deeds thereof be acknowledged and recorded in manner aforesaid."

Here again a bargain and sale is recognized as a valid mode of conveyance.

But it is said, that this last mentioned clause in the statute has abolished all the former modes of conveying real estate, and that no conveyance remains, except that prescribed by the statute. We have attentively examined the statute, but have sought in vain to find any thing indicating such an intention in the legislature. It is a well settled rule, in the construction of statutes, that affirmative words do not take away the common law, nor a former statute, unless it be in cases, where the affirmative words in sense contain a negative.

The statute, now under consideration, declares what shall constitute a valid conveyance; but it contains no negative, either in its terms, or in sense. On the contrary, it in express terms recognizes "*bargains and sales, and other conveyances,*" and declares, that they shall not be good against any, but the grantors, and their heirs, unless recorded. Nothing can afford a clearer demonstration, that it was not the intention of the legislature to abolish the modes of conveyance, which had been in common use, than the language used in this statute. Whoever attentively examines this subject will find, that the object of this statute was to take away the necessity of livery of seisin, and to substitute a deed, executed in a particular manner, and acknowledged and recorded, in its place. Nothing more than this is believed to have been intended; and this purpose the statute has most conveniently fulfilled. 4 Mass.Rep. 64, Wells vs. Prince. . . .

But it is further contended, in this case, that no deed can operate here as a covenant to stand seised, or as a bargain and sale, because the statute of uses was never adopted in this state. If the premises, upon which this argument is founded, are true, the conclusion is without doubt a sound one. These conveyances cannot exist without the statute of uses. But what seems to us to be a decisive answer to this argument is, that our present statute, as well as the ancient provincial act, expressly recognizes a bargain and sale as a mode of conveyance, and thus, by necessary implication, recognizes the adoption of the statute of uses. . . .

It is clearly the duty of the court to give such construction to every instrument, as will give effect to the intention of the parties, if, by law, it can be done. In this case we are clearly of opinion, that this deed may be construed as a covenant to stand seised, and pass the land without the aid of the statute. The consideration of blood appears upon the face of the deed. . . .

The contract of the grantor in this instance, made upon the consideration of blood, is sufficient to raise a use, and that use is executed by the statute of uses. We are, therefore, of opinion, that there be

Judgment for the demandant.

1. Sara Mallary was a wonderful lady—everyone in the community said so. Nevertheless, at forty-eight, life had passed her by. She had refused her "many" suitors to remain at home caring for her aged, cantankerous father. It was her duty and she asked little in return. In fact, she got nothing. She had always assumed that the small farm on which she and her father lived belonged to her, but when he died after a long illness, in 1975, a will was discovered in his personal papers. It had been executed in 1970 and left the entire estate of Mr. Mallary to a Eugene Planeton. Research of an elementary sort disclosed that Eugene was the product of an illicit love affair of old Mallary. Eugene had not known the name of his sire, but willingly accepted the farm as his due for having been so rudely brought into a cruel and unfeeling world.

Sara lays this tale of woe at your feet. Questioning reveals the following facts:

1. Daddy was mighty queer at the end but he was sound as a dollar in 1970.

2. Daddy never made a deed or gave any kind of writing to Sara.

3. Daddy owned the farm in fee simple absolute and the abstract of title discloses this fact.

4. Sara began taking care of Daddy on a full-time basis in 1967 and worked at it until his death in 1975.

5. In 1968 the following episode occurred: Sara, Daddy, and two friends (both of whom are still alive and verify the story) were walking through the garden after a Sunday dinner. Daddy picked up a clod of dirt, crumbled it in his hand and, giving it to Sara, said: "Gal, this here farm is yourn—see that you take proper care of it." Sara said nothing but smiled in her usual sweet way.

6. Since that date Sara has paid the taxes on the farm out of her own meager savings, has painted once and papered twice. On both occasions she told the workmen the place was hers and that Mallary was living with her.

Can you be of any professional assistance to Sara? Explain how you would approach the problem and the various possibilities involved. See Hill v. Bowen, 8 Ill.2d 527, 134 N.E.2d 769 (1956); Comment, 1956 U.Ill.L.F. 513; Hayes v. Hayes, 126 Minn. 389, 148 N.W. 125 (1914); McFadden, Oral Transfers of Land in Illinois, 1988 U.Ill.L.Rev. 667.

2. In Montoya v. New Mexico Human Services Department, 108 N.M. 263, 771 P.2d 196 (App.1989), the land in question had been the subject of an attempted oral gift to Mrs. Montoya by her parents in 1973. They told her the property was hers; in so doing, they were observing longstanding northern New Mexico tradition in orally declar-

ing, prior to their death, their children's portions. In keeping with that tradition, they intended not only that the land should be part of her inheritance but also that it was to be presently enjoyed by her. She took possession, and after both her parents had died in 1976, her brothers quitclaimed their interests to her. Mrs. Montoya then elected to observe the same tradition and told her two children that the property belonged to them. The children relied upon the "oral conveyance" and built major permanent improvements on their respective portions of the property. They also paid the taxes from 1976, and Mrs. Montoya exercised no further authority or control over the property.

In 1987, the Human Services Department declared Mr. and Mrs. Montoya ineligible for further food stamps after finding the land in question to be "an accessible resource valued in excess of the $3,000 permitted for program eligibility." The court reversed the agency's decision, holding that Mrs. Montoya's "attempted oral gift of land to her children created an equitable cloud on the title, and therefore the land was not an accessible resource." After citing the doctrine of part performance as an exception to the statute of frauds, the court said, "[T]here is no essential difference between the circumstances that make it inequitable to deny enforcement to an oral contract to sell real property and those that make it inequitable to refuse to enforce a promise to give real property. Thus, we hold that if there is proof of the elements of promissory estoppel, an oral gift of real property is enforceable in New Mexico."

SECTION 2. THE MODERN DEED—TYPES AND ELEMENTS

Like the "standard contract", the term "modern deed" is a misnomer. No one form of deed is in universal use in this country, and you must familiarize yourself with the types employed in the jurisdiction where you plan to practice. "Modern deed" is used here to distinguish our present methods of conveyancing from those available at common law. Bargain and sale deeds have been used extensively in the United States, and the words "bargain and sell" are still much in evidence in the modern deed. Some of the deeds are still prolix and contain the quaint language of the Pennsylvania common-law warranty deed, "has granted, bargained, sold, aliened, enfeoffed, released, conveyed and confirmed, and by these presents does grant, bargain, sell, alien, enfeoff, release, convey and confirm unto the said party of the second part, his heirs and assigns." This should be sufficient to transfer any interest the grantor may happen to have! Fortunately, most of the states have statutes which permit the transfer of land by a simple form, usually referred to as a statutory short-form deed.

There are two basic types of deeds—warranty and quitclaim. The warranty deed [1] contains personal covenants of the grantor relating to

1. Covenants for title are treated in detail hereafter, pages 1305 to 1337.

the nature of the estate conveyed and usually covenanting that the grantor has an indefeasible estate in fee simple. Quitclaim deeds take their name from a word typically used in a common-law release. They purport to transfer only such interest as the grantor may have and usually exclude any implication that he has a good title, or even any title at all. They contain no covenants for title but they are just as effective as a warranty deed in conveying any interest which the grantor *presently* has.[2] Of course, it is possible to use a deed which contains some covenants but not all of the so-called usual ones, and this may be referred to as a special warranty deed or a limited warranty deed. There are also specialized deeds for use in conveying a security interest (mortgage deed or trust deed, depending on the form used) or for use in setting up a trust (deed in trust), etc.

Regardless of the jurisdiction, there are certain essentials of a conveyance that are of importance to all lawyers. These essentials are described by one of the leading text writers as follows.

TIFFANY, REAL PROPERTY

Pages 670–672, 674–681 (New Abridged Edition, 1940).

DEEDS IN GENERAL

All conveyances of freehold or leasehold interests other than leases for three years or less, must be in writing under the Statute of Frauds as originally enacted in England and as re-enacted in this country. This statute does not, however, interfere with surrenders by operation of law.

At common law, all written conveyances, as well as most other written instruments, were in the form of deeds (instruments under seal) and a deed was either a "deed of indenture" or a "deed poll." A deed of indenture was a deed executed by all the parties to it, while a deed poll was executed by the grantor only.

A carefully drawn conveyance usually consists of the following parts: First the names of the parties are stated, and the date may be added, though it is frequently placed at the end. Next come the recitals, if any, being statements of fact explanatory of the transaction. A statement of the consideration and of its payment and receipt follows, and after this come the operative words of conveyance, followed by a description of the land conveyed and any exceptions or reservations. These elements constitute the "premises" and are followed by the "habendum," which limits the estate to be taken by the grantee, and is usually introduced by the words "to have and to hold." Any declaration of trust sought to be made is inserted at this place. A statement of any condition or power affecting the grant follows, and the covenant or covenants of title are last. The conclusion is a formal reference to the execution, and the signatures and seals of the parties are then placed at the foot of the instrument and one, two or more witnesses (usually

2. As to the doctrine of after-acquired title see pages 1331 to 1337.

required by the recording statutes) sign their names opposite that of the parties. A certificate of acknowledgment signed (and sealed if he has a seal) by an officer authorized to take acknowledgments completes the instrument. The officer, if a notary public, may also be required to state when his commission expires.

Though a well-drawn conveyance usually contains all or most of these parts, a conveyance containing merely the names of the parties, a statement of the consideration, and words of conveyance, with a description of the land, if duly executed, may be sufficient.

DESIGNATION OF PARTIES IN DEED

A conveyance should at the beginning name the grantor. If the name as given is sufficient to enable him to be identified, the fact that it appears in the instrument different from his actual name, or from that signed, does not invalidate the deed. A conveyance by the "heirs" of a decedent is sufficient, if they can be identified.

When two or more persons join in a conveyance, only such as are named in the body of the instrument are parties. In a conveyance by a husband, the mere joinder of his wife in the execution, therefore, is insufficient to release her dower; and the rule applies, for stronger reasons, to strangers merely joining in the execution. Where there is only one grantor it is not so necessary that he be named in the instrument, since his name is put in "but to make certainty of the grantor."

The grantee or grantees must be named or means for their identification furnished. A deed to a deceased person is void, but a conveyance to his heirs is sufficient, since their identity can be determined. Of course, a deed to the heirs of a living person is void since they cannot be identified. . . .

HABENDUM IN DEED

The purpose of the habendum is to limit the estate to be taken by the grantee. In construing it, the purpose, of course, is to arrive at the intention of the parties. It will, if possible, be construed to harmonize with the premises, thus giving effect to both.

Where the premises are inconsistent with the habendum, the premises will prevail to the extent that an estate created in the granting clause cannot be cut down or invalidated by the habendum. If the estate limited in the habendum, however, is greater than that named in the premises, the habendum prevails. An estate granted to A for life may, by the habendum, be enlarged to a fee simple.

If there is no express limitation of an estate in the premises the habendum may determine its quantum. Though a grant without words of limitation creates an estate for life only, it may be shown by the habendum that an estate in fee or for years is intended. Where, under statutes, a grant to A creates a fee simple, or passes whatever estate the grantor has, the habendum may show that an estate for life only is intended. . . .

EXCEPTIONS AND RESERVATIONS IN DEED

An exception excludes from the operation of a conveyance some actually existing part of the thing described (e.g., an orchard or houses on the land conveyed), and must be less extensive than such thing. The part excepted must be described with sufficient certainty to be identified. It may cover not only a particular piece of land measured horizontally, but also fixtures on the land conveyed, or timber growing thereon, or minerals underneath. It may also limit the purpose for which it is made.

A reservation, on the other hand, is a clause by which the grantor secures to himself a new thing "issuing out of" the thing granted, and not in esse before.

Since an exception is merely a part of the description of the thing granted, its subject remains in the grantor and no words of inheritance or other words of limitation are necessary to enable him to retain the same state as he had before. A reservation, on the other hand, since it creates a new thing, must contain words of inheritance, except where the common-law rule has been changed by statute. Both exceptions and reservations operate exclusively in favor of the grantor. . . .

In construing conveyances creating, or attempting to create, rights in the land granted in favor of the grantor, the courts construe the language used as an exception or a reservation, according to the nature of the rights sought to be created, and hold that a "reservation" is an exception and that an "exception" is a reservation.

In states where the word "heirs" is still necessary to create a fee, the question whether the language of the conveyance is to be construed as an exception or a reservation may determine the question whether the grantor has an easement in fee or for life only. In some of these states, however, the courts refuse to apply this requirement to a reservation of an easement, holding that since the reservation is evidently intended for the benefit of the land retained by the grantor, he will have an easement of like duration with his estate in such land.[3]

CONSIDERATION IN DEED

A conveyance is not a contract, though it is the result of an agreement, and hence a consideration is not necessary except when the conveyance operates under the Statute of Uses. The owner of land has the same right to give it away as he has to sell it, and the only persons who may question the validity of such a gift are creditors who may thereby lose their debts.

3. Much ancient learning is involved in the exception-reservation controversy, but it has relatively little current significance. Judge Lindley summed it up in Adkins v. Arsht, 50 F.Supp. 761, 764 (E.D.Ill.1943): "Irrespective of their exact meanings, the words 'exception' and 'reservation' have been used indiscriminately as synonymous in meaning, and courts quite generally have held that the legal intent will be determined, not by the word used, but by the purport indicated in the entire grant."

Most conveyances expressly acknowledge the receipt of a consideration, which frequently is merely nominal.[4] The purpose is to rebut any implication of a resulting use or trust in favor of the grantor, and to furnish support for the conveyance as a bargain and sale. Such acknowledgment, while not conclusive as to the amount of the consideration, is conclusive upon the parties for the purpose of supporting the conveyance and vesting a beneficial interest in the grantee. The absence of such a recital does not affect the right of the grantee to show its payment for the purpose of supporting the conveyance.

REALITY OF CONSENT TO DEED

While a conveyance is presumed to have been made with the free consent of the parties, it may be shown that such consent was wanting. This want may arise from a mistake of fact concerning the subject-matter of the contract (e.g., the quantity of land embraced in the description is materially different from what the parties supposed and with reference to which the price was fixed). That the parties ignorantly fail to agree on the land to be conveyed is ground for a rescission of the conveyance. A mistake in the words describing the interest conveyed may be corrected (e.g., an omission of words of inheritance). Relief may be obtained when the legal nature and effect of the conveyance as written does not correspond with the agreement of the parties.

The want of consent may arise from the fact that the conveyance was procured by fraudulent representations, or by duress, or undue influence.

NOTE

Many states provide by statute a short form of deed that may be used. The form contains all elements necessary for a valid conveyance: names of grantor and grantee, words of conveyance, description of the land conveyed, and signature of grantor. The short form warranty deed authorized by Ill.—S.H.A. ch. 30, § 9 (1985), is as follows:

> The grantor [name] for and in consideration of [consideration] conveys and warrants to [grantee] the following described real estate [description], situated in the county of _______, in the State of Illinois.
>
> Dated _______, 19__.
>
> [signature of grantor]

Concerning the significance of the word "warrants," see Chapter 26, Section 2, at pages 1305–1308 and 1315–1318 infra.

---

4. Typically, the consideration in a deed is recited as being "one dollar ($1.00) and other good and valuable consideration." Does this mean that the courts presume that only $1.00 was in fact paid? In Walliker v. Escott, 608 P.2d 1272 (Wyo. 1980), the court noted: "We do not think it can be seriously argued that a recitation of a consideration of One Dollar in a deed demonstrates that the consideration underlying the deed was in fact One Dollar and was, therefore, insufficient consideration to support the contract." Is a deed a contract in any case? Why do parties continue to recite a nominal as opposed to the true consideration?

FIRST NATIONAL BANK OF OREGON v. TOWNSEND

Court of Appeals of Oregon, 1976.
27 Or.App. 103, 555 P.2d 477.

TANZER, JUDGE. This is an appeal by the State of Oregon, asserting the interests of the grantor, from a declaratory judgment decree construing a deed as creating a fee simple title in the grantee.

The matter was tried upon stipulated facts. The grantee died on May 14, 1974. The following witnessed and notarized deed was thereafter discovered among his personal effects and was recorded by plaintiff, the decedent's personal representative, in the Jackson County Deed Records on September 11, 1974.

"WARRANTY TIMBER AND MINERAL DEED

"This indenture made and entered into this the first day of February, 1955 between John Townsend, the party to the first part, and Claude J. Miller and [sic: name obliterated], Parties of the second part.

"WITNESSETH

"The said party to the first part, for and in consideration of Two Hundred and No/100 Dollars, to him in hand paid on all Trees and Minerals removed from his property.

"Does hereby grant and convey unto the said parties of the second part, their heirs and assigns, the said tract of land in Jackson County, Oregon. Described as follows to wit:

"The South West Quarter of the North East Quarter of Section 35 Township 40, Range 2, East the Willamette Meridian

"The right to enter upon said land, cut and remove trees, mine and remove minerals, and make such alteration on said property as may be required in the removal of said trees of [sic: or] the mining of said ores or minerals. Said party of the first covenanting not to enter on said lands during said term in any manner which would prevent the relogging removal of trees or ores and minerals of commercial value of the second parties.

"All back taxes and taxes hereafter levied on said land will be paid by the parties of the second part, their heirs or assigns.

"And the above described lands and property in quiet, peaceable, and exclusive possession of the said parties of the second part, their heirs or assigns against all persons lawfully claiming or to claim the whole or any part thereof, the said party of the first part will warrant and defend.

"In witness whereof I have hereunto set my hand and seal the day, and year first above written.

"/s/ John Townsend"

The sole issue is the legal effect to be given this deed. If the instrument made a conveyance of fee title, the land therein described is included in the grantee's estate. If, however, the instrument conveyed only a limited right to remove timber and minerals from the land, then the grantor retained the underlying fee. The grantor is deceased and has no known heirs. Thus any interest retained by him is subject to escheat to the State of Oregon.

In support of its contention that the deed conveyed only timber and mineral rights, the state points to the title of the instrument. The language "timber and mineral deed" is, it contends, an express limitation on the otherwise all-inclusive word "warranty." The state also relies on the recital of consideration. That the grantor acknowledges, in this clause, receipt of payment for trees and minerals removed from "his" land indicates, it is urged, an intent by the parties that the grantor retain title. Moreover, it is argued, if a fee were to be conveyed, there would have been no mention of trees and minerals, the rights to which are implicitly included in a fee simple. Similarly, if the parties contemplated the transfer of a fee, there would have been no reason to include in the instrument express provisions that the grantee would have the right to enter upon the land or that the grantor would not enter on the land in a manner which would interfere with grantee's operation. Finally the state points out that the parties referred to a "term" in the instrument. Such a reference is inconsistent with the grant of an unlimited estate.

The grantee's representative bases its claim that the deed conveys a fee simple on the unequivocal language of the granting clause which purports to convey "the said tract of land" to the grantee and "their heirs and assigns." Reliance is also placed upon the clause requiring the grantee "and their heirs and assigns" to pay all "taxes hereafter levied" without time limitation and upon the final clause which purports to warrant "quiet, peaceable, and exclusive possession" to the grantee.

When, as here, a deed is patently ambiguous, the court must first attempt to determine the intent of the parties from the language of the deed itself, taken as a whole, and from the surrounding circumstances. Wirostek v. Johnson, 266 Or. 72, 511 P.2d 373 (1973), Doyle v. Gilbert, 255 Or. 563, 469 P.2d 624 (1970). Palmateer et al. v. Reid, 121 Or. 179, 254 P. 359 (1927). However, this record is devoid of any extrinsic evidence which might shed light on the parties' intent, and the language of the deed itself is so contradictory, and the inferences for either construction equally strong, that we cannot reasonably discern from it what legal effect its maker contemplated. Reference to established rules of construction is appropriate in such a situation.

When there is doubt as to whether the parties intended that a deed transfer a fee simple or a lesser interest in land, that doubt should be resolved in favor of the grantee and the greater estate should pass. Palmateer et al. v. Reid, supra. Stated differently, "all doubts are resolved against restrictions on the use of property by the grantee . . . ." Gange et ux. v. Hayes et al., 193 Or. 51, 61, 237 P.2d 196, 200 (1951). The apparent intent of the rule is to avoid undue fragmentation of ownership and to deter quiet title suits.

There is also authority for the more technical proposition that if the intent of the parties cannot be discerned from the deed and there is, as here, an irreconcilable conflict between the granting clause and other parts of the deed, the estate conveyed in the granting clause will prevail. Palmateer et al. v. Reid, supra, 121 Or. at 185, 254 P. 359.

Both of these constructional preferences support a conclusion that the deed conveyed title in fee simple.

There is yet another principle of construction: that escheat is not favored by the law. It has been held that doubt as to whether property is subject to escheat should be resolved against the state. See 7 Powell, Real Property ¶ 988, at 621 (1975). This tenet has its typical application in escheat proceedings when it is uncertain whether the intestate died without heirs. Since the issue here is resolved through other rules of construction, we note the rule regarding escheat, but need not consider whether it is controlling in this type of proceeding.

Affirmed.

NOTES

1. The deed in the principal case was obviously poorly drafted and does not follow the statutory form. Unfortunately, this is a common occurrence and litigation frequently results. Note, however, the canon of construction which resolves all doubts in favor of the grantee. Read the next case before you give too much credence to the other canon that the granting clause prevails in case of a conflict among the parts of the deed.

Frequently a court will uphold a deed which, at first glance, appears to be some other form of legal document. See, e.g., Hinchcliffe v. Fischer, 198 Kan. 365, 424 P.2d 581 (1967), where the court held an instrument entitled "Private Annuity Contract" to be, in fact, a deed of land with a duty to pay an annuity to the grantor for her natural life.

2. The grantor's attorney usually prepares the deed, but the results of poor drafting may be felt primarily by the grantee. Is the grantor's attorney liable to the grantee for damages caused by negligent drafting? See Collins v. Binkley, 750 S.W.2d 737 (Tenn.1988), holding the attorney liable despite the lack of an attorney-client relationship between him and grantee.

GRAYSON v. HOLLOWAY

Supreme Court of Tennessee, 1958.
203 Tenn. 464, 313 S.W.2d 555.

NEIL, CHIEF JUSTICE. This appeal involves the proper construction of a deed duly executed by A.J. Holloway and wife "Manervy" Holloway to G.P. Holloway, purporting to convey to him a certain tract of land (70) acres more or less), the consideration being "the said G.P. Holloway is to take care of the said A.J Holloway and Manervy Holloway as long as they live and at their death to pay all funeral and burial expenses, and said deed is to become a warranty deed." The foregoing is the "granting clause in the deed".

The "habendum" clause is "To have and to hold the same to the said G.P. Holloway and wife Mae Holloway and their heirs and assigns forever".

The complainants filed their original bill in the Chancery Court against Mae Holloway charging that they are the lawful heirs of A.J. Holloway,[5] now deceased, and that the defendant, Mae Holloway, is the widow of G.P. Holloway; that under the aforesaid deed they own the fee simple title to the land in question subject to homestead and dower of the defendant. The prayer of the bill is that the lands be sold for partition.

The defendant, Mae Holloway, filed an answer and cross-bill in which she denied that she is entitled to only "homestead and dower", as charged in the original bill. She insists in her answer that the deed in question conveyed an estate by the entireties and that she, having survived her said husband, is the owner of a fee simple title to the land. She therefore denies "that the complainants have a right to have the property sold in lieu of partition."

The cross–bill charges that she paid the purchase price of $700 and that, under the terms of the deed, the grantors intended to convey an estate by the entireties. She charges that A.J. Holloway and wife, Minerva, were advanced in years and that prior to the execution of the deed they discussed with defendant and her deceased husband their personal needs and it was agreed that cross-complainant and her husband "would move onto the farm" and care for the old people; that the draftsman of the deed was instructed by A.J. Holloway and wife, Minerva, to make the deed to cross-complainant and her husband "so that upon the death of either the title would vest in the survivor." The cross-bill charges that she, Mae Holloway, "cared for them when they were sick, cooked their meals and spent much time and made many sacrifices in their care and providing for their comfort."

The complainants demurred to the cross-bill (1) on the ground of laches, and (2) because "the cross-bill shows on its face that it is a plenary suit seeking construction of a written instrument based upon extrinsic facts which can be made to appear only through evidence of conversations, agreements" etc. rather than from words and language found within the four corners of the same, and that the cause of action

5. How could the complainants, heirs of A.J. Holloway, have any possible interest, regardless of the estate of Mae Holloway, since A.J. Holloway had clearly conveyed away his interest in the land? Correspondence with one of the attorneys in the case explains the puzzle. "This came about by an inadvertent statement in the opinion of the Supreme Court whereby complainants were designated as the heirs of A.J. Holloway, the grantor in the deed before the Court making absolute conveyance to G.P. Holloway. The original bill filed in Chancery Court identified and described complainants as follows: 'The said G.P. Holloway, Jr., did not have any children and complainants, as surviving children of his deceased sisters constitute his next of kin and heirs at law and as such are the owners of the same as tenants in common, subject to the aforesaid rights of defendant and are owners of respective shares and interests as hereinafter set out. . . . ' " [We are indebted to Professor James E. Starrs of the George Washington University for the inquiry which resulted in this letter of explanation.]

accrued more than ten years before the bill in this cause was filed; (3) because the cross-bill shows on its face that it is in fact a suit for reformation of a deed rather than a suit for construction.

The answer to the cross-bill denies that Mae Holloway and her deceased husband were entitled to any relief based upon any alleged service to A.J. Holloway and wife, Minerva.

The Chancellor held that the habendum clause in the deed is repugnant to the granting clause; that the granting clause conveys in fee the property to G.P. Holloway. "The habendum on the other hand limits it to a tenancy by the entirety by including the name of his wife, Mae Holloway.

"' . . . the granting clause creating a fee simple estate will prevail over the subsequent habendum clause granting a less estate.'" Citing Teague v. Sowder, 121 Tenn. 132, 114 S.W. 484; Simpson v. Simpson, 160 Tenn. 645, 28 S.W.2d 349; and Hicks v. Sprankle, 149 Tenn. 310, 257 S.W. 1044.

The Chancellor further held: "The second ground of the demurrer ' . . . that the cause of action accrued more than ten years before the bill in this case was filed' has been many times sustained by the Supreme Court in cases of this type." The demurrer to the cross-bill was sustained. "The original bill and answer thereto is remanded to the rules for proof."

The assignment of error is, as follows:

"The Court erred in sustaining the demurrer and dismissing the cross bill for the following reasons:

"A. It was error not to consider the whole instrument in its construction and in limiting the finding to the determination that the granting clause and habendum clause were in conflict and the granting clause was controlling, thus failing to apply the modern rules of construction making it the duty of courts to ascertain the intention of the makers of the deed and give effect to all its provisions regardless of the technical parts of the instrument.

"B. It was error not to find and decree that the deed when construed as a whole, giving effect to all its provisions, created a tenancy by the entireties in Green P. Holloway and wife, Mae Holloway."

The pleadings presented two aspects for consideration by the Chancellor. But the appellees, complainants below, say that the only issue is as to the correctness of his decision in holding that the deed in question vested the fee simple title in G.P. Holloway.

The learned Chancellor decided the case based upon the supposed irreconcilable conflict between the granting clause and the habendum clause. No consideration was given to the issue as to the *intention of the grantors,* based upon the recitals in the deed and "extrinsic facts". He thus states the problem before him: "A construction in its strict sense and in the only sense open to the court, in view of the 10 year statute, would be upon the instrument itself devoid of extrinsic facts."

We find no merit in the contention that the cross-complainant should be repelled on account of "laches". She had the right to rely on her title; nor can the statute of 10 years be invoked to bar her right to a proper construction of the deed considered in all its parts and aspects. The contention that the cross-bill by the defendant, Mae Holloway, is for a reformation of the deed is a conclusion and is without merit.

We readily agree with the Chancellor that under the common law the vendee, G.P. Holloway, acquired a fee simple title to the land conveyed. The case of Teague v. Sowder, 121 Tenn. 132, 114 S.W. 484, seems to sustain the contention of the complainants in the court below where the common-law rule was applied to the effect that the "granting clause prevails over habendum, if they are irreconcilable by the context failing to show grantor's intention." But in the same case it is held:

"The rule of construction of a deed, when it is sought to determine what estate was conveyed thereby, is to ascertain the intention of the grantor, if possible, by giving to every word of the deed its appropriate meaning, and to enforce that intention regardless of the mere formal divisions of the instrument."

In Higginson v. Smith, 38 Tenn.App. 223, 272 S.W.2d 348, 349, the Court of Appeals speaking through Judge Felts held, as follows:

"The technical rules of the common law as to the division of deeds into formal parts have long since been disregarded in this state, and the rule now is that all parts shall be examined as to ascertain the intention. Lockett v. Thomas, 179 Tenn. 240, 243, 165 S.W.2d 375; Archer v. Culbertson, 28 Tenn.App. 52, 185 S.W.2d 912; McCord v. Ransom, 185 Tenn. 677, 207 S.W.2d 581; Hall v. Crocker, 192 Tenn. 506, 241 S.W.2d 548."

The facts as they appear in the foregoing decision by the Court of Appeals are similar in all respects to the case at bar, except that in the former "the consideration was paid by Dudley Smith", the vendee, while in the case at bar the principal consideration was the obligation of the grantees to care for his father and mother and pay the cost of their "funeral and burial" expenses.

In the Higginson case, supra, the Chancellor construed the deed *in its entirety* and held that the *intention of the grantors* was to convey a fee simple estate to Dudley Smith, and not an estate by the entirety.

We think it was the duty of the Chancellor to construe the deed in question by giving effect to *all its parts* and thus determine the true intention of the grantors therein.

When the granting clause, and the habendum clause, are construed in determining the true intention of the grantors as to the quantum of the estate conveyed we think and so hold, that the deed vested in G.P. Holloway and Mae Holloway an estate by the entireties for the following reasons. The deed shows on its face that these old people (grantors) contemplated that *both of the grantees* would render personal services. It would be most unusual for them to contemplate a situation where their son alone could attend to all their needs without the active assistance of his wife, Mae Holloway. She, of necessity, was the one who was the main dependence to see that these old people had enough food properly cooked, clean clothing and bedding. It certainly was not contemplated that the son, G.P. Holloway, would do any washing and ironing, cooking and serving meals, making up beds or perform other household duties which usually devolve upon the wife. In other words this, in our opinion, was a joint undertaking by the grantees.

With further reference to the cross-bill and the demurrer thereto, if the cross-bill were a suit to *reform the deed* so as to conform to the intention of the parties then the 10–year statute of limitations (section 28–310, T.C.A.) would apply. Lee v. Harris, 188 Tenn. 373, 219 S.W.2d 892; Henderson v. Henderson, 158 Tenn. 452, 14 S.W.2d 714. But we do not construe the cross-bill as an action to reform the deed, and for this reason we hold that the Chancellor was in error in holding that the cross-bill was barred by the 10–year statute of limitations. Compare Alsobrook v. Orr, 130 Tenn. 120, 169 S.W. 1165, and cases cited therein, and Clarke v. Walker, 25 Tenn.App. 78, 150 S.W.2d 1082.

The assignment of error is sustained, and the cause remanded to the Chancery Court for further proceedings consistent with this opinion.

WOMACK v. STEGNER

Court of Civil Appeals of Texas, 1956.
293 S.W.2d 124.

HAMILTON, CHIEF JUSTICE. This was a suit in trespass to try title, filed by appellant D.R. Womack against the appellee, Harold Stegner, involving an undivided interest in the minerals in a tract of land in Reeves County. The case came on for trial before a jury. At the close of plaintiff's case the appellee moved for an instructed verdict which motion was sustained by the court, resulting in a "take nothing" judgment against appellant.

The plaintiff claimed title to the premises involved in a deed executed and delivered to him by his brother, W.B. Womack, dated and acknowledged on December 17, 1951, and alleged to have been delivered to plaintiff in February 1952, complete in every respect except that the name of the grantee was not filled in. W.B. Womack died testate on November 30, 1952, and his will was duly probated and would have passed title to the property in the suit to his wife, Louise S. Womack, but for the deed previously executed to plaintiff. Prior to the filing of this suit Louise S. Womack died testate, leaving her property, insofar as material to this case, to her brother, Harold Stegner, the defendant in this suit.

Testimony was offered by D.R. Womack, appellant, that at the time of delivery of said deed by W.B. Womack to D.R. Womack, W.B. Womack authorized D.R. Womack to fill his name or any name he desired in the blank as grantee. The testimony further showed that there was no consideration for said deed, that it was a gift.

All of appellant's points of error complain of the court granting an instructed verdict when, as contended by appellant, he had made out a prima facie case showing title to said minerals to be in him.

It is our opinion that the court was in error in granting the instructed verdict. It appears to be well settled in Texas that when a deed with the name of the grantee in blank is delivered by the grantor with the intention that the title shall vest in the person to whom the deed is delivered, and that person is expressly authorized at the time of delivery to insert his own or any other name as grantee, title passes with the delivery. . . .

In Threadgill v. Butler, supra, the court said that the effect of such a transaction is to vest an irrevocable power coupled with an interest in the person to whom the deed is delivered. It appears that where there is failure to fill in the blank, the instrument coupled with the power, that is, the authority, to fill in the blank, is sufficient to vest equitable title in a person to whom the deed is delivered. Schleicher v. Runge, supra.

It is contended by appellee that since the grantor W.B. Womack, died before the grantee, D.R. Womack, exercised his authority by filling in the blank that the authority given D.R. Womack ended with the death of the grantor, as is the case with an ordinary power of attorney. We cannot agree with appellee's contention, because if the authority given by the grantor to fill in the blank is an irrevocable power, coupled with an interest, it does not terminate with the death of the grantor. The equitable title passed at the time of the delivery of the deed, and the subsequent death of W.B. Womack before the authority was exercised is immaterial.

Appellee also contends that since there was no consideration for the deed no equitable title passed at the time of the delivery of the instrument and the oral authority given to fill in the name of the grantee was not an irrevocable power coupled with an interest. We cannot follow the reasoning of appellee on such contention because a deed does not have to be supported by a consideration to be a valid deed. We see no reason why there could not be an irrevocable power, coupled with an interest, vested in the person to whom a deed of gift is delivered just the same as when the deed is supported by a consideration. We find that none of the decisions which support our position herein were based on the fact that a consideration was paid for the deed involved—in fact in the case of Dallas Joint Stock Land Bank v. Burck, Tex.Civ.App., 102 S.W.2d 1074 it does not appear there was any consideration passing from the recipient of the deed to the grantor. However, the court did not discuss in its opinion the matter of consideration or the lack thereof.

Believing that the appellant made out a prima facie case, the court was in error in instructing a verdict for the appellee, and we reverse and remand the case for a new trial.

NOTE

For a comment criticizing the principal case see 35 Tex.L.Rev. 435 (1957). The cases abound with statements like this one from Hedding v. Schauble, 146 Minn. 95, 97 177 N.W. 1019, 1020 (1920): "The deed was a nullity until the name of a grantee was lawfully inserted therein." In the light of Womack v. Stegner what does such a statement mean?

WILLARD v. FIRST CHURCH OF CHRIST, SCIENTIST, PACIFICA

Supreme Court of California, In Bank, 1972.
7 Cal.3d 473, 102 Cal.Rptr. 739, 498 P.2d 987.
[printed at page 586, supra.]

NOTES

1. Some states still follow the common law rule that a grantor cannot reserve a title in a stranger to the grant. See, e.g., Leidig v. Hoopes, 288 P.2d 402 (Okl.1955) where the court said: "A reservation in a deed does not create title or enlarge the vested rights of a grantor; it merely reserves the specific interest named therein from the operation of the grant, and leaves that interest vested in the grantor to whom it belonged at and before the execution of the deed . . .." In order to remove all doubt and avert the possibility of litigation, how should a transaction like that in the principal case be handled?

2. In Hummelman v. Mounts, 87 Ind. 178, 179 (1882) a deed read "I, Jacob Smith, of Washington County, warrant and defend unto Christena Smith . . . the following real estate." The court held that the deed was void. "While it is true that, if in any part of the instrument apt words of conveyance are used, the instrument will be treated as a deed, it is also true that if no such words can be found in any part it will be deemed utterly devoid of force. . . . The rule that courts will so construe an instrument as to make it effective does not mean that courts shall inject into it new and distinct provisions. The instrument before us contains no words of conveyance, and we have no authority to put any into it."

3. The following deed was written in verse and is actually recorded on page 215 of Volume No. 40, Cass County, Illinois, deed records.

I, J. Henry Shaw, the grantor, herein
Who lives at Beardstown the county within,
For seven hundred dollars to me paid today
By Charles E. Wyman do sell and convey
Lot two (2) in Block forty (40), said county and town,
Where Illinois River flows placidly down,
And warrant the title forever and aye,
Waiving homestead and mansion to both a goodbye,

And pledging this deed is valid in law
  I add here my signature, J. Henry Shaw
(Seal) Dated July 25, 1881

The justice of peace may have been in a poetic mood the day when he certified the acknowledgment, but it is more likely that the latter was also written by Shaw as follows:

I, Sylvester Emmons, who lives at Beardstown,
  A Justice of Peace of fame and renown,
Of the county of Cass in Illinois state,
  Do certify here that on the same date
One J. Henry Shaw to me did make known
  That the deed above and name were his own,
And he stated he sealed and delivered the same
  Voluntarily, freely, and never would claim
His homestead therein, but left all alone,
  Turned his face to the street and his back to his home.
(Seal) S. Emmons, J.P.
Dated August 1, 1881

Is this a valid deed? If you wished to contend that it was invalid what arguments could you make to support your position?

SECTION 3. EXECUTION OF THE DEED

"Don't worry, the deal is all signed, sealed, and delivered!" How many times have you heard that phrase? Like many another old expression (e.g., possession is nine points of the law) it contains a great deal of truth but not the whole truth. The execution of a deed comprises all the acts necessary to make the instrument effective as a conveyance of land. Hence, the term includes those essentials which were discussed in the preceding section. However, most of those matters are usually thought of as a part of the drafting of deeds, and in common parlance execution covers signing, sealing, attesting, acknowledging, delivering, and accepting the deed. The first four of these are sometimes referred to as the formalities of execution and, except for signing, the necessity for and effect of these acts varies from state to state.

At one time a seal was necessary, but not a signature. Today, however, the signature of the grantor, or of someone acting in his behalf in a manner authorized by the local law, is required. The place of the signature is not important unless a statute requires that the instrument be "subscribed." The signature of the grantee is not required and usually does not appear.

At common law the seal was the very essence of the deed, and its omission was fatal to the conveyance, at least in a court of law. The seal retained its significance in American law and was even highly praised by some courts: "This venerable custom of sealing is a relic of ancient wisdom and is not without its real use at this day. There is yet some degree of solemnity in this form of conveyance. A seal attracts attention and excites caution in illiterate persons, and thereby operates as a security against fraud." Jackson ex dem. Gouch v. Wood, 12 Johns. (N.Y.) 73, 76 (1815). Gradually, however, the importance of the seal declined and it appeared solely as the mystical letters (L.S.) or the word (Seal) following the grantor's signature. Moreover, courts of equity held that an unsealed deed passed at least equitable title, and by proper legal proceedings the defect could be corrected. Most states have now abolished the private seal, and there is no distinction between sealed and unsealed instruments. Nonetheless, many of the forms which you will use continue to bear the printed (Seal).

Attestation refers to the practice of having witnesses sign the deed as a means of assuring its authenticity. The common law does not require attestation; this aspect of execution is entirely statutory. Many states have no such requirement; others treat it only as a prerequisite to recording; and still others make it essential to the transfer of legal title. You should consult the statutes in your own jurisdiction, as well as the cases construing the legal effect of attestation.

Acknowledgment is also a creature of local statutory law, and its importance and legal effect vary from jurisdiction to jurisdiction. It really amounts to attestation by a public officer, usually a notary public or a justice of the peace, but it is supposed to be more formal in character than ordinary attestation. Some statutes require that certain instruments be acknowledged; e.g., tax deeds, homestead deeds, deeds from husband to wife, deeds of married women, and sheriff's deeds. Usually, however, the acknowledgment is not considered part of the deed, and title passes between the parties even if the acknowledgment is defective or omitted entirely. It may be required as a prerequisite to recording or as a condition to use of a deed in evidence without further proof of execution.

ACKNOWLEDGMENT FORM[6]

State of ____________ }
County of ____________ }

Be it remembered that on this ______ day of ______ 19__, before me,the undersigned [*official title*], personally came ______, who is personally known to me to be the same person who executed the foregoing instrument of writing, and, as such person, duly acknowledged the execution of the same.

6. Absence of acknowledgment to a deed or instrument of conveyance does not affect its validity or render it void as between parties. Deeds are required to be acknowledged only for recordation and to protect the grantee against subsequent purchasers in good faith and without notice. New Mexico Properties, Inc. v. Lennox Industries, Inc., 95 N.M. 64, 618 P.2d 1228 (1980).

In witness whereof I have hereunto set my hand and affixed my official seal at ______, on the day and year last above written.

[*Signature and title of officer.*]

The foregoing aspects of execution are usually "cut and dried"; at most they raise simple questions of statutory construction. On the other hand, the remaining items—delivery and acceptance—can raise complicated issues. Since both delivery and acceptance create problems in gratuitous transfers also, we have chosen to give the detailed treatment in Part Two of the book. At this point you should refresh your recollection of the materials covered in pages 166 to 207. Our principal emphasis here will be on the escrow device and the delivery problems related to it, since escrow is used so frequently in commercial transactions.

CRIBBET AND JOHNSON, PRINCIPLES OF THE LAW OF PROPERTY*

Pages 213–215, 225–227 (3d ed. 1989).

THE ESCROW AGREEMENT

The sale of real property can be conducted without the use of an escrow agreement. In rural areas and in smaller communities it is not usually involved because the parties know and trust each other and the title questions tend to be less complex. In big metropolitan centers it is much more likely to be a part of the transaction and frequently is as common as the contract and the deed. Also, an understanding of escrow will throw considerable light on the always troublesome issue of delivery. . . .

For at least five centuries, the escrow has served as a convenient mechanism for closing real estate transactions. The use of this familiar device involves the deposit of a deed or other document with a third party to be held by the latter pending performance of certain conditions. When those conditions have been performed, the third party is authorized to deliver the deed or other document to the person then entitled thereto.

Perhaps the simplest illustration of such an escrow transaction is the deposit by the vendor of his deed with a third party to be delivered over to the purchaser upon payment of the purchase price. Thus a nonresident vendor of an Illinois farm may forward his deed to an Illinois bank or trust company in the city where the purchaser resides with instructions to deliver the deed to the purchaser if and when the purchase money has been duly deposited for the vendor's account. In this way the vendor can guard against delivery of the deed without concurrent receipt of the purchase price. Or a vendee who has entered into a contract for the purchase of a home where the purchase price is to be paid in monthly installments over a period of years may insist

* The author's footnotes have been omitted.

that the vendor deposit his deed with a bank or trust company to be delivered if and when the purchase price has eventually been paid in full. The deed will thus be available for delivery when the last installment is paid some years later, even though the vendor may have died in the interim.

Generally this basic type of escrow transaction between vendor and purchaser, sometimes referred to as a "Deed and Money Escrow," involves conditions relating to title. Thus it may be provided that the third party is to deliver the deed to the purchaser and turn over the purchase money to the vendor only if and when the abstract of title has been examined and approved by the purchaser's attorney. In Cook County, where the great volume of instruments continuously passing through the recorder's office makes it impossible to check the status of a title as of any current date, the third party is frequently authorized to record the vendor's deed as soon as the purchase money has been deposited by the purchaser and before any investigation has been made with respect to title. In addition to the purchase money, the purchaser also deposits with the third party a quitclaim deed back to the vendor. After the vendor's deed has been recorded, a title examination is made up to and including the recording of that deed, and if the title is ready to be guaranteed in the purchaser or is otherwise approved, the third party disburses the purchase money to the vendor and returns the quitclaim deed to the purchaser. If the title cannot be guaranteed or is not found good in the purchaser, the third party records the latter's quitclaim deed in order to put the vendor back in status quo and returns the purchase money to the purchaser.

There may, of course, be many variations in the form of a "Deed and Money Escrow," depending upon the facts of the particular case. For example, the third party is frequently authorized to use a part of the purchase money in discharging liens and encumbrances on the property so that the purchaser will receive an unencumbered title, as agreed.

Another common type of escrow transaction is that known as a "Money Lender's Escrow." In general this involves deposit of the proceeds of a mortgage loan with a third party to be disbursed as directed when satisfactory evidence has been furnished showing the mortgage to be a valid first lien. This type of escrow transaction not only provides the mortgagee with a convenient method of protecting its interests, but it may also be used to advantage by an owner who has made a mortgage loan for the purpose of refunding an existing mortgage or of paying accumulated taxes and special assessments, judgments, mechanic's liens, or other encumbrances on the property. . . .

The foregoing illustrate only a few of the varied forms which escrow transactions may assume. In essence, however, they involve as their basic framework the deposit of deeds and other documents with a third party to be delivered upon the performance of specified conditions.

It is well settled, of course, that the use of escrows is not restricted to real estate transactions. Instruments other than deeds for the conveyance of real estate may legally be deposited as escrows. Indeed, the Illinois Supreme Court has said that "the term 'escrow,' though usually applied to deeds, is equally applicable to all written instruments." . . .

WHEN DEED TAKES EFFECT

Where a sale of real estate between vendor and purchaser is to be closed by means of an escrow, with final delivery of the deed by the escrowee dependent upon the performance of some uncertain future condition, the general rule is that the escrow will have no effect as a conveyance, and no estate will pass until the event has happened and the second delivery has been made, or at least until the grantee has become absolutely entitled to such a delivery.

This general rule is, however, subject to the important qualification that where the condition has been fully performed, and the deed delivered by the escrowee, it will under certain circumstances be treated as relating back to and taking effect at the time of its original deposit as an escrow. Thus the Illinois Supreme Court has said that "the instrument will be treated as relating back to and taking effect at the time of its original deposit in escrow, where a resort to this fiction is necessary to give the deed effect to prevent injustice, or to effectuate the intention of the parties."

INSTANCES OF RELATION BACK

The operation of this doctrine of "relation back" can be illustrated best by reference to certain concrete situations.

Death of grantor. Where the grantor dies before the condition is performed, his death would, if the doctrine of "relation back" were not employed, operate as a revocation of the escrowee's authority to make a valid delivery to the grantee upon subsequent performance. Accordingly in such a case, the rule is universal that the transaction will be effectuated by holding the conveyance operative as of the time when the deed was originally deposited as an escrow, and the grantee's title will for such purpose relate back to that date.

Dower of grantor's widow. Likewise, where the grantor dies before the condition is performed, the doctrine of "relation back" has been applied to protect the grantee against a claim of dower by the grantor's widow where such a claim could not have been properly asserted had the grantor's deed been unconditionally delivered at the time it was deposited as an escrow.

Incompetency of grantor. The doctrine of "relation back" is also applied to effectuate the escrow transaction where the grantor becomes incompetent before the condition has been performed.

Death of grantee. Where the grantee dies after the deed has been deposited as an escrow but before the condition has been performed, the doctrine of "relation back" will be applied to sustain the transaction, and the deed may, after the condition has been performed, be delivered by the escrowee to the grantee's heirs.

Conveyance by grantor to a third party. Where the grantor has deposited his deed as an escrow but thereafter, pending performance of the condition, he conveys to a third-party purchaser with notice, it has been held that the doctrine of "relation back" will be applied to protect the title of the grantee under the deed previously deposited as an escrow. However, it appears that the doctrine will not be so applied where the third party to whom the grantor conveys is a bona fide purchaser for value without notice of the escrow.

. . .

"Relation back" for one purpose and not others. The fact that the doctrine of "relation back" is applied for one purpose does not necessarily mean that it must be applied for all other purposes in the same transaction.

The fiction of "relation back" would seem to afford an apt illustration of the flexibility of the common law in adapting itself to practical situations. The escrow has long been a convenient mechanism which serves a useful and practical end. The doctrine of "relation back" is the method by which the common law has exempted that particular transaction from certain general rules governing delivery of instruments so that parties may avail themselves of the escrow as a useful, workable device.

NOTES

1. Although the foregoing analysis of when a deed in escrow takes effect and the various instances of relation back are frequently used by the courts to rationalize the cases, this is not the only way of looking at the problem. Note that in Val Verde Hotel Co. v. Ross (cited on page 1175 infra) a court pointed out that no second delivery is required where all of the conditions of an escrow have been met. This suggests that there is actually no need for a second delivery and that its only significance is to give the grantee tangible evidence of title. Some writers have suggested that there can be only one legal delivery, that into escrow. However, the conditions must be met before the title passes. If there is no compliance with the conditions, then the effect of the delivery into escrow dissipates and no title has passed. See Bogert, Trusts and Escrows in Credit Conveyancing, 21 Ill.L.Rev. 655 (1927). The result would probably be the same under either analysis. Which view is better in clarifying your own thinking about this useful legal tool?

2. The prevailing view is that there cannot be a valid conditional delivery, or delivery in escrow, directly to the grantee. In State, By Pai v. Thom, 58 Hawaii 8, 563 P.2d 982 (1977), grantors delivered their deed to grantee but later denied its effectiveness and sought rescission, claiming that "the alleged delivery of said deed was merely a conditional delivery subject to [grantors] receiving payment of the purchase price by the Due Date in accordance with" the terms of the land contract. The court held that grantee's failure to pay the consideration was not a ground for rescission because such a result "would render real estate titles dangerously uncertain." The court said, "[A] delivery in escrow

may be made only to a third person not a party to the transaction, and there can be no such delivery to the grantee on a condition not expressed in the instrument. Accordingly, while there is some authority to the contrary, it is generally held that the delivery to the grantee of a deed absolute on its face will pass complete title to him regardless of any condition or contingency on which its operative effect is made to depend."

For a particularly fascinating case to the contrary, see Chillemi v. Chillemi, 197 Md. 257, 78 A.2d 750 (1951). H, going overseas on military duty, delivered a deed directly to W, subject to two oral conditions: (1) W was not to record unless H was killed and (2) if H came back the deed was to be returned to him and destroyed. One month after H's return and following major marital discord (described in detail in the case), W recorded the deed, thus showing title in her. [The facts have been simplified since a tenancy by the entirety was involved but this does not affect the result.] The court recognized the oral conditions and annulled the deed. Said the court: "[t]here is actually no logical reason why a deed should not be held in escrow by the grantee as well as by any other person. The ancient rule is not adapted to present-day conditions and is entirely unnecessary for the protection of the rights of litigants. After all, conditional delivery is purely a question of intention, and it is immaterial whether the instrument, pending satisfaction of the condition, is in the hands of the grantor, the grantee, or a third person." Clearly, the court's sympathies were with H but is it true that there is no logical reason for the "ancient" rule? What are some of the problems with allowing conditional delivery to the grantee? If W, after recording, had conveyed to a b.f.p. would the latter prevail over H?

In ITT Industrial Credit Company v. R.T.M. Development Co., Inc., 512 N.E.2d 201 (Ind.App.1987), sellers signed a warranty deed, wrote the words "Not valid until receipt of full payment" across the top, and gave it to buyer's agent with instructions not to release it to buyer until the full purchase price was received at the closing. Thereafter, the closing was held without notice to sellers, and the agent surrendered the deed even though buyer made only a partial payment and signed a promissory note for the balance. The court held that the deed was ineffective to convey any interest to the buyer.

3. The cases generally support the proposition that a valid commercial escrow must be based on an enforceable contract of sale, i.e., the deed must be placed beyond the control of the vendor by a contract capable of being specifically enforced in equity. If the contract fails because it violates the Statute of Frauds, for example, the vendor can repudiate the contract and successfully demand the return of the deed from the escrowee, prior to the time when the escrowee actually delivers the deed to the grantee. See Jozefowicz v. Leickem, 174 Wis. 475, 182 N.W. 729 (1921).

4. Granting that an enforceable contract is required as the basis of a commercial escrow, can the deed itself serve as a memorandum of the transaction? "The weight of authority holds an undelivered deed is

not a sufficient memorandum in writing of the contract to answer the requirements of the statute of frauds. Other authorities hold an undelivered deed will satisfy the requirements . . . where such deed embodies the substance of the parol contract, giving the parties, consideration, description, and terms of sale, and a few authorities hold an undelivered deed itself is a sufficient memorandum in writing." Main v. Pratt, 276 Ill. 218, 225, 114 N.E. 576, 578 (1916).

If the contract of sale is in writing the escrow agreement may be verbal although it is obviously better practice to have both documents in writing. In the absence of a written contract, the escrow agreement can satisfy the statute of frauds if the written instructions meet the usual requirements. See Wood Building Corp. v. Griffitts, 164 Cal.App. 2d 559, 330 P.2d 847 (1958).

5. "The theory that a specifically enforceable contract is necessary has been criticized Tiffany, Conditional Delivery of Deeds, 14 Col. L.Rev. 389, 399 (1914); Aigler, Is a Contract Necessary to Create an Effective Escrow? 16 Mich.L.Rev. 569 (1918). Professor Aigler points out that in many of the cases purporting to follow the rule that an underlying contract is necessary for a valid escrow, the facts show that the grantor did not deliver his deed with the intention that it should be considered as immediately operative. In other words, the deed was not in fact delivered. . . . There can be no delivery in escrow, or otherwise, if the deed is transferred with the understanding that it remain subject to the demand of the grantor." Burby, Real Property 445, n. 30 (2d ed. 1954).

6. You should compare the commercial escrow with the gratuitous transaction where the deed is delivered to a third party to hold until the death of the donor. See pages 199 to 207 supra. In that situation no writing other than the deed is required since the first delivery normally places the deed beyond the grantor's control (indeed, if it does not the transaction will be inoperative) and the second delivery is based on a condition certain to occur, to wit the grantor's death. In a sense, therefore, the delivery is not conditional at all and it is a misnomer to call such a gift device an escrow. It is not clear just when title passes in such a case although if necessary to protect the grantor's rights he will be held to have retained a life estate, even if he did not expressly reserve one, and the grantee's claim will be viewed as a future interest, vesting in possession on the donor's death. For an expanded treatment of this point see Mann, Escrows—Their Use and Value, 1949 U.Ill.L.F. 398, 418–422. See also Milligan v. Milligan, 161 Neb. 499, 74 N.W.2d 74 (1955).

CLEVENGER v. MOORE

Supreme Court of Oklahoma, 1927.
126 Okl. 246, 259 P. 219, 54 A.L.R. 1237.

DIFFENDAFFER, C. This is an action brought by the plaintiff for the possession of lot 15, block 10, in the original town of Bartlesville, and for the cancellation of a deed therefor from plaintiff to defendant J.D.

Simmons, and also for cancellation of a deed made by J.D. Simmons to defendant D.F. Moore.

[The evidence for the plaintiff, Mrs. Clevenger, was as follows: In September, 1922, she owned a building in Bartlesville. Peay asked her if she would trade the building for an apartment house in Tulsa, owned by Simmons. At Peay's instigation she executed a deed to Simmons, which was given to Peay to hold pending her inspection of the Tulsa property. If she did not approve the trade the deed was to be returned to her. This was not done, although she did not approve the transaction. In December her tenant vacated the building, and she left Bartlesville for about a month. When she returned she discovered that the deed to Simmons had been recorded and that Simmons had executed a deed to the defendant, Moore. The trial court sustained a demurrer to the plaintiff's evidence and dismissed the action.]

The plaintiff sets up five assignments of error, but presents them here in three propositions:

First. That where a deed is placed in escrow and the same is delivered to the grantee without performance of the conditions for delivery, such deed is absolutely void.

Second. That the first proposition applied to an innocent purchaser. In other words, the deed being obtained without performance of the condition, the same is absolutely void, passes no title, and the said title remains in the grantor. Therefore the grantee has no title which he can pass to an innocent purchaser, and there can be no innocent purchaser thereof.

Third. That in passing upon a demurrer to the evidence, the court must give to the evidence of plaintiff all reasonable inferences, presumptions, and deductions, and must consider all evidence favorable to said defendant as withdrawn, and when so done, if there is any evidence whatsoever, however slight, justifying a recovery in favor of the said plaintiff, the demurrer should be overruled.

We think the evidence clearly shows that the deed to plaintiff's property was placed in escrow and was delivered to defendant Simmons without the fulfillment of the conditions, and without any authority whatever from plaintiff, and in violation of the escrow agreement, which is sufficient to make out a clear case in favor of plaintiff as against the defendant Simmons, and that the only question for us to consider in this case is: First, where a deed is placed in escrow and the same is delivered to the grantee without performance of the conditions for delivery, is such a deed absolutely void? And, second, what are the rights of one claiming to be an innocent purchaser for value of the property from such grantee, where such grantee is in possession of the property without the knowledge or consent of the grantor? The first question, we think, is well settled in this state. In Hunter Realty Co. v. Spencer et al., 21 Okl. 155, 95 P. 757, 17 L.R.A.,N.S., 622, this court in the second syllabus said:

"No title will pass by a deed which is not delivered by the grantor or some one duly authorized by him."

And in the case of Taylor v. Harkins, 74 Okl. 206, 178 P. 117, it was held that a deed does not operate to convey title until delivered, and that, where the possession of a deed placed in escrow is obtained without the performance of the condition upon which delivery thereof was to be made, no title passes therefor.

We think these cases clearly state the rule in cases of this character where the question is between the grantor and grantee.

In the case of Wood v. French, 39 Okl. 685, 136 P. 734, this court said:

"We are of opinion that where the grantor retains the actual possession of the land, as in the present case, although such possession be not notice of his adverse claim (Smith v. Phillips, 9 Okl. 297, 60 P. 117; Flesher v. Callahan, 32 Okl. 283, 122 P. 489), an escrow deed is utterly invalid to transfer any right, in the absence of performance of the condition, so that the wrongful yielding of possession of the deed to the grantee by the person with whom it is deposited transfers no title, even though the claimant thereunder be an innocent purchaser for value."

It will be observed that in that case, the court went so far as to say that where a grantor retains possession of the land, though his possession is not notice of his adverse claim, the escrow deed is utterly invalid to transfer any right, in the absence of performance of the conditions, even though the claimant thereunder be an innocent purchaser for value.

The second proposition of plaintiff's brief is that the deed, being obtained from escrow, without performance of the conditions, is absolutely void, passes no title, and the title remains in the grantor. Therefore the grantee has no title which he can pass to an innocent purchaser, and that there can be no innocent purchaser.

In considering this proposition, it must be borne in mind that this class of cases is to be distinguished from those in which the signature to the deed or consent to its delivery from the escrow holder is obtained by fraud. In the latter class, the rule is everywhere recognized to be that an innocent purchaser from such grantee will be protected, and the distinction seems to be made on the ground that where the instrument is obtained from the escrow in violation of the terms thereof, and without the knowledge or consent of the grantor, it is equivalent to taking the instrument from his possession by theft. While in the other class the grantor consents thereto and has knowledge of such delivery, and where it is a question of whether he or another innocent person must suffer from the fraud, he will be held to suffer the loss rather than the innocent purchaser who takes without knowledge.

It is conceded by defendant that the case of Wood v. French, supra, cited by counsel for plaintiff, at least tends to support plaintiff's claim in this case, but defendant insists that Wood v. French, supra, was based upon the fact that the grantor remained in possession of the land. Defendants' counsel state that, so far as their research has led, in no case has it been held that an innocent purchaser from a record owner of land in possession thereof fails to acquire title thereto, by reason of the fact that his grantor's title came through a deed which had been delivered out of escrow before performance of the conditions of the escrow agreement. The general rule, as stated in 21 Corpus Juris, 885, is:

"A transfer to a subvendee of an instrument, wrongfully delivered to the grantee or obligee, confers no right or title upon him where he has notice of such delivery or is put upon inquiry regarding it. Further, although there is some authority to the contrary, according to the weight of authority the same rule applies even in the case of an innocent subvendee without notice of the conditions or event stipulated in the escrow contract, and is especially applied in cases where the escrow has been obtained or delivered through fraud."

There is some authority to the contrary: Hubbard v. Greely, 84 Me. 340, 24 A. 799, 17 L.R.A. 511, and Blight v. Schenck, 10 Pa. 285, 51 Am. Dec. 478. In support of the majority rule, cases are cited from Colorado, Georgia, Illinois, Indiana, Iowa, Kansas, Nebraska, New Jersey, Oregon, Texas, Vermont, Wisconsin, and also the case of Wood v. French, supra.

We have read all the cases cited, and one of the earliest cases on the subject seems to be the case of Smith v. South Royalton Bank, 32 Vt. 341, 76 Am.Dec. 179, where it is held that a deed delivered in escrow to be delivered to the grantee, after the performance of some other act, will not be valid for any purpose until the condition upon which it is to be delivered to the grantee has been performed, and the fact that the deed has since come into the hands of an innocent purchaser for value will not change the rule in that case. However, it does not appear that the grantor had surrendered possession of the property. In that case, the court, however, after discussing the principle of the rule as applied to commercial paper, says:

"But let the principle be as it may, in regard to commercial papers, no question can be made as to a void deed. The case of Van Amringe v. Morton, 4 Whart. [pa.] 382, 34 Am.Dec. 517, is ruled expressly on the distinction between a void and a voidable deed, and it was there held that a bona fide purchaser for a valuable consideration, from the person holding a void deed, stands in no better situation than such fraudulent holder. The distinction is fully recognized in Price v. Junkin, 4 Watts [pa.] 85, 28 Am.Dec. 685, and the case decided upon that distinction. So in Arrison v. Armstead, 2 Pa.St. 191, 195, it was held that a deed having been rendered void by an alteration, a purchaser without notice and for valuable consideration was in no better situation than the original parties. The case in 4 Wharton, as in the case at bar, was one where there had been no valid delivery of the deed. So in the case of Pawling v. United States, 4 Cranch, 219 [2 l.ed. 601], there had been no delivery of the deed. It hardly need be remarked that if a deed wants delivery, it is void ab initio. . . .

Another early case on the subject is the case of Everts v. Agnes, 4 Wis. 343, 65 Am.Dec. 314, which case was again before the court on a second appeal in Everts v. Agnes, 6 Wis. 453. That case was one where the facts are almost identical with those disclosed in the record in the case before us. . . .

In that case Everts, the plaintiff, was the maker of the deed. Agnes, one of the defendants, was the one to whom the deed had been wrongfully delivered from escrow, and Swift, the other defendant, was the one to whom Agnes had conveyed the property and made his defense upon the ground that he was an innocent purchaser for value without notice, and set up in his answer, as did Moore in the instant case, that at the time he made the purchase he caused the record to be examined, obtained full abstract of Agnes' title, and believed he (Agnes) had a good title, and gave him, Swift, one, except as to the balance due on a mortgage, subject to which Swift made the purchase. Also, that before he made the purchase he visited the premises and found Agnes and Bender in possession, that Agnes had been in undisputed possession there the preceding summer, and assured Swift his title was good, denies all notice, at the time of the purchase and payment of consideration money, as to the manner in which Agnes got the deed from Zettler (the escrow holder), and all notice of the conditions under which the deed was left by Everts with Zettler. He further alleges in his answer, that Everts, before any of these transactions, resided in the neighborhood of the premises, and saw Agnes in possession without objection, that the possession was given Agnes at the date of the contract between Everts and Agnes, and that Agnes held possession until he sold the premises to Swift. It will thus be seen that, in that case, the facts appeared more strongly against the plaintiff than in the instant case, for the reason that the evidence in this case, as the record now stands, is that the plaintiff did not know that Simmons ever was in possession, did not know how he obtained possession, if he was in possession, and that such possession was without her knowledge or consent. The court in the case of Everts v. Agnes, supra, held:

"We have not the slightest doubt that the deed of Everts to Agnes was delivered to Zettler as an escrow, to be delivered only upon the performance of the conditions prescribed. That Agnes fraudulently obtained possession of the deed, and fraudulently procured it to be recorded. That no title passed to Agnes, and hence he could convey none to Swift. The latter has his remedy upon his covenant against Agnes if any there be. This is the only point necessary to be considered at this time, and we adhere to the language and the conclusion adopted when this case was under consideration before, viz.: that the fraudulent procurement of a deed, deposited as an escrow, from the depositary, by the grantee named in the deed, would not operate to pass the title; and that a bona fide purchaser from such grantee so fraudulently procuring the deed, could derive no title from him, and would not be protected."

. . .

The rule laid down in the Wisconsin case (Everts v. Agnes, supra) seems to have been followed in the following cases: Chipman v. Tucker, 38 Wis. 43, 20 Am.Rep. 1, Tyler v. Cate, 29 Or. 515, 45 P. 800, and Weghorst v. Clark, 66 Colo. 535, 180 P. 742, where it is said:

"The only way, if any, in which a grantee of a grantee of a recorded undelivered deed can claim anything against the grantor in such deed is by estoppel in pais through the grantor's neglect to take immediate measures to recover his land, thus leaving an apparently good title shown by the record." . . .

We have given due consideration to the cases cited by defendant wherein third persons claiming as innocent purchasers have been protected under circumstances somewhat similar to those in the instant case, but we think the great weight of authority, as well as better reasoning, is found in those cases holding the other way. The defendant in his brief says:

"In passing upon a demurrer to the evidence the court does not weigh the evidence. The demurrer admits every fact which the evidence in the slightest degree tends to prove and all inferences and conclusions that may be reasonably and logically drawn from the same, and, where there is any conflict in the plaintiff's evidence that would make any part of it unfavorable to the plaintiff or sustains the defense, the court in passing upon such demurrer should consider such evidence withdrawn."

Applying this rule, we think the trial court committed error in sustaining the demurrer to plaintiff's evidence, and that for the reasons stated this cause should be reversed and remanded for a new trial.

BENNETT, P.C., and HALL, HERR, and JEFFREY, CC., concur.

PER CURIAM. Adopted in whole.

NOTES

1. Oklahoma reaffirmed the view of the principal case in Blakeney v. Home Owners' Loan Corp., 192 Okl. 158, 135 P.2d 339 (1943), where the purchaser without paying the full price obtained the deed, recorded it, and mortgaged the land to a b.f.p. In the absence of ratification or estoppel, the vendor's title was held not subject to the mortgage lien. See, however, Mann, Escrows—Their Use and Value, 1949 U.Ill.L.F. 398, 417. "There are strong considerations, it would seem, to support the view that the bona fide purchaser should be protected. . . . The first is based on the familiar doctrine that when a loss has occurred which must fall on one of two innocent persons, it should be borne by him who is the occasion of the loss. . . . Secondly, a contrary view would tend to render title insecure. Many real estate transactions are today closed by means of escrows with nothing of record to indicate that fact. If a purchaser could acquire such a title only at his peril, the merchantability of real estate generally as an article of daily commerce would be impaired."

2. Suppose a deed has been placed in escrow and all of the conditions have been met but the deed has not yet been handed physically to the grantee. Who has the legal title to the land? Val Verde Hotel Co. v. Ross, 30 N.M. 270, 272, 231 P. 702 (1924), answers as follows: "This action was begun February 18, 1920. Long prior thereto, to wit, September 28, 1918, the conveyance was executed and placed in

escrow, and within seven months thereafter all of the conditions of the escrow had been performed. It therefore appears that long prior to the bringing of the action, plaintiff was entitled to the delivery of the deed by the escrow holder. The deed belonged to the plaintiff, and the grantor no longer had any power or control over the same. Under such circumstances, the delivery of the deed was complete, and title vested in the grantee, notwithstanding the manual delivery of the paper had not been made." See also Osborn v. Osborn, 42 Cal.2d 358, 267 P.2d 333 (1954).

3. It is important that escrow agreements or instructions tell the escrow agent what to do with documents and money entrusted to him or her if the escrow conditions are not met, and that the agent follow the instructions. In Miller v. Craig, 27 Ariz.App. 789, 558 P.2d 984 (1976), involving the sale of a tavern, the escrow agreement provided that the agent should give purchaser's $5,000 earnest money to vendors upon their transfer of the beer and wine license to purchaser, and that vendors should receive the $5,000 as liquidated damages if purchaser failed to comply with the sales contract. There were no other provisions authorizing the agent to disburse funds. Prior to the closing, purchaser filed suit against vendors seeking rescission of the contract, and the trial court entered a judgment in her favor directing that she recover $5,000. Purchaser presented the escrow agent with a copy of the judgment, and he, without notifying vendors or attempting to determine whether they would appeal, disbursed the earnest money to purchaser. Vendors thereafter obtained a reversal and a new judgment in their favor for the $5,000. After unsuccessful efforts to collect from purchaser, they sued the escrow agent for breach of his fiduciary duty. The court held the agent liable despite a provision in the escrow agreement that the agent "shall not become liable to either [party] for anything whatsoever so long as said Agent acts with reasonable prudence." The court said, "The judgment in favor of [purchaser] dealt not with a specific res, the earnest money deposit, but merely entitled her to recover $5,000 *from the [vendors].* It did not authorize a disbursement of funds held in escrow. . . . [T]he duties of an escrow agent are defined in the escrow agreement and will be strictly construed. Any deviation therefrom without the requisite authority is per se unreasonable and cannot be done with 'reasonable prudence.'"

4. Most of the escrow work in real estate transactions is handled by corporations (title insurance companies, banks, etc.) which maintain escrow departments. Their service is usually professional and efficient but they do make mistakes. In Akin v. Business Title Corp., 264 Cal. App.2d 153, 70 Cal.Rptr. 287 (1968) the escrowee recorded a mortgage in the wrong county. The corporation attempted to rely on an exculpatory clause intended to insulate it from its own ordinary negligence. The court held that the escrow agreement was a contract of adhesion, that the corporation was one suitable for public regulation, and that the transaction was one that "affects the public interest." The exculpatory clause was held to be invalid and the escrowee was liable for its negligence. "While the general rule still is that an exculpatory clause

relieving individuals of liability from their own ordinary negligence does not contravene public policy, a contract entered into between two parties of unequal bargaining strength, expressed in the language of a standardized contract written by the more powerful bargainer to meet its own needs and offered to the weaker party on a 'take it or leave it' basis carries some consequences that extend beyond orthodox implications. When the public interest is affected the exculpatory clause will be held invalid."

5. In Edwards v. Stewart Title & Trust of Phoenix, Inc., 156 Ariz. 531, 753 P.2d 1187 (App.1988), sellers and buyer agreed that title would be conveyed to buyer, that buyer would give sellers a purchase-money installment note and mortgage, and that if buyer died before completing all payments, the house would revert to Sellers. The parties engaged Stewart Title as escrow agent, and escrow officer Robinson agreed to prepare the necessary documents for the transaction. Sellers and buyer signed the documents, including escrow instructions and a warranty deed. The instructions provided that in the event buyer died before paying the full purchase price, "Buyer directs that this property is to revert to the Sellers." However, the warranty deed prepared by Robinson made no mention of sellers' intended reversionary interest. Robinson recorded the deed but not the escrow instructions or any other document referring to the reversionary interest. Thereafter, before having paid the full purchase price, buyer died after conveying the house to a bona fide purchaser. The court held that Stewart Title had breached its instructions by "failing to properly record the reverter clause" and therefore was liable to sellers for the fair market value of the house at the time of buyer's death, less the payments made by buyer.

SECTION 4. SUBJECT MATTER CONVEYED

MALEY AND THUMA, LEGAL DESCRIPTIONS OF LAND

Pamphlet published by Chicago Title and Trust Co. (1955).
Pages 1–3.

The subject "Legal Descriptions of Land" defines itself. It is a description in words deemed legally sufficient to locate and identify a particular parcel of land. It is to be differentiated from the term "common description," which means the designation of location by a commonly known name as, for example, "the Jones farm," or a commonly accepted address as, for example, "the property at 100 North Doe Street."

To those who daily work with real estate matters the subject of legal descriptions should be of great interest. In any event, an understanding of the subject should be considered of prime importance because all titles depend upon a legally sufficient description.

Your client tells you he wants to sell his property at "100 North Doe Street." You prepare the contract or deed. When you hand him the document and he reads it, he may not know what you mean when you describe his property as being in a "subdivision of Government lot 1 in fractional Section 1, Township 39 North, Range 9 East of the Third Principal Meridian"; but he rightfully will expect that you understand these words and that you know the description you have placed in the document properly describes his property at 100 North Doe Street. . . .

THE FUNDAMENTALS OF LEGAL DESCRIPTIONS

Every legal description is based upon a survey of the land. In order to prepare a legal description of a parcel or tract of land someone at some time must have gone upon the particular land and made some sort of a survey upon which the description is based.

The subject of land descriptions and of surveys is not new; it is centuries old. The earliest records of man refer to skillful measurements and calculations with respect to land, but it is impossible to assign the birth of the science of surveying to any particular year or even country. Clark, in his work on "Surveying and Boundaries" (2d ed.) says that it seems well established that the Chinese, at an early date, and the Egyptians, long before Christ's time, practiced the art of surveying. In the case of the Egyptians it appears it was necessary every spring to re-establish corners and boundary lines obliterated by floods of the Nile River. It required the application of established rules for the re-establishment of such corners and boundaries.

1. *Metes and bounds descriptions.* The metes and bounds description is the oldest known manner of describing land. Literally this term means the measurements and boundaries of a tract of land. This method of description consists of beginning at some point in the boundary of the tract to be described and then reciting the courses (that is, the directions) and the distances from point to point entirely around the tract.

Two things are of prime importance in a metes and bounds description. First, the description must begin at some known point that can be readily identified, that is of substantial character and is so established and witnessed that it can be relocated with certainty if the marker (or, as we say, the monument) that identifies the point should be destroyed or removed. Second, the description must close; that is, if the courses and distances of the description are followed step by step from corner to corner, one must come back to the place of beginning.

2. *Monuments.* Monuments are of various kinds, some natural and some artificial. Natural monuments, as the term signifies, are those created by nature; such, for example, as trees, rivers and lakes. Artificial monuments, as the term signifies, are those created by man; as for example, highways, section corners, quarter corners and boundaries, or a stone or other permanent marker, properly located and witnessed.

3. *The original 13 colonies.* The metes and bounds method of description was followed by the colonists in the early settlement of this country. An example of a legal description of property in Vermont contained in a deed of October 3, 1784, reads in part as follows: "Begin at the middle of a large white pine stump standing in the west side line of Simon Vender Cook's land on the south side of the main road that leads to the new city,—and there is also a fense that stands a little to the west of Simon Vendor Cook's barn, which said fense if it was to run across the said road southerly, would run to the middle of said stump; and running thence north 2 degrees east 19 chains and 50 links to a small white oak tree;" etc. This particular description continues with courses that run to trees and to stakes and piles of stones, and concludes with a course that reads "thence north 9 chains 16 links to the middle of the stump where it first begun."

Such a description, although probably legally sufficient, had the failing of a lack of permanency both as to the monument that identified the initial place of beginning and as to those that marked the ends of the various courses. Destruction or removal of such monuments would obviously make a resurvey of the property difficult, if not impossible.

This description is typical of the early descriptions used in the colonial states. The references to monuments that lacked permanency—the surveying of large and irregular tracts of land without regard to any system or uniformity—the failure of the surveyors to make their survey notes a matter of public record, created a situation that gave rise to frequent boundary line disputes and litigation.

RECTANGULAR SURVEY SYSTEM

After the close of the Revolution and the adoption of the Federal Constitution the greater part of the land in this country outside the original 13 colonies became the property of the Federal Government, either as a result of cession by the original 13 states or by trades, purchase or treaty.

The Federal Government found itself with vast tracts of undeveloped and uninhabited land, with few natural characteristics suitable for use as monuments in metes and bounds descriptions. The metes and bounds system, in any event, was not satisfactory; and it was determined to be necessary to devise some new standard system of describing land so as to make parcels readily and forever locatable and easily available for land office sales. To meet this need a committee headed by Thomas Jefferson evolved a plan which the Continental Congress, on April 26, 1785, adopted for dividing the land into a series of rectangles. It appears that the system adopted was truly American. It was designated the Rectangular System (also called the Government System) of survey. It is the system we use today.[7]

7. This system was not applied to Texas, since that state retained its public lands when annexed to the Union. Much Texas land had been surveyed in connection with grants by former sovereigns—the Spanish Crown, Mexican States, and the Republic of Texas. Those surveys authorized by the State of Texas, were not based upon a uniform statewide system.

WARD, ILLINOIS LAW OF TITLE EXAMINATION

Pages 69–74 (2d ed. 1952).

GOVERNMENT SURVEYS

All of Illinois is subdivided by Government Survey into townships, and they are surveyed into 36 sections one mile square and containing approximately 640 acres except that the sections on the North and West sides contain a greater or lesser number of acres in order that the lines may be adjusted to the meridian lines, as subsequently explained.

The system of survey requires that a starting point be the intersection of a Base Line and a Principal Meridian as in the first illustration below.

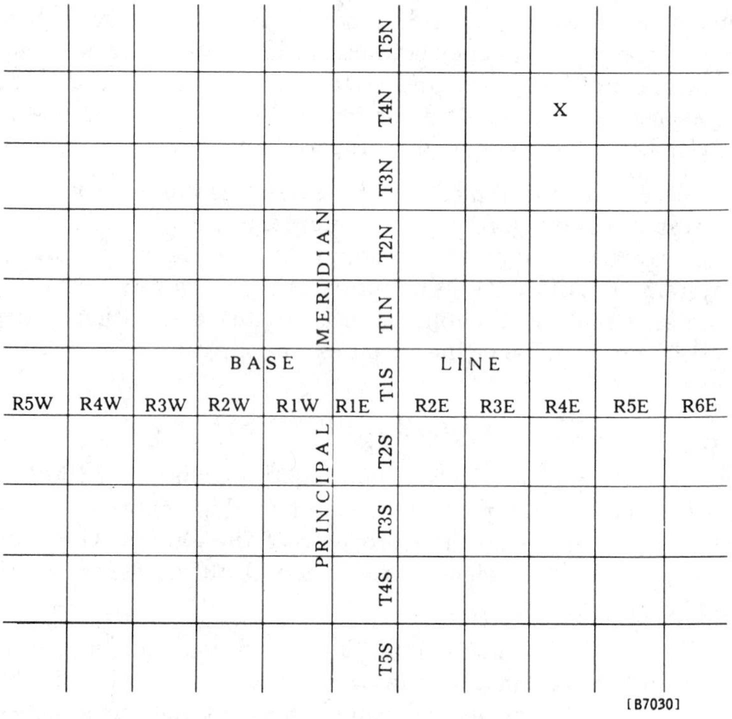

T5N
T4N X
T3N
T2N
T1N
BASE LINE
PRINCIPAL MERIDIAN
T1S
R5W R4W R3W R2W R1W R1E R2E R3E R4E R5E R6E
T2S
T3S
T4S
T5S

[B7030]

The numbers increasing North or South from the Base line are the Township numbers. Those increasing East or West of the Meridian are the Range numbers. So in the diagram the square marked X is Township 4 North, Range 4 East of the Principal Meridian.

The sections of a Township are numbered 1 to 36 as shown in the following illustration:

6.	5.	4.	3.	2.	1.
7.	8.	9.	10.	11.	12.
18.	17.	16.	15.	14.	13.
19.	20.	21.	22.	23.	24.
30.	29.	28.	27.	26.	25.
31.	32.	33.	34.	35.	36.

TOWNSHIP [B7029]

To aid in learning to designate the portion of a normal section so it may be quickly identified, the following plat gives the acreage, dimensions and also the correct legal description of each subdivision marked upon the plat.

N½ of NW¼—80 acres
¼ m 20 ch
2640 ft. 160 r. 40 ch. ½ mile
NORTHEAST QUARTER
160 acres
1980 ft. 30 ch. 120 r
1320 ft 80r 20ch
W 3/4 of S½ of NW¼
60 a
660 ft
40 rd
10 ch
E¼ of S½
of NW¼
or
E½ of SE¼
of NW¼
20 a
1320 ft. 20ch 80r
1/4 mile
80 a
W½ of SW¼
330f
5 ch
20r
20a
W½
W½
E½
SW¼
990 ft 15 ch
60 r
60a
E 3/4 SW¼
½ mile 40 ch
NW¼ of SE¼
40 acres
¼ m 20 ch
E½ SE¼
80 a
N½N½SW¼ SE¼
10a
5 ch
S½N½SW¼ SE¼
10a
330f
SW¼
SW¼
SE¼
10a
N½SE
SWSE
5 a
10 ch
2½a
X
330f

[B7031]

The correct legal description of the tract marked X is the Southeast one quarter of the Southeast one quarter of the Southwest one quarter of the Southeast one quarter of Section O in Township O, etc.

MALEY AND THUMA, LEGAL DESCRIPTIONS OF LAND

Page 13 (1955).

Under the Government survey, as we have seen, fractions of a section, containing 40 acres or multiples thereof, are easily describable. Now what does the owner of a large acreage tract do who desires to split it up into much smaller parcels or lots? He subdivides the tract.

To accomplish the subdivision he employs a surveyor to survey the tract and to draw a plat dividing the tract into blocks separated by streets and alleys, and then dividing the blocks in turn into smaller areas called lots.

Such blocks are given consecutive numbers or letters, and the lots in each block are likewise given consecutive numbers, thus enabling identification of a particular area of land within the subdivision by a lot and block number. For further identification it is common practice to give the subdivision a name.

The surveyor's map (or plat, as it is more commonly called) is captioned with the legal description of the land surveyed, shows all the boundary lines of the land, all necessary monuments and the lines dividing it into blocks, lots and streets and the numbering and dimension of each lot, etc.

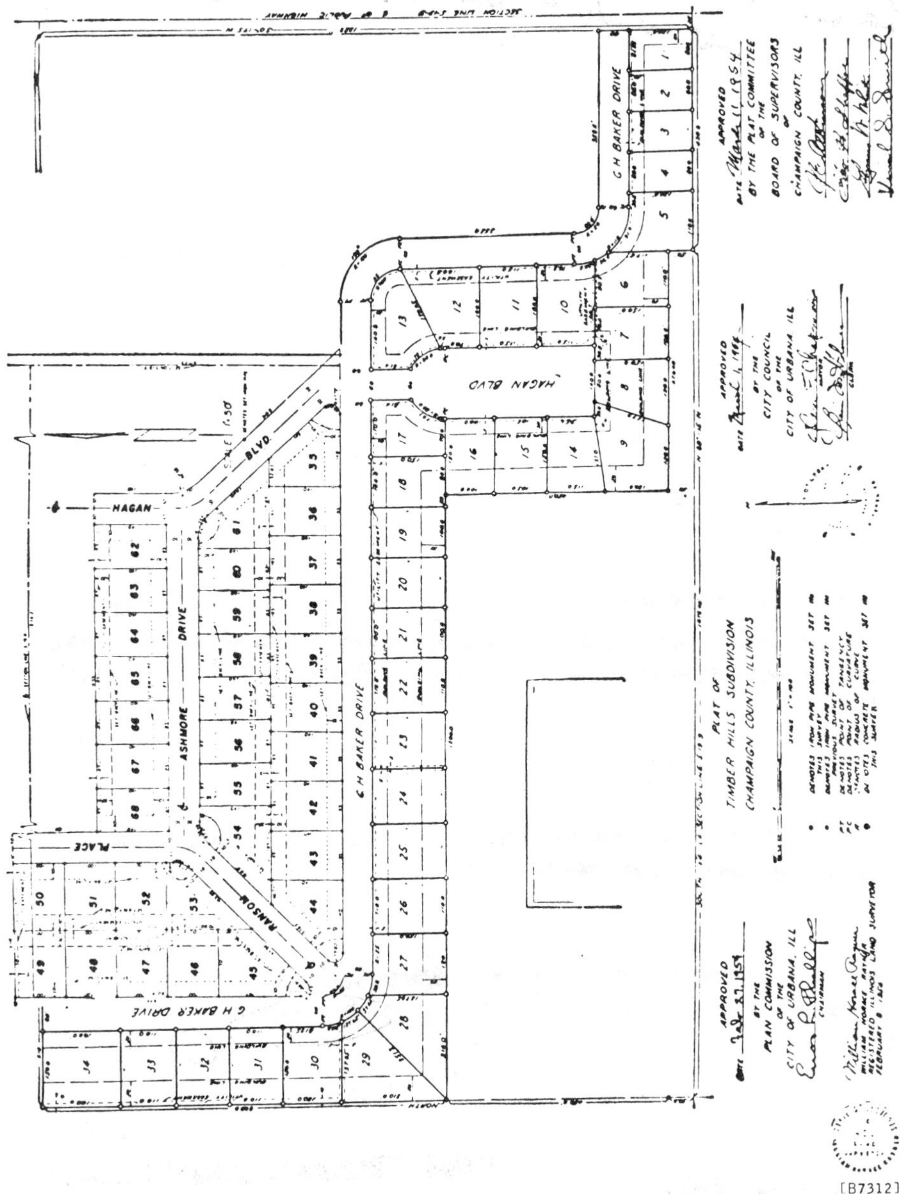

If the owner desires to establish easements and restrictions he may do so by indicating the same on the plat and by spelling out the easements and restrictions by legends on the plat. The plat is then certified by the surveyor and signed by the owners, and upon approval by the proper authorities is recorded in the Recorder's Office. Of course, the governing statutes should be carefully followed.

Upon recordation the lots in the subdivision may be easily identified in a deed of conveyance by merely using the lot and block number, the subdivision name, and the section, township and range wherein the entire subdivision falls on the Government survey.

BYBEE v. HAGEMAN

Supreme Court of Illinois, 1873.
66 Ill. 519.

This was a bill in chancery, by Adam Hageman, against John Ewald, Elizabeth Ewald, James Manly, Abner E. Barns, Rebecca Barns, and Thomas T. Bybee, to foreclose a mortgage on the premises described in the opinion, executed to the complainant by Ewald and wife. After the execution of the mortgage sought to be foreclosed, Ewald and wife executed a second mortgage on the lands in question to James Manly, to secure the payment of a promissory note of said Ewald to Manly, which was assigned by the latter to Bybee. Bybee, after answering the original bill, filed his cross bill to foreclose the junior mortgage. The court decreed the foreclosure of the prior mortgage, declaring it a valid lien on the premises. From this decree Bybee appealed.

MR. CHIEF JUSTICE LAWRENCE delivered the opinion of the Court:

If the description contained in the first mortgage was sufficient to pass the title, the record was notice to the subsequent mortgagee. The description was as follows: "one acre and a half in the northwest corner of section five (5), together with the brewery, malthouse, all buildings thereon and fixtures contained therein." The mortgage also described the land as situated in the county of McDonough, and State of Illinois.

It is objected by appellant that the description is void for uncertainty, inasmuch as it specifies neither township nor range.

If there had been but one section five in McDonough county, the description as to the section would have been perfectly certain. The ambiguity arises from the fact that there are several sections bearing that number. The ambiguity, then, is a latent ambiguity, arising, not upon the face of the deed, but when it is ascertained dehors the deed what are the boundaries of McDonough county, and that they are such as to include several. This was the view of a similar description taken by this court in Dougherty v. Purdy, 18 Ill. 206, which case was followed in Clark v. Powers, 45 Ill. 283. Being a latent ambiguity it is susceptible of explanation.

The explanation was made, in this case, by proof that at the time the mortgagor executed the mortgage he was living on the north-west quarter of section five, in township six north, and range one west, and that he had a dwelling house, malt-house and brewery in the north-west corner of the quarter section. It also appeared that he had no brewery elsewhere, and that he had a parol contract for an acre and a half of land in the north-west corner, and subsequently bought two and a half acres more, and received a deed from the owner for the four acres. If the description in the mortgage was sufficient, the title to the acre and a half inured to the mortgagee. There can be no doubt, under the cases above cited as to the sufficiency of this proof to remove the latent ambiguity. The calls in the mortgage were answered by the particular tract in controversy, and could be answered by none other. In the cases referred to, less proof was held sufficient. If the mortgage was sufficient to pass the title as between the parties, its record was good as notice to the second mortgagee.

It is also objected that the description of "one acre and a half in the north-west corner" of the section is too uncertain, as it might refer either to an acre and a half in the form of a square or a triangle. Under our system of congressional surveys all lands were originally surveyed and laid out into rectangular forms, except fractional sections. Hence, it has become common to apply that form to all subdivisions where the description is of a certain number of acres in the corner of a larger tract. Thus, the north-east forty acres of a quarter section would be as definitely understood by all persons in this State, familiar with our local conveyancing, to describe forty acres in a square form, as if the tract had been described by metes and bounds. It is a form of description growing naturally and almost inevitably out of our system of surveys, and being universally understood, should be recognized by the courts. In Walsh v. Ringer, 2 Ham. (Ohio) 327, the same rule is held, and the court, in that case, remark that this is also the Kentucky rule.

In the view we have taken of this case it is unnecessary to discuss any further questions.

The decree of the court below is affirmed.

NOTES

1. A mortgage described land as follows: "A certain piece or tract of land, grist mill and all fixtures thereunto, and one storehouse, 28 by 100 feet long, lying and being in Brassfield township, Granville County, N.C. and adjoining the lands of Anderson Breedlove, J.C. Usry and Dora Harris, said lot to contain three acres." There were forty acres in the tract where the store and grist mill were located. The court said: "There is nothing to segregate this three acres out of the forty, nothing to indicate a beginning, nor where or in what direction the lines are to be run—nothing whatever beyond the inference—for it is not expressly stated that the grist mill and store-house are to be located somewhere upon the said three acres when laid off. . . . [h]ere there is only an uncertain, indefinite, undefined and undefinable three acres out of a

tract of forty, and the court properly held that this was too indefinite to be a conveyance of any three acres, and the mortgage was therefore, void as to the land." Harris v. Woodard, 130 N.C. 580, 41 S.E. 790, 791 (1902).

Compare Miracle Construction Co. v. Miller, 251 Minn. 320, 87 N.W.2d 665 (1958) where the court sustained a contract for sale of certain land (correctly described) "excepting house, out-buildings and approx. 3½ acres surrounding same." Extrinsic evidence disclosed that the parties knew the physical location of the boundaries of the excepted area and the court allowed parol evidence to identify the 3½ acres. See also O'Dwyer v. Ream, 390 Pa. 474, 136 A.2d 90 (1957) where the court sustained an exception of "one hundred acres of coal bed geologically known and designated as 'E' to be hereafter surveyed from the northeast end of the farm. . . ."

In Peterson v. Taylor, 226 Mont. 400, 735 P.2d 1120 (1987), the owners of four acres referred to as the "Mill Site" on an 1877 plat deeded a portion of it described as "that part . . . lying at and within the southerly end of [the Mill Site], together with all buildings, improvements and machinery, including water wheel, generators, motors and equipment therefor, held, owned and used for . . . the electric lighting and power plant of the grantors. . . ." The court held that the description was "sufficient to permit the use of extrinsic evidence to determine the boundaries of the property."

2. A warranty deed conveyed "all that certain premises described as: "twenty (20) acres out of the southwest quarter of Section 7, etc." No attempt was made to describe a specific twenty acres. The trial court concluded that the deed conveyed no title due to the defective description. In reversing, the appellate court said: "The one rule that holds true as to any conveyance is that 'a deed should be held to pass some interest if such effect may be given to it consistently with the law and the terms of the instrument.' . . . [s]uch a conveyance operates to give the grantee an undivided interest in the land as a tenant in common. . . . [t]he extent of the undivided interest is measured by the proportion which the number of acres conveyed bears to the whole number of acres in the tract." Mounce v. Coleman, 133 Ariz. 251, 650 P.2d 1233 (App.1982).

3. In Pettigrew v. Dobbelaar, 63 Cal. 396, 397 (1883) the following description was held good: "All lands and real estate belonging to the said party of the first part, wherever the same may be situated." To the same effect is Roeder Company v. Burlington Northern, Inc., 105 Wash.2d 567, 716 P.2d 855 (1986), referring to such catchall or "omnibus" clauses as "Mother Hubbard" descriptions. See Cunningham, Stoebuck & Whitman, The Law of Property 728 (1984), where it is noted that, because such descriptions are difficult for title examiners to find, instruments containing them may be treated as unrecorded or "outside the chain of title" for purposes of the recording acts.

4. How useful is the patent-latent test referred to in the principal case? Professor McBaine gives it the following evaluation: "Problems of interpretation must be solved the hard way. A maxim or a neatly

phrased rule covering all situations is quite likely to be a snare and a delusion. Various attempts have been made to lay down a rule for the interpretation of writings. One was a rule attributed to Sir Francis Bacon. In this rule, which was widely used in the United States, a distinction is made between *latent* and *patent* ambiguities. Bacon's distinction between *latent* and *patent* ambiguities—Maxim 25—as misunderstood for a general rule of interpretation nearly two centuries after he wrote it, was that oral evidence is admissible to aid in the interpretation of a writing if there is a *latent* ambiguity, but where there is a *patent* ambiguity it can only be cured by the writing itself. This concept of interpretation, which has been thoroughly discredited, may not be so fallacious as the idea that parol evidence is admissible if the writing is ambiguous on its face, but not admissible where the writing is plain on its face, yet the difference in the amount of error embodied in the two rules is not very great." McBaine, The Rule Against Disturbing Plain Meaning of Writings, 31 Cal.L.Rev. 145, 147 (1943).

In a footnote Professor McBaine points out a statement from 20 Am.Jur. § 1155 that the distinction "is gradually disappearing" and adds the hope that the time will soon come "when it will be of interest only to students engaged in tracing the history of law through periods of formalism to a period of realism."

5. The cases involving the adequacy and meaning of legal descriptions of land are legion. A true understanding of the difficulties involved would require a knowledge of surveying techniques and of the canons of construction plus an exposure to a range of decisions which are impossible to include in a basic property course. The cases and notes in this section are designed to give you some *feel* for the nature of the problems.

WALTERS v. TUCKER

Supreme Court of Missouri, 1955.
281 S.W.2d 843.

HOLLINGSWORTH, JUDGE. This is an action to quiet title to certain real estate situate in the City of Webster Groves, St. Louis County, Missouri. Plaintiff and defendants are the owners of adjoining residential properties fronting northward on Oak Street. Plaintiff's property, known as 450 Oak Street, lies to the west of defendants' property, known as 446 Oak Street. The controversy arises over their division line. Plaintiff contends that her lot is 50 feet in width, east and west. Defendants contend that plaintiff's lot is only approximately 42 feet in width, east and west. The trial court, sitting without a jury, found the issues in favor of defendants and rendered judgment accordingly, from which plaintiff has appealed.

The common source of title is Fred F. Wolf and Rose E. Wolf, husband and wife, who in 1922 acquired the whole of Lot 13 of West Helfenstein Park, as shown by plat thereof recorded in St. Louis

County. In 1924, Mr. and Mrs. Wolf conveyed to Charles Arthur Forse and wife the following described portion of said Lot 13:

"The West 50 feet of Lot 13 of West Helfenstein Park, a Subdivision in United States Survey 1953, Twp. 45, Range 8 East, St. Louis County, Missouri, ..."

Plaintiff, through mesne conveyances carrying a description like that above, is the last grantee of and successor in title to the aforesaid portion of Lot 13. Defendants, through mesne conveyances, are the last grantees of and successors in title to the remaining portion of Lot 13.

At the time of the above conveyance in 1924, there was and is now situate on the tract described therein a one-story frame dwelling house (450 Oak Street), which was then and continuously since has been occupied as a dwelling by the successive owners of said tract, or their tenants. In 1925, Mr. and Mrs. Wolf built a 1½-story stucco dwelling house on the portion of Lot 13 retained by them. This house (446 Oak Street) continuously since has been occupied as a dwelling by the successive owners of said portion of Lot 13, or their tenants.

Despite the apparent clarity of the description in plaintiff's deed, extrinsic evidence was heard for the purpose of enabling the trial court to interpret the true meaning of the description set forth therein. At the close of all the evidence the trial court found that the description did not clearly reveal whether the property conveyed "was to be fifty feet along the front line facing Oak Street or fifty feet measured Eastwardly at right angles from the West line of the property . . ."; that the "difference in method of ascertaining fifty feet would result in a difference to the parties of a strip the length of the lot and approximately eight feet in width"; that an ambiguity existed which justified the hearing of extrinsic evidence; and that the "West fifty feet should be measured on the front or street line facing Oak Street." The judgment rendered in conformity with the above finding had the effect of fixing the east-west width of plaintiff's tract at about 42 feet.

Plaintiff contends that the description in the deed is clear, definite and unambiguous, both on its face and when applied to the land; that the trial court erred in hearing and considering extrinsic evidence; and that its finding and judgment changes the clearly expressed meaning of the description and describes and substitutes a different tract from that acquired by her under her deed. Defendants do not contend that the description, on its face, is ambiguous, but do contend that when applied to the land it is subject to "dual interpretation"; that under the evidence the trial court did not err in finding it contained a latent ambiguity and that parol evidence was admissible to ascertain and determine its true meaning; and that the finding and judgment of the trial court properly construes and adjudges the true meaning of the description set forth in said deed.

Attached hereto is a reduced copy of an unchallenged survey of Lot 13, as made by plaintiff's witness, Robert J. Joyce, surveyor and graduate (1928) in civil engineering at Massachusetts Institute of Technology, for use in this litigation. Inasmuch as the two properties here in question front northward on Oak Street, the plat is made to be viewed from the bottom toward the top, which in this instance is from north to south:

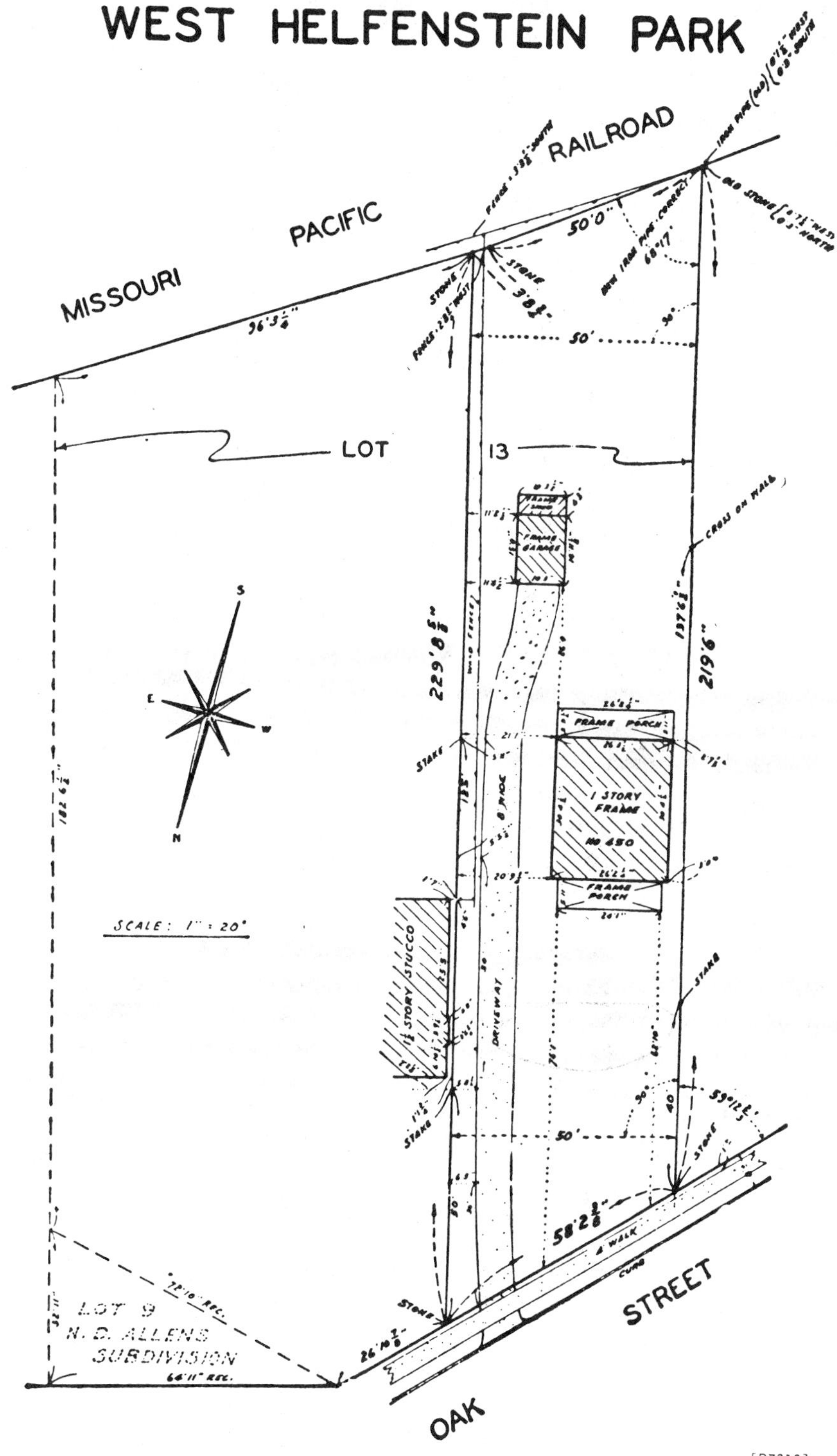

[B7313]

It is seen that Lot 13 extends generally north and south. It is bounded on the north by Oak Street (except that a small triangular lot from another subdivision cuts off its frontage thereon at the northeast corner). On the south it is bounded by the Missouri Pacific Railroad right of way. Both Oak Street and the railroad right of way extend in a general northeast-southwest direction, but at differing angles.

Joyce testified: The plat was a "survey of the West 50 feet of Lot 13 of West Helfenstein Park". In making the survey the west boundary line of Lot 13 was first established. Lines 50 feet in length (one near the north end and one near the south end of the lot, as shown by the plat) were run eastwardly at right angles to the west line of the lot, and then a line was run parallel to the west line and 50 feet, as above measured, from it, intersecting both the north and south boundaries of the lot. This line, which represented 50 feet in width of Lot 13, made a frontage of 58 feet, 2⅜ inches, on Oak Street, and 53 feet, 8¾ inches, on the railroad right of way. The line, as thus measured, comes within 1 foot, 1¾ inches, of the west front corner of the stucco house (446 Oak Street), within 1 foot, 7 inches, of the west rear corner thereof, and within less than 1 foot of a chimney in the west wall.

The trial court refused to permit the witness to testify, but counsel for plaintiff offered to prove that, if permitted, witness would testify that the methods used by him in making the survey were in accordance with the practices and procedures followed in his profession in determining the boundaries of lots such as was described in the deed. The witness further testified that the method used by him was the only method by which a lot such as that described in the deeds in question could be measured having precisely and uniformly a width of 50 feet; and that a 50 foot strip is a strip with a uniform width of 50 feet.

Defendants also introduced in evidence a plat of Lot 13. It was prepared by Elbring Surveying Company for use in this litigation. August Elbring, a practicing surveyor and engineer for 34 years, testified in behalf of defendants: "In view of the fact that the deed (to the west 50 feet of Lot 13) made reference to the western 50 feet, and in view of the fact that the line which would have been established construing the dimension to be 50 feet at right angles, coming within a foot or so of an existing building (the stucco house), we felt that the line was intended to have been placed using the frontage of 50 feet on Oak Street and thence running the line (southward) parallel to the western line of Lot 13." The line so run, as being the east line of plaintiff's tract, was 8.01 feet west of the northwest corner of the stucco house and 8.32 feet west of its southwest corner. The Elbring plat does not show the actual width of plaintiff's tract as thus measured. But, concededly, there is no point on it where it approximates 50 feet in width; and, while it "fronts" 50 feet on Oak Street, its actual width is between 42 and 43 feet.

Both plats show a concrete driveway 8 feet in width extending from Oak Street to plaintiff's garage in the rear of her home, which, the testimony shows, was built by one of plaintiff's predecessors in title. The east line of plaintiff's tract, as measured by the Joyce (plaintiff's) survey, lies 6 or 7 feet east of the eastern edge of this driveway. Admittedly, the driveway is upon and an appurtenance of plaintiff's property. On the Elbring (defendants') plat, the east line of plaintiff's lot, as measured by Elbring, is shown to coincide with the east side of the driveway at Oak Street and to encroach upon it 1.25 feet for a distance of 30 or more feet as it extends between the houses. Thus, the area in dispute is essentially the area between the east edge of the driveway and the line fixed by the Joyce survey as the eastern line of plaintiff's tract.

Plaintiff adduced testimony to the effect that she and several of her predecessors in title had asserted claim to and had exercised physical dominion and control over all of the 50 feet in width of Lot 13, which included the concrete driveway and 6 or 7 feet to the east thereof. Defendants adduced testimony to the effect that they and their predecessors in title had asserted claim to and had exercised physical dominion and control over all of Lot 13 east of the driveway. The view we take of this case makes it unnecessary to set forth this testimony in detail.

The description under which plaintiff claims title, to wit: "The West 50 feet of Lot 13 . . .", is on its face clear and free of ambiguity. It purports to convey a strip of land 50 feet in width off the west side of Lot 13. So clear is the meaning of the above language that defendants do not challenge it and it has been difficult to find any case wherein the meaning of a similar description has been questioned. See Mississippi County v. Byrd, 319 Mo. 697, 4 S.W.2d 810, 812[5]; Adkins v. Quest, 79 Mo.App. 36.

The law is clear that when there is no inconsistency on the face of a deed and, on application of the description to the ground, no inconsistency appears, parol evidence is not admissible to show that the parties intended to convey either more or less or different ground from that described. But where there are conflicting calls in a deed, or the description may be made to apply to two or more parcels, and there is nothing in the deed to show which is meant, then parol evidence is admissible to show the true meaning of the words used. . . . "The office of extrinsic evidence as applied to the description of a parcel is to explain the latent ambiguity or to point out the property described on the ground. *Such evidence must not contradict the deed, or make a description of other land than that described in the deed.*" (Emphasis ours.) Thompson on Real Property, Vol. 6, § 3287, p. 468.

No ambiguity or confusion arises when the description here in question is applied to Lot 13. The description, when applied to the ground, fits the land claimed by plaintiff and cannot be made to apply to any other tract. When the deed was made, Lot 13 was vacant land except for the frame dwelling at 450 Oak Street. The stucco house (446 Oak Street) was not built until the following year. Under no conceivable theory can the fact that defendants' predecessors in title (Mr. and Mrs. Wolf) thereafter built the stucco house within a few feet of the east line of the property described in the deed, be construed as competent evidence of any ambiguity in the description. Neither could the fact, if it be a fact, that the Wolfs and their successors in title claimed title to and exercised dominion and control over a portion of the tract be construed as creating or revealing an ambiguity in the description.

Whether the above testimony and other testimony in the record constitute evidence of a mistake in the deed we do not here determine. Defendants have not sought reformation, and yet that is what the decree herein rendered undertakes to do. It seems apparent that the trial court considered the testimony and came to the conclusion that the parties to the deed did not intend a conveyance of the "West 50 feet of Lot 13", but rather a tract fronting 50 feet on Oak Street. And, the decree, on the theory of interpreting an ambiguity, undertakes to change (reform) the description so as to describe a lot approximately 42 feet in width instead of a lot 50 feet in width, as originally described. That, we are convinced, the courts cannot do.

The judgment is reversed and the cause remanded for further proceedings not inconsistent with the views expressed.

All concur.[8]

PRITCHARD v. REBORI

Supreme Court of Tennessee, 1916.
135 Tenn. 328, 186 S.W. 121.

WILLIAMS, J. The bill of complaint filed by Pritchard was to recover for the breach of a covenant against incumbrances incorporated in a deed executed to him by defendant, Rebori.

It appears that the Southern Railway Company owns between Madison and Monroe avenues in the city of Memphis a right of way that extends 50 feet westward from the center of its track. This easement was acquired by its predecessor in title in the year 1855. The tracks of the railway at the place in question lie in a cut, the western slope of which does not take up the entire distance of 50 feet; that is to say, the top edge of the slope runs east of the true western limit of the right of way.

However, at the base of the slope the company has constructed a fence of heavy timbers which was evidently built for the purpose, in part at least, of holding back the dirt that might slide from the slope. This fence is about 15 feet from the track. There was nothing in the way of fence, posts, or markers in the western margin of the right of way to indicate where it was.

Pritchard was desirous of acquiring a site near the railroad track on which to build a warehouse, and purchased a parcel of land from defendant for that purpose. The distance calls of the deed run to the fence at the base of the cut, considerably beyond the record showing as to the real western line of the right of way.

8. On retrial issues of reformation of the deed and adverse possession were introduced and judgment was entered for the plaintiff. The case was again appealed, resulting in another reversal. See Walters v. Tucker, 308 S.W.2d 673 (1957).

When Pritchard began to construct the warehouse he was notified by the railway company of its rights and his invasion thereof. On taking legal advice, he found that the building was being erected several feet within the limits of the legal right of way.

In order to remove the incumbrance and continue building operations, Pritchard conveyed two pieces of realty to the railway company, in return for which it quitclaimed to him that portion of the right of way which was covered by both the deed from defendant, Rebori, and the building, paying what is contended to be a fair price for the same.

To fairly set forth the points in dispute, it may be well to quote the description of the parcel contained in the deed executed by Rebori. The particularity and nicety of the distance calls will be noted.

"Beginning at a point, the intersection of the east line of South Lauderdale street with the north line of the first alley south of Madison avenue; running thence eastwardly with said alley forty (40) feet to the southwest corner of lot No. 13; thence continuing east with the south line of lots Nos. 11, 12 and 13 one hundred forty-six (146) feet, to a point in the west line of lot No. 10; thence south with the west line of lot No. 10 sixteen (16) feet; thence east fifty-two (52) feet to the Scroggins subdivision; thence northwardly with the west line of the Scroggins subdivision *thirty (30) feet to the right of way of the Southern Railroad;* thence northwestwardly with the line of said right of way two hundred sixteen (216) feet, to the northwest corner of lot No. 13; thence southwardly with the west line of lot No. 13 one hundred fifty-eight and five-tenths (158.5) feet to the northeast corner of lot No. 7 of the Armour subdivison; thence westwardly with the north line of lot No. 7, forty-seven and eight-tenths (47.8) feet to South Lauderdale street; thence south with South Lauderdale street fourteen and two-tenths (14.2) feet to the point of beginning."

The prime contention of Rebori is, that the line of the parcel that is underscored must stop at the real or record line of the right of way, and that, so stopping, the deed did not convey any land east of that line; therefore, that there is no incumbrance.

We are brought to a consideration of the rules of construction applicable in this action between the immediate vendor and vendee.

The general rule is that in determining boundaries resort is to be had, first, to natural objects or landmarks, because of their very permanent character, next, to artificial monuments or marks, then to boundary lines of adjacent owners, and then to courses and distances. But this general rule, as to the relative importance of these guides to the ascertainment of a boundary of land, is not an inflexible or absolute one.

The use of the rule is as a means to the discovery of the intention of the parties. To arrive at the intention of the parties to the instrument is the purpose of all rules of construction, and this applies to the description of premises conveyed as well as to other parts of the instrument.

It is not true, as appellant supposes, that there is such magic in a monument called for that it will be made to control in construction invariably. If it controls it is only because it is to be regarded as more certain than course or distance.

"If it should in a given case be less certain, the rule would fail with the reason for it and the monument would yield to the course and distance and an artificial monument will yield more readily than a natural one." Note 30 Am.Dec. 734, 740.

It is manifest that a mere adjacent boundary line would be caused to yield more readily to course and distance than would an artificial monument:

"When the call is for the line of another, it has also been held that course and distance may yield to it. But it is, obviously, not so decisive as the call for a natural boundary; and the mind may be under perfect conviction, from other circumstances, that the mistake is not in the course and distance, but in supposing that the other had a line at the end of the course and distance. If that conviction exists, there ought to be no deviation from course and distance." Carson v. Burnett, 18 N.C. 546, 30 Am.Dec. 143; 1 Jones, Real Prop. § 383.

The rule that course and distance yield to monuments or adjacent boundary lines is usually applied in fuller force to large boundaries of land in the country, where mistakes in the use of a surveyor's chain may easily occur, and with less potency to land in towns or cities. This for a manifest reason:

"Where the lines are so short as evidently to be susceptible of entire accuracy in their measurement, and are defined in such a manner as to indicate an exercise of care in describing the premises, such a description is regarded with great confidence as a means of ascertaining what is intended to be conveyed." White v. Luning, 93 U.S. 514, 23 L.Ed. 938.

Ordinarily surveys are not so loosely made where small and very valuable parcels are to be conveyed as in case of large boundaries, where the surveys are made on rough land or in forests; and there is not equal occasion for the application of the general rule that courses and distances are to be regarded as more uncertain, and must, therefore, give place to known monuments or boundaries, referred to as identifying the land. Where in such case it appears that courses and distances were intended by the parties to control they will be given that effect. The object in all boundary questions is to find, as nearly as may be, certain evidences of what particular land was meant to be included for conveyance. The natural presumption is that the conveyance is made after and with reference to an actual view of the premises by the parties to the instrument. The reason why a monument or adjacent line is ordinarily given preference over courses and distances is that the parties so presumed to have examined the property have, in viewing the premises, taken note of the monument or line.

In the case at bar the outer limit of the real right of way was not marked in any way; and the parcel was so small that it could be taken in by the contracting parties at a glance. The outer limit, therefore, lacked the element of open or manifest definiteness and fixity to constitute a boundary line that ought to be held to override the call of courses and distances. There were no right of way stakes or marks on the west boundary of the right of way to be visible, for purpose of demarcation, to the parties to the deed; and the right of way should be deemed to be undefined and without the characteristics of a monument, as against the call for distance. When a street or right of way is, as to limits, so unmarked and indefinite, it should not overrule the courses and distances of so small a parcel as this, every distance call of which would be changed in event of conformity thereto.

"Where, as in the infancy of a town, streets are only undefined portions of land dedicated to public use and themselves required to be located, they cannot be given controlling effect in fixing boundaries of other lands." 4 Rul.C.L. p. 103; 5 Cyc. 923; Doe v. Riley, 28 Ala. 164, 65 Am.Dec. 334; Dolphin v. Klann, 246 Mo. 477, 151 S.W. 956.

The fence, in the nature of a retaining wall, at the base of the slope of the cut, gave the contracting parties the impression that it marked the limit of the right of way on the west. The distances called for by the deed reach and terminate at this fence. The grantor, Rebori, had previously had the parcel surveyed so as to reach the fence. He supposed the fence to be the east line of his property, and it appeared that he so treated of it in the negotiations with Pritchard, who testifies that he would not have purchased unless the fence was in fact the line. Rebori admits that this is true. Both parties proceeded, therefore, on the assumption that the fence stood on the western line of the railway right of way, if proof of the facts may be looked to.

That it may not, is a contention of appellant, Rebori.

The rule in such case is well stated by Mr. Jones in his work on Real Property, § 466:

"A grant of land bounded upon a public street will be referred to the street as actually built and used, rather than to the street as shown upon a recorded plat or map. . . . It is like any other monument described as a boundary, a monument existing in fact. But where land is conveyed bounded by the line of a highway, parol evidence is admissible to show whether, by such description, the parties meant the surveyed line of the highway or the line actually used and occupied."

See, also, 2 Devlin on Deeds (3d Ed.) § 1015(a); 5 Cyc. 867; Wead v. St. Johnsbury, etc., R. Co., 64 Vt. 52, 24 A. 361.

The existence of the right of way constituted a valid outstanding incumbrance on the land, which the covenantee had a right to remove; and the rule is that he is entitled on doing so, as damages for the breach of the covenant against incumbrances, to recover the amount necessarily paid in the discharge, with interest, provided the expenditure was fair and reasonable. Kenney v. Norton, 10 Heisk. (57 Tenn.) 384; Robinson v. Bierce, 102 Tenn. 428, 52 S.W. 992, 47 L.R.A. 275; 3 Sedg.Damages (9th Ed.) § 978.

Other assignments of error are disposed of in a memorandum for decree. Affirmed.

NOTE

A common difficulty in a metes and bounds description is the failure of the various calls to enclose a specific area. Consider the following description and accompanying diagram.

"Beginning on Market street, between the lot hereby intended to be conveyed and a lot confirmed by the government of the United States to Ambrose R. Davenport; thence north, 62 degrees 15 minutes west, 158.96 feet; thence south, 31 degrees west, 60 feet; thence south, 62 degrees 15 minutes west, 158.96 feet, to Market Street; thence along said street north, 27 degrees 55 minutes east, to the place of beginning." Note how the description looks on the accompanying diagram.

Give the arguments for and against the validity of a deed containing this description. How do you think a court would decide the issue? See Hoban v. Cable, 102 Mich. 206, 60 N.W. 466 (1894). Assuming that a court would sustain such a deed if the description were directly in issue, what effect would this sloppy draftsmanship have on merchantability of title?

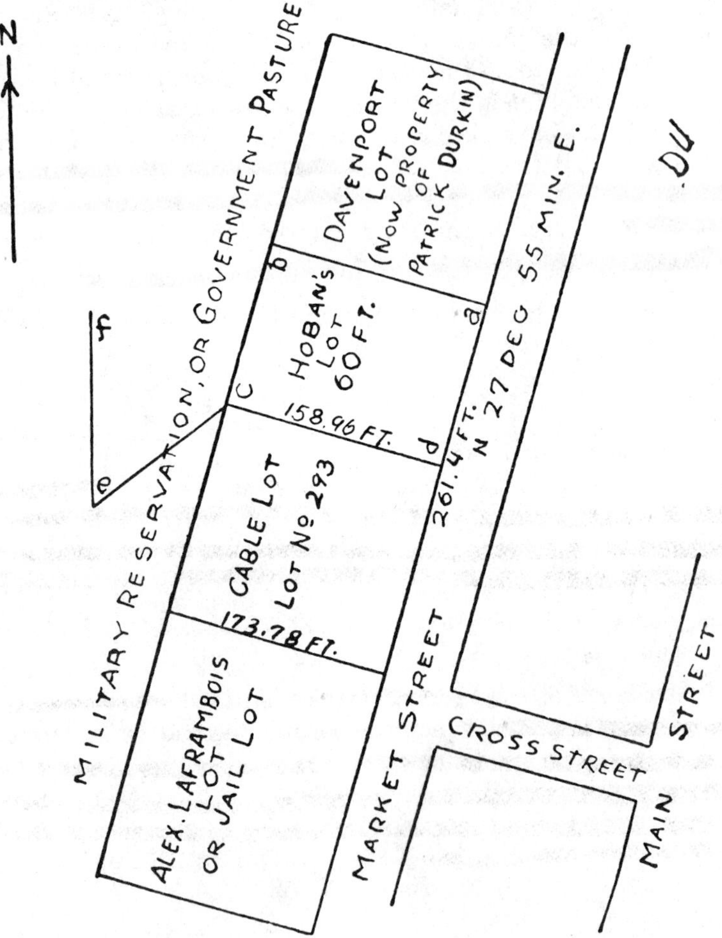

[B7315]

PARR v. WORLEY

Supreme Court of New Mexico, 1979.
93 N.M. 229, 599 P.2d 382.

EASLEY, JUSTICE.

Parr sued Worley to quiet title to the mineral interest in land occupied by a public highway. Worley counterclaimed to quiet title in himself. The court granted summary judgment for Parr. We reverse.

The questions are whether a deed conveying land "lying to the East of" the highway includes the east one-half of the highway and whether a designation of the acreage is controlling in determining the intent of the grantor.

In 1949, Parr conveyed to Worley a portion of land described as "lying to the East of" the highway, "containing 25 acres, more or less." The actual area of the land, as disclosed by a survey prepared for this action, was 25.80 acres if measured from the eastern edge of the highway right-of-way, and 31.57 acres if measured from the center of the highway. Parr later purported to convey to a third party the mineral interest under both sides of the highway with a description of the land as "lying west of the east right-of-way line of" the highway.

The trial court found no facts in dispute, and we therefore discuss whether, as a matter of law, the mineral interest in the eastern portion of the highway right-of-way was vested in Worley.

> It is a rule practically without exception that a conveyance of land abutting on a road, highway, alley, or other way, is presumed to take the fee to the center line of the way. The presumption, however, is a rebuttable one. After all, it depends upon the intention of the parties to the deed, to be ascertained from its language, viewed in the light of the surrounding circumstances. The presumption may be overcome either by express words or by the use of such words as necessarily exclude the highway from the description of the premises conveyed; but in case the language is of doubtful meaning, the presumption will prevail (Citations omitted.) . . . See also Tagliaferri v. Grande, 16 N.M. 486, 493, 120 P. 730, 732, (1911) where a deed calling for an acequia as a boundary was held to carry title to the center of the acequia in which this court stated:
>
> > We deem it, therefore, the law of this jurisdiction that a boundary call for an irrigating ditch goes, in the absence of some contrary intent manifested in the instrument, to the middle of the ditch.

Parr makes three arguments: (1) the reasons which justify the presumption do not exist in the present case; (2) the deed to Worley contains language that expressly excluded the highway from the conveyance, thus, the presumption is rebutted; and (3) Worley had constructive notice that Parr claimed title to the mineral interest under the highway and acquiesced thereto. We discuss the first two arguments together since they involve construction of the deed.

Parr cites Stuart v. Fox, 129 Me. 407, 409, 152 A. 413, 415 (1930) as authority that the presumption is justified "on the theory that the grantor could not have intended to retain the ownership in a long narrow strip of land of no apparent benefit to himself." Parr argues that the retention of mineral interest is of clear apparent benefit, and therefore the presumption should not apply. However, Parr could have, but did not, reserve the mineral interest in his deed to Worley.

There are other reasons which support the presumption.

> The reasons for the rule are variously assigned as public policy to prevent disputes and litigation over narrow gores of land, that a highway being a momument, the call should run to the center, or that the small strip is of little value to the grantor as compared with the grantee. (Footnotes omitted.) . . .

Generally, the theory that a small, narrow strip of land was of little value to the grantor grew out of a line of cases involving, essentially, subdivisions where larger plots of land were sold by lot, usually with provisions for alleys, highways, roads, etc. See e.g., Pilkington v. Fausone, 11 Cal.App.3d 349, 90 Cal.Rptr. 38 (1970); Hixson v. Jones, 253 Cal.App.2d 860, 61 Cal.Rptr. 883 (1967). Frequently in these cases, the roadways or alleys were later abandoned, and questions then arose concerning title to them. We note that, as Thompson, supra, has phrased the issue, the question goes to the "value to the grantor *as compared with the grantee.*" In the present case, the mineral interest in question is clearly of as much value to the grantee as to the grantor. However, we need not rely solely on this fact, because another theory which justifies this presumption is also present in this case.

The deed in question described the property as "[a]ll that part of the Southeast Quarter [of a certain section] lying to the East of United States Highway No. 62 and 180. . . ." Similar references in deeds to highways or streets have been considered to indicate monuments, and the general rule is that the line runs through the center of a monument. *Tagliaferri,* supra. "The statement in the deed that the land was all north of the pike has reference to a well known highway, which we may regard as a monument." . . .

The area, as stated in the deed, is the only other fact, either from the deed or from the surrounding circumstances, which could arguably indicate that the reference to the highway was not intended by the parties as a monument indicating the boundary. This fact alone is not sufficient. "[a]n order of precedence has been established among different calls for the location of boundaries, and other things being equal, resort is to be had first to natural objects or landmarks, next to artificial monuments, then to adjacent boundaries, then to courses and distances, and *lastly to quantity.*" *Haverstick,* 37 N.E.2d at 654–55 (emphasis in original; citation omitted). Accord, 23 Am.Jur.2d, Deeds, § 240 (1965); 26 C.J.S. Deeds, § 100 (1956). In *Haverstick,* the issue was whether a call for area in a deed extended the conveyance *beyond* the center line of a highway which was called for as a monument. The court held that it did not overcome the presumption that the center line of the highway was the true boundary. See Askins v. British-American Oil Producing Co., 201 Okl. 209, 203 P.2d 877, 880–81 (1949), in which the court stated:

> We are unwilling to hold that the mere statement of quantity in the deeds clearly and plainly disclosed that such was the intention of the parties, and in such case the doubt should be resolved against the grantor. (Citation omitted.)

See also Bowers v. Atchison, T. & S.F. Ry. Co., 119 Kan. 202, 237 P. 913 (Kan.1925).

We subscribe to the above language in *Askins* and hold that the Parr deed did not clearly and plainly disclose an intention to exclude the east side of the highway from the description. We construe the deed to refer to the highway as a monument, and as such, the deed passes title to the center line. Cordova v. Town of Atrisco, 53 N.M. 76, 201 P.2d 996 (1949); *Tagliaferri, supra.*

Parr argues that, in the phrase "lying to the East of [the highway]", the word "to" was intended to be a word of exclusion; and thus, the highway is excluded from the grant. However, the cases cited by Parr to support this point are clearly distinguishable on their facts.

Parr makes two arguments based on the subsequent acts of the parties: (1) that the subsequent acts are relevant to the practical construction which the parties gave to the deed, and (2) that the subsequent acts constitute acquiescence. The subsequent acts relied on are the actions of just one party, Parr. He relies on the later mineral leases, filed of record, which purported to cover the disputed area. Parr argues that Worley should have been aware of these leases, and yet he did nothing.

Acquiescence in a boundary line requires some form of knowledge. Platt v. Martinez, 90 N.M. 323, 563 P.2d 586 (1977). In the absence of some indication that Worley was or should have been aware of the subsequent filing of mineral leases by Parr, the doctrine of aquiescence does not apply.

We reverse and remand this case to the trial court for entry of judgment in favor of Worley.

IT IS SO ORDERED.

Sosa, C.J., and Payne, J., concur.

NOTES

1. In Roeder Company v. Burlington Northern, Inc., 105 Wn.2d 567, 716 P.2d 855 (1986), grantor owned land abutting, and extending to the center of, a railroad right of way. The deed from grantor described, in part, the land conveyed as extending "thence North [353 feet] to the South line of the Railroad Right–of–Way . . .; thence Easterly along said Right–of–Way South line [160 feet]; thence South. . . ." The court concluded, "When . . . a deed refers to the right of way as a boundary but also gives a metes and bounds description of the abutting

property, the presumption of [a conveyance] to the center of the right of a way is rebutted."

For an interesting case involving a conveyance of land by a city for a state university campus see City of Albany v. State of New York, 28 N.Y.2d 352, 321 N.Y.S.2d 877, 270 N.E.2d 705 (1971). The land was bordered by an unopened street and, while the court approved of the general rule of a presumption that the grant carries to the center line, it refused to apply it where the original grantor was a municipality. Said the court: "There is an obvious and material distinction between the case of a conveyance by an individual of lands bounded upon, or by, a street and that of a similar conveyance by municipal authorities. The presumption that obtains ordinarily in the one case, I think, should be regarded as offset in the other by another presumption—that the municipality would not part with the ownership and control of a public street once vested in it for public benefit."

Despite the general presumption followed in the principal case, note that because of the diverse statutory provisions and municipal ordinances relating to highways and streets and because of the terms, conditions and express language of particular grants in deeds, each case must be considered on the basis of its own particular facts and circumstances. For a more detailed discussion of the problems involved see 1 Flick, Abstract and Title Practice 232–236 (1958).

2. As the principal case indicates, the list of priorities sometimes relied on by courts to resolve inconsistencies in descriptions is, in descending order with the most reliable first: (1) natural monuments, (2) artificial monuments and marked or surveyed lines, (3) adjacent tracts or boundaries, (4) courses or directions, (5) distances, and (6) area or quantity. See Cunningham, Stoebuck & Whitman, The Law of Property 731 (1984). However, these priorities may be disregarded in light of extrinsic evidence of contrary intent. Also, other rules of construction may come into play. In Bernard v. Nantucket Boys' Club, Inc., 391 Mass. 823, 465 N.E.2d 236 (1984), the court decided, in light of the particular facts, not to resolve the inconsistency by preferring natural monuments over artificial ones, but rather to apply "a long-established rule of construction . . . not cited by the parties," i.e., "that the language, being the language of the grantor, is to be construed most strongly against him."

3. In many parts of the country water frequently forms a boundary line for real property. The boundary-changing propensities of a stream furnish a constant source of litigation. For a brief discussion of the issues presented by variable boundary lines see Burby, Real Property 51–53 (3d ed. 1965).

4. Although a reference to the area or quantity of land conveyed may be given low priority in the construction of a deed, it sometimes is of importance to the parties, especially in calculating the sale price. In Hagenbuch v. Chapin, 149 Ill.App.3d 572, 102 Ill.Dec. 886, 500 N.E.2d 987 (1986), both the public auction advertisement and the warranty deed for a farm described it as containing "129 acres, more or less." Bids were accepted "on a per acre basis," and plaintiff's successful offer

was "$2610.00 per acre × 129 acres = $336,690.00." After the closing, plaintiff had the land surveyed, learned that it contained only 123 acres, and sued vendor to recover for the deficiency. After finding that there had been no fraudulent misrepresentation by vendor, the court still held for the buyer. "Where the sale is in gross—for a lump sum regardless of the acreage—the vendor is not liable for any deficiency in the acreage except for fraud. By contrast, where the sale is by the acre, the vendor will be held liable for such deficiency. . . . Where a farm is sold and described as containing any certain number of acres, a presumption arises that the sale is by the acre and not in gross."

5. Even though the boundaries to land may appear to be clearly fixed in the deed they are subject to change in fact due to the doctrines of acquiescence and adverse possession.

The distinction between acquiescence and adverse possession is clear in theory but clouded in practice. The former is based on an oral agreement following a bona fide dispute between the parties, a taking of possession in accordance with the agreement, and a long acquiescence in the agreed line. Some authorities do not require the long acquiescence, apparently resting the doctrine on estoppel, and even those cases which require the passage of a period of time do not necessarily equate it with the period of the statute of limitations. See Burby on Real Property 310–311 (3d ed. 1965).

See also Stith v. Williams, 227 Kan. 32, 605 P.2d 86 (1980) where a syllabus by the court noted: "Where the parties by mutual agreement fix boundary lines and thereafter acquiesce in the lines so agreed upon, they must be considered as the true boundary lines between them, even though the period of acquiescence falls short of the time fixed by statute for gaining title by adverse possession."

Adverse possession (treated in detail on pages 1392 to 1419, infra) is based on a statutory period and requires a proof of adverseness which is the antithesis of agreement. Frequently the courts confuse the two doctrines or sustain the boundary without clarifying the real basis of the opinion. For a case illustrating this point see Tull v. Ashcraft, 231 Ark. 928, 333 S.W.2d 490 (1960) where the majority of the court sustained a boundary after thirty-five years by presuming an agreement and acquiescence although the minority would have defeated it because there was lack of adverseness as shown by evidence that the claimant was willing to give up the disputed strip until he learned of the statute of limitations shortly before the trial.

Whatever the basis for decision in these boundary line disputes, it is clear that the courts are prone to sustain long-established boundaries even when they conflict with the language of the deed. See Sobol v. Gulinson, 94 Colo. 92, 95, 28 P.2d 810, 811 (1933), where the judge quotes with approval the following statement of a Texas court: "These settlements of disputed, conflicting, or doubtful boundaries should be encouraged by the courts as a means of suppressing spiteful and vexatious litigation, and thus banishing from peaceful communities a fruitful source of discord. 'Convenience, policy, necessity, justice—all unite in sustaining such an amicable agreement.'"

6. Under proper circumstances it is possible to grant or to reserve certain property interests by a conveyance and never mention the interest in the deed. This is the area of easements created by implication (necessity or easements implied from quasi easements) and materials covering the problems are frequently inserted at this point. We have chosen to cover this material under creation of easements, pages 601 to 613. "As to the effect of a conveyance of land, not as creating an easement, but as conveying an easement already existing, it is well settled that such an easement will pass on a conveyance of the land to which it appertains, that is, the dominant tenement, even though there is no reference to the specific easement, or any statement that all the 'appurtenances' or 'privileges' belonging to the land shall pass therewith." 4 Tiffany, Real Property 122–123 (3d ed. 1939).

Chapter 25

THE RECORDING SYSTEM

The recording system lies at the heart of the modern commercial transaction affecting land. In contrast, recording plays an insignificant role in the transfer of personal property and is important only where chattel mortgages or conditional sales contracts are involved.[1] By now you are well aware that "title" to real estate is a slippery concept, yet every purchaser is eager to receive full value for his money and certainly does not wish to buy a defective title. In the next chapter we will explore the methods of title assurance so that you may understand the lawyer's role in protecting the purchaser of land, but first we must take a look at the mechanics and operation of the recording system, since the two principal methods of assurance (abstract examination and title insurance) are based on recording.

"Apart from the recording acts priority between deeds, mortgages, judgments and other liens or titles, is determined by the order in point of time in which they become effective. Where A conveys land by a valid deed to B, and conveys or mortgages the same land to C, nothing passes to C since A had nothing to convey to him, having already conveyed the same property to B. So, if A mortgages the land to B and later conveys or mortgages it to C, the right secured by C is subject to B's mortgage. This is true though C be a purchaser for value without notice of B's deed or mortgage. The doctrine that a purchaser for value without notice will be protected against prior claims applies only to cases where the legal title has passed to such purchaser and the prior claims are equitable and not legal rights. This doctrine is purely equitable, equity refusing to disturb the legal title by enforcing a prior equity where such title is held by a purchaser for value without notice. Apart from the statutes, therefore, a valid title or lien existing and enforceable at law is never cut off or affected by a subsequent deed or mortgage executed by the same vendor or owner to another person, whether a purchaser for value or not."[2]

There is logic in the "first in time, first in right" scheme of priority, but it is the logic of theory, not of practice. In a complex society purchasers have no way of checking on the status of title unless they can rely on some official record which shows all of the transactions in regard to the land in question. In the United States[3] the recording system has furnished the solution to the purchaser's dilemma by

1. For these problems see the course in Sales or Commercial Law.

For an excellent symposium on notice and recordation see 47 Iowa L.Rev. 221–495 (1962). Several of the leading articles and notes are directly relevant to the materials of this chapter and should be consulted for a more detailed treatment of individual issues.

2. 2 Walsh, Commentaries on the Law of Real Property 487, 488 (1947).

3. "Except as registration of title under a Torrens law obtains in the city and county of London, and except lands affected by the registry acts for the counties of Middlesex and York, proof of title in England is to this day by possession of the property and by exhibition of the original title deeds.

creating a permanent record which can be examined by anyone wishing to buy land or lend money on it as a security interest. The net effect of the system is to introduce by statute the equitable concept of bona fide purchaser for value without notice so that the b.f.p. takes free of prior deeds, mortgages, leases, etc., if they are not recorded as required by the particular act.

The acts set forth the instruments which are authorized to be recorded, and while there is considerable variation they generally include deeds, mortgages, assignments of mortgages, leases, and executory contracts. Some acts are broad enough to include virtually any document: "Deeds, mortgages, powers of attorney, and other instruments relating to or affecting the title to real estate." [4] These instruments are copied (originally in a flowing script unknown today and now by photostatic means) into books kept in a public office in the local unit of government (usually a county) where the land is located. Typically the instruments go into the record as tendered, without regard to the names of the parties or the location of the tracts being conveyed. (Indeed in some areas little attention is paid to the instruments themselves and one wag tells of the county clerk who would put a menu on record if a fee were tendered.) Since in many counties there will be hundreds of books and thousands of instruments, it is apparent that careful indexing is required if the recording system is to make any sense whatever.

There are two basic systems of indexing—the grantor-grantee system and the tract system. The present trend is to reduce the number of indexes and use only one grantor-grantee index, but many states have a separate index for each type of instrument (mortgagor-mortgagee, mechanic's lien, index to miscellaneous documents, etc.) The next excerpt explains the two systems of indexing and describes the complicated process of searching a title.

NELSON AND WHITMAN, REAL ESTATE TRANSFER, FINANCE AND DEVELOPMENT

Pages 196–203 (2d ed. 1981).

Searching a Title. With the foregoing basic knowledge of recording acts, we are now ready to discuss how titles are searched. If you practice law on the eastern seaboard, there is a good chance that you will use this information directly in your practice. In other areas of the country, abstract or title insurance companies perform most searches, but an understanding of the process is still very helpful to real estate attorneys.

All privately-held land titles (except those derived from accretion or adverse possession) can be traced back through a chain of owners to some original conveyance from a sovereign, typically the federal gov-

. . . But, with the exception first noted, there has never been any provision in England by which proof of title may be made from public and semipublic records alone, as is now so universally the case in this country." 1 Patton, Titles 8 (1957). England is now moving to the Torrens system throughout the nation. See pages 1355 to 1366, infra.

4. Ill.Rev.Stat., c. 30, § 27 (1981).

ernment or a state. Let us invent a simple chain of title which we can use as the basis for illustration of title search problems. You may wish to sketch it out on a separate piece of paper so you can keep it before you as you read the remainder of this section. It appears [below].

The patent is merely a grant of title by the state. The present owner of the land is Davis, and we will assume that he proposes to sell it to your client, who has asked you to search and examine the title. When you receive this assignment, you know nothing about the prior title history of the land; you are merely told its legal description, (Lot 4, Block G, Suburban Acres) and the fact that Donald Davis presently claims to own it.

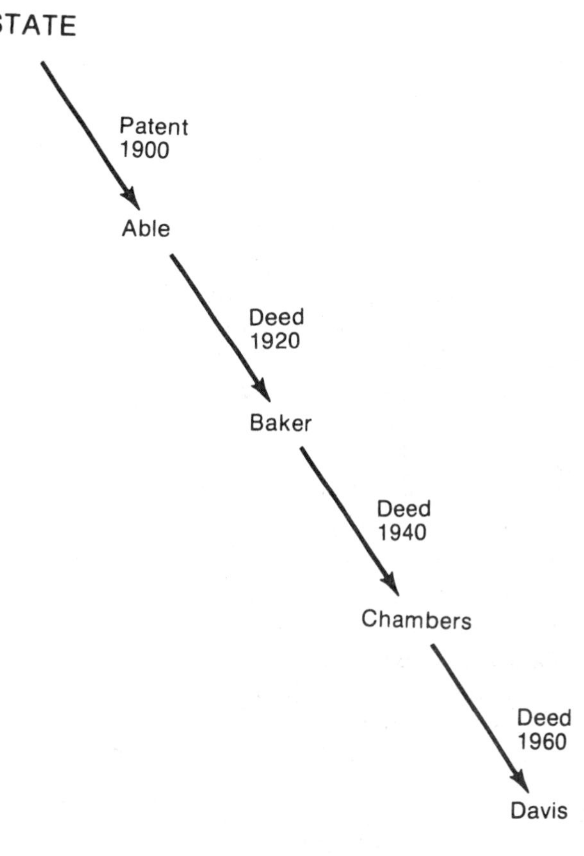

[C3060]

How will you proceed? The answer depends on the type of indexing which is employed by the recorder in your jurisdiction. From the searcher's viewpoint, indexing by tract or parcel is by far the better method. This approach allocates a separate page or set of pages in the index books to each parcel of land, or perhaps to each tract (such as a quarter-quarter section) even though it might contain several parcels. As each instrument is brought into the courthouse for recordation, an entry is made on the appropriate page for the parcel which the instrument affects. Below is a brief section of a typical page:

Parcel Index Lot 3, Block L, Eastlawn Estates Subdivision					
Type of Instrm't	Grantors, etc.	Grantees, etc.	Doc. No.	Date Filed	Book & Page
[Note: for prior instruments, see SE¼ of NW¼, T4N, R2E.]					
Subdiv. Plat	Eastlawn Devel. Co.	-------	45872	9–15 1949	34–17 Plat Bk
Deed of Trust	Eastlawn Devel. Co.	Fourth State Bank	47339	10–10 1949	117–667
Reconv.	Fourth State Bank	Eastlawn Devel. Co.	48960	5–12 1950	119–88
Deed	Eastlawn Devel. Co.	Shaw, Harry & Betty	48961	5–12 1950	119–89
Deed of Trust	Shaw, Harry & Betty	Last Federal Sav. & Loan	48962	5–12 1950	119–90
Lis Pen.	Shaw, Harry & Betty	Gotcha, George	53964	8–30 1952	124–733

[C3058]

This particular page represents the title history of the land commencing at the time it was subdivided by the filing of an approved plat. The reference at the top of the page shows where the same land's pre-subdivision records would be indexed. You should be able to follow the imposition and later satisfaction of the construction loan deed of trust given by the developer, the deed to the first owners of the house which the developer built on the land, and their deed of trust to the lender who made the loan with which they bought the house. Finally, you can see that they apparently had a dispute concerning title to their land, and were sued in connection with it by George Gotcha in 1952.

With this sort of index, the construction by the searcher of a chain of title is relatively easy, for all of the information is on a single page. Of course, it may be necessary to consult other records in other offices (e.g., for wills, intestacies, judgments, property taxes, etc.), but in most cases the chain can be determined without much trouble. The searcher must then pull the books from the shelves and examine the actual copies of the instruments themselves to see if they appear to be regular and indeed affect the land in question. The references in the last column on the right in the index book tell the searcher where each document will be found. If any prior owner has made an "adverse conveyance"—one which impairs the present quality of the title or makes it unmarketable—that fact will also be easy to see. The lis pendens would be considered such an adverse conveyance unless it had been removed later or a statute of limitations had cut it off.

The tract index is very convenient for searchers, but it does require a reasonable amount of skill on the part of the recording office personnel, since they must read every instrument with some care to determine what land it affects, so that it can be properly indexed. This is not hard when the legal description is based on a recorded subdivision plat as in our example, but it can be formidable with descriptions based on natural monuments (e.g., "to the old white oak tree", etc.) Perhaps for this reason, only a few American states provide in their recording statutes for the maintenance of tract or parcel indexes.[5] In the great majority of states, the only official indexes available to searchers in the courthouse are "name" indexes—those based on the names of the parties to a given instrument. They are easier to construct and maintain, but much harder to search in. There is little pressure from any organized group—recorders, lawyers, title companies, or the public—for reform. Hence there is only modest movement toward the establishment of public tract indexes in this country. The overall advantages of the tract index are attested by the fact that virtually every privately-owned set of title records ("title plant") in the nation employs tract indexing!

Suppose you are not fortunate enough to practice in a state with an official tract index. (Ironically, in those states few lawyers perform searches in the public records.) Instead, you find that you must search in the name indexes in your courthouse. How can you construct a chain of title to the land your client wishes to buy from Davis? There are dual sets of name indexes; one set is arranged alphabetically by the name of the grantee(s) to each instrument, and the other alphabetically by the name of the grantor(s). You will begin your work in the grantee index, which might take a form like this:

Grantee Index Year 1960 Grantee's Names beginning with Da						
Type of Instrm't	Grantee's Name	Grantor's Name	Doc. No.	Date Filed	Book & Page	Brief Legal Description
Release of Easm't	Davis, Abner	Voltzman Elect. Power Co.	2243	5-22 1960	344-221	Lt. 14, Block B Ridge Estates
Mech's Lien	Damion Plumbing & Heating	Fish, Frederick	4322	8-16 1960	346-132	E ½ of SE ¼ Sec. 22, R2E T3N
Deed	Davis, Donald	Chambers, Elaine	2089	8-19 1960	346-367	Lot 4, Block G Suburban Acres
Lease	Dalton's Men's Wear	Watson Real Estate, Inc.	4531	8-28 1960	346-451	Lots 3-4, Brown's Addition No. 2

[C3061]

There are several interesting features of the grantee index page above. The grantee's names are not in exact alphabetical order, since they are entered on the page (this one labeled "Da") as they come into the office for recordation. In some sophisticated offices, a computer program may be used to resort and reprint the pages periodically in accurate alphabetical order. Note that all entries are during the year

5. All of the states authorizing tract indexing are in the area of the nation covered by the government survey system, which tends to minimize the difficulties of land descriptions. States which have tract indexes in all counties include Nebraska, North Dakota, Oklahoma, South Dakota, Utah, and Wyoming. States which permit tract indexing on a county option basis include Kansas, Ohio, Wisconsin, and Minnesota. New York City has a "block index" system. See generally Note, The Tract and Grantor-Grantee Indices, 47 Iowa L.Rev. 481 (1962). USLTA mandates a tract index, but it has not yet been adopted by any state legislature; see § 6–207. It also contains an interesting and apparently unprecedented feature requiring those who present instruments for recordation to supply "information fixing the location sufficiently to enable the recording officer to determine where in the geographic index the document is to be indexed;" § 2–302(a)(4). [The authors' footnotes have been renumbered.]

1960. In large urban counties, a new set of index books is generally made up each year; if this were not done, the books would soon become so large as to be physically unmanageable. In rural counties with few transactions, the indexes might be allowed to accumulate over a five-year or even ten-year period before a new set is begun.

Now, to search Donald Davis' title, we must begin by looking for his name in the grantee index, since if he owns the land he must have been a grantee under a deed at some past time. Unless we can get a copy of Davis' deed from him or he tells us when he acquired the land, we will not know in which of the (possibly yearly) grantee books to check, so we must start with the present year and work our way backwards, looking for Davis' name as a grantee. When we finally get to 1960 and read the page reproduced above, we will find him. Scanning across to the "Brief Legal Description" column will verify that the entry does in fact affect the land we are searching. (Unfortunately, in some states there is no such column, and we would have to look up in the actual record books each deed which is indexed with Davis as a grantee to see what land it covered. If Davis had bought a good deal of real estate in the county, this could become exceedingly tedious. Even where the indexes carry this column, there may be a serious but rarely litigated question as to whether a searcher can safely rely upon it; as a practical matter, searches obviously do so.)

We must now look for the next link (going backward in time) in the chain of title. We do so by looking for Elaine Chambers' name in the grantee index, since the entry which we found under Davis' name told us that Chambers was Davis' grantor. We assume that Chambers received title to the land prior to the time she deeded it to Davis (although this need not always be true under the doctrine of estoppel by deed), and begin looking for her name as a grantee in 1960. Searching back year by year, we will find her as a grantee from Baker in 1940. We then search for Baker as a grantee, and so on, until we come back to the original patent from the state in 1900.

We now have a complete chain of title to the land, but that is only the first of three major steps in searching the record title. The second step involves determining whether any of the owners we have identified has made any adverse conveyances. Suppose, for example, that Able (who obtained the land in 1900) granted an easement to Zoller in 1910. You might wish to pencil in such a grant on the diagram of the chain. We would certainly want to advise our client that the easement exists. How can we discover such conveyances? We must use the other set of name indexes, those arranged alphabetically by the name of the grantor. A part of a typical page might look as follows:

Grantor Index Year 1910 Grantor's Names beginning with Aa through Ac						
Type of Instrm't	Grantor's Name	Grantee's Name	Doc. No.	Date Filed	Book & Page	Brief Legal Description
Mortg.	Ackerman, Alan	Third Nat'l Bank	2276	1–14 1910	22–889	Pt. of N ½ Sec. 5 R3E T6S
Grant of Easement	Able, Abner	Zoller, Charles	2298	2–21 1910	22–970	Lot 4, Block G Suburban Acres
Assign. of Mtg.	Abbott Mortgage Co.	Philadelphia Soc. for Savings	2375	4–12 1910	23–29	Lot 18, Summit Ridge Add'n
Release of Mtg.	Abbott Mortgage Co.	Weller, Frank & Martha	2418	7–7 1910	23–445	S ½ of NE ¼ Sec. 12, R3E T5S

[C3062]

We will begin with Able's name.[6] Since he acquired the land in 1900 and deeded it away to Baker in 1920, we will look for any conveyances with Able as a grantor during that period. (We reserve for later discussion whether we need to look under his name prior to 1900 or after 1920). Again we check year by year, this time in the grantor index. The page reprinted above shows that in 1910 Able was a grantor to Zoller of an easement. Unless we subsequently find a release of the easement by Zoller (which we can find by looking in the grantor index under his name), we will conclude that the easement still exists and will report it to our client as affecting the current state of the title. Of course, some off-record circumstances, such as a stone wall which has blocked the path of the easement for 30 years, might convince us that despite the records the easement is no longer viable but has been terminated by prescription.

We must check the grantor index in a similar fashion for Baker, Chambers, and Davis to see if any of them made adverse conveyances. We are very likely to find, for example, that one or more of them gave mortgages or deeds of trust on the land. We must then use the grantor

6. Why not begin with the state itself? It is surely possible that the state land office inadvertently issued two patents on the same land. If our chain of title derives from the second, then it presumably has no validity at all. In some states, the recording acts or other statutes specifically treat state patents in the same manner as other deeds; thus, if the first patent were unrecorded in the county records, the second one would prevail in the hands of a BFP. See 2 Patton, Titles § 296 (2d ed.1957), listing 16 states with such statutes; Meacham v. Stewart, 19 Or. 285, 24 P. 241 (1890). In other jurisdictions there is no applicable statute, and the records of the state land office are sufficient to sustain the first patent even against a BFP holder of the second. See, e.g., United States v. Buras, 332 F.Supp. 1017 (E.D.La.1970), rev'd, 458 F.2d 346 (5th Cir.1972); Moran v. Palmer, 13 Mich. 367 (1865). In these states, a careful title searcher ought to review the records in the land office to make certain that no earlier patent covers the land in question. The same is true of federal patents, since state recording statutes cannot divest them; Patton, supra; Lomax v. Pickering, 173 U.S. 26, 19 S.Ct. 416, 43 L.Ed. 601 (1899); Sayward v. Thompson, 11 Wash. 706, 40 P. 379 (1895); 8A Thompson, Real Property § 4348 (1963). Even though the records of the United States patent offices are constructive notice to subsequent purchasers, and many states would probably take the same position with respect to state-issued patents, it is doubtful that many title searchers attempt to check for duplicate or overlapping patents. See also United States v. Eaton Shale Co., 433 F.Supp. 1256 (D.Colo. 1977), in which the court held that a BFP was not on constructive notice of records in the Department of the Interior which indicated that his title was based on a mistakenly-issued patent. The court noted that the records in question were not readily accessible to the public. On federal patent procedures generally, see III Am.L.Prop. § 12.20 (1952).

index to trace any further transfers or releases of these interests in order to determine whether they still affect the title today. We might even discover that Baker was a crook, and gave a deed to some person outside our chain of title (say, Zobell), in 1930. Zobell, in turn, might have started a chain of further conveyances leading down to a present owner who would claim title as

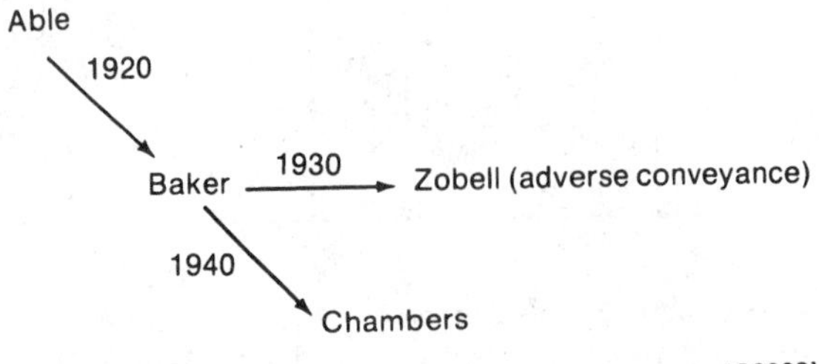

against Davis. If the deed from Baker to Zobell were recorded, it (and persons claiming under it) would have priority over the chain of title we have discovered from Baker through Chambers to Davis, and Davis would own nothing. Fortunately, since the deed to Zobell was recorded, we will be able to find it by our normal search process, and thus can warn our client not to buy the land from Davis. On the other hand, if the deed from Baker to Zobell were not recorded, then we would need only to show that Chambers, Davis, or our own client was a BFP in order to cut off Zobell by operation of the recording acts. Incidentally, if Chambers, for example, were a BFP, then Davis (and our client) could take the land safely even though they were aware of the unrecorded adverse conveyance to Zobell. This is so because of the "shelter" or "BFP filter" theory, which says that once title has come into the hands of a BFP who is protected by the recording acts, he or she can pass that protection on to grantees even if they have notice of the adverse conveyance.[7] If this were not the rule, and if the news of Baker's adverse conveyance to Zobell became common knowledge in the community after Baker's conveyance to Chambers, she might find that she owned the land but could not as a practical matter sell it to anyone, since no one could qualify as a BFP.

We have now completed the second major step in the search process, checking for adverse conveyances. We're ready to proceed to the third step, which requires that we look at the full copies of each of the instruments we have thus far identified. We will check them for the necessary formalities, consistency of legal descriptions, etc., and we will also be alert for any references in them to unrecorded documents or interests. Assuming that no problems develop in this area, we will check for adverse interests in relevant sources outside the county land records, such as tax and assessment liens, bankruptcies, judgment liens, and so on. Finally, we are ready to prepare an opinion of title for

7. See Hendricks v. Lake, 12 Wash.App. 15, 528 P.2d 491 (1976); IV Am.L.Prop. § 17.11 nn. 18–20 (1952); 3 Pomeroy, Equity Jurisprudence 55–57 (5th ed.1941). The one exception is that if title is transferred back to one who had previously held it with notice of the adverse conveyance before it was "cleansed" by the BFP, he will not be protected. Thus, one cannot "clean up" his own title merely by running it through a BFP. See Rose v. Knapp, 153 Cal.App.2d 379, 314 P.2d 812 (1957).

transmission to our client. Since we have only performed a search in the records, we cannot deny the possible existence of some off-record claims, such as those of parties in possession, undisclosed spouses of prior owners, etc. Many careful lawyers use "boilerplate" language in their title opinions to exclude such matters from coverage.

In the present chapter we shall explore some of the problems created by the recording system and note the judicial construction of the recording acts. You must keep constantly in mind that we are dealing with *statutes* and that there will be variations from jurisdiction to jurisdiction. Obviously, you should become familiar with the recording act of your own state. We shall look first at the general operation of the system, then at the persons who are entitled to protection by the system, and finally at the theory and application of the chain of title concept.

SECTION 1. GENERAL OPERATION OF THE SYSTEM

MOUNTAIN STATES TELEPHONE & TELEGRAPH CO. v. KELTON

Supreme Court of Arizona, 1955.
79 Ariz. 126, 285 P.2d 168.

[The telephone company brought an action against property owners and a contractor for damage to an underground cable laid across land under a perpetual easement which had been duly recorded. Only so much of the opinion as deals with constructive notice to the contractor is reproduced here. The property owners who had actual knowledge of the cable were held guilty of negligence in failing to take proper precautions.]

UDALL, JUSTICE. This action, brought to recover damages for injuries inflicted by defendants to plaintiff's underground telephone cable, was tried to the court sitting without a jury, resulting in a judgment for the defendants, and plaintiff appeals. The parties will be designated the same as they were in the lower court.

. . .

LIABILITY OF CONTRACTOR

Plaintiff contends that the court erred in finding the contractor exercised reasonable care for the reason "that the undisputed evidence shows that defendants John C. Kelton and Son entered upon the property of plaintiff with heavy digging equipment without making any inquiry as to what might lay below the surface of the premises although the right of way for the placing of the conduit and a cable was matter of record . . . ."

From the record it appears that the court's finding hereinbefore set forth, that defendants Kelton by the exercise of due care were unable to learn of plaintiff's cable, is supported by competent evidence and hence cannot be disturbed upon appeal. It is admitted that the contractor had no actual notice that there was a buried cable, nor was this fact apparent from the visible inspection made by them of the premises prior to commencing the contracted work. We cannot agree with the implication that the contractor was bound to search the records and is charged with constructive notice of the contents thereof. While this court has often said ". . . instruments authorized to be recorded, . . . when recorded, became notice to the world", First National Bank of Yuma v. Yuma Nat. Bank, 30 Ariz. 188, 245 P. 277, 278, see, also, Valley Products, Inc., v. Kubelsky, 49 Ariz. 500, 68 P.2d 69, it is apparent this statement is not wholly accurate. As stated by the Supreme Court of Pennsylvania:

> "It is sometimes said that the record of a deed is constructive notice to all the world. That, it is evident, is too broad and unqualified an enunciation of the doctrine. *It is constructive notice only to those who are bound to search for it* . . . ." (Emphasis supplied.)

Maul v. Rider, 59 Pa. 167, 171. For a good statement of the rule, see 66 C.J.S., Notice, § 13c, page 650. We do not believe the contractor in the instant case was bound to search the record to learn of plaintiff's easement. He had no interest in the title to the land. We have been cited to no cases where constructive notice was applied to such a situation, nor has an independent search revealed such an extension of the doctrine. We hold defendants Kelton were not charged with notice of plaintiff's easement, hence this assignment of error is without merit.

. . .

Judgment affirmed in part and reversed in part with directions.

LA PRADE, C.J., and WINDES, PHELPS and STRUCKMEYER, JJ., concur.

STONE v. FRENCH

Supreme Court of Kansas, 1887.
37 Kan. 145, 14 P. 530, 1 Am.St.Rep. 237.

VALENTINE, J. This was an action for the partition of 200 acres of land in Neosho county, Kansas, brought in the district court of that county on October 16, 1884, by Luther C. French against John Stone and others. The case was tried before the court and a jury, and judgment was rendered for the partition of the property, giving to the plaintiff, Luther C. French, one-seventh thereof, and to the defendant John Stone one-seventh thereof, and to the other defendants the remainder thereof; and to reverse this judgment the defendant John Stone, as plaintiff in error, brings the case to this court, making the plaintiff, Luther C. French, and all the defendants, except himself, defendants in error.

It appears that on March 1, 1878, and prior thereto, the property in controversy belonged to Francis B. French, although he had not yet entirely paid for the same. At that time he formed the intention of giving this land at his death to his brother, Dudley S. French, unless he should sell the same during his life-time. On March 1, 1878, he wrote a letter to his brother, Dudley S. French, in which he stated, among other things, the following: "In case I should drop off, you can take possession of the land, and do with it as you please. When I have paid the land out, if not sold, I will make a deed to it to you, inclose it in envelope, direct it to you, to be mailed in event of death, which would make it sure to you without expense or trouble." Nearly one year afterwards, and on February 18, 1879, Francis B. French signed a warranty deed for the property to Dudley S. French, and on April 4, 1879, acknowledged the deed before S. Michaels, a justice of the peace in said county. The deed also contained the words: "Signed, sealed, and delivered in the presence of S. Michaels." The deed, however, never was in fact delivered.

On August 2, 1879, Francis B. French died, in the possession of and owning the land in controversy. During all this time he was a single man, and did not leave at his death any wife or child, or father or mother, but left several brothers, including the plaintiff, Luther C. French, and Dudley S. French. It does not appear that any person except Michaels and Francis B. French ever saw the aforesaid deed, or had the slightest knowledge thereof until about half an hour before French died, when it was found by William Welch inclosed in an envelope, with a letter, in a cigar box, in the drawer of a table in the house occupied as a residence by French. The following words were indorsed upon this envelope: "This deed to be placed in the recorder's office at Erie, Kansas, for record, and the accompanying letter to be mailed as per direction thereon." At the time this deed was found, French was speechless and unconscious, and remained in that condition until he died, about half an hour afterwards. Welch immediately telegraphed to Dudley S. French, who resided at Clinton, Illinois, and French came to Kansas, arriving at the place where Francis B. French died on August 4, 1879. Shortly afterwards, Welch delivered to French the aforesaid deed. This is the first time that French ever saw the deed, and he never heard of it until after the death of Francis B. French. On August 6, 1879, Dudley S. French filed the deed for record in the office of the register of deeds of Neosho county, Kansas. Dudley S. French then took possession of the land, and remained in the possession thereof until he sold the same to John Stone, the plaintiff in error. Dudley S. French was a brother-in-law to Stone, and for a time lived at his house. He was weak in body and in mind, and a part of the time could scarcely dress himself. On June 10, 1882, he sold and conveyed this land by warranty deed to Stone for the expressed consideration of $2,000, but for the real consideration of only $800. He was a single man at the time. The land was worth about $3,000. Stone at the time did not know that there was an infirmity in the title of Dudley S. French, and for the purposes of this case he must be considered as *in fact a bona fide purchaser,* whatever the law may be.

The deed from Dudley S. French to Stone was recorded on June 16, 1882. At some time during the summer of 1882, Stone took possession of the land, and has remained in the possession thereof ever since. This action was commenced on October 16, 1884. All the heirs at law of Francis B. French, including the plaintiff below, Luther C. French, and Dudley S. French, were made parties to the action, so, also, were the defendant, John Stone, and S. Michaels and others. Dudley S. French died on January 7, 1885, after this action was commenced, but before the trial was had.

It is conceded by all parties that John Stone is entitled to one-seventh of the land in controversy, that amount being admitted to be the share inherited by Dudley S. French from Francis B. French; but Stone claims that he is entitled to all the land, and whether he is entitled to only one-seventh thereof or to all the land is the only substantial question involved in this case. The principal questions presented by counsel to this court are as follows: (1) Was the deed from Francis B. French to Dudley S. French ever delivered so as to make it a valid deed? (2) If not, then, is John Stone, for any reason, entitled to more than one-seventh of the land in controversy?

There is no room for even a pretense that the deed was ever in fact delivered to Dudley S. French, or to any one else, and there is scarcely any room for even a pretense that it was ever in law delivered. The only grounds upon which it is claimed that it was ever delivered is the letter of Francis B. French to Dudley S. French, dated March 1, 1878; the indorsement on the envelope found in the cigar box on August 2, 1879; and the words contained in the deed, to-wit: "Signed, sealed, and delivered in the presence of S. Michaels." Now, it may be conceded that these things constitute some evidence of a delivery; but, when it is shown conclusively by the other evidence that there was no delivery, these things can have no force. Besides, the letter itself shows that there was no present intention on the part of Francis B. French of conveying the land, or delivering a deed to Dudley S. French; and it also shows that Francis B. French contemplated that he might before his death sell the land to some other person. Francis B. French never had any intention of conveying the land immediately, but it was always his intention, unless he sold the land, to retain the title thereto in himself as long as he lived, and to let the property go to Dudley S. French only after his death. This does not constitute a delivery of a deed or a conveyance of the land. Of course, there are cases where it is not necessary that there should be any actual manual delivery of the deed. A recording of the deed is sometimes considered as a delivery. So, also, is a delivery to a third person sometimes considered as a delivery to the grantee. And where a deed is executed by a father to an infant child, with the intention that the title shall immediately pass and vest in the child, and the father retains the custody of the deed as the natural guardian of the child, the title may pass. But none of these cases is the present case; nor is the present case anything like them. Dudley S. French was not an infant, and, although he was a man of weak mind, yet he was not *non compos mentis.* The deed was not delivered or recorded by Francis B. French, nor during his life-time, and he never had any intention that the title should pass until after his death. The deed never was a deed in law, and Dudley S. French never had any right to it; nor had he any right to have it recorded; nor did it convey any title, interest, or estate to him. It was not merely voidable, but it was absolutely void. . . .

Taking this view of the case, John Stone obtained no title from Dudley S. French; for Dudley S. French had none whatever to convey.

This is unlike a case where a deed is only voidable, and a bona fide purchaser obtains title from the holder of the same without any notice of its infirmity. In such a case he may obtain a good title; but, where the deed is absolutely void, he cannot. It seems to be admitted that if the deed were forged, that no person could obtain any title under it, however innocent he might be, but a forged deed is no more void than this deed. Both, in this respect, are precisely alike. Both are equally void. And neither the record of a forged deed, nor the record of an absolutely void deed, can be invoked to support or bolster up a disputed title; for the record is worth no more than the original deed itself. It is only instruments that have some validity, and that may in some manner affect real estate, that can be recorded legally. There is no statute authorizing the recording of a void instrument, and it is an error to suppose that the statutes can have the effect of making valid an absolutely void instrument by permitting the void instrument to be recorded. The instrument is still void, although recorded. The record can give it no validity. As tending to support the view that a purchaser of real estate from a person holding under a void recorded deed, although in fact a bona fide purchaser, cannot obtain a good or valid title, or, indeed, any title, we would refer to the following authorities: Everts v. Agnes, 6 Wis. 453; Tisher v. Beckwith, 30 Wis. 55; Chipman v. Tucker, 38 Wis. 43, 20 Amer.Rep. 1; Van Amringe v. Morton, 4 Whart. 382; Smith v. South Royalton Bank, 32 Vt. 341; Harkreader v. Clayton, 56 Miss. 383; Berry v. Anderson, 22 Ind. 37, 40. The case of Lewis v. Kirk, 28 Kan. 497, 505, has no reference to void deeds, or to the record of void deeds.

A deed not delivered at all is a very different thing from a deed actually delivered, even though the delivery of the same may have been procured through fraud; and a deed not delivered, but wrongfully in the hands of the apparent grantee, without fault or negligence on the part of the owner of the land, is unlike a deed not delivered, but through the fault or negligence of the owner has been permitted to get into the hands of the apparent grantee. In the present case the deed was never delivered, and was not permitted to get into the hands of Dudley S. French, the apparent grantee, while Francis B. French was the owner of the land; but after Francis B. French died, and after the title to the land had passed, from him to his heirs, the deed did get into the hands of Dudley S. French, the apparent grantee, but not through any fault or negligence on the part of the heirs, who were then the owners of the land.

Other points are raised in this case, but they are technical and unsubstantial and require no comment. To reverse the judgment of the court below for any of them would be a violation of the spirit of the Civil Code, and especially of sections 140 and 304. We think no substantial error has been committed in this case, and it is unnecessary to prolong this opinion.

The judgment of the court below will be affirmed.

(All the Justices concurring.)

NOTES

1. What about a deed given by a grantor who is in fact insane and hence lacks the capacity to convey land? What about an infant whose minority does not appear of record? How can a purchaser rely on the record if an apparently valid instrument may be shown to be void in fact? Would it be fair to a grantor to make recording conclusive evidence of the validity of a deed? Note the following Massachusetts statute: "The record of a deed, lease, power of attorney or other instrument, duly acknowledged or proved as provided in this chapter, and purporting to affect the title to land, shall be conclusive evidence of the delivery of such instrument, in favor of purchasers for value without notice claiming thereunder." Massachusetts Gen.Laws Ann. c. 183 § 5.

What should the owner of land do if a deed is mistakenly delivered and recorded thereby making it possible for a b.f.p. to be misled by the state of the record? See W.L. Schautz Co. v. Duncan Hosiery Mills, Inc., 218 Ga. 729, 130 S.E.2d 496 (1963) where the court indicated that equity would cancel the record of a deed which was never actually delivered but which was filed by mistake of the attorney for the grantor.

2. Generally, recording does not make an invalid instrument valid, nor is recording necessary for the validity of a deed or mortgage as between the parties. The grantor and his heirs are bound whether the grantee records or not; it is the b.f.p. who receives the protection of the acts. Two or three states have an express statutory provision that instruments of conveyance are void until recorded, but it is not clear how such a provision would be interpreted by the courts.

3. Since the recording system is statutory, a question arises as to the legal effect of a recorded deed which is defective in some respect under the specific statutes of the jurisdiction involved. Illustrative of this problem is the recorded deed which has no acknowledgment or is defectively acknowledged. Does such a deed give notice to a subsequent purchaser? The answers are far from uniform and depend largely on the wording of the state's recording act. For an interesting case see Messersmith v. Smith, 60 N.W.2d 276 (N.D.1953) where the acknowledgment was taken over the telephone, instead of in person as required by the North Dakota statute. The court treated the acknowledgment as a nullity and, because the recording act provided "an instrument is deemed to be recorded when, being duly acknowledged or proved and certified, it is deposited in the register's office with the proper officer for record", held that the recorded deed gave no notice to a subsequent purchaser who would therefore prevail over the prior grantee. Said the court: "It may be stated as a general rule that the recording of an instrument affecting the title to real estate which does not meet the statutory requirements of the recording laws affords no constructive

notice." For a comment on this case see 52 Mich.L.Rev. 927 (1954). See also Nordman v. Rau, 86 Kan. 19, 119 P. 351 (1911).

Although the court refused to protect the holder of the unacknowledged instrument, there was a strong dissent which stated, in part: "My own view of the question presented is this: Where a prospective buyer of land sees upon the record what purports to be the copy of an instrument bearing no certificate of acknowledgment (or a defective one, for the rule would necessarily be the same), the inference which he would naturally and almost necessarily draw would be that the record was made at the instance of the grantee; and that the grantee claimed to have an interest in the land under an instrument in the language of the copy. The record would not be competent legal evidence that such an instrument had been executed, but it would suggest that probability so strongly that a prudent person having knowledge of it would be put upon inquiry. It would give him a definite and tangible clue which, if diligently followed up, would ordinarily bring the truth of the matter to light." For a thorough analysis of acknowledgment problems, see Maxwell, The Hidden Defect in Acknowledgment and Title Security, 2 U.C.L.A.L.Rev. 83 (1954).

Despite the general rule that no record notice is given by instruments which fail to meet certain statutory requirements (acknowledgment, attestation, etc.) some statutes are to the contrary. See, for example, Ill–S.H.A. ch. 30, § 30 (1981): "Deeds, mortgages, and other instruments of writing relating to real estate shall be deemed, from the time of being filed for record, notice to subsequent purchasers and creditors, though not acknowledged or proven according to law; but the same shall not be read as evidence, unless their execution be proved in manner required by the rules of evidence applicable to such writings, so as to supply the defects of such acknowledgment or proof." Even in states following the general rule curative acts have made a defective instrument sufficient to give notice after a specified date.

The extreme importance of specific statutes is illustrated by Flexter v. Woomer, 46 Ill.App.2d 456, 197 N.E.2d 161 (1964). Despite Illinois' liberal position in regard to acknowledgments, the court held that a recorded mortgage was not constructive notice to a subsequent b.f.p. when it did not state the maturity date or the amount of the note. The statute required the mortgage to recite the nature and amount of the indebtedness. Should not the defectively recorded mortgage at least put the purchaser on notice of a prior lien and force him to make inquiry as to the date and amount?

After following for 135 years the general rule that documents not entitled to be recorded do not impart constructive notice, the Supreme Court of Indiana held that a mortgage recorded improperly due to the absence of the preparer's name, as required by statute, was not subject to the general rule. The court reasoned that the purpose of the 1959 "preparer statute" probably was to prevent unauthorized practice of law and that erroneous recordation of the noncomplying mortgage still gave "that kind of clear, undoubted notice of the state of legal title which the recording act contemplates." In re Sandy Ridge Oil Co., 510 N.E.2d 667 (Ind.1987).

EARLE v. FISKE

Supreme Judicial Court of Massachusetts, 1870.
103 Mass. 491.

Writ of Entry against Elizabeth L. Fiske (wife of Benjamin Fiske) and Mary E. Fiske, to recover land in Malden. Writ dated April 14, 1868. Plea, nul disseisin.

At the trial in the superior court, before Putnam, J., these facts appeared: Nancy A. Fiske, being owner of the demanded premises, conveyed them to Benjamin and Elizabeth for their lives, and, subject to their life estate, to Mary E. Fiske, by deeds dated April 22, 1864, but not recorded till 1867, and died in 1865, leaving said Benjamin, her son, as sole heir, and he in 1866 executed and delivered to the demandant a deed of the premises, which was recorded in the same year. Upon these facts, the judge ruled that Nancy A. Fiske "had no seisin, at her death, which would descend to Benjamin Fiske, so as to enable him to convey a good title" to the demandant. Upon this ruling, the demandant, who made no claim to any estate less than a fee simple, submitted to a verdict for the tenants, and alleged exceptions.

AMES, J. The formalities which shall be deemed indispensable to the valid conveyance of land are prescribed and regulated by statute. A deed duly signed, sealed and delivered is sufficient, as between the original parties to it, to transfer the whole title of the grantor to the grantee, though the instrument of conveyance may not have been acknowledged or recorded. The title passes by the deed, and not by the registration. No seisin remains in the grantor, and he has literally nothing in the premises which he can claim for himself, transmit to his heir at law, or convey to any other person. But when the effect of the deed upon the rights of third persons, such as creditors or bona fide purchasers, is to be considered, the law requires something more, namely, either actual notice, or the further formality of registration, which is constructive notice. It may not be very logical to say that, after a man has literally parted with all his right and estate in a lot of land, there still remains in his hands an attachable and transferable interest in it, of exactly the same extent and value as if he had made no conveyance whatever. But, for the protection of bona fide creditors and purchasers, the rule has been established that although an unrecorded deed is binding upon the grantor, his heirs and devisees, and also upon all persons having actual notice of it, it is not valid and effectual as against any other persons. As to all such other persons, the unrecorded deed is a mere nullity. So far as they are concerned, it is no conveyance or transfer which the statute recognizes as binding on them, or as having any capacity adversely to affect their rights, as purchasers or attaching creditors. As to them, the person who appears of record to be the owner is to be taken as the true and actual owner, and his apparent seisin is not divested or affected by any unknown and unrecorded deed that he may have made. Gen.Sts. c. 89, § 3.

It is argued, however, that, as the unrecorded deed from Nancy A. Fiske was valid and binding upon herself and her heirs at law, nothing descended from her to her son Benjamin, and he had no seisin or title which he could convey to the plaintiff. A case is cited (Hill v. Meeker, 24 Conn. 211) in which the supreme court of Connecticut (Hinman and Storrs, JJ.) in 1855 decided that a deed of land, not recorded until after the death of the grantor, is valid against a purchaser from his heir at law, although such purchaser has no knowledge of the existence of the deed. From this decision the chief justice (Waite) dissented, saying, "So far as my researches have extended, this is the first case in the whole history of our jurisprudence, in which it has ever been holden that an unrecorded deed shall defeat the title of a bona fide purchaser or mortgagee, having no knowledge of the existence of any such deed, unless it were recorded within a reasonable time." The cases cited from the decisions of the supreme court of Kentucky are to the effect also that the protection afforded by their registration laws against an unrecorded deed only extend to purchasers from the grantor himself, and not to purchasers from his heirs or devisees. Ralls v. Graham, 4 T.B.Monr. 120. Hancock v. Beverly, 6 B.Monr. 531. That court however in a more recent case, decided in 1857, say that, if it were a new question, "and had not been heretofore decided," they should be strongly inclined to give to the statute a liberal construction, and make it operate as a remedy for the whole evil which it was intended to guard against. They add, however, that as the previous decision had become a settled rule of property, it is better that the law should remain permanent, "although settled originally upon doubtful principles." Harlan v. Seaton, 18 B.Monr. 312.

We do not, under the circumstances, incline to yield to the authority of these cases in the construction of a local statute of this Commonwealth. It appears to us that the plain meaning of our system of registration is, that a purchaser of land has a right to rely upon the information furnished him by the registry of deeds, and in the absence of notice to the contrary he is justified in taking that information as true, and acting upon it accordingly. It is impossible to see why the unrecorded deed of Nancy A. Fiske should have any greater weight or force after her demise than it had immediately after it was first delivered. It could not be any more or less binding on her heir at law than it was upon herself; he was as much the apparent owner of the land as she had been during her lifetime. The manifest purpose of our statute is, that the apparent owner of record shall be considered as the true owner, (so far as subsequent purchasers without notice to the contrary are concerned,) notwithstanding any unrecorded and unknown previous alienation. As against the claim of this plaintiff, the unrecorded deed of Nancy A. Fiske had no binding force or effect, and the objection of the defendants, that in consequence of her having given that deed nothing descended to her son Benjamin from her, is one of which they cannot avail themselves. As a purchaser without notice, the plaintiff is in a position to say that the unrecorded deed had no legal force or effect; that she died seised; that the property descended to Benjamin, her son and sole heir at law. Upon that assumption his deed would take precedence over the unrecorded deed of his mother, in exactly the same manner as a deed from his mother in her lifetime would have done over any unrecorded or unknown previous deed from herself. The ruling at the trial was therefore erroneous, and the plaintiff's exceptions are sustained.

MUGAAS v. SMITH [8]

Supreme Court of Washington, 1949.
33 Wn.2d 429, 206 P.2d 332, 9 A.L.R.2d 846.

HILL, JUSTICE. This is an action by Dora B. Mugaas, a widow, to quiet title to a strip of land 135 feet in length and with a maximum width of 3½ feet which she claims by adverse possession, and to compel Delmar C. Smith and his wife to remove therefrom any and all buildings and encroachments. From a judgment quieting title to the strip in Mrs. Mugaas and directing the removal of any and all buildings and encroachments, the Smiths appeal.

The appellants contend that the respondent has failed to establish adverse possession of the tract in question. The character of the respondent's possession over the statutory period is one of fact, and the trial court's finding in that regard is to be given great weight and will not be overturned unless this court is convinced that the evidence preponderates against that finding. We are of the opinion that the evidence was sufficient to sustain the trial court's findings, and the conclusions based thereon, that the respondent had acquired title to the strip in question by adverse possession. The evidence would have warranted a finding that her adverse possession dated back to 1910.

The only serious questions raised by this appeal are attributable to the fact that the fence which between 1910 and 1928 clearly marked the boundary line for which respondent contends, disappeared by a process of disintegration in the years which followed, and, when appellants purchased the property in 1941 by a legal description and with a record title which included the disputed strip, there was no fence and nothing to mark the dividing line between the property of appellants and respondent, or to indicate to the appellants that the respondent was claiming title to the strip in question.

We have on several occasions approved a statement which appears in Towles v. Hamilton, 94 Neb. 588, 143 N.W. 935, 936, that:

"... It is elementary that, where the title has become fully vested by disseisin so long continued as to bar an action, it cannot be divested by parol abandonment or relinquishment or by verbal declarations of the disseizor, nor by any other act short of what would be required in a case where his title was by deed."

See McInnis v. Day Lumber Co., 102 Wash. 38, 172 P. 844; King County v. Hagen, Wash., 194 P.2d 357.

8. For treatment of titles acquired by adverse possession see pages 1392 to 1419, infra.

The fact that the respondent had ceased to use the strip in question in such a way that her claim of adverse possession was apparent did not divest her of the title she had acquired.

Appellants' principal contention is that we have held, in a long line of cases, that a bona fide purchaser of real property may rely upon the record title. The cases cited by appellants construe our recording statute, Rem.Rev.Stat. §§ 10596—1 to 10596—2, and involve contests between those relying upon the record title and those relying upon a prior unrecorded conveyance as conveyances are defined by Rem.Rev. Stat. § 10596—1. The holdings in the cases cited give effect to that provision of § 10596—2 which states that any unrecorded conveyance ". . . is void as against any subsequent purchaser or mortgagee in good faith and for a valuable consideration from the same vendor, his heirs or devisees, of the same real property or any portion thereof whose conveyance is first duly recorded. . . ."

Appellants cite no cases, and we have found none, supporting their contention that, under a recording statute such as Rem.Rev.Stat. §§ 10596—1, 10596—2, a conveyance of the record title to a bona fide purchaser will extinguish a title acquired by adverse possession. The trial judge, in his admirable memorandum decision, quoted the following from the opinion in Ridgeway v. Holliday, 59 Mo. 444, 454:

". . . But it is contended by the defendant that he is a purchaser for value from Voteau who appeared from the record to be the owner, and was in possession, without any notice of the prior adverse possession which passed the title to Ridgeway, or of any claim on his part to the premises; and that as against him, the defendant, Ridgeway, cannot assert his title; that to permit him to do so, would be giving to an adverse possession greater force and efficacy than is given to an unrecorded conveyance. These objections, it must be admitted, are very forcible. The registry act, however, cannot, in the nature of things, apply to a transfer of the legal title by adverse possession, and such title does not stand on the footing of one acquired and held by an unrecorded deed, and of such title, the purchaser may not expect to find any evidence in the records."

He quoted, also, the following from Schall v. Williams Valley R. Co., 35 Pa. 191, 204:

"An unrecorded paper title does not affect a purchaser without actual notice, and the learned judge pronounced a title by the statute of limitations, if unaccompanied by a continued possession, as no more than an unrecorded paper title. If this be sound doctrine, then the claimant under the statute, however he may have perfected his right, must keep his flag flying for ever, and the statute ceases to be a statute of *limitations.*

"The first observation we have to make on his ruling is, that titles matured under the statute of limitations, are not within the recording acts. However expedient it might be to require some public record of such titles to be kept, and however inconvenient it may be to purchasers to ascertain what titles of that sort are outstanding, still we have not as yet any legislation on the subject, and it is not competent for judicial decision to force upon them consequences drawn from the recording acts. Those acts relate exclusively to written titles."

These cases seem to us to be directly in point, and to afford a complete answer to appellants' contention. However, appellants say that these and other cases are not applicable because legislation has been enacted, i.e., Rem.Rev.Stat. § 10577, to bring possessory titles within the recording act. That section reads as follows:

"Whenever any person, married or single, having in his or her name the legal title of record to any real estate, shall sell or dispose of the same to an actual bona fide purchaser, a deed of such real estate from the person holding such legal record title to such actual bona fide purchaser shall be sufficient to convey to and vest in such purchaser the full legal and equitable title to such real estate free and clear of any and all claims of any and all persons whatsoever not appearing of record in the auditor's office of the county in which such real estate is situated."

The appellants contend that, under this section of the statute, the full legal and equitable title is vested in them as bona fide purchasers from the record title holder, and that the title acquired by adverse possession is thereby extinguished. We again quote a sentence from the Pennsylvania decision:

". . . If this be sound doctrine, then the claimant under the statute, however he may have perfected his right, must keep his flag flying for ever, and the statute ceases to be a statute of *limitations.*"

If Rem.Rev.Stat. § 10577 has the effect claimed for it by the appellants, the only way in which a person who has acquired title by adverse possession could retain it against the purchaser of the record title is to make his possession and use of the property so continuous, so open, and so notorious as to prevent anyone from becoming a bona fide purchaser.

Immediately following this section in Rem.Rev.Stat., this statement appears in italics: "This section relates to community property only." It was § 1 of chapter 151 of the Laws of 1891, and the title of the act was "An Act to protect innocent purchasers of community real property." The other three sections of that act appear in Rem.Rev.Stat. as §§ 10578, 10579, and 10580; and the act in its entirety, in accordance with its title, is for the protection of innocent purchasers against undisclosed community interests. It is too clear for argument that the act never was intended to have, and could not have, constitutionally, in view of its restricted title, any such application as that for which appellants contend.

It is true that there is language in McIver v. Hilstad, 80 Wash. 206, 141 P. 306, and Ashton v. Buell, 149 Wash. 494, 271 P. 591, which could be construed as giving the statute a broader effect. The limited application of this enactment was not called to the court's attention in the briefs in those cases, and there was no question of adverse possession involved. The statute's limited application was recognized in Sengfelder v. Hill, 21 Wash. 371, 58 P. 250, 254, where it was said:

". . . An examination of the act will show that the legislature intended by it to protect bona fide purchasers of community property only. The title of the act is, 'An act to protect innocent purchasers of community real property,' which, under section 19 of article 2 of the state constitution, is too narrow to include within the terms of the act property held by a title other than that specially mentioned."

Appellants have placed too great a weight on too frail a reed.

There is no merit in the appellants' claim of estoppel. They do not plead it, nor support it with any apropos authority. It is clear that there was no admission, statement, or act on the part of the respondent which could be construed as inconsistent with her present position. No inquiry was made of her as to the boundary line before the appellants made their purchase. They were notified as to her claim before doing any work on the strip in question and before setting in place the house which encroaches on that strip. Title to real property is a most valuable right and will not be disturbed by estoppel unless the evidence is clear and convincing. Tyree v. Gosa, 11 Wash.2d 572, 119 P.2d 926.

The judgment is affirmed.

JEFFERS, CHIEF JUSTICE, and BEALS, STEINERT, and MALLERY, JJ., concur.

MORTENSEN v. LINGO

United States District Court, D.Alaska, 1951.
99 F.Supp. 585.

FOLTA, DISTRICT JUDGE. This is an action for damages for breach of covenants of title.

On February 20, 1941, Harry G. McCain conveyed the real property involved to E.M. Anglin. The deed was recorded in the office of the recorder for the Anchorage recording district, in which the land lies, but not indexed as the statute directs. It is not contended that the defendant had actual notice of this conveyance. On August 18, 1947, McCain conveyed the identical property to the defendant who in turn on April 16, 1948 conveyed it by warranty deed to the plaintiffs who now allege that Anglin threatens to evict them.

The plaintiffs contend that the index to deeds is no part of the recording thereof, whereas the defendant contends to the contrary and asserts that recording alone was insufficient to constitute constructive notice, particularly where the records of deeds consist, as in the Anchorage District, of more than 100 large volumes.

The pertinent statutory provisions of the Alaska Compiled Laws Annotated, 1949, are as follows:

"Separate books shall be provided by the commissioner in each recording district or precinct for the recording of deeds and mortgages, in one of which books all deeds left with such commissioner shall be recorded at full length, with the certificates of acknowledgment or proof of the execution thereon, and in the other all mortgages left with the commissioner shall in like manner be recorded.

"The commissioner shall certify upon each conveyance recorded by him the time when it was received and the reference to the book and the page where it is recorded, and every conveyance shall be considered as recorded at the time it was so received.

"The commissioner shall also keep a proper index, direct and inverted, to the books for the recording of deeds, and also one to the books for the recording of mortgages, in which he shall enter alphabetically the name of every party to each and every instrument recorded by him, with a reference to the book and page where the same is recorded.

"Every conveyance of real property within the Territory hereafter made which shall not be filed for record as provided in this chapter shall be void against any subsequent innocent purchaser in good faith and for a valuable consideration of the same real property, or any portion thereof, whose conveyance shall be first duly recorded". A.C.L.A.1949, §§ 22–3–22 to 22–3–25.

These provisions were taken from the Code of Oregon and adopted without change by the Act of Congress of June 6, 1900, 31 Stat. 321, 505.

The question presented is whether a deed properly recorded in the office of the district where the land lies but not indexed is constructive notice as against subsequent innocent purchasers for value. It is obvious that this question cannot be determined without imposing a great hardship on an innocent party.

It must be presumed that in adopting these provisions for Alaska, Congress knew that in Board of Commissioners for the Sale of School Lands v. Babcock, 1875, 5 Or. 472, 473, where the identical question was involved, the Supreme Court held that the index was not a part of the record. The conflict among the authorities on this question cannot be entirely accounted for by differences in statutory provisions. What appears to be the leading case in support of the opposing view is Ritchie v. Griffiths, 1890, 1 Wash. 429, 25 P. 341, 343, 12 L.R.A. 384. The statutory provisions, so far as pertinent, provided that:

"'The auditor of each county in this territory shall record, in a fair and legible handwriting, in books to be provided by him for that purpose, at the expense of the county, all deeds, mortgages, and other instruments of writing required by law to be recorded, and which shall be presented to him for that purpose, and the same shall be recorded in regular succession, according to the priority of their presentation, and, if a mortgage, the precise time of the day in which the same was presented shall also be recorded. . . . Upon the presentation of any deed, or other instrument of writing, for record, the auditor shall indorse thereon the date of its presentation, . . . and, when such deed, or other instrument of writing, shall be recorded, the recorder shall indorse thereon the time when recorded, and the number or letter and page of the book in which the same is recorded.' . . . Each auditor shall, upon the written demand of any person, make out a statement in writing, certified under his hand and the seal of his office, of all mortgages, liens, and incumbrances of any kind of record in his office, in relation to any real or personal property, in relation to which the demand shall be made; and, if said statement shall be incorrect, he, and the sureties upon his official bond, shall be liable to the person aggrieved for all damages sustained by him in consequence of such incorrect statement, to be recovered in a civil action. . . . Each county auditor shall keep a general index, direct and inverted. The index direct shall be divided into seven columns, with heads to the respective columns, as follows: (Here is a diagram of the column headings.) He shall correctly enter into such index every instrument concerning or affecting real estate, the names of the grantors being in alphabetical . . . columns precisely similar, only that the names of the grantees shall be alphabetically arranged, and occupy the second column." [Laws Wash.Terr.1869, p. 313, §§ 18, 19, 23, 24.]

It was held that these constituted a system of registration; that they must be construed together and that when so construed all the prescribed steps, including indexing, had to be performed before the record could constitute constructive notice. The Court took occasion to point out that as records accumulate the only practical way of imparting notice to the public or finding the record affecting any particular piece of property is through the index.

The reasoning of that Court appeals to me. Not only does it seem unreasonable to require each person interested in ascertaining the status of the title to any piece of property to examine every page of a great number of volumes, but to hold that the index, notwithstanding that it is required to be kept by statute, is no part of the record is to deny any effect to the provision requiring the maintenance of an index. I am of the opinion, therefore, that a single decision rendered 76 years ago should not be deemed controlling in an age when the tempo of life is much faster, the population more transient and real property transactions occur with such frequency that, it takes hundreds of large volumes to contain the records thereof. In this situation the observation of the Court in Barney v. McCarty, 1864, 15 Iowa 510, 521, 83 Am. Dec. 427, that "a deed might as well be buried in the earth as in a mass of records without a clue to its whereabouts" seems particularly apt.

I conclude, therefore, that the recording of the deed to Anglin without indexing was insufficient to give constructive notice to the defendant.

NOTES

1. In Gregor v. City of Fairbanks, 599 P.2d 743 (Alaska 1979), the Supreme Court of Alaska took a contrary view. "In reaching this conclusion, we have implicitly rejected the line of cases which holds that where the record of a conveyance is either incorrectly or never transcribed by the actions of a careless recording officer, the grantee must suffer the consequences, regardless of the fact that she has done all she can do to ensure that the deed is properly recorded. These cases would remit the unfortunate recording grantee to a remedy against the recording officer or his sureties." The court did not cite Mortensen v.

Lingo. Why would they fail to do so? What is the current law in Alaska?

See Haner v. Bruce, 146 Vt. 262, 499 A.2d 792 (1985), where a misindexed real estate attachment was held to be valid against a subsequent bona fide purchaser who had no knowledge of the attachment despite having conducted a title search. The court said, "Although the result reached by Vermont (and most other states) has been criticized, e.g., 4 A. Casner, American Law of Property § 17.25, at 604–05 (1952), 'the rule appears to be well established that in the absence of statutory provision to that effect, an index is not an essential part of the record.' . . . The recently developed Uniform Simplification of Land Transfers Act (not as yet enacted in Vermont) gives priority to the attaching party when his interests conflict with those of subsequent purchasers." The Chief Justice dissented, saying, "[T]he parties were equally blameless for the error that led to this action . . . The filer should suffer the consequences of improper indexing as he is usually the only one who can make certain that it was done right."

2. In the principal case could Anglin have sued McCain for the loss resulting from the latter's subsequent sale to the defendant? Could Anglin have done so if he had failed to record at all? If so, on what legal theory? The next principal case deals with a similar problem.

3. "In spite of the fact that the whole doctrine of record notice has been developed on the basis of what a prospective purchaser will find if he makes a proper search in the indices of grantors and grantees, only a few of the statutes make the index an essential part of the record. Since the latter is the case in Iowa, North Carolina, Pennsylvania, Washington, and Wisconsin, a record in these states is ineffective for imparting constructive notice if it is not indexed or if there is a material defect in the indexing. . . . [t]he rule appears to be well established that in the absence of statutory provision to that effect, an index is not an essential part of the record. In other words, a purchaser is charged with constructive notice of a record even though there is no official index which will direct him to it. In most communities no harm will result in that searches are no longer made by the aid of the alphabetical indices but instead by the use of private or public indices compiled by tracts." 4 American Law of Property 603–605 (1952).

4. A similar problem can arise where the recorder makes an error in transcribing the deed, mortgage, etc. Who will be protected in this case—the recording party, who did all that the statute required of him in leaving the document in the recorder's office, or the b.f.p., who relied on the records, which he assumed were accurate? See Mangold v. Barlow, 61 Miss. 593, 48 Am.Rep. 84 (1884). Is such a problem likely to arise if modern photostatic methods of recording are used?

PATTERSON v. BRYANT

Supreme Court of North Carolina, 1939.
216 N.C. 550, 5 S.E.2d 849.

The plaintiff complained, and the evidence tended to show, that the defendant conveyed to him the timber located on a certain tract of land in Pender County, described in the complaint, and received the purchase price therefor. The plaintiff did not immediately cause his deed to be registered. Meantime, the defendant, for a valuable consideration, included the same timber in a deed made to other parties, who promptly registered their deed. The last mentioned deed was recorded on September 7, 1937; ten days later the plaintiff's deed was recorded. The time given the plaintiff to cut the timber had not expired.

In the course of the trial a judgment of nonsuit was entered as to the grantees under the deed last executed, from which order the plaintiff did not appeal, and the suit proceeded against Bryant.

In the evidence supporting the contentions of the plaintiff it was developed that the defendant at the time of the execution of the second deed hesitated about making it, recalled and spoke of the transaction he had had with the plaintiff about the timber, and raised some question as to whether the deed made to the plaintiff ought to have included certain timber which he was then about to convey under the second deed, and appealed to the recollection of persons standing by to verify his impression of the transaction theretofore made with Patterson.

In his answer to the complaint the defendant Bryant alleged that he had been defrauded by the plaintiff in the inclusion in the first deed to plaintiff of the timber in dispute, and in his testimony reviewed the transaction with Patterson leading to the execution of the deed, claimed that he had been deceived as to the conditions on the land as being unfavorable to the cutting of the timber, and as to the quantity of timber in the swamp, and claimed that he only intended to give the plaintiff the right to cut not exceeding fifteen trees upon the area afterward included in the deed made to Grimes, Worthy, and others. He claimed that at the time of the execution of the deed to Patterson he was sick in bed and signed the deed only at the insistence of Patterson.

In apt time the defendant moved for judgment as of nonsuit, both at the conclusion of the plaintiff's evidence and at the conclusion of all the evidence, which motion was declined.

Upon the issues submitted to the jury a judgment was entered awarding $350 damages to the plaintiff in compensation for the injuries done him through the alleged wrongful acts of the defendant, from which judgment defendant appealed, assigning errors.

John J. Best, of Burgaw, for defendant-appellant.

Hackler & Allen, of Wilmington, and C.E. McCullen, Jr., of Burgaw, for plaintiff-appellee.

SEAWELL, JUSTICE. The only question argued by the defendant in this court relates to the refusal of the trial judge to allow his motion for judgment as of nonsuit made at the conclusion of the plaintiff's evidence and renewed at the conclusion of all the evidence.

Defendant's counsel contends that the motion for judgment as of nonsuit should have been allowed (1) because there was no allegation or evidence of the breach of any covenant in the deed from defendant to plaintiff; (2) that there was no allegation or evidence of any unjust enrichment of the defendant; and (3) that there was no allegation or evidence of fraud or guilty knowledge or intentional unfair dealings on the part of the defendant. It is further pointed out that the plaintiff was negligent or guilty of laches in recording his deed, and that his loss or injury, if any, was due to that cause.

The deed does not, in fact, contain any covenants or warranties, but the rights of the plaintiff in this suit are not predicated upon a breach of any warranty in the deed, but upon a broader principle; the breach of duty which he conceives the defendant owed him of refraining from the deliberate selling of the land a second time, with the knowledge that he was jeopardizing the rights of plaintiff, and thus setting in motion a chain of events that defeated the title of the plaintiff, while it left the defendant enriched by the purchase price paid to him by the plaintiff, as well as that paid to him by his subsequent grantees of the same property.

The single question before us is whether in equity the defendant may be allowed to retain the money received as a purchase price from both of these parties, and, if not, to whom restitution should be made.

It is true in a general sense that the plaintiff lost the title to his land by his failure to record his deed promptly. For reasons of public policy C.S. § 3309, in cases coming within its purview, undertakes to determine the question of title upon the fact of registration, making the unregistered title ineffective as against a subsequent holder from the same grantor for a valuable consideration except from registration. For the same reasons of public policy, actual knowledge on the part of the holder of the registered title of the execution of the prior deed, in the absence of fraud or matters creating an estoppel, will not avail to defeat his title as a purchaser for a valuable consideration.

The statute is intended to render titles certain and secure and to prevent confusion, mistake, and fraud growing out of the existence of unregistered and unknown titles which might defeat a subsequent purchaser for value. Warren v. Williford, 148 N.C. 474, 62 S.E. 697; Weston v. J.L. Roper Lumber Co., 160 N.C. 263, 75 S.E. 800. It is objective in its character and does not attempt to settle any equities which might exist between a grantor and those to whom he has sold his land, and those to whom he has resold it either mistakenly or deliberately and fraudulently. The deed made by him in the first instance is good inter partes. Hargrove v. Adcock, 111 N.C. 166, 16 S.E. 16; Warren v. Williford, supra; Weston v. J.L. Roper Lumber Co., supra. Whether it is registered at all is of no consequence to the grantor, and the statute requiring conveyances to be registered is not for his protection, but, as stated, for protection of a subsequent purchaser with whom he has seen fit to deal; therefore, laches on the part of his first grantee in recording his deed is not availble to defendant as an equitable defense. The first grantee is not bound to anticipate that the grantor would sell the property again and rush off to the registry office to forestall such a breach of faith. As between the parties, any loss sustained by the plaintiff in the transaction complained of must be regarded as the result of the defendant's conduct in dealing doubly with the plaintiff and with subsequent grantees to whom he successfully transferred the timber.

It cannot be said that the defendant was unaware of the fact that he was selling his timber a second time and a second time receiving pay for it. According to witnesses present when the deed to Grimes and others was signed, the defendant there sought to justify his action by raising a question as to the fairness and validity of the former transaction between himself and this plaintiff,—hesitating to sign the deed until he could receive assurances that witnesses might remember phases of the former transaction agreeable to his present purpose. The evidence was sufficient to sustain an inference that the act was deliberate and that the defendant might at the time have known that he was violating a duty either to the plaintiff or to the persons who were then about to receive title to the land. That was a violation of duty, the consequences of which will be referred to the act of the defendant himself, without whose wrongful act the plaintiff would not have sustained his loss.

But to sustain this action it is not necessary for the plaintiff to maintain it as one of tort. If we wish to be technical about the forms of action, which we consider wholly unnecessary in this case, it may be regarded as an action of assumpsit, involving the principles of quasi contract, which are broad enough to include practically every instance where a defendant has received money which he is "obliged by the ties of natural justice and equity to refund." 41 C.J. p. 29, note 7(c). "A person who has been unjustly enriched at the expense of another is required to make restitution to the other". Restatement of the law; Restitution. Am.Law Inst.1937, p. 27.

According to the facts found by the jury, the plaintiff has paid to the defendant a sum of money for which he received no value. The defendant has in his hands this money, as well as the price paid to him for the same thing by his subsequent grantees. Equity will not permit him to retain both. Restitution must be made to the plaintiff, whose present condition is in part, at least, due to the conduct of the defendant. In this case the amount of restitution was properly left to the jury, upon the evidence.

The judgment is affirmed.

NOTE

Observe that the principal case indicates that the second grantee who records first would prevail over the first, non-recording grantee, even if the former had actual notice of the prior deed so long as he is a purchaser for a valuable consideration. Does this seem fair? What type of recording act did North Carolina have? race

---

Classification of Recording Acts

As the last question in the preceding Note suggests, there is more than one type of recording act. It would be pleasant if all recording acts were based on a uniform statute so that the problems could be resolved by an analysis of the basic pattern. As you know, however, statutes are not drafted to give pleasure to law students and the recording acts are far from uniform. Fortunately, there are not fifty separate types. Most modern commentators have classified the acts into three categories, as follows:

(1) *Pure race.* Under an act of this type the grantee who first places his deed on the proper records prevails over other conveyances from the common source of title. The first grantee for value to record is protected even though he took with notice of a prior unrecorded conveyance.

(2) *Race-notice.* Acts of this type require that the subsequent purchaser be without notice at the time the conveyance is made and the consideration paid. In addition, the subsequent buyer without notice must record first.

(3) *Notice.* Acts following this pattern protect the junior conveyee against a prior unrecorded conveyance if he has paid value and is without notice. They differ from race-notice acts, since the junior conveyee is protected even though the senior conveyee records after the grant to the junior and before the junior records, or even if the junior does not record at all.

Professor Simes, in his Handbook for More Efficient Coveyancing, page 18 (1961) stated it this way: "In the first type, it is a pure question of race to the records; the purchaser who first records wins. In the [third] type, the subsequent purchaser wins if he purchases without notice of the prior deed and before the prior deed is recorded. In the [second] type, the subsequent purchaser wins if he purchases without notice of the prior deed, and also records his deed before the prior deed is recorded."

Some commentators have included a fourth category—the period of grace type, which declared a deed invalid against a good faith purchaser unless recorded within a certain number of days (typically fifteen) of the closing. This type was common in an earlier day when it took some time to travel to the county seat and when such trips might be infrequent for a landowner. It provided protection to the first purchaser during the grace period but left the title in a state of limbo for that same period. Delaware seems to have been the last state with such a statute and, since it was repealed by 56 Del. Laws Ch. 318 (1968), this type is of historical interest only.

Now, can you answer the question, what type of recording act does North Carolina have? For a direct answer, see Dulin v. Williams, 239

N.C. 33, 38, 79 S.E.2d 213, 217 (1953) where a grantor allegedly executed a timber deed to a grantee who failed to record. Later the grantor conveyed the same land to a husband and wife for a valuable consideration. They recorded their deed although apparently they had actual knowledge of the prior deed.

"The Connor Act provides that 'no conveyance of land, or contract to convey, or lease of land for more than three years shall be valid to pass any property, as against creditors or purchasers for a valuable consideration, from the donor, bargainor, or lessor, but from the registration thereof within the county where the land lies'. G.S. § 47–18.

"The decisions applying the Connor Act establish these propositions:

"1. The registration of a deed to an interest in land is essential to its validity as against a purchaser for a valuable consideration title as a purchaser for value. . . .

"2. Standing timber is an interest in land. . . .

"3. As between two purchasers for value of the same interest in land, the one whose deed is first registered acquires title. Combes v. Adams, 150 N.C. 64, 66, 63 S.E. 186.

"4. Actual knowledge on the part of the grantee in a registered deed of the existence of a prior unregistered deed will not defeat his title as a purchaser for value. . . .

"When the pleadings of the plaintiff are read in the light of these decisions, they show that under the Connor Act, the title to the timber standing on the 25 acres is in the male defendant and his wife, whose subsequent deed was registered before their grantor's prior deed to the plaintiff, even though the male defendant and his wife took their subsequent deed with actual knowledge of the prior deed to the plaintiff. Lanier v. John L. Roper Lumber Co., 177 N.C. 200, 98 S.E. 593."

North Carolina still has a pure race statute, see Simmons v. Quick-Stop Food Mart, Inc., 307 N.C. 33, 296 S.E.2d 275 (1982). Despite the fact that a pure race statute is the easiest to apply, North Carolina and Louisiana are the only states which have this type for conveyances generally, although a few other states use it for mortgages. Do you see why the pure race statute is not a popular model?

Nearly all of the states now have either a notice or a race-notice statute and the two categories are about equally divided in popularity. See 4 American Law of Property section 17.5 (A.J. Casner ed. 1952) for a listing of states by types of recording acts. The Uniform Simplification of Land Transfers Act, section 3–202, provides for a race-notice statute.

It is not always easy to fit the recording acts into the correct category even if you understand those categories. All statutes are subject to interpretation by the courts and the "judicial gloss" may change what appears to be the plain meaning of a recording act. The next principal case is a classic example of this point.

SIMMONS v. STUM

Supreme Court of Illinois, 1882.
101 Ill. 454.

MR. CHIEF JUSTICE CRAIG delivered the opinion of the Court.

This was a bill to foreclose a mortgage, executed on the 22d day of September, 1874, by Isaiah McHenry, to the complainant in the bill, John W. Stum, to secure the payment of seven promissory notes, of $100 each, due, respectively, on the 1st day of March, 1876, 1877, 1878, 1879, 1880, 1881, and 1882, which were given for the purchase money of the mortgaged premises, consisting of 80 acres of land in White County. The bill was brought to foreclose the mortgage for the non-payment of the note due March 1, 1879, the notes which became due before that time having been paid.

It is alleged in the bill that the mortgage was recorded on the 15th day of March, 1879; that on the 7th day of November, 1878, Isaiah McHenry conveyed the mortgaged premises to William R. Cochran and Samuel Strong; that the grantees were informed, at the time of the conveyance, of the existence of complainant's mortgage, and that they took the deed subject to the mortgage. It is also alleged in the bill, that on the 13th day of March, 1879, Cochran and Strong conveyed the premises to Isabelle Simmons; that the conveyance was made without consideration, and for the purpose of defrauding complainant.

Cochran and Strong, and Isabelle Simmons, and the mortgagor, Isaiah McHenry, were made parties defendant to the bill. The defendants Cochran, Strong and Simmons, put in an answer to the bill. A replication was filed, and a hearing had on the evidence, which resulted in a decree in favor of complainant, as prayed for in the bill, and the defendant Isabelle Simmons appealed.

There is no controversy in regard to the fact that Cochran and Strong had notice of the existence of complainant's mortgage at the time they obtained a deed to the mortgaged premises. The evidence upon this point is clear and undisputed. But it is claimed that Isabelle Simmons purchased the premises in good faith, without notice, and that she is entitled to hold the premises as an innocent purchaser. The circumstances under which Isabelle Simmons obtained a deed for the land are calculated to create a strong suspicion that she knew, or had good reason to know, of the existence of complainant's mortgage, although there is no direct proof in the record that she had notice of the mortgage, or notice of such facts as might put a prudent person on inquiry.

But we do not find it necessary to determine whether appellant, at the time of the alleged purchase of the premises, knew of the existence of the mortgage or not, as the decree will have to be affirmed on another ground. It is alleged in the bill, and shown by the evidence, that the deed to Isabelle Simmons was executed on the 13th day of March, 1879. There is also proof in the record that the deed was recorded, but the deed was not introduced in evidence, and the record contains no evidence, in regard to the date, that the instrument was recorded. Conceding, then, that appellant purchased the mortgaged premises without notice of the existence of complainant's mortgage, if she failed to record her deed until after March 15, 1879, the date of the record of the mortgage, the deed would stand subordinate to the prior lien of the mortgage. Under our recording laws, the instrument first on record takes priority. Brookfield v. Goodrich, 32 Ill. 363.

The statute declares: "All deeds, mortgages and other instruments of writing which are authorized to be recorded, shall take effect, and be in force, from and after the time of filing the same for record, and not before, as to all creditors and subsequent purchasers without notice; and all such deeds and title papers shall be adjudged void as to all such creditors and subsequent purchasers without notice, until the same shall be filed for record." Rev.Stat.1874, p. 278. The deed made to appellant could not take effect so as to cut off the mortgage unless it was first on record, and this fact appellant was bound to establish by the evidence. It may be, that under the allegations of the bill appellant could not be required to prove the date of her purchase as that was alleged, but the bill contained no allegation in regard to the date of the record of the deed, and that was a vital fact, which appellant was bound to establish.

As the evidence fails to show that the deed was recorded prior to the mortgage, the decree giving the mortgage a prior lien must be affirmed.

Decree affirmed.

NOTES

1. If Isabelle Simmons had recorded at once, would it have become important to know whether she was a b.f.p.? Why?

2. What type of recording act does Illinois have as a result of Simmons v. Stum? Professor Aigler, commenting on the case, wrote: "It will be noticed that this statute in terms avoids the unrecorded instrument 'as to all such creditors and subsequent purchasers without notice.' The California statute contains, in essence, the same language, but with this significant addition—'whose conveyance is first duly recorded.' Thus, under the California legislation, and a considerable number of states have recording acts with similar provisions, the subsequent, innocent purchaser, etc., must beat the claimant under the earlier instrument to the record office. The Illinois court, however, has interpreted their statute as leading to the same result . . . .. Surely the Illinois court has read something into the statute." Aigler, Cases on Titles 848, n. 17 (3d ed. 1942).

In Daughters v. Preston, 131 Ill.App.3d 723, 86 Ill.Dec. 944, 476 N.E.2d 445 (1985), grantor purported to convey the same land to A in 1958 and again to B, a bona fide purchaser, in 1980. Four days after delivery of the latter deed, A at last recorded his 1958 deed, one hour before B recorded his. Citing not Simmons v. Stum but an even earlier, 1843 decision of the Illinois Supreme Court, affirming a trial court judgment by Stephen A. Douglas, the appellate court held that A had priority over B.

3. As the preceding materials illustrate, priority of right depends on the wording of the particular recording act, subject to judicial construction. You have already been exposed to the acts in North Carolina and Illinois. Now read those in California and Massachusetts.

West's Ann.Cal. Civil Code § 1214 (1980).

Every conveyance of real property, other than a lease for a term not exceeding one year, is void as against any subsequent purchaser or mortgagee of the same property, or any part thereof, in good faith and for a valuable consideration, whose conveyance is first duly recorded . . . .

Massachusetts General Laws Ann. c. 183, § 4 (1987).

A conveyance of an estate in fee simple, fee tail or for life, or a lease for more than seven years from the making thereof, or an assignment of rents or profits from an estate or lease, shall not be valid as against any person, except the grantor or lessor, his heirs and devisees and persons having actual notice of it, unless it . . . is recorded in the registry of deeds for the county or district in which the land to which it relates lies.

What type of statute does California have? Massachusetts?

Assume that O held record title in fee simple to Blackacre. O made a conveyance of Blackacre to X, followed two months later by a conveyance of the same land to Y. Both paid value and neither had notice of the conveyance to the other. At the time Y purchased, X had not recorded but he did so later and prior to Y's ultimate recording.

At common law, without any recording acts, which grantee would be preferred? Which would be preferred in North Carolina? Illinois? California? Massachusetts?

You should try your hand at making additional assumptions and solving the resulting problems in light of the various types of recording acts.

SECTION 2. PERSONS PROTECTED BY THE SYSTEM

EASTWOOD v. SHEDD

Supreme Court of Colorado, 1968.
166 Colo. 136, 442 P.2d 423.

DAY, JUSTICE. We will refer to the parties as they appeared in the trial court. Defendant in error was the plaintiff there and successfully obtained a judgment and decree quieting title in her name to certain real property situated in Green Mountain Falls, Colorado. Plaintiff in error, the defendant against whom the quiet title suit was brought, was by the decree deprived of any right or claim to the property.

This is a dispute between two recipients of a gift of property. Both of the parties were grantees of the disputed property by warranty deed from one Cleo Alexander at different times. On December 2, 1958,

Mrs. Alexander deeded the property to the defendant who did not record the instrument until October 16, 1964. On October 15, 1963, Mrs. Alexander executed a warranty deed to the property to her daughter—the plaintiff—who recorded it on *October 23, 1963*. Plaintiff had no actual or constructive notice of the deed to defendant until it was placed of record a year after plaintiff had recorded her deed.

The question presented by this writ of error is strictly one of law, and may be stated as follows:

IS THE DONEE OF REAL PROPERTY, WHO HAS DULY RECORDED THE INSTRUMENT OF CONVEYANCE, ENTITLED TO THE PROTECTION OF THE PROVISIONS OF C.R.S.1963, 118–6–9, OF THE COLORADO CONVEYANCING AND RECORDING ACT?

We answer the question in the affirmative.

Section 118–6–9 was enacted in 1927, and reads as follows:

"All deeds, powers of attorney, agreements or other instruments in writing, conveying, encumbering or affecting the title to real property, certificates and certified copies of orders, judgments and decrees of courts of record may be recorded in the office of the recorder of the county where such real property is stituated and no such instrument or document shall be valid as against any class of persons with any kind of rights, except between the parties thereto, and such as have notice thereof, until the same shall be deposited with such recorder. In all cases where by law any instrument may be filed, the filing thereof with such recorder shall be equivalent to the recording thereof."

In enacting the law of that year, the legislature made a very substantial and significant change in the wording of the recording act as it had existed previously thereto. Stricken from the former act were the words, "shall take effect as to subsequent bona fide purchasers and encumbrancers by mortgage, judgment or otherwise not having notice thereof" and substituted therefor were the words, "shall be valid as against any class of persons with any kind of rights."

Notwithstanding this change in the law, defendant argues that a review of all of the recording acts in the United States reveals that in 39 of the states acts specifically protect only bona fide purchasers for value and without notice, i.e., an unrecorded deed is invalid only against such claims. Defendant further argues that in the remaining states with statutes of the same general nature as that of Colorado the courts which have considered the question have also limited the protection of the recording act to bona fide purchasers for value and without notice even though such limitation does not appear in the statute itself. Waterman v. Buckingham, 79 Conn. 286, 64 A. 212; Kruse v. Conklin, 82 Kan. 358, 108 P. 856, 36 L.R.A.,N.S., 1124; Hayden v. Russell, 119 Me. 38, 109 A. 485; Potter v. Aiden Lair Farms Ass'n, 225 Mass. 97, 113 N.E. 1035; Strong v. Whybark, 204 Mo. 341, 102 S.W. 968, 12 L.R.A.,N.S., 240; Whitehead v. Garrett, 199 Okl. 278, 185 P.2d 686; Spaulding v. H.E. Fletcher Co., 124 Vt. 318, 205 A.2d 556; 45 Am.Jur. Records and Recording Laws § 148. Therefore, defendant argues that C.R.S.1963, 118–6–9, should be construed so as to bring it within the "universal rule that a person must be a bona fide purchaser for value in order to be protected by the recording act . . . ."

This matter is one of first impression in Colorado since the 1927 enactment. We believe that the wording of the Colorado statute is unique compared with recording acts in other jurisdictions which limit the protected claims to "bona fide purchasers for value and without notice." See Storke & Sears, The Perennial Problem of Security and Recordation, 24 Rocky Mt.L.Rev. 180.

The trial court, aptly we think, labeled the Colorado statute as a "race-notice statute" granting priority to a second grantee only if he takes the instrument without notice of the prior conveyance and gets his instrument recorded ahead of the prior instrument. 6 R. Powell, The Law of Real Property § 913.

Colorado appears to be the only state which broadly protects "any class of persons with any kind of rights." To adopt the argument of the defendant would be to give no recognition to and to rule as inconsequential the very drastic and substantial amendment to the then existing statute by the state legislature. It appears to us that with full knowledge of the prevailing law with reference to the limitation of protection to subsequent bona fide purchasers for valuable consideration without notice the legislature intentionally removed such limitation from the statute and inserted therein the broad class enumerated therein.

The judgment is affirmed.

STRONG v. WHYBARK

(good holding)

Supreme Court of Missouri, 1907.
204 Mo. 341, 102 S.W. 968.

This is a bill in equity, instituted in the circuit court of Butler county, wherein plaintiff seeks to have her title quieted to 520 acres of land. John R. Boyden was one of the several defendants named in the bill. He filed an answer, claiming an interest in and to 160 acres of said land, and also denied generally the allegations of the bill. No point is made against the pleadings, and he is the only defendant whose interest is involved in this appeal.

The facts in the case are undisputed, and are as follows: Seth D. Hayden was the common source of title, and on March 6, 1861, by his warranty deed, for a recited consideration in the deed of $640, conveyed said land to William A. Moore, and on August 26, 1863, said Hayden, by his quitclaim deed, for a recited consideration of "natural love and affection and five dollars," conveyed the same land to Josephine Hayden. The deed to Hayden was recorded April 11, 1868, and the one to Moore was recorded December 14, 1874. The plaintiff's title is derived through mesne conveyances from Josephine Hayden, while defendant's title is derived through similar conveyances from William A. Moore. It was admitted that the land was wild and unoccupied. This was all the evidence in the case. The court found for defendant, and rendered judgment for him. The plaintiff in due time filed his motion for a new trial, which was overruled by the court, and to the action of the court in overruling said motion the plaintiff duly excepted, and has appealed the cause to this court.

Woodson, J. (after stating the facts). The sole question involved in this case is: Did the subsequently executed quitclaim deed of Seth D. Hayden to Josephine Hayden, dated August 26, 1863, by virtue of its prior recordation, have the force and effect of conveying to her the title to the land in controversy by force and operation of the registry act, and thereby render invalid and inoperative the prior warranty deed made by him to William A. Moore, dated March 6, 1861, but not filed for record until December 14, 1874?

There is no evidence whatever in this record tending to show that Josephine Hayden had any notice or knowledge of the execution of the prior unrecorded warranty deed from Seth D. Hayden to said Moore at the time he made the quitclaim deed to her, nor is there any evidence of fraud or collusion between Seth D. Hayden and Josephine Hayden. Both William A. Moore and Josephine Hayden neglected for years to file their deed for record, as provided for by section 923, Rev.St.1899, yet the latter filed her deed about six years prior to the time when he filed his.

The statute provides that "no such instrument in writing shall be valid, except as between the parties thereto and such as have actual notice thereof until the same shall have been deposited with the recorder for record." Rev.St.1899, § 925 [Ann.St.1906, p. 847]. According to the provisions of this section, the deed from Hayden to Moore was invalid and conveyed no title to the land in controversy in so far as Josephine Hayden was concerned, because she had no notice of its execution at the time she filed her deed for record. If the exception mentioned in the section just quoted was the only exception or limitation to that statute, then there would be no question as to the title of Josephine Hayden and those claiming under her, but the courts upon principles of equity and justice have repeatedly held that if the subsequent purchaser either had notice of the prior unrecorded deed or if he was a purchaser without having paid a good and valuable consideration for the land, then he would take nothing by his purchase and deed. Maupin v. Edmonds, 47 Mo. 304; Aubuchon v. Bender, 44 Mo. 560.

The question now presenting itself is: Was Josephine Hayden a purchaser of the land in question for a good and valuable consideration? The deed recites that the conveyance was made for and in "consideration of natural love and affection and five dollars to him in hand paid by the party of the second part, the receipt of which is hereby acknowledged." A valuable consideration is defined to be money or something that is worth money. 2 Washburn on Real Prop. (4th Ed.) p. 394. 1 Chitty on Contracts (11th Am.Ed.) 27. It is not necessary that the consideration should be adequate in point of value. Although small or even nominal, in the absence of fraud, it is enough to support a contract entered into upon the faith of it. . . . It seems to us that it would be a useless waste of time and energy to cite authorities in support of the proposition that $5 or any other stated sum of money is a valuable consideration within the meaning of the law of conveyancing.

It has been suggested that a quitclaim deed is notice of pre-existing equities, and that those who claim under Josephine Hayden had notice that her title to this land was questionable, and that neither she nor they could defend upon the ground that they were bona fide purchasers for a valuable consideration without notice of the title of the true owner. Stivers v. Horne, 62 Mo. 473; Mann v. Best, 62 Mo. 491; Ridgeway v. Holliday, 59 Mo. 444. But the rule last suggested has no application to a case where the grantee under a subsequent quitclaim deed from the same grantor acquired the title for value and without notice of the former unrecorded deed. Fox v. Hall, 74 Mo. 315, 41 Am. Rep. 316. "A purchaser for value by quitclaim deed is as much within the protection of the registry act as one who becomes a purchaser by a warranty deed." . . .

Where the controversy is between the vendee of a duly recorded deed and the vendee of a prior unrecorded deed from the same vendor, the settled rule of law in this state seems to be that the consideration in the latter must be such as the law denominates a valuable consideration as distinguished from a good consideration. We know of no case which has gone farther and holds that the purchaser under the recorded deed must have paid a full and adequate consideration for the land. If fraud is made an issue in the case, then the inadequacy of the consideration paid may be taken into consideration with all the other facts and circumstances in the case for the purpose of establishing fraud; but, in the absence of fraud, a want of consideration cannot be shown against a recital of a consideration for the purpose of defeating the operative words of a deed. . . . In the case at bar, however, there was no evidence introduced tending to prove the recited consideration of $5 was not in fact paid.

Counsel for defendant, in both his oral and written arguments, contends that Josephine Hayden procured her deed from Seth D. Hayden by fraud. It is a sufficient answer to that to say that no such issue is made by the pleadings in the case, nor was there a word of evidence introduced at the trial tending to establish that fact. If defendant wished to rely upon fraud as a defense, he should have alleged and proved it. The burden of proving such an issue is upon the defendant. . . .

It follows from what has been said that the judgment of the circuit court must be reversed, and the cause remanded for a new trial. All concur.

NOTES

1. The American Law of Property states that a valuable consideration does not mean a consideration equal to the market value of the property. However, Mr. Patton, who wrote the material on priorities, recording and registration, concludes that a nominal consideration or a mere recital of value in a deed is insufficient. He notes that Strong v.

Whybark was approved in Hays v. Pumphrey, 226 Mo. 119, 125 S.W. 1109 (1908) but states it "must be considered to have been erroneously decided". 4 Am.Law Prop. § 17.10, at 558 n. 9 (Casner ed. 1952).

2. Concerning a grantee under a quitclaim deed, note the following statement from Morris v. Wicks, 81 Kan. 790, 791, 106 P. 1048, 1049 (1910): "Many courts hold that, regardless of the consideration paid, one who accepts a quitclaim deed cannot invoke the benefit of the registration act against the holder of an unrecorded warranty deed. In a note in 105 Am.St.Rep. 859 it is said: 'The argument has generally prevailed that as a quitclaim deed purports to convey only the interest of the grantor, it cannot have any operation when he has already parted with his interest, and that it is not material that his grantee had no actual notice of that fact; that the restricted language of the conveyance is equivalent to notice, and, as a final result, that he who accepts such a conveyance cannot, within the meaning of the registry acts, be a bona fide purchaser and as such entitled to protection against prior conveyances or encumbrances made by his grantor or equities existing against him.' " Which view seems more in accord with the spirit of the recording system?

Despite the arguments made in Morris v. Wicks, most of the modern cases protect a grantee under a quitclaim deed if he or she is otherwise a b.f.p. See Note, Deeds—Quitclaim Grantee as a Bona Fide Purchaser, 28 Or.L.Rev. 258 (1949); Annot. 162 A.L.R. 556 (1946); and IV Am.L.Prop. s. 17.16 (1952).

3. Suppose a purchaser has paid only a portion of the contract price when he discovers that there was a prior deed or mortgage. "Under these circumstances he was entitled to protection only to the extent that he was—to use the expression of Lord Hardwicke—'hurt.' The rule therefore applies 'that where a part only of the price or consideration has been paid before notice, either the defendant should be entitled to the position and protection of a bona fide purchaser pro tanto, or that the plaintiff should be permitted to enforce his claim to the whole land only upon condition of his doing equity by refunding to the defendant the amount already paid before receiving the notice: (Pomeroy's Equity Jurisprudence, sec. 750)." Davis v. Ward, 109 Cal. 186, 41 P. 1010, 50 Am.St.Rep. 29 (1895). The rule of pro tanto protection for a b.f.p. is easy to state but hard to apply; for a good statement of the principles involved see Durst v. Daugherty, 81 Tex. 650, 17 S.W. 388 (1891).

What constitutes notice to the b.f.p. under these circumstances? In Alexander v. Andrews, 135 W.Va. 403, 64 S.E.2d 487 (1951) the court held that a purchaser who was paying the price in installments received notice of a prior unrecorded deed as soon as it was recorded. This places an intolerable burden on the buyer since he would have to examine the records immediately before paying each installment. It would seem preferable to require actual notice to the b.f.p. similar to that required of a subsequent judgment creditor.

Is a lessee a purchaser under the recording system? The answer is yes, according to Egbert v. Duck, 239 Iowa 646, 32 N.W.2d 404 (1948).

"Although a lessee is considered a purchaser, as a practical matter this means very little to the lessee, since he is protected only to the extent of rent paid to notice and must vacate the premises at the end of the period for which such rent was paid. This may result in a great hardship when the lessee has made expensive improvements or has otherwise substantially changed his position, as a lessee for a long term may well have done." Johnson, Purpose and Scope of Recording Statutes, 47 Iowa L.Rev. 231, 235 (1962).

4. The doctrine of bona fide purchaser for value without notice plays a leading role in the operation of the recording system. The following is a classic statement of the doctrine: "There are two special rules on the subject which have been settled since an early day; one being a mere application of the general doctrine, and the other a necessary inference from it. The first is, that if a second purchaser for value and without notice purchases from a first purchaser who is charged with notice, he thereby becomes a bona fide purchaser, and is entitled to protection. This statement may be generalized. If the title to land, having passed through successive grantees, and subject in the hands of each to prior outstanding equities, comes to a purchaser for value and without notice, it is at once freed from these equities; he obtains a valid title, and, with a single exception, the full power of disposition. This exception is, that such a title cannot be conveyed, free from the prior equities, back to a former owner who was charged with notice. If A, holding a title affected with notice, conveys to B, a bona fide purchaser, and afterwards takes a reconveyance to himself, all the equities revive and attach to the land in his hands, since the doctrine requires not only valuable consideration and absence of notice, but also *good faith.* The second rule is, that if a second purchaser with notice acquires title from a first purchaser who was without notice, and bona fide, he succeeds to all the rights of his immediate grantor. In fact, when land once comes, freed from equities, into the hands of a bona fide purchaser, he obtains a complete *jus disponendi,* with the exception last above mentioned, and may transfer a perfect title even to volunteers." 3 Pomeroy, Equity Jurisprudence 55–57 (5th ed.1941).

GABEL v. DREWRYS LIMITED, U. S. A., INC.

Supreme Court of Florida, 1953.
68 So.2d 372, 39 A.L.R.2d 1083.

DREW, JUSTICE. McCaffrey was a beer distributor and became indebted to Drewrys Limited, U. S. A., Inc., for beer in a sum exceeding $20,000. Drewrys received several "rubber" checks from McCaffrey and stopped beer shipments to him. A conference was arranged and as a result McCaffrey gave Drewrys a demand note for $10,000 of the debts, secured by a mortgage dated June 30, 1950, on the property involved in this suit. The mortgage was in the usual form and contained a provision for the payment, by the mortgagor, of "costs, charges and expenses . . . including reasonable attorney's fees . . . ." The record discloses that at the same time additional notes, secured by chattel mortgages, were given to make up the balance of the debt.

Concurrently, McCaffrey and Drewrys entered into an agreement which recited the debt due from McCaffrey to Drewrys, the fact that the former did not then have assets to pay it, and that Drewrys had "agreed to accept a note, or notes, payable to its order in the above amount together with certain securities consisting of lien on real and personal property, and to *forbear for the time being any action to enforce the collection of said sum due and owing it* . . . said forbearance, however, to be conditioned upon (McCaffrey) making the payments as provided in said notes . . ." (Emphasis supplied).

Prior to the time of giving the notes and mortgage, Drewrys had caused the public records to be examined to see that there were no liens against the properties encumbered by the mortgage and found none.

There is some evidence as to the oral statements on forbearance which took place at the time the mortgage was given. Drewrys' attorney testified:

"Q. Now, what period of time did you agree to forbear suit against him? A. *Well, there was no specific date fixed in there.* It was depending on what activity Mr. McCaffrey made in taking care of his obligations and how soon he was able to get this money he was counting on that he said he was going to have. We were going to let him get started with his new operations and capital. *I think within a reasonable time. We have nothing we could lose.* We could have gone ahead into Court and filed an attachment and gotten the advantage through a prior lien through an attachment suit, and he begged almost with tears in his eyes, he begged us to not put him out of business, if we would give him a chance." (Emphasis supplied).

Drewrys' agent testified:

"Q. How much time did you extend to him in not filing suit if he would give you this security? A. *There was no element of time involved in the filing of a suit.* There was no conversation about filing of a suit.

. . .

"Q. You didn't extend any time to him then? A. *There was no extension time, as you put it, and there was no demand made at the same time."* (Emphasis added).

The Drewry mortgage was then promptly recorded although Drewrys did not resume beer shipment to McCaffrey as he said Drewrys had agreed to. McCaffrey became more involved and a few months later appellant Gabel, who held a note from McCaffrey in the principal sum of $2,750, secured by a mortgage on the same real estate as covered by the Drewrys mortgage, said note and mortgage being dated March 14, 1950, but not filed for record, read in the paper that McCaffrey "was in trouble." Whereupon Gabel recorded his mortgage.

Later, Drewrys filed suit to foreclose its mortgage, making Gabel a party. The latter filed a cross-claim to foreclose his mortgage. The learned Circuit Judge, after personally hearing the evidence, entered a final decree holding the Drewrys' mortgage to be superior to the Gabel lien and finding:

"2. The consideration for the note executed by the defendant, James McCaffrey and the mortgage executed by the defendants, James McCaffrey and Mary C. McCaffrey, his wife, to the plaintiff *was the forbearance on the part of the plaintiff* to prosecute any legal action against the said defendant, James McCaffrey, for the enforcement of his obligation to the plaintiff at the time of the execution thereof, for an indebtedness in amount of Ten Thousand Dollars ($10,000.00) as represented by said note, as well as an additional indebtedness of approximately Eleven Thousand Dollars ($11,000.00), said note and mortgage being the basis of the plaintiff's complaint.

"3. The plaintiff had no notice of the mortgage held by the defendant, L.A. Gabel, and that the failure of said defendant, L.A. Gabel, to have his mortgage recorded at the time of the execution and recording of the mortgage held by the plaintiff, misled the plaintiff in accepting security for the indebtedness due it, or a portion thereof, in lieu of taking legal action at said time to secure the collection of said indebtedness from the defendant, James McCaffrey, to the plaintiff." (Emphasis added).

Def.'s arg

Gabel argues that since the agreement to forbear was for no definite time, it amounted to no enforceable right on the part of McCaffrey, hence it was of no benefit to him or detriment to Drewrys, and did not constitute sufficient consideration, and in support cites Strong v. Sheffield, 144 N.Y. 392, 39 N.E. 330. Also cited by appellant were Mitchell v. Harper, 80 Fla. 338, 86 So. 246; Kreiss Potassium Phosphate Co. v. Knight, 98 Fla. 1004, 124 So. 751, regarding consideration to support extension of time for payment. On the other hand, Drewrys says whether the agreement to forbear was for any definite time, or was enforceable by McCaffrey, is immaterial, because in fact there was a forbearance of benefit to the debtor and a detriment to Drewrys. . . . Drewrys also cites Sweeney v. Bixler, 69 Ala. 539, where the general rule is well summarized in the following language:

"It has long been settled, both in this court and elsewhere, that the inquiry, whether a mortgagee is a purchaser, depends on the question, whether he parted with anything valuable, surrendered an existing right, incurred a fixed liability, or submitted to a loss or detriment, contemporaneously with the execution of the mortgage, or with the agreement, afterwards performed, to execute the mortgage. If either of these several categories be shown to exist, then the law presumed such act of the mortgagee was done or suffered in consideration of the mortgage executed, or to be executed. In any such case the mortgagee is a purchaser. He is a bona fide purchaser, if, at the time he so took the mortgage, he was without notice, actual or constructive, of an older, latent equity in another. What is sufficient notice to put him on inquiry, we do not propose to consider in this case. *On the other hand, if the mortgage be taken to secure a pre-existing debt, and no new contemporaneous consideration passes, either of benefit to the mortgagor, or detriment to the mortgagee, then the mortgagee does not thereby become a purchaser."* (Emphasis supplied).

The authorities cited by Drewrys do not support its contention that it is immaterial whether a definite enforceable time extension is made, if there is forbearance in fact. 36 Am.Jur. 795, § 205, states only that ". . . if a mortgage is taken for a pre-existing debt, and the creditor *at the time* agrees to extend the time of payment, this additional consideration will entitle the mortgagee to protection as a purchaser for value." (Emphasis supplied). And Jones on Mortgages (8th Ed.), Vol. 1, page 769, states: ". . . *A definite extension time for the payment* of an existing debt, by a valid agreement, for any period however short, though it be for a day only, is a valuable consideration, and is sufficient to support a mortgage, or a conveyance, as a purchase for a valuable consideration." (Emphasis supplied).

In those cases cited, where the creditor mortgagee was allowed priority over a prior mortgage, it appears in each case that there was given a *definite extension of time* of the pre-existing debt contemporaneously with the taking of the mortgage. In Van Cleve v. Meyers, supra, priority was given two mortgages for each of which was granted a one year extension time, but priority was denied another mortgage where the six months note extending time was taken eight days *before* the mortgage. In O'Brien v. Fleckenstein, supra, the creditor mortgagee was allowed priority where one month's extension of time was granted. In Douglas v. Miller, supra, priority was allowed where three months' extension of time and surrendering right of action against an indorser was given. And in Sweeney v. Bixler, supra, the court declined to give creditor mortgagee of personal property priority for taking note due one day after date, stating it did not consider that extension, being the usual form in closing accounts, to be sufficient to constitute the mortgagee a purchaser for value.

We are impressed by the closing sentence in the quotation (by appellee Drewrys) from Sweeney v. Bixler, supra, which we have emphasized. It seems to us that this case falls squarely within the situation there described. The instant after Drewrys accepted the demand note and mortgage, it was in a better position than before because, not only had it the right instantly to sue, but it also reduced a claim to a sum certain and secured a mortgage on the property of the debtor and an additional covenant to pay attorney fees and costs if it should bring action thereon. Instead of "a detriment to the mortgagee" there was a benefit to it. Instead of "a benefit to the mortgagor" there was a detriment to him. In reality, Drewrys' attorney summed it up when he testified it had "nothing to lose."

While we are impressed with the care and caution taken by Drewrys in examining the public records, the facts simply do not place Drewrys in the position of an innocent purchaser for value.

The cause is hereby reversed with directions to enter a final decree in accordance with this opinion.

Reversed.

ROBERTS, C.J., and THOMAS and MATHEWS, JJ., concur.

NOTE

The role of the pre-existing debt in the drama between purchasers is an old and troublesome one. Not surprisingly the courts have disagreed on the casting, and cases can be found on both sides of the issue. In the personal property area the matter has received legislative attention. Section 76(1) of the Uniform Sales Act provides: " 'Value' is any consideration sufficient to support a simple contract. An antecedent or pre-existing claim, whether for money or not, constitutes value where goods or documents of title are taken either in satisfaction thereof or as security therefor." Section 25 of the Uniform Negotiable Instruments Act reads: "Value is any consideration sufficient to support a simple contract. An antecedent or pre-existing debt constitutes value; and is deemed such whether the instrument is payable on demand or at a future time." Similarly the Uniform Commercial Code, Section 1–204(44) provides: "Value. A person gives 'value' for rights if he acquires them . . . (b) as security for or in total or partial satisfaction of a pre-existing claim. . . ."

OSIN v. JOHNSON

United States Court of Appeals, District of Columbia Circuit, 1957.
243 F.2d 653.

BURGER, CIRCUIT JUDGE. Appellant, a woman of more than average business experience, agreed to sell a parcel of improved real estate to appellee Johnson and subsequently executed and delivered a deed, taking back a note for the full purchase price of $30,000. There was no down payment. Johnson represented to appellant that he would prepare, execute and record a trust on the property to secure his purchase money note.

After delivery of the deed to him, Johnson recorded the deed but did not prepare and record the trust instrument as he had promised appellant he would do. For this breach of faith and fraud Johnson was thereafter indicted, tried and convicted and testimony in the criminal case forms part of the record in this case.

Without disclosing appellant's prior unrecorded lien against his title, Johnson borrowed $11,000 from appellee Perpetual Building Association, executing deeds of trust against the property. Later Johnson borrowed an additional $3300 on second deeds of trust from appellee Glorius. Thereafter, creditors of Johnson obtained judgments which became liens on the real estate under D.C.Code, § 15–103 (1951 ed.) [1]

1. "Every final judgment at common law . . . for the payment of money from the date when the same shall be rendered, every judgment of the municipal court when docketed in the clerk's office of the District Court . . . shall be a lien on all the freehold . . . estates, legal and equitable, of the defendants bound by such judgment . . . in any lands, tenements, or hereditaments in the District . . .".

Appellant's Brief urges us to take judicial notice of certain facts of record in the cases of Umbricht v. Johnson, No. M–7187–55, Municipal Court of District of Columbia, and Hakim v. Johnson, No. 771–55, United States District Court for the District of Columbia, to wit: Umbricht sold

When foreclosure proceedings were commenced under the trust deeds executed by Johnson, appellant brought this suit for equitable relief, joining the trust holders, with the judgment creditors of Johnson subsequently intervening.

The trial court properly heard the case without a jury since this suit was plainly addressed to the equity jurisdiction of the court. The trial judge found that appellant conveyed title to Johnson knowingly and in reliance on Johnson's assurances that he would record all the documents including the deed of trust which secured the purchase money note. Upon this finding the court concluded that appellee trust holders and judgment creditors had acquired interests in the property superior to that of appellant's unrecorded claim.

Appellant contends she did not knowingly execute and deliver the deed, and that Johnson fraudulently procured her signature on an instrument represented to be a sales contract. Cf. Baker v. Morton, 1870, 12 Wall. 150, 79 U.S. 150, 20 L.Ed. 262; Brown v. Pierce, 1868, 7 Wall. 205, 74 U.S. 205, 19 L.Ed. 134. Compare Restatement, Contracts § 494 with § 495 (1932). However, appellant's pre-litigation actions and letters expressly refute this contention and provide ample basis for the trial court's finding contrary to her testimony.[2] Nor do we find merit in appellant's other allegations of error on the part of the trial court.

I.

The trial court apparently did not consider whether Johnson's fraudulent conduct might give rise to the imposition of a constructive trust on the real estate in appellant's favor, although appellant's prayer for equitable relief, while not specifically requesting this remedy, was sufficiently broad to enable a court of equity to impress a trust upon the property.[3]

A constructive trust is a purely equitable device which can be applied with great flexibility.[4] It arises by operation of law from the occurrence of an unconscionable act for which no traditional relief is

Johnson an Oldsmobile car taking Johnson's note for $1875, against which Johnson later paid $400. Hakim sold a Cadillac car to Johnson taking the latter's note for $4,500 upon which he later defaulted.

It would appear from the nature of these transactions that neither judgment creditor dealt with Johnson in reliance on the state of the record title as to the realty. [Footnotes in the case by the Court and numbered accordingly.]

2. The trial judge, in finding number 7, recited: "Plaintiff [mrs. osin], shortly after [the date she executed and delivered the deed], sought, and received, return of her deposits with the several utility companies for service to the aforesaid houses. She agreed that defendant Johnson should receive the rents for said properties thereafter and she no longer received them herself. She made no further efforts to sell the property and later went to Florida from which place, she wrote letters on March 30, 1955, stating that she had sold the properties and had received back a purchase money deed of trust."

3. Mrs. Osin's complaint "to set aside deed; for injunctive relief, accounting and other relief" concluded with a general prayer "(6) And for such other and further relief as the case may require and to the court may seem meet and proper."

4. For instances in which this court has approved the application of a constructive trust, see Harrington v. Emmerman, 1950, 88 U.S.App.D.C. 23, 186 F.2d 757; Cahill v. Bryan, 1950, 87 U.S.App.D.C. 271, 184 F.2d 277; Mandley v. Backer, 1941, 73 U.S.App. D.C. 412, 121 F.2d 875. See also Restatement, Restitution § 166 (1937).

available. A constructive trust can be imposed wherever one unfairly holds title or a property interest and where the holder would be unjustly enriched if permitted to retain such interest. Specifically, the acquisition of property through the fraudulent misrepresentation of a material fact has been held sufficient grounds to fasten a constructive trust on the property. Howard v. Howe, 7 Cir., 1932, 61 F.2d 577, certiorari denied, 1933, 289 U.S. 731, 53 S.Ct. 527, 77 L.Ed. 1480. Since the District Court in the instant case found that appellant was induced to convey her title to the real estate by a fraudulent promise of Johnson that he would execute and record a deed of trust, the court could have properly considered whether, under all the circumstances, a constructive trust should have been imposed. It thus becomes necessary to consider whether the existence of a constructive trust would give appellant a superior claim to the interests of the trust holders and Johnson's judgment creditors, should it be found that a constructive trust exists.

II.

We turn first to the holders of the first and second deeds of trust. Whatever the nature of appellant's interest, the District Court was correct in holding the fraud in the relationship between appellant and Johnson did not give appellant a claim superior to that of the trust holders who occupy the position of bona fide purchasers. Colorado Coal and Iron Co. v. United States, 1887, 123 U.S. 307, 314, 8 S.Ct. 131, 31 L.Ed. 182; Davison v. Morgan, 1931, 60 App.D.C. 161, 50 F.2d 311.

The record demonstrates, and the lower court so found, that the holders of the trust deeds were innocent purchasers for value without notice of appellant's prior equity, and thus they clearly fall within the purview of the recording act, D.C.Code, § 45–501 (1951 ed.), protecting bona fide purchasers against unrecorded conveyances.[5] The logical and rational basis for preferring the bona fide purchaser over the grantor of the record title holder is that as between two innocent parties, i.e., appellant and the bona fide lenders such as Perpetual and other trust holders, appellant must yield to those who in good faith relied on the state of the record which her negligence allowed to exist. It would manifestly defeat the whole point of recording statutes to permit Mrs. Osin to assert her admitted equities at the expense of those who relied in good faith on a state of the record title which her acts created.

Even in the absence of recording acts or, as discussed under point III infra, if the recording statute is inapplicable a bona fide purchaser's

5. "Any deed conveying real property in the District, or interest therein . . . executed and acknowledged and certified as provided in sections 30–216, 45–106, 45–302, 45–401 to 45–404 and delivered to the person in whose favor the same is executed, shall be held to take effect from the date of the delivery thereof, except that as to creditors and subsequent bona fide purchasers and mortgagees without notice of said deed, and others interested in said property, it shall only take effect from the time of its delivery to the recorder of deeds for record."

D.C.Code, § 45–601 (1951 ed.) provides that deeds of trust are to be recorded and to take effect as against "bona fide purchasers and mortgagees and creditors" in the same manner as absolute deeds under § 45–501.

rights have always been held superior to prior equitable interests. A purchaser for value without notice of the facts which lead to the creation of a constructive trust, will cut off the trust beneficiary's rights. Restatement, Restitution, § 172 (1937); 4 Scott, Trusts § 468 (2d ed. 1956). Therefore, the holders of the deeds of trust would prevail over appellant even if a constructive trust were to be imposed on the property.

III.

The same rationale does not have equal validity when applied to judgment creditors of the fraudulent grantee. A judgment creditor possessing a statutory lien on property does not occupy a position equivalent to that of a purchaser for value and thus "if the land of the debtor is subject to equities, the judgment creditor's lien is subject to such equities." 3 Scott, Trusts § 308.1, p. 2276 (2d ed. 1956). See also Restatement, Restitution § 173, comment j (1937). As a matter of simple ordinary fairness, which is the essence of equity, there is every reason why a defrauded grantor of title should command a higher priority than creditors of the fraudulent grantee since such creditors usually do not rely on the record title in their extension of credit. The equitable considerations dictating the priority of an equitable right over subsequently acquired judgment liens was aptly summarized by this court many years ago:

"Unless precluded by the terms of some statute expressly intended to change it, the rule has always prevailed that the equity under a trust or a contract *in rem* is superior to that under a judgment lien. The claimant under the contract *in rem* has an equity to the specific thing which binds the conscience of his grantor; whilst the judgment creditor, who has advanced nothing on the faith of the specific thing, is entitled only to that which his debtor really has, at the time, or could honestly convey or encumber; his beneficial interest and nothing more." Hume v. Riggs, 1898, 12 App.D.C. 355, 367.

The appellee judgment creditors, however, point to the recording acts as altering the equitable rule and giving them a preference over appellant's unrecorded interest. This jurisdiction, like approximately half of the states,[6] has adopted a recording statute which specifically lists "creditors" among those classes given precedence to prior interests not recorded.[7] Despite early intimations to the contrary,[8] it is now well settled that the statutory reference to "creditors" includes a good faith judgment creditor holding a statutory lien obtained under D.C. Code, § 15–103, without the necessity of such creditor executing his lien by attachment or by "filing a bill in equity." Hitz v. National Metropolitan Bank, 1884, 111 U.S. 722, 4 S.Ct. 613, 28 L.Ed. 577; Atlas Portland Cement Co. v. Fox, 1920, 49 App.D.C. 292, 265 F. 444, 266 F. 1021. See also 4 American Law of Property § 17.29 (Casner ed. 1952); 1919, 4

6. For a summary of the applicable state statutes, see 4 American Law of Property § 17.29 n. 1 (Casner ed. 1952).

7. See note 5 supra.

8. Crosby v. Ridout, 1906, 27 App.D.C. 481, 494–495. See also Arlington Brewing Co. v. Wyvill, 1910, 35 App.D.C. 589, 593; Ohio National Bank v. Berlin, 1905, 26 App.D.C. 218, 225, 227.

A.L.R. 434. Thus, as to instruments required to be recorded *and capable of being recorded,* the recording act elevates a judgment creditor to the same legal plane as a bona fide purchaser for value.

But since the preference accorded a judgment lien depends upon the statute, it extends only to such interests as the statute requires to be recorded. It has long been acknowledged that recording acts similar to that enacted in the District of Columbia do not apply to interests incapable of record. Where an equitable interest is not created by a written instrument or conveyance but rather arises by operation of law, such an interest "is not within the statute and is not subject to the lien of a judgment [creditor] . . ." 2 Freeman, Judgments 2043 (5th ed. 1925). Other jurisdictions have recognized that a constructive trust, by its nature not susceptible of record, is not within the reach of recording acts and thus retains priority over judgment liens. In re Rosenberg, D.C.S.D.Tex.1925, 4 F.2d 581; East St. Louis Lumber Co. v. Schnipper, 1923, 310 Ill. 150, 141 N.E. 542; School District No. 10 v. Peterson, 1898, 74 Minn. 122, 76 N.W. 1126.[9]

This jurisdiction has never passed directly on the question whether a creditor holding a statutory lien takes preference over an earlier equity incapable of being recorded. In American Savings Bank v. Eisminger, 1910, 35 App.D.C. 51, this court held the lien of a judgment creditor equal to the lien of a bona fide purchaser and thus superior to any secret trust *capable of being recorded,* but not so recorded. This qualification of recordability was carefully and precisely delineated by the court by repetition in these words: "We say, trust capable of being placed upon record, for that is the case here. *Whether* a resulting or constructive trust, *incapable of record,* and in the assertion of which there has been no laches, would yield to the lien also, *we intimate no opinion.*" American Savings Bank v. Eisminger, supra at 55. (Emphasis added). The case now before us gives rise to precisely the possible situation envisaged by this court in the American Savings Bank case and as to which the court would then "intimate no opinion." We say "possible situation" for it is not the function of this court to resolve whether the facts warrant the imposition of a constructive trust since appellant failed to point out the possibility of such a course to the District Court. We decide only the question pointedly left open in American Savings Bank v. Eisminger, supra. For the reasons indicated above, and in line with the authority cited, we now supply that gap and hold if a new trial discloses (1) a constructive trust inherently incapable of recording and (2) no laches on the part of appellant in the assertion of her rights, that in such case Mrs. Osin's constructive trust will have priority over the judgment creditors of Johnson. But we qualify the above holding to this extent: a judgment creditor who is able to show affirmative reliance on the state of the record without notice of any infirmity should be entitled to the same standing as a bona fide purchaser. See 2 Freeman, Judgments 2043–44 (5th ed. 1925). Thus if a judgment creditor can satisfy the District Court that he, like the trust holders, extended credit on faith of Johnson's record title, he should be

9. See also 3 Scott, Trusts § 308.2 (2d ed. 1956).

entitled to the same priority enjoyed by other bona fide purchasers, unless when the debt arose he had actual or constructive notice of Johnson's fraud on Mrs. Osin. D.C.Code, § 45–501 (1951 ed.).

The judgment of the District Court also provided that appellant could elect to take a reconveyance of the property upon her returning to Johnson (for the benefit of Johnson's judgment creditors) the $680 Johnson had paid appellant on his purchase money note. We think that part of the judgment should be vacated and the ultimate disposition of the $680 abide the determination of the equities on a new trial.

The judgment below is affirmed as to the trust holders, Perpetual Building Association, Scrivener, Crowell, Laughlin, Sinclitico, Glorius and Sherman; reversed as to the intervenor judgment creditors Hakim and Umbricht, and the case is remanded for further proceedings.

Affirmed in part; reversed in part.

NOTES

1. Suppose a grantor conveys Blackacre to a grantee who fails to record and does not enter possession; later X obtains a valid judgment against the grantor and seeks to levy execution on Blackacre. Who prevails, the judgment creditor or the non-recording grantee? Many courts, following the logic of the principal case, prefer the grantee, holding that a judgment creditor is not a b.f.p. "[d]oes the lien of an execution levy extend only to the actual, or does it also reach the apparent, title of the judgment debtor? Is the inquiry restricted to the face of the record, or may it pass to the actual facts? Authorities are not wanting to support either view. . . .

"With much hesitation, and after a long and careful examination of the question in its various relations, we have reached the conclusion that the lien of the mortgage must be adjudged prior and paramount. These are the reasons which have controlled us: It gives exact force to the statute declaring to what a judgment lien and an execution levy extend. Judgments 'shall be liens on the real estate of the debtor within the county.' Dass: Comp.Laws 1879, p. 656, § 419. This evidently contemplates actual and not apparent ownership. The judgment is a lien upon that which is his, and not that which simply appears to be his." . . .

"Again, it may be laid down as familiar law that a judgment creditor is not a bona fide purchaser. He parts with nothing to acquire his lien. He is in a very different position from one who has bought and paid or has loaned on the face of a recorded title. The equities are entirely unlike. One has, and the other has not, parted with value upon the face of the record. If the real prevails over the apparent title, the one is no worse off than before he acquired his lien,—has lost nothing; while the other loses the value paid or loaned. Hence equity will help the latter, while it cares nothing about the former." Holden v. Garrett, 23 Kan. 98 (1879). See also Kartchner v. State Tax Commission, 4 Utah 2d 382, 294 P.2d 790 (1956).

Note, however, that many jurisdictions take the opposite position, usually based on statutory language. See, e.g., Ill.–S.H.A., ch. 30, § 29 (1975) "All deeds, mortgages, or other instruments of writing, which are authorized to be recorded, shall take effect and be in force after the time of filing the same for record, and not before, as to *all creditors* and subsequent purchasers without notice; and all such deeds and title paper shall be *adjudged void* as to *all such creditors* and subsequent purchasers without notice, *until the same shall be filed for record.*" (Emphasis added.) Which position seems better to you?

2. While it is clear that the b.f.p. is entitled to the protection of the recording acts, it is not so easy to determine the persons who will fit under that protective cloak. Assume that the state in question does not protect the judgment lienholder on the basis of his lien alone. If he forecloses the lien and purchases in the judicial sale for the amount of his indebtedness, will he then be protected as a b.f.p.? See Sternberger and Willard v. Ragland, 57 Ohio St. 148, 48 N.E. 811 (1897) and Shirk v. Thomas, 121 Ind. 147, 22 N.E. 976, 16 Am.St.Rep. 381 (1889). Suppose a stranger purchases at the judicial sale, having no notice of any prior claims and paying approximately the amount of indebtedness? If the stranger would be protected, what would be the judgment lienholder's status if he took a conveyance from the stranger?

WINEBERG v. MOORE

United States District Court, N. D. California, S. D., 1961.
194 F.Supp.12.

OLIVER J. CARTER, DISTRICT JUDGE. This is an action by William J. Wineberg, a citizen of Washington, for quiet title and other relief upon 880 acres of timber land in Humboldt County, located in northern California. The amount in controversy exceeds the sum or value of $3,000, exclusive of interest and costs, and is between citizens of different states; therefore, jurisdiction is established on the basis of diversity of citizenship as provided by Title 28 U.S.C. § 1332. The real property and transactions critical to the disposition of this matter occurred in California, and it is deemed that California law is controlling. See Erie R. R. Co. v. Tompkins, 304 U.S. 64, 58 S.Ct. 817, 82 L.Ed. 1188.

Wineberg alleges that he purchased the property from O. O. Barker in May, 1948, for $6,000, but he failed to record his deed in Humboldt County until May, 1951. In the interim Barker, the seller, made a contract for the sale of the timber on the land to the defendant, Construction Engineers, which contract was recorded in 1950; in 1951 Barker sold the property again, deeding it this time to the defendant, Natural Resources, Inc., and this deed was also recorded before the Wineberg deed. Throughout this period, several judgments were obtained against O. O. Barker, and some of these judgment creditors are also defendants.

At the outset, this Court must resolve the difficult factual question of whether or not Wineberg ever actually purchased the property from

Barker. It is urged that the $6,000 advanced to Barker was intended as a loan, with the deed given to Wineberg serving only as security for the loan. . . .

The question to be ascertained is whether or not the parties intended this deed to be a security device, or to convey an absolute estate as the deed purported to do. See Greene v. Colburn, 160 Cal. App.2d 355, 325 P.2d 148. The deed from Barker to Wineberg purported to convey a fee simple absolute, but "a deed absolute on its face may in equity be shown by parol evidence to have been intended as security for a debt, and hence only a mortgage." . . .

The circumstances surrounding the deed from Barker to Wineberg is not without doubt as to the true intent of the parties in respect to the interest created, but this Court is not persuaded that this transaction was merely a security device to secure a loan to Barker. And since the evidence of a loan was not clear and convincing, it follows that this deed must stand as a conveyance of the fee simple absolute.

This Court must now ascertain whether or not failure to record by Wineberg makes his legal title subject to the prior recordings by Construction Engineers and Natural Resources, Inc. or whether these defendants were put on notice by conduct of Wineberg so as to preclude a subsequent good faith purchase of any interest in the property by said defendants.

Construction Engineers seeks to defeat Wineberg's right to the timber on the property by virtue of its 1950 contract with Barker for the sale of the timber on the land, which contract was recorded prior to the time that Wineberg recorded his deed. All other defendants who actively participated in the trial and who filed briefs seek to defeat Wineberg's title on the additional ground of Barker's 1951 deed of this property to Natural Resources, Inc., said deed being recorded subsequent to the timber contract of Construction Engineers, but before the deed to Wineberg. Wineberg's superiority of title as against all defendants named rests upon the outcome of the issues between Wineberg, Construction Engineers, and Natural Resources, Inc., respectively, since there is no other assertion of a superior title being made.

It must first be established that the timber contract of Construction Engineers was such an interest as to be within the scope of the recording statute. . . . This Court is persuaded that the timber contract in question was a recordable document, and, as such, if the vendee was without notice at the time of purchase and recordation of any outstanding equities, his claim would be superior to that of Wineberg.

The critical factual question for resolution is whether or not Wineberg's possession was sufficient to impart notice to Construction Engineers, Inc. and Natural Resources, Inc. which would prevent them from establishing a superior right pursuant to Section 1214 of the Civil Code of California.

The common law rule was that once a grantor conveyed all his interest in a parcel of real property he could create no further rights in the property in a third person absent any elements of estoppel. The recording statutes have altered this rule for it is now possible for a grantor to make a second conveyance divesting the first grantee so long as the second grantee pays a valuable consideration, records first, and is in good faith. The California recording statute requires the second purchaser to be without notice, actual or constructive, of the interest of the prior purchaser. A deed that is not recorded is nevertheless valid between the parties thereto, and persons who have notice thereof. § 1217 Civil Code of California. Section 18 of the Civil Code of the State of California defines notice as follows:

"1. Actual—which consists in express information of a fact; or, 2. Constructive—which is imputed by law."

Section 1107 of the Civil Code of the State of California provides:

"Every grant of an estate in real property is conclusive against the grantor, also against every one subsequently claiming under him, except a purchaser or incumbrancer who in good faith and for a valuable consideration acquires a title or lien by an instrument that is first duly recorded."

A party purchasing real property from a title holder of record where a third person is in possession is presumed to purchase "with full notice of all the legal and equitable rights in the premises of such party in possession and in subordination to these rights, and this presumption is only to be overcome or rebutted by clear and explicit proof on the part of such purchaser, or those claiming under him, of diligent, unavailing effort by the vendee to discover or obtain actual notice of any legal or equitable rights in behalf of the party in possession." Pell v. McElroy, 36 Cal. 268, 271. It is incumbent upon a subsequent purchaser to ascertain who is in possession. Scheerer v. Cuddy, 85 Cal. 270, 271, 24 P. 713. In absence of actual inquiry a person is still chargeable with the notice imparted by possession—such notice is akin to, if not equivalent to constructive notice.

California Civil Code § 19 provides:

"Every person who has actual notice of circumstances sufficient to put a prudent man upon inquiry as to a particular fact, has constructive notice of the fact itself in all cases in which, by prosecuting such inquiry, he might have learned such fact."

In Pacific Gas & Electric Co. v. Minnette, 1953, 115 Cal.App.2d 698, 705, 252 P.2d 642, 646, the court applies the following rule:

"'Possession of land is notice to the world of every right that the possessor has therein, legal or equitable; it is a fact putting all persons on inquiry as to the nature of the occupant's claims.' (39 Am.Jur. 242.)"

The same court approvingly quoted from 66 C.J.S., Notice § 11, pp. 646, 647, as follows:

"'The presumption is that inquiry of the possessor will disclose how and under what right he holds possession, and, in the absence of such inquiry, the presumption is that, had such inquiry been made, the right, title, or interest under which the possessor held would have been discovered. The notice which the law presumes has been held to be actual, and not merely constructive, notice. Possession is notice not only of whatever title the occupant has but also of whatever right he may have in the property, and the knowledge chargeable to a person after he is put on inquiry by possession of land is not limited to such knowledge as would be gained by examination of the public records.' . . . The foregoing rules are applied by California courts." 115 Cal. App.2d 705–706, 252 P.2d 646.

Thompson in his treatise on real property states that:

"It is held that the law will impute to a purchaser all information which would be conveyed to him by an actual view of the premises." Thompson on Real Property (permanent edition), Vol. 8, § 4464 at page 318.

This "view of the premises" is by actual visit to the property and not by looking at an aerial map of the terrain nor by flying over the property, even if this is customary with some persons who do not conduct themselves in a prudent manner. This approach may be suitable in an inaccessible terrain, but not as here, where the property is readily accessible by automobile.

The possession required to impart notice to a subsequent purchaser in California must be "open, notorious, exclusive and visible, and not consistent with the record title." Randall v. Allen, 180 Cal. 298, 303, 180 P. 941. And in Gibbons v. Yosemite Lumber Co., 190 Cal. 168, 172, 211 P. 4, 5, it is further stated: "'. . . the acts of dominion must be adapted to the particular land, its condition, locality, and appropriate use.'"

The burden of proof as to what acts of dominion will suffice to establish notice by possession rests with the person claiming such possession. Dreyfus v. Hirt, 82 Cal. 621, 23 P. 193.

The acts of dominion exercised by Wineberg do not present the strongest case possible in his favor, but, nevertheless, in viewing all the acts and circumstances surrounding the timber contract from Barker to Construction Engineers, Inc. and the conveyance from Barker to Natural Resources, Inc., these acts were sufficient to prevent these defendants from claiming that they purchased their respective interests "in good faith".

This 880 acre parcel of real property is primarily suited to logging operations and secondarily as a recreational facility, with the prime attraction consisting of hunting and fishing. At the time Wineberg purchased the property, there was a dwelling suitable for residence or summer recreational activities and a garage. These buildings were also present on the property at the time defendants consummated their respective transactions. A woven wire fence extended along two sides of the property, but it did not encompass the whole 880 acres. The road leading to the property was obstructed by a locked gate. There was a no trespassing sign posted upon the gate with Wineberg's name and Portland, Oregon, address.

Wineberg paid the taxes upon the property. He visited the property occasionally for recreational purposes, and friends of Wineberg's also utilized the property for like purposes. The occupancy by Wineberg's guests is deemed that of Wineberg for the purpose of establishing possession, for if an inspection of this property had been made such persons would have identified Wineberg as owner. Further indicia of ownership was present in the form of personal property located in the residence structure identifiable as Wineberg's. There were several no trespassing signs in the near vicinity of the dwelling, and along a trail leading to the stream. These signs all identified Wineberg as claiming an interest in the property inasmuch as he was advising all other persons not to trespass.

The fact that the whole of the property was not enclosed does not prevent Wineberg's possessory acts from extending over the whole 880 acre parcel. As stated in Andrus v. Smith, 1901, 133 Cal. 78, 80, 65 P. 320, 321:

"It has been held that where the property is in some way subjected to the will and control of the claimant, that an inclosure is not always necessary."

And at page 81 of 133 Cal., at page 321 of 65 P. the same court said:

"And where a party enters, under color of title, and has actual possession of a part of the whole tract, he has constructive possession of the whole."

Another factor that lessens the need for a complete enclosure is that the point of recognized ingress and egress to this property was by a road that led to the dwelling, and the dwelling and surrounding area was posted with Wineberg's no trespassing signs. Anyone inspecting this property would have begun at this location and be made immediately aware of the fact that some third person was exercising rights therein. A prudent person would have made an inquiry as to the rights of this party.

The use of this property from 1948 through 1950 and 1951 (the critical years as to notice) was occasional, but this, nevertheless, was an adaptation of use in accordance with the secondary utility of the parcel; namely, recreational purposes such as hunting and fishing. This use has particular meaning when considering the fact that timber, although considered a crop, does not ripen in a given year as far as a logger is concerned, nor is there any demand that it be harvested at a particular time, other than restrictions as to access because of weather conditions. It seems wholly unrealistic to say that logging activities would be the only acts that would be sufficient exercise of dominion over this property to put these defendants on notice of Wineberg's title. This Court does not require that kind of showing, which view is consistent with the controlling California decisions.

The recording system is intended to make secure real property transactions and to protect bona fide purchasers for value from secret liens. This does not mean that a subsequent purchaser may close his eyes to everything but the record title. Beach v. Faust, 2 Cal.2d 290, 40 P.2d 822. . . .

Under the conditions existing when the defendants negotiated their respective deals with Barker, they were bound to inspect the property. In the absence of such inspection, they are chargeable with all facts such inspection would have revealed, as well as with facts discoverable by inquiry suggested by such inspection. Such inquiry would have revealed Wineberg's fee simple interest. Good faith demanded this inquiry by these defendants.

In view of this holding it is unnecessary to pass on Wineberg's other contentions.

Judgment is awarded to plaintiff on the issue of title. The issue of damages may be set down for hearing upon the request of any of the parties.

[Affirmed 349 F.2d 685, 9th Cir. 1965.]

NOTE

In Strong v. Strong, 128 Tex. 470, 473, 98 S.W.2d 346, 348, 109 A.L.R. 739 (1936), it was contended that "the existence in the community in which the land lies of common reputation or notoriety that some person other than the person in possession has an interest in or claim to the land is of itself sufficient to put a purchaser on inquiry and to charge him with knowledge of the facts which inquiry would disclose." The court refused to sustain the contention. "We know of no rule of law which requires one who is about to purchase land to make inquiries of persons living near it. It is the duty of the purchaser to inquire of the party in possession by what right he holds, and hence the law affects him with notice of the claim of such possessor. But, in the absence of some information that some particular person knows of an adverse claim to the premises in dispute, there is no duty resting upon the purchaser to make inquiries of such person, although he may live in the neighborhood in which the land lies." The court then distinguished a prior case saying: "The case holds that evidence of notoriety is admissible as a circumstance tending to show actual notice and not that notoriety of which a purchaser knows nothing will of itself charge the purchaser with notice or put him on inquiry."

In the Strong case a son who claimed an interest in the property was living with his father and helping to cultivate the land. He claimed this was sufficient possession to give notice of his rights. "The visible possession was that of the father, Manuel Strong, who held legal title. If the presence of T. B. Strong as a member of the family may be considered possession, it is apparent that his possession was not of the character or quality that gives constructive notice. The essential elements of that character or quality are thus clearly defined . . .:

" 'So it may safely be said that the character of possession referred to as constituting constructive notice, with respect to the character of case we have under consideration, must consist of open, visible, and unequivocal acts of occupancy in their nature referable to exclusive dominion over the property, sufficient upon observation to put an intending purchaser on inquiry as to the rights of such possessor; and that ambiguous or equivocal possession which may appear subservient or attributable to the possession of the holder of the legal title is not sufficiently indicative of ownership to impute notice as a matter of law of the unrecorded rights of such possessor.' "

Although the Strong case seems correct in not imputing notice from the son's "possession", it is never safe to rely on the test stated in the decision. If a purchaser knows, from the record or some other source, that the possessor is a lessee or a cotenant it might be supposed that further inquiry would be useless. However, in some states he would be charged with notice of additional unrecorded interests of the possessor. See Miller v. Green, 264 Wis. 159, 58 N.W.2d 704, 37 A.L.R.2d 1104 (1953); Dengler v. Fowler, 94 Neb. 621, 143 N.W. 944 (1913); Contra, Central Bank v. Downtain, 162 Ark. 46, 257 S.W. 746 (1924).

KINDRED v. CROSBY

Supreme Court of Iowa, 1959.
251 Iowa 198, 100 N.W.2d 20.

THOMPSON, JUSTICE. On March 28, 1938, the plaintiff and one Scott Crosby, also known as Bonny S. Crosby, were owners of real estate in Polk County described as: "Lot One (1) U.S.S., all West Half (W ½) South of River, Section Three (3), Township Eighty (80), Range Twenty-five (25) West of the Fifth P. M., Iowa." On this date Crosby executed a quitclaim deed of his interest in the realty, with the name of the grantee blank, and delivered it to the plaintiff. The deed was not recorded until December 19, 1957.

On December 11, 1953, Bonny S. Crosby, with his then wife, Mildred A. Crosby, the defendant herein, executed and delivered a joint tenancy deed of the same interest to Bonny S. Crosby and Mildred A. Crosby. This deed was recorded on December 14, 1953. Crosby died during the month of October, 1956, and the defendant now claims to be the owner of an undivided one-half interest in the real estate above described by virtue of the deed last referred to.

It is evident that the case turns upon the priority of the two deeds: the first, delivered to the plaintiff, but not of record when the second deed was executed creating the joint tenancy and recorded. The defendant, as appellant here, makes in substance two contentions: the first deed was invalid because the name of the grantee was not filled in when it was delivered; and second, she is an innocent purchaser for value without notice of the prior unrecorded conveyance. The trial court found all issues with the plaintiff.

I. It is not disputed that Crosby executed the first deed in the presence of plaintiff, and delivered it to him. And it is conceded by the plaintiff that the name of the grantee was not filled in at the time of execution and delivery. He testifies that his own name was filled in as grantee, by his authority, shortly before the deed was recorded in 1957. But we think this avails the defendant nothing. The law is well settled in Iowa that equitable title passes by the delivery of a deed which leaves the name of the grantee blank. . . .

II. Defendant's further reliance is upon her claim that when she received the deed creating a joint tenancy between herself and her husband Bonny S. Crosby, she had no notice of the earlier unrecorded deed and so became a purchaser for value and entitled to priority under Section 558.41 of the Code of 1958, I.C.A., which has appeared in substantially identical form in the Iowa law for many years past. She denies any knowledge of the existence of the unrecorded deed under which the plaintiff claims, and testifies that she paid her husband $200 for the execution of the joint tenancy deed upon which her rights rest.

It cannot be disputed that a bona fide purchaser for value without notice of an existing unrecorded conveyance obtains priority. But there are some things a claimant to such priority must do before it will be upheld in the courts of Iowa. First, he must plead and prove his status as such purchaser. In Young v. Hamilton, 213 Iowa 1163, 240 N.W. 705, the question was discussed at length. Certain Iowa cases holding that the burden of proof is upon the holder of the unrecorded instrument were overruled, and we concluded: "Plaintiff had the burden of pleading and proof that he was a subsequent purchaser for valuable consideration without notice." See at page 1173 of 213 Iowa, at page 710 of 240 N.W. In 107 A.L.R. annotations, pages 503, 504, Iowa is listed among the jurisdictions which place the burden of proof to show good faith upon the party claiming to be a purchaser without notice, and many Iowa cases, including Young v. Hamilton, supra, are cited. At pages 513, 514 of the same volume is this: "In accord with the general rule . . . the numerical weight of authority is to the effect that one claiming to be a bona fide purchaser as against the holder of a prior unrecorded conveyance or encumbrance has the burden of showing that he paid a valuable consideration for the conveyance to him, and this by other evidence than the recitals in the deed." Iowa cases are again cited as following this rule.

An examination of the record shows that the defendant here has failed to carry the burden required of her. Her answer is no more than a general denial of the material allegations of plaintiff's petition in equity praying that title be quieted in him. She has not met the first requirement, that she plead her status as a purchaser for value without notice.

Nor do we think she has carried the burden of proof. Her testimony is that she paid $200 in cash for the survivor deed. On cross-examination she was asked where she obtained the money, and she said she had saved it in small amounts while she was employed in Omaha some five or six years before the execution of the deed. She says that she came to the premises whose title is in question here on March 10, 1952. The plaintiff and Crosby were then living there together. Kindred's wife had died in 1951, and Crosby had never been married, so far as the record shows. On June 10, 1952, the defendant and Crosby were married. The joint tenancy deed was dated December 11, 1953. So the sum which defendant says she paid for the deed was earned some years before. Upon cross-examination she testified that it was in small bills; and the record shows this: "Q. Where did you have the money just before you gave it to Mr. Crosby? A. My mother. Q. Where did she have it? A. She carried it in her purse. Q. You mean she carried this $200.00 for some five or six or eight years? A. Yes."

The defendant's mother, who was still living at the time of the trial so far as the record shows, and who might have corroborated her possession of the money, was not called as a witness. We have followed the rule set out in 58 Am.Jur., Witnesses, Section 864, page 493, where it is said: "However, while the jury is not warranted in arbitrarily or capriciously rejecting the testimony of a witness, neither is it required to accept and give effect to testimony which it finds to be unreliable, although it may be uncontradicted. Testimony may be unimpeached by any direct evidence to the contrary and yet be so contrary to natural laws, inherently improbable or unreasonable, opposed to common knowledge, inconsistent with other circumstances established in evidence, or so contradictory within itself, as to be subject to rejection by the court or jury as a trier of the facts." We have ourselves said: "The court is not required to accept as a verity uncontradicted testimony, but might well scrutinize closely such testimony as to its credibility, taking into consideration all the circumstances throwing light thereon, such as the interest of the witnesses, remote or otherwise." Gregory v. Gregory, 248 Iowa 672, 682, 82 N.W.2d 144, 150. See also Gilmer v. Neuenswander, 238 Iowa 502, 507, 28 N.W.2d 43, 46.

We measure the testimony of the defendant as to her payment for the joint tenancy deed by the yardstick of her interest in the matter, and the reasonableness or improbability of the story she told, and the availability of corroboration which was not produced. Her whole case depended upon establishing a consideration for the deed; her interest is apparent and strong. We think her story so evidently out of line with reason and probability that, as triers of the facts, we cannot accept it. It is possible that she had saved this money as she says; it is possible her mother carried it in her purse for "five or six or eight years" as she testified. But it is not in accord with the way people usually conduct their affairs. It is a story which cries for corroboration, if it is to be believed; but the one possible witness who knew the facts as to the saving of the money and its possession during those "five or six or eight years", defendant's mother, was not called, and no reason appears in the record why she could not have appeared and testified. It was obviously impossible for the plaintiff to contradict defendant's testimony at this point; and her counsel therefore assume it must be accepted as true. But we think as triers of the facts, her interest in the case and the patent improbability of her story furnish sufficient contradiction, and destroy its weight.

The burden was upon the defendant to plead and prove her status as a purchaser for value without notice. She did not plead it; and we think, in view of our reluctance to believe her evidence as to payment for the deed under which she claims, it must be held she has failed to prove it. . . .

Affirmed and remanded.

All Justices concur.

NOTES

1. "The measure of protection actually afforded by the recording system in operation is significantly affected by location of the burden of proof[9] on the issues of notice and valuable consideration. If possible, this question should be resolved by reference to the underlying purposes of recordation. It would be reasonable to say that if the dominant purpose of the recording system is to encourage recording by penalizing failure to record, the burden of proof should be upon the one who did not record. On the other hand, if protection of designated groups is the aim, it might follow that the burden should be upon those seeking to bring themselves within the favored categories. An analysis in terms of policy produced the conclusion by one authority that the burden should be placed 'squarely in all cases on the holder of the prior unrecorded instrument.'[10] Unfortunately, the decided cases in the main are not characterized by a purpose-oriented approach to the problem. Authority can be found for almost every conceivable position: burden on one who failed to record;[11] burden on one claiming to be a subsequent purchaser without notice;[12] burden on one who failed to record if his interest was equitable rather than legal;[13] burden on purchasers but not on creditors;[14] and burden on purchasers as to consideration but not as to notice.[15]

"The rationalizations offered are as diverse as the results. One technique is to attach great significance to the structure of statutory phrases, in a manner reminiscent of the refinements of the distinction between vested and contingent remainders. If the statute provides that 'no deed . . . shall take effect as regards the interests and rights of third parties [subsequent purchasers] until presented . . . for the recording,' this means that the legislature intended the burden to be on the one who failed to record, while a statutory declaration that an unrecorded deed is 'void as to . . . subsequent purchasers' reveals intent to put the burden on the purchaser.[16] A related approach is to indulge in a question-begging analysis of the operation of the recording acts upon property interests: Do these acts divest the unrecorded title or do they confer upon subsequent purchasers a title never owned by the party who failed to record? If a title is being divested, it is thought that the burden should be upon the divestor.[17] Along somewhat more

9. The term "burden of proof" as used here is meant to refer to the burden of persuasion rather than to the burden of going forward with the evidence. See McCormick, Evidence §§ 306–07 (1954).

10. Osborne, Mortgages § 208, at 531 (1951).

11. Cessna v. Hulce, 322 Ill. 589, 153 N.E. 679 (1926).

12. E.g., Kindred v. Crosby, 251 Iowa 198, 100 N.W.2d 20 (1959); Young v. Hamilton, 213 Iowa 1163, 240 N.W. 705 (1932).

13. Delay v. Truitt, 182 S.W. 732 (Tex. Civ.App.1916) (error refused).

14. Turner v. Cochran, 94 Tex. 480, 61 S.W. 923 (1901).

15. Steinman v. Clinchfield Coal Co., 121 Va. 611, 93 S.E. 684 (1917).

16. Kimball v. Houston Oil Co., 100 Tex. 336, 99 S.W. 852 (1907).

17. Turner v. Cochran, 94 Tex. 480, 61 S.W. 923 (1901); 4 American Law of Property s. 17.35, at 633 (Casner ed. 1952).

realistic lines, concern about the reasonableness of the burden has led to the conclusions that the burden should not be on one to "prove the negative" but that the burden should be upon one within whose knowledge the proof peculiarly lies.[18] But the assumptions upon which these conclusions are based are doubtful and, with respect to the notice issue, these conclusions would tend to cancel each other." Johnson, Purpose and Scope of Recording Statutes, 47 Iowa L.Rev. 237–238 (1962). [Footnotes by the author.]

2. The proper location of the burden of proof continues to plague the courts. In Nelson v. Hughes, 290 Or. 653, 625 P.2d 643 (1981) the court was faced with a simple fact situation but the decision turned on the burden of proof. The defendants were contract purchasers whose land sale contract for undeveloped lots was prior in time, but unrecorded. The plaintiff claimed, by mesne conveyances, through a deed to some of the same lots which, though subsequent in time, was recorded. The plaintiff would clearly prevail under the Oregon recording act if she were a bona fide purchaser. While she alleged bona fide purchaser status, there was no evidence in the trial court record beyond her own testimony that she was a grantee under the deed, that the lots were undeveloped, and that she claimed ownership under the recorded chain of title.

After a detailed analysis of the problem, including extensive quotations from Professor Johnson's article in the Iowa Law Review (see Note 1), the court concluded: "We have found no Oregon case that states, as between a party who failed to record his interest in land and a subsequent purchaser of the same property, which party has the burden of alleging and proving whether the subsequent purchase was or was not 'in good faith, and for a valuable consideration.' However, prior decisions of this court indicate that the burden should be placed on the subsequent purchaser." Since that burden of proof had not been sustained, the plaintiff lost the case.

Does this result seem fair? Did not the defendant cause the problem by failure to record? How does the plaintiff prove her status as a bona fide purchaser for value?

SECTION 3. THE CHAIN OF TITLE

This section could be omitted if all American jurisdictions made tract indices the official method of indexing. Under the tract system, every document affecting title to land (and entitled to be recorded) is indexed under the specific tract of land involved. Therefore, a title searcher would find the document, regardless of when recorded, so long as it was indexed before he purchased or took a mortgage on the land. Of course, if he failed to make a search he would have constructive notice in any case. Unfortunately, many states do not have tract indexing, or do not make it the official system, and reliance must be

18. Kruse v. Conklin, 82 Kan. 358, 108 P. 856 (1910).

placed on the outmoded grantor-grantee system. (Since the latter system was the original method and is "in place" it has been thought too costly for many local governmental units to make the shift to the admittedly superior technique.) Under the older system, documents affecting title may be recorded and indexed and still fail to bind a subsequent grantee if they fall outside the chain of title. This paradox results because the recorded instrument may be, for all practical purposes, lost in the vastness of the recorder's office. The materials in this section explore the meaning of the chain-of-title concept and demonstrate the legal consequences of retaining an obsolete system in a complex, modern society.

CRIBBET & JOHNSON, PRINCIPLES OF THE LAW OF PROPERTY

320–322 (3d ed.1989).

The chain of title concept is illustrated by the following case. *A* leases to *B*, who neither records nor takes possession. *B* assigns the lease to *C* who records the assignment but does not enter into possession. *A* then gives a warranty deed to *D*, a b.f.p., who records. *D* will take free of the lease, even though its assignment was recorded, because it is outside the chain of title. In using the grantor-grantee index, *D* would find no prior conveyance indexed under the name of *A* as grantor. How could he ever discover the assignment since it would be indexed under names that are strangers to his chain of title? A contrary holding would make the system unworkable since no one could search every document in the recording office. Note that if a tract system were in use all instruments relating to that particular piece of property would be indexed in the same place and the assignment would then be discovered, giving notice of the prior unrecorded lease. If, under the above facts, *A*, prior to the warranty deed to *D*, had given an option to purchase (recorded) to *E* and that option had recited that it was subject to a prior lease to *B* that would have been sufficient to bind *D*. This is so, because the option is in the chain of title and the subsequent purchaser takes subject to all facts disclosed by the terms of the option, i.e., he is put on inquiry notice by the recital.[1]

There are many variations of the basic situation just discussed but it is safe to conclude that any time a document affecting title is left unrecorded, subsequent transactions based on that document will be out of the chain of title and hence will not give constructive notice to a subsequent b.f.p. from the original owner.[2] Of course, if the claimants

1. Guerin v. Sunburst Oil and Gas Co., 68 Mont. 365, 218 P. 949 (1923). The reference to claims outside the chain, in recitals in documents inside the chain, has clouded many titles. This is particularly troublesome if the reference is vague and gives no real clue as to the nature of the claim or the identity of the claimant. This problem has been dealt with by statutes in some states, and the acts tend to protect the b.f.p. and promote merchantability of titles. See L.C. Stroh and Sons, Inc. v. Batavia Homes and Develop. Corp., 17 A.D.2d 385, 234 N.Y.S.2d 401 (1962).

2. Capper v. Poulsen, 321 Ill. 480, 152 N.E. 587 (1926), is another variation on the theme in which a recorded affidavit, which would have put the subsequent purchaser

under the unrecorded instrument enter into possession that will be constructive notice in itself.

Must a purchaser search the records for a conveyance recorded *after* a prior grantor in the chain parted with title? *A* conveys to *B* but the latter does not record. *A* then conveys to *C* who promptly records but is not a protected party because he knew of the prior deed to *B*. *B* then records, but some time after the recorded conveyance to *C*. *C* then conveys to *D*, a b.f.p., who records. Who has priority? The better view would prefer *D*, since he is a b.f.p. and the deed to *B* is now out of the chain of title.[3] A contrary position, based on the fact that *B's* deed was recorded before the conveyance to *D*, has been adopted in some states.[4] The importance of the problem lies in the light it throws on the chain of title concept. It is impractical for a purchaser to search the grantor index for a period after the title has been conveyed because there would literally be no place to stop, short of the day when the purchaser's deed is recorded, and this would have to be done for every title holder in the chain, back to the patent deed from the government.

The converse of the situation discussed in the preceding paragraph is also interesting. Must a purchaser search the records for a conveyance recorded *before* a prior grantor in the chain acquired title? *A* conveys by warranty deed to *B*, who promptly records. Unfortunately, *A* has no title at the time since the land is really owned by *X*. Subsequently, *A* acquires *X's* interest and the deed is recorded. *A* then conveys to *C*, a b.f.p., who records. Who has priority? Again, the better view prefers *C* since he is a b.f.p. and the deed to *B* is out of the chain of title.[5] However, since this situation involves the doctrine of estoppel by deed it is possible to argue that the title acquired by *A* from *X* passed immediately to *B* under the warranties in the deed and hence left nothing for *C*. Several cases have so held[6] but this position has been vigorously attacked by Professor Walsh. "This obsolete doctrine of estoppel by deed has been applied . . . in obvious disregard of the recording acts and the necessary rule incident to their application that the recorded instrument must be in the chain of title. They have held that estoppel by deed binds all subsequent purchasers, though for value and without notice, and therefore the recording acts do not protect them—a shocking exhibition of technicality and ignorance of legal history. . . . Though the principle of legal estoppel is recognized, its application in these cases to defeat the recording acts by the fiction of relation is without any reasonable basis."[7] This latter view, which prefers *B*, would require the purchaser to search the grantor index for conveyances by the grantor clear back to the beginning—again, a hopeless task since it would have to be done for every grantor in the

on notice, failed to have that effect because it was out of the chain of title.

3. Morse v. Curtis, 140 Mass. 112, 2 N.E. 929 (1885).

4. Woods v. Garnett, 72 Miss. 78, 16 So. 390 (1894).

5. Richardson v. Atlantic Coast Lumber Corporation, 93 S.C. 254, 75 S.E. 371 (1912).

6. Ayer v. Philadelphia and Boston Face Brick Co., 159 Mass. 84, 34 N.E. 177 (1893); Tefft v. Munson, 57 N.Y. 97 (1875).

7. Walsh, Commentaries on the Law of Real Property 511 (1947).

chain. Of course, a tract index would solve both of these knotty problems.

One final illustration should be sufficient to clarify the chain of title problem. *A* subdivides a tract of land into numerous lots, putting restrictive covenants (set back lines, limitations to residential use, etc.) in most of the deeds to his grantees. He fails to put any such covenants in a deed to *B*, a b.f.p., who is unaware of the restricted nature of the area. All of the prior deeds are recorded so that if they give constructive notice *B* is bound by the restrictions. Once more the cases split, with some courts taking the position that the prior deeds are out of the chain of title since "subsequent purchaser" in the recording acts means purchaser of the same tract of land, *not* purchaser from the same grantor.[8] Other courts, claiming to represent the weight of authority, say that the "grantee is chargeable with notice of everything affecting his title which could be discovered by an examination of the records of the deeds or other muniments of title of his grantor."[9] Strict chain of title logic favors the former position, but the latter may be more practical since usually the restricted nature of the subdivision is apparent to the purchaser so that he may be put on inquiry notice as to the covenants.[10]

SABO v. HORVATH

Supreme Court of Alaska, 1976.
559 P.2d 1038.

BOOCHEVER, CHIEF JUSTICE. This appeal arises because Grover C. Lowery conveyed the same five-acre piece of land twice—first to William A. Horvath and Barbara J. Horvath and later to William Sabo and Barbara Sabo. Both conveyances were by separate documents entitled "Quitclaim Deeds." Lowery's interest in the land originates in a patent from the United States Government under 43 U.S.C.A. § 687a ("Alaska Homesite Law"). Lowery's conveyance to the Horvaths was prior to the issuance of patent, and his subsequent conveyance to the Sabos was after the issuance of patent. The Horvaths recorded their deed in the Chitna Recording District on January 5, 1970; the Sabos recorded their deed on December 13, 1973. The transfer to the Horvaths, however, predated patent and title, and thus the Horvaths' interest in the land was recorded "outside the chain of title." Mr. Horvath brought suit to quiet title, and the Sabos counterclaimed to quiet their title.

In a memorandum opinion, the superior court ruled that Lowery had an equitable interest capable of transfer at the time of his conveyance to the Horvaths and further said the transfer contemplated more than a "mere quitclaim"—it warranted patent would be transferred. The superior court also held that Horvath had the superior claim to the

8. Glorieux v. Lighthipe, 88 N.J.L. 199, 96 A. 94 (1915).

9. Finley v. Glenn, 303 Pa. 131, 136, 154 A. 299, 301 (1931).

10. For a more detailed analysis of this point see 4 Am.L.Prop. § 17.24, p. 602 (Casner ed.1952).

land because his prior recording had given the Sabos constructive notice for purposes of AS 34.15.290.[1] The Sabos' appeal raises the following issues:

1. Under 43 U.S.C.A. § 687a, when did Lowery obtain a present equitable interest in land which he could convey?

2. Are the Sabos, as grantees under a quitclaim deed, "subsequent innocent purchaser[s] in good faith"?

3. Is the Horvaths' first recorded interest, which is outside the chain of title, constructive notice to Sabo?

We affirm the trial court's ruling that Lowery had an interest to convey at the time of his conveyance to the Horvaths. We further hold that Sabo may be a "good faith purchaser" even though he takes by quitclaim deed. We reverse the trial court's ruling that Sabo had constructive notice and hold that a deed recorded outside the chain of title is a "wild deed" and does not give constructive notice under the recording laws of Alaska.[2]

The facts may be stated as follows. Grover C. Lowery occupied land in the Chitna Recording District on October 10, 1964 for purposes of obtaining Federal patent. Lowery filed a location notice on February 24, 1965, and made his application to purchase on June 6, 1967 with the Bureau of Land Management (BLM). On March 7, 1968, the BLM field examiner's report was filed which recommended that patent issue to Lowery. On October 7, 1969, a request for survey was made by the United States Government. On January 3, 1970, Lowery issued a document entitled "Quitclaim Deed" to the Horvaths; Horvath recorded the deed on January 5, 1970 in the Chitna Recording District. Horvath testified that when he bought the land from Lowery, he knew patent and title were still in the United States Government, but he did not rerecord his interest after patent had passed to Lowery.

Following the sale to the Horvaths, further action was taken by Lowery and the BLM pertaining to the application for patent[3] and culminating in issuance of the patent on August 10, 1973.

Almost immediately after the patent was issued, Lowery advertised the land for sale in a newspaper. He then executed a second document also entitled "quitclaim" to the Sabos on October 15, 1973. The Sabos duly recorded this document on December 13, 1973.

Luther Moss, a representative of the BLM, testified to procedures followed under the Alaska Homesite Law [43 U.S.C.A. § 687a]. After numerous steps, a plat is approved and the claimant notified that he

1. AS 34.15.290 states:

A conveyance of real property in the state hereafter made, other than a lease for a term not exceeding one year, is void as against a subsequent innocent purchaser or mortgagee in good faith for a valuable consideration of the property or a portion of it, whose conveyance is first duly recorded. An unrecorded instrument is valid as between the parties to it and as against one who has actual notice of it. [Footnotes in the case are by the Court and numbered accordingly.]

2. Because we hold Lowery had a conveyable interest under the Federal statute, we need not decide issues raised by the parties regarding after-acquired property and the related issue of estoppel by deed.

3. [The court's footnotes 3 through 11 are omitted.]

should direct publication of his claim. In this case, Lowery executed his conveyance to the Horvaths after the BLM field report had recommended patent.

The first question this court must consider is whether Lowery had an interest to convey at the time of his transfer to the Horvaths. [The court's discussion of this question is omitted.]

Since the Horvaths received a valid interest from Lowery, we must now resolve the conflict between the Horvaths' first recorded interest and the Sabos' later recorded interest.

The Sabos, like the Horvaths, received their interest in the property by a quitclaim deed. They are asserting that their interest supersedes the Horvaths under Alaska's statutory recording system. AS 34.15.290 provides that:

> A conveyance of real property . . . is void as against a subsequent innocent purchaser . . . for a valuable consideration of the property . . . whose conveyance is first duly recorded. An unrecorded instrument is valid . . . as against one who has actual notice of it.

Initially, we must decide whether the Sabos, who received their interest by means of a quitclaim deed, can ever be "innocent purchaser[s]" within the meaning of AS 34.15.290. Since a "quitclaim" only transfers the interest of the grantor, the question is whether a "quitclaim" deed itself puts a purchaser on constructive notice. Although the authorities are in conflict over this issue, the clear weight of authority is that a quitclaim grantee can be protected by the recording system, assuming, of course, the grantee purchased for valuable consideration and did not otherwise have actual or constructive knowledge as defined by the recording laws.[12] We choose to follow the majority rule and hold that a quitclaim grantee is not precluded from attaining the status of an "innocent purchaser."

In this case, the Horvaths recorded their interest from Lowery prior to the time the Sabos recorded their interest. Thus, the issue is whether the Sabos are charged with constructive knowledge because of the Horvaths' prior recordation. Horvath is correct in his assertion that in the usual case a prior recorded deed serves as constructive notice pursuant to AS 34.15.290, and thus precludes a subsequent recordation from taking precedence. Here, however, the Sabos argue that because Horvath recorded his deed prior to Lowery having obtained patent, they were not given constructive notice by the recording

12. See Note, Deeds—Quitclaim Grantee as a Bona Fide Purchaser, 28 Ore.L.Rev. 258 n. 1 (1949) and the many cases cited therein. See generally, Annot., 59 A.L.R. 632 (1929); Annot., 162 A.L.R. 556, 560–62 (1946); 77 Am.Jur.2d, Vendor and Purchaser, §§ 711–13. On the other hand, there is also authority which holds that a quitclaim grantee cannot be a good faith purchaser. See 28 Ore.L.Rev. 258, at 259 n. 2. See also the territorial case of Crossly v. Campion Mining Co., 1 Alaska 391 (1901). There it was held that a grantee accepting a quitclaim deed with *full knowledge* of a prior unrecorded deed was not a subsequent innocent purchaser in good faith. This case would not be conclusive with respect to quitclaim grantees who record under a recording system and without actual knowledge. See also Wickwire v. City and Borough of Juneau, 557 P.2d 783, fn. 7 (Alaska, 1976), holding that the right to recover damages for condemnation is not an interest in real property which passes by quitclaim deed.

system. They contend that since Horvaths' recordation was outside the chain of title, the recording should be regarded as a "wild deed".

It is an axiom of hornbook law that a purchaser has notice only of recorded instruments that are within his "chain of title."[13] If a grantor (Lowery) transfers prior to obtaining title, and the grantee (Horvath) records prior to title passing, a second grantee who diligently examines all conveyances under the grantor's name from the date that the grantor had secured title would not discover the prior conveyance. The rule in most jurisdictions which have adopted a grantor-grantee index system of recording is that a "wild deed" does not serve as constructive notice to a subsequent purchaser who duly records.[14]

Alaska's recording system utilizes a "grantor-grantee" index. Had Sabos searched title under both grantor's and grantee's names but limited his search to the chain of title subsequent to patent, he would not be chargeable with discovery of the pre-patent transfer to Horvath.

On one hand, we could require Sabo to check beyond the chain of title to look for pretitle conveyances. While in this particular case the burden may not have been great, as a general rule, requiring title checks beyond the chain of title could add a significant burden as well as uncertainty to real estate purchases. To a certain extent, requiring title searches of records prior to the date of a grantor acquired title would thus defeat the purposes of the recording system. The records as to each grantor in the chain of title would theoretically have to be checked back to the later of the grantor's date of birth or the date when records were first retained.

On the other hand, we could require Horvath to rerecord his interest in the land once title passes, that is, after patent had issued to Lowery. As a general rule, rerecording an interest once title passes is less of a burden than requiring property purchasers to check indefinitely beyond the chain of title.

It is unfortunate that in this case due to Lowery's double conveyances, one or the other party to this suit must suffer an undeserved loss. We are cognizant that in this case, the equities are closely balanced between the parties to this appeal. Our decision, however, in addition to resolving the litigants' dispute, must delineate the requirements of Alaska's recording laws.

13. 1 R. Patton & C. Patton, Patton on Land Titles § 69, at 230–33 (2d ed. 1957). Cities Service Oil Co. v. Adair, 273 F.2d 673, 676 (10th Cir. 1959); Stafford v. Ballinger, 199 Cal.App.2d 289, 18 Cal.Rptr. 568, 572 (1962); Pierson v. Bill, 138 Fla. 104, 189 So. 679, 684 (1939); Jenkins v. Bates, 230 Miss. 406, 92 So.2d 655, 657 (1957); Baker v. Koch, 114 Ohio App. 519, 183 N.E.2d 434, 437 (1960); Portman v. Earnhart, 343 S.W.2d 294, 297 (Tex.Civ.App.1960); Lone Star Gas Co. v. Sheaner, 297 S.W.2d 855, 857 (Tex.Civ.App.1957); Hyson v. Dodge, 198 Va. 792, 96 S.E.2d 792, 796 (1957).

14. 1 R. Patton & C. Patton, Patton on Land Title § 69, at 230–33 (2d ed. 1957); Lacey v. Humphres, 196 Ark. 72, 116 S.W.2d 345, 347 (1938); Etchison v. Dail, 182 Ark. 350, 31 S.W.2d 426, 427 (Ark. 1930); Brown v. Copp, 105 Cal.App.2d 1, 232 P.2d 868, 871 (1951); Hawley v. McCabe, 117 Conn. 558, 169 A. 192, 194 (1933); Ward v. Parks, 166 Ga. 149, 142 S.E. 690, 692 (1928); Manson v. Berkman, 356 Ill. 20, 190 N.E. 77, 79 (1934); Blumenthal v. Serota, 129 Me. 187, 151 A. 138, 141 (1930); Smith v. Williams, 132 Okl. 141, 269 P. 1067, 1073 (1928); Brown v. Ackerman, 17 S.W.2d 771 (Tex.Civ.App.1929).

Because we want to promote simplicity and certainty in title transactions, we choose to follow the majority rule and hold that the Horvaths' deed, recorded outside the chain of title, does not give constructive notice to the Sabos and is not "duly recorded" under the Alaskan Recording Act, AS 34.15.290. Since the Sabos' interest is the first duly recorded interest and was recorded without actual or constructive knowledge of the prior deed, we hold that the Sabos' interest must prevail. The trial court's decision is accordingly

Reversed.

NOTE

Although the Sabo case reveals an unusual problem—a conveyance prior to the issuance of a federal patent deed—it clearly illustrates the nature of the chain of title concept. While the spread of title insurance, which typically relies on company-owned tract indexes, eliminates much of the potential difficulty, cases continue to arise. In Ryczkowski v. Chelsea Title & Guaranty Co., 85 Nev. 37, 449 P.2d 261 (1969), a title insurance company relied on the concept and the court held that "an instrument executed by an owner which is recorded before acquisition or after relinquishment of title is outside the chain of title." In Spring Lakes, Ltd. v. O.F.M. Co., 12 Ohio St.3d 333, 467 N.E.2d 537 (1984), the court used the concept to protect a purchaser who did not have actual notice of an easement. The court held he could not be charged with constructive notice of the easement on the basis that it was recorded in a deed from one who was also a grantor in purchaser's chain of title. Said the court, "The rationale for this rule is apparent. It was stated in the syllabus in Glorieux v. Lighthipe, 88 N.J.Law 199, 96 A. 94 (1915): 'A purchaser of other land from the same grantor is not charged with notice of building restrictions contained in an earlier deed not in his chain of title. . . . It would impose an intolerable burden to compel him to examine all conveyances made by every one in his chain of title.'" See also Skidmore, Owings & Merrill v. Pathway Financial, 173 Ill.App.3d 512, 123 Ill.Dec. 395, 527 N.E.2d 1033 (1988) and Schuman v. Roger Baker & Associates, 70 N.C.App. 313, 319 S.E.2d 308 (1984).

For a good analysis of the entire problem, with suggestions as to how many of the difficulties could be resolved, see Cross, The Record "Chain of Title" Hypocrisy, 57 Col.L.Rev. 787 (1957).

Chapter 26

THE METHODS OF TITLE ASSURANCE

Most contracts for the sale of real estate require the vendor to convey a merchantable title to the purchaser. Unfortunately this does not solve the buyer's problem because the ownership of real property is so complex a matter that the seller frequently does not know whether his title is "good" or "bad." Moreover, once the deed is delivered, the doctrine of merger ends most of the purchaser's rights under the contract, and he must assure himself that the deed in fact conveys what he wants. Much of the law of real property involves man's search for a reliable way to obtain title security.

The most obvious and the oldest method of title assurance is to require the personal promise of the grantor that he is seised in fee simple absolute. In Section 2 we will explore the effectiveness of these personal covenants for title. Whatever their virtues, they have two obvious limitations: (1) they are no better than the personal solvency rating of the grantor, and (2) they require the willingness of the grantor to pay in event of breach or resort must be had to litigation. As the cases disclose, the covenants are subject to other technical limitations that leave much to be desired.

The inadequacy of the personal covenants led to the recording system and thence to two other methods of title assurance—examination of the records or of a specially prepared abstract of the records (Section 3) and title insurance (Section 5). These two methods account for the bulk of the present commercial transfers. Defects in the recording system in turn led to title registration (the Torrens system) (Section 4), which is used in a small minority of real estate transactions.

This chapter also presents the various statutes of limitation which have served as aids in assuring the possessor of land that his title is good (Section 6). These statutes are not methods of title assurance in the usual sense, but they do bolster the weak or non-existent paper title and hence are a valuable adjunct to this phase of the law.

You should note that the problems in this chapter are peculiar to real property. No similar general development has been necessary for chattels. Basically, the buyer's remedy for the failure of title to a watch, for example, is found in a cause of action against the jeweler who sold it to him. There are some parallels in the area of personal property, e.g., registration of title to an automobile and implied warranty of title, but these will be covered in Commercial Law or Sales courses.

SECTION 1. IMPLIED COVENANTS OF HABITABILITY AND SOME RELATED DOCTRINES

Before we analyze covenants for title and other methods of title assurance, we must familiarize ourselves with the doctrine of *caveat emptor* and the growing exceptions to this ancient precept. Traditionally, there were no implied covenants in a conveyance of land. The purchaser's "eyes were his bargain" and he had the "gracious protection of *caveat emptor.*" You should ponder the reason for this doctrine and its hardy survival into the twentieth century. Whatever its merits, the doctrine was easy to apply and had the effect of reducing litigation. Even today, the quitclaim deed contains no title covenants (express or implied) and the warranty deed is strictly limited in its warranties as Section 2 discloses. The heavy emphasis on the importance of the title overshadows the very real losses a purchaser could suffer even if he has a merchantable title. What shall it profit a man to gain a fee simple absolute if he loses the roof over his head due to faulty construction, termites, etc.?

The trend away from *caveat emptor* toward implied covenants of habitability is long overdue. The first two cases, and the notes which follow, analyze the present state of the law. The third case explores the periphery of the growing law and, while not strictly an implied warranty case, raises an even broader issue. Should the law, via traditional doctrine, allow the purchaser to suffer a loss where the builder of tract housing is insolvent but his principal financier and collaborator is solvent and may bear a part of the responsibility for the damage? By discussing the non-title covenants first, we should be able to illuminate the extreme technicality of the covenants for title which follow.

PETERSEN v. HUBSCHMAN CONSTRUCTION CO., INC.

Supreme Court of Illinois, 1979.
76 Ill.2d 31, 27 Ill.Dec. 746, 389 N.E.2d 1154.

RYAN, JUSTICE:

This case involves the dual issues of "implied warranty of habitability" and "substantial performance" as they apply to a contract of sale of a new home by a builder-vendor. The purchasers, Raymond S. Petersen and Delores E. Petersen, sued the builder-vendor, Hubschman Construction Company, Inc., in the circuit court of Lake County for the return of the $10,000 earnest money they had paid on the contract for the purchase of a new house, and for the value of the labor and materials supplied by Petersen. The trial court entered judgment in favor of the plaintiffs for $19,000. The appellate court affirmed. (53 Ill.App.3d 626, 11 Ill.Dec. 436, 368 N.E.2d 1044.) We granted leave to appeal.

In April 1972, the plaintiffs, Raymond and Delores Petersen, entered into a $71,000 contract with the defendant, Hubschman Construction Company, Inc., for the purchase of a piece of land and for the construction of a new home on that land. Later, the parties agreed to an offset from the contract price for work to be done on the home by Petersen. The plaintiffs paid $10,000 earnest money. In the fall of 1972 the Petersens became dissatisfied with Hubschman's performance, and Hubschman later agreed to repair or correct numerous items on a "punch list" but failed to satisfactorily carry out this agreement. The trial court found that the defects included: a basement floor pitched in the wrong direction away from a drain; improperly installed siding; a defective and ill-fitting bay window; a seriously defective front door and the door frame; and deterioration and "nail-popping" in the drywall on the interior. Testimony at the trial by the Petersens and by one of Hubschman's former employees indicated that repair of these items would involve major amounts of work. However, no one disputes that the house was at least habitable in that the Petersens could live in it and it was not dangerously unsafe. The Petersens proposed that Hubschman deposit $1,000 in escrow to guarantee completion of the repairs, but the suggestion was rejected. The Petersens refused to accept the home, and no closing of the transaction occurred; that is, the balance of the purchase price was not paid and no deed was delivered. Hubschman then invoked the contract forfeiture provision and notified the Petersens that they had forfeited both the $10,000 deposit and approximately $9,000 worth of labor and materials supplied by Petersen. The Petersens sued Hubschman. The trial court ruled that there were "defects in substance in the construction" of the house and that Hubschman had not substantially performed and could not declare a forfeiture. The court held that the Petersens were entitled to recover the earnest money and the value of the labor and materials provided.

Usually it is the builder-vendor who urges that, by reason of *caveat emptor* or merger, there is no warranty which the vendee of a new house can assert against a builder-vendor. In our case, however, it is the builder-vendor who urges the existence of the implied warranty of habitability. Hubschman, however, asserts that the implied warranty of habitability can be asserted by a vendee of a new house only if the defects in the structure render it unfit for habitation. Since in our case the defects complained of did not render the house uninhabitable, Hubschman contends that the trial court erred in ruling in favor of the Petersens. In this regard, Hubschman relies on Goggin v. Fox Valley Construction Corp. (1977), 48 Ill.App.3d 103, 8 Ill.Dec. 271, 365 N.E.2d 509. In that case the court, after remanding the case to the trial court, stated, in *dicta,* what that court conceived to be the nature of the warranty of habitability as follows:

> "The primary function of a new home is to shelter its inhabitants from the elements. If a new home does not keep out the elements because of a substantial defect of construction, such a home is not habitable within the meaning of the implied warranty of habitability. [citation.] Another function of a new home is to provide its inhabitants with a reasonably safe place to live, without fear of injury to person, health, safety, or property. If a new home is not structurally sound because of a substantial defect of construction, such a home is not habitable . . . . If a new home is not aesthetically satisfying because of a defect of construction, such a defect should not be considered as making the home uninhabitable." Goggin v. Fox Valley Construction Corp. (1977), 48 Ill.App. 3d 103, 106, 8 Ill.Dec. 271, 273, 365 N.E.2d 509, 511.

Ordinarily, it is the position of the buyer that *caveat emptor* or merger does not prohibit recovery from a builder-vendor for latent defects in a new house because of the warranty of habitability. However, in our case, the Petersens contend that the warranty of habitability is not involved since title to the property had not passed to them. It is their position that the builder-vendor had not substantially performed the contract to construct the new house and therefore they were entitled to repudiate the contract and to recover a money judgment.

This court has not considered the implied warranty of habitability as it relates to a contract for sale of a new house by a builder-vendor. That question was involved in Coutrakon v. Adams (1964), 31 Ill.2d 189, 201 N.E.2d 100, but this court decided that case on other grounds. This court has recognized an implied warranty of habitability in a landlord-tenant relationship. (Jack Spring, Inc. v. Little (1972), 50 Ill.2d 351, 280 N.E.2d 208.) The appellate courts of this State, however, have had the opportunity on several occasions to consider the implied warranty of habitability in cases involving the sale of new homes by a builder-vendor, but the results have not been uniform. . . .

The implied warranty of habitability in cases involving the sale of new homes by a builder-vendor is a judicial innovation of rather recent origin used to avoid the harshness of *caveat emptor* and the doctrine of merger and to afford a degree of relief to vendees of new homes who subsequently discover latent defects in the structure. This represents a distinct departure from accepted principles of real estate law that were based on reasons founded in antiquity. The vendee took the property at his risk. If he failed to discover defects, *caveat emptor* prevented him from maintaining an action against the vendor. The principle of merger produced the same result. All agreements between a vendee and the vendor were said to have merged in the deed, and if reservations were not contained in that instrument the doctrine of merger would prevent relief to the aggrieved vendee after receipt of the deed. (See Roeser, The Implied Warranty of Habitability in the Sale of New Housing: The Trend in Illinois, 1978 S.I.U.L.J. 178.) In Illinois, however, certain exceptions to the merger doctrine have been created. Reasoning that the merger doctrine evolved solely to protect the security of land titles, the Illinois courts have held that when the deed embraced and contained all of the subjects of the executory contract, the contract merged with the deed. However, an executory agreement for the performance of separate and distinct provisions did not merge with the deed. The prior contract is superseded only as to such of its provisions as are covered by the conveyance made pursuant to its terms. . . .

Although of recent origin, the implied warranty of habitability has found substantial acceptance in the various jurisdictions, and the commentators have voiced their approval and have examined the nature and basis of the implied warranty. See cases collected in Annot., 25 A.L.R.3d 383 (1969); see also Bearman, Caveat Emptor In Sales of Realty—Recent Assaults Upon The Rule, 14 Vand.L.Rev. 541 (1961); Roberts, The Case Of The Unwary Home Buyer: The Housing Merchant Did It, 52 Cornell L.Q. 835 (1967); Haskell, The Case For An Implied Warranty Of Quality In Sales Of Real Property, 53 Geo.L.J. 633

(1965); Jaeger, The Warranty of Habitability, 46 Chi.-Kent L.Rev. 123 (1969); 47 Chi.-Kent L.Rev. 1 (1970).

Because of the vast change that has taken place in the method of constructing and marketing new houses, we feel that it is appropriate to hold that in the sale of a new house by a builder-vendor, there is an implied warranty of habitability which will support an action against the builder-vendor by the vendee for latent defects and which will avoid the unjust results of *caveat emptor* and the doctrine of merger. Many new houses are, in a sense, now mass produced. The vendee buys in many instances from a model home or from predrawn plans. The nature of the construction methods is such that a vendee has little or no opportunity to inspect. The vendee is making a major investment, in many instances the largest single investment of his life. He is usually not knowledgeable in construction practices and, to a substantial degree, must rely upon the integrity and the skill of the builder-vendor, who is in the business of building and selling houses. The vendee has a right to expect to receive that for which he has bargained and that which the builder-vendor has agreed to construct and convey to him, that is, a house that is reasonably fit for use as a residence.

Many of the cases have held that the warranty of habitability will be applied for the protection of the vendee only when the house he contracts to purchase is not completed at the time of the execution of the contract. The reasoning is that, if it is a completed house, the vendee has an opportunity to make a complete inspection for defects before signing the contract. We do not agree with this reasoning. In most instances, the latent defects would not be discoverable by a vendee whether the house is complete or incomplete at the time the contract is entered into. The same reliance must be placed on the integrity and skill of the builder-vendor in the purchase of a completed house as in the purchase of an uncompleted one. The vendee should be permitted to recover for latent defects in either case. In both instances the builder-vendor is selling a house which he knows will be used as a home. The vendee's expectation that it will be reasonably suitable for that purpose is a reasonable one, whether or not the house is completed at the time the contract is executed.

In this court the vendees (the Petersens) urge that the implied warranty of habitability is not involved and that it is not needed, since in our case the deed has not been delivered and the contract has not merged in the deed. The implied warranty does not arise as a result of the execution of the deed. It arises by virtue of the execution of the agreement between the vendor and the vendee. If that agreement would have contained express covenants concerning the quality of construction they would not have merged in the deed, but would have continued as a collateral undertaking. In Brownell v. Quinn (1964), 47 Ill.App.2d 206, 208–09, 197 N.E.2d 721, it was held that a covenant to construct a building in a "neat and workmanlike" manner did not merge in the deed because the delivery of the deed did not fulfill that provision of the contract. The implied warranty, in a similar manner, exists as an independent undertaking collateral to the covenant to convey. As a matter of public policy it relaxes the rule of *caveat emptor* and the doctrine of merger in the special situation we are now discussing. It is implied as a separate covenant between the builder-vendor and the vendee because of the unusual dependent relationship of the vendee to the vendor. The implied warranty arises with the execution of the contract and survives the delivery of the deed. It is an implied covenant by the builder-vendor that the house which he contracts to build and to convey to the vendee is reasonably suitable for its intended use.

What we have just said evidences our disagreement with the narrow interpretation of the implied warranty of habitability urged by Hubschman and stated by the appellate court in *Goggin.* The mere fact that the house is capable of being inhabited does not satisfy the implied warranty. The use of the term "habitability" is perhaps unfortunate. Because of its imprecise meaning it is susceptible of misconstruction. It would more accurately convey the meaning of the warranty as used in this context if it were to be phrased in language similar to that used in the Uniform Commercial Code, warranty of merchantability, or warranty of fitness for a particular purpose. See Ill.Rev.Stat.1977, ch. 26, pars. 2–314, 2–315.

In fact, by drawing an analogy to the provisions of the Uniform Commercial Code, it has been suggested:

> "A solution to the problems created by the structural and habitability limitations is provided by characterizing the warranty as one of merchantability rather than one of habitability. Using the Uniform Commercial Code by analogy, the builder-vendor would guarantee that, upon sale, the house would be of fair average quality, that it would pass without objection in the building trade, and that it would be fit for the ordinary purpose of living in it.
>
> This warranty would suit the expectations and needs of both parties. . . . Some courts have already moved in this direction.
>
> . . .

Applying the reasoning of the above suggestion to the limited context of our case, we hold that implied in the contract for sale from the builder-vendor to the vendees is a warranty that the house, when completed and conveyed to the vendees, would be reasonably suited for its intended use. This implied warranty, of course, extends only to latent defects which interfere with this legitimate expectation.

Reference to the Uniform Commercial Code concerning the nature of the implied warranty invites consideration of the effect of provisions in a contract disclaiming the existence of such an implied warranty. (See Ill.Rev.Stat.1977, ch. 26, par. 2–315 for disclaimers under the Code.) Although the implied warranty of habitability is a creature of public policy, we do not consider a knowing disclaimer of the implied warranty to be against the public policy of this State. However, we do hold that any such a disclaimer must be strictly construed against the builder-vendor. (See Conyers v. Molloy (1977), 50 Ill.App.3d 17, 7 Ill. Dec. 695, 364 N.E.2d 986.) We refer to the well-reasoned opinion of the Supreme Court of Missouri in Crowder v. Vandendeale (Mo.1978), 564 S.W.2d 879, where it was held that "boilerplate" clauses, however worded, are rendered ineffective in such a disclaimer (564 S.W.2d 879, 881), and the court further stated:

> "[o]ne seeking the benefit of such a disclaimer must not only show a conspicuous provision which fully discloses the consequences of its inclusion but also that such was *in fact* the agreement reached. The heavy burden thus placed upon the builder is completely justified, for by his assertion of the disclaimer he is seeking to show that the buyer has relinquished protection afforded him by public policy. A knowing waiver of this protection will not be readily implied." (Emphasis in original.) Crowder v. Vandendeale (Mo. 1978), 564 S.W.2d 879, 881 n. 4.

Hubschman argues that since the house was habitable the Petersens must fulfill the contract to purchase and are only entitled to have the defects repaired or to damages if the builder fails to repair. We stated above that the implied warranty arose out of the execution of the contract for sale. At the time the Petersens repudiated the contract, it was executory and substantial performance of it, including the implied warranty, by Hubschman was a constructive condition to performance by the Petersens. The trial court found that "there were defects in substance in the construction" of the house and held that, under the circumstances of the case, Hubschman could not rely on substantial performance in declaring a forfeiture. It would be manifestly unjust to require the Petersens to accept a house in which "there were defects in substance in construction" and to settle for damages. That is not what they had bargained for. They contracted to pay for a house reasonably fit for its intended use, not for a house with substantial defects plus damages. "It is substantial performance of what the builder promised to do, of the construction work, . . . that is the 'condition' of the [vendee's] duty to pay." (3A A. Corbin, *Contracts* 314 (1960).) If a contractor builds a house on his own land for sale to a buyer, a departure from the plans will more readily be held to be sufficient reason for justifying rejection by the buyer than if the house would have been built on the "buyer's" land. If the defective house is built on the land of the contractor it belongs to him and depriving him of the contract price does not deprive him of the value of his labor and materials. (3A A. Corbin, *Contracts* 314, 344–45 (1960).) We do not decide in this case what the appropriate remedy would have been if the defects had not been discovered until after the deed had been delivered. We also do not decide whether there is an implied warranty when the builder builds the house for another on the "buyer's" land.

The question of whether there has been substantial performance of the terms and conditions of a contract sufficient to justify a judgment in favor of the building for the contract price is always a question of fact. (3A A. Corbin, *Contracts* 314, 318 (1960).) In this case the court held that Hubschman had not substantially performed, and the facts recited by the court in its order support that determination. Since the house was constructed on land owned by Hubschman, he was in a position to recover for his labor and materials through the resale of the house. There is some indication in this case that Hubschman has, in fact, resold the house. The circuit court of Lake County therefore did not err in treating the contract as repudiated by the Petersens and in entering a money judgment in their favor. The judgment of the appellate court is therefore affirmed.

Judgment affirmed.

NOTES

1. The principal case illustrates the continuing capacity of the common law to change and grow as social conditions are altered. For several decades courts have recognized implied warranties in cases of houses sold before the completion of construction but they had held fast to the doctrine of *caveat emptor* in all other cases.

As recently as 1961 an American court could say: "The great weight of authority does not support implied warranties in real estate transactions but requires any purported warranties to be in written contractual form . . . . No decision has come to our attention which permitted recovery by the vendee of a house upon the theory of implied warranty." Druid Homes, Inc. v. Cooper, 272 Ala. 415, 131 So.2d 884 (1961). By 1971, Alabama had reversed its position. See Cochran v. Keeton, 252 So.2d 313 (Ala.1971).

The implied warranty of habitability was first recognized in the English case of Miller v. Cannon Hill Estates, Limited, 2 K.B. 113 (1931). In 1957 an Ohio court in Vanderschrier v. Aaron, 103 Ohio App. 340, 140 N.E.2d 819 (1957) applied the Miller rule for the first time in the United States. Then, in 1964 the Colorado Supreme Court extended the implied warranty to a completed house. Carpenter v. Donohoe, 154 Colo. 78, 388 P.2d 399 (1964). (The Miller case involved the purchase of an unfinished house.) In the last two decades, there has been an apparently irresistable tide flowing toward the implication of covenants of habitability in the sale of new homes. While there has been an occasional defection, as in Bruce Farms, Inc. v. Coupe, 219 Va. 287, 247 S.E.2d 400 (1978) where the court preferred to wait for legislative action, the majority view now clearly favors the doctrine of the principal case. So far, however, the trend toward implied covenants is restricted to housing and does not extend to commercial structures. Thus, in Dawson Industries, Inc. v. Godley Construction Co., 29 N.C.App. 270, 224 S.E.2d 266 (1976) the court said the warranty applied "only to contracts for the sale of a new dwelling when the vendor is in the business of building dwellings." What is the rationale for this distinction? Does the vendor have to be in the "*business* of building dwellings?" In Park v. Sohn, 89 Ill.2d 453, 60 Ill.Dec. 609, 433 N.E.2d 651 (1982) the Illinois Supreme Court thought not. In that case, the defendant asserted that the warranty of habitability applied only to mass producers of new houses. The court found that the defendant need not be a full-time professional builder. He had built one house prior to construction of the one at issue and later built six more. However, where an individual who was not a professional builder constructed a house with the intent that it was to be his personal residence, but then sold it, no warranty of habitability was found. Dryden v. Bell, 158 Ariz. 164, 761 P.2d 1068 (App.1988); Siders v.

Schloo, 188 Cal.App.3d 1217, 233 Cal.Rptr. 906 (1987). Even professional builders of apartment complexes for their own ownership were held not to have warranted the habitability of a complex which they agreed to sell when approached by an offeror without having put the property on the market. Frickel v. Sunnyside Enterprises, Inc., 106 Wash.2d 714, 725 P.2d 422 (1986).

While the dam of *caveat emptor* has been broken, note that many sub-issues remain for judicial exploration. For example, in the principal case, the Illinois Supreme Court stated: "We do not decide in this case what the appropriate remedy would have been if the defects had not been discovered until after the deed had been delivered." Should the delivery of the deed make any difference? In Tavares v. Horstman, 542 P.2d 1275 (Wyo.1975) the Supreme Court of Wyoming thought not, and the Illinois Supreme Court subsequently agreed in Redarowicz v. Ohlendorf, 92 Ill.2d 171, 65 Ill.Dec. 411, 441 N.E.2d 324 (1982). What is the "appropriate remedy" when the implied warranty of habitability is breached? In Gaito v. Auman, 313 N.C. 243, 327 S.E.2d 870 (1985), the court found that the defect complained of could be remedied "without destroying a substantial part of the dwelling" and therefore awarded money damages equal to the cost of bringing the property into compliance with the warranty; however, the court said that "where, in order to conform the work to the contract requirements, a substantial part of what has been done must be undone, and the contractor has acted in good faith, or the owner has taken possession, the latter is not permitted to recover the cost of making the change, but may recover the difference in value," i.e., the difference between the reasonable market value of the property as warranted and its reasonable market value in its actual condition. In Finke v. Woodard, 122 Ill.App.3d 911, 78 Ill.Dec. 297, 462 N.E.2d 13 (1984), buyers who had taken possession of a badly built house were granted rescission. Does the implied warranty of habitability extend to duplexes purchased solely for income-producing purposes and never occupied by the plaintiff-purchasers? Hopkins v. Hartman, 101 Ill.App.3d 260, 56 Ill.Dec. 791, 427 N.E.2d 1337 (1981) said no, limiting the benefits of the warranty to "the relatively unsophisticated buyer, making a large investment, in a structure to be used by him as a residence." But the court in Tusch Enterprises v. Coffin, 113 Idaho 37, 740 P.2d 1022 (1987) disagreed: "It is of no matter *who* ultimately inhabits the home after purchase, be it the buyer, a relative or lessee. The implied warranty is that the *structure* will be fit for habitation. . ." Can there be a breach of the warranty if the construction defects are not so serious as to render the dwelling unfit for human habitation? In Gaito v. Auman, supra, involving a defective air conditioning unit, the court said the test was not whether a fixture is an "absolute [sic] essential utility to a dwelling house" but whether there is "a failure to meet the prevailing standard of workmanlike quality." In Evans v. J. Stiles, Inc., 689 S.W.2d 399 (Tex.1985), where the builder used faulty brick in the house, the court said, "[A] builder/vendor impliedly warrants that a building constructed for residential use is constructed in a good workmanlike manner and is suitable for human habitation. . . . The implied warranty of construction in a good workmanlike manner is independent of the implied warranty of habitability. . . ." To the same effect is Aronsohn v. Mandara, 98 N.J. 92, 484 A.2d 675 (1984).

Two of the most important sub-issues relate to the sale of "used" housing and to the right of a successor in interest of the first purchaser to sue on the implied warranty. The breakthrough on the first sub-issue came in the "termite cases" where the buyers of older dwellings were given relief even though there were no express warranties against termites. See Maser v. Lind, 181 Neb. 365, 148 N.W.2d 831, 22 A.L.R.3d 965 (1967) and Halpert v. Rosenthal, 107 R.I. 406, 267 A.2d 730 (1970). The extension of the doctrine to "used" housing was given impetus by Section 2–309 of the Uniform Land Transactions Act (see Note 2 below) and various cases are beginning to explore the problem. See Posner v. Davis, 76 Ill.App.3d 638, 32 Ill.Dec. 186, 395 N.E.2d 133 (1979) and Redarowicz v. Ohlendorf, 92 Ill.2d 171, 65 Ill.Dec. 411, 441 N.E.2d 324 (1982), both of which indicated the doctrine should be extended to used housing. See generally, Note, Builders' Liability for Latent Defects in Used Homes, 32 Stan.L.Rev. 607 (1980). It is still too early to tell how far this extension will go, but the winds of doctrine seem to be blowing in the direction of more protection for the consumer even if the dwelling is not completely new. What are the relevant policy considerations?

The second sub-issue is closely related to the first and entwined in that hardy favorite—privity. Although the issue is still open in many states, "[t]he current trend . . . extends protection to remote purchasers who have no contractual relationship or privity with the builder-vendor." Keyes v. Guy Bailey Homes, Inc., 439 So.2d 670 (Miss.1983) (overruling three earlier decisions requiring privity). In Terlinde v. Neely, 275 S.C. 395, 271 S.E.2d 768 (1980), a defendant builder constructed a house for speculative sale. The house settled and the first purchaser made a claim against the builder which was satisfied. The house was then sold to the present plaintiff and it settled again. This time the builder refused to pay and the trial court granted summary judgment for the builder. The court reversed and held that a subsequent purchaser of a house could pursue a course of action in contract or tort against the builder for a reasonable period of time after the construction, without privity. An implied warranty for latent defects extends to subsequent purchasers for a reasonable period. The key inquiry is foreseeability not privity. By placing the house in the stream of commerce, the builder owes a duty of care to those who will use it and renders him accountable for negligent workmanship. What is a reasonable period of time?

A related problem is when the statute of limitations begins to run. Does the cause of action arise when the defective construction occurs or when it is discovered? If the defect is latent, which is typically the case, the builder may be sued years after the construction occurred. See McAllister v. Stoeco Homes, Inc., 740 F.2d 957 (3d Cir.1984), where a claim based on a latent defect in an eighteen year old home was held not actionable. There was a ten year statute of limitations. In Gaito v.

Auman, supra, the court concluded that a home should be considered "new" throughout the ten year period of limitations.

In Arvai v. Shaw, 289 S.C. 161, 345 S.E.2d 715 (1986), defendant builder constructed a house for Farr, according to Farr's plans and specifications, on land which defendant previously had conveyed to Farr. In 1971 Farr moved in, was dissatisfied with the septic tank system, and reconveyed the house to defendant. Defendant then sold it to Semones, who conveyed it to plaintiff in 1976. Plaintiff experienced flooding problems and sued for breach of the implied warranty of habitability, claiming that the house was badly designed so as to be susceptible to flood damage. Although it concluded that lack of privity does not bar a remote purchaser from suing the initial vendor, the court nevertheless held in favor of defendant: "[T]he implied warranty of habitability has its roots in the *execution of a contract for sale*. . . . Holding the custom builder liable . . . where he is not also involved in the *sale* of the house, would be incompatible with the law of warranty. . . . At the time of the sale to [Semones], the house was not *new*, but *used*. [N]o warranty attaches to sales of used homes." Does this decision make sense? Did defendant not sell Farr a new house? Would the decision have been different if defendant had built the house before conveying the land to Farr? Should it be significant that defendant was an intervening owner between Farr and Semones? Is it important that the house was built according to Farr's plans and specifications? See Young v. DeGuerin, 591 S.W.2d 296 (Tex.Civ.App. 1979) where a contractor built a townhouse on a lot owned by another. The contractor contended that an implied warranty did not exist in such a case. The court held that a sale of realty was not a prerequisite, because to hold otherwise would deny recovery to a consumer who proved faulty workmanship and materials if the consumer owned his lot and hired a contractor, but would allow recovery under the same fact situation to a consumer who bought his lot and house in a package deal. See also Herlihy v. Dunbar Builders Corp., 92 Ill.App.3d 310, 47 Ill.Dec. 911, 415 N.E.2d 1224 (1980) holding that the implied warranty could attach to the sale of a new condominium and that such a warranty could extend to defects in the common elements of the condominium.

In Kramp v. Showcase Builders, 97 Ill.App.3d 17, 52 Ill.Dec. 749, 422 N.E.2d 958 (1981), the court extended the doctrine to cover vacant property where a developer had installed a septic system which was inadequate due to underlying soil conditions. On the other hand, in a similar case, where no septic tank had yet been installed but where the purchasers alleged breach of warranty because the soil would not support a septic system, a South Carolina court denied recovery, saying *caveat emptor* applied to the sale of unimproved land. The purchaser of such land has to have an express covenant to protect whatever special rights or interests he would presume to acquire in the land. Jackson v. River Pines, Inc., 276 S.C. 29, 274 S.E.2d 912 (1981). To the same effect is Lehmann v. Arnold, 137 Ill.App.3d 412, 91 Ill.Dec. 914, 484 N.E.2d 473 (1985).

If the builder-vendor becomes insolvent, can the initial home purchaser—or remote purchasers—maintain an implied warranty action against the builder's subcontractors? Minton v. Richards Group of Chicago, 116 Ill.App.3d 852, 72 Ill.Dec. 582, 452 N.E.2d 835 (1983), held that despite the lack of contractual privity the initial purchaser could recover from the painting subcontractor for defective exterior painting. "[W]here the innocent purchaser has no recourse to the builder-vendor and has sustained loss due to the faulty and latent defect in their new home caused by the subcontractor, the warranty of habitability applies to such subcontractor."

2. The Uniform Land Transactions Act in Section 2–309 adopts the strongest position so far suggested for implied covenants. The act refers to an implied warranty of quality and applies to all real estate, not merely housing. The warranty also arises in the case of used, as well as new, buildings or other improvements on the real estate. Section 2–309 reads as follows:

Section 2–309. [implied warranty of quality]

(a) Subject to the provisions on risk of loss (Section 2–406), a seller warrants that the real estate will be in at least as good condition at the earlier of the time of the conveyance or delivery of possession as it was at the time of contracting, reasonable wear and tear excepted.

(b) A seller, other than a lessor, in the business of selling real estate impliedly warrants that the real estate is suitable for the ordinary uses of real estate of its type and that any improvements made or contracted for by him will be:

(1) free from defective materials;

(2) constructed in accordance with applicable law, according to sound engineering and construction standards, and in a workmanlike manner.

(c) In addition, a seller in the business of selling real estate warrants to a protected party that an existing use, continuation of which is contemplated by the parties, does not violate applicable law at the earlier of the time of conveyance or delivery of possession.

(d) Warranties imposed by this section may be excluded or modified as specified in the provisions on exclusion or modification of warranties of quality (Section 2–311).

(e) For purposes of this section, improvements made or contracted for by a person related to the seller (Section 1–204) are made or contracted for by the seller.

(f) A person who extends credit secured by real estate and thereafter acquires the real estate by foreclosure, or in lieu of foreclosure, does not become a person in the business of selling real estate by reason of selling that real estate.

It will be interesting to watch the fate of this language both in the legislatures and in the trend of court decisions.

It is already clear, however, that this Section will have an impact on the developing doctrine. Thus, in Redarowicz v. Ohlendorf, 92 Ill.2d

171, 65 Ill.Dec. 411, 441 N.E.2d 324 (1982), the Illinois Supreme Court said: "While the warranty of habitability has roots in the execution of the contract for sale . . . we emphasize that it exists independently. . . . Privity of contract is not required." The court further stated that the safeguards which have evolved to protect home owners should not be frustrated because of the short intervening ownership of the "first purchaser," and the defects in a new house should be the responsibility of the builder or vendor who created the problems. Going beyond the analogy to the UCC, used in the principal case, the court adopted the standard of the Uniform Land Transactions Act. "[w]e do not believe it is logical to arbitrarily limit that protection to the first purchaser of a new house," and latent defects, which are noticed within a reasonable time of purchase, whether by an initial or a subsequent purchaser, can be the basis of an implied warranty of habitability.

3. There is a clear distinction between covenants relating to title to the land and covenants as to improvements on the land. As to the former, the old rule of no implied covenants still prevails. Whittemore v. Farrington, 12 Hun 349, 76 N.Y. 452, 457 (1879) shows the full impact of the common-law rule against implied covenants in deeds. "The question is then reduced to this. A party who, under a verbal agreement for the conveyance to him of lands, is entitled to insist upon a good title, and a deed with covenants, pays the consideration and is then tendered a deed without covenants. He demands a deed with covenants and this is refused. He then accepts the deed without covenants, and, believing the title to be clear, records it, and continues to occupy and improve the property. An incumbrance unknown at the time to both parties is afterwards discovered. Both parties are innocent of any fraud. It is conceded that no legal liability rests upon the grantor in such a case. . . ." [the court also denied relief in equity.] "If the grantor and grantee had both intended that the deed should contain covenants, and supposed at the time of its delivery that it did contain them, but through a mistake of the scrivener they had been omitted, the court might insert them. But no such case is made out here."

4. In Humber v. Morton, 426 S.W.2d 554, 25 A.L.R.3d 372 (Tex. 1968), referred to in the principal case, the defendant attempted to rely on the doctrine of merger, arguing that even if a covenant of habitability were implied in the contract it was not included in the deed and hence was lost due to the merger of the contract into the deed. The court rejected the argument.

The doctrine of merger is an old but misleading concept. Briefly stated, it means that any covenants in the contract merge into the deed on the execution of the deed and are no longer enforceable. Actually, the contract covenants are terminated rather than merged and the parties must then look to the deed for any cause of action. It is basically a titles doctrine designed to prevent the grantee from going behind the deed to earlier promises. There are many exceptions to the doctrine when title is not directly involved and when the covenant is collateral to the promise to convey land. See, for example, Re v.

Magness Construction Co., 49 Del. 377, 10 Terry 377, 117 A.2d 78 (1955) where the suit was for breach of a construction contract due to the defendant's failure to build in accordance with written plans and specifications. The deed to the property had been accepted although the work was not completed and was improperly done. The court allowed recovery saying, "Clearly the agreement calls for the performance of two separate acts, the conveyance of land improved by a dwelling and the building of a house in accordance with certain plans and specifications. This contract falls within the exception to the rule. There is no merger." See also Rhenish v. Deunk, 193 N.E.2d 295, 26 O.O.2d 416 (1963) and Richmond Homes, Inc. v. Lee-Mar, Inc., 20 Ohio App. 27, 251 N.E.2d 637 (1969). Even in title situations there is some chipping away at the doctrine, and in Mayer v. Sumergrade, 111 Ohio App. 237, 167 N.E.2d 516 (1960) the court allowed a purchaser to sue on a covenant against special tax assessments in the contract after delivery of the deed. There was a vigorous dissent, however, and the case represents a minority position on the title issue.

The merger doctrine continues to be discussed in the recent cases but it seldom prevails to defeat a suit by the purchaser. In Mallin v. Good, 93 Ill.App.3d 843, 49 Ill.Dec. 168, 417 N.E.2d 858 (1981) the court said: "While no Illinois reviewing court has considered the specific question of whether a vendor's covenant to make repairs will be merged into the subsequent deed, the weight of authority in other jurisdictions is that such agreements are collateral to the deed and are not merged into it. . . . In our view, an examination of the analogous authority in this state leads to a similar conclusion." On the other hand, in Bakken v. Price, 613 P.2d 1222 (Wyo.1980), the court held that a covenant to provide title insurance was merged into the deed and that after conveyance the deed controlled the rights of the parties. Note, however, that this was a title matter not collateral to the deed. The court held that the purchaser's remedy for the vendors' breach was in damages for breach of warranty rather than rescission.

The Uniform Land Transactions Act would abolish the doctrine of merger entirely:

Section 1–309. [Effect of Acceptance of Deed on Contract Obligations]

Acceptance by a buyer or a secured party of a deed or other instrument of conveyance is not of itself a waiver or renunciation of any of his rights under the contract under which the deed or other instrument of conveyance is given and does not of itself relieve any party of the duty to perform all his obligations under the contract.

G-W-L, INC. v. ROBICHAUX

Supreme Court of Texas, 1982.
643 S.W.2d 392.

SONDOCK, JUSTICE.

This is a suit brought under the Texas Deceptive Trade Practices Act by John and Merila Robichaux because of alleged defects in a new house purchased from builder-vendor G-W-L, Inc. d/b/a Goldstar Builders ("Goldstar"). The trial court rendered judgment for the Robichaux after a jury trial. The court of appeals affirmed. 622 S.W.2d 461. We reverse the judgments of the courts below and render judgment that plaintiff take nothing.

The Robichaux contracted with Goldstar for the construction of a house. The contract provided that Goldstar would design, build, and provide the materials for the house. The construction was completed by Goldstar but the roof of the house had a substantial sag in it. The Robichaux sued for breach of express and implied warranties. The jury found that no express warranties were breached, but found that Goldstar had failed to construct the roof in a good workmanlike manner and that the house was not merchantable at the time of completion. Judgment was rendered awarding the Robichaux damages under the Deceptive Trade Practices Act, plus attorney fees.

Goldstar's first point of error is that the court of appeals erred in holding that the implied warranty of fitness created by Humber v. Morton, 426 S.W.2d 554 (Tex.1968) was not waived because the parties agreed that there were no express or implied warranties. The promissory note signed by the Robichaux contained this provision:

> This note, the aforesaid Mechanic's and Materialmen's Lien Contract and the plans and specification signed for identification by the parties hereto constitute the entire agreement between the parties hereto with reference to the erection of said improvements, there being no oral agreements, representations, conditions, warranties, express or implied, in addition to said written instruments.

In Humber v. Morton, supra, this Court held that a builder-vendor who built and conveyed a house impliedly warranted that the house was constructed in a good workmanlike manner and was suitable for human habitation. Both parties acknowledge that the *Humber* warranty applies to real estate transactions of this nature. Additionally, both parties agree that this implied warranty can be waived by proper language. The question presented, therefore, is what is sufficient to exclude the implied warranty of fitness created in Humber v. Morton, supra. This question was reserved in Watel v. Richman, 576 S.W.2d 779 (Tex.1978), and has not been addressed by this Court.

The court of appeals stated that the language waiving the implied warranty must be "clear and free from doubt." 622 S.W.2d 464. We agree. This standard is consistent with the better-reasoned decisions in other states addressing the exclusion of the implied warranty of habitability. . . .

The court of appeals held, however, that the language of disclaimer in this case did not meet that test. With this we do not agree. The language in the contract that states "no . . . warranties, express or implied, in addition to said written instruments" could not be clearer. The parties to a contract have an obligation to protect themselves by reading what they sign. Thigpen v. Locke, 363 S.W.2d 247 (Tex.1962). Unless there is some basis for finding fraud, either actual or constructive, the parties may not excuse themselves from the consequences of failing to meet that obligation. . . .

Although this is a question of first impression, we do not write on an entirely clean slate. In Pyle v. Eastern Seed Co., 198 S.W.2d 562, 563 (Tex.1946), this Court faced a similar question. In the *Pyle* case, a seed buyer sued the seed company for breach of warranty when the seed delivered was not the variety provided for in the contract. The seed company argued that the contract contained a waiver of all warranties because the contract provided that "Eastern Seed Co. gives no warranty, express or implied, as to description, purity, productivity, or any other matter of any seed we may send out. . . ." Id. at 563. In holding that the buyer could not recover for breach of warranty, this Court stated:

> Neither of the parties here are under guardianship or incompetent to contract. There is no claim that the contract signed was not the one agreed upon, or that both parties did not fully understand what they were agreeing to. Plaintiff [seed seller] plainly undertook to relieve itself from liability in case of intermixture, and defendant agreed that it should be relieved. It is not claimed that the contract is void, because contrary to public law or to public policy, and, if not, effect should be given to it. . . . If it be conceded that the contract is one-sided, it must also be conceded that the parties had a right to make a one-sided contract if they saw fit.

See also Allright, Inc. v. Elledge, 515 S.W.2d 266 (Tex.1974) (limitation of liability in bailee's written parking contract need not be called to consumer/bailor's attention); W.R. Weaver Co. v. Burroughs Corp., 580 S.W.2d 76 (Tex.Civ.App.—El Paso 1979, writ ref'd n.r.e.) (disclaimer in an equipment lease agreement need not meet the conspicuousness requirement of Tex.Bus. & Com.Code Ann. § 2.316).

The Robichaux cite MacDonald v. Mobley, 555 S.W.2d 916 (Tex.Civ. App.—Austin 1977, writ ref'd n.r.e.), for the proposition that the provisions in the Texas Business and Commerce Code for exclusions or modifications of warranties should be applicable to the implied warranty of fitness created in Humber v. Morton, supra. See Tex.Bus. & Com. Code Ann. § 2.316 (1968). In MacDonald v. Mobley, supra, the builder-vendor defended on the grounds that the sales contract excluded the *Humber* warranty pursuant to § 2.316 of the Business and Commerce Code. The court of appeals agreed that the provisions of § 2.316 were applicable, but held that the language used was not effective to exclude the warranty of fitness because it was not "conspicuous," as required by § 2.316(b). Id. at 919.

The provisions of Chapter 2 (Sales) of the Business and Commerce Code are not applicable to the construction and sale of a house. The Legislature thus far has not included real estate transactions within the scope of Chapter 2. Chapter 2 is limited to transactions involving the sale of "goods." Tex.Bus. & Com.Code Ann. § 2.102 (1968). Goods are defined as "all things . . . that are *movable* . . . at the time of identification to the contract. . . ." Tex.Bus. & Com.Code Ann. § 2.105 (1968). The Code additionally makes it clear that the sale of a home is not normally "movable." Section 2.107 provides that "a contract for the sale of . . . a structure or its materials to be removed from realty is a contract for the sale of goods within this chapter if they are to be severed by the seller."

Additionally, building contracts involve the sale of both services and materials. In such hybrid transactions, the question becomes whether the dominant factor or "essence" of the transaction is the sale of the materials or the services. See Freeman v. Shannon, 560 S.W.2d 732 (Tex.Civ.App.—Amarillo 1977, writ ref'd n.r.e.). The contract in this case provided that Goldstar would "build, construct, and complete . . . and furnish and provide all labor and material to be used in the construction and erection thereof." Clearly, the "essence" or "dominant" factor of the transaction was the furnishing of labor and the performance of work required for constructing the house. See Robertson Lumber Co. v. Stephens Farmers Co-op Elevator, 274 Minn. 17, 143 N.W.2d 622 (1966); Markman v. Hefner, 252 Iowa 118, 106 N.W.2d 59 (1960).

Goldstar's second point of error complains that the court of appeals erred in holding that the implied warranty of merchantability could be applied to this transaction. Since we conclude that Chapter 2 of the Business and Commerce Code is not applicable to this real estate transaction, we hold that the trial court and court of appeals erred in applying the implied warranty of merchantability contained therein.

The judgments of the courts below are reversed and judgment is rendered that plaintiff take nothing.

SPEARS, J., dissents with an opinion in which RAY and ROBERTSON, JJ., Join

SPEARS, JUSTICE, dissenting.

I respectfully dissent.

I do not agree with the majority that the language "no warranties, express or implied" is sufficient to exclude the builder's implied warranty of fitness. The better rule is the waiver must be in *clear and unequivocal* language specifically naming the warranty that is being disclaimed. See Sloat v. Matheny, 625 P.2d 1031 (Colo.1981); Herlihy v. Dunbar Builders Corp., 92 Ill.App.3d 310, 47 Ill.Dec. 911, 415 N.E.2d 1224 (1980).

In analogous areas of contract law this court has held clauses ineffective if not clear and specific, and I see no reason not to apply that same rule here. For example, in order for an indemnity agreement to protect an indemnitee from its own negligence the obligation must be expressed in clear and unequivocal terms. Eastman Kodak v. Exxon Corp., 603 S.W.2d 208 (Tex.1980); Fireman's Fund Insurance Co. v. Commercial Standard Insurance Co., 490 S.W.2d 818 (Tex.1972). Similarly, in McMillan v. Klingensmith, 467 S.W.2d 193 (Tex.1972), we held unless a party is expressly named in a release, he is not released.

The warranty of habitability is implied in law to protect innocent consumers, and to hold builders accountable for their work. To effectuate the public policies underlying the implied warranty, a court should not consider the warranty waived except by very express and specific language which clearly reflects that the buyer knew the implied warranty did not attach to the sale of his home.

In the sale of a new home, the builder warrants that the house is constructed in a good and workmanlike manner, and is suitable for human habitation. Humber v. Morton, 426 S.W.2d 554 (Tex.1968). An effective waiver must give the buyer notice that he is waiving his warranty of habitability. The ordinary consumer when signing a contract for sale would not even conceive of the possibility that his house would not be built in a good and workmanlike manner. For that reason the waiver must at least be specific and express enough to inform the buyer specifically what he is waiving. An effective waiver of the implied warranty of fitness in the sale of a new home should refer to a warranty of "habitability" or disclaim "good and workmanlike manner." In this case the language "no warranties express or implied" is not sufficient to notify the purchaser that he is waiving his implied warrant of habitability.

Other states have various requirements for effectively waiving the implied warranty of habitability. I believe the better reasoned authorities are those that at least require specific and express language. E.g., Sloat v. Matheny, 625 P.2d 1031, 1034 (Colo.1981); Peterson v. Hubschman Construction Co., 76 Ill.2d 31, 27 Ill.Dec. 746, 748, 389 N.E.2d 1154, 1156 (1979); Crowder v. Vandendale, 564 S.W.2d 879, 881 (Mo.1978); Casavant v. Campopiano, 114 R.I. 24, 327 A.2d 831, 834 (1974).

I would, therefore, affirm the judgments of the court's below.

RAY and ROBERTSON, JJ., join in this dissenting opinion.

NOTES

1. Now that the housing consumer's battle against *caveat emptor* has been nearly won, it is inevitable that the vendor-builders will strike back via a disclaimer or waiver of any implied warranty of habitability in the contract or deed. The principal case indicates that this counterattack may be successful, at least against the unwary consumer.

The Illinois courts have taken a position more nearly in line with the dissenting justices in the principal case. Refer to the Petersen case and see also Herlihy v. Dunbar Builders Corp., 92 Ill.App.3d 310, 47 Ill. Dec. 911, 415 N.E.2d 1224 (1980). The court there recognized that a knowing disclaimer of an implied warranty of habitability did not violate public policy but that such a disclaimer should be strictly construed against the condominium developer. A disclaimer clause located near the end of a standard form contract in the same print size and type as other clauses, and which did not mention or refer to a warranty of habitability nor explain the consequences of disclaimer, was not necessarily a sufficiently valid disclaimer. Briarcliffe West Townhouse Owners Association v. Wiseman Construction Co., 107 Ill.App.3d 402, 89 Ill.Dec. 351, 480 N.E.2d 833 (1985), found no effective disclaimer of the implied warranty of habitability despite prominently displayed, bold-faced contractual language that "THESE [express] WARRANTIES ARE GIVEN IN LIEU OF ANY OTHER WARRANTIES, EXPRESSED OR IMPLIED, AND ALL SUCH WARRANTIES INCLUDING WARRANTIES OF MERCHANTABILITY AND FITNESS FOR A PARTICULAR PURPOSE ARE HEREBY EXCLUDED." However, a subsequent decision by a different appellate court reached an apparently contrary result where the contract said, "SELLER DISCLAIMS ANY AND ALL IMPLIED WARRANTIES OF MERCHANTABILITY AND FITNESS AS TO THE PROPERTY." Country Squire Homeowners Association v. Crest Hill Development Corp., 150 Ill.App.3d 30, 103 Ill.Dec. 477, 501 N.E.2d 794 (1986).

2. Purchasers of defective housing may have other causes of action against their vendors besides breach of warranty. Among the most common are fraudulent or negligent misrepresentation of the condition of the premises, fraudulent concealment of defects, and breach of a duty to disclose facts materially affecting the value of the property.

In Wagner v. Cutler, 757 P.2d 779 (Mont.1988), the corporate defendant, as an accommodation, bought the house of one of its employees, who was being transferred to another state, and listed it for sale with a realtor. Defendant, which did not know of latent defects in the chimney, insulation, sewage pump, and lawn sprinkler system, signed a listing agreement which stated, "To the best of my knowledge, the following items are in good repair and working condition, and I am unaware of anything wrong with the foundation, roof, siding, wiring, drainage, heating, plumbing or sanitation system except: none." The realtor thereafter told plaintiff purchaser that the house was "well built" according to "code." Although the earnest money receipt signed by plaintiff said, "Purchaser agrees to accept property and appliances in 'as is' condition [and] enters into this agreement in full reliance upon his independent investigation and judgment," the court found that plaintiff had relied on the representations by defendant's agent, the realtor. Defendant was held liable for negligent misrepresentation because it had failed to exercise reasonable care in obtaining information about the latent defects in the house.

In Hill v. Jones, 151 Ariz. 81, 725 P.2d 1115 (App.1986), the issue was whether the seller of a used house had an affirmative duty to disclose to the buyer the existence of termite damage known to the seller but not to the buyer, which was not readily observable and materially affected the value of the property. The court held that there was such a duty, saying that "nondisclosure may be equated with and given the same legal effect as fraud and misrepresentation." In Mancini v. Gorick, 41 Ohio App.3d 373, 536 N.E.2d 8 (1987), the court said, "Although a claim of nondisclosure will not overcome an 'as is' clause, a claim of fraudulent concealment will. Nondisclosure will become the equivalent of fraudulent concealment when it becomes the duty of a person to speak in order that the party with whom he is dealing may be placed on an equal footing with him." Seller had told the buyer that seller was an architectural engineer and had personally designed and built the house. Buyer claimed that he did not have the house inspected because he relied on seller's professional expertise in believing the house to have been constructed in a workmanlike manner, free of latent defects. The court concluded that it was a "question of fact as to whether [buyer's] confidence in what [seller] implied was reasonable and sufficient to nullify the effect of the 'as is' clause."

In an especially interesting case, a California court held that purchaser had stated a cause of action for rescission or damages by alleging that seller had failed to disclose that the house had been the site of a multiple murder ten years earlier. Referring to "the nettlesome problem of the duty of disclosure of blemishes on real property which are not physical defects or legal impairments to use," the court said, "In general, a seller of real property has a duty to disclose: 'where the seller knows of facts *materially* affecting the value or desirability of the property which are known or accessible only to him and [not] to the buyer.'" Reed v. King, 145 Cal.App.3d 261, 193 Cal.Rptr. 130 (1983).

CONNOR v. GREAT WESTERN SAVINGS AND LOAN ASSOCIATION

Supreme Court of California, In Bank, 1968.
69 Cal.2d 850, 73 Cal.Rptr. 369, 447 P.2d 609.

TRAYNOR, CHIEF JUSTICE. These consolidated appeals are from a judgment of nonsuit in favor of defendant Great Western Savings and Loan Association in two actions consolidated for trial.

Plaintiffs in each action purchased single-family homes in a residential tract development known as Weathersfield, located on tracts 1158, 1159, and 1160 in Ventura County. Thereafter their homes suffered serious damage from cracking caused by ill-designed foundations that could not withstand the expansion and contraction of adobe soil. Plaintiffs accordingly sought rescission or damages from the various parties involved in the tract development.

Holders of promissory notes secured by second deeds of trust on the homes filed cross-complaints, alleging that their security had been impaired by the damage to the homes. They sought to impose liens on any recovery plaintiffs might obtain from other defendants.

There was abundant evidence that defendant Conejo Valley Development Company, which built and sold the homes, negligently constructed them without regard to soil conditions prevalent at the site. Specifically, it laid slab foundations on adobe soil without taking proper precautions recommended to it by soil engineers. When the adobe soil expanded during rainstorms two years later, the foundations cracked and their movement generated further damage.

In addition to seeking damages from Conejo, plaintiffs sought to hold Great Western liable, either on the ground that its participation in the tract development brought it into a joint venture or a joint enterprise with Conejo, which served to make it vicariously liable, or on the ground that it breached an independent duty of care to plaintiffs.

A brief review of the negotiations leading to Great Western's role in the development of the Weathersfield tract is essential to a clear perspective of the issues. Since the appeals are from a judgment of nonsuit, such a review must give to plaintiffs' evidence all the value to which it is legally entitled, must recognize every legitimate inference that may be drawn from that evidence, and must disregard conflicting evidence. (Raber v. Tumin (1951), 36 Cal.2d 654, 656, 226 P.2d 574; Blumberg v. M. & T., Inc. (1949) 34 Cal.2d 226, 229, 209 P.2d 1.) If there is evidence that would support a recovery against Great Western on either of the grounds set forth by plaintiffs, the judgment of nonsuit must be reversed.

The Weathersfield project originated in December 1958, when Harris Goldberg, president of South Gate Development Company, undertook negotiations to purchase for South Gate 547 acres of the McRea ranch, a parcel of approximately 1,600 acres of undeveloped real property in the Conejo Valley, which was then undergoing the beginnings of large-scale development. Goldberg and Keith Brown together owned and controlled South Gate Development Company. They planned to develop the property with the goal of creating a community of approximately 2,000 homes.

Neither Goldberg nor Brown had any significant experience in large-scale construction of tract housing. Goldberg had left the men's apparel business in 1955 to begin a career in real estate. He subsequently established a number of companies that engaged principally in subdividing raw acreage. In 1958 he undertook the construction of a 31-home development called Waverly Manor; when 15 or 20 homes had been partially completed under the supervision of a South Gate employee, he engaged Brown to supervise completion of the job. This task was Brown's first experience with tract construction, although he had been licensed as a general contractor in 1950 and had built approximately 50 single-family dwellings on an individual custom basis before 1958.

In January 1959 South Gate signed an agreement to purchase 100 acres of the McRea ranch for $340,000 within 120 days, and a conditional sales agreement to purchase 447 adjoining acres for $2,500 per acre over a 10-year period. Neither South Gate nor Goldberg had the financial resources to perform these agreements, and in March Goldberg approached Great Western for the necessary funds to purchase the 100-acre parcel on which Weathersfield was to be constructed.

Great Western processed between 8,000 and 9,000 loans each year, amounting to more than $100,000,000, but had not previously made loans in Ventura County. It expressed an interest to Goldberg in developing a volume of new construction loan business and in providing long-term financing in the form of first trust deeds to the buyers of the homes to be built. By the end of April, the general outlines of an agreement with Goldberg had been developed, and they were recorded in the minutes of Great Western's Loan Committee.

During the ensuing four months the parties and their lawyers worked out the details of a transaction whereby Great Western would supply the funds necessary to enable Goldberg to purchase the 100-acre parcel and construct homes thereon. In return, Great Western was given the right to make construction loans on the homes to be built and the right of first refusal to make long-term loans to the buyers of the homes. Before agreeing to provide money for the purchase of the land, Great Western also demanded and received a "gentleman's agreement" that it would have the right of first refusal to make construction loans on the homes to be built on the adjoining 477-acre parcel.[1]

Great Western employed a geologist to determine whether an adequate quantity and quality of water would be available in the area. As a result of the geologist's report and its own investigations, Great Western further demanded and received a guarantee from South Gate, Goldberg, and Mr. and Mrs. Brown that if Great Western held title to the 100-acre parcel in September 1960, adequate water service lines from a new or existing public utility would be available at the property line for consumer use.

In July, Great Western provided the necessary funds for the purchase of the Weathersfield tract. Goldberg had deposited $190,000 of the $340,000 purchase price with the escrow agent on behalf of South Gate. He apparently obtained the money by draining assets from his corporations, leaving a combined net worth in those enterprises of $36,000 as of July 31.

Goldberg, by amended escrow instructions, substituted Conejo Development Company in place of South Gate as purchaser of the land from the McReas, and all funds deposited theretofore by South Gate were credited to Conejo. Conejo had been incorporated several months earlier, though with only $5,000 capital to handle the tract development.

Great Western deposited the remaining $150,000 of the purchase price in a second escrow opened between Conejo as seller and Great Western as buyer, took title to the land from Conejo, and granted South Gate a one-year option to repurchase the land in three parcels for a total of $180,000. South Gate, Goldberg, and Mr. and Mrs. Brown agreed to repurchase the property from Great Western on demand for $200,000 if the option were not exercised and adequate water facilities were not available by September 1960.

The arrangement for the purchase of the land by Great Western was an early example of what has come to be known as "land warehousing." Under such an arrangement, a financial institution holds land for a developer until he is ready to use it. Unlike a normal bailee

1. Although Goldberg testified at the trial that he rejected Great Western's demand for such a right of first refusal, his testimony was to the contrary in a 1965 deposition that was also introduced. [All footnotes in the case are by the court.]

of personal property, however, the institution retains title to the property as well as the right to possession.

At the outset Great Western confronted the problem that it could not lend Goldberg $150,000 outright and still retain the land as security, for section 7155 of the Financial Code prohibited it from lending more than 33⅓ percent of the appraised value of unimproved property.[2] It therefore sought to circumvent the specific statutory prohibition by disguising what was in substance admittedly a loan as the kind of investment in real property that was sanctioned by section 6705 of the Financial Code.[3]

Great Western agreed to make the necessary construction loans to Conejo only after assuring itself that the homes could be successfully built and sold. During the negotiations on the terms of the contemplated construction loans to Conejo and the long-term loans to be offered to the buyers of homes in the proposed development, Great Western investigated Goldberg's financial condition and learned that it was weak. Moreover, Great Western received, without comment or inquiry, an August 1959 financial statement from Conejo that set forth capital of $325,000, of which $320,000 was accounted for as estimated profits from the sales of homes when the sales transactions, then in escrow, were completed. Such an entry was far outside the bounds of generally accepted accounting principles. The estimated profits, representing 64/65 of the total purported capital, were not only hypothetical, but were hypothesized on the basis of houses that had not yet been constructed.

Great Western delved no deeper into the proposed foundations of the houses than into the conjectural bases of Conejo's capital. It did require Conejo to submit plans and specifications for the various models of homes to be built, cost breakdowns, a list of proposed subcontractors and the type of work each was to perform, and a schedule of proposed prices. Conejo, which at no time employed an architect, purchased plans and specifications from a Mr. L.C. Majors that he had prepared for other developments, and submitted them to Great Western.

Great Western departed from its normal procedure of reviewing and approving plans and specifications before making a commitment to provide construction funds. It did not examine the foundation plans and did not make any recommendations as to the design or construction of the houses. It was preoccupied with selling prices and sales. It suggested increases in Goldberg's proposed selling prices, which he accepted. It also refused any formal commitment of funds to Conejo until a specified number of houses were pre-sold, namely, sold before they were constructed.

Prospective buyers reserved lots after inspecting three landscaped and furnished model homes standing on 1.6 acres of the otherwise

2. In 1961 the statute was amended to allow savings and loan associations to lend up to 70 percent of the appraised value of unimproved property.

3. In 1959 section 6705 read in part: "An association may invest in real property and such investment may include subdividing and developing real property and building homes and other buildings on such property principally for residential use by veterans on such property. An association may own, rent, lease, manage, operate for income, or sell such property."

barren tract. The model homesites as well as a 60-foot wide access road had been granted by the McReas directly to Conejo "without consideration and as an accommodation" two weeks before the close of the land-purchase escrows.[4]

When Conejo sold the lots, its sales agents informed the buyers that Great Western was willing to make long-terms secured by first trust deeds to approved persons, and obtained credit information for later submission to Great Western. This procedure was dictated by the right of first refusal that Conejo agreed to give Great Western to obtain the construction loans. If an approved buyer wished to obtain a long-term loan elsewhere, Great Western had 10 days to meet the terms of the proposed financing; if it met the terms and the loan was not placed with Great Western, Goldberg, Brown, and South Gate were required to pay Great Western the fees and interest obtained by the other lender in connection with the loan. Most of the buyers of homes in the Weathersfield tract applied to Great Western for loans. They obtained approximately 80 percent of the purchase price in the form of 24-year loans from Great Western at 6.6 percent interest secured by first trust deeds. Great Western charged Conejo a 1 percent fee for loans made to qualified buyers, and a 1½ percent fee for loans made to Conejo on behalf of buyers who, in Great Western's opinion, were poor risks.

By September, the specified number of houses had been reserved by buyers, and Great Western accordingly made approximately $3,000,000 in construction loans to Conejo. Conejo agreed to pay Great Western a 5 percent construction loan fee and 6.6 percent interest on the construction loans as disbursed for six months and thereafter on the entire amount. Great Western had originally demanded 6.6 percent interest on the entire amount without regard to the disbursement of the funds, and its 5 percent loans fee was higher than normal because it assessed the loan as one involving a substantial risk. When the construction loans were recorded, Conejo became entitled to advances on the loans and to "land draws," lump sums calculated as a percentage of the value of the land. Conejo received advances on the construction loans and land draws in the sum of $148,200. It turned this sum together with $31,800 over to South Gate, which in turn paid the total of $180,000 back to Great Western in the exercise of its option to repurchase the 100-acre tract from Great Western. South Gate simultaneously transferred the land to Conejo.

Conejo accepted notes secured by second trust deeds from the buyers of homes for the balance of the purchase price that was not provided by Great Western. Goldberg planned to discount the notes at 50 percent of their face value and to use the proceeds to pay the interest and fees to Great Western and provide a profit to Conejo. The evidence indicates, however, that in his enthusiasm to develop the first 100 acres of his projected community, Goldberg pared estimated profits to the dangerously thin margin of $500 per house, and that he exceeded his depth in expertise and finances, with a resulting deterioration in his

4. The record does not disclose the source of the $111,000 supplied by Conejo to build and landscape the model homes. A permanent loan covering the cost of construction was eventually received from Great Western.

financial position as construction progressed. Conejo ultimately pledged the notes as security for a $300,000 loan, 43 percent of their face value, forfeiting profits in the urgent need for liquid capital. This loan was obtained from cross-complainants Meyer Pritkin et al. seven business acquaintances of Goldberg who at his suggestion organized a joint venture in December 1959 to purchase 382 acres of land in the Conejo Valley.

A subcontractor employed by Conejo began grading the property before Great Western made a final commitment to provide construction loan funds, and while Great Western still nominally owned the land. During the course of construction, Great Western's inspectors visited the property weekly to verify that the pre-packaged plans were being followed and that money was disbursed only for work completed. Under the loan agreement, if construction work did not conform to plans and specifications, Great Western had the right to withhold disbursement of funds until the work was satisfactorily performed; failure to correct a nonconformity within 15 days constituted a default. Representatives of Great Western remained in constant communication with the developers of the Weathersfield tract until all the houses were completed and sold in mid-1960.

The evidence establishes without conflict that there was no express agreement either written or oral creating a joint venture or joint enterprise relationship between Great Western and Conejo or Goldberg. Without exception the testimony of the principal witnesses discloses specific disclaimers of all intention that any such relationship should exist, and the written documents provided only for typical option and purchase agreements and loan and security transactions. Plaintiffs contend, however, that the evidence of the conduct of the parties demonstrates that neither the documents nor the testimony as to the parties' intentions accurately reflect their legal relationship. They assert that such evidence of conduct supports an inference that a joint venture or joint enterprise relationship existed. (See Civ.Code, § 1621; Universal Sales Corp. v. California Press Mfg. Co. (1942), 20 Cal.2d 751, 764–765, 128 P.2d 665; Nelson v. Abraham (1947), 29 Cal.2d 745, 749–750, 177 P.2d 931; Holtz v. United Plumbing & Heating Co. (1957), 49 Cal.2d 501, 506–507, 319 P.2d 617.)

A joint venture exists when there is "an agreement between the parties under which they have a community of interest, that is, a joint interest, in a common business undertaking, and understanding as to the sharing of profits and losses, and a right of joint control." (Holtz v. United Plumbing & Heating Co., supra, 49 Cal.2d 501, 506–507, 319 P.2d 617, 620. See also Nelson v. Abraham, supra, 29 Cal.2d 745, 749, 177 P.2d 931; Spier v. Lang (1935) 4 Cal.2d 711, 716, 53 P.2d 138; Quinn v. Recreation Park Ass'n (1935), 3 Cal.2d 725, 728, 46 P.2d 144.) Although the evidence establishes that Great Western and Conejo combined their property, skill, and knowledge to carry out the tract development, that each shared in the control of the development, that each anticipated receiving substantial profits therefrom, and that they cooperated with each other in the development, there is no evidence of a community or joint interest in the undertaking. Great Western participated as a buyer and seller of land and lender of funds, and Conejo participated as a builder and seller of homes. Although the profits of each were dependent on the overall success of the development, neither was to share in the profits or the losses that the other might realize or suffer. Although each received substantial payments as seller, lender, or borrower, neither had an interest in the payments received by the other.[5] Under these circumstances, no joint venture existed. . . .

Even though Great Western is not vicariously liable as a joint venturer for the negligence of Conejo, there remains the question of its liability for its own negligence. Great Western voluntarily undertook business relationships with South Gate and Conejo to develop the Weathersfield tract and to develop a market for the tract houses in which prospective buyers would be directed to Great Western for their financing. In undertaking these relationships, Great Western became much more than a lender content to lend money at interest on the security of real property. It became an active participant in a home construction enterprise. It had the right to exercise extensive control of the enterprise. Its financing, which made the enterprise possible, took on ramifications beyond the domain of the usual money lender. It received not only interest on its construction loans, but also substantial fees for making them, 20 percent capital gain for "warehousing" the land, and protection from loss of profits in the event individual home buyers sought permanent financing elsewhere.

Since the value of the security for the construction loans and thereafter the security for the permanent financing loans depended on the construction of sound homes, Great Western was clearly under a duty of care to its shareholders to exercise its powers of control over the enterprise to prevent the construction of defective homes. Judged by the standards governing nonsuits, it negligently failed to discharge that duty. It knew or should have known that the developers were inexperienced, undercapitalized, and operating on a dangerously thin capitalization. It therefore knew or should have known that damage from attempts to cut corners in construction was a risk reasonably to be foreseen. (See Lefcoe & Dobson, Savings Associations as Land Developers (1966) 75 Yale L.J. 1271, 1293.)[6] It knew or should have known of the expansive soil problems,[7] and yet it failed to require soil tests, to examine foundation plans, to recommend changes in the prepackaged

5. We need not consider plaintiffs' contention that some of the testimony of Judge Alfred Gitelson, Goldberg's former counsel in real property matters, was improperly struck from the record; consideration of the testimony would not alter the conclusion that there is no evidence of a community or joint interest in the undertaking.

6. For example, Goldberg refused to follow the suggestion of soil engineers that Conejo comply with FHA grading standards requiring all homes to drain to the street, because the cost would be an extra $200 per lot.

7. Adobe soil is common in southern California. Tests conducted by Conejo's soil engineers indicated the presence of adobe soil. Such soil is distinguished easily by the naked eye in dry weather in areas where the ground cover is sparse; when it dries and contracts, the surface cracks into plates, frequently hexagonal in shape and 10 or 12 inches in diameter. Several Conejo employees noticed the characteristic cracks during the summer of 1959, as did the geologist hired by Great Western to investigate water supply problems.

plans and specifications, or to recommend changes in the foundations during construction. It made no attempt to discover gross structural defects that it could have discovered by reasonable inspection and that it would have required Conejo to remedy. It relied for protection solely upon building inspectors with whom it had had no experience to enforce a building code with the provisions of which it was ignorant. The crucial question remains whether Great Western also owed a duty to the home buyers in the Weathersfield tract and was therefore also negligent toward them.

The fact that Great Western was not in privity of contract with any of the plaintiffs except as a lender does not absolve it of liability for its own negligence in creating an unreasonable risk of harm to them. "Privity of contract is not necessary to establish the existence of a duty to exercise ordinary care not to injure another, but such duty may arise out of a voluntarily assumed relationship if public policy dictates the existence of such a duty." . . . The basic tests for determining the existence of such a duty are clearly set forth in Viakanja v. Irving, supra, 49 Cal.2d 647, 650, 320 P.2d 16, 19, as follows: "The determination whether in a specific case the defendant will be held liable to a third person not in privity is a matter of policy and involves the balancing of various factors, among which are [1] the extent to which the transaction was intended to affect the plaintiff, [2] the foreseeability of harm to him, [3] the degree of certainty that the plaintiff suffered injury, [4] the closeness of the connection between the defendant's conduct and the injury suffered, [5] the moral blame attached to the defendant's conduct, and [6] the policy of preventing future harm."

In the light of the foregoing tests Great Western was clearly under a duty to the buyers of the homes to exercise reasonable care to protect them from damages caused by major structural defects.

[1] Great Western's transactions were intended to affect the plaintiffs significantly.

The success of Great Western's transactions with South Gate and Conejo depended entirely upon the ability of the parties to induce plaintiffs to buy homes in the Weathersfield tract and to finance the purchases with funds supplied by Great Western. Great Western's agreement to supply funds to Conejo to build homes in return for a 5 percent construction loan fee and 6.6 percent interest, was on condition that a sufficient number of persons first made commitments to buy homes. Great Western agreed to warehouse land for Conejo on the understanding that the land would be used for a residential subdivision. Great Western also stipulated that advances from its construction loans would be used by Conejo to exercise repurchase options, thereby affording Great Western the opportunity for a $30,000 capital gain. Finally, Great Western took steps to have Conejo channel buyers of homes to its doors for loans, extracting a 1 percent loan fee from Conejo in the process.

[2] Great Western could reasonably have foreseen the risk of harm to plaintiffs.

Great Western knew or should have known that neither Goldberg nor Brown had ever developed a tract of similar magnitude. Great Western knew or should have known that Conejo was operating on a dangerously thin capitalization, creating a readily foreseeable risk that it would be driven to cutting corners in construction. That risk was enlarged still further by the additional pressures on Conejo ensuing from its onerous burdens as a borrower from Great Western.

[3] It is certain that plaintiffs suffered injury.

Counsel stipulated that each of the plaintiff homeowners, if called, would testify that their respective homes sustained damage in varying degrees "of the character of which we have been concerned in this action." Sufficient evidence was presented to show by way of example the existence of damage to the homes and therefore injury to plaintiffs. Under the terms of the pretrial order, the extent of each plaintiff's injury is to be litigated in further proceedings after the question of Great Western's liability is determined.

[4] The injury suffered by plaintiffs was closely connected with Great Western's conduct.

Great Western not only financed the development of the Weathersfield tract but controlled the course it would take. Had it exercised reasonable care in the exercise of its control, it would have discovered that the pre-packaged plans purchased by Conejo required correction and would have withheld financing until the plans were corrected.[8]

[5] Substantial moral blame attaches to Great Western's conduct.

The value of the security for Great Western's construction loans as well as the projected security for its long-term loans to plaintiffs depended on the soundness of construction, Great Western failed of its obligation to its own shareholders when it failed to exercise reasonable care to preclude major structural defects in the homes whose construction it financed and controlled. It also failed of its obligation to the buyers, the more so because it was well aware that the usual buyer of a home is ill-equipped with experience or financial means to discern such structural defects. (Cf. Schipper v. Levitt & Sons, Inc. (1965), 44 N.J. 70, 207 A.2d 314, 325–326.) Moreover a home is not only a major investment for the usual buyer but also the only shelter he has. Hence it becomes doubly important to protect him against structural defects that could prove beyond his capacity to remedy.

[6] The admonitory policy of the law of torts calls for the imposition of liability on Great Western for its conduct in this case. Rules that tend to discourage misconduct are particularly appropriate when applied to an established industry.

By all the foregoing tests, Great Western had a duty to exercise reasonable care to prevent the construction and sale of seriously defec-

8. The vice-president in charge of Great Western's tract loan development activities testified that had Great Western known of the soil condition it would have required soil tests and the correction of plans before approving a construction loan. Although Conejo had the right to seek another lender at any time to continue as financier of the project, there is no reason to assume that such lender would not have exercised reasonable care and imposed similar requirements.

tive homes to plaintiffs. The countervailing considerations invoked by Great Western and amici curiae are that the imposition of the duty in question upon a lender will increase housing costs, drive marginal builders out of business, and decrease total housing at a time of great need. These are conjectural claims. In any event, there is no enduring social utility in fostering the construction of seriously defective homes. If reliable construction is the norm, the recognition of a duty on the part of tract financiers to home buyers should not materially increase the cost of housing or drive small builders out of business.[9] If existing sanctions are inadequate, imposition of a duty at the point of effective financial control of tract building will insure responsible building practices.[10] Moreover, in either event the losses of family savings invested in seriously defective homes would be devastating economic blows if no redress were available.

Defendants contend, however, that the question of their liability is one of policy, and hence should be resolved only by the Legislature after a marshalling of relevant economic and social data. There is no assurance, however, that the Legislature will undertake such a task, even though tract financing grows apace. In the absence of actual or prospective legislative policy, the court is free to resolve the case before it, and indeed must resolve it in terms of common law.

Great Western contends that lending institutions have relied on an assumption of nonliability and hence that a rule imposing liability should operate prospectively only. In the past, judicial decisions have been limited to prospective operation when they overruled earlier decisions upon which parties had reasonably relied and when considerations of fairness and public policy precluded retroactive effect. (Forster Shipbuilding Co. v. County of Los Angeles (1960), 54 Cal.2d 450, 458–459, 6 Cal.Rptr. 24, 353 P.2d 736.) Conceivably such a limitation might also be justified when there appeared to be a general consensus that there would be no extension of liability. Such is not the case here. At least since MacPherson v. Buick Motor Co. (1916) 217 N.Y. 382, 111 N.E. 1050, there has been a steady expansion of liability for harm caused by the failure of defendants to exercise reasonable care to protect others from reasonably foreseeable risks. (See generally Pros-

9. In 1965 a state legislative committee found that hundreds of homes built upon expansive soil in California had cracked to such an extent as to make continued habitation uncomfortable or unsafe, that the existence of such soil could be easily and cheaply identified, that the cost of engineering solutions was minimal and easily financed by the builder and homebuyer, and that "local ordinances requiring soil analysis prior to home construction are virtually nonexistent," leaving the potential homebuyer "without minimum assurance that his purchase will be a safe and habitable home." (6 Assembly Interim Com. Report No. 21, Municipal and County Government (1965) p. 9, "Problems of Construction Upon Expansive Soil.") In 1965 soil analysis and precautionary measures were required by state statute. (Health & Saf.Code, §§ 17953, 17954.)

10. The residential construction industry is composed principally of small builders, most of whom have so little equity that they must borrow money in order to finance the production of new homes. (See Gillies and Mittelbach, Management in the Light Construction Industry (1962) pp. 15–16, 19, 21; Gillies & Curtis, Institutional Residential Mortgage Lending in Los Angeles County (1956) 41–42.) Savings and loan associations are bound by market forces and legal restraints to be a major supplier of funds to such small builders. (Lefcoe and Dobson, supra, 75 Yale L.J. 1271, 1284–1286.)

ser, The Law of Torts (3d ed. 1964) ch. 19.) By the time of the decision in Sabella v. Wisler (1963), 59 Cal.2d 21, 27 Cal.Rptr. 689, 377 P.2d 889, such liability had been imposed on a builder who negligently constructed a seriously defective home. (See also Stewart v. Cox, supra, 55 Cal. 2d 857, 13 Cal.Rptr. 521, 362 P.2d 345.) Those in the business of financing tract builders could therefore reasonably foresee the possibility that they might be under a duty to exercise their power over tract developments to protect home buyers from seriously defective construction. Moreover, since the value of their own security depends on the construction of sound homes, they have always been under a duty to their shareholders to exercise reasonable care to prevent the construction of defective homes. Given that traditional duty of care, a lending institution should have been farsighted enough to make such provisions for potential liability as would enable it to withstand the effects of a decision of normal retrospective effect.

Great Western contends finally that the negligence of Conejo in constructing the homes and the negligence of the county building inspectors in approving the construction were superseding causes that insulate it from liability. Conejo's negligence could not be a superseding cause, for the risk that it might occur was the primary hazard or one of the hazards which makes the actor negligent, such likelihood that a third person may act in a particular manner is the hazard or one of the hazards which makes the actor negligent, such an act whether innocent, negligent, intentionally tortious or criminal does not prevent the actor from being liable for harm caused thereby. (Richardson v. Ham (1955) 44 Cal.2d 772, 777, 285 P.2d 269, 272, quoting Rest. Torts, 449; see also Rest.2d Torts, § 449; Weaver v. Bank of America (1963) 59 Cal.2d 428, 433–434, 30 Cal.Rptr. 4, 380 P.2d 644.) The negligence of the building inspectors, confined as it was to inspection, could not serve to diminish, let alone spirit away, the negligence of the lender. Great Western's duty to plaintiffs was to exercise reasonable care to protect them from seriously defective construction whether caused by defective plans, defective inspection, or both, and its argument that there was a superseding cause of the harm "is answered by the settled rule that two separate acts of negligence may be the concurring proximate causes of an injury. (Fennessey v. Pac. Gas & Elec. Co., 20 Cal.2d 141, 145, 124 P.2d 51; Lacy v. Pacific Gas & Elec. Co., 220 Cal. 97, 98, 29 P.2d 781; . . ..)" (Merrill v. Buck, supra, 58 Cal.2d 552, 563, 25 Cal.Rptr. 456, 463.)

The question remains whether granting a nonsuit in favor of Great Western against cross-complainants was also erroneous. As pledgees of promissory notes secured by second deeds of trust, cross-complainants seek to hold Great Western liable for the impairment to their security caused by the damage to the homes and to impose liens on any recovery plaintiffs may obtain from Great Western or other defendants. By stipulation and pretrial order the parties agreed that the issue of Great Western's liability should be determined first and that thereafter the rights and liabilities of the other parties among themselves should be determined. The question whether cross-complainants are entitled to liens on any recoveries plaintiffs may obtain from Great Western has therefore not yet been litigated. (Cf. American Sav. & Loan Assoc. v. Leeds (1968), 68 A.C. 637, 68 Cal.Rptr. 453, 440 P.2d 933.) Accordingly, it was error to grant a nonsuit against cross-complainants as well as against plaintiffs, for in further proceedings cross-complainants may be able to establish some basis for sharing in plaintiffs' recoveries.

For the purposes of such proceedings, however, we also hold that Great Western owed no independent duty of care to cross-complainants. The balance of the factors set forth in the *Biakanja* case is significantly different when an investor in or pledgee of notes secured by second deeds of trust is substituted for a member of the home-buying public as the party claiming a duty of care on the part of the tract financier. Although some factors may indicate no difference between plaintiffs and cross-complainants insofar as Great Western's duties are concerned, others point toward a duty to plaintiffs but not toward a duty to cross-complainants.

The foreseeability of harm to cross-complainants as a result of defective construction was substantially less than in the case of plaintiffs. As security cross-complainants had notes from the home owners as well as second deeds of trust. Furthermore, they assured themselves of a substantial margin of safety against the risk that the notes would not be paid or that the homes would be worth less than the purchase price when they lent only 43 percent of the face value of the notes. Plaintiffs, on the other hand, were powerless to protect their equities in their homes from reduction or extinction by diminution of the value of the property as a result of defective construction.

Likewise, Great Western's negligence was more closely connected with plaintiffs' injuries than cross-complainants' injuries. Plaintiffs were injured by the diminution of value of their homes as a result of defective construction. Cross-complainants will be injured only if plaintiffs default on their notes and the diminution in value of the homes leaves insufficient security to protect the second trust deeds.

Finally, substantially less moral blame attached to Great Western's conduct with respect to cross-complainants than attached to its conduct with respect to plaintiffs. The roles played by cross-complainants and plaintiffs in the transaction were crucially different. Like Great Western itself, cross-complainants were investors in a business enterprise and dealt with Conejo as creditors, not as purchasers of the homes it built. As substantial creditors of Conejo, cross-complainants were voluntary co-participants with Great Western and Conejo in the enterprise of building and selling homes to the general public. Cross-complainants did not have Great Western's power to prevent defective construction through control of construction loan payments; but, unlike plaintiffs, who had no practical alternative to accepting Conejo's qualifications and responsibility on faith, cross-complainants as substantial investors were in a position to protect themselves.[11] Under

11. Goldberg's accountant is one of four cross-complainants who are co-partners doing business as Pritkin-Finkel Investment Company. He testified that the partnership made investments on the advice of accounting clients without previous investigation, that it had made approximately a dozen investments in the last several years totalling less than a million dollars, and that the deals in which it had invested

these circumstances, we do not believe that either Great Western or cross-complainants were under a duty to exercise reasonable care to protect the other from negligence on the part of Conejo. Accordingly, Great Western's duty to exercise reasonable care to prevent Conejo from constructing defective homes was limited to the members of the public who bought those homes.

The parties stipulated that the homes of plaintiffs Elwood and Evelyn Guest and plaintiffs John and Grace Whitaker are not located in tract 1158, 1159, or 1160. As to them, the nonsuit is affirmed. In all other respects the judgment is reversed.

PETERS, TOBRINER and SULLIVAN, JJ., concur.

MOSK, JUSTICE (dissenting).

I dissent.

The evidence is overwhelming, and the majority concede, that as between the lender of funds and the tract developer there was no agency, no joint venture, no joint enterprise. It is clear there was merely a lender-borrower relationship. Nevertheless, the majority here hold the lender of funds vicariously liable to third parties for the negligence of the borrower. This result is (a) unsupported by statute or precedent; (b) inconsistent with accepted principles of tort law; (c) likely to be productive of untoward social consequences. (The dissent of Justice Mosk is well worth reading but is omitted here because of its great length.) . . .

For all of the foregoing reasons, I would affirm the judgment.

BURKE, JUSTICE (dissenting).

I dissent. I agree with the Chief Justice that despite the extensive activities of Great Western here the evidence, viewed most favorably to plaintiffs, falls short of establishing the existence of a joint venture between Great Western and Conejo or Goldberg. However, I would hold a joint venture relationship to be the only basis for imposing liability upon Great Western. Its position vis-a-vis plaintiffs differs materially from the relationships between plaintiffs and defendants in the four cases upon which the majority opinion relies. (Merrill v. Buck (1962), 58 Cal.2d 552, 561–562, 25 Cal.Rptr. 456 [defendant real estate agent showed and rented to injured plaintiff lessee a house with latent dangerous defect]; Biakanja v. Irving (1958), 49 Cal.2d 647, 650, 320 P.2d 16, 65 A.L.R.2d 1358 [defendant notary public drew invalid will, thereby depriving plaintiffs of intended benefits thereunder]; Lucas v. Hamm (1961), 56 Cal.2d 583, 588, 15 Cal.Rptr. 821, 364 P.2d 685 [attorney charged with drafting will with invalid trust provisions, causing loss to intended beneficiaries]; Stewart v. Cox (1961), 55 Cal.2d 857, 863, 13 Cal.Rptr. 521, 362 P.2d 345 [defendant subcontractor

involved total dollar amounts of approximately one hundred million dollars. Goldberg's former counsel in real property matters is one of two cross-complainants who are co-partners doing business as K. G. & Company.

installed defective and leaking concrete work for swimming pool built for plaintiff].)

In each of the cited cases defendant behaved negligently in carrying out a duty of care *undertaken by defendant toward another.* But in the present case Great Western *undertook no duty* toward Conejo, Goldberg, plaintiffs, or any one else, any violation of which resulted in plaintiffs' losses. The majority opinion speaks of a negligent failure by Great Western of "a duty of care to its shareholders . . . to prevent the construction of defective homes" (ditto pp. 376, 378–379), and on such asserted failure appears to predicate the pronouncement of an obligation to protect plaintiff home buyers from structural defects. (Ditto p. 378). Even assuming that certain officers or employees of Great Western were derelict in their duties of care toward Great Western and its shareholders, those officers or employees *are not the corporation;* more logically, in such a context it is the shareholders themselves who might be said to constitute the corporate entity. In my view negligent performance by corporate officers or employees of their duty of care toward the corporation and its shareholders provides no basis for imposing upon the corporation (and therefore upon its shareholders, who must bear the loss) a duty toward others (here, plaintiffs). The fallacy of such an approach is readily perceived by substituting an individual financier for Great Western. In that situation could it be said that the individual's failure to exercise prudence and care in protecting *himself* gives rise to a duty of care to others? I think not. Similarly it would appear as sound to rule that an agent's violation of his obligations to his principal would in and of itself render the principal liable to others injured in the same transaction, and up to now such has not been the law.

I would affirm the judgment.

McComb, J., concurs.

Rehearing denied; McComb, Mosk and Burke, JJ., dissenting.

NOTES

1. See also Bradler v. Craig, 274 Cal.App.2d 466, 79 Cal.Rptr. 401 (1969) where the purchasers sued the general contractor and the construction and purchase money lender to recover damages for alleged negligent construction of a house. The court cited the principal case with apparent approval but held that any legal duty to protect the purchasers had expired by lapse of time. The plaintiffs had purchased the house eighteen years after its construction.

The principal case became one of the most widely noted and debated California civil cases of the '60's. See for example Comment, "New Liability in Construction Lending: Implications of Connor v. Great Western Savings and Loan," 42 S.Calif.L.Rev. 353 (1969) and Comment, "Liability of Institutional Lender for Structural Defects in New Housing," 35 U. of Chi.L.Rev. 739 (1968). The latter comment was prepared while the case was at the intermediate appellate level.

In 1969, the California legislature passed the following statute: "Liability of lender financing design, manufacture, construction, repair, modification or improvement of real or personal property.

"A lender who makes a loan of money, the proceeds of which are used or may be used by the borrower to finance the design, manufacture, construction, repair, modification or improvement of real or personal property for sale or lease to others, shall not be held liable to third persons for any loss or damage occasioned by any defect in the real or personal property so designed, manufactured, constructed, repaired, modified or improved or for any loss or damage resulting from the failure of the borrower to use due care in the design, manufacture, construction, repair, modification or improvement of such real or personal property, unless such loss or damage is a result of an act of the lender outside the scope of the activities of a lender of money or unless the lender has been a party to misrepresentations with respect to such real or personal property. (Added by Stats.1969, c. 1584, p. 3222 § 1.)" West's Ann.Cal.Civ.Code § 3434.

What impact will this statute have on future cases? See Lascher, "Lending-Institution Liability for Defective Home Construction," 45 State Bar of Calif.J. 338 (1970).

2. In Jeminson v. Montgomery Real Estate and Co., 396 Mich. 106, 240 N.W.2d 205 (1976) the lender was so involved with a fraudulent real estate broker that the lender was held potentially liable. However, the Connor case has not been widely followed, usually because the courts have found that the lender was less closely involved with the builder-vendor than in the California situation. See, for example, Butts v. Atlanta Federal Savings and Loan Association, 152 Ga.App. 40, 262 S.E.2d 230 (1979). Note that the Uniform Land Transactions Act, Sect. 2–310, provides that a construction lender is not liable for defects "solely by reason of making the loan."

3. If a developer of tract housing is strictly liable in tort to a purchaser for a defective structure, does it follow that a mortgage lender can also sue the developer for the impairment of his security interest? United States Financial v. Sullivan, 37 Cal.App.3d 5, 112 Cal. Rptr. 18 (1974) held no. Said the court: "The doctrine of manufacturers' and suppliers' strict liability in tort was developed primarily to protect individual consumers. . . . A lender is not in such a vulnerable position. Without its money, the mass production of homes could not proceed. When it is called upon to lend its money, a lender is in a position to require of the developer not only plans and specifications but engineering reports of all sorts, including a soil test report. Thus, the historical reason for imposing strict liability is absent when sought by a lender whose resources are loaned to facilitate the mass construction of homes. . . . Unlike the consumer . . . the lender is itself a link in the marketing chain of mass-produced homes and residential lots and is itself in a position to spread the risks of harm resulting from a defective lot or home."

4. Congress' enactment in 1980 of the Comprehensive Environmental Response, Compensation, and Liability Act (CERCLA) 42 U.S.

C.A. § 9601 et seq., has created an entirely new and exceedingly broad field of liability for owners—including both vendors and purchasers—of real property. They, along with "generators" and transporters of hazardous substances, may be strictly liable for "releases" of such substances from disposal sites. Because § 107(a) of CERCLA extends liability for cleanup costs to all owners of contaminated properties, regardless of the circumstances of their ownership, parties who involuntarily or innocently acquired former disposal sites have been required to pay for cleanup, even when the cost exceeded the value of the land. Several well publicized cases helped to focus Congress' attention on this aspect of CERCLA's liability scheme. In United States v. Maryland Bank & Trust Co., 632 F.Supp. 573 (D.Md.1986), a bank made a mortgage loan of $335,000 on a piece of land. The borrower defaulted, and the bank instituted a foreclosure suit. After the bank took title to the property, state and federal authorities determined that it was a contaminated waste site requiring cleanup under CERCLA. The bank was held liable for response costs of more than $550,000.

Prompted by the perceived unfairness of such results, Congress in 1986 added a new defense to protect "innocent landowners." Now, persons who acquire property without "reason to know" that hazardous substances have been disposed of there are not liable under § 107. However, innocent owners who learn of hazardous substance releases at the site and then transfer ownership without disclosing such information to subsequent purchasers are fully liable under § 107(a).

Some states have enacted even stronger statutes than CERCLA. The most prominent is the New Jersey Environmental Cleanup Responsibilities Act (ECRA), N.J.Stat.Ann. 13:1K–6 et seq., effective December 31, 1983. ECRA was intended to guarantee that no industrial property will be transferred until the state Department of Environmental Protection (DEP) is satisfied that the property is free from serious contamination by hazardous substances. ECRA applies to the sale or transfer of, or cessation of operations at, any "industrial establishment." It also applies to other transactions such as termination of a lease, transfer of a controlling interest in a corporate owner, initiation of bankruptcy proceedings, and transfer of title through foreclosure. If a transaction is subject to ECRA, the owner or operator of the industrial establishment must notify DEP of the transaction and either (1) submit a "negative declaration" and secure DEP's approval, or (2) submit a cleanup plan (with adequate financial security guaranteeing performance), secure DEP's approval, and implement the plan. A "negative declaration" is a written statement that there has been no discharge of hazardous substances or wastes at the site, or that any such discharge has been cleaned up so that no hazardous substances or wastes remain. DEP will not approve a negative declaration or a cleanup plan based on the owner's or operator's statement alone. A detailed description of operations, a description of the uses and storage of hazardous substances, and a detailed sampling plan are among the items that must be submitted before DEP will give its approval. The penalties for failure to comply with ECRA are severe. The sale or transfer of the property may be voided, the transferee may recover damages, and the owner or operator is strictly liable for all cleanup costs. A civil penalty of $25,000 per day also may be imposed.

The following case illustrates the application of CERCLA where land is sold and the purchaser subsequently discovers the presence of hazardous substances on the site.

SUNNEN PRODUCTS CO. v. CHEMTECH INDUSTRIES, INC.

United States District Court, E.D. Missouri, 1987.
658 F.Supp. 276.

GUNN, DISTRICT JUDGE.

IT IS HEREBY ORDERED that the motion of plaintiff Sunnen Products Company for partial summary judgment be and it is granted. The Court concludes on the basis of stipulated facts of record and the applicable law that defendant Chemtech Industries, Inc. is strictly liable for "necessary costs of response incurred by [Sunnen Products Company] consistent with the national contingency plan" pursuant to § 107(a)(4)(B) of the Comprehensive Environmental Response, Compensation and Liability Act, 42 U.S.C. § 9607(a)(4)(B) (1983).

Plaintiff Sunnen Products Company (Sunnen) brought this action pursuant to § 107(a)(4)(B) of the Comprehensive Environmental Response, Compensation and Liability Act (CERCLA), 42 U.S.C. § 9601 et seq., to recover "necessary costs of response incurred" in remedying the environmental contamination of property located at 7882 Folk Avenue in Maplewood, Missouri (the Site).

The parties have stipulated to the following facts: Defendant Chemtech Industries, Inc. (Chemtech) transferred the Site to Sunnen through a property exchange agreement in 1978. Between 1956 and 1978 Chemtech operated a chemical manufacturing industry at the Site and stored chemicals in above-ground and underground tanks on the property. Sunnen has used the Site to house administrative, research, warehousing and light manufacturing facilities. In 1982 the owners of the adjacent property notified Sunnen of chemical seepage in the soil. Sunnen advised Chemtech of the complaint, seeking information with regard to the origin of the chemicals. Chemtech collected and analyzed samples of the chemicals found on the adjacent property and notified the Missouri Department of Natural Resources (MDNR), in accordance with § 9603(c) of CERCLA, that a potential release of hazardous substances had occurred at the Site.

During 1983 and 1984, Sunnen and Chemtech jointly undertook action to investigate and remedy the hazardous waste contamination at the Site. The investigation revealed that the chemicals contaminating the Site matched those handled and stored by Chemtech in its operations there. The actions undertaken jointly by the parties were described in advance in Remedial Action Plans (RAP) approved by MDNR.

In 1985 Sunnen entered into a consent decree with the Missouri Hazardous Waste Commission, pursuant to which Sunnen would submit a revised RAP providing for removal of the hazardous substances from the Site. In June 1985 MDNR issued an order declaring that a hazardous waste emergency existed at the Site and ordering Sunnen to complete the revised RAP.

Sunnen brought this private CERCLA action against Chemtech seeking a declaration of liability for costs incurred and to be incurred in the future in complying with the revised RAP. Chemtech has not participated in continuing clean-up efforts at the Site since 1985.

Section 107(a) of CERCLA creates a private cause of action to recover from responsible parties the costs of responding to hazardous waste conditions. Wickland Oil Terminals v. Asarco, Inc., 792 F.2d 887 (9th Cir.1986); Wehner v. Syntex Corp., 622 F.Supp. 302 (E.D.Mo.1983). The section establishes liability on the part of

> (2) any person who at the time of disposal of any hazardous substance owned or operated any facility at which such hazardous substances were disposed of. . . .

The liability imposed has been construed by the courts to be strict, subject only to three causation defenses enumerated in subsection (b). State of New York v. Shore Realty Corp., 759 F.2d 1032, 1042 (2d Cir. 1985); Wehner, 622 F.Supp. at 304.[1]

Plaintiff has moved the Court for partial summary judgment on the issue of defendant Chemtech's liability. This Court concludes that the stipulated facts establish that Chemtech operated a facility at which hazardous wastes were disposed of, and hence that there exists no genuine issue of material fact with respect to Chemtech's strict liability under § 107(a)(2). Chemtech has not sought to establish any of the § 107(b) enumerated defenses, nor would the facts of record support them.[3] Summary judgment is therefore appropriate on this issue.

1. There shall be no liability under subsection (a) of this section for a person otherwise liable who can establish by a preponderance of the evidence that the release or threat of release of a hazardous substance and the damages resulting therefrom were caused solely by—

(1) an act of God:

(2) an act of war;

(3) an act or omission of a third party other than an employee or agent of the defendant, or than one whose act or omission occurs in connection with a contractual relationship, existing directly or indirectly, with the defendant . . ., if the defendant establishes by a preponderance of the evidence that (a) he exercised due care with respect to the hazardous substance concerned, taking into consideration the characteristics of such hazardous substance, in light of all relevant facts and circumstances, and (b) he took precautions against foreseeable acts or omissions of any such third party and the consequences that could foreseeably result from such acts or omissions; or

(4) any combination of the foregoing paragraphs.

3. Chemtech filed a motion in limine seeking a ruling from the Court that certain common law defenses are cognizable in a CERCLA action. The Court has reviewed the case law on this issue and concludes that it does not unsettle the strict liability standard imposed by § 107(a). Courts have upheld agreements to transfer liability for potential toxic contamination from sellers to purchasers of property to defeat private claims under CERCLA, see Mardan v. C.G.C. Music, Ltd., 804 F.2d 1454 (9th Cir.1986); Pinole Point Properties v. Bethlehem Steel, slip op., No. C–83–5893 (March 31, 1986, N.D.Cal.), without ruling that the liability standard imposed by the statute is less than strict. This case does not involve such an express agreement. Courts have also recognized equitable defenses in fashioning appropriate remedies. Mardan v. C.G.C. Music, Ltd., 600 F.Supp. 1049 (D.Ariz.1984) (unclean hands). No court has accepted the defense of *caveat emptor,* which would improperly shift liability for environmental contamination

The Court cautions that its ruling on the liability issue represents solely a judgment that Chemtech is liable for "necessary costs of response . . . consistent with the national contingency plan." The Court declines to find on the basis of the record before it that the expenditures already made by Sunnen fit this statutory requirement or that future costs are "necessary." Accordingly, the Court will hear testimony on this issue as this case proceeds to trial on the appropriate measure of damages.

SECTION 2. COVENANTS FOR TITLE AND AFTER-ACQUIRED TITLE (ESTOPPEL BY DEED)

In feudal times the grantor of a fee was typically a lord with large estates at his disposal. He owed protection to the grantee, his vassal, in return for homage and other feudal services. If the vassal happened to be ousted from possession the lord simply furnished another fief of equal value. This feudal warranty operated rather like specific performance of a contract in equity, but it was not based on contract at all; it arose out of the tenurial relationship between the lord and his vassal. The warranty could be enforced either by a real action against the disseisor, where the warrantor was impleaded and forced to defend the title, or by a writ of *warrantia chartae* brought by the grantee directly against the grantor. If the warrantor lost he was forced to give up land of equal value (the value of the original land at the time of the grant) or, if he did not possess sufficient land for this purpose, he was assessed damages to make up the difference. This feudal warranty had a complicated history and was subjected to many statutory modifications. It gradually became too cumbersome for modern times, fell into disuse, and finally was abolished in 1834.

Modern covenants find their genesis in the feudal warranty, but they are quite different in scope and operation. The basic difference is that today's covenants are contractual in nature; hence they can be molded to fit the needs of the particular case. While this section will deal only with the traditional or so-called usual covenants, you should remember that the lawyer can draft any covenant which suits his purpose so long as it does not run counter to public policy. Legislation has played a major role in this area so that you must always check the statutes before attempting to draft a deed in an unfamiliar jurisdiction. Typically, the statutes provide for a short-form warranty deed, the usual covenants, or some of them, being implied from the use of such key words as "grant, bargain and sell" or "warrant." This means that in present-day practice you may never run into the exact language of a covenant set forth in the deed itself.

from the responsible party to an unwitting purchaser. The District Court in *Mardan* expressly rejected the defense. 600 F.Supp. at 1055.

The restitution remedy sought under CERCLA is equitable in nature, and the Court will utilize its equitable discretion in fashioning relief. None of Chemtech's proffered defenses, however, bar plaintiff's claim. The Court rejects the *caveat emptor* defense as a matter of law.

In the present section we are concerned with the operation of these covenants and with the answers to several crucial questions. Why should there be more than one covenant? What is the meaning of each covenant? Do the covenants in fact overlap? Can the same act breach more than one covenant? Do they run with the land; i.e., do they protect successors in interest or only the original warrantee? How much protection do they actually give to a purchaser?

But first it is important that we try to define and classify the six usual covenants. They are as follows: (1) the covenant of seisin; (2) the covenant of right to convey; (3) the covenant against incumbrances; (4) the covenant for further assurance; (5) the covenant of quiet enjoyment; and (6) the covenant of warranty. Collectively they are called covenants for title to distinguish them from restrictive covenants of the type discussed in Chapter 17 of this book. The first three are called present covenants because they are breached, if ever, as soon as the deed is delivered. The last three are referred to as future covenants because they may be breached at some future date when actual injury accrues to the warrantee.

While there is much ancient, technical learning involved in covenants for title, we will concern ourselves primarily with those aspects which have modern significance. The following case sets the stage for the still important role of the covenants, despite the growth of title insurance and other methods of title assurance.

BROWN v. LOBER

Supreme Court of Illinois, 1979.
75 Ill.2d 547, 27 Ill.Dec. 780, 389 N.E.2d 1188.

UNDERWOOD, JUSTICE:

Plaintiffs instituted this action in the Montgomery County circuit court based on an alleged breach of the covenant of seisin in their warranty deed. The trial court held that although there had been a breach of the covenant of seisin, the suit was barred by the 10-year statute of limitations in section 16 of the Limitations Act (Ill.Rev.Stat. 1975, ch. 83, par. 17). Plaintiffs' post-trial motion, which was based on an alleged breach of the covenant of quiet enjoyment, was also denied. A divided Fifth District Appellant Court reversed and remanded. (63 Ill.App.3d 727, 20 Ill.Dec. 286, 379 N.E.2d 1354.) We allowed the defendant's petition for leave to appeal.

The parties submitted an agreed statement of facts which sets forth the relevant history of this controversy. Plaintiffs purchased 80 acres of Montgomery County real estate from William and Faith Bost and received a statutory warranty deed (Ill.Rev.Stat.1957, ch. 30, par. 8), containing no exceptions, dated December 21, 1957. Subsequently, plaintiffs took possession of the land and recorded their deed.

On May 8, 1974, plaintiffs granted a coal option to Consolidated Coal Company (Consolidated) for the coal rights on the 80-acre tract for the sum of $6,000. Approximately two years later, however, plaintiffs "discovered" that they, in fact, owned only a one-third interest in the subsurface coal rights. It is a matter of public record that in 1947, a prior grantor had reserved a two-thirds interest in the mineral rights on the property. Although plaintiffs had their abstract of title examined in 1958 and 1968 for loan purposes, they contend that until May 4, 1976, they believed that they were the sole owners of the surface and subsurface rights on the 80-acre tract. Upon discovering that a prior grantor had reserved a two-thirds interest in the coal rights, plaintiffs and Consolidated renegotiated their agreement to provide for payment of $2,000 in exchange for a one-third interest in the subsurface coal rights. On May 25, 1976, plaintiffs filed this action against the executor of the estate of Faith Bost, seeking damages in the amount of $4,000.

The deed which plaintiffs received from the Bosts was a general statutory form warranty deed meeting the requirements of section 9 of "An Act concerning conveyances" (Ill.Rev.Stat.1957, ch. 30, par. 8). That section provides:

> "Every deed in substance in the above form, when otherwise duly executed, shall be deemed and held a conveyance in fee simple, to the grantee, his heirs or assigns, with covenants on the part of the grantor, (1) that at the time of the making and delivery of such deed he was lawfully seized of an indefeasible estate in fee simple, in and to the premises therein described, and had good right and full power to convey the same; (2) that the same were then free from all incumbrances; and (3) that he warrants to the grantee, his heirs and assigns, the quiet and peaceable possession of such premises, and will defend the title thereto against all persons who may lawfully claim the same. And such covenants shall be obligatory upon any grantor, his heirs and personal representatives, as fully and with like effect as if written at length in such deed." Ill.Rev.Stat.1957, ch. 30, par. 8.

The effect of this provision is that certain covenants of title are implied in every statutory form warranty deed. Subsection 1 contains the covenant of seisin and the covenant of good right to convey. These covenants which are considered synonymous (McNitt v. Turner (1873), 83 U.S. (16 Wall.) 352, 21 L.Ed. 341), assure the grantee that the grantor is, at the time of the conveyance, lawfully seized and has the power to convey an estate of the quality and quantity which he professes to convey. Maxwell v. Redd (1972), 209 Kan. 264, 496 P.2d 1320.

Subsection 2 represents the covenant against incumbrances. An incumbrance is any right to, or interest in, land which may subsist in a third party to the diminution of the value of the estate, but consistent with the passing of the fee by conveyance. Marathon Builders, Inc. v. Polinger (1971), 263 Md. 410, 283 A.2d 617; Aczas v. Stuart Heights, Inc. (1966), 154 Conn. 54, 221 A.2d 589.

Subsection 3 sets forth the covenant of quiet enjoyment, which is synonymous with the covenant of warranty in Illinois. Biwer v. Martin (1920), 294 Ill. 488, 128 N.E. 518; Barry v. Guild (1888), 126 Ill. 439, 18 N.E. 759; Bostwick v. Williams (1864), 36 Ill. 65.) By this covenant, "the grantor warrants to the grantee, his heirs and assigns, the possession of the premises and that he will defend the title granted by the terms of the deed against persons who may lawfully claim the same, and that such covenant shall be obligatory upon the grantor, his heirs, personal representatives, and assigns." Biwer v. Martin (1920), 294 Ill. 488, 497, 128 N.E. 518, 522.

Plaintiffs' complaint is premised upon the fact that "William Roy Bost and Faith Bost covenanted that they were the owners in fee simple of the above described property at the time of the conveyance to the plaintiffs." While the complaint could be more explicit, it appears that plaintiffs were alleging a cause of action for breach of the covenant of seisin. This court has stated repeatedly that the covenant of seisin is a covenant *in praesenti* and, therefore, if broken at all, is broken at the time of delivery of the deed. Tone v. Wilson (1876), 81 Ill. 529; Jones v. Warner (1876), 81 Ill. 343.

Since the deed was delivered to the plaintiffs on December 21, 1957, any cause of action for breach of the covenant of seisin would have accrued on that date. The trial court held that this cause of action was barred by the statute of limitations. No question is raised as to the applicability of the 10-year statute of limitations (Ill.Rev.Stat. 1975, ch. 83, par. 17). We conclude, therefore, that the cause of action for breach of the covenant of seisin was properly determined by the trial court to be barred by the statute of limitations since plaintiffs did not file their complaint until May 25, 1976, nearly 20 years after their alleged cause of action accrued.

In their post-trial motion, plaintiffs set forth as an additional theory of recovery an alleged breach of the covenant of quiet enjoyment. The trial court, without explanation, denied the motion. The appellate court reversed, holding that the cause of action on the covenant of quiet enjoyment was not barred by the statute of limitations. The appellate court theorized that plaintiffs' cause of action did not accrue until 1976, when plaintiffs discovered that they only had a one-third interest in the subsurface coal rights and renegotiated their contract with the coal company for one-third of the previous contract price. The primary issue before us, therefore, is when, if at all, the plaintiffs' cause of action for breach of the covenant of quiet enjoyment is deemed to have accrued.

This court has stated on numerous occasions that, in contrast to the covenant of seisin, the covenant of warranty or quiet enjoyment is prospective in nature and is breached only when there is an actual or constructive eviction of the covenantee by the paramount titleholder. Biwer v. Martin (1920), 294 Ill. 488, 128 N.E. 518; Barry v. Guild (1888), 126 Ill. 439, 18 N.E. 759; Scott v. Kirkendall (1878), 88 Ill. 465; Bostwick v. Williams (1864), 36 Ill. 65; Moore v. Vail (1855), 17 Ill. 185.

The cases are also replete with statements to the effect that the mere existence of paramount title in one other than the covenantee is not sufficient to constitute a breach of the covenant of warranty or quiet enjoyment: "[t]here must be a union of acts of disturbance and lawful title, to constitute a breach of the covenant for quiet enjoyment, or warranty . . . ." (Barry v. Guild (1888), 126 Ill. 439, 446, 18 N.E.

759, 761.) "[t]here is a general concurrence that something more than the mere existence of a paramount title is necessary to constitute a breach of the covenant of warranty." (Scott v. Kirkendall (1878), 88 Ill. 465, 467.) "A mere want of title is no breach of this covenant. There must not only be a want of title, but there must be an ouster under a paramount title." Moore v. Vail (1855), 17 Ill. 185, 189.

The question is whether plaintiffs have alleged facts sufficient to constitute a constructive eviction. They argue that if a covenantee fails in his effort to sell an interest in land because he discovers that he does not own what his warranty deed purported to convey, he has suffered a constructive eviction and is thereby entitled to bring an action against his grantor for breach of the covenant of quiet enjoyment. We think that the decision of this court in Scott v. Kirkendall (1878), 88 Ill. 465, is controlling on this issue and compels us to reject plaintiffs' argument.

In *Scott,* an action was brought for breach of the covenant of warranty by a grantee who discovered that other parties had paramount title to the land in question. The land was vacant and unoccupied at all relevant times. This court, in rejecting the grantee's claim that there was a breach of the covenant of quiet enjoyment, quoted the earlier decision in Moore v. Vail (1855), 17 Ill. 185, 191:

> " 'Until that time, (the taking possession by the owner of the paramount title,) he might peaceably have entered upon and enjoyed the premises, without resistance or molestation, which was all his grantors covenanted he should do. They did not guarantee to him a perfect title, but the possession and enjoyment of the premises.' " 88 Ill. 465, 468.

Relying on this language in *Moore,* the *Scott* court concluded:

> "We do not see but what this fully decides the present case against the appellant. It holds that the mere existence of a paramount title does not constitute a breach of the covenant. That is all there is here. There has been no assertion of the adverse title. The land has always been vacant. Appellant could at any time have taken peaceable possession of it. He has in no way been prevented or hindered from the enjoyment of the possession by any one having a better right. It was but the possession and enjoyment of the premises which was assured to him, and there has been no disturbance or interference in that respect. True, there is a superior title in another, but appellant has never felt 'its pressure upon him.' " 88 Ill. 465, 468–69.

Admittedly, *Scott* dealt with surface rights while the case before us concerns subsurface mineral rights. We are, nevertheless, convinced that the reasoning employed in *Scott* is applicable to the present case. While plaintiffs went into possession of the surface area, they cannot be said to have possessed the subsurface minerals. "Possession of the surface does not carry possession of the minerals . . . . [citation.] To possess the mineral estate, one must undertake the actual removal thereof from the ground or do such other act as will apprise the community that such interest is in the exclusive use and enjoyment of the claiming party." Failoni v. Chicago & North Western Ry. Co. (1964), 30 Ill.2d 258, 262, 195 N.E.2d 619, 622.

Since no one has, as yet, undertaken to remove the coal or otherwise manifested a clear intent to exclusively "possess" the mineral estate, it must be concluded that the subsurface estate is "vacant." As in *Scott,* plaintiffs "could at any time have taken peaceable possession of it. [they have] in no way been prevented or hindered from the enjoyment of the possession by any one having a better right." (88 Ill. 465, 468.) Accordingly, until such time as one holding paramount title interferes with plaintiffs' right of possession (e.g., by beginning to mine the coal), there can be no constructive eviction and, therefore, no breach of the covenant of quiet enjoyment.

What plaintiffs are apparently attempting to do on this appeal is to extend the protection afforded by the covenant of quiet enjoyment. However, we decline to expand the historical scope of this covenant to provide a remedy where another of the covenants of title is so clearly applicable. As this court stated in Scott v. Kirkendall (1878), 88 Ill. 465, 469:

> "To sustain the present action would be to confound all distinction between the covenant of warranty and that of *seizin,* or of right to convey. They are not equivalent covenants. An action will lie upon the latter, though there be no disturbance of possession. A defect of title will suffice. Not so with the covenant of warranty, or for quiet enjoyment, as has always been held by the prevailing authority."

The covenant of seisin, unquestionably, was breached when the Bosts delivered the deed to plaintiffs, and plaintiffs then had a cause of action. However, despite the fact that it was a matter of public record that there was a reservation of a two-thirds interest in the mineral rights in the earlier deed, plaintiffs failed to bring an action for breach of the covenant of seisin within the 10-year period following delivery of the deed. The likely explanation is that plaintiffs had not secured a title opinion at the time they purchased the property, and the subsequent examiners for the lenders were not concerned with the mineral rights. Plaintiffs' oversight, however, does not justify us in overruling earlier decisions in order to recognize an otherwise premature cause of action. The mere fact that plaintiffs' original contract with Consolidated had to be modified due to their discovery that paramount title to two-thirds of the subsurface minerals belonged to another is not sufficient to constitute the constructive eviction necessary to a breach of the covenant of quiet enjoyment.

Finally, although plaintiffs also have argued in this court that there was a breach of the covenant against incumbrances entitling them to recovery, we decline to address this issue which was argued for the first time on appeal. It is well settled that questions not raised in the trial court will not be considered by this court on appeal. Kravis v. Smith Marine, Inc. (1975), 60 Ill.2d 141, 324 N.E.2d 417; Ray v. City of Chicago (1960), 19 Ill.2d 593, 169 N.E.2d 73.

Accordingly, the judgment of the appellate court is reversed, and the judgment of the circuit court of Montgomery County is affirmed.

Appellate court reversed; circuit court affirmed.

NOTES

1. The plaintiff still owns only one-third of the subsurface coal rights and presumably the paramount title holder will someday assert his claim. In the meantime, the plaintiff cannot lease that two-thirds because he has no title. When will there be a breach of the covenant of quiet enjoyment? When will the statute of limitations bar a suit on that covenant? Has there been a breach of the covenant against incumbrances? What would you advise the plaintiff to do now?

If a grantee is subjected to suit and a judgment is entered against him, he may be said to be constructively evicted without waiting for actual loss of possession. Even there, however, he must notify his grantor of the suit and give him an opportunity to defend (since the grantor might have a good defense to the title, unknown to the grantee) or the prior suit will not be res judicata and the grantee may have to prove that the grantor's title was actually defective before he can recover on his covenant. See Morgan v. Haley, 107 Va. 331, 58 S.E. 564 (1907).

Suppose the grantee pays a third party on the strength of that party's claim without resorting to litigation? See Brewster v. Hines, 155 W.Va. 302, 185 S.E.2d 513 (1971), where the court held that a grantee was not required to prove actual physical eviction but could rely on constructive eviction by alleging and proving that the grantor's deed passed no valid legal title and that he (the grantee) had, in good faith, surrendered possession to persons holding under paramount title. The grantee acts at his peril, however, and if he fails to prove that the third party's claim was valid he will lose his suit for breach of covenant.

2. If the grantee under a warranty deed receives land which is not served by a public way or private easement and is accessible only pursuant to a license from a neighbor, is the grantor liable for breach of the covenant of quiet enjoyment if the license is revoked? Sinks v. Karleskint, 130 Ill.App.3d 527, 85 Ill.Dec. 807, 474 N.E.2d 767 (1985), said no because "[l]ack of access does not defeat [grantee's] right to possession."

3. The principal case illustrates some of the general problems associated with covenants for title. It does not, however, raise the question of whether the covenants run with the land i.e., whether successors in interest can sue on covenants included in deeds to their predecessors. Suppose the plaintiff in the principal case conveyed by quitclaim deed to X and then X was ousted from the two-thirds mineral interest by the paramount title holder. Could X sue the warrantor on the basis of the warranty deed given to the plaintiff? This is the stuff of covenants running with the land.

Cribbet and Johnson, Principles of the Law of Property *

Pages 296–298 (3d ed. 1989).

RUNNING OF COVENANTS WITH THE LAND

You will recall our earlier discussion of this problem in connection with leases. There the principal difficulty was "touch and concern", a matter of no great moment here since a promise relating to title clearly "touches and concerns" the land. But the basic question remains, how can a subsequent purchaser of the land sue on a promise never made to him? So far as the three present covenants were concerned the answer of the common law was clear—he could not! These covenants, being breached as soon as made—i.e., when the deed was delivered the grantor either was or wasn't seised, either did or didn't have a right to convey, and the land was either incumbered or it wasn't—became choses in action and hence unassignable at common law.[1] The original grantee could sue for breach but when he sold the land his grantee's sole cause of action was against him, not the remote grantor. The non-assignability of choses in action has largely disappeared into the limbo it so richly deserves, but the bulk of American courts still follow the common-law doctrine. England and some American states, both by decision and by statute, have abandoned this "technical scruple" and allowed even the present covenants to run with the land.[2]

The future covenants do not raise this problem since they are not breached until an eviction occurs, which may be years and many grantees in the future. Granting, however, that the particular covenant runs with the land there must be privity of estate, i.e., the remote grantee must prove that he now owns the estate once conveyed from

* The author's footnotes have been renumbered.

1. Mitchell v. Warner, 5 Conn. 498 (1825).

For a good analysis of California law, which is fairly typical, see Comment, Covenants of Title Running with the Land in California, 49 Calif.L.Rev. 931, 945 (1961). The writer concludes: "Present covenants cannot run with the land however, for the whole concept of present and future covenants precludes this. Nevertheless, there is no reason why virtually the same result could not be accomplished by holding that covenants of title are assigned by operation of deed. If this were done the only reason for distinguishing between present and future covenants would be to determine when the statute of limitations begins to run." See also Comment, Covenants for Title—Protection Afforded Buyer of Realty in Florida, 7 U.Miami L.Rev. 378 (1953).

2. Schofield v. The Iowa Homestead Co., 32 Iowa 317, 7 Am.Rep. 197 (1871).

Some states have solved the runability problem by a simple statute. See, for example, Colorado Revised Statutes, c. 118, art. 1–21 (1953): "Covenants of seisin, peaceable possession, freedom from incumberances, and of warranty, contained in any conveyance of real estate, or of any interest therein, shall be held to run with the premises, and to inure to the benefit of all subsequent purchasers and incumbrancers."

Such a statute does not solve the problem of the time of breach and the resulting difficulty as to when the statute of limitations will bar a suit by the covenantee. See Bernklau v. Stevens, 150 Colo. 187, 189, 371 P.2d 765, 768, 95 A.L.R.2d 905 (1962). "The purpose of C.R.S. '53, 118–1–21, as to such covenants, is not to change the time of the accrual of the cause of action, but rather to extend the benefit of such covenants to subsequent purchasers and incumbrancers. Wheeler v. Roley, 105 Colo. 116, 118, 95 P.2d 2 (1939). Thus the accrual of a cause of action still depends upon the time of breach; and the time of breach varies with the particular covenant. Consequently whether defendants' counterclaim is barred by the statute of limitations depends upon the particular covenants alleged to have been breached."

the remote grantor to the first grantee. If he fails to so prove or must rely on the Statute of Limitations to take the place of a missing link in his title chain, he cannot sue.[3] A more serious problem arises when there is a total failure of title from the start. If the grantor never owned an estate to convey to the grantee, how can the covenants attach to nothing and run with a non-existent estate? This may sound like another quibble, but it appealed to courts, not too happy with the "runability" of covenants anyway, and many of them held that this barred a suit by a remote grantee. If possession passed, although no title, the covenants could latch onto the possession, but if neither title nor possession was transferred the paradox was complete. Nevertheless, some courts were friendly to suits by the remote grantee even in these cases.[4] One court stated it this way: "We should be inclined rather to say, that although the covenant of warranty is attached to the land, and for that reason is said in the books, to pass to the assignee, yet this certainly does not mean that it is attached to the paramount title, nor does it mean that it is attached to an imperfect title, or to possession, and only passes with that, but it means simply, that it passes by virtue of the privity of estate, created by the successive deeds, each grantor being estopped by his own deed from denying that he has conveyed an estate to which the covenant would attach."[5]

Assuming that the particular covenant will run with the land, it is not essential that all of the deeds in the chain be warranty deeds. Thus, if *A* delivers a warranty deed to *B*; *B*, a quitclaim deed to *C*; *C*, a warranty deed to *D*; and the title is now in *E* by virtue of a sheriff's deed coming through a mortgage foreclosure against *D*; *E* may have the following choices, in event of a title failure which antedates *A*'s conveyance. He may sue *C* or *A* on the covenants running with the land, but he cannot sue *B* or *D* who gave no covenants for title.

LEACH v. GUNNARSON

Supreme Court of Oregon, 1980.
290 Or. 31, 619 P.2d 263.

HOWELL, JUSTICE.

This action involves the question whether an irrevocable license to use a spring on a grantee's land is a breach of the grantor's covenant against encumbrances if the license is an open, notorious and visible physical encumbrance. Petitioners (hereinafter "plaintiffs") are third-party plaintiffs seeking damages for breach of the warranty deed from their grantor, the third-party defendant (hereinafter "defendant"). It was established at trial that plaintiffs' neighbors, Henry and Betty Leach (hereinafter "the Leaches"), have an irrevocable license to use and maintain a spring on plaintiffs' property. The trial court instructed the jury that, if they found the license to be an open, notorious and

3. Deason v. Findley, 145 Ala. 407, 40 So. 220 (1906).

4. Solberg v. Robinson, 34 S.D. 55, 147 N.W. 87 (1914).

5. Wead v. Larkin, 54 Ill. 489, 499 (1870).

visible physical encumbrance, then there was no breach of the covenant against encumbrances in the grantor's warranty deed. The jury found for defendants. The Court of Appeals affirmed, 43 Or.App. 761, 604 P.2d 419 (1979), and we granted review.

Defendant and her husband (who died prior to trial) were the original owners of a 20-acre parcel of land in Douglas County on which was located a spring. Around 1954, they sold a small piece of an adjoining parcel, which they also owned, to defendant's brother-in-law and his wife, Henry and Betty Leach. Defendant and her husband also orally granted the Leaches the right to locate, construct and maintain a facility to draw water from the spring on defendants' land. The Leaches built a concrete dam one foot high by three feet long and installed a 370-gallon storage tank with a plastic pipe running for 175 feet across defendants' land to convey the water to the Leaches' homesite.

In May, 1975, defendant and her husband sold their 20-acre parcel to plaintiffs. Plaintiff Ove Gunnarson admitted that he knew the Leaches were using the spring, but he also testified that defendant's husband had assured him that the Leaches had no right to use the spring. The warranty deed from defendant and her husband to plaintiffs, after describing the parcel of property, states that the grantors ". . . covenant to and with the grantees that [the parcel] is free and clear of all encumbrances, and that grantors will warrant and defend the same against all persons who may lawfully claim the same."

In June of 1977, the Leaches filed a suit in circuit court seeking a decree that they own in fee simple an easement for installing and maintaining a domestic water supply line and water basin and tank located at the spring on plaintiffs' land. Plaintiffs filed an answer denying that the Leaches have a right to use the spring. Plaintiffs also filed a third-party complaint against defendant alleging that, if the Leaches do establish a right to use the spring, then defendant is in breach of her covenant in the warranty deed that the parcel was free and clear of all encumbrances. Defendant denied any breach of warranty.

The circuit court, in a separate trial, first determined that the Leaches are owners in fee simple of an irrevocable license to use the spring for domestic water supply. The court then held a separate trial on the issue of defendant's breach of warranty.

Plaintiffs contended at trial that, because defendant had covenanted against encumbrances in her warranty deed and had not excepted the Leaches' irrevocable license to use the spring on plaintiffs' property, defendant was in breach of her warranty deed. Defendant filed an answer denying that the Leaches' irrevocable license to use the spring is an encumbrance on plaintiffs' property. Defendant alleged as an affirmative defense that the Leaches' use of the spring was an open, notorious and visible encumbrance known to plaintiffs, that the license did not constitute an encumbrance, and that plaintiffs knew of the license.

Plaintiffs' motion to strike defendant's affirmative defense was denied. Plaintiffs also moved for a directed verdict on the grounds that the allegations did not constitute a defense. The court denied that motion also.

Plaintiffs requested jury instructions to the effect that their knowledge of the Leaches' use of the spring does not relieve the defendant of her liability under her covenant against encumbrances in her warranty deed. The trial court failed to give plaintiffs' requested instructions and, instead, gave the following instructions:

> "A covenant in a deed conveying real property that the same is free from encumbrances except those listed therein is not breached by the existence upon the property described in said deed by an open, notorious and visible, physical encumbrance.
>
> "The mere existence of one or more irrevocable licenses owned by the Henry Leaches, . . . as are admitted by all parties, do [sic] not constitute an encumbrance which is a breach of any covenant in the deed from Defendant and her husband as grantors to the Plaintiffs as grantees, if you find that any of such irrevocable licenses were open, notorious and visible, physical encumbrances capable of being seen and known to the Plaintiffs before they took delivery of said deed."

The jury returned a verdict for defendant, and the circuit court entered a judgment dismissing plaintiffs' complaint.

Plaintiffs appealed, assigning as error: the trial court's failure to strike defendant's affirmative defense, the court's failure to direct a verdict in plaintiffs' favor, the court's failure to give plaintiffs' requested instructions, and the court's instructions to the jury that the covenant against encumbrances is not breached by the existence of an open, notorious and visible physical encumbrance.

The Court of Appeals affirmed the trial court, citing the case of Ford v. White, 179 Or. 490, 495–96, 172 P.2d 822 (1946), for the proposition that a covenant to convey real property free from encumbrances is not breached by the existence of an open, notorious and visible physical encumbrance.

Before turning to plaintiffs' reasons for reversal, we should review the law regarding warranty deeds and a grantor's covenant against encumbrances.

Historically, a warranty deed would include covenants of title, which typically are the covenant of seisin, the covenant of good right to convey, the covenant of quiet enjoyment, and the covenant against encumbrances. See generally Powell, Real Property ¶ 904 (1979); Tiffany, Real Property § 999 (1975). If the warranty deed contains the grantor's covenant that the real property is free and clear of all encumbrances, that covenant protects the grantee against all encumbrances that exist as of the date of the delivery of the deed, whether the encumbrance was known or unknown to the grantee at that time. . . .

Because the deed is a document containing the grantor's covenants, courts generally construe the deed against the grantor and in favor of the grantee. . . . When a grantor covenants against encumbrances, the grantor is expected to clearly state in his deed what, if any, encumbrances are accepted by the grantee, will continue in existence and are therefore excluded from the scope of his covenant against encumbrances. . . .

In 1973 the legislature enacted ORS 93.850 which provides a form for the warranty deed. 1973 Or.Laws, ch. 194 § 1. The warranty deed form in ORS 93.850 is permissive and not mandatory, and other warranty deed forms may be used. See ORS 93.870. ORS 93.850 reads as follows:

"(1) Warranty deeds may be in the following form:

______, Grantor, conveys and warrants to ______ Grantee, the following described real property free of encumbrances except as specifically set forth herein: (Describe the property conveyed.)

(If there are to be exceptions to the covenants described in paragraph (c) of subsection (2) of this section, here insert such exceptions.) The true consideration for this conveyance is $______. (Here comply with the requirements of ORS 93.030.)

Dated this ______ day of ______, 19__.

"(2) A deed in the form of subsection (1) of this section shall have the following effect:

"(a) It shall convey the entire interest in the described property at the date of the deed which the deed purports to convey.

"(b) The grantor, his heirs, successors and assigns, shall be forever estopped from asserting that the grantor had, at the date of the deed, an estate or interest in the land less than that estate or interest which the deed purported to convey and the deed shall pass any and all after acquired title.

"(c) It shall include the following covenants, each of which shall run in favor of the grantee and his successors in title as if written in the deed:

"(A) That at the time of the delivery of the deed the grantor is seized of the estate in the property which the grantor purports to convey and that he had good right to convey the same.

"(B) That at the time of the delivery of the deed the property is free from encumbrances except as specifically set forth on the deed.

"(C) That the grantor warrants and will defend the title to the property against all persons who may lawfully claim the same.

"(3) If the grantor desires to exclude any encumbrances or other interests from the scope of his covenants, such exclusions must be expressly set forth on the deed."

Legislative history indicates that ORS 93.850 was intended to provide practioners with a modern simplified form of the warranty deed and also to codify the law in this state with regard to the effect of a conveyance of real property by a warranty deed in the statutory form.

The warranty deed used by defendant to convey the real property to plaintiffs reads, in pertinent part, as follows:

> "KNOW ALL MEN BY THESE PRESENTS, that CLIFFORD LEACH and WILMA LEACH, husband and wife, grantors, convey to OVE K. GUNNARSON and INGA-LILL GUNNARSON, husband and wife, grantees, for and in consideration of the sum of THIRTY THOUSAND DOLLARS ($30,000) to them in hand paid, all that real property situated in the County of Douglas, State of Oregon, described as:
>
> [Legal description omitted]
>
> and covenant to and with the grantees that it is free and clear of all encumbrances, and that grantors will warrant and defend the same against all persons who may lawfully claim the same.
>
> "DATED this 12 day of May, 1975.
>
> "/s/ Clifford A. Leach"

Comparing the warranty deed used by defendant to the form in ORS 93.850, we find them to be similar, if not identical, in all essential respects. Defendant's warranty deed warrants that the real property is "free . . . of . . . encumbrances" and states in dollars the amount of consideration paid by plaintiffs. Defendant's warranty deed may contain more language than contained in the form in the statute, but defendant's deed does not limit or except any of the covenants of title specified in ORS 93.850(2)(c). We therefore hold that the warranty deed used by defendant is in the form of ORS 93.850(1) and that therefore ORS 93.850(1) and ORS 93.850(3) apply.

ORS 93.850(3) requires a grantor who uses a warranty deed and covenants against encumbrances to expressly exclude any encumbrance or other interests from the scope of the covenant against encumbrance. Otherwise, ORS 93.850(2)(b) has the effect of estopping the grantor, her heirs, successors and assigns, from asserting that the grantor had an estate or interest in the land less than that estate or interest which the deed purported to convey. Thus ORS 93.850 and the prior case law of this state require a grantor who covenants against encumbrances in a warranty deed to be liable to the grantee if the real property, as of the date of the deed, is encumbered by any interest not expressly excluded from the scope of the covenant against encumbrances.

Turning now to plaintiffs' argument for reversal, plaintiffs assign as error the failure of the trial court to strike defendant's affirmative answer, alleging that (1) the irrevocable license did not constitute an encumbrance; (2) the plaintiffs knew of the Leaches' rights in the spring; and (3) the license was open, notorious and visible.

ORS 93.850 does not define the term "encumbrance" but our prior cases have done so. An "encumbrance," as the term is used in a grantor's covenant that the premises are free and clear of all encumbrances, generally means "any right to or interest in the land, subsisting in a third person, to the diminution of the value of the land, though consistent with the passing of the fee by conveyance." . . .

Because the question of whether the license diminished the value of the property was an issue in the case, the trial court did not err in refusing to strike defendant's allegation that the license did not constitute an encumbrance.*

Plaintiffs contend also that defendant was not entitled to allege in her affirmative defense that plaintiffs knew of the existence of the Leaches' rights and that the Leaches' irrevocable license was an "open, notorious and visible encumbrance."

ORS 93.850 does not distinguish between types of encumbrances and does not state a rule regarding a grantee's knowledge of the encumbrance. Our prior decisions, however, clearly state that a grantor's covenant against encumbrances in a warranty deed protects the grantee against all encumbrances existing at the time of the delivery of the deed even if the grantee knew about the encumbrance. . . . In some jurisdictions, however, a different rule applies with respect to encumbrances that affect the physical condition of the real property and that are open, notorious and visible. See generally Powell, supra at ¶ 907; 20 Am.Jur.2d, Covenants § 84. With respect to known easements for a public highway or a railroad right-of-way, courts are in conflict, and some have held that such an easement does not constitute a breach of the covenant against encumbrances. This court has previously considered this rule with respect to physical encumbrances in two cases: Ford v. White, supra, and Barnum v. Lockhart, 75 Or. 528, 146 P. 975 (1915).

In *Barnum* a vendor of real property, in an installment contract, promised to provide his purchaser with a deed covenanting against encumbrances. The vendor provided the purchaser with an abstract of title which showed that the Coos Bay Roseburg Eastern Railway & Navigation Company owned a railroad right-of-way across the property. The purchaser refused to continue making the installment payments on the contract, claiming that the vendor's abstract did not show marketable title free and clear of encumbrances. This court held that the vendor's title was not unmarketable because the railroad right-of-way was an encumbrance of such a character that the parties could not have contemplated that the vendor would remove the encumbrance prior to conveying the deed.

The *Barnum* court relied on a rule of law stated in Maupin on Marketable Title 197 (2d ed.1889):

> "As a general rule, the existence of an open, notorious, and visible physical encumbrance upon the estate, such as a public highway, forms no objection to the title, because it is presumed that the purchaser was to take subject to such encumbrance. Neither

* We recognize that diminution in value may not always be a necessary element of plaintiff's proof of an encumbrance where plaintiff seeks rescission rather than damages. There may be instances where the encumbrance has a substantial effect on the buyer's use of the land so he would not have purchased it had he known the condition existed, although the condition did not, in a general sense, diminish the market value of the land. [Other footnotes by the Court have been omitted.]

does such encumbrance entitle the purchaser to . . . a conveyance with a covenant against the encumbrance, because it is presumed that in fixing the purchase price the existence of the encumbrance was taken into consideration." 75 Or. at 540, 146 P. 975.

Mr. Justice McBride, writing for the court in *Barnum* went on to explain:

"Nothing can be more public than a railway over a tract of land, and *it is inconceivable that defendant [purchaser] could have contemplated that plaintiff [vendor] would remove it before tendering an abstract,* and equally inconceivable that he was ignorant of its existence. Without reference to authority it seems reasonable that where the existence of so palpable a physical easement as a railroad is urged as an objection to the title, the burden of pleading and proof should be upon the purchaser to show that he was in fact ignorant of its existence. . . ." 75 Or. at 541, 146 P. 975. (Emphasis added.)

In Ford v. White, supra, the purchasers of real property sought to rescind their executory contract because the vendor, who had promised to convey the premises free and clear of encumbrances, furnished an abstract of title that showed that the California Oregon Power Company owned an easement on the land. The easement affected the real property only to the extent that two guy wires, attached to a pole not on the property, extended about 20 feet onto the property where they were anchored. The trial court found that the purchasers had observed the power line and the two guy wires prior to entering into the contract. Citing *Barnum,* this court held that

"[a] covenant to convey real property free from incumbrances is not breached by the existence upon the property of an open, notorious, and visible physical incumbrance, as it is presumed that, in fixing the purchase price, the existence of the incumbrance was taken into consideration." 179 Or. at 495–96, 172 P.2d 822.

The court then concluded that the encumbrance, known to the purchasers, did not render the vendor's title unmarketable.

It is unnecessary for us to decide whether the decisions in *Barnum* and *Ford* are correct today, especially in light of ORS 93.850, because we hold that the Leaches' use of the spring on plaintiffs' property is not the type of an open and notorious encumbrance to which the *Barnum* and *Ford* decisions apply. The exception carved out in those decisions is limited to known easements for public highways, powerlines, railroads and the like. An irrevocable license to use a spring is neither so palpable nor so physically permanent as to come within the exception.

We therefore hold that the trial court erred in not striking from defendant's answer her affirmative defense alleging that the Leaches' irrevocable license was an open, notorious and visible encumbrance. We also hold that the trial court erred in not striking from defendant's answer her allegation that plaintiffs knew of the Leaches' irrevocable license.

Plaintiffs contend that the trial court erred in not granting their motion for directed verdict. They argue that, because the *Ford* and *Barnum* decisions do not apply to this case, the only issue properly presented for resolution by the jury was the amount of damages to be awarded. We disagree. In an action for damages for breach of a warranty against encumbrances, an issue is whether or not the encumbrance diminished the value of the land. As previously mentioned, defendant properly raised the issue for the jury as to whether the Leaches' irrevocable license resulted in a diminution of the value of the land and thereby constituted an encumbrance. The trial court instructed the jury that if they found the plaintiff had not sustained any damages they should find for defendant. The trial court therefore properly denied plaintiffs' motion for directed verdict.

Finally, plaintiffs contend that the trial court erred in instructing the jury that the defendant's covenant against encumbrances was not breached if it found that the Leaches' irrevocable license to use the spring was an open, notorious and visible physical encumbrance. We agree. For the reasons previously stated, defendant was not entitled to a defense based on the *Ford* and *Barnum* decisions. We hold that the trial court therefore erred in so instructing the jury.

Accordingly, we remand for a new trial.

Reversed and remanded.

PETERSON, JUSTICE, specially concurring. [Justice Peterson's concurring opinion is well worth reading but is too long to reprint here. It is more nearly a dissent than a concurrence.]

NOTES

1. The issue presented in the principal case is a troublesome one. Is it not reasonable to contend that a purchaser who views the land and sees an easement across it does not intend that his grantor shall covenant against that very encumbrance? Some courts have certainly thought so, as see Merchandising Corp. v. Marine National Exchange Bank, 12 Wis.2d 79, 84, 106 N.W.2d 317, 320 (1960) where a prescriptive easement was involved and the court said: "That an easement is an incumbrance of course cannot be denied; but, where it is open, obvious, and notorious, it is not such an incumbrance as constitutes a defect upon the vendor's title nor can the purchaser under a warranty deed with full covenants maintain an action for breach of the covenants of seizin and against incumbrances by reason of the existence of such an easement."

2. Although an easement is clearly an encumbrance, it is not always easy to determine whether a particular interference with a purchaser's rights amounts to breach of the covenant against encumbrances. The mere existence of use restrictions by way of zoning or building codes does not constitute an encumbrance but violation of these restrictions prior to sale may be sufficient to cause a breach of the covenant in the warranty deed. Thus in Lohmeyer v. Bower, 170 Kan. 442, 227 P.2d 102 (1951), the court decided that the location of a

structure in violation of a zoning ordinance specifying a minimum distance from the rear lot line exposed the owner to the hazard of litigation and made the title doubtful and unmarketable. Similarly, Brunke v. Pharo, 3 Wis.2d 628, 89 N.W.2d 221 (1958), held that violation of a building code, prescribing standards of safety to be met by apartment buildings, constituted an encumbrance violative of the grantor's covenant, where the agency charged with enforcement of the code had begun official action before conveyance and such action was thus imminent when the deed was delivered; and First American Federal Savings & Loan Association v. Royall, 77 N.C.App. 131, 334 S.E.2d 792 (1985), held that the failure of a subdivision developer to install a water line extension required by law before a certificate of occupancy could be issued to the purchaser violated the covenant against encumbrances.

On the other hand, in Fahmie v. Wulster, 81 N.J. 391, 408 A.2d 789 (1979) a prior owner had constructed a culvert on the land which did not conform to government specifications. The plaintiff acquired title by a warranty deed which included a covenant against encumbrances. He was than notified by the state that the culvert was inadequate in size and would have to be replaced. The court held that while breach of a covenant against encumbrances can involve physical conditions concerning the property, such as a building encroachment, this concept would not be extended to the condition of a structure on the property which is in violation of some governmental law or regulation. The court cited Brunke v. Pharo but distinguished that case because the conveyance there was made after violations of the building code had been found and official action begun to compel compliance. The court then concluded: "The present situation is different and, in any event we are not inclined to follow the Wisconsin approach. To expand the concept of encumbrance as urged by the plaintiffs would create uncertainty and confusion in the law of conveyancing and title insurance. A title search would not have disclosed the violation, nor would a physical examination of the premises. The better way to deal with violations of governmental regulations, their nature and scope being as pervasive as they are, is by contract provision which can give the purchaser full protection in a situation such as here presented." Could the doctrine of implied covenants of quality be extended to a case like this?

In Brewer v. Peatross, Utah, 595 P.2d 866 (1979) the court allowed a suit based on an encumbrance created by a special improvement district. Wrote the court: "In regard to the defendant's argument that there was no encumbrance on the property because the assessment ordinance had not become effective nor created as a lien by the statute, it is appropriate to note that the term 'encumbrance' is more comprehensive than 'lien.' For instance, mortgages, tax liens, labor and materialmen's liens, are encumbrances but without expatiating thereon, there are some encumbrances upon property which are not liens. An encumbrance may be said to be any right that a third person holds in land which constitutes a burden or limitation upon the rights of the fee title holder." In the case, there was evidence that the purchaser had inquired as to whether the price of the lots included the improvements to be made by the special district and the vendor assured him that it did. This represents a situation where the parties should be especially careful and put their agreement in writing because it can be a prime source of litigation.

3. "A covenant against encumbrances is breached as soon as made if an encumbrance in fact exists. In an action based on such a breach, only nominal damages can be recovered unless the covenantee has removed the encumbrance, had his possession disturbed, or had his use or enjoyment of the land interfered with by reason of the encumbrance." Stockman v. Yanesh, 68 Ohio St.2d 63, 428 N.E.2d 417 (1981).

DAVIS v. SMITH

Supreme Court of Georgia, 1848.
5 Ga. 274, 48 Am.Dec. 279.

[The estate of N.H. Harris, deceased, was partially insolvent, and the administrator brought a bill in equity, seeking directions for the payment of debts. Among the debts was a claim by the heirs of Noah Laney, deceased, for breach of a covenant of warranty in a deed by Harris to Laney. The case was remanded for further proceedings, and the Supreme Court, in the following excerpt from a long opinion, considered the measure of damages, assuming that proof of breach would be forthcoming.]

NESBET, J. . . . The question as to the measure of damages upon the breach of a covenant of warranty, has divided the most learned jurists of this country. Some have held that the vendee is entitled to recover the value of the land, at the time of eviction, including its natural appreciation of course, and no more than its value than, if it has depreciated; others have held that he is entitled to recover the value of the land at the time of eviction, including the improvements which may have been put upon it; whilst the majority of jurists, and of the courts of this country, and of the courts of England, have adopted, as the most equitable, most permanent and expedient rule, the purchase money with interest from the time of the purchase. A great deal may be said in favor of allowing the vendee, the value of the premises at eviction. Forcible illustrations are given in the books of its equity. On the contrary, equally striking illustrations are furnished of its hardships. In relation to which, I remark that no rule of law can be safe which is founded upon extreme cases. The best rules are those which, upon general principles, operate, in the main, most beneficially to entire communities; which are uniform, and by their simplicity are most easily understood. The rule last adverted to has not these elements of optimism, perhaps I should say, of utility. It is not uniform, for in some cases, under its operation, as in case of great appreciation in the value of the land, the vendee gets more than is equitable, and in others, as where there is a great depreciation, he gets less. So also, vice versa, it is not uniform as to the vendor. In favor of the purchase money with the interest, it may be said, that it is a uniform rule; it is easy of comprehension; easy of proof; and more than all this, it is a criterion of recovery and liability, which the parties may always establish for themselves. It is right upon principle; it is the rule of the common law, and has received the sanction of the courts of a majority of the states of our union. The history of it, at common law, will show that it has and does obtain in England.

The ancient covenant of warranty was a real covenant, binding upon the covenantor and the heir. In suits upon this covenant, the recovery was in other lands equivalent in value to the lands sold, at the time of the sale. There is no doubt but this was the mode and measure of recovery upon the old covenants of warranty. In feudal times, lands were esteemed more highly than money, for reasons growing out of feudal institutions, and the anti-commercial tendencies of the age. Hence, the recovery was in lands. But what is important to notice, is that in the earliest days of the common law, the *measure of recovery was the value of the land at the time the warranty was made.* . . .

Inasmuch as a personal action would not lie upon the covenant of warranty, and when the value of money relatively to lands had risen, in consequence of the revival of commerce and the giving way of feudal institutions and policy, and after the introduction of alienations by bargain and sale, a new species of covenant was devised, to wit: the personal covenants of this day. Purchasers of land desired the personal security of the vendor, and hence are covenants of warranty, of seisin, and covenants for quiet enjoyment, &c. Although we thus find engrafted upon the common law, a new security and a new remedy, yet we find no alteration made in the rule, as to the measure of the covenantor's liability upon a breach. That continued the same. I believe there is no case in the English books to show the contrary. The recovery, instead of being in lands, as formerly, is now in money, yet the amount of it is regulated by the value of the land at the time of the sale, and that is considered to be, what the parties estimated it at, to wit: the purchase money. Upon eviction, the grantee recovers the purchase money, with interest, the interest being allowed to countervail his liability for mesne profits. . . .

Such is the rule of the Common Law, and it is right upon principle. The covenant in this case was a covenant of warranty of title. There was no covenant for quiet enjoyment, none against incumbrances. And as before stated, there was an eviction by judgment in ejectment. The decision we now make, therefore, is in reference alone to the case—that is, it applies to a covenant of warranty upon eviction. What would be the measure of damages upon a breach of a covenant for quiet enjoyment, when the breach does not extend to a breach of a covenant of seisin in the same deed, or in a case where there is only a covenant for quiet enjoyment, we do not now determine. I will only remark, that in case there is only a covenant for quiet enjoyment, and the breach of that amounts to a total failure of title, Chancellor Kent holds, (and many other eminent men,) that the rule of damages is the purchase money, with interest, and no more. And further, that when the covenant for quiet enjoyment follows a covenant of seisin in the same deed, the intent of the instrument appears to be, that the one covenant is merely auxiliary to the other; one referring to the title, and the other to the enjoyment of that title. A breach of the latter involves a breach of the former. It would seem to be unreasonable, that a purchaser should recover upon the covenant of seisin the full value of the estate, and also additional damages for being disturbed in the enjoyment of that estate. There are no precedents at common law for the recovery of more damages in the covenant for quiet enjoyment, than under a covenant of seisin. The covenant of seisin draws after it, the covenant for quiet enjoyment. "*Omne majus continet in se minus.*"

I say, however, that to my mind the rule of the common law is right on principle. In this contract, as in all others, the rule of construction is the *intention of the parties.* What is that? The grantor covenants that the grantee shall be undisturbed in his title. He undertakes that the title in the hands of the grantee is good, and will continue good. The land and its value is the subject matter of the contract. The grantor does not look beyond the immediate transaction; that is perfect in itself. It embraces a sale—a transfer of title—a payment of a fair equivalent by the purchaser, and an undertaking by the vendor, to save him harmless from a failure of title. He, (the vendor,) cannot be presumed to contract in reference to any future condition of the estate which he sells, either to his loss by its natural appreciation, or its actual improvement, or to his gain by its depreciation. He does not submit himself and his heirs to the contingencies which run through many years, much less can he be understood as contracting for a liability to pay for improvements, which rest altogether within the discretion, or caprice, or folly of the purchaser. Wise men do not so contract. They avoid future chances of loss or disturbance, and repose upon what is written. A vendor, for example, bona fide, sells for a fair price one hundred acres of wild land. It becomes the site of a city, and its appreciation rises to millions, and the title fails. It is to be presumed that he guaranteed to the purchaser, upon a contract which, perhaps, did not involve a thousand dollars, the payment of millions. In this country, and at this day, such a case is not merely hypothetical. It would seem that if he were thus liable when the title fails, there would be some equity in allowing him, in case of such appreciation, the title remaining good, to share it with the purchaser. Yet such an idea has never received the least countenance.

On the other hand, the purchaser takes the title for what that is worth *at the time.* The future appreciation, or depreciation, is a chance which he takes with it. The improvements are with him, but he has the right to ask security against the failure of the title. He may ask security in any amount; covenants of any kind; but he asks and takes security against the failure of title alone. It is a personal security—it is available to him in money. He estimates the value of the title in the sum he agrees to pay for it; *he makes, by his contract, the purchase money the measure of the value of the title,* and takes security in that amount. Such seems to me to be the *intention* of the parties, and they ought to be held to their contract. It is right that the vendor should pay interest, because he has had the use of the purchaser's money, and is presumed to have made interest; it is right that the purchaser should receive interest, for although he has had the use of the land, its rents, issues and profits, yet he is liable to refund them to him who has the paramount title. He seems to be the favored person; for at law *he* gets the land and the improvements. Yet, not always so in equity, for it is settled, that if he is compelled to go into a Court of Equity, to assert his title, (upon the principle that equity must be done by him who asks it,) an allowance will be made in favor of the purchaser, in most cases, for his improvements. If he has acted *bona fide,* without notice of the owner's title, a court of equity, in decreeing an account, will allow him to deduct, therefrom, a due compensation for them. . . .

In the United States, the weight of authority is in favor of the rule as enforced at common law. . . .

NOTES

1. The principal case restricts the damages for breach of a covenant of warranty to the purchase price paid to the grantor plus interest, depending on the circumstances. This seems clear enough if the grantee is suing his grantor but, since a covenant of warranty runs with the land, what is the measure of damages if a remote grantee is suing? Assume the following facts. A delivers a warranty deed to B for $50,000. The price of land declines due to an economic depression and B delivers a warranty deed of the same land to C for $40,000. X, a claimant under a title paramount to A, successfully ousts C. C can recover $40,000 from B but, since A's covenant runs with the land, he can also sue A. He is, of course, restricted to one satisfaction, but how much can C recover from A? In Brooks v. Black, 68 Miss. 161, 8 So. 332, 24 Am.St.Rep. 259 (1890), the court allowed C to recover the amount A received ($50,000 in this hypothetical), even though C paid less to his own grantor. The court noted: "The value at the time of the sale by the first vendor is the measure prescribed. It ought to operate both ways. If the vendor be not liable for more, he ought not to be for less. I understand it to be admitted that, if his immediate vendee be evicted, he is still liable for that. I do not see why he should not be equally so to the assignee as his vendee. Does the assignment change his covenant? It runs with the land, and he who buys the land buys the covenant. He gets the whole of it. But it is said that the assignor in such case cannot recover from the first vendor more than the evicted vendee gave for the land, because this is all the assignor would be obliged to pay the assignee, and therefore he has complete indemnity. This is changing the rule essentially. It puts it upon the amount of the loss, not the price paid. It would seem to me that whoever buys land with a covenant adhering to it takes it with all the advantages it conferred on his assignor."

Does this seem fair? Other courts have not thought so and have restricted the recovery to the amount paid by the grantee to his own grantor. See, for example, Taylor v. Wallace, 20 Colo. 211, 37 P. 963 (1894); Taylor v. Allen, 131 Ga. 416, 62 S.E. 291 (1908); and King v. Anderson, 618 S.W.2d 478 (Tenn.App.1981). It is not an easy question, however. If the remote grantee is a donee, could he recover nothing under the latter view? If the remote grantee drove a hard bargain and bought the land for considerably less than its actual value, should he be deprived of the benefit of his bargain if the title fails? The remote grantor gave a covenant of warranty and knew (or should have known) that it would run with the land. If the title fails due to a claimant with title paramount to his, shouldn't he be liable for the amount he received? On the other hand, does this give the remote grantee a windfall which he had no right to expect? It is odd that the problem has not arisen with greater frequency but this may be due to several factors: The extensive use of title insurance and less reliance on the warranties in a deed, the generally rising price of land, and the difficulty of locating a solvent, remote grantor in an increasingly mobile society.

In some situations grantees have recovered from convenantors amounts expended in unsuccessful title litigation against paramount titleholders. For example, Rauscher v. Albert, 145 Ill.App.3d 40, 99 Ill. Dec. 84, 495 N.E.2d 149 (1986), held that the grantees under a warranty deed who attempted to establish clear title against an adverse possessor could recover from their grantor the attorney fees and other costs incurred in the unsuccessful suit against the adverse possessor; however, grantees could not recover attorney fees or costs incurred in their action against the grantor. In Groves v. First National Bank of Valparaiso, 518 N.E.2d 819 (Ind.App.1988), grantor not only had given grantees a warranty deed but knowingly had misrepresented that the property was free of liens and mortgages. When a third party claimant filed a quiet title suit against the grantees, they did not tender the defense to their grantor but hired their own attorney. In their subsequent action against their grantor to recover attorney fees and other expenses from the quiet title suit, the court held that although "the general rule requires tender of the defense to the warranting party . . ., we find an exception . . . where the covenantor defrauds the covenantee."

Where the grantee under a warranty deed successfully defends a title suit brought by a third party, the original grantor is not required to indemnify the grantee for costs of defeating the unsuccessful claim. Chaney v. Haeder, 90 Or.App. 321, 752 P.2d 854 (1988).

2. Damages for breach of a covenant against encumbrances are typically limited by the amount which was fairly and necessarily paid to extinguish the encumbrance, not to exceed, however, the amount of the purchase price, plus attorneys' fees reasonably incurred in contesting the encumbrance, interest at the legal rate from the date of eviction, and court costs. Attorneys' fees incident to the action for breach of covenant are not recoverable. Forrer v. Sather, 595 P.2d 1306 (Utah 1979). In New York, "[t]he general rule is that damages for a breach of covenant against encumbrances or a breach of a warranty of title are measured by subtracting the value of the property after the defect is discovered from its value before the defect existed." Yonkers City Post No. 1666, V.F.W. v. Josanth Realty Corp., 67 N.Y.2d 1029, 503 N.Y.S.2d 321, 494 N.E.2d 452 (1986).

3. What are the legal rights of a possessor of land who makes improvements in good faith, relying on his supposed ownership, and

later discovers that a stranger is the owner? He may recover from his grantor, if a warranty deed was used, but the principal case indicates that the measure of damages will fall short of his real loss. Can he recoup from the stranger? The next case deals with a problem of that type.

MADRID v. SPEARS

United States Court of Appeals, Tenth Circuit, 1957.
250 F.2d 51.

MURRAH, CIRCUIT JUDGE. Appellee, Spears, a nonresident of New Mexico, brought this diversity action to cancel a deed and quiet her title to an undivided one-half interest in 320 acres of land in New Mexico, on the grounds that her name to the deed was forged. The appellant Madrids, occupying claimants under the deed, denied the forgery, but pleaded alternatively that they had made valuable improvements in good faith under color of title, and that Spears was estopped by laches to assert her title. By responsive pleading, Spears admitted the valuable improvements for which the Madrids were entitled to credit, but alleged that they had also realized large profits from the land during the years 1952, 1953, 1954 and 1955, and that they should be made to account for them.

On a trial without a jury, the court found that the deed was a forgery and that the plaintiff, Spears, was entitled to a one-half interest in the land; but it also found that the Madrids had, prior to notice of the forgery, made valuable improvements in the good faith belief that they were the fee owners; and that the Madrids were entitled to restitution for one-half of the cost of such improvements in the agreed amount of $14,214.42. Finding no evidence of the rental value of the land without the improvements, the court concluded that Spears was not entitled to share in the profits in the agreed amount of $17,453 realized from the use of the land for the years 1952 through 1955. The court ordered the land partitioned; the Madrids made an election which the court confirmed and imposed a lien against Spears' interest and the rents and profits therefrom for the amount of the agreed one-half cost of the improvements until discharged.

The Madrids have appealed from that part of the judgment limiting their recovery for the improvements to the actual cost thereof, contending that the amount of their recovery in this equitable proceedings is not measured by "the cost of the improvements, but by the amount they have enhanced the value of the land, less the net profits derived therefrom since the filing of the plaintiff's complaint." In that connection, it is agreed that one-half of the difference between the value of the land at the time the Madrids occupied it under the forged deed, and the time they were dispossessed, was $39,150. The appellee, Spears, has appealed from that part of the judgment which denied her any credit or set-off for the rents and profits received by the Madrids after notice of appellee's claim in October 1953.

Like most states, New Mexico has long since enacted a statutory scheme under which an occupying claimant in an ejectment action may plead and prove the value of the good faith improvements under color of title. And, the plaintiff in such action may, after prescribed notice, in like manner prove the amount of the mesne profits of the said premises; provided, however, that no improvements shall be valued or allowed which were made after the execution of the original summons in the suit or after service of written notice of claim of title to the land, and the nature of such claim; and provided also that no mesne profits shall be valued and recovered except those which accrued after the commencement of the suit or after notice given as prescribed in the statute. N.M.Stat.Annot.1953, § 22–8–14. When the verdict is for the plaintiff in the action, the jury must also find the "value of the improvements" in favor of the defendant "proved in the manner aforesaid" and also the amount of the mesne profits "proved to have been accrued as aforesaid, as also the value of the land in its natural state without the improvements, and if the value of the improvements should exceed the amount of the mesne profits, the balance or overplus thereof shall be found by the jury in favor of the defendant or tenant in possession . . . ." If the mesne profits shall exceed the value of the improvements, the jury shall find the amount of such sale or overplus against the defendant or tenant in possession, and judgment shall be rendered for such balance or overplus so found against the defendant or tenant in possession. § 22–8–15.

The statutes also further provide that if, upon the rendition of the judgment in the suit, the value of the good faith improvements shall exceed the mesne profits, the plaintiff in such suit shall elect whether he shall take his judgment and pay for the improvements assessed against him, or take the pay from the defendant for the net profits and the value of the land in its natural state without the improvements. If he elects to take pay for the net profits and the value of the land without the improvements, he shall tender a warranty deed to the defendant for the said lands upon the payment of the value as found by the jury in its natural state without the improvements, the said payment to be made in such reasonable time as the court may allow. See § 22–8–16. Sections 22–8–17 and 22–8–18, which immediately follow, also provide a remedy for good faith improvers, but such remedies are less comprehensive and not entirely consistent with the foregoing provisions. And, the compiler suggests that these latter sections may be superseded by the former.

These statutes are intended to modify and ameliorate the rigid common-law rule under which even an innocent improver was considered an interloper without legal remedy. They have their genesis in and are based upon the maxim that one who seeks equity must do equity; and the equally, yet more complex doctrine of restitution, as for unjust enrichment. See Restatement Restitution, Introductory Note p. 4, Topic 1, p. 11, § 1, p. 12. They have the designed effect of balancing the equities between the parties and enabling the court to do complete justice in the premises.

Appellant Madrids deny that the statutes have application in this equitable action. But, under New Mexico procedure, like federal procedure, there is only one form of action known as a "civil action", in which the pleader is required only to plead facts entitling him to relief on any legally sustainable theory. See Rules 21–1–1(2) and 21–1–1(8)(a)(2). And while the rules do not purport to abolish the distinction between equity and law, no distinct forms of action are necessary or permissible to state a claim under either. Applicability does not depend upon the form of action, either here or in the state court. The statutes, while procedural in form, are substantive and restitutory in nature and effect. And, their "principles . . . apply and extend to all suits in equity when the object of the complaint or answer is for the recovery of lands and tenements." § 22–8–3. We have then a good faith improver admittedly entitled to recover the statutory value of his improvements, and the question is by what criteria shall we measure it. The actual cost of the improvements is admitted and it was the basis of the trial court's judgment.

From the welter of cases collected at 24 A.L.R.2d 14, 31, based both on equitable and statutory considerations, the editors have evolved the rule that a good faith improver is entitled to compensation for his improvements "measured not by the cost of the improvements, but by the amount to which they have enhanced the value of the owner's estate, less the mesne profits or rental value of the land." And, enhanced value is usually determined by the difference between the value of the land with and without the improvements at the time of dispossession. In most cases, of which Reimann v. Baum, 115 Utah 147, 203 P.2d 387, is typical, the cost of the improvements exceeds the enhanced value of the land, and the court is concerned lest the improver recoup more than the owner is unjustly enriched. And see Greer v. Stanolind Oil & Gas Co., 10 Cir., 200 F.2d 920. But, cost is usually a factor in determining value, and in some cases is a limitation upon the improver's recovery, as where enhancement exceeds cost, and the court is again concerned lest the improver's recovery exceed the amount of the unjust enrichment to the owner. This is so for the test of recovery is not how much the owner is enriched by the improvements, but how much he is unjustly enriched. And, the owner is not unjustly enriched more than the improver's cost. In short, where enhancement exceeds cost, unjust enrichment equals cost. See cases Annot., supra, page 37; Meyers v. Canute, 242 Iowa 692, 46 N.W.2d 72, 24 A.L.R.2d 1. It was these considerations which undoubtedly led the Restatement to adopt the "whichever is the least rule" to the effect that "where the improver is permitted to recover for the improvements, he is entitled to the reasonable value of his labor and materials or to the amount which his improvements have added to the market value of the land, whichever is smaller." Restatement on Restitution, § 42, Comment on Subsection (1).

The land has enhanced in value during the Madrids' occupancy from $4,800 to $83,100. The enhancement was undoubtedly attributable in part to natural economic factors, and part to the good faith improvements. The proof does not show the extent to which the improvements enhanced the gross value, but we may concede that such enhancement greatly exceeded the agreed cost. But even so, since the owner cannot be said to have been unjustly enriched in excess of the improver's cost, the trial court's judgment based thereon is correct.

CROSS APPEAL

The trial court based its denial of a setoff for the agreed mesne profits derived from the premises during the Madrids' occupancy squarely on the premise that Spears' recovery therefor was limited to the "rental value of the land in its raw state without its improvements", and in the absence of any such proof, the plaintiff was not entitled to recover any of the rents and profits. And, this is undoubtedly the prevailing rule. See cases collected Annot. 24 A.L.R.2d 52, § 19.

As we have seen, the applicable statutes contemplate and provide for an equitable setoff of the mesne profits which accrue after the prescribed statutory notice, and for judgment for the balance or overplus, whichever is greater. The statute also provides for the determination of the value of the land in its natural state, and it does not specifically provide that the rental value or mesne profits shall be based thereon. But we can find nothing in the equalizing provisions of the statute which would require us to construe it differently from the prevailing rule. Certainly we cannot say that the trial court's construction in that regard is clearly erroneous, and the judgment is affirmed.

NOTES

1. In City of Poplar Bluff v. Knox, 410 S.W.2d 100 (Mo.1966) the court discussed the so-called "betterment acts" or "occupying claimants laws" and stated: "The compensation to which a good faith occupant is entitled for improvements he makes on the land of another is generally held to be the amount by which the owner is benefited, i.e., the amount by which the value of the land has been enhanced by the improvements and *not* the actual value of the improvements themselves or the amount the improvements cost the occupant." The court held the act did not apply, however, in a case where a city sought to eject a defendant from a portion of the street purportedly conveyed to the defendant years earlier. The defendant was allowed to remove her improvements from the street.

2. Previous materials have made some reference to the doctrine of estoppel by deed or, as it is frequently called, after-acquired title. While the doctrine is not confined strictly to warranty deeds, it seems best to explore it in connection with covenants for title, since it is most frequently applied where a warranty deed has been used. Moreover, it has a role in assuring the grantee's title.

The basic problem is this: A, having no title or a defective one, purports to convey an indefeasible estate to B. Later A acquires a good title from some source. What are B's rights as against A or A's transferee or successor?

ROBBEN v. OBERING

United States Court of Appeals, Seventh Circuit, 1960.
279 F.2d 381.

Castle, Circuit Judge. This appeal involves a declaratory judgment action removed to the District Court on grounds of diversity. The controversy concerns who holds a valid oil and gas lease covering an undivided ¼ interest in a certain 21 acre tract of land in Clinton County, Illinois. Both plaintiff-appellee and defendants-appellants claim to hold a valid lease covering the interest. The District Court found the issue in favor of and entered judgment for Robert H. Robben, plaintiff-appellee. E.A. Obering and Helen Bailey Obering, defendants-appellants appealed.

The main contested issue is whether the District Court erred in holding the doctrine of after-acquired title inapplicable.

On November 7, 1953 Ed Meirink, as grantor, executed an oil and gas lease covering the tract to E.A. Obvering as lessee. Obering conveyed a one-half interest in the lease to his wife, Helen Bailey Obering, on November 23, 1953. The lease contained a covenant of warranty as follows:

"Lessor hereby warrants and agrees to defend the title to the lands herein described . . .."

A leasing agent for Obering testified that prior to the execution of the lease Ed Meirink informed him, in response to a telephone inquiry, that he owned the tract and probably would lease it. Meirink testified that at the time he executed the lease he considered himself the owner "of the entire 21 acres". In June of 1956 an oil well was brought in on an adjacent tract. Meirink notified Obering's office and requested a local attorney to have a title search made. Meirink found out that he owned but a ¼ interest in the tract; that his brother, Arthur, his sister, Laura, and a nephew, each owned a ¼ interest. Meirink attempted to acquire these interests. He obtained a quitclaim deed from his brother, Arthur, on July 20, 1956. It was recorded the next day. Meirink learned that he could not obtain a conveyance from his nephew because of the latter's minority, nor from his sister, who was then incompetent. Meirink quitclaimed an undivided ¼ interest back to Arthur Meirink and the latter's wife, Dorothy, in joint tenancy. This quit-claim deed is dated July 20, 1956 and was recorded August 7, 1956. On November 2, 1956 Arthur and Dorothy Meirink, as grantors, executed an oil and gas lease of the tract to plaintiff-appellee, Robben. Arthur Meirink testified that the purpose of his quit-claim deed to Ed Meirink was to get the lease drilled; that Ed promised that "he would give me my share"; and that Ed Meirink quitclaimed back the next day. Ed Meirink testified that he "gave it back to Arthur because I had promised him that even with me holding the paper I would still give him his fractional part".

The District Court rejected defendants' contention that the interest acquired by Ed Meirink by the quit-claim deed from Arthur passed to defendants under the doctrine of after-acquired title and that Arthur Meirink thereafter had no interest to lease to Robben.

Illinois law governs the issue here involved. In the course of oral argument before us both parties conceded that there is no Illinois case directly in point as to the application of the doctrine of after-acquired title to an oil and gas lease.

The doctrine of after-acquired title or estoppel by deed stems from the common law rule of implied warranties. Although the common law rule of implied warranties is not in existence in Illinois unless all of the words of the statute are used (Wheeler v. County of Wayne, 132 Ill. 599, 24 N.E. 625) express warranties are given the same effect as implied warranties at common law. See Biwer v. Martin, 294 Ill. 488, 500, 128 N.E. 518, in which the doctrine of after-acquired title was recognized as applicable in Illinois where an express warranty is made by the grantor. The court stated (294 Ill. at page 496, 128 N.E. at page 522):

"It is likewise the rule in this state that where one who has no interest, or but a part thereof, in the land he undertakes to convey, and afterwards acquires title, the interest he acquires passes to the grantee by way of estoppel, and, if there be a warranty, it not only estops the grantor but a subsequent purchaser from him. Frisby v. Ballance, 2 Gilm. 141; 4 Kent's Com. * 98; Phelps v. Kellogg, 15 Ill. 131; Bennett v. Waller, 23 Ill. 97; Walton v. Follansbee, supra; Williams v. Esten, 179 Ill. 267, 53 N.E. 562; Tiedeman on Real Prop. § 728".

Unless repealed by statute the common law is in full force and effect in Illinois. Illinois Bell Telephone Co. v. Slattery, 7 Cir., 102 F.2d 58, 67; Fergus v. Russel, 270 Ill. 304, 377, 110 N.E. 130 and Wunderle v. Wunderle, 144 Ill. 40, 33 N.E. 195, 19 L.R.A. 84.

The common law doctrine of after-acquired title or estoppel by deed applies to leases. In Poultney v. Emerson, 117 Md. 655, 658, 84 A. 53, 54, it was said in this connection:

"It is a well-recognized rule that if a lease is made by one who has no present interest in the demised property, but acquires an interest during the term, the lease will operate upon his estate as if vested at the time of its execution. 1 Tiffany on Landlord and Tenant, § 76; Rawle on Covenants for Title (5th Ed.) §§ 258–273; Bigelow on Estoppel (5th Ed.) 384–390; 1 Taylor's Landlord and Tenant (8th Ed.) § 87; Williams on Real Property (18th Ed.) p. 476; 24 Cyc. 923; Cunningham v. Pattee, 99 Mass. 248; Austin v. Ahearne, 61 N.Y. 6."

The doctrine has been applied to oil and gas leases. Columbian Carbon Co. v. Kight, 207 Md. 203, 114 A.2d 28, 51 A.L.R.2d 1232. See also cases cited in the annotation in 51 A.L.R.2d commencing at page 1238.

In Summers Oil & Gas, Vol. 3, Sec. 552, p. 577 (1958 Ed.) it is stated:

"The principle that the after-acquired title passes to the grantee where grantor warrants the title or represents that he conveys the land, operates in assignment of oil and gas leases as in other conveyances."

We see no reason why an oil and gas lease in which the lessor warrants title should be excluded from the scope of the doctrine of after-acquired title.

Plaintiff argues that Ill.Rev.Stat.1959, Ch. 30, Par. 6 (Sec. 7 of "An Act concerning conveyances", approved March 29, 1872) restricts and limits the scope of the common law doctrine to conveyances "in fee simple absolute." The statute provides:

"If any person shall sell and convey to another, by deed or conveyance, purporting to convey an estate in fee simple absolute, in any tract of land or real estate, lying and being in this state, not then being possessed of the legal estate or interest therein at the time of the sale and conveyance, but after such sale and conveyance the vendor shall become possessed of and confirmed in the legal estate to the land or real estate so sold and conveyed, it shall be taken and held to be in trust and for the use of the grantee or vendee; and the conveyance aforesaid shall be held and taken, and shall be as valid as if the grantor or vendor had the legal estate or interest, at the time of said sale or conveyance."

The language of the statute above is substantially that of R.S.1833, p. 131, considered in Frink v. Darst, 14 Ill. 304, 308, where the Illinois Supreme Court quoted with approval (at pages 309, 310) the following statement from Bogy v. Shoab, 13 Mo. 365, 366 with respect to a precisely similar statute:

"It may be, then that our statute was intended to settle a question which had been much discussed, and about which there was certainly great conflict of opinion whether a general warranty would operate to transfer a subsequently acquired legal title. It undoubtedly settles this question in the affirmative, and I think, it goes further. It puts the whole question upon principles of sound sense and strict justice. It does not limit its operation to deeds containing covenants of general warranty, but it extends to every deed which purports to convey a fee-simple absolute whether it contains a general warranty or not. It is easy to imagine numerous cases in which there are conveyances obviously intended, and purporting to convey absolute titles, but which omit any covenants of warranty".

It is our opinion that the Illinois statute was intended to remove, in cases of conveyances in fee simple absolute, any uncertainty which may have existed as to whether an express warranty was required to invoke the doctrine of after-acquired title. This view is in harmony with the general principle that statutes are not presumed to alter the common law further than that expressly declared and will not be construed to repeal by mere implication a rule of common law, unless the implication is absolutely imperative. Cadwallader v. Harris, 76 Ill. 370; Smith v. Laatsch, 114 Ill. 271, 2 N.E. 59. Repeal of the common law by implication is not favored. People ex rel. Nelson v. West Englewood Trust & Savings Bank, 353 Ill. 451, 187 N.E. 525.

The Illinois statute discloses no intent, express or implied, to restrict the application of the common law rule. Nor do the terms and provisions of the statute require such a result. This conclusion is further borne out by the Illinois decisions recognizing the applicability of the doctrine of after-acquired title to mortgages which contain the words "and warrants". Lagger v. Mutual Union Loan Association, 146 Ill. 283, 300, 33 N.E. 946, and cases therein cited.

We are of the opinion, in this setting, that the view taken by the Kansas District Court in O'Connor v. J.H. Huber, Corp., D.C.Kan., 85 F.Supp. 381 can have no controlling effect in Illinois. In that case the *provisions* of a similar Kansas statute were relied upon rather than the common law rule. We conclude that in Illinois the doctrine of after-acquired title is applicable to an oil and gas lease which contains an express warranty of title.

The lease to defendants contains a "lesser interest" clause under which if the lessor owns a less interest in the land therein described than the entire undivided fee simple estate, then the royalties and rentals are to be paid to the lessor only in the proportion which his interest bears to the whole and undivided fee. Plaintiff contends that the presence of the lesser interest clause renders the warranty of title ambiguous and so limits and qualifies the warranty as to make it ineffective except as to the interest which the lessor was able to lease or grant. We find no merit to this contention. The purpose of each clause is different and there is no ambiguity nor any conflict between them.

In the instant case the estoppel arises by warranty. No attempt to assert an estoppel *in pais* is involved. Consequently cases such as Bradley v. Lightcap, 202 Ill. 154, 67 N.E. 45 and Perry Coal Co. v. Richmond, 287 Ill.App. 298, 4 N.E.2d 891 relied upon by plaintiff are not applicable and any failure of defendants to utilize means of ascertaining the condition of the title by referring to the public land records is not a factor for consideration. Such failure would not preclude operation of the rule of after-acquired title.

Plaintiff's final contention is that the doctrine of after-acquired title is inapplicable for the reason that the conveyance from Arthur to Ed Meirink constituted a trust and Ed Meirink took title as trustee. We are of the opinion that the record does not support a conclusion that the title to Arthur's 1/4 interest in the property was held by Ed Meirink in a fiduciary capacity. It is unquestioned that Ed Meirink was to see that Arthur got "his share". It is equally evident that the Meirinks intended at the time of the quit-claim by Arthur that the Obering lease should attach to Arthur's 1/4 interest. The Obering lease was the only lease of the tract then in existence in which anyone could have received a "share" and the conveyance was to "get him to drill". The application of the doctrine of after-acquired title would defeat no trust. Nor does it in any manner affect any rights Arthur Meirink may have against Ed Meirink to receive 1/4 of the royalty interest.

We conclude that the doctrine of after-acquired title applies to the 1/4 interest conveyed by the quit-claim deed of Arthur Meirink to Ed Meirink; that by operation of law the Obering lease attached to said interest and that the subsequent attempt to lease to plaintiff was ineffectual as against the Obering lease as so enlarged.

The judgment order of the District Court is reversed and the cause is remanded with directions that appropriate findings and judgment be entered for defendants in conformity with the views herein expressed.

Reversed and remanded with directions.

NOTES

1. There is one curious aspect of the principal case which was not discussed by the court. Wasn't the Obering lease out of the chain of title since it was given *before* Ed Meirink acquired title to more than one-quarter of the land? Robben was a b.f.p. who was entitled to rely on the records and, in Illinois, the grantor-grantee index is the official system. Moreover, Illinois follows the chain-of-title reasoning, see Capper v. Poulsen, 321 Ill. 480, 152 N.E. 587 (1926). See also discussion on page 1431 supra. Did Robben's attorney simply overlook this argument or is there some other explanation?

2. The true basis for the doctrine of estoppel by deed is not always apparent from the cases. A common saw states that the doctrine is designed to avoid circuity of action. If the grantor is not estopped, he is liable on the covenants of the deed. If he is estopped, the breach of covenant vanishes. This avoids circuity of action, but it means that the doctrine applies only when the deed contains covenants. It is true that a warranty deed is *usually* involved, but not *always*. Some courts have limited the doctrine to cases involving a breached covenant, and some have even required that it be a covenant of warranty. But the view seems better that the doctrine is based on the parties' intention as gathered from all the terms of the conveyance. See, for example, Hagensick v. Castor, 53 Neb. 495, 73 N.W. 932 (1898), where a quitclaim deed was used but it contained a recital that the grantor therein "being one of the three heirs of George H. Ohler" quitclaimed and conveyed. In fact, George H. Ohler, although missing, was not then dead. He died later and the court held that after-acquired title passed under the deed. It was more than a mere quitclaim since the grantor recited that he was an heir, thereby representing that he had an interest to convey. This is often referred to as "estoppel by representation" and operates even in absence of an express warranty. Some states have reached this same result by statute as see Ill.Rev.Stat. ch. 30, § 6 (1985): "If any person shall sell and convey to another, by deed or conveyance, *purporting to convey an estate in fee simple absolute*, in any tract of land or real estate, lying and being in this state, not then being possessed of the legal estate or interest therein at the time of the sale and conveyance, but after such sale and conveyance the vendor shall become possessed of and confirmed in the legal estate to the land or real estate so sold and conveyed, it shall be taken and held to be in trust and for the use of the grantee or vendee; and the conveyance aforesaid shall be held and taken, and shall be as valid as if the grantor or vendor had the legal estate or interest, at the time of said sale or conveyance." [Emphasis added.] See also 44 Ill.Bar J. 263 (1955). For some additional light on this problem see Sorenson v. Wright, 268 N.W.2d 203 (Iowa 1978) and Dixieland Realty Co. v. Wysor, 272 N.C. 172, 158 S.E.2d 7 (1967).

3. Even if we know the basis for the doctrine not all problems are solved, for the courts also differ as to the method of operation of the doctrine. Does the after-acquired interest pass *eo instante* to the conveyee or his successor in title, or does the grantee simply have an equitable interest which he can assert if he so desires?

In Perkins v. Coleman, 90 Ky. 611, 14 S.W. 640 (1890), the court took the position sometimes referred to as "feeding the estoppel" and held that the legal title passed instantly to the grantee once it was acquired by the grantors, thus allowing the former to sue a stranger in ejectment without first bringing a bill in equity to acquire the title from the grantor. This is the usual view and is a great help to title examiners since it allows them to assume that the title has been "fed" down the chain to the present owner. However, this is not an absolute rule and in the proper circumstances the grantee may have a choice as to whether he will assert the doctrine. In Resser v. Carney, 52 Minn. 397, 404, 54 N.W. 89, 90 (1893) the grantee brought suit for breach of warranty and then the grantor acquired title from a third party and claimed this ended P's suit. "If the grantee acquires nothing by the deed to him, and has and asserts a legal cause of action for covenant broken, no principle of estoppel operates against him to compel him, perhaps years afterwards, as in this case, to accept, in satisfaction of that legal cause of action, wholly or partially, a title which his covenantor may then procure. The latter, whose covenant has been wholly broken, has no right to elect, as against the covenantee, and to his prejudice, whether he will respond in damages for the breach by repaying the purchase money, or buy in the paramount title, when the value of the property may be greatly depreciated, and compel the plaintiff to accept that title. The right of election is, and should be, with the other party. He has the benefit of the estoppel but it is not to be imposed upon him as a burden, at the will of the party who alone is subject to the estoppel."

For an interesting case in which the majority of the court thought the doctrine should be automatically applied while three dissenting judges felt this led to an inequitable result see Erickson v. Wahlheim, 52 Wn.2d 15, 319 P.2d 1102, 1105 (1958). "The after-acquired-title doctrine, applied by the majority, originated in the common law as the equitable doctrine of estoppel by deed. . . . The following quotation from the Harvard Law Review (22:136–7), concerning this doctrine, is especially apropos in this case: 'it should always be recognized that in essence the cases on this general subject demand the application of equitable principles and that a court of law in entertaining them can be justified only as it reaches an equitable result. *Recognition of the doctrine as a hard and fast rule of law has inevitably led to inequitable results.* . . .' (Emphasis supplied.)"

4. Courts have divided over whether the grantor in a warranty deed can later claim to have obtained title from the grantee or the grantee's successor by adverse possession. Lewicki v. Marszalkowski, 455 A.2d 307 (R.I.1983), held that the specific language of Rhode Island's statutorily implied covenants of warranty and quiet enjoyment estopped a grantor from making such a claim. The court acknowledged

that in other states the general rule was that if good title was conveyed by the warranty deed, there was no breach of covenant and no ground for estoppel since the acts of disseisin occurred after the transfer of title. Even in such other states, however, where a grantor retains possession of the land conveyed, such possession usually is presumed to be subordinate to the title of the grantee and thus not adverse unless the grantor by some affirmative action indicates to the grantee that the possession is hostile to the grantee's title.

SECTION 3. EXAMINATION OF THE RECORDS OR OF AN ABSTRACT OF TITLE

The recording system was designed to protect a purchaser or a mortgagee of an interest in land. That individual has constructive notice of all that appears in the records, and he would be most foolish to invest his money without a careful check at the appropriate offices in the county court house. He has constructive notice of matters other than those in the recorder's office; he must check the court records for judgments that may be liens against the land, the probate records for proceedings in an intestate or a testate succession, the tax and special assessments records, etc. All of these have indexes, and since they are public records the purchaser himself could make the examination. Obviously this would be a waste of his time since, even if he found the relevant documents, he would have some difficulty in interpreting them. Therefore, the lawyer performs this service and renders his opinion as to the state of the title.

In some areas of the country the lawyer still makes the search, prepares his chain of title, and then gives his opinion. This is slow, detailed work, virtually impossible in large population centers because of the sheer bulk of the records. Private abstract companies have been developed to ease the lawyer's load (and make a good profit). These companies typically keep a duplicate set of records based on the tract index principle. They then prepare an abstract of the record for each piece of property, as the need develops, and the lawyer can examine this abstract in the privacy of his own office, then give his opinion of the title. The abstract company keeps its records up to date by a daily transfer from the various public records to the private set kept by the company. This is usually done by a "take-off man" who operates between the courthouse and the company office.

Once the initial abstract has been prepared, usually starting with the patent deed from the United States or the state, it is relatively easy to keep it up to date by a continuation each time the land is transferred. The abstracter need cover only the period from the last continuation down to date and add this to the constantly-increasing bulk of the abstract. Needless to say, the abstract will become a valuable piece of personal property in its own right, frequently being worth several hundred dollars.

The examining attorney does not assume any responsibility for the correctness of the astract but limits his opinion to the title disclosed by the abstracted records. Any error in the abstract itself, such as the miscopying of a deed or the omission of a mortgage, is the fault of the company. Both the lawyer and the abstracter may be liable to the client for any negligence in the areas of their respective responsibilities.

As the term indicates, the abstract is not a reproduction of the original documents but consists of a condensed statement of the key facts in each transfer. Normally the abstracter expresses no opinion as to the legal significance of the instruments but simply sets them forth for the lawyer's judgment.

The best way to acquaint you with this method of title assurance would be to have you examine an actual abstract of title. Most of them are too long to include in these materials, however, and any given abstract could scarcely illustrate the broad range of problems, from the mundane to the sophisticated, that occur in actual practice. We have compromised by reprinting, at this point, a truncated abstract that is too brief to be typical but which will give you some feel for this method of title assurance. You should try your hand at examining it and, after you have reached a conclusion as to the state of the title, you may wish to compare your conclusion with that of an experienced property lawyer. If so, see 1 Flick, Abstract of Title Practice 34–40 (2d ed. 1958).

FLICK, ABSTRACT AND TITLE PRACTICE

Vol. 1, Pages 22–40 (2d ed. 1958).

Abstract of Title

. . .

This abstract, taken from actual records by an experienced abstracter, will indicate one way in which the various entries are set out in an abstract of title; however, no two abstracters ever set out their material in precisely the same manner. The manner of setting up the abstract depends upon the experience of the particular abstracter, the size of his plant and on other matters which lead to dissimilarity.

ABSTRACT OF TITLE

1.

CAPTION

Situated in the Township of Audrain, in the County of Dore and in the State of Ohio, and Being the Northwest quarter of the Southeast quarter, and the Northeast fraction of the Southwest (fractional) quarter of Section 34, Township one South, of Range five East, containing 83 acres of land, more or less.

2.

The State of Ohio

TO

John Glander

STATE DEED

Date of instrument? August 5, 1835

Filed: December 16, 1842

Recorded in Volume 12, Page 236 of the Record of Deeds of Dore County, Ohio

Consideration $132.33

Estate conveyed:

What if any defect in instrument? None.

DESCRIPTION: The Southeast fraction of the West half of Section No. 34, Township one South of Range five East within the land and containing 105 acres of land, more or less.

Regularly signed, sealed, witnessed and acknowledged.

1-A-PLAT.

Section 34 Tp. 1 South R. 5 East

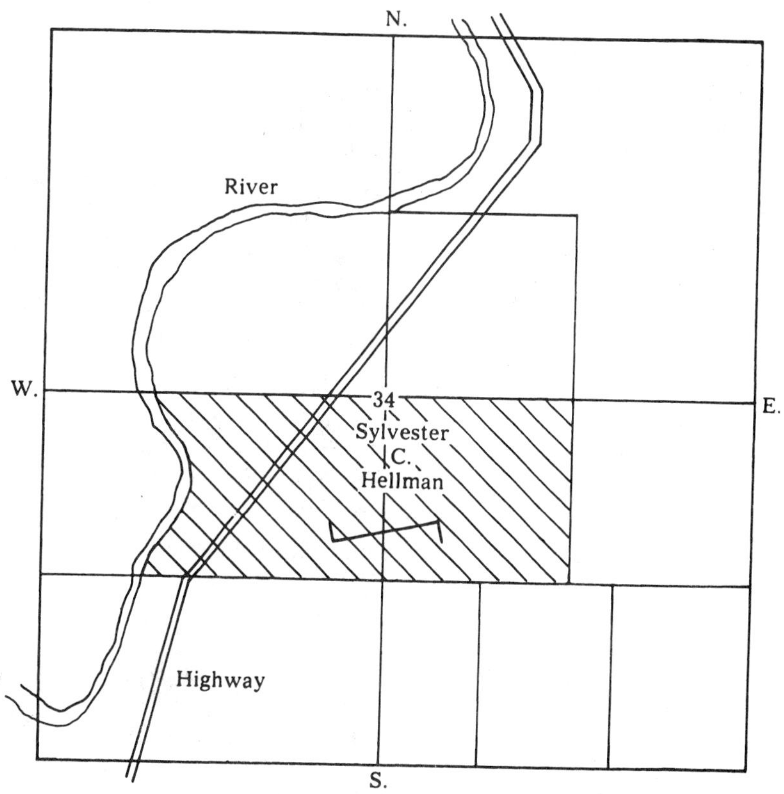

Audrian Township, Dore County, Ohio

[B7184]

3.

John Glander and Elizabeth Glander, his wife

TO

Henry Joseph Boehmer

WARRANTY DEED

Date of instrument? September 4, 1847
Filed: June 4, 1848
Recorded in Volume 2, Page 315 of the Record of Deeds of Dore County, Ohio
Consideration $390.00
Estate conveyed: Fee simple
What if any defect in instrument? None.

DESCRIPTION: Situated in the County of Dore and State of Ohio and bounded and described as follows, to-wit: The Southeast fraction of the West half of Section No. 34, Township one South, Range five East, containing 105.86 acres, more or less.

Also the Northeast fraction of Section No. 34, Township one South, Range five East, containing 71.51 acres of land, more or less.

Regularly signed, sealed, witnessed and acknowledged.

4.

Henry Joseph Boehmer and Mary Boehmer his wife

TO

Mathias Hellman

WARRANTY DEED

Date of instrument? January 29, 1848
Filed: November 28, 1848
Recorded in Volume 2, Page 405 of the Record of Deeds of Dore County, Ohio
Consideration $155.00
Estate conveyed: Fee simple
What if any defect in instrument? None.

DESCRIPTION: Situated in the County of Dore and State of Ohio and bounded and described as follows, to-wit: The Northeast fraction of the Southwest quarter of Section 34, Township one South, Range five East, containing 43.20 acres of land, more or less.

Regularly signed, sealed, witnessed and acknowledged.

5.

The State of Ohio

TO

J.C. McCowen

STATE DEED

Date of instrument? September 16, 1853
Filed: January 7, 1854 at 12:30 P.M.

Recorded in Volume 87, Page 93 of the Record of Deeds of Dore County, Ohio
Consideration $160.00
Estate conveyed:
What if any defect in instrument? None.

DESCRIPTION: The Southeast quarter of Section No. 34, Township one South, Range five East, containing 160 acres of land.

Regularly signed, sealed, witnessed and acknowledged.

6.

John McCowen and Drucilla McCowen, his wife
TO
Mathias Hellman

WARRANTY DEED
Date of instrument? August 10, 1854
Filed: November 9, 1854
Recorded in Volume 11, Page 164 of the Record of Deeds of Dore County, Ohio
Consideration $120.00
Estate conveyed: Fee simple
Defects: None.

DESCRIPTION: The West half of the Northwest quarter of the Southeast quarter of Section 34, Twp 1 S of R 5 E, in the County of Dore, Ohio, containing 20 acres of land.

Regularly signed, sealed, witnessed and acknowledged.

7.

John McCowen and Drucilla McCowen, his wife
TO
Mathias Hellman

WARRANTY DEED
Date of instrument? January 14, 1860
Filed: September 12, 1860
Recorded in Volume 14, Page 221 of the Record of Deeds of Dore County, Ohio
Consideration $140
Estate conveyed: Fee simple
What if any defect in instrument? None.

DESCRIPTION: Situated in the County of Dore in the State of Ohio and in ______ and bounded and described as follows: Being the East half of the Northwest quarter [of Southeast 1/4?] of Section 34, Township one South, Range five East, containing 20 acres of land in the County of Dore, Ohio.

Regularly signed, sealed, witnessed and acknowledged.

8.

Mathias Hellman

TO

Joseph Hellman

WARRANTY DEED

Date of instrument? April 2, 1883

Filed: May 11, 1883

Recorded in Volume 42, Page 426 of the Record of Deeds of Dore County, Ohio

Consideration $3500.00

Estate conveyed: Fee simple

What if any defect in instrument? None.

DESCRIPTION: Situated in the Township of Audrain, in the County of Dore and State of Ohio and being the Northeast fraction of the Southwest fractional quarter, and the Northwest quarter of the Southeast quarter of Section 34, Township one South of Range five East, containing 80 acres of land, more or less.

Regularly signed, sealed, witnessed and acknowledged.

9.

Joseph Hellman and Bernadina Hellman, husband and wife

TO

Sylvester C. Hellman

WARRANTY DEED

Date of instrument? October 17, 1929

Filed: April 28, 1930 at 4:15 P.M.

Recorded in Volume 139, Page 398 of the Record of Deeds of Dore County, Ohio

Consideration $1.00

Estate conveyed: Fee simple

What if any defect in instrument? None.

DESCRIPTION: Situated in the Township of Audrain, County of Dore and State of Ohio, and being the Northeast fraction of the Southwest fractional quarter, and the Northwest quarter of the Southeast quarter of Section 34, Township one South, of Range five East, and containing 80 acres of land, more or less.

Regularly signed, sealed, witnessed and acknowledged.

10.

CERTIFICATE TO RECORDER

REAL ESTATE DEVISED BY WILL

Probate Court, Dore County, Ohio
To the County Recorder of said County:

I the undersigned, Probate Judge of said County, do hereby certify that on the 18th day of March, A.D. 1930, the Last Will and Testament of Joseph Hellmann, late of said County, was duly admitted to probate in this Court, and the same has been duly recorded in Volume P Page 159 of the Records of Wills in this office.

That by the terms of said Will certain real estate was devised to Bernadina Hellmann and Sylvester Hellman.

That the following is a description of said real estate as is contained in the Will, to-wit:

Second: I give, devise and bequeath to my beloved wife, Bernadina, the farm on which we now reside together with all chattel property I may have at the time of my decease. She to have full possession of same during her natural life. After the death of my beloved wife, I give to my son, Sylvester, the aforementioned farm located in Section 34, Audrain Township, Dore County, Ohio, containing 83 acres of land, together with all chattels. He, however, must pay all funeral expenses and debts contracted by my said wife. Also to pay my following named children within three years after the death of my said wife as follows:

Witness my signature and the seal of said Court, this 6th day of January, 1931.

W.M. Bunge,
Probate Judge
By Mary McLeasure,
Deputy Clerk

[*Seal*]
Recorded in Vol. 141, Page 191
Record of Deeds of said County

11.

APPLICATION FOR PROBATE OF WILL

Probate Court, Dore County, Ohio

In the Matter of The Last Will and Testament of Joseph Hellmann, Deceased.	Application To Admit To Probate

To the Probate Court of said County:

Your petitioner respectfully represents that Joseph Hellmann, late a resident of the Township of Audrain in said County, died on or about the 4th day of March, A.D., 1930, leaving an instrument in writing, herewith produced, purporting to be his last Will and Testament;

That the said Joseph Hellmann died leaving Bernadina Hellmann, widow, who resides at Fort Audrain, Ohio, and the following named persons his only next of kin, to-wit:

Name	Degree of Kinship	P.O. Address
Mathias Hellmann	Son	Fort Audrain, Ohio
Otto Hellmann	"	Delton, Ohio
Christina Brinkman	Daughter	Fort Audrain, O.
Bernadina Beining	"	Fort Audrain, "
Mary Hellmann	"	" " "
Sylvester Hellman	Son	" " "

Your petitioner offers said Will for Probate and prays that a time may be fixed for the proving of the same, and that said above named persons resident in this State may be notified according to law of the pendency of said proceedings.

Sylvester Hellmann,
Petitioner

Properly verified

12.

LAST WILL AND TESTAMENT

In the Name of the Benevolent Father of All: Amen.

I, Joseph Hellmann, of the Township of Audrain, County of Dore and State of Ohio, being about 70 years of age and of sound and disposing mind and memory, do make, publish and declare this my last will and testament, hereby revoking and annulling any and all will or wills by me made heretofore:

First: My will is that all my just debts and funeral expenses be paid out of my estate as soon after my decease as shall be found convenient.

Second: I give, devise and bequeath to my beloved wife Bernadina the farm on which we now reside together with all chattel property I may have at the time of my decease. She to have full possession of same during her natural life. After the death of my beloved wife I give to my son Sylvester the aforementioned farm located in Section Thirty-four, Audrain Township, Dore County, Ohio, containing eighty-three (83) acres of land together with all chattels. He, however, must pay all funeral expenses and debts contracted by my said wife. Also to pay my following named children within three years after the death of my said wife as follows:

Item 3. My son Mathias to get Seven Hundred ($700.00) Dollars, I having paid him Eight Hundred ($800.00) Dollars.

Item 4. My son Otto to get Fifteen Hundred ($1500.00) Dollars.

Item 5. My daughter Christina Brinkman to get Fourteen Hundred ($1400.00) Dollars. She having been paid One Hundred ($100.00) Dollars.

Item 6. My daughter Bernadina Beining to get Fourteen Hundred ($1400.00) Dollars. She having been paid One Hundred ($100.00) Dollars.

Item 7. My daughter Mary to get Eighteen Hundred ($1800.00) Dollars and the privilege of remaining and living on said farm with my son Sylvester, as long as she lives, and to occupy the East upstairs room. However in case Sylvester is forced to sell, then my daughter may so give up the aforesaid privileges.

Item 8. I desire that there be no appraisement of my property and ask that the court omit the same.

Item 9. I hereby revoke any and all wills formerly made by me.

In Testimony Whereof, I have set my hand to this my last will and testament at Fort Audrain, Ohio, this 8th day of April in the year of our Lord one thousand nine hundred and twenty-four.

JOSEPH HELLMANN

The foregoing instrument was signed by the said Joseph Hellmann in our presence, and by him published and declared as and for his last will and testament and at his request, and in his presence, and in the presence of each other, we hereunto subscribe our names as attesting witnesses, at Fort Audrain, Ohio, this 8th day of April, A.D., 1924.

Anton J. Berelman resides at Fort Audrain, Ohio

Rudolph Rasbe resides at Fort Audrain, Ohio

Filed March 18, 1930

13.

Note: The order for hearing, the admission to probate and record, the waiver of notice and consent to probate, the testimony of witnesses to the will, the application for letters, the issuance of letters; the order for bond; and the proof of publication of notice to creditors are all regular and complete and are not set out.

14.

JOURNAL ENTRY

In the Probate Court of Dore County, Ohio May 13, 1930

In the matter of the Estate of Joseph Hellman,* Deceased.	Estate Not Subject to Tax

DETERMINATION OF INHERITANCE TAX

Sylvester C. Hellman as Administrator of the estate of Joseph Hellman, deceased, having filed an application duly verified, for a finding and order that said estate and the succession therein are exempt from any inheritance tax under the laws of Ohio, the same came on for hearing.

And the Court being fully advised in the premises, finds and determines that the gross value of said estate is $885.86; the debts and costs of administration are $585.00, and the net actual market value thereof is $300.86, (a) Said decedent died leaving three sons and three daughters, and that as a result said estate and the successions therein are exempt from such inheritance tax.

It is ordered that the court costs on this proceeding taxed at $3.00 be certified to the County Auditor to be paid and credited in the manner provided by law.

W.M. Bunge, *Probate Judge*

Filed May 13, 1930.

15.

In the Matter of the Estate of Joseph Hellman, Deceased.	IN PROBATE COURT Dore County, Ohio Saturday May 2, 1931.

The first and final account of Sylvester Hellman, Administrator with will annexed of the estate of Joseph Hellman, deceased, herein filed on the 23rd day of March, A.D., 1931, came in this day for hearing and settlement, due notice thereof having been published according to law. No exceptions having been filed thereto, and no one now appearing to except or object to the same; and the Court having carefully examined said account and the vouchers therewith and all matters pertaining thereto, and being fully advised in the premises, finds the same to be in all respects just and correct and in conformity to law.

It is ordered that the same be and hereby is approved, allowed and confirmed.

* The various spellings of the name "Hellmann" are as they appeared in the original documents.

The Court further finds said Administrator with will annexed chargeable with the assets of the estate of said Joseph Hellman to the amount of $929.11 and that he is entitled to the credits in the sum of $929.11 and that there is no balance due to said estate.

And the Court further finding that said estate has been duly and fully settled, it is ordered that said Administrator with will annexed be discharged and his bond released from further liability. It is ordered that said account and the proceedings herein be recorded in the records of this office, and that said Administrator with will annexed pay the costs herein taxed at $5.00

W.M. Bunge, *Probate Judge*

Filed May 2, 1931

16.

Sylvester Hellman	EASEMENT
TO	Date of instrument. April 22, 1933
The General Utilities Co. of Deshler, Ohio	Recorded May 17, 1933 in Volume 143 at Page 596
	No defects in instrument

Grants the right to construct, operate and maintain its lines through and along the following described property: The Northeast 43.1 acres of the Southwest quarter of section 34, Township one South, Range five East.

17.

TAX STATEMENT

The tax duplicates of the Treasurer's Office and the records of the Auditor's Office and Surveyor's Office of Dore County, Ohio, show the following in connection with the taxes levied against caption lands:

AMOUNT OF SPECIAL ASSESSMENTS AND TERMS: No specials

DESCRIPTION OF LAND AS IT APPEARS ON THE DUPLICATES:

Sec. 34	NW¼ SE¼	40A
Sec. "	N½ SE fr. SW¼	43.10A

ASSESSED VALUE OF

Land	$4390.00
Buildings	$2340.00
Total	$6730.00

CURRENT TAXES:

Paid	Taxes for the first half of the year 1937, due and payable in December 1937	$33.65
Unpaid	Taxes for the last half of the year 1937, due and payable in June 1938	$33.65

18.

STATE OF OHIO
COUNTY OF DORE

I hereby certify that the annexed abstract, which is furnished ______, as prospective mortgagee for use in passing on the title to premises covered thereby, is a correct abstract of the title to the land described in the caption thereof, to-wit:

CAPTION LANDS

in the said county and state: that said abstract correctly shows all matters affecting or relating to the said title which are of record or on file in said county, including conveyances, deeds, trust deeds, land and other liens, attachments and foreign or domestic executions in the hands of the sheriff, certificates of authority to pay taxes, suits pending by or against owners of record within the last two years or against Sylvester Hellman, notices of Federal liens, tax sales, tax deeds, probate proceedings, special proceedings, and unsatisfied judgments and transcripts of judgments from United States and State courts against owners of record or against Sylvester Hellman, notices of liens on bail bonds or recognizances filed against said premises, or against owners of record on or since April 1, 1929, or against Sylvester Hellman, under chapter 14, section 13435–5, of laws of Ohio of 1929; that said abstract also shows all bankruptcy proceedings and certified copies of orders of adjudication and orders approving bonds of trustee in bankruptcy proceedings by or against any party who, within three years past, has been an owner of record of said land or against Sylvester Hellman on file or of record in said county; that all taxes and special assessments against said premises are paid in full to and including the first instalment of the taxes for the year 1957 and that there are no outstanding instalments of special assessments to become due in the future.

Dated at ______, Ohio this 2nd day of May A.D. 19__ at 10:00 o'clock A.M.

C. W. McLain
Abstracter

Continued to this date and recertified as above, this ______ day of ______ A.D. 19__ at ______ o'clock __.M.

FIRST AMERICAN TITLE INSURANCE COMPANY, INC. v. FIRST TITLE SERVICE COMPANY OF THE FLORIDA KEYS, INC.

Supreme Court of Florida, 1984.
457 So.2d 467.

BOYD, JUSTICE.

This cause is before the Court on petition for review of a district court of appeal decision reported as First American Title Insurance Co.

v. First Title Service Co., 423 So.2d 600 (Fla.3d DCA 1982). The district court properly followed established precedent, see Hoffman v. Jones, 280 So.2d 431 (Fla.1973), in holding that an abstracter can be held liable for negligent preparation of an abstract only to a party, such as the purchaser of the abstract, in privity with the abstracter. See Sickler v. Indian River Abstract & Guaranty Co., 142 Fla. 528, 195 So. 195 (1940). The district court certified that its decision directly conflicts with Kovaleski v. Tallahassee Title Co., 363 So.2d 1156 (Fla. 1st DCA 1978). We have jurisdiction. Art. V, § 3(b)(4), Fla.Const. Although we decline to recognize an abstracter's liability in tort for negligence to any and all foreseeable injured parties, we hold that the plaintiff here stated a cause of action as a third-party beneficiary of the contract of employment of the abstracter.

First American Title Insurance Company brought this action against First Title Service Company of the Florida Keys alleging that First Title Service Company had prepared abstracts for the sellers of two lots and that First American Title Insurance Company, relying on the abstracts, had issued owners' and mortgagees' title insurance policies to the buyers of the two lots and their lender. The complaint went on to allege that the abstracts had failed to note the existence of a recorded judgment against a former owner of the lots; that the holder of the judgment had made demand on the new owners for payment of the judgment; and that First American, pursuant to the policies of title insurance it had issued, had been obliged to pay and had paid approximately $75,000 to satisfy the judgment and obtain releases. The complaint did not allege any privity of contract between the plaintiff insurer and the defendant abstracter, but did allege that at the time the defendant prepared the abstracts for the sellers of the lots the defendant knew that a person other than the person ordering the abstracts would rely on them as providing an accurate and complete summation of all recorded instruments affecting title to the lots in question.

The defendant abstracting company moved to dismiss the complaint for failure to state a cause of action upon which relief may be granted. The trial court granted the motion and the plaintiff title insurer appealed. As has already been stated, the district court of appeal relied on Sickler v. Indian River Abstract & Guaranty Co., and affirmed the dismissal.

. . .

Petitioner argues that the proper test for liability is not the existence of a contractual relationship between the parties but rather the foreseeability of the plaintiff's reliance on the defendant's abstract. The cause of action, petitioner maintains, is not based on breach of contract but on negligence. Petitioner cites numerous cases illustrating the transition from the privity doctrine to the theory of liability in tort to foreseeably injured persons. All of these cases involved bodily harm or injury caused by negligently designed or produced manufactured products or negligently prepared or packaged food products. . . .

. . .

Petitioner relies on numerous cases from other jurisdictions as illustrating the wisdom of recognizing an abstracter's liability for injury to any foreseeably relying parties, the most notable of which is Williams v. Polgar, 391 Mich. 6, 215 N.W.2d 149 (1974). There an abstract prepared in 1926 had failed to note the existence of a deed executed in that year. Several continuations of the abstract were made thereafter, and as extended the abstract was exhibited by the seller and relied upon by the buyer in a conveyance that occurred in 1959. Subsequently the ownership interest the abstracter had failed to discover in 1926 was asserted and the 1959 purchaser suffered financial losses because of it. So, in 1971, the purchaser brought an action for damages against the successor in interest to the firm that had prepared the 1926 abstract and subsequent continuations. Pointing out that Michigan law already recognized that an abstracter is liable for negligence causing damages to a third party whom the abstractor *knows* is relying on the abstract, the Supreme Court of Michigan framed the issue thus: "The question boils down to whether there should be liability for *foreseeable* as well as *known* reliance." 391 Mich. at 9, 215 N.W.2d at 150. The court embraced the foreseeability theory and held that there was liability in tort. In holding that the defense of privity was no bar to the action, the court reasoned as follows:

> The early common-law rule restricting liability to those in contractual privity with an abstracter was based on a system where abstracts would only be used by real estate owners. 1 Fitch, Abstracts and Titles to Real Property, § 9, p. 9; and see § 3. As time went on the actual usage of abstracts and the class of people relying on them expanded. This historical change in circumstance and the corresponding change in law is noted in numerous cases. . . . Brown v. Sims, 22 Ind.App. 317, 325; 53 N.E. 779; 72 Am.St.Rep. 308 (1899) illustrates a judicial expansion of liability to a known third party beneficiary:
>
> > "It is very well known that the owner of real estate seldom incurs the expense of procuring an abstract of the title from an abstracter, except for the purpose of thereby furnishing information to some third person or persons who are to be influenced by the information thus provided. If the abstracter in all cases be responsible only to the person under whose employment he performs the service, it is manifest that the loss occasioned thereby must in many cases, if not in most cases, be remediless."
>
> . . .

391 Mich. at 11–13, 215 N.W.2d at 151–52 (footnotes omitted). The court went on to discuss the concept that one who undertakes by contract to perform a service not only owes a duty of diligence to his contracting counterpart, but also owes a general duty to perform the service with reasonable care, and that this latter duty may, if breached, give rise to liability in tort to a person injured even if the injured person is a stranger to the contract. After discussing the several other

possible theories of recovery (fraud, deceit, warranty, and strict liability) and finding them all unsatisfactory, the court concluded that the tort of negligent misrepresentation "precisely fits this situation." Id. at 20, 215 N.W.2d at 156. The court concluded:

> Thus, we adopt the tort action of negligent misrepresentation in this context. See 1 Harper & James, The Law of Torts, § 7.6; 17 C.J.S., Contracts, § 154(c). It should be noted that this action is premised on negligence in title search; an abstracter is not converted into a title insurer by virtue of our decision today. We repeat that the only liability an abstracter has to an injured third-party is with respect to negligent performance of his or her contractual duty.
>
> As to the measure of the duty required to be exercised by the abstracter, Chief Justice T.M. Kavanagh noted in Nash v. Sears, Roebuck & Co., supra, [383 Mich. 136], at page 142 [174 N.W.2d 818]:
>
> > "Every contract of employment includes an obligation, whether express or implied, to perform in a diligent and reasonably skillful workmanlike manner."
>
> This is clearly a form of the traditional negligence standard. Since the legal duty which, when breached, gives rise to a tort cause of action, springs from the contractual duty imposed, this *Nash* standard governs an abstracter's legal obligation to non-contracting parties. Because an abstracter is hired to determine what is in the public record, misstatements of, or failure to include, relevant items contained in that record are obviously examples of acts constituting failure to perform abstracting services in a diligent and reasonably skillful workmanlike manner.
>
> This cause of action arising from breach of the abstracter's contractual duty runs to those persons an abstracter could reasonably foresee as relying on the accuracy of the abstract put into motion. The particular expert-client relationship accruing to a professional contract to certify the condition of the record of title reposes a peculiar trust in an abstracter which runs not only to the original contracting party. There is a clearly foreseeable class of potential injured persons which would obviously include grantees where his or her grantor or any predecessor in title of the grantor has initiated the contract for abstracting services with the abstracter.

391 Mich. at 21–23, 215 N.W.2d at 156–57 (footnotes omitted).

We decline the petitioner's invitation to approve a completely open-ended kind of abstracter's liability based on a duty of care to any and all persons who might foreseeably use and rely on the abstract. The petitioner urges us to adopt this foreseeability theory as a matter of public policy. It is indeed a public policy question, but we do not agree with the wisdom of the policy urged upon us.

We find the attempted analogy to products liability situations unpersuasive. The privity doctrine was gradually eliminated in that field because of a recognition that manufacturers and distributors release products into the commercial marketplace which the ultimate users and consumers thereof are in no position to test, examine, or evaluate for design safety or fitness. The ultimate purchaser relies on the manufacturer for assurance that the product is safe and the manufacturer knows of this reliance. The consumer has no other alternative but reliance on the manufacturer for the fitness of the product. A prospective purchaser of real estate, on the other hand, is not so restricted in his quest for assurances that he is getting what he is paying for. Rather than rely on the abstract of title prepared for the seller or for a previous owner, the purchaser can order his own abstract and an attorney's title opinion based thereupon.

. . .

On the question of whether an abstracter owes a duty of due care to any and all persons who might foreseeably see, use, and rely on the abstract, we believe the analysis made in Ultramares Corp. v. Touche, 255 N.Y. 170, 174 N.E. 441 (1931), pertaining to a negligence action against an accounting firm, is highly persuasive.

> If liability [to third parties] for negligence exists, a thoughtless slip or blunder, the failure to detect a theft or forgery beneath the cover of deceptive entries, may expose accountants to a liability in an indeterminate amount for an indeterminate time to an indeterminate class. The hazards of a business conducted on these terms are so extreme as to enkindle doubt whether a flaw may not exist in the implication of a duty that exposes to these consequences.

Id. at 179–80, 174 N.E. at 444. To hold an abstracter liable to every stranger to the contract of employment who might happen to come to see and rely on the abstract would be like holding a title insurer liable to anyone who knows of the issuance of an insurance policy but who has not paid a premium. For the reasons stated we decline to expose abstracters to liability to any person who foreseeably relies on a negligently prepared abstract to his detriment.

While the policy arguments put forth by the petitioner, and so well expressed in Williams v. Polgar, do not persuade us to adopt open-ended liability for negligence to any foreseeably relying persons, they do convince us that, when an abstract is prepared in the knowledge or under conditions in which an abstracter should reasonably expect that the employer is to provide it to third persons for purposes of inducing those persons to rely on the abstract as evidence of title, the abstracter's contractual duty to perform the service skillfully and diligently runs to the benefit of such known third parties. As was said in Brown v. Sims, 22 Ind.App. 317, 53 N.E. 779 (1899), and quoted by the Michigan Supreme Court in Williams v. Polgar, "It is very well known that the owner of real estate seldom incurs the expense of procuring an abstract of title from an abstracter, except for the purpose of thereby furnishing information to some third person or persons who are to be influenced by the information thus provided." 22 Ind.App. at 325, 53 N.E. at 781.

. . . [W]hen an abstracter knows that his employer or customer is ordering the abstract for the use of a purchaser of the property, reliance on the abstract by the purchaser is "the end and aim of the transaction." We therefore hold that such a known third-party user is owed the same duty and is entitled to the same remedy as the one who ordered the abstract.

It clearly follows that the purchasers here, as intended and known beneficiaries of the contract for the abstract service, may recover damages from the abstract company for its negligent performance. But the purchasers, of course, are not the plaintiffs. The plaintiff in this case, and the petitioner before us, is First American Title Insurance Company. The purchasers of the property, and their lender-mortgagee, have been fully protected from harm and made whole by their title insurer's satisfaction of the judgment that threatened their title and security interests. But we believe it is fair to say, and we so hold, that the title insurer stands in the place of its insured under principles of subrogation. Having held the owner harmless from the negligently omitted title defect, the insurer may pursue the purchaser's cause of action against the abstracter. . . .

The effect of our holding in this case will be to change the law of abstracter's liability, but not so drastically as the petitioner would have us change it. Where the abstracter knows, or should know, that his customer wants the abstract for the use of a prospective purchaser, and the prospect purchases the land relying on the abstract, the abstracter's duty of care runs, as we have said, not only to his customer but to the purchaser. Moreover, others involved in the transaction through their relationship to the purchaser—such as lender-mortgagees, tenants and title insurers—will also be protected where the purchaser's reliance was known or should have been known to the abstracter. But a party into whose hands the abstract falls in connection with a subsequent transaction is not among those to whom the abstracter owes a duty of care.

Applying these new principles of Florida law to the facts of this case, we conclude that the petitioner's complaint stated a cause of action. Of course, our recitation of facts above was based on the allegations of the complaint which we took to be true but which remain to be proven. Thus it remains to be established that the abstracter knew or reasonably should have known that the abstract was ordered for the use of the purchasers or others likely to rely upon it in the near future. This can be shown by inference from circumstances. Most importantly, it must be shown that the fault in the abstract was due to the negligence of the abstracting company or its agent or employee.

Although the district court of appeal was correct in following and applying an established principle of law embodied in a prior and standing precedent from this Court, see Hoffman v. Jones, 280 So.2d 431 (Fla.1973) our holding today necessarily requires that we overturn the district court's decision. We note that the case in conflict, Kovaleski v. Tallahassee Title Co., 363 So.2d 1156 (Fla. 1st DCA 1978), adopted the foreseeability approach of Williams v. Polgar and is therefore also inconsistent with our decision here.

The decision of the district court of appeal is quashed and the case is remanded for further proceedings consistent with this opinion.

It is so ordered.

ALDERMAN, C.J., OVERTON, MCDONALD, EHRLICH and SHAW, JJ., concur.

ADKINS, JUSTICE, Dissenting:

"I would not modify the rule in Sickler v. Indian River Abstract & Guaranty Co., 142 Fla. 528, 195 So. 195 (1940)."

NOTES

1. Shortly after deciding the principal case, the Florida Supreme Court held that a complaint against two abstracters failed to state a cause of action because "[t]he complaint included no allegation that the abstracts were prepared for [plaintiff's] immediate predecessors in title nor that the abstracters furnished the abstracts in the actual or constructive knowledge of their intended prospective use by [plaintiff]." Abstract Corp. v. Fernandez Co., 458 So.2d 766 (Fla.1984).

2. In Chun v. Park, 51 Hawaii 501, 462 P.2d 905 (1969), the court held a title company liable to the buyers and a lending institution where the seller had ordered the title search. The title company was said to owe a duty to those parties, whose identity was known, to use reasonable care in making the search and preparing the certificate of title. The company, however, was liable only for those damages for which its negligence was the proximate cause of the loss. Loss of anticipated profits from resale of the premises and sums expended for plans and specifications for a new building on the land were thus held not to be recoverable. What would be the measure of the plaintiff's damages?

For a lengthy and informative discussion of the liability of an abstract company see Ford v. Guarantee Abstract & Title Co., Inc., 220 Kan. 244, 553 P.2d 254 (1976). Dictum in the case indicates that the company may be liable to all persons who purchase or invest in land relying on an abstract furnished for that purpose. The court also allowed punitive damages against the company for "reckless indifference" toward the rights of the plaintiff.

3. The courts hold abstract companies to high standards of care in the preparation of abstracts for those parties who are entitled to rely on them. For example, in Wichita Great Empire Broadcasting, Inc. v. Gingrich, 4 Kan.App.2d 223, 604 P.2d 281 (1979), the court held that an abstracter was negligent as a matter of law when he relied solely on the judgment docket in the office of the clerk of the district court. The judgment docket was erroneous and the abstracter was liable for the damages caused by his failure to refer to the judgment itself. Similarly, in Tipton County Abstract Co., Inc. v. Heritage Federal Savings and Loan Association, 416 N.E.2d 850 (Ind.App.1981), the court held that a savings and loan association's knowledge, actual or constructive, of a

prior mortgage was irrelevant if the association, in fact, relied on the abstracter's representation that the prior mortgage did not exist.

4. If the contract is silent as to who must furnish the abstract (normally the contract provides that the vendor must do so), who must bear the burden of preparing such a document? See Department of Public Works and Buildings v. Halls, 35 Ill.2d 283, 220 N.E.2d 167 (1966). "The option here was to buy certain property for $25,000. There was no reference therein to an abstract of title or a warranty deed, and it is clear that a seller is under no obligation to furnish an abstract (Turn Verein Eiche v. Kionka, 255 Ill. 392, 99 N.E. 684, 43 L.R.A.,N.S. 44), or a warranty deed (Morris v. Goldthorp, 390 Ill. 186, 60 N.E.2d 857) in the absence of a specific agreement to do so."

SECTION 4. TITLE REGISTRATION (TORRENS SYSTEM)—AN ALTERNATIVE TO THE RECORDING SYSTEM?

The abstract examination system has long been criticized as a wasteful, inefficient method, and many suggestions for improving or replacing it have been forthcoming. The registration of title, first developed by an Australian, Sir Robert Torrens, is the most far-reaching of these reforms. "The basic principle of the system is the registration of the *title* of land, instead of registering as the old system requires, the evidence of title. In the one case only the ultimate fact or conclusion that a certain named party has title to a particular tract of land is registered, and a certificate thereof is delivered to him. In the other the entire evidence, from which proposed purchasers must, at their peril, draw the conclusion, is registered. Necessarily the initial registration of the title—that is, the conclusive establishment of a starting point binding upon all the world—must rest upon judicial proceedings."[1]

The operation of title registration, outlined below, has an appealing simplicity which made it the fair-haired child of the land reformers of the 1920's, but it has never fulfilled its youthful promise and as one writer puts it, "its future is dubious." The system is in operation in only a fraction of the states, and even in those it has not replaced the recording system but exists as an additional method of title assurance. Moreover, it is not compulsory and in the bulk of land transfers purchasers must, therefore, reply upon the recording system. Nor does it operate throughout the state, in many instances; e.g., in Illinois it is available only in Cook County (the Chicago area).

"Explanations of this failure of registration to take hold are manifold. Much is to be attributed to inertia and ignorance, coupled with the fact that registration of land titles is entirely optional. Initial expense and time must have deterred some, and insufficient assurance funds may have discouraged others. Title companies, which feel that

1. State v. Westfall, 85 Minn. 437, 89 N.W. 175 (1902).

they have only to lose by the adoption of the Torrens system, have done much to oppose stringent Torrens legislation, and by their refusal to extend loans or registered titles have prevented the successful operation of the system.[2]

In contrast to the atrophy of the Torrens system in the United States, title registration has had remarkable success in the British Commonwealth. In reply to a question in the House of Commons, Sir Reginald Manningham—Buller, Attorney General of England stated: "Approximately a quarter of all conveyancing transactions in England and Wales are now registered in the Land Registry. Registration of title is compulsory on sale in [a number of counties]. Elsewhere large areas of land are being registered voluntarily. . . . It is intended to extend the compulsory area further as fast as the availability of up-to-date ordinance survey maps and the recruitment and training of staff permits."[3]

The failure of the Torrens system to take root in the United States is not because of widespread satisfaction with the recording system. On the contrary, there have been numerous attempts to reform the present system without abolishing it. The most ambitious attempt has been made by the National Conference of Commissioners on Uniform State Laws and has resulted in the Uniform Simplication of Land Transfers Act (USOLTA), designed to reduce transfer costs for buyers and sellers of real property. See Maggs, Land Records of the Uniform Simplication of Land Transfers Act, 1981 So.Ill.L.J. 491 (1981). Professor Maggs writes: "It (USOLTA) attempts to achieve this reduction (of costs) by reducing the costs of entering and maintaining land records, by eliminating discretionary functions of the recording office in order to open the way to automated recording, by shortening the extent of necessary search and reducing the risk of title defects, such as incompetency of a grantor, which are not shown by the public records. . . . The Act is not a radical reform document, rather it is the culmination of many years of work to repair the existing recording system without supplanting it with a completely different system such as a Torrens Title act." Although USOLTA was approved by the Commissioners in 1976 and by the House of Delegates of the American Bar Association in 1978, it has yet to be adopted *in toto* by any state. The pace of reform in this area is glacial, due to a number of factors, but USOLTA is a step in the right direction.

In connection with the general problems of the American system of title assurance and the impact of technology, see "Land Information Systems For the Twenty-First Century," 15 Real Property, Probate and Trust Journal 890 (1980). This Report of the Committee on the Improvement and Modernization of Land Records states: "The need for land information is essential to social and political innovation. . . . The public depends upon such systems for the marketing, valuation and conveyancing of land, but the system becomes more impractical with each additional transfer of title. . . . Technology will force examina-

2. Handler, Cases and Materials on Vendor and Purchaser 674 (1933).

3. London Times, June 3, 1959, p. 6, Col. 4.

tion of values, preferences, interests and ideals, with reference to definition of rights in land." Why will technology force such an examination? What will the land information system of the future look like? For some light on answers to these questions, see Patterson and Alexander, Land Title Records Modernization: An Update On The RESPA Section 13 Research, 16 Real Property, Probate and Trust Journal 630 (1981). This excellent analysis of research activity in the area of land title records also describes a number of demonstration projects across the nation that hold promise for the future.

FLICK ABSTRACT AND TITLE PRACTICE

Vol. 1, Pages 188–189, 199–201 (2d ed. 1958).

REGISTERED TITLES: IN GENERAL

The certificate system is in world-wide use for the purpose of showing ownership of merchant vessels. Every ship is listed in a national registry. A page in the Register is devoted to each ship and on that page there appears its name and description, the name of the owner, and any encumbrances. A duplicate of this page in the form of a certificate is given to the owner and is his evidence of ownership no matter where he may be. It is usually kept on the ship and accordingly is frequently spoken of in literature as the "ship's papers." Any lien or claim against a ship is required to be noted on the original register page so that it is possible for any interested person to tell at a glance exactly the condition of the title. To make a transfer, the owner assigns the certificate which he has and takes it to the registry office whereupon the old certificate is cancelled, the old page is closed, a new page is opened, and a duplicate certificate of the new page is given to the new owner.

In fact the Torrens system grew out of the fact that its originator, Robert R. Torrens, had been connected with the shipping industry for a number of years before he was appointed Registrar General of the Province of South Australia and given charge of registering all instruments affecting the title to real estate in that province. His experience in his former office led him to speculate on the subject of why the title to a tract of land could not be registered with the same simplicity as the title to a ship. He demonstrated that this was entirely possible and the system for which he drafted the law in Australia has proven to be a very efficient method of keeping track of the ownership of real property and of simplifying every transaction concerned with transferring the title or of using that type of property as security.

EXAMPLE OF REGISTERED TITLE: OWNER'S CERTIFICATE (FORM)

Folio 128208 Volume 10 Page 1205 No. 128208

UNITED STATES OF AMERICA

STATE OF WASHINGTON
KING COUNTY

Owner's Duplicate Certificate of Ownership

FIRST CERTIFICATE OF TITLE

Pursuant to order of the Superior Court of the State of Washington, in and for King County.

STATE OF WASHINGTON, County of King of Seattle STATE OF WASHINGTON	ss.	THIS IS TO CERTIFY THAT Alice S. Potter County of King

is now the owner of the following described land situated in the County of King and State of Washington, to-wit:

Lot Eighteen (18) in Block Eighty-one (81) of a plat of an Addition to the Town (now city) of Seattle as laid off by A. A. Arnheim.

KING COUNTY AUDITOR'S SEAL STATE OF WASHINGTON

subject to the encumbrances, liens and interests noted by the memorial underwritten or indorsed thereon subject to the exceptions and qualifications mentioned in the thirtieth section of "An Act Relating to the Registration and Confirmation of Titles to Land" in the session laws of Washington, for the year 1907.

IN WITNESS WHEREOF, I have hereunto set my hand and affixed the official seal of my office this 17th day of August, A. D., 1958.

James Thurber
Registrar of Titles
King County, Washington.

MEMORIAL OF ENCUMBRANCES, LIENS AND INTERESTS ON THE LANDS IN THIS CERTIFICATE OF TITLE

File No.	Kind	Running in Favor of	Amount
18732	Mortgage	Equitable Life Assurance Society	$104,000
951097	Tax	General	593.10
83942	Judgment	Brink Co.	2,319.58

Date of Instrument			Date of Registration					Signature of Registrar
Mo.	Day	Year	Mo.	Day	Yr.	Hr.	A.M. P.M.	
11	25	1956	12	3	29	11	A.M.	Henry Behnke, Asst. Registrar
		1956			Due and Unpaid			Henry Behnke, Asst. Registrar
5	6	1956	5	6	32	2	P.M.	Henry Behnke, Asst. Registrar

UNITED STATES v. RYAN

United States District Court, D.Minnesota, 1954.
124 F.Supp. 1.

BELL, DISTRICT JUDGE. This suit involves real estate registered under the Torrens System of land registration in Minnesota. It is to establish and enforce certain liens and claims, for the foreclosure thereof and to obtain a judgment and decree of this Court that the defendants Ralph D. Piltz and Edward C. Engdahl purchased the real estate subject to the lien claimed by the United States. . . .

The only issues remaining for determination by the Court involve questions of law. The ultimate issue can be resolved into a single question. Does plaintiff have a lien against the property?

It is the claim of the defendants that the plaintiff in the first instance, did not take proper steps to perfect a lien as required by the laws of the United States and the State of Minnesota, and that, because of its failure properly to file notice of its alleged lien, the plaintiff did not acquire a lien against the property. It is also the claim of the defendants that by virtue of the foreclosure of the prior mortgage held by Minnesota Federal Savings and Loan Association, followed by a decree of the State District Court directing the issuance of a new certificate of title, the plaintiff has lost its right to perfect a claim of lien and is estopped from asserting any interest in the property.

Plaintiff contends that the filing of a notice of tax lien, by name only, in the office of the register of deeds was sufficient to create a lien against property registered under the Torrens System.

As this action involves the title to property registered under the Torrens System of land registration, adopted by the State of Minnesota in 1901, Chapter 237, Laws of Minnesota 1901, and amendments thereof, now Chapter 508, Minnesota Statutes Annotated, a brief history of the Torrens System and its purpose is deemed necessary and in order.

The Torrens System, so called, is a result of an idea and the work of Sir Robert Richard Torrens, born in Ireland in 1814, educated in Trinity College, Dublin, collector of customs at Adelaide in 1841, and afterwards the first premier of South Australia. His idea was to apply the principles of registration of ownership in ships under the English law known as the "Merchants Shipping Act" to registration of title to lands. That is, to have land ownership conclusively evidenced by certificate and thereby made determinable and transferable quickly, cheaply and safely.

The idea gained favor in Australia, resulting in the framing of what became known as the Torrens Act and the adoption of the system in practically all Australia not later than 1870.

The Torrens Law, as originally drafted, has been greatly modified in the statutes enacted in the United States, but the salient feature of registration by certificate has been retained, and the law is usually referred to as the Torrens Law wherever statutes providing for registration of title to land have been enacted in this country. Statutes embodying the basic principles of the Torrens System of land registration by certificate have been enacted in nineteen states of the United States.

The registration of the title to property results in the transferring of a title from the recording act system to the certificate system, provided by the Torrens Law, by a judicial proceeding in the nature of a suit to quiet title against all persons, both known and unknown, who could by any possibility assert an adverse interest. In the State of Minnesota the registration of titles is under the jurisdiction of the District Court. The original registration, and all subsequent involuntary transfers of title, is accomplished by obtaining a decree of the Court followed by the issuance of a certificate of title thereunder.

"The official certificate will always show the state of the title and the person in whom it is vested. The basic principle of the system is the registration of the title to the land, instead of registering, as under the old system, the evidence of such title." In re Bickel, 301 Ill. 484, 134 N.E. 76, 80.

In the case of an involuntary transfer, such as a mortgage foreclosure, there is a radical difference from the procedure which applies to a voluntary transfer in that the registrar cannot, upon the filing with him of documents purporting to make an involuntary transfer, recognize any such transfer unless and until he receives an order of court directing the action which he shall take. These orders are all based upon a final adjudication determining the rights of all parties involved. The conclusiveness of the certificate is based upon an order or decree of court and upon statutes of limitation. M.S.A. §§ 508.26 and 508.28. It is clearly evident that, when a certificate of title has been issued by the registrar of titles pursuant to a decree of the District Court the decree is binding upon the entire world, subject only to the right of appeal allowed for a period of six months by M.S,A. § 508.28.

The purpose of the Torrens Law is to establish an indefeasible title free from any and all rights or claims not registered with the registrar of titles, with certain exceptions not important here, M.S.A. § 508.25, to the end that anyone may deal with such property with the assurance that the only rights or claims of which he need take notice are those registered. The law was framed to accomplish that purpose, and it establishes rules in respect to registered land which differ widely from those which apply in case of unregistered land. It provides that the holder of a certificate of title to registered land "shall hold the same free from all encumbrances and adverse claims," excepting only those noted on the last certificate of title.

At the outset it should be pointed out that under 26 U.S.C.A. § 3672, as amended in 1942, it is provided that a federal tax lien shall not be valid as against any mortgagee, pledgee, purchaser or judgment creditor until notice thereof has been filed by the Collector. The pertinent part of this section is:

"a. Invalidity of lien without notice. Such lien shall not be valid as against any mortgagee, pledgee, purchaser, or judgment creditor until notice thereof has been filed by the collector—

"(1) . . . In the office in which the filing of such notice is authorized by the law of the State or Territory in which the property subject to the lien is situated, whenever the State or Territory has by law authorized the filing of such notice in an office within the State or Territory".

The State of Minnesota has by statute authorized the filing of such notices, and the laws of the State of Minnesota must be complied with if a valid lien is to be obtained in any case. Because the property involved in this action is registered property, the laws of the State of Minnesota which deal with registered property have application and are controlling here.

M.S.A. § 272.48, provides as follows:

"The filing and recording in the office of the register of deeds of any county in this state of notices of liens for taxes due the United States and discharges and releases of such liens is hereby authorized."

M.S.A. § 508.48, provides as follows:

"Every conveyance, lien, attachment, order, decree, or judgment, or other instrument or proceeding, which would affect the title to unregistered land under existing laws, if recorded, or filed with the register of deeds, shall, in like manner, affect the title to registered land if filed and registered with the registrar in the county where the real estate is situated, and shall be notice to all persons from the time of such registering or filing."

M.S.A. § 508.64, provides as follows:

"Attachments and *liens of every description* upon registered land shall be continued, reduced, discharged, and dissolved by any method sufficient therefor in the case of unregistered land. All certificates, writings, or other instruments permitted or required by law to be filed or recorded to give effect to the enforcement, continuance, reduction, discharge, or dissolution of attachments *or other liens* upon unregistered land or to give notice of the same, shall, in the case of like liens upon registered land, be filed with the registrar."

M.S.A. § 508.30, provides as follows:

"Registers of deeds shall be the registrars of titles in their respective counties."

The form of certificate of title prescribed by M.S.A. § 508.25, contains six exceptions. The plaintiff contends that one of the exceptions applies to the issue involved herein. That exception reads as follows:

"(1) Liens, claims, or rights arising or existing under the laws or the constitution of the United States, which the state cannot require to appear of record".

However, the claim of lien involved in this action is not such a lien or claim, in that 26 U.S.C.A. § 3672, provides a method by which the State may require that it be made a matter of local record and if this is not done a federal tax lien shall not be valid as against any mortgagee, pledgee, purchaser, or judgment creditor, namely not unless nor until notice thereof has been filed by the collector in accordance with the laws of the State.

Under said statutes, M.S.A. §§ 508.48 and 508.64, in order to effect the registration by memorial upon a certificate of title the lien instrument must designate the land affected by the lien or claim of lien, such as is possible in the case of mechanics' lien claims and judgment entries creating specific liens on described real estate, or the party filing a claim of general lien, such as a personal judgment, or a federal tax lien, must designate the land upon which it is claimed so that the registrar may know the certificate of title upon which it can be memorialized. The mere filing of a notice, by debtor's name only, in the office of the register of deeds cannot, and does not, create a lien on registered land. It is plainly evident to this Court that the liens authorized by M.S.A. § 272.48, to be filed with the register of deeds, must, in the case of registered property, be filed with the register of deeds in his capacity as registrar of titles, and to be effective, they must be noted as memorials on the certificate of title covering the specific parcel of registered land intended to be affected by such filing, M.S.A. §§ 508.48 and 508.64.

The office of the register of deeds, in Minnesota, is made up of two component parts. The office of the register of deeds as originally created by Chapter 21, Sec. 1, Laws of Minnesota, 1849, which has to do with the recording of all instruments affecting unregistered property, and the office of the registrar of titles created by Chapter 237, Laws of Minnesota 1901, which is part and parcel of the original office, but which office has special functions to perform in connection with property registered under the Torrens System. . . .

An identical situation is presented in Minnesota in connection with old age assistance liens. . . .

The same situation exists with reference to the Minnesota Statutes dealing with mechanics' liens, M.S.A. §§ 514.08 and 514.12. . . .

Plaintiff contends that "Minnesota cannot require the United States to memorialize notice of federal tax lien on a certificate of title", and that, "it can do no more than designate in what office the notice of lien shall be filed". As hereinbefore pointed out Minnesota has designated the office in which the notice shall be filed, and, by virtue of the statutory procedure relative to the operation of that office in respect to registered titles, the notice must contain a description of the land on which the lien is claimed, and the only method for filing it is by memorializing it on the certificate of title. . . .

The Supreme Court of the State of Minnesota has taken a very definite stand in upholding the validity of titles registered under the Torrens System, and in particular with reference to the necessity for filing notices of claim of lien with the registrar of titles.

"A memorial of a mortgage, lien, or other charge against registered land, entered by the registrar of titles upon the original certificate of title in his office and upon the owner's duplicate, becomes a part of the certificate of title and is made conclusive evidence of the matters therein contained." Horgan v. Sargent, 182 Minn. 100, 233 N.W. 866.

"Unregistered deeds or contracts do not affect Torrens titles nor create any interest in land. The Torrens Law intends that all titles registered thereunder shall be free from all unregistered rights or claims except those specifically named . . ..

"The purpose of the Torrens Law is to establish an indefeasible title free from any and all rights or claims not registered with the registrar of titles, with certain unimportant exceptions, to the end that any one may deal with such property with the assurance that the only rights or claims of which he need take notice are those so registered. The law was framed to accomplish that purpose; and it establishes rules in respect to registered land which differed widely from those which apply in the case of unregistered land. It provides that the holder of a certificate of title to registered land 'shall hold the same free from all incumbrances, and adverse claims, excepting only' those noted on the last certificate of title and certain other specified rights or claims not important here. . . .

"Torrens Law abrogates doctrine of constructive notice, except as to matters noted on certificate". In re Juran, 178 Minn. 55, 226 N.W. 201. See also, Cook v. Luettich, 191 Minn. 6, 252 N.W. 649, and Carl v. DeToffol, 223 Minn. 24, 25 N.W.2d 479.

In State ex rel. Douglas v. Westfall, 85 Minn. 437, 89 N.W. 175, 176, 57 L.R.A. 297, the Court held that the Laws 1901, c. 237, providing for the Torrens System of registering land titles, is not unconstitutional in that it is special legislation; nor that it deprives the owner of his interest in land without due process of law, in violation of both state and federal constitutions. In this case the Court said:

"Any person who has any interest in the land, and who has not actually been served or notified of the filing of the application, may at any time within 60 days from the entry of such decree appear, and file his sworn answer, providing no innocent purchaser for value has acquired an interest. If there is any such purchaser, the decree of registration remains in full force forever, subject only to the right of appeal, ... Every person receiving a certificate of title and every subsequent purchaser in good faith takes the same free from all incumbrances, except such as are noted thereon."

In Kane v. State, 237 Minn. 261, 55 N.W.2d 333, 337, the Court held that a purchaser was not bound by restrictions which were not noted on the certificate of title. The Court said:

"The question before us is whether a good-faith purchaser, for value, of registered land obtains such land free and clear of a restrictive covenant or encumbrance which is not referred to in the certificate of title under the memorial of estates, easements, or charges on the land described. In other words, must a purchaser of registered land, in addition to being charged with notice of estates, mortgages, liens, charges, and interests noted on the previous owner's certificate of title, also go directly to the plat to ascertain whether there may be any other restrictive covenants or encumbrances noted on the plat which are not shown on the certificate of title? Under § 508.25, it is our opinion that he is not required to do so. It seems to us that if we were to hold otherwise, under the facts and circumstances of the instant case, it would tend to create confusion which would jeopardize the stability and purpose of the Torrens law. The manifest purpose of the Torrens system, as stated in 3 Devlin, Real Estate, Deeds (3 ed.) § 1439, is—'first, to secure by a decree of court, or other similar proceeding, a title which will be impregnable against any attack, and, when this title is once determined, to provide that all subsequent transfers, encumbrances, or proceedings affecting the title shall be placed on a page of the register and marked on the memorial of title. A purchaser may accept this memorial as truly stating the title, and may disregard any claim not so appearing.' "

The United States is not exempt from the provisions of the state statutes. The laws of the United States definitely provide that the tax lien here asserted will not become a valid lien unless notice thereof is filed as by state law prescribed. A state law affecting the title to property must be followed, and is binding upon the United States. See Custer v. McCutcheon, 283 U.S. 514, 51 S.Ct. 530, 75 L.Ed. 1239. . . .

For more than fifty years the people of the State of Minnesota have been buying and selling properties registered under the Torrens System with full and complete reliance upon the certificate of title and in the firm belief that the certificate of title disclosed the true nature of the status of the title, and that they were amply and fully protected under the laws of the State of Minnesota. A judgment in this action, in favor of the plaintiff, having as it does a claim of lien which was not filed in accordance with the laws of the State of Minnesota, and which claim of lien was never at any time filed with the registrar of titles and noted as a memorial on the certificate of title, would completely defeat what has been a permanent rule of property in Minnesota for more than half a century.

To sustain the Torrens System of registration in Minnesota will not burden the United States. It could have established a lien on the land involved by merely following the plain and simple requirements of the applicable federal and state statutes. This it did not do.

The Court, therefore, concludes that the defendants Minnesota Federal Savings and Loan Association, Ralph D. Peltz and Edward C. Engdahl are entitled to a summary judgment of dismissal, and that the motion of the plaintiff for a summary judgment should be denied. It is so ordered.

NOTES

1. The principal case was reversed in United States v. Rasmuson, 253 F.2d 944 (8th Cir. 1958). The Circuit Court of Appeals for the Eighth Circuit held that under statutes establishing a federal lien upon all property and rights to property, whether real or personal, belonging to a taxpayer at the time an assessment list against him is received by the Collector of Internal Revenue, Torrens-title property was subject to such a lien, without regard to requirements of state statutes for memorializing. The Collector of Internal Revenue is a tough guy to beat even by the Torrens system!

2. The basic idea of the Torrens System is that the certificate of registration is more than just evidence of title; it *is* title. Any claims not noted on the memorial are invalid as against a subsequent purchaser. (There may be statutory exceptions to this broad statement, such as local real estate tax liens.) A little reflection, however, will disclose situations in which the absolute validity of the certificate will run counter to established principles of law, such as the operation of constructive or actual notice. Suppose that a stranger to the registered title is in possession at the time the original certificate is issued. Assume that a power company has electric lines on the property but lacks a properly recorded deed of the easement, and that its interest is purportedly foreclosed at the registration hearing without any notice to the company. Should the power company lose its interest in the land as against a subsequent purchaser for value?

Or suppose that after the initial registration the owner makes a lease to X, who does not register the nonfreehold estate but does take possession, so that a subsequent purchaser could readily learn of the lease. Who should be preferred, X or a subsequent purchaser for value who claims to take free of the lease? Should it make any difference whether the subsequent purchaser actually knew of the lease or had only constructive notice?

Assume that you are a judge and must pass on these situations as matters of first impression. What are the various policy considerations which you must take into account in reaching your decision? How would you decide them?

For cases in which courts wrestled with similar problems see Follette v. Pacific Light & Power Corp., 189 Cal. 193, 208 P. 295 (1922); Abrahamson v. Sundman, 174 Minn. 22, 218 N.W. 246 (1928); Killam v. March, 316 Mass. 646, 55 N.E.2d 945 (1944).

In Tetrault v. Bruscoe, 398 Mass. 454, 497 N.E.2d 275 (1986), the Donnises, owners of a tract of land, filed a petition in the Land Court to register and confirm their title. As abutting owners, the Bruscoes were notified by registered mail of the registration petition, but they made no objection and raised no claims concerning the land. The Donnises' title was confirmed and registered, and no encumbrances involving Bruscoes were listed on the certificate of title. Thereafter, the Tetraults purchased a seven-acre lot of the registered land from the Donnises, obtaining a transfer certificate of title. The Bruscoes then claimed a right to use a roadway across the lot, and the Tetraults filed suit to enjoin the Bruscoes from doing so. Defendants claimed a prescriptive easement antedating registration of the land by the Donnises. The trial court, without finding that plaintiffs had prior actual knowledge of the roadway or defendants' use of it, held that plaintiffs nevertheless had acquired their lot subject to defendants' preexisting unregistered and unrecorded easement. On appeal, the Supreme Judicial Court reversed: "The Bruscoes do not contend that the original registration decree was procured by the plaintiffs' predecessor in title through fraud. Therefore, that decree extinguished the Bruscoes' easement as against the plaintiffs' predecessors. The Bruscoes should not be able to revive their interest in the land by the happenstance that a subsequent purchaser of the property had knowledge at some unascertainable time of the easement's prior existence."

3. Whatever the virtues of the Torrens System, and they are many if we were writing on a clean slate, it is now relatively clear that Torrens is not a viable alternative to the antiquated recording system in the United States. "The areas of largest use in the United States are Hennepin County Minnesota (Minneapolis), with 40% to 45% of the parcels registered under the system; Cook County, Illinois, with about one-third of the land registered; the Southern District Registry of Middlesex County, Massachusetts (Cambridge) with about 20% registered; and Hawaii, with about 45% registered. The system is legislatively authorized today in Colorado, Georgia, Hawaii, Illinois, Massachusetts, Minnesota, New York, North Carolina, Ohio, Virginia, and Washington, but in several of those states activity under it is virtually nil."[4]

California once had the system but a judgment against the state assurance fund left the system in debt. See Gill v. Johnson, 21 Cal. App.2d 649, 69 P.2d 1016 (1937). New registrations virtually ceased after this decision and the statute itself was repealed in 1955.

The system still has its advocates as well as its opponents. See Fiflis, English Registered Conveyancing: A Study in Effective Land Transfer, 59 N.W.L.Rev. 468 (1964) and Shick and Plotkin, Torrens in the United States (1978). The latter book's authors were employed as consultants to the title insurance industry, historically opposed to Torrens for obvious reasons. Of course, no system is perfect and even if Torrens did sweep the nation it would leave a detritus of unresolved issues. See, for example, Hoffman v. Schroeder, 38 Ill.App.2d 20, 186 N.E.2d 381 (1962) for an imaginative scam worked out by a fraud-bent husband.

These brief materials on Torrens are included here for two reasons. First, you may practice in an area of the nation where the system is in use and, while you will then need to study it in more detail, you should be aware of its existence and understand the general principles. Second, it is a valuable example of comparative methods of title assurance (after all, it is in wide use in most English-speaking nations except the United States) and, who knows, it may be the wave of the future in the People's Republic of China or on the moon if we ever move to that new frontier. In the meantime, the search for a truly efficient system of title assurance goes on!

4. Nelson and Whitman, Real Estate Transfer, Finance and Development 213 (2d ed. 1981). See also pages 212–215 of Nelson and Whitman for a good, brief description of the Torrens System.

SECTION 5. TITLE INSURANCE

FITCH, ABSTRACTS AND TITLES TO REAL PROPERTY

Vol. 2, Pages 445–446 (1954).

TITLE INSURANCE GENERALLY

Due to the hidden risks involved in the purchase of a title or the taking of a mortgage thereon, there has been in recent years a large increase in the use of title insurance. The largest growth in the use of title insurance has been in the larger urban communities where the buyer or mortgagee, or his attorney, is not so apt to know the seller or mortgagor personally; but the advantages of this form of title protection have also become apparent in the smaller urban communities and in rural areas throughout the United States.

In connection with any title, the following dangers must be considered:

(1) defects in the title of record;

(2) hidden defects not disclosed by the record;

(3) cost of defending the title against attack.

Some of the hidden defects, also called hidden risks, no notice of which will ordinarily appear of record, are:

(1) the disability of a grantor in the chain of title;

(2) forgery of a deed, mortgage or other instrument in the chain of title;

(3) fraudulent representation of marital status by a grantor in the chain of title;

(4) mistaken identity of a record titleholder and a grantor due to similar or identical names;

(5) errors in the record;

(6) errors in the examination of the record;

(7) undisclosed heirs;

(8) exercise of a power of attorney after death of the creator of the power;

(9) defects in conveyances in the chain of title due to lack of delivery.

To these risks should be added two others; namely, unjustifiable attack, and interpretation. In the former case, one having a good title may be forced to pay the expense of defending it, though the ultimate decision is in his favor. In the latter case, differences of opinion may arise between lawyers successively examining the abstract for successive buyers or mortgagees in the chain of title. Thus, a lawyer examining the title at the present time will be forced to take a conservative view of the matters of construction arising in the chain of title. If he fails to raise an objection, a subsequent examiner of the abstract may raise it. Thus, partition suits, suits to quiet title, and suits to construe wills are often required.

In order to meet these problems, many persons buy title insurance policies. The title may be purchased with confidence that the insurer will not, in subsequent transactions, raise objections it has previously waived. Further, title companies undertake to defend the title of the person named as owner in the policy, if the attack arises out of a defect which is not excepted by the terms of the policy.

AMERICAN LAND TITLE ASSOCIATION
OWNER'S POLICY (10-21-87)

CHICAGO TITLE INSURANCE COMPANY

SUBJECT TO THE EXCLUSIONS FROM COVERAGE, THE EXCEPTIONS FROM COVERAGE CONTAINED IN SCHEDULE B AND THE CONDITIONS AND STIPULATIONS, CHICAGO TITLE INSURANCE COMPANY, a Missouri corporation, herein called the Company, insures, as of Date of Policy shown in Schedule A, against loss or damage, not exceeding the Amount of Insurance stated in Schedule A, sustained or incurred by the insured by reason of:

1. Title to the estate or interest described in Schedule A being vested other than as stated therein;
2. Any defect in or lien or encumbrance on the title;
3. Unmarketability of the title;
4. Lack of a right of access to and from the land.

The Company will also pay the costs, attorneys' fees and expenses incurred in defense of the title, as insured, but only to the extent provided in the Conditions and Stipulations.

In Witness Whereof, CHICAGO TITLE INSURANCE COMPANY has caused this policy to be signed and sealed as of Date of Policy shown in Schedule A, the policy to become valid when countersigned by an authorized signatory.

CHICAGO TITLE INSURANCE COMPANY
By:

SPECIMEN

President

CHICAGO TITLE INSURANCE COMPANY CORPORATE SEAL

By:

Secretary

[F5110]

ALTA Owner's Policy (10-21-87)

EXCLUSIONS FROM COVERAGE

The following matters are expressly excluded from the coverage of this policy and the Company will not pay loss or damage, costs, attorneys' fees or expenses which arise by reason of:

1. (a) Any law, ordinance or governmental regulation (including but not limited to building and zoning laws, ordinances, or regulations) restricting, regulating, prohibiting or relating to (i) the occupancy, use, or enjoyment of the land; (ii) the character, dimensions or location of any improvement now or hereafter erected on the land; (iii) a separation in ownership or a change in the dimensions or area of the land or any parcel of which the land is or was a part; or (iv) environmental protection, or the effect of any violation of these laws, ordinances or governmental regulations, except to the extent that a notice of the enforcement thereof or a notice of a defect, lien or encumbrance resulting from a violation or alleged violation affecting the land has been recorded in the public records at Date of Policy.

(b) Any governmental police power not excluded by (a) above, except to the extent that a notice of the exercise thereof or a notice of a defect, lien or encumbrance resulting from a violation or alleged violation affecting the land has been recorded in the public records at Date of Policy.

2. Rights of eminent domain unless notice of the exercise thereof has been recorded in the public records at Date of Policy, but not excluding from coverage any taking which has occurred prior to Date of Policy which would be binding on the rights of a purchaser for value without knowledge.

3. Defects, liens, encumbrances, adverse claims or other matters:

(a) created, suffered, assumed or agreed to by the insured claimant;

(b) not known to the Company, not recorded in the public records at Date of Policy, but known to the insured claimant and not disclosed in writing to the Company by the insured claimant prior to the date the insured claimant became an insured under this policy;

(c) resulting in no loss or damage to the insured claimant;

(d) attaching or created subsequent to Date of Policy; or

(e) resulting in loss or damage which would not have been sustained if the insured claimant had paid value for the estate or interest insured by this policy. [F5111]

OWNERS

SCHEDULE A

FORM 3529

1 OFFICE FILE NUMBER	2 POLICY NUMBER	3 DATE OF POLICY	4 AMOUNT OF INSURANCE

1. Name of Insured:

2. The estate or interest in the land which is covered by this policy is:

3. Title to the estate or interest in the land is vested in:

4. The land referred to in this policy is described as follows:

Countersigned SPECIMEN

Authorized Signatory

This Policy valid only if Schedule B is attached.

[F5112]

OWNERS

FORM 3528

SCHEDULE B

Policy Number ______________________
Owners

EXCEPTIONS FROM COVERAGE

This policy does not insure against loss or damage (and the Company will not pay costs, attorneys' fees or expenses) which arise by reason of:

General Exceptions:

1. Rights or claims of parties in possession not shown by the public records.
2. Encroachments, overlaps, boundary line disputes, and any other matters which would be disclosed by an accurate survey and inspection of the premises.
3. Easements or claims of easements not shown by the public records.
4. Any lien, or right to a lien, for services, labor, or material heretofore or hereafter furnished, imposed by law and not shown by the public records.
5. Taxes or special assessments which are not shown as existing liens by the public records.

Countersigned

SPECIMEN

____
Authorized Signatory

Schedule B of this Policy consists of pages. [F5113]

CONDITIONS AND STIPULATIONS

1. DEFINITION OF TERMS

The following terms when used in this policy mean:

(a) "insured": the insured named in Schedule A, and, subject to any rights or defenses the Company would have had against the named insured, those who succeed to the interest of the named insured by operation of law as distinguished from purchase including, but not limited to, heirs, distributees, devisees, survivors, personal representatives, next of kin, or corporate or fiduciary successors.

(b) "insured claimant": an insured claiming loss or damage.

(c) "knowledge" or "known": actual knowledge, not constructive knowledge or notice which may be imputed to an insured by reason of the public records as defined in this policy or any other records which impart constructive notice of matters affecting the land.

(d) "land": the land described or referred to in Schedule A, and improvements affixed thereto which by law constitute real property. The term "land" does not include any property beyond the lines of the area described or referred to in Schedule A, nor any right, title, interest, estate or easement in abutting streets, roads, avenues, alleys, lanes, ways or waterways, but nothing herein shall modify or limit the extent to which a right of access to and from the land is insured by this policy.

(e) "mortgage": mortgage, deed of trust, trust deed, or other security instrument.

(f) "public records": records established under state statutes at Date of Policy for the purpose of imparting constructive notice of matters relating to real property to purchasers for value and without knowledge. With respect to Section 1(a)(iv) of the Exclusions From Coverage, "public records" shall also include environmental protection liens filed in the records of the clerk of the United States district court for the district in which the land is located.

(g) "unmarketability of the title": an alleged or apparent matter affecting the title to the land, not excluded or excepted from coverage, which would entitle a purchaser of the estate or interest described in Schedule A to be released from the obligation to purchase by virtue of a contractual condition requiring the delivery of marketable title.

2. CONTINUATION OF INSURANCE AFTER CONVEYANCE OF TITLE

The coverage of this policy shall continue in force as of Date of Policy in favor of an insured only so long as the insured retains an estate or interest in the land, or holds an indebtedness secured by a purchase money mortgage given by a purchaser from the insured, or only so long as the insured shall have liability by reason of covenants of warranty made by the insured in any transfer or conveyance of the estate or interest. This policy shall not continue in force in favor of any purchaser from the insured of either (i) an estate or interest in the land, or (ii) an indebtedness secured by a purchase money mortgage given to the insured.

3. NOTICE OF CLAIM TO BE GIVEN BY INSURED CLAIMANT

The insured shall notify the Company promptly in writing (i) in case of any litigation as set forth in Section 4(a) below, (ii) in case knowledge shall come to an insured hereunder of any claim of title or interest which is adverse to the title to the estate or interest, as insured, and which might cause loss or damage for which the Company may be liable by virtue of this policy, or (iii) if title to the estate or interest, as insured, is rejected as unmarketable. If prompt notice shall not be given to the Company, then as to the insured all liability of the Company shall terminate with regard to the matter or matters for which prompt notice is required; provided, however, that failure to notify the Company shall in no case prejudice the rights of any insured under this policy unless the Company shall be prejudiced by the failure and then only to the extent of the prejudice.

4. DEFENSE AND PROSECUTION OF ACTIONS; DUTY OF INSURED CLAIMANT TO COOPERATE

(a) Upon written request by the insured and subject to the options contained in Section 6 of these Conditions and Stipulations, the Company, at its own cost and without unreasonable delay, shall provide for the defense of an insured in litigation in which any third party asserts a claim adverse to the title or interest as insured, but only as to those stated causes of action alleging a defect, lien or encumbrance or other matter insured against by this policy. The Company shall have the right to select counsel of its choice (subject to the right of the insured to object for reasonable cause) to represent the insured as to those stated causes of action and shall not be liable for and will not pay the fees of any other counsel. The Company will not pay any fees, costs or expenses incurred by the insured in the defense of those causes of action which allege matters not insured against by this policy.

(b) The Company shall have the right, at its own cost, to institute and prosecute any action or proceeding or to do any other act which in its opinion may be necessary or desirable to establish the title to the estate or interest, as insured, or to prevent or reduce loss or damage to the insured. The Company may take any appropriate action under the terms of this policy, whether or not it shall be liable hereunder, and shall not thereby concede liability or waive any provision of this policy. If the Company shall exercise its rights under this paragraph. it shall do so diligently.

(c) Whenever the Company shall have brought an action or interposed a defense as required or permitted by the provisions of this policy, the Company may pursue any litigation to final determination by a court of competent jurisdiction and expressly reserves the right, in its sole discretion, to appeal from any adverse judgment or order.

(d) In all cases where this policy permits or requires the Company to prosecute or provide for the defense of any action or proceeding, the insured shall secure to the Company the right to so prosecute or provide defense in the action or proceeding, and all appeals therein, and permit the Company to use, at its option, the name of the insured for this purpose. Whenever requested by the Company, the insured, at the Company's expense, shall give the Company all reasonable aid (i) in any action or proceeding, securing evidence, obtaining witnesses, prosecuting or defending the action or proceeding, or effecting settlement, and (ii) in any other lawful act which in the opinion of the Company may be necessary or desirable to establish the title to the estate or interest as insured. If the Company is prejudiced by the failure of the insured to furnish the required cooperation, the Company's obligations to the insured under the policy shall terminate, including any liability or obligation to defend, prosecute, or continue any litigation, with regard to the matter or matters requiring such cooperation.

5. PROOF OF LOSS OR DAMAGE

In addition to and after the notices required under Section 3 of these Conditions and Stipulations have been provided the Company, a proof of loss or damage signed and sworn to by the insured claimant shall be furnished to the Company within 90 days after the insured claimant shall ascertain the facts giving rise to the loss or damage. The proof of loss or damage shall describe the defect in, or lien or encumbrance on the title, or other matter insured against by this policy which constitutes the basis of loss or damage and shall state, to the extent possible, the basis of calculating the amount of the loss or damage. If the Company is prejudiced by the failure of the insured claimant to provide the required proof of loss or damage, the Company's obligations to the insured under the policy shall terminate, including any liability or obligation to defend, prosecute, or continue any litigation, with regard to the matter or matters requiring such proof of loss or damage.

In addition, the insured claimant may reasonably be required to submit to examination under oath by any authorized representative of the Company and shall produce for examination, inspection and copying, at such reasonable times and places as may be designated by any authorized representative of the Company, all records, books, ledgers, checks, correspondence and memoranda, whether bearing a date before or after Date of Policy, which reasonably pertain to the loss or damage. Further, if requested by any authorized representative of the Company, the insured claimant shall grant its permission, in writing, for any authorized representative of the Company to examine, inspect and copy all records, books, ledgers, checks, correspondence and memoranda in the custody or control of a third party, which reasonably pertain to the loss or damage. All information designated as confidential by the insured claimant provided to the Company pursuant to this Section shall not be disclosed to others unless, in the reasonable judgment of the Company, it is necessary in the administration of the claim. Failure of the insured claimant to submit for examination under oath, produce other reasonably requested information or grant permission to secure reasonably necessary information from third parties as required in this paragraph shall terminate any liability of the Company under this policy as to that claim.

6. OPTIONS TO PAY OR OTHERWISE SETTLE CLAIMS; TERMINATION OF LIABILITY

In case of a claim under this policy, the Company shall have the following additional options:

(a) To Pay or Tender Payment of the Amount of Insurance.

To pay or tender payment of the amount of insurance under this policy together with any costs, attorneys' fees and expenses incurred by the insured claimant, which were authorized by the Company, up to the time of payment or tender of payment and which the Company is obligated to pay.

Upon the exercise by the Company of this option, all liability and obligations to the insured under this policy, other than to make the payment required, shall terminate, including any liability or obligation to defend, prosecute, or continue any litigation, and the policy shall be surrendered to the Company for cancellation.

(b) To Pay or Otherwise Settle With Parties Other than the Insured or With the Insured Claimant.

(i) to pay or otherwise settle with other parties for or in the name of an insured claimant any claim insured against under this policy, together with any costs, attorneys' fees and expenses incurred by the insured claimant which were authorized by the Company up to the time of payment and which the Company is obligated to pay; or

(ii) to pay or otherwise settle with the insured claimant the loss or damage provided for under this policy, together with any costs, attorneys' fees and expenses incurred by the insured claimant which were authorized by the Company up to the time of payment and which the Company is obligated to pay.

[F5115]

Upon the exercise by the Company of either of the options provided for in paragraphs (b)(i) or (ii), the Company's obligations to the insured under this policy for the claimed loss or damage, other than the payments required to be made, shall terminate, including any liability or obligation to defend, prosecute or continue any litigation.

7. DETERMINATION, EXTENT OF LIABILITY AND COINSURANCE

This policy is a contract of indemnity against actual monetary loss or damage sustained or incurred by the insured claimant who has suffered loss or damage by reason of matters insured against by this policy and only to the extent herein described.

(a) The liability of the Company under this policy shall not exceed the least of:

(i) the Amount of Insurance stated in Schedule A; or,

(ii) the difference between the value of the insured estate or interest as insured and the value of the insured estate or interest subject to the defect, lien or encumbrance insured against by this policy.

(b) In the event the Amount of Insurance stated in Schedule A at the Date of Policy is less than 80 percent of the value of the insured estate or interest or the full consideration paid for the land, whichever is less, or if subsequent to the Date of Policy an improvement is erected on the land which increases the value of the insured estate or interest by at least 20 percent over the Amount of Insurance stated in Schedule A, then this Policy is subject to the following:

(i) where no subsequent improvement has been made, as to any partial loss, the Company shall only pay the loss pro rata in the proportion that the amount of insurance at Date of Policy bears to the total value of the insured estate or interest at Date of Policy; or

(ii) where a subsequent improvement has been made, as to any partial loss, the Company shall only pay the loss pro rata in the proportion that 120 percent of the Amount of Insurance stated in Schedule A bears to the sum of the Amount of Insurance stated in Schedule A and the amount expended for the improvement.

The provisions of this paragraph shall not apply to costs, attorneys' fees and expenses for which the Company is liable under this policy, and shall only apply to that portion of any loss which exceeds, in the aggregate, 10 percent of the Amount of Insurance stated in Schedule A.

(c) The Company will pay only those costs, attorneys' fees and expenses incurred in accordance with Section 4 of these Conditions and Stipulations.

8. APPORTIONMENT

If the land described in Schedule A consists of two or more parcels which are not used as a single site, and a loss is established affecting one or more of the parcels but not all, the loss shall be computed and settled on a pro rata basis as if the amount of insurance under this policy was divided pro rata as to the value on Date of Policy of each separate parcel to the whole, exclusive of any improvements made subsequent to Date of Policy, unless a liability or value has otherwise been agreed upon as to each parcel by the Company and the insured at the time of the issuance of this policy and shown by an express statement or by an endorsement attached to this policy.

9. LIMITATION OF LIABILITY

(a) If the Company establishes the title, or removes the alleged defect, lien or encumbrance, or cures the lack of a right of access to or from the land, or cures the claim of unmarketability of title, all as insured, in a reasonably diligent manner by any method, including litigation and the completion of any appeals therefrom, it shall have fully performed its obligations with respect to that matter and shall not be liable for any loss or damage caused thereby.

(b) In the event of any litigation, including litigation by the Company or with the Company's consent, the Company shall have no liability for loss or damage until there has been a final determination by a court of competent jurisdiction, and disposition of all appeals therefrom, adverse to the title as insured.

(c) The Company shall not be liable for loss or damage to any insured for liability voluntarily assumed by the insured in settling any claim or suit without the prior written consent of the Company.

10. REDUCTION OF INSURANCE; REDUCTION OR TERMINATION OF LIABILITY

All payments under this policy, except payments made for costs, attorneys' fees and expenses, shall reduce the amount of the insurance pro tanto.

11. LIABILITY NONCUMULATIVE

It is expressly understood that the amount of insurance under this policy shall be reduced by any amount the Company may pay under any policy insuring a mortgage to which exception is taken in Schedule B or to which the insured has agreed, assumed, or taken subject, or which is hereafter executed by an insured and which is a charge or lien on the estate or interest described or referred to in Schedule A, and the amount so paid shall be deemed a payment under this policy to the insured owner.

12. PAYMENT OF LOSS

(a) No payment shall be made without producing this policy for endorsement of the payment unless the policy has been lost or destroyed, in which case proof of loss or destruction shall be furnished to the satisfaction of the Company.

(b) When liability and the extent of loss or damage has been definitely fixed in accordance with these Conditions and Stipulations, the loss or damage shall be payable within 30 days thereafter.

13. SUBROGATION UPON PAYMENT OR SETTLEMENT

(a) The Company's Right of Subrogation.

Whenever the Company shall have settled and paid a claim under this policy, all right of subrogation shall vest in the Company unaffected by any act of the insured claimant.

The Company shall be subrogated to and be entitled to all rights and remedies which the insured claimant would have had against any person or property in respect to the claim had this policy not been issued. If requested by the Company, the insured claimant shall transfer to the Company all rights and remedies against any person or property necessary in order to perfect this right of subrogation. The insured claimant shall permit the Company to sue, compromise or settle in the name of the insured claimant and to use the name of the insured claimant in any transaction or litigation involving these rights or remedies.

If a payment on account of a claim does not fully cover the loss of the insured claimant, the Company shall be subrogated to these rights and remedies in the proportion which the Company's payment bears to the whole amount of the loss.

If loss should result from any act of the insured claimant, as stated above, that act shall not void this policy, but the Company, in that event, shall be required to pay only that part of any losses insured against by this policy which shall exceed the amount, if any, lost to the Company by reason of the impairment by the insured claimant of the Company's right of subrogation.

(b) The Company's Rights Against Non-insured Obligors.

The Company's right of subrogation against non-insured obligors shall exist and shall include, without limitation, the rights of the insured to indemnities, guaranties, other policies of insurance or bonds, notwithstanding any terms or conditions contained in those instruments which provide for subrogation rights by reason of this policy.

14. ARBITRATION

Unless prohibited by applicable law, either the Company or the insured may demand arbitration pursuant to the Title Insurance Arbitration Rules of the American Arbitration Association. Arbitrable matters may include, but are not limited to, any controversy or claim between the Company and the insured arising out of or relating to this policy, any service of the Company in connection with its issuance or the breach of a policy provision or other obligation. All arbitrable matters when the Amount of Insurance is $1,000,000 or less shall be arbitrated at the option of either the Company or the insured. All arbitrable matters when the Amount of Insurance is in excess of $1,000,000 shall be arbitrated only when agreed to by both the Company and the insured. Arbitration pursuant to this policy and under the Rules in effect on the date the demand for arbitration is made or, at the option of the insured, the Rules in effect at Date of Policy shall be binding upon the parties. The award may include attorneys' fees only if the laws of the state in which the land is located permit a court to award attorneys' fees to a prevailing party. Judgment upon the award rendered by the Arbitrator(s) may be entered in any court having jurisdiction thereof.

The law of the situs of the land shall apply to an arbitration under the Title Insurance Arbitration Rules.

A copy of the Rules may be obtained from the Company upon request.

15. LIABILITY LIMITED TO THIS POLICY; POLICY ENTIRE CONTRACT

(a) This policy together with all endorsements, if any, attached hereto by the Company is the entire policy and contract between the insured and the Company. In interpreting any provision of this policy, this policy shall be construed as a whole.

(b) Any claim of loss or damage, whether or not based on negligence, and which arises out of the status of the title to the estate or interest covered hereby or by any action asserting such claim, shall be restricted to this policy.

(c) No amendment of or endorsement to this policy can be made except by a writing endorsed hereon or attached hereto signed by either the President, a Vice President, the Secretary, an Assistant Secretary, or validating officer or authorized signatory of the Company.

16. SEVERABILITY

In the event any provision of the policy is held invalid or unenforceable under applicable law, the policy shall be deemed not to include that provision and all other provisions shall remain in full force and effect.

17. NOTICES, WHERE SENT

All notices required to be given the Company and any statement in writing required to be furnished the Company shall include the number of this policy and shall be addressed to the Company at the issuing office or to:

Chicago Title Insurance Company
Claims Department
111 West Washington Street
Chicago, Illinois 60602

[F5114]

Form No. 3658 (10/87)

WHITE v. WESTERN TITLE INSURANCE CO.

Supreme Court of California, 1985.
40 Cal.3d 870, 221 Cal.Rptr. 509, 710 P.2d 309.

BROUSSARD, JUSTICE.

Plaintiffs Brian and Helen White filed suit against defendant Western Title Insurance Company for breach of contract, negligence, and breach of implied covenants of good faith and fair dealing. A jury found for plaintiffs, awarding damages of $8,400 for breach of contract and negligence, and an additional $20,000 for breach of the covenants of good faith and fair dealing. We affirm the judgment.

In 1975, William and Virginia Longhurst owned 84 acres of land on the Russian River in Mendocino County. The land was divided into two lots, one unimproved, the other improved with a ranchhouse, a barn and adjacent buildings. It contained substantial subsurface water.

On December 29, 1975, the Longhursts executed and delivered an "Easement Deed for Waterline and Well Sites," conveying to River Estates Mutual Water Corporation an "easement for a right-of-way for the construction and maintenance of a water pipeline and for the drilling of a well or wells within a defined area and an easement to take water, up to 150 [gallons per minute], from any wells within said defined area." The deed was recorded the following day.

In 1978 plaintiffs agreed to purchase the property from the Longhursts. Plaintiffs, who were unaware of the water easement, requested preliminary title reports from defendant. Each report purported to list all easements, liens and encumbrances of record, but neither mentioned the recorded water easement.

Plaintiffs and the Longhursts opened two escrows, one for each lot. Upon close of escrow defendant issued to plaintiffs two standard CLTA title insurance policies, for which plaintiffs paid $1,467.55. Neither policy mentioned the water easement.

The title insurance policies provided: "SUBJECT TO SCHEDULE B AND THE CONDITIONS AND STIPULATIONS HEREOF, WESTERN TITLE INSURANCE COMPANY . . . insures the insured . . . against loss or damage, . . . and costs, attorneys' fees and expenses . . . incurred by said insured by reason of:

"1. Title to the estate or interest described in Schedule A being vested other than as stated therein;

"2. Any defect in or lien or encumbrance on such title; . . ."

"SCHEDULE B" provided in part that "[t]his policy does not insure against loss or damage . . . which arise[s] by reason of the following: . . .

"3. Easements, liens or encumbrances, or claims thereof, which are not shown by the public records. . . .

"5. (a) Unpatented mining claims; (b) reservations or exceptions in patents or in Acts authorizing the issuance thereof; (c) *water rights, claims or title to water.*" (Italics added.)

About six months after the close of escrow, River Estates Mutual Water Corporation notified plaintiffs of its intention to enter their property to implement the easement. Plaintiffs protested, and River Estates filed an action to quiet title to the easement. Plaintiffs notified defendant, who agreed to defend the proceeding. Plaintiffs, however, declined defendant's offer, preferring representation by an attorney who was then representing them in an unrelated action. River Estates eventually decided not to enforce its easement and dismissed the suit.

Plaintiffs' appraiser estimated the loss in value of their lots resulting from the potential loss of groundwater at $62,947. Plaintiffs then made a demand on defendant for that sum. Defendant acknowledged its responsibility for loss of value due to the easement (the loss attributable to the occupation of plaintiffs' land by wells and pipes, and to the water company's right to enter the property for construction and maintenance). It maintained, however, that any loss in value attributable to loss of groundwater was excluded by the policy, and since plaintiffs' claim of loss was based entirely on diminution of groundwater, declined to pay their claim.

Plaintiffs filed suit in October of 1979, alleging causes of action for breach of the insurance contract and negligence in the preparation of the preliminary title reports. Defendant moved for summary judgment; after briefing and argument the motion was denied. Defendant then retained an appraiser, who estimated plaintiffs' loss at $2,000. Assertedly based on this estimate, defendant in May of 1980 offered to settle the case for $3,000. Defendant did not furnish plaintiffs with a copy of the appraisal, and plaintiffs rejected the offer. In June defendant served a written offer to compromise for $5,000 pursuant to Code of Civil Procedure section 998.[2] Plaintiffs, having already incurred litigation expenses exceeding this figure, rejected the offer. Plaintiffs then obtained leave of court to amend their complaint to state a cause of action for breach of the covenant of good faith and fair dealing.

The trial court separated the issues of liability and damages. The issue of liability under the original complaint was presented to the court without a jury in January of 1981; in August of that year the court rendered an interlocutory judgment finding defendant liable for breach of contract and negligence. Defendant then furnished plaintiffs with a copy of their appraisal, and filed a new offer to compromise for $15,000. Plaintiffs rejected the offer, and the remaining issues were tried to a jury in February of 1982.

The parties first presented evidence of the loss in value to plaintiffs' property; the jury returned a special verdict fixing the loss at $100 per acre, or a total of $8,400. The court then turned to the cause of action for breach of the covenant of good faith and fair dealing. Plaintiffs indicated their intention to present evidence of defendant's conduct, including settlement offers, during the whole course of the litigation. In response to defendant's objection, the court ruled that such evidence would be admissible only as to events occurring before the interlocutory judgment of August 1981. Plaintiffs' former attorney then testified to defendant's settlement offers of $3,000 and $5,000, its failure to provide plaintiffs with a written appraisal to support those offers, and the attorney's fees paid and incurred in prosecuting the suit. The jury returned a special verdict finding defendant in breach of the covenant, awarding compensatory damages of $20,000, and denying punitive damages. Defendant appeals from the judgment.

2. Under section 998, if a plaintiff rejects a defendant's offer and fails to obtain a more favorable judgment, he cannot recover costs, is liable for defendant's costs from the time of the offer, and in the discretion of the court liable for defendant's prior costs.

1. *LIABILITY UNDER THE TERMS OF THE INSURANCE CONTRACTS*

The insurance policies purport to insure a "fee" interest, free from any defect in title or any lien or encumbrance on title, subject to the exceptions listed in schedule B of the policies. A fee interest includes appurtenant water rights. (See City of San Diego v. Sloane (1969) 272 Cal.App.2d 663, 77 Cal.Rptr. 620.) Thus the only question is whether coverage under the present case is excluded by schedule B.

Schedule B contains two parts. Part two lists specific exceptions, generally encumbrances of record discovered by the title company and therefore excluded from coverage under the policy. The easement of River Estates Mutual Water Corporation was not listed in part two. Part one describes nine kinds of title defects excluded generally from coverage. The first four paragraphs describe interests which should have been, but were not, recorded; item 3, for example, excludes coverage of "[e]asements, liens, or encumbrances . . . which are not shown by the public records. . . ." The remaining five paragraphs exclude interests of a type which are ordinarily not recorded, including, in paragraph 5, "(a) Unpatented mining claims; (b) reservations or exceptions in patents or in Acts authorizing the issuance thereof; (c) water rights, claims or title to water." Defendant relies on this last exclusion to avoid coverage in the present case.

Construction of the policy, however, is controlled by the well-established rules on interpretation of insurance agreements. As described most recently in Reserve Insurance Co. v. Pisciotta (1982) 30 Cal.3d 800, 807–808, 180 Cal.Rptr. 628, 640 P.2d 764: " '[A]ny ambiguity or uncertainty in an insurance policy is to be resolved against the insurer and . . . if semantically permissible, the contract will be given such construction as will fairly achieve its object of providing indemnity for the loss to which the insurance relates.' The purpose of this canon of construction is to protect the insured's reasonable expectation of coverage in a situation in which the insurer-draftsman controls the language of the policy. Its effect differs, depending on whether the language to be construed is found in a clause providing coverage or in one limiting coverage. 'Whereas coverage clauses are interpreted broadly so as to afford the greatest possible protection to the insured . . . exclusionary clauses are interpreted narrowly against the insurer.' " (Citations omitted.)

The Court of Appeal in Jarchow v. Transamerica Title Ins. Co. (1975) 48 Cal.App.2d 917, 941, 122 Cal.Rptr. 470, reiterated these rules in the title insurance context: "In determining what benefits or duties an insurer owes his insured pursuant to a contract of title insurance, the court may not look to the words of the policy alone, but must also consider the reasonable expectations of the public and the insured as to the type of service which the insurance entity holds itself out as ready to offer. (Barrera v. State Farm Mut. Automobile Ins. Co.; 71 Cal.2d 659, 669, 79 Cal.Rptr. 106, 456 P.2d 674.) Stated in another fashion, the provisions of the policy, ' "*must be construed so as to give the insured the protection which he reasonably had a right to expect,* . . ."' (Original italics.) (Gray v. Zurich Insurance Co., 65 Cal.2d 263, 270, fn. 7, 54 Cal.Rptr. 104, 419 P.2d 168.)"

In the present context, these rules require coverage of water rights shown in public records within the scope of an ordinary title search. The structure of the policy itself creates the impression that coverage is provided for claims of record, while excluded for unrecorded claims. This impression is reinforced by the specific language of the policy. Paragraph 3, by excluding easements, liens, and encumbrances "not shown by public records," implies inclusion of such interests when recorded. Paragraph 5, the exclusion of water rights on which defendant relies, joins that exclusion with exclusion of unpatented mining claims and exceptions in patents or authorizing legislation—interests which would not appear in the records ordinarily searched by a title company.

Coverage of claims of record also accords with the purpose of the title policies and the reasonable expectations of the insured. This standard CLTA policy is a policy based upon an inspection of records and, unlike more expensive policies, does not involve inspection of the property. The purchaser of such a policy could not reasonably expect coverage against unrecorded claims, but he could reasonably expect that the title company had competently searched the records, disclosed all interests of record it discovered and agreed to protect him against any undisclosed interests. Nothing in the policy makes it clear that there may be interests of record undisclosed by the policy yet excluded from coverage.

We conclude that the title insurance policies here in question, construed to carry out their purpose of protecting against undisclosed recorded interests, provide coverage for water rights which appear of record within the scope of the ordinary title search. The trial court reached the same conclusion, but by a different route. It reasoned that the water rights here at issue are inseparable from the recorded easement permitting River Estates Mutual Water Corporation to construct and maintain wells and pipelines. No provision of the policies excluded such easement, and defendant from the beginning has acknowledged liability for any loss in value attributable to the easement. The loss of water rights, the trial court concluded, is a loss attributable to the easement. We raise no objection to this line of reasoning, but prefer to rest our holding upon the broader ground that a purchaser of a title policy could reasonably expect protection against recorded water rights even if they were not connected to an easement for wells or pipes.

2. *LIABILITY FOR NEGLIGENCE*

Plaintiffs' cause of action for negligence rests on long-established principles concerning the duties of a title insurer. As explained in Jarchow v. Transamerica Title Ins. Co., supra, 48 Cal.App.3d 917, 938–939, 122 Cal.Rptr. 470: "When a title insurer presents a buyer with both a preliminary title report and a policy of title insurance, two distinct responsibilities are assumed. In rendering the first service, the insurer serves as an abstractor of title—and must list *all* matters of public record regarding the subject property in its preliminary report. [Citations.] The duty imposed upon an abstractor of title is a rigorous one: 'An abstractor of title is hired because of his professional skill, and when searching the public records on behalf of a client he must use the degree of care commensurate with that professional skill. . . . [T]he abstractor must report all matters which could affect his client's interests and which are readily discoverable from those public records ordinarily examined when a reasonably diligent title search is made.' [Citations.] Similarly, a title insurer is liable for his negligent failure to list recorded encumbrances in preliminary title reports. [Citations.]" These principles find support in the numerous cases cited in *Jarchow,* and also in the more recent decision of Wilkinson v. Rives (1981) 116 Cal.App.3d 641, 650, 172 Cal.Rptr. 254, where the court said that "[w]hen a title insurer furnishes a preliminary title report to a prospective buyer, the insurer serves as an abstractor of title and has a duty to list all matters of public record regarding the subject property in its preliminary report."

It is undisputed that the preliminary title report failed to list the recorded easement of River Estates Mutual Water Corporation. The failure of a title company to note an encumbrance of record is prima facie negligent. Defendant has made no attempt to rebut this inference of negligence.

Defendant relies instead on the language of the preliminary title reports and on the enactment of Insurance Code section 12340.11. Each report states that it "is issued solely for the purpose of facilitating the issuance of a policy of title insurance and no liability is assumed thereby." This statement, however, appears in the report itself, not in a contract under which defendant agreed to prepare that report. Moreover, even if we viewed the title report as a contract, the quoted provision would be ineffective to relieve defendant of liability for negligence. A title company is engaged in a business affected with the public interest and cannot, by an adhesory contract, exculpate itself from liability for negligence. (Akin v. Business Title Corp. (1968) 264 Cal.App.2d 153, 70 Cal.Rptr. 287.)

Insurance Code section 12340.11, effective January 1, 1982, provides: " 'Preliminary report', 'commitment', or 'binder' are reports furnished in connection with an application for title insurance and are offers to issue a title policy subject to the stated exceptions set forth in the reports and such other matters as may be incorporated by reference therein. The reports are not abstracts of title, nor are any of the rights, duties or responsibilities applicable to the preparation and issuance of an abstract of title applicable to the issuance of any report. Any such report shall not be construed as, nor constitute, a representation as to the condition of title to real property, but shall constitute a statement of the terms and conditions upon which the issuer is willing to issue its title policy, if such offer is accepted."

Whatever the effect of this statute upon preliminary title reports prepared after January 1, 1982, it has no effect upon the present case. " 'It is a general rule of construction . . . that, unless the intention to make it retrospective clearly appears from the act itself, a statute will not be construed to have that effect.' " (Western Pioneer Ins. Co. v. Estate of Taira (1982) 136 Cal.App.3d 174, 180–181, 185 Cal.Rptr. 887; see Balen v. Peralta Junior College Dist. (1974) 11 Cal.3d 821, 830, 114 Cal.Rptr. 589, 523 P.2d 629; Battle v. Kessler (1983) 149 Cal.App.3d 853, 858, 197 Cal.Rptr. 170; Carr v. State of California (1976) 58 Cal. App.3d 139, 147, 129 Cal.Rptr. 730.) This rule is particularly applicable to a statute which diminishes or extinguishes an existing cause of action. (Cf. Robinson v. Pediatrics Affiliates Medical Group, Inc. (1979) 98 Cal.App.3d 907, 159 Cal.Rptr. 791.) Nothing in the language or legislative history of section 12340.11 suggests an intention to apply that statute to a preliminary title report procured prior to its effective date.

Defendant finally argues that the trial court refused to permit it to introduce evidence of plaintiffs' contributory negligence. Defendant offered only to prove that plaintiffs by diligent investigation could have discovered the water easement. Since plaintiffs had no duty to investigate, but were entitled to rely on the preliminary title report, such evidence is insufficient to show contributory negligence. (See J.H. Trisdale Inc. v. Shasta etc. Title Co. (1956) 146 Cal.App.2d 831, 839, 304 P.2d 832.) Defendant did not offer to prove that plaintiffs had actual knowledge of the easement.

3. *LIABILITY FOR BREACH OF THE COVENANT OF GOOD FAITH AND FAIR DEALING*

A covenant of good faith and fair dealing is implied in every insurance contract (Gruenberg v. Aetna Ins. Co. (1973) 9 Cal.3d 566, 575, 108 Cal.Rptr. 480, 510 P.2d 1032), including title insurance contracts (Jarchow v. Transamerica Title Ins. Co., supra, 48 Cal.App.3d 917, 940, 122 Cal.Rptr. 470; see Kapelus v. United Title Guaranty Co. (1971) 15 Cal.App.3d 648, 653, 93 Cal.Rptr. 278). The jury found defendant breached the covenant, and awarded compensatory damages of $20,000. Defendant argues on appeal that the court erred in admitting, as evidence of breach, settlement offers and other matters occurring after commencement of litigation. It also asserts that no substantial evidence supports the jury's verdict.

Defendant first contends that all evidence relating to events after plaintiffs filed suit should have been excluded on the ground that, once suit has been filed, the insurer stands in an adversary position to the insured and no longer owes a duty of good faith and fair dealing. The issue is one of first impression. The parties review the numerous cases which discuss first-party good faith litigation: plaintiffs point out that none of the cases suggest that the insurer's duty of good faith terminates when suit is filed; defendant points out that all involve acts which in fact occurred before litigation commenced. But neither can point to any case which has considered the issue raised here, and we have discovered none.

We believe, however, that the issue can be resolved as a matter of principle. It is clear that the contractual relationship between insurer and the insured does not terminate with commencement of litigation. In an automobile liability policy, for example, even if the insurer and insured were engaged in litigation concerning coverage of one accident, if the insured were involved in another accident within the policy terms and coverage he would certainly be protected. In the present setting, if some third party today were to assert title to plaintiff's land—or if River Estates Mutual Water Corporation were to reassert its right to a pipeline easement—there is no doubt that defendant would be obliged to provide a defense and possible indemnity. And it is not unusual for an insurance company to provide policy benefits, such as the defense of litigation, while itself instituting suit to determine whether and to what extent it must provide those benefits. It could not reasonably be argued under such circumstances either that the insurer no longer owes any contractual duties to the insured, or that it need not perform those duties fairly and in good faith.

Defendant's argument is less unreasonable in a case in which the insured filed suit (obviously the insurer could not be permitted to terminate its own obligations by initiating litigation), and the issue is limited to the insurer's duty of good faith and fair dealing in regard to the specific subject matter of the suit. But even here a sharp distinction between conduct before and after suit was filed would be undesirable. Defendant's proposed rule would encourage insurers to induce the early filing of suits, and to delay serious investigation and negotiation until after suit was filed when its conduct would be unencumbered by any duty to deal fairly and in good faith. Defendant responds that such delay would itself be a breach of the implied covenant, but the incentive would remain, especially since the insured would find it difficult to prove the prelitigation conduct unreasonable if it could not present evidence of the postlitigation conduct by way of contrast. The policy of encouraging prompt investigation and payment of insurance claims would be undermined by defendant's proposed rule.

Defendant argues that imposing a duty of good faith after litigation has begun will make it difficult for the insurer to defend the suit. It claims that investigation of the factual circumstances would be hampered by an obligation to reveal to the insured any material facts it discovers favorable to his claim, and that the attorney who prepares the case for trial could not conduct the trial because he would be a critical witness to the insurer's good faith during the pretrial period. Neither of these concerns, however, justify a distinction between the period before suit is filed and the period after it is filed. Certainly the insurer should have investigated the factual basis of the claim before suit is filed, and may well have utilized counsel to evaluate that claim. The issue of contractual liability can be tried separately, and prior to the trial on the good faith claim, as was done in the present case. In any event, what constitutes good faith and fair dealing depends on the circumstances of each case, including the stage of the proceedings and the posture of the parties. We trust that the jurors will be aware that parties to a lawsuit are adversaries, and will evaluate the insurer's conduct in relation to that setting.

Defendant next contends that the admission of the two settlement offers violated Evidence Code section 1152. That section states that "[e]vidence that a person has, in compromise or from humanitarian motives, furnished or offered or promised to furnish money . . . to another who has sustained . . . loss or damage, as well as any conduct or statements made in negotiation thereof, is inadmissible to prove his liability for the loss or damage or any part of it." The Law Revision Commission comment to this section states that "[t]the rule excluding offers is based on the public policy in favor of the settlement of disputes without litigation."

The language of this section does not preclude the introduction of settlement negotiations if offered not to prove liability for the original loss but to prove failure to process the claim fairly and in good faith. . . .

. . .

Both defendants' offers of compromise were submitted before plaintiffs had filed a claim for damages for breach of the covenant of good faith and fair dealing. Both sought only to compromise plaintiffs' original contractual and negligence claims. Under our construction of the statutes, those offers were inadmissible to prove liability on plaintiffs' original causes of action, but were admissible to prove liability for breach of the covenant. That is exactly how matters proceeded: the trial court bifurcated the trial, and admitted the offers into evidence only on the issue of liability for breach of the covenant.

. . .

The entire pattern of conduct shows a clear attempt by defendant to avoid responsibility for its obvious failure to discover and report the recorded easement of River Estates Mutual Water Corporation. We conclude that the evidence is sufficient to permit the jury to find a breach of the covenant of good faith and fair dealing.

4. *DAMAGES FOR BREACH OF THE COVENANT OF GOOD FAITH AND FAIR DEALING*

We agree with the Court of Appeal that there is no "merit in the . . . argument that damages for emotional distress were not permitted because that issue was unraised by the pleadings. Such an issue is reasonably, perhaps necessarily, raised by the pleaded issue of an insurer's bad faith in rejecting settlement of a meritorious claim. And here we observe that the issue of damages for emotional distress was fully and fairly tried and presented for adjudication, in the superior court."

The remaining question concerns recovery of attorney fees and other litigation expense as an element of damage. The Court of Appeal held that attorney fees were recoverable under the terms of the title insurance policies, which insure against "costs, attorney's fees and expenses sustained or incurred by said insured by reason of . . . any lien or encumbrance on . . . title." Defendant contends that this provision covers only actions against third parties in defense of title, and does not apply to suits against the title insurer itself. (See Jesko v. American–First Title and Trust Co. (10th Cir.1979) 603 F.2d 815, 819.)

The trial court, however, did not award attorney fees as a separate item of damage under the quoted policy provision, but as an element of the damages for breach of the covenant of good faith and fair dealing. A subsequent decision by this court, Brandt v. Superior Court (1985) 37 Cal.3d 813, 210 Cal.Rptr. 211, 693 P.2d 796, supports the trial court's position. We there stated that " 'when the insurer's conduct is unreasonable, a plaintiff is allowed to recover for all detriment proximately resulting from the insurer's bad faith, which detriment . . . includes those attorney's fees that were incurred to obtain the policy benefits and that would not have been incurred but for the insurer's tortious conduct.' " (37 Cal.3d 813, 819, 210 Cal.Rptr. 211, 693 P.2d 796.) The same reasoning supports inclusion of witness fees and other litigation expenses as an element of damage.

The judgment is affirmed.

BIRD, C.J., and MOSK and REYNOSO, JJ., CONCUR.

GRODIN, JUSTICE, concurring.

I agree with the majority that an insurer's duty to deal with its insured fairly, and not to withhold payment of claims unreasonably and in bad faith, does not evaporate with the onset of litigation. . . .

What bothers me in this case—and, I take it our dissenting colleagues as well—is that the two settlement offers which *were* admitted in evidence support plaintiff's theory of bad faith only weakly, and a third settlement offer, which might have been helpful to the jury's evaluation despite its somewhat disparate context, was excluded. Once the trial court decided to admit the first two offers, I believe (unlike the majority) that it should have allowed the defendant to complete the picture. However, in light of the relatively modest verdict I do not believe there has been such a miscarriage of justice as to require reversal and a new trial.

Subject to these reservations, I concur.

LUCAS, JUSTICE, concurring and dissenting.

I respectfully dissent from the affirmance of the judgment as to plaintiff insured's good faith cause of action. Scylla and Charybdis had nothing on my colleagues for making life difficult—if not impossible. An insurer who refuses to pay its insured on a disputed claim is now not only at risk that its refusal will subject it to damages for breach of the covenant of good faith and fair dealing, but must also be conscious that any aspect of its conduct during litigation of the original claim of coverage may be used as significant evidence in an ensuing breach of good faith action. An insurer's unsuccessful attempts to settle during the course of the initial litigation may now be presented to a second jury, along with all other aspects of its defense. Confronted with such evidence and unfamiliar with the vagaries of litigation the jury will, I submit, in all likelihood regard any settlement attempts as prejudgment admissions of liability, and standard defense tactics as indications of a lack of good faith. . . .

NOTES

1. Not all courts are as eager as California's to expand the tort liability of title insurers. In Brown's Tie & Lumber Co. v. Chicago Title Co. of Idaho, 115 Idaho 56, 764 P.2d 423 (1988), defendant's commitment to issue the title insurance policy failed to report a recorded deed of trust. Plaintiff-insured appealed a partial summary judgment in which the trial court, saying that plaintiff had an action in contract, not tort, dismissed claims of negligence, negligent misrepresentation, and insurer's bad faith. In affirming the judgment, the Supreme Court said that negligence liability should not be imposed unless "the act complained of was a direct result of duties voluntarily assumed by the insurer in addition to the mere contract to insure title." Although a recent statute provided that no title insurance should be issued unless and until the insurer or its agent "[h]as caused to be made a search and examination of the title and a determination of insurability of title in accordance with sound title underwriting practices," the court held that the statute "does not create a duty in tort upon the part of title insurers to conduct a reasonable search and inspection of title."

2. As in the case of abstract companies, there is a growing tendency by the courts to impose high standards on title insurance companies. In a case of first impression, the Court of Appeals of New York held that an insured was under no duty to disclose to the insurer the facts as to a condemnation proceeding which were readily ascertainable from the public records. Even the insured's intentional failure to disclose a matter of public record did not result in the loss of title insurance protection. L. Smirlock Realty Corp. v. Title Guarantee Co., 52 N.Y.2d 179, 437 N.Y.S.2d 57, 418 N.E.2d 650 (1981). The court added: "Of course, an intentional failure by the insured to disclose material information not readily discernable from the public records will render the policy void."

TRANSAMERICA TITLE INSURANCE CO. v. JOHNSON

Supreme Court of Washington, 1985.
103 Wn.2d 409, 693 P.2d 697.

BRACHTENBACH, JUSTICE.

Plaintiff issued title insurance policies for three parcels of real estate. The defendant corporation was the seller-grantor. The insureds were the purchasers-grantees. Plaintiff failed to except from coverage a sewer assessment lien on each parcel. It paid the assessments and sued the seller-grantor corporation under its policy subrogation rights. The trial court granted summary judgment against the defendant corporation. The Court of Appeals affirmed by an unpublished opinion. Transamerica Title Ins. Co. v. Johnson, noted at 37 Wash.App. 1005 (1984). We affirm.

The facts are not disputed. The defendant corporation, a developer/homebuilder, purchased vacant lots for the purpose of building residences thereon. At the time of purchase preliminary sewer district assessments had been made. The preliminary assessments were disclosed in title insurance policies issued by another title company, which the corporation, as the purchaser, received.

The corporation's president testified by deposition:

Q. When you purchased those three parcels of property, did you know about the sewer assessments?

A. Yes.

Q. And when you purchased those three parcels, they would have been subject to that assessment, I take it?

A. That's right.

Clerk's Papers, at 111–12.

Soon after purchase the corporation listed the properties for sale. The listing agreements provided that the "buyer [is] to assume sewer assessment for U.L.I.D. # 22, Cascade Sewer District". Later the listing agreements were amended to delete the requirement that the buyer assume the assessment. The earnest money agreements, signed by defendant corporation as seller, provided that title was to be free of encumbrances. These listing agreements and earnest money agreements were signed long before any involvement by or with plaintiff title company. Finally, the conveying statutory warranty deeds did not make title subject to the assessments.

When the plaintiff issued its "preliminary commitment for title insurance" for each of the parcels, the preliminary sewer assessments had become final and were liens on the parcels. Neither the preliminary commitments nor the policies, ultimately insuring the purchasers' title, disclosed the assessments.

There is no dispute that (1) the plaintiff was negligent in not disclosing the assessments and (2) the defendant corporation breached its warranty of title and its contractual obligations to its purchasers.

The policies issued to the purchasers provided:

> When the Company [plaintiff] shall have paid a claim hereunder it shall be subrogated to all rights and remedies which the insured [the purchaser-grantee] may have against any person or property with respect to such claim, or would have if this policy had not been issued, and the insured shall transfer all such rights to the Company.

Clerk's Papers, at 292.

The main thrust of defendant's argument is that the plaintiff, in issuing a preliminary commitment for title insurance, acts as an abstractor of title with a duty to disclose all discoverable defects. The defendant asserts that this case presents the typical transaction in which the seller pays the premium even though the purchaser is ultimately the insured under the title insurance policy. Therefore, the defendant argues that in addition to the duties under the policy to insure the purchaser subject to the exceptions, terms and conditions of the preliminary report, the title insurer owes the duties of search and disclosure to the seller.

It is apparent that the defendant seeks to impose liability upon the title insurance company which is beyond that contained in the policy itself. The defendant is not an insured under that policy and is not provided coverage therein. It, therefore, does not seek to impose liability based on a theory of contractual liability. Rather, defendant would have us impose an abstractor's duty upon the title insurance company and would extend that duty to the seller-applicant. Necessarily the existence of that duty depends upon an analysis of the expectations and obligations running from the title insurance company to the seller-applicant, the noninsured grantor who has previously contractually agreed to provide its buyer with a specified form of title insurance policy. Regardless of the label given the ultimate theory relied upon, the suggested action sounds in tort. The measure of damages would not be limited to policy limits and the title company's risk or premium would not be limited to a traditional risk of loss vis-a-vis an actuarial determination of premium.

. . .

Potential liability would be based on a duty of the plaintiff to advise the defendant of the existence of encumbrances. . . . Some jurisdictions have held that no duty is owed to vendors who pay title insurance premiums for the protection of the insured vendees and that any search actually undertaken was for the protection of the insurance company. Horn v. Lawyers Title Ins. Corp., 89 N.M. 709, 557 P.2d 206 (1976); Wolff v. Commercial Standard Ins. Co., 345 S.W.2d 565 (Tex.Civ. App.1961). Although the title insurer may be negligent, where no duty is owed the vendor, there is no liability extending to the vendor.

Other jurisdictions have recognized a duty on the part of the title insurance company extending to other than the insured. Malinak v. Safeco Title Ins. Co., 661 P.2d 12 (Mont.1983); Kovaleski v. Tallahassee Title Co., 363 So.2d 1156 (Fla.Dist.Ct.App.1978); Williams v. Polgar, 391 Mich. 6, 215 N.W.2d 149 (1974); Transamerica Title Ins. Co. v. Ramsey, 507 P.2d 492 (Alaska 1973); Chun v. Park, 51 Hawaii 462, 462 P.2d 905 (1969). However, even assuming that we were to recognize such a duty, we would not impose liability here. In the cases cited by defendant, in addition to those cited herein, the courts have held a title insurance company liable on a duty to search and disclose only when the noninsured has shown foreseeable *reliance* upon the preliminary commitment or upon the representations of the title insurance company. Where it cannot be shown that the noninsured relied upon the search and disclosure and that this reliance was foreseeable, no liability based on such a duty can be imposed.

There is no showing, on this record, of reliance, damage or an expectation of a search and disclosure. This defendant knew of the assessments long before the plaintiff ever issued a preliminary commitment. . . . Again, long before asking the plaintiff to insure title, the defendant had contractually agreed with its purchasers (the only insureds) to convey title free of the assessments. There is no showing that this defendant expected an "abstract" of title or that even if it had, that it relied thereon in any manner. In fact, had the assessments been disclosed, the defendant would have had to pay them from the closing proceeds. The defendant is merely paying, through subrogation, that which it had knowledge of and had agreed to pay long before the plaintiff became involved.

. . .

Lastly, defendant asserts that a violation of the Consumer Protection Act (C.P.A.), RCW 19.86, occurs where the vendor purchases a title search, opinion and policy and the title company is negligent in its duty to perform a reasonable search. A cause of action for a per se violation of the C.P.A. may be brought only by the insured. Green v. Holm, 28 Wash.App. 135, 622 P.2d 869 (1981). Therefore, defendant, as a noninsured, must rely on the public interest test for a violation of the C.P.A. In view of our disposition that there was no reliance shown by the defendant, any injury that defendant may have incurred was not the result of an act or practice of the plaintiff. Therefore, a cause of action under the public interest test would also fail.

The judgment is affirmed.

WILLIAM H. WILLIAMS, C.J., and UTTER, DOLLIVER, DIMMICK, DORE, PEARSON and ANDERSEN, JJ., concur.

NOTES

1. Would a New York court reach the same decision as the Washington court did? Does the Smirlock case, discussed in the note immediately preceding the principal case, suggest that New York would favor the person ordering and paying for the title insurance, even if he or she had knowledge of the encumbrances? Of what relevance are cases holding that abstracters' liability is not restricted to persons in privity of contract with the abstracters? See First American Title Insurance Co. v. First Title Service Co. of the Florida Keys, page 1348 supra. Would the result in the principal case have been different if defendant had not previously known about the encumbrances? Even in that situation, would the Washington court have held for plaintiff because defendant already had contracted to convey title free of encumbrances before receiving plaintiff's preliminary commitment for title insurance?

2. Most of the cases involving suits on title insurance policies are by the insured against the insurer while the former still owns the land but has suffered a loss. Suppose the insured sells the land, unaware of any defect in title, and gives a warranty deed to his grantee. A defect in the title, paramount to the insured's interest, then appears and the insured is successfully sued on his warranty deed. Does the insured have a cause of action against the insurance company? See Stewart Title Guaranty Co. v. Lunt Land Corp., 162 Tex. 435, 347 S.W.2d 584 (1961). Under the language of the policy, the court held that upon the sale of the land the title policy ceased to be an owner's policy and became a warrantor's policy. The court denied recovery, however,

because the insured knew of the defect before he sold the land but failed to notify the company and did not cooperate with them so that they would have the opportunity to reduce any subsequent loss. The court noted: "[W]hen the [insured] knows of the title defect, [he] must give notice or take some appropriate action to prevent automatic conversion of the contract from an owner's to a warrantor's policy. He cannot, having such knowledge, remain silent, sell the property, execute a full warranty deed thereto and then contend that the policy remained in effect as an owner's policy despite the specific wording thereof."

. . .

BEAULLIEU v. ATLANTA TITLE & TRUST CO.

Court of Appeals of Georgia, 1939.
60 Ga.App. 400, 4 S.E.2d 78.

STEPHENS, PRESIDING JUDGE. C.B. Beaullieu brought suit against The Atlanta Title & Trust Company for an alleged breach of a contract of title insurance to the plaintiff's damage. In the petition plaintiff alleges that he bought from B.P. Hancock a certain described parcel of real estate in the County of Fulton and State of Georgia and contracted to pay therefor the purchase price of $8,000, that the defendant on March 18, 1937, for a consideration of $60 paid to it, issued to plaintiff its title guaranty policy by which it insured the plaintiff against all loss or damage not exceeding $7,000, which the plaintiff should sustain by reason of any defect or defects of title affecting the property which the plaintiff had contracted to purchase, that the plaintiff entered into the possession of the land and after proceeding to build thereon a house early in the month of March, 1937, he ascertained that Mrs. Hal Padgett had an easement in and over the property, that plaintiff notified defendant of this fact, that defendant admitted the validity of the easement and requested plaintiff to allow it to bring suit in plaintiff's name against Hancock in order to minimize the damage which plaintiff had sustained, that plaintiff agreed to this, that on the date of the issuance of the policy the true market value of the property, if unencumbered by the easement, was $15,000, that on this date the true market value of the property, encumbered by the easement, was $5,000, and that in order to extinguish the easement plaintiff would be obliged to purchase the land to which the easement is appurtenant at a cost of $50,000. Plaintiff alleges that the defendant has, on demand of plaintiff, failed and refused to pay the loss which plaintiff sustained by the easement upon the property, to the plaintiff's damage of $7,000, for which plaintiff prays.

The defendant filed no general demurrer to the petition, but specially demurred thereto on the ground, among others, that the allegation as to the market value of the property was irrelevant and immaterial and that the plaintiff in alleging his damage to be the difference between the market value of the property, namely, $15,000, without the easement or encroachment thereon, and the value with the easement or encroachment thereon, namely, $5,000, alleges the wrong measure of damage by reason of the defendant's breach of its contract of title insurance, and that the correct measure of plaintiff's damage is the difference between the purchase money of the property, namely, $8,000, and the market value of the property, with the easement or encroachment thereon. The defendant also specially demurred to the allegations in the petition that prior to the purchase of the land plaintiff had been engaged in the business of selling building supplies, that the land purchased was adapted to plaintiff's business, and what land of this character would cost. The court sustained all these demurrers and gave to the plaintiff 20 days in which to amend by alleging damages "in reduction of the price paid according to the relative value of the interest lost", citing Code, § 29–202, and in default of such amendment that the petition should stand dismissed. Before the expiration of the 20 days the court passed a subsequent order amendatory thereof which provided that the case should not stand dismissed in default of an amendment to the petition until 10 days after the remittitur from the appellate court had been made the judgment of the trial court. Plaintiff did not amend the petition in accordance with the order sustaining the demurrers, but on the date of the passage of the second order tendered and had certified his bill of exceptions, excepting to the judgment sustaining the special demurrers.

The court properly sustained the special demurrers except the two which are first above referred to.

The sole question for determination is what is the plaintiff's measure of damage for the defendant's breach of its contract of title insurance. The plaintiff contends that the measure is the difference between the true market value of the land, as it would be without the easement upon it, and the true market value of the land encumbered with the easement. The defendant contends that the true measure of damage is the difference between the purchase price of the land and the market value of the land with the easement upon it. The suit is against the title insurer and not against the vendor for breach of warranty.

In respect to a breach of covenant in a deed to land by the covenantor and vendor it is stated in 14 Am.Jur. 604, § 186, as follows: "Where an encumbrance is a servitude or easement which cannot be removed at the option of either the grantor or grantee, damages will be awarded for the injury proximately caused by the existence and continuance of the encumbrance, the measure of which is deemed to be the difference between the value of the land as it would be without the easement and its value as it is with the easement. This is the rule applicable where the covenant against encumbrances is broken by the existence, at the time of the execution of the deed, of a continuing right of way over the land granted in favor of a third person, which materially affects the value of the land." The plaintiff alleges the existence of a servitude or easement upon his property which cannot be removed either at his option or at the option of the grantor or the defendant. It can only be removed by agreement with the owner of the dominant tenement.

For a breach by a vendor of a contract for the sale of land the measure of damage to the vendee is the amount equal to the difference between the value of the land when the contract was broken and the contract price. Mobley v. Lott, 127 Ga. 572, 56 S.E. 637. In 2 Sutherland on Damages, 4th ed., § 669, "A loss of property through a want of title is precisely the same to the vendee as a loss of it because the vendor fails to deliver, and the latter, by violating his contract, is the cause of the loss in either case. The value of the property at the time the vendee is dispossessed has been held to be the measure of damages." This is the rule with reference to personalty. As to realty where there is an outstanding easement of a permanent nature see 2 Sutherland on Damages, 4th ed., §§ 627, 628.

As stated by the Supreme Court of this State in Mobley v. Lott, supra [127 ga. 572, 56 s.e. 638] "The law aims to place the injured party, so far as money can do it, in the position he would have occupied if the contract had been fulfilled. Such is the rule as recognized in this state." In City of New York v. New York & South Brooklyn etc. Co., 231 N.Y. 18, 131 N.E. 554, 16 A.L.R. 1059, the defect in the title was a servitude on the land, and the court held that the damages for a breach of warranty was the difference between the value of the land without the servitude and the value of the land with the servitude or the money reasonably expended by the owner in freeing the land by extinguishing the burden. The decrease in the market value of the land may usually be taken as a proper criterion by which to measure the damages caused by the existence of an easement. . . .

A contract of title insurance is an agreement whereby the insurer, for a valuable consideration, agrees to indemnify the assured in a specified amount against loss through defects of title to real estate, wherein the latter has an interest, either as purchaser or otherwise; a contract to indemnify against loss through defects in the title to real estate or liens or encumbrances thereon. 62 C.J. 1053, § 1.

Whatever may be the rule as to the measure of damages in a suit by a vendee against the vendor of land with reference to a breach of warranty of title, and by section 29–202 of the Code, which refers to the measure of damages against the vendor of realty where the vendee loses a part of the land from a defect in the title warranted, the measure of damage for a breach by an insurer under a policy insuring the title against encumbrances or encroachments is the difference between the value of the property when purchased with the encumbrance or encroachment thereon, and the value of the property as it would have been if there had been no such encumbrance or encroachment. 62 C.J. 1070, § 103. The rule as laid down in Glyn v. Title Guarantee & Trust Co., 132 App.Div. 859, 117 N.Y.S. 424, 428, is that, for a breach of the policy, the insured who purchased the property to which the title was insured by the insurer, "is entitled to recover the difference between the value of the property when purchased, as it was with the encroachments, and its value as it would have been if there had been no such encroachments."

The court erred in sustaining the demurrers directed to the allegations as to the measure of damage.

Judgment reversed.

SUTTON, J., concurs.

FELTON, J., dissents.

NOTES

1. Coverage is a major issue in insurance of any kind. The layman is apt to think that he is protected against all conceivable losses: "I bought protection didn't I? The company is just relying on technicalities." The lawyer knows that he must read the terms with care, for the technicalities may be the heart of the matter. Consider the case of the lady from the city of Palm Springs, county of Riverside, state of California.

California's Subdivision Map Act reads: "Except as provided in Section 11537 (not material here), no final map of a subdivision shall be accepted by the county recorder for record unless there has been a compliance with all provisions of this chapter and of any local ordinance." A Palm Springs ordinance provided that the City Council should not approve or accept a subdivision map of any property without first obtaining from the owners of the subdivision certain agreements and bonds providing for the grading and paving of streets in the subdivision. In spite of these provisions, the City Council approved a subdivision without the agreements and bonds required by ordinance, and the county official recorded the subdivision map showing the streets.

The plaintiff purchased two unimproved lots for $13,550 and received a deed therefor in reliance on the subdivision map. Later the defendant company insured her, in a sum not to exceed $13,550, against loss (1) "by reason of title to the lots not being vested in plaintiff in fee simple, (2) by reason of unmarketability of plaintiff's title, (3) by reason of any defect, lien or encumbrance on such title." The legal description of the lots in the policy was "Lots 5 and 10 of Vista Del Cielo No. 3, as shown by Map on file in Book 21 page 55 of Maps, records of Riverside County, California." The policy stated five exceptions, including: "The Company does not, by this policy, insure against loss by reason of . . . 5. Any governmental acts or legal actions restricting, regulating, or prohibiting the occupancy or use of said land or any building or structure thereon."

The city denied the plaintiff a building permit because the subdivision did not comply with the ordinance. Apparently the subdivider was not going to comply with his agreement to build the streets, and he had filed no bond on which he could be sued. The plaintiff alleges that she is now the sad owner of two small areas of vacant, unimproved desert land and that it would cost her more than $13,550 to make the necessary improvements so that she could secure city approval and build on the lots. Says she: "Street improvements obviously enhance the value of subdivision lots, and the sale value of my property [without streets] is a long ways from the sum of $13,550."

She sues the defendant company alleging, among other things, that her title is unmarketable. The company takes the position that the plaintiff confuses title with physical condition of the property and of the adjacent streets: "One can hold perfect title to land that is valueless; or can have marketable title to land while the land itself is unmarketable."

Is the plaintiff entitled to recover? If so, how much should she receive? Explain the lawyer's role in this transaction, if the plaintiff had consulted one at the time of the original purchase. See Hocking v. Title Insurance & Trust Co., 37 Cal.2d 644, 234 P.2d 625 (1951).

See also Title and Trust Co. of Florida v. Barrows, 381 So.2d 1088 (Fla.App.1979). In that case, a platted street which bordered on one side of the insured's lot was at times impassable. Furthermore, the county had no plans for making any street improvements. Consequently, as a practical matter, the insured had no vehicular access to its property since the abutting street was covered by high water during each spring and fall. The trial court awarded money damages for breach of a title insurance policy.

In reversing, the appellate court found that the property abutted a properly dedicated right of way. Therefore, the cause of action was founded on the impassable condition of a platted street. In accepting the title insurer's view that it indemnifies only against defects in the record title, the court held that the title insurance policy only insured against record title defects and not against physical infirmities of the platted street.

2. Property lawyers should be aware of the full implications of title insurance since it is playing a growing role in modern real transactions. For two excellent practical analyses of title insurance see Rooney, Title Insurance: A Primer For Attorneys, 14 Real Property, Probate and Trust Journal 608 (1979) and Kuklin, Commercial Title Insurance And The Lawyer's Responsibility, 15 Real Property, Probate and Trust Journal 557 (1980). Mr. Kuklin correctly concludes that: "As long as we have a title system dependent upon searches in local recording offices rather than registered title, title insurance will play an increasing role. It insures risks which an attorney's opinion does not, both because of legal limitations on the attorney's liability and because of the economic stability and continuity of existence of the corporate insurer. This does not make title insurance the *sine qua non* of every real estate closing or, even when it is in order, the solution to all title problems, but it is a very limited vision which excludes it from the major title role in our ever burgeoning real estate market."

3. Title insurance is of two basic types—commercial title insurance and bar-related title insurance. The former operates much like any for-profit corporation; the latter is more complicated. The latter is essentially like a lawyers' cooperative and was developed to maintain the lawyers' role in the title aspects of real estate transactions—a role which the bar was steadily losing as fewer individuals relied on the

lawyer's direct search of the records or on the examination of an abstract. For a good discussion of the latter type, by an admittedly biased advocate, see Rooney, Bar-Related Title Insurance: The Positive Perspective, 1980 S.Ill.U.L.J. 263.

SECTION 6. STATUTES OF LIMITATION AND RELATED LEGISLATION AS AIDS TO TITLE ASSURANCE

At various points in the course we have referred to title by adverse possession, to prescriptive rights, and to the role of statutes of limitation. However, we have not taken a detailed look at the operation of the statutes, and it is appropriate that we do so in this chapter, since the *principal* role of such legislation is to strengthen the title of the possessor of land. The interest obtained by the adverse possessor is frequently referred to as an original title—i.e., a new title obtained in opposition to the former record owner—as distinct from a derivative title, which is obtained by descent, devise, or purchase. It is possible to obtain an original title in this way, but it would be a rare case in which an individual would set out deliberately to acquire title by adverse possession. He may quite frequently, however, purchase what he thinks is a valid paper title only to find a major flaw in the chain. In this situation each year of possession adds to his claim and may thus be said to give him added title assurance. Mr. Justice Holmes, in a letter to William James, stated the "reason behind the rule" with his usual succinctness: "The true explanation of title by prescription seems to me to be that man, like a tree in the cleft of a rock, gradually shapes his roots to his surroundings, and when the roots have grown to a certain size, cannot be displaced without cutting at his life. The law used to look with disfavor on the Statute of Limitations, but I have been in the habit of saying it is one of the most sacred and indubitable principles that we have, which used to lead my predecessor Field to say that Holmes didn't value any title that was not based on fraud or force." [5]

The statutes are of many types and naturally vary from state to state. It is the purpose of this section to explore the principal varieties and to study their operation. As usual, the roots must be traced to the English common law. From an early date numerous English statutes limited the time within which an action could be brought for a disseisin, but instead of stating a gross period they named a specific year beyond which the pleader could not go. For example, a statute enacted in 1275 barred the remedy by writ of right where the pleader relied upon the seisin of an ancestor before the first year of the reign of Richard I (1189). The modern method of measuring limitation was adopted in 1540, and in 1623 it was provided that no person should thereafter make any entry into any lands, tenements, or hereditaments but within twenty years next after his or their right or title accrued.

5. Lerner, The Mind and Faith of Justice Holmes 417 (1953).

While this act is the model for most of the statutes in the United States, it has been replaced in England by acts which bar any action to recover land after the statutory period has elapsed, without reference to the character of the defendant's possession. Many difficult questions plague the real estate lawyer in this country as he attempts to discern the character of the possession which the claimant must have for the statutory period in order to bar the rights of the original owner. It is clear that it must be adverse, but what does the term adverse mean? [6]

The Statute of James [7] adopted a gross period of twenty years after the cause of action accrued, and most states have used the same measuring stick, although a few require a greater or a lesser period. Many states have "short limitations" acts where the claimant is in possession under "color of title"; e.g., a judicial decree falsely purporting to vest title in him. Usually these acts require not only "color of title" but also payment of taxes for each year of possession.

While statutes of limitation have had a profound effect on land titles and have partially achieved the objective of "quieting men's estates", the traditional statutes have been deficient because, in general, they do not apply to future interests, to persons under legal disability, to governmental units, or, in many cases, to cotenants or to mineral interests. This has led to more specialized statutes, some of them not true statutes of limitations, to title standards and curative legislation, and has culminated in the most useful statutes of all—the marketable title acts. In the materials which follow we will explore these various techniques in the long search for title security, and you should form your own opinion as to their effectiveness and as to what further steps are required. For an excellent discussion of statutes of limitation, and marketable title generally, see Bayse, Clearing Land Titles 175–213 (2d ed. 1970).

HOWARD v. KUNTO

Court of Appeals of Washington, 1970.
3 Wn.App. 393, 477 P.2d 210.

PEARSON, JUDGE. Land surveying is an ancient art but not one free of the errors that often creep into the affairs of men. In this case, we are presented with the question of what happens when the descriptions in deeds do not fit the land the deed holders are occupying. Defendants

6. For a fascinating exposition of the complexity of adverse possession see Callahan, Adverse Possession (1961). This short book contains three lectures given at the Law Forum of the Ohio State University College of Law on the subjects of Property, Policy and Possession; Adverse Possession: The Law; and The Question of Purpose. At one point Professor Callahan notes: "Inertia, mistakes, a mixture of contradictory theories. . . . Adverse possession may have had even more than its fair share." Id. at 27.

7. James I, c. 16 (1623). The preamble reads: "For quieting of men's estates, and avoiding of suits be it enacted . . . ." It is significant that this basic English statute recognizes that most titles by adverse posession are honestly acquired and the statute is designed to protect persons relying on such honest claims. Of course, the statute may incidentally protect the dishonest individual as well but that is a price that must be paid for a meaningful doctrine of adverse possession. Do you see why?

appeal from a decree quieting title in the plaintiffs of a tract of land on the shore of Hood Canal in Mason County.

At least as long ago as 1932 the record tells us that one McCall resided in the house now occupied by the appellant-defendants, Kunto. McCall had a deed that described a 50-foot-wide parcel on the shore of Hood Canal. The error [1] that brings this case before us is that the 50 feet described in the deed is not the same 50 feet upon which McCall's house stood. Rather, the described land is an adjacent 50-foot lot directly west of that upon which the house stood. In other words, McCall's house stood on one lot and his deed described the adjacent lot.[2] Several property owners to the west of defendants, not parties to this action, are similarly situated.

Over the years since 1946, several conveyances occurred, using the same legal description and accompanied by a transfer of possession to the succeeding occupants. The Kuntos' immediate predecessors in interest, Millers, desired to build a dock. To this end, they had a survey performed which indicated that the deed description and the physical occupation were in conformity. Several boundary stakes were placed as a result of this survey and the dock was constructed, as well as other improvements. The house as well as the others in the areas continued to be used as summer recreational retreats.

The Kuntos then took possession of the disputed property under a deed from the Millers in 1959. In 1960 the respondent-plaintiffs, Howard, who held land east of that of the Kuntos, determined to convey an undivided one-half interest in their land to the Yearlys. To this end, they undertook to have a survey of the entire area made. After expending considerable effort, the surveyor retained by the Howards discovered that according to the government survey, the deed descriptions and the land occupancy of the parties did not coincide. Between the Howards and the Kuntos lay the Moyers' property. When the Howard's survey was completed, they discovered that they were the record owners of the land occupied by the Moyers and that the Moyers held record title to the land occupied by the Kuntos. Howard approached Moyer and in return for a conveyance of the land upon which the Moyers' house stood, Moyer conveyed to the Howards record title to the land upon which the Kunto house stood. Until plaintiffs Howard obtained the conveyance from Moyer in April, 1960, neither Moyer nor any of his predecessors ever asserted any right to ownership of the property actually being possessed by Kunto and his predecessors. This action was then instituted to quiet title in the Howard and Yearlys. The Kuntos appeal from a trial court decision granting this remedy.

1. Plaintiff's survey, the validity of which is challenged by defendant, demonstrates the error. [Footnotes in the case are by the court and numbered accordingly.]

2. Defendant's deed and chain of title purported to convey

"The West fifty (50) feet of the East two hundred (200) feet of Government Lot two (2), Section nineteen (19); and the West fifty (50) feet of the East two hundred (200) feet of Government Lot one (1), Section thirty (30); all in Township twenty-two (22); North, of Range two (2) West, W.M.; . . . ."

The land defendants and their predecessors occupied, according to the survey, was the "West 50 feet of the east 150 feet of Government Lot 2, in Section 19, Township 22 North, of Range 2 West of W.M. . . ."

At the time this action was commenced on August 19, 1960,[3] defendants had been in occupance of the disputed property less than a year. The trial court's reason for denying their claim of adverse possession is succinctly stated in its memorandum opinion: "In this instance, defendants have failed to prove, by a preponderance of the evidence, a continuity of possession or estate to permit tacking of the adverse possession of defendants to the possession of their predecessors."

Finding of fact 6,[4] which is challenged by defendants, incorporates the above concept and additionally finds defendant's possession not to have been "continuous" because it involved only "summer occupancy."

Two issues are presented by this appeal:

(1) Is a claim of adverse possession defeated because the physical use of the premises is restricted to summer occupancy?

(2) May a person who receives record title to tract A under the mistaken belief that he has title to tract B (immediately contiguous to tract A) and who subsequently occupies tract B, for the purpose of establishing title to tract B by adverse possession, use the periods of possession of tract B by his immediate predecessors who also had record title to tract A?

In approaching both of these questions, we point out that the evidence, largely undisputed in any material sense, established that defendant or his immediate predecessors did occupy the premises, which we have called tract B, as though it was their own for far more than the 10 years as prescribed in RCW 4.16.020.[5]

3. The inordinate delay in bringing this matter to trial appears from the record to be largely inexcusable. However, neither counsel who tried the case was at fault in any way. We have intentionally declined to consider defendant's motion (probably well founded) to dismiss this case for want of prosecution (Rules of Pleading, Practice and Procedure 41.04W (1950)) for the reason that a new trial of the same issues would be inevitable and in light of our disposition of the case on the merits, defendants are not prejudiced by disregarding the technical grounds.

4. In the instant case the defendants' building was not simply over the line, but instead was built wholly upon the wrong piece of property, not the property of defendants, described in Paragraph Four (4) of the complaint herein, but on the property of plaintiffs, described in Paragraph Three of the complaint and herein. That the last three deeds in the chain of title, covering and embracing defendants' property, including defendants' deed, were executed in other states, specifically, California and Oregon. And there is no evidence of pointing out to the grantees in said three deeds, aforesaid, including defendants' deed, of any specific property, other than the property of defendants, described in their deed, and in Paragraph Four (4) of the complaint, and herein; nor of any immediate act of the grantees, including defendants, in said Three (3) deeds, aforesaid, of taking possession of any property, other than described in said three (3) deeds, aforesaid; and the testimony of husband, defendant, was unequivocally that he had no intention of possessing or holding anything other than what the deed called for; and that there is no showing of any continuous possession by defendants or their immediate predecessors in interest, since the evidence indicates the property was in the nature, for use, as a summer occupancy, and such occupancy and use was for rather limited periods of time during comparatively short portions of the year, and was far from continuous."

5. This statute provides:

"4.16.020 Actions to be commenced within ten years. The period prescribed in RCW 4.16.010 for the commencement of actions shall be as follows:

"Within ten years;

"Actions for the recovery of real property, or for the recovery of the possession thereof; and no action shall be maintained for such recovery unless it appears that the plaintiff, his ancestor,

We also point out that findings of fact 6 is not challenged for its factual determinations but for the conclusions contained therein to the effect that the continuity of possession may not be established by summer occupancy, and that a predecessor's possession may not be tacked because a legal "claim of right" did not exist under the circumstances.

We start with the oft-quoted rule that:

> [t]o constitute adverse possession, there must be actual possession which is *uninterrupted*, open and notorious, hostile and exclusive, and under a *claim of right* made in good faith for the statutory period.

(Italics ours.) Butler v. Anderson, 71 Wash.2d 60, 64, 426 P.2d 467, 470 (1967). Also see Fadden v. Purvis, 77 Wash.Dec.2d 22, 459 P.2d 385 (1969) and cases cited therein.

We reject the conclusion that summer occupancy only of a summer beach home destroys the continuity of possession required by the statute. It has become firmly established that the requisite possession requires such possession and dominion "as ordinarily marks the conduct of owners in general in holding, managing, and caring for property of like nature and condition." Whalen v. Smith, 183 Iowa 949, 953, 167 N.W. 646, 647 (1918). Also see Mesher v. Connolly, 63 Wash.2d 552, 388 P.2d 144 (1964); Skoog v. Seymour, 29 Wash.2d 355, 187 P.2d 304 (1947); Butler v. Anderson, supra; Fadden v. Purvis, supra.

We hold that occupancy of tract B during the summer months for more than the 10-year period by defendant and his predecessors, together with the continued existence of the improvements on the land and beach area, constituted "uninterrupted" possession within this rule. To hold otherwise is to completely ignore the nature and condition of the property. See Fadden v. Purvis, supra.

We find such rule fully consonant with the legal writers on the subject. In F. Clark, Law of Surveying and Boundaries, § 561 (3d ed. 1959) at 565: "Continuity of possession may be established although the land is used regularly for only a certain period each year." Further, at 566:

> This rule [which permits tacking] is one of substance and not of absolute mathematical continuity, provided there is no break so as to sever two possessions. It is not necessary that the occupant should be actually upon the premises continually. If the land is occupied during the period of time during the year it is capable of use, there is sufficient continuity.

We now reach the question of tacking. The precise issue before us is novel in that none of the property occupied by defendant or his predecessors coincided with the property described in their deeds, but was contiguous.

In the typical case, which has been subject to much litigation, the party seeking to establish title by adverse possession claims *more* land

predecessor, or grantor was seized or possessed of the premises in question within ten years before the commencement of the action."

than that described in the deed. In such cases it is clear that tacking is permitted.

In Buchanan v. Cassell, 53 Wash.2d 611, 614, 335 P.2d 600, 602 (1959) the Supreme Court stated:

This state follows the rule that a purchaser may tack the adverse use of its predecessor in interest to that of his own where the land was intended to be included in the deed between them, but was mistakenly omitted from the description.

El Cerrito, Inc. v. Ryndak, 60 Wash.2d 847, 376 P.2d 528 (1962).

The general statement which appears in many of the cases is that tacking of adverse possession is permitted if the successive occupants are in "privity." See Faubion v. Elder, 49 Wash.2d 300, 301 P.2d 153 (1956). The deed running between the parties purporting to transfer the land possessed traditionally furnishes the privity of estate which connects the possession of the successive occupants. Plaintiff contends, and the trial court ruled, that where the deed does not describe *any* of the land which was occupied, the actual transfer of possession is insufficient to establish privity.

To assess the cogency of this argument and ruling, we must turn to the historical reasons for requiring privity as a necessary prerequisite to tacking the possession of several occupants. Very few, if any, of the reasons appear in the cases, nor do the cases analyze the relationships that must exist between successive possessors for tacking to be allowed. See W. Stoebuck, The Law of Adverse Possession In Washington in 35 Wash.L.Rev. 53 (1960).

The requirement of privity had its roots in the notion that a succession of trespasses, even though there was no appreciable interval between them, should not, in equity, be allowed to defeat the record title. The "claim of right," "color of title" requirement of the statutes and cases was probably derived from the early American belief that the squatter should not be able to profit by his trespass.[6]

However, it appears to this court that there is a substantial difference between the squatter or trespasser and the property purchaser, who along with several of his neighbors, as a result of an inaccurate survey or subdivision,[7] occupies and improves property exactly 50 feet to the east of that which a survey some 30 years later demonstrates that they in fact own. It seems to us that there is also a strong public policy favoring early certainty as to the location of land ownership which enters into a proper interpretation of privity.

On the irregular perimeters of Puget Sound exact determination of land locations and boundaries is difficult and expensive. This difficulty is convincingly demonstrated in this case by the problems plaintiff's engineer encountered in attempting to locate the corners. It cannot be expected that every purchaser will or should engage a surveyor to ascertain that the beach home he is purchasing lies within the bounda-

6. The English common law does not require privity as a prerequisite for tacking. See F. Clark, Law of Surveying and Boundaries, § 561 (3d ed. 1959) at 568.

7. Defendants' deed and chain of title had an alternate description referring to an unrecorded plat called the Navy Yard Additions 1 and 2.

ries described in his deed. Such a practice is neither reasonable nor customary. Of course, 50-foot errors in descriptions are devastating where a group of adjacent owners each hold 50 feet of waterfront property.

The technical requirement of "privity" should not, we think, be used to upset the long periods of occupancy of those who in good faith received an erroneous deed description. Their "claim of right" is no less persuasive than the purchaser who believes he is purchasing *more* land than his deed described.

In the final analysis, however, we believe the requirement of "privity" is no more than judicial recognition of the need for some reasonable connection between successive occupants of real property so as to raise their claim of right above the status of the wrongdoer or the trespasser. We think such reasonable connection exists in this case.

Where, as here, several successive purchasers received record title to tract A under the mistaken belief that they were acquiring tract B, immediately contiguous thereto, and where possession of tract B is transferred and occupied in a continuous manner for more than 10 years by successive occupants, we hold there is sufficient privity of estate to permit tacking and thus establish adverse possession as a matter of law.

We see no reason in law or in equity for differentiating this case from Faubion v. Elder, 49 Wash.2d 300, 301 P.2d 153 (1956) where the appellants were claiming *more* land than their deed described and where successive periods of occupation were allowed to be united to each other to make up the time of adverse holding. To the same effect see Naher v. Farmer, 60 Wash. 600, 111 Pac. 768 (1910), and cases cited therein; Buchanan v. Cassell, 53 Wash.2d 611, 335 P.2d 600 (1959) and cases cited therein; El Cerrito, Inc. v. Ryndak, 60 Wash.2d 847, 376 P.2d 528 (1962); see 17 A.L.R.2d 1128 (1951). This application of the privity requirement should particularly pertain where the holder of record title to tract B acquired the same with knowledge of the discrepancy.

Judgment is reversed with directions to dismiss plaintiffs' action and to enter a decree quieting defendants' title to the disputed tract of land in accordance with the prayer of their cross-complaint.

ARMSTRONG, P. J., and PETRIE, J., concur.

NOTES

1. "The general rules of law respecting successive disseisins are well settled. To make a disseisin effectual to give title under it to a second disseisor, it must appear that the latter holds the estate under the first disseisor, so that the disseisin of one may be connected with that of the other. Separate successive disseisins do not aid one another, where several persons successively enter on land as disseisors, without any conveyance from one to another, or any privity of estate between them other than that derived from the mere possession of the estate; their several consecutive possessions cannot be tacked, so as to make a

continuity of disseisin of sufficient length of time to bar the true owners of their right of entry. To sustain separate successive disseisins as constituting a continuous possession and conferring a title upon the last disseisor, there must have been a privity of estate between the several successive disseisors. To create such privity, there must have existed as between the different disseisors, in regard to the estate of which a title by disseisin is claimed, some such relation as that of ancestor and heir, grantor and grantee, or devisor and devisee. In such cases, the title acquired by disseisin passes by descent, deed or devise. But if there is not such privity, upon the determination of the possession of such disseisor, the seisin of the true owner revives and is revested, and a new distinct disseisin is made by each successive disseisor." Sawyer v. Kendall, 10 Cush. (Mass.) 241, 244 (1852).

The general rules laid down in Sawyer v. Kendall are still valid today. For example, in Stith v. Williams, 227 Kan. 32, 605 P.2d 86 (1980) the court said: "The tacking must evidence a continuous adverse possession for the statutory period. In addition, there must be no abandonments or other interruptions between those periods of possession that might return seisin to the owner."

Note that "the possession necessary to establish title by adverse possession need not always be personal possession by the adverse claimant, but in some circumstances may be established by conduct of another which the adverse claimant has authorized. . . . The trial court found that defendant's sons used the property with consent of the defendants." Holland v. Sutherland, 635 P.2d 926 (Colo.App. 1981). What are other examples of possession of this genre?

2. Can a possessor successfully claim title to land which he occupied without muniment of title for the statutory period in the mistaken belief that it was his own? The Supreme Court of Wyoming gave the following answer: "The main point in dispute herein is the point that has given rise to the greatest controversy in the law of adverse possession; namely, the rule that possession must be taken and held under a claim of right, or title, or ownership. The controversy has been fiercest in cases where possession of the land has been taken under a mistake, which, we may admit, as heretofore stated, was true in the case at bar. The contentions are perhaps not to be wondered at, for in the absence of specific legislation on the subject, courts would naturally attempt to protect the title of the real owner on the one hand, and to protect a truly adverse possession for the period fixed by the statute on the other. It is admitted by the authorities that it is difficult, if not impossible, to reconcile the various holdings of the courts on this subject, although we are inclined to think that a greater uniformity, in results at least, has been attained by the courts within the last few years. And it would seem to be true, as stated in the note to 33 L.R.A.,N.S., 930, that 'the trend of opinion is against disturbing him whose visible boundaries have existed for the period of the statute of limitations, which is illustrated in many cases where the possession has been held sufficient.'" City of Rock Springs v. Sturm, 39 Wyo. 494, 273 P. 908, 97 A.L.R. 1 (1929).

While the Wyoming court may be correct about "the trend of opinion" there are many cases which continue to point in the other direction. See, for example, Boyle v. D–X Sunray Oil Co., 191 F.Supp. 263, 267 (1961) in which a federal court, applying Iowa law, laid down a strict test for both adverse possession and acquiescence. The claimant admitted that the present boundary line was based on a mistake as to the true line and this was held to be fatal to his cause of action. "The principle just discussed operates so as to render impossible any acquisition of title by adverse possession in the majority of boundary line disputes because, in such cases, encroachment is ordinarily the result of mistake as to the location of the true line. This doctrine has been criticized as placing a premium on bad faith and as encouraging the possessor to falsely assert a hypothetical intention (to hold beyond the true line *if* that should be necessary) when only in rare cases would such a hypothetical intention be formed. . . . Nonetheless, this doctrine remains as the established law of Iowa which this Court is bound to follow."

Many of the cases dealing with this issue are discussed in Helmholz, Adverse Possession and Subjective Intent, 61 Wash.U.L.Q. 331 at 337–345 (1983). He confirms that the "newer, but now majority view" is that possession is "hostile even though the possessor would not have used the land had he known the location of the record boundary." However, the author concludes that "the cases which reject . . . the [older] 'subjective' test . . . stop well short of embracing a purely 'objective' test. . . . Indeed it appears that it is the importance of good faith which has fueled development in this area. . . . [T]he cases show that it is the very absence of a desire to trespass upon another's land that makes the [newer] rule preferable."

3. In a 1984 opinion which expressly overruled, in whole or in part, Howard v. Kunto and fifty-one other appellate decisions, the Supreme Court of Washington held in favor of defendant adverse possessors who had had actual notice of a contract provision in which an earlier possessor in their chain of title acknowledged both that his possession encroached upon adjacent land owned by plaintiffs' predecessors and that he would make no legal claim thereto. The court said, "[W]e are convinced that the dual requirement that the claimant take possession in 'good faith' and not recognize another's superior interest does not serve the purpose of the adverse possession doctrine. The 'hostility/claim of right' element . . . requires only that the claimant treat the land as his own as against the world throughout the statutory period. The nature of his possession will be determined solely on the basis of the manner in which he treats the property. His subjective belief regarding his true interest in the land and his intent to dispossess or not dispossess another is irrelevant to his determination." The court also held that defendants' possession, though not very conspicuous with respect to a portion of the land in question, was open and notorious because "the requirement of open and notorious is satisfied if the title holder has actual notice of the adverse use throughout the statutory period." Chaplin v. Sanders, 100 Wn.2d 853, 676 P.2d 431 (1984).

Four years later, a Washington appellate court denied the claim of an alleged adverse possessor on the grounds that his possession had not been "exclusive" (other houseboat owners, like him, also having moored their boats to the land in question and used it for an outhouse, gardens and firepits) and that he did not "believe that he had title to this property or any claim of right to it. . . . [H]is claim cannot be said to have been made in good faith. . . . [T]he *Chaplin* court did not indicate that the good faith of the possessor is no longer an element of adverse possession." ITT Rayonier, Inc. v. Bell, 51 Wn.App. 124, 752 P.2d 398 (1988).

Professor Helmholz, in the article cited in note 2 above, says that although many courts and scholars have stated that the motive of the possessor is legally irrelevant, that position is "undermined by the great majority of recent cases where there was actual evidence showing that the adverse possessor knew he was trespassing on the land of another at the time of the initial appropriation. Most such cases hold that the willful trespasser has acquired no title." Courts reached this result by various means, such as by saying "claim of right" requires more than "squatter's rights" or by characterizing the knowing trespasser's possession as permissive or lacking the requisite hostility.

4. If A's possession of O's land is permissive, and A purports to convey it to B who believes that A had good title, can B's possession qualify as hostile and adverse? For an affirmative answer, see Vanasdal v. Brinker, 27 Ohio App.3d 298, 500 N.E.2d 876 (1985).

5. Most statutes of limitation do not run against nonpossessory interests. Therefore, A might occupy Blackacre for twenty years adversely to B; but if B had only a life estate, the statute would not have run at all against the remainder interest of C, and A would have only an estate *pur autre vie*. See Annot., 58 A.L.R.2d 299, 302–05 (1958).

6. Most statutes of limitation also have disability provisions, so that the interests of minors, insane persons, etc., may survive well beyond the basic period.

"The exemption clause is applicable only as to the disability, or disabilities, existing when the cause of action accrued. If land was held adversely when the owner died the disability of one who succeeds to the estate will not interrupt the running of the statute. If the owner was under a disability at the time of his death the statute will start to run regardless of a disability in the new owner. There can be no 'tacking of disabilities' either with respect to successive disabilities in the same owner or with respect to disabilities in successive owners. However, if an owner is under two or more disabilities when the cause of action first accrues, the disability of longest duration will control.

"If land is held in trust the disability of a beneficiary is not controlling because the statute runs against the legal owner. This is also true with respect to an executor or administrator if he is considered to be the legal owner of the property. However, if he merely has possession of the land for purpose of administration the statute will not operate to bar the claim of an heir or devisee under a disability at the time of the death of the ancestor.

"Some statutes provide that the record owner may maintain his action within a stated period of time after the disability has been removed. Other statutes provide that the duration of disability is not computed as a part of the statutory period. Statutes frequently provide a maximum time during which the disability exemption will be allowed." Burby, Real Property 277–278 (3d ed. 1965) [The author's footnotes have been omitted.]

Can a person who has been in adverse possession of another's land for the period of limitations have a marketable title without having obtained a quiet title decree against the record owner? In Simis v. McElroy, 160 N.Y. 156, 54 N.E. 674 (1899), the defendant, purchaser under an executory land contract, refused to perform because a conveyance more than thirty years earlier had failed to give plaintiff-vendor's remote grantor the title of all the heirs of the deceased landowner. The court rejected plaintiff's breach of contract claim, saying, "Nonresidence, infancy, or other disabilities sometimes operate to prevent the statute of limitations from running. The difficulty with plaintiff's case is that she has not negatived the possibility of an outstanding claim to this land, or some interest in it, by the heirs. . . . [T]he proof must be of such a character as to exclude to a moral certainty any right or claim on their part. . . ." However, in Rehoboth Heights Development Co. v. Marshall, 15 Del.Ch. 314, 137 A. 83 (1927), the court granted a forty-year adverse possessor a decree of specific performance against the contract purchaser because the disability of infancy could not extend beyond thirty-one years and "other disabilities founded on insanity or imprisonment . . . can be founded on nothing more than conjecture without a shred of evidence to support them."

7. "There are undoubted instances where one may safely disregard an ancient title or claim appearing of record where there has been no assertion thereof against a subsequent title supported by possession. But the solicitude of the statute for persons under disabilities makes it relatively ineffective to accomplish its great purpose, viz., to quiet titles. We need to reexamine the basis for these exceptions. The period of general statutes of limitations applying to real property in the different states varies from five to thirty years, with a considerable number providing for ten, fifteen or twenty years. Within fifteen or twenty years most minors attain their majority and many others overcome their disabilities. The following question is then in order and deserves a fair answer: how often will minors, insane persons and other incompetents be deprived of their property if this exception in their favor were not contained in the statute? Will not relatives and friends of such persons ordinarily be sufficiently apprised of their interests to see that they are not lost? Legal action is always possible by a guardian. If actual loss should occasionally occur, will it not be more than compensated for by the greatly improved security given to all titles by casting the exception from the limitation chart? . . .

"In view of the relatively long periods of time allowed in many states for those not under disability to commence actions to recover land, it may be seriously doubted whether there is any justification for extending such periods in favor of persons under disabilities. A legislative movement to delete altogether or to shorten the additional period customarily allowed to incompetents may be observed in recent years. The desired objective may be accomplished either by shortening the general period of limitations permitted to enforce outstanding rights, or by limiting the period of additional time allowed persons under disabilities. More than ten or fifteen years seems unnecessary for the general period; five years more for persons who are under disabilities and who have no guardian would appear ample for the additional period. If there is a guardian, such additional period could well be omitted entirely. One immediate benefit would appear in the reduced volume of title litigation involving old claims. The larger benefits in greater stability of titles would be more than sufficient to justify these changes in legislation.

"While statutes of the kind discussed in the preceding paragraphs are not in themselves sufficient to bar all outstanding claims, they constitute the first step and an essential part of a thorough program to streamline conveyancing and eliminate old defects as perpetual impairments on titles." Basye, Clearing Land Titles 183, 188–189 (2d ed.1970) [The author's footnotes have been omitted.]

8. Besides adverse possession, there are at least four other doctrines that have been employed by the courts to settle boundary disputes, especially where uncertainty over the precise location of a boundary on the ground results from an ambiguous or confusing description in a deed or other document: (1) boundaries by agreement, (2) boundaries by acquiescence, (3) estoppel, and (4) boundary determination by a common grantor. None of these doctrines requires a writing to satisfy the statute of frauds, yet all of them have the effect of reducing the size of one owner's parcel while enlarging another's. The courts say not that a transfer takes place, but rather that the boundary has been redefined or reconstrued by the parties' actions. See Cunningham, Stoebuck and Whitman, The Law of Property 764–73 (1984); Piotrowski v. Parks, 39 Wn.App. 37, 691 P.2d 591 (1984) (boundary by agreement); Drake v. Claar, 339 N.W.2d 844 (Iowa App.1983) (boundary by acquiescence).

FAILONI v. CHICAGO & NORTH WESTERN RAILWAY CO.

Supreme Court of Illinois, 1964.
30 Ill.2d 258, 195 N.E.2d 619.

DAILY, JUSTICE. Chicago and North Western Railway Company, defendant, appeals from a declaratory judgment of the circuit court of Macoupin County which found that title to the mineral rights, except coal, under some 130 acres of Macoupin County land was held in fee simple by the surface owner, Catterina Failoni, the plaintiff. The jurisdiction of this court has been properly invoked since a freehold is involved.

The subject real estate consists of two separate parcels, composed 76 acres and 54 acres, respectively. The larger tract was f owned by John Ottersburg and Janna Ottersburg, who veyed "all coal and other minerals" thereunder to B.C. Dorsey by warranty deed. By mesne conveyances of "all coal and other minerals," record title thereto became vested in defendant in 1956. In 1921 Tony Failoni, plaintiff's husband, received an administrator's deed for the Ottersburg tract which apparently made no reference to the mineral interest, and upon his death in 1956, his heirs quitclaimed the property to plaintiff.

The smaller tract was formerly owned by John McKeone, who in 1903 conveyed by warranty deed to B. C. Dorsey "all coal and other minerals" thereunder. By mesne conveyances, record title to this mineral interest also became vested in defendant in 1956. However, by deed which referred only to a prior sale of the underlying "coal," McKeone later conveyed this tract to Ernest Busse, who in turn sold it in 1939 to Tony Failoni and Catterina Failoni, as joint tenants and not as tenants in common.

It appears that for some years prior to 1942, Superior Coal Company, being then the record owner of the mineral interest, mined the coal from under the land, and during this time the coal rights were separately assessed against and taxes thereon paid by Superior Coal Company. After the coal was removed, however, no further assessment of coal rights was made. It also appears that it was the practice in Macoupin County to assess no mineral interest other than coal, and no such assessment was made at any time against the subject property even though the property was in recent years leased for the production of gas.

The plaintiff testified that she had lived on the land for the past 40 years and claimed the mineral rights as well as the surface interest. She and her husband executed oil and gas leases thereon in 1923, 1940, and 1942, but at no time did anyone except Superior Coal Company ever remove, or attempt to remove, coal or minerals therefrom. Plaintiff and her family farmed the surface, however, and paid taxes assessed by government survey description.

It is admitted that record title to the surface interest and to the mineral interest is now held by plaintiff and defendant, respectively. Nevertheless, plaintiff contends that because the conveyances in her chain of title did not except the mineral interest she acquired color of title to the mineral interest which has since ripened into fee ownership under the provisions of section 7 of the Limitations Act. (Ill.Rev.Stat. 1961, chap. 83, par. 7.) This is the sole question presented upon appeal.

Section 7 states: "Whenever a person having color of title, made in good faith, to vacant and unoccupied land, shall pay all taxes legally assessed thereon for seven successive years, he or she shall be deemed and adjudged to be the legal owner of said vacant and unoccupied land, to the extent and according to the purport of his or her paper title." We have construed this to mean that one claiming the benefit of this statute must prove not only that he holds vacant and unimproved land under color of title but also that he has paid taxes thereon for seven successive years and has since taken possession thereof. Chicago Title and Trust Co. v. Drobnick, 20 Ill.2d 374, 169 N.E.2d 792; Anderson v. Village Homebuilders, Inc., 401 Ill. 60, 81 N.E.2d 430; White v. Harris, 206 Ill. 584, 69 N.E. 519.

It has long been recognized that the mineral estate may be severed from the surface estate by a grant specifically of the minerals, reserving the surface, or by a grant of the surface while reserving the minerals, and when this has been accomplished, both estates are subject, to independent ownership and separate taxation, and both constitute "land" within the meaning of section 7. (Pyle v. Ferrell, 12 Ill.2d 547, 147 N.E.2d 341; Shell Oil Co. v. Moore, 382 Ill. 556, 48 N.E.2d 400.) Oil and gas, by the overwhelming weight of authority, are minerals, and when the mineral interest is severed from the surface estate, the former may also be regarded as "vacant and unoccupied land." (Catlin Coal Co. v. Lloyd, 176 Ill. 275, 52 N.E. 144.) Although deeds may in certain instances provide color of title, (Bergesen v. Clauss, 15 Ill.2d 337, 155 N.E.2d 20, 68 A.L.R.2d 446; Belunski v. Oakes, 6 Ill.2d 176, 128 N.E.2d 689) they do not in and of themselves operate as adverse possession, or even notice thereof where the severance of the mineral and surface estates was prior thereto. (Uphoff v. Trustees of Tufts College, 351 Ill. 146, 184 N.E.2d 213, 93 A.L.R. 1224; Jilek v. Chicago, Wilmington & Franklin Coal Co., 382 Ill. 241, 47 N.E.2d 96, 146 A.L.R. 871.) Possession of the surface does not carry possession of the minerals, nor does nonuse or abandonment of the mineral interest terminate said estate. (Jilek v. Chicago, Wilmington & Franklin Coal Co., 382 Ill. 241, 47 N.E.2d 96, 146 A.L.R. 871.) To possess the mineral estate, one must undertake the actual removal thereof from the ground or do such other act as will apprise the community that such interest is in the exclusive use and enjoyment of the claiming party. (Pickens v. Adams, 7 Ill.2d 283, 131 N.E.2d 38, 56 A.L.R.2d 605; Towle v. Quante, 246 Ill. 568, 92 N.E. 967.) Furthermore, payment of taxes by government survey description after severance of title between minerals and surface does not constitute payment of taxes under section 7 of the Limitations Act, regardless of whether the minerals were in fact separately assessed. Uphoff v. Trustees of Tufts College, 351 Ill. 146, 184 N.E. 213, 93 A.L.R. 1224; Catlin Coal Co. v. Lloyd, 176 Ill. 275, 52 N.E. 144.

In the present case, neither plaintiff nor her predecessors in title actually removed any minerals so as to gain possession thereof, the mere executing of oil and gas leases not being sufficient for this purpose, nor did they ever pay taxes upon the separate mineral estate. In fact it appears that no minerals, except coal, were ever assessed or were intended to be assessed under the policy then in force in Macoupin County. Although plaintiff resided upon and farmed these premises, such use related only to the surface and not to the mineral interest which she now claims. Therefore, the provisions of section 7 of the Limitations Act were not complied with, and the ownership of the mineral estate rests not with the plaintiff but with defendant, the record title holder.

The judgment of the circuit court of Macoupin County is reversed and the cause remanded to that court, with directions to enter judgment for the defendant in accordance with this opinion.

Reversed and remanded, with directions.

NOTE

For a later case on the same point, see Payne v. Williams, 91 Ill. App.3d 336, 46 Ill.Dec. 783, 414 N.E.2d 836 (1980). "The court in *Failoni* was presented with a controversy virtually identical to the instant case, and our supreme court there held that where the surface and mineral estates have been severed, possession of the estate has been treated as an additional requirement for adverse possession and that possession of the surface does not carry with it possession of the minerals."

MERCER v. WAYMAN (Cotenancy)

Supreme Court of Illinois, 1956.
9 Ill.2d 441, 137 N.E.2d 815.

DAVIS, JUSTICE. Plaintiffs, widow and children of Fred L. Mercer, deceased, filed this suit in the circuit court of Marion County against the defendants, the surviving sons of Lora Wayman, deceased, and the widow and daughter of Verne Wayman, deceased, to set aside certain oil and gas leases executed by defendants and to have themselves declared the sole owners of the land in question. The circuit court granted the relief prayed for in the complaint and a freehold being involved, defendants appealed directly to this court.

The facts in the record are undisputed. The 40-acre tract of land was originally owned in fee simple by John W. Mercer who died intestate prior to 1920, leaving him surviving as his sole heirs-at-law his widow, five sons and two daughters.

Shortly thereafter one of the daughters, Lora Wayman, died intestate, leaving her surviving, Oscar T. Wayman, her husband, and three minor sons, Verne Wayman, June Wayman and Paul Wayman.

Thereafter, on May 7, 1920, the widow of John W. Mercer, four of the sons, and the surviving daughter, together with their spouses, joined in a quitclaim deed conveying the 40-acre tract to the remaining son, Fred L. Mercer and M. Hattie Mercer, his wife. Oscar T. Wayman, the husband of the deceased Lora Wayman, also joined in the conveyance, both individually and as "father and natural guardian of Verne Wayman, June Wayman, Paul Wayman, children of Lora Wayman, deceased." This deed purported to grant to Fred and Hattie Mercer "all interest" in the 40-acre tract. The consideration for the deed was the assumption of an existing mortgage on the property.

Fred L. Mercer and M. Hattie Mercer entered upon the property and farmed it continuously until the present time. The property was assessed in the name of Fred L. Mercer and they paid all taxes when due. They leased land, collected crop rentals, and were generally reputed to be the owners thereof. They executed mortgages on the property in April, 1920, December, 1920, and April, 1926, and thereby warranted their fee simple title to the premises. All of these mortgages were recorded.

Both the plaintiffs and the defendants, or their predecessors in title, executed oil and gas leases on the entire tract. The plaintiffs executed such leases in 1938, 1939, and 1953. Subsequent to the execution of the latter oil and gas lease by plaintiffs, wherein J. T. Thompson was lessee, the defendants also executed oil and gas leases on the same tract to the said J. T. Thompson. These are the leases which the plaintiffs seek to set aside. On April 4, 1939, June Wayman, Paul Wayman, and Verne Wayman, now deceased, executed an oil and gas lease to the Texas Company, which was thereafter recorded. This lease was subsequently released by the Texas Company.

The youngest of the children of Lora Wayman attained his majority on July 1, 1926. Neither the defendants nor any deceased member of the Wayman family ever made claim to any right, title or interest in the tract of land in question, nor have they sought an accounting of the rents and profits; and neither the plaintiffs nor any deceased member of their family ever asserted to the defendants or their predecessors in title any claim of possession adverse to them.

The plaintiffs contend that their possession of the tract in question has ripened into title and defendants are barred from any claim as to the premises by reason of both the 20-year Statute of Limitations (Ill. Rev.Stat.1953, chap. 83, par. 1) and the 7-year Statute of Limitations (Ill.Rev.Stat.1953, chap. 83, par. 6). Defendants insist that they are tenants in common of an undivided one seventh of the tract and as such, are not barred by the 20-year Statute of Limitations because there has been no actual disseizin or ouster. They further contend that the deed to Fred L. Mercer was not good color of title as to the interests of the minor sons of Lora Wayman.

The sole issue presented to this court is whether defendants are, as the trial court held, barred from their claim by virtue of the Statute of Limitations.

While the plaintiffs exercised such control and dominion over the property as to be hostile and adverse to all strangers, the rules with regard to adverse possession are different in the case of one cotenant who claims adversely to other cotenants. The doctrine was well stated in Simpson v. Manson, 345 Ill. 543, 551, 178 N.E. 250, 253: "The rule is well settled that the mere possession by one tenant in common who receives all the rents and profits and pays the taxes assessed against the property, no matter for how long a period, cannot be set up as a bar against the cotenants. In such case the possession of one tenant in common is in contemplation of law the possession of all the tenants in common. Such possession, however, may become adverse if the tenant in common by his acts and conduct disseizes his cotenants by repudiating their title and claiming adversely to them. . . . Before the possession of one tenant in common can be adverse to the cotenant there must be a disseizin or ouster by some outward act of ownership of an unequivocal character, overt and notorious, and of such nature as to impart information and notice to the cotenant that an adverse possession and disseizin are intended to be asserted by the tenant in possession. . . . Such notice need not, however, be formal in its nature

(Roberts v. Cox, 259 Ill. 232, 102 N.E. 204) and if one tenant in common holds exclusive possession, claiming the land as his and his conduct and possession are of such a character as to give notice to his cotenant that his possession is adverse, the statute of limitations will run." . . .

These rules have been consistently followed in this State. As recently as Williams v. Fulton, 4 Ill.2d 524, 123 N.E.2d 495, we held that in order to start the running of the Statute of Limitations against a cotenant, it must be shown that the tenant in possession gave actual notice to the tenant out of possession that he was claiming adversely, or that the tenant out of possession had received notice of such claim of the tenant in possession by some act which would amount to an ouster or disseizin. In White v. Harris, 206 Ill. 584, at page 592, 69 N.E. 519, at page 522, we stated: "'A party claiming title by adverse possession always claims in derogation of the right of the real owner. He admits that the legal title is in another. He rests his claim, not upon a title in himself, as the true owner, but upon holding adversely to the true owner for the period prescribed by the statute of limitations. Claiming a benefit from his own wrong his acts are to be construed strictly.' Cornelius v. Giberson, 25 N.J.L. 1, 31. 'Adverse possession cannot be made out by inference or implication, for the presumptions are all in favor of the true owner, and the proof to establish it must be strict, clear, positive and unequivocal.' Zirngibl v. Calumet Dock Co., 157 Ill. 430, 42 N.E. 431. The rule is that every presumption will be made in favor of the holder of the legal title, and no presumption will be made in favor of the holder of color of title only. Kurz v. Miller, 89 Wis. 426, 62 N.W. 182." In Dunlavy v. Lowrie, 372 Ill. 622, at page 632, 25 N.E.2d 67, at page 72, we held that: "Mere knowledge of the obvious fact of possession cannot be converted into proof of knowledge that those in possession were claiming adversely."

The pertinent statutes of limitations have likewise been held inapplicable to cases where there was possession in a cotenant and no actual ouster or disseizin. . . . In Stowell v. Lynch, 269 Ill. 437, at pages 443 and 444, 110 N.E. 51, at page 54 we held: "To establish a title under section 1 of the Limitation Act . . . not only must there be 20 years' continuous uninterrupted possession, but such possession must be hostile in its inception, and so continue. It must be visible, exclusive, and notorious, and be acquired and retained under claim of title inconsistent with that of the true owner. All these elements must concur."

Fred L. Mercer was a cotenant of the defendants at the time of the delivery of the quitclaim deed which purported to convey the premises therein described to him and Hattie Mercer, his wife. Tested by the above rule, the original taking and holding possession of the land by Fred L. Mercer and Hattie Mercer was not hostile or adverse as required by the 20-year Limitation Act. This deed, signed by Oscar Wayman as father and natural guardian of Verne Wayman, June Wayman, and Paul Wayman, minor children of Lora Wayman, deceased, was ineffective to convey the interests of said minor children. It did not constitute color of title as against the minor children because of the defects appearing on the face of the deed showing that their interests had not been conveyed. Consequently, the 7-year Statute of Limitations was inapplicable. Allen v. Allen, 292 Ill. 453, 127 N.E. 85, 27 A.L.R. 1.

While the plaintiffs have, for thirty-four years, occupied the premises, paid the taxes, and improved the property, they at no time affirmatively did anything that would serve as notice to their cotenants that they were claiming adversely to them. Such adverse claim as against cotenants cannot be established by inference. Stowell v. Lynch, 269 Ill. 437, 110 N.E. 51. The execution of mortgages, warranting complete ownership, would not be of a nature to impart information and notice to a cotenant that adverse possession or disseizin was intended. There is no evidence that defendants had notice of the execution of oil leases by plaintiffs, and, in any event, such oil leases could have been executed by a cotenant. Plaintiffs rely on Simpson v. Manson, 345 Ill. 543, 178 N.E. 250, but in that case there was actual notice to the majority of the cotenants, in both number and interest, that the tenant in possession claimed title to the land in question. Other cases cited by the plaintiffs . . . are all cases where there was an ouster by a deed of the entire property from one cotenant to a stranger, or where it was proved that there was actual knowledge on the part of the cotenant out of possession that the cotenant in possession was claiming to hold the same adversely.

The burden was upon the plaintiffs to prove facts which would cause the provisions of the Statute of Limitations to bar the defendants from asserting any claim of ownership to the property. This they have failed to do.

The decree of the trial court is accordingly reversed.

Decree reversed.

NOTES

1. For a comment on the principal case see 1957 U.Ill.L.F. 120.

As the principal case indicates, concurrent ownership causes special problems for the cotenant who is claiming the full fee simple title based on adverse possession. See, for example, City and County of Honolulu v. Bennett, 57 Haw. 195, 552 P.2d 1380 (1976) where the court stated: "Following in the line of *Yin* and *Poka*, we lay down in this case the rule that, because of the general fiduciary relationship between cotenants, a tenant in common claiming by adverse possession must prove that he acted in *good faith* towards the cotenants during the statutory period. In most circumstances, this requirement of good faith will in turn mandate that the tenant claiming adversely must *actually notify* his cotenants that he is claiming against them. In the following exceptional circumstances, however, good faith is satisfied by less than actual notice: where the tenant in possession has *no reason to suspect* that a cotenancy exists; or where the tenant in possession makes a *good faith, reasonable effort to notify* the cotenants but is unable to locate them; or where the tenants out of possession already have *actual knowledge* that the tenant in possession is claiming adversely to their interests. In these limited circumstances, the notice requirement will be satisfied by constructive notice and 'open and notorious possession'." This principle was reiterated in Matter of Keamo, 3 Hawaii App. 360, 650 P.2d 1365 (1982).

An Idaho court put it more simply. "A cotenant (brothers and sisters were involved) who claims to have adversely possessed the interest of his cotenants must prove that the fact of adverse possession was 'brought home' to the cotenants." Tremayne v. Taylor, 101 Idaho 792, 621 P.2d 408 (1980).

Did the plaintiffs in the principal case have any reason to suspect that a cotenancy existed?

In this connection, see McCree v. Jones, 103 Ill.App.3d 66, 58 Ill. Dec. 644, 430 N.E.2d 676 (1981). The court, in a case very similar on the facts, cited Mercer v. Wayman but distinguished it and held for the claimant who had been in possession for thirty years under a quitclaim deed which purported to give title to the entire property. There was a vigorous dissent, based on Mercer v. Wayman, an Illinois Supreme Court case which of course the Illinois Appellate Court could not overrule. The Illinois law in this area remains murky. Do you think Mercer v. Wayman was rightly decided?

2. In Nicholas v. Cousins, 1 Wn.App. 133, 459 P.2d 970 (1969) the cotenants of the plaintiff were out of possession but they questioned the competency of the mother at the time of the probate of the mother's will. The court held the cotenants had received constructive notice of the plaintiff's claim to the property devised to him and when they failed to examine the history of the transaction and allowed the plaintiff to remain in possession for more than seven years and pay taxes on the property, the plaintiff acquired title by adverse possession. "The knowing cotenant out of possession who has notice or is held to have notice of the hostile acts of a 'stranger' to his title, must act to protect his position, or suffer the consequential loss of his title. . . . But the acts of a cotenant in possession which appear hostile to the world at large do not place an obligation to act upon the cotenant out of possession, until he learns—actually or constructively—of the accompanying hostile intent."

3. Could a forged deed, which is an absolute nullity, operate to give color of title? For an affirmative answer see Bergesen v. Clauss, 15 Ill.2d 337, 341, 155 N.E.2d 20, 22, 68 A.L.R.2d 446 (1960) where the court said: "Color of title is not a claim of ownership that is defective for some technical reason, nor is it meant to be something just short of absolute title. Rather, color of title is an instrument or a record that in fact does not convey title but appears to have the effect of a conveyance. Color of title, then, need not be an imperfect title of a sort that could, without aider, ripen into absolute title. Color of title need only show some evidence of claimed ownership by the grantee. It need be only some semblance of title, however invalid may be that claim. . . . A forged deed, when taken in good faith, may constitute color of title if, at the time of the purchase of the deed, the grantee believed it to be genuine."

4. Can a remainderman obtain title by adverse possession against a life tenant? Can a life tenant do so against a remainderman? In Lucas v. Brown, Ala., 396 So.2d 63 (1981), the court held that since a remainderman has no right to possession during the life of the life tenant, the possession by a remainderman would be adverse to the possession of the life tenant. The doctrine of prescription clearly applied, even though a life tenant could not adversely possess against a remainderman. Why not?

5. Statutes of limitation have been a great boon to merchantability of title, and they scrape a few of the staler barnacles from the title chain. The benefits of such statutes tend to be illusory, however. With few exceptions they do not bar a future interest, since the cause of action will not accrue until the estate becomes possessory; parties under disability are usually given preferred treatment and their interests may survive even an extended period; and the statutes do not normally bar the claims of the federal, state or even local governments.

Because of the deficiencies of the traditional statutes of limitation, many states have passed specialized statutes which bar particular interests, such as mineral estates, mortgages, possibilities of reverter, rights of entry for condition broken, restrictive covenants, etc. These statutes are typically more than the usual limitation acts, since they may terminate interests which are not in fact in the adverse possession of another or they may cut off future interests which have not yet become possessory. See, for example, the leading Illinois case, Trustees of Schools of Township No. 1 v. Batdorf, 6 Ill.2d 486, 130 N.E.2d 111 (1955), which held constitutional a Reverter Act which limited the duration of possibilities of reverter and rights of entry for condition broken to fifty years (later reduced to forty years by the Illinois legislature), unless a claim preserving the future interest was filed within one year after the effective date of the Act. The Act was designed to clear titles to "little red school house" tracts at a time when consolidated school districts were coming into existence. The Illinois Supreme Court said at one point: "It has been said that the Reverter Act was passed in recognition of the operation of possibilities of reverter as 'clogs on title, withdrawing property thus encumbered from the commercial mortgage market long after the individual, social or economic reason for their creation had ceased, and at a time when the heirs from whom a release could be obtained will be so numerous as to be virtually impossible to locate.'" Note that these future interests would not become possessory until the land was no longer used for school purposes and in some cases that had not occurred at the time the Reverter Act was passed. Nonetheless, the future interests would be barred unless the owners filed the necessary claims in the recorder's office within the one year period. Since very few owners of the future interests would do so, either because they did not know of the passage of the Reverter Act or because they did not even know they owned the interests (many were heirs of long-since deceased grantors of the original defeasible fee), the practical effect of the Reverter Act and the court's decision was to limit the duration of these future interests to forty years. This means that the title examiner could confine his search for such interests to the forty year period. Similarly, the effect of the statute applied and upheld in Manning v. New England Mutual Life Insurance Co., 399 Mass. 730, 506 N.E.2d 870 (1987), was to limit the duration of restrictive covenants to fifty years unless notices of restriction were filed, thus confining title searches.

The future interests affected by the Batdorf case were, at best, "remotely expectant" (the court's language) and the economic stakes were not particularly significant. The same cannot be said of the mineral interests involved in the next case, which goes as far as any decision to date in upholding legislation of this genre.

SHORT v. TEXACO, INC.

Supreme Court of Indiana, 1980.
273 Ind. 518, 406 N.E.2d 625.

DEBRULER, JUSTICE.

The trial court declared Ind.Code §§ 32–5–11–1 through 32–5–11–8, the Mineral Lapse Act, unconstitutional. The Act puts an end to interests in coal, oil, gas or other minerals which have not been used for twenty years. The "use" of a mineral interest which continues it in force includes actual production, payment of rents, royalties or taxes, or the filing of a claim in the dormant mineral interest record in the recorder's office. It granted owners of mineral interests a two year period of grace after its effective date in which to file the claim and preserve the interest. This is an appeal from two judgments below, consolidated here, that termination of an interest under the Act is contrary to due process, equal protection, and the guarantee of just compensation for property taken by the State.

The Act reflects the legislative belief that the existence of a mineral interest about which there has been no display of activity or interest by the owners thereof for a period of twenty years or more is mischievous and contrary to the economic interests and welfare of the public. The existence of such stale and abandoned interests creates uncertainties in titles and constitutes an impediment to the development of the mineral interests that may be present and to the development of the surface rights as well. The Act removes this impediment by returning the severed mineral estate to the surface rights owner. There is a decided public interest to be served when this occurs. The extinguishment of such an interest makes the entire productive potential of the property again available for human use.

The trial court concluded that the legislative purpose of the Act is to facilitate the exploitation of energy sources and accepted such purpose as legitimate. While all its conclusions are not entirely clear, it went on to void the entire statute because it determined among other things that due process of law required the divestiture of the vested mineral interest to be preceded by due process notice and an opportunity to be heard.

Interests or estates in oil, gas, coal and other minerals lying beneath the surface of the land are interests in real estate for our purposes here, and as such are entitled beyond question to the firmest protection of the Constitution from irrational state action. They are vested property interests separate and distinct from the surface ownership. The State has no power to deprive an owner of such an interest without due process of law. They are entitled to the same protection as are fee simple titles. They are themselves of great utility and benefit to the society as a means of facilitating the development of natural resources.

Courts of this state and nation have always given due regard to constitutional constraints upon their authority to void statutes. In doing so in Noel v. Ewing, (1857) 9 Ind. 37, we said:

> "It is due from the judiciary to sustain and reconcile their enactments, if possible. We will not lightly conclude that the law-making power has either ignorantly or wilfully violated the constitution. To justify the Courts in declaring an act void, it must be clearly subversive of that instrument. (Citations omitted.)
>
> They who claim that the legislature has, in this particular, transcended its constitutional power, should be prepared to make a strong and clear case. All doubts must fall in favor of the validity of the law." 9 Ind. at 43.

We reaffirm again now in this case our adherence to this vital principle.

In Chicago and North Western Transportation Co. v. Pedersen, (1977) 80 Wis.2d 566, 259 N.W.2d 316, the Supreme Court of Wisconsin voided a similar act which directed that mineral rights revert to the surface fee ownership if they were not registered or taxes had not been paid on them. That statute was deemed contrary to procedural due process in that the mineral interest owner was not given notice or an opportunity to be heard prior to the reversion of his interest to the surface rights owner. That court relied upon Mullane v. Central Hanover Bank & Trust Co., (1950) 339 U.S. 306, 70 S.Ct. 652, 94 L.Ed. 865, and Bell v. Burson, (1971) 402 U.S. 535, 91 S.Ct. 1586, 29 L.Ed.2d 90. The court below took the same tack in voiding the Indiana Act.

In *Mullane,* supra, primarily relied upon by the trial court, the United States Supreme Court said:

> "Many controversies have raged about the cryptic and abstract words of the Due Process Clause but there can be no doubt that at a minimum they require that deprivation of life, liberty or property by adjudication be preceded by notice and opportunity for hearing appropriate to the nature of the case.
>
> . . .
>
> An elementary and fundamental requirement of due process *in any proceeding* which is to be accorded finality is notice reasonably calculated, under all the circumstances, to apprise interested parties of the pendency of the action and afford them an opportunity

> to present their objections." (Emphasis added.) 339 U.S. at 313, 314, 70 S.Ct. at 656, 657.

In *Mullane* the bank petitioned a court for settlement of an account of a trust fund, and the sufficiency of publication notice to beneficiaries was the issue. Notice was due to the beneficiaries because a tribunal was about to adjudicate upon their property. The Mineral Lapse Act in contrast is self-executing and does not contemplate an adjudication before a tribunal before a lapse occurs. When the statutory conditions exist the lapse occurs. *Mullane* does not support the trial court conclusion that notice and hearing are due to a mineral interest owner prior to the occurrence of an extinguishment.

Bell v. Burson, supra, relied upon by the trial court does not support the conclusion either. There a Georgia law provided that the drivers license of an individual motorist involved in an accident is to be automatically suspended without notice or hearing if security was not posted to cover the damages claimed by aggrieved parties in the accident reports. In the course of holding this system violative of procedural due process the court specifically noted:

> "If the statute barred the issuance of licenses to all motorists who did not carry liability insurance or who did not post security, the statute would not, under our cases, violate the Fourteenth Amendment. (Citations omitted.) It does not follow, however, that the amendment also permits the Georgia statutory scheme where not all motorists, but rather only motorists involved in accidents, are required to post security under penalty of loss of the licenses." 402 U.S. at 539, 91 S.Ct. at 1589.

Thus, even in *Bell,* a case involving a different complex of social concerns, there is this language supportive of the Act under consideration. It would support as consistent with procedural due process a legislative enactment which declared no more than that all licenses issued by the state would cease to be valid on a date certain in the future unless proof of financial responsibility were filed. Cf. Frost & Frost Trucking Co. v. Railroad Commission, (1926) 271 U.S. 583, 46 S.Ct. 605, 70 L.Ed. 1101. Such a hypothetical statute would be very similar in operation to the Act being questioned in this case.

The Act under question does not provide for any adjudicatory process by a court or administrative agency. The absence of such a provision is not, we think, invalidating. The Act simply spells out the conditions which when existing mandate the extinguishment of an interest. If a court should be called upon to determine whether such conditions arose in a particular case so as to have effected the loss of an interest, the owner of such interest would be entitled to notice and an opportunity to be heard. Prior to any extinguishment the owner of an interest will have had notice by reason of the enactment itself of the conditions which would give rise to an extinguishment and at a minimum a two year opportunity to prevent those conditions from occurring by filing a statement of claim. Anderson National Bank v. Luckett, (1944) 321 U.S. 233, 64 S.Ct. 599, 88 L.Ed. 692. That procedure is both simple and inexpensive. Based upon the foregoing analysis we do not find the case of Chicago & North Western Transportation Co. v. Pedersen, supra, persuasive.

The reasoning of the trial court and the cases relied upon by it do not warrant the conclusion that the Act is unconstitutional because it fails to afford notice and hearing to mineral interest owners required by procedural due process.

The trial court also concluded that the extinguishment of mineral interests under the Act constituted a taking of property without due process of law. Judge Young for the Fourth District Court of Appeals summarized the due process analysis applicable here in Foreman v. State ex rel. Department of Natural Resources, (1979) Ind.App., 387 N.E.2d 455:

> "The government has the inherent power or 'police power' to enact laws, within constitutional limits, to promote order, safety, health, morals, and the general welfare of society. . . . Property rights are not absolute and may be restricted by legislation which constitutes a proper exercise of the State's police power. . . . Legislation is a proper exercise of the police power when the collective benefit to the general public outweighs the restraint imposed. . . . The methods or means used to protect the public order, health, morals, safety or welfare must have some reasonable relation to the purpose or end sought." 387 N.E.2d at 460.

Study of this Act reveals that its outstanding feature is its declaration that mineral interests are terminable. Whatever may be the exact legal dimensions of such interests, they are not greater than fee simple titles. Under the statute of limitations and the law of adverse possession a fee simple title to land is terminable. The Mineral Lapse Act can be viewed as vesting legal title in the owner of the surface rights which is free of the mineral servitude when the conditions required by it exist. A statute of limitations vests legal title in an adverse possessor as against the true legal owner when the conditions required by it exist. Brown v. Anderson, (1883) 90 Ind. 93. Statutes of limitation are statutes of repose founded upon a rule of necessity and convenience and the well-being of society. Chase Securities Corp. v. Donaldson, (1945) 325 U.S. 304, 65 S.Ct. 1137, 89 L.Ed. 1628. This Act is also based upon the same rule. Cf. Love v. Lynchburg National Bank and Trust Co., (1965) 205 Va. 860, 140 S.E.2d 650. We do not disregard the distinctions between the two types of statutes. The element of possession is different. No cause of action has arisen in the owner of the mineral interest which is required to be prosecuted. Given these differences and aforementioned similarities, we believe that this Act is, according to its principal intent and effect, and for the purpose of constitutional analysis, analogous to acts of limitation which vests title to real and personal property.

Acts of limitation are not per se unconstitutional as impairing the obligation of contracts or as denying a person property without due process of law. This is so even though they extinguish the right of the party having a true title and vest a perfect title in the adverse holder. Hawkins v. Barney's Lessee, (1831) 5 Pet. 457, 8 L.Ed. 190, is an early case upholding the validity of a seven year limitation upon actions to recover possession of land in Kentucky. In the course of that opinion it is said:

> "It is argued, that limitation laws although belonging to the lex fori, and applying immediately to the remedy, yet indirectly they effect a complete divesture and even transfer of right. This is unquestionably true, and yet in no wise fatal to the validity of this law. The right to appropriate a derelict is one of universal law, well known to the civil law, the common law, and all law; it existed in a state of nature, and is only modified by society, according to the discretion of each community."

The transfer of right upheld by the court was deemed the indirect product of the limitation law. The transfer or right effected by the Indiana Act under consideration is its direct product. That minor difference would not support a contrary evaluation of our Act.

In Terry v. Anderson, (1877) 95 U.S. 628, 24 L.Ed. 365, Chief Justice Waite stated the general rule regarding the manner in which statutes of limitation are received by courts:

> "This court has often decided that statutes of limitation affecting existing rights are not unconstitutional, if a reasonable time is given for the commencement of an action before the bar takes effect. . . .
>
> In all such cases, the question is one of reasonableness, and we have, therefore, only to consider whether the time allowed in this statute is, under all the circumstances, reasonable. Of that the legislature is primarily the judge; and we cannot overrule the decision of that department of government, unless a palpable error has been committed." 95 U.S. at 632–633.

Indiana is in accord with the rule stated and the reasoning behind it. Guthrie v. Wilson, (1959) 240 Ind. 188, 162 N.E.2d 79; Sansberry v. Hughes, (1910) 174 Ind. 638, 92 N.E. 783. In *Terry* the court held that the period of nine months and seventeen days given to sue upon a cause of action was not unconstitutional. In Turner v. People of State of New York, (1897) 168 U.S. 90, 18 S.Ct. 38, 42 L.Ed. 392, a statute declaring that past sales and conveyances by a comptroller for nonpayment of taxes would be conclusively presumed regular six months after the effective day of the statute was upheld as providing a reasonable period for bringing an action. Pursuant to Ind.Code § 32–5–11–4, owners of mineral interests are granted a minimum of two years in which to act to preserve their interests. Such a period of grace would constitute a reasonable time as contemplated by these cases.

In Wilson v. Iseminger, (1902) 185 U.S. 55, 22 S.Ct. 573, 46 L.Ed. 804, the United States Supreme Court upheld a statute which barred actions to recover ground rents and extinguished totally the right to recover further such rents, after twenty-one years had expired during which no declaration or acknowledgment of the existence of the right or claim had been made. The statute provided that the bar and extinguishment would not be effective until three years after the passage of the act. The court held that the act gave a reasonable time to the owners of the ground rents for preserving their rights. This case strongly supports the validity of our Act, because it upheld a statute having an extinguishment feature similar to the Indiana Act under consideration.

The purposes of this Act as stated above at the beginning of this opinion are to remedy uncertainties in titles and to facilitate the exploitation of energy sources and other valuable mineral resources. The dependence of local economies upon the mineral recovery industry and the entire State upon limited fossil fuel resources illustrates the public nature of these purposes. The objectives are valid and similar to those served by acts of limitation and the law of adverse possession. In limiting its incursion upon mineral rights to those which have been unused in the statutory sense for as long as twenty years, and in granting a two year period of grace after the enactment of the statute to preserve interests, the Legislature adopted means which are rationally related to such objectives, and which themselves provide a reasonable time and a simple and inexpensive method, taking into consideration the nature of the case, for preserving such interests. We find that this Act is within the police power of the states and does not unconstitutionally impair the obligation of contracts.

The trial court's judgment is arguably based upon the conclusion that the statute effectuates a taking of property without just compensation contrary to the mandate of Art. I, § 21, of the Indiana Constitution. We agree with appellant that extinguishment of mineral interests under this statutory scheme does not involve an exercise by the State of its power of eminent domain. The State through this statute is not actually taking the mineral interest for its own use and benefit. Consequently, Art. I, § 21, does not provide an applicable standard for review of this statute. Buckler v. Hilt, (1936) 209 Ind. 541, 200 N.E. 219; Foreman v. State ex rel. Department of National Resources, supra. Appellees point to Evansville & Crawfordsville R.R. Co. v. Dick, (1857) 9 Ind. 433, in which this Court stated:

> "[t]he legislature have no power to authorize, in any case, either a direct or consequential injury to private property, without compensation to the owner." 9 Ind. at 436.

This statement in context gave support to the court's ruling that the power of eminent domain cannot serve as a source of immunity from suits for damages for injury to private property. The Mineral Lapse Act does not involve the injury to private property through conduct or activities of governmental agents or others having and exercising the power of eminent domain. It declares instead that a lapse of a mineral interest will occur in the event of specified conditions and circumstances. We are satisfied that substantive due process provides the proper standard for constitutional review of it.

Appellant next contends that the trial court erred in concluding that the Act is violative of the guarantees of Art. I, § 23, of the Indiana Constitution and the Fourteenth Amendment of equal protection of the law by reason of the special treatment afforded certain owners of mineral interests described in Ind.Code § 32–5–11–5. That provision states:

> "Failure to file a statement of claim within the time provided in section 4 shall not cause a mineral interest to be extinguished if the owner of such mineral interest:
>
> (1) was at the time of the expiration of the period provided in section four, the owner of ten or more mineral interests, as above defined, in the county in which such mineral interest is located, and;
>
> (2) made diligent effort to preserve all of such interests as were not being used, and did within a period of ten years prior to the expiration of the period provided in section 4 preserve other mineral interests, in said county, by the filing of statements of claim as herein required, and;
>
> (3) failed to preserve such interest through inadvertence, and;
>
> (4) filed the statement of claim herein required, within sixty days after publication of notice as provided in section seven herein, if such notice is published, and if no such notice is published, within sixty days after receiving actual knowledge that such mineral interest had lapsed."

By declaring the mineral interest terminable under the conditions set forth in the other sections of the Act, the Legislature sought to create an environment in which mineral interests will be promptly exploited or abandoned. If achieved, this objective would create economic benefits for the people and industries within local communities where actual development activities result and would create other land development where abandonment results. The criteria in Ind.Code § 32–5–11–5, can be rationally conceived as establishing a border line beyond which strict application of the Act's extinguishment standards would become destructive of these goals. Minerals exist within the earth in strata and formations which do not necessarily coincide with the manner in which man has chosen to divide the surface area. Consequently it is commonly necessary to assemble several mineral interests in order to render the extraction of minerals safe and profitable. The Legislature could reasonably have concluded that those meeting the criteria set forth above include those most likely to assemble such interests and actually produce minerals. The separate classification of interests so held within these essential clusters is rationally related to the legitimate objectives of the enactment and is consequently not contrary to the requirements of state and federal equal protection.

The Act seeks to remedy a situation thought to retard economic activity vital to the welfare of local communities and the general public as well. The classification erected does not involve a suspect classification or an impingement upon the exercise of a fundamental right, and consequently the traditional fair and substantial relation test is applicable to it. Johnson et al. v. St. Vincent Hospital, Inc. et al., Ind., 404 N.E.2d 585 (1980); Steup, et al. v. Indiana Housing Authority, Ind., 402 N.E.2d 1215 (1980). In this area of economic and social concern, legislative choices are entitled to a large degree of deference from the court. They are not required to be made with mathematical precision or along entirely logical lines. Williamson v. Lee Optical of Oklahoma, (1955) 348 U.S. 483, 487, 75 S.Ct. 461, 464, 99 L.Ed. 563; Indiana Aeronautics Com'n v. Ambassadair Inc., (1977) 267 Ind. 137, 368 N.E.2d 1340.

> "In short, the judiciary may not sit as a superlegislature to judge the wisdom or desirability of legislative policy determinations made in areas that neither affect fundamental rights nor proceed along suspect lines, see, e.g., Day-Brite Lighting, Inc. v. Missouri, 342 U.S. 421, 423, [72 s.ct. 405, 407, 96 l.ed. 469] (1952); in the local economic sphere, it is only the invidious discrimination, the wholly arbitrary act, which cannot stand consistently with the Fourteenth Amendment." City of New Orleans v. Dukes, (1976) 427 U.S. 297, 303–304, 96 S.Ct. 2513, 2517, 49 L.Ed.2d 511.

There has been no demonstration made which convinces us that the classification of Ind.Code § 32–5–11–5 is invidiously discriminatory or wholly arbitrary.

The judgments of the trial court here appealed from declaring the statute unconstitutional are reversed and the cases remanded to the trial court for enforcement of the Act.

GIVAN, C.J., and HUNTER, PRENTICE and PIVARNIK, JJ., concur.

NOTES

1. Not surprisingly, the principal case was immediately appealed to the United States Supreme Court. The judgment of the Indiana Supreme Court was affirmed in Texaco, Inc. v. Short, 454 U.S. 516, 102 S.Ct. 781, 70 L.Ed.2d 738 (1982). It was a five to four decision with Justice Brennan filing a rigorous dissent in which he was joined by Justices Marshall, Powell, and White. Justice Brennan concluded: "In the exercise of a State's police powers, perhaps particularly with respect to matters involving the regulation of land, we owe the judgments of state legislatures great deference. Nevertheless, the Due Process Clause of the Fourteenth Amendment was designed to guard owners of property from the wholly arbitrary actions of state governments. As applied retrospectively to extinguish the rights of mineral interest owners for their failure to have made use of their interests within a prior 20 year period, Indiana's statutory scheme would likely effect an unlawful taking of property absent the proviso that such mineral interest owners could preserve their rights by filing a notice of claim within the two year grace period. Given the nature of the scheme established, there is no discernable basis for failing to afford those owners such notice as would make the saving proviso meaningful. As applied to mineral interest owners who were without knowledge of their legal obligations, and who were not permitted to file a saving statement of claim within some period following the giving of statutory notice by the surface owner, the statute operates unconstitutionally. In my view, under these circumstances, the provision of no process simply cannot be deemed due process of law. I respectfully dissent." The

United States Supreme Court opinion plus the dissent is a lengthy one but it is well worth reading in its entirety.

2. Although statutes of limitation do not normally apply to governmental units, the doctrine of laches may be used even against the state. See Hickey v. Illinois Central Railroad Co., 35 Ill.2d 427, 220 N.E.2d 415 (1966) where for more than fifty years the state and the city of Chicago had disclaimed any interest in the air rights over the Illinois Central Railroad and acted as if the lands were owned in fee by the railroad. The court held the state and city were estopped from asserting any claim in such lands.

3. These specialized statutes are most helpful, and when collected into one comprehensive table they form an impressive array of weapons for merchantability. But they do not cover nearly all of the possible claims, and still other devices are resorted to in the quest for merchantability; e.g., uniform title standards adopted by state and local bar associations,[13] and curative acts of various types. Title standards have been particularly useful because they provide a uniform set of guidelines for title examiners and eliminate many of the petty objections which would otherwise plague the commercial transfer of land. For a good discussion of the philosophy and utility of the standards see Bayse, Clearing Land Titles (2d ed. 1970). Professor Bayse notes that the standards have covered several different areas. "These include (1) attitudes and relationships between examiners themselves and between examiners and the public; (2) the duration of search; (3) the effect of lapse of time on record title defects; (4) presumptions of fact which should be ordinarily applied by examiners; and (5) the law applicable to commonly recurring situations. Some have specified the form and content of abstracts and their certificates, the form of certificates of title, the effect of wild deeds, and sometimes the effect of legislation itself."

Typically, the title standards do not have the force of law but operate as custom and as an agreed convention among title examiners. Unfortunately, this view is reinforced by a recent Indiana case, Staley v. Stephens, 404 N.E.2d 633 (Ind.App.1980), where the court held that title standards adopted by a county bar association have no legal effect unless a contract specifically incorporates them. The title defect was almost de minimis (a 1 to 1.6 of a foot violation of a setback line and the house had been located over the line for about ten years, making it inconceivable that a court would have required removal of the improvements) but the court said that, although the defect was small, it was a cloud on title that might expose the purchaser to the possibility of litigation and thus the title was not merchantable. An earlier Indiana case had used the phrase "probable" litigation. This decision used the language "possible" litigation and puts a difficult burden on the examining attorney since many otherwise good titles may be subject to the "possibility" of litigation.

13. For a good example see Recommended Uniform Rules for the Examination of Abstracts of Title, published by the Illinois State Bar Association in 1977 with Commentary by Michael J. Rooney of the Illinois Bar.

The curative or validating acts do have the force of law, and they have been useful in removing some of the minor objections to land titles, such as the failure to affix a seal or trivial defects in acknowledgments.

4. The most ambitious statutes are those which attempt to define merchantability or to provide for really effective periods of limitation. These statutes vary considerably in their language and approach to the problem, but they all have the same goal—to improve merchantability of land titles. Note how effective they can be in a case like the following one.

PRESBYTERY OF SOUTHEAST IOWA v. HARRIS

Supreme Court of Iowa, 1975.
226 N.W.2d 232.

RAWLINGS, JUSTICE. Plaintiff commenced a quiet title action. Some of the named defendants, as alleged holders of a reversionary interest, challenge applicability and constitutionality of The Code 1971, Section 614.24, quoted infra. On motion by plaintiff a summary judgment was ultimately entered adverse to defendants and those appearing now appeal. We affirm.

By petition filed July 28, 1971, the Presbytery of Southeast Iowa, a Corporation, asserts in relevant part: (1) H.B. and Elizabeth Cline, by warranty deed bearing date November 18, 1898, conveyed lots 9 and 10, Block 5, Cline's Addition to Hills Siding, Johnson County, Iowa to the First Presbyterian Church of Iowa City; (2) the aforesaid conveyancing instrument contains this pivotal provision:

"It is further agreed that if said church building is not erected on said premises within two years from Nov. 1st, 1898, or if erected and services shall be permanently discontinued, then said premises shall revert to the grantors or their heirs and assigns."

(3) Presbytery acquired title to said property January 17, 1970, under warranty deed given by the First Presbyterian Church of Iowa City; (4) defendants, as holders of an alleged reversionary interest under the aforesaid 1898 deed, claim a right in the real estate therein described by reason of a breach of the quoted provision which apparently occurred sometime after July 4, 1965; and (5) any such claim asserted by defendants stands extinguished because of their failure to comply with the provisions of Code § 614.24.

Five of the named defendants, as heirs of H.B. and Elizabeth Cline, allege by answer they possess a reversionary interest in the above described property. They also thereby aver Code § 614.24 is inapplicable to their interest and alternately, if applicable, is "unconstitutional as far as any extinguishment of the rights and interests of these Defendants in the above described real estate is concerned for the reason that it deprives these Defendants and other owners or holders of reversionary interests in real estate of their property and rights without notice and without due process of law contrary to the provisions of the Fourteenth Amendment of the Constitution of the United States and Section 9 of Article I of the Constitution of the State of Iowa."

May 11, 1972, plaintiff moved for an adjudication on law points (Iowa R.Civ.P. 105) regarding the constitutionality of Code § 614.24.

June 19th trial court adjudged said enactment constitutional and applicable to defendants.

July 17, 1973, plaintiff filed motion for summary judgment thereby alleging defendants had not filed notice as to any claimed reversionary interest within one year after July 4, 1965, as required by § 614.24.

August 21st trial court entered summary judgment for plaintiff from which this appeal is taken.

In support of a reversal defendants Faye Amish, H. Ray Cline, Robert Cline, Thomas B. Cline, William Cline and Marjorie Harr, here contend § 614.24(1) unconstitutionally impairs contract rights; (2) is unconstitutionally vague; (3) authorizes a divestment of property rights in violation of substantive due process; (4) is violative of procedural due process in that no reasonable notice is afforded a claimant, owning a reversionary interest, of his obligation to record said interest in order that the same may not be extinguished.

Since the first two assignments above set forth are here asserted for the first time they will not be entertained save and except as incident to a determination of other issues properly presented. See Schnabel v. Display Sign Service, Inc., 219 N.W.2d 546, 548 (Iowa 1974); State v. Willis, 218 N.W.2d 921, 923 (Iowa 1974).

As to the first contention see, however, Jackson v. Lamphire, 3 Pet. 280, 290, 7 L.Ed. 679 (1830); Trustees of Schools of Township No. 1 v. Batdorf, 6 Ill.2d 486, 130 N.E.2d 111 (1955); Evans v. Finley, 166 Or. 227, 111 P.2d 833, 836–837 (1941).

And with regard to the second assertion see generally Iron Workers Local No. 67 v. Hart, 191 N.W.2d 758, 772 (Iowa 1971); "Marketable Title Legislation—A Model Act for Iowa", 47 Iowa L.Rev. 389 (1962); Code §§ 4.1(2), 4.2, 4.4.

The third and fourth assignments will be considered in their respective order.

I. At the threshold it is understood the above stated 1898 deed proviso created what is known as a "possibility of reverter." . . .

II. In approaching the task at hand we accord recognition to some other statutes not here directly involved because a reading thereof will disclose an underlying motivating purpose common to all. See Chicago & North Western Ry. Co. v. City of Osage, 176 N.W.2d 788, 792–793 (Iowa 1970); 2A Sutherland, Statutory Construction, § 56.02 (4th ed. 1973); 73 Am.Jur.2d, Statutes, §§ 155–158; 82 C.J.S. Statutes § 366, p. 801.

Code § 614.17, has been described as the first of our "Marketable Title Acts." See 2 Patton, Titles, § 563 at 443 (2d ed. 1957); 1 Flick,

Abstract and Title Practice, § 357 at 345 (2d ed. 1958). In material part said statutory enactment recites:

"No action based upon any claim arising or existing prior to January 1, 1960, shall be maintained . . . to recover any real estate . . . or establish any interest therein or claim thereto . . . against the holder of the record title to such real estate in possession, when such holder of the record title and his grantors immediate or remote are shown by the record to have held chain of title to said real estate, since January 1, 1960, unless such claimant . . . shall within one year from and after July 1, 1970, file in the office of the recorder of deeds of the county wherein such real estate is situated, a statement in writing . . . describing the real estate involved, the nature and extent of the right or interest claimed, and stating the facts upon which the same is based."

Standing under the spotlight in the case at hand is Code § 614.24, which provides:

"*No action based upon any claim arising or existing by reason of the provisions of any deed* or conveyance or contract or will reserving or providing for any reversion, reverted interests or use restrictions in and to the land therein described *shall be maintained either at law or in equity* in any court to recover real estate in this state or to recover or establish any interest therein or claim thereto, legal or equitable, against the holder of the record title to such real estate in possession *after twenty-one years from the recording of such deed of conveyance* or contract or after twenty-one years from the admission of said will to probate *unless the claimant* shall, by himself, or by his attorney or agent, or if he is a minor or under legal disability, by his guardian, trustee, or either parent or next friend, *shall file a verified claim with the recorder of the county wherein said real estate is located within said twenty-one year period. In the event said deed was recorded or will was admitted to probate more than twenty years prior to July 4, 1965, then said claim may be filed on or before one year after July 4, 1965.* Such claims shall set forth the nature thereof, also the time and manner in which such interest was acquired. For the purposes of this section, the claimant shall be any person or persons claiming any interest in and to said land or in and to such reversion, reverter interest or use restriction, whether the same is a present interest or an interest which would come into existence if the happening or contingency provided in said deed or will were to happen at once. Said claimant further shall include any member of a class of persons entitled to or claiming such rights or interests." (Emphasis supplied).

And Code §§ 614.29, 614.38, collectively referred to as our "Marketable Record Title Act", constitute the most recent and comprehensive legislative effort to simplify land transfers in this jurisdiction. See Marshall, Iowa Title Opinions and Standards, at 77–81 (Cum.Supp. 1970).

We are persuaded the aforesaid statutes clearly represent a salutary attempt on the part of our General Assembly to keep pace with public demands for needed reforms in the field of land title conveyancing practices. As this court observed in Chicago & North Western Ry. Co. v. City of Osage, 176 N.W.2d at 793, they are "designed to shorten the period of search required to establish title in real estate and give effect and stability to record titles by rendering them marketable and alienable—in substance to improve and render less complicated the land transfer system." See also Basye, Trends and Progress—The Marketable Title Acts, 47 Iowa L.Rev. 261 (1962); Aigler, Constitutionality of Marketable Title Acts, 50 Mich.L.Rev. 185 (1951); American Bar News, Vol. 19, No. 10, at p. 1 (November 1974).

The necessity for such reformational action has been vigorously articulated by distinguished members of the legal profession. In a 1974 Report of the Special Committee on Residential Real Estate Transactions of the American Bar Association is this relevant statement at 14–16:

"Our system of public land title records was designed to fit the needs of a rural community. It was invented by the Massachusetts colonists and has not been essentially changed in the interim. The records are so scattered in different offices or so badly indexed, or both, as to make the task of separating the relevant from the irrelevant long and arduous. Where lawyers resort to direct examination of these records the cost, in terms of their time, is clearly apparent.

". . .

"A second means of reducing title costs can be achieved by shortening the period of search. While the invention of the recording system was a great improvement over the then existing English system, or non-system, it would have been a greater improvement if a limit had been placed on the duration of the notice created by recording. While the various statutes of limitations can be relied upon to bar many ancient claims, there are other interests as to which the applicable statute does not begin to run until the interest has been violated. A purchaser needs, of course, to know about these. As a consequence, in theory, it is necessary to trace every title back to its origin in the state. To do so is already impracticable in much of our country and will ultimately become so elsewhere. As a consequence, conveyancers conventionally limit search to an arbitrary number of years. Aside from the fact that this practice is resorted to at the risk of the lawyer's client, the periods set, ranging up to sixty or more years, result in an enormous and unnecessary input of labor. What is needed is a theory of title which will permit the examining attorney to take title back for only a relatively short number of years with complete confidence that his client will be protected from all adverse claims antedating a record root of title. Much legislation is developing piece-meal, in a number of states, some based on shortening the applicable statutes of limitations, others based on a periodic re-recording requirement for certain specific interests, and others based on marketable title acts. All these approaches can be improved and extended. The Committee draws special attention to the need to amend the existing marketable title acts. Many commentators consider these acts the cornerstone for any systematic program of reform. However, all of the existing acts need strengthening and there are available no adequate models. The creation of effective models should therefore be given high priority."

Also pointing up the demands of the times are these unpublished remarks by the Honorable Warren E. Burger to the opening session of the American Law Institute, May 21, 1974, at Washington, D.C.:

"When I began to practice law the newest associate in the firm was assigned the task of examining titles and closing real estate purchases, and he continued in that role until another new man came along. In that apprenticeship I examined many hundreds of land titles and closed an almost equal number of purchase and financing transactions.

"The cost at that time ranged from $15 to $30 for the purchase of the typical home. There is a growing practice of using title insurance either as a substitute for or in addition to the lawyer's title opinion.

"Today, we know that in many states the incidental costs of acquiring a new home, even in the $40,000 category, can run into a very large sum. We know that, in common with others, the operating costs of lawyers have skyrocketed in recent years, but the very cost of the procedure today dictates that we examine the whole business closely.

". . . The basic system of real estate titles and transfers and the related matters concerning financing and purchase of homes cries out for reexamination and simplification. In a country that transfers not only expensive automobiles but multimillion dollar airplanes with a few relatively simple pieces of paper covering liens and all, I believe that if American lawyers will put their ingenuity and inventiveness to work on this subject they will be able to devise simpler methods than we now have."

It is thus apparent the statutes heretofore noted were enacted in furtherance of the general welfare. See Evans v. Finley, 111 P.2d at 837, 838; 47 Iowa L.Rev. at 426.

But this is not alone instantly dispositive.

III. We therefore turn to defendant's claim that § 614.24 serves to divest them of property rights in violation of constitutional due process standards.

At the outset this court has repeatedly held a strong presumption of constitutionality attends statutes regularly enacted by our General Assembly. See e.g., Keasling v. Thompson, 217 N.W.2d 687, 689–690 (Iowa 1974) and citations.

Referring again to Chicago & North Western Ry. Co. v. City of Osage, 176 N.W.2d at 792, we said Code § 614.24: "'. . . is a true statute of limitations designed to bar claims which have no longer any social or economic utility and, at the same time, to provide for periodic renewal of active claims.' . . .."

And, since § 614.24 permits extinguishment of an existing reverter interest in the absence of a recordation thereof, it clearly operates retrospectively as well as prospectively. . . .

Furthermore, retrospective applicability of the statute in question does not render it unconstitutional per se. See Van Voorhis v. District of Columbia, 236 F.Supp. 978, 981 (D.D.C.1965); Thompson v. Thompson, 78 N.W.2d 395, 399 (N.D.1956); Adelman v. Adelman, 58 Misc.2d 803, 296 N.Y.S.2d 999, 1004 (1969); Yoli v. Yoli, 55 Misc.2d 416, 285 N.Y.S.2d 470, 472 (1967).

IV. Defendants take the position that since their reverter interests did not vest until after enactment of § 614.24, the Act served to unconstitutionally deny them a vested future interest before right of enforcement thereof matured. We find no viability in that contention.

It is conceded this court has not heretofore been called upon to resolve the precise constitutional question now before us. Therefore, pertinent authorities from other jurisdictions, though not binding on this court, will be considered. See Simpson v. Low-Rent Housing Agency of Mount Ayr, Iowa, 224 N.W.2d 624 (Iowa, 1974).

In Wichelman v. Messner, 250 Minn. 88, 83 N.W.2d 800 (1957), the Minnesota Marketable Title Act was found to be a constitutionally permissible limitations enactment barring a reverter interest. The statute there involved, M.S.A. § 541.023, stated in relevant part:

"As against a claim of title based upon a source of title, which source has then been of record at least 40 years, no action affecting the possession or title of any real estate shall be commenced by a person, . . . after January 1, 1948, to enforce any right, claim, interest, incumbrance or lien founded upon any instrument, event or transaction which was executed or occurred more than 40 years prior to the commencement of such action, unless within 40 years after such execution or occurrence there has been recorded in the office of the register of deeds [the required notice] . . .."

Plaintiff Wichelman's right of reverter had not been recorded as statutorily required and in holding as aforesaid the court stated, 83 N.W.2d at 820, 821:

"*We* must *reject the construction suggested by counsel amici curiae for plaintiff that the 40-year period does not begin to run in favor of a determinable fee or a fee subject to a condition subsequent until after a breach of the restriction.* Applying that construction to the facts of the instant case, where the restrictions were created in 1897 and broken in 1946, the 40-year period would not expire until 1986; and if a restriction were created in 1800 and not breached until 2000, the 40-year period would not expire until the year 2040. Some other statute of limitations, or adverse possession, or laches would probably operate within 40 years after breach and § 541.023 would be unnecessary. The economic reason for which the original grantor imposed the restriction in either of these cases would probably have ceased long before its breach; yet unless it is breached the restriction has an indefinite duration. We may assume that in enacting this statute the legislature adopted the view that such a restriction on the fee is probably so scattered among numerous heirs and assignees that it is almost impossible to locate them. In the case before us the plaintiff who purchased quit-claims from the heirs was himself unable to acquire the total interest. Outstanding interests of this nature are likely to have merely nuisance value 40 years after their creation. They are the type of clogs at which the provisions of the act are aimed. Obviously the policy of preventing ancient records from fettering the marketability of the fee is frustrated by the construction contended for by the plaintiff. (Emphasis supplied).

". . .

"The plaintiff argues that the right of reentry or reverter is an enforceable and vested right in land and asserts that the application of the statute as between parties to the same instrument may produce consequences in violation of the contract and due process of law provisions of our state and Federal Constitutions. In Scanlan v. Grimmer, 71 Minn. 351, 74 N.W. 146, where the purchaser of real estate assumed a mortgage and took title and then attempted to repudiate the mortgage on the property he had purchased, the court held that one cannot accept the benefits conferred by a deed and repudiate the burden imposed by it. On this authority the plaintiff contends that the Marketable Title Act does not relieve the record owner of a fee simple title from the burdens and restrictions outstanding against such fee where the fee title itself is predicated upon the instrument which contains the right or condition to be extinguished.

"As we have heretofore noted, a statute of limitations necessarily deprives a person of an interest which he would be able to assert in the absence of the statute if he fails to commence action in the stated period. *Marketable title acts merely require filing notice rather than comencing an action; hence they may apply to vested future interests.* If § 541.023 *automatically* barred a vested right retroactively without providing an opportunity to protect that interest, the plaintiff's argument that vested substantial rights cannot be barred would have considerably more force. On the contrary, however, § 541.023 allowed nine months for any outstanding interest to be protected by the easy expediency of recording notice. No one has a vested right in any particular remedy and the legislature may change or modify the existing remedies for the enforcement and protection of the contract rights as long as an adequate remedy remains. (Authorities cited)." (Emphasis supplied).

Parenthetically we note this observation by Professor Basye as to the significance of *Wichelman,* supra. "Over 60 lawyers and law firms throughout the state appeared and filed briefs and amici curiae because of the decision's obvious potential effect on land titles." Basye, Clearing Land Titles, § 180 at 417 (2d ed. 1970).

Hiddleston v. Nebraska Jewish Education Society, 186 Neb. 786, 186 N.W.2d 904 (1971), involved the question as to whether a statute limiting duration of a possible reverter and right of entry or reentry for breach of a condition subsequent violated the United States and Nebraska constitutional due process or contract provisions. Noticeably the Nebraska statute did not afford owners of such barred estates an opportunity to file claims in order to preserve their reverter interests. Yet the court determined the enactment did not impinge on any constitutional due process or contract rights held by owners of reverter interests. In so holding the court declared, 186 N.W.2d at 907:

"The Legislature may reasonably have intended the reverter act to increase utility of land and marketability of titles by methods that were certain, uniform and inexpensive. See Note, 65 Colum.L.Rev. 1272 (1965). Section 76–2, 102, R.R.S.1943, either on its face or in its application to plaintiffs, did not violate the due process or the contract clause of the United States or the Nebraska Constitution."

See also Hart and Wechsler, The Federal Courts and the Federal System, at 467 (1953).

. . .

Defendants urge us to accept, as controlling in this case, the decision in Board of Education of Central Sch. Dist. No. 1 v. Miles, 15 N.Y.2d 364, 259 N.Y.S.2d 129, 207 N.E.2d 181 (1965). Briefly stated, we respectfully decline defendants' invitation and in so doing adopt the position taken by Marshall, Iowa Title Opinions and Standards at 80, n. 1 (Cum.Supp.1970):

"In Board of Education of Central School Dist. No. 1 v. Miles, 15 N.Y.2d 364, [259 n.y.s.2d 129,] 207 N.E.2d 181 (1965) the New York Court of Appeals held a statute similar to Iowa Code §§ 614.24 to 614.28 unconstitutional when applied to a possibility of reverter. The court expressed the view that the legislature could not bar a remedy before the right to enforce it had matured. The lower court had held the statute constitutional, citing Wichelman v. Messner, 250 Minn. 88, 83 N.W.2d 800 (1957) (sustaining validity of Marketable Title Act) and Tesdell v. Hanes, 248 Iowa 742, 82 N.W.2d 119 (1957). Board of Education of Central School Dist. No. 1 v. Miles, 18 App.Div.2d 87, 238 N.Y.S.2d 766, 772 (1963). The New York Court of Appeals attempted to distinguish Wichelman on the unconvincing ground that the reverter matured in 1946 and the action to enforce the reverter was not commenced until 1952. This analysis overlooks the fact that the Minnesota court emphasized the reversion claimant failed to file a claim as required by the Minnesota statute. No attempt was made by the court of appeals to distinguish Tesdell since it is unlikely a logical argument could be made to support the view that Tesdell's rationale would not be controlling. Certainly Tesdell, interpreting Iowa Code, § 614.17 (a statute of limitations) was relevant to the issue before the court.

"Finally, the New York Court of Appeals cites two law review articles, purportedly critical of the analysis in Wichelman. Aigler, A Supplement to 'Constitutionality of Marketable Title Acts'—1951–1957, 56 Mich.L.Rev. 225, 232, 237 (1957); Basye, Trends and Progress—The Marketable Title Acts, 47 Iowa Law Review, 261, 279 (1962). The citations are suspect when viewed in light of the conclusions of each author.

" 'Though one may have doubts as to the soundness of the court's construction and application of the act, the value of the decision on the constitutional question is not lessened. Indeed, if the court is right on the matter of construction, the case is an even more striking one on the constitutional phase.

" 'The same public policy that was found to be back of the Iowa and Minnesota statutes is behind the Michigan act. As well said by the Minnesota court, the obvious objectives sought to be effectuated by the legislature should be given significant weight in settling questions of construction. It is difficult to see how a Michigan court could fail to follow the lead of those recent decisions and do otherwise than conclude that the act is within the legislative power.' Aigler, supra at 233.

" 'If it is felt that possibilities of reverter or rights of entry are not sufficiently desirable interests to deserve recognition, their duration can *easily* be made a matter of statutory control.' Basye, supra at 279. (Emphasis added).

"The impact of the Court of Appeals decision is softened somewhat by the court's observation that it was not ruling on the constitutionality of marketable title acts in general."

. . .

We also recognize the numerous commentators who persuasively argue that statutes premised on the theory the legislature may require periodic filing in order to preserve rights do not run afoul of constitutional limitations. See Basye, Clearing Land Titles, at 384, 385, 476–508; Simes and Taylor, The Improvement of Conveyancing by Legislation, at 268–270, 289–292 (1960); Aigler, A Supplement to "Constitutionality of Marketable Title Acts"—1951–1957, 56 Mich.L.Rev. 225 (1957); Marshall, Reforming Conveyancing Procedure, 44 Iowa L.Rev. 75 at 80 (1958).

. . .

It is to us evident the above cited authorities reasonably and logically establish the constitutional propriety of marketable title statutes which operate retrospectively to bar an action on reverter interests. Furthermore, Wichelman and Town of Nahant, both supra, uphold this bar even where the reverter interest is contingent at time of expiration of the limitation period allowed for preservation thereof. We subscribe to these views. Code, § 614.24 requires nothing more than the filing of a notice of claim after which enforceability thereof is extended for an additional 21 years. "In other words, we do not have before us a statute which operates to bar the claimant's remedy before he has had an opportunity to assert it." Wichelman v. Messner, 83 N.W.2d at 822.

Therefore, § 614.24 does not abolish or alter any vested right. Rather, it modifies the procedure for effectuation of the remedy by conditionally limiting the time for enforcement of the right.

This court is therefore satisfied and now holds, Code § 614.24 did not serve to unconstitutionally deprive defendants of any vested rights.

VII. It is further apparent the time period allowed defendants for the preservation of their remedy under § 614.24 is not constitutionally unreasonable. See Selectmen of Town of Nahant v. United States, 293 F.Supp. at 1078; Wichelman v. Messner, 83 N.W.2d at 818; Trustees of

Schools of Township No. 1 v. Batdorf, 130 N.E.2d at 115; 51 Am.Jur.2d, Limitation of Actions, §§ 31–35.

VIII. The remaining issue to be considered is whether Code § 614.24 denied defendants procedural due process because vested property rights were extinguished, without adequate notice and opportunity for hearing.

Despite dicta contained in Board of Education of Central Sch. Dist. No. 1 v. Miles, 15 N.Y.2d 364, 259 N.Y.S.2d 129, 207 N.E.2d 181, 183 (1965), we conclude, enactments of our state legislature and publication thereof constitute adequate notification to all concerned as to what they contain. See Woodruff & Son v. Rhoton, 251 Iowa 550, 554, 101 N.W.2d 720 (1960); 58 Am.Jur.2d, Notice, § 21; 66 C.J.S. Notice § 13.

Defendants' contention, regarding absence of notice is without substance.

IX. In summary we conclude and accordingly hold, defendants' contentions that § 614.24 authorizes a divestment of property rights in violation of (1) substantive and (2) procedural due process, are each and both devoid of merit.

Costs are taxed to appealing defendants Faye Amish, H. Ray Cline, Robert Cline, Thomas B. Cline, William Cline and Marjorie Harr.

Affirmed.

MOORE, C.J., and MASON, LEGRAND, UHLENHOPP and MCCORMICK, JJ., concur.

REES, REYNOLDSON and HARRIS, JJ., dissent.

REES, JUSTICE (dissenting).

I am unable to agree with the majority in this case and respectfully dissent.

The majority views § 614.24 as a "'true statute of limitations designed to bar claims . . .' (citing Chicago & Northwestern Ry. Co. v. City of Osage, 176 N.W.2d 788, 792 (Iowa 1970), [which] does not abolish or alter any vested right [but merely] modifies the procedure for effectuation of the remedy by conditionally limiting the time for enforcement of the right." This, the classic defense of a statute such as § 614.24, involves no small measure of semantic gymnastics. See Wichelman v. Messner, 250 Minn. 88, 83 N.W.2d 800. It is a defense I cannot abide.

A possibility of reverter is not simply a claim or right but an interest in property. Jacobs v. Miller, supra. See Simes, Law of Future Interests, 2d Ed., 1966, § 13, p. 28 et seq. Section 614.24 attempts to convert that interest in property into a mere right of action subject to defeasance if not timely asserted. Once that is recognized, it is clear the statute operates not simply to "bar claims" but to divert persons such as these defendants of existing property interests. It is not therefore a true statute of limitations. See Simes, Law of Future Interests, supra, § 51, pp. 111–112.

Even assuming a possibility of reverter is but a claim or right and not an interest in property, the characterization of § 614.24 as a statute of limitations does not stand close scrutiny under circumstances such as those presented here. Defendants' "claim" to the real estate in question "accrued" only when the condition in the 1898 deed was "breached". That breach apparently occurred sometime after July 4, 1965. As applied, § 614.24 would have required defendants to assert their "claim" before it accrued and operates potentially to bar their remedy before the "right" to enforce it matured. I know of no true statute of limitation which operates in that fashion. See Board of Education of Central School District No. 1 v. Miles, 15 N.Y.2d 364, 207 N.E.2d 181; Simes, Law of Future Interests, supra at 111. Town of Brookline v. Carey, 355 Mass. 424, 245 N.E.2d 446, which held an act limiting enforcement of reversionary interests that have "accrued" can constitutionally be applied to reverters which occurred *prior* to its enactment, supports this position.

Because § 614.24 does far more than simply bar claims, and in effect divests persons of their existing property interests, it cannot in the end be justified as a mere statute of limitation. Accordingly, the question must be whether the statutory procedure designed to forestall divestiture comports with constitutional guarantees of due process.

The statute contains no provision for notice. Statutory enactment alone was evidently deemed sufficient notice for those persons whose interests in property would be affected. I am not persuaded that manner of notice is "such as one desirous of actually informing . . . might reasonably adopt to accomplish it" (the constitutional standard for due process). Mullane v. Central Hanover Bank & Trust Co., 339 U.S. 306, 315, 70 S.Ct. 652, 657, 94 L.Ed. 865. Cf. Lane v. Traveler's Ins. Co., 230 Iowa 973, 299 N.W. 553 (decided nine years before Mullane).

Moreover, I am frankly unable to reconcile recent decisions broadening the due process rights of persons possessing interests in personalty with the procedural burden placed on persons under § 614.24 to take affirmative action to protect their interests in realty. See Sniadach v. Family Finance Corp., 395 U.S. 337, 89 S.Ct. 1820, 23 L.Ed.2d 349. Fuentes v. Shevin, 407 U.S. 67, 92 S.Ct. 1983, 1997–1998, 32 L.Ed.2d 556; Thorp Credit, Inc. v. Barr, 200 N.W.2d 535 (Iowa 1972). See also North Georgia Finishing, Inc. v. Di-Chem, Inc. (opinion announced by United States Supreme Court, 1975; appearing in 419 U.S. 601, 95 S.Ct. 719, 42 L.Ed.2d 751). Surely owners of interests in personalty are entitled to no more due process protection in Iowa than are owners of interests in realty.

The majority characterizes the Iowa marketable title legislation as "a salutary attempt on the part of our General Assembly to keep pace with public demands for needed reforms in the field of land title conveyancing practices." I agree with that characterization. The majority goes on to justify § 614.24 as a statute "designed to bar claims which have no longer any social or economic utility and, at the same time, to provide for periodic renewal of active claims." (citing Chicago

& Northwestern Ry. Co. v. City of Osage, supra, at 792). There we part company.

Whatever its social utility, § 614.24 operates to deprive persons of their interests in property without due process. Paraphrasing a legislative commission report quoted by the New York Court of Appeals in Board of Education v. Miles, supra, where a similar statute was found unconstitutional as applied to a possibility of reverter, it is almost certain that an appreciable number of persons owning ancient but useful restrictions and other valuable interests in property similar to that owned by these defendants will lose them without compensation through failure to file claims under § 614.24, a prerequisite to their continued vitality. Such failure may occur under a variety of circumstances. Unless the owner of the interest has regular occasion to be on the watch for new legislation or unless he is regularly engaged in transactions involving real estate, he might never have learned of the requirement for filing a claim under the statute.

For the foregoing reasons I am satisfied § 614.24 of the Code violates both substantive and procedural constitutional guarantees of due process. Trial court erred in upholding the statute and in refusing to recognize defendants' interest in the subject property.

I would reverse trial court.

REYNOLDSON and HARRIS, JJ., join this dissent.

NOTES

1. Although the principal case deals with that old favorite—a possibility of reverter--note that the merchantability of title acts cover all types of interests in land, except those specifically exempted from coverage. See, for example, Semachko v. Hopko, 35 Ohio App.2d 205, 64 O.O.2d 316, 301 N.E.2d 560 (1973), where the court held that certain restrictive covenants were unenforceable because barred by the Ohio Marketable Title Act.

For a recent case interpreting the Ohio Marketable Title Act see Heifner v. Bradford, 4 Ohio St.3d 49, 446 N.E.2d 440 (1983). The Ohio Act was taken primarily from the Model Marketable Title Act and provided protection for an owner with an unbroken title of record for forty years or more. In 1916, the owners of a tract of land in fee simple conveyed their interest, reserving the oil and gas rights in the land. In 1936, the grantees in the 1916 deed conveyed by warranty deed to the predecessors in interest of the present claimants to all of the land. This deed was recorded and there was no mention of the reservation of the oil and gas rights. Thus, the present claimants had a record chain of title to all of the land which had existed for more than forty years. However, in 1957, the survivor of the original grantors died testate leaving the oil and gas rights to individuals who now claim to own those interests. The will was filed for record. The court held that the Marketable Title Act did not protect the claimants and that they owned the surface rights only. "The recording of an instrument of conveyance subsequent to the effective date of the root of title has the same effect in preserving any interest conveyed as the filing of the notice provided for in section 4 of the Act." There were two independent chains of title. "Thus, the 1957 conveyance under the terms of [the will] was a title transaction which the meaning of R.C. 5301.49(D), and appellants' interest was not extinguished by operation of the Marketable Title Act."

What would have been the result if Ohio had had a statute like that in the Indiana case of Short v. Texaco, Inc.?

Part Six

A CONCLUDING NOTE

Casebooks do not have a Conclusion, only a Preface. This is because casebooks do not tell a story (at least in the conventional sense) nor do they normally expound a thesis. You are left to draw your own conclusions and shape your own conceptions about the nature and function of law. We do ask you, however, to review Part One of this casebook as you conclude your study of basic property law and to ask again some timeless questions: What is property? What has been its past? What does it look like in the present? Above all, what will be its future? For some reflections on this latter question see Cribbet, Property in the Twenty-First Century, 39 Ohio St.L.J. 671 (1978). In that article, one of the editors of these materials gazed into the crystal ball and opined: "I foresee a property law more nearly fashioned to serve the needs of a relatively free people, with less reification of the 'thing' (land or chattel) and more emphasis on the rights of society as a whole. The winds of doctrine are not all blowing in that direction, but enough of the signs are emerging so that I, for one, do not despair."

We hope you share that optimism as you prepare to play a professional role in the year 2001 and beyond.

INDEX

References are to Pages

ABANDONMENT
Chattels, 97, 113
Easements, 644

ABSTRACT OF TITLE
Generally, 1337–1355
Example of an abstract, 1338–1348

ACCESSION
See also Accretion
Good faith improvers of chattels, 157
Good faith improvers of land, 163

ACCRETION
Riparian land, 95

ACKNOWLEDGMENT
Effect of, 1164
Form of, 1164

ADVERSE POSSESSION
See Statutes of Limitation

AFTER-ACQUIRED TITLE
See Estoppel By Deed

AIRSPACE
Aircraft flights, liability to landowners, 764
Light and air, interference with, 771
Solar energy, 771
Weather modification, 783

ATTRIBUTES OF PROPERTY
Generally, 32–55
Animals and property, 32–33
Primitive societies, 34–36
Private property, 3–5, 44–55
Soviet view, 41–44

BAILMENTS
Creation of, 119
Damages recoverable by bailee from tort-feasor, 142
Distinguished from sales, 126

BONA FIDE PURCHASER
See also Recording System
Chattels, 128

BROKERS
Generally, 1122–1140
Commission, 1132–1137
Exclusive listing, 1122–1123
Multiple listing service, 1123

BROKERS—Cont'd
Regulation of, 1123–1132
Role of, 1122–1140
Tort liability, 1137–1140

CERCLA
See Hazardous Substances

COMMUNITY PROPERTY
Generally, 336–338

CONCURRENT OWNERSHIP
See also Cotenancy
Generally, 322–425
Introduction to, 322–332

CONDOMINIUMS
See also Covenants Affecting Land Use; Landlord and Tenant
Generally, 415–425

CONTRACTS
See Real Estate Contracts

CONVEYANCING
See Deeds

COTENANCY
Accounting for rents and profits, 346–363
Creation and attributes, 371–415
Creditor's rights, 330–332
Destruction by fire, 398–401
Four unities, 371–398
Intent to sever, 408–411
Joint tenancy, 323–327
Mining, accountability for, 354–363
Murder of one cotenant by another, 411–415
Relationship between cotenants, 346–354
Right to partition, 363–371
Severance, 379–398
Tax aspects, 414–415
Tax sale, 348–350
Tenancy by the entirety, 327–331, 398–408
Tenants in common, 322–323
Types, 322–332

COVENANTS AFFECTING LAND USE
Affirmative covenants, 663–666, 668
Anticompetitive, 673
Benefit in gross, 662–663, 669
Building design, discretion to control, 703
Building schemes, scope of, 685
Conditions distinguished, 690

COVENANTS AFFECTING LAND USE—Cont'd
Constructional bias against, 717
Easements distinguished, 710
Equitable servitudes recognized, 667
Group homes forbidden by, 691
Implied, 681
In esse rule, 649
Intent requirement, 649
Liability of covenantor after transfer, 649
Parties who can enforce, 685
Privity of estate requirement, 649–662
Property owners associations, enforcement by, 659
Racial discrimination, 77, 691
Reservation of power to modify, 691, 702
Statute of Frauds, 679
Termination,
Changed circumstances, 706–712
Eminent domain, 709
Zoning, 710
Terminology, simplification of, 713
Third party, for benefit of, 685
Touch and concern requirement, 649–657, 663–666, 673
Unenforceability,
Constitutional grounds, 77–84, 691
Public policy, 691
Unification of concepts, 713

COVENANTS FOR TITLE
Generally, 1305–1337
Against encumbrances, 1313–1322
Caveat emptor, 1268–1269
Damages, 1322–1326
Disclaimer, 1282–1286
Estoppel by deed, 1331–1337
Implied covenants of habitability, 1268–1287
Merger doctrine, 1280–1281
Occupying claimant's acts, 1327–1330
Related doctrines, 1287–1305
Running with the land, 1312–1313
Usual covenants, 1305–1311

COVENANTS RUNNING WITH THE LAND
See Covenants Affecting Land Use; Covenants for Title; Landlord and Tenant

CURTESY
Generally, 332–334

DEEDS
See also Gifts
Generally, 1141–1202
Acknowledgment, 1164
Bargain and sale, 1144–1149
Consideration, 1152
Construction, 1184–1202
Covenant to stand seised, 1144–1149
Delivery, 199, 1165–1177
Descriptions, 1177–1184
Escrow agreements, 1165–1177
Exceptions and reservations, 1152, 1162
Execution of, 1163
Habendum, 1150–1151
History, 1141–1149

DEEDS—Cont'd
Latent and patent ambiguities, 1184–1187
Monuments, 1197–1200
Parties, 1150, 1160
Relation back, 1167–1168
Reservations in third parties, 586–591
Statutory forms, 1153
Subject matter conveyed, 1177–1202
Survey systems, 1179–1183
Types and elements, 1149–1163
Warranty and quitclaim, 1149

DEFEASIBLE ESTATES
Generally, 248–268
Construction, 248
Effect of changed circumstances, 265, 709
Fee simple determinable vs. fee simple subject to condition subsequent, 248
Possibilities of reverter and rights of entry, 254
Role of Rule against Perpetuities, 265, 315
Termination of possibilities of reverter and rights of entry, 264–265

DEVELOPMENT OF ESTATES DOCTRINE
Generally, 208–220
English History, 209–217
United States history, 217–220

DOCTRINE OF WORTHIER TITLE
Generally, 285–291
Abolition of Doctrine, 289–291

DOWER
Generally, 334–336

EASEMENTS
Categories, 612
Customary, 621
Defined, 580
Equitable, 593
Fee, distinguished from, 591
Formalities for creation, 582
Implied, By necessity, 601
Implied, Pre-existing use, 604
In gross, 638
Lease, distinguished from, 593
License, distinguished from, 593–600
Negative reciprocal, 681
Prescription, creation by, 613–630
Public easements, 621
Real covenants and servitudes distinguished, 710–712
Reservation of, 582–591
Right-of-way deed, construction of, 591
Scenic, 611
Scope, 630–638
Termination, 644, 710
Transferability, 638

ECONOMIC ANALYSIS
Broadcast frequencies, 8–10
Conversion to condominiums, 50
Economic theory of property, 6–8, 36–37
Future rights, 10–12
Housing codes and implied warranty of habitability, 474

ECONOMIC ANALYSIS—Cont'd
Nuisance doctrines, 730

EMINENT DOMAIN
Public purpose or use, 813
Regulatory takings, 887

ENVIRONMENTAL PROTECTION
See Hazardous Substances; Land Use Control; Nuisance

EQUITABLE CONVERSION
Generally, 1091–1122
Concurrent estates, 1101
Debtor-creditor relationship, 1096
Devolution on death, 1097–1107
Dower, 1100
Effect of rezoning, 1091–1095
General nature, 1091–1097
Insurance, 1111–1121
Mortgages, 1096–1097
Options, 1104–1107
Relation back, 1104–1107
Risk of loss, 1107–1122
Uniform Vendor and Purchaser Risk Act, 1111

EQUITABLE SERVITUDES
See Covenants Affecting Land Use

ESCHEAT
Chattels, 114
Land, 218–220
Personal property, 114

ESCROW
See Deeds

ESTOPPEL BY DEED
Generally, 1331–1337
Oil and gas deed, 1331–1335
Theory and operation, 1335

EXAMINATION OF THE RECORDS
See Abstract of Title; Recording System

EXECUTORY INTERESTS
Generally, 291–321
Doctrine of uses, 291–293
Modern trust, 295
Racial restrictions, 310–313
Rule Against Perpetuities, 302–304
Springing and shifting interests, 299–302
Statute of Uses, 293–294
Unexecuted uses, 295

FEE SIMPLE ABSOLUTE
Generally, 224–227
Meaning of word "heirs", 227
Modern statute of descent, 231–236
Requirement of words of art, 224

FEE SIMPLE CONDITIONAL
See Fee Tail

FEE SIMPLE DETERMINABLE
See Defeasible Estates

FEE SIMPLE SUBJECT TO CONDITION SUBSEQUENT
See Defeasible Estates

FEE TAIL
Generally, 268–272
Conveyance of, 270
Historical development, 268–270
Statutory changes, 269–270

FINDING
Legislation, 116
Mislaid things, 108–113
Place of finding, 92, 101–118
Possession by finder, protection of, 100

FIXTURES
See Accession; Landlord and Tenant

FREEHOLD ESTATES
Generally, 221–272
Classification of interests in real property, 222–224
Historical development, 221–222

FUTURE INTERESTS
Generally, 273–321
Doctrine of Worthier Title, 285–291
Executory interests, 291–321
Possibilities of reverter, 273
Remainders, 273
Reversions, 273
Rights of entry (powers of termination), 273
Rule in Shelley's Case, 281–285
Vested and contingent remainders, 273–281

GIFTS
Causa mortis, 177–189
Delivery, 166–187
Joint bank accounts, 187, 197
P.O.D. bank accounts, 196, 197
Totten trusts, 195
Uniform Probate Code, 197

HAZARDOUS SUBSTANCES
Landowners' liability for cleanup, 1301–1305

HISTORIC PRESERVATION
See Land Use Control

HOMESTEAD RIGHTS
Generally, 336
Enforceability of lien to secure maintenance fees, 698

INHERITANCE
Generally, 227–237
At common law, 228–231
Modern statute of descent and distribution, 231–236

INSTITUTION OF PROPERTY
Generally, 1–90
Economic theory, 6–12, 36

INSTITUTION OF PROPERTY—Cont'd
Institution defined, 1
Legal theory, 3–5, 12–31
What is property, 1–31

JOINT TENANCY
See Cotenancy

LAND USE CONTROL
See also Zoning
Aesthetic goals, 796
Architectural design, 797
Comprehensive plans, 829
Deregulation, 973
Development rights transfer, 881
Exclusion of non-affluent, 958
Family, definition of, 943
Group homes, 951
Growth control, 965
Historic preservation, 881
Official maps, 805
Planned unit development, 859
Racial discrimination, 934
Signs, 797
Subdivision regulation, 801
Takings,
Compensation for, 919
Criteria, 877

LANDLORD AND TENANT
Generally, 426–579
Abandonment by tenant, 551
Assignment and sublease, 564–579
Covenant of continued operation, 576–579
Damages, duty of landlord to mitigate, 551
Demolition of single occupancy rooms, 520–528
Discrimination in selection of tenants, 436–446
Distress, 559
Dumpor's case, rule in, 576
Duration,
Generally, 503–531
Hold-over tenant, 503–507
Periodic tenancy, 434–436
Statutory entitlement, 508–520
Eminent domain, effect of, 477
Eviction,
Actual partial, 476
Constructive, 477
Conversion to condominium, 529–531
Dwellings subject to rent control, 496–503, 528
Good cause required, 508
Procedures for, 545–551
Public and publicly assisted housing, 473, 508–520
Retaliatory, 545
Single occupancy rooms, 520
Fitness of premises,
Annoying conduct by other tenants, 453
Exculpatory clause, effect of, 494
Housing codes, effect of, 457–472
Implied warranty, habitability, 459–477
Injuries to person or property, 481
Security against crime, 487
Fixtures, 534

LANDLORD AND TENANT—Cont'd
Formalities required for creation of relation, 426
Implied duty of landlord to put tenant in possession, 446
Implied warranty, suitability for commercial use, 477–481
Interesse termini, 430
Licensee distinguished from tenant, 427
Percentage rent, 495, 540
Periodic tenancy, 434–436
Prohibition against assignment, 576–579
Rent control, 496–503
Security deposits, 559–564
Statute of frauds, 429
Surrender, 551
Tenancy at will, 431
Tenant at sufferance, 507
Term for years, 431
Uses by tenant, 532

LEGAL DESCRIPTIONS
See Deeds

LICENSE
Defined, 582
Easement, distinguished from, 593–600
Irrevocable, 595
Lease, distinguished from, 427

LIFE ESTATE
Generally, 237–248
Creation and construction, 238–244
Reservation by grantor, 237
Waste, 244–248

MARITAL ESTATES
Generally, 332–342
Community property, 336–338
Curtesy, 332–334
Dower, 334–336
Homestead rights, 336
Jure uxoris, 332
Marital Property Act, 338–342

MARITAL PROPERTY ACT
Generally, 338–342

MERCHANTABLE TITLE
Generally, 1059–1071
Contract calling for, 1059–1062
Courts' role, 1063–1067
Definition, 1062
Installment land contract, 1068–1070
Tax title, 1071

MORTGAGES
See also Cotenancy; Landlord and Tenant
Generally, 1037–1043
Equity of redemption, 1037–1038
Foreclosure, 1039
History, 1037
Relationship to installment land contracts, 1042–1059
Statutory redemption, 1040
Types of, 1040–1041

NUISANCE
Generally, 716–733
Distinction between private and public nuisance, 727
Economic analysis, 730
Noise levels, 716
Remedies, 721
Right-to farm statutes, 729

OBJECTS AND CLASSIFICATIONS OF PROPERTY
Generally, 56–70
Classes of property, 56–59
Fixtures, 59–60
"New" property, 67–70
Ownership of caves, 60–67
Real and personal property distinguished, 56–60
Water as property, 67

OIL AND GAS
Interests of overlying landowners, 96

PART PERFORMANCE
See Statute of Frauds

PARTITION
See Cotenancy

PLANNED UNIT DEVELOPMENT
See Land Use Control

POSSIBILITY OF REVERTER
See Defeasible Estates

POSSESSION
See also Bailments; Deeds; Finding; Gifts; Statutes of Limitation
Defined, 97
Unauthorized possession deemed ownership, 139

POWER OF TERMINATION
See Defeasible Estates

POWERS OF APPOINTMENT
Generally, 301–302

PRESCRIPTION
See Easements

PROFIT A PRENDRE
Defined, 581

REAL COVENANTS
See Covenants Affecting Land Use

REAL ESTATE CONTRACTS
Generally, 980–1122
Assignment, 1076–1081
Construction and performance, 1021–1090
Damages, 1081–1090
Equitable conversion, 1091–1122
Financing arrangements, 1032–1059
Forfeiture, 1042–1059
Installment land contracts, 1042–1059
Merchantable title, 1059–1071
Mortgages, 1037–1043

REAL ESTATE CONTRACTS—Cont'd
Remedies for breach of contract, 1081–1090
Role of real estate broker, 1022–1040
Specific performance, 1081
Standard written contract, 1021
Statute of Frauds, 981–1020
Tender, 1071–1075
Time for performance, 1022–1032

RECORDING SYSTEM
Generally, 1203–1267
Acknowledgments, 1216–1217
Adverse possession, effect of, 1220–1223
Bona fide purchaser for value, 1236–1240
Burden of proof, 1256–1260
Chain of title, 1260–1267
Classification of recording acts, 1230–1234
Donees, 1234
Failure to index, 1223–1226
General operation, 1211–1232
Lessees, 1239–1240
Persons protected by system, 1234–1260
Possession as notice, 1250–1256
Pre-existing debt, 1240–1244
Quitclaim deed, 1239
Searching title, 1204–1211

REMAINDERS
Alienability, 277
Destructibility, 277–280
Distinguished from executory interests, 306–310
Vested or contingent, 273–277

RESTRAINTS ON ALIENATION
Generally, 302–304

RIGHT OF ENTRY
See Defeasible Estates

ROLE OF PROPERTY
Generally, 71–87
Changing nature, 84–87
Lawyers' role, 88–90
Rights of Indians, 71–77
Rights of minorities, 77–84

RULE AGAINST PERPETUITIES
Generally, 302–304
Application of the Rule, 315–321

RULE IN SHELLEY'S CASE
Generally, 281–285
Abolition of Rule, 284
Applicability of Rule, 285

STATUTE OF FRAUDS
Generally, 981–1020
Brokerage contracts, 1009
Differing views of part performance, 982–1000
Easements, 618
Elements of written memorandum, 1006–1009
English statute, 981
Equitable estoppel, 994–998
Leases, 429

STATUTE OF FRAUDS—Cont'd
Parol modification and rescission, 1016–1020
Part performance and equitable estoppel, 982–1000
Unequivocal referability, 990–994
Written memorandum, 1001–1016

STATUTES OF LIMITATION
Generally, 1392–1433
Color of title, 1403–1405
Constitutionality of specialized statutes, 1411–1419
Cotenancy, 1406–1410
Disabilities, 1401–1403
Forged deed as color of title, 1410
Merchantability of title acts, 1421–1433
Mistake, effect of, 1399–1401
Possession of mineral interest, 1403–1406, 1412–1419
Role as aids to title assurance, 1392–1393
Specialized statutes, 1411–1433
Tacking, 1394–1399
Title standards compared, 1420

STATUTE OF USES
Generally, 291–306

SUBDIVISION REGULATION
See Land Use Control

SUPPORT OF LAND
Disrepair of supporting wall, 733
Ground water, removal of, 740
Lateral or subjacent soil, removal of, 733
Mining operations, 739

TAKING
See Eminent Domain

TENANCY BY THE ENTIRETY
See Cotenancy

TENANCY IN COMMON
See Cotenancy

TESTATE AND INTESTATE SUCCESSION
Common law and early English statutes, 228–231
Modern statute, 231–236
Problems, 235

TIME-SHARE ARRANGEMENTS
Generally, 416

TITLE ASSURANCE
Generally, 1268–1433
Abstract of title, 1337–1355
Covenants for title, 1305–1377
Statutes of limitation as aids to, 1392–1433
Title insurance, 1367–1392
Title registration (Torrens system), 1355–1366

TITLE INSURANCE
Generally, 1367–1392
Damages, 1373–1391

TITLE INSURANCE—Cont'd
Description, 1367–1368
Forms, 1368–1373
Title search, necessity for, 1373–1387
Types, 1391–1392

TITLE REGISTRATION
Generally, 1355–1366
Form, 1357–1358
History, 1355–1357
Tax liens, 1359–1364

TITLES
See Deeds; Recording System; Title Assurance

TORRENS SYSTEM
See Title Registration

UNIFORM LAND TRANSACTIONS ACT
Generally, 978–979
Implied warranty of quality, 1279
Land contract,
Formal requirements, 1016
Modification or rescission, 1020
Time of performance, 1031
Tender,
Deed, 1075
Purchase money, 1075

UNIFORM SIMPLIFICATION OF LAND TRANSFERS ACT
Generally, 978–979

UNIFORM VENDOR AND PURCHASER RISK ACT
Generally, 1111

URBAN RENEWAL
See Eminent Domain

WASTE
Generally, 244–248
Meliorating, 248
Voluntary or permissive, 246

WATER
Diversion, 752
Drainage of surface water, 740
Eastern states, 358
Groundwater rights, 758–764
Prior appropriation, 754, 763
Riparian rights, 748–758
Watercourses, 748
Weather modification, 783

WILD ANIMALS
Ownership, 96, 99

ZONING
Amendments, 829
Comprehensive plan, 829
Conditional uses, 852
Constitutionality established, 788
Contract zoning, 853
Development rights transfer, 881
Effect on covenants, 710

ZONING—Cont'd
Family, definition of, 943
Floating zones, 859
Initiative and referendum, 870
Nonconforming uses, 820
Planned unit development, 859

ZONING—Cont'd
Racial discrimination, 934
Special exceptions, 848
Variances, 848
Vested rights and estoppel, 826

†

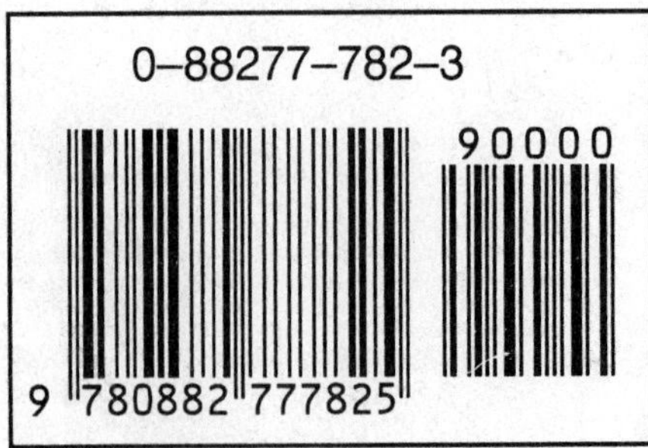

0–88277–782–3
90000
9 780882 777825